THE YEAR'S

The Year's Work in English Studies Volume 89

Covering work published in 2008

Edited by
WILLIAM BAKER
and
KENNETH WOMACK
with associate editors

OLGA FISCHER
MARY SWAN
ANNALIESE CONNOLLY
KIRSTIE BLAIR
CHRIS HOPKINS
THERESA SAXON
JAMES DECKER
PAUL SHARRAD

Published for
THE ENGLISH ASSOCIATION

by

OXFORD JOURNALS
OXFORD UNIVERSITY PRESS

OXFORD

UNIVERSITY PRESS

Great Clarendon Street, Oxford OX2 6DP, UK

Oxford University Press is a department of the University of Oxford.
It furthers the University's objective of excellence in research, scholarship,
and education by publishing worldwide in

Oxford New York

Athens Auckland Bangkok Bogotá Buenos Aires Cape Town
Chennai Dar es Salaam Delhi Florence Hong Kong Istanbul Karachi
Kolkata Kuala Lumpur Madrid Melbourne Mexico City Mumbai Nairobi
Paris São Paulo Shanghai Taipei Tokyo Toronto Warsaw

British Library Cataloguing in Publication Data
Data available
ISSN 0084-4144
ISBN 9780199602421
1 3 5 7 9 10 8 6 4 2
Typeset by Cepha Imaging Pvt. Ltd., Bangalore, India
Printed in Great Britain on acid-free paper by the MPG Books Group,
Bodmin and King's Lynn

The English Association

The object of The English Association is to promote the knowledge and appreciation of English language and its literatures.

The Association pursues these aims by creating opportunities of co-operation among all those interested in English; by furthering the recognition of English as essential in education; by discussing methods of English teaching; by holding lectures, conferences, and other meetings; by publishing several journals, books, and leaflets; and by forming local branches overseas and at home. English Association Fellowships recognize distinction and achievement in the field of English worldwide.

Publications

The Year's Work in English Studies. An annual narrative bibliography which aims to cover all work of quality in English studies published in a given year. Published by Oxford University Press.

The Year's Work in Critical and Cultural Theory. An annual narrative bibliography which aims to provide comprehensive cover of all work of quality in critical and cultural theory published in a given year. Published by Oxford University Press.

Essays and Studies. A well-established series of annual themed volumes edited each year by a distinguished academic.

English. This internationally-known journal of the Association is aimed at teachers of English in universities and colleges, with articles on all aspects of literature and critical theory, an extensive reviews section and original poetry. Four issues per year. Published by Oxford University Press.

Use of English. The longest-standing journal for English teachers in schools and colleges. Three issues per year.

English 4–11. Designed and developed by primary English specialists to give practical help to primary and middle school teachers. Three issues per year.

English Association Studies. A new monograph series published in association with Liverpool University Press.

Issues in English. Occasional pamphlet series.

Membership

Membership information can be found at http://www.le.ac.uk/engassoc or please write to The English Association, University of Leicester, University Road, Leicester LE1 7RH, UK or email: engassoc@le.ac.uk.

The Year's Work
in English Studies

Subscriptions for Volume 89

Institutional (combined rate to both *The Year's Work in English Studies* and *The Year's Work in Critical and Cultural Theory*) print and online: £320.00/$560.00/ €480.00. *Institutional* (*The Year's Work in English Studies* only) print and online: £216.00/$400.00/€324.00.

Please note: £/€ rates apply in Europe, US$ elsewhere. All prices include postage, and for subscribers outside the UK delivery is by Standard Air. There may be other subscription rates available. For a complete listing, please visit www.ywes.oxford journals.org/subinfo.

Online Access

For details please email Oxford University Press Journals Customer Services on: jnls.cust.serv@oxfordjournals.org.

Order Information

Full prepayment, in the correct currency, is required for all orders. Orders are regarded as firm and payments are not refundable. Subscriptions are accepted and entered on a complete volume basis. Claims cannot be considered more than FOUR months after publication or date of order, whichever is later. All subscriptions in Canada are subject to GST. Subscriptions in the EU may be subject to European VAT. If registered, please supply details to avoid unnecessary charges. For subscriptions that include online versions, a proportion of the subscription price may be subject to UK VAT.

Methods of payment. (i) Cheque (payable to Oxford University Press, Cashiers Office, Great Clarendon Street, Oxford OX2 6DP, UK) in GB£ Sterling (drawn on a UK bank), US$ Dollars (drawn on a US bank), or EU€ Euros. (ii) Bank transfer to Barclays Bank Plc, Oxford Group Office, Oxford (bank sort code 20-65-18) (UK), overseas only Swift code BARC GB 22 (GB£ Sterling to account no. 70299332, IBAN GB89BARC20651870299332; US$ Dollars to account no. 66014600, IBAN GB27BARC20651866014600; EU€ Euros to account no. 78923655, IBAN GB16BARC20651878923655). (iii) Credit card (Mastercard, Visa, Switch or American Express).

Back Issues

The current plus two back volumes are available from Oxford University Press. Previous volumes can be obtained from the Periodicals Service Company, 11 Main Street, Germantown, NY 12526, USA. Email: psc@periodicals.com; tel: +1 (518) 537 4700; fax: +1 (518) 537 5899.

Further information. Journals Customer Service Department, Oxford University Press, Great Clarendon Street, Oxford OX2 6DP, UK. Email: jnls.cust.serv@oxfordjournals. org; tel (and answerphone outside normal working hours): +44 (0) 1865 353907; fax: +44 (0) 1865 353485. *In the US, please contact:* Journals Customer Service Department, Oxford University Press, 2001 Evans Road, Cary, NC 27513, USA. Email: jnlorders@oxfordjournals.org; tel (and answerphone outside normal working hours): 800 852 7323 (toll-free in USA/Canada); fax: 919 677 1714. *In Japan, please contact:* Journals Customer Services, Oxford Journals, Oxford University Press, Tokyo, 4-5-10-8F Shiba, Minato-ku, Tokyo 108-8386, Japan. Email: custserv.jp@ oxfordjournals.org; Tel: +81 3 5444 5858; Fax: +81 3 3454 2929.

The Year's Work in English Studies (ISSN 0084 4144) is published annually by Oxford University Press, Oxford, UK. Annual subscription price is £320.00/$560.00/ €480.00. *The Year's Work in English Studies* is distributed by Mercury International, 365 Blair Road, Avenel, NJ 07001, USA. Periodicals postage paid at Rahway, NJ and at additional entry points.

US Postmaster: send address changes to *The Year's Work in English Studies*, c/o Mercury International, 365 Blair Road, Avenel, NJ 07001, USA.

The Table of Contents email alerting service allows anyone who registers their email address to be notified via email when new content goes online. Details are available at http://ywes.oxfordjournals.org/cgi/alerts/etoc.

Permissions

For permissions requests, please visit www.oxfordjournals.org/permissions.

Advertising

Inquiries about advertising should be sent to Oxford Journals Advertising, Oxford University Press, Great Clarendon Street, Oxford, OX2 6DP, UK. Email: jnlsadvertising@oxfordjournals.org; tel: +44 (0) 1865 354767; fax: +44 (0) 1865 353774.

Disclaimer

Contents

Abbreviations

1. Journals, Series and Reference Works

19	*Interdisciplinary Studies in the Long Nineteenth Century*
1650–1850	*1650–1850 Ideas, Aesthetics, and Inquiries in the Early Modern Era*
A&D	*Art and Design*
A&E	*Anglistik und Englishunterricht*
AAA	*Arbeiten aus Anglistik und Amerikanistik*
AAAJ	*Accounting, Auditing and Accountability Journal*
AAR	*African American Review*
ABäG	*Amsterdamer Beiträge zur Älteren Germanistik*
ABC	*American Book Collector*
ABELL	*Annual Bibliography of English Language and Literature*
ABM	*Antiquarian Book Monthly Review*
ABQ	*American Baptist Quarterly*
ABR	*American Benedictine Review* (now *RBR*)
ABSt	*A/B: Auto/Biography Studies*
AC	*Archeologia Classica*
Academy Forum	*Academy Forum*
AcadSF	*Academia Scientiarum Fennica*
ACar	*Analecta Cartusiana*
ACF	*Annuli, Facolta di Lingue e Litterature Straniere di Ca'Foscari*
ACH	*Australian Cultural History*
ACLALSB	*ACLALS Bulletin*
ACM	*Aligarh Critical Miscellany*
ACR	*Australasian Catholic Record*
ACS	*Australian-Canadian Studies: A Journal for the Humanities and Social Sciences*
Acta	*Acta* (Binghamton, NY)
Adaptation	*Adaptation*
AdI	*Annali d'Italianistica*
ADS	*Australasian Drama Studies*
AEB	*Analytical and Enumerative Bibliography*
Æstel	*Æstel*
AF	*Anglistische Forschungen*
AfricanA	*African Affairs*
AfrSR	*African Studies Review*
AfT	*African Theatre*
AgeJ	*Age of Johnson: A Scholarly Annual*
Agenda	*Agenda*
Agni	*Agni Review*
AGP	*Archiv für Geschichte der Philosophie*
Ahornblätter	*Ahornblätter: Marburger Beiträge zur Kanada-Forschung*
AH	*Art History*

AHR	*American Historical Review*
AHS	*Australian Historical Studies*
AI	*American Imago*
AICRJ	*American Indian Culture and Research Journal*
AILA	*Association Internationale de Linguistique Appliqué*
AIQ	*American Indian Quarterly*
AJ	*Art Journal*
AJGLL	*American Journal of Germanic Linguistics and Literatures*
AJIS	*Australian Journal of Irish Studies*
AJL	*Australian Journal of Linguistics*
AJP	*American Journal of Psychoanalysis*
AJPH	*Australian Journal of Politics and History*
AJS	*American Journal of Semiotics*
AKML	*Abhandlungen zur Kunst-, Musik- and Literaturwis-senschaft*
AL	*American Literature*
ALA	*African Literature Association Annuals*
ALASH	*Acta Linguistica Academiae Scientiarum Hungaricae*
Albion	*Albion*
AlexS	*Alexander Shakespeare*
ALH	*Acta Linguistica Hafniensia; International Journal of Linguistics*
Alif	*Journal of Comparative Poetics* (Cairo, Egypt)
ALitASH	*Acta Literaria Academiae Scientiarum Hungaricae*
Allegorica	*Allegorica*
ALN	*American Literary Nationalism Newsletter*
ALR	*American Literary Realism, 1870–1910*
ALS	*Australian Literary Studies*
ALT	*African Literature Today*
Alternatives	*Alternatives*
AmasJ	*Amerasian Journal*
AmDram	*American Drama*
Americana	*Americana*
AmerP	*American Poetry*
AmerS	*American Studies*
AmLH	*American Literary History*
AmLS	*American Literary Scholarship: An Annual*
AMon	*Atlantic Monthly*
AmPer	*American Periodicals*
AmRev	*Americas Review: A Review of Hispanic Literature and Art of the USA*
Amst	*Amerikastudien/American Studies*
AN	*Acta Neophilologica*
Anaïs	*Anaïs*
AnBol	*Analecta Bollandiana*
ANCH	*American Nineteenth Century History*
ANF	*Arkiv för Nordisk Filologi*
Angelaki	*Angelaki*
Anglia	*Anglia: Zeitschrift für Englische Philologie*
Anglistica	*Anglistica*
Anglistik	*Anglistik: Mitteilungen des Verbandes Deutscher Anglisten*
AnH	*Analecta Husserliana*
AnL	*Anthropological Linguistics*
AnM	*Annuale Mediaevale*
Ann	*Annales: Économies, Sociétés, Civilisations*

ANQ	*ANQ: A Quarterly Journal of Short Articles, Notes and Reviews* (formerly *American Notes and Queries*)
AntColl	*Antique Collector*
Anthurium	*Anthurium: A Caribbean Studies Journal*
AntigR	*Antigonish Review*
Antipodes	*Antipodes: A North American Journal of Australian Literature*
ANStu	*Anglo-Norman Studies*
ANZSC	*Australian and New Zealand Studies in Canada*
ANZTR	*Australian and New Zealand Theatre Record*
APBR	*Atlantic Provinces Book Review*
APL	*Antwerp Papers in Linguistics*
AppLing	*Applied Linguistics*
APR	*American Poetry Review*
AQ	*American Quarterly*
Aquarius	*Aquarius*
AR	*Antioch Review*
ArAA	*Arbeiten aus Anglistik und Amerikanistik*
ARAL	*Annual Review of Applied Linguistics*
Arcadia	*Arcadia*
Archiv	*Archiv für das Stadium der Neueren Sprachen und Literaturen*
ARCS	*American Review of Canadian Studies*
ArdenS	*Arden Shakespeare*
ArielE	*Ariel: A Review of International English Literature*
Arion	*Arion: A Journal of the Humanities and the Classics*
ArkQ	*Arkansas Quarterly: A Journal of Criticism*
ArkR	*Arkansas Review: A Journal of Criticism*
ArQ	*Arizona Quarterly*
ARS	*Augustan Reprint Society*
ARSR	*Australian Religion Studies Review*
ArtB	*Art Bulletin*
Arth	*Arthuriana*
ArthI	*Arthurian Interpretations*
ArthL	*Arthurian Literature*
Arv	*Arv: Nordic Yearbook of Folklore*
AS	*American Speech*
ASch	*American Scholar*
ASE	*Anglo-Saxon England*
ASInt	*American Studies International*
ASoc	*Arts in Society*
Aspects	*Aspects: Journal of the Language Society* (University of Essex)
AspectsAF	*Aspects of Australian Fiction*
ASPR	*Anglo-Saxon Poetic Records*
ASSAH	*Anglo-Saxon Studies in Archaeology and History*
Assaph	*Assaph: Studies in the Arts (Theatre Studies)*
Assays	*Assays: Critical Approaches to Medieval and Renaissance Texts*
ASUI	*Analele Stiintifice ale Universitatii 'Al.I. Cuza' din Iasi (Serie Noua), e. Lingvistica*
AteneaPR	*Atenea: A Bilingual Journal of the Humanities and Social Science*
Atlantis	*Atlantis: A Journal of the Spanish Association for Anglo-American Studies*
ATQ	*American Transcendental Quarterly: A Journal of New England Writers*

ATR	*Anglican Theological Review*
AuBR	*Australian Book Review*
AuFolk	*Australian Folklore*
AuFS	*Australian Feminist Studies*
AuHR	*Australian Humanities Review*
AuJL	*Australian Journal of Linguistics*
AUMLA	*Journal of the Australasian Universities Language and Literature Association*
Aurealis	*Australian Fantasy and Science Fiction Magazine*
AuS	*Australian Studies*
AuSA	*Australian Studies* (Australia)
AusCan	*Australian-Canadian Studies*
AusPl	*Australian Playwrights*
AusRB	*Australians' Review of Books*
AustrianS	*Austrian Studies*
AuVSJ	*Australasian Victorian Studies Journal*
AuWBR	*Australian Women's Book Review*
AvC	*Avalon to Camelot*
AY	*Arthurian Yearbook*
BakhtinN	*Bakhtin Newsletter*
BALF	*Black American Literature Forum*
BandL	*Borrowers and Lenders: The Journal of Shakespeare and Appropriation*
BAReview	*British Academy Review*
BARS Bulletin	*British Association for Romantic Studies Bulletin & Review*
BAS	*British and American Studies*
BASAM	*BASA Magazine*
BathH	*Bath History*
BaylorJ	*Baylor Journal of Theatre and Performance*
BayreuthAS	*Bayreuth African Studies*
BB	*Bulletin of Bibliography*
BBCS	*Bulletin of the Board of Celtic Studies*
BBCSh	*BBC Shakespeare*
BBN	*British Book News*
BBSIA	*Bulletin Bibliographique de la Société Internationale Arthurienne*
BC	*Book Collector*
BCan	*Books in Canada*
BCMA	*Bulletin of Cleveland Museum of Art*
BCS	*B.C. Studies*
BDEC	*Bulletin of the Department of English* (Calcutta)
BDP	*Beiträge zur Deutschen Philologie*
Belfagor	*Belfagor: Rassegna di Varia Umanità*
Believer	*Believer*
Bell	*Belgian Essays on Language and Literature*
BEPIF	*Bulletin des Itudes Portugaises et Brésiliennes*
BFLS	*Bulletin de la Faculté des Lettres de Strasbourg*
BGDSL	*Beiträge zur Geschichte der Deutschen Sprache and Literatur*
BH	*Book History*
BHI	*British Humanities Index*
BHL	*Bibliotheca Hagiographica Latina Antiquae et Mediae Aetatis*
BHM	*Bulletin of the History of Medicine*
BHR	*Bibliothèque d'Humanisme et Renaissance*
BHS	*Bulletin of Hispanic Studies*

BI	*Books at Iowa*
Biblionews	*Biblionews and Australian Notes and Queries: A Journal for Book Collectors*
Bibliotheck	*Bibliotheck: A Scottish Journal of Bibliography and Allied Topics*
Biography	*Biography: An Interdisciplinary Quarterly*
BioL	*Biolinguistics*
BIS	*Browning Institute Studies: An Annual of Victorian Literary and Cultural History*
BJA	*British Journal of Aesthetics*
BJCS	*British Journal of Canadian Studies*
BJDC	*British Journal of Disorders of Communication*
BJECS	*British Journal for Eighteenth-Century Studies*
BJHP	*British Journal for the History of Philosophy*
BJHS	*British Journal for the History of Science*
BJJ	*Ben Jonson Journal*
BJL	*Belgian Journal of Linguistics*
BJPS	*British Journal for the Philosophy of Science*
BJRL	*Bulletin of the John Rylands* (University Library of Manchester)
BJS	*British Journal of Sociology*
Blake	*Blake: An Illustrated Quarterly*
BLE	*Bulletin de Littérature Ecclésiastique*
BLJ	*British Library Journal*
BLR	*Bodleian Library Record*
BMC	*Book and Magazine Collector*
BMJ	*British Medical Journal*
BN	*Beiträge zur Namenforschung*
BNB	*British National Bibliography*
BoH	*Book History*
Bookbird	*Bookbird*
Borderlines	*Borderlines*
Boundary	*Boundary 2: A Journal of Postmodern Literature and Culture*
BP	*Banasthali Patrika*
BPMA	*Bulletin of Philadelphia Museum of Art*
BPN	*Barbara Pym Newsletter*
BQ	*Baptist Quarterly*
BRASE	*Basic Readings in Anglo-Saxon England*
BRH	*Bulletin of Research in the Humanities*
Brick	*Brick: A Journal of Reviews*
BRMMLA	*Bulletin of the Rocky Mountain Modern Language Association*
BRONZS	*British Review of New Zealand Studies*
BS	*Bronte Studies*
BSAL	*Beckford Society Annual Lecture*
BSANZB	*Bibliographical Society of Australia and New Zealand Bulletin*
BSE	*Brno Studies in English*
BSEAA	*Bulletin de la Société d'Études Anglo-Américaines des XVIIe et XVIIIe Siècles*
BSJ	*Baker Street Journal: An Irregular Quarterly of Sherlockiana*
BSLP	*Bulletin de la Société de Linguistique de Paris*
BSNotes	*Browning Society Notes*
BSRS	*Bulletin of the Society for Renaissance Studies*
BSSA	*Bulletin de la Société de Stylistique Anglaise*
BST	*Brontë Society Transactions*
BSUF	*Ball State University Forum*

BTHGNewsl	*Book Trade History Group Newsletter*
BTLV	*Bijdragen tot de Taal-, Land- en Volkenhunde*
Bul	*Bulletin (Australia)*
Bullán	*Bullán*
BunyanS	*Bunyan Studies*
BuR	*Bucknell Review*
BurlM	*Burlington Magazine*
BurnsC	*Burns Chronicle*
BWPLL	*Belfast Working Papers in Language and Linguistics*
BWVACET	*Bulletin of the West Virginia Association of College English Teachers*
ByronJ	*Byron Journal*
CABS	*Contemporary Authors Bibliographical Series*
CahiersE	*Cahiers Élisabéthains*
CAIEF	*Cahiers de l'Association Internationale des Études Françaises*
Caliban	*Caliban* (Toulouse, France)
Callaloo	*Callaloo*
CalR	*Calcutta Review*
CamObsc	*Camera Obscura: A Journal of Feminism and Film Theory*
CamR	*Cambridge Review*
CanD	*Canadian Drama/L'Art Dramatique Canadienne*
C&L	*Christianity and Literature*
C&Lang	*Communication and Languages*
C&M	*Classica et Medievalia*
CanL	*Canadian Literature*
CAnn	*Carlyle Annual*
CanPo	*Canadian Poetry*
CapR	*Capilano Review*
CARA	*Centre Aixois de Recherches Anglaises*
Carib	*Carib*
Caribana	*Caribana*
CaribW	*Caribbean Writer*
CarR	*Caribbean Review*
Carrell	*Carrell: Journal of the Friends of the University of Miami Library*
CASE	*Cambridge Studies in Anglo-Saxon England*
CathHR	*Catholic Historical Review*
CatR	*Catalan Review*
CaudaP	*Cauda Pavonis*
CBAA	*Current Bibliography on African Affairs*
CBEL	*Cambridge Bibliography of English Literature*
CCL	*Canadian Children's Literature*
CCor	*Cardiff Corvey: Reading the Romantic Text*
CCRev	*Comparative Civilizations Review*
CCS	*Comparative Critical Studies*
CCrit	*Comparative Criticism: An Annual Journal*
CCTES	*Conference of College Teachers of English Studies*
CCV	*Centro de Cultura Valenciana*
CDALB	*Concise Dictionary of American Literary Biography*
CDCP	*Comparative Drama Conference Papers*
CDIL	*Cahiers de l'Institut de Linguistique de Louvain*
CdL	*Cahiers de Lexicologie*
CDS	*Critical Discourse Studies*

CE	College English
CEA	CEA Critic
CEAfr	Cahiers d'Études Africaines
CE&S	Commonwealth Essays and Studies
CentR	Centennial Review
Cervantes	Cervantes
CF	Crime Factory
CFM	Canadian Fiction Magazine
CFS	Cahiers Ferdinand de Saussure: Revue de Linguistique Générale
CH	Computers and the Humanities
Chapman	Chapman
Chasqui	Chasqui
ChauR	Chaucer Review
ChauS	Chaucer Studion
ChauY	Chaucer Yearbook
ChE	Changing English
ChH	Church History
ChildL	Children's Literature: Journal of Children's Literature Studies
ChiR	Chicago Review
ChLB	Charles Lamb Bulletin
CHLSSF	Commentationes Humanarum Litterarum Societatis Scientiarum Fennicae
CHR	Camden History Review
ChRC	Church History and Religious Culture
CHum	Computers and the Humanities
CI	Critical Idiom
CILT	Amsterdam Studies in the Theory and History of the Language Sciences IV: Current Issues in Linguistic Theory
Cinéaste	Cinéaste
CinJ	Cinema Journal
CIQ	Colby Quarterly
CISh	Contemporary Interpretations of Shakespeare
Cithara	Cithara: Essays in the Judaeo Christian Tradition
CJ	Classical Journal
CJE	Cambridge Journal of Education
CJH	Canadian Journal of History
CJIS	Canadian Journal of Irish Studies
CJL	Canadian Journal of Linguistics
CJR	Christian–Jewish Relations
CK	Common Knowledge
CL	Comparative Literature (Eugene, OR)
CLAJ	CLA Journal
CLAQ	Children's Literature Association Quarterly
ClarkN	Clark Newsletter: Bulletin of the UCLA Center for Seventeenth- and Eighteenth-Century Studies
ClassW	Classical World
CLC	Columbia Library Columns
CLE	Children's Literature in Education
CLet	Confronto Letterario
CLIN	Cuadernos de Literatura
ClioI	Clio: A Journal of Literature, History and the Philosophy of History
CLQ	Colby Library Quarterly

CLS	Comparative Literature Studies
Clues	Clues: A Journal of Detection
CMCS	Cambridge Medieval Celtic Studies
CML	Classical and Modern Literature
CN	Chaucer Newsletter
CNIE	Commonwealth Novel in English
CogLing	Cognitive Linguistics
Cognition	Cognition
Cog&Em	Cognition and Emotion
ColB	Coleridge Bulletin
ColF	Columbia Forum
Collections	Collections
CollG	Colloquia Germanica
CollL	College Literature
Colloquy	Colloquy: Text Theory Critique
Com	Commonwealth
Comitatus	Comitatus: A Journal of Medieval and Renaissance Studies
Commentary	Commentary
Comparatist	Comparatist: Journal of the Southern Comparative Literature Association
ComparativeCS	Comparative Critical Studies
CompD	Comparative Drama
CompLing	Contemporary Linguistics
ConcordSaunterer	Concord Saunterer: Annual Journal of the Thoreau Society
Configurations	Official Journal of the Society for Literature, Science and the Arts
ConfLett	Confronto Letterario
ConL	Contemporary Literature
Connotations	Connotations
ConnR	Connecticut Review
Conradian	Conradian
Conradiana	Conradiana: A Journal of Joseph Conrad Studies
ContempR	Contemporary Review
ConTR	Contemporary Theatre Review
Coppertales	Coppertales: A Journal of Rural Arts
Cosmos	Cosmos
Costume	Journal of the Costume Society
CP	Concerning Poetry
CQ	Cambridge Quarterly
CR	Critical Review
CRCL	Canadian Review of Comparative Literature
CRev	Chesterton Review
CRevAS	Canadian Review of American Studies
Crit	Critique: Studies in Modern Fiction
CritI	Critical Inquiry
Criticism	Criticism: A Quarterly for Literature and the Arts
Critique	Critique (Paris)
CritQ	Critical Quarterly
CritT	Critical Texts: A Review of Theory and Criticism
CrM	Critical Mass
CRNLE	CRNLE Reviews Journal
Crossings	Crossings
CRUX	CRUX: A Journal on the Teaching of English
CS	Critical Survey

CSASE	*Cambridge Studies in Anglo-Saxon England*
CSCC	*Case Studies in Contemporary Criticism*
CSELT	*Cambridge Studies in Eighteenth-Century Literature and Thought*
CSLBull	*Bulletin of the New York C.S. Lewis Society*
CSLL	*Cardozo Studies in Law and Literature*
	Critical Studies in Media Communication
CSML	*Cambridge Studies in Medieval Literature*
CSNCLC	*Cambridge Studies in Nineteenth-Century Literature and Culture*
CSPC	*Cambridge Studies in Paleography and Codicology*
CSR	*Cambridge Studies in Romanticism*
CSRev	*Christian Scholar's Review*
CStA	*Carlyle Studies Annual* (previously CAnn)
CTC	
CTR	*Canadian Theatre Review*
Cuadernos	*Cuadernos de Literatura Infantil y Juvenil*
CulC	*Cultural Critique*
CulS	*Cultural Studies*
CulSR	*Cultural Studies Review*
CUNY	*CUNY English Forum*
CultGeo	*Cultural Geographies*
Current Writing	*Current Writing: Text and Reception in Southern Africa*
CV2	*Contemporary Verse 2*
CVE	*Cahiers Victoriens et Edouardiens*
CW	*Current Writing: Text and Perception in Southern Africa*
CWAAS	*Transactions of the Cumberland and Westmorland Antiquarian and Archaeological Society*
CWS	*Canadian Woman Studies*
Cycnos	
DA	*Dictionary of Americanisms*
DAE	*Dictionary of American English*
DAEM	*Deutsches Archiv für Erforschung des Mittelalters*
DAI	*Dissertation Abstracts International*
DAL	*Descriptive and Applied Linguistics*
D&CN&Q	*Devon and Cornwall Notes and Queries*
D&S	*Discourse and Society*
Daphnis	*Daphnis: Zeitschrift für Mittlere Deutsche Literatur*
DC	*Dickens Companions*
DerbyM	*Derbyshire Miscellany*
Descant	*Descant*
DFS	*Dalhousie French Studies*
DHLR	*D.H. Lawrence Review*
DHS	*Dix-huitième Siècle*
Diac	*Diacritics*
Diachronica	*Diachronica*
Dialogue	*Dialogue: Canadian Philosophical Review*
Dickensian	*Dickensian*
DicS	*Dickinson Studies*
Dictionaries	*Dictionaries: Journal of the Dictionary Society of North America*
Dionysos	*Dionysos*
Discourse	*Discourse*
DisS	*Discourse Studies*

DLB	*Dictionary of Literary Biography*
DLN	*Doris Lessing Newsletter*
DM	*Dublin Magazine*
DMT	*Durham Medieval Texts*
DNB	*Dictionary of National Biography*
DOE	*Dictionary of Old English*
Dolphin	*Dolphin: Publications of the English Department* (University of Aarhus)
DOST	*Dictionary of the Older Scottish Tongue*
DownR	*Downside Review*
DPr	*Discourse Processes*
DQ	*Denver Quarterly*
DQR	*Dutch Quarterly Review of Anglo-American Letters*
DQu	*Dickens Quarterly*
DR	*Dalhousie Review*
Drama	*Drama: The Quarterly Theatre Review*
DrS	*Dreiser Studies*
DS	*Deep South*
DSA	*Dickens Studies Annual*
DSNA	*DSNA Newsletter*
DubJJJ	*Dublin James Joyce Journal*
DU	*Der Deutschunterricht: Beiträge zu Seiner Praxis und Wissenschaftlichen Grundlegung*
DUJ	*Durham University Journal*
DVLG	*Deutsche Vierteljahrsschrift für Literaturwissenschaft und Geistesgeschichte*
DWPELL	*Dutch Working Papers in English Language and Linguistics*
EA	*Études Anglaises*
EAL	*Early American Literature*
E&D	*Enlightenment and Dissent*
E&S	*Essays and Studies*
E&Soc	*Economy and Society*
EarT	*Early Theatre*
EAS	*Early American Studies*
EASt	*Englisch Amerikanische Studien*
EBST	*Edinburgh Bibliographical Society Transactions*
EC	*Études Celtiques*
ECan	*Études Canadiennes/Canadian Studies*
ECCB	*Eighteenth Century: A Current Bibliography*
ECent	*Eighteenth Century: Theory and Interpretation*
ECF	*Eighteenth-Century Fiction*
ECI	*Eighteenth-Century Ireland*
ECIntell	*East-Central Intelligencer*
ECLife	*Eighteenth-Century Life*
ECN	*Eighteenth-Century Novel*
ECon	*L'Époque Conradienne*
ECr	*L'Esprit Créateur*
ECS	*Eighteenth-Century Studies*
ECSTC	*Eighteenth-Century Short Title Catalogue*
ECW	*Essays on Canadian Writing*
ECWomen	*Eighteenth-Century Women: Studies in their Lives, Work, and Culture*
EDAMN	*EDAM Newsletter*

EDAMR	*Early Drama, Art, and Music Review*
EDH	*Essays by Divers Hands*
EdL	*Études de Lettres*
EdN	*Editors' Notes: Bulletin of the Conference of Editors*
	of Learned Journals
EDSL	*Encyclopedic Dictionary of the Sciences of Language*
EEMF	*Early English Manuscripts in Facsimile*
EF	*Études Francaises*
EHL	*English Historical Linguistics*
EHR	*English Historical Review*
EI	*Études Irlandaises* (Lille)
EIC	*Essays in Criticism*
EinA	*English in Africa*
EiP	*Essays in Poetics*
EIRC	*Explorations in Renaissance Culture*
Éire	*Éire-Ireland*
EiTET	*Essays in Theatre/Études Théâtrales*
EIUC	
EJ	*English Journal*
EJES	*European Journal of English Studies*
EL	*Études lawrenciennes*
ELangT	*ELT Journal: An International Journal for Teachers of English*
	to Speakers of Other Languages
ELet	*Esperienze Letterarie: Rivista Trimestrale di Critica e Cultura*
ELH	*English Literary History*
ELing	*English Linguistics*
ELL	*English Language and Linguistics*
ELN	*English Language Notes*
ELR	*English Literary Renaissance*
ELS	*English Literary Studies*
ELT	*English Literature in Transition*
ELWIU	*Essays in Literature* (Western Illinois University)
EM	*English Miscellany*
Embl	*Emblematica: An Interdisciplinary Journal of English Studies*
EMD	*European Medieval Drama*
EME	*Early Modern Europe*
EMedE	*Early Medieval Europe* (online)
EMLS	*Early Modern Literary Studies* (online)
EMMS	*Early Modern Manuscript Studies*
EMS	*English Manuscript Studies, 1100–1700*
EMu	*Early Music*
EMW	*Early Modern Englishwomen*
Encult	*Enculturation: Cultural Theories and Rhetorics*
Encyclia	*Encyclia*
English	*English: The Journal of the English Association*
EnT	*English Today: The International Review of*
	the English Language
EONR	*Eugene O'Neill Review*
EPD	*English Pronouncing Dictionary*
ER	*English Review*
ERLM	*Europe-Revue Littéraire Mensuelle*
ERR	*European Romantic Review*
ES	*English Studies*

ESA	*English Studies in Africa*
ESC	*English Studies in Canada*
ESQ	*ESQ: A Journal of the American Renaissance*
ESRS	*Emporia State Research Studies*
EssaysMedSt	*Essays in Medieval Studies*
EST	*Eureka Street*
Estudios Ingleses	*Estudios Ingleses de la Universidad Complutense*
ET	*Elizabethan Theatre*
Etropic	*Etropic*
EurekaStudies	*Eureka Studies*
EuroS	*European Studies: A Journal of European Culture, History and Politics*
EWhR	*Edith Wharton Review*
EWIP	*Edinburgh University, Department of Linguistics, Work in Progress*
EWN	*Evelyn Waugh Newsletter*
EWPAL	*Edinburgh Working Papers in Applied Linguistics*
EWW	*English World-Wide*
Excavatio	*Excavatio*
Exemplaria	*Exemplaria*
Exit	
Expl	*Explicator*
Extrapolation	*Extrapolation: A Journal Science Fiction and Fantasy*
FC	*Feminist Collections: A Quarterly of Women's Studies Resources*
FCEMN	*Mystics Quarterly* (formerly *Fourteenth-Century English Mystics Newsletter*)
FCS	*Fifteenth-Century Studies*
FDT	*Fountainwell Drama Texts*
FemR	*Feminist Review*
FemSEL	*Feminist Studies in English Literature*
FemT	*Feminist Theory*
FFW	*Food and Foodways*
FH	*Die Neue Gesellschaft/Frankfurter Hefte*
Fiction International	*Fiction International*
FilmJ	*Film Journal*
FilmQ	*Film Quarterly*
FilmS	*Film Studies*
Fiveb	*Fivebells*
FiveP	*Five Points: A Journal of Literature and Art* (Atlanta, GA)
FJS	*Fu Jen Studies: Literature and Linguistics* (Taipei)
FLH	*Folia Linguistica Historica*
Florilegium	*Florilegium: Carleton University Annual Papers on Classical Antiquity and the Middle Ages*
FLS	*Foreign Literature Studies* (Central China Normal University, Wuhan, People's Republic of China)
FMLS	*Forum for Modern Language Studies*
FNS	*Frank Norris Studies*
Folklore	*Folklore*
FoLi	*Folia Linguistica*
Forum	*Forum*
FranS	*Franciscan Studies*
FreeA	*Free Associations*
FrontenacR	*Revue Frontenac*

Frontiers	*Frontiers: A Journal of Women's Studies*
FS	*French Studies*
FSt	*Feminist Studies*
FT	*Fashion Theory*
FuL	*Functions of Language*
Futures	*Futures*
GAG	*Göppinger Arbeiten zur Germanistik*
GaR	*Georgia Review*
GBB	*George Borrow Bulletin*
GBK	*Gengo Bunka Kenkyu: Studies in Language and Culture*
GEGHLS	*George Eliot–George Henry Lewes Studies*
GeM	*Genealogists Magazine*
Genders	*Genders*
Genre	*Genre*
GER	*George Eliot Review*
Gestus	*Gestus: A Quarterly Journal of Brechtian Studies*
Gettysburg Review	*Gettysburg Review*
GG@G	*Generative Grammar in Geneva* (online)
GHJ	*George Herbert Journal*
GissingJ	*Gissing Journal*
GJ	*Gutenberg-Jahrbuch*
GL	*General Linguistics*
GL&L	*German Life and Letters*
GlasR	*Glasgow Review*
Glossa	*Glossa: An International Journal of Linguistics*
GLQ	*A Journal of Lesbian and Gay Studies* (Duke University)
GLS	*Grazer Linguistische Studien*
GPQ	*Great Plains Quarterly*
GR	*Germanic Review*
Gramma	*Gramma: Journal of Theory and Criticism*
Gramma/TTT	*Tijdschrift voor Taalwetenschap*
GrandS	*Grand Street*
Granta	*Granta*
Greyfriar	*Greyfriar Siena Studies in Literature*
GRM	*Germanisch-Romanische Monatsschrift*
Grove	*The Grove: Working Papers on English Studies*
GSE	*Gothenberg Studies in English*
GSJ	*Gaskell Society Journal*
GSN	*Gaskell Society Newsletter*
GURT	*Georgetown University Round Table on Language and Linguistics*
HamS	*Hamlet Studies*
H&T	*History and Theory*
HardyR	*Hardy Review*
Harvard Law Review	*Harvard Law Review*
Haskins Soc Jnl	*Haskins Society Journal*
HatcherR	*Hatcher Review*
HazlittR	*The Hazlitt Review*
HBS	*Henry Bradshaw Society*
HC	*Hollins Critic*
HCM	*Hitting Critical Mass: A Journal of Asian American Cultural Criticism*
HE	*History of Education*

HEAT	*HEAT*
Hecate	*Hecate: An Interdisciplinary Journal of Women's Liberation*
HEdQ	*History of Education Quarterly*
HEI	*History of European Ideas*
HeineJ	*Heine Jahrbuch*
HEL	*Histoire Épistémologie Language*
Helios	*Helios*
HEng	*History of the English Language*
Hermathena	*Hermathena: A Trinity College Dublin Review*
HeroicA	*Heroic Age: A Journal of Early Medieval Northwestern Europe*
HeyJ	*Heythrop Journal*
HFR	*Hayden Ferry Review*
HistJ	*Historical Journal*
History	*History: The Journal of the Historical Association*
HistR	*Historical Research*
HJEAS	*Hungarian Journal of English and American Studies*
HJR	*Henry James Review* (Baton Rouge, LA)
HL	*Historiographia Linguistica*
HLB	*Harvard Library Bulletin*
HLQ	*Huntingdon Library Quarterly*
HLSL	(online)
HNCIS	*Harvester New Critical Introductions to Shakespeare*
HNR	*Harvester New Readings*
HOPE	*History of Political Economy*
HopRev	*Hopkins Review*
HPT	*History of Political Thought*
HQ	*Hopkins Quarterly*
HR	*Harvard Review*
HRB	*Hopkins Research Bulletin*
HSci	*History of Science*
HSE	*Hungarian Studies in English*
HSELL	*Hiroshima Studies in English Language and Literature*
HSJ	*Housman Society Journal*
HSL	*University of Hartford Studies in Literature*
HSN	*Hawthorne Society Newsletter*
HSSh	*Hunganan Studies in Shakespeare*
HSSN	*Henry Sweet Society Newsletter*
HT	*History Today*
HTR	*Harvard Theological Review*
HudR	*Hudson Review*
HumeS	*Hume Studies*
HumLov	*Humanistica Lovaniensia: Journal of Neo-Latin Studies*
Humor	*Humor: International Journal of Humor Research*
HUSL	*Hebrew University Studies in Literature and the Arts*
HWJ	*History Workshop*
HWS	*History Workshop Series*
Hypatia	*Hypatia*
IAL	*Issues in Applied Linguistics*
IAN	*Izvestiia Akademii Nauk SSSR* (Moscow)
I&C	*Ideology and Consciousness*
I&P	*Ideas and Production*
ICAME	*International Computer Archive of Modern and Medieval English*
ICS	*Illinois Classical Studies*

IEEETrans	*IEEE Transactions on Professional Communications*
IF	*Indogermanische Forschungen*
IFR	*International Fiction Review*
IGK	*Irland: Gesellschaft and Kultur*
IJAES	*International Journal of Arabic-English Studies*
IJAL	*International Journal of Applied Linguistics*
IJB	*International Journal of Bilingualism*
IJBEB	*International Journal of Bilingual Education & Bilingualism*
IJCL	*International Journal of Corpus Linguistics*
IJCT	*International Journal of the Classical Tradition*
IJECS	*Indian Journal for Eighteenth-Century Studies*
IJES	*Indian Journal of English Studies*
IJL	*International Journal of Lexicography*
IJPR	*International Journal for Philosophy of Religion*
IJSL	*International Journal of the Sociology of Language*
IJSS	*Indian Journal of Shakespeare Studies*
IJWS	*International Journal of Women's Studies*
ILR	*Indian Literary Review*
ILS	*Irish Literary Supplement*
ILStud	*Interdisciplinary Literary Studies: A Journal of Criticism and Theory*
Imaginaires	*Imaginaires*
Imago	*Imago: New Writing*
IMB	*International Medieval Bibliography*
Imprimatur	*Imprimatur*
Indexer	*Indexer*
IndH	*Indian Horizons*
IndL	*Indian Literature*
InG	*In Geardagum: Essays on Old and Middle English Language and Literature*
Inklings	*Inklings: Jahrbuch für Literatur and Ästhetik*
Ioc	*Index to Censorship*
Inquiry	*Inquiry: An Interdisciplinary Journal of Philosophy*
Interactions	*Interactions: Aegean Journal of English and American Studies*
InteractionsAJ	*Interactions: Aegean Journal of English and American Studies/ Ege Ingiliz ve Amerikan Incelemeleri Dergisi*
Interlink	*Interlink*
Interpretation	*Interpretation*
Intertexts	*Intertexts*
Interventions	*Interventions: The International Journal of Postcolonial Studies*
IowaR	*Iowa Review*
IRAL	*IRAL: International Review of Applied Linguistics in Language Teaching*
Iris	*Iris: A Journal of Theory on Image and Sound*
IS	*Italian Studies*
ISh	*Independent Shavian*
ISJR	*Iowa State Journal of Research*
Island	*Island Magazine*
Islands	*Islands*
Isle	*Interdisciplinary Studies in Literature and Environment*
ISR	*Irish Studies Review*
IUR	*Irish University Review: A Journal of Irish Studies*
JAAC	*Journal of Aesthetics and Art Criticism*

JAAR	*Journal of the American Academy of Religion*
Jacket	*Jacket*
JADT	*Journal of American Drama and Theatre*
JAF	*Journal of American Folklore*
JafM	*Journal of African Marxists*
JAIS	*Journal of Anglo-Italian Studies*
JAL	*Journal of Australian Literature*
JamC	*Journal of American Culture*
JAmH	*Journal of American History*
JAmS	*Journal of American Studies*
JAP	*Journal of Analytical Psychology*
JAPC	*Journal of Asian Pacific Communication*
JArabL	*Journal of Arabic Literature*
JAS	*Journal of Australian Studies*
JASAL	*Journal of the Association for the Study of Australian Literature*
JAStT	*Journal of American Studies of Turkey*
JBeckS	*Journal of Beckett Studies*
JBS	*Journal of British Studies*
JBSSJ	*Journal of the Blake Society at St James*
JCAKSU	*Journal of the College of Arts* (King Saud University)
JCanL	*Journal of Canadian Literature*
JCC	*Journal of Canadian Culture*
JCERL	*Journal of Classic and English Renaissance Literature*
JCF	*Journal of Canadian Fiction*
JCGL	*Journal of Comparative Germanic Linguistics*
JChL	*Journal of Child Language*
JChLS	*Journal of Children's Literature Studies*
JCL	*Journal of Commonwealth Literature*
JCP	*Journal of Canadian Poetry*
JCPCS	*Journal of Commonwealth and Postcolonial Studies*
JCSJ	*John Clare Society Journal*
JCSR	*Journal of Canadian Studies/Revue d'Études Canadiennes*
JCSt	*Journal of Caribbean Studies*
JDECU	*Journal of the Department of English* (Calcutta University)
JDHLS	*Journal of D.H. Lawrence Studies* (formerly *The Journal of the D.H. Lawrence Society*)
JDJ	*John Dunne Journal*
JDN	*James Dickey Newsletter*
JDTC	*Journal of Dramatic Theory and Criticism*
JEBS	*Journal of the Early Book Society*
JECS	*Journal of Eighteenth-Century British Studies (formerly British Journal …[BJECS])*
JEDRBU	*Journal of the English Department* (Rabindra Bharati University)
JEEBS	
JEGP	*Journal of English and Germanic Philology*
JEH	*Journal of Ecclesiastical History*
JELL	*Journal of English Language and Literature*
JEMCS	*Journal of Early Modern Cultural Studies*
JEn	*Journal of English* (Sana'a University)
JEngL	*Journal of English Linguistics*
JENS	*Journal of the Eighteen Nineties Society*
JEP	*Journal of Evolutionary Psychology*

JEPNS	*Journal of the English Place-Name Society*
JES	*Journal of European Studies*
JETS	*Journal of the Evangelical Theological Society*
JFR	*Journal of Folklore Research*
JGE	*Journal of General Education*
JGenS	*Journal of Gender Studies*
JGH	*Journal of Garden History*
JGL	*Journal of Germanic Linguistics*
JGN	*John Gower Newsletter*
JH	*Journal of Homosexuality*
JHI	*Journal of the History of Ideas*
JHLP	*Journal of Historical Linguistics and Philology*
JHP	*Journal of the History of Philosophy*
JHPrag	*Journal of Historical Pragmatics*
JHSex	*Journal of the History of Sexuality*
JHu	*Journal of Humanities*
JHuP	*Journal of Humanistic Psychology*
JIEP	*Journal of Indo-European Perspectives*
JIES	*Journal of Indo-European Studies*
JIL	*Journal of Irish Literature*
JIPA	*Journal of the International Phonetic Association*
JIWE	*Journal of Indian Writing in English*
JJ	*Jamaica Journal*
JJA	*James Joyce Annual*
JJB	*James Joyce Broadsheet*
JJLS	*James Joyce Literary Supplement*
JJQ	*James Joyce Quarterly*
JKS	*Journal of Kentucky Studies*
JL	*Journal of Linguistics*
JLC THEMA	*Journal of Language and Contact*
JLH	*Journal of Library History, Philosophy and Comparative Librarianship*
JLLI	*Journal of Logic, Language and Information*
JLP	*Journal of Linguistics and Politics*
JLS	*Journal of Literary Semanitcs*
JLSP	*Journal of Language and Social Psychology*
JLVSG	*Journal of the Longborough Victorian Studies Group*
JmedL	
JMemL	*Journal of Memory and Language*
JMEMS	*Journal of Medieval and Early Modem Studies*
JMGS	*Journal of Modern Greek Studies*
JMH	*Journal of Medieval History*
JMJS	*Journal of Modern Jewish Studies*
JML	*Journal of Modern Literature*
JMMD	*Journal of Multilingual and Multicultural Development*
JMMLA	*Journal of the Midwest Modern Language Association*
JModH	*Journal of Modern History*
JMRS	*Journal of Medieval and Renaissance Studies*
JMS	*Journal of Men's Studies*
JNLH	*Journal of Narrative and Life History*
JNPH	*Journal of Newspaper and Periodical History*
JNT	*Journal of Narrative Theory* (formerly *Technique*)
JNZL	*Journal of New Zealand Literature*

JNZS	Journal of New Zealand Studies
Jouvert	Jouvert: A Journal of Postcolonial Studies
JoyceSA	Joyce Studies Annual
JP	Journal of Philosophy
JPC	Journal of Popular Culture
JPCL	Journal of Pidgin and Creole Languages
JPhon	Journal of Phonetics
JPJ	Journal of Psychology and Judaism
JPolR	Journal of Politeness Research: Language, Behavior, and Culture
JPrag	Journal of Pragmatics
JPRAS	Journal of Pre-Raphaelite and Aesthetic Studies
JPsyR	Journal of Psycholinguistic Research
Jpub	
JPW	Journal of Postcolonial Writing
JQ	Journalism Quarterly
JR	Journal of Religion
JRAHS	Journal of the Royal Australian Historical Society
JRH	Journal of Religious History
JRMA	Journal of the Royal Musical Association
JRMMRA	Journal of the Rocky Mountain Medieval and Renaissance Association
JRSA	Journal of the Royal Society of Arts
JRT	Journal of Religion and Theatre
JRUL	Journal of the Rutgers University Libraries
JSA	Journal of the Society of Archivists
JSaga	Journal of the Faculty of Liberal Arts and Science (Saga University)
JSAS	Journal of Southern African Studies
JScholP	Journal of Scholarly Publishing
JSem	Journal of Semantics
JSoc	Journal of Sociolinguistics
JSP	Journal of Scottish Philosophy
JSPNS	
JSSE	Journal of the Short Story in English
JSTWS	Journal of the Sylvia Townsend Warner Society
JTheoS	Journal of Theological Studies
JVC	Journal of Victorian Culture
JWCI	Journal of the Warburg and Courtauld Institutes
JWH	Journal of Women's History
JWIL	Journal of West Indian Literature
JWMS	Journal of the William Morris Society
JWSL	Journal of Women's Studies in Literature
KanE	Kansas English
Ka Mate Ka Ora	Ka Mate Ka Ora: A New Zealand Journal of Poetry and Poetics
KanQ	Kansas Quarterly
KB	Kavya Bharati
KCLMS	King's College London Medieval Series
KCS	Kobe College Studies (Japan)
KDNews	Kernerman Dictionary News
KJ	Kipling Journal
KN	Kwartalnik Neoflologiczny (Warsaw)
KompH	Komparatistische Hefte
Kotare	Kotare: New Zealand Notes and Queries

KPR	*Kentucky Philological Review*
KR	*Kenyon Review*
KSJ	*Keats-Shelley Journal*
KSMB	
KSR	*Keats-Shelley Review*
Kuka	*Kuka: Journal of Creative and Critical Writing* (Zaria, Nigeria)
Kunapipi	*Kunapipi*
KWS	*Key-Word Studies in Chaucer*
L&A	*Literature and Aesthetics*
L&B	*Literature and Belief*
L&C	*Language and Communication*
L&E	*Linguistics and Education: An International Research Journal*
Landfall	*Landfall: A New Zealand Quarterly*
L&H	*Literature and History*
L&L	*Language and Literature*
L&LC	*Literary and Linguistic Computing*
L&M	*Literature and Medicine*
L&P	*Literature and Psychology*
L&S	*Language and Speech*
L&T	*Literature and Theology: An Interdisciplinary Journal of Theory and Criticism*
L&U	*Lion and the Unicorn: A Critical Journal of Children's Literature*
Lang&S	*Language and Style*
LangF	*Language Forum*
LangQ	*USF Language Quarterly*
LangR	*Language Research*
LangS	*Language Sciences*
Language	*Language* (Linguistic Society of America)
LanM	*Les Langues Modernes*
La Revue LISA	*La Revue LISA*
LATR	*Latin American Theatre Review*
LaTrobe	*La Trobe Journal*
LawL	*Law and Literature*
LawLi	*Law and the Literary Imagination*
LB	*Leuvense Bijdragen*
LBR	*Luso-Brazilian Review*
LCrit	*Literary Criterion* (Mysore, India)
LCUT	*Library Chronicle* (University of Texas at Austin)
LDOCE	*Longman Dictionary of Contemporary English*
LeedsSE	*Leeds Studies in English*
LeF	*Linguistica e Filologia*
Legacy	*Legacy: A Journal of Nineteenth-Century American Women Writers*
Le Journal	*Le Journal*
Lemuria	*Lemuria: A Half-Yearly Research Journal of Indo-Australian Studies*
L'EpC	*L'Epoque Conradienne*
LeS	*Lingua e Stile*
Lexicographica	*Lexicographica: International Annual for Lexicography*
Lexicography	*Lexicography*
LFQ	*Literature/Film Quarterly*
LH	*Library History*
LHY	*Literary Half-Yearly*

LI	*Studies in the Literary Imagination*
Library	*Library*
Library Review	*Library Review*
LibrQ	*Library Quarterly*
LIN	*Linguistics in the Netherlands*
LingA	*Linguistic Analysis*
Ling&P	*Linguistics and Philosophy*
Ling&Philol	*Linguistics and Philology*
LingB	*Linguistische Berichte*
LingI	*Linguistic Inquiry*
LingInv	*Linvisticæ Investigationes*
LingP	*Linguistica Pragensia*
LingRev	*Linguistic Review*
Lingua	*Lingua: International Review of General Linguistics*
Linguistics	*Linguistics*
LinguisticT	
Linguistique	*La Linguistique*
LiNQ	*Literature in Northern Queensland*
LiRevALSC	*Literary Imagination: The Review of the Association of Literary Scholars and Critics*
LIT	*LIT: Literature, Interpretation, Theory*
LitComp	*Literature Compass*
LiteratureC	*Literature Compass*
LitH	*Literary Horizons*
LitI	*Literary Imagination: The Review of the Association of Literary Scholars and Critics*
LitR	*Literary Review: An International Journal of Contemporary Writing*
LittPrag	*Litteraria Pragensia: Studies in Literature and Culture*
LJCS	*London Journal of Canadian Studies*
LJGG	*Literaturwissenschaftliches Jahrbuch im Aufrage der Görres-Gesellschaft*
LJHum	*Lamar Journal of the Humanities*
LMag	*London Magazine*
LockeN	*Locke Newsletter*
LocusF	*Locus Focus*
Logos	*Logos: A Journal of Catholic Thought and Culture*
LongR	*Long Room: Bulletin of the Friends of the Library* (Trinity College, Dublin)
Lore&L	*Lore and Language*
LP	*Lingua Posnaniensis*
LPLD	*Liverpool Papers in Language and Discourse*
LPLP	*Language Problems and Language Planning*
LR	*Les Lettres Romanes*
LRB	*London Review of Books*
LSE	*Lund Studies in English*
LSLD	*Liverpool Studies in Language and Discourse*
LSoc	*Language in Society*
LSp	*Language and Speech*
LST	*Longman Study Texts*
LTM	*Leeds Texts and Monographs*
LTP	*LTP: Journal of Literature Teaching Politics*
LTR	*London Theatre Record*

LuK	*Literatur und Kritik*
LVC	*Language Variation and Change*
LW	*Life Writing*
LWU	*Literatur in Wissenschaft und Unterricht*
M&Lang	*Mind and Language*
MÆ	*Medium Ævum*
MAEL	*Macmillan Anthologies of English Literature*
MaComere	*MaComère: Journal of the Association of Caribbean Women Writers and Scholars*
Magistra	*Magistra: A Women's Spirituality in History*
MagL	*Magazine Littéraire*
Mana	*Mana*
MAS	*Modern Asian Studies*
M&H	*Medievalia et Humanistica*
M&L	*Music and Letters*
M&N	*Man and Nature/L'Homme et la Nature: Proceedings of the Canadian Society for Eighteenth-Century Studies*
M&Sym	*Metaphor and Symbol*
M&T	
Manuscripta	*Manuscripta*
MAR	*Mid-American Review*
Margin	*Margin: Life and Letters in Early Australia*
MarkhamR	*Markham Review*
Matatu	*Matatu*
Matrix	*Matrix*
MBL	*Modern British Literature*
MC&S	*Media, Culture and Society*
MCI	*Modern Critical Interpretations*
MCJNews	*Milton Centre of Japan News*
McNR	*McNeese Review*
MCRel	*Mythes, Croyances et Religions dans le Monde Anglo-Saxon*
MCV	*Modern Critical Views*
MD	*Modern Drama*
ME	*Medieval Encounters*
Meanjin	*Meanjin*
MED	*Middle English Dictionary*
MedFor	*Medieval Forum* (online)
MedHis	*Media History*
Mediaevalia	*Mediaevalia: A Journal of Mediaeval Studies*
MedPers	*Medieval Perspectives*
MELUS	*MELUS: The Journal of the Society of Multi-Ethnic Literature of the United States*
Meridian	*Meridian*
MES	*Medieval and Early Modern English Studies*
MESN	*Mediaeval English Studies Newsletter*
MET	*Middle English Texts*
Met&Sym	
METh	*Medieval English Theatre*
MFF	*Medieval Feminist Forum* (formerly *Medieval Feminist Newsletter*)
MFN	*Medieval Feminist Newsletter* (now *Medieval Feminist Forum*)
MFS	*Modern Fiction Studies*
MH	*Malahat Review*

MHL	*Macmillan History of Literature*
MHLS	*Mid-Hudson Language Studies*
MichA	*Michigan Academician*
MiltonQ	*Milton Quarterly*
MiltonS	*Milton Studies*
MinnR	*Minnesota Review*
MissQ	*Mississippi Quarterly*
MissR	*Missouri Review*
Mittelalter	*Das Mittelalter: Perspektiven Mediavistischer Forschung*
MJLF	*Midwestern Journal of Language and Folklore*
ML	*Music and Letters*
MLAIB	*Modern Language Association International Bibliography*
MLing	*Modelès Linguistiques*
MLJ	*Modern Language Journal*
MLN	*Modern Language Notes*
MLQ	*Modern Language Quarterly*
MLR	*Modern Language Review*
MLRev	*Malcolm Lowry Review*
MLS	*Modern Language Studies*
M/M	*Modernism/Modernity*
MMD	*Macmillan Modern Dramatists*
MMG	*Macmillan Master Guides*
MMisc	*Midwestern Miscellany*
MOCS	*Magazine of Cultural Studies*
ModA	*Modern Age: A Quarterly Review*
ModCult	*Modernist Cultures*
ModET	*Modern English Teacher*
ModM	*Modern Masters*
ModSp	*Moderne Sprachen*
Mo/Mo	*Modernism/Modernity*
Monist	*Monist*
MonSP	*Monash Swift Papers*
Month	*Month: A Review of Christian Thought and World Affairs*
MOR	*Mount Olive Review*
Moreana	*Moreana: Bulletin Thomas More* (Angers, France)
Mosaic	*Mosaic: A Journal for the Interdisciplinary Study of Literature*
Moving Worlds	*Moving Worlds*
MoyA	*Moyen Age*
MP	*Modern Philology*
MPHJ	*Middlesex Polytechnic History Journal*
MPR	*Mervyn Peake Review*
MPsych	*Media Psychology*
MQ	*Midwest Quarterly*
MQR	*Michigan Quarterly Review*
MR	*Massachusetts Review*
MRDE	*Medieval and Renaissance Drama in England*
MRTS	*Medieval and Renaissance Texts and Studies*
MS	*Mediaeval Studies*
MSC	*Malone Society Collections*
MSE	*Massachusetts Studies in English*
MSEx	*Melville Society Extracts*
MSh	*Macmillan Shakespeare*
MSNH	*Mémoires de la Société Néophilologique de Helsinki*

MSpr	*Moderna Språk*
MSR	*Malone Society Reprints*
MSSN	*Medieval Sermon Studies Newsletter*
MT	*Musical Times*
MTJ	*Mark Twain Journal*
Multilingua	*Multilingua: Journal of Cross-Cultural and Interlanguage Communication*
MusR	*Music Review*
MW	*Muslim World* (Hartford, CT)
MWQ	*Mid-West Quarterly*
MysticsQ	*Mystics Quarterly*
Mythlore	*Mythlore: A Journal of J.R.R. Tolkein, C.S. Lewis, Charles Williams, and the Genres of Myth and Fantasy Studies*
NA	*Nuova Antologia*
Names	*Names: Journal of the American Name Society*
NAmR	*North American Review*
N&F	*Notes & Furphies*
N&Q	*Notes and Queries*
Narrative	*Narrative*
Navasilu	*Navasilu*
NB	*Namn och Bygd*
NCaS	*New Cambridge Shakespeare*
NCBEL	*New Cambridge Bibliography of English Literature*
NCC	*Nineteenth-Century Contexts*
NCE	*Norton Critical Editions*
NCFS	*Nineteenth-Century French Studies*
NCI	*New Critical Idiom*
NCLE	*Nineteenth-Century Literature in English*
NConL	*Notes on Contemporary Literature*
NCP	*Nineteenth-Century Prose*
NCS	*New Clarendon Shakespeare*
NCSR	*New Chaucer Society Readings*
NCSTC	*Nineteenth-Century Short Title Catalogue*
NCStud	*Nineteenth-Century Studies*
NCT	*Nineteenth-Century Theatre*
NDQ	*North Dakota Quarterly*
Nebula	*Nebula*
NegroD	*Negro Digest*
NELS	*North Eastern Linguistic Society*
Neoh	*Neohelicon*
Neophil	*Neophilologus*
NEQ	*New England Quarterly*
NERMS	*New England Review*
NewA	*New African*
NewBR	*New Beacon Review*
NewC	*New Criterion*
New Casebooks	*New Casebooks: Contemporary Critical Essays*
NewComp	*New Comparison: A Journal of Comparative and General Literary Studies*
NewF	*New Formations*
NewHibR	*New Hibernian Review*
NewHR	*New Historical Review*
NewR	*New Republic*

NewSt	*Newfoundland Studies*
NewV	*New Voices*
Nexus	*The International Henry Miller Journal*
NF	*Neiophilologica Fennica*
NfN	*News from Nowhere*
NF&LS	*Newfoundland and Labrador Studies*
NFS	*Nottingham French Studies*
NGC	*New German Critique*
NGS	*New German Studies*
NH	*Northern History*
NHR	*Nathaniel Hawthorne Review*
NIS	*Nordic Irish Studies*
NJES	*Nordic Journal of English Studies*
NJL	*Nordic Journal of Linguistics*
NL	*Nouvelles Littéraires*
NLAN	*National Library of Australia News*
NL&LT	*Natural Language and Linguistic Theory*
NLH	*New Literary History: A Journal of Theory and Interpretation*
NLitsR	*New Literatures Review*
NLR	*New Left Review*
NLS	*Natural Language Semantics*
NLWJ	*National Library of Wales Journal*
NM	*Neuphilologische Mitteilungen*
NMAL	*NMAL: Notes on Modern American Literature*
NMer	*New Mermaids*
NMIL	*Notes on Modern Irish Literature*
NML	*New Medieval Literatures*
NMS	*Nottingham Medieval Studies*
NMW	*Notes on Mississippi Writers*
NN	*Nordiska Namenstudier*
NNER	*Northern New England Review*
Nomina	*Nomina: A Journal of Name Studies Relating to Great Britain and Ireland*
NoP	*Northern Perspective*
NOR	*New Orleans Review*
Nordlit	*Nordlit: Arbeidstidsskrift i litteratur og kultur*
NorfolkA	*Norfolk Archaeology*
NortonCE	*Norton Critical Edition*
Novel	*Novel: A Forum on Fiction*
Novitas-ROYAL	*Research on Youth and Language*
NOWELE	*North-Western European Language Evolution*
NPEC	*New Perspectives on the Eighteenth Century*
NPS	*New Penguin Shakespeare*
NR	*Nassau Review*
NRF	*La Nouvelle Revue Française*
NRRS	*Notes and Records of the Royal Society of London*
NS	*Die neuren Sprachen*
NSS	*New Swan Shakespeare*
NTQ	*New Theatre Quarterly*
NTU	*NTU: Studies in Language and Literature*
NVSAWC	*Newsletter of the Victorian Studies Association of Western Canada*
NwJ	*Northward Journal*

NWR	*Northwest Review*
NWRev	*New Welsh Review*
NYH	*New York History*
NYLF	*New York Literary Forum*
NYRB	*New York Review of Books*
NYT	*New York Times*
NYTBR	*New York Times Book Review*
NZB	*New Zealand Books*
NZJAS	*New Zealand Journal of Asian Studies*
NZListener	*New Zealand Listener*
NZW	*NZWords*
OA	*Oxford Authors*
OB	*Ord och Bild*
Obsidian	*Obsidian II: Black Literature in Review*
OBSP	*Oxford Bibliographical Society Publications*
OED	*Oxford English Dictionary*
OEDNews	*Oxford English Dictionary News*
OENews	*Old English Newsletter*
OELH	*Oxford English Literary History*
OET	*Oxford English Texts*
OH	*Over Here: An American Studies Journal*
OHEL	*Oxford History of English Literature*
OhR	*Ohio Review*
OL	
OLR	*Oxford Literary Review*
OnCan	*Onomastica Canadiana*
OPBS	*Occasional Papers of the Bibliographical Society*
OpenGL	*Open Guides to Literature*
OpL	*Open Letter*
OPL	*Oxford Poetry Library*
OPLiLL	*Occasional Papers in Linguistics and Language Learning*
OPSL	*Occasional Papers in Systemic Linguistics*
OralT	*Oral Tradition*
Orbis	*Orbis*
OrbisLit	*Orbis Litterarum*
OS	*Oxford Shakespeare*
OSS	*Oxford Shakespeare Studies*
OT	*Oral Tradition*
Outrider	*Outrider: A Publication of the Wyoming State Library*
Overland	*Overland*
PA	*Présence Africaine*
PAAS	*Proceedings of the American Antiquarian Society*
PacStud	*Pacific Studies*
Paideuma	*Paideuma: A Journal Devoted to Ezra Pound Scholarship*
PAJ	*Performing Art Journal*
P&C	*Pragmatics and Cognition*
P&CT	*Psychoanalysis and Contemporary Thought*
P&L	*Philosophy and Literature*
P&P	*Past and Present*
P&R	*Philosophy and Rhetoric*
P&SC	*Philosophy and Social Criticism*
P&MS	
PAns	*Partial Answers*

PAPA	*Publications of the Arkansas Philological Association*
Papers	*Papers: Explorations into Children's Literature*
PAPS	*Proceedings of the American Philosophical Society*
PAR	*Performing Arts Resources*
Parabola	*Parabola: The Magazine of Myth and Tradition*
Paragraph	*Paragraph: The Journal of the Modern Critical Theory Group*
Parergon	*Parergon: Bulletin of the Australian and New Zealand Association for Medieval and Renaissance Studies*
ParisR	*Paris Review*
Parnassus	*Parnassus: Poetry in Review*
PastM	*Past Masters*
PaterN	*Pater Newsletter*
PAus	*Poetry Australia*
PBA	*Proceedings of the British Academy*
PBerLS	*Proceedings of the Berkeley Linguistics Society*
PBSA	*Papers of the Bibliographical Society of America*
PBSC	*Papers of the Biographical Society of Canada*
PCL	*Perspectives on Contemporary Literature*
PCLAC	*Proceedings of the California Linguistics Association Conference*
PCLS	*Proceedings of the Comparative Literature Symposium* (Lubbock, TX)
PCP	*Pacific Coast Philology*
PCRev	*Popular Culture Review*
PCS	*Penguin Critical Studies*
PEAN	*Proceedings of the English Association North*
PE&W	*Philosophy East and West: A Quarterly of Asian and Comparative Thought*
PELL	*Papers on English Language and Literature* (Japan)
Pequod	*Pequod: A Journal of Contemporary Literature and Literary Criticism*
Performance	*Performance*
PerfR	*Performance Review*
Peritia	*Peritia: Journal of the Medieval Academy of Ireland*
Perspicuitas	*Perspicuitas: Internet-Periodicum für Mediävistische Sprach-, Literatur- und Kulturwissenschaft*
Persuasions	*Persuasions: Journal of the Jane Austen Society of North America*
Persuasions On-Line	*The Jane Austen Journal On-Line*
Philament	*Philament: Online Journal of the Arts and Culture Phonology*
Philosophy	*Philosophy*
PhilRev	*Philosophical Review: A Quarterly Journal*
PhiN	*Philologie im Netz*
PHist	*Printing History*
Phonetica	*Phonetica: International Journal of Speech Science*
Phonology	*Phonology*
PHOS	*Publishing History Occasional Series*
PhRA	*Philosophical Research Archives*
PhT	*Philosophy Today*
PiL	*Papers in Linguistics*
PIMA	*Proceedings of the Illinois Medieval Association*
PinterR	*Pinter Review*
PJCL	*Prairie Journal of Canadian Literature*

PLL	*Papers on Language and Literature*
PLPLS	*Proceedings of the Leeds Philosophical and Literary Society, Literary and Historical Section*
PM	*Penguin Masterstudies*
PMHB	*Pennsylvania Magazine of History and Biography*
PMLA	*Publications of the Modern Language Association of America*
PMPA	*Proceedings of the Missouri Philological Association*
PNotes	*Pynchon Notes*
PNR	*Poetry and Nation Review*
PoeS	*Poe Studies*
Poetica	*Poetica: Zeitschrift fur Sprach- und Literaturwissenschaft* (Amsterdam)
PoeticaJ	*Poetica: An International Journal of Linguistic-Literary Studies* (Tokyo)
Poetics	*Poetics: International Review for the Theory of Literature*
Poétique	*Poétique: Revue de Théorie et d'Analyse Littéraires*
Poetry	*Poetry* (Chicago)
PoetryCR	*Poetry Canada Review*
PoetryNZ	*Poetry New Zealand*
PoetryR	*Poetry Review*
PoetryW	*Poetry Wales*
POMPA	*Publications of the Mississippi Philological Association*
PostS	*Past Script: Essays in Film and the Humanities*
PoT	*Poetics Today*
PP	*Penguin Passnotes*
PP	*Philologica Pragensia*
PPA	*Philosophical Perspectives Annual*
PPMRC	*Proceedings of the International Patristic, Mediaeval and Renaissance Conference*
PPR	*Philosophy and Phenomenological Research*
PQ	*Philological Quarterly*
PQM	*Pacific Quarterly* (Moana)
PR	*Partisan Review*
Pragmatics	*Pragmatics: Quarterly Publication of the International Pragmatics Association*
PrairieF	*Prairie Fire*
Praxis	*Praxis: A Journal of Cultural Criticism*
PRep	
Prépub	*(Pré)publications*
PRev	*Powys Review*
PRIA	*Proceedings of the Royal Irish Academy*
PRIAA	*Publications of the Research Institute of the Abo Akademi Foundation*
PRMCLS	*Papers from the Regional Meetings of the Chicago Linguistics Society*
Prospects	*Prospects: An Annual Journal of American Cultural Studies*
Prospero	*Prospero: Journal of New Thinking in Philosophy for Education*
Proteus	*Proteus: A Journal of Ideas*
Proverbium	*Proverbium*
PrS	*Prairie Schooner*
PSt	*Prose Studies*
PsyArt	*Psychological Study of the Arts* (hyperlink journal)

PsychR	*Psychological Reports*
PTBI	*Publications of the Sir Thomas Browne Institute*
PubH	*Publishing History*
PULC	*Princeton University Library Chronicle*
PURBA	*Panjab University Research Bulletin (Arts)*
PVR	*Platte Valley Review*
PWC	*Pickering's Women's Classics*
PY	*Phonology Yearbook*
QDLLSM	*Quaderni del Dipartimento e Lingue e Letterature Straniere Moderne*
QE	*Quarterly Essay*
QI	*Quaderni d'Italianistica*
QJS	*Quarterly Journal of Speech*
QLing	*Quantitative Linguistics*
QQ	*Queen's Quarterly*
QR	*Queensland Review*
QRFV	*Quarterly Review of Film and Video*
Quadrant	*Quadrant* (Sydney)
Quarendo	*Quarendo*
Quarry	*Quarry*
Quidditas	*Journal of the Rocky Mountain Medieval and Renaissance Association*
QWERTY	*QWERTY: Arts, Littératures, et Civilisations du Monde Anglophone*
RadP	*Radical Philosophy*
RAL	*Research in African Literatures*
RALS	*Resources for American Literary Study*
Ramus	*Ramus: Critical Studies in Greek and Roman Literature*
R&C	*Race and Class*
R&L	*Religion and Literature*
Raritan	*Raritan: A Quarterly Review*
Rask	*Rask: International tidsskrift for sprong og kommunikation*
RB	*Revue Bénédictine*
RBPH	*Revue Belge de Philologie et d'Histoire*
RBR	*Rare Book Review* (formerly *ABR*)
RCEI	*Revista Canaria de Estudios Ingleses*
RCF	*Review of Contemporary Fiction*
RCPS	*Romantic Circles Praxis Series* (online)
RDN	*Renaissance Drama Newsletter*
RE	*Revue d'Esthétique*
Reader	*Reader: Essays in Reader-Oriented Theory, Criticism, and Pedagogy*
ReAL	*Re: Artes Liberales*
REALB	*REAL: The Yearbook of Research in English and American Literature* (Berlin)
ReAr	*Religion and the Arts*
RecBucks	*Records of Buckinghamshire*
RecL	*Recovery Literature*
REPCS	*Review of Education, Pedagogy and Cultural Studies*
RECTR	*Restoration and Eighteenth-Century Theatre Research*
RedL	*Red Letters: A Journal of Cultural Politics*
REED	*Records of Early English Drama*
REEDN	*Records of Early English Drama Newsletter*

ReFr	*Revue Française*
Reinardus	*Reinardus*
REL	*Review of English Literature* (Kyoto)
RELC	*RELC Journal: A Journal of Language Teaching and Research in Southeast Asia*
Ren&R	*Renaissance and Reformation*
Renascence	*Renascence: Essays on Values in Literature*
RenD	*Renaissance Drama*
Renfor	*Renaissance Forum* (online)
RenP	*Renaissance Papers*
RenQ	*Renaissance Quarterly*
Rep	*Representations*
RePublica	*RePublica*
RES	*Review of English Studies*
Restoration	*Restoration: Studies in English Literary Culture, 1660–1700*
Rev	*Review* (Blacksburg, VA)
RevAli	*Revista Alicantina de Estudios Ingleses*
Revels	*Revels Plays*
RevelsCL	*Revels Plays Companion Library*
Revista Canaria	*Revista Canaria De Estudios Ingleses*
RevelsSE	*Revels Student Editions*
RevR	*Revolution and Romanticism, 1789–1834*
RFEA	*Revue Française d'Études Américaines*
RFR	*Robert Frost Review*
RG	*Revue Générale*
RH	*Recusant History*
Rhetorica	*Rhetorica: A Journal of the History of Rhetoric*
Rhetorik	*Rhetorik: Ein Internationales Jahrbuch*
RhetR	*Rhetoric Review*
RHist	*Rural History*
RHL	*Revue d'Histoire Littéraire de la France*
RHT	*Revue d'Histoire du Théâtre*
RIB	*Revista Interamericana de Bibliografia: Inter-American Reviews of Bibliography*
Ricardian	*Ricardian: Journal of the Richard III Society*
RJ	*Richard Jefferies Society Newsletter*
RJES	*Romanian Journal of English Studies*
RL	*Rereading Literature*
RLAn	*Romance Languages Annual*
RLC	*Revue de Littérature Comparée*
RL&C	*Research on Language and Computation*
RLing	*Rivista di Linguistica*
RLit	*Russian Literature*
RLM	*La Revue des Lettres Modernes: Histoire des Idées des Littératures*
RLMC	*Rivista di Letterature Moderne e Comparate*
RLT	*Russian Literature Triquarterly*
RM	*Rethinking Marxism*
RMR	*Rocky Mountain Review of Language and Literature*
RM	*Renaissance and Modern Studies*
RMSt	*Reading Medieval Studies*
ROA	*Rutgers Optimality Archive*
Romania	*Romania*

Romanticism	*Romanticism*
RomN	*Romance Notes*
RomQ	*Romance Quarterly*
ROMRD	
RomS	*Romance Studies*
RomText	*Romantic Textualities: Literature and Print Culture, 1780–1840 (formerly Cardiff Corvey)*
RoN	*Romanticism on the Net* (now *Romanticism and Victorianism on the Net*)
ROO	*Room of One's Own: A Feminist Journal of Literature and Criticism*
RORD	*Research Opportunities in Renaissance Drama*
RPT	*Russian Poetics in Translation*
RQ	*Riverside Quarterly*
RR	*Romanic Review*
RRDS	*Regents Renaissance Drama Series*
RRestDS	*Regents Restoration Drama Series*
RS	*Renaissance Studies*
RSQ	*Rhetoric Society Quarterly*
RSV	*Rivista di Study Vittoriani*
RUO	*Revue de l'Université d'Ottawa*
RUSEng	*Rajasthan University Studies in English*
RuskN	*Ruskin Newsletter*
RUUL	*Reports from the Uppsala University Department of Linguistics*
R/WT	*Readerly/Writerly Texts*
SAC	*Studies in the Age of Chaucer*
SAD	*Studies in American Drama, 1945–Present*
SAF	*Studies in American Fiction*
Saga-Book	*Saga-Book (Viking Society for Northern Research)*
Sagetrieb	*Sagatrieb: A Journal Devoted to Poets in the Pound–H.D.–Williams Tradition*
SAIL	*Studies in American Indian Literatures: The Journal of the Association for the Study of American Indian Literatures*
SAJL	*Studies in American Jewish Literature*
SAJMRS	*South African Journal of Medieval and Renaissance Studies*
Sal	*Salmagrundi: A Quarterly of the Humanities and Social Sciences*
SALALS	*Southern African Linguistics and Applied language Studies*
SALCT	*SALCT: Studies in Australian Literature, Culture and Thought*
S&P	*Script and Print (formerly BSANZB, Bibliographical Society of Australia and New Zealand Bulletin)*
S&Prag	*Semantics and Pragmatics*
S&S	*Sight and Sound*
SAntS	*Studia Anthroponymica Scandinavica*
Salt	*Salt: An International Journal of Poetry and Poetics*
SAP	*Studia Anglica Posnaniensia*
SAQ	*South Atlantic Quarterly*
SAR	*Studies in the American Renaissance*
SARB	*South African Review of Books*
SARev	*South Asian Review*
Sargasso	*Sargasso*
SASLC	*Studies in Anglo-Saxon Literature and Culture*
SatR	*Saturday Review*
SB	*Studies in Bibliography*

SBHC	*Studies in Browning and his Circle*
SC	*Seventeenth Century*
Scan	*Scandinavica: An International Journal of Scandinavian Studies*
ScanS	*Scandinavian Studies*
SCC&HTLJ	*Santa Clara Computer and High Technology Law Journal*
SCel	*Studia Celtica*
SCER	*Society for Critical Exchange Report*
Schuylkill	*Schuylkill: A Creative and Critical Review* (Temple University)
Scintilla	*Scintilla: Annual Journal of Vaughan Studies and New Poetry*
SCJ	*Sixteenth Century Journal*
SCL	*Studies in Canadian Literature*
ScLJ	*Scottish Literary Journal: A Review of Studies in Scottish Language and Literature*
ScLJ(S)	*Scottish Literary Journal Supplement*
SCLOP	*Society for Caribbean Linguistics Occasional Papers*
SCN	*Seventeenth-Century News*
ScotL	*Scottish Language*
ScottN	*Scott Newsletter*
SCR	*South Carolina Review*
Screen	*Screen* (London)
SCRev	*South Central Review*
Scriblerian	*Scriblerian and the Kit Cats: A Newsjournal Devoted to Pope, Swift, and their Circle*
Scripsi	*Scripsi*
Scriptorium	*Scriptorium: International Review of Manuscript Studies*
ScTh	*Scottish Journal of Theology*
SD	*Social Dynamics*
SDR	*South Dakota Review*
SECC	*Studies in Eighteenth-Century Culture*
SECOLR	*SECOL Review: Southeastern Conference on Linguistics*
SED	*Survey of English Dialects*
SEDERI	*Journal of the Spanish Society for Renaissance Studies (Sociedad Española de Estudios Renacentistas Ingleses)*
SEEJ	*Slavic and East European Journal*
SEL	*Studies in English Literature, 1500–1900* (Rice University)
Selim	*SELIM: Journal of the Spanish Society for Medieval English Language and Literature*
SELing	*Studies in English Linguistics* (Tokyo)
SELit	*Studies in English Literature* (Tokyo)
SELL	*Studies in English Language and Literature*
Sem	*Semiotica: Journal of the International Association for Semiotic Studies*
SEMC	*Studies in Early Medieval Coinage*
Semiosis	*Semiosis: Internationale Zeitschrift für Semiotik und Ästhetik*
SER	*Studien zur Englischen Romantik*
Seven	*Seven: An Anglo-American Literary Review*
SF&R	*Scholars' Facsimiles and Reprints*
SFic	*Science Fiction: A Review of Speculative Literature*
SFNL	*Shakespeare on Film Newsletter*
SFQ	*Southern Folklore Quarterly*
SFR	*Stanford French Review*
SFS	*Science-Fiction Studies*
SH	*Studia Hibernica* (Dublin)

Shakespeare	
ShakB	*Shakespeare Bulletin*
ShakS	*Shakespeare Studies* (New York)
Shandean	*Shandean*
Sh&Sch	*Shakespeare and Schools*
ShawR	*Shaw: The Annual of Bernard Shaw Studies*
Shenandoah	*Shenandoah*
SherHR	*Sherlock Holmes Review*
ShIntY	*Shakespeare International Yearbook*
Shiron	*Shiron*
ShJE	*Shakespeare Jahrbuch* (Weimar)
ShJW	*Deutsche Shakespeare-Gesellschaft West Jahrbuch* (Bochum)
ShLR	*Shoin Literary Review*
ShN	*Shakespeare Newsletter*
ShortS	
SHPBBS	*Studies in the History of Philosophy of Biological and Biomedical Sciences*
SHPS	*Studies in the History and Philosophy of Science*
SHR	*Southern Humanities Review*
ShS	*Shakespeare Survey*
ShSA	*Shakespeare in Southern Africa*
ShStud	*Shakespeare Studies* (Tokyo)
SHW	*Studies in Hogg and his World*
ShY	*Shakespeare Yearbook*
SiAF	*Studies in American Fiction*
SIcon	*Studies in Iconography*
SidJ	*Sidney Journal*
SidN	*Sidney Newsletter and Journal*
Signs	*Signs: Journal of Women in Culture and Society*
SiHoLS	*Studies in the History of the Language Sciences*
SIL	*Studies in Literature*
SiMed	*Studies in Medievalism*
SIM	*Studies in Music*
SiP	*Shakespeare in Performance*
SIP	*Studies in Philology*
SiPr	*Shakespeare in Production*
SiR	*Studies in Romanticism*
SJC	
SJS	*San José Studies*
SL	*Studia Linguistica*
SLang	*Studies in Language*
SLCS	*Studies in Language Companion Series*
SLI	*Studies in the Literary Imagination*
SLJ	*Southern Literary Journal*
SLJH	*Sri Lanka Journal of the Humanities*
SLRev	*Stanford Literature Review*
SLSc	*Studies in the Linguistic Sciences*
SMART	*Studies in Medieval and Renaissance Teaching*
SmAx	*Small Axe: A Caribbean Journal of Criticism*
SMC	*Studies in Medieval Culture*
SMed	*Studi Medievali*
SMELL	*Studies in Medieval English Language and Literature*
SMLit	*Studies in Mystical Literature* (Taiwan)

SMRH	*Studies in Medieval and Renaissance History*
SMRT	*Studies in Medieval and Renaissance Teaching*
SMS	*Studier i Modern Språkvetenskap*
SMy	*Studia Mystica*
SN	*Studia Neophilologica*
SNNTS	*Studies in the Novel* (North Texas State University)
SO	*Shakespeare Originals*
SOA	*Sydsvenska Ortnamnssällskapets Årsskrift*
SoAR	*South Atlantic Review*
SoC	*Senses of Cinema* (online)
Sociocrit	*Sociocriticism*
Socioling	*Sociolinguistica*
SocN	*Sociolinguistics*
SocSem	*Social Semiotics*
SocT	*Social Text*
SohoB	*Soho Bibliographies*
SoQ	*Southern Quarterly*
SoR	*Southern Review* (Baton Rouge, LA)
SoRA	*Southern Review* (Adelaide)
SoSt	*Southern Studies: An Interdisciplinary Journal of the South*
Soundings	*Soundings: An Interdisciplinary Journal*
Southerly	*Southerly: A Review of Australian Literature*
SovL	*Soviet Literature*
SP	*Studies in Philology*
SPAN	*SPAN: Newsletter of the South Pacific Association for Commonwealth Literature and Language Studies*
SPAS	*Studies in Puritan American Spirituality*
SPC	*Studies in Popular Culture*
Spectrum	*Spectrum*
Speculum	*Speculum: A Journal of Medieval Studies*
SpeechComm	
SPELL	*Swiss Papers in English Language and Literature*
Sphinx	*Sphinx: A Magazine of Literature and Society*
Spiritus	*Spiritus: A Journal of Christian Spirituality*
SpM	*Spicilegio Moderno*
SpNL	*Spenser Newsletter*
Sport	*Sport*
Sprachwiss	*Sprachwissenschalt*
SpringE	*Spring: The Journal of the e.e. cummings Society*
SPub	*Studies in Publishing*
SPWVSRA	*Selected Papers from the West Virginia Shakespeare and Renaissance Association*
SQ	*Shakespeare Quarterly*
SR	*Sewanee Review*
SRen	*Studies in the Renaissance*
SRSR	*Status Report on Speech Research* (Haskins Laboratories)
SSEL	*Stockholm Studies in English*
SSELER	*Salzburg Studies in English Literature: Elizabethan and Renaissance*
SSELJDS	*Salzburg Studies in English Literature: Jacobean Drama Studies*
SSELPDPT	*Salzburg Studies in English Literature: Poetic Drama and Poetic Theory*
SSELRR	*Salzburg Studies in English Literature: Romantic Reassessment*

SSEng	*Sydney Studies in English*
SSF	*Studies in Short Fiction*
SSILA Newsletter	*Newsletter of the Society for the Study of the Indigenous Languages of the Americas*
SSL	*Studies in Scottish Literature*
SSLA	*Studies in Second Language Acquisition*
SPap	*Sydney Papers*
SSR	*Scottish Studies Review*
SSt	*Spenser Studies*
SStud	*Swift Studies: The Annual of the Ehrenpreis Center*
Staffrider	*Staffrider*
StaffordS	*Staffordshire Studies*
STAH	*Strange Things Are Happening*
StCH	*Studies in Church History*
STGM	*Studien und Texte zur Geistegeschichte des Mittelalters*
StHR	*Stanford Historical Review*
StHum	*Studies in the Humanities*
StIn	*Studi Inglesi*
StLF	*Studi di Letteratura Francese*
STP	*Studies in Theatre and Performance*
StQ	*Steinbeck Quarterly*
StrR	*Structuralist Review*
StTCL	*Studies in Twentieth-Century Literature*
StTW	*Studies in Travel Writing*
StudiesAmNaturalism	
StudUBBPhil	*Studia Universitatis Babeş-Bolyai Philologia*
StudWF	*Studies in Weird Fiction*
STUF	*Sprachtypologie und Universalienforschung*
Style	*Style* (De Kalb, IL)
SUAS	*Stratford-upon-Avon Studies*
SubStance	*SubStance: A Review of Theory and Literary Criticism*
SUS	*Susquehanna University Studies*
SussexAC	*Sussex Archaeological Collections*
SussexP&P	*Sussex Past & Present*
SVEC	*Studies on Voltaire and the Eighteenth Century*
SWPLL	*Sheffield Working Papers in Language and Linguistics*
SWR	*Southwest Review*
SwR	*Swansea Review: A Journal of Criticism*
Sycamore	*Sycamore*
Symbolism	*Symbolism: An International Journal of Critical Aesthetics*
TA	*Theatre Annual*
Tabu	*Bulletin voor Taalwetenschap, Groningen*
Takahe	*Takahe*
Talisman	*Talisman*
TC	*Textual Cultures: Texts, Contexts, Interpretation*
T&C	*Text and Context*
T&L	*Translation and Literature*
T&P	*Text and Performance*
T&S	*Theology and Sexuality*
T&T	*Text & Talk*
TAPS	*Transactions of the American Philosophical Society*
TCBS	*Transactions of the Cambridge Bibliographical Society*
TCE	*Texas College English*

TCL	Twentieth-Century Literature
TCS	Theory, Culture and Society: Explorations in Critical Social Science
TCWAAS	Transactions of the Cumberland and Westmorland Antiquarian and Archaeological Society
TD	Themes in Drama
TDR	Drama Review
TEAMS	Consortium for the Teaching of the Middle Ages
TEAS	Twayne's English Authors Series
Telos	Telos: A Quarterly Journal of Post-Critical Thought
TennEJ	Tennessee English Journal
TennQ	Tennessee Quarterly
TennSL	Tennessee Studies in Literature
TeReo	Te Reo: Journal of the Linguistic Society of New Zealand
TSLL	Texas Studies in Language and Literature
Text	Text: Transactions of the Society for Textual Scholarship
Textus	
TH	Texas Humanist
THA	Thomas Hardy Annual
Thalia	Thalia: Studies in Literary Humor
ThC	Theatre Crafts
Theater	Theater
TheatreS	Theatre Studies
Theoria	Theoria: A Journal of Studies in the Arts, Humanities and Social Sciences (Natal)
THES	Times Higher Education Supplement
Thesis	Thesis Eleven
THIC	Theatre History in Canada
THJ	Thomas Hardy Journal
ThN	Thackeray Newsletter
ThoreauQ	Thoreau Quarterly: A Journal of Literary and Philosophical Studies
Thought	Thought: A Review of Culture and Ideas
Thph	Theatrephile
ThreR	Threepenny Review
ThS	Theatre Survey: The American Journal of Theatre History
THSJ	Thomas Hardy Society Journal
THSLC	Transactions of the Historic Society of Lancashire and Cheshire
THStud	Theatre History Studies
ThTop	Theatre Topics
THY	Thomas Hardy Yearbook
TiLSM	Trends in Linguistics: Studies and Monographs
Tip	Theory in Practice
Tirra Lirra	Tirra Lirra: The Quarterly Magazine for the Yarra Valley
TJ	Theatre Journal
TJS	Transactions (Johnson Society)
TJAAWP	Text: Journal of the Australian Association of Writing Programs
TkR	Tamkang Review
TL	Theoretical Linguistics
TLJ	The Linguistics Journal
TLR	Linguistic Review
TLS	Times Literary Supplement
TMLT	Toronto Medieval Latin Texts

TN	*Theatre Notebook*
TNWSECS	*Transactions of the North West Society for Eighteenth Century Studies*
Torre	*Torre*
TP	*Terzo Programma*
TPLL	*Tilbury Papers in Language and Literature*
TPQ	*Text and Performance Quarterly*
TPr	*Textual Practice*
TPS	*Transactions of the Philological Society*
TR	*Theatre Record*
Traditio	*Traditio: Studies in Ancient and Medieval History, Thought, and Religion*
Transition	*Transition*
TRB	*Tennyson Research Bulletin*
TRHS	*Transactions of the Royal Historical Society*
TRI	*Theatre Research International*
TriQ	*TriQuarterly*
Trivium	*Trivium*
Tropismes	*Tropismes*
TSAR	*Toronto South Asian Review*
TSB	*Thoreau Society Bulletin*
TSLang	*Typological Studies in Language*
TSLL	*Texas Studies in Literature and Language*
TSWL	*Tulsa Studies in Women's Literature*
TTR	*Trinidad and Tobago Review*
TUSAS	*Twayne's United States Authors Series*
TWAS	*Twayne's World Authors Series*
TWBR	*Third World Book Review*
TWQ	*Third World Quarterly*
TWR	*Thomas Wolfe Review*
Txt	*Text: An Interdisciplinary Annual of Textual Studies*
TYDS	*Transactions of the Yorkshire Dialect Society*
Typophiles	*Typophiles* (New York)
UCrow	*Upstart Crow*
UCTSE	*University of Cape Town Studies in English*
UCWPL	*UCL Working Papers in Linguistics*
UDR	*University of Drayton Review*
UE	*Use of English*
UEAPL	*UEA Papers in Linguistics*
UES	*Unisa English Studies*
Ufahamu	*Ufahamu*
ULR	*University of Leeds Review*
UMSE	*University of Mississippi Studies in English*
Untold	*Untold*
UOQ	*University of Ottawa Quarterly*
URM	*Ultimate Reality and Meaning: Interdisciplinary Studies in the Philosophy of Understanding*
USSE	*University of Saga Studies in English*
UtopST	*Utopian Studies*
UTQ	*University of Toronto Quarterly*
UWR	*University of Windsor Review*
VCT	*Les Voies de la Création Théâtrale*
VEAW	*Varieties of English around the World*

Verbatim	*Verbatim: The Language Quarterly*
VIA	*VIA: The Journal of the Graduate School of Fine Arts* (University of Pennsylvania)
Viator	*Viator: Medieval and Renaissance Studies*
Views	*Viennese English Working Papers*
VIJ	*Victorians Institute Journal*
VLC	*Victorian Literature and Culture*
VN	*Victorian Newsletter*
Voices	*Voices*
VP	*Victorian Poetry*
VPR	*Victorian Periodicals Review*
VQR	*Virginia Quarterly Review*
VR	*Victorian Review*
VS	*Victorian Studies*
VSB	*Victorian Studies Bulletin*
VWB	*Virginia Woolf Bulletin*
VWM	*Virginia Woolf Miscellany*
WAJ	*Women's Art Journal*
WAL	*Western American Literature*
W&I	*Word and Image*
W&L	*Women and Literature*
W&Lang	*Women and Language*
Wasafiri	*Wasafiri*
WascanaR	*Wascana Review*
WBEP	*Wiener Beiträge zur Englischen Philologie*
WC	*World's Classics*
WC	*Wordsworth Circle*
WCR	*West Coast Review*
WCSJ	*Wilkie Collins Society Journal*
WCWR	*William Carlos Williams Review*
Wellsian	*Wellsian: The Journal of the H.G. Wells Society*
WEn	*World Englishes*
Westerly	*Westerly: An Annual Review*
WestHR	*West Hills Review: A Walt Whitman Journal*
WF	*Western Folklore*
WHASN	*W.H. Auden Society Newsletter*
WHR	*Western Humanities Review*
WI	*Word and Image*
WLA	*Wyndham Lewis Annual*
WL&A	*War Literature, and the Arts: An International Journal of the Humanities*
WLT	*World Literature Today*
WLWE	*World Literature Written in English*
WMQ	*William and Mary Quarterly*
WoHR	*Women's History Review*
WolfenbütteleB	*Wolfenbüttele Beiträge: Aus den Schätzen der Herzog August Bibliothek*
Women	*Women: A Cultural Review*
WomGY	*Women in German Yearbook*
WomHR	*Women's History Review*
WorcesterR	*Worcester Review*
WORD	*WORD: Journal of the International Linguistic Association*
WPW	*Working Papers on the Web*

WQ	*Wilson Quarterly*
WRB	*Women's Review of Books*
WS	*Women's Studies: An Interdisciplinary Journal*
WSIF	*Women's Studies: International Forum*
WSJour	*Wallace Stevens Journal*
WSR	*Wicazo Sa Review*
WstA	*Woolf Studies Annual*
WTJ	*Westminster Theological Journal*
WTW	*Writers and their Work*
WVUPP	*West Virginia University Philological Papers*
WW	*Women's Writing*
WWR	*Walt Whitman Quarterly Review*
XUS	*Xavier Review*
YCC	*Yearbook of Comparative Criticism*
YeA	*Yeats Annual*
YER	*Yeats Eliot Review*
YES	*Yearbook of English Studies*
YEuS	*Yearbook of European Studies/Annuaire d'Études Européennes*
YFS	*Yale French Studies*
Yiddish	*Yiddish*
YJC	*Yale Journal of Criticism: Interpretation in the Humanities*
YLS	*Yearbook of Langland Studies*
YM	*Yearbook of Morphology*
YNS	*York Note Series*
YPL	*York Papers in Linguistics*
YR	*Yale Review*
YREAL	*The Yearbook of Research in English and American Literature*
YULG	*Yale University Library Gazette*
YWES	*Year's Work in English Studies*
ZAA	*Zeitschrift für Anglistik and Amerikanistik*
ZCP	*Zeitschrift für celtische Philologie*
ZDA	*Zeitschrift für deutsches Altertum und deutsche Literatur*
ZDL	*Zeitschrift für Dialektologie und Linguistik*
ZGKS	*Zeitschrft für Gesellschaft für Kanada-Studien*
ZGL	*Zeitschrift für germanistische Linguistik*
ZPSK	*Zeitschrift für Phonetik Sprachwissenshaft und Kommunikationsforschung*
ZSpr	*Zeitschrift für Sprachwissenshaft*
ZVS	*Zeitschrift für vergleichende Sprachforschung*

Volume numbers are supplied in the text, as are individual issue numbers for journals that are not continuously paginated through the year.

2. Publishers

AAAH	Acta Academiae Åboensis Humaniora, Åbo, Finland
AAH	Australian Academy of Humanities
A&B	Allison & Busby, London
A&R	Angus & Robertson, North Ryde, New South Wales
A&U	Allen & Unwin (now Unwin Hyman)
A&UA	Allen & Unwin, North Sydney, New South Wales
A&W	Almqvist & Wiksell International, Stockholm
AarhusUP	Aarhus UP, Aarhus, Denmark

ABC	ABC Enterprises
ABC CLIO	ABC CLIO Reference Books, Santa Barbara, CA
Abbeville	Abbeville Press, New York
ABDO	Association Bourguignonne de Dialectologie et d'Onomastique, Dijon
AberdeenUP	Aberdeen UP, Aberdeen
Abhinav	Abhinav Publications, New Delhi
Abingdon	Abingdon Press, Nashville, TN
ABL	Armstrong Browning Library, Waco, TX
Ablex	Ablex Publishing, Norwood, NJ
Åbo	Åbo Akademi, Åbo, Finland
Abrams	Harry N. Abrams, New York
Academia	Academia Press, Melbourne
Academic	Academic Press, London and Orlando, FL
Academy	Academy Press, Dublin
AcademyC	Academy Chicago Publishers, Chicago
AcademyE	Academy Editions, London
Acadiensis	Acadiensis Press, Fredericton, New Brunswick, Canada
ACarS	Association for Caribbean Studies, Coral Gables, FL
ACC	Antique Collectors' Club, Woodbridge, Suffolk
ACCO	ACCO, Leuven, Belgium
ACLALS	Association for Commonwealth Literature and Language Studies, Canberra
ACMRS	Arizona Center for Medieval and Renaissance Studies
ACP	Another Chicago Press, Chicago
ACS	Association for Canadian Studies, Ottawa
Adam Hart	Adam Hart Publishers, London
Adam Matthew	Adam Matthew, Suffolk
Addison-Wesley	Addison-Wesley, Wokingham, Berkshire
ADFA	Australian Defence Force Academy, Department of English
Adosa	Adosa, Clermont-Ferrand, France
AEMS	American Early Medieval Studies
AF	Akademisk Forlag, Copenhagen
Affiliated	Affiliated East–West Press, New Delhi
AFP	Associated Faculty Press, New York
Africana	Africana Publications, New York
A–H	Amold-Heinemann, New Delhi
Ahriman	Ahriman-Verlag, Freiburg im Breisgau, Germany
AIAS	Australian Institute of Aboriginal Studies, Canberra
Ajanta	Ajanta Publications, Delhi
AK	Akadémiai Kiadó, Budapest
ALA	ALA Editions, Chicago
Al&Ba	Allen & Bacon, Boston, MA
Albatross	Albatross Books, Sutherland, New South Wales
Albion	Albion, Appalachian State University, Boone, NC
Alderman	Alderman Press, London
Aldwych	Aldwych Press
AligarhMU	Aligarh Muslim University, Uttar Pradesh, India
Alioth	Alioth Press, Beaverton, OR
Allen	W.H. Allen, London
Allied Publishers	Allied Indian Publishers, Lahore and New Delhi
Almond	Almond Press, Sheffield
AM	Aubier Montaigne, Paris

AMAES	Association des Médiévistes Angliciste de l'Enseignement Supérieur, Paris
Amate	Amate Press, Oxford
AmberL	Amber Lane, Oxford
Amistad	Amistad Press, New York
AMP	Aurora Metro Press, London
AMS	AMS Press, New York
AMU	Adam Mickiewicz University, Posnan
Anansi	Anansi Press, Toronto
Anderson-Lovelace	Anderson-Lovelace, Los Altos Hills, CA
Anma Libri	Anma Libri, Saratoga, CA
Antipodes	Antipodes Press, Plimmerton, New Zealand
Anvil	Anvil Press Poetry, London
APA	APA, Maarssen, Netherlands
APH	Associated Publishing House, New Delhi
API	API Network, Perth, Australia
APL	American Poetry and Literature Press, Philadelphia
APP	Australian Professional Publications, Mosman, New South Wales
Applause	Applause Theatre Book Publishers
Appletree	Appletree Press, Belfast
APS	American Philosophical Society, Philadelphia
Aquarian	Aquarian Press, Wellingborough, Northants
ArborH	Arbor House Publishing, New York
Arcade	Arcade Publishing, New York
Archon	Archon Books, Hamden, CT
ArchP	Architectural Press Books, Guildford, Surrey
Ardis	Ardis Publishers, Ann Arbor, MI
Ariel	Ariel Press, London
Aristotle	Aristotle University, Thessaloniki
Ark	Ark Paperbacks, London
Arkona	Arkona Forlaget, Aarhus, Denmark
Arlington	Arlington Books, London
Arnold	Edward Arnold, London
ArnoldEJ	E.J. Arnold & Son, Leeds
ARP	Australian Reference Publications, N. Balwyn, Victoria
Arrow	Arrow Books, London
Arsenal	Arsenal Pulp Press
Artmoves	Artmoves, Parkdale, Victoria
ASAL	Association for the Study of Australian Literature
ASB	Anglo-Saxon Books, Middlesex
ASchP	Australian Scholarly Publishing, Melbourne
ASECS	American Society for Eighteenth-Century Studies, c/o Ohio State University, Columbus
Ashfield	Ashfield Press, London
Ashgate	Ashgate, Brookfield, VT
Ashton	Ashton Scholastic
Aslib	Aslib, London
ASLS	Association for Scottish Literary Studies, Aberdeen
Asmara	Audio Visual Institute of Eritrea (AVIE)
ASP	Australian Scholarly Publishing
AStP	Aboriginal Studies Press, Canberra
ASU	Arizona State University, Tempe

Atheneum	Atheneum Publishers, New York
Athlone	Athlone Press, London
Atlantic	Atlantic Publishers, Darya Ganj, New Delhi
Atlas	Atlas Press, London
Attic	Attic Press, Dublin
AuBC	Australian Book Collector
AucklandUP	Auckland UP, Auckland
AUG	Acta Universitatis Gothoburgensis, Sweden
AUP	Associated University Presses, London and Toronto
AUPG	Academic & University Publishers, London
Aurum	Aurum Press, London
Auslib	Auslib Press, Adelaide
AUU	Acta Universitatis Umensis, Umeå, Sweden
AUUp	Acta Universitatis Upsaliensis, Uppsala
Avebury	Avebury Publishing, Aldershot, Hampshire
Avero	Avero Publications, Newcastle upon Tyne
A-V Verlag	A-V Verlag, Franz Fischer, Augsburg, Germany
AWP	Africa World Press, Trenton, NJ
Axelrod	Axelrod Publishing, Tampa Bay, FL
BA	British Academy, London
BAAS	British Association for American Studies, c/o University of Keele
Bagel	August Bagel Verlag, Dusseldorf
Bahri	Bahri Publications, New Delhi
Bamberger	Bamberger Books, Flint, MI
B&B	Boydell & Brewer, Woodbridge, Suffolk
B&J	Barrie & Jenkins, London
B&N	Barnes & Noble, Totowa, NJ
B&O	Burns & Oates, Tunbridge Wells, Kent
B&S	Michael Benskin and M.L. Samuels, Middle English Dialect Project, University of Edinburgh
BAR	British Archaelogical Reports, Oxford
Barn Owl	Barn Owl Books, Taunton, Somerset
Barnes	A.S. Barnes, San Diego, CA
Barr Smith	Barr Smith Press, Barr Smith Library, University of Adelaide
Bath UP	Bath UP, Bath
Batsford	B.T. Batsford, London
Bayreuth	Bayreuth African Studies, University of Bayreuth, Germany
BBC	BBC Publications, London
BClarkL	Bruccoli Clark Layman Inc./Manly Inc.
BCP	Bristol Classical Press, Bristol
Beacon	Beacon Press, Boston, MA
Beck	C.H. Beck'sche Verlagsbuchhandlung, Munich
Becket	Becket Publications, London
Beckford Society	Beckford Society, UK
Belin	Éditions Belin, Paris
Belknap	Belknap Press, Cambridge, MA
Belles Lettres	Société d'Édition les Belles Lettres, Paris
Bellew	Bellew Publishing, London
Bellflower	Belflower Press, Case University, Cleveland, OH
Benjamins	John Benjamins, Amsterdam
BenjaminsNA	John Benjamins North America, Philadelphia
BennC	Bennington College, Bennington, VT

Berg	Berg Publishers, Oxford
BFI	British Film Institute, London
BGUP	Bowling Green University Popular Press, Bowling Green, OH
BibS	Bibliographical Society, London
BilinguaGA	Bilingua GA Editions
Bilingual	Bilingual Press, Arizona State University, Tempe
Bingley	Clive Bingley, London
Binnacle	Binnacle Press, London
Biografia	Biografia Publishers, London
Birkbeck	Birkbeck College, University of London
Bishopsgate	Bishopsgate Press, Tonbridge, Kent
BL	British Library, London
Black	Adam & Charles Black, London
Black Cat	Black Cat Press, Blackrock, Eire
Blackie	Blackie & Son, Glasgow
Black Moss	Black Moss, Windsor, Ontario
Blackstaff	Blackstaff Press, Belfast
Black Swan	Black Swan, Curtin, UT
Blackwell	Basil Blackwell, Oxford
BlackwellR	Blackwell Reference, Oxford
Blackwood	Blackwood, Pillans & Wilson, Edinburgh
Bl&Br	Blond & Briggs, London
Blandford	Blandford Press, London
Blaue Eule	Verlag die Blaue Eule, Essen
Bloodaxe	Bloodaxe Books, Newcastle upon Tyne
Bloomsbury	Bloomsbury Publishing, London
Blubber Head	Blubber Head Press, Hobart
BM	Bobbs-Merrill, New York
BMP	British Museum Publications, London
Bodleian	Bodleian Library, Oxford
Bodley	Bodley Head, London
Bogle	Bogle L'Ouverture Publications, London
BoiseSUP	Boise State UP, Boise, Idaho
Book Enclave	Book Enclave, Shanti Nagar, Jaipur, India
Book Guild	Book Guild, Lewes, E. Sussex
BookplateS	Bookplate Society, Edgbaston, Birmingham
Booksplus	Booksplus Nigeria Limited, Lagos, Nigeria
Boombana	Boombana Press, Brisbane, Queensland
Borealis	Borealis Press, Ottawa
Borgo	Borgo Press, San Bernardino, CA
BostonAL	Boston Athenaeum Library, Boxton, MA
Bouma	Bouma's Boekhuis, Groningen, Netherlands
Bowker	R.R. Bowker, New Providence, NJ
Boyars	Marion Boyars, London and Boston, MA
Boydell	Boydell Press, Woodbridge, Suffolk
Boyes	Megan Boyes, Allestree, Derbyshire
Br&S	Brandl & Schlesinger
Bran's Head	Bran's Head Books, Frome, Somerset
Braumüller	Wilhelm Braumüller, Vienna
Breakwater	Breakwater Books, St John's, Newfoundland
Brentham	Brentham Press, St Albans, Hertfordshire
Brepols	Brepols, Turnhout, Belgium
Brewer	D.S. Brewer, Woodbridge, Suffolk

Brewin	Brewin Books, Studley, Warwicks
Bridge	Bridge Publishing, S. Plainfield, NJ
Brill	E.J. Brill, Leiden
BrillA	Brill Academic Publishers
Brilliance	Brilliance Books, London
Broadview	Broadview, London, Ontario and Lewiston, NY
Brookside	Brookside Press, London
Browne	Sinclair Browne, London
Brownstone	Brownstone Books, Madison, IN
BrownUP	Brown UP, Providence, RI
Brynmill	Brynmill Press, Harleston, Norfolk
BSA	Bibliographical Society of America
BSB	Black Swan Books, Redding Ridge, CT
BSP	Black Sparrow Press, Santa Barbara, CA
BSU	Ball State University, Muncie, IN
BuckUP	Bucknell UP, Lewisburg, PA
Bulzoni	Bulzoni Editore, Rome
BUP	Birmingham University Press
Burnett	Burnett Books, London
Buske	Helmut Buske, Hamburg
Butterfly	Butterfly Books, San Antonio, TX
BWilliamsNZ	Bridget Williams Books, Wellington, New Zealand
CA	Creative Arts Book, Berkeley, CA
CAAS	Connecticut Academy of Arts and Sciences, New Haven
CAB International	Centre for Agriculture and Biosciences International, Wallingford, Oxfordshire
Cadmus	Cadmus Editions, Tiburon, CA
Cairns	Francis Cairns, University of Leeds
Calaloux	Calaloux Publications, Ithaca, NY
Calder	John Calder, London
CALLS	Centre for Australian Language and Literature Studies, English Department, University of New England, New South Wales
Cambria	Cambria Press, Amherst, NY
CambridgeSP	Cambridge Scholars Publishing, Newcastle upon Tyne, United Kingdom
Camden	Camden Press, London
CamdenH	Camden House (an imprint of Boydell and Brewer), Rochester, NY
C&G	Carroll & Graf, New York
C&W	Chatto & Windus, London
Canongate	Canongate Publishing, Edinburgh
Canterbury	Canterbury Press, Norwich
Canterbury UP	Canterbury University Press, Christchurch, New Zealand
Cape	Jonathan Cape, London
Capra	Capra Press, Santa Barbara, CA
Carcanet	Carcanet New Press, Manchester, Lancashire
Cardinal	Cardinal, London
CaribB	Caribbean Books, Parkersburg, IA
CarletonUP	Carleton UP, Ottawa
Carucci	Carucci, Rome
Cascadilla	Cascadilla Press, Somerville, MA
Cass	Frank Cass, London

Cassell	Cassell, London
Cavaliere Azzurro	Cavaliere Azzurro, Bologna
Cave	Godfrey Cave Associates, London
CBA	Council for British Archaeology, London
CBS	Cambridge Bibliographical Society, Cambridge
CCEUCan	Centre for Continuing Education, University of Canterbury, Christchurch, New Zealand
CCCP	Critical, Cultural and Communications Press, Nottingham
CCP	Canadian Children's Press, Guelph, Ontario
CCS	Centre for Canadian Studies, Mount Allison University, Sackville, NB
CDSH	Centre de Documentation Sciences Humaines, Paris
CENS	Centre for English Name Studies, University of Nottingham
Century	Century Publishing, London
Ceolfrith	Ceolfrith Press, Sunderland, Tyne and Wear
CESR	Société des Amis du Centre d'Études Supérieures de la Renaissance, Tours
CETEDOC	Library of Christian Latin Texts
CFA	Canadian Federation for the Humanities, Ottawa
CG	Common Ground
CH	Croom Helm, London
C–H	Chadwyck–Healey, Cambridge
Chambers	W. & R. Chambers, Edinburgh
Champaign	Champaign Public Library and Information Center, Champaign, IL
Champion	Librairie Honoré Champion, Paris
Chand	S. Chand, Madras
Chaucer	Chaucer Press
ChelseaH	Chelsea House Publishers, New York, New Haven, and Philadelphia
ChLitAssoc	Children's Literature Association
Christendom	Christendom Publications, Front Royal, VA
Chronicle	Chronicle Books, London
Chrysalis	Chrysalis Press
ChuoUL	Chuo University Library, Tokyo
Churchman	Churchman Publishing, Worthing, W. Sussex
Cistercian	Cistercian Publications, Kalamazoo, MI
CL	City Lights Books, San Francisco
CLA	Canadian Library Association, Ottawa
Clarendon	Clarendon Press, Oxford
Claridge	Claridge, St Albans, Hertfordshire
Clarion	Clarion State College, Clarion, PA
Clark	T. & T. Clark, Edinburgh
Clarke	James Clarke, Cambridge
Classical	Classical Publishing, New Delhi
CLCS	Centre for Language and Communication Studies, Trinity College, Dublin
ClogherHS	Clogher Historical Society, Monaghan, Eire
CLUEB	Cooperativa Libraria Universitaria Editrice, Bologna
Clunie	Clunie Press, Pitlochry, Tayside
CMAP	Caxton's Modem Arts Press, Dallas, TX
CMERS	Center for Medieval and Early Renaissance Studies, Binghamton, NY

CML	William Andrews Clark Memorial Library, Los Angeles
CMST	Centre for Medieval Studies, University of Toronto
Coach House	Coach House Press, Toronto
Colleagues	Colleagues Press, East Lansing, MI
Collector	Collector, London
College-Hill	College-Hill Press, San Diego, CA
Collins	William Collins, London
CollinsA	William Collins (Australia), Sydney
Collins & Brown	Collins & Brown, London
ColUP	Columbia UP, New York
Comedia	Comedia Publishing, London
Comet	Comet Books, London
Compton	Compton Press, Tisbury, Wiltshire
Constable	Constable, London
Contemporary	Contemporary Books, Chicago
Continuum	Continuum Publishing, New York
Copp	Copp Clark Pitman, Mississuaga, Ontario
Corgi	Corgi Books, London
CorkUP	Cork UP, Eire
Cormorant	Cormorant Press, Victoria, BC
Cornford	Cornford Press, Launceston, Tasmania
CornUP	Cornell UP, Ithaca, NY
Cornwallis	Cornwallis Press, Hastings, E. Sussex
Coronado	Coronado Press, Lawrence, KS
Cosmo	Cosmo Publications, New Delhi
Coteau	Coteau Books, Regina, Saskatchewan
Cowley	Cowley Publications, Cambridge, MA
Cowper	Cowper House, Pacific Grove, CA
CPP	Canadian Poetry Press, London, Ontario
CQUP	Central Queensland UP, Rockhampton
Crabtree	Crabtree Press, Sussex
Craftsman House	Craftsman House, Netherlands
Craig Pottoon	Craig Pottoon Publishing, New Zealand
Crawford	Crawford House Publishing, Hindmarsh, SA
Creag Darach	Creag Durach Publications, Stirling
CreativeB	Creative Books, New Delhi
Cresset	Cresset Library, London
CRNLE	Centre for Research in the New Literatures in English, Adelaide
Crossing	Crossing Press, Freedom, CA
Crossroad	Crossroad Publishing, New York
Crown	Crown Publishers, New York
Crowood	Crowood Press, Marlborough, Wiltshire
CSAL	Centre for Studies in Australian Literature, University of Western Australia, Nedlands
CSLI	Center for the Study of Language and Information, Stanford University
CSP	Canadian Scholars' Press, Toronto
CSU	Cleveland State University, Cleveland, OH
CTHS	Éditions du Comité des Travaux Historiques et Scientifiques, Paris
CUAP	Catholic University of America Press, Washington, DC

Cuff	Harry Cuff Publications, St John's, Newfoundland
CULouvain	Catholic University of Louvain, Belgium
CULublin	Catholic University of Lublin, Poland
CUP	Cambridge UP, Cambridge, New York, and Melbourne
Currency	Currency Press, Paddington, New South Wales
Currey	James Currey, London
Cushing	Cushing Memorial Library & Archives
CV	Cherry Valley Edition, Rochester, NY
CVK	Cornelson-Velhagen & Klasing, Berlin
CWU	Carl Winter Universitätsverlag, Heidelberg
Da Capo	Da Capo Press, New York
Dacorum	Dacorum College, Hemel Hempstead, Hertfordshire
Daisy	Daisy Books, Peterborough, Northampton
Dalkey	Dalkey Archive Press, Elmwood Park, IL
D&C	David & Charles, Newton Abbot, Devon
D&H	Duncker & Humblot, Berlin
D&M	Douglas & McIntyre, Vancouver, BC
D&S	Duffy and Snellgrove, Polts Point, New South Wales
Dangaroo	Dangaroo Press, Mundelstrup, Denmark
Daniel	Daniel & Daniel Publishers Inc., California
DavidB	David Brown Books
Dawson	Dawson Publishing, Folkestone, Kent
DawsonsPM	Dawsons Pall Mall
DBAP	Daphne Brasell Associates Press
DBP	Drama Book Publishers, New York
Deakin UP	Deakin UP, Geelong, Victoria
De Boeck	De Boeck-Wesmael, Brussels
Dee	Ivan R. Dee Publishers, Chicago, IL
De Graaf	De Graaf, Nierwkoup, Netherlands
Denoël	Denoël S.A.R.L., Paris
Dent	J.M. Dent, London
DentA	Dent, Ferntree Gully, Victoria
Depanee	Depanee Printers and Publishers, Nugegoda, Sri Lanka
Deutsch	André Deutsch, London
Didier	Éditions Didier, Paris
Diesterweg	Verlag Moritz Diesterweg, Frankfurt am Main
Dim Gray Bar Press	Dim Gray Bar Press
Doaba	Doaba House, Delhi
Dobby	Eric Dobby Publishing, St Albans
Dobson	Dobson Books, Durham
DodoP	Dodo Press, Gloucester
Dolmen	Dolmen Press, Portlaoise, Eire
Donald	John Donald, Edinburgh
Donker	Adriaan Donker, Johannesburg
Dorset	Dorset Publishing
Doubleday	Doubleday, London and New York
Dove	Dove, Sydney
Dovecote	Dovecote Press, Wimborne, Dorset
Dovehouse	Dovehouse Editions, Canada
Dover	Dover Publications, New York
Drew	Richard Drew, Edinburgh
Droste	Droste Verlag, Düsseldorf
Droz	Librairie Droz SA, Geneva

DublinUP	Dublin UP, Dublin
Duckworth	Gerald Duckworth, London
Duculot	J. Duculot, Gembloux, Belgium
DukeUP	Duke UP, Durham, NC
Dundurn	Dundurn Press, Toronto and London, Ontario
Duquesne	Duquesne UP, Pittsburgh
Dutton	E.P. Dutton, New York
DWT	Dr Williams's Trust, London
EA	English Association, London
EAS	English Association Sydney Incorporated
Eason	Eason & Son, Dublin
East Bay	East Bay Books, Berkeley, CA
Ebony	Ebony Books, Melbourne
Ecco	Ecco Press, New York
ECNRS	Éditions du Centre National de la Recherche Scientifique, Paris
ECW	ECW Press, Downsview, Ontario
Eden	Eden Press, Montreal and St Albans, VT
EdinUP	Edinburgh UP, Edinburgh
Edizioni	Edizioni del Grifo
Educare	Educare, Burnwood, Victoria
EEM	East European Monographs, Boulder, CO
Eerdmans	William Eerdmans, Grand Rapids, MI
EETS	Early English Text Society, c/o Exeter College, Oxford
1890sS	Eighteen-Nineties Society, Oxford
Eihosha	Eihosha, Tokyo
Elephas	Elephas Books, Kewdale, Australia
Elibank	Elibank Press, Wellington, New Zealand
Elm Tree	Elm Tree Books, London
ELS	English Literary Studies
Ember	Ember Press, Brixham, South Devon
EMSH	Editions de la Maison des Sciences de l'Homme, Paris
Enitharmon	Enitharmon Press, London
Enzyklopädie	Enzyklopädie, Leipzig
EONF	Eugene O'Neill Foundation, Danville, CA
EPNS	English Place-Name Society, Beeston, Nottingham
EPURE	Editions et Presses universitaires de Reims
Epworth	Epworth Press, Manchester
Eriksson	Paul Eriksson, Middlebury, VT
Erlbaum	Erlbaum Associates, NJ
Erskine	Erskine Press, Harleston, Norfolk
EscutchP	Escutcheon Press
ESI	Edizioni Scientifiche Italiane, Naples
ESL	Edizioni di Storia e Letteratura, Rome
EUFS	Editions Universitaires Fribourg Suisse
EUL	Edinburgh University Library, Edinburgh
Europa	Europa Publishers, London
Evans	M. Evans, New York
Exact Change	Exact Change, Boston
Exeter UP	Exeter UP, Devon
Exile	Exile Editions, Toronto, Ontario
Eyre	Eyre Methuen, London
FAB	Free Association Books, London

Faber	Faber & Faber, London
FAC	Federation d'Activites Culturelles, Paris
FACP	Fremantle Arts Centre Press, Fremantle, WA
Falcon Books	Falcon Books, Eastbourne
FALS	Foundation for Australian Literary Studies, James Cook University of North Queensland, Townsville
F&F	Fels & Firn Press, San Anselmo, CA
F&S	Feffer & Simons, Amsterdam
Farrand	Farrand Press, London
Fay	Barbara Fay, Stuttgart
F–B	Ford–Brown, Houston, TX
FCP	Four Courts Press, Dublin
FDUP	Fairleigh Dickinson UP, Madison, NJ
FE	Fourth Estate, London
Feminist	Feminist Press, New York
FictionColl	Fiction Collective, Brooklyn College, Brooklyn, NY
Field Day	Field Day, Derry
Fifth House	Fifth House Publications, Saskatoon, Saskatchewan
FILEF	FILEF Italo–Australian Publications, Leichhardt, New South Wales
Fine	Donald Fine, New York
Fink	Fink Verlag, Munich
Five Leaves	Five Leaves Publications, Nottingham
Flamingo	Flamingo Publishing, Newark, NJ
Flammarion	Flammarion, Paris
FlindersU	Flinders University of South Australia, Bedford Park
Floris	Floris Books, Edinburgh
FlorSU	Florida State University, Tallahassee, FL
FOF	Facts on File, New York
Folger	Folger Shakespeare Library, Washington, DC
Folio	Folio Press, London
Fontana	Fontana Press, London
Footprint	Footprint Press, Colchester, Essex
FordUP	Fordham UP, New York
Foris	Foris Publications, Dordrecht
Forsten	Egbert Forsten Publishing, Groningen, Netherlands
Fortress	Fortress Press, Philadelphia
Francke	Francke Verlag, Berne
Franklin	Burt Franklin, New York
FreeP	Free Press, New York
FreeUP	Free UP, Amsterdam
Freundlich	Freundlich Books, New York
Frommann-Holzboog	Frommann-Holzboog, Stuttgart
FS&G	Farrar, Straus & Giroux
FSP	Five Seasons Press, Madley, Hereford
FW	Fragments West/Valentine Press, Long Beach, CA
FWA	Fiji Writers' Association, Suva
FWP	Falling Wall Press, Bristol
Gale	Gale Research, Detroit, MI
Galilée	Galilée, Paris
Gallimard	Gallimard, Paris
G&G	Grevatt & Grevatt, Newcastle upon Tyne
G&M	Gill & Macmillan, Dublin

Garland	Garland Publishing, New York
Gasson	Roy Gasson Associates, Wimbourne, Dorset
Gateway	Gateway Editions, Washington, DC
GE	Greenwich Exchange, UK
GIA	GIA Publications, USA
Girasole	Edizioni del Girasole, Ravenna
GL	Goose Lane Editions, Fredericton, NB
GlasgowDL	Glasgow District Libraries, Glasgow
Gleerup	Gleerupska, Lund
Gliddon	Gliddon Books Publishers, Norwich
Gloger	Gloger Family Books, Portland, OR
GMP	GMP Publishing, London
GMSmith	Gibbs M. Smith, Layton, UT
Golden Dog	Golden Dog, Ottawa
Gollancz	Victor Gollancz, London
Gomer	Gomer Press, Llandysul, Dyfed
GothU	Gothenburg University, Gothenburg
Gower	Gower Publishing, Aldershot, Hants
GRAAT	Groupe de Recherches Anglo-Américaines de Tours
Grafton	Grafton Books, London
GranB	Granary Books, New York
Granta	Granta Publications, London
Granville	Granville Publishing, London
Grasset	Grasset & Fasquelle, Paris
Grassroots	Grassroots, London
Graywolf	Graywolf Press, St Paul, MI
Greenhalgh	M.J. Greenhalgh, London
Greenhill	Greenhill Books, London
Greenwood	Greenwood Press, Westport, CT
Gregg	Gregg Publishing, Surrey
Greville	Greville Press, Warwick
Greymitre	Greymitre Books, London
GroC	Grolier Club, New York
Groos	Julius Groos Verlag, Heidelberg
Grove	Grove Press, New York
GRP	Greenfield Review Press, New York
Grüner	B.R. Grüner, Amsterdam
Gruyter	Walter de Gruyter, Berlin
Guernica	Guernica Editions, Montreal, Canada
Guilford	Guilford, New York
Gulmohar	Gulmohar Press, Islamabad, Pakistan
Haggerston	Haggerston Press, London
HakluytS	Hakluyt Society, c/o British Library, London
Hale	Robert Hale, London
Hall	G.K. Hall, Boston, MA
Halstead	Halstead Press, Rushcutters Bay, New South Wales
HalsteadP	Halstead Press, c/o J. Wiley & Sons, Chichester, W. Sussex
Hambledon	Hambledon Press, London
H&I	Hale & Iremonger, Sydney
H&L	Hambledon and London
H&M	Holmes & Meier, London and New York
H&S	Hodder & Stoughton, London
H&SNZ	Hodder & Stoughton, Auckland

H&W	Hill & Wang, New York
Hansib	Hansib Publishing, London
Harbour	Harbour Publishing, Madeira Park, BC
Harman	Harman Publishing House, New Delhi
Harper	Harper & Row, New York
Harrap	Harrap, Edinburgh
HarrV	Harrassowitz Verlag, Wiesbaden
HarvardUP	Harvard UP, Cambridge, MA
Harwood	Harwood Academic Publishers, Langhorne, PA
Hatje	Verlag Gerd Hatje, Germany
HBJ	Harcourt Brace Jovanovich, New York and London
HC	HarperCollins, London
HCAus	HarperCollins Australia, Pymble, New South Wales
Headline	Headline Book Publishing, London
Heath	D.C. Heath, Lexington, MS
HebrewUMP	Hebrew University Magnes Press
Heinemann	William Heinemann, London
HeinemannA	William Heinemann, St Kilda, Victoria
HeinemannC	Heinemann Educational Books, Kingston, Jamaica
HeinemannNg	Heinemann Educational Books, Nigeria
HeinemannNZ	Heinemann Publishers, Auckland (now Heinemann Reed)
HeinemannR	Heinemann Reed, Auckland
Helm	Christopher Helm, London
HelmI	Helm Information
Herbert	Herbert Press, London
Hermitage	Hermitage Antiquarian Bookshop, Denver, CO
Hern	Nick Hem Books, London
Hertfordshire	Hertfordshire Publications
Heyday	Heyday Books, Berkeley, CA
HH	Hamish Hamilton, London
Hilger	Adam Hilger, Bristol
HM	Harvey Miller, London
HMSO	HMSO, London
Hodder, Moa, Beckett	Hodder, Moa, Beckett, Milford, Auckland, New Zealand
Hodge	A. Hodge, Penzance, Cornwall
Hogarth	Hogarth Press, London
HongKongUP	Hong Kong UP, Hong Kong
Horsdal & Schubart	Horsdal & Schubart, Victoria, BC
Horwood	Ellis Horwood, Hemel Hempstead, Hertfordshire
HoughtonM	Houghton Mifflin, Boston, MA
Howard	Howard UP, Washington, DC
HREOC	Human Rights and Equal Opportunity Commission, Commonweath of Australia, Canberra
HRW	Holt, Reinhart & Winston, New York
Hudson	Hudson Hills Press, New York
Hueber	Max Hueber, Ismaning, Germany
HUL	Hutchinson University Library, London
HullUP	Hull UP, University of Hull
Humanities	Humanities Press, Atlantic Highlands, NJ
Humanities-Ebooks	Humanities Ebooks, Penrith
Huntington	Huntington Library, San Marino, CA
Hurst	C. Hurst, Covent Garden, London

Hutchinson	Hutchinson Books, London
HW	Harvester Wheatsheaf, Hemel Hempstead, Hertfordshire
HWWilson	H.W. Wilson, New York
Hyland House	Hyland House Publishing, Victoria
HyphenP	Hyphen Press, London
IAAS	Indian Institute of Aveanced Studies, Lahore and New Delhi
Ian Henry	Ian Henry Publications, Homchurch, Essex
IAP	Irish Academic Press, Dublin
Ibadan	Ibadan University Press
IBK	Innsbrucker Beiträge zur Kulturwissenschaft, University of Innsbruck
ICA	Institute of Contemporary Arts, London
IHA	International Hopkins Association, Waterloo, Ontario
IJamaica	Institute of Jamaica Publications, Kingston
Imago	Imago Imprint, New York
Imperial WarMuseum	Imperial War Museum Publications, London
IndUP	Indiana UP, Bloomington, IN
Inkblot	Inkblot Publications, Berkeley, CA
IntUP	International Universities Press, New York
Inventions	Inventions Press, London
IonaC	Iona College, New Rochelle, NY
IowaSUP	Iowa State UP, Ames, IA
IOWP	Isle of Wight County Press, Newport, Isle of Wight
IP	In Parenthesis, London
Ipswich	Ipswich Press, Ipswich, MA
IrishAP	Irish Academic Press, Dublin
ISI	ISI Press, Philadelphia
Italica	Italica Press, New York
IULC	Indiana University Linguistics Club, Bloomington, IN
IUP	Indiana University of Pennsylvania Press, Indiana, PA
Ivon	Ivon Publishing House, Bombay
Jacaranda	Jacaranda Wiley, Milton, Queensland
JadavpurU	Jadavpur University, Calcutta
James CookU	James Cook University of North Queensland, Townsville
Jarrow	Parish of Jarrow, Tyne and Wear
JBPC	John Benjamins Publishing Company, Amsterdam, The Netherlands
Jesperson	Jesperson Press, St John's, Newfoundland
JHall	James Hall, Leamington Spa, Warwickshire
JHUP	Johns Hopkins UP, Baltimore, MD
JIWE	JIWE Publications, University of Gulbarga, India
JLRC	Jack London Research Center, Glen Ellen, CA
J-NP	Joe-Noye Press
Jonas	Jonas Verlag, Marburg, Germany
Joseph	Michael Joseph, London
Journeyman	Journeyman Press, London
JPGM	J. Paul Getty Museum
JT	James Thin, Edinburgh
Junction	Junction Books, London
Junius-Vaughan	Junius-Vaughan Press, Fairview, NJ
Jupiter	Jupiter Press, Lake Bluff, IL

JyväskyläU	Jyväskylä University, Jyväskylä, Finland
Kaibunsha	Kaibunsha, Tokyo
K&N	Königshausen & Neumann, Würzburg, Germany
K&W	Kaye & Ward, London
Kangaroo	Kangaroo Press, Simon & Schuster (Australia), Roseville, New South Wales
Kansai	Kansai University of Foreign Studies, Osaka
Kardo	Kardo, Coatbridge, Scotland
Kardoorair	Kardoorair Press, Adelaide
Karia	Karia Press, London
Karnak	Karnak House, London
Karoma	Karoma Publishers, Ann Arbor, MI
Katha	Katha, New Delhi
KC	Kyle Cathie, London
KCL	King's College London
KeeleUP	Keele University Press
Kegan Paul	Kegan Paul International, London
Kenkyu	Kenkyu-Sha, Tokyo
Kennikat	Kennikat Press, Port Washington, NY
Kensal	Kensal Press, Oxford
KentSUP	Kent State University Press, Kent, OH
KenyaLB	Kenya Literature Bureau, Nairobi
Kerosina	Kerosina Publications, Worcester Park, Surrey
Kerr	Charles H. Kerr, Chicago
Kestrel	Viking Kestrel, London
K/H	Kendall/Hunt Publishing, Dubuque, IA
Kingsley	J. Kingsley Publishers, London
Kingston	Kingston Publishers, Kingston, Jamaica
Kinseido	Kinseido, Tokyo
KITLV	KITLV Press, Leiden
Klostermann	Vittorio Klostermann, Frankfurt am Main
Kluwer	Kluwer Academic Publications, Dordrecht
Knopf	Alfred A. Knopf, New York
Knowledge	Knowledge Industry Publications, White Plains, NY
Kraft	Kraft Books, Ibadan
Kraus	Kraus International Publications, White Plains, NY
KSUP	Kent State UP, Kent OH
LA	Library Association, London
LACUS	Linguistic Association of Canada and the United States, Chapel Hill, NC
Lake View	Lake View Press, Chicago
LAm	Library of America, New York
Lancelot	Lancelot Press, Hantsport, NS
Landesman	Jay Landesman, London
L&W	Lawrence & Wishart, London
Lane	Allen Lane, London
Lang	Peter D. Lang, Frankfurt am Main and Berne
Latimer	Latimer Trust
Learning Media	Learning Media Ltd, Wellington, New Zealand
LehighUP	Lehigh University Press, Bethlehem, PA
LeicAE	University of Leicester, Department of Adult Education
LeicsCC	Leicestershire County Council, Libraries and Information Service, Leicester

LeicUP	Leicester UP, Leicester
LeidenUP	Leiden UP, Leiden
Leopard's Head	Leopard's Head Press, Oxford
Letao	Letao Press, Albury, New South Wales
LeuvenUP	Leuven UP, Leuven, Belgium
Lexik	Lexik House, Cold Spring, NY
Lexington	Lexington Publishers
LF	LiberFörlag, Stockholm
LH	Lund Humphries Publishers, London
Liberty	Liberty Classics, Indianapolis, IN
Libris	Libris, London
LibrU	Libraries Unlimited, Englewood, CO
Liffey	Liffey Press, Dublin
Liguori	Liguori, Naples
Limelight	Limelight Editions, New York
Lime Tree	Lime Tree Press, Octopus Publishing, London
LincolnUP	Lincoln University Press, Nebraska
LINCOM	LINCOM Europa, Munich, Germany
LIT	Lit Verlag
LITIR	LITIR Database, University of Alberta
LittleH	Little Hills Press, Burwood, New South Wales
Liveright	Liveright Publishing, New York
LiverUP	Liverpool UP, Liverpool
Livre de Poche	Le Livre de Poche, Paris
Llanerch	Llanerch Enterprises, Lampeter, Dyfed
Locust Hill	Locust Hill Press, West Cornwall, CT
Loewenthal	Loewenthal Press, New York
Longman	Pearson Longman Wesley, Harlow, Essex
LongmanC	Longman Caribbean, Harlow, Essex
LongmanF	Longman, France
LongmanNZ	Longman, Auckland
Longspoon	Longspoon Press, University of Alberta, Edmonton
Lovell	David Lovell Publishing, Brunswick, Australia
Lowell	Lowell Press, Kansas City, MS
Lowry	Lowry Publishers, Johannesburg
LSUP	Louisiana State UP, Baton Rouge, LA
L3	L3: Liege Language and Literature, University of Liege, Belgium
LundU	Lund University, Lund, Sweden
LUP	Loyola UP, Chicago
Lutterworth	Lutterworth Press, Cambridge
Lymes	Lymes Press, Newcastle, Staffordshire
Lythrum	Lythrum Press, Adelaide
MAA	Medieval Academy of America, Cambridge, MA
Macleay	Macleay Press, Paddington, New South Wales
Macmillan	Macmillan Publishers, London
MacmillanC	Macmillan Caribbean
Madison	Madison Books, Lanham, MD
Madurai	Madurai University, Madurai, India
Maecenas	Maecenas Press, Iowa City, Iowa
Magabala	Magabala Books, Broome, WA
Magnes	Magnes Press, The Hebrew University, Jerusalem
Mainstream	Mainstream Publishing, Edinburgh

MaIP	Marymount Institute Press, Tsehai Publishers, Los Angeles, CA
Maisonneuve	Maisonneuve Press, Washington, DC
Malone	Malone Society, c/o King's College, London
Mambo	Mambo Press, Gweru, Zimbabwe
ManCASS	Manchester Centre for Anglo-Saxon Studies, University of Manchester
M&E	Macdonald & Evans, Estover, Plymouth, Devon
M&S	McClelland & Stewart, Toronto
Maney	W.S. Maney & Sons, Leeds
Mango	Mango Publishing, London, United Kingdom
Manohar	Manohar Publishers, Darya Gan, New Delhi
Mansell	Mansell Publishing, London
Manufacture	La Manufacture, Lyons
ManUP	Manchester UP, Manchester
Mardaga	Mardaga
Mariner	Mariner Books, Boston, MA
MarquetteUP	Marquette UP, Milwaukee, WI
Marvell	Marvell Press, Calstock, Cornwall
MB	Mitchell Beazley, London
McDougall, Littel	McDougall, Littel, Evanston, IL
McFarland	McFarland, Jefferson, NC
McG-QUP	McGill-Queen's UP, Montreal
McGraw-Hill	McGraw-Hill, New York
McIndoe	John McIndoe, Dunedin, New Zealand
McPheeG	McPhee Gribble Publishers, Fitzroy, Victoria
McPherson	McPherson, Kingston, NY
MCSU	Maria Curie Skłodowska University
ME	M. Evans, New York
Meany	P.D. Meany Publishing, Port Credit, Ontario
Meckler	Meckler Publishing, Westport, CT
MelbourneUP	Melbourne UP, Carlton South, Victoria
Mellen	Edwin Mellen Press, Lewiston, NY
MellenR	Mellen Research UP
Menzies	Menzies Centre for Australian Studies
MercerUP	Mercer UP, Macon, GA
Mercury	Mercury Press, Stratford, Ontario
Merlin	Merlin Press, London
Methuen	Methuen, London
MethuenA	Methuen Australia, North Ryde, New South Wales
MethuenC	Methuen, Toronto
Metro	Metro Publishing, Auckland
Metzler	Metzler, Stuttgart
MGruyter	Mouton de Gruyter, Berlin, New York, and Amsterdam
MH	Michael Haag, London
MHRA	Modern Humanities Research Association, London
MHS	Missouri Historical Society, St Louis, MO
MI	Microforms International, Pergamon Press, Oxford
Micah	Micah Publications, Marblehead, MA
MichSUP	Michigan State UP, East Lansing, MI
MidNAG	Mid-Northumberland Arts Group, Ashington, Northumbria
Miegunyah	Miegunyah Press, Carlton, Victoria, Australia

Mieyungah	Mieyungah Press, Melbourne University Press, Carlton South, Victoria
Milestone	Milestone Publications, Horndean, Hampshire
Millennium	Millennium Books, E.J. Dwyer, Newtown, Australia
Millstream	Millstream Books, Bath
Milner	Milner, London
Minuit	Éditions de Minuit, Paris
MIP	Medieval Institute Publications, Western Michigan University, Kalamazoo
MITP	Massachusetts Institute of Technology Press, Cambridge, MA
MLA	Modern Language Association of America, New York
MIM	Multilingual Matters, Clevedon, Avon
MLP	Manchester Literary and Philosophical Society, Manchester
MnaN	Mkuki na Nyota Publishers, Dar es Salaam, Tanzania
Modern Library	Modern Library (Random House), New York
Monarch	Monarch Publications, Sussex
Moonraker	Moonraker Press, Bradford-on-Avon, Wiltshire
Moorland	Moorland Publishing, Ashbourne, Derby
Moreana	Moreana, Angers, France
MorganSU	Morgan State University, Baltimore, MD
Morrow	William Morrow, New York
Mosaic	Mosaic Press, Oakville, Ontario
Motilal	Motilal Books, Oxford
Motley	Motley Press, Romsey, Hampshire
Mouton	Mouton Publishers, New York and Paris
Mowbray	A.R. Mowbray, Oxford
MR	Martin Robertson, Oxford
MRS	Medieval and Renaissance Society, North Texas State University, Denton
MRTS	MRTS, Binghamton, NY
MSUP	Memphis State UP, Memphis, TN
MtAllisonU	Mount Allison University, Sackville, NB
MTP	Museum Tusculanum Press, University of Copenhagen
Mulini	Mulini Press, ACT
Muller	Frederick Muller, London
MULP	McMaster University Library Press
Murray	John Murray, London
Mursia	Ugo Mursia, Milan
NAL	New American Library, New York
Narr	Gunter Narr Verlag, Tübingen
Nathan	Fernand Nathan, Paris
NBB	New Beacon Books, London
NBCAus	National Book Council of Australia, Melbourne
NCP	New Century Press, Durham
ND	New Directions, New York
NDT	Nottingham Drama Texts, c/o University of Nottingham
NEL	New English Library, London
NELM	National English Literary Museum, Grahamstown, S. Africa
Nelson	Nelson Publishers, Melbourne
NelsonT	Thomas Nelson, London
New Endeavour	New Endeavour Press
NeWest	NeWest Press, Edmonton, Alberta

New Horn	New Horn Press, Ibadan, Nigeria
New Island	New Island Press
NewIssuesP	New Issues Press, Western Michigan University
NH	New Horizon Press, Far Hills, NJ
N-H	Nelson-Hall, Chicago
NHPC	North Holland Publishing, Amsterdam and New York
NicV	Nicolaische Verlagsbuchhandlung, Berlin
NIE	La Nuova Italia Editrice, Florence
Niemeyer	Max Niemeyer, Tübingen, Germany
Nightwood	Nightwood Editions, Toronto
NIUP	Northern Illinois UP, De Kalb, IL
NUSam	National University of Samoa
NLA	National Library of Australia
NLB	New Left Books, London
NLC	National Library of Canada, Ottawa
NLP	New London Press, Dallas, TX
NLS	National Library of Scotland, Edinburgh
NLW	National Library of Wales, Aberystwyth, Dyfed
Nodus	Nodus Publikationen, Münster
Northcote	Northcote House Publishers, Plymouth
NortheastemU	Northeastern University, Boston, MA
NorthwesternUP	Norhwestem UP, Evanston, IL
Norton	W.W. Norton, New York and London
NorUP	Norwegian University Press, Oslo
Novus	Novus Press, Oslo
NPF	National Poetry Foundation, Orono, ME
NPG	National Portrait Gallery, London
NPP	North Point Press, Berkeley, CA
NSP	New Statesman Publishing, New Delhi
NSU Press	Northern States Universities Press
NSWUP	New South Wales UP, Kensington, New South Wales
NT	National Textbook, Lincolnwood, IL
NUC	Nipissing University College, North Bay, Ontario
NUP	National University Publications, Millwood, NY
NUSam	National University of Samoa
NUU	New University of Ulster, Coleraine
NWAP	North Waterloo Academic Press, Waterloo, Ontario
NWP	New World Perspectives, Montreal
NYPL	New York Public Library, New York
NYUP	New York UP, New York
OakK	Oak Knoll Press, New Castle, DE
O&B	Oliver & Boyd, Harlow, Essex
Oasis	Oasis Books, London
OBAC	Organization of Black American Culture, Chicago
OberlinCP	Oberlin College Press, Oberlin, OH
Oberon	Oberon Books, London
O'Brien	O'Brien Press, Dublin
OBS	Oxford Bibliographical Society, Bodleian Library, Oxford
Octopus	Octopus Books, London
OdenseUP	Odense UP, Odense
OE	Officina Edizioni, Rome
OEColl	Old English Colloquium, Berkeley, CA
Offord	John Offord Publications, Eastbourne, E. Sussex

OhioUP	Ohio UP, Athens, OH
Oldcastle	Oldcastle Books, Harpenden, Hertfordshire
Olms	Georg Ohms, Hildesheim, Germany
Olschki	Leo S. Olschki, Florence
O'Mara	Michael O'Mara Books, London
Omnigraphics	Omnigraphics, Detroit, MI
Oneworld	Oneworld Classics, Surrey
Open Books	Open Books Publishing, Wells, Somerset
Open Court	Open Court Publishing, USA
OpenUP	Open UP, Buckingham and Philadelphia
OPP	Oxford Polytechnic Press, Oxford
Orbis	Orbis Books, London
OregonSUP	Oregon State UP, Corvallis, OR
Oriel	Oriel Press, Stocksfield, Northumberland
Orient Longman	Orient Longman, India
OrientUP	Oriental UP, London
OriginalNZ	Original Books, Wellington, New Zealand
ORP	Ontario Review Press, Princeton, NJ, United States
Ortnamnsarkivet	Ortnamnsarkivet i Uppsala, Sweden
Orwell	Orwell Press, Southwold, Suffolk
Oryx	Oryx Press, Phoenix, AR
OSUP	Ohio State UP, Columbus, OH
Other	Otherland, Kingsbury, VC, Australia
OTP	Oak Tree Press, London
OUCA	Oxford University Committee for Archaeology, Oxford
OUP	Oxford UP, Oxford
OUPAm	Oxford UP, New York
OUPAus	Oxford UP, Melbourne
OUPC	Oxford UP, Toronto
OUPI	Oxford UP, New Delhi
OUPNZ	Oxford UP, Auckland
OUPSA	Oxford UP Southern Africa, Cape Town
Outlet	Outlet Book, New York
Overlook	Overlook Press, New York
Owen	Peter Owen, London
Owl	Owl
Pace UP	Pace University Press, New York
Pacifica	Press Pacifica, Kailua, Hawaii
Paget	Paget Press, Santa Barbara, CA
PAJ	PAJ Publications, New York
Paladin	Paladin Books, London
Palgrave	Palgrave, NY
Pan	Pan Books, London
PalMac	Palgrave Macmillan, Hampshire, UK
PanAmU	Pan American University, Edinburgh, TX
P&C	Pickering & Chatto, London
Pandanus	Pandanus Press, Canberra, Australia
Pandion	Pandion Press, Capitola, CA
Pandora	Pandora Press, London
Pan Macmillan	Pan Macmillan Australia, South Yarra, Victoria
Pantheon	Pantheon Books, New York
ParagonH	Paragon House Publishers, New York
Parnassus	Parnassus Imprints, Hyannis, MA

Parousia	Parousia Publications, London
Paternoster	Paternoster Press, Carlisle, Cumbria
Patten	Patten Press, Penzance
Paulist	Paulist Press, Ramsey, NJ
Paupers	Paupers' Press, Nottingham
Pavilion	Pavilion Books, London
PBFA	Provincial Booksellers' Fairs Association, Cambridge
PCP	Playwrights Canada Press, Ontario, Canada
Peachtree	Peachtree Publishers, Atlanta, GA
Pearson	David Pearson, Huntingdon, Cambridge
Peepal Tree	Peepal Tree Books, Leeds
Peeters	Peeters Publishers and Booksellers, Leuven, Belgium
Pelham	Pelham Books, London
Pembridge	Pembridge Press, London
Pemmican	Pemmican Publications, Winnipeg, Canada
PencraftI	Pencraft International, Ashok Vihar II, Delhi
Penguin	Penguin Books, Harmondsworth, Middlesex
PenguinA	Penguin Books, Ringwood, Victoria
PenguinNZ	Penguin Books, Auckland
Penkevill	Penkevill Publishing, Greenwood, FL
Pentland	Pentland Press, Ely, Cambridge
Penumbra	Penumbra Press, Moonbeam, Ontario
People's	People's Publications, London
Pergamon	Pergamon Press, Oxford
Permanent	Permanent Press, Sag Harbor, NY
Permanent Black	Permanent Black, Delhi, India
Perpetua	Perpetua Press, Oxford
Petton	Petton Books, Oxford
Pevensey	Pevensey Press, Newton Abbot, Devon
PH	Prentice-Hall, Englewood Cliffs, NJ
Phaidon	Phaidon Press, London
PHI	Prentice-Hall International, Hemel Hempstead, Hertfordshire
PhilL	Philosophical Library, New York
Phillimore	Phillimore, Chichester
Phoenix	Phoenix
Piatkus	Piatkus Books, London
Pickwick	Pickwick Publications, Allison Park, PA
Pilgrim	Pilgrim Books, Norman, OK
PIMS	Pontifical Institute of Mediaeval Studies, Toronto
Pinter	Frances Pinter Publishers, London
Plains	Plains Books, Carlisle
Plenum	Plenum Publishing, London and New York
Plexus	Plexus Publishing, London
Pliegos	Editorial Pliegos, Madrid
Ploughshares	Ploughshares Books, Watertown, MA
PlovdivUP	Plovdiv University Press
Pluto	Pluto Press, London
PML	Pierpont Morgan Library, New York
Polity	Polity Press, Cambridge
Polygon	Polygon, Edinburgh
Polymath	Polymath Press, Tasmania, Australia
Poolbeg	Poolbeg Press, Swords, Dublin
Porcepic	Press Porcepic, Victoria, BC

Porcupine	Porcupine's Quill, Canada
PortN	Port Nicholson Press, Wellington, NZ
Potter	Clarkson N. Potter, New York
Power	Power Publications, University of Sydney
PPUBarcelona	Promociones y Publicaciones Universitarias, Barcelona
Praeger	Praeger, New York
Prakash	Prakash Books, India
Prestel	Prestel Verlag, Germany
PrestigeB	Prestige Books, New Delhi
Primavera	Edizioni Primavera, Gunti Publishing, Florence, Italy
Primrose	Primrose Press, Alhambra, CA
PrincetonUL	Princeton University Library, Princeton, NJ
PrincetonUP	Princeton UP, Princeton, NJ
Printwell	Printwell Publishers, Jaipur, India
Prism	Prism Press, Bridport, Dorset
PRO	Public Record Office, London
Profile	Profile Books, Ascot, Berks
ProgP	Progressive Publishers, Calcutta
PSUP	Pennsylvania State UP, University Park, PA
Pucker	Puckerbrush Press, Orono, ME
PUF	Presses Universitaires de France, Paris
PULM	Presses Universitaires de la Mediterranee, Université Paul-Valéry - Montpellier III, France
PUPV	Publications de l'université Paul-Valéry, Montpellier 3
PurdueUP	Purdue UP, Lafayette, IN
Pushcart	Pushcart Press, Wainscott, NY
Pustet	Friedrich Pustet, Regensburg
Putnam	Putnam Publishing, New York
PWP	Poetry Wales Press, Ogmore by Sea, mid-Glamorgan
QED	QED Press, Ann Arbor, MI
Quarry	Quarry Press, Kingston, Ontario
Quartet	Quartet Books, London
Quaternary	The Quaternary Institute
QUT	Queensland University of Technology
RA	Royal Academy of Arts, London
Rainforest	Rainforest Publishing, Faxground, New South Wales
Rampant Lions	Rampant Lions Press, Cambridge
R&B	Rosenklide & Bagger, Copenhagen
R&L	Rowman & Littlefield, Totowa, NJ
Randle	Ian Randle, Kingston, Jamaica
RandomH	Random House, London and New York
RandomHAus	Random House Australia, Victoria
RandomHNZ	Random House New Zealand Limited, Auckland, New Zealand
Ravan	Ravan Press, Johannesburg
Ravette	Ravette, London
Ravi Dayal	Ravi Dayal Publishers, New Delhi, India
Rawat	Rawat Publishing, Jaipur and New Delhi
Reaktion	Reaktion Books, London
Rebel	Rebel Press, London
Red Kite	Red Kite Press, Guelph, Ontario
Red Rooster	Red Rooster Press, Hotham Hill, Victoria
Red Sea	Red Sea Press, NJ

Reed	Reed Books, Port Melbourne
Reed NZ	Reed Publishing NZ Ltd., Auckland, New Zealand
Reference	Reference Press, Toronto
Regents	Regents Press of Kansas, Lawrence, KS
Reichenberger	Roswitha Reichenberger, Kessel, Germany
Reinhardt	Max Reinhardt, London
Remak	Remak, Alblasserdam, Netherlands
RenI	Renaissance Institute, Sophia University, Tokyo
Research	Research Publications, Reading
RETS	Renaissance English Text Society, Chicago
RH	Ramsay Head Press, Edinburgh
RHS	Royal Historical Society, London
RIA	Royal Irish Academy, Dublin
RiceUP	Rice UP, Houston, TX
Richarz	Hans Richarz, St Augustin, Germany
RICL	Research Institute for Comparative Literature, University of Alberta
Rivers Oram	Rivers Oram Press, London
Rizzoli	Rizzoli International Publications, New York
RobartsCCS	Robarts Centre for Canadian Studies, York University, North York, Ontario
Robinson	Robinson Publishing, London
Robson	Robson Books, London
Rodopi	Rodopi, Amsterdam
Roebuck	Stuart Roebuck, Suffolk
RoehamptonI	Roehampton Institute London
Ronsdale	Ronsdale Press
Routledge	Routledge, London and New York
Royce	Robert Royce, London
RS	Royal Society, London
RSC	Royal Shakespeare Company, London
RSL	Royal Society of Literature, London
RSVP	Research Society for Victorian Periodicals, University of Leicester
RT	RT Publications, London
Running	Running Press, Philadelphia
Russell	Michael Russell, Norwich
RutgersUP	Rutgers UP, New Brunswick, NJ
Ryan	Ryan Publishing, London
SA	Sahitya Akademi, New Delhi
Sage	Sage Publications, London
SAI	Sociological Abstracts, San Diego, CA
Salamander	Salamander Books, London
Salem	Salem Press, Englewood Cliffs, NJ
S&A	Shukayr and Akasheh, Amman, Jordon
S&D	Stein & Day, Briarcliff Manor, NJ
S&J	Sidgwick & Jackson, London
S&M	Sun & Moon Press, Los Angeles
S&P	Simon & Piere, Toronto
S&S	Simon & Schuster, New York and London
S&W	Secker & Warburg, London
Sangam	Sangam Books, London
Sangsters	Sangsters Book Stores, Kingston, Jamaica

SAP	Scottish Academic Press, Edinburgh
Saros	Saros International Publishers
Sarup	Sarup & Sons, New Delhi
SASSC	Sydney Association for Studies in Society and Culture, University of Sydney, New South Wales
Saur	Bowker-Saur, Sevenoaks, Kent
Savacou	Savacou Publications, Kingston, Jamaica
S-B	Schwann-Bagel, Düsseldorf
ScanUP	Scandinavian University Presses, Oslo
Scarecrow	Scarecrow Press, Metuchen, NJ
Schäuble	Schäuble Verlag, Rheinfelden, Germany
Schmidt	Erich Schmidt Verlag, Berlin
Schneider	Lambert Schneider, Heidelberg
Schocken	Schocken Books, New York
Scholarly	Scholarly Press, St Clair Shores, MI
ScholarsG	Scholars Press, GA
Schöningh	Ferdinand Schöningh, Paderborn, Germany
Schwinn	Michael Schwinn, Neustadt, Germany
SCJP	Sixteenth-Century Journal Publications
Scolar	Scolar Press, Aldershot, Hampshire
SCP	Second Chance Press, Sag Harbor, NY
Scribe	Scribe Publishing, Colchester
Scribner	Charles Scribner, New York
SDSU	Department of English, South Dakota State University
Seafarer	Seafarer Books, London
Seaver	Seaver Books, New York
Segue	Segue, New York
Semiotext(e)	Semiotext(e), Columbia University, New York
SePA	Self-Publishing Association
Seren Books	Seren Books, Bridgend, mid-Glamorgan
Serpent's Tail	Serpent's Tail Publishing, London
Sessions	William Sessions, York
Seuil	Éditions du Seuil, Paris
7:84 Pubns	7:84 Publications, Glasgow
Severn	Severn House, Wallington, Surrey
SF&R	Scholars' Facsimiles and Reprints, Delmar, NY
SH	Somerset House, Teaneck, NJ
Shalabh	Shalabh Book House, Meerut, India
ShAP	Sheffield Academic Press
Shaun Tyas	Paul Watkins Publishing, Donington, Lincolnshire
Shearsman	Shearsman Books, Exeter
Shearwater	Shearwater Press, Lenah Valley, Tasmania
Sheba	Sheba Feminist Publishers, London
Sheed&Ward	Sheed & Ward, London
Sheldon	Sheldon Press, London
SHESL	Société d'Histoire et d'Épistemologie des Sciences du Langage, Paris
Shinozaki	Shinozaki Shorin, Tokyo
Shinshindo	Shinshindo Publishing, Tokyo
Shire	Shire Publications, Princes Risborough, Buckinghamshire
Shoal Bay Press	Shoal Bay Press, New Zealand
Shoe String	Shoe String Press, Hamden, CT
SHP	Shakespeare Head Press

SIAS	Scandinavian Institute of African Studies, Uppsala
SIL	Summer Institute of Linguistics, Academic Publications, Dallas, TX
SIUP	Southern Illinois University Press
Simon King	Simon King Press, Milnthorpe, Cumbria
Sinclair-Stevenson	Sinclair-Stevenson, London
SingaporeUP	Singapore UP, Singapore
Sismel	Società Internazionale per lo Studio del Medioevo Latino. Published by Edizione del Galluzo, Florence.
SIUP	Southern Illinois UP, Carbondale, IL
SJSU	San Jose State University, San Jose, CA
Skilton	Charles Skilton, London
Skoob	Skoob Books, London
Slatkine	Éditions Slatkine, Paris
Slavica	Slavica Publishers, Columbus, OH
Sleepy Hollow	Sleepy Hollow Press, Tarrytown, NY
SLG	SLG Press, Oxford
Smith Settle	Smith Settle, W. Yorkshire
SMUP	Southern Methodist UP, Dallas, TX
Smythe	Colin Smythe, Gerrards Cross, Buckinghamshire
SNH	Société Néophilologique de Helsinki
SNLS	Society for New Language Study, Denver, CO
SOA	Society of Authors, London
Soho	Soho Book, London
SohoP	Soho Press, New York
Solaris	Solaris Press, Rochester, MI
SonoNis	Sono Nis Press, Victoria, BC
Sorbonne	Publications de la Sorbonne, Paris
SorbonneN	Publications du Conseil Scientifique de la Sorbonne Nouvelle, Paris
Souvenir	Souvenir Press, London
SPA	SPA Books
SPACLALS	South Pacific Association for Commonwealth Literature and Language Studies, Wollongong, New South Wales
Spaniel	Spaniel Books, Paddington, New South Wales
SPCK	SPCK, London
Spectrum	Spectrum Books, Ibadan, Nigeria
Split Pea	Split Pea Press, Edinburgh
Spokesman	Spokesman Books, Nottingham
Spoon River	Spoon River Poetry Press, Granite Falls, MN
SRC	Steinbeck Research Center, San Jose State University, San Jose, CA
SRI	Steinbeck Research Institute, Ball State University, Muncie, IN
SriA	Sri Aurobindo, Pondicherry, India
Sri Satguru	Sri Satguru Publications, Delhi
SSA	John Steinbeck Society of America, Muncie, IN
SSAB	Sprakförlaget Skriptor AB, Stockholm
SSNS	Scottish Society for Northern Studies, Edinburgh
StanfordUP	Stanford UP, Stanford, CA
Staple	Staple, Matlock, Derbyshire
Starmont	Starmont House, Mercer Island, WA
Starrhill	Starrhill Press, Washington, DC

Station Hill	Station Hill, Barrytown, NY
Stauffenburg	Stauffenburg Verlag, Tübingen, Germany
StDL	St Deiniol's Library, Hawarden, Clwyd
Steel Rail	Steel Rail Publishing, Ottawa
Steele Roberts	Steele Roberts Publishing Ltd, Wellington, New Zealand
Steiner	Franz Steiner, Wiesbaden, Germany
Sterling	Sterling Publishing, New York
SterlingND	Sterling Publishers, New Delhi
Stichting	Stichtig Neerlandistiek, Amsterdam
St James	St James Press, Andover, Hampshire
St Martin's	St Martin's Press, New York
StMut	State Mutual Book and Periodical Source, New York
Stockwell	Arthur H. Stockwell, Ilfracombe, Devon
Stoddart	Stoddart Publishing, Don Mills, Ontario
StPB	St Paul's Bibliographies, Winchester, Hampshire
STR	Society for Theatre Research, London
Strauch	R.O.U. Strauch, Ludwigsburg
Streamline	Streamline Creative, Auckland, New Zealand
Stree	Stree/Bhatkal, Kolkata, India
Studio	Studio Editions, London
Stump Cross	Stump Cross Books, Stump Cross, Essex
Sud	Sud, Marseilles
Suhrkamp	Suhrkamp Verlag, Frankfurt am Main
Summa	Summa Publications, Birmingham, AL
SUNYP	State University of New York Press, Albany, NY
SUP	Sydney University Press
Surtees	R.S. Surtees Society, Frome, Somerset
SusquehannaUP	Susquehanna UP, Selinsgrove, PA
SussexAP	Sussex Academic Press
SussexUP	Sussex UP, University of Sussex, Brighton
Sutton	Alan Sutton, Stroud, Gloucester
SVP	Sister Vision Press, Toronto
S–W	Shepheard–Walwyn Publishing, London
Swallow	Swallow Press, Athens, OH
SWG	Saskatchewan Writers Guild, Regina
Sybylla	Sybylla Feminist Press
SydneyUP	Sydney UP, Sydney
SyracuseUP	Syracuse UP, Syracuse, NY
Tabb	Tabb House, Padstow, Cornwall
Taishukan	Taishukan Publishing, Tokyo
Talonbooks	Talonbooks, Vancouver
TamilU	Tamil University, Thanjavur, India
T&F	Taylor & Francis Books
T&H	Thames & Hudson, London
Tantivy	Tantivy Press, London
Tarcher	Jeremy P. Tarcher, Los Angeles
Tartarus	Tartarus Press
Tate	Tate Gallery Publications, London
Tavistock	Tavistock Publications, London
Taylor	Taylor Publishing, Bellingham, WA
TaylorCo	Taylor Publishing, Dallas, TX
TCG	Theatre Communications Group, New York
TCP	Three Continents Press, Washington, DC

TCUP	Texas Christian UP, Fort Worth, TX
TEC	Third Eye Centre, Glasgow
Tecumseh	Tecumseh Press, Ottawa
Telos	Telos Press, St Louis, MO
TempleUP	Temple UP, Philadelphia
TennS	Tennyson Society, Lincoln
TexA&MUP	Texas A&MUP, College Station, TX
Text	Text Publishing, Melbourne
TextileB	Textile Bridge Press, Clarence Center, NY
TexTULib	Friends of the University Library, Texas Tech University, Lubbock
The Smith	The Smith, New York
Thimble	Thimble Press, Stroud, Gloucester
Thoemmes	Thoemmes Press, Bristol
Thornes	Stanley Thornes, Cheltenham
Thorpe	D.W. Thorpe, Australia
Thorsons	Thorsons Publishers, London
Times	Times of Gloucester Press, Gloucester, Ontario
TMP	Thunder's Mouth Press, New York
Tombouctou	Tombouctou Books, Bolinas, CA
Totem	Totem Books, Don Mills, Ontario
Toucan	Toucan Press, St Peter Port, Guernsey
Touzot	Jean Touzot, Paris
TPF	Trianon Press Facsimiles, London
Tragara	Tragara Press, Edinburgh
Transaction	Transaction Publishers, New Brunswick, NJ
Transcendental	Transcendental Books, Hartford, CT
Transworld	Transworld, London
TrinityUP	Trinity UP, San Antonio, TX
Tsar	Tsar Publications, Canada
TTUP	Texas Technical University Press, Lubbock
Tuckwell	Tuckwell Press, East Linton
Tuduv	Tuduv, Munich
TulaneUP	Tulane UP, New Orleans, LA
TurkuU	Turku University, Turku, Finland
Turnstone	Turnstone Press, Winnipeg, Manitoba
Turtle Island	Turtle Island Foundation, Berkeley, CA
Twayne	Twayne Publishing, Boston, MA
UAB	University of Aston, Birmingham
UAdelaide	University of Adelaide, Australia
UAlaP	University of Alabama Press, Tuscaloosa
UAlbertaP	University of Alberta Press, Edmonton
UAntwerp	University of Antwerp
UArizP	University of Arizona Press, Tucson
UArkP	University of Arkansas Press, Fayetteville
UAthens	University of Athens, Greece
UBarcelona	University of Barcelona, Spain
UBCP	University of British Columbia Press, Vancouver
UBergen	University of Bergen, Norway
UBrno	J.E. Purkyne University of Brno, Czechoslovakia
UBrussels	University of Brussels
UCalgaryP	University of Calgary Press, Canada
UCalP	University of California Press, Berkeley

UCAP	University of Central Arkansas Press, Conway
UCapeT	University of Cape Town Press
UChicP	University of Chicago Press
UCDubP	University College Dublin Press
UCL	University College London Press
UCopenP	University of Copenhagen Press, Denmark
UDelP	University of Delaware Press, Newark
UDijon	University of Dijon
UDur	University of Durham, Durham, UK
UEA	University of East Anglia, Norwich
UErlangen-N	University of Erlangen-Nuremberg, Germany
UEssex	University of Essex, Colchester
UExe	University of Exeter, Devon
UFlorence	University of Florence, Italy
UFlorP	University of Florida Press
UFR	Université François Rabelais, Tours
UGal	University College, Galway
UGeoP	University of Georgia Press, Athens
UGhent	University of Ghent
UGlasP	University of Glasgow Press
UHawaiiP	University of Hawaii Press, Honolulu
UHertP	University of Hertfordshire Press
UHuelva	Universidad de Huelva Publicaciones
UIfeP	University of Ife Press, Ile-Ife, Nigeria
UIllp	University of Illinois Press, Champaign
UInnsbruck	University of Innsbruck
UIowaP	University of Iowa Press, Iowa City
UKanP	University of Kansas Press, Lawrence, KS
UKL	University of Kentucky Libraries, Lexington
ULavalP	Les Presses de l'Université Laval, Quebec
ULiège	University of Liège, Belgium
ULilleP	Presses Universitaires de Lille, France
ULondon	University of London
Ulster	University of Ulster, Coleraine
U/M	Underwood/Miller, Los Angeles
UMalta	University of Malta, Msida
UManitobaP	University of Manitoba Press, Winnipeg
UMassP	University of Massachusetts Press, Amherst
Umeå	Umeå Universitetsbibliotek, Umeå
UMichP	University of Michigan Press, Ann Arbor
UMinnP	University of Minnesota Press, Minneapolis
UMirail-ToulouseP	University of Mirail-Toulouse Press, France
UMIRes	UMI Research Press, Ann Arbor, MI
UMissP	University of Missouri Press, Columbia
UMontP	Montpellier University Press
UMP	University of Mississippi Press, Lafayette
UMysore	University of Mysore, India
UNancyP	Presses Universitaires de Nancy, France
UNCP	University of North Carolina Press, Chapel Hill, NC
Undena	Undena Publications, Malibu, CA
UNDP	University of Notre Dame Press, Notre Dame, IN
UNebP	University of Nebraska Press, Lincoln
UNevP	University of Nevada Press, Reno

UNewE	University of New England, Armidale, New South Wales
UnEWE, CALLS	University of New England, Centre for Australian Language and Literature Studies
Ungar	Frederick Ungar, New York
Unicopli	Edizioni Unicopli, Milan
UnisaP	University of South Africa Press, Muckleneuk, South Africa
Unity	Unity Press, Hull
UnityP	Unity Press Woollahra
Universa	Uilgeverij Universa, Wetteren, Belgium
UNMP	University of New Mexico Press, Albuquerque
UNorthTP	University of North Texas Press
UNott	University of Nottingham
UNSW	University of New South Wales
Unwin	Unwin Paperbacks, London
Unwin Hyman	Unwin Hyman, London
UOklaP	University of Oklahoma Press, Norman
UOslo	University of Oslo
UOtagoP	University of Otago Press, Dunedin, New Zealand
UOttawaP	University of Ottawa Press
UPA	UP of America, Lanham, MD
UParis	University of Paris
UPColorado	UP of Colorado, Niwot, CO
UPennP	University of Pennsylvania Press, Philadelphia
UPFlorida	University Press of Florida
UPittP	University of Pittsburgh Press, Pittsburgh
UPKen	University Press of Kentucky, Lexington
UPMissip	UP of Mississippi, Jackson
UPN	Université de Paris Nord, Paris
UPNE	UP of New England, Hanover, NH
Uppsala	Uppsala University, Uppsala
UProvence	University of Provence, Aix-en-Provence
UPSouth	University Press of the South, NO
UPSouthDen	University Press of Southern Denmark
UPValéry	University Paul Valéry, Montpellier
UPVirginia	UP of Virginia, Charlottesville
UQDE	University of Queensland, Department of English
UQP	University of Queensland Press, St Lucia
URouen	University of Rouen, Mont St Aignan
URP	University of Rochester Press
USalz	Institut für Anglistik and Amerikanstik, University of Salzburg
USantiago	University of Santiago, Spain
USCP	University of South Carolina Press, Columbia
USFlorP	University of South Florida Press, Florida
USheff	University of Sheffield
Usher	La Casa Usher, Florence
USPacific	University of the South Pacific, Institute of Pacific Studies, Suva, Fiji
USQ, DHSS	University of Southern Queensland, Department of Humanities and Social Sciences
USydP	University of Sydney Press
USzeged	University of Szeged, Hungary
UtahSUP	Utah State UP, Logan

UTampereP	University of Tampere Press, Knoxville
UTas	University of Tasmania, Hobart
UTennP	University of Tennessee Press, Knoxville
UTexP	University of Texas Press, Austin
UTorP	University of Toronto Press, Toronto
UTours	Université de Tours
UVerm	University of Vermont, Burlington
UVict	University of Victoria, Victoria, BC
UWalesP	University of Wales Press, Cardiff
UWAP	University of Western Australia Press, Nedlands
UWarwick	University of Warwick, Coventry
UWashP	University of Washington Press, Seattle
UWaterlooP	University of Waterloo Press, Waterloo, Ontario
UWI	University of the West Indies, St Augustine, Trinidad
UWIndiesP	University of West Indies Press, Mona, Jamaica
UWiscM	University of Wisconsin, Milwaukee
UWiscP	University of Wisconsin Press, Madison
UWoll	University of Wollongong
UYork	University of York, York
Valentine	Valentine Publishing and Drama, Rhinebeck, NY
V&A	Victoria and Albert Museum, London
VanderbiltUP	Vanderbilt UP, Nashville, TE
V&R	Vandenhoeck & Ruprecht, Göttingen, Germany
Van Gorcum	Van Gorcum, Assen, Netherlands
Vantage	Vantage Press, New York
Variorum	Variorum, Ashgate Publishing, Hampshire
Vehicule	Vehicule Press, Montreal
Vendome	Vendome Press, New York
Verdant	Verdant Publications, Chichester
Verso	Verso Editions, London
VictUP	Victoria UP, Victoria University of Wellington, New Zealand
Vieweg	Vieweg Braunschweig, Wiesbaden
Vikas	Vikas Publishing House, New Delhi
Viking	Viking Press, New York
VikingNZ	Viking, Auckland
Virago	Virago Press, London
Vision	Vision Press, London
VLB	VLB Éditeur, Montreal
VP	Vulgar Press, Carlton North, Australia
VR	Variorum Reprints, London
Vrin	J. Vrin, Paris
VUP	Victoria University Press, Wellington, New Zealand
VUUP	Vrije Universiteit UP, Amsterdam
Wakefield	Wakefield Press
W&B	Whiting & Birch, London
W&N	Weidenfeld & Nicolson, London
Water Row	Water Row Press, Sudbury, MA
Watkins	Paul Watkins, Stanford, Lincsolnshire
WB	Wissenschaftliche Buchgesellschaft, Darmstadt
W/B	Woomer/Brotherson, Revere, PA
Weaver	Weaver Press
Webb&Bower	Webb & Bower, Exeter
Wedgestone	Wedgestone Press, Winfield, KS

Wedgetail	Wedgetail Press, Earlwood, New South Wales
WesleyanUP	Wesleyan UP, Middletown, CT
West	West Publishing, St Paul, MN
WHA	William Heinemann Australia, Port Melbourne, Victoria
Wheatsheaf	Wheatsheaf Books, Brighton
Whiteknights	Whiteknights Press, University of Reading, Berkshire
White Lion	White Lion Books, Cambridge
Whitston	Whitston Publishing, Troy, NY
Whittington	Whittington Press, Herefordshire
WHP	Warren House Press, Sale, Cheshire
Wiener	Wiener Publishing, New York
Wildwood	Wildwood House, Aldershot, Hampshire
Wiley	John Wiley, Chichester, New York and Brisbane
Wilson	Philip Wilson, London
Winter	Carl Winter Universitätsverlag, Heidelberg, Germany
Winthrop	Winthrop Publishers, Cambridge, MA
WIU	Western Illinois University, Macomb, IL
WL	Ward Lock, London
WLUP	Wilfrid Laurier UP, Waterloo, Ontario
WMP	World Microfilms Publications, London
WMU	Western Michigan University, Kalamazoo, MI
Woeli	Woeli Publishing Services
Wolfhound	Wolfhound Press, Dublin
Wombat	Wombat Press, Wolfville, NS
Wo-No	Wolters-Noordhoff, Groningen, Netherlands
Woodstock	Woodstock Books, Oxford
Woolf	Cecil Woolf, London
Words	Words, Framfield, E. Sussex
WP	Women's Press, London
WPC	Women's Press of Canada, Toronto
WSUP	Wayne State UP, Detroit, MI
WUS	Wydawnictwo Uniwersytetu Slaskiego
WVT	Wissenschaftlicher Verlag Trier
WVUP	West Virginia UP, Morgantown
W-W	Williams-Wallace, Toronto
WWU	Western Washington University, Bellingham
Xanadu	Xanadu Publications, London
XLibris	XLibris Corporation
YaleUL	Yale University Library Publications, New Haven, CT
YaleUP	Yale UP, New Haven, CO and London
Yamaguchi	Yamaguchi Shoten, Kyoto
YMP	York Medieval Press
YorkP	York Press, Fredericton, NB
Younsmere	Younsmere Press, Brighton
Zed	Zed Books, London
Zell	Hans Zell, East Grinstead, W. Sussex
Zena	Zena Publications, Penrhyndeudraeth, Gwynedd
Zephyr	Zephyr Press, Somerville, MA
Zomba	Zomba Books, London
Zwemmer	A. Zwemmer, London

3. Acronyms

AAVE	African-American Vernacular English
AmE	American English
AusE	Australian English
BrE	British English
DP	Determiner Phrase
ECP	Empty Category Principle
EFL	English as a Foreign Language
EIL	English as an International Language
ELF	English as a Lingua Franca
ELT	English Language Teaching
eModE	early Modern English
ENL	English as a Native Language
EPNS	English Place-Name Society
ESL	English as a Second Language
ESP	English for Special Purposes
HPSG	Head-driven Phrase Structure Grammar
LF	Logical Form
LFG	Lexical Functional Grammar
ME	Middle English
MED	*Middle English Dictionary*
NZE	New Zealand English
ODan	Old Danish
OE	Old English
OED	*Oxford English Dictionary*
OF	Old French
ON	Old Norse
OT	Optimality Theory
PDE	Present-Day English
PF	Phonological Form
PP	Prepositional Phrase
SABE	South African Black English
SAE	South African English
SingE	Singapore English
TESOL	Teaching English to Speakers of other Languages
TMA	Tense, Mood and Aspect
UG	Universal Grammar

Preface

The Year's Work in English Studies is a narrative bibliography that records and evaluates scholarly writing on English language and on literatures written in English. It is published by Oxford University Press on behalf of the English Association.

The Editors and the English Association are pleased to announce that this year's Beatrice White Prize has been awarded to Douglas Gray for *Later Medieval Literature* (Oxford University Press; ISBN 9 7801 9812 2180).

The authors of *YWES* attempt to cover all significant contributions to English studies. Writers of articles can assist this process by sending offprints to the journal, and editors of journals that are not readily available in the UK are urged to join the many who send us complete sets of current and back issues. These materials should be addressed to The Editors, *YWES*, The English Association, The University of Leicester, University Road, Leicester LEI 7RH, UK.

Our coverage of articles and books is greatly assisted by the Modern Language Association of America, who annually supply proofs of their *International Bibliography* in advance of the publication of each year's coverage.

The views expressed in *YWES* are those of its individual contributors and are not necessarily shared by the Editors, Associate Editors, the English Association, or Oxford University Press.

We are especially grateful to Kira Condee-Padunova for her superlative work on behalf of this issue. We also wish to thank Michele Kennedy at Penn State Altoona and Jayne Crosby at Northern Illinois University for their kindness, professionalism, and unwavering support.

Last year's prize was awarded to Robert E. Lewis, Mary Jane Williams, and Marilyn S. Miller for the second edition of *Middle English Dictionary: Plan and Bibliography* (University of Michigan Press; ISBN 9 7804 7201 3104).

The Editors

I

English Language

VERENA HASER, ANITA AUER, BERT BOTMA,
MARION ELENBAAS, WIM VAN DER WURFF,
BEÁTA GYURIS, JULIE COLEMAN, EDWARD CALLARY,
LIESELOTTE ANDERWALD, ANDREA SAND,
MARCUS CALLIES AND ROCÍO MONTORO

This chapter has twelve sections: 1. General; 2. History of English Linguistics; 3. Phonetics and Phonology; 4. Morphology; 5. Syntax; 6. Semantics; 7. Lexicography, Lexicology and Lexical Semantics; 8. Onomastics; 9. Dialectology and Sociolinguistics; 10. New Englishes and Creolistics; 11. Pragmatics and Discourse Analysis; 12. Stylistics. Section 1 is by Verena Haser; section 2 is by Anita Auer; section 3 is by Bert Botma; sections 4 and 5 are by Marion Elenbaas and Wim van der Wurff; section 6 is by Beàta Gyuris; section 7 is by Julie Coleman; section 8 is by Edward Callary; section 9 is by Lieselotte Anderwald; section 10 is by Andrea Sand; section 11 is by Marcus Callies; section 12 is by Rocío Montoro.

1. General

In recent years there has been an upsurge of interest in evolutionary linguistics. *The Origin of Speech* by Peter F. MacNeilage is a stimulating addition to research in the field. As indicated in the title, the author's major concern is to elucidate the question how speech developed, based on an intriguing discussion how speech is produced. The book presents a neo-Darwinian theory of speech evolution, which is sharply opposed to generativist models. Following a succinct outline of the overall train of argument (part I), part II sets forth an account of speech production as a process involving two independently represented components: 'overarching syllable structure frames' and 'segmental content elements'. This conception is motivated by psycho-linguistic research on tip-of-the-tongue experiences, where subjects are unable to recall a word as a whole, even though they can remember some of the word's characteristic features (e.g. sounds occurring in the word). Many readers will be surprised to learn that the notion of distinctive features does

Year's Work in English Studies, Volume 89 (2010) © *The English Association; all rights reserved*
doi:10.1093/ywes/maq001

not figure in MacNeilage's exposition of how speech is produced. The roots of speech production are argued to lie in part in the changes of mouth position (close–open) that are involved in ingestion—a type of alternation in motor action which instantiates the biphasic cycles that form the basis of human speech. MacNeilage dubs such opening–closing cycles 'frames'. Syllables constitute a paradigm example of a close–open alternation, with syllable nuclei characterized by a more or less open vocal tract, and margins, which involve a comparatively closed vocal tract (p. 89). 'Segmental content elements' result from the movement of specific articulators and are superimposed on frame structures. On MacNeilage's view, the development of a capacity for motor mimesis (re-production of actions) in our ancestors marks the transition from a system restricted to the 'frame' to a system which superimposes a content level on frame structures, and hence enables humans to express an almost infinite number of meanings. A general increase in the ability to perform sophisticated motor action thus forms the basis of speech. Part III takes up 'The Relation between Ontogeny and Phylogeny', elaborating on the idea that hominid speech was initially comparable to child babbling, and that its evolutionary trajectory is mirrored in the steps leading to children's command of speech. A key idea is that evolution of human speech can be explained without recourse to the notion of 'speech-specific innateness' (p. 132) as suggested by generativist accounts. The distinctive properties of speech, such as its syllable structure, are ultimately due to and constrained by the 'affordances' offered by the human body. Part IV, 'Brain Organization and the Evolution of Speech', considers language evolution in relation to the specialization of the left brain hemisphere. Similar to the author's proposals in earlier chapters, his line of reasoning offers support for the embodied cognition view which pervades much of present-day linguistics and cognitive science: the specialization of the hemispheres is first and foremost seen as a means of ensuring successful action, with speech being an 'offshoot of a more general left-hemisphere specialisation for the control of the whole body under routine circumstances' (p. 210). Part V contrasts MacNeilage's neo-Darwinian view with the generative linguistic account, outlining the author's arguments against the generativist conception of an specifically linguistic innate capacity that arose suddenly due to genetic mutation. Further arguments designed to undermine the generativist account relate to the hypothesized flaws in generativist models of distinctive features and markedness. Part VI provides a thought-provoking 'Perspective on Speech from Manual Evolution', while the final part recapitulates and expands on the basic hypotheses and traces their implications for, inter alia, the embodied cognition view.

Another stimulating account of linguistic evolution has been developed by Boban Arsenijević in his paper 'From Spatial Cognition to Language' (*BioL* 2[2008] 3–23). Arsenijević conjectures that language may have emerged from spatial cognition, a development which was possible due to the 'the extension of the spatial computation into non-spatial domains leading to a domain-general use of the computation' (p. 19). Similar to MacNeilage's work, the idea of a link between language and more basic 'bodily' aspects of human thought is particularly intriguing from an embodied cognition perspective as espoused by cognitive linguists and many other scholars.

The nineteen papers collected in *Symbols and Embodiment: Debates on Meaning and Cognition*, edited by Manuel de Vega, Arthur M. Glenberg and Arthur C. Graesser, present another significant contribution to the embodied cognition framework. As noted by the editors, this volume figures importantly as the first concerted effort by proponents of embodied cognition and rivalling symbolist approaches to elucidate meaning and thought. The collection is framed by two chapters contributed by the editors ('Framing the Debate', pp. 1–10, and 'Reflecting on the Debate', pp. 397–440). The editors' account of meaning and embodiment is grounded in their survey of key arguments found in the main body of the book and accommodates findings from both symbolist and embodied theories. The remaining papers span a wide variety of issues. Chapter 2 ('The Limits of Covariation', pp. 11–32), by Arthur M. Glenberg and Sarita Mehta, is a critical discussion of the limits of theories that attempt to ground meaning in co-variation, such as Latent Semantic Analysis, a highly sophisticated statistical method for describing the meaning of words in terms of the contexts in which they occur. In 'Body and Symbol in AutoTutor: Conversations that are Responsive to the Learners' Cognitive and Emotional States' (pp. 33–56), Arthur Graesser and G. Tanner Jackson approach the issue of symbolic representations and embodiment from the perspective of AutoTutor, a computer which is designed to have conversations with humans, featuring synthesized speech and facial expressions. Lawrence Shapiro, in 'Symbolism, Embodied Cognition, and the Broader Debate' (pp. 57–75), throws light on the differences between symbolist and embodied accounts, arguing that from an embodied perspective, the role of symbols in cognition is limited, with action playing a far more important role in shaping cognition. Marcel Adam Just ('What Brain Imaging Can Tell Us about Embodied Meaning', pp. 75–84) presents evidence from functional magnetic resonance imaging studies (fMRI) suggesting that sensory and motor areas are activated during the processing of language. Friedemann Pulvermüller ('Grounding Language in the Brain', pp. 85–116) proposes an elaborate model of how words are grounded in neuronal structures. The neural patterns underpinning language and cognition are approached from a rather different point of view by Andreas Knoblauch ('Symbols and Embodiment from the Perspective of a Neural Modeller', pp. 117–44). Walter Kintsch, in 'Symbol Systems and Perceptual Representations' (pp. 145–65) opts for a modified version of the symbolist position. Kintsch submits that 'the meaning of a symbol is not defined through its reference to another level of representation, but through its relationship with other symbols' (p. 147). He also emphasizes a fundamental fact about arbitrary symbols: They are *not* invariably more difficult to process than iconic representations. According to Kintsch, symbolic representations are essentially separate from, but 'interact with', perceptual representations. Chapter 9 by Rolf Zwaan ('Experiential Traces and Mental Simulations in Language Comprehension', pp. 165–80) offers an overview of crucial findings by proponents of the embodied cognition approach, focusing inter alia on the notion of multimodal experiential traces and their role in mental simulation and language use. Experiential traces encompass both referential traces ('records of experience') and linguistic traces; if instances of the two types of traces co-occur, they come to be associated ('L-R associations'; p. 165).

Anthony J. Sanford ('Defining Embodiment in Understanding', pp. 181–94) is concerned with real-time embodied processes and the question whether they are involved in comprehension. Possibly, the author suggests, 'embodied aspects of understanding are not real-time components of comprehension, but in some sense effects correlated with necessary processing' (p. 190). Deb Roy ('A Mechanistic Model of Three Facets of Meaning', pp. 195–222) sketches a computational model of the referential, functional, and connotative meaning conveyed by speech acts. Chapter 12 by Luc Steels ('The Symbol Grounding Problem Has Been Solved, So What's Next?', pp. 223–44) elaborates on why he believes that the question of how symbols are mapped onto referents in the real world has been solved. In 'Language and Simulation in Conceptual Processing' (pp. 245–84) Lawrence W. Barsalou, Ava Santos, W. Kyle Simmons and Christine D. Wilson tackle conceptual processing, setting forth their LASS (language and situated simulations) theory on how concepts are processed and represented. The general thrust of their account is that knowledge representation and processing engage both linguistic processing and mental simulation, with the former being rather superficial (at least when executed on its own), and the latter inducing deeper comprehension. Chapter 14 by Manuel de Vega ('Levels of Embodied Meaning: From Pointing to Counterfactuals', pp. 285–308) takes on the task of investigating three types of reference that seem to rely, albeit to different extents, on embodied comprehension. Chapter 15 ('Language Comprehension Is Both Embodied and Symbolic', pp. 309–26), by Max Louwerse and Patrick Jeuniaux, is one of the contributions that most clearly purports to negotiate a compromise between embodied and symbolic frameworks, summarizing evidence in favour of both models and offering illuminating comments on pertinent experiments in the field. The contribution by Robert Goldstone, David Landy and Ji Y Son (pp. 327–56) considers the embodied cognition view in the context of instructions in science and mathematics. Antoni Gomila (pp. 357–74) adopts a more radical stance, urging us to abandon not merely the notion of abstract symbols as key elements of cognition, but also other aspects of the computational theory of thought. Finally, Mitchell J. Nathan (pp. 375–96) demonstrates that embodied cognition theories and research on gesture can cross-fertilize each other.

The tenet that human thought is 'embodied' is no less prominent in the work of one of the pioneers of cognitive linguistics: Ronald Langacker. *Cognitive Grammar: A Basic Introduction* presents Langacker's own exposition of the principal ideas associated with his framework. In light of the book's 560-odd pages, the title 'basic' is to be taken with a grain of salt. In fact, the monograph is the first introduction of this scope that provides a detailed account of the theory without eschewing rather technical issues. For this reason, it will appeal not only to students of cognitive linguistics but to all scholars who want to familiarize themselves with Langacker's theory.

That frequency asymmetries motivate many aspects of language structure is one of the cardinal hypotheses of usage-based models of grammar embraced by many cognitive linguists. In 'Frequency vs. Iconicity in Explaining Grammatical Asymmetries' (*CogLing* 19[2008] 1–33) Martin Haspelmath sets out compelling arguments why structural asymmetries between expressions should not be attributed to iconicity of quantity, complexity or cohesion. The relevant phenomena should rather be traced to frequency effects.

LOT2: The Language of Thought Revisited by Jerry A. Fodor presents a stance which contrasts starkly with the embodiment perspective that pervades much of the above-discussed works. The book is a relatively brief update on Fodor's seminal ideas dating back to the 1970s and highlights his advocacy of a computational theory of mind—i.e., the idea that thought should be described in terms of computations on mental representations, which in turn require a kind of mental 'language'. Particularly intriguing is Fodor's contention that 'the whole notion of concept learning is per se confused' (p. 130), which elaborates his well-known tenet that lexical concepts cannot be learned. Of similar interest to many linguists will be his account of the nature of lexical items as indefinable, and his rejection of Frege's notion of sense.

Several books published in 2008 testify to the growing impact of M.A.K. Halliday's Systemic Functional Theory (SFT) on linguistic research. The first is *Intonation in the Grammar of English* by Halliday himself and William S. Greaves, a work which provides a fascinating analysis of English intonation against the backdrop of SFT. Language in SFT is put to the service of expressing four types of meaning or meta-functions: experiential (describing the world), logical (used for establishing relations between events, such as hypotaxis and parataxis), interpersonal (negotiating social relations), and textual (relating to text/discourse structuring and the link between language and context). The first two types of meaning are often referred to as the ideational meta-function of language. The book examines how intonation contributes to the creation of these various types of meaning. Part I is concerned with 'The Study of Speech Sound', part II develops the authors' account of how intonation creates the different types of meaning, and part III offers a very helpful guide for analysing texts along the lines suggested in the book. The book comes with a CD that contains not only additional material, but also the printed text in a pdf file, accompanied by numerous sound files. These features, as well as the detailed examples provided, make this book an indispensable addition to the existing literature on this topic.

Systemic Functional Linguistics is also the foil for David Banks's monograph on *The Development of Scientific Writing: Linguistic Features and Historical Context*. The author expounds scientific writing and its evolution from the first English scientific text to modern works in the genre. The book covers distinctive features of scientific works such as frequent use of passives and nominalization, and low incidence of first person pronoun subjects. Banks's study is largely based on a corpus of thirty scientific writings from 1700 to 1980, and is designed to complement Halliday's seminal research. While the latter's work is largely concerned with qualitative analyses, Banks's account is far more detailed, offering a wealth of examples to illustrate his points. Even though the author emphasizes that his results are presented in quantified form, he does not use any statistical methods, a decision one might possibly quibble with.

Yet another book which documents the growing endorsement of Halliday's framework is the collection of papers edited by Carys Jones and

Eija Ventola: *From Language to Multimodality: New Developments in the Study of Ideational Meaning.* The first section is concerned with theoretical developments relating to the experiential function. It includes three contributions: Geoff Thompson's 'Methodological Considerations in Analysing Transitivity in Text' (pp. 17–34) and two papers concerned with assigning clauses/verbs to different process types, authored by Lynne Flowerdew (pp. 35–46), and Mick O'Donnell, Michele Zappavigna and Casey Whitelaw (pp. 47–64), respectively. The second section of the book throws light on 'Interactions among Ideational, Interpersonal and Textual Meanings'. Julia Lavid (pp. 67–86) is engaged with the conceptualization and expression of emotion in English and Spanish, Claire Scott (pp. 87–110) scrutinizes experiential and attitudinal meanings, and Nick Moore (pp. 111–30) examines the ideational and textual meta-function, having a look at the concept of bridging inferences. Finally, Sridevi Sriniwass's contribution (pp. 131–52) explores the experiential and logical meta-function in scientific texts. The third section encompasses various studies concerned with academic texts. Ann Montemayor-Borsinger (pp. 155–68) investigates papers written by a physicist, while the remaining three contributions in this section concentrate on student writing: Sheena Gardner's paper investigates the ideational meta-function in student writing, Anne McCabe and Christopher Gallagher focus on 'The Role of the Nominal Group in Undergraduate Academic Writing' (pp. 169–88), and Ana Martín-Úriz, Rachel Whittaker, Susana Murcia and Karina Vidal (pp. 209–28) have a look at experiential meaning in student texts. Part IV moves beyond the confines of linguistic analysis, featuring five contributions which shed light on multi-semiotic representation: Kay L. O'Halloran (pp. 231–54) studies mathematics discourse, while Birgit Huemer is concerned with digital art (pp. 255–74), and Arianna Maiorani with promotional posters (pp. 275–96). The final two papers deal with multimodal text (Dai Fei Yang, pp. 297–312) and political cartoons (Maria J. Pinar Sanz, pp. 313–34), respectively.

The relation between universals of language and linguistic change has long been a prominent research agenda especially in functional linguistics. *Linguistic Universals and Language Change*, edited by Jeff Good, is a collection of twelve papers by eminent functionalist and formalist linguists. The following questions take centre stage: How should linguistic universals be explained? Should they be traced to synchronic principles, such as Chomskian universal grammar, or should explanations be framed in terms of functionalist principles, notably the forces at work in grammaticalization processes? What is the role of grammar-external principles, such as discourse constraints, with regard to the emergence of universal grammatical patterns? What kinds of universals should be accepted in the first place? For instance, should the term 'universal' be restricted to (near-)absolute universals, or do probabilistic patterns fit the bill? Finally, how should we characterize the link between diachronic change and synchronic structures? The volume addresses both general issues and specific domains which feature linguistic universals. Key topics and problems are thrown into sharp relief by the editor's introduction as well as by the contribution by Johanna Nichols, which closes the volume

('Universals and Diachrony: Some Observations', pp. 287–94), commenting on the various papers and opening up avenues for further research.

The first contributor, Paul Kiparsky ('Universals Constrain Change; Change Results in Typological Generalizations', pp. 23–53), finds that the functionalist and formalist research agendas are not necessarily incompatible, given that the two models suggest a rather neat division of tasks. According to Kiparsky, 'true' universals (and their impact on linguistic change) are the principal domain of generative linguistics, whereas 'typological generalizations' can be attributed to recurrent historical trajectories as proposed by many functionalists. Kiparsky suggests a number of criteria for singling out true universals, e.g. true universals are exceptionless. Diametrically opposed to such absolute universals are typologically rare patterns, which are the major focus of Alice Harris's contribution ('On the Explanation of Typologically Unusual Structures', pp. 54–78). Typologically rare patterns can frequently be explained in terms of 'uncommon combinations of common changes' (p. 76).Two studies are concerned with phonological universals: Juliette Blevins's paper on 'Consonant Epenthesis: Natural and Unnatural Histories' (pp. 79–107) and Joan Bybee's investigation of 'Formal Universals as Emergent Phenomena: The Origins of Structure Preservation' (pp. 108–24). Blevins's conclusion that substantive phonological universals are (at least) very rare represents a counterpoint to Kiparsky's stance. Bybee's paper centres on the principle of Structure Preservation in Lexical Phonology. The author elucidates recurrent diachronic developments which account for this principle, and identifies a number of central mechanisms underlying trajectories of phonological change, such as automatization due to repeated use. Universals relating to morphological paradigms are discussed by Andrew Garrett ('Paradigmatic Uniformity and Markedness', pp. 125–43) and Adam Albright ('Explaining Universal Tendencies and Language Particulars in Analogical Change', pp. 144–84). Garrett argues that paradigm uniformity cannot be traced to universal grammar, while Albright suggests that a synchronic model of the structure and acquisition of paradigms can accommodate analogical change. Universal morphosyntactic patterns figure importantly in Martin Haspelmath's contribution ('Creating Economical Morphosyntactic Patterns in Language Change', pp. 185–214) as well as in Tania Kuteva and Bernd Heine's article ('On the Explanatory Value of Grammaticalization', pp. 215–30). Based on a wide range of examples, Haspelmath demonstrates that 'morphosyntactic asymmetries' (i.e., cases where differences in coding do not amount to differences in meaning) are invariably due to economy—'more frequent patterns are coded with less material' (p. 185). Kuteva and Heine throw light on the interplay between language-internal grammaticalization processes and grammaticalization due to language contact. Based on close scrutiny of definiteness marking in Scandinavian and Bulgarian, the authors show that the explanatory value of grammaticalization theory is enhanced once contact-induced grammaticalization is taken into consideration as a major force shaping both regular and apparently irregular grammatical patterns. Finally, two chapters are devoted to syntactic constructions. John Whitman ('The Classification of Constituent Order Generalizations and Diachronic Explanation', pp. 233–52) is concerned with different types of constituent order universals. He argues that cross-categorial universals—which are invariably statistical rather than absolute universals—should be attributed to diachronic processes rather than synchronic factors such as Universal Grammar or constraints on language processing. By contrast, two other types of constituent order generalizations—including hierarchical generalizations, which relate to the position of two different categories in a particular syntactic arrangement—can be linked to synchronic syntactic structure. In his paper on 'Emergent Serialization in English: Pragmatics and Typology' (pp. 253–84), Paul Hopper elucidates how discourse principles have shaped the development of the English *take NP and* construction, which he analyses from a typological perspective. Evidence is provided for the fact that the construction is 'emergent' rather than a stable part of grammar.

The state of the art in work on linguistic universals and the status of historical or functionalist as opposed to synchronic or formalist accounts is also the topic of a special theme issue of the *Linguistic Review*, which encompasses five thought-provoking contributions. The introductory paper by Harry van der Hulst (*LingRev* 25[2008] 1–34) is a concise and highly informative exposition of the fundamental concepts and issues in work pertinent to this topic, covering, inter alia, different types of universals, functional and formal approaches to universals, and historical and evolutionary explanations. Four papers are specifically devoted to different types of universals. Jonathan David Bobaljik's contribution takes up absolute morphological universals (*LingRev* 25[2008] 203–30), focusing on generalizations about person marking inventories. Bobaljik finds that certain potential morphological contrasts in this domain are never found, a pattern which lends itself to a formal explanation in terms of a universal feature inventory that constrains the possible types of morpheme inventories that can occur in languages. In his contribution on phonological universals, Larry M. Hyman notes the relative scarcity of absolute universals in this domain (*LingRev* 25[2008] 83–137). Historical explanations, the author contends, are well suited to accommodating untypical features of phonological systems, but when it comes to explaining absolute universals, it is synchronic accounts which are called for. Frederick J. Newmeyer (*LingRev* 25[2008] 35–82) delineates the different strands of investigation characterizing formalist and functionalist studies of universals. One of the questions raised in his paper is whether formalist and functionalist approaches to universals can be reconciled with each other. While not receiving a completely negative answer, Newmeyer's discussion inspires little optimism that the principal disagreements at the heart of the debate (such as the validity of the concept of UG as an explanatory factor) could be settled in the near future. In a timely paper on a comparatively neglected subject, Kai von Fintel and Lisa Matthews (*LingRev* 25[2008] 139–201) address semantic and pragmatic universals. As for the former, there are very few noteworthy examples of meanings that are universally lexicalized. On the other hand, the prospects for identifying universal principles of semantic composition are much higher. In the area of pragmatics, Gricean maxims seem to qualify as universal principles. As noted by the authors, '[w]e know of only one attempt in the literature to argue against the universality of Gricean pragmatics' (p. 189). Incidentally, the year 2008 has seen the publication of another paper which pursues this goal. Scepticism concerning the universality of Gricean pragmatics may well receive new impetus in light of Gunter Senft's proposal that speakers of Kilivila (an Austronesian language) do not conform to the Gricean principles of Manner and Quality (*Anthropos* 103[2008] 139–47).

Universals which can in some sense be classified as 'semantic' take centre stage in another article published in 2008 by Stephen Crain and Drew Khlentzos: 'Is Logic Innate?' (*BioL* 2[2008] 24–56)—a question which receives an affirmative answer from the authors. The main focus of their account is on the interpretation of disjunction ('or'). Empirical evidence as well as philosophical arguments are advanced to the effect that children obey universal semantic principles and that logic is innate.

The nature of reference has given rise to a bewildering number of controversies across diverse scientific traditions. The collection of papers in *Reference: Interdisciplinary Perspectives*, edited by Jeanette Gundel and Nancy Hedberg, does justice to the interdisciplinary nature of much research in this area. Contributors include linguists, cognitive and computer scientists, philosophers and psychologists. The four parts of the book address fundamental puzzles such as 'What is Reference' (part I), 'What is the Appropriate Linguistic Analysis of Different Forms of Referring Expression?' (part II), 'How Is Reference Resolved' (part III), and 'How Do We Select Forms of Referring Expressions? (part IV). Contributors who approach these issues from a philosophical perspective include Kent Bach ('On Referring and Not Referring', pp. 13–58) and Barbara Abbott ('Issues in the Semantics and Pragmatics of Definite Descriptions in English', pp. 61–72). Bach challenges some time-honoured assumptions about reference, putting forward some persuasive observations to the effect that many putative cases of referring are better analysed in terms of descriptions or allusions. Abbott's paper takes on the task of refuting the idea that the notion of familiarity is part and parcel of the semantics of English definite determiners. The author makes a case for the view that it is, rather, uniqueness which constitutes the core semantic meaning of these items. A primarily linguistic methodology and approach is adopted in the papers by Gregory Ward, Andrew Kehler and Maite Taboada. Gregory Ward ('Equatives and Deferred Reference', pp. 73–92) focuses on metonymic reference, revisiting and critically assessing familiar accounts of deferred reference. Andrew Kehler ('Rethinking the SMASH Approach to Pronoun Interpretation', pp. 95–122) is occupied with psycholinguistic and computational models of pronoun interpretation, uncovering weaknesses of the SMASH ('Search, Match, and Select Using Heuristics') procedure which is commonly assumed to underlie pronoun resolution. Maite Taboada ('Reference, Centers, and Transitions in Spoken Spanish', pp. 176–215) applies Centering Theory to spoken dialogue in Spanish. Centering Theory is a model designed to account for the choice of referring expressions (e.g. pronouns, names, or descriptions) in particular discourse contexts. According to this model, the type of transition between adjacent utterances has an impact on the kind of referring expression selected. Taboada's analysis suggests some revisions of the Centering Model. This theory also figures prominently in another chapter, authored by computer/cognitive scientist Massimo Poesio ('Linguistic Claims Formulated in Terms of Centering', pp. 216–45). His findings shed light on the link between choice of expression (pronoun, full NPs) in subject position and transition type, as well as the relation between global and local coherence. A primarily psycholinguistic perspective informs the contribution by Sungryong Koh, Anthony J. Sanford, Charles Clifton Jr and Eugene J. Dawydiak ('Good-Enough Representation in Plural and Singular Pronominal Reference', pp. 123–39). The authors investigate the processing of plural and singular pronouns which relate to one or two referents mentioned in a preceding sentence.

Donna K. Byron, Sarah Brown-Schmidt and Michael K. Tanenhaus ('The Overlapping Distribution of Personal and Demonstrative Pronouns', pp. 143–75) investigate the factors that impact on speaker's choice of a personal versus a demonstrative pronoun. The authors present both a corpus study and a psycholinguistic experiment, which uncover intriguing facts about the relation between a referent's salience and the choice of pronoun. A joint paper by psychologist Alan Garnham and linguist H. Wind Cowles ('Looking Both Ways', pp. 246–72) concludes the book. The authors offer a reassessment of previous work on the processing of anaphoric expressions, setting forth their JANUS model, according to which a satisfactory account of co-referential NP anaphora requires scrutiny of both the preceding and the following text.

Two classics among introductory textbooks to psycholinguistics have been published in new editions in 2008. The fifth edition of Jean Aitchison's *The Articulate Mammal: An Introduction to Psycholinguistics* features several new topics that are absent from previous editions, including spatial cognition, aphasia, construction grammar, and the question of 'language genes'. Readers will be hard pressed to find a more entertaining or accessible guide to the subjects covered in this monograph. Hardly an easy read for beginners, on the other hand, is Trevor A. Harley's far more hefty *The Psychology of Language: From Data to Theory*. The third edition presents a wealth of cutting-edge research in the field. Harley offers a comprehensive introduction to the major fields of enquiry in psycholinguistics, including first- and second-language acquisition, word recognition, syntactic processing and language processing, to name but a few of the topics covered. The book is an invaluable source of information for aspiring psycholinguists, or indeed all linguists concerned with language and cognitive processes.

Students of psycholinguistics and related fields will also profit from close perusal of a volume edited by Jeanette Altarriba and Roberto R. Heredia. *An Introduction to Bilingualism: Principles and Processes* is aimed at under-graduate and graduate students of psycholinguistics with a special interest in bilingualism. The volume is divided into five parts. Part I includes the editors' introduction, a paper on methodological issues by Viorica Marian ('Bilingual Research Methods', pp. 13–38), and a contribution by Roberto R. Heredia which surveys some important milestones in bilingualism research, focusing on how the different languages are represented in bilinguals' memory ('Mental Models of Bilingual Memory', pp. 39–67). Part II ('Cognitive and Neurological Mechanisms') encompasses three contributions. The first, by

Jennifer L. Gianico and Jeanette Altarriba ('The Psycholinguistics of Bilingualism', pp. 71–104), is a digest of crucial findings that have emerged from studies of bilingualism. Robert W. Schrauf focuses on 'Bilingualism and Aging' (pp. 105–28), while Jyotsna Vaid ('The Bilingual Brain: What Is Right and What Is Left'?, pp. 129–46) discusses neuro-imaging studies, research on aphasia in bilinguals, and other types of methods pertinent to the study of the bilingual brain. Part III ('Creativity and Developmental Principles') contains a chapter by Dean Keith Simonton on the relationship between 'Bilingualism and Creativity' (pp. 147–66), delineating different methods for addressing this issue. A contribution by Elena Nicoladis centres on the impact of bilingualism on language acquisition and cognitive development ('Bilingualism and Language Cognitive Development', pp. 167–81). Part IV ('Social and Sociocultural Processes') contains a paper by Luis A. Vega on 'Social Psychological Approaches to Bilingualism' (pp. 185–98) as well as a contribution by Flavia C. Peréa and Cynthia García Coll on 'The Social and Cultural Contexts of Bilingualism' (pp. 199–241). The final section ('Linguistic Principles and Applied Perspectives') features four papers. Vivian Cook (pp. 245–64) deals with the relation between general linguistics and research on SLA and bilingualism. Susan Gass and Margo Glew (pp. 265–94) also take a look at SLA, focusing on fundamental concepts and insights from this field of enquiry. Another intriguing topic takes centre stage in Kathryn Kohnert's contribution, which investigates language disorders in bilinguals (pp. 295–320). The final chapter by Eugene E. Garcia investigates 'Bilingual Education in the United States' (pp. 321–43).

Turning to the field of applied linguistics, Jane Jackson's monograph *Language, Identity and Study Abroad: Sociocultural Perspectives* discusses adult learners of English as a foreign language, more specifically Hong Kong university students who stayed in England for five weeks. Jackson's analysis takes as its foil pertinent theories by Lev Vygotsky, Mikhail Bakhtin and Pierre Bourdieu, expounding their relevance to her study of L2 sojourners. Poststructuralist accounts of language and identity are also taken into consideration.

Vygotsky's theory also features in James P. Lantolf and Matthew E. Poehner's collection of papers on *Sociocultural Theory and the Teaching of Second Languages*. The book includes thirteen chapters that present research on adult second/foreign language teaching, taking their inspiration from Sociocultural Theory as championed by Vygotsky. The book is divided into three parts plus the editors' introduction. Part I, 'Mediation and the Zone of Proximal Development', encompasses papers by, inter alia, Rumia Ableeva, Tony Erben, Ruth Ban and Robert Summers. The notion of mediation captures Vygotsky's tenet that higher cognitive processes and cognitive development are mediated by signs or other cultural tools; cognitive development thus arises through interaction with others. 'Zone of proximal development' is another key term in Vygotsky's theory, which relates to the difference between the cognitive achievement a child is capable of without the guidance of others and the higher level of achievement possible in cases where learning results from the collaborative efforts of instructor and child. Part II is concerned with 'Concept-Based Instruction', i.e., a type of instruction which is geared to the 'scientific understanding of the L2 as the focus of classroom learning' (p. 22). This section includes papers by Eduardo Negueruela, Sharon Lapkin, Merrill Swain and Ibtissem Knouzi, to name but a few. The third part focuses on 'The Classroom–World Nexus', featuring contributions by Sally Sieloff Magnan and Howard Grabois. Both of them propose that the contexts for learning of foreign languages should not be restricted to classrooms.

Already published in 2007, *Learning English*, edited by Neil Mercer, Joan Swann and Barbara Mayor, is predicated on assumptions that also inform some previously mentioned works. The various authors favour a functional view of language acquisition and language learning, emphasizing that learning arises through the interaction between learners and instructors or other persons. The book comprises seven chapters. The first one, by Dennis Bancroft, concentrates on 'English as a First Language' (pp. 5–42). Barbara Mayor's contribution (pp. 43–78) discusses the acquisition of English in bilinguals as well as mastery of different varieties in monolingual children. A chapter by Pam Czerniewska expounds the development of reading and writing skills (pp. 79–116). The following chapter, by Neil Mercer, turns to English as a medium of instruction used in classrooms (pp. 117–50), while Frank Monaghan focuses on English as part of the curriculum in English-speaking countries (pp. 151–88). English as a foreign language is the topic of Jill Bourne's contribution (pp. 189–226). The concluding chapter by Ann Hewings, Theresa Lillis and Barbara Mayor focuses on 'Academic Writing in English' (pp. 227–65).

Two rather different, but equally successful introductions to linguistics have been published by OUP in 2008. Barry Blake's *All About Language* is an engaging introduction to a wide variety of topics in linguistic research. The book falls into five parts plus a general introduction. Part I ('Words') deals with word classes, word-formation processes and word meaning. The following section (Part II, 'Syntax and Discourse') examines basic syntactic concepts (such as predicate, argument, phrase structure, etc.). A separate chapter is devoted to language use, covering topics such as given vs. new information, speech acts and Grice's co-operative principle. Part III ('Speech and Writing') contains chapters on phonetics and phonology as well as a separate chapter on writing that runs the whole gamut from Egyptian hieroglyphs and Sumerian cuneiform to English spelling idiosyncrasies ('English has the worst relationship between sound and spelling of any language', p. 175). Part IV focuses on variation and change, including short and highly readable sections on different types of language change (sound change, morphological change, syntactic change, semantic change), a topic which is frequently omitted from comparable textbooks. Even more untypical for general introductory works are some of the themes broached in the final chapter ('The Brain'): language acquisition, language processing and language evolution. A very helpful glossary rounds off this valuable primer in linguistics. A major asset for many students will be the availability of solutions to the various exercises, which can be found online.

No less stimulating reading is offered in Daniela Isac and Charles Reiss's *I-Language: An Introduction to Linguistics as Cognitive Science*. The authors present an accessible introduction to topics that are at the core of generative approaches, tackling both linguistic analyses and pertinent psychological, ethological and philosophical issues. Divided into four parts, the book expounds four major areas of generativist research: the notion of I-language (part I), linguistic representation (part II), universal grammar (part III), and social and philosophical implications (part IV). The authors do not shy away from intricate issues—such as finite state languages or ergative languages, to name but two—which are expounded with great lucidity. Linguists will be hard pressed to find a better introduction to a wide variety of topics that have proved elusive for generations of students in linguistics and related fields.

Let us finally glance at a subject which many students approach with some trepidation: statistics. Yet proficiency in quantitative methods is the order of the day for linguists and cognitive scientists of different persuasions, which explains the plethora of statistics textbooks that have appeared in recent years. Many linguists will welcome two recent additions to the literature, both of which are targeted at a scholarly audience willing to use the increasingly popular statistical software package R. The more voluminous of the two— R.H. Baayen's *Analyzing Linguistic Data: A Practical Introduction to Statistics Using R*—presents a thorough introduction to basic and more sophisticated statistical methods, including many examples and exercises (plus solutions). What makes the book particularly valuable is a discussion of mixed effect models that are increasingly replacing some older statistical techniques. Baayen's exposition largely dispenses with mathematical background information.

In a similar vein, Keith Johnson's *Quantitative Methods in Linguistics* covers both long-established and more modern statistical methods for linguists, complemented by 'R notes', which describe how the examples found in the text can be analysed with the help of R. Most of the chapters centre on specific linguistic subdisciplines and popular quantitative methods used in the respective fields (phonetics, psycholinguistics, sociolinguistics, historical linguistics and syntax). Because of its relative brevity this book is most profitably read in conjunction with further textbooks on R and statistical methods.

2. History of English Linguistics

In the year 2008 a lot of attention has been paid to the role that grammars and grammarians played in the history of the English language. An important contribution to this field of study is the volume *Grammars, Grammarians and Grammar-Writing in Eighteenth-Century England* edited by Ingrid Tieken-Boon van Ostade. The contents of the book are subdivided into four parts, namely 'Background', 'Reception and the Market for Grammars', 'The Grammarians' and 'The Grammars', all of which contain a brief introduction by the editor. The first part—'Background'—contains Don Chapman's paper 'The Eighteenth-Century Grammarians as Language Experts' (pp. 21–36), which sheds light on the professional background of these grammarians. Most of these language experts were not linguists as we think of them today, but clergymen, schoolmasters or booksellers who had an interest in language, for instance in 'the structure of vernacular grammar or universals that all languages share' (p. 35). Very importantly, Chapman points out that prescriptivism did not start with the beginning of grammar writing, but when grammarians were no longer critical of their predecessors' accounts of particular language features and instead started passing on the ideas of these earlier grammarians. The second paper in part I is Richard J. Watts's 'Grammar Writers in Eighteenth-Century Britain: A Community of Practice or a Discourse Community?' (pp. 37–56). Watts discusses the two socio-linguistic concepts of community of practice and discourse community and tries to apply them to eighteenth-century grammarians. He concludes that discourse community is the more appropriate concept because it 'implies a community of common interests, goals and beliefs rather than a community of individuals' (p. 52) that interact with each other. The third paper, 'Eighteenth-Century Grammars and Book Catalogues' by Anita Auer (pp. 57–75), is concerned with tracing the dissemination and the popularity of grammars in order to shed some light on the influence of these works. The author's analysis of sale, book auction and library catalogues reveals that book catalogues, even though they provide a lot of interesting and useful information, cannot contribute to solving the question of the normative grammarians' influence. What can be inferred from catalogues, however, is which grammars were considered prestigious and therefore saleable.

Part II of this volume deals with issues of publishing and trade. The first paper here, '*Bellum Grammaticale* (1712)—A Battle of Books and a Battle for the Market' (pp. 81–100) by Astrid Buschmann-Göbels, is concerned with the publication history and the function of the anonymous book *Bellum Grammaticale*. The author argues that the publication of the book, which criticized three contemporary grammars, namely Brightland and Gildon's *Grammar of the English Tongue* [1711], Greenwood's *Essay towards a Practical English Grammar* [1711] and Maittaire's *English Grammar* [1712], may 'be seen as an effort to launch the Brightland grammar, of which Gildon was one of the authors [and probably also the author of the *Bellum Grammaticale*], onto the market' (p. 100). Moreover, she notes that a shift from rational to practical grammar for the education of a larger public can be observed. The following paper by Ingrid Tieken-Boon van Ostade, 'The 1760s: Grammars, Grammarians and the Booksellers' (pp. 101–24), deals with the publication of grammars in the eighteenth century, in particular the role of publishers and booksellers, on the one hand, and their relationships to grammarians on the other. She illustrates these relationships by taking a closer look at the publication history of Robert Lowth's grammar and concludes that '[t]he grammars that developed into the most popular ones of the eighteenth century were first and foremost booksellers' projects' (p. 124). What follows the publication of a grammar, namely the reception, is the topic of an article by Carol Percy, 'Mid-Century Grammars and their Reception in the *Monthly Review* and the *Critical Review*' (pp. 125–42). The author notes that periodical reviews can also be regarded as a publishing phenomenon in the eighteenth century, which means that some reviews consisted of summaries only and therefore reflected the author's rather than the reviewer's judgement. However, 'by synthesizing and contextualizing the most common opinions articulated in the reviews, modern scholars can still attempt to gain some insight into the contemporary reception of the grammars' (p. 127). Reviews do not only show how newly published grammars were received by the contemporary scholarly community, but, when viewed in a more general historical context, they also shed light on the role that the English language played in the socio-political environment, most notably the effect that the Seven Years War had on the status of English.

Part III, concerned with specific grammarians, first deals with the female grammarian Ann Fisher (1717–78) (María E. Rodríguez-Gil, 'Ann Fisher's *A New Grammar*, or Was It Daniel Fisher's Work?', pp. 149–76). The paper is concerned with the authorship of *A New Grammar*. A systematic investigation of the roles that Ann Fisher as well as Daniel Fisher played in the production of the grammar leads to the conclusion that Ann Fisher was primarily responsible for writing the grammar, but that Daniel Fisher may have contributed 'with the spelling rules and probably also in the discussion of the use of the "double accent"' (p. 175). 'Joseph Priestley's two *Rudiments of English Grammar*: 1761 and 1768' is the title of Jane Hodson's contribution (pp. 177–89). The paper deals with (a) changes that Priestley carried out in the second edition of this grammar, and (b) finding out about Priestley's reasons for altering the text. Hodson argues that while the 1761 edition was of a pedagogical nature, the 1768 edition reflects how Priestley's grammatical thought had developed. The principles of the English language were a lot more complicated than Priestley had envisaged at first. In the 1768 edition he therefore tried to combine the instruction of beginning language learners with the discussion of complex language issues. The following paper, 'Eighteenth-Century Teacher-Grammarians and the Education of "Proper" Women', by Karen Cajka (pp. 191–221), takes a look at six female teacher-grammarians, namely Ellin Devis, Mrs M.C. Edwards, Mrs Eves, Jane Gardiner, Mrs Taylor and Blanch Mercy, whose 'educational goal was the education of girls into "proper" women' (p. 220). Cajka shows that the main aim of teacher-grammarians was to stimulate the intellectual development of girls, which includes academic, moral and social knowledge, through the study of English grammar. Another female grammarian is the topic of Karlijn Navest's paper, '"Borrowing a Few Passages": Lady Ellenor Fenn and her Use of Sources' (pp. 223–43). As the title suggests, Navest traces Fenn's use of sources in her grammatical works. Rather than condemning Fenn for unacknowledged copying, the attitude to which was not as strict as it is today, Navest emphasizes the originality of Fenn's grammars and defends the choices the female grammarian made for pedagogical reasons. Navest also has an article on the same grammarian in *Perspectives on Prescriptivism* (edited by Joan C. Beal, Carmela Nocera and Massimo Sturiale, pp. 59–82) entitled 'Ash's *Grammatical Institutes* and "Mrs Teachwell's Library for her Young Ladies"'. Ellenor Fenn, also known as Mrs Teachwell, greatly relied on John Ash's *Grammatical Institutes* [1760] in writing her own grammatical treatises, and encouraged her readers to consult Ash's work. Navest ascertains that, even though Fenn was undoubtedly strongly influenced by Ash's work, differences in their accounts of grammatical features reveal that Fenn 'did not copy his works uncritically' (p. 70). As for choosing Ash's work as a model, the author suggests that a change of title to *The Easiest Introduction to Dr. Lowth's English Grammar* [1766], instigated by John Collett Ryland, made Ash's work seem the ideal pedagogical grammar.

The fourth and final part of the book deals with the treatment of specific linguistic features in eighteenth-century grammars. Nuria Yáñez-Bouza's contribution, 'Preposition Stranding in the Eighteenth Century: *Something to Talk About*' (pp. 251–77), focuses on 'the various ways in which preposition stranding was understood and commented upon within the eighteenth-century normative grammatical tradition' (p. 252). The author shows that the proscriptive comments on preposition stranding, which were until then strongly associated with Lowth's grammar, were in fact much older and not restricted to grammars but found in other text types of a normative nature. Moreover, the paper reveals that the use of preposition stranding was not only stigmatized in grammatical works but also simply mentioned and sometimes even advocated. Randy Cliffort Bax's paper, '*Foolish, Foolisher, Foolishest*: Eighteenth-Century English Grammars and the Comparison of Adjectives and Adverbs' (pp. 279–88), analyses twenty-seven grammars, investigating their rules on the comparison of adjectives and adverbs. Bax shows that rules on the selected language feature changed over time: when grammatical production increased in the course of the century, 'greater attention was paid to formal characteristics of adjectival and adverbial comparison that would help to determine what forms to use' (p. 287). This change in approach coincided with a change in readership, i.e. from boys in the upper layers of society to everyone who wanted to climb the social ladder. The final paper is Victorina González-Díaz's 'On Normative Grammarians and the Double Marking of Degree' (pp. 289–310). The author traces the development of double periphrastic comparatives, in particular *worser* and *lesser*, in both meta-linguistic comments by grammarians in the ModE period and actual language use from MiE to PDE. The investigation reveals for instance that *lesser* 'acquired a differential linguistic value from that of *less*', which 'must have guaranteed its lexicalization' (p. 309). González-Díaz emphasizes the importance of combining corpus-based studies of linguistic features with meta-linguistic comments in order to identify whether prescriptive grammarians played a role in the development of the particular feature.

The proceedings of the colloquium with the same title, *Perspectives on Prescriptivism* edited by Joan C. Beal et al., which was hosted by the University of Catania (Sicily) contains several articles, next to the one already discussed above, that are concerned with the history of English linguistics. Joan C. Beal's contribution, '"Shamed by your English?": The Market Value of a "Good" Pronunciation' (pp. 21–40), traces the history of guides on 'correct' pronunciation from the eighteenth to the twenty-first centuries. Her main aim is to find out whether the social forces that created a market for usage guides in the eighteenth century are the same as those in the twenty-first century. While 'linguistic insecurity' can always be found 'in some sector of British society' (p. 35), in all centuries under investigation, the late twentieth and early twenty-first centuries stand out with regard to the proliferation as well as popularization of a great variety of 'prescriptive' texts. In the twentieth century, which witnessed both the pinnacle and the decline of RP, the market value of good pronunciation diminished. In the twenty-first century, however, a new market for lessons on elocution has been created 'under the guise of "business communication"' (p. 31). The grammarian Joseph Priestley is the focus of attention of Giuliana Russo's 'Joseph Priestley's *The Rudiments of English Grammar; Adapted to the Use of schools. With Observations on Style* (1761)' (pp. 165–79). The author aims to assess Priestley's supposed descriptivism by 'analyzing his grammar and assessing its internal coherence' (p. 167). Most of the examples that Russo provides do support the view that Priestley adhered to descriptivism. The author is, however, sceptical of 'Priestley's unconditioned adherence to descriptivism' (p. 175) and argues for instance that a grammar aimed at teaching needs to be clear, systematic and authoritative in order to coincide with the norms of a community. Ingrid Tieken-Boon van Ostade's contribution, 'The Codifiers and the History of Multiple Negation in English, Or, Why Were the 18th-Century Grammarians So Obsessed with Double Negation?' (pp. 197–214), discusses the perennial 'problem' of multiple negation. The author suggests that grammars contained a stricture against multiple negation because its use was associated with lower social classes and therefore carried a social stigma. She also shows that Lowth's comment on multiple negation was 'strictly descriptive' (p. 202) as opposed to Priestley's comment, which 'must be labeled as proscriptive' (pp. 202–3). Tieken-Boon van Ostade thus suggests that this stricture, which had for a long time been associated with Lowth, had been turned into a prescription not by Lowth but 'by those who came after him' (p. 210). Larisa Oldireva Gustafsson's 'Phonoaesthetic Assessment of Words in 18th-Century Prescriptions and Later' (pp. 83–112) analyses phono-aesthetic prescriptions with respect to choice of words as found in style guides and works by rhetoricians. For instance, monosyllables such as pronouns and prepositions in sentence-final position were proscribed by late eighteenth-century rhetoricians arguing that the last word would stick in the reader's mind. In order to find out whether prescriptions were also put into practice, Gustafsson analyses words in sentence-final position in a selection of sermons by the Scottish rhetorician Hugh Blair. The results of this investigation make her conclude that rhetoricians' comments can be seen as 'tentative recommendations, not rules, despite the fact they were often formulated as rules' (p. 101). Gustafsson then continues to investigate comments regarding word choice as found in twentieth-century style guides. She notes that the latter preferred short words and recommended the avoidance of Latinate borrowings. The paper by Laura Pinnavaia is concerned with 'Charles Richardson: Prescriptivist or Descriptivist? An Analysis Based on *A New Dictionary of the English Language* (1836–37)' (pp. 147–63). A thorough comparison of the dictionary entries for *abominate, abominable* and *abominably* in Samuel Johnson's *Dictionary*, Richardson's *Dictionary* and the *OED* reveals that Richardson's approach does to some extent fit with the prescriptive line taken by his predecessors but at the same time shows the descriptive method that the *OED* adopted. Pinnavaia's paper nicely illustrates how difficult it is to make a clear-cut dichotomy between a descriptive and a prescriptive approach when investigating Late ModE grammars and dictionaries. Massimo Sturiale's contribution to the volume is entitled 'Prescriptivism and Eighteenth-Century

Bilingual Dictionaries: William Perry's *The Standard French and English Pronouncing Dictionary* (1795)' (pp. 181–95). Perry followed Sheridan and Walker in correcting 'his countrymen of "vicious" and "provincial" pronunciation' (p. 188). Sturiale shows that prescriptivism was not only restricted to monolingual dictionaries but can also be found in bilingual dictionaries published in Late ModE. In fact, by applying the prescriptive line to a bilingual dictionary, Perry found a new market niche. Pronunciation, namely 'Social Attitudes towards Londoners' Front-Glide Insertion after Velar Consonants and before Front Vowels' is the topic of Laura Wright's paper (pp. 215–35). Wright traces the trajectory of this sound change over time and also takes into consideration comments, which were both of a positive and negative prescriptive nature. It is difficult to say whether this particular linguistic feature had turned into a shibboleth as '[c]omments about social class are usually coded in metaphor, and it is not easy to judge precisely who might have been polite, fashionable or elegant speakers in a given generation' (p. 231). Nuria Yáñez-Bouza's 'To End or Not to End a Sentence with a Preposition: An 18th-Century Debate' (pp. 237–64) is concerned with contemporary attitudes to another shibboleth. A thorough analysis of a self-compiled corpus of meta-linguistic comments on this grammatical feature reveals that 'end-placed prepositions were not only criticized but were occasionally advocated and often just mentioned' (p. 256). By studying the specific labels used in connection with preposition stranding, Yáñez-Bouza is able to show how attitudes evolved throughout the eighteenth century.

The article '*A Key to the Art of Letters*: An English Grammar for the Eighteenth Century' (*Neophil* 92[2008] 545–57) by Robert W. Rix provides the first detailed study of A. Lane's grammar [1700], with a particular focus on the innovative methods contained and its radical proposals for a new national curriculum. In fact, Lane's grammar is advertised as providing 'the universal building blocks of language, which will help the intellectual development of the nation by enabling the easy acquisition of proficiency in Latin and French' (p. 549). Rix emphasizes the strong relationship between vernacular grammar, education, empire and manners in the eighteenth century. Moreover, he shows that both A. Lane and V.J. Peyton in his *History of the English Language* [1771] were keen on propagating English as a world language—an idea strongly associated with cultural imperialism.

'The Rise of Prescriptive Grammars on English in the 18th Century' is the title of Miriam A. Locher's article in the volume *Standards and Norms in the English Language* edited by Miriam A. Locher and Jürg Strässler (pp. 127–47). The author aims to (a) answer the question of why there was such an enormous increase of English grammars from the middle of the eighteenth century onwards, and (b) illustrate the topicality of eighteenth-century grammars for linguistics today by taking a closer look at John Fell's grammar [1784]. Locher identifies four interrelated reasons for the rise of prescriptive grammars, namely: (1) a new market situation directed at social climbers, (2) a process of language standardization, (3) the notion of politeness, and (4) new developments in the printing trade. The investigation of Fell's grammar shows the dilemma that eighteenth-century grammarians found themselves in, namely whether to describe actual language use that was considered the ultimate authority or whether to propagate the 'best language' and thereby preserve the Saxon heritage. Rather than trying to reconcile these contradictory views, Fell emphasizes the importance of education in his grammar. Another paper dealing with grammarians' views, in the same volume, is Anita Auer's '*Lest* the Situation Deteriorates—A Study of *Lest* as Trigger of the Inflectional Subjunctive' (pp. 149–73). The author traces the development of the conjunction *lest* in combination with the inflectional subjunctive in a range of multi-genre corpora from 1570 to 1994 and shows that the use of the construction strongly decreased between 1570 and 1700, that it had almost disappeared between 1700 and 1984, and that a revival can be observed between 1984 and 1994. Auer tentatively suggests that the revival of the construction, which can first be observed in AmE, strongly resembles the recent development, i.e. rise, of the mandative subjunctive. An analysis of meta-linguistic comments by grammarians revealed that the *lest*-subjunctive construction was only recognized and advocated by grammarians in the second half of the eighteenth century; later grammarians emphasized that the meaning of the entire sentence decides which mood should be used rather than the choice of conjunction. Jürg Rainer Schwyter's contribution to the volume, 'The BBC Advisory Committee on Spoken English or How (Not) to Construct a "Standard" Pronunciation' (pp. 175–93), traces the language policy of the BBC Advisory Committee on Spoken English and thus its attempt to fix and diffuse a uniform pronunciation standard during the period 1926–39. The author convincingly shows that the original intention of the committee was not only to achieve consistency among BBC announcers and newsreaders but also to teach the public good and correct English. The next step in the development was a so-called 'listening BBC', i.e. provisional decisions on pronunciation until feedback was given by advisers as well as the public. As a last step, alternative pronunciations were gradually admitted and 'eventually found to be "equally good"' (p. 187).

Eighteenth-century grammars also feature in two articles on social network theory. Anni Sairio's paper, 'A Social Network Study of the Eighteenth-Century Bluestockings: The Progressive and Preposition Stranding in their Letters' (*HLSL* 8[2008]), discusses the diachronic development of the two selected linguistic features during the period 1738 to 1778. The author successfully shows that network ties were not particularly influential in the epistolary use of both the progressive and preposition stranding. The central character of the study, Elizabeth Montagu, was rather hesitant in using the progressive. As for preposition stranding, this stigmatized grammatical feature was also largely avoided by Montagu, in particular once she had established herself as a hostess and author of the Bluestocking circle. Sairio suggests that the condemnation of preposition stranding in language treatises since 1749 must have influenced Montagu's usage of the language feature. Froukje Henstra's article, 'Social Network Analysis and the Eighteenth-Century Family Network: A Case Study of the Walpole Family' (*TPS* 106[2008] 29–70), investigates three linguistic features that were in the process of changing during the Late ModE period, namely (a) *you was/you were* variation, (b) *be/have* in perfective constructions with mutative intransitive verbs, and (c) variation in the use of preterite forms for the past participle in perfective and passive constructions in the irregular verb paradigm. Even though not many instances of all three language features occur in the data, Henstra can, based on the first two features, tentatively conclude that 'Lady Waldegrave, Duchess of Gloucester may have been an early adopter and linguistic leader in this network' (p. 61). With regard to the use of preterite forms for the past participle, the author finds that Horace Walpole consistently uses *written* instead of the commonly found *wrote* in a past participle context. This strongly suggests that Walpole was an innovator in his network and possibly even set the norm for the form that was prescribed in contemporary grammars. Henstra's article is interesting not only from the point of view of linguistic analysis but also for her critical assessment of the social network model, and in particular the network strength scale.

3. Phonetics and Phonology

In recent years there has been renewed interest in the role of paradigms in shaping the phonological form of words. One reason for this is that in OT, still the dominant framework in phonology, paradigmatic effects can be formalized in terms of constraints which force surface forms to be 'faithful' to morphologically related forms. Two of the contributions to Laura J. Downing, T. Alan Hall and Renate Raffelsiefen, eds., *Paradigms in Phonological Theory*—published in 2004 but not previously mentioned in *YWES*—deal with paradigm uniformity effects in English from an OT perspective. In 'The Paradigm Uniformity Effect Reconsidered' (pp. 107–21) Stuart Davis focuses on AmE, which has a difference between *capitalistic*, with a flapped /t/, and *militaristic*, with an unflapped aspirated /t/. The latter demands an explanation since flapping normally occurs at the beginning of unstressed syllables (e.g. *writer*, *pity*). One possibility, suggested by Donca Steriade in an earlier paper, is that the closure duration of the unflapped /t/ makes *militaristic* more similar to *military*, which also has an unflapped /t/. This view has important consequences not just for the relation between phonology and morphology, but also for the relation between phonology and phonetics: the fact that such durational aspects are not normally thought of as being relevant to the phonology suggests that paradigm uniformity may also involve non-contrastive properties. For the case at hand, however, Davis observes that unflapped /t/ is also found in words that are metrically identical to *militaristic*, but morphologically different (e.g. *Mediterranean*, *Navratilova*). Thus an explanation is required not so much for the unflapped /t/ in *militaristic* but for the flapped /t/ in *capitalistic*. Davis accounts for this in terms of a constraint which requires the foot structures of *capitalistic* and *capital* to be uniform. In both words /t/ is foot-internal, the appropriate context for flapping.

In which cases is an appeal to paradigm uniformity justified? This question is addressed by Renate Raffelsiefen in her contribution to this volume, 'Paradigm Uniformity Effects versus Boundary Effects' (pp. 211–62). She starts out by observing that the words *shyness* and *minus* are not perfect rhymes: the diphthong in *shyness* is longer, and the /n/ in *shyness* has greater amplitude than the one in *minus*. These differences could be due to paradigm uniformity (the length of the diphthong in *shyness* is like that in *shy*), but they can also be viewed as a boundary effect (the diphthongs are long because both *shy*s form prosodic words, and the morpheme-initial /n/ in *shyness* is more prominent than the morpheme-internal /n/ in *minus*). Raffelsiefen examines a wide range of morphological combinations and concludes that an appeal to paradigm uniformity should be reserved for those cases which involve 'genuine violations of regular phonology' (p. 237). This is the case for instance in a word such as *vinegarish*, which violates the generalization that stress always falls on one of the last three syllables of a word. This violation is arguably the result of paradigmatic pressure from the base *vinegar*. The lengthening of the diphthong in *shyness*, on the other hand, is a perfectly regular phenomenon and hence better accounted for by reference to morphological boundaries.

Paradigm uniformity also plays a role in Donka Minkova's article, 'Prefixation and Stress in Old English—in Memoriam Richard Hogg (1944–2007)' (*WS* 1[2008] 21–52). Minkova observes, as others have before her, that the category of OE prefixes is difficult to delineate, given that morphosyntactic, semantic and phonological criteria for prefixhood do not converge. She focuses on the question of whether the prosodic behaviour of OE prefixes must be lexically specified or whether it is derivable from the morphological structure of the base to which they attach. Minkova argues that the prosodic behaviour of prefixes depends on both morphosyntactic and phonological properties. Morphosyntactically, a distinction can be made between nouns and adjectives, on the one hand, and verbs and adverbs on the other: the former have main stress on the prefix (e.g. *ýmb-sìttend* 'neighbour'), the latter on the root (e.g. *ỳmb-séttan* 'to surround'). Phonologically, a distinction can be made between *be-* and *ge-*, which are invariably unstressed (e.g. *be-hólen* 'hidden'), and other prefixes, which are variably stressed. Minkova contends that *be-* and *ge-* do not form independent prosodic words, and as such cannot be stressed. While these generalizations account for most prefixed forms, some irregularity remains (e.g. *for-géfenesse* 'forgiveness', *ánd-swarode* 'answered'). Minkova suggests that these exceptions are due to paradigmatic analogy in that 'the prosodic contour of one, presumably the most frequently used, member of a derivational set, is preserved throughout the paradigm' (p. 37).

As a further showcase of paradigmatic pressure we may mention Peter Trudgill's 'English Dialect "Default Singulars", *Was* versus *Were*, Verner's Law, and Germanic Dialects' (*JEngL* 36[2008] 341–52). Although more concerned with morphology than phonology, this article offers a nice illustration of how paradigmatic levelling can undo the irregularity caused by sound change, in this case the voicing and subsequent rhotacization of pre-Germanic intervocalic /s/, which has given rise to such ModE alternations as *was* and *were*. Trudgill provides cross-linguistic support for the view that *r*-generalization was initially dominant in both English and other Germanic languages. In English this process was later supplanted by *s*-generalization, under the influence of the English south-east.

Which syllables do English speakers stress in pseudo-words like *potabovoo* and *tabovoo*? In 'Word Length and the Location of Primary Word Stress in

Dutch, German and English' (*Linguistics* 46[2008] 507–40) Mirjam Ernestus and Anneke Neijt take as their starting point the observation that primary stress in Germanic tends to fall on one of the last three syllables in the word, and the claim, made by many phonologists, that the assignment of primary stress is independent from that of secondary stress. The authors show that this claim is problematic. The results of their experiments indicate that speakers of English show a greater preference for penultimate stress in *potabovoo* than in *tabovoo*, suggesting that the length of a word affects the position of primary stress. More specifically, the authors assert that the greater preference for penultimate stress in *potabovoo* is due to the fact that English prefers word-initial syllables with primary or secondary stress, and an alternating pattern of stressed and unstressed syllables. This strongly suggests that the assignment of primary and secondary stress is not independent. Ernestus and Neijt find the same effect in German and Dutch. They also observe that in each of the three languages speakers show both inter-speaker and intra-speaker variation. Here, too, paradigmatic analogy may be relevant. They point out that one way to account for the variation would be to take a 'data-oriented' approach according to which speakers base the stress pattern of new words on that of existing words which are phonologically, morphologically or semantically similar.

Recent work in psycholinguistics has suggested that paradigm uniformity may aid lexical access. In 'English Stress Preservation: The Case for "Fake Cyclicity"' (*ELL* 12[2008] 505–32) Sarah Collie notes that this is arguably the reason why some suffixed words in English retain the prosodic contour of their base (e.g. *accèptabílity*, where the primary stress of *accéptable* is retained as secondary stress). However, Collie observes that the status of this 'relative prominence preservation' is controversial since it occurs in some words but not others (e.g. *repátriate*, with stress on the second syllable, versus *répatriation*, with initial stress). The results of Collie's corpus study show that relative prominence preservation is probabilistic: stress is preserved more often in derivatives whose frequency is lower than that of their bases—or, as she puts it, 'lower embedding frequency and higher embedded frequency favour stress preservation' (p. 516). Collie concludes from this that relative prominence preservation is not the result of a mechanism of the grammar, e.g. the phonological cycle, but a usage-based phenomenon.

Frequency of use also plays a role in the West Yorkshire English lenition of /t/ to [ɹ]. In '*t*-to-*r* in West Yorkshire English' (*ELL* 12[2008] 141–68) Judith Broadbent observes that this lenition is lexically restricted and as such likely to be a remnant of a once fully productive process (which once affected /d/ as well as /t/); this process has been gradually superseded by glottal replacement over the course of the twentieth century. What makes *t*-to-*r* synchronically interesting is that it applies productively in connected speech (e.g. *get it* [gɛɹ ɪt], *put it* [pʊɹ ɪt]), where it interacts with processes such as *h*-dropping (e.g. *get her* [gɛɹ əɹ]). Broadbent notes that the restricted application of *t*-to-*r* is difficult to account for in Lexical Phonology and OT, unless one is willing to assume that forms like *put* and *get* are lexically marked. The *t*-to-*r* facts appear to be more amenable to a usage-based account: *t*-to-*r* has remained in a group of high-frequency words that are related to each other on account of their similar phonological shape. The high frequency with which these words are used ensures the continued survival of the process.

Another process affecting /t/ is frication, as found in many varieties of Irish and north-eastern BrE. In 'Fricated Realisations of /t/ in Dublin and Middlesbrough English: An Acoustic Analysis of Plosive Frication and Surface Fricative Contrasts' (*ELL* 12[2008] 419–43), Mark Jones and Carmen Llamas examine to which extent frication in these localities is a general property of the voiceless plosives /p, t, k/, and in which respects fricated /t/ is different from other voiceless fricatives, such as /s, ʃ/. Their experiments show that some speakers of Dublin English have categorical frication of /t/ but sporadic frication of /p, k/. In Middlesbrough, where frication of stops is a more recent phenomenon, frication of /t/ is on the whole a gradient. In addition, frication here affects stops regardless of place, suggesting that it is a general phonetic effect. Jones and Llamas conclude from this that the Middlesbrough pattern is unlikely to be the result of Irish English influence. The authors further find that the fricated /t/ of Dublin English is closer to /ʃ/ than to /s/ while that of Middlesbrough English is closer to /s/ than to /ʃ/. Neither variety shows any sign of neutralization of an existing fricative contrast.

Moving across the Atlantic to the United States, the 2008 issue of *American Speech* contains a range of articles dealing with ongoing vowel changes in American varieties of English—a topic which is also of obvious interest to dialectologists (hence these are also discussed in section 9 below). In 'Prevelar Raising and Phonetic Conditioning: The Role of Labial and Anterior Tongue Gestures' (*AS* 83[2008] 373–402), Thomas C. Purnell reports on an articulatory investigation into the raising of low front /æ/ before /g/. For some speakers, particularly in the Upper Midwest of the US, this has led to a merger or near-merger with /eɪ/ or /ɛ/. Purnell's study shows that raised /æ/ has three consistent articulatory correlates, viz. a higher jaw position, a more anterior gesture and a more forward lip position than non-raised /æ/. The author conjectures that children may acquire prevelar raising by correlating the jaw position and lip readjustment with the auditory cues of a raised /æ/.

The raising of /æ/ before voiced velars is also the topic of Matt Bauer and Frank Parker's '/æ/-Raising in Wisconsin English' (*AS* 83[2008] 403–31). Bauer and Parker observe that raising in this dialect does not lead to a merger with either /e/ or /ɛ/ although a few words with original /eg/ have been reanalysed as containing /æg/ (e.g. *plague, bagel*). The authors note that raising is a natural co-articulatory effect, resolving as it does an intrinsic conflict between the low front tongue body gesture of the vowel and the following high back tongue body gesture of the stop. The fact that it occurs before /g/ but not /k/ is attributed to the voiceless stop having a raised larynx, with the resulting higher F1 producing an acoustically lower vowel. Bauer and Parker interpret the data as supporting the view on sound change espoused in the work of John Ohala: speakers of Wisconsin English have failed to correct for the co-articulatory effects of /g/, as a result of which the raised variant of /æ/ has become phonologized. This has caused some /eg/ words (which are on the whole relatively rare) to have been reanalysed as having /æg/ instead.

In 'Patterns of /uw/, /ʊ/ and /ow/ Fronting in Reno, Nevada' (*AS* 83[2008] 432–54) Valerie Fridland discusses the phenomenon of back vowel fronting in the western region of the US. Fridland observes that this shift is found in many US dialects and is relatively uniform as compared to other vowel shifts. Back vowel fronting minimally involves /uw/; in those dialects where /ʊ/ and /ow/ are also affected, as in Nevada English, the change is most advanced for /uw/. As one would expect, fronting is most prominent before alveolars and is inhibited by following labials and velarized laterals. The ubiquity and regularity of back vowel fronting lead Fridland to suggest that the change is internally motivated rather than driven by regional or social factors. The exact nature of this internal motivation remains unclear, but cross-linguistic evidence suggests that fronting of back vowels is more typical of languages with relatively large vowel systems.

Maeve Eberhardt's 'The Low-Back Merger in the Steel City: African American English in Pittsburgh' (*AS* 83[2008] 284–311) and David Bowie's 'Acoustic Characteristics of Utah's *Card-Cord* Merger' (*AS* 83[2008] 35–61) deal with similar vowel mergers. Eberhardt asserts that the merger of /ɑ/ and /ɔ/, a widespread sound change in white vernaculars of AmE, also occurs in the variety of AAE spoken in Pittsburgh. The interest in AAE vowel systems is of relatively recent origin. Eberhardt notes that the previously dominant view was that these varieties were by and large immune to vowel changes in white vernaculars. Recent studies suggest that this view is incorrect. Indeed, Eberhardt shows that in Pittsburgh AAE the low-back vowel merger was already well established by the end of the nineteenth century, a time when there was extensive contact between African Americans and whites.

David Bowie's article discusses the variable merger of /ɔɹ/ and /ɑɹ/ into [ɑɹ] in certain varieties of Utah English. Bowie observes that the phonetic characteristics of this merger have never been made explicit. The results of his acoustic measurements bear out the variable nature of the merger, which is characterized by a raised F1 and F2 and, crucially, a lowered F3 of merged /ɔɹ/ tokens. Bowie conjectures that these changes are the result of multiple gestures, including lip rounding and palatal constriction, though the exact articulatory correlates of the merger remain as yet unclear.

Mention must also be made of a number of articles in which phonological concepts and constructs are supported on the basis of data from English. An interesting and ambitious specimen is Andries Coetzee's 'Grammaticality and Ungrammaticality in Phonology' (*Language* 84[2008] 218–57). Interesting, because it argues for a model that combines a formal OT grammar with insights from usage-based approaches; ambitious, because OT is probably not the first framework that leaps to mind when considering the psychological reality of formal linguistic theorizing. Coetzee's aim is to add support to the OT assumption that phonological surface forms may violate some constraints of the language, and to show that ungrammaticality, rather than absolute, is a matter of degree. The article's empirical focus is the observation that some languages do not permit forms like /kek/ and /pop/. This kind of restriction is usually attributed to a constraint banning consonants with identical places of articulation (in some domain or other). In English we find a rather more specific restriction: while words like *cake* and *pope* are obviously fine, **scake* and *spope* are not. *State*, on the other hand, is fine, as is *taut*. Coetzee shows that this pattern can be straightforwardly formalized in terms of violable constraints. However, such an analysis raises two general questions: Is there any reason to suggest that a surface form like *state* is still relatively ill formed? And is there any indication that *scake*, while ungrammatical, is less ill formed than *spope*? In addressing these questions, Coetzee first observes that in the CELEX database [tVt] occurs much more often than [kVk], which in turn occurs more often than [pVp]. This leads him to suggest that English speakers acquire the ranking *pVp > > *kVk > > *tVt on the basis of these syllables' respective frequencies. Coetzee assumes that this basic ranking is maintained in more specific phonotactic patterns; that is, the relative preference for [tVt] is reflected by the grammaticality of *state*, whereas the relative dispreference of [kVk] and [pVp] is reflected by the ungrammaticality of *scake* and *spope*. Coetzee supports this with experimental evidence. First, the results of a phoneme identification experiment suggest that English speakers have a perceptual bias against [stVt] as compared to [stVk] and [stVp], showing that despite its grammaticality [stVt] is relatively ill formed. Second, the results of a word-likeness experiment show that English speakers prefer [skVk] to [spVp], even though both are ungrammatical. Coetzee's article offers a new and fascinating direction of research which, as the author himself notes, yields two testable predictions: 'a grammatical form that violates more, or more serious, constraints should show a processing deficit relative to a grammatical form that violates fewer, less serious, constraints [and] an ungrammatical form that violates more or more serious constraints should show a deficit relative to a form that violates fewer or less serious constraints' (pp. 218–19).

In 'Variation and Opacity in Singapore English Consonant Clusters' (*Phonology* 25[2008] 181–216), Arto Anttila, Vivienne Fong, Štefan Beňuš and Jennifer Nycz focus on the notion of opacity in OT, against the backdrop of a complex array of cluster reduction processes in SingE. Some of these processes are opaque. For instance, SingE speakers delete the second consonant in a coda obstruent cluster (e.g. [tes] 'test'). Final /sp/ clusters, however, undergo metathesis (e.g. [lips] 'lisp'), and some speakers in fact also metathesize /sp/ before inflectional suffixes (e.g. [lipsiŋ] 'lisping'). The authors provide a detailed account of the attested patterns of cluster reduction, which display both opacity and variation. They show that the observed variation is systematic and that all cases of previously observed opaque interactions involve the 'interleaving of phonology and morphology' (p. 212), or else are falsified by new data.

Another theoretical article which draws on English is 'The Syllabic Affiliation of Postvocalic Liquids: An Onset-Specifier Approach' (*Lingua* 118[2008] 1250–70), by Bert Botma, Colin Ewen and Erik Jan van der Torre. The authors argue for the existence of a specifier position in the onset constituent of the syllable, which brings their government-based approach to syllable structure more in line with the X-bar schema as used in syntax. The authors argue that the onset-specifier in English is restricted to /s, l, n/. These sounds have in common that when followed by a homorganic stop, they permit a preceding vowel-length contrast (e.g. *feast* vs. *fist*, *mint* vs. *paint* but not *leemp*, *leesp*). Botma et al. argue that the final cluster in a word like *feast* forms the onset of an empty-headed syllable, with the first consonant occupying the onset-specifier. They go on to show that initial three-consonant clusters, whose first element is predictably /s/ (e.g. *strong*, but **ftrong*) can be straightforwardly analysed if /s/ occupies the onset-specifier.

Laurie Bauer gives a short, accessible and up-to-date discussion of the notion of contrast in his article 'Contrast in Language and Linguistics' (*JEngL* 36[2008] 93–8). Most of Bauer's examples are phonological, and most of these are taken from English. Aside from clear-cut instances of contrastive sounds (e.g. the initial stops in *tin* and *din*), Bauer discusses more problematic cases where a contrast is extremely marginal, as in the 'minimal stress pair' *below* vs. *billow*, or sometimes suspended, as in the variable fronting of /θ/ to [f], giving rise to occasional homophones such as *free* and *three*. In other cases a contrast is neutralized in specific contexts, e.g. stops after /s/, while in yet other cases a contrast cannot be reduced to a property of a single phoneme. This is arguably the case in a pair such as *writer* and *rider*, where each of the sounds in *writer* differs slightly from those in *rider*. These examples show that languages employ different degrees of contrast, with some more thoroughly integrated in the language than others.

Another short and accessible discussion is Donka Minkova and Robert Stockwell's 'Phonology: Segmental Histories' (in Momma and Matto, eds., *A Companion to the History of the English Language*, pp. 29–42). The authors present a concise overview of the various vocalic and consonantal changes that have occurred in the development from OE to PDE.

An article that is also worth mentioning is Daniel Sanford's 'Metaphor and Phonological Reduction in English Idiomatic Expressions' (*CogLing* 19[2008] 585–603), if only to show that the phonological spectrum is always broader than you think. Sanford reports on an experiment which shows that a word like *spill* has a shorter duration in *Don't spill the beans* than in *Don't spill the peas*. This, he argues, is in line with the observation that words inside idiomatic expressions are typically highly predictable, given the restricted nature of the 'source domain' from which metaphorical idioms take their meaning. Sanford's experiment shows that this predictability correlates with phonological reduction.

Phonology textbooks tend to devote a lot of attention to English. Geoffrey S. Nathan's *Phonology: A Cognitive Grammar Introduction* is no exception. The book offers a critical and refreshingly theory-neutral introduction to some of the core concepts of phonological theory, including phonemes, features, syllables and alternations. Nathan makes an effort to show that these concepts have a 'long and honorable' tradition (p. ix), with some of them pre-dating the modern era by more than 2,000 years. The title of the book deserves some comment, as there are about as many linguists as there are meanings of 'cognitive'. For Nathan, the term seems more or less synonymous with 'psychologically plausible'. This textbook, then, is not an introduction to phonology from the perspective of Cognitive Grammar (the framework associated first and foremost with Ronald W. Langacker).

It is fitting to end this overview with a word or two about the seventh, updated edition of Alan Cruttenden's *Gimson's Pronunciation of English*, a classic textbook on phonetics. If you don't already own a copy, I urge you to get one now. The new edition includes among other things new articulatory diagrams based on MRI scans and a discussion of the idea of a global pronunciation standard as an alternative to Received Pronunciation and General American. Another book that is warmly recommended is Phil Carr's *A Glossary of Phonology*. Good glossaries are up to date, exhaustive in their coverage and useful for both practitioners and students of the field. *A Glossary of Phonology* is all of these things.

4. Morphology

There are several articles describing aspects of morphology from a typological point of view in *Grammatical Categories and the Lexicon*, volume 3 of the work *Language Typology and Syntactic Description*, edited by the late Timothy Shopen, of which a second edition has appeared. Like all the chapters in this work (we review some more in section 5) they contain a wealth of cross-linguistic material but they also include English data, and the general typological points made are often relevant to the analysis of English as well. Alexandra Aikhenvald contributes 'Typological Distinctions in Word-Formation' (pp. 1–65), which considers the following issues in the field of word building: morphological typology (analytic, agglutinating, fusional and polysynthetic systems), noun incorporation, iconicity in word formation, compounding, derivation, factors determining a pattern's productivity, grammaticalization and lexicalization. The chapter on 'Inflectional Morphology' by Balthasar Bickel and Johanna Nichols (pp. 169–240) discusses inflectional categories, head and dependent marking, the position of inflectional markers in the word (with prefixes, infixes and suffixes as the basic categories), paradigms, markedness, the differences between layered and template morphology and the interaction of inflection and syntax. Some further detail is provided on person and number marking, which are used as extended examples of the various notions discussed. There is more on this in Jonathan Bobaljik's 'Missing Persons: A Case Study in Morphological Universals' (*LingRev* 25[2008] 203–30). After showing that, cross-linguistically, certain logically possible person markings in fact never occur, without there being any good functional reason for the gaps, he argues that they can be explained if person marking universally and innately involves a two-valued system, [±speaker] and [±hearer], without a category of third person.

Martin Maiden, in 'Lexical Nonsense and Morphological Sense: On the Real Importance of "Folk Etymology" and Related Phenomena for Historical Linguists' (in Eythórsson, ed., *Grammatical Change and Linguistic Theory: The Rosendal Papers*, pp. 307–28), argues that formatives sometimes act as morphological units without their meaning playing any role in this. The main data come from the process of folk etymology, which Maiden argues involves a desire by speakers to endow a single opaque word with structure (often of the compound type), whether or not this results in a recognizable meaning. Thus, when French *mousseron* was folk-etymologized into English *mushroom*, there was a gain in morphological but not semantic transparency. A further extension is suggested to cases of lexical replacement, where often a new word replaces the older one across the board even if the old word has several widely divergent meanings. Here too, things appear to happen to lexical formatives regardless of their meanings. This of course is not to deny the existence of meaning-based processes. Thus Antonio Lillo, 'Covert Puns as a Source of Slang Words in English' (*ES* 89[2008] 319–38), discusses the formation of what the author calls 'covert puns', in which the punning element and its target (which are homophonous) 'are indirectly connected by means of sense relations and/or cultural associations' (p. 320). In 'Architecture and Blocking' (*LingI* 39[2008] 1–53) David Embick and Alec Marantz are also concerned with big questions. They reject the standard interpretation of blocking, whereby two forms (one regular, one memorized) compete for the same semantic/syntactic slot, which involves evaluation of ill-formed words (such as *gived*). Instead they argue that the locus of observable blocking effects is the point at which allomorphs are inserted at terminal nodes (as when the zero allomorph, but not /ed/, is inserted in the context of *give*). To implement these ideas, the model of distributed morphology is used.

Relations between morphology and phonology come to the fore in two contributions. Martin Hilpert, 'The English Comparative: Language Structure and Language Use' (*ELL* 12[2008] 395–417), argues that the choice between the morphological form (*-er* suffixation) and the periphrastic form (*more* + adjective) is mostly governed by phonological factors, with a smaller role for syntax and frequency of usage. Kumiko Tanaka-Ishii and Zhihui Jin go 'From Phoneme to Morpheme: Another Verification in English and Chinese Using Corpora' (*SL* 62[2008] 224–48), test the hypothesis, first formulated by Zellig Harris, that a phoneme at a morpheme boundary can potentially be followed by a greater number of different phonemes than a phoneme inside that morpheme. To implement this, they use the notion of branching enthropy, defined as (hold on to your seats) $H\left(X|X_n = x_n\right) = -\sum_{x \varepsilon \chi} P\left(X = x|X_n = x_n\right) \log P\left(X = x|X_n = x_n\right)$. The results of their counting show that this idea is correct, in both English and Chinese (though in the latter it does not hold for word boundaries). As the authors point out, this finding helps shed some light on the question of how language can be understood, in spite of its double articulation.

On matters derivational, there is Zeki Hamawand's study, *Morpho-Lexical Alternation in Noun Formation*, which describes the semantic relationship between noun pairs that share a single root but end in different suffixes, e.g. *dispersal/dispersion*, *emergence/emergency*. Hamawand approaches this topic from a Cognitive Semantic and usage-based point of view, making use of data from the BNC and the internet. Hamawand proposes a new approach in which the choice between two alternative nominal suffixes is related to the meaning of each alternative, specifically the conceptual content of each alternative and the construal of content it represents. This approach is applied to a number of nominalizers, de-verbal, de-adjectival, de-nominal and agent-forming. For each type of suffix, Hamawand provides a semantic description according to which the suffixes are polysemous and their senses constitute a semantic network in which all the senses are organized around a primary sense. Hamawand further argues that the two derived nouns in a noun pair represent two different conceptualizations or construals of their common root, each of which is coded by a different suffix. Throughout the book, ample examples are given to illustrate and test the hypotheses put forward. In the concluding chapter, tables are given that summarize the multiple senses of the noun-forming suffixes in English, as well as the semantic distinctions these nominal suffixes show and the discriminating collocates of the noun pair.

The topic of 'Lexical Nominalization' is discussed from a typological perspective by Bernard Comrie and Sandra Thompson (in Shopen, ed., vol. 3, pp. 334–81), who give an overview of methods used to create nouns from other words, sometimes other nouns but more often verbs or adjectives (with the resultant nominalization designating the activity or state described by the base word or naming one of its arguments). The authors point out that the relevant processes are often irregular and unpredictable and that nouns derived from verbs can vary in their degree of 'nouniness', with some verbal or clausal properties often surviving. Indeed, in some languages, nouns can be formed by adding a nominalizer to an entire clause (though this clause may have somewhat reduced marking of clausal categories, such as tense). More on the topic of derivation, this time verbal, can be found in Robert M.W. Dixon's article, 'Deriving Verbs in English' (*LangS* 30[2008] 31–52), which shows that the way in which verbs are derived from nouns and adjectives (e.g. by *-ize* or *-(i)fy* suffixation or zero-derivation) is guided by a combination of etymology, semantics and phonological form.

On compounds, in particular the psycholinguistic issues they raise, there is the volume *The Representation and Processing of Compound Words*, edited by Gary Libben and Gonia Jarema. It opens with Gary Libben's 'Why Study Compound Processing? An Overview of the Issues' (pp. 1–22). As Libben points out, compounding appears to be a fundamental property of language, and insight into its processing promises to shed light on basic issues in the mental representation of language. The available evidence suggests that during processing of a compound all possibly relevant items in the lexicon are accessed, so both the constituent elements and the compound as a whole. In the case of *cranberry* and *strawberry*, the first element would have to be deactivated again, perhaps through it being more weakly linked with the compound or perhaps through consideration of the entire *berry* family, in which semantic opacity is widespread. In 'Compound Types' (pp. 23–44), Wolfgang Dressler is concerned with the definition and linguistic properties of different types of compounds, with a view to informed decisions on stimuli words in psycholinguistic experiments. Among the properties considered are the degree of lexicalization, polysemy, internal word classes, the absence of agreement, recursivity, productivity, headedness, the position of the head and the normally word-based (but sometimes stem-based) nature of compounds. Gonia Jarema contributes 'Compound Representation and Processing: A Cross-Language Perspective' (pp. 45–70), culling convergent findings on this topic from existing studies. A firm finding, again, is that a compound's constituents are activated during processing. Moreover, the first constituent appears to be activated most strongly, even if this is not the head. Studies of linking elements suggest that during processing these are interpreted as signals of compound structure.

In 'The Neuropsychology of Compound Words' (pp. 71–95), Carlo Semenza and Sara Mondini begin by arguing that the study of aphasics may be expected to shed light on compound processing more easily than that of normal subjects, because results from the former group will typically show much greater differences—i.e. aphasics make many more errors. Findings confirm that full and simultaneous decomposition of compounds takes place and show that different types of lexical knowledge (phonological, order-related, rule-based) are accessed independently of each other. Elena Nicoladis addresses 'Preschool Children's Acquisition of Compounds' (pp. 96–124), finding that high frequency appears to promote early acquisition but that ordering in synthetic compounds often remains difficult (leading to forms like *breaker-bottle*, perhaps based on ordinary verb-object order, even among children that already know words like *dishwasher*). Erika Levy, Mira Goral and Loraine Obler tackle a little-researched topic in 'Doghouse/Chien-Maison/Niche: Approaches to the Understanding of Compound Processing in Bilinguals' (pp. 125–44). The authors review what is known about bilingual processing in general and suggest several methods and caveats for work on bilingual compound processing. Christina Gagné and Thomas Spalding write about 'Conceptual Combination: Implications for the Mental Lexicon' (pp. 145–68), focusing on the meaning relation between first and second element in compounds. They argue that it is the modifier that is crucial here and that the relation preferentially selected is the one that this modifier has most often in other (existing) compounds. Thus *mountain village* is readily interpreted as 'village LOCATED on a mountain', because 80 per cent of the *mountain X* compounds in a corpus show this relation. Finally, James Myers considers 'Processing Chinese Compounds: A Survey of the Literature' (pp. 169–96), which again confirms the reality of decomposition during processing (but also yields an unexpected finding: that written form influences processing not only in the visual but also in the spoken medium).

Vincent Renner's article, 'On the Semantics of English Coordinate Compounds' (*ES* 89[2008] 606–13), offers a typology of the complex semantic behaviour of English co-ordinate compounds such as *player-manager*. Another issue regarding English compounds is addressed by Sara Gesuato in 'Co-Text of Use of Forty English Nominal Premodifiers' (*LingInv* 31[2008] 143–57), in which she shows that plural premodification (e.g. *tribesman*) contributes significant numbers of compounds, although singular premodification (e.g. *armchair*) is favoured.

Historical developments in English morphology are the focus of Robert McColl Millar's 'History of English Morphology' (in Momma and Matto eds., pp. 43–56). McColl Millar concentrates on changes in noun phrase inflectional morphology, providing a clear overview of the simplification that has taken place in this area. A method of studying the fine details of OE morphology (but also spelling and some simple syntax) is described by Antonio Miranda García, Javier Calle Martín, David Moreno Olalla and Gustavo Muñoz González in 'The Old English Apollonius of Tyre in the Light of the Old English Concordancer' (in Renouf and Kehoe, eds., *The Changing Face of Corpus Linguistics*, pp. 81–98). They explain how the concordancer works and what can be achieved if it is applied to an OE corpus that has vowel-length marking, lemmatization and morphological tagging. Part of an *English Language and Linguistics* special issue on English intensifiers, Ursula Lenker's 'Booster Prefixes in Old English—An Alternative View of the Roots of ME *Forsooth*' (*ELL* 12[2008] 245–65) presents an analysis of the Old English booster (i.e. upward scaling) prefix *for-*, on the basis of which it is concluded that ME *forsoothe* derived from the OE accusative singular neuter form of the adjective *forsoþ*.

Ewa Ciszek, in her book *Word Derivation in Early Middle English* (a revised version of her Ph.D. dissertation), provides a detailed description and analysis of seven suffixes forming abstract nouns in Early ME: the native suffixes *-dom*, *-s(c)hip(e)*, *-hed(e)* and *-nes(se)*, and the suffixes of French origin *-āge*, *-(e)rīe* and *-ment*. The analysis presented covers the productivity of the suffixes, their semantics (both synchronically and diachronically) and their dialect distribution in Early ME (excluding the north, due to a lack of available written sources). Ciszek devotes a separate chapter to a discussion of the notion of productivity, 'a controversial concept in word-formation in general and in historical linguistics in particular' (p. 6). She establishes the productivity of a given suffix on the basis of type frequency, token frequency and transparency. The native suffixes (*-dom*, *-s(c)hip(e)*, *-hed(e)* and *-nes(se)*) are all shown to be productive and to occur in all dialect areas in Early ME. The suffix *-hed(e)* is considered by Ciszek to be a suffix of Continental Germanic (most likely Frisian) origin, which was functionally and semantically equivalent to OE *-hād*. The semantic development of *-s(c)hip(e)* shows that it mostly derives abstract nouns from adjectives in Early ME, whereas it mostly formed denominal nouns in OE. The three suffixes of French origin (*-āge*, *-(e)rīe* and *-ment*) receive less attention. Ciszek measures their productivity on the basis of their appearance in hybrid formations (native stem + foreign suffix), transparent borrowings from which the suffix was extracted, and the frequency of the suffix. Using these indicators, Ciszek concludes that *-āge* and *-(e)rīe* but not *-ment*, were productive in Early ME.

Juan Manuel Hernández-Campoy, in 'Overt and Covert Prestige in Late Middle English: A Case Study in East Anglia' (*FLH* 29[2008] 1–26), reports on a study of *was/were* variation in the *Paston Letters*, finding some signs of replacement of standard *was* by *were* in the language of William Paston II. Since William seems to have been aware of standard norms (as developed, amongst others, in Chancery English), the author interprets the shift as a possible case of a form with covert prestige winning out against a form with overt prestige. Isabel Moskowich, '"To lerne sciences touching nombres and proporcions": The Proportion of Affixation in Early Scientific Writing' (*ES* 89[2008] 39–66), presents a corpus study of affixation patterns in the scientific register of the late Middle Ages, showing that scientific texts responded to the needs of the readership. Also in the *ELL* special issue on English intensifiers is Terttu Nevalainen's 'Social Variation in Intensifier Use: Constraint on *-ly* Adverbialization in the Past?' (*ELL* 12[2008] 289–315), which shows that social conditioning played a role in the choice of form (*-ly* suffix or zero) of de-adjectival intensifiers between 1400 and 1600, and that the *-ly* suffix was less grammaticalized than it is today.

5. Syntax

(a) Modern English
There are several textbooks to report on—some in new editions and some from earlier years: it is not easy to keep up with the steady stream of introductory publications. In *Discovering Language: The Structure of Modern English,* Lesley Jeffries offers first-year students engaging with English language the tools that they need to 'pull it to pieces' (p. 7). There are seven chapters, on phonetics, phonology, words (i.e. their morphology and classes), phrases, clauses/sentences, lexical semantics and 'theory, text and context' (dealing with text structure but also general properties and conceptualizations of language). Exercises (with suggested answers) and a quite full glossary of terms complete the book. The overall approach is practical but students will also acquire some feeling for more theoretical reflection.

A second, extended, edition has appeared of Jim Miller's *An Introduction to English Syntax,* which offers a clear and concise introduction to its topic. In the foreword, we read that the second edition features two major changes: non-finite clauses are discussed in more detail in a separate chapter, and a chapter has been added on discourse and syntax (replacing the chapter on case, gender and mood included in the first edition). The book deals with all the major concepts and topics of English syntax, including constituent structure, word classes, clause types, subcategorization and dependency relations (e.g. grammatical functions, agreement, government). It also pays attention to recurring syntactic patterns ('constructions'), including active/ passive, declarative/interrogative and oblique object/double object. Thematic roles are also discussed, and the last two chapters of the book are devoted to syntax and discourse, including topics such as focus, aspect, tense and voice. As in the first edition, this second edition contains useful exercises at the end of each chapter, as well as a discussion of the exercises at the end of the book.

The year 2008 saw the publication of a third edition of another textbook on English syntax: *English Syntax and Argumentation* by Bas Aarts. The foreword informs us that the main changes incorporated in the third edition are the addition of a chapter on grammatical indeterminacy (inspired by the author's work on syntactic gradience, see below) and the addition of a case study, as well as some new exercises. Another change is the replacement of the term *determiner* by the term *determinative* (for which no motivation is given). The book is subdivided into four parts: the first part contains chapters about form and function, the second part, entitled 'Elaboration', delves deeper into a number of syntactic issues, including X-bar syntax, clausal syntax and movement, the third part is specifically concerned with syntactic argumenta-tion, and the fourth part contains a chapter on grammatical indeterminacy and one with a number of case studies. Each chapter comes with a useful list of the key concepts discussed there, a set of exercises and suggestions for further reading. There is a glossary of important terms at the end of the book as well as a list of reference works that are useful to anyone studying English syntax. The work is written in a lucid style, and its emphasis on argumentation offers the beginning student of English syntax a solid basis for further study.

Geoffrey Leech, Margaret Deuchar and Robert Hoogenraad have written a second edition of their *English Grammar for Today: A New Introduction* (first edition 1982). There has been some streamlining of chapter divisions, updating of examples and exercises, and adjustments of explanations, but the book's overall structure and content have remained largely similar and the grammatical framework is still resolutely Quirkian. The intended audience consists of students in higher secondary or first-year university courses, and we feel that the book is pitched at exactly the right level for them. After some general discussion of notions of grammar and an explanation of basic morphological concepts, there are six chapters dealing with the usual syntactic phenomena: sentence parts, word classes, phrases, clauses, clause linking through subordination and co-ordination, and non-basic constructions (involving displacement and empty elements). The third part of the book contains five chapters in which grammatical knowledge is applied to phenomena such as differences between speech and writing, registers, literary texts, questions of good usage and problems of writing.

A comparable work, but addressed to an American audience, is *The Uses of Grammar*, by Judith Rodby and W. Ross Winterowd. Though with sometimes slightly different terminology (and the use of Reed-Kellogg diagrams in addition to tree diagrams), it also covers the basic elements of grammar, including simple morphological concepts, sentence types, the word classes, verbal groups, noun phrases, complement clauses, adjectives, relative clauses, adverbials, prepositional phrases and conjoined clauses. A difference is that this book pays somewhat greater attention to practical matters of usage and prescription, advice on which is integrated in the analytical chapters. Furthermore, some modern linguistic concepts are introduced (though sometimes so briefly that their usefulness must be doubted) and explicit attention is devoted to issues of English learnt as a second language. There is a separate teacher's guide, which also contains answers to the exercises, and the book has an accompanying website, which the authors promise will be extended over the coming years.

For students in search of information on the cross-linguistic properties and distinguishing characteristics of word types and sentence types, there are two articles with a typological slant. A comprehensive introduction to 'Parts-of-Speech Systems' is provided by Paul Schachter and Timothy Shopen (in Shopen, ed., *Language Typology and Syntactic Description*, vol. 1: *Clause Structure*, pp. 1–60). The open classes of nouns, verbs, adjectives and adverbs are discussed, as are the closed classes of pro-forms, noun adjuncts (such as case markers, adpositions, quantifiers and articles), verb adjuncts (auxiliaries and particles) and conjunctions. Ekkehard König and Peter Siemund have written 'Speech Act Distinctions in Grammar' (in Shopen, ed., vol. 1, pp. 276–324), replacing the chapter by Jerrold Sadock and Arnold Zwicky in the first edition of this work [1985]. The new chapter still deals with the grammatical categories reflecting speech-act types, i.e. with declaratives, interrogatives and imperatives. For the latter two, several subtypes are distinguished (polar and constituent interrogatives, positive, negative and indirect imperatives) and the range of cross-linguistic realizations is discussed.

We also mention here Edwin Battistella's *Bad Language: Are Some Words Better than Others?*, a work on language prescription and description addressed to a general (American) audience. After an introductory chapter, the author deals with what the two approaches have to say about written English, about rules of grammar, about vocabulary (focusing on offensive language, slang and politically correct usage), about the use in the USA of languages other than English and about native English varieties (regional dialects as well as AAVE). A concluding chapter sets out what assumptions should be avoided and what mind frame should be adopted when wishing to engage in fruitful discussion of linguistic issues of this type. The author is careful not to dismiss popular attitudes and feelings about linguistic usage, but does expose their often shaky foundations and undesirable consequences.

Another work that non-specialists may also find useful is John Algeo's *British or American English? A Handbook of Word and Grammar Patterns*. Based on a large collection of Briticisms collected over several decades and supplemented by data from the Cambridge International Corpus, this book contains masses of information about differences in grammatical usage between the two varieties. There are chapters on each of the parts of speech and on grammatical patterns, i.e. complementation, mandative constructions, expanded predicates, concord, pro-forms and tag questions. Each section starts with a general characterization of the relevant difference between BrE and AmE, followed by detailed information about specific words/phrases, arranged alphabetically, with a brief explanation, an example sentence, frequency figures for the two varieties, and any other relevant differences in meaning or usage. To help the user locate information, there is an index of words. All in all, this is an impressive work. Although many of the differences dealt with have been described in general terms before, this book gathers them all together, adds a host of further differences and provides detailed corpus-based information not only about general patterns but also about the behaviour of the individual words and phrases making up the pattern.

There are three dictionary-glossary type of works to report on. Michael Pearce has written *The Routledge Dictionary of English Language Studies*. It contains some 600 entries on grammar, vocabulary, phonetics, phonology, semantics, sociolinguistics, pragmatics and discourse. There are descriptions of the main characteristics of many varieties of English, and, in addition, the history of English, stylistics, and literary discourse studies are well covered. The entries are clear, accessible and often include examples (many of them corpus-based). We can easily imagine undergraduates in introductory modules turning to this book and finding relevant information, even enlightenment. For more advanced students, there is now a sixth edition of David Crystal's *Dictionary of Linguistics and Phonetics*, with some 3,000 entries. Some of them have been updated, minimalism now has a stronger presence, but overall the book remains the same—very full in coverage, very well informed but often somewhat too compact for our taste. Further useful materials for advanced students of syntax are provided by Silvia Luraghi and Claudia Parodi in *Key Terms in Syntax and Syntactic Theory*. A first section deals with 'Key Theories', devoting one to two pages each to the major general frameworks that students might come across (such as case grammar, cognitive grammar, the extended standard theory, functional sentence perspective, head-driven phrase structure, tagmemics, etc.). The second section, the bulk of the book, provides definitions, examples and explanations of 'Key Terms', from A-position, actant, cataphora, complement, copy theory, and covert movement to variables, voice, weak features, *Wh-* in situ, word order and X-bar theory. The entries here range from a few lines to two pages, and many cross-references are given. The people behind the theories and terms are introduced in the section on 'Key Thinkers', where the careers and major achievements of about fifty syntacticians are briefly summarized.

If your students want to know more about the ideas of one of these fifty linguists (guess who), you can send them to *Chomsky: A Guide for the Perplexed* by John Collins. But better do this only with quite advanced students: this work requires a good familiarity with Chomsky's own writings and the ability to keep focused when reading philosophical discourse. In the first chapter, Collins introduces the different strands in Chomsky's work, discussing their general significance and the misunderstandings they have engendered (a theme sustained throughout the book). Chapter 2 deals with 'Methodological Foundations', as built up in Chomsky's early work. In the third chapter, the introduction of transformations is dealt with, while chapter 4 discusses the cognitive basis of Chomsky's work. Going back slightly in time, chapter 5 considers Chomsky's review of Skinner, what it entailed and what many people erroneously think it entailed. Chapter 6 deals with Chomsky's conviction, voiced from the 1970s onwards, that grammar, not language, is the true object of linguistic study. Chapter 7 reviews the nuts and bolts of Chomskyan syntax and the changes it has undergone from the early 1960s into the 1980s. The final chapter deals with the minimalist turn, explaining its conceptual foundations and giving some idea of the concrete implementation of the ideas in actual analyses.

The three major grammars of English that all students are likely to use at some point (the 1985 *Comprehensive Grammar of the English Language*, see *YWES* 66[1988] 91; the 1999 *Longman Grammar of Spoken and Written English*, *YWES* 80[2001] 20, and the 2002 *Cambridge Grammar of the English Language*, *YWES* 84[2005] 25) are compared by Joybrato Mukherjee in 'Corpus Linguistics and English Reference Grammars' (in Renouf and Kehoe, eds., pp. 337–54). He considers the first and the second work together the best corpus-based reference grammars currently available (the third work being more theoretical in many places) and makes several recommendations for future grammars with respect to overall corpus design and the use of register-specific corpora. Other opinions on what the impact of corpus studies should be on reference grammars are represented in 'Corpus Linguistics, Grammar and Theory: Report on a Panel Discussion at the 24th ICAME Conference', written up by Jan Aarts (in Renouf and Kehoe, eds., pp. 391–408). It contains position statements by panel members Bas Aarts, Geoffrey Leech, Christian Mair, Joybrato Mukherjee and Elena Tognini Bonelli, followed by an account of the discussion that ensued. For want of a better place, we also mention here *Monograph: Software Aided Analysis of Language*, edited by Mike Scott, Pascual Pérez-Paredes and Purificación Sánchez-Hernández. In spite of its main title, this is a collection of eight articles on software for corpus analysis, with five articles focusing on its development and three on its application (for purposes of establishing authorship, studying writing processes and analysing levels of complexity in student writing).

We have imperceptibly moved up a couple of floors to reach the more advanced materials, though we are still in the student union shop. Mira Ariel has written *Pragmatics and Grammar*, a textbook that addresses the question: what is the division of labour between pragmatics and grammar? Ariel distinguishes the two by saying that grammar embraces meanings expressed by the linguistic code while pragmatics is all about inferences. She shows in detail how this works in concrete terms using the case of referential expressions as an example. Furthermore, she distinguishes explicated, implicated and truth-compatible inferences, illustrated by analyses of clause-linking *and* and the scalar expression *most*. The second part of the book is devoted to the ways in which grammar and pragmatics interact, which Ariel argues is mainly visible in historical change through grammaticization (as in the by now standard idea that inferential meaning can over time become semanticized). She proposes that the input to such grammaticization cannot be just anything but only a salient discourse pattern—an example being the development of reflexive pronouns in English, which originally expressed marked co-reference in a salient manner. The final chapter considers what exactly the level of meaning is at which pragmatics and grammar interact.

Another advanced-level textbook is Patrick Farrell's *Grammatical Relations*, which deals with syntactic functions and thematic/semantic roles, and the relations between them. Farrell first describes the main categories, highlighting problematic cases such as the status of the indirect object. This is followed by an overview of the main systems found cross-linguistically, paying attention to basic function marking (as in accusative, ergative and split-intransitive languages) and relational alternations such as passive, antipassive and applicative. Having established the facts—much as in F.R. Palmer's [1994] *Grammatical Roles and Relations* (*YWES* 75[1997] 46), though in somewhat less detail and with greater discursive scaffolding—Farrell then goes on to describe the way these facts are analysed in three major theories of syntax: Relational Grammar, Role and Reference Grammar and Transformational Grammar. Each of these three chapters includes several case studies, thus giving a good impression of how the relevant theory deals with the phenomena. Throughout, Farrell emphasizes the complexity of the facts, which makes it possible for three very different approaches to these facts to all claim some degree of success (while also leaving various questions open).

Writing on *Syntactic Gradience: The Nature of Grammatical Indeterminacy*, Bas Aarts proposes that two types should be distinguished: subsective gradience, where a grammatical category has core and peripheral members, and intersective gradience, where elements of one category can have certain properties more characteristic of another category (though this does not mean the categories overlap). After usefully surveying earlier work on (linguistic) categorization, gradience and gradience-related phenomena, Aarts applies his ideas to a wide range of grammatical categories in English, including word classes (particularly interesting areas being prepositional subsection and noun–adjective intersection), noun phrases, clauses and constructions (such as passives, possessives, co-ordination and subordination). The third part of the book offers a formalization of the central notions and applies this to several cases, such as the gerund, the behaviour of *near* and *like*, and *to*-infinitival constructions. The conclusion drawn is that gradience is real but less widespread than some other accounts have claimed—an important method of distinguishing true from spurious gradience is a close consideration of the categories being proposed and the criteria being used for them. Overall, we feel that this book, thanks to its systematic and level-headed approach to a potentially slippery topic, will be required reading for any linguist tempted to appeal to notions of overlap, fuzziness, squishiness and prototypicality. In a separate article, 'Approaches to the English Gerund' (in Trousdale and Gisborne, eds., *Constructional Approaches to English Grammar*, pp. 11–31; see also below), Aarts shows in more detail why it is not necessary to assume a 'mixed category' in order to account for verbal gerunds (which appear to be a type of noun and a type of verb at the same time): they can be dealt with by assuming they show intersective gradience.

Anna Wierzbicka continues her quest to uncover relations between language and culture in *English: Meaning and Culture*. Where other work in ethno-grammar is circumspect to the point of coyness, Wierzbicka is nothing if not forthright, stating that English reflects many features of Anglo (i.e. Anglo-American-Australian-New Zealand) culture and ways of thinking. After demonstrating that this culture, its scripts and its manners of speaking are very different from what people from other societies are used to, she argues that Anglo culture is directly reflected in the meanings expressed by English words such as *right*, *wrong*, *reasonable* and *fair* (a thesis that many linguists might agree with) and also in grammatical patterns (here, of course, eyebrows will be raised, as Wierzbicka herself is only too aware). The specific grammatical phenomena she analyses are causative constructions and epistemic adverbs (*evidently*, *obviously*, *probably* etc.) and phrases (*I think*, *I suppose*, *I gather*, *I imagine* etc.). With respect to the former, she argues that the wide range of such constructions in English (with matrix verbs like *get*, *cause*, *have*, *let*, *force* etc., each of them occurring in several distinct patterns) reflects the Anglo preoccupation with personal freedom from interference (presumably via a close attention to ways of verbalizing any infringement of this autonomy). With regard to the second phenomenon, she shows that these expressions arose mainly after the eighteenth century, when the modern concern with the uncertainty of knowledge emerged, with John Locke being a driving force behind their development and spread. To describe the meanings of the various elements she analyses, Wierzbicka employs the natural semantic meta-language that she has developed in earlier work. Whatever one's reaction to her overall thesis, her semantic analyses of the relevant phenomena strike us as sensitive and compelling.

Adele Goldberg continues her exploration of Construction Grammar in *Constructions at Work: The Nature of Generalization in Language*. After three introductory chapters (on the nature of constructions, their essential role in describing and explaining surface generalizations and the relation between item-specific knowledge and generalizations), she considers in more detail the way generalizations are learned and the way generalizations can be explained in a construction framework. Adopting a usage-based model of acquisition, she argues that generalizations are learned on the basis of specific tokens, and that generalizations as well as tokens are stored. To explain generalizations, no innate principles are invoked: instead, an appeal is made to processing constraints and pragmatic (e.g. information-structural) factors. Specific cases analysed in this way are island constraints, scope phenomena and subject–auxiliary inversion (a construction argued to signal 'non-canonical sentence type'). After considering a number of constructions cross-linguistically, Goldberg ends by comparing the construction approach with several similar and not so similar alternatives, a helpful exercise that brings out well the precise impact of some of the basic constructional ideas. For further appreciation of Goldberg's book, there is Mira Ariel's review of it (*Language* 84[2008] 632–6), which supports many of the findings, encourages further usage-based work on constructions, but also cautions that certain elements of grammar may be arbitrary, representing unmotivated relics of earlier usage. For further detail on one of the points in the book, there is Ben Ambridge and Adele Goldberg's 'The Island Status of Clausal Complements: Evidence in Favor of an Information Structure Explanation' (*CogLing* 19[2008] 357–89), where it is shown that the island status of clausal complements can be predicted by their discourse function: there exists a correlation between islandhood and backgroundedness.

Graeme Trousdale and Nikolas Gisborne have edited the volume *Constructional Approaches to English Grammar*. The volume is thematically arranged into three parts: 'The English Gerund' (part I), 'Constructions and Corpora' (part II) and 'Constructions and Lexicalism' (part III). Part III contains three papers in which Construction Grammar and Word Grammar are compared. Andrew Rosta's 'Antitransitivity and Constructionality' (pp. 187–217) discusses the basis of the notion 'construction' and challenges some key Construction Grammar views. Nikolas Gisborne's contribution 'Dependencies are Constructions: A Case Study in Predicative Complementation' (pp. 219–55) is concerned with the symbolic nature of Word Grammar dependency and argues that dependencies are constructions. Richard Hudson's 'Word Grammar and Construction Grammar' (pp. 257–302) compares the Construction Grammar treatment of the ditransitive construction with (his own) Word Grammar analysis. The papers in part I and part II are discussed separately elsewhere in this section.

The journal *Linguistics* has a special issue on two important distinctions in functional grammatical theory: that between ideational and interpersonal, and that between syntactic, semantic and pragmatic. The issue's guest editors, Christopher Butler and Miriam Taverniers, contribute 'Layering in Structural-Functional Grammars' (*Linguistics* 46[2008] 689–756), in which they provide a survey of the way these distinctions are operationalized in older and more recent work within three functional models that give due attention to formalization as well: systemic-functional (i.e. Hallidayan) grammar, functional (i.e. Dikkian) grammar and role-and-reference (i.e. Van Valinian) grammar. The second of these models is investigated in more detail in Matthew Anstey's 'Functional Discourse Grammar: Multifunctional Problems and Constructional Solutions' (*Linguistics* 46[2008] 831–59).

The author notes several problems in the model and suggests that they can be solved by adoption of features of the architecture of Construction Grammar.

William Croft and Keith Poole propose a method of 'Inferring Universals from Grammatical Variation: Multidimensional Scaling for Typological Analysis' (*TL* 34[2008] 1–37). When faced, for example, with several indefinite pronouns which between them cover the functional-conceptual contexts of 'irrealis non-specific' (1), 'question' (2), 'conditional' (3) and 'indirect negative' (4), linguists have responded by trying to discover which form associates with which meaning(s), so that implicational statements can be formulated. Thus, it has been found that any form having functions 1 and 4 also has function 2. The authors now propose that this procedure, as used in the semantic map model, should be replaced by a multidimensional scaling procedure. The advantages are that this procedure has a clear mathematical interpretation and also works when many functions in many languages are studied. They demonstrate in detail how this works for the areas of indefinite pronouns and tense-aspect. As is usual in *Theoretical Linguistics*, this paper is followed by several responses, in this case authored by Johan van der Auwera, Michael Cysouw, Östen Dahl, Asifa Majid and Joost Zwarts. Among the points they raise are that perfectly natural diachronic changes can lead to situations not envisaged in Croft and Poole's model; that the model can only deal with binary data, not with continuous frequency data; that the model cannot deal with default forms; that there are other suitable and mathematically grounded models that may provide different types of insight; and that Croft and Poole's use of two-dimensional visual displays of the data may suggest that conceptual space is Euclidean, which it perhaps is not. In 'Multidimensional Scaling and Other Techniques for Uncovering Universals' (*TL* 34[2008] 75–84), Croft and Poole address these criticisms; they welcome the use of additional procedures and note that the visual display is only part of their results.

There is more on universals in a special issue of this year's *Linguistic Review*. In an extensive introduction by the editor, Harry van der Hulst reflects 'On the Question of Linguistic Universals' (*LingRev* 25[2008] 1–34), surveying them from various theoretical angles and considering various possible explanations for them. In his contribution on 'Universals in Syntax' (*LingRev* [2008] 35–82) Frederick Newmeyer explores the relation between work on universals of the Greenbergian type and of the generative type. It might be thought that the latter should provide explanations for the former, but Newmeyer is sceptical, arguing that the divide between the two traditions is currently too wide, with typologists being satisfied with very surface-based statements and generativists claiming deep structural connections on the basis of extremely limited cross-linguistic data.

Though Fritz Newmeyer may not like all the goods on display, we are clearly in the generative shop now. Indeed, we see there Stephen R. Anderson addressing 'The Logical Structure of Linguistic Theory' (*Language* 84[2008] 795–814), arguing that it can be hard to distinguish between the effects of innate principles and other factors, such as historical accident, processing requirements, pragmatic regularities and the like. Moreover, there is also the possibility that some of these other factors at some point in prehistory have become incorporated into the genome shaping the language faculty.

The conclusion is obvious: determining what is and what is not in the language faculty is an even more challenging job than previously recognized. However, in 'The Differential Sensitivity of Acceptability Judgments to Processing Effects' (*LingI* 39[2008] 686–94), Jon Sprouse reports on sentence-processing experiments that suggest syntactic factors have a different effect on acceptability than processing and semantic ones, so there may be ways of meeting the challenge.

Some quick scouting around reveals that the generative shelves are well stocked. Editors Martin Everaert and Henk van Riemsdijk have deposited there the five hefty volumes of *The Blackwell Companion to Syntax*, with its seventy-seven substantial chapters on areas of syntax whose analysis has at some point played an important role in theoretical debate. Space forbids summary—and even simple listing—of all of the papers, but we can say that here is indeed syntax galore, going from 'The Accusative Plus Infinitive Construction in English' (Jeffrey Runner, vol. 1, pp. 1–15), 'Adjectival Passives' (Joseph Emonds, vol. 1, pp. 16–60), 'Adjectives: Order within DP and Attributive APs' (Daniel Valois, vol. 1, pp. 61–82), 'Adverb Classes and Adverb Placement' (Denis Delfitto, vol. 1, pp. 83–120), 'Affectedness' (Mona Anderson, vol. 1, pp. 121–41), 'Analytic Causatives' (Maria Teresa Guasti, vol. 1, pp. 142–72), 'A-not-A Questions' (Paul Hagstrom, vol. 1, pp. 173–213) to 'Unexpected Wide-Scope Phenomena' (E.G. Ruys, vol. 5, pp. 175–228), 'Verb Clusters, Verb Raising, and Restructuring' (Susi Wurmbrand, vol. 5, pp. 229–343), 'Verb Particle Constructions' (Martin Haiden, vol. 5, pp. 344–75) and '*Wh-* In Situ' (Josef Bayer, vol. 5, pp. 376–438). In each paper, the emphasis is on empirical generalizations and their (generative) theoretical explanations. We see great potential use for this resource, both in teaching (at an advanced level) and in research (for getting a quick fix on a topic or phenomenon and its analysis—the overall aim of the work ensures that many topics are included that have sparked great controversy). Usefully, the hundred-page-plus index to the entire work is printed in each volume, and references are given after each paper but also in a consolidated bibliography in the last volume. In a review of this work, Olga Fischer asks, 'Is There Life Beyond Generative Syntax?' (*BGDSL* 130[2008] 199–235). While acknowledging the value of the work, she points out that it may create the quite erroneous impression that there is no syntax beyond generative syntax. She goes on to argue in some detail, for such cases as the accusative plus infinitive, the ordering of adjectives and the presence or absence of agreement in Italian participles, that consideration of semantic, pragmatic and diachronic factors, as taken into account in other models of language, can sometimes shed more light on the facts than generative analyses—which, moreover, often take a rather narrow view of what the data are that need to be accounted for.

That there is much wrong with mainstream generative grammar is also argued by Paul M. Postal in the entertaining collection *Skeptical Linguistic Essays*. In fourteen chapters, he takes aim at what he considers two persistent and objectionable features of generative work: a frequent disregard for empirical adequacy, with many properties of many phenomena not being properly investigated, and linked to this a frequent disregard for scholarly standards, where the importance of empirical adequacy is downplayed or dismissed, counter-arguments are ignored and insights known to be incomplete (or wrong) are paraded as if they are major successes. The first part of the book contains essays in which Postal addresses questions of empirical fact and their analysis. In each case he advances empirical arguments for the incorrectness of some claim in the literature. Among the topics dealt with here are the subject of locative inversions (argued to be an invisible expletive, not the initial PP), raising to the complement position of a preposition (argued to exist), the correct analysis of complex DP shift and right node raising, a previously unrecognized subclass of DPs (including *something, anything, what, who, when,* etc.) which shows several special properties (such as inability to occur in pseudo-clefts: *What I need is something/anything/what*), the word *squat* in sentences like *He knew squat about it* (argued not to be negative but to feature the unexpressed numeral zero). While the above essays all focus on the issues under consideration, part II of the book directly criticizes ideas and practices that Postal labels 'junk linguistics'—linguistics that he thinks fails (sometimes blatantly) to observe scholarly standards of rational enquiry. Particular targets of his wrath are the rhetorical style found in some of the work of Chomsky and his followers and the idea that certain features of minimalist theory are conceptually necessary. In the final, brief, chapter Postal gives several lists with pieces of advice, some addressed to all linguists, some to referees, some to editors and publishers, some to authorities in departments of linguistics and some to students (who are simply advised to 'Beware' and 'Be skeptical', p. 338).

In reviewing this year's work on minimalist theory, we start with the journal *Language*, which has introduced a feature called 'Alternate (Re)views', where one and the same book is independently reviewed by two linguists of different persuasions. The first book receiving this treatment is Cedric Boeckx's 2006 *Linguistic Minimalism* (*YWES* 88[2009] 32–3). The verdict given in Frederick J. Newmeyer's review (*Language* 84[2008] 387–95) is: 'Nice try, but minimalism just isn't convincing.' In particular, Newmeyer is less than impressed by the results achieved to date in minimalist work on concrete phenomena and by minimalism's fundamental claim that the language faculty embodies the perfect (i.e. maximally economical) solution to linking sound with meaning. Like Postal above, he is also not convinced by claims that phenomena fall out just like that from the architecture of minimalist theory. Naoki Fukui's review (*Language* 84[2008] 395–400) sees greater promise in minimalism, though here too it is noted that the number of phenomena on which minimalism has succeeded in shedding light is as yet small. Moreover, Fukui points at the lack of significant mathematization in minimalism and linguistics in general as a worrying feature for a discipline that likes to compare itself to the exact sciences—a fair point, we think (though we wonder what effect thoroughgoing mathematization would have on the discipline's popularity if each formula in a publication indeed halves its potential readership). Also reviewed in *Language* (84[2008] 411–15) is Richard Kayne's 2005 *Movement and Silence* (*YWES* 88[2009] 32). Reviewer Andrew Carnie focuses on the way Kayne's linear correspondence axiom forces movement analyses of many phenomena, noting that '[t]he quantity and extent of the movement posited will surprise most syntacticians' (p. 412). Nevertheless,

Carnie commends the book for its detailed exploration of a wide range of facts and is also largely in agreement with its invocation of a range of zero categories.

Minimalist theory is further explored in Jordi Fortuny's *The Emergence of Order in Syntax*. After a wide-ranging tour of phenomena and analyses, the author comes to the conclusion that I and C are intimately related, with specific features being associated not with just one of these positions, but with both. He also suggests that the cartographic approach, which seeks to identify all functional positions and their relative order, is on the right track, but that the ordering need not be attributed to UG and can instead be made to follow from quite general principles, such as full interpretation. The final innovative proposal is that feature matching is maximized, i.e. matching operations are combined where possible and take place across the smallest possible structural space. Principles or mechanisms that are not needed include Kayne's linear correspondence axiom, the extended projection principle and the vacuous movement hypothesis.

In *Mind Design and Minimal Syntax*, a work addressed to both philosophers and linguists, Wolfram Hinzen addresses the relationship between language and the human mind. Taking issue with standard assumptions in the philosophy of the mind, which are based on externalism, metaphysical naturalism and functionalism, Hinzen proposes a view that is based on internalism and methodological naturalism, which he suggests represents a continuation of seventeenth- and eighteenth-century thinking. He argues that the design of the mind can be fruitfully compared with the design of language as envisaged in minimalist theory: in both cases, the relevant principles and processes should not be seen as deriving from functional adaptation to external conditions but as the inevitable outcome of the operation of internal structures. In language, this is argued to be true not only of formal syntactic patterning but also of meaning. Hinzen is aware that these claims may sound startling but believes they can be viewed as a natural extension of minimalist ideas. His message to philosophers is that it is worthwhile to pay more attention to the nature of language, and to linguists that it is necessary to keep sight of the philosophical underpinnings of their theories and practices.

Pieter Muysken takes a wide-ranging look at *Functional Categories*, understood as those elements that mark notions such as definiteness, possession, gender, case, number, person, tense, aspect, mood, modality, negation, focus, voice and so forth. The book has eighteen relatively short chapters, which investigate the behaviour and interpretation of functional categories in such diverse fields as language typology, lexis, morphology, phonology, semantics, pragmatics, generative theory, grammaticalization, linguistic reconstruction, speech production, language development, language disorders, attrition, sign languages, code-switching, borrowing, pidgins and foreigner talk. As this list suggests, a lot of ground is covered but this is because in each of these fields the lexical–functional distinction is an important one. For example, the chapter on reconstruction considers standard hypotheses about Proto-Indo-European, Proto-Uralic, Afro-Asiatic and Amerind, and interprets the findings from the perspective of the stability or otherwise through time of various types of functional categories, which may or may not be susceptible to replacement by borrowing, to phonological erosion and to grammaticalization. The chapter on language development reviews several studies intent on determining possible differences in the acquisition of functional and lexical categories, an important focus of much work in both FLA and SLA. The chapter on code-switching devotes attention to the structural conditions on switching points, which again have been argued to involve the functional–lexical distinction. Muysken's conclusion from all the material is that a differentiated perspective on functional categories is called for, where some are seen to be more integrated into the clausal structure than others and where there are also differences in the relations they have with the lexical categories of nouns, verbs and adverbs.

Arguments and Agreement, edited by Peter Ackema, Patrick Brandt, Maaike Schoorlemmer and Fred Weerman, is a collection of articles on the link between agreement and the possibility of having non-overt arguments. The starting point is the traditional recognition that rich agreement of the verb with the subject tends to go together with the option of not expressing the subject argument (i.e. having *pro*-drop), but the nine contributions modify, develop or replace this idea with various more precise and empirically adequate hypotheses. The approach in most of the papers is of the principles-and-parameters type, with some use of minimalist ideas. English features in many of the chapters as a non-*pro*-drop entity usefully contrasted with various 'dropping' languages. In addition, some of the papers deal with facts that can also be found in historical stages of English, inviting extension of the relevant analyses (in particular Olaf Koeman's 'Deriving the Difference between Full and Partial Pro-Drop', pp. 76–100) while others (Hans Bennis's 'Agreement, Pro, and Imperatives', pp. 101–23, and Cecilia Poletto's 'Asymmetrical Pro-Drop in Northern Italian Dialects', pp. 159–91) address the licensing of null subjects in imperatives, a puzzling feature for non-*pro*-drop languages in general.

Having looked at a host of textbooks, other introductory materials, general works and theory-specific items, it is now time to turn to the main elements of the clause, starting with nominals and subjects, from there on to auxiliaries and verbs, complements, adjuncts and non-finites, until we arrive at phenomena and processes that involve several clausal elements. To begin with, Avery Andrews gives a thorough overview of 'The Major Functions of the Noun Phrase' (in Shopen, ed., vol. 1, pp. 132–223), discussing their semantic roles, pragmatic functions (topic, focus, thetic element), coding and grammatical functions. In discussing the latter, Andrews also deals with subject ellipsis, switch reference, reflexivization and ergative systems. The internal elements of the NP are surveyed by Matthew Dryer in 'Noun Phrase Structure' (in Shopen, ed., vol. 2: *Complex Constructions*, pp. 151–205). The emphasis is on the cross-linguistic diversity in what elements occur and what form they take. The elements discussed include articles, demonstratives, numerals, adjectives, nouns modifying nouns, possessives of various types (pronominal, multiple, (in)alienable, non-referential), adpositional phrases and relative clauses. A separate section is devoted to NPs without a head noun, including headless relatives. Also concerned with inner NP structure is Jan Rijkhoff in 'Descriptive and Discourse-Referential Modifiers in a Layered

Model of the Noun Phrase' (*Linguistics* 46[2008] 789–829). Distinguishing several categories of descriptive elements, as found in NPs like *those three black sniffer dogs in the corner*, he contrasts them with discourse-related elements like the definite article and discusses how all of them can be represented formally in the structure of the NP within the framework of functional grammar. Julia Schlüter's 'Constraints on the Attributive Use of "Predicative-Only" Adjectives: A Reassessment' (in Trousdale and Gisborne, eds., pp. 145–79) focuses on a specific class of English adjectives ('*a*-adjectives' such as *adrift*, *awake*, *afraid*), whose occurrence in attributive position has recently become more frequent. Schlüter argues that this is connected to the general increase in grammatical complexity of attributive constructions.

More than 600 pages on the internal structure of the NP can be found in *Noun Phrase in the Generative Perspective* by Artemis Alexiadou, Liliane Haegeman and Melita Stavrou. Taking a cartographic approach, i.e. trying to determine exactly the position and order of all modifying elements, and using data from Germanic, Romance, Slavic, Semitic and Greek, the authors provide detailed structural analyses and semantic characterizations of a wide range of NP-based phenomena. There are chapters on the DP hypothesis, NPs without a determiner, functional projections inside DP, the status and position of adjectives, pseudo-partitives, the argument structure of nominals, possessors and genitives. In quite a number of sections, the authors first provide a brief presentation of the theoretical concepts or hypotheses that will be needed and then proceed to the data and analysis. Throughout, references are given to relevant theoretical proposals or generalizations, making the bibliography into a virtual checklist for the generative study of NP syntax.

You might not think that the predicate in a sentence like *He was smartest* contains an NP, but Ora Matushansky, in 'On the Attributive Nature of Superlatives' (*Syntax* 11[2008] 26–90) argues that there is universally a zero noun in such cases. One piece of evidence in English is the regular occurrence of the definite article (*He was the smartest*), and Matushansky provides several further ones from other languages. He attributes the need for a noun to the semantics of the superlative. The same author makes another surprising claim in 'On the Linguistic Complexity of Proper Names' (*Ling&P* 31[2008] 573–627), where he argues that proper names are underlyingly predicates, with an argument slot for a naming convention (i.e. a relation between individuals and proper names). Chris Collins, Simanique Mooday and Paul Postal have studied AAVE sentences like *I saw his ass* [= *him*] *yesterday*, analysing such NPs as 'An AAE Camouflage Construction' (*Language* 84 [2008] 29–68). After arguing that the NP is not a complex pronoun (thus, adjectives can intervene, *his stupid ass*, and the possessor need not be pronominal, *Pete('s) ass*), they show that it sometimes behaves as if the possessor is the head (e.g. it can bind an object: *His ass done messed himself up*) but sometimes not (e.g. it does not determine agreement: **your ass are dreaming*). To explain this, they suggest that the possessor moves into the NP from a higher position. For parallels to such movement, they consider another AAVE construction (*Mary need to sit down with her stupid ass*) and various cross-linguistic data.

Null and overt determiners are the focus of Isaiah Won Ho Yoo's article 'A Corpus Analysis of *(the) Last/Next* + Temporal Nouns' (*JEngL* 36[2008] 39–61), which presents a detailed account of when *last* and *next*, followed by singular temporal nouns (and not by plural temporal nouns or non-temporal nouns), combine with a null determiner or with the overt determiner *the*. Kristin Davidse, Lieselotte Brems and Liesbeth De Smedt, in their article 'Type Noun Uses in the English NP: A Case of Right to Left Layering' (*IJCL* 13[2008] 139–68), consider all the intra-NP uses of type nouns (*sort, kind* and *type*) from right to left (head, modifier, post-determiner, qualifier, quantifier), viewed in the light of subjectification. Anette Rosenbach's 'Animacy and Grammatical Variation: Findings from English Genitive Variation' (*Lingua* 118[2008] 151–71) shows that animacy plays a genuine role in English genitive variation, mirroring a broader typological pattern. Antoinette Renouf and Jayeeta Banerjee's article 'The Phenomenon of Lexical Repulsion in Text' (*LingInv* 31[2008] 213–25) investigates the forces of attraction (preference) and repulsion (dispreference or even non-occurrence) that are at work in collocations (e.g. *impeccable* + *manners*, but not *spotless* + *manners*).

The journal *Syntax* has a special issue on binding, the central question addressed being: does binding (broadly construed) take place in the narrow syntax or at the level of LF? In the recent literature, various arguments have been given for the latter answer, but the papers make clear that the question is not yet settled. Guest editor Jonny Butler's introduction (*Syntax* 11[2008] 251–4) sketches the main issues and summarizes the papers. It is followed by four articles: 'Why the Binding Theory Doesn't Apply at LF' by Glyn Hicks (*Syntax* 11[2008] 255–80), with arguments coming from a critical re-examination of the data for each of the traditional binding conditions; 'Binding, Phases, and Locality' by Vera Lee-Schoenfeld (*Syntax* 11[2008] 281–98), which uses data from German to argue that binding is phase-based; 'Anaphora by Phase' by Carlos Quicoli (*Syntax* 11[2008] 299–329), who on the basis of English reconstruction facts and Romance clitic data similarly argues for the crucial role of phases; and finally 'Coconstrual and Narrow Syntax' by Ken Safir (*Syntax* 11[2008] 330–55), who comes to the rather different conclusion that binding must take place not in the narrow syntax but at an interpretative level (presumably LF).

A special case of co-reference is analysed by Tania Strahan in '"They" in Australian English: Non-Gender-Specific or Specifically Non-Gendered?' (*AuJL* 28[2008] 17–29). She shows that, in both spoken utterances and in students' essays, *they* is sometimes used not only to refer to singular indefinites but also definites whose gender is known (as in *Did Helen$_i$ resign, or is that their$_i$ signature?*). She suggests that its function is to signal that the referent's gender is not relevant to the proposition being expressed. Another type of dependency between NPs is the focus of Ilan Hazout's 'On the Relation between Expletive *There* and its Associate: A Reply to Williams' (*LingI* 39 [2008] 117–28). The author objects to claims by Williams, most recently in 2006 (*YWES* 87[2006] 55), that the associate assigns a thematic role to *there*; instead, Hazout argues that the relation involves agreement.

There has been some attention to subjects of special kinds. The well-known idea that the subject of an unaccusative verb originates as an object is put to the test by Naama Friedmann, Gina Taranto, Lewis P. Shapiro and David Swinney in 'The Leaf Fell (the Leaf): The Online Processing of Unaccusatives' (*LingI* 39[2008] 355–77). The method they use is cross-modal lexical priming, where respondents hear a sentence and at the point of the putative trace or copy are presented with a visual stimulus word semantically related to the moved NP. A fast response then is a sign that the relevant NP has been reactivated at its trace site, confirming the initial movement hypothesis. The results of the experiment indeed show reactivation of surface subjects after unaccusative (but not unergative) verbs. With regard to subjects of imperative clauses, Raffaella Zanuttini, in 'Encoding the Addressee in the Syntax: Evidence from English Imperative Subjects' (*NL&LT* 26[2008] 185–218), proposes that 'the syntactic representation of imperatives contains a functional projection not present in other clause types' (p. 185) labelled JussiveP, which accounts for the peculiar properties of imperative subjects. Peter Culicover and Susanne Winkler, in 'English Focus Inversion' (*JL* 44[2008] 625–58), argue that the syntax of comparative inversion is characterized by 'suspension of the EPP', which means that the subject (which receives contrastive focus) is *in situ*, rather than in its canonical position Spec,IP.

'Functional Relations in the English Auxiliary System' have been inspected by Yehuda Falk (*Linguistics* 46[2008] 861–89), who proposes that not all auxiliaries should be treated in the same way: some are heads (taking V as a complement; *will/would*, *do* and *have* are of this type) and some are feature-bearing modifiers of V (all other auxiliaries are like this). Leiv Egil Breivik and Ana Martinez-Insua, in 'Grammaticalization, Subjectification and Non-Concord in English Existential Sentences' (*ES* 89[2008] 351–62), argue that the frequent occurrence of non-concord in existential *there*-constructions in contemporary spoken English can be seen as the result of subjectification in grammaticalization, by which it has become a fixed pragmatic formula. The modal *shall* comes under scrutiny in Alexander Bergs's '*Shall* and *Shan't* in Contemporary English—A Case of Functional Condensation' (in Trousdale and Gisborne, eds., pp. 113–43). Bergs presents a corpus study of the positive and negative forms of *shall*, which are shown to have decreased in number, having become restricted to particular contexts.

Alan Timberlake provides a useful and accessible introduction to the categories of 'Aspect, Tense, Mood' from a typological perspective (in Shopen, ed., vol. 3, pp. 280–333). The chapter starts by comparing how painting and language can express images of reality, using Breughel's *Hunters in the Snow* as an example, and finishes by demonstrating how aspect, tense and mood operate in the connected discourse of an Old Russian tale (though, puzzlingly, the text of the tale is not provided). In between, there is a general characterization of the main categories, precise semantic analysis of the many subcategories and presentation of cross-linguistic data. The standard concepts and distinctions are all dealt with (with mood being defined as 'modality crystallized as morphology', p. 326) and attention is also paid to sequence of tense phenomena and modality in conditionals. Bridget Copley's 'The Plan's the Thing: Deconstructing Futurate Meanings' (*LingI* 39[2008] 261–74) examines sentences like *The Red Sox play the Yankees tomorrow*. She argues that its planned-event interpretation derives from two more basic modal concepts, i.e. ability and desire/commitment (to bring about the relevant eventuality). The former is presupposed, while the latter is asserted.

Björn Rothstein has studied *The Perfect Time Span: On the Present Perfect in German, Swedish and English*. Taking an enriched Reichenbachian approach to the analysis of tense, the author argues that the perfect has one single meaning. To explain cross-linguistic variation in usage, it is assumed that the perfect introduces a time interval, the perfect time span, with a right-hand boundary whose location can vary: in English, it is the moment of speech, in Swedish it is the reference time of the auxiliary, while in German its default location is the event time (thus licensing definite past time adverbials like *yesterday*, which are not possible in English and Swedish). To account for the different readings of the perfect (extended-now, universal, experiential, etc.), Rothstein makes use of discourse representation theory. A discourse time point is posited that is established in one sentence and then used to calculate the temporal location of the eventuality in the next sentence through a temporal antecedent–anaphor relation. Further factors that enter into this calculation are situation type, the nature of adverbials and context.

Marie-Eve Ritz and Dulcie Engel continue their exploration of tense in '"Vivid Narrative Use" and the Meaning of the Present Perfect in Spoken Australian English' (*Linguistics* 46[2008] 131–60). Using data from Australian live radio, they show that the present perfect is there sometimes used in innovative ways: it occurs in narrative contexts, with definite time adverbials and in clauses describing temporal progression, none of which is among the standard uses of the perfect. The authors note the frequent co-occurrence of such perfects with narrative present tenses, leading them to interpret the phenomenon as one of a set of strategies used by speakers to create vividness. Hamida Demirdache and Myriam Uribe-Etxebarria, 'Scope and Anaphora with Time Arguments: The Case of "Perfect Modals"' (*Lingua* 118[2008] 1790–1815), present a unified account of the temporal readings of perfect modals, making use of the model of temporal interpretation in which tense and aspect are assigned isomorphic structural representations.

The aim of Carl Bache's *English Tense and Aspect in Halliday's Systemic Functional Grammar: A Critical Appraisal and an Alternative* is to offer an alternative approach to M.A.K. Halliday's description of tense and aspect in *An Introduction to Functional Grammar* (Halliday [1994], Halliday and Matthiessen [2004]: see *YWES* 86[2007] 38–9). Bache first points out some advantages of Halliday's model of tense, aspect and phase. The most attractive feature of the model according to Bache is the fact that it makes use of the notion of choice: it focuses on the native speaker's motivation for choosing a particular tense in a given situation. But Bache also sees problems with Halliday's model, such as the fact that it is not truly functionalist in nature. More specifically, Bache criticizes Halliday and Matthiessen's description of the tense category as a simple tripartite system generating a large number of tenses by means of recursion. He proposes to adapt the model in such a way that it is more sensitive to function, the role of context and the basic semiotics of each tense marker. He presents an alternative model of tense in English, which is inspired by the Cardiff Grammar approach and Peter Harder's [1996] work on functional semantics. In Bache's model, the core tense system consists of four ordered choices where each choice has scope over subsequent choices. An adequate description of the choice relations is made possible by viewing tense forms as realizations of a number of different semantic categories, including aspect, action and modality. Bache also shows that the core tense system is affected by higher-level communicative considerations, which is shown to offer support for the alternative model.

In another book-length study, Olga Borik investigates *Aspect and Reference Time*, developing her analysis for Russian but making frequent comparisons with the interpretation of aspect in English. After a brief introductory chapter, Borik considers but then rejects theories that posit a link or even complete identity between (a)telicity and (im)perfectivity. Her conclusion is that the two types of aspect need to be kept strictly apart. Like Rothstein above, she adopts a Reichenbachian system, whereby event time is included within a Reference Time interval, the temporal interpretation is determined by the relation between Speech Time and Event Time, and the relation between Speech Time and Reference Time determines aspectual differences of the (im)perfective type. A formalization of the relations is given, and various correlations are derived, such as that between imperfectivity and progressive meaning.

An analysis of aspect using functional projections is proposed by Jonathan MacDonald in 'Domain of Aspectual Interpretation' (*LingI* 39[2008] 128–47). Whereas earlier proposals had posited that telicity involved movement to an AspP above vP, MacDonald adduces data showing that certain types of NPs affect the telicity of a predicate when they are objects but not when they are subjects. His conclusion is that AspP is located in between VP and vP, where the subject cannot access it. Karen Zagona, in 'Perfective Aspect and "Contained Perfectivity"' (*Lingua* 118[2008] 1766–89), claims that mismatches between event telicity and temporal boundedness arise vP-externally in (Viewpoint) Aspect and concern the mapping from Event Time to Reference Time. Also writing on perfective and telic aspect is Jacqueline Guéron, 'On the Difference between Telicity and Perfectivity' (*Lingua* 118[2008] 1816–40), who argues that 'the difference between telicity and perfectivity falls out from the interaction of morphology and syntactic structure in temporal construal' (p. 1816).

Cristiano Broccias, in 'Imperfectivity and Transience: The Two Sides of the Progressive Aspect in Simultaneity *As*- and *While*-Clauses' (*JEngL* 36[2008] 155–78), shows that progressive aspect in *as*-clauses is used as an imperfectivization mechanism, whereas in *while*-clauses it marks that the described event is a temporary state (cf. main clauses). Hiromi Onozuka, in 'On the Resultative Reading of the Imperfective Aspect in English' (*AuJL* 28[2008] 1–16), argues against the idea that the English progressive can express resultative aspect, as has been suggested—somewhat implausibly, we agree— to be the case in sentences like *Your drink is sitting on the table*. In 'The Progressive Aspect in World Englishes: A Corpus-based Study' (*AuJL* 28 [2008] 225–49), Peter Collins examines progressive usage in nine varieties of English. His detailed analysis of data from the ICE corpus reveals, amongst many other things, that the progressive is clearly more frequent in spoken than written texts, that AusE and NZE have particularly high frequencies, and that these two varieties also have the highest proportions of innovative uses, such as futurate and interpretative use (as in *I am going for the ballet tonight* and *What the government is trying to do is...*). Ute Römer has been 'Looking at *Looking*: Functions and Contexts of Progressives in Spoken English and "School" English' (in Renouf and Kehoe, eds., pp. 231–42), aiming to establish whether spoken-type discourse in German textbooks of English successfully approximates actual English speech with respect to progressive forms of the verb *looking*. Investigation of rates of contraction of the auxiliary, complementation by *at* and *for* and the precise aspectual meaning of the verb shows that the textbooks either over-represent or under-represent specific uses, thus failing to offer learners 'real English'.

On modality in PDE, all we have seen this year is Ilse Depraetere and An Verhulst's 'Source of Modality: A Reassessment' (*ELL* 12[2008] 1–25), which shows, on the basis of a corpus study of *have to* and *must*, that the traditional distinction in meaning for these modals ('objective' vs. 'subjective' respectively) is not as outspoken as is normally assumed, and offers a more accurate description of the sources of necessity.

Lexical verbal meanings are investigated by Leonard Talmy in 'Lexical Typologies' (in Shopen, ed., vol. 3, pp. 66–168). He considers the question: what types of meanings are cross-linguistically expressed by verbs and their satellites (i.e. sister dependents of the verb, such as particles, prefixes and bare nouns, as in English *start over, misfire, test-drive*)? Among the meanings distinguished are Figure, Ground, Path, Motion and Co-event (e.g. manner or cause). The results show that there are definite and detailed typologies in the linking of form to meaning in this area. The findings also make it possible to compare the degrees of salience of particular meanings, depending on the nature of the forms by which they are expressed. Dilin Liu, 'Intransitive or Object Deleting? Classifying English Verbs Used without an Object' (*JEngL* 36[2008] 289–313), offers a new classification of English verbs used without an object (e.g. *deliver, read, know, eat, understand*), based on semantic, syntactic and pragmatic properties.

Having come now to the area of verbal complements, we first consider Matthew Dryer's 'Clause Types' (in Shopen, ed., vol. 1, pp. 224–75), which specifically deals with the classification of clauses according to the type of complementation found in them. Thus, it includes discussion of copular and locational/existential clauses as well as intransitive, transitive, ditransitive and other types. As Dryer's presentation makes clear, there is considerable variety in the marking and patterning of each of these in the world's languages. Coming at complements from a radically different direction, Michaela Mahlberg says 'But It Will Take Time...Points of View on a Lexical Grammar of English' (in Renouf and Kehoe, eds., pp. 377–90). Her study of the word *time* used as a direct object reveals the existence of several patterns (*to devote/dedicate/give time, to have time, to need time, to spend time* and *to take time*), each of which is found in several different lexico-grammatical contexts.

The dative alternation is the topic of Joan Bresnan and Jennifer Hay's 'Gradient Grammar: An Effect of Animacy on the Syntax of *Give* in New Zealand and American English' (*Lingua* 118[2008] 245–59). The authors show that the effect of animacy on the dative alternation with *give* varies between different dialects of English, which is suggested to be consistent with probabilistic models of grammar (according to which grammars are quantitative and learned from exposure to other speakers). Beth Levin, 'Dative Verbs: A Crosslinguistic Perspective' (*LingInv* 31[2008] 285–312), argues that the ditransitive predicate *give* and the ditransitive predicates *throw* and *send* do not behave in a uniform way: *give* only bears the meaning of 'caused possession', whereas *throw* and *send* convey the meaning of caused 'possession' and 'caused motion'. In 'Ditransitives, the *Given Before New* Principle, and Textual Retrievability: A Corpus-Based Study Using ICECUP' (in Renouf and Kehoe, eds., pp. 243–62), Gabriel Ozón examines the behaviour of ditransitive verbs in the ICE-GB corpus. It is found that the double object variant is over two times more frequent than the prepositional one; that this proportion is the same in speech and writing; and that the 'given before new' principle is operative in the double object variant but not the prepositional alternative (though this may be due to the way it was operationalized for this study).

David Basilico, 'Particle Verbs and Benefactive Double Objects in English: High and Low Attachments' (*NL&LT* 26[2008] 731–73), proposes a Distributed Morphology analysis in which the difference between the benefactive double object construction and the particle verb construction is the result of a difference in the timing of the merger of a functional element with the Root. Particle verbs with the particle *up* are investigated by Peter A. Machonis, 'Disambiguating Phrasal Verbs' (*LingInv* 31[2008] 200–12), in which he addresses the problem of semantic ambiguity found in these combinations.

Kristin Davidse and Kathleen Rymen, in 'Cognate and Locative Complements: Their Effect on (A)Telicity and their Semantic Relation to the Verb' (*LingInv* 31[2008] 256–72), examine whether M.A.K. Halliday's thesis that cognate complements (e.g. *dance a waltz*) and locative complements (e.g. *climb a mountain*) express the same semantic role is correct. Seizi Iwata argues that 'A Door that Swings Noiselessly Open May Creak Shut: Internal Motion and Concurrent Changes of State' (*Linguistics* 46[2008] 1049–1108). After investigating the syntax and semantics of the relevant sentences, the author proposes a constructional analysis whereby they are differentiated from other resultatives.

Included in the broad category of adverbs are Giuliana Diani's 'Emphasizers in Spoken and Written Academic Discourse: The Case of *Really*' (*IJCL* 13[2008] 296–321). The author shows that the use of *really* is more frequent in spoken than in written academic discourse, and observes an ambiguity in the functions of *really* relating to its syntactic role/scope. Another article on an intensifying adverb can be found in an *ELL* special issue on English intensifiers: Sali Tagliamonte's 'So Different and Pretty Cool! Recycling Intensifiers in Toronto, Canada' (*ELL* 12[2008] 361–94) investigates the role of a number of contextual and social factors in the development of intensifiers in Toronto English and finds evidence of ongoing delexicalization, specifically recycling and renewal of intensifiers. Liu Dilin, 'Linking Adverbials: An Across-Register Corpus Study and its Implications' (*IJCL* 13[2008] 491–518), presents findings about the frequency of linking adverbials in a number of registers and about the usage patterns of some specific linking adverbials. The linking adverb *indeed* is the topic of Paloma Núñez Pertejo's article 'The Multifunctionality of *Indeed* in Contemporary Spoken and Written English' (*ES* 89[2008] 716–36), which shows, on the basis of examples from ICE-GB, that *indeed* clearly functions as a discourse marker with a procedural meaning, the end stage of the path Clause-internal adverb > Sentence adverb > Discourse marker. John Taylor and Kam-Yiu Pang, in 'Seeing as Though' (*ELL* 12[2008] 103–39), present a study of the relatively new causal conjunction *seeing as though*, noting that it is highly subjective and speaker-oriented, and as such can be said to fill a gap in the paradigm of causal connectives.

It is not surprising to see a challenge to Peter Culicover and Ray Jackendoff [2005] (*YWES* 88[2009] 32), who had argued that VPs have a flat structure encompassing both arguments and adjuncts. Nicholas Sobin, in '*Do So* and VP' (*LingI* 39[2008] 147–60), critically examines Culicover and Jackendoff's account of *do so* and comes to the conclusion that the standard view is after all correct, i.e. VPs are not flat but layered. Two other VP-related phenomena are addressed in Jason Merchant's 'An Asymmetry in Voice Mismatches in VP-Ellipsis and Pseudogapping' (*LingI* 39[2008] 169–79), which homes in on the following grammaticality contrast: *The system can be used by anyone who wants to* [i.e. *use it*] (VP-ellipsis) versus **Roses were brought by some, and others did lilies* [i.e. *bring lilies*] (pseudo-gapping). Merchant suggests that the two processes are similar in involving deletion, but that what gets deleted is different: a projection higher than VoiceP in the case of pseudo-gapping but lower in the case of VP-ellipsis. Also looking at VP-ellipsis is Paul Elbourne's 'Ellipsis Sites as Definite Descriptions' (*LingI* 39[2008] 191–220). The author considers several problems for the standard view of ellipsis (e.g. the availability of sloppy readings where no binding can take place, as in *If John has trouble at school, I'll help him, but if Bill does, I won't*) and proposes a solution that treats silent VPs and NPs as definite descriptions. We also slip in here Rui P. Chaves's 'Linearization-Based Word-Part Ellipsis' (*Ling&P* 31[2008] 261–307), which proposes a uniform account of peripheral ellipsis of word-parts and peripheral ellipsis of phrases, rejecting sub-lexical and movement-based approaches.

Because it provides a wealth of ideas and analyses on a somewhat neglected area of grammar, we were happy to see *Syntax and Semantics of Spatial P*, edited by Anna Asbury, Jakub Dotlačil, Berit Gehrke and Rick Nouwen. It starts off with a substantial introduction in which Anna Asbury, Berit Gehrke, Henk van Riemsdijk and Joost Zwarts provide a survey of earlier work on the topic, focusing on gradient phenomena (though not employing the useful subsection/intersection distinction proposed by Aarts, discussed above), the lexical/functional distinction, the fine structure of PPs, locative and directional semantics, and the difference between satellite-framed and verb-framed languages (with the former allowing sentences like *the ball floated into the cave*, while the latter use constructions of the type *the ball went into the cave, floating*). The fourteen papers that follow address these issues in more detail. Some of them primarily deal with languages other than English, but we note here Marcus Kracht on 'The Fine Structure of Spatial Expressions' (pp. 35–62), who analyses spatial P-semantics using a Cartesian co-ordinate frame imposed on the relevant space; Peter Svenonius on 'Projections of P' (pp. 63–84), which takes a cartographic approach, arguing that P has several extended projections mirroring aspects of its semantic composition; Joost Zwarts on 'Priorities in the Production of Prepositions' (pp. 85–102), which closely examines the kinds of situations describable by the Ps *in*, *on*, *over* and *around*, interestingly casting the results in terms of OT faithfulness constraints; Bert Cappelle on 'The Grammar of Complex Particle Phrases in English' (pp. 103–45), who first addresses questions of general structure (arguing against the two—separate—ideas that particle and direct object form a constituent and that particles are intransitive prepositions) and then provides analyses for particle sequences and modifiers (as in *It fell several metres right back on down to the bottom*); Sander Lestrade on 'The Correspondence between Directionality and Transitivity' (pp. 149–74), arguing that the complement of a directional P is more proto-patient-like than that of a locative P; Tatiana Nikitina on 'Pragmatic Factors and Variation in the Expression of Spatial Goals: The Case of *Into* vs. *In*' (pp. 175–95), proposing on the basis of corpus data that the choice between *into* and directional *in* (the latter only possible when some other element in the clause already signals directional meaning) depends on conceptual profile, with prominence of the path leading to *into* and prominence of the resultant location triggering use of *in*; Ivano Caponigro and Lisa Pearl on 'Silent Prepositions: Evidence from Free Relatives' (pp. 365–85), who suggest that silent Ps, occasionally proposed for phrases like *that day*, *this way* and (*go*) *places* used as adjuncts, are also present in sentences like *I live* [P ø] *where you used to live* and *Lily cried* [P ø] *when Jack left*. With further articles contrasting English with Italian, German and Japanese, this is a valuable volume (though the editors have not been particularly careful in proofreading: spot-checks of just a few pages yielded errors on page 23, where examples (45a,b), meant to illustrate a crucial locative vs. directional difference, are the same; page 64, where *from* and *front* are confused in (2b), not very helpful in discussing questions about the (non-) overtness of these elements; and page 195, where a linguist well known for her meticulous work is sloppily referred to as both van der Leek and van der Leer in one and the same bibliographical entry).

   Two shorter items also consider prepositional elements. Evelien Keizer, 'English Prepositions in Functional Discourse Grammar' (*FuL* 15[2008] 216–56), offers a unified Functional Discourse Grammar analysis of English prepositions and prepositional phrases which differs radically from previous Functional Grammar treatments of English prepositions. In '*Construction After Construction* and its Theoretical Challenges' (*Language* 84[2008] 8–28) Ray Jackendoff looks at units like *day by day*, *dollar for dollar*, *face to face*, *picture after picture* and *argument upon argument*. After exploring their lexico-syntax and semantics (which exhibit a mixture of regularity and idiosyncrasy), he argues that they are best analysed using a Construction Grammar approach, whereby they are classed as semi-idiomatic constructions having quantificational force and involving reduplication of the noun.

   A typological survey of 'Relative Clauses' has been written by Avery Andrews (in Shopen, ed., vol. 2, pp. 206–36). It considers the way the relative clause relates to the matrix clause (distinguishing internal, external and free relatives), the way the relativized NP in the relative clause is treated (e.g. with special marking, pronominalization or omission, all of them instantiated in English), constraints on the choice of relativized NP (due, for example, to island constraints or the accessibility hierarchy) and further special properties of the relative clause (such as formal reduction and/or nominalization). Louise McNally has investigated 'DP-Internal *Only*, Amount Relatives, and Relatives out of Existentials' (*LingI* 39[2008] 161–9). She argues against the proposal that relatives such as *They're overwhelmed by (all) the visitors there are* resemble so-called amount relatives, such as *It would take days to drink the champagne they spilled* in its most natural reading. One argument for saying they are different hinges on the possibility of inserting *only*, which blocks an amount reading (*the only people there were were . . .*).

Non-restrictive relatives continue to puzzle and delight. Barbara Citko responds to recent claims that they involve a Kaynian co-ordination phrase with a null head (i.e. [&P DP [& ø] [DP [D ø] [CP rel cl]]]) by presenting 'An Argument against Assimilating Appositive Relatives to Coordinate Structures' (*LingI* 39[2008] 633–55). Using evidence from case marking, relative pronoun selection and extraction, she argues that the standard adjunction analysis of non-restrictives is to be preferred. Goran Kjellmer, '"Troublesome Relatives": On *Whose Her* and Others' (*ES* 89[2008] 482–94), presents a study of the use of *whose* + resumptive possessive pronoun based on internet data, showing that the construction is not infrequent and fulfils a number of functions, such as the marking of animacy. Thomas Hoffmann's article 'English Relative Clauses and Construction Grammar: A Topic which Preposition Placement Can Shed Light on?' (in Trousdale and Gisborne, eds., pp. 77–112) examines variation in the position of prepositions in various types of English relative clauses and explores how entrenchment can be supported in a corpus-based approach to constructions.

Many aspects of sentential complementation, viewed cross-linguistically, are dealt with in Michael Noonan's 'Complementation' (in Shopen, ed., vol. 2, pp. 52–150). It includes discussion of the form of complement clauses (e.g. indicative, subjunctive, infinitival, nominalized, participial), issues in their syntax (e.g. equi, raising, verb serialization, negative raising, sequence of tenses) and semantics (of both the complement-taking verb and the complement itself). Complementation involving reported speech is investigated in more detail by Mark de Vries in 'The Representation of Language within Language: A Syntactico-Pragmatic Typology of Direct Speech' (*SL* 62[2008] 39–77). Pragmatically, de Vries views quotation as a type of demonstration, following a well-established view. Syntactically, he proposes that quoting is a function turning a previous utterance into a nominal category which, in accordance with current X-bar thinking, can function as an entire NP or as a N head, much in the same way as a name. We note, though, that not all languages allow quotation in the same contexts as Dutch, from which all examples are drawn, so de Vries's claim of the general applicability of the model may need to be tempered. Cédric Fairon and John Singler report on a corpus study of quotation in 'I'm like, "Hey, It Works!": Using GlossaNet to Find Attestations of the Quotative (*BE*) *Like* in English-Language

Newspapers' (in Renouf and Kehoe, eds., pp. 325–36). It turns out that, in American newspapers from the year 2001, *be like* is used, but only inside quotations. It sometimes occurs with negation (but never in questions) and has a low proportion of subjects referring to a living person—perhaps because of fear of litigation for incorrect attribution of words. On the relation between sentential semantics and complement choice, there is Mark Jary's 'The Relevance of Complement Choice: A Corpus Study of "Believe"' (*Lingua* 118[2008] 1–18), which shows that the *to-*/*that*-complement alternation with *believe* is sensitive to whether the proposition of the embedded clause or the proposition of the entire sentence is in focus.

In a comprehensive investigation of *Non-Finite Complementation: A Usage-Based Study of Infinitive and -ing Clauses in English*, Thomas Egan first provides a semantic classification of matrix verbs taking non-finite complements, then reviews the voluminous earlier literature on this topic and draws on it to propose his own characterization of the meaning of the various non-finites. He suggests that the bare infinitive expresses a situation profiled as one whole and certain to occur; the *-ing* form views a situation as being extended and existing in some (mental or physical) domain; while the *to*-infinitive profiles a unitary situation that is being targeted from among various alternatives. The next three chapters put these ideas to the test by examining the complement choices made after various verbs allowing two or more non-finite options. Data come from the BNC; an appendix contains a useful list of all verbs investigated with information about their semantics, frequency in the various construction types, example sentences for each type and, where relevant, page references to the main text. The theoretical framework used is that of cognitive grammar, though the discussion nowhere becomes overly abstract. With its more than 400 pages, packed with information and solidly grounded in corpus data while also taking full account of previous work, this is a major contribution to the study of its topic.

A more structure-focused approach to non-finite complementation is taken by John Bowers in 'On Reducing Control to Movement' (*Syntax* 11[2008] 125–43). He agrees with the idea that control should be so reduced but, contra earlier work by Norbert Hornstein and others, does not believe the movement is triggered by θ-features. Instead, he proposes that ordinary c-selection features can do the job. A welcome result is that syntactic theory can be entirely derivational, with no need for a level of LF. Vikki Janke, in her article 'Control without a Subject' (*Lingua* 118[2008] 82–118), similarly offers an account of obligatory control without recourse to null subject PRO, claiming that it is the interpretation of the infinitival's subject (not its case) that is relevant to the control relation. A well-known but still puzzling alternation in non-finite complements, that between *He saw them leave* and *They were seen to leave*, is addressed by Norbert Hornstein, Ana Maria Martins and Jairo Nunes in 'Perception and Causative Structures in English and European Portuguese: Φ-Feature Agreement and the Distribution of Bare and Prepositional Infinitives' (*Syntax* 11[2008] 198–222). Using a minimalist approach, they derive the need to insert *to* in the passive version from the licensing requirements of the infinitive. In 'English C Moves Downward as well as Upward: An Extension of Bošković and Lasnik's (2003) Approach' (*LingI*

39[2008] 295–307), Kwang-sup Kim argues that there is only one head C in English, that it is an affix which attaches to V either in the matrix or embedded clause, and that the overt complementizers *that* and *for* are last-resort options only used when affixation of C is barred. The latter two claims are certainly surprising, but Kim points out that they make the English C-system comparable to the I-system, where affix hopping can be upward or downward and auxiliary *do* is a last-resort filler. The complex distribution of *that* and *for* is shown to follow from the analysis proposed.

Sandra Thompson, Robert Longacre and Shin Ja Hwang have written 'Adverbial Clauses' (in Shopen, ed., vol. 2, pp. 237–300). This typological survey has two parts: the first part deals with the characteristics of adverbial clauses defined semantically (such as time clauses, locative clauses, purpose and reason clauses, circumstantial clauses and conditionals), while the second part considers the discourse functions of adverbial clauses, with many of them contributing to cohesiveness of one kind or another between sentences or paragraphs. Exemplification in part II is mostly from English, so it is clear there is still plenty of scope for further work in the field of cross-linguistic cohesion marking. Part of the preparatory work is done in Robert Longacre's 'Sentences as Combinations of Clauses' (in Shopen, ed., vol. 2, pp. 372–420), which looks at the semantic notions that are cross-linguistically expressed through clause combination (e.g. contrast, comparison, alternation, causation, conditionality, paraphrase, illustration and defeated expectation) and the ways in which clause combination is implemented, some also familiar from English but others being rather different in nature.

Adverbial clauses that in some respects behave like complement clauses form the topic of Jean-Christophe Verstraete's 'The Status of Purpose, Reason, and Intended Endpoint in the Typology of Complex Sentences: Implications for Layered Models of Clause Structure' (*Linguistics* 46[2008] 757–88). He notes that the subordinate clause in sentences like *He set the alarm because there might be burglars in the area* resembles a reported clause in adopting another person's perspective (and, in many languages, taking formal marking associated with speech reporting). On the basis of these facts, he proposes a formal representation of such clauses involving layering. Undoubted adverbial clauses are analysed in 'Three Types of Conditionals and their Verb Forms in English and Portuguese', by Gilberto Gomes (*CogLing* 19[2008] 219–40). The author argues that a distinction should be made between three types of conditionals instead of the usual two: counter-factual conditionals (replacing the term 'subjunctive conditionals'), uncertain-fact conditionals and accepted-fact conditionals (replacing the term 'indicative conditionals'). Analysing ordering tendencies involving adverbial clauses is Holger Diessel's 'Iconicity of Sequence: A Corpus-Based Analysis of the Positioning of Temporal Adverbial Clauses in English' (*CogLing* 19[2008] 465–90). Diessel shows that there is a clear iconicity relation between meaning and clause order, with temporal clauses denoting a prior event preceding the main clause more often than temporal clauses of posteriority.

A wide range of ordering phenomena in many languages is discussed in Matthew Dryer's chapter on 'Word Order' (in Shopen, ed., vol. 1, pp. 61–131). After discussing methods of identifying the major clausal constituents as well as problems that can arise in establishing what the canonical word order of specific elements in a language is, Dryer's main focus is on the extent to which the order of the object and verb in a language correlates (bidirectionally or unidirectionally) with the order of other elements, Thus verb–adposition order, auxiliary–main verb order, complementizer–clause order, article–noun order and noun–relative clause order all correlate with object–verb order, but demonstrative–noun, and negative particle–verb do not. Ken Ramshøj Christensen investigates word-order differences between the Germanic languages in 'Neg-Shift, Licensing, and Repair Strategies' (*SL* 62[2008] 182–223). The focus is on sentences like *He has seen nothing*, where PDE shows the usual VO order but some of the Scandinavian languages, though otherwise firmly VO, allow or require the object to be preverbal (as does ME, we note). The analysis proposed is minimalist but incorporates optimality-type violable constraints.

William Foley offers 'A Typology of Information Packaging in the Clause' (in Shopen, ed., vol. 1, pp. 362–446). The author shows that, cross-linguistically, there are strong links between the marking of an element's information status and the overall grammatical system of the language as well as the element's position on the animacy hierarchy. The packaging functions of the passive antipassive are discussed, as are various linear displacements, such as topicalization and right/left dislocation. A good introduction to the comparative study of passives is given in Edward Keenan and Matthew Dryer's 'Passive in the World's Languages' (in Shopen, ed., vol. 1, pp. 325–61). The authors discuss the syntax and semantics of basic passives and various types of non-basic passives, make comparisons with several constructions resembling passives (such as middles and unspecified subject constructions) and point out that the passive plays a more central role in the grammar of some languages than others.

Andrea Calude's 'Clefting and Extraposition in English' (*ICAME* 32[2008] 7–34) shows that a word-order rearrangement test can disambiguate between clefts and extraposition, using evidence from a corpus of spoken NZE (*Wellington Corpus*). The same author examines 'Demonstrative Clefts and Double Cleft Constructions in Spontaneous Spoken English' (*SL* 62[2008] 78–118), using data from the same corpus. She reports that sentences such as *That's what he said* are the most frequent type of cleft (it has even spawned a double version, as in *This is where he went is Auckland*), and she presents a detailed analysis of their discourse function. One of her conclusions is that the construction is ideally geared to use in online spoken production, being low in informational content and cognitive load.

Susi Wurmbrand considers the word '*Nor*: Neither Disjunction nor Paradox' (*LingI* 39[2008] 511–22). She notes that the meaning of a sentence such as *Leo ate neither the rice nor the carrots* can be represented either as a disjunction ('the following does not hold: Leo ate the rice or the carrots') or as a conjunction ('[Leo didn't eat the rice] AND [Leo didn't eat the carrots]'). However, she goes on to argue that only the conjunctive representation is correct. Crucial evidence comes from the ambiguity of the first clause in *Everyone didn't talk to the king nor did they/anyone/John call the queen* and the lack of ambiguity in *Someone didn't talk to the king nor did they/anyone call the queen*. Timothy Osborne considers constraints on co-ordination in 'Major Constituents and Two Dependency Grammar Constraints on Sharing in Coordination' (*Linguistics* 46[2008] 1109–65). In an example like *An old [man] and [woman] arrived*, the words *old* and *arrived* are said to be 'shared'; Osborne's proposals relate to the question in what contexts such sharing is (im)possible. A typological perspective is taken in Martin Haspelmath's overview article on 'Coordination' (in Shopen, ed., vol. 3, pp. 1–51). The author discusses properties of co-ordinators, the different syntactic and semantic types of co-ordination (and the ways in which they can be identified), ellipsis in co-ordination and several problems in distinguishing co-ordination from subordination.

Benjamin Spector has discovered 'An Unnoticed Reading for WH-Questions: Elided Answers and Weak Islands' (*LingI* 39[2008] 677–86). It involves questions such as *Which books must Jack read?*, answered elliptically by *The French or the Russian novels*. Spector argues that the ambiguity of the answer is due to the fact that the question has two LF representations. When the WH element originates in a weak island (as in *Which books didn't Jack read?*), the ambiguity disappears. Ewa Dąbrowska's 'Questions with Long-Distance Dependencies: A Usage-Based Perspective' (*CogLing* 19[2008] 391–425) shows that prototypical instances of long-distance dependency questions (i.e. *WH do you think S-GAP*, S-GAP being a missing constituent in a subordinate clause) are judged to be most acceptable, suggesting they are conventional units with an unusual form. And finally, because we cannot think of another place for it, there is Jack Hoeksema and Donna Jo Napoli's 'Just for the Hell of It: A Comparison of Two Taboo-Term Constructions' (*JL* 44[2008] 347–78). The authors shows that the taboo-term *get the hell out* (labelled the 'G-construction') and the taboo-term *beat the hell up* (labelled the 'B-construction'), which share the surface string VERB + TABOO TERM + PP, differ syntactically and semantically and should be analysed in terms of constructions as building blocks.

(b) Early Syntax

First, there are several general works on language change to report on. John McWhorter's *Language Interrupted: Signs of Non-Native Acquisition in Standard Language Grammars* puts forward the argument that languages are not equally complex overall and that a marked lack of complexity is always a sign of non-native acquisition at some point in history. McWhorter is aware that these ideas go against standard thinking in linguistics and presents a detailed case for nevertheless accepting them. He first proposes a complexity metric which is based on the occurrence of cases of overspecification (where a communicatively redundant feature, such as gender, is obligatorily marked), structural elaboration (the number of basic elements and/or rules in phonology and syntax) and irregularity. Next, he addresses three possible objections to his enterprise (that it flies in the face of linguistic egalitarianism, that it ignores crucial data and that it does not address questions of formal structure or sociolinguistic implementation) and defuses them. The next five chapters show that English, Mandarin Chinese, Persian, colloquial Arabic and Malay are all characterized by reduced complexity compared with their closest sister languages. In each case, the loss of complexity is argued to be attributable to the occurrence of large-scale non-native acquisition of the language. In English, the relevant foreigners were the Scandinavians settlers during the Middle Ages. While the book as a whole has a strong persuasive effect, we feel that the large sweep of data, often presented without significant analysis, makes it difficult to evaluate its claims. On the other hand, we also recognize that more traditional historical work, while quite successful at explaining innovations, has never been very good at dealing with disappearance and loss—and those are exactly the processes that McWhorter addresses here.

Joan Bybee's *Frequency of Use and the Organization of Language* contains fifteen articles that she has (co-)written over a period of more than twenty-five years, all of them dealing with the effects that frequency has on language form and structure. Among the many topics dealt with are the role of frequency in determining morphological structure, in shaping patterns of lexical diffusion, in reinforcing constituency boundaries (and sometimes breaking them up), and in triggering grammaticalization. Data are drawn from historical developments, present-day corpora and also experimental studies. The overall conclusion is that frequency effects are everywhere, but that their precise nature depends on the specifics of the frequency profile (type vs. token, high vs. low, high vs. extremely high) and the nature of the processes investigated. Not surprisingly given all this, Bybee advocates a strongly usage-based view of language, where much of syntax and morphology is emergent and stable patterns of grammar often derive their motivation from patterns of (frequent) usage found in earlier historical stages.

Issues of frequency are also crucial in 'Priming and Unidirectional Language Change' (*TL* 34[2008] 85–113) by Gerhard Jäger and Anette Rosenbach. After reviewing several psycholinguistic studies showing that priming leads to reduced pronunciations and that it can be asymmetric (for example, words with spatial meaning prime ones with temporal meaning, but not vice versa), the authors put forward the idea that priming is behind such frequently observed historical changes as phonetic erosion and grammaticalization of space into time expressions. Three responses follow: Franklin Chang, in 'Implicit Learning as a Mechanism of Language Change' (*TL* 34[2008] 115–22), notes that priming effects are often very short (less than one second) and suggests a greater role for his model of implicit learning; Regine Eckardt, in 'Concept Priming in Language Change' (*TL* 34[2008] 123–33), shows that traditional semantic changes like metaphor, narrowing and generalization are not easily interpretable as being due to priming effects; and Elizabeth Traugott, in 'Testing the Hypothesis that Priming is a Motivation for Change' (*TL* 34[2008] 135–42), considers the question whether there are any clear effects of priming in ordinary speech (as opposed to experiments). Jäger and Rosenbach respond in 'Priming as a Testing Ground for Historical Linguists? A Reply to Chang, Eckardt, and Traugott' (*TL* 34[2008] 143–56).

A different explanation for unidirectionality is proposed by Jan Terje Faarlund in 'A Mentalist Interpretation of Grammaticalization Theory' (in Eythórsson, ed., pp. 221–44). After pointing out that many practitioners of grammaticalization theory fail to consider the role of the mind in language change, Faarlund proposes that grammaticalization often involves failure by language learners to assign a morpheme boundary. Since insertion of a boundary is less likely, it follows that grammaticalization is usually unidirectional. The latter idea is supported by John Ole Askedal, who in the same volume considers ' "Degrammaticalization" versus Typology' (pp. 45–77). He investigates eight changes that have been held to be convincing examples of degrammaticalization. Among them are the development of English possessive -s from case marker to clitic and infinitival to from prefix to more loosely connected element (as evidenced by the rise of split infinitives of several types from ME onwards). Aksedal is not convinced by any of these cases, which is not entirely surprising since he believes that, depending on the overall typology of a language, the change from word to clitic to affix does not always signal a more grammaticalized status of the element. In a wide-ranging contribution, 'Grammaticalization in a Speaker-Oriented Theory of Change' (pp. 11–44), Henning Andersen does not hide the fact that he thinks there is much wrong with a great deal of grammaticalization work. He finds some of it conceptually muddled and all of it neglectful of the precise ways in which change is initiated and spread among language users. In addition, he argues that there are many important types of change other than grammaticalization. Still in the same volume, Elly van Gelderen studies 'Linguistic Cycles and Economy Principles: The Role of Universal Grammar in Language Change' (pp. 245–64). Building on her earlier work in this area, she proposes that there are three general economy-motivated principles that guide language acquirers: it is preferable to merge an element late rather than early in the derivation; to analyse it as a head rather than a phrase; and to analyse it as a specifier rather than an adjunct. She illustrates their operation with examples of changes in negative marking, marking of completive aspect and the development of elements in the CP area. A reformulation of one of the principles is proposed by the same author in, 'Where Did Late Merge Go? Grammaticalization as Feature Economy' (*SL* 62[2008] 287–300). Here, van Gelderen addresses the problem that the principle of Late Merge is not really compatible with the most recent minimalist thinking. As a solution, she proposes that Late Merge should be reformulated as a feature economy condition. The reformulation is in accord with current minimalist principles and can still successfully explain historical developments such as grammaticalization of verbs as auxiliaries or prepositions as complementizers.

Montserrat Batllori, Maria-Lluïsa Hernanz, Carme Picallo and Francesc Roca have edited *Grammaticalization and Parametric Variation*. Most of the articles focus on change in Romance languages, but Cristina Guardiano and Giuseppe Longobardi contribute 'Parametric Comparison and Language Taxonomy' (pp. 149–74), which investigates the possibility of using parameter settings as a tool in estimating degrees of historical relatedness of languages. Fifteen languages (fourteen European ones and Arabic) are investigated with respect to their settings for thirty parameters operating in the field of nominal syntax. The results are encouraging, since the groupings that emerge from this syntactic comparison (Romance, Germanic, Slavic, Greek and Arabic) are also the ones traditionally recognized as forming historical language families, as established on the basis of lexical and phonological methods. It thus appears that settings for (certain) parameters tend to be historically stable.

Turning now to the early history of English, we welcome the book *From Proto-Indo-European to Proto-Germanic*, volume 1 of Don Ringe's planned *A Linguistic History of English*. This volume provides a detailed introduction to the major properties reconstructed for Proto-Indo-European, PIE (in phonology, inflectional and derivational morphology, and the lexicon), an account of the phonological and morphological changes it underwent to produce Proto-Germanic, PG, and a description of the overall properties of this language (in phonology, inflection, word-formation patterns, syntax, and lexicon). The author points out in his introduction that this volume addresses readers without a background in IE studies but with a general knowledge of linguistic concepts and analysis and of general principles of language change. He also notes that some knowledge of an ancient language (Sanskrit, Latin, Greek, OE) or even modern German or Russian would be helpful too. We think this actually understates the case: in view of the author's expectation that students will be able to cope with large amounts of detailed information about cognates, historical sequences of forms and the interaction of sound changes, we think a good working knowledge of at least one of the early Germanic languages and one classical language is essential. Any reader meeting these criteria here finds a book breaking with the long tradition of histories of English that deal with its PIE and PG roots only in the most general terms. That is excellent. Our only qualm about the book concerns the short shrift given to syntax: the subsections on this aspect of PIE and PG together take up less than one page. It is true that syntactic reconstruction is difficult but surely there are by now enough interesting proposals about PIE and PG syntax to further flesh out these parts of the book.

For OE, Paul Remley, Carole Biggam, Simon Keynes, Carole Hough, Rebecca Rushforth, Mark Blackburn, Martha Bayless, Felicity Clark and Fiona Edmonds contribute a 'Bibliography for 2007' (*ASE* 37[2008] 233–366) with section 2 b (pp. 248–57) containing items on the linguistics of OE, including several on syntax. An overview of historical changes in English syntax can be found in Olga Fischer's 'History of English Syntax' (in Momma and Matto, eds., pp. 57–68). An extensive table included in the chapter provides a convenient overview of the main changes English has undergone between OE and PDE. Dolores González-Álvarez and Javier Pérez-Guerra, in 'Grammere = Grammar? Syntaxe = Syntax? Early Modern English = Present-Day English?' (*ICAME* 32[2008] 47–68), explore various kinds of grammatical variation between EModE and PDE, using the English Constraint Grammar Parser.

Last year we missed Simon Horobin's *Chaucer's Language* [2007], but we hasten to repair the omission because this is a book that deserves to be widely known and used. It offers the reader an accessible yet linguistically well-informed introduction to all aspects of Chaucer's language. The traditional linguistic levels are dealt with (spelling, pronunciation, vocabulary and grammar) and in addition there are chapters on pragmatics and discourse (covering features such as forms of address, politeness, the use of discourse markers), Chaucer's style and the sociolinguistics of English in Chaucer's time. All of these are crucial to an appreciation of Chaucer's artistry, and although they have been written about at length before, we cannot easily think of a book pre-Horobin that deals with all of them and manages to present the material in a form comprehensible to literature students doing Chaucer while also containing enough to interest language students focusing on the period. If, after finishing Chaucer, students move on some 200 years, they may want to read David Crystal's *Think on My Words: Exploring Shakespeare's Language*. This work too is introductory and deals with orthography (including punctuation), pronunciation (covering both prosody and segmental phonology), vocabulary, grammar, and varieties of language. There is a separate chapter on the sources for Shakespeare's language, i.e. the printed editions and also the few examples of his handwriting. The tone throughout the book is light and there are plenty of anecdotes and interesting titbits of language-related information, yet a good amount of solid linguistic material is also covered. One recurrent theme is the possible discrepancy between a modern reader's expectations and Shakespeare's intentions; another one is the extent to which Shakespeare's language conforms to general usage in his time. All of this is copiously illustrated with analysis of Shakespearian passages.

Several items investigate the NP through time. Tine Breban, in 'Grammaticalization, Subjectification and Leftward Movement of English Adjectives of Difference in the Noun Phrase' (*FoLi* 42[2008] 259–306), observes that the association between leftward-movement and grammaticalization and subjectification can also be observed with grammaticalizing adjectives of difference (*different, distinct, divers(e), several, sundry* and *various*) at the level of the NP. Mikko Laitinen has investigated 'Sociolinguistic Patterns in Grammaticalization: *He, They*, and *Those* in Human Indefinite Reference' (*LVC* 20[2008] 155–85). Two changes took place: *he* yielded ground to *they* when referring anaphorically to an indefinite (*If anyone thinks he/they can do it*) and *he/they* yielded ground to *those* when functioning as the antecedent of a relative clause (*he/they/those that think(s) so*). Using the Corpus of Early English Correspondence, covering the period 1500–1800, Laitinen finds that the first change was slow, led by women and sensitive to some other sociolinguistic factors, while the second change was rapid and showed no signs of social conditioning. Judy Bernstein, in 'The Expression of Third Person in Older and Contemporary Varieties of English' (*ES* 89[2008] 571–86), argues that word-initial *th-* as found in grammatical forms like *the, this/that*, etc. was (and still is) a marker of third person rather than definiteness.

The monograph *English Adjective Comparison: A Historical Perspective* by Victorina González-Díaz offers an in-depth diachronic study of English adjective comparison. The study is set within a broadly functional perspective and is corpus-based, the data having been collected from an impressive range of corpora. The first issue González-Díaz discusses is that of the origin of the periphrastic construction with *more* and *most*, aiming to remedy the lack of a completely satisfactory account of this. Her data show that the adjectival periphrastic construction was already present in the ninth century, much earlier than the thirteenth century that has always been cited. It is further shown that the periphrastic construction is a native development and not a Latin borrowing. González-Díaz also looks at the rise of the periphrastic comparative marker *ma* 'more' and the disappearance of *bet* and *swiðor* and suggests that the success of *ma* was due to its more general semantics, allowing it to combine more harmoniously with participles as well as adjectives. The rise of the adjectival periphrastic construction as a whole is explained as a process of grammaticalization. With regard to the spread of the construction, González-Díaz suggests that this process may have been favoured by contact with French, as English speakers show an (initial) preference for using the construction with Romance loans, possibly to maintain the morphological integrity of the foreign adjectival base. Another issue addressed in detail by the author is whether there is any difference in use between the inflectional comparison with *-er* and the periphrastic one. Focusing on Early and Late ModE and PDE, González-Díaz examines syntactic and semantic-pragmatic factors; her data analysis suggests that the position of the comparative adjective is the factor that has the greatest influence on the choice of strategy across periods. A further case study on double periphrastic comparatives reveals that their historical development was not simply influenced by linguistic factors, but was also sensitive to social factors. With this clear and thorough study, González-Díaz's provides new insight into the origin and development of adjective comparison in English.

Ilse Wischer has studied '*Will* and *Shall* as Markers of Modality and/or Futurity in Middle English' (*FLH* 29[2008] 125–43), with a view to establishing how and why these two words grammaticalized as pure markers of future meaning. Close inspection of examples in the early ME part of the Helsinki Corpus suggests that both words acquired future meanings through reinterpretation of sentences with a modal meaning (with *will* expressing possibility or habit and *shall*—which was more frequent—necessity). The further history of these words is studied by Maurizio Gotti in 'Prediction with SHALL and WILL: A Diachronic Perspective' (in Renouf and Kehoe, eds., pp. 99–116), where Late ME, EModE and PDE corpus data are analysed. The findings are that in ME *will* had a range of modal meanings, including that of intention, naturally leading to a prediction sense; that it became more frequent than *shall* in EModE; and that it gradually shed its deontic meanings.

Meiko Matsumoto's study *From Simple Verbs to Periphrastic Expressions: The Historical Development of Composite Predicates, Phrasal Verbs, and Related Constructions in English* offers a descriptive exploration of the history of periphrastic verbal constructions. The study presents a varied range of data spanning the period from OE to PDE. Matsumoto makes use of a number of grammatical criteria, including passivization, relativization and presence of an article in order to investigate the relation between the elements of the periphrastic verbal construction. She also considers the functional character-istics of periphrastic verbal constructions, such as active/passive use and state/event distinction. The study includes a characterization of composite predicates in PDE, a description of the historical development of composite predicates with *do/make/give*, as well as the composite predicates (and phrasal verbs) with *have* and *take*. Matsumoto also discusses some other periphrastic verbal constructions: *used to*, periphrastic constructions meaning 'happen', and periphrastic constructions with *have* and *be*.

Ines Lareo and María-José Esteve Ramos, in '18th Century Scientific Writing: A Study of *Make* Complex Predicates in the *Coruña Corpus*' (*ICAME* 32[2008] 69–96), show that *make* complex predicates are used in eighteenth-century life science texts, although the scientists show an overall preference for verbs rather than complex predicates. More on the history of a specific example of a composite predicate can be found in Graeme Trousdale's 'Constructions in Grammaticalization and Lexicalization: Evidence from the History of a Composite Predicate Construction in English' (in Trousdale and Gisborne, eds., pp. 33–67). He argues that the historical development of *give*-gerund constructions is part of a larger grammaticalization process of composite predicate constructions. Christiano Broccias, 'Towards a History of English Resultative Constructions: The Case of Adjectival Resultative Constructions' (*ELL* 12[2008] 27–54), shows that the evolutionary path of English adjectival resultative constructions is characterized by an extension of the set of verbs that these constructions can occur with.

Marianne Hundt reports on '"*Curtains like these are selling right in the city of Chicago for $1.50*": The Mediopassive in American 20th-Century Advertising Language' (in Renouf and Kehoe, eds., pp. 163–83). She finds an increase in frequency, especially in the period 1920–50 (with an attendant decrease in passive usage). Contra earlier suggestions, Hundt found no evidence that the medio-passive played any special role in sentences with persuasive function.

Belén Méndez-Naya's introductory article, 'Special Issue on English Intensifiers' (*ELL* 12[2008] 213–19), provides some background to the topic and briefly looks ahead at the articles in this issue, which are mostly historical in outlook. First there is Victorina González-Díaz's 'Recent Developments in English Intensifiers: The Case of *Very Much*' (*ELL* 12[2008] 221–43), which shows, on the basis of a corpus study, that *very much* has been developing sentence-modifier functions since Late ModE, and can therefore be seen to be moving along the 'Internal Adverb > Sentence Adverb > Discourse Particle' path. Belén Méndez-Naya's own 'On the History of *Downright*' (*ELL* 12[2008] 267–87) shows that the origin and development of the low-frequency intensifier *downright* involves lexicalization as well as grammaticalization, that the development of its degree function concurs with the Invited Inferencing Theory of Semantic Change, and that the developments of the adjective and adverb *downright* intertwine. Matti Rissanen contributes 'From "Quickly" to "Fairly": On the History of *Rather*' (*ELL* 12[2008] 345–59), showing that the semantic development of the moderator *rather* involves a loss of the connotation of comparison and contrast, and that its syntactic development is from adjunct to subjunct to modifier.

OE prepositions have so far not attracted the attention they deserve, but this year sees an excellent paper by Ann Taylor on 'Contact Effects of Translation: Distinguishing Two Kinds of Influence in Old English' (*LVC* 20[2008] 341–65). She shows that the pronoun–preposition order that OE allows is less usual in texts translated from the Latin (which basically has head-initial

PPs)—interestingly, in biblical translations this affects not only PPs directly corresponding to a Latin PP but all PPs, while in non-biblical translations the effect is restricted to directly corresponding PPs. Taylor relates this finding to the different attitudes held by Anglo-Saxon translators to biblical and non-biblical texts.

There are two items on non-finite argument clauses. Dirk Noël, in 'The Nominative and Infinitive in Late Modern English: A Diachronic Constructionist Approach' (*JEngL* 36[2008] 314–40), demonstrates that the development of the different types of the nominative and infinitive construction does not involve grammaticalization, He also shows that a diachronic construction grammar approach can reveal other changes, such as the distribution of the construction across different genres. Hendrik de Smet's 'Functional Motivations in the Development of Nominal and Verbal Gerunds in Middle and Early Modern English' (*ELL* 12[2008] 55–102) suggests that the greater syntactic flexibility of verbal gerunds and the competition between verbal gerunds and nominal gerunds helped promote the use of verbal gerunds. Adverbial clauses introduced by *seeing* and *considering* are studied by Anneli Meurman-Solin and Päivi Pahta in 'Circumstantial Adverbials in Discourse: A Synchronic and a Diachronic Perspective' (in Renouf and Kehoe, eds., pp. 117–41). The authors analyse their use and functions in PDE and then turn to two EModE corpora to trace their origin and functioning in that period. It turns out that the clauses often have argumentative function, though there are several register-specific uses as well.

On OE word order, Susan Pintzuk has written 'The Syntax of Objects in Old English' (in Batllori et al. eds., pp. 251–66). Using quantitative evidence from the parsed corpus of OE, she argues that the increase in VO order seen in the period is not due to increased frequency of rightward movement but to an increase in the use of underlying VO order. Moreover, she shows that negative and quantified objects behave differently from other objects, due to a leftward movement process that these elements can undergo. In the same volume (pp. 267–83), Eric Haeberli investigates 'Clause Type Asymmetries in Old English and the Syntax of Verb Movement'. The asymmetries are those between main, subordinate and conjoined clauses, in which finite verbs appear to occupy different positions. Haeberli provides a full analysis of the facts, using exploded CP and IP structures and exploring the idea that the verb moves to Agr in main clauses but to T in subordinate and (some conjoined) clauses. Remus Gergel, 'Comparative Inversion: A Diachronic Study' (*JCGL* 11[2008] 191–211), argues that the derivation of comparative inversion involves a non-moved T and a low subject, contra the traditional account which assumes verb movement to C in comparative inversion structures.

A long-term view of word order and other changes in English is taken by Theresa Biberauer and Ian Roberts in 'Cascading Parameter Changes: Internally-Driven Change in Middle and Early Modern English' (in Eythórsson, ed., pp. 79–113). Among the phenomena they consider are the shift from OV to VO word order, V-Aux to Aux-V order, the loss of V2 order, the development of the modals and dummy *do*, and the rise of contracted negation. In each case, they formulate the change as one of parameter setting, with one change leading to the following one. Apart from specific details of the grammatical system at the time, what also appears to play a role in this 'cascading' is a general drive towards narrowing of formerly more widely occurring options—due to the Subset Principle, the authors suggest.

Junichi Toyota's *Diachronic Change in the English Passive* offers insight into the historical development of the passive voice in English. Toyota begins his investigation with an analysis of the *be*-passive and argues that the passive developed out of an adjectival perfect construction which had a stative meaning to begin with, developing a dynamic meaning in the ME period. When the perfect came to be associated with the auxiliary *have* only, the construction with *be* developed into the passive. Toyota also provides an analysis of the components of the *be*-passive, '*be* + past participle' and the development these components have undergone in the history of English. Toyota views the development of *be* in terms of gradience, i.e. assuming that there exists a continuum between auxiliary verb and lexical verb. The functions of the *be*-passive are also discussed, in particular the related functions of topicalization and impersonalization, including the historical changes in the functions of the passive. Toyota argues that the establishment of SVO word order coincided with some important changes in the passive, such as the development from stative to dynamic aspect and the topicality assignment to the passive subject. He also discusses the notion of 'voice continuum', which expresses the idea that the different grammatical voices do not exist independently. Other types of passives in English are also included in the study: the *get*-passive, passive diathesis, and the quasi-passive. Toyota argues that the *get*-construction is still developing, and that it shows passive behaviour when there is no subject control, causing the subject to be interpreted as an undergoer. Passive diathesis has the same orientation as the passive, but lacks the overt grammatical marking of the passive. Two cases of passive diathesis are discussed: potential and necessitative passive, both related to modality. It is shown that while necessitative modality follows the unidirectional pattern of change from deontic to epistemic, potentiality does not. Quasi-passives have the same function as the passive, but have a different orientation. Toyota discusses two cases of quasi-passives: inversion and the use of an indefinite pronoun. It is argued that politeness can be an indicator of position in the voice continuum.

After a couple of meagre years, there is a reasonable crop of work on negation again. Yoko Iyeiri, in 'Unsupported Negative *Ne* in Later Middle English' (*N&Q* 55[2008] 21–3), shows that *ne* unaccompanied by another negative word is found particularly with the auxiliary verbs *be*, *will* and *witen* in the prose parts of Chaucer's *Boece* and *The Canterbury Tales*. Iyeiri notes a striking contrast between main clauses and subordinate clauses: the majority of the unsupported *ne* cases are found in subordinate clauses. Phillip Wallage's 'Jespersen's Cycle in Middle English: Parametric Variation and Grammatical Competition' (*Lingua* 118[2008] 643–74) evaluates two syntactic models of Jespersen's Cycle, concluding that a morphosyntactic feature-based approach can best handle the proposed distinction between two types of *ne*. Uses such as *He was bigger nor* [i.e. 'than'] *me* are investigated in Stephen Laker's 'The English Negative Comparative Particle' (*TPS* 106[2008] 1–28). The history of the particle is examined (it first appears in ME), earlier explanations for its origin are reviewed, and the possibility is put forward that its use is due to borrowing from Celtic (not entirely unproblematic, since the comparative particle of early Welsh is not clearly negative).

Negative contraction is the topic of three papers that appeared in *Neuphilologische Mitteilungen*. Two of those are by the same author: Linda van Bergen's 'Negative Contraction and Old English Dialects: Evidence from Glosses and Prose. Part I' (*NM* 109[2008] 275–312) shows that uncontracted forms are more frequent in Anglian than in West Saxon, with the exception of some particular verb forms. Her second paper, 'Negative Contraction and Old English Dialects: Evidence from Glosses and Prose. Part II' (*NM* 109[2008] 391–435), confirms Samuel Levin's [1958] conclusion about negative contraction in OE: it is regular in West Saxon and much more variable in Anglian, However, van Bergen proposes several refinements to this conclusion. The third article is Michiko Ogura's 'Negative Contraction and Noncontraction in Old English' (*NM* 109[2008] 313–29), also showing that negative contraction was widely used in OE, especially in West Saxon.

Various changes of different types taking place in PDE are described in 'Recent Grammatical Change in Written English 1961–1992: Some Preliminary Findings of a Comparison of American with British English' by Geoffrey Leech and Nicholas Smith (in Renouf and Kehoe, eds., pp. 185–204). Comparison of the Brown, Frown, LOB and FLOB corpora reveals increased use of semi-modals, the present progressive, *that*-relatives, nouns, *s*-genitives and negative contraction, and a decline in the use of the core modals, passives, *wh*-relatives and *of*-genitives. The authors also discuss the adequacy of explanations for these developments in terms of Americanization and colloquialization. In the same volume, Christian Mair writes about 'Tracking Ongoing Grammatical Change and Recent Diversification in Present-Day Standard English: The Complementary Role of Small and Large Corpora' (pp. 355–76), arguing that even the closed and carefully balanced BNC is too small to provide sufficient data on ongoing changes such as the extension of the *get* passive. However, he also shows that use of the open and unbalanced Web has its own problems and that data drawn from it need careful interpretation. How addition of a date restriction option has made WebCorp suitable for the study of (short-term) diachronic change is described by Andrew Kehoe in 'Diachronic Linguistic Analysis on the Web with WebCorp' (in Renouf and Kehoe, eds., pp. 297–307); Kehoe discusses the ways the date facility can be used and the limitations users have to be aware of. This may also be the best place to note Barry Morley's 'WebCorp: A Tool for Online Linguistic Information Retrieval and Analysis' (in Renouf and Kehoe, eds., pp. 283–96), where several features are discussed that have been added to WebCorp to increase its usefulness for accessing the Web as a linguistic corpus.

6. Semantics

Quantifiers in Language and Logic, by Stanley Peters and Dag Westerståhl, is a must-read for any student or scholar working on any aspect of natural language quantification. Although the hardcover version of the volume appeared in 2006, it was unfortunately not available for review then. We therefore discuss it now with the publications for the year 2008, which saw the appearance of the paperback version. Although the title might suggest otherwise, Peters and Westerståhl's impressive handbook-style overview is a very accessible read even for the non-logician linguist: it combines careful presentation of relevant natural language data, precise definition of new concepts and the properties thereof, and rigorous proofs of the results. It provides impressively clear overviews of previous theoretical approaches to many burning issues in the field of natural language quantification, and a substantial number of new proposals to solve old or new puzzles. After an introduction presenting some basic data and theoretical concepts, part I, 'The Logical Conception of Quantifiers and Quantification', outlines the historical development of the concept of quantification from Aristotle through the Middle Ages and Frege to the twentieth century, when the concept of generalized quantifiers appeared. Part II, 'Quantifiers of Natural Language', introduces ways of analysing quantifier meanings with the help of model theory, providing an overview of the logical properties of types $\langle 1 \rangle$ and $\langle 1,1 \rangle$ quantifiers, with special attention devoted to monotonicity properties and polarity-sensitive items in natural languages, symmetry and restrictions on quantificational expressions in existential *there*-sentences, quantifiers involved in the interpretation of possessive expressions and exceptive constructions, the question of the logicality of natural language quantifiers, and the constructions that can only be formalized by irreducibly polyadic quantifiers such as those requiring quantification over pairs or triples, branching constructions, as well as reciprocals. Part III, 'Beginnings of a Theory of Expressiveness, Translation, and Formalization', presents an abstract account of concepts related to the expressivity of languages (synonymy, translation, definition), and applies the results regarding the expressivity of logical languages to the investigation of natural languages, whereas part IV, 'Logical Results on Expressibility with Linguistic Applications', presents logical tools and techniques for demonstrating non-expressibility and undefinability in logical languages.

Individual issues of natural language quantification are dealt with in various other publications. 'A Multi-Dimensional Treatment of Quantification in Extraordinary English' (*Ling&P* 31[2008] 101–27), by Paul Dekker, presents, discusses and defends a multi-dimensional architecture for the interpretation and use of quantifying expressions in natural language, which builds on the Montagovian paradigm but also takes pragmatic insights into account. Richard Breheny takes 'A New Look at the Semantics and Pragmatics of Numerically Quantified Noun Phrases' (*JSem* 25[2008] 93–139) and claims that the NPs in the title, which have traditionally been assigned an *at least* interpretation, should rather be assumed to unambiguously encode an *exactly* interpretation, the *at least* cases being due to independently motivated pragmatic inferences. 'The Question–Answer Requirement for Scope Assignment' by Andrea Gualmini, Sarah Hulsey, Valentine Hacquard and Danny Fox (*NLS* 16[2008] 205–37) looks at the question of why children interpret sentences containing negation and a quantifier such as *The detective didn't find some guys* with an inverse scope reading in a smaller number of cases than adults, and attribute the phenomenon to a requirement according to which interpreters take a sentence they evaluate as an answer to a question that is made salient by the discourse based on experimental evidence.

Rick Nouwen's 'Upper-Bounded No More: The Exhaustive Interpretation of Non-Strict Comparison' (*NLS* 16[2008] 271–95) argues that expressions of non-strict comparison, primarily as illustrated by constructions of the form [*no(t)* . . . *-er than*] in modified numerals, can give rise to scalar implicatures, as opposed to their positive counterparts, which is attributed to the exhaustification of non-strict comparatives with respect to a dense scale. 'A Universal Scale of Comparison', by Alan Clinton Bale (*Ling&P* 31[2008] 1–55), proposes a unified theory of direct and indirect comparison (illustrated in *Seymour is taller than he is wide* versus *Esme is more beautiful than Einstein is intelligent*) based on the use of the conceptual tool called 'Universal Scale', which contains degrees that are isomorphic to the rational numbers between 0 and 1, representing the position an individual occupies on a more primary scale such as beauty, intelligence, height, or width, thus making direct comparisons possible even when the primary scales for two individuals are different.

The papers in the collection *Reference: Interdisciplinary Perspectives*, edited by Jeanette K. Gundel and Nancy Hedberg, discuss various issues related to reference from the perspectives of linguistics, philosophy, psychology and computer science. Reference, according to the editors, 'comprises the ability to think of and represent objects . . . to indicate to others which of these objects we are talking about, and to determine what others are talking about when they use a (pro)nominal expression' (pp. 3–4). The most general question, 'What is reference?', is addressed by Kent Bach's contribution, 'On Referring and Not Referring' (pp. 13–58). He supports Peter F. Strawson's [1950] position, saying that referring is not what an expression does but what a speaker does; he emphasizes that the so-called referring expressions (indexicals, demonstratives, proper names and definite descriptions) can be used in non-referential ways, too, and that a given singular term means the same thing whether it is used referentially or not. Questions concerning the appropriate linguistic analysis of different forms of referring expression are addressed by, among others, Barbara Abbott's 'Issues in the Semantics and Pragmatics of Definite Descriptions in English' (pp. 61–72), which argues for taking uniqueness as the essence of definiteness, as opposed to familiarity or givenness. Several intriguing contributions in the volume address the questions of how reference is resolved and how speakers select forms of referring expression, based on corpus research and experimental studies.

Further important issues of NP semantics are investigated by David Nicolas, 'Mass Nouns and Plural Logic' (*Ling&P* 31[2008] 211–44), who makes a case for a non-singularist account treating mass nouns as non-singular terms, which may refer to several things at once, and by Paul Elbourne, who provides a unified semantics for the English demonstrative determiners *that* and *this* in 'Demonstratives as Individual Concepts' (*Ling&P* 31[2008] 409–66), claiming that the latter are both definite articles of a certain kind introducing existence and uniqueness presuppositions, and that DPs headed by demonstrative determiners are interpreted as individual concepts.

Ora Matushansky, 'On the Linguistic Complexity of Proper Names' (*Ling&P* 21[2008] 573–627), looks at the syntax and semantics of proper names in the naming construction, as in *Call me Al*, arguing for an approach that assumes that proper names have an argument slot for a naming convention. Friederike Moltmann, in 'Intensional Verbs and their Intentional Objects' (*NLS* 16[2008] 239–70), argues that whenever transitive intensional verbs have 'special quantifier' or 'special pronoun' complements such as *something, the same thing* or *what*, as in *John thinks something*, they should be taken to introduce entities that one would refer to with the corresponding nominalization.

'Donkey Anaphora Is In-Scope Binding', by Chris Barker and Chung-chieh Shan, appeared in the very first issue of the new peer-reviewed open-access online journal *Semantics and Pragmatics* (*S&Prag* 1[2008] 1–46), edited by David Beaver and Kai von Fintel. Barker and Shan argue, contradicting Garrett Evans [1977] and all the literature on the subject ever since, that the reason why donkey pronouns, that is, pronouns lying outside the antecedent of a conditional (*If a farmer owns a donkey, he beats it*) or the restrictor of a quantifier (*Every farmer who owns a donkey beats it*), co-vary with a quantificational element in the two domains above is because they are bound by them in the ordinary way, assuming that indefinites can take scope wider than their minimal clause, as known since Donka F. Farkas [1981]. Staying with donkeys, Adrian Brasoveanu, 'Donkey Pluralities: Plural Information States versus Non-Atomic Individuals' (*Ling&P* 31[2008] 129–209), proposes that two distinct and independent notions of plurality play a role in natural language anaphora and quantification, namely plural reference (the usual non-atomic individuals), and plural discourse reference, that is, a quantificational dependency between sets of objects established and elaborated upon in discourse, motivated by the existence of relative-clause donkey sentences with multiple instances of singular donkey anaphora that have mixed (weak and strong) readings. In 'Towards a Uniform Analysis of *Any*' (*NLS* 16[2008] 297–315), Robert van Rooij analyses Universal *any* and NPI *any* as 'counterfactual' donkey sentences in disguise, and attributes the difference in their meaning to the distinction between strong and weak readings of donkey sentences. This would also explain the universal and existential character of Universal- and NPI-*any*, respectively, and why they are licensed in positive vs. negative contexts. 'NPI *Any* and Connected Exceptive Phrases' (*NLS* 16[2008] 69–110), by John Gajewski, proposes a solution to two puzzles related to the interpretation of connected exceptive phrases (EP), as in *No one but Bill ate the herring*, namely, the compatibility of EPs modifying noun phrases headed by the NPI determiner *any* and the ability of a negative universal quantifier modified by an EP to license strong NPIs. Anna Szabolcsi, Lewis Bott and Brian McElree put the scalar approach to NPI licensing to the test, which assumes that NPIs are allowed in contexts where the introduction of the NPI leads to proposition strengthening, in 'The Effect of Negative Polarity Items on Inference Verification' (*JSem* 25[2008] 411–50). They find that NPIs do not facilitate inference verification from sets to subsets, which is predicted by the above approach in a straightforward way.

The papers in the collection *Existence: Semantics and Syntax*, edited by Ileana Comorovski and Klaus von Heusinger [2007], discuss three types of

phenomena, in the interpretation of which the notion of 'existence', claimed by
the editors to have a solid intuitive grounding, plays a central role, namely,
copular clauses, existential sentences and (in)definite noun phrases. Claudia
Maienborn, 'On Davidsonian and Kimian States' (pp. 107–30), addresses two
possible arguments against her earlier proposal (Maienborn [2005], reviewed in
YWES 86[2007] 75–6) saying that some statives, including all copular clauses,
do not denote Davidsonian eventualities but what she refers to as 'Kimian
states', that is, temporally bound property exemplifications: combinability
with manner adverbials and Terence Parsons's [2000] so-called time travel
argument. Ronnie Cann, 'Towards a Dynamic Account of *Be* in English'
(pp. 13–48), claims that elliptical, predicative and existential focus constructions involving *be* can be straightforwardly accounted for in the framework of
Dynamic Syntax if the copular verb is assumed to project a semantically
underspecified one-place predicate, and that the different possible interpretations of *there be* constructions depend on the interaction of pragmatic and
syntactic processes mediated by the properties of the expressions with which
the string is correlated. Ileana Comorovski, 'Constituent Questions and the
Copula of Specification' (pp. 49–77), looks at the specificational reading of
interrogative and declarative copular clauses (like *The guests are Jane and
Tom*) from a cross-linguistic point of view, and argues that this reading is
induced by the copula of specification, and that specificational subjects are
non-rigid designators that are contextually anchored, established with the help
of a referential expression contained in the NP. Francis Corblin, 'Existence,
Maximality, and the Semantics of Numeral Modifiers' (pp. 223–52), argues
that expressions like *at least n Ns*, *at most n Ns* and *exactly n Ns* express a
relation between two sets: a set of cardinality *n* and the maximal set of
individuals satisfying the conditions expressed by the sentence. Bart Geurts,
'Existential Import' (pp. 253–71), makes a case for extending Peter F.
Strawson's [1964] proposal—a sentence with a non-referring definite description is considered false or infelicitous depending on whether the definite
description is interpreted as topical—to quantifying expressions, thus
accounting for the difference in acceptability between the sentences: *The
Exhibition was visited yesterday by all Swiss matadors* vs. *All Swiss matadors
visited the Exhibition yesterday*. Klaus von Heusinger, 'Referentially Anchored
Indefinites' (pp. 273–92), argues that a specific indefinite introduces a
discourse item that has a (pragmatically salient) link to an already given
discourse item, which accounts for both the wide and narrow scope readings of
specific indefinites.

    We turn now to VP semantics. The contributions to the collection *Event
Structures in Linguistic Form and Interpretation*, edited by Johannes Dölling,
Tatjana Heyde-Zybatow and Martin Schäfer, take the existence of
Davidsonian arguments for granted, and explore how the assumption that
linguistic expressions encode conceptual information about event structure
contributes to providing better explanations to a wide range of problems.
These include the nature of the verbal information that plays a role in syntactic
derivation, exemplified by studies on various less-studied languages, or the
interpretation of adverbial modifiers, particularly depending on their syntactic
position, which was one of the main motivations for Donald Davidson [1967]

to introduce event variables into semantic representations. In 'Unifying *Illegally*' (pp. 81–102), Kyle Rawlins proposes one lexical representation for the clausal use of the adverb in the title, and type-shifting mechanisms to account for its manner uses and two pre-adjectival uses. Marcin Morzycki, 'Adverbial Modification of Adjectives: Evaluatives and a Little Beyond' (pp. 103–26), claims that evaluative adverbs like *remarkably* and *surprisingly* are to be interpreted as arguments of an unrealized degree morpheme, and have the same denotation as the corresponding adjectives. Kjell Johan Sæbø investigates 'The Structure of Criterion Predicates' (pp. 127–48), illustrated by *obey doctor's orders*, or *do me a favour,* as well as that of so-called causative predicates like *create a fiction* or *ruin my reputation,* claiming that they both involve a predication over sets of events, and that the interpretation of constructions where they are complemented with an instrumental *by* adjunct also involves a second, indeterminate predicate. Marcus Egg, 'Reference to Embedded Eventualities' (pp. 149–72), looks at modification of deverbal nouns (*beautiful dancer*) and restitutive readings of *again*-sentences, claiming that these modifiers apply only to a part of the semantic contribution of the modified expression.

Another set of papers in this volume is concerned with the role of event structure in the determination of situation aspect. Susan Rothstein, in her discussion of 'Two Puzzles for a Theory of Lexical Aspect: Semelfactives and Degree Achievements' (pp. 175–98), argues that the best criterion for setting the Vendlerian verb classes apart is whether or not the event in their denotation is inherently temporally extended, and whether or not it denotes an event of change. She argues furthermore that telicity (characterized by compatibility with modifiers of the form *in α time*) cross-cuts the above classification. This explains why semelfactives (e.g. *kick, knock, jump, flap (its wings)* and *skip*), which have natural beginnings and endpoints, are compatible with telic modifiers. The author also accounts for why degree achievements, illustrated by *cool, brighten, redden, widen and darken*, which are verbs of change, can also have atelic interpretations. John Beavers, in 'Scalar Complexity and the Structure of Events' (pp. 245–65), discusses the factors governing durativity in predicates that involve some 'change' in one participant, integrating it into previous work on telicity.

A further group of papers, still in the same volume, is concerned with the role of event structure in accounting for distributive, collective and cumulative readings. Angelika Kratzer, 'On the Plurality of Verbs' (pp. 269–300), argues that there are at least two pluralization mechanisms at work in English, one being Lexical Cumulativity ('all verb stems are born as plurals', p. 269), and the other being due to the inflectional feature [plural], which always originates within a DP. She illustrates that event-less accounts of plurality pose several conceptual problems that are avoided elegantly in some version of a Davidsonian event semantics. Alexis Dimitriadis looks at 'The Event Structure of Irreducibly Symmetric Reciprocals' (pp. 327–54), such as *meet* appearing in discontinuous constructions, where the logical subject of the reciprocal verb is split between the syntactic subject and a comitative *with*-phrase. Sheila Glasbey studies 'Existential Readings for Bare Plurals in Object Position' (pp. 355–85), arguing that these readings are made available by a localizing situation provided by either the event argument of the verb (which is argued to be missing for psychological verbs with experiencer subjects) or by an appropriate context. The relation between event structure and temporal location is investigated by Cornelia Endriss and Stefan Hinterwimmer, in 'Tense and Adverbial Quantification' (pp. 389–412). They compare adverbially quantified sentences containing indefinites modified by a relative clause with sentences containing corresponding quantificational NPs modified by relative clauses. Alice G.B. ter Meulen's 'Cohesion in Temporal Context: The Role of Aspectual Verbs' (pp. 435–46) analyses the relation between the objective content of English aspectual adverbs (*not yet, already, still* and *not anymore*), which are claimed by her to constitute a logical polarity square in the temporal domain of events, and the subjective information that can also be conveyed by them.

The last set of papers in the collection is concerned with event structure as reflected in natural language ontology. Regine Eckardt, 'The Lower Part of Event Ontology' (pp. 477–92), looks at an apparent conflict between two ways in which event ontology has been applied to natural language semantics. Research concerned with the distinction between telic and atelic predicates traditionally assumes that certain properties of events are inherited by all their parts, whereas recent accounts of the interpretation of negative polarity items assume that from a certain level onwards events are so small that they cannot possibly inherit any property that can be denoted by a natural language predicate. Christopher Piñón proposes a new analysis of 'Verbs of Creation' (pp. 493–521) that does equal justice to the three subclasses of this class, which are distinguished on the basis of the semantic character of their direct internal arguments: those denoting the creation of a physical object, those denoting the creation of an event ('performance verbs of creation'), and those denoting the creation of an abstract entity.

A large number of studies appeared again on tense, aspect and modality. The central claim of Henk J. Verkuyl's monograph *Binary Tense* is that the well-known tense system proposed by Hans Reichenbach in 1947, in which the English tenses are arranged in a 3×3 matrix constructed from two temporal tripartitions, should be replaced by a $2 \times 2 \times 2$ system that was proposed originally to describe the eight forms of the Dutch tense system in 1866 by the Dutch grammarian L.A. te Winkel. The three oppositions on which Te Winkel's system is based are the following: the opposition between two time points referred to as Present and Past, taken by Verkuyl as signalling whether the 'deictic point' i is situated in the present or the past; the opposition between two relations between temporal units referred to as Synchronous and Posterior, taken by the author to signal whether a 'reference point' j is located synchronously to i or later to i; and the opposition between whether the action expressed by a verb is thought of as going on (as an action in progress) or as having been done (as a completed action), taken to mark whether the 'eventuality point' k is located synchronously to j or earlier than j. After formalizing the interpretation of Te Winkel's oppositions, which can easily be connected to the contribution of particular auxiliaries in Dutch and English in a compositional manner, the author extends it, in order to capture the interpretation of different kinds of temporal adverbials, to the analysis of the tense structure of complex sentences, and shows how it can be applied to languages with poor as well as rich tense systems (Mandarin and Russian vs. French, Bulgarian and Georgian).

'The English Resultative Perfect and its Relationship to the Experiential Perfect and the Simple Past Tense' (*Ling&P* 31[2008] 323–51), by Anita Mittwoch, aims to sharpen the criteria for distinguishing between Resultative and Experiential readings of the perfect, but argues against the truth-conditional nature of the distinction. Marie-Eve A. Ritz and Dulcie M. Engel, '"Vivid Narrative Use" and the Meaning of the Present Perfect in Spoken Australian English' (*Linguistics* 46[2008] 131–60), report on uses of the present perfect (PP) in spoken Australian English that are considered unusual or unacceptable in other English varieties, and would normally be expressed by the narrative present. Atsuko Nishiyama and Jean-Pierre Koenig discuss the results of a corpus study of English and Japanese in 'The Discourse Functions of the Present Perfect' (in Benz and Kühnlein, eds., *Constraints in Discourse*, pp. 201–23) that aimed to find out why speakers or writers choose the present or non-past perfect forms in these languages to describe a past eventuality. They argue that the use of the perfect serves the aim of maximizing discourse coherence by introducing a state that allows the establishment of additional discourse relations between discourse segments.

The papers in the volume *Theoretical and Crosslinguistic Approaches to the Semantics of Aspect*, edited by Susan Rothstein, address the questions of whether the Vendler characterization is a characterization of verbs or of VPs, what the correct characterization of telic predicates is, what grammatical operators there are and what their interpretation is. The book consists of three parts, with contributions discussing general issues in the semantics of aspect, issues in Slavic aspect and in the aspectual properties of non-Indo-European languages. Malka Rappaport Hovav, 'Lexicalized Meaning and the Internal Temporal Structure of Events' (pp. 13–42), claims that the Vendler classification is not relevant at the verb level but possibly more relevant at the level of VPs, and proposes a new feature for classifying verbs that explains their aspectual potential, i.e. whether they lexically specify a scale or not. Susan Rothstein, 'Telicity, Atomicity and the Vendler Classification of Verbs' (pp. 43–78), proposes that telicity/atelicity is a property of VPs, and that, assuming that all VPs have their denotation in the count domain, telic and atelic VPs differ in that only the former includes an explicit measure of what counts as one event in the set. The significance of Vendler classes on the verb level is that they contribute in different ways to the telicity of the VP. Joost Zwarts, 'Aspects of a Typology of Direction' (pp. 79–106), offers a two-dimensional typology of directional prepositions and shows that many analogies between directional prepositions and aspectual verbal classes can be found if the semantics of verbs is viewed in spatial terms, as places and paths in conceptual spaces. Fred Landman, in '1066: On the Differences between the Tense-Perspective-Aspect Systems of English and Dutch' (pp. 107–66), puts forth an account of the semantics of grammatical aspectual operators in English and Dutch. Anita Mittwoch, 'Tenses for the Living and the Dead: Lifetime Inferences Reconsidered' (pp. 167–87), argues that lifetime inferences from one-place, individual-level predicates in the present and the past tenses are presuppositional, and that lifetime inferences involving two-place predicates where the referent of one of the arguments is alive and the other is dead depend on whether the predicate denotes a relation that requires some input from the participants or not.

The contributions to *Modality–Aspect Interfaces: Implications and Typological Solutions*, edited by Werner Abraham and Elisabeth Leiss, present synchronic and diachronic studies on how the expression of perfective and imperfective aspect vs. root (or deontic) and epistemic modality interact in a wide range of languages. The individual studies confirm, to a great extent, the generalization formulated in the editors' introduction, that '[m]odal verbs are aspect sensitive as regards their infinitival complement—embedded infinitival perfectivity implies root modal readings, whereas embedded infinitival imperfectivity (and sentence negation) triggers epistemic readings' (p. xxi), and that 'paradigmatically manifested modality and morphologically manifest aspect systems are complementarily represented among languages' (p. xxii).

Still on the topic of modality, in a special issue of the *Journal of Semantics* on modality and evidentiality (edited by Takao Gunji, Stefan Kaufmann and Yukinori Takubo), Tim Fernando's 'Branching from Inertia Worlds' (*JSem* 25[2008] 321–44) proposes that the concept of inertia worlds as used to describe the semantics of modal expressions referring to alternative courses of events, such as the progressive and temporal *before*, should be replaced by an account in which simple event descriptions, called *fluents*, form the basic building blocks of a formal language for describing complex processes and their interactions. In this account, inertia is taken to be the tendency of some fluents to continue indefinitely until they are acted upon by a *force*. In the same special issue, James Isaacs and Kyle Rawlins provide, in 'Conditional Questions' (*JSem* 25[2008] 269–319), an analysis of conditional sentences with interrogative consequents, as in *If Alfonso comes to the party, will Joanna leave*, combining a dynamic semantics for conditionals with a partition semantics for questions. Mikhail Kissine, 'Why *Will* is not a Modal' (*NLS* 16[2008] 129–55), argues against the common assumption that the auxiliary verb *will* has a modal component within its semantics or is ambiguous between modal and temporal meanings, and claims that the only semantic contribution it makes is a forward expansion of the evaluation time.

A considerable number of studies discuss the semantic (and pragmatic) effects of information structuring in natural languages. The most significant among these from the point of view of originality is *Sense and Sensitivity: How Focus Determines Meaning*, by Daniel I. Beaver and Brady Z. Clark, an authoritative work on the semantic/pragmatic effects on focus in general and on the interpretation of expressions that have traditionally been assumed to be particularly affected by the position of focus in particular; it is bound to become an important reference point for future research in the field. The central claim of the work is that, as opposed to general opinion prevalent in the literature, the class of such focus-sensitive expressions is not homogeneous: there is a class of expressions, exemplified by exclusives (*only*), additives (*too*) and scalar additives (*even*), which lexically encode a conventional (albeit pragmatic) association with focus, whereas in other cases association with focus is a non-conventional epiphenomenon. 'Quasi association' with focus is characteristic of a broad range of expressions, including propositional operators (like negation and *either...or*) where the interaction between focus and the operator gives rise only to cancellable implicatures, whereas 'free association' affects a class of operators that perform quantification over or comparison within an implicit domain (such as quantificational adverbs, modal operators and superlatives), in the case of which the placement of focus can correlate with relatively robust truth-conditional differences. Foci associated with the three classes of focus-sensitive expressions outlined above are shown to display systematic phonological, syntactic, and semantic differences. The authors propose a new interpretation for exclusives that captures their focus sensitivity and the complex inference patterns associated with them, claiming that they comment 'on the Current Question, stating that some partial answer is all there is to say' (p. 282). These novel claims are evaluated against the vast number of theoretical proposals made on focus in the last thirty years, such as Alternative Semantics, Structured Meanings, event-based theories of focus, as well as purely pragmatic approaches.

Michaela Ippolito, 'On the Meaning of *Only*' (*JSem* 25[2008] 45–91), proposes a different account on the English exclusive particle, claiming that in a sentence of the form *only A is B*, it triggers the conditional presupposition that *if something is B, A is B*. In a positive-only sentence, the prejacent (the *only*-less sentence) is a conversational implicature and is therefore cancellable, but it is entailed in a context that satisfies the above presupposition and to which a negative-*only* sentence is added.

Topic and Focus: Cross-Linguistic Perspectives on Meaning and Intonation, edited by Chungmin Lee, Matthew Gordon and Daniel Büring, is a collection of papers presenting the results of phonetic research on the expression of topic and focus, discussing the semantics and pragmatics of topic and focus, as well as being concerned with the interface between intonation and meaning in a wide range of languages. Among the papers discussing English, Nancy Hedberg and Juan M. Sosa, 'The Prosody of Topic and Focus in Spontaneous English Dialogue' (pp. 101–20), present convincing evidence against the claim that information structure categories like topic and focus are correlated with specific types of contours, whereas Carlos Gussenhoven, 'Types of Focus in English' (pp. 83–100), argues that the wide variety of focus types that can be distinguished, based on how the information in the speaker's expression is related to the hearer's information about the world, do have identifiable prosodic correlates. Manfred Krifka, 'The Semantics of Questions and the Focusation of Answers' (pp. 139–50), claims that the Alternative Semantics approach to the meaning of questions and to the focus of corresponding answers (cf. Mats Rooth [1992]) does not predict the correct patterns of answer focus, neither does the theory of Roger Schwarzschild [1999], whereas the Structured Meaning Theory does not face these problems. Mark Steedman, 'Information-Structural Semantics for English Intonation' (pp. 245–64), develops a new semantics for information structure that is fully integrated into the author's Combinatory Categorial Grammar (Steedman [2000]), which includes intonation structure in the surface derivational structure. He associates Montague-style semantic representations with the resulting surface structures, where the different types of pitch accents and boundaries are assumed to correspond to three primitive meaning components: theme/rheme status, contentiousness, and speaker/hearer commitment, claiming that more complex discourse meanings can be derived from these by means of conversational implicatures.

The domain of information structure research is laden with terminological differences between the various subdisciplines of linguistics. A special issue of *Acta Linguistica Hungarica*, edited by Caroline Féry, Gisbert Fanselow and Manfred Krifka, has undertaken the respectable task of reviewing and clarifying the major terminological distinctions for the benefit of future cooperation between phonology, syntax, semantics and pragmatics. Manfred Krifka's important contribution, 'Basic Notions of Information Structure' (*ALASH* 55[2008] 243–76), provides a transparent system of interconnected definitions for the basic information-structural notions of focus, givenness, and topic. According to Krifka, 'focus indicates the presence of alternatives that are relevant for the interpretation of linguistic expressions' (p. 247), '[a] feature X of an expression α is a Givenness feature iff X indicates whether the denotation of α is present in the CG or not, and/or indicates that degree to which it is present in the immediate CG' (p. 262), whereas '[t]he topic constituent identifies the entity or set of entities under which the information expressed in the comment constituent should be stored in the CG content' (p. 265). The special issue features contributions discussing relevant information-structural distinctions from a formal semantic perspective by Mats Rooth, 'Notions of Focus Anaphoricity' (*ALASH* 55[2008] 277–85), Cornelia Endriss and Stefan Hinterwimmer, 'Direct and Indirect Topics'(*ALASH* 55[2008] 297–307), Satoshi Tomioka, 'Information Structure as Information-Based Partition' (*ALASH* 55[2008] 309–17), and Dorit Abusch, 'Focus Presuppositions' (*ALASH* 55[2008] 319–30). From a discourse semantic perspective there is a contribution by Malte Zimmermann, 'Contrastive Focus and Emphasis' (*ALASH* 55[2008] 347–60). The perspective of syntax is represented by Gisbert Fanselow, 'In Need of Mediation: The Relation Between Syntax and Information Structure' (*ALASH* 55[2008] 397–413), that of phonology by Elisabeth O. Selkirk, 'Contrastive Focus, Givenness and the Unmarked Statues of "Discourse-New"' (*ALASH* 55[2008] 331–46), Caroline Féry, 'Information Structural Notions and the Fallacy of Invariant Correlates' (*ALASH* 55[2008] 361–79) and Carlos Gussenhoven, 'Notions and Subnotions of Information Structure' (*ALASH* 55[2008] 381–95).

'Functional Similarities between Bimanual Coordination and Topic/ Comment Structure' (in Eckardt, Jäger and Veenstra, eds., *Variation, Selection, Development: Probing the Evolutionary Model of Language Change*, pp. 307–36), by Manfred Krifka, presents and discusses the consequences of the intriguing observation that there are striking similarities between the asymmetric contributions of the non-dominant versus the dominant hand in bimanual actions and the structuring of utterances into topic and comment, and suggests that 'bimanual coordination might have been a preadaptation in the development of information structure in human communication' (p. 307), thus outlining new directions for the interdisciplinary investigation of the human language capacity.

The monograph *Accentuation and Interpretation*, by Hans-Christian Schmitz, presents a new approach to a key problem that semantic theories of focus are also concerned with: how does the interpretation of the sentence depend on its accentuation in languages where focusing is expressed with the help of prosody? Whereas semantic theories of focus assume that the relation between stress pattern and interpretation is grammatical, Schmitz argues that the accentuation and/or the interpretation of the sentence depends on the context of the utterance. The author hypothesizes that a recipient will always be able to grasp the entire meaning of an uttered sentence if he recognizes the words that are critical to correct interpretation; this forms the basis of his theory of optimal accentuation. The main ingredients of the theory are: (1) a formal model of co-operative information exchange based on a classical update system (cf. Frank Veltman [1996]) for the modification of the common ground for formal languages; (2) criteria of adequacy for uttering complete sentences and interpreting them, defined for a formal language and then for a fragment of English; and (3) operations for the reconstruction of incompletely recognized messages. The resulting model of active interpretation specifies the interpretation of incomplete sentences in a given context, and also which words in a sentence must be recognized in a given context in order for the sentence to be interpreted correctly. He compares the theory of optimal accentuation to semantic theories of focus, Alternative Semantics (cf. Mats Rooth [1992]) and the Structured Meaning Approach to Focus (Manfred Krifka [1992]), and shows that the predictions of the latter do not correspond with the experimental evidence for at least two phenomena: the non-accentuation of second-occurrence foci and the interpretational properties of sentences with focused constituents consisting of more than one word.

We turn now to interface studies. The range of publications exploring the syntax–semantics interface includes *Differential Subject Marking*, a collection of papers edited by Helen de Hoop and Peter de Swart, which aims to integrate formal approaches and typological studies of the phenomenon called Differential Subject Marking (DSM). DSM, attested in many languages, refers to a range of phenomena, all having to do with the fact that certain 'subjects have a different Case, agree differently, or occur in a different position than others' (p. 17). Paul Elbourne, 'Ellipsis Sites as Definite Descriptions' (*LingI* 39[2008] 191–220), investigates three notoriously problematic cases of ellipsis: the existence of sloppy readings when the relevant pronouns cannot possibly be bound; cases where the antecedent of ellipsis does itself contain an ellipsis site; and cases where an ellipsis site draws upon material from two or more separate antecedents. The author proposes to handle these data in a uniform way by making silent VPs and NPs into higher-order definite descriptions that can be bound into. Benjamin Schnieder's '"By": A Refutation of the Anscombe Thesis' (*Ling&P* 31[2008] 649–69) proposes a new argument against the Anscombe Thesis (if x φ-s by ψ-ing, then x's φ -ing $= x$'s ψ -ing) that rests on a cleverly chosen counterexample.

A special issue of *Synthèse*, edited by Isidora Stojanovic, is devoted to how the domains of semantics and pragmatics should be delineated. 'Linguistic Communication and the Semantics/Pragmatics Distinction', by Robyn

Carston (*Synthèse* 165[2008] 321–45), argues that the dividing line between semantics and pragmatics should be drawn between (context-invariant) encoded linguistic meaning and speaker meaning. Brendan S. Gillon, 'On the Semantics/Pragmatics Distinction' (*Synthèse* 165[2008] 373–84), looks at the question of whether the semantics/pragmatics distinction is important from the point of view of context-sensitive expressions such as relational words with implicit arguments and phenomena involving so-called quantifier-domain restriction. In 'The Semantics/Pragmatics Interface from an Experimental Perspective: The Case of Scalar Implicature' (*Synthèse* 165[2008] 385–401), Napoleon Katsos reviews various accounts giving different answers to the question of whether scalar implicatures fall within the domain of semantics or pragmatics, and proposes a new, empirically testable criterion to decide the issue. In 'Zero Tolerance for Pragmatics' (*Synthèse* 165[2008] 359–71), Christopher Gauker claims that the proposition that a speaker's words express in context never depends on the speaker's intentions (which he considers to be the essence of pragmatics).

In his monograph *Between Saying and Doing: Towards an Analytic Pragmatism*, Robert B. Brandom lays out a programme for a pragmatically grounded (formal) semantics. His starting-point is the (Frege-inspired) assumption that nothing counts as a linguistic (discursive) practice that does not involve assertive use of declarative sentences expressing propositions. The foundational component of this practice is the ability to ask for and to give reasons. It is then shown how such a practice relates to ('can be elaborated into') one involving the normative categories of commitment and entitlement, which in turn underlies a practice involving full-fledged standard modality. At the same time, the relations of such practices to language fragments called 'vocabularies' are explored. Certain practices are said to be necessary/ sufficient for the deployment of certain vocabularies and—conversely—certain vocabularies are considered necessary/sufficient for the (explicit) specification of certain practices. In addition to applying his method to vocabularies containing logical connectives and indexical expressions, Brandom provides a formal semantics replacing the notion of the incompatibility (of propositions) with the notion of truth.

Commitment is the title of a collection edited by Philippe de Brabanter and Patrick Dendale as a special issue of the *Belgian Journal of Linguistics*. In their introduction, the editors reflect on the range of uses of the term 'commitment' in the fields of speech-act theory, formal modelling of dialogue, and linguistic analysis of modality. Important differences concern common-sense vs. technical, as well as psychologizing vs. conventionalizing, usages. The eleven articles in the volume reveal a variety of interests such as the linguistic description of discourse particles, 'cognition verbs', and expressions of futurity and intention. Discourse analysis is the topic of 'Legal Norms as Objects of (Non-)Commitment' (*BJL* 22[2008] 83–100) by Karen Deschamps, while a broader philosophical enquiry is central in 'Assertoric Commitments' by Mikhail Kissine (*BJL* 22[2008] 155–77). Two studies deal with declarative questions, aka 'rising declaratives'. In 'A Question of Commitment' (*BJL* 22[2008] 101–36) Christine Gunlogson argues that rising intonation signals that an utterance is '*contingent* upon some discourse condition obtaining'

(p. 101). In declarative questions like *The server is down?*, the speaker's commitment to the truth of the declarative is taken to be intonationally marked as contingent on ratification by the addressee, whence the question-like effect. Claudia Poschmann, 'All Declarative Questions are Attributive?' (*BJL* 22[2008] 247–69), suggests that further progress in this area can be made by distinguishing 'echo' usages from 'confirmative' ones and by being more sensitive to variability in intonation. According to her, declarative questions when used as confirmative questions show falling intonation quite regularly and suspend speaker commitment to a lesser degree.

Another collection surveying a broad issue of central concern to studies of the semantics/pragmatics interface is *Perspectives on Contexts*, edited by Paolo Bouquet, Luciano Serafini, and Richmond H. Thomason. In their introduction the editors optimistically state that the eleven chapters presented in the body of the collection 'clearly show how insights from all the areas of cognitive science can be combined to improve our understanding of this important topic' (p. x). Accordingly, we find some papers written from the perspectives of artificial intelligence, philosophy, and logic, as well as (formal) semantics and pragmatics. Other studies ('The Search for the Semantic Grail' by John Perry, pp. 56–77; 'On a Proposal of Strawson Concerning Context vs. "What Is Said"' by Varol Akman, pp. 97–49; and 'Truth-Conditional Pragmatics: An Overview' by François Recanati, pp. 171–88) grapple with the well-known puzzle of distinguishing (narrow) semantic content ('what is said') from broader pragmatic content ('what is communicated'). A highly technical study is provided by Richmond H. Thomason in his 'Contextual Intensional Logic: Type-Theoretic and Dynamic Considerations' (pp. 43–63). Among the crucial technical assumptions of this paper belongs the introduction of a type i for (contextual) indices in addition to the familiar type w for possible worlds. This allows the implementation of ideas by David Kaplan according to which sentential expressions are interpreted as functions from contexts to (propositional) contents. 'Fictional Contexts' (pp. 215–49) by Andrea Bonomi formalizes the meaning of referential expressions figuring in fictional discourse as well as in discourse about fiction. This involves among other things (type-)shifting from any character α within a story H (e.g. Buck Mulligan in *Ulysses*) to α_H, the set of properties attributed to Buck Mulligan in *Ulysses*. The inside and outside of fictional worlds as well as their overlap with the real world can then be captured as compatibility relations between sets of properties attributable to fictional and real individuals. The approach allows formal statements of 'double identity' and can account for the oddness of statements like *Andrea Bonomi and Sancho Panza love Don Quixote*.

We finish with studies addressing fundamental questions of semantics, such as the place of semantics within linguistics, the structure of a semantic theory and the availability of semantic universals. The first topic is discussed in the classic Festschrift for Sir John Lyons, *Grammar and Meaning*, edited by Frank R. Palmer, which appears, thirteen years after its first edition, in a digitally printed version, and features contributions by an impressive range of eminent scholars on topics intimately connected to Lyons's work, including Adam Kilgariff and Gerald Gazdar, Adrienne Lehrer and

Keith Lehrer, Peter Matthews, Ruth M. Kempson, Stephen Levinson, Jim Miller, Peter Trudgill, Bernard Comrie, John Anderson, R.M.W. Dixon and John Lyons himself.

Donald Davidson's Truth-Theoretic Semantics, by Ernest Lepore and Kirk Ludwig [2005], examines the foundations and applications of Davidson's programme for truth-theoretic semantic theory for natural languages, the foundations of which are laid in Davidson [1966, 1967], and which rests on two basic assumptions: a meaning theory for natural language should be a compositional one, and 'the most philosophically perspicuous way of doing this is by adapting a Tarski-style axiomatic truth theory for the purpose' (p. 16). After laying the philosophical foundations of the general programme outlined above, and addressing and answering some criticisms against it, the authors discuss the applications of the programme to various natural-language constructions like quantifiers, referring terms and quotation, adverbial and adjectival modification, tense, opaque contexts, and non-declarative sentences, by considering Davidson's own solutions but also by suggesting new proposals that avoid problems arising in the course of carrying out Davidson's own suggestions. A chapter is devoted to the questions of how to give a general characterization of the notion of logical form as semantic form, and another one to the discussion of Davidson's views on the relative primacy of the concept of truth and criticisms of traditional theories of truth (coherence, redundancy, correspondence theories). Miklós Erdélyi-Szabó, László Kálmán and Agi Kurucz propose, in their article 'Towards a Natural Language Semantics without Functors and Operands' (*JLLI* 17[2008] 1–17), to do away with the Fregean approach to semantic theory, according to which syntactic 'completeness' vs. 'incompleteness' is replicated in a corresponding semantic distinction. They argue for a compositional semantic theory that uses models where the basic entities are neither individuals, nor eventualities, nor their properties, but 'pieces of evidence', which are combined by means of a binary constructor used for creating structured complex terms representing arbitrary phenomena.

'Universals in Semantics', by Kai von Fintel and Lisa Matthewson (*LingRev* 25[2008] 139–201), investigates the possibility of finding semantic universals within the inventory of lexical/content morphemes among the mechanisms that compose meanings (the inventory of functional 'glue' morphemes, and of composition principles), and among the mechanisms of pragmatics. They argue that there are few promising constraints at the level of the lexicon, that there are more at the level of functional morphemes and composition principles, and that Gricean mechanisms are universal although the precise nature of presuppositions is subject to cross-linguistic variation. Robert van Rooij's 'Evolutionary Motivations for Semantic Universals' (in Eckardt, Jäger and Veenstra, eds., pp. 103–42) aims to give motivations for semantic universals that encode which of a set of meanings potentially expressible in natural languages are expressed in simple or lexicalized terms in all languages, within the domain of connectives, property- and proposition-denoting expressions and quantifiers, using the apparatus of evolutionary game theory.

7. Lexicography, Lexicology and Lexical Semantics

There were a number of interesting publications on lexicology this year. M. Lynne Murphy's *Semantic Relations and the Lexicon* approaches the subject from a variety of theoretical and methodological frameworks, taking into account developments in psychology, philosophy, education, anthropology and computer science as well as linguistics. Her main aim is 'to provide an account of how individuals know (or determine) whether words are semantically related or not' (p. 4), arguing that the pervasive metaphors describing the mental lexicon as either a dictionary or a thesaurus in our heads are not always useful or entirely sufficient. Differences between beliefs and facts about language use reveal that although our meta-linguistic knowledge about words is extensive, it is not always correct. Murphy explores approaches to semantic relations in a variety of different disciplines in light of their different motivations, and considers whether they have produced compatible results. Philosophical discussions have been interested more in things than in the words that denote them, while linguistic approaches have generally been structural in various ways, attempting to study the structure of the lexicon on semantic, syntactic, morphological, or contextual grounds. Anthropological studies are often interested in folk taxonomies, but Murphy finds that 'word meanings and concepts are completely intertwined in most theoretical discussions' (p. 75) among some groups of psychologists, and that others are more interested in categorization than word meaning. Computer science is interested in semantic relations from the perspective of natural language processing and is thus less concerned with the linguistic/conceptual division that interests those studying human cognition. Murphy suggests that the mental lexicon is not organized semantically: relations between concepts are present outside the lexicon and are, therefore, part of general cognition. She argues that their production in meta-linguistic activities, such as word-association tests, does not disprove this.

Martine Vanhove's edited collection *From Polysemy to Semantic Change: Towards a Typology of Lexical Semantic Associations* brings together papers on a variety of language groups to explore the possibility of cross-linguistic studies of the lexicon. Using data from the '45 languages for which we could rely on first-hand data collected by the linguists of the research team, or on their mother tongues' (p. x), the papers explore various features of polysemy across and within language groups. For example, Vanhove's own chapter, 'Semantic Associations between Sensory Modalities, Prehension and Mental Perceptions: A Crosslinguistic Perspective' (pp. 341–70), explores semantic associations between words for hearing, sight, prehension ('taking'), and mental perception, to determine whether the connection between vision and knowledge is universal. She finds that there is an association between hearing and mental perception in all the languages sampled from Indo-European, Afro-Asiatic, Niger-Congo, Nilo-Saharan, Austronesian, Eskimo [*sic*] Sino-Tibetan, and Creole groups, and also that the semantic association between vision and understanding is very strong, but that the association between taking and cognition is rather less so. Vanhove concludes that literacy is not, as had been suggested, a decisive factor favouring the semantic association between vision and mental perception, and argues that 'a typological classification of this association needs to examine, for each lexical item in each language, the details of the semantic networks, morpho-syntactic frames, contextual uses, and historical data or reconstructions' (p. 369). The ultimate outcome of this type of work is the identification of semantic universals.

Howard Jackson and Etienne Zé Amvela published a second edition of their *Words, Meaning and Vocabulary: An Introduction to Modern English Lexicology* [2007], covering etymology, word formation, lexical semantics, style and register, investigating vocabulary, and words in dictionaries. Exercises are provided in each chapter, with a key to the exercises at the back, and the text has also been updated. James Pustejovsky and Anna Rumshisky's 'Between Chaos and Structure: Interpreting Lexical Data through a Theoretical Lens' (*IJL* 21[2008] 337–55) explores the tension inherent in the relationship between corpus data and linguistic theory.

The following publications are listed chronologically according to the historical provenance of the words they discuss. Alfred Bammesburger argues that the question 'Is There an Old English Adjective *Scrid* "Swift"?' (*N&Q* 55[2008] 117–19) should be answered in the negative. In 'Æthelberht's *Fedesl* Revisited' (*N&Q* 55[2008] 125–6), Lisi Oliver suggests that *fedesl* refers to an assessed payment due rather than to a fine. Christine F. Cooper-Rompato finds an example of 'Sugar-Cane: Antedating the Entry in the *Oxford English Dictionary*' (*N&Q* 55[2008] 136–7), pushing the date back from 1568 to 1424. Andrew Breeze identifies Celtic influence in '*Art* "Direction" in *St Erkenwald*' (*N&Q* 55[2008] 273). Richard Levin argues against a suggestion that *back* was used with the sense 'phallus' in 'Early Modern English "Back": Erotic But Not Phallic Uses' (*N&Q* 55[2008] 135–6). Colin Wilcockson's '"One Foot in the Grave": Antedating the *Oxford English Dictionary*' (*N&Q* 55[2008] 360) antedates the phrase by twenty-seven years, to 1605. Sophie Tomlinson finds 'A Jacobean Dramatic Usage of "Actress"' (*N&Q* 55[2008] 282–3) that antedates the first *OED* citation by ninety-two years, to 1608. Edward Pickering identifies an 'Unidentified First Use of *Self-Esteem:* Milton's *An Apology for Smectymnuus* (1642)' (*N&Q* 55[2008] 287–9), antedating an *OED* first citation by fifteen years. Carol Hough finds 'An Ante-Dating of the *OED* Entry for *Nanny* Goat' (*N&Q* 55[2008] 134–5) in place-name evidence dating from *c*.1700.

A number of publications dealt with contemporary lexis this year, including Vincent B.Y. Ooi's 'The Lexis of Electronic Gaming on the Web: A Sinclairian Approach' (*IJL* 21[2008] 311–23), which uses material available online as a corpus. Welby Ings discusses 'From the Beat to the Soob: The Language of the Male Sex Worker in New Zealand' (*NZW* 12[2008] 2–5). Lynn Grant considers words and phrases used in cricket commentaries, and Cherie Connor words in fishing magazines in 'It's Just Not Cricket ... or Is It?' and 'Creating Fishing Mates' (*NZW* 12[2008] 5–6, 8). Dianne Bardsley explores New Zealand usage of *rotunda* for 'bandstand' in 'How Round is a Rotunda?' (*NZW* 12[2008] 6–7). Elisa Mattiello's *An Introduction to English Slang* is a wide-ranging account that moves happily between American slang, Australian slang and rhyming slang in a single sentence. She provides an extensive selection of examples of informal trends in word formation and characterizes her wide-ranging forms of slang as a 'slang system' independent from 'the standard system' (pp. 201–2). It is not hard to find details to take issue with. For instance, Mattiello asserts that *big-mouth* and *motor-mouth* are perfect synonyms (p. 162), but while *motor-mouth* is used to indicate that someone talks too much, *big-mouth* refers more specifically to an individual guilty of revealing a secret. We are told that *mug* 'a (usually) large earthenware vessel or bowl; a pot' (*OED n^1* sense 2) is 'not polysemous in the standard language' (p. 204), and that slang senses may be distant from those found in standard English, but the slang examples given (*OED n^3*) share an uncertain etymological relationship with the standard term. This is an interesting and ambitious study, but it ranges too widely to present a convincing account of slang usage.

A number of interesting books dealt with metaphor and idiom. In *Rethinking Idiomaticity: A Usage-Based Approach*, Stefanie Wulff adopts a bottom-up approach to her corpus material, whereby definitions arise from her data rather than being applied to it, assuming a causal relationship between corpus-linguistic definitions of the different idiomatic variation parameters (representing usage) and speakers' idiomaticity judgements. She argues that data from the BNC confirms existing theoretical assumptions about cognitive processes, but that it also allows the identification of systematic patterns not otherwise apparent. Wulff argues that in V-NP constructions, flexibility operates at the level of individual words rather than across the phrase as a whole, and emphasizes in particular the morphological flexibility of verbs with regard to number and mood but not tense and person. Accordingly, she visualizes idiomaticity by means of a three-dimensional graph rather than a continuum, with idiomaticity on the X-axis, schematization on the Y, and compositionality (e.g. how far the phrase is formally frozen and semantically opaque) on the Z. This Z-axis represents the information that speakers draw upon when judging idiomaticity.

Elena Semino's *Metaphor in Discourse* applies the insights of Cognitive Metaphor Theory to texts of various types as well as to corpus material, and thus studies genuine manifestations of conceptual metaphors, both conventional and creative, rather than 'artificially constructed examples' (p. 10), concentrating on the metaphoricity of individual words rather than of phrases as a whole. She begins by setting out the 'metaphor identification procedure' (MIP), conceding that it might seem 'a large analytical sledgehammer to crack a very small textual nut' (p. 14), but arguing that it is necessary to deal with problematic cases in a consistent and systematic manner. Metaphors are patterned in discourse in a variety of ways: by repetition, recurrence, clustering, extension, combination, literal-metaphorical oppositions, signalling, and intertextual relations, but Semino is also interested in the functions of metaphors, and applies her analysis to texts belonging to the fields of literature, politics, science, education and advertising. She notes that metaphors in advertising are often represented visually as well as textually. Although many rely on conventional metaphors and represent them visually in novel ways, others present images that cannot be decoded without detailed reference to the text. In an interesting analysis of a radio phone-in, Semino found considerable use of metaphorical language to depict depression as a physical object, either on top of or inside the sufferer, that can be controlled by putting it in a box. Other callers described themselves as contained within depression, or saw their depression as a phase or obstacle in a journey. Contributors involved in treating or caring for those suffering from depression typically used a different range of metaphors: presenting depression as a problem with seeing (particularly in the perception of colours) and as the result of an elastic band (the mind) being over-stretched (by stress). In contrast to metaphors used by sufferers from depression, those used by carers depict the condition as part of the patient and as something, to some extent, within their control.

Alan Cienki and Cornelia Müller's edited volume, *Metaphor and Gesture*, brings together a variety of linguistic and disciplinary perspectives on the metaphorical use of gestures and the gestural revelation of metaphorical thinking. Cienki's 'Why Study Metaphor and Gesture?' (pp. 5–25) reviews research into gestures representing abstract notions, supporting the view that metaphor is a cognitive phenomenon. Geneviève Calbris's 'From Left to Right...: Coverbal Gestures and their Symbolic Use of Space' (pp. 27–53) finds that the gestures used by a French prime minister, Lionel Jospin, confirm the existence of mental image schemas independent of language production. In 'Gesture as a Conceptual Mapping Tool' (pp. 56–92), Robert F. Williams finds that in teaching children to tell the time, gestures were used both to guide the mapping of conceptual elements to environmental structures (the clock face) and in adding structure to an existing conceptualization. Rafael Núñez takes 'A Fresh Look at the Foundation of Mathematics: Gesture and the Psychological Reality of Conceptual Metaphors' (pp. 93–114), and finds that professional mathematicians use gesture to characterize fundamental metaphorical concepts not adequately captured by verbal definitions. In 'Piercean Semiotics Meets Conceptual Metaphor: Iconic Modes in Gestural Representations of Grammar' (pp. 115–54), Irene Mittelberg studies the gestures used by four linguistics professors during introductory courses. David McNeill's 'Unexpected Metaphors' (pp. 155–70) concentrates on gestures used in describing the content of cartoons or films that do not draw on canonical or cultural metaphorical schemas. Jacques Montredon, Abderrahim Amrani, Marie-Paule Benoit-Barnet, Emmanuelle Chan You, Régine Llorca and Nancy Peuteuil. examine 'Catchment, Growth Point, and Spatial Metaphor: Analyzing Derrida's Oral Discourse on Deconstruction' (pp. 171–94), while Fey Parrill explores 'Form, Meaning and Convention. A Comparison of a Metaphoric Gesture with an Emblem' (pp. 195–217), concentrating on observers' response to variations in commonly used PRESENTING and OKAY gestures. Cornelia Müller asks 'What Gestures Reveal about the Nature of Metaphor?' (pp. 219–45), and concludes that metaphors are products of a general cognitive process rather than just a linguistic phenomenon, and that they are dynamic in several respects. A series of commentaries by Ronald W. Langacker ('Metaphoric Gesture and Cognitive Linguistics', pp. 249–51), Naomi Quinn ('Metaphoric Gestures and Cultural Analysis', pp. 253–7), Jürgen Streeck ('Metaphor and Gesture: A View from the Microanalysis of Interaction', pp. 259–64), Anders R. Hougaard and Gitte R. Hougaard ('Implications   of   Cognitive   Metaphor   and   Gesture   Studies   for

Ethnomethodology and Conversation Analysis and Vice Versa', pp. 265–72), Sherman Wilcox ('Sign and Gesture: Towards a New Paradigm', pp. 273–5), Paul Bouissac ('The Study of Metaphor and Gesture: A Critique from the Perspective of Semiotics', pp. 277–82), George Lakoff ('The Neuroscience of Metaphoric Gestures. Why they Exist', pp. 283–9) and Raymond W. Gibbs, Jr ('Metaphor and Gesture: Some Implications for Psychology', pp. 291–301) are an effective way of demonstrating the importance of the fascinating studies in this volume from the perspective of a wide variety of disciplines.

The theory and practice of lexicography received considerable attention this year. B.T. Sue Atkins and Michael Rundall's *The Oxford Guide to Practical Lexicography* offers 'a complete introduction to the job of creating a dictionary' (p. 1), which they carefully distinguish from meta-lexicography (the writing of books about dictionaries) or theoretical lexicography (of which they deny the existence). They divide their discussion into three parts: 'Pre-Lexicography', 'Analysing the Data' and 'Compiling the Entry'. The first part discusses dictionary types, corpus construction ('all good dictionaries take corpus data as their starting point', p. 3), software, style guides, and macro- and micro-structure. It also considers the points where 'linguistic theory meets lexicography', dealing particularly with semantic relationships and frame semantics. The second part explains how to extract data from a corpus, considering particularly the division into senses and the provision of information. This section is briefer than the others, perhaps in reluctant recognition of the fact that '[y]ou learn about lexicography by doing it' (p. 9). Part III looks at finalized dictionary entries in monolingual dictionaries but concentrates particularly on issues relevant to bilingual dictionaries. Although it is unlikely that an untrained lexicographer would be asked to make all or any of these decisions, the format is a useful way of exploring lexicographical issues systematically. Atkins and Rundall concede that 'there is ... no "right" way to produce a dictionary' (p. 2), but they are not afraid to offer advice and guidelines based on their own experience. For example: 'You won't always be able to avoid the "act of/state of/quality of ..." formulae, but it is worth trying every other option before you reach this point. Applying these formulae as a sort of automatic, default approach suggests a lack of concern for the needs of users' (p. 447). Exercises in each chapter encourage the reader to apply their knowledge to carefully defined tasks. This remarkably thorough and clearly written handbook will undoubtedly provide aspiring lexicographers with an invaluable grounding in the tools and methodologies of their trade. While it may not be as relevant to those working on well-established dictionaries for native speakers, this book nevertheless represents a salutary challenge to traditional practice.

Thierry Fontenelle's *Practical Lexicography: A Reader*, a companion volume to Atkins and Rundall, reprints a collection of papers recommended by them on various aspects of dictionary-making for the benefit of trainee lexicographers and students in other branches of linguistics. The focus on contemporary lexicography is clear in the emphasis on the contribution that computers now make to dictionary production, but Johnson's plan is reprinted in an isolated concession to dictionary history. Fontenelle asks whether dictionaries and lexicographers are actually necessary in the era of the World

Wide Web, and responds by offering a range of approaches now encompassed in the discipline of lexicography. Papers by various authors discuss 'Metalexicography, Macrostructure, Microstructure, and the Contribution of Linguistic Theory', 'Corpus Design', 'Lexicographical Evidence', 'Word Senses and Polysemy', 'Collocations, Idioms, and Dictionaries', 'Definitions', 'Examples', 'Grammar and Usage in Dictionaries', 'Bilingual Lexicography', 'Tools for Lexicographers', 'Semantic Networks and Wordnets' and 'Dictionary Use', but several sections include only one paper. This volume will be of great interest and use to students of lexicography, and offers scholars the convenience of having twenty-two important papers in a single volume.

Sven Tarp's *Lexicography in the Borderland between Knowledge and Non-Knowledge* is the English translation of his doctoral dissertation. Unlike Atkins and Rundall, who deny the existence of purely theoretical lexicography, Tarp argues that theory and practice are not as closely related as they ought to be, commenting that 'Danish learner's [*sic*] dictionaries . . . in lexicographical terms are still living in the Stone Age' (p. 2). It is learners' dictionaries on which Tarp focuses, and he concludes that producers of learners' dictionaries for Danish could learn a lot from the 'big five' British learners' dictionaries. A 'large Danish core dictionary' would be the sun around which 'many bilingual immigrant dictionaries could revolve like planets' (p. 280), and Tarp argues that although text reception and text production would be important functions of these dictionaries, they also have a role to play in the acquisition of knowledge. This is a densely written account of lexicographical theory, with numerous examples from existing dictionaries. It is enlivened by its uncompromising assessments of earlier work in the field: Wiegend's general lexicographical theory was 'useless from a lexicographical, user-oriented perspective' (p. 37), Zgusta and Landau 'based their ideas more on intuition than on convincing scientific arguments' (p. 114), and nowhere in his 'relatively large production' does Hartmann provide a 'clear definition of the concept of ⟨⟨learner's [*sic*] dictionary⟩⟩' (p. 126). Tarp argues that 'lexicographical theory must never . . . allow itself to be limited by pragmatic considerations' (p. 176); this, in fact, denies the reality of the circumstances in which most dictionaries are produced. Although there is a detailed table of contents, an index would have been an invaluable feature in this book; the fact that I could not locate a concise description of 'function theory' does not necessarily mean that Tarp did not provide one.

Definition in Theory and Practice: Language, Lexicography and the Law, by Roy Harris and Christopher Hutton [2007], begins by looking at ways in which writers use stipulative definitions to identify and delineate their subjects, providing a useful reminder that definitions do not exist solely in dictionaries. However, James Murray and his successors are set up as straw men in the development of Harris and Hutton's argument. Without a proper understanding of *langue* and *parole*, and without appreciating the difference between a synchronic and diachronic approach, *OED* lexicographers 'perpetuate[d] a confusion about meaning that had been commonplace in the Western tradition [since ancient Greece] . . . that the "true" or "proper" definition of a word is revealed by its etymology' (p. 97). Murray is particularly taken to task for failing to maintain the distinction between real definition (describing the thing) and lexical definition (explaining the meaning of the word). At one point, Murray is criticized for omitting from his definition for *crocodile* the information that crocodiles are sometimes referred to using the word *alligator* ('Presumably Murray did not know this, or regarded Australian English as falling outside his remit', p. 82). This criticism betrays the same confusion between real and lexical definitions for which Murray is being taken to task: although this is a fact about crocodiles, it regards the use of the word *alligator*, and Murray did record the information under that headword. Having established that 'in the present state of lexicography, a systematic "communicational" definition of words is nowhere to be found' (p. 130), Harris and Hutton move on to the subject of 'The Definition of Law and Legal Definition', noting that the US Supreme Court is tending to turn to dictionaries more often now than in the past.

Juri Apresjan's *Systematic Lexicography* first appeared in its English translation in 2000. It was reissued as a paperback this year, without change.

Papers on dictionaries and lexicology from the third International Conference on Historical Lexicology and Lexicography in Leiden in 2006 are collected in Marijke Mooijaart and Marijke van der Wal's *Yesterday's Words: Contemporary, Current and Future Lexicography*. In 'John Wilkins' Metalinguistic Lexicon in the Panorama of Linguistic Terminology' (pp. 160–72), Natascia Leonardi explores the linguistic meta-language employed in the *Essay Towards a Real Character and a Philosophical Language* [1668]. Joseph T. Farquharson's 'Using Historical Dictionaries to Reconstruct Language History: The Case of Jamaican Creole' (pp. 148–59) asks whether Cassidy and Page's *Dictionary of Jamaican English* supports its authors' claims about the undocumented early history of Jamaican Creole. Noel Osselton's 'The *Glossographia Anglicana Nova* (1707, 1719) and the Royal Society' (pp. 88–95) argues that this anonymous dictionary represents a unique account of scientific vocabulary in the early eighteenth century. Starting with Johnson's *Dictionary* [1755], Laura Pinnavaia explores the treatment of 'Food and Drink Idioms in Two Hundred and Fifty Years of English Monolingual Lexicography' (pp. 173–83). In 'The *Electronic Jamieson:* Towards a Bicentenary Celebration' (pp. 333–40), Susan Rennie describes the work involved in producing an online edition of John Jamieson's *Etymological Dictionary of the Scottish Language* [1808] and *Supplement* [1825]. Julie Coleman's 'Lost Between Hotten and Henley: Barrère and Leland's *Dictionary of Slang Jargon and Cant*' (pp. 29–40) explains why the neglect of this late nineteenth-century dictionary is entirely justifiable. Maggie Scott looks to 'Unsung Etymologies: Lexical and Onomastic Evidence for the Influence of Scots on English' (pp. 187–98), tracing the interplay between language policy and lexicography. In two journal articles, Monique C. Cormier analyses the application of 'Usage Labels in *The Royal Dictionary* (1699) by Abel Boyer' (*IJL* 21[2008] 153–71), while Michael H. Whitworth explores the use of dictionaries in literature, in 'Hugh MacDiarmid and *Chambers's Twentieth Century Dictionary*' (*N&Q* 55[2008] 78–80).

Neil Johnson's *Dr Johnson's Reliquary of Rediscovered Words* was not, as I had expected, a compilation of entries from Johnson's dictionary, but a collection of obscure and obsolete terms, many with examples suggesting their applicability to contemporary government and related institutions. The *Reliquary* is unlikely to appeal to a scholarly audience, because it gives no indication of dates or frequency of usage, and although citations are provided, there are no other references to facilitate further research. Of the first ten words under the letter O, nine were listed in the *OED* with the same meaning (*obelise, oblocution, obreption, obsecrate, obstringe, obtenebrate, obtestation, Od, olid*), and only one (*oblicate*, perhaps for *obliquate*) was not. Nevertheless, for a popular audience interested in words this is a handsomely bound and diverting volume. Another readable book for a popular audience that draws more overtly on material found in the *OED* is Ammon Shea's *Reading the OED*. It describes his experience of reading the twenty volumes of the dictionary from cover to cover including, rather reluctantly, the bibliography. Eye strain, backache and caffeine dependency are interspersed between diverting lexicological and lexicographic facts. This is an engaging account of an odd feat and an enjoyable read even if the *OED* anecdotes are familiar.

Papers focusing on the *OED* this year included Peter Gilliver's 'The Philological Society's First New English Dictionary: Frederick Furnivall's Sub-Editors and their Work' (in Mooijaart and van der Wal, eds., pp. 67–76), which describes progress towards the Concise Dictionary proposed by Furnivall as a step towards what was to become the *OED*. In 'The Oxford Quarto Dictionary' (*Henry Sweet Society Bulletin* 51[2008] 25–39), Charlotte Brewer outlines H.W. Fowler's work towards a prescriptive Oxford dictionary to appease readers dissatisfied with the *OED*. It never reached publication. Valerie Creelman compares the treatment of 'Margaret Paston's Use of *Captenesse*' (*N&Q* 55[2008] 275–7) in the *MED* and *OED*. Sarah Ogilvie's 'Rethinking Burchfield and World Englishes' (*IJL* 21[2008] 23–59) uses statistical data derived from the *OED*'s supplements to disprove the commonly held view that Burchfield expanded the dictionary's coverage of World Englishes, and suggests that the misconception was promoted by misleading self-publicity. In 'The Mysterious Case of the Vanishing Tramlines: James Murray's Legacy and the 1933 *OED Supplement*' (*Dictionaries* 29[2008] 1–22), Ogilvie explores the deletion between proofs and publication of tramlines marking non-naturalized words and argues that this resulted from the influence of the Society for Pure English. Anthea Fraser Gupta considers 'English Words from the Malay World' (*N&Q* 55[2008] 357–60) from the perspective of an *OED* consultant, and identifies improvements under way in the third edition. R.M.W. Dixon similarly considers 'Australian Aboriginal Words in Dictionaries: A History' (*IJL* 21[2008] 129–52), but refers mainly to the *Random House Dictionary* [1987], the *Australian National Dictionary* [1988], and *Australian Words* [1990].

Work on bilingual lexicography included Włodzimierz Sobkowiak's 'Pronunciation of Acronyms and Abbreviations in e-LDOCE and e-MEDAL' (*IJL* 21[2008] 61–8), which finds that these two CD-ROM dictionaries are weak in this aspect of their presentation and coverage. B.L. Fraser's 'Beyond Definition: Organising Semantic Information in Bilingual Dictionaries' (*IJL* 21[2008] 69–93) describes the approach adopted by a diachronic Greek–English dictionary on which work is currently under way.

A special issue of *IJL* focused on the work of John Sinclair. Geoffrey Williams explores the influence of linguistic corpora on bilingual dictionaries in 'A Multilingual Matter: Sinclair and the Bilingual Dictionary' (*IJL* 21[2008] 255–66), and Gilles-Maurice de Schryver looks in particular at Sinclair's influence on African bilingual dictionaries in 'Why Does Africa Need Sinclair?' (*IJL* 21[2008] 267–91). In 'Lexicography, Grammar, and Textual Position' (*IJL* 21[2008] 293–309), Michael Hoey and Matthew Brook O'Donnell suggest that learners' dictionaries ought to provide information about not just grammatical contexts, but also textual position. Hai Xu's 'Exemplification Policy in English Learners' Dictionaries' (*IJL* 21[2008] 395–417) examines the use of the 'big five' English learners' dictionaries, and sets out criteria for the use of exemplification. In 'The Lexicographical Legacy of John Sinclair' (*IJL* 21[2008] 219–29), Patrick Hanks argues for a synthesis between corpus linguistics and construction grammar. Ramesh Krishnamurthy traces the influence of corpus-driven lexicography on EFL, native-speaker and national dictionaries in 'Corpus-Driven Lexicography' (*IJL* 21[2008] 231–42). Rosamund Moon's contribution deals with 'Sinclair, Phraseology, and Lexicography' (*IJL* 21[2008] 243–54), observing that the implications of Sinclair's approach have not yet been fully realized in the study of phraseology. Kenneth W. Church's 'Approximate Lexicography and Web Search' (*IJL* 21[2008] 325–36) argues that this compromise between linguistics and engineering was another product of Sinclair's work.

8. Onomastics

The year under review (2008) was not a particularly robust one for the publication of major onomastic works. A scant three books account for the extended publications, but these meagre offerings were bolstered by the appearance of the long-delayed volume 40 of *Onoma* and the continued timely publication of *Names*, *Onomastica Canadiana* and the *Journal of the English Place-Name Society*.

Of the three books reviewed the one which is likely to have the greatest impact on onomastics is Michael McCafferty's *Native American Place-Names of Indiana*. By any measure this is an impressive and important publication which makes a major contribution to an area of toponymy that has long been neglected and patronized as an 'insignificant' part of the namescape and unworthy of study since Native American naming was primitive by definition and 'merely descriptive' by nature. McCafferty has sifted through scores of primary and secondary documents searching for geographical names in Indiana which were created and used by Native Americans. These are the names found on maps, itineraries, letters and reports of French explorers, priests and administrators in the seventeenth and eighteenth centuries and later by English and other European travellers, settlers and entrepreneurs. The author has identified several dozen such names, traced each one to its language source, phonemicized each one, given a morphological analysis of each one and given each one a meaning. The scholarship demonstrated here is prodigious: McCafferty deals not only with English and French but in depth with Potawatomi and Miami-Illinois, as well as several Delaware and Iroquois languages. As McCafferty notes in the introduction, Native American place-names in Indiana (and indeed elsewhere) fall mainly into three categories, whereby they refer to a physical or spiritual attribute of the referent, to noteworthy flora or fauna associated with the location, or to the location of a tribe. Furthermore, 'Most Native American place-names in Indiana tend to be descriptive expressions related to the immediate physical environment, labels created by hunting-gathering-farming peoples specifically for practical geo-locational purposes within a complex natural world. In fact, the penchant that such names possess for communicating direct, meaningful, and typically very useful information, most often geophysical, biological, or ethnonymic in nature, is their most common characteristic' (p. xxiv). What distinguishes this book from others is the fact that this is primarily a linguistic rather than a cultural or historical study of the names. History enters in only in so far as it provides a chronology for the various name forms and as a means of reconstructing the physical surroundings (particularly the hydrology and botany of the area when the name was created and used). Hydrology is especially relevant since hydronyms are by far the most common Native American names in Indiana. This book is especially welcome since so much nonsense has been written about Native American names, so many incorrect interpretations have been mindlessly copied from one writer to the next, and so many folk etymologies have been offered as meanings for a name (most often involving an Indian princess and a love triangle) that Native American names have been brushed aside as trivial or marginal to the larger naming picture. McCafferty's work should go a long way towards righting this sorry situation since it opens a window onto what was once a rich, vital and sophisticated namescape.

Peter Bernhardt's *Gods and Goddesses in the Garden* is a book which will appeal to anyone interested in classical mythology or botany as well as those interested primarily in names. Bernhardt, a professor of botany at St Louis University as well as a fellow of the Royal Botanical Gardens in Sydney, Australia, has written a scholarly but approachable book on the names of flora which derive from Greek or Roman mythological figures. An idea of the coverage can be gathered from the chapter headings, (e.g. 'The Gods of Olympus', 'The Triumph of Zeus', 'Troy and its Aftermath'), and sub-chapters (e.g. 'The Muses', 'Chaste or Constant Nymphs', 'The Household of Aphrodite'). Each chapter begins with a short retelling of the relevant parts of a classical myth, which leads to a discussion of the plant names derived from the story, along with some most interesting asides on the circumstances surrounding the naming (in which Carolus Linnaeus figures prominently, as we would expect). As someone not particularly interested in botany beyond the heritage tomatoes I plant each spring and also not particularly interested in mythology beyond the one class I was forced to take as an undergraduate, I approached this book as more a chore than an opportunity, but I was pleasantly surprised on almost every page by the author's grasp—of botany and mythology, of course, but also of the history surrounding each name. I learned that rheumatism root (for which, by the way, no commercial use has been found), is named for Thomas Jefferson, as we can gather from the scientific name of the herb, *Jeffersonia diphylla*; that Jesus was denied the customary glass of wine and myrrh at his crucifixion because this induced a trancelike euphoria; and that acanthus, distinguished by the spines along its leaves, is named for the nymph Acantha, who used her nails to scratch the face of Apollo, who was forcing his affections upon her. This is all set in a luminous historical, cultural and literary background which includes references to Charles Darwin, Emily Dickinson and William Shakespeare. Bernhardt is an exceptionally talented writer, and his graceful sentences make this book a delight to read. One example of many, again on Acantha: 'Acantha continues to defend her honour in gardens all over the world, although she has been reduced to the status of a formal perennial groundcover' (p. 132).

The final book to be mentioned is Philip Gooden's *Name Dropping*. Although this is more derivative than the books mentioned above, it is a serious study nonetheless and deserves to be in their company. *Name Dropping* is a dictionary of some 400 adjectives derived from the names of persons, with citations drawn from British newspapers showing their current meanings, followed by a paragraph by Gooden setting the name in historical and social context. The entries range from the familiar (Puckish, Machiavellian, Sadistic) to the lesser known (Stepfordian, from the robotic Stepford Wives of the Ira Levin novel and movie; Humbert Humbertish, from the narrator of Vladimir Nabokov's *Lolita*) to the esoteric (Basil Fawlty-like, from the manic, snobbish John Cleese character on the television show *Fawlty Towers*; Blofeld-Style, for James Bond's nemesis, the brilliantly villainous Ernst Stavro Blofeld; Clouseauesque, for the bumbling Peter Sellers character, Inspector Clouseau of the Pink Panther movies). Gooden's compilation is current, with entries for Spielbergian (from director Steven Spielberg), meaning 'calculating, visually dazzling' (p. 182); Rumsfeldian (from former US Secretary of Defense Donald Rumsfeld), meaning 'tough, aggressive, verbally tortuous' (p. 169); Oprah-esque (no identification needed since Oprah is a world icon), meaning 'successful, influential, unpretentious' (p. 139); and Bushite (from immediate past president of the United States George W. Bush), meaning 'folksy, verbally inept' (p. 30). In fact, almost anyone with a distinctive characteristic risks having their name adjectivized with an appropriate derivational morpheme. The particular suffixes employed are interesting in their own right as they range from Elgarian to Eeyoreish to Fellini-esque to Midas-like to Miltonic to Miss Havisham-style to Nietzschean to Oedipal, all with suffix or suffix-like derivation, to Mickey Mouse with zero derivation. There is little that is original here, but this book does good service by bringing together many of the adjectivized eponyms which resonate with contemporary language users, along with actual illustrations of their use and a great deal of interesting historical and cultural background.

Moving from books to articles, an especially significant and welcome arrival was that of *Onoma*, the journal of the International Council of Onomastic Sciences (ICOS). Originally scheduled for publication in 2005, volume 40 appeared in late 2008. Each of the past several issue of *Onoma* has been given over to a single topic: volume 37 was devoted to Nordic onomastics, volume 38 to onomastics in North America, and volume 39 to teaching onomastics. Volume 40 is devoted to literary onomastics, the study of the use of names in literature, guest-edited by Grant Smith from the US and Friedhelm Debus from Germany. It is impossible to summarize the variety of essays found here; suffice to say that they range from theory of literary onomastics (articles by W.F.H. Nicolaisen and Benedicta Windt), to the use of names by particular authors (Alleen and Don Nilsen on names in the Harry Potter series), to overviews of literary onomastic research in the Netherlands (Karina van Dalen-Oskam), Poland (Irena Sarnowska-Giefing) and Russia (Natalija Vasil'eva). I should mention that, although ICOS is an international organization and various nations are represented in this collection, there is an obvious and decided skew towards English-speaking cultures, likely explained by the fact that literary onomastics has a longer and more extensive history in these than those in other parts of the world. Furthermore, English is apparently seen as the language of literary onomastics, regardless of the literary or cultural focus. Of the nineteen essays in this volume, thirteen are in English (even those dealing with literary onomastics in Poland and in Russia). Of the remaining six, four are in German and two are in French. For anyone in search of a general introduction to the field of literary onomastics I would recommend Grant Smith's preface, 'Names as Art: An Introduction to Essays in English' (*Onoma* 40[2005] 7–27).

In last year's review I introduced in the onomastics section the term 'forensic linguistics'. The current year brings an excellent overview of that topic, 'Trademarks and Other Proprietary Terms', by Ronald R. Butters, one of the foremost practitioners of forensic linguistics. In this chapter (in Gibbons and Turell, eds., *Dimensions of Forensic Linguistics*, pp. 231–47), Butters lays out the basic outlines of the field. Forensic linguistics, for the moment at least since this is a developing and dynamic area, finds its primary justification in such legal domains as statutes and contracts, death penalty appeals, and names, especially trademark litigation and in the litigation of associated marks and proprietary slogans, such as that of Maxwell House coffee, 'good to the last drop'. The bibliography appended to this article is an especially valuable introduction to forensic linguistics. Butters notes that in trademark litigation concerning names, forensic linguists consider primarily three things: the likelihood of confusion between competing marks specifically in terms of their sight, sound, and meaning; the strength of a mark (on a scale ranging from arbitrary through suggestive to generic); and their propriety (the lack of propriety being defined by federal statute as a name which is immoral, deceptive, scandalous, disrespectful, and the like). Butters richly illustrates these concepts with examples drawn from cases in which he has been involved, such as those dealing with the names 'Kettle Chips' and 'Washington Redskins'.

In a related article (*SCC&HTLJ* 24[2007–2008] 507–19), Butters discusses the potential contribution of forensic linguists to trademark (name) dilution, where a plaintiff claims that its trademark is being diluted (becoming generic) by the existence of a similar mark. Butters feels that linguists can contribute to the legal process concerning dilution of trademarks by providing evidence assisting in determining the 'fame' of a name; providing evidence for determining the location of a mark on the 'strength' scale from 'arbitrary' to 'generic'; and providing evidence with respect to the likelihood of the blurring and tarnishing of a mark.

In a revision of an article with the same title, which was reviewed in this section for 2004 (*YWES* 85[2006] 64), Michael McCafferty, "'Kankakee": An Old Etymological Puzzle' (*Le Journal* 24[2008] 1–6) updates the origin of the Native American 'Kankakee', the name of the river which heads in Indiana and joins with the Des Plaines to form the Illinois River near Chicago. Some investigators had claimed that the name meant 'wolf land', others that it derived from a Potawatomi word meaning 'swampy ground'. McCafferty, a Miami–Illinois language specialist, argues that the source is to be found in a Miami–Illinois form reconstructed as *teeyaahkiki*, meaning 'open country' or 'exposed land', an interpretation supported by reconstructions of the river's eighteenth- and even nineteenth- century biological and botanical ecosystems. For McCafferty, *Théakiki*, as the name was first recorded by La Salle in 1679, became *Tiakiki* and subsequently *Kiakiki* through regressive assimilation, then evolved to *Kinkiki* and ultimately to *Kankakee*.

Comments on Etymology, the journal devoted to the origins and derivations of (primarily informal) English words and phrases, and edited by Gerald Cohen, professor in the Department of Arts, Languages, and Philosophy at the Missouri University of Science and Technology in Rolla, has a full serving of etymological information relating to names. In '*Dallas* (Texas)' (*CoE* (37[2008] 12–13) etymologist Barry Popick, a frequent contributor to CoE, has unearthed an 1876 article from the Galveston (Texas) Daily News which provides confirming evidence, lacking until now, that the city and county of Dallas, Texas (and indeed most of the other sixty or so communities or civil divisions in the US named Dallas) were named for George Mifflin Dallas, vice president of the US under John Tyler, serving from 1845 to 1849. In addition the article contains a major surprise by presenting evidence that the namer of Dallas was not the city's founder, John Neely Bryan, as previously assumed, but another of the early settlers, a Mrs Gilbert, who suggested the name in honour of her fellow Pennsylvanian, George M. Dallas.

Gerald Cohen, in "'Fiddy Cent'" (*CoE* 37[2008] 32–6), following the lead of Ben Zimmer, reports on rap artist Curtis Jackson's performance name, '50 Cent'. At one time Jackson apparently said he chose '50 Cent' because this name represented change, a very lame play on words. Later, in a more fully elaborated version, he claimed that he took the name in honour of Calvin '50 Cent' Martin, because, as Jackson put it, the name 'says everything I want it to say. I'm the same kind of person 50 Cent was. I provide for myself by any means' (p. 37). Calvin Martin, the namesake 50 Cent, in the 1980s was one of Brooklyn, New York's most notorious gangsters, an armed robber, an extortionist and a killer or presumed killer of at least thirty people. The origin of Martin's *nom de guerre* is unknown.

A new eponym has made its way into at least one sector of society. Gerald Cohen, in 'Marsha Bradys' (*CoE* 37[2008] 10), reports on a kind of footwear which is now mandatory in the Joliet, Illinois, prison. The design and brand of shoes worn in this (and other) correctional institutions have long been status symbols among inmates. Joliet prison has responded to the resulting status competition by requiring all inmates to wear the plain, white, slipper-type shoes that both prisoners and guards call Marsha Bradys, named for the teenage, oldest daughter of the long-running television show *The Brady Bunch*. The shoes are supposed to be copies of or very similar to the shoes Marsha Brady wore on the show.

The *Journal of the English Place-Name Society* (*JEPNS* 40[2008]), under the general editorship of Richard Coates, contains five articles in addition to the usual reviews, notes, comments, corrections and the bibliography for 2007, prepared by Carole Hough. Duncan Probert (*JEPNS* 40[2008] 7–22) takes what appears to be a settled issue and shows that its simplicity may have contributed to a less than complete analysis. Probert considers the origins of the sixty or so Kingstons in England and finds that a simple gloss of 'the king's town' is inadequate. He concludes 'it remains likely that most "Kingston" names arose as a consequence of some not-yet-properly-defined function or functions of the places concerned at the time of coining' (p. 19), and that 'we need to consider each "Kingston" name not only in terms of its immediate historical, administrative and tenurial context... but also with regard to the wider patterns of local landscape organization within which it existed' (p. 19). (Good advice for dealing with names in general.)

In a similar investigation, Keith Briggs (*JEPNS* 40[2008] 97–111) re-examines the etymology of Freemantle, traditionally held to be a direct translation of French for 'cold cloak'. Briggs points out that usages in France have to do with grain production and derive from Fromentel 'wheat field'. The 'cold cloak' derivation is seen to be an instance of folk-etymology.

Other articles in *JEPNS* are 'Upton, Thurgarton Wapentake, Nottinghamshire', by Jean Cameron with Paul Cavill and Richard Jones (*JEPNS* 40[2008] 23–33), 'The Domesday Book Castle *LVVRE*' by Keith Briggs (*JEPNS* 40[2008] 113–18), and the extensive 'Reflections on Some Major Lincolnshire Place-names Part 1: Algarkirk to Melton Ross' by Richard Coates (*JEPNS* 40[2008] 35–95), in which the author comments—often at length—on some fifty Lincolnshire names, largely those of parishes, manors and districts. Because of the sheer number of entries and their variety, an attempt to characterize Coates's work would not be appropriate here; suffice to say that they are informed by and suffused with an impressive display of linguistic, social, historical and cultural information.

Several times in recent years I have reported on the work of D.K. Tucker, a statistician at Carleton University in Ottawa. Tucker continues his investigations into large-scale onomastic databases in 'Reaney & Wilson Redux: An Analysis and Comparison with Major English Surname Data Sets' (*Nomina* 31[2008] 5–44), in which he compares statistically the contents of the first edition of Percy Hide Reaney's *A Dictionary of British Surnames*, published in 1958, with those of the third edition, revised by Richard Middlewood Wilson and updated in 1997. The contents of both were then compared with the names found in the 1881 Census of England and Wales and with the 1998 electoral roll of Britain. Tucker finds that Reaney's work, begun in the early 1940s and obviously without the assistance provided by the digital availability of large corpora and the data-handling capacity of desktop computers, corresponded remarkably well with the information found in the 1881 census (also not available to Reaney), matching 93 per cent of the names, covering more than

72 per cent of the population. The 1997 edition showed a match rate of 89 per cent with the census and 88 per cent with the electoral roll, but interestingly this latter covered only 77 per cent of the population, due in large part to what Tucker calls 'the surge in immigrant names' (*Nomina* 31[2008] 31). These are of considerable interest in their own right. Tucker appends a list of 100 surnames found in the electoral roll of 1998 but absent from the 1881 census. Patel, from Hindu and Parsi for 'village headman', is the most frequent of the non-traditional surnames (and is the forty-third most common name overall), followed by Begum (an honorific for a Muslim woman), Hussain, Bibi, Mistry, Iqbal, Malik, Bi, Uddin and Khatun.

The recent availability of large digital databases of names and their analysis by modern statistical methods have resulted in studies such as those of Tucker which have identified and elaborated patterns of incidence and relationships among names previously unknown or even suspected. Not only considerations of name etymologies, the evolution of names and the like are possible, but also possible are insights into more abstract social dimensions of naming. Looking at recent naming practices in the Netherlands and the UK from 1985 through the mid-2000s, Gerrit Bloothooft and Loek Groot of Utrecht University, in 'Name Clustering on the Basis of Parental Preferences' (*Names* 56[2008] 111–63), consider naming patterns within families. Starting from the premise that 'parents do not choose first names for their children at random (p. 111), Bloothooft and Groot find 'coherent sets of names that have a high probability to be found in the same family (p. 111). Given an older child's name, there is a likelihood that a sibling will have a name from the same name set or 'cluster' that was tapped into by the parents for the older child. Parents 'can choose names for all of their children from a single cluster, from one or more related clusters, but also definitely *not* from certain clusters' (p. 113). Names from Western and Arabic clusters are rarely if ever found in the same family, for instance. Names are shown to be linked in clusters and even in pairs. In the Netherlands, for instance, if an older brother is named Lars, the likelihood of his having a younger brother named Niels is more than four and a half times greater than the probability of finding the name Niels in general. In the UK the probability of an older brother Ben having a younger brother Sam is more than eight times greater than finding Sam in the general male population. And there are some provocative cross-cultural comparisons. The English name set consisting of Ann, Anna, Elizabeth, and Catherine corresponds directly to the Dutch set Anna, Elisabeth and Catharina.

The March 2008 *Names* was a special issue devoted to 'Names and Ethnicity', edited by American Name Society co-presidents, Don and Alleen Nilsen. The articles therein, as in any such collection, are highly varied and, rather than attempt to summarize all or even a few of the more substantial contributions, I will simply list the authors and titles of the essays dealing with English names and ethnicity so they can be retrieved by interested readers: Lindsey N. Chen, 'Ethnic Marked Names as a Reflection of United States Isolationist Attitudes in *Uncle $crooge* [*sic*] Comic Books' (*Names* 56[2008] 19–22); Cynthia Lyles-Scott, 'A Slave By Any Other Name: Names and Identity in Toni Morrison's *Beloved*' (*Names* 56[2008] 23–8); Frank Nuessel, 'A Note on Ethnophaulisms and Hate Speech' (*Names* 56[2008] 29–31);

Cleveland Kent Evans, 'A Note on US Immigrants' Choice of Baby Names' (*Names* 56[2008] 39–40); Karen Sands-O'Connor, 'After Midnight: Naming, West Indians, and British Children's Literature' (*Names* 56[2008] 41–6); Anjanette Darrington, 'A Note on Perceived Male/Female Differences in the Giving of Less-Than-Perfect Names' (*Names* 56[2008] 54–6).

Onomastics, as is often noted, is a discipline which knows few boundaries. Onomasts, people who investigate names and naming practices, come from many walks of life and from many persuasions and diverse academic disciplines—linguistics, literature, sociology and psychology come immediately to mind. But there are outliers as well, and practitioners in the outlying areas have contributed significantly to the growth of the field and the body of knowledge which has accrued to it. This in prologue to introducing an article by Ernest Abel, who is a professor in the Department of Obstetrics and Gynecology at Wayne State University in Detroit, Michigan. Abel's research has appeared several times in these annual summaries of onomastic research and it is a pleasure to welcome him once again, this time with his article 'Going to the Devil' (*Names* 56[2008] 95–105), co-authored with Michael L. Kruger, who contributed the statistical analyses. Abel and Kruger examined the distribution and designation of 'Heavenly' geographical names such as 'Heaven', 'Angel' and 'Chielo' versus 'Hellish' names such as 'Hell', 'Satan' and 'Diablo'. Overall, 'Hellish' place names were more frequent than 'Heavenly' names by more than three to one, especially for natural features such as mountains and lakes. As Abel and Kruger put it, '[T]he devil has the greatest fondness for canyons...followed by creeks...holes...dens...and kitchens.... [A]ngels have a similar preference for creeks...and canyons...but shun dens, holes, and kitchens,...gaps...and passes' (p. 100). And, as we might expect, these names are unevenly distributed, with a considerably higher percentage of 'Devil' and 'Hell' place-names in the southern and western states than in the rest of the country. Although 'Heavenly' and 'Hellish' names are generally found as the names of natural rather than artificial features, there have been at least two dozen communities in the US named 'Hell'. These include the well-known Hell's Kitchen area of New York City, the lesser-known Hellhole Palms in California (although it is hard for me to think of Hellhole Palms as ever becoming a major tourist destination), and the most famous of all Hells, Hell, Michigan, where the mayor's office gets a flood of enquiries every winter asking if, indeed, Hell has frozen over. (The local legend is that the founder of Hell, Michigan, George Reeves, was asked repeatedly what the name of the town was to be to the point where he piquedly replied 'you can call it Hell for all I care'.)

It is well known that George W. Bush is an inveterate nicknamer, giving nicknames not only to family and friends and those within his inner circle but also to political associates, members of the media and world leaders as well. Political strategist Karl Rove was Boy Genius when a plan of his succeeded and Turd Blossom or just Turd when one failed; former Attorney General Alberto Gonzales was Fredo, former Secretary of State Colin Powell was Balloonfoot; former UK Prime Minister Tony Blair was Landslide, and Russian president and later Prime Minister Vladimir Putin was Pooty-Poot. Michael Adams, in 'Nicknames, Interpellation, and Dubya's Theory of the

State' (*Names* 56[2008] 206–20), argues that Bush's obsession with tagging everyone with whom he interacts with a nickname is more subtle, more complex and more significant than it appears. Adams feels that nicknaming such as this is an act of interpellation as that term is used by the Marxist philosopher Louis Althusser, whereby the subject is the effect rather than the cause of social relations. Such nicknaming is far from innocent language play; rather it is a 'complex onomastic maneuvre . . . a means of "hailing" actors within the state and converting them into subjects of state ideology, which . . . collapses state authority and the executive power of the American presidency' (p. 206). Adams's premise is tightly and convincingly argued, and I highly recommend this article to anyone who feels that nicknaming is little more than innocuous linguistic bantering and that little can be gained from exploring its social (and political) context.

Marc Picard, in 'The Assimilation of English Surnames in French Canada' (*OnCan* 90[2008] 15–24), makes the important point that while large numbers of French names were modified under the influence of English, very few English names were modified because of contact with Canadian French. He lists, however, some forty English names (including anglicized Irish and Scottish) which were so affected, and these are quite remarkable as they illuminate a number of processes of linguistic change in multi-language communities, as when O'Brennan becomes Aubry, Perry becomes Perré, and Dicker becomes Dicaire.

For the past few years Donna Lillian has been tracking the fluctuation in the use of Ms as a courtesy title for all women, irrespective of marital status, corresponding to the use of Mr for men in general. In 'Ethnicity and Women's Courtesy Titles' (*Names* 56[2008] 231–8), Lillian reports on an online survey using ethnicity of respondents as the independent variable and the acceptability of addressing a woman with the title Ms as the dependent variable. Lillian presented respondents with descriptions of fifteen hypothetical women and asked how they would address the women so described (e.g. 'Elaine Parker is a 35-year-old lawyer, married to Alex Wilson. Would you address her as Miss Parker, Miss Wilson, Miss Parker-Wilson, Ms. Parker, Ms. Wilson, Ms. Parker-Wilson, Mrs. Parker, Mrs. Wilson, or Mrs. Parker-Wilson?'). Lillian reports a slight difference (which she calls tentative and to be approached with caution) whereby black respondents (who were overwhelmingly women) 'tend[ed] to prefer the more traditional titles Miss and Mrs. at a higher rate than Whites' (p. 231). This is an intriguing although preliminary result and one would hope a larger and more detailed investigation would allow more nuanced findings.

In a replication of an earlier study ('The Geography of Personal Name Forms', *Professional Geographer* 49[1997] 494–500), Edward Callary, in 'Presentation Names: Their Distribution in Space and Time' (*Names* 56[2008] 195–205), considers how politicians are increasingly choosing to present themselves through informal names—shortened versions of their full names, familiar forms, or nicknames—rather than formal names or initials as was common practice in the past. In the original study conducted in 1997 slightly more than 29 per cent of state legislators in the US used an informal name when interfacing with the public; by 2007 this number had increased to more than 35 per cent. The distribution was uneven, with informal names characteristic of most of the country except the north-east. The increasing use of informal presentation names was seen as part of a societal shift towards informality in language as well as behaviour in general.

9. Dialectology and Sociolinguistics

This year has seen its share of new, or new editions of, general textbooks that deal with sociolinguistics and/or variation studies. Janet Holmes's *Introduction to Sociolinguistics* is now in its third edition (first edition 1992), and the most notable change is the addition of a chapter on analysing discourse (chapter 14), arguably moving into some fields of pragmatics. Holmes takes a rather broad view of sociolinguistics, and the book is divided into more macro-sociolinguistic concerns (section A: 'Multilingual Speech Communities') before looking at more traditional variationist categories (section B: 'Language Variation: Focus on Users'), and at variation conceived of more widely (section C 'Language Variation: Focus on Uses'), where she deals with politeness, cross-cultural communication, gender, language and cognition, attitudes, and, as mentioned above, discourse analysis. The wide scope is laudable, but for a one-semester course probably too extensive. Nevertheless, since chapters are mostly self-contained, this book is very well suited for teaching, using only authentic examples, mostly deriving from Holmes's own extensive fieldwork, exercises interspersed with the text, including model answers, a collection of key words for each chapter and a helpful further reading section.

Martin Montgomery's *An Introduction to Language and Society* (also the third edition; first edition 1986) has a different focus in that his account also includes language learning (part I), a chapter on language and subculture concentrating on 'Anti-Language', and he discusses the rather contentious topic of 'Restricted and Elaborate Speech Variants' (chapter 7). What Montgomery calls 'Language and Social Interaction' (part III) again straddles the border between sociolinguistics more narrowly conceived, and pragmatics, and covers speech acts as well as discourse analysis. In part IV ('Language and Representation') more philosophical topics are dealt with, in particular universalist and relativist ideas about language and thought, but he also analyses 'The Vocabulary of Modern Warfare', and in particular (in 'After 9/11') language use in the 'war against terror'—not variationist topics per se, but clearly a relevant example of how to analyse the use of language in a society that will also fascinate students, and that replaces the older analyses of the language of the Cold War in earlier editions. Montgomery's book is less activity-centred than Holmes's and more text-based, but he does suggest follow-up activities after each chapter that are intended to consolidate the reading by applying the key concepts to example texts. With its different focus clearly this book will also find its readers.

Discourse Analysis is the topic of Barbara Johnstone's updated (second) edition (first edition 2002). She differs from other authors in that she regards discourse analysis not as a separate field of (socio)linguistics, but as a research method that might clearly be relevant beyond linguistic concerns (e.g. to cultural studies, anthropology, sociology, psychology, etc.), hinging on the multi-faceted use of *discourse*. Johnstone looks in particular at 'Discourse and World', also including a discussion of culture and ideology, and then examines constituting elements of discourse more specifically, such as 'Discourse Structure', 'Participants in Discourse', 'Prior Texts, Prior Discourses', 'Discourse and Medium' and 'Intention and Interpretation'. Johnstone's examples come from a wide variety of languages and cultures, and her text is clearly written with also a non-native English audience in mind. The chapters are regularly interrupted by discussion exercises that force readers to apply and reflect what they have read, and chapters are supplemented by a very helpful extended annotated further reading section. A very welcome new version of an excellent introduction to the field.

A general introduction to *Quantitative Methods in Linguistics* is provided by Keith Johnson this year. Himself a phonetician, Johnson guides the reader through working with the sophisticated (and free) statistics programme R, giving first an introduction to the 'Fundamentals of Quantitative Analysis' and 'Patterns and Tests' (chapters 1 and 2), while the following chapters contain working with 'real' data from several domains of linguistics, among them sociolinguistics (chapter 5). In particular, results from R are compared to Varbrul, and Johnson points out that a general statistics programme has several advantages over a specialist programme like Varbrul when it comes to general data handling, graphs, flexibility, etc. However, despite its claims that this book is 'an ideal text for students', it is hardly suitable for the beginner.

Quite the opposite can be said for the very basic introduction to *Language Matters* [2006] by Laurie Bauer, Janet Holmes and Paul Warren, which dedicates one of four parts to 'Language and Society'. Strangely, the first question the authors pose is related to language death; other topics they cover are address terms, gender differences, sexism, contextual variation (in a chapter called 'What Language Do You Use to Your Grandmother?') and regional variation ('Why Can't People in Birmingham Talk Right?'). As these chapter titles indicate, this text is aimed at the absolute beginner, but it makes entertaining and thought-provoking introductory reading nevertheless, appropriately with 'Some Points to Ponder' after each chapter. Probably quite suitable as a first approach to this (admittedly restricted) set of sociolinguistic topics if followed up by some more in-depth studies. That 'language matters' is also stressed in Jane H. Hill's detailed investigation of *The Everyday Language of White Racism*. Hill argues convincingly that racism is 'an active, productive and dynamic contemporary reality' of life in the US today, constituted by everyday discourse, indeed by people who would not describe or see themselves as racists. Hill shows the underlying mechanisms of this societal racism in 'The Social Life of Slurs'—ironically, any critical public debate (or ritualized routine) of the use of racial slurs also serves the purpose of keeping these words in active use: 'the very arguments over the word continually reinscribe both the label and the racializing stigma that it imposes', and even doubly ironically this is also what happens in this serious and disturbing book when Hill discusses racial slurs that may not be very well known outside the US. Similar to slurs, 'gaffes' also attract considerable attention in the media, where they are typically defended, or explained, as being uttered by someone who is not a racist 'really' (but as Hill correctly points out, 'one person's racial slur is the other person's gaffe'). Even more interesting, Hill also looks at 'Covert Racist Discourse: Metaphors, Mocking, and the Racialization of Historically Spanish-Speaking Populations in the United States', covert discourses being those that are not immediately visible as being racist, such as the (increasing?) use of mock-Spanish. Globally well-known examples include the Terminator's use of 'hasta la vista, baby', which requires access to the stereotype of Spanish speakers as treacherous and insincere, or the joking reference to 'cerveza' instead of 'a few glasses of beer', which accesses the nasty stereotype of the lazy Mexican, etc. (It is not quite clear in how far this mechanism is restricted to the US, since the use of Spanish carries quite different connotations in Continental Europe.) The actual use of Spanish on the other hand is often violently opposed in the US, under the heading of 'English First', 'English Only', or 'This is America, We Speak English Here'. Hill also notes that what sometimes goes under the label of lexical 'borrowing' might actually constitute a kind of theft—by 'reshaping the meaning of the borrowed material into forms that advance their own interest, making it useless or irrelevant, or even antithetical' to the donor community, and then imposing these new meanings in return on the donor speakers. As already said, a disturbing book, since its case is made convincingly, and therefore a must-read, not just for sociolinguists.

Sociolinguistics and Linguistic Anthropology is the title of a special issue of the *Journal of Sociolinguistics* (*JSoc* 12:iv[2008]) this year, edited by Mary Bucholtz and Kira Hall, a topic that is justified by the editors in their programmatic paper 'All of the Above: New Coalitions in Sociocultural Linguistics' (*JSoc* 12[2008] 401–31) and which can indeed be linked to Hill's book above since Bucholtz and Hall identify 'race talk in sociolinguistic interviews' as an exemplary area where the 'creative combinations of diverse methodological and conceptual tools' may be helpful, necessary or even indispensable for analysis, constituting the field they call socio-cultural linguistics. Penelope Eckert in the same issue discusses 'Variation and the Indexical Field' (*JSoc* 12[2008] 453–76), going back to Silverstein's notion of indexical order (as does Johnstone and Kiesling's analysis below). Eckert argues that variables constitute 'a [fluid] field of potential meanings' (p. 453) that inscribes ideology into language and that is used in return to constitute ideologies. To make this less abstract, she cites the well-known case of *-ing*, variably realized as /ɪn/, a variant that is (mistakenly) perceived as a reduced form (hence the popular denotation as G-dropping), and through this mistaken perception connotes lack of education, rebellion, laziness, but also relaxedness, easygoingness, or unpretentiousness (from this list it is already clear that the connotations differ in moral value, and can be situated in different locations in this indexical field). The advantage of grouping these evaluations in an indexical field is that it allows a more multi-dimensional analysis than, say, a two-dimensional analysis in terms of scales, or axes. The study Eckert refers to is actually Kathryn Campbell-Kibler's paper from last year (cf. *YWES* 88[2009] 93), expanded upon this year in 'I'll Be the Judge of That: Diversity in Social Perceptions of (ING)' (*LSoc* 37[2008] 637–59).

Again relating to her matched guise experiments, Campbell-Kibler concentrates on three speakers who elicited rather contradictory evaluations from different listeners (such as more intelligent *and* less intelligent; compassionate *and* condescending; less masculine *and* a 'jock'), or rather, while the variants are understood in a similar way, they are integrated differently into listeners' indexical fields (as either an actual reflection of speakers' traits, or the failed attempt to convey these traits), drawing our attention to the fact that 'listeners have options in how they engage with a sociolinguistic performance' (p. 645).

Much more critical is Beverley Skeggs in two contributions to Angel M.Y. Lin's edited book on *Problematizing Identity: Everyday Struggles in Language, Culture, and Education*. In 'The Problem with Identity' (pp. 11–34), Skeggs shows that identity is an unequal resource, basically centred on bourgeois middle-class white males (you may have guessed that this is a neo-Marxist analysis); only recently have white middle-class *females* also been permitted to participate in identity construction, but identity is necessarily based on 'exclusion, authority and morality' (p. 11). The point is important, since if 'race, class, or femininity as a resource only exists for those who are NOT positioned by it' (p. 25), then social constructivism will probably work only for the privileged. Returning to one of these factors, Skeggs also discusses 'Making Class through Fragmenting Culture' (pp. 35–47). Some elements of (working-class) culture are 'convertible and propertisable' (p. 44) and can thus be appropriated (Skeggs says 'plundered') in particular by the middle class, whereas others remain essentialized and fixed. This reviewer was left wondering whether this view of identity might explain the persistent pattern of language change from below.

The Milroys' important concept of social networks is refined and extended by Mieko Ogura and William S.Y. Wang in 'Dynamic Dialectology and Social Networks' (in Dossena, Dury, and Gotti, eds., *English Historical Linguistics*, pp. 131–51). The authors model different types of (idealized) networks (regular, random, small-world, or scale-free), developed in the field of network theory, and simulate processes of language change in them which show markedly different trajectories. These models in turn can be used diagnostically to throw light on historical processes of change, such as the ON influence on English (the result of massive immigration, as the authors claim), which patterns quite differently from the development of third person singular -*s* (resulting from a small-scale network in the north).

Sociolinguistic variation seems to play an increasing part in introductory textbooks on phonetics and phonology (and quite rightly so, we would want to add here)—one example is this year's *Practical Phonetics and Phonology: A Resource Book for Students* by Beverley Collins and Inger M. Mees (now in its second edition). As with other books in the series, this book is divided into four sections that are to be used more or less simultaneously, and it is section C, 'Exploration', that deals with accent variation—clearly a central topic for any self-respecting phonetician! The accents introduced are General American, as opposed to modern British NRP (not 'new RP' or 'non-RP', as one might think, but an abbreviation apparently of 'non-regional pronunciation', although we are not sure whether this term will have much of a future), various regional English accents, plus 'Celtic-Influenced Varieties', and 'World

Accent Varieties'. In fact, the tracks (available on the accompanying CD) include speakers from London, Bristol, Birmingham, Lancashire, Newcastle, Liverpool, Edinburgh, Dublin, Belfast and Glamorgan, whereas different American varieties are—slightly curiously—grouped with 'World Accents'—speakers here come from Texas, Kentucky and New York. This accent section alone is already worth purchasing the book for, as the collection of short, comparable audio samples is of very good quality and will be eminently useful in the classroom. (Also, the mini-narratives make rather addictive listening, so beware . . .) There are also interesting, well-thought-through activities, such as comparing 'Estuary English' with Cockney and 'NRP', or spotting the *interviewers'* dialects, that will be welcome additions to any class on varieties. Speaking of resources for the classroom, we also note here the paperback edition of Kortmann and Schneider's monumental *Handbook of the Varieties of English* of four years ago. Since the articles have remained completely unchanged, they will not be discussed in the individual regional sections again; the interested reader is referred to the detailed appraisal in *YWES* 85[2006]. What is worth knowing, however, is the attractive repackaging of the rather bulky (and prohibitively expensive) original hardcover volumes, which apparently also entailed a redistribution of editors. Instead of the two volumes (phonology vs. morphology and syntax), the articles are now ordered according to rough world regions, and the title *Varieties of English* is followed in each case by a regional subtitle. Thus volume 1, edited by Bernd Kortmann and Clive Upton, collects all articles (both on the phonology and the morphosyntax) on *The British Isles*, volume 2, edited by Edgar W. Schneider, is on *The Americas and the Caribbean*, volume 3, edited by Kate Burridge and Bernd Kortmann, is on *The Pacific and Australasia*, and volume 4, edited by Rajend Mesthrie, on *Africa, South and Southeast Asia*. Individual volumes can now be purchased separately, making this collection affordable even for students (as well as their lecturers). (In fact, the best deal is volume 2, since it is the longest with 800 pages of running text, while all cost the same!) Each volume also contains the CD with audio samples for all regions and extra material (although it has to be said that varieties here are rather unevenly covered), which makes this edition a fine resource for teaching advanced students.

Linking variation and the history of the English language (but also dealing with many other topics besides), the enormous *Companion to the History of the English Language*, edited by Haruko Momma and Michael Matto, contains fifty-nine(!) articles, almost 700 pages of text, and deals with some expected historical topics (e.g. on historical phonology, morphology, syntax, lexicon, on individual periods from the pre-history of English to present-day English), but also moves beyond these historical concerns. For instance, for each period there is also an article on language variation. Thus, Lucia Kornexl presents 'Topics in Old English Dialects' (chapter 16), Jeremy J. Smith discusses 'Varieties of Middle English' (chapter 19), and Jonathan Hope deals with 'Varieties of Early Modern English' (chapter 21). After EModE the sections are split between BrE and AmE. In the British section, Carey McIntosh deals with the 'long' eighteenth century until 1830, Richard W. Bailey with what is left over, before Lynda Mugglestone tries to cover 'The Rise of Received

Pronunciation' in no more than eight pages. (Remember she wrote a highly acclaimed monograph on the topic, cf. *YWES* 84[2003].) The section on AmE draws the dividing line slightly later at the Civil War, with David Simpson covering 'American English to 1865', Walt Wolfram dealing with 'American English Since 1865', and Gavin Jones covering 'American English Dialects'. After this historical overview, the *Companion* deals with various 'Topics in History', among them 'Issues of Gender in Modern English' by Deborah Cameron, a good introduction to the various facets of the topic, or the thorny issue of 'Class, Ethnicity and the Formation of "Standard English"' by Tony Crowley, where again different aspects of earlier chapters are taken up. Part VI then moves beyond England and the US and deals with English in Wales, Scotland and Ireland, and the overseas varieties of English in Canada, Australia and New Zealand, and in South Asia, in the Caribbean and in Africa—curiously almost completely without mentioning any distinguishing linguistic features. 'Literary Languages' is the topic of part VII, not so relevant to sociolinguistics, and part VIII deals with some more varieties: the development of AAVE (by Mary B. Zeigler), 'Latino Varieties of English' (by Robert Bayley), with learner varieties, with 'Creoles and Pidgins' (by Salikoko S. Mufwene), and with 'World Englishes in World Contexts' (by Braj B. Kachru). Under the heading of 'Further Approaches to Language Study' we finally also find an overview chapter of 'Sociolinguistics' (by Robin Tolmach Lakoff, no less), but also a chapter on style and stylistics, on corpus approaches, and on cognitive linguistics. As this overview already indicates, this *Companion* is quite a curious collection of diverse topics and to this reviewer it is not quite clear whether it can really serve as a 'meeting ground for students of language and literature', as the blurb claims. Certainly from a linguistic point of view, as general introductions, many chapters are too short and restricted (as an example, the chapter on AAVE contains one page summarizing its phonetic and morphosyntactic features, surely not doing justice to the intricacies of this variety, neither does the chapter on 'English in Scotland' or 'English in Ireland'; the chapter on 'English in Wales' even manages completely without linguistic features!). As an overview, this *Companion* is too long and internally diverse, as a course companion it is probably too expensive. Perhaps it is really meant as a book just sitting on your shelf, perhaps with other *Companions* in the series, looking impressive—this it does well.

Historical sociolinguistics proper is exemplified by Terttu Nevalainen's study on 'Social Variation in Intensifier Use: Constraint [*sic*] on *-ly* Adverbialization in the Past?' (*ELL* 12[2008] 289–315). With the help of data from the Corpus of Early English Correspondence, Nevalainen is able to close the gap between modern varieties (in the majority without *-ly* adverbs) and the standard (with obligatory use of *-ly* adverbs) by showing that the change in variable (dual) adverbs took place in the pre-normative era (i.e. before the eighteenth century) and, as Nevalainen puts it carefully, 'was not promoted by the lower end of the literate section of the language community' (p. 312), so can probably be regarded as one of the (rare) changes from 'above' in the history of English.

Turning now to studies concentrating on present-day Britain, Joan C. Beal asks whether you are "'Shamed by your English?'": The Market Value of a "Good" Pronunciation' (in Beal, Nocera and Sturiale, eds., *Perspectives on Prescriptivism*, pp. 21–40). Beal traces the recent resurgence of a demand for elocution lessons (that have been on offer basically since the eighteenth century) to changes in British society linked to the growth of the service sector, the culture of 'self-improvement', a more general backlash against the 1960s, especially in 'post-feminism', and a continuing discrimination against the 'underclass', as Beal writes: 'the last bastion of bigotry' where discrimination is not culturally frowned upon (yet?).

A general feature of English dialects is taken up by Peter Trudgill, who discusses 'English Dialect "Default Singulars", Was versus Were, Verner's Law, and Germanic Dialects' (*JEngL* 36[2008] 341–53). Trudgill claims that the interpretation of *was* as a default singular (e.g. by Chambers [2004]) 'has no explanatory value' (p. 342); instead, what we can observe is competition between *r*- and *s*-forms in the past tense paradigm of *be* (which also includes dialectal variants *war*, *wor* vs. *wiz*, *wuz*), which—at least in principle—can be levelled in either direction, as a comparison with other Germanic languages makes clear (this is where Verner's law comes in). Indeed, Trudgill claims that in dialects, *r*-forms were predominant until rather recently, and that the *s*-forms may have started out from London and the Home Counties, and have spread world-wide from there.

Historical dialects will perhaps in the future be easier to study with the help of an electronic version of Joseph Wright's monumental *English Dialect Dictionary* (originally published between 1898 and 1905, so too early for a *YWES* review), an undertaking that is currently under way in Innsbruck, Austria, under the guidance of Manfred Markus. He reports on this enterprise in 'Joseph Wright's *English Dialect Dictionary* Computerized: A Platform for a New Historical English Dialect Geography' (in Amano, Ogura and Ohkado, eds., *Historical Englishes in Varieties of Texts and Contexts*, pp. 335–53), certainly a resource we look forward to using once it is up and running.

Moving to regional studies more generally, Katie Wales prophesies 'Regional Variation in English in the New Millennium: Looking to the Future' (in Locher and Strässler, eds., *Standards and Norms in the English Language*, pp. 47–67), cautioning researchers against simply extending current trends into the future. In particular, Wales notes that the current predominance of London and the south-east is not God-given, and that variants can lie 'dormant' and emerge at different places at the same time. Relating to the north (quite generally speaking), Sali A. Tagliamonte proceeds with her 'Roots' project on comparing northern dialects in 'Conversations from the Speech Community: Exploring Language Variation in Synchronic Dialect Corpora' (in Nevalainen, Taavitsainen, Pahta and Korhonen, eds., *The Dynamics of Linguistic Variation: Corpus Evidence on English Past and Present*, pp. 107–28). She gives a quantitative analysis of verbal -*s*, causal conjunctions, relative clauses, necessity modals, stative possessives, and future reference (yes, all in twenty pages) and claims that despite surface differences, 'internal linguistic constraints are typically shared' across the Scottish, northern English and Northern Irish varieties under investigation, due to their common history. Inter-dialectal differences are due to the differential speed with which individual changes proceed in the speech communities, and Northern Ireland in particular comes out as a very conservative dialect area—something that we could only suspect before, but now have evidence of.

Raymond Hickey deals with rather the reverse, 'Feature Loss in 19th Century Irish English' (in Nevalainen et al., eds., pp. 229–43), due to the emergence of a native middle class in Ireland in the nineteenth century, which produced a more supra-regional variety of Irish English, more influenced by southern British forms and in particular, Hickey claims, by prescriptive middle-class judgements. Arguing in the same vein, Hickey also discusses 'Exceptions to Sound Change and External Motivation' (in Dossena et al., eds., pp. 185–94). Both historically in the emergence of a more supra-regional variety of Irish English and at present, with the evolution of the trendy 'Dartspeak', speakers' motivation is the dissociation (becoming dissimilar) from vernacular (working-class) Dublin English, as evidenced by the failure of complete lenition in general Irish English, and non-retraction of vowels before /r/ today (as in the emblematic 'Dortspeak' (pronounced today as 'Dartspeak').

Moving to the new subfield of *Variational Pragmatics* (to quote the title of a new collection of essays, edited by Klaus P. Schneider and Anne Barron this year), Anne Barron analyses 'The Structure of Requests in Irish English and English English' (pp. 35–67) on the basis of a text production questionnaire administered to twenty-seven schoolgirls in Ireland and the same number of schoolgirls in southern England. Both groups of speakers use few imperatives (as perhaps might be expected in an English-language community), but the Irish girls use more mitigation and perhaps even more indirectness than the English informants. In the same volume, Anne O'Keeffe and Svenja Adolphs count 'Response Tokens in British and Irish Discourse: Corpus, Context and Variational Pragmatics' (pp. 69–98) and find that BrE speakers use them far more, whereas the Irish use more items involving religious reference, or swear words—an intriguing result that would call for an analysis in terms of the wider cultural differences between the two countries.

English and Celtic in Contact is discussed in much more detail by Markku Filppula, Juhani Klemola and Heli Paulasto. In the monograph of just this title, the authors try to counter the common impression that Celtic has only had minimal influence on English. They trace possible Celtic influence through time and identify a large number of standard and non-standard areas of English morphosyntax where an analysis in terms of contact with Celtic languages seems plausible, if not compelling. Countering what they call 'the ideology of Anglo-Saxonism' (p. 2) prevalent in historical studies since the nineteenth century, in chapter 2, 'The Linguistic Outcomes of the Early Contacts', they trace the stem of the verb *be* to Celtic influences, as well as the rise of the progressive, DO-periphrasis, clefting, reflexivization, and internal possessor constructions for PDE, and the non-standard features of zero relatives, the Northern Subject Rule, the (northern) use of comparative *nor*, and south-western pronoun exchange—admittedly all constructions that make English and its varieties markedly different from other Germanic languages. For each feature, alternative accounts are carefully discussed. Chapter 4 becomes more regional since it discusses 'The Linguistic Outcomes of the Modern Contacts', in particular common features of the 'Celtic Englishes', concentrating on the divergent definite article use, absolute use of reflexive pronouns, extended use of the progressive, different perfect markers, habitual markers, lack of inversion in polar questions, focusing constructions, prepositional usage, as well as some phonological and lexical features. The authors concede that modern influences can best be observed in the contact varieties but claim that 'the CEs [Celtic Englishes] may well have provided a springboard for the spread of these features into other varieties of English, mediated through generations of emigrants to Britain, America and other parts of the world' (p. 219). In the light of this partly new, partly old evidence the authors call for a 'reassessment of the extent of Celtic influence on English' (p. 244) more generally, making this book a most welcome, well-argued contribution to a very controversial area of variationist linguistics these days. Also in a separate publication, Markku Filppula claims that 'The Celtic Hypothesis Hasn't Gone Away: New Perspectives on Old Debates' (in Dossena et al., eds., pp. 153–70), presenting some of the book-length arguments in a condensed form. In particular, Filppula cautions the reader against looking for evidence of language contact in the wrong places, since a paucity of Celtic loanwords is expected, given the circumstances. However, English contains many 'odd' morphosyntactic constructions that make it distinctly un-Germanic and that 'cannot be satisfactorily explained as independent developments' (p. 155), such as internal possessor constructions, periphrastic *do*, the progressive, and cleft-constructions. One other construction, the Northern Subject Rule, is taken up by Nynke de Haas in the same volume. Haas discusses 'The Origins of the Northern Subject Rule' (in Dossena et al., eds., pp. 111–30), offering additional textual evidence for substrate influence from Cumbrian for this construction, arguing against Lukas Pietsch's internally motivated explanation of several years ago (cf. *YWES* 86[2005]). Indeed, Pietsch seems to have come around; at least he sets the Irish *after*-perfect in relation to other similar 'Prepositional Aspect Constructions in Hiberno-English' and also in Irish Gaelic (in Siemund and Kintana, eds., *Language Contact and Contact Languages*, pp. 213–36), claiming that 'interlingual identification' of similar constructions across languages was at work here, supporting and strengthening these constructions in both languages. Moving more specifically to Mid-Ulster English, Una Cunningham instrumentally investigates 'Vowel Quality and Quantity in the English Spoken in Rural Southwest Tyrone' (*NIS* 7[2008] 41–55), a transitional zone between the Ulster Scots north-east, and the southern Irish English. The four young rural speakers (all siblings) she investigates show striking evidence of the Scottish Vowel Length Rule (or Aitken's Law), merge GOOSE with FOOT, and sometimes pronounce *pull* with /ʌ/, a quite frequent (though stigmatized) pronunciation.

A non-Celtic contact zone is found in the very north of Scotland on the Shetland and Orkney islands, and Sebastian Seibert's study of the *Reception and Construction of the Norse Past in Orkney* makes interesting complementary reading to the few linguistic studies there are to date. Seibert concentrates on the cultural construction of a Norse heritage up to the present day, but references to the distinct linguistic variety of Orkney are unfortunately missing—apart from a few marginal remarks on intonation and rhythm—although they could obviously be linked well to his overall argument. As if complementing Seibert, Robert McColl Millar tries to shed light on 'The Origins and Development of Shetland Dialect in Light of Dialect Contact Theories' (*EWW* 29[2008] 237–67). He employs Trudgill's dialect formation model and claims that the dialect we encounter in the Shetland Islands today was formed in the nineteenth century from an earlier *koiné* based on Scots, but also heavily influenced by Norn. This explains the, at first glance, rather unexpected presence of some southern Scots features in this otherwise Northern Scots variety.

Dealing with mainland Scots, Lynn Clark 'Re-Examin[es] Vocalic Variation in Scottish English: A Cognitive Grammar Approach' (*LVC* 20[2008] 255–73), which, Clark argues, can incorporate sociolinguistic patternings. Clark investigates (au) as in OUT, undergoing OUT-fronting in Scotland, and (o) as in COT or COAT, undergoing a merger or near-merger. Interestingly, 'the monophthong variant is used more often in words that occur more frequently' (p. 262), whereas (o) is more variable. Nevertheless, speakers can choose to select linguistic variants to 'project social meaning' (p. 269).

Mark J. Jones and Carmen Llamas connect Ireland and Northern England and look at 'Fricated Realizations of /t/ in Dublin and Middlesbrough English: An Acoustic Analysis of Plosive Frication and Surface Fricative Contrasts' (*ELL* 12[2008] 419–43). From this acoustic analysis, the authors conclude that although fricated /t/ is distinctive (compared to other plosives) in both cities, it is not identical: in Dublin English, fricated /t/ has more in common with /ʃ/, whereas in Middlesbrough it is more similar to /s/. Middlesbrough fricated /t/ is therefore probably not a transfer feature of Irish immigrants, but an independent development.

Judith M. Broadbent investigates '*t*-to-*r* in West Yorkshire English' (*ELL* 12[2008] 141–68), stereotypically depicted in set phrases like *shurrup* (for *shut up*) or *gerroff* (for *get off*). Broadbent argues that this stigmatized feature is fossilized today and restricted to a few lexemes, but was productive during the nineteenth century. (Wells presents it as the reinterpretation of a tap or flap, not unlike US American T-flapping.) Broadbent links the decline to the increase in T-glottalling which would 'overshadow *t*-to-*r* usage' (p. 141). Where it does persist, this is probably due to usage frequency.

Coming to our favourite quotative, *be like*, this qualifies as undergoing what Isabelle Buchstaller calls 'The Localization of Global Linguistic Variants' (*EWW* 29[2008] 15–44). In particular, Buchstaller investigates *be like* and quotative *go* and compares the original US development with data from the English towns of Derby and Newcastle from the 1990s, a time when *be like* is reported to enter British varieties. Buchstaller shows how speakers on the one hand participate in global trends and use *be like* and *go* in largely similar ways for mimesis or reporting linguistic material, and on the other hand adapt the variants to their local needs and 'creatively adapt ... linguistic innovations' (p. 15). Thus, British speakers can use *go* with an explicit addressee (*and she's going **to me**: 'will you speak to her today?'*), and *like* can also be used with *say* (*and then you **say like** ...*), whereas US speakers prefer the collocation *feel like*.

Similarly (and as reported before), the social evaluations are not imported wholesale. In this way, Buchstaller claims, 'the surface form...indeed globalizes but their social and functional realities are re-created by localized groups of speakers' (p. 37).

The south of England is not often the subject of a detailed variationist study, but this year an exception to this rule is represented by Christina Laurer's investigation of L-vocalization in *Poor Paul: L Vocalisation and the Process of Syllable-Coda Weakening*. (The language play of the title hinges on concomitant vowel changes that make *poor* and *Paul* homophones in this variety.) The vocalization of post-vocalic dark /l/ is a purported (and much criticized) feature of Estuary English, and Laurer investigates the geographical spread on the basis of data from 124 interviews in seven southern counties. Interestingly, the rate of L-vocalization does not correlate with region in her data. L-vocalization is led by men, and by younger speakers, but social class is not relevant in her data either, nor is the formality of the situation. In terms of intra-linguistic context, most of the expected phonetic correlations again do not hold (however, it would have been interesting to have a multi-variate analysis here of the many different variables to test for cross-dependencies). This may be an indication that L-vocalization has moved beyond the stage of being a noticeable innovation and has become a rather unmarked general feature of the south of England. Staying with the south, London vowels are the subject of Paul Kerswill, Eivind Nessa Torgersen and Sue Fox in 'Reversing "Drift": Innovation and Diffusion in the London Diphthong System' (*LVC* 20[2008] 541–91). In particular, they look at the diphthongs in PRICE, MOUTH, FACE, and GOAT, diphthongs that are undergoing the London vowel shift but now seem to show 'diphthong shift reversal' (p. 541) in the direction of variants resembling RP, caused by social forces such as contact with ethnic minorities, dialect contact, and gender (again we see one of the rare cases where males lead this development).

Even further south lies a dialect area not, to our knowledge, studied much so far: the British enclave of Gibraltar. This oversight is set right this year by David Levey's monograph on *Language Change and Variation in Gibraltar*. Levey takes the reader through the socio-historical background of the area and then spends two chapters on the phonetics and phonology of this variety, one chapter declining Gibraltarian (yes, that is the adjective) vowels, one concentrating on consonants. Obviously, the interesting question is the question of possible transfer from Spanish, since most speakers only come into contact with English in school, and indeed Spanish influence can be detected in older speakers in vowel mergers of KIT-FLEECE, FOOT-GOOSE, BULL-TOOL and LOT-THOUGHT, and features like a short START vowel, a front vowel in NURSE, and the non-reduction of LETTER. Interestingly, for vowels the traditional local pronunciations seem to be on the wane, giving way to more 'British' pronunciations. Similarly in the field of consonants, potential areas of transfer seem to be in the process of convergence with BrE norms, such as a labiodental realization of /v/, voiced TH or the realization of /r/. One noticeable difference that persists is clear /l/ in all positions. In the realm of consonants, even some non-standard BrE features are taken over, such as vocalized L, TH-fronting or T-glottalling. Apparently, the change towards a more British norm is led by the (more mobile) middle class.

Across the ocean, Stefan Dollinger contributes an in-depth study of the development of English modals in the formative period of CanE in the monograph *New-Dialect Formation in Canada: Evidence from the English Modal Auxiliaries*, testing Trudgill's thesis of new-dialect formation. Dollinger looks in particular at Ontario English between 1776 and 1850, when the two main waves of immigration (first by American loyalists, arguably the 'founder' population in Mufwene's terms, and then by English immigrants) took place. Based on the *Corpus of Early Ontario English*, consisting mainly of letters, diaries and newspapers, Dollinger investigates in detail the modals *can/could, may/might, must, have to, shall, will, should, would* and *ought to* and compares results to BrE (and, more marginally, AmE) control corpora. Dollinger finds that *can* and *may* 'are subject to drift' both in CanE and BrE (p. 191), *can* being used more in negative, *may* in positive contexts. *Have to* patterns more with AmE than with BrE and is thus a progressive feature, making statements of wholesale 'colonial lag' difficult to maintain. The prescriptive distinction between *will* and *shall* (used only in the first person singular) is not maintained; probably the high number of immigrants from Scotland, Ireland and northern England, who did not have this distinction in their dialects, 'swamped' the loyalists in this case. *Would* specialized as 'the modal auxiliary in hypothetical contexts' (p. 266), whereas *should* was increasingly disfavoured. Dollinger stresses that, at least based on these modals, 'no simple statement as to the conservatism or progressivism of the modal auxiliaries seems possible' (p. 272), and Peter Trudgill's model of new-dialect formation (e.g. Trudgill [2004]) probably has to be modified in his stage I to include 'extreme variability' (p. 280). Dollinger also discusses modals in 'Taking Permissible Shortcuts? Limited Evidence, Heuristic Reasoning and the Modal Auxiliaries in Early Canadian English' (in Fitzmaurice and Minkova, eds., *Studies in the History of the English Language IV: Empirical and Analytical Advances in the Study of English Language Change*, pp. 357–85). Dollinger exemplifies his heuristic with the modals *can* and *may*, which, being involved in slow change, do not reach sufficient token frequencies for shorter time spans, but we can infer the direction of change from present-day situations. (However, as Dollinger points out, this method cannot discover reversals of trends.)

Present-day CanE is the subject of Hélène Blondeau and Naomi Nagy, who investigate 'Subordinate Clause Marking in Montreal Anglophone French and English' (in Meyerhoff and Nagy, eds., *Social Lives in Language: Sociolinguistic and Multilingual Speech Communities: Celebrating the Work of Gillian Sankoff*, pp. 273–313). In particular, they investigate the use of *that* vs. zero as complementizer (and the equivalent *que* in the speakers' L2 French). This is an interesting comparison since COMP-deletion is unmarked in English, but stigmatized in French. The detailed phonological, syntactic and lexical analysis reveals that speakers seem to have separate grammars for the two languages. In an interesting addition, the authors also find that *like* occasionally functions as a complementizer, a lexeme that this chapter regularly traces in its quotative use. In just an aside, quotative *like* (of course also used by self-respecting younger Montrealers) seems to be making inroads in their L2 French in the shape of *comme*, and may even currently be spreading to L1 French there.

Intensifiers, recently much studied, are taken up (again) by Sali A. Tagliamonte, who thinks they're 'So Different and Pretty Cool! Recycling Intensifiers in Toronto, Canada' (*ELL* 12[2008] 361–94) because they are undergoing rapid language change—however, not as 'part of a continual longitudinal process' (p. 361), but in a cyclical movement. In particular, *very* is declining rapidly, especially with speakers under 50, whereas *really* shows the opposite development, with *so* and *pretty* as minority variants. Interestingly, *so* is promoted by young females, while *pretty*, contrary to expectations, is promoted by young male speakers—perhaps a reaction against female-dominated *so*, a form that, according to Tagliamonte, has been 'lurking in the corners and cubby-holes of the grammar' in order to 'come and go and come again' (p. 391).

Pronunciation is the concern of Charles Boberg, who discusses 'Regional Phonetic Differentiation in Standard Canadian English' (*JEngL* 36[2008] 129–54). Based on data from eighty-six middle-class speakers, Boberg refines and alters data from the *Atlas of North American English* (*ANAE*; =Labov, Ash and Boberg [2006], cf. *YWES* 87[2008]) and proposes splitting the 'Inland Canada' region into a western and an eastern half, resulting in six Canadian accent areas: British Columbia, the Prairies, Ontario, Quebec, the Maritimes, and Newfoundland. The distinguishing factors are, in particular, the Canadian Shift, the MARY-MERRY-MARRY merger, /ahr/-fronting (e.g. in *car* or *hard*), and /æ/-raising (before nasals as opposed to before velars). Some of these are stable features, but the Canadian Shift and /uw/ fronting in particular seem to be changes in progress. It would be fascinating to see a similar investigation repeated for working-class speakers, since this might relativize the accepted wisdom of Canada having no interior variation even further. Speaking of *ANAE* and vowel shifts (definitely the most discussed topic of the year!), William Labov discusses the rather general topic of 'Triggering Events' (in Fitzmaurice and Minkova, eds., pp. 11–54), claiming, probably uncontroversially, that 'th[e] sequence of preceding causes is not a smooth and uniform sequence' (p. 11). Taking six chain shifts as the basis (the Canadian Shift, the Pittsburgh Shift, the Northern Cities Shift [NCS], the Southern Shift, the Back Upglide Shift, and the Back Chain Shift before /r/), Labov tries to find internal reasons, the main one being the low back merger, that can be argued to set in motion the Pittsburgh and the Canadian shifts. /uw/ fronting was perhaps caused by YOD-dropping and the collapse of /iu/ and /u:/. The NCS on the other hand is traced by Labov to a *koiné* formed in New York State, then expanding westward along the Erie Canal.

Adrian Pablé takes the reader 'From "Standard" to "Nonstandard" Grammar: New England in the Days of *Salem Witchcraft* and the Civil War' (in Locher and Strässler, eds., pp. 105–26), basically claiming that many (morphosyntactic) forms that are today considered non-standard in American English have only become so relatively recently, whereas they are regularly attested in early colonial New England and at the time of the Civil War. Some examples of these morphosyntactic constructions are finite *be*, non-concord *was* and -*s*, unmarked tensed verbs, third person singular *don't*, verb paradigm levelling, unmarked plurals, demonstrative *them*, adverbs without *-ly* (remember Nevalainen's discussion above), *a*-prefixing of participles, and subject relative zero. Unfortunately this short study is little more than an enumeration, but it can give a first indication that the general non-standard features we find today in varieties of AmE (and, incidentally, BrE) are probably due to a common source and are historical retentions.

Barbara Johnstone and Scott F. Kiesling discuss 'Indexicality and Experience: Exploring the Meanings of /aw/-Monophthongization in Pittsburgh' (*JSoc* 12[2008] 5–33). Interestingly, the perception of /aw/-monophthongization as a marker (or index) of local speech does not go together with the actual use of this feature, at least not in the same speakers, which suggests that hearer-meaning and speaker-meaning may be quite distinct, perhaps even harking back to Skegg's cautioning analysis of identity work above. In fact, Johnstone and Kiesling explicitly exclude a social constructivist analysis, claiming that 'the people who do monophthongize in unselfconscious speech may not link monophthongal /aw/ with local identity and so cannot be monophthongizing to express or claim such an identity' (p. 23), a result which surely calls for more careful sociolinguistic interpretations generally. Robin Dodsworth investigates a phenomenon that 'resists traditional sociolinguistic explanations', /o/-fronting in Worthington, Ohio, and proposes instead 'Sociological Consciousness as a Component of Linguistic Variation' (*JSoc* 12[2008] 34–57). /o/-fronting patterns only weakly according to age, sex, or attitude towards the locality. Instead, the results correlate with 'sociological consciousness', i.e. 'the ability to conceive of connections between personal experiences and social structures or processes' (p. 46), and speakers who have this ability in this study tend not to use the very local variants. (Granted, there are only two of them.) Matt Bauer and Frank Parker investigate '/æ/-Raising in Wisconsin English' (*AS* 83[2008] 403–31)—a feature of the Midwest in particular before velars, such that *bag* is perceived as *beg*. The authors can show experimentally that, contrary to received dialectological wisdom, this is not an incidence of a merger, but rather /æ/ is raised due to co-articulation. The same phenomenon is taken up by Thomas C. Purnell in 'Prevelar Raising and Phonetic Conditioning: Role of Labial and Anterior Tongue Gestures' (*AS* 83[2008] 373–402), who supports and extends Bauer and Parker's analysis: even in non-raising speakers, /æ/ before velars is more anterior and has 'statistically significant lip repositioning associated with the raising gesture' (p. 373) (for these two *AS* articles, see also section 3).

Moving further west, David Bowie discusses the 'Acoustic Characteristics of Utah's *Card–Cord* Merger' (*AS* 83[2008] 35–61), which necessitates an analysis of F1, F2 and F3 formants to distinguish merged from unmerged instances. Bowie tentatively puts forward the suggestion merged that this might be due to the 'simultaneous manipulation of multiple articulatory features' by speakers (or, to be more precise, the one Utahn [yes, that is the adjective] under investigation), which clearly calls for more research. Valerie Fridland moves to the desert and investigates back vowel fronting, more specifically 'Pattern of /uw/, /ʊ/, and /ow/ Fronting in Reno, Nevada' (*AS* 83[2008] 432–54). Fronting in the BOOT, BOAT and BOOK vowels is sometimes linked to Californian 'Valley Girl' talk and is in fact found in particular in the ten younger speakers under investigation here, with the BOOT class most advanced. Fridland argues that back vowel fronting is internally motivated and thus 'of a truly global nature' (p. 448) and is not directly linked to back vowel fronting in the South, as might perhaps be suspected (for these two articles, see also section 3).

The internal dialect geography of California, or rather its perception, continues to play a role in Mary Bucholtz, Nancy Bermudez, Victor Fung, Rasalva Vargas and Lisa Edwards's contribution on 'The Normative North and the Stigmatized South: Ideology and Methodology in the Perceptual Dialectology of California' (*JEngL* 36[2008] 62–87), building on last year's investigation (cf. *YWES* 88[2007] 91), and again a hot contender for the prize for the most co-authors! Whereas last year's article was based on map-labelling tasks, this year's paper concentrates on an evaluation of open-ended questions eliciting evaluative judgements. The clear stigmatization of the Californian south can perhaps be linked to a (perceived) 'lack of education and access to English' (p. 69), as the authors claim, but this seems to be a polite way of referring to the presence of Chicano English speakers, and to the stigmatized southern neighbour Mexico, harking back to Hill's investigation of societal racism above. Indeed this fits well with answers that can be grouped under the heading of 'I'm not a racist but . . .'. Dialect perception, this time by Nevadans, but of the South, is also discussed by Valerie Fridland in 'Regional Differences in Perceiving Vowel Tokens on Southerness [*sic*], Education, and Pleasantness Ratings' (*LVC* 20[2008] 67–83). Fridland compares results from Reno informants (on Southern vowel-shifted speakers and non-vowel-shifted speakers) with her informants from Memphis, Tennessee (i.e., Memphians). She finds that the recognition of southernness, not surprisingly, has 'traveled far outside the South' (p. 80) and that the Reno informants are in fact better at recognizing shifted vowel variants, irrespective of actual experience of (other) regional dialects.

Allison Burkette looks at three verb paradigms in '"The Lake Frozed Over": Non-Standard Past Tense Forms in LAMSAS and LAGS' (*SJoL* 32[2008] 60–82), namely *freeze*, *blow*, and *rise*, and examines in particular the social distribution of core and peripheral responses. The most frequent responses (after the StE forms) were the regularized *blowed* or *freezed* (but doubly marked forms like *blewed* or *frozed*, or unmarked forms like *blow* or *freeze* also occur). For *freeze* Burke also finds the minority variants *friz* and *frizzed*, paralleled by *riz*, which was in fact the majority non-standard choice. In geographical terms, the most non-standard forms are found in rural areas, used by men and women alike (although there seem to be subtle gender factors in the choice of variant), and clearly related to educational status, although even here some non-standard variants persist with higher education. Maciej Baranowski deals with 'The Fronting of the Back Upgliding Vowels in Charleston, South Carolina' (*LVC* 20[2008] 527–51). As Baranowski claims, Charleston 'has lost most of the distinctive features of the traditional dialect' (p. 527), including the traditional feature /ow/ and /uw/. Instead, /ow/ (as in GOAT) and /uw/ (as in GOOSE) are fronted. GOOSE- and GOAT-fronting is clearly led by the highest status group, leading Baranowski to claim that GOAT-fronting is an instance of change from above, i.e. introduced from outside the speech community. These changes result in making Charleston more like the general south-eastern 'superregion' (p. 546). The differences between Charleston and the 'Deep South' also play a role in William A. Kretzschmar Jr's introductory article on 'Language in the Deep South: Southern Accents Past and Present' (*SoQ* 45[2008] 9–27), clearly written with a lay audience in mind. In a very personal way, Kretzschmar presents traditional and changing features of a 'Southern' accent, and distinguishes Plantation from non-Plantation speech. His paper includes many anecdotes and popular references, encouraging readers that 'there is absolutely no need to apologize for one's accents' (p. 18). Moving to the Appalachians in West Virginia, Kirk Hazen analyses '(ING): A Vernacular Baseline for English in Appalachia' (*AS* 83[2008] 116–40). Contrary to popular perceptions, the sixty-seven speakers under investigation do not use the alveolar variant invariably; this variable patterns according to gender (with women slightly in the lead), social class and region (internally), confirming the stereotype in so far as southern Appalachians had a higher rate of /ɪn/ than northern ones (in West Virginia). Kirk Hazen and Sarah Hamilton also discuss 'A Dialect Turned Inside Out: Migration and the Appalachian Diaspora' (*JEngL* 36[2008] 105–28), comparing the language of family members who moved from West Virginia to Ohio and Michigan, to those who stayed behind. In particular, they investigate eighteen phonological and seventeen(!) morphosyntactic features and find gradience across speakers. Clearly, migrants retain many features, but better educational opportunities also play a role here, so that the authors can show that 'Appalachian migrants negotiate their sociolinguistic identities by drawing on the norms both of their family members and of their adopted homes' (p. 105). This in turn might influence Appalachia as many migrants eventually return and bring new norms with them.

The theme of migration is also taken up by Bridget L. Anderson, who looks at language change (or lack of it) in *Migration, Accommodation and Language Change: Language at the Intersection of Regional and Ethnic Identity*; in particular she investigates the vowel systems in (descendants of) Southern migrants in Detroit, both black and white. Crucially, the variables under investigation behave in very different ways: /ai/ monophthongization is still employed to index local orientation to the South and has even expanded in linguistic contexts, whereas /u/ fronting is found in many more varieties of English world-wide and is therefore not as useful (and, consequently, abandoned) to index a non-Midwestern identity. Anderson proposes that this (Hickey would say: dissociation) is the main motivation behind the continuing distinctiveness of black and white Appalachian migrants in Detroit: they do not want to sound like white Midwesterners, but are oriented to Southern culture in many ways, one of which is linguistic. (The question remains: how do speakers know that /u/ fronting is used much more widely in English varieties around the world, given that they have probably never met speakers from South Africa, New Zealand, or southern Britain?) Nevertheless, Anderson's study is an impressive reminder that language ideologies may play an important part in language change. Also discussing AAE in a 'northern' town, Maeve Eberhardt concentrates on 'The Low-Back Merger in the Steel City: African American English in Pittsburgh' (*AS* 83[2008] 284–311), a phenomenon also known as the *cot-caught* merger. This is noteworthy because this feature has so far been reported to be a white feature, but Eberhardt can show that the thirty-four African American native Pittsburghers(?) under investigation here share this pan-American development—in contrast to /aw/-monophthongization discussed by Johnstone and Kiesling above (see also section 3).

Earlier AAE is discussed by Gerard Van Herk in 'Letter Perfect: The Present Perfect in Early African American Correspondence' (*EWW* 29[2008] 45–69). In nineteenth-century letters from Liberian settlers investigated here, the present perfect occurs surprisingly frequently, whereas preverbal *done* is most noticeable by its absence. Van Herk proposes that the perfect may be a genre feature (caused by the 'news-giving function' of letters). Since the linguistic factors governing the choice of the present perfect (vs. the simple past) match those of historical varieties of English, Van Herk's paper can be seen as support for an English origin of earlier AAE. The contrary position is defended by Arthur Spears. He gives a new summary of those features of AAVE that could be called 'creolisms' in 'Pidgins/Creoles and African American English' (in Kouwenberg and Singler, eds., *The Handbook of Pidgin and Creole Studies*, pp. 512–42), although he is careful to stress that he uses this term only to relate to parallels in form and meaning and does not necessarily imply 'claims of creole sources'. In his list, we find features like disapproving *come* and *go*, the associate plural *and them*, stressed BIN, absence of 3sg -*s* and possessive -*s*, absence of plural marking on nouns, auxiliary *done*, habitual *be*, *be done*, remote BIN, unstressed *been*, copula absence, complementizer *say*, and the use of bare nouns (another impressive list this year). Spears points out that as camouflaged forms, many of these forms may have gone undetected in their specific creole meanings, which, despite his initial claim of form-function parallels only, 'suggests interesting possibilities for formulating new hypotheses on AAE origins' (p. 536). One of Spears's items is also taken up by Chris Collins, Simanique Moody and Paul M. Postal in 'An AAE Camouflage Construction' (*Language* 84[2008] 29–68), although their analysis is not a sociolinguistic one, and indeed they do not use *camouflage* in Spears's meaning! The construction the authors analyse is the metonymic *ass* construction as in *I saw his ass* [=*him*] *yesterday*, where, they claim, the possessor behaves as if it were external to the construction on some criteria, but internal on some others, a phenomenon that is relatively well attested across languages, but little studied so far. Although this study does not shed light on AAE as such, it is surely important to note that AAE data has found its way into very mainstream theoretical discussions these days.

Jacquelyn Rahman discusses a group of speakers not frequently under investigation, 'Middle-Class African Americans: Reactions and Attitudes toward African American English' (*AS* 83[2008] 141–76), employing subjective reaction tests, interviews, and an online questionnaire. Not surprisingly, since these speakers have to 'function in a number of vastly distinct social worlds', their attitude to AAVE is rather ambivalent; on the one hand, it is seen as their heritage language, and speakers 'value and appreciate their ethnic identity' (p. 144), and using Standard English is denigrated as 'talking white'; on the other hand these speakers are clearly aware of the heavy stigmatization that goes hand in hand with using AAVE. A form of standard AAE could be an alternative, since it combines standard grammar with a 'moderate' use of AAVE phonological features and manages to convey ethnically identifiable speech that at the same time 'meets establishment requirements' (p. 170).

An ethnic dialect that has encountered at least some discussion before, although not on the same scale as AAVE, is Lumbee English, the variety of a group of Native American speakers who have long ago lost their native language. Chris Scott and Kathleen Brown this year discuss 'Rising Above my Raisin'? Using Heuristic Inquiry to Explore the Effects of the Lumbee Dialect on Ethnic Identity Development' (*AIQ* 32[2008] 485–521). Heuristic Inquiry distinguishes phases (initial engagement, immersion, incubation, illumination, explication, creative synthesis, and validation of the heuristic inquiry), and Scott and Brown apply these phases to the very personal development of identity construction of Scott, a Lumbee Indian, and some other speakers from this community. Scott and Brown do not concentrate on the linguistic features themselves, but on the changes speakers undergo from realizing that they spoke rather differently and were often the laughing stock in class, to a lack of interest in matters ethnic, to (in this case) turning the insider position into an academically rewarding research project. But also for non-linguists, the painful 'transition to and experience in college often result in identity transformation' (p. 509), a transformation one can only hope results in as much pride in the ethnic heritage as shown in this article.

One study this year focuses explicitly on the variable 'age'. This is Federica Barbieri's article on 'Age-Based Variation in American English' (in *JSoc* 12[2008] 58–88). It is slightly ironic (probably unintentionally so) that she bases her analysis of 'linguistic variation across the life span' (p. 59) on a *synchronic* corpus of natural speech, covering varying age groups. Investigating a large number of lexico-grammatical features, Barbieri finds that 'stance is a more prominent feature of the language of the youth' (p. 78); this includes the use of slang, inserts, polite speech-act formulae, first and second person reference, attitudinal adjectives, intensifiers, or discourse markers. However, Barbieri does not address the question whether we are looking at change in progress, or age-grading for these features (and indeed, the answers might be different from feature to feature). Teenagers more specifically are the subject of Sali A. Tagliamonte and Derek Denis's article on 'Linguistic Ruin? Lol! Instant Messaging and Teen Language' (*AS* 83[2008] 3–34), drawing on an impressive corpus of over a million words of instant messaging, and comparing this with authentic colloquial interactions by the same participants. Rather than ruining 'the' language, Tagliamonte and Denis show that instant messaging (IM) is 'firmly rooted in the model of the extant language' (p. 25). The much-maligned abbreviations (like the stereotypical *lol* for 'laughing out loud' in the title) are strikingly rare (together they do not make up more than 3 per cent of the corpus). An analysis of innovative features like intensifier *so* and quotative *be like*, and of still ongoing changes like the *going to* future and deontic *have to* shows that IM is essentially a hybrid medium that 'mixes innovative trends alongside an overarching conservative nature' (p. 18), and that teenagers might 'abandon the "funky" IM features at a very young age' (p. 24). Stance is also expressed differently by men and women, or so Kristen Precht claims in 'Sex Similarities and

Differences in Stance in Informal American Conversation' (*JSoc* 12[2008] 89–111). The 180 stance expressions she investigates cannot be enumerated here for obvious reasons of space, but it is important to note that her investigation is one of the few to date that combine large-scale computer corpora and gender. And of course she wins the prize for highest number of features investigated, hands down! Interestingly, Precht finds no significant differences between men's and women's use of affect, evidentiality or quantification (except in the use of expletives)—but this of course does not mean that we do not perceive as different what may, in fact, be identical.

The field of gender has now also brought forward a *Beginner's Guide to Language and Gender*, by Allyson Jule, and as the title implies this book is really very short, at just over a hundred pages, and very, *very* basic. It introduces the reader to some general ideas in gender studies, looks at gender in the media, in education, in the workplace, in church and in relationships and thus has a clearly non-variationist focus. The chapters are short (between nine and fifteen pages) and are summarized by three statements each. After each summary, three discussion points ask the reader to consider some possible applications of what she has read. However, many important sociolinguistic aspects are left out, which makes this book(let) too short to be really useful in class at university level.

More academic in nature and more comprehensive is Kate Harrington, Lia Litosseliti, Helen Sauntson and Jane Sunderland's edited collection of papers on *Gender and Language Research Methodologies*. The book shows the rich diversity of the field, covering more traditional approaches like 'Sociolinguistics and Ethnography', 'Corpus Linguistics', or 'Conversation Analysis', but also including articles on 'Discursive Psychology', 'Critical Discourse Analysis', 'Feminist Post-Structuralist Discourse Analysis' and 'Queer Theory'. Each approach is laid out in an introductory chapter and then exemplified by several contributions drawing on contributors' own empirical work. This collection thus puts the approaches themselves at the centre, something that was (to a large degree) left implicit in Holmes and Meyerhoff's *Handbook of Language and Gender* [2003] (cf. *YWES* 84[2005]). This collection makes fascinating reading in itself and can, in part or in whole, be sincerely recommended for classroom use.

Helene A. Shugart and Catherine Egley Waggoner are *Making Camp: Rhetorics of Transgression U.S. Popular Culture*. Contrary to expectations, their book deals with female camp artists, 'Xena', Karen Walker, Macy Gray and Gwen Stefani (who represent the 'Camped Crusader', 'Drag Hag', 'Venus in Drag' and 'Camp Vamp' respectively). 'Camp' is characterized as the exaggerated, ostentatious, outrageous, artificial performance of hyper-femininity obviously displayed visually, but also by linguistic means, and the authors' detailed analyses of the construction of female camp in these four cases is insightful and convincing, and calls for an investigation of female camp in more narrowly linguistic investigations too. One such linguistic investigation (though not of the female camp) is Veronika Koller's study on *Lesbian Discourse: Images of a Community*, where she traces the shift in the lesbian community in Britain and the US from the 1970s to today. According to Koller, the 1970s saw the creation of the lesbian community, linked to feminist concerns; the 1980s were characterized by challenges to that community by minority groups that felt excluded, e.g. butch/femme couples, S/M advocates, or older working-class women, curiously pre-empting discussions in queer theory decades later; the 1990s, according to Koller, saw 'Contradicting Voices within the Community', with a fragmentation of the community, and inter-generational conflict, but also the commercialization of lesbianism, embodied for example in glossy lifestyle magazines; whereas the 2000s are in many instances characterized by the importation of 'corporatism and consumerism' (p. 148). Koller analyses a variety of paradigmatic texts using Critical Discourse Analysis, relating the close linguistic analysis back to wider socio-political developments.

Finally, Mary Bucholtz investigates 'Shop Talk: Branding, Consumption, and Gender in American Middle-Class Youth Interaction' (in McElhinny, ed., *Words, Worlds, and Material Girls: Language, Gender, Globalization* [2007], pp. 371–402). Bucholtz argues that rather than a deterministic top-down view, researchers should pay attention to teenagers' inside perspective on branding and consumption since these commodities are employed to 'make, and make sense of their social world' (p. 373), and in a rather local way. Examples are white (middle-class) boys who appropriate African American hip hop style, engaging with global brands in ways not necessarily envisaged by the makers, or a group of nerd girls who reject trendy consumerism. Interestingly, in the group of high-school teenagers Bucholtz investigates, all are oriented to middle-class values, so that upper-class children tend to dress down, and working-class children tend to dress up, often wearing more expensive brand-name clothing than upper-class children. Bucholtz makes it quite clear that rather than the actual brands, it is the discourse about brands, shopping and consuming that shapes adolescents' view of themselves and others. In this way, 'gendered youth styles were simultaneously classed and racialized' (p. 394).

10. New Englishes and Creolistics

There are a number of book-length publications on English as a world language this year which are all geared towards a textbook audience. My personal favourite is *World Englishes: The Study of New Linguistic Varieties* by Rajend Mesthrie and Rakesh M. Bhatt because of the very sound and transparent discussion of the structural properties of the New Englishes, based on recent research in the field. After a more theoretical introduction dealing with the spread of English, models of English and the native-speaker debate, the authors discuss the morphology and syntax of the New Englishes, their lexis and phonology, but also discourse-related features, such as speech acts, cross-cultural discourse, literary discourse and code-switching at length and with many illuminating examples. Two further chapters explore issues of language contact and language acquisition with regard to the New Englishes and English-based pidgins and creoles, as well as current trends in the spread of English, such as developments in the expanding circle, the role of the call-centre industry and other global players. All chapters are accompanied by study questions and suggestions for further reading, and the glossary in the appendix will also be very useful for a student readership.

The textbook on *Cultures, Contexts and World Englishes* by Yamuna Kachru and Larry E. Smith also discusses shared features of the New Englishes, but places a much stronger emphasis on discourse, text type and cultural background, as can be gleaned from chapters on conversational interaction, interaction in writing, or World Englishes literatures. The two introductory chapters focus on the present-day situation of English as a world language and a more general introduction to the principles of pragmatics, with a focus on discourse analysis, politeness and intelligibility. This textbook contains fewer examples but is also supplemented by suggestions for further reading and activities.

Andy Kirkpatrick's textbook *World Englishes: Implications for International Communication and English Language Teaching* [2007] is firmly rooted in a sociolinguistic framework and takes a more traditional approach, presenting individual varieties from the British Isles, the United States, Australia, South Asia, Africa and South-East Asia. There is also a chapter on English as a lingua franca, especially in the context of ASEAN and the EU. A summary of key themes and some thoughts on implications on teaching round off this very readable textbook. In the appendix, readers can access the transcripts of the soundtracks from the accompanying CD-ROM, which include interviews and readings of poetry.

The paperback textbook edition of Kortmann et al., eds., *Handbook of Varieties of English* [2004] (cf. *YWES* 85[2006] 86–7) has made this extremely useful reference work more accessible to a wider readership. In contrast to the two-volume hardback edition, the present edition is organized into four volumes according to region. Each volume is prefaced by a general introduction outlining the organization of the collection and the features discussed in the contributions. This is followed by an introduction on the region presented in the volume and rounded off by two synopses summarizing the most characteristic features of the varieties spoken there. While the first volume *Varieties of English: The British Isles*, edited by Bernd Kortmann and Clive Upton, is probably of less interest to those working on World Englishes, the other three volumes certainly offer the same insightful and lucidly written contributions on the phonology and morpho-syntax of a large number of standard and non-standard varieties as the hardback edition. The second volume, *Varieties of English: The Americas and the Caribbean* is edited by Edgar W. Schneider and covers a large number of North American varieties, including Gullah, as well as Jamaican Creole, the eastern Caribbean varieties, Bajan, and the creoles of Trinidad, Tobago and Suriname. In the third volume, edited by Bernd Kortmann and Kate Burridge, the *Varieties of English: The Pacific and Australasia* are presented, including various varieties of AusE and NZE, as well as the pidgins and creoles from Vanuatu, the Solomon Islands, Papua New Guinea, Hawai'i, Fiji, Pitcairn and Norfolk. Rajend Meshtrie has edited the fourth volume, *Varieties of English: Africa, South and Southeast Asia*, dealing with the varieties spoken in Nigeria, Ghana, Liberia, Cameroon, East Africa, South Africa, St Helena, India, Pakistan, Singapore, Malaysia and the Philippines. The textbook edition is also accompanied by an interactive CD-ROM with sound samples and maps showing the distribution of individual linguistic items. Additional features of this edition, which will be appreciated by students and scholars alike, are the exercises and study questions at the end of each contribution and the list of 'General References' (pp. 8–22), a selection of classic studies on varieties of English around the world. Unfortunately, the editors have not seen fit to remedy the gaps in the coverage, with regard to both the contributions and the sound samples on the CD-ROM, which were pointed out in the review of the 2004 edition. Nevertheless, this more affordable edition will enable a larger number of interested linguists to include this important reference work in their personal library.

A number of articles deal with the globalization of English. David Crystal provides 'Two Thousand Million? Updates on the Statistics of English' (*EnT* 24:i[2008] 3–6) in comparison to an earlier publication from 1985, and also ventures some predictions on the structural consequences of the increased number of speakers world-wide. Rajend Mesthrie reassesses Braj Kachru's model of 'English Circling the Globe' (*EnT* 24:i[2008] 28–32), pointing out changes since the first publication of the concentric circles model in 1988. Philip Sergeant examines the interplay of 'Language, Ideology and "English within a Globalized Context"' (*WEn* 27[2008] 217–32), cautioning linguists to pay close attention to the relationship between politics and language in the study of English as a world language as they are inextricably linked.

A number of studies also deal with individual features of the New Englishes. Thomas Biermeier presents a study of *Word-Formation in New Englishes: A Corpus-Based Analysis* using data from the ICE from Great Britain, New Zealand, East Africa, Jamaica, India, Singapore and the Philippines. Setting out to discover quantitative and qualitative differences with regard to the productivity of common English word-formation processes, Biermeier encounters the problem of how to discover instances of, for example clippings or endocentric compounds in the corpora. He proceeds by selecting certain test items, for example frequent prefixes and suffixes or parts of compounds, but also by running searches for two-letter sequences in the hope of turning up interesting forms. While this shows certain trends which characterize individual varieties in terms of word-formation preferences, overall there are immense difficulties in accounting for all forms, especially if the author is not familiar with certain varieties. For example, Biermeier claims that the Jamaican English form *bandoolooism* means 'sale of illegal overseas phone-calls' (p. 84), but a look into any recent Jamaican reference work would have told him that *bandooloo* is any kind of scam or illegal activity. Similarly, the clipping *lab* for *Labrador (dog)* is widespread among dog-lovers in the English-speaking world and not particularly noteworthy when encountered in the Philippine corpus (p. 149). However, despite these shortcomings, Biermeier's study illustrates that the ICE corpora are also useful tools for investigations into the lexicon.

Peter Collins examines 'The Progressive Aspect in World Englishes: A Corpus-Based Study' (*AuJL* 28[2008] 225–49) on the basis of American corpus data and nine ICE corpora from ENL and ESL countries and comes to the conclusion that according to the variables under analysis (functions,

contractions, verb semantics, grammatical environment), the southern hemisphere varieties take the lead with regard to the spread of the progressive,
while the other varieties tend to pattern into regional groups. Andrea Sand
looks at 'Morphosyntactic Parallels in Englishes around the World' (in
Thormählen, ed., *English Now: Selected Papers from the 20th IAUPE
Conference in Lund 2007*, pp. 248–66) on the basis of six ICE corpora and
two corpora of Irish English, pointing out striking similarities in subject–verb
concord and interrogative patterns between the contact varieties under
analysis.

Two further publications focus on aspects of World Englishes that have
been quite neglected so far. Peter Trudgill explains 'The Role of Dialect
Contact in the Formation of Englishes' (in Locher and Strässler, eds.,
pp. 69–83) and provides a plausible explanation for the presence of a feature
like Canadian raising in colonial Englishes from Tristan da Cunha to the
Bahamas. Sarah Ogilvie is 'Rethinking Burchfield and World Englishes' (*IJL*
21[2008] 23–59), and comes to the conclusion that Charles Onions, rather than
Robert Burchfield, who was considered by many 'the champion of World
Englishes', included most lexemes from the New Englishes in the *OED*.

As in 2007, a large number of publications this year deal with the use of
English as a lingua franca (ELF). *English as a Lingua Franca: A Corpus-Based
Study* by Luke Prodromou is concerned with the uses and functions of multi-
word units and idioms by native speakers and highly competent speakers of
ELF. His very thorough analysis is based on a corpus of 200,000 words from
twenty-four speakers from various European and South American countries
which he compared to a North American corpus of conversation and the
BNC. Prodromou provides an excellent survey of previous research and
presents his data in a very readable way. While there are definitely differences
between the L1 and the L2 speakers represented in his study, he succeeds in
showing that the L2 speakers are by no means deficient in putting their point
across and using the English language creatively.

Mario Saraceni's article 'English as a Lingua Franca: Between Form and
Function' (*EnT* 95:ii[2008] 20–6) criticizes current ELF research, especially the
underlying assumption that ELF is most often used in interactions of non-
native speakers. Alessia Cogo counters Saraceni's arguments in 'English as a
Lingua Franca: Form Follows Function' (*EnT* 95:iii[2008] 58–61), pointing
out the common ground of present ELF research. Anna Mauranen and Elina
Ranta provide a brief update of 'English as an Academic Lingua Franca—the
ELFA Project' (*NJES* 7[2008] 199–202), presenting research presently under
way in Finland on the basis of a million-word corpus of ELF in academic
contexts. Allan James discusses 'New Englishes as Post-Geographic Englishes
in Lingua Franca Use: Genre, Interdiscursivity and Late Modernity' (*EJES*
12[2008] 97–112), applying Critical Discourse Analysis and Bakhtinian notions
of genre to examples from ELF corpora to show how genre and
interdiscursivity interact in ELF discourse.

Three articles are concerned with specific linguistic features of ELF.
Christiane Meierkord investigates 'Coherence Devices in the Englishes of
Speakers in the Expanding Circle' (in Kraft and Geluykens, eds., *Cross-
Cultural Pragmatics and Interlanguage English* [2007], pp. 201–19), such as

conjunctions which are reanalysed as discourse markers. Juliane House examines '(Im)Politeness in English as Lingua Franca Discourse' (in Locher and Strässler, eds., pp. 351–66) by presenting three case studies which illustrate the irrelevance of native-speaker politeness norms in ELF communication. Andy Kirkpatrick investigates 'English as the Official Working Language of the Association of Southeast Asian Nations (ASEAN): Features and Strategies' (*EnT* 24:ii[2008] 27–34).

A number of publications are concerned with the issue of intelligibility in World Englishes and ELF. Cecil L. Nelson reviews studies and concepts of 'Intelligibility since 1969' (*WEn* 27[2008] 297–308), illustrating a shift in research from attention to native-speaker norms to the demands of intercultural communication. Yamuna Kachru discusses the cultural factors relevant for the interpretability of utterances in her article 'Cultures, Contexts, and Interpretability' (*WEn* 27[2008] 309–18). Margie Berns compares views on intelligibility expressed by researchers working within the ELF and the World Englishes paradigm in her article 'World Englishes, English as a Lingua Franca, and Intelligibility' (*WEn* 27[2008] 327–34), coming to the conclusion that they do not have much in common, as their underlying attitude towards variability and varieties is very different.

Matthew Watterson investigates 'Repair of Non-Understanding in English in International Communication' (*WEn* 27[2008] 378–406) on the basis of videotaped data of Korean and Mongolian ELF speakers followed by interviews eliciting the participants' degree of comprehension in various sequences of the recorded data analysed according to CA methodology. Watterson discusses a number of verbal and non-verbal strategies of signalling non-understanding and the following negotiation of meaning. Paroo Nihalani discusses 'Globalization and Multicultural Communication: Unity in Diversity' (*RELC* 39[2008] 242–61), arguing on the basis of quantitative acoustic data from various expanding, outer- and inner-circle varieties that intelligibility is not so much hampered by phonetic differences as by intonation. As a consequence, she recommends no longer using RP or GAm phonetic features as teaching standards in outer- and expanding-circle countries.

As in previous years, we will begin the survey of the individual varieties with those from the southern hemisphere. We welcome the publication of Daniel Schreier's *St Helenian English: Origins, Evolution and Variation*, which sheds some light on a variety spoken in the South Atlantic, of whose development and present form very little is known so far. Schreier has conducted extensive fieldwork on the island and also analysed a large number of historical documents from its archives. He is thus able to trace the development of St Helenian English since the eighteenth century and account for its present-day structure and internal variation. As Schreier's informants were all born before the Second World War, the study covers the twentieth century, but the question remains as to how far recent socio-economic changes have affected the variety since. Schreier presents a very careful account of his data and typological accounts of other varieties of English, and concludes by stating that St Helenian English may be classified as a creole on the basis of its development and present features, albeit one relatively low on the cline of 'creoleness'. A much shorter account of the development of St Helenian English by Daniel Schreier can also be found in his chapter on 'Non-Standardization' (in Locher and Strässler, eds., pp. 85–103).

Continuing with AusE, the bulk of publications this year deal with issues of pronunciation. Seyed Ghorshi, Saeed Vaseghi and Qin Yan provide a 'Cross-Entropic Comparison of Formants of British, Australian and American Accents' (*SpeechComm* 50[2008] 564–79) on the basis of large speech databases. Jeanette McGregor and Sallyanne Palethorpe discuss 'High Rising Tunes in Australian English: The Communicative Function of L* and H* Pitch Accent Onsets' (*AuJL* 28[2008] 171–93) on the basis of data produced by four adolescents from the same peer group in an interactive speech-production task. They found that high-rising tones are significantly more frequent in their data than in previous studies of AusE and fulfil a number of discourse functions, such as providing information and checking understanding. Marija Tabain reports on the 'Production of Australian English /ʉː/: Language-Specific Variability' (*AuJL* 28[2008] 195–224), considering acoustic and articulatory data from three speakers of AusE. Kimiko Tsukada provides 'An Acoustic Comparison of English Monophthongs and Diphthongs Produced by Australian and Thai Speakers' (*EWW* 29[2008] 194–211), showing significant differences in the production of diphthongs between these two speaker groups. Jennifer Price investigates 'New News Old News: A Sociophonetic Study of Spoken Australian English in News Broadcast Speech' (*AAA* 33[2008] 285–310), showing that the former RP-oriented speech of newscasters in Australia has been replaced by a range of accents since the 1950s, including Broad Australian and—in the case of some commercial stations—even American-sounding intonations.

Two articles deal with discourse features of AusE. Marie-Eve Ritz and Dulcie Engel examine '"Vivid Narrative Use" and the Meaning of the Present Perfect in Spoken Australian English' (*Linguistics* 46[2008] 131–60) on the basis of stories recorded from radio chat-shows and news reports. They find that speakers of AusE often replace the narrative present with the present perfect, especially when the verb in question is durative and contains a process part. Tania E. Strahan looks at '"They" in Australian English: Non-Gender-Specific or Specifically Non-Gendered?' (*AuJL* 28[2008] 17–29) in essays written by first-year university students. She found that the students also use *they* when the gender of the referents is known but irrelevant in the present context.

There are also a number of publications concerned with Australian Aboriginal English. Diana Eades's study of *Courtroom Talk and Neocolonial Control* is a very careful investigation into how speakers of Aboriginal English are systematically disadvantaged in Australian courts because of the different communicative strategies employed by them. The study draws on the micro-analysis of legal cross-examinations and interviews conducted with three juvenile speakers of Aboriginal English in a court hearing in Queensland in 1994, but also includes a very detailed analysis of the relationships between Aboriginal and white Australians, especially with regard to interaction in the courtroom.Michael Walsh also examines '"Which Way?" Difficult Options for Vulnerable Witnesses in Australian Aboriginal Land Claim and Native Title

Cases' (*JEngL* 36[2008] 239–65), pointing out similar communicative problems of Aboriginal witnesses as discussed by Eades. Andrew Butcher provides information on 'Linguistic Aspects of Australian Aboriginal English' (*CLP* 22[2008] 625–42), discussing phonetics and phonology, grammar and lexis in comparison to non-standard English, the Australian creoles and Australian Aboriginal languages. Finally, Patrick McConvell looks at 'Language Mixing and Language Shift in Indigenous Australia' (in Simpson and Wigglesworth, eds., *Children's Language and Multilingualism: Indigenous Language Use at Home and School*, pp. 237–60), examining various social contexts for code-switching between indigenous languages and English, code-mixing or language shift in Australia.

Moving on to New Zealand, there is still an ongoing scholarly debate about the origins of NZE. David Britain asks 'When Is a Change Not a Change? A Case Study on the Dialect Origins of New Zealand English' (*LVC* 20[2008] 187–223), examining the diphthong /au/ in great detail on the basis of contemporary conversational data from various social and ethnic groups in comparison with historical data. He argues that the present realizations of the vowel are not the result of language change, but rather of dialect levelling of earlier variants. Peter Trudgill puts forward a claim about 'Colonial Dialect Contact in the History of European Languages: On the Irrelevance of Identity to New-Dialect Formation' (*LSoc* 37[2008] 241–54), using evidence from other languages to refute claims about the origins of NZE. His contribution is followed by a number of responses and a rejoinder by Peter Trudgill, providing a lively debate on the role of identity in dialect formation in general and in the case of NZE in particular. Salikoko S. Mufwene discusses 'Colonization, Population Contacts, and the Emergence of New Language Varieties: A Response to Peter Trudgill' (*LSoc* 37[2008] 254–8), Donald N. Tuten explores 'Identity Formation and Accommodation: Sequential and Simultaneous Relations' (*LSoc* 37[2008] 259–62), Edgar W. Schneider compares 'Accommodation versus Identity? A Response to Trudgill' (*LSoc* 37[2008] 262–7) and Nikolas Coupland looks at 'The Delicate Constitution of Identity in Face-to-Face Accommodation: A Response to Trudgill' (*LSoc* 37[2008] 267–70). Laurie Bauer, 'A Question of Identity: A Response to Trudgill' (*LSoc* 37[2008] 270–3), as well as Janet Holmes and Paul Kerswill, 'Contact Is Not Enough: A Response to Trudgill' (*LSoc* 37[2008] 273–7), particularly refer to the situation in New Zealand. Finally, Peter Trudgill writes 'On the Role of Children, and the Mechanical View: A Rejoinder' (*LSoc* 37[2008] 277–80).

Four publications are concerned with the syntax and pragmatics of NZE. Joan Bresnan and Jennifer Hay report on 'Gradient Grammar: An Effect of Animacy on the Syntax of *Give* in New Zealand and American English' (*Lingua* 118[2008] 245–59). They compare the probability of the double object construction versus the prepositional dative after *give* on the basis of a large number of syntactic and semantic features, coming to the conclusion that while there are similarities between AmE and NZE, the NZE speakers appear to be more sensitive to animacy in this context. Sabine Jautz compares 'Gratitude in British and New Zealand Radio Programmes: Nothing but Gushing?' (in Schneider and Barron, eds., *Variational Pragmatics: A Focus on*

Regional Varieties in Pluricentric Languages, pp. 141–78) on the basis of data from the BNC and the Wellington Corpus. She comes to the conclusion that speakers of both varieties are polite, but use different strategies in different contexts in the discourse. Finally, Shie Sato examines the 'Use of "Please" in American and New Zealand English' (*JPrag* 40[2008] 1249–78) on the basis of conversational corpus data, coming to the conclusion that while there are differences with regard to the various forms of occurrence and the preferred position of *please* in these two varieties, the functions in the various positions are quite similar.

The ethnolects of NZE have also received some scholarly attention this year. Margaret Maclagan, Jeanette King and Gail Gilson introduce 'Maori English' (*CLP* 22[2008] 658–70), presenting the history of the variety as well as its phonetics and phonology, morpho-syntax and pragmatics and their implications for language testing and speech therapy in New Zealand. Donna Starks discusses 'National and Ethnic Identity Markers: New Zealand Short Front Vowels in New Zealand Maori English and Pasifika Englishes' (*EWW* 29[2008] 176–93), showing that the pan-ethnic label 'Pasifika' is problematic as all the ethnic groups under analysis differed with regard to the realization of this vowel set. Meredith Marra and Janet Holmes investigate 'Constructing Ethnicity in New Zealand Workplace Stories' (*Te&Ta* 28[2008] 397–419) and show how Maori New Zealanders use stories in a work-related meaning to co-construct ethnic group identity. Donna Starks, Laura Thompson and Jane Christie wonder 'Whose Discourse Particles? New Zealand *eh* in the Niuean Migrant Community' (*JPrag* 40[2008] 1279–95) and conclude that Niuean speakers of NZE use this particle less frequently than the other ethnicities analysed so far.

Moving on to Asia, Kingsley Bolton addresses 'English in Asia, Asian Englishes and the Issue of Proficiency' (*EnT* 24:ii[2008] 3–12), surveying the development of English in both outer- and expanding-circle countries in Asia. Beginning my review of work on individual Asian Englishes with India, I would like to point out the very positive evaluation of *Biliteracy and Globalization: English Language Education in India* by Viniti Vaish. The author has conducted a long-term qualitative study at a state-run English-medium school in New Delhi and shows how teachers and students use strategies like translation, code-switching or code-mixing to cope with the multilingual environment. A much more critical view of 'English in India: The Privilege and Privileging of Social Class' (in Tan and Rubdy, eds., *Language as Commodity: Global Structures, Local Marketplaces*, pp. 122–45) is presented by Rani Rubdy, who considers English a means of closing off the elite in India. Rakesh M. Bhatt analyses the use of Hindi in English newspapers in India in his article 'In Other Words: Language Mixing, Identity Representations, and *Third Space*' (*JSoc* 12[2008] 177–200) on the basis of a newspaper corpus spanning five years, showing how code-mixing and code-switching are employed to create a distinctly Indian communication style.

With regard to South-East Asian Englishes, it is Hong Kong English phonology and prosody which has received most scholarly attention this year. Winnie Cheng, Chris Greaves and Martin Warren present *A Corpus-Driven Study of Discourse Intonation* based on a prosodic transcription of the Hong

Kong Corpus of Spoken English. They employ Brazil's Discourse Intonation system to analyse four different genres, namely academic discourse, conversation, business and public communication. The book is accompanied by a complete listing of all quantitative data and a CD-ROM containing the complete corpus along with the specifically designed retrieval software, *iConc*. As the corpus contains utterances by Hong Kong Chinese speakers as well as native speakers of English from various countries, it offers the opportunity to compare the two groups. For example, it was found that the Hong Kong speakers make a wider use of level tone. These analyses are particularly interesting as Cantonese, their L1, is a tone language and has long been considered to influence the local variety of English in terms of intonation. It is thus most surprising that overall the patterns of discourse intonation of the two groups are remarkably similar.

David Deterding, Jennie Wong and Andy Kirkpatrick provide a detailed description of 'The Pronunciation of Hong Kong English' (*EWW* 29[2008] 148–75) on the basis of data recorded from fifteen undergraduate students, looking at features such as consonant clusters, /l/-vocalization or the realization and reduction of vowels. Jane Setter investigates 'Consonant Clusters in Hong Kong English' (*WEn* 27[2008] 502–15) and their underlying phonotactics, showing that Hong Kong English speakers produce fewer syllable types than BrE speakers. Andy Kirkpatrick, David Deterding and Jennie Wong also report on 'The International Intelligibility of Hong Kong English' (*WEn* 27[2008] 359–77). They played recordings of six Hong Kong English speakers to university students in Singapore and Australia and found that overall intelligibility was unproblematic despite L1-interference from Cantonese. Lian-Hee Wee compares 'Phonological Patterns in the Englishes of Singapore and Hong Kong' (*WEn* 27[2008] 480–501) within a generative framework, focussing on /l/-vocalization and tone assignment.

Arto Anttila, Vivienne Fong, Štefan Beňuš and Jennifer Nycz discuss 'Variation and Opacity in Singapore English Consonant Clusters' (*Phonology* 25[2008] 181–216), showing very convincingly the interaction of phonology and morphology in the realization of clusters. Jock Wong compares 'Anglo English and Singapore English Tags: Their Meaning and Cultural Significance' (*P&C* 16[2008] 88–117) within Wierzbicka's framework of natural semantic meta-language, focusing on the Singaporean English tag *is it* and its equivalents in other varieties of English. Peter K.W. Tan and Daniel K.H. Tan examine 'Attitudes towards Non-Standard English in Singapore' (*WEn* 27[2008] 465–79) with the help of a questionnaire survey among secondary-school students, including a matched-guise experiment. They find that while StE is held in high esteem, the non-standard variety, Singlish, is favourably rated in terms of intimacy and identity. Viniti Vaish reports on 'Mother Tongues, English, and Religion in Singapore' (*WEn* 27[2008] 450–64) on the basis of the 2006 Sociolinguistic Survey of Singapore, showing that while the so-called mother tongues (Tamil, Malay and Mandarin) dominate in the domain of religion, English is dominant in the workplace, education and the public sphere and competes with the mother tongues in the sphere of friendship and family. Rani Rubdy, Sandra Lee McKay, Lubna Alsagoff and Wendy D. Bokhorst-Heng investigate 'Enacting English Language Ownership in the Outer Circle: A Study of Singaporean Indians' Orientations to English Norms' (*WEn* 27[2008] 40–67) on the basis of an acceptability judgement test administered to Singaporeans of various social backgrounds and education levels. The results show significant differences between younger speakers who use English also in the private sphere, and older speakers whose use of English is restricted to very few formal contexts. Lionel Wee discusses 'Linguistic Instrumentalism in Singapore' (in Tan and Rubdy, eds., pp. 31–43), mainly concentrating on the government's language policy. Chng Huang Hoon ventures 'Beyond Linguistic Instrumentalism: The Place of Singlish in Singapore' (in Tan and Rubdy, eds., pp. 57–69), presenting the government's attempts to eradicate the use of Singlish and the various functions it fulfils for its speakers.

Hajar Abdul Rahim presents 'The Evolution of Malaysian English: Influences from Within' (in Manan and Sinha, eds., *Exploring Space: Trends in Literature, Linguistics and Translation*, pp. 1–19) in a corpus-based study of local lexis which is based on sections of ICE-Malaysia which is currently being compiled. Peter K.W. Tan presents 'The English Language as a Commodity in Malaysia: The View through the Medium-of-Instruction Debate' (in Tan and Rubdy, eds., pp. 106–21). Stefanie Pillai is concerned with 'Speaking English the Malaysian Way—Correct or Not?' (*EnT* 96[2008] 42–5), and discusses the pedagogical implications of the development of a characteristic Malaysian accent of English.

To round off this section on Asian Englishes, there are two publications on the varieties spoken in Macau and on the Philippines. Andrew Moody introduces 'Macau English: Status, Functions and Forms' (*EnT* 24:iii[2008] 3–15), a lesser-known variety which functions as a de facto official language in this rather small special administration region. Finally, T. Ruanni F. Tupas discusses 'Anatomies of Linguistic Commodification: The Case of English in the Philippines vis-à-vis Other Languages in the Multilingual Marketplace' (in Tan and Rubdy, eds., pp. 89–105).

With regard to English in Africa, two publications take a comparative approach. Edgar W. Schneider's contribution 'Towards Endonormativity? African English and the Dynamic Model of the Evolution of Postcolonial Englishes' (in Harrow and Mpoche, eds., *Language, Literature and Education in Multicultural Societies: Collaborative Research on Africa*, pp. 283–305) elaborates on the development of African Englishes within the framework of his previous publications, e.g. Schneider [2007] (cf. *YWES* 88[2009] 95–6). Mungai Mutonya examines 'African Englishes: Acoustic Analysis of Vowels' (*WEn* 27[2008] 434–49). This careful quantitative analysis of speakers from Kenya, Ghana and Zimbabwe tests previous claims about the realization of vowels in African Englishes, pointing out similarities between the accents as well as country-specific differences.

A number of studies deal with West African Englishes. Aloysius Ngefac presents a book-length study of *Social Differentiation in Cameroon English: Evidence from Sociolinguistic Fieldwork*. He looks at differentiation with regard to phonological features according to education, gender, age, occupation, region, ethnicity and mood (anger, fear, joy) on the basis of word-list, reading and conversational styles. While the study is undoubtedly an important contribution to the description of the socio-phonology of Cameroon English and possibly even the eventual standardization of the variety, there are some serious issues to be raised with regard to the author's methodology. While the informants' consent was obtained for the recordings of the reading list, the conversations were recorded surreptitiously, and for the sampling of data produced in different moods Ngefac manipulated his students, making them believe they had failed an exam. Such breaches of research ethics should not be endorsed by supervisors or publishers. Aloysius Ngefac has also summarized the chapter on phonological variation in correlation to education, in his article 'The Social Stratification of English in Cameroon' (*WEn* 27[2008] 407–18).

Further publications dealing with Cameroon English include Edmund Biloa and George Echu's chapter on 'Cameroon: Official Bilingualism in a Multilingual State' (in Simpson, ed., *Language and National Identity in Africa*, pp. 199–213), which is mainly concerned with the present socio-linguistic situation and current language policy. A. Neba Fontem and S.O. Oyetade look at 'Declining Anglophone English Language Proficiency in Cameroon: Which Factors Should Be Considered?' (in Harrow and Mpoche, eds., pp. 121–38). They find considerable differences in proficiency test results of secondary students who claimed Cameroon Pidgin as their L1 and those who claimed English. Camilla A. Tabe examines 'Orality and Literacy in Cameroon E-Mail Discourse' (in Harrow and Mpoche, eds., pp. 194–209) on the basis of a rather small set of data. It seems to me that some of the features claimed to be unique to Cameroonian e-mail discourse can also be found elsewhere in the English-speaking world, for example ellipsis, creative uses of punctuation, abbreviations and colloquialisms, even code-switching. Daniel Nkemleke discusses the 'Frequency and Use of Modals in Cameroon English and Application to Language Education' (in Harrow and Mpoche, eds., pp. 242–61) on the basis of corpus data of Cameroon English, BrE and AmE, pointing out that modals and semi-modals are used less frequently in Cameroon English and for a smaller range of functions.

Andrew Simpson and B. Akíntúndé Oyètádé survey 'Nigeria: Ethno-Linguistic Competition in the Giant of Africa' (in Simpson, ed., pp. 172–98), providing an overview of the historical development and the present-day linguistic situation. Adeyemi Daramola studies 'A Child of Necessity: An Analysis of Political Discourse in Nigeria' (*Pragmatics* 18[2008] 355–80) on the basis of a small number of important political speeches and the responses they elicited in 1993 within the framework of functional-semiotic discourse analysis. I.N. Ohia investigates the development 'Towards Standard Nigerian English: The Acceptability of Some Popular Nigerian English Expressions' (in Bagwasi, Alimi and Ebewo, eds., *English Language and Literature: Cross Cultural Currents,* pp. 224–32) on the basis of a questionnaire survey of 100 lexical items, such as *boys' quarters* 'servants' lodgings', gleaned from a variety of written sources. Of these, fifty-nine were judged highly acceptable by the thousand-plus respondents, suggesting that they are indeed part of standard Nigerian English. Innocent Chiluwa is 'Assessing the Nigerianness of SMS Text-Messages in English' (*EnT* 24:i[2008] 51–6) on the basis of sixty-one SMS messages, both private and business-related. While Chiluwa does not consider personal messages with a Christian content to be specifically Nigerian, social and business messages contain local lexemes and abbreviations. Finally in this section on West African Englishes, there is one contribution on the linguistic situation of Ghana. Akosua Anyidoho and M.E. Kropp Dakubu present 'Ghana: Indigenous Languages, English, and an Emerging National Identity' (in Simpson, ed., pp. 141–57), focusing on language policy and the status and functions of the major language families and English, but not Ghanaian Pidgin English.

East Africa has not received much attention this year, with only Chege Githiora's chapter on 'Kenya: Language and the Search for a Coherent National Identity' (in Simpson, ed., pp. 235–51) to show for, a brief survey of the present-day sociolinguistic profile of the country and a discussion of the functions of Swahili and English with regard to national identity.

The bulk of publications is concerned with Southern African Englishes. Lutz Marten and Nancy C. Kula report on 'Zambia: One Zambia, One Nation, Many Languages' (in Simpson, ed., pp. 291–313), looking at present linguistic make-up and the role of English, the historical development and current language policy. M.M. Bagwasi debates 'English Acculturating to African Culture: A Truism or Fallacy' (in Bagwasi et al., eds., pp. 2–14), considering the situation in Botswana in particular and coming to the conclusion that even an Africanized English cannot be considered adequate for the expression of African experience, values and culture. H.M. Batibo contemplates 'Anglicization or Tswanalization: Which Way Botswana?' (in Bagwasi et al., eds., pp. 15–26), and points out that on the basis of the present situation a number of developments are possible. J.T. Mathangwane assesses 'English in Botswana: A Blessing or a Curse?' (in Bagwasi et al., eds., pp. 27–37), arguing strongly in favour of the latter. R.O.B. Nhlekisana investigates 'The Coexistence of English and Setswana in Botswana Judiciary System' (in Bagwasi et al., eds., pp. 54–9), outlining some of the difficulties arising from the bilingual proceedings. N.N. Kgolo provides 'An Analysis of the Discourse of Botswana Parliamentary Proceedings' (in Bagwasi et al., eds., pp. 62–77) within the framework of Systemic Functional Linguistics on the basis of the parliamentary *Hansard*s, covering 1994 to 2004. Kgolo outlines various discourse strategies, for example code-switching or the use of Setswana kinship terms as terms of address in parliamentary speeches and debates. G.H. Kamwendo looks at 'English, Globalization and Botswana's Revised National Policy on Education' (in Bagwasi et al., eds., pp. 172–85), critically evaluating current policy and practice in the education system.

Finex Ndhlovu examines 'The Conundrums of Language Policy and Politics in South Africa and Zimbabwe' (*AuJL* 28[2008] 59–80), comparing *de jure* policies with the de facto situation in these two countries, which do not support the use of indigenous languages as much as is claimed in official statements, favouring English instead. Rajend Mesthrie surveys the situation in 'South Africa: The Rocky Road to Nation Building' (in Simpson, ed., pp. 314–38) from colonial times to the present day. Rajend Mesthrie also discusses '"Death of the Mother Tongue"—Is English a Glottaphagic Language in South Africa?' (*EnT* 24:ii[2008] 13–19), painting a more differentiated picture than most of the sources he is referring to. His arguments are backed by Charlyn Dyers's study of 'Truncated Multilingualism or Language Shift? An Examination of Language Use in Intimate Domains in a New Non-Racial Working Class Township in South Africa' (*JMMD* 29[2008] 110–26), whose author encountered 'vibrant multilingualism' among her informants in Wesbank Township, Capetown. Stephanie Rudwick conducted an ethnographic study of '"Coconuts" and "Oreos": English-Speaking Zulu People in a South African Township' (*WEn* 27[2008] 101–16) in KwaZulu-Natal where speaking English, especially with a 'white accent', is stigmatized by the community and not considered appropriate for Zulus, hence the derogatory terms.

Three publications deal with linguistic features of SAE varieties. Ana Deumert and Sibabalwe Oscar Masinyana report on 'Mobile Language Choices—The Use of English and isiXhosa in Text Messages (SMS)' (*EWW* 29[2008] 117–47), pointing out differences with regard to encoding conventions between English and isiXhosa messages of twenty-two bilingual South Africans. While the English messages exhibit most of the features found in SMS messages internationally, the isiXhosa messages contain no abbreviations, changed spellings or paralinguistic restitutions, such as emoticons. In fact, the informants did not respond favourably to one of the co-authors' attempts to introduce such features. This hints at two completely separate sociolinguistic norms for these bilinguals. Bertus van Rooy provides 'A Multidimensional Analysis of Student Writing in Black South African English' (*EWW* 29[2008] 268–305), comparing data from a Tswana Learner Corpus and the LOCNESS corpus containing essays by BrE university students. He concludes that the differences observable in the data with regard to information density and presentation justify the classification of black SAfE as a variety in its own right. Further evidence is provided in his paper 'An Alternative Interpretation of Tense and Aspect in Black South African English' (*WEn* 27[2008] 335–58), which contains quantitative and qualitative analyses of a corpus of roughly 200,000 words of various spoken and written text types. While the quantitative analysis does not reveal significant differences to other varieties, the qualitative analysis of text samples shows different uses of the forms under analysis.

Moving on to the Caribbean, we welcome Alison Irvine's study of 'Contrast and Convergence in Standard Jamaican English: The Phonological Architecture of the Standard in an Ideologically Bidialectal Community' (*WEn* 27[2008] 9–25) outlining phonological features of acrolectal Jamaican English, such as the stopping of the voiced dental fricative or the palatalization of the velar stops in certain environments, based on the data used in Irvine [2004] (cf. *YWES* 85[2006] 99). Korah Belgrave has conducted a matched-guise experiment to investigate 'Speaking the Queen's English: Attitudes of Barbadians to British, American and Barbadian Accents' (*Torre* 13[2008] 429–44), concluding that the preference for foreign accents reflects the exonormative orientation of Barbadians. Rhoda Arindell, Micah Corum and Mervyn Alleyne 'Locat[e] St. Martin in Caribbean Sociolinguistic Typology' (*Torre* 13[2008] 591–614), outlining the history and present form of St Martin English, which is comparable to Bajan in that is shows very little restructuring and can be located quite low on the cline of 'creoleness'. Jack Sidnell provides

'Alternate and Complementary Perspectives on Language and Social Life: The Organization of Repair in Two Caribbean Communities' (*JSoc* 12[2008] 477–503), namely in Bequia, an island belonging to St Vincent and the Grenadines, and Cailander, a coastal village in Guyana, in comparison to AmE data. Miriam Meyerhoff uses data from the same fieldwork in Bequia for her analysis of 'Bequia Sweet/Bequia Is Sweet: Syntactic Variation in a Lesser-Known Variety of Caribbean English' (*EnT* 24:i[2008] 33–40), discussing possible environments for copula deletion in this variety. As Bequia English has a number of such creole features, it provides the link to the section on creolistics.

A number of publications deal with creole languages in general or provide a comparative analysis. We welcome the publication of the *Handbook of Pidgin and Creole Studies*, edited by Silvia Kouwenberg and John Victor Singler. It contains a wealth of very informative contributions written by some of the leading experts in the field, and represents in many ways the state of the art in pidgin and creole linguistics, particularly with regard to the ongoing creole genesis debate. The handbook is divided into five parts, of which the most relevant contributions for scholars of English-based creoles will be mentioned. The first part contains contributions on the linguistic properties of pidgins and creoles, for example Donald Winford's account of 'Atlantic Creole Syntax' (pp. 19–47) focusing on the shared features of the Atlantic creoles; Miriam Meyerhoff's contribution on 'Forging Pacific Pidgin and Creole Syntax: Substrate, Discourse, and Inherent Variability' (pp. 48–73); Terry Crowley's discussion of 'Creole Morphology' (pp. 74–97), and Norval Smith's summary of 'Creole Phonology' (pp. 98–129), which includes synchronic as well as diachronic information. The second part is concerned with perspectives on pidgin and creole genesis. Jeff Siegel discusses 'Pidgins/Creoles, and Second Language Acquisition' (pp. 189–218); Tonjes Veenstra critically assesses 'Creole Genesis: The Impact of the Language Bioprogram Hypothesis' (pp. 219–41); Sarah G. Thomson looks at the relationship of 'Pidgins/ Creoles and Historical Linguistics' (pp. 242–62), while Rajend Mesthrie provides a larger typological context in his contribution 'Pidgins/Creoles and Contact Languages: An Overview' (pp. 263–86). The late Jacques Arends takes 'A Demographic Perspective on Creole Formation' (pp. 309–31); John Victor Singler examines 'The Sociohistorical Context of Creole Genesis' (pp. 332–58), while Christine Jourdan investigates 'The Cultural in Pidgin Genesis' (pp. 359–81). The third part of the handbook is concerned with the linguistic differentiation and explanation of pidgins and creoles, for example in Adrienne Bruyn's account of 'Grammaticalization in Pidgins and Creoles' (pp. 385–410); Peter L. Patrick's contribution on 'Pidgins, Creoles, and Variation' (pp. 461–87); or George Huttar's very interesting 'Semantic Evidence in Pidgin and Creole Genesis' (pp. 440–60), which suggests different degrees of semantic complexity due to different communicative needs in pidgins and creoles. The fourth part is concerned with related languages (see section 9 above), while the fifth part contains contributions illuminating the role of pidgins and creoles in society. Geneviève Escure examines 'Pidgins/ Creoles and Discourse' (pp. 567–92); Dennis Craig reports on 'Pidgins/Creoles and Education' (pp. 593–614); Hubert Devonish discusses 'Language Planning in Pidgins and Creoles' (pp. 615–36); and, finally, Hélène Buzelin and Lise Winer look at 'Literary Representations of Creole Languages: Cross-Linguistic Perspectives from the Caribbean' (pp. 637–65). Because of the high quality of the individual contributions, the handbook will serve as a ready reference in a research as well as in a teaching context.

Two monographs address the issue of pidgin and creole genesis in more detail. Salikoko S. Mufwene's *Language Evolution: Contact, Competition and Change* provides further arguments in favour of his view of language change as selection from a feature pool (cf. *YWES* 82[2003] 85), supplemented by a chapter on globalization, language death and language maintenance. These issues are illustrated with an account of the linguistic changes in sub-Saharan Africa since the pre-colonial period and the case of Gullah in the US. Jeff Siegel's monograph *The Emergence of Pidgin and Creole Languages* is based on his work on the Pacific pidgins and creoles, but his conclusions are of a general nature. Siegel discusses morphological simplicity in pidgins, and simplicity and expansion in creoles, then proceeds to elaborate on the role of transfer in SLA and substrate influence in pidgins and creoles. A final chapter is dedicated to the discussion of decreolization and the notion of the creole continuum. Siegel presents the material in a very careful way and supports his arguments with a wealth of examples from a large number of Pacific pidgins and creoles, both English-lexifier, such as Tok Pisin, Melanesian Pidgin, Hawai'ian Creole English, or Roper Kriol, but also varieties with other lexifiers, such as Tayo (French) or Pidgin Fijian (Fijian). Summarizing his results, Siegel makes a strong claim against most current models of creole genesis, including the superstratist hypothesis, relexification, the two-target model, the bioprogram hypothesis or any other universalist claim. He sees the strongest evidence in SLA and transfer, stressing that each pidginization is the product of individuals acquiring language. Without doubt, his thought-provoking book will further fuel the ongoing creole genesis debate.

Along similar lines, Ingo Plag argues in favour of regarding 'Creoles as Interlanguages: Inflectional Morphology' (*JPCL* 23[2008] 114–35) and 'Creoles as Interlanguages: Syntactic Structures' (*JPCL* 23[2008] 307–28), providing counter-evidence to the language bioprogram hypothesis, but also to John McWhorter's position on creole simplicity. Donald Winford stresses the similarities between 'Processes of Creole Formation and Related Contact-Induced Phenomena' (*JLC THEMA* 2[2008] 124–45), also stressing the role of transfer in all of the processes under analysis, as bilinguals have been shown not to operate the two grammatical systems completely separately.

Claire Lefebvre has also published on her model of relexification. Her current focus is on processes of relabelling, as introduced in her paper 'On the Principled Nature of the Respective Contributions of Substrate and Superstrate Languages to a Creole's Lexicon' (in Michaelis, ed., *Roots of Creole Structures: Weighing the Contribution of Substrates and Superstrates*, pp. 196–222) of which a revised version on 'Relabelling: A Major Process in Language Contact' (*JLC THEMA* 2[2008] 91–111) is also available.

Various publications deal with the features of creoles in general. Mikael Parkvall discusses 'The Simplicity of Creoles in a Cross-Linguistic Perspective' (in Miestamo, Sinnemäki and Karlsson, eds., *Language Complexity: Typology,*

Contact, Change, pp. 265–85), using a large typological database to lend support to the claim that creoles are indeed less complex than other languages. Sarah J. Roberts and Joan Bresnan look at 'Retained Inflectional Morphology in Pidgins: A Typological Study' (*LinguisticT* 12[2008] 269–302) based on data from pidgins and jargons with lexifiers other than English. They find that inflections that carry important semantic distinctions are not necessarily abandoned in pidginization and that the sweeping claim that pidgins are languages without inflections cannot be upheld in the light of the evidence. Marco Nicolis examines 'The Null Subject Parameter and Correlating Properties: The Case of Creole Languages' (in Biberauer, ed., *The Limits of Syntactic Variation*, pp. 271–94) within the framework of generative grammar. Harald Hammarström reports on 'Complexity in Numeral Systems with an Investigation into Pidgins and Creoles' (in Miestamo et al., eds., pp. 287–304), comparing the number of irregular forms in the numerals of pidgins, creoles and other languages world-wide.

I would like to point out one publication on a shared feature of many Atlantic creoles from the Caribbean before we proceed to a discussion of work on individual varieties. Ian F. Hancock investigates 'Scots English and the English-Lexifier Creole Relativizer *We*' (*EWW* 29[2008] 1–14), claiming that the etymon of the relativizer *we* is not English *what*, as this form is not attested before the nineteenth century. He suggests Scottish or northern English variants of *who* as more likely sources of *we*.

Stephanie Durrleman-Tame has published *The Syntax of Jamaican Creole: A Cartographic Perspective*, a recent version of the generative Principles and Parameters framework. In a way, her book is a more recent version of Bailey's [1966] first attempt to capture basilectal creole syntax within a generative framework, especially as she expresses the same motivation as Bailey, namely to prove that Jamaican Creole is a language in its own right, not a kind of 'broken English'. Durrleman-Tame begins with an overview of the linguistic situation in Jamaica and the theoretical framework of her work. The following chapters introduce the realizations of inflectional categories, different clause types, including focusing constructions, and a very thorough treatment of the structure of nominals. Once the reader gets used to the notation conventions of the cartographic approach, the discussion of the hierarchical structure of various constructions is enlightening. Durrleman-Tame's work will be important to linguists working on Jamaican Creole, but is definitely not ideal for a lay audience.

Silvia Kouwenberg tackles 'The Problem of Multiple Substrates' (in Michaelis, ed., pp. 1–27) in the case of Jamaican Creole, for which Akan had been claimed as dominant substrate. She argues very convincingly that there must have been widespread multilingualism among the slaves in the seventeenth century, and that therefore a different, typological methodology needs to be applied in assessing substrate influence. Celia Brown-Blake discusses 'The Right to Linguistic Non-Discrimination and Creole Language Situations: The Case of Jamaica' (*JPCL* 23[2008] 32–74), exploring the legal ramifications if the constitution of Jamaica were to be changed in order to prevent discrimination on linguistic grounds.

A number of articles are concerned with the Suriname creoles. Bettina Migge and Laurence Goury provide information on processes 'Between Contact and Development: Towards a Multi-Layered Explanation for the Development of the TMA System in the Creoles of Suriname' (in Michaelis, ed., pp. 301–31), summarizing the historical development of the Maroon creoles and comparing their TMA system with that of the West African substrate language Gbe. Norval Smith explores 'The Origin of the Portuguese Words in Saramaccan' (in Michaelis, ed., pp. 153–68), looking at different paths of transmission. Heiko Narrog provides 'A Note on Modality and Aspect in Saramaccan' (in Abraham and Leiss, eds., *Modality–Aspect Interfaces*, pp. 359–68), looking at combinations of tense and aspect marking, especially in the case of *musu* 'must'. John McWhorter's article 'Hither and Thither in Saramaccan Creole' (*SLang* 32[2008] 163–95) is concerned with two verb constructions which have received little attention so far, *túwe* 'throw' and *púu* 'remove, pull', which he interprets as evidence against the relexification hypothesis. Claire Lefebvre and Virginie Loranger provide 'A Diachronic and Synchronic Account of the Multifunctionality of Saramaccan *táa*' (*Linguistics* 46[2008] 1167–1228), which can be used as a verb, a complementizer, a conjunction, and to introduce direct quotes. Finally, Christian Uffmann is concerned with 'Vowel Epenthesis and Creole Syllable Structure' (in Michaelis, ed., pp. 123–52) in Sranan, applying an OT approach to historical and present-day data to evaluate the respective contributions of the substrate and superstrate languages.

There are also a number of publications dealing with other Caribbean creoles. Stephanie Hackert is involved in 'Counting and Coding the Past: Circumscribing the Variable Contact in Quantitative Analyses of Past Inflection' (*LVC* 20[2008] 127–53), comparing the definitions of the variable in a large number of studies of Atlantic creoles and her own data from the Bahamas, showing how easily categories and their semantics can be mismatched with regard to this well-studied variable. Paula Prescod reports on 'The Formation of Deverbal Nouns in Vincentian Creole' (in Michaelis, ed., pp. 333–55), an eastern Caribbean creole spoken on St Vincent. Prescod gives a detailed account of the socio-historical circumstances leading to the formation of this creole, linking the unusual presence of derivational morphology and other word-formation processes to the different contact situation on the island. Finally, Shelome Gooden explores 'Discourse Aspects of Tense Marking in Belizean Creole' (*EWW* 29[2008] 306–46) based on interview and elicitation data from Bermuda Landing and Belize City, carefully linking reference to past events to strategies of foregrounding and backgrounding in narrative context.

Moving on to the pidgins and creoles on the other side of the Atlantic, we welcome the publication of Jean-Paul Kouega's *Dictionary of Cameroon Pidgin Usage: Pronunciation, Grammar and Vocabulary*, which includes chapters on the development and present status and function of Cameroon Pidgin, its phonological and morpho-syntactic features, the structure of its lexicon, followed by a dictionary section of Cameroon Pidgin–English and an appendix containing transcriptions and translation of spoken media discourse (news, reports, interviews), based on data recorded from a large number of radio and television broadcasts between 2006 and 2007. The dictionary thus provides a complete survey of Cameroon Pidgin as used in a public domain by skilled users.

George Echu investigates 'Forms of Address as a Politeness Strategy in Cameroon Pidgin English' (in Farenkia, ed., *Linguistic Politeness in Cameroon: Pragmatic, Comparative and Intercultural Approaches*, pp. 121–33) based on data recorded at meetings of a multi-ethnic organization which has adopted Cameroon Pidgin as its working language, and on various written sources, discussing a range of terms used in symmetrical and asymmetrical communicative settings. Herbert Igboanusi is concerned with 'Empowering Nigerian Pidgin: A Challenge for Status Planning?' (*WEn* 27[2008] 68–82), analysing language attitudes of 200 informants and proposing possible ways of implementing Nigerian Pidgin as an officially recognized language. B. Akíntúndé Oyètadé and Victor Fashole Luke report on 'Sierra Leone: Krio and the Quest for National Integration' (in Simpson, ed., pp. 122–40), providing a brief historical overview and discussing the role of Krio in Ghana and the language attitudes connected to it.

To round off this section on individual pidgins and creoles, there are a number of publications dealing with various Pacific varieties. Jeff Siegel writes 'In Praise of the Cafeteria Principle: Language Mixing in Hawai'i Creole' (in Michaelis, ed., pp. 59–82) putting forth strong arguments against Derek Bickerton's criticism of the so-called 'cafeteria principle', which refers to possible influences of the various substrates involved and was renounced by Bickerton. Mikaela L. Marlow and Howard Giles discuss 'Who You Tink You, Talking Propah? Hawaiian Pidgin Demarginalised' (*JMD* 3[2008] 53–68), reporting on language attitudes and practices of Hawaiians and pointing out how Hawaiian Pidgin acts as a marker of group solidarity.

Bambi B. Schieffelin examines 'Tok Bokis, Tok Piksa: Translating Parables in Papua New Guinea' (in Meyerhoff and Nagy, eds., *Social Lives in Language*, pp. 111–34), focusing on this particular aspect of Bible translations to show how translation practices have changed over the years. Stuart Robinson explains 'Why Pidgin and Creole Linguistics Needs the Statistician: Vocabulary Size in a Tok Pisin Corpus' (*JPCL* 23[2008] 141–6), showing how statistical analysis can contribute to the debate on simplicity and complexity by analysing a Tok Pisin folk-tale corpus. Peter Mühlhäusler investigates 'Multifunctionality in Pitkern-Norf'k and Tok Pisin' (*JPCL* 23[2008] 75–113), and comes to the conclusion that the processes in Ptikern-Norf'k are very different from those of Tok Pisin, as they are a mere subset of the English system.

Christine Jourdan comments on 'Language Repertoires and the Middle-Class in Urban Solomon Islands' (in Meyerhoff and Nagy, eds., pp. 43–67), elaborating on how the urban middle class on the Solomon Islands has been shifting from one or more vernacular languages plus Solomon Pidgin to solely Pidgin and a more standard form of English. Miriam Meyerhoff looks at 'Empirical Problems with Domain-Based Notions of "Simple"' (in Meyerhoff and Nagy, eds., pp. 327–55), discussing three features of Bislama which can be traced to influences of the substrate, the lexifier and cognitive constraints. Felicity Meakins reports on 'Land, Language and Identity: The Socio-Political

Origins of Gurindji Kriol' (in Meyerhoff and Nagy, eds., pp. 69–94) spoken in northern Australia, and discusses some of its features. Finally, Ronald Kim introduces 'California Chinese Pidgin English and its Historical Connections: Preliminary Remarks' (*JPCL* 23[2008] 329–44), shedding light on the historical background and development of a little-known variety which might have also played a role in the formation of Hawaiian Pidgin English.

11. Pragmatics and Discourse Analysis

This year, several edited collections were published that address the wider scope of pragmatics and its application to other disciplines. To begin with, three volumes explore the relationship between pragmatics and corpus linguistics. First, *Pragmatics and Corpus Linguistics: A Mutualistic Entente*, edited by Jesús Romero-Trillo, aims to go beyond the limits of both disciplines to shed light on their intricate relationship. The editor argues that pragmatics and corpus linguistics are joint forces in the common cause to work with real-usage data, more convincingly addressing some specifics of language usage by combining the methodologies that underlie both disciplines. The ten papers in the volume are organized around two research topics that have turned out to be essential in the emergence of corpus pragmatics: corpus linguistics and conversational pragmatics, and corpus linguistics and interlanguage pragmatics, i.e. pragmatics in language learning. Four papers investigate discourse and hesitation markers: 'At the Interface between Grammar and Discourse—A Corpus-Based Study of Some Pragmatic Markers' by Karin Aijmer; 'The Subjectivity of *Basically* in British English—A Corpus-Based Study' by Chris Butler; 'Hesitation Markers Among EFL Learners: Pragmatic Deficiency or Difference?' by Gaëtanelle Gilquin; and 'Discourse Markers and the Pragmatics of Native and Non-Native Teachers in a CLIL Corpus' by Ana Llinares-García and Jesús Romero-Trillo. Two papers focus on specific types of speech act: 'The Use(fulness) of Corpus Research in Cross-Cultural Pragmatics: Complaining in Intercultural Service Encounters' by Ronald Geluykens and Bettina Kraft and 'A Cross-Linguistic Study on the Pragmatics of Intonation in Directives' by Maria Dolores Ramírez-Verdugo. The remaining four papers study broader discourse phenomena: 'Variation in Advanced Oral Interlanguage: The Effect of Proficiency on Style Choice' by Jean-Marc Dewaele; 'The Discourse-Grammar Interface of Regulatory Teacher Talk in the EFL Classroom' by Silvia Riesco Bernier; 'Evidentiality in Discourse: A Pragmatic and Empirical Account' by Leo Francis Hoye; and 'Multi-Modal Corpus Pragmatics: The Case of Active Listenership' by Dawn Knight and Svenja Adolphs.

Another collection that surveys the use of corpora in the study of discourse and discourses is *Corpora and Discourse*, edited by Annelie Ädel and Randi Reppen, bringing together eleven contributions from a diverse group of scholars who explore different ways of combining corpus linguistics and discourse analysis. The volume provides a rich sample of English-language discourse from around the world (including international, learner, and non-standard varieties of English), and covers a broad range of topics and methods. Both spoken and written discourse are investigated at the prosodic, lexical and textual levels. Nine papers explore discourse in a variety of settings, with three each focusing on academia, the workplace, and news and entertainment, while the remaining two contributions explore discourse through specific linguistic features.

The third book-length treatment of corpora and pragmatics is Svenja Adolphs's monograph *Corpus and Context: Investigating Pragmatic Functions in Spoken Discourse*. The book comprises seven chapters, discussing possible frameworks for the analysis of utterance function on the basis of spoken corpora. It addresses the challenges and opportunities associated with a change of focus in spoken corpus research, from the purely textual analysis of lexical units and concordance lines to the multi-modal analysis of functional units in extended stretches of discourse. Chapters 1 and 2 provide a general introductory overview of major issues in the analysis of spoken corpora and related methodological questions, while chapters 3–5 include a close analysis of contextual variables in relation to lexico-grammatical and discourse patterns that emerge from the corpus data. The analysis is based on a number of transcript-only, but also multimodal spoken corpora, including the Cambridge and Nottingham Corpus of Discourse in English (CANCODE). Chapter 3 examines the significance of collocation and co-text of individual speech-act expressions for the purpose of functional disambiguation, and also develops functional profiles for these speech-act expressions. Chapter 4 discusses the role of electronic corpora in the relationship between text and context in relation to utterance function, and establishes the link between lexico-grammar and context in relation to speech-act expressions. Chapter 5 provides a wider discussion of the role of context in spoken corpus research, focusing on the co-text of individual speech acts. Finally, chapter 6 explores the impact of multi-modal corpus analysis, i.e. the analysis of corpora with aligned data streams combining text, sound and video.

Two edited collections appeared that deal with contrastive and intercultural pragmatics. The first is *Languages and Cultures in Contrast and Comparison*, edited by María de los Ángeles Gómez González, J. Lachlan Mackenzie and Elsa M. González Álvarez. It covers a wide variety of languages such as Akan, Dutch, English, Finnish, French, German, Italian, Norwegian, Spanish and Swedish, and aims to explore various hitherto under-researched relationships between these languages and their discourse-cultural settings. The papers are organized in three thematic sections. While parts II and III focus on lexis in contrast and contrastive perspectives on language teaching and learning respectively, the four papers in part I focus on structural options in syntax and deal with information structure, and are thus the more relevant contributions for the present review: 'Theme Zones in Contrast: An Analysis of their Linguistic Realization in the Communicative Act of a Non-Acceptance' by Anita Fetzer; 'Last Things First: An FDG Approach to Clause-Final Focus Constituents in Spanish and English' by Mike Hannay and Elena Martínez Caro; 'Contrastive Perspectives on Cleft Sentences' by Jeanette K. Gundel; and 'The Position of Adverbials and the Pragmatic Organization of the Sentence: A Comparison of French and Dutch' by Ilse Magnus.

The second collection, *Developing Contrastive Pragmatics: Interlanguage and Cross-Cultural Perspectives*, edited by Martin Pütz and JoAnne Neff-van Aertselaer, grew out of the 32nd LAUD Symposium held at the University of Koblenz-Landau (Germany) in 2006, and primarily addresses issues of contrastive pragmatics, involving research on interlanguage and cross-cultural perspectives with a focus on SLA contexts. Pragmatics is seen from a multilingual and multicultural perspective, contributing to an emerging field of study (i.e. intercultural pragmatics) which can fruitfully be applied to contrastive analysis and contexts of second-language learning and teaching. The contributions to this volume are organized into three sections that reflect the various approaches employed in studying contrastive pragmatics. Section I focuses on 'Intercultural Pragmatics and Discourse Markers', section II on 'Interlanguage Pragmatics: Strategies and Identity in the Foreign Language Classroom', and section III on the 'Development of Pragmatic Competence in Foreign Language Learning: Focus on "Requests"', which includes contributions on Japanese, German, Turkish, Persian and Dutch learners of English as a foreign language, as well as a study on patterns of variation in requests in two inner-circle varieties of English, i.e. Irish English and English English.

Variation is also the topic of *Variational Pragmatics: A Focus on Regional Varieties in Pluricentric Languages*, a collection edited by Klaus P. Schneider and Anne Barron that bears witness to the emergence and establishment of Variational Pragmatics, a new research field situated at the interface of pragmatics and dialectology. By systematically examining pragmatic variation across geographical and social varieties of a language, this new sub-discipline aims at determining the impact of such factors as region, social class, gender, age and ethnicity on communicative language use. In their introductory chapter ('Where Pragmatics and Dialectology Meet: Introducing Variational Pragmatics'), the editors lay out the rationale for studying Variational Pragmatics as a separate field of enquiry, systematically sketching the broader theoretical framework and also presenting a framework for further analysis. They highlight the problem that much research in the field of contrastive and cross-cultural pragmatics is based on the assumption that language communities of native speakers are homogeneous wholes, while language variation is abstracted away. However, cultural norms reflected in speech acts differ not only across different languages and cultures, but also between regional and/or social varieties of only one language. The contributions in this book address the current research gap in sociolinguistics for variation on the pragmatic level and are divided into three sections that focus on English (part I), Dutch and German (part II), and Spanish and French (part III). The four papers on English are 'The Structure of Requests in Irish English and English English' by Anne Barron; 'Response Tokens in British and Irish Discourse: Corpus, Context and Variational Pragmatics' by Anne O'Keeffe and Svenja Adolphs; 'Small Talk in England, Ireland, and the USA' by Klaus P. Schneider; and 'Gratitude in British and New Zealand Radio Programmes: Nothing but Gushing?' by Sabine Jautz. Another paper that addresses pragmatic variation across Englishes is Shie Sato's 'Use of "Please" in American and New Zealand English' (*JPrag* 40[2008] 1249–78), which examines the politeness marker *please* and its positional and functional variability within turn-constructional units in spoken AmE and NZE.

Two book-length discussions and a special journal issue have put research on impoliteness phenomena in language on the agenda, and their publication reflects the enormous imbalance that has existed between research on politeness phenomena compared to impoliteness phenomena. While for more than three decades, pragmatic and sociolinguistic studies of interaction have considered politeness a central explanatory concept underlying and governing face-to-face interaction, impoliteness has largely been neglected until only very recently. Derek Bousfield's pioneering monograph *Impoliteness in Interaction* addresses the nature of impoliteness in face-to-face spoken interaction, considering its role in a wide range of discourse types (from car-parking disputes, army and police training and police–public interactions to kitchen discourse). Chapters 1–4 discuss impoliteness in interaction, implicature, face within a model of (im)politeness, and perspectives on politeness and impoliteness, while chapters 5–8 examine the realization of impoliteness and its dynamics on the levels of utterance, discourse and turn-taking.

Together with Miriam A. Locher, Bousfield has also co-edited *Impoliteness in Language: Studies on its Interplay with Power in Theory and Practice*, a collection which explores the concept of linguistic impoliteness, the crucial differences and interconnectedness between lay understandings of impoliteness, and the academic concept within a theory of facework/relational work, as well as the exercise of power that is involved when impoliteness occurs. It should provide a strong impetus for research on impoliteness in other fields of research. The contributions are organized into five parts on the basis of the issues they address and the types of empirical data they draw on. Part I, 'Theoretical Focus on Research on Impoliteness', includes two more theoretically oriented papers: 'Reflections on Impoliteness, Relational Work and Power' by Jonathan Culpeper, and 'Toward a Unified Theory of Politeness, Impoliteness, and Rudeness' by Marina Terkourafi. Parts II–IV consist of studies that present data from political interaction ('Relational Work and Impoliteness: Negotiating Norms of Linguistic Behaviour' by Miriam A. Locher and Richard J. Watts, and 'Political Campaign Debates as Zero-Sum Games: Impoliteness and Power in Candidates' Exchanges' by Maria Dolores Garcia-Pastor); interaction with legally constituted authorities ('Impoliteness in the Struggle for Power' by Derek Bousfield; 'Threats in Conflict Talk: Impoliteness and Manipulation' by Holger Limberg and 'Verbal Aggression and Impoliteness: Related or Synonymous?' by Dawn Archer); and workplace interaction in the factory and the office ('Impoliteness as a Means of Contesting Power Relations in the Workplace' by Stephanie Schnurr, Meredith Marra and Janet Holmes and '"Stop Hassling Me!" Impoliteness, Power and Gender Identity in the Professional Workplace' by Louise Mullany). Finally, part V includes two further empirical studies on code-switching and internet practices.

The special issue on 'Impoliteness: Eclecticism and Diaspora' published in the *Journal of Politeness Research* (4:ii[2008]), co-edited by Derek Bousfield and Jonathan Culpeper, surveys the variety of approaches that constitute the field and aims to bring together researchers with different backgrounds and different perspectives on the notion of impoliteness in order to show the diversity of directions that research into the phenomenon can take. In their introduction to the special edition the editors point out that the 'classic' politeness theories of Robin T. Lakoff, Penelope Brown and Stephen C. Levinson, and Geoffrey Leech focused on harmonious interactions, and hence largely ignored impoliteness. Thus it appears that these are generally not well equipped to account for impoliteness phenomena since they tend to give the impression that impoliteness either constitutes some kind of pragmatic failure or merely anomalous behaviour not worthy of further consideration. The special issues includes six case studies on different aspects of impoliteness such as interruptions, rudeness and swearing: '"Reasonable Hostility": Situation-Appropriate Face-Attack' by Karen Tracy; 'Impoliteness and Ethnicity: Māori and Pākehā Discourse in New Zealand Workplaces' by Janet Holmes, Meredith Marra and Stephanie Schnurr; 'Participants' Orientations to Interruptions, Rudeness and Other Impolite Acts in Talk-In-Interaction' by Ian Hutchby; 'Impoliteness and Emotional Arguments' by Manfred Kienpointner; 'The Pragmatics of Swearing' by Timothy Jay and Kristin Janschewitz; and 'Rudeness, Conceptual Blending Theory and Relational Work' by Richard J. Watts.

As far as overview textbooks on pragmatics are concerned, this year the updated second edition of *Culturally Speaking: Culture, Communication and Politeness Theory* was published, a comprehensive introduction to cross-cultural and intercultural pragmatics for undergraduate and postgraduate students edited by Helen Spencer-Oatey. The book examines the theoretical, methodological and practical issues in the analysis of talk across cultures and includes several empirical case studies from a variety of languages such as German, Greek, Japanese and Chinese. The five thematic sections of the book are: part I, 'Basic Concepts' (face, (im)politeness and rapport, culture and communication); part II, 'Cross-Cultural Pragmatics: Empirical Studies' ('Apologies in Japanese and English', 'British and Chinese Reactions to Compliment Responses', 'Interactional Work in Greek and German Telephone Conversations'); part III, 'Processes in Intercultural Interaction' (pragmatic transfer, communication accommodation theory, adaptation and identity); and part IV, 'Intercultural Pragmatics: Empirical Studies' ('Negotiating Rapport in German–Chinese Conversation', 'Negative Assessments in Japanese–American Workplace Interaction', 'Impression Management in Intercultural German Job Interviews', 'Issues of Face in a Chinese Business Visit to Britain'). The final section on methodology deserves special mention as it includes three practical and most useful chapters introducing students to the wide range of research methods and data-collection techniques in pragmatics research, the recording and analysis of data, and projects in intercultural pragmatics.

The year 2008 has also seen the publication of some substantial research on historical pragmatics. *Methods in Historical Pragmatics*, edited by Susan M. Fitzmaurice and Irma Taavitsainen (which in fact appeared in 2007) is a critical review and assessment of the assumptions and practices underlying research on English historical pragmatics and historical discourse analysis. It thus reflects and contributes to historical pragmatics as an established and maturing field of research in that it exemplifies and extends its range of research approaches and methods. The eleven contributions examine various topics and offer insights into earlier communicative practices, registers, and linguistic functions. The first chapter by the editors, 'Historical Pragmatics: What It Is and How to Do It', gives a survey of the approaches and methods that continue to shape this extending research field, which is still in development. The next two chapters represent case studies on individual expressions ('The Development of *I mean*: Implications for the Study of Historical Pragmatics' by Laurel J. Brinton and '*Soþlice, Forsoothe, Truly*— Communicative Principles and Invited Inferences in the History of Truth-Intensifying Adverbs in English' by Ursula Lenker), whereas the following four contributions shift to the level of speech acts and address methodological challenges more specifically, also exemplifying the significance of corpora in the study of historical pragmatics ('Speech Act Verbs and Speech Acts in the History of English' by Irma Taavitsainen and Andreas H. Jucker; 'Text Types and the Methodology of Diachronic Speech Act Analysis' by Thomas Kohnen; 'Developing a More Detailed Picture of the English Courtroom (1640–1760): Data and Methodological Issues Facing Historical Pragmatics' by Dawn Archer; and 'What Do You Lacke? What Is It You Buy? Early Modern English Service Encounters' by Birte Bös). Finally, four papers provide stimulating impulses for collaborative efforts between linguists and literary scholars in the study of narrative discourse ('A Pragmatics for Interpreting Shakespeare's Sonnets 1 to 20: Dialogue Scripts and Erasmian Intertexts' by Lynne Magnusson; 'Letters as Narrative: Narrative Patterns and Episode Structure in Early Letters, 1400 to 1650' by Monika Fludernik; 'Historical Linguistics, Literary Interpretation, and the Romances of Margaret Cavendish' by James Fitzmaurice; and 'Discoursal Aspects of the *Legends of Holy Women* by Osbern Bokenham' by Gabriella Del Lungo Camiciotti).

The second collection on the pragmatics of earlier stages of English, *Speech Acts in the History of English*, is also co-edited by Irma Taavitsainen, this time with Andreas H. Jucker. It includes eleven case studies that explore similarities and differences in the use of speech acts from OE to PDE, and are organized into three thematic sections. The first part of the volume is devoted to directives and commissives, i.e. speech acts such as requests, commands and promises, and comprises five papers: 'Directives in Old English: Beyond Politeness?' by Thomas Kohnen; 'Requests and Directness in Early Modern English Trial Proceedings and Play-Texts, 1640–1760' by Jonathan Culpeper and Dawn Archer; 'An Inventory of Directives in Shakespeare's *King Lear*' by Ulrich Busse; 'Two Polite Speech Acts from a Diachronic Perspective: Aspects of the Realisation of Requesting and Undertaking Commitments in the Nineteenth-Century Commercial Community' by Gabriella Del Lungo Camiciotti; and '"No Botmeles Bihestes": Various Ways of Making Binding Promises in Middle English' by Mari Pakkala-Weckström. The second part consists of three papers that deal with expressives and assertives, focusing on greetings, compliments and apologies: '*Hāl, Hail, Hello, Hi*: Greetings in English Language History' by Joachim Grzega; '"Methinks you seem more beautiful than ever": Compliments and Gender in the History of English' by Irma Taavitsainen and Andreas H. Jucker; and 'Apologies in the History of

English: Routinized and Lexicalized Expressions of Responsibility and Regret'
by Andreas H. Jucker and Irma Taavitsainen. Finally, part III, 'Methods of
Speech Act Retrieval', features three technical reports that deal primarily with
the problem of extracting speech acts from historical corpora: 'Showing a
Little Promise: Identifying and Retrieving Explicit Illocutionary Acts from a
Corpus of Written Prose' by Petteri Valkonen; 'Fishing for Compliments:
Precision and Recall in Corpus-Linguistic Compliment Research' by Andreas
H. Jucker, Gerold Schneider, Irma Taavitsainen and Barb Breustedt; and
'Tracing Directives through Text and Time: Towards a Methodology of
Corpus-Based Diachronic Speech-Act Analysis' by Thomas Kohnen.

In addition to these two edited collections, several papers on the historical
pragmatics of English have appeared in the *Journal of Historical Pragmatics*.
In '"You belly-guilty bag": Insulting Epithets in Old English' (*JHPrag* 9[2008]
1–19), Don Chapman examines epithets used as insults that accompany the
second person pronouns *þu* and *þin* in the *Dictionary of Old English Corpus*.
Chapman shows that nearly all these insulting epithets are highly conventional, both in their use of well-established words from the OE lexicon and in
their reuse of typical epithets, with only a handful of them showing originality
and creativity. In 'From Proper Name to Primary Interjection: The Case of
Gee!' (*JHPrag* 9[2008] 71–88), Elke Gehweiler deals with interjections that
have evolved from nouns, specifically expletives like *gee!*, *jeeze!*, *gosh!*, or
crikey! Using the *OED* and the *BNC* for diachronic and synchronic corpus
data respectively, she shows that a four-stage model can explain how primary
interjections regularly evolve from religious names via secondary interjections
and phonological modifications. In 'Linguistic Politeness in Anglo-Saxon
England? A Study of Old English Address Terms' (*JHPrag* 9[2008] 140–58),
Thomas Kohnen uses the *Dictionary of Old English Corpus* to examine the
most prominent OE terms of nominal address associated with polite or
courteous behaviour. Analysing their distribution, typical communicative
settings of use and basic pragmatic meaning, Kohnen argues that politeness as
facework may not have played a major role in Anglo-Saxon England, but that
the use of address terms may rather reflect accommodation to the overriding
importance of both mutual obligation and kin loyalty, as well as obedience to
the basic Christian ideals of *humilitas* and *caritas*.

In the same journal, Francisco Alonso-Almeida's 'The Pragmatics of *and*-
Conjunctives in Middle English Medical Recipes: A Relevance Theory
Description' (*JHPrag* 9[2008] 171–99) seeks to explore the multiple meanings
of the conjunction *and* in ME medical recipes in the *Corpus of Middle English
Medical Texts*. Sigi Vandewinkel and Kristin Davidse's 'The Interlocking
Paths of Development to Emphasizer Adjective *Pure*' (*JHPrag* 9[2008] 255–87)
presents a close analysis of synchronic and diachronic data on the basis of
which the authors argue that the peculiarities of the emphasizer *pure* in PDE
are the result of two distinct but mutually reinforcing paths of development.
Emphasizing *pure* first appeared as a subjective heightener of emotion nouns
in the syntactic environment *pure* + noun, in which it subsequently spread to
other collocational sets, while in the pattern *pure* and adjective + noun, the
emphasizing use occurred only at the end of Late ModE. Finally, Hélène
Margerie provides a 'A Historical and Collexeme Analysis of the Development

of the Compromiser *Fairly*' (*JHPrag* 9[2008] 288–314), arguing that *rather*, which had already developed into a compromiser by the time *fairly* started going down the same cline, provides the background for the study of the grammaticalization of *fairly*. Margerie carries out a distinctive collexeme analysis based on electronic corpora, focusing on the collocational preferences of the two compromisers when combining with an adjective. The difference in the polarity of the adjectives they modify indicates their complementary distribution.

The remainder of this review will very briefly highlight a number of special issues of journals that have appeared this year. The *Journal of Pragmatics* alone published three special issues in 2008. 'Questions of Context in Studies of Talk and Interaction—Ethnomethodology and Conversation Analysis' (*JPrag* 40:v[2008]), edited by Alex Houl, features papers that take on the issue of context within, and between, ethnomethodology and conversation analysis. 'Empirical Data and Pragmatic Theory' (*JPrag* 40:viii[2008]), edited by Salvador Pons Borderia, highlights the advantages of a strictly empirical approach which takes the use of language into account in order to explain language in use. In order to stress the connection between pragmatic theory and data, all papers in this volume start with precise hypotheses within a theoretical framework, analyse tokens of naturally occurring samples of language (either spoken or written), show that the data reveal that some aspect(s) of a previous theoretical assumption ought to be changed, and provide a new theoretical reformulation of (any of) the idea(s) in the initial framework. Most of the contributions discuss discourse markers, but differ in their theoretical approaches, ranging from politeness theory or grammaticalization studies to neo-Gricean pragmatics or construction grammar.

'Pragmatic and Discourse-Analytic Approaches to Present-Day English' (*JPrag* 40:ix[2008]), edited by Anita Fetzer and Karin Aijmer, examines the interrelation between linguistic form, communicative function and context by focusing on the question of how context may influence, if not determine, the use of themes, non-congruently configured linguistic forms, adjectival constructions, adverbials, interrogative forms and concessive repair. The contributions investigate a variety of contexts such as computer-mediated interaction (chat and forum discussions), media discourse (newspapers), dialogic genre (interview), and picture books, examining the function(s) and context of morphological (adjectives, adverbs) and syntactic (themes, rhetorical questions) forms, as well as communicative practices (concessive repair). Special attention is given to the accommodation of sequentiality, information packaging and narrative patterns, to multimodality and to the status of English as an international language. Further special issues appeared in *Pragmatics* on 'The Discourse of News Management' (*Pragmatics* 18:i[2008]), edited by Geert Jacobs and Henk Pander Maat, and *Intercultural Pragmatics* (*IPrag* 5:iv[2008]), the latter focusing on negation and context by studying both the processing and production of negation in various languages such as German, Hebrew, Spanish, English and French.

Turning to special journal issues in the field of discourse analysis, *Critical Discourse Studies* published an issue on 'Class and Discourse' (*CDS* 5:iv[2008]), and *Discourse Processes* features a special edition on 'Cognitive and Linguistic Factors in Interactive Knowledge Construction' (*DPr* 45:iv–v[2008]), which aims to identify some models of the cognitive discourse and linguistic processes that underlie knowledge construction and to analyse how such processes are supported in technologies with diverse channels of communication. *Text & Talk* has a special issue on 'Narrative Analysis in the Shift from Texts to Practices' (*T&T* 28:iii[2008]), guest-edited by Anna De Fina and Alexandra Georgakopoulou, which reflects on and critically assesses a 'new' turn to narrative that is part of a more general shift from texts to social practices in language-focused enquiry: a move away from narrative as a well-defined and delineated genre with an identifiable structure (narrative as text) to narrative as practice within social interaction, focusing on the multiplicity, fragmentation, and irreducible situatedness of its forms and functions in a wide range of social arenas.

Finally, a special issue of *Discourse Studies* (*DisS* 10:i[2008]) features papers that, from a broadly conversation-analytic methodological approach, address questions and questioning as a social practice that has real-life consequences in a variety of settings (everyday talk between friends and relatives, meetings, therapy, televised political discussions, survey interviews, home help, calls to an ambulance call centre, emergency calls, service encounters and police interrogations), and in a variety of European languages (German, Finnish, Danish, Italian and British English).

12. Stylistics

The year 2008 has witnessed the publication of a healthy number of studies written either by long-established practitioners of stylistics or by other scholars whose work has some bearing on the research of the former. The following pages review significant publications by stylisticians and other influential works.

The Language and Literature Reader, edited by Ronald Carter and Peter Stockwell, is one of those works which any discipline is in need of from time to time. The editors have managed to put together a comprehensive array of chapters of previously published work by scholars who have nurtured stylistics to take it to what it is today. The volume is divided into three sections ('Foundations', 'Developments' and 'New Directions') which encompass various sub-branches of stylistics (for instance, the corpus stylistics take of Michael Stubbs or the cognitive stylistics perspective of Elena Semino and Joanna Gavins); various linguistic models, such as M.A.K. Halliday's now canonical analysis of William Golding's *The Inheritors*; or William Nash's application of tools from discourse analysis and speech-act theory to drama. A second key publication is Geoffrey Leech's *Language in Literature: Style and Foregrounding*. Leech has also contributed to the previous collection as his research can be considered seminal in stylistics. The chapters in Leech's book are not all original work. In his far-reaching career spanning over four decades, Leech has had the opportunity to develop various and distinctive approaches to the analysis of English in general, and stylistics in particular, and this volume gathers some of that work in chapters 2 to 9. Chapters 1, 10,

11 and 12 are original contributions including some frameworks not investigated before, sometimes simply because the technology required was yet not available (as in corpus stylistics). Leech's work relies heavily on the notion of foregrounding, which has been the focus of extensive analysis in stylistics.

Another comprehensive volume that attempts to provide an overview of stylistic approaches from the 1960s to current trends is Andrew Goatly's *Explorations in Stylistics*. Starting with the theoretical principles defended by Roman Jakobson, Goatly looks at William Golding's *Pincher Martin*, J.K. Rowling's *Harry Potter and the Philosopher's Stone* and Harold Pinter's *The Birthday Party*, among other works, from the perspectives of systemic-functional linguistics, corpus linguistics, and pragmatics respectively. The great asset of this volume is, undoubtedly, its hands-on approach. Goatly has eschewed dense theoretical accounts of the principles and frameworks he applies to texts in favour of practical applications, emphasizing the pedagogical potential of this monograph. Greg Watson's edited collection, *The State of Stylistics*, is another good example of the inherently practical nature of most stylistic analyses. This is the last volume to be published by Rodopi as part of the Poetics and Linguistics Association series; it originates in the twenty-sixth PALA conference that took place in Joeensuu, Finland, in 2006 and presents a selection of the papers given there. As the title suggests, the conference organizer and editor of the volume intended stylisticians to reflect on the state of the discipline. The result is a collection of twenty-four papers organized around five sections roughly corresponding to sub-branches currently favoured by stylisticians: the theoretical outlook, cognitive stylistics, corpus stylistics, pragmatic stylistics and stylistics in the classroom. Of the five sections, only the first pertains specifically to the theme of the conference, as contributors were requested to 'define' the remit of stylistics. Among the chapters dealing with cognitive aspects, for instance, Katerina Vassilopou investigates the applicability of 'possible worlds' theory to drama, a genre which has generally escaped the attention of possible worlds theorists. Merja Kytö and Suzanne Romaine, in turn, use the CONCE (Corpus of Nineteenth-Century English) and the BNC to track down the semantic evolution of the adjective 'dear' as an affect marker in nineteenth-century English letters. A general concern as to where the boundaries of stylistics lie is also dealt with in David Gugin's 'The Uses of Literature: Towards a Bidirectional Stylistics' (*L&L* 17[2008] 123–36). Gugin proposes the term 'bidirectional stylistics' to describe the twofold way in which stylistics can be used. The bidirectionality of stylistics emerges, on the one hand, from the primarily linguistic basis which stylistics has not only made extensive use of but which, Gugin defends, should not cease to be part of its basic tenets; on the other hand, Gugin argues that stylistics can also help linguistics by strengthening and expanding traditional discussions of certain syntactic structures, such as the pseudo-cleft sentence, which he analyses in relation to Flannery O'Connor's fiction.

Concerning general studies on the nature of language, several publications deserve space in this review, among them David Crystal's *Txtng: The Gr8 Db8*. Following the trends set by his previous *Language and the Internet* [2001] and *Glossary of Netspeak and Textspeak* [2004], Crystal sets out to describe the phenomenon of texting. Using very accessible language not solely aimed at the scholarly community, Crystal approaches the issue from a linguistic perspective. Despite some stern animadversion (especially in the media) towards the negative influence of texting on language in general, Crystal insists that there are some linguistic aspects of texting worth highlighting such as, for instance, the combination of standard and non-standard features, the use of pictograms and emoticons, or the special way the apostrophe is dealt with. The rejection expressed by the media, which have sometimes referred to this variety of language as 'textese', 'slanguage', 'a new high-tech lingo', 'a hybrid shorthand' or 'a digital virus' (p. 13) fails to acknowledge that, in other ways, texting is extremely creative. Crystal also emphasizes that texting, like other forms of language, is capable of displaying sociolinguistic markers such as register, formality or even gender. For instance, institutions (schools, associations, big companies) use texts to communicate with a large community and maintain a high level of conventionality in their messages; similarly, gender can also be typographically realized in text-messaging as women are considered to use more exclamation marks than men.

On a different topic, Ludovic De Cuypere's *Limiting the Iconic: From the Metatheoretical Foundations to the Creative Possibilities of Iconicity in Language* revisits the well-debated issue of whether language is to be defined as arbitrary or iconic. After Saussure declared that languages are, by and large, mainly arbitrary in nature, the last two decades have seen a surge of studies that have questioned this fundamental linguistic tenet. These studies are based on the Peircean notion of iconicity, that is, on the belief that languages do reflect reality to some extent and are not merely arbitrary or conventionally established. De Cuypere calls into question the empirically oriented findings of these studies and suggests that the issue of whether language is arbitrary or iconic might never be resolved. The book summarizes the proposals of the main thinkers that have discussed the theory of signs, starting with Aristotle, moving on to Saussure's arbitrariness and ending with the semiotic perspective put forward by Peirce. Stylistics, very much dependent on the new developments of linguistic theoretical proposals, has a lot to gain from debates such as this As a complement to this volume, Klaas Willems and Ludovic De Cuypere's *Naturalness and Iconicity in Language* gathers together a series of articles presenting a state-of-the-art view on the issue of iconicity and what is generally known as 'naturalness' in language. Although both terms are sometimes used interchangeably, the editors clarify that iconicity is but one aspect of naturalness. According to them: 'The fundamental tenet of Naturalness Theory is that distinctions in language may be mapped onto naturalness scales founded in extralinguistic reality, that is, the physical or cognitive foundations of language' (p. 2). This volume brings together theoretical papers on both notions. Of special interest for stylistics is Juliette Blevins's 'Natural and Unnatural Sound Patterns: A Pocket Field Guide' (pp. 121–48). Stylistic analyses of poetic texts have thoroughly discussed phonetic issues such as rhyme, rhythm, assonance and consonance and have also considered the effect of 'sound-symbolism' in the creation of meaning. Theoretical examinations of the nature of phonetic naturalness, thus, can augment our understanding of stylistics as a discipline. Finally, an article dealing with general issues of dialect representation is Katy M. Wright's 'The Role of Dialect Representation in Speaking from the Margins: "The Lesson" of Toni Cade Bambara' (*Style* 42[2008] 73–83).

Research built upon narratological principles should be considered in a review of stylistic work. Although viewed as two distinct disciplines, there are, nevertheless, not just plenty of commonalities between the two approaches but also plenty of practitioners who work as easily in one camp as in the other. There have been some interesting publications in this area in 2008, some of which have direct resonance in more clearly defined stylistic publications. One such trans-disciplinary volume is *Theorizing Narrativity*, edited by John Pier and José Ángel García Landa. The editors claim that this collection presents a number of chapters that collectively aim to answer the (otherwise elusive and not easily resolvable) question of what narrative is. Questions such as 'What makes a narrative more or less narrative?' or 'What features of a discourse otherwise considered a description, an argument or a dialogue can legitimately be regarded as narrative?' (p. 7) are two of the issues that this volume addresses. Two contributions are particularly relevant for stylistics, one written by a stylistician, Michael Toolan's 'The Language of Guidance', (pp. 307–30), and another by a narratologist whose work is often quoted by stylisticians, Monica Fludernik's 'Narrative and Drama' (pp. 355–84). Toolan's chapter is concerned with the reading process because, according to Toolan, that is where the notion of narrativity actually lies. He points out how the text guides the reader by using corpus linguistic methods, but he does not consider those as the ultimate or only tool that can help the narrative stylistician gain an insight into how narrativity is constructed. For instance, he openly maintains that corpus techniques totally miss out those aspects of the text whose significance does not lie in their recurrence but in the implicatures that the various collocations may create. Fludernik, on the other hand, investigates the narrative aspects of drama. Dramatic texts, she argues, have traditionally been associated with narratives in as much as the plot component is always present, but they differ as far as the absence of a narrating entity is concerned. The difference between narratives and drama texts, she adds, lies not simply at the level of presentation via a mediator (the narrator) but at discourse level, where drama texts exploit visual elements more clearly or use elliptical methods where narrative would probably opt for summary or description techniques.

A second publication falling well within the remit of narratology is Hilary Dannenberg's *Coincidence and Counterfactuality: Plotting Time and Space in Narrative Fiction*. Dannenberg presents an overview of two basic mechanisms for devising narrative plot, coincidence and counterfactuality. She analyses the convergence and divergence of characters' trajectories in plots across a wide range of texts, as well as across various periods. She also proposes a cognitive, reader-oriented model to explain why these techniques are so ingrained in fictional narratives. Many other linguistic and stylistic aspects have been discussed from a narratological perspective, such as a study on the use of the first person plural in Amit Marcus's 'A Contextual View of Narrative Fiction in the First Person Plural' (*Narrative* 16[2008] 46–64). David Herman's 'Description, Narrative, and Explanation: Text-Type Categories and the

Cognitive Foundations of Discourse Competence' (*PoT* 29[2008] 437–72) is an attempt at defining 'description, narration and explanation' as text types, while a reading of Wordsworth's *The Prelude* through the prism of narrative theory is the subject of Monique R. Morgan's 'Narrative Means to Lyric Ends in Wordsworth's *Prelude*' (*Narrative* 16[2008] 298–330).

A year's worth of stylistic work is not complete without considering publications on poetry. To begin with, a paperback version of a hardback monograph needs to be mentioned. Shira Wolosky's *The Art of Poetry: How to Read a Poem* is a volume whose contents suit the basic needs of undergraduates as it describes classic notions such as syntax and the poetic line, metaphors and similes, poetic forms such as the sonnet, rhetoric and gender. The introductory nature of Wolosky's study is not mirrored in Nigel Fabb and Morris Halle's *Meter in Poetry: A New Theory*. This volume contains an extremely detailed account of metre and its exploitation in various poetic forms in languages as diverse as English, Spanish, Galician-Portuguese, French, Greek, Classical Arabic, Sanskrit and Latvian as well as in the Old Testament. Proof of the undying interest in poetry is supplied by articles that have appeared in *Language and Literature* and the *Journal of Literary Semantics*, the two main journals for stylistic studies. Martin J. Duffell's 'Some Observations on English Binary Metres' (*L&L* 17[2008] 5–20) and Matthew B. Winn and William J. Idsardi's 'Musical Evidence Regarding Trochaic Inversion' (*L&L* 17[2008] 335–49) specialize in metre too, whereas Karen Sullivan's 'Genre-Dependent Metonymy in Norse Skaldic Poetry' (*L&L* 17[2008] 21–36) discusses the poetic forms used by skalds (court poets) in Iceland and Norway from the ninth to the fourteenth centuries. In turn, Gareth Twose's 'What's in a Clause? Milton's Participial Style Revisited' (*L&L* 17[2008] 77–96) deftly revisits claims made by Seymour Chatman in the 1960s concerning Milton's poetic style by applying new corpora techniques, and James Carney's '"Unweaving the Rainbow": The Semantic Organization of the Lyric' (*JLS* 37[2008] 33–53) applies the mathematical resources of 'catastrophe theory' to develop a semantic model of lyric poetry. Finally, Iris Yaron's 'What Is a "Difficult Poem"? Towards a Definition' (*JLS* 37[2008] 129–50) bravely attempts to provide a definition of how to understand the notion 'difficult poem' by proposing to incorporate a reader's perspective in such an arduous and rather controversial enterprise.

Metaphor studies are another important source for stylistic analyses. The variety of approaches, trends and versions of models that deal with metaphor is sufficiently ample to allow new perspectives to be generated all the time. The year 2008 has not let us down in this respect either and, more importantly, seems to be highlighting a trend among metaphor scholars that signals a move away from the theoretical tenets that characterized some studies of the past towards more contextualized approaches that should disclose actual uses of metaphors by speakers. The first of these publications is a collection edited by Mara Sophia Zanotto, Lynne Cameron and Marilda Cavalcanti, *Confronting Metaphor in Use: An Applied Linguistic Approach*. It contains fourteen chapters grouped into four sections, all sharing an eminently practical definition of how metaphorical patterns and structures need to be understood. Of special interest is the section devoted to the conflation of cognitive and corpus approaches: 'Examining Metaphors in Corpora'. Alice Deignan's chapter, 'Corpus Linguistic Data and Conceptual Metaphor Theory' (pp. 149–62), for instance, argues for the complementarity of corpus linguistics and conceptual metaphor theory. She states that both disciplines share specific aspects of the definition of metaphor, such as the ubiquity and patterned structure of its use. She also suggests that the original cognitivist view of metaphor based largely on data provided by the analyst should, by now, have been made obsolete. In 'Metaphor Shifting in the Dynamics of Talk' (pp. 45–62), Lynne Cameron investigates linguistic metaphors in naturally occurring conversations in the contexts of school classrooms and conciliation talk. She concludes that metaphor use in conversation is dynamic, which necessarily entails that a certain degree of adaptation and reformulation of the original in the hands of its users is to be expected. Cameron further argues (p. 61) that, viewed from a primarily practical perspective, the cognitive basis of metaphors only acts as 'way-routed paths' that might somehow indicate the direction the metaphor will take, but that contextual factors such as speakers' 'experience of the world, their socio-cultural contexts and, their discourse purposes' dictate the actual realization of the metaphor in use. Another volume devoted to metaphor in use is Erich Berendt's *Metaphors for Learning: Cross-Cultural Perspectives*. Although the theoretical position that informs most of the papers in this volume is the traditional cognitivist stance of George Lakoff and Mark Johnson, these chapters go on to investigate the role of metaphor in academic discourse, education and rhetorical studies as well as in languages as diverse as Arabic, Chinese, English, Hungarian, Japanese, Malay, Polish and Russian.

Elena Semino's *Metaphor in Discourse* shares the same urge to claim the need for a fully contextualized approach to the study of metaphor. This volume concurs, in fact, with quite a few of the proposals made in the previous collections. Semino is part of the Pragglejaz Group, which has brought together a series of metaphor scholars interested both in devising an accurate procedure for metaphor identification and in understanding the peculiarities of contextualized metaphor in use. The term Pragglejaz is an acronym made up of the initial letters of the members' first names: Peter Crisp, Ray Gibbs, Alan Cienki, Gerard Steen, Graham Low, Lynne Cameron, Elena Semino, Joseph Grady, Alice Deignan and Zoltan Kövecses, some of whom are editors and contributors to the collections discussed above. As a group they have come up with the so-called Metaphor Identification Procedure (MIP) which they propose as a more rigorous way of identifying metaphorical use in discourse. Semino's monograph is a further contribution to the Pragglejaz Group's endeavours in that the MIP is taken as the basis to determine the patterns that linguistic metaphors display in discourses as diverse as literature, politics, science, education, advertising, and health and illness discourse. The application of corpus linguistic methods (*Wordsmith* tools) to the textual material chosen as data for comparison (the BNC) again brings this publication in line with the research of Cameron and Deignan described above. Although acknowledging that metaphor studies are clearly indebted to the efforts of cognitive theorists such as Lakoff and Johnson, Semino still maintains that an understanding of the real nature of what it means to comprehend something in terms of something else can only be truly achieved by paying very close attention to those that actually use, modify, reformulate or borrow metaphors (this study is also discussed in section 7).

A further publication on the nature of linguistic metaphor, similarly informed by rigorous methods of analysis, is Cornelia Müller's *Metaphors Dead and Alive, Sleeping and Waking*. Müller wants to challenge the commonly held view that verbal metaphors may be dead or alive by proving, through empirical evidence, that 'conventional verbal metaphors are for the most part dead and alive' (p. 1). She is interested in supporting her view with empirically tested analyses, echoing Semino's, Deignan's and Cameron's views on this matter. Müller also looks at 'verbal, pictorial and gestural contexts of conventionalized verbal metaphors' (p. 2), which allows her to see that the activation of particular source domains varies from speaker to speaker, writer to writer and moment to moment. Furthermore, the successful marriage of a cognitive and empirical perspective also shows that metaphoricity is gradable and not an absolute category, so it may be more active in one context and less so in others. Dynamicity and gradability are two characteristics that seem to make the dichotomy 'dead' versus 'alive' redundant. The varying degree of activation, that is, 'low or no degree' versus 'high degree', explains the existence of 'sleeping' and 'waking' metaphors. To back up her dynamicity and gradability theory she implements a multimodal analysis of verbo-pictorial adverts; the verbal expression 'in the shade', for instance, is brought to life when the specific producer of the metaphor (a journalist in this case) chooses a particular visual manifestation to accompany that text, which, literally, places one of the participants under the shadow of somebody else. The multimodal domains that Müller examines as part of her analysis are language, pictures, sculpture and gestures, which turn this volume into an extremely thorough, well-researched piece of work, surely long overdue.

More work on metaphor can be found in Markus Tendahl and Raymond W. Gibbs's 'Complementary Perspectives on Metaphor: Cognitive Linguistics and Relevance Theory' (*JPrag* 40[2008] 1823–64), who defend an interdisciplinary and collaborative take on metaphor analysis. This article shows how previously antagonistic views on metaphor emerging from cognitive science and relevance theory seem to be not only complementary but even 'marriageable'. Yesim Aksan and Dilek Kantar look at the linguistic realization of love metaphors in two unrelated languages such as English and Turkish in 'No Wellness Feels Better than this Sickness: Love Metaphors from a Cross-Cultural Perspective' (*M&Sym* 23[2008] 262–91).

One area to which stylistic studies are beginning to turn unabashedly is that of emotion, both as a linguistic realization and as the embodiment of readers' sentiments when processing literature. In this respect, Ayako Omori's 'Emotion as a Huge Mass of Moving Water' (*M&Sym* 23[2008] 130–46) raises extremely interesting issues worth considering from a stylistic perspective, such as the need to bring in empirical methodologies to the manifestation of emotions and the accuracy of previous proposals in relation to attributes of the emotion prototype. The journal also includes a reply by Zoltán Kövecses, 'On Metaphors for Emotion: A Reply to Ayako Omori'

(*M&Sym* 23[2008] 200–3), who disagrees with some of the conclusions drawn by Omori.

Another volume to be discussed in this section on metaphor nicely combines metaphor studies and an area of research that stylisticians are also turning to more and more, that of multimodality. Alan Cienki and Cornelia Müller's *Metaphor and Gesture* investigates a particular realization of metaphor, namely that found in gestures, which is comprehensively examined by a range of scholars from the US, France and Germany. The relationship between metaphor and gestures is examined from a variety of perspectives, among them a conceptual and a semiotic point of view. From a semiotic perspective, the focus is on the 'metaphoric use of different forms of iconic structures in gesture' (p. 1). Other perspectives are also brought in, such as that of gesture understood as a window onto the thought process of speakers or gesture as a tool used by the hearer to construct the speaker's intended meaning. Furthermore, there are papers relating to the use of gesture in pedagogic contexts. Rafael Núñez, for instance, looks at how gestures used by lecturers in mathematics 'provide additional evidence of metaphoric conceptualization' (p. 2). Additionally, Irene Mittelberg's chapter focuses on the gestures of linguistics teachers and brings together Peircean semiotic theory and conceptual metaphor theory. The second part of the book is made up of comments from practitioners drawn from a diversity of disciplines regarding the viability of the application of theoretical tenets on metaphor and gesture in their own fields of study. These disciplines include cognitive linguistics, anthropology, conversation analysis, ethno-methodology, sign language, semiotics, conceptual metaphor theory and psychology. Paul Bouissac's contribution, 'The Study of Metaphor and Gesture: A Critique from the Perspective of Semiotics' (pp. 277–82) needs some consideration, for its dissenting voice stands out among the rest. Bouissac criticizes the way in which gesture scholars interpret the embodiment of particular metaphorical meanings in gestures. He suggests that these gestures work as 'cases of semantic supplementation rather than the redundant expressions of a metaphor in two modalities' (p. 279) and distinguishes between those gestures that are 'mere' illustrators and metaphorical gestures proper. Another criticism concerns the 'a-cultural' nature attributed by scholars to gestures. It seems, though, that the volume is but a first attempt to look at these two basic aspects of human communication and that further work is much needed. (For more details on other studies in this volume, see section 7.)

As pointed out above, more and more stylisticians acknowledge the advantage of embracing a broader understanding of the notions of text and discourse as conventional ways of realizing literature, for instance, are being subverted (in multimodal novels or hypertext fiction) or simply reformulated in formats other than the written one (cinematic adaptations, for example). John Bateman's *Multimodality and Genre: A Foundation for the Systematic Analysis of Multimodal Documents* illustrates this broad conceptualization of the notion of 'text'. The book has three main audiences in mind: researchers and students looking for methods to analyse communication forms that combine several semiotic modes, document scholars and multimodal scholars. As the title of the book suggests, the core focus lies in the 'written document', which encompasses 'any piece that uses writing as a means of communication: bus ticket, doctoral dissertation, supermarket sales offer, legal contracts' (p. 1). Bateman argues that nowadays documents no longer rely simply on the written mode as their main mode of communication. Instead there are a myriad different modes combined with the written one in what he calls the 'multimodal document'. The aim is, thus, to consider how such modes are combined and deployed simultaneously 'in order to fulfil an orchestrated collection of interwoven communicative goals' (p. 1). Furthermore, the book attempts to present a series of analytical methods to explain how such orchestration has been achieved.

Another contribution to multimodality is Kay O'Halloran's *Mathematical Discourse: Language, Symbolism and Visual Images*. At first glance, the title might appear to convey a lack of resonance with stylistic concerns, but that view would be rather short-sighted. The choice of mathematics as an example of both multisemiotic and multimodal discourse is indicative of the range of discourses that multimodal approaches can encompass. O'Halloran uses Systemic Functional Grammar and communicative principles put forward by M.A.K. Halliday to account for the multifaceted aspects of mathematics. For instance (written) mathematical discourse is commonly characterized by a combination of semiotic modes such as textual elements, graphics in the form of equations and visual display. Mathematics discourse, nonetheless, can also manifest itself multimodally when used in academic lectures or presentations. The fact that literature is, similarly, one type of discourse easily transposed to various other media (film, audio-books, radio readings) presents stylisticians with vast scope for further research. Systemic Functional Grammar/ Linguistics and social semiotics are also the theoretical frameworks of Len Unsworth's *Multimodal Semiotics Functional Analysis in Contexts of Education*. This is a collection of essays that extends the application of systemic functional principles to semiotic systems other than language with an added underlying concern for pedagogical issues. The collection is divided into four parts, each with a specific textual focus in mind: space, film, news and public media, and school curricula. For instance, Betty O.K. Pun's 'Metafunctional Analysis of Sound in Film Communication' (pp. 105–21) highlights the importance of analysing cinema as an inter-semiotic event in which the presence of sound is to be understood in relation to other semiotic forms such as the visual or camera movement.

The relationship between literary and cinematic forms is, in fact, a rich source of material for multimodal analysis, and one that is being taken up by stylisticians too. This year has witnessed the launch of the Oxford journal *Adaptation* devoted specifically to the transposition of literary forms into cinematic versions. As Deborah Cartmell, Timothy Corrigan and Imelda Whelehan (editors) explain: 'The journal offers an opportunity for the two disciplines to "talk to each other", not as Literature and Film, but as literature on screen and "screen" on literature, not demonstrating how the two arts are or are not similar, but how they contribute to and enrich each other through an understanding of the translation of one art into another and the commingling of the 'literary' and the 'cinematic' across both' (*Adaptation* 1[2008] 1–4). A traditional take on cinema studies is evidenced in David

Bordwell's *Poetics of Cinema*, which gathers essays written by the author over a period of thirty years and mostly published elsewhere. Bordwell's monograph is formalist in nature, and stylisticians might find commonalities with some of the tools they use in their own analyses. For instance, Bordwell discusses narration, plot structure and point of view. Among publications on cinematic issues, Dan McIntyre's 'Integrating Multimodal Analysis and the Stylistics of Drama: A Multimodal Perspective on Ian McKellen's *Richard III*' (*L&L* 17[2008] 309–34) is especially illustrative of the growing number of analyses that are specifically applying stylistic tools to cinematic texts. The publication of this article in *Language & Literature* also shows the variety of journals (apart from those specifically devoted to film studies) that host articles on cinema, such as *Media Psychology* (e.g. Melanie C. Green, Sheryl Klass, Jana Carrey, Benjamin Herzig, Ryan Feeney and John Sabini's 'Transportation across Media: Repeated Exposure to Print and Film', *MPsych* 11[2008] 512–39), *Narrative* (e.g. Tony Jackson's 'Writing, Orality, Cinema: The "Story" of *Citizen Kane*', *Narrative* 16[2008] 29–45) or *Poetics Today* (e.g. Silke Horstokke and Nancy Pedri's 'Introduction: Photographic Interventions', *PoT* 29[2008] 1–29).

The interface of corpus linguistics and more traditional stylistic analyses is no longer a new trend or a 'fad' among stylisticians but a well-established discipline, whose principles and methodologies are currently being embraced and exploited in the branch known as corpus stylistics. Volumes on corpus linguistics, consequently, are always welcomed by the stylistics community, especially when they try to move away from those initial tentative approaches that used to only deal with relatively small texts towards the analysis of longer stretches of language. Such is the case in *Corpora and Discourse: The Challenges of Different Settings*, edited by Annelie Ädel and Randi Reppen. This collection of essays concerns the analysis of language in general, but can potentially be significant for stylistics in that the various contributors are interested in using corpus tools to look at discourse phenomena. The book contains four general sections reflecting the type of discourse they attempt to describe: academic settings, workplace settings, news and entertainment, and exploring discourse through specific linguistic features. Among the various chapters, Elaine Vaughan's '"Got a date or something?": An Analysis of the Role of Humour and Laughter in the Workplace Meetings of English Language Teachers' (pp. 95–116) exemplifies the way discourse as opposed to lexical or grammatical matters can be investigated. It focuses on the naturally occurring interactions taking place among university staff during meetings. The data was recorded in two different institutions, a public university in Mexico and a private language school in the west of Ireland. The recordings were duly transcribed and run through *Wordsmith* tools; the results highlight that the extralinguistic element of 'laughter' featured rather prominently. The author rightly concludes that corpus linguistic methods can help the analyst focus not only on lexical patterns but also on discoursal features not always previously considered in corpus studies. Vaughan goes on to also examine how humour is used as a politeness strategy to mark both positive and negative politeness instances. In *Emotion Talk across Corpora*, on the other hand, Monica Bednarek excellently combines studies on emotion and the systematic perspective of corpus analysis. The book stems from the assumption (later proven) that our 'emotion talk' (p. 4) can reveal not only personal but also cultural experience and attitudes. Bednarek summarizes previous theories on emotion as considered mainly in psychology, sociology and linguistics, and deals with issues such as 'What is an emotion?', 'How can emotions be defined?', 'What is the structure of emotions?', 'How can emotions be distinguished from each other?', and 'How can emotions be studied, measured, and described?' (p. 5). The answers to such questions emphasize the complexity of the relationship between language and emotion: 'we can express feelings that we have, we can have feelings that we do not express, we can express feelings that we do not have' (p. 7). Although in linguistics there are several ways of approaching the notion of emotion (a cognitive, cross-linguistic, linguistic-anthropological and a functional approach, among others), they all basically handle the relationship between language and emotion as either 'language about emotion (linguistic expressions denoting emotions) or language as emotion (linguistic expressions as conventionalized reflexes or indices of speakers' emotions)' (p. 10). In order to contextualize all of the linguistic and emotional connections, Bednarek looks into the occurrence of emotion terms in four varieties of BrE in a large corpus that includes casual conversation, fiction, news reportage and academic discourse. The particularly salient feature of this monograph is its successful contextualization of emotion talk, thanks to a quantitative approach which allows her to look at the spread of emotion terms in what she calls 'emotion profiles' (p. 17) in each variety. The end result is a well-written, excellently researched and informative monograph that succeeds in combining two aspects of text analysis that stylistics is always keen to investigate.

The analysis of historical data is, perhaps, one area that stylistics has always found challenging. The earlier lack of studies is now rapidly being addressed. Patrick Studer's *Historical Corpus Stylistics: Media, Technology and Change* focuses mainly on early modern news discourse, that is, the media genres of the eighteenth and nineteenth centuries. These forms are investigated with the aid of computerized methodologies which, once more, highlight the advantages of empirical approaches. Studer calls his approach 'historical corpus stylistics' but, somewhat disappointingly, he also points out that his aim is not to be understood simply as an extension of 'corpus stylistics as defined by Mahlberg (2007: 355–398)' (p. 1). Studer seems to be of the opinion that stylistics in general, and corpus stylistics in particular, exclusively engage in the characterization of literary texts. As more and more stylistics research proves, this might have been the case when the discipline first developed, but such a notion no longer describes the reality of what goes on among practitioners of stylistics. Since Studer actually uses the principles described in the work of linguists such as M.A.K. Halliday and Norman Fairclough to account for the stylistic variations of the media genre of the eighteenth century, it could be argued that he is, in fact, utilizing the same linguistic frameworks that stylisticians apply in sub-branches such as functionalist stylistics, feminist stylistics or critical stylistics.

If there is a stylistician who, over the years, has become the bastion of empiricism, that is Willie van Peer, as *Directions in Empirical*

Literary Studies: In Honor of Willie van Peer edited by Sonia Zyngier, Marisa Bortolussi, Anna Chesnokova and Jan Auracher demonstrates. This volume was published on the occasion of van Peer's sixtieth birthday and contains the work of established and budding scholars alike. The editors aimed to pay homage to van Peer's unremitting defence of empiricism by presenting a multidisciplinary collection that shows how empirical perspectives can aid the study of literature. Part III, devoted to the interface of computer methodologies and the humanities, again echoes the viability of such a combination (cf. the volumes by Studer and Bednarek discussed above). Other sections underscore that empirical perspectives do not necessarily always have to rely on the exclusive use of computerized tools. Van Peer has also edited the collection *The Quality of Literature: Linguistic Studies in Literary Evaluation.* On this occasion the focus veers away from exclusively considering empiricism, to reflect on issues of evaluation and literary quality instead. In the introduction, the editor spells out that, of the three elements that influence literary evaluation (i.e. the text, the reader and the context), context seems to have been selected as the most likely, almost exclusive, factor by many analysts. Contextual factors include, according to van Peer, the readers' immediate surroundings, their gender, social class, race, etc., so context is here viewed as a notion loaded with strong ideological content. The approaches and viewpoints in this volume are rather varied, ranging from considerations of the formation of the canon in van Peer's 'Canon Formation: Ideology or Aesthetic Quality?' (pp. 17–30), poetic forms, such as Laurence Lerner's 'Poetic Value: Political Value' (pp. 83–94), and philosophical takes, as in Paisley Livingston's 'Philosophical Perspectives on Literary Value' (pp. 209–22).

The empirical and corpus-assisted trend comes also to the fore in Michael Toolan's 'Narrative Progression in the Short Story: First Steps in a Corpus Stylistic Approach' (*Narrative* 16[2008] 105–20) and in Marcella Corduas, Salvatore Attardo and Alysson Eggleston's 'The Distribution of Humour in Literary Texts is not Random: A Statistical Analysis' (*L&L* 17[2008] 253–70). Corduas and her co-authors argue that humorous instances in two novels (Oscar Wilde's *Lord Arthur Savile's Crime* and Douglas Adams's *The Hitchhiker's Guide to the Galaxy*) follow a particular pattern that can be identified by using statistical methods such as time-series analysis. The thoroughly detailed and rigorous tools used to explain humour distribution might certainly not be to every analyst's taste. However, they build up a solid argument as to why stylistic studies should consider more seriously empirical and even mathematical techniques to analyse language. The study of humour described in this article has also received attention, albeit not from an empirical perspective, in Isabel Ermida's *The Language of Comic Narratives: Humor Construction in Short Stories.* Ermida shows how a linguistic approach informs the way humour works; her theoretical considerations are comple-mented by an analysis of short stories by Woody Allen, Cory Ford, Evelyn Waugh, Dorothy Parker, Graham Greene and David Lodge.

The article by Alison Johnson, '"From where we're sat…"': Negotiating Narrative Transformation through Interaction in Police Interviews with Suspects' (*T&T* 28[2008] 327–49) is written from a discourse-analytical perspective, with a subtle but underlying critical stance. It is a fascinating analysis of police interviews and of the creation, remodulation and reshaping of the narrative accounts provided by suspects. Johnson argues that the 'negotiation' techniques utilized by police interviewers can have several political and judicial readings. From the point of view of the defence of victims, police interviewers attempt to gain the suspect's trust by establishing a false relationship, which will hopefully encourage the suspect to supply the desired account of events. From the point of view of civil liberties, however, the false sense of camaraderie and trust purportedly manufactured by the police can be conceived simply as a 'con' tactic on the part of the interviewers to gain information that might even be untrue. This sense of manipulation, nonetheless, also works from the perspective of the suspect, who can similarly fail to articulate accurate accounts of events for fear of punishment and incarceration. Johnson's engaging analysis highlights the powerful nature of narrative construction by also emphasizing the usefulness of critical discourse techniques to elucidate what might be uncomfortable truths for institutional discourse tactics such as those of the police. Institutional discourse is also the topic of Andrea Mayr's edited volume, *Language and Power: An Introduction to Institutional Discourse*. According to Mayr, the contributors to this volume all work within a 'general critical discourse/multimodal framework' (p. 1), and each presents the theoretical tenets and demonstrates the practical and analytical tools corresponding to the study of the discourse of universities, prisons, the media and the military in British contexts. Thus, the chapter on university discourse, for instance, describes the linguistic manifestations of the increasing 'commercialization' of universities potentially viewed as 'money-making' machinery that needs to generate income and make profits; the chapter on prison discourse, in turn, studies the assigning of criminal blame to the individual and conversely eschewing societal or system responsibility.

The last publications to be discussed are those with a cognitive orientation. Todd Oakley and Anders Hougaard's *Mental Spaces in Discourse and Interaction* conflates two separate frameworks for the understanding of meaning construction, mental spaces theory and conceptual integration, also known as blending theory, which the editors of this volume call the 'mental spaces and conceptual integration framework' (hereafter MSCI). Despite the fact that not all cognitive linguists, nor indeed all stylisticians, concur with the tenets defended in either framework, there is no doubt that the exploration of human understanding still requires much investigative work to be done. This volume certainly contributes to providing just that as there is a distinct variety of approaches all employing the MSCI framework. For instance, the connections with literary stylistics are clear in Barbary Dancygier's 'The Text and the Story: Levels of Blending in Fictional Narratives' (pp. 51–78), where the author looks at narrative discourse and analyses extracts from Ian McEwan's novel *Atonement* and Margaret Atwood's *The Blind Assassin*. But the assortment of applications in this volume also includes an analysis of courtroom settings, of clinical experiences and of instructional discourse.

Blending theory, in particular, has proven particularly popular in 2008, receiving special attention from many authors. For instance, Sarah Copland writes 'Reading in the Blend: Collaborative Conceptual Blending in the Silent Traveller Narratives' (*Narrative* 16[2008] 140–62) and analyses characters', narrators' and readers' thought processes as blending phenomena. Two further studies are Patricia Canning's '"The bodie and the letters both"': "Blending" the Rules of Early Modern Religion' (*L&L* 17[2008] 187–203) and Peter Crisp's 'Between Extended Metaphor and Allegory: Is Blending Enough?' (*L&L* 17[2008] 291–308). Canning uses blending theory to explain how Reformation principles were understood in an early modern context, which differs from the usual contemporary take of most blending theory analyses. Crisp, on the other hand, convincingly argues that the 'healthy' state of a discipline is, more often than not, proven by those situations in which contrasting opinions are set in motion. Crisp does that here by considering the validity of blending theory. Although he acknowledges that few, if any, philosophers or psychologists would ever question the fact that cognitive processes generally involve bringing together existing concepts to create new ones, he also points out that (following Ray Gibbs) not much experimental evidence has been brought to the table just yet. Other articles characterized by a cognitive orientation are Skye Ochsner Margolies and L. Elizabeth Crawford, 'Event Valence and Spatial Metaphors of Time' (*Cog&Em* 22[2008] 1401–14); Lesley Jeffries, 'The Role of Style in Reader-Involvement: Deictic Shifting in Contemporary Poems' (*JLS* 37[2008] 69–85); and Eduard Sioe-Hao Tan, 'Entertainment is Emotion: The Functional Architecture of the Entertainment Experience' (*MPsych* 11[2008] 28–51).

In conclusion, I would like to echo and adopt Crisp's suggestions in relation to the way scholarly enquiry should be conducted if stale and sterile work is to be avoided. He writes that constant and inquisitive debate forms part of stylistics, and stylistics-informed research is proof of the conviction among its practitioners that circular, self-indulging and self-aggrandizing work can only prevent the discipline from evolving positively. Similarly, the fact that stylistics does not shy away from feeding from and incorporating models, frameworks and tools from other cognate areas is proof of the maturity and self-assurance that has been achieved by this discipline.

Books Reviewed

Aarts, Bas. *English Syntax and Argumentation*. 3rd edn. Palgrave. [2008] pp. 344. hb £60 ISBN 9 7802 3055 1206, pb £22.99 ISBN 9 7802 3055 1213.

Aarts, Bas. *Syntactic Gradience: The Nature of Grammatical Indeterminacy*. OUP. [2007] pp. xiv + 280. hb £84 ISBN 9 7801 9921 9261, pb £27 ISBN 9 7801 9921 9278.

Abraham, Werner, and Elisabeth Leiss, eds. *Modality–Aspect Interfaces: Implications and Typological Solutions*. Benjamins. [2008] pp. xxiv + 422. €110 ISBN 9 7890 2722 9922.

Ackema, Peter, Patrick Brandt, Maaike Schoorlemmer, and Fred Weerman, eds. *Arguments and Agreement*. OUP. [2006] pp. vii + 349. £89 ISBN 9 7801 9928 5730.

Ädel, Annelie, and Randi Reppen, eds. *Corpora and Discourse*. Studies in Corpus Linguistics 31. Benjamins. [2008] pp. vi + 295. €105 ($158) ISBN 9 7890 2722 3050.

Adolphs, Svenja. *Corpus and Context: Investigating Pragmatic Functions in Spoken Discourse*. Studies in Corpus Linguistics 30. Benjamins. [2008] pp. xi + 151. €99 ($149) ISBN 9 7890 2722 3043.

Aitchison, Jean. *The Articulate Mammal: An Introduction to Psycholinguistics*. 5th edn. Routledge. [2008] pp. ix + 302. hb £70 ISBN 9 7804 1542 0167, pb £19.99 ISBN 9 7808 0585 1359.

Alexiadou, Artemis, Liliane Haegeman, and Melita Stavrou. *Noun Phrase in the Generative Perspective*. Studies in Generative Grammar 71. Mouton. [2007] pp. xxii + 664. hb €98 ISBN 9 7831 1017 6841, pb €39.95 ISBN 9 7831 1017 6858.

Algeo, John. *British or American English? A Handbook of Word and Grammar Patterns*. Studies in English Language. CUP. [2006]. pp. xii + 348. hb £55 ISBN 9 7805 2137 1377, pb £20.99 ISBN 9 7805 2137 9939.

Altarriba, Jeanette, and Roberto R. Heredia, eds. *An Introduction to Bilingualism: Principles and Processes*. Psychology Press. [2008] pp. xix + 388. hb £60 ISBN 9 7808 0585 1342, pb £34.50 ISBN 9 7808 0585 1359.

Amano, Masachiyo, Michiko Ogura, and Masayuki Ohkado, eds. *Historical Englishes in Varieties of Texts and Contexts*. Lang. [2008] pp. xi + 403. €68.50 ISBN 9 7836 3158 1902.

Anderson, Bridget L. *Migration, Accommodation and Language Change: Language at the Intersection of Regional and Ethnic Identity*. Macmillan. [2008] pp. xviii + 196. £45 ISBN 9 7802 3000 8861.

Apresjan, Juri. *Systematic Lexicography*. trans. Kevin Windle. OUP. [2000/2008] pp. xviii + 304. pb £21.99 ISBN 9 7801 9955 4256.

Ariel, Mira. *Pragmatics and Grammar*. Cambridge Textbooks in Linguistics. CUP. [2008]. pp. xviii + 343. hb £65 ISBN 9 7805 2155 0185, pb £24.99 ISBN 9 7805 2155 9942.

Asbury, Anna, Jakub Dotlačil, Berit Gehrke, and Rick Nouwen, eds. *Syntax and Semantics of Spatial P*. Linguistik Aktuell 120. Benjamins. [2008] pp. vi + 416. €120 ISBN 9 7890 2725 5037.

Atkins, B.T. Sue, and Michael Rundall. *The Oxford Guide to Practical Lexicography*. OUP. [2008] pp. xii + 545. £90 ISBN 9 7801 9927 7704.

Baayen, R.H. *Analyzing Linguistic Data: A Practical Introduction to Statistics using R*. CUP. [2008] pp. xiii + 353. hb £55 ISBN 9 7805 2188 2590, pb £21.99 ISBN 9 7805 2170 9187.

Bache, Carl. *English Tense and Aspect in Halliday's Systemic Functional Grammar: A Critical Appraisal and an Alternative*. Discussions in Functional Approaches to Language. Equinox. [2008] pp. ix + 229. hb £50 ISBN 9 7818 4553 3519, pb £16.99 ISBN 9 7818 4553 3540.

Bagwasi, Mompoloki Mmangaka, Modupe Moyosore Alimi, and Patrick James Ebewo, eds. *English Language and Literature: Cross Cultural Currents*. Cambridge SP. [2008] pp. xii + 295. £39.99 ($59.99) ISBN 9 7818 4718 9523.

Banks, David. *The Development of Scientific Writing: Linguistic Features and Historical Context*. Equinox. [2008] hb £50 ISBN 9 7818 4553 3168, pb £16.99 ISBN 9 7818 4553 3175.

Bateman, John. *Multimodality and Genre: A Foundation for the Systematic Analysis of Multimodal Documents*. Palgrave. [2008] pp. 336. £60 ISBN 9 7802 3000 2562.

Batllori, Montserrat, Maria-Lluïsa Hernanz, Carme Picallo, and Francesc Roca, eds. *Grammaticalization and Parametric Variation*. OUP. [2005] pp. xvii + 313. £85 ISBN 9 7801 9927 2129.

Battistella, Edwin L. *Bad Language: Are Some Words Better than Others?* OUP. [2005] pp. ix + 230. hb £16 ISBN 9 7801 9517 2485, pb £12.99 ISBN 9 7801 9533 7457.

Bauer, Laurie, Janet Holmes, and Paul Warren. *Language Matters*. Macmillan. [2006] pp. 280. pb £17.99 ISBN 9 7814 0393 6288.

Beal, Joan C., Carmela Nocera, and Massimo Sturiale, eds. *Perspectives on Prescriptivism*. Lang. [2008] pp. 269. pb €47 (£42.30, $72.95) ISBN 9 7830 3911 6324.

Beaver, David I., and Brady Z. Clark. *Sense and Sensitivity: How Focus Determines Meaning*. Blackwell. [2008] pp. xiv + 307. hb £50 (€57.50) ISBN 9 7814 0511 2635, pb £24.99 (€28.80) ISBN 9 7814 0511 2642.

Bednarek, Monica. *Emotion Talk across Corpora*. Palgrave. [2008] pp. 256. £50 ISBN 9 7802 3055 1466.

Benz, Anton, and Peter Kühnlein, eds. *Constraints in Discourse*. Benjamins. [2008] pp. vii + 292. €105 ISBN 9 7890 2725 4160.

Berendt, Erich A. *Metaphors for Learning: Cross-Cultural Perspectives*. Benjamins. [2008] pp. ix + 249. €105 ISBN 9 7890 2722 3760.

Bernhardt, Peter. *Gods and Goddesses in the Garden*. RutgersUP. [2008] pp. xix + 239. $24.95. ISBN 9 7808 1354 2669.

Biberauer, Theresa, ed. *The Limits of Syntactic Variation*. Benjamins. [2008] pp. vii + 521. €115 ($173) ISBN 9 7890 2725 5150.

Biermeier, Thomas. *Word-Formation in New Englishes: A Corpus-Based Analysis*. LIT. [2008] pp. xiv + 292. pb €29.90 ISBN 9 7838 2581 3727.

Blake, Barry J. *All About Language*. OUP. [2008] pp. xvii + 322. hb $110 ISBN 9 7801 9923 8392, pb $29.95 ISBN 9 7801 9923 8408.

Bordwell, David. *Poetics of Cinema*. Routledge. [2008] pp. xi + 499. pb £30.99 ISBN 9 7804 1597 7791.

Borik, Olga. *Aspect and Reference Time*. Oxford Studies in Theoretical Linguistics 13. OUP. [2006] pp. xii + 226. hb £70 ISBN 9 7801 9929 1281, pb £21.99 ISBN 9 7801 9929 1298.

Bouquet, Paolo, Luciano Serafini, and Richmond H. Thomason, eds. *Perspectives on Contexts*. CSLI Publications. [2008] pp. xiv + 285. hb $70 ISBN 9 7815 7586 5379, pb $32.50 ISBN 9 7815 7586 5386.

Bousfield, Derek. *Impoliteness in Interaction*. Pragmatics & Beyond New Series 167. Benjamins. [2008] pp. xiii + 281. €105 ($158) ISBN 9 7890 2725 4115.

Bousfield, Derek, and Miriam A. Locher, eds. *Impoliteness in Language: Studies on its Interplay with Power in Theory and Practice*. Language, Power and Social Process 21. MGruyter. [2008] pp. viii + 346. pb €34.95 ($49.95) ISBN 9 7831 1020 2670.

Brandom, Robert B. *Between Saying and Doing: Towards an Analytic Pragmatism.* OUP. [2008] pp. xxi + 251. £21 ISBN 9 7801 9954 2871.

Burridge, Kate, and Bernd Kortmann, eds. *Varieties of English, vol. 3: The Pacific and Australasia.* MGruyter. [2008] pp. xxxiii + 618. pb/CD-ROM €29.95 ($29.95) ISBN 9 7831 1019 6375. For the complete set of four volumes, see Kortmann and Schneider.

Bybee, Joan. *Frequency of Use and the Organization of Language.* OUP. [2007] pp. viii + 365. pb £40 ISBN 9 7801 9530 1571.

Carr, Phil. *A Glossary of Phonology.* EdinUP. [2008] pp. 216. hb £45 ISBN 9 7807 4862 4041, pb £9.99 ISBN 9 7807 4862 2344.

Carter, Ronald, and Peter Stockwell, eds. *The Language and Literature Reader.* Routledge. [2008] pp. x + 306. pb £24.99 ISBN 9 7804 1541 0038.

Cheng, Winnie, Chris Greaves, and Martin Warren. *A Corpus-Driven Study of Discourse Intonation: The Hong Kong Corpus of Spoken English (Prosodic).* Benjamins. [2008] pp. xi + 325. hb/CD-ROM €105 ($158) ISBN 9 7890 2722 3067.

Cienki, Alan, and Cornelia Müller, eds. *Metaphor and Gesture.* Gesture Studies 3. Benjamins. [2008] pp. ix + 306. €99 ($149) ISBN 9 7890 2722 8437.

Ciszek, Ewa. *Word Derivation in Early Middle English.* Lang. [2008] pp. 141. pb £19.30 (€25.70) ISBN 9 7836 3158 3722.

Collins, Beverley, and Inger M. Mees. *Practical Phonetics and Phonology: A Resource Book for Students.* 2nd edn. Routledge. [2008] pp. xix + 305. hb £58.50 ISBN 9 7804 1542 2666, pb £17.99 ISBN 9 7804 1542 5148.

Collins, John. *Chomsky: A Guide for the Perplexed.* Continuum. [2008] pp. xii + 229, pb £12.99 ISBN 9 7808 2648 6639.

Comorovski, Ileana, and Klaus von Heusinger, eds. *Existence: Semantics and Syntax.* Springer. [2007] pp. vii + 332. hb €124.95 ISBN 9 7814 0206 1967, pb €49.95 ISBN 9 7814 0206 1981.

Cruttenden, Alan. *Gimson's Pronunciation of English.* 7th edn. Hodder Education. [2008] pp. 384. pb £24.99 ISBN 9 7803 4095 8773.

Crystal, David. *Dictionary of Linguistics and Phonetics.* 6th edn. Blackwell. [2008] pp. 560. hb £60 ISBN 9 7814 0515 2969, pb £19.99 ISBN 9 7814 0515 2976.

Crystal, David. *Think On My Words: Exploring Shakespeare's Language.* CUP. [2008] pp. xii + 254. hb £40 ISBN 9 7805 2187 6940, pb £12.99 ISBN 9 7805 2170 0351.

Crystal, David. *Txtng: The Gr8 Db8.* OUP. [2008] pp. 256. £9.99 ISBN 9 7801 9954 4905.

Dannenberg, Hilary. *Coincidence and Counterfactuality: Plotting Time and Space in Narrative Fiction.* UNebP. [2008] pp. 304. £33 ISBN 9 7808 0321 0936.

De Cuypere, Ludovic. *Limiting the Iconic: From the Metatheoretical Foundations to the Creative Possibilities of Iconicity in Language.* Benjamins. [2008] pp. xiii + 286. €110 ISBN 9 7890 2729 0779.

De Hoop, Helen, and Peter de Swart, eds. *Differential Subject Marking.* Springer. [2008] pp. xii + 305. €123 ISBN 9 7814 0206 4982.

De Vega, Manuel, Arthur Glenberg, and Arthur Graesser, eds. *Symbols and Embodiment: Debates on Meaning and Cognition*. OUP. [2008] pp. ix + 445. $79.95.

Dölling, Johannes, Tatjana Heyde-Zybatow, and Martin Schäfer, eds. *Event Structures in Linguistics: Form and Interpretation*. MGruyter. [2008] pp. xxii + 531. €118 ISBN 9 7831 1019 0663.

Dollinger, Stefan. *New-Dialect Formation in Canada: Evidence from the English Modal Auxiliaries*. Benjamins. [2008] pp. xxii + 355. €110 ISBN 9 7890 2723 1086.

Dossena, Marina, Richard Dury, and Maurizio Gotti, eds. *English Historical Linguistics, vol. 3: Geo-Historical Variation in English*. Benjamins. [2008] pp. xiii + 197. €105 ISBN 9 7890 2724 8121.

Downing, Laura J., T. Alan Hall, and Renate Raffelsiefen, eds. *Paradigms in Phonological Theory*. OUP. [2004] pp. 360. hb £95 ISBN 9 7801 9926 7705, pb £33 ISBN 9 7801 9926 7712.

Durrleman-Tame, Stephanie. *The Syntax of Jamaican Creole: A Cartographic Perspective*. Benjamins. [2008] pp. xii + 190. €110 ($165) ISBN 9 7890 2725 5105.

Eades, Diana. *Courtroom Talk and Neocolonial Control*. MGruyter. [2008] pp. xix + 389. hb €98 ($125) ISBN 9 7831 1020 4827, pb €34.95 ($49.95) ISBN 9 7831 1020 4834.

Eckardt, Regine, Gerhard Jäger, and Tonjes Veenstra, eds. *Variation, Selection, Development: Probing the Evolutionary Model of Language Change*. MGruyter. [2008] pp. viii + 408. €98 ISBN 9 7831 1019 8690.

Egan, Thomas. *Non-Finite Complementation: A Usage-Based Study of Infinitive and -ing Clauses in English*. Language and Computers: Studies in Practical Linguistics 65. Rodopi. [2008] pp. xi + 432. €87 ($122) ISBN 9 7890 4202 3598.

Ermida, Isabel. *The Language of Comic Narratives: Humor Construction in Short Stories*. MGruyter. [2008] pp. xii + 261. €98 ISBN 9 7831 1020 5145.

Everaert, Martin, and Henk Van Riemsdijk, eds. *The Blackwell Companion to Syntax*. vols 1–5. Blackwell. [2006] pp. 3,285. £700 ISBN 9 7814 0511 4851.

Eythórsson, Thórhallur, ed. *Grammatical Change and Linguistic Theory: The Rosendal Papers*. Linguistik Aktuell 113. Benjamins. [2008] pp. vi + 441. €120 ISBN 9 7890 2723 3776.

Fabb, Nigel, and Halle Morris. *Meter in Poetry: A New Theory*. CUP. [2008] pp. 312. pb £25.99 ISBN 9 7805 2171 3252.

Farenkia, Bernard Mulo, ed. *Linguistic Politeness in Cameroon: Pragmatic, Comparative and Intercultural Approaches / De la politesse linguistique au Cameroun: Approches pragmatiques, comparatives et interculturelles*. Lang. [2008] pp. viii + 194. pb €40.40 ($62.95) ISBN 9 7836 3157 1583.

Farrell, Patrick. *Grammatical Relations*. Oxford Surveys in Syntax and Morphology. OUP. [2005] pp. x + 234. hb £90 ISBN 9 7801 9926 4018, pb £27 ISBN 9 7801 9926 4025.

Filppula, Markku, Juhani Klemola, and Heli Paulasto. *English and Celtic in Contact*. Routledge. [2008] pp. xix + 312. £70 ISBN 9 7804 1526 6024.

Fitzmaurice, Susan M., and Donka Minkova. *Studies in the History of the English Language IV: Empirical and Analytical Advances in the Study of*

English Language Change. Mouton. [2008] pp. viii + 433. €98 ISBN 9 7831 1020 5879.

Fitzmaurice, Susan M., and Irma Taavitsainen, eds. *Methods in Historical Pragmatics.* TiEL 52. MGruyter. [2007] pp. vi + 313. €118 ($183) ISBN 9 7831 1019 0410.

Fodor, Jerry. *LOT 2: The Language of Thought Revisited.* OUP. [2008] pp. 228. $37.95 ISBN 9 7801 9954 8774.

Fontenelle, Thierry. *Practical Lexicography: A Reader.* OUP. [2008] pp. x + 405. £85. ISBN 9 7801 9929 2332.

Fortuny, Jordi. *The Emergence of Order in Syntax.* Linguistik Aktuell 119. Benjamins. [2008] pp. viii + 211. €105 ISBN 9 7890 2725 5020.

Gibbons, John, and M. Teresa Turell, eds. *Dimensions of Forensic Linguistics.* Benjamins. [2008] pp. vi + 316. €99 ($149). ISBN 9 7890 2720 5216.

Goatly, Andrew. *Explorations in Stylistics.* Equinox. [2008] pp. ix + 233. £50 ISBN 9 7818 4553 2963.

Goldberg, Adele. *Constructions at Work: The Nature of Generalization in Language.* OUP. [2006] pp. vii + 280. hb £85 ISBN 9 7801 9926 8511, pb £19 ISBN 9 7801 9926 8528.

Gómez González, María de los Ángeles, J. Lachlan Mackenzie, and Elsa M. González Álvarez, eds. *Languages and Cultures in Contrast and Comparison.* Pragmatics & Beyond New Series 175. Benjamins. [2008] pp. xxii + 364. €105 ($158) ISBN 9 7890 2725 4191.

González-Díaz, Victorina. *English Adjective Comparison: A Historical Perspective.* Benjamins. [2008] pp. xix + 252. €110 ($165) ISBN 9 7890 2724 8152.

Good, Jeff, ed. *Linguistic Universals and Language Change.* OUP. [2008] pp. xvi + 339. pb $50 ISBN 9 7801 9922 8997.

Gooden, Philip. *Name Dropping.* St Martin's. [2008] pp. vi + 213. $21.95. ISBN 9 7803 1237 7397.

Gundel, Jeanette K., and Nancy Hedberg, eds. *Reference: Interdisciplinary Disciplines.* OUP. [2008] pp. vii + 279. £40 ISBN 9 7801 9533 1639.

Halliday, M.A.K., and William S. Greaves. *Intonation in the Grammar of English.* Equinox. [2008] pp. 224. hb £65 ISBN 9 7819 0476 8142, pb £14.99 ISBN 9 7819 0476 8159.

Hamawand, Zeki. *Morpho-Lexical Alternation in Noun Formation.* Palgrave. [2008] pp. 200. £53 ISBN 9 7802 3053 7385.

Harley, Trevor A. *The Psychology of Language: From Data to Theory.* 3rd edn. Psychology Press. [2008] pp. xvii + 602. hb £49.46 ISBN 9 7818 4169 3811, pb £26.96 ISBN 9 7818 4169 3828.

Harrington, Kate, Lia Litosseliti, Helen Sauntson, and Jane Sunderland, eds. *Gender and Language Research Methodologies.* Palgrave. [2008] pp. xii + 332. pb £18.99 ISBN 9 7802 3055 0698.

Harris, Roy, and Christopher Hutton. *Definition in Theory and Practice: Language, Lexicography and the Law.* Continuum. [2007] pp. ix + 238. £80 ISBN 9 7808 2649 7055.

Harrow, Kenneth, and Kizitus Mpoche, eds. *Language, Literature and Education in Multicultural Societies: Collaborative Research on Africa.*

Cambridge SP. [2008] pp. vii + 381. hb £39.99 ($59.99) ISBN 9 7818 4718 5631, pb £19.99 ($39.99) ISBN 9 7814 4380 3441.

Hill, Jane H. *The Everyday Language of White Racism*. Blackwell. [2008] pp. ix + 224. pb £26.99 ISBN 9 7814 0518 4533.

Hinzen, Wolfram. *Mind Design and Minimal Syntax*. OUP. [2006] pp. xvi + 297. hb £89 ISBN 9 7801 9927 4413, pb £26 ISBN 9 7801 9928 9257.

Holmes, Janet. *An Introduction to Sociolinguistics*. Longman. [2008] pp. xviii + 482. £31.95 ISBN 9 7814 0582 1315.

Horobin, Simon. *Chaucer's Language*. Palgrave. [2007] pp. x + 198. hb £50 ISBN 9 7814 0399 3557, pb £16.99 ISBN 9 7814 0399 3564.

Isac, Daniela, and Charles Reiss. *I-Language: An Introduction to Linguistics as Cognitive Science*. OUP. [2008] pp. xiii + 318. hb $120 ISBN 9 7801 9953 4197, pb $39.95 ISBN 9 7801 9953 4203.

Jackson, Howard, and Etienne Zé Amvela. *Words, Meaning and Vocabulary: An Introduction to Modern English Lexicology*. Continuum. [2007] pp. xii + 248. pb £19.99 ISBN 9 7808 2649 0186.

Jackson, Jane. *Language, Identity and Study Abroad: Sociocultural Perspectives*. Equinox. [2008] pp. ix + 267. hb £65 ISBN 9 7818 4553 1416, pb £16.99 ISBN 9 7818 4553 1423.

Jeffries, Lesley. *Discovering Language: The Structure of Modern English*. Palgrave. [2006] pp. xvii + 252. hb £50 ISBN 9 7814 0391 2619, pb £16.99 ISBN 9 7814 0391 2626.

Johnson, Keith. *Quantitative Methods in Linguistics*. Wiley-Blackwell. [2008] pp. xv + 277. hb £60 ISBN 9 7814 0514 4247, pb £25.99 ISBN 9 7814 0514 4254.

Johnson, Neil. *Dr Johnson's Reliquary of Rediscovered Words*. Marius. [2008] pp. xii + 180. £9.99 ISBN 9 7818 7162 2348.

Johnstone, Barbara. *Discourse Analysis*. 2nd edn. Blackwell. [2008] pp. xvii + 311. pb £22.99 ISBN 9 7814 0514 4278.

Jones, Cary, and Eija Ventola, eds. *From Language to Multimodality: New Developments in the Study of Ideational Meaning*. Equinox. [2008] pp. xii + 341. £50 ISBN 9 7818 4553 3472.

Jucker, Andreas H., and Irma Taavitsainen, eds. *Speech Acts in the History of English*. Pragmatics & Beyond New Series 176. Benjamins. [2008] pp. viii + 318. €105 ($158) ISBN 9 7890 2725 4207.

Jule, Allyson. *A Beginner's Guide to Language and Gender*. Multilingual Matters. [2008] pp. ix + 104. hb £49.95 ISBN 9 7818 4769 0562, pb £12.95 ISBN 9 7818 4769 0555.

Kachru, Yamuna, and Larry E. Smith. *Cultures, Contexts, and World Englishes*. Routledge. [2008] pp. xxii + 234. hb £95 ($145) ISBN 9 7808 0584 7321, pb £27.99 ($43.95) ISBN 9 7808 0584 7338.

Kirkpatrick, Andy. *World Englishes: Implications for International Communication and English Language Teaching*. CUP. [2007] pp. x + 258. hb/CD-ROM £61.50 ($91) ISBN 9 7805 2185 1473, pb/CD-ROM £27.70 ($41) ISBN 9 7805 2161 6874.

Koller, Veronika. *Lesbian Discourse: Images of a Community*. Routledge. [2008] pp. xii + 226. £85 ISBN 9 7804 1596 0953.

Kortmann, Bernd, and Edgar W. Schneider, eds. *Varieties of English.* vols. 1–4. MGruyter. [2008] pp. c.2,000. pb/CD-ROM €98 ($98) ISBN 9 7831 1017 2690.

Kortmann, Bernd, and Clive Upton, eds. *Varieties of English, vol. 1: The British Isles.* MGruyter. [2008] pp. xxix + 512. pb/CD-ROM €29.95 ($29.95) ISBN 9 7831 1019 6351. For the complete set of four volumes, see Kortmann and Schneider.

Kouega, Jean-Paul. *A Dictionary of Cameroon Pidgin English Usage: Pronunciation, Grammar and Vocabulary.* LINCOM. [2008] pp. iv + 150. pb €62 ($86.80) ISBN 9 7838 9586 2045.

Kouwenberg, Silvia, and John Victor Singler, eds. *The Handbook of Pidgin and Creole Studies.* Blackwell. [2008] pp. xvi + 688. €125 ($199.95) ISBN 9 7806 3122 9025.

Kraft, Bettina, and Ronald Geluykens, eds. *Cross-Cultural Pragmatics and Interlanguage English.* LINCOM. [2007] pp. 260. pb €74 ($91) ISBN 9 7838 9586 7767.

Langacker, Ronald W. *Cognitive Grammar: A Basic Introduction.* OUP. [2008] pb $39.95 ISBN 9 7801 9533 1967.

Lantolf, Hames P., and Matthew E. Poehner, eds. *Sociocultural Theory and the Teaching of Second Languages.* Equinox. [2008] pp. xii + 422. hb £70 ISBN 9 7818 4553 2499, pb £18.99 ISBN 9 7818 4553 2505.

Laurer, Christina. *Poor Paul: L Vocalisation and the Process of Syllable-Coda Weakening.* Lang. [2008] pp. 232. £29.80 ISBN 9 7836 3156 9139.

Lee, Chungmin, Matthew Gordon, and Daniel Büring, eds. *Topic and Focus: Cross-Linguistic Perspectives on Meaning and Intonation.* Springer. [2007] pp. ix + 290. hb €109.95 ISBN 9 7814 0204 7954, pb €59.95 ISBN 9 7814 0204 7978.

Leech, Geoffrey. *Language in Literature: Style and Foregrounding.* Longman. [2008] pp. xi + 222. pb £20.99 ISBN 9 7805 8205 1096.

Leech, Geoffrey, Margaret Deuchar, and Robert Hoogenraad. *English Grammar for Today: A New Introduction.* 2nd edn. Palgrave. [2006] pp. xvii + 238. hb £55 ISBN 9 7814 0391 6419, pb £17.99 ISBN 9 7814 0391 6426.

Lepore, Ernest, and Kirk Ludwig. *Donald Davidson's Truth-Theoretic Semantics.* OUP. [2005] pp. xii + 346. hb £55 ISBN 9 7801 9925 1346, pb £25 ISBN 9 7801 9929 0932.

Levey, David. *Language Change and Variation in Gibraltar.* Benjamins. [2008] pp. xxii + 192. €105 ISBN 9 7890 2721 8629.

Libben, Gary, and Gonia Jarema, eds. *The Representation and Processing of Compound Words.* OUP. [2006] pp. xv + 242. £60 ISBN 9 7801 9928 5068.

Lin, Angel M.Y., ed. *Problematizing Identity: Everyday Struggles in Language, Culture, and Education.* Lawrence Erlbaum. [2008] pp. viii + 239. £20.99 ISBN 9 7804 1544 4293.

Locher, Miriam A., and Jürg Strässler, eds. *Standards and Norms in the English Language.* MGruyter. [2008] pp. xxv + 412. €98 ($152) ISBN 9 7831 1020 3981.

Luraghi, Silvia, and Claudia Parodi. *Key Terms in Syntax and Syntactic Theory.* Key Terms. Continuum. [2008] pp. xii + 265. pb £16.99 ISBN 9 7808 2649 6560.

MacNeilage, Peter. *The Origin of Speech.* OUP. [2008] pp. xi + 389. $50 ISBN 9 7801 9923 6503.

Manan, Shakila Abdul, and Lalita Sinha, eds. *Exploring Space: Trends in Literature, Linguistics and Translation.* Cambridge SP. [2008] pp. xiii + 169. £29.99 ($44.99) ISBN 9 7818 4718 4726.

Matsumoto, Meiko. *From Simple Verbs to Periphrastic Expressions: The Historical Development of Composite Predicates, Phrasal Verbs, and Related Constructions in English.* Lang. [2008] pp. 231. pb £32.90 (€43.80) ISBN 9 7830 3911 6751.

Mattiello, Elisa. *An Introduction to English Slang.* Polimetrica. [2008] pp. 320. pb €25 ISBN 9 7888 7699 1134.

Mayr, Andrea, ed. *Language and Power: An Introduction to Institutional Discourse.* Continuum. [2008] pp. vi + 204. pb £24.99 ISBN 9 7808 2648 7445.

McCafferty, Michael. *Native American Place-Names of Indiana.* UIllP. [2008] pp. xxxi + 299. $50 ISBN 9 7802 5203 2684.

McElhinny, Bonnie, ed. *Words, Worlds, and Material Girls: Language, Gender, Globalization.* Mouton. [2007] pp. vi + 454. hb €98 ISBN 9 7831 1019 5743, pb €34.95 ISBN 9 7831 1019 5750.

McWhorter, John. *Language Interrupted: Signs of Non-Native Acquisition in Standard Language Grammars.* OUP. [2007] pp. 332. £40. ISBN 9 7801 9530 9805.

Mercer, Neil, Joan Swann, and Barbara Mayor, eds. *Learning English.* 2nd edn. Routledge. [2007] pp. iv + 296. hb £70 ISBN 9 7804 1537 6860, pb £21.99 ISBN 9 7804 1537 6877.

Mesthrie, Rajend, ed. *Varieties of English, vol. 4: Africa, South and Southeast Asia.* MGruyter. [2008] pp. xxix + 655. pb/CD-ROM €29.95 ($29.95) ISBN 9 7831 1019 6382. For the complete set of four volumes, see Kortmann and Schneider.

Mesthrie, Rajend, and Rakesh M. Bhatt. *World Englishes: The Study of New Linguistic Varieties.* CUP. [2008] pp. xviii + 276. hb £45 ($81) ISBN 9 7805 2179 3414, pb £19.99 ($39.99) ISBN 9 7805 2179 7337.

Meyerhoff, Miriam, and Naomi Nagy, eds. *Social Lives in Language: Sociolinguistics and Multilingual Speech Communities: Celebrating the Work of Gillian Sankoff.* Benjamins. [2008] pp. ix + 365. €105 ($158) ISBN 9 7890 2721 8636.

Michaelis, Susanne, ed. *Roots of Creole Structures: Weighing the Contribution of Substrates and Superstrates.* Benjamins. [2008] pp. xvii + 425. €105 ($158) ISBN 9 7890 2725 2555.

Miestamo, Matti, Kaius Sinnemäki, and Fred Karlsson, eds. *Language Complexity: Typology, Contact, Change.* Benjamins. [2008] pp. xiv + 356. €110 ($165) ISBN 9 7890 2723 1048.

Miller, Jim. *An Introduction to English Syntax.* EdinUP. [2008] pp. 224. hb £45 ISBN 9 7807 4863 3609, pb £14.99 ISBN 9 7807 4863 3616.

Momma, Haruko, and Michael Matto, eds. *A Companion to the History of the English Language.* Wiley-Blackwell. [2008] pp. xxxiii + 690. £100 ISBN 9 7814 0512 9923.

Montgomery, Martin. *An Introduction to Language and Society.* 3rd edn. Routledge. [2008] pp. xx + 314. hb £58.50 ISBN 9 7804 1538 2991, pb £17.99 ISBN 9 7804 1538 2748.

Mooijaart, Marijke, and Marijke van der Wal, eds. *Yesterday's Words: Contemporary, Current and Future Lexicography.* Cambridge SP. [2008] pp. viii + 376. £39.99 ISBN 9 7818 4718 4693.

Mufwene, Salikoko S. *Language Evolution: Contact, Competition and Change.* Continuum. [2008] pp. xv + 354. hb 91.99 ($150) ISBN 9 7808 2649 3699, pb 31.99 ($34.95) ISBN 9 7808 2649 3705.

Müller, Cornelia. *Metaphors Dead and Alive, Sleeping and Waking.* UChicP. [2008] pp. xix + 272. £24 ISBN 9 7802 2654 8258.

Murphy, M. Lynne. *Semantic Relations and the Lexicon.* CUP. [2008] pp. x + 292. pb £21.99 ISBN 9 7805 2107 0584, hb [2003] £55 ISBN 9 7805 2178 0674.

Muysken, Pieter. *Functional Categories.* Cambridge Studies in Linguistics 117. CUP. [2008] pp. xxi + 297. hb £60 ISBN 9 7805 2185 3859, pb £23.99 ISBN 9 7805 2161 9981.

Nathan, Geoffrey S. *Phonology: A Cognitive Grammar Introduction.* Benjamins. [2008] pp. x + 171. hb €105 ISBN 9 7890 2721 9077, pb £25 ISBN 9 7890 2721 9084.

Nevalainen, Terttu, Irma Taavitsainen, Päivi Pahta, and Minna Korhonen, eds. *The Dynamics of Linguistic Variation: Corpus Evidence on English Past and Present.* Benjamins. [2008] pp. viii + 339. €105 ISBN 9 7890 2723 4827.

Ngefac, Aloysius. *Social Differentiation in Cameroon English: Evidence from Sociolinguistic Fieldwork.* Lang. [2008] pp. xiv + 163. €41.20 ($63.95) ISBN 9 7814 3310 3902.

Oakley, Todd, and Hougaard Anders. *Mental Spaces in Discourse and Interaction.* Benjamins. [2008] pp. vi + 262. €105 ISBN 9 7890 2729 1455.

O'Halloran, Kay. *Mathematical Discourse Language, Symbolism and Visual Images.* Continuum. [2008] pp. viii + 226. pb £24.99 ISBN 9 7818 4706 4219.

Palmer, Frank R., ed. *Grammar and Meaning.* CUP. [2008] xii + 265. pb €17.99 ($32.99) ISBN 9 7805 2105 4775.

Pearce, Michael. *The Routledge Dictionary of English Language Studies.* Routledge. [2007] pp. xi + 211. hb £50 ISBN 9 7804 1535 1874, pb £12.99 ISBN 9 7804 1535 1720.

Peters, Stanley, and Dag Westerståhl. *Quantifiers in Language and Logic.* OUP. [2006] pp. xix + 528. hb £65 ISBN 9 7801 9929 1250, pb £27 ISBN 9 7801 9929 1267.

Pier, John, García Landa, and José Ángel. *Theorizing Narrativity.* MGruyter. [2008] pp. 464. €98 ISBN 9 7831 1020 2441.

Postal, Paul M. *Skeptical Linguistic Essays.* OUP. [2004] pp. 414. £60 ISBN 9 7801 9516 6729.

Prodromou, Luke. *English as a Lingua Franca: A Corpus-Based Analysis.* Continuum. [2008] pp. xiv + 295. hb £75 (€92.99, $150) ISBN 9 7808 2649 7758, pb £24.99 (€29.99, $44.95) ISBN 9 7808 2642 5850.

Pütz, Martin, and JoAnne Neff-van Aertselaer, eds. *Developing Contrastive Pragmatics: Interlanguage and Cross-Cultural Perspectives.* SOLA 31. MGruyter. [2008] pp. xviii + 437. €98 ($152) ISBN 9 7831 1019 6702.

Renouf, Antoinette, and Andrew Kehoe, eds. *The Changing Face of Corpus Linguistics.* Language and Computers: Studies in Practical Linguistics 55. Rodopi. [2006] pp. vii + 408. €84, $105 ISBN 9 7890 4201 7382.

Ringe, Don. *A Linguistic History of English, vol. 1: From Proto-Indo-European to Proto-Germanic.* OUP. [2006] pp. x + 355. hb £95 ISBN 9 7801 9928 4139, pb £24.99 ISBN 9 7801 9955 2290.

Rodby, Judith, and W. Ross Winterowd *The Uses of Grammar.* OUP. [2005] pp. xiv + 274. £32.99 ISBN 9 7801 9517 5080.

Romero-Trillo, Jesús, ed. *Pragmatics and Corpus Linguistics: A Mutualistic Entente.* Mouton Series in Pragmatics 2. MGruyter. [2008] pp. vi + 276. €98 ($152) ISBN 9 7831 1019 5804.

Rothstein, Björn. *The Perfect Time Span: On the Present Perfect in German, Swedish and English.* Linguistik Aktuell 125. Benjamins. [2008] pp. xi + 170. €115 ISBN 9 7890 2725 5082.

Rothstein, Susan, ed. *Theoretical and Crosslinguistic Approaches to the Semantics of Aspect.* Benjamins. [2008] pp. viii + 453. €120 ISBN 9 7890 2723 3745.

Schmitz, Hans-Christian. *Accentuation and Interpretation.* Palgrave. [2008] pp. vii + 226. £50 ISBN 9 7802 3000 2531.

Schneider, Edgar W., ed. *Varieties of English, vol. 2: The Americas and the Caribbean.* MGruyter. [2008] pp. xxix + 800. pb/CD-ROM €29.95 ($29.95) ISBN 9 7831 1019 6368. For the complete set of four volumes, see Kortmann and Schneider.

Schneider, Klaus P., and Anne Barron, eds. *Variational Pragmatics: A Focus on Regional Varieties in Pluricentric Languages.* Benjamins. [2008] pp. vii + 371. €105 ($158) ISBN 9 7890 2725 4221.

Schreier, Daniel. *St Helenian English: Origins, Evolution and Variation.* Benjamins. [2008] pp. xv + 312. €115 ($173) ISBN 9 7890 2724 8978.

Scott, Mike, Pascual Pérez-Paredes, and Purificación Sánchez-Hernández, eds. *Monograph: Software Aided Analysis of Language.* International Journal of English Studies 8/1. Universidad de Murcia. [2008] ISSN 1578 7044.

Seibert, Sebastian. *Reception and Construction of the Norse Past in Orkney.* Lang. [2008] pp. 341. £39.60 ISBN 9 7836 3157 2955.

Semino, Elena. *Metaphor in Discourse.* CUP. [2008] pp. xii + 247. hb £55 ISBN 9 7805 2186 7306, pb £19.99 ISBN 9 7805 2168 6969.

Shea, Ammon. *Reading the OED.* Lane. [2008] pp. 224. pb £12.99 ISBN 9 7818 4614 1980.

Shopen, Timothy, ed. *Language Typology and Syntactic Description, vol. 1: Clause Structure; vol. 2: Complex Constructions; vol. 3: Grammatical Categories and the Lexicon.* 2nd edn. CUP. [2007] vol. 1, pp. xx + 477, vol. 2, pp. xxii + 465, vol. 3, pp. xxii + 426. hb £160 ISBN 9 7805 2185 8564 (set of 3 vols.), pb. £65 ISBN 9 7805 2167 5284. (set of 3 vols.).

Shugart, Helene A., and Catherine Egley Waggoner. *Making Camp: Rhetorics of Transgression U.S. Popular Culture.* UAlaP. [2008] pp. 189. £32.03 ISBN 9 7808 1731 6075.

Siegel, Jeff. *The Emergence of Pidgin and Creole Languages*. OUP. [2008] pp. xiv + 320. hb £74 ($130) ISBN 9 7801 9921 6666, pb £27 ($50) ISBN 9 7801 9921 6673.

Siemund, Peter, and Noemi Kintana, eds. *Language Contact and Contact Languages*. Benjamins. [2008] pp. x + 358. €75 ISBN 9 7890 2721 9275.

Simpson, Andrew, ed. *Language and National Identity in Africa*. OUP. [2008] pp. 448. hb £84 ($150) ISBN 9 7801 9928 6744, pb £29 ($55) ISBN 9 7801 9928 6751.

Simpson, Jane, and Gillian Wigglesworth, eds. *Children's Language and Multilingualism: Indigenous Language Use at Home and School*. Continuum. [2008] pp. 336. hb £75 ($150) ISBN 9 7808 2649 5167, pb €32 ($49.95) ISBN 9 7808 2649 5174.

Spencer-Oatey, Helen, ed. *Culturally Speaking: Culture, Communication and Politeness Theory*. 2nd edn. Continuum. [2008] pp. 384. pb $39.95 ISBN 9 7808 2649 3101.

Studer, Patrick. *Historical Corpus Stylistics: Media, Technology and Change*. Continuum. [2008] pp. xii + 267. £75 ISBN 9 7808 2649 4306.

Tan, Peter K.W., and Rani Rubdy, eds. *Language as Commodity: Global Structures, Local Marketplaces*. Continuum. [2008] pp. xiv + 228. hb £75 ($150) ISBN 9 7818 4706 4226, pb £24.99 ($39.95) ISBN 9 7818 4706 4233.

Tarp, Sven. *Lexicography in the Borderland between Knowledge and Non-Knowledge*. Niemeyer. [2008] pp. viii + 308. pb £84 ISBN 9 7834 8329 1345.

Thormählen, Marianne, ed. *English Now: Selected Papers from the 20th IAUPE Conference in Lund 2007*. LundUP. [2008] pp. xx + 354. €127.99 (SEK 400, $149.50) ISBN 9 7891 9769 3509.

Tieken-Boon van Ostade, Ingrid, ed. *Grammars, Grammarians and Grammar-Writing in Eighteenth-Century England*. MGruyter. [2008] pp. ix + 361. €98 ($152) ISBN 9 7831 1019 6276.

Toyota, Junichi. *Diachronic Change in the English Passive*. Palgrave. [2008] pp. 304. £55 ISBN 9 7802 3055 3453.

Trousdale, Graeme, and Nikolas Gisborne. *Constructional Approaches to English Grammar*. Mouton. [2008] pp. vi + 310. £123 (€88) ISBN 9 7831 1019 6269.

Unsworth, Len. *Multimodal Semiotics Functional Analysis in Contexts of Education*. Continuum. [2008] pp. 272. £75 ISBN 9 7808 2649 9462.

Vaish, Viniti. *Biliteracy and Globalization: English Language Education in India*. MlM. [2008] pp. x + 126. hb £54.95 ($109.95) ISBN 9 7818 4769 0333, pb £21.95 ($44.95) ISBN 9 7818 4769 0326.

Van Peer, Willie, ed. *The Quality of Literature: Linguistic Studies in Literary Evaluation*. Benjamins. [2008] pp. ix + 243. €99 ISBN 9 7890 2723 3363.

Vanhove, Martine, ed. *From Polysemy to Semantic Change: Towards a Typology of Lexical Semantic Associations*. Benjamins. [2008] pp. xiv + 404. £92 ISBN 9 7890 2720 5735.

Verkuyl, Henk J. *Binary Tense*. CSLI. [2008] pp. xii + 289. hb $80 ISBN 9 7815 7586 5638, pb $37.50 ISBN 9 7805 7586 5645.

Watson, Greg, ed. *The State of Stylistics*. Rodopi. [2008] pp. xxii + 517. €108 ISBN 9 7890 4202 4281.

Wierzbicka, Anna. *English: Meaning and Culture*. OUP. [2006] pp. ix + 352. pb £22.50 ISBN 9 7801 9517 4755.

Willems, Klaas, and Ludovic De Cuypere, eds. *Naturalness and Iconicity in Language*. Benjamins. [2008] pp. ix + 249. €105 ISBN 9 7890 2724 3430.

Wolosky, Shira. *The Art of Poetry: How to Read a Poem*. OUP. [2008] pp. 248. pb £9.99 ISBN 9 7801 9537 1185.

Wulff, Stefanie. *Rethinking Idiomaticity: A Usage-Based Approach*. Research in Corpus and Discourse. Continuum. [2008] pp. x + 240. £75 ISBN 9 7818 4706 4202.

Zanotto, Mara Sofia, Lynne Cameron, and Marilda C. Cavalcanti, eds. *Confronting Metaphor in Use: An Applied Linguistic Approach*. Benjamins. [2008] pp. vii + 315 €105 ISBN 9 7890 2725 4177.

Zyngier, Sonia, Marisa Bortolussi, Anna Chesnokova, and Jan Auracher, eds. *Directions in Empirical Literary Studies: In Honor of Willie van Peer*. Benjamins. [2008] pp. xii + 357. €105 ISBN 9 7890 2723 3370.

II

Early Medieval

STACY S. KLEIN AND MARY SWAN

This chapter has the following sections: 1. Bibliography; 2. Manuscript Studies, Palaeography and Facsimiles; 3. Social, Cultural and Intellectual Background; 4. Literature: General; 5. The Exeter Book; 6. The Poems of the Vercelli Book; 7. The Junius Manuscript; 8. The *Beowulf* Manuscript; 9. Other Poems; 10. Prose. Sections 1 and 2 are by Mary Swan; section 3 is by Mary Swan with a contribution by Stacy Klein; sections 4, 5, 7 and 9 are by Stacy Klein with contributions by Mary Swan; sections 6 and 8 are by Stacy Klein; section 10 is by Mary Swan.

1. Bibliography

Old English Newsletter 41:i (Fall 2007) was published in 2008. It includes notes on forthcoming conferences and workshops, news of publications, reports and essays. The reports are 'Dictionary of Old English: 2007 Progress Report', by Joan Holland (*OENews* 41:i[2008] 21–33); 'Anglo-Saxon Plant Name Survey (ASPNS): Ninth Annual Report, for 2007', by C.P. Biggam (*OENews* 41:i[2008] 34–5); 'The Production and Use of English Manuscripts 1060 to 1220: Report on the First Project Symposium, Leicester, July 2007', by Mary Swan (*OENews* 41:i[2008] 35–8); and 'ISAS 2007, London' (*OENews* 41:i[2008] 39–41). Essays in this volume are 'Old English, New Media: Blogging *Beowulf*', by Mary Kate Hurley (reviewed in section 8 below); and 'Circolwyrde 2007: New Electronic Resources for Anglo-Saxon Studies', by Edward Christie (*OENews* 41:i[2008] 47–50).

Volume 41:ii (Winter 2008) contains the *Year's Work in Old English Studies* 2006. Volume 41:iii (Spring 2008) includes news of conferences, publications and research projects and calls for conference papers. Reports included are 'Anglo-Saxon Plant Name Survey (ASPNS): Tenth Annual Report, for 2008', by C.P. Biggam (*OENews* 41:iii[2008] 18); 'Palaeography and Codicology: A Seminar on Medieval Manuscript Studies, University of New Mexico Institute for Medieval Studies, June 9–July 3, 2008', by Rhonda McDaniel (*OENews* 41:iii[2008] 19–21); and 'Dictionary of Old English 2008 Progress Report', by Joan Holland (*OENews* 41:iii[2008] 22–5). The essays are '*Beowulf: Prince of*

Year's Work in English Studies, Volume 89 (2010) © *The English Association; all rights reserved*
doi:10.1093/ywes/maq017

the Geats, Nazis, and Odinists', by Richard Scott Nokes (reviewed in section 8 below); and 'Anglo-Saxon Women Before the Law: A Student Edition of Five Old English Lawsuits', by Andrew Rabin (reviewed in section 10 below). This volume of *OEN* also contains Abstracts of Papers in Anglo-Saxon Studies. Volume 41:iv (Summer 2008) contains the Old English Bibliography for 2007 and the Research in Progress listings.

Beginning with volume 42 (2009), *OEN* is to return to its original publishing schedule of two issues a year. From this volume, it will print only the Bibliography (spring) and *Year's Work in Old English Studies* (fall); all other content will be published on the *OEN* website (< www.oenewsletter.org/ OEN/ >)

Anglo-Saxon England (37[2008] 233–66) includes a report by Mary Swan on the thirteenth conference of the International Society of Anglo-Saxonists in London in July 2007 (pp. 1–5) and the bibliography for 2007 (pp. 233–66).

2. Manuscript Studies, Palaeography and Facsimiles

Six volumes of the Anglo-Saxon Manuscripts in Microfiche Facsimile series have been made available for review this year: Michael Wright and Stephanie Hollis, *Manuscripts of Trinity College, Cambridge* (volume 12 in the series); Rolf H. Bremmer Jr and Kees Dekker, *Manuscripts in the Low Countries* (volume 13); Sarah Larratt Keefer, David Rollason and A.N. Doane, *Manuscripts of Durham, Ripon, and York* (volume 14); A.N. Doane, *Grammars/Handlist of Manuscripts* (volume 15), which includes a complete list of the manuscripts the project has covered and plans to cover; Peter J. Lucas and Jonathan Wilcox, *Manuscripts Relating to Dunstan, Ælfric, and Wulfstan; The 'Eadwine Psalter' Group* (volume 16); and Jonathan Wilcox, *Homilies by Ælfric and Other Homilies* (volume 17). As usual with this series, each volume includes a full description of every manuscript, bibliography and microfiche facsimiles of every folio.

Helmut Gneuss makes a most welcome offering of 'More Old English from Manuscripts' (in Blanton and Scheck, eds., *Intertexts: Studies in Anglo-Saxon Culture Presented to Paul E. Szarmach*, pp. 411–21). The texts described here supplement the additions to Ker's *Catalogue of Manuscripts Containing Anglo-Saxon* published by Ker and Mary Blockley, and they include an Old English prayer; a further seven fragments of Ælfrician prose from the Arnamagnaean Institute in Copenhagen; an Old English sentence in a copy of Orderic Vitalis's *Historia Ecclesiastica*, now in Paris; Old English glosses to Latin texts now in Paris and Sondershausen; an Old English colophon to a now lost manuscript from the St Petersburg Imperial Public Library; and the Taunton Fragments of Gospel pericopes. Gneuss also provides some supplementary notes to Blockley's addenda.

Jonathan Wilcox's contribution to the same volume, 'New Old English Texts: The Expanding Corpus of Old English' (in Blanton and Scheck, eds., pp. 423–36), is a bibliographical review essay which gathers and contemplates discoveries made in recent years, including new manuscripts and fragments, discoveries from transcriptions, and new readings in known manuscripts.

Gifford Charles-Edwards and Helen McKee introduce 'Lost Voices from Anglo-Saxon Lichfield' (*ASE* 37[2008] 79–89), in the form of drypoint glosses added to the Lichfield Gospels in the tenth or eleventh century. The glosses include personal names, presumably of members of the Lichfield community. Charles-Edwards and McKee demonstrate that the glosses were added to the Lichfield Gospels after the book had left Llandeilo Fawr, and provide an edition of them as the appendix to the article.

Jane Roberts examines '*The Finnsburh Fragment*, and its Lambeth Provenance' (*N&Q* 55[2008] 122–4) in the light of Hickes's report that he found the fragment in a '*Semi-Saxonicarum*' homiletic collection in Lambeth Palace Library. Roberts proposes that, instead of speculating about which of the two surviving Old English homiletic manuscripts from this library— Lambeth Palace 489, from the third quarter of the eleventh century, and Lambeth Palace 487, from around 1200—might have contained the fragment, we should consider a third, early eleventh-century manuscript, of which only two leaves now survive, bound into manuscript 427 as folios 210 and 211 and labelled by Ker as 'History of the Kentish royal saints'. A detailed examination of these two leaves in terms of dimensions and quantity of writing is provided and compared with the *Finnsburh Fragment* leaf, and Roberts proposes that all three once belonged to the same manuscript, and that they came to Lambeth Palace from Lanthony Priory in the early seventeenth century.

Richard Gameson's *The Earliest Books of Canterbury Cathedral: Manuscripts and Fragments to c.1200* is the first thorough catalogue of Canterbury manuscripts, which include the holdings of the important Anglo-Saxon foundations of St Augustine's Abbey and Christ Church Cathedral. The catalogue proper is preceded by a summary list of manuscripts, a concordance of shelfmarks and catalogue numbers, and a substantial discursive introduction to the collection. Forty-two items are catalogued in detail, with high-quality colour photographs of each, and a bibliography, index of manuscripts and index of people and places aid reference. Many of the items catalogued can be shown to have been at Canterbury in the pre-Conquest period.

Benjamin C. Withers's *The Illustrated Old English Hexateuch, Cotton Claudius B. iv: The Frontier of Seeing and Reading in Anglo-Saxon England,* published in 2007, was made available for review this year. Via a detailed study of the manuscript, including its design and construction, iconography, and of notions of authority, audience and social reading and viewing, Withers argues that the book unites past and present, orality and textuality and a common Christian heritage, and that it 'can be seen to function as both "domain" (a subject for political and social action) and "scene" (a space for an unfolding drama)' (p. 288).

Susan Rankin's splendid facsimile edition of *The Winchester Troper* was published in 2007. The Troper—Cambridge, Corpus Christi College MS 473— was copied at Winchester in the early eleventh century, and used there and added to until the early twelfth. Rankin's introduction covers the book's production and liturgical design, and provides a detailed study of its fifty-plus scribes and of Anglo-Saxon neume notation, and the facsimile makes available this important manuscript to experienced scholars and those new to the field.

'Viking Invasions and Marginal Annotations in Cambridge, Corpus Christi College 162' (*ASE* 37[2008] 151–71), by Kathryn Powell, is an excellent demonstration of the value of scrutinizing texts in their manuscript context. Powell examines an early eleventh-century marginal annotation to Ælfric's Ash Wednesday homily in this manuscript, and shows that it refers to Viking attacks in Æthelred's reign. Comparison with other marginalia in the manuscript enables Powell to argue that they might be by the same scribe, and to show that this scribe is revising the homiletic texts in the manuscript for use in preaching, possibly at St Augustine's Canterbury, between 1009 and 1012.

3. Social, Cultural and Intellectual Background

The focus of John H. Arnold's *What Is Medieval History?* is, of course, much wider than Anglo-Saxon England, but its treatment of important topics, including historiography, types of sources—including different sorts of text, images, archaeology and material culture—and different theoretical approaches, makes it a lively and thorough introduction for students embarking on the study of the period.

Important new work on mainland Europe in the Early Middle Ages is of great interest to Anglo-Saxonists. None of the individual essays in *The Long Morning of Medieval Europe: New Directions in Early Medieval Studies*, edited by Jennifer R. Davis and Michael McCormick, has an Anglo-Saxon focus, but overall the collection includes much of interest in terms of new approaches to key questions: the economy, holiness, literature, power and intellectual artistic culture. Rosamond McKitterick's *Charlemagne: The Formation of a European Identity* offers an equally important context for Anglo-Saxon studies. McKitterick's chapters cover representations of Charlemagne; Pippinids, Arnulfings and the Agilolfings: the creation of a dynasty; the royal court; the king and kingdom: communications and identities; and *Correctio*: knowledge and power.

The essays in *Frankland: The Franks and the World of the Early Middle Ages. Essays in Honour of Dame Jinty Nelson*, edited by Paul Fouracre and David Ganz, are equally important for understanding the European context of much elite culture of the mid-Anglo-Saxon period, and five of them have a specifically English focus: 'Gallic or Greek? Archbishops in England from Theodore to Ecgbert', by Alan Thacker (pp. 44–69); 'Making a Difference in Tenth-Century Politics: King Athelstan's Sisters and Frankish Queenship', by Simon MacLean (pp. 167–90); '*Absoluimus uos uice beati petri apostolorum principi*: Episcopal Authority and the Reconciliation of Excommunicants in England and Francia *c*.900–*c*.1100', by Sarah Hamilton (pp. 209–41); 'The Death of Burgheard Son of Ælfgar and its Context', by Stephen Baxter (pp. 266–84); and 'The Representation of Queens and Queenship in Anglo-Norman Royal Charters', by David Bates (pp. 285–303).

Christopher Daniell's *Atlas of Medieval Britain* includes a number of very useful maps: 'Kingdoms in the British Isles *c*.AD 800', 'Viking Settlement and Anglo-Saxon Burhs', 'Anglo-Saxon Dioceses in the 9th Century', 'Anglo-Saxon Dioceses 900–1066', 'New Boroughs in Anglo-Saxon England', 'Mints of Edward the Confessor', 'Anglo-Saxon Earldoms in 1065', '1066: Campaigns of August to October', and 'William the Conqueror's Conquest of England 1066–72'.

New work continues to add to our understanding of Anglo-Saxon ecclesiastical culture. Several essays in *The Cambridge History of Christianity*, volume 3: *Early Medieval Christianities, c.600–c.1100*, edited by Thomas F.X. Noble and Julia M.H. Smith, are of interest to Anglo-Saxonists. Of particular relevance are Lesley Abrams's 'Germanic Christianities' (pp. 107–29) and Julia Barrow's 'Ideas and Applications of Reform' (pp. 345–62).

Joyce Hill writes on 'The Transmission of Christian Learning in Early Medieval Europe: A Northern Perspective' (in Martino, ed., *L'identità europea: lingua e cultura*, pp. 121–38). Her starting-point is Boniface and his contribution to the establishment of centres of learning and ecclesiastical administration in his missionary work. Hill uses this example to emphasize the strong link between learning and Christianity, monastic foundations as centres of scholarship, and the Anglo-Saxon role in transmitting Christian learning, themes which she then traces through early medieval western Europe with examples, including Ælfric's teaching texts, drawn from Anglo-Saxon England.

In 'Paganism in Conversion-Age Anglo-Saxon England: The Evidence of Bede's *Ecclesiastical History* Reconsidered' (*History* 93[2008] 162–80), S.D. Church reminds us of the importance of reading Bede's and Gregory I's descriptions of pagan practices in England as expressions of an evangelical Christian conversionary ideology rather than as accurate reports of the situation. Ian Wood's *The Priest, the Temple and the Moon in the Eighth Century*, his 2007 Brixworth Lecture, is a thought-provoking comparison of Pre-Columbian Maya civilization and early Anglo-Saxon England which aims to 'break away from a Euro-centric viewpoint' (p. 2). Wood compares Mayan and Anglo-Saxon temples and churches, monoliths and observation of the heavens and the calendar. His concluding point—that, in studying the early Middle Ages, 'we think of the reckoning of time and the calculation of Easter as no more than a matter of abstruse calculus, not a ritual on which a people's relation with God depended', is a timely reminder.

In 'Aldhelm of Malmesbury and High Ecclesiasticism in a Barbarian Kingdom' (*Traditio* 63[2008] 47–88), G.T. Dempsey examines three aspects of Aldhelm's career at Malmesbury: his scholarly output, administration, and participation in the wider English church and the kingdom.

Richard Gem's 2007 Deerhurst Lecture, *Deerhurst and Rome: Æthelric's Pilgrimage c. 804 and the Oratory of St Mary Mediana*, is published this year. Gem tracks the pilgrimage of Æthelric, son of Æthelmund, who was buried at Deerhurst and in whose name Æthelric donated lands to the community there. The political situation of the papacy at this date is then discussed, as is the pilgrim route through Old St Peter's, and Gem makes a case for the position and decoration of the west porch at Deerhurst, which originally had an image of the Virgin Mary holding an oval panel on which was painted the Christ Child, being inspired by Æthelric's Roman visit, and perhaps being furnished with a panel painting which he had brought back with him.

James F. LePree presents new evidence for the influence of an important source in 'Two Recently Discovered Passages of the Pseudo-Basil's *Admonition to a Spiritual Son* (*De admonitio ad filium spiritualem*) in Smaragdus' *Commentary on the Rule of St. Benedict* (*Expositio in regulam s. Benedicti*) and the *Letters* (*Epistolae*) of Alcuin' (*HeroicA* 11[2008] 8 paras).

Helene Scheck's fascinating new monograph, *Reform and Resistance: Formations of Female Subjectivity in Early Medieval Ecclesiastical Culture*, will greatly enrich scholarly understanding of gender, identity and ecclesiastical culture in the early Middle Ages. Scheck's interest lies in the various kinds of subject positions available to women during three different periods of reform: the early Carolingian reform movement under Charlemagne (*c*.742–814), the Alfredian and Benedictine reform movements in late ninth- through early eleventh-century England, and the Ottonian renaissance and monastic reforms of tenth-century Saxony. Scheck's study moves across a range of texts and traditions, both Latin and vernacular, and draws on contemporary critical theory to show how each of these historical moments created different possibilities for the emergence of female subjectivity. [SK]

Mary Frances Giandrea offers a 'Review Article: Recent Approaches to Late Anglo-Saxon Episcopal Culture' (*EMedE* 16[2008] 89–106), in which she surveys work on Wulfstan of York, Wulfstan II of Worcester and Wulfsige of Sherborne, ponders the nature of the evidence for each individual, and notes the post-Conquest date of many of the key texts and their pro-Reform ideology.

Elizabeth O'Brien presents 'Literary Insights into the Basis of some Burial Practices in Ireland and Anglo-Saxon England in the Seventh and Eighth Centuries' (in Karkov and Damico, eds., *Aedificia Nova: Studies in Honor of Rosemary Cramp*, pp. 283–99). With reference to Bede, the Penitential of Theodore and assorted other Anglo-Saxon texts and to funerary archaeology, O'Brien stresses the value of an interdisciplinary approach to the topic. Kelly M. Wickham-Crowley's contribution to the same volume, 'Buried Truths: Shrouds, Cults, and Female Production in Anglo-Saxon England' (pp. 300–24), draws out women's contribution to the development of saints' cults through the production of textile gifts. The examples she explores include the cults of Æthelburh, Cuthbert, Æthelthryth, Edmund and Guthlac, and she concludes that 'the status of the dead, male or female, was confirmed and made visible at the hands of women' (p. 324). More work on textiles from the same volume is reviewed below.

Zoe Devlin draws on recent work on social memory and technologies of memory to offer an interdisciplinary study, *Remembering the Dead in Anglo-Saxon England: Memory Theory in Archaeology and History* (BAR British Series 446 [2007]), which examines grave goods and landscape at a number of sites to chart changes across time and the impact of Christianization and literacy on attitudes to the past. Angela A. Redmond adds to the work on death and burial with a geographically focused study of *Viking Burial in the*

North of England (BAR British Series 429 [2007]) which explores the effect on cultural continuity of contact between the Scandinavian migrants and resident groups. Redmond's conclusions argue for a much higher number of Viking burials than has been assumed to be the case, and for the importance of recognizing cultural assimilation.

Patrick W. Conner draws on theory about the public sphere to examine 'Public Guilds and the Production of Old English Literature in the Public Sphere' (in Blanton and Scheck, eds., pp. 255–71). He notes evidence of parish guilds in England from the seventh century onwards and considers in detail evidence, in the form of guild statutes and guild-lists, for Exeter from the early tenth to early twelfth centuries. Guild feasts, or banquets, are proposed as events which might include literary performance, including poetry.

Cross and Culture in Anglo-Saxon England: Studies in Honor of George Hardin Brown, edited by Karen Louise Jolly, Catherine E. Karkov and Sarah Larratt Keefer, is a stimulating collection of studies on a wide range of aspects of the use and interpretation of the Christian cross in Anglo-Saxon England. Its contents are grouped into three sections: part I, 'Reading and Speaking the Cross': 'Bede and the Cross', by George Hardin Brown; 'Preaching the Cross: Texts and Contexts from the Benedictine Reform', by Joyce Hill; and 'At Cross Purposes: Six Riddles in the Exeter Books', by Jill Frederick; part II, 'The Cross as Image and Artifact': '*In Hoc Signo*: The Cross on Secular Objects and the Process of Conversion', by Carol Neuman de Vegvar; 'The Cross in the Grave: Design or Divine?', by Gale R. Owen-Crocker and Win Stephens; 'A Chip off the Rood: The Cross on Early Anglo-Saxon Coinage', by Anna Gannon; and 'Crosses and Conversion: The Iconography of the Coinage of Viking York ca.900', by Mark Blackburn. Part III, 'Performing the Cross': 'The Performance of the Cross in Anglo-Saxon England', by Sarah Larratt Keefer; 'Hallowing the Rood: Anglo-Saxon Rites for Consecrating Crosses', by Helen Gittos; 'Prayers and/or Charms Addressed to the Cross', by Roy M. Liuzza; and 'Reading the Cross in Anglo-Saxon England', by William Schipper.

Political, legal and administrative aspects of Anglo-Saxon culture are the focus of new work this year. Catherine Hills tracks 'Roman to Saxon in East Anglia' (in Karkov and Damico, eds., pp. 268–82) from archaeological evidence, with particular reference to the Spong Hill and Icklingham sites and an emphasis on the complexity of the picture and the dangers of over-interpreting evidence. *Edgar King of the English, 959–975: New Interpretations*, edited by Donald Scragg, is a timely reassessment of this monarch and his reign. Its contents are divided into four parts. Part I, 'Documentary Evidence', contains two essays by Simon Keynes: 'Edgar: *Rex admirabilis*' and 'A Conspectus of the Charters of King Edgar, 957–975'. Part II, 'Edgar before 959', contains Shashi Jayakumar, 'Eadwig and Edgar: Politics, Propaganda, Faction'; C.P. Lewis, 'Edgar, Chester, and the Kingdom of the Mercians, 957–9'; and Frederick M. Biggs, 'Edgar's Path to the Throne'. Part III, 'Edgar, 959–975', contains Barbara Yorke, 'The Women in Edgar's Life'; Julia Crick, 'Edgar, Albion and Insular Dominion'; Lesley Abrams, 'King Edgar and the Men of the Danelaw'; and Hugh Pagan, 'The Pre-Reform Coinage of Edgar'. Part IV, 'Edgar and the Monastic Revival', contains Julia Barrow, 'The

Chronology of the Benedictine "Reform"'; Catherine E. Karkov, 'The Frontispiece to the New Minster Charter and the King's Two Bodies'; Alexander M. Rumble, 'The Laity and the Monastic Reform in the Reign of Edgar'; and Mercedes Salvador-Bello, 'The Edgar Panegyrics in the *Anglo-Saxon Chronicle*'.

Pauline Stafford addresses the central question of the relationship between 'The Anglo-Saxon Chronicles, Identity and the Making of England' (*Haskins Soc Jnl* 19[2007] 28–550). Opening by noting the relative lack of use made by historians of the Chronicles as texts 'involved in the production of England and English identity' (p. 30), Stafford goes on to examine terminology related to the concept of English identity, and makes important points about the reshaping of the text to include Norman history in version F and the Northern Recension, and about the chronological and geographical and social specificity of each version.

Judith Green gave the R. Allen Brown Memorial Lecture on the topic of 'Kingship, Lordship, and Community in Eleventh-Century England' (*ANStu* 31[2008] 1–16), with a focus on the impact of the Conquest on these social roles and formations. Like Stafford, Green emphasizes that her central concepts are 'multifaceted, locally varied, exercised through differing channels, and through the medium of differing discourses', and she ends by calling for an altered timescale, so that 'our view of eleventh-century England is not dominated by the knowledge of the events of 1066' (p. 16).

Three of the essays in *People and Space in the Middle Ages, 300–1300*, edited by Wendy Davies, Guy Halsall and Andrew Reynolds ([2006]; made available for review this year), are on Anglo-Saxon topics. Andrew Reynolds and Alex Langlands explore 'Social Identities on the Macro Scale: A Maximum View of Wansdyke' (pp. 13–44); Stephen Bassett traces 'Boundaries of Knowledge: Mapping the Land Units of Late Anglo-Saxon and Norman England' (pp. 115–42); and Grenville Astill's focus is on 'Community, Identity and the Later Anglo-Saxon Town: The Case of Southern England' (pp. 233–54). Recent publications in the British Archaeological Reports British Series continue to drive forward our understanding of the physical and social landscape of Anglo-Saxon England. Stuart Brookes's study of *Economics and Social Change in Anglo-Saxon Kent AD 400–900* (BAR British Series 431 [2007]) examines physical landscapes of habitation and communication and human landscapes of consumption and distribution to map the development of the kingdom of Kent. Ryan Lavelle's focus is *Royal Estates in Anglo-Saxon Wessex: Land, Politics and Family Strategies* (BAR British Series 439 [2007]), and on the period from the end of the tenth century to the Conquest. Estate organization in Hampshire and Dorset, and in particular three categories of royal land—lands providing the 'farm of one night', lands granted to queens and other relatives, and lands held by royal agents—are analysed to investigate 'the organisation of landed resources, the very basis of royal power' (p. 126).

Sutton Hoo and its Landscape: The Context of Monuments, by Tom Williamson, draws on a detailed examination of the landscape context of the burial mounds, and on new phenomenological approaches to landscape archaeology, to track the area over time. Williamson's conclusion—that 'the cemeteries at Sutton Hoo and Tranmer House were positioned where they were, not to ensure that they could be viewed from the river, but so that the river could be seen from them' (p. 142)—moves away from the view that the burial site was selected in order to create a display, and towards an understanding of the centrality of the river Deben to the lives of local people, and a reintegration of environmental factors into our thinking on the significance of place.

Robert Cowie and Lyn Blackmore publish *Early and Middle Saxon Rural Settlement in the London Region*, in the Museum of London Monograph series. The results of excavations and surveys of thirty sites between 1945 and 2005, and evidence from place-names, topography, texts and material culture are drawn on to provide a detailed overview of the topic. Specialist appendices are provided on the pottery, accessioned finds, plant remains, animal bone, radiocarbon dating, archaeomagnetic dating and place-names.

Ian Wood offers two important new studies of monastic sites. In 'Monasteries and the Geography of Power in the Age of Bede' (*NH* 45[2008] 11–25) he makes particular reference to Northumbria and to the cluster of monastic communities in the Vale of Pickering—Lastingham, Kirkdale, Gilling, Crayke, Coxwold, Stonegrave, Hovingham—and on the lower Tyne—Jarrow, *Donamutha*, Tynemouth, Gateshead, Bywell, Hexham and Corbridge. The relationship of these foundations, and of Streanshalch, to the Deiran and Bernician dynasties is explored, and the centrality of monasticism to the political life of early Anglo-Saxon Northumbria is emphasized. In *The Origins of Jarrow: The Monastery, the Slake and Ecgfrith's Minster*, the first in the new Bede's World Studies series, Wood scrutinizes the textual accounts of the foundation of St Paul's monastery, Jarrow, and draws attention to differences between the dedication stone; which dates the foundation with reference to Abbot Ceolfrid and King Egfrith, Bede's account in his *History of the Abbots*, which foregrounds Benedict Biscop as builder of the new monastery; and the anonymous *Life of Ceolfrid*, usually considered to be Bede's source, which further emphasizes Ceolfrid's role. Through detailed examination of these texts, of the politics of the final years of Ecgfrith's life, and of the landscape of the harbour of Jarrow Slake and the lower Tyne and its royal and monastic connections, Wood constructs a convincing argument for textual attempts to mask political crisis in the period of the foundation of St Paul's and tensions in monastic–royal relationships, and in passing he makes important suggestions about the location of a nunnery for Iurminburg, Ecgfrith's queen, and about the possible role of St Paul's as a royal mausoleum.

Anne V. Ellis reconstructs *The Estates of Winchcombe Abbey, Gloucestershire: A Preliminary Landscape Archaeological Survey* (BAR British Series 474 [2008]) through an examination of textual and physical evidence. Ellis charts the extent of the estates as it changes over time, and traces in today's landscape of historical endowments. An appendix gives a full gazetteer of locations where Winchcombe Abbey held assets.

Eric G. Stanley examines Old English words for household based on *hiw*, and argues for 'The *familia* in Anglo-Saxon Society: "household", Rather Than "Family, home life" as now Understood' (*Anglia* 126[2008] 37–64). He notes that 'The Anglo-Saxons seem not to have understood any of their words in terms of close relationship tied by blood or affinity, and seem not to have succumbed to the sentimental belief...that this group of close relatives is always held together by love' (p. 63).

James T. McIlwain compares 'Theory and Practice in the Anglo-Saxon Leechbooks: The Case of Paralysis' (*Viator* 39[2008] 65–73). Drawing on the Old English Leechbook chapters on paralysis and their Latin sources, he shows the influence of classical theories of the humours.

Much new work on material and artistic culture is included in *Aedificia Nova: Studies in Honor of Rosemary Cramp*, edited by Catherine E. Karkov and Helen Damico. Rosemary Cramp herself contributes the text of her Rawlinson Lecture of 2000: 'The Changing Image, Divine and Human, in Anglo-Saxon Art' (pp. 3–32), in which she examines three aspects of her topic: mask, icon and dramatic actor, with reference to a wide range of images on stone, metal, wood and parchment, and to textual evidence from Bede onwards. The distinctive traits of Anglo-Saxon art which emerge from this study are 'fancifulness and ambiguity...surface texturing, a lack of "volume," and above all...a lack of pomposity and grandiose settings' (p. 32).

Gale R. Owen-Crocker's 'Embroidered Wood: Animal-Headed Posts in the Bayeux "Tapestry"' (in Karkov and Damico, eds., pp. 106–38) notes thirty-eight zoomorphic or grotesque human heads on wooden posts in the first half of the Tapestry, discusses the different settings in which they are placed, and argues that they serve to connect scenes, fill spaces, and reflect a human protagonist's situation or emotion. Elizabeth Coatsworth's 'Design in the Past: Metalwork and Textile Influences on Pre-Conquest Sculpture in England' (pp. 139–61) draws on data from the Manchester Medieval Textiles Project to show the close links between art in different media. Coatsworth takes edges and trimmings as her case-study, and shows how frames and edges in paintings, sculpture, ivories, wood, metalwork and textiles influence each other and speak to stylistic trends and their adaptation to new media. Kelly R. Wickham-Crowley's essay on textiles in the same volume is reviewed above.

Susan Youngs concentrates on metalwork in 'Missing Material: Early Anglo-Saxon Enameling' (pp. 162–75). She notes that almost all surviving evidence is for enamelling on dress items, re-evaluates some examples and proposes that the earliest ones are 'badges of success' (p. 175), but that this form of decoration was not widespread in England until the ninth century. Leslie Webster's 'Apocalypse Then: Anglo-Saxon Ivory Carving in the Tenth and Eleventh Centuries' (pp. 226–53) explores signs of the belief that the world would end 1,000 years after the time of Christ. Webster surveys eschatological ideas in Anglo-Saxon England in texts and images and then offers detailed studies of a number of ivory carvings to stress their function as 'images to be dwelled upon in the heart...encapsulations of eternal truths about life and death' (p. 253).

Carol Neuman de Vegvar's 'Reading the Franks Casket: Contexts and Audiences' (in Blanton and Scheck, eds., pp. 141–59) contemplates the interpretative skills needed to read the images and inscriptions. She notes that 'for the casket to continue to function as a transmitter of any form of information or message, it would have had to be at least partially accessible to an audience of high-status individuals with unpredictable and possibly widely differing levels of literacy, let alone intellectual training' (p. 148), points out parallels between the Casket and Old English wisdom poetry in terms of structure and content, and suggests that the Casket's original contents might have been a psalter rather than a gospel book.

Gale R. Owen-Crocker's 2007 article on the Bayeux Tapestry, 'The Bayeux Tapestry: The Voice from the Border' (in Keefer and Bremmer, eds., *Signs on the Edge: Space, Text and Margins in Medieval Manuscripts*, pp. 235–58), was omitted from last year's *YWES*. In it, Owen-Crocker reads the border of the tapestry in counterpoint to the main register, and offers many insights into the way in which the two parts play off against each other and into the border's sometimes ironic comment on the main actions depicted.

Another splendid volume in the *Corpus of Anglo-Saxon Stone Sculpture*, volume 8: *Western Yorkshire*, by Elizabeth Coatsworth, appears this year. As usual in this series, the historical context of the sculpture and the regional geology are discussed in the opening chapters. Anglian and Anglo-Scandinavian period forms and ornament, figural sculpture, the distribution and dating of the sculptures, and the inscriptions are also assessed. The catalogue proper is supported by an extraordinary 870 plates, giving photographs and sketches of the items catalogued and also comparative examples from elsewhere.

The Alfred Jewel and Other Late Anglo-Saxon Decorated Metalwork, by David A. Hinton, is a richly illustrated handbook guide to objects, mostly from the Ashmolean Museum, which represent this art form. Its sections cover the Jewel, other possible *aestels*, royal gifts and finger-rings, hoards, swords and other weapons, brooches, other personal fittings, riding equipment, enamel mounts, coins and the Sandford hanging reliquary. 'Re-evaluating Base-Metal Artefacts: An Inscribed Lead Strap-End from Crewkerne, Somerset', by Gabor Thomas, Naomi Payne and Elisabeth Okasha (*ASE* 37[2008] 173–81), considers a recently discovered, and male-owned, example of this most common type of dress accessory, and explores the use of lead dress accessories to advertise status.

Several of the essays in *Health and Healing from the Medieval Garden*, edited by Peter Dendle and Alain Touwaide, are on Anglo-Saxon topics: Maria Amalia d'Aronco, 'Gardens on Vellum: Plants and Herbs in Anglo-Saxon Manuscripts' (pp. 101–27); Philip G. Rusche, 'The Sources for Plant Names in Anglo-Saxon England and the Laud Herbal Glossary' (pp. 128–44); and Marijane Osborn, 'Anglo-Saxon Ethnobotany: Women's Reproductive Medicine in *Leechbook III*' (pp. 145–61).

'A Picture of Paul in a Parker Manuscript' by Frederick M. Biggs (in Blanton and Scheck, eds., pp. 169–89) adds to our understanding of representations of the apostles in Anglo-Saxon art. The picture in question is on folio ii^r of Cambridge, Corpus Christi College 198, and Biggs identifies the scene in the lower register as Paul approving Luke's book, and relates the image to Ælfric's *Lives of Saints* homily on Mark, which is included in the manuscript

Robert L. Schichler studies iconography in manuscript illustration and coins in 'Ending on a Giant Theme: The Utrecht and Harley Psalters, and the Pointed-Helmet Coinage of Cnut' (in Blanton and Scheck, eds., pp. 241–54). The illustration of Psalm 143 on folio 73^v of the Harley Psalter shows Goliath in a pointed helmet, unlike the Utrecht Psalter but similar to images of Cnut on Anglo-Saxon pennies from c.1023–30. Schichler notes the Viking resonance of this depiction of Goliath, and suggests that this and its positioning on the page relative to a textual reference to foreigners would evoke memories of recent Viking raids and Cnut's foreignness.

The first volume of a new journal, *Studies in Early Medieval Coinage* (*SEMC*), appears this year. This is a most welcome development for Anglo-Saxon studies, since it brings together work by numismatists, art historians and textual scholars. The volume opens with the proceedings of the International Sceatta Symposium of 2006: 'Sceattas: Twenty-One Years of Progress', by Michael Metcalf (*SEMC* 1[2008] 7–15); 'Sceattas in East Anglia: An Archaeological Perspective', by John Newman (*SEMC* 1[2008] 17–22); 'Thrynmsas, Sceattas and the Cult of the Cross', by Ian Wood (*SEMC* 1[2008] 23–30); 'Some New Types', by Tony Abramson (*SEMC* 1[2008] 31–44); 'Series K: Eclecticism and *Entente Cordiale*', by Anna Gannon (*SEMC* 1[2008] 45–52); 'Series X and Coin Circulation in Ribe', by Claue Feveile (*SEMC* 1[2008] 53–67); and 'The 2006 Symposium and Beyond', by Mark Blackburn (*SEMC* 1[2008] 69–72). Additional papers follow: 'The Sceattas of Series D', by Wybrand Op Den Velde (*SEMC* 1[2008] 77–90); 'Sceattas from a Site in Essex', by Mike Bonser and Tony Carter (*SEMC* 1[2008] 91–5); 'Orthographic Standardization and Seventh- and Eighth-Century Coin Inscriptions', by Philip Shaw (*SEMC* 1[2008] 97–112); 'Fifty Years after Dunning: Reflections on Emporia, their Origins and Development', by Richard Hodges (*SEMC* 1[2008] 113–18); and 'A New Sceat of the Dorestat/Madelinus-Type', by Arent Pol (*SEMC* 1[2008] 119–22). Finally, significant collections are described by Tony Abramson in 'The Beowulf Collection' (*SEMC* 1[2008] 125–53) and 'The Patrick Finn Sceatta Index and Analysis: A Collector's Perspective' (*SEMC* 1[2008] 155–96).

New work throws interesting light on Anglo-Saxonism as a discipline. Janet L. Nelson's 2006 Henry Loyn Memorial Lecture, 'Henry Loyn and the Context of Anglo-Saxon England' (*Haskins Soc Jnl* 19[2007] 154–70) is an 'exploration into the imaginative world which framed and shaped Henry's scholarly work on Anglo-Saxon England' (p. 169) which emphasizes the importance of his insights into the European context of his subject. In 'Anglo-Saxonism and Victorian archaeology: William Wylie's *Fairford Graves*' (*EMedE* 16[2008] 49–88), Howard Williams examines a mid-nineteenth-century report on an early medieval cemetery and shows how it contributed to constructions of English identity. 'Anglo-Saxon and Related Entries in the *Oxford Dictionary of National Biography* (2004)' are surveyed and listed by Helen Foxhall Forbes and others (*ASE* 37[2008] 183–232).

Kathleen Davis's *Periodization and Sovereignty: How Ideas of Feudalism and Secularization Govern the Politics of Time* is an important book about the making of history, and a timely challenge to the construction of the Middle Ages in opposition to the modern. Addressing aspects of medieval and postcolonial studies, Davis examines concepts of feudalism and secularization, with extensive reference to Bede as 'an ambitious and influential historian and theorist of temporality, as well as a powerful synthesizer of previous traditions' (p. 101).

Haruko Momma and Michael Matto's *A Companion to the History of the English Language* includes several essays on Old English which will serve students well as introductions to the subject: Daniel Donoghue, 'Early Old English (up to 899)' (pp. 156–64); Mechthild Gretsch, 'Late Old English (899–1066)' (pp. 165–71); Lucia Kornexl, 'Topics in Old English Dialects' (pp. 172–9); and Fred C. Robinson, 'The Anglo-Saxon Poetic Tradition' (pp. 435–44).

4. Literature: General

The year 2008 saw the publication of an impressive array of texts and materials on Anglo-Saxon literature. *Intertexts: Studies in Anglo-Saxon Culture Presented to Paul E. Szarmach*, edited by Virginia Blanton and Helene Scheck, contains a wealth of essays on early medieval literature and culture. The volume's contents are: 'Sharing Words with *Beowulf*', by Roberta Frank; 'Old English Poetic Compounds: A Latin Perspective', by Michael Lapidge; 'Working the Boundary or Walking the Line? Late Old English Rhythmical Alliteration', by Joseph B. Trahern Jr; 'Reconstructing *The Ruin*', by Andy Orchard; 'The Baby on the Stone: Nativity as Sacrifice (The Old English *Christ III*, 1414–1425)', by Thomas D. Hill; '*Hnescnys*: Weakness of Mind in the Works of Ælfric', by Rhonda L. McDaniel; 'Bede's *Ecclesiastical History*: Numbers, Hard Data, and Longevity', by Joel T. Rosenthal; 'A Context for *Resignation A*?', by Mechthild Gretsch; 'A Man "boca gleaw" and his Musings', by Jane Roberts; 'Reading the Franks Casket: Contexts and Audiences', by Carol Neuman de Vegvar; 'Why the Left Hand is Longer (or Shorter) than the Right: Some Irish Analogues for an Etiological Legend in the Homiliary of St. Père de Chartres', by Charles D. Wright; 'A Picture of Paul in a Parker Manuscript', by Frederick M. Biggs; 'King and Counselor in the Alfredian Boethius', by M.R. Godden; '*Beowulf*'s Foreign Queen and the Politics of Eleventh-Century England', by Helen Damico; 'Ending on a Giant Theme: The Utrecht and Harley Psalters, and the Pointed-Helmet Coinage of Cnut', by Robert L. Schichler; 'Parish Guilds and the Production of Old English Literature in the Public Sphere', by Patrick W. Conner; 'Pictured in the Heart: The Ediths at Wilton', by Catherine E. Karkov; 'The Armaments of John the Baptist in Blickling Homily 14 and the Exeter Book *Descent into Hell*', by Thomas N. Hall; 'Spiritual Combat and the Land of Canaan in *Guthlac A*', by David F. Johnson; 'Ciceronianism in Bede and Alcuin', by George Hardin Brown; 'Ælfric and Haymo Revisited', by Joyce Hill; 'Eugenia before Ælfric: A Preliminary Report on the Transmission of an Early Medieval Legend', by E. Gordon Whatley; 'The Vercelli Homilies and Kent', by Donald G. Scragg; 'Archbishops, Lords, and Concubines: Words for People and their Word-Formation Patterns in Early English (*Épinal-Erfurt Glossary* and Ælfric's *Glossary*)—A Sketch', by Hans Sauer; 'More Old English from Manuscripts', by Helmut Gneuss; and 'New Old

English Texts: The Expanding Corpus of Old English' by Jonathan Wilcox. Essays in this volume that focus on individual texts are reviewed in the appropriate sections above and below.

Nicholas Howe's groundbreaking book, *Writing the Map of Anglo-Saxon England: Essays in Cultural Geography*, constitutes a major contribution to our understanding of place, space and home in Anglo-Saxon literature and culture. Howe's elegantly written monograph demonstrates that the Anglo-Saxons possessed a remarkable body of geographical knowledge in written rather than cartographic form, and explores the complex ways in which the Anglo-Saxons located themselves, both literally and imaginatively, in the world. By examining a range of Latin and Old English writings on place and homeland, as well as the single map of the known world found in Cotton Tiberius B. v, Howe reveals that the Anglo-Saxons tended to view themselves and their homeland as being far from the centre of the world, and he discusses how they attempted to narrow that distance and to redefine themselves. *Writing the Map of Anglo-Saxon England* is a powerful and important book whose impact will be felt both in and beyond the field of Anglo-Saxon studies.

Coverage of the pre-Conquest period in *The Oxford History of Literary Translation in English*, volume 1: *To 1500*, edited by Roger Ellis, is much stronger in some sections than others. The opening section, 'Contexts of Translation', consists of three essays, all of which cover the pre-Conquest period: 'The Languages of Medieval England', by John Burrow (pp. 7–28), 'Manuscript Culture', by Tim William Machan (pp. 29–44), and 'Nation, Region, Class, and Gender', by Helen Phillips (pp. 45–69). Also containing material of relevance are 'The Developing Corpus of Literary Translation', by Edward Wheatley (pp. 171–89); 'Chronicles and Historical Narratives', by Thea Summerfield with Rosamund Allen (pp. 332–63); 'Classical Authors', by Stephen Medcalf (pp. 364–89), which includes analyses of the Alfredian Boethius and *Apollonius of Tyre*; and 'Scientific and Medical Writing', by Paul Acker (pp. 407–20); and 'The Translators: Biographical Sketches', by a number of the book's contributors (pp. 423–45). Robert Stanton's essay on the Alfredian translations is reviewed in section 10, below. [MS]

Mary Dockray-Miller surveys 'Old English Literature and Feminist Theory: A State of the Field' (*LitComp* 5/6[2008] 1049–59), and tracks an important paradigm shift brought about by such work 'so that women must now be regularly included in discussions of Anglo-Saxon cultural agency' (p. 1049). Dockray-Miller notes trends in the scholarship, including the blurring of the dividing line between pre- and post-Conquest textual production and reception, and the influence of work on later medieval women as readers and on their devotional practices. [MS]

Janie Steen's new monograph, *Verse and Virtuosity: The Adaptation of Latin Rhetoric in Old English Poetry*, provides a rich commentary on the complex ways in which Latin models have shaped Old English poetic style. Steen's interest lies in understanding which figures in vernacular verse are inherited or borrowed from Latin rhetoric, and in elucidating the various channels through which Latin rhetorical devices reached Old English poetry. She analyses a range of vernacular texts, including *The Phoenix*, *Judgment Day II*, Exeter Book Riddles 35 and 40, *Elene*, *Christ II* and *Juliana*, and contends that 'for an aspiring vernacular poet, the gulf between Latin rhetoric and the vernacular tradition would have made the task of translation a daunting challenge, one that required not only faithfulness to the Latin authority, but also flexibility in adapting its style and substance to a very different idiom' (p. 3). Matthew S, Kempshall reads 'The Virtues of Rhetoric: Alcuin's *Disputatio de rhetorica et de uirtutibus*' (*ASE* 37[2008] 7–30) against its sources to argue that 'Alcuin's understanding of rhetoric ... was central to his understanding of how wisdom should be applied by individuals within human society' (p. 29).

Michael Lapidge offers 'Old English Poetic Compounds: A Latin Perspective' (in Blanton and Scheck, eds., pp. 17–32), with a particular focus on compounds in the work of the Latin poets studied in Anglo-Saxon schools from the late seventh century until beyond 1066—Virgil, Juvencus, Caelius Sedulius, Alcimus Ecdicius Avitus, Arator and Cyprianus Gallus—and in the work of Aldhelm and Bede and Old English verse. Lapidge identifies strong similarities in the coining and use of tetrasyllabic compounds in Latin and Old English verse. [MS]

Two new studies of texts produced for Wilton appeared this year. Elizabeth M. Tyler's 'The *Vita Ædwardi*: The Politics of Poetry at Wilton Abbey' (*ANStu* 31[2008] 135–56) adds to our understanding of the eleventh century as 'a rich and vibrant period of creativity for English literature' (p. 135). With a focus on the Roman story-world of the *Vita Ædwardi*—a text written 'in Latin, by a foreign cleric working under the patronage of a woman' (p. 155)—Tyler emphasizes influence on mainland Europe, the importance of the court, the use of Latin, and poetry as a medium for the writing of history. Catherine E. Karkov's 'Pictured in the Heart: The Ediths at Wilton' (in Blanton and Scheck, eds., pp. 273–85) asks whether Goscelin's description of the wooden chapel which Edith had built and decorated with a cycle of wall-paintings in the late tenth century is an accurate eye-witness account. The metaphorical and ideological force of architectural and artistic description are emphasized, and Karkov suggests that Goscelin's aim may have been to turn 'his audience's minds and eyes away from the problematic Queen Edith and the economic troubles that followed the Conquest, back to what in retrospect could be portrayed as an idyllic period of growth for the monastery' (p. 285). [MS]

In 'Working the Boundary or Walking the Line? Late Old English Rhythmical Alliteration' (in Blanton and Scheck, eds., pp. 34–44), Joseph B. Traherne notes that 'we continue to debate the place where we should put that literature which we assign to "the borderland between verse and prose"' (p. 34). He surveys contributions to this debate, and then turns to an analysis of four late texts which fall into this category: excerpts from homilies Napier 30 and 49, an excerpt from Vercelli Homily 21, and the passage known as *The Judgement of the Damned*. Gabriella Corona's analysis of Ælfric's rhythmic prose is reviewed in section 10 below. [MS]

Ian Kirby surveys 'Gradual Revelation as Narrative Strategy in Medieval Literature' (in Thormählen, ed., *English Now: Selected Papers from the 20th IAUPE Conference in Lund 2007*, pp. 14–22), with reference to a range of Old English poetry, including *Beowulf*, the Exeter Book Riddles, *Wulf and Eadwacer*, *The Seafarer*, *The Wife's Lament* and *The Husband's Message*. [MS]

A good number of the essays in volume 2 of '... *un tuo serto di fiori in man recando*': *Scritti in onore di Maria Amalia D'Aronco*, edited by Patrizia Lendinara, are on Anglo-Saxon literature: Peter Bierbaumer, Hans Sauer, Helmut W. Klug and Ulrike Krischke, 'Old English Plant Names Go Cyber: The Graz–Munich Dictionary Project' (pp. 43–62); Rolf H. Bremmer, 'The Reception of Defensor's *Liber scintillarum* in Anglo-Saxon England' (pp. 75–89); Claudia di Sciacca, in 'Every Cloud Has a Silver Lining: A Note on OE *sceo*' (pp. 123–46); Dora Faraci, 'L'ineffabilità della creazione nel *Physiologus* antico inglese' (pp. 167–81); Renato Gendre, ' "Cibi di carne" nell'Inghilterra anglosassone' (pp. 195–210); Joyce Hill, 'Reflections on the Rood: Paradox and Enigma in Text and Artefact' (pp. 223–334); Michael Lapidge, 'The Latin Exemplar of the Old English *Bede*' (pp. 235–46); Loredana Lazzari, 'La *Regularis Concordia* e la lettera ai monaci di Eynsham: implicazioni politiche della riforma monastica' (pp. 247–8); Patrizia Lendinara, 'I donestri, pericolosi indovini delle *Meraviglie dell'Oriente*' (pp. 259–73); Anna Maria Luiselli Fadda, 'Il testo fluttuante e la *restitution textus*. Per una edizione genetica del *Sermo Lupi ad Anglos*' (pp. 275–93); Marcello Meli, '*Beowulf*, la madre di Grendel e *Hárbarðzljóð*, strofa 56' (pp. 295–306); Maria Vittoria Molinari, 'Retorica dell'ironia in *Beowulf*' (pp. 307–17); Carla Morini, 'A Revision of the So-Called Old English "Brontologium"', CCCC 391, ff. 714 and 715' (pp. 319–31); Katherine O'Brien O'Keeffe, 'Inside, Outside, Conduct and Judgement: King Alfred Reads the *Regula pastoralis*' (pp. 333–45); Donald Scragg, 'London, British Library, Royal 2 B. V, Christ Church, Canterbury, and the English Language in the Eleventh Century' (pp. 381–93); and Loredana Teresi, 'Which Way Is the Wind Blowing? Meteorology and Political Propaganda in the OE *Metres of Boethius*' (pp. 427–46). [MS]

Several essays published in 2008 focus on interiority and emotion. Britt Mize investigates 'Manipulations of the Mind-as-Container Motif in *Beowulf*, *Homiletic Fragment II*, and Alfred's *Metrical Epilogue to the Pastoral Care*' (*JEGP* 107[2008] 25–56). Mize begins from the premise that Old English poetry regularly represents the mind as a metaphysical enclosure, and he explores the creative uses to which Anglo-Saxon poets put this traditional motif, as well as the various contexts in which it was deployed. Dirk Geeraerts and Caroline Gervaert study 'Hearts and (Angry) Minds in Old English' (in Sharifian, Dirven, Yu and Niemeier, eds., *Culture, Body, and Language: Conceptualizations of Internal Body Organs across Cultures and Languages*, pp. 319–47). They analyse 'heart' and 'mood' compounds in Old English and draw three main conclusions: that 'mood' represents an integrated conception of mental life in which cognition, emotion and volition occur side by side; that Anglo-Saxon writers depict the heart as an embodied seat of the mind and soul; and that this second point is importantly qualified by the fact that figurative 'heart' imagery is far less prevalent in Old English texts than literal 'mood' denominations. Don Chapman writes on ' "You belly-guilty bag": Insulting Epithets in Old English' (*JHPrag* 9[2008] 1–19). He uses the *Dictionary of Old English* corpus to examine all uses of the second person pronouns *þu* and *þin*. He finds that almost all insulting epithets in Old English are highly conventional, both in their use of well-established words from the Old English lexicon and in their reuse of typical epithets from context to context, but that a handful of epithets exhibit much originality and creativity. These are mainly found in addresses to devils and in complaints between the body and soul. Thomas Kohnen studies 'Linguistic Politeness in Anglo-Saxon England? A Study of Old English Address Terms' (*JHPrag* 9[2008] 140–58). Kohnen's interest lies in examining Anglo-Saxon address terms associated with polite or courteous behaviour (e.g. *leof, broþor, hlaford, hlæfdige*). He argues that politeness as 'face work' may not have played a major role in Anglo-Saxon England and that the use of address terms that appear to be associated with polite behaviour 'may reflect accommodation to the overriding importance of mutual obligation and kin loyalty on the one hand, and obedience to the basic Christian ideals of *humilitas* and *caritas* on the other' (p. 140).

Jordi Sánchez-Martí writes on 'Age Matters in Old English Literature' (in Lewis-Simpson, ed., *Youth and Age in the Medieval North*, pp. 205–25). The focus here is on the life cycle of the Anglo-Saxon male as portrayed in the Anglo-Saxon literary corpus. Sánchez-Martí argues that Anglo-Saxon writers depicted cognitive development and the gaining of wisdom as crucial aspects of male development, and that the prime of life for men is the time after the completion of cognitive training but before the onset of physical decrepitude.

The 2008 volume of *The Heroic Age* contains two essays that focus on developments in the study of Anglo-Saxon literature. Michael D.C. Drout, Tom Shippey, Richard Scott Nokes and Eileen A. Joy discuss 'State of the Field in Anglo-Saxon Studies' (*HeroicA* 11[2008] 73 paras). They present a range of ideas about the current state of Anglo-Saxon studies, with attention to the status of language teaching, the field's strength and vitality, recognition of that strength in the form of employment opportunities and resources, and the future of Anglo-Saxon studies within the academy at large. This same volume features Martin K. Foys's essay on 'The Reality of Media in Anglo-Saxon Studies' (*HeroicA* 11[2008] 34 paras). This essay is a digital version of an excerpt from Foys's 2007 monograph, *Virtually Anglo-Saxon: Old Media, New Media, and Early Medieval Studies* (see *YWES* 88[2009] 164). Foys argues that the change in media and the essay's unlinked endnotes contribute to the sense that 'other paths within this text beyond the uni-linear remain to be found, imagined, or invented' (p. 2).

Four of the essays in *Historical Englishes in Varieties of Texts and Contexts*, edited by Masachiyo Amano, Michiko Ogura, and Masayuki Ohkado, focus on Old English language and literature. Kousuke Kaita investigates 'Distribution of OE *mid rihte* as an Adverbial of Propriety—with Special Reference to the Textual Variation' (pp. 33–47). Kaita examines how the Old English adverbials *mid rihte* 'rightfully' and *rihtlice* 'rightly' vary, and discusses which words they collocate with as a sign denoting the notion of obligation or propriety. Aurelijus Vijunas studies 'The Old English Adjective *siht*' (pp. 135–41), with particular attention to its synchronic meaning and structure, as well as its derivation. Vijunas concludes that the hapax word-form *sihtre*, attested in the *Corpus Diplomaticus Aevi Saxonici*, could be glossed as either 'drained' or 'wet'. Tomonori Yamamoto provides 'A Reconsideration of the Reliability of Alliterative Evidence for the Sound System of Old English: Does Old English Poetry Work Aurally or Visually?' (pp. 157–68). Yamamoto considers whether 'eye-rhyme' (e.g. love: prove, forth: worth) is appropriate when considering alliteration in Old English, and then turns to the broader question of whether alliteration in Old English is set up primarily on an aural or on a visual basis. He concludes that alliteration is phonemically based in Old English and can thus be used as reliable evidence for reconstructing the sound system. Hans Sauer's 'Interjection, Emotion, Grammar, and Literature' (pp. 387–403) touches briefly on these topics in a variety of Old English texts. Of particular interest is Sauer's point that *c*.35–40 interjections are attested for Old English, with approximately eight of them appearing in Ælfric's *Grammar*, as well as his broader argument that interjections not only express emotions, but are also used for other purposes such as greetings and farewells, attention- and response-getters, hesitators, polite formulas, expletives and commands.

Michiko Ogura studies 'Old English Verbs of Tasting with Accusative/Genitive/*Of*-Phrase' (*Neophil* 92[2008] 517–22). Ogura's interest lies in showing that the genitive object of Old English verbs of tasting was in the process of being replaced by the *of*-phrase during the Anglo-Saxon period.

5. The Exeter Book

Six of the essays in Blanton and Scheck, eds., *Intertexts: Studies in Anglo-Saxon Culture Presented to Paul E. Szarmach*, discuss poems found in the Exeter Book. Andy Orchard offers new insights into 'Reconstructing *The Ruin*' (pp. 45–68). Orchard reviews the textual difficulties that confront any serious scholar of this fragmentary poem, provides a careful assessment of the lines that remain, and concludes by suggesting possible literary models (both Latin and vernacular) that might have influenced the *Ruin*-poet. Thomas D. Hill discusses 'The Baby on the Stone: Nativity as Sacrifice (The Old English *Christ III*, 1414–1425)' (pp. 69–77). Hill draws our attention to the rather unusual presentation of the Nativity in *Christ III* as a dark moment of sacrifice and a time of poverty, solitude and hardness. He contends that this depiction of the Nativity finds parallels not in literary texts but in Anglo-Saxon art, specifically, *The Benedictional of Æthelwold*. Mechthild Gretsch provides 'A Context for *Resignation A*?' (pp. 103–17). She surveys the critical history of *Resignation A* and argues that the repetitive nature and formal peculiarities of the poem suggest that it may have originated in a classroom as a kind of 'student's exercise'. Gretsch concludes that if her hypothesis is correct, poems such as *Resignation A* may provide valuable evidence that the Anglo-Saxons considered pragmatic devotional literature worthy of rhetorical and poetical embellishment and that this skill may have been taught in schools.

Jane Roberts studies 'A Man "boca gleaw" and his Musings' (pp. 119–37), and proposes that *Vainglory* should be read as both wisdom literature and also a piece of meditative writing which seeks to impart wisdom, affirm true humility and exhort audiences to meditation on fear of the Lord. Thomas N. Hall examines 'The Armaments of John the Baptist in Blickling Homily 14 and the Exeter Book *Descent into Hell*' (pp. 289–306). Hall traces the appearance and transmission of this biblical motif, in which John the Baptist seizes weapons and leaps up prepared to fight while still in his mother's womb, from early Eastern sources, to Blickling Homily 14, and to *The Descent into Hell*. Hall contends that the poet who composed *The Descent into Hell* consistently thinks in terms of parallels and tends to associate events typologically, and that his depiction of John the Baptist receiving armour and weapons in hell is meant to recall the image of John seizing weapons in the womb. David F. Johnson provides a fascinating account of 'Spiritual Combat and the Land of Canaan in *Guthlac A*' (pp. 307–17). His focus is on the *Guthlac A* poet's almost obsessive interest in Guthlac's land and *beorg* 'barrow', and he contends that the poet uses the theme of the land and its possession to symbolize Guthlac's spiritual struggle.

Two essays published in 2008 focus on gnomic poetry in the Exeter Book. David Robert Howlett studies 'The Gnomic Collection of Verse in the Exeter Book' (*PhilRev* 34[2008] 51–78), with particular attention to the prosody of *Maxims I*. Howlett argues that his analysis of prosody and style in the Exeter Book's gnomic verses points to the court of Æthelstan as a possible milieu for their composition. Rafał Borysławski's essay, '*Wordhordes cræft*: Confusion and the Order of the Wor(l)d in Old English Gnomes' (in Krygier and Sikorska, eds., *The Propur Langage of Englische Men*, pp. 119–31) sets out to understand the sense of confusion, turmoil, and mystery that is present in Old English gnomic texts such as *The Order of the World*. He argues that this confusion provides evidence of God's magnificence and also reflects the political turmoil and confusion of Alfred's reign.

Sarah Downey examines 'Too Much of Too Little: Guthlac and the Temptation of Excessive Fasting' (*Traditio* 63[2008] 89–127). Downey seeks to show that, although Guthlac is not generally remembered among modern readers for his food asceticism or resistance to demonic temptations to excessive fasting, these features were of great significance to his biographer Felix and to medieval English audiences. She points out that many different versions of Guthlac's life, including the prose excerpt appearing as Vercelli Homily 23, Felix's Latin *Vita Sancti Guthlaci*, and the 'full' Old English prose rendition of Felix's *Vita* that appears in British Museum Cotton Vespasian D. xxx, contain elaborate accounts of diabolic temptations to excessive fasting in which the Devil and his minions try to convince Guthlac to fast beyond ecclesiastically sanctioned standards of asceticism. She concludes that, although food asceticism is not employed as an object of demonic temptation in *Guthlac A* or *B*, it is nevertheless an important part of the Guthlac tradition and a rich source of information regarding Anglo-Saxon cultural attitudes towards asceticism, the homiletic form, methods of diabolic temptation, and sanctity.

Glenn Davis considers 'Corporeal Anxiety in *Soul and Body II*' (*PQ* 87[2008] 33–50). Davis argues that the gruesome depiction of the decaying body in *Soul and Body II* ought to be read in the context of Anglo-Saxon medical texts, and he concludes that 'the poem's use of graphic bodily imagery can be understood as a sophisticated response to a prevalent cultural anxiety about the health and integrity of the human body' (p. 36).

Two essays published in 2008 focus on the Exeter Book elegies. Melissa J. Wolfe's '*Swa cwæð snottor on mode*: Four Issues in *The Wanderer*' (*Neophil* 92[2008] 559–65) asks four central questions: how many speakers there are in the poem; who or what is set up in opposition to the *wis wer* in line 64; how the virtue of reticence is reconciled with the existence of the poem; and how the Wanderer experiences grace in the midst of his sufferings. She contends that the poem has only one speaker, that hastiness stands in opposition to the wisdom of the *wis wer*, that the use of third-person narrative enables reticence to coexist with emotional expression, and that *ar* in the poem must be understood by recognizing the multiple kinds of grace encompassed by the term. Sebastian I. Sobecki writes on 'The Interpretation of *The Seafarer*: A Re-examination of the Pilgrimage Theory' (*Neophil* 92[2008] 127–39). He claims that the standard interpretation of *The Seafarer* as an account of a sea pilgrimage, or *peregrinatio pro amore Dei*, fails to consider early medieval pilgrimage patterns, and proposes that the narrator of the poem may have been a fisherman.

The Exeter Book riddles continue to inspire new scholarship. Brian McFadden writes on 'Raiding, Reform, and Reaction: Wondrous Creatures in the Exeter Book Riddles' (*TSLL* 50[2008] 329–51). McFadden contends that the riddles 'serve as a site for the expression of cultural anxiety' (p. 329), particularly with respect to actual or potential threats posed by Viking incursions and the blurring of civil or ecclesiastical affairs in the wake of the Benedictine reforms. Mark Griffith writes on 'Exeter Book Riddle 74 *Ac* "Oak" and *Bat* "Boat"' (*N&Q* 55[2008] 393–6). Griffith seeks to refine John Niles's recently proposed solution to Riddle 74 as an oak tree that has been cut down to make a boat. Griffith's research suggests possible connections between Riddle 73 and Riddle 74, and that these two riddles might have their origin in a lost Old English rune poem.

In '*Leo ond beo*: Exeter Book Riddle 17 as Samson's lion' (*ES* 89[2008] 371–87), Patrick J. Murphy offers a very thorough rereading of the riddle and of previous interpretations of it, and proposes that the rhyming doublet *leo ond beo* 'lion and bee' 'seems a nice fit for both runes and Riddle' (p. 385). [MS]

Valentine A. Pakis provides 'A Note in Defense of "The Partridge" (Exeter Book 97v)' (*Neophil* 92[2008] 729–34). Pakis reviews recent criticism that argues that the fragmentary third poem of the Old English *Physiologus* series in the Exeter Book is about the phoenix rather than the partridge, and concludes that grounds for such arguments are highly speculative.

An important item from last year that escaped notice is Allen J. Frantzen's 'Drama and Dialogue in Old English Poetry: The Scene of Cynewulf's *Juliana*' (*ThS* 48[2007] 99–119). Frantzen begins by pointing out that Anglo-Saxon narrative poems, and the performative tradition to which these texts belong, have been excluded from drama criticism and theatre history, which have tended to focus on texts and productions involving fixed elements of the tradition, such as actors, paying audiences, costumes and stages. Frantzen analyses previous scholarly assessments of drama in Old English literature, and explores the complex relationships between semiotics, narrative poetry and oral performance. His study concludes with a thorough analysis of drama and performance in *Juliana*, with some attention to *Beowulf*.

6. The Poems of the Vercelli Book

A small but noteworthy amount of criticism has appeared in 2008 on the poetry in the Vercelli Book. Two essays focus on Cynewulf's poems. Nicole Marafioti writes on 'The *Siðgeomor* Speaker and his Sources, in Cynewulf's *The Fates of the Apostles* (*N&Q* 55[2008] 119–22). She calls attention to the introductory lines in Cynewulf's *Fates*, in which the speaker refers to his own maladies and afflictions, and contends that these bodily infirmities point to a monastic infirmary as a possible setting for the poem's composition. Laurence Erussard writes on 'Language, Power, and Holiness in Cynewulf's *Elene*' (*M&H* 34[2008] 23–41). Erussard focuses on Elene's styles of speaking and emotional expression and concludes that, 'by the end of the poem, Judas and Elene's common hieratic and impersonal style stands in drastic contrast with the devil's personal language' (p. 24).

Alfred Bammesberger asks 'Is There an Old English Adjective *Scrid* "Swift"?' (*N&Q* 55[2008] 117–19), with particular attention to the term's use in *Andreas*. Bammesberger points out that the basic meaning of *scrydan* is 'clothe', that *fulscrid* (*Andreas*, line 496b) is best translated as 'completely equipped', and that there is hardly any reason to posit an Old English adjective *scrid* 'swift'.

7. The Junius Manuscript

2008 has been a relatively quiet year for work on poetry in the Junius manuscript. Miranda Wilcox discusses '*Meotod*, the Meteorologist: Celestial Cosmography in *Christ and Satan*, lines 9–12a' (*LeedsSE* 39[2008] 17–32). Wilcox opens her essay by noting that the first six lines of *Christ and Satan* imagine a cosmographic map, with the Creator framing the dimensions of a cosmos formed out of the four elements. She shows that the poet diverges markedly from the chronology of creation as recounted in the first chapter of Genesis, and that the account of creation here must be understood as derived from 'a syncretic model which was developed in the scriptural exegesis of Basil, Ambrose, Augustine, and seventh-century Irish monks, codified in scientific handbooks by Isidore and Bede, and authorized in the liturgy' (p. 27).

W.B. Lockwood examines 'OEng. *scūrboga* and the Provenance of *Genesis A*' (*N&Q* 55[2008] 2–3). The word, in line 1540 of the poem, literally translates as 'shining bow', and means 'rainbow'; this is its only attestation, and Lockwood argues that it is a loan translation from Gaelic, via the Irish mission to Anglo-Saxon England, that it is thus 'inconceivable that such a partisan term ... could have remained in living use after 663' (p. 3), and that *Genesis A* might have been 'composed in Northumbria during the period of Celtic ascendancy' (p. 3). [MS]

8. The *Beowulf* Manuscript

The year 2008 has been extraordinarily fruitful for *Beowulf* studies. Leading the way is the publication of the long-awaited fourth edition of *Klaeber's Beowulf and the Fight at Finnsburg*, edited by R.D. Fulk, Robert E. Bjork, and John D. Niles, with a foreword by Helen Damico. This edition, which was awarded the International Society of Anglo-Saxonists' 2009 biennial publication prize for 'Best Edition', constitutes a major contribution to Anglo-Saxon scholarship. The editors have brought Klaeber's third edition (published in 1936) up to date, while preserving its integrity, range, and exceptionally thorough notes and glossary. A revised Introduction and Commentary incorporate the vast quantity of *Beowulf* scholarship that has been published since 1936, and the lightly revised text incorporates the best textual criticism of the intervening years. The fourth edition of Klaeber's *Beowulf* is an essential resource for students of Anglo-Saxon literature and offers a model of what can be achieved through scholarly collaboration.

A number of new monographs focus on *Beowulf*. John M. Hill's *The Narrative Pulse of Beowulf: Arrivals and Departures* argues against critics who believe that *Beowulf* lacks a steady narrative advance and that the poem's numerous digressions complicate and/or halt the poem's movement. Hill contends that the poem's many scenes of arrival and departure create a distinct 'narrative pulse', and contribute to the structural density, social drama and aesthetic cohesiveness of the poem. Hill also writes on 'Episodes Such as the Offa of Angeln Passage and the Aesthetics of *Beowulf*' (*PhilRev* 34[2008] 29–49), with a particular focus on the ways in which digressions such as the Offa of Angeln passage work to create an aesthetic standard in *Beowulf*. Scott Gwara's new monograph, *Heroic Identity in the World of Beowulf*, begins from the question of Beowulf's motivations and temperament, and considers how audiences can judge a character who seems at once so heroic and so utterly reckless. Gwara argues that this tension can be productively resolved by understanding Beowulf as a foreign fighter seeking glory abroad. Individual chapters of Gwara's monograph focus on the poem's digressions, use of flyting rhetoric and heroic vocabulary. Gwara has also published two essays this year on *Beowulf*. A version of his 'The Foreign Beowulf and the "Fight at Finnsburg"' (*Traditio* 63[2008] 185–233) is published as chapter 2 of his monograph. This essay focuses on the complex relationship between the Finnsburg digression and the rest of *Beowulf* and contends that the digression 'represents the first time in English literature that characters can be shown to evaluate and react to intradiegetic narrative that analogizes their circumstances and guides their conduct' (p. 233). In '*Beowulf* 3074–75: Beowulf Appraises his Reward' (*Neophil* 92[2008] 333–8), Gwara begins from John Tanke's reading of the word *goldhwæte* as a feminine noun which means 'luck with gold'. Gwara seeks to demonstrate that in lines 3074–5 Beowulf is dying and thus stares at the treasure Wiglaf has brought more keenly than he has ever done in the past and that Beowulf's appraisal of the treasure 'evokes an ambivalence and invites an observer's assessment of Beowulf's deeds in the dragon fight' (p. 333).

A number of new monographs contain individual chapters on *Beowulf*. The first chapter of Andrew James Johnston's *Performing the Middle Ages from 'Beowulf' to 'Othello'* is intent on 'chart[ing] the discrepancy between *Beowulf*'s ostensible idealization of the heroic warrior and the complex power struggles going on beneath the text's heroic surface' (p. 21). Johnston examines images of royal succession in the poem, and uses modern critical theory to 'offer a deconstructive reading of *Beowulf*'s ideological manoeuvres and the role that gender plays in their service' (p. 21). The second chapter of J.A. Burrow's *The Poetry of Praise* focuses mainly on *Beowulf*. Burrow's interest lies in understanding how Old English poets use verse to distribute praise and blame, and he contends that critical remarks in *Beowulf* may still redound to the hero's praise. Chapter 4 of E.L. Risden's *Heroes, Gods and the Role of Epiphany in English Epic Poetry* argues that Beowulf's encounters with monsters serve as a means of 'fix[ing] audience attention on the poem's themes: the need for steadfast courage, the glory of devotion to duty, immortality through *lof* or *dom*, praise or fame and glory' (pp. 65–6).

The monsters in *Beowulf* and issues of monstrosity continue to generate new scholarship. M. Wendy Hennequin argues that 'We've Created a Monster: The Strange Case of Grendel's Mother' (*ES* 89[2008] 503–23). Hennequin's aim is to describe the complex intersections of gender, humanity and monstrosity that are evident in the case of Grendel's mother. By drawing on contemporary theories of gender as performance, Hennequin seeks to show that reading Grendel's mother as a human (as opposed to monstrous) avenger opens up new and productive lines of critical enquiry. James Phillips reflects on being 'In the Company of Predators: *Beowulf* and the Monstrous Descendants of Cain' (*Angelaki* 13[2008] 41–51). He provides a wide-ranging discussion of the monsters in *Beowulf*, with particular attention to the ways in which they assist in defining the boundaries of humanity and the limits of community. Janice Hawes considers 'The Monstrosity of Heroism: Grettir Ásmundarson as an Outsider' (*ScanS* 80[2008] 19–50). Hawes's main interest lies in understanding the portrayal of the hero Grettir in *Grettis saga Ásmundarsonar*, but her analysis also contains an interesting comparison of Beowulf and Grettir in which she seeks to show that the two heroes differ in temperament—Grettir is far more rash than Beowulf—and in their relationships to outlawry.

Beowulf scholarship and critical methodologies continue to inspire interesting new work. James Cahill's 'Reconsidering Robinson's *Beowulf*' (*ES* 89[2008] 251–62) offers a detailed critique of Fred Robinson's *Beowulf and the Appositive Style* (see *YWES* 66[1985] 122), and explores the kind of poet that emerges from Robinson's 'appositional' reading of *Beowulf*. Cahill focuses on two passages in *Beowulf* (lines 2794a–7b and 3180b–2b), and argues that Robinson's appositional readings of these passages cannot be substantiated. Cahill contends that 'these failed readings are symptomatic of an overarching commitment [on Robinson's part] to discerning in *Beowulf* a consistent, rational, and authorial theology that runs contrary to the language of the poem itself' (p. 253). Andrew Scheil writes on 'The Historiographic Dimensions of *Beowulf*' (*JEGP* 107[2008] 281–302). He begins by noting that the lack of any sure historical mooring for *Beowulf* has both isolated it from traditional forms of historicization and also allowed the poem to generate its own historical context. Scheil urges scholars to read *Beowulf* as 'an exercise in historiography' (p. 284), and contends that the *Beowulf*-poet invites us to marvel at the causes and ramifications of unexpected moments in history. Scheil concludes that the poem stands between the traditions of poetic composition and those of narrative history. Tom Shippey considers 'The Case of *Beowulf*' (*EuroS* 26[2008] 223–39), with particular interest in *Beowulf* as a contested site for nationalist scholarship. He explores the ways in which interpretations of the poem have been affected by nationalist sympathies, as well as by sub-national and supra-national sentiments, and contends that the poem's early politicization continues to affect scholarship to the present day.

Issues of editing and translation continue to provide fodder for new scholarship. Magnús Fjalldal's essay, 'To Fall by Ambition: Grímur Thorkelín and his *Beowulf* Edition' (*Neophil* 92[2008] 321–32), focuses on Thorkelín's unusually swift rise in the world of Danish scholarship. Fjalldal contends that Thorkelín was essentially a fraud as a scholar, that he was well aware that he might not have the ability to produce a respectable scholarly edition from his transcripts and that, when his edition finally appeared in 1815, it 'was a predictable disaster which exposed the editor for what he was and brought him misery rather than scholarly fame' (p. 321). Dongill Lee investigates 'Korean Translation of *Beowulf*: Variety and Limitation of Archaic Words' (*MES* 16[2008] 19–42). Lee's interest lies in the challenges of rendering particular Old English words into their Korean equivalents while preserving the Old English appositive style and conveying some sense of Anglo-Saxon heroic culture. He focuses on the following terms and phrases: *heard under helme*, *wlenco*, *oferhygd*, *dolgilp* and *mapelian*.

Jennifer Anh-Thu Tran Smith writes on 'Fidelity in Versification: Modern English Translations of *Beowulf* and *Sir Gawain and the Green Knight*' (in Fitzmaurice and Minkova, eds., *Studies in the History of the English Language*, vol. 4: *Empirical and Analytical Advances in the Study of English Language Change*, pp. 121–52). Smith studies alliterative verse translations of *Beowulf* by Charles W. Kennedy, Burton Raffel, Michael Alexander, Howell D. Chickering, Ruth Lehmann and Seamus Heaney. By drawing on quantitative modes of linguistic analysis, she seeks to understand what it means to be faithful to the metrical requirements of alliterative verse and whether changes in fidelity in versification are due mainly to prosodic differences between Old English and modern English or to changes in the philosophical climate in which the particular translation was produced. Preceding Smith's essay in this same volume is a brief discussion by Thomas Cable, 'The Elusive Progress of Prosodical Study' (pp. 101–19), in which Cable overviews Smith's essay (among others), suggests that we might wish to reconsider the priority given to alliteration in any ranking of translations and also the rules for metrical positions that Smith posits, and concludes that Smith offers us a valuable opportunity to rethink our assumptions about Old English metre. This volume also includes Smith's 'Response to Tom Cable's Comments' (pp. 153–4), in which she challenges Cable's contention that widespread lack of alliteration is something that may not register for the casual reader and also provides additional discussion of her scansion of *Beowulf*, line 736a.

Two of the essays in *Aedificia Nova: Studies in Honor of Rosemary Cramp*, edited by Catherine E. Karkov and Helen Damico, shed new light on the complex relationships between *Beowulf* and material culture. Roberta Frank provides an important study of 'The Boar on the Helmet' (pp. 76–88). Frank situates the image of the boar-helmet in *Beowulf* in the context of medieval Latin and Continental literature. She considers whether the material world exhibited in *Beowulf* may have its roots in North Sea culture and concludes that references to boar-helmets in *Beowulf* are closely aligned with those found in tenth- and eleventh-century skaldic verse. This same volume also features John Hines's characteristically insightful study of '*Beowulf and Archaeology—Revisited*' (pp. 89–105). Hines seeks to understand how the study of Old English literature and archaeology may be integrated. He argues against an 'overtextual approach' to the poem and concludes that 'archaeology, as an intellectual and scientific appreciation of the systemic role played by material culture in human life in both the past and the present, is truly fundamental to the conception and achievement of *Beowulf*' (p. 105).

Two of the essays in Blanton and Scheck, eds., *Intertexts: Studies in Anglo-Saxon Culture Presented to Paul E. Szarmach*, discuss *Beowulf*. In a brief but characteristically thought-provoking essay, Roberta Frank considers 'Sharing Words with *Beowulf*' (pp. 3–15). Frank begins by discussing the very broad issue of style in Old English verse. She then focuses our gaze on the Old English term *bune* 'vessel' as it appears in *Beowulf*, and on Dennis Cronan's recent discussion of poetic simplexes (see *YWES* 85[2006] 140). Frank's essay concludes by returning to broad questions of style and philology, with particular attention to the complex relationships between the poetics of *Beowulf* and Anglo-Saxon culture. This same volume features Helen Damico's essay on '*Beowulf*'s Foreign Queen and the Politics of Eleventh-Century England' (pp. 209–40). Damico compares representations of queenship in *Beowulf* and in the *Encomium Emmae Reginae*, finds striking similarities between Wealhtheow and Emma, and contends that 'in *Beowulf*, then, we are most probably looking at the Old English poetic version of that same queen, Emma of Normandy' (p. 240).

The poem's numerous cruces continue to stimulate new research. J.D. Thayer focuses on 'Resolving the "Double Curse" of the Pagan Hoard in Beowulf' (*Expl* 66[2008] 174–7). Thayer's aim is to argue against critics who claim that the hoard in *Beowulf* receives two conflicting burials and curses: the burial by the Last Survivor and the poet's later reference to a group of nobles who bury the treasure. He contends that any confusion on the part of critics is due to a failure to note the timing of the two burials and the fact that the poet has offered a very compact view of narrative past and present. Earl R. Anderson writes on 'Beow the Boy-Wonder (*Beowulf* 12–25)' (*ES* 89[2008] 630–42). He examines what we can know about the figure Beow and argues that the *Beowulf*-poet most likely did not have access to a particular story about Beow and thus 'created a generalized portrait of Beow with reference to a migratory oral-compositional typescene that sometimes was used as part of the profile of a boy-wonder or prodigious child-hero' (p. 637). Murray

McGillivray asks 'What Kind of a Seat is Hrothgar's *Gifstol*?' (*SP* 105[2008] 265–83). His goal is to focus our attention not on the crux in lines 168–9 but on the nature of the *gifstol* itself, and he concludes that *gifstol* does not refer to a throne but instead to the hall Heorot. J.R. Hall studies '*Beowulf* 1741a: *we‡* . . . and the Supplementary Evidence' (*ANQ* 21:i[2008] 3–9). Hall begins by pointing out that the word with which most editors begin line 141a, *weaxeð*, does not occur in the manuscript. Hall's aim is to indicate precisely what can still be read in the manuscript, and to adduce new evidence that will place ð on a secure palaeographical footing. Valentine Anthony Pakis investigates 'The Meaning of Æshere's Name in *Beowulf* (*Anglia* 126[2008] 104–13), and contends that Æschere is a kenning for 'cremation' or 'funeral pyre'.

'Old English *þa* "now that" and the Integrity of *Beowulf*', by R.D. Fulk (*ES* 89[2008] 623–31), examines, with comparison to other Old English poetry, occurrences of *þa* in *Beowulf* which could be translated 'now that'. He notes that only *Beowulf* and *Genesis A* use *þa* in this way, and that its distribution in *Beowulf* 'argues for the integrity of the composition of the poem' (p. 629). [MS]

Graham D. Caie writes on '*Ealdgesegena worn*: What the Old English *Beowulf* Tells Us about Oral Forms' (in Mundal and Wellendorf, eds., *Oral Art Forms and their Passage into Writing*, pp. 109–20). His interest lies in asking what *Beowulf* may be able to tell us about oral forms of composition and delivery. He concludes that the use of formulas, in *Beowulf* and in other Old English poems, should not be confused with oral composition. Two of the essays in Amano, Ogura, and Ohkado, eds., *Historical Englishes in Varieties of Texts and Contexts*, focus on language issues in *Beowulf*. Yookang Kim studies 'The Prenominal Prefix *ge-* in *Beowulf*' (pp. 49–61), with a focus on *ge-* nouns in *Beowulf*. Kim argues against the traditional view that the nominal prefix *ge-* is either meaningless or collective, and contends that the prefix instead points to something which either results from or causes an action. This same volume also features Hideki Watanabe's study of 'The Ambiguous or Polysemous Compounds in *Beowulf* Revisited: *Æsholt* and *Garholt*' (pp. 143–55). Watanabe reviews critical interpretations of *æsholt* and *garholt* over the past two centuries and concludes that a metaphorical reading of the two compounds contributes to a stronger understanding of the thematic resonances and verbal coincidences in *Beowulf*.

The 2008 *Old English Newsletter* contains two short but fascinating essays on *Beowulf*. Richard Scott Nokes writes on '*Beowulf: Prince of the Geats*, Nazis, and Odinists' (*OENews* 41[2008] 26–32). Nokes focuses on Scott Wegener's recent film, *Beowulf: Prince of the Geats*, which features the African-American actor Jayshan Jackson as Beowulf. Although the film was intended as a fundraiser for cancer research, *Beowulf: Prince of the Geats* nevertheless found itself at the centre of heated controversies over national identity, ethnicity and religion. Nokes discusses these controversies and concludes that academics might do well to remember that the poem has an ardent popular audience whose responses must be acknowledged as part of *Beowulf*'s cultural heritage. Mary Kate Hurley reflects on 'Old English, New Media: Blogging *Beowulf*' (*OENews* 41[2008] 42–6). Hurley shares her experiences in the academic 'blogosphere', and contends that developing one's academic voice is one of the most valuable and rewarding aspects of academic blogging. She makes a strong case that blogging enables the connection of 'ideas, people, cultures and texts in a network that might, in the end, be best described not only as human but also as humane' (p. 44).

Hülya Tafli studies 'Number, Colour and Animal Mysticism in *Beowulf* and *The Book of Dedem Korkut*' (*Turkish Studies* 3[2008] 96–120). Tafli examines key similarities and differences in the use of numbers, colours, and animal imagery in *Beowulf* and *The Book of Dedem Korkut*, and concludes that pre-Christian and pre-Islamic legends, myths, and sagas influenced both texts. Daniel M. Murtaugh considers 'Absent Beowulf' (*HeroicA* 11[2008] 31 paras). By drawing on insights from contemporary critical theory and modern popular culture, Murtaugh reflects on the complex relations among myth and history in *Beowulf*. Allen J. Frantzen's 'Drama and Dialogue in Old English Poetry: The Scene of Cynewulf's *Juliana*' (*ThS* 48[2007] 99–119) contains a brief discussion of performance in *Beowulf* and is reviewed in section 5 of this chapter.

9. Other Poems

Two essays this year expand our understanding of *Caedmon's Hymn*. Rochelle Altman focuses on 'Hymnody, Graphotactics, and "Cædmon's Hymn"' (*PhilRev* 34[2008] 1–27), with particular interest in understanding *Caedmon's Hymn* as a song. She first situates *Caedmon's Hymn* in the context of early hymnody, and then examines the *Hymn* through graphotactic analysis of the manuscripts in which it appears. By focusing on the incidence and measure of spacing between strings of written text, Altman concludes that *Caedmon's Hymn* is a perfect example of a hymn in both the medieval and modern senses of hymnody. Alfred Bammesberger studies '*Nu Scylun Hergan* (*Caedmon's Hymn*, 1a)' (*ANQ* 21:iv[2008] 2–6). He argues that 'if *scylun* in *Nu Scylun Hergan* ("Now [they] must be praised [...]") is originally the form for third person plural, and lines 1b, 2a, 2b, and 3a contain the syntactically parallel subjects of the clause, then it is quite possible that the early stages of the *Hymn*'s development already evidence a reinterpretation of the Old English text' (p. 5).

Éamonn Ó Carragáin asks 'Who Then Read the Ruthwell Poem in the Eighth Century?' (in Karkov and Damico, eds., pp. 43–75). He studies the runic poem and Latin inscriptions on the Ruthwell cross, argues for the integrity of design and liturgical purpose of the cross and contends that the designer of the cross was subject to Roman influence. Ó Carragáin concludes his essay by arguing for the intentional and contemporaneous carving of the runic passages on the cross for use in both prayer and worship.

Patrick W. Conner sets out to 'disturb the status quo' (p. 26) on the Ruthwell poem. In 'The Ruthwell Monument Runic Poem in a Tenth-Century Context' (*RES* 59[2008] 25–51) he explores questions of language choice and literacy in Roman and runic scripts, and argues that the poem is influenced by developments in the Passion liturgy which were probably not available in England before the late tenth century, and which are reflected in the prayers for the adoration of the cross referred to in the *Regularis Concordia*. [MS]

Sara M. Pons-Sanz examines 'Norse-Derived Terms and Structures in *The Battle of Maldon*' (*JEGP* 107[2008] 421–44). She begins by establishing that, out of all of the terms and structures in *The Battle of Maldon* that have been identified as Norse-derived or that have somehow been associated with Norse usage, the terms *ceallian, dreng, eorl* and *griδ* are the only ones that ought to be seriously considered. Even in these cases, Pons-Sanz argues, Norse derivation or influence is not certain. She then turns to the poem itself and concludes that Norse-derived terms in *The Battle of Maldon* cannot be taken as clear indication of the *Maldon*-poet's dialectal origin and that 'these terms may be best taken as examples of the deep integration of some Norse-derived items in Old English dialects or technolects by the early eleventh century' (p. 444).

Two essays published in 2008 focus on *The Battle of Brunanburh*. Paul Cavill sheds new light on '*Eorodcistum* in *The Battle of Brunanburh*' (*LeedsSE* 39[2008] 1–15). Cavill's focus is on determining the meaning of the compound *eorodcistum*. He argues that an accurate analysis and gloss for *eorodcistum* and variants would be 'adverb; *en masse*, in bands' (p. 10), and that *eorodcistum* does not necessarily refer to West Saxon 'elite cavalry' or 'mounted companies'. Scott Herring focuses on ' "A Hawk from a Handsaw": A Note on the Beasts of *The Battle of Brunanburh*' (*ANQ* 21:i[2008] 9–11). The interest here is on the *guδ-hafoc*, or war-hawk, of line 64, and Herring contends that *guδ-hafoc* is a kenning renaming the eagle in the previous line, and not an unprecedented fourth beast.

Katrin Rupp sheds welcome light on 'The Anxiety of Writing: A Reading of the Old English *Journey Charm*' (*OralT* 23[2008] 255–66). Rupp's goal is to examine what happens to the *Journey Charm*'s originally performative nature when it is brought to parchment and thus transformed from an oral performance into a written text. She considers the charm in its manuscript context, Cambridge Corpus Christi College 41, and concludes that the scribe uses visual cues in order to shift readers' attention away from the words with which the charm is written down in an effort to preserve its original power and efficacy. Yoon-hee Park writes on 'The Meaning of the Cotton "Wulf" Maxim in the Context of Anglo-Saxon Popular Thought and Culture' (*MES* 16[2008] 247–63). Park's interest lies in exploring the Anglo-Saxon concept of *wulf* and in identifying the specific meaning of *sceal* so as to better understand line 18b, *Maxims II*, 'wulf sceal on bearowe'. Park concludes that this line is correctly read as 'The wolf ought to be in the forest' as opposed to 'The wolf is typically in the forest'. Heide Estes provides 'A Note on *Solomon and Saturn I*, Lines 107b–108a' (*N&Q* 55[2008] 260–2). Estes contends that new digitized images of CCCC 422 reveal earlier emendations of lines 107b–108a to be erroneous, and suggests that a better translation of lines 107–10 might read: 'Then the twins of the church, [and] brave "I", repudiate him. Each of them brings affliction through a scythe; {he} sorrows for a while, hostile to the body, does not mourn the spirit' (p. 262).

Kathryn Wymer writes on 'A Poetic Fragment on the Soul's Address to the Body in the *Trinity Homilies*' (*N&Q* 55[2008] 399–400). Wymer contends that a previously unidentified poetic fragment appears in the collection known as the *Trinity Homilies* (Trinity College, Cambridge MS B.14.52; James no. 335).

The fragment can be found in the homily 'De Sancto Andrea', and is part of the soul's address to the wicked body. Wymer concludes that the fragment does not stylistically match the rest of the homily and could conceivably represent the homilist recalling lines of a poem from memory.

Several essays on Old Norse poetics published in 2008 will be of interest to Anglo-Saxonists. Yelena Sesselja Helgadóttir Yershova writes on 'Egill Skalla-Grímsson: A Viking Poet as a Child and an Old Man' (in Lewis-Simpson, ed., pp. 285–304). Yershova's emphasis is on Egill's poetic career and on the different kinds of imagery that Egill used to describe himself as a Viking poet during different periods of his life. Three of the essays in Mundal and Wellendorf, eds., *Oral Art Forms and their Passage into Writing*, focus on Old Norse poetry and poetic form. Bernt Øyvind Thorvaldsen studies 'The Eddic Form and its Contexts: An Oral Art Form Performed in Writing' (pp. 151–62). Thorvaldsen's interest lies in understanding how Old Norse poetry represents performance, and the essay argues that orality and literacy must be understood as integrated aspects of expression. Bergsveinn Birgisson asks 'What Have We Lost by Writing? Cognitive Archaisms in Skaldic Poetry' (pp. 163–84). Birgisson contends that in the oldest skaldic poetry, composed before the arrival of writing and Christianity, we find archaisms that the learned and converted Norse skalds did not adapt and bring forth in their later poetry. Else Mundal studies 'Oral or Scribal Variation in *Voluspá*: A Case Study in Old Norse Poetry' (pp. 209–27). Mundal compares two versions of the Eddic poem *Voluspá* and tries to determine whether the different versions of the poem are the result of oral or scribal variation, a question that she views as having important consequences for the stability of oral eddic tradition.

A small portion of Rafał Borysławski's essay '*Wordhordes cræft*: Confusion and the Order of the Wor(l)d in Old English Gnomes' (in Krygier and Sikorska, eds., pp. 119–31) focuses on the *Metres of Boethius*, and is reviewed in section 5 of this chapter. Jane Roberts provides a brief discussion of '*The Finnsburh Fragment*, and its Lambeth Provenance' (*N&Q* 55[2008] 122–4), reviewed in section 2 of this chapter. Sarah Downey's 'Too Much of Too Little: Guthlac and the Temptation of Excessive Fasting' (*Traditio* 63[2008] 89–127) discusses *The Seasons for Fasting* and is reviewed in section 5 of this chapter.

10. Prose

This was a rich year for new work on the Anglo-Saxon transmission of Isidore of Seville's *Synonyma*. Claudia di Sciacca's *Finding the Right Words: Isidore's 'Synonyma' in Anglo-Saxon England* examines Isidore's life and culture; the structure, style and sources of the *Synonyma*; their vernacularization in Vercelli XXII and the *ubi sunt* topos; and their place in Anglo-Latin literature. In her conclusion, di Sciacca offers support to Donald Scragg's suggestion that St Augustine's, Canterbury, is the most likely location for the production of the Vercelli Homilies, and that this library included a copy of the *Synonyma*. In '*Transmarinis litteris*: Southumbria and the Transmission of Isidore's

Synonyma' (*JEGP* 107[2008] 141–68), Matthew T. Hussey makes a case for Southumbrian missionaries, perhaps including Boniface, disseminating Isidore's *Synonyma* from Merovingian Gaul to Fulda, Würzburg, and other Anglo-Saxon mission areas. Drawing on textual evidence, including the works of Aldhelm and Boniface, and surveying *Synonyma* manuscripts from Anglo-Saxon centres in Germany, Hussey also shows the roots of the later Anglo-Saxon use of the *Synonyma* in Latin and vernacular Anglo-Saxon literature.

As ever, Bede has generated a number of new studies. Calvin B. Kendall's translation of *Bede, 'On Genesis'*, adds to the admirable range of scholarly translations of Bede's works, and supplements its text with an introduction on the context and themes of the text, appendices which address specific textual points, a bibliography and an index of sources and parallels. Eric Knibbs offers a re-examination of 'The Manuscript Evidence for the *De octo quaestionibus* Ascribed to Bede' (*Traditio* 63[2008] 129–83), a series of discussions of scripture which survives in nine manuscripts. Knibbs describes each manuscript and a reconstructed lost tenth version, reconstructs the textual tradition, and argues that the first four *Solutiones* are probably by Bede. The article concludes with a new edition of the first four *Solutiones*, the *Interim quaesisti*, the *Putant quidam*, the *Quod interrogasti* and the *Congregauit autem*. 'Bede's *Ecclesiastical History*: Numbers, Hard Data, and Longevity', by Joel T. Rosenthal (in Blanton and Scheck, eds., pp. 91–102) notes Bede's 'predilection for precise information' (p. 91), discusses the types of quantitative information he provides and ponders the insight this gives us into Bede's conception of history-writing.

George Hardin Brown continues to offer important insights into Bede and his work. He draws our attention to 'Quotations in Bede's Exegetical Commentaries Misinterpreted as Autobiographical' (*N&Q* 55[2008] 116–17), with particular reference to a quotation in *In Lucae euangelium* which he shows Bede to have derived from John Cassian's *Collatio*. In 'Ciceronianism in Bede and Alcuin' (in Blanton and Scheck, eds., pp. 319–29), Brown compares the style of these two influential authors, noting that, despite the fact that Ciceronian rhetoric was not promoted in northern English monastic schools in the seventh and early eighth centuries, Bede shows signs of admiring and emulating Cicero's prose, and Alcuin 'resolutely sanctions both Ciceronian rhetoric and doctrine' (p. 326). And in 'Bede and Change' (in Karkov and Damico, eds., pp. 33–42), Brown examines Bede's treatises on time and his historical works for signs of how he depicts and directs the depiction of change in human history, the church and society.

Leofranc Holford-Strevens surveys 'Paschal Lunar Calendars up to Bede' (*Peritia* 20[2008] 165–208), starting with Hippolytus, to reconstruct the lunar calendars underlying the computistical cycles and to explore the ways in which the same reconstruction was done by medieval scholars. An appendix to the article surveys pagan and Christian lunar dates in Christian inscriptions.

A number of Paul Meyvaert's essays on Bede are reprinted in *The Art of Words: Bede and Theodulf*. The relevant items in the collection are 'Bede and Church Paintings at Wearmouth-Jarrow', 'Bede's *Capitula Lectionum* for the Old and New Testaments', '"In the Footsteps of the Fathers": The Date of Bede's *Thirty Questions on the Book of Kings to Nothelm*', 'Discovering the

Calendar (*annalis libellus*) Attached to Bede's Own Copy of *De temporum ratione*', 'Bede, Cassiodorus, and the Codex Amiatinus', 'The Date of Bede's *In Ezram* and his Image of Ezra in the Codex Amiatinus', Dissension in Bede's Commentary Shown by a Quire of Codex Amiatinus' and 'Medieval Notions of Publication: The "Unpublished" *Opus Caroli Regis contra synodum* and the Council of Frankfurt (794)'.

David Howlett analyses 'Willibrord's Autobiographical Note and the "Versus Sybillae de iudicio Dei"' (*Peritia* 20[2008] 154–64). The note, usually accepted to be in Willibrord's hand, is in the margin of manuscript Paris, Bibliothèque nationale, latin 10837, folio 39ᵛ. Howlett presents a transcription and translation and a study of the note's spelling, Willibrord's name, dates, and numbers and gematria (the calculation of the numerical values of names), and suggests that Willibrord may have written the poem 'Versus Sybillae de iudicio Dei' while at Rath Melsege from 678.

Recent work on prose associated with the Alfredian translation project continues to address, whether directly or implicitly, the question of authorship. David Pratt's *The Political Thought of King Alfred the Great* [2007] was made available for review this year. Aiming to set Alfredian prose—'this supremely material realization of learned kingship' (p. 349)—in its ninth-century context, the book opens with a detailed examination of 'The West Saxon Political Order' in its first part, with attention paid to resources and power, lordship and secular and ecclesiastical office-holding, Alfred's predecessors and the Viking impact. 'Alfredian Discourse and its Efficacy' is the focus of the second, central, part of the book. Here, Pratt examines the shift to vernacular prose, distinctive features of Alfredian discourse, book production, the *Hierdeboc*, the *Domboc*, the Old English Psalms, *Boethius* and *Soliloquies*. The appendix provides editions of West Frankish texts which use Solomon's dream.

Robert Stanton's essay on 'King Alfred' (in Ellis, ed., pp. 116–25) offers an overview of the historical context of the Alfredian translations, Alfredian translation theory, and the impetus for the project and Asser's presentation of the connections between this and Alfred's own development as teacher and translator. Stanton's view is that Alfred 'clearly supervised the translations and put his *imprimatur* on them' (p. 124). A different perspective is offered in 'King and Counselor in the Alfredian Boethius', by M.R. Godden (in Blanton and Scheck, eds., pp. 191–207), which re-examines the political resonance of the presentation of these figures in the text in the light of contemporary glosses on it and of the Latin *vitae*—introductory accounts—added to the *Consolation* in the ninth and tenth centuries. Godden notes parallels between the Old English Boethius and the Old English *Soliloquies*, and concludes that the author of the Old English Boethius is 'fascinated by kings, counselors, and favourites' and that this is an unlikely text for King Alfred to have produced. An appendix to the article provides a transcription of the version of Vita 1 in Paris, Bibliothèque nationale lat. 16093, folio 68ᵛ.

Nicole Guenther Discenza contemplates 'Alfred the Great and the Anonymous Prose Proem to the *Boethius*' (*JEGP* 107[2008] 57–76). Starting with a reminder of the problematic nature of this text as a source of information on the circumstances or authorship of the translation, Discenza agrees with those who believe that it is not the work of Alfred, and then sets about analysing style and vocabulary to demonstrate this, and to contrast the Prose Proem, which she judges to be 'thoroughly undistinguished, *boring*' (p. 38) with the Verse Proem, which she categorizes as 'joyous' (p. 75) and self-confident.

Irmeli Valtonen's *The North in the Old English 'Orosius': A Geographical Narrative in Context* explores this text in the context of concepts of the North from ancient to early medieval times. Her analysis includes the *Vita Willibrordi*, the *Historia Brittonum*, the *Anglo-Saxon Chronicle*, *Æthelweard's Chronicon*, *Beowulf*, *Widsith*, the *mappa mundi* and Sutton Hoo, and in her concluding remarks she observes that 'travel accounts reflect the Anglo-Saxon society's faith in the power of the written word, the vernacular, and authority' (p. 572).

Myth, Rulership, Church and Charters: Essays in Honour of Nicholas Brooks, edited by Julia Barrow and Andrew Wareham, is an excellent collection of new work on the topics of its title. The contents are: Julia Barrow, 'Introduction: Myth, Rulership, Church and Charters in the Work of Nicholas Brooks'; Christopher Dyer, 'Nicholas Brooks at Birmingham'; Barbara Yorke, 'Anglo-Saxon Origin Legends'; James Campbell, 'A Nearly, but Wrongly, Forgotten Historian of the Dark Ages'; Simon Keynes, 'Anglo-Saxon Charters: Lost and Found'; Susan Kelly, 'Reculver Minster and its Early Charters'; Margaret Gelling, 'Stour in Ismere'; Alex Burghart and Andrew Wareham, 'Was There an Agricultural Revolution in Anglo-Saxon England?'; Pauline Stafford, '"The Annals of Æthelflæd": Annals, History and Politics in Early Tenth-Century England'; Janet L. Nelson, 'The First Use of the Second Anglo-Saxon *Ordo*'; Sarah Foot, 'Where English Becomes British: Rethinking Contexts for *Brunanburh*'; Catherine Cubitt, 'Archbishop Dunstan: A Prophet on Politics?'; Alicia Corrêa, 'A Mass for St Birinus in an Anglo-Saxon Missal from the Scandinavian Mission-Field'; Barbara E. Crawford, 'The Saint Clement Dedications at Clementhorpe and Pontefract Castle: Anglo-Scandinavian or Norman?'; Nick Webber, 'England and the Norman Myth'; Julia Barrow, 'What Happened to Ecclesiastical Charters in England 1066–*c*.1100?'. A list of Nicholas Brooks's publications and an index close the volume.

Stefan Jurasinski explores 'Germanism, Slapping and the Cultural Contexts of Æthelberht's Code: A Reconsideration of Chapters 56–58' (*Haskins Soc Jnl* 18[2006] 51–71). The chapters in question deal with penalties for injuries inflicted without weapons, and Jurasinski suggests a revised understanding of the significance of wounds, presents some potential analogues for chapter 58.1, proposes that the blow described at this point is one with an open hand, and offers a new translation of chapters 58.1 and 59. Lisi Oliver contributes 'Æthelberht's *Fedesl* Revisited' (*N&Q* 55[2008] 125–6), in which she argues that this clause concerns 'a simple assessment rather than a punitive fine' (p. 126); a payment to be made by noblemen for the king's support.

Oliver also examines 'Sick-Maintenance in Anglo-Saxon Law' (*JEGP* 107[2008] 303–26). She seeks to distinguish inheritance, borrowing and innovation in the development of legal rulings set down in Anglo-Saxon texts. She discusses examples of each category in laws on sick-maintenance: the penalty to be paid by a person who injures another, to cover compensation and medical fees; notes that this practice is not recorded in later Anglo-Saxon England; and concludes that Alfredian personal injury laws are innovative and that they lay the basis for common law.

The latest volume in the British Academy Anglo-Saxon Charters series is Julia Crick's *Charters of St Albans*, which makes accessible important records for the Benedictine re-foundation of the house and the later Anglo-Saxon reconstruction of its foundation. The introductory section of the volume provides a thorough overview of the history of St Albans Abbey, its archive, the manuscripts and the claims they record. The Will of Æthelgyfu is discussed in some detail, and editions of the charters are followed by appendices which include lists of benefactions, lost charters and extracts from the *Miracula S. Albani* and the *Tractatus de inuencione siue translacione beati Albani*. Indexes include personal and place-names, words used in boundary marks, a Latin glossary and a diplomatic index.

Peter A. Stokes re-examines 'King Edgar's Charter for Pershore (AD 972)' (*ASE* 37[2008] 31–78), one of the *Orthodoxorum* charters. His focus is on the little-studied copy of the charter which survives in a copy made by Joscelyn. Stokes compares this version with the much-studied tenth-century one, translates the Jocelyn copy and translates and edits a twelfth-century letter which refers to the charter. He shows that the later version of the charter is not a copy of the earlier one, but that it includes three new charter bounds.

An interesting aspect of the continuity of Old English textual production across the Conquest is explored by Kathryn A. Lowe in 'Post-Conquest Bilingual Composition in Memoranda from Bury St Edmunds' (*RES* 59[2008] 52–66). The texts in question were added, in Old English and Latin, to MS Oxford, Corpus Christi College 197 from around 1066 to the mid-twelfth century. Lowe presents an analysis of the Old English, and shows that the 'scribes had Latin, if not in front of them, then certainly in their mind as they were copying', but that also 'every one of the scribes ... is connected in some way to the vernacular, either by writing Old English or by undertaking translation work from it' (p. 64). Her study is a useful addition to our understanding of the complex set of choices behind the use of Old English into the twelfth century.

'Anglo-Saxon Women before the Law: A Student Edition of Five Old English Lawsuits', by Andrew Rabin (*OENews* 41:iii[2008] 33–56) is a most useful resource for teaching. Rabin provides an introductory overview of Old English lawsuits and their records, and of women and the law, and then sets out an edition of charters S1211 (Queen Eadgifu), S1377 (The 'Peterborough Witch'), S1454 (Wynflæd), S1242 (Queen Ælfthryth) and S1462 (a Herefordshire Widow). Textual notes follow each charter, and a glossary to all five texts concludes the edition.

Homiletic and hagiographic prose is still generating a quantity of new scholarship. The Henry Bradshaw series *Saints in English Kalendars before A.D. 1100*, by Rebecca Rushforth, is an invaluable resource for those working on Anglo-Saxon hagiography and its context in the cult of saints. Rushforth's introduction gives an overview of Kalendars as a genre and the criteria for dating and localizing manuscripts. The main body of the book is a set of detailed descriptions of twenty-seven Kalendar manuscripts, and this is followed by notes on manuscripts not included, and then a series of double-page tables showing saints in English Kalendars. The volume's indices list manuscripts and names. It is to be hoped that the tables might also be issued in electronic format, since the resulting searchability would facilitate many other research projects.

Christine Rauer scrutinizes 'Old English *Blanca* in the *Old English Martyrology*' (*N&Q* 55[2008] 396–9). *Blancan* is used to refer to the governor of Rome's horses in the *OE Martyrology*'s description of the humiliation of Marcellus I, and Rauer argues that it is the result of a misunderstanding of a Latin source which read *plancas*, 'planks'.

New editions of Anglo-Latin hagiographic texts are an important resource. In 2006 Andrew J. Turner and Bernard J. Muir published *Eadmer of Canterbury, Lives and Miracles of Saints Oda, Dunstan, and Oswald*, an edition and translation of these post-Conquest lives of Anglo-Saxon saints. A detailed introduction covers Eadmer's life and writings, and sets out the date, sources, manuscript tradition and use of each of the three lives. Facing-page editions and translations of each follow, and an index of sources is a useful supplement to the general index.

The Fursey Pilgrims aim to promote knowledge of the cult of Fursey, and two of their recent publications will be of interest to Anglo-Saxonists. Oliver Rackham's '*Transitus beati Fursei': A Translation of the 8th Century Manuscript Life of Saint Fursey* [2007] is a most welcome edition and translation of the Anglo-Latin life of Fursey, based on the northern French copy of the text in London, British Library, MS Harley 5041. Marilyn Dunn's *The Vision of St. Fursey and the Development of Purgatory* [2007], is the text of a lecture delivered in 2005. Dunn traces the development of the concept of intercession on behalf of souls in the afterlife, and its effect on monastic life.

Charles D. Wright tells us 'Why the Left Hand is Longer (or Shorter) than the Right: Some Irish Analogues for an Etiological Legend in the Homiliary of St. Père de Chartres' (in Blanton and Scheck, eds., pp. 161–8). This homiliary is the 'Pembroke Homiliary', the source of six Old English anonymous homilies, and Wright's focus is on sermon 30 and its reference to Eve taking the fruit with her left hand and to this resulting in humans having shorter left than right hands. Several Irish vernacular analogues are presented, and Wright proposes that the Pembroke compiler's source might be a Hiberno-Latin Genesis commentary.

In 'Sulpicius Severus and the Medieval *Vita Martini*' (*Peritia* 20[2008] 28–58), Juliet Hewish explores the relationship between insular and mainland European manuscript traditions of the *Vita Martini* and related works by Sulpicius Severus. Included in her examination of the Anglo-Saxon tradition are the Vercelli Life of Martin homily and those in Ælfric's *Catholic Homilies* and *Lives of Saints*. E. Gordon Whatley's 'Eugenia before Ælfric: A Preliminary Report on the Transmission of an Early Medieval Legend' (in Blanton and Scheck, eds., pp. 349–67) outlines the earliest known version of the legend, guides the reader through the two printed editions of it, and offers a close comparison of one episode to show how it is revised at an early stage of the legend's development.

In 'The Vercelli Homilies and Kent' (in Blanton and Scheck, eds., pp. 369–80), Donald G. Scragg explores evidence for the place of production of other manuscripts which contain whole or part texts from the Vercelli Homilies to show that, until the mid-eleventh century, the items in the Vercelli Homilies remained in a group available to other scribes, and a large number of the items were in a south-eastern English library. He concludes by proposing that a library in Canterbury contained the source-books for the Vercelli Homilies for three-quarters of a century after the writing of the Vercelli manuscript, and that copies of the source-materials had moved to Rochester by the twelfth century.

Mary Swan's 'Constructing Preacher and Audience in Old English Homilies' (in Andersson, ed., *Constructing the Medieval Sermon* [2007], pp. 177–88) compares three Old English homilies for the first Sunday in Lent—Blickling Homily III, Ælfric's First Series *Catholic Homilies* item 'Dominica I in Quadragesima', and Bodley 343 Homily V—in terms of the construction of their preaching voice and its relationship to the audience. Swan shows how all three homilies carefully manipulate the positions of preacher and audience, and that the Blickling and Bodley 343 examples have more similarities with each other than they do with Ælfric's homily, which 'implies a much greater perceived need for the performance of very precisely defined, and text-controlled, identities for both preacher and audience' (p. 188).

'Rhetoric and Politics in Archbishop Wulfstan's Old English Homilies' is the subject of Jonathan Davis-Secord's study (*Anglia* 126[2008] 65–96). Through an analysis of nominative compounds, especially those which feature in lists, in a number of Wulfstan's homilies, including one which is adapted from Ælfric, Davis-Secord shows how Wulfstan's rhetoric promotes the cause of social stability. A Wulfstan connection is explored by Mary Clayton, in 'The Old English *Promissio regis*' (*ASE* 37[2008] 91–150). The *Promissio regis* gives the threefold promise made by tenth- and eleventh-century Anglo-Saxon kings at their coronation, and it survives in two versions. Clayton focuses on the two paragraphs of the text which follow the promises, and which outline the duties of kingship. She notes the prevailing assumption that it is a sermon for Æthelred's coronation, and the relatively common view that Dunstan was its author, and then sets out to test whether or not the ways in which the text has been noted as similar to elements of Wulfstan's writing might in fact indicate that Wulfstan composed it. The manuscripts of the text, its sources and analogues, and its potential function are discussed in some detail, and a case is made, based on vocabulary and style, for Wulfstan as its author. A new edition of the text is provided as an appendix to the article.

Work on a variety of aspects of Ælfric's corpus appeared this year. Scholars will particularly welcome the first volume of Richard Marsden's EETS edition of *The 'Old English Heptateuch' and Ælfric's 'Libellus de Veteri Testamento et Novo'*. Marsden's introduction gives a thorough account of the manuscripts and the relationships between them and of editorial conventions, and the edited texts have on-page collation. Volume 2 will contain the notes and glossary. Aaron J Kleist's 'The Ælfric of Eynsham Project: An Introduction' (*HeroicA* 11[2008] 26 paras) gives an overview of plans to make available printed and electronic editions of Ælfric's homilies from Easter to Pentecost in his First Series of *Catholic Homilies*.

'Ælfric and Haymo Revisited', by Joyce Hill (in Blanton and Scheck, eds., pp. 331–47), reassesses identifications of Haymo's homiliary as a source for Ælfric, and emphasizes the importance of taking into account Ælfric's immediate sources, often compilations. An appendix sets out a comparison of the work of Smetana and Haymo in identifying instances in the *Catholic Homilies* where Ælfric draws on Haymo. Gabriella Corona tracks 'Ælfric's (Un)Changing Style: Continuity of Patterns from the *Catholic Homilies* to the *Lives of Saints*' (*JEGP* 107[2008] 169–89) and addresses the question of the poetry–prose continuum in Old English literature. The patterns under investigation are sound- and word-play; in particular lexical assonance and consonance, and Corona suggests that 'Ælfric's fluid style provides a spectrum of rhetorical possibilities which are more easily enjoyed when the non-rhythmical/rhythmical form is seen as a transition rather than a break' (p. 188). In 'Ælfric, St Edmund, and St Edwold of Cerne' (*MÆ* 77[2008] 1–9), Mark Faulkner examines Ælfric's possible motivation in writing his *Life of Edmund* and proposes that his posting to Cerne is significant. The relics of Edmund's brother, Edwold, were translated to Cerne shortly after its foundation, and Faulkner suggests that 'Ælfric is likely to have had some involvement in the management' of Edwold's cult (p. 5).

Hans Sauer offers a comparative study of 'Archbishops, Lords, and Concubines: Words for People and their Word-Formation Patterns in Early English (*Épinal-Erfurt Glossary* and Ælfric's *Glossary*)—a Sketch' (in Blanton and Scheck, eds., pp. 381–409), which traces continuity and change in this area of Old English vocabulary and in how words are formed over about 300 years. Mary Clayton looks at 'Temperance as the Mother of Virtues in Ælfric' (*N&Q* 55[2008] 1–2), with reference to his *Lives of Saints* Christmas homily and the composite *De octo uitiis. Et de duodecim abuisiuis gradus*. Clayton proposes that Haymo is Ælfric's source for this idea, and that Ælfric combines two separate Latin phrases from Haymo. Rhonda L. McDaniel's focus is '*Hnescnys*: Weakness of Mind in the Works of Ælfric' (in Blanton and Scheck, eds., pp. 79–90). Taking her starting-point from studies of the Latin terms *molles* as used of unmanly or feminized men, and of the use of *hnesclic* in similar contexts in Old English texts, McDaniel examines Ælfric's use of the term and shows that he restricts this to its meaning of moral weakness, for example an inability to resist sexual gratification, and that, when working with sources which use *molles* to mean 'effeminate men', he filters out this element of its meaning in his Old English translation, and presents it as a generalized and ungendered reference to moral weakness. She concludes that 'effeminate' is not part of the semantic range of OE *hnesce*, and calls for a reassessment of the association between femininity and moral weakness in Anglo-Saxon vernacular textual culture. In 'Ælfric's Zoology' (*Neophil* 92[2008] 141–53), Emily Thornbury shows how he presents human power over the natural world, and identifies Isidore, Ambrose and perhaps a *Physiologus*-book as the sources for his animal descriptions.

Elaine Treharne tracks 'The Canonisation of Ælfric' (in Thormählen, ed., pp. 1–13) in scholarship of the last few decades, where he has been a prominent subject of new work. Through an analysis of his prefaces, Treharne shows that 'Ælfric's own declared position of "authority" has often caused scholars to take him at his word to the detriment of the tradition within which he worked' (p. 3), and that this has resulted in a neglect of much of the rest of the corpus of religious prose. In conclusion, Treharne suggests that Ælfric may have been constructing his own identity as that of a confessor saint, and contrasts what she sees as his unsuccessful attempt to secure canonization in the Anglo-Saxon period with the prestige afforded him by modern scholarship.

Books Reviewed

Amano, Masachiyo, Michiko Ogura, and Masayuki Ohkado, eds. *Historical Englishes in Varieties of Texts and Contexts: The Global Coe Programme, International Conference 2007*. Lang. [2008] pp. xi + 403. £48 ($99.95) ISBN 9 7836 3158 1902.

Andersson, Roger, ed. *Constructing the Medieval Sermon*. Brepols. [2007] pp. xiii + 334. €60 ISBN 9 7825 0352 5891.

Arnold, John. *What Is Medieval History?* Polity. [2008] pp. ix + 155. £13.99 ISBN 9 7807 4563 9338.

Barrow, Julia, and Andrew Wareham, eds. *Myth, Rulership, Church and Charters: Essays in Honour of Nicholas Brooks*. Ashgate. [2008] pp. xiv + 271. £60 ISBN 9 7807 5465 1208.

Blanton, Virginia, and Helene Scheck, eds. *Intertexts: Studies in Anglo-Saxon Culture Presented to Paul E. Szarmach*. ACMRS. [2008] pp. xvi + 448. $58 (€50) ISBN 9 7825 0352 8939.

Bremmer Jr, Rolf H., and Kees Dekker. Manuscripts in the Low Countries. Anglo-Saxon Manuscripts in Microfiche Facsimile 13. ACMRS. [2006] pp. x + 117. $90 ISBN 9 7808 6698 3662.

Brookes, Stuart. *Economics and Social Change in Anglo-Saxon Kent AD 400–900*. BAR British Series 431. Archaeopress. [2007] pp. viii + 243. £36 ISBN 9 7814 0730 0160.

Burrow, J.A. *The Poetry of Praise*. CUP. [2008] pp. vii + 196. £47 ISBN 9 7805 2188 6932.

Coatsworth, Elizabeth. *Corpus of Anglo-Saxon Stone Sculpture, vol. 8: Western Yorkshire*. BA/OUP. [2008] pp. xiv + 514 + 870 plates. £140 ISBN 9 7801 9726 4256.

Cowie, Robert, and Lyn Blackmore. *Early and Middle Saxon Rural Settlement in the London Region*. Museum of London Archaeology Service. [2008] pp. xviii + 239. £14.95 ISBN 9 7819 0199 2779.

Crick, Julia, ed. *Charters of St Albans*. OUP. [2008] pp. xxxii + 265. £55 ISBN 9 7801 9726 3969.

Daniell, Christopher. *Atlas of Medieval Britain*. Routledge. [2008] pp. viii + 160. £50 ISBN 9 7804 1534 0694.

Davies, Wendy, Guy Halsall, and Andrew Reynolds. *People and Space in the Middle Ages, 300–1300*. Brepols. [2006] pp. xv + 366. €75 ISBN 9 7825 0351 5267.

Davis, Jennifer R., and Michael McCormick, eds. *The Long Morning of Medieval Europe: New Directions in Early Medieval Studies*. Ashgate. [2008] pp. xix + 345. £60 ISBN 9 7808 5466 2549.

Davis, Kathleen. *Periodization and Sovereignty: How Ideas of Feudalism and Secularization Govern the Politics of Time*. UPennP. [2008] pp. 189. $42.50 (£28) ISBN 9 7808 1224 0832.

Dendle, Peter, and Alain Touwaide, eds. *Health and Healing from the Medieval Garden*. Boydell. [2008] pp. xiii + 256. £50 ISBN 9 7818 4383 3635.

Devlin, Zoe. *Remembering the Dead in Anglo-Saxon England: Memory Theory in Archaeology and History*. BAR British Series 446. Archaeopress. [2007] pp. vii + 1148. £36 ISBN 9 7814 0730 1440.

Di Sciacca, Claudia. *Finding the Right Words: Isidore's 'Synonyma' in Anglo-Saxon England*. UTorP. [2008] pp. xvi + 323. $85 (£48) ISBN 9 7808 0209 1291.

Doane, A.N. *Grammars/Handlist of Manuscripts*. Anglo-Saxon Manuscripts in Microfiche Facsimile 15. ACMRS. [2007] pp. xii + 123. $90 ISBN 9 7808 6698 3808.

Dunn, Marilyn. *The Vision of St. Fursey and the Development of Purgatory*. Fursey Pilgrims. [2007] pp. 32. £3 ISBN 0 9544 7731 6.

Ellis, Anne V. *The Estates of Winchcombe Abbey, Gloucestershire: A Preliminary Landscape Archaeological Survey*. BAR British Series 474. Archaeopress. [2008] pp. v + 120. £28 ISBN 9 7814 0730 3758.

Ellis, Roger, ed. *The Oxford History of Literary Translation in English, vol. 1: To 1550*. OUP. [2008] pp. x + 485. £105 ISBN 9 7801 9924 6205.

Fitzmaurice, Susan M., and Donka Minkova, eds. *Studies in the History of the English Language, vol. 4: Empirical and Analytical Advances in the Study of English Language Change*. Gruyter. [2008] pp. xi + 433. €98 ($152) ISBN 9 7831 1020 5879.

Fouracre, Paul, and David Ganz, eds. *Frankland: The Franks and the World of the Early Middle Ages*. Essays in Honour of Dame Jinty Nelson. ManUP. [2008] pp. xvi + 340. £55 ISBN 9 7807 1907 6695.

Fulk, R.D., Robert E. Bjork, and John D. Niles eds., with a foreword by Helen Damico. *Klaeber's Beowulf and the Fight at Finnsburg*, 4th edn. UTorP. [2008] pp. cxc + 497. hb £65 ($100) ISBN 9 7808 0209 8436, pb £22.95 ($39.95) ISBN 9 7808 0209 5671.

Gameson, Richard. *The Earliest Books of Canterbury Cathedral: Manuscripts and Fragments to c.1200*. BibS. [2008] pp. 414. £60 ISBN 9 7809 4817 0166.

Gem, Richard. *Deerhurst and Rome: Æthelric's Pilgrimage of c.804 and the Oratory of ST Mary Mediana*. Deerhurst Lecture 2007. Friends of Deerhurst. [2008] pp. 32. £3 ISBN 9 7809 5494 8405.

Gwara, Scott. *Heroic Identity in the World of Beowulf*. Brill. [2008] pp. xvi + 419. €135 ($199) ISBN 9 7890 0417 1701.

Hill, John M. *The Narrative Pulse of Beowulf: Arrivals and Departures*. UTorP. [2008] pp. x + 119. hb £25 ($40) ISBN 9 7808 0209 3295, pb $21.95 ISBN 9 7814 4261 0873.

Hinton, David A. *The Alfred Jewel and Other Late Anglo-Saxon Decorated Metalwork*. Ashmolean. [2008] pp. 94. £12.95 ISBN 1 8544 4229 5.

Howe, Nicholas. *Writing the Map of Anglo-Saxon England: Essays in Cultural Geography*. YaleUP. [2008] pp. xiv + 278. $45 ISBN 8 7803 0011 9336.

Johnston, Andrew James. *Performing the Middle Ages from 'Beowulf' to 'Othello'*. Brepols. [2008] pp. viii + 344. €70 ISBN 9 7825 0352 7550.

Jolly, Karen Louise, Catherine E. Karkov, and Sarah Larratt Keefer, eds. *Cross and Culture in Anglo-Saxon England: Studies in Honor of George Hardin Brown*. WVUP. [2008] pp. x + 356. $44.95 ISBN 9 7819 3320 2235.

Karkov, Catherine E., and Helen Damico, eds. *Aedificia Nova: Studies in Honor of Rosemary Cramp*. PIP. [2008] xv + 427. $80 ISBN 9 7815 8044 1100.

Keefer, Sarah Larratt, and Rolf H. Bremmer Jr. *Signs on the Edge: Space, Text and Margin in Medieval Manuscripts*. Peeters. [2007] pp. viii + 319. €62 ISBN 9 7890 4291 9808.

Keefer, Sarah Larratt, David Rollason, and A.N. Doane *Manuscripts of Durham, Ripon, and York*. Anglo-Saxon Manuscripts in Microfiche Facsimile 14. ACMRS. [2007] pp. x + 156. $90 ISBN 9 7808 6698 3723.

Kendall, Calvin B., and trans. *Bede, 'On Genesis'*. LiverUP. [2008] pp. xii + 359. £18.50 ISBN 9 7818 4631 0881.

Krygier, Marcin, and Liliana Sikorska, eds. *The Propur Langage of Englische Men*. Lang. [2008] pp. 147. pb SFR53 (€33.80) ISBN 9 7836 3157 5345.

Lavelle, Ryan. *Royal Estates in Anglo-Saxon Wessex: Land, Politics and Family Strategies*. BAR British Series 439. Archaeopress. [2007] pp. ix + 153. £31 ISBN 9 7814 0730 0993.

Lendinara, Patrizia, ed. '... *un tuo serto di fiori in man recando': Scritti in onore di Maria Amalia D'Aronco*, vol. 2. Forum. [2008] pp. 462. €45 ISBN 9 7888 8420 4639.

Lewis-Simpson, Shannon, ed. *Youth and Age in the Medieval North*. Brill. [2008] pp. ix + 308. €109 ($174) ISBN 9 7890 0417 0735.

Lucas, Peter J., and Jonathan Wilcox. *Manuscripts Relating to Dunstan, Ælfric, and Wulfstan; The 'Eadwine Psalter' Group*. Anglo-Saxon Manuscripts in Microfiche Facsimile 16. ACMRS. [2008] pp. x + 118. £90 ISBN 9 7808 6698 3914.

Marsden, Richard, ed. *The 'Old English Heptateuch' and Ælfric's 'Libellus de Veteri Testamento et Novo'*, vol. 1. EETS OS 330. OUP. [2008] pp. clxxix + 230. £60 ISBN 9 7801 9956 1438.

Martino, Paolo, ed. *L'identità europea: lingua e cultura*. Edizioni Studium. [2008] pp. 262. €22 ISBN 9 7888 3824 0782.

McKitterick. *Charlemagne: The Formation of a European Identity*. CUP. [2008] pp. xviii + 460. hb £45 ($90) ISBN 9 7805 2188 6727, pb £15.99 ($29.99) ISBN 9 7805 2171 6451.

Meyvaert, Paul. *The Art of Words: Bede and Theodulf*. Ashgate. [2008] pp. xvii + 11 essays. £70 ISBN 9 7807 5465 9778.

Momma, Haruko, and Michael Matto, eds. *A Companion to the History of the English Language*. Wiley-Blackwell. [2008] pp. xxxiii + 690. £95 ISBN 9 7814 0512 9923.

Mundal, Else, and Jonas Wellendorf, eds. *Oral Art Forms and their Passage into Writing*. MTP. [2008] pp. vi + 241. DKK298 ($52) ISBN 9 7887 6350 5048.

Noble, Thomas F.X., and Julia M.H. Smith, eds. *The Cambridge History of Christianity, vol. 3: Early Medieval Christianities, c.600–c.1100.* CUP. [2008] pp. xxix + 846. £105 ISBN 9 7805 2181 7752.

Pratt, David. *The Political Thought of King Alfred the Great.* CUP. [2007] pp. 434. £63 ($123) ISBN 9 7805 2180 3502.

Rackham, Oliver. *'Transitus beati Fursei': A Translation of the 8th Century Manuscript Life of Saint Fursey.* Fursey Pilgrims. [2007] pp. 68. £9.95. ISBN 0 9544 7732 4.

Rankin, Susan, ed. *The Winchester Troper.* Stainer & Bell. [2007] pp. 206. £120 $219 ISBN 9 7808 5249 8941.

Redmond, Angela A. *Viking Burial in the North of England.* BAR British Series 429. Archaeopress. [2007] pp. x + 127. £42 ISBN 9 7814 0730 0504.

Risden, E.L. *Heroes, Gods and the Role of Epiphany in English Epic Poetry.* McFarland. [2008] pp. v + 204. pb $39.95 ISBN 9 7807 8643 5418.

Rushforth, Rebecca. *Saints in English Kalendars before A.D. 1100.* Boydell. [2008] pp. ix + 79. £35 ($70) ISBN 9 7818 7025 2232.

Scheck, Helene. *Reform and Resistance: Formations of Female Subjectivity in Early Medieval Ecclesiastical Culture.* SUNYP. [2008] pp. xi + 238. $70 ISBN 9 7807 9147 4893.

Scragg, Donald, ed. *Edgar, King of the English 959–975: New Interpretations.* Boydell. [2008] pp. xix + 274. £55 ($105) ISBN 9 7818 4383 3994.

Sharifian, Farzad, René Dirven, Ning Yu, and Susanne Niemeier, eds. *Culture, Body, and Language: Conceptualizations of Internal Body Organs across Cultures and Languages.* MGruyter. [2008] pp. x + 431. €98 ($152) ISBN 9 7831 1019 6221.

Steen, Janie. *Verse and Virtuosity: The Adaptation of Latin Rhetoric in Old English Poetry.* UTorP. [2008] pp. xii + 237. £45 ($70) ISBN 9 7808 0209 1574.

Thormählen, Marianne, ed. *English Now: Selected Papers from the 20th IAUPE Conference in Lund 2007.* Centre for Languages and Literatures, LundU. [2008] pp. xx + 354. €127.99 (SEK 400, $149.50) ISBN 9 7891 9769 3509.

Turner, Andrew J., and Bernard J. Muir, eds. *and trans. Eadmer of Canterbury, Lives and Miracles of Saints Oda, Dunstan, and Oswald.* Clarendon. [2006] pp. cxxxiv + 333. £100 ISBN 9 7801 9925 3870.

Valtonen, Irmeli. *The North in the 'Old English Orosius': A Geographical Narrative in Context.* SNH. [2008] pp. xvi + 672. €55 ISBN 9 7895 1904 0295.

Wilcox, Jonathan. *Homilies by Ælfric and Other Homilies.* Anglo-Saxon Manuscripts in Microfiche Facsimile 17. ACMRS. [2008] pp. x + 142. $90 ISBN 9 7808 6698 4072.

Williamson, Tom. *Sutton Hoo and its Landscape: The Context of Monuments.* Windgather. [2008] pp. xi + 154. £20. ISBN 9 7819 0511 9257.

Withers, Benjamin C. *The Illustrated Old English Hexateuch, Cotton Claudius B. IV: The Frontier of Seeing and Reading in Anglo-Saxon England.* UTorP. [2007] pp. xvi + 429 + 115 plates. $90 ISBN 9 7808 0209 1048.

Wood, Ian. *The Origins of Jarrow: The Monastery, the Slake and Ecgfrith's Minster*. Bede's World, Jarrow. [2008] pp. 40. £7.50 ISBN 9 7809 5582 3404.

Wood, Ian. *The Priest, the Temple and the Moon in the Eighth Century*. 25th Brixworth Lecture, 2007. Friends of All Saints' Church, Brixworth. [2008] pp. 33. £4 ISBN 0 9544 0926 4.

Wright, Michael, and Stephanie Hollis. *Manuscripts of Trinity College, Cambridge*. Anglo-Saxon Manuscripts in Microfiche Facsimile 12. ACMRS. [2004] pp. x + 95. $90 ISBN 0 8669 8317 1.

III

Later Medieval: Excluding Chaucer

JENNIFER N. BROWN, CARRIE GRIFFIN, JURIS LIDAKA,
RALUCA RADULESCU, MICHELLE M. SAUER AND
GREG WALKER

This chapter has the following sections: 1. General and Miscellaneous; 2. Women's Writing; 3. Alliterative Verse and Lyrics; 4. The *Gawain*-Poet; 5. *Piers Plowman*; 6. Romance; 7. Gower, Lydgate, Hoccleve; 8. Malory and Caxton; 9. Middle Scots Poetry; 10. Drama. Sections 1 and 7 are by Juris Lidaka; sections 2 and 9 are by Jennifer N. Brown; section 3 is by Carrie Griffin; sections 4 and 5 are by Michelle M. Sauer; sections 6 and 8 are by Raluca Radulescu; section 10 is by Greg Walker.

1. General and Miscellaneous

Among reference works this year, we should note Ann Eljenholm Nichols's *Cambridge*, vol. 1: *Christ's College, Clare College, Corpus Christi College, Emmanuel College, Gonville and Caius College, and The Fitzwilliam Museum*, the fifth volume in the series *An Index of Images in English Manuscripts from the Time of Chaucer to Henry VIII c.1380–c.1509*. It includes 321 manuscripts, mostly in Latin of course, from Duns Scotus with historiated initials or simply a drawing of a scroll, to highly illustrated books of Hours, to illustrated copies of Chaucer, Langland, Lydgate (and Benedict Burgh), Hoccleve, Ranulph Higden's *Polychronicon*, Trevisa's Higden, Walton's Boethius, Wyclif, John Mirk's *Festial*, the *Brut*, Stephen Scrope's *Dicts and Sayings of the Philosophers*, the *Prick of Conscience*, *Mandeville's Travels*, Richard Rolle, Nicholas Love, the *South English Lectionary* (*sic*, actually the *South English Legendary*), Henry Lovelich, Geoffrey of Monmouth, William Worcester, and miscellanies with contents ranging from 'Richard Coeur de Lion' and 'Bevis of Hampton' to the 'Doctrine of the Heart', with one literary miscellany having no contents listed at all (no. 245, Gonville and Caius 215/230). Since the focus is artistic, less attention to other aspects is to be expected, such as the lack of detail on contents (as just noted), as well as unfamiliar conventions such as indexing by authors' first names (Lydgate and Trevisa under 'John') and even silent translations (Guillaume Deguileville among the Williams). A short introduction surveying the scope of the volume precedes the latest version of the various editors' 'User's Manual' for the series and lists of manuscripts and abbreviations, before the catalogue itself. A template at the beginning notes that the outline of each description is basically shelfmark, author/contents, date, pictorial information (much subdivided), and odd details at the end; in practice and as expected, the pictorial information is the focus of attention throughout. At the end are: a glossary of subjects and terms; indices of authors and texts, incipits, pictorial subjects (the longest and most detailed), and manuscripts with coats of arms; and twenty-three highly selected illustrations preceded by a list, five of which are in Middle English and one of which shows a scroll configured like a Möbius strip.

Ralph Hanna's edition of the *Speculum Vitae: A Reading Edition* proved too large for EETS to issue it as a single volume, as previously announced, and requires two hefty tomes. As Hanna graciously notes, many have preceded him in studying English works stemming from Lorens of Orleans's *Somme le roi*, and he has benefited directly and indirectly from their studies. The anonymous Yorkshire translator followed Lorens's plan of using linked septenaries to provide a basic, educational book of vices and virtues, and tied this to the seven petitions of the Pater Noster, rather like the well-known Pater Noster table immediately preceding the *Speculum Vitae* in the Vernon manuscript. Hanna describes the forty-five manuscripts or substantial fragments of the *Speculum Vitae*, adding notes on extracts, and presents the usual EETS discussion of dialect, concluding that the northern features are unmistakable and Yorkshire seems the most likely location, but admitting that northern traditionalism hinders much closer localization. Five early Yorkshire manuscripts seem to offer the best text, so they are collated for this edition, using British Library MS Additional 33995 as the base (as in previous editions), with two others to compare, spot checks among the other manuscripts, and recourse to two manuscripts of the *Somme le roi*. The text presented reproduces the copy manuscript's marginalia and running heads; the heads are likely to strike readers as section titles because the printed format spreads them around in the text columns, but one must remember that they are indeed running heads or titles, as the marginal folio references should make clear. Following the commentary notes after the end of the text in the second volume, we find a brief edition of a Latin septenary tract from which the *Speculum Vitae* derives its early portions, the glossary, a list of proper names, and an index of biblical references.

TEAMS continues its fine work with Anne B. Thompson's edition of *The Northern Homily Cycle* (*NHC*), albeit not complete, for it contains only twenty-three of the fifty-two Sunday sermons for the year, to which must be added sermons for the Purification, the Annunciation and the Ascension, even before the various expansions. Recent work casts serious doubt upon assertions that the laity 'could understand so little of what they heard' in the Mass (p. 1), but the value of the vernacular in their spiritual education is not doubted now, nor was it *c*.1300, when an unknown hand—probably an Austin canon—composed the core of the *NHC*. That date is also consistent with the trickle-down effect of the Fourth Lateran Council's stressing education and the consequent emphasis at the University of Paris on preaching, both of which respond to late twelfth-century heretical sermonizing, partially addressed in the introduction. It is good to see continental and learned matters affecting insular vernacular literature receive attention. Like other TEAMS volumes, difficult words are glossed to the side, longer passages at the bottom of the page—conveniently including more of the pericope, very shortly given in Latin in the text—and miscellaneous explanatory notes follow, before short textual notes, a bibliography and a brief glossary.

Many readers will enjoy George Shuffelton's TEAMS edition of *Codex Ashmole 61: A Compilation of Popular Middle English Verse* for its wide variety of verse. This familiar verse anthology from the end of the fifteenth century by an otherwise unidentified 'Rate' (a plate showing Rate's trademark fish is included) ranges across romances (*Sir Isumbras, Lybaeus Desconus, Sir Orfeo,* etc.), Lydgate (*Right as a Ram's Horn,* an altered *Stans puer ad mensam,* etc.), hagiography (*St Eustace, St Margaret*), and religious works ranging as broadly as the *Northern Passion,* Maidstone's *Seven Penitential Psalms,* and a tale of *The Incestuous Daughter.* The introduction begins with codicological matters but keeps them in a smoothly flowing narrative, no doubt so as not to put off the students for whom the series is designed, and moves into surveying the genres and themes covered by the forty-two items. Shuffelton suggests that Rate's goal was simply to collect poems of instruction and of entertainment (which he seems to have revised to his taste as he copied), and that the collection may potentially have been used for group entertainment at various times of the year. As a diplomatic edition of one manuscript, the edition does not compare multiple copies of the poems and emend for a 'best text', but emends conservatively to correct where Rate's texts seem inadequate, and adds modern punctuation. The texts are presented first in the usual TEAMS style, followed by commentaries for each item with a set format of origin, genres, and themes; manuscript context; text; references to printed editions and reference works; and individual items by line.

Jennifer N. Brown's *Three Women of Liège: A Critical Edition of and Commentary on the Middle English Lives of Elizabeth of Spalbeek, Christina Mirabilis, and Marie d'Oignies* presents these late twelfth- and thirteenth-century beguines' lives, written by men, from the Middle English translation in Bodleian Library MS Douce 114, which Brown dates to around the second quarter of the fifteenth century. The manuscript shows signs of being a copy of some earlier exemplar, but no other copies have come to light for comparison. A short introduction discusses the Latin *vitae,* their authors and transmission, including manuscripts surviving in England, then the target manuscript's audience and reception, and closes with an overview of editorial practice, which is to modernize thorns and yoghs but not i/j/y or u/v, modernize compounds, expand abbreviations, and modernize capitalization and punctuation except for retaining paraphs, with some adaptations. Then come the editions: Elizabeth of Spalbeek by Philip of Clairvaux, Christina Mirabilis by Thomas of Cantimpré, and Marie d'Oignies by Jacques de Vitry. Footnotes combine textual and explanatory materials, sources, glosses and miscellaneous matters. Thereafter come discursive essays, one for each life. Elizabeth of

Spalbeek re-enacted Christ's Passion daily and received stigmata on a Friday; her re-enactments were dramatic performances in public, complete with ecstatic dancing and rhythmic body-slapping, interspersed with catatonic ravishment. Her hagiographer organizes what he saw and learned according to the liturgical hours, with additional material afterward. Christina Mirabilis was not visited by her biographer, who probably got much of his information from his mentor, Jacques de Vitry, who had known Christina. She had a habit of rising from the dead (two or three times), she saw and learned from Purgatory, she fed herself from her virgin breasts for nine weeks, and she threw herself into ovens, fires and boiling or freezing water with no physical effects but pain. Marie d'Oignies's *vita* seems to be a vehicle for of Jacques de Vitry's self-promotion, begun safely after her death and ornately embellished with allusions and flourishes; de Vitry draws attention to some elements of her excess or, at least, qualifies them, but his aim is to emphasize her devotion, submission (to God, not her husband), frequent crying fits, fasting, self-mortification and more to pave the way for her canonization.

More *Fachliteratur* is being made available. In 'A Middle English Treatise on Comets in Cambridge, Trinity College MS O.5.26' (*ANQ* 21:i[2008] 11–22), Jill Fitzgerald edits the short treatise and provides some background material for placing it in the context of vernacular science and ideas about comets. Dirk Schultze's 'Hippocras Bag, Oil of Exeter and Manus Christi: Recipes in BL Harley 1706' (*Anglia* 126[2008] 429–60) diplomatically edits and discusses thirteen previously unpublished recipes from the late fifteenth or early sixteenth centuries, adding a convenient glossary. 'Three Short Anglo-Norman Texts in Leeds University Library Brotherton Collection MS 29' (*NMS* 52[2008] 81–112) are briefly discussed, edited and translated by Diana B. Tyson, who also provides a fulsome description of the manuscript's contents: a *Political Genealogy*, *A prayer for victory*, and *Against the Queen*. A.S.G. Edwards edits and briefly describes a text at the edge of the end of our coverage—'A Verse Chronicle of the House of Percy' (*SP* 105[2008] 226–44)—surviving in a professionally copied roll from the early sixteenth century but earlier in origin; seeming more like a late Middle English work.

Religious texts also continue to be published in articles. For example, Ralph Hanna's 'Verses in Sermons Again: The Case of Cambridge, Jesus College, MS Q.A.13' (*SB* 57[2005–6] 63–83) discusses and presents the seven sets of verses in Latin sermons from late fourteenth-century west Norfolk, related to those in John of Grimestone's book and others; copied by a continental scribe who did not understand the English, the verses make good sense only when read in their Latin context. Palti edits and discusses seven late, mostly macaronic carols in 'An Unpublished Fifteenth-Century Carol Collection: Oxford: Lincoln College MS Lat. 141' (*MÆ* 77[2008] 260–78), probably from Norfolk and an educational environment; the discussion contextualizes these carols among others and in their cultural milieu. Marlene Villalobos Hennessy offers an edition with extensive discussion of 'Three Marian Texts, including a Prayer for a Lay-Brother, in London, British Library, MS Additional 37049' (*EMS* 14[2008] 163–79), a northern Carthusian miscellany *c*.1460–70, that may very well have been compiled for the education of lay brothers. In 'A Marian Lyric from Bodleian MS. Add. A. 268' (*ANQ* 21:ii[2008] 4–7), Melissa Mayus also edits another short Marian verse in twenty-two couplets and briefly discusses the early fifteenth-century poem.

Not an edition but a translation is Siegfried Wenzel's *Preaching in the Age of Chaucer: Selected Sermons in Translation*, a highly informative teaching text designed to illustrate how sermons might be developed and what varieties existed. The first section opens with the Gospel reading for the third Sunday of Lent and adds the commentary from the *Glossa Ordinaria*, then follows with three sermons on that reading, to show the variety of ways in which a single reading might be interpreted. The second section follows the liturgical year from Advent through Christmas and Easter to the first Sunday after Trinity. The third turns to saints, with one sermon on the Annunciation, one on the Assumption, two by Richard FitzRalph on St Katherine, and John the Baptist from John Mirk's *Festial* (the only Middle English sermon). The fourth part is for 'Special Occasions': a funeral, a convocation, a sermon to the clergy rather than the laity, a monastic visitation, a nun's enclosure and introducing a new university lecturer. As Wenzel notes in his introduction, the styles are of particular interest; perhaps for this reason he also includes two 'reported sermons' (*reportationes*) so that their peculiarities can be seen, for those who have read passing references to such *reportationes* but have not seen any or been accorded the chance to compare them with full sermon texts. Most surviving sermons are anonymous, but those selected here are often by known writers: Thomas Brinton, John Dygon, John Felton, Richard FitzRalph, one Frisby, John Mirk, Nicholas Philip and John Wyclif are responsible for eleven of the twenty-three sermons, and Thomas Wimbledon (of the famous sermon *Redde rationem villicationis tue*) may have written one of the others. To help learners understand the structure of the scholastic sermon, one is presented with its sections numbered so as to match the outline presented in its introduction (no. 4). Throughout, we find familiar literary features and topoi: exempla, the Seven Deadly Sins, alliteration, dialogues, allegories, imagery, verse (and some sermons are macaronic), allusions to external events and works (e.g., Ovid, Bartholomæus Anglicus, and the fable of belling the cat, familiar from *Piers Plowman*) and even puns. The liveliness of these sermons serves well to remind us that literary endeavours did not stop short of sermons and their oral delivery.

The most important volume in manuscript studies this year must be M.B. Parkes's *Their Hands before our Eyes: A Closer Look at Scribes. The Lyell Lectures Delivered in the University of Oxford 1999*, which focuses on how scribal hands write and how their choices determine the final product to be read. Three short chapters on scribal environments precede the texts of the lectures: one from antiquity in Rome to about 1100 in England, and then two on later periods, one on the religious orders and one on secular scribes, generously supported with details of individuals and groups, so much so that one is grateful that the publisher provided footnotes rather than endnotes so one can immediately see what to consult when a detail strikes a chord of interest. Then begin the Lyell lectures, which use the subsequent plates carefully. The first examines the relationship between writing and reading, starting again with Roman antiquity but swiftly moving on to medieval Europe, touching on letter formation, spelling, and other matters; covering mostly Latin materials but also referring to a scribe's altering the dialect of Rolle's *Form of Living*. The second lecture surveys the development of faster, cursive scripts typical of documentary and personal writing but also appearing in literary materials, such as a Middle English *Secreta secretorum*, while the third turns to more set, bookish hands of *c*.800–1200. The fourth examines more closely issues of style *c*.1200–1500; there were varieties and sub-varieties, illustrated here mostly by scribes of Latin texts but also of Gower's *Vox clamantis*, *Mirrour de l'homme*, and *Confessio amantis*, Higden's *Polychronicon*, Gaytrigge's *Lay Folks' Catechism*, Chaucer's *Canterbury Tales*, Lydgate's *Fall of Princes*, *Le songe du vergier*, Benedict Burgh's *Disticha Catonis*, Nicholas Love's *Mirrour of the Blessid Lyf of Jesu Christ*, and other English texts. The final lecture is on the resulting image of the script or page, for over time scripts developed a hierarchy and layout identifying relationships between texts on a page and what their roles might be while not losing track of the fact that the texts were to be read, not viewed. Following these are a glossary of technical terms, indices of scribes and manuscripts cited, a select bibliography of works cited, and a short general index; these precede the plates, given in order of examination in the lectures, though some are referred to briefly outside that order in other lectures.

Design and Distribution of Late Medieval Manuscripts in England, edited by Margaret Connolly and Linne R. Mooney, is largely the product of the 2005 York Manuscripts Conference, and so varies somewhat from the implied unity of the collection's title, although the contents are often fascinatingly valuable and well designed and illustrated. The first three articles concern 'Designing the *Canterbury Tales*: Chaucer's Early Copyists'. First, in ' "Chaucer's Scribe", Adam, and the Hengwrt Project' (pp. 11–40), Daniel W Mosser makes a case for thinking that Adam expected corrections, clarifications, and supplements from Chaucer, and thus that the Hengwrt MS was begun before his death and finished after it. Second, in 'The Trinity Gower D Scribe's Two *Canterbury Tales* Manuscripts Revisited' (pp. 41–60), Jacob Thaisen goes over the linguistic and codicological aspects of, principally, Oxford, Corpus Christi College MS 198 to propose that the first third had one exemplar, but that another or others were used after the *Squire's Tale*, which was copied after the *Wife of Bath's Prologue*. Third, Takako Kato analyses the types of 'Corrected Mistakes in MS Gg. 4. 27' (pp. 61–87) to find that arrhythmia (where the mind thinks it has written what the hands have not yet done) is the most common type, meaning that the scribe memorized and understood passages for copying as he worked.

The next four articles are appropriately grouped together under the heading 'Designing Devotion: Individual and Institutional'. Not all Sarum rites were the same, so in 'Late Medieval Efforts at Standardization and Reform in the Sarum Lessons for Saints' Days' (pp. 91–117), Sherry L. Reames reports on her collation of selected texts, finding there may have been at least three attempts to make a standard lectionary of saints and that short lessons may indeed have been more official than personal in nature. Amelia Grounds's 'Evolution of a Manuscript: The Pavement Hours' (pp. 118–38) examines how the text is reflected in the original and later, inserted images taken often from disassembled manuscripts (and a woodcut) and how the whole illustrates the buying public and what the market could offer it. Alexandra Barratt looks into a number of questions in 'Singing from the Same Hymn-Sheet: Two Bridgettine Manuscripts' (pp. 139–60), British Library MS Harley 494 and Lambeth Palace MS 3600, both from the early sixteenth century and related to Syon Abbey. Julian Luxford's '"Secundum originale examinatum": The Refashioning of a Benedictine Historical Manuscript' (pp. 161–79) looks at British Library MS Additional 36985, a reproduction of the earlier Tewksbury Abbey Founders' Book (Bodleian Library MS Top. Glouc. d.2), both of the sixteenth century, wondering about the origins of and reasons for the later reproduction.

The last six articles are gathered under the generic label 'Development and Distribution: Mapping Manuscripts and Texts'. In 'Locating Scribal Activity in Late Medieval London' (pp. 183–204), Linne R Mooney uses her experience in compiling a database of scribes who wrote multiple manuscripts (available at < http://www.medievalscribes.com >) to reveal where their desks probably were (monastic scribes and clerics excepted), since they did not work in scriptoria. Michael Sargent's 'What Do the Numbers Mean? Observations on Some Patterns of Middle English Manuscript Transmission' (pp. 205–44) is a well-nuanced interpretation of survival rates of vernacular texts. Taking advantage of the recent 'mapping' metaphor, in 'The Middle English Prose *Brut* and the Possibilities of Cultural Mapping' (pp. 245–60), John J. Thompson draws on his 'Imagining History' project (< http://www.qub .ac.uk/imagining-history/ >) to range over provenance, copying histories, and thereby a reception history of the work in its many forms, especially in the fifteenth and sixteenth centuries. Continuing this metaphor, Margaret Connolly sets about 'Mapping Manuscripts and Readers of *Contemplations of the Dread and Love of God*' (pp. 261–78), extending provenance into the sixteenth century and adding comments on printed variations. The alleged originator of the metaphor, Ralph Hanna, does not bring it up in his 'Yorkshire Manuscripts of the *Speculum Vitae*' (pp. 279–91), a work as popular as *Piers Plowman* but less studied; Hanna gives a prolegomenon, as it were, to his edition, for which see above. Finally, in 'Vernacular Herbals: A Growth Industry in Late Medieval England' (pp. 292–307), George R. Keiser uses the herbal in British Library MS Sloane 5 and four related copies to look into the text's sources, related texts, and the development of vernacular herbals.

More closely focused on the fourteenth and fifteenth centuries is the collection of essays edited by Denis Renevey and Graham D. Caie, *Medieval Texts in Context*, a product of sessions at the 2002 sixth European Society for the Study of English conference. Graham D. Caie opens with 'The Manuscript Experience: What Medieval Vernacular Manuscripts Tell Us about Authors and Texts' (pp. 10–27), offering some scattered comments on material, script, and layout before turning to a discussion of Gower and Chaucer as *compilatores* rather than *auctores*, with some notes on marginal glosses. Matti Peikola details quite a few 'Aspects of *Mise-en-page* in Manuscripts of the Wycliffite Bible' (pp. 28–67), from 127 copies examined and with an emphasis on ruling patterns; double-column layouts are most common, perhaps due to copying of exemplars or shared production networks. Simon

Horobin's 'Harley 3954 and the Audience of *Piers Plowman*' (pp. 68–84) notes that the switch from a B to an A text and use of reading from the other version within each point to the manuscript's audience being within an East Anglian religious house and very much concerned with confession, penance, and pastoral care. In ' "Cy ensuent trois chaunceons": Groups and Sequences of Middle English Lyrics' (pp. 85–95), Julia Boffey swiftly surveys some sequences (Gower, Audelay and Ryman, Charles d'Orléans, and Fairfax 16) to raise questions about other real or possible sequences (e.g. TCC R. 3. 19).

Richard Beadle's 'Sir John Fastolf's French Books' (pp. 96–112) reviews how Fastolf may have obtained some of the French royal library bought by the duke of Bedford in 1425, and moves on to discuss a previously unpublished book list from 1448, with observations on the books' used by Ricardus Franciscus, Stephen Scrope, and William Worcester. In 'Journeyman Manuscript Production and Lay Piety: The Hopton Hall Manuscript' (pp. 113–21), A.S.G. Edwards describes the manuscript now at Keio University and discusses its contents, principally John Gaytryge's *Lay Folks' Catechism* and *The Charter of the Abbey of the Holy Ghost*. Marleen Cre's 'Contexts and Comments: *The Chastising of God's Children* and *The Mirror of Simple Souls* in MS Bodley 505' (pp. 122–35) wonders about the joining of these quite dissimilar texts in one manuscript, finding them a useful pair as a contemplative tool urging discretion as the readers (probably Carthusians) read one against the other. In 'The Haunted Text: Reflections in *The mirror to deuout people*' (pp. 136–66), Vincent Gillespie ponders the work's Sheen/Syon origin, with a view to enhancing our understanding of works of spiritual advice with roots in Sheen and even the Syon Brethren. Ripon is Ralph Hanna's focus in 'Some North Yorkshire Scribes and their Context' (pp. 167–91), working with four manuscripts that share eleven or more hands; he assembles local materials to describe a literate milieu with a network of notables and others whose literary interests and relationships extend from Laurence Minot to Hoccleve, Chaucer, and Charles of Orléans. In 'Looking for a Context: Rolle, Anchoritic Culture and the Office of the Dead' (pp. 192–210), Denis Renevey contextualizes Rolle's *Expositio super novem lectiones* and its focus on the book of Job within the broader historical readership of Job, the influence anchoritic culture may have had on Rolle for this work, and the popularity of Rolle's work among clergy and laity in fifteenth-century York. The final item is Jeremy J. Smith's 'Issues of Linguistic Categorisation in the Evolution of Written Middle English' (pp. 211–24), which reviews the post-Conquest shifts by which graphemic and phonemic values re-coincided to varying degrees, depending on local habits, even as graphemic alterations need not have followed phonemic ones.

Mary-Jo Arn's study of *The Poet's Notebook: The Personal Manuscript of Charles d'Orléans (Paris BnF MS fr. 25458)* is a codicological examination broken down by the manuscript's four stints of copying from *c.*1440 to *c.*1465, after Charles returned from twenty-five years of captivity in England. Most of the poems in the manuscript are in French, with some Latin, and it is curious that the English poems seem copied much later than they were composed. The first chapter provides a detailed description of the manuscript, its various hands, limning, the poems' numbering, and the like, with a good number of plates inserted to illustrate various points. The next four chapters detail each of the varying stints of copying, with some analysis of the nature of the lyrics in each (also with illustrative plates). A number of tables and charts are appended—and even a larger one included on a CD in Microsoft Access 2000 format; for those without Access, an installation file of OpenOffice 2.3.1 (only the Windows version) is included. The contents of these supporting materials and many key phrases or abbreviations are used throughout, so careful cross-referencing is required by the reader. The conclusion observes that the order of poems was confused due to disordering of quires, scribal mislabelling, lack of numbering, and copying of lyrics physically before, not after, chronologically earlier lyrics. Restoring the order and the omitted English poems, Arn proposes, would help reveal Charles's complex conception of larger wholes, for he saw an organic structure, not a formal one, mingling forms as he kept his eye on the poems' *gravitas*, grouping love poems against ones on other subjects, and inadvertently but necessarily revealing his development as a poet while adding poems over the years.

Quiring also receives some attention. Phillipa Hardman's 'A Note on the Collation of BL MS Add. 37492 (The Fillingham Manuscript)' (*JEBS* 11[2008] 217–21) uses the medieval quire signatures to reconstruct how much is lost from *The Eremyte and the Owtelawe*; the manuscript also contains *Firumbras*, *Otuel and Roland*, *The Fendys Parlement*, and *The Myrour of Mankind*, the first and last incomplete.

Daniel Wakelin and Christopher Burlinson describe the 'Evidence for the Construction of Quires in a Fifteenth-Century Manuscript' (*Library* 9[2008] 383–96), St John's College, Cambridge, MS S.54, a collection of carols and lyrics, probably from Norfolk, in nested quadrifolia. Oliver Pickering briefly describes 'Two Pynson Editions of the Life of St Katherine of Alexandria' (*Library* 9[2008] 471–8), a third fragment having been found of the printed versions of the fifteenth-century life. Vincent Gillespie's 'Chapter and Worse: An Episode in the Regional Transmission of the *Speculum Christiani*' (*EMS* 14[2008] 86–111) analyses the contents of the work in Cambridge University Library MS Dd. 14. 26 and the prime source, *Cibus Anime*, arguing for a very complicated and Carthusian origin quite early in the fifteenth century. Juliana Dresvina offers 'A Note on a Hitherto Unpublished Life of St Margaret of Antioch from MS Eng. th. e 18: Its Scribe and its Source' (*JEBS* 10[2007] 217–31), incomplete in a probable booklet from the late fifteenth century and coming from the little-known Rebdorf version of *Passio Sanctæ Margaritæ* from between the eighth and eleventh centuries. 'Ricardus Franciscus Writes for William Worcester', asserts Catherine Nall (*JEBS* 11[2008] 207–12), on the basis of the script in a Cambridge manuscript; adding that manuscript to the others written by Franciscus shows that his clientele extended beyond Sir John Fastolf to others associated with him. In 'Newly Discovered Booklets from a Reconstructed Middle English Manuscript' (*EMS* 14[2008] 112–29), Kathleen L. Scott adds six further, now scattered, booklets to the vernacular manuscript with Lydgate, Burgh, Hoccleve, Mandeville, Gower, the *Awnters of Arthur*, hunting and hawking treatises, and more, describing what it must have looked like when written, probably just after the middle of the fifteenth century.

This supplements her original article, 'A Fifteenth-Century Vernacular Manuscript Reconstructed' (*BLR* 7[1966] 235–41).

Abandoning paper, the *British Library Journal* is now electronic (<http://www.bl.uk/eblj/>) and offers three articles relating to various Harleian manuscripts. Laura Nuvoloni's 'The Harleian Medical Manuscripts' (*BLJ* [2008] article 7) provides an overview of the collection of 153 manuscripts which the Harley Medieval Medical Manuscripts Project has now catalogued online (<http://www.bl.uk/catalogues/manuscripts/>), noting that more than a third are of British origin, containing medical texts in Old and Middle English. Peter Murray Jones lays out three 'Witnesses to Medieval Medical Practice in the Harley Collection' (*BLJ* [2008] article 8), texts of which are in Latin, Middle English, and French, with notes on actual cases and treatments, some of which are based on academic sources and others evidently on experience, owned and partly written by Thomas Fayreford, John Crophill, and William Worcester. And in 'Wolfenbüttel HAB Cod. Guelf. 51. 9. Aug. 4° and BL, Harley MS. 3542: Complementary Witnesses to Ralph Hoby's 1437 Treatise on Astronomical Medicine' (*BLJ* [2008] article 10), Linda Ehrsam Voigts compares the known and newly found copies of this Latin treatise, one of which was in the hands of the royal physician Roger Marchall (fl. 1436–77).

New work across the Conquest includes Eric Gerald Stanley's 'Judgment Day: Hopes, Joys, and Sorrows in Medieval England' (*SMRH* 5[2007] 1–53), a combination of selections from Old and Middle English literary works, with observations upon their vocabulary and themes, seeking cultural values. We must not forget all the Latin literature shortly after the Conquest. 'Yes' is Jill Mann's answer to her question 'Does an Author Understand his Own Text? Nigel of Longchamp and the *Speculum Stultorum*' (*Journal of Medieval Latin* 17[2007] 1–37), using a close reading of the poem with its seemingly fatuous allegorizing epistle and a careful dip into the historical background, which she finds urges a redating to perhaps the 1190 s. In 'Eleanor of Aquitaine, Twelfth-Century English Chroniclers and her "Black Legend"' (*NMS* 52[2008] 17–42), Ralph V. Turner examines the likes of Walter Map, Gerald of Wales, Ralph Niger, John of Salisbury, William of Newburgh, and others to argue that it was their tradition-bound anti-feminism that made them portray Eleanor's self-determination as sexual impropriety. Rebecca Rushforth argues for an ownership connection between 'The Crowland Psalter and Gundrada de Warenne' (*BLR* 21[2008] 156–68 + 2 plates), finding her an example of female aristocratic piety in the late eleventh century, before the psalter went to Lewes in Sussex, for Hours added to the psalter use feminine forms and she had a Lewes connection.

The Vatican Mythographers have been translated by Ronald E. Pepin. That much said, it is necessary to point out that they are actually not 'Vatican' mythographers except by accident of modern publication. That is, the texts were first published in 1831 from Vatican manuscripts by Angelo Mai, prefect of the Vatican library, who called them Vatican mythographers, and the term stuck. The myths and tales are not unique to these mythographers or Vatican manuscripts, and such works were used in the schools, and also used by Chaucer, Gower, Jean de Meun for the *Roman de la Rose*, and Petrarch, amongst others. The first mythography survives in a unique manuscript and—even with about 230 brief chapters—is the shortest of the three; its author might be an Irish writer from the ninth century or later. The second can be found in at least eleven manuscripts, has about 275 brief chapters, and seems somewhat later. The third mythography is different: surviving in over forty manuscripts, its fifteen chapters are lengthy and prone to digressions and personal opinions as well as longer allegorical comments; the author is claimed in many copies to be one Alberic of London, who might have been a canon of St Paul's *c.*1160, but some copies refer instead to Alexander Neckam. Recent decades have produced new editions of the first and second mythographers' works, but not the third. Pepin's translation uses these newer editions, and aims to make all three more readily available for easy reading as well as for further research; as such, it is a welcome addition to the bookshelf.

J.S. Mackley's *The Legend of St Brendan: A Comparative Study of the Latin and Anglo-Norman Versions* looks into elements of the fantastic following Tzvetan Todorov's model, dividing the discussion into parts representing the *Legend*'s own tripartite structure in the Anglo-Norman version, a translation of which is conveniently added in an appendix. First, some background information on authorship, audience, manuscripts, sources, and subsequent heritage is presented. Mackley notes that supernatural elements are added gradually for verisimilitude; accordingly, the second chapter, 'Accepting the Fantastic: From the Familiar to the Fantastic-Uncanny', summarizes Todorov's model and traces these steps. 'The Marvels of the Ocean: From the Fantastic-Uncanny to the Marvellous' looks deeper into how the unnatural may be treated as if it were natural, into the patently implausible scenes concerning conflicts of monsters, and into scenes which are in the Latin but not the Anglo-Norman. 'The Mirrors of Salvation' turns to the final sections, the Crystal Pillar and the Smithy of Hell, and then to the paired opposites, Judas Iscariot and Paul the Hermit, before considering Paradise, whose treatment differs between the Latin and the Anglo-Norman. The general conclusion notes that the Latin text seems more like hagiography directed towards a clerical audience, emphasizing an Irish connection, while the Anglo-Norman includes elements of romance and may be more suitable for a secular, courtly audience, especially one in England.

Concentrating on roughly the first two centuries after the Conquest, C.S. Watkins ranges widely through chronicles for evidence of his *History and the Supernatural in Medieval England*, with forays into penitentials, sermons, *vitae*, *miracula*, and other types of material, and expands at times into Normandy, Wales, and Scotland because the written materials do not respect political boundaries. Typical chronicles used are those by Gerald of Wales, William of Newburgh, Orderic Vitalis, and Walter Map. The opening chapter enquires into what the conceptual categories were, looking at the background of several chroniclers and considering the interplay between the natural and supernatural according to human experience, then providing a few types of the supernatural beliefs. The next chapter ranges over various aspects of surviving paganism, including the possibility that events may be neither Christian nor pagan survivals, especially if the churchmen writing about them did not identify them as such. A constant danger was that the laity viewed holy things as useful charms to protect them against worldly misfortunes: holy water or ritual words could banish demons, regardless of a person's faith, so some chroniclers included stories that emphasized true belief, at times overseen by an intercessionary saint. Thinking that things have secret properties that could be exploited led to an understandable concern with magic, necromancy, divination, prophecy, and astrology. Wondering about the dead seemed to bring about not just visions of the afterlife but a growing sense of a possibility of purgation, even a Purgatory, as well as concerns about revenants and ghosts. Since chroniclers recorded all these wonders but seemed sometimes to have difficulty coming to terms with them, Watkins looks more closely at treatments by Walter Map, Gerald of Wales, and Gervase of Tilbury, and then moves on to clerical appropriation of wonders. School-trained churchmen in the late twelfth and early thirteenth centuries entered service in parishes where, unavoidably, parochial beliefs were to varying degrees inconsistent with or simply outside orthodox faith; coming from those very parishes, the churchmen shared concepts with the laity and helped the church adjust to them at the same time they worked to correct them.

Two most welcome articles are published this year on the thirteenth-century poem 'Judas'. First, John C. Hirsch proffers 'The Earliest Known English Ballad: A New Reading of "Judas" ' (*MLR* 103[2008] 931–9), presenting a new transcription with editorial suggestions that three marginal Roman numeral 'glosses' tell the performer to repeat passages, and putting the poem in a Franciscan preaching perspective and a penitential context. Second, Thomas D. Hill's 'The Middle English "Judas" Ballad and the Price of Jesus: Tradition and the Legendary History of the Cross' (*ES* 89[2008] 1–11) identifies the platen of the ballad as the thirty hoops, or circles, that David placed around the Rood Tree in the well-known *Legend of the Cross* before the crucifixion.

In 'Mood Imperative: The Cuckoo, the Latin Lyrics, and the "Cuckoo Song" ' (*PQ* 85[2006] 207–22), James M. Dean asks how 'Sumer is icumen in' relates to the tune's alternative lyric 'Perspice, Christicola', showing thematic completion and arguing that both texts should be presented, for the worldliness of one is balanced by the contemplative reminder of the other. In ' "The werste lay that euer harper sange with harp": The Forms of Early Middle English Satire' (*Comitatus* 39[2008] 113–35), Ben Parsons reviews the scholarship on satire and uses 'Sinners Beware', 'A Lutel Soth Sermun', the *Land of Cokayne*, and the 'Satire on the Consistory Courts' to conclude that the satires often ironically deflate multiple values and are not simple complaints or supports of social norms.

Dealing with Latin materials, John Haines poses but does not resolve the question 'Did John of Tilbury Write an *Ars notaria*?' (*Scriptorium* 62[2008] 46–73). Haines uses internal and external evidence to show the hermetic *Ars notoria scribendi* is far more likely to date from after *c*.1220 and to be possibly by Edmund of Canterbury or, better yet, Roger Bacon, who was interested in magical and hermetic works. And in 'Ein Kommentar aus dem frühen 14. Jahrhundert zu Geoffrey von Monmouth "Prophetiæ Merlini" ' (*Mittellateinisches Jahrbuch* 43[2008] 223–40), Carl Lukas Bohny briefly describes the commentary in Trinity College, Dublin, MS 496 (E.6.2), written probably *c*.1284–1307, and the backgrounds and sources of the sixth and eighteenth prophecies. We should also note Donald Matthew's 'The Incongruities of the St Albans Psalter' (*JMH* 34[2008] 396–416), which examines a number of features, notably the inclusion of the *Chanson d'Alexis*, to observe that the connection to Christina of Markyate is probably unprovable, for Richard, abbot of St Albans, is most likely responsible for inclusion of that verse life. According to John Spence in 'Anglo-Norman Prose Chronicles and their Audiences' (*EMS* 14[2008] 27–59), the early provenance of the manuscripts and their contents support the conclusion that their readers were primarily English, and fairly well off, and that they favoured a wide variety of works in Latin and French.

Jennifer Arch reads Thomas Usk's poem as 'The Boethian *Testament of Love*' (*SP* 105[2008] 448–62) and argues that Usk may have been understanding Boethius differently from what we expect on four points: the process of education, politics, heroism, and life and death. In ' "A good reder and a deuout": Instruction, Reading, and Devotion in the *Wise Book of Philosophy and Astronomy*' (*JEBS* 10[2007] 107–27), Carrie Griffin describes the fourteenth-century work's contents and many manuscript environments, professional and popular, to show the author's awareness of a widely varying readership, with an eye on how the *Wise Book* resembles popular devotional texts. Niamh Pattwell focuses on 'Providing for the Learned Cleric: Schemas and Diagrams in *Sacerdos Parochialis* in British Library MS Burney 356' (*JEBS* 10[2007] 129–49), the vernacular work made professional. Lay piety is further explored in studies of the psalms. Annie Sutherland surveys the 'English Psalms in the Middle Ages' (*BLR* 21[2008] 75–92): Rolle's, the Wycliffite, the fourteenth-century Midland Prose Psalter, and the earlier Metrical or Surtees Psalter, putting these in the context of *The Chastising of God's Children* with its awkward stance between the Vulgate and the vernacular, and observing other works accompanying these in the manuscripts. Eamon Duffy's 'The Psalms and Lay Devotion in the Late Middle Ages' (*BLR* 21[2008] 93–105) turns to the psalms in books of hours continuing into the Tudor period, and considers what psalms people read and how they read and understood them in a devotional way; he finds a rift around the 1530s, when Latin turned to bilingual and then just English texts for the pious.

Coincidentally following the same linguistic shift, Richard Newhauser surveys the tradition of 'Preaching the "Contrary Virtues" ' (*MS* 70[2008] 135–62), in which various sins are matched with opposing virtues, not always with only one per sin; this is not an English tradition only, but Newhauser does stress materials from late medieval England, in Latin or English, including the likes of John Mirk, Chaucer's *Parson's Tale*, Reginald Pecock, and Wyclif. (See above for Hanna's edition of another relevant text, the *Speculum Vitae*.) Wycliffite materials have been the subject of close scrutiny in recent years. Asking 'Could the Gospel Harmony *Oon of Foure* Represent an Intermediate Version of the Wycliffite Bible?' (*SN* 80[2008] 160–76), Paul Smith closely examines translations and syntax to decide in favour, adding that it is independent of the Wycliffite Bible. Stephen Shepherd collects a variety of information to argue the provenance for 'A Wycliffite Bible Possibly Owned by Sir Henry Spelman and Ole Worm' (*N&Q* 55[2008] 269–73), now in Texas. The difficulty of expressing certain ideas through language is the focus of Rick

McDonald's 'The Perils of Language in the Mysticism of Late Medieval England' (*MysticsQ* 34:iii–iv[2008] 45–70), which works through the *Ancrene Wisse*, Walter Hilton, Julian of Norwich, the *Cloud of Unknowing*, Margery Kempe, *The Book of Privy Council*, and Richard Rolle, all of whom decry their inability to express the ineffable well, and tend to resort to sensual terms to describe their experiences and intents.

Two essays in *What Nature Does Not Teach: Didactic Literature in the Medieval and Early-Modern Periods*, edited by Juanita Feros Ruys, are of interest in reminding us of several important works. First, Anne M. Scott's '"For lewed men y vndyr toke on englyssh tonge to make this boke": *Handlyng Synne* and English Didactic Writing for the Laity' (pp. 377–400) reviews Mannyng's choice of English and his intended audience, both within the Sempringham Gilbertine community and extending to the laity outside its walls (such as midwives), and shows how his exempla, use of dialogue, cross-references, and local references further his ends. Second, as Philippa Bright describes in 'Anglo-Latin Collections of the *Gesta Romanorum* and their Role in the Cure of Souls' (pp. 401–24), the Anglo-Latin versions were often used as resources for the clergy: the tales have greater authority, verisimilitude, character motivation, drama, and audience appeal thanks to a variety of textual differences; the moralizations share some features of sermons; tales and moralizations are enhanced for didactic effect; and the manuscript environments support such an interpretation.

Scientific works can help illuminate literary texts. According to *Sidrak and Bokkus*, Karl Steel observes in 'How To Make a Human' (*Exemplaria* 20[2008] 3–27), resemblances between humans and animals are made in order to subject the animals and dominate them, acts which effectively define 'the human'. In 'From Popular Science to Contemplation: The Clouds of *The Cloud of Unknowing*' (*E&S* 61[2008] 13–34) Gillian Rudd views the clouds through *Sidrak and Bokkus* and Trevisa's translation of Bartholomæus Anglicus, *On the Properties of Things*; their perceived natural qualities are reflected in and influence the *Cloud*'s discussion, naturally so because the author worked within contemporary understanding of the properties of clouds. 'Jolly Jankin Meets Aristotle' (*JEBS* 11[2008] 223–9) is Ralph Hanna's way of showing how an unrecorded fourteenth-century Middle English couplet glosses and is explained by a passage in Michael Scot's Latin translation of Aristotle's *De animalibus*, and how this fragment adds to the world of 'Jolly Jankin' and 'A Midsummer Day's Dance' while staying within the academic world. Peter Murray Jones describes 'The *Tabula medicine*: An Evolving Encyclopedia' (*EMS* 14[2008] 60–85), created in England in the fifteenth century in Latin for mendicants and scholars who seemed active in adding to it, an easy task since it is alphabetical and left space for supplementing the practical medical information. Physical and spiritual travel are brought out in A.C. Spearing's 'The Journey to Jerusalem: Mandeville and Hilton' (*EssaysMedSt* 25[2008] 1–17), touching on the authorial 'I' and style, and devoting more space to method, goals, and a kind of relativism. (See also Susanna M. Yeager's *Jerusalem in Medieval Narrative*, below.)

In 'Image, Ideology, and Form: The Middle English *Three Dead Kings* in its Iconographic Context' (*ChauR* 43[2008] 48–81), Ashby Kinch delves into the poem whose manuscript is *De tribus regibus mortuis* (by which it is better known) and explores how it mirrors and alters specific visual motifs; the poem and tradition may well have been meant to remind patrons of the need for intercessory prayers for ancestors. Images include maps, which need to be read in special ways. Thus, two articles in Bork and Kann's *The Art, Science, and Technology of Medieval Travel* should be noted. First, on the analogy of *Arma Christi* and *Exultet* rolls, in 'Informal Catechesis and the Hereford *Mappa Mundi*' (pp. 127–41), Dan Terkla takes ekphrasis as the pedagogical use of the map, which he believes was installed next to the shrine of St Thomas Cantilupe and used for instruction of the laity, including pilgrims. Nick Millea prefers not to answer his question 'The Gough Map: Britain's Oldest Road Map, or a Statement of Empire?' (pp. 143–56), but he notes that the map may now be viewed for free at the Oxford digital library (<http://www.odl.ox.ac.uk>), and surveys the map's many features, commenting on recent cartographic work and pointing out that the most accurately depicted areas seem to be north-west of London.

For additional thoughts on the Peasants' Revolt and other political matters, we might consider Helen Lacey's '"Grace for the Rebels": The Role of the Royal Pardon in the Peasants' Revolt of 1381' (*JMH* 34[2008] 36–63), on understandings of royal mercy in various quarters. A reaction to the revolt may also explain 'John de Cobham and Cooling Castle's Charter Poem' (*Speculum* 83[2008] 884–916), Cristina Maria Cervone explains, reading it in the recent 'documentary culture' frame, since Cobham's ambiguous but highly visible quatrain requires a document-based reading ability among passers-by, for whom it was intended. Brantley L. Bryant's 'Talking with the Taxman about Poetry: England's Economy in "Against the King's Taxes" and *Wynnere and Wastoure*' (*SMRH* 5[2007] 219–48) contrasts the anti-tax Anglo-Norman poem with the pro-tax Middle English one—both of the fourteenth century—and fine-tunes their sentiments to show the rationales behind them as reflecting changed national issues and thus perceived moral obligations.

Derek G. Neal's *The Masculine Self in Late Medieval England* is not about swordplay, power, and status so much as a closer investigation of how masculinity was understood more typically in daily affairs. Accordingly, most of the book is devoted to a historical examination of documents of various sorts, with occasional literary references (all texts are given in modern English, unless some special feature in the original is noted). The first chapter is devoted to establishing that truth and openness were primary and opposed to guile (like the main characters of *Gamelyn* and *Amis and Amiloun*); the second focuses on responsibility with regard to the managing of household and property, whether one's own or another's (three romances are mentioned briefly); and the third turns to the body and to fashion and the social status it could confer. The fourth looks at a number of romances to see how the documentary evidence might be revealed through literature interpreted psychoanalytically, since they are often concerned with identity. Texts examined are *Partenope of Blois, Bevis of Hampton, Lybeaus Desconus, Of Arthour and of Merlin, Sir Perceval of Galles, Sir Gawain and the Green Knight,* and *Ywain and Gawain.*

Nicole R. Rice's *Lay Piety and Religious Discipline in Middle English Literature* begins in the late fourteenth century and closes in the early fifteenth. At its heart lie the *Abbey of the Holy Ghost*, *Fervor amoris*, *Book to a Mother*, *The Life of Soul*, and Walter Hilton's *Mixed Life*, and these are interpreted with a firm eye on their lay audience. The first two are 'claustral' works intending to translate terms and understandings of cloistered devotion to that audience, while the last three are 'clerical' ones aiming to imbue the laity with a priestly mode of study and pastoral care. After introductory groundwork on lay devotion after the Black Death, with some emphasis on Wyclif's writings, the opening chapter discusses the *Abbey of the Holy Ghost* and *Fervor amoris* as revisions of their predecessors within a fairly traditional communal environment; in the light of this, Chaucer's *Shipman's Tale* is a cautionary tale of a merchant and monk uneasily passing between spiritual and worldly riches. Thereafter, the latter three works are viewed as laying out a new orthodoxy via a dialogue between the reader and a priestly author, identifying Christ with the Bible and allowing unmediated contact between scripture and the reader. A closer look at Hilton's *Mixed Life* and its wealthy reader brings out further issues of lay pastoral care, notably charity, also reflected in Langland. Whether women could assume the clerical role of preaching is a difficult issue; accordingly, Rice looks at what Wyclif has to say about it, explores the *Book to a Mother* with its widow-reader, and casts an eye on the *Wife of Bath's Prologue* to show the complicated nature of the issue. The conclusion carries these many concerns into the the period after Arundel's Constitutions and Nicholas Love's *Mirror of the Blessed Life of Jesus Christ*, noting the continued circulation of the five basic works of concern and remarking on their persistent and mutable orthodoxy in a curious time of change.

In *Later Medieval English Literature*, Douglas Gray presents a literary guide for appreciating the fifteenth century (and early sixteenth). Varying degrees of depth are employed, and the emphasis throughout is to entertain as well as instruct. His introduction covers England in its European and global context, popular and learned beliefs, book ownership and patronage, and language change and use. Prose, which occupies nearly half the tome, opens with ' "Practical" Prose' (amusing bits from the Paston letters, more general *Fachliteratur*, and histories and chronicles) before moving on through Malory and later prose romances, tales and jests (Reynard the fox, *Solomon and Marcolfus*, etc.), exempla and moral learning (for example *Dicts and Sayings of the Philosophers*, William Worcester's *Boke of Noblesse*, Reginald Pecock), Lollards, their opponents, sermons and religious instruction and devotion, mystics, and more. 'Poetry' surveys Hoccleve, Lydgate, assorted didactic verse (for example Capgrave, Bokenham, *Stans puer ad mensam*), Chaucerian poems like *The Floure and the Leafe* and *The Court of Love*, secular and sacred lyrics, romances and tales (Arthurian, Gawain stories, Thomas Chestre, outlaw tales, and so on), and the rather late poets Stephen Hawes, Alexander Barclay, and John Skelton. Scottish writing gets its own introduction, covering international perceptions and relations, languages, and other subjects. Gray then turns to Wintoun's *Original Chronicle*, Hary's *Wallace*, *The Kingis Quair*, *The Quare of Jelusy*, and Holland's *The Buke of the Howlat* in one chapter, with many other poets or poems brought up in passing. Then follow discussions of Henryson, Dunbar, and Douglas. For drama, Gray draws upon many plays, remnants, and references to lay a groundwork of dramatic and comedic presentations into the early sixteenth century, before he turns to the Old and New Testament cycles, the morality plays, and interludes.

Simon Horobin and Alison Wiggins's 'Reconsidering Lincoln's Inn MS 150' (*MÆ* 77[2008] 30–53) discusses textual changes and additions in *Piers Plowman* and *Merlyn* that heighten setting and a dramatic sense between characters; enhanced conventional formulae in the *Seege of Troye*, *Merlyn*, and *King Alisaunder*; and other features that imply adaptation for some kind of performance, if only reading aloud. Lawrence Warner ponders the significance of 'Latin Verses by John Gower and "John of Bridlington" in a *Piers Plowman* Manuscript (BL Add. 35287)' (*N&Q* 55[2008] 127–31), in that their Leonine form unites them and implies reception of Gower and political verse that extended beyond the works themselves, as is supported to some extent by the manuscript's link to other London manuscripts of Gower, Chaucer, or Langland.

George Shuffelton has a companion essay to his TEAMS edition (for which see above): 'Is There a Minstrel in the House? Domestic Entertainment in Late Medieval England' (*PQ* 87[2008] 51–76), wherein he argues that antiquarian Romantic nostalgia did not create the idea of wandering minstrels but that medieval myth created it or at least maintained it, such as in Ashmole 61, but also Thornton's manuscripts, or the Findern anthology—the household book and its uses seem to have recalled what was perceived as private minstrel performances.

Simon Horobin's 'A Manuscript Found in the Library of Abbotsford House and the Lost Legendary of Osbern Bokenham' (*EMS* 14[2008] 130–62), describes the manuscript and its language, compares its structure and contents to the *Gilte Legende*, reconciles the contents with Bokenham's comments about the lost work, notes the significance of changes from the *Legends of Holy Women* version, and argues that it was owned by Cecily Neville, duchess of York. In 'Usurping "Chaucers dreame": *Book of the Duchess* and the Apocryphal *Isle of Ladies*' (*SP* 105[2008] 207–25), Annika Farber takes the *Isle* as a conscious imitation, just good enough to be in the Chaucer canon for two centuries and mysterious enough on its own. In 'Urbane Boys and Obedient Stonemasons: An Adapted Courtesy Poem in British Library Royal MS 17.A.I' (*JEBS* 11[2008] 213–16), Michael Foster briefly describes a Middle English 'Urbanitas' poem in a Shropshire manuscript. The poem was created by joining three prior poems: one on the history of stonemasonry, an extract from John Mirk's Instructions for Parish Priests, and an 'Urbanitas' in two other manuscripts. Kathleen Kamerick's 'Shaping Superstition in Late Medieval England' (*MRW* 3[2008] 29–53) surveys the varying attitudes towards superstition in court cases and selected works such as Reginald Pecock's *The Repressor of Over Much Blaming of the Clergy*, *The Pore Caitif*, *Speculum Christiani*, *Dives and Pauper*, Alexander Carpenter's *Destructorium viciorum*, *The Doctrinal of Sapience*, the *Apology for Lollard Doctrines*, and Thomas More's *Dialogue*.

Piety continues to be a concern in fifteenth-century studies. A.I. Doyle surveys 'The *Speculum Spiritualium* from Manuscript to Print' (*JEBS* 11[2008] 145–53), a compilation made probably in the very early fifteenth century, mostly in Latin but with some text from Rolle's *Form of Living* and two Middle English poems, which was widely owned not just in England but also on the continent; its sources include Hilton and William Flete in addition to the usual patristic and medieval theologians. Jenny Rebecca Rytting examines 'The Literary and Devotional Contexts of Julian of Norwich's ABCs' (*MysticsQ* 34:iii–iv[2008] 71–84), for the alphabet was the beginning of knowledge and therefore signified much more than itself, as well as being an ordering principle and a mnemonic tool. Additional background for lay piety may be found in Peter D. Clarke's 'New Evidence of Noble and Gentry Piety in Fifteenth-Century England and Wales' (*JMH* 34[2008] 23–35), which uses registers of the papal penitentiary to study what requests the gentry made of the pope for their souls' sake.

Chris Nighman's 'Citations of "Noster" John Pecham in Richard Fleming's Sermon for Trinity Sunday: Evidence for the Political Use of Liturgical Music at the Council of Constance' (*MSSN* 52[2008] 31–41) urges that the 1417 sermon and music were used to keep the English delegation from losing its status as a 'nation' at the council. Susan Powell's 'Cox Manuscript 39: A Rare Survival of Sermons Preached at Syon Abbey?' (*MSSN* 52[2008] 42–62) notes that the manuscript was donated by a brother of Syon, bound there, and entered into the library register, but that performance is uncertain. Margaret Connolly gives a good reminder, in 'Practical Reading for Body and Soul in Some Later Medieval Manuscript Miscellanies' (*JEBS* 10[2007] 151–74), of how modern distinctions between medical and devotional materials do not apply to the past, and that scientific, spiritual, and superstitious works were gathered together as they appealed and were found fitting and convenient. Similarly, Nicole R. Rice presents a case study of mercantile literary culture in 'Profitable Devotions: Bodley MS 423, Guildhall MS 7114, and a Sixteenth-Century London Pewterer' (*JEBS* 10[2007] 175–83), focusing on vernacular works like *Pore Caitiff*, *Fervor amoris*, and an *Ars moriendi*. That *Pore Caitiff* enhanced doctrinal understanding of the Creed and Decalogue is the argument of Moira Fitzgibbons's 'Poverty, Dignity, and Lay Spirituality in *Pore Caitiff* and *Jacob's Well*' (*MÆ* 77[2008] 222–40); even as the former stresses individuality and charity towards the poor, the latter urges communal participation and reminds the audience than the poor and elderly deserve dignity as well as charity. Atsushi Iguchi's 'Translating Grace: The *Scala Claustralium* and *A Ladder of Foure Rongs*' (*RES* 59[2008] 659–76) compares the original with the fifteenth-century translation, which seems more fully explanatory and affective, less intellectual, than the Latin, and perhaps intended for a wider readership including the laity, not just Carthusians.

The most recent *Florilegium* (23:i[2006]) is a Festschrift, *Confronting the Present with the Past: Essays in Honour of Sheila Delany*, with only a few articles relevant here, the first actually at the very edge of our coverage. Brenda M. Hosington's 'Translation, Early Printing, and Gender in England, 1484–1535' (*Florilegium* 23:i[2006] 41–67) dips into fourteen translations, such as *The Book of the Knight of the Tower*, *The Dictes and Sayengs of the*

Philosophres, and *The fyftene joyes of maryage*—noting a slight shift to fewer misogynistic satires, some association with Chaucer, and a growth in home-grown works, both pro- and anti-feminine. In 'The Authorship of the Poems of Laurence Minot: A Reconsideration' (*Florilegium* 23:i[2006] 145–53), A.S.G. Edwards reviews the manuscript and poems for clues to the poems' transmission history; since Minot identifies himself in only two poems and since the works cover nearly two decades of historically separated events, he may not have authored them all. Lawrence Besserman's '*Imitatio Christi* in the Later Middle Ages and in Contemporary Film: Three Paradigms' (*Florilegium* 23:i[2006] 223–49) outlines the several focuses on physical suffering (e.g. *Meditations on the Life of Christ*, translated for lay use by Nicholas Love), on sexuality (e.g. the *Meditations* and an earlier verse translation, *Meditations on the Supper of Our Lord*), and on humility and teaching (e.g. Walter Hilton's *Scale of Perfection* and Wyclif).

Several new articles deal with chronicles and chroniclers. James Wade's 'Abduction, Surgery, Madness: An Account of a Little Red Man in Thomas Walsingham's *Chronica maiora*' (*MÆ* 77[2008] 10–29) concerns a young man deprived of his brain for six years by a mysterious beautiful lady, placing it in the context of other marvels reported in chronicles and literature, and wondering why Walsingham included it. In 'The Unoriginality of Tito Livio Frulovisi's *Vite Henrici Quinti*' (*EHR* 123[2008] 1109–31), David Rundle argues that Frulovisi used the *Vita et Gesta Henrici Quinti*, not vice versa, and tries to explain various features through Frulovisi's relationship with Humfrey, duke of Gloucester. More focused, Anne Curry studies 'The Battle Speeches of Henry V' (*RMSt* 34[2008] 77–97)—mainly Agincourt—across fifteenth- and sixteenth-century chronicles and histories, for their themes, motifs, borrowings, and revisions. Anne F. Sutton assembles materials for a remarkably detailed biography of 'Robert Bale, Scrivener and Chronicler of London' (*EMS* 14[2008] 180–206), working to strengthen the likelihood that he was indeed the author of 'Bale's Chronicle' but also providing a good picture of fifteenth-century scriveners' life. And Philip Caudrey's 'William Worcester, the *Boke of Noblesse*, and Military Society' (*NMS* 52[2008] 191–211) sets William as an antiquarian in East Anglia to establish the historical background for his lamentation of the decline of chivalry in the *Boke*.

Robin Hood is still a popular topic. Anthony J. Pollard attempts to trace the early fictional development of 'Robin Hood, Sherwood Forest and the Sheriff of Nottingham' (*NMS* 52[2008] 113–30) in the fourteenth and fifteenth centuries, surveying a number of points and reminding us that real-world references grant verisimilitude to imaginary works. Extending closer to the present are the essays in Lois Potter and Joshua Calhoun's collection of papers from the fifth International Association for Robin Hood Studies conference: *Images of Robin Hood: Medieval to Modern*, broadly divided in two parts and illustrated with thirty-nine plates, six in colour. The first part is described as being 'Medieval', and its opening section, 'Origins and Others', contains Stephen Knight's 'Robin Hood: The Earliest Contexts' (pp. 21–40) on the play-games, their frequent location in seaports, and the French *bergerie* as the origin; Stuart Kane's '*The Outlaw's Song of Trailbaston*, the Green Man, and the Facial Machine' (pp. 41–50) on how the Anglo-Norman poem's outlaw is faceless in 'the medieval imaginary' (p. 49); Stephen D. Winick's 'Reynardine and Robin Hood: Echoes of an Outlaw Legend in Folk Balladry' (pp. 51–9), which argues that the eighteenth-century ballad 'Reynardine' is an outlaw ballad related to Robin Hood ballads; and John Marshall's 'Picturing Robin Hood in Early Print and Performance: 1500–1590' (pp. 60–81), mostly on pictorial representations and with some emphasis on hat and garb.

Another section, 'Image and Society', contains '"Merry" and "Greenwood": A History of Some Meanings' by Helen Phillips (pp. 83–101), looking at reverberations of those terms in the Middle Ages and later; 'The Late Medieval Robin Hood: Good Yeomanry and Bad Performances' by Kimberly A. Thompson (pp. 102–10), noting how Robin's shifting identities are a reaction to attempts to identify him; and '"From the Castle Hill they came with violence": The Edinburgh Robin Hood Riots of 1561' by Michael Wheare (pp. 111–20), an exploration of reactions against the Protestant banishing of every Robin Hood parade and game, with its 'Abbott of vnressoun' and May queen. The 'Postmedieval' part opens with a section entitled 'Image and Word', containing Henry Griffy's 'The Work of Robin Hood: Art in an Age of Mechanical Reproduction' (pp. 123–37), on the 1947 *Song of Robin Hood*; and Jill May's 'Robin Hood's Home Away from Home: Howard Pyle and his Art Students' (pp. 138–51)—the students in question are N.C. Wyeth and Charlotte Harding. The next section, 'Word and Image', has '"There was something about him that spoke of other things than rags and tatters": Howard Pyle and the Language of Robin Hood' by Alan T. Gaylord (pp. 153–73), enjoying the voices, especially the mirth, in Pyle's Oldë English; 'The Play's the Thing: Tom Sawyer Re-enacts Robin Hood' by Patricia Lee Yongue (pp. 174–87), with some comparison to the 1844 *Robin Hood* by Stephen Percy (Joseph Cundall); '"A Song of Freedom": Geoffrey Trease's *Bows Against the Barons*' by Michael R. Evans (pp. 188–96), a 1934 socialistic version, pioneering for its revisionism; and 'Picturing Marian: Illustrations of Maid Marian in Juvenile Fiction' by Sherron Lux (pp. 197–207), noting how the pictures show conventional gender roles, no matter what the text might indicate. The last section, 'Image and Performance', has Yoshiko Uéno's 'Male Cross-Dressing in Kabuki: Benten the Thief' (pp. 209–216), about a late nineteenth-century thief whose leader Daemon is the chivalric thief; Jianguo Chen's 'Figures of "Robin Hood" in the Chinese Cultural Imaginary' (pp. 217–33), where bandits can just be those who have lost to prevailing powers; Judy B. McInnis's 'The Images of Robin Hood and Don Juan in George Bernard Shaw's *Man and Superman*' (pp. 234–41), which is much more on the Don Juan image; Orly Leah Krasner's 'To Steal from the Rich and Give to the Poor: Reginald de Koven's *Robin Hood*' (pp. 242–55), on an opera premiering in 1890 and receiving some success; and Lorraine Kochanske Stock's 'Recovering Reginald de Koven's and Harry Bache Smith's "Lost" Operetta *Maid Marian*' (pp. 256–65), which opened in 1891 and survives in three typescript librettos.

Third to appear in its series but chronologically the first is *The Oxford History of Literary Translation in English*, volume 1: *To 1550*, edited by Roger Ellis. The thick vade mecum is divided into six unequally sized parts, the first of which is an almost obligatory 'Contexts of Translation', in which we find John Burrow surveying 'The Languages of Medieval England' (pp. 7–28) before and after the Conquest, with comments on knowledge of Hebrew and Greek, as well as the Celtic languages, and well-nuanced coverage of French and Latin. Next, Tim William Machan briefly discusses 'Manuscript Culture' (pp. 29–44), ranging across content, layout, mark-up, and issues of value in a small space; and Helen Phillips contemplates 'Nation, Region, Class, and Gender' (pp. 45–69) before and after the Conquest, with special attention to translations before and after 1350. The second part consists solely of Nicholas Watson's 'Theories of Translation' (pp. 71–91), summarizing the traditional notions and casting an eye on particular cases like Capgrave, the Wycliffite Bible, and Gavin Douglas, among others. The third part turns to 'The Translator', with an overview preceding chapters on the main figures, including Robert Grosseteste, because, as Ellis explains in the introduction to this part (pp. 95–7), 'study of translation in English in the Middle Ages runs a risk of distortion if it ignores the wider context of translation represented by the important activity of translation into Latin' (p. 96). Ellis opens with an overview of 'Patronage and Sponsorship of Translation' (pp. 98–115) before the chapters on individual translators: Robert Stanton takes on 'King Alfred' (pp. 116–25), Philipp W. Rosemann discusses 'Robert Grosseteste' (pp. 126–36), Barry Windeatt covers 'Geoffrey Chaucer' (pp. 137–48), Traugott Lawler delves into 'William Langland' (pp. 149–59); and A.E.B. Coldiorn covers 'William Caxton' (pp. 160–9).

The fourth part is Edward Wheatley's 'The Developing Corpus of Literary Translation' (pp. 171–89), a swift survey before and after 1300, followed by observations on ownership. The fifth part, 'Subjects of Translation', opens with David Lawton's complex yet engaging look at versions of 'The Bible' (pp. 193–233). This is followed by Vincent Gillespie on 'Religious Writing' (pp. 234–83), Alexandra Barratt on 'Women Translators of Religious Texts' (pp. 284–95), Rosalind Field on 'Romance' (pp. 296–331), Thea Summerfield, with Rosamund Allen, on 'Chronicles and Historical Narratives' (pp. 332–63), Stephen Medcalf on 'Classical Authors' (pp. 364–89), Karla Taylor on 'Writers of the Italian Renaissance' (pp. 390–406), and Paul Acker on 'Scientific and Medical Writing' (pp. 407–20). Finally, the sixth part is 'The Translators: Biographical Sketches' (pp. 421–45), comprising forty-three brief lives plus four references to individuals named in this volume but described in volume 2. The articles represent great learning and extend broadly, and occasionally, deeply, into many aspects one would gladly learn more about; thankfully, each chapter has a bibliography for further reading to aid the student.

In *Jerusalem in Medieval Narrative*, Suzanne M. Yeager looks at the various views the English had of Jerusalem, from travellers' curiosity all the way to crusading zeal, as these were displayed in nine texts from the fourteenth to the sixteenth centuries. Pilgrim narratives discussed include the anonymous *Itinerarium cuiusdam Anglici, 1344–45*, the itineraries of William Wey about a century later, and Sir Richard Torkington's sixteenth-century *Diarie of Englysshe Travell*, as well as several other texts. More literary texts transform Jerusalem into a devotional goal for England or the individual. *Richard, Coeur de Lion*, presents the English in the thirteenth century as superior to the French despite facing the difficulties of the third crusade and European opposition. Readers of *The Siege of Jerusalem* see themselves as the conquering Christians, yet the partly sympathetic treatment of the Jews offers a reminder that even the virtuous must redeem themselves through moral exemplariness in the eyes of God. *The Book of Sir John Mandeville* similarly chastises its readers, offering a spiritual Jerusalem that can be used to enhance national moral fibre. The same kind of crusading rhetoric employed to further personal morality with a spiritual Jerusalem as the goal is found in the translation *The Pilgrymage of the Lyfe of the Manhode*. In a slightly different form in his *Songe du vieil pèlerin* and *Epistre au Roi Richard*, Philippe de Mézière urges that peace between France and England and righteous crusading will obtain the physical Jerusalem even as the city represents a spiritual goal for the individuals striving for it.

Jennifer Bryan's *Looking Inward: Devotional Reading and the Private Self in Late Medieval England* also spans from the late fourteenth to the mid-sixteenth centuries, but mostly restricts itself to before the middle of the fifteenth century. To look inward, one must have an idea of interiority, and the opening chapter concerns itself not with establishing a medieval concept of interiority but with the variety and complexity of approaches Middle English readers and writers themselves had. The introduction and first chapter trace the development of vernacular religiosity in this period and lay out the cultural complications that urge us not to oversimplify medieval lives, working from theory as well as from Richard Rolle, Nicholas Love's *Mirror of the Blessed Lyf of Jesu Crist*, the *Pricke of Conscience*, and many instances of orthodox and even Lollard opinion. The second chapter focuses more on writers and how they used the metaphorical concept of the mirror to approach interiority; first Augustine and then Middle English mirror-tropes, such as the *Myroure of Oure Ladye*, with its conflict between self-consciousness and monastic self-effacement, and the *Cloud of Unknowing*, with its goal of eliminating the self. Through the powerful affective emotion of Passion meditations—such as the late fourteenth-century *A Talkynge of the Love of God* and *The Prickynge of Love* and *Lydgate's Testament*—readers might transform themselves. With these works covered, Bryan then discusses Julian of Norwich's *Showings* as an example of how personal introspection and transformation could assist others in their own search for enlightenment and, second, how Thomas Hoccleve's shorter devotional works, the *Regement of Princes*, and his personal involvement played a role in instructing readers.

J.A. Burrows's *The Poetry of Praise* is not specific to medieval literature but scans from classical to modern works, with special attention to *Beowulf*, Chaucer, and some other Middle English works. His concern is that modern literary audiences are uncomfortable with encomia, preferring to pick out flaws or uncover irony. We are taken on a tour of the historical background from Aristotle through the rhetoricians (and back to Aristotle once his works are made available to the medieval reader) and the poetic theorists, such as John of Garland, Geoffrey of Vinsauf, Benvenuto on Dante, and Dante himself. In Old English, Cædmon's Hymn in praise of God is a logical starting point, to which Burrow adds further examples of paeans to God, to saints, kings, and warriors—and some blame—before moving on to *Beowulf*, including many comments on critical reactions, as well as not a few references to more recent works. Various Middle English lyrics show differing attitudes to ruling monarchs, with increasing positivity as the centuries pass, and the Marian poems are notable in themselves. Longer alliterative works tend to be concerned with martial ability, such as Layamon's *Brut*, the *Morte Arthure*, and the *Wars of Alexander*; *Sir Gawain and the Green Knight*, however, is more subtly executed, so that the praise is tinged with varying degrees of doubt, often best seen in retrospect. This is perhaps best known from Chaucer's epideictic descriptions in the *General Prologue* to the *Canterbury Tales*, where all are praised, but in such a way that the careful reader perceives ironies, not all of which are easily defined—a practice Chaucer seems to have learned from French poets like Machaut and Guillaume de Lorris. Taking into account *Troilus and Criseyde*, the *House of Fame*, and other works shows that simple irony is not typical of Chaucer, though he may use it.

Siân Echard's *Printing the Middle Ages* is not a history of when and how medieval texts were printed; rather, it considers selected texts and visual elements as responding to the desires of various ages. Thus, although it ranges from early printing ventures to the present, it does not organize medieval works chronologically. The introduction, 'Plowmen and Pastiche: Representing the Medieval Book', considers how reproductions carried a special fascination, so that both facsimiles and forgeries found impetus in a willingly receptive audience that appreciated the creation of even *faux* verisimilitude, which develops a life of its own. 'Form and Rude Letters: The Representation of Old English' looks more closely at the re-creation or imitation of fonts (such as by Parker and Junius) for Old English texts, particularly in the sixteenth century, but later in a more generalized visual fashion extending beyond fonts. 'The True History of Sir Guy (and What Happened to Sir Bevis?)' notes that *Bevis of Hampton* had slightly earlier success in print, probably thanks to certain illustrations—for it and its printed contemporary *Guy of Warwick*, a telling illustration may become more authentic than the original text. 'Aristocratic Antiquaries: Gower on Gower' surveys what has been done with the Trentham Manuscript (British Library Add. MS 59495) of Gower's works, from Earl Gower in the eighteenth century to the Roxburghe Club in the nineteenth, amid a broader study of Gower's poetic reception in print. 'Bedtime Chaucer: Juvenile Adaptations and the Medieval Canon' moves outwards from the 1877 *Chaucer for Children* by Mary Haweis, which views medieval times as a childhood long before adult contemporary society; her work and that of others typifies contemporary tastes for named authors who can be pictured and whose lives can be written from the viewpoint of a more advanced, grown-up culture that knows how to present medieval works properly. 'Froissart's Not French (or Flemish): The Travels of a Medieval History' follows those travels as the text of Froissart's *Chroniques* is appropriated to serve any period's self-interest, whether through translation into English or through marginal notes emphasizing English matters, with the text designed to offer authenticity in appearance. The coda, 'The Ghost in the Machine: Digital Avatars of Medieval Manuscripts', must be largely hypothetical, despite the ready examples of digital editions and facsimiles, since technologies tend to change swiftly; popular influences continue to affect scholarly presentation, and competing interests from the market and other spheres cast a shadow between intentions and acts.

Peter Brears's thick volume on *Cooking and Dining in Medieval England* is an informative treat, with documentary and archaeological evidence, many dozens of recipes (with imperial and metric measurement), and many drawings to illustrate features ranging from how to cook a boar's head to how the feast for the archbishop of York's enthronement in 1466 was served (in seventy panels). As often as possible, relevant snippets from Chaucer, Langland, Walter de Bibbesworth, *Gawain and the Green Knight*, Lydgate, and others are inserted into the descriptions of buildings, rooms, cooking and eating utensils, supplies, furniture, preparation, and foods. Institutional arrangements (colleges, monasteries, and so forth) are not Brears's concern, but domestic ones are, principally those of castles and manors, with a continual eye kept on the surviving evidence for cottages. Brears begins with the counting house since household finances determine meals, and devotes individual chapters to such topics as water, the brewhouse, the bakehouse, pottage utensils, leaches, frying, the ewery, table manners, dining in the chamber, and feasts. For those of us who read texts that refer to such matters, the detailed comments with additional information are most useful.

Postcolonialisms: Caribbean Rereading of Medieval English Discourse, by Barbara Lalla, is an interesting survey from Old to Middle English times of history, vocabulary, and literature that confuses and illuminates in various ways, not least through assertions such as 'Middle English verse is outposted to the cultural and historical margins of enlightenment' (p. 1). Using the technical vocabulary of linguistics and literary history, but not fully working within these fields, the volume endeavours to find parallels between the Caribbean and England thanks to the multiple invasions and conquests that were formative to both. The intended audience seems to be Caribbean readers, for references to Jamaican literary works and figures are explained less than those to English ones. The theoretical bounds blinker the discussion: the study 'must restrict itself to strands of development relevant to postcoloniality' (p. 7) and it invokes 'postcolonialism, rather than post-colonialism' (p. 20, the hyphen coinciding with a line-end). The introduction establishes the theoretical bases for the subsequent chapters, and is followed by 'Ancestral Paths', tracking what happened when the Celts and Romans met, then pagan, Germanic Anglo-Saxons, who subsequently interfaced with Christianity and then were confronted by the Vikings and Scandinavian rule; works discussed here range from *The Wanderer* and 'The Wife's Lament' to *Beowulf*. and *The Battle of Maldon*. 'Terms of Contact' balances conquests with language and poetic discourse, finding Middle English to be a conflation of Germanic with Latin, French, Danish, and Celtic, as if lexical borrowing identified linguistic history (pp. 128–9). 'Confrontation and Colonial Sensibility' turns to how the Norman and Angevin kings rewrote history and how romances created tensions between heroes in battle and in faith, such as in Geoffrey of Monmouth, *Havelok the Dane*, Langland, and the *Dream of the Rood*. 'Psychic Fracture' seeks depression in the Middle English lyrics and Chaucer. 'Contending for Discourse' aims to see revision of 'imperial texts' in works such as *Sir Orfeo*, Langland's *Piers Plowman*, and the *Wife of Bath's Tale*. 'Masquerade' views threatening realities and playful burlesques as portrayed in *Sir Gawain and the Green Knight* and the *Canterbury Tales*. 'The Trickster and Disclosure: Postcolonial Rereading and "The Pardoner's Tale"' delves into the various dichotomies of the popular text. Finally, the conclusion attempts to find closure even as it expands its purview to medieval verse more broadly.

Owen Davies's *Grimoires: A History of Magic Books* stretches from ancient times to modern in the Western tradition, is aimed at the general reader, has numerous informative and entertaining illustrations, and surveys the first 2,000 years or so of magic books in the West in thirty-five pages, granting the last 500 years well over 200 pages. For the medieval period (fairly accurately in broad terms), we are referred to Albertus Magnus's comments on works ascribed to Solomon, to the *Ars Notoria*, the *Clavicula Salomonis*, Simon Magus (particularly in post-medieval texts), the *Picatrix*, kabbalah, and quite a few sixteenth-century figures. For that period, we are naturally brought to Hermes Trismegistus, Agrippa, Trithemius, and other figures, who continue their tradition in later periods, together with a number of medieval names or works. As the Old World colonized the New, so old and new magic books spread, and Davies surveys cases in both worlds across time, with heavy emphasis on Romance countries and even a chapter on the US. As the volume approaches the present, more British references are mentioned.

The language of texts continues to be informative and thought-provoking. What bothers Ralph Hanna in 'Lambeth Palace Library, MS 260, and the Problem of English Vernacularity' (*SMRH* 5[2007] 130–99) is separating English works (notably verse) from their trilingual origins and environment, whether macaronic, as in snatches in Latin sermon materials, or interpretative, as in glosses, *ordinatio* (the manuscript's *Northern Homily Cycle* and *Prick of Conscience*), or even authorial guides (e.g. Gower's *Confessio Amantis*, *Piers Plowman*). Examining vocabulary closely in ' "I shalle send word in writing": Lexical Choices and Legal Acumen in the Letters of Margaret Paston' (*MÆ* 77[2008] 241–59), Alison Spedding shows that Margaret—and thus women like her in general—was familiar with a broad array of legal and administrative vocabulary, no doubt greater than the surviving documents reveal, and thus helps uncover the social involvement of women in several areas. Francisco Alonso-Almeida sets out to characterize 'The Middle English Medical Charm: Register, Genre, and Text Type Variables' (*NM* 109[2008] 9–38), with a functional and linguistic base, finding that charms have the general reader as audience, give factual (not affective) information, and are more ritualistic or religious than are recipes. Emphasizing the value of versions of the *OED* before the online version dropped headwords or materials, Merja Stenroos teases out the meaning of 'A-Marscled in "The Man in the Moon"' (*N&Q* 55[2008] 400–4): it could come from a metathesized *malscren*, so *a-marscled in-to þe mawe* is like 'crazy to the core'. Phrases that become common expressions can affect the direction of literary texts, Sarah H. Peverley argues in 'Political Consciousness and the Literary Mind in Late Medieval England: Men "Brought up of nought" in Vale, Hardyng, *Mankind*,

and Malory' (*SP* 105[2008] 1–29); Henry VI's counsellors were the targets of
the charge, which had wider currency in chronicles, politics, and literature.

Christopher Cannon's *Middle English Literature: A Cultural History* is
organized according to five cultural aspects, with less frequently read works
alongside the familiar. 'Technology' views how culture shaped literature: the
stirrup seems responsible for romances and related works, such as Geoffrey of
Monmouth, *King Horn*, and Malory; writing is somehow responsible for
'confessional' works such as the *Ancrene Wisse*, *Prick of Conscience*, and
Mannyng's *Handlyng Synne*. 'Insurgency' reverses this view: literature could
alter the culture around it. Thus complaints arose, such as the *Song of the
Husbandman*, *The Simonie*, *Piers Plowman* and related texts, and several plays;
satires were common, such as the *Satire on the Retinues of the Great*, that *on
the Consistory Courts*, Chaucer, and *Winner and Waster*. 'Statecraft' considers
the interrelationships between literature and politics, well illustrated by
Langland's rodent parliament; censorship is perceptible in Usk's *Testament of
Love*, William Thorpe's *Testimony*, *Mum and the Sothsegger*, and works by
prisoners like Malory and Ashby. Propaganda is obvious in Laurence Minot,
Reginald Pecock, Nicholas Love, and Hoccleve, while counsel is commonplace, as in Lydgate's *Fall of Princes* and Ashby. 'Place' limits its purview;
thus, the schoolroom crops up in the *Proverbs of Alfred*, Chaucer's *Melibee*,
How the Good Wife Taught her Daughter, and *Stans puer ad mensam*; religious
communities are foregrounded in *Ancrene Wisse*, Richard Rolle, and Julian of
Norwich, while the household reigns in *Havelok the Dane* and fifteenth-
century dream visions. Urban features manifest in the *South English
Legendary*, *Pearl*, *London Lickpenny*, and some plays, while roadways and
travel are reflected in Chaucer, *The Stacions of Rome*, *Mandeville's Travels*,
and Margery Kempe. 'Jurisdiction' actually refers to how Middle English
literature obtained autonomy relative to the 'jurisdiction' of other cultural
concerns: the church (the *Northern Passion*, the *South English Legendary*, and
Lydgate), laughter (*The Land of Cockaygne*, beast fables, and fabliaux), and
the aesthetic (*Owl and the Nightingale*, *Pearl*, and Chaucer).

Roger Rosewell's *Medieval Wall Paintings in English and Welsh Churches* is
a visual treat that means to entertain as well as inform, covering in six chapters
the history, subjects, patrons and painters, method of production, interpretation, and history from the Reformation onwards. The history begins with a
fourth-century chi-rho painting in Kent and then explains, peculiarly, that
Anglo-Saxon wall paintings are rare because the collapse of the western
Roman empire meant the end of its occupation of Britain. Romanesque
churches show stories and ideas from across Europe and even from
Constantinople, although apparently 'They were built when books were
scarce, few priests could read Latin and universities did not exist' (p. 12). The
real strengths are liveliness of style and the illustrations, with interesting
discussions of developments in the art. Subjects are divided into nine broad
areas: Old Testament scenes, devotional images of Christ, the life of Christ,
saints, death and the Last Judgement, the Seven Deadly Sins and Seven Works
of Mercy, transgressions, and various allegories and symbols, to which is
appended a brief discussion of subjects expected but not found. While evidence
for patrons is widespread, that for painters tends to be tucked inside

documents of many kinds not prima facie relevant to art. After the discursive text are two appendices that should be of great value to travellers: first, a gazetteer of the main paintings visible to the public at large, listed by by county and location with guides to viewing inside the building and subjects imaged; second, useful also to researchers, a list of those subjects imaged, with brief descriptions followed by lists of locations. Thus, anyone researching St Thomas Becket can quickly find fifty-three locations to visit (listed by name, but not grouped into counties to ease travelling), and in this case asterisks identify the eighteen with paintings of his martyrdom.

2. Women's Writing

Middle English, in the series Oxford Twenty-First Century Approaches to Literature appeared in 2007 in cloth, and in paperback in 2008. This anthology approaches its subject from various perspectives and thematic points of- view, and, as its editor Paul Strohm writes in the introduction, is not mean to be a 'Companion' to Middle English literature, but rather a collection of exploratory essays about 'the less than fully understood' (p. 1). Many of the essays touch on medieval women's writing, including Margery Kempe, Julian of Norwich, and Marie de France. Carolyn Dinshaw's contribution to the volume, 'Temporalities' (pp. 107–23), looks at time in Kempe's *Book*, starting with her understanding of Christ's death as something she immediately experiences, but quickly turns to the time of the *Book*'s editing and its editor Hope Emily Allen. Dinshaw weaves through the essay queer theory and her own sense of time as a scholar of both Allen and Kempe, the people and their writings. In 'Vision, Image, Text' (pp. 315–34), Jessica Brantley looks at what Julian of Norwich and Margery Kempe 'see' in their visions and how religious visions both intersect with and depart from other literary discourses of seeing, such as medieval dream visions. Brantley argues that what she terms literary 'imagetexts' (p. 316) are central to medieval concepts of reading and seeing both. In Nancy Bradley Warren's 'Incarnational (Auto)biography' (pp. 369–85), Julian's 'afterlife' is looked at while Warren examines the seventeenth-century Benedictine nun Margaret Gascoigne's copy of Julian's writings and narratives of Margaret's own contemplation recorded by sister nuns. Warren shows how Julian's text has been read as part of shared mystical experience and extends this idea of a subject 'paradoxically individual and plural at once' (p. 372), extending her discussion to other Middle English texts, including Margery Kempe's *Book* and *Piers Plowman*.

Vincent Gillespie also situates Kempe and Julian's writings among other texts in 'Vernacular Theology' (pp. 401–20), examining the debates and definitions of the terms of his title, as well as the literature both associated with and disenfranchised by the category, focusing especially on the issue of translation and vernacularity. Karen Winstead likewise turns to devotional texts in 'Saintly Exemplarity' (pp. 335–51), evaluating the assumption that 'saints, where meant as exemplars, are always meant as exemplars of the good and not the bad' (p. 336), as well as the assumption that saints' lives are mainly directed at readers of the same gender as the saint. She argues that the fifteenth century provides important generic departures from previous hagiographies that challenge traditional notions of the audience and purpose of Middle English saints' lives. Finally, Marie de France gets her due in Robert M. Stein's 'Multilingualism' (pp. 23–37). Stein examines the manuscript tradition of some of Marie's texts, noting that the trilingualism of post-Conquest England is reflected in these codices, which provide information about both compiler and audience and how they 'read' the languages.

The most significant contribution to Julian studies in 2008 was the publication of *A Companion to Julian of Norwich*, edited by Liz Herbert McAvoy. In her introduction ' "God forbede … that I am a techere": Who, or What, Was Julian?' (pp. 1–16), McAvoy questions what about both Julian's person and her writings has made her such a figure of fascination, to scholars, certainly, but also through popular novels and other ideas of the anchoress and who she is. She nicely situates the current scholarly discussions about Julian in dialogue with the essays in the volume, suggesting that we cannot truly 'know' Julian but that the multitudes of approaches gathered in the collection begin to create a fuller picture, contextualizing her in networks and structures of the Middle Ages and today. McAvoy also situates the scholarly debates surrounding both Julian and her literary production, and lays out some of the issues raised and conclusions drawn by Nicholas Watson and Jacqueline Jenkins in their influential 2006 edition of Julian's texts.

After the introduction, the collection is divided into two parts: 'Julian in Context' and 'Manuscript Tradition and Interpretation'. The essays in the first section of the book aim to place Julian within a social, religious, and historical context; the group of articles is coherent and nicely ordered. The opening essay, 'Femininities and the Gentry in Late Medieval East Anglia: Ways of Being', by Kim M. Phillips (pp. 19–31), proposes for Julian a lower aristocratic upbringing. Cate Gunn's ' "A recluse atte Norwyche": Images of Medieval Norwich and Julian's Revelations' (pp. 32–41) also looks at contemporary Norwich and the culture by which Julian would have been surrounded. In ' "No such sitting": Julian Tropes the Trinity' (pp. 42–52), Alexandra Barratt looks at Julian's environs and suggests that Julian may have known the Ormesby Psalter (which had been displayed at Norwich Cathedral) and that the image of the Trinity therein could have influenced Julian's conception of it, particularly in regard to gender.

Denise N. Baker's 'Julian of Norwich and the Varieties of Middle English Mystical Discourse' (pp. 53–64) places Julian in contrast to traditionally considered 'English mystics', including Margery Kempe, arguing that Julian most likely did not know her contemporaries' texts, but rather participated in a common and 'rich discourse of the contemplative tradition' (p. 55). 'Saint Julian of the Apocalypse', by Diane Watt (pp. 64–74), by contrast, looks at Julian's affinity with her contemporaries, particularly Margery Kempe and Christina of Markyate, placing her within the context of a female spiritual legacy in English culture. Watt argues that Julian resists placing herself within this community of feminine spirituality, but that her theology and comprehension of God are significantly influenced by the tradition. E.A. Jones, in 'Anchoritic Aspects of Julian of Norwich' (pp. 75–87), argues for envisioning Julian in another context—that of the anchorites. The final essay of the section, Annie Sutherland's 'Julian of Norwich and the Liturgy' (pp. 88–98), discusses contemporary liturgy and liturgical practice and how these are reflected in Julian's texts. Sutherland points to textual moments where Julian markedly departs from liturgical teaching, showing how she simultaneously grounds herself in the orthodox and familiar, while allowing for a departure from these things.

The second part of the volume is more textually based, examining the manuscript tradition of Julian's texts as well as new ways it may be approached and interpreted. Barry Windeatt's 'Julian's Second Thoughts: The Long Text Tradition' (pp. 101–15) opens the section, closely comparing the short to the long text and seeing the movement from one to the other as a way to 'chart the development of a mystic mind and a contemplative writer' (p. 101). Windeatt looks particularly at the interpolations and expansions between the two versions. Marleen Cré follows Windeatt with ' "This blessed beholdyng": Reading the Fragments from Julian of Norwich's *A Revelation of Love* in London, Westminster Cathedral Treasury, MS 4' (pp. 116–26), where she looks at both her titular late fifteenth-/early sixteenth-century manuscript which has one text compiled of fragments of several devotional pieces (including Julian's long text) and the mid-fifteenth-century London, British Library MS Additional 37790 (Amherst), a devotional anthology which contains Julian's short text. Focusing on the former, Cré examines the Julian fragments in the context of the whole piece and its juxtaposed texts. Elizabeth Dutton turns to later manuscripts in 'The Seventeenth-Century Manuscript Tradition and the Influence of Augustine Baker' (pp. 127–38), noting that the seventeenth century marks the first surviving appearance of the long text in its entirety (its only, and partial, medieval witness being the manuscript Cré discusses in the previous article). Dutton examines all of the seventeenth-century versions of the long text, including MS St Joseph's College, Upholland, and what influence Augustine Baker, the spiritual adviser to the Cambrai nuns who owned the text, may have had—an issue that McAvoy suggests is 'becoming a contentious contemporary debate' (p. 13).

The final essays in the volume turn away from specific manuscripts and towards matters of interpretation. In 'Julian of Norwich's "Modernist Style" and the Creation of Audience', by Elizabeth Robertson (pp. 139–53), Julian's audience, both intended and incidental, is examined in the context of modernist literature and narrative technique. Robertson argues that Julian eschews linear narrative and erases any distinction between author and audience, and that she is 'committed above all to showing rather than telling her audience what she has seen' (p. 139). Laura Saetveit Miles follows with 'Space and Enclosure in Julian of Norwich's *A Revelation of Love*' (pp. 154–65), where, using Foucault as a theoretical backdrop, she applies the literal space and confinement of the anchorhold to the perception of mystical space and authority presented in the text. Miles also draws on the writings of Bridget of Sweden and Margery Kempe as points of comparison for mystical treatment and comprehension of space.

McAvoy follows Miles with her own contribution to the collection: ' "For we be doubel of God's making": Writing, Gender and the Body in Julian of Norwich' (pp. 166–80). Here, McAvoy turns to Kristeva and semiotics to look at Julian's linguistic choices, arguing that the phallocentrism of the language disallows Julian from fully realizing her mystical experience through text until she moves beyond the corporeal body as metaphor. Ena Jenkins likewise discusses Julian's language in 'Julian's *Revelation of Love:* A Web of Metaphor' (pp. 181–91), analysing the poetic devices of Julian's words, in particular her complex use of metaphor as theological expression. Vincent Gillespie's ' "[S]he do the police in different voices": Pastiche, Ventriloquism and Parody in Julian of Norwich' (pp. 192–207) sees Julian's texts as a heteroglossic expression, drawing on different contemporary styles and elements in her writing. Gillespie points to differences between the short and long texts to elucidate how this pastiche and original expression work throughout Julian's writings. The final essay in the volume, 'Julian's Afterlives' by Sarah Salih (pp. 208–18), turns the reader to post-medieval Norwich and how Julian has been co-opted and incorporated into the modern era, through various media and with different purposes. Salih attempts to grasp what is the essential 'Julian' that continues to fascinate its audience, both academic and non-academic. The volume concludes with a very helpful bibliography, and as a whole is indispensable to scholars working on Julian.

Another important publication regarding Julian this year is Elisabeth Dutton's *Julian of Norwich: The Influence of Late-Medieval Devotional Compilations.* In her introduction Dutton lays out the ways that miscellanies, anthologies, and compilations were used in a devotional context in medieval England. She covers the scholarly debates about Julian: who she was, what literacy and education she may have had, and what access she had to reading and books. Dutton concludes that, while the answers to these questions will forever be in debate, it is clear that the cultural and spiritual milieu in which Julian lived was one that was heavily invested in the idea of the devotional compilation and what that meant. Dutton observes that these texts were intended to blur 'the distinctions between compiler and source, in which the compiler's own voice may be disguised as that of an *auctor*, or the voice of an *auctor* appropriated by the ventriloquism of the compiler' (p. 5). She suggests that Julian's *Revelations* consciously construct God as *auctor* using the techniques of compilation. Julian also uses the elements of compiling for didactic purposes, making the text open to different readers through its construction.

Dutton first looks at the *Revelations* itself and how the short and long texts gesture towards compilations through the structuring principles and order of the text. She discusses the different manuscripts as well, careful to point out what may or may not be Julian's own invention, as there are no autograph copies. The chapter and revelation divisions, she argues, allow for either an 'academic' or a 'devotional' reading and invite the reader to take the text as a whole or in pieces. She also examines how unattributed sources may be worked into the *Revelations*, and how Julian interweaves these into her own authorial control. Dutton elaborates her thesis through chapters that look at Julian's *Revelations* alongside important contemporary compilations, including *The Chastising of God's Children, Speculum Christiani,* and *Contemplations of the Dread and Love of God.* She examines how authors are appropriated or unattributed in these texts and in what ways they construct a reader response to the works at hand. She ends with chapters that look closely at the *Revelations* in relation to *The Lyf of Soule* and *Book to a Mother*, and how their physical and literary forms may illuminate the principles behind the *Revelations'* own layout, imagery, and technique.

The conclusion of Dutton's book focuses on the idea of authorship and authority in medieval devotional texts, examining how Julian may have understood herself in relation to her learning and her writing. Dutton suggests that Julian positions herself as a student of God, and that this humility shows through her work and the way in which she presents it. She turns the focus from Julian's structural practice to her readers' reading practices, and suggests that the culture of compilation which influenced Julian would also direct readers through her *Revelations*.

Julian is central to Carmel Bendon Davis' monograph *Mysticism and Space: Space and Spatiality in the Works of Richard Rolle, 'The Cloud of Unknowing' Author, and Julian of Norwich*. Davis sets up her theoretical and contextual framework over the course of a short introduction and three full chapters, treating 'Physical Space', 'Social Space', and 'The Space of the Text and the Language of Space' before turning to the three authors of the title. Drawing on a wide variety of theorists, including Henri Lefebvre, Michel Foucault, Mikhail Bakhtin, and Pierre Bourdieu, Davis takes 'space' not only to signify a physical environment but also to be implicated in cosmological and philosophical comprehension, both medieval and modern. In her chapter on Julian, 'The Mystical Space of Julian of Norwich', the concluding chapter of the book, Davis examines both the physical questions of Julian's space (here, not the space of the anchorhold, but rather the space of the sickbed in which she has her visions) and the spatiality and metaphor of space in her texts. She argues that the medieval conceptions of space—that it is both receptacle to be filled and that which is contained—are given full expression in Julian's understanding of love and the divine.

Amy Appleford places Julian in the context of the culture of death and dying in 'The "Comene course of prayers": Julian of Norwich and Late Medieval Death Culture' (*JEGP* 107[2008] 190–214). She argues that the constant critical search for Julian's sources should include a closer look at wider devotional culture, such as the death practices of late medieval England. In 'The Literary and Devotional Contexts of Julian of Norwich's ABCs' (*MysticsQ* 34.iii–iv[2008] 71–84), Jenny Rebecca Rytting reads the passage in which Julian writes that her revelations were like receiving 'the beginning of an ABC' in understanding God. Rytting describes all the ways in which ABC primers were used (including in several devotional contexts) and analyses how this may illuminate our comprehension of Julian's analogy.

Julian's rhetoric and comprehension of atonement are explored in George Tolley's short article, '"Love was his meaning" Julian of Norwich and Atonement' (*Theology* 111[2008] 102–7). Bradley Herzog also addresses Julian's theology in 'Somatic Pathways to Christ: Passion, Travail, and Julian of Norwich's Challenge to Christian Neoplatonism' (*Magistra* 14[2008] 34–49), where he suggests that Julian challenges Neoplatonic ideals through her understanding of the body and how it relates both to Christ and to herself.

Many women's texts figure in Jennifer Bryan's *Looking Inward* (also discussed above), where she particularly looks at the kinds of devotional books circulating among the laity and what kind of reader these books construct. Bryan suggests that many late medieval devotional texts construct an interiority in their audiences and that the readers are drawn to the works not necessarily out of piety but out of a desire to understand that inner self. Although she discusses books directed at women (the *Ancrene Wisse*, for example) and Margery Kempe throughout the volume, her concentration on Julian of Norwich will probably be most useful to discuss here. Her chapter 'Profitable Sights: The *Showings* of Julian of Norwich' examines Julian both as a reader and as the author of devotional texts. Bryan shows how, although Julian is clearly indebted to and affected by contemporary Passion meditations, she departs from their descriptive nature and engages in the subjective quality of the idea of a meditation itself, demonstrating this in her writings. She suggests that Julian is deeply aware of and invested in the discourses of inwardness in devotional writings, and that she consciously turns these towards herself and her understanding of Christ and the Trinity.

Throughout Beth Allison Barr's *The Pastoral Care of Women in Late Medieval England*, Margery Kempe is referred to mainly as an example or as evidence to illustrate the relationship between lay people and their clerics. Of course, Barr recognizes that Margery is an exceptional case, but she suggests her *Book* is rich with anecdotes that give some clues as to how women were treated and what was expected of them by their priests and parishes. A letter of Agnes Paston's is likewise used as an example in Katherine L. French's *The Good Women of the Parish: Gender and Religion after the Black Death* to illustrate how important families were both separate from (in terms of seating) and integrated within their parish community. French's book intentionally steers away from discussing aristocratic and noble women, whose experiences, she argues, are markedly different from those of common laywomen, but her excellent monograph will still be of use to anyone studying women between the time of the Black Death and the Reformation, the period she covers.

Sarah Stanbury's fascinating book *The Visual Object of Desire in Late Medieval England* opens with a discussion of the medieval 'fetish' for the devotional object and form. Looking closely at medieval texts, including saints' lives, Chaucer, and Nicholas Love's *Mirror*, Stanbury examines how the devotional object is described and utilized, linking these literary representations to the performance and ritual of medieval devotion and the church, as well as examining how and why the Lollard reaction to devotional visual culture manifested itself. Although she discusses Margery Kempe throughout, she focuses on her most in the final chapter, 'Arts of Self-Patronage in *The Book of Margery Kempe*'. Stanbury opens the chapter by discussing how medieval England gave a kind of 'cultic status' to identified benefactors (through names, images, and coats of arms in plaques, art, and wills), and how Margery's book is a type of record of one benefactor, Margery, with her prayers as currency and donation. With Margery seen as a donor, her role shifts from private to a different kind of public image and voice. Stanbury suggests that Margery's dialogues with Christ reflect the contractual language of patronage: one interested in exchange, naming and heavenly reward for material actions. Margery figuratively paints herself, like a medieval donor in a tableau, into her descriptions of Christ: a Pietà–Man of Sorrows hybrid where Margery is witness and display. Stanbury closes the chapter by linking Margery's conceptions and descriptions to the devotional art and architecture surrounding her in late medieval East Anglia, showing how the medieval culture of the visual permeates the *Book* and its meanings.

Andrew Cole's book on medieval England and Lollardy, *Literature and Heresy in the Age of Chaucer*, also devotes a significant chapter to the study of Margery Kempe and her *Book*. Cole aims to challenge many of the assumptions made about Wycliffism and Lollardy, and, like Stanbury, primarily uses the literary record as source material for his study, searching for what he terms a 'post-Wycliffite character' (p. xiii) in the texts. Also like Stanbury, Cole focuses on Margery Kempe in the final chapter of his book, as a way to both challenge and pull together the other authors studied therein, such as Langland, Chaucer, Hoccleve, and Lydgate. Cole claims that 'Kempe is among the authors who both declare their differences from the juridical forms of orthodoxy that would condemn Wycliffism as heresy and who uses the social typology of the "Lollard" to offer a new perspective on late medieval religiosity' (p. 155). He argues that the idea and vocabulary of the Lollard is used in Kempe's text affectively, a 'new discourse of shame' (p. 156). Kempe uses this concept of shame as part of her own affective piety and mysticism, as well as a way to position herself in orthodox opinions in opposition to the shame associated with the Lollard. Cole also juxtaposes Kempe to Philip Repingdon, a former Wycliffite who recants and is ultimately held up as a figure of orthodoxy. Cole suggests that Margery identifies with Repingdon because it allows an embracing of both her heterodox and orthodox tendencies and a model for effectively erasing those binaries.

Valerie Allen discusses Margery's role as pilgrim in 'As the Crow Flies: Roads and Pilgrimage' (*EssaysMedSt* 25[2008] 27–38). Allen argues that there is meaning inherent in the pilgrimage roads that is separate from their intended destination, and uses Kempe's description of her travels to Jerusalem as her primary example of this. Ruth Summar McIntyre also addresses questions of pilgrimage along with generic conventions in Kempe's *Book* with 'Margery's "Mixed Life": Place Pilgrimage and the Problem of Genre in *The Book of Margery Kempe*' (*ES* 89[2008] 643–61), where she examines Margery's public and private identities and how these correspond to the ideas of 'pilgrim', 'mystic', and her authorial identity. María Beatriz Hernández Pérez further examines genre in 'Both Human and Divine: The Conflict between Confession and Gossip in *The Book of Margery Kempe*' (*Selim* 14[2007] 163–95) and argues that, although Kempe's *Book* can be read as an autobiographical confession, and through the lens of confessional practice, it is most fruitful to see it as a combination of confession and gossip. Gossip allows for a wider communal view of the text that includes some fictionalization and subversion.

Autobiography is also the subject of Alysia Kolentsis's 'Telling the Grace that She Felt: Linguistic Strategies in *The Book of Margery Kempe*' (*Exemplaria* 20[2008] 225–43), where she analyses Kempe's text through 'the practices of women's life writing' (p. 225). Kolentsis focuses on Kempe's linguistic choices, including naming and syntax, to demonstrate how Kempe is consciously interested in her own authority and subjectivity. Roger Ellis similarly looks closely at language in 'Translation and Frontiers in Late Medieval England: Caxton, Kempe, and Mandeville' (in Merisalo and Pahta, eds., *Frontiers in the Middle Ages: Proceedings of the Third European Congress of Medieval Studies*, pp. 559–83). In this expansive article, Ellis suggests that medieval geographical, cultural, and linguistic frontiers are crossed and erected through the practice of translation, using the many frontiers Kempe crosses (both literally and figuratively) as one of his primary illustrative examples.

Translation is key to Sif Rikhardsdottir's 'The Imperial Implications of Medieval Translations: Old Norse and Middle English Versions of Marie de France's *Lais*' (*SP* 105[2008] 144–64). Rikhardsdottir suggests that the translations of Marie's *lais* into Old Norse and Middle English raise issues about the cultural dominance and influence of Anglo-Norman. John Beston looks at Marie de France's *Lai le Fresne* in relation to Renaut's text in ' "Une bele conjointure": The Structure of *Galeran de Bretagne*' (*Neophil* 92[2008] 19–33), arguing that the latter is a careful and deliberate departure from the former, not a simple expansion of it. Marie's *Guigemar* is the subject of Nicole D. Smith's ' "Estreitement Bendé": Marie de France's *Guigemar* and the Erotics of Tight Dress' (*MÆ* 77[2008] 96–117). Smith examines twelfth-century women's dress and how this is translated into markers of aristocracy and power in Marie's *lais*, using *Guigemar* as her exemplar. Marie de France's *L'Espurgatoire Seint Patriz* is one of the primary subjects of Margaret Burrell's 'Hell as a Geological Construct' (*Florilegium* 24[2007] 37–54). She also looks at Benedeit's *Le Voyage de Saint Brendan* and addresses the geological features of both hell and purgatory as they are described in the two texts.

All of Marie's works are considered in Logan E. Whalen's monograph, *Marie de France and the Poetics of Memory*: her *lais*, fables, the *Espurgatoire* and *La vie seinte Audree* (the last of which Whalen considers to be Marie's work, although this is still constantly in debate). Whalen is interested in how Marie's narrative style incorporates the rhetoric and technique of medieval memory, as reflected in the ways in which her texts use source material and are elaborated in Marie's own style. Central to Whalen's argument is the fact that although Marie 'had no access to the *artes memorativae*, treatises devoted solely to the art of memory that were to develop in the centuries following her own, she nonetheless exemplifies some of the same techniques' (p. 4). Throughout the book, Whalen looks at explicit references to memory, for example in Marie's prologues, but also at the ways in which it is subtly incorporated into the narrative itself through structure, rhetoric, and use of detail.

In 2007 Glyn S. Burgess's *Marie de France Supplement 3* was published. This updates a list of all translations, editions, and studies (including theses and dissertations) related to Marie de France; the original volume was published in 1977, with a two supplements following in 1986 and 1997. This comprehensive supplement will be very useful to readers who are Marie de France scholars, especially as *YWES* did not include work on Marie (or any Anglo-Norman writings) until its 2006 volume.

June Hall McCash takes on an important topic in 'The Role of Women in the Rise of the Vernacular' (*CL* 60[2008] 45–57), suggesting that women's interest in romances, *lais*, and lyric poetry is partly responsible for the increase of vernacular literature in the high Middle Ages. She writes that the move from a heroic culture to a courtly one is necessarily intertwined with the move from Latin to vernacular. Julian, Margery, and Marie de France, among other women writers, are discussed in a comprehensive overview. In ' "I shalle send word in writing": Lexical Choices and Legal Acumen in the Letters of Margaret Paston' (*MÆ* 77[2008] 241–59), Alison Spedding looks closely at the legal vocabulary used in Margaret Paston's letter, suggesting that she had a firm grasp on legal terms and procedures.

Medieval women's writing is the subject of some discussion in *Historical Englishes in Varieties of Texts and Contexts*, edited by Masachiyo Amano, Michicko Ogura, and Masayuki Ohkado. The heavily linguistic-oriented collection includes Akinobu Tani's 'The Word Pairs in *The Paston Letters and Papers* with Special Reference to Text Type, Gender and Generation' (pp. 217–31), where Tani examines the language of the Paston letters separately from other papers (such as legal documents or recipes) related to the Pastons. Tani breaks the words up into useful graphs that categorize different usage by the different writers. This essay is followed by Fumiko Yoshikawa's 'Discourse Strategies in Late Middle English Women's Mystical Writing' (pp. 233–44), where she examines the language of time and place in Julian of Norwich's *Revelations* and Margery Kempe's *Book*. Yoshikawa closely reads the two texts and compares the adverbial phrases of time or place that being sentences throughout the narratives.

Texts written for and about women were also important subjects of study this year. Karen Bollerman and Cary J. Nederman discuss the *vita* of Christina of Markyate in 'King Stephen, the English Church, and a Female Mystic: Christina of Markyate's *Vita* as a Neglected Source for the Council of Winchester (August 1139) and its Aftermath' (*JMH* 34[2008] 433–44), suggesting that the *vita* may be the earliest and potentially most accurate description of the Council of Winchester. Two essays look at women in the *Devotio Moderna*. Christoph Burger's 'Late Medieval Piety Expressed in Song Manuscripts of the Devotio Moderna' (*Church History and Religious Culture* 88[2008] 320–45) discusses models of female piety and erotic imagery in a booklet associated with a female Augustinian canon, and perhaps even written by her. Hermina Joldersma, ' "Alternative Spiritual Exercises for Weaker Minds"? Vernacular Religious Song in the Lives of Women of the Devotio Moderna' (*Church History and Religious Culture* 88[2008] 371–93), suggests ways in which song may have been incorporated into the devotional and meditative life of religious women.

Alexandra Barratt's 'English Translations of Didactic Literature for Women to 1550' (in Ruys, ed., pp. 287–301), explores the 'niche market' (p. 287) of translations intended for medieval women. Barratt focuses primarily on religious texts, including saints' lives and religious rules, but also includes some of the non-religious instructional texts such as *The Book of the Knight of La Tour-Landry* in her helpful survey.

Mary Dockray-Miller presents the first edition of 'The Middle English Verse of Boston Public Library MS 124' (*W&Lang* 20[2008] 23–6). The verse in question is prayers from the fourteenth-century Mohun Hours, a woman-owned text whose female audience is reflected in the poems themselves. Monica Green also looks at women's manuscript culture in 'Rethinking the Manuscript Basis of Salvatore de Renzi's *Collectio Salernitana*: The Corpus of Medical Writings in the "Long" Twelfth Century' (in Jacquart and Bagliani, eds., *La Scuola Medica Salernitana: gli autori e i testi*, pp. 15–60) and in 'Reconstructing the *Oeuvre* of Trota of Salerno' (in Jacquart and Bagliani, eds., pp. 183–233). In the first article Green looks at the *Trotula,* a twelfth-century text on women's medicine and cosmetics, and its relation to the school of Salerno, and also examines how this manuscript affects the manuscript tradition of the *Trotula* throughout western Europe (many of the Trotula-related manuscripts were English). In the second article Green looks at the medical texts attributed to 'Trota', assessing the evidence that comes from collating and editing many of these pieces; the essay includes some useful editions of Trota's work.

Monica Green also contributes a monograph, *Making Women's Medicine Masculine: The Rise of Male Authority in Pre-Modern Gynaecology*, which further examines the writings of Trota of Salerno, as well as other women medical practitioners and writers through to the early modern era. The comprehensive volume gives an invaluable overview of women's medical history, complete with references to several texts in both Latin and the vernacular as well as some noteworthy medical images. It will be very helpful for those studying women's bodies, women's writing, or medieval medical history. Laura Jose looks at the male medical tradition and its intersections with gender and madness in medical texts in 'Monstrous Conceptions: Sex, Madness and Gender in Medieval Medical Texts' (*CCS* 5[2008] 153–63).

Cate Gunn's monograph, *Ancrene Wisse: From Pastoral Literature to Vernacular Spirituality*, serves as an excellent introduction to and contextualization of this important thirteenth-century text. The volume is broken into three parts, with the first two placing the *Ancrene Wisse* into its broader, medieval context: 'The Religious Context' and '*Pastoralia* and Vernacular Pastoral Literature'. The first of these is a very helpful historical overview, touching on the Fourth Lateran Council, eucharistic theology, and the spirituality and lifestyle of the beguines and anchorites. The second section places the *Ancrene Wisse* in its literary context, looking at *pastoralia*, devotional literature dedicated 'to the care of souls' (p. 92), as well as sermons and pastoral literature. In the third part, '*Ancrene Wisse*: Text and Context', Gunn turns to the text itself. She begins with a subsection on 'the rhetoric of *Ancrene Wisse*', looking closely at its structure, allusions, and citations. Gunn uses contemporary texts both in comparison with and in contrast to the *Ancrene Wisse*'s rhetorical and structural devices, again making the book especially useful as an introduction to the text. The final two subsections—'*Ancrene Wisse*: Asceticism and Contemplation' and 'Reading *Ancrene Wisse* as Vernacular Spirituality'—turn to a more theoretical interpretation of the work, although this in large part also works as a survey of the criticism done on the text and what it suggests. Overall, the book is a coherent overview of an important and often neglected text of women's spiritual writings.

In the same University of Wales Press series, Religion and Culture in the Middle Ages, is Jane Cartwright's *Feminine Sanctity and Spirituality in Medieval Wales*. The Welsh tradition is generally under-studied, particularly when it comes to the role of women in medieval Welsh texts. Cartwright discusses poetry dedicated to the Virgin Mary and the cult of the Virgin's larger role in Wales, as well as various hagiographical traditions, including those of native Welsh saints such as Non (St David's mother), Dwynwen, and Melangell. She also focuses on the Middle Welsh lives of Mary Magdalene, Martha, and Katherine of Alexandria. Cartwright places all of this in the context of medieval Wales, which had a surprisingly small number of convents and therefore very few nuns. She situates this reality in contrast to the literary tradition of female sanctity, and considers the questions of audience and reception that it raises.

3. Alliterative Verse and Lyrics

Perhaps a good place to begin is with a familiar work, since 2008 saw the welcome publication of the second edition of J.A. Burrow's *Medieval Writers and their Work: Middle English Literature 1100–1500*. First issued in 1982 (*YWES* 63[1985] 74–5) this work remains one of the best introductions for students—and teachers—of the period, and Burrow has revised and updated the text and references. For our purposes, the section on Middle English lyrics remains one of the most succinct and useful general statements on the genre, with Burrow noting that 'lyric...usually means no more than a short poem...in stanzas', observing too, however, that 'it is hardly possible to speak in general about lyrics so loosely defined' (p. 64). Lyric, ballade, and virelay, developed in the earlier fourteenth century by Machaut and others, were first taken up by Chaucer, beginning a mode of writing that would endure in popularity until the sixteenth century, and that would extend the scope of the lyric beyond the theme of love (p. 65). Burrow's survey, which is restricted to poems in the first person addressing an other, foregrounds the problem of definition in the sense that medieval lyrics relate to other styles of writing, such as dream vision, and with respect to the narrative modes, and the tensions between first-person and personal verse; Burrow states that 'the poet's own thoughts and expressions found direct expression *less* often in lyrics' than in many other kinds of writing (p. 64). As such, we must imagine the speaker not necessarily as representative of the authorial voice but as a 'type', allowing us to imagine the lyric in use by any reader for amorous, devotional or penitential purposes, or performed generally or particularly (p. 65). What survives is verse that is at once stable and fixed yet fluid, blurring the lines between devotional and amorous sentiments, but that has a common submissive speaker. On religious lyrics proper, Burrow revisits the thirteenth century, noting that from quite early on lyrics allowed the reader to be meditative, powerfully combining the physical and the metaphysical (p. 67). Some dramatic lyrics—such as the *chansons de femme*, which give voice to women who have been rejected in love—require the reader not to identify with, but rather to identify, the speaker, and are generally thought to contrast with courtly love lyrics not because they are written by and for people of different class but, as Burrow observes, because they are different kinds of poem (p. 69).

Burrow uses the term 'narrative poetry' to classify verse that includes alliterative forms, acknowledging that the 'variety defies summary' (p. 71). Nonetheless (and noting that modern distinctions are imperfect with regard to Middle English narrative verse), Burrow distinguishes three categories: histories, lives, and tales. Layamon's *Brut* falls into the first category, following the history of the kings of Britain chronologically and 'producing a linear sequence of stories strung out in order of time on the thread of the topic' (p. 72). Burrow writes convincingly of contemporary and historical attitudes towards alliterative verse; in his final chapter 'The Afterlife of Middle English Literature' (pp. 125–38) he cites Chaucer's Parson's apparent reference to the mode as evidence of southern English attitudes towards the alliterative as opposed to the syllabic forms of verse (p. 132). Chaucer, of course, largely avoids alliteration, it being associated with the north and west, and Burrow points to the late revival of the genre in the Victorian period as an extension of late medieval southern attitudes to linguistically challenging literature (pp. 132–4).

In the same vein, but a new publication, is Douglas Gray's superb *Later Medieval English Literature*. Gray has an extensive and comprehensive section on lyrics (pp. 355–80) that opens with the assertion that lyrics have suffered from 'the idea of the cultural decay of the Middle Ages ... and the notion that individual literary genres must necessarily follow a pattern of a gradual rise to a high point of excellence and then decline and become degenerate' (p. 355). He does not deny the poor quality of some surviving pieces, but focuses on the developments in the genre, including those of carol and verse epistle; the prolific nature of lyrics in the works of major authors; their preservation— sometimes incidental—in margins and miscellanies; and the complex nature of European crossover and influence. Gray traces the types while wisely noting that 'courtly' ought not to be considered 'a literary kind totally separate from other kinds of less "courtly" lyric' but ' "courtly" and "popular" need to be seen as the extremes of a continuum rather than opposed concepts' (pp. 356– 7). Gray also—like Burrow—claims it rash to suppose that such verse never emerged out of personal experience, but even more rash to suppose that it always did (p. 357). This chapter extends beyond the scope of Burrow's book, treating bawdy lyrics, verse on mortality, erotic and seductive lyric, and laments, and tracing them and their various allusions into the song- and chapbooks of the sixteenth century. Gray's chapter on romances and tales (pp. 381–410) is also relevant here, with a substantial discussion of ballads (related to verse romances and lyric), in particular those concerned with Robin Hood. Gray examines this definition, allowing for 'generic overlap' and for the need to recognize that 'contemporary terminology is flexible rather than fixed', to the extent that a 'short narrative poem may be called "ryme", "song", "talking", or "gest" ' (p. 393). He also examines the outlaw ballad tradition in Scotland (pp. 521–4).

Gray's work, of course, also considers alliterative verse, albeit less extensively, and at assorted points in different chapters. Of most relevance here is probably the section entitled 'Romances and Tales', in which alliterative verse is considered *passim*. The alliterative *Morte Arthure* (described by Gray as 'excellent', p. 381) is highlighted for its influence on Malory and its preservation in the famous Thornton MS. Indeed Gray questions arguments for the early composition of this work, since the alliterative *Morte* is transmitted in a fifteenth-century manuscript and—like *The Wars of Alexander* which survives in two copies, the earliest being MS Ashmole 44 (dated *c.*1450)—is assumed by modern editors on 'conjectural grounds', to have been composed in the previous century (pp. 381–2). Gray's point may seem pedantic, but it is important in the context of the chapter which treats of romances and tales 'which can be placed in the fifteenth century with some certainty' (p. 382). Elsewhere, the Scottish penchant for alliterative verse—frequently humorous and bawdy—in the sixteenth century is discussed (pp. 143–5, 465).

Andrew Cole's *Literature and Heresy in the Age of Chaucer* refers to familiar alliterative protest texts throughout, despite his focus being on Margery Kempe, John Lydgate and Thomas Hoccleve, as well as on Langland. Cole argues that, when Wycliffism appeared in late medieval England, 'writers began to engage in older topics in new ways, conferring onto the resulting literatures an indelibly post-Wycliffite character' (p. xiii). He finds a difference between earlier, pre-Wycliffite moments and the post-Wycliffite age of the late fourteenth and the fifteenth centuries, the latter of which he sees as novel. Cole delves into the literature to uncover evidence of attitudes, developments and patterns; *Pierce the Ploughman's Crede*, for example, is discussed with reference to the invention of Lollardy, since the poet sees 1382 as a 'seminal year' for Lollardy. Wyclif, according to the poet, tried to warn friars about their bad living, but he was 'lollede'—charged with heresy—effectively 'lollardized' (p. 33).

Thomas D. Hill studies 'The Middle English *Judas* Ballas and the Price of Jesus: Ballad Tradition and the Legendary History of the Cross' (*ES* 89:i[2008] 1–11). Hill's article on this important text—important not least because it is the earliest attested English ballad—addresses some philological issues in order to better understand the 'legendary context' and 'narrative logic' of the poem (p. 4). Hill quotes the poem in its entirety, and goes on to examine specific semantic moments—including the description of the selling of Jesus by Judas—to argue for a medieval popularizing and rewriting of the story through the rewriting and reimagining of 'some the central problems of the Christian history of the Passion' (p. 10).

Samantha J. Rayner's nicely crafted *Images of Kingship in Chaucer and his Ricardian Contemporaries* uses the literature of the late fourteenth century— specifically for our purposes that of the *Gawain*-poet—to investigate the 'shifting nature' of the world from which they emerge (p. 1). The 'presumed author' of the four texts preserved in British Library MS Cotton Nero A. x, Rayner argues, displays a consistency in his treatment of the court and kingship (p. 61); Rayner highlights the regal language of *Pearl* which, though relating to the God as king, 'implies a comparison with social organisation on earth' (p. 63). In *Cleanness*, the treatment of kingship 'becomes vitally integrated with the poem's theme of purity' (p. 72), while *Patience*, though having less obvious references to royalty and kingship, offers some 'illuminating insights into the hierarchy of power' (p. 75). Ultimately, Rayner concludes, the *Gawain*-poet has 'reverence' at the core of his work, which displays 'a transcendence of earthly concerns that try to reconcile the responsibilities owed to both realms' (p. 161).

Ralph Hanna's excellent edition of *The Knightly Tale of Golagros and Gawane*, published in 2008 and reprinted in 2009 for the Scottish Text Society, is the result of his collaborative research with the late W.R.J. Barron, and is an important re-examination of this anonymous alliterative romance which has one source: the imprint of 1508 by Chepman and Myllar, surviving together with ten other small early printed books as National Library of Scotland Advocates Library 19.1.16. Hanna spends some valuable time on the history of the book and its production, and constructs a rich and layered history of a text composed sometime between the 1420s and the printing date of 1508, the upper limit established by the text's indebtedness to *The Awntyrs of Arthure at the Terne Wathelyn* (p. xxiv); its sources include Chrétien de Troyes' *Perceval*, and the poem replaces the chivalric quest with a penitential pilgrimage (p. xxxi). Hanna's textual work is exemplary: close, detailed, and thorough, treating Chepman and Meyer's imprint as a 'copy-text to be critically analysed' (p. xlii).

Finally, a return to J.A. Burrow, and to his new work *The Poetry of Praise*, in which he examines the poetics of praise not just in panegyric, love-song, and hymn, but also in 'narrative texts' that 'speak the language of praise, though more indirectly' (p. 2). Poetry addressed to 'a variety of individual subjects, male and female, human and divine, public and private', Burrow notes, is more frequently found in the Middle Ages than the *laudes* to the deeds of a hero (p. 61). Lyrics offer a prime opportunity for the former distinction; Burrow gives an example from Harley 2253, 'Annot et Johon', in which Annot is compared variously with jewels, flowers, birds, spices, and heroes and heroines (p. 66). Some lyrics used ironic praise, for example 'The Lover's Mocking Reply', which describes the lady as 'crabbed of kynde' (p. 67). Burrow looks also at Marian lyrics, which flourished after the Conquest in line with the increased popularity of the cult of the Virgin (pp. 68–9), and notes that praise of Mary is found also in the alliterative *Pearl* ('Quen of cortasysye'). The alliterative *Morte* portrays Arthur as so impressive as to solicit the praise of a Roman emissary. However, despite the encomiastic tendencies, the poem has 'given rise to differing interpretations in recent time, especially where the portrayal of the hero is concerned' (p. 79); Burrow's treatment sets out to refute what he sees as overly moralistic interpretations of Arthur's wars and their conduct and of his dream of Fortune (p. 78). *The Wars of Alexander* also finds its way into Burrow's section on Middle English; it is described as an 'accomplished' alliterative poem with a high auxetic style, although the poet portrays Alexander, too, 'as a man who can feel pity and show mercy, most memorably in his final exchanges with the defeated and dying Darius' (p. 89). Burrow states that poems such as the *Morte* and the

Wars 'present their own challenges to modern interpretation' (p. 92); challenges which are both expressed and answered very lucidly in this work.

4. The *Gawain*-Poet

Scholarship on the *Gawain*-poet was less active this year than last. The bulk of articles this year addressed *Sir Gawain and the Green Knight*, one of which claimed the Allen D. Breck Award for the most distinguished paper given by a junior scholar at the annual Rocky Mountain Medieval and Renaissance Association conference. Alice Blackwell's 'Gawain's Five Wits: Technological Difficulties in the Endless Knot' (*Quidditas* 29[2008] 8–25) proposes that the five wits, misunderstood and poorly remembered, are the source of Gawain's mistakes, and that the endless knot, which is dependent upon them, is unknowingly unravelled before the journey. The five wits are reassessed as 'internal wits' instead of the five senses, which then automatically calls into question Gawain's self-identity, since he cannot rely on the faultlessness of the wits.

'*Sir Gawain and the Green Knight*, Stanzas 32–34' (*Expl* 67[2008] 22–5), by Paul Battles, is a close examination of Gawain's approach to the castle, in which the subjective point of view dominates. More specifically, Gawain's 'state of mind is expressed especially through his feeling of physical insignificance' (p. 22). Thus the forest surroundings first serve to increase Gawain's sense of unease, while the sudden appearance of the castle brings relief. The viewpoint of the passage is specifically Gawain's, not the narrator's, as demonstrated by diction.

Conor McCarthy, in '*Luf-talkyng* in *Sir Gawain and the Green Knight*' (*Neophil* 92[2008] 155–62), discusses the debate regarding courteous behaviour between Gawain and Lady Bertilak in the third fit. Both *luf* and *luf-talkyng* are used, and together they represent the wide range of possible meanings related to both courtly courtesy and love. McCarthy points out that limiting translation of *luf-talkyng* to 'conversation about love' reduces the meaning to a singular one that could be seen as ironic in the context of the discussion itself, and prevailing concentration on the sexual interpretations of both discussion and kiss should be carefully examined in light of the poem's emphasis on chasteness.

In 'Hiding the Harm: Revisionism and Marvel in *Sir Gawain and the Green Knight*' (*PLL* 44:ii[2008] 168–93), Manish Sharma looks at the Green Knight's 'gomen', the Christmas beheading game, and its significance to the poem and its world. The Arthurian court's availability for and acceptance of such a game might suggest a disregard for life that goes against Christian dignity. Moreover, the poem's structure and narrative trajectory render the results of the Green Knight's challenge farcical. The most significant point about this failure on Gawain's part, however, is that, in writing this scene and its consequences, the poet opened up a space for imagination and experimental ideas and techniques, an effect often overlooked in modern criticism.

Jennifer Anh-Thu Tran Smith's study of 'Fidelity in Versification: Modern English Translations of *Beowulf* and *Sir Gawain and the Green Knight*' (in Fitzmaurice and Minkova, eds., *Studies in the History of the English Language*, vol. 4: *Empirical and Analytical Advances in the Study of English Language Change*, pp. 121–54) is fascinating, and it relates directly to university teaching. She examines *Beowulf* and *Sir Gawain and the Green Knight* as old texts resurrected and 'made cool' by new translations, in such a way that the translations are made, in effect, more significant than the originals. She chose these two poems because they are frequently taught and anthologized, and also because each survives in only one manuscript. I will exclude her comments on *Beowulf* here. First, she notes that there are numerous violations of alliteration in *Gawain* translations, although older texts (e.g. Tolkien's) tend towards alliterative fidelity more than later versions. Most notably, all the translations achieve at least some 'pure' lines, where the alliteration, scansion, and metre all work. Numerous graphs and charts follow, delineating each of her tests and the results in various comparative fashions. Though she makes few value judgements, she asks her audience to consider what they want—good poetry or a good translation.

Three articles address *Pearl*. Julie Fifelski, in 'Two *Loci Amoeni* in *Pearl* and the *Roman de la Rose*' (*N&Q* 55[2008] 17–19), acknowledges that numerous scholars recognize the connection between the opening scenes of *Pearl* and the *Romance of the Rose*, and continues by pointing out a further connection—*Cleanness* specifically mentions Jean de Meun. Moreover, there are additional similarities in two *loci amoeni*: the opening pleasure-garden, and the other which the narrator encounters but cannot join. Both created spaces reflect heavenly glory. The two poems are also linked through ideas of time and space and in the image of the rose as mutable beauty.

In 'Rethinking the "corse in clot": Cleanness, Filth, and Bodily Decay in *Pearl*' (*SIP* 105:iv[2008] 429–47), Katherine H. Terrell argues that the poem's examination of death and grief depends on the juxtaposition of the pearl and corpse. Both Maiden and Dreamer link these images together despite their disagreement on what each means. The Pearl Maiden sees both pearls and corpses as pure and incorrupt; the dreamer sees pearls as spotless, but corpses as impure and putrefied. Terrell sees both as valuable positions, and also seeks to rectify a lack of scholarly enquiry into the corpse. Originally, the Dreamer is earthbound, which forces his view of corruption. However, when he becomes focused on the Eucharist he is given a new place from which to see the grave, one that elevates his thought to heaven, and allows him to share the Maiden's viewpoint. The Maiden has already described death and decay in the context of original sin, but also as requirements for salvation. The Eucharist, a perpetual symbol of death and regeneration, becomes a source of spiritual cleanness and allows the Dreamer to reconcile the two positions.

H.L. Spencer's '*Pearl*: "God's Law" and "Man's Law"' (*RES* 59[2008] 317–41) begins by affirming the commonly held date of composition—the late 1380s—and seeks to do this through an examination of the legal and political theory embedded in the poem. Overall, Spencer argues that the audience would likely have been bilingual in French and English, and noble, but not royal. The political and theological arguments are expressed in legal terms that may signal a developing trend in vernacular writing in the late fourteenth century. Moreover, in legal terms, the author describes God as an absolute but not tyrannical ruler—like Richard II. This fusion of legal terms and political ideas produces a particularly 'English' poem, with the monarchy being traced to Roman law. Overall, then, the poem reflects contemporary doctrine and theological positioning, while expressing those stances in legal and political terms.

Four pieces address *St. Erkenwald*: two short notes and two longer articles. In 'Art "Direction" in St Erkenwald' (*N&Q* 55[2008] 273), Andrew Breeze rejects both standard glosses of the word 'art' in favour of a proposed third notion—direction, specifically related to a compass point. This is found in other northern and Middle Scots texts. Thus, while the historical figure Eorcenwold was from southern England, the poem exhibits Celtic and northern influences.

Thorlac Turville-Petre, in 'St Erkenwald and the Judicial Oath' (*N&Q* 55[2008] 19–21), draws on Burrow's exploration of the word 'declynet', further expanding the discussions through reliance upon the Burton Annals of 1257 and oaths recorded therein. Turville-Petre also discusses the use of the word in Latin translations of the Old Testament, *The Troy Book*, and *De Miseria Conditionis Humane*, with further references to legal use of the term in Anglo-Norman oaths and ecclesiastical sources. He raises the possibility that the author had legal training or influence.

David Coley's 'Baptism as Eucharist: Orthodoxy, Wycliffism, and the Sacramental Utterance in Saint Erkenwald' (*JEGP* 107:iii[2008] 327–47) focuses on the sacrament of baptism and its association with orthodoxy, Wycliffism, and sacramental utterance. The poem is aligned with orthodoxy in eucharistic theology, especially in regard to the judge's conversion, and demonstrates how its orthodoxy is constructed through its baptismal imagery.

In 'Sight and Sound in *St Erkenwald*: On Theodicy and the Senses', John Bugbee (*MÆ* 77[2008] 202–21) discusses, in a somewhat pedantic manner, the opposing roles of sight and sound in *St Erkenwald*. The article opens with an overview of the poem that somewhat highlights images of sight and sound to some degree, but ends up reading more like a summary. This segues into a theological overview of sources and analogues: the Gregory–Trajan legend, but also the Jesus and Lazarus legend, and the healing of the blind man from John, chapter 9. Finally, Bugbee presents the requirements for salvation, pointing out that hearing is a humble, dependent sense, while sight is an active sense. The moral of the poem in this sense, then, seems to be that vision is what humans have to look forward to in heaven, but that it cannot be obtained on earth.

5. *Piers Plowman*

This is a very active year in *Piers Plowman* studies. Several books address *Piers Plowman* in whole or part, including one edition. Derek Pearsall's *Piers Plowman: A New Annotated Edition of the C-Text* is a complete revision of his version originally published in 1974 (*YWES* 59[1978] 84). Most welcome is the updated introduction, providing overviews of key concepts and historical context, including Lollardy, poverty, and salvation. In addition to this, the completely redone bibliography is fully updated to reflect recent scholarship. The footnote annotations have also been revised to incorporate new scholarship and evidence, making this edition one of the most valuable tools available.

The massive and monumental *Piers Plowman: A Parallel-Text Edition of the A, B, C, and Z Versions*, volume 2: *Introduction, Textual Notes, Commentary, Bibliography, and Indexical Glossary*, by A.V.C. Schmidt, is a companion to the volume published by Longman in 1995 (*YWES* 76[1995] 145). This new volume is an amazing accomplishment representing years of careful work, and it is indispensable for dedicated *Piers* scholars. The 'Textual Notes' section is specifically directed towards the C-text; however, that does not necessarily impede its usefulness, as important textual issues are discussed with reference to the other versions. The volume offers a full glossary that reflects all four versions, as well as an extensive bibliography. The substantive introduction covers the manuscripts, the editorial tradition, editing techniques, the textual traditions, and the context of the poem within its own and contemporary times. Finally, the collection of appendices is extremely useful, covering such things as language, rubrics, metre, and errata.

Sarah A. Kelen, in *Langland's Early Modern Identities* [2007], focuses on early modern reactions to *Piers Plowman* from the viewpoint of editors, writers, and readers, tying these to the idea of early modern medievalism. The first two chapters concentrate on the sixteenth century. Despite the relative ease with which early modern audiences accepted anonymous texts, the search for the *Piers* author was ongoing, and Robert Crowley even went so far as to add the life of 'Robert' Langland to his editions. Kelen also looks carefully at the usurpation of the poem as a unified whole, primarily through the adaptation of the protagonist into works of social satire and religious reform. Both of these practices reflect the editorial wishes, rather than the real Langland or even the real Middle Ages. Sixteenth-century responses see Langland as a political and religious writer. Later chapters unpack this idea further, with contextualized nods towards the seventeenth and eighteenth centuries, in which Langland was understood within the linguistic and literary history of his own day and cast as a major figure of poetic development rather than religious reform. The closing chapter looks at Chaucer's relationship with Langland by specifically tackling a series of texts that connect the authors as Londoners who may have moved within the same circles. The book provides an important perspective on early modern views of medieval literary and religious history, as well as the identity of medieval poets as constructed by early modern readers.

Mary Clemente Davlin's *A Journey into Love: Meditating with 'Piers Plowman'* is a most unusual volume. Selected passages from the poem are drawn out and combined with photography, commentary, and introspective questions in order to create a template for meditation. The brief introduction provides just enough background to inform a non-specialist while not overwhelming the reader with too many details. The passages selected are carefully chosen to reflect inner spirituality, biblical connections, and contemporary appeal. Davlin provides original translations and narrative summaries along with the meditative portions, lending a scholarly air to this spiritual guidebook.

Rebecca L. Schoff both builds on and revises previous work in a chapter of her 2007 book *Reformations: Three Medieval Authors in Manuscript and Moveable Type*, which uses *Piers* as a case study for the way a medieval text's tradition influenced its transition from manuscript to print. She initially examines Crowley's print version, but then turns to C-text revisions and John But's continuation of the A-text, all of which, she believes, are constructed in such a way as to present the readers with Will as an author-figure. The final portion of the chapter investigates the lingering hold that early print interpretations have on modern ideas about the poem.

Scott Lightsey devotes the first chapter of his 2007 book *Manmade Marvels in Medieval Literature and Culture* to examining an automaton used in the coronation pageant of 1377 and its connections to a scene in *Piers Plowman*. Lightsey suggests that this not only reflects contemporary chroniclers' reactions to such a marvel but also helps explain the textual complication in B. Prol. 113–32. He suggests, for instance, that the allegorical image might demonstrate a voice for the craftsmen of the realm who would otherwise go unheard during a kingly prerogative. Thus the image might reflect both an 'advice to princes' moment, and a solace to guildsmen such as the goldsmiths.

Wendy Scase's 2007 *Literature and Complaint in England 1272–1553* successfully combines literary and archival research into the investigation of a new genre she calls the 'literature of clamour' and, while it does not devote a large portion of its discussion to *Piers*, the study provides valuable background information for *Piers* studies. Scase posits that medieval writers, in a type of literary recycling, use the same medieval complaints for different purposes and goals. The initial chapters look at historical and legal context for complaints, examining documentary process, petitions, and related lyrics. From these, Scase turns to Lollardy, among other troublesome activities, focusing on the literary consequences of political actions and documents. The middle chapters look more specifically at the literature of clamour, including the *Piers* pamphlets that appeared at the same time as Crowley's editions—all of which are shown to have origins in the medieval art of clamour-writing.

In *Excrement in the Late Middle Ages: Sacred Filth and Chaucer's Fecopoetics*, Susan Signe Morrison devotes most of a chapter to an overview of 'waste studies', in which she relies upon Chaucer and Langland for examples. In particular, she examines wasted production and wasted resources in *Piers*, with emphasis on the idea that a working society will produce the correct amounts of sustenance, while an improperly functioning society will result in flawed expenditures. Gluttony, wealth, and society are set against the poor and helpless.

Andrew Cole, in *Literature and Heresy in the Age of Chaucer* devotes two chapters to William Langland, *Piers Plowman*, and the (re)invention of Lollardy. Lollard studies are experiencing something of an upswing in interest recently, which in turn has prompted a spate of new scholarship on how *Piers* relates to that tradition. Cole's work is an interrogation of the term 'Lollard' along with the historical and literary context surrounding it. To some degree,

Cole is hesitant about the term itself since the meaning, as he adeptly discusses, is flexible. Much of his argument rests on the late medieval vernacular literary canon, including Langland, Chaucer, Lydgate, and Margery Kempe, with attention paid to vernacular translation and the effect on various audiences. For instance, Cole suggests that the C-text is, at least in part, a reaction to the ambiguous term 'Lollard', and provides evidence of a spirited debate. The debate is embodied throughout the work, but especially in the Wasters and the poor priests. Cole puts forth the notion that Wycliffite ideas were at the centre of late medieval vernacular literature, and argues his case rather convincingly.

Although Nicole R. Rice, in *Lay Piety and Religious Discipline in Middle English Literature*, does not devote an individual chapter to *Piers*, the work informs several ideas within her book, particularly the idea of dialogic form and its connection to clerical understanding. The dialogues in *Piers*, she writes, both 'demonstrate and widen the gap between "lewed" and clerical subjects' (p. 48). She connects *Piers* predominantly with the genre she identifies as 'spiritual guide as dialogic text,' in that each uses literary means to enhance and extend clerical understanding. The dialogue provides Langland with a framework within which he can interrogate lay–clerical relations, as well as related issues such as charity and community. Ultimately, however, Rice concludes that Langland's disillusionment with clergy is too overwhelming even for a perfected figure like Will to overcome.

Indulgences in Late Medieval England: Passports to Paradise? by R.N. Swanson offers some valuable insights on the medieval view of pardons and salvation. In fact, Swanson suggests that Langland directly challenges the doctrine of indulgences in the pardon scene (A-text, passus 8; B-text, passus 9; C-text, passus 7). He also notes the prevalence of pardoners within the landscape of *Piers*, many of whom move without purpose towards undefined goals. The only way to secure salvation, according to Swanson's reading of Langland, is to live without need of pardon, which is a subversive position, since the implication is that the church need not provide such pardons.

The Piers Plowman Electronic Archive: 6; San Marino, Huntington Library HM 128 (Hm. Hm²), edited by Michael Calabrese, Hoyt N. Duggan, and Thorlac Turville-Petre, continues the excellent resource series, this time concentrating on Huntington manuscripts. As with previous volumes, this CD features a full-colour facsimile. This volume proves the series editors' commitment to publishing all witnesses to *Piers Plowman*, as the manuscript in question is a second-generation B-text with numerous emendations. Hyperlinks connect to the variants and additions, and highlight the scribal contributions, making this volume particularly fascinating, as well as a valuable tool in understanding how authorial, scribal, and audience perceptions interconnect. As with the other volumes in this series, the major drawback is that Macintosh users encounter great difficulty in using this resource, which will not work without a Windows emulator.

Several essay collections covered *Piers* as well. Macklin Smith, in 'Did Langland Read the Lignum Vitae?' (in Smarr, ed., *Writers Reading Writers: Intertextual Studies in Medieval and Early Modern Literature in Honor of Robert Hollander*, pp. 149–82), examines the indebtedness of Langland to

Bonaventure's *opusculum* as well as to the *Lignum vitae*, both of which concentrate on episodes in the Life of Christ. This connection may be seen both in the broader theme and scope and in the structural similarities.

In '"Nede ne hath ne lawe": The Pleas of Necessity in Medieval Literature and Law' (in Hanawalt and Grotans, eds., *Living Dangerously: On the Margins in Medieval and Early Modern Europe*, pp. 9–30), Richard Firth Green focuses on the phrase 'nede ne hath no lawe', contending that this constituted a recognized medieval legal principle intended to allow those who committed crimes such as theft in order to sustain themselves to remain unpunished. Both canon and secular law seemingly uphold this attitude, which then casts a new perspective on Langland's allegorical figure Need as potentially one that justifies theft.

Kathleen Cawsey, in '"I Playne Piers" and the Protestant Plowman Prints: The Transformation of a Medieval Figure' (in Cawsey and Harris, eds., *Transmission and Transformation in the Middle Ages*, pp. 189–206), looks at the possible audience and reception of sixteenth-century 'plowman prints', focusing especially on how the medieval ploughman was transformed into a new early modern application, which may or may not have borne a resemblance to the figure found in *Piers Plowman*.

Old age is proposed as a crucial element to understanding *Piers Plowman* in 'Old Age, Narrative Form, and Epistemology in Langland's *Piers Plowman*: The Possibility of Learning' (in Classen, ed., *Old Age in the Middle Ages and the Renaissance: Interdisciplinary Approaches to a Neglected Topic*, pp. 393–405) by Daniel F. Pigg. The varying personifications, primarily of Will and Elde, demonstrate differing positions on the elderly. On one hand, those still hale and hearty should avoid the elderly since they can be objects of ridicule. On the other hand, the elderly can also be sources of wisdom, and should thus be respected. Will, who loses his hair, hearing, and sexual capacity, is victimized by old age. More interestingly, his impotence may have signalled to contemporary audiences that he was oversexed, and thus deserved to have his ageing process hastened. Pigg concludes by positing *Piers* as presenting a unique approach to old age, seeing it as an opportunity for renewal, not simply death.

In 'Being a Man in *Piers Plowman* and *Troilus and Criseyde*' (in Pugh and Smith Marzec, eds., *Men and Masculinities in Chaucer's 'Troilus and Criseyde'*, pp. 161–82), Michael Calabrese addresses what he terms the 'strangely parallel stories of men, Troilus and Will' who journey in search of truth (p. 162). Moreover, he focuses on the male body as a site of this construction. Calabrese's take on the poems includes a look at sickness and healing in connection to the male body, creating a 'sexual biography' of sorts, through which each poem demonstrates what it means to be a man, both in relation to love, and in connection to the medieval world.

A unique approach is taken by Dídac Llorens-Cubedo in 'Building and Plowing: Some Connections between T.S. Eliot's *The Rock* and William Langland's *Piers Plowman*' (in Prado-Pérez and Llorens-Cubedo, eds., *New Literatures of Old: Dialogues of Tradition and Innovation in Anglophone Literature*, pp. 105–15). After a brief overview of the works in question, Llorens-Cubedo turns to the connections he sees between passus 6 (the ploughing of the half-acre) and Eliot's writing concerning performances of *The Rock*. One of the main associations Llorens-Cubedo points out is the shared view of building as a reflection of an evangelical spirit of creation, which is, in turn, tied to writing. Another, perhaps more important, connection is the view of communal life and the importance of communal work. For instance, Llorens-Cubedo compares Eliot's Unemployed with Langland's Wasters. Finally, he sees a desire for spiritual perfection in both works, accomplished through ploughing and building. While interesting, and contextualized to some degree, the argument lacks both specific and direct connections and evidence that Eliot relied upon Langland as a source.

J.A. Burrow published two pieces on *Piers* this year. The shorter, '*Piers Plowman* B XIII 190' (*N&Q* 55[2008] 124–5), concerns a passage in the B-text where Conscience decides to leave his own dinner party. Some editions, including Kane and Donaldson, include 'of' in a passage concerning the dinner guests, while others do not. The manuscript evidence is not in agreement on the point. Burrow points out that the inclusion changes the passage's meaning, for without the 'of', the whole company is seen as errant, not just the Friar. In the longer piece, 'The Structure of *Piers Plowman* B XV–XX: Evidence from the Rubrics' (*MÆ* 77[2008] 306–12), Burrow tackles the rubrics associated with the Three Lives—Dowel, Dobet, and Dobest. Several manuscript copies have what Burrow calls 'split rubrics', meaning headings which contain more than one of the *Do*s. These splits can be interpreted in two ways: either as obvious transitions between passus, or as mixed passus. Burrow then proceeds to look for evidence of transitions, eventually calling for further examination of the rubrics and a reavowal of the traditional position of Coghill and Skeat.

Another short article, by Cristina Maria Cervone, 'Christ the Falcon' (*N&Q* 55[2008] 277–82), addresses Langland's use of *iouken*, a hawking term, in connection with the Incarnation. Cervone traces this usage not only to biblical passages, but also to a parallel sermon found in MS Harley 2268. The various arguments rely on nature ('kynde') as well as authority, and are further connected to the trope of Christ as Knight, and build up to eucharistic imagery, thus explaining how Will can taste the fruit.

'Langland's Rats Revisited: Conservatism, *Commune*, and Political Unanimity' (*Viator*1:xxxix[2008] 127–55), by Nicole Lassahn, addresses political and religious concerns, particularly parliament and Lollardy, as contextualized within the idea of the *commune*, and as set against the traditionally accepted view that Langland was a conservative. Towards that end, Lassahn undertakes an examination of Langland's view set against not only materials about the Good Parliament of 1376, but also other accounts from that same year, using all of the texts, including *Piers*, as a source. Part of the discussion concerns separating a master-narrative from the idea of the collective, especially as contextualized within medieval social order. Using the rolls of parliament, Thomas Walsingham's accounts, and the *Anonimalle* chronicle as rhetorics of community alongside *Piers*, Lassahn suggests that the late fourteenth century exhibited a great deal of anxiety about political communities and social classification, especially as linked to laws and governance.

In 'Latin Verses by John Gower and "John of Bridlington" in a *Piers Plowman* Manuscript (BL ADD. 35287)' (*N&Q* 55[2008] 127–31) Lawrence Warner points out three items that have yet to be definitively identified in the manuscript in question, and addresses two of them. These two passages are written in Latin. The first is from the *Prophecy of John of Bridlington* and the second is from John Gower's *Cronica Tripertita*. Warner suggests that the inclusion of these passages in one of the most important manuscripts containing the B-text demonstrates the circulation patterns of major fourteenth-century works. In particular, he suggests production in a 'tight metropolitan circle' (p. 129), and that they testify to both the reader's activities and to the transmission of the works themselves.

In 'The Book of the World as I Found It: Langland and Wittgenstein's *Tractatus Logico-Philosophicus*' (*Exemplaria* 20:iv[2008] 341–60), Sarah Tolmie addresses how *Piers* can be considered Tractarian, focusing especially on allegory as a logical manner of mapping language in which it gains meaning from form rather than content. She insists that, despite the difference in era and origin, Langland is readable through Wittgenstein because *Piers* 'concerns logical constitution of the subject' (p. 341). As with Tolmie's other work in this area, the article is intriguing, especially in its attempts to examine logic and the transcendental subject. However, the material here seems to primarily be a retread of her article in two issues of the *Yearbook of Langland Studies* (the earlier of which is reviewed in *YWES* 88[2009] 243 and the more recent below). A slight shift here incorporates the formation of wonder as a cognitive process.

Simon Horobin and Alison Wiggins, in 'Reconsidering Lincoln's Inn MS 150' (*MÆ* 77[2008] 30–53), discuss the 'textual idiosyncrasies' of the manuscript in question, which contains an early version of the A-text along with several Middle English romances. In particular, the article examines the manuscript for evidence of fifteenth-century readership, while investigating the potential use of these texts as well. Beginning with a description of the manuscript itself, the authors then contextualize the rather surprising appearance of *Piers Plowman* among the romances, suggesting that this could be due to anything from circumstance to popularity. Next they consider the unique aspects of the A-text version found in the Lincoln's Inn manuscript. Most significantly, the additions provide a more explicit dramatic framework, particularly in passages that concentrate on dialogue. The authors next turn to the deliberate and progressive revisions found especially in *Merlyn*. Among the conclusions is the suggestion that these revisions are parallel in tone and scope, and that the scribal errors seemingly confirm that the texts were copied from written exemplars.

Roger A. Ladd's ' "My condicion is mannes soule to kill"—Everyman's Mercantile Salvation' (*CompD* 41[2007] 57–78) focuses, of course, on the play *Everyman*. However, Ladd uses *Piers* as a point of reference for one of his main ideas. *Everyman*, he argues, suggests a tension between salvation and 'sins of profit'. The solution, according to the play, lies in church and charity—the position Ladd believes is 'abandoned' by *Piers Plowman*, which demonstrates a distinctly anti-mercantile stance. *Everyman* instead shows that, by the end of the fifteenth century, profit and salvation could be merged.

As always, the *Yearbook of Langland Studies* provided a wealth of essays on a variety of topics, ranging from close readings to theoretical investigations. Larry Scanlon, in 'Personification and Penance' (*YLS* 21[2007] 1–29), argues that personification, as part of allegory, was the true centre of Langland's writing. In particular, the portrait of Glutton (B.5) illustrates how Langland views the intersection of penance, a major theme of *Piers*, and personification, a major technique used in *Piers*. This convergence results in an instability, which in turn demonstrates Christ's unlimited capacity for forgiveness. Moreover, Langland's reliance on personification as a device of allegory disrupts the Coleridgean perspective that allegory is a feature of the Middle Ages. Finally, Scanlon suggests that the portrait of Glutton is part of the tradition known as the Liar's Paradox, discussed by Lacan, and exhibited also by Chaucer's Pardoner.

Sarah Wood's '"Ecce Rex": *Piers Plowman* B.19.1–212 and its Contexts' (*YLS* 21[2007] 31–56) looks at analogues for Conscience's speech (B.19) naming Christ as 'knight, king, and conqueror'. These are found mostly found in Advent sermons. Moreover, additional Advent materials provide inspiration for Langland's discussions of kingship, especially in the Prologues of the B-text and C-text. These similarities, then, suggest a connection between the composition of B.19 and the Prologues. Amanda Walling, 'Friar Flatterer: Glossing and the Hermeneutics of Flattery in *Piers Plowman*' (*YLS* 21[2007] 57–76), sees Langland's treatment of friars and minstrels as particularly indicative of examining the intersections between glossing and flattery—one an interpretative practice, the other a rhetorical one. This idea is contextualized within the mendicant tradition, particularly looking at pastoral care and social corruption. The validity of friars is called into question, but even more intriguing is Langland's effort to define minstrelsy within a spiritual framework. Thomas D. Hill, in 'God's Tower: *Piers Plowman* B, Prologue 11–16' (*YLS* 21[2007] 77–82), investigates analogues concerning God dwelling in a high tower, as presented in the prologue of the B-text. Many early authors, including Jerome, Aquinas, and Boethius, use this image demonstrating that Langland drew on both biblical and exegetical sources.

In '*Pier Plowman*, Pastoral Theology, and Spiritual Perfectionism: Hawkyn's Cloak and Patience's *Pater Noster*' (*YLS* 21[2007] 83–118), Nicholas Watson looks at *Piers* B.13–14—the encounter among Patience, Conscience, and Hawkyn—as Langland's response to the medieval theological tension between the universal ideal and perfectionism, a conundrum not readily satisfied. *Piers* can be viewed as an attempt to merge these differing perspectives. Piers himself represents a way to reform Christianity from within, and beyond this, the connection between Patience and Hawkyn demonstrates pastoral theology at work. This attempt, too, fails. Ultimately, Watson argues that, despite the aura of pessimism, Langland continues to insist that all Christians can be saved.

Lawrence Warner, in 'An Overlooked *Piers Plowman* Excerpt and the Oral Circulation of Non-Reformist Prophecy, *c*.1520–55' (*YLS* 21[2007] 119–42), looks at an excerpt from *Piers Plowman* B.6 found in the so-called Winchester Anthology—London, British Library, MS Additional 60577—that has, until now, been virtually ignored. This excerpt provides an important overview of Tudor-era reception of *Piers*, including a particular emphasis on prophecy.

In 'Robert Crowley and the Editing of *Piers Plowman* (1550)' (*YLS* 21[2007] 143–70), R. Carter Hailey examines the three Crowley editions, which mark a significant moment in the poem's critical reception despite criticism of Crowley's meddling with textual content. Hailey argues by contrast that Crowley attempted to present an accurate rendition, including a completely revised and re-edited second edition that included additional manuscript evidence. Most valuable here is the consideration of the extant manuscripts that Crowley used, most notably Cambridge, Cambridge University Library, MS Gg. iv. 31.

Wendy Scase also addresses Crowley's editions in '*Dauy Dycars Dreame* and Robert Crowley's Prints of *Piers Plowman*' (*YLS* 21[2007] 171–98), but in a unique manner. Traditional scholarship holds that Crowley's 1550 edition was the first published version, and that its publication demonstrates the relaxation of censorship laws, and inspired imitative works, such as *Dauy Dycars Dreame*. Scase, on the other hand, suggests that *Piers* was treated as prophecy in manuscript before and during the same era as Crowley's editions. *Dauy Dycars Dreame* and other printed broadsides deliberately use the same language as *Piers* in order to construct a proper way to read medieval prophetic works. Scase also suggests that, contrary to prior claims, *Dauy Dycars Dreame* actually antedates Crowley's editions.

In this year's *Yearbook of Langland Studies* Christopher Cannon notes that his article, 'Langland's *Ars Grammatica*' (*YLS* 22[2008] 1–25), is drawn from a larger project on 'the relationship of the grammar school and grammar school texts to the practices and habits of thought of Middle English writers' (p. 1). Here Cannon concentrates on the third vision, which, he claims, proceeds according to traditional schoolroom form, with a tutor guiding Will away from errors. He uses Chaucer's *Tale of Melibee* to suggest the wider significance of the project, outlining how it illustrates grammar-school training as a template for his discussion of *Piers*. Both rely, for instance, on citing typical schoolroom texts, and where the texts are not cited directly, the language used is clearly reminiscent of school texts. In particular, Langland treats Latin quotations (e.g. his repeated phrase 'patientes vincunt') in a manner similar to *latinates*, the model sentences used in school texts.

In 'Langland and the Truelove Tradition' (*YLS* 22[2008] 27–55), Cristina Maria Cervone argues that Langland's references to 'trewe loue' (C.1.136 and C.18.9) are connected to the medieval traditions surrounding the true-love plant. Traditionally, the plant often symbolizes Christ, or, more broadly, divine love and salvation. If the references overlap with Christ as lover–knight, sexualized puns occur. Cervone investigates *Piers* in the context of contemporary botanical lyrics that utilize the double entendre of 'spring' (leap v. botanical growth). Langland associates such passages with the Incarnation and, subsequently, with grace. Cervone ends by urging Langland scholars to make more close readings of the C-text.

Turning to alliterative metrics, Macklin Smith's 'Langland's Unruly Caesura' (*YLS* 22[2008] 57–101) examines Langland's 'unruly' techniques in order to highlight the rhythmic complexity of *Piers Plowman*, with special attention paid to the caesura. Smith discusses this in terms of clerical versification which, in turn, asks for a clerical reading. As he points out, 'here Langland's lines with multiple, uncertain, or shifting pauses are especially instructive' (p. 99). Readers are invited to evaluate the force and meaning of the caesurae, thus altering the balance of meaning, and demonstrating a subtle, yet powerful, method of poetic licence.

Sarah Tolmie, in 'Langland, Wittgenstein, and the Language Game' (*YLS* 22[2008] 103–29), suggests that Ludwig Wittgenstein's language game in *Philosophical Investigations* can be used as a model for understanding some of the ambiguities of *Piers Plowman*. In particular, Langland's use and reuse of specific words in varying ways (termed 'proprietary' and 'separate') demonstrates this game. For instance, the 'recurrence of the words *life* and *live*' reveals a 'new preoccupation with the immediacy of lived experience' (p. 105). In a manner similar to Wittgenstein, Langland moves from a search for perfect logical language to an understanding of actual human usage. Tolmie sees this as part of Langland's allegorical strategy as well as promoting *Piers* as a 'poem of serious philosophical claims' (p. 129).

Katherine Zieman, author of 'The Perils of *Canor*: Mystical Authority, Alliteration, and Extragrammatical Meaning in Rolle, the *Cloud*-Author, and Hilton' (*YLS* 22[2008] 131–63), focuses on the idea of religious experience as a valuable site of vernacular literary production, and suggests that this provides new contexts for the study of *Piers*. One such area of study is extragrammatical language, which could be seen as a way of accessing the divine. Extragrammatical language was more difficult to regulate than vernacular theology and thus it could be a powerful tool. Hilton and *The Cloud of Unknowing* are the two main focuses of this essay, but Zieman does conclude that the 'idea of extragrammaticality might shed new light on complex Langlandian lines' (p. 163). Langland may have capitalized on ambiguity whenever possible, and scholars should be alert to this.

In 'The Rise of English Printing and Decline of Alliterative Verse' (*YLS* 22[2008] 165–97), Timothy Stinson purports to correct a scholarly oversight: while the rise of the Alliterative Revival has been studied, the decline has not enjoyed the same treatment. Stinson seeks to connect this decline with the rise of printing. Of the alliterative texts, only *Piers Plowman* contains all the elements printers found appealing: orthodoxy, popularity, availability, local copies, varied audience, and sustained appeal. Thus *Piers* secured its place as a favourite of printers into the sixteenth century.

Nicolette Zeeman, in 'Tales of Piers and Perceval: *Piers Plowman* and the Grail Romances' (*YLS* 22[2008] 199–236), argues for the existence of analogues between *Piers* and the French Grail romances, particularly *Perlesvaus* and *Queste del saint graal*. Zeeman begins by successfully explaining how Langland would have encountered these texts. For instance, there were numerous copies of the *Queste* in England, including readers' copies. Next, she establishes shared literary iconography, including the harrowing of hell and the Good Samaritan, discussing how these scenes are constructed in romance rhetoric. Besides Christ the lover–knight, Zeeman further sees that 'Langland's *semyvif*, the post-lapsarian "wounded man" who can only be cured with the *plastre* of a child's blood, recalls a number of romance protagonists whose sickness can only be cured by the blood of others' (p. 213). In particular, Langland's *semyvif* recalls the wounded knights of the *Queste*. Moreover, the Good Samaritan sequence recalls the Grail romances in larger ways—uncertain commentary by various narrators, prophecy and foretelling, a focus on travellers and questers, and a preoccupation with failure. Ultimately, 'like the grail romances, *Piers Plowman* situates theological and moral events within a shifted and unbounded landscape' (p. 235), but also shares a focus on a recuperative agenda.

6. Romance

This year work on medieval romance tended to focus on genre and classification and, with regard to specific texts, *Havelok* clearly dominates the debate, with no fewer than six articles dedicated to its study, and *Bevis of Hampton*, which received a full-volume treatment. Another, though minor, trend follows the re-emergence of performance in relation to the popular romances, examined both in manuscript mark-up and within a broader framework in two articles.

Understanding Genre and Medieval Romance represents well the recent return to defining the genre. Kevin S. Whetter's book is an investigation of the vexed question of romance, a genre that is notoriously hard to define, due partly to the multi-faceted nature of the extant corpus, and to the too broad or too narrow labels used so far. Following a range of chapters and articles that have explored this issue, the most recent being Yin Liu's article (*YWES* 87[2008] 255), Whetter sets out to explore the notion of genre, which was as crucial to medieval audiences as it is to modern ones, and the troubled relationship between romance and epic, particularly in relation to Malory's *Morte*. The book consists of three uneven parts: the first deals with romance expectations, in terms of author–audience contracts and recognizable features; the second focuses on redefining medieval romance primarily by contrast with epic, problematic as this latter genre might be to define in Middle English literature; and the last is dedicated exclusively to defining Sir Thomas Malory's *Morte Darthur* as a tragic romance (dealt with in section 8(*a*) below). In his review of generic features (chapter 1), Whetter argues in favour of returning to analysing genre, and looking at generic hybrid forms in order to understand the place of medieval romance in literature, while pointing out the danger of using Alastair Fowler's 'kinds' and 'modes'. In chapter 2 Whetter challenges Northrop Frye's 'mode' as a way to analyse romance, and again argues in favour of the return to genre and its demands. Here Whetter suggests three main definitive categories: chivalric adventures (for their own sake), love (and the prominent place given to ladies), and happy endings. Epic and romance are discussed in contrast to each other, and *Beowulf* is used as a counterpoint to romances such as, among others, *Sir Gawain and the Green Knight*, *Guy of Warwick*, *Launfal*, and *Orfeo*. While it can be argued that the epic–romance binary has long been challenged in relation to Arthurian romance (W.R.J. Barron famously drew attention to the inevitable 'historical shading' of Arthurian romance), Whetter's analysis of tragic romance in

Malory is very persuasive. Indeed, the last chapter is the most detailed, and indicates that the main focus of this monograph is the analysis of Malory's prose romance.

Another monograph, Rhiannon Purdie's *Anglicising Romance: Tail-Rhyme and Genre in Medieval English Literature*, explores in fascinating detail the origins, characteristics, and geographical distribution (in manuscript and printed format) of this poetic form, establishing the parameters within which we need to view the development of insular romance. Taking as a starting point Chaucer's famous parody of tail-rhyme romance in his *Tale of Sir Thopas*, included in the *Canterbury Tales*, Purdie's meticulous survey covers, in five chapters and an appendix (containing a very detailed analysis of the provenance of each romance in the corpus), the challenging and hitherto unanswered question of where the tail-rhyme stanza came from, and how its popularity might be justified. The origins of the stanza are traced back to continental and Anglo-Norman lyrics, as well as Latin hymnody and the Victorine sequence. In chapter 2 Purdie demonstrates that the development of tail-rhyme romance is an insular phenomenon, an argument amply supported by evidence from a variety of religious and secular poetry of a predominantly didactic character. Chapters 3 and 4 contain fascinating and authoritative investigations of the complex web of relationships between the production, transmission, and readership of manuscripts containing tail-rhyme romances, with a case study of the Auchinleck manuscript and numerous insights into the graphic impact of manuscript presentation of the tail-rhyme and its links with musical performance. Finally, chapter 5 focuses on the geographical distribution of the extant corpus of romances, closely linked to the evidence provided in the appendix, primarily by means of dialect analysis. In Purdie's view, some general trends might be identified, in particular the flourishing of such romances in the area broadly defined as the north and central/east Midlands (p. 144). Meticulously researched and thoroughly enjoyable, Purdie's monograph offers a rare and valuable addition to this developing area of study.

Medieval romance also takes central stage in Jane Bliss's monograph *Naming and Namelessness in Medieval Romance*. This study focuses on the insular tradition, both in Anglo-Norman and Middle English productions, though not excluding French romances. The book is structured in two parts: in part I Bliss explores the 'Context and Content', while part II focuses on 'Themes and Meanings'. In part I Bliss briefly reviews romance definitions against other genres before she moves on to a thorough investigation of the naming patterns and tendencies evident in the extant corpus. The main thesis of the book is that 'naming is a distinguishing theme of romance, and it is also profoundly interwoven with other defining themes ... it is not so essentially interwoven in other genres' (p. 196), and Bliss successfully demonstrates it via a range of excellent examples, ranging from the well-known romances of *Sir Orfeo* and *Guy of Warwick* to less studied texts such as *Octavian*. Alternating between verse and prose, the examples chosen in this study transcend the boundaries commonly established by previous criticism (verse/prose; Anglo-Norman/English/French), which results in a fresh appraisal of the validity of thematic approaches, and an awareness that medieval audiences dealt with verse and prose in a similar manner. The sections on 'Disguise or Incognito', 'Doubles', 'Love-Madness', and 'Anonymous Women' will prove useful for students of romance. In part II more focused analyses of individual texts that are not usually treated together are grouped under subsections: 'The Power of Name' includes both *Horn* and *Generydes* alongside *Amis and Amiloun* and *Merlin*; while the Fair Unknown and women receive treatment in two subsections, alternating between Middle English, Anglo-Norman, and French examples. The challenges imposed by the extant corpus and its variety are in evidence here, as Bliss tends to select texts to fit in with her chosen categories both in the body of her discussion and in the appendix.

Neil Cartlidge edits proceedings from the biennial conference 'Romance in Medieval England', held in Dublin in 2004, in *Boundaries in Medieval Romance*. 'Boundaries' are defined here in the widest context, not confined to geographical, racial, religious, gender, or other traditional divides. The collection contains eleven selected essays from the conference, in addition to Helen Cooper's Royal Irish Academy lecture given at the time of the conference. Aptly entitled 'When Romance Comes True', Cooper's chapter presents a lively discussion of the boundaries (or lack of them) between romance and history or historical events, including social and political changes. The romances investigated in this chapter look at the beginning and end of the Middle Ages: *Melusine* and *Havelok* and, at the other end, *Blanchardyn and Eglantine*, and *Olyuer of Castille*. Rosalind Field, in 'The Curious History of the Matter of England', offers a much-needed assessment of this modern label and the variety of romances grouped under it, and reveals that it is a product of American scholarship at the beginning of the twentieth century; the relationship of this 'matter' with the older (medieval) matters of France, Rome, and Britain is also discussed (the chapter also includes a discussion of *Havelok*). Marianne Ailes and Phillipa Hardman ask 'How English Are the English Charlemagne Romances?', in which they offer a timely review of this group, in particular of their unifying, formal elements, which assist with speeding up the pace of the narrative and smoothing over inconsistencies. Elizabeth Berlings, in 'The *Sege of Melayne*—A Comic Romance; or, How the French Screwed Up and "Oure Bretonns" Rescued Them', directs attention to the parodic treatment of the little-studied *Sege* text by comparison with the serious tone she identifies in *Richard Coeur de Lion*, while Simon Meecham-Jones, in 'Romance Society and its Discontents: Romance Motifs and Romance Consequences in *The Song of Dermot and the Normans in Ireland*', amply demonstrates the boundaries between romance and history in this text. Elizabeth Williams, in 'England, Ireland and Iberia in *Olyuer of Castille*: The View from Burgundy', examines the boundaries between folk-tale, romance, and historical elements, and Arlyn Diamond returns scholarly attention to the 'Alliterative *Siege of Jerusalem*: The Poetics of Destruction', in particular the blurring of boundaries between romance and religious writing.

The next group of essays in this collection focuses on the origins of romance and links some of its motifs to earlier literature, in particular connections (and boundaries) with the Anglo-Saxon period. Robert Rouse explores 'The Peace of the Roads: Authority and *Auctoritas* in Medieval Romance', while Laura

Ashe provides an investigation of 'The Hero and his Realm in Medieval English Romance'. Judith Weiss, in '"The Courteous Warrior": Epic, Romance and Comedy in *Boeve de Haumtone*', revisits the popular hero from the perspective of comic elements, and investigates the potential audience for this romance, and Ivana Djordjeviç, in 'Rewriting Divine Favour', investigates the potential for transformation in the romances of *Amis and Amiloun* and *Bevis of Hampton*, seen from the perspective of rationalizing God's intervention in human affairs. Corinne Saunders's 'Bodily Narratives: Illness, Medicine and Healing in Middle English Romance' ends the collection with an investigation of the power of magic, in particular through women, and a review of the boundaries between health and illness in medieval romance, in a variety of texts.

The Anglo-Norman and Middle English hero Bevis of Hampton and associated romance versions receive full treatment in this year's collection *Sir Bevis of Hampton in Literary Tradition*, edited by Jennifer Fellows and Ivana Djordjeviç. The collection consists of eleven chapters, and several themes may be identified: the genre and evolution of the Anglo-Norman version, in Marianne Ailes's 'The Anglo-Norman *Boeve de Haumtone* as a *Chanson de Geste*' and Judith Weiss's '*Mestre* and Son: The Role of Sabaoth and Terri in *Boeve de Haumtone*'; Bevis in a number of other languages, in 'Rewriting Bevis in Wales and Ireland', by Erich Poppe and Regine Reck, and Christopher Sanders's '*Bevers Saga* in the Context of Old Norse Historical Prose'; and the manuscript and print context of this romance, and the translation process from Anglo-Norman to Middle English, in Ivana Djordjeviç's 'From *Boeve* to *Bevis*: The Translator at Work', and Jennifer Fellows's 'The Middle English and Renaissance *Bevis*: A Textual Survey'.

The next couple of chapters deal with thematic approaches, ranging from national, racial, and religious boundaries in Robert Allen Rouse's 'For King and Country? The Tension between National and Regional Identities in *Sir Bevis of Hampton*' and Siobhain Bly Calkin's 'Defining Christian Knighthood in a Saracen World: Changing Depictions of the Protagonist in *Sir Bevis of Hampton*', followed by two analyses of discrete topics in Melissa Furrow's 'Ascopard's Betrayal: A Narrative Problem', and Corinne Saunders's 'Gender, Virtue and Wisdom in *Sir Bevis of Hampton*'. Andrew King's essay on '*Sir Bevis of Hampton*: Renaissance Influence and Reception' concludes the collection. As the aptly chosen titles of each chapter reveal, the variety of approaches employed by this group of scholars displays the versatility of *Bevis* in all its incarnations, across language and geographical boundaries, and in both manuscript and print. Traditional, manuscript-based, and linguistic analyses sit well alongside political, racial, and gender readings; students and scholars alike will find the collection rewarding, and a comprehensive guide to this rich romance and its traditions, while new directions for further research are also well represented.

Several chapters in *Authority and Subjugation in Writing of Medieval Wales*, edited by Ruth Kennedy and Simon Meecham-Jones, deal with medieval romance. Tony Davenport explores 'Wales and Welshness in Middle English Romances' (pp. 137–58), with particular reference to *Sir Perceval of Galles*,

Sir Cleges, brief references to *Emaré*, and an extended discussion of *King Horn*, alongside *Sir Tristrem* and *Lybeaus Desconus*. In her chapter 'Crossing the Borders: Literary Borrowing in Medieval Wales and England' (pp. 159–73), Ceridwen Lloyd-Morgan briefly refers to a number of Middle English and Anglo-Norman romances, Arthurian and non-Arthurian, in the broader contexts of Welsh writing (such romances are the Anglo-Norman *Boeve of Haumtone*, *Amis et Amiloun*, and *Fouke le Fitz Waryn*).

Sebastian I. Sobecki writes persuasively about the romance of *King Horn* in his book *The Sea and Medieval English Literature* (pp. 100–13), unsurprisingly giving precedence to the links between land, sea, and identity in this romance (in both Anglo-Norman and Middle English versions), but also to the motif of being set adrift in an inadequate boat, a recurrent motif in the Arthurian and non-Arthurian romances. The secular implications of these voyages on the sea are explored in detail, as is the 'far greater prominence' of the sea in the Middle English version by comparison with Anglo-Norman variants (p. 107).

As mentioned at the beginning of this section, in many ways 2008 looks to be a *Havelok* year; as many as six articles deal with this romance at length, while several other articles and studies refer to it. Two companion articles published in the same issue of *Parergon* demonstrate the results of collaboration between two scholars on the manuscript context for one of the extant versions of *Havelok the Dane*: Kimberly K. Bell, 'Resituating Romance: The Dialectics of Sanctity in MS Laud Misc. 108's *Havelok the Dane* and Royal *Vitae*' (*Parergon* 25:i[2008] 27–51), and Julie Nelson Couch, 'Defiant Devotion in MS Laud Misc. 108: The Narrator of *Havelok the Dane* and Affective Piety' (*Parergon* 25:i[2008] 53–79). In these two substantial studies, both authors make a case for reading this text as a hagiographical romance; while Bell looks closely at the religious implications of the manuscript context, Nelson Couch redirects attention to the links between affective piety and a return to secular values, in particular worldly power and kingship. Julie Nelson Couch also offers 'The Vulnerable Hero: *Havelok* and the Revision of Romance' (*ChauR* 42:iii[2008] 330–52), in which she makes the case for reading this romance from the point of view of childhood and its associated anxieties about vulnerability. Richard Moll focuses on the reception of *Havelok* in a substantial study, '"Nest pas autentik, mais apocrophum": Haveloks and their Reception in Medieval England' (*SP* 105[2008] 165–206). Here Moll revisits medieval audience responses to the variants of this romance, drawing attention to the connections between Gaimar, *Lai d'Haveloc*, and the Anglo-Norman and Middle English *Brut* chronicles, Mannyng's *Chronicle*, Gray's *Scalacronica* and a series of other historical chronicles and the versions of Havelok's story they contain, reaching the conclusion that 'Havelok may very well be found more often in the chronicles than in romances, and this may imply that medieval readers felt that his story was more history than fiction' (p. 183). Raluca L. Radulescu, in 'Insular Romance and Genealogy' (in Radulescu and Kennedy, eds., *Broken Lines: Genealogical Literature in Medieval Britain and France*, pp. 7–25), similarly argues in favour of reading romances and historical chronicles together, specifically for their genealogical discourse which can be identified in both ancestral, Anglo-Norman romances and in later reworkings in Middle English. Radulescu's article includes an extended discussion of *Havelok*, read from the perspective of genealogical concerns, and an exploration of the connections between romance and genealogy in Malory's Grail story, as a response to an insular perception of history and politics (see section 8(*a*) below).

June Hall McCash, 'The Role of Women in the Rise of the Vernacular' (*CL* 60:i[2008] 45–57), examines the prominence of the place assigned to women as both readers and patrons of romances, in a broad overview of literary production, and more specifically of the production of romances, from Wace's *Roman de Brut* to Christine de Pisan. Alison Wiggins and Simon Horobin propose 'Reconsidering Lincoln's Inn MS 150' (*MÆ* 77[2008] 30–53), in which they make a case for the versions of different literary texts, including the romances *Merlyn* (a later version of *Of Arthour and of Merlin*), *King Alisaunder*, *Seege of Troye*, and *Lybeaus Desconus* alongside the A-text of *Piers Plowman* as performance texts in the light of scribal intervention in the manuscript variants. Their argument is based on the visual mark-up and linguistic variation in the manuscript versions of these texts, and the links between the presentation of *Piers Plowman* and that of the romances. They suggest that scribal intervention assisted with adapting these texts to suit the tastes of an early fifteenth-century audience. In another article focused on the performance of medieval romance, 'Is There a Minstrel in the House? Domestic Entertainment in Late Medieval England' (*PQ* 87[2008] 51–76), George Shuffelton tackles the oft-debated question of performance from the viewpoint of medieval nostalgia—he even goes as far as to say that 'nostalgia may have even been a necessary precondition for enjoying minstrel performance' (p. 54). Shuffelton then applies his idea to a household miscellany, Oxford, Bodleian Library, MS Ashmole 61 (or the 'Rate Manuscript', after its scribe), and the best-known romances contained in it: *Lybeaus Desconus*, *Sir Isumbras*, and *Sir Orfeo*.

Michael Johnston, in 'Knights and Merchants Unite: *Sir Amadace*, the Grateful Dead, and the Moral Exemplum Tradition' (*Neophil* 92[2008] 735–44), focuses on this little-studied romance from a broader perspective than that afforded by its usual label of 'didactic' or 'homiletic' romance. Johnson argues that the dialogue between a knight and a merchant draws attention to a non-aristocratic approach to the virtue of *largesse*, which appears even more striking when one compares this text with its closest source, identified by Johnson as chapter 499 in a fourteenth-century moral compilation, *Ci nous dit*. This identification, and the comparison with *Sir Amadace*, supports the view that this romance is part of the exemplum tradition. Sergi Mainer, 'The Singularity of *Sir Tristrem* in the Tristan Corpus' (*LeedsSE* 39[2008] 95–115), explores the extant variants of this romance and their relationships, and Phillipa Hardman writes 'Speaking of Roland: The Middle English *Roland* Fragment in BL MS Lansdowne 388' (*RMSt* 34[2008] 99–121).

Several Grail romances in French and English are mentioned in passing in Juliette Wood's *Eternal Chalice: The Enduring Legend of the Holy Grail*, among which are *Joseph of Arimathea*, Henry Lovelich's *History of the Holy Grail*, and Malory's Grail quest (see also section 8(*a*) below).

7. Gower, Lydgate, Hoccleve

(a) Gower
Lordship and Literature: John Gower and the Politics of the Great Household by Elliot Kendall, a revised thesis, looks at how the networks of power and influence in royal and aristocratic great households are reflected or employed, whether explicitly or implicitly, in the *Confessio Amantis*. Unofficial politics influenced public life and relationships, and while the *Confessio* avoids its overt political thought it cannot avoid displaying the more generalized social politics that are also seen in other works, including parliamentary texts, other literary works, annals, administrivia, and artistic materials. Kendall founds his work on Pierre Bourdieu's economic theory of practice and its understanding of exchange, and turns to describing contemporary loci of power, neatly illustrated by the whole business of the Merciless Parliament and the Lords Appellant in 1388, including how this might have been viewed by landowners such as Gower. He then turns to the frame, exploring the household as a 'geography' for Avarice, as well as the other Seven Deadly Sins, and ethics portrayed through allegory, and then politicizing how Amans views himself and his life as reflected through notions of courtly love. The fifth chapter looks at arranged marriages, so important to aristocratic families (particularly Medea and the Princess of Pantapolis), and the use by fathers of women in the various tales. This is followed by a look at how judicial and other disputes are settled, which extends to several senses of justice or retribution. Finally *Confessio Amantis* Book 7 is found to focus 'on kingship as a means to fix a system that depends on internal play' (p. 262), although the other books are broader in intent when it comes to kingship.

Amanda M. Leff examines women who write in 'Writing, Gender, and Power in Gower's *Confessio Amantis*' (*Exemplaria* 20[2008] 28–47), seeing how they find power and social freedom by doing so. Mike Rodman Jones's '"Of depe ymaginaciouns and strange interpretaciouns": Sorcery and Politics in Gower's *Confessio Amantis*' (*NML* 10[2008] 115–36) takes a picaresque view of the *Confessio* as a better guide to how to read it and Gower's explicit treatments of magic, in parallel with passages in Walsingham's *Chronicle* that link politics to occult activities. In 'Gower *pia vota bibit* and Henry IV in 1399 November' (*ES* 89[2008] 377–84), David R. Carlson follows Fisher's suggestion that one version of a stanza of 'O recolende' thanks the king for an annuity of two pipes of Gascon wine, and ties that gift to 'In Praise of Peace' and the *Cronica tripertita*. Conrad van Dijk's 'Simon Sudbury and Helenus in John Gower's *Vox clamantis*' (*MÆ* 77[2008] 313–18) notes that Gower's sources let him understand Helenus as a wise, prophetic priest or bishop, not as a traitor, so modern critics' labelling of Helenus/Sudbury as a traitor is mistaken, perhaps relying on a mistranslation in Stockton.

(b) Lydgate

Lydgate Matters: Poetry and Culture in the Fifteenth Century opens with an introduction by the editors, Lisa H. Cooper and Andrea Denny-Brown, which takes the title's pun to spring into the broad reaches of the collection, on materiality and the many connections between literature and society. Claire Sponsler follows with 'Lydgate and London's Public Culture' (pp. 13–33), arguing that his work was actually directed to and read only by a small urban elite (cf. Floyd's and Ganim's offerings, below). In 'Lydgate's Golden Cows: Appetite and Avarice in *Bycorne and Chychevache*' (pp. 35–56), Andrea Denny-Brown continues in the vein of abandoning old views by arguing that this beast fable is not about marriage and misogyny but material appetite, literal and spiritual. Paul Strohm's 'Sovereignty and Sewage' (pp. 57–70) presents an idealized London in the *Troy Book* with covered walkways, rain gutters, a sewer system and other means of protecting the health and appearance of citizens: most praiseworthy civil engineering. According to Maura Nolan, 'Lydgate's Worst Poem' (pp. 71–87) is the 'Tretise for Lauanders', but its polyvalent nature and manuscript environment reveal a different mode of reading than we are used to assuming for Lydgate and his readers, from literal through allegorical. Lisa H. Cooper's ' "Markys . . . off the workman": Heresy, Hagiography, and the Heavens in *The Pilgrimage of the Life of Man*' (pp. 89–111) aims to show a changed cultural environment from Deguileville to Lydgate, with respect to views of artisanry as a response to Lollardy.

In 'Lydgate, Lovelich, and London Letters' (pp. 113–38), Michelle R. Warren seeks common ground between the two poets based on interests and values, notably serving attempts by the merchant elite to use art to establish their civic centrality. Jennifer Floyd's 'St. George and the "Steyned Halle": Lydgate's Verse for the London Armourers' (pp. 139–64) finds such common ground in the verses Lydgate made for the illustrated tapestries or hanging panels commissioned to enhance the armourers' public image. John M. Ganim explores social spaces and urban landscapes in 'Lydgate, Location, and the Poetics of Exemption' (pp. 165–83), using the mummings, other commissioned works, the entries, and the *Life of St. Edmund* as test cases for a communal topography. Finally, D. Vance Smith closes with an 'Afterword. Lydgate's Refrain: The Open When' (pp. 185–95), seeing Lydgate's reworking of matters as a hindrance to his re-evaluation and a key to a new view, such as the relationship between the material and the abstract, as in the subject of death.

J. Allan Mitchell argues that an allegory lies between 'Queen Katherine and the Secret of Lydgate's *Temple of Glass*' (*MÆ* 77[2008] 54–76), for Lydgate had come to sympathize with Henry V's widow and to approve her independent self-determination in marrying Owen Tudor. Andrew Galloway links 'John Lydgate and the Origins of Vernacular Humanism' (*JEGP* 107[2008] 445–71), applying historicism to *The Serpent of Division* and exploring the grounds of the connection. Lisa H. Cooper's ' "His guttys wer out shake": Illness and Indigence in Lydgate's *Letter to Gloucester* and *Fabula duorum mercatorum*' (*SAC* 30[2008] 303–34) seizes upon the image of the poet's purse as an ailing body and follows it through typically Lydgatean images of inversion or reversal, seeing in the *Letter* patronage turned to commerce and in the *Fabula* commerce turned to affection.

Shannon Gayk's ' "Among psalms to fynde a cleer sentence": John Lydgate, Eleanor Hull, and the Art of Vernacular Exegesis' (*NML* 10[2008] 161–89) inspects contemporary exegeses of 'De profundis' for their intellectual nature and in their search for a reformist milieu that did not rely on affective devotion, and that was supported by social and institutional authority. In 'The Dance of Death in London: John Carpenter, John Lydgate, and the *Daunce of Poulys*' (*JMEMS* 38[2008] 285–314), Amy Appleford reads Carpenter's commissioned *Daunce* as an attempt to picture the political community of London in its variety and changeability, with the B version of Lydgate's poem as that intended for the paintings.

(c) Hoccleve

Once again, this is a year of few Hoccleve studies. Richard Firth Green and Ethan Knapp make a correction concerning 'Thomas Hoccleve's Seal' (*MÆ* 77[2008] 319–21) to Linne Mooney's account (see *YWES* 88[2009] 258): it should read '† : VA : MA : VOLUNTEE :' meaning 'Go, my will [to God or heaven]' as reflected in the *Regiment of Princes* and the *Series*. Nicholas Perkins's 'Haunted Hoccleve? *The Regiment of Princes*, the Troilean Intertext, and Conversations with the Dead' (*ChauR* 43[2008] 103–39) discusses a number of new or under-discussed borrowings from or allusions to Chaucer, adding a tabular list of such passages, including shared proverbs.

8. Malory and Caxton

(a) Malory

Malorian criticism this year tended to focus on the Grail and political uses of Arthurian romance and a number of shorter studies on his sources, questions of genre and themes. P.J.C. Field's newly revised edition of *Le Morte Darthur: The Seventh and Eighth Tales* provides both students and scholars with a revised text and new ancillary material, including a very thorough introduction to the Arthurian tradition and Malory's place in it. In *Malory's Library: The Sources of the Morte Darthur*, Ralph Norris focuses primarily on the minor sources Malory used, and makes a persuasive case for the inclusion of Malory's own early tales in the list of minor sources for his last ones. The book consists of an introduction and one chapter for each of the eight tales that form the *Morte*. Norris takes account of previous criticism, ranging widely from Oscar Sommer's late nineteenth-century edition through to the present day. Malory's method of translation and adaptation is, as expected, given prominent place in the discussion, with particular reference to his invention or reuse of Arthurian names, one of the most appealing features of his narrative. John Hardyng's *Chronicle* is shown to function as a minor source in more than one tale, while the Vulgate *Suite de Merlin* and the *Alliterative Morte Arthure*, Malory's main sources for Tale I ('The Tale of King Arthur') and Tale II

('The Tale of King Arthur and the Emperor Lucius') respectively, are, Norris argues, minor sources for the same tales (the *Suite* for Tale II, and the alliterative poem for Tale I). In his analysis of 'The Tale of Sir Gareth' Norris presents fresh evidence about the geographical location of the castle of 'Kyng Kenadon', and in the discussion of 'The Tale of Sir Tristram' he reviews and corrects previous criticism of the links between Malory's tale and the two romances *Sir Orfeo* and *Sir Tristrem*. Chaucer, Lydgate, and, once again, Hardyng are minor sources in Malory's last tales, while the chapter on the Holy Grail quest only warrants a few pages, given the prominence of a major source (but see the article by P.J.C. Field, reviewed below, with regard to several possible sources for this tale). Well researched, though not always well presented (incomplete references and typos abound), Norris's book will inform all new studies of Malory's sources.

Roberta Davidson also focuses on Malory's engagement with his sources in her article 'The "Freynshe booke" and the English Translator: Malory's "Originality" Revisited' (*T&L* 17:ii[2008] 133–49); Davidson reviews previous criticism on Malory and Caxton's print, and uses some of Malory's well-known original passages, concluding that Malory was 'a redactor, a creative adaptor, and compiler of Arthurian narratives' (p. 149).

Kevin Whetter's *Understanding Genre and Medieval Romance* (reviewed section 6 above) contains an investigation of the vexed question of the romance genre, working through a variety of texts, and leading to Malory's late romance. In the last and longest chapter of his monograph, 'Generic Juxtapositioning in Malory's *Morte Darthur*' (pp. 99–149), Whetter contends that Malory's work was conceived of as a tragedy. He carefully investigates the tragic dimension throughout the *Morte*, in particular with reference to the trajectory followed by Balin, the quintessential tragic hero, whose 'dolorous stroke' both kills his brother and triggers a series of unfortunate events with devastating consequences for the Round Table fellowship.

Norris J. Lacy edits *The Grail, the Quest and the World of Arthur*, in which two chapters focus on Malory's work. In 'Grail and Quest in the Medieval English World of Arthur' (pp. 126–40), Phillip C. Boardman returns scholars' attention to Middle English retellings of the Grail quest, which he notes is well represented in the alliterative *Joseph of Arimathea*, Henry Lovelich's *History of the Holy Grail*, John Hardyng's section of the Grail quest in his *Chronicle*, and Malory's version, alongside the lesser romance *Sir Percyvell*. Boardman concludes, in agreement with earlier criticism, that Galahad's life is '*only* an episode in his father's [Launcelot's]' (p. 129; author's italics). In the same collection, P.J.C. Field's 'Malory and the Grail: The Importance of Detail' (pp. 141–55), draws attention to the fact that the sources Malory used in his *Sankgreal* story are of a more complex nature than previously thought; Field discusses at least other four sources, including the *Vulgate*, the *Post-Vulgate*, the *Prose Tristan*, and *Perlesvaus* (p. 147). Among other points of great interest in Malory's version of the Grail story is the difference between the Winchester manuscript and Caxton's print in the passage of the last vision of the Grail; in the Winchester, Field argues, Malory replaced his source's reference to Maundy Thursday with Easter Day, which leads to 'a unique moment of illumination' for Malory (p. 155), though one which was lost on readers who, for 400 years, had access to Caxton's edition, since Caxton corrected what he thought was a mistake, and restored the original 'Maundy Thursday'.

In a study of Malory's Grail quest, 'Malory's Lancelot and the Key to Salvation' (*ArthL* 25[2008] 93–118), Raluca L. Radulescu argues that Malory's treatment of Lancelot in the Grail quest and the 'Healing of Sir Urry' alters the overall presentation of the Arthurian story in three significant ways: it shows that Lancelot's spiritual state is developing, not declining, after the quest; that the 'Healing' is an open miracle, for the whole fellowship, and a contrast to the private world of quest experiences; and that the phrase 'best knight of the world' acquires new meanings in the episode of the 'Healing'. In 'Insular Romance and Genealogy' (in Radulescu and Kennedy, eds., pp. 7–25), Raluca L. Radulescu also addresses the political implications of Malory's use of the Grail story, in relation to an insular interest in genealogy and the writing of national history. Malory's Grail story features, albeit briefly, in Juliette Wood's *Eternal Chalice: The Enduring Legend of the Holy Grail*, while Jon Whitman's 'Transfers of Empire, Movements of Mind: Holy Sepulchre and Holy Grail' (*MLN* 123[2008] 895–923) and 'National Icon: The Winchester Round Table and the Revelation of Authority' (*Arth* 18:iv[2008] 33–65) include references to the development of the Grail stories, including Malory's.

Sarah L. Peverley, in 'Political Consciousness and the Literary Mind in Late Medieval England: Men "Brought Up of Nought" in Vale, Hardyng, *Mankind*, and Malory' (*SP* 105[2008] 1–29), explores the commonplace motif of the evil counsellors to the king in fifteenth-century political and non-political texts against the contemporary background of civil war, while Colin Richmond reassesses Malory's work in the context of the transition between the medieval political state to the early modern state in his 'Malory and Modernity: A Qualm about Paradigm Shifts' (*CK* 14:i[2008] 34–44).

In his chapter on 'Malory's Divided Wales' (in Kennedy and Meecham-Jones, eds., 175–89), Cory James Rushton argues persuasively that 'Malory testifies to [a] continuing English fear of the margins when he notes that Arthur's enemies hail from every possible border region' (p. 177); Rushton's meticulous analysis sheds light on many relevant, though little studied, passages in a number of Malory's tales.

(b) Caxton

Alison Wiggins explores the uses of Caxton's printed copies of Chaucer's work in her 'What Did Renaissance Readers Write in their Printed Copies of Chaucer?' (*Library* 7th series 9:i[2008] 3–36), and Caxton's work also features, albeit briefly, in a number of other scholarly articles not primarily focused on Caxton: Roberta Davidson, 'The "Freynshe booke" and the English Translator: Malory's "Originality" Revisited' (*T&L* 17:ii[2008] 133–49), reviewed in section 8(*a*) above; Robert Epstein, '"Fer in the north; I kan nat telle where": Dialect, Regionalism, and Philologism' (*SAC* 30[2008]

95–124); Daniel Wakelin, Possibilities for Reading: Classical Translations in Parallel Texts ca. 1520–1558' (*SP* 105[2008] 463–86); and Jon Whitman, 'National Icon: The Winchester Round Table and the Revelation of Authority' (*Arth* 18:iv[2008] 33–65), reviewed in section 8(*a*) above.

9. Middle Scots Poetry

This year the Scottish Text Society published *The Poems of Walter Kennedy*, edited by Nicole Meier, and the hefty tome belies Kennedy's modest known production of only six poems. This welcome edition contains a thorough introduction covering what is known of Kennedy's life, his manuscript tradition, and critical analyses of The *Passioun*, his Marian poem, his shorter poems, and *The Flyting of Dunbar and Kennedie*. The introduction is followed by the texts themselves, which are only glossed with textual variations and emendations. Following the texts are complete explanatory notes on the poems, as well as appendices covering editorial emendations concerning capitalization and punctuation, and textual notes on the *Passioun* and the *Flyting*. The volume concludes with a glossary, certain to be helpful to all scholars of Middle Scots language, an index of names, and a bibliography.

Only one essay in the 2007 volume *Middle English* touches on Middle Scots poetry, and that is Nicolette Zeeman's 'Imaginative Theory' (in Strohm, ed., pp. 222–40). Zeeman focuses on the genre of the *chanson d'aventure*, arguing that it constructs its own figurative expression of literary theory. Among her literary examples, Zeeman turns to Henryson's *Fables*, in particular 'The Lion and the Mouse' and 'The Preaching of the Swallow'. She writes that these juxtaposed *chansons d'aventure* postulate a kind of exemplary 'seeing' (p. 239) of the moral lessons they narrate.

Only one monograph in 2008 concentrates on Middle Scots poetry, Joanna Martin's *Kingship and Love in Scottish Poetry, 1424–1540*. This focused volume covers aspects of Dunbar, Henryson, James I, Sir David Lyndsay, and under-studied texts such as *Lancelot of the Laik* and *King Hart*, among others. Martin argues that much of Middle Scots poetry is concerned with the 'the impact of sexual desire on the king's governance of his realm and therefore establish[es] a connection between the moral order of the self and good political rule' (p. 1). Indeed, she suggests that the little 'love poetry' that survives from late medieval Scotland is almost always tied up in a political theme as well—that the two are inextricably linked for writer and audience. In her introduction, 'The Wooing of the King', Martin surveys the political and instructional texts contemporary to the Middle Scots poets, such as *The Buke of the Governaunce of Princis* and *The Buke of the Order of Knychthede*, highlights the principles of these texts, and speculates how they may have influenced the poets themselves.

In the chapters that follow, Martin uses this basis to look closely at specific texts and authors and how kingship and desire are intertwined. The first chapter, '*The Kingis Quair* and *The Quare of Jelusy*', examines the most overtly political of the Middle Scots poems, James I's *Kingis Quair*, along with another poem preserved in MS Selden B. 24 (the only witness to the *Quair*),

The Quare of Jelusy. She follows this with a chapter on *Lancelot of the Laik*, the Middle Scots translation and rewriting of the French prose romance of the same name, suggesting that the poet's focus on Lancelot and Arthur plays out a complex relationship between the amatory and the political. Martin then turns to *The Buik of King Alexander the Conquerour*, an Alexander romance that greatly expands on any surviving Middle English texts. She suggests that here love is used primarily as a vehicle in order to fully explain Alexander's heroism and kingship. Martin turns to Henryson's *Orpheus and Eurydice* in her chapter 'Robert Henryson's "traite of Orpheus kyng" ', examining Orpheus as a young and susceptible king in the light of James IV. She also includes a chapter on the under-studied *The Thre Prestis of Peblis*, a poem whose date of composition is in dispute, but whose first surviving witness is early sixteenth-century. The poem comprises three separate tales, each of which receives a subsection in the chapter. Martin's final chapter is on the allegorical *King Hart*, which Martin reads closely in relation to its larger political themes. The book closes with an epilogue on the 'Poetry and the Minority of James V', looking at some of the poems of David Lyndsay, John Bellenden, and William Stewart in relationship to the court that they served. Each chapter helpfully lays out the manuscript and historical tradition of the works studied therein, and overall this is an extremely welcome study for students of Middle Scots literature.

William Dunbar received much critical attention in 2008. Priscilla Bawcutt's 'Dunbar and his Readers: From Allan Ramsay to Richard Burton' (*SSL* 35[2007] 362–81) addresses Dunbar's reputation, from the eighteenth century and beyond. Bawcutt looks at editors, anthologists, and poets, as well as literary critics, but suggests towards the end of her discussion that much work still needs to be done on the reception of Dunbar among the other *makars*. In 'Reconsidering Dunbar's *Sir Thomas Norny* and Chaucer's Tale of *Sir Thopas*' (*SSL* 35[2007] 444–54), Deanna Delmar Evans challenges the view that Dunbar's *Sir Thomas Norny* may be derivative of *Sir Thopas*, and indeed works from the assumption that it is not at all indebted to Chaucer, and that it ultimately differs in its content, authorial intent, and genre.

Dunbar's *Tretis of the Tua Mariit Wemen and the Wedo* is discussed, along with Suero de Ribera's 'En una linda floresta', in Alan Deyermond's 'Three Ladies in a Garden: Suero de Ribera and Dunbar' (*CL* 60[2008] 29–44), where he examines close thematic, generic, and linguistic similarities between the two poems, and suggests reasons for these analogues. Gregory A. Foran's 'Dunbar's Broken Rainbow: Symbol, Allegory, and Apocalypse in "The Golden Targe" ' (*PQ* 86[2007] 47–65) looks at the generic conventions of the dream vision, but also at the ways in which the 'Targe' departs from genre. He is particularly interested in what he considers to be critically ignored complex religious allegories and symbolism throughout the poem.

This year's *Fifteenth-Century Studies* yields one essay on Middle Scots poetry: Alessandra Petrina's 'Robert Henryson's "Orpheus and Eurydice" and its Sources' (*FCS* 33[2008] 198–217). Petrina takes as her point of departure the lack of a named source in Henryson's poem, in contrast to his other major works, which readily name the basis for their narratives, and what this means in terms of the poem and Henryson's conception and construction of it. She argues that Henryson relies heavily on allegory and allusion to much of the Greco-Roman tradition and that this sometimes makes the poem difficult to navigate, but that his incorporation of *auctoritas* is rather nuanced and worthy of critical unpacking.

George Edmondson turns to Robert Henryson in 'Henryson's Doubt: Neighbors and Negation in *The Testament of Cresseid*' (*Exemplaria* 20[2008] 165–96), placing the poem in contrast to Chaucer's *Troilus and Criseyde* using the psychoanalytic concept of *Nebenmensch* (positioning one text as a neighbour to another). Edmondson suggests that Henryson is negating Chaucer's *Troilus* through the choices he makes in constructing his poem, and that he offers it as a kind of response to England's increased hostility towards neighbouring Scotland. Richard Firth Green similarly positions Chaucer next to a Middle Scots poet in 'Did Chaucer Know the Ballad of *Glen Kindy*?' (*Neophil* 92[2008] 351–8), where he argues that Gavin Douglas's *The Palice of Honour* and Chaucer's *The House of Fame* both refer to a Welsh harper, Glascurion, whose legend, he suggests, may have come down to both of them in a ballad entitled *Glasgerion* or *Glen Kindy*.

Two articles examine the international influences on medieval Scottish writing. Iain Macleod Higgins, in 'Shades of the East: Orientalism, Religion, and Nation in Late Medieval Scottish Literature' (*JMEMS* 38[2008] 197–228), looks at 'shades' of the East, a word that deliberately invokes both colour and ghosts, in Richard Holland's *Buke of the Howlat* and the *Flyting of Dunbar and Kennedie*. William Calin explores closer influences in 'The French Presence in Medieval Scotland: Le Roi René and *King Hart*' (*Florilegium* 24[2007] 11–20), where he argues the French *dit amoureux* had a crucial impact on Middle Scots courtly narratives, especially the allegorical *King Hart*.

Darragh Greene contributes ' "Sum newe thing": Autobiography, Allegory and Authority in the *Kingis Quair*' (in Carr, Clarke and Neivergelt, eds., *On Allegory: Some Medieval Aspects and Approaches*, pp. 70–86). Greene approaches the question of genre in James I's *Kingis Quair*, which is part-autobiography and part-dream vision, looking specifically at structure and rhetorical strategies through close reading.

Finally, while none of its essays deals directly with the Middle Scots poets and their writings, the collection *Finding the Family in Medieval and Early Modern Scotland*, edited by Elizabeth Ewan and Janay Nugent, would be useful to scholars of Middle Scots literature. In particular Katie Barclay's ' "And four years space, being man and wife, they lovingly agreed": Balladry and Early Modern Understandings of Marriage' (in Ewan and Nugent, eds., pp. 23–33), which discusses medieval Scottish ballads, and Dolly MacKinnon's ' "I have now a book of songs of her writing": Scottish Families, Orality, Literacy and the Transmission of Musical Culture *c*.1500–*c*.1800' (in Ewan and Nugent, eds., pp. 35–48), which looks at medieval and early modern Scottish families and their relationship to text and music.

Ralph Hanna's edition of *The Knightly Tale of Golagros and Gawane* is reviewed in section 3 above.

10. Drama

Among the best of the new books on the early drama published this year is *Visualizing Medieval Performance: Perspectives, Histories, Contexts*, edited by Elina Gertsman, a fascinating collection of essays on various aspects of the performed and the witnessed in late medieval art and culture. Poised productively on the boundaries of optics, the history of art, bibliography, and theatre studies, Gertsman's collection is a valuable addition to studies of pre-modern drama and performance from a richly interdisciplinary angle. Setting 'performance' in its broadest context, the contributors range across the fields of preaching, the liturgy, church architecture, manuscript illumination, sculpture and narrative as well as the dramatic, quasi-dramatic, ritual, and ceremonial. All of the chapters are worthy of close scrutiny by drama scholars, but those most obviously and directly focused on the drama itself (albeit largely on continental examples) are Erika Fischer-Lichte's thought provoking piece, 'The Medieval Religious Plays—Ritual or Theatre?' (pp. 249–62) and Glenn Ehrstine's 'Framing the Passion: Mansion Staging as Visual Mnemonic' (pp. 263–78). Further essays look productively at music and dance in late medieval Europe.

Also much to be welcomed is a revised second edition of *The Cambridge Companion to Medieval English Theatre*, edited by Richard Beadle and Alan J. Fletcher. This is a substantial revision of the groundbreaking original collection, published in 1994 and edited by Beadle alone (*YWES* 75[1997] 161–2). All of the chapters have been updated, and the select bibliography and 'Guide to Criticism of Medieval English Theatre', written by Peter Happé (pp. 326–60), has been expanded and rewritten to incorporate the wealth of critical studies published in the field since the early 1990s. One chapter in the earlier volume, that on Cornish drama, has been removed, and three new ones have been specially commissioned. The first of these, 'An Introduction to Medieval English Theatre' (pp. 1–25) by Alexandra F. Johnston, surveys the history, geographical spread, and generic range of 'early drama', drawing on the author's rich experience of the drama records. In the second, 'The Cultural Work of Early Drama' (pp. 75–98), Greg Walker reflects on the 'performative turn' in drama studies and its implications for work on the later medieval and early modern periods, examining the range of responses that plays from the civic religious cycles to the moralities and Sir David Lyndsay's *Ane Satyre of the Thrie Estaitis* seem designed to provoke in their diverse audiences. The third new piece, John McKinnell's 'Modern Productions of Medieval English Drama' (pp. 287–325), reviews a broad spectrum of twentieth- and twenty-first-century productions of early plays, from spectacular professional pieces such as the National Theatre's *Mysteries*, directed by Bill Bryden and scripted by Tony Harrison, and the South African *Yiimimangaliso*, to more modest community and academic productions on reconstructed pageant wagons in city streets or in the halls of university buildings.

Two of the essays in Pauline Blanc, ed., *Selfhood on the Early Modern English Stage* also look closely at the early drama. André Lascombe's 'The Selfhood of Stage Figures and their Spectacular Efficacy in Early English Plays (*c.*1450–1528)' (pp. 8–20) scrutinizes allegorical personifications as the nexus of intellectual and theatrical energy in the interludes and moralities. Meanwhile, in 'Wit and Will and the Cohesion of the Human Self in the English Moral Drama' (pp. 21–32), Jean-Paul Debax examines the treatment of 'mankind' figures in the *humanum genus* plays, specifically exploring the representation of free will through the Reformation period as an index of these plays' variously successful attempts to represent human selfhood. References to the drama are also liberally scattered through Jon Robinson's excellent study, *Court Politics, Culture and Literature in Scotland and England, 1500–1540*. This book's focus on politics and literature on both sides of the Anglo-Scottish border makes it a particularly interesting comparative study of the role of texts and performances in court and popular politics in the first half of the sixteenth century. The Scottish dramatic material draws heavily, as one might expect, on Sir David Lyndsay's *Ane Satyre of the Thrie Estaitis*, but George Buchanan's work also features strongly, while the sparser English examples are largely taken from Skelton's *Magnyfycence* and the polemical work of John Bale. In each case Robinson uses the plays, alongside courtly poetry and prose writing, to point up the complexities of both the representations of political culture and the courtly politics with which they engage.

Among the specialist journals, this year's *Medieval English Theatre* (*METh* 28[2008 for 2006]) maintains its excellent record for publishing new work on a wide range of plays, performances, festivals and the various pre-modern cultures of playing. Its lead essay, James McBain's ' "By example and gode reason": Reconsidering Commonplaces and the Law in *Fulgens and Lucrece*' (*METh* 28[2008 for 2006] 3–28) is a splendid reading of the debate on nobility in that play, which identifies its debts (and those of its source texts—John Tiptoft's *The Declamacion of Noblesse* [*c*.1460] and Buonaccorso da Montemagno's *Controversia de Nobilitate* [1428] to classical oratorical precedents. Gordon Kipling's weighty and wide-ranging essay, '*Le Régisseur toujours sur les planches*: Gustave Cohen's Construction of the Medieval "*meneur de jeu*" ' (*METh* 28[2008 for 2006] 29–130), uses visual and textual evidence to cast doubt on the long-cherished idea of the 'always on-stage director' in large-scale French drama. Louis Peter Grijp's 'Boys and Female Impersonators in the Amsterdam Theatre of the Seventeenth Century' (*METh* 28[2008 for 2006] 131–70) is equally suggestive, attesting as it does to the range of approaches to the representation of female roles in the Dutch drama of the period. Finally, Priscilla Bawcutt's brief 'A Note on the Term "Morality" ' (*METh* 28[2008 for 2006] 171–4) draws attention to the intriguing early reference to 'playing' a 'morality' in the records of the visit of John Inglish and his players to Edinburgh in the entourage of Margaret Tudor in August 1503.

In other journals, Holly Dugan's article, 'Scent of a Woman: Performing the Politics of Smell in Late Medieval and Early Modern England' (*JMEMS* 38[2008] 229–52) looks productively at a trio of 'remarkably odiferous plays' (p. 229) in which the central female roles are strongly associated with smells: *Antony and Cleopatra*, *Twelfth Night*, and, most interestingly from an early drama perspective, the Digby *Mary Magdalene*. Noting how the Digby play represents both the Magdalene's initial fall into sin and debauchery and her subsequent repentance and life of asceticism in terms of a complex array of

pungent odours—frankincense, musk, gillyflowers—Dugan skilfully demonstrates how 'the play stages both the sinful nature of a luxurious touch and the
venerating touch of salvation' (p. 236) through sensual representations of
femininity performed by an all-male cast.

A number of articles in this year's *Early Theatre* (*ET* 11[2008]) address the
earlier period covered by this chapter. Ernst Gerhardt's ' "We pray you all ...
to drink ere ye pass": Bann Criers, Parish Players and the Henrician
Reformation in England' (*ET* 11:i[2008] 57–88) discusses the decline of parish
plays, primarily in the south-west of Kent, during the sixteenth century,
finding the origins of the phenomenon in the 1520s rather than later, and so
arguing that the Reformation may have had a rather less significant impact
upon the viability of such plays than some accounts have suggested. In place of
the growth of radical religious reform and official censorship or indifference,
Gerhardt suggests that the gradual disappearance of a sense of 'associative
connection', *communitas*, or social capital among the parishes may have sown
the seeds of the plays' decline in the longer term. In 'A Crisis of Gerontocracy
and the Coventry Plays' (*ET* 11:ii[2008] 13–32), Sheila K. Christie also dwells
upon the notion of decline. Building on the work of Charles Phythian-Adams,
Theresa Coletti, and others, Christie explores the representations of youth and
age in the surviving texts of the Coventry pageants, seeing in them a communal
reflection on the city's demographic crisis of the early sixteenth century as well
the religious changes of the later Henrician period. The religious and cultural
world of the mid-Tudor drama is also vividly portrayed in a number of the
essays in *The Church of Mary Tudor*, edited by Eamon Duffy and David
Loades, which offer accounts of the political, theological, and literary culture
of the Marian period. Another book that helpfully adds complexity and
nuance to our understanding of the religious and bibliographical culture of the
Reformation years and their aftermath, in which the urban religious plays
experienced their last florescence, is Anne Overell's *Italian Reform and English
Reformations, c.1535–c.1585*. Overell tells the fascinating story of the
interactions between Italian religious reform—the would-be architects of
Italy's never-to-happen reformation—and English thought and practice,
suggesting that the influence of Italian ideas on English Protestantism was
considerably more substantial and significant than previous studies have
allowed.

Readers interested in the Bakhtinian culture of the folk plays and popular
drama and festival will gain considerable benefit and a good deal of pleasure
from reading Alison G. Stewart's *Before Bruegel: Sebald Beham and the
Origins of Peasant Festival Imagery*. This book is a fascinating analysis of a
series of around a dozen prints of scenes of misrule in peasant festivals
produced in Nuremberg between 1524 and 1535 by Sebald Beham, a one-time
apprentice of Albrecht Dürer. Stewart's persuasive case is that, through these
prints, Beham effectively invented the peasant festival as a subject of early
modern visual art, thus (as her title suggests) paving the way for the later, and
much better-known, work of Peter Bruegel the Elder. In the course of the book
Stewart demonstrates both the richness and the variety of Beham's bawdy,
scatological representations of peasant celebrations, cautionary images, and

visualizations of proverbs, the influence of which lasted well beyond the sixteenth century.

Unavailable for review for this chapter were William Kuskin, *Symbolic Caxton: Literary Culture and Print Capitalism* (Notre Dame [2008]); Suzanne M. Yeager, *Jerusalem in Medieval Narrative* (CUP [2008]); and Katherine Zieman, *Singing the New Song: Literacy and Liturgy in Late Medieval England* (UPennP [2008]).

Books Reviewed

Amano, Masachiyo, Michicko Ogura, and Masayuki Ohkado, eds. *Historical Englishes in Varieties of Texts and Contexts: The Global COE Program, International Conference 2007*. Lang. [2008] pp. xi + 403. £48 $99.95 ISBN 9 7836 3158 1902.

Arn, Mary-Jo. *The Poet's Notebook: The Personal Manuscript of Charles d'Orléans (Paris BnF MS fr. 25458)*. Texts & Transitions 3. Brepols. [2008] pp. xxii + 202 + CD. €80 (£78, $116) ISBN 9 7825 0352 0704.

Barr, Beth Allison. *The Pastoral Care of Women in Late Medieval England*. Boydell. [2008] pp. 171. £50 ($95) ISBN 9 7818 4383 3734.

Beadle, Richard, and Alan J. Fletcher, eds. *The Cambridge Companion to Medieval English Theatre*, 2nd edn. CUP. [2008] pp. xxi + 398. hb £47 ISBN 9 7805 2186 4008, pb £18.99 ISBN 9 7805 2168 2541.

Blanc, Pauline, ed. *Selfhood on the Early Modern English Stage*. CambridgeSP. [2008] pp. 225. £34.99 ISBN 9 7818 4718 4511.

Bliss, Jane. *Naming and Namelessness in Medieval Romance*. CUP. [2008] pp. xii + 253. £50 ISBN 9 7818 4384 1593.

Bork, Robert, and Andrea Kann, eds. *The Art, Science, and Technology of Medieval Travel*. AVISTA Studies in the History of Medieval Technology, Science, and Art 6. Ashgate. [2008] pp. xiv + 226. £55 ($99.95) ISBN 9 7807 5466 3072.

Brears, Peter. *Cooking and Dining in Medieval England*. Prospect. [2008] pp. 560. £30 ($60) ISBN 9 7819 0301 8552.

Brown, Jennifer N., ed. *Three Women of Liège: A Critical Edition of and Commentary on the Middle English Lives of Elizabeth of Spalbeek, Christina Mirabilis, and Marie d'Oignies*. Medieval Women: Texts and Contexts 23. Brepols. [2008] pp. viii + 348. €70 (£61.90, $102) ISBN 9 7825 0352 4719.

Bryan, Jennifer. *Looking Inward: Devotional Reading and the Private Self in Late Medieval England*. UPennP. [2008] pp. 288. £32.50 ($49.95) ISBN 9 7808 1224 0481.

Burgess, Glyn S. *Marie de France: Supplement 3*. Research Bibliographies and Checklists: NS 8. Tamesis. [2007] pp. xi + 135. £50 ($85) ISBN 9 7818 5566 1547.

Burrow, J.A. *Medieval Writers and their Work*. OUP. [2008] pp. 156. £16 ISBN 9 7801 9953 2049.

Burrow, J.A. *The Poetry of Praise*. CUP. [2008] pp. viii + 200. £47 ($90) ISBN 9 7805 2188 6932.

Cannon, Christopher. *Middle English Literature: A Cultural History*. Polity. [2008] pp. xii + 256. hb £55 ($69.95) ISBN 9 7807 4562 4419, pb £17.99 ($26.95) ISBN 9 7807 4562 4426.

Carr, Mary, K.P. Clarke, and Marco Nievergelt, eds. *On Allegory: Some Medieval Aspects and Approaches*. CambridgeSP. [2008] pp. 269. £34.99 ($69.99) ISBN 9 7818 4718 4009.

Cartlidge, Neil, ed. *Boundaries in Medieval Romance*. CUP. [2008] pp. x + 198 £50 ISBN 9 7818 4384 1555.

Cartwright, Jane. *Feminine Sanctity and Spirituality in Medieval Wales*. UWalesP. [2008] pp. xv + 301. £75 ($85) ISBN 9 7807 0831 9994.

Cawsey, Kathleen, and Jason Harris, eds. *Transmission and Transformation in the Middle Ages*. FCP. [2007] pp. 257. €55. ISBN 9 7818 5182 9903.

Classen, Albrecht, ed. *Old Age in the Middle Ages and the Renaissance: Interdisciplinary Approaches to a Neglected Topic*. Gruyter. [2007] pp. vii + 575. $152. €98. ISBN 9 7831 1019 5484.

Cole, Andrew. *Literature and Heresy in the Age of Chaucer*. CUP. [2008] pp. xix + 297. £52 ($93) ISBN 9 7805 2188 7915.

Connolly, Margaret, and Linne R. Mooney, eds. *Design and Distribution of Late Medieval Manuscripts in England*. York Medieval Press. [2008] pp. xiv + 338. £60 $115 ISBN 9 7819 0315 3246.

Cooper, Lisa H., and Andrea Denny-Brown, eds. *Lydgate Matters: Poetry and Culture in the Fifteenth Century*. The New Middle Ages. Palgrave. [2007] pp. viii + 224. £42.50 $79.95 ISBN 9 7814 0397 6741.

Davies, Owen. *Grimoires: A History of Magic Books*. OUP. [2008] pp. xii + 372. £14.99 ($29.95) ISBN 9 7801 9920 4519.

Davis, Carmel Bendon. *Mysticism and Space: Space and Spatiality in the Works of Richard Rolle, 'The Cloud of Unknowing' Author, and Julian of Norwich*. CUAP. [2008] pp. xiii + 271. £67.50 ($74.95) ISBN 9 7808 1321 5228.

Davlin, Mary Clemente. *A Journey into Love: Meditating with 'Piers Plowman'*. MaIP. [2008] pp. x + 170 + 16 plates. $14.95 ISBN 9 7815 9907 0315.

Duffy, Eamon, and David Loades, eds. *The Church of Mary Tudor*. Ashgate. [2008] pp. xxi + 348. £65 ISBN 9 7807 5463 0708.

Dutton, Elisabeth. *Julian of Norwich: The Influence of Late-Medieval Devotional Compilations*. Brewer. [2008] pp. 189. £50 ($95) ISBN 9 7818 4384 1814.

Echard, Siân. *Printing the Middle Ages*. UPennP. [2008] pp. xviii + 318. £42.50 ($65) ISBN 9 7808 1224 0917.

Ellis, Roger, ed. *The Oxford History of Literary Translation in English, vol 1: To 1550*. OUP. [2008] pp. x + 486. £100 ($190) ISBN 9 7801 9924 6205.

Ewan, Elizabeth, and Janay Nugent, eds. *Finding the Family in Medieval and Early Modern Scotland*. Ashgate. [2008] pp. xv + 190. £55 ($99.95) ISBN 9 7807 5466 0491.

Fellows, Jennifer, and Ivana Djordjeviç, eds. *Sir Bevis of Hampton in Literary Tradition*. CUP. [2008] pp. xii + 207. £50 ISBN 9 7818 4384 1739.

Field, P.J.C., ed. *Sir Thomas Malory: Le Morte Darthur: The Seventh and Eighth Tales*. Hackett. [2008] pp. lxxxvii + 218. $14.95 ISBN 9 7808 7220 9466.

Fitzmaurice, Susan M., and Donka Minkova. *Studies in the History of the English Language, vol. 4: Empirical and Analytical Advances in the Study of English Language Change.* Gruyter. [2008] pp. ix + 433. $152. (€98) ISBN 9 7831 1020 5879.

French, Katherine L. *The Good Women of the Parish: Gender and Religion after the Black Death.* UPennP. [2008] pp. xi + 336. £45.50 ($69.95) ISBN 9 7808 1224 0535.

Gertsman, Elina, ed. *Visualizing Medieval Performance: Perspectives, Histories, Contexts.* Ashgate. [2008] pp. xii + 348. £60 ISBN 9 7807 5466 4369.

Gray, Douglas. *Later Medieval English Literature.* OUP. [2008] pp. xiv + 712. £65 ($130) ISBN 9 7801 9812 2180.

Green, Monica. *Making Women's Medicine Masculine: The Rise of Male Authority in Pre-Modern Gynaecology.* OUP. [2008] pp. xx + 409. £74 ($120) ISBN 9 7801 9921 1494.

Gunn, Cate. *Ancrene Wisse: From Pastoral Literature to Vernacular Spirituality.* UWalesP. [2008] pp. 243. £75 ($85) ISBN 9 7807 0832 0341.

Hanawalt, Barbara A., and Anna Grotans, eds. *Living Dangerously: On the Margins in Medieval and Early Modern Europe.* UNDP. [2007] pp. 184. $27 ISBN 9 7802 6803 0827.

Hanna, Ralph, ed. *The Knightly Tale of Golagros and Gawane.* B&B. [2008] pp. xlv + 145. £35 ISBN 9 7818 9797 6296.

Hanna, Ralph, ed. *'Speculum Vitae': A Reading Edition.* EETS OS 331–2. OUP. [2008] pp. xcvi + 674. £70 ($150) ISBN 9 7801 9956 3999 (vol. 1), ISBN 9 7801 9956 4002 (vol. 2), ISBN 9 7801 9956 4019 (set).

Jacquart, Danielle, and Agostino Paravicini Bagliani, eds. *La 'Collectio Salernitana' di Salvatore de Renzi.* Sismel. [2008] pp. xviii + 262. €45 ISBN 9 7888 8450 3169.

Jacquart, Danielle, and Agostino Paravicini Bagliani, eds. *La Scuola Medica Salernitana: gli autori e i testi.* Sismel. [2007] pp. xiv + 588. €68 ISBN 9 7888 8450 2322.

Kendall, Elliot. *Lordship and Literature: John Gower and the Politics of the Great Household.* Oxford English Monographs. Clarendon. [2008] pp. xii + 302. £50 ($99) ISBN 9 7801 9954 2642.

Kennedy, Ruth, and Simon Meecham-Jones, eds. *Authority and Subjugation in Writing of Medieval Wales* Palgrave Macmillan. [2008] pp. xv + 289. £39.99 ISBN 9 7802 3060 2953.

Lacy, Norris J., ed. *The Grail, the Quest and the World of Arthur.* B&B. [2008] pp. xvii + 214. £50 ISBN 9 7818 4384 1708.

Lalla, Barbara. *Postcolonialisms: Caribbean Rereading of Medieval English Discourse.* UWI. [2008] pp. xvi + 440. pb £31.50 ($35) ISBN 9 7897 6640 2013.

Mackley, J.S. *The Legend of St Brendan: A Comparative Study of the Latin and Anglo-Norman Versions.* Brill. [2008] pp. xiv + 350. €99 (£89.10) $147 ISBN 9 7890 0416 6622.

Martin, Joanna. *Kingship and Love in Scottish Poetry, 1424–1540.* Ashgate. [2008] pp. 212. £50 ($99.95) ISBN 9 7807 5466 2730.

McAvoy, Liz Herbert, ed. *A Companion to Julian of Norwich.* Brewer. [2008] pp. 249. £50 ($95) ISBN 9 7818 4384 1722.

Meier, Nicole, ed. *The Poems of Walter Kennedy*. Scottish Text Society. [2008] pp. cxvii + 449. £35 ($70) ISBN 9 7818 9797 6289.

Merisalo, O., and P. Pahta, eds. *Frontiers in the Middle Ages: Proceedings of the Third European Congress of Medieval Studies*. Brepols. [2006] pp. 766. £80 ($160) ISBN 9 7825 0352 4207.

Morrison, Susan Signe. *Excrement in the Late Middle Ages: Sacred Filth and Chaucer's Fecopoetics*. Palgrave. [2008] pp. xiii + 271. $95 ISBN 1 4039 8488 3.

Neal, Derek G. *The Masculine Self in Late Medieval England*. UChicP. [2008] pp. xiv + 304. hb £40 ($68) ISBN 9 7802 2656 9550, pb £14.50 ($25) ISBN 9 7802 2656 9574.

Nichols, Ann Eljenholm. *Cambridge, vol.1: Christ's College, Clare College, Corpus Christi College, Emmanuel College, Gonville and Caius College, and the Fitzwilliam Museum*. Vol. 5 of *An Index of Images in English Manuscripts from the Time of Chaucer to Henry VIII c.1380–c.1509*. HM. [2008] pp. 234. pb €60 ($87) ISBN 9 7819 0537 5370.

Norris, Ralph. *Malory's Library: The Sources of the Morte Darthur*. CUP. [2008] pp. viii + 187. £45 ISBN 9 7818 4384 1548.

Overell, Anne. *Italian Reform and English Reformations, c.1535–c.1585*. Ashgate. [2008] pp. xii + 250. £60 ISBN 9 7807 5465 5794.

Parkes, M.B. *Their Hands before our Eyes: A Closer Look at Scribes, The Lyell Lectures Delivered in the University of Oxford 1999*. Ashgate. [2008] pp. xx + 190 + 69 plates. £65 ($124.95) ISBN 9 7807 5466 3379.

Pearsall, Derek. *Piers Plowman: A New Annotated Edition of the C-Text*. UExeP. [2008] pp. 432. $95 ISBN 9 7808 5989 7839.

Pepin, Ronald E. trans. *The Vatican Mythographers*. Medieval Philosophy: Texts and Studies. FordUP. [2008] pp. x + 358. £58.50 ($65) ISBN 9 7808 2322 8928.

Potter, Lois, and Joshua Calhoun, eds. *Images of Robin Hood: Medieval to Modern*. UDelP. [2008] pp. 288. $65 ISBN 9 7808 7413 0034.

Prado-Pérez, José Ramón, and Dídac Llorens-Cubedo, eds. *New Literatures of Old: Dialogues of Tradition and Innovation in Anglophone Literature*. CambridgeSP. [2008] pp. 194. $52.99 (£34.99) ISBN 9 7818 4718 6232.

Pugh, Tison, and Marcia Smith Marzec, eds. *Men and Masculinities in Chaucer's 'Troilus and Criseyde'*. B&B. [2008] pp. 212. $95 (£50) ISBN 9 7818 4384 1609.

Purdie, Rhiannon. *Anglicising Romance: Tail-Rhyme and Genre in Medieval English Literature*. CUP. [2008] pp. xii + 272. £50 ISBN 9 7818 4384 1623.

Radulescu, Raluca L., and Edward Donald Kennedy, eds. *Broken Lines: Genealogical Literature in Medieval Britain and France*. Brepols. [2008] pp. xiv + 295. € 60 ISBN 9 7825 0352 4856.

Rayner, Samantha J. *Images of Kingship in Chaucer and his Ricardian Contemporaries*. Brewer. [2008] pp. 177. $90 ISBN 9 7818 4384 1746.

Renevey, Denis, and Graham D. Caie, eds. *Medieval Texts in Context*. Routledge. [2008] pp. xii + 260. £70 ($140) ISBN 9 7804 1536 0258.

Rice, Nicole R. *Lay Piety and Religious Discipline in Middle English Literature*. CUP. [2008] pp. xviii + 254. £50 ($90) ISBN 9 7805 2189 6078.

Robinson, Jon. *Court Politics, Culture and Literature in Scotland and England, 1500–1540*. Ashgate. [2008] pp. 186. £50 ISBN 9 7807 5466 0798.

Rosewell, Roger. *Medieval Wall Paintings in English and Welsh Churches*. Boydell. [2008] pp. viii + 382. £39.95 ($80) ISBN 9 7818 4383 3680.

Ruys, Juanita Feros, ed. *What Nature Does Not Teach: Didactic Literature in the Medieval and Early-Modern Periods*. Disputatio 15. Brepols. [2008] pp. xiv + 530. €90 (£60.94, $131) ISBN 9 7825 0352 5969.

Scase, Wendy. *Literature and Complaint in England, 1272–1553*. OUP. [2007] pp. xii + 216. £50 ($95) ISBN 0 1992 7085 6.

Schmidt, A.V.C. *Piers Plowman: A Parallel-Text Edition of the A, B, C, and Z Versions, vol. 2: Introduction, Textual Notes, Commentary, Bibliography, and Indexical Glossary*. MIP. [2008] pp. xiv + 950. $100. ISBN 9 7815 8044 1414.

Schoff, Rebecca L. *Reformations: Three Medieval Authors in Manuscript and Moveable Type*. Brepols. [2007] pp. 200. $87. ISBN 9 7825 0352 3163.

Shuffelton, George, ed. *Codex Ashmole 61: A Compilation of Popular Middle English Verse*. TEAMS Middle English Texts. MIP. [2008] pp. viii + 664. $30 ISBN 9 7815 8044 1292.

Smarr, Janet Levarie, ed. *Writers Reading Writers: Intertextual Studies in Medieval and Early Modern Literature in Honor of Robert Hollander*. UDelP. [2007] pp. 255. $51.40. ISBN 9 7808 7413 9761.

Sobecki, Sebastian I. *The Sea and Medieval English Literature*. CUP. [2008] pp. xii + 205. £45 ISBN 9 7818 4384 1371.

Stanbury, Sarah. *The Visual Object of Desire in Late Medieval England*. UPennP. [2008] pp. 320. £42.50 $65 ISBN 9 7808 1224 0382.

Stewart, Alison G. *Before Bruegel: Sebald Beham and the Origins of Peasant Festival Imagery*. Ashgate. [2008] pp. xx + 358. £55 ISBN 9 7807 5463 3082.

Strohm, Paul, ed. *Middle English*. OUP. [2007] pp. xii + 521. hb £104 ISBN 9 7801 9928 7666, pb £27.50 $55 ISBN 9 7801 9955 9398.

Swanson, R.N. *Indulgences in Late Medieval England: Passports to Paradise?* CUP. [2008] pp. xiv + 579. $110 (£62) ISBN 9 7805 2188 1203.

Thompson, Anne B., ed. *The Northern Homily Cycle*. TEAMS Middle English Texts. MIP. [2008] pp. viii + 296. $20 ISBN 9 7815 8044 1261.

Watkins, C.S. *History and the Supernatural in Medieval England*. CUP. [2007] pp. xii + 276. £55 ($99) ISBN 9 7805 2180 2550.

Wenzel, Siegfried. *Preaching in the Age of Chaucer: Selected Sermons in Translation*. CUAP. [2008] pp. xviii + 334. $34.95 ISBN 9 7808 1321 5297.

Whalen, Logan E. *Marie de France and the Poetics of Memory*. CUAP. [2008] pp. xii + 208. £53.95 ($59.95) ISBN 9 7808 1321 5099.

Whetter, Kevin S. *Understanding Genre and Medieval Romance*. Ashgate. [2008] pp. 205. £55 ISBN 9 7807 5466 1429.

Wood, Juliette. *Eternal Chalice: The Enduring Legend of the Holy Grail*. I.B. Tauris. [2008] pp. ix + 244. $37 ISBN 9 7818 4511 3605.

Yeager, Suzanne M. *Jerusalem in Medieval Narrative*. CUP. [2008] pp. x + 260. £50 ($99) ISBN 9 7805 2187 7923.

IV

Later Medieval: Chaucer

SUSANNAH MARY CHEWNING, ORIETTA DA ROLD AND
KATHARINE JAGER

This chapter is divided into four sections: 1. General; 2. *The Canterbury Tales*; 3. *Troilus and Criseyde*; 4. Other Works. The ordering of individual tales and poems within the sections follows that of the Riverside Chaucer.

1. General

Allen and Bowers make an invaluable contribution to the Chaucer community by publishing their yearly bibliographical compendium 'An Annotated Chaucer Bibliography 2006' (*SAC* 30[2008] 425–509). This includes all material published in 2006 with additional entries from previous years, as always on the New Chaucer Society web page: < http://artsci.wustl.edu/~chaucer/bibliography.php > .

In *Symbolic Caxton*, William Kuskin describes the introduction of printing from a material culture perspective and looks at the impact of mass production and patronage on the consumption of Caxton's books. Chapters 3 and 4 consider the treatment of Caxton's Chaucer. Kuskin argues that the significance of printing to Chaucer lies in bringing together the differentiations and textual variations of the manuscript culture. Thus, printing acts as a unifying force which brings to Chaucer new and 'appropriate authority and identity' (p. 154). Chapter 4 reconsiders in particular Caxton's aristocratic patronage, arguing that the nobility was as involved in creating commerce as the middle or mercantile class. Kuskin revisits those people who supported Caxton at the initial stages of setting the press, from Margaret of York to the earl of Arundel, focusing in particular on Anthony Woodville and Alice Chaucer de la Pole (p. 189), and evaluating their interest in the development of the press and their literary tastes.

Daniel W. Mosser, in ' "Chaucer's Scribe": Adam and the Hengwrt Project' (in Connolly and Mooney, eds., *Design and Distribution of Late Medieval Manuscripts in England*, pp. 11–40) reviews scholarly opinions on the involvement of Chaucer in the creation of 'Hengwrt' (Aberystwyth, National Library of Wales MS Peniarth 392 D) in the light of the recent

Year's Work in English Studies, Volume 89 (2010) © *The English Association; all rights reserved*
doi:10.1093/ywes/maq009

identification of Adam Scriveyn as Adam Pinkhurst. By looking at the structural evidence, the textual variants and supplementary hands, Mosser argues that most of the gaps and codicological uncertainties have all the makings of authorial decisions taken while compiling a first version of the *Canterbury Tales*, and thus argues that Hengwrt could be 'the first real attempt to arrange the tales and groups of tales into a coherent whole' (p. 360).

Amanda Holton, in 'Which Bible Did Chaucer Use? The Biblical Tragedies in the *Monk's Tale*' (*N&Q* 55[2008] 13–17), contributes a short note on which bible Chaucer may have used. She immediately dismisses the Wycliffite Bible on chronological grounds, and then considers the Vulgate and the *Bible historiale*. Her argument is mainly developed as a response to J.H. Ramsey's famous article 'Chaucer and Wycliffe's Bible' (*Academy* 22[1882]), which argued that Chaucer used Wyclif, and to Johnson's claim that Chaucer exclusively owes the biblical inspiration in the *Monk's Tale* to the *Bible historiale*. Holton's comparative analysis suggests that Chaucer could have used the French Bible in writing the *Monk's Tale*, and that it is more reasonable to suggest that 'Chaucer used the *Bible historiale*, perhaps along the Vulgate' (p. 17).

In 'Manuscript Studies, Literary Value and the Object of Chaucer Studies' (*SAC* 30[2008] 1–37), Robert J. Meyer-Lee argues for a reappraisal of the study of Chaucer's texts based on new work on textual layout and other textual information such as glosses, questioning what constitutes the object of literary study. The edition-based approach, he suggests, may have some limitations for the study of Chaucer's works, and his theoretical approach touches on the uses of philology and new historicism to negotiate the value of creating new editions.

Alison Wiggins meticulously researches Renaissance marginalia to look for Chaucer's readers in her 'What Did Renaissance Readers Write in their Printed Copies of Chaucer?' (*Library*, 7th series 9[2008] 3–36). Wiggins looks at specific aspects of book history and readership: the reception of Chaucer's works as a trustworthy author, the attitude of female readers towards Chaucer's texts, the household as the communal space for reading Chaucer, and the keen antiquarian interest that some readers had in these works. Antonia Harbus looks similarly to Renaissance readership of Chaucer in 'A Renaissance Reader's English Annotations to Thynne's 1532 Edition of Chaucer's Works' (*RES* 59[2008] 342–55). Her focus is Thynne's 1532 edition of the works of Chaucer. The annotation on authorship seems to be of particular interest, Harbus notes, because even though the annotator does not seem to be concerned with the Chaucerian canon of the edition he recognizes that the metre of Henryson's *Testament of Cresseid* is not Chaucer's.

Ayumi Miura considers the use of impersonal verbs in Old and Middle English texts, focusing in particular on '*methinks*-type of impersonal constructions', in 'New Impersonal Verbs in Some Late Fourteenth-Century English Texts' (in Amano, Ogura and Ohkado, eds., *Historical Englishes in Varieties of Texts and Contexts*, pp. 187–200). She notes that this usage is more common in Chaucer than in Gower, the *Gawain*-poet and Langland.

This linguistic influence in Chaucer is also noted by Young-Bae Park in his 'Multilingualism in English Literature: Applicable to the Study of the History of English?' which appears in the same volume (pp. 371–86). Here Park places Chaucer's language in the multilingual discourse often considered by scholars, arguing that Chaucer's linguistic features contain traditional and modern linguistic traits and that they have an impact on the development of modern English.

Peggy A. Knapp examines Chaucer's approaches to beauty in her *Chaucerian Aesthetics*. She lays out her theoretical frame in her first chapter, 'Why Aesthetics?', by using Kant, Williams, Adorno, Gadamer and Jauss, and argues for a rationale that claims beauty has a social purpose as much as it has a value in and of itself. Her second chapter, 'Chaucerian Resoun Ymaginatyf', considers the contribution of later thinkers to medieval aesthetic production and offers an analysis of medieval conceptions of beauty, noting that, along with thinkers like Bonaventure, Thomas Aquinas and Boethius, 'Augustine is everywhere aware of beauty' (p. 18). Her term 'resoun ymaginatyf' pertains to the verisimilitudinous representation of poetic writing. She argues that 'literary verisimilitude is made possible by the power of imagination to form mental pictures and interpret the world actually before us, causing us to *see* what we experience *as* a specific something, something already carrying meaning' (p. 33). 'Playing with Language Games', Knapp's third chapter, posits that 'Chaucer does not so much play language games' within the Canterbury project as much as 'he plays with them' (p. 45), primarily through allegory. Knapp's fourth chapter, 'Beautiful Persons', 'addresses the interpretive and aesthetic effects of allowing the characters of Chaucer's fictions to appear before us as genuine subjects with rich, complex interior lives on the one hand, or enjoying them for the striking alterity of their presentation as types on the other' (p. 70). 'The Beauty of Women', the fifth chapter, examines representations of feminine beauty and the 'contradictions of aesthetic attitudes' endemic to these gendered representations (p. 99). Knapp reads representations of the seductress, the victim and the inspiration (pp. 102–12); she focuses primarily on Criseyde and the ways in which her beauty is associated with victimhood, seduction and inspiration (pp. 112–24). As Knapp notes, the pleasure that feminine beauty and the aesthetic in general provides 'can either fatally ensnare rectitude or inspire it' (p. 125). The sixth chapter, 'The Aesthetics of Laughter', examines 'the breadth and inclusiveness of Chaucer's distinctive humor and the aesthetic effects it evokes' (p. 128). Knapp reads the *Miller's Tale*, the *Reeve's Tale* and the *Summoner's Tale* as part of the fabliau tradition (pp. 133–44), and she discusses the parody and satire in the *Thopas–Melibee* link, the *Nun's Priest's Tale* and the Wife of Bath (pp. 144–52). Her final chapter, 'Imagining Community', asserts that via all of the aesthetic games that Chaucer plays with language, 'the broadest effects' of his inclusiveness of style and approach can be found in the 'creation of an image English community' (p. 156), but one that accommodates art at its core. Community in the *Canterbury Tales* is created textually, via language (pp. 159–65).

Dolores L. Cullen's *Ensnared by his Words: My Chaucer Obsession*, is less a scholarly approach to Chaucer and more a manifesto of Cullen's personal journey through academia, including a biographical review of her other works, the best known of which, *Chaucer's Host: Up-So Down*, identifies the Host of the *Canterbury Tales*, allegorically, as Christ.

2. The Canterbury Tales

William F. Woods discusses the many manifestations of space in medieval culture and society in *Chaucerian Spaces: Spatial Poetics in Chaucer's Opening Tales*, defining space as 'an area of characteristic potential' (p. 4). For Woods, 'the experiential world of the tale derives from our sense of how characters respond to, but at the same time create, their unique emplacement in space and place' (p. 5). Space thus becomes a locus of identity and social recognition for both the characters in the works and, perhaps, for Chaucer himself. In his study, Woods examines the *Knight's Tale*, the *Miller's Tale*, the *Reeve's Tale*, the *Man of Law's Tale*, the *Wife of Bath's Prologue and Tale* and the *Shipman's Tale*, deconstructing notions of space and place as he examines the various dimensions of space and spatial theory in relation to Chaucer's works. Woods seeks to examine how space is understood by both Chaucer and his readers. Chaucer's work leads to an examination of various articulations of space and place, 'thus, the study of narrative space leads to a sense of narrative affect, giving us a richer, more sensible appreciation of the medieval subjects in Chaucer's poetry, and how, through Chaucer's eyes, they saw their world' (p. 133). Woods argues for a re-examination of the various binaries of space (small and large, internal and external, inhabited and uninhabited, public and private, narrative space and others) in order to rethink Chaucer's pilgrims as characteristic of medieval people and their various cultural identities.

Thomas J. Farrell introduces a new reading of the portraits of the *General Prologue* in his 'Hybrid Discourse in the *General Prologue* Portraits' (*SAC* 30[2008] 39–93). He acknowledges that the 'free indirect discourse' theory is an unsuitable methodology for approaching Chaucer's speech and characterization. He frames his reading of the portraits within the Bakhtinian 'hybrid' discourse which takes the reader away from an interpretation based solely on direct voices to a more complex understanding of Chaucer's sophisticated narratological flair. In his discussion of the Friar, Farrell argues that 'the narrative strategy reinserts the Friar into a social order that radically devalues his protestations' (p. 63). Chaucer's experimentation with a hybridized discourse is unusual in the literature of this time, and yet would become very popular afterwards.

Andrew H. Jucker looks at the use of pronominal address in Chaucer's *Canterbury Tales* and compares it with early modern usage in 'Politeness in the History of English' (in Dury, Gotti and Dossena eds, English Historical Linguistics [2006], pp. 3–29). His argument shows that the pronominal forms have changed the culture of politeness in English from a positive to a negative politeness culture. Through various case studies Jucker demonstrates that, on the one hand, the forms 'you' and 'thou' are markers, respectively, of negative and positive differentiations of polite culture. On the other hand, this association can be interpreted as situational and genre-specific.

Siân Echard, in *Printing the Middle Ages*, looks at the impact of printing across periods, but her focus is on how medieval texts were received and reinterpreted by editors and printers. Considering the book as a symbol, she takes a different view from Kuskin inasmuch as she chooses to study how later individuals decided to represent the medieval book as an object but also as a development of aesthetic tastes and of the cultural understanding of what a book should look like. In her own words, 'this book is about books' (p. 1) and the transmission of books from early medieval to modern times. Chapter 4 considers the reception and transmission of the *Canterbury Tales* in the nineteenth century, looking at adaptations for children. Echard argues that Chaucer was particularly popular in children's adaptations because of the associations medieval literature had for the Victorians. For them, she argues, the Middle Ages were the cradle of the European nations. She also notes that most of these adaptations sprang from a sense of medievalism which was associated with simplicity and innocence, and that authors would thus select what they considered the most suitable tales from amongst the *Canterbury Tales*, often providing their own images. For instance, in 1878 Mary Eliza Haweis's *Chaucer for Children: A Golden Key* excludes the beast fables, such as the *Nun's Priest's Tale*, but includes her own illustrations to the texts. Naturally decisions about including or excluding certain texts are based on a perception of what the child-reader can or cannot read, and there is a marked preference in this period for tales with a moral or virtuous ending. The 1930s, Echard explains, saw a decline in Chaucerian adaptations for children, due partly to a change in taste and mainly to historical circumstances. Chaucer is again revisited in the final chapter, in which Echard looks at how the electronic media have influenced the representation of, for example, the *Canterbury Tales*.

In 'Overlooked Variants in the Orthography of British Library, Additional MS 35286' (*JEEBS* 11[2008] 121–43), Jacob Thaisen looks at Additional MS 35286 and summarizes the structure of the manuscript with specific reference to the tale-order to argue that it was copied without much planning. The orthographical distribution, for instance of y/i, which is not usually considered in dialectal analysis, can be used to refute Manly and Rickert's suggestions that Ad3 was copied using multiple exemplars; rather, it argues that Additional MS 35286 is copied progressively from the '*General Prologue* to the *Parson's Tale* and is based on a single exemplar' (p. 133).

In 'Companies, Mysteries and Foreign Exchange: Chaucer's Currency for the Modern Reader' (in Bishop, ed., *The Canterbury Tales Revisited: 21st-Century Interpretations*, pp. 256–80), Nancy M. Reale chooses to read Chaucer in his economic and social context, arguing that the *General Prologue* can be interpreted as real and mundane 'companies', and that it portrays medieval 'occupations and organizations of businessmen' (p. 275). The language of the pilgrims then reinforces the diverse socio-economic background and stratification that they are meant to represent.

Charity Jensen takes the *Canterbury Tales* and *Troilus and Criseyde* back to the question of authority, interpreting the relationship that Chaucer has with *auctoritas* and with his own understanding of being an author, in her 'Spaces of Authority: *Troilus and Criseyde* and the *Canterbury Tales*' (in Bishop, ed., pp. 281–99). Jensen looks at extracts from *Troilus* to note how Chaucer defines himself as a translator while also emulating classical authorial techniques. In the *Canterbury Tales*, Jensen observes, Chaucer continues this topos, but does step up the auctorial voice by allowing individual characters to reappropriate their own authority by 'reporting [the author's] authority' (p. 294). Jensen contends that it is the retraction which sanctions Chaucer as an author. By recanting some and yet naming all his works, Chaucer can 'establish his own place as an auctor' (p. 297).

A reconsideration of the poem 'New Fanglenesse' is presented in Sonya Veck's 'Chaucerian Counterpoise in the *Canterbury Tales*: Implications of Newfangleness and Suffisaunce for the 21st Century Reader' (in Bishop, ed., pp. 300–13). In this short poem, which takes the form of a complaint, Chaucer associates 'newfangleness' with mankind's lust and materialism and explains that honour ought to be upheld regardless of material promises and vainglory. Veck observes that this vice is further deployed by Chaucer in the *Canterbury Tales* to 'illustrate newfangleness through extreme greed and infidelity' (p. 303), and sets out an analysis of the textual evidence to argue that Chaucer juxtaposes newfangleness with 'suffisaunce' to demonstrate that neither extreme works and that both can be 'equally destructive' (p. 311). Thus Veck concludes that a modern reader finds morality in these thematic considerations of the extremes of Chaucer's narrative, which also 'provokes necessary inquiry into the ways humans often desire to live at the extremes' (p. 312).

Kevin Teo Kia-Choong, in 'Noise, *Terminus* and *Circuitus*: Performing Voices in Chaucer's *Canterbury Tales*' (in Bishop, ed., pp. 314–33) develops an analysis of the dialogic technique of Chaucer's voices. The author argues that the voices in the *Canterbury Tales* do not represent an organic, aesthetically organized continuum, but that they mirror the polyphonic conglomeration of noise and voices which the pilgrims encounter on their way to Canterbury. Rather than being on pilgrimage to the ideal city of Jerusalem, they are in pursuit of the 'earthly' city of Babel (p. 331).

Meredith Clermont-Ferrand focuses her attention on another manuscript of the *Canterbury Tales* in her edition of *Jean d'Angoulême's Copy of the Canterbury Tales: An Annotated Edition of Bibliothèque Nationale's Fonds Anglais 39 (Paris)*. This is a diplomatic edition which aims at making available the text of a less well known, but nevertheless unique, copy of the *Canterbury Tales*. In her introduction, Clermont-Ferrand offers information on the manuscript history. This manuscript contains a copy of the text which was written by a known scribe, Duxworth, for Jean d'Angoulême, brother to Charles d'Orléans. Thus the textual corrections and annotations reflect Jean's interest in Chaucer's work, and as such Clermont-Ferrand argues that making available the content of this text goes beyond editorial judgements of the merit of the text itself (good versus bad versions), and addresses the variation in the textual tradition of this poem, 'deliberately defamiliarizing what we believe is known' and 'submitting to the indeterminacy of all the variants of the *Canterbury Tale*' (p. xxi). She also argues that this edition stands against editorial approaches which champion definitive versions and authorial intention; what she finds interesting is what this text demonstrates from a cultural viewpoint. The preface to the edition is a defence of the value of looking at the text of the *Canterbury Tales* as a multifaceted production within each manuscript context.

In 'The Trinity Gower D Scribe's Two *Canterbury Tales* Manuscripts' (in Connolly and Mooney, eds., pp. 41–60), Jacob Thaisen looks at the orthographic evidence of the so-called scribe D, so named as the third scribe who copied Cambridge, Trinity College MS R.3.2 which contains Gower's *Confessio Amantis*, and numerous other medieval literary manuscripts, including two copies of Chaucer's *Canterbury Tales*: London, British Library MS Harley 7334 and Oxford, Corpus Christi College MS 198. Focusing in particular on the Corpus manuscript, Thaisen discusses the relationship between linguistic aspects of the D scribe's language and the make-up of the manuscript in order to investigate a number of textual exemplars used to copy the text. He discovers that there are two main linguistic systems in the manuscript, and that this is a reflection of how the scribe may be influenced by the language of the source being used.

Takako Kato closely analyses the scribal mistakes in an early copy of Chaucer's *Canterbury Tales*. In her 'Corrected Mistakes in Cambridge University Library MS Gg.4.27' (in Connolly and Mooney, eds., pp. 61–87), she questions the reliability of the scribe and the exemplars. Kato has collected and categorized scribal corrections according to different criteria, from scribal habits to verbal, auditory and visual memory, and offers a complete survey of these categories. By addressing questions such as how accurate the scribe was, whether the scribe understood what he was copying and whether he edited the text he was transcribing, she demonstrates that many of the uncorrected and corrected mistakes in MS Gg.4.27 are of a careless nature, and that this scribe does not seem to have had problems with the understanding of the language, as has been previously argued.

Graham D. Caie's 'The Manuscript Experience: What Medieval Vernacular Manuscripts Tell Us about Authors and Texts' (in Caie and Renevey, eds., *Medieval Texts in Context*, pp. 10–27) argues for the need to look at the physical context of medieval texts, because what surrounds the text can be significant for the interpretation of the text itself. 'Material', 'Layout and Presentation' and 'Script', together with 'Vernacular Poets and their Manuscripts', are discrete sections in which Caie explains why it is important to look at these physical aspects; paper, parchment and slates are all viable materials which can be use to transmit text, and their use is distinctive.

Jamie C. Fumo, in 'John Metham's "Straunge Style": Amoryus and Cleopes as Chaucerian Fragment' (*ChauR* 43:ii[2008] 216–36), makes a case for Chaucerian influence on John Metham. He posits that there is a connection between Fragment V of the *Canterbury Tales* and Metham's *Amoryus and Cleopes*, due perhaps to Metham's reading habits as an East Anglian (pp. 217–18).

While praise has long been a subject of poetry, it has been out of fashion since at least the seventeenth century. Thus J.A. Burrow's objective, in his *The Poetry of Praise*, is 'to pay more sympathetic attention to the auxetic character of [medieval English] poetic idiom and to the laudatory function that such idiom commonly serves' (p. 4). Chapter 1 discusses 'The Poetics of Praise', outlining the trajectory of praise-poetry from Aristotle to the medieval, and focuses specifically on the medieval reception of Aristotle's discussion of *auxesis* in his *Poetics* (pp. 6–28). Of particular interest is chapter 4, 'Geoffrey Chaucer', where Burrow observes that 'from the moment when the pilgrim checks in at the Tabard Inn, he strikes the note of praise' by mentioning the wide, fine stables and the way that guests 'esed atte beste' (p. 102). Burrow notes that that the majority of the pilgrims 'are represented as nonesuches in their particular walks of life, and eleven of them are said to have no rivals there' (p. 103). Burrow is careful to point out that Chaucer has long been known for his use of irony, a device usually at odds with praise, and he asserts that praise in the *General Prologue* is 'often ironically inflected, but determination of the ironies can prove elusive' (p. 104). He observes that Chaucer's use of magnification, particularly in the term 'al', can be used to create hyperbole (pp. 117–19). He also examines Chaucer's laudatory treatment of noble women in the *Book of the Duchess* and the *Legend of Good Women* (pp. 127–31), as well as his focus on praiseworthy men in the *General Prologue* (pp. 132–5). Burrow treats *Troilus and Criseyde* separately, due to its 'extravagance' of praise (p. 135), and he notes that, unlike the *Gawain*-poet, Chaucer is painfully reluctant to use description in this text, instead focusing his efforts on his characters (pp. 136–48).

In her essay, 'The Host, his Wife and their Communities in the *Canterbury Tales*' (*ChauR* 42:iv[2008] 383–408), Tara Williams discusses the narrative frame around the *Canterbury Tales* and the representation of Harry Bailly and his wife, Goodelief, within that frame. She posits that Bailly 'suggests that, far from being isolated, the Wife of Bath belongs to a community of wives that includes Goodelief and other wives from the frame and tales' (p. 383). This community is 'textual rather than social or historical' (p. 389). Williams analyses the Host's re-creation of his wife's speech in the frame in Fragment VII, arguing that Bailly's ventriloquism fails because 'his own voice slips in, revealing the narrator behind the curtain', and that his repeating her complaints 'reveals his own faults as much as hers' (p. 400).

In 'Chaucer and the War of the Maidens' (in Cohen, ed., *Cultural Diversity in the British Middle Ages: Archipelago, Island, England*, pp. 191–208) John Ganim suggests a fascinating approach to the *Knight's Tale* by comparing the context and background of the tale to the history and cultural background of Richard II's queen, Anne of Bohemia. Ganim examines Chaucer's sources, especially *Teseida*, and includes possible sources based on the 'legendary origins of Bohemia in a female leader who surrenders her authority at the same time that a concomitant Amazon-like insurrection of maidens who refuse to surrender is suppressed' (p. 191).

Carl C. Curtis offers a new interpretation of the *Knight's Tale*, contemplating the influences of the pagan past on Chaucer's narrative. His discussion goes beyond a historicist approach, delving into philosophical influences and the medieval conception of human microcosms. In *Chaucer's 'The Knight's Tale' and the Limits of Human Order in the Pagan World: Athenian Order, Theban Love, Christian Cosmos*, Curtis begins with a discussion of the medieval understanding of paganism, contextualizing Chaucer's classical influences. Chapter 2 considers the idea of heroism and the allegory of rule and love. The last two chapters focus on Athens and the values and issues which are attached to this symbolic place. Curtis looks at mercy, fortune, reason, passion and imagination, ultimately to consider how the Knight feels about the pagan world. He suggests that providence and human salvation are central to Chaucer's argument in the *Knight's Tale*. The Knight's vision of the pagan world is portrayed as a failure which has to surrender to the biblically based medieval understanding of the universe.

In 'Chaucer's Knight as Revisionist Historian: Anachronism in the *Knight's Tale*' (in Bishop, ed., pp. 194–208), Art Zilleruelo reads the *Knight's Tale* as an outdated text in which the Knight uses historical details inaccurately with the aim of manipulating his audience's temporal and factual knowledge and expectations. Building on Terry Jones's argument in *Chaucer's Knight* (*YWES* 59[1980] 107), which views the Knight as a mercenary, Zilleruelo notes that the Knight betrays the lower class he originally belonged to. The threatening dissolution of the chivalric status quo, Zilleruelo argues, make the Knight consider a narrative which conveys a strong message: 'military action might preclude rebellion by ending lives and instilling fear' (p. 206).

Jim Casey takes a different approach to the *Knight's Tale* in his ' "Love should end with hope": Courting and Competition in the *Knight's Tale*' (in Bishop, ed., pp. 209–27). At the beginning of the essay he poses the question: 'How does Chaucer matter now?' (p. 209). He then structures his discussion to elucidate the modernity of the themes and the alterity of the plot. Casey suggests that the courting of Emelye goes hand in hand with the chivalric themes of the tale, because 'love arouses chivalry and chivalry encourages love' (p. 217). This circular discourse and the display of violence in medieval cultural relationships offers continuities between medieval and modern times. Drawing on the attacks of 11 September 2001, Casey concludes by further demonstrating that 'men are still devoured by war, and they still endure intense physical pain and privation in order to "prove" their love' (p. 222).

In her fascinating analysis of images, *The Visual Object of Desire in Late Medieval England*, Sarah Stanbury offers several readings of Chaucer's use of icons and images. Her third chapter, 'Chaucer and Images', argues that the late medieval controversy over images acts as a 'discursive backdrop against which to look at [Chaucer's] construction of textual bodies, or his arts describing the human form' (p. 100). Stanbury asks of Chaucer's representations of visual art, 'does the act of looking risk idolatry or even animate its object?' (p. 101), and she focuses her analysis on the pagan temple images in the *Knight's Tale* and the multiple gazes and the image of a wraith-like grieving Troilus, in *Troilus and Criseyde* (pp. 102–10). She also examines the issue of icons, specifically the daisy, in the Prologue to the *Legend of Good Women* (pp. 110–16) and explores the role of the Pardoner's relics and veronica image (pp. 117–20). Chaucer, she argues, 'imbues devotional images, though in pagan or atavistic form, with vivacity, bringing them to life when he looks at them' (p. 120); he is able to 'assert their deadness', thereby giving voice to anti-iconic late medieval ethics, 'but as a writer Chaucer kneels before' aesthetic images and allows them to 'do what they will' (p. 121). Stanbury's fourth chapter, 'Translating Griselda', explores the ways in which Chaucer creates 'a sacramental poetic' (p. 151). She argues that the transformative 'translation' of

Griselda 'from peasant girl into sacred site or sign, a devotional image of sorts, attributed with cultic powers' acts as 'a commentary on marital sacrament and on the related problematic of private trust and verbal contracts' (p. 127). When Griselda is translated from peasant girl into nobleman's wife, her transformation 'plays to familiar structures or performances of faith that share, as a central motif in their visual theophany, the placement of a miraculous body at the center of a group of spectators' (p. 132). In other words, Griselda becomes a relic, an object of pilgrimage. Stanbury goes on to read Griselda's status as object as indicative of her passive role in her marriage to the tyrannical Walter (pp. 137–9), and her plain speaking as being 'the chief voice of ethical accountability in the tale' (p. 147). Indeed, Stanbury notes that 'if we hear in Griselda's language an idealized form of plain speaking, it is also a voice of poetic resistance, or of the poet whose choices both to translate and to speak plainly in the vernacular can subject him, if not to violence, at least to critical censure' (p. 150). 'The Clergeon's Tongue', Stanbury's fifth chapter, reads the *Prioress's Tale* and its images of immortal singing tongues. She notes that 'as the producer of language, the tongue is sacred, the organ that most closely allies the sexual body to the speaking soul' (p. 154), and sees in the clergeon's singing, and in the grain lifted from his dead, still musical tongue, a strong allusion to the liturgy (p. 169). As she wisely points out, in this tale Chaucer uses 'liturgical spectacle' to serve as 'a performance that masks collusive practices of power, the central metaphor for which is usury' (p. 171), and she argues that Chaucer makes in this tale a kind of shrine.

In *The Canterbury Tales Revisited*, Kathleen A. Bishop brings together eighteen essays to discuss a number of issues relating to critical approaches to the reading and interpretation of the *Canterbury Tales*. The foreword by David Matthews offers an eloquent appraisal of Chaucer study in the twenty-first century, and argues for the integration of Chaucerian scholarship into, rather than its separation from, other Middle English literature. The following essays are, not surprisingly, short theoretical pieces which focus on interpretations of single tales, reflecting on new ideas and critical frameworks. Heidi Breuer, in her 'Being Intolerant: Rape Is Not Seduction (in the *Reeve's Tale* or Anywhere Else)' (in Bishop, ed., pp. 1–15), argues that lines 344–9 and 378–82 of the *Reeve's Tale* ought to be considered a 'rape' scene. Her reading is pursued as a response to a personal experience as a student, in which a male professor strongly denied that Chaucer's students perpetrated any sort of violence against the family of the Reeve. Drawing on the legal context for violence against women in thirteenth- and fourteenth-century England, she believes that in these scenes Chaucer's language is clearly drawing on legalistic terminology to describe an act of violence against Malyne and her mother. One of the points of contention is that neither Malyne nor her mother consented to have intercourse with Aleyne and John. Kathleen A. Bishop takes a historical angle when she analyses the *Miller's Tale* in the light of the death of King Edward II of England in her 'Queer Punishments: Tragic and Comic Sodomy in the Death of Edward II and in Chaucer's *Miller's Tale*' (in Bishop, ed., pp. 16–24). She notes that Chaucer could not fail to be aware of what had happened to Edward II by virtue of his connection with the court of Edward III and Prince Lionel. Concluding, she argues that Chaucer draws on the familiarity of the audience with the historical events which befell Isabella, Edward and Hugh and thus that Chaucer was trying to using a clear parallelism between the historical and the fictional characters: Alison, Nicholas and Absolon. The thematic resonance is of course the 'comic sodomy via a red hot poker' (p. 21), and she argues that there is a clear connection between 'the sodomitic execution of Edward and the sodomitic comedy of Chaucer' (p. 22).

Henry Ansgar Kelly, in 'Canon Law and Chaucer on Licit and Illicit Magig' (in Karras, Kaye and Matter, eds., *Law and the Illicit in Medieval Europe*, pp. 211–24), discusses the canon law that may or may not have been broken by John the Carpenter in the *Miller's Tale*. Ansgar creates a series of charges that might have been made against John regarding his treatment of Nicholas, ultimately finding that, although some aspects seem to cross the line of magic and the supernatural, they can all be viewed as orthodox and unthreatening to John (and, presumably, to Chaucer). Erica L. Zilleruelo offers a linguistic reading of the *Miller's Tale* in her 'The Churlish Nature of Chaucer's *Miller's Tale*: How Language Can Define Genre' (in Bishop, ed., pp. 27–43). She analyses the lexical choices made by Chaucer to describe the ending of the story. She departs from the theory proposed by Thomas J. Farrell in 'Privacy and Boundaries of Fabliau in the *Miller's Tale*' (*ELH* 56[1989] 773–83; see *YWES* 70[1992] 220) that Chaucer stops working within the parameters of the fabliau at the end of the tale (line 3798 onwards), and argues that Chaucer offers a new way of distributing justice, but still 'exemplifies the fabliaux spirit of vengeance' (p. 40).

Robert Epstein takes up the issue of the northernism in the *Reeve's Tale* and discusses it in the light of the Wakefield master's work on the *Second Shepherds' Play*. In '"Fer in the north; I kan nat tell where": Dialect, Regionalism and Philologism' (*SAC* 30[2008] 95–124) he uses Pierre Bourdieu's linguistic theory to argue that the *Canterbury Tales* reflects a linguistic hierarchy in which 'Chaucerian dialect functions as dominant competence in that it is not universally accessible' (p. 106). Epstein sees Chaucer as a writer who is engaged in the 'construction of Northernness as a state of physical, linguistic, economic, social, political and geographical otherness' (p. 116).

In 'Women's Secrets: Childbirth, Pollution and Purification in Northern Octavian' (*SAC* 30[2008] 235–68), Angela Florshuetz, in her detailed study of *Octavian*, discusses the violation of the birth chamber in medieval romances and the role that the mother-in-law has in this violation. The role of the ill-natured female relationship is naturally compared in passing with Constance's mother-in-law. Here the *Man of Law's Tale* is offered as an analogy.

Celia Lewis reads the complicated and painful history of crusade against the backdrop of the *Man of Law's Tale* and the *Knight's Tale* in her 'History, Mission and Crusade in the *Canterbury Tales*' (*ChauR* 42:iv[2008] 353–82). She argues that the figure of the Knight is an ambivalent one, given the late medieval English concerns over crusades and battlefield murder (p. 360), and that, despite the violence in the *Man of Law's Tale*, for fourteenth-century readers 'the violent and destructive side of crusade did not go unnoticed any more than did the sins shared by the faiths' (p. 373). Elizabeth Edwards also reads the *Knight's Tale*, in her 'Chaucer's *Knight's Tale* and the Work of Mourning' (*Exemplaria* 20[2008] 361–84). She argues that the acts of public mourning that follow the death of Arcite act as a 'kind of cultural work, a labor which solves, or perhaps dissolves, the problem of unbridled male competition, hostility and jealousy' (p. 363). Edwards points out the ways in which late medieval English society was invested in public displays of mourning and grief, observing that the 'enormous social investment' of such public acts 'represents a way to turn mourning from waste into a productive economy, to set loss to work, to convert wild expenditure to debt and exchange' (p. 375); or a way to make mourning useful and meaningful—a question of particular importance to the chivalric culture in which the *Knight's Tale* is set.

Of interest to Chaucer studies in the volume *Medievalisms: The Poetics of Literary Re-Reading*, edited by Liliana Sikorska, is Joanna Maciulewicz's essay, 'Translations and Imitations of Medieval Texts in Neoclassicism: Chaucer as a 'Rough Diamond' that 'Must be polished ere he shines' (pp. 113–31). Maciulewicz reads eighteenth-century adaptations of Chaucer, noting that they frequently sought to 'improve' upon their original medieval sources, translating and omitting at will (p. 118). Indeed, she observes that Dryden decided 'to omit from the *Canterbury Tales* the indecent material', thus translating the *Wife of Bath's Tale* but leaving out her Prologue (p. 121). Both Dryden and Pope were convinced of the 'progress of poetry', but Dryden 'looks upon the medieval poet as too crude and thus amplifies the original text, whereas Pope cuts short its prolixity' (p. 124). Maciulewicz sagely notes that eighteenth-century writers cut and pasted, translated at will and frequently excised those portions that were salacious, the better to fit their own concepts of proper poetry. She points out that 'no matter how fond of their father neoclassical poets claim to be, they approach his works in a conspicuously patronizing manner' (p. 130).

In 'The Wife of Bath's Urinary Imagination' (*Exemplaria* 20[2008] 244–63) Shawn Normandin explores the representations of urine in the *Wife of Bath's Tale*, observing that she mentions urine 'more frequently than any other pilgrim' (p. 244). He argues that 'Chaucer's urinary games scapegoat the Wife but also ridicule the desire of his audience to make her a scapegoat' (p. 245), and parses the ways in which medieval femininity is associated with urine (pp. 247–8). References to urine in the text further the implications that the Wife cannot employ verbal, theological or rhetorical continence (p. 253).

Alastair Minnis's *Fallible Authors: Chaucer's Pardoner and Wife of Bath* is a magisterially historicized account of the religious and moral context out of which the Pardoner and the Wife of Bath are made. For both characters, who they are and the public, moral efficacy of what they say are at odds; each is a fallible author who does not possess any authority to preach in public. Minnis's first chapter, '*De officio praedicatoris*: Of Preaching, Pardon and Power', historicizes the medieval context of preaching and the development of the system of pardons. Preaching was given power by a tradition of theological and moral thinking, and served as a public act. Minnis argues that 'to preach was to address oneself directly and publicly to a congregation in order to instruct its members in the basics of Christianity and to encourage them to act well' (p. 39). 'Moral Fallibility: Chaucer's Pardoner and the Office of the Preacher', Minnis's second chapter, discusses the character who emerges from this English context: the corrupt but brilliant Pardoner. The Pardoner exists squarely within the conundrum Minnis raises in his first chapter: what to do with 'bad' preachers? He describes the Pardoner as 'a layman or at best a man in minor orders... a figure who has taken upon himself, with no legal warrant, the *officium praedicatoris* and certain other functions properly reserved for those in major orders, particularly the power to absolve which is reserved to priests alone' (p. 118). Minnis's third chapter, '*De impedimento sexus*: Women's Bodies and the Prohibition of Priestly Power', historicizes the situation for medieval women who might be accused of preaching in public, and lays the foundation for his discussion of the Wife of Bath. Minnis argues that Chaucer's 'Bible-quoting, argument-toting Wife of Bath... was a highly topical construct' (p. 243). His final chapter, 'Gender as Fallibility: Chaucer's Wife of Bath and the Impediment of Sex', analyses and historicizes the Wife and her tale. Married and female, thereby occupying an 'inferior subject position', the Wife nonetheless is able, via her tale, 'to offer genuinely impressive instruction which centers on the nature of true nobility, this coming from the mouth of an old woman who thereby exercises pedagogical dominion over the immoral man who is her reluctant pupil' (p. 245). What the Wife and her tale offer is a perspective that accommodates the theological frailty of femininity while also urging deeper and quite radical moral complexity. The Wife—corporeal, carnal, obscene—depicts a loathly old woman, also corporeal, carnal, obscene, who presents an unethical knight with words of wisdom, what Minnis calls 'a wonderful homily on true nobility' (p. 310).

Al Walzem's central argument in ' "Peynted by the lion": The Wife of Bath as Feminist Pedagogue' (in Bishop, ed., pp. 44–59) focuses on the Wife of Bath as a teacher, noting that what matters is what the audience is learning from Alison's experience. She also notes that many of the events accruing to the Wife of Bath's Prologue, when read simultaneously with her tale, offer evidence in support of the rhetorical skills of the wife, who argues all along that 'when men attempt to control women, a battle of the sexes results in which neither can sustain happiness' (p. 58), but that in granting 'maistrie' to their wife, men 'will win their love and loyalty and both can find lasting peace and harmony' (p. 58). Jennifer L. Martin also writes on the *Wife of Bath's Tale* in her 'The Crossing of the Wife of Bath' in the same volume (pp. 60–74). She argues that the Wife plays with professional roles, cross-dressing as a clerk and using patriarchal sources to construct her discourse and supporting her experience using male texts. This crossing over of roles and discourses leads to a consistent reading of both Prologue and tale, Martin notes, which both have at the centre of their discussion the question of gender.

William Rossiter considers the *Clerk's Tale* and the intertextual influences which are provided by Chaucer's sources in his ' "to Grisilde agayn wol i me dresse": Readdressing the *Clerk's Tale*' (in Bishop, ed., pp. 166–93). He persuasively argues that Chaucer's ability to 'form a textual mosaic' (p. 167) offers readers a multifaceted canvas of interpretative material. Chaucer's manipulation of the source material, in particular regarding the portrayal of Griselda as perhaps a symbol for Queen Anne and the possible political parallelism between Walter and Richard II, leads to a variety of hermeneutical approaches and to a 'critique of political abuse' (p. 183). 'The heteroglossia' present in the *Clerk's Tale*, Rossiter argues, allow the engagement of the medieval and the modern audience alike.

In another short note, 'The Merchant, the Squire and Gamelyn in the Christ Church Chaucer Manuscript' (*N&Q* 55[2008] 265–9), Jacob Thaisen looks at another manuscript of the *Canterbury Tales*, Oxford, Christ Church, MS 15, which is written on paper, to discuss the peculiar make-up of quire 12. This quire includes three bifolia which belong to a different paper stock from the one used elsewhere in the quire. Thaisen argues that this anomaly is most probably a substitution which is a consequence of the scribe obtaining the longer version of the *Merchant's Tale* (from line E2319 onwards) and L17 (Merchant End-Link and Squire Head-Link) at a later stage in the progress of copying. He corroborates this suggestion by looking at the colour of the ink.

Susan Signe Morrison devotes the second of three sections of her book, *Excrement in the Late Middle Ages: Sacred Filth and Chaucer's Fecopoetics*, to the *Canterbury Tales*, most notably the *Pardoner's Tale*, the *Prioress's Tale* and the *Nun's Priest's Tale*. Morrison's thesis is based on 'a cultural poetics of excrement'—what she calls 'fecopoetics'—which serves to explain the symbolic and physical means by which excrement was 'disciplined by humans' in the Middle Ages (p. 2). Morrison argues that Chaucer's works are 'touchstones for understanding the multiple roles excrement played materially and figuratively in the late Middle Ages' (p. 3). Her argument is very thorough with respect to her knowledge and articulation of 'fecopoetics' and the pervasiveness and significance of these images in medieval literature. When she gets specific about Chaucer, she continues to emphasize the historical position of his works and their relationship to her thesis. For example, when she discusses the *Prioress's Tale*, it is not so much the tale itself as the 'boundaries of what is sacred and what is filth' (p. 87), discussing the tale in the context of 'Host desecration accusation tales'. Morrison's treatment of the *Pardoner's Tale* further addresses the paradox of the sacred and filth, pointing out that 'waste reminds us of the enfleshing of God. Excrement reminds us not only of our bodily nature, but of Christ's. Excrement actually brings us closer to God' (p. 89). Morrison's argument about the *Nun's Priest's Tale* outlines the concept of the 'wasteway' and the relationship of where food comes from and how it ends up, with the cycle of consumption and waste and civilization as an allegory of Chaunticleer's barnyard. Morrison concludes with a argument for waste studies as a new field, arguing that it can open up new roads into the study of medieval culture and society.

Will Stockton, in his 'Cynicism and the Anal Erotics of Chaucer's Pardoner' (*Exemplaria* 20[2008] 143–64), situates the Pardoner's cynicism within his figuration as a critically queer character. Stockton argues that 'by inviting the pilgrims to kiss the relics he freely admits are fraudulent, the Pardoner does not try to bring the pilgrims out from beneath the veil of false consciousness' (p. 144), instead allowing them to occupy a privileged space. He observes that the Pardoner is 'cynically cognizant of the relationship between ideology and reality, yet he seeks only to preserve the status quo' (p. 157), thereby complicating recent analyses of the Pardoner that view him as a rabble-rousing truth teller. Gabriele Cocco likewise reads the Pardoner, in his ' "I trowe he were a gelding or a mare": A Veiled Description of a Bent Pardoner' (*Neophil* 92[2008] 359–66), but as a trickster figure akin to the Icelandic Loki. Loki is able to change sex, has extreme cunning, and is associated with mares and geldings, Cocco observes (pp. 363–5). He urges a reconsideration of Scandinavian and Germanic sources in Chaucer's characterization, pointing out that it was unlikely that 'Anglo-Saxon England turned in an instant into an ersatz of romance background' upon the Norman Conquest (p. 365).

Miriamne Ara Krummel, in 'The Pardoner, the Prioress, Sir Thopas and the Monk: Semitic Discourse and the Jew(s)' (in Bishop, ed., pp. 88–109), considers the question of Jewishness and medieval Semitisms in the *Pardoner's Tale*, the *Prioress's Tale*, *Sir Thopas* and the *Monk's Tale*. Remarking on the thematic variation within each tale, Krummel considers the dynamic use of these themes by Chaucer and, for example, reads the Prioress's narrative in a Christian, anti-Judaic context which empowers the Prioress and allows her to conclude the tale with the 'language of authority' (p. 97).

Elaine Brown discusses the duality of public and private in the *Shipman's Tale* in 'An Exploration of the Public and Private in Chaucer's *Shipman's Tale*' (in Bishop, ed., pp. 75–87). She sets the context of her investigation within the fabliau genre and argues that the game-play set up by Chaucer allows the wife to seem in control of the adulterous relationship, and yet opens the issue of 'the appropriate role of the medieval husband to the reader' (p. 84); this issue is not resolved because of the interference of the public demands of the church and the private bond of the marriage.

Winter S. Elliott, in 'Eglentyne's Mary/Widow: Reconsidering the Anti-Semitism of the *Prioress's Tale*' (in Bishop, ed., pp. 110–26) also reflects on the *Prioress's Tale* from an anti-Semitic perspective. Elliott acknowledges the difficulties that modern critics face when they attempt 'to reconcile modern integrity with medieval prejudice' (p. 110), but argues that beyond the obvious anti-Semitic tone the Prioress has a unique position as a female narrator and that the tone integral to the genre (Mariology) seems to be essential to the empowering of the Prioress yet embedded in cultural and religious prejudices. This sense of 'violent anti-Semitism' (p. 127) is again considered by Bronwen Welch in ' "Gydeth my song": Penetration and Possession in Chaucer's *Prioress's Tale*' (in Bishop, ed., pp. 127–50). She argues that the *Prioress's Tale* can be appreciated beyond its anti-Semitic tone. Modern readers can find meaning in the rich metaphorical language and the story itself, although the miracle at the end only produces a silence which is difficult to fill—it is not easy for modern readers to believe in miracles. Welch notes that it is indeed this tension between believing the Prioress and the anti-Semitic tone of the text which limits and at the same time enriches the reading of the text.

Leona Fisher, in her ' "No man ne truste upon hire favour longe": Fortune and the Monk's Other Women' (in Bishop, ed., pp. 151–65), points out that Fortune in this tale works as a unifying figure against which Chaucer mirrors the female protagonists of some of his tragedies. Fortune is portrayed alongside women such as Zenobia, Dianarah, Judith and Phanye, who are, Fisher notes, always represented in traditional medieval misogynistic vocabulary. Fisher argues that this is another cunning Chaucerian ploy to invite the reader not to take these discussions seriously; the Monk is not a trustworthy character and, in his mouth, these tragedies subvert the grave message, giving instead an ironic twist.

Alice Spencer, in her 'Dialogue, Dialogics and Love: Problems of Chaucer's Poetics in the *Melibee*' (in Bishop, ed., pp. 228–55), reconsiders the manipulations of Chaucer's sources and suggests that Melibee is presenting an 'Aristotelian/Thomistic argument in a form which is essential Platonic/ Augustinian' (p. 229). Spencer bases her argument on the Bakhtinian dialogic theories of heteroglossia, polyphony and carnival, compares Chaucer's text with both Albertano da Brescia and Renaud de Louens's works, and considers the place of the tale in the sequence of the *Canterbury Tales*. She argues that, in *Melibee*, Chaucer fails to employ a Boethian dialogue which is aimed at focusing readers' attention on an absolute truth; rather, he follows his source in 'associating his feminine teacher persona with rhetoric rather than dialectic and presenting his text as a *compilatio*' (p. 250). In doing so, Spencer argues, Chaucer moves away from Socratic dialogues by introducing polyphony and heteroglossia to his text.

The *Tale of Melibee* is scrutinized anew in 'Violence, Law and Ciceronian Ethics in Chaucer's *Tale of Melibee*' (*SAC* 30[2008] 125–69) by Patricia DeMarco. DeMarco argues for a critical appraisal of the role of Prudence in the text beyond the scholarly opinion that the text is learned and speaks for itself. She places Chaucer's *Tale of Melibee* in a juridical context and prefaces this argument by asserting that 'Christian virtue is strongly marked as feminine virtue' (p. 130); she then elaborates on the importance of the virtuous women in Chaucer as ambassadors of 'Christian theology' (p. 131). Her discussion of Chaucer's sources and influences spans Albertano of Brescia, Justinian and of course Cicero. DeMarco concludes that Chaucer makes Prudence consider carefully these learned influences to argue that 'Romanist legal thinking and Ciceronian ethics' lead to 'harmonious communal relationships, and Christian salvation' (p. 169).

3. *Troilus and Criseyde*

Colin Fewer, in his 'The Second Nature: Habitus as Ideology in the *Ars amatoria* and *Troilus and Criseyde*' (*Exemplaria* 20[2008] 314–39), reads Chaucer's uses of Ovid in his *Troilus and Criseyde* as providing a 'habit of thought' (p. 318) consonant with Chaucer's historical moment as well as with current philosophical enquiry, and notes that *Troilus and Criseyde* provides an example of 'the forms of subjection that are possible and necessary outside the sphere of sovereign power' (p. 334). William A. Quinn argues, in his 'Chaucer's Recital Presence in the *House of Fame* and the Embodiment of Authority' (*ChauR* 43:ii[2008] 171–96), that Chaucer's narratorial stance in the *House of Fame* serves as a kind of bridge between dreaming and waking, fantasy and reality (pp. 172–3). He observes that the narrator never wakes, in the text, and he posits that the text itself 'provides an outline for the imaginative reconstruction of the thereby immortalized poet' (p. 190).

Mari Pakkala-Weckström analyses the speech act of promising, focusing in particular on Chaucer's *Canterbury Tales* and *Troilus and Criseyde*, in '"No botmeles bihestes": Various Ways of Making Binding Promises in Middle English' (in Jucker and Taavitsainen, eds., *Speech Acts in the History of English*, pp. 133–61). She argues that pledging and promising are important in medieval literature and, in particular, essential in binding and establishing relationships in chivalric literature. Pakkala-Weckström offers an overview of Chaucer's lexical choices, contextualizing them within the broader context of medieval literature. She concludes by arguing that there are 'magic words', which entrap speakers, whether they are sincere or not in their promise, and make them fulfil whichever promise or agreement they have entered, whether voluntary or not.

Anita Helmbold reconsiders the numerous opinions on the commissioning of the famous frontispiece in Corpus Christi College Cambridge MS 61, which represents a poet reading in front of an audience, and argues, in 'Chaucer Appropriated: The Troilus Frontispiece as Lancastrian Propaganda' (*SAC* 30[2008] 205–34), that the manuscript may have been a commission for Henry V. She adduces as evidence the specific interests of Henry V in multilingualism, highly decorated manuscripts and French direct inspiration. Furthermore this type of book would fit in with the Lancastrian agenda of elevating the status of Chaucer as a national poet. Additional evidence, she argues, can be found in the close personal relationships to Henry V that some of the names in the manuscript suggest: from John Shirley to the Nevilles, dukes of Westmorland.

Men and Masculinities in Chaucer's Troilus and Criseyde, edited by Tison Pugh and Marcia Smith Marzec, brings together twelve essays on its topic. In the introduction (pp. 1–8) Pugh, Michael Calabrese and Smith Marzec open the debate by asking: 'What is a man? What groups together approximately half of the humans on this planet, in contrast to the other half?' (p. 1). This set of questions introduces the main issues explored in the book on the characterization of medieval male personalities in both literary fiction and historical figures, analysing *Troilus* 'through the hermeneutics of medieval and modern conceptions of masculinity' (p. 2), gender and sexuality. This is a hard task as masculinity in Chaucer's *Troilus* is defined by various mythologies of masculinity, from the classical Trojan through to the French romance traditions, which contribute to a complex web of interpretative material.

In turn each contributor looks at such material in an imaginative way. John M. Bowers historicizes the character of Troilus in his '"Beautiful as Troilus": Richard II, Chaucer's *Troilus* and Figures of (Un)Masculinity' (pp. 9–27). Starting with a quotation from Richard Maidstone, who commented on the beauty of Richard II when he entered London in 1392, Bowers sets up a series of parallels between Chaucer's text and the life of Richard II. Bowers notes that the poem was very popular in the mid-1380s and that authors from Chaucer to Gower to Usk often refer to the tragic love of Troilus and Criseyde. Within notions of medieval masculinities, Chaucer's Troilus is not a patriarchal figure, and is still a virgin when he meets Criseyde. Thus, Bower argues, Maidstone's comment must have drawn from a set of parallels with Richard II's biography which the medieval audience would have recognized. In particular, Bower focuses on key historical facts, such as the inability to father a successor and the allegations of an illicit relationship with de Vere, to demonstrate the level on which this association must have worked. Robert S. Sturges investigates the place of sovereignty in his chapter on 'The State of Exception and Sovereign Masculinity in *Troilus and Criseyde*' (pp. 28–42). He defines sovereignty in the light of Giorgio Agamben's view that it is 'the biopolitical power of life and death' (p. 29), and thus argues that sovereignty in the poem is reciprocally charged via the lovers' love-relationship. Male sovereignty is not exclusive to male characters, because of the intrinsic duality of reciprocal power between the lovers; thus the poem can be read, Sturges notes, as both reinforcing and resisting male sovereignty. Gretchen Mieszkowski looks in detail at the characterization of Troilus. Reconsidering modern theories of genre and genre role and performance, she contextualizes the accepted understanding that Troilus is 'effeminate, emasculated, even impotent' (p. 45). In her essay, 'Revisiting Troilus's Faint' (pp. 43–57), she discusses the compelling medieval evidence for male loss of consciousness, which authors usually employ in conjunction with extreme suffering or strong emotion, and she argues that Chaucer has Troilus faint in the bedroom scene not because he is a feminized character but to express the strong emotions capturing his body and the great love he feels for Criseyde.

Marcia Smith Marzec, in 'What Makes a Man? Troilus, Hector and the Masculinities of Courtly Love' (in Pugh and Smith Marzec, eds., pp. 58–72), considers the juxtaposition of the characters of Troilus and the almost absent Hector, noting that Chaucer's message is fairly traditional. The poet does not associate masculinity with sexual prowess; rather, sex outside marriage 'weakens and feminizes a knight' (p. 59). This ultimately, Marzec comments, is the fate of Troilus. James J. Paxson's essay on 'Masculinity and its Hydraulic Semiotics in *Troilus and Criseyde*' (pp. 73–96) takes the reader into Pandarus's house, describing its architectural features and analysing the symbolic meaning of spatial representations of Chaucer's 'hydraulic' imagery and its function in 'masculine symbolic action' (p. 77). In 'Masochism, Masculinity and the Pleasures of Troilus' (pp. 82–96), Holly A. Crocker and Tison Pugh negotiate the pain that Troilus suffers as a lover, defined by them as masochistic, and the reader's appreciation of the poem. Crocker and Pugh show that *Troilus* is a poem centred on pain and suffering which is transferred to the audience. Thus the poem becomes an enjoyable reading-act which can be best appreciated at a philosophical level through the suffering of Troilus.

Kate Koppelman examines the relationships of Criseyde with her dominant male characters in ' "The dreams in which I'm dying": Sublimation and Unstable Masculinities in *Troilus and Criseyde*' (in Pugh and Smith Marzec, eds., pp. 97–114). Koppelman looks at Criseyde as the object of desire by Troilus, and at how Criseyde's own voice emerges in subliminal forms such as her dreams. It is also Koppelman's contention that the role of Criseyde in the poem is active and supportive of Troilus's masculinity, to the definition of which she contributes. The motif of female masculinity is then taken up further by Angela Jane Weisl in the following essay, ' "A mannes game": Criseyde's Masculinity in *Troilus and Criseyde*' (pp. 115–31), in which she argues that Criseyde performs 'both traditional defined femininity...and a female masculinity' (p. 115) as an act of self-preservation. Thus Weisl shows that

Criseyde is condemned in the poem precisely for her act of self-preservation. Molly A. Martin, in 'Troilus's Gaze and the Collapse of Masculinity in Romance' (pp. 132–4), considers the use of the 'visual gender/genre trope' (p. 135) in Chaucer's romance. Focusing in particular on gaze, visions and sight patterns, Martin analyses how the romance is constructed around these motives and argues that the genre is not entirely successful because it implodes when Troilus is elevated to heaven and his visions are not concerned any more with the earthly world. Richard E. Zeikowitz looks at the relationship between Troilus and Pandarus and at their potential homoerotic associations in his 'Sutured Looks and Homoeroticism: Reading Troilus and Pandarus Cinematically' (pp. 148–60). Zeikowitz explores other male friendships in medieval literature and then considers closely Book 1 using gaze gender theory. He argues that there is a 'homosocial love story' in Book 1 between the characters and in his concluding remarks he suggests that a similar relationship can also be found in Books 2 and 3.

Michael Calabrese's essay, 'Being a Man in Piers Plowman and Troilus and Criseyde' (in Pugh and Smith Marzec, eds., pp. 161–82), considers Chaucer's Troilus alongside Langland's Piers and analyses shared features such as their journey, their quest and their suffering. These are qualities of 'men in search of truth' (p. 162), which are shared by men. Masculinity studies, Calabrese notes, can thus help to interpret these associations anew. His reading enters into a series of vivid textual parallels in which he admirably demonstrates that central to both poems are two main themes: sickness and healing. These unifying forces bring together two diametrically different texts in which Chaucer and Langland explore religious love for the sake of truth. The final essay of the book investigates another perhaps distant authorial relationship, offering a parallel analysis of the versions by Chaucer and Shakespeare. R. Allen Shoaf, in ' "The Monstruosity in Love": Sexual Division in Chaucer and Shakespeare' (pp. 183–94), considers the sexual or erotic influence that Chaucer had on Shakespeare, and the transformation of Troilus across history. Shoaf maintains that Shakespeare collapses gender roles after drawing on the intricate complexities of the genders in Chaucer.

4. Other Works

Malte Urban analyses authority, history and poetics in his Fragments: Past and Present in Chaucer and Gower. Balancing Chaucer and Gower, he argues that 'Chaucer does not offer fixed moral or political solutions, but rather urges his audience to realize the potential as well as the limitations of the discursive construction of meaning, stressing fragmentation and dialogue where Gower emphasizes division and singular authority' (p. 224). He accommodates historicism as well as queer theory in his own critical approach, emphasizing both Chaucer's and Gower's 'strategies of approaching history as a cultural construct influencing all aspects of culture' (p. 49). Chapter 3, 'Chaucer's Dreams: Authority in Writing and Society', discusses Chaucer's rendering of the 1381 rebellion, as seen in his Nun's Priest's Tale, the House of Fame and the Parliament of Fowls. The tale is composed of 'various contesting voices', which

Urban sees as an 'abundance' in which no one voice dominates (p. 91). He argues that, although these texts were written over a decades-long period, all three are 'concerned with the notion of authority and its significance for human actors in historically-bound circumstances' (p. 115). He analyses the *House of Fame*, and the moment when the eagle in that text names the Milky Way after a London street, using this as a springboard for positing that the text might be read as 'the work of an author who found himself in the midst of an urban metropolis, whose professional life was divided between the coming and going of merchants from everywhere around the known world and the possibly no less hectic environment of the royal court, and whose intellectual curiosity evidently introduced him to a vast array of writings' (pp. 100–1). And he argues that, in the *Parliament of Fowls*, 'the weight of the narrative is squarely set on the way a reader . . . has to appropriate a kind of authority that is valuable in the given context' (p. 104). His fourth chapter, 'Time Past and Time Present in Chaucer's *Troilus and Criseyde*', argues that Chaucer uses the poem as 'a negotiation of conflicting theoretical notions of history and historiography, both Christian and pagan', and ultimately posits that Chaucer pairs Troy and London as mirror images (p. 118). He observes that, across the poem, 'there is a constant concern about the time past of Chaucer's fictional Trojans and the time present of Ricardian London', and that the connections between the two are emphasized as strongly as the gap the separates them (p. 134). Urban posits that Chaucer uses Troy as a setting to parse the 1381 rebellion, the difficulties in Richard II's rule, and the parliamentary conflicts of the 1380s and 1390s, and that his doing so allows him to critique both historiography and the ways by which London (and Trojan) society was engaged in faulty decision-making processes (p. 144). His sixth chapter, '*The Tale of Melibee* and *Confessio Amantis* VII: What To Do with Knowledge', discusses authority and knowledge. He argues that, in the *Melibee*, 'the meaning of counsel, and by extension that of authorities, has to be constantly checked against the continually changing context of the present' (p. 179). The *Melibee* is one voice among many, and 'it illustrates how source material in the hand of a prudent reader can turn a hierarchy . . . almost upside down', while ultimately strengthening authority (pp. 181–2). Authoritative sources inform good counsel in the *Melibee*, but they do not dominate oppressively (pp. 193–4). 'Tales of Virginia', Urban's seventh chapter, focuses on Gower's 'Tale of Virginia' and Chaucer's *Physician's Tale*, and he points out that these are only a few of the many versions of the same story (p. 198). He asserts that the *Physician's Tale* is a story 'concerned with kingship, but does not directly allude to it in the narrative', largely because Chaucer has erased much of the political content of his source material from Livy (p. 209). Overall, Chaucer focuses on the disjunctions in his sources, decapitating Virginia (where Gower kills her by stabbing) as a metonym for 'fragment[ing] the body of history' itself' (p. 218). Urban generally posits that Chaucer's texts present us with a poet uneasy with 'unambiguous statements', whereas Gower's texts reveal him to be a poet who rigorously pursues certainty (p. 224).

In his *Chaucer's Narrators and the Rhetoric of Self-Representation*, Michael Foster discusses the ways by which Chaucer's narrators reflect his presence while also deflecting attention away from him. Foster argues that Chaucer's 'self-representation as an asocial bibiliophile is surprisingly consistent' (pp. 175–6), and that Chaucer attempts rhetorically to create both an image of himself and a flattering, communal image of his audience (p. 176). He sees Chaucer's depiction of a narrator as a figure that is 'best understood as the author's textual representative' (p. 178). Overall, Foster here seeks 'to map Chaucer's rhetorical construction of his identity as an author who presents ideas and stories and the identities of his audiences, who are invited to interpret those ideas and stories in an open, public forum' (p. 14). His first chapter, 'Chaucer's Voice', explores Chaucer's role as translator, audience-pleaser, author and narrator, and argues that 'the narrator should be understood as a reflection of the author, and that Chaucer expected his audience to conflate the narrator with the author' (p. 15). Foster deftly points out that Chaucer's reception and his narrators are inextricably linked with orality and prelection, a term which refers 'both to one's performance of one's own work and to one's performance of a text written by someone else' (p. 23). Chapter 2, 'The Consoler: *Book of the Duchess*', reads Chaucer's narrative role as consoler in the *Book of the Duchess*; a figure who is a master empathizer but who is 'ambiguously melancholic', the combination of which puts him 'in the perfect position to console the Man in Black without appearing' to be smarter than him (p. 48). In his first original narrative, Chaucer makes his narrator a bit of a bumbler, a man with 'qualified, limited knowledge and analytical tools', a manoeuvre that at once made him look quite at odds with his courtly audience while allowing him 'the space to write an inoffensive, sensitive poem to help console England's second most powerful man as he mourned the death of his first wife' (p. 78).

Chapter 3, 'The Scholar of Love: The Dream Visions', explores Chaucer's representations of reading in the dream visions. Foster argues here that 'the narrator's reading habits characterize Chaucer as a maker of poetry, but his reading is to be preferred and . . . books, ultimately, are merely the representations of their author's voices, best debated openly among a community of readers' (p. 82). Chapter 4, 'The Servant of Servants: *Troilus and Criseyde*', discusses narrative authority in *Troilus and Criseyde*, arguing that, unlike Boccaccio, Chaucer 'presents his poem to a larger community, a group of lovers who experience poetry together' (p. 118). Chaucer may initiate the narrative, but his communal audience must complete the task of interpretation (p. 129). Chapter 5, 'The Storyteller: The *Thopas–Melibee* Link' analyses the role of the narrator in the *Canterbury Tales*, identifying him as 'ambiguously situated between the text's real-world audience and the fictional pilgrims on their way to Canterbury' (p. 131). Chapter 6, 'The Border between Reputation and Repentance', reads Chaucer's later compositions, *The Second Nun's Tale* and the *Retraction*. Foster sagely points out that Chaucer's social status among his contemporaries, as well as his self-representation in the literary canon, was 'ambiguous and malleable' (p. 157). He notes that, in the *Retraction*, Chaucer's ownership of religious texts (and his rejection of his secular ones) serves to identify him as a writer whose 'social function' was 'virtuous and significant' (p. 161). Foster then reads the *Second Nun's Tale* as an example of Chaucer's pious presentation of an appropriate religious text. What is unique in both of these examples for Chaucer, Foster notes, is the 'non-ironic, non-comical presentation of himself as an established English writer' (p. 173).

In *The Sources of Chaucer's Poetics*, Amanda Holton explores Chaucer's poetic technique and its varieties through a comparative study of the poet's sources. Her work is a contribution to the recent revival of scholarly work on Chaucer's sources. Holton's analysis encompasses 'Chaucer's use of narrative, speech, rhetorical device and figurative language' (p. 4) in a selection of texts from *The Legend of Good Women* and the *Canterbury Tales*. Her discussion is developed over four chapters which shed new interpretative light on these issues. Chapter 1, on narrative, looks closely at the structure of Chaucer's text and at how the poet works with his sources to organize his narrative and the events therein. Holton argues that, from a narratological perspective, Chaucer seems 'to be governed by the unities of space, time and character' (p. 43), and that he thus modifies his sources accordingly and keeps events in chronological order, rearranging his sources should he need to, as in the case of Ovid's *Heroides*. The chapter on speech starts with the observation that Chaucer prefers long speeches over shorter ones regardless of his sources, and they can often take the form of complaints. This mode of speech is central to Chaucer's poetics, Holton argues, as he uses it extensively. Rhetoric and figurative language are considered in the two impressive final chapters, in which Holton lucidly demonstrates the influences that authors such as Guido and Ovid had on Chaucer, but also the differences between them. In particular, Chaucer is not influenced by Ovid's flair for ornamental rhetoric; his similes are quite short and his metaphors often unique, and Chaucer's original metaphorical language often departs from his sources. Holton's study brings together a new assessment of Chaucerian style in close comparison with his sources. In her concluding remarks Holton expounds on how Ovid, Virgil and Guido influence Chaucer, but argues that Boccaccio is perhaps the author stylistically closest to Chaucer.

A discussion on the declining use of *ne* in Middle English appears in a note by Yoko Iyeiri in 'Unsupported Negative *Ne* in Later Middle English' (*N&Q* 55[2008] 21–3). Iyeiri looks in particular at Middle English prose, including Chaucer's *Boece* and the *Tale of Melibee* and the *Parson's Tale*. In her analysis, she demonstrates that auxiliary verbs, for instance 'be, will and witen are . . . more inclined to yield unsupported *ne* than other types of verbs' (p. 22), and that much of this use depends on the syntactical construction, as unsupported *ne* seems to be associated with subordinate clauses, at least in *Boece*.

Jessica Brantley, in 'Venus and Christ in Chaucer's Complaint of Mars: The Fairfax 16 Frontispiece' (*SAC* 30[2008] 171–204), reconsiders the frontispiece of Oxford, Bodleian Library MS Fairfax 16 in medieval sacred and classical pictorial contexts. The frontispiece precedes Chaucer's 'Complaint of Mars' (fo. 14^v) and Brantley notes that the artist chooses to represent Chaucer's secular love-lament as an iconographical 'crossover' between 'classical narrative' and 'the traditions of Christian complaint' (p. 174). Brantley takes the reader through the background of the artist known as the Abingdon Missal Master and expands on her interpretation of the relationship between text and image to argue that the frontispiece itself has a narrative of its own which combines classical, astrological and Christian conventions (p. 204).

Bodleian MS Fairfax 16 is also considered in Victoria Louise Gibbons's 'The Manuscript Titles of Truth: Titology and the Medieval Gap' (*JEEBS* 11[2008] 197–206), a preliminary study of titology in Chaucer's works. Gibbons notes that titles in Chaucer's *Short Poems* are few and far between and that only a nineteenth-century editorial desire for uniformity standardizes the nomenclature of some of Chaucer's poetry. She observes that seven manuscript copies ('one third', p. 197) of the poem *Truth* do not have a title. This is a problem, she argues, which can be extended to many other Chaucerian lyrics and to his longer poetry (*ABC* and *The Legend of Good Women*, for instance), for it seems that 'Titles . . . did not always constitute part of a Middle English manuscript's ordination' (p. 198). This of course is not a generalized practice, as some manuscripts, such as Fairfax 16, offer a variety of labels for the two versions of *Truth*: 'Explicit le bon Counseill de G. Chaucer' and 'Balde'. This manuscript evidence, Gibbons suggests, points to a complex theoretical understanding of what titling meant in the Middle Ages: on the one hand titles do not conform with modern theories of titling, 'textual integrity, completeness and authorial authority' (p. 203), but on the other they could be understood as 'polyvalent and occasionally arbitrary mechanisms of the chirographic paratext' (p. 203).

Michael Foster offers a nuanced reading of the *Book of the Duchess* in 'On Dating the Duchess: The Personal and Social Context of *Book of the Duchess*' (*RES* 59[2008]185–96), arguing that it is essential to establish a precise date for the composition of the poem in light of the affair between John of Gaunt and Katherine Swynford. Dating the poem before or after the affair has important implications for how we interpret the poem itself. After reviewing previous opinions of possible chronological termini, Foster argues that, if the poem was written before the affair, one could interpret it as an attempt on Chaucer's part to establish a stronger relationship with Gaunt, and that if the poem is dated to after the relationship, it can be seen as an attempt by Gaunt to state his love for Blanche and to counter rumours of infidelity.

Chaucer's Boece: A Critical Edition Based on Cambridge University Library, MS Ii.3.21, ff.9r–180v, edited by Tim William Machan as the companion to the 2005 edition *Source of the Boece* edited by Machan and A.J. Minnis (see *YWES* 86[2007] 306), includes an appraisal of the scholarship and a review of former editorial practices relating to Chaucer's *Boece* and a short introduction with information about the manuscripts and printed editions which Machan has used in establishing the text. In 'Textual Affiliations', Machan reviews the work of other editors, including Skeat and Robinson, and corrects some of their assumptions; for instance, he clarifies that there are only twelve 'authorities' which contain a copy of Chaucer's *Boece*, rather than thirteen, because Phillipps MS 9472 (Cambridge, University Library MS Additional 3573) is in fact an early fifteenth-century copy of Walton's 'verse translation of the *Consolation*' (pp. xxvii–xxviii). Thus he sets out his rationale for choosing his base-text. The archetype of the whole tradition is once removed from the holograph, and thus all manuscripts seem to go back to a finished translation. According to Machan, an analysis of the variants of the surviving witnesses points to two main traditions: α, which includes more scribal 'improvements', and β, which is more authoritative. The β stemmatic branch is 'the more original' and thus 'C[2] [Cambridge, University Library MS ii.3.21] is the extant, manuscript with the most authentically Chaucerian text' (pp. xxxvii–xxxviii). Thus Machan's edition of the manuscript is only lightly emended 'to preserve, whenever possible, the integrity of any one of the many individual and sometimes idiosyncratic witnesses to this tradition—in this case the English text of C[2]' (p. xxxix). The edition also contains an apparatus criticus with main textual variants (pp. 99–161) and a commentary (pp. 163–88).

Andrew Cole devotes a chapter of his *Literature and Heresy in the Age of Chaucer* to what he calls 'Chaucer's Wycliffite text': the Prologue to the *Treatise on the Astrolabe*. He begins with a discussion of the well-known encounter between the Host and the Parson, a moment 'when "lollardy" is free of heresy...just before the Shipman rushes in to collapse the meaning of "lollard" and "heretic" into one' (p. 78). Cole goes on to discuss the Prologue to the *Treatise on the Astrolabe* in the context of the 'circle' of Wycliffite writers known to Chaucer, connecting it to the well-known heretical work, the Wycliffite vernacular Bible, and arguing that the Bible serves as a source for Chaucer in his composition of the Prologue. Cole asserts that the Wycliffite text 'ends with a signal statement about new forms of idiomatic translation that Chaucer...found useful for his own purposes...namely, to explain his own idiomatic translation of the *Treatise*, which shows a marked improvement in method over the earlier and more literally rendered *Boece*' (p. 81).

Not available for review this year were Edward I. Condren, *Chaucer from Prentice to Poet: The Metaphor of Love in Dream Visions and Troilus and Criseyde* (UPFla [2008]); Eva Nunez Mendez, *A Spanish Version of Chaucer's Troilus and Criseyde* (Mellen [2008]); Esther Casier Quinn, *Geoffrey Chaucer and the Poetics of Disguise* (UPA [2008]); and Samantha J. Rayner, *Images of kingship in Chaucer and his Ricardian Contemporaries* (Boydell [2008]).

Books Reviewed

Amano, Masachiyo, Michiko Ogura, and Masayuki Ohkado, eds. *Historical Englishes in Varieties of Texts and Contexts: The Global Coe Programme, International Conference 2007*. OUP. [2008] pp. xi + 403. £48 ISBN 9 7836 3158 1902.

Bishop, Kathleen A., ed. *The Canterbury Tales Revisited: 21st-Century Interpretations*. CambridgeSP. [2008] pp. xvi + 337. £39.99 ISBN 9 7818 4718 6133.

Burrow, J.A. *The Poetry of Praise*. CUP. [2008] pp. vii + 196. £47 ISBN 0 5218 8693 7.

Caie, Graham D., and Denis Renevey, eds. *Medieval Texts in Context*. Routledge. [2008] pp. ix + 257. £70 ISBN 9 7804 1536 0258.

Clermont-Ferrand, Meredith. *Jean d'Angoulême's Copy of The Canterbury Tales: An Annotated Edition of Bibliothèque Nationale's Fonds Anglais 39 (Paris)*. Mellen. [2008] pp. xxxv + 473. £84.95 ISBN 9 7807 7345 3272.

Cohen, Jeffrey Jerome, ed. *Cultural Diversity in the British Middle Ages: Archipelago, Island, England*. Palgrave. [2008] pp. 240. $57.95 ISBN 9 7802 3060 3264.

Cole, Andrew. *Literature and Heresy in the Age of Chaucer*. CUP. [2008] pp. xx + 297. $93 ISBN 0 5218 8791 7.

Connolly, Margaret, and Linne R. Mooney, eds. *Design and Distribution of Late Medieval Manuscripts in England*. YMP. [2008] pp. xiii + 336. £70 ISBN 9 7819 0315 3246.

Curtis, Carl C. *Chaucer's 'The Knight's Tale' and the Limits of Human Order in the Pagan World: Athenian Order, Theban Love, Christian Cosmos*. Mellen. [2008] pp. x + 262. £69.95 ISBN 9 7807 7345 0592.

Cullen, Dolores L. *Ensnared by his Words: My Chaucer Obsession*. Daniel. [2008] pp. 155. $12.95 ISBN 9 7815 6474 4722.

Dury, Richard, Maurizio Gotti, and Marina Dossena, eds. *English Historical Linguistics 2006. Selected papers from the fourteenth International Conference on English Historical Linguistics (ICEHL 14), Bergamo, 21–25 August 2006 Volume II: Lexical and Semantic Change*. John Benjamins. [2008] pp. xiii + 264. EUR 110; $165. ISBN 9 7890 2724 8114.

Echard, Siân. *Printing the Middle Ages*. UPennP. [2008] pp. xvi + 314. £42.50 ISBN 9 7808 1224 0917.

Foster, Michael. *Chaucer's Narrators and the Rhetoric of Self-Representation*. Lang. [2008] pp. 196. £30 ISBN 9 7830 3911 1213.

Holton, Amanda. *The Sources of Chaucer's Poetics*. Ashgate. [2008] pp. x + 168. £50 ISBN 9 7807 5466 3942.

Jucker, Andreas H., and Irma Taavitsainen, eds. *Speech Acts in the History of English*. JBPC. [2008] pp. viii + 318. €105 ISBN 9 7890 2725 4207.

Karras, Ruth Mazo, Joel Kaye, and E. Ann Matter, eds. *Law and the Illicit in Medieval Europe*. UPennP. [2008] pp. xviii + 315. $59.95. ISBN 9 7808 1224 0801.

Knapp, Peggy. *Chaucerian Aesthetics*. Palgrave. [2008] pp. x + 242. $85 ISBN 9 7802 3060 6685.

Kuskin, William. *Symbolic Caxton: Literary Culture and Print Capitalism*. UNDP. [2008] pp. xxvi + 390. $40. ISBN 9 7802 6803 3170.

Machan, Tim William. *Chaucer's Boece: A Critical Edition Based on Cambridge University Library, MS Ii.3.21, ff.9r–180v*. UWH. [2008] pp. xli + 193. €58 ISBN 9 7838 2535 4329.

Minnis, Alastair. *Fallible Authors: Chaucer's Pardoner and Wife of Bath*. UPennP. [2008] pp. xvi + 510. $69.95 ISBN 9 7808 1224 0306.

Morrison, Susan Signe. *Excrement in the Late Middle Ages: Sacred Filth and Chaucer's Fecopoetics*. Palgrave. [2008] pp. xiii + 271. $95 ISBN 1 4039 8488 3.

Pugh, Tison, and Marcia Smith Marzec, eds., Men and Masculinities in Chaucer's Troilus and Criseyde. CUP. [2008] pp. ix + 202. $95 (£50) ISBN 9 7818 4384 1609.

Sikorska, Liliana, ed. *Medievalisms: The Poetics of Literary Re-reading*. Lang. [2008] pp. 229. $46.95 ISBN 9 7836 3157 2177.

Stanbury, Sarah. *The Visual Object of Desire in Late Medieval England*. UPennP. [2008] pp. 290. $65 ISBN 9 7808 1224 0382.

Urban, Malte. *Fragments: Past and Present in Chaucer and Gower*. Lang. [2008] pp. 248. $66.95 ISBN 9 7830 3911 3767.

Woods, William F. *Chaucerian Spaces: Spatial Poetics in Chaucer's Opening Tales*. SUNYP. [2008] pp. xi + 203. $21.95 ISBN 9 7807 9147 4877.

V

The Sixteenth Century: Excluding Drama after 1550

ROS KING AND JOAN FITZPATRICK

This chapter has three sections: 1. General; 2. Sidney; 3. Spenser. Section 1 is by Ros King; sections 2 and 3 are by Joan Fitzpatrick.

1. General

From the books and articles that are reviewed here this year it is possible to discern something of a shift in early modern studies. There is some dissatisfaction with previous methodologies, and an acknowledgement (unsurprisingly in our current circumstances) of a need for interdisciplinary study. There are, accordingly, a number of attempts not only to expand our knowledge but to change the basis of our approaches to the period, and a real interest in uncovering the conscious strategies whereby Renaissance writers and artists constructed their ideas of the world and communicated these to their contemporaries. Writers are thus beginning to overturn the most powerful critical taboo of the last forty years by suggesting that it is both necessary and, through a careful examination of the structure of a work, possible to establish authorial or artistic intention.

Several books, perhaps inspired by the continuing popular vogue for biography, attempt to unpick our assumptions about early modern ideas of the self and of the individual by attempting to reconstruct non-elite lives, or to examine early modern life-writing—a genre which is not necessarily identical with modern biography or autobiography. In *Life Writing in Reformation Europe: Lives of Reformers by Friends, Disciples and Foes*, Irena Backus makes a well-historicized approach to the topic of capturing a life in words, which also pays close attention to the ways in which those lives were written. She begins her book by surveying the lives written by classical writers, including Plutarch, observing that Plutarch in particular is interested in the psychological make-up of his subjects. Rather than assuming that an interest in the individual consciousness is a modern invention, she insists that life-writing can have a variety of purposes. She is interested in the different ways in which

Year's Work in English Studies, Volume 89 (2010) © *The English Association; all rights reserved*
doi:10.1093/ywes/maq010

major figures of the Reformation—Luther, Calvin, Beza and others—were written about by both friends and foes, and she explores the philosophical, social, and political reasons why the writers thought it important to undertake this task. The one thing that most of the lives she describes have in common, and the aspect that differentiates these texts from modern biography, is that they concentrate less on events and chronology than on ethos and moral imperative. It may be this feature of the genre that has made both the existence of an idea of self in the period, and the value of these texts for modern history writing, invisible to modern historians. Backus cites Josiah Simler, for example, who wrote about Vermigli and Bullinger, and who also wrote a life of the naturalist Conrad Gesner. Clearly he felt the need to explain this choice: 'given that the life of Gesner was full of piety, humanity and all sorts of moral values, I do no doubt that its account would be welcome to very many people' (p. 98). Simler's Gesner is an example of how (and also how not) to study; in his opinion, his subject did not use his student days wisely since he was too undisciplined in his reading, but this seems to have paid off in later life when his scientific investigations were meshed with close reading of both classical philosophy and the Bible in order, as he says, to 'be of use to the church' (p. 101). Simler was in turn the subject of a life, this time written by Johann Wilhelm Stucki. Backus finds that, while Stucki still stresses the Christian moral lesson to be learnt from observing the lives of great men, he takes a rather more classicizing approach: 'in Stucki's view, biographies of eminent Zurich Protestants contain all the characteristics of antique *Lives*. The only difference is that being Christian, they are better and contain more moral truth than the efforts of Xenophon or Suetonius' (p. 104). Backus ends each chapter with a conclusion summing up the characteristics of a particular type of life-writing. She distinguishes between the purposes of lives written in Geneva from those emanating from Zurich, but stresses that in both cases writers had to distance themselves from the traditional hagiographical 'Lives of the Saints' models, while still treating their subjects as models of piety to be imitated. Thus the various biographies of Luther she considers are often telling a story of 'nascent nationalism' combined with 'eschatology'. A concluding chapter argues that we should pay more attention to these early lives as historical documents of the 'various Reformations' of the sixteenth century and 'an important source of information about the changes in religious climate, the reputation and image of different reformers, the obstacles they encountered, and their relations with civil authorities' (p. 229).

Early Modern English Lives: Autobiography and Self-Representation 1500–1660, by Ronald Bedford, Lloyd Davis and Philippa Kelly, is dedicated to the memory of Lloyd Davis, whose untimely death is a great loss. The authors begin by commenting on the lack of words to describe emotional states at this period—confirming that the *OED*'s first recorded use of 'emotional' dates from 1857. But they also draw attention to a number of words from passages of early life-writing, which were commonly used to express health, including mental health and what we would call emotional states—'affliction', 'deliverance', and particularly 'cheerfulness' and 'content'. Their contention is not that people living 'four centuries ago had a different language to express the same emotions that we might entertain today' or that people then were 'without loneliness and despair, or emotional equivalencies' but that 'the absence of a language to describe the intricacies of emotion means also that such intricacies are largely implicit, unanalyzed and therefore not recorded as a part of individual self-identity' (p. 2). This is partly to do with the ways in which 'people wanted their lives to be recorded' and a sense of 'what is fit and unfit for expression', as in the pejorative sense of the expression 'self-conceit' found commonly in this period (p. 3). The opening chapter, on the autobiography of the musician, lute teacher and social aspirant Thomas Whythorne, develops this concept in ways which interestingly complement Backus's book: Whythorne 'abandons the day-of-the-week, date and year chronology of the customary diary or journal. At a stroke he generates instead what appears as a more 'novelistic' narrative mode structured upon 'events', circumstantial and psychological, extended over large temporal units, and providing opportunities for cross-reference, reflection and didacticism. These temporal units are both familiar and ancient, deriving from the division of a life into ages' (p. 15). Thus by abandoning conventional journal chronology, Whythorne paradoxically shapes his life as lived in and affected by time in a number of wider senses. Thereafter the book criss-crosses lives from different moments in the period 1550–1660 with contemporary references to concepts such as the measurement of time, memorialization, framing and gender. It is a rich and suggestive tapestry, through which reference to Whythorne recurs like a connecting thread. But these later chapters are less lucidly written and a long section on mirrors and the conflicting images, vices and virtues that various characters in both life and in literature saw in them needs more careful literary analysis to be successfully brought into an argument about the construction and communication of *self*-representation.

The most daring of these books on life-writing is *Six Renaissance Men and Women: Innovation, Biography and Cultural Creativity in Tudor England c.1450–1560*, by Elisabeth Salter. This seeks to reconstruct six less well-known lives, commenting on the strategies for doing so, and on both the limitations and the opportunities of such an undertaking. Salter's six men and women all hail from the 'middling sort' although the opportunity to talk about them stems from the fact that they are mostly connected in some way with the Tudor court. Their activities, both as individuals and as representatives of their respective professions, are accordingly rather more visible than those of most people of their class. The individuals concerned, Gilbert Banaster, Elizabeth Philip, William Cornysh, Katherine Styles, William Buckley and one 'anonymous witness', are not in fact equally unknown. Both Banaster and Cornysh were members of the Chapel Royal (Cornysh indeed was Master), and both warrant entries in the *DNB* as composers. William Buckley was a schoolmaster, scientist and scientific instrument maker (likewise known to *DNB*). Elizabeth Philip, however, is known simply because she appears repeatedly as a payee in the Revels accounts for her work as a silk woman and supplier of textiles for court masques and entertainments. The sixth individual in the book is the anonymous author of an account of the arrival in England of Catherine of Aragon and the ceremonies associated with her marriage to Henry VII's eldest son, Prince Arthur. It is, like many such documents, composed from several points of view, or rather no one person could have seen all the events described, and one part of the account would require a 'witness' privy to the plans rather than the execution, since Catherine landed at Plymouth and not at Southampton, as described in the book. The book seems to have been put together by one of the royal heralds, but rather than exploring this group of people as a class (and there is a good deal of biographical evidence for at least one of them at about this time) it switches rather inexplicably from the writer to the countless readers of all social classes who might have bought the book as a souvenir of the event. Salter recounts the story told by the 'eyewitness', but how this constitutes a life of either the teller or his even more unknown readers is not clear. The connecting thread for Salter's book is that all her subjects lived or worked in Greenwich—the location, of course, of a royal palace. Several of them, including Dame Katherine Styles, left wills in that jurisdiction, and Salter claims to have read some 2,000 of these. Salter's other methodological link is likewise serendipitous: in the main, the reason their stories can be pieced together is through the recent chance discovery of some extra document. The book begins with an explication of this methodology and the rationale for it, although the principle that by focusing on a little-known life we might gain new perspectives on the cultural context in which that person lived is surely now sufficiently well established as 'micro-history' that it does not warrant the defensiveness that Salter brings to it. Salter's introduction engages in a critique of Greenblatt's *Renaissance Self-Fashioning,* which begins tentatively but becomes something of a denunciation of the 'arbitrary connectedness' of new historicism (pp. 8–12). She then briefly toys with the idea of using creative writing. Some experiments with students over the last few years have convinced me that creative writing—for example constructing an 'eyewitness' account of preparations for an early modern play performance—can indeed be a productive method for releasing the information locked up in apparently unpromising dry financial or other official records. It forces one to ask the questions about both practical and social organization often ignored or glossed over in more conventional historical analyses, and can be insightful. But instead of trying out this method for herself, Salter quotes from two popular novels published some forty years apart, both of which she refers to repeatedly as belonging to a 'Mills and Boon' genre. Indeed, both might qualify as candidates for the 'Bad Sex' award, but they have little to tell us about the kind of social networks in which Salter's sextet might have participated. The idea behind this book is promising, but the result is sadly disappointing.

The kinds of ceremonial events in which some of Salter's men and women played an important though backstage role are the subject of *The Drama of Coronation*, Alice Hunt's careful and illuminating investigation of changes in coronation practice across the Tudor period. She asks the deceptively simple question, 'Why crown a king?', which reveals that there is a problem at the heart of English kingship; the new monarch accedes to the throne by right of birth at the moment the old monarch dies, and yet is simultaneously deemed not to acquire the true status of kingship until anointed with holy oil at the coronation. This fundamental contradiction was not lost on medieval writers, but perhaps became ever more glaringly problematic with the successive accessions of an under-age boy, Edward VI, and two women, the first acknowledged queens regnant, Mary I and Elizabeth I. Hunt's book accordingly explores coronation 'occupying as it does that hybrid space between religious rite and political contract, complicated further by the supremacy and its amplification of sacred monarchy' (p. 83). She describes the coronation of Anne Boleyn as a ceremony that 'was reclaimed from papal authority and inscribed as the space where the truth of a supreme English monarchy is sanctioned and even, via the collaborative and multivocal coronation pageants of the procession, defined and negotiated' (p. 75). And she reconsiders *Respublica*, Nicholas Udall's accession play (whether or not it was actually performed for Mary's coronation), in the context of Mary's status not only as the first woman to be crowned as a monarch and the first monarch to be crowned as supreme head of the church in England, but also as a 'parliamentary queen' who 'would owe her authority to Parliament first, not to God'. As the Council declared in an unsuccessful attempt to 'delay her coronation until after her first Parliament had sat...only Parliament—and not sacred ceremony—can retract Edward [VI]'s will and the declaration of bastardy' (pp. 111, 124–5).

Two books that are designed primarily as contributions to art history, James Hall's *The Sinister Side: How Left–Right Symbolism Shaped Western Art* and Tatiana C. String's *Art and Communication in the Reign of Henry VIII* are worth considering here because of their implications for interpretation and performance in other disciplines. String argues that the art (and therefore the artists) associated with the court of Henry VIII are consciously trying to communicate a political message and, secondly, that there is more evidence than has hitherto been thought for a conscious awareness of the processes of aesthetic appreciation and analysis in England at this period. Her thesis complements Hunt's work (above) by contrasting the woodcuts used to decorate the accounts of the coronation ceremonies of Catherine of Aragon and Anne Boleyn. Her starting point, however, is the treatise *A perswasion to the Kyng that the laws of the realm should be in Latin*, written by Richard Morison, who served under Thomas Cromwell in the 1530s. This advocates the use of visual forms such as plays by communicators since 'into the comon people thynges sooner enter by theeies, then by the eares, remembryng moche better that they see, then that they heare' (pp. 2, 32). Unfortunately, String's book is marred by repetition—particularly of the ugly phrase 'communicative loading', which recurs incessantly in her attempt to avoid the unhelpful term 'propaganda'. More successful are the later chapters, where she considers ways in which we might uncover ideas of reception. She suggests that the new architectural feature of the long gallery is designed as much as a place to hang works of art as a place for exercise in inclement weather. The order in which works are recorded in inventories of the same gallery from different periods, with the occasional new work interspersed in the middle of otherwise identical lists, seems to suggest a hanging order, revealing which pictures were grouped together. The inclusion of religious images amongst secular pictures in these new secular spaces is, she finds, significant: 'pictures formerly known as devotional were redeployed to create the shock of the new. The novelty of their setting was effectively a cue for how people should attach meaning to the collection as a whole' (p. 131).

A noticeable feature of many of the most apparently realistic Renaissance paintings is that the principal subject is lit from their right. Gombrich attempted to explain this through reference to the practicality of painting and the shadow that might be cast on a canvas by a right-handed painter. James Hall's elegant, witty and copiously illustrated book *The Sinister Side* explains why this does not add up and shows instead that the feature is iconographical. The basic thesis is simple enough: the still lingering prejudice against left-handedness apparent in the very word 'sinister' is not only a reflection of the physiological norm in humans, 90 per cent of whom are right-handed, but also performed in social practice: the place of status is on the right side of the protagonist. More than that, however, there are widespread symbolic resonances, stemming from Aristotle's association of the right side of the human body with the sun and the left side with the moon, which mean that throughout Renaissance art and literature the right side is associated with the spiritual power that comes from God, while the left side is linked to physicality and, because it is the side of the heart, to earthly love, sexuality and carnal appetite. Countless crucifixions show the dead Christ leaning to his right, but the convention is powerfully broken in later pictures showing the still living Christ, leaning to his left as if loath to leave the world. Three portraits of Hanseatic merchants by Holbein, which otherwise seem compellingly realistic, show his sitters with a right eye noticeably and puzzlingly larger than the left. Hall's theory provides the convincing explanation that Holbein is implying that 'the spiritual side of these successful merchants is more powerful than their worldly side' (p. 88). Similar iconography of light and shade, this time combined with a very slightly closed left eye, characterizes Signior Arnolfini in his marriage portrait, and adds depth to utterances connected with both Claudius and Paulina in *Hamlet* and *The Winter's Tale* respectively, when mingled joy and sorrow is expressed by one auspicious or elevated eye and one dropping or declined.

The language and iconography with which sixteenth-century Englishmen and Spaniards expressed their relations with each other is the subject of a collection of essays edited by Anne J. Cruz, *Material and Symbolic Circulation between Spain and England, 1554–1604*. This is a multidisciplinary rather than an interdisciplinary collection, and in contrast to some of the other items considered here this year takes a more traditional top-down approach to history-writing. The first part of the book nevertheless stresses the large numbers of people who, despite constant rivalry and intermittent hostilities, travelled between the two countries for reasons of family, education, religion or trade, and invites us to see English–Spanish relations—both across the Channel and across the Atlantic—in a more nuanced way than through the usual lens of post-Armada polarization. The second part looks at the ways in which both countries created and circulated fictions of the other, in drama and in romance.

A bottom-up approach to the question of not only Iberian but also black African relations in sixteenth-century England is offered by Gustav Ungerer in 'The Presence of Africans in Elizabethan England and the Performance of

Titus Andronicus at Burley-on-the-Hill, 1595/96' (*MRDE* 21[2008] 19–55). This article combines research in Spanish and English archives, including: a case heard by the English High Court of Admiralty associated with the exiled Don Antonio, heir to the Portuguese throne; the English government's connivance in the slave trade under the auspices of the Guinea charter, which stated that 'exporting slaves from Guinea was a legal enterprise provided the European exporter secured a licence from the native kings or chieftains' (p. 28); the activities of Portuguese Jewish converso merchants in London; a publication by the printer Richard Field; and speculation as to why *Titus* might have been an interesting choice of play for the Chamberlain's men to perform at Burley, the seat of Sir John Harington, during a Christmas in which he was 'royally' entertaining 200 family members and friends and as many as 900 locals. Harington had close female relatives who had married into the Spanish aristocracy but who continued to communicate with the family in England. Ungerer has unearthed some fascinating information about the operation of the slave trade in both England and Spain. In England, it was then unregulated, with the effect that the courts could do nothing to force a black slave to work for the person who had bought him—as one Dr Hector Nunes, a Portuguese merchant and slave owner living in London, found to his surprise and cost. Elizabethan anxiety about the numbers of 'blackamoors' living in England was sufficient for the queen to issue edicts for their expulsion, twice in 1596 and again in 1601, although since the Africans had no legal status this could not be enforced. The Africans that Ungerer has identified working as servants in English households, however, seem to have been treated no differently from their white counterparts: one Grace Robinson worked as part of a team of five laundresses at Knole House in Kent, while Widow Stokes of All Hallows, Barking, 'paid an annual per capita tax of 8d for her servant "Clare, a Negra". The majority of the Africans [living in England] were black domestic slaves, a few were freedmen, and some of them were Moors, mostly Berbers from North Africa' (p. 20). Richard Hakluyt knowingly, it seems, edited out of his accounts of English seafaring all reference to English merchants as slave traders, but 'It emerges from the documents retrieved from Spanish archives that all the English merchants residing in lower Andalusia after 1480 were potential owners of domestic slaves, black Africans and Moors, and that they were deeply immersed in the slave trade as dealers in human merchandise' (p. 42).

Jeanne H. McCarthy, ' "The sanctuarie is become a plaiers stage": Chapel Stagings and Tudor "Secular" Drama' (*MRDE* 21[2008] 56–86), consolidates recent suggestions arising from REED archival work to rethink our presumption that secular drama before and after the Reformation would inevitably be played in halls. On the contrary, she suggests, a number of interludes of the Henrician era, such as *Youth* and *Hick Scorner*, 'long considered "household plays" performed by small professional troupes in halls and deemed "unquestionably" part of the popular canon by Bevington, bear signs of performance by household chapel personnel in a chapel setting'. She therefore considers that the repeated references to children and to schools in Munday's *A Second and Third Blast of Retrait from Plaies and Theatres* [1580] is directed primarily against the practice of playing in schools and chapels (pp. 56–7). She observes that architecturally the household chapel's central location in domestic architecture allowed for fluid movement for the different feast-day or other celebratory events between chapel, great hall, antechamber, and outdoor locations, and argues that 'use of child choristers to impersonate clerics and priests in both *Youth* and *Hick Scorner* would, moreover have mitigated any then-current hostility to priestly theatricality...[avoiding] accusations of impropriety' (p. 77).

Ursula Potter, in 'To School or Not to School: Tudor Views on Education in Drama and Literature' (*Parergon* 25:i[2008] 103–21), argues that the middle years of the sixteenth century probably marked a high point for literacy. She observes that girls as well as boys might have a petty school education and that the provision for differential fees, including free school places, meant that, particularly in towns, schools would attract boys from across the social spectrum. By the 1580s, the limitations of the traditional grammar-school curriculum were being keenly felt, and schools had begun to offer an education in mathematics as well as in reading and writing in English. Unsurprisingly, perhaps, she discerns anxiety amongst the traditionally ruling classes about 'the rapid growth in public education and the apparent upward mobility it facilitated' (p. 119). The end of the century saw an increase in private, or 'venture', schools, and a decline in new grammar schools; 'Poor families, of course, must have been the most disadvantaged by this development; being unable to afford the fee-paying schools, they were left with the traditional but impractical Latin, Greek, and rhetoric-based curriculum taught in the free grammar schools' (p. 118). She suggests that plays dating from that period, such as *Hamlet* or '*Tis Pity She's a Whore*, tend 'to associate scholars with dangerous melancholy...or with politically dangerous conceit' and quotes a father's opinion in *Patent Grissill*: 'I thought by learning thou hadst been made wise, | But I perceive it puffeth up thy soule' (p. 76).

An interesting insight into reactions to the inequality experienced by upper-class women comes in George McClure's 'Women and the Politics of Play in Sixteenth-Century Italy: Torquato Tasso's Theory of Games' (*RQ* 61[2008] 750–91). This is an analysis of Tasso's two versions of his *Theory of Games*, written in 1581 and revised the following year. McClure suggests that the new fashion for parlour games, particularly those involving wit and verbal dexterity, 'might at times have been an experimental venue to challenge [the] realities of normal social relations between the sexes' (p. 751). Set at the court of Ferrara during the festivities surrounding the marriage of Alphonso II to Margherita Gonzaga in 1579, the *Theory of Games* is presented as an earlier conversation between male courtiers reported to one Margherita as she watches her husband play cards. In the second version of the treatise, this Margherita is identified as Margherita Bentivoglia. On being told that men might courteously allow women to win, she sturdily replies 'if we [women] cede to fortune, this happens because we cede by force, although we are equal in ability; and the violence of men is the maker of this fortune, which, even if it is anything (which I doubt), is nothing other than the result of their tyranny' (p. 758). McClure charts the differences between the two versions, though he could perhaps give more consideration to the effect on the reader of the double reportage structure of Tassos's text, and the doubtful identity of Margherita.

Gerard Passanante's study of one of Gabriel Harvey's letters, 'The Art of Reading Earthquakes: On Harvey's Wit, Ramus's Method, and the Renaissance of Lucretius' (*RQ* 61[2008] 792–832), also begins in the realm of game and play. The occasion for this letter is the famous earthquake of 1580, which prompted a large number of ballads and sermons which sought to explain it as the wrath of God visited on an immoral society. Harvey claims, perhaps deliberately unconvincingly for one of notoriously humble stock, that he was playing cards with aristocratic friends when the event occurred, and that, far from being portentous, it sounded to them as if someone had been moving heavy furniture in an upstairs room; no one was hurt, despite the levity and even immorality of their proceedings. Passanante convincingly demonstrates that Harvey's satire is aimed at Puritan poet Arthur Golding, who was one of those claiming the vengeance of God, and relies for its force on a close reading of Lucretius, allied to a Ramist sense of logic. Not only had Ramus argued for the teaching of Lucretius in the schools, but Lucretius had 'also played a role in the way Ramus conceived of the central relation between philosophy and eloquence' (p. 817). It is probably time that we allowed for a far greater appreciation of Lucretius's great poem in some quarters in the sixteenth century—and we should perhaps encourage a wider knowledge of it now.

Gary G. Gibbs and Florinda Ruiz, 'Arthur Golding's *Metamorphoses*: Myth in an Elizabethan Political Context' (*RS* 22[2008] 557–75) also touch on the earthquake of 1580 but this time in Arthur Golding's account of the event; worryingly for such a committed Christian, the only fatalities had been two innocent children attending a sermon. They go on to examine Golding's more famous work, his translation of Ovid's *Metamorphoses* in the light of his Calvinism, paying particular attention to his censorious treatment of unconventional sexuality in both the Byblis and Orpheus myths. They suggest that his object was to speed the rate of religious reform in England. 'The fantastic stories of ancient people and several lustful deities in the Roman pantheon would by their bad example only enlighten those who had been predestined by God for salvation.... But in an England ruled by a queen who loved entertainments and flirted with courtiers and rulers—even Catholic ones—and who delayed action for further church reforms, these myths could aim at potential crises at the very heart of the English regime' (pp. 574–5).

A similarly veiled attack on Elizabeth's resistance to necessary reform, but this time in the case of the law, is identified by Gregory Kneidel in 'Coscus, Queen Elizabeth, and Law in John Donne's "Satyre II"' (*RQ* 61[2008] 92–121). Kneidel argues that the poem's 'poet-turned-lawyer Coscus' is probably Sir Edward Coke, while the two female protagonists may be representations of Elizabeth herself. The poem, he suggests, is an attack on Coke's and Elizabeth's connivance in enshrining backward-looking feudal ideas in the project to codify common law, while Donne emerges as 'a much more astute, sophisticated, and skeptical observer of the law, as it was being practiced and institutionalized, than literary critics and legal historians have previously allowed' (p. 94). His account of the increasingly impenetrable attempts to counter Henry VIII's statute against 'uses'—a form of trust whereby a landholder could prevent his estate reverting to the crown on his death—is both intriguing and illuminating; 'the terms and practices of early modern land law were constantly evolving to confront new threats, less like the current collection of standardized forms with which most of us are familiar and more like computer system software. Landholders could choose what operating system to use—the common law, like Windows, controlled but did not monopolize the market—and these systems were constantly being updated to prevent new virus threats, to add desirable new features, and to compete better with other systems' (pp. 104–5).

2. Sidney

There were two important monographs on Philip Sidney this year. Regina Schneider's *Sidney's (Rewriting) of the Arcadia* tackles the complexities of Sidney's *Arcadia*, specifically the relationship between Sidney's original work, the *Old Arcadia*, and the revision that he undertook to produce the *New Arcadia*. In chapter 1 Schneider usefully establishes the differences between the two texts, specifically in relation to the coherence of plot and Sidney's progress as a writer of fiction. Schneider moves on to the work's pastoral origins in chapter 2, explaining how Sidney adapted his sources so as to best utilize a particularly versatile genre. Chapter 3 considers the speeches in the *Old Arcadia*, which Schneider argues are indebted to Jorge de Montemayor's *Siete Libros de la Diana* [1559], a philosophical dialogue that encouraged Sidney to develop 'the rather static pastoral scene of the Eclogues into a full-blown narrative with a didactic intention' (p. 87). Chapter 4 indicates the influence of Aristotelian precepts when revising the *Old Arcadia* so as to achieve dramatic unity in the revised work, and chapter 5 is focused on the various representations of Sidney's voice in the *Arcadia* and what this tells us about the author's involvement with his text. As Schneider notes, the revisions that characterize the *New Arcadia* are 'the dramatic unities of time, place and action with its resulting pseudo-epic *in medias res* beginning and retrospective narratives' (pp. 215–16). Sidney was thoroughly eclectic in utilizing a number of genres so as to present the reader with a work described by Northrop Frye as 'tragical-comical-historical-pastoral', one that is a 'combination of fantasy and morality'. The *Arcadia* is clearly difficult to define but, as Schneider points out in her conclusion, by expanding the narrative Sidney created his own poetics; although the *New Arcadia* anticipates the novel, Schneider contends that Sidney was trying to write the perfect poem.

Robert E. Stillman's *Philip Sidney and the Poetics of Renaissance Cosmopolitanism* argues that the value of knowledge, best gained by reading, is central to Sidney's *Defence of Poetry* and this was influenced by Sidney's own education. Stillman explores the nature of Sidney's education by the followers of Philip Melanchthon, a continental group termed the Philippists. He then moves on to consider how this education shaped Sidney's attitude to poetics, piety and politics. Stillman argues that witnessing the St Bartholomew's Day Massacre as a young man 'helped to determine the course of Sidney's education and the character of his piety and politics' (p. 2). This experience did not encourage anti-Catholic rhetoric; indeed, Sidney is unusual among his contemporaries in not attacking Catholicism in his writings, but rather expressed a desire for unity amongst Christians. According to Sidney, piety, for one committed to Christian unity and defence of the church, could only come about through knowledge. This knowledge, gained specifically through books, would also facilitate justice through natural law, which would free humankind from the acts of violence and tyranny that resulted from confessionalism. In his *Defence* Sidney privileges poetry above the more traditionally accepted forms of knowledge; above all, argues Stillman, Sidney emphasized the importance of poetry in public life since poetry was 'a vehicle of liberation' (p. 171) from tyrannical power.

A collection of essays with a historic trajectory and in honour of the critic Arthur Kinney appeared this year, and in it an essay by Christopher Martin should be of interest to Sidneians: 'Sidney's Exemplary Horse Master and the Disciplines of Discontent' (in Dutcher and Prescott, eds., *Renaissance Historicisms: Essays in Honor of Arthur F. Kinney*, pp. 85–102). Martin considers the anecdote with which Sidney begins his *Defence of Poetry*, that involving John Pietro Pugliano, Sidney's riding master, during a brief visit to the Viennese court. As Martin points out, Arthur Kinney read the anecdote as a parody of Stephen Gosson's *Schoole of Abuses*, a work that also opened with autobiography. Whilst acknowledging the value of this reading, Martin suggests that the reference to Pugliano is of more consequence. By examining Sidney's letters to his brother Robert and his friend Edward Denny in the context of Sidney's increasingly marginal position at court, Martin detects Sidney's compassion for, and affinity with, Pugliano, who also had to contend with disrespect and disappointment.

One essay that appeared in a collection considering the sacred and profane in English literature should also be of interest to Sidneians. Robert Kilgore, in 'Poets, Critics, and the Redemption of Poesy: Philip Sidney's *Defence of Poesy* and Metrical Psalms' (in Papazian, ed., *The Sacred and Profane in English Renaissance Literature*, pp. 108–31), is concerned with the secular and theological in Sidney's poetry and prose. Sidney's *Psalms* are clearly religious but, as Kilgore points out, critics have paid less attention to the religious thrust of the *Defence of Poetry*. Kilgore argues that knowledge of the *Psalms* can increase our understanding of the *Defence* since the *Psalms* functions as a defence for Sidney's treatise on poetry. In the *Psalms* Sidney attacks the critics, arguing that their failure to think carefully and reasonably about poetry is a thoughtlessness that leads to wickedness. Poetry is inspired by God, and the outcome for those 'who trust and believe in God, and thus *poetry*, is much better than the fate of the critics' (p. 127). The point Sidney makes is that both poetry and criticism will benefit from spiritual faith.

This year's *Sidney Journal* contained some fascinating essays about Philip Sidney's attitudes to art, class, sexuality and the textual, history, philosophy and story-telling. Adam McKeown, 'Class Identity and Connoisseurship in Sidney's *New Arcadia*' (*SidJ* 26:i[2008] 17–34), argues that attention to the visual arts in Sidney's *New Arcadia*, a topic that has recently been given less attention than hitherto by critics, is bound up with social class, a topic that has increasingly interested critics but is usually considered as being quite distinct from art. McKeown contends that throughout the *New Arcadia* 'class identity—both of the culturally empowered and the disenfranchised—is established through and around visual artworks' (p. 26) and the text subverts rather than reinforces aristocratic ideals. An important moment occurs in Kalander's gallery when two members of the cultural elite 'establish their subjective domain by sniggering at a vulgar artist' (p. 26), another when an artist who paints a violent insurrection is punished as one of the rebels. Here, and in other episodes, Sidney suggests that art is not distinct from the political realm: in the presence of a work of art a gentleman will behave differently from a peasant. However, argues McKeown, the notion of connoisseurship is destabilized throughout the *New Arcadia* since 'by allowing erotic desire and class tensions to accumulate around it and challenge its fundamental assumptions' it is exposed 'not as a natural expression of a noble character but as a set of actions and attitudes that serve to demarcate a subjective domain for the people who are empowered to do so' (p. 30). Thus the question of how to interpret art and how to judge those doing the interpreting lies at the very heart of the text.

Stephen Guy-Bray, in ' "Unknowne Mate": Sidney, Motion, and Sexuality' (*SidJ* 26:i[2008] 35–56), considers the homosocial dimension to the relationship between the characters Strephon and Klaius, who appear three times in Sidney's *Arcadia*. He argues that Sidney uses these characters, both in the *Old Arcadia* and in the unfinished 'Lamon's Tale', in order to comment upon sexuality and narratives in general. Most early modern friendship narratives highlight the difference between same-sex and male–female relations, with the usual outcome being marriage and an assertion of the value of friendship between men. According to Guy-Bray, Sidney equates sexual matters with the textual, and Strephon and Klaius are excluded from the usual narrative movement. Although both love Urania, Sidney 'stresses the excellence of their friendship and the mutuality of their pursuit' rather than any conclusion in marriage. Guy-Bray perceives 'an equivalence between a kind of sexuality that does not result in children and a kind of movement that does not result in either literal or metaphorical progress' (p. 39). In telling the story of the two men Sidney chooses poetic forms 'that make extensive use of repetition', namely the double sestina and the corona. The narrative involving these two friends thus stalls in sexual and textual terms. Guy-Bray also explores the sources to which Sidney was indebted in the creation of Strephon and Klaius, namely Jorge de Montemayor's unfinished *Los Siete Libros de la Diana* [1559] and *Diana Enamorada* [1564], a continuation of this text by Gaspar Gil Polo.

Robert E. Stillman's monograph on the influence of the Philippists on Sidney's view of poetics, piety and politics is reviewed above. In his article for the *Sidney Journal*, 'Philip Sidney and the Idea of Romance' (*SidJ* 26:ii[2008] 17–32), Stillman further develops Sidney's approach to poetry and how this relates to the *Old Arcadia*. Considering Sidney's views on history and philosophy, specifically those gained from the historian Hubert Languet and the philosopher Philippe Duplessis-Mornay, Stillman argues that Sidney shared Mornay's view of philosophy as especially enabling for the poet. Mornay used philosophy in applying natural law theory against tyranny and pondered contemporary political debates without reference to specific historical or religious phenomena. Free from history, the poet too could explore the problem of how best to rule. But history had its place also: in his *Defence* Sidney claimed that the perfection of the poets 'consists in their coupling of the philosopher's "general notion" with the historian's "particular example"' (p. 30). In the *Old Arcadia* the reader is presented with 'a syncresis of history and philosophy' (p. 28) by which Sidney reveals his romance as the best means of examining the body politic.

Staying with Sidney's debt to his continental mentors is Richard Wood's essay, '"If an excellent man should err": Philip Sidney and Stoical Virtue' (*SidJ* 26:ii[2008] 33–48), which explores how Sidney's *New Arcadia* was influenced by his philosophical inheritance. Hubert Languet's defence of Guy du Faur de Pibrac's public defence of the St Bartholomew's Day Massacre was a rejection of the stoical judgements of those who considered Pibrac the most wicked of men. Wood contends that the portrayal of Amphialus in the *New Arcadia* is similarly informed by a recognition of human potential, specifically corrigibility. He argues that, by reading the *New Arcadia* via Languet's anti-stoical ethos, apparently distinct scholarly interpretations of Sidney's philosophical inheritance can be successfully unified. What becomes clear is that while Sidney displays his knowledge of stoicism he does not advocate this particular philosophical outlook.

Alex Davis, '"The web of his story": Narrating Miso's Poem and Mopsa's Tale in Book 2 of the *New Arcadia*' (*SidJ* 26:ii[2008] 49–64), explores the stories that make up the second book of Sidney's *New Arcadia*, specifically those narrated by Miso and Mopsa. As Davis points out, these figures are unlike the other story-tellers in the book since this mother and daughter are identified as being of low rank and Miso is especially uncouth. Taking as his starting point Clare Kinney's view of the episode as interrogatory and self-reflexive, Davis further considers the self-reflexive nature of these episodes, examining not only how they relate to the narrative as a whole but also what they reveal about Sidney's depiction of culture, class, gender, narrative style and history. He concludes that, far from being distinct from the rest of the narrative, they are remarkably similar. The episodes also reveal something about Sidney himself since Sidney 'chooses to have his own literary practice reflected back to him' via these story-tellers (p. 63); the nature of the reflection is ambivalent and playful but also suggests a degree of self-revulsion.

Moving to other journals, Sidney's debt to Stephen Gosson was of interest to Christopher Martin (above), and Kent R. Lehnhof, 'Profeminism in Philip Sidney's *Apologie for Poetrie*' (*SEL* 48[2008] 23–43), also considers the influence of Stephen Gosson's *School of Abuses* on Sidney by offering a valuable corrective to the feminist view that Sidney shared Gosson's misogyny, specifically in his *Apology for Poetry*. Although Gosson and Sidney agreed that poetry could be beneficial, Lehnhof argues convincingly that they do not share anti-feminist ideas. According to Lehnhof, feminist critics have repeatedly made the mistake of attributing ideas presented by Sidney as his own, for example his reference to poetry as 'the Nurse of abuse, infecting vs with many pestilent desires'. As Lehnhof succinctly puts it, 'Although Sidney's treatise invokes anti-feminist ideas and images, it does not endorse them' (p. 26). Gosson and Sidney both perceive poetry as inherently feminine, but they do not come to the same conclusion about the effects of that femininity: Gosson fears poetry's influence upon what he perceives as proper masculinity, characterized by hardness, whereas 'Sidney consistently valorizes poetry for performing the 'feminine' functions of delighting, softening, seducing, and enchanting' (p. 29). Lehnhof examines at length the views of both men on pleasure and on poetry itself, arguing that where Gosson portrays poetry 'as an emasculating woman' (p. 29), Sidney associates it with motherhood and its 'life-giving and life-sustaining functions'. Although Sidney is a product of his time, and so not entirely blameless in his attitudes to women, Lehnhof regards these infractions as relatively minor; moreover, the view of Sidney as proto-feminist is in keeping with his attitude to women in the *Old Arcadia*, for example in Pyrocles' response to the misogynist words of Musidorus.

Jane Kingsley-Smith, 'Cupid, Idolatry, and Iconoclasm in Sidney's *Arcadia*' (*SEL* 48[2008] 65–91), considers Sidney's conception of Cupid in his *Arcadia*, specifically the ambivalence with which Sidney apparently regarded the figure and what it stood for in the period. Kingsley-Smith traces Sidney's debt to the visual arts in his conception of Cupid, via visits to Italy in the early 1570s and a fine-art collection belonging to Sidney's uncle, Robert Dudley, earl of Leicester. In Book II of the *Arcadia* Sidney presents Pyrocles as an idol, a living image, and Philoclea as idol-worshipper, an episode that anticipates the anti-Catholic iconoclasm that took place in early modern England, and yet Sidney also suggests a distinct sympathy for Catholic idolatry since 'Philoclea's prayers before the statue are not uttered in vain' (p. 73). As Kingsley-Smith points out, 'Pyrocles brings Love to life. He is one of Cupid's artifacts—an emblem, a tragedy, a statue—that testifies to the greatness of Love' (p. 74). In the first Eclogue of the *Old Arcadia*, Dicus, the shepherd, is an enemy of Cupid and 'a potential iconoclast', suggesting 'the deliberate demystification of idols that was a feature of much anti-Catholic writing of the period' (p. 75), yet in the narrative of Plangus and Erona, Sidney presents 'the dangerous effects of blasphemy and iconoclasm against Cupid' (p. 76), which contradicts the notion of Sidney as a Calvinist. Kingsley-Smith compares Sidney's apparent ambivalence in his treatment of Cupid in the episode featuring Plangus and Erona with the Reformative spirit of Francis Beaumont and John Fletcher's play *Cupid's Revenge* based on the same story. She also compares Sidney to Spenser, since the Plangus and Erona episode is distinctly Spenserian, arguing that both writers are ambivalent about religion, but where Spenser puts the focus squarely on the idolater or iconoclast rather than the idol itself, Sidney 'appears unwilling to separate the love of art from erotic love and from the impulse to worship, uniting all three within the figure of Cupid' (p. 82).

In an essay focusing on marginalia, Fred Schurink, ' "Like a hand in the margine of a booke": William Blount's Marginalia and the Politics of Sidney's *Arcadia*' (*RES* 59[2008] 1–24), provides a fascinating analysis of a copy of the 1593 edition of Sidney's *Arcadia* in the Folger Shakespeare Library, probably annotated by William Blount, seventh Lord Mountjoy. Some of the marginalia attend to the political dimension of Sidney's work, and here Blount draws upon a variety of historical sources, especially Tacitus and specifically the first and fourth books of the *Histories* and the *Agricola*, which influenced Essex and his circle at court. As Schurink points out, Blount's defence of rebellion against an unjust king is quite remarkable for its time. Yet most of the marginalia demonstrate Blount's interest in other subjects, specifically ethics and love. Via the fourth book of Virgil's *Aeneid*, Blount comments on the feelings of characters, especially female characters. Blount's comments regarding female subjectivity are mostly taken from Book IV of the *Aeneid*, which deals with the love relationship of Dido and Aeneas, and although Blount was interested in Sidney's 'sympathetic portrayal of the feelings of women in love' (p. 19) there is clear evidence also of misogyny in some of his annotations. Blount objectifies female figures, focusing on their bodies, even invoking similar descriptions of Queen Elizabeth, and at one point women are compared to several kinds of animals. Other marginalia by Blount comment on the literary and rhetorical qualities of the *Arcadia* using non-verbal signs such as underlining, flowers, maniculae and quotations from other literary authors, and Blount also provides notes explaining references to classical mythology and natural history. As Schurink shows, these marginalia suggest that, although early modern readers were interested in the political dimension of the *Arcadia*, they did not necessarily notice the same political parallels as modern readers. In general their responses would likely have been more complex than critics usually allow and, judging by Blount's article, they were also drawn to other aspects of the text.

3. Spenser

D.K. Smith's monograph, *The Cartographic Imagination in Early Modern England: Re-writing the World in Marlowe, Spenser, Raleigh and Marvell*, deals with the literary representation of maps in the late medieval and early modern period. He is specifically concerned with what he terms 'the cartographic imagination', that is, the effect of 'technological changes and imaginative transformations' (p. 10) that underpinned the new maps. The book contains chapters on a range of texts, amongst them the anonymous *Mary Magdalen*, an English saints' play surviving from the fifteenth century, Christopher Marlowe's *Tamburlaine*, and Andrew Marvell's *Bermudas*. There is also a chapter devoted to the growing consciousness about maps that developed in the 1500s, a development culminating in the 1579 atlas of the counties of England and Wales by Christopher Saxton. Of particular interest to Spenserians is chapter 3, 'From Allegorical Space to a Geographical World: Mapping Cultural Memory in *The Faerie Queene*'. Focusing on Books I–III of Spenser's epic poem, Smith argues that Spenser's Faerieland is indebted to Saxton's atlas; as Smith puts it, 'In creating his land of Faerie as a template of Elizabethan England, the poet was necessarily positioning that new poetic landscape—whether deliberately or not—alongside an almost equally new, and precisely visualized, map of the nation' (p. 75). Although the poem's protagonists wander in Faerieland, Smith argues that the reader is guided through a distinct terrain, for example in Guyon's travels through Book II 'Spenser suggests a spatial plan that continues to plot both allegorical characteristics and character development within an organized landscape'

(p. 100). Both Saxton and Spenser were concerned with mapping England, the former in literal and the latter in conceptual terms; where Saxton presented 'a unified, imaginable shape to his country', namely England (p. 124), Spenser gave shape to his country, namely Faerieland.

A book of essays on Shakespeare and Spenser, *Shakespeare and Spenser: Attractive Opposites*, appeared this year, the first in a new series entitled the Manchester Spenser, published by Manchester University Press. The editor, J.B. Lethbridge, suggests in his preface to the volume that by focusing on historical and textual approaches to Spenser and his contemporaries the series will eschew theoretically informed criticism, a rather odd position since most critics would acknowledge that history is theoretically informed. The introduction to the volume makes little mention of the essays therein, which is disappointing, but the essays themselves provide a valuable analysis of Shakespeare's debt to Spenser and, moreover, do engage with theory.

The first essay in the volume is Judith Anderson's 'Beyond Binarism: Eros/ Death and Venus/Mars in Shakespeare's *Antony and Cleopatra* and Spenser's *Faerie Queene*', in which she argues that critics are wrong to conclude that these works are pulling in opposite directions. She denies the notion that the relationship between Shakespeare and Spenser was one of 'mocking rivalry' (p. 59) and argues for an affinity between rhetorical poetry and embodied drama, using as her point of reference the exploration of hermaphroditism that occurs in both these texts. Robert L. Reid's essay, 'Spenser and Shakespeare: Polarized Approaches to Psychology, Poetics, and Patronage', is focused on how Spenser and Shakespeare differ. Reid considers Spenser less protean than Shakespeare and more concerned with fixed identities and moral authorities. He argues that the position each writer takes on self-love was influenced by his patrons and reveals their religious preferences: Spenser equated self-love with pride and sin, unlike the more morally ambivalent Shakespeare. Patrick Cheney, in 'Perdita, Pastorella, and the Romance of Literary Form: Shakespeare's Counter-Spenserian Authorship', considers Shakespeare's debt to Book VI of *The Faerie Queene* when creating the Perdita story in *The Winter's Tale*, arguing that various author-figures in the play, including Autolycus and Perdita, are indebted to, and also critique, Spenser's depiction of himself as Colin Clout.

One of the best essays in the collection is Karen Nelson's 'Pastoral Forms and Religious Reform in Spenser and Shakespeare', which considers Shakespeare's *As You like It* and Book VI of *The Faerie Queene* in the light of reform and counter-reform. Nelson usefully provides a survey of religious debates in the 1590s, specifically the use of pastoral literature for religious education and polemic. Catholic authors tended to associate the figure of the hermit with the Church Fathers, but reformers saw the figure as indicative of cannibalistic savagery, an allusion to the Catholic belief in transubstantiation. Spenser's Serena episode is typical of the tendency to equate Catholicism with a lack of culture, yet the scene of her torture also suggests the imprisonment and the torture of Catholic priests. In another fine essay, '*Hamlet*'s Debt to Spenser's *Mother Hubberds Tale*: A Satire on Robert Cecil?', Rachel E. Hile argues that Shakespeare may have been influenced by Spenser's satire on Lord Burghley and his son Robert Cecil, where the former was compared to an ape and the latter a fox. These images appear in the Folio *Hamlet*, printed after the death of Burghley and Cecil, which connects Claudius to the ape and Polonius to the fox. Hile considers the possibility that Claudius was modelled on Cecil and Old Hamlet on Essex, since Old Hamlet is compared to Hyperion and sun imagery was often used to describe Essex.

In 'The Equinoctial Boar: Venus and Adonis in Spenser's Garden, Shakespeare's Epyllion, and *Richard III*'s England' Anne Lake Prescott considers the boar in Spenser's Garden of Adonis in Book III of *The Faerie Queene* alongside the mythological tradition concerning the boar in the period and Shakespeare's use of the boar in *Richard III*. Michael L. Hays, in 'What Means a Knight? Red Cross Knight and Edgar', argues that in his depiction of Redcrosse, Spenser departs from chivalric convention by suggesting that chivalry is inadequate, whereas Shakespeare, via Edgar in *King Lear*, suggests the opposite to be true. Susan Oldrieve's essay, 'Fusion: Spenserian Metaphor and Sidnean Example in Shakespeare's *King Lear*', compares Shakespeare's play with Spenser's Ruddymane episode in Book II of *The Faerie Queene*, arguing that both focus on intemperance. In the final essay from the volume, 'The Seven Deadly Sins and Shakespeare's Jacobean Tragedies', Ronald Horton considers Shakespeare's considerable debt to Spenser's procession of sins in Book I of *The Faerie Queene*, arguing that Shakespeare might have misread the serpentine order of Spenser's vices and explored them out of sequence.

Another collection of essays emerged this year that includes essays on Spenser, specifically on the topic of gender. The volume explores the gendered meanings of material associated with oral traditions, and the first essay to deal with Spenser, by Jacqueline T. Miller, considers the figure of the nurse and stories told by nurse-figures in *The Faerie Queene*: 'Telling Tales: Locating Female Nurture and Narrative in *The Faerie Queene*' (in Lamb and Bamford, eds., *Oral Traditions and Gender in Early Modern Literary Texts*, pp. 3–12). Miller focuses on a range of bad and good nurse-figures such as Clarinda, Radigund's handmaid, and Glauce, Britomart's nurse, pointing out that the words of such women are not to be trusted. Those rare moments when women who are not the enemies of virtue get to tell their own stories 'are often hedged by constraints and haunted by a sense that only in very circumscribed situations can women be invoked as narrators' (p. 7). Miller considers at length the figure of Samient, who defines herself as Mercilla's messenger in Book V of the poem; Samient tells her story but 'is reduced to a voiceless victimized female in distress' (p. 12) by the male knights who hear it and, argues Miller, the male poet is implicated in thus making her voiceless.

Staying with the figure of the nurse, Kate Giglio explores Spenser's *Mother Hubberds Tale* in 'Female Orality and the Healing Arts in Spenser's *Mother Hubberds Tale*' (in Lamb and Bamford, eds., pp. 13–24). Giglio contends that Spenser reveals respect for knowledge of the female healer, the 'hard-working but formally unlearned woman' (p. 13) when he adopts her voice to tell the fable of the Fox and the Ape. Yet despite respect for her story, there is 'insistence upon their differences' and the unlearned woman is effectively dismissed after the tale's framing narrative when literacy is clearly prioritized over oral knowledge. This reviewer cannot help but wonder why Spenser would have done otherwise; it is rather ironic that literary scholars should complain about authors privileging literacy over ignorance, a worryingly common view amongst some feminist critics. Marianne Micros considers Spenser's use of folk tales in *The Faerie Queene*, specifically in the Busirane and Isis church episodes from Book III of the poem, in 'Robber Bridegrooms and Devoured Brides: The Influence of Folktales on Spenser's Busirane and Isis Church Episodes' (in Lamb and Bamford, eds., pp. 73–84). In tales that Spenser probably knew via an oral tradition he would have come across 'descriptions of the process of maturation undergone by women' (p. 75) and, argues Micros, in the episodes featuring Britomart, Spenser's work is informed by tales 'supporting a woman's active participation in courtship and marriage rituals' (p. 76). However, in written versions of the tales and in *The Faerie Queene* she detects 'signs of the transition from the oral tradition that respects and empowers women to a literary tradition that warns women to obey men' (p. 76). Micros argues that Britomart will learn to become the kind of woman her society will accept, but the background presence of Elizabeth I, the unmarried Virgin Queen, serves to problematize any neat conclusion.

In a collection of essays with a historic trajectory, in honour of the critic Arthur Kinney (also mentioned in the Sidney section above), there were two essays that should appeal to Spenserians. The first of these, 'Seventeen Ways of Looking at Nobility: Spenser's Shorter Sonnet Sequence' (in Dutcher and Prescott, eds., pp. 103–19), is by William A. Oram and, like the essay by Christopher Martin on Sidney, considers how disappointment can impact upon an author's work. Oram focuses upon the seventeen sonnets that appear in some copies of the 1590 edition of *The Faerie Queene*, sonnets that were written before Spenser's keen sense of disappointment in Queen Elizabeth took hold. Oram argues that although some of the sonnets ask for patronage most do not, and he concurs with Judith Owens's assessment of the sequence as demonstrating 'an edgy independence' (p. 106). The dedications indicate not 'dependence and humility' but, rather, 'a dramatic self-announcement and self-justification' (p. 116). Spenser's disappointment is relevant, argues Oram, because these poems, which reveal 'maximum exuberance' were written after he had read his poem aloud to Queen Elizabeth but before he realized that she was not terribly interested in what she heard. The second essay in this volume likely to interest Spenserians is by Donald Cheny, 'Spenser's Undergoing of Ariosto' (in Dutcher and Prescott, eds., pp. 120–36), and interrogates Spenser's engagement, or rather his lack of engagement, with Ariosto's *Orlando Furioso*. Cheney lists four of the Italian poet's strengths that Spenser 'seems to ignore completely' (p. 121): the intricate plot, the careful mapping of a fictive landscape, fully rounded characters, and fully developed family relationships. He argues that Spenser's refusal to emulate Ariosto in these ways suggests that 'he was more deeply engaged by the internalized actions of dream romance' and thus presents a poem that is more concerned with the psychological; the appearance of earlier knights in later episodes indicates his interest in 'an elusive, dreamlike logic' whereby allusion and echo, rather than clear delineation, dominate.

This year's *Spenser Studies* saw a welcome focus on Spenser's minor poetry as well as *The Faerie Queene*. F.W. Brownlow's article, 'The British Church in

The Shepheardes Calender' (*SSt* 23[2008] 1–12), is the first of three essays to focus on the English and British context of Spenser's *Shepheardes Calender*. Brownlow notes how the so-called 'ecclesiastical eclogues' of Spenser's pastoral poem (February, May, July and September) reflect discussions about religion that were taking place in Pembroke, Spenser's Cambridge college, when he was a student. According to Brownlow, the eclogues promote the notion of an ancient British Church, one that considered the true religion to have been established in England by Joseph of Arimathaea, Simon Zelotes, St Peter and others. As Brownlow points out, this myth of origins, invented during the reign of Henry VIII and influential through the reign of Elizabeth I and into the seventeenth century, 'provided necessary comfort for Protestants under Catholic attack on charges of novelty and schism' (p. 4). It is not only invoked in the conversation between Spenser's shepherds but provided inspiration for Spenser's depiction of British Protestant history in *The Faerie Queene*.

Staying with English nationalism, Steven K. Galbraith's essay, '"English" Black-Letter Type and Spenser's *Shepheardes Calender*' (*SSt* 23[2008] 13–40), ponders the book as object and how the object itself, as well as what it contains, might promote an English agenda. As Galbraith demonstrates, in the early modern period black-letter type was known as 'English' type, where foreign works used roman and italic type. This is important, argues Galbraith, because the decision to set the *Shepheardes Calender* in English type, a decision that might well have involved Spenser, reinforces 'a literary project that promoted English language and literature' (p. 33). S.K. Heninger showed that Sannazaro's Italian *Arcadia* functioned as a bibliographical model for the 1579 edition of Spenser's poem; the decision to replace the roman and italic type was a deliberate act suggesting not so much 'an intentional bit of antiquarianism', as Ronald McKerrow put it, but a growing sense of English nationalism. Galbraith usefully provides two illustrations at the end of this fascinating essay, showing texts set in roman and black-letter type.

Also focusing on England and Englishness but also on Ireland, Catherine Nicholson, 'Pastoral in Exile: Spenser and the Poetics of English Alienation' (*SSt* 23[2008] 41–71), argues that Spenser's pastoral poem, like the Virgilian eclogue, invokes England as a place of exile and encourages a distinct sense of estrangement, for example by making no mention of the author on its title page and by E.K.'s comments on the strangeness of the poem's language and his own strange glossing. Nicholson attributes what she terms 'the poem's embrace of strangeness' (p. 60) not only to the pastoral tradition embodied in Virgil but to the fact that Spenser lived and worked in Ireland, 'in a state of literal proximity to and alienation from his native land and fellow English poets' (p. 64). Although life in Ireland constitutes 'displacement and estrangement' (p. 64), it is this alienation that has enabled Spenser's pastoral vision.

Sean Henry's essay, 'How Doth the Little Crocodile Improve his Shining Tale: Contextualizing the Crocodile of *Prosopopeia*: Or *Mother Hubberds Tale*' (*SSt* 23[2008] 153–80), is a fascinating analysis of the significance of the rapacious crocodile in Spenser's *Mother Hubberds Tale*, but it extends far beyond this one text. Drawing upon the appearance of the crocodile in other works by Spenser, as well as on natural history and art, specifically a church painting commemorating the English defeat of the Spanish Armada, Henry suggests that the crocodile invokes the Egyptian tyrant Pharaoh, 'which in biblical symbolism is a type for all tyrants whether those of Egypt, Babylon, or Rome' (p. 163). According to Henry, the figure of the crocodile facilitates misogynist rhetoric regarding deceit and hypocrisy and also invokes the dragon of Catholicism that threatens to swallow Protestant England.

Fred Blick detects a hitherto unnoticed punning on the name of Elizabeth Boyle, Spenser's second wife, in his *Amoretti* and Elizabeth's playful references to Spenser in her embroidery in 'Spenser's *Amoretti* and Elizabeth Boyle: Her Names Immortalized' (*SSt* 23[2008] 309–15). Blick makes a powerful case for puns in a number of the sonnets from the sequence, and suggests that Elizabeth took up Spenser's use of spider symbolism in her handiwork, with 'SP' or 'S' depicting Spenser as a spider and 'B' herself as a bee.

As is usual for this journal, a number of essays concentrated on Spenser's most famous work, *The Faerie Queene*. Daniel Moss 'Spenser's Despair and God's Grace' (*SSt* 23[2008] 73–102), considers the episode from Book I featuring Redcrosse and Despair when, during the conversation between the knight and the demon, Una remains silent until the end and then speaks only briefly. Una's failure to respond to Despair earlier in the episode, by which she remains invisible to Redcrosse and the reader, allowing Despair to rehearse his temptation of Redcrosse in full, has long proved perplexing to readers. Moss notes that Redcrosse's response to Despair's temptation 'is so feeble' that critics and readers 'are tempted to respond with superior claims, to answer for Redcrosse with appropriate Scriptural citations, or to ventriloquize Una's answer to Despair with their own timing and on their own terms' (p. 79). For Moss however, this misses the point. Contextualizing the episode via Protestant teachings about salvation and despair, Moss argues that Despair embodies incomplete scripture and that Una's 'redemptive argument' at the end of the episode offers not only hope and grace but 'coherent and complete scriptural citations to supersede the demon's incomplete and insufficient ones' (p. 93). Una's rebuttal is brief, but it represents 'an instant of grace' (p. 93), like the small of amount of grace from God that can redeem sinners, and thus is sufficient.

Judith Anderson, 'Flowers and Boars: Surmounting Sexual Binarism in Spenser's Garden of Adonis' (*SSt* 23[2008] 103–18), focuses on the description of the Garden of Adonis that occurs in Book III of *The Faerie Queene*. According to Anderson, the reader is here presented not with strict gender binaries but the bisexual, not in the human and physical sense, which would personify the garden, but, rather, in the sense of the symbolic. Providing a detailed reading of canto vi, within which the episode appears, she contends that 'This landscape is everywhere imbued with bisexuality', for example 'the myth of Chrysogone's conception, with its all-inclusive perspectives' and in 'Venus's Actaeon-like surprisal of the disarrayed Diana', which transfers 'the role of mythic male hunter to Venerean goddess, aptly and anticipatively mixes sexes/genders in approaching the Garden' (p. 107). The flowers within the garden are those 'of metamorphosis, at once of death and life, of mutability and perpetuity', whilst the coexistence of art and nature is the garden's 'commitment to conjunctive generations that at once contain and surmount doubleness and difference' (p. 108). The boar is also a bisexual figure: the animal is clearly masculine but Venus is his captor, thus demonstrating typical masculine traits, and Anderson invokes Lauren Silberman's reading of the boar as symbolic of *vagina dentata*.

Staying with Book III of *The Faerie Queene*, Brad Tuggle considers the House of Busirane episode in 'Memory, Aesthetics, and Ethical Thinking in the House of Busirane' (*SSt* 23[2008] 119–52). Tuggle is indebted to the work of Mary Carruthers 'on the emotive and memorial significance of sacred architecture in medieval monasticism', specifically the ancient rhetorical concept of architectural ductus, which Tuggle describes as 'the way we are led through a composition, be it poetic or architectural' (p. 122). Tuggle argues that the House of Busirane reveals Spenser's debt to the *ductus*, specifically via the biblical Temple of Solomon, 'the traditional memorial space par excellence' (p. 124). Tuggle also considers Spenser's attitude to art in the episode via the writing of Bernard of Clairvaux, a medieval writer with reforming impulses and one of the early sponsors of the Knights Templar, also known as the Knights of the Temple of Solomon. Tuggle suggests that 'the Knights Templar provide one of the vital foundations of Spenser's memory work in *The Faerie Queene*' (p. 135) and that in the House of Busirane episode Spenser presents 'a Bernardian meditation on the way that art and architecture nurture the ethical thinking of its readers' (p. 144).

Rachel E. Hile, 'Louis du Guernier's Illustrations for the John Hughes Edition' (*SSt* 23[2008] 181–214), is concerned with the first illustrated edition of the works of Spenser, published in 1715. Of particular focus are the illustrations themselves by the French engraver Louis du Guernier which, Hile contends, have been unfairly neglected or disparaged because of anti-French bias. Du Guernier's allegorical illustrations for Hughes's edition suggest not just collaboration between the two men but the significant influence of Hughes upon his illustrator. Hile provides detailed descriptions of a number of these illustrations, noting that she does not have the space here to consider them all; further analysis of all nineteen illustrations, here reprinted, would surely be warmly welcomed by Spenserians interested in the visualization of Spenser's allegory.

David Scott Wilson-Okamura, 'Errors About Ovid and Romance' (*SSt* 23[2008] 215–34), asks a number of questions about epic and romance in Spenser's writing, specifically whether some of the preconceptions about these genres and how they relate to Spenser ought to be reconsidered. Crucially, as Wilson-Okamura points out, Spenser did not use either term and his contemporaries did not agree about definitions. This essay usefully interrogates the notion that Ovid was anti-Virgil, that he provided Spenser with a model for 'honourable exile' (p. 218), and that Ovid's narrative, and the genre of romance in general, are characterized by the deferral of closure.

In a section entitled 'On the Margins of *The Faerie Queene*', *Spenser Studies* presents two 'paired but independent essays' (p. 257) that comment on marginalia in copies of Spenser's epic poem. The first essay, Tianhu Hao's 'An Early Modern Male Reader of *The Faerie Queene*' (*SSt* 23[2008] 257–60), surveys a 1609 copy of the poem with marginalia by an unidentified male reader whom Hao describes as 'a spontaneous editor, an active reader and writer at the same time' (p. 259), in other words the most exciting kind of annotator one examining marginalia could hope for. Hao points out that the reader interprets the allegory and is especially concerned with metrical regularity; showing little respect for authorial intention, he plays an active role in the writing process. Hao claims that the reader is male 'on paleographical grounds', but does explain what these are, which is rather disappointing.

Anne Lake Prescott offers the second essay in this section on marginalia, 'Two Copies of the 1596 *Faerie Queene*: Annotations and an Unpublished Poem on Spenser' (*SSt* 23[2008] 261–71). Prescott considers two 'badly damaged or partial copies' (p. 261) of the 1596 edition of the poem, both of which contain annotations and one of which also contains a poem praising Spenser. One of the copies is a volume that seems to have been repaired with some cropped pages from a 1590 copy. The annotations in this copy show a reader keen to interpret Spenser as primarily didactic, and descriptions of certain episodes appear as they might in an index. This volume also has annotations in two different inks and, Prescott thinks, two different hands. The other copy, one that similarly reveals an interest in rhetoric, has post-1700 notes, which might indicate that it was used for the purpose of teaching, perhaps by a student trying to remember instruction. This volume contains a poem about Spenser that takes the form of a Spenserian stanza and is signed by 'John Sheridan', probably an Irish barrister living in London. The poem is here reproduced, as is the cover of the book from which it is taken, and Prescott provides a thoughtful reading of it.

In the first of several items in the 'Gleanings' section of the journal, David Scott Wilson-Okamura, in 'When Did Spenser Read Tasso?' (*SSt* 23[2008] 277–82), concludes that Spenser read Torquato Tasso's *Gerusalemme liberata* in Ireland, the same place in which he wrote *The Faerie Queene*. It would not have been easy to find such a book as *Gerusalemme liberata* in Ireland, but Spenser managed to get hold of a copy, perhaps with the help of his friend and benefactor Lodowick Bryskett. Lauren Silberman, '"Perfect Hole": Spenser and Greek Romance' (*SSt* 23[2008] 283–92), concentrates on the conclusion to Book III of *The Faerie Queene*, a book that is also of interest to other critics in this section. She argues that the reference to Amoret being restored to a 'perfect hole' is not a bawdy pun, as some critics have thought, but rather a bilingual pun on a Greek word translated as 'perfect whole', suggesting Spenser's debt to the Greek romance *Clitophon and Leucippe* by Achilles Tatius.

William E. Bolton, 'Anglo-Saxons in Faerie Land? A Note on Some Unlikely Characters in Spenser's *Britain Moniments*' (*SSt* 23[2008] 293–302), explores the historical sections of *Faerie Queene* II.x and III.iii, specifically the Anglo-Saxons who are described therein. As Bolton points out, these figures have not hitherto been considered by critics in any detail, other than amidst studies of the *Britain moniments* sections of the poem, in which they appear. Bolton notes that the Anglo-Saxons are generally depicted as aggressive and lacking in loyalty, and yet Angela, the Anglo-Saxon warrior, is a model for Britomart, who resembles Elizabeth I. Bolton concludes that depicting the Anglo-Saxons in negative terms presents them as a foil to the virtuous

Elizabeth, who invoked Arthurian legend to legitimize her rule, whilst comparison between Angela and Britomart reinforces the sense of Britomart as a transgressive figure.

Rebecca Olson, 'A Closer Look at Spenser's "Clothes of Arras and of Toure"' (*SSt* 23[2008] 303–8), concentrates on the reference to the 'clothes of Arras and of Toure' that Britomart encounters in Castle Joyous in Book III of *The Faerie Queene*. She observes that Spenser is 'working from specific contemporary models when he describes these Ovidian tapestries' (p. 303). Whilst it is accepted that 'Arras' refers to the city that famously produced tapestries and thus the hangings themselves, critics disagree over what is meant by 'Toure'. Olson suggests that the reference is to tapestries from 'Tournai' that were commonly displayed in English courts and homes of the nobility. Spenser's truncation of the word allows for a pun on 'tower', the tower being a symbol of quality on tapestries and perhaps alluding to the Tower of London, where many tapestries were hung.

In this year's *Sidney Journal* Jean Brink, 'Spenser's Romances: From 'Lying Shepherd's Tongues' to Wedded Love' (*SidJ* 26:ii[2008] 101–10), presents a well-researched and convincing essay that warns against reading Spenser's literary work as autobiographical. She argues that critics have underestimated the importance of Spenser's first marriage to Machabyas Chylde, specifically in his choice of career. Brink attacks the notion that Spenser lived for a time in the north of England where he met and wooed Rosalind (the love-interest who appears in *The Shepheardes Calender*) as a 'manufactured fiction' (p. 107), contending that there is no evidence Rosalind was a real person. But we do know for sure that Spenser married Machabyas Chylde in 1579. Crucially, Brink asserts, the marriage to Machabyas probably influenced Spenser's career choice: as a married man he could no longer be employed in the church or university and this would have influenced his decision to accept the job of secretary to Lord Grey in Ireland.

A number of other important journal articles on Spenser also appeared this year on a number of his poetical writings. James Harmer, 'Spenser's "Goodly Thought": Heroides 15 and *The Teares of the Muses*' (*RS* 22[2008] 324–37), considers Spenser's debt to Ovid's *Heroides* in his complaint poem *The Teares of the Muses*, specifically *Heroides* 15, 'Sappho to Phaon'. As Harmer points out, 'a basic question that runs through many of the queries thrown out by the *Heroides* is this: what is it like to think a really new thought?' (p. 326), and it is an attention to self-consciousness and a first-person presence that intrigues Spenser also. Spenser makes use of the *Heroides* in what Harmer terms 'an intertextual poetics', a process that was part of an early modern debate over the significance of poetic invention. Harmer denies that *The Teares of the Muses* are repetitive, arguing that the work develops in an intriguing fashion, revealing to the reader the process by which the consciousness of the thinking subject is formed.

In the first of a number of essays on Spenser to appear in the journal *Studies in Philology*, M.L. Stapleton, 'Edmund Spenser, George Turberville, and Isabella Whitney Read Ovid's *Heroides*' (*SP* 105[2008] 487–519), also traces Spenser's debt to Ovid's *Heroides*. In Ovid's text legendary women lament at length about the wrongs they have suffered at the hands of the men they love, their lamentations taking an epistolary form. As Stapleton points out, in Spenser's *Faerie Queene* only one woman reads aloud a lamentation and that is the evil Duessa, but he argues that other female figures in the poem present 'impassioned speeches... that closely resemble many of the epistles of Ovid's heroines' (p. 489). Amongst the speeches considered by Stapleton are Britomart's Petrarchan speech by the sea-shore (III.iv.8–10), Scudamour's lament for Amoret in the House of Busirane (III.xi.9–11), Florimell's complaint for Marinell (IV.xii.6–11), and Una's complaint to Arthur (I.vii.41–51). As Stapleton notes, Spenser does not merely absorb and repeat uncritically what he finds in Ovid but, rather, presents what he terms 'an ethical correction' of his predecessor. Crucially, Spenser's female speakers use their speeches in a positive manner; where Ovid presents laments heard by no one and proclamations full of despair, Spenser uses his to liberate, to educate and to vanquish wrongdoers. Stapleton compares Spenser's treatment of Ovid with George Turberville's English translation of Ovid's text and, briefly, with Isabella Whitney's epistles, both of which 'serve as important precedents for the use of different poetical forms and meters and for women's voices' (p. 492) in Spenser's work.

Jenny Walicek, in ' "Strange Showes": Spenser's Double Vision of Imperial and Papal Vanities' (*SP* 105[2008] 304–35), disagrees with those critics who regard Spenser's 'Visions of the worlds Vanitie', beast fables published in his *Complaints*, as being of little historical interest. Taking as her starting point the suggestion by Francesco Viglione that the 'Visions' may be interpreted as referring to the demise of the Church of Rome, Walicek regards Spenser as a visionary poet, 'duty-bound to tell the unpleasant truth' to those in power (p. 306), specifically Queen Elizabeth. In this work Spenser's describes Roman political and papal empires, focusing on 'the absent virtues that ruined their leaders' (p. 310). In the final allegorical stanza, 'The Lion and the Wasp', the lion represents Queen Elizabeth and the stanza functions as 'a warning to the lion of England not to rely on her power lest she, too, be stung by the unexpected and underestimated' (p. 330). The wasp also represents Spenser, who 'has made himself a Virgilian insect', an irritant but a necessary one who speaks the truth to power and, moreover, one that survives. Walicek argues that Spenser's *Visions* was written in what proved to be a difficult year for Spenser: it constitutes a response to Queen Elizabeth's engagement in 1579 to the French Catholic duke of Alençon and those who opposed the match, one of whom was his patron, Robert Dudley, the earl of Leicester. This was also the year in which Stephen Gosson published his *Schoole of Abuse*, in which he criticized poets and which triggered a response from Thomas Lodge (*Reply*) and probably also Philip Sidney (*Defence of Poetry*). Importantly, Walicek contents that the *Visions* is the poem under discussion in letters between Harvey and Spenser and that this is Spenser's 'Dreames', a poem critics generally believe to have been lost. Spenser's self-censorship can be explained by his new position in Ireland, which would have made the publication of a poem critical of the queen offensive.

Thomas Herron, 'Reforming the Fox: Spenser's *Mother Hubberds Tale*, the Beast Fables of Barnabe Riche, and Adam Loftus, Archbishop of Dublin' (*SP* 105[2008] 336–87), proposes a new identity for the object of Spenser's satire in

Mother Hubberds Tale. Herron claims that the fox in the first and fourth parts of the tale primarily represents the archbishop of Dublin and Armagh and Lord Chancellor of Ireland, Adam Loftus, rather than the Lord Treasurer of England, William Cecil, Lord Burghley, as is usually argued. The archbishop, described by Herron as 'the most powerful administrator in Ireland after the lord deputy and the most powerful churchman in the country' (p. 342), was one of a group of moderate Protestants who held in check the more militant impulses of Protestants like Spenser who advocated a reintroduction of martial law in Ireland. After providing a useful overview of the political situation in early modern Ireland, Herron traces verbal clues in *Mother Hubberds Tale* that seem to identify the fox with Loftus (also criticized by Spenser in *A View of the Present State of Ireland*). He points out that the allusions to Loftus are also paralleled by Barnabe Riche in his beast fables, which he argues further reinforces the notion that Lofus was Spenser's main target.

Staying with identifying particular people alluded to by Spenser, Katherine Duncan-Jones, in 'MS Rawl. Poet. 185: Richard Tarlton and Edmund Spenser's "Pleasant Willy"'' (*BLR* 20[2008] 76–101), presents an analysis of a small manuscript notebook from the Bodleian that will engage Spenserians since it provides evidence for dating Spenser's composition of *The Teares of the Muses*. After describing the notebook in detail, Duncan-Jones focuses on a ballad entitled *Willie and Peggie*, often thought to be about the death of the player Richard Tarlton, but which is attributed to Tarlton himself in the manuscript. Critics have identified the 'pleasant Willy' mourned by Spenser in *The Teares of the Muses* with Richard Tarlton, but Duncan-Jones argues that both works allude to a dead player, William Knell, a member of the Queen's men. Since it is suggested that less than a year has elapsed since the death of 'pleasant *Willy*', this part of *The Teares of the Muses*, and perhaps the whole collection, can be dated late 1587 or early 1588. Duncan-Jones usefully provides the full text of Tarlton's ballad as an appendix to the essay.

Thomas A. Prendergast, 'Spenser's Phantastic History, *The Ruines of Time*, and the Invention of Medievalism' (*JMEMS* 38[2008] 175–96), considers Spenser's creation of history via the chronicle in Book II of *The Faerie Queene*, which he argues ought to be considered in the context of *The Ruines of Time*, a work that appeared a year after the publication of Books I–III of Spenser's epic poem. During the Reformation many valuable records and documents had been lost, feared destroyed, and those that did survive were often dismissed as non-historical romances. As Prendergast demonstrates, Spenser 'made the case for an occulted form of historicism', presenting 'a melancholic history, born of the loss of material medieval monuments and based on the phantasmatic recreation of that which was lost' (p. 176). His history was neither 'the truth-based history of the humanists' nor the fictitious history of the poets, but a third kind of history that can be called medievalism. Prendergast argues convincingly that the phantastic history Spenser presents in *The Faerie Queene*, one that is justified in *The Ruines of Time*, endeavours to re-create the past by engaging in a melancholia that communes with the dead through fantasy and dreams visions; Spenser thereby generates a story of the past that could also speak to a Protestant, Elizabethan present.

Benjamin P. Myers, in 'Spenser's *Faerie Queene*, 6.10.1–4' (*Expl* 66[2008] 237–40), suggests that critics have misread the episode when Calidore, the hero of Book VI of *The Faerie Queene*, disappears from the narrative in canto iii and does not re-emerge until canto ix. Critics have usually assumed that this gap, what J.C. Maxwell termed 'The Truancy of Calidore', signals the poem's condemnation of Calidore for leaving his quest or, as Paul Alpers claimed, signals the poem's dismissal of its previous commitment to action. Myers argues that, unlike Redcrosse, Calidore has committed no sin before his departure and that it ought to be viewed not as a dereliction of duty 'but rather as a necessary interlude toward the end of a long struggle' (pp. 238–9). His time in a pastoral environment is clearly positive since it facilitates his view of the dance of the Graces, a symbol of virtue, and he does not laze about but, rather, partakes in physical work, which serves as a reminder to the reader of the value of labour.

This year's *Notes and Queries* contained a number of essays on Spenser, specifically *The Faerie Queene*. Chris Butler, '"Pricking" and Ambiguity at the Start of *The Faerie Queene*' (*N&Q* 55[2008] 159–61), explores the ambiguous meanings behind the word 'pricking' in Book I of the epic poem. Butler suggests that the concept of pricking is metaphorical as well as metonymic: the word does not just mean 'riding fast' but connotes a number of meanings, not least the book's focus on Holiness via the mortification of Redcrosse's pride. Additionally, the term could refer to writing and the ambiguity that 'belongs to all signs' (p. 161), specifically the ambiguity of allegory.

As we have seen, marginalia proved a popular topic this year, and this continues with Andrew Fleck's 'Early Modern Marginalia in Spenser's *Faerie Queene* at the Folger' (*N&Q* 55[2008] 165–70), an examination of marginalia in a copy of *The Faerie Queene* currently located in the Folger Shakespeare Library. The reader, who identified himself as Brook Bridges, made extensive notes commenting on the poem and gave particular attention to the first three books. Political annotations occur only on Book V, where Bridges identifies the Seneschall who appears in V.x with the Duke of Alva and provides explication of the Belge episode, thus giving us an insight into what one particular Jacobean reader made of Spenser's political allegory.

James H. Runsdorf, 'Weaker Vessels: Spenser's Abessa and Propertius's Tarpeia' (*N&Q* 55[2008] 161–5), proposes a classical source for the depiction of Abessa in Book I of *The Faerie Queene*. The figure of Abessa, 'the deaf-mute daughter of spiritually blind Corceca, and church-pillaging Kirkrapine's well-compensated whore' (p. 161), is usually considered to be drawn from biblical references, but Runsdorf argues convincingly that Spenser was thinking of Tarpeia, the Vestal Virgin who was said to have betrayed Rome to the Sabine army of Titus Tatius before being slain by the Sabines. The story was available to Spenser in the writing of Livy, Ovid and Plutarch and, for early modern writers, was synonymous with treachery and greed, but it seems likely that Spenser was specifically indebted to Sextus Propertius, whose account 'uniquely associates her perfidy with erotic transgression' (p. 162) and thus corresponds to Abessa's relationship with Kirkrapine.

For those critics interested in comparative literary study, Simon Humphries, in 'Christina Rossetti's *Goblin Market* and Spenser's *Malbecco*' (*N&Q* 55[2008] 51–4), suggests that Spenser's Malbecco episode from Book III of *The Faerie Queene* influenced the Victorian poet Christina Rossetti when writing her poem *Goblin Market*. Humphries notes that the unusual term 'succous pasture' meaning 'juicy food' is used in both works. Humphries also claims that Rossetti's Laura is modelled upon the figure of Malbecco, one who wastes away with desire for something they can no longer have and is overwhelmed by jealousy, which Humphries argues is apparent in Laura's jealousy towards her sister Lizzie. As Humphries points out, little has been observed about the debt Rossetti, and other nineteenth-century poets, owed to Spenser; this short essay is a good start.

Books Reviewed

Backus, Irena. *Life Writing in Reformation Europe: Lives of Reformers by Friends, Disciples and Foes*. Ashgate. [2008] pp. vii + 259. £60 ISBN 9 7807 5466 0552.

Bedford, Ronald, Lloyd Davis, and Philippa Kelly. *Early Modern English Lives: Autobiography and Self-Representation 1500–1660*. Ashgate. [2007] pp. vii + 241. £55 ISBN 9 7807 5465 2953.

Cruz, Anne J., ed. *Material and Symbolic Circulation between Spain and England, 1554–1604*. Ashgate. [2008] pp. 178. £55 ISBN 9 7807 5466 2150.

Dutcher, James M., and Anne Lake Prescott, eds. *Renaissance Historicisms: Essays in Honor of Arthur F Kinney*. UDelP. [2008] pp. 355. £60.95 ISBN 9 7808 7413 0010.

Hall, James. *The Sinister Side: How Left–Right Symbolism Shaped Western Art*. CUP. [2008] pp. 489. £16.99 ISBN 9 7801 9923 0860.

Hunt, Alice. *The Drama of Coronation: Medieval Ceremony in Early Modern England*. CUP. [2008] pp. x + 242. £52 ISBN 9 7805 2188 5393.

Lamb, Mary Ellen, and Karen Bamford, eds. *Oral Traditions and Gender in Early Modern Literary Texts*. Ashgate. [2008] pp. 250. £55 ISBN 9 7807 5465 5381.

Lethbridge, J.B., ed. *Shakespeare and Spenser: Attractive Opposites*. ManUP. [2008] pp. 320. £50 ISBN 9 7807 1907 9627.

Papazian, Mary A., ed. *The Sacred and Profane in English Renaissance Literature*. UDelP. [2008] pp. 377. $75 ISBN 9780 87413 0256.

Salter Elizabeth. *Six Renaissance Men and Women: Innovation, Biography and Cultural Creativity in Tudor England c.1450–1560*. Ashgate. [2007] pp. viii + 167. £55 ISBN 9 7807 5465 4407.

Schneider, Regina. *Sidney's (Rewriting) of the Arcadia*. AMS. [2008] pp. xx + 238. $86 ISBN 9 7804 0462 3432.

Smith, D.K. *The Cartographic Imagination in Early Modern England: Re-writing the World in Marlowe, Spenser, Raleigh and Marvell*. Ashgate. [2008] pp. 214. £55 ISBN 9 7807 5465 6203.

Stillman, Robert E. *Philip Sidney and the Poetics of Renaissance Cosmopolitanism*. Ashgate. [2008] pp. 284. £55 ISBN 9 7807 5466 3690.

String, Tatiana C. *Art and Communication in the Reign of Henry VIII*. Ashgate. [2008] pp. xi + 157. £50 ISBN 9 7807 5466 3058.

VI

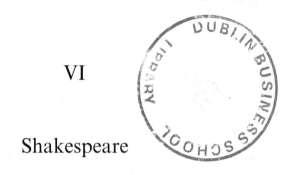

Shakespeare

GABRIEL EGAN, PETER J. SMITH, ELINOR PARSONS,
CHRIS BUTLER, ANNALIESE CONNOLLY,
RICHARD WOOD, STEVE LONGSTAFFE, JON ORTEN AND
NAOMI McAREAVEY

This chapter has four sections: 1. Editions and Textual Matters; 2. Shakespeare in the Theatre; 3. Shakespeare on Screen; 4. Criticism. Section 1 is by Gabriel Egan; section 2 is by Peter J. Smith; section 3 is by Elinor Parsons; section 4(a) is by Chris Butler; section 4(b) is by Annaliese Connolly; section 4(c) is by Richard Wood; section 4(d) is by Steve Longstaffe; section 4(e) is by John Orten; section 4(f) is by Naomi McAreavey.

1. Editions and Textual Matters

Three major critical editions of Shakespeare appeared in 2008: Anthony B. Dawson and Gretchen E. Minton edited *Timon of Athens*, Keir Elam edited *Twelfth Night* for the third series of the Arden Shakespeare, and Roger Warren edited *The Two Gentlemen of Verona* for the Oxford Shakespeare. This year there were no monographs, no major collections of essays, and few journal articles on the subject of Shakespeare's texts. Since the three editions are of plays for which the 1623 Folio is the only authority—relieving editors of the task of deciding between the readings of competing early editions—there is not a great deal to be said about them and this section is somewhat shorter than usual.

The cover and the half-title page of Dawson and Minton's *Timon of Athens* make no mention of the shared authorship, but the title page prints 'and Thomas Middleton' under Shakespeare's name. Their 145-page introduction (average for an Arden these days) covers a number of thematic topics, and when making interpretative arguments Dawson and Minton's footnotes frequently discuss what particular productions chose to do for the moment under discussion. The editors acknowledge the collaborative nature of the play right away and connect it with the distinct possibility that the play was not staged when first written; until the last century productions were rare indeed.

Year's Work in English Studies, Volume 89 (2010) © *The English Association; all rights reserved*
doi:10.1093/ywes/maq018

Perhaps, they speculate, Shakespeare turned to Middleton because he wanted to write a gritty urban satire and knew it was not his forte (pp. 3–4). We know that sometimes collaborative labour was divided by scene or act units, but otherwise—and most famously with Francis Beaumont and John Fletcher—the collaborators worked closely with one another and cross-fertilized. Dawson and Minton think the latter happened with *Timon of Athens*, with Shakespeare forming the initial plan and writing two-thirds of the dialogue. Dawson and Minton summarize which writer did which bit, noting that while some parts can be ascribed with confidence to one or other writer, other parts seem to blend their labours (pp. 5–6).

There is no early performance history, and together with the unfinished nature of the script we have and the original intention to leave it out of the Folio this suggests that the play was abandoned; it survives only because it was slotted in to fill a gap that opened when it looked like *Troilus and Cressida* would have to be withdrawn from the collection (p. 10). Why leave it out of the Folio? Maybe, the editors suggest, because it was not acted and was only dimly remembered (p. 11). There is an obvious danger of circular logic here, since its not being in the Folio was one of the reasons for supposing it was not acted. Alternatively, it might have been omitted because it was co-written, and we know that the co-written plays *Pericles* and *The Two Noble Kinsmen* were omitted; on the other hand, Dawson and Minton admit, co-written *All is True* was included in the collection. (Indeed, and co-written *Titus Andronicus*, *1 Henry VI*, *Macbeth*, and *Measure for Measure* were included too.) The usual evidence for dating a play is missing in this case: there is no Stationers' Register entry, no quarto, no records of or allusions to early performance. Dawson and Minton's best guess is that the play was composed in 1607. However, there is a likely allusion to the Gunpowder Plot of November 1605 in 'set whole realms on fire' (III.iii.34). If Shakespeare returned to Plutarch's *Lives* (used in 1599 for *Julius Caesar*) in order to write *Antony and Cleopatra* and *Coriolanus* in 1607–8, he would have found there the story of *Timon of Athens* (pp. 15–16). Coriolanus is like Timon in detesting ingratitude and leaving his city, and like Alcibiades in attacking his city and then giving it a reprieve. An upper limit to the date is set by *Timon of Athens*'s avoidance of a five-act structure, which the King's men started using once they got the Blackfriars in 1608. There is something like an act-division structure to the first half of the play, but it ceases with the Timon-in-the-woods scene. Dawson and Minton explain that they retain the 'conventional act breaks (though we acknowledge their arbitrariness), partly for convenience of reference, and partly because the first half of the play really does reflect that kind of structure' (p. 17 n.1).

The sources are discussed concisely (pp. 18–27). One source is the anonymous comedy *Timon* based on one of Lucian's *Dialogues*, which itself also influenced *Timon of Athens*. The Lucian strain accounts for the character of misanthropic Timon being ridiculous, and Plutarch for him being tragic: *Timon of Athens* neatly combines this material. Only Lucian explains why Timon became a misanthrope and says that he found gold while in exile. Dawson and Minton outline the debt to the anonymous comedy *Timon*, and pose the awkward question of which came first. *Timon* seems to echo *King*

Lear, so perhaps it was a parody of Shakespeare written after *King Lear* and before *Timon of Athens*, hence *Timon of Athens* borrows bits from *Timon*. In genre *Timon of Athens* is mixed: sort of tragedy-cum-satire, but the audience is not given many reasons to like the tragic hero. Where it is satirical the play explores the perennial problem that satire is always caught up in the criticisms it makes. Dawson and Minton acknowledge that with certain exceptions (such as the Poet who is at once a scourge of flattery and a flatterer) the characterization is largely abstract, and the power of the play lies elsewhere (pp. 45–54). Timon's benevolence is actually 'an urge to undo reciprocity' (p. 52) because he hates his own dependence, and Dawson and Minton offer an excellent summary of the psychoanalytical ideas of Melanie Klein in which envy is central, and they persuasively link these to the idea of Fortune as a fickle mother, giving and then withholding her bounty (pp. 82–4).

Dawson and Minton's introduction is superb on matters of interpretation and language and there are few obvious errors. One is that they repeat, four times in all, the familiar assertion that Lear appears on a 'heath'; there is no heath mentioned in *King Lear* (pp. 87–8). In the same discussion they refer to the 'so-called "inner stage" at the Globe', a phrase and concept that has long been abandoned by theatre historians, not all of whom even accept that there was a permanent discovery space between the two stage doors whose existence is vouchsafed by a contemporary drawing of the Swan. Discussing the taking in wax of an impression of what is written on Timon's tomb, they ask why the soldier who does this cannot read the epitaph yet apparently reads something else that he finds around the tomb. Perhaps on Timon's tomb there are two epitaphs, one in English that he can read and one in Latin that he cannot; this is the explanation Dawson and Minton reluctantly settle for, but they explore the other possibilities, including the authorial manuscript containing first and second thoughts (pp. 102–9). When the wax impression is brought to Alcibiades in the next scene, it contains two epitaphs, so there are three in all. The two on wax contradict one another, the first telling the reader not to seek the name of the dead man. This first one also contradicts what the soldier read near Timon's tomb ('Timon is dead . . .') in the preceding scene, so Dawson and Minton cut it to leave the second epitaph from the wax, which they also prefer as more in keeping with the tone of the ending of the play. The editors go to great lengths to justify their editorial intervention of cutting one epitaph, apparently in fear of being judged too interventionist. As they point out, the manuscript from which the Folio text of the play was printed was probably authorial and in two hands. The evidence for this is that it was typeset by one man, compositor B, perhaps with a little help from compositor E, and the variations in certain spellings across the play fall into two groupings that follow the division into Shakespeare's and Middleton's writing.

The account of the play in performance (pp. 109–45) contains the familiar story of Restoration adaptation and the putting back of Shakespeare's material in the nineteenth century, and Dawson and Minton are particularly attentive to important twentieth-century productions on stage and on television. Their extensive account of the BBC television production neglects to mention that the Poet and Painter were played by the eminent British satirists John Fortune and John Bird, a casting decision suggesting that the director—Bird and Fortune's fellow satirist from the 1960s, Jonathan Miller—took much the same line as Dawson and Minton on the play's essentially satirical purpose. In a surprising and most welcome innovation, the edition offers a 'Note on the Text' with the following explanation of its purpose: 'Since the textual notes are rather cryptic and hard to make out for the non-specialist, it might be helpful to the reader to provide a few guidelines' (p. 147). It would be commendable for Arden to adopt this note for all subsequent editions as even specialists might appreciate practical guidance on decoding the Arden's typographical conventions.

There being only the Folio text as authority for this play, what follows here is consideration of the most noteworthy emendations adopted or invented by Dawson and Minton. In the opening stage direction, Dawson and Minton cut the Folio's entrance for a 'ghost' Merchant who never speaks. They follow Samuel Johnson in printing 'Our poesy is as a gum which oozes' (I.i.22) for F's absurd 'Our Poesie is as a Gowne, which vses' but defend F's having the Poet say that his creative flow moves 'In a wide sea of wax' (I.i.48), rejecting the common emendations ('of tax', 'of verse') on the grounds that F either means a sea that is growing (on the wax) or else the Poet is referring to the wax tablet he writes his poems on. At I.i.89 Dawson and Minton use a common emendation (from Nicholas Rowe) in having the Poet say that Timon's flatterers will let him 'slip down', rather than F's bizarre 'sit downe'. Using F3's reading, Dawson and Minton have Timon say that he will not shake off Ventidius when he 'most needs me' (I.i.104) rather than F's 'must neede me'. Both make sense but F3 is, they say, 'more idiomatic' and in any case 'must needs' is 'always followed by a verb': the only other 'must need' in Shakespeare (2 Henry IV V.i.22–3) is also followed by a verb. (In fact that moment in 2 Henry IV is not an occurrence of 'must need' at all: it is 'must needes be had' in Q1 and F.) Dawson and Minton stick with Apemantus's 'That I had no angry wit to be a lord' (I.i.238–9) which is F's reading, rejecting all emendations. They admit that it is 'obscure' but they find none of the emendations plausible. As it stands, the line means either that if he were a lord he would hate himself, or better still that in order to be a lord he would have to give up his 'angry wit' which is what defines him, and that is why he would hate himself.

Dawson and Minton use William Warburton's emendation to have Apemantus say that Timon's meat would 'choke me 'fore I should flatter thee' (I.ii.38–9) where F has 'choake me: for I should nere flatter thee', which they admit makes reasonable sense: your meat would stick in my throat because I cannot flatter you. They also stay with F in printing 'There taste, touch, all, pleased from thy table rise' (I.ii.125) instead of emendations that try to make 'all' into 'smell': they point out that 'all' covers the missing senses. (Cupid has just mentioned the five senses, and editors generally want to fit as many as possible into this line in order to fulfil his promise; sight is covered by the next line's offer to 'feast thine eyes' so hearing is the obvious omission.) Dawson and Minton dispute John Jowett's claim—made in his Oxford Shakespeare edition reviewed in *YWES* 85[2006]—that the phrase 'methinks I could' (I.ii.225) appears nowhere in Shakespeare and is likely to be Middleton's. They claim that there are four occurrences of 'methinks I could' and four of 'methinks I should' in Shakespeare, and they are quite right.

Jowett's counting, presumably automated by computer, seems to have been thrown off by the frequent use of a space between 'me[e]' and 'think[e]s' in the early printings. For dropping the line in F where the Senator repeats Caphis's 'I go sir' (II.i.33) by saying 'I go sir? | Take the Bonds along with you', Dawson and Minton offer the argument (shared with the *Oxford Complete Works*) that this is a serious scene and the Senator's line introduces incongruous humour. They turn F's 'With clamorous demands of debt, broken Bonds' into 'With clamorous demands of broken bonds' (II.ii.39) on the grounds that it not only fits the meaning better and avoids a clash with 'debts' in the next line, but it also fits the metre. (In fact F's reading would be metrically acceptable, albeit not so regular, with 'clamorous' spoken as a disyllable.)

Since the Fool says he serves a mistress not a master, Dawson and Minton emend F's apparently erroneous references to his master to make them refer to his mistress (II.ii.73, 101). At II.ii.99–102 they print 'When men come to borrow of your masters, they approach sadly and go away merry, but they enter my mistress's house merrily and go away sad' in place of F's '. . . go away sadly'. This is a suggestion made by the Arden general editor Richard Proudfoot and it balances the chiasmus by creating the sequence adverb (*sadly*), adjective (*merry*), adverb (*merrily*) and adjective (*sad*). Dawson and Minton use F2's reading where Flavius complains that whenever he showed Timon the domestic accounts Timon would say he 'found them in mine honesty' (II.i.135), meaning that Timon took his honesty as proof the accounts were in order. This they prefer to F, in which Flavius claims that Timon would say he 'sound them in mine honestie', which can just about be made meaningful ('sound' meaning 'take the measure of') but is the wrong tense (the past tense is needed). The editors adopt Alexander Pope's emendation to print 'This slave | Unto this hour has my lord's meat in him' (III.i.54–5) instead of F's '. . . vnto his Honor . . .' which makes a sort of awkward sense: he was honoured by being allowed eat at Timon's. For a notorious crux at III.ii.39, Dawson and Minton punctuate 'He cannot want fifty—five hundred talents' and explain that Lucius means that Timon is so wealthy he cannot be short of even as much as 500 talents, let alone the 50 talents the note asks for.

Dawson and Minton accept Lewis Theobald's emendation so that the stranger, observing Lucius's refusal of Timon's plea for money, says that such ingratitude is 'every | Flatterer's spirit' (III.ii.67) where F has the perfectly serviceable 'euery Flatterers sport'. By contrast, F has the very peculiar lines 'So fitly? Go, bid all my Friends againe, | *Lucius, Lucullus*, and *Sempronius Vllorxa*: All' (III.iv.5–6), and the problem is explaining where the meaningless '*Vllorxa*' comes from. Dawson and Minton reject all previous editors' attempts to explain it (such as F.G. Fleay's that it is a misreading of 'all luxors', meaning leeches) and they simply cut it, saying that we cannot tell what it is doing in F. They print 'He did behave his anger ere 'twas spent' (III.vi.22), using Rowe's emendation of F's 'behoove his anger', which seems to make no sense (he had need of his anger?); they point out that Edmund Spenser's *The Faerie Queene* has such a transitive use of the verb *to behave*. Dawson and Minton emend F's stage direction so that the 'divers Friends' of Timon who enter to be entertained include the ones we have seen being false friends (III.vii.0). F's speech prefixes for these characters do not name them specifically (F uses numbers only) and Dawson and Minton think it better to keep this vagueness so they call them '1 LORD' and '2 LORD'. They reject Jowett's assigning of the speeches to numbered 'Senators' on the grounds that two of them seem ignorant of Alcibiades' banishment, and since the previous scene showed the Senators agreeing on this they would know about it if they really are supposed to be Senators.

Like Thomas Hanmer, Dawson and Minton have Timon's curse be 'The rest of your foes, O gods...make suitable for destruction' (III.vii.78–81) where F has 'The rest of your Fees, O Gods...'. Charles Jasper Sisson defended 'fees' as meaning 'properties', that is the people Timon wants destroyed, who are the properties of the gods. Against this Dawson and Minton object that it makes poor sense to ask the gods to destroy their own property. Also from Hanmer comes their 'This is Timon's last, | Who, stuck and spangled with your flatteries, | Washes it off' (III.vii.89–91) where F has 'This is *Timon's* last, | Who stucke and spangled you with Flatteries, | Washes it off', which as they say leaves 'Washes' without a subject and weirdly makes Timon accuse himself, rather than his false friends, of flattery. Hanmer is again followed in turning F's 'And yet Confusion liue' to 'And let confusion live' (IV.i.21), which Dawson and Minton admit is not really necessary. F has 'Raise me this Beggar, and deny't that Lord' (IV.iii.9), and the trouble is that to make sense of 'deny't', which has no antecedent, it needs to mean something opposite to 'raise'. Dawson and Minton go for J.C. Maxwell's emendation of 'deny't' to 'deject'. Where F has the puzzling line 'It is the Pastour Lards, the Brothers sides', Dawson and Minton accept the emendation first enacted by John Payne Collier to print 'It is the pasture lards the rother's sides' (IV.iii.12). They point out—but without saying why it is relevant—that there is a Rother Street in Stratford-upon-Avon; Collier himself joined the dots by noting that oxen are rothers and these were sold at Rother Market in Stratford, so Shakespeare would have known the word. For this edition Proudfoot came up with a fresh analogue to support the emendation's dropping of an initial letter B: 'Ravish'd' is misread as 'Bravishd' in *The Two Noble Kinsmen*.

Samuel Weller Singer was the first to emend F's 'the wappen'd Widdow wed againe' to 'the wappered...' (IV.iii.39), and again *The Two Noble Kinsmen* provides an analogue in Palamon calling himself young and 'unwappered'. Dawson and Minton follow Johnson in their emendation to 'spare not the babe...Think it a bastard whom the oracle | Hath doubtfully pronounced thy throat shall cut' (IV.iii.118–21), because it alludes to Oedipus, whereas F has the more generalized '...the throat shall cut', which can be defended. Dawson and Minton accept the *Oxford Complete Works* emendation of F's curse on the prostitutes 'your paines six months | Be quite contrary' to 'your pain-sick months...' (IV.iii.143). Like Nicholas Rowe they have Apemantus accuse Timon with 'This is in thee a nature but affected' (IV.iii.201), meaning that he is putting on an act of misanthropy, in preference to F's '...infected' which would not be an accusation but a condolence. In order to conform to the play's wider debate about Fortune, Dawson and Minton follow Rowe in having Apemantus attribute Timon's behaviour to a 'change of fortune' (IV.iii.203) rather than F's 'change of future' (that is, prospects), which makes perfect sense on its own. Another such relatively under-motivated change is their following Hanmer in having Apemantus refer to 'mossed trees' (IV.iii.222) in preference to F's equally acceptable 'moyst Trees'. Only occasionally do Dawson and Minton acknowledge how finely balanced such decisions are: they adopt Singer's emendation of F's 'that poore ragge' (that is, your father) to 'that poor rogue' (IV.iii.270) on the grounds that 'Poore Rogue' occurs three lines later, but admit that 'stuff' in the next line may have been suggested by 'rag'.

Dawson and Minton print 'APEMANTUS Here, I will mend thy feast. [*Offers food.*] | TIMON First mend my company, take away thyself' (IV.iii.282) where F has '...mend thy company ...', which perhaps makes better sense in a kind of misanthropically contrary way: improve your companionship by leaving me. The emendation is Rowe's. On Pope's precedent, Dawson and Minton delete 'If not' from F's 'Is not thy kindnesse subtle, couetous, | If not a Vsuring kindnesse, and as rich men deale Guifts' (IV.iii.503–4), on the grounds that it came from eyeskip to 'Is not' in the previous line and harms the sense. However, one could make a case for 'If not' meaning 'I'd even go so far as to say', although as Sisson noted when admitting this as a possibility (*New Readings in Shakespeare*, pp. 177–8), the subtle covetousness is already indicated before 'If not', so calling it usury does not amplify the point but only rephrases it. F has the Senator say that the Senate 'hath since withall | Of it owne fall' (V.ii.32–3) and Dawson and Minton follow Rowe in emending 'since' to 'sense'—needed for the meaning to be clear: we know we have done wrong, he is saying—but they also follow Pope in emending 'it' to 'its'. This second change is unnecessary because, as Sisson remarked (*New Readings in Shakespeare*, p. 178), 'it own' is perfectly good early modern English.

With some misgivings, Dawson and Minton follow Rowe's emendation of F's 'let foure words go by' to 'let sour words go by' (V.ii.105), on the grounds that Timon means 'let me say these last few bitter things and then die'. Dawson and Minton point out that the Soldier's 'The character I'll take in wax' (V.iv.106) might not be an impression but only copying onto a wax table. While usefully removing a troublesome detail that an impression would be back to front when later read, this raises another in having the Soldier copy something written in a language he cannot read; I suppose this would be plausible if the alphabet were familiar, so Latin perhaps but not Greek. Dawson and Minton print 'These walls of ours | Were not erected by their hands from whom | You have received your griefs; nor are they such | That these great towers, trophies and schools should fall | For private faults in them' (V.v.22–6), where F has 'your greefe' in place of 'your griefs'. The problem is in understanding the referents of 'they' (the griefs?) and 'them' (also the griefs? or the people who caused the griefs?) As Dawson and Minton point out, not emending 'greefe' to 'griefs' as Theobald did would prevent 'they' referring to the griefs and hence it would have to refer to the causers of Alcibiades' singular grief, meaning that these people who hurt him are not so important that he should destroy the city. But, as Dawson and Minton insist, Alcibiades has been saying that these people *are* so important in Athens that their city should fall, so the Senator would only be making a weak denial of his claim if F is thus left unemended, whereas with the emendation the Senator is able to make the more powerful claim that the griefs are not so great as the consequence Alcibiades intends. Well worked out. At V.v.28–9 the Senator says of those who hurt Alcibiades '(Shame that they wanted, cunning in excesse) | Hath broke their hearts', and Dawson and Minton follow a suggestion of Johnson's to emend 'cunning' to 'coming' and lose the brackets, which should have run all the way from 'Shame' to 'hearts'.

As can be seen from this survey of their interventions, Dawson and Minton are not particularly conservative and make no strenuous effort to retain Folio readings where previous editors have come up with plausible emendations that remove difficulty. They offer few new readings of their own. Their edition contains seven appendices. The first, entitled 'Sources', gives just what one would expect from Plutarch's *Lives of the Noble Grecians and Romans* (modernized from Thomas North's early modern English translation), plus relevant bits of the anonymous play *Timon*. The second appendix, 'Authorship', largely summarizes previous scholarship and simply declares bits of it to be unconvincing without saying why. Dawson and Minton are cautious about ascribing certain passages to one or other writer, which results in ascribing them 'Ambiguous'. The appendix on 'The Printed Text and its Anomalies' details Charlton Hinman's working out of how *Timon of Athens* came to replace *Troilus and Cressida* in the Folio and how *Troilus and Cressida* was then reintroduced. The fourth appendix simply details 'Changes to Lineation' and the fifth deals with 'Currency' in the play. Dawson and Minton outline the apparent fluctuations in the value of money, especially the talent, and survey the explanations that editors have come up with: self-correction by an author who realized he had undervalued the talent, confusion between two authors, contradiction in the sources, deliberate currency fluctuation to make the point that money is unstable, and the fact that dramatists were often simply inconsistent about talents. Dawson and Minton settle on three combined causes: multiple authorship, discrepancies in the sources, and indifference to the precise value of a talent. In the sixth appendix, a 'Doubling Chart', Dawson and Minton reckon that with at least thirty lines allowed for a quick change, the minimum cast is eleven men and four boys (plus some supernumeraries). The final appendix, 'Notable Performances of *Timon of Athens* in the Past Century', puts their notes into tabulated, potted descriptions.

The cover for Keir Elam's Arden edition calls his play *Twelfth Night*, but the half-title and title pages also give it its alternative title, *What You Will*. Elam's introduction is around the same length as Dawson and Minton's, 153 pages, but unusually it contains no section on the text and its editing: these matters are handled by appendix I. There is a common mistake early in Elam's introduction (p. 3 n. 1) when he discusses the difference between the Old Style and New Style (that is, Julian and Gregorian) calendars, which is a matter of asking 'What day is it today?', and elides it with the difference between incrementing the year number on 1 January (as we do now) and incrementing it on 25 March, Lady Day, as pious people used to do in deference to Christ's conception. It so happens that Pope Gregory's bill introducing his dating also moved the increment day from 25 March to 1 January and the bill that introduced New Style dating into England did the same. Nonetheless, the matters are distinct, and contrary to Elam's assertion some Elizabethans incremented the year number on 1 January.

Elam reckons that John Manningham wrote in his diary that he saw 'Mid 'Twelfth night' because he started to write the title of *A Midsummer Night's Dream*, and that he thought Olivia was a widow because he was probably confused by her dressing in black (p. 4). James 1 saw *Twelfth Night* in 1623 (according to Henry Herbert) and Charles 1 wrote the name 'Malvolio' beside the title *Twelfth Night* in his copy of F2 (p. 5). The highly quotable Samuel Pepys disliked the productions of *Twelfth Night* he saw, but things picked up for the play on the stage in the mid-eighteenth century (pp. 6–7). In a long series of relatively short sections organized thematically, Elam covers questions that are frequently asked about the play. How come Viola does not present herself to Orsino as a eunuch and does not sing, as she said she would? How come Maria says that Feste will be one of the spectators at the gulling of Malvolio, but Fabian in the event takes his place? These are essentially loose ends in the plot (pp. 10–17). Elam gives readings of the play's peculiar title in relation to its content—misrule, wassailing, gifting, epiphany, characters named after saints—and explores the parallels (in experiences and names) between the characters. He makes an excellent point about Viola-as-Cesario imitating her brother because she is bereaved, and he is fascinating on narcissism in general (pp. 17–32). On clothing (pp. 38–50), Elam repeats the familiar (but unreferenced and problematic) claim that 'companies received clothing from their noble patrons' (p. 45), but he gets cross-gartering right and shows a picture. Many productions get it wrong and have the garters running the length of the calf rather than being confined to the knees.

Returning to one of the familiar problems, Viola's plan to present herself as a eunuch, Elam wonders if Cesario's name (from *caesus*, cut) means 'castrated'; he finds castratedness in Viola-as-Cesario's role and points to John Astington's observation that the aphorism beginning 'some are born great...' is based on Christ's discourse on eunuchs (pp. 57–68). The introduction is studded with startling contextual knowledge, such as the fact that Illyria (roughly modern Albania) was a place where rituals of same-sex unions of non-sexual love were long practised (p. 73). This knowledge is matched with sound interpretations, such as the idea that Antonio's advice to Sebastian to visit the southern suburbs—Southwark, where the dangerous pleasures are—and to lodge at the Elephant Inn, the name of a notorious brothel on Bankside, suggests that he is leading him into temptation (p. 75). It is odd, though, that in his discussion of the 'Performances Virtual and Actual' (pp. 87–96) Elam covers the means by which the 'dark house' scene was staged without mentioning Astington's seminal essay on it. Elam buys the idea that the play was performed in honour of the real Duke Orsini visiting Elizabeth's court at the time (or at least Shakespeare remembered the name when he came to write *Twelfth Night*), but not Anthony Arlidge's idea that Shakespeare had close connections with the Middle Temple and wrote the play for it, and hence that Manningham saw the first performance. There is not much in it, but Elam goes for first performance on the twelfth night preceding Manningham's viewing on 6 February 1602, so that would be 6 January 1602. The venue, he decides, was another private hall, not Middle Temple since there is no record of a performance there on that day. The history of adaptations and rearrangements (pp. 96–106) shows not quite the extraordinary rewriting that befell other Shakespeare plays in the seventeenth to nineteenth centuries, but some considerable rearrangements, often driven by the staging requirements of the day. In the nineteenth and twentieth centuries there were a number of musical adaptations. Productions in the past fifty years can conveniently be divided into the temporal—those that give it winter or spring settings—and the spatial ones that try to capture Illyria as a specific place (pp. 106–10).

A considerable part of Elam's introduction is taken up with a survey of particularly noteworthy performances in each of the play's major roles (pp. 122–45), followed (as with Dawson and Minton's edition of *Timon of Athens*) by a table giving the basic details of 120 productions. In the text of the play itself, a lot of the explanatory notes tell the reader the stage business choices for certain productions. A few explanatory notes are on different pages from the lines they gloss. This can easily happen when there is real difficulty fitting all the notes for one page onto that page, but here it seems to happen too often and looks like a typesetting error. Twice a collation note appears on the page preceding the one holding that line: for 'Toby' V.i.353 and 'against' V.i.356. The following is not an exhaustive list of emendations, just some notable ones. At I.i.5 Elam prints 'O, it came o'er my ear like the sweet south [that is, wind]', which is Pope's emendation of F's '... sweet sound'; Elam objects that F is tautologous. Elam has the Captain say of Olivia that 'she hath abjured the company | And sight of men' (I.ii.37–8) where F has 'sight | And company'. The switch is Hanmer's and Elam thinks it improves the metre in the second line, so that Viola's response, 'O that I served that lady', completes a regular line with feminine ending. The *Oxford Complete Works* editors argue for expanding 'prethee' into 'pray thee' (I.ii.49) on the grounds that Folio compositor B had a habit of shortening it, and in agreeing to this Elam notes that here it enables an internal rhyme with 'pay thee'. On page 171 something goes wrong in the collation section of the review copy: there are unwanted underscoring characters that look like a relic from a typescript that used underlining to represent italicization.

For a famous crux, Elam has Andrew Aguecheek say his leg looks good in a 'flame-coloured stock' (I.iii.130), which is Rowe's emendation of F's 'dam'd colour'd stocke'. Elam offers nothing to overcome the objection that it is hard to see how a compositor would set 'dam'd' where his copy had 'flame', yet he objects to the *Oxford Complete Works* emendation of 'divers-coloured' on precisely this ground. Collier's emendation to 'dun-coloured' is no good, says Elam, because the stockings need to be flamboyant. His alteration of F's entrance for Cesario and Malvolio 'at seuerall doores' to 'at separate doors' (II.ii.0) seems fussy: the quality of being apart is still one of the ordinary meanings of 'several'. Elam prints 'Alas, our frailty is the cause, not we, | For such as we are made of, such we be' (II.ii.31–2) for F's 'Alas, O frailtie is the cause, not wee, | For such as we are made, if such we bee', adopting F2 change of 'O' to 'our' and Joseph Rann's emendation (first proposed by Thomas Tyrwhitt) for 'if' to 'of'. Elam turns F's 'Some are become great, some atcheeues greatnesse, and some haue greatnesse thrust vponn em' into the familiar 'Some are born great, some achieve greatness and some have greatness thrust upon them' (II.v.141–2), which is Rowe's emendation of 'become' to 'born' based on the observation that the word 'born' is twice used later in the play when the contents of the letter are reiterated. As Proudfoot notes, 'borne' could easily be misread as 'become'. Elam makes no comment on Patricia Parker's essay of 2006 (reviewed in *YWES* 87[2008]), which pointed out that those later reiterations of the letter's contents deviate in other ways too from this first reading: here Malvolio is told to smile, but at III.iv.71 he says that the letter told him to be sad.

At III.iii.14–15, F has 'I can no other answer make, but thankes, | And thankes: and euer oft good turnes', which second line is short one iambic foot. Elam adopts Theobald's emendation to make the second line 'And thanks, and ever thanks; and oft good turns'. This is a tricky problem, as the awkwardness of the short line could be intended to show that Sebastian is embarrassed at Antonio's over-solicitousness. Elam alters F's 'for | t comes to passe' to 'for it comes to pass' (III.iii.174), saying that 'for't comes to pass' is another possibility, but he makes no mention of the 't' starting a new line in F. Since it is always an error to start a new line with a space—unless you mean to indent the line, and this is the middle of a prose paragraph—it looks like a letter has come out of the forme of type. It would be odd to start a line with ''t', as would be needed for the reading 'for't', so it is almost certain that a letter 'i' has come out; thus Elam's 'for it' seems right. Strangely enough, however, his collation wrongly records that F's reading is 'For't' and his explanatory note says that F's reading is 'For t', with a 'wide space between "for" and "t" ', but does not mention the decisive matter of the line-break.

Elam's first appendix is a substantial one concerned with 'The Text and Editorial Procedures' (pp. 355–79), and it begins with the simple facts. The 1623 Folio is basic for this play, and to print a manuscript a publisher needed 'authority' (sometimes called 'allowance') from the church or state as well as permission ('licence') from the Stationers' Company. In the printshop of Isaac and William Jaggard, the Folio was printed concurrently with at least four other books, identified here, and compositor B set all of *Twelfth Night*. Elam reports that the play occupied twenty-one pages in the Folio, 'signed Y2 to Z6' (p. 361). This is not quite right, since the fourth, fifth, and sixth leaves of each regular gathering in the Folio are unsigned: he means that if they were signed those would be their signatures. Hinman's reconstruction of the order of presswork in the Folio showed that, having finished most of *All's Well That Ends Well*, the printers did not proceed to gatherings Y and Z (the end of *All's Well That Ends Well* and all of *Twelfth Night*) but turned instead to the Histories section. Presumably, copy for *Twelfth Night* was not available since with no preceding edition there could not have been a copyright problem, as with the fuss over *Troilus and Cressida*. What was the Folio compositor's copy? W.W. Greg thought *Twelfth Night* was printed from a promptbook, but admitted that there was little to go on to make such a determination. There are literary-scribal features to *Twelfth Night*, such as Latinate markers of intervals, but it is impossible to say what this manuscript was a transcript of.

As is fashionable these days, Elam calls the printer's copy a 'purely virtual object' and says that we should be careful about 'reifying it' (p. 367). In truth there is nothing virtual about the copy: it is merely a lost document. It is our conception of it, not the thing itself, that is 'virtual'. Reification is a particularly inappropriate term, because it implies that without someone doing the reifying the document would never have had physical existence, and that is not true. Elam concludes that the most we can say is that the copy was a transcript of either authorial papers or a theatrical document. In a useful subsection on punctuation, Elam is concerned with discourse markers: semantically empty words and phrases that add colour such as 'By my troth', 'Fie', and 'I warrant'. When these are used at the start of an assertion they receive too much weight if followed by a comma. Elam withholds the comma so that Andrew Aguecheek's 'By my troth I would not undertake her' (I.iii.56) is not a 'solemn pledge', as it would be if rendered as 'By my troth, I would not undertake her'. A second appendix on 'Casting' reports others' conclusions and offers a fresh calculation of its own with a doubling chart: eleven men and three boys (plus supernumeraries) are all that are needed. The last appendix covers music, reprinting musical transcriptions from the second Arden series edition.

Roger Warren's Oxford Shakespeare edition of *The Two Gentlemen of Verona* is like this year's two Arden editions in a number of ways. Although the introduction is much shorter (sixty-two pages totalling around 20,000 words), it too is highly performance-centred: virtually every discussion of the problems of certain lines and scenes is fleshed out with a consideration of how practitioners have handled them. Particular praise is given Edward Hall's company, to which Warren is an adviser. The central staging problem, according to Warren, is how to reconcile the attempted rape of Sylvia and its aftermath with the regularly comic material, and he offers a brief survey of the history of attempts to do this (pp. 2–14). Regarding 'Origins' (pp. 14–18), the main sources are *Diana* by Portuguese writer Jorge de Montemayor, first published in Spanish in 1559 (translated into French in 1578 and English in 1598), and Boccaccio's *Decameron* 10.8, coming to Shakespeare not directly but via Thomas Elyot's retelling of it in *The Governor*. It is possible that Shakespeare was not the first to dramatically combine these stories: the title of a lost Queen's men's play suggests that it might just have been such a combination and hence an ur-*The Two Gentlemen of Verona*. Other minor sources are uncertain and the links tenuous at best. There must be some connection with a scene in John Lyly's play *Midas*, and since *The Taming of the Shrew* also has parallels with that scene it seems more likely that Shakespeare in different places drew on Lyly than Lyly combined bits from different plays by Shakespeare (pp. 19–20).

In all likelihood *The Two Gentlemen of Verona* was Shakespeare's first play, so Warren explores what the dramatist might have been doing to acquire the ability to write it (pp. 21–7). Possibly Julia's reference to taking part in an amateur play at Pentecost (IV.iv.155–60) glances at Stratford Corporation's payment to 'Davy Jones [who later married into the Hathaways] and his company' for a 'pastime', which the young Shakespeare was involved in. We know that the Queen's men's Richard Tarlton performed with a dog, and they played in Stratford and Coventry in the late 1580s, so perhaps Shakespeare wrote it for them some time before Tarlton's death on 3 September 1588.

However, Lyly's *Midas* (to which *The Two Gentlemen of Verona* is indebted) is usually dated 1589 or 1590, and if that dating is accepted then the idea that Shakespeare wrote it in Stratford for the visiting Queen's men collapses. Warren turns to connections with Shakespeare's later work and finds that the Silvia–Proteus–Valentine love triangle is similar to the one in the sonnets; parallels with *Twelfth Night* are, of course, obvious (pp. 29–38).

The remainder of Warren's introduction is largely concerned with the staging of particular scenes and the nature of particular characters. The scene where Valentine's elopement is discovered by the Duke (III.i) is particularly clunky, he finds. Possibly, Julia deliberately gives to Silvia the wrong letter at IV.iv.119—the one she tore up earlier and has now stuck back together?—so perhaps she also deliberately hands over the wrong ring in the final scene. If so she wants her identity to be discovered (pp. 42–8). Lance's loyalty to his undeserving dog is paralleled in Julia's loyalty to the undeserving Proteus, and the scenes of Lance's berating Crab are brilliantly designed so that if the dog does not react to the accusations it is funny and if he does it is funny (pp. 48–53). Concerning the notorious problems of the final scene (pp. 53–9), Warren reckons that Valentine does not give Silvia to Proteus, but rather extends to Proteus the love he feels for Silvia; Warren explores how this has been handled in performance. Does Julia really faint, or just pretend to, at this point? Warren links this moment to Julia's other accidentally-on-purpose acts with the letter and ring.

It takes just four pages to deal with 'The Text' (pp. 59–62). The Folio, which is basic, was printed from a Ralph Crane transcript with massed entrance directions, which means he was making it for readers, not actors. This is awkwardly put by Warren, who writes that Crane was 'not transcribing a prompt-book' (p. 59), meaning not making one, although Warren could be misread as meaning not copying from one. Crane's copy may have been foul papers, which might explain his relatively heavy imposition of his own editorial habits: those massed entrances and what editors calls swibs, single words in brackets. Where there is a stop-press correction in F, such as 'heauily' to 'grieuously' (III.ii.14, TLN 1459), Warren reports that Charlton Hinman thought that copy was 'almost certainly' (p. 62) consulted, for this and other corrections on the same page. True, but it would be worth noting that Peter W.M. Blayney disagreed and thought it just as likely a printshop sophistication. Furthermore, in an insufficiently explained point of some importance, Warren asserts that the proof correction of 'heauily' to '*grieuously*' was made by consultation of 'Shakespeare's foul papers' (p. 62), which must mean he thinks the printer had access to two kinds of copy: Crane's transcript made from foul papers, and the foul papers themselves.

According to Warren, Crane probably made F's list of characters and imposed 'the division into acts and scenes' (p. 62). He must mean only the division into acts, since the scene breaks were doubtless an intrinsic part of the original writing. Crane may also have cut the play, since it is rather short, but Warren is not strongly convinced of this. For an explanation, in his 'Editorial Procedures' (pp. 63–5) Warren sends the reader back to the Oxford Shakespeare *Henry V* [1982], which seems a little dismissive. (Is not the reader of this edition entitled to at least a summary of those procedures?

There is plenty of space in this short volume.) Warren confines himself to remarking that passages from non-Shakespearian works used in the introduction and commentary are modernized, that indications of lines spoken 'aside', or 'to' another character, are editorial, and that disputable emendations to stage directions are shown in broken brackets.

In the text of the play itself there are few emendations, mostly consisting of added stage directions. What follows is, as usual, not an exhaustive list: I have omitted the fairly indisputable corrections of obvious error. At I.i.43–4 F has 'The eating Canker dwels; so eating Loue | Inhabits in the finest wits of all', but Warren, following Stanley Wells, changes the second 'eating' to 'doting' on the grounds that F is weak and the misreading is graphically highly plausible. Warren adopts Pope's 'I leave myself, my friends, and all, for love' (I.i.65) in place of F's absurd 'I loue my selfe . . .'. Lance describes his mother as like 'a wood woman' (II.iii.26–7) where F has 'a would-woman', which is an adoption of Theobald's suggestion and a rejection of Wells's innovative emendation to 'moved', which assumes that minim error made 'm' look like 'w' and that an 'e' can easily look like an 'l'. The problem with Theobald's suggestion, of course, is its graphic implausibility, but Warren counters this by suggesting that 'would' was an acceptable spelling of 'wood'; the *OED* agrees, but its only example is this very moment from *The Two Gentlemen of Verona*. Warren has additional evidence: in Q1 *The Merry Wives of Windsor* 'wood' is a spelling of the verb 'would', but of course he needs the opposite evidence ('wood' spelt as 'would') to clinch the argument.

At II.iii.46–8 Warren prints 'PANTHINO Where should I lose my tongue? | LANCE In thy tale. | PANTHINO In my tail!', whereas F has Panthino simply repeat Lance's line back to him by saying 'In thy Taile'. Warren points out that the pun is on tale/tail: Lance says that Panthino will lose (and loosen) his tongue from too much talking (of his tale) but Panthino 'takes him to mean "rimming", anal penetration with the tongue'; the alteration of 'my' to 'thy' was Crane's censorship of this bawdy joke. Following Theobald, Warren has a servant come in and tell Silvia that her father wishes to speak to her (II.iv.113–15), whereas F has Thurio, who has been on stage a while, suddenly blurt out this servant-like news without giving him the means to acquire it. In one of his few original emendations, Warren makes Proteus say 'Why, Valentine, what braggartism's this?' (II.iv.162) where F has 'Why *Valentine*, what Bragardisme is this?' Crane had the peculiar habit of putting in an apostrophe to show elision and yet including the elided vowel, so Warren reckons Crane wrote Bragardisme'is (meaning braggartism's) but the compositor omitted the apostrophe rather than the 'i'. In another adoption of Theobald, Warren has Proteus ask himself 'Is it mine eye, or Valentine's praise' (II.iv.196) that makes him, Proteus, suddenly love Silvia, where F has 'It is mine, or *Valentines* praise'. Sisson found a couple of similarly dropped eyes, including one in Sonnet 113. There is an error in the collation at II.iv.208: the word 'dazzlèd' in the dialogue is wrongly given the lemma 'dazzelèd', doubtless because Warren was thinking of its pronunciation.

At the beginning of II.v, F has Speed welcome Lance to 'Padua', but they are in Milan so Warren follows Pope in making that correction. Similarly at III.i.81 the Duke says that there is a lady 'in Verona here' but since they are in

Milan it just takes a switch of 'in' to 'of' to fix that. Warren follows Gary Taylor's decision for the *Oxford Complete Works* in printing 'she is not to be broken with fasting, in respect of her breath' (III.i.316–17), where F has 'shee is not to be fasting in respect of her breath'. The joke relies on a broke/break pun with the next line: 'that fault may be mended with a breakfast'. Rowe printed 'kissed' where Taylor has 'broken with', although F's reading could easily be accepted without emendation. For F's 'I often had beene often miserable' (IV.i.34), Warren gives 'I had often been miserable', which is Collier's emendation (dropping the second 'often' and reversing the order of 'had' and 'often'). Where F has the Third Outlaw say that the lady he abducted was 'heire and Neece, alide vnto the Duke' (IV.i.47), Warren has him say she was 'heir, and near allied unto the Duke' which is Theobald's emendation. Finally, at V.iv.67–8 F has 'Who should be trusted, when ones right hand | Is periured to the bosome?' but Warren follows Johnson in inserting the extra syllable to make it metrically regular as 'Who should be trusted, when one's own right hand'. There are two appendices to the edition. The first, 'Music', notes that there is just one song in the play, 'Who is Silvia?', the wooing sung by Proteus. Warren presents a setting prepared for this edition by Guy Wolfenden from a book of tunes published in 1601. The second appendix shows 'Alterations to Lineation'.

There were no monographs this year. The closest to our topic was Patrick Cheney's brilliant literary-critical work, *Shakespeare's Literary Authorship*, on the ways in which bookishness functions in Shakespeare's poems and plays, the study of which illuminates Shakespeare's own ideas on authorship. However, it is not strictly relevant to a survey of work on Shakespeare's texts and cannot be noticed here. The most important article this year was Zachary Lesser and Peter Stallybrass's superb account of how commonplacing—the marking of *sententiae* in a text—was used in a tussle to establish the literary validity of drama, and how Shakespeare side-stepped this tussle and reinvented himself as a tragic-comic writer with no classical pretensions ('The First Literary *Hamlet* and the Commonplacing of Professional Plays', *SQ* 59[2008] 371–420). They start with the peculiar claim on the title page of Q1 *Hamlet* that it was performed at universities; this claim is unique in pre-Restoration printed drama. Moreover, the title page claims that the play was performed in the 'Cittie of London' (instead of the suburban amphitheatres), which also puts it outside the commercial theatre industry. Yet this edition is traditionally seen as unliterary, as a botched-up acting version in contrast to the authorially derived Q2. Indeed, Nicholas Ling, publisher of Q1, implicitly castigated his own product as imperfect when he published Q2 with a title-page boast of being better than Q1. Q2's reference to its 'true and perfect Coppie' sounds like a boast of authoriality, and yet Q2 closely copies Q1's title-page layout, even in its unusual hanging indent. Was he trying to pass off to undiscerning buyers the remainder of his Q1 stock as Q2 while hoping that discerning ones (who might already have Q1) would spot the improvements and be encouraged to have both? If so, the theatrical Q1 as was not quite so unlike the literary Q2 as we have thought.

The status of Q1 is all the more strange because it contains a rare, new literary feature: 'sententiae or commonplaces that are pointed out to the reader, either by commas or inverted commas at the beginning of each line or by a change in font (usually from roman to italic)' (p. 376), which arose first in prestigious and classical plays. The marks highlight Corambis's (= Polonius's) lines of advice to his son and daughter, and they make Q1 literary despite its memorial link to performance (which Lesser and Stallybrass accept). When first discovered in the nineteenth century, Q1 was taken to be Shakespeare's first stab at the drama. Although he gave a convoluted, and universally rejected, theory of the early *Hamlet* editions, John Dover Wilson realized that the commonplace markers were a writerly phenomenon, not one that could be attributed to a stenographer or actor or to the workings of anyone's memory; Albert Weiner spotted that too. But the success of the theory of memorial reconstruction caused these scholars to be ignored, even by editors who write about the same features appearing in Q2 *Hamlet*. If compositors would not introduce the commonplace markers, and actors would not, who did? Lesser and Stallybrass make a highly convincing case for their suspects.

Frances Mere's *Palladis Tamia* [1598] was the second part of *Politeuphuia: Wits Commonwealth*, published in 1597 by Ling—the publisher of Q1 and Q2 *Hamlet*—and was itself based on John Bodenham's compilation of classical authors. Bodenham and his circle also laboured to collate work by contemporary vernacular writers, resulting in *Bel-vedere or the Garden of the Muses* [1600], including 214 quotations from Shakespeare. Nearly half of these 214 were from *The Rape of Lucrece* [1594], the only Shakespeare book before Q1 *Hamlet* to have commonplace markers in it. Furthermore, Ling was also the co-publisher of Robert Allott's *England's Parnassus* [1600], another collection of contemporary vernacular writers. The appearance of commonplace markers in literature was sporadic before 1594, but then took off and Ling, James Roberts and John Busby were the key figures in this development. Roberts printed for Ling and/or Busby five commonplaced books in 1594–8 whose excerpts ended up in *England's Parnassus* or *Bel-vedere*, so quite possibly these five were printed from the same manuscripts that Bodenham, Allott and Ling used to make their collections. In the preliminaries to *Bel-vedere* Bodenham writes in praise of the universities at Oxford and Cambridge, but of course in 1601 or 1602 students at St John's College Cambridge put on the play *2 The Return from Parnassus* as the third part of a trilogy starting with *The Pilgrimage to Parnassus* and *1 The Return from Parnassus*. The students gave an unflattering view of Shakespeare, and made an onstage mockery of *Bel-vedere* for its temerity in suggesting that vernacular authors should be commonplaced. The student Ingenioso who leads the mockery is usually taken to represent Thomas Nashe, a Cambridge graduate whose experiences paralleled Ingenioso's in the plays and who likewise attacked modern writers, especially dramatists.

Yet around this time Gabriel Harvey, a Cambridge don, wrote that *Hamlet* had in it matter 'to please the wiser sort' (to judge from his annotation to his copy of Chaucer's works), and he paired it with *The Rape of Lucrece*, the only other Shakespeare work to have been printed with commonplace markers. *2 The Return from Parnassus* presents Shakespeare as a poet, but at just this time one of his plays, *Hamlet*, was singled out by Harvey as being worth putting alongside the English greats and it was printed in Q1 with commonplace markers; simultaneously Bodenham and Allott were putting not just Shakespeare's poems but his plays too into their commonplace books. In the first decade of the new century, plays suddenly started to predominate amongst the printed books containing commonplace markers. Jonson's *Every Man In His Humour* was printed with commonplace markers in 1601, but it had already appeared in Bodenham's *Bel-vedere*.

Thus Bodenham and Allott were commonplacing a lot of drama, and indeed Lesser and Stallybrass reckon that it was their activity in putting extracts from plays in their commonplace books that led to the widespread publication of plays (many published by Ling) with commonplace markers in the first decade and a half of the new century. Before Bodenham and Allott's books were published no plays appeared with commonplace markers, after them came a flurry of plays printed with commonplace markers. There was in the compositor's typecase no sort for quotation marks: printers used inverted commas (or indeed non-inverted ones) to represent the variety of marginal marks indicating sententiae that they found in their manuscript and printed copy. However, shifts in printed font to note sententiae seem to indicate marks present in the body of a manuscript (not marginalia) or a change from italic to secretary hand (or vice versa). Marginalia and underlining could of course be added to a manuscript by anyone, but a change in handwriting (secretary/italic) is a feature of a writer, whether scribe or author.

Lesser and Stallybrass reckon that marginal commas are much less likely to be authorial (more likely to be added by a reader) than use of italics, but mid-line commas (inverted or not) that mark off more than one line's-worth of material are, they reckon, likely to be authorial. This is because they require more intervention than the marginal marks typically made be readers, and because we find Jonson doing them. All the material in *Every Man Out Of His Humour* that ended up in Allott's *England's Parnassus* is also marked up as commonplace using marginal commas in the 1600 quarto of Jonson's play. Perhaps Allott simply excerpted all the bits so marked in the quarto, or alternatively Allott's manuscript of the play (in which he marked the bits he wanted to excerpt) was used to print the play. Lesser and Stallybrass think the latter more likely because the play quarto also has commonplaces marked by change of font—presumably authorial ones—that Allott did not put into *England's Parnassus*, as we would expect him to do if he were simply copying from the quarto. There are also examples of highlighting words like 'proverb', 'saying', 'axiom' and so on in the dialogue of printed plays and these are typically associated with a font change too: presumably the author changed hand to highlight the commonplace.

The authors who most marked commonplaces in their own plays were Jonson and John Marston, and for other commonplaced dramatists Lesser and Stallybrass reckon that Bodenham and Ling were the driving force. After all, if Shakespeare was responsible for the commonplacing in *Hamlet*, why did he do so much more of it in Q1 than in Q2? It were better to suppose the differences arise from different readers' commonplacing of the play. Looking at all the plays up to 1642 (something that Lesser's previous scholarly surveys make him expertly equipped to do), no obvious pattern emerges concerning which type of commonplacing marker—change of font, marginal commas, mid-line commas—is used, except that marginal commas are almost exclusively reserved for vernacular plays while font-changing is used for Latin and vernacular commonplacing. Lesser and Stallybrass decide that the marginal comma method arose as a compositorial indicator of the kind of commonplacing practice that Bodenham initiated and that quickly took off, and that was consciously trying to argue against the university view that English writing should not be commonplaced at all.

There is evidence in plays that have commonplace markers of a publisher's attempt to distance the work from the theatre. For example, instead of mentioning performance as Q1 does, Q2 *Hamlet* emphasizes its origin in the author's 'true and perfect Coppie', and the second issue of *Troilus and Cressida* in 1609 cancels the reference to performance and asserts that the play was never performed. Importantly, however, these distancing gestures are not the norm: 'Overall, about three-quarters of these playbooks [containing commonplace markers] advertise theatricality and performance on their title pages—by naming the playing company or the venue, or both' (p. 409). Thus, literariness emerges not in distinction from theatricality but in consort with it, and indeed professional plays are more often given commonplace markers than other vernacular writings are. (Although it is not mentioned here, this conclusion is consistent with earlier work by Lesser on the ways that drama was marketed.) Q1 *Hamlet* is squarely within this literary-theatrical (as opposed to literary-versus-theatrical) tradition: it is commonplaced and associated with the universities. *2 Return from Parnassus* attacks Bodenham for trying to get vernacular poetry accepted as good enough to commonplace (and in that play Shakespeare appears only as a poet, not a dramatist) but Bodenham and his circle had already moved on and were trying, even more audaciously, to get professional stage plays accepted as literature. Q1 *Hamlet* was a manoeuvre in this struggle.

What kinds of writing were commonplaced in a printed play? Leaving aside *Sejanus's Fall*, which Jonson was commonplacing in order to deny it was topical (which is the opposite of commonplace) and hence escape censure for its political satire, it was writing concerned with love and women, the very things the university men agreed were not worth commonplacing. Whereas Lukas Erne sees the rising literariness of drama as an effort made by authors, Lesser and Stallybrass see it as an effect of the activities of readers like Bodenham and spreading from them to publishers. With the sole exception of one moment in *Troilus and Cressida*, Shakespeare does not seem to have marked the commonplaces in his plays. Moreover, where Erne sees increasing literariness in drama accompanying an interest in characters' interiority and psychology, Lesser and Stallybrass see the literariness witnessed in commonplacing as an interest in lines 'extracted from the dramatic situation and from the character who speaks them' (p. 416); that is to say, the lines of special interest are not individuals' thoughts but shared ones.

According to Lesser and Stallybrass's narrative, around 1607 Shakespeare decided to relearn his trade and apprenticed himself to George Wilkins and John Fletcher in order to get the hang of tragicomedy; this was instead of trying to establish himself as a writer (like Jonson) in the sententious style. It worked, and *Pericles* was the biggest hit of his career. By the time of Leonard

Digges's encomium to Shakespeare prefacing John Benson's 1640 edition of the sonnets, his not being commonplaced was part of his greatness. The same distancing from the classics—in order to laud a new vernacular classic, Shakespeare—is apparent in John Suckling's portrait of himself reading *Hamlet* and in Nicholas Rowe's story that Suckling thought Jonson too indebted to the classical writers and Shakespeare wonderfully, imperiously, free of them. This should not distract us from seeing that, around 1600, Bodenham and Ling and others were aggressively asserting the place of vernacular dramatists alongside the classics.

The foremost journal in its field, *Studies in Bibliography*, has begun to catch up with itself after a hiatus. The volume published in 2008 is 'for 2005–6' and in it R. Carter Hailey throws light on the likely order of presswork in the Pavier Shakespeare quartos of 1619 ('The Shakespearian Pavier Quartos Revisited', *SB* 57[2008] 151–95). His primary evidence is the patterns of paper stock usage, which he derives from the reappearances of watermarks and characteristic chainline intervals, on the principles that a paper mould had distinctive intervals, was used constantly until it wore out in under a year, and that a printer bought a stock of paper for a job and used it up fairly quickly rather than mixing it with other stock over many years. Hailey set out to look at more exemplars of the Pavier quartos than W.W. Greg examined for his groundbreaking essays in *The Library* in 1908 (the ones that proved that the title-page dates were false), and he has found over fifty watermark pairs in them. This enables Hailey to speak more authoritatively about pairs (of which Greg was ignorant) and to track individual wireforms (that make the watermarks) as they get damaged from use.

Hailey begins by politely correcting an error in a standard textbook on the topic, Philip Gaskell's *New Introduction to Bibliography*, which claims that a book would usually be printed on just one stock of paper. Hailey's investigations show that this might happen, or else the book might be printed on a variety of paper stocks: there is no rule. David Vander Meulen came up with the technique of identifying stocks of paper even when there is no watermark: the intervals between chainlines form a kind of fingerprint. You have to measure the intervals at one place on the sheet each time—best to go for the centre of a sheet as it is the easiest spot to identify—because the lines wander a little in their intervals across the sheet. Hailey standardizes on always looking and representing watermarks from the felt side, that is the side you can see when looking down into the mould; the other side—the one into which the chainlines will impress—is known as the mould side. The details of how Hailey does his measuring are impressively complete, if a little daunting for all but the expert. I found only one error, and it is simply a slip of expression: 'If a mark is centered between chainlines . . .', Hailey writes, then his record has to identify the chainline intervals to the left and right of it (p. 160). He means that this, the specification of intervals on either side, is given if the chainline is centred on (not 'between') chainlines.

Hailey describes how his survey of the Pavier quartos refines Greg's identifications of watermarks and puts them into pairs: with his chainline interval measurement he can tell when marks that by eye Greg thought were made by one wireform in one mould were in fact made by different wireforms in different moulds. Importantly, Allan Stevenson's continuation of Greg's work (published in *Studies in Bibliography* in 1951–2) was wrong in identifying the dates 1608 and 1617 written into a couple of watermarks in the Pavier quartos. Hailey has found these watermarks' twins, and unless they both were damaged in identical ways (an unlikely coincidence) the patterns can best be read not as numerals but as decorations in the watermark (p. 172). Regarding the order of presswork, the pattern of paper stock use implied by the watermarks show 'a complex production system that utilized cast-off copy and the concurrent printing of multiple plays to keep Jaggard's two presses busy' (p. 175). The evidence from paper is consistent with Blayney's inferences of the order of presswork from skeleton forme reuse, where one skeleton was used for both sides of each sheet but a different skeleton was used for alternate sheets. However, the paper evidence contradicts W.J. Neidig's determination, published in *Modern Philology* in 1910–11, of the order of printing of the title pages (and by inference the plays themselves), which was arrived at by tracking the changes around the bits the title pages have in common, which are the printer's device and 'Written by W. Shakespeare'. Hailey's trick is to show that the end of a particular book is printed on a mix of, say, two paper stocks, which two stocks appear together again only at the start of another book. The logical inference is that the second book was begun when the first was finished or was done concurrently with it; it is most unlikely that these two books were printed with a time interval between them, since that would require the printer to set aside the peculiar mix of two stocks that shows up in both. Hailey is also able, by the same procedure, to identify other books going through Jaggard's shop at the time: the anonymous *Troubles in Bohemia* [1619] and *The Second Part of the Booke of Christian Exercise* [1619], and just possibly John Selden's *The Historie of Tithes* that was begun by William Stansby but suppressed during production at the end of 1617.

Brian Vickers continues his reattribution of plays that Shakespeare had a hand in, and shows that Thomas Kyd was one of the authors of *Arden of Faversham* ('Thomas Kyd: Secret Sharer', *TLS* 5481(18 April)[2008] 13–15). (That Shakespeare had a hand in it was demonstrated by MacDonald P. Jackson in an article reviewed in *YWES* 87[2008].) On points of detail inessential to his claim Vickers is disturbingly misleading or mistaken. He writes that the Red Lion project of 1567 was a 'conversion' of a building into a playhouse, but, as has been known since Janet Loengard uncovered a lawsuit about it in the 1980s, the venue was a free-standing addition to the courtyard of a farm, without foundations. Vickers misleads on how scripts were delivered by freelance dramatists, claiming that 'Payment was on delivery' whereas in fact payment could be piecemeal, as sections were completed, as is clear from letters the dramatist Robert Daborne wrote to Philip Henslowe between March and December 1613, recorded as Articles 73 to 97 in Greg's edition of Henslowe's papers. He asserts that 'Having delivered their manuscript, most dramatists never saw a play again, and moved on to the next project', without addressing Grace Ioppolo's claim (reviewed in *YWES* 87[2008]) that dramatists worked closely with the actors on subsequent reshapings of a play; admittedly Ioppolo offered no clinching evidence to support her claim.

There are few works attributed to Kyd, yet his contemporaries said he was industrious, and claims that he wrote *Arden of Faversham* have emerged from time to time. Vickers has tested these claims using plagiarism-detection software that finds three-word collocations in order to compare the play to *The Spanish Tragedy*, *Soliman and Perseda* and the English translation of Robert Garnier's closet tragedy in French, *Cornelie*, these being three widely accepted Kyd attributions. Having found the collocations, the trick is then to eliminate the ones that occur in others' writing. Using a self-built machine-readable corpus of seventy-five plays from before 1596—there is no explanation why he does not use the Literature Online texts—Vickers was able to whittle the list of collocations down to thirty-two that appear only in *Arden of Faversham* and *The Spanish Tragedy*, thirty-six that appear only in *Arden of Faversham* and *Soliman and Perseda*, and eight that appear only in *Arden of Faversham* and the English translation of *Cornelie*. At this point in the argument, Vickers gives a URL to where he claims his raw data can be downloaded, but it resolves to simply the home page of the University of London's School of Advanced Study, and the data cannot be found from there. (In a subsequent issue of the journal the correct URL was given.) The evidential bottom line is that only Kyd and *Arden of Faversham* use 'And faine would have', 'Ile none of that', 'there is no credit in', 'thou wert wont to', 'on/ upon your left hand', 'then either thou or', 'have your company to', 'sit with us', 'give it over', 'heaven is my hope', and 'there he lyes'.

Two of these pieces of evidence are easily dismissed: 'thou wert wont to' appears in John Lyly's *Love's Metamorphosis* (performed by the boys of St Paul's in 1590) and 'sit with us' appears in Thomas Garter's play *Susanna* (published 1578), as *Literature Online* readily reveals. Vickers's rule of looking for matches only in plays before 1596 serves no obvious purpose: if we want to exclude sayings in common usage we need to check that around this time no one else was using these phrases. In fact, 'thou wert wont to' also appears in Anonymous's *The Wisdom of Doctor Dodypoll* (performed 1599) and Samuel Daniel's *The Queen's Arcadia* (performed 1605). If we widen the net a little to include variant forms and thereby admit 'thou wast wont to' we find it in Christopher Marlowe's *2 Tamburlaine* (performed 1588), Shakespeare's *A Midsummer Night's Dream* (performed 1595), Anonymous's *Timon* (performed 1602), John Marston's *The Malcontent* (performed 1604), Thomas Heywood's *The Rape of Lucrece* (performed 1607), Anonymous's *Tom a Lincoln* (performed around 1611), Thomas Middleton's *A Chaste Maid in Cheapside* (performed 1611) and *No Wit, No Help Like a Woman's* (performed 1613), John Fletcher's *Monsieur Thomas* (performed 1615), and John Webster's *A Cure for a Cuckold* (performed 1625). The phrase, then, was not in the least unusual. Vickers goes on to discuss looser verbal parallels between *Arden of Faversham* and the Kyd canon, and also claims *King Leir* for Kyd's authorship. He ends by arguing for Kyd's share in *1 Henry VI*, showing how many of its phrases are loosely mirrored in the Kyd canon and nowhere else before 1596. As before, the logic of limiting the search to plays before 1596 needs stronger justification than it gets in the essay. Jackson's work in the same field provides more secure scholarly procedures for the kinds of argument Vickers wishes to make, and produces results that are harder to critique.

Jackson's own contribution to the field this year was substantial, and in two articles he disproves Brian Vickers's attribution of the poem *A Lover's Complaint* to John Davies of Hereford. The first uses unusual spellings that are characteristic of an author and, despite scribal and compositorial interference, make it into print ('The Authorship of *A Lover's Complaint*: A New Approach to the Problem', *PBSA* 102[2008] 285–313). Jackson's method was to search in plays in Literature Online from the period 1590 to 1614 that contain the unusual spellings in *A Lover's Complaint* as it appears in the 1609 quarto of the sonnets, and then repeat the process for Literature Online's poetry. One of the wrinkles is that Literature Online tags drama by date of composition and first performance, but poetry only by date of publication. Of the hits he found, Jackson recorded the rare spellings, defined as ones appearing in no more than five dramatists' plays, and he prints the complete list (identifying the plays and poems they occur in) from 'doble' to 'spungie'. The technical details of how he handled capitals, hyphenated words, inflections and conjugations, and apostrophes marking elision are well explained and reasonable. The plays having three or more rare-spelling links to *A Lover's Complaint* are *Hamlet*, *2 Henry IV*, *Love's Labour's Lost*, *King Lear* and *Romeo and Juliet* (all by Shakespeare) and Middleton's *The Second Maiden's Tragedy*. Of the nineteen plays having two links to *A Lover's Complaint*, twelve are by Shakespeare, and of the sixty-one plays having one link, ten are by Shakespeare. Not only does Shakespeare dominate the top of the table of links, but the five Shakespeare plays with three or more links to *A Lover's Complaint* are all ones that on other grounds are thought to have been printed from authorial papers. The cross-check with the words' occurrences in poetry eliminates the danger that these are otherwise common spellings that happen to be rare in drama.

In all, Shakespeare's work comprises 8 per cent of the text searched by Jackson yet provides one in every three of the links to *A Lover's Complaint* he discovered. To counter Vickers's claim (made in works reviewed in *YWES* 84[2005] and *YWES* 88[2009]) that *A Lover's Complaint* was written by John Davies of Hereford, Jackson points out that his works' links to *A Lover's Complaint* are few. The rarest spellings of all, those occurring in *A Lover's Complaint* and only one other writer's work, are 'twaine', 'didde', 'sheelded', 'beseecht', and 'filliall', all Shakespeare's, and 'laundring' (Jonson), 'satte' (Giles Fletcher), 'addicions' (William Rowley), 'hewd' (George Chapman), 'subdewe' (William Warner) and 'brynish' (Nathaniel Baxter). It is obvious that no one is named twice except Shakespeare, who is responsible for five of the spellings. Broadening the net to look at the rarest spellings across the whole of Literature Online, Shakespeare still predominates: these are genuinely rare spellings in absolute terms, and they are common to *A Lover's Complaint* and Shakespeare. Jackson shows that a number of apparent errors in early editions of Shakespeare can be explained if we accept that the spellings uncovered in this study really are Shakespeare's idiosyncratic habits.

It occurs to Jackson that if Shakespeare were just an abnormally frequent user of peculiar spellings, then any searches for peculiar spellings in a work of unknown authorship, like *A Lover's Complaint*, would be likely to make links with Shakespeare for that reason alone, no matter who wrote it. To discount this possible bias, Jackson repeated the whole exercise of this article but using as his suspect text a work known to be by John Davies of Hereford. It turned out to have most links with Davies's other works, not with Shakespeare; this extra step is described in an appendix to the present article made available online by the Bibliographical Society of America. A key advantage of spelling studies is that they are not likely to be skewed by poets' imitations of one another. Jackson ends with a couple of touchstones. Arguing against Davies's authorship of *A Lover's Complaint* is his liking for *sith* (= *since*), which Shakespeare does not show, and likewise Davies has a preference for using an apostrophe to indicate elision within a word, which Shakespeare does not. Shakespeare's and not Davies's preferences show up in *A Lover's Complaint*. Likewise with the preferences for abbreviating *it is* to *it's/its* or *'tis/tis* and spelling *ere* (meaning before) as *yer*. As Jackson points out, the evidence in his study covers too many printers (whose habits would average out) for them to be the cause of bias: these are authorial habits coming through in print.

Jackson's second article buttresses the first using not rare spellings but simply rare words ('*A Lover's Complaint*, *Cymbeline*, and the Shakespeare Canon: Interpreting Shared Vocabulary', *MLR* 103[2008] 621–38). As was already known, there are rare words—those used no more than five times by Shakespeare—that cluster in *Cymbeline* and *A Lover's Complaint*: *gyves* (as a noun), *physic* (as a verb), *amplify*, *blazon* (as a verb), *ruby*, *outwardly*, *tempter*, *aptness*, *commix*, *spongy*, *slackly*, *feat*, *rudeness*, *usury* and *pervert* (as a verb). Vickers reckons they are either common words in the language or Shakespeare copied them from John Davies of Hereford's *A Lover's Complaint* that was published, wrongly, under Shakespeare's name. These explanations Jackson finds improbable because in *Cymbeline* and *A Lover's Complaint* several of these words collocate with specific other words or occur in situations of similar action or feeling. Jackson has two more words to add to the above list: *seared* (as an adjective) and *outward* (as a noun). Searching for these seventeen words in Literature Online for 1598–1614 shows that four of them are almost never used outside Shakespeare: *physic*, *slackly*, *seared* and *outward*. However, Davies uses eleven of these seventeen words, so we need a test for whether it is more likely that Shakespeare got his from Davies (as writer of *A Lover's Complaint*) or simply wrote *A Lover's Complaint* himself. It is noticeable that fifteen of these seventeen words occur in other Shakespeare works besides *Cymbeline*, and predominantly in the later ones, and appear there more often than they do in the Davies canon. So it seems that Shakespeare in *Cymbeline* was not getting these words from reading Davies's work in the 1609 quarto of the sonnets; rather, he was simply repeating himself. The poetical use of the idea of something peeping through something else comes up frequently in Shakespeare and is in *A Lover's Complaint*, but is not in other writers' work nor in Davies's, other than as the commonplace idea of the sun peeping out. In Sonnet 69 and in *A Lover's Complaint* the rare noun *outward* is used of a man's appearance, which is uncommon. At this point in his article Jackson departs from the quantitative approach and starts showing how poetical conceits are shared between *A Lover's Complaint* and Shakespeare works. This approach is less persuasive than his quantitative method because it does not show that no one else was using these conceits. When Jackson challenges Vickers on his reading of poetry, the contest is likewise inconclusive. But when he shows that the characteristic words of Davies that Vickers offers as evidence of his composition of *A Lover's Complaint* are truly commonplaces, the scales tip again in Jackson's favour.

In a third, slighter, article, Jackson gives his views on a clutch of well-known Shakespearian cruxes ('Three Disputed Shakespeare Readings: Associations and Contexts', *RES* 59[2008] 219–31). In Q2 *Romeo and Juliet* Romeo refers to the winged messenger of heaven travelling on 'lazie puffing Cloudes' in II.ii, but Jackson prefers Q1's 'lasie-pacing' (that is, lazy-pacing) clouds. The argument is essentially linguistic: the image is one of horse-riding, and Shakespeare repeatedly brings together words regarding pace (be)striding, horsemanship and supernatural beings riding in the air. Jackson thinks that Q1 *Romeo and Juliet* is 'perhaps' and Q1 *Hamlet* 'probably' based on memorial reconstruction. In *Hamlet*, the question is whether to accept a 'good kissing carrion' (as Q2/F have it), or Warburton's emendation to a 'god kissing carrion'. In favour of the latter is the idea that Hamlet is likening himself to a much-elevated thing (the sun) making a lowly thing conceive life, and so is deliberately activating Polonius's anxiety that the prince pursues Ophelia only for sex. The clincher in favour of Warburton is the frequency of other gods kissing lowly things in Shakespeare. For the 'dram of eale...of a doubt' problem, Jackson declares himself convinced that the *Oxford Complete Works* editors hit on the solution: it is 'The dram of evil...over-daub'.

Paul Werstine explains how the digital version of the *New Variorum Shakespeare* (*NVS*) will make readers' use of the edition, and especially of its collation information, much easier than hitherto, mainly because of Alan Galey's technical wizardry ('Past is Prologue: Electronic New Variorum Shakespeares', *Shakespeare* 4[2008] 208–20). Werstine refers to the series' electronic text of *The Winter's Tale* released on a CD-ROM accompanying the print version as 'protected' because it is in PDF format, but in fact anyone with a full version of the Acrobat software, or indeed of the many rival PDF-editing packages, can edit the document at will. The amazing visual representations of the collation data in the online *NVS* are possible because the project uses eXtensible Markup Language (XML) for encoding. The *NVS* has always been rigorous in its checking of volumes for accuracy, but Werstine reports that the discipline of tagging for XML has enforced even greater rigour. On the downside, however, editors find themselves going back and fixing errors after they thought they were done with an edition, simply because the electronic medium allows you to do this.

New Textualist objections to the regularizing of speech prefixes continue to resurface periodically, as when John Drakakis and Leah S. Marcus complained (in essays reviewed in *YWES* 88[2009]) that modern editors fail to follow the variations between the personal name 'Shylock' and the generic label 'Jew' and between the personal name 'Aaron' and the generic label 'Moor' in *The Merchant of Venice* and *Titus Andronicus* respectively. Lina Perkins Wilder likewise objects to the regularizing of Bottom's speech prefixes in *A Midsummer Night's Dream*, since this Protean figure should be allowed break all constraints and be at once lover and tyrant, the company clown inhabiting various roles, and Bottom the artisan ('Changeling Bottom: Speech Prefixes, Acting, and Character in *A Midsummer Night's Dream*', *Shakespeare* 4[2008] 45–64). To editorially reduce the multiplicity of 'Clowne', 'Pyramus', and 'Bottom' (as in the early editions) to just 'BOTTOM' is to efface the expression at a paratextual level of the phenomenon of changeability that the play is concerned with. This argument presupposes that someone's (the author's?) agency is expressed in the various names, but in fact there are good reasons to suspect that speech-prefix variation emerged in the printshop to solve problems of type shortage. Even if not, there is no reason to suppose that actors changed their performances for scenes where the speech prefixes change, so it is hard to see what is lost by regularizing the prefixes for the convenience of modern readers, who have enough work to do making sense of 400-year-old dramatic verse.

Last among the articles is John Felce's argument that Q1 *Hamlet* was written before Q2 or F ('Riddling Q1: Hamlet's Mill and the Trickster', *ShS* 61[2008] 269–80). Q1 is generally thought to derive from the play better represented in Q2 and F, but if so how come Q1 is closer than the others to the play's sources? Felce surveys the Hamlet story in Norse poetry and in the Danish oral tradition, which share the idea of sand as a kind of flour milled by the sea. (It never became clear to me why that idea matters; perhaps it emerges within the several untranslated foreign-language quotations offered here.) In the Norse tradition Hamlet is essentially a trickster, as he is in Q1; he is less so in Q2 and F. In Q1 the nunnery scene, Felce alleges, is more sexual than it is in Q2/F, more like the equivalent scene (a seductive ambush in the forest) in the sources. In Q1's nunnery scene, Hamlet says he never loved Ophelia, whereas in Q2/F he says he did and then says he did not, so Felce sees him as more obviously a deceiver in Q1. Because of where it appears in the action of Q1, the rejection of Ophelia is more important to the story, more a reason for her madness, than it is in Q2/F. Gertrude's knowledge of Hamlet's plan and her going along with it in Q1 also show it to be closer to the sources than Q2/F, in which versions we are allowed into Hamlet's mind. In the sources and in Q1 he keeps us out. Thus, according to Felce, the trickster of Q1 and the sources becomes the thinker of Q2/F.

Just two chapters in collections of essays were relevant to this survey. In the first, Leah S. Marcus offers a history of theories about the badness of Shakespeare's text, from the 1623 Folio through the intervening centuries to now, with lots of generalizations about how people felt about printing and about the theatre, but with no evidence offered to support the claims ('Who's Afraid of the Big 'Bad' Quarto?' in Dutcher and Prescott, eds., *Renaissance Historicisms: Essays in Honor of Arthur F. Kinney*, pp. 147–58). She focuses rather pointlessly on lectures given by Roger Chartier on French literature and then switches attention to a New Variorum Shakespeare editor who would not let his edition go online for fear that it would be corrupted. From there Marcus moves to Web 2.0 and the attacks of 9/11. The essay is a string of non sequiturs. Much more substantial is Anthony B. Dawson's reflection on editing, 'What Do Editors Do and Why Does It Matter?' (in Maguire, ed. *How To Do Things with Shakespeare: New Approaches, New Essays*, pp. 136–59). Dawson critiques Lukas Erne's *Shakespeare as Literary*

Dramatist as it applies to Folio *Hamlet*: if the underlying manuscript were, as Erne claims, an intermediate document in which were marked preliminary cuts for performance, but nowhere near all the cuts needed, what did John Heminges and Henry Condell think they were doing in using it for this prestigious book? They could easily have simply reprinted Q2 or Q3, which presented no rights problems. Good point. Dawson maintains that drama is not antithetical to literature: the scene in *Hamlet* where the Player recites the death of Priam neatly illustrates this by drawing on Virgil's *Aeneid* and alluding to bookish Marlowe, and it survives relatively unscathed across Q1, Q2 and F. We need not, Dawson counsels, be afraid of the concept of authorial intention. He ends by discussing the problems he faced editing *Timon of Athens* for the Arden edition reviewed above.

And so to the round-up from *Notes & Queries*. In Q1 *A Midsummer Night's Dream*, Cupid aims an arrow 'At a faire Vestall, throned by west', but most editors prefer F's 'At a faire Vestall, throned by the West'. Richard F. Kennedy reckons that Q1 is better if we just emend it to 'At a fairy vestal, throned by west'; there are *faire/fairie* and *aire/airie* errors in F1 *A Midsummer Night's Dream* and 'by west' for 'by the west' was not unusual in early modern English ('*A Midsummer Night's Dream* II.I.157: A Proposed Emendation', *N&Q* 55[2008] 176). John Flood has an additional biblical source for Portia's claim that mercy 'droppeth as the gentle rain': it is Isaiah 45:8, which in the Geneva Bible is 'Ye heavens, send the dewe from aboue, & let ye cloudes drop downe righteousnes' and in the Bishops Bible is 'Ye heauens from aboue drop downe, and let the cloudes rayne righteousness' ('"It droppeth as the gentle rain": Isaiah 458:8 and *The Merchant of Venice* IV.1.181', *N&Q* 55[2008] 176–7). Flood does not know which bible Shakespeare used (maybe both, he says) but judges Isaiah a particularly relevant book for this play and notices that the disadvantage of the Genevan reading in having dew instead of rain is counterbalanced by its pun on dew/Jew. In the first of two notes on Falstaff's speech about honour in *1 Henry IV* V.i, Christopher M. McDonough reads the 'scutcheon' to which he likens it as not merely the symbolic shield on which heraldic devices were drawn, but also the real weapon that in classical writings a coward throws away to save himself ('"A mere scutcheon": Falstaff as Rhipsaspis', *N&Q* 55[2008] 181–3).

Joaquim Anyó weighs the evidence for a number of possible sources for *Much Ado About Nothing*, and decides (as he did in a note reviewed in *YWES* 87[2008]), that *Tirante il Bianco*, first published in Valencia in 1490, is a neglected source ('More on the Sources of *Much Ado About Nothing*', *N&Q* 55[2008] 185–7). In Sonnet 46 the 1609 quarto reads 'To side this title is impannelled | A quest of thoughts', meaning that to decide whether the eye or the heart has a stronger claim of possession ('title') over the image of the love object a jury ('quest') has been established. The problem is the use of 'side' as a verb, and some editors go for "cide" (= decide). What if, suggests Paul Hammond, the manuscript copy read 'finde' but 'f' was misread as 's' and 'n' omitted ('A Textual Crux in Shakespeare's Sonnet 46', *N&Q* 55[2008] 187–8)? The sense works well (find = determine) and graphically such a minim error is common in Shakespeare and can be paralleled from compositorial mistakings of 'n' minims elsewhere in the sonnets. For the purpose of goading Achilles back into action, Ulysses in *Troilus and Cressida* imagines aloud a scene of Ajax with his foot on Hector's breast, accompanied by 'great Troy shriking [shrieking]' (Q) or 'great Troy shrinking' (F). Both make sense, but because they are so similar MacDonald P. Jackson thinks that one must be wrong: Shakespeare would not revise one to make the other ('Great Troy Shrieking: *Troilus and Cressida*, III.iii.136', *N&Q* 55[2008] 188–91). (This is debatable: E.A.J. Honigmann's classic *The Stability of Shakespeare's Text* argued that such inconsequential tweaking is just the sort of thing he would do.) Jackson argues that elsewhere in this play and in Shakespeare, shrieking is what happens when disaster strikes, and it is often spelt 'shrike'. Also, Literature Online shows that John Ogle's poem 'Troy's Lamentation for the Death of Hector' (published 1594) uses various forms of 'shrike' much more often than other writings of the period. Ogle's account of the destruction of Troy has parallels with the destruction imagined in *Troilus and Cressida* and the destruction of Harfleur conjured up in *Henry V*. Thus 'great Troy shrieking' is the reading Jackson prefers.

In *Measure for Measure*, Elbow calls brothels 'common houses' and this is the *OED*'s only occurrence of the term. Is it an Elbowism? Kenji Go thinks not, as it appears as 'common base houses' in the *Second Book of Homilies* of 1563 ('On the Origin of the "Common Houses" as Brothels in *Measure for Measure*', *N&Q* 55[2008] 191–4). Unfortunately, what goes on in these 'common base houses' was said in the homily to be 'low occupying', which was probably innocuous in the 1560s (it meant simply a debased practice), but by the 1590s the work *occupy* was synonymous with *fuck* and the homily must have sounded terribly (unintentionally) vulgar by then; the offending passage was later reworded to avoid this. Perhaps, ponders Go, that is why 'common houses' appealed to Shakespeare and was put in the mouth of a constable who utters a stream of unintentionally vulgar words by mistake: it reminded everyone of an unintentional vulgarity in the homilies. David George has two sources for *Coriolanus*: the attack on Corioles is like the attack upon Orléans in *1 Henry VI*—similar actions, similar rhetoric—and a pamphlet on *The Great Frost* [1608] has phrases and ideas that come up in various places in *Coriolanus* ('Two New Sources for *Coriolanus*', *N&Q* 55[2008] 194–7). Actually, they are not unusual phrases or ideas, so accepting that they came from this pamphlet depends on accepting that so many everyday things accumulating in one place is unlikely; the odds for that are hard to calculate. George confuses the Arden Shakespeare and the New Cambridge Shakespeare, thinking that Michael Hattaway, editor of the latter's *1 Henry VI*, edited the former's (p. 195 n. 1).

According to Herbert W. Benario, the entry of Richard to London in shame, following Bolingbroke, in *Richard II* has parallels of phrasing and action with the death of emperor Vitellius in Tacitus's *Histories* ('Shakespearean Debt to Tacitus' *Histories*', *N&Q* 55[2008] 202–5). He thinks there may also be a parallel between the death of emperor Otho in Tacitus and the dignified death of the Thane of Cawdor in *Macbeth*, but he rejects a claimed parallel between Tacitus and *Richard III*. David McInnis is keen to dismiss the idea that *The Tempest* is an American play ('Old World Sources for Ariel in *The Tempest*', *N&Q* 55[2008] 208–13). There is a passage in George Wilkins, John Day and William Rowley's *The Travails of Three*

English Brothers in which bees are commented upon for their foraging abroad and taking home their booty. This McInnes thinks was in Shakespeare's mind when he wrote the song for Ariel 'Where the bee sucks', because Ariel will spend elsewhere the liberty he earns on the island and because the word 'industrious' is applied to the bees (and to Ariel at IV.iii.33) and the bees are 'merry' (as Ariel says he will be at V.i.93). McInnis finds a source for Ariel's ventriloquism in III.ii in Richard Eden's 1553 translation of Sebastian Münster's *Cosmographia*, which tells how spirits in the region of Tangut use ventriloquism and music to waylay and dissever groups of travellers, just as Ariel splits the shipwrecked men across the island. The same claim arises in Marco Polo's writing, although whether Münster got the idea from Polo or learnt of it independently is impossible to say. Somebody ought to advise journal publishers that printing the long URLs that scholars cut and paste into their essays is pointlesss. Here is one that is 129 characters long, much more than can be retyped accurately. Even those who access McInnis's essay as a PDF document will find that the hyperlink does not work because in typesetting certain characters have been changed: the ASCII hyphen in the URL has become an en-line dash. An indefatigable reader who corrects and retypes the URL will find it still does not work, unless she happens to be a member of the University of Melbourne: the quoted URL contains the string 'unimelb.edu.au' showing that it relies upon McInnis's prior authentication as a member of that institution.

In a note reviewed in *YWES* 86[2007], Thomas Merriam argued that the 31-line segment in the middle of *All is True* II.iii, in which the Lord Chamberlain enters and speaks to Anne Bullen, is Fletcher's interpolation in a scene otherwise by Shakespeare. Merriam now adds further evidence for the claim in the form of parallels between Fletcher's play *The Valentinian* and *All is True* ('A Fletcher Interpolation in *Henry VIII*, II.iii', *N&Q* 55[2008] 213–15). The alleged interpolation shares with Fletcher's play the phrase 'from this lady'. True, but the phrase also appears in Webster's *The Devil's Law Case* [1617] and Thomas Randolph's *The Jealous Lovers* [1632], and is in any case not unusual; it pops ups in Spenser's *The Faerie Queene*. There are thematic parallels between *All is True* and *The Valentinian* as well as some looser one-word verbal parallels. As so often with these cases, the cumulative weight of individually insignificant pieces of evidence has to be determined before assent is given to the proposition. The statistical analyses needed to make such determinations are highly complex and almost never feature in the arguments being made.

2. Shakespeare in the Theatre

Consider the following quotations: 'Once disguise playfully dissociates any unitary cast of character, the closure of representation in the characterization of given standards of worthiness itself is ruptured', and 'Shakespeare would explore the actor's grappling with cross-dressed disguise in several comedies'. While the latter quotation is comprehensible, it tells us nothing we don't already know. The former quotation, by contrast, if it is telling us something original or important, masks that something beneath a style so opaque as to render it beyond assimilation. Now the fact that these two quotations come from the same page (p. 126) of *Shakespeare and the Power of Performance: Stage and Page in Elizabethan Theatre* only goes to show how much of a curate's egg the book is. Robert Weimann and Douglas Bruster have produced a volume that is by turns suggestive, exciting, bland and infuriatingly nonsensical.

Unfortunately for readers of the volume, it is the latter quality which is most extensively represented and conspicuous in a prose style that relishes formulations which demand to be read three or four times and, even then, without always making sense: 'a thick performative is jostling side by side with representations of personal and sometimes national plight' (p. 5) or 'a stage-centred approach is scarcely qualified for probing more deeply into the *énoncé/ énonciation* relations in question, even when ultimately bifold authority wants to have a verbal correlative in the theatre itself' (p. 21). Elsewhere the pronouncements are so patent as to be virtually pointless: 'Shakespeare was immersed ... within a dense network of theatricality' (p. 188); 'live actors [are] involved in a communication situation' (p. 190); the word 'ha!' as printed cannot capture 'the performer's explosive breath, the airstream's vibrations in his vocal cords, or the membranes in his glottis' (p. 40).

The book comprises several theses but it never successfully sustains or clinches any of them. To begin with, and as its subtitle indicates, it is concerned to heal or at least, address 'a renewed or ... growing rift between page and stage in Shakespeare studies' (p. 13). While the Oxford edition of *The Complete Works* sought to prioritize the plays' theatricality, more recent work by Lukas Erne and others has sought to stress the literariness of Shakespeare's composition—to suggest that the playwright had page as much as stage in mind when writing. For Weimann and Bruster the plays are not consumed in different places by different audiences/readerships but rather manifest and sustain a parity between stage and page. The plays' significance is in the ways 'in which the script and the show mutually engaged and intensified one another' (p. 25) and the authors are intent on exploring 'from how *in the theatre* the specific form and force of each medium defines, and is defined by the other' (p. 3, my emphasis). But notice the force of that 'in the theatre'— while the argument is made for a reciprocity that suggests a relationship among equals, stage is finally more equal than page.

Since the authors are primarily interested in the practicalities of performing rather than reading, this asymmetry should not shock us. In fact reading takes a back seat as they explore such theatrical phenomena as personation, character, clowning and cross-dressing. The argument is that basic persona-tion gives way to a more complicated staging of character as 'a more comprehending image of subjectivity' (p. 160). This is said to occur 'at about the turn of the century' (p. 161) though there is no specific evidence offered for this timing. Indeed the authors cite Anthony Dawson on the ineluctable quality of the actor under the character, as it were, what Dawson refers to as 'a mingling of representational or mimetic acting and "presentational" acting whereby the actor ... calls attention to his own skill and invites the audience to admire it' (quoted on p. 162) which rather gives the lie to the argument that we graduate from latter to former, let alone 'at about the turn of the century'. Rather, as Dawson insists, both styles are maintained on the early modern stage, a thesis which, in spite of their earlier claim, Weimann and Bruster are forced to acknowledge, conceding that 'the person who is actually speaking is neither the actor nor the character but the actor-character' (p. 176).

Given their greater interest in stage rather than page, it is unsurprising that the latter term doesn't really get a look-in until page 180 (of a 223-page discussion). When it does appear, it means a bewildering number of things: early modern printing (i.e. the book trade), the relationship of prose and verse (i.e. prosody), printed and written matter within the plays—such as letters, tavern bills and other documents (i.e. hand properties). The authors attempt to account for the term's multiplicity: ' "pages" ' (their quotation marks) is 'a term under which we could loosely gather all the materials in question here'— precisely the problem: the term is used so broadly, it ceases to be useful.

The volume ends not with a bang but with a whimper. One of the most textually intriguing and problematic of Shakespeare's dramas which exists, as the Oxford editors and others have argued, as two distinct plays, *King Lear*, is here given short shrift. There is hardly any discussion of different texts but a series of weird suggestions: 'the middle scenes of *King Lear* offer . . . a display of what we could anachronistically think of as the early modern playhouse's green room' (p. 200); 'As long as something would stand for something else, the register of what is representative makes representation tick' (p. 200). Both Weimann and Bruster are undisputed heavyweights of the Shakespeare world and one is loath to sound so waspish about their volume. The trouble is that in its eccentricity, its magpie-mindedness and its obfuscatory critical discourse, it clouds rather than illuminates the complex relationship between stage and page in early modern England.

In his elegant summation of the various essays that comprise *Shakespeare and the Cultures of Performance* (in Yachnin and Badir, eds., *Shakespeare and the Cultures of Performance*, pp. 169–88), forming the collection's afterword, Edward Pechter points up the diversity of two of the terms used in its title: *performance* is no longer circumscribed by the theatre but is commonly used to refer to cultural, religious, social, even gender rituals and roles. *Culture*, similarly, 'bounces around a sometimes bewilderingly wide and varied range of reference' (p. 176). The terms' polysemic nature accounts for the enormous variance of critical positions and stances taken by the nine contributors. David Bevington, in 'Shakespeare and the Theatrical Performance of Rusticity' for instance, adopts a straightforwardly biographical approach. He argues that the plays' rural know-how suggests a rural playwright: 'the sylvan and pastoral world of Shakespeare's imagination [was that] from which he came and to which he would return again and again' (p. 22). The essay is not unsentimental, including expressions such as 'self-effacement' or 'good-natured laughter' (p. 17). However at one point he is forced to concede that the biographical reading is 'speculation' and may even be 'unproductive' (p. 23). By contrast, both Gretchen E. Minton and Huston Diehl prioritize literary sources (classical and biblical respectively), the former suggesting that performances of *Troilus and Cressida* are complicated by 'the enormous weight of literary history' (p. 119) to do with sources about the Trojan wars which are no longer familiar to contemporary audiences, while Diehl demonstrates how *The Winter's Tale* appropriates and deploys 'an unsettling dimension of Pauline rhetoric: the rebuke' (p. 72) and, furthermore, 'By deliberately mingling preaching and playing in the character of Paulina, Shakespeare may be audaciously claiming Paul as a model for the playwright' (p. 74).

One play is the topic of two essays. In 'Payback Time: On the Economic Rhetoric of Revenge in *The Merchant of Venice*' Linda Woodbridge insists that early modern England 'witnessed an epidemic of personal and family indebtedness' (p. 29) and goes on to illustrate how the discourse of economic dependence is inseparable from that of revenge, arguing for an equivalence between 'monetary and retaliatory payment' (p. 29). In '"To give and to receive": Performing Exchanges in *The Merchant of Venice*' Sean Lawrence takes a broadly anthropological stance in his assertion that 'any apparent gesture of goodwill is . . . an effort to impose an obligation' (p. 44). From here he arrives at the not too unfamiliar conclusion: 'The play does not contrast amorous and financial economies, but conflates them into a single system of exchanges' (p. 45).

In 'To "gase so much at the fine stranger": Armado and the Politics of English' Lynne Magnusson reads the parodic Spaniard in terms of a contemporary linguistic xenophobia. Citing early modern tracts such as Thomas Wilson's *The Arte of Rhetorique* [1553], she argues for the existence of a cultural anxiety concerned with 'the damage from verbal invasion' (p. 62), though she concludes that Armado is not a 'despised alien' but rather 'an aspiring immigrant, eager to assimilate' (p. 68). In 'Shakespeare and Secular Performance' Anthony B. Dawson uses *Measure for Measure* as his test case in order to answer the question, 'in what ways does religion . . . enter into theatrical discourse?' (p. 83). It is in the cultivation and manipulation of audience pleasure that theatre resembles the rituals of worship—'religious language and feelings enter deeply into the performance on the public stage' (p. 89)—and he goes so far as to argue that the theatre was 'Brimful of religious thinking and sacramental allusion' (p. 97). Coppélia Kahn focuses on mid-nineteenth-century performance in her consideration of minstrelsy, in particular, Thomas Dartmouth Rice's *Otello, a Burlesque Opera*, performed in Philadelphia. Her treatment in 'Forbidden Mixtures: Shakespeare in Blackface Minstrelsy, 1844' is broadly sympathetic and she goes as far as to assert that 'Rice used blackface as a complex language of satire and critique, not to be confused with the demeaning caricature to which it was later reduced' (p. 122). The essay is especially cogent on ideas of the burlesque, and demonstrates that the knee-jerk reaction of modern criticism against minstrelsy may be founded on insufficient appreciation of its complexity and its combination of 'original and copy, authentic and spurious, elite and popular, tragic and comic' (p. 124). In '*The Tempest* and the Uses of Late Shakespeare in the Cultures of Performance: Prospero, Gielgud, Rylance', Gordon McMullan reflects imaginatively on the kinds of assumptions made about painters, composers, poets and other artists as they are evaluated in terms of their late work. He attributes the 'invention of lateness' (p. 150) to the Romantic period and notes that, perhaps not surprisingly, the confluence of 'the artist's life and the progress of his...style' (p. 150) was a Romantic concern in particular. McMullan then goes on to show how 'the appropriation of Shakespearean lateness [has been deployed] as a vehicle for the self-conscious structuring of theatrical careers' (p. 147). By tracing the triangular relationship of Prospero, John Gielgud and Mark Rylance, McMullan demonstrates the mystical force of the role with the actors on the one hand and Shakespeare himself on the other. Yet in spite of the empathy between actor and playwright, McMullan notes wryly that Rylance is a vehement anti-Stratfordian (as was Gielgud before him). McMullan's pseudo-Greenblattian opening aside—flicking through a magazine on a train journey in Spain—this is a deft and persuasive essay. In their introduction (pp. 1–12), the editors propose that this diversity of approaches and topics is a strategy designed to confront the 'totalizing bent' (p. 3) of new historicism's understanding of culture. This is a wide-ranging and engaging collection but that such diversity is, in itself, sufficient to urge us to reappraise new historicism's homogenizing tendency is not convincing.

In 'Audience and Actor Response to a Staged Reading of Nahum Tate's *The History of King Lear* (directed by Joe Curdy) at the Shakespeare Institute, Stratford-upon-Avon, 27 January 2008' (*Shakespeare* 4[2008] 302–8), Curdy provides a vivid and fascinating account of his resurrection of Tate's all but extinct animal and details the responses of both cast and spectators. Having briefly summarized Romantic and post-Romantic critical positions and theatrical histories, he then poses the questions as to how a modern acting company and audience might respond and, perhaps more interestingly, whether the audience would be capable of viewing Tate's version free of the shadow cast by Shakespeare's play. (Curdy notes that the last professional stage version of Tate's *Lear* was in 1845.) Curdy's research method is refreshingly 'hands on', assembling a company comprising seasoned RSC actors (including Richard Cordery and Clifford Rose), academics and interested amateurs. By means of a series of interviews, he establishes that the performers were pleasantly surprised by the quality of Tate's writing and that they were willing to determine the 'performance potential of a text based on its theatricality' (p. 304) as opposed to the tyranny of language associated with Shakespeare. Curdy had also prepared a questionnaire which he circulated among the audience. Having prefixed his assimilation of these results with an informed analysis of the audience demographic—'roughly 75% were female...a statistic that corresponded to the high number of postgraduate students in attendance' (p. 305)—Curdy, with the aid of a couple of bar charts, demonstrates that 'overall the response was more optimistic than I [had] anticipated' (p. 305). The fraught question remains, however, whether the audience were responding positively to the play in its own terms or whether 'Tate's adaptation might merit interest from a modern audience simply as a notorious footnote in the performance history of Shakespeare's *Lear*' (p. 305). Although Curdy is unable to answer that question definitively, his raising it in the first place, as well as his empirical approach, are unusual and praiseworthy.

Sticking with the eighteenth century, Laura Engel describes not merely the performance but the cultural implications of Sarah Siddons's long association with the role of Lady Macbeth. In 'The Personating of Queens: Lady Macbeth, Sarah Siddons and the Creation of Female Celebrity in the Late Eighteenth Century' (in Moschovakis, ed., *Macbeth: New Critical Essays*, pp. 240–57), she argues that Siddons invented a new 'category of identity...the modern female superstar' (p. 240). This seems, at first, to be a bold claim, but Engel constructs a rigorous and convincing argument. As the essay's title suggests, Siddons took on the mantle of several queens. Chief among these politically was Queen Charlotte, with whom an association was facilitated by the similarities between Siddons and Charlotte in the portraiture of Thomas Gainsborough (who painted both women): 'Just as Gainsborough created the idea of status, wealth, and noble bearing with his portrait of Siddons, Queen Charlotte appears magically beautiful in his representation of her' (p. 246). Engel argues that Siddons and Charlotte 'invoked similar images of royalty and maternity' (p. 242). The second queen Siddons inhabited, as it were, is Lady Macbeth, an account of which is still accessible through Siddons's own 'Remarks on the Character of Lady Macbeth' in which she empathizes with her heroine and considers her as being noble and compassionate in nature. Engel explains that the murder of her own child, hypothetically alluded to by Lady Macbeth, indicates not a violent streak but just the opposite, and she cites Siddons herself: 'The very use of such a tender allusion in the midst of her dreadful language, persuades one unequivocally that she has really felt the maternal yearnings of a mother towards her babe, and that she considered this action the most enormous that ever required the strength of human nerves for its perpetration' (quoted on p. 249). This would have been powerfully envisioned when, in April 1794, Siddons played the role while heavily pregnant. The final queen Engel describes is a product of the first two, Siddons's own 'status as a celebrity diva' (p. 242). Engel concludes effectively, 'For Siddons, "personated Queens"—real and imagined—made it feasible for her to embody an unprecedented form of female celebrity, and to transform one of the most ruthless stage heroines into an exemplar of femininity' (p. 254).

3. Shakespeare on Screen

Despite fewer book-length considerations of Shakespeare on screen this year, several journal issues focused upon performance and helped ensure that the research area continues to evolve. In 2008 two edited collections of essays were added to the University of Rouen's Shakespeare on Screen series, Anthony R. Guneratne focused upon Shakespearian films in his monograph *Shakespeare, Film Studies, and the Visual Cultures of Modernity*, and Frank Occhiogrosso's edited collection *Shakespearean Performance: New Studies* embraces screen versions within a performance-orientated study. *Gothic Shakespeares*, edited by John Drakakis and Dale Townshend, includes in its enquiry one essay analysing the connections between Shakespearian films and the horror film.

The *Shakespeare International Yearbook* granted space to 'European Shakespeares' in its special section, and the guest editors, Ton Hoenselaars and Clara Calvo, contributed an article examining the BBC's 2005

ShakespeaRe-Told series (*ShIntY* 8[2008] 82–96). Special issues in three other journals focused more exclusively upon Shakespeare on screen. The customary 'Shakespeare on Film' issue of *Literature/Film Quarterly* (*LFQ* 36:ii[2008]) contains six articles and, this year, that number is exceeded with fourteen screen-related essays in *Shakespeare Survey*: 'Shakespeare, Sound and Screen' (*ShS* 61[2008]). The summer issue of *Shakespeare Bulletin* includes four articles centring upon 'Shakespearean Screen Adaptations for the Teen Market' (*ShakB* 26:ii[2008]).

Anthony R. Guneratne's *Shakespeare, Film Studies, and the Visual Cultures of Modernity* seeks to 'tell a different kind of film history' (p. xiii) of film adaptations of Shakespeare's plays. Guneratne's emphasis is upon the cultural history of film adaptation, and he seeks to explore the intersections between film and other media. His study consists of five chapters, organized thematically, and a distinctive narrative style is established, with chapter titles and summaries in the style of an eighteenth-century novelist. These summaries signal the somewhat episodic nature of the text, which subtitles and section breaks maintain. Each individual chapter offers a focused case-study in response to the book's opening thesis. Guneratne begins his introduction with a consideration of 'Shakespeare', the man and the work. He signals the number of firsts (within Shakespearian adaptation on film) which can be attributed to Mélies's *Shakespeare Writing Julius Caesar* [1907] and then jumps decades to consider *Shakespeare in Love* [1998]. Both films establish that biographical genres 'are reflective of contemporary concerns and preoccupations' (p. 5). Guneratne moves on to consider the cult of Shakespeare in connection with geographical place, and he analyses three Russians adaptations: Yutkevich's *Othello* [1956], and Kozintsev's *Hamlet* [1964] and *King Lear* [1970]. These films are united by their use of Boris Pasternak's translation and Guneratne explores linguistic translation as cultural translation.

The American film industry is then considered, and Hitchcock's involvement in the British *Elstree Calling* [1930] prompts reflection upon Hollywood's ability 'to assimilate, and in doing so, transform varied sources of influence' (p. 19). Chapter 2 explores in more detail this suggestion of cultural continuity in Anglo-American culture. In his consideration of the 'film studies' of the book's title, Guneratne identifies 'the three simultaneous registers of adaptation' (p. 31): the movement from medium to medium; the movement from text to text; and that of culture to culture. He summarizes 'Tendencies in Film Adaptations' in tabular form and promotes a personal formula (A+ to E–) as a logical way of considering Shakespeare adaptations. The exploration of adaptations ranges widely to include *Theater of Blood* [1973], *Tempest* (Mazursky [1982]) and *Fanny and Alexander* [1982]. In his third chapter Guneratne focuses upon versions of *Hamlet* as a way of extending his consideration of film acting and stardom.

Guneratne's interest in 'visual cultures' ensures that Shakespeare has generated 'an artistic efflorescence that has continued to influence theatrical productions, photography and film' (p. 49). These introductory ideas are secured with consideration of the cinematography in Olivier's *Henry V* [1944] and *Richard III* [1955] alongside the contrasting style of Kurosawa's

Shakespearian adaptations. Chapter 4 then concentrates on Orson Welles's visual language. Guneratne focuses upon 'the inequalities of modernity', and a geographical distinction is drawn between 'voluntary modernity' in Japan and 'imposed modernity' in Africa, Latin America and the Indian subcontinent (p. 62). The Merchant–Ivory *Shakespeare Wallah* [1965] and Vishal Bhardwaj's *Maqbool* [2004] are considered initially, and Guneratne uses the 'myth' invented in Salman Rushdie's 1995 novel *The Moor's Last Sigh* 'to sum up the legacies of Shakespeare, of film, and of the visual cultures that through, from, into, and out of languages, inform adaptations' (p. 73). The final chapter of Guneratne's study shifts between places, periods and texts in its consideration of the Shakespearian film work of Van Sant, Branagh, Godard, Pasolini, Greenaway and Luhrmann.

Sarah Hatchuel and Nathalie Vienne-Guerrin edited two collections of essays to extend their Shakespeare on Screen series. In contrast with the series' previous publications (*A Midsummer Night's Dream* [2005] and *Richard III* [2005]), both collections of essays this year broaden their focus beyond one specific text. *Shakespeare on Screen: The Henriad* is genre-driven in its focus upon 'filming *history* plays' (p. 15), and there is some interrogation of cinema's avoidance of *Richard II* and enthusiasm for *Henry V*. Interest in the former play on television helps redress the balance and signals one way in which the collection of essays negotiates different screens. The volume is also interested in the way that filmed versions might be valued as useful, as 'tools to explore the texts' in contrast with scholarly assessment of stage productions (p. 17). The essays move between 'macro-analysis' and 'micro-analysis' and the editors make a virtue of these contrasting approaches. They encourage their readers to consider the way in which a connection between methodologies and technological advances might illuminate 'what Shakespeare's contrasting afterlives keep saying, not only about the dramatic texts but also about ourselves' (p. 18).

The essays which include some discussion of versions only commercially available in recent years are of greatest interest. Michael Hattaway's piece considers different kinds of non-cinematic versions in 'Politics and Mise-en-Scène in Television Versions of *King Richard II*' (pp. 59–74). Here the versions are categorized as made for television (Giles, 1978 and Woodman, 1981); televised theatrical performances which include an audience (Bogdanov and Carroll in 2003) and theatrical productions radically reworked for the screen (Deborah Warner's 1995 production). Hattaway's argument centres upon the importance of critics and producers recognizing these categories. Lois Potter focuses upon the 1954 version of *Richard II* in her 'The Royal Throne of Kings and the American Armchair: Deconstructing the Hallmark *Richard II*' (pp. 75–98). Potter situates the version in a theatrical context (on both sides of the Atlantic), considers the version alongside the 'real' coronation of Elizabeth II and looks closely at the tone of the reception to Maurice Evans's performance. Both Hattaway's and Potter's essays can be usefully set alongside Russell Jackson's article in *Shakespeare Survey* which considers: 'Maurice Evans's *Richard II* on Stage, Television and (Almost) Film' (*ShS* 61[2008] 36–56).

Hatchuel and Vienne-Guerrin's collection of essays is usefully concluded with José Ramón Díaz Fernández's '*The Henriad* on Screen: An Annotated

Filmo-Bibliography' (pp. 269–348). He develops a recent trend in 'Shakespeare on screen' publications by granting space to the reference materials and ordering them in a helpfully interpretative way. Six categories (film adaptations; television adaptations; filmed staged performances; derivatives and citations; educational films; documentary films) contain chronological lists of the screen versions with relevant books and articles positioned beneath their respective film. Selected entries are annotated to clarify the nature of the relationship, and the detail here ensures the usefulness of the scholarly resource. Fernández also contributed the detailed 'Teen Shakespeare Films: An Annotated Survey of Criticism' to *Shakespeare Bulletin* this year (*ShakB* 26:ii[2008] 89–133).

Sarah Hatchuel and Nathalie Vienne-Guerrin's other publication in the same series, *Shakespeare on Screen: Television Shakespeare*, is dedicated to Michèle Willems. Their text celebrates Willems's influential 1987 collection of essays, and responding to that seminal text prompts the question: 'Is there still such a thing as "Television Shakespeare"?' (p. 18). Some contributors respond to that question by moving beyond productions originally conceived to be broadcast on the small screen and therefore suggesting that television is now perhaps 'a hybrid object that seems to escape definition and apprehension' (p. 18).

One such example is Peter Holland's 'Afterword: What(ever) Next?' (pp. 271–7), which considers YouTube recordings of the 'RST Demolition' and suggests that the brief clip 'produces strange linkings of forms and of timescales' (p. 272). Holland's piece encourages reflection upon the relationship between the small screen, cinema and theatre. It is suggested that the YouTube community, whose roles can shift between producers (through uploading clips and comments) and receivers, 'requires a reformulation of what it means to watch or to share watching Shakespeare on screen as well as redefining what Shakespeare on screen might include' (p. 274).

Peter Hutchings directs attention towards a genre-inflected consideration of Shakespeare films in 'Shakespeare and the Horror Film' (in Drakakis and Townshend, eds., *Gothic Shakespeares: Accents on Shakespeare*. pp. 153–66). His assessment begins with the citation of *Hamlet* in Universal's 1931 *Dracula*, 'a founding text in horror cinema' (p. 153) and that film's use of *Hamlet* establishes an enquiry which negotiated cultural hierarchies in its consideration of *Macbeth* (Polanski [1971]), *Hamlet* (Branagh [1996]) and *Titus* (Taymor [1999]). The idea that 'Shakespeare's *Macbeth* concludes with a clear sense that a just rule has been restored' (p. 160) typifies Hutchings's at times uncomplicated perspective on the playtexts which constrains his analysis of the films. More interesting is his consideration of *Theatre of Blood* [1973] and *The Flesh and Blood Show* [1972]. The latter film explores less familiar Shakespeare on screen territory. The engagement with that film's theatricality and the suggested allusion to *A Double Life* (Cukor [1947]) deserve development.

Russell Jackson's essay is, in part, a consideration of Branagh's 2000 film in the context of critical responses. In 'Filming Shakespeare's Comedies: Reflections on *Love's Labour's Lost*' (in Occhiogrosso, ed., *Shakespearean Performance: New Studies* pp. 62–73), Jackson's personal tone reflects an engagement with that which has shaped his own perspective upon the film. His defence of the film is cautious, and throughout the piece he considers the possible bias produced by his role as a collaborator in the film's production. His suggestion that 'From my own point of view... *Love's Labour's Lost* remains an enjoyable and testing experience' (p. 71) points to the self-conscious conflation of process and product in the assessment of the film.

Mark Thornton Burnett's essay provides a stark contrast to Russell Jackson's piece in its content and approach. 'Madagascan Will: Cinematic Shakespeares/Transnational Exchanges' (*ShS* 61[2008] 239–55) focuses upon two screen adaptations which document journeys to Madagascar: Alexander Abela's *Makibefo* (a version of *Macbeth* [2000]) and his *Souli* (inspired by *Othello* [2004]). Limited global exhibition and distribution mean that these versions have received little critical attention. Thornton Burnett raises questions about these processes as part of his engagement with concepts of transnationalism. An unexpected connection between Russell Jackson's article and Mark Thornton Burnett's piece can be found in the latter's suggestion that an emerging element within Shakespeare on screen scholarship lies in a consideration of 'the producers as well as the products, the creative forces as well as the final statements' (p. 255).

Ton Hoenselaars and Clara Calvo seek to emphasize the spatial and temporal locations in screen versions of Shakespeare's plays, and they suggest that the multiple labels used for screen versions can obscure that process of relocation. In 'Shakespeare Uprooted: The BBC and *ShakespeaRe-Told*' (*ShIntY* 8[2008] 82–96) decisions about time and space are defined as inextricably linked. The essay concludes by considering the series as a redefinition of contemporary Britain, and Hoenselaars and Calvo worry about the degree of Europhobia reflected in some of the series' specific choices.

The performance-orientated issue of *Shakespeare Survey*, 'Shakespeare, Sound and Screen', includes fourteen screen-related articles. Several of these pieces offer 'micro-analysis'. Anna K. Nardo discusses Branagh's adaptation of Shakespeare's text in *Love's Labour's Lost* [2000] (*ShS* 61[2008] 13–22), Peter Donaldson analyses the musicality of Michael Hoffman's 1999 *A Midsummer Night's Dream* (*ShS* 61[2008] 13–22), Alfredo Michale Modenessi considers the violence in Tim Supple's 2003 television film of *Twelfth Night* (*ShS* 61[2008] 91–103) and Lindsey Scott focuses upon Polanski's 1971 *Macbeth* (*ShS* 61[2008] 104–15). Two articles consider *Hamlet* versions. Simon J. Ryle uses the 'sense of rupture implicit in Jacques Lacan's theory of the gaze' (p. 116) to explore Olivier, Branagh and Almereyda's film adaptations of *Hamlet*. Catherine Grace Canino interrogates John Frankenheimer's suggestion that his film *The Manchurian Candidate* is 'a modern-day retelling of *Hamlet*' (p. 135). Canino places the film and the play alongside Foucault's and Meerloo's ideas about the 'coercive nature of power and the resultant reconstruction of self-agency' (p. 134). Her piece reads *Hamlet* with these theories in mind and 'through Frankenheimer's lens' (p. 146). The connections between the political context of Shakespeare's play, the protagonist's journey and the plot structure are set against the 1962 film in an, at times, thought-provoking way. Canino's piece is a useful illustration of the way that an adaptation might be used as a tool for looking again at Shakespeare's text.

The boundaries of Shakespeare on screen are pushed by Thomas Cartelli's 'Channelling the Ghosts: the Wooster Group's Remediation of the 1964 Electronovision *Hamlet*' (*ShS* 61[2008] 147–60). Cartelli begins his essay with a consideration of the cultural context of Richard Burton's 1964 theatrical performance as Hamlet, which moved from Toronto to New York and was then filmed. An engagement with the technology used to make this 'Theatrofilm' means that Cartelli considers the recorded *Hamlet* to be 'both an anomalous and nostalgic throwback to the already superseded days of live television recording' (p. 148). The article then jumps forward to 2007 and considers the Wooster Group's 'sustained "emulation" of the 1964 "theatrofilm" of *Hamlet*' (p. 149). Cartelli is particularly interested in the effects of the Wooster Group's use of video footage 'as a visual prompt or model for their own efforts of imitation or emulation' (p. 150) and he notes that the film has been re-edited aurally and visually with the effect of displacing and colonizing the 1964 broadcast. In contrast, two other *Hamlet* films (Branagh [1995] and Almereyda [2000]) were briefly 'granted a freedom to speak directly to the audience seldom allowed the Burton production' (p. 151). Cartelli identifies the Wooster Group's *Hamlet* project as distinct in relation to their previous productions and he proposes that one problem lies in the way that Shakespeare's play has 'been largely emptied out of any point or purpose beyond studied and sustained replication' (p. 157). His article attests to the compelling presence of the screen images in the closing moments of the Wooster Group's piece, and questions are therefore asked about the result of the 2007 theatre production's 'increasingly fevered competition with the film itself' (p. 152).

Evelyn Tribble seeks to break with the critical tradition of analysing the 'extraordinarily dense rendering of the visual field' (p. 161) in her article 'Listening to *Prospero's Books*' (*ShS* 61[2008] 161–9). Michael Nyman's score for the film prompts Tribble to suggest that 'the acoustic dimension of *Prospero's Books* is one of the most complex areas of intersection between the play and the film' (p. 161). A comparable emphasis can be found in David L. Kranz's article on 'Tracking the Sounds of Franco Zeffirelli's *The Taming of the Shrew*' (*LFQ* 36:ii[2008] 94–112). While Nino Rota's score is given attention, Kranz does work hard to situate the scored music as one part of the 'sonic motifs, sound effects, volume, pitch, rhythm and mixing' (p. 94). Kranz's piece sensitively engages with the film's aural subtlety, and he makes a very strong case for the way that the soundtrack helps direct attention towards 'a mix of realism and artifice' (p. 95). The sustained attention to laughter as working variously, 'undercutting...appearances' and expressing 'positive emotion', is thoughtfully detailed, and existing critical ideas about the film and the play are challenged in a usefully precise way.

The customary special Shakespeare issue of *Literature/Film Quarterly* includes five other essays, all of which are grouped under the Barthesian heading 'Image/Music/Shakespeare'. Despite the bold decision of placing Shakespeare third in the title, the prioritization of 'image' supports Krantz's observation that visual enquiries dominate film scholarship. The articles which look at visual imagery are less exciting than Krantz's aurally attentive piece. Monique L. Pittman's genre-inflected analysis of Shakespeare's uneasy position in Andy Fickman's version of *Twelfth Night* seems to continue the concerns emerging from last year's *LFQ* (35:ii[2007]). In 'Dressing the Girl/ Playing the Boy: *Twelfth Night* Learns Soccer on the Set of *She's The Man*' (*LFQ* 36:ii[2008] 122–36) Pittman places the film securely in the context of teen movies. She persuasively justifies her disappointment that after the film's initial demonstration of 'the permeable boundaries between gender identities' it 'reverts to conservatism' (p. 123). In *Shakespeare Bulletin* both Elizabeth Klett and Laurie Osborne chose to situate *She's The Man* [2006] within the teen movie genre. Klett sets Fickman's film alongside *Lost and Delirious* [2001] and considers Viola's 'identity crisis' (p. 69) in 'Reviving Viola: Comic and Tragic Teen Film Adaptations of *Twelfth Night*' (*ShakB* 26:ii[2008] 69–87). Laurie Osborne's essay considers more closely the way that *She's The Man* was framed as a Shakespearian adaptation, in '*Twelfth Night's* Cinematic Adolescents: One Play, One Plot, One Setting, and Three Teen Films' (*ShakB* 26:ii[2008] 9–36). Her piece explores 'intertextual and intercinematic connections created by the film itself and its marketing' (p. 10). Her argument then shifts to consider *Just One of the Guys* [1985], *Motocrossed* [2001] and *She's The Man* as 'intertexts' which demonstrate 'evolving gender politics' (p. 32).

Michael J. Friedman's introduction to the teen-focused *Shakespeare Bulletin* makes a strong case for dating the genre from the 1960s rather than as a mid-1990s, post-Luhrmann phenomenon: 'Introduction: '"To think o' the' teen that I have turned you to": The Scholarly Consideration of Teen Shakespeare Films' (*ShakB* 26:ii[2008] 1–7). He contends that, rather than thinking in terms of a cinematic shift in recent years, it is more useful to connect scholarly analysis of films aimed at the teen market with 'a willingness on the part of Shakespeare critics to take teen Shakespeare adaptations seriously as an object of study' (p. 1). Friedman's definition of the study of Shakespeare's plays and their cinematic counterparts can, I think, extend beyond teen Shakespeare adaptations and define the relationship between Shakespeare and screen as offering, potentially, 'a mutually productive process' (p. 5).

4. Criticism

(a) General

By focusing on the brief period Shakespeare spent as a lodger with French Huguenot exiles in *The Lodger: Shakespeare on Silver Street*, Charles Nicholl dispenses with the usual journey from cradle to grave, and goes into detail about matters often neglected in standard biographies. Part I relates the basic facts regarding Shakespeare's involvement with his former hosts the Mountjoys, their daughter Mary and their son-in-law Stephen Belott. The book's second section describes the physical environment around Silver Street, where Shakespeare lodged with the Mountjoys. As you would expect from Nicholl, the rendering of concrete detail—the churches, streets and shops—is superb. Admirably, Nicholl prefers not to pad out his reconstruction with guesswork, stressing the value of *known* presence over 'might have been present'. Part III tells us everything knowable about the Mountjoys, who made head-tires (delicate and fancy head-dresses), lingering on evidence relating Mrs Mountjoy's visits to the quack doctor/astrologer Simon Forman (at times one is inclined to suspect Nicholl himself has a crush on this invisible French lady). The social and cultural relevance of head-tires is then examined at length. One thing emerges between the lines: the material details of head-tiring would be just the kind of ephemera Shakespeare would have gluttonously relished. Nicholl traces references to head-tires in Shakespeare's works and explores Marie Mountjoy's links to Queen Anne, noting that both Shakespeare and Marie were court servants. Analysing Shakespeare's representations of 'aliens', Nicholl surmises that foreignness was exciting to the poet-playwright. Then comes an absorbing chapter on George Wilkins, whose brothel Mary Mountjoy went to live in after she married her father's apprentice Stephen Belott in 1605. Nicholl relates these events to the composition of *Pericles* by Wilkins and Shakespeare. Included here is some very welcome discussion of other works by Wilkins from this period, including the play *The Miseries of Enforced Marriage*. Shakespeare seems to have felt in some way responsible for Mary's married situation. Thus, the comparable plight of Marina in *Pericles* receives due attention. At one point, Nicholl suggests that Shakespeare teamed up with Wilkins because he was not able to write an effective city comedy by himself. This might be more plausible if the end result of their collaboration were something more like a city comedy than *Pericles*. By part VII of the book it is clear that the crucial element is the hand-fasting. What exactly was Shakespeare's role in the troth-plight of Mary Mountjoy and Stephen Belott? It is said he 'made [the couple] sure'. The witness Daniel Nicholas apparently deposed that Shakespeare did this by 'giving each other's hand to hand' (p. 253), but this last phrase is deleted in the court record. Someone objected. Perhaps Shakespeare. In any case, as Nicholl suggests. Shakespeare played something like a directorial role in the ceremony. During a very pertinent discussion of *Measure for Measure*. Nicholl notes that Juliette and Claudio's betrothal is not in Shakespeare's source for the play. In sum, Nicholl's thesis—that here for once we can really follow Shakespeare's use of real-life experience in his work, *circa* 1603 and after—is amply sustained.

Like Nicholl's book, Germaine Greer's biographical study, *Shakespeare's Wife*, has a novel focus, as indicated by the title. Unlike Nicholl, though, Greer *is* prepared (indeed, obliged) to pad out material evidence with speculation because, of course, even less is known about Anne Hathaway than about her husband. The vast majority of (male) Shakespearian biographers, says Greer, have tended to be disparaging about Anne because, let's face it (they imply), wives of great men just do not understand their husbands. Thus, these scholars have supposed the Shakespeares' marriage was unhappy. The problem with Greer's attempt to counter this misogynist tide, of course, is that Shakespeare did spend the vast majority of his adult life away from his wife (and children) and blatantly snubbed Anne in his will. Greer chooses to play down these uncomfortable facts. Likewise, throughout the book, Greer insists that Shakespeare was never as prosperous as scholars customarily suggest. Again, the facts regarding his purchases of property simply do not uphold

Greer's argument. It is also odd that, having rightly attacked some stereotyping of Hathaway, Greer caricatures Anne's Catholic mother-in-law, suggesting that Mary Arden 'may have been something of a social climber' and was lazy in the house (p. 32). One begins to think there is something going on here. Declaring that 'the one resounding exception to the rule that wives of great men must all have been unworthy' is the case of 'wives of protestant reformers' (p. 9), Greer provides a list of housewife superstars (Anna Zwingli, Idelette Calvin and so on). The suspicion of special pleading is confirmed when Greer dismisses theories regarding Shakespeare's Catholicism as 'modish brouhaha' (p. 29). Apparently, Greer wishes to read Anne as a model Protestant housewife. It is a plausible supposition, but, on the other hand, for all we know, Anne was as slatternly as Greer's version of her mother-in-law. With some of the polemics out of the way, however, Greer's skills as a historical researcher come to the fore in chapters 5 and 6. Customs surrounding marriage are analysed with clarity and economy. There is, moreover, a healthy side to Greer's scepticism towards received wisdom. For example, she pays close attention to the marriage licence of 'Wm Shaxpere et Annam Whateley de Temple Grafton', challenging the usual view that this apparent oddity is the result of scribal error (p. 81). In line with her thesis, Greer speculates that Anne Hathaway was working in Temple Grafton, *perhaps* 'apprenticed to a skilled craftswoman or artisan' (p. 84). While this is by no means conclusive (after all, Anne Hathaway was never called Whateley and has no known connection with Temple Grafton), it at least demonstrates how complacently the Whateley document is dispensed with in conventional biographies. Another intriguing point made by Greer, consequent upon her notion of Hathaway as the industrious manager of a thriving cottage industry, is that Anne may have been the malt-hoarder rather than William ('Ungentle Hathaway'?). Unfortunately, however, the book ends with some examples of Greer at her most reckless. Discussing the poet-playwright's final years, Greer argues that Shakespeare *may* have died of syphilis. Therefore, she suggests, his son-in-law John Hall *probably* wrote the epitaph to prevent anyone digging up Shakespeare and finding evidence of his terminal disease. In addition, Anne's 'epitaph was probably written by John Hall, ventriloquising for Susanna' (p. 343). It is astonishing to find Greer denying authorship of a text to an early modern female and awarding it to her husband. Finally, Greer suggests that Anne Hathaway may have had a hand in preparing the First Folio. Once more, this is an interesting idea, but, again, there is no evidence to support it.

Though René Weis's biography *Shakespeare Revealed* has received less attention than Nicholl's and Greer's volumes, it does have its own claims to distinction. Its thesis is that Shakespeare was a real person, like any other author, and real people leave traces of their lives in their works. In addition, the book pays more attention than is customary in scholarly biographies to traditional anecdotes, evidently regarding these as valuable traces of actual events, relationships and personalities. This is not to say that Weis takes such tales at face value. Far from it, but he does not dismiss them as having no basis in historical reality. This offers a valuable corrective to new historicist reliance on material textual traces, for the latter approach inevitably gives greater air time to an institutional version of history. Notwithstanding this openness to unorthodox material, Weis's book has been criticized for refusing to tackle the issue of whether Shakespeare spent his 'lost years' in Lancashire. This seems an unfair charge, for to explore this issue properly would commit Weis to devoting a large section of his book to a speculative area that has already been well served by previous biographers. However, Weis does not rubbish the Lancastrians. He acknowledges their existence (unlike Greer), allows the possibility of their case, notes the lack of hard evidence, and turns to matters about which he feels he has something new to add. For example, Weis re-examines the circumstances surrounding Shakespeare's marriage[s]. He points out that on 2 September 1582, just under three months before William Shakespeare married Anne Whateley, his father John Shakespeare voted at a Stratford council meeting for the first time since January 1577. As he was under virtual house arrest for debt at the time, John must have had a particular reason for doing this, Weis argues, noting also that Shakespeare senior did not vote again until September 1586. Weis posits that John was voting to snub one of the two losing candidates, George Whateley, head of the 'grand' Henley Street Whateleys, who had 'strong Catholic connections', including George's brothers who were both fugitive recusant priests (pp. 58–9). Weis does not go on to speculate what connection there may be between George and the otherwise non-existent Anne Whateley, but the matter certainly calls for further investigation. Elsewhere, though, Weis does allow himself to get a little carried away with speculation. For example, he seems quite certain that the 'dark lady' of the sonnets was Emilia Lanyer. I would be happy to be persuaded that Lanyer is in the mix, but it is a big leap from claiming Shakespeare was a human being who left traces in his work to making a case for one-to-one identifications of actual people with fictional characters.

The Shakespeare International Yearbook 8, special section, *European Shakespeares*, is edited by Ton Hoenselaars and Clara Calvo. As the subtitle indicates, the bulk of this volume is taken up with essays examining Shakespeare in European contexts. These include a study of Shakespearian reception in relation to mid-twentieth-century Portuguese academic politics by Rui Carvalho Homem in 'The Chore and the Passion: Shakespeare and Graduation in mid-Twentieth Century Portugal' (15–31), and an absorbing account by Tina Krontiris in 'Henry V and the Anglo-Greek Alliance of World War II' (32–50) of a 1941 Greek production of *Henry V*. Krontiris notes that '[w]hen Greece entered World War II in October 1940, all the theatre companies changed their repertories, turning to satirical revues and war plays' (p. 38). These might involve an implied critique of what was seen as weak French resistance to the Nazis. The staging of *Henry V*, therefore, which had not been popular outside England prior to then, was 'an interventionist act' (p. 39). Krontiris concludes by examining the reasons why this production failed to do well at the box office. Alexander C.Y. Huang's contribution 'Asian Shakespeares in Europe: From the Unfamiliar to the Defamiliarised' (165–182), meanwhile, deals with Asian Shakespeares, exploring the benefits of defamiliarization. Asian acting conventions, for example, being less 'realistic', may, when applied to Shakespeare, lead Europeans to question how appropriate 'realistic' conventions are to the performance of early modern drama. In 'The BBC and *Shakespeare Re-Told* (2005)' (82–96), the volume's editors Clara Calvo and Ton Hoenselaars provide close analysis of the BBC's *Shakespeare Re-Told* series of adaptations, pointing out how these versions relocate Shakespeare's comedies to Britain. Making Shakespeare accessible seems to entail insularity. In section III of the volume, dedicated to romance, Steve Mentz in 'Shipwreck and Ecology: Toward a Structural Theory of Shakespeare and Romance' (165–182), complains of the critical distortions created by career narratives. Nonetheless, he restricts the term 'romance' to the Shakespeare plays from *Pericles* and *Cymbeline* on. Mentz considers shipwreck as a major Renaissance trope. What makes his approach distinct, however, is the use of ecology as a key frame of reference for understanding what Shakespeare is up to in presenting fallible heroes. In the following essay, Tiffany J. Werth in 'Great Miracle or Lying Wonder? Janus-Faced Romance in *Pericles*' (183–203), reads *Pericles* as an example of Shakespeare exploiting 'the Janus-like aspects of early modern romance' (p. 183). That is, romance looks back nostalgically at a Catholic past but is also a big crowd-pleaser in the commercial present. Section IV contains two excellent review essays. The first, '(Re)Presenting Shakespeare's Co-Authors: Lessons from the *Oxford Shakespeare*' (219–237) by Tom Rooney, considers how the various recent collected editions of Shakespeare have dealt with the issue of collaboration. *Oxford 2* [2005] (Stanley Wells et al. eds) comes out the winner, but Rooney points out different ways in which the various editions excel. In the second review essay, Laurence Wright defends Harold Bloom's *The Invention of the Human* [1998] in "Inventing the Human: Brontosaurus Bloom and 'the Shakespeare in us'" (238–260). Wright emphasizes Bloom's Emersonian inheritance, viewing this as a counter-weight to Greenblattian determinism. Wright admits that Bloom can put people off, especially new young students, with his bardolatry. Accordingly, Bloom is perhaps best read as an antidote to unbridled cultural materialism.

Shakespeare and Spenser: Attractive Opposites, edited by J.B. Lethbridge, is a valuable collection of new essays offering a detailed consideration of the two Elizabethan authors in relation to each other. Lethbridge's 'Introduction: Spenser, Marlowe, Shakespeare: Methodological Investigations' is amply footnoted, functioning as a bibliographical guide to the topic. He stresses the collection's methodological rigour: Shakespeare and Spenser have been compared before, but this time it will be done *better*. Karen Nelson, in her essay 'Pastoral Forms and Religious Reform in Spenser and Shakespeare', argues that 'English authors of pastoral literature, along with their continental counterparts, were often engaged in "figuring forth" debates about reform and counter-reform with their shepherds and shepherdesses' (p. 143). She compares Spenser's use of Faerieland with Shakespeare's employment of Arden as exile states of wilderness, focusing also on the figure of the hermit. Catholic authors tended to associate hermits with the Church Fathers, while reformers surrounded the hermit-figure with wild men and cannibalistic savages. Nelson, moreover, sees Shakespeare as offering a *politique* version of the more aggressive (albeit coded) radicalism of Lodge's *Rosalind*. Anne Lake Prescott, 'The Equinoctial Boar: Venus and Adonis in Spenser's Garden,

Shakespeare's Epyllion, and *Richard III*'s England', supplies an erudite assessment of the allegorical/mythographical renderings of the Venus and Adonis story, and equinoctial boar imagery, in *The Faerie Queene*, Shakespeare's epyllion and *Richard III*. In a similarly beast-tropic vein, Rachel E. Hile, '*Hamlet*'s Debt to Spenser's *Mother Hubberds Tale*: A Satire on Robert Cecil?', considers *Hamlet*'s debt to Spenser's *Mother Hubberds Tale*, with regard to covert attacks upon the Cecils. Hile argues that 'Claudius' murder of Old Hamlet in order to woo his queen is reminiscent of Robert Cecil's role in the trial and execution of Essex and his concomitant increase in political power under Elizabeth' (p. 200). The heart of the collection, though, is Robert L. Reid's magisterial essay, 'Spenser and Shakespeare: Polarized Approaches to Psychology, Poetics and Patronage'. Reid stresses the 'peculiar Christian–Classical synthesis in each poet's work' (p. 82). He then compares Spenser's elaborate and overt use of pattern, structure and numerology with Shakespeare's concealed 'dramaturgical structure' (p. 83). Reid also considers Essex allusions in *Henry V* and *Julius Caesar*; the latter play offers 'a complex anatomy of Essex's militaristic quest for honour and power' (p. 94). Shakespeare, then, like Spenser, is attempting to fashion Essex, but the dramatist offers a 'socially inclusive...epic [i.e. the *Henriad*] to replace Spenser's refined intellectual allegory' (p. 95). Reid, however, does not restrict his focus to a consideration of Essex's fortunes. He develops his argument to present a finely nuanced comparative study of Spenser's and Shakespeare's concepts of self-love and the action of grace.

Phebe Jensen's *Religion and Revelry in Shakespeare's Festive World* updates Barber's work on festivity in the wake of revisionist history. Jensen argues for the 'importance of the continued association between traditional pastimes and Catholic "superstition" in early modern culture' (p. 5). However, Shakespeare, according to Jensen, aligns his work with festive energies on aesthetic rather than theological grounds. Jensen seeks to supplement recent scholarship in exploring devotional identity in a way that 'rejects the sharp devotional categorization' that, say, asking if Shakespeare was a Catholic assumes. But she also declares that Shakespeare 'clearly conformed to Protestantism' (p. 6). Some categories, it appears, are able to retain their form. The main body of the study, however, has less polemical positioning and much informative historicist analysis. After chapters examining attitudes to popular festivity in Reformation England and calendrical reform respectively, Jensen offers a reading of *As You Like It* in relation to the anti-clericalism of earlier Robin Hood texts. *As You Like It*, she avers, redirects Robin Hood-style anti-clerical satire, targeting mainstream Church of England clerics, thereby suggesting 'the unreliability of officially sanctioned marriage rituals' (p. 142). Jensen's conclusion to this chapter conflicts somewhat with statements in her introduction: 'When *As You Like It*'s spectacles become sacramental, they reflect a belief in the salvific function of festivity' (p. 148). Presumably, Shakespeare is not pursuing merely aesthetic aims, therefore. After a chapter on Shakespeare's festive use of Falstaff and Falstaffian representations in *Twelfth Night*, the book concludes with an excellent chapter on *The Winter's Tale*. Jensen suggests that the play's statue scene implies one should not trust in Catholic spectacle. On the other hand, the scene is miraculous in terms of its human effect. Again, it might be objected that such a humanist recuperation of the superstitious is not an exclusively aesthetic project. Jensen astutely notes, though, that Perdita herself 'reveals a profound . . . unease with festive play' (p. 218). With experience, Perdita learns that devotion must be ritualized to some extent. Consequently, she becomes more festive and playful, coming to resemble her father less and her mother more. Thus, as a hybrid figure blending secular pastoral with religious festivity, Perdita can be seen as an embodied appropriation, rather than nostalgic iteration, of 'the energies of ancient Catholic rituals' (p. 224).

The general (introductory) chapters of Bradin Cormack's *A Power To Do Justice: Jurisdiction, English Literature, and the Rise of Common Law, 1509–1625*, though not concerned directly with Shakespeare, might well be of great interest to scholars investigating the socio-cultural context of Shakespeare's works. In a densely theoretical, but hugely rewarding, prologue Cormack posits that jurisdiction, being improvised and, therefore, always provisional, is 'the sign under which literary and legal aesthetics are legible' (p. 5). Cormack demonstrates that jurisdiction is the performative phase of legality, and, therefore, as perfect implementation of the law is impossible, jurisdiction is the means by which a legal system can be challenged (deformed) from within. In other words, jurisdiction reveals law as flux, just as gender-as-performance, for example, reveals sexual identity as flux. The relevance of Cormack's insights into the importance of jurisdiction to Shakespeare's political contexts is readily apparent: the contest between canon law and common law may well turn out to be no less significant for the understanding of the nascent nation-state of England than the battle between religious confessions. For one thing, the importance of Ireland, as a liminal zone where the provisional nature of jurisdiction is most patent, here looms larger than ever before (chapter 3 deals with Ireland in relation to Spenserian texts). In chapter 4 Cormack examines the relationship between Shakespeare's second tetralogy and English law. As Cormack says, the French background of English law tended to undermine its function as a prop for the nascent nation-state. Accordingly, Cormack sees the insistence on the *non*-immemorial origins of common law as having pro-absolutist implications. That is, 'the Conquest was saved for English common law by becoming an iterative structure more than a discrete event'. Consequently, Shakespeare's history plays are 'deeply concerned with the trope of reiterative conquest' (p. 181). In his discussion of Thomas Starkey's *Dialogue between Reginald Pole and Thomas Lupset* [*c*.1530], though, Cormack's focus on legal implications perhaps prevents his readings from achieving a suppleness comparable to the theoretical sophistication of the book's opening chapters. As Cormack notes, Starkey's Pole proposes the adoption of Roman civil law in England in order to do away with common law and its Norman taint. Doing so would remove the potential for tyranny. Cormack, however, considers only the classical aspect of Starkey's emphasis on the need for an overarching *Roman* system of jurisdiction. Given the historical context of Starkey's dialogue, the argument for a papal role in determining sovereignty has at least to be acknowledged. Be that as it may, Cormack conducts some insightful close reading, especially in his discussion of the relationship between Shakespeare's kings and iconography in John

Rastell's 1529 chronicle history of England. In chapter 5 Cormack argues that Shakespeare questions the equation of jurisdiction with territory by exploiting ambiguities arising not only from the union under James I, but also from the attempted mapping of the sea. Pondering how an empire can maintain its jurisdiction across distance and borders, Cormack looks at the 1608 *Post-Nati* case, concerned with the problem of whether James's Scottish subjects, born after his accession, could inherit land in England. Cormack also examines how far allegiance and fidelity can be said to transcend distance and time. *Cymbeline* and *Pericles* are key texts here.

In the introduction to *Shakespeare in French Theory: King of Shadows*, Richard Wilson claims that ' "Shakespeare in French theory" emerged as a site of defiance of America's dream of the "end of history" in neo-liberal capitalism' (p. 5). Having established this, Wilson then pits Bourdieu's less rhapsodic version of Shakespeare against Foucault's romanticization of madness (for Foucault, Shakespeare's fools are a source of truth). Bourdieu locates Shakespeare in relation to power and commerce. Thus, 'Shakespeare pretended to serve the prince [or noble patrons] . . . not out of deference, but to protect his own creative freedom by playing off the playhouse against the palace' (p. 11). Wilson, however, complains that Bourdieu privileges the aesthetic over the political, and points out that Bourdieu lacked a perception of the religious dimension of Shakespeare's situation. The question then becomes, if Shakespeare is neither romantic truth-teller nor game-playing aesthete, what *was* he doing? Playing to (apparently) lose, suggests Wilson. Shakespeare seeks ways of surviving (by changing) until things change, as they inevitably must. Hence, he seems always to anticipate the positions of poststructuralism because he is never exactly anywhere. Thus, Wilson argues against claiming Shakespeare for any religion (which is odd because that is what critics tend to accuse Wilson of doing!). Shakespeare's optimism involves a resistance to religious finality, and is compatible with Derrida's spirituality of endless deferral. Wilson then offers a splendid (Derrida-influenced) account of Shakespeare's boundless hospitality to whatever 'guests' the future may bring. That is why all subsequent readings find such a warm welcome waiting in his plays. As in the mumming tradition (discussed in the Epilogue), the sincerely hospitable host becomes, in a sense, the captive of his guests, but, by the same token, the truly gracious guest becomes the adapted host of his host. In addition, the guest always brings a gift, an element of difference which rubs off on the host. (It is interesting to recall that Shakespeare was himself at times a lodger, a house-guest, for instance, of Huguenot exiles.) Wilson's first chapter includes a history of French response to Shakespeare, starting with the reaction of Henri IV's spy Jacques Petit to a performance of *Titus Andronicus* in Sir John Harington's house in 1596, and going on through neoclassical French dislike of Shakespeare, Shakespeare as revolutionary hero of the people, Lyotard's appropriation of Shakespeare for postmodernism, Deleuze's happy Hamlet and Derrida's glimpse of Shakespeare as a sentinel on the night watch at Elsinore, always ready for the Messiah (the future) whatever monstrous form it takes. Chapter 2 discusses Foucauldian Shakespeare: a Shakespeare on the border between changing epistemes. A lengthy discussion of *Measure for Measure* reads the play in relation to Foucault's theories of surveillance as the control technique *par excellence* of the modern state. Wilson also includes the somewhat startling claim that modern idealizations of romantic love and companionate marriage derive their power from improvements in cereal farming. Once we can grow more, we can feed more people, so we can safely let subjects procreate. This provides a fascinating economic context for the loosening of the Catholic stranglehold on the sex lives of the faithful. One problem with this argument, as I see it, is that it equates reproduction with marriage. In chapter 5, Wilson registers the fact that Bataille was troubled by 'the gratuitousness of the sacrifice' (p. 174). Of course, it is precisely that gratuitousness which allows the sacrifice to escape from the economy of need. Wilson considers aspects of *Julius Caesar* in this regard, citing Richard Marienstras's comparison of Brutus to a priest. Duelling as a French import is investigated in the following chapter, bringing to light buried Essex allusions in *Twelfth Night*. Finally, in the Epilogue, Wilson distinguishes between carnival, as a defensive expression of insularity, and mumming, 'a more open, dialogic form of masquerade' (p. 247), suggesting that Shakespeare was more influenced by the mumming tradition, in which parties of disguised mummers invade houses. Accordingly, in his plays Shakespeare exaggerates the alterity of Moors, Jews, Egyptians and so on in order to test and extend his audience's hospitality.

Laurie Maguire's *Shakespeare's Names* is a (mostly) formalist study investigating the function of names in Shakespeare's works. The importance of names with regard to a broader theory of language is stressed by pointing out that Adam, before the Fall, effectively named the animals. True names, therefore, offer access to unfallen language. Accordingly, *Richard II* is concerned with a world that speaks a fallen language, where patience equals despair. A double standard of language, however, remains available. As the same play's Duchess of Gloucester says, that which in 'mean men' is 'patience' is 'pale cold cowardice in noble breasts' (p. 46). Chapter 2 looks at *Romeo and Juliet*. The lovers are damned because they live in a fallen world. 'What's in a name?' emerges as a crucial line: 'one of the two lovers must relinquish a surname if their love is to be feasible' (p. 51). But love is also about language— i.e. about learning to speak the language of the beloved. Achieving this selfless skill, one translates fallen into unfallen language. *Romeo and Juliet*, therefore, is about translation: Romeo into Juliet, Juliet into Romeo, comedy into tragedy, etc. Chapter 3 demonstrates the significance of characters' names in *A Midsummer Night's Dream*, especially 'Helen' and 'Theseus'. Maguire brings out very well the disturbing undertones of this romantic comedy: 'a world ruled by Theseus is a frightening place for a character named Helen'. However, '[t]he story shall be changed', Helen announces (p. 82). She means the story of Apollo and Daphne, but Shakespeare means, argues Maguire, the story of Helen of Troy. In another section, Maguire argues for the influence of Euripides' strange *Helen* play on *All's Well That Ends Well*. Thus, she questions scholars' continuing scepticism as to Shakespeare's familiarity with Greek originals. Chapter 5 shows that the rampant doubling of Euripides' play is also recalled in *The Comedy of Errors*: Pauline/Plautine; Christian/Pagan; the Temple of Diana/the Abbey; and of course the play's two sets of twins, whose names cease to guarantee identity. Maguire discusses Paul's letter to the

Ephesians, in particular the advice given about marriage. She notes that marriage in the play is treated as a commercial transaction and a spiritual action. This is 'no more paradoxical' than the dramatic hybrid Shakespeare creates, implying thereby that the play effectually marries the sacred and the profane (p. 165).

Literary culture in Tudor–Stuart England was, in many respects, European culture, so studies which explore the relationship between Shakespeare and European literature, being thin on the ground, presumably because scholars focus on texts written in their native language, are always welcome. *Italian Culture in the Drama of Shakespeare and his Contemporaries: Rewriting, Remaking, Refashioning* is one such artefact, being a collection of new essays, edited by Michele Marrapodi. In his introduction 'Appropriating Italy: Towards a New Approach to Renaissance Drama', Marrapodi stresses a desire to resist simplistic models of appropriation. Rather, 'the ideological appropriation of Italy may become a disruptive force which serves as a cover for political dissent' (p. 4). Thus, in the opening essay 'Pastoral Jazz from the Writ to the Liberty', Louise George Chubb celebrates the fact that continental pastoral works are now being taken more seriously as political allegory. With regard to pastoral drama, she argues that 'the very fact of dramatization offered the possibility of representing ... intangible [concepts]'. Moreover, the development of the '3rd genre' of tragicomedy within pastoral drama 'authorized a venue for liberty of imagination', allowing jazz-like exploration of new doctrines and ideas (p. 16). This relative freedom was vital to Italian exponents of reformation within a Catholic context. Chubb considers the importance of these issues with regard to plays such as *As You Like It*. Robert Henke in 'Virtuosity and Mimesis in the *Commedia dell'arte* and *Hamlet*' also discusses Italian developments of hybrid genres, arguing that the ancient satyr play provided Italian classicists with useful hints in this regard. After tracing the development of the *buffone* tradition in early sixteenth-century Venice, Henke turns to the first organized professional performances of *commedia dell'arte* (from 1545). He stresses the importance of the actress Flamina's decision to convert the tragedy of Dido into a tragicomedy. In doing so, Flamina anticipates the generic morphologies of Shakespeare's Polonius. The Italian actresses, however, work in a mimetic tradition committed to self-contained illusion, distinct from the *buffone* style. Henke, then, finds a polyvocal Italian influence in the way Shakespeare's *Hamlet*, for example, oscillates between the poles of mimesis and buffoonery. In a seemingly related vein, Keir Elam in "'At the cubiculo': Shakespeare's Problems with Italian Language and Culture" finds that 'a great deal of the comic energy in Shakespeare's plays derives precisely from the grotesque failure to assimilate Italianate culture' (p. 105). To argue this case, Elam explores links between John Florio and Shakespeare, noting the use Shakespeare seems to have made of Florio's Italian dictionary *A World of Words* [1598] in writing *Twelfth Night*. Elsewhere, Adam Max Cohen in 'The Mirror of All Christian Courtiers: Castiglione's *Cortegiano* as a Source for *Henry V*' examines Castiglione's *Cortegiano* as a possible source for *Henry V*. The claim by one of Castiglione's speakers that a true courtier has the 'ability to appropriate traits of either gender when the circumstances require' is read as informing

Shakespeare's portrayal of Henry's rhetorical conquests (p. 41). Henry, moreover, applies the principle of *sprezzatura* even in battle at Agincourt. Thus, whatever his failings, Henry to some extent embodies a courtly ideal.

B.J. Sokol's *Shakespeare and Tolerance* reassesses the meaning of tolerance in the early modern period. Noting that post-Enlightenment definitions read 'tolerance' as implying a prior dislike of the tolerated person or belief, Sokol argues that Shakespeare 'dramatises circumstances in which tolerance is required *before* any dislike is established' (p. xii). After all, if tolerance only means 'forbearance from harming' then only the dominant can practise it (p. xiv). Shakespeare, however, says Sokol, regularly represents mutual tolerance between parties within a power relationship. The book's first chapter is concerned with humour. Sokol suggests that 'Shakespeare's representations of poor or failed jokes...need not be...inartistic' (future editors of Shakespeare plays take note!). Seemingly poor jokes may be included not to win easy laughter but 'to make salient points about individual or group relations'. Thus, humour in Shakespeare's works should always be assessed within the immediate fictional context. As Sokol says, 'a true joke must be capable not only of succeeding but also of failing' (p. 10). Thus, while tyrants command obedient laughter for their worst jokes, other characters may manage power-dynamics and affirm inter-subjectivity by making poor jokes *without* impunity. Turning to *The Merchant of Venice*, Sokol argues that Shylock initially did not intend to obtain his pound of flesh. The joke was on humourless Antonio. Thus, Shylock initially demonstrates his superiority through humour only to lose this superiority by succumbing to an urge for bloody revenge. Sokol's second chapter focuses on gender issues. *The Taming of the Shrew*, suggests Sokol, is mindful of the impossibility of any marriage being truly happy. However, the marriage of Katherine and Petruchio may turn out to be uniquely happy, the play implies, as a result of their having achieved mutual tolerance. Furthermore, Sokol stresses that the practice of toleration is not about finding some bland middle way. Tolerance is rather about becoming flexible, rather than retaining fixity in one's own character and beliefs albeit while professing one's tolerance of difference. In his chapter on religion, Sokol likewise argues that *Hamlet* and *All's Well That Ends Well* promote a 'tolerantly syncretic' viewpoint (p. 102). In the second of two chapters on race, Sokol discusses geohumoral theories, suggesting that Prospero's island is appropriately utopian in that it offers a temperate meeting place for different (geographically figured) humours. The final chapter considers Shakespeare's Antony (in *Antony and Cleopatra*) in relation to Aristotle's description of *megalopsychia*. The ups and downs of Antony's career and relationship with Cleopatra are linked to his ability to practise true tolerance.

Shakespeare's Book: Essays in Reading, Writing and Reception, edited by Richard Meek, Jane Rickard and Richard Wilson, pursues the idea that Shakespeare *did* care about the publication of his plays (as well as his poems). The introduction ponders Shakespeare's cryptic reference to the printer Richard Field in *Cymbeline*, concluding that Field (who sold his interest in *Venus and Adonis* after issuing one edition) did not value Shakespeare's dramatic work. Stanley Wells in 'A New Early Reader of Shakespeare' discusses William Scott, secretary to Sir John Davies and a hitherto neglected early reader of Shakespeare. Scott gave evidence at the 1601 Essex inquiry, and in his remarks on Shakespeare, in his manuscript [*The Model*] *of Poesy* (to which Wells has had access), show particular interest in *Richard II*. Patrick Cheney in "'An Index and Obscure Prologue': Books and Theatre in Shakespeare's Literary Authorship" argues that Shakespeare challenges the binary of page versus stage via his characteristic use of hendiadys. Duncan Salkeld's account of *Henry V*'s publication history in "'As Sharp as a Pen': *Henry V* and its Texts" scans familiar terrain from a neglected viewpoint, asking whether the play's Choruses were, in fact, designed to help a reader re-create the play's theatrical performance in his or her imagination. Salkeld diagnoses his own reluctance to accept this hypothesis, for it conflicts with one's received opinions regarding the dramatic (albeit metatheatrical) effect of the prologues. However, such thought-experiments demonstrate the advantage of emphasizing a print-conscious Shakespeare, in that doing so challenges settled viewpoints.

Tom Rutter's *Work and Play on the Shakespearean Stage* is a thematic study, exploring the notion of work in relation to different aspects of Elizabethan and Jacobean culture. Chapter 1 demonstrates the relevance of late medieval and early modern religious upheavals to this topic, while the second chapter details how the display of superior acting skills served as a refutation of charges of idleness once actors had formed into companies under the protection of noblemen and justices. In this context, Rutter compares and contrasts the presentation of actors-as-characters in Shakespeare's *Shrew* and *A Midsummer Night's Dream* with the presentation of same in *The Taming of a Shrew* [*c.*1588–93]. In chapter 3, Rutter endorses Phyllis Rackin's view that Shakespeare's histories themselves engaged in the debate as to whether drama was capable of subversion, representing this debate as a contest between secular agency and divine providence. This insight, observes Rutter, acknowledges the fact that while players had noble backing they still needed civic approval and citizens' money. Rutter then reads *2 Henry VI*, *Richard II* and *Henry V* for traces of tension arising from the players' desire to please a plural audience. Chapter 4 includes discussion of Dekker's use of the figure of St Hugh in *The Shoemakers' Holiday* [1599]. This, notes Rutter, appears related to the invocation of St Crispian in Shakespeare's *Henry V*. Deloney (Dekker's principal source) mentions Crispin and Crispianian as preachers in Gaul who practised the art of shoemaking. Dekker replaces Crispin/Crispian with Hugh and gives more voice to the workers, whereas Henry suppresses Crispian's shoemaker association. All of which supports Rutter's argument that the Admiral's men sought the city audience, whereas the Lord Chamberlain's men remained cagier around 1599/1601. Chapter 5 continues the comparative study of different theatre companies' interactions with their cultural environment, in relation to the theme of work, covering the period 1599–1610.

Shakespeare as Children's Literature: Edwardian Retellings in Words and Pictures, by Velma Bourgeois Richmond, would be a useful purchase for any department running children's literature courses. This is not to ghettoize the study, for it contains much material of interest to the general Shakespeare scholar as well. Chapter 1 provides a mini-history of children's literature (as it developed from chapbooks intended for the emerging literate poor) in order to provide a context for the achievement of the innovators in the field of Shakespeare adaptations for children: Charles and Mary Lamb. Subsequent chapters examine the Lambs' adaptations in detail before turning to Victorian and Edwardian developments. A pleasing feature of the book is the close attention paid to (and the many reproductions of) illustrations. This is hugely relevant to the history of the reception of Shakespeare, for illustrations reflect Edwardian reception no less than do textual adaptations. Focusing on pedagogical issues, the final chapters examine the use of Shakespeare in schools, analysing editors' intentions as stated in prefaces to adaptations for children and for schools, revealing much about educational attitudes and socio-cultural models in general.

In the opening contribution, "'A System of Oeconomical Prudence': Shakespearean Character and the Practice of Moral Inquiry", to *Shakespeare and the Eighteenth Century*, a collection of new essays edited by Peter Sabor and Paul Yachnin, Michael Bristol investigates Theobald's view that Shakespeare's most significant achievement was the creation of characters with fictional agency. Given this emphasis on character, figures such as Angelo in *Measure for Measure* raised critical issues for literary scholars of the eighteenth century, as Bristol shows. Jean Marsden's essay, 'Shakespeare and Sympathy' meanwhile, discusses how eighteenth-century readers expected great literature to communicate 'sympathy'. Marsden sees this expectation as distinct from the early modern focus on 'art's responsibility to "please and instruct"' (p. 29). According to Marsden, Adam Smith's first book, *The Theory of Moral Sentiments* [1759], was a main instigator of the sympathy craze. Smith saw sympathy as 'the founding principle for all moral behaviour' (p. 31). As a result of this emphasis, tragedy was valued more than comedy. Moreover, eighteenth-century audiences were expected to show sympathy 'through highly visible tears' (p. 33). Nicholas Hudson discusses in "The 'Vexed Question': Shakespeare and the Nature of Middle-Class Appropriation" the question of middle-class appropriation of Shakespeare. In the eighteenth century, the middle classes 'increasingly made up the main audience at the theatres'. This class-conscious audience responded enthusiastically to Garrick's 'naturalness' because it was not linked to his character as king, but to his character's presumed individuality. Audiences and critics, moreover, projected their class anxiety onto the dramatist himself. Shakespeare's 'low birth and lack of education' enabled him to forgo the 'erroneous lenses of a classical . . . tradition'. He 'merely described what he saw before him' (p. 45). This approach, however, opened up a can of worms. For example, Maurice Morgan extended Johnson's empirical method to absurdity, insisting that, because we like him, Falstaff cannot really be a coward. Hudson concludes by observing, however, that Shakespeare was also valued for expressing contempt for the bourgeoisie. This suggests that the sentimentality associated with eighteenth-century empiricism tends to involve an element of self-loathing. A chapter by Fiona Ritchie, 'The Influence of the Female Audience on the Shakespeare Revival of 1736–1738: The Case of the Shakespeare Ladies Club', meanwhile, provides an account of the role of the Shakespeare Ladies Club in reviving interest in Shakespeare in 1736–8.

In the face of popular adaptations, the club campaigned for original versions to be performed and for the revival of neglected plays. Marcus Walsh's contribution, 'George Stevens and the 1778 Variorum: A Hermeneutics and a Social Economy of Annotation', compares the annotational styles of Steevens and Malone. For anyone interested in the history of the annotation of Shakespeare, this chapter is essential reading. It also contains amusing discussion of Steevens's use of fictional editorial personae to satirize his own endeavours. Paul Yachnin in 'Looking for *Richard II*' investigates how modern interpretations of Shakespeare's history plays have been influenced by the Enlightenment's emphasis on character-motivation as the guide to a play's meaning. In contrast, Yachnin argues, Shakespeare himself saw concepts such as Providence as having 'motives of its own' (p. 130). Thus, Yachnin concludes, Richard II's character is not necessarily the centre of gravity of the play bearing his name as title. Rather, that centre may be the cultivation in the audience of 'a sceptical spirit of historical enquiry that is inseparable from an enfolding awareness of themselves as a sacramental political community' (p. 134). Amanda Cockburn's chapter, 'Awful Pomp and Endless Diversity: The Sublime Sir John Falstaff' reveals that the main flaw with Adam Smith's view that moral behaviour is learned by observing and adopting established rules is that this model leads not to the purging of negative passions but only to their effective masking. This understanding helps to account for the ambivalent attitude to the masquerade in eighteenth-century England. Hence, the character of Sir John Falstaff, being a similar conflation of the immoral and the pleasurable, was a challenging problem for literary critics of the time. Gefen Bar-On Santor in "Looking for 'Newtonian' Laws in Shakespeare: The Mystifying Case of the Character of Hamlet" finds that Shakespeare was regarded in the eighteenth century as being great in so far as, like a humanities version of Newton, he comprehended the hidden workings of human nature. Consequently, Enlightenment critics set about trying to find the underlying principles of characters such as Hamlet. When these characters proved to be incoherent, the plays were suspected of being at fault, and in need of editorial fixing. Thus, while for readers today 'the association of *Hamlet* with ambiguity may seem like a commonplace', for editors such as Malone it was 'a revolutionary idea'. Ultimately, 'the Newtonian search for underlying principles produced the ironic effect of highlighting the limitations of the scientific worldview in relation to literary character' (p. 163). Finally, Jenny Davidson's essay 'Why Girls Look Like their Mothers: David Garrick Rewrites *The Winter's Tale*' compares early seventeenth- and eighteenth-century concepts of heredity, and discusses relevant aspects of *The Winter's Tale*.

In *Shakespeare, the Earl, and the Jesuit*, John Klause explores the links between Shakespeare, Henry Wriothesley and Robert Southwell. Copious evidence of Shakespeare's verbal debts to the Jesuit poet is provided in table form and examined in detail, revealing an ongoing virtual debate between the two authors regarding contentious issues for English Catholics. Klause's work evidently has connections with aspects of Richard Wilson's *Secret Shakespeare* [2004]. However, where Wilson found Southwell responding to Shakespeare's *Venus and Adonis*, Klause reverses the direction of intercourse, arguing that it is unlikely that Southwell read Shakespeare's epyllion in manuscript.

Consequently, where Wilson interprets Shakespeare's Venus as an analogue for Queen Elizabeth, Klause's Venus figures coercive Rome and its Jesuit emissary. On the one hand, Klause's version makes sense: Venus does resemble 'a Mother church who would possess a subject entirely' (p. 55). On the other hand, where Southwell notoriously exhorted English Catholics to embrace martyrdom, Shakespeare's Venus clearly does not seek martyrdom for her beloved Adonis. Possibly where both Wilson and Klaus lack suppleness in this regard is their seeming commitment to one-to-one identifications of literary characters with real people. An appreciation of the allegorical nature of early modern literature does not have to entail such an approach. Venus might be better read as presenting the possessive nature of any coercive religious institution. Notwithstanding his difference from Wilson with regard to *Venus and Adonis*, Klause by no means finds Shakespeare to be pro-Elizabeth. For example, discussing the 'fair vestal' speech in *A Midsummer Night's Dream*, which is often taken to allude to Queen Elizabeth, Klause stresses its negative connotations. Thus, by tracing the abundant echoes of Southwell's writings in Shakespearian texts (*A Midsummer Night's Dream*, *The Rape of Lucrece*, *The Comedy of Errors*, *Titus Andronicus*, *Hamlet* and *All's Well That Ends Well*), Klause reveals a Shakespeare who is highly critical of both the Elizabethan regime and the Jesuit poet's 'stern moralizings' (p. 60). Nonetheless, given the evident extent of Shakespeare's borrowings from Southwell, says Klause in conclusion, it becomes more likely that the 'W.S.' to whom, it is supposed, the Jesuit poet dedicated a collection of poems in the early 1590s was the Stratford man (this dedication, it should be noted, appeared only in a 1616 Saint-Omer manuscript).

The late A.D. Nuttall provides a highly stimulating formalist account of Shakespeare's mental processes in *Shakespeare the Thinker*. Nuttall's Shakespeare is suspicious of language's (and, therefore, his own) capabilities to simulate and manage feeling. Accordingly, the monastery-like academy of *Love's Labour's Lost* is portrayed as an ultimately self-indulgent, self-deceiving institution. Nonetheless, Shakespeare is clearly not an anti-intellectual. Nuttall emphasizes throughout the book Shakespeare's profound knowledge of Latin classical works. However, Nuttall appears unconcerned as to where Shakespeare acquired such extreme familiarity with the classics. (It is sometimes claimed young Will could have easily learned all he knew from his local grammar school; if this is true we need look no further for a template for educational reform.) Working doggedly through the canon, Nuttall supplies countless insights and challenging, but always well-supported, readings. Extensive discussions of key speeches and scenes are rigorously self-interrogating. In particular, Nuttall shows how Shakespeare deployed complex rhetorical methods to interrogate Stoicism, nominalism, determinism and so forth. Over the course of the book, Nuttall demonstrates that Shakespeare was committed to a view of human identity as utterly dependent on social relations. In addition, Nuttall's Shakespeare often emphasizes the artificiality of his play-worlds, as if implying that a transcendent reality is the true one, but this does not make him a Platonist: 'the severe separation of the Form from the turbulent half-reality of the sensuously available world, is not there, in Shakespeare's mind. All remains this-worldly, fully human'

(p. 253). Though he skirts the issue of Shakespeare's faith, Nuttall by no means always plays safe in his readings. For example, he offers a full-blown (and extremely plausible) Gnostic interpretation of *Measure for Measure*. Nuttall admits, though, that he cannot say how Shakespeare accessed Gnosticism. He settles for assuming not a continuous textual tradition but 'the continuing *availability of the thought*' (p. 264). This is where a more historicized, intertextual approach might yield further dividends.

Kenneth Burke on Shakespeare, edited by Scott L. Newstok, usefully gathers the maverick intellectual's essays on the poet-playwright into one place. The book's insights come thick and fast, often from unexpected angles. For example, in a footnote to an article on 'Imagery', Burke surmises that 'corrective hypocrisy' would be the likely response of an author to an awareness of his or her habitual patterns of metaphorization. Thus, Shakespeare may have been aware of his habits, indeed 'deliberately coached himself to cultivate them'. This might represent a form of 'secular prayer'; i.e. by consciously employing certain metaphors, the poet can alter his or her subjective state—and, therefore, that of his or her spectator/reader (p. 50). Especially refreshing is Burke's view that Shakespeare was not so much a creator of characters who seem like individuals as a writer able to translate ideas into (and disperse them throughout) 'a scattering of personalities' (p. 8). Obviously such a view predisposes Burke to a theme-based approach. Accordingly, he insists that we pay attention to the opening lines (or scenes) of Shakespearian drama, as, in a sense, they contain the whole play. Intriguingly, like Nuttall (given that both scholars generally follow a formalist procedure), Burke finds himself obliged to posit a Shakespeare who remembered ideas, in the Platonic sense, rather than learned them. Burke, moreover, sees Shakespeare as translating the religious into the aesthetic, with the usual emphasis on the major tragedies that invariably accompanies this assertion. The aesthetic of course cannot give adequate meaning to a tragic universe. Thus, overwhelmed by a perception that words threatened to become mere 'words, words, words', Shakespeare botched *Hamlet* (p. 50). In his essay on *Othello*, however, Burke anticipates the return of historicism by asking the excellent question: why, at this time, does this play deal with the particular tension arising from a sense of one's wife as one's possession? Burke reads this tension against the transition from feudalism to capitalist nation-state, noting the probable relevance of enclosure acts. Hence, the significance of Desdemona being strangled—the fear of communal possession leading the jealous 'owner' to destroy the thing or person he seeks to profit from or claims to love. Similarly, Burke reads *Antony and Cleopatra* as demonstrating that 'love is in essence an empire'. Love becomes greater, the greater its territory. Shakespeare thus converts his spectators (who all 'own some shares in love') into budding empire-builders (p. 115). I could continue at length, but the wealth of insight embarrasses selection. Suffice to say, this collection would be a valuable addition to any library of Shakespeare criticism.

Ehsan Azari, in the introduction to *Lacan and the Destiny of Literature: Desire, Jouissance and the Sinthome in Shakespeare, Donne, Joyce and Ashbery*, observes that Lacan's theories, being often inadequately understood, are frequently misapplied in literary criticism. His book, therefore, is divided into two sections, the first providing a comprehensive exposition of Lacanian theory, including its later formulations, the second offering examples of that theory being applied to works of literature. For those of us who struggle with some of the more complicated reaches of Lacan's thought, Azari's first section is obviously useful. Indeed, Azari admits that certain aspects of Lacanian theory remain obscure to him. However, Azari believes it is worthwhile getting to grips with Lacan, as his theories may, for instance, serve to deconstruct deconstructivism (i.e. manage to explain what deconstruction leaves as rubble in its wake). Azari maintains, moreover, that unlike Freudianism, the application of Lacan's theories does not commit the scholar to predetermined readings. I would object here that this precisely is one problem with Lacanian theory. It may not seek to impose the Freudian Oedipal model onto literary texts, but it does necessarily impose its presupposition that desire is always an expression of lack. I was hoping to see Azari tackle this problem, perhaps by acknowledging, say, the formidable attack made upon Freud and Lacan in Deleuze and Guattari's *Anti-Oedipus*, but for Azari, apparently, Lacan is right, desire equals lack, and that is that. Thus, literary texts may be read as illustrations of this theory. Nonetheless, Azari does address other challenges to Lacan, notably feminist charges made by Irigaray and Cixous. Scholars interested in these debates will find useful discussion in the book's second chapter. Chapter 5 discusses Shakespeare's 'theatre of desire', focusing on *Hamlet* as an articulation of male desire, and on *Coriolanus*, *Macbeth* and *The Merchant of Venice* as articulations of female desire. Azari applies Lacan's theories in an orthodox manner, incorporating the later ideas. This results in Azari arguing, for example, that, since we no longer desire an object once we attain it, when Ophelia is in reach of Prince Hamlet, 'he sends her to a convent to become a nun' (p. 12). Whatever the merits of this reading, it may be seen that Azari is applying psychoanalytical theory to the character of Prince Hamlet as though he were self-evidently an individual. Kenneth Burke's observation that Shakespeare's characters are not so much individuals as particles of ideas in action might offer an appropriate basis for proposing that it could be theoretically sounder to apply Lacanian psychoanalytical concepts to plays as a whole. Notwithstanding this, Azari's readings are multi-faceted and complex, so any reader with fewer qualms about the fundamental Lacanian model than myself is sure to find his book useful.

The *Cambridge Companion to Shakespeare and Popular Culture*, states editor Robert Shaughnessy, is not only concerned with contemporary manifestations but also features a broader historical assessment of the interactions between Shakespeare's texts and 'popular culture'. Consequently, several of the volume's essays offer chronological accounts of ways in which Shakespeare and his texts have been recycled and referenced in different media: in popular music, in digital formats, upon Stratford theatre playbills and posters. Often it is debatable how far these essays treat of popular culture rather than, say, middle-brow manifestations. For example, Peter Holland in 'Shakespeare Abbreviated' provides an excellent account of abbreviated versions of Shakespeare plays, reading them as 'deliberate intervention[s] in a history of cultural reception that negotiates concepts of high/low and popular/elite cultural formations' (p. 28). The 'popular' aspect of this formulation holds good, however, only for pre-cinema eras. Be that as it may, the coverage of illegal performances of versions of Shakespeare plays, such as the Interregnum 'drolls', is especially welcome (pp. 33 ff.). Holland also describes Robert Elliston's 1809 staging of a balletic/quasi-operatic *Macbeth*. Only two theatre companies were allowed to perform spoken drama at the time, so the adaptation replaced spoken dialogue with mime and singing. Likewise, Pavel Kohout's 1977 abbreviated version of *Macbeth* 'was a response to legal restrictions, in Soviet-controlled Prague in 1977'. Unable to perform in theatres, Kohout's cast of five performed 'Living Room Theatre' (p. 40). Holland includes discussion of the Reduced Shakespeare Company's *The Complete Works of William Shakespeare (Abridged)*. Needing to represent Ophelia economically, the cast invite sections of the audience to play the 'roles' of Ophelia's 'id', 'ego' etc—a hint perhaps of some fundamental link between audience participation and psychomachy (p. 42)? As mentioned, I am not sure how 'popular' this really is. This version of Shakespeare was debuted at the Edinburgh Festival and in the 'To be or not to be' speech, 'Hamlet' worries about having to 'make guacamole for twelve' (p. 43). In any case, Holland also mentions a wonderful-sounding 1987 production of *Hamlet* by the Cambridge Educational Theatre in which 'every actor played each "character"' . . . denying narrative and creating non-linear theatre' (p. 42). In the following essay, 'Shakespearean Stars: Stagings of Desire', Barbara Hodgdon investigates how the concept of stardom has been configured at different cultural moments by describing contemporary responses to famous Shakespearian actors from Burbage onwards. She claims that 'the notion of stardom is alien to early modern thinking' but refutes herself somewhat by pointing out the 'social significance' of clowns such as Tarlton and Kempe (p. 48). Stephen Orgel in 'Shakespeare Illustrated' performs close readings of illustrations of Shakespeare texts, paying particular attention to Rowe's 1709 edition, in which each play had a frontispiece illustration. He stresses the oddity of the omission of illustrations from earlier English publications of dramatic texts, for their continental equivalents had been illustrated during the sixteenth and seventeenth centuries. Laurie Osborne's essay 'Narration and Staging in *Hamlet* and its Afternovels' uses *Hamlet* as a vehicle for exploring how the concept of narrativity relates to popular assimilation(s) of Shakespeare. Osborne is interested in the 'competition between narration and action, between telling a story and staging it' (p. 117). Thus, she observes that 'Old Hamlet's story is a counter-narrative from the start, challenging the current report of his death' (pp. 117–18). Noting how Gertrude's seemingly eyewitness description of Ophelia's death raises the question of why the queen did not intervene, Osborne concludes that things narrated are always doubtful. Consequently, there is always room for further tellings, and licence for simplification or alteration to make things more comprehensible to people who were not present. In conclusion, Osborne argues that, by turning Shakespeare into new fiction, 'popular novelists rework Shakespeare's own creative process' (p. 128). Emma Smith's contribution, 'Shakespeare Serialized: *An Age of Kings*', ponders whether Shakespeare was in fact an author of serialized cliff-hangers. Smith analyses the 1960 BBC serial *An Age of Kings*, stressing the importance of structure for the reception of

Shakespeare's plays. The series-makers' decision to cut each featured play into two episodes created new emphases, implying in turn of course that the plays themselves had been conceived within modifying structures. In a presentist vein, Smith suggests that the articulations made available by such approaches (i.e. comparing modern serialized modes with Shakespearian drama) may serve 'to challenge the hegemony of historicism' (p. 147). Finally, investigating radio Shakespeare in 'Shakespeare Overheard: Performances, Adaptations, and Citations on Radio', Susanne Greenhalgh demonstrates how the maximum suggestiveness of the radio medium offers incitement to engage in the kind of imaginary activity that the Prologue in *Henry V* calls upon the audience to perform.

In *Shakespeare and the Rise of the Editor*, Sonia Massai pursues connections between the first committed publishers of English commercial drama (John and William Rastell) and the humanist project of Sir Thomas More. More required a high level of accuracy in the printing of his works, on a par with standards developed on the continent in preparing reliable editions of classical texts. However, unlike his opponent Tyndale, More allowed that his text might contain errors and, therefore, careful readers could function as agents of necessary correction—editors after the fact. As Massai shows, More's English printer of preference, William Rastell, applied the same high standards to the printing of commercial drama. This humanist combination of a commitment to accuracy and submission to correction by readers came, in due course, to inform the publication of Shakespeare's quartos (and the Folios). Thus, Massai contends, when scholars regard Nicholas Rowe as the first 'proper' editor of Shakespeare, dismissing earlier 'editions' as products of a process of decay, they do so because (like Rowe) they wish to retain potential access to an authorial text. Massai does not rule out authorial agency in the preparation of early modern quartos, but, given her findings concerning the Rastells et al., insists that readers' annotations were commonly incorporated by publishers within subsequent editions of a printed play, those publishers being keen to advertise their wares as 'perfected' editions. By comparing variant readings in extant multiple edition quartos, Massai demonstrates that neither compositors nor *theatrical* annotators are likely to have been responsible for such variants. Thus, early modern editing appears to have been a collective process, carried out by publishers working in tandem with a community of careful readers. The use of the term 'perfected', moreover, turns out to be strategic. With reference to printing, 'to perfect' had two meanings in the period: 'to correct' and 'to complete'. Massai shows that publishers and authors took full advantage of the slippage between these significations. If their works contained mistakes (either formal errors or offensive matter) then these were the results of human fallibility. Therefore, sensitive correction (rather than punishment) was called for, with appropriate changes to be incorporated in subsequent editions. In her conclusion, Massai considers the implications of her findings for current editorial practice, pointing out flaws with both the copy-text and the facsimile approaches to producing editions of early modern plays.

Laura Shamas's *We Three: The Mythology of Shakespeare's Weird Sisters* opens with a concise, detailed account of the stage history of the 'Weird Sisters' from *Macbeth*, including the useful reminder that the only extant contemporary description of their on-stage appearance comes from the diarist and astrologer Simon Forman, who refers to them as 'nymphs and fairies' (p. 2). This provides Shamas with a solid base for launching her investigation into what Shakespeare was up to in presenting these ambiguous figures to James I. Shamas pays close attention to probable sources for Shakespeare's depiction of the witches, including Holinshed's *Chronicles*, 'The Original Chronicle of Andrew of Wyntoun' (*c*.1420) and Matthew Gwinn's *Tres Sibyllae* (performed 1605). Shamas also considers the mythological background of female triads at length and discusses the witch as a scapegoat-figure.

Nina Taunton's *Fictions of Old Age in Early Modern Literature and Culture* examines the contradiction between (classical-influenced) Renaissance prescriptive literature's praise of old age and customary fictional representations of the negative aspects of that condition. In addition, the book explores paradoxical attitudes to gender with regard to the pros and cons of old age. In the opening chapter, Taunton argues that, in *The Comedy of Errors*, Shakespeare transforms classical material in order to show that age is 'as much a state of mind as an inevitable condition defined by chronology' (p. 13). Chapter 2 investigates the notion that 'the old have a moral responsibility to prepare the young spiritually and temporally', noting that this issue 'becomes increasingly complex and ambivalent as it migrates...from prescriptive to imaginative writing' (pp. 35, 37). Thus, respect for age belongs to the ideal world, but inheritance issues generate uncertainty which finds expression in more 'realistic' scenarios. Accordingly, plays such as *The Merchant of Venice* and *King Lear*, by focusing on inter-generational relationships, manage to register debates derived from the world of realpolitik upon a dramatically engaging domestic scale. Taunton's discussion of *Lear* is particularly suggestive, as she interrogates the period's anxieties about inheritance and demonstrates the growing early modern conviction that testaments require written forms to secure their observation. Lear's vain need for, and naive commitment to, old-fashioned spoken avowals of love and loyalty lead him to undermine the commonwealth, losing all claim to respect for his age, wisdom and (former) sovereignty in the process. By failing to realize the extent to which his identity was bound up with his role as king, he exposes his newly naked self to ingratitude and loss. Hence, 'old' Lear emerges as equivalent to 'the poor'. It becomes clear from the book's analysis that Shakespeare used terms such as young/old and rich/poor as dialectical categories. For example, in *All's Well*, as Taunton notes, the positive qualities of old age are projected onto Helena, so that she emerges as metaphorically 'old' and wise. However, Taunton focuses on the material implications of such poetic treatments by contrasting them with prescriptive texts. At times, this approach results in a feeling of mismatch between the imaginative and non-fictional categories. On the other hand, since it is obviously impossible to separate these categories, Taunton's rigorously materialist approach yields a rich sociocultural analysis of early modern attitudes to old age. Nonetheless, Taunton herself registers this categorical difference in her concluding observation that prescriptive manuals seem to be more obdurate in their positions whereas drama (by Shakespeare, Middleton, Ford et al.) offers scope for the presentation of plural voices, occasioning a complex play of meaning.

In *Sacramental Poetics at the Dawn of Secularism: When God Left the World*, Regina Mary Schwartz argues that after Reformers rejected the doctrine of transubstantiation '[a]spects of the Eucharist began showing up in the poetry of the Reformation, albeit in completely unorthodox ways' (pp. 7–8). Both poetry and the sacrament of the Eucharist, notes Schwartz, are engaged in making present what is absent. Therefore, a sacramental notion of poetry entails that a reader/spectator is not just a passive recipient of a poem or play but is changed by his or her encounter with it. Furthermore, although Reformers insisted that the Mass only commemorates Christ's sacrifice, 'Shakespeare is clearly preoccupied with representing the *sacrifice* of the Eucharist'. Consequently, Schwartz sees Othello as a version of a priest sacrificing at the altar. Thus, the tragedy 'draws a troubling relation between murder and sacrifice' (p. 17). Schwartz devotes a chapter to *Othello*, noting, however, that Shakespeare's plays generally acknowledge a desire for redemption which the secular theatre cannot satisfy. In stating that '[t]he theatre cannot *do* anything to other humans', though, Schwartz seems to contradict her earlier assertion of the transformational power of a sacramental poetics. Nonetheless, Schwartz then makes the excellent point that it was the Reformers' very insistence upon the illusionism of the Catholic Mass which 'brought the Mass closer to the theatre'. If, therefore, the theatre successfully offered a cleansing and affecting ritual, without engaging in actual sacrifice, perhaps it became 'the first truly Reformed church' (p. 42). Moreover, as Schwartz deftly argues, if Othello's killing of Desdemona is regarded as murder, it becomes emptied of significance—pointless slaughter. The audience, however, is encouraged to reinvest Desdemona's death with ritual meaning and regard it as an efficacious sacrifice. Hence the play insists upon Desdemona's purity, and gives prominence to her final forgiveness of Othello.

Rather than presume that early modern literature expresses any 'spirit of the age' in the use of archaeological themes, Philip Schwyzer, in *Archaeologies of English Renaissance Literature*, contends that archaeological concepts appear in specific alignments with political, religious and cultural crises; tracing these links allows us to interrogate the relationship between the past and the present. Thus, the book's third chapter considers how monastic ruins manifest in Elizabethan literary texts. For Schwyzer, such ruins figure doubleness. Elizabethan poetic descriptions of them are common but also stereotypical and imprecise. The resulting combination of declared emotional effect and optical disconnection results in ambiguity whenever monastic ruins feature in plays and poems. Schwyzer, moreover, finds an analogue to this doubleness in the figure of Aaron the Moor in *Titus Andronicus*: Aaron is a gleeful murderer but also a devoted parent. Therefore it is significant that Aaron is found cradling his son 'behind a crumbling monastic wall' (p. 101). Sonnet 73 ('Bare ruined choirs') also comes up for inspection in this context. Again there is doubleness in the treatment: the sonnet represents the monasteries' dissolution as analogous to a natural phenomenon (a tree's annual loss of leaves), but, while we know that spring will come again, how can the monasteries ever be restored? Schwyzer compares the sonnet to Maarten van Heemskerck's painting *Self-Portrait, with the Colosseum Behind* [1553]. The middle ground of this work is said to show the artist's younger self, busily painting the monument, while the artist's bearded, mature self stands in the foreground and stares out at the viewer. 'The ruin stands between Heemskerck's two selves' (p. 104). By means of this comparison, Schwyzer effectively demonstrates the exploded representation of time in Shakespeare's sonnet. Chapter 4, meanwhile, reads the poem inscribed upon Shakespeare's burial monument ('Good friend, for Jesus' sake forbear . . .') as much less conventional than is usually claimed. Epitaphs written after the prohibition—during Edward VI's reign—of prayers for the dead 'rarely exhort the living to do anything for Jesus's sake' (pp. 117–18). On the other hand, the use of the verb 'forebear' actually reverses Catholic assumptions: the poem asks the reader *not* to do something. With this ambivalence in mind, Schwyzer goes on to discuss the significance of private family crypts in *Titus Andronicus* and *Romeo and Juliet*. He also seeks to contrast Shakespeare's apparent aversion to the promiscuous mingling of bodies after death with John Donne's declared appetite for it. This approach works well with regard to Shakespeare's tomb inscription, but Schwyzer then reads *Hamlet* in the light of this distinction, treating Prince Hamlet's views as equivalent to Shakespeare's own. Schwyzer thus argues for a Shakespeare who valued privacy, in this life and in the grave.

Simon Palfrey and Tiffany Stern's *Shakespeare in Parts* proposes looking at early modern actors' parts (portions of playscripts provided to individual actors containing all their character's dialogue) as a new way of approaching Shakespeare's plays, arguing that doing so will enable scholars to move away from the Romantic conception of the author as commanding genius. The book is divided into four sections, examining the history of the 'part'; the function of cues (lines which actors had to listen out for as signals for their next utterance); Shakespeare's use of premature and repeated cues; and directions for acting contained within dialogue. In section I, following analysis of the only extant English professional theatre part (Orlando from Green's *Orlando Furioso*), Palfrey and Stern explain that early modern playwrights designed parts for particular actors. Since there were no directors, the argument runs, casting was carried out within the writer's mind while he wrote. During a useful discussion of ways in which adult actors instructed boy performers, Palfrey and Stern stress how disastrous the closure of the theatres during the Interregnum appeared to the actors, removing as it did the practical need for the passing on of valuable acting skills. Explaining the function of cues, Palfrey and Stern claim that Shakespeare includes many repeated cues in his texts in order to generate surprises. The actor listening for his cue could be tricked into speaking at the wrong moment by treating the first appearance of a particular word or phrase as his cue to speak, when in fact, a subsequent repetition of that word or phrase was the proper cue. Examples of this technique 'invariably coincide with moments of decision for the character'. Thus, 'the score is subjected to . . . jazz-like peril' (p. 78). To the objection that such 'surprises' would only occur in rehearsal, Palfrey and Stern insist that whole-cast rehearsals were rare. In any case, the generation of surprise in early recitals provided the actor with hints for spontaneous-seeming performance.

Palfrey and Stern also claim that Shakespeare's use of cues in general was often meaningful and is a neglected area in interpretative studies.

Rebecca Steinberger's study, *Shakespeare and Twentieth-Century Irish Drama: Conceptualizing Identity and Staging Boundaries*, begins with a familiar proposition: Shakespeare gives a voice to the Other in his works (here it is the Irish Other). The book's opening chapter thus contrasts Shakespeare's ambivalent representation of the Irish in *Richard II* and *Henry V* to what Steinberger sees as Spenser's more univocal position in his *A View of the Present State of Ireland*. The chapter does, however, contain some factual errors: Steinberger wrongly states that *A View* was published (as opposed to probably written) in 1596, and refers to it as a 'state-supported' text (p. 5). However, chapter 2 reveals that the preceding section is best read as a necessary preliminary to the book's main focus: modern Irish drama's appropriation of Shakespeare, and the concomitant facilitation of Irish dramatists' escape from binary models. Steinberger discusses plays by Synge and O'Casey, making an interesting comparison between the Abbey Theatre and the Globe. In particular, Steinberger notes that Synge shared with Shakespeare the ability to juxtapose the comic and the tragic, a skill Steinberger maintains had been lost to the English-speaking stage for over two centuries. Furthermore, Steinberger compares the anti-clericalism she finds in *2 Henry IV* with O'Casey's anti-clerical discourse, observing that both dramatists wrote against a backdrop of exhortations to martyrdom uttered by charismatic figures. Thus, the Irish activist Padraic Pearse's demagoguery is discussed in relation to Henry V's 'band of brothers' speech. The book's third and final chapter focuses on the activities of the Field Day Theatre Company (formed in 1980) in Northern Ireland. The company's board of directors was selected to form a 50:50 balance of Protestants and Catholics. Nonetheless, its activities were not apolitical, but 'polypolitical' (p. 68). Field Day, notes Steinberger, set out to 'invent...an audience'. If nationalism 'invents nations where they don't exist', then it follows that the theatre can fashion its own audiences (p. 71). Field Day was also associated with polemical pamphlet production (three publications every six months). Here is much scope for presentist exploration. One wonders if Shakespeare's company operated in comparable ways.

Jane K. Brown begins her ambitious volume, *The Persistence of Allegory: Drama and Neoclassicism from Shakespeare to Wagner*, with a forthright statement: 'Between the cultural materialism of much recent scholarship in the English Renaissance and the rear guard of those who consider Shakespeare above all a dramatist of character...there is little space left for those who see a plurality of discourses operating in the plays' (p. 3). As might be expected, Brown's book seeks to occupy and expand that 'little space'. One of the strengths of Brown's approach is her perception that mimesis is not the opposite but rather the ground of allegory. For Brown, allegory is 'a mode of perception which renders the supernatural visible, by mimesis, a mode which imitates the natural' (p. 5). The discovery of perspective in the visual arts, argues Brown, meant that visual images became more 'realistic', without programmatically jettisoning their allegorical qualities, and, therefore, literary fictions had to keep up. Nonetheless, as a result of the secularization of

European culture, and the rise of empiricism, the allegorical basis of mimesis began to be devalued or ignored. Allegory (as the ground of mimesis) inevitably persisted, but without always being recognized. With regard to the development of English drama in particular, Brown insists on the importance of distinguishing between the mystery and morality traditions: mystery plays tended to relate centrally to the Passion, 'by typological reference if not directly' (p. 49), whereas morality plays, being more homiletic, are analogous to sermons. Brown also traces the development of pastoral drama from Poliziano to Shakespeare via Guarini and Tasso. This recovery of Shakespeare's allegorical heritage enables Brown to argue that modern scholarly perceptions of 'implausibility' in Shakespeare's works arise from 'the assumption that [a given] play's Gestalt is determined by its mimesis of human actions; if, however [the play is] understood as an experiment in blending dramaturgies, the problems become opportunities to examine the interaction of Aristotelian, Platonist and morality modes to create a more sophisticated allegorical dramaturgy' (p. 67). Brown then applies this insight, offering credible readings of *King John*, *Julius Caesar* and *Twelfth Night*. Brown's knowledge of classical texts stands her in good stead here. For instance, with regard to her discussion of *Twelfth Night* as a sophisticated variation upon the conventions of the morality play's representations of Vices and Virtues, Brown points out that disguise is not typical of Latin comedy, but has its origins as a dramatic device in the morality tradition, where it sustains a Vice's trickery. The transplantation of disguise to a neoclassical context in itself serves to foreground the device (such foregrounding is a common signal of allegorization). Moreover, 'Viola turns the disguise tradition inside out, since she is a rescuing Virtue not a Vice' (p. 99). From this it may be inferred that virtue must be disguised in some historical contexts (committed to a formalist approach, Brown does not explore the historical implications of her arguments in detail). Brown also provides a confessedly schematic run-through of the major tragedies, mapping a particular cardinal sin onto each. Subsequently, in a chapter on the illusionist stage, Brown makes the significant point that the development of a perspectivist stage during the seventeenth century had more to do with the installation of 'realism' as the governing dramatic mode than the sophistication of Shakespeare's powers of characterization. For, with a perspectival arrangement, 'stage actions "begin necessarily to take on the quality of empirical data"' (p. 17; quoting Stephen Orgel's *The Complete Masques of Ben Jonson*, p. 28). Moreover, the fact that the perspectival stage was first used for emphatically allegorical masques offers impressive support for Brown's case that allegory is the engine of mimetic development.

Power and Imagination: Studies in Politics and Literature by Leonidas Donskis has its peculiarities. It lacks an outline of structure (the general editor of the New Studies in Aesthetics series to which the book belongs feels obliged to provide a schematic outline in a foreword). In addition, the declared thesis—literature often says as much, if not more, about forms of power and authority than do works of political philosophy—is one which probably few readers would care to contest. At the same time, statements are made in the course of chapter 1 which lack adequate support, and so might themselves function better as thesis statements. For example, on pages

2–3 Donskis says: 'If we consider love and friendship to be the primary forms and expressions of a modern society … then we will have to acknowledge that Shakespeare reveals the birth of the modern person.' That seems a big 'if' and Donskis has not shown that 'love and friendship' were not well represented in earlier literature. This quotation also provides an example of Donskis's apparently bullying tone ('we will have to'). The reason I start with all this negativity, though, is to get it out of the way, for by the end of the book I was convinced of the profundity of Donskis's arguments. Thus, I feel inclined to attribute the organizational and stylistic problems to cultural differences and limitations on Donskis's management of tone in English (he is Lithuanian). It is only fair, though, to warn the prospective reader that Donskis's book is not an easy one for the academic to use, accustomed as we are to be led by the hand through complex arguments. Donskis begins by pointing out that Machiavelli's comedy *Mandragola* (written in 1518) does basically the same political work as *The Prince*. Therefore it is clear that early modern literary works have a serious political dimension. After an excellent chapter on Vico, Donskis compares and contrasts the representation of love and friendship in *Don Quixote* and *Romeo and Juliet*. In *Romeo and Juliet*, in Donskis's view, 'a fundamental conflict takes places between the premodern and modern mentalities' (p. 51). Basically, the play represents the dawning of the modern age when people will choose their own loves and friends, thus rejecting tribal obligations which result in blood-feuds and maintain the traditional hierarchy. *Don Quixote*, likewise, takes place against a seismic shift in cultures—from the feudal to the modern. Thus it is all the more telling that, whereas Shakespeare seems able to imagine mutually satisfying friendships as existing only between social equals, Don Quixote and Sancho Panza develop a profound friendship by the end of Cervantes' novel. Donskis also compares Don Quixote to Prince Hamlet, finding that both characters belong to 'a transitional period in which the values and ideas of a previous age had stopped operating, but in which [reliable] new ones … had yet to appear' (p. 46). The chapter then concludes with an apparent about-turn, endorsing Louis Dumont's positive valorization of hierarchy. According to Dumont, hierarchy 'is precisely what allows the creation of bonds between people, because any social whole is prior to a disconnected individual who is a typical modern invention' (p. 67). Of course, it is not an about-turn at all. Rather, Donskis here completes the dialectical framework behind the statement from the book's opening which I had (wrongly) read as coercive (rather than as contingent on the argument that was to follow).

In *Shakespeare Films in the Making: Vision, Production and Reception*, Russell Jackson focuses on the complexities of film-making processes, with regard to three distinct kinds of Shakespearian film. Chapter 1 provides an exhaustively researched account of the Warner Brothers studio's attempt to acquire cultural prestige by making *A Midsummer Night's Dream* [1935] with director Max Reinhardt. The second chapter sites Olivier's *Henry V* [1944] firmly in its wartime milieu, examining Anglo-American behind-the-scenes politics. Jackson also supplies detailed analyses of other wartime films in order further to contextualize Olivier's labours. In addition, Jackson demonstrates how Olivier's use of elaborate framing devices exploited the metatheatricality of Shakespeare's play. This approach enabled Olivier to 'side-step the debates of the 1930s about the compatibility of Shakespearean drama and the cinema' (p. 71). As a result of Olivier's manoeuvre, Jackson suggests, the viewer's imagination deals with the unrealities of film in a manner analogous to (but also quite different from) the way in which the Globe audiences' imaginations pieced out the bare stage. The final chapter investigates representations of Renaissance Italy in three film versions of *Romeo and Juliet*.

Shakespeare Now is a series of 'minigraphs', i.e. short works attempting to bridge the gap between general readers and specialized studies. Three volumes from the series are up for consideration. Eric S. Malin's *Godless Shakespeare* argues that Shakespeare explores and endorses an atheistic viewpoint in his works. Malin opens with the assertion that Shakespeare's 'faith or spiritual inclinations cannot be predicted or bound by the religious habits of thought endemic to much of his culture' (p. 3). The potential hazards of such a disregard for cultural context, however, are evidenced by a lack of subtlety in Malin's readings. Discussing the speech in *Romeo and Juliet* where Juliet asks 'gentle night' to cut Romeo into pieces and make stars of him to inspire worship, for example, Malin feels it is surprising that 'for a girl with a good religious education' her lines 'have nothing of Christianity about them'. This is well observed, but Malin then claims that Juliet thus 'takes surprisingly little account of divinity', her speech being 'innocently pagan' (p. 8). Yet a pagan speech *does* take account of divinity: it projects it upon or finds it immanent in nature. Another distracting feature of the book is Malin's habit of referring to 'believers' as 'unthinking' (p. 23). This attitude posits 'believer' and 'non-believer' as fixed categories in a way that ignores the function of doubt in early modern religious thought.

Philip Davis's *Shakespeare Thinking* represents a more positive expression of the series' aims. If we have lost the way of thinking common to Shakespeare's period, Davis argues, then there is 'a license for help wherever we can get it, in the alternative and less orthodox histories of human thinking' (p. 2). The first of the book's three sections is a historical survey of process-based ways of thinking, using Hazlitt. Carlyle, Montaigne, Goethe and Pico de Mirandola as reference points. In the middle chapter Davis offers readings of particular Shakespearian passages, suggesting that they show Shakespeare's unorthodox habits of thought in action, where any grammatical part of speech may be called upon to perform the function of a different one (such as prepositions taking the place of verbs). One weakness here is that the author never explains why he is using Shakespeare to illustrate his case, and not, say, Marlowe or anyone else. In chapter 3, Davis discusses Edwin A. Abbot's work, especially his *Shakespearean Grammar*, noting Abbot's argument that the loss of inflectional endings in the Middle Ages liberated and empowered Shakespeare. Abbot claimed that, though no longer represented, the converting power of inflection was retained in early modern English. This all fits with Davis's invigorating notion of a non-human 'it' as a conspicuous presence in Shakespeare's works: a '3rd thing'—the space between characters and words. By way of conclusion, Davis describes an ongoing project at the University of Liverpool. The brains of willing students are monitored as they are read items of language. Davis admits that there is little point reading passages of Shakespeare to these subjects yet, but the observers are trying to analyse what happens in the brain when it is offered, for example, a noun being used as a verb. Commendably, Davis is out to champion the positive aspects of what other observers might consider to be anomalous thinking, with Shakespeare as his major ca[n]non. He even argues that, by revealing the extent of literature's capacity to act upon the brain, his team at Liverpool could help to put literary criticism back 'at the forefront of human critical thinking' (p. 91).

A third volume in this series, *Shakespeare's Double Helix*, by Henry S. Turner, presents two essays: one, focusing on hybrid forms in *A Midsummer Night's Dream*, occupies the book's left-hand pages; the other essay, on the right-hand pages, argues that modern science is a new form of radical mimesis, and thus the rightful humanistic heir to early modern poetry. In the left-hand essay, Turner suggests that theatres replaced monasteries as machines for fabricating truths, prior to the construction of the first scientific laboratories. He also suggests that early modern anti-theatricalists feared that theatres were constructing 'a monstrous man-woman' (p. 10). These are juicy statements and invite further development. Turner's close reading of Shakespearian passages is sometimes less impressive, though. For example, he offers a stretched reading of Titania's speech on eco-breakdown, arguing that the described natural disasters lack a stated cause—this despite the fact that Titania identifies the cause of the bad weather as her ongoing debate with Oberon. Also, Turner sometimes gets carried away using scientific jargon; for instance, Helena is described as a cyborg because her heart is 'true as steel' (p. 96). A more focused use of a scientific concept occurs when Turner suggests that metaphors are akin to genetic modification (a topic Shakespeare, with his interest in the science of grafting, would probably have been intrigued by). Another quibble is that Turner equates Shakespeare's anti-poetic Theseus with church and state as a totality. A probable motive for this reductive attitude becomes apparent in the closing remarks of the left-hand essay, 'Theseus occupies the White House' (p. 108). There is a danger that modern arguments are being too casually mapped onto early modern culture here. The book's right-hand essay, however, makes a very strong case for modern science as a form of radical mimesis, continuing thereby the early modern humanist project. Turner argues this case eloquently, yet it remains doubtful whether the rank and file of scientists *really* view what they do in such a manner. The amusing example he gives of science creating by naming in fact works against his argument. Scientists, he reveals, have labelled two new fibroblast growth factor genes in *Drosophilia*, the common fruit fly, 'Pyramus' and 'Thisbe' because they govern the development of cardiac tissue (p. 21). I take the point that poetry and science have here interacted, but surely the poetic language is being used descriptively. The genes were causing heart failure before they were named. More seriously, Turner fails to mention that in the modern corporate science world, new names get patented and make their authors a lot of money. To claim, therefore, that scientific acts of description are really acts of creation may easily be put to service in the corporate science world. Indeed, one wonders if Shakespeare is not being recruited as a potential PR man here. Turner's book also has a tendency to contradict itself in rather queasy territory. For example, Turner stresses at one point that the human species should not 'retain a monopoly on ... dignity' (p. 103). Just a few pages earlier, however, he had waxed lyrical regarding the modern genetic experiments being conducted on laboratory animals, such as the growing of human ears 'on the backs of mice for use in plastic surgery' (p. 99). Admittedly, Turner seems aware of this contradiction, seeing the need for the category 'human' as merely 'contingent' (p. 101). Despite my qualms in this area, I was fully convinced of the importance of the issues Turner raises. Thus, I would emphasize that this book certainly fulfils the stated aims of the series, engaging one's interest in perhaps unfamiliar spheres of specialist research. It should also be noted that the book concludes with a highly readable and wide-ranging bibliographical mini-essay.

In the following section, which discusses journal articles, I have generally omitted pieces offering readings of a single text. Rather, I summarize articles seeming to contain broader implications for the current understanding of Shakespeare's works.

In 'Finding *Cardenio*' (*ELH* 74[2007] 957–87), Howard Marchitello compares the cultural function of the lost Shakespeare and Fletcher play *Cardenio* to that of a funeral monument, i.e. a structure which fails to contain its nominal occupant. In short, the *Cardenio* concept is an occasionally manifesting ghost haunting the official canon, in that the play represented by that title continues to be lost only to be found again. Accordingly, Marchitello contends that Theobald's *Double Falsehood* (published 1728) was indeed based, as its editor/adaptor claimed, on Shakespeare-authored manuscripts of *Cardenio*. Pursuing links between textual and familial legitimacy, the article also finds in *Hamlet* expressions of the prince's anxiety with regard to his begetting. According to this reading, Hamlet is Claudius's bastard. Since *Double Falsehood* is often viewed as an illegitimate copy of the lost *Cardenio*, and yet (at the time of writing) is about to appear as an Arden edition, Marchitello's essay can be said to achieve its ambitious aim of demonstrating that the story of *Cardenio*-as-textual-ghost is intimately linked to the story of Shakespeare-as-author.

Also concerned with canon-formation is Stephen Orgel's 'The Desire and Pursuit of the Whole' (*SQ* 58[2007] 290–310). Orgel diagnoses the modern obsession with completeness with regard to Shakespeare's canon, in the case of both individual works and collected editions. Arguing against the excessive desire for integral artefacts, Orgel points out that the pains taken by Shakespeare's texts to declare their state of incompletion are at least equal to those taken by modern editors to 'repair' perceived omissions. The article maintains that the drive for completion has manifested itself differently at different times. Thus, Magna Carta scenes were sometimes added to *King John* in the nineteenth century because, according to history, they really *should* be there. This is certainly a healthy reminder that modern editors are probably engaged in analogous distortions when they emend Shakespeare's text in line with what they suppose should be present. Orgel also recalls Garrick's wearing of a pneumatic wig as Prince Hamlet so that his hair could stand on end upon seeing the ghost. Orgel claims that this is a symptom of the desire to expand on the text to imply a fuller psychological life for the characters. Here the argument threatens to become a little dogmatic, for surely all playscripts are recipes for 'fuller' performances, always with the proviso that each performance is not an attempt at completion but the enactment of one version in an endless series of possible interpretations. Pursuit of difference is not the same as pursuit of the whole. That said, Orgel's main argument is sound: completion is a self-defeating goal, the pursuit of which may obscure our view of the material texts as we have them.

In 'Canonizing Shakespeare: *The Passionate Pilgrim, England's Helicon* and the Question of Authenticity' (*ShS* 60[2007] 252–67), James P. Bednarz reprises arguments in defence of William Jaggard, the publisher of *The Passionate Pilgrim* [1599]. However, Bednarz differs from previous defenders of Jaggard, such as Joseph Loewenstein, who suggested that the name 'Shakespeare' functioned as a generic marker for high-quality poetry and that Jaggard was, therefore, only describing his product (*Pilgrim*) in good faith, in claiming (falsely) it was all written by Shakespeare. Bednarz points out that no other writer's name was used in this fashion in the period. Nevertheless, the article then recounts how Nicholas Ling (assumed to be the main editor of *England's Helicon*) reprinted four of the poems from Jaggard's 1599 collection but either reattributed them or left them anonymous. What emerges from Bednarz's analysis is that, whatever Shakespeare felt about all this, the editors involved were striving to publicize a Shakespeare of their own. For example, the poem from *Love's Labour's Lost* which Jaggard had entitled 'On a day' appears in Ling's collection as 'The passionate Sheepheards Song'. Ling, moreover, appears to have replaced the word 'lover' in line 7 with 'Sheepheard' to 'fit the design of his pastoral collection'. Since Jaggard ended up as one of the principal publishers of the First Folio, it is fair to assume that the contest among Shakespeare's contemporaries to eternize a particular version of the poet-playwright continued with the creation of that volume.

June Schlueter summarizes recent debates as to which Martin Droeshout out of the two likely candidates executed the Folio engraving of Shakespeare, in 'Martin Droeshout *Redivivus*: Reassessing the Folio Engraving of Shakespeare' (*ShS* 60[2007] 237–51). In 1991, Schlueter recalls, Mary Edmond put the case for the older candidate, who is known to have been a painter, while Christiaan Schuckman argued for the younger man. Admitting that she set out to argue on behalf of Edmond, Schlueter concludes by acknowledging that the evidence now suggests the younger Droeshout was indeed the engraver. Schuckman found ten further Droeshout engravings in Madrid, all signed, with four of them labelled as executed in Madrid. There may be an interesting lead here for Shakespeare scholars, with reference to continuing debates as to the mix of confessional allegiances among the people responsible for the publication of the First Folio: the younger Droeshout's earliest (extant) commission in Spain was the coat of arms of a major player in the Spanish Counter-Reformation, Gaspar de Guzmán. Other Spanish Droeshout engravings portray Catholic saints and Counter-Reformation iconography.

Alan D. Lewis, in 'Shakespearean Seductions, or, What's with Harold Bloom as Falstaff?' (*TSLL* 49:ii[2007] 125–54) is bothered by Bloom's agonistic Shakespeare. Bloom, Lewis observes, has argued that alone among authors Shakespeare is untroubled by the anxiety of influence. The Stratford man may have seen Marlowe as a threat but dealt with that by creating Falstaff (who, implausibly, Bloom sees as a version of Marlowe) and then killing him off. One problem with Bloom's approach is that it appears to be 'underwritten by a distinctly Freudian notion of an anxious, melancholic masculinity beset with lack', according to which the mother (or the female) is denied a role in artistic creation (p. 128). Thus, Lewis concludes that Bloom wants a Shakespeare who is 'a self-sending god—free of emasculating literary influence' (p. 138). For his part, Lewis prefers Oscar Wilde's notion of Shakespeare's art as seduction not agon. In fairness to his target, however, Lewis acknowledges that, in *The Anxiety of Influence*, Bloom allows that Shakespeare clearly had extra-poetic influences.

Brian Vickers's article 'Coauthors and Closed Minds' (*ShakS* 36[2008] 101–13) opens with much polemical positioning before settling down to make its point that, while the single-author paradigm is appropriate for classical authors (despite Foucault's claim it is a bourgeois invention) and, not coincidentally, for classicist writers such as Spenser, Milton and Fielding, it does not work for drama written in London between 1579 and 1642. Vickers, here as elsewhere, makes excellent cases for *1 Henry VI*, *Titus Andronicus* and *Pericles* having been extensively co-written. However, one wonders if the majority of scholars really question these findings. Furthermore, there is a big gap between arguing the case for the three plays mentioned, and declaring that all of Shakespeare's plays are typical of Vickers's totalizing model. As said, though, where Vickers argues for specific plays, he makes a very persuasive case. For his thorough analysis of *1 Henry VI* in this regard, see 'Incomplete Shakespeare: Or, Denying Coauthorship in *1 Henry VI*' (*SQ* 58[2007] 311–52).

In 'A Partial Theory of Original Practice' (*ShS* 61[2008] 302–17) Jeremy Lopez discusses issues arising from the growth of the original practices movement over the past twenty years or so. Unusually, he draws upon related websites' promotional material as the best available documents of original practice in action, justifying this by pointing out that critics friendly to original practice tend to be divorced from the activity itself. After noting the (understandable) optimism of the promotional material, he goes on to observe that original practice, on closer scrutiny, turns out not to be about finding out (and repeating) how it was done back then. What is being offered, he infers from the promotional material, is the promise of infinite scholarship, for new historicist scepticism about the possibility of recovering the past is to be imported into theatrical production. More generally, Lopez is concerned that the material reality of theatre itself is being neglected by new historicism, hidden beneath the latter's stylistic elegance: body-text is being turned into literature. Thus, the message of the cited promotional material dismays him in that it suggests the original practices movement is not primarily committed to emphasizing theatre's material reality.

In 'Terms of "Indearment": Lyric and General Economy in Shakespeare and Donne' (*ELH* 75[2008] 241–62), Barbara Connell resists the usual tendency to conflate the term 'economy' with 'restrictive economy', using

Bataille's work on 'general economy', which accommodates the notion of 'unproductive or sacrificial expenditure', as found in gift-giving cultures (p. 241). Bataille saw the break between feudalism and the bourgeois period as related to the decline of the archaic gift economy. However, where Bataille used modernist poetic works as signifiers of general economy, Connell here discusses early modern amatory lyrics: Shakespeare's Sonnet 31 ('Thy bosom is indeared with all hearts') and Donne's Elegy 10 ('Image of her whom I love more than she'). According to Connell, both Shakespeare and Donne use and transform Petrarchan cultural capital; both authors play with discourse in a way that may be read (following Adorno) as resisting the restrictive economy of sonnet conventions. Donne, however, seems more concerned than Shakespeare to resolve conflict and contain uncertainty. Donne's poetry, therefore, is markedly committed to restrictive economy, being obsessed with gauging losses and gains. By contrast, Shakespeare seems more prodigal in his expenditure. Connell includes discussion of *King Lear* in this regard, citing Richard Halpern's argument that the tragedy is concerned with the historical transition from 'Do you love me?' to 'How much?' The play, moreover, throws feudalism over the precipice (squandering it, in effect), in order to reassemble it in a tragic guise.

In 'From Revels to Revelation: Shakespeare and the Mask' (*ShS* 60[2007] 58–71) Janette Dillon protests critical neglect of the Tudor mask. (For the less spectacular Tudor version of this cultural phenomenon, Dillon rejects the 'masque' spelling as a misguided attempt to dignify what has tended to be perceived as a childish entertainment.) Dillon also points out the overlooked importance of Hall as a historical source (albeit often via Holinshed) for our knowledge of early Tudor masking. Scholarly attitudes to the mask of course impinge on Shakespeare studies, given the dramatist's evident commitment to the mask as an enabling device. Dillon discusses relevant aspects of Elizabethan Shakespeare plays: *Richard III*, *The Merchant of Venice*, *Titus Andronicus*, *Love's Labour's Lost*, *The Merry Wives of Windsor*, *Much Ado About Nothing* and *As You Like It*. She then turns to Jacobean works: *Timon of Athens*, *The Winter's Tale* and *Henry VIII*. This division allows for nuanced comparisons to be made between the cultural milieus of the two regimes. With regard to *As You Like It*, Dillon points out, however, that 'the very fact that *As You Like It* . . . already contains the germ of the later, spectacular form indicates that there can be no absolute separation between "mask" and [Stuart] "masque" ' (p. 66).

In 'Protesting Too Much in Shakespeare and Elsewhere, and the Invention/ Construction of the Mind' (*ELR* 37:iii[2007] 337–59), Richard Levin looks at characters from Shakespeare's plays (and the works of other dramatists) who seem to protest too much, thus indicating their hypocrisy. Such representations may be read as satirical attacks upon puritanical two-facedness. However, Levin interrogates this at first glance straightforward verdict. Is puritanical Malvolio (one of the over-protesters) actually insincere? Does he not just protest too much for other characters' and, presumably, the audience's taste? Likewise, though Angelo in *Measure for Measure* seems to fit the bill of hypocritical Puritan, Levin notes that he is shown to be surprised by his alteration. Similarly, Romeo and Orsino are portrayed as immature

Petrarchans, but are not depicted as insincere. It turns out that the overwhelming majority of the over-protesters are in earnest. Why, then, do we tend to suspect their honesty? Levin suggests that over-protesting seems insincere because it is usually done for an audience, or by characters seeking to convince themselves while denying natural impulses. The latter aspect indicates a certain amount of divided self-consciousness. Hence, Levin considers whether this representation in Shakespeare's plays of people discovering that they have been fooling themselves does not indicate that, just like us, early modern people had a sense of continuous selfhood. Yet Greenblatt claims, says Levin, that this was unthinkable in the sixteenth century, while Dollimore says it came with the Enlightenment. However, Levin observes, these scholars provide no real evidence. Nonetheless, the *content* of one's over-protesting does derive from the cultural environment. The essay has not finished yet. In order to test Freud's theory of the unconscious, Levin next ponders whether early modern gynophobia might not be equivalent to modern homophobia. That is, where, according to Freudianism, homophobes reveal unconscious anxieties about their own homoerotic impulses, over-protesting early modern gynophobes may likewise really be anxious about their desire for women. Levin declares, however, that he can find no evidence in early modern texts that this is the case (he invites scholars to provide him with possible examples). Given this, Levin concludes that the Freudian unconscious does not really exist, but is rather a 'story we tell ourselves'.

In 'Rereading Shakespeare: The Example of Richard Braithwait' (*ShS* 60[2007] 268–83) Richard Abrams pays close attention to the First Folio preface by Heminge and Condell. The latter authors' reference to 'Friends, whom...can bee [readers'] guides if necessary' implies, argues Abrams, that 'Shakespeare's first editors imagined a community of readers helping each other to understand' the Bard's works, something akin, that is, to a Bible-reading group (p. 268). Evidence of Stuart-era Shakespeare reading groups is thin on the ground, so Abrams turns to the writings of the poet Richard Braithwait for inferential support. After a detailed description of his use of Literature Online (LION) to police his allusion-hunting, Abrams embarks on a compelling analysis of Shakespearian allusions in Braithwait's works. For example, Braithwait sets out to 'redeem' Pyramus and Thisbe in 'Loves Labyrinth' [1615], his declared subject being 'The disastrous fals of two star-crost | Louers' (p. 272). Also of interest is the fact that, when Braithwait's first wife died, the poet evidently found the funeral rites inadequate, for he resolved to dedicate annual poems of commemoration to his deceased spouse. In these poems, Braithwait alludes to Shakespeare's *Hamlet*, the question of sincere mourning being of obvious relevance. As Abrams observes, it is significant that Braithwait chose to allude to a secular work in such a context. In addition, Abrams quotes Braithwait on the value of post-reading discussion with good friends (such activity can soothe a 'distemperd' mind). Where the Folio editors quite fit with regard to Braithwait's activities as Shakespeare-reader, however, is left largely to our surmise (if they knew 'Loves Labyrinth', comments Abrams, 'they may well have read the poem as a gloss on *Romeo and Juliet*', p. 277).

(b) Problem Plays

The majority of scholarship produced on the problem plays this year is to be found in a series of edited collections on a range of subjects, including Renaissance justice, Shakespearian performance studies and European politics, and it is *Measure for Measure* and *All's Well* which continue to dominate the critical discussion. In the first of these collections *Justice, Women, and Power in English Renaissance Drama*, Andrew Majeske and Emily Detmer-Goebel provide a useful introductory essay which surveys the development of the interdisciplinary approach to law and literature over the past twenty years (pp. 11–26), while the collection itself contains essays on plays by Shakespeare and his contemporaries including *Arden of Faversham* and the tragedies of John Webster. The first of two essays on *Measure for Measure*, 'Shakespeare's Bed-Tricks: Finding Justice in Lies?' (in Majeske and Detmer-Goebel, eds., pp. 118–39), Detmer-Goebel argues that while the bed-tricks appear to offer solutions to the difficulties facing characters such as Helena, Mariana and Isabella, the plays ultimately tap into cultural anxieties about women and their perceived propensity for lying about sex. By contrast David Evett offers a less sceptical reading of the marriages depicted at the end of Measure in ' "What is yours is mine": Sexual and Social Complementarity in the Trial Scenes of *Measure for Measure*' (pp. 140–52) as he considers the ways in which marriage and the domestic household offered a model for the running and organization of the state. *Measure*, Evett argues, is unusual amongst Shakespeare's plays as it lacks the usual domestic households or relationships and so must build them from scratch. The marriages at the end of the play therefore serve to provide the building blocks to establish Viennese society and the couples themselves provide a model of complementarity, with male and female characters bringing qualities to their union which make it a complete unit.

Familial relationships in the final scene of *Measure* are also the focus for Corinne S. Abate's essay, 'Missing the Moment in *Measure for Measure*' (in Occhiogrosso, ed., pp. 19–39), which seeks to challenge the critical emphasis placed upon the Duke's proposal to Isabella and his role as stage manager in V.i by redirecting our attention to Isabella's relationship with her brother Claudio and their reunion at the close of the play. *Shakespeare and European Politics* contains two essays on *Measure for Measure* and, like *Justice, Women, and Power in English Renaissance Drama*, also provides a stimulating introductory chapter which considers 'European Shakespeare' as a research area in its own right. The first essay, by Roderick J. Lyall, ' "Here in Vienna": The Setting of *Measure for Measure* and the Political Semiology of Shakespeare's Europe' (in Delabastita, de Vos and Franssen, eds., *Shakespeare and European Politics*, pp. 74–89) responds to work by Gary Taylor and John Jowett in the early 1990s, who argued that Shakespeare originally set his play in the Italian city of Ferrara and that Thomas Middleton substituted Vienna for Ferrara in 1621 when he revised the play. Lyall challenges the view that the play's initial setting was Ferrara rather than Vienna and goes on to consider the political and religious significance of the Austrian city in the late 1590s and early 1600s. In an essay from the second section of the collection, which examines twentieth-century performances of Shakespeare's plays in a European context, Veronika Schandl's essay, 'Measuring the "Most Cheerful Barrack": Shakespeare's *Measure for Measure* in Hungary under the Kádár Regime (1964–85)' (pp. 158–68), offers an important overview of landmark productions of the play, particularly in the wake of the failed revolution in 1956. Schandl traces the ways in which different directors sought to utilize the play's darker, more troubling aspects as the means of reflecting contemporary political anxieties in Hungary. The final essay from an edited collection is the jointly authored essay by Gale H. Carrithers Jr and James D. Hardy Jr, 'Rex Absconditus: Justice Presence and Legitimacy in *Measure for Measure*' (in Shami, ed., *Renaissance Tropologies: The Cultural Imagination of Early Modern England*, pp. 23–41). This collection was inspired by the monograph *Age of Iron: English Renaissance Troplogies of Love and Power* by Carrithers and Hardy, in which they identify and discuss Renaissance literature in the light of the following tropes: 'Journey', 'Theatre', 'Moment' and 'Ambassadorship'. The essay on *Measure* draws on the tropes of 'Moment' and 'Theatre' and examines the Duke's exercise of power in the context of royal coronation and public displays of royal power. The essay suggests that ultimately the Duke's role in the play is a benign one and that the marriages arranged in the final scene of the play offer a just and optimistic conclusion.

Another performance criticism essay on *Measure* comes from Pascale Aebischer, 'Silence, Rape and Politics in *Measure for Measure*: Closer Readings in Performance History' (*ShakB* 26:iv[2008] 1–23), who considers the handling of the silences in the play, particularly the silence of Isabella in recent productions, using the archival material of the RSC at the Shakespeare Birthplace Trust. Aebischer looks at six productions between 1970 and 1998 and, like Veronika Schandl's essay on the production of the play in twentieth-century Hungary, suggests ways in which each production encodes contemporary cultural and political concerns in Britain during this period. The 1987 production directed by Nicholas Hytner clearly engages with the sexual politics of that decade 'at the height of Thatcherism, the conclusion of the play pointed even less ambiguously towards recognition of the link between state repression and the challenge to sexual integrity. Isabella's right to her body and her chastity, within a society coming to terms with the implications of AIDS for the sexual revolution, was never in doubt' (p. 9). The plague of 1603–4 provides the context for Catherine I. Cox's essay, ' "Lord have mercy upon us": The King, the Pestilence, and Shakespeare's *Measure for Measure*' (*Exemplaria* 20[2008] 430–57). The essay explores the association between disease and civic excess and degeneracy beginning with Shakespeare's source, Boccaccio's *Decameron*, before moving on to Shakespeare's other plays, such as the histories, *Romeo and Juliet* and *Measure for Measure*. In '*Measure for Measure* and the (Anti-)Theatricality of Gascoigne's *The Glasse of Government*', Richard Hillman develops the work of Charles T. Prouty, who argued that Gascoigne's morality play, based on the story of the Prodigal Son, had been an influence on Shakespeare's play. Hillman goes on to consider the triangulated relationship between Gascoigne's play, George Whetstone's

Promos and Cassandra and Shakespeare's *Measure for Measure* (*Comp D* 42[2008] 391–408).

As publications in 2008 on *All's Well That Ends Well* were scarce, this year's survey will consider an edited collection overlooked in last year's entry, published by Routledge in the New Critical Essays series. The play, as Gary Waller points out in his detailed yet incisive introduction, is one of the least popular of Shakespeare's plays, is rarely performed and tends to prompt strong reactions from readers. Waller provides a clear overview of the play's critical and performance history in a chapter which is usefully divided by subheadings including: 'Genre: *All's Well* as a Problem Play', Old and New Historicisms', 'Fistulas, Receipts and the Learned Woman' and 'Shakespeare's Critique of Masculinity'. In the first essay of the collection, which begins by focusing on the sources of the play, Steven Mentz considers the value of 'source study' in his essay 'Revising the Sources: Novella, Romance, and the Meanings of Fiction in *All's Well, That Ends Well*' (pp. 57–70), and argues that the two narrative forms which influence the play, the Italian novella and the romance, help to account for the characterization of Helena as witty Doctor She and the passive Patient Grissel. Mentz concludes that 'The double source underwrites *All's Well*'s fundamental division: the play is both comedy of wit and romance of suffering' (p. 58). Regina Buccola also considers Boccaccio's *Decameron* the source for *All's Well* in '"As sweet as sharp": Helena and the Fairy Bride Tradition' (pp. 71–84), as she reflects on observations made by Robert S. Miola on the parallels between *All's Well* and *The Merry Wives of Windsor*. Both plays, according to Miola, blend elements of romance, comedy and folk tale and examine themes of transformation. Buccola builds on Miola's observations and locates her discussion of the play in the context of the fairy lore and the folk tales available to a contemporary audience which involved the intervention of the Fairy Queen in human relationships. Paul Gleed takes issue with the reputation of *All's Well* in the light of the more traditional ideas about festive comedy developed in the 1960s in 'Tying the (K)not: The Marriage of Tragedy and Comedy in *All's Well That Ends Well*' (pp. 85–97). Gleed resituates the play in the context of the festivals of ancient Greece, the Pharmakos and the Eiresione, to argue that the play captures the essence of Greek comedy through its blending of pleasure and suffering, life and death (p. 87).

In a fascinating essay '*All's Well That Ends Well* and the Art of Retrograde Motion' (in Waller, ed., pp. 98–110), Deanne Williams begins with a close reading of the exchanges between Helena and Parolles in Act I, scene i, when Helena suggests that Parolles was born under the sign of Mars when it was in retrograde. The planet in this aspect was associated with introspection, depression, irrationality and retrospectivity. Williams uses this discussion of planetary motion to argue that it provides insights into the character of Parolles as well as the relationship between Helena and Bertram. Kent R. Lehnhof provides another context for Helena's role as Doctor She as she examines the role of women in the medicine shows of Italian and English mountebanks in 'Performing Woman: Female Theatricality in *All's Well That Ends Well*' (pp. 111–24). Lehnhof illustrates the parallels between the routines of the mountebank and the staged comedy in the public theatre, making the point that the Italian word for medicines was also the same word used for street actor, thus blurring the distinction between the two professions. The focus of Ellen Belton's essay, ' "To make the 'not' eternal": Female Eloquence and Patriarchal Authority in *All's Well That Ends Well*' (pp. 125–39), is Helena's verbal dexterity and she argues that Helena's eloquence establishes her authority in the play as it surpasses that of the male characters.

Helen Wilcox offers another generic label for *All's Well* in her essay 'Shakespeare's Miracle Play? Religion in *All's Well That Ends Well*' (pp. 140–54), where she argues that her choice of label is used 'not to imply a reliance upon medieval dramatic traditions, but rather to assert that devotion, faith and redemption are among its chief concerns' (p. 140). Michele Osherow continues the religious theme by locating the play in the context of Old Testament stories found in the book of Proverbs concerning biblical heroines known as women of valour, in 'She Is in the Right: Biblical Maternity and *All's Well That Ends Well*' (pp. 155–68). Osherow establishes parallels between Helena's story and those of these biblical women, and insists that 'the complexities surrounding Helena establish her as part of a biblical tradition of women who, in the name of motherhood, risk modesty and honesty to achieve their goals' (p. 155).

David Bergeron shifts the focus to the absent fathers in the play and argues that *All's Well* is full of dead, ageing and inadequate fathers in ' "The credit of your father": Absent Fathers in *All's Well That Ends Well*' (pp. 169–82). Here Bergeron considers Shakespeare's handling of this theme in other comparable plays such as *Hamlet* to argue that both Helena and Bertram are coming to terms with the loss of their fathers. The erotic potential of the rings which circulate in the play is the subject of Nicholas Ray's essay, ' "Twas mine, 'twas Helen's": Rings of Desire in *All's Well That Ends Well*' (pp. 183–92), while Catherine Field, in ' "Sweet practicer, thy physic I will try": Helena and her "Good Receipt" in *All's Well That Ends Well*' (pp. 194–208), continues the focus upon the medical, but situates her discussion of the play in the context of medical cures and the female housewife as medical practitioner to consider Helena's part in the curing the king. The play's interest in medicine and the body reflects a wider concern with 'the empiric in a world increasingly less magical and less religious and where bodies of kings and upstarts are subject to the cold eye and hand of "how to" science recorded in the form of the receipt' (p. 201).

Terry Reilly's contribution turns attention from the medical to the legal profession as he considers the legal status of wards and their guardians and argues that, like *Cymbeline*, *All's Well* is concerned with the relationship between the two. The precise context is the debate surrounding the abolition of the Court of Wards and Liveries in 1604, and Reilly provides fascinating case studies of those members of the nobility who were wards themselves, including the earl of Southampton and Robert Devereux, the second earl of Essex. The influence of new historicism on Shakespeare criticism is examined in Craig Dionne's essay, 'Parolles and Shakespeare's Knee-Crooking Knaves' (pp. 221–33), as he examines the theme of self-fashioning in *All's Well* and how 'Shakespeare uses the courtly rogue as a vehicle to parody the radically ersatz, or depthless depthless quality of the genuinely scripted self' (p. 224).

Finally, Bob White discusses Elijah Moshinsky's production of *All's Well* for the BBC. One of the valuable features of this collection is the inclusion of stills from recent productions of the play by Purchase Repertory, Ark Theatre Company and Washington University to illustrate a number of the essays. Unfortunately this final piece lacked any additional visual material, which would have been helpful to its discussion of the director's interest in 'pictorial art' (p. 236).

(c) Poetry

Of the publications on Shakespeare's poems that appeared this year by far the majority were on the sonnets. In an article entitled 'Will Will's Will Be Fulfilled? Shakespeare's Sonnet 135' (*Expl* 66:ii[2008] 66–8), Erica L. Zilleruelo asks if the speaker of the poem 'has the same success with [spoken] language' as the writer does with the written word (p. 68). Zilleruelo explores 'the poet's eloquence' in the 'intertwining of four possible interpretations of "will"', but also notes the speaker's inability to achieve *his* goal, to 'have' the poem's addressee, the infamous Dark Lady of Shakespeare's sequence. This 'juxtaposition' of poetic success and sexual failure 'creates an interesting quandary for readers, who must reconcile the ironic discrepancy Shakespeare creates' (pp. 67–8).

Similarly admiring of the poet's skill, Regula Hohl Trillini's article, 'The Gaze of the Listener: Shakespeare's Sonnet 128 and Early Modern Discourses of Music and Gender' (*M&L* 89:i[2008] 1–17), corrects the previous critical perception of cruxes and mixed metaphors as 'authorial oversights' (p. 17) in Shakespeare's Sonnet 128. In a particularly enlightening essay, Trillini examines the early modern ambivalence towards musical performers and performances, noting the acknowledgement by writers in the period of 'music's dual potential as a force for good and evil' and the 'gendered aspects' of this discourse, which has significant consequences for reading Sonnet 128 (pp. 2–3). Where earlier critics may have dismissed the poem's invocation of musical performance as (besides an extended erotic metaphor) a jokey allusion to the Dark Lady's ability as a performer, Trillini, employing a sound knowledge of the virginals, finds a series of 'fascinating transgressions' that go beyond the clumsy metaphorical language of lesser poets towards a literal sense of the 'hands-on' that has Shakespeare displaying a more intimate acquaintance with the instrument than he has been credited with previously (p. 10). Indeed, Trillini's reading finds the virginals an apt device for a poet who wishes to represent 'the role of confusion inherent in the situation of a female performer before a male listener. He is being seduced by her, but is also tempted to seduce her himself, while the woman is both dangerous and victimized, simultaneously man-eater and sweetmeat' (p. 12). This essay includes a reading of that other famous 'musical' sonnet, Sonnet 8, in which the consequences of Trillini's work for reading the 'Young Man' sonnets are made apparent: in Sonnet 8, unlike the 'conflicted and thrilling eroticism' of Sonnet 128, an 'almost cloying harmony is established' as another male listener takes the place of the female performer (p. 13).

Turning from musical to legal matters, Paul Hammond, in a note on Sonnet 46, 'A Textual Crux in Shakespeare's Sonnet 46' (*N&Q* 55[2008] 187–8), makes a strong case for emending 'fide' to 'finde' in line 9. As part of the poem's legal conceit, a jury, a 'quest of thoughts' (l. 10), is asked to settle a dispute between the speaker's eye and heart over the ownership of the lover's image: they, the jury, are, it appears, in the only authority for the poem, asked 'to side this title'. Previously, 'fide' has either been read straightforwardly as 'side' (meaning 'to assign to one of two sides') or interpreted less persuasively as ''cide', meaning 'decide'. Hammond, noting that Sonnet 46 is the only example of the former meaning cited in the *OED* and that the compositors of *Shake-speares Sonnets* [1609] were wont to omit the letter 'n', judges 'finde' to be a more fitting choice for the legal context of the poem.

Barbara Everett's article in the *London Review of Books*, 'Shakespeare and the Elizabethan Sonnet' (*LRB* 30:ix[2008] 12–15), is much broader in scope, reading the sonnet sequence as a whole against the Elizabethan courtly fashion for sonnet-writing. Everett welcomes the uncertainty surrounding Shakespeare's authorship of *A Lover's Complaint* for the consequent doubt that this casts on what she terms the 'Elizabethanising' of the sonnets. This 'scholarly falling back on convention', which includes the case for the inseparability of the *Complaint* from the sonnets on the grounds of Elizabethan custom, prevents the full play of all the mysteries the poems contain; for Everett, a central theme of the sonnets 'is the defeat of the mere social moment and its transmutation into an eternal landscape' (p. 13). Compared to other Elizabethan sonneteers, such as Sidney, whose sonnets can be 'sterile' (p. 15), Shakespeare looks 'to move through and beyond the whole utilitarianism of the Tudor ethos, the concept of goodness as use, as profit, which unites the Elizabethan farmyard to the guild and the court: to find an innate metaphysic in human love itself' (p. 14).

Joshua Cohen's short article for the *Shakespeare Newsletter*, 'Ovid Inverted: Shakespeare's Sonnet 20 and the Metamorphoses of a Metamorphosis' (*ShN* 58:iii[2008] 93, 97) is interested in the conceit of Sonnet 20, which is characterized as a 'story in a line of female-to-male sex change scenarios stretching back to Ovid's tale of Iphis and Ianthe' (p. 93). For Cohen, Shakespeare and Ovid are alert to the mysteries of desire and identity: 'what we desire does not necessarily correspond with who we think we are'. In this provocative essay, Cohen extrapolates from the speaker's imagined transfor-mation of a female love-object into a male in Sonnet 20 to the sonnet sequence as a whole, such that 'the speaker/poet pursues...two desires: one, a sublimated, idealized, but sexually charged passion for the young man; and the other, a tempestuous physical relationship with a sensual and promiscuous woman' (p. 97).

Another article that addresses the whole sequence of sonnets is Georgia Brown's 'Time and the Nature of Sequence in Shakespeare's *Sonnets*: "In sequent toil all forwards do contend"' (in Maguire, ed., *How To Do Things with Shakespeare*, pp. 236–54). Inspired by a visit to the Landesmuseum in Zurich, where, among other artefacts, Renaissance clocks are exhibited, Brown's essay displays the ways in which 'the *Sonnets* do show Shakespeare thinking about the mechanisms of time' and goes some way to answering 'the question of why sonnet sequences...[became] such a resonant and popular form in the 1590s' (p. 237). For Brown, Shakespeare's poet/lover experiences time in a peculiarly postlapsarian way: he is hurried and subject to the pressure of inexorable change, unlike his prelapsarian counterparts, represented by Milton's Adam and Eve, who may 'Sleep on' (*Paradise Lost*, IV.773). His motto is, inevitably, *carpe diem* (pp. 237–8). Alighting on individual sonnets as she goes, Brown includes several insightful close readings. Sonnet 60 (the source of the essay's title) is notable for its allusions to both natural and 'artificial, or mechanical, ways of telling time', suggesting the 'parallels projected by geometry onto charts of the earth and the sky' via the deepening lines on a human face. In the same sonnet, the word 'nativity' (l. 5) 'invokes the zodiac' and the whole Ptolemaic system of astronomy (pp. 239–40). The sonnet sequence's (both Shakespeare's and those of others) preoccupation with time is conceived as a reaction to 'the real intrusion of time into people's private lives' (p. 247); the sixteenth century saw a rise in indoor timepieces as technology advanced and mechanical clocks grew smaller. Moreover, Brown notes a tension between the idea of a poetic sequence, which implies the linearity of narrative so often sought by critics, and the 'oscillation, and backwards and forwards motion', of actual sonnet sequences. Happily, this tension is resolved in the shape of those Renaissance clocks in which time, that conventionally 'continuous and unidirectional phenomenon', is marked by an oscillating regulator (p. 248).

Not unlike the clockwork sonnets in Georgia Brown's reading, Michael C. Clody's study of the 'Young Man' sonnets, 'Shakespeare's "Alien Pen": Self-Substantial Poetics in the Young Man Sonnets' (*Criticism* 50:iii[2008] 471–500), relies on the 'perpetual movement' of poetic mimesis. Drawing on the work of Philippe Lacoue-Labarthe (*Typography: Mimesis, Philosophy, Politics*, ed. Christopher Fynsk [1989]), William West ('Nothing as Given: Economies of the Gift in Derrida and Shakespeare', *CL* 48:i[1996] 1–18) and Susan Stewart ('Lyric Possession', *CritI* 22:i[1995] 34–63), Clody develops an elegant way of 'reading for general mimesis' in which one must 'listen to the *way* that language brings forth rather than the ideas it artistically represents' (p. 475). Clody characterizes his own method, quoting Stewart, as a consideration of 'the "many springs of a poem's generation" in the active mode in which language brings forth—its "perpetual movement of presentation"' (p. 476). This theoretical approach inherits something from each of the mimetic theories of Aristotle, Sidney (*The Defence of Poesy*) and Shakespeare's Polixenes ('that art | Which you say adds to Nature, is an art | That Nature makes': *Winter's Tale*, IV.iv.90–2). In beginning to read the Young Man sonnets, Clody focuses on the speaker's pleas to the addressee to encourage procreation, in which Shakespeare employs the language of economic growth. In the absence of real offspring, as Clody argues, the poems' metaphorical 'economy' is founded on a void, leading the critic to find 'the value of the poems' economy...in their perpetual fluctuations', 'as a model of [their] movement rather than a fund for its metaphors' (pp. 477–8). This is exemplified by lines such as, 'I must each day say o'er the very same' (l. 6), from Sonnet 108, in which the repetition of the addressee's 'fair name' (l. 8) 'incarnates the thin substance of love, ever fresh, and each...*insistence*...extends that substance into the future' (p. 478). Ultimately, the poems' absent core cannot realize a consummation; the young man declines 'from occasion to muse', and the poet becomes 'present-absent to himself during the act of conception'. It is this state of oscillation (so to speak) between presence and absence that defines literary subjectivity in this reading of poiesis (pp. 486–7); it is a reading that, in Clody's concluding words, 'gestures towards an immanent force of linguistic alterity that drives, but cannot be captured by, representation' (p. 495).

Páraic Finnerty's essay, 'Queer Appropriations: Shakespeare's Sonnets and Dickinson's Love Poems' (*BandL* 3:ii[2008] no pagination), discusses the afterlife of the sonnets, particularly their use by Emily Dickinson in her own poems as an 'authoritative and...controversial resource for her construction of love'. Finnerty offers 'an antidote to the intrusive and spurious biographical readings' of both poets' lyrics. Here, Dickinson and Shakespeare are shown to be poets similarly capable of treating 'the gender of the speaker or addressee...as an interchangeable alternative', thereby 'unsettling...the naturalness of the male or female position within the lover's discourse', but neither is seen, to paraphrase Robert Browning, to 'unlock his or her heart'. Using many of Shakespeare's tropes, Dickinson turns their metaphorical force to her own ends. In one of several readings that delineate the precise parallels and divergences between the two poets' poems, Finnerty compares the love triangle and 'the imagery of light and darkness' in Shakespeare's sonnets with Dickinson's 'That Malay—took the Pearl', in which a 'Pearl' is lost to a 'Swarthy fellow'. In both scenarios, the speakers feel their losses deeply because of a sense of their own unworthiness and lose out to rivals—Shakespeare's 'woman coloured ill' (Sonnet 144) and Dickinson's Malay—whose 'darkness' is repeatedly invoked. Moreover, in terms of sexuality, as Finnerty notes, Dickinson appears to be using Shakespeare's homoerotic discourse for the expression of lesbian love.

A notable book-length work on Shakespeare's sonnets is Robert Matz's *The World of Shakespeare's Sonnets: An Introduction*. It is divided into four sections, containing eight, seven, nine and seven short chapters (some shorter than three pages) respectively; a 'Coda' entitled 'Universal Shakespeare?' concludes the study. As Matz asserts in his preface, although this book, like other recent publications (Paul Edmondson and Stanley Wells, *Shakespeare's Sonnets* [2004] and Dympna Callaghan, *Shakespeare's Sonnets* [2007]), is an introduction, 'it offers a more particular argument'. In wishing to place the emphasis on 'the relationship between the sonnets and Renaissance culture' rather than the 'many riches that formal literary analysis' can reveal (which is not to say that there is a lack of strong literary analysis here), Matz certainly brings a freshness to this kind of publication (p. 3). Matz's particular method is perhaps most readily evident in the titles of some of the thirty-one chapters: 'Love, or Literary Credential?', 'But Did They Have Sex?', and 'Gynerasty'. The first two of these three examples illustrate one aspect of Matz's style: he asks (and answers) many questions in a direct and lucid manner. The third, while also indicating the same directness, is typical of the author's determination not to separate the sonnets from the social milieu of their time. In this case, he considers 'how Shakespeare portrays his black mistress through the lens of negative Renaissance stereotypes about women'. Such expositions invariably raise even more questions ('Does the magnificent fairness of Shakespeare's young man depend on locating anything that's black somewhere else—in the mistress?', for example), which Matz hardly ever fails to broach himself (p. 113). The later chapters of the book, included within the section headed 'So Long Lives This', which covers the afterlife of the sonnets, have some of the most enlightening content. The graphs and pie charts showing the varying degrees of anthologization of individual sonnets and groups of sonnets in the twentieth and twenty-first centuries are effectively utilized to tell a story of the ebbing and flowing of the significance of Matz's avowedly historicist approach to reading the sonnets (pp. 199–202). Perhaps, with the publication of this introduction, predominantly targeted at the sonnets' new readership, it could be said that 'history [has] come back' (p. 202).

Kathryn Schwarz's article, ' "Will in overplus": Recasting Misogyny in Shakespeare's Sonnets' (*ELH* 75[2008] 737–66), like Matz, engages with the 'conventions of a hegemonic misogyny' on which Shakespeare draws. Nevertheless, Schwarz, interested as much in literary subjectivity (see the discussion on Clody above) as in 'misogynist clichés', highlights the operation of the 'will' ('the agent that mediates between reason and passion') in the final twenty-eight sonnets, including that pivotal meditation on 'Will' that is Sonnet 136 (p. 739). Yet, unlike other critics, Schwarz sees a 'circulation of will across lines of gender' that 'demystifies' the 'totalizing claims' of misogyny (p. 738); the last twenty-eight sonnets are shown to 'dismantle the assumptions that define women and will as instrumental, and construct instead a system of intersubjective exchange' (p. 741). Schwarz builds on this insight, enlisting the work of Paul de Man to describe the process by which both the speaker and the addressee 'construct an autobiography not of a privileged . . . solipsism but of heterosocial relations' (p. 743); in de Man's words, 'they determine each other by mutual reflexive substitution' ('Autobiography as De-Facement', in *The Rhetoric of Romanticism* [1984]). This leads quite naturally to further observations on the notions of beauty and truth that are invoked in the sonnets. As the earlier conclusions suggest, these 'effects' are seen to be produced by 'heterosocial' forces as opposed to any 'discretely possessed' will: 'Beauty is not something that God does to women for men, or that men do to women for God or for men, or that women do to women for women or for men or for God; or rather it is never only one of these things' (p. 754). Nevertheless, Schwarz is ultimately justified in claiming that the last twenty-eight sonnets clearly show 'the participation of feminine subjects in the strategies that define them' (p. 759).

Manfred Pfister's essay, ' "Bottom, thou art translated": Recent Radical Translations of Shakespearean Sonnets in Germany' (in Dente and Soncini, eds., *Crossing Time and Space: Shakespeare Translations in Present-day Europe*, pp. 21–36), acknowledges the 'literary ritual' that translating Shakespeare's sonnets into German has become in Germany, as well as noting the 'gamut of critical questions' that this raises for the discipline of Translation Studies, but is most interested in the complexities of 'the triangulation between source text, previous translation and new translation'

(p. 22). But not just any new translation qualifies for attention here. It has to
fall into Pfister's most extreme category (of seven categories in total):
Radikalübersetzung, a term originating with Ulrike Draesner ('Twin Spin:
Acht Shakespeare-Sonette', *ShJE* 136[2000] 160–70) and translated as 'radical
translation' (p. 26). Indeed, Pfister chooses Draesner's translation of Sonnet 3
for analysis, along with Franz Josef Czernin's two versions of Sonnet 62. In
these latter poems, Czernin complicates Pfister's triangulation even further by
adding an even more radical translation—'a translation to the second
power... *Übertragung der Übersetzung*'—to his first (p. 31).

Both publications on *A Lover's Complaint* are by MacDonald P. Jackson,
and continue the scholarly debate about the poem's authorship. Responding in
both instances to Brian Vickers's attribution of the poem to John Davies of
Hereford (*Shakespeare, A Lover's Complaint, and John Davies of Hereford*
[2007]) and the decision of Jonathan Bate and Eric Rasmussen to exclude it
from the Royal Shakespeare Company's *Complete Works* (*The RSC
Shakespeare: William Shakespeare. Complete Works* [2007]), Jackson contends
that they are wrong. The most extensive evidence is presented in Jackson's
essay, 'The Authorship of *A Lover's Complaint*: A New Approach to the
Problem' (*PBSA* 102:iii[2008] 285–313). Using the Chadwyck-Healey electronic database Literature Online (LION), Jackson aims to counter the
'superficially impressive' evidence of earlier studies, in which 'the search for
similarities has been uncontrolled'. Jackson prefers 'to search a predetermined
range of texts, by a variety of authors, for a carefully defined category of
features that they share with the disputed work'. This more obviously scientific
approach has been made possible, Jackson notes, by the 'advent of searchable
electronic databases' (p. 287). Initially, Jackson searches the drama of 1590–
1614 for instances of rare spellings of words in *A Lover's Complaint* and finds
that five out of six plays that have 'three or more rare spelling links to *LC*'
were written by Shakespeare; twelve out of nineteen of those with two links
were Shakespeare's; and 'a further ten Shakespeare plays, plus Hand D of
Sir Thomas More, and fifty-one non-Shakespearean plays register one link'
(pp. 294–5). As Jackson states, 'It is hard to see why, if Shakespeare did not
write *LC*, three of his plays should each share more rare spellings with it than
does any play by another playwright, and why plays by Shakespeare should so
dominate the list of those with two or more spelling links to the poem' (p. 296).
Shakespeare also 'dominates... [Jackson's] list of rare spelling links to poetry
and drama texts no less clearly than the... list of links to drama alone', even
though his 'canon covers only about eight per cent of the amount of text
searched' (p. 300). Jackson goes on to reduce his list to 'those [spellings]
employed by a single writer and those employed by no more than two writers',
and then even further still, and Shakespeare's dominance becomes more and
more evident (pp. 302–3). After five sections of Jackson's essay in which he
makes the positive case for Shakespeare's authorship of *A Lover's Complaint*,
he reserves a sixth for challenging John Davies of Hereford's authorship. Here,
with reference to Davies's preference for '*sith* as an alternative to *since*', for
'apostrophes to indicate metrical elision in various words', for *yer* instead of
'ere', and for *it's* in place of 'it is', Jackson makes an equally persuasive case
(pp. 308–11). Precluding 'a gigantic conspiracy among printing-house

workers', Jackson appears to have established strong links between *A Lover's Complaint* and Shakespeare (p. 312). In the other article on the same authorship question, '*A Lover's Complaint, Cymbeline,* and the Shakespeare Canon: Interpreting Shared Vocabulary' (*MLR* 103:iii[2008] 621–38), Jackson again uses Literature Online to contest Brian Vickers's account (in his case for Davies's authorship, *Shakespeare, A Lover's Complaint, and John Davies of Hereford* [2007]) of why *A Lover's Complaint* and *Cymbeline* have a lot of 'rare-in-Shakespeare words' in common (p. 637). Jackson finds, contrary to Vickers's assertion, that several of the words were 'in general usage in London between 1603 and 1609' (Vickers, p. 213), that they were 'used by no non-Shakespearian writer during those years', but were used by Shakespeare in works of this period other than *Cymbeline* (pp. 637–8).

Lois Potter's article, 'Involuntary and Voluntary Poetic Collaboration: *The Passionate Pilgrim* and *Love's Martyr*' (in Drábek, Kolinská and Nicholls, eds., *Shakespeare and his Collaborators over the Centuries*, pp. 5–19), is part of a collection arising from papers given at a conference (with the same title) at the Faculty of Arts, Masaryk University in Brno, Czech Republic in February 2006. Potter makes an interesting connection between Shakespeare and the 'rich variety of collaborative and combative verse' found in the early modern period, including the 'commendatory' verses published (at Prince Henry's behest) with Thomas Coryate's travel book, *Coryate's Crudities Hastily Gobbled Up* [1611], which were humorously and satirically composed by Coryate's associates at the 'elite Mermaid Club' (p. 9). *The Passionate Pilgrim* is suggested as a possible contribution to the fashion for such collaborative collections; in answer to the question of 'how so many sonnets on the Venus and Adonis theme came to be written', Potter suggests that writers might have competed or collaborated on them as part of 'a tribute to Shakespeare's early erotic poems and plays' (p. 12). Indeed, it is also postulated that, in contributing some examples of his own work, Shakespeare might have been 'using this opportunity [in 1599] to test the waters before deciding whether to publish the mainly misogynistic and bawdy poems that constitute 126–152 of the 1609 edition [of *Shake-speares Sonnets*]' (pp. 12–13). In the case of *Love's Martyr* [1601], and the 'The Phoenix and the Turtle' contained therein, Potter argues for Shakespeare's poem being part of another significant collaborative project, in which Shakespeare and his fellow dramatists (Marston, Chapman and Jonson), as well as the anonymous 'Ignoto' and *Vatum Chorus*, would have been more than willing to add their poems to Robert Chester's volume in honour of Sir John Salusbury. What has often been considered a tenuous relationship between authors and patron might, in fact, have been quite significant, not least because of the prior existence of a 'cooperative poetic circle' of Welsh bards, who had benefited from the restoration of the Salusbury family fortunes (after the damage incurred as a result of the Babington plot) and the munificent literary patronage that followed. Potter's essay chimes with the suggestion made by Colin Burrow (*William Shakespeare: The Complete Sonnets and Poems* [2002], p. 89) that, after the execution of the earl of Essex, new patrons were being sought by poets such as these.

Judith H. Anderson includes a chapter in her book, *Reading the Allegorical Intertext: Chaucer, Spenser, Shakespeare, Milton,* on the intertextual relationship between Shakespeare's *Venus and Adonis* and Spenser's *The Faerie Queene*. Entitled '*Venus and Adonis*: Spenser, Shakespeare, and the Forms of Desire' (pp. 201–13), it characterizes Shakespeare's poem as 'a seriocomic meditation on the landscape of desire, or wanting—on passion and grief—and on the kinds of figures desire generates in the third book of Spenser's *The Faerie Queene*'. This is achieved by Shakespeare's 'folding into characters' of several allegorical figures taken from Spenser's epic (p. 201). Adopting a method in opposition to a posited 'critical tradition [that] has too often assumed rivalry or anxiety as the only possible relation between poets and precursors', Anderson sees Shakespeare performing 'at once an act of reading and of (in)habitation' (p. 204). If Shakespeare is 'inhabiting' anywhere in Anderson's reading, it is Spenser's Garden of Adonis from Book III. In response to Ellen April Harwood's article, 'Venus and Adonis: Shakespeare's Critique of Spenser' (*JRUL* 39[1977] 44–60), Anderson expands what she sees as Harwood's 'too selective' reading to take into account the fullest 'implication of [Spenser's] Garden' and recognize the way Spenser 'often uses a kind of refraction to relate largely disparate figures to a single type, such as Venus' (p. 206). More specifically, Shakespeare is shown to deploy the topos of a 'landscape of erotic desire' found in the Garden of Adonis, but whereas Spenser retains an atmosphere of myth—'Right in the middest of that Paradise | There stood a stately Mount . . .' (III.vi.43)—Shakespeare's landscape is more suggestive and comic: 'Within this limit is relief enough, | Sweet bottom grass and high delightful plain | Round rising hillocks, brakes obscure and rough' (ll. 235–7) (Anderson, p. 208). Ranging more widely, and in keeping with her recognition of Spenser's relating of 'disparate figures to a single type', Anderson notes the 'figure of a female bending over a recumbent male'— Acrasia, Cymoent, Belphoebe, Venus, Argante and Britomart—that recurs from the end of Book II to almost the close of Book III of *The Faerie Queene* and is central to the representation of Venus in Shakespeare's narrative poem (p. 209). The Giantess Argante is a significant 'Venerean figure' for Anderson; her 'taste for boys', her incestuous character and her 'manhandling' all have parallels in the nature of the Shakespearian goddess (pp. 210–11). In the end, the huge variety of Spenser's allegorical figures that Shakespeare would have had to 'fold' into his characters leads Anderson to suggest that it 'actually exceeds and challenges such a concentration, defying containment' (p. 212).

W.P. Weaver's article, '"O teach me how to make mine own excuse": Forensic Performance in *Lucrece*' (*SQ* 59[2008] 421–49), is the final publication to be considered here. It takes as its subject Lucrece's speeches following her rape, and offers a corrective to the critical consensus on the poem that likens these speeches to the early modern genre of female complaint. Weaver's thesis is that 'the primary formal models of Lucrece's speeches are to be found in the rhetorical exercises and textbooks of Elizabethan grammar schools' (p. 422). Crucially, Weaver reveals the dark irony of a schoolboy's lessons in rhetoric being used to speak eloquently of the inadequacy of words when a woman must narrate her own violation. In a compelling conclusion to a persuasive essay, the representation of the 'hyperarticulate Lucrece' is compared to the 'silent Lavinia' of *Titus Andronicus* in order to suggest that 'Lavinia's dismemberment is Shakespeare's first image of the insufficiency of words alone to narrate such a crime' and that 'Lucrece's rhetorical exercise and judicial speech are his proofs' (p. 448–9). Shakespeare is shown drawing on an education in 'late antique and early modern rhetoric' (p. 423), as well as his own canon.

(d) Histories

Robert A Logan's *Shakespeare's Marlowe* ranges widely across the canon in its consideration of the latter's influence on the former; its discussions of the histories focus on *Richard III, Richard II* and *Henry V*. Beyond the level of verbal or strong character echoes, 'Marlowe' here functions rather as 'republicanism' sometimes does in Andrew Hadfield's 2005 book: in both, analogues are treated as, effectively, sources, though there may be any number of other analogous elements outside the remit of the book which remain unexplored. So Logan asks, of Henry's response to the tennis balls insult, whether Shakespeare is trying to make him sound authoritative in the epic manner of a Tamburlaine. It is an interesting question, but to answer it the book would have to address how we might tell simple authoritative language from language which might be 'authoritative in [an] epic [but non-Marlovian] manner' from language 'authoritative in the epic manner of a Tamburlaine'. Logan's discussion of Marlowe's dramaturgy above the verbal level focuses on the ways in which he seems to have invented 'prototypes'—or, in the case of *Edward II*, what we might call a 'proto-prototype' which didn't particularly catch on—to which Shakespeare responded. A later chapter on the 'deep' influence of *Tamburlaine* on *Henry V* suggests that Shakespeare acknowledges through his protagonist the prototypical nature of Tamburlaine, finally coming round to the heroical history paradigm Marlowe's two-parter established. Logan interestingly explores the ways that Shakespeare's Henry negotiates with the Tamburlaine type, rather in the manner that earlier criticism suggested Falstaff negotiated with the *miles gloriosus*. However, most of what Shakespeare learned from Marlowe, it appears, is uncontroversial aesthetic techniques such as unsettling the audience's desire to experience a fixed, idealized image of the protagonists in order to create and sustain dramatic tension. The book's focus is resolutely aesthetic—neither writer's use of or attitudes towards the chronicles, for example, get much attention, and nor do historical or theatrical contexts.

David N Beauregard's *Catholic Theology in Shakespeare's Plays* focuses on the relationship between papal authority and the English monarch in the two non-tetralogical histories, arguing that the Catholic Church's authority is comparatively sympathetic when held next to the absolutisms of the two titular monarchs in *King John* and *Henry VIII*. John's legitimacy is in question by the time he produces his anti-papal speech at III.i, and his words consequently are arrogant—an arrogance which is transferred by association to Henry VIII through the use of phrases such as 'supreme head'. The flipside of establishing the absolutist tendencies of the monarch is a defence of the papacy. Here Beauregard's defence of the papal legate in *King John* deals in some very fine distinctions indeed—for example, he mitigates Pandulph's threat that an assassin of John would be canonized on the grounds, first, that assassination was never an official papal policy, second, that saints are venerated rather than worshipped (so he is off-message politically and doctrinally) and third, that this is in the context of a heated exchange of views. Pandulph, in a formulation that might raise the odd eyebrow, he sees as a conciliatory and finally benevolent figure who brings about peace. Similarly, Beauregard suggests that, though Katherine, Wolsey and Campeius in *Henry VIII* provide some suggestion of Shakespeare's theological positioning (and he admits that the latter two are 'corrupt'), papal authority is never unequivocally attacked—in fact coming off rather well. Henry, on the other hand, is neglectful, hypocritical and manipulative. For this reader, the limitation of Beauregard's approach is his neglect of politics and nationalism; his generous interpretation of Pandulph's character proposes a writer (and theatre company, and audience) extraordinarily remote from the usual understanding of the immediate post-Armada context into which the play came.

Patricia Cahill's *Unto the Breach: Martial Formations, Historical Trauma, and the Early Modern Stage* considers the way the history play—broadly conceived to include *Tamburlaine* and *The Triumph of Chivalry*—shapes and is shaped by the 'new military rationalities' of the *fin de siècle*, theorizing both labouring bodies and trauma. 'Trained bands' were a late Elizabethan innovation requiring selection from the more established 'musters' (hence, Cahill notes, 'pass muster'), and as such foreshadow the kind of taxonomies satirized in Dickens's *Hard Times* more than two centuries later. The Gloucestershire scene in *2 Henry IV*—properly a representation of an impressment 'muster' rather than a voluntarist 'recruitment'—focuses critical attention on such Foucauldian scrutiny, and for Cahill is fatal to the chivalric ideals represented most obviously via Hotspur. Such impressments were also important factors in a national 'proletarianization', as once economically independent workers took up places within a strict command hierarchy. But where other stagings of impressments 'imagine this as 'a kind of primal moment when a man is torn from his home and transformed into someone else's goods, the Gloucestershire one re-enacts that rupture five times as five men fend off Falstaff's inquiries' (pp. 84–5). Cahill's attention here is not on the corruption of the process, but its relationship to incipient knowledges of enumeration, discipline and normativity. Cahill sums it up as one of 'riotous particularity' (p. 92), which at the same time disrupts the scene's satirical impulses. The play's answer to this is not what Dover Wilson identified as the 'chivalry, of the old anarchic kind' of Hotspur, but the calculative and indeed bureaucratic rationality of Hal, influentially anatomized by Greenblatt's 'Invisible Bullets'. This continues to operate in Eastcheap throughout the second play, as through the first; however, the play does end with the lean and Lenten king subjected to the appraising gaze of the lean Shallow.

A short epilogue on *Richard III* returns to the issue of trauma. Even before the ghosts appear near the end of the play, the 'integrity of space' convention of the amphitheatre stage has been 'shattered' by having two 'places' represented at once (in contrast, the 'French' and 'English' tents are never on stage at the same 'time' in *Henry V*). This is all the more disorienting because it is accompanied by the forms of the new military science, with both leaders plotting their battle formations, both writing, and Richard's need for precision about the time. The ghosts themselves are assimilable to the repetition compulsions of trauma, and doing so leads Cahill to oppose 'redemptive' readings of the scene by claiming that they 'evoke the eeriness of history itself' (p. 217); her reading of trauma seems to depend on eternal repetition, committing her to the position that 'movement forward—literal succession—[is] an impossibility'. This point demonstrates the incompatibility of Cahill's reading with a reading like Greenblatt's in *Hamlet in Purgatory*. However, it does not in itself demonstrate its superiority.

Hugh Grady's superb work on the *Henriad* has found its reader. David Schalwyk considers the two *Henry IV* plays' representations of 'service' in *Shakespeare, Love and Service*. 'Service' is defined as 'a commingling of affect and structure, devotion and self-interest, abandon and control' (p. 172), and Schalwyk takes it as a master-concept for understanding affective bonds between nobility and royalty, and its wider distribution among other social milieux—the 'ungoverned' services of tavern or brothel, and the 'more settled reciprocities of rural Gloucestershire' (p. 165). The chapter opens with a keynote reading of the tormenting of Francis and of Shallow and Davy in Act V of *2 Henry IV*. Of the former, Schalwyk perceptively remarks that 'the cruelty of the joke lies in the way in which Hal tortures the young man with the suggested promise of release' while being constantly reminded of his immediate 'servile obligations' from the other room, and the indifference with which the 'wayward royal apprentice' then abandons him (p. 166). In a sense, Falstaff is a 'loyal servant...calling in...debts' (p. 168), and Schalwyk reads him here as 'characteristically Janus-like' (p. 169), aware of the self-interest in service relationships while blind to what this will mean for himself. In another sense, of course, Falstaff's structural position in regard to the prince is occluded, certainly in comparison with his affective bonds. Theatrically, too, the millennia-old 'master–servant' double act is given a new twist, with the master undermining the servant (so that, in Weimann's terminology, he takes the *platea* to the servant's *locus*).

But 'master' and 'servant' are not simply roles to be adopted or shucked off. Schalwyk argues, against Grady, that Hal is 'contaminated' by the self-imposed but structurally servile positions he occupies—his 'inventory' of Poins's shirts and silk stockings is rather closer to the laundry than the panopticon, as it were. Schalwyk argues also that Grady's perception of the play as anticipating a modern 'shifting nature of subjectivity' (p. 180) is effectively a reading of the tavern scenes between Hal and Falstaff. Elsewhere, 'the parameters of variation in subjectivity are relatively constrained'—Hal certainly moves between roles, but 'each of these roles restricts the possibilities of fully inhabiting the others or another' so that 'the heir-apparent finds that he can never recover the affective tenderness of the loving son' (p. 192). It is only in the tavern that forms of identity can be 'tried without consequence'. Schalwyk points, too, to the downside of 'modern' freedom in comparison to the obligations on the early modern master, noting the 'utterly unreciprocal' (p. 187) nature of Falstaff's relationships with Quickly, Feeble and Shallow, and the 'profound sense of loss' when the new king leaves Falstaff as merely his pensioner.

Schalwyk remarks, in passing, that the plays 'offer a sustained *realistic* representation, sometimes parodic, of service as it might have touched the drawer or ostler' (p. 165). Ostlers, carriers, tapsters and others are the focus of Alan Stewart's *Shakespeare's Letters* (and the virtually identical article 'Shakespeare and the Carriers', *SQ* 58[2008] 431–64). Focusing on the Gadshill robbery, he proposes that it shows how 'an unholy alliance between career criminals and their high-ranking protectors preyed on a crucial infrastructure of early modern England...the network of carriers and carriers' inns on which so much communication depended' (p. 117). Carriers typically travelled between specific provincial locations and specific London inns, carrying letters and goods, and accompanying people, in both directions, and as such provided a crucial link between recent London immigrants and their origins. The Tarlton part in *The Famous Victories* is a carrier, fittingly in the light of Tarlton's 'rustic in the city' persona. Though he is robbed at Gadshill this is not staged, and the audience does not see Dericke until he reaches Deptford. In contrast, Shakespeare gives us a detailed representation of the inn at Rochester, as well as the nearby Gadshill, and anatomizes both 'corrupt' and 'good, exploited' inn servants, the former in league with the robbery. In common law, losses at an inn were the liability of the innkeeper (hence the Hostess's indignation when Falstaff asks her 'have you enquired yet who picked my pocket?' at III.iii). Similarly, if a carrier was robbed he was responsible for compensating the owner, which explains the carrier's virtually non-speaking presence with the sheriff when he investigates the robbery in Eastcheap at II.iv. The play emphasizes, in other words, that robbery affects not only the rich but vulnerable (indeed, 'victimized') figures like the carrier. In doing so it 'refuses an easy separation between evil lowly villains and the reckless, dashing elite characters' (p. 149). Falstaff's progress towards battle parodies that of a carrier, mapped against inns and staging points, and amongst his 'food for powder' are both ostlers and tapsters. Hal's implication in the robbery, and continuing indulgence of Falstaff, must be read in this light, for his victims ultimately are the carriers—the figure who for provincial immigrants into London is nothing less than 'the face of home' (p. 154).

An altogether different view of the carriers informs Harry Berger Jr's 'A Horse Named Cut: *1 Henry IV*, 2.1' (in Dutcher and Prescott, eds., pp. 193–205). Berger claims that this scene is less about '"objective" circumstances' and more about 'the speakers' condition as they represent it to themselves' (p. 195). Berger does mean speakers rather than characters, 'more the objects than the subjects of their discourse' (p. 196), and thus 'sitting ducks for social parody' (p. 195). What speaks through them is 'their delight in the victims' discourse' (p. 196): 'victimization has its pleasures, chief of which is the delight in mastering the expressive conventions of the discourse that represents it' (p. 199). However, what follows this rather reductive reading of the scene is an extremely subtle close reading of verbal ducking and diving between Gadshill and the Chamberlain, whose 'victim' status is far more complex than Berger initially implied, showing in the tension between 'rhetorical bluster and syntactical uncontrol' (p. 203).

Colin Burrow's 'Reading Tudor Writing Politically: The Case of *2 Henry IV*' (*YES* 38:i–ii[2008] 234–50) provides yet another example of the rewards that focusing on a seemingly marginal element can bring. He sees the Gloucestershire scenes of that play speaking 'in a mode attuned with incredible precision to sensing awkward and potentially settling interactions between different projects and affinities within the Tudor commonwealth' (p. 250). Burrow then provides an appropriately precise reading, showing how the elusiveness of the scenes' effects is a function of these interactions. Shallow in a sense 'speaks' from a position of overlap between different spheres and roles, 'interlaced fragments of his affinity, his juridical being, his household' (p. 242), and Burrow persuasively argues that this kind of position was a function of the many networks, structures and positions within which many people situated themselves. But this is no Whitmanesque hymn to multiplicity; Shallow is 'repeatedly *not quite* performing responsibilities that were explicitly those of JPs in this period' (p. 245).

Phebe Jensen considers the ways in which Falstaff might be said to 'haunt' the cakes and ale of *Twelfth Night* in *Religion and Revelry in Shakespeare's Festive World*. The Illyrian play itself is a response to the Admiral's men's 'splitting' in *Sir John Oldcastle* of the complexly Puritan-and-festive Falstaff of *1 Henry IV* into two characters, a 'good' proto-Protestant Sir John (Oldcastle) and a festive Catholic priest, Sir John of Wrotham, and his paramour Doll. The latter Sir John is twice referred to as 'Master Parson', a standard term of derision for Catholic priests—and what both Sir Toby and Feste call Sir Topas in Act IV of *Twelfth Night*. Jensen sees the encounter between the secular Lord of Misrule, the Lenten jester and the 'kind of Puritan' as both a theatrical in-joke and a clear clue to the further distribution of the Falstaff-function of *1 Henry IV* (as it were) amongst several characters. Malvolio's Puritanism is not 'hypocritical attachment to holiday excess' (p. 169) (which Jensen sees as a Falstaffian characteristic), but opposition to festive revelry. Festivity itself is detached from its Admiral's men, anti-Falstaff association with corrupt Catholicism. The effect is to revisit the festive tradition, defending the theatre as its current institutional base. A rather different take on Falstaff and festivity comes in Robert Shaughnessy's closely historicized reading of post-war British performances of the Henry plays, ' "I do, I will": Hal, Falstaff and the Performative' (in Henderson, ed., *Alternative Shakespeares 3*, pp. 14–33). Shaughnessy traces the ways in which Hal's line 'I do, I will', in a theatre under the influence of Beckett and Pinter, came to be performed as enacting an irreversible transition between play and 'confessional frankness'. Shaughnessy contrasts the kind of self-present subjectivity this reading presents us with to Michael Gambon's Protean performance as Falstaff, as 'just possibly . . . the embodiment of a kind of oppositional politics' (p. 32). Alexander Welsh provides a short but incisive analysis of Falstaff's 'honour' speech in *1 Henry IV* in *What is Honor? A Question of Moral Imperatives*. Honour 'thrusts the body into the path of danger' (p. 53), testing the body on behalf of the self, yet is also 'word' (bodily courage alone is not honour); it cannot be certain until death, when 'the possibility of any further actions is at an end and the pledge has been surrendered for good' (p. 53). E.P. Lock's 'Thouing the King in Shakespeare's History Plays' (*EIC* 58[2008] 120–42) explores the transgressiveness of Falstaff addressing king Henry as 'thou' in his appeal to him at the end of *2 Henry IV*. The essay surveys the various categories of breaking the general grammatical rule that 'you' is used to an equal or superior; it does not consider the play in depth, but finds that the majority of such rule breaches are not, in context, direct challenges to royal legitimacy.

Elena Levy-Navarro investigates fatness and leanness in the *Henry IV* plays in *The Culture of Obesity in Early and Late Modernity*, taking aim at 'essentialist' readings of such categories. Falstaff is the 'before', and Hal the 'after', in an image familiar to contemporary diet culture; he is also the 'before' of psychoanalytic readings, a stage to be passed through or past to be mastered, and 'the excesses of old civilization' (p. 75). But she points out that Falstaff's fatness is to an extent constructed by Hal in the service of his own project of predatory 'virtuous self-restraint' (p. 68), and in that sense takes its place on one side of the binary oppositions many critics see operating between Falstaff and Hal. While Levy-Navarro attends very closely to the linguistic constructions of fatness and leanness, showing convincingly that neither is conclusively privileged by the plays, some of her readings seem rather literal. Hal's language 'characterizes' rather than, for example, plays with Falstaff. I'm not sure how well the fat/thin binary as here constructed could cope with, for example, the martial and heroic body of single combat that is the focus at the end of the first play (Falstaff's body is un-modern and 'feudal' but there is no mention of Hotspur's to speak of), or indeed the thinness of Shallow, who is here programmatically lined up, with the thin beadles leading Doll and the Hostess away, on the side of the new *civilité*.

Lauren M. Blinde seeks to uncover the place of rumour in Shakespeare's idea of history in 'Rumored History in Shakespeare's *2 Henry IV* (*ELR* 38:i[2008] 34–54). The essay's leaps of logic are at times disconcerting. I can see that 'By presenting Rumor as our historian, Shakespeare encourages the audience members to include a fundamental sense of unreliability in their thinking about history', but I can't see how that entails the very next sentence's claim that 'Rumor is history's foundation, and thus for Shakespeare history is, in many ways, rumor' (p. 35). I found Blinde's argument, when it diverged from the critics whose work she competently surveys, extremely difficult to understand, and when I did understand it I found it tendentious and over-fond of sweeping assertions ('Rumor's creative potential allows the dramatist to transcend both class and historicity', p. 37). An example from early in the essay, seeking to introduce one of the ideas to follow, will allow the reader a taste of the effort (and, for some no doubt, the rewards) involved in engaging with it: 'By embodying the conflict between narrative and display, Rumor transcends the split between aural and visual epistemologies in order for Shakespeare to argue that history is fundamentally imaginative. Although narrative and display seem to compete with, rather than reinforce, each other, Shakespeare's Rumor undoes the conflict by replacing narrative and display with anatomy to present a theory of history that transcends notions of true and false' (p. 35). Enough transcendence, already.

Ian McAdam's 'Masculine Agency and Moral Stance in *King John*' (*PQ* 86:i–ii[2007)] 431–64) proposes that the play offers a distinctly less religiously engaged sensibility than recent accounts find. He suggests that the play's central concern is 'individual moral and rational agency' (p. 68), and that both

Catholic and Protestant forms of Christianity are subjected to scrutiny from this point of view. This 'self-possession' (the right kind of 'strong possession') is most clearly located, and therefore gendered, in the Bastard. John's nobles and the Citizen at Angiers are judged by his standards and found wanting. Here McAdam equates manliness with assertive and consistent political commitment, and naturally enough finds John a 'precarious...manly role model' (p. 88). Paul Quinn, on the other hand, argues that John is a 'full-blown Protestant martyr' in ' "Thou shalt turn to ashes": Shakespeare's *King John* as Protestant Martyrology (*Moreana* 45:clxxv[2008] 189–207). Shakespeare's play is the culmination of decades of Protestant revisionism, beginning with Simon Fish in the 1520s, and his distinctive contribution is to reconceive John's death, turning away from Foxe's account of it to draw instead on the deaths of Foxe's Marian martyrs. Where *The Troublesome Reigne* presented 'reconfigured Protestant history masquerading as political allegory' Shakespeare writes 'Foxe inspired martyrology' (p. 199). John's protracted exit from the world via poison is accompanied by an unusual number of references to burning, so much so that he 'appears to burn to death' (p. 201). John's fate in the second half of the play even mirrors the Foxean sequencing of accusation, confirmation, condemnation and sentence, beginning with Pandulph in III.i.

Paul Hammer returns to the question of Essex and *Richard II* last broached by Blair Worden in 'Shakespeare's Richard II and the Essex rising' (*SQ* 59[2008] 1–35). Hammer is an expert on Essex (and is writing a monograph on 1601). Here he offers a revisionist account of Essex's final years as a way of freshly contextualizing the issues. There is no space to delineate the detailed and fascinating narrative Hammer provides in his discrediting of the interpretation of this experienced military leader's last throw of the dice as a 'pathetically incompetent coup' (p. 18). He concludes that Essex, beset by plots, and with his enemies at court having gained the upper hand, plotted to force his way into Elizabeth's presence to justify himself, but was instead panicked into throwing himself on the mercy of the London authorities who, however, had already been primed to rebuff him. Hammer then takes aim at Worden's suggestion that the Globe play performed on the eve of Essex's action was not *Richard II*. He plausibly suggests that Essex was 'present at the playing of' not a lost play based on Hayward's history of *Henry IV* but at the playing of the *character*, perhaps in plays we still have. Hayward's book was seeking to capitalize on Essex's public association with plays featuring Bolingbroke, not the inspiration for a new play about him. Finally, Hammer investigates the ways in which the play was 'a coterie performance on a public stage' (p. 26), with a range of privately available significances for Essex's followers, some of whom were descendants of the aristocrats portrayed in the play. The play, Hammer suggests, would have built on Essex's associations with Bolingbroke, but also functioned as a cautionary example of how things could go wrong if the faction had its way and confronted Elizabeth. A bare summary doesn't do justice to the patient, scholarly and comprehensive case Hammer assembles. This essay is, quite simply, essential reading for anybody interested in historicizing Shakespeare.

(e) Tragedies

Shakespeare's tragedies received a great deal of attention in 2008. The critical output in the subject is impressive, and much new insight is provided by experts within the field. The studies represent various critical schools and approaches, and the resulting totality is rather intriguing. Questions regarding Shakespeare's ideas as revealed in his works are addressed, relations between text and performance are explored, and issues concerned with interpretation and authorship are discussed. Other studies throw new light on attitudes to race in *Titus Andronicus* and *Othello*. Some few plays have been revised or updated. Several studies of scholarly high standard have described the tragedies as part of Shakespeare's work as a whole, and their contribution to our understanding of the tragedies specifically should not be overlooked. Finally, there are numerous illuminating articles that focus on more limited topics. Collectively the scholars in Shakespeare studies have provided considerable new insight into the tragedies. The following survey will first deal with more general studies, then turn to specific tragedies.

Shakespeare's Book: Essays in Reading, Writing and Reception, edited by Richard Meek, Jane Rickard and Richard Wilson, is a collection of essays on various aspects of Shakespeare study, with a focus on the question whether his plays work as well on the page as on the stage. Of immediate interest to a review of Shakespeare's tragedies is Richard Meek's article on '"Penn'd speech": Seeing and Not Seeing in *King Lear*' (pp. 79–102). Meek refers to the description of dramatic utterances as 'penn'd speech' (from *Love's Labour's Lost* V.ii.146–8), indicating the paradoxical nature of the spoken words in dramatic texts, the fact that they are penned as well as spoken. Meek pursues this by asking how readers and audiences conceive of dramatic works. He subsequently explores 'the textuality of Shakespearean drama via a reading of *King Lear*, a play that—like *Love's Labour's Lost*—contains an unusually large number of epistles and other stage documents' (p. 79). Meek argues that *King Lear* is concerned with relations between seeing, hearing and reading, experiences which are relevant to our appreciation of the play. Meek's approach to *King Lear* involves questions related to text and performance, for example whether his plays work equally well on the page as on the stage. As Meek notes, there are many examples of 'seeing' in *King Lear* and much emphasis on literal as well as metaphorical blindness. The analysis comments on several instances of this, particularly in IV.vi. In Meek's opinion, we should not try to decide whether Shakespeare is pro- or anti-theatrical in a simple sense, but 'we should think more about the ways in which his works themselves explore the relationship between text and performance, and even dismantle the distinction between the two' (p. 97).

Some related questions are dealt with in Robert Weimann and Douglas Bruster's book, *Shakespeare and the Power of Performance: Stage and Page in the Elizabethan Theatre*, which sets out to redefine the relationship between language and performance on the early modern stage, with special reference to Shakespeare's achievement. According to the authors, Shakespeare fore-grounds the power of performance through his use of clowns and fools, Vice descendants, gendered disguise, and 'secretly open' types of role-playing.

In Shakespeare's plays there is, therefore, a drive towards a dynamic relationship between show and language. Stage–page relations are addressed with reference to a great many Shakespeare plays, including most of the tragedies. In addition to specific chapters on *Richard III* and *King John*, a special chapter is devoted to *King Lear*, which is seen as containing a dynamic inventory of modes of playing in the early modern theatre. 'These modes range from Lear's madness, Edgar's excessive role-playing, Kent's threadbare disguise, and the "all-licensed Fool" to the lower, more earthy "new pranks" (Goneril's phrases [*King Lear* I.iv.201, 238]) that recur so frequently in the tragedy' (p. 199). The play is saturated with performance tricks and practices. To the authors, *King Lear* communicates the freedom to reveal the solemnization as well as the loss of royal power, and the division, oppression, and corruption caused by criminal acts of self-interest. The discussion contains many illuminating observations on 'the play's most radical "practicers," Edmund and Edgar' (p. 203). As the authors note, most criticism of *King Lear* puts emphasis on the act and consequences of dividing the kingdom, while 'the underlying politics and poetics of authority in representation have received considerably less notice' (p. 216). The authors commendably point out linkage among different dimensions in *King Lear* and thus increase our appreciation of the interplay between text and stage.

The Norton Shakespeare has appeared in a second edition, still with Stephen Greenblatt as general editor. The work continues to be based on the Oxford edition. The new edition has drawn on reactions from the thousands of readers that have made use of the book, and recent scholarship has been taken into account. As a result, there are some minor changes to the general introduction, as well as to the introductions to individual plays, textual notes have been made to reflect new findings, and new notes and glosses have been included. The general bibliography and the selected bibliographies have been extended and updated. The genealogies have been revised, and new annotated film lists follow the introductions to the plays. The filmographies reveal that all Shakespeare's tragedies have been filmed. This new edition of the *Norton Shakespeare* is published in three different formats. Of these there are four genre paperbacks, including one on the tragedies. The publisher's online resource, Norton Literature Online, has been extended, giving access to a great number of useful general resources.

While the second edition at first glance appears little changed from the first edition (after all only six pages have been added), some alterations should be noted. The excerpt from Henry Jackson's comments on *Othello* [1610] has been removed. The same applies to Nicholas Richardson's comments on *Romeo and Juliet* [1620].

To the students of Shakespearian tragedy, the new edition of the *Norton Shakespeare*, like the old, continues to provide illuminating introductions to each of the tragedies, from *Titus Andronicus* to *Coriolanus*. *Titus Andronicus* 'differs strikingly from most Renaissance tragedies' (p. 400), *Romeo and Juliet* has become one of the greatest love stories 'by means of the incandescent brilliance of its language' (p. 989), *Julius Caesar* 'dramatizes incidents that seem . . . of world-historical significance' (p. 1549), while the introduction to *Hamlet* at once declares that *Hamlet* is an enigma (p. 1683). And for the last tragedy, Katharine Eisaman Maus tries to answer the question, "What goes wrong in *Coriolanus*?" To the editors, *Othello* today 'speaks to readers and audiences alike with unusual power, largely because it explores race and racism in unsettled fashion' (p. 2109). *Timon of Athens* is seen as having 'strong affinities to *The Merchant of Venice* in its concern with the connections between affectional and monetary bonds, and between material and intangible goods' (p. 2263). Just as in the first edition, *King Lear* is presented with Q1 and F on facing pages for ease of comparison. In addition, a conflated version is offered, prepared by Barbara K. Lewalski. The *Norton Shakespeare* has for a number of years proved a useful resource for students and teachers alike. The collaboration with the readers reflected in the new edition, and the updating that has taken place, seem to have led to an even better Shakespeare resource.

Shakespeare in Theory and Practice, by Catherine Belsey, is a collection of essays written over a long period. The original articles appeared in a variety of publications but are now put together in a slightly revised form. Two interesting essays deal specifically with a Shakespeare tragedy; chapter 9 is devoted to *Hamlet* ('In the case of Hamlet's Conscience') and chapter 10 to *Othello* ('Iago the Essayist'). Looking back on her Hamlet essay, Belsey notes that, 'Contrary to the widespread account of a prince required to kill Claudius but impeded by his own psychological inadequacy, my view is that Hamlet confronts an ethical question: what *ought* he to do?' (p. 13). She observes a dissatisfaction with the binary oppositions central to the criticism when the essay originally appeared in 1974. To Belsey, Hamlet's obligations were 'less resolved, more equivocal, than commentators were ready to acknowledge' (p. 13). Belsey's essay on Hamlet's conscience includes interesting comments on the Protestant science of casuistry, with specific reference to William Perkins's influential work. As regards *Hamlet*, the ambiguities remain, and the question 'What ought Hamlet to have done?' (p. 156) is supplemented with 'What else could he have done?'

Belsey's other essay with relevance for the tragedies, 'Iago the Essayist', is an approach to *Othello* from a formal perspective, seeing the tragedy as a clash of genres, where heroic poetry encounters a sceptical type of prose, reminiscent of Montaigne. In Belsey's view Iago becomes so destructive because he betrays the genre he mimics. Iago's style masks his intense passion, 'prosaic skepticism confronts passionate poetry and prevails, taking possession of the hero to his own destruction' (p. 167).

Four tragedies are discussed in David Schalkwyk's *Shakespeare, Love and Service*. *Timon of Athens* is considered in a chapter ('More Than a Steward') that also encompasses the sonnets and *Twelfth Night*. *Antony and Cleopatra* is commented upon in the chapter on 'Office and Devotion' with *1* and *2 Henry IV*, which includes another look at the sonnets. Finally, *King Lear* and *Othello* are treated in the chapter 'I Am Your Own Forever'. The book reveals the interaction of two concepts, love and service, and was written on the assumption that all relationships can be seen as love relationships. Schalkwyk considers service 'the world we have lost' (p. 3) and love 'the word we have lost' (p. 5). He sets the unpolished *Timon of Athens* beside *Twelfth Night*, using the sonnets as a bridge, and unravelling a darker view of love, duty and sacrifice. For the treatment of *Antony and Cleopatra*, the author places the

Henriad alongside it to illuminate the similarities between relationships of friends in service, including Henry and Falstaff, on the one hand, and Antony and Enobarbus, on the other. As Schalkwyk makes perfectly clear, questions relating to love, friendship and service pervade all levels of the play. He remarks that '*Antony and Cleopatra* is an exception to my earlier claim that love has disappeared from the critical vocabulary of Shakespeare critics in the past two decades' (p. 197). In the course of the play, Antony and Cleopatra extend the concept of *eros*, making infusing it 'with the subjectivities of soldiership, mastery, service, beggary, play, friendship, and transcendence' (p. 198). The chapter on *King Lear* and *Othello* sees the two as being united by their empowerment of the qualities, as well as uncertainties, of service. In different ways, both plays are preoccupied with showing love and service. Schalkwyk describes service in *King Lear* as a dynamic concept which changes shape from one type of relationship to another, at one time approaching love, later an instrument of hatred. The play may therefore be read partly as emphasizing structural forms of power, and partly as a type of agency that transforms ideological instrumentality into an irrational devotional quality of love. Schalkwyk finds that *King Lear* and *Othello*, for all their differences, 'have much in common, not least their shared social framework of service and love, warped and self-negating' (p. 245). What follows is an interesting discussion of *Othello*, including comments on the master–servant dialectic involving Othello and Iago and a discussion of Emilia's counter-service. Schalkwyk's book represents scholarly work of a high standard, and greatly illuminates its subject.

David Crystal's *'Think on my words': Exploring Shakespeare's Language* contains references to most of Shakespeare's work, including the tragedies, but the book explores the playwright's overall use of language, rather than the language of particular plays. The book is highly relevant as an excellent exploration of Shakespeare's language, and Crystal's question 'What does it do?' implies a semantic as well as a pragmatic approach.

Jonathan Bate's book, *Soul of the Age: The Life, Mind and World of William Shakespeare*, is an extensive treatment of Shakespeare's world. For our purposes its references to the tragedies are highly relevant, and all examples of the genre receive some comment. For example, *Hamlet* is discussed with dilemmas and duality in mind; *Othello* is approached with observations on the bawdy court and occasional comments on the charismatic villain. There are also references to Othello as soldier and Othello as Christian. The author's discussion of *King Lear* particularly comments on allusions to philosophers and on the Fool. Bate's discussions of aspects of the tragedies are illuminating, and he reveals an excellent grasp of Shakespeare's world.

David Bevington has explored the ideas prevalent in Shakespeare's work in his book *Shakespeare's Ideas: More things in Heaven and Earth*. While the book reflects Shakespeare's political and moral philosophy as revealed in the plays as well as the poems, the student of Shakespeare's tragedies will find that all the tragedies are referred to repeatedly. *Julius Caesar*, *Hamlet*, *King Lear* and *Othello* receive more attention than the others within the genre. Thus Bevington sees *Julius Caesar* as 'the story of great philosophical ideas in conflict' (p. 160), and he aptly discusses Brutus's divided state of mind.

His discussion of *King Lear* is equally interesting, containing a focus on deliberate evil and finding 'the existential challenge in *King Lear* . . . especially acute' (p. 171). *Hamlet* is referred to repeatedly in the book, incorporating comments on the theological distinctions needed to understand what the Ghost is telling his son. Bevington also discusses interestingly the—in Calvinist terms edifying—contrast between Hamlet's dead father and Claudius. The discussion of *Othello* includes illuminating commentary on Iago as a consummate deceiver. In Bevington's view, there is in both *King Lear* and *Othello* a clash of ideologies that 'centres to a considerable extent on the existential challenges posed by Iago and Edmund to conventional ideas of moral order' (p. 162). Although mirroring what plays as well as poems suggest about a great many topics, Bevington's book on Shakespeare's moral and intellectual commitment is rewarding reading for the general reader as well as the expert. It is especially commendable that Bevington presents a finely balanced account, avoiding extreme interpretation.

In an article devoted to a somewhat related topic entitled 'Who Do the People Love?' (*ShS* 61[2008] 289–301), Richard Levin discusses Shakespeare's opinions on politics. According to Levin, Shakespeare's views on art, justice, love, marriage, friendship, sex and religion are implied in his works. Shakespearian critics have had no problems in showing, by supporting evidence from the plays, what were Shakespeare's views on subjects such as justice, nature, war and honour. In Levin's experience, it is more difficult for critics to point out Shakespeare's attitude to politics. Levin notes that in Shakespeare there are only three extended treatments of 'the people' as a separate political agency: the Roman plebeians in the first three acts of *Julius Caesar* and *Coriolanus*, as well as Jack Cade's rebels in Act IV of *2 Henry VI*. In all three plays they appear as a mindless, fickle and murderous 'rabble'. Levin thus clearly demonstrates that while critics have wanted Shakespeare to favour democracy, there is every reason to believe that he did not.

A special issue of *Shakespeare* (4:ii[2008]) is devoted to 'Shakespeare and Islam', and in the 'Introduction' (pp. 102–111), Mark Hutchings, guest editor, states that the publication is not concerned with approaching doctrinal questions but with questions of adaptation and appropriation, staging and interpretation. The issue thus contributes to central fields within contemporary Shakespeare studies, including the tragedies. The term 'Islam' is used to cover the Ottoman empire as well as the Persian, and the early modern as well as more recent periods are considered.

The Review of English Studies (*RES* 59[2008] 219–31) contains an article by MacDonald P. Jackson on 'Three Disputed Shakespeare Readings: Associations and Contexts'. The author acknowledges the careful work involved in the preparation of a critical edition of a Shakespeare play: selecting from variants in the earliest printed texts or later conjectural emendations. The article is focused on two passages in *Romeo and Juliet* (II.ii.26–32 in *The Riverside Hamlet*) and two in *Hamlet* (I.iv.36–8 and II.ii.174–86), arguing that in practically all recent editions the editors have made the wrong choices. These views are based on examinations of context and of associations, not least concerning imagery, with similar situations in other Shakespeare plays.

John W. Velz, who passed away in 2008, has an engaging article on 'Eschatology in the Bradleian Tragedies: Some Aesthetic Implications' (*ShN* 58:ii[2008] 41, 62, 64, 74). The illuminating discussion on the eschatological motif deals with the four plays that A.C. Bradley said defined the genre, *Hamlet*, *Othello*, *Macbeth* and *King Lear*. Velz notes that in the 'Bradleian tragedies' the judge and his judgement are absent, while in plays with comedic resolutions judgements seemingly based on Doomsday pageants and moralities abound. In another article John W. Velz presents 'Notes on Shakespeare's Sources for Four Plays' (*ShN* 57:iii[2007/8] 87–8, 96). The author examines a few passages from *Julius Caesar*, *Othello*, *Antony and Cleopatra* and *Cymbeline* in relation to passages in North's Plutarch, in order to demonstrate that 'even the least prominent of source questions can throw light on the creative process' (p. 87). To illustrate his point, Velz uses an example from *Julius Caesar* IV.iii. Shakespeare is establishing a conflict between private grief and military necessity. Plutarch employs three different numbers to indicate military strength in the various Lives of Brutus, Marcus Antonius and Cicero. In Velz's view, Shakespeare, when writing *Othello* five years later, borrowed from *Julius Caesar* IV.iii the uncertainty about numbers that Plutarch had prompted.

In *Shakespeare Jahrbuch* (*ShJE* 144[2008] 47–65) Jerzy Limon writes about 'The Fifth Wall: Words of Silence in Shakespeare's Soliloquies and Asides'. Limon advocates that acoustic silence on the stage does not necessarily mean silence in fictional space. Making use of a great many examples from Shakespeare's plays, including *King Lear* (I.i.60) and *Titus Andronicus* (Acts II and V), the author shows that 'in theatre verbal signs do not necessarily have to be the signs of verbal utterances in the fictitious realm, and *vice versa*' (p. 48). In the theatre there are, according to Limon, at least two semiotic orders in constant play. Each of these is distinguished by a hierarchy of functions, in Charles Peirce's terminology named for example iconic, indexical and symbolic. Limon's subsequent comments on *King Lear* I.i.60 concern the question whether the single sentence is a short soliloquy or an aside.

Addressing the question of authorship, David Scott Kastan, in ' "To think these trifles some-thing": Shakespearean Playbooks and the Claims of Authorship' (*ShakS* 36[2008] 37–48), comments informatively on several of the tragedies. Kastan assumes that 'all agree that nineteen of Shakespeare's plays were individually published before the Folio appeared in 1623. By 1603, fifteen of these were already in print' (p. 41). Six of them, including *Romeo and Juliet* and *Hamlet*, first appeared as 'bad quartos', and, as Kastan notes, these seem to have been printed without Shakespeare's initiative or knowledge. In order to replace deficient printings, *Romeo and Juliet* and *Hamlet* were soon followed by new versions. As Kastan cautiously puts it, the other six plays, including *Titus Andronicus*, 'appeared in editions that might plausibly be thought to reflect the desire or at least a willingness of Shakespeare to see them in print in the form they were published' (p. 42).

Turning to treatments of individual plays, we start with *Titus Andronicus*, noticing that in *Medieval and Renaissance Drama in England* Gustav Ungerer has an informative article on 'The Presence of Africans in Elizabethan England and the Performance of *Titus Andronicus* at Burley-on-the-Hill,

1585/96' (*MRDE* 21[2008] 19–56). Ungerer's discussion is an illuminating contribution to our knowledge of Africans in Elizabethan England. As Ungerer points out, Shakespeare in 1594 confronted the Elizabethans with Aaron, a literate African and a dramatic figure trained in the classics. The dramatist thereby presented a marked departure from the notion of black inferiority. However calculated such a move may have been, this was not, in Ungerer's view, surprising to the educated classes, to courtiers and noblemen whose views had been shaped by the Portuguese and Spanish experience. In addition, the author refers to the descendants of English merchants who had slaveholdings in Andalusia from 1480 to 1572. Ungerer unravels the history of the black presence in Elizabethan England, then turns to the performance of *Titus Andronicus* on 1 January 1596. Ungerer's survey of the presence of Africans in Elizabethan England includes fascinating comments on the English female slaveholders and English merchant slaveholders. The Guinea Charter of 1588–98 is specifically discussed, as are the Mediterranean traders and the Portuguese New Christians as slaveholders in England. The performance of *Titus Andronicus* is seen as breaking 'new ground in its attempt to cast doubt on the conventional perception of the African other as an inferior being' (p. 39). Ungerer observes that the racial discourse of the time was an immediate concern, as the founding of the Guinea Company in 1588 caused a great influx of black Africans, reaching a peak around 1593/4, when Shakespeare was writing *Titus Andronicus*.

In *New Literary History* Tzachi Zamir has an article on *Titus Andronicus* entitled 'Wooden Subjects' (*NLH* 39:ii[2008] 277–300). Zamir presents a literary criticism of the play discussing the great many examples of atrocities inflicted on characters. The topics treated include tree imagery, pain and its aesthetic experience, and grief. Zamir concludes that *Titus Andronicus* is a tragedy about the genre of tragedy.

Moving on to *Romeo and Juliet*, we find an article on the European Herbal Medicines Directive, seemingly outside our area, in which Philip A. Routledge asks the titillating question, 'Could It Have Saved the Lives of Romeo and Juliet?' (*Drug Safety* 31:v[2008] 416–18). As Routledge points out, herbal medicines have a long history of therapeutic use. They may, however, occasionally cause dose-related or idiosyncratic toxicity. *Romeo and Juliet* contains many references to herbal medicines. In Routledge's view, Shakespeare recognized that therapeutic benefit and toxicity could come from the same herbal source. Thus, in *Romeo and Juliet* II.iii Friar Laurence states that 'Within the infant rind of this weak flower, Poison hath residence, and medicine power'. Romeo himself knew about the effects of herbal medicines, informing Benvolio that plantain leaf would help his 'broken shin' (I.ii). Routledge argues that what puts Juliet into a deep sleep was almost certainly a type of herbal medicine (distilled liquor). Also, what Romeo uses to take his own life thinking that Juliet is dead is a poison which might be of herbal origin. Routledge advocates that what seems to cause the chain of events ending with the death of the two lovers is poor communication. As he concludes, the fate of the lovers is sealed when Juliet, in Act III scene v, decides 'I'll to the friar to know his remedy, if all else fails I can but die'.

A discussion of the name Rosalind, as used by Spenser in *The Shepheardes Calender* and Shakespeare in *Romeo and Juliet*, appears in *TLS* (12:xii[2008] 13–14). As the author Andrew Hadfield points out, the character Rosalind never appears although she is referred to in both texts. The article contains scholarly speculations concerning who the character might be or what she represents.

'The Taming of Romeo in Shakespeare's *Romeo and Juliet*' is the subject of a short article in *Explicator* (*Expl* 66:iv[2008] 206–8) by Wisam Mansour. The author argues that Juliet is a stronger person than is customarily assumed. To prove that point Mansour focuses on the balcony scene in II.ii, which 'illuminates Juliet's depth of personality and accentuates her struggle for selfhood' (p. 206). Juliet wants to control her destiny by manipulating and taming Romeo. In support of this view, the author points to Shakespeare's use of falconry and falconer imagery.

Among the tragedies, *Hamlet* continues to receive more critical attention than any other Shakespeare play. Harold Bloom's edition of *Hamlet* has appeared in the Bloom's Shakespeare through the Ages series. The book is a study guide to the play: it does not contain the text but presents a selection of excellent criticism of *Hamlet* through the centuries. The introductory chapters contain a biography of the playwright, a summary of the play, key passages in *Hamlet*, and a list of characters. The main portion of the book contains criticism of the play by writers as different as Ben Jonson and Samuel Pepys from the seventeenth century, Voltaire, Fielding, Sterne and Goethe from the eighteenth century, and Schlegel, Lamb, Hazlitt, Coleridge, Edgar Allan Poe, Hugo, Nietzsche, Swinburne, Arnold, Twain and Wilde from the nineteenth century. Of critical views meant to represent the twentieth century, we find Chesterton, de la Mare, Bradley, Eliot, Joyce, Wilson Knight, Empson and Bloom himself. It is a pity that most of the authors are represented by very short excerpts. Those that are given most attention, or space, from the seventeenth century are Francois de Belleforest from 1608, with his *The Hystorie of Hamblet*, and John Dryden, for remarks in his preface to *Troilus and Cressida*. From the eighteenth century Samuel Johnson receives a comparatively large amount of attention. Of nineteenth-century criticism Nietzsche's *The Birth of Tragedy* is one of several excerpts that make an impression. It is to be expected, as well as commended, that A.C. Bradley's *Shakespearean Tragedy* has been included. Other interesting comments are found in Joyce's *Ulysses*. G. Wilson Knight is represented by 'The Embassy of Death: An Essay on Hamlet', from *The Wheel of Fire*. One of the most extensive examples of criticism is William Empson's 'Hamlet When New', from the *Sewanee Review*. Similarly, Harold C. Goddard's comments from *The Meaning of Shakespeare*, Stephen Booth 's 'On the Value of *Hamlet*', and Margaret Ferguson's '*Hamlet*: Letters and Spirits' are allowed some development. Graham Bradshaw's contribution, 'Hamlet and the Art of Grafting', from *Shakespeare's Scepticism*, is intriguing for his rejection of much new historicist and cultural materialist Shakespeare criticism. From the present century only one source of criticism has been deemed worthy of representation: James Shapiro's two half-page comments on *Hamlet* in *A Year in the Life of William Shakespeare*. As an overview of *Hamlet* criticism

Bloom's book is insightful and serves a useful purpose. But for in-depth studies, including more exemplifications from the twenty-first century, other publications might be better suited.

Michael Davies has written a book on *Hamlet: Character Studies* in the series Continuum Character Studies. This is a small volume containing interesting views on the character Hamlet, primarily, but also comments on the other characters. It is a student-friendly book which makes accessible a fairly sophisticated type of literary analysis. Initially, Davies gives an overview of *Hamlet* and discusses dramatic character as perceived in Shakespeare's time as well as in more recent criticism. A separate chapter deals with Shakespeare's way of introducing us to Hamlet's character and considers complexities concerning Hamlet's first appearance. Hamlet is described as 'a compendium of selves: an early modern man of no fixed identity' (p. 50). In a chapter on *Hamlet*'s other characters, Davies notes that these other characters do not detract from the impression that the tragedy 'has been constructed through or around the consciousness of its hero, as if its action is somehow taking place within and without Hamlet's own mind' (p. 75), as he is the subject of others' conversations and speculations. Particular attention is paid to the rivalry between the polarized characters of Prince and King, while the other characters, Polonius, Laertes, Gertrude and Ophelia, are seen as reflecting the nature of Claudius's court, family, and affairs of state. The conclusion moves from characters to the key themes and issues, ending on the unsettling realization that '*Hamlet* appears to be full of doubles with whom Shakespeare twins his Prince in complex dramatic and rhetorical ways' (p. 115).

The question of *Hamlet* as a literary and professional version of the First Quarto is considered in *Shakespeare Quarterly*. In the article 'The First Literary *Hamlet* and the Commonplacing of Professional Plays' (*SQ* 59[2008] 371–420), Zachary Lesser and Peter Stallybrass address the use of commonplace markers, commas or inverted commas at the beginning of each line. The discussion includes the use of commonplaces by those responsible for the publication of both Q1 and Q2 of *Hamlet*, publisher John Bodenham and stationer Nicholas Ling. The authors' interesting conclusion is as follows: 'Reading Q1 *Hamlet* with the commonplace markers in mind suggests, in what may now seem a paradox, that if we want to historicize this playbook in its own moment, we need to see it not simply as a theatrical abridgment but rather as a *literary text for reading*' (pp. 379–80).

Another article on *Hamlet* focuses on the character Horatio. In 'Specters of Horatio' (*ELH* 75[2008] 1023–50), Christopher Warley finds that Horatio embodies rationality as well as objectivity and justness. The character of Gertrude is approached in Richard Levin's article, 'Gertrude's Elusive Libido and Shakespeare's Unreliable Narrators (*SEL* 48[2008] 305–26). The article discusses the nature and role of the characters involved in the play, with special emphasis on Gertrude's sexuality and her relationship with her husband. In *Critique*, Shuli Barzilai compares *Hamlet* and one of Margaret Atwood's novels in the article ' "Tell my story": Remembrance and Revenge in Atwood's *Oryx and Crake* and Shakespeare's *Hamlet*' (*Critique* 50:i[2008] 87–110). The author notes that several of Atwood's novels share multiple elements with revenge tragedy. An intertextual reading comparing Atwood's novel with

Hamlet demonstrates that both texts contain a revenge plot involving a murdered father, a mother marrying the murderer, and an only son dedicated to vengeance. Insight into a psychoanalytical interpretation of *Hamlet* is provided in the article 'On the Ghostly Father: Lacan on *Hamlet*', by Stefan Polatinsky and Derek Hook (*Psychoanalytic Review* 95:iii[2008] 359–85). A Lacanian psychoanalytical reading of the play suggests that *Hamlet* is a tragedy of desire.

In a lengthy essay using as a point of departure Walter Benjamin's 1928 *Ursprung des deutschen Trauerspiele* (translated as *The Origin of German Tragic Drama*), Hugh Grady discusses '*Hamlet* as Mourning-Play: A Benjaminesque Interpretation' (*ShakS* 36[2008] 135–65). Grady presents Benjamin's theory of allegory and discusses aspects of the play with allegory in mind, among them the role of the Ghost, Hamlet's vision of the emptiness of the world, Ophelia's madness, and the graveyard scene. In Grady's view, the play goes beyond the limitations of the *Trauerspiel* in its complex hero, while it follows the typical *Trauerspiel* in its conclusion. The ending of *Hamlet* is characterized by the ambiguity of catastrophe, involving a balance between continuing emptiness and redemption, even triumph.

Versions of the printed text of *Hamlet* are focused on in Ian Felce's article on 'Riddling Q1: *Hamlet*'s Mill and the Trickster' (*ShS* 61[2008] 269–80). The author notes the questionable shape of the First Quarto of *Hamlet* when it was rediscovered in Henry Bunbury's closet 200 years after the publication of the First Folio. Felce points out that Q1 was printed in 1603 and Q2 appeared in 1604–5, while it took twenty years before the First Folio version was published in 1623. With the exception of some telling differences, Q2 and F are close, sharing some celebrated verse, characters behaving similarly and a similar chronology of scenes. Q1, the 'bad' quarto, stands out, however. It is considerably shorter than the other two, characters are different with regard to name and action, the chronology of scenes is dissimilar, and the verse is frequently patchy. On the basis of this, Felce argues that it is doubtful that Shakespeare could have been responsible for Q1 as it stands. The Q1 *Hamlet* text may therefore be viewed as a skilful theatrical abridgement. He refers to Thomas Clayton's opinion that Q1 is a memorial reconstruction by a player. Textual comparison between the texts of Q1, Q2 and F may indicate that Q1 most closely approaches the Hamlet tradition and was written before Shakespeare's re-creation of the play.

In the article 'Eclipse of Action: *Hamlet* and the Political Economy of Playing' (*SQ* 59[2008] 450–82), Richard Halpern addresses a few old problems in Hamlet and presents a new approach to character, action and temporality. Halpern contends that '*Hamlet* reworks the Aristotelian discrimination between *poiesis* and *praxis*, making and doing, in a way that not only produces a major philosophical statement on the nature of human action but also fundamentally recasts the relation between the tragic and the political' (p. 450). He argues that this creates a major philosophical affirmation of the nature of human action and reshapes the relationship between the political and the tragic. To Halpern, Adam Smith's work on political economy is a threat to Aristotle's understanding of action. The ethical and political dimensions of this crisis are remade by Hannah Arendt in the twentieth century.

Stimulating work on *Othello* is represented by, for example, Nicholas Potter's book *Othello: Character Studies*, which has appeared as one of the Continuum Character Studies, a series aiming 'to promote sophisticated literary analysis through the concept of character' (p. ix). After an introduction to the play, Potter deals with the character Othello in three consecutive chapters, followed by three chapters on Iago and one on Desdemona. There is also a chapter on the minor characters, including the Duke, Brabantio, Roderigo, Emilia, Montano and Ludovico, then a short conclusion and further reading. Commenting on the close of the play, Potter instructively notes that so far the postcolonial position has not been sufficiently explored, and in his view, 'It is perhaps this perspective that offers the most poignant view of the play' (p. 118). In one version *Othello* is the tale of an idealistic member of a subaltern race in the service of a colonial power intent on exploiting his people. While Potter finds that new historicism and psychological accounts have problems accommodating a tragic perspective, feminism can unravel the tragedies of Desdemona and Emilia and may develop Othello's tragedy as being of a constructed masculinity. Potter categorically states that tragedies are about endings. Significantly, Cassio has the last word of the play, 'it was he who was the cause, in great part, of Iago's anger; it was he who, next to Desdemona and before Roderigo, was most wronged' (p. 121). Potter's study is that of a well-read author who opens our eyes to new aspects of the characters of the play.

Speaking of the Moor: From Alcazar to Othello is another fascinating study of *Othello*. In her book, Emily C. Bartels tries to show that speaking of the 'Moor of Venice' is not as straightforward as one would think. Othello represents many and culturally divergent images, and this is apparent in the diversity of narratives of Africa. The multiplicity of images makes it hard to draw the line between them. Although Othello bids the audience to 'speak of me as I am; nothing extenuate, | Nor aught set down in malice' (V.ii.341–2), it is difficult to speak clearly of his ethnicity. Bartels focuses on and emphasizes the place of Africa in the early modern English imagination, and through her study she reveals the openness with which the Moor was treated in the period: as she points out, the Moor became a central character on the stage. This applies to *Othello* as it does to *Titus Andronicus*. Bartels makes clear that there is no single attitude to blackness. 'In *Titus*, as in *Othello*, interpretations of the Moor happen *inside*, not *outside*, the cultural moment' (p. 99). The variables with regard to geography and history, religion, and skin colour contribute to making the Moor truly intriguing. Tellingly, the chapter devoted to the character Othello is called 'The "stranger of here and everywhere"' (p. 155). More than anything, *Othello* the play, at its core a domestic tragedy, is the staging of a cross-cultural exchange, in which 'we cannot really tell where Venice's story stops and the Moor's story begins' (p. 190). The book places Moor plays alongside texts containing Moorish figures. Besides interesting chapters on *Othello* and *Titus Andronicus*, Bartels's study includes comments on Hakluyt's *Navigations*, John Pory's translation of *The History and Description of Africa*, and Queen Elizabeth's letters suggesting the deportation of 'blackamoors'. *Speaking of the Moor* increases our understanding of the diversity of attitudes to people of African descent in early modern England and contributes to our appreciation of the divergent images of the Moor.

Othello is also addressed by Lena Cowen Orlin in her article on 'The Domestication of *Othello*' (*ShJE* 144[2008] 132–47). Orlin focuses her discussion on III.iii.213, 'to seel her father's eyes up, close as oak'. She argues that this should be read in the context of the materialistic culture of Elizabethan England. In Orlin's view, Othello's material imagination is reconfigured under the malign influence of Iago. Othello in turn internalizes paranoias and superstitions that are detrimental to him. There is a striking change in Othello from the role of being leading general to that of being domesticated. Orlin concludes: 'By falling subject to suspicion of a blocked peephole, by phrasing his belief in his own betrayal as the constituting of a corner, Othello confirms his domestication' (p. 146).

An extensive essay by Shawn Smith in *Papers on Language and Literature* discusses 'Love, Pity, and Deception in *Othello*' (*PLL* 44:i[2008] 3–51). The point of departure for the article is Henry Jackson's reaction to the performance of *Othello* at Oxford in 1610, where he was moved by the image of Desdemona's dead body on the stage, an image Smith describes as non-verbal but not unrhetorical. This raises questions about the dramatic economy of *Othello*. Smith notes that 'much of the play's dialogue draws on the vocabulary and rhetorical forms of forensic debate' (p. 4). Legal contexts, including the 'court of love', are important for an understanding of the treatment of pity as a token of Desdemona's love for Othello, a love questioned as a feigned response when Iago later makes Othello raise doubts about her fidelity. Smith's article discusses *Othello*'s dual mode of verbal and visual expression as reflected in two currents of *Othello* criticism, one concerned with the importance of speech and narrative in the play, and the other with a focus on the visual power of its final scene. The article contains a thorough discussion of pity, love and deception, ending on an ominous note that Iago, although 'censured', will remain 'outside the world of justice and mercy that he has helped to impose upon Othello and through which he has succeeded in achieving his goal—revenge upon Othello' (p. 48).

A.R. Braunmuller has edited an updated edition of *Macbeth*. This edition, which replaces that of 1997, appears in the New Cambridge Shakespeare series and is, according to the publisher, 'the most extensively annotated edition of *Macbeth* currently available, offering a thorough reconsideration of one of Shakespeare's most popular plays' (p. i). The updated, lengthy introduction of 110 pages considers the contexts of the composition of the play. More particularly, the introduction deals with the character Macbeth in legend and the play *Macbeth* in history, *Macbeth* in the mind, and *Macbeth* in performance. Possible new sources are mentioned, including Thomas Middleton's writing. There are also comments on filmed versions of the play. The part on recent criticism and scholarship lists a few of the many contributions to our understanding of *Macbeth* from the two most recent decades. There is also a section on *Macbeth* since 1700. The page-by-page commentary on the text is unusually full. The comments make frequent references to the *OED* and other lexical sources and draw attention to the play's verbal inventiveness. Following the dramatic text, there is a section on textual analysis, which deals with different aspects of the Folio, including comments on Thomas Middleton's contribution to the Folio. Here it is stated that Folio *Macbeth* 'may print passages not written by Shakespeare but (most probably) by Thomas Middleton; Act I, Scene ii, has been especially controversial' (p. 271). This updated edition of *Macbeth* reveals thorough research, it is conscientiously annotated, and it appears a superb tool for researchers and students involved in Shakespeare scholarship.

'Shakespearean Debt to Tacitus' Histories' is the topic of an article by Herbert W. Benario (*N&Q* 55[2008] 202–5). In addition to drawing on *Richard II*, Benario also comments on *Macbeth*, suggesting several parallels of dramatic narrative between Tacitus and Shakespeare.

Sofie Kluge has written 'An Apology for Antony: Morality and Pathos in Shakespeare's *Antony and Cleopatra* (*OrbisLit* 63:iv[2008] 304–34). Kluge initially observes that critical opinion about *Antony and Cleopatra* has varied a great deal. The study starts off with a discussion of the play as being a mixture of pathetic and moral tragedy. The author sets out 'to demonstrate how the play's peculiar combination of morality and pathos results in a dialectical critique of both moral and pathetic concepts of the tragic (p. 305). According to Kluge, Shakespeare created in *Antony and Cleopatra* an 'apology' for Antony, exploring the beauty of perdition and greatness in a person having become an image of corruption. In the author's view, the play fundamentally relies on the Christian moral concept of tragedy, and this interferes with the apologetic direction contained in the play. A consequence of this is that 'the character of Antony appears in an ambiguous chiaroscuro whose somber moral tones have their origin in Roman and medieval historiography while the lighter, more comprehensive ones stem from the poet's Renaissance heritage, Petrarchan philography, Humanist anthropology, and Neoplatonic transcendental philosophy' (p. 305). The ambiguity inherent in Shakespeare's characterization of Antony's role as tragic hero will, in Kluge's opinion, by implication lead to questioning the view of Shakespeare as a modern dramatist and of Renaissance drama as breaking away from the medieval heritage.

'Two New Sources for *Coriolanus*' is the title of an article by David George (*N&Q* 55[2008] 194–7). George sees battle-scene influences on *Coriolanus* issuing from the staging of *1 Henry VI*, with regard to both rhetoric and action. The author also finds textual similarities between the anonymously written pamphlet 'The Great Frost' and *Coriolanus*, concluding that Shakespeare was influenced by the pamphlet.

In a thought-provoking article on 'Shakespeare as Coauthor' (*ShakS* 36[2008] 49–59), Jeffrey Knapp looks into Shakespeare's return to co-authorship at the end of his career. Knapp notes that, according to current histories of authorship in Renaissance drama, 'collective playwriting was both the practical and the theoretical norm in English theaters until around 1600, when the idea of single dramatic authorship first began to surface' (p. 49). To Knapp it makes sense to suggest that Shakespeare might have had a co-author in plays such as *Henry VI* and *Coriolanus*. He looks for reasons why Shakespeare would have returned to collaborative writing towards the end of his career, and after he had become famous as a single author. Knapp looks for other genres of collective writing in the book market at the time, and states that, interestingly, Shakespeare returned to collective playwriting at a time when there was a substantial change in his dramaturgy from tragedy to romance. Three or four years before *Pericles*, Shakespeare wrote his great tragedies *Othello, King Lear, Macbeth, Antony and Cleopatra, Coriolanus* and *Timon of Athens*. These tragedies, and especially the last two, with protagonists who overvalue their singleness, 'offered little hope that a new generation might continue or complete the work of the generation before it' (p. 52). With *Pericles*, as an example of one of his late co-authored plays, Shakespeare envisioned 'a future of "new joy" beyond the single life of his protagonist, which in turn created a future for himself beyond the single genre of tragedy' (p. 52).

As should be amply revealed in this review of scholarship on Shakespeare's tragedies published in 2008, critics continue to be strongly attracted to the genre. The multiplicity of approaches to Shakespearian tragedy is stimulating and truly impressive. This remarkable interest in Shakespeare's tragedies and the resulting wealth of competent scholarship testify, in the final analysis, to the greatness of Shakespeare's artistry.

(f) Late Plays

Gordon McMullan's *Shakespeare and the Idea of Late Writing: Authorship in the Proximity of Death* [2007] was discussed in detail in last year's review. His contribution to this year's *Shakespeare and the Cultures of Performance*, edited by Paul Yachnin and Patricia Badir, also merits attention, if only to show that the concept of 'late' writing continues to be debated. '*The Tempest* and the Uses of Late Shakespeare in the Cultures of Performance: Prospero, Gielgud, Rylance' (a version of the concluding chapter of his monograph) explores 'the appropriation of Shakespearean lateness as a vehicle for the self-conscious structuring of theatrical careers' (p. 147). Focusing on John Gielgud's and Mark Rylance's involvement with *The Tempest* at various stages of their careers, McMullan argues that both actors use the idea of late Shakespeare—and specifically *The Tempest* as Shakespeare's last play, and the assumption that Prospero is Shakespeare's alter ego—to validate their theatrical careers. In this lively and engaging essay, McMullan draws attention to the '*utility*' (p. 153) of the idea of lateness in Shakespeare, and exposes our investment in the idea of lateness as 'a final flowering' (p. 150). While it is for this that the essay is most valuable, it also makes a significant contribution to our understanding of Shakespearian theatrical careers.

In contrast to McMullan's revisionary work on lateness, the concluding chapter of Patrick Cheney's monograph, *Shakespeare's Literary Authorship*, presupposes a 'late or mythic phase' (p. 234) of Shakespeare's literary career. Picking up on an idea raised in the epilogue of his 2004 book, *Shakespeare, National Poet-Playwright*, Cheney reads in Shakespeare's work the assertion of a 'counter-laureate authorship', which he brings to a close with an examination of *Cymbeline*:

> *Cymbeline* helps conclude a study of Shakespeare's literary authorship— his historic role as national poet-playwright—because it is the only late

romance formally set in Britain. It therefore affords a unique opportunity to wed the political topic of nationalism to the literary topic of romance, especially since late in his career Shakespeare rescripted this emergent stage genre by fusing a discourse of theatre to a discourse of poetry (p. 234).

In an appealing analysis of Imogen's conversation with Pisano about her plan for reuniting with Posthumous at Milford Haven, Cheney sums up his approach to *Cymbeline*: 'The conversation turns out to be about "Britain", but it also combines an ancient trope for lyric poetry, the discourse of print culture, and theatre, and so forms a memorable miniature of Shakespeare's literary authorship near its close' (p. 238). Cheney identifies *Cymbeline* as a play about Shakespearian authorship, and specifically a play about the author's writing of Britain: 'As a late national romance about Shakespeare's counter-laureate career, *Cymbeline* functions as a testament to his historic authorship' (p. 242). In what he calls his *'intertextual intratextuality'* (p. 246), Cheney demonstrates that in *Cymbeline* Shakespeare alludes to the work of other ancient and contemporary poets specifically concerned with the writing of nation through self-conscious references to his own previous work. Cheney thus suggests that Shakespeare presents himself as 'self-conscious counter to the Western art of laureate self-presentation' (p. 263) as he reviews his literary authorship towards the end of his career. Following McMullan's challenge to the idea of lateness, the notion of 'late Shakespeare' must be accepted with caution. Still, in 'Venting Rhyme for a Mockery: *Cymbeline* and National Romance', Cheney's concept of 'counter-laureate authorship' offers a fresh reading of *Cymbeline* and Shakespeare's literary canon as a whole. Within this, a particular highlight is his persuasive reading of the bedroom scene, which for the first time interprets the Ovidian allusions through Imogen and not Iachimo, and thus focuses 'on the author's literary representation of female consciousness and identity' (p. 246).

Also highlighting *Cymbeline*'s preoccupation with nation but taking a very different approach, Andrew Escobedo's 'From Britannia to England: Cymbeline and the Beginning of Nations' (*SQ* 59[2008] 60–87) considers the idea of England, Britain, and the question of national origins in the play. Observing that *Cymbeline* 'registers a transition from conceiving the nation as a community of deep-rooted *nati* to conceiving it as a community of rather recent origin' (p. 62), he argues that it 'dramatizes the tension between a sense of a British nation, awkwardly heterogeneous but linked to antiquity, and an English nation, potentially pure but severed from tradition' (p. 63). Reading *Cymbeline* as a response to the question 'What is a nation?', Escobedo argues that the play offers two answers: '(1) the (British) nation is a community that tries to make the best of the heterogeneity of deep roots, or (2) the (English) nation is a community that eschews roots for the sake of purity in the present' (p. 65). In this carefully researched and persuasively argued essay, Escobedo demonstrates the complexity of *Cymbeline*'s representation of nation and makes a significant contribution to the continuing debate about national consciousness in the early modern period, and the question of 'Britain' in particular.

In a second essay on *Cymbeline* in *Shakespeare Quarterly*, Bonnie Lander challenges the conflation of Imogen with the idea of nation that has characterized much criticism of the play. 'Interpreting the Person: Tradition, Conflict, and *Cymbeline*'s Imogen' (*SQ* 59[2008] 156–84) focuses on the 'person' of Imogen, and argues that the play explores two different models of personhood—the culturally determined and the self-determined—through its representation of Imogen, and imagines her as 'a philosophical adventurer who interrogates these opposed conceptions of character in order to achieve a satisfying definition of personhood in which both conceptions exist in dynamic interrelationship' (p. 158). Taking this approach, Lander produces an interesting new reading of the ending of the play and the circumstances in which Imogen can proclaim 'I am nothing', and she concludes: 'The contradictory position [Imogen] embodies confirms the necessity of dismantling the immensely powerful structures governing identity formation, even if such structures can never ultimately be discarded. The defining nature of identity must not be allowed a tyrannical hold, yet such definitions can and must never be wholly overthrown; selfhood itself relies on them' (p. 181). The essay makes its argument through a detailed discussion of the play's performance history and, more importantly, its reception, and for this it is particularly useful.

In the first of two pieces on service in the late plays, David Schalkwyk's *Shakespeare, Love and Service* looks at the ways in which the personal, affective relations of love are informed by the social, structural interactions of service. His concluding chapter, ' "Something more than man": *The Winter's Tale*', identifies Camillo, Antigonus, Paulina, Hermione and Autolycus among the servants who populate *The Winter's Tale* (and offers insightful overviews of their particular representations of service), but focuses on Paulina, who, as the play's 'chief agent of resistance, healing, and restoration' (p. 263), he understands as the epitome of service in the Shakespearian canon. Maintaining that *The Winter's Tale* represents the crisis of service in the face of tyranny more than any other Shakespearian play, he identifies 'disobedience, critical opposition, and judicious counsel' (p. 263) as the essential qualities of service. And while he challenges the assumption that service is inherently conservative, Schalkwyk argues that 'Shakespeare's concern with the affective ethics of *continued* service even in the face of tragic obduracy, represents a dimension that cannot be encompassed by the mere politics of resistance' (p. 263). In this richly nuanced analysis of representations of service in *The Winter's Tale*, the subtle reading of Camillo's relationship with his two masters, Leontes and Polixenes, is a particular strength. Also noteworthy is its penetrating reading of the statue scene in which, Schalkwyk concludes, 'What we witness through the inversion of master and servant in Act Five [i.e. Leontes' transferral of power to Paulina] are the transformations of desire into love and of power into service' (p. 296).

The theme of service is also taken up in Melissa E. Sanchez's 'Seduction and Service in *The Tempest*' (*SP* 105:i[2008] 50–82), which situates the play in the context of Jacobean debates on the duties and responsibilities of kingship, and specifically the continuing struggles between king and parliament that the Great Contract of 1610 failed to resolve. She argues that *The Tempest* reflects upon these debates, and reminds its audience that 'indulgence and assault, seduction and force, are not opposites but simply different expressions of the claim to erotic, and hence political, agency' (p. 81). Focusing on Miranda, the article is most interesting for its questioning of her subjugation, and its exploration of her relationship with both other subjects (Caliban, Ariel) and other women (Sycorax, Claribel). Sanchez also provides an intriguing analysis of Prospero's epilogue, which, she argues, aligns the audience with Prospero's other subjects.

In her informative article on Caliban and Miranda's education, 'Single Parenting, Homeschooling: Prospero, Caliban, Miranda' (*SEL* 48[2008] 373–93), Hiewon Shin questions the interpretation of Prospero as a patriarchal imperialist and offers a more sympathetic analysis of his relationship with Caliban and Miranda as both father and educator. She argues that Caliban received good schooling from Prospero until his attempted rape of Miranda, after which he was denied a masculine education, made to engage in domestic chores, and trained only for feminine service. This view is broadly compatible with colonial readings of the play, of course, but this is not Shin's primary focus. She then argues that the education of Miranda is untypical for the period, and persuasively suggests that her training allows her to challenge traditional gender roles. Anchoring her analysis of *The Tempest* with a detailed discussion of the education and training of children in the early modern period, Shin's essay draws upon writers such as Thomas Elyot, Thomas Salter, Henry Smith, and Juan Luis Vives. While it sometimes implies that ideas about children's education were straightforward and accurately reflected children's educational experiences, the essay's argument that Prospero offered a progressive education to Miranda is convincing, and its alternative reading of Caliban's education and training is interesting (if potentially controversial).

Katherine Steele Brokaw turns her attention to Ariel in her captivating essay on Ariel's performance history. 'Ariel's Liberty' (*ShakB* 26:i[2008] 23–42) has at its heart Julian Bleach's celebrated performance for the RSC, but situates Bleach's Ariel in the context of other performances of *The Tempest*. In doing so, Brokaw delightfully shows how the best Shakespearian adaptations always shed new light on the play. Making her case through detailed textual analysis, she argues that Shakespeare deliberately left the role of Ariel open to the actor's interpretation. Emphasizing the richly metatheatrical nature of *The Tempest*, Brokaw argues that 'this textually ambiguous, wide-open, liberated role pushes hard on questions of who creates meaning in theatre, inviting an actor's body to exceed the disciplines of the text' (p. 39). Reflecting on the fertile ambiguity of the play's construction of Ariel, this article brings Ariel and *The Tempest* vividly to life through its detailed discussion of the history of Ariel in performance.

Ariel is also the focus in the first of two essays on sources for *The Tempest* published in 2008. David McInnis, in 'Old World Sources for Ariel in *The Tempest*' (*N&Q* 55[2008] 208–13), posits Wilkins, Day and Rowley's *The Travels of the Three English Brothers* [1607] and Richard Eden's *A treatyse of the newe India with other new founde landes and islandes* [1553], a translation of portions of Sebastian Munster's Latin text, *Cosmographia*, as possible Old World sources for the play. In doing so, he challenges the assumption that the play is about America, and instead argues that *The Tempest* is 'a *generic* travel play, concerned simply with the unknown and the psychology of exploration' (p. 210). Reading Ariel in the context of stories of malignant spirits coming from Old World travel, McInnis's essay makes a significant contribution to the continuing debate about *The Tempest*'s colonial contexts, and offers a fresh perspective on the play. Alden T. Vaughan, on the other hand, returns to more familiar New World sources for *The Tempest*, contending, in 'William Strachey's "True Reportory" and Shakespeare: A Close Look at the Evidence' (*SQ* 59[2008] 245–73), that critics such as Roger Stritmatter and Lynne Kositsky have been incorrect in rejecting Strachey's letters as a source for Shakespeare's play. Vaughan sets out his evidence carefully—the letter reaching London in September 1610; at least two copies circulating widely; as well as the thematic and verbal parallels with the play—and makes a good case for the legitimacy of the 'True Reportory' as a source for *The Tempest*; I wonder if this marks an end to this particular debate.

Michael Neill certainly assumes the influence of the 'True Reportory' when he draws attention to the acoustic effects in the representation of the Bermuda shipwreck in his discussion of the uses of sound in Shakespeare's play. Reminding us that *The Tempest* 'is equipped with an elaborate soundtrack, in which episodes of violent, discordant, and chaotic noise are set against the harmonious songs and instrumental music performed by Ariel and his consort of spirits' (p. 36), '"Noises, / Sounds, and sweet airs": The Burden of Shakespeare's *The Tempest*' (*SQ* 59[2008] 36–59) focuses on the play's representation of concord and discord, exploring how the play's meaning is expressed through aural effects. Focusing on its elaborate play on the word 'burden' in its musical and other senses, Neill shows how *The Tempest* challenges the binary of ordered speech and disordered noise and links this to Prospero's exercise of power on the island. This complex and beautifully written essay offers a meticulous reading of the play's orchestration of sound and shows again the value of attending to aural effects in Shakespeare's plays.

While Neill observes that *The Tempest* is 'steeped . . . in the language and motifs of scripture' (p. 58), Huston Diehl's essay, '"Does not the stone rebuke me?": The Pauline Rebuke and Paulina's Lawful Magic in *The Winter's Tale*' (in Yachnin and Badir, eds., pp. 69–82), focuses in detail on theological allusions in *The Winter's Tale* to explore Paulina's connection with her namesake, the apostle Paul, and in doing so argues that she is situated at the centre of Reformation debates about 'the nature of representation, the power of words, the status of images, and the legitimacy of the theatre' (p. 71). In particular, Diehl reads the statue scene as a 'visual rebuke' that completes the work of Paulina's earlier verbal rebukes, and thus shows how Paulina's theatrical spectacle does Leontes good. Showing how Shakespeare 'appropriates Paul for his own theatrical purposes' (p. 75), the chapter offers a persuasive analysis of the statue scene. It promotes a more nuanced understanding of Protestantism and theatre, arguing that through the play Shakespeare develops 'a Protestant aesthetic of the theatre in direct response to attacks by Protestant clergy' (p. 76).

David N. Beauregard, in contrast, relocates Shakespeare to a Catholic context in his monograph, *Catholic Theology in Shakespeare's Plays*. Based on the contention that Shakespeare was Catholic, the book attempts to uncover evidence of Catholic theology in the plays. 'Nature and Grace in *The Winter's Tale*' argues that the action of the play 'is structured along the lines of the three "parts" of the Roman Catholic sacrament of penance, following the movements of contrition, confession, and satisfaction' (p. 109). Taking a similar approach, '"Let your indulgence set me free": Prospero's Farewell in *The Tempest*' argues that Prospero's epilogue 'contains a peculiar series of references to sin, grace, and pardon that are the expressions of a sensibility rooted in Roman Catholic doctrine' (p. 145). Beauregard's evidence of 'non-explicit' (p. 146) Catholic theology in the two plays is more or less convincing, even if he has a tendency to homogenize diverse reformist theologies and practices in order to assert Catholic particularity. And while the implications of his arguments could be teased out further—reading such references as 'essentially mimetic' (p. 109) is a little unsatisfying—Beauregard's work does help to uncover the plays' theological underpinning.

The next three essays on *The Winter's Tale* explore issues of gender and sexuality in the play. In 'Framing Wifely Advice in Thomas Heywood's *A Curtaine Lecture* and Shakespeare's *The Winter's Tale*' (*SEL* 48[2008] 131–46), Kathleen Kalpin revisits the issue of Leontes' jealousy and links it, as many others have done, to Hermione's persuasive speech. In a detailed reading of Act I, scene ii, Kalpin argues that Leontes reads Hermione's conversation with Polixenes as a curtain lecture (persuasive speech between a wife and her husband that takes place in bed), and immediately reaches the conclusion that his wife has been unfaithful with his friend. By making the same conceptual leap that she accuses Leontes of making (from private speech to curtain lecture), Kalpin perhaps overstates her case. Nevertheless, treating the curtain lecture as a distinct genre (her discussion moving from Pepys to Erasmus to Heywood), Kalpin suggests that its representation of persuasive female speech is ambivalent, 'complicating any simple causal relationship between women's speech and their sexual actions' (p. 132). With broad implications for the play's debate about female speech and sexuality, this is the essay's significant achievement.

In 'Siring the Grandchild in *The Winter's Tale* and *The Fawn*' (*SEL* 48[2008] 349–71), Robert W. Reeder moves from the relationship between husbands and wives to explore the intergenerational tensions between fathers and sons (Polixenes and Florizel, primarily, but also Leontes and Mamillius), which, he suggests, come to a head 'when the *next* generation is in view' (p. 351). 'Prospective grandchildren', argues Reeder, 'serve as a site of conflict between father and son: are they going to reflect the father's will or the grandfather's?' (p. 350), and he offers a nuanced reading of the father's sexual jealousy implicit in Polixenes' relationship with Florizel and Perdita, and Leontes' relationship with Mamillius, Hermione and Perdita. Reading *The Winter's Tale* as prodigal son drama, Reeder argues that Leontes and Florizel's embrace at the end of the play offers the hopeful possibility that conflict between father and son can be resolved because 'the scene stages the fact that the same person can—and, in time, will—stand in the place of son and father' (p. 350). This is a rich and carefully argued essay that sheds important light on the struggles between men that are dramatized in the play.

Shifting from sons to daughters in *The Winter's Tale*, Diane Purkiss's provocative essay, 'Fractious: Teenage Girls' Tales in and out of Shakespeare' (in Lamb and Bamford, eds., *Oral Traditions and Gender in Early Modern Literary Texts*, pp. 57–72), reads *The Winter's Tale* primarily as 'the romance of the discovery of the daughter' (p. 57), and focuses on Perdita, the daughter whose story, she claims, is subordinated to that of her parents in both the play itself and its critical reception. Uncovering traces of folk tales told by adolescent girls in the play's representation of parent–child relationships, she shows how Perdita's story chimes with stories told by real teenage girls in the early modern period. Reading the play through detailed analysis of depositions given by adolescent girls in witch trials, Purkiss maintains that these young women had 'a storyteller's stake in the tale of the lost girl because it was a story they told about themselves, a story that could be a tale of rebellion and subversion of all that being a teenage girl meant' (p. 57). Specifically, she reads girls' fairy tales as fantasies by which they both express and relieve their anxieties around their relationships with mothers/mistresses. However, she points out that in *The Winter's Tale* it is Leontes who 'becomes a nightmare version of the teenage girls' nightmares about their mothers' (p. 68), which, she claims, oddly legitimates his passions. Purkiss's essay is less about *The Winter's Tale* than the marginalized voices of teenage girls that are fleetingly glimpsed in the play, but this is the key strength of the essay, which ably demonstrates how the play is steeped in an oral tradition, and she helps us to return to the voices that speak through the play.

Two student-orientated guides to Shakespeare's most-studied late plays were published in 2008, both of which focus on the plays in performance. The first, Ros King's *The Winter's Tale: A Guide to the Text and the Play in Performance*, is the latest addition to Palgrave Macmillan's Shakespeare Handbooks series. As with other titles in the series, at the core of the book is a detailed scene-by-scene commentary, which gently guides students through the play as it raises thought-provoking issues and questions, especially around performance. A student-friendly overview of critical assessments of the play showcases its richness and helps students formulate their own responses to the play. A particular highlight is the book's sections on key productions of the play on stage and screen, which illuminate the play through its performance history and open up for the student new interpretative possibilities. Also useful, in its discussion of the play's sources and cultural context, is its comparison with Robert Greene's *Pandosto*, which is helpfully illustrated with generous excerpts from the text.

The second student guide is Lisa Hopkins's *Shakespeare's The Tempest: The Relationship between Text and Film*, which like the other books in Methuen's Screen Adaptations series, provides in-depth analysis of how *The Tempest* has been adapted for the screen—specifically, in Fred Wilcox's *Forbidden Planet* [1956], Derek Jarman's *The Tempest* [1979], and Peter Greenaway's *Prospero's Books* [1991]—and shows how the alternative readings demonstrated in each of the films represent new interpretations of the original text. The opening part of the book, 'Literary Contexts', provides an overview of responses to the play by literary critics. Focusing on William Strachey's pamphlet as source for the play, and then raising issues of colonization and exploration, and their connection with gender and sexuality, Hopkins prioritizes postcolonial readings of the play; however, she also introduces other interpretations, such as psychoanalytical and genre-based readings. She then finishes the first part by showcasing the many ways in which the play has been adapted in a variety of media, and very usefully raises key issues inherent in the process of adapting the play (considering a variety of topics from setting, time-frame and genre to back story and music). The main part of the book, 'From Text to Screen', introduces the three substantial case studies via a detailed history of the play on screen, which is then followed by a conclusion that compares their different takes on the play through the readings they emphasize or subordinate. Hopkins's comparison of film adaptations of the play with the perspectives of literary critics is particularly useful. On the question of Caliban's blackness, for example, she writes: 'Although literary criticism may not have all the answers, this is one area in which it has at least attempted to bring an informed political awareness to the play' (p. 144). Finally, a discussion of critical responses to each of the films, supplemented with generous quotation, brings the book to a conclusion. Accessibly written and bursting with ideas for studying *The Tempest* through film, this is an excellent resource for film and literature students and their teachers. Its crowning achievement is in showing students how screen adaptations of the play represent interpretations rather than offering transparent access to the play, and it helps bring the play to life through a consideration of filmic performance.

Another exciting volume aimed primarily at students is Laurie Maguire's *How To Do Things with Shakespeare: New Approaches, New Essays*. In this creative and innovative collection, Shakespearian scholars were asked to preface specially commissioned essays with a short description of what prompted them to embark on their particular research project, with the aim of helping students to develop their own critical approaches to Shakespeare. Three essays are included on the late plays: Tanya Pollard examines *Cymbeline* in the context of Greek romance; Chris R. Kyle explores *Henry VIII*'s specific use of history; and Paul Yachnin reads *The Winter's Tale* in terms of Renaissance ideas about animals: 'it is sheep all the way down' (p. 216). An engaging collection of essays in their own right, this volume introduces students to contemporary approaches to Shakespeare in a stimulating and accessible way. Its particular strength lies in its self-consciousness about the process of literary research, which will be both inspiration and invaluable resource to students as they begin to formulate and develop their own research projects.

Books Reviewed

Anderson, Judith H. *Reading the Allegorical Intertext: Chaucer, Spenser, Shakespeare, Milton*. FordUP. [2008] pp. 436. £49.50 ISBN 9 7808 2322 8478.

Azari, Ehsan. *Lacan and the Destiny of Literature: Desire, Jouissance and the Sinthome in Shakespeare, Donne, Joyce and Ashbery*. Continuum. [2008] pp. 205. £60 ISBN 1 8470 6379 3.

Bartels, Emily C. *Speaking of the Moor: From Alcazar to Othello*. UPennP. [2008] pp. vii + 252. $55 ISBN 9 7808 1224 0764.

Bate, Jonathan, *Soul of the Age: The Life, Mind and World of William Shakespeare*. Viking. [2008] pp. xii + 500. £25 ISBN 9 7806 7091 4821.

Beauregard, David N. *Catholic Theology in Shakespeare's Plays*. UDelP. [2008] pp. 226. $49.50 ISBN 9 7808 7413 0027.

Belsey, Catherine. *Shakespeare in Theory and Practice*. EdinUP. [2008] pp. 224. £60 ISBN 9 7807 4863 3012.

Bevington, David. *Shakespeare's Ideas: More Things in Heaven and Earth*. Blackwell. [2008] pp. 248. £45 ISBN 9 7814 0516 7956.

Bloom, Harold, and Brett Foster, eds. *Hamlet*. ChelseaH. [2008] pp. 464. $50 ISBN 9 7807 9109 5928.

Braunmuller, A.R., ed. *Macbeth*, 2nd edn. The New Cambridge Shakespeare. CUP. [2008] pp. xxi + 297. hb £40 ISBN 9 7808 6240 0, pb £8.99 ISBN 9 7805 2168 0981.

Brown, Jane K. *The Persistence of Allegory: Drama and Neoclassicism from Shakespeare to Wagner*. UPennP. [2007] pp. 304. £39. ISBN 0 8122 3966 0.

Cahill, Patricia. *Unto the Breach: Martial Formations, Historical Trauma, and the Early Modern Stage*. OUP. [2008] pp. x + 227. £50 ISBN 9 7801 9921 2057.

Cheney, Patrick. *Shakespeare's Literary Authorship*. CUP. [2008] pp. xxv + 296. £57 ISBN 9 7805 2188 1661.

Cormack, Bradin. *A Power To Do Justice: Jurisdiction, English Literature, and the Rise of Common Law, 1509–1625*. UChicP. [2008] pp. 406. £24 ISBN 0 2261 1624 2.

Crystal, David. *'Think on my words': Exploring Shakespeare's Language*. CUP. [2008] pp. 272. hb £40 ISBN 9 7805 2187 6940, pb £ 12.99 ISBN 9 7805 2170 0351.

Davies, Michael. *Hamlet*. Character Studies. Continuum. [2008] pp. viii + 141. hb £50 ISBN 9 7808 2649 5914, pb £11.99 ISBN 9 7808 2649 5921.

Davis, Philip. *Shakespeare Thinking*. Continuum. [2007] pp. 105. £14.99 ISBN 0 8264 8695 0.

Dawson, Anthony B., and Gretchen E. Minton, eds. *Timon of Athens. William Shakespeare and Thomas Middleton*. Arden3. [2008] pp. 480. hb £60 ISBN 9 7819 0343 6967, pb £17 ISBN 9 7819 0343 6974.

Delabastita, Dirk, Jozef de Vos, and Paul Franssen, eds. *Shakespeare and European Politics*. AUP. [2008] pp. 385. £70.50 ISBN 9 7808 7413 0041.

Dente, Carla, and Sara Soncini, eds. *Crossing Time and Space: Shakespeare Translations in Present-Day Europe*. PLUS/Pisa University Press. [2008] pp. 128. €14 ISBN 9 7888 8492 5404.

Donskis, Leonidas. *Power and Imagination: Studies in Politics and Literature*. Lang. [2008] pp. 170. £32.90 ISBN 1 4331 0125 0.

Drábek, Pavel, Klára Kolinská, and Matthew Nicholls, eds. *Shakespeare and His Collaborators Over the Centuries*. CambridgeSP. [2008] pp. xii + 242. £76. ISBN 9 7818 4718 9783.

Drakakis, John, and Dale Townshend, eds. *Gothic Shakespeares: Accents on Shakespeare.* Routledge. [2008] pp. 243. pb £19.99 ISBN 0 4154 2066 0.

Dutcher, James M, and Anne Lake Prescott, eds. *Renaissance Historicisms: Essays in Honor of Arthur F. Kinney.* UDelP. [2008] £57.50 ISBN 9 7808 7413 0010.

Elam, Keir, ed. *Twelfth Night.* Arden. Methuen. [2008] pp. 428. £8.99 ISBN 9 7819 0343 6998.

Greenblatt, Stephen, et al., eds. *The Norton Shakespeare,* based on the Oxford edn.; 2nd edn. Norton. [2008] pp. xviii + 3,419. $60.99 ISBN 9 7803 9392 9911.

Greer, Germaine. *Shakespeare's Wife.* Bloomsbury. [2007] pp. 406. £8.99 ISBN 0 7475 9300 3.

Guneratne, Anthony R. *Shakespeare, Film Studies, and the Visual Cultures of Modernity.* Palgrave. [2008] pp. 346. £45 ISBN 9 7814 0396 7886.

Hatchuel, Sarah, and Nathalie Vienne-Guerrin, eds. *Shakespeare on Screen: The Henriad.* URouen. [2008] pp. 358. pb €21 ISBN 2 8777 5454 5.

Hatchuel, Sarah, and Nathalie Vienne-Guerrin, eds. *Shakespeare on Screen: Television Shakespeare. Essays in Honour of Michèle Willems.* URouen. [2008] pp. 315. pb €21 ISBN 9 7828 7775 4507.

Henderson, Diana E, ed. *Alternative Shakespeares 3.* Routledge. [2008] pp. x + 310. £62 ISBN 0 4154 2332 5.

Hopkins, Lisa. *Shakespeare's The Tempest: The Relationship between Text and Film.* Methuen. [2008] pp. 224. £12.99 ISBN 9 7807 1367 9106.

Jackson, Russell. *Shakespeare Films in the Making: Vision, Production and Reception.* CUP. [2007] pp. 280. £53 ISBN 0 5218 1547 5.

Jensen, Phebe. *Religion and Revelry in Shakespeare's Festive World.* CUP. [2008] pp. xii + 267. £50 ISBN 9 7805 2150 6397.

King, Ros. *The Winter's Tale: A Guide to the Text and the Play in Performance.* Shakespeare Handbooks. Palgrave. [2008] pp. 168. £42.50 ISBN 9 7802 3000 8519.

Klause, John. *Shakespeare, the Earl, and the Jesuit.* FDUP. [2008] pp. 339. £59.95 ISBN 9 7808 3864 1378.

Lamb, Mary Ellen, and Karen Bamford, eds. *Oral Traditions and Gender in Early Modern Literary Texts.* Ashgate. [2008] pp. 276. £55 ISBN 9 7807 5465 5381.

Lethbridge, J.B., ed. *Shakespeare and Spenser: Attractive Opposites.* ManUP. [2008] pp. 320. £50 ISBN 9 7807 1907 9627.

Levy-Navarro, Elena. *The Culture of Obesity in Early and Late Modernity: Body Image in Shakespeare, Jonson, Middleton and Skelton.* Palgrave. [2008] pp. xii + 238. £40 ISBN 9 7802 3060 1239.

Logan, Robert A. *Shakespeare's Marlowe.* Ashgate. [2007] pp. vii + 251. £55 ISBN 9 7807 5465 7637.

Maguire, Laurie. *How To Do Things with Shakespeare: New Approaches, New Essays.* Blackwell. [2007] pp. 320. £60 ISBN 9 7814 0513 5269.

Maguire, Laurie. *Shakespeare's Names.* OUP. [2007] pp. 256. £28 ISBN 9 7801 9921 9971.

Majeske, Andrew, and Emily Detmer-Goebel, eds. *Justice Women, and Power in English Renaissance Drama.* AUP. [2008] pp. 193. £40.50 ISBN 9 7808 3864 1699.

Malin, Eric S. *Godless Shakespeare.* Shakespeare Now. Continuum. [2007] pp. 132. £14.99 ISBN 9 7808 2649 0421.

Marrapodi, Michele, ed. *Italian Culture in the Drama of Shakespeare and his Contemporaries: Rewriting, Remaking, Refashioning.* Ashgate. [2007] pp. 300. £55 ISBN 9 7807 5465 5046.

Massai, Sonia. *Shakespeare and the Rise of the Editor.* CUP. [2007] pp. 254. £53 ISBN 9 7805 2187 8050.

Matz, Robert. *The World of Shakespeare's Sonnets: An Introduction.* McFarland. [2008] pp. 240. £29.95 ISBN 9 7807 8643 2196.

Meek, Richard, Jane Rickard, and Richard Wilson, eds. *Shakespeare's Book: Essays in Reading, Writing and Reception.* ManUP. [2008] pp. vii + 273. £55 ISBN 9 7807 1907 9054.

Moschovakis, Nick, ed. *Macbeth: New Critical Essays.* Routledge. [2008] pp. xi + 363. £65 ISBN 9 7804 1597 4042.

Newstok, Scott L, ed. *Kenneth Burke on Shakespeare.* Parlor Press. [2006] pp. 368. £35 ISBN 9 7816 0235 0038.

Nicholl, Charles. *The Lodger: Shakespeare on Silver Street.* Lane. [2007] pp. 378. £20 ISBN 9 7807 1399 8900.

Nuttall, A.D. *Shakespeare the Thinker.* YaleUP. [2007] pp. 428. £10.99 ISBN 0 3001 3629 6.

Occhiogrosso, Frank, ed. *Shakespearean Performance: New Studies.* FDUP. [2008] pp. 211. $47.50 ISBN 9 7808 3864 1286.

Palfrey, Simon, and Tiffany Stern. *Shakespeare in Parts.* OUP. [2007] pp. 416. $45. ISBN 0 1992 7205 0.

Potter, Nicholas. *Othello: Character Studies.* Continuum. [2008] pp. 152. hb £50 ISBN 9 7808 2649 4320, pb £11.99 ISBN 9 7808 2649 4337.

Richmond, Velma Bourgeois. *Shakespeare as Children's Literature: Edwardian Retellings in Words and Pictures.* McFarland. [2008] pp. 363. £29.92 ISBN 0 7864 3781 8.

Rutter, Tom. *Work and Play on the Shakespearean Stage.* CUP. [2008] pp. x + 205. £50 ISBN 9 7805 2188 4860.

Sabor, Peter, and Paul Yachnin, eds. *Shakespeare and the Eighteenth Century.* Ashgate. [2008] pp. 189. £55 ISBN 0 7546 6295 2.

Schalkwyk, David. *Shakespeare, Love and Service.* CUP. [2008] pp. 336. £52 ISBN 9 7805 2188 6390.

Schwartz, Regina Mary. *Sacramental Poetics at the Dawn of Secularism: When God Left the World.* Stanford. [2008] pp. 187. £49.50 ISBN 9 7808 0475 6679.

Schwyzer, Philip. *Archaeologies of English Renaissance Literature.* OUP. [2007] pp. 256. £59 ISBN 9 7801 9920 6605.

Shamas, Laura. *We Three: The Mythology of Shakespeare's Weird Sisters.* Lang. [2007] pp. 140. £34.90 ISBN 0 8204 7933 0.

Shami, Jeanne, ed. *Renaissance Tropologies: The Cultural Imagination of Early Modern England.* Duquesne. [2008] pp. 382. £49.99 ISBN 9 7808 2070 4098.

Shaughnessy, Robert, ed. *The Cambridge Companion to Shakespeare and Popular Culture*. CUP. [2007] pp. 291. £48 ISBN 9 7805 2184 4291.

Sokol, B.J. *Shakespeare and Tolerance*. CUP. [2008] pp. 260. £50 ISBN 9 7805 2187 9125.

Steinberger, Rebecca. *Shakespeare and Twentieth-Century Irish Drama: Conceptualizing Identity and Staging Boundaries*. Ashgate. [2008] pp. 132. £50 ISBN 9 7807 5463 7806.

Stewart, Alan. *Shakespeare's Letters*. OUP. [2008] pp. xvi + 405. £26 ISBN 9 7801 9954 9276.

Taunton, Nina. *Fictions of Old Age in Early Modern Literature and Culture*. Routledge. [2007] pp. 210. £95 ISBN 0 4153 2473 1.

Turner, Henry S. *Shakespeare's Double Helix*. Continuum. [2007] pp. 129. £13.99 ISBN 0 8264 9120 6.

Waller, Gary ed. *All's Well That Ends Well*. New Critical Essays. Routledge. [2007] pp. xix + 258. £70 ISBN 9 7804 1597 3250.

Warren, Roger ed. *The Two Gentlemen of Verona*. OUP. [2008] pp. 208. £7.99 ISBN 9 7801 9283 1422.

Weimann, Robert, and Douglas Bruster, *Shakespeare and the Power of Performance: Stage and Page in the Elizabethan Theatre*. CUP. [2008] pp. x + 266. £52 ISBN 9 7805 2189 5323.

Weis, René. *Shakespeare Revealed: A Biography*. Murray. [2008] pp. 444. £10.99 ISBN 0 7195 6574 8.

Welsh, Alexander. *What is Honor? A Question of Moral Imperatives*. YaleUP. [2008] pp. xxiv + 228. £25 ISBN 9 7803 0012 5641.

Wilson, Richard. *Shakespeare in French Theory: King of Shadows*. Routledge. [2007] pp. 336. $37.95. ISBN 0 4154 2165 9.

Yachnin, Paul Edward, and Patricia Badir, eds. *Shakespeare and the Cultures of Performance*. Studies in Performance and Early Modern Drama. Ashgate. [2008] pp. 224. £55 ISBN 9 7807 5465 5855.

VII

Renaissance Drama: Excluding Shakespeare

SARAH POYNTING, ELEANOR COLLINS, JESSICA DYSON,
ANDREW DUXFIELD AND SAM THOMPSON

This chapter has three sections: 1. Editions and Textual Scholarship; 2. Theatre History; 3. Criticism. Section 1 is by Sarah Poynting; section 2 is by Eleanor Collins; section 3(a) is by Jessica Dyson; section 3(b) is by Andrew Duxfield; section 3(c) is by Sam Thompson.

1. Editions and Textual Scholarship

After last year's flood of material, publication of critical editions this year diminished to a trickle. Leah Scragg's fine edition of John Lyly's short pastoral drama *Love's Metamorphosis* is, therefore, particularly welcome, though it would have been so whenever it appeared. It follows her editions of *Euphues* and *The Woman in the Moon*, and means that of Lyly's plays only *Mother Bombie* has not yet been re-edited for the Revels series. The text itself is uncomplicated, there being only one, well-printed, early edition, a quarto of 1601 probably based on authorial copy; four more recent editions (including one in an unpublished Ph.D. thesis) are collated with the quarto in the textual apparatus. More problematic are the dates of writing and first performance, and the contentious question of whether the play has been abridged or revised for a revival or for publication. Scragg proposes a date of *c*.1588, rejecting arguments based on 'tenuous' topical references for a later one (pp. 9, 29–31), and similarly finds no proof that the length of *Love's Metamorphosis* might be the result of censorship. She examines the evidence concerning performance, taking into account information on the quarto title page that the play was staged by both children's companies, and suggests that it may well have been revived in the late 1590 s. In considering its brevity, she describes the uneven layout of the increasingly widely spaced quarto text and assesses the possible reasons behind it. The annotation of the text itself is as helpful as might be expected, being notably strong in its consideration of the play's staging: Scragg

Year's Work in English Studies, Volume 89 (2010) © *The English Association; all rights reserved*
doi:10.1093/ywes/maq011

draws attention, as in the introduction, to the emblematic and spectacular effects achieved by scenic devices and properties.

In her rich and thoughtful critical introduction, Scragg discusses *Love's Metamorphosis* in relation both to its sources, and in particular Ovid's tale of Erisichthon (*Metamorphoses*, Book VIII), and to the corpus of Lyly's own plays. She delineates his variations from Ovid, and demonstrates how these contribute to Lyly's exploration, as in other of his plays, of the tensions between love and chastity. Typically he works through a pattern of oppositions in language, character and staging, which is especially clear in this play, as she shows, owing to the tightness and clarity of its dramatic structure with its lack of sub-plot. His employment of the 'courtly Pastorall' mode, as the title page has it, is at its purest in *Love's Metamorphosis* in Lyly's adherence to genre conventions, but he challenges audience expectations in its resolution. Ambiguity is inherent to Lyly's representation of characters who take up fixed positions in a mutable and unstable world, and it is this ambiguity which has led to the very varied critical responses to the play, and especially to its denouement, which Scragg outlines. These disagreements are also found in judgements as to the extent of its contemporary references, which Scragg looks at in a very interesting section on 'Gender Politics and the Elizabethan Court', finding contemporaneity less in specific topical allusions than in the play's distinction between virginity and chastity, and in its dismissal of misogyny and patriarchal assumptions.

The second play from ManUP is a Middleton I missed in 2007, though it is one that may well get more use than that year's hefty *Collected Works*, being a Revels Student edition of *Women Beware Women* by J.R. Mulryne. This is based on his full edition of 1975, and has both gained and lost in adaptation. The new introduction is particularly strong in siting the social attitudes and morality expressed in the play in the context of Middleton's city comedies, and in examining links between Florence and London, assessing the effects of the collection of Florentine art on contemporary London culture. Staging is well considered—indeed Mulryne's discussion resembles, at times, notes for budding directors—in relation to location, scenic space and properties. Mulryne perceptively analyses individual 'inset' scenes that provide 'crucial insights' (p. 19) without necessarily furthering the plot (the chess game, for example, and the Ward's inspection of Isabella), and draws out the final masque's possible parallels with Jonson's *Hymenaei*. The examination of characterization, however, is a little cursory, and the list of further reading a little elderly. There is no section on performances of the play, but a reference to the 1969 RSC production suggests that the introduction was, rather regrettably, written prior to the 2006 revival. The annotation of the text has unavoidably shrunk from the 1975 version, but is still informative and reasonably full for this kind of edition.

The Malone Society Reprint for 2007 (published 2008) again comes from ManUP, to which the society migrated after many years with OUP. It is a full-colour facsimile edition on glossy paper of the Lambarde manuscript of John Fletcher's *The Woman's Prize* (perhaps better known as *The Tamer Tamed*), and a handsome, if unwieldy, volume it is. It is prepared and introduced by Meg Powers Livingston, who briefly discusses the uncertain provenance of the manuscript before it turned up at the Folger Shakespeare Library, the print history of the play, its authorship and date. On the latter she disagrees with Gary Taylor's and Celia Daileader's dating of late 1609 to early 1610 in their Revels Student edition *The Tamer Tamed*, preferring the slightly later (and traditional) 1611. She then gives us a very clear description of the physical state of the manuscript, pointing out that cracking in its margins means that the Folger has been forced to restrict access to it, making this edition all the more useful. She describes in great detail the hands to be found in it, drawing attention to idiosyncratic letter forms, punctuation and contractions, and analysing the emendation of errors, which includes a second correcting hand. The three seventeenth-century texts of *The Woman's Prize* are compared, together with their relationship to the activities of the censor, Sir Henry Herbert. In discussing the text of the manuscript, Livingston challenges the argument put forward by R.C. Bald and Fredson Bowers that its omissions, as compared with the Folio text, indicate that cuts had been made to accommodate a touring company, arguing rather that overall the manuscript has a closer relationship to Fletcher's play as performed in 1611 than does F1. She suggests that the copy-text for it was probably a prompt copy, and proposes a date earlier than the 1633 revival which caused such problems with the censor, and probably between 1611 and 1623. Appendix A lists the corrections made by the original scribe (those made by the second hand are included in the description of the copying of the manuscript), while appendix B gives us the differences between the manuscript and F1 that are attributable to censorship, defined according to Herbert's objections as 'Oaths', 'Ribaldry' and 'Profanity'. These are, usefully, keyed not only to the line numbers of this version, but to the act, scene and line numbers of Bowers's edition. A final appendix provides a table of references between Malone (by line number and folio number), F1 (by page numbers and signatures) and Bowers. The facsimile itself is beautifully and very clearly produced, the finely written manuscript shown actual size, with discreet marginal line numberings. It is a most valuable addition to the Malone collection (though I wish I had a bookshelf big enough for it).

Martin Wiggins adds to the World's Classics collection of early modern drama with his useful edition, *A Woman Killed with Kindness and Other Domestic Plays*, the others being the anonymous *The Tragedy of Master Arden of Faversham*, *The Witch of Edmonton* (Dekker, Rowley and Ford), and *The English Traveller* (Heywood). The introduction briefly outlines the nature of the genre in its attribution to largely non-aristocratic, contemporary characters of the potential for tragedy, before looking at each play in more detail in terms of action, characters and themes. These individual discussions are helpfully cumulative, so each one builds on and refers back to what has been said about the previous play(s). The social standing of the protagonists is given particular attention, Wiggins showing in relation to *Arden of Faversham* that, whatever their status, the drive of all the characters is upwards, their individualistic aspirations leading to a ruthless—if sometimes incompetent— willingness to destroy others. Ironically, it is Arden's one kindly act that leads to the success of the plot against him. By contrast, he argues, hospitality and social bonds are central to Heywood's more introspective *A Woman Killed with Kindness.* Wiggins demonstrates the thematic 'contrasts and continuities' between the main action and the sub-plot (otherwise tenuously connected), being especially illuminating on 'the shaming power of kindness' (pp. xiv, xx), and the ways in which in both threads of the play it is women who suffer by it. He is, though, more inclined to find Frankford a generally benign figure than experience suggests most students do. In discussing *The Witch of Edmonton*, Wiggins suggests that the development of the 'domestic' genre by the 1620s had led to a shift in dramatic language, achieving greater realism and an effective apparent artlessness by largely abandoning the openly rhetorical style that still characterized the earlier plays. He concentrates on issues of human moral responsibility and guilt in relation to the 'devil-dog', while demonstrating how both are affected less by the supernatural than by social status. It is, perhaps, slightly odd to draw attention to plot inconsistencies without ever referring to collaborative authorship, and it might have been helpful for student readers to be given some idea of how this operated. *The English Traveller* is probably the least well known of the plays, and it is good to have it easily available, especially as Paul Merchant's Revels edition *Three Marriage Plays*, in it was which included, is now out of print. As Wiggins shows, the English world of the play is markedly different from that in the preceding plays, being 'strikingly stable' (p. xxvii). Characters become complacent about the courtesies and contentment of their social life, seeing danger as external and foreign: as a result the tragic denouement is all the more shocking. The four plays are then drawn together again by Wiggins, who concludes that, far from being homiletic, as might be expected, they all 'resist easy moral classifications' (p. xxxiv).

The endnotes (bookmark, as always, required) are helpful, and like Leah Scragg's edition, particularly so in making stage 'business' clear. The first appendix examines the authorship of *Arden of Faversham*, Wiggins arguing firmly that whoever it was, he was not a professional dramatist since it 'shows a striking disregard for the techniques and limitations of the theatre' (p. 285); Marlowe, Kyd, Shakespeare et al. are decisively rejected. In the second appendix, he looks again at the date of *The English Traveller*, proposing that it was written at the end of 1624. In addition there is a very useful descriptive bibliography; a list of domestic plays 1590–1642 (which indicates that this was, whatever its development, quite a rare genre); and a chronological catalogue of the four plays' source material, publication, adaptation and production, including casts. I wasn't entirely sure about the purpose of it all, but it was good to be reminded of David Bradley's Shakebag and Miles Anderson's gleefully wriggling Dog. A revival of all the first three plays would be welcome, but a first modern production of *The English Traveller* would be even better.

Articles of textual interest were almost equally rare this year. MacDonald P. Jackson, presumably recovered from his exertions on Middleton and Webster, has turned his attention to 'New Research on the Dramatic Canon of Thomas Kyd' (*ROMRD* 47[2008] 107–27). In it he takes issue with Brian Vickers's attribution to Kyd, in an article in the *TLS*, of three anonymous plays (*Arden of Faversham*, *The True Chronicle History of King Leir*, and *Fair Em the Miller's Daughter of Manchester*), as well as a substantial part of *1 Henry VI*. He challenges Vickers's methodology, suggesting that he 'has entered Kyd in a one-horse race, which Kyd cannot fail to win' (p. 108). Using *Arden* as an example and employing a more rigorous system of comparison, he finds that 'unique matches' (listed) with *2 Henry VI* and *The Taming of the Shrew* outnumber those with Kyd's drama. Jackson states that his purpose is not to argue for Shakespeare's authorship of *Arden* (though, unlike Martin Wiggins, he seems to favour it), nor even to claim that Kyd had no hand at all in these plays, but to demonstrate that Vickers's case for expanding the Kyd canon is inadequate.

Wiggins himself returns in 'When Did Marlowe Write *Dido, Queen of Carthage?*' (*RES* 59[2008] 521–41). In this he disputes the assumption, based, he argues, on no better proof than impressionistic value judgements about style, that *Dido* was Marlowe's first play: he places it rather after *Tamburlaine 1* and *2*, and close to the composition of *Faustus*. He assesses the problems posed by the title page of the 1594 quarto in assigning the play to the Children of her Majesty's Chapel as performers, and to Marlowe and Nashe as joint authors, suggesting that we should be prepared to take its evidence seriously. The idea that *Dido* is no more than a translation of the *Aeneid* is challenged by demonstrating the effects of the modifications made to Virgil's text, while arguments that the play was written by Marlowe when a student at Cambridge for a university production are similarly rejected on the grounds both of language (not in Latin) and of the demands of staging. The history of the children's companies is re-examined, along with the date and language of *The Wars of Cyrus*, which like *Dido* was published in 1594 as acted by the Children of the Chapel. Wiggins analyses similarities between the two plays before sketching out his own narrative for how Marlowe might have come to write *Dido* for the company. It is unlikely to be the last word on the subject, but it certainly shakes up traditional thinking.

Dating is again the subject of David Nicol's 'The Date of *The Thracian Wonder*' (*N&Q* 55[2008] 223–5). Rowley's pastoral romance has gone through a number of proposed datings, the most recent placing it in 1611–12. Nicol argues that the late 1610s or even early 1620s may be more accurate, on the grounds that the play is probably a collaboration with Heywood (and therefore likely to be later rather than earlier), and reveals striking similarities with *The Changeling*. Internal evidence, he suggests, is supported by connections with the publication of other plays by Rowley and/or Webster, all written in the early 1620s.

Jonson makes his only appearance this year in Holger Schott Syme's subtle and interesting article, 'Unediting the Margin: Jonson, Marston, and the Theatrical Page' (*ELR* 38[2008] 142–71), in which he argues that, far from the publication of his drama signalling a deliberate removal of his plays from a theatrical to a literary context, both the process and form of their printing constitute their reinscription within the performative community of the stage. He focuses on 'the non-verbal signifiers of the page' (p. 149)—primarily the typographical use of margins—in the works of Marston, Webster and, especially, Jonson. The first of these, as he shows, was one of the earliest dramatists to have a play, *The Malcontent*, printed in 1604 with marginal stage directions, while Jonson moved from the literary glosses of *Sejanus* to a similar concern with textual representation of stage action. The result is that what characters *do* is shown simultaneously with what they *say*, rather than the two being separated, as they are when stage directions are printed within the body of the text, as was normal. This is clearly illustrated with passages from early editions of *The Malcontent*, *Sejanus*, *The Alchemist* (both of them from Q and F1) and *Bartholomew Fair*. He looks closely at the playwrights' relationships with individual printers to demonstrate that this must have been the result of a collaboration that mimicked that of the theatre. In this account of Jonson's printing strategies, he emerges as a writer who was not only not hostile to the public theatre throughout his career, as he is commonly represented as being, but actively engaged, from the 1612 quarto of *The Alchemist* up until the publication of *The New Inn* in 1631, in reproducing its visual effects on the page as an essential element in his text.

Winner of most popular playwright of the year emerges as Heywood, who reappears in the final article, 'Foul Papers, Promptbooks, and Thomas Heywood's *The Captives*' by James Purkis (*MRDE* 21[2008] 128–56). Paying particular attentions to cuts, annotations and corrections, Purkis offers a 'micro-narrative of early modern textual revision' (p. 129) through a detailed analysis of Heywood's holograph manuscript, which he compares with Munday's *John a Kent and John a Cumber* to reassess past and current thinking on the nature of playbooks in general. He challenges the commonly held view that the manuscript is too messy and illegible to have been used by a bookkeeper during performance (I would have appreciated the opportunity to have an opinion on this by some illustrations), arguing that this is based on a misunderstanding of bookkeeping duties, which did not include those of the modern prompter. In asserting that it is quite possible for the manuscript to have been thus used, he complicates (not for the first time, of course) Greg's division between 'foul papers' and 'promptbooks', as well as Gurr's explanation of licensing by the Master of the Revels. As he recognizes, his own account constitutes an alternative but still speculative narrative: it is not an unfamiliar disclaimer.

2. Theatre History

An emphasis on the study of hitherto neglected non-Shakespearian plays and dramatists characterizes a large proportion of recent work in early modern theatre history. David Nicol's fresh interpretation of William Rowley's gender politics leads the way, in ' "My little what shall I call thee": Reinventing the Rape Tragedy in William Rowley's *All's Lost by Lust*' (*MRDE* 19[2006] 175–93). He argues that Rowley radically breaks with convention in his attempt to 'shift the blame for rape away from the victim and onto ideological admonitions to female silence' in the play (p. 180). Rather than subscribe to tragic theatrical convention, in which rape victims are either murdered as a direct result of their rape or commit suicide, Rowley keeps Jacinta 'noisily and energetically alive' (p. 175) until the closing scene, in which her tongue is cut out before she is stabbed and killed, in circumstances unrelated to her violation, by her father Julianus. Following the play's emphasis on the phallic symbolism of swords, Nicol reads the scene as a stark reminder of Julianus's failure to protect her; her murder becomes a 'metaphorical rape' enacted by her own father. Rowley's final rendering of Jacinta in the 'traditional image' of a 'tongueless rape victim' hereby serves 'to remind the audience of her powerlessness *before* the event, as well as after it, and to criticize that powerlessness' (p. 186). Most interesting in this analysis is Nicol's contention that Rowley's social criticism, and his support of female subjectivity through the manipulation of the conventions of genre, are indebted to his theatrical role as an actor as well as a playwright. If Rowley's acting experience as a clown, a character who 'specializes in holding up social conventions for ridicule', provided him with a perspective that enabled him to depart from the 'strict ideologies underpinning conventional dramatic structures' (p. 186), Nicol makes a convincing argument that we should look for exceptions to the rule in the 'popular' dramatists rather than the 'learned' (p. 186), and search for 'radical answers' at the margins (p. 176).

It is in something of this spirit that Kirk Melnikoff and Edward Gieskes frame their collection, *Writing Robert Greene: Essays on England's First Notorious Professional Writer*—though the outcome is perhaps less radical than might be expected. The essays here provide a new critical context for the playwright and pamphlet-writer, and assess his impact upon both the theatrical and literary professions. The editors compare Greene to Dekker and Middleton, as dramatists 'whose positions in and relation to a broader cultural market have been obscured by a sustained focus on other writers' (p. 12), and in so doing establish that the shortcoming is our own, and not Greene's; his marginality to early modern drama is a consequence of the critical tendency to dismiss Greene as '*the* Elizabethan "hack writer" who wrote prolifically, lived profligately, and died squalidly' (p. 12). In its attempt to redress the balance, the collection emphasizes that Greene's professional commitments and ambitions placed him between the 'two very different burgeoning economies' of print and professional theatre, but that his work for either should be treated as part of a 'continuum' (pp. 6–7). The means by which Greene straddled both worlds, and the ways in which his role as a writer of pamphlets and romances framed his approach to playwriting, is the subject of many of the essays collected here. The strategies by which Greene 'engages in the struggle for authority within the [dramatic] profession', and Greene's 'negotiations with the idea of dramatic authorship', are two such recurring themes (p. 19). Alan Dessen explores the specifics of Greene's 'theatrical vocabulary' in a move to establish dramatic distinctiveness and innovation in Greene's work, while Ronald A. Tumelson's essay explores Greene's 'renegotiation of the cultural status of the early modern English playwright' and the construction of literary authorship, years before the publication of Jonson's 1616 Folio. Much energy is also expended in dispelling the orthodox critical assumption of Greene's 'antitheatrical bias', by revising the contexts for Greene's infamous 'upstart crow' comment in *Greene's Groats-Worth of Wit,* and reclaiming the writer from dominant narratives that unquestioningly accept the straightforward polarization of Shakespeare and Greene.

In complicating the received wisdom on Greene, one of the book's collective contentions is to argue for his professionalism and skill in negotiating different markets, audiences and authorial constructions of himself as a writer.

Noting that the charge of sensationalism applies to many biographical accounts of Greene (which, it must be said, the subtitle's description of Greene as a 'notorious' writer does little to avert), Melnikoff and Gieskes argue for a departure from Greene's 'bohemian' reputation towards an appreciation of his acute professionalism. They suggest that Greene's 'multiple engagements with the literary field index authorial and literary sophistication rather than bohemian disinterest or pecuniary desperation' (p. 24), and propose that his writerly practice 'was structured by a distinctly "professional" space of cultural production' (p. 13). This is a useful context in which to place Greene, though one cannot help but feel that his 'professionalism' is summoned in order to compensate for both the quality and significance of his work. The suspicion is strengthened in a discussion of the extent to which Greene's success is thought to have ultimately depended on whether there was room for him in the cultural economy: on 'a combination of his cultural capacity and the availability of positions in [the literary or dramatic] field' (p. 14). The argument finds itself in difficult territory here in terms of the process of justification for critical attention to Greene, though this is not borne out by the essays that follow. Perhaps this lack of conviction in the strength of Greene's 'cultural capacity' alone explains the sense in which the book does not make a strenuous argument for Greene's role at the centre of things; its resistance to overstating the case for Greene is admirably temperate. Though Greene's writing and professional practices are described, and his role in early modern drama and authorship is properly examined, his contribution remains somehow anticipatory—and therefore preliminary. The upshot is that Greene remains curiously marginal despite this renewed attention, though the collection helps us recognize the importance of that marginality, and is instrumental in rethinking the reasons behind it.

Paul Whitfield White also looks outwards in his *Drama and Religion in English Provincial Society, 1485–1660*, a wide-ranging but carefully considered examination of 'the ways in which drama engaged with religious culture in provincial England' (p. 7). In one of the first book-length studies to organize the material collected by REED according to a particular narrative angle, White continues to address the 'anti-provincial bias in modern theatrical scholarship' (p. 2) and focuses on the relationship between drama outside London and the social, cultural and religious contexts in which it was performed. White's ambitions are modest, and he is anxious to stress that the present study is by no means definitive or exhaustive—in either archival or methodological terms. But the engaging anecdote with which he introduces the work, which describes an ill-fated provincial performance in Witney, Oxfordshire, dispels two commonly held myths about early modern theatre: first, that drama was unperformed after 1642, and second, that provincial drama was mainly performed by travelling professional companies. To the contrary, this performance was acted in 1652 by a group of countryside parishioners. White also raises the important issue of the critical 'period-ization' of drama, for his study challenges the understanding of parish drama as a primarily medieval phenomenon, with predominantly Catholic associations. Instead, he examines the complicated ways in which drama continued to be connected with religious practice and community, and the processes of revision and negotiation that it underwent in order to retain its popularity, relevance and viability under changing religious and political circumstances.

Consistent with his criticism of periodization, White's organizing principle is predicated on the 'local conditions of sponsorship, production, and reception' of the drama, rather than its chronology (p. 5). His resistance to the structural convention of telling an ordered 'history' of drama makes the book a challenge to navigate at times, but it does give the work a focus that it might otherwise lack, spanning as it does such a broad time-frame. The book's distinctive local focus also enables White to pose meaningful questions about the reception of plays originally performed in London, as he does with respect to the 1635 performance of *The Late Lancashire Witches* in Oxford, reading into Nathaniel Tomkyns's famous account of the Globe performance 'a level of sophistication and astuteness that we normally do not associate with provincial spectatorship' (p. 188). White's work is an important development in the understanding of the intricate social and religious engagements and responsibilities of provincial drama, and an indicator of the kind of work that the REED project is now enabling.

Moving back into the mainstream, and at the other end of the spectrum, is Darryll Grantley's *London in Early Modern English Drama*, which describes the sixteenth-century commercial theatre as 'an overwhelmingly metropolitan phenomenon' (p. 1). Grantley's focus is 'on how geographical localities in the capital are talked about . . . on how they function as settings for narratives and on how the incorporation of local geography becomes part of the theatre's range of staging conventions' (p. 2). The emphasis on geographical specificity and representation in the drama is not in itself new, but Grantley's engagement with the 'social texturing' of drama through topographical reference is interesting in the way that it endows early modern audiences with 'imaginative ownership of the terrain on which the theatrical narratives were being played out', as well as contributing to perceptions of their 'actual habitat' (pp. 5, 7). In this way, Grantley analyzes the fictive city—which 'inserts itself into the drama as a player more than as merely the setting of dramatic narratives' (p. 5)—within the framework of theatrical convention, and also with an eye to the streets and stone amongst which the audiences made their way to the playhouses. He explores the powerful and pervasive influence of the 'moralized geography' of London (p. 7), and the ways in which theatre helped to define specific relations between fictionalized place, actual space, and social and political meaning.

Affirming a strong sense of periodization, the book is divided into analysis of the 'pre-commercial theatre interlude drama', late Elizabethan drama, Jacobean drama and Caroline drama. This chronological span enables an appreciation of the 'shift from the moralized geography of the earlier religious dramas to the much greater tangibility of topography in the secular plays of the commercial theatre', though Grantley remains sensitive to the 'residual presence of mythic or quasi-mythic associations of place' (p. 13). There are potential difficulties with the project—both methodological and practical—as Grantley willingly admits: first, of 'trying to get to grips with the way in which drama represents a larger spatial entity such as a metropolis' (p. 14), and second, the acknowledgement of the 'considerable divergence in the extent to which early modern drama incorporates a sense of familiar place in its narratives' (p. 20). The breadth of drama available for analysis is as daunting for the project as it is enabling, though the chapter on pre-commercial interlude drama, which includes the plays of George Gascoigne, John Skelton, John Bale and Robert Wilson, covers drama that, for the most part, has remained beyond the remit of early modern theatre criticism. It is perhaps inevitable that the further Grantley progresses in the period, the more familiar the plays become, and the usual suspects in discussion of London 'place' all make their appearance: *The Shoemaker's Holiday*, *Eastward Ho!*, *The Weeding of Covent Garden*, *The Sparagus Garden* and *Hyde Park*. Grantley rehearses a fairly familiar narrative, tracing the move from representations of a moralized and allegorized city in the Elizabethan period to the more complexly social and specific topographical references in Jacobean city comedies and, finally, the 'current of self-congratulation' in Caroline drama that was concerned with 'fashionable' and 'modish' pastimes, and which provided 'definition of the elite urbanite' by juxtaposing the city with the country (p. 187). It is, however, an important and substantiated account of that narrative, taking into consideration the contribution of the physical venues of the theatre and the changing topography of the city as determining processes.

Two essays return to the core issue of theatrical practice and company operation. Robert Barrie interrogates the 'rarely challenged' assumptions that underpin our understanding of boy players as 'apprentices' to the theatrical profession (p. 238), in 'Elizabethan Play-Boys in the Adult London Companies' (*SEL* 48[2008] 237–57). The problem is our commonly accepted comparison of the boy-players' contractual arrangements with the guild system model, which has governed the context and capacity of the boys' work and conditions for too long. Barrie finds instead that arrangements were often on a more short-term basis than has been recognized, and that labour rights in boys could be rented out in 'sales or lease transactions' to theatrical companies (p. 244). He also offers the surprising discovery that some of these 'apprentice boys' were, rather than pre-pubescent dependants, in fact married men. Barrie's detailed historical analysis concerns itself with the minutiae of theatrical employment, but he is quick to emphasize the importance of such processes of subtle differentiation. The apprentice analogy 'so oversimplifies the conditions of the play-boys that it distorts the nature of the drama in which they played such vital roles' (p. 250); these 'vital' (and often female) roles were regularly performed by 'expendable commodities', rather than by 'apprenticed' boys who would go on to 'become hired men or even company sharers' (pp. 250, 251, 252). Barrie both effects a necessary factual correction and, in the same vein as William Ingram's research, shows how close biographical work has far-reaching and striking repercussions for analysis of company dynamics and, in this case, performance.

Christopher Matusiak's essay, 'Christopher Beeston and the Caroline Office of Theatrical "Governor"' (*EarT* 11:ii[2008] 39–56), is similarly concerned with the analysis of company operation, though from a managerial perspective. The essay considers the circumstances under which Queen Henrietta's Men broke in 1636, leading to the formation of a new company, the 'King's and Queen's boys', of which Beeston was appointed governor.

Matusiak attributes Beeston's promotion in theatrical status to his connections with the Herbert family—particularly the Lord Chamberlain and Henry Herbert, Master of the Revels—arguing that Beeston's non-theatrical involvement in prominent London building projects provided him with social and financial leverage, while his gifts to Herbert acted as a series of 'carefully encoded' reminders 'of the obligation to bestow favour upon a client' (p. 42). The identification of networks of patronage at work is helpful, if not necessarily surprising, but many of the ideas and readings offered by Matusiak in the process are original and invite more exposition and attention; for instance, the ranking of 'governor' as something like 'an adjunct position in the Revels Office' (p. 49), and the attribution of the disintegration of Queen Henrietta's Men to an internal 'dysfunction' that consisted of the younger actors' usurpation of veteran roles in the company (p. 46). According to Matusiak, it is only in the role of governor that Beeston acquired 'the authority to make and break acting companies', and this new reading of the breaking of the Queen's Men and formation of Beeston's Boys 'requires us to modify the conventional image of the impresario as a ruthless, market-driven autocrat' (p. 51). Instead, Beeston is recast as 'an amphibious creature, as carefully adapted to the courtly ambit of Whitehall as to the theatrical marketplace of Drury Lane' (p. 51)—in many ways an altogether less pleasant construction of character, though with suggestive implications for the future understanding of Beeston's theatrical ventures.

3. Criticism

(a) General

To begin with single-authored monographs: in her excellent *The Drama of Coronation: Medieval Ceremony in Early Modern England*, Alice Hunt offers an assessment of the ceremony of monarchical coronation in the Tudor period. This highly original study views the documents and texts that survive from the reigns of the Tudor monarchs as both literary works and as historical evidence and allows us a detailed view of these fascinating elite spectacles. Separate chapters deal with the coronations of Henry VIII, Anne Boleyn, Edward VI (including new work on John Bale's *King Johan*), Mary I (including a discussion of *Respublica*) and, of course, the ceremony for Elizabeth I. Hunt has had to show great skill in weaving this together thematically, and the result is an innovative and groundbreaking study of ceremony in early modern England. The introduction carefully contextualizes the Tudor ceremonies, because, as Hunt makes clear, they 'were not...limited to the ceremony of anointing and crowning that took place in Westminster Abbey, before a select audience on a chosen day. Indeed it is the counterpart to the sacred, private rite—the monarch's procession through the city of London on the eve of the coronation—that has been more commonly studied' (p. 7). Furthermore, because of the historical scope of this monograph, Hunt is able to synthesize neglected areas of literary research, such as the reign of Mary, alongside more 'popular' critical work on Elizabeth, such as the wealth of scholarship on the cult of Elizabeth and the related field of progress studies. This is an extremely valuable study for research into all of the Tudor reigns mentioned above, and will be particularly fruitful for those interested in elite and courtly cultures as well as to researchers of spectacle, ceremony and even the later Stuart masques.

Michelle Ephraim's monograph *Reading the Jewish Woman on the Elizabethan Stage* examines the ways in which a wide variety of dramatic texts, both less well known, such as George Buchanan's *Jephthes Sive Votum Tragoedia*, and the more popular *The Jew of Malta* and *The Merchant of Venice*, present the figure of the Jewish woman. Ephraim's main focus is on the ways in which the body of the Jewish woman on the Elizabethan stage can be read as an embodiment of the Hebrew scriptures to which the Elizabethan, Christian, Protestant audience sought access, and over which they sought interpretative control. The book's argument is divided into two parts. In the first part, Ephraim discusses the body of Queen Elizabeth herself as such a scriptural body, arguing that, in *The Godly Queen Hester* (possibly written under Henry VIII, but published during Elizabeth's reign) and *The Historie of Jacob and Esau*, in chapters 1 and 2 respectively, 'by figuring the queen as Deborah, Rebecca and Esther, writers position Elizabeth within the history of God's chosen people, confirming her connection to the text that became the Protestant *prisca veritas*' (p. 21). Concluding this first part, Ephraim discusses Thomas Garter's *The Virtuous and Godly Susanna* and George Peele's *The Love of King David and Fair Bethsabe* in chapter 3, arguing that the sinful voyeurism in these plays is a form of misreading the scripture figured in Bethsabe and Susanna. In the second part, Ephraim shifts the focus to the archetype of the sacrificed daughter. In her discussion of George Buchanan's *Jephthes Sive Votum Tragoedia*, she establishes the paradigm of the sacrificed virgin body as a site of Christological transformation, going on in the following chapters to discuss the ways in which Marlowe and Shakespeare use and trouble the archetype of Jephthes' virgin daughter. She concludes that the idea of the Jewish woman's virgin body and the maternal body to which they are connected is overdetermined, simultaneously presented as the means to possessing scriptural *veritas* and the method of occluding it from the eyes of the Protestant suitors of Abigail and Jessica. Although highly specific in its focus, the broad range of texts Ephraim covers makes this book a valuable addition to discussions of religion on the Elizabethan stage.

Staying with the theme of religion, but moving away from religious truth to the efficacy and representation of religious practice and ritual, we have Thomas Rist's monograph, *Revenge Tragedy and the Drama of Commemoration in Reforming England*, which provides a strong and valuable reassessment of the genre of revenge tragedy. Taking Roland Broude's arguments that revenge tragedy is an anti-Catholic genre as his point of departure, Rist explores the representation of funeral and mourning rites and rituals in the plays, arguing that such a focus on remembrance suggests a much less 'Reformed' genre. Rist takes the fascinating approach of offering 'a historical method of interpreting such remembrance in each play, and hence an analysis of how each play interprets it' (p. 2). It is this interaction between the critic's and the plays' interpretation that makes this book a lively and interesting read. Beginning, in his first chapter, with a discussion of whether 'Outrage Fits' as commemoration of the dead in *The Spanish Tragedy*, *Titus Andronicus* and *Hamlet*, Rist goes on in chapter 2 to consider the interaction between mourning, commemoration and the location of the theatrical performance in John Marston's *Antonio's Revenge*, performed at Paul's Theatre, where the audience would enter and exit past real gravestones. In the third and final chapter Rist explores 'Melodrama and Parody: Remembering the Dead in *The Revenger's Tragedy*, *The Atheist's Tragedy*, *The White Devil* and *The Duchess of Malfi*'. Here, he argues that 'all but one of these plays address the performance of remembrance self consciously' by juxtaposing real and parodic, extended and restricted remembrances, so that each 'reflects uncertainly on the other' (p. 97). The exception is *The Revenger's Tragedy*, which Rist argues empties the sacred from religious rituals, and it is in this emptying that the play comments on commemoration of the dead.

While Bradin Cormack's *A Power To Do Justice: Jurisdiction, English Literature, and the Rise of Common Law, 1509–1625* is not solely concerned with Renaissance drama, dramatic texts form the majority of its literary content. Central to this wide-ranging book is division of legal jurisdiction, as Cormack argues that 'Even if jurisdiction is already a principle of distribution that dramatizes the law's operations from within, still it is the fictive encounter with that principle that brings the drama to light and to life' (p. 4). After an introduction which lays out the relationship between jurisdiction, legal ideology and literature, the book is divided into three parts, 'Centralization', 'Rationalization' and 'Formalization', and these stages in the establishment of the common law correspond to the Henrician, Elizabethan and Jacobean periods. In part I, chapter 1 takes as its jurisdictional focus debates over bureaucratic feudalism, and explores these in John Skelton's *Magnyfycence*, and chapter 2 examines Thomas More's writings as engaged with ideas of equity and the conflict of jurisdiction between church and state. In part II, Cormack explores 'the manufacture of English legal identity' (p. 227), by examining the crisis of jurisdiction in Ireland through Spenser's *Faerie Queene* in chapter 3, and in chapter 4 discussing the relationship between conquest and jurisdiction in France in Shakespeare's *Henry V* and *Richard III*. In part III, Cormack takes account of the complex ideas of *imperium* in chapter 5, as he considers Shakespeare's *Cymbeline* and *Pericles* as exploring 'the fragility of authority over distance' (p. 227), and finally, in chapter 6, he brings his discussion back to London, discussing Webster, Rowley and Heywood's *A Cure for a Cuckold* as a play in which the comedy is created through a clash of jurisdictions. Each chapter includes a detailed discussion of the jurisdictional problems with which it engages, and explores the dynamic relationship between the law and literary texts. This is an ambitious and useful intervention not only in early modern literary criticism, but also in the realms of law and literature.

Also relevant to this year's section on monographs is Todd Butler's *Imagination and Politics in Seventeenth-Century England*, although only two of the four chapters (2 and 3) deal with Renaissance drama. In chapter 2, entitled 'The "Immaginacy" of the Caroline Court Masque', Butler examines the roles of Ben Jonson and Inigo Jones in this crucial generic form of the 1630 s and then turns attention to the masques of 1632, as Jones went on to work with Aurelian Townsend on *Albion's Triumph* and *Tempe Restored* (p. 64). Furthermore, Butler examines the masques of 1634–5 under the subtitle 'Cracks in the Facade' (p. 73), including discussion of the *Triumph of Peace, Coelum Britannicum* and *The Temple of Love*, and concludes this chapter with a section on the last Caroline masques and 'The Collapse of a Genre' (p. 84). As Butler puts it, 'Beginning with William Devenant's *Britannia Triumphans* (17 January 1638)...the later masques of Charles's reign bear witness to...royal struggle and the increasing uncertainty of Caroline politics during the late 1630s' (p. 87). This textual and historical approach continues with a third separate chapter on John Milton, which includes a thought-provoking discussion of his *Mask at Ludlow* (*Comus*), as Butler examines 'The Revisioning of the Caroline Masque' (p. 97).

Staying with the Caroline years, we come to an excellent collection of essays edited by Adam Zucker and Alan B. Farmer which should have appeared in an earlier volume of *YWES*. Taken as a whole, the collection, entitled *Localizing Caroline Drama: Politics and Economics of the Early Modern Stage, 1625–1642* [2006] seeks to contextualize the drama of the 1630s, and opens with an excellent foreword by R. Malcolm Smuts and then, as the editors put it, 'present[s] a series of short-focus views of England's theatrical culture between the years 1625 and 1642' (p. 1). This introduction then goes on to justify expertly the need for this collection of essays and makes fascinating points about the printing of plays compared to the earlier Elizabethan and Jacobean reigns, including several useful tables. Further chapters by leading critics of the period include Kathleen E. McLuskie's discussion of 'Politics and Aesthetic Pleasure in 1630s Theater', a piece which is well positioned at the start of the collection. Lauren Shohet then continues her work on court drama in her 'Reading Triumphs: Localizing Caroline Masques', while Martin Butler revisits his earlier work on the period in his discussion of 'The Caroline Hall Theaters' (chapter 4). The collection's interest in theatre history continues with Richard Dutton's interesting examination of 'The St. Werburgh Street Theater' in Dublin, including a discussion of work by James Shirley (p. 137) in chapter 5, while Mario DiGangi offers critical work on 'The Monstrous Favorite in Caroline Drama' (chapter 6). Chapter 7 allows Jean E. Howard to offer a sustained critical reading of the neglected topic of Caroline town comedy, before the collection concludes with a detailed approach to Philip Massinger's *The Renegado* by Benedict S. Robinson in chapter 8. Overall, this is an extremely valuable collection of essays that simply has to be read by all scholars and students of both Renaissance drama and the Caroline period more particularly.

The year 2008 also witnessed the publication of Martin Butler's *The Stuart Court Masque and Political Culture* by Cambridge University Press. In this highly original, deeply significant and important study of the Stuart court and its accompanying theatre, Butler takes a chronological sweep through the years 1603 to 1641 and so tackles the masques in order of performance, while at the same time expertly organizing his discussion into ten chapters of separate but interlocking topics. As Butler makes clear in his introduction, 'This book studies English court festival under James I and Charles I in relation to the changing political and cultural climate of the time. It considers virtually the complete run of royal masques, from Queen Anne's first show at Winchester in 1603 to the last Whitehall festival, *Salmacida Spolia*, danced by Charles and Henrietta Maria in 1640 as the court geared up to confront rebellion in Scotland and the first parliament for eleven years. It presents the story of the form while integrating it into an encompassing narrative of political and cultural transformation. The masques are a vehicle through which we can read the early Stuart court's political aspirations and the changing functions of royal culture in a period of often radical instability' (p. 1). As this opening makes clear, this is certainly not an easy or straightforward task, but Butler then proceeds to justify the scope of the project by both offering fascinating discussions of the leading Stuart masques and simultaneously contextualizing them in terms of the politics and cultural debates of the times. Thus, the book charts the importance of the masque to literary criticism (including the breakthrough work of Stephen Orgel), the importance of new historicism, and the recent work of James Knowles, Karen Britland and Clare McManus. As is to be expected of twenty-first-century scholarship on the masque, the study is interdisciplinary in nature, as Butler examines these literary artefacts in the light of theory, politics, performance and staging, history, costume, gender (including new work on the two consorts), political factionalism and favouritism, spectacle, history of art, and ceremony. Owing to this, the study is of crucial importance to both students and scholars of the masque from a range of subject areas, but literary scholars are particularly indebted to Butler for his new calendar of all of the entertainments at the end of the book. Overall, this is a fine work of scholarship from one of the leading experts in the history of masque criticism.

Continuing with the activities of the Caroline court, the final book for inclusion here is a collection of essays edited by Erin Griffey, *Henrietta Maria: Piety, Politics and Patronage*. This volume, the editor argues, 'insists...on Henrietta Maria's importance as a political figure who attempted to shape court politics through her cultural patronage of representation in art, drama and music...based on the understanding that her piety was, ironically, her principal political tool' (p. 6). The book provides new and insightful perspectives on Henrietta Maria's patronage, although only two of the essays are concerned with drama. In chapter 3, 'Queen Henrietta Maria's Theatrical Patronage', Karen Britland continues her work on the queen's play-going, performance and patronage, arguing that in the 1633–4 season, Henrietta Maria and Charles's choices of drama for the court were aligned in promoting a type of 'exemplary drama' as part of Charles's 'reformatory project' for drama (p. 64), whereas her sponsorship of Floridor's French troupe in the 1634–5 season indicated her awareness of the possibilities for her own political influence through drama. Sarah Poynting's essay, '"The rare and excellent partes of Mr Walter Montague": Henrietta Maria and her Playwright' (chapter 3), discusses the political position of Montague in Charles's court, and the reasons for the queen's choice of this particular playwright, '[if] Montagu lacked dramatic experience, his sympathetic knowledge of the interests and problems of powerful, and would-be powerful, women was second to none' (p. 77). Poynting goes on to discuss

The Shepherd's Paradise in more detail, exploring the play's political positioning of women and desire. Overall, this is a valuable collection for anyone wishing to develop their understanding of Henrietta Maria's significance for Caroline arts.

Moving on now to shorter studies in scholarly journals, we begin with three different articles on the production and staging of theatrical entertainments. The first of these is Barbara D. Palmer's essay 'Staging Invisibility in Early Modern Drama' (*EarT* 11:ii[2008] 113–28). Taking the 'robe for to goo invisibell' purchased by Henslowe in 1598 as its starting point, this essay explores the different methods of staging invisibility from the early mystery cycles through to Elizabethan productions. Palmer gives five different modes: verbal markers, physical markers, prescribed and proscribed playing spaces, instruments, devices and, finally, deceptions or distractions. In the final section of the essay, Palmer goes on to suggest possible fabrics and designs for Henslowe's robe itself. Next we come to Jeanne H. McCarthy's essay, ' "The Sanctuarie is become a plaiers stage": Chapel Stagings and Tudor "Secular" Drama' (*MRDE* 21[2008] 56–86), which attempts to question prevailing orthodoxy that most secular plays of the Henrician and Elizabethan periods were performed in halls rather than chapels. McCarthy finds evidence within such plays as *The Godly Queen Hester*, *Youth*, *The Pardoner and the Frere* and *Hickscorner* that a chapel setting, and the youths of chapel companies, would be more appropriate and indeed more effective for the performance than adult companies in halls. These comments on boy actors leads us on to Robert Barrie's article, 'Elizabethan Play-Boys in the Adult London Companies' (*SEL* 48[2008] 237–57), which discusses the connections between boy actors and the playing companies, re-examining the 'apprentice' status of the boys. Barrie argues that the guild-style system, while the most common analogy, does not fit the evidence, and suggests a more plausible alternative might be employing the boys as covenant servants or Parish apprentices, paid and temporary, to take women's roles which may have been rejected by the company's free men.

Moving on to items concerned with plays of political interest, we begin with Allyna E. Ward's article in the *Early Modern Literary Studies* special edition 18 on George Gascoigne, ' "If the head be evill the body cannot be good": Legitimate Rebellion in Gascoigne and Kinwelmershe's *Jocasta*' (*EMLS* 14:i[2008] 33 paras). This interesting essay discusses the 1566 Inns of Court play in relation to resistance theories, arguing that although Creon is described as a tyrant at the beginning of the play, he does not act as such, and in refusing to take any real action against the rightful rulers until providence allows him the throne, he is shown to be the only legitimate ruler of Thebes. Following this, we have another discussion of rebellion, as Stephen Schillinger's article, 'Begging at the Gate: *Jack Straw* and the Acting Out of Popular Rebellion' (*MRDE* 21[2008] 87–125), seeks to re-examine the anonymous history play *Jack Straw* both as a play and as printed text. Schillinger argues that cursory glances at the play have led critics to argue that it is royalist in its political leanings, but that a closer examination of its content and paratexts in the 1604 printed edition suggests a play and an expected readership sympathetic to the rebels. Finally on history plays we have Miles Taylor's article, 'The End of the

English History Play in *Perkin Warbeck*' (*SEL* 48[2008] 395–418). This carefully argued essay considers the ways in which Ford's Caroline play *Perkin Warbeck* revives the outmoded history play genre in order to play out on the stage 'as a central concern its own obsolescence' (p. 415). Taylor explores the changes in historiography from the height of the Elizabethan history play to the Caroline presentation of *Perkin Warbeck* and argues that Ford's pragmatic Henry VII represents the more modern, factual, understanding of history as an embodiment of political practice, whereas the more theatrical Warbeck presents to us the rhetorical practices of earlier studies of history. In failing to include in the play Warbeck's confession (found in all of his sources) of counterfeiting his claim to the throne, Taylor argues, Ford allows issues of Warbeck's legitimacy, and so also Henry's, to remain unresolved. Thus, by analogy, the legitimacy of each branch of history also remains in the balance. This article is an important and interesting addition not only to scholarship on Ford, but also to that of the history play genre more broadly.

Staying with challenges to rulers, next we come to revenge tragedy in '*Oeconomia* and the Vegetative Soul: Rethinking Revenge in *The Spanish Tragedy*' (*ELR* 38[2008] 3–33). In this essay Christopher Crosbie examines the idea of revenge in Kyd's *The Spanish Tragedy* through ideas of class, particularly economic and social gain through good household management (*oeconomia*) and through the lens of Aristotelian tripartite psychology, arguing that revenge is shown as a natural, if dark, diversion of the soul's 'vegetative' part, which seeks personal advancement in a world structured by inflexible and unnatural class boundaries.

Ideas of class bring us on to Bradley D. Ryner's discussion of 'Commodity Fetishism in Richard Brome's *A Mad Couple Well Matched* and its Sources' (*EMLS* 13:iii[2008] 1–26). Ryner usefully places Brome's play in its literary context of 'lovers' gifts regained', arguing that this play combines pre-Chaucer versions of this tale, in which women are punished for turning sex into a saleable commodity by losing out on their expected economic gain, with Chaucer's *Shipman's Tale* version where, although the lady is not punished and is in fact able to sell sex twice, the reader is shocked by the lack of punishment. Ryner, using the Marxian idea of commodity fetishism, argues that Brome's play attempts to make a distinction between licit economic transactions and illicit sexual ones, but this distinction is undermined through the interchangeability of all commodities in money, when commodities are valued not on a fixed exchange rate, but through the fluctuations of desire. Also on this play, and complementing Ryner's work, we have Rachel E Poulsen's article, 'The "plentifull Lady-feast" in Brome's *A Madd Couple Well Matcht*' (*EarT* 11:i[2008] 77–97), which explores the economic relationships in the play in relation to the circulation of desire, suggesting that 'the play, which seems on the surface to be primarily about female transgression via adultery, is also a profound examination of credit, service, and the circulation of wealth and affect between women' (p. 91). Taking Eve Kosofsky Sedgwick's ideas of the homosocial triangle as a starting point, Poulsen argues that this play places women in the more powerful financial and erotic position, as the money and influence are taken into and remain in the hands of the female characters throughout the play.

Another item which deals with ideas of female agency is Keith Botelho's 'Maternal Memory and Murder in Early-Seventeenth-Century England' (*SEL* 48[2008] 111–30). Botelho discusses the threat to the patriarchal order embodied in the representation of the murdering mother. While the pamphlet and ballad discussed at the beginning of the article present women who murder their children as outcast not only by patriarchy, but also by any female community, Ford's *Love's Sacrifice*, Botelho argues, reverses this idea, in presenting a strong domestic community of women moving against patriarchy, as the women murder the father of their illegitimate children, making the private a matter for public concern.

Andrew Gurr and Karoline Szatek's article, 'Women and Crowds at the Theatre' (*MRDE* 21[2008] 157–69), attempts to take account of the influence of women in early modern theatre audiences. The authors take as their literary focus Heywood's *A Wise-Woman of Hogsdon* and Middleton and Dekker's *The Roaring Girl* and argue, based on the influential women in these plays, that theatre-going women of the period, despite the primarily negative contemporary accounts, could play a positive and significant role in forming crowd reaction to a play. Robert Tittler explores female agency in the early modern world outside the playhouse in his interesting article, 'Thomas Heywood and the Portrayal of Female Benefactors in Post-Reformation England' (*EarT* 11:i[2008] 33–52). Here, Tittler discusses Heywood's *If You Know Not Me You Know Nobody* as a social document, drawing attention to portraiture as a form of recognition for secular benefactors, particularly women of the middling classes, and suggests that Heywood may not only be commenting on contemporary activity, but encouraging such benefactions. Also concerned with female agency post-Reformation is Nandra Perry's carefully argued article, 'The Sound of Silence: Elizabeth Cary and the Christian Hero' (*ELR* 38[2008] 106–41). Perry critically intertwines the complex relationship between Cary's biography and her play *The Tragedy of Mariam* by means of the figure of the Christian martyr. Using Catholicism's and Protestantism's different modes of hagiography, and early modern understandings of the 'appropriateness of "public" language as a vehicle for Christian heroism', she argues that 'Mariam's emergence in the last act as a silent, stoical heroine marks her successful transformation from an eloquent, "Protestant" dissident into a reticent, "Catholic" martyr, whose ineffable, saintly interior is both signified and stabilized by her withdrawal from the sphere of "public" speech' (p. 122).

Next we have two articles considering gender, crime and cross-dressing. In 'The Theatricality of Transformation: Cross-Dressing, Sexual Misdemeanour and Gender/Sexuality Spectra on the Elizabethan Stage, Bridewell Hospital Court Records, and the Repertories of the Court of the Alderman, 1574–1607' (*EMLS* 13:iii[2008] 37 paras), Sara Gorman uses records from Bridewell to reconsider cross-dressing on the Elizabethan stage. She argues that male cross-dressing was considered and punished in the same way as female cross-dressing, so acts of female cross-dressing on the stage should not be considered as a comment made specifically on patriarchy's concerns about unruly women or female sexuality. Rather, Gorman moves away from female sexual transgression to a more inclusive idea of a fascination with the potential for transformation embodied in the cross-dressed figure. She argues that the stage was a perfect platform for 'prolonged speculation on . . . transitional states of being, whether they were embodied in the boy, the virgin, the transvestite of the actor himself' (para. 34). The next article is concerned with a more specific cross-dresser, Moll Cutpurse (Mary Frith). Alicia Tomasian's 'Moll's Law: *The Roaring Girl*, Mary Frith, and Corrupt Justice from the Streets to the Star Chamber' (*BJJ* 15[2008] 205–31) examines what purposes might have been served by Dekker and Middleton's presentation of Mary. In doing so, she compares the play's construction of its heroine with that of a Star Chamber case report, and her supposed posthumously published diaries, exploring Mary Frith's position in law as criminal or negotiator, and as having friends in high and low places.

Staying with Dekker, Meg F. Pearson's article, 'A Dog, a Witch, a Play: *The Witch of Edmonton*' (*EarT* 11:ii[2008] 89–111), explores the role of Dog in Dekker, Middleton and Rowley's play, highlighting the lack of agency the witch herself, Elizabeth Sawyer, has in comparison with the witches of other witch plays. Pearson emphasizes, through a comparison with Frank of the play's main plot, that it is Sawyer's social circumstances which cause her to turn to the Devil. However, the main focus of this article is the question posed to the audience through their interest in the theatrical abilities and agency of Dog. Pearson argues that the play leaves the audience to consider the moral dilemma of condemning the Devil and his acts, while at the same time finding the static world dull without him. It seems logical here also to mention Derek B. Alwes's 'The Secular Morality of Middleton's City Comedies' (*CompD* 42:ii[2008] 101–19), which re-examines the ways in which Middleton's plays, particularly *A Chaste Maid in Cheapside* and *A Mad World, My Masters* have been understood by critics, and proposes that a spiritually moral/immoral, or irreligious/diabolical framework is unhelpful in understanding the more problematic aspects of these plays. Rather, he suggests that Middleton advocates a human integrity, highlighted by oath-taking in the plays, to secure and maintain human community.

Another item concerned with human agency is Wendy Ribeyrol's 'The Character as Text in Philip Massinger's *A New Way to Pay Old Debts*' (*La Revue LISA* 6[2008] 208–16). Invoking the idea that man is a clean page on which he may write his own story, Ribeyrol discusses the literal and metaphorical uses of papers and texts in Massinger's *A New Way to Pay Old Debts*. She explores the idea of character as text in linking the characters' notions of honour with what may be written about them, and in doing so makes distinctions in gender between the possibilities that men might write themselves, but women are to be pure white sheets to be imprinted by men. In her discussion of the epilogue, she concludes that, in its allowance that Welbourne, whose slate is 'both literally and metaphorically wiped clean' (p. 216), may write himself anew, Massinger links the process of writing 'character as text' with that of writing the playtext itself. In the same way, given a second chance, both character and playwright might do better next time.

To finish this year, we have two articles which consider the relationship between theatre drama and its sale in print. In his excellent essay, ' "Follow the

Money": Sex, Murder, Print, and Domestic Tragedy' (*MRDE* 21[2008] 170–88), Peter Berek 'follows the money' both within the domestic tragedies he discusses, such as *Arden of Faversham*, *A Warning for Fair Women* and *Two Lamentable Tragedies*, and in the world of marketing printed plays of the 1590s and early 1600s. In the drama, he argues, contemporary anxieties of social mobility are displaced onto transgressive female sexuality, until financial acquisitiveness becomes more socially acceptable and therefore is shown more explicitly. In these later plays, it is the 'patient Griselda'-type women who can repair the damage done to society through the financial profligacy of men. In following the money in print, Berek argues that, as it became more acceptable to present social mobility on the stage and the printed play became 'secure enough not to need decking out in generic emblems of merit' (p. 181), domestic tragedy itself was established as a legitimate genre, and the generic marker of 'tragedy' was dropped from title pages. Finally, John Pendergast's ' "Comedies for Commodities": Genre and Early Modern Dramatic Epistles' (*ELR* 38[2008] 483–505) discusses the ways in which epistles accompanying printed texts sought to legitimize their playtexts as serious literature rather than common public theatre. Commenting on Fletcher's *The Faithful Shepherdess*, Shakespeare's *Troilus and Cressida* and Ford's '*Tis Pity She's a Whore*, Pendergast ranges through issues of genre, patronage and public/private performance spaces in his exploration of the ways in which playwrights and printers turned their texts into saleable commodities, at a time 'when playwrights were becoming professionals and plays were becoming literature' (p. 505).

(b) Marlowe

The most substantial contribution to research on Christopher Marlowe in 2008 came in the form of *Placing the Plays of Christopher Marlowe: Fresh Cultural Contexts*, a collection of essays arising from the proceedings of the Marlowe Society of America and edited by two of its former presidents, Sara Munson Deats and Robert Logan. This collection, which states in its introduction the aim of diverting critical attention away from biographically focused readings of Marlowe's work and towards analysis of it in newly considered cultural contexts, is divided into four sections: 'Marlowe and the Theater', 'Marlowe and the Family', 'Marlowe, Ethics, and Religion' and 'Marlowe and Shakespeare'.

The first of these sections begins with Sara Munson Deats's ' "Mark this show": Magic and Theatre in Marlowe's *Doctor Faustus*'. The essay notes a similarity between the rhetoric of anti-theatrical and anti-occult polemic before going on to identify a similar relationship between language pertaining to magic and that pertaining to theatre in Marlowe's play. After establishing these relationships, Deats proposes that the ultimate doom of Faustus might suggest a correlative scepticism on Marlowe's part regarding the future of his own brand of subversive theatre; in other words, his fear that 'the established forces of society might finally eradicate the rebellious playwright even as the authoritarian theological powers destroy the mutinous magician in the play'

(p. 24). In 'Marlowe's *Edward II* and the Early Playhouse Audiences', Ruth Lunney focuses on the role of the early modern theatre audience, highlighting the importance of reception and participation, and arguing that critical accounts of probable audience responses to Marlowe's works (usually figuring them as ambivalent) are too ready to accept the audience as passive. Discussions of Marlowe's manipulation of his audience, Lunney argues with reference to *Edward II*, need to take into account complex expectations, derived from their own cultural and theatrical experience, that they take into the theatre. The first section is brought to a close by Stephanie Moss, with her essay 'Edmund Kean, Anti-Semitism and *The Jew of Malta*'. Moss draws attention to actor/director Edmund Kean's controversial production of the play at Drury Lane in 1818, which, after reviews praising Kean's performance as Barabas but berating his choice of play as unsuitable for an enlightened liberal age, came to an abrupt halt after only eleven performances. The violent response to the production, Moss suggests, was the result of a hypersensitivity brought on by a contemporary tension between idealistic conceptions of society as enlightened and egalitarian and the very real existence of prejudice that those idealistic conceptions strove to conceal.

The second section contains three essays, each dealing with a specific type of familial relationship in Marlowe's plays, the first being Lagretta Tallent Lenker's 'The Hopeless Daughter of a Hapless Jew: Father and Daughter in Marlowe's *The Jew of Malta*'. Lenker challenges the critical commonplace that the play descends into 'savage farce' after Abigail's murder, arguing that Barabas's apparently nonchalant response to her death actually represents an instance of 'writing beyond words', a device which has an eloquent character reduced to 'staccato-like, mad ravings' (p. 72) in response to extreme emotional upheaval. Despite this, however, Lenker acknowledges the increased inclination to cruelty in the play once Abigail is no longer there, and argues that Marlowe 'creates a provocative and subversive comment on the sins of the father and, by extension, the rulers in the patriarchal system' (p. 73). In 'A Study in Ambivalence: Mothers and their Sons in Christopher Marlowe', Joyce Karpay discusses the bifurcated attitudes towards motherhood in early modern society, suggesting that the mother tended to be perceived either as socially powerless or as a threatening wielder of influence in the home. With this as a context, Karpay goes on to discuss the representation of mothers in several of Marlowe's plays, arguing that the dramatist 'expose[s] the ambivalent nature of our relationship with our first love object' (p. 91). In the third and final chapter of the section, 'Masculinity, Performance, and Identity: Father/Son Dyads in Christopher Marlowe's Plays', Merry G. Perry examines the relationships between fathers and sons in the plays through the lens of modern masculinity studies. Rebellion against paternal authority, Perry suggests, always fails in Marlowe, but the excessive severity with which the perpetrators of such rebellion are punished in his plays problematizes the patriarchal system. As such, Marlowe 'offers his audience the simultaneous opportunity to valorize, accept, or critique patriarchy' (p. 110).

The third section of the book begins with a postmodernist reading of *Dr Faustus* which identifies its relevance to modern academia. Rick Bowers's 'Almost Famous, Always Iterable: *Doctor Faustus* as Meme of Academic

Performativity' argues that while to its contemporary audience the play parodied religious conformity and promoted humanist learning, today it is humanist knowing that is satirized in the play, and promoted instead is 'open-ended academic performativity' (p. 121). In 'Misbelief, False Profession and *The Jew of Malta*', William H. Hamlin discusses the play's use of the word 'misbelief', a rare word in early modern English which 'oscillates in meaning between "erroneous belief" and "absence of belief," with connotations of incredulity, distrust, and doubt' (p. 128). Barabas's misbelief initially lends him a cultural flexibility which serves him well, but it eventually results in a self-deceit of which Ferneze is able to take advantage. Barabas's role as both knave and gull, Hamlin suggests, secures for him our sympathy. Deborah Willis, in '*Doctor Faustus* and the Early Modern Language of Addiction', reads the decline of Faustus in the B-text of the play in the context of early modern discourses of addiction, and discusses the related (and more heavily trodden) issue of free will in the play. Willis suggests that our modern understanding of addiction bears a resemblance to medieval and Renaissance conceptions of religious despair, and allows us to conceive of Faustus's fall as 'the spectacle of a free agent manipulated into the repetition of acts that, over time, produce a changed inner nature and a diminishment of agency' (p. 148). Christine McCall Probes's essay, entitled 'Rhetorical Strategies for a *Locus Terribilis*: Senses, Signs, Symbols, and Theological Allusion in Marlowe's *The Massacre at Paris*', examines Marlowe's use of signs, rhetorical tendencies and biblical allusions in order to construct the sense of a *locus terribilis* (terrible event) in *The Massacre at Paris*. The play, Probes argues, 'may be an indictment not only of the atrocities that occurred on St. Bartholomew's Day in 1572, but of all religious terror, and, as such, is relevant not only to sixteenth century France and England but also to our own post-9/11 age' (pp. 151–2). John Parker's 'Barabas and Charles I' is the final essay in the third section, and draws a parallel between Protestant polemic against the Catholic Church and Barabas's grievances with the Christian knights of Malta. Parker suggests this as a rationale behind the printing of the play in the 1630 s, when Charles's I's apparent lack of reformist zeal led to a spate of revivals of old anti-Catholic plays.

The final section of the book opens with Constance Brown Kuriyama's 'Marlowe, Shakespeare, and the Theoretically Irrelevant Author'. Kuriyama challenges the theoretical approaches to authorship by writers such as Barthes and Foucault, and also the idea that interiorized characterization was the invention of Shakespeare. Kuriyama compares *The Jew of Malta* with *The Merchant of Venice*, and *Dr Faustus* with *Hamlet*, arguing that in both cases such complex characterization appears in Marlowe's earlier play, and also suggesting that the inherent differences between the two dramatists' work illustrate the point that it is not helpful to conceive of the author as dead. In ' "Glutted with conceit": Imprints of *Doctor Faustus* on *The Tempest*', Robert Logan stakes a claim for a Marlovian influence on Shakespeare that was maintained long after the traditional model of interplay between the two playwrights' early works tends to suggest. Logan traces Marlowe's influence in the metadramatic nature of the two works, arguing that in both of them 'the figure of the magician can be seen to stand for the author who, in playing God the Creator, uses his imagination to become glutted with conceit' (p. 203). The final essay of the volume is David Bevington's 'Christopher Marlowe: The Late Years', which examines the development of the history play and argues that the genre, as we are familiar with it, originates with Marlowe and Shakespeare. Bevington identifies the key factors in *Edward II* and a selection of Shakespeare's histories—highlighting in particular an episodic yet sustained structures and patterns of rise and fall—that set those plays apart from the roistering of comedies by writers such as Peele and Nashe and the specifically courtly concerns of earlier works such as *Gorboduc*.

The other notable full length volume this year was Lisa Hopkins's *Christopher Marlowe: Renaissance Dramatist*, which offers a student-aimed introduction to the playwright and his works. The volume begins with a brief chronology which lists the composition dates of works by Marlowe and his contemporaries alongside the significant political and theatrical events of the period. The main body of the text begins with a biography, entitled 'Marlowe's Life and Death', before chapter 2—'The Marlowe Canon'—gives a brief account of the major concerns central to each of the plays (including a section on plays of doubtful authorship), the poems and the translations. In chapter 3, 'Marlowe on Stage, 1587–2007', Hopkins first provides an account of both early modern theatre culture and the dramatic traditions from which Marlowe's drama arose before discussing how each of the plays works in performance (with particular attention being paid to Derek Jarman's film adaptation of *Edward II* and David Farr's 2005 production of *Tamburlaine* at the Barbican, which caused controversy by adapting the scene in which the protagonist burns the Qur'an). The fourth chapter, 'Marlowe as Scholar', examines the intellectual contexts that inform Marlowe's work, first by discussing the influence of classical knowledge on each of the plays and then by devoting a section each to representations of contemporary developments in geography, cosmology and medicine. The fifth chapter, 'Marlowe the Horizon Stretcher', concentrates on the transgressive elements of the Marlowe oeuvre, including formal innovations, religious subversion, 'Marlovian psychology' and the representation of his overreaching heroes. In the final chapter of the volume Hopkins gives a compact history of the major issues that have tended to occupy Marlowe criticism.

Hopkins is also the author of one of a small number of articles published in 2008 which provide commentary on several of Marlowe's works. 'Christopher Marlowe and the Succession to the English Crown' (*YES* 38[2008] 183–98) argues the case for a Marlowe with a keen interest in the issue of succession. After pointing out particular aspects of the *Tamburlaine* plays, *The Jew of Malta*, *The Massacre at Paris* and *Edward II* which directly speak to concerns about succession, Hopkins goes on to identify associations of Marlowe with other people, and of his plays with other plays, that are clearly concerned with royal succession; the writer William Warner, whose anti-Scottishness was topical at a time when James VI of Scotland appeared to be the prime contender for the throne, is posited as an associate of Marlowe's (Kyd's reference to a 'Warner' who was friends with Marlowe being the basis for this), and Marlovian resonances are identified in plays such as *Gorboduc* and *King Lear*. Hopkins acknowledges the tenuousness inherent in tracing an author's dramatic interest in a topic the discussion of which was strictly forbidden, but argues that, at the least, Marlowe's plays ask us to think about the destiny of the English throne. In 'Oedipal Marlowe, Mimetic Middleton' (*MP* 105:iii[2008] 417–36), Lars Engle offers a brief reading of a selection of plays by Marlowe and Thomas Middleton according to two models of demystification, namely an Oedipal model, which highlights repression (sexual, psychological or political) as a legacy of something past and dramatizes the possibility of casting it off, and a mimetic model, which exposes a society as described by Girard, in which all desire is occasioned by imitation of another's desire, thus necessitating human rivalry (and the construction of a social hierarchy in order to avoid all-out conflict). While suggesting that there are elements of both models at work in each playwright, Engle goes on to argue that Middleton's plays concern themselves more with the exposition of mimetic rivalry, while Marlowe's demonstrate a preoccupation with an Oedipal desire to throw off repression, before finally adding as something of an afterthought that Shakespeare might be seen as occupying a position somewhere between the two. Graham Hammill's 'Time for Marlowe' (*ELH* 75[2008] 259–81) conducts a political reading of *Tamburlaine* and *The Massacre at Paris*. First, by looking at early modern accounts of absolute sovereign power by authors such as Niccolò Machiavelli, Jean Bodin and Giovanni Botero, and secondly by examining the use of the word 'massacre' in the two plays, Hammill presents Marlowe as offering a critique of the sovereign state's use of violence in order to prevent the danger of the potential unifying of the multitude; 'Marlowe proposes that massacre is a necessary, not incidental, component of sovereignty—part of its broader political logic' (p. 292). Through both his choice of title and his conclusion, Hammill suggests that readings of Marlowe which engage with his use of political terms imbue his work with a particular aptness for the current time. D.K. Smith, using as a context the new, mathematically precise early modern mode of cartography, identifies, in his essay 'Conquering Geography: Sir Walter Raleigh, Christopher Marlowe, and the Cartographic Imagination' (in Smith, *The Cartographic Imagination in Early Modern England: Re-writing the World in Marlowe, Spenser, Raleigh and Marvell*, pp. 125–55), key resonances between Marlowe's *Dr Faustus* and *Tamburlaine*, and Walter Raleigh's account of his discoveries in Guiana. Raleigh, Smith suggests, attempts to emulate the rhetoric and manipulation of cartography exemplified by Tamburlaine, who enacts domination simply by mapping and naming. Raleigh, however, falls short, hamstrung as he is (and as Tamburlaine isn't) by his grounding in a real world in which the majority of his claims about his discoveries in the New World simply aren't true. Raleigh's use of cartography, then, more resembles that of Faustus, who 'remains a creature of illusion and appearance' (p. 151).

Of all of the canon, the *Tamburlaine* plays were those that received the most individual attention, including two more that, like Smith, consider the play in the context of early modern geography. In ' "A world of ground": Terrestrial Space in Marlowe's *Tamburlaine* Plays' (*YES* 38[2008] 168–82), Emrys Jones focuses closely on the fascination shown in the *Tamburlaine* plays with physical, geographical space, and with arduous movement through it. Besides proposing a two-part structure for each of the plays, Jones addresses

Marlowe's apparent confusion as to what is in Africa and what is in Asia, suggesting that he is in fact employing poetic licence to 'set up a symmetrical Asia-Africa scheme' (p. 180), and more generally articulates how Marlowe's interest in cartography and evocation of place and movement lend the play its sense of monumental scale. The essay also attempts to place this facet of Marlowe's work in its cultural context, highlighting both its debt to Ariosto's *Orlando Furioso*, and its correlation with a new fascination with geographical scale in the visual arts, most notably in the work of Albrecht Altdorfer. Paige Newmark's 'Marlowe, Maps, and Might' (in Lynch and Scott, eds., *Renaissance Poetry and Drama in Context: Essays for Christopher Wortham*, pp. 129–44) examines the dualistic role of the map in the *Tamburlaine* plays, arguing that the play marks a transition point between the tripartite medieval world map and the beginnings of modern cartography as exemplified by the likes of Abraham Ortelius. Newmark argues that Tamburlaine and Marlowe make both symbolic (in the medieval tradition) and more fundamentally practical (and thus modern) use of maps, helping to achieve, amongst other things, a fine balance in the characterization of the protagonist between murderous efficiency and romantic exoticism. Similarly, the map serves as a justification of and means to imperial domination for Tamburlaine, yet also serves as an ironic reminder of his limitations, highlighting as it does in the plays' climactic scene the boundaries to his success by bringing to the attention of the audience that which remains unconquered. Two other essays on the *Tamburlaine* plays suggest hitherto unconsidered classical sources, or at least inspirations, for them. Allyna E. Ward's 'Lucanic Irony in Marlowe's *Tamburlaine*' (*MLR* 103:ii[2008] 311–29) aligns the plays, both temporally and thematically, with Marlowe's translation of Lucan's *Pharsalia*. Ward argues that Marlowe echoes Lucan in the *Tamburlaine* plays in order to comment on the irony inherent in the Reformation doctrine that posited sovereignty as divinely ordained, whether tyrannical or not—tyrants were inflicted upon sinful peoples as a punishment by God, and should no more be the object of rebellion than benign monarchs. Lucan's epic bears a relation to these Reformation ideas in that it simultaneously asserts Julius Caesar's predestined greatness and disparages the civil war he initiates in enacting that destiny. Marlowe, Ward suggests, identifies this relationship and imitates it in his similarly ironic representation of the Scythian conqueror who, despite his insatiable appetite for cruelty and destruction, remains unpunished throughout the plays. In 'Seneca's Influence on the Construction of Bajazeth in Marlowe's *Tamburlaine*' (*N&Q* 55[2008] 152–4), Arnd Bohm identifies passages from the moral essays of Seneca as sources for the ritual humiliation of Bajazeth in *Tamburlaine 1*. Seneca's account of the cruelty meted out by Lysimachus, a friend of Alexander the Great, on his own friend Telesphorus— he maims him and keeps him half-starved in a cage—is shown to resonate with the episode from Marlowe's play not just in its detail but also in the fact that it is later cited by Seneca as an example of a situation in which suicide is the desirable course of action. Bajazeth's self-annihilation in the face of abject humiliation adheres to Seneca's stoic code, and, Bohm argues, contributes to the play's irony; just as Seneca highlights the degradation of Telesphorus in order to illustrate the moral decrepitude of Lysimachus, in Marlowe's play the shame attached to Bajazeth's torture and suicide belongs to Tamburlaine. Finally, in 'English Renaissance Drama: The Imprints of Performance' (*LitComp* 5:iii[2008] 529–40), Paul J. Gavin gives a brief account of the development of the relationship between the play in performance and the play in print in the early modern period, offering commentary on the ancillary matter (paratexts) of the 1590 octavo of *Tamburlaine* in the process. The essay examines the gradual conceptual bifurcation of page and stage, as exemplified by Richard Jones's preface to *Tamburlaine*, which details the excision from the octavo of various performance elements of the play that he deems unsuitable for the serious reader. Gavin also, however, maintains that a fluid relationship pertains between the two media, exemplified by the development of stage directions, which 'situate the reader in the interpretive, transitional and meaning-making space between page and stage' (p. 539).

Dr Faustus was the subject of four articles. First is David Wootton's 'Marlowe's *Doctor Faustus* and the *English Faustbook*' (in Fitzsimmons, ed., *Lives of Faust: The Faust Theme in Literature and Music. A Reader*, pp. 145–55). After first offering a comparison of the varying eschatological systems implied by the endings of the *English Faustbook* and the two texts of *Faustus*, Wootton proceeds to make a case for Reginald Scot's *The Discoverie of Witchcraft* as a text which informs the theology employed by Marlowe in his play. Scot's sceptical argument is that all astonishing acts which purport to be magic (and, by extension, those which purport to be miracles) can be explained as the product of human legerdemain. This scepticism, Wootton states, is reflected both in the dismissal of the miraculous feats of Moses, attributed to Marlowe by Richard Baines, and in the stage trickery performed by Faustus. The essay further states that, rather than deriving from the medieval tradition as is commonly asserted, the good and bad angels have their inspiration in Scot, who argued, to use Wootton's paraphrase, 'that within each of us there is a constant tension between good and evil that can be described as a constant conflict between a good spirit and an evil spirit' (p. 153). In '*The verie paines of hell: Doctor Faustus* and the Controversy over Christ's Descent' (*ShakS* 36[2008] 166–81), Heather Anne Hirschfeld examines the play against the backdrop of the sixteenth-century Protestant theological debates that centred around the question of whether or not Christ's soul actually descended to hell upon his death. While the idea of a descent was commonplace, the debate centred upon the extent to which it was a literal or a metaphorical one, fundamentally balancing on the issue of *how much* sacrifice by Christ was sufficient to save mankind: was an earthly death sufficient or was spiritual torment required as well? Hirschfeld argues that this question of sufficiency—of how much is enough—informs *Dr Faustus*, which features both an inexpressible Hell and a protagonist who repeatedly invokes vast numerical quantities in order to (vainly) illustrate, amongst other things, his commitment to Mephostophiles or his desire for salvation. Another essay which suggests a new classical source for a Marlowe play is Arnd Bohm's 'Global Dominion: Faust and Alexander the Great' (in Fitzsimmons, ed., *International Faust Studies: Adaptation, Reception, Translation*, pp. 17–35), which argues the case for Alexander the Great (or at least classical and medieval mythically infused conceptions of Alexander the Great) as a basis for the Faust figure, as exemplified in the Faustbooks, Marlowe's *Dr Faustus* and Goethe's *Faust*. Bohm draws attention both to events described in Christian accounts of Alexander's life, such as visiting paradise and the underworld and flying with the help of griffins, and to moral judgements made of him in those accounts, which tend to chastise him for his excessive curiosity and ambition. Drawing upon the clear resonance between these moral objections and the central themes of the Faust myth, Bohm goes on to identify specific allusions to or similarities with the mythography of Alexander in the chapbooks and the famous works of Marlowe and Goethe. In the case of Marlowe's *Faustus*, this mainly surrounds the protagonist's ambitious vaunts early in the play and his summoning of the simulacrum of Alexander for the entertainment of Emperor Charles V. Lastly, Sarah Wall-Randell's '*Doctor Faustus* and the Printer's Devil' (*SEL* 48[2008] 259–81) offers a reading of *Dr Faustus* in the light of the early history of the printed book. First highlighting the fact that the invention of the printing press was attributed by John Foxe in the 1570 edition of *Actes and Monuments* to a man named 'Joan Faustus', the essay goes on to discuss in relation to Marlowe's play why this Faust of the print world would by the latter part of the seventeenth century be synonymous with the Faust of the occult myth. Highlighting the play's interest in books, and in particular books which contain universal knowledge, Wall-Randell draws a parallel with contemporary encyclopaedic texts and voluminous English histories like Foxe's, which often contain a preface in which the author expresses their anxiety about the possibility that they might be unleashing too much information. This anxiety brings the essay neatly onto the subject of bibliolatry, closing by suggesting that the kind of contemporary anxiety about books that is dramatized in *Dr Faustus* might have a lot to do with a Protestant ideology that condemns idolatry in all its forms, but which places the book—itself a physical object—at the centre of its mode of worship.

Edward II was also, directly or indirectly, the subject of four commentaries. Mark Dooley's 'Queer Teaching/Teaching Queer: Renaissance Masculinities and the Seminar' (in Knights, ed., *Masculinities in Text and Teaching*, pp. 59–74) offers a markedly personal account of the influence of cultural models of masculinity on the author's trajectory into the study of English literature, and later of how the same models influenced a series of seminar discussions on early modern sexuality and gender (including readings of Marlowe's *Edward II*) which culminated in a scene in which two male students confronted and intimidated Dooley while he was working late in his office. Dooley uses this episode and the build-up to it, as well as his own youth, to illustrate the complexity inherent in the teaching of literature, 'a subject more profoundly engaged with the process of identity formation than any other' (p. 73), arguing that it is important for teachers to be aware of what is at stake for participants in the literature classroom. In 'The Aristocracy in *Edward II*' (*MES* 16:ii[2008] 311–27), Byung-Eun Lee offers a critical survey of the play's themes, touching upon various established readings of the play, and ultimately argues both that the central catalyst of the drama is aristocratic pride and that central to Edward II's downfall is his lack of family loyalty, a trait that Lee suggests is amply displayed by the weak king's patently more capable son. What happens to sons when fathers or father figures are out of the way is the subject of David

H. Brumble's 'Personal, Paternal, and Kingly Control in Marlowe's *Edward II*' (*EIRC* 34:i[2008] 56–70). Starting by noting the parallel between the opening of the first two acts of the play, in which the deaths of Edward I and Gloucester are referred to respectively, Brumble argues that, rather than representing a subversive exposition of power politics, the play bemoans the moral chaos that ensues when people in positions of power abandon the kind of reasoned control that is exemplified by these two dead father figures. Contemporary cultural commentary, he points out, suggests a widespread belief that those not capable of keeping their own impulses in check should be kept in check by someone else. It is in this way that Spencer and Baldock, prior to the death of Gloucester, and Edward II, prior to the death of Edward I, are kept from harming themselves or the state. The removal of these checks gives full rein to avaricious desire, with, of course, disastrous results. Thus, Brumble argues, Marlowe's play does not make a case for levity, but rather demonstrates the need for control. Mathew Martin's 'Plays of Passion: Pain, History and Theater in *Edward II*' (in Papazian, ed., *The Sacred and Profane in English Renaissance Literature*, pp. 84–107) draws on the representation of pain in Edward II, focusing specifically on Elaine Scarry's conception of pain as separating the voice, or articulating subject, from the body in pain. In this configuration, pain 'resists objectification in language' (p. 85), and as such is erased from history. Drawing a contrast with the story of Christ—'one subject in whom pain and being are reconciled' (p. 86)—Martin notes the correlation between the suffering of Edward and that of Actaeon, whose own plight is evoked in Gaveston's description of his masque for Edward at the play's opening: in both cases the victim is left voiceless. Noting also the similarly metatheatrical nature of the deaths of Acteon in Gaveston's masque and of Edward in Marlowe's play, Martin goes on to suggest that the moment of extreme violence in the play's penultimate scene is ultimately erased from history by the restorative effect of the succession of the boy king at the close.

The year 2008 also saw work from Martin on *The Jew of Malta*. 'Maltese Psycho: Tragedy and Psychopathology in *The Jew of Malta*' (*LIT* 19[2008] 367–87) offers a Lacanian reading of the play, arguing that, in contrast to the neurosis of the protagonist of *Hamlet*, Barabas provides an example of psychosis—of the defiant disavowal of the threat of castration. Martin reads Barabas's apparently unwitting reference to two figures associated with child sacrifice—Abraham and Agamemnon—as illustrating his own repeated refusal of sacrifice, and goes on to discuss his confessions of a constitutionally murderous past, his perpetration of repetitive killings in the play itself and his unstinting defiance of the society in which he lives as constructive of a world 'in which he is the castrating agent and not the castrated victim' (p. 380). Finally, drawing a parallel between the hyperbolic crimes of Marlowe's protagonist and the fallout of economic and technological transformations taking place in, and changing the face of, early modern Europe, Martin argues that the ultimately laughable Barabas is claimed by the audience as 'its fetish' (p. 385)—a protection against its own threat of castration. Other commentary on *The Jew of Malta* consisted largely of brief discussion in essays that were concerned mainly with *The Merchant of Venice*. These included Aaron Kitch's 'Shylock's Sacred Nation' (*SQ* 59[2008] 131–55), which examines the significance of the Jewish trading nations—centres of commerce like Venice and Amsterdam where Jews who had been banished from the Iberian peninsula by the Inquisition were offered limited citizen's rights in return for the benefits their mercantile expertise would reap for the community—on Marlowe's *The Jew of Malta* and Shakespeare's *The Merchant of Venice*. Kitch first offers a useful account of the position of trading Jews in the early modern Mediterranean before moving on to discuss Marlowe's play. *The Jew of Malta*, the essay argues, refuses to adhere to stereotypes about Jewish usury, or even, as is often argued, to deliver a fully fledged commentary on the use of religion to conceal financial corruption, instead asserting the fundamental importance of mercantile trade, as exemplified by Barabas and historical Jewish speculators, to statecraft. Lara Bovilsky's 'Exemplary Jews and the Logic of Gentility' (in Bovilsky, *Barbarous Play: Race on the English Renaissance Stage*, pp. 67–102) similarly makes limited reference to *The Jew of Malta*, discussing primarily the representation of Jewishness and gentility in Shakespeare's *The Merchant of Venice*. Bovilsky considers the implications of Shylock's claim that he had rather his daughter married anyone from 'the stock of Barabas' than a Christian. Taking this as a reference to Marlowe's protagonist, the chapter suggests *Merchant* as contributing to, rather than initiating, an already vibrant tradition of representations of English conceptions of Jewishness. In 'Early Modern Dietaries and the Jews: *The Jew of Malta* and *The Merchant of Venice*' (in Fotheringham, Jansohn and White, eds., *Shakespeare's World/ World Shakespeares*, pp. 98–107), Joan Fitzpatrick analyses the relationship between Jewish dietary law, early modern dietary treatises and Shakespeare's *The Merchant of Venice*, with some reference to *The Jew of Malta*. Fitzpatrick identifies the importance of food in both plays, suggesting that, while Barabas fulfils a more stereotypical Jew/villain role as poisoner of other people's food (and accordingly meets his end in his own cooking pot), Shylock's relationship with food—which Fitzpatrick associates with his melancholy—is altogether more complex.

While discussion of *Dido, Queen of Carthage* gave rise to only two publications in 2008, these two essays represent consecutive winners of the Hoffman Prize for distinguished publication on Christopher Marlowe (2006 and 2007 respectively). In 'When Did Marlowe Write *Dido, Queen of Carthage?*' (*RES* 59[2008] 521–41), Martin Wiggins sets out to answer the question plainly raised in the essay's title. Wiggins takes aim at the standard critical position that *Dido* represents the earliest extant dramatic work by Marlowe, and probably one produced in the mid-1580s while the dramatist was still at Cambridge, arguing that this perception is maintained by questionable aesthetic judgements of the play and by its convenience to standard conceptions of the trajectory of Marlowe's development as a writer. The essay also discusses the generally disregarded involvement of Nashe in the authorship of the play that is asserted by its title page, suggests that an academic theatre group would have neither the materials nor the inclination to stage the play and finally goes on to discuss the activity of the Children of the Chapel (also cited on the title page) during the 1580s. Wiggins comes to the hypothetical conclusion that *Dido* was in fact written after the *Tamburlaine* plays, and represented an attempt by the Children of the Chapel to cash in on their runaway success. Timothy Crowley's 'Arms and the Boy: Marlowe's Aeneas and the Parody of Imitation in *Dido, Queen of Carthage*' (*ELR* 38:iii[2008] 408–38) focuses on Marlowe's use of *imitatio* (rhetorical imitation of classical literary sources) in *Dido*, and its central role in establishing the ironic tone of the play. Through persistent echoing of Ovidian and Lucanian rhetorical models, Crowley suggests, Marlowe undermines the heroic persona 'Aeneas', putting in its place a vacillating and underwhelming hero, and problematizes the epic's investment in martial conquest and imperial power by divesting the play's accounts of violence of their Virgilian dignity. Crowley ultimately argues, however, that Marlowe's play parodies the process of *imitatio*, in that to whatever extent the imitation of more subversive accounts of the myth undercuts the epic dignity of the play's protagonist, the Virgilian source (of both Marlowe's play and those other versions of the myth which it imitates) necessitates the eventual downfall of Dido and the successful creation of an imperial legacy by Aeneas; for all its irony the play 'flaunts the fact that it cannot change the shared parameters of that source material upon which it feeds, thus remaining knowingly bound to Vergil's *Aeneid* as if to an antagonist' (p. 438).

The only piece to pay sole attention to *The Massacre at Paris* was Richard Hillman's note 'Marlowe's Guise: Offending against God and the King' (*N&Q* 55[2008] 154–9), which tackles an editorial quandary in the play, namely to whom the 'Him/him' refers in the Guise's dying lines: 'Trouble me not, I ne'er offended Him, | Nor will I ask forgiveness of the King' (p. 155). Hillman suggests that two French works which he posits as sources for Marlowe's play, both of which are sympathetic to Catholicism, encourage differing readings of the ambiguous pronoun. Pierre Mathieu's *La Guisiade* [1589] has a pious Guise admit, though a messenger reporting his death, that he has offended God, suggesting that Marlowe in response has his Machiavellian Guise petulantly deny that he has done any such thing. Conversely, Simon Belyard's *Le Guysien* has a similarly upstanding Guise assailed with strictly political accusations by his murderers, which, read in connection with Marlowe's play, suggests that the 'him' in question is not God but the king. Hillman takes the availability of both readings to allow Marlowe to simultaneously answer both sympathizers with the historical Guise who attribute him with piety and those who attribute him with political loyalty.

This entry is concluded by three essays on *Hero and Leander*, which continues to generate healthy debate. Bruce Boehrer and Trish Thomas Henley's 'Automated Marlowe: *Hero and Leander* 31–36' (*Exemplaria* 20:i[2008] 98–119) applies close attention to the artificiality of Hero's buskins, as described in Marlowe's blazon of her early in the poem. The elaborate mechanical birds, which sing when Hero's handmaids fill the boots' apparently portable reservoirs with water, are placed in their historical and theoretical contexts by Boehrer and Henley; having established the presence of such mechanisms in contemporary scientific texts and decorative gardens, the article highlights the association of such automata with other cultural examples of artificiality, such as theatre, 'juggling' and Catholic ceremony. In more specific relation to the poem, Boehrer and Henley observe the tension between the natural and the artificial in Marlowe's epyllion that is exemplified by Hero's boots; they contribute, the authors argue, to Marlowe's depiction of Hero's suppression of her sexual desire as unnatural, and 'help mark out a continuum of desire' (p. 115) which culminates in the figuring of Hero as a vulnerable bird wrung in a pair of hands upon the scene of consummation. Thus is identified the misogynistic double bind into which Marlowe places Hero: for a female to repress sexual desire is unnatural; for her to give in to it is to put herself completely at the mercy of a man. In 'The Implications of Tucker Brooke's Transposition in *Hero and Leander*' (*SP* 105[2008] 520–32), Vincenzo Pasquarella draws attention to what he argues is a long-standing oversight in editorial approaches to Marlowe's epyllion, namely the (often unacknowledged) retention of a transposition of several lines of the poem made by C.F. Tucker Brooke in 1910. Tucker Brooke shifted eleven lines of verse from the poem's culminating scene to an earlier position on aesthetic grounds, arguing by way of explanation that a leaf of Marlowe's manuscript may have been misordered at some point in the publication process. Pasquarella questions the likelihood of this account, citing evidence to the effect that all of the earliest editions of the poem show signs of a level of meticulous attention to detail that would make such an oversight anomalous. The essay then goes on to suggest that the poem does not require the transposition in order to make sense; while Tucker Brooke and subsequent editors have preferred the transposition on the basis that it creates a more coherent narrative, Pasquarella suggests that the apparently contradictory sense of the un-transposed quartos actually enacts Hero's conflicting feelings regarding her sexual experience with Leander in a way that is characteristic of Renaissance non-linear narrative. 'Marlowe's Fable: Hero and Leander and the Rudiments of Eloquence' (*SP* 105[2008] 388–408), by William Weaver, makes a case for the history of the book as an illuminating context for the network of influences and imitations in which early modern authors worked. Paying particular attention to *Hero and Leander*, Weaver identifies the form in which Musaeus's (shorter) version of the poem was made available to a sixteenth-century English audience, namely as a minor supplementary in an apparently disparate collection, the main attraction of which was a translation of Aesop's fables. By looking at Quintilian's writing on grammatical and rhetorical training, however, Weaver establishes that the collection is in fact representative of the 'rudiments of eloquence', a group of grammar-school exercises which involved the translation and imitation of, among other things, fables and poetic myths. The essay goes on to argue that Marlowe's poem represents a 'mock heroic amplification of a fable' of the kind that students of the Elizabethan grammar school would be encouraged to produce.

(c) Jonson

Space is a prominent topic in this year's Jonson scholarship. James D. Mardock's monograph *Our Scene Is London: Ben Jonson's City and the Space of the Author* is a study in 'the history of authorship' (p. 2) which argues that, while Jonson constructed himself as an author through the monumentalizing textual project of the 1616 *Workes*, he also pursued a parallel 'authorial strategy' based on 'establishing control over the spatial laboratory that the playhouse provided, and over the theatrically represented space of his city' (p. 2). Mardock suggests that Jonson's experience of contributing to the 'Magnificent Entertainment' of 1604, in which he vied with Dekker to interpret the royal entry, taught him that authorship could be asserted through 'the poet's interpretive and transformative power over London's places' (p. 21). Building on work such as Henry S. Turner's *The English Renaissance Stage: Geometry, Poetics and the Practical Spatial Arts 1580–1630* [2006], and Jean E. Howard's *Theater of a City: The Places of London Comedy, 1598–1642* [2007], which explore how the concept of theatrical space was shaped by urbanization and by new knowledge-making practices, Mardock reads *Every Man In His Humour, Eastward Ho, Epicoene, The Alchemist* and *Bartholomew Fair* as plays in which Jonson creates himself as an author by representing his city in the theatre. Mardock concludes that, while the publication of the *Workes* 'exhausted his primary authorial strategy', Jonson continued to experiment with 'space-based authorial strategies' (p. 111), entering into interpretative competition with his own characters and audiences over the meaning of theatrical space in the late plays.

Peter Happé, 'Jonson's Management of Space in his Later Plays' (*BJJ* 15[2008] 1–18), argues that the plays Jonson wrote from 1626 create meaning from the tension between 'the actuality of the theatre' (p. 3) and the imaginary spaces that are superimposed on it through language. For Happé, too, the 'enveloping presence of London is a persistent factor' (p. 17). The meaning of space is also at issue in John Shanahan's 'Ben Jonson's *Alchemist* and Early Modern Laboratory Space' (*JEMCS* 8[2008] 35–66), which relates Jonson's neoclassical dramaturgy to the development of early modern science, arguing that *The Alchemist* helps lay the conceptual groundwork for public laboratory spaces and corporate knowledge-making. Shanahan stresses 'the pre-disciplinary fluidity' (p. 37) which meant natural philosophy and drama belonged within a broad group of practices (also including masques, anatomy demonstrations, wonder-cabinets and forensic rhetoric) which were simultaneously epistemological and performative. Laboratories, like theatres, are places in which time, space and human skill are tightly organized 'to produce truths of various kinds' (p. 38), and the dramaturgy of *The Alchemist* can be seen as 'a means of conceiving the very possibility of the space . . . for the Royal Society's later synthesis of fact production and social decorum' (p. 56).

For Peter Womack, 'The Comical Scene: Perspective and Civility on the Renaissance Stage' (*Rep* 101[2008] 32–56), Jonson's representation of urban space demonstrates his allegiance to a European tradition of humanist drama, and his refusal of 'the "Shakespearean" fluidity of the English theater' (p. 32). Rather than a 'dissenting pedant', Jonson is the English translator of a theatrical tradition whose centre is 'the Teatro Olimpico rather than the Globe' (p. 46). His neoclassical stage, aspiring to a neo-Aristotelian ideal of imitation, is 'essentially a mentalistic space' (p. 44): a system for knowing about reality by simulating it. This signals a key difference between Shakespearian and Jonsonian representation, since whereas Shakespeare (for instance in the Chorus to *Henry V*) solicits the audience's belief in what it cannot see, Jonson instead requires detachment, discrimination and judgement of what *is* present on stage. Holger Schott Syme, 'Unediting the Margin: Jonson, Marston, and the Theatrical Page' (*ELR* 38[2008] 142–71), addresses a different kind of spatial awareness, arguing that some early modern printed playtexts develop a kind of 'mise-en-page' (p. 163): playwrights like Marston and Jonson, aided by printers and publishers, 'used the page's specific signifying systems to recreate a set of effects characteristic of the stage... they found a way of making the book a theater' (p. 144). Paradoxically, this also makes the book more 'literary': for instance, the layout of Doll's 'fit of talking' in the Folio text of *The Alchemist* would be unhelpful in a performance script, but strengthens the 'conceptual correlation' (p. 162) between what we see on the page and hear in the theatre. Syme offers a qualified account of Jonson's anti-theatricalism: in turning to print, he does not escape from the social, collaborative, craft-based world of performance into a realm of isolated authorship, but instead reconstructs theatricality in the equally collaborative and technical professional context of print.

The other Jonsonian monograph of 2008 is Richard Dutton's *Ben Jonson, Volpone and the Gunpowder Plot*, which synthesizes an array of Dutton's previous published work on *Volpone* into a compelling account of the play's links with the Gunpowder Plot, and argues that it is 'in important ways "about" Robert Cecil' (p. 4). Jonson could not address such sensitive matters directly—(hence the fact that *Volpone* has 'very largely passed under the radar of successive "new historicisms"' (p. 6)—but the elaborate paratextual apparatus of the 1607 quarto signalled the play's contentious subtexts to readers with eyes to see, while retaining 'plausible deniability' (p. 9). Dutton examines the quarto as a complete textual artefact, giving generous attention to the contemporary significance of the Epistle and the commendatory poems, while also arguing that Sir Pol, who offers teasing hints of personation, fixes the play precisely to the time-frame of the Plot, and that the setting suggests 'a significant element of London-in-Venice' (p. 12). A fascinating discussion of the play's beast-fable elements shows how Jonson invokes a tradition of coded political satire, and links his drama with the genre of fox-fable, such as Spenser's *Mother Hubberds Tale*, which had become 'a recognized mode of satire on the Cecils' (p. 134).

A variety of other approaches to *Volpone* is on offer in the periodical literature. Alison V. Scott, 'Censuring Indulgence: Volpone's "Use of Riches" and the Problem of Luxury' (*AUMLA* 110[2008] 1–15), considers the implications of Dryden's observation that Volpone is a 'voluptuary' as well as a miser, in a cultural context in which habits of self-indulgent, conspicuous consumption were emerging as a greater social threat than mere avarice. Volpone's luxurious self-transformations reflect contemporary fears about the fluidity of value. Early modern capitalism is also Oliver Hennessey's topic in 'Jonson's Joyless Economy: Theorizing Motivation and Pleasure in *Volpone*' (*ELR* 38[2008] 83–105), which reads the play as an investigation of the 'individual's pursuit of happiness in a society increasingly concerned with commodification and the circulation of consumer goods' (pp. 84–5). Drawing on Stephen Greenblatt's article 'The False Ending in *Volpone*' (*JEGP* 75[1976] 90–104), and on twentieth-century economic and psychoanalytic theorists, Hennessey argues that the play explores the boredom and anxiety attendant on excessive material wealth in a proto-capitalist culture. Charlotte Scott, 'Still Life? Anthropocentrism and the Fly in *Titus Andronicus* and *Volpone*' (*ShS* 61[2008] 256–68), compares Jonson's 'complex symbolic' staging of a fly in the shape of Mosca with Shakespeare's 'fly scene' in *Titus Andronicus* (p. 256): citing Donna Haraway's 'cyborg' theory of how the concept of the human is constructed, Scott argues that the trope of the fly challenges 'the traditional binaries between man and (his) nature' (p. 257).

Purificación Ribes turns to Spanish adaptations of *Volpone* in a two-part article on 'Enrique Llovet's Versions of *Volpone* and Increasing Freedom of Expression in Spain' (*BJJ* 15[2008] 79–97, 194–204). Llovet adapted the play twice for the Spanish theatre, in 1969 and 1997. Ribes argues that the earlier version, although constrained by the censors of Franco's regime, was a contentious production with satirical relevance to a contemporary financial scandal involving the administration: it was part of 'the struggle for freedom that was all-pervading in Spain at the time' (p. 80). The 1997 version, free of censorship, was a 'wholly updated and experimental stagepiece' (p. 195), a Brechtian farce with Mosca as the protagonist. Performance history is also the focus of Clare McManus's essay, '*Epicene* in Edinburgh (1672): City Comedy beyond the London Stage' (in Henke and Nicholson, eds., *Transnational Exchange in Early Modern Theater*, pp. 181–96), which asks how a play with such a detailed, self-conscious relationship with Jacobean London might produce new meanings when performed in Restoration Edinburgh, as it was in 1672. McManus acknowledges that this question can be answered only speculatively, but she assembles illuminating evidence of the conditions of Scottish Restoration theatre, and argues that in watching the production 'a London-focused aristocratic Scottish elite creates itself against and through the theatrical fashions of the Restoration Whitehall court' (p. 196).

Similarly learned and persuasive is McManus's article, 'When Is a Woman Not a Woman? or, Jacobean Fantasies of Female Performance (1606–1611)' (*MP* 105[2008] 437–74), which traces the emergence in the English theatre of the 'trope' of the 'Jacobean theatrical woman': the 'staging of the elite female body in the early years of the Jacobean masque' gives rise to an idea of female performance that feeds back into the meanings of theatre at the level of dramatic texts. For instance, the antimasque to *The Masque of Queens*, performed by professional players, 'tropes male performers...as textual women, thereby...positioning women in roles that at this point in the genre's development they could not have undertaken' (p. 454). Also on the masques, Jean Lambert, 'Expounding the Owl: Ben Jonson's the *Masque of Owls*' (*BJJ* 15[2008] 19–53), gives a fine-grained reading of the relations between the 'politicized satire' (p. 19) of the *Masque of Owls*, the traditions of owl tales in folklore and literature, the politics of the close of the Jacobean era, and Jonson's career as poet-counsellor to the monarch. In this masque, performed before Prince Charles at Kenilworth in August 1624 in the king's absence, Jonson articulates 'a quasi-state-of-the-nation speech on the eve of Charles's succession' (p. 19), creating carefully managed ambiguities to shore up his own position at the same time as guiding Charles away from James's faults as a ruler.

Edel Lamb's article 'Becoming Men: The Child Player in Jonson's *Epicene*' (*BJJ* 15[2008] 175–93) proposes that the existence of child players gave rise to a 'trope of childhood' (p. 175) which became a theatrical signifier in itself (an idea cognate with McManus's 'theatrical woman'). Through readings of Marston's *Antonio and Mellida* and *What You Will*, Lamb argues that in the ten years between the revival of the two major children's companies in 1599–1600 and the first performance of *Epicoene*, the concept of the boy player took root as a 'discursive and institutional identity' (p. 176) which informs Jonson's play. The links between Jonson's practices and those of other playwrights also concern Tom Rutter in '*Patient Grissil* and Jonsonian Satire' (*SEL* 48[2008] 283–303). Rutter argues that Dekker, Chettle and Haughton's *Patient Grissil*, which includes echoes of *Every Man Out of His Humour*, can be seen as a prelude to the plays of the Poets' War, attacking the principles of comical satire as articulated in *Every Man Out* and rejecting Jonson's attempts to define a position of disinterested moral authority for the satirist. Catherine Rockwood, '"Know Thy Side": Propaganda and Parody in Jonson's *Staple of News*' (*ELH* [2008] 135–49), argues that *The Staple of News* involves a satirical assault on the politics and morality of Middleton's *A Game at Chess*, when, in Act III, scene ii, Pennyboy Junior enjoys warmongering propaganda in the spirit of Middleton's play. For Jonson, the allegory of the black and white Houses is a dangerous simplification, and in *The Staple of News* he parodies such strategies of political polarization, and asks his Blackfriars audience to reflect on their consequences.

Michael Lee Manous, 'An Eagle's Wing and a Vulture's Wing: Poetic Journey and Wager Journey in Jonson's "Famous Voyage"' (*BJJ* 15[2008] 54–78), suggests that Jonson transforms the social game of the wager-journey into 'a literary motif conducive to the requirements of mock-heroic, carnivalesque poetry' (p. 71): the voyage is in tune with the didactic purpose of the rest of the *Epigrammes*, because its levelling scatology 'demonstrates that the path to true virtue in life as well as in poetry inevitably winds through the "Hell" of human physicality, or human nature and human everydayness' (p. 72).

The everyday hell of the plague is foregrounded in two articles by Mathew Martin. In 'Wasting Time in Ben Jonson's *Epicoene*' (*SP* 105[2008] 83–102), Martin argues that Jonson's neoclassical poetics are centred on a concept of 'nature' as benign, productive and in harmony with an idealized patriarchal social order. However, in the urban world of *Epicoene*, this concept buckles under the pressure of the plague, a minatory form of 'nature' antithetical to Jonson's poetics. The threat is literally unspeakable in the play: *Epicoene*'s tight classical unities form an ordered, rational universe of art that excludes the plague, but it intrudes figuratively, in the hostile invasion of Morose's home. Similarly, in 'The Name of the Father in "On My First Son": Ben Jonson and the Work of Mourning' (*BJJ* 15[2008] 159–74), Martin emphasizes the unspoken cause of the death of Jonson's son, calling on psychoanalytical theory and cultural history to argue that the poem records the failure of the structure of patriarchal authority to which Jonson's poetry is committed. 'The plague strikes at the heart of Jonson's poetics not only by presenting a virulent form of nature...but also by destabilizing Jonson's position as father'

(p. 166), and undermining the entire 'patriarchal symbolic order' (p. 168): 'O, could I lose all father, now' (l. 5).

Finally, the *Ben Jonson Journal* continues its series of summary guides to scholarship on particular texts and topics within Jonson studies, 'Jonson and his Era: Overviews of Modern Research', with entries from Eric Sterling on *The Alchemist* (*BJJ* 15[2008] 112–22) and Robert C. Evans on *Bartholomew Fair* (*BJJ* 15[2008] 271–89).

Books Reviewed

Bovilsky, Lara. *Barbarous Play: Race on the English Renaissance Stage.* UMinnP. [2008] pp. x + 218. $67.50 cloth. $22.50 pb ISBN 9 7808 1664 9648.

Butler, Martin. *The Stuart Court Masque and Political Culture.* CUP. [2008] pp. 462. £60 ISBN 9 7805 2188 3542.

Butler, Todd. *Imagination and Politics in Seventeenth-Century England.* Ashgate. [2008] pp. 214. £55 ISBN 9 7807 5465 8832.

Cormack, Bradin. *A Power To Do Justice: Jurisdiction, English Literature, and the Rise of Common Law.* UChicP [2008] pp. 424. $55 ISBN 9 7802 2611 6242.

Deats, Sara Munson, and Robert A. Logan. *Placing the Plays of Christopher Marlowe: Fresh Cultural Contexts.* Ashgate. [2008] pp. xi + 249. £55 ISBN 9 7807 5466 2044.

Dutton, Richard. *Ben Jonson, Volpone and the Gunpowder Plot.* CUP. [2008] pp. 216. £52 ISBN 9 7805 2187 9545.

Ephraim, Michelle. *Reading the Jewish Woman on the Elizabethan Stage.* Ashgate. [2008] pp. 192. £55 ISBN 9 7807 5465 8153.

Fitzsimmons, Lorna, ed. *International Faust Studies: Adaptation, Reception, Translation.* Continuum. [2008] pp. 320. £75 ISBN 9 7818 4706 0044.

Fitzsimmons, Lorna, ed. *Lives of Faust: The Faust Theme in Literature and Music: A Reader.* DeGruyter. [2008] pp. 508. $29.95 ISBN 9 7831 1019 8232.

Fotheringham, R., C. Jansohn, and R.S. White, eds. *Shakespeare's World/ World Shakespeares: The Selected Proceedings of the International Shakespeare Association World Congress, Brisbane, 2006.* UDelP. [2008] $69.50 ISBN 9 7808 7413 9891.

Grantley, Darryll. *London in Early Modern English Drama.* Palgrave [2008] pp. xii + 231. £50 ISBN 9 7802 3055 4290.

Griffey, Erin, ed. *Henrietta Maria: Piety, Politics and Patronage.* Ashgate. [2008] pp. 240. £55 ISBN 9 7807 5466 4208.

Henke, Robert, and Eric Nicholson, eds. *Transnational Exchange in Early Modern Theater.* Ashgate. [2008] pp. 286. £55 ISBN 0 7546 6281 0.

Hopkins, Lisa. *Christopher Marlowe: Renaissance Dramatist.* EdinUP. [2008] pp. x + 179. £50 ISBN 9 7807 4862 4737.

Hunt, Alice. *The Drama of Coronation: Medieval Ceremony in Early Modern England.* CUP. [2008] pp. 256. £52 ISBN 9 7805 2188 5393.

Knights, Ben, ed. *Masculinities in Text and Teaching.* Palgrave Macmillan. [2008] pp. 264. £53 ISBN 9 7802 3000 3415.

Livingston, Meg Powers, ed. *The Woman's Prize, by John Fletcher.* Malone 172. ManUP. [2008] pp. xxviii + 52. £40 ISBN 9 7807 1907 7104.

Lynch, Andrew, and Anne M. Scott, eds. *Renaissance Poetry and Drama in Context: Essays for Christopher Wortham.* CambridgeSP. [2008] pp. 353. £39.99 ISBN 9 7818 4718 6102.

Mardock, James D. *Our Scene Is London: Ben Jonson's City and the Space of the Author.* Routledge. [2008] pp. 164. £22.50 ISBN 0 4159 7763 0.

Melnikoff, Kurt, and Edward Gieskes, eds. *Writing Robert Greene: Essays on England's First Notorious Professional Writer.* Ashgate. [2008] pp. x + 248. £55 ISBN 9 7807 5465 7019.

Mulryne, J.R., ed. *Women Beware Women, by Thomas Middleton.* RevelsSE. ManUP. [2007] pp. 170. pb £5.99 ISBN 9 7807 1904 3505.

Papazian, Mary A., ed. *The Sacred and Profane in English Renaissance Literature.* UDelP. [2008] p. 377. $75 ISBN 9 7808 7413 0256.

Rist, Thomas. *Revenge Tragedy and the Drama of Commemoration in Reforming England.* Ashgate [2008] pp. 176. £50 ISBN 9 7807 5466 1528.

Scragg, Leah, ed. *Love's Metamorphosis, by John Lyly.* Revels. ManUP. [2008] pp. xv + 135. £50 ISBN 9 7807 1907 2468.

Smith, D.K. *The Cartographic Imagination in Early Modern England: Rewriting the World in Marlowe, Spenser, Raleigh and Marvell.* Ashgate. [2008] £55 ISBN 9 7807 5465 6203.

White, Paul Whitfield. *Drama and Religion in English Provincial Society, 1485–1660.* CUP. [2008] pp. xii + 247. £52 ISBN 9 7805 2185 6690.

Wiggins, Martin, ed. *A Woman Killed with Kindness and Other Domestic Plays.* OUP. [2008] pp. xlviii. + 344. pb £10.99 ISBN 9 7801 9282 9504.

Zucker, Adam, and Alan B. Farmer, eds. *Localizing Caroline Drama: Politics and Economics of the Early Modern Stage, 1625–1642.* Palgrave. [2006] pp. 280. £39.99 ISBN 9 7814 0397 2828.

VIII

The Earlier Seventeenth Century: General and Prose

JOHN R. BURTON

Work on women's writing for both 2008 and 2009 will be covered in next year's *YWES*.

While the early modern literary exploration of human misdeeds so often invoked biblical mandate, how did the early modern writer represent a female murderer? With few biblical precedents, and with a reading public eager to learn of society's ugly exceptions, writers of murder pamphlets exposed the uncharted territory of female villainy, according to Lynn Robson's valuable article ' "Now farewell to the lawe, too long have I been in they subjection": Early Modern Murder, Calvinism, and Female Sexual Authority' (*L&T* 22[2008] 295–312). The article centres its analysis on the Calvinist framework used by pamphleteers of the period to 'interpret and expose' (p. 295) the interplay between female subjection to social and judicial authority and the spiritual command granted the spoken and written word of the female accused, in this case Elizabeth Caldwell.

While attitudes to authority were changing in the period, notions of rebellion were equally in a state of transition, particularly when they concerned Satan, as Evan Labuzetta demonstrates with the case of the Ranters, a group largely defined by oppositional pamphlets, in ' "This diabolical generation": The Ranters and the Devil' (*LitComp* 5[2008] 591–602). Labuzetta's article, which won the 2007 *Literature Compass* Graduate Essay Prize for the Seventeenth Century Section, focuses on the use of Satan in the texts, a figure who gains a new revolutionary guise, significant given the civil war. Surveying anti-Ranter pamphlets, the study argues that denunciation itself resulted in a new complex perception of opposing, and indeed what it meant to be a devil.

Seventeenth-century queer studies are alive and well according to Jeremy W. Webster's 'Queering the Seventeenth Century: Historicism, Queer Theory, and Early Modern Literature' (*LitComp* 5[2008] 376–93). Surveying work on the history of sexuality by scholars such as Mario DiGangi, Jonathan Goldberg, David Halperin, Bruce Smith and Valerie Traub, Webster declares that despite

Year's Work in English Studies, Volume 89 (2010) © *The English Association; all rights reserved*
doi:10.1093/ywes/maq012

claims of its demise, historicism proves itself to be a 'significant and vital factor' in queer seventeenth-century scholarship (p. 379).

Anna Suranyi explores the genesis of English nationalism and imperialism in her study of early modern travel writing, *The Genius of the English Nation: Travel Writing and National Identity in Early Modern England*. The study surveys English national identity as represented to early modern readers in travel and ethnographic literature, and particularly how such literature portrays Irish, continental European, and Ottoman cultures in relation to the emerging English nation. Naturally, Suranyi's work responds to the travel writing of Sir Thomas Palmer, Thomas Coryate, Henry Blount and George Sandys. The study extends to incorporate a large number of works treating foreign cuisine, dress and the cultural and political position of women, a point particularly enlarged upon in the final section, which addresses gendered references to nations by writers of the period, leaving Suranyi to conclude that early modern writers attempted to articulate a national identity between 'the two extreme poles of the absolute liberty of the Irish, and the absolute control of the Turks' (p. 167).

The incorporation or renunciation of foreign ideas, language and practices is taken up in the collection of essays edited by Helen Ostovich, Mary Silcox and Graham Roebuck, *The Mysterious and the Foreign in Early Modern England*, which explores literary reactions to "otherness". Divided into three sections, 'The Foreign Journey', 'Profiting from the Mysterious', and 'The Domestication of the Mysterious and Foreign', the book draws from a range of works throughout the period, including dramatic, poetic and non-literary texts. Of particular note for this section is Sandra Bell's chapter, 'The Subject of Smoke: Tobacco and Early Modern England' (pp. 153–69), which surveys the literary praise and condemnation of the use of the imported herb, and Graham Roebuck's article (pp. 170–86), on England's relatively short-lived interest in the Sassafras tree, an episode which illustrates both attitudes towards America and the socio-political consequences of receiving the new and apparently better.

While medieval writers generally understood lovesickness and its attendant maladies as masculine, eighteenth-century authors perceived the reverse; amorous melancholy and physical ailments resulting from unfulfilled passions were feminine disorders. Lesel Dawson's *Lovesickness and Gender in Early Modern English Literature* examines the intervening period during the Renaissance, in which a series of transitions occurred in how lovesickness was regarded. The study is not limited to texts discussing the emotional trauma of problematic love, but concerns itself with how such traumas are rooted in the body, providing a illuminating treatment of early modern perceptions of desire. Furthermore, Dawson addresses the gendering of illness, challenging early models of critical discourse in which men are intellectually and creatively enriched by their lovesickness and women sufferers are conversely read as lacking in reason, numbed by overwhelming erotic impulses. In contrast she posits an alternative, reading a series of texts throughout the period as evidence of feminine pleasure or empowerment derived from lovesickness. Richard Burton's *Anatomy of Melancholy* is considered, along with Shakespeare's depiction of Ophelia, Fletcher's *The Maid's Tragedy*, John

Ford's *The Broken Heart*, and several other dramatic works, providing a substantial reading of the impassioned subject.

The value and place of dreams is considered in the collection of essays *Reading the Early Modern Dream: The Terrors of the Night*, edited by Katharine Hodgkin, Michelle O'Callaghan and S.J. Wiseman. Covering the whole of the early modern period from the late medieval to the dawn of Freud and Jung, the collection centres on the question of what seventeenth-century writers understood of dreams and the question of whether dreams are meaningful. Of particular interest in this section is the essay by Erica Fudge, 'Onely Proper Unto Man: Dreaming and Being Human' (pp. 31–43), which considers the problematic distinction, often vigorously drawn, between human and animal. Fudge appeals to a number of texts to demonstrate that certainties over the primacy of human reason over animal instinct are far from absolute when dreams are considered. Michelle O'Callaghan adds to the discussion with her chapter, 'Dreaming the Dead: Ghosts and History in the Early Seventeenth Century' (pp. 81–95), in which the political dream and the historical ghostly visitor are read together as an intimately related literary concept. Concluding that both the ghost and the dream inhabit the same textual interpretative space, one which speaks in figurative ways, O'Callaghan places the early modern recipient of ghostly visits and the dreamer in the position of recollecting histories and unfolding political meaning.

Despite an ongoing interest in Sir Thomas Browne, it has been some years since a major publication has appeared. *Sir Thomas Browne: A World Proposed* is a significant collection of essays edited by Reid Barbour and Claire Preston, divided into three sections. 'Habits of Thought' addresses a central question—where, in an age of political and religious reformations, should one place Browne? The section explores Browne's intellect as a writer, philosopher and historian. His capacity to adopt numerous literary styles is considered by Sharon Cadman Seelig, and Browne's theology is picked up by Deborah Shuger, who surveys his works in relation to religious texts by Herbert and Digby, thus considering Browne's proximity to Laudianism. Graham Parry surveys Browne's use of antiquity, while Brent Nelson draws from contemporary accounts of Browne's family life to complete the impression of a man of immense intellectual appetite and an infectious curiosity. Despite the lack of direct evidence of Browne's connection to his contemporary John Milton, Karen L. Edwards considers the handling of an issue both authors addressed: the question of the pygmy race, mentioned by Milton in the *Animadversions* and in Book I of *Paradise Lost*, and confronted by Browne in his *Pseudodoxia Epidemica*. Victoria Silver concludes the opening section by investigating Browne's role as an expert witness in a witch trial of 1662, extending her survey of the anonymous 1682 trial pamphlet in which Browne is named, to explore his standing on the detection of supernatural and spiritual wonders.

The second section considers his works, and Brooke Conti's contribution on the *Religio Medici* examines the 'leisurely expansiveness' (p. 150) of the volume, for which Browne has become known as a writer at ease with his faith. However, Conti's appraisal reveals 'a significant degree of doctrinal anxiety'

(p. 150). Conti senses Browne's unease in his approach to reason—at times making bold assertions for reason's place in religious experience, yet at other times 'discounting its operation entirely' (p. 156), concluding that the *Religio* constitutes an anxious self-examination rather than merely a relaxed and amiable autobiography. Both William N. West and Kevin Killeen approach the *Pseudodoxia Epidemica*, though from different perspectives. While West suggests that Browne's digressions (something he quips metaphorically as Brownean motion) are more than idle wanderings, and are suggestive of Browne's approach to knowledge and the interconnectedness of things, Killeen reads the *Pseudodoxia* as a critique of idolatry and the political background of iconoclasm from which the work emerges and with which it engages. Further chapters on the medical narrative in *A Letter to a Friend* by Claire Preston and on Browne's religious toleration in *Urne-Buriall* by Achsah Guibbory are followed by Kathryn Murphy's reading of the *Garden of Cyrus*, which incorporates the *Timaeus* in order to unravel the complexities of Browne's mysticism, and, lastly, by Jonathan F.S. Post's analysis of *The Miscellaneous Writings*.

The book closes with a section on Browne's reception and interpretation, 'Life and Afterlives', with Reid Barbour considering Browne's many references—medical and otherwise—to skin, and Roy Rosenstein contributing with an intertextual reading of Jorge Luis Borges as a modern Browne, while Sir Thomas's antiquarian credentials are brought under spotlight in Peter N. Miller's reading of German English writer W.G. Sebald. In all the book well illustrates the worthy position Browne scholarship deserves in studies of the period.

A further work on Browne emerged this year. Ronald Huebert's article, 'Reading, Writing, and *Religio Medici*' (*PSt* 30[2008] 109–23), concerns itself with the question of Browne's position in the history of reading. Acknowledging the work done by Lisa Jardine, William H. Shurman, Kevin Sharpe and Anthony Grafton, in which they demonstrate the political basis of early modern reading, Huebert begins by demonstrating that, for Browne, 'reading and writing are primarily epistemological and political engagements' (p. 110). This argument is extended by Huebert, who concludes that, for Browne, writing and reading are a means of engaging with the problem of knowledge—of both scientific and divine truth.

Books Reviewed

Dawson, Lesel. *Lovesickness and Gender in Early Modern English Literature*. OUP. [2008] pp. 244. £53 ISBN 9 7801 9926 6128.
Barbour, Reid, and Claire Preston. *Sir Thomas Browne: The World Proposed*. OUP. [2008] pp. 368. £63 ISBN 9 7801 9923 6213.
Hodgkin, Katharine, Michelle O'Callaghan and S.J. Wiseman. *Reading the Early Modern Dream: The Terrors of the Night*. Routledge. [2008] pp. 176. £85 ISBN 0 4153 8601 2.

Ostovich, Helen, Mary V. Silcox, and Graham Roebuck. *The Mysterious and the Foreign in Early Modern England.* UDelP. [2008] pp. 318. $63.50 ISBN 9 7808 7413 9549.

Suranyi, Anna. *The Genius of the English Nation: Travel Writing and National Identity in Early Modern England.* UDelP. [2008] pp. 242. $52.50 ISBN 9 7808 7413 9983.

IX

Milton and Poetry, 1603–1660

DAVID AINSWORTH, ALVIN SNIDER, HOLLY FAITH NELSON, PAUL DYCK AND NOAM REISNER

This chapter has five sections: 1. General; 2. Milton; 3. Donne; 4. Herbert; 5. Marvell. Section 1 is by David Ainsworth; section 2 is by Alvin Snider; section 3 is by Holly Faith Nelson; section 4 is by Paul Dyck; section 5 is by Noam Reisner.

1. General

The year 2008 saw a cluster of articles on Michael Drayton. The general poetry area saw historicist approaches predominate in published articles and books. I begin with Bruce Boehrer's 'Inviting a Friend to Supper' (*BJJ* 14[2007] 255–9). Boehrer examines Jonson's epigram of the same name, discussing a range of scholarly perspectives on the piece. Boehrer summarizes the position of scholars who see the epigram as both emulation and invocation of Martial, matching gustatory receptivity to receptivity for the classical tradition. He situates other readings within humanist festivity, suggesting that the poem generates an atmosphere of trust and free discourse. And he offers up the views of other critics who read the poem biographically, politically or as a redefinition of the social dynamics of festivity. This article is part of an overview of research and does not introduce new ideas.

The year's articles on Jonson are quite eclectic. Mathew Martin examines the place of mourning in Jonson's poetry in 'The Name of the Father in "On My First Son:" Ben Jonson and the Work of Mourning' (*BJJ* 15[2008] 159–74). Martin establishes the patriarchal overtones of funeral rites in the period, suggesting first that Jonson himself embraces and endorses this paternalist order, but then that 'On My First Son' breaks the pattern. The breakdown of patriarchal symbolism in the poem stems, Martin writes, from the tension between Jonson's role as public poet and the private character of this particular poem. Construing this breakdown along psychoanalytic lines, Martin argues that the poem sets versions of fatherhood at odds in a way which avoids Lacanian psychosis only by replacing mourning with the fetish of poetry itself. The plague which took Benjamin Jonson's life threatens the

Year's Work in English Studies, Volume 89 (2010) © *The English Association; all rights reserved*
doi:10.1093/ywes/maq013

model of a productive and stable natural world, like that of 'To Penshurst', and Jonson cannot position his child as the fruit of an abundant natural world without confronting nature's destructive side. Jonson thus drives his poem, not towards a transcendent heaven, but towards a preserving poetic power. He compensates for his physical absence at the time of his son's death by constituting his poem as a surrogate, asserting an authorizing power over his son which the plague deprived him of in a literal sense. But Martin also acknowledges a reading of the poem as a resignation, an acknowledgement both of human mortality and of poetic mortality. That tension, Martin argues, renders this poem a fetishistic defence against psychosis, an attempt to reconstitute a destabilized paternal metaphor, or, at the least, insist upon it. Barbara Mather Cobb takes up the topic of Jonson's investment in his own literary worth in ' "Excribe"-ing, Esteem, and Estimation: Jonson as Window to the "Soule of the Age" ' (*CEA* 71:i[2008] 1–11). She argues that Jonson himself defines a standard for literary success as lasting worth. Through examination of Jonson's memorial poem to Shakespeare, his sonnet to Mary Wroth and an elegy from *Underwood*, Cobb establishes how Jonson positions himself in his literary age as poet and as peer to other literary figures. She argues that Jonson's interest in his own literary worth holds primacy over his pursuit of patronage. Discussing the sonnet to Wroth, she argues for Jonson's ambivalence towards her, making the poem one intended to distance him from Wroth as much as to praise her. In Jonson's poem to Shakespeare, he employs and echoes Shakespearian tropes, demonstrating not only his familiarity with Shakespeare's work but also his own literary merit. Cobb compares *Underwood 22* to Donne's 'The Expostulation' to again demonstrate how Jonson situates himself consciously within a poetic community, setting himself in relation to Donne and not to their respective patrons.

In 'Less Well-Wrought Urns: Henry Vaughan and the Decay of the Poetic Monument' (*ELH* 75[2008] 197–217), William N. West takes up the Cleanth Brooks's *The Well Wrought Urn*, establishing Donne's passage from 'The Canonization' as a significant New Critical metaphor for poetic power and then arguing that Vaughan qualifies the metaphor and calls poetry's power into question. Brooks begins with a wide-ranging discussion of the claim that verse endures like a monument, considering Donne, Keats, Greek lyric and epic, Ovid's *Metamorphoses*, Herrick's 'His Poetrie His Pillar' and Milton's 'On Shakespeare'. West identifies a historical shift in seventeenth-century poetry towards the poem as a written object, a shift which reinforces New Critical assumptions. He suggests that this idea of the lyric is written, not sung, a lapidary lyric instead of an Orphic one. A poem as a material text can be equated with a physical monument with ease, but the very materiality of the book potentially complicates the claim that verse is timeless. West identifies John Weever's *Ancient Funerall Monuments* [1631], Herrick's 'To Live Merrily, and to Trust to Good Verses' [1648] and Waller's 'English Verse' [1664] as examples of poems in the period which suspect the enduring power of language and meaning. Turning to Vaughan, West reads 'An Elegie on the Death of Mr R.W.' and 'Upon a Cloak Lent Him by Mr J. Ridsley' as poems which suggest that poetry can preserve and endure only so long as it remains absent of form. The material of the poem endures, but the shape which the poet forms out of that material fades. Reading a range of poems from *Silex Scintillans*, West argues that Vaughan ultimately transforms his own poetry into parts of the material book which it inhabits. Thus Vaughan offers up the material book as the means for shared experience and thus as a facilitator for spiritual (specifically, Anglican) community. This community is one which emerges out of such shared experience, and thus the poem does not commemorate what is past but provides the raw materials for what is to come. West concludes by suggesting that the path of literary criticism has followed the path of seventeenth-century poetry, increasingly linking the material and the communal. Alan Rudrum addresses the link between peace and theology in 'Bringing Peace Back to Life: The Anglican Irenicism of Lancelot Andrewes, Henry Vaughan and Rowan Williams' (*Scintilla* 12[2008] 111–20). He examines Andrewes's Easter sermon of 1609, which associates Christ's resurrection to the general concept of peace, and he associates this message with Williams's theology. He emphasizes the political dimensions of Vaughan's poetry, but stresses his concern for forgiveness as a facilitating gesture of peace. In 'Easter-Day', Vaughan locates Christ, not in Jerusalem, but in the Usk Valley, opening the possibility that peace might come with him to Britain. In 'Henry Vaughan, Jeremy Taylor, Edward Sparke, and the Preservation of the Anglican Communion' (*Scintilla* 12[2008] 141–59), Robert Wilcher characterizes Vaughan as an Anglican survivalist, who aims *Silex Scintillans* at friends in order to preserve the communion of the Anglican Church. His poetry could hold the church together through a private communion of believers, united through Vaughan's lyric power. Unlike West, Wilcher emphasizes the literary and aesthetic power of Vaughan's poetry as that which generates shared experiences, not the material book itself. Wilcher relates Vaughan to Taylor, whose work he describes as more schematic than Vaughan's, but he concentrates on how the two poets play off one another. He also briefly considers Edward Sparke's volume of prose and verse, *Scintillula Altaris*, relating it to Vaughan's work and suggesting that Vaughan's influence on it suggests the workings of the Anglican communion all three poets strove to protect.

In 'Richard Crashaw's Poem on Matthew 22 and the *Ars Memorativa*' (*ANQ* 21:iii[2008] 28–35), Sean McDowell quotes Beaumont to establish Crashaw's mastery of the rhetorical art of memory, offering the epigram on Matthew 22 as evidence that Crashaw himself deliberately situates his poetry within memorial practices. McDowell acknowledges the devotional work of memory, with reference to Augustine and to Martz's *The Poetry of Meditation*, but argues that the poem draws only upon the rhetorical traditions of memory. He argues that the 'stonied' Pharisees and Sadducees in the epigram function as memory images, both of their own passionate astonishment and of the affective power of Christ's response to their questions. Drawing upon the work of Charles Le Brun, First Painter to Louis XIV, McDowell argues that the facial registering of strong emotions generates meaning by capturing expressions which, individually, represent multiple responses and which, collectively, set themselves in comparison with alternative expressions. McDowell concludes that Crashaw's devotional poetry should be read with attention to the Renaissance rhetorical theory which provides its foundation.

Matthew Horn discusses Crashaw's employment of lyric and emblem traditions to evoke the affect of a Catholic chapel in his essay, 'A Safe Space for the Texted Icon: Richard Crashaw's Use of the Emblem Tradition in his Devotional Lyrics' (*Exemplaria* 20:iv[2008] 410–29). Horn concentrates on Crashaw's sacred verse, arguing that it should be read in the context of the Catholic understanding of iconography and physicality. This iconic materiality stands in the face of English iconoclasm over the late sixteenth and early seventeenth centuries, with both relics and images retaining their devotional and political power across the period. Horn argues for a reconfigured icon, one which replaces or tries to replace the sense of Catholic community interrupted by the need to meet and worship in secret. Symbols and emblems become substitutes or disguises for Catholic iconography. But by the middle of the seventeenth century, Horn argues, the religious lyric becomes a more powerful place to conceal iconography meaningful to literate Catholic readers. Crashaw's poetry is thus full of imagery and of literal references to colour, which alone or in conjunction with Crashaw's emblems and illustrations act as sacred iconography. The materiality of the book of poetry acts as substitute for the material prayerbook, while the content of the poems acquires iconographic force through association with the visual and physical.

Garth Bond suggests, in 'Expanding the Canon of Lady Mary Wroth's Poetry' (*N&Q* 55[2008] 283–6), that the poetry from her romance *Love's Victory* ought to be included in her poetic canon. He notes that Josephine Roberts had only an incomplete edition of the play when she compiled Wroth's poetry for her 1983 edition, although he notes that she also deliberately omits several other poems from the text along with some poetic fortunes and riddles. Bond also draws our attention to two 'hidden' poems in the play, which are presented as regular dramatic dialogue and marked only marginally in the manuscripts of the play. Bond suggests that one of these sonnets in particular would be a valuable canonical addition because it exhibits characteristics of Wroth's fictional voice, evoking *Urania* through references to ciphers and to a retreat into the woods to grieve. Bond concludes with a warning about errors in the Cerasano–Wynne-Davies edition of *Love's Victory*.

Carol Blessing discusses Lanyer's poetic interpretation of the Bible in '"Most blessed daughters of Jerusalem": Aemilia Lanyer's *Salve Deus Rex Judaeorum* and Elizabethan and Jacobean Bible Commentary' (*BJJ* 15[2008] 232–47). Blessing suggests that close attention to Lanyer's work as biblical commentary will help situate her positions on a feminized Christ, the women in his life, and Eve within a scriptural dialogue, placing her in an appropriate historical context instead of rendering her as a modern feminist. Arguing that Lanyer writes along Anglican lines, Blessing challenges the assumption that her depictions of Christ are revolutionary. She discusses a range of earlier works which present Christ in feminine terms: Markham's *The Tears of the Beloved* and *Mary Magdalens Lamentations for the Losse of her Master Jesus* [1600], and the anonymous *The Song of Mary the Mother of Christ* [1601]. She relates Markham's verse form to Lanyer's, as well as suggesting that Lanyer adopts and expands upon a section of Markham's poetry which blames a long list of men for Christ's crucifixion. She also demonstrates how the earlier works employ the same connection between Christ's suffering and women's tears. Examining Lanyer's defence of Eve, Blessing associates this portion of the *Salve Deus* with Willet's *Hexpla in Genesin* [1608] and *Adams Tragedie* [1608], both of which direct blame for the Fall away from Eve. These works also emphasize Eve's weakness as part of their defence of her, which may provide a useful context for Lanyer's own repeated emphasis of that weakness. Blessing challenges assertions of Lanyer's complete originality, situating her within a larger discourse about biblical women.

Bart van Es's 'Michael Drayton, Literary History and Historians in Verse' (*RES* 59[2008] 255–69) begins with Drayton's verse assessment of Samuel Daniel as too much a historian in verse, moving into an argument that Drayton himself writes verse history despite the problems it caused him with patronage. Van Es begins with Drayton's nostalgia, in 1621, for the Elizabethan tradition of verse history going back to Baldwin's *Mirror for Magistrates*. He compares Daniel's *The Complaint of Rosamond* to Drayton's revision of the story in his *Heroicall Epistles*. Drayton draws strongly upon Ovid's *Heroides* to complicate the relationship between female chastity and male persuasion, and uses that complication to examine the crisis between the individual conscience and duty to one's king. In the process, he constructs a poem which reflects the suspension of history between actual events and myths. Van Es indicates that Drayton's attempt at a new kind of exchange between poetry and history also directs itself as instruction and warning for Lucy, countess of Bedford. Drayton relies upon a discerning audience for his poetry which can reflect upon its moral and literary messages. Lucy's shift of patronage from Drayton to Donne thus demonstrates a strong trend away from the former's historical verse. Drayton insists upon a balance between history, moral instruction and poetry, which he sees as violated in Donne's works. Drayton's poems can be seen as transitional, worth study from a historicist perspective as examples of period negotiations of historical accounts.

The influence of Ovid on Drayton received considerable attention in 2008. In ' "Large complaints in little papers": Negotiating Ovidian Genealogies of Complaint in Drayton's *Englands Heroicall Epistles*' (*RS* 22:iii[2008] 368–85), Alison Thorne suggests that Drayton develops a distinctive feminine epistolary voice in his poem by reworking the Heroidean topos of a heroine's self-conscious reflection on her own letter-writing. These poetic characters deliberately position themselves against Ovidian tropes in ways which grant them textual authority. Thorne analyses how the male and female writers in the *Heroicall Epistles* deploy allusions to Ovid in ways that reflect their gender positions. Drayton's heroines thus develop their voices in dialogue with the male correspondents and with Ovidian models. Thorne concentrates on the interplay between the intertwined personas of Drayton's poem and their Ovidian counterparts, alongside the interplay between Ovid and Drayton himself. Drayton's remaking of Ovid empowers his female characters as his attempt to establish a distinctive voice permits them their own distinctive voices within his text. The act of writing itself becomes the focal point of these female letter-writers' anxieties, which in turn draws readers' attention to those cultural factors which inhibit female expression in the period. While partially inscribed in their Ovidian models, these women seek to rewrite themselves by means of their own articulated ideas, putting forward ethical arguments which also express Drayton's critique of Ovid's rhetoric. Danielle Clarke also examines Drayton's *Heroicall Epistles* in 'Ovid's *Heroides*, Drayton and the Articulation of the Feminine in the English Renaissance' (*RS* 22:iii[2008] 385–400). She argues that Drayton adopts Ovid's poetic model to invest the female voice with authority and political meaning. This investment turns upon the consequences of sexual and dynastic desire as they work themselves out through the poem. Drayton not only includes female voices within his work, he also situates them within political, especially dynastic, power structures. The dynamics of the epistolary form, coupled with the moral and ethical standing of the female voices within the text, grants an authority to these female figures while inviting us to judge the powerful men in relation to them. Drayton thus presents characters invested in public and political roles and concentrates upon their agency within the public sphere. Drayton founds his epistles on the idea of presence as manifested through the act of writing, embodying his heroines through their own textual production. Danijela Kambaskovic-Sawers addresses Ovid's *Metamorphoses* and its reworking in Drayton and Daniel in her article, '"Bugbears in Apollo's Cell": Metamorphoses of Character in Drayton's *Idea* and Daniel's *Delia*' (*Parergon* 21:i[2008] 123–48). Situating Daniel's and Drayton's use of Ovid in its cultural context, she presents their semantic use of Roman mythology as a way to engage readers in a mental debate. By twisting Ovidian figures, the poets develop characterization in part through deliberate disjuncture with these textual models. Addressing both works as sequences, Kambaskovic-Sawers discusses how references to and variations from Ovid generate readerly interest in the speakers of the poems. She argues that ambiguity and duality within character is necessary to construct complex and captivating first-person speakers. While she limits her examination to specific creative changes to Ovidian texts, she does map out Drayton's revisions of *Idea's Mirrour* and *Idea* as part of her project. Arguing that Daniel and Drayton adopt Ovidian characterization in similar ways, she suggests that both use Ovid to comic effect and to produce overtly erotic, attention-seeking figures of interest in their sequences.

In '"Bake'd *in the* oven *of* applause": The Blazon and the Body in Margaret Cavendish's Fancies' (*WW* 15:i[2008] 86–106), Elizabeth Scott-Baumann argues that Cavendish fuses recipes and scientific images to provide an alternative representation of the female body, drawing upon Cavalier imagery along corporeal and consumptive lines. Evoking the blazon tradition alongside the kitchen in her recipe poems, Cavendish opens up space in each. Scott-Baumann suggests that kitchens and scientific laboratories cannot be readily distinguished in the period, making work on recipes scientific work. Cavendish challenges the blazon tradition by breaking down gender binaries, drawing upon lyric poetry to feminize science and scientific practices. She contests eroticized desire and the blazon's anatomization through scientific anatomization. Scott-Baumann situates Cavendish's work within the Petrarchan tradition, as well as Cavalier poetry, showing how she draws upon natural philosophy and images of food and cooking to challenge the traditional gender hierarchies of the lyric tradition. By associating women with Nature, Cavendish resists the object–subject model of love poetry and seventeenth-century science, uniting subject and object within Nature herself. Yaakov Mascetti also examines the intersections between science and the cultural place of women in 'A "World of nothing, but pure wit": Margaret Cavendish and the Gendering of the Imaginary' (*PAns* 6:i[2008] 1–31). He argues that Cavendish opposes the crude world of fact offered by male thinkers of her time, offering instead imagination and wit as the central elements of science. This opposition promises liberation from the masculine valuation of reason and natural interpretation as male and the association of the female mind with imagination, fancy and superstition. His heavily theorized examination addresses Cartesian dualism, both in the work of Descartes himself and in Hobbes's *Leviathan*, as well as setting Bacon's methods of direct observation against Aristotle's 'organon' of logic and speculation. Associating this new scientific framework with cultural understandings of gender in the period, Mascetti presents the new science as an assertion of culturally masculine approaches to knowledge over culturally feminine ones. The association of the masculine and the divine, the feminine and Nature, affirms a directive masculine sphere and a confined, responsive feminine sphere. Cavendish pursues a proto-feminist agenda in her work by offering feminine fancy as the parallel to male wisdom. Mascetti positions Cavendish against Hobbes, with Cavendish praising and privileging wit, fancy and delight over sombre materialism and the plodding 'authentic' knowledge of the masculine mind.

In 'Joyce and Herrick' (*NConL* 38:ii[2008] 2), Jeffrey Meyers lists a few of Herrick's poems evoked by Joyce's *Chamber Music*. He also identifies Herrick's poems 'North and South' and 'Delight in Disorder' as influences on *Ulysses*, pointing in particular to Bloom's clothing fetish and to Bloom and Molly's sleeping positions. His examination will probably interest Joyce scholars more than Herrick scholars, though.

Heather Dubrow's book *The Challenges of Orpheus: Lyric Poetry and Early Modern England* represents both a wide-ranging exploration of lyric poetry in the early modern period and a plea for scholars to emphasize multivalent ideas and inclusive taxonomies over hierarchical and sharply argumentative approaches. Dubrow's work embodies that which she advocates for other scholars, offering a complex but close examination of lyric poems which could well be described as a theory of the lyric. Basing her work on the Orpheus myth, Dubrow offers a field of enquiry on lyric, contextualized and defined predominantly by her analysis of period poetry, but incorporating comparative terms and approaches ranging from cultural studies to discussions of architecture and space. Her first chapter follows mythic narratives and figurative language in early modern English lyric to consider the question: how do English lyricists write about lyric? Taking mythic tropes and figuration as her means to discuss lyric, Dubrow offers a deliberatively suggestive definition, one grounded upon loss, gender, power, agency and its absence and the musical elements of lyric poetry, all themes figured through various Orphean myths. Chapter 2 examines audiences and audience positions in relation to lyric poetry, discussing the instability of an audience position which can

involve reading poetry as something both overheard and specifically aimed at
the reader. Dubrow's discussion ranges from narratology and Bakhtinian
discourse analysis to the communal elements of singing. Chapter 3 discusses
the dynamic of immediacy and distance in lyric, taking up Orpheus's
dismemberment as a representation of poetry's scattering, while suggesting
that a process of reclaiming keeps the poem whole. This chapter focuses on the
place of the author within the lyric tradition. Chapter 4 considers lyric
linkages, from the potential of the stanza's stability and restraint to the
authorial possibilities of grouped poems. This chapter again considers
authorial matters, but takes a predominantly structuralist approach.
Dubrow takes up lyric and narrative in chapter 5, situating lyric meditation
in a dynamic relationship with narrative. She suggests that lyric can intensify
narrative force, examines the place of lyric poetry within prose romances and
Shakespeare's plays, and concludes with a look towards future work, arguing
for an imbalance between study of the lyric and the dramatic in our profession.
Her open-ended conclusion defends interlocking, dynamic argumentation over
the simple thesis, while her own work typifies the 'both/and' approach she
advocates. Dubrow also defends broad-based critical engagement, especially
close reading, and proposes a new formalism. Authors whose poems receive
attention include Herrick, Donne, Milton, Dryden, Sir Thomas Wyatt,
Petrarch, Michael Drayton, Philip Sidney, Spenser, Puttenham, Shakespeare,
Jonson, Herbert, Vaughan, Fletcher, Gascoigne, Wroth, Crashaw and Daniel,
as well as Wordsworth and Keats. As that list indicates, Dubrow offers no
comprehensive analysis of a single author, instead interweaving her examinations into a broader tapestry of interpretative meaning.

Where Dubrow's approach employs a range of formal and structural
theoretical approaches, Edward Holberton's *Poetry and the Cromwellian
Protectorate: Culture, Politics, and Institutions* takes a historicist approach
influenced by the work of Pocock and Skinner. Holberton examines the
complexity of shifting cultural institutions and the ways in which these shifts
come through some of the poetry of the period, focusing upon the occasions
for poetry. He challenges the centrality of republican thinking in interpretations of poems in the period, as well as suggesting that poetry about Oliver
Cromwell presents a nuanced and ambivalent version of the man, influenced
as much or more by the circumstantial commitments of poets than by
Cromwell's own mastery or public image. In effect, he suggests reading poems
about Cromwell by placing the wider political and cultural entanglements of
the period at the centre, rather than a charismatic Cromwell. His first chapter
addresses Whitelocke's embassy to Sweden, concentrating on the three Latin
poems he presented to Queen Christina in manuscript. Using Whitelocke's
journal to establish the circumstances of the embassy, Holberton reads poems
by Whistler, Wolseley and Marvell as rhetorical efforts which complement
Whitelocke's own droll plainness and ironic self-presentation. In particular, he
suggests how these poets bring out mythic references to render Christina
poetically manipulable through comparison, and he suggests ways in which
these poems emphasize the Protectorate's progressive humanism while
mitigating its radical revolutionary elements. Chapter 2 examines London's
civic societies, suggesting that the ebb and flow of political power within the

livery companies which formed London's body politic is captured in and reflected by the poetic products of the city. Examining the poetry of civic pageants, especially Tatham's work, Holberton argues that these poems link civic virtue to a humanist understanding of republics, rendering London as a counterpart to the Roman republic and thus embodying the tension between the republican enterprise and the inherent elitism of the livery companies. Chapter 3 examines the Oxford collection of poetry, *Musarum Oxoniensium Elaiophoria*, as a production contingent upon the range of identities within the anthology, capturing the pressures and perspectives of the moment. These poems present peace as a return to old forms, disempowering the military's role in maintaining a peace in favour of the civil arts which constitute the university's ethos. The collection thus justifies Oxford's existence while appealing to Cromwell and friends as a new elite, and it configures Britain's economic potential as part of a larger promise of Reformation emerging from the Protectorate. In chapter 4, Holberton closely reads Waller's *Panegyrick to My Lord Protector* and Marvell's *The First Anniversary*. Waller offers a portrait of Cromwell as an Augustan moderate, able to reconcile royalists to the Protectorate through his leadership. Parliament is rendered a subordinate body, eliding political tensions and offering the chance of a cultural unity with many yoked together through Cromwell's leadership. Marvell's poem engages more directly than Waller's with the problems between Cromwell and parliament, capturing a sense of a fissure between the people and their leadership while offering a promise of a greater restoration to come out of the present crisis. Chapter 5 looks at poetry about the New World generally and the conflict with Spain particularly, reading poetry by Waller and Davenant's works as well as a poem by 'R.F.'. Again, this poetry is conditional and circumstantial, offering an alterative telos of economic expansion and trade in place of a baldly imperial narrative at odds with a republican Britain. Political and religious moderation become poetically linked with wrangling against Spain in the New World. In chapter 6, Holberton concentrates on the historical circumstance of the wedding entertainments for Cromwell's young-est daughters, interpreting occasional poetry by Marvell and Waller. These poems reshape the masque tradition, addressing the problematic revival of courtly forms in the occasion. Waller deals with Cromwell's lack of courtly manners in comparison to his daughter Frances by contrasting her courtliness with his plainness, as if the latter produced the former, referring to Samson's lion to balance Cromwell's godliness with Frances's greater stateliness. In contrast, Marvell maintains the tensions between courtliness and puritanical republicanism by fashioning a new pastoral space. He places Mary Cromwell as a slightly passive Cynthia to Fauconberg's unusually active Endymion, who courts the goddess. The result is an ironic tension between the great promise of the Protectorate and its yet-to-be-fulfilled state, with Cromwell's place not yet settled. Chapter 7 discusses elegies written after Cromwell's death, by Marvell, Waller, Dryden and Thomas Sprat. Holberton reads these poems as positioning or negotiating new boundaries and borders on expectations of the Protectorate, setting Cromwell's deeds—finished or unfinished—against an uncertain future. In his epilogue Holberton briefly examines reception of Cromwell and poetry of the period, with particular focus on how each era's version of Cromwell reflects its own expectations or agendas. He suggests that the rich contexts of contingent poetry in the period offers a corrective to history's distorted portraits of Cromwell, while arguing that reading of the poetry should not over-stress Cromwell's centrality or influence.

2. Milton

Over the centuries since his birth, biographers have treated Milton as a subject of inexhaustible interest, and 2008, Milton's quatercentenary, supplied an occasion for fresh appraisals. Few seventeenth-century literary lives are better documented, and scholars need look no further than Barbara Lewalski's *The Life of John Milton* [2001] for a comprehensive biography. The once standard life by William Riley Parker (revised by Gordon Campbell in 1996) has not yet outlived its usefulness, and readers can turn to dozens of earlier biographies as well. Although certain local mysteries remain unresolved, together with the perennial issue of accounting for discontinuities in Milton's political and religious identities, biographers need not trouble to set the basic record straight. Absent the discovery of a trove of lost letters or manuscripts, biographical and bibliographical researches into Milton's life have produced a comprehensive documentary record of extant sources scattered across many archives. With the appearance of a new full-dress biography, by Campbell and Thomas N. Corns, *John Milton: Life, Work, and Thought*, we now have an account that sifts through all the available archival evidence, incorporating many recent discoveries. The authors also claim to have benefited from revisionist Stuart historiography, which 'has developed in the last thirty years with a vigour and subtlety in comparison with which even historically informed literary criticism sometimes seems jejune' (p. 2). Avoiding a tone of uncritical adulation for their subject, the John Milton who emerges here, perhaps unsurprisingly, is a bundle of contradictions. The study takes shape around the phases of Milton's radicalization 'as he moves from a culturally advanced but ideologically repressive young manhood into the struggle for a new reformation of the church and on to defence of regicide and republicanism, finally working out how to retain political and spiritual integrity in the threatening context of the Restoration' (p. 3).

Readers who choose to read through the chapters consecutively will discover an accessible, scholarly and judicious account in just under 500 pages. Some will succumb, as I did, to the temptation of jumping to particular moments in the poet's life and reading Campbell and Corns back to back with Lewalski. Campbell and Corns's treatment will strike many as less 'literary' than Lewalski's, less concerned to synthesize the reach of modern scholarship. Its undoubted value lies in its handling of fact and detail, in its revelation of particulars pertinent to our understanding of the poems and prose. If the 'history' the authors invoke sometimes has a positivist tinge to it—high politics, war, great men, relentless linear development and so forth—one can return to the biography again and again for leads, for clarification and insight into the social, religious and political life of the period. With this entry in the crowded field of Milton biography, the authors have succeeded in making an indispensable and probably enduring contribution to Milton studies.

Anna Beer's *Milton: Poet, Pamphleteer and Patriot*, which also appeared in the red-letter year of 2008, offers a seamless popular narrative of the life that stays clear of conjecture, Blackadderish anachronism or faux-novelistic detail. Scholarly but written to satisfy the interests of a non-specialist audience (in Britain perhaps a more realistic aspiration than elsewhere in the anglophone world), the biography occasionally falls back on one-dimensional generalizations about seventeenth-century culture: Milton's anxious attitude towards chastity in the 1630s, for example, becomes the expression of 'a prevalent view in his society, where the sexual act with a woman was often viewed with disgust', a view 'fuelled by the Church's anxiety about sex, even within marriage' (p. 78). Such displacements onto seventeenth-century religious culture at large can perform as a sort of pseudo-explanation, whereby Milton becomes 'representative' of a monolithic historical 'background'. For the most part, however, Beer (who also blogs on the arts for the *Guardian*) deftly depicts Milton in his various public roles as writer, controversialist and patriot, combining the art of the professional biographer with the wide-ranging curiosity of a cultural historian.

Thomas N. Corns looks back to 'The Early Lives of John Milton' in his contribution to Kevin Sharpe and Steven N. Zwicker's *Writing Lives*, pointing out that 'all the lives are to an extraordinary degree concerned with a small number of topics while silent on issues of massive significance' (p. 78). Milton's sex life and marriage hold a particular fascination for the biographers, as does the tour of the continent and experience as a teacher; the biographers also pay 'obsessive attention both to the aetiology of his blindness and to his coping strategies' (p. 79). The silences in these accounts seem deafening now, frustrating our curiosity about Milton's political transformation, how he escaped retribution at the Restoration and other such questions. Corns concludes that 'the early lives, at least before Toland's, show an imperfect engagement with Milton's writing, and none systematically connects biography and even the most rudimentary critical insight' (p. 88), sounding a note of exasperation familiar to students of early modern literary culture.

Nigel Smith's provocatively titled *Is Milton Better than Shakespeare?* also celebrates the 400th birthday and seeks a new audience for the poet. To the rhetorical question posed by the title, the common reader might respond that the playwright has a distinct advantage, that only when directors can cast Jude Law or Ethan Hawke in *Comus* or *Samson Agonistes* will the later writer stand much of a chance in this contest. What should draw us to Milton, Smith argues, is his continuing relevance, his utility 'in our current predicaments', in particular, his views on 'religious, political, and civil liberty, including divorce and a theology of free will' (p. 5). We can compare this to another brief introductory study, published twenty years ago: Catherine Belsey's *John Milton: Language, Gender, Power*. While Belsey read Milton's writings for contested meanings, for the unresolved conflicts that define modernity, Smith responds to more immediate events, specifically 'the terrorists of Al-Qaeda', who 'do not care for Western liberalism' (p. 1), 'the world-wide spread of computer-driven information technology' (p. 3), and other developments snatched from the headlines. In seven chapters of appreciation, with ample block quotations and minimal citation, Smith's bold agenda articulated in the introduction gradually ebbs away. Whether we can (or would want to) draft Milton to serve a somewhat beleaguered liberalism finally seems beside the point. When Christopher Hill strove to recover Milton as a figure deserving of our attention, making him a fellow-traveller of Ranters and Muggletonians and treating sectarian radicals as proto-Bolsheviks, his agenda lay square-ly within the parameters of a particular radical tradition, that of the Communist Party Historians' Group. When Smith claims that Milton, because of his commitment to liberty, furnishes a key to what it means 'to be quintessentially American', he directs our attention to the Liberty Fund, an Indianapolis-based libertarian foundation which, he inaccurately claims, 'devotes a sizable part of its website to Milton's poetry and prose and a discussion of his work' (p. 4). The non-specialist (implicitly American) reader the book hopes to attract will find Smith an engaging and learned cicerone in this conducted tour of the Miltonic corpus, but the positioning of Milton—politically, vis-à-vis American liberalism, and even within popular culture (p. 185)—sometimes darkens as much as it illuminates. You do not have to agree with everything Smith says about the present, however, to find the book a useful introduction.

A very different and far more oblique approach to the issue of what 'makes the reading of Milton so relevant today' (p. 12) emerges in Claire Colebrook's *Milton, Evil and Literary History*. Colebrook takes up the issue of the figuration of evil in Milton, less the old problem of Satan than theoretical questions following mainly from deconstruction and having to do with historicist knowledge. Misreadings, Colebrook contends, historically have 'depended upon the two figures of evil against which Western thought has defined life: evil as detached self-enclosure, and evil as chaotic unboundedness' (p. 10). Colebrook ingeniously draws a line connecting Milton's own polarized conception of good as renewal and evil as incoherence with literary theories that treat reading as a restoration of an original act or the recovery of life-giving contexts and meaningful order. Milton's ethics of reading, according to Colebrook, 'his own opposition between good (as expansive life) and evil (as non-relation or absence of sense)' (p. 13), makes a strong case for the value of poststructuralist modes of thought as an alternative to thinking about literature historically. In his refusal to look beyond relations, 'Satan is the first new historicist', incapable of seeing beyond the autotelic self to a vitalistic source of life and being. Readers might find themselves taken aback at how Colebrook analogizes the turn to interiority as a movement towards evil: 'Like Stephen Greenblatt, when Satan looks to find the subject he looks for an interior and self-present truth; he, not surprisingly, finds nothing and a hell opens within him' (p. 85). Such moments aside, my summary cannot do justice to the intricacy of Colebrook's analysis, which puts at its centre a critique of new historicism, of Satan as 'the proto new historicist' (p. 74) who has boned up on his Foucault and Nietzsche to represent the self merely as an effect of power, and presents Milton as a necessary corrective. If the general tone of her work owes something to Jacques Derrida, no figure apart from Milton bulks large enough to lay a special claim on Colebrook's argument about the figuration of evil.

A second book on Milton published by Continuum also adopts a presentist programme of seeing Milton 'as a genuinely important resource for our time', as a thinker who launched a liberal Protestant tradition that makes allies out of 'secular liberalism and Christianity' (p. ix). Focusing mainly on the prose and raising a *cri de cœur* against academic critics—'with their inherited sneer towards his thought, their lack of interest in theology' (p. xi), and other faults too numerous to list—Theo Hobson's *Milton's Vision: The Birth of Christian Liberty* paints the writer, for the benefit of believers, as a secularist, libertarian, foe of literalism and proponent of toleration. The much-discussed question of Milton's implacable anti-Catholicism elicits the illiberal comment that 'Islamic extremism has reminded us that liberalism...has to reject its opposite—this ought to make us sympathise with Milton's stand against Catholicism' (p. 163). Let me put in a word for professional Miltonists here, many of whom have offered perspectives on the liberal intolerance of intolerance that Hobson might have found useful in writing such a study, had he stopped to consult them.

The shadow cast by the World Trade Center towers also falls over the late Douglas A. Brooks's introduction to *Milton and the Jews,* which opens with a discussion of *Samson Agonistes* in relation to terrorism. Through the centuries Jews have served to represent everything from rampant traditionalism to existential homelessness, and the Jews who appear in this Cambridge collection of eight essays are called on to do some heavy metaphorical and historical lifting. Achsah Guibbory's 'England, Israel, and the Jews in Milton's Prose, 1649–1660' studies Milton's opinions of Jews in the prose and concludes that Milton probably did not favour the readmission of the Jews, held out little hope for their conversion, and tended to identify Judaism with such disfavoured belief systems as monarchism, Catholicism and Laudianism. Elizabeth M. Sauer's 'Milton's Peculiar Nation' investigates the Judaism/Hebraism dichotomy in Milton's writings and the familiar conflation of ancient Israel and early modern England. Sauer finds that Milton moves from embracing an elect England to lamenting 'both the ancient and the new Israelites' unworthiness'. Election eventually marks the boundaries of a special preserve for 'those who have become heart-circumcised Christians (i.e., Gal. 5.6), or, in the language of seventeenth-century dissenters to whose thinking Milton subscribes, for those who have become "Jews inward"' (p. 38). Nicholas von Maltzahn's chapter on 'Making Use of the Jews: Milton and Philo-Semitism' turns to biographical details such as Milton's profit from money-lending and his exposure to arguments for and against the Jews. He finds, as others have before him, a half-hidden resemblance between anti-Semitic and philo-Semitic discourses, a convergence in Milton's work with consequences for *Samson Agonistes, Paradise Regained* and the psalm translations. Milton, he speculates, might have worried that the readmission of the Jews, a focal point for anti-Semitic sentiment, would fuel competition among London usurers: 'For money-lending was not just part of Milton's youth, some immediate legacy of his father's business, but rather his own lifelong means of making a living, a source of income more lasting than the salaries he drew as a teacher and then state servant' (p. 72). Douglas Trevor's essay on 'Milton and Solomonic Education' reanimates traditional work on Milton and biblical exegesis to study the morally ambiguous figure of Solomon, who exemplifies how a 'learned man can nonetheless become spiritually corrupted when he fails to avoid perilous forms of love' (p. 86), and who functions in *Paradise Lost* 'as the paradigmatic example of the limitations of knowledge when it is not accompanied by spiritual faith' (p. 93). Matthew Biberman's 'T.S. Eliot, Anti-Semitism, and the Milton Controversy' sees the famous dispute as commencing with a series of appropriations whereby Milton comes to stand in for 'the Jew'. By reconstructing its intricate 'backstory' (p. 117) Biberman persuasively discloses the role of philo- and anti-Semitism in Milton's reception history. Linda Tredennick, in her chapter on the 'metaphorical Jew', notes that what looks like increased tolerance for Jews 'has very little to do with actual Jews and is, not surprisingly, about the category of Christian identity' (p. 135), an insight productively applied to Milton's poetry. Rachel Trubowitz's chapter explores the connection between Asians and Jews, and Benedict S. Robinson looks at Jewishness in relation to Turkishness, two religious and cultural constructions that 'in their various supposed relations and differences' operate as 'paired, mutually exclusive but reciprocally dependent categories' (p. 182). If Milton occasionally gets nudged to the sidelines in these essays, his writings indeed stand at the confluence of the intriguing issues discussed in the volume.

Guibbory and von Maltzahn also make appearances in the outstanding collection of essays on Milton published in 2008, David Loewenstein and Paul Stevens's edited volume on *Early Modern Nationalism and Milton's England*. Fourteen contributors from Canada, Britain and the US address themselves to questions of Milton's English nationalism, its distinctive and representative qualities, its consistency, and the overarching question of 'how useful a category is "nations and nationalism" in explaining the imaginative achievements, religious polemics, and political tensions of Milton's poetry and prose' (p. 5). In an adroit introduction the editors point out that their collaborative undertaking emerges at a time when globalization and the alleged demise of the nation-state have forced a reconceptualization of nationalism across many disciplines, including literary studies. For whatever reason, studies of Milton's politics and republicanism have crowded off the stage any sustained exploration of his nationalism, although the editors note some important exceptions (and I would refer the reader to the Victorian-sounding 'patriot' in the subtitle of Beer's biography, mentioned above). To be sure, no earlier study has emphasized the significance of the nation as an 'imaginative and political construct' (p. 9) in Milton's writings as these contributors do, or has looked deep below the surface of his Protestant nationalism. In a singularly sceptical contribution to this volume, 'Look Homeward Angel: Guardian Angels and Nationhood in Seventeenth-Century England', Joad Raymond suggests a reason for the neglect, that the English in the sixteenth and seventeenth centuries embraced identities—'local, archipelagic, international' (p. 155)—that made any sort of self-conscious 'Englishness' (a word introduced in the nineteenth century) an impossibility and imperialism an obvious anachronism. 'Nationalism' (itself a late eighteenth-century term) assumes the existence of a fixed notion of English identity, based on ethnicity and bolstered by a belief in a providential destiny. Raymond looks elsewhere for a sense of patriotism, apart from the ideology of the 'nation-state' (a term from the late nineteenth century), and towards the local guardian angels of *Lycidas* for 'another way of thinking about belonging to a place, the idea of home' (p. 160). With Raymond's arrow in the collection's quiver, the editors daringly have equipped readers with a ready-made critique of their basic assumptions.

Loewenstein's opening essay in the volume, 'Milton's Nationalism and the English Revolution: Strains and Contradictions', shows how 'Milton the controversialist reconfigured the language and concept of nationhood in striking ways' (p. 26), emerging as 'an anguished nationalist who struggled deeply with his conflicted national feelings and with the nation itself as it went through uncertain permutations' (p. 43) during the revolutionary period. In 'Milton and the Struggle for the Representation of the Nation: Reading *Paradise Lost* through *Eikonoklastes*', Andrew Hadfield explores Milton's steadfast belief, despite shifts in his thinking about nationhood over the course of his career, 'that it is the people as represented by Parliament who should have the power to fashion the nation as they see fit' (p. 52). Hadfield contends that, just as Milton in *Eikonoklastes* criticizes monarchy for degrading a free people, Book II of *Paradise Lost* 'contains a fable of national political decay, a process of degeneration that happens before our eyes' (p. 65), when Satan seduces the masses in Pandemonium to install his absolute rule. The Son, by contrast, steps forward as a true democrat and republican hero. In 'Victory's Crest: Milton, the English Nation, and Cromwell', Warren Chernaik writes on Milton's ambivalence (and that of some contemporaries) towards military conquest and Oliver Cromwell. Achsah Guibbory's 'Israel and English Protestant Nationalism: "Fast Sermons" during the English Revolution' explores the familiar England–Israel analogy, particularly in the fast sermons preached to parliament in the 1640s and 1650s. Against scholars such as Patrick Collinson, who downplay any English tendency to think of themselves as a chosen people, Guibbory treats the analogy as central to English identity in the period, and argues that the image of rebuilding the Temple creates a sense of kinship between England and Israel rather than casting Jews as 'other'. In 'The Invisible Nation: Church, State, and Schism in Milton's England', Andrew Escobedo argues that although the state did not exist in its present form in the 1640s and 1650s, for Milton and his contemporaries the imagined community of England 'bears the trace of religious affect in its analogical relation to the invisible church of Christ' (p. 176), in particular, to the intimacy and voluntarism of Congregationalism.

Protestantism often took on an internationalist coloration, and nothing in Milton's writing suggests that he harboured any simple notion of Britain's inevitable ascent to greatness. The editors gather four more strong essays under the rubric 'Ethnicity and International Relations', the first of which, by Thomas N. Corns, deals with 'Milton and the Limitations of Englishness'. Milton's history, Corns affirms, 'abandons the myth of England as a chosen and privileged nation', avoiding altogether the providential view of history that we associate with John Foxe and John Bale (p. 212). In a shrewd assessment, John Kerrigan enlarges our sense of Milton's connections to the British Isles as an 'archipelagic' assemblage, studying 'The Anglo-Scoto-Dutch Triangle: Milton and Marvell to 1660', and correcting 'the residually Whig view of both writers as narrowly English patriots' (p. 223). Victoria Kahn writes with great insight on 'Disappointed Nationalism: Milton in the Context of Seventeenth-Century Debates about the Nation-State', which explores tensions between international law and national sovereignty, a theme that resonates loudly in our own time (Kahn explicitly invokes Guantánamo Bay detention camp). When *Samson Agonistes* sets Dalila's belief that she has conducted herself as a patriot against Samson's denunciation of her for violating the law of nature and of nations, the characters stake out the ground of this controversy. Treating Dalila as representative of Milton's disillusioned nationalism, Kahn concludes that Milton's own disappointed nationalism came as a consequence of political failures he had witnessed and of fissures in his own discourse of the nation, a position that undermines the claim that any single nation stands as 'the bearer of God's word' (p. 266). Paul Stevens's piece on 'How Milton's Nationalism Works: Globalization and the Possibilities of Positive Nationalism' affirms the importance of situating Milton in the context of an idealistic civic nationalism, while defending the value of politically committed literary criticism. The echo of Stanley Fish in the title is entirely deliberate, and the essay articulates a critique of Fish's current devaluation of the political in favour of aesthetic value.

Willy Maley's witty essay on 'That Fatal Boadicea: Depicting Women in Milton's *History of Britain*, 1670', looks at representations of the British warrior queen to argue for Milton's 'militantly masculine nationalism' (p. 307), in other words, for his gendering of the elect and anxiety about powerful women. Laura Lunger Knoppers's 'Consuming Nations: Milton and Luxury' explores how the idea of a corrupting luxury shapes Milton's nationalism throughout his career. Mary Nyquist's superb analysis of 'Slavery, Resistance, and Nation in Milton and Locke' will garner a good deal of attention, not only from Miltonists but from everyone concerned to understand the philosophical basis of slavery and racism. The essay takes a nuanced view of the 'vexed, complex relations between representations of actual bondage and its rhetorical counterpart, political "slavery"' (p. 357) in Milton and Locke, foregrounding the glaring contradiction between a passionate attachment to a universal liberty and the brutality of the Atlantic slave trade. Setting Locke's *Second Treatise of Government*, which explicitly defends chattel slavery, alongside *Paradise Lost* gives Milton the advantage, yet Milton sometimes implicitly elides the differences among classical, biblical and Euro-colonial versions of slavery. Nicholas von Maltzahn winds the volume to a satisfying conclusion with an extended essay on the late seventeenth- and eighteenth-century reception of Milton's blank-verse tradition ('Milton: Nation and Reception'), and the assimilation of *Paradise Lost* into the sort of militaristic nationalism his work supposedly undercut.

Von Maltzahn and most of the other scholars mentioned above (Loewenstein, Stevens, Knoppers, Guibbory) contribute to a special volume in celebration of the Milton quatercentenary, one of two volumes of *Milton Studies* for 2008. The spotlight in this volume falls on 'Milton and

Historicism', and the collection concludes with an essay by Annabel Patterson, 'His Singing Robes' (*MiltonS* 48[2008] 178–94), that repudiates the historicist credo associated with Patterson's own earlier work and that of other scholars who appear alongside her. This collection too makes room for auto-critique even in the midst of laying out a critical agenda. Patterson claims that Milton placed poetry 'in a different sphere from other kinds of human utterance' (p. 179) and when he turned to polemic effectively gave up poetry. His return to publishing poetry after the Restoration involved disambiguating the work of the left hand from the work of the right, drawing a thick dividing line between the prose and poetry. Patterson's accommodation of a traditional view of Milton seems more startling than Stanley Fish's long-standing hostility to historicism, since she now thinks 'almost the opposite of what I thought before' (p. 178), and makes a full confession as 'one of the worst offenders' (p. 191). Other old offenders (and some not so old) include Sharon Achinstein, whose excellent introductory essay 'Cloudless Thunder: Milton in History' (*MiltonS* 48[2008] 1–12) notes that 'historicist inquiry is often undertaken to explain our current predicament's contradictions and complexities' (p. 3), a move Patterson might see as a rationalization by those who find themselves baffled by the defeat of causes (secularism and toleration among them) that they hold dear. Achinstein also notes, with her usual acuity, that literary criticism has recently seen a backlash against historicism, wanting to replace it with a more ethically engaged 'presentism', a new formalism, or a grab box of other critical approaches. Ann Baynes Coiro's essay on 'Milton & Sons: The Family Business' (*MiltonS* 48[2008] 13–37) enters Milton through a biographical passageway, pursuing the connection between writing and money in the Milton family. Nicholas von Maltzahn discusses relations between Marvell and Milton, taking 'Lycidas' as his focal point, in 'Death by Drowning: Marvell's *Lycidas*' (*MiltonS* 48[2008] 38–52). In 'Late Milton: Early Modern Nationalist or Patriot?' (*MiltonS* 48[2008] 53–71), David Loewenstein pursues his interest in Milton's conflicted patriotism, and Paul Stevens in 'Milton's Polish Pamphlet and the Duke of Monmouth: Longing for a Hero' (*MiltonS* 48[2008] 72–94), probes Milton's *Declaration, or Letters Patents* [1674] for a hidden topicality, associating John III Sobieski, king of Poland, with the duke of Monmouth. Martin Dzelzainis's 'Dating and Meaning: *Samson Agonistes* and the "Digression" in Milton's *History of Britain*' (*MiltonS* 48[2008] 160–77) raises a classic historicist methodological issue when he explores Samson's 'rousing motions' in light of an earlier date proposed for the poem, 1647–53, the very period 'when divine incitements to action were at the epicenter of political debate' (p. 163), and investigates the ways in which chronology shapes interpretation.

The regular 2008 volume of *Milton Studies* presents a Milton Who Matters to the twenty-first century, in a vein similar to studies cited elsewhere in this review. Michael Lieb's 'Brotherhood of the Illuminati: Milton, Galileo, and the Poetics of Conspiracy' (*MiltonS* 47[2008] 54–95) takes a page from Dan Brown to discuss how accounts of the relationship between Milton and Galileo give rise to various interpretative problems, even while Milton's own perspective remains elusive and even indecipherable. Lara Dodds's essay ' "Great things to small may be compared": Rhetorical Microscopy in

Paradise Lost' (*MiltonS* 47 [2008] 96–117) looks once again at Milton's comparison of great things to small and turns to Robert Hooke's use of the topos in microscopy, his comparisons, for example, of moss to cedar, and his use of simile. Rather than seeing Milton's comparisons as attempts to overreach his classical predecessors, Dodds finds an implicit measuring where 'the truth of science' (p. 114) stands in proportional contrast to the minutiae of literary tradition. Eric B. Song's astute essay on 'Nation, Empire, and the Strange Fire of the Tartars in Milton's Poetry and Prose' (*MiltonS* 47[2008] 118–44) looks at Milton's allusions to Tatars, a trope in which he uncovers anxiety about English regression to barbarism. Song concludes that Milton deploys an Orientalist discourse of Tatars 'to question the unity, primacy, and wholeness of all political formations', including the normally privileged sites of Israel and England, thus establishing 'a global outlook that is deeply critical about its own Anglocentric perspective' (p. 139).

In the same issue David Loewenstein writes on 'The War against Heresy in Milton's England' (*MiltonS* 47[2008] 185–218), drawing in particular on the heresy hunters Thomas Edwards (author of *Gangraena*) and Ephraim Pagitt (whose *Heresiography* went through six editions), as well as on William Walwyn, an early advocate of religious toleration. Loewenstein explores the propaganda campaign against heresy, the polemical savagery unkennelled by what Milton in *Areopagitica* calls the 'fantastic terrors of sect and schism', with the goal of considering 'how the topic speaks to us today with a new kind of immediacy' (p. 186). Walwyn, according to Loewenstein, registers the protean nature of language used to revile opponents and warns against stoking fear and hatred within the Protestant community. Milton responded to the heresiographers by arguing in *Areopagitica* that a man who accepts religious doctrines on the authority of his pastor or the Westminster Assembly 'may be a heretick in the truth'. Milton speaks to us today, Loewenstein argues, because he challenges us to rethink derogatory labels and 'to think more skeptically about the terms of anathematization that may close off or silence probing debate about the religious conflicts that have made our own world so unstable and dangerous in recent years' (p. 212). Jeffrey S. Shoulson's article on 'Milton and Enthusiasm: Radical Religion and the Poetics of *Paradise Regained*' (*MiltonS* 47[2008] 219–57) offers a reading of the brief epic in light of the author's encounter with messianism and radical sectarianism, in particular the critique of enthusiasm and religious zeal. Taking up the question of style in *Paradise Regained*, Shoulson concludes that apocalyptic prophecy, a mode associated with Quakers, Fifth Monarchists, Ranters and Sabbatians, finds expression 'more frequently within the temptations to power offered by the Adversary than in the responses of the Son' (p. 249), with important consequences for Milton's poetics and late style.

Paul Stevens co-edits (with Patricia Simmons) and introduces a special issue of *University of Toronto Quarterly* on 'Milton in America', which also addresses the self-flagellating question, currently the rage among Miltonists, of 'why Milton matters'. Stevens contends that 'Milton lives in the way he continues to enable us to think through the complexities of our culture, whether it be American, British, or even Canadian' (p. 798), and to this end he has assembled an international group of contributors who place Milton in

American political contexts, broadly defined. David Hawkes, 'Milton among the Pragmatists' (*UTQ* 77[2008] 923–39) looks at pragmatist readings of Milton, including Stanley Fish's, a line of interpretation, Hawkes argues, that 'does violence to Milton's original meanings and intentions' (p. 923)—a critique unlikely to ruffle the feathers of critics who consider intentions inaccessible and interpretative validity a matter of political and aesthetic utility (p. 935). Christopher Kendrick's 'Un-American Milton: Milton's Reputation and Reception in the Early United States' (*UTQ* 77[2008] 903–22) considers the literary reception of Milton in Joel Barlow's *The Columbiad* [*c*.1810] and Melville's 'Bartleby the Scrivener', finding Milton's radicalism and anti-monarchism less congenial to the American mainstream than earlier critics have maintained. Catherine Gimelli Martin's 'Milton and the Pursuit of Happiness' (*UTQ* 77[2008] 876–902) reconstructs Milton's influence on shifting the concept of happiness from a species of virtue to a sort of idealized hedonism, and notes, among other intellectual links, the prestige in America of the representation of connubial bliss in Book IV of *Paradise Lost*. Feisal G. Mohamed's 'Liberty before and after Liberalism: Milton's Shifting Politics and the Current Crisis in Liberal Theory' (*UTQ* 77[2008] 940–60) explores the distance between Milton's early pamphlets, including *Areopagitica*, and his later writings, which he treats as spanning the distance between a liberalism of speech and a liberalism of faith. The latter, he notes (with a keen eye for the contradictions of liberal political theory), 'cannot be called liberalism at all', but rather 'a liberty of conscience quite menacing to liberal notions of freedom of religious expression' (p. 953). Sharon Achinstein's fascinating 'Cold War Milton' (*UTQ* 77[2008] 801–36) looks back to 1953, the year the first volume of Yale University Press's landmark *Complete Prose Works of John Milton* appeared under the editorship of Don M. Wolfe. Wolfe's Milton was a man of the hour, a 'polemicist, politically engaged, a man of action and decision as much as a great poet' (p. 803), drafted to serve the cause of civil liberties in a period of Cold War paranoia and McCarthyism. Miltonists of that generation, we learn, opposed the New Criticism in part for its complicity in promoting scholarship that decontextualized and depoliticized the great writers.

In these compelling essays readers will find abundant confirmation of the insight that American politics and religion owe a sizeable debt to Milton. They might also note the absence of sexuality and gender as significant categories of analysis in the pieces printed here. Given the significance of biopolitics, reproductive rights, same-sex marriage, and other hot-button issues to the political and religious discourses of American public life, the 'politics' invoked in this collection can seem somewhat bloodless, abstracted from the messy realities and bruising cultural warfare experienced on the ground. Taken on their own terms and as an ensemble, however, the pieces deserve to become required reading by anyone concerned with the long afterlife of seventeenth-century thought.

Another Canadian Miltonist, James Dougal Fleming, offers an innovative and basically theoretical argument, in *Milton's Secrecy and Philosophical Hermeneutics*, that Milton's 'writings are notable, not for their utilization of secrecy, but for their root-and-branch opposition to secrecy as a moral, political, and hermeneutic category' (p. 6). Writing a book on Milton's ethos of anti-secrecy and anti-esotericism sometimes commits Fleming to arguing from absence, but he scores a good point when he reminds us that in the culture of the period secrecy functioned as the antithesis of political and social life in their utopian forms, and that Milton considers hiddenness a divine attribute, not the soul of statecraft. Fleming's first chapter, on *Lycidas* and Milton's autobiographical writings, argues that 'Milton's self-presentational texts are casuistical representations' (p. 33), which turns on its head the notion that casuistry functions as a vehicle for systematic dissimulation and the internalization of truth. Fleming suggests that in conceptualizing the forma-tion of conscience—a key concern for casuists—Milton substitutes an external audience for the calling of God to witness. Two chapters on *A Mask* and *Samson* pursue the argument into the domain of the drama, where Milton, he argues, thematizes the idea of not retreating to an inward and secret self and embraces an exoteric conception of minds and words. A chapter on *Paradise Lost* continues to skirmish with intentionalist theory and offers a series of comments on Milton's hermeneutics and anti-intentionalism, making a series of forays into philosophical hermeneutics without necessarily addressing the issue of secrecy directly. Fleming's argument, in the final analysis, attempts to deconstruct the practice of reading 'below the surface' and makes Milton a laboratory for testing the theory that any hermeneutics that depends on secrecy and esoteric intention will inevitably fail. Put baldly, Fleming attempts to show that 'Milton redirects our hermeneutic attention from intentions to expressions, minds to texts … from the esoteric to the exoteric, and from discovery to recognition' (p. 172), thus redirecting our attention to dialogue and textuality as keys to literary understanding.

Phillip J. Donnelly revisits the problem of Milton's rationalism in *Milton's Scriptural Reasoning: Narrative and Protestant Toleration*, locating his position in Scripture and aligning it with a theory of difference. What Milton means by 'reason' or 'freedom' is no simple matter, and critics have clashed over such key words in the past. Donnelly distances Milton from modern views of reason as violent, calculative and coercive, preferring to root assumptions about reason in Renaissance educational theory, logic and rhetoric. Working initially with Milton's Ramist logic, *Of Education* and *Areopagitica*, he treats reason as the cement that binds together Milton's monism and a sort of limited tolerationism that upholds the unity of human beings: 'Milton's view of right reason, his anthropological monism, and his ontological monism are insep-arable from one another and, through that unity, inform his arguments for Protestant toleration' (p. 68). To some extent, the key terms at stake here strike me as conceptually undernourished, as if Cartesian rationalism boils down to nothing more than the domination of nature, or a tightly circumscribed 'Protestant toleration' resembles the familiar bedrock liberal value in more than just name. Moving to *Paradise Lost* and highly attuned to the complexities of biblicist rhetoric, Donnelly focuses, in three closely argued chapters, on the Son as the image of divine reason, on divine kingship, and on the war in heaven. Chapter 7 shifts the argument about Milton's peaceful, non-coercive and non-calculative conception of reason to the issue of gender, contending that gender difference in *Paradise Lost* arises from Milton's notions of rationality and harmony between the sexes. Donnelly hopes to leapfrog arguments over whether the epic endorses a hierarchical or an egalitarian position by arguing that 'amid the layers of allegorical ambivalence, Milton weaves a typological disclosure of ontic charity that subverts the customary assumption that the *archē* in hier*archy* is necessarily coercive' (p. 143). Peaceful reason and ontic charity propel the readings in three final chapters, on Books XI and XII of *Paradise Lost, Paradise Regained* and *Samson Agonistes,* which together address the problem of how an ethical praxis can arise from irenic values. Among several arresting claims made in these chapters, the one I find most productive addresses the ethics of religious compulsion in *Samson,* that the tragedy does not put forward arguments for religious violence or toleration, but 'offers implicit guidance to those religious Dissenters during the Restoration who were subject to coercion by a state church' (p. 202).

The role of gender in Christian religious thought receives a more sustained treatment in Theresa M. DiPasquale's *Refiguring the Sacred Feminine,* which knits together three more or less self-contained studies of John Donne, Aemilia Lanyer and Milton. The long chapter on Milton examines his handling of archetypes that incorporate figures of the sacred feminine and divine wisdom, drawing Milton into the orbit of the book of Proverbs and the deuterocanonical Wisdom of Solomon. In *Arcades* DiPasquale finds a formulation of a blessed female Sapientia, and (extending John M. Wallace's insight of fifty years ago) associates this mother-goddess with the dowager countess of Derby. Building upon and revising his early deployment of a female Wisdom figure, Milton transforms the chaste Lady of *A Mask* into a type of the Church who embodies 'both the sapient "discipline" of a nonconformist Ecclesia and the wise mixture of valor and vulnerability that, according to Milton's Arminian theology of grace and works, preserves the spiritual virginity of the regenerate soul' (p. 233). When DiPasquale reaches *Paradise Lost* the gears of her argument fully mesh as she advances a view of Adam and Eve's connubial love as a type of King Solomon's union with Wisdom, and of Eve as a type of Sapientia, especially in her acts of loving self-sacrifice. The chapter's final segment, on *Paradise Regained,* positions Jesus as Mary's devoted son, an apt pupil whose association with feminine wisdom adds to his perfection.

Shannon Miller's *Engendering the Fall: John Milton and Seventeenth-Century Women Writers* also mixes feminism with Milton studies, operating in an eclectic critical mode that draws on new historicism and early modern intellectual history while offering a rethinking of conventional assumptions about literary influence. In eight densely packed chapters she juxtaposes *Paradise Lost* with texts by women writers, among them Aemilia Lanyer's *Salve Deus Rex Judaeorum,* Lucy Hutchinson's *Order and Disorder,* Margaret Cavendish's *Blazing World* and Mary Chudleigh's *The Song of the Three Children Paraphras'd.* According to the map of influence Miller charts, intellectual exchange among writers flows in multiple directions: not only can we trace, as Joseph Wittreich and others have, the enabling presence of Milton in texts by later women writers, but within *Paradise Lost* Miller descries the outlines of various seventeenth-century debates over gender, Eve and the Fall. The bridges Miller builds accommodate multi-lane traffic. Part I reads Milton's epic against writings from earlier in the century, taking note of how the issue of culpability for the Fall serves to legitimize early modern family structure and the gendered organization of the state. Beyond direct linguistic parallels, Miller analyses the *querelle des femmes* and conventional disputations about Eve in female-authored defences, 'to which Milton appears to respond with his apology-offering Eve' (p. 48). Noting multiple points of contact between Lanyer and Milton, Miller centres her reading within a thematics of gender, power and specularity. Part II offers readings of Milton and his younger contemporaries Hutchinson and Cavendish that treat how their texts 'expose different aspects of the political imaginary generated through the events of the Civil War, the Interregnum, and then the Restoration' (p. 77), paying particular attention to republican theory and gendered hierarchies. The sort of intercultural influence Miller has in mind permits her to range freely over large discursive frameworks and within the ideologies gathered around gender and power, facilitating the claim, for example, that 'Milton's and Cavendish's stories of the Garden event negotiate Restoration practices of controlling knowledge in the period' (p. 136), thus linking Milton to the emergent practices of the Royal Society. Reaching to the far end of the century in her closing chapters on Chudleigh, Aphra Behn and Mary Astell, Miller takes up how Milton's representation of Edenic marriage served later interrogations of the patriarchalist family and (setting aside obvious political differences among these writers) the authoritarian state that took its warrant from it.

Drawing some intellectual sustenance from feminism and theories of subject formation, but more from anthropology and psychoanalysis, William Shullenberger's *Lady in the Labyrinth: Milton's 'Comus' as Initiation* reads *Comus* by highlighting Alice Egerton's ritual passage from girlhood into womanhood. Shullenberger examines, from various perspectives, how Alice's initiation reconfigures a particular notion of womanhood, how 'cultural protocols and rituals as well as political contexts order and inform the *Maske*'s drama' (p. 34). In a series of refreshingly unconventional chapters (some of which allude in their titles to film and popular culture), Shullenberger argues that Milton feminizes the discourse of virtue as it figured in the Stuart masque; that the Attendant Spirit is a demiurge who guides the children and the audience through the maze of the masque's poetic and ethical byways; that the Lady's soliloquy reveals a process of self-discovery and dawning awareness of the world's complexity; and that Comus, as the offspring of Bacchus and Circe, has a double inheritance that spells trouble in its fusion of shapeshifting energy and dehumanizing power. Chapter 5, 'Girl Power: The Profession of Virginity', attends carefully to the passage where the Lady extols virginity (lines 779–99), arguing, among other points, that the speech expounds 'a mode of erotic self-determination' (p. 188) that far exceeds Comus's limited comprehension and enacts the doctrine's rhetorical potency. In the three chapters following, Shullenberger re-evaluates the issues of Milton's identification with the Lady, her enthralment in Comus's chair and release by the river goddess Sabrina, and her final re-entry into her father's household, where her body becomes 'a this-worldly figure for a redeemed and redemptive sexuality and for the vitally reconfigured cosmos in which it flourishes' (p. 42). The first book-length study of *Comus* to appear in some years, *Lady in the*

Labyrinth fills several gaps in the criticism and accomplishes its goals, perhaps unexpectedly, by treating ritual structures, mythology and psychological processes as keys to unlocking the masque's meaning.

David Ainsworth's *Milton and the Spiritual Reader* differs from recent work on Milton and early modern reading, for example that of Sharon Achinstein, by looking past politics to make religion the paramount concern and describing a reading practice that puts sacred truths before worldly knowledge. In his first chapter, on *Areopagitica*, Ainsworth finds Milton advocating a mode of spiritual reading that demands a 'strenuous' (p. 15), 'collaborative' and 'contentious' (p. 24) engagement with texts, while a chapter on *Eikonoklastes* argues that Milton outlines a process by which readers can interrogate the 'unsoundness' (p. 35) of books such as *Eikon Basilike* for themselves. Ainsworth finds this same quality of 'strenuous' critical reading promoted in *De Doctrina Christiana,* which in another chapter he treats as a treatise that models exegetical technique and teaches how to read Scripture with an 'unflinching willingness to engage with controversial points of doctrine' (p. 63). When Ainsworth comes to *Paradise Lost* and *Paradise Regained*, in the following two chapters, he studies how reading and interpretation animate those poems, focusing on Eve's dream, the biblical narratives that Michael distils in Books XI and XII, and the importance of proof and misunderstanding in Satan's temptation of Jesus. To my mind, the most rewarding chapter comes at the end: it compares Milton's 'spiritual reading' to the approaches of Richard Baxter, George Fox and Gerrard Winstanley (representing Presbyterian, Quaker and radical millenarian practices respectively). Ainsworth concludes by finding Milton's interpretative methodology unique, especially in its placing a 'heavy burden of interpretation' (p. 167, echoing Dayton Haskin) upon the individual Christian. The book has relatively little to say about actual readers—humanist readers, the reading styles of different religious communities and so forth—yet shines some light on Milton's ideal spiritual reader as something embedded within his texts.

Erik Gray's elegantly written and thoroughly persuasive reception study, *Milton and the Victorians*, also deals with the act of reading, in particular by writers such as Elizabeth Barrett Browning, Christina Rossetti, Gerard Manley Hopkins, Matthew Arnold, Alfred Tennyson and Anthony Trollope, not ordinarily regarded as fervent admirers of Milton in the manner of the Romantic poets. The barricade thrown up by an artificial Romantic/Victorian divide has no doubt obscured the importance of Milton to Victorian poetry. Gray shows 'how Milton can continue to exert a powerful influence while largely disappearing from view' (p. 24), how Milton's distinctive strain melds with other voices, and how he functions as a modern classic, pervasive but invisible. A chapter on 'Milton, Arnold, and the Might of Weakness' shows how Milton's influence paradoxically appears strongest when withdrawn and triumphantly weak, a typically Miltonic posture. Understated and arrayed in muted colours, Milton appears inconspicuously in Tennyson's poetry, visible 'everywhere and nowhere' (p. 117), yet still manages to play a key role. Milton steps forth into broad daylight in George Eliot's *Middlemarch*, yet figures there mainly as an embodiment of failed communication. A final chapter reviews how Milton's writings furnish models of intertextuality: his impact on the Victorians, Gray argues, derives from something similarly diffuse in Milton's own poetry and prose. The study of intertextuality, allusion and influence has staged a comeback in recent years, after decades of neglect, and Gray makes a signal contribution to the debate: the central paradox in Milton—that he appears most himself when 'most dispersed amongst other texts and contexts' (p. 167)—has a field of application far larger than any single canonical author.

The appearance of volume 2 of the Oxford *Complete Works of John Milton, The 1671 Poems: Paradise Regain'd* and *Samson Agonistes*, edited by Laura Lunger Knoppers, will facilitate study of Milton's work in the context of Restoration England. The first to be published of a projected eleven volumes, the edition supplies a substantial introduction, with sections on the text's publishing history and discussions of the literary, political and religious contexts surrounding its publication. Knoppers has uncovered new archival materials in the course of assembling this edition, and includes a section on 'Early Readers and Marginalia', which takes up the task of describing historical reading practices and interpretative notes connected to the 1671 volume.

Contributing to recent scholarship on Milton's ecological awareness, Ruth Summar McIntyre's '"Flowers Worthy of Paradise": Milton and the Language of Flowers' (*MiltonS* 47[2008] 145–67) goes deeper than many of her predecessors in examining Milton's depiction of flowers, detecting in it evidence of the poet's imaginative conversion of the physical into an immaterial and abstract force. McIntyre's work remains well within the parameters of traditional studies of poetic imagery, presenting a florid rather than a green Milton. Assuming a different position, Ken Hiltner's avowedly green collection, *Renaissance Ecology: Imagining Eden in Milton's England*, looks to Milton as a resource in confronting the current environmental crisis. Hiltner describes the volume's baseline assumption thus: 'As a contemporary of [John] Evelyn and other protoecologists, it is perhaps not surprising that Milton would not only weigh in on debates over issues such as deforestation, but also actually prescribe a way for human beings to more successfully interact with the natural world in an Edenic way' (pp. 6–7). Not every contributor to the volume, however, comes to Milton through ecopoetics, and a good deal of the analysis makes gender and source study its twin poles. Barbara Lewalski's 'Milton's Paradises' considers the multiple meanings of 'paradise' in all its literary and theological complexity. Stella P. Revard's 'Eve and the Language of Love in *Paradise Lost*' pays close attention to Milton's classical sources, tracing the gender equality of their speech to the Greek epigrammatist Asclepiades of Samos and a variety of other classical poets. Similarly focused on Eve and gender, Ann Torday Gulden's 'A Walk in the Paradise Garden: Eve's Influence in the "Triptych" of Speeches, *Paradise Lost* 4.610–88' suggests that 'Eve creatively shows Adam an alternative to his rather monolithic, linear way of thinking based on pragmatically understood lines of authority, as she guides him toward a more comprehensive understanding of his surroundings' (p. 45). William Shullenberger's 'Milton's *Primavera*' presents a version of an argument made at greater detail in his book-length study discussed above. Jane Sturrock's 'Eve, Eden, and the Flowers of

Experience: Milton, Blake, and Botany' contributes an influence study that explores the relationship between William Blake's flower poems and *Paradise Lost,* supplemented with some interesting material on eighteenth-century botany and the eroticization of plants. In ' "Earth Felt the Wound": Gendered Ecological Consciousness in Illustrations of *Paradise Lost*', Wendy Furman-Adams and Virginia James Tufte read Milton against visual art, arguing that before 1820 illustrators of *Paradise Lost* tended to overlook the poem's ecological subtext as well as 'the visual nature of the "landskip" he had delineated in such bountiful detail' (p. 108). Jeffrey S. Theis's ' "The Purlieus of Heaven": Milton's Eden as a Pastoral Forest' asks us, quite reasonably, 'to think more consciously about why Milton repeatedly describes paradise as a forest and why he does so in distinctly pastoral terms' (p. 231), adding significantly to recent literary accounts of sixteenth- and seventeenth-century woodland ecologies. Karen L. Edwards's 'Eden Raised: Waste in Milton's Garden' shifts the field of vision from woodlands to 'waste', the startling topographical feature invoked in Book IV of *Paradise Lost* (line 538). Tracing the use of the word in agricultural and legal history, Edwards shrewdly discloses the significance of *waste* 'as land not yet under the plough, arable land-in-waiting' (p. 262), inescapably calling to mind disputes over landholding associated with enclosure, depopulation, Levellers and Diggers. With this strategic word, economic relations and material conditions impinge, as they often do, on the paradisal world of the poem. Writing at a time when a growing segment of the US public considers environmental activism an outright hoax or a liberal power-grab orchestrated by Al Gore, the essayists gathered here sometimes seem to depoliticize their concerns, speaking a language of aesthetic appreciation and utopian longing rather than engaging in a shared agenda. Some of the pieces have relatively little to say about the natural world, as if more pressing religious and literary concerns have edged it out of the picture, but all encourage a redrawing of the shifting borders around Eden, England, pastoral poetry and spiritual regeneration.

I have accounted for some substantial part of the Milton criticism published in 2008 but far from all of it, and have passed over much fine work (for which omissions I apologize). A comprehensive review, however, would run to many more pages than the present section. Neither could I put my hands on every item cited in the online databases, nor have I examined scholarship in languages other than English (see the retrospective in Hiroko Sano, 'Japanese Milton Scholarship, 1980–2006', *MiltonQ* 42[2008] 197–210). I have tried to include books from smaller presses, but could not incorporate the great wealth of journal scholarship that appeared last year, some of it in periodicals that do not publish on Milton routinely. In response to the burning question 'Does Milton Matter?' let me conclude by saying that the sheer weight of publication on Milton proves that he matters a good deal to scholars around the world. Milton criticism marches forward on many fronts and in many countries. Miltonic intertextuality remains a subject apparently illimitable and without bound. Editorial and biographical projects undergo renewal from generation to generation. We see in this year's work evidence of a resurgence (not quite yet a boomlet) of theoretical approaches, and the historicist enterprise, long at the epicentre of Milton studies, continues apace.

3. Donne

Though scholarship on Donne this year reflects a range of interests, a great many of the more than fifty journal articles, book chapters, and monographs address the complexity of classifying Donne's thought, given his penchant for transgressing boundaries. In 'Donne, Imperfect' (*JDJ* 27[2008] 1–20), Jeffrey Johnson convincingly presents Donne as a man of the 'in-between', a restless thinker who gladly occupies ideological borderlands (p. 1). Though Donne's 'pervasive' and 'profound rest-lessness' can be viewed as an 'imperfection', Johnson believes that this trait drives Donne towards inclusiveness and expansiveness, inspiring him to react to the irresolvable tensions of life with 'both/and' rather than with 'either/or' (pp. 9, 2). It is Donne's 'free-ranging' mind that allows him to imagine an expansive church that can contain various forms of Christianity without denying their differences (p. 19).

Donne's indebtedness to both Catholic and Protestant thought is raised in five of the twelve essays in *The Reformation Unsettled: British Literature and the Question of Religious Identity, 1560–1660*, edited by Jan Frans van Dijkhuizen and Richard Todd. The focus of this suggestive collection is the hybridity of the spiritual imagination in early modern Britain. In ' "She on the Hills": Traces of Catholicism in Seventeenth-Century English Protestant Poetry' (pp. 9–33), Helen Wilcox uncovers in the devotional lyrics of Donne and his contemporaries vestiges of the Catholic faith related to religious rituals; the doctrine of transubstantiation; sensual spiritual experience; hagiographic and Marian figures; and human agency in salvation. In 'The Speaking Picture: Visions and Images in the Poetry of John Donne and George Herbert' (pp. 99–113), Francis Cruickshank contends that images play a crucial role in the faith of Donne and Herbert: 'each poet's work registers a strangely visual apprehension of the doctrines of Christianity and a desire to explore the religious landscape through the conceit of the eyes of faith' (p. 100). The scene of the crucified (and resurrected) Christ in Donne's poetry mediates encounters between an apprehensive subject and an unseen God, thereby allowing the former to experience divine grace more fully.

In his evocative essay, 'In Thy Passion Slain: Donne, Herbert, and the Theology of Pain' (in Dijkhuizen and Todd, eds., pp. 59–84), Jan Frans van Dijkhuizen examines the conflict between medieval and Reformed theologies of pain in Donne's work. Though van Dijkhuizen views Donne as more Calvinist than Catholic in his propensity to diminish or deny the salvific value of physical suffering, he notes that Donne periodically presents bodily affliction as spiritually productive, even redemptive. In ' "No rule of our beleef"? John Donne and Canon Law' (pp. 45–57), Hugh Adlington reasons that Donne does not so much reject canon law as 'papal and Tridentine interpolations' that endeavour to render papal and scriptural authority equivalent (p. 57). Still, Donne privileges conscience 'and its associated law of nature' over canon law, Adlington explains (p. 57). In 'Was Donne Really

Apostate' (pp. 35–43), Richard Todd proposes that Donne has been misidentified as an apostate because modern critics approach his life and works with eighteenth-century notions of Britishness and Protestantism in mind. Todd speculates that Donne would have been seen by contemporary Catholics as a type of heretic rather than an apostate.

In Roberta J. Albrecht's *Using Alchemical Memory Techniques for the Interpretation of Literature: John Donne, George Herbert, and Richard Crashaw*, Donne is also seen to operate within competing structures of religious belief. What interests Albrecht is the response of Donne, Herbert and Crashaw to the Protestant interdiction of the Catholic doctrine of purgatory. Despite the official abandonment of purgatory, and related doctrines, in the English Church, Albrecht believes that a deep-seated fear of purgatory and a longing to utter prayers of intercession and weep tears of penance (rather than contrition) remained. Albrecht theorizes that Donne, Crashaw and Herbert deploy Lullian spiritual logic and alchemical symbols—especially 'the fiery sword, mercurial tears, and the nurturing breast'—as a code that readers will decipher to discover the poets' views on 'purgatory, penance, and intercessory prayer' (p. 2). In the case of Donne, Albrecht asserts that he structured his sequence of twelve Holy Sonnets according to Ramon Lull's principles of spiritual logic and filled them with 'alchemico-Lullian signs' so that it would become a purgatorial site (p. 39). Albrecht determines that the coded symbols in each pair of related sonnets in the sequence reveal the speaker's place in the purgatorial process. In the sequence as a whole, 'a psychological version of Roman purgatory' is portrayed, in which we observe 'a fearful soul buried alive in time' (pp. 41, 89). However, Albrecht discovers in Donne's funeral sermon on Magdalen Herbert 'a new Protestant version of intercession', by which worthy 'saints' can improve the spiritual state of the living (p. 192).

At one point in her analysis of Donne, Albrecht associates his sonnet sequence with montage, and this term could also be applied to *Using Alchemical Memory Techniques for the Interpretation of Literature* itself. To read the monograph is to encounter a series of verbal pictures set side by side and supplemented with commentary. The benefit of this method is that Albrecht covers a great deal of ground, introducing and explaining a substantial number of Lullian concepts and alchemical symbols, and offering some intriguing readings of Donne's works. The thirty illustrations included in the book complement the verbal pictures she paints. However, the ideas presented do not always unfold in an orderly fashion, and a measure of coherence is lost.

Two of the essays in *The Sacred and Profane in English Renaissance Literature*, edited by Mary A. Papazian, also envision Donne negotiating apparently differing forces. Though the volume's theme is not especially original, its innovative essays shed new light on the ways in which the secular and sacred coalesce in early modern literature. In 'John Donne's Secular and Sacred Reactions to Loss: From Nothingness to God's Tender Jealousy' (pp. 159–82) Papazian appeals to Aristotle's theory of mimesis and Sidney's conception of poetry as an ethical medium to argue that Donne's poems dramatize the experiences of 'men in action' to model for the reader debasing or ennobling responses to troubling life events (p. 160). Papazian contrasts the response of speakers in the secular and religious poems to loss through exemplary texts, 'A nocturnall upon S. Lucies Day' and 'Since she whome I loved', finding in the former a 'negative spiritual condition' and in the latter a sense of spiritual peace and assurance worthy of imitation (p. 171). In 'Poetic Re-creation in John Donne's "A Litanie"' (in Papazian, ed., pp. 183–210), Hannibal Hamlin reminds us that 'A Litanie' is not a liturgical text but rather an aesthetic work that should be read as such. Detailing the poem's complex structure (which suggests it is not a devotional piece), Hamlin posits that Donne makes use of the litany genre to establish 'the proper role for the religious poet', a secular and sacred ambition (p. 200).

Feisal G. Mohamed's noteworthy monograph, *In the Anteroom of Divinity: The Reformation of the Angels from Colet to Milton* offers an absorbing and incisive portrait of angelology in the works of Colet, Hooker, Spenser, Donne and Milton. Mohamed not only considers how these post-Reformation writers, inevitably influenced by 'Dionysian angelology', visualize angels, but also how they conceptualize, more generally, mediation between the human and the divine (p. 11). He aligns the angelology of Donne with that of Calvin inasmuch as Donne dwells on the believer's access to God through Scripture, grace, and pastoral care, while remaining dubious about 'angelic mediation' (p. 79). When Donne does play with the Dionysian tradition in context-specific ways, he offers a range of views on angels; yet even in these cases, Mohamed suspects that some aspect of the tradition is subjected to Donne's 'destabilizing scepticism' (p. 167).

Gary Kuchar focuses on Donne's tempering of Reformation thought in 'Petrarchism and Repentance in John Donne's *Holy Sonnets*' (*MP* 105:iii[2008] 535–69), which also appears as chapter 5 in his *Poetry of Religious Sorrow in Early Modern England*. Kuchar interestingly argues that Petrarchism allows Donne to distance himself from the traumatic effects of divine 'overpresence' in his contrite soul, a sublime experience that both frightens and comforts him (p. 550). The Petrarchan discourse of grief converges with the Pauline and Lutheran rhetoric of 'godly sorrow' in 'O might those sighes', 'If faithfull soules' and 'What if this present were the worlds last night?' to allow the speaker to avoid self-eradication in the process of repentance (p. 541). In 'John Donne and the Poetics of Belatedness: Typology, Trauma and Testimony in *An Anatomy of the World*', chapter 6 of *The Poetry of Religious Sorrow*, Kuchar also interrogates the adequacy of 'godly sorrow' in the Reformed sense, arguing that the *Anatomy* is 'a meditation on belatedness that puts on trial the redemptive power of Reformation typology and soteriology' (p. 184).

Donne's concern with the effect of Reformation theology is again taken up by Kuchar in 'Ecstatic Donne: Conscience, Sin, and Surprise in the *Sermons* and the Mitcham Letters' (*Criticism* 50:iv[2008] 631–54), which explores the 'strangely interior-exterior modality of the Protestant conscience as an inward voice that is not directly one's own' (p. 637). For Protestants, Kuchar recounts, the conscience was an 'agency of judgement within the soul' which yielded 'knowledge of one's actions' (p. 631). Donne portrays the preacher in his sermons as the 'Pauline-Reformed conscience' of his listeners, who are startled by his nearness; yet he also presents himself as an auditor, subject to the scrutiny of a God who is uncannily near (p. 634). Kuchar again observes this 'nearness effect' in the Mitcham letters, which encode the disquieting experience of 'being unable to control a phenomenon that happens within us' (pp. 631, 649).

In 'The Picture of Christ Crucified: Lutheran Influence on Donne's Religious Imagery' (in Carr, Clarke and Nievergelt, eds., *On Allegory: Some Medieval Aspects and Approaches*, pp. 42–55), Kirsten Stirling imagines Donne negotiating Reformed and Roman thought, 'poised between image and iconoclasm' in 'What if this present were the worlds last night?' (p. 43). She delves more fully into Donne's fascination with visual images in 'Dr. Donne's Art Gallery and the *Imago Dei* (*JDJ* 27[2008] 67–80), in which she alleges that Donne uses the trope of an internal art gallery to illuminate humanity's relation to God. In the sermons, Stirling writes, the trope is used to depict the spiritual experience of believers (viewers) who look at God (the image) and find their gaze returned; they are known and watched over by God. However, in some devotional poems the trope exposes Donne's fear that fallen humans, imperfect images of God, may be unable to look upon Christ as they should, preventing the return of his gaze.

In Cottegnies et al., eds., *Les Voix de Dieu: Littérature et prophétie en Angleterre et en France à l'âge baroque*, two essays examine the potentially destabilizing force of Donne's complex religious sensibility. In 'Donne, Crashaw, and Prophetic Conversion' (pp. 101–12), Robert V. Young asserts that the authentic conversions of Donne and Crashaw reflect the 'Protestant principle' that individuals, guided by conscience, must discover their own religious truth, which anticipates a modern view of faith as 'a matter of personal choice' (pp. 107, 101). However, Young suggests that the expression of this principle in their poetry undercuts their belief in the need to submit to the sovereign will of God and weakens ecclesiastical authority. In '"The Minister of God, the Preacher of God, the Prophet of God"': aspects du prophétisme de John Donne' (pp. 243–58), Pascal Caillet argues that in his sermons Donne presents his role as priest and preacher as comparable to that of the Old Testament prophet. In probing Donne's sermons on the Gunpowder Plot and the Directions for Preachers, however, Caillet notes the irony of a 'man of God' called to denounce immorality at all levels who is also a servant of the king, called on to defend Jacobean policies that restrict the liberty of preachers (p. 256). For Caillet, Donne's role as an agent of the state curtails the radical potential of his prophetic voice.

In *John Donne: Body and Soul*, Ramie Targoff examines Donne's fascination with an 'in-between' moment when the soul must leave the body at death. Though Targoff identifies this leave-taking as the overriding theme in Donne's work, her study considers many facets of the relation of body and soul in his prose and verse. In her introduction, Targoff explores the metaphysical foundation of Donne's interest in body and soul, reviewing texts he may have read on the subject as well as theories he considered on the origin and nature of the soul and the state of the resurrected body. Targoff maintains that Donne moves between two theories of the soul's origin, traducianism and infusionism, but commits fully to the view that the earthly body and the resurrected body are almost indistinguishable. In chapter 1, Donne's prose and verse letters are read in relation to each other, as in both Targoff discovers

Donne imagining ways to 'overcome the problems of separation and absence that haunt him' (p. 27). In the prose letters, Donne seeks to transmit to friends his soul *and* body, while in the verse letters he imagines that to write or read epistles is possibly to 'resurrect' friends (p. 45). In chapter 2, Targoff claims that the relationship of the lovers in much of Donne's amatory verse is analogous to that of body and soul, particularly in terms of 'the difficulty of sustaining ... a union' (p. 49). For Targoff, 'Donne's poetics of love is a poetics of taking leave' often marked by intense anxiety and antagonism (p. 50). Separation of the lovers, Donne fears, will cause 'a potentially irreversible injury' because, though 'inherently distinct', they are 'essential to each other's existence' (pp. 50, 51).

In chapter 3, Targoff challenges the critical consensus that the 'Second Anniversarie' is a 'traditional celebration of the soul's passage to heaven', arguing instead that it is an account of the soul's natural and unyielding desire to remain with the body at death, a desire linked with Traducian thought (p. 80). In examining the Holy Sonnets in chapter 4, Targoff admits that their focus is the outcome of God's judgement of the soul. However, she is convinced that when Donne writes on the state of the soul in these poems, angst about his fleshly condition is not far off, and that when Donne implores God to mend him in the sonnets, he seeks the restoration of soul and body. Targoff reads Donne's *Devotions* in chapter 5 against the backdrop of typical Protestant prose meditations on illness, contrasting Donne's focus on disease as a spiritual and physical state in the *Devotions* with the emphasis on the condition of the soul in standard works, in which bodily affliction is usually set aside (p. 132). When the illness of his body and soul coincide, Donne is better able to comprehend, and seek treatment for, the 'chronic and willful' sickness of his soul (p. 141). While this process leads to a sometimes desired 'intimacy with God', it also grants Donne the 'devotional autonomy' to 'dilate and shape his reckoning with God' (pp. 144, 145). Targoff ends in chapter 6 with a close reading of *Deaths Duell*, in which she pictures Donne dramatically rehearsing or performing his death, while the listener joins him on a harrowing rhetorical voyage in which life and death are not distinguishable, the grotesque dissolution of the flesh takes centre stage, and the 'material continuity of the self' is ultimately affirmed (p. 169).

In *John Donne: Body and Soul*, Targoff offers a perceptive and penetrating reading of a grand and emotionally fraught theme in Donne's oeuvre. It is an immensely readable scholarly study that is never dull or pedantic. Aspects of Targoff's thesis may be less original than she suggests, and past scholarship relevant to her research goes unnoticed at times. However, she reveals, in delightful, well-paced prose, the metaphysical core of many of Donne's works.

Donne's tendency to resist closed categories and move between forms and concepts is assessed in aesthetic and philosophical terms by Victoria Moul in 'Donne's Horatian Means: Horatian Hexameter Verse in Donne's *Satyrs* and *Epistles*' (*JDJ* 27[2008] 21–48). Moul explains that Donne was drawn to both the generic hybridity and the ethical perspective that he found in Horace's verse. She explores the ways in which 'Satyre I', 'Upon Mr Thomas Coryats Crudities' and 'To Mr R.W.' are indebted to the ideas of Horace (as well as Persius) on 'the poet's choice ... of genre, of behavior, of religion' and on the need to eschew extremes (p. 47). In his verse epistles and satires, Moul concludes, Donne conflates these classical values with Christian principles in his pursuit of an ethical 'mature poetic mode' (p. 47).

The attention dedicated this year to Donne as a creature of the 'in-between', as one 'neither here nor there', is matched by an emphasis on his tropological imagination (see Johnson, 'Donne, Imperfect', p. 1; reviewed above). Ceri Sullivan explores the intersection of rhetorical figures and theological views in *The Rhetoric of the Conscience in Donne, Herbert, and Vaughan*, in which she identifies key tropes used by the three authors to depict the workings of the conscience: *antanaclasis, aposiopesis, chiasmus*, enigma and *subjectio*. Sullivan first describes the flawed conscience as a syllogism missing a term, before turning to the treatment of God's torture of the resistant conscience in the poets' works, associating such divine intervention with *subjectio*, 'a monologue that presents itself as a dialogue but where...the speaker answers himself' (p. 5). Sullivan notes that the admissions of tortured consciences are rarely authentic. Accounts of God writing the law on the believer's heart in the poems of Herbert and Vaughan are then examined and linked with enigma because the conscience chooses not to grasp the meaning of the engraved words to avoid compliance. Sullivan next considers the conscience's 'self-selective reading' of Scripture in the poets' works, connecting the repetition of biblical fragments with *antanaclasis* (the altering of a word's meaning as it is restated in new contexts) and recalling that 'conscientious repetition is not always self-abnegating' (p. 156). The easily bored conscience that halts dialogue before any moral resolution can be made, most evident in the poets' poems on distraction, is then related by Sullivan to a futile 'melancholic humour' and to *aposiopesis*, 'breaking off from discussion' (pp. 159, 157). Sullivan ends her study by presenting more rewarding 'models of the conscience' that are associated with *chiasmus* (p. 8). Though the conscience invokes this trope in the works of Donne, Herbert and Vaughan, it fails 'to leap over the *chiasmus* into God's position' as it wishes to preserve 'a space for a self which is other than God' (pp. 193, 219).

The Rhetoric of the Conscience undeniably expands our knowledge of theological and tropological connections in early modern devotional texts. By reading the idiom of the conscience in the works of Donne, Herbert and Vaughan in light of contemporary casuistry manuals, legal records, accounts of interrogation, torture, and tattooing, and educational and religious treatises, Sullivan provides us with surprising and valuable insights into how the conscience was 'engineered' at the time (p. 220). However, Sullivan's fascination with diverse cultural phenomena, sometimes only tangentially related to Donne, Herbert and Vaughan, leaves her with less space to produce fully developed readings of their works.

Donne's tropological practice is also the subject of half of the essays in *Renaissance Tropologies: The Cultural Imagination of Early Modern England*, edited by Jeanne Shami, a thematically unified volume dedicated to Gale Carrithers. The collection concentrates on the tropes that Carrithers and James D. Hardy believe governed the early modern imagination: 'journey, theatre, moment, and ambassadorship' (p. 1). In 'Salvific Moments in John Donne's *Devotions upon Emergent Occasions*' (pp. 45–62), Eric Brown traces

Donne's movement in the *Devotions* from a terrible moment of illness to a redemptive moment associated with 'occasional time', during which he enjoys the 'eternal expansiveness of communion' with God (pp. 46, 59). In 'Donne and the State of Exception' (pp. 63–88), Greg Kneidel makes a controversial claim: that Donne's works can be usefully read alongside those of the German conservative political philosopher (and Nazi polemicist) Carl Schmitt, because Donne and Schmitt share an understanding of the 'state of exception' (when laws are suspended). Kneidel theorizes that Donne's conservative impulse to normalize the state of exception in his amatory verse results from his desire to 'rule by arresting and suspending thought' (p. 87). In 'Troping Religious Identity: Circumcision and Transubstantiation in Donne's Sermons' (pp. 89–120), Jeanne Shami conjectures that Donne selects, transforms, and rescues the potentially divisive tropes of transubstantiation and circumcision in his sermons to inspire his auditors to take up genuine 'religious identities' (p. 90). Shami contends that by releasing in his sermons the surplus of meaning made possible through metaphor (an ontological and epistemological device), Donne facilitates the spiritual transformation of his listeners.

Alexandra Mills Block's striking essay, 'Eucharistic Semiotics and the Representational Formulas of Donne's Ambassadors' (in Shami, ed., pp. 169–85), proposes that in employing the trope of ambassadorship, Donne scrutinizes 'the viability of various representational models' (p. 170). Block suggests that Donne is drawn to this trope because he conceives of his ministerial role in ambassadorial terms, sees his poems as his representatives, and worries about 'the challenge of crafting a text that represents *himself*' (p. 185). Block finds in 'To Sir Henry Wotton, at his going Ambassador to Venice' and 'To Mr T.W.' the desire for representational resemblance or 'semiotic transparency' via 'textual investiture' or mystical transposition (pp. 177, 171). Donne, however, is well aware of the unstable nature of the relationship between the represented and representative, and ponders the consequences of 'ambassadorship gone wrong' (p. 176). In 'Donne and Diplomacy' (pp. 187–216), Hugh Adlington also assesses the figure of ambassadorship in Donne's works, but relates it to Donne's role as chaplain to Doncaster, ambassador to Bohemia. Adlington highlights Donne's reliance on 'the methods and language of diplomacy' in his 1619 sermons, especially in the Heidelberg sermon (p. 189). Adlington draws parallels between the diplomatic rhetoric used by Donne in these sermons and that used by Doncaster in letters written in the same period, speculating that the sermons 'served as spiritual adjuncts to the temporal diplomacy of Doncaster's embassy' and recognizing that Donne's diplomatic irenicism served both religious and political ends (p. 215).

In 'Dangerous Liaisons: "Spider Love" in Donne's "Twicknam Garden"' (in Shami, ed., pp. 219–28), Albert C. Labriola wittily and credibly argues that Donne borrows the metaphor of 'spider love' from Mary Wroth's *Urania*, in which it signifies 'amorous intrigue and marital infidelity' (p. 227). The speaker of 'Twicknam Garden', Labriola asserts, feels such 'spider love' for the lady in the poem who, as a paragon of virtue, will not yield to his advances; he is left in 'an approach-avoidance conflict' because he must draw near, yet he longs to evade her refusal (p. 224). The speaker's only hope is to sublimate his 'spider love' to remain in her presence. Labriola conjectures that here Donne tropes his relationship with his patron, the countess of Bedford, offering her a triple compliment inasmuch as she is simultaneously portrayed as an object of sexual desire, a worthy woman uncontaminated by adulterous romantic liaisons and one who amiably permits men 'to commune transcendently with her' (p. 228).

Heather Dubrow considers a single trope in Donne's works in 'Paradises Lost: Invaded Houses in Donne's Poetry' (in Lynch and Scott, eds., *Renaissance Poetry and Drama in Context: Essays for Chris Wortham*, pp. 241–55). Dubrow remarks that Donne regularly fixates on 'scenarios of invasion', which she attributes to broader cultural anxieties about intrusion into domestic space and to political concerns about foreign invasion, and which she associates with the classical figure of *paraklausithyron* in section I.6 of Ovid's *Amores* (p. 241). Donne's appropriation of the biblical trope of the adulterous woman is the subject of Kimberly Johnson's 'John Donne's Adulteries: Spiritual Uncertainty and the Westmoreland Sonnets' (in Johnson, Schoenfeld and Strier, eds., *Divisions on a Ground: Essays on English Renaissance Literature in Honor of Donald M. Friedman*, pp. 28–44). Johnson claims that in the Holy Sonnets found only in the Westmoreland manuscript, Donne figures adultery as the perfect spiritual state because it arouses 'divine steadfastness' (p. 39). This trope comforts Donne, who sees himself as a spiritual adulterer because of his 'uncertain' faith. Johnson assumes that Donne chose not to circulate these poems because, as a priest, he should censure rather than embody 'spiritual uncertainty' (p. 41).

Donne's willingness to style himself an adulterous woman in the Westmoreland sonnets brings to mind the much-debated issue of gender in his works, a subject addressed in a book and six articles this year. In her cogently argued and compelling monograph, *Refiguring the Sacred Feminine: The Poems of John Donne, Aemilia Lanyer, and John Milton*, Theresa M. DiPasquale scrutinizes the audacious and provocative transformation of the 'Judeo-Christian tradition of the sacred feminine' in the works of three early modern poets who view the relation of the human and the divine in distinctly gendered terms; tackle the sacred significance of gendered roles; abandon the Calvinist doctrine of total depravity; testify to the feminine in the divine; depict women as potentially redemptive agents and instruments of divine grace; and view their poetry as Marian, inasmuch as it brings forth or incarnates the Word (pp. 1–2). DiPasquale first establishes that Donne can only move from Ovidian misogyny to the sacred feminine after the death of the Virgin Queen. She then undertakes aesthetically, theologically and politically sensitive close readings of 'The Annuntiation and Passion', select Holy Sonnets, and *The Anniversaries*, to explore Donne's view of the holy woman as a 'mortal sacrament' through whom God is made known and of the 'female flesh and feminine virtue' as a vehicle of God's grace, which she reads, in part, as Donne's gendered reaction to private loss and public religious controversy (pp. 35, 5).

In 'John Donne and the Debate about Women' (in Johnson et al., eds., pp. 92–113), Cristina Malcolmson links Donne's complex treatment of gender with his humanist education, which trained him to 'argue on both sides of a question' in order to prepare him for success in a ruthless male world (p. 93). She identifies in Donne's writings conflicting positions on 'the nature of women' and recognizes that in 'A Valediction: of the Booke' and 'Valediction: of my Name in the Window' Donne is 'at his most insightful about early modern gender dynamics' (pp. 94, 109). Yet she warns that Donne may take on the 'woman question' only to solidify masculine identity and authority. In 'Donne and Ovid: Two Valedictory Poems in Relation to *Metamorphoses* ll. 410–748' (*RES* 59[2009] 677–700), Misako Himuro argues that Donne, with an atypical Petrarchan tone of gentle adoration, presents a vision of mutual, unending love in 'On his Mistress' and 'Sweetest love, I do not goe' because he is indebted to the episode of Alcyone and Cex in *Metamorphoses*, not because these poems are addressed to his wife. In 'Intertextuality and the Female Voice after the *Heroides*' (*RS* 22:iii[2008] 307–23), Raphael Lyne studies the unruly voices of early modern female literary creations who speak back to and challenge the authority of their male authors. She hears such voices in the poems of John Donne and the plays of Francis Beaumont and John Fletcher. Reading against the grain, Lyne argues of Donne's 'Sappho to Philaenis' that Sappho engages with other Donnean texts in such a way as to privilege her own authority. Intertextuality becomes a means for Sappho to usurp Donne's authorial power, allowing the reader to witness a woman's 'disruptive creative autonomy' (p. 315).

That the female voice in Donne's poems is more assertive or authoritative than is generally believed, or the male voice less aggressive or potent, is supported by three articles this year. In 'Hearing the "harmonious chime" in Donne's "To his Mistress going to bed"' (*ANQ* 21:iii[2008] 19–28), Theresa M. DiPasquale cleverly argues that the 'harmonious chime' of the timepiece in the poem functions as the 'surrogate voice' of the mistress, to whose command the speaker responds; that it sounds 'an erotic call to prayer', irreverently recalling a rhythmic monastic time structured by 'canonical hours' (pp. 20, 22); that it marks, not the decaying process of the mistress's body nor the power of the poet to immortalize, but rather that the lover's erection may soon 'time out' (p. 23); and that it suggests (scandalously) that the mistress, like Christ, is the 'determiner of another kind of time' during which she will incarnate by 'clothing herself' in the speaker's flesh (pp. 24, 25). While DiPasquale attends to the authority of the female in 'To his Mistress going to bed', Martin Dodsworth pauses over the fear and nervousness of its male speaker. In 'Donne, Drama and Despotism in "To his Mistress going to bed"' (*EIC* 58[2008] 210–36), Dodsworth challenges the claims made by John Carey and Thomas M. Greene, among others, that the male speaker of the poem is an Ovidian or Marlovian despot caught up in a 'pornographic' 'fantasy' that reflects lewd authorial longings (pp. 211–13). Dodsworth believes that the subject of the elegy is the speaker's anxious imaginings about the anticipated 'sexual encounter' (p. 214). The speaker's mental state drives him to doubt that his mistress shares his desire and leads him to question the ethics of his own behaviour. As Dodsworth determines, the speaker is therefore ultimately 'incapacitated by his own sensibility' (p. 233).

In 'Donne's "Valediction of the booke" as a Performative Action' (*ANQ* 21:ii[2008] 25–34), Raymond-Jean Frontain is also persuaded that the silent female in a Donne poem is more potent than the male speaker who petitions her. Frontain avers that in the 'Valediction of the booke' the woman addressed by the male lover is godlike since she has the authority to grant him 'a sign of his election' (p. 26). It is she who can memorialize his name and their love and assure him that her affection will survive his absence. The 'speech act' of the male lover, the matter of the poem, is intended to will her to assent, but as Frontain points out, all he can do is wait to see if 'she will deign to deliver the word by which her will can be known and done' (p. 31).

Donne's conception of gender is tied to his notions of identity or selfhood, the focus of Nancy Selleck's perceptive study *The Interpersonal Idiom in Shakespeare, Donne, and Early Modern Culture*. In sketching a fascinating '"prehistory" of the modern self', Selleck abandons the notion that a version of modern subjectivity, marked by individualism, cropped up in early modern England (p. 1). To the contrary, she proposes that early modern writers understood selfhood to be fundamentally interpersonal as well as embodied, contextually informed, contingent and thus unstable. In Donne's *Devotions* and poems, Selleck finds a corporeal, particularly humoral, understanding of selfhood that presents both body and spirit as fluid, permeable and penetrable, and in which the self is often objectified in relation to, and (re)constituted by, a divine or human other. Existing as an incomplete self produces in Donne, Selleck suspects, a spiritually positive and productive anxiety because he longs for connection with the other and is 'committed to an interpersonally participant selfhood': to 'selfhood as exchange' (pp. 88, 144). For Selleck, Donne yearns for 'association' not 'autonomy', as is sometimes claimed, and he is therefore willing to risk 'engagement' (pp. 83, 84, 150). Although this well-written study contains some profound insights, and its reading of the Donnean self is convincing, Selleck tends to elide any overlap between early modern and modern notions of identity. She works within a binary in which the categories of interpersonal early modern selfhood and modern individual selfhood are insufficiently troubled.

The various identities that Donne assumed, or unsuccessfully sought, during the course of his life are investigated in several articles this year. Donne's exposure to particular cases during his training in the law at the Inns of Court, and its influence on his perception of contemporary statutes on land use, is discussed by Gregory Kneidel in 'Coscus, Queen Elizabeth, and Law in John Donne's "Satyre II"' (*RenQ* 61[2008] 92–121). Kneidel argues that Donne mocks in 'Satyre II' the 'antiquarian ideology' of Sir Edward Coke and the self-serving 'fiscal feudalism' of Queen Elizabeth, which led to the enactment of statutes, particularly the Statute of Uses, that 'pitted the crown against the landholding gentry' (pp. 117, 94). Piers Brown highlights Donne's contribution to 'secretarial culture' (p. 844) in ' "*Hac ex consilio meo via progredieris*": Courtly Reading and Secretarial Mediation in Donne's *The Courtier's Library*' (*RenQ* 61[2008] 833–66). He considers the stance taken in *The Courtier's Library* on the role played by 'secretaries, tutors, and professional readers' as knowledge mediators in a courtly context. He focuses on Donne's understanding of the thorny relationship between 'knowledge production', 'courtly display' and social advancement in this poem and elsewhere (pp. 844, 834).

Donne's effort to secure a permanent place for himself at court is taken up by Cedric C. Brown in 'Presence, Obligation and Memory in John Donne's Texts for the Countess of Bedford' (*RS* 22:i[2008] 63–85). The 'communication system' employed by Donne in his epistolary exchanges with the countess of Bedford are analysed by Brown, who detects in Donne's letters a drive to make certain he is on the countess's mind; a fear that he may soon be forgotten; a longing to enter her presence; the use of a 'proxy' to maintain himself in her memory; an account of her transcendent qualities and his material needs; and the employment of the language of 'gifts', 'services' and 'exchange' to indirectly request 'financial payment' (pp. 63, 71, 83). Attempts by rival poets to secure the countess of Bedford as a patron are discussed by Jean R. Brink in 'Michael Drayton and John Donne' (*JDJ* 27[2008] 49–66). Brink suspects that Drayton did not become the countess's client because of testimony he gave in support of Thomas Goodyear and his mother in a property case against Sir Henry Goodyear, a friend and neighbour of the countess. Powerless to secure a place at court, and angered at inequitable patronage practices, Drayton censures 'elitist' coterie poets, especially clients of the countess, and presents himself as a 'spokesman for public values' (p. 62). Brink conjectures that Drayton's criticism of the 'jetting *Jay*' who defiles the Muses in *The Owle* [1604] and his attacks on Cerberon, 'a beastly clowne to[o] vile to be spoken of' in the revised *Shepheards Garland* [1606] may be directed at Donne (pp. 60, 61). Drayton's final insult, Brink gathers, may be his exclusion of Donne from his otherwise comprehensive elegy 'Of poets and poesie' [1627].

The uneasy intersection of economic and amatory discourse in epistles written by Donne to his patron is present elsewhere in his works, as Barbara Cornell indicates in 'Terms of "Indearment": Lyric and General Economy in Shakespeare and Donne' (*ELH* 75:ii[2008] 241–62). Drawing on George Bataille's theory of a 'general or unrestricted economy', Cornell compares the discourses of love and money in Donne's Elegy 10 ('Image of her whom I love') and Shakespeare's Sonnet 31 ('Thy bosom is indeared') (p. 241). She claims that, while both poems reveal 'an awareness of the alienating and plurally signifying potential of early modern market and material culture', Donne shows a preference for a 'restrictive economy of mastery' in his elegy, while Shakespeare creates a place for a general economy of 'expenditure, nonproductive excess, and loss' in his sonnet (pp. 255, 256). Albert C. Labriola also examines the intersection of the languages of love and finance in 'Altered States in Donne's "The Canonization": Alchemy, Mintage, and Transmutation' (*JDJ* 27[2008] 120–30). Labriola suggests that the alchemical terms in 'The Canonization' allude not simply to alchemy per se, but rather to coin production in the London Mint as an alchemical operation; if this allusion is properly understood, Labriola believes the complexity, even irony, of the 'rhetorical imprint' left by the poem's speaker will come to light (p. 130).

Donne's transition from would-be courtier to priest is the subject of John Wall's important article, 'The Irregular Ordination of John Donne' (*JDJ* 27[2008] 81–102). Wall has found three documents in the Diocese of London and the University of Cambridge which suggest that the ordination of Donne, as well as the trajectory of his career, were more controversial than once thought; these manuscripts are the bishop of London's Register of

Ordinations; Cambridge's Grace Books, volume E; and a letter from King James to Cambridge University (17 December 1624). These documents reveal that the date and place of Donne's ordination, and his same-day ordination as priest and deacon, did not conform to the canons or regular practices of the church, which caused some strife, evident in the way the event is recorded in the Register; that the king forced administrators and faculty members at Cambridge to confer a doctorate of divinity on Donne; and that the king planned to grant Donne the deanship of Canterbury Cathedral shortly thereafter, but was thwarted by those who felt Donne was being fast-tracked in the church without the requisite education and experience. That Donne was finally appointed dean of St Paul's six years after his ordination, and that the king later wrote a conciliatory letter to the administrators of Cambridge restricting his own authority in their awarding of degrees, is evidence, to Wall, of the 'limitations of royal power in the early seventeenth century' (p. 97).

As Wall emends Donne's biography in the light of new evidence, Lara M. Crowley seeks to emend the Donne canon on the same terms in 'Donne, not Davison: Reconsidering the Authorship of "Psalme 137"' (*MP* 105:iv[2008] 603–36). Crowley attributes 'Psalm 137' to Donne rather than Francis Davison for the following reasons: that only one seventeenth-century scribe, Ralph Crane, attributes it to Davison; that Davison collected Donne's poetry; that it is attributed to Donne in every seventeenth-century printed edition of his collected poems and in several contemporary manuscripts; that Davison's tutor, Edward Smyth, apparently attributed it to Donne; that Herbert J. Griersen denied Donne's authorship for subjective reasons; that there are thematic and semantic similarities between 'Psalme 137' and 'The Lamentations of Jeremy'; that about 20 per cent of Donne's sermons are based on a psalmic text, so the absence of a psalm translation in his works is peculiar; and that Donne's experiences of spiritual and social exile would draw him to Psalm 137.

In 'New Manuscript Texts of Sermons by John Donne' (in Beal, ed., *English Manuscript Studies*, pp. 77–119), Jeanne Shami recalls her significant discovery of three manuscripts in the British Library containing unknown versions of Donne's sermons (p. 77). In 1995 she published her findings on one manuscript that contained a version of Donne's sermon on the Gunpowder Plot with authorial corrections, but in this article she turns to the contents of the two other manuscripts. Shami notes that Harley MS 6946 (H1) contains five Donne sermons on the following texts: Proverbs 8:17, Genesis 2:18, Hosea 2:19, John 11:35 and 1 Thessalonians 5:16; each sermon is written in a distinct secretary hand. In Harley MS 6356 (H2), Shami discovered a wide assortment of printed, as well as handwritten, tracts; the handwritten material was produced by multiple scribes. The two sermons by Donne that are included (copied by different scribes, but revised by only one of them) are on Ecclesiastes 12:1 and Matthew 21:44. Shami records with great care the physical appearance of these manuscripts, along with their transmission history and textual significance.

Three articles this year consider the limitations of certain critical approaches to, or readings of, Donne's poems. In 'Going in the Wrong Direction: Lyric Criticism and Donne's "Goodfriday, 1613. Riding Westward"' (in Johnson et al., eds., pp. 13–27), Richard Strier rejects two standard approaches to 'Goodfriday, 1613. Riding Westward': those that treat the poem's speaker as a 'persona' and those that weigh the poem down with 'scholarly baggage' (p. 14). A.B. Chambers's ' "Goodfriday, 1613. Riding Westward": The Poem and the Tradition' [1961], is acknowledged as the source of these faulty interpretative methods. Strier maintains that the poem should be taken at face value as 'a re-creation of an "occasional meditation" performed or begun while Donne was actually "riding westward" possibly to Sir Edward Herbert's, in 1613' (p. 19). Strier declares that, on this occasion, Donne gladly turns his face from God because he hopes to encounter God 'on his own terms' when he is 'made perfect' to avoid facing his 'imperfection and finitude' (pp. 23, 24)

In 'Dar la luz: Illuminating John Donne's "A nocturnall upon S. Lucies day, Being the shortest day" ' (JDJ 27[2008] 103–20), Lauren La Torre argues that the subject of 'A nocturnall upon S. Lucies day' is not the countess of Bedford, but rather the death of Anne Donne in childbirth. She bases her argument on the 'cross-cultural' pun she observes in the poem. Donne, she states, indirectly plays on the phrase dar la luz ('to give the light') in 'A nocturnall', which in Spanish means 'to give birth', referring to the light the infant is pushed toward as it leaves the womb (pp. 104, 106). The poem's emphasis on the 'extinction of light' suggests an 'inverted birth' as well as a 'reversed alchemy'—how Donne imagined the death of his wife and child (pp. 107, 109). The pun is expanded, La Torre alleges, when Anne is strangely aligned with the Virgin Mary: Mary gave birth to the Light while Anne 'died dando la luz' (pp. 114–15).

Leslie Brisman, in 'The Wall Is Down: New Openings in the Study of Poetry' (PoT 29:ii[2008] 245–75), wonders if new critical methods lead to more sophisticated or insightful readings of familiar poems. Brisman applies methods associated with new historicist and intertextual criticism to Donne's 'A Valediction Forbidding Mourning' and Wallace Stevens's 'Puella Parvula' and finds they allow him to see these texts in fresh ways. However, in terms of Donne's poem, he concludes that any new interpretation can do little more than 'add ... a footnote to the erudite reach and humanistic grasp' of John Freccero's reading of 'A Valediction Forbidding Mourning' in an article published in English Literary History in 1963 (p. 272).

Discovering productive ways to teach Donne in the classroom continues to be a concern of the Donne Society, which held a colloquium on 'Upon the translation of the Psalmes by Sir Philip Sydney, and the Countess of Pembroke his Sister' in 2007, the proceedings of which were published in the John Donne Journal this year. In 'Teaching Donne on the Sidney Psalms' (JDJ 27[2008] 153–60), Anne Lake Prescott recalls asking English majors in a compulsory course on Renaissance literature what information they required to comprehend 'Upon the translation of the Psalmes'. She discovered that students needed instruction on biblical and theological matters to make sense of specific terms in the text; that Donne's association of Mary and Philip with Miriam and Moses had to be unpacked for students, especially as it relates to gender roles; that while students benefit from information on the politics, spirituality and aesthetics of psalm translation, the 'mysterious energies' accessed in the act of translation should also be accentuated (p. 156); that students find fascinating the politics of music as it relates to the singing of psalms in the period; that the genre(s) of the poem should be reviewed with students; and that students might profitably speculate about why the poem was not circulated.

In 'Donne's "Upon the translation of the Psalmes" and the Challenge to "Make all this All"' (*JDJ* 27[2008] 161–74), Raymond-Jean Frontain reports that when he teaches Donne, postmodern students (comfortable with the idea that life is incoherent) have difficulty accepting that Donne is driven by an anxiety 'to achieve coherence' (p. 162). To bridge this cognitive gap between Donne and his students, Frontain turns to 'Upon the translation of the Psalmes', which allows him to discuss Donne's recognition of the unifying force of speech; to situate Donne within literary and spiritual tradition; to trace Donne's association of the personal and public voice; and to introduce Donne's activation of multiple meanings of 'translation', many of which imply movement from the solitary and fractional to the communal and coherent.

In 'Upon Donne's "Upon the translation of the Psalmes"' (*JDJ* 27[2008] 175–96), Hannibal Hamlin first reviews the limited criticism published on the poem before identifying its genre, detailing its aesthetic strengths and intellectual complexity, and addressing its important place in literary tradition. Hamlin attends to the text's sophisticated scriptural allusions and musical references as well as to its consideration of biblical imitation, acts of translation, liturgical practices, ecclesiastical reformation and religious doctrine. Because the poem thematizes 'the nature of Psalms and Psalm translation', 'the relationship between earthly and heavenly music', and 'the vocational dilemma of the religious poet', Hamlin argues that it belongs to a sub-genre of poems that introduce metrical psalms, and he identifies Francis Davison's 'An Introduction to the Translation of the Psalms', Mary Sidney Herbert's 'To the Angell spirit of the most excellent Sir Phillip Sidney' and Milton's 'At a Solemn Music' as other examples of the literary form (p. 188).

In 'Donne's Dedication of the Sidney Psalter' (*JDJ* 27[2008] 197–211), Gary A. Stringer traces the history of the poem's transmission, sets out the relationship of the printed copy of the poem in the 1635 edition of Donne's *Poems* (B) to the version of the poem in the O'Flahertie manuscript (H6), and rejects claims that 'B derives from H6', asserting that the exact opposite is true (p. 200). Stringer declares that early modern versions of the poem are extremely rare and that the only 'authoritative source' for the text is B (p. 203). He speculates that Donne wrote the poem around 1625, that he envisioned it as part of the prefatorial material for a new edition of the Sidney Psalter, and that he probably did not circulate the poem for political reasons.

Donne's influence on early modern and modernist poets is sketched in concise, lucid, and discerning terms by P.G. Stanwood in *John Donne and the Line of Wit: From Metaphysical to Modernist*, the 2008 Garnett Sedgewick Memorial Lecture. Stanwood first rehearses efforts to define, censure, and/or defend metaphysical poetry by Carew, Dryden, Johnson, H.G.C. Grierson and T.S. Eliot, reminding us that early criticism of metaphysical poetry applied less to Donne than to his disciples. In comparing the poems of Donne to those of his first imitators, Stanwood exposes the 'elaborate' tropes and 'wayward wit' of Cowley, the 'clotted' conceits of Cleveland, and the 'sensible and flat' idiom of Lord Herbert of Cherbury (pp. 15, 20). Stanwood next considers Donne's influence on the Fugitives, American modernist poets drawn to 'metaphorical ingenuity', 'metrical formality' and authorial 'impersonality', which they found in Donne's poems (p. 25). As the Fugitives inspired the New Critics, it is no surprise that Donne played a central role in this school of criticism; but Stanwood is more interested in how the Fugitive poets, especially John Crowe Ransom, Robert Penn Warren and Allen Tate, imitate Donne, which he explores in readings of Ransom's 'History of Two Simple Lovers', Warren's 'Bearded Oaks' and 'Love's Parable', and Tate's 'Ode to the Confederate Dead'. Stanwood concludes by charting the path of this 'line of wit' from the 'Fugitive-New Critics' to John Berryman, Randall Jarrell and Robert Lowell, offering a reading of 'Mr. Edwards and the Spider', Lowell's parodic imitation of Donne's 'A nocturnall upon S. *Lucies* Day' (p. 31).

The reception of Donne in China has lately become a topic of some interest. In 'A Survey of and Comments on Twenty-First Century Donne Studies' (*FLS* 30[April 2008] 165–72), Li Zhengshuan and Liu Luxi identify recent trends in Donne scholarship in China. These include an increase in Chinese translations of Donne's work; the application of literary theories to his poetry; the emergence of comparative studies of Donne and Chinese poets; and the analysis of Donne's influence on later writers. There is a desire to move forward in the field, but a sense that this can only be achieved with a stocktaking of past research.

4. Herbert

Kristine A. Wolberg's *'All Possible Art': George Herbert's The Country Parson* was the only monograph devoted solely to Herbert this year. Wolberg's project is to read *The Country Parson* not as a cultural or theological background to Herbert's poetry, but on its own merits as a literary text. She does so by situating it in relation both to courtesy manuals (primarily those by Baldassare Castiglione and Stefano Guazzo) and to clerical manuals (including those by William Perkins and Richard Bernard). Wolberg notes that, while Herbert's work has often been linked to courtesy literature, no one has previously done a thorough study of *The Country Parson* as a unique combination of the two popular forms. Wolberg demonstrates that Herbert, unlike Puritan clerical manual writers, pays relatively little attention to the inner state of the minister, and great attention to details of external form. While Puritan manuals agree that if the heart is right, all else will follow, Herbert gives instruction on all matters of the minister's life, from the way he prays and preaches, to his clothing, to his friendly conversation. In this emphasis on outer form, Herbert's manual more closely resembles courtesy manuals than clerical ones. Likewise, most clerical manuals were sermonic in method, many of them in fact beginning as sermons. Herbert's, however, works nothing like a sermon, but is rather an orderly calculation of all that comprises the minister's life as God's courtier. Wolberg poses the question of how the openly manipulative and self-serving form of the courtesy manual could inform pastoral ministry, and moves to Guazzo for her answer. In Guazzo she finds an apt source for Herbert's manners, for Guazzo alone of the great Italian courtesy writers integrally linked manners and holiness. Not only did Guazzo's project aim at social edification rather than the raising of the self, he also insisted that one should strive to seem a gentleman and also be one. This generative interplay between seeming and being was, Wolberg argues, a great resource for Herbert, giving him a position between a court that put its efforts into seeming and a Puritan movement that insisted that seeming must follow being. For Herbert, rather, one could learn to be a good parson by learning how to act like one.

Michael Schoenfeldt's 'George Herbert's Divine Comedy: Humour in *The Temple*' (*GHJ* 29[Fall 2005/Spring 2006] 45–66), published in 2008, aims to recover the laughter in Herbert's work from the unrelenting solemnity with which religion is usually approached. Schoenfeldt notes that, for Herbert, humour is a potential danger, but also a potential occasion for pastoral instruction. The pleasure of mirth in right measure participates in a Pauline 'holy folly', paradoxically both recognizing that heavenly and earthly values are utterly disparate, but also allowing insight into the heavenly via the quotidian. Schoenfeldt investigates the many sources and forms of Herbert's humour, noting that he tends most to amiable 'impractical jokes' on speakers who, like him and the reader, struggle to get the foolishness of the Gospel (p. 57).

In 'Devoted Forms: Reading George Herbert' (*SWR* 93[2008] 428–47), poet Rick Barot powerfully reminds us of the poetic force of Herbert's work. Delightfully, he begins by locating Herbert not in the hagiographical distance of Bemerton, but in an urban dance club, full of bodies moving in time to Madonna covering 'Love' (III). The readings that follow lean a bit too much on Fish—'one of the costs of God's grace is the abdication of the self' (p. 432)—but are charged with poetic life, considering Herbert's poetics from his rhythms to his acrostics.

Anne-Marie Miller-Blaise, in ' "Priests and Yet Prophets"? The Identity of the Poetic Voice in the Shorter Religious Lyric of Robert Southwell and George Herbert' (in Cottegnies et al., eds., pp. 113–24) takes on the question of prophetic utterance in the work of these two poets. Noting that prophetic speech was met with great suspicion at the time, Miller-Blaise nonetheless observes Southwell and Herbert employing it, particularly in their use of prospopoeia and sermocinatio, in which biblical speakers declare things already accomplished. Thus, these poets use the power of predictive speech by employing it within ritualized memory. Miller-Blaise also published an article the previous year, ' "*Oratio nostra est silentium*" Silence in George Herbert's Holy Rhetoric' (*Cahiers Charles V* 43[2007] 43–67), in which she argues that silence is a positive and persuasive poetic tool for Herbert. In light of the ambivalence towards rhetoric within the Augustinian tradition, Miller-Blaise proposes that Herbert's silence, which on the face of it abrogates his own art, at the same time creates a visual rhetoric that was otherwise in ill repute, in which verbal eloquence gives way to the living picture.

In ' "Thy glorious household-stuffe": Doctrinal (Re)Inscription in George Herbert's Church Furnishing Poems' (in Papazian, ed., pp. 211–35), David L. Orvis argues that Herbert's church furnishing poems neither conform to an untroubled *via media*, nor to either Low Church or High Church militancy, but rather, in a 'self-consciously nonsectarian' way, reinscribe church objects with Herbert's 'own doctrine' (pp. 215, 213). Orvis persuasively demonstrates Herbert's attraction to controversial places such as 'The Altar' and 'The Windows', and, once there, to Herbert's displacement of that controversy through devotional engagement. At the same time, Orvis seems too ready to assume both the polarity of church politics and the individuality of 'Herbert's doctrine'.

Patricia Canning, in her article ' "The bodie and the letters both" ': 'Blending' the Rules of Early Modern Religion' (*L&L* 17[2008] 187–203), uses blending theory to shed light on the highly complex operations of one of Herbert's most deceptively simple-seeming poems, 'JESU', ultimately arguing that the poem demonstrates the contradiction at the heart of Reformation iconoclasm. Canning argues that only blending, or conceptual integration, can trace the multiple relations between the six 'input spaces' of the poem, concluding that the word 'JESU' in the poem has value not only as a sign, but as a thing in itself, thus inadvertently portraying the sort of 'fetishistic consciousness' supposed to belong to Catholics but also inherent in Protestant word-centredness (p. 200).

5. Marvell

Studies of poetry in the later seventeenth century continued apace in 2008 along the critical trajectory of previous years, with a pronounced emphasis on historicist and bibliographical analyses. Throughout, the complex political, cultural and material conditions of writing in the period remain the focus of critical attention. In Marvell studies specifically, political, biographical or sexual 'ambiguity' continues to be the watchword as critics attempt to solve the mystery of Marvell's real and imagined persona. In *Poetry and Allegiance in the English Civil Wars: Marvell and the Cause of Wit*, Nicholas McDowell takes a novel historicist-biographical approach in attempting to reconstruct a complex network of socio-historical contexts in post-civil war London which purport to shed new light on some of Marvell's most famous and politically enigmatic lyrics. In effect, McDowell submits Marvell to a process of biographical contextualization very similar to that which Milton underwent in the late 1980s and the 1990s. Having exposed the historical fallacy of critics who see in a Marvell a private, solitary figure, McDowell situates many of his major lyrics, including 'To His Coy Mistress' and the 'Horatian Ode', in a London-based literary circle which formed in 1647 under the patronage of the wealthy royalist Thomas Stanley. As McDowell shows, membership in the circle included not only Marvell, but men like the parliamentarian propagandist John Hall and 'Cavalier' poets such as Richard Lovelace. Such men were united, argues McDowell, by a shared interest in lyric poetry that could negotiate the new possibilities of patronage, power, and social-political commentary following the upheavals of the civil war, regicide and the creation of the Commonwealth. Although the book contains intriguing historical analyses of the literary fortunes of Lovelace and Hall as two opposed, yet strangely complementary, aspects of the Stanley circle, Marvell's elusive political and ideological loyalties and commitments remain at the heart of

McDowell's investigation. The opening chapter situates Marvell's lyrics composed between 1646 and 1648 in the context of the Stanley circle's network of friendships. McDowell then presents 'To His Coy Mistress' as a test case for proving his claim that Marvell was associated with the Stanley circle and its friendly exchange of literary and political, essentially royalist, ideas and sympathies. These themes are developed in much greater detail in the fourth chapter, where a close analysis of Marvell's 'An Elegy Upon the Death of My Lord Francis Villiers' and the verse epistle 'To His Noble Friend Mr Richard Lovelace' demonstrate McDowell's central claim that following the dissolution of the monarchy as a centre of political power and patronage Marvell was negotiating with his friends the future for poetry and wit in a Puritan society. What emerges is a view of Marvell whose final allegiance was not to the cause of the defeated king, or the emerging Commonwealth, but to what McDowell identifies as the post-war, post-regicide 'cause of wit'. To cement this thesis, McDowell next explores the 'Horatian Ode' as a poem which re-examines the new climate of patronage following regicide, and, in a concluding chapter, the contextually elusive satire 'Tom May's Death', whose implicit loyalties, according to McDowell, are neither royalist nor republican, but finally literary and witty. McDowell's methodology is certainly unique and raises at times difficult questions, especially in his analysis of 'To His Coy Mistress', where a detailed examination of echoes of other poets is used to argue for the poem's place in the Stanley circle. It is never sufficiently clear, for example, if the internal evidence McDowell detects in a given poem justifies its place in the emerging socio-historical context, or is used a priori to justify the existence of the context itself. It is certainly a novel idea to examine the value and content of poetry strictly in terms of its putative reception by historically specific readers. The historical analysis depends here not on the usual new historicist assumption that a literary work can shed light on a given historical moment, but on the assumption that a reconstruction of what the poems possibly meant to individual readers living and acting *in* a given historical moment can in turn resolve many of their apparent historical ambiguities. Needless to say, such a methodological assumption is assuming very much indeed. However, notwithstanding the conceptual difficulties such a method raises, McDowell succeeds comprehensively in enriching and complicating the age-old debate about Marvell's political and literary loyalties. The book is a significant contribution to the field which all subsequent investigations of Marvell's historical situation will have to contend with.

Many of the historical issues raised by McDowell also feature indirectly in the proceedings from the International Marvell Conference held in Rheims on 13–14 May 2005, edited and published this year by Gilles Sambras as *New Perspectives on Andrew Marvell*. Despite Sambras's attempt to present a coherent structure for the volume, the essays have little in common with one another beyond their common preoccupation with Marvell's poetry. The collection simply offers what are evidently the best pickings from a typically diverse range of conference papers. Klaudia Laczynska opens the collection with a meditation on 'Upon Appleton House' which reads the poem's perplexities and architectural-pastoral itinerary in terms of the scientific discoveries of the sixteenth and seventeenth centuries. Gabriella Gruder-Poni next contributes an intriguing essay which reads the implied crucifixion scene in 'Upon Appleton House' in terms of its possible echoes of a poem by Ausonius as an example of the classical-Renaissance topos of the fugitive Cupid. Estelle Haan surveys Marvell's reliance on and indebtedness to contemporary pedagogical methods as it is manifested in his Anglo-Latin bilingualism, teasing out the much-neglected image of Marvell as a teacher. Out of Marvell's innovative and didactically informed bilingualism, argues Haan, the poet's vernacular singularity asserts itself. Jon Stainby reflects on the intellectual affinities and ideological similarities (as well as important differences) between Marvell and John Harrington. Stainby makes a case for a common philosophical 'ground' between the two writers where notions of political power are inseparable from the economics underlying contemporary practices of landowning. Art Kavanagh examines conflicting notions of divine justice in relation to several textual ambiguities in 'Upon the Death of Lord Hastings', while Warren Chernaik, in a compelling piece, examines the rhetorical strategies of the post-Restoration, polemical Marvell which allow him to avoid censorship and keep in the king's good graces by deflecting legitimate criticism of the restored monarch to his advisers. On the other hand, Chernaik argues that Marvell's satires also reveal a more sober, conflicted view of the monarch, where disaffection with royal authority allows for the re-emergence of Marvell's republican commitments. The familiar subject of Marvell's divided political loyalties is also treated by Charles-Edouard Levillain, who next documents in great detail Marvell's politics along the fault-lines of French, papist and court interests, putting into focus Marvell's possible view on international affairs. Martin Dzelzainis, in a piece that has appeared in slightly altered form elsewhere, then continues in this vein by submitting to close analysis the clandestine print history of Marvell's political satires. The final section of the volume sees George Klawitter offering a provocative reading of 'The Nymph Complaining for the Death of Her Fawn' by situating the poem in the context of seventeenth-century erotica. Gilles Sambras, the editor, next contributes an essay which offers a contextual political reading for the dilemma confronting the speaker of 'The Coronet'. Sambras argues that the Christian pastoral abstractions of the poem can be read as a commentary on topical strife between Catholics and Protestants. Nigel Smith concludes the volume with an overall review of the critical and editorial history of Marvell's poems and highlights the manner in which our view of Marvell and his literary influence has developed and changed in recent decades.

Other than the two books mentioned above there were very few articles of note in 2008 which dealt with Marvell. Nicholas von Maltzahn is author of two such articles. In 'Death by Drowning: Marvell's *Lycidas*' (*MiltonS* 48[2008] 38–52), Maltzahn reflects on the profound influence of Milton's *Lycidas* on Marvell's development as a lyrical poet. Isolating 'Drinking, drowning, and a death wish' (p. 41) as a recurring motif in Marvell's poetry, Maltzahn traces the influence of *Lycidas* as an example of the Pindaric elegy which Marvell repeatedly echoed and rewrote in his own elegies for Francis Villiers and Cromwell, and in other, more complex, poetical contexts as produced for example in Marvell's *The First Anniversary*, 'Bermudas' or his later Restoration satires. Finally, however, Maltzahn argues that Marvell outgrew *Lycidas*, or rather that its hold on him diminished as a more prosaic Marvell 'was no longer drowning in Milton or any other of his literary forebears' (p. 49). Maltzahn continues his comparative assessment of Milton and Marvell in a companion piece, 'Liberalism or Apocalypse? John Milton and Andrew Marvell' (in Thormählen, ed., *English Now: Selected Papers from the 20th IAUPE Conference in Lund 2007*, pp. 44–58). Taking Milton and Marvell as the precursors of a modern tradition of 'liberalism', Maltzahn draws the important distinctions between the two poets' respective ideological positions as a way to highlight the tensions underlying the British liberal tradition from its inception. Surveying Milton's and Marvell's respective political careers as state servants under the Protectorate, Maltzahn draws out a tension between Milton's apocalyptic, or confessional, approach to international politics and Marvell's secular, and therefore 'liberal', one. For the apocalyptic Milton, politics on a grand, international scale—especially where the Thirty Years War was concerned—is addressed in the confessional context of divine providence and the final victory of (Protestant) truth. But in a geopolitical reality where Lutheran states such as Sweden and Denmark can also be at war, it is Marvell's pragmatic view of politics as an expression of interest and relativism which emerges as the more sober assessment. Maltzahn traces these two opposing world-views first in the political career of either poet, and finally in samples from their literary and polemical work, concluding that it was Milton's apocalyptic sublimity which was to shape his subsequent literary as well as political influence on posterity. Conversely, it was on this account that Marvell was supposedly deemed less appealing in the eyes of 'posterity' even as, with the advent of multiculturalism in the twenty-first century, it appears that it is Marvell's version of secular 'liberalism' that is winning, and has been in fact for a long time.

Another historicist meditation on Marvell is offered up in David Norbrook's 'Bards and Republicans: Marvell's "Horatian Ode" and the Wars of the Three Kingdoms' (in Dutcher and Prescott, eds., *Renaissance Historicisms: Essays in Honor of Arthur F. Kinney*, pp. 291–312). Returning to the ever enigmatic 'Horatian Ode' and its depiction of the Irish who, despite being 'asham'd | To see themselves in one Year tam'd' by Cromwell, nevertheless 'can affirm his Praises best' (ll. 72–7), Norbrook unpacks the political and historical complexity of these lines by questioning the Anglocentric point of view which encodes Irish identity in terms of such stereotypical binaries as the effeminate, traditional, local Irish Catholic Other, as opposed to the masculine, militant, universal English Protestant. Taking the lead from recent trends in postcolonial and postmodern theory, Norbrook compares Marvell's poem to three contemporary Irish literary works which deal with the same event from a different, and at times alarmingly similar, perspective. Comparing Marvell's Tacitist political ambiguity with similar expressions of ambivalence in the prose speech of the poet Richard Fanshaw, addressed on 28 November to the marquis of Inchiquin at a Council of War, an anonymous manuscript history of the wars in Ireland dating between 1652 and 1660 and known as the *Aphorismical Discovery of Treasonable Faction*, and a bardic Irish poem dated as the 'Horatian Ode' to 1650, rendered in

English as 'The Roman Visionary'. The analysis of Fanshaw's prose and the treacherous political waters it was attempting to navigate highlights the extent to which, according to Norbrook, we need to qualify Marvell's use of the word 'Irish' from an English Protestant perspective. The subsequent analysis of the *Discovery* and the Gaelic poem and their respective treatment of English Protestant aggression then serve to demonstrate just how complex and ambivalent perceptions were on the Irish side, not only of the English, but of the Irish themselves.

On the bibliographical front, Martin Dzelzainis continued to bring out more of his insights into the printing history of the satirical 'Advice to a Painter' poems, two of which (the third and second 'Advices') are widely presumed to be the work of Marvell. In 'L'Estrange, Marvell and the *Directions to a Painter*: The Evidence of Bodleian Library, MS Gough London 14' (in Dunan-Page and Lynch, eds., *Roger L'Estrange and the Making of Restoration Culture*, pp. 53–66), Dzelzainis first reconstructs the extent of L'Estrange's involvement with the *Directions* volume as Surveyor of the Press. According to Dzelzainis, L'Estrange was far more anxious about seditious scribal literature than print publication, and this is borne out, indirectly enough, by the clandestine print history of the *Directions* volume and the movement of the scandalous 'Advice to a Painter' poems from manuscript to contraband print and back to manuscript again. Dzelzainis then presents the Bodleian's Gough manuscript as a test case for his theory, a close analysis of which reveals that, contrary to perceived wisdom, it was in fact transcribed from a prior printed edition not for private use, but to prepare a new underground print publication that never materialized. Whatever other conclusions one might draw from Dzelzainis's bibliographical work, it certainly bears the overall conclusion which Dzelzainis ventures, namely that such a complex printing history testifies to 'the sheer potency of Marvellian state satire' (p. 66).

Another bibliographical reflection on Marvell's poetry is offered by Ian C. Parker in two notes. In 'Marvell's "A Dialogue between the Soul and Body": Probable Sources and Implications' (*N&Q* 55[2008] 290–9) Parker demonstrates that Marvell's reliance on James Howell's prose work *The Vision* [1651], especially in the Soul's speeches, is far more extensive than previously assumed. Parker argues that the use of Howell and other sources in fact forms a critique of these sources, and that Marvell's model for such a critique was Sylvester's translation of Du Bartas's *Divine Weeks* and its portrayal of the Tower of Babel and the construction of Solomon's temple. Such appropriations, according to Parker, give to the body's complaint in the poem a 'deeper theological significance' (p. 298) which extends to other references to this theme elsewhere in Marvell's poetry. Continuing the same argument in a subsequent note, 'Marvell and the "Tygress Fell": A Supplementary Note' (*N&Q* 55[2008] 299–300), Parker reinforces previous notes which argued that an epic simile from 'The Last Instructions to a Painter' depicting a 'Tygress' separated from her cubs by the swelling Euphrates river is again based in large part on Du Bartas. By cementing the argument for this allusion, Parker claims to shed light on Marvell's uniquely eclectic compositional process and argues for the authority of Bodleian MS Eng. poet. d. 49 in deciding on a variant reading in these lines of the poem.

Not all articles on Marvell this year dealt with politics or historical/ bibliographical contexts. In ' "The Garden" and Marvell's Literal Figures' (*CQ* 37[2008] 224–52), Dominic Gavin explores the intellectual implications of Marvell's drive towards literalism in his natural and pastoral imagery. Using 'The Garden' as prooftext, Gavin demonstrates how Marvell does not merely borrow from a rich Neoplatonic, hermetic and emblematic tradition when thinking about the cultural commonplace of a 'book of nature', but comments on and critiques these traditions and their spent allegorical forces. The resulting critique never devolves into pure parody; as Gavin shows, Marvell elevates the trope of the 'book of nature' beyond (or above) the dualism of allegory to the level of experienced truth which 'forestalls awareness of the allegorical mode' and 'eschews exegesis' (p. 236) beyond what it offers in the vicarious world of perception and imagination.

Michael John Disanto offers, in 'Andrew Marvell's Ambivalence towards Adult Sexuality' (*SEL* 48:i[2008] 165–82), a reassessment of Marvell's putative anticipation of Nabokov in exploring, to quote *Lolita*, 'the perilous magic of nymphets' (p. 165). Analysing the representation of youthful virgins and garden nymphs alongside imagery suggesting castration and sterility in such poems as Marvell's 'The Picture of Little T.C. in a Prospect of Flowers', 'Young Love', 'Upon Appleton House', 'The Garden' or the four 'Mower' poems, Disanto argues for a view of Marvell as a man threatened by adult women and adult sexuality and seeking refuge from these in the erotic, but finally asexual pastoral embrace of imagined or idealized virginal 'nymphets'.

Books Reviewed

Ainsworth, David. *Milton and the Spiritual Reader: Reading and Religion in Seventeenth-Century England*. Routledge. [2008] pp. ix + 233. $108 ISBN 9 7804 1596 2513.

Albrecht, Roberta J. *Using Alchemical Memory Techniques for the Interpretation of Literature: John Donne, George Herbert, and Richard Crashaw*. Mellen. [2008] pp. xvi + 234. $109.95 ISBN 9 7807 7345 1988.

Beal, Peter, ed. *English Manuscript Studies: New Texts and Discoveries in English Manuscripts*, vol. 13. English Manuscript Studies 1100–1700. BL. [2008] pp. 272. $85 ISBN 9 7807 1234 9772.

Beer, Anna R. *Milton: Poet, Pamphleteer, and Patriot*. Bloomsbury. [2008] pp. xvii + 458. $34.99 ISBN 9 7815 9691 4711.

Brooks, Douglas A., ed. *Milton and the Jews*. CUP. [2008] pp. xii + 226. $93 ISBN 9 7805 2188 8837.

Campbell, Gordon, and Thomas N. Corns. *John Milton: Life, Work, and Thought*. OUP. [2008] pp. xiii + 488. $39.95 ISBN 9 7801 9928 9844.

Carr, Mary, K.P. Clarke, and Marco Nievergelt, eds. *On Allegory: Some Medieval Aspects and Approaches*. CambridgeSP. [2008] pp. ix + 269. £34.99 ISBN 9 7818 4718 4009.

Colebrook, Claire. *Milton, Evil and Literary History*. Continuum. [2008] pp. 158. $120 ISBN 9 7808 2648 4925.

Cottegnies, Line, Claire Gheeraert-Graffeuille, Tony Gheeraert, Anne-Marie Miller-Blaise and Gisèle Venet, eds. *Les Voix de Dieu: Littérature et prophétie en Angleterre et en France à l'âge baroque.* SorbonneN. [2008] pp. 315. £20 ISBN 9 7828 7854 4183.

Dijkhuizen, Jan Frans van, and Richard Todd, eds. *The Reformation Unsettled: British Literature and the Question of Religious Identity, 1560–1660.* Brepols. [2008] pp. 244. £53 ISBN 9 7825 0352 6249.

DiPasquale, Theresa M. *Refiguring the Sacred Feminine: The Poems of John Donne, Aemilia Lanyer, and John Milton.* Duquesne. [2008] pp. xiii + 392. $60 ISBN 9 7808 2070 4050.

Donnelly, Phillip J. *Milton's Scriptural Reasoning: Narrative and Protestant Toleration.* CUP. [2009] pp. x + 267. $90 ISBN 9 7805 2150 9732.

Dubrow, Heather. *The Challenges of Orpheus: Lyric Poetry and Early Modern England.* JHUP. [2008] pp. x + 293. £33.50 ISBN 0 8018 8704 8.

Dunan-Page, Anne, and Beth Lynch, eds. *Roger L'Estrange and the Making of Restoration Culture.* Ashgate. [2008] pp. xvii + 236. £60 ISBN 9 7807 5465 8009.

Dutcher, James M., and Anne Lake Prescott, eds. *Renaissance Historicisms: Essays in Honor of Arthur F. Kinney.* UDelP. [2008] pp. 355. $60.95 ISBN 9 7808 7413 0010.

Fleming, James Dougal. *Milton's Secrecy and Philosophical Hermeneutics.* Ashgate. [2008] pp. x + 196. £55 ISBN 9 7807 5466 0675.

Gray, Erik. *Milton and the Victorians.* CornUP. [2009] pp. ix + 183. $39.95 ISBN 9 7808 0144 6801.

Hiltner, Ken, ed. *Renaissance Ecology: Imagining Eden in Milton's England.* Duquesne. [2008] pp. xi + 356. $62 ISBN 9 7808 2070 4029.

Hobson, Theo. *Milton's Vision: The Birth of Christian Liberty.* Continuum. [2008] pp. xiv + 178. $29.95 ISBN 9 7818 4706 3427.

Holberton, Edward. *Poetry and the Cromwellian Protectorate: Culture, Politics, and Institutions.* OUP. [2008] pp. ix + 249. £50 ISBN 0 1995 4458 5.

Johnson, Kimberly, Michael C. Schoenfeldt, and Richard Strier. *Divisions on a Ground: Essays on English Renaissance Literature in Honor of Donald M. Friedman.* George Herbert Journal Special Studies and Monographs. [2008] pp. x + 142. $25 ISBN 9 7818 8811 2177.

Knoppers, Laura Lunger, ed. *The Complete Works of John Milton,* vol. 2: *The 1671 Poems: Paradise Regain'd and Samson Agonistes.* OUPAm. [2008] pp. civ + 170. $135 ISBN 9 7801 9929 6170.

Kuchar, Gary. *The Poetry of Religious Sorrow in Early Modern England.* CUP. [2008] pp. xi + 241. £52 ISBN 9 7805 2189 6696.

Loewenstein, David, and Paul Stevens, eds. *Early Modern Nationalism and Milton's England.* UTorP. [2008] pp. xi + 470. $80 ISBN 9 7808 0208 9359.

Lynch, Andrew, and Anne M. Scott, eds. *Renaissance Poetry and Drama in Context: Essays for Christopher Wortham.* CambridgeSP. [2008] pp. xii + 353. £39.99 ISBN 9 7818 4718 6102.

McDowell, Nicholas. *Poetry and Allegiance in the English Civil Wars: Marvell and the Cause of Wit.* OUP. [2008] pp. 295. £53 ISBN 9 7801 9927 8008.

Miller, Shannon. *Engendering the Fall: John Milton and Seventeenth-Century Women Writers.* UPennP. [2008] pp. viii + 280. $65 ISBN 9 7808 1224 0863.

Mohamed, Feisal G. *In the Anteroom of Divinity: The Reformation of the Angels from Colet to Milton.* UTorP. [2008] pp. xiv + 242. £35 ISBN 9 7808 0209 7927.

Papazian, Mary. A., ed. *The Sacred and Profane in English Renaissance Literature.* UDelP [2008] pp. 377. $75 ISBN 9 7808 7413 0256.

Sambras, Gilles, ed. *New Perspectives on Andrew Marvell.* EPURE. [2008] pp. 194. £16.65 ISBN 9 7829 1527 1218.

Selleck, Nancy. *The Interpersonal Idiom in Shakespeare, Donne, and Early Modern Culture.* Palgrave. [2008] pp. ix + 214. £50 ISBN 9 7814 0369 9061.

Shami, Jeanne, ed. *Renaissance Tropologies: The Cultural Imagination of Early Modern England.* Duquesne. [2008] pp. x + 382. $49.99 ISBN 9 7808 2070 4098.

Sharpe, Kevin, and Steven N. Zwicker, eds. *Writing Lives: Biography and Textuality, Identity and Representation in Early Modern England.* OUP. [2008] pp. xii + 369. $99 ISBN 9 7801 9921 7014.

Shullenberger, William. *Lady in the Labyrinth: Milton's 'Comus' as Initiation.* FDUP. [2008] pp. 361. $65 ISBN 9 7808 3864 1743.

Smith, Nigel. *Is Milton Better Than Shakespeare?* HarvardUP. [2008] pp. xvii + 214. $22.95 ISBN 9 7806 7402 8326.

Stanwood, P.G. *John Donne and the Line of Wit: From Metaphysical to Modernist. The 2008 Garnett Sedgewick Memorial Lecture.* Ronsdale. [2008] pp. 42. $9.95 ISBN 9 7815 5380 0651.

Sullivan, Ceri. *The Rhetoric of the Conscience in Donne, Herbert, and Vaughan.* OUP. [2008] pp. 275. £53 ISBN 9 7801 9954 7845.

Targoff, Ramie. *John Donne: Body and Soul.* UChicP. [2008] pp. xiv + 213. $29 ISBN 9 7802 2678 9637.

Thormählen, Marianne, ed. *English Now: Selected Papers from the 20th IAUPE Conference in Lund 2007.* Centre for Languages and Literatures. LundU [2008] pp. xx + 354. $149.50 ISBN 9 7891 9769 3509.

Wolberg, Kristine A. *'All Possible Art': George Herbert's The Country Parson.* Madison. [2008] pp. 165. $43.50 ISBN 9 7808 3864 1705.

X

The Later Seventeenth Century

NOAM REISNER, LESLEY COOTE, HELEN BROOKS AND
JAMES OGDEN

This chapter has three sections: 1. Poetry. 2. Prose. 3. Drama. Section 1 is by
Noam Reisner; section 2 is by Lesley Coote; section 3(a) is by Helen Brooks;
section 3(b) is by James Ogden.

1. Poetry

Compared with previous years, 2008 was a lean year for Dryden studies as
such, but there were a number of articles and essays worth noting where
Dryden features either directly or indirectly at the heart of a sustained
cultural-literary analysis of the later seventeenth century. Dryden's implicit
politics in later years is the subject of Abigail Williams's 'The Politics of
Providence in Dryden's *Fables Ancient and Modern*' (*T&L* 17[2008] 1–20).
Taking as her starting point the much-debated political ambiguity of Dryden's
translations in *Fables*, which despite topical references appear to resist the
imposition of political readings along allegorical lines, Williams argues for an
emerging critique in *Fables* of contemporary providential theory. According to
Williams, the apparent resistance of Dryden's *Fables* to fixed political readings
is a calculated feature of the translations, which offer 'explanations of events
that confirm divine order, or justice, and then refuse to provide evidence of
that order' (p. 10). Keenly aware that her argument veers at times into
intractable realms of intentional fallacy, Williams finally hedges her bets and
merely concludes that Dryden creates in *Fables* an 'interpretative uncertainty'
(p. 20) which operates by offering an elusive narrative design that points to its
own illusory nature as mere fiction, or, indeed, a fable.

Two closely related articles published alongside each other examine the
reception and sexual politics of Ovidian erotica in the later seventeenth
century, as reflected in the fortunes of the Dryden–Tonson collaboration on
the collection of Ovid's *Heroides* [1680]. In 'The Early Modern Afterlife of
Ovidian Erotics: Dryden's *Heroides*' (*RS* 22:iii[2008] 401–13) Harriette
Andreadis surveys the print history of the *Heroides* and its numerous editions
and revisions and reflects in the process on changing male attitudes to female

same-sex sexuality and the cultural changes in 'gender dynamics' as they are filtered through the emergence of literary coteries in Restoration London. Using Sir Carr Scrope's translation for Dryden of the epistle 'Sappho to Phonon' as a test case for the trajectory of Ovidian erotics evolving within a changing literary and cultural context, Andreadis demonstrates how each successive translation (almost all by men) reveals its own sexual bias towards female sapphism. The varying responses to the Ovidian epistle, argues Andreadis, show the extent to which emerging literary coteries reflected the sexual prejudices of their times, but also shaped these prejudices in recognizing an Ovidian Sappho as a valid, if suspect, embodiment of female sexuality. Andreadis's piece is followed by Susan Wiseman's complementary ' "Perfectly Ovidian"? Dryden's *Epistles*, Behn's "Oenone", Yarico's Island' (*RS* 22:iii[2008] 417–33). Taking the *Heroides* collection of 1680 as her starting point, Wiseman explores the satirical and pathetic reactions to the collection and meditates on the overall literary and cultural reception of Ovidian sensibilities in the Restoration. Using Dryden's theory of the free 'paraphrase' from the preface to the collection as a theoretical metonym for the looseness of parody and satire on the one hand, and the 'looseness' of female sexuality celebrated in the translations by 'various hands' on the other, Wiseman explores a number of possible trajectories of this literary influence. She moves from the invitation to satire in Behn's supposedly inept paraphrase of Oenone's epistle, through a wider reflection on gender politics and how the *Heroides* came to be considered either suitable or unsuitable for female readers, all the way to a more ambitious argument about the possible, and very tentative, links between the 'sexually transgressive' nature of the Ovidian heroines and the 'language of enslavement' (p. 427) in the early eighteenth century. Analysing various treatments in contemporary literature of the story of Inkle and Yarico, Wiseman demonstrates how the Indian maid Yarico, a victim of slavery, is drawn in the contemporary imagination ethically and formally as an Ovidian heroine.

Finally, in 'Restoration Poetry and the Failure of English Tangier' (*SEL* 48:iii[2008] 547–67), Adam R. Beach considers Dryden's little-considered 'Epitaph on Sir Palmes Fairborne' alongside the anonymous satire 'Rochester's Farewell' and a broadside ballad found in Pepys's collection called 'The English Courage Undaunted' for their respective engagement with the colonial and imperial politics of English Tangier, which was finally abandoned as an English colony in 1684. Beach considers these three poems as a test case for examining the 'relationship between literary production and the colonial system in the Restoration' (p. 549), where it emerges that even when panegyrics are intended, as in Dryden's epitaph to the late governor of the colony, the resulting ambivalence of rhetoric points to the breakdown of English imperial ideology in the period.

2. Prose

In a relatively lean year for work on later seventeenth-century prose, the 'standout' work is David Appleby's *Black Bartholomew's Day: Preaching,*

Polemic and Restoration Nonconformity. The 'day' of the title is the deadline on which those ministers ejected from their livings for refusing to conform to the terms of the 1662 Act of Uniformity were to preach their last sermon to their congregations. In that year, and subsequent years (Appleby concentrates on the years 1662–5), selections from these sermons were published, and in some cases republished. The book is much more than a study of the nature of the sermons, although Appleby does survey their content in some detail, teasing out hidden meanings in discourses which had to be encoded in order to disguise challenges to royal and governmental authority, and to avoid allegations of socio-political radicalism, disloyalty, and sectarianism. Appleby examines the sermons for evidence of the nature of post-Restoration 'puritanism', what made clergy into 'non-conformists' at great cost to themselves, and what can be revealed about their preaching methods—for example, he notes that many sermons were prepared in advance, not extempore, and that these preachers also exhibited a balance of rationality and emotion in their performance. Most clergy did not want to separate from the Church of England, but having done so they sometimes remained as members of the same congregation. Many survived by combinations of mutual support, patronage and publishing, leading to a decline in the charismatic nature of preaching. One of the most interesting factors surrounding the ejections, uncovered from sermon evidence, is the onus placed upon congregations to remain faithful to their principles, and to take responsibility for the spiritual content of their future devotions and the quality of ministry in their churches. Surveying polemical responses to the sermons in print, Appleby notes the growing gulf which this ultimately created between the conforming and non-conforming, and how individuals such as Sir Roger L'Estrange were able to exploit the situation created by the controversy to oust rivals and establish supremacy in their field; in L'Estrange's case, licensing and censorship. This is much more than a monograph on a collection of sermons. With a bibliography of source material, detailed analysis and scholarly critical work, Appleby's book is a mine of inspiration and information.

Another, somewhat 'left field' book on John Bunyan is *Reception, Appropriation, Recollection: Bunyan's Pilgrim's Progress*, a collection of papers from the fourth Triennial Conference of the Bunyan Society in Bedford, 1–5 September 2004, edited by W.R. Owens and Stuart Sim. Beginning with later seventeenth-century editions such as the translation into French in 1685, the essays capture the essence of different interpretations of Bunyan's most famous work through the centuries, culminating with the Bunyan character in Powell and Pressburger's film *A Matter of Life and Death* in 1946. Along the way, the writers examine the reception and use of Bunyan's work by authors such as Scott and Macaulay, Kipling, Hardy and Ward, MacNeice and Beckett, leading to a discussion of potentially troubling interpretations of *Pilgrim's Progress* in the light of contemporary anxieties over revived fundamentalism. It is always valuable to consider why we read 'classical' texts as we do, and this book has great value as an aid to the epistemology of scholarship.

In an article centred on *Pilgrim's Progress* and *Grace Abounding*, ' "As blood forced out of the flesh": Spontaneity and the Wounds of Exchange in *Grace*

Abounding and *The Pilgrim's Progress*' (*ELH* 74[2008] 271–99), Lori Branch discusses the tension in reformed 'covenant theology' as espoused by Bunyan between the commercial and contractual discourse of redemption and the emotional discourse of faith as a personal relationship with Christ, and therefore with God. She argues that Bunyan himself found this dichotomy almost impossible to bear, but that in *Pilgrim's Progress*, his later work, he managed to find a discursive method of reconciliation by means of allegorical narrative (Branch has written on this theme before), one of the reasons for the great popularity of the latter work. The article contains an excellent exposition of the Vanity Fair episode in *Pilgrim's Progress*. A similar theme is covered by Hilary Hinds in '"And the Lord's power was over all": Calvinist Anxiety, Sacred Confidence, and George Fox's Journal' (*ELH* 75[2008] 841–70), but in this case examining the tension between predestination and faith in personal salvation and being elect, in the context of early Quakerism (or, maybe, one 'branch' of it) as evidenced by the *Journal* of George Fox. In both articles, a central feature is the experienced need of the 'elect' to continually seek out and evaluate evidence in daily life for God's favour, with the subsequent impulse to doubt its validity.

On the subject of early Quaker unity, or lack of it, Matthew Horn's 'Texted Authority: How Letters Helped Unify the Quakers in the Long Seventeenth Century' (*SC* 23[2008] 290–314) provides evidence for considerable divergence of theological and devotional interpretation among early Quaker groups. He examines the nature of the difficult relationship between George Fox's group and those of other Quaker preachers, and how the idea of the Divine Light at the centre of the Quakers' individually and experientially based theology made uniformity impossible. In the face of this, Horn traces the gradual imposition of Fox's authority on the movement by use of the Pauline example of letter-writing. His study culminates in the conflict between James Nayler, his colleague Martha Simmonds and Fox over hat-wearing. Perversely, there are similarities with Appleby's work on L'Estrange and Berkenhead in *Black Bartholomew's Day*.

Before leaving the subject of religion, mention should be made of articles by David Loewenstein and Bas van Fraassen. The first section of Lowenstein's 'The War Against Heresy in Milton's England' (*MiltonS* 47[2008] 185–218) is a scholarly assessment of discourses of heresy and heretics, demonstrating that Thomas Edwards's famous *Gangraena* was not an isolated work, but part of a culture in which heresy was a terminology of moral judgement and religious authorization. Loewenstein's study takes in other such works (for example, Ephraim Pagitt's *Heresiography* of 1645), and a discussion of William Walwyn's sceptical response, before progressing to the work of Milton. Van Fraassen, in 'Sloughs of Despond, Mountains of Joy' (*CritQ* 50[2008] 74–87), takes a philosophical, theological view of the epistemology of seventeenth-century 'reformed' theological thought, a 'left field' piece of value for its thought-provoking, epistemological qualities rather than for the detail of its seventeenth-century scholarship.

On the subject of natural philosophy, Christopher Carter, in '"A constant prodigy"? Empirical Views of an Unordinary Nature' (*SC* 23[2008] 265–89), examines the nature of marvels and prodigies, and how they were perceived by natural philosophers, in the later seventeenth century. He notes that there were two kinds of 'recognized' prodigy, signal and penal, and that the study of them was considered to be a relevant aspect of natural philosophy. Scholars such as Isaac Newton and Robert Boyle were in favour of alchemy as a fit subject for natural philosophers, and alchemists flourished at the court of Charles II. Empirical methodologies and discourses dictated, however, that prodigies should be investigated, witnessed, collected, collated and evaluated. The findings were expressed in discourse such as that used to describe other experimentation and observation. Glanville and Boyle compiled lists of prodigies, which were considered to be part of nature, which was itself prodigious. Carter concludes with the notorious case of Glanville and the 'Demon Drummer of Tedworth', which is illustrative, salutary, a scholarly exposition and well worth reading. Also well worth a read is Raymond Anselment's article on 'Robert Boyle, Izaak Walton and the Art of Angling' (*P St* 30[2008] 124–41), a study of meditation and its divergent uses by two apparently similar characters. Walton's reflections are more pastoral and poetic, while Boyle's reflections on the pastoral and the Edenic (Walton shares with John Evelyn a pastoral-religious view of interaction with the natural world, food-gathering and provision) are more humanistic, with stronger socio-political connotations. The whole is an extremely interesting, well written and valuable study of a literary 'episode' in later seventeenth-century culture.

Adam Smyth's 'Almanacs, Annotators, and Life-Writing in Early Modern England' (*ELR* 38[2008] 200–44) is less an article than a mini-monograph on later seventeenth-century almanacs, their content and their uses, both as texts in themselves and as texts-as-objects. In the years from 1640 to 1700, Smyth notes, almanacs were the most popular form of published literature in England, but because they were ephemeral literature only a relatively small number have survived. This important study concentrates on almanac reception, examining not only their use as texts of an episodic, predictive nature, but also the way in which readers would interpolate and annotate their own marginalia, glosses and notes into the text, with 'blanks' being deliberately left in anticipation of such interpolations. Calendars from almanacs, as well as other sections of the text, were selected, cut and pasted by readers into other works, notably into their own diaries, and Smyth examines some examples of this, including that of a woman, Lady Isabella Twysden. This seems to be part of a larger work; hopefully, a larger volume will appear in the future.

Finally, Evan Labuzetta's essay on ' "This diabolical generation": The Ranters and the Devil' (*LitComp* 5[2008] 591–602) casts fresh light upon the nature of 'ranting', and on the formation of the idea of 'ranterism'. Labuzetta defines the critical period for the formation of Ranter identity as between October 1650 and June 1651. He examines the evidence of contemporary polemic, and charts how the idea of Ranters as a definable sect was built up by their opponents, and how these perceptions then helped to shape the development of this identity. The 'ranters' themselves had little to do with this, but in the process certain 'ranting' characteristics came to be generally accepted by those who feared and opposed the likes of Coppe, Salmon and

Clarkson, and these 'ranters' came to be associated with the Devil. Satan must have been a ranter, opponents argued, as both he and the 'ranters' shared qualities of demonism. This is a really interesting essay on the operation of the processes of demonization by polemic—a winner of the *Literature Compass* Essay Prize.

3. Drama

(a) General

While there was a notable scarcity of edited collections or monographs on Restoration drama this year, the diversity and range of journal articles, considering not only the plays but also the economic and material contexts and conditions of Restoration dramatic production, provides ample material for consideration. One of the highlights of 2008 was a special issue of *Comparative Drama* (42:i[2008]) devoted to Restoration and eighteenth-century drama. More specifically, as Robert Markley highlights in his introduction to the issue, 'Rethinking Restoration and Eighteenth-Century Drama' (CompD 42:i[2008] 15 1–6), the issue seeks to resituate 'the theatre as an integral part of literary history rather than as a "background" for the novel' (p. 5). Markley's introduction raises important and timely questions over the status and value of drama within the wider field. It reflects upon the shift in understandings of 'history' and 'literary history', in the twenty-five years since James Thompson's seminal essay 'Histories of Restoration Drama' (*ECent* 24[1983] 163–72) urged the need to rethink the problems of history and interpretation in order to understand the literary culture of the period. Markley reminds us of the continuing necessity for such reflexivity. He draws attention to the ways in which changing understandings of literary history, cultural context and reception continue to problematize the relationship between dramatic litera- ture and history of the period, as well as prompting us to rethink how such critical shifts have impacted upon the placement of drama within the wider field. Despite, he argues, 'or perhaps because of, the critical revolutions of the last few decades, drama remains a sideshow for many critics of the long eighteenth century, who continue to revisit and recast the late twentieth- century project of examining the history of the novel' (p. 2). Drama, he concludes, is either treated as a 'retrograde showcase for declining aristocratic ideology or assimilated to a narrative of incipient modernization' (p. 3). It is this dichotomy which the essays in this special issue seek to resist, both by disrupting existing narratives and proposing alternative ones.

Diana Jaher's essay, 'The Paradoxes of Slavery in Thomas Southerne's *Oroonoko*' (*CompD* 42:i[2008] 51–71), does this by offering an alternative reading of this well-known play through the lens of contemporary discourses on slavery. She focuses not on Oroonoko, nor on Imoinda, but rather on the oft-ignored character of the slave, Aboan. Through a close reading of Southerne's play, and by drawing on Behn's novella, in which Aboan does not appear, Jaher argues that Southerne introduces this character to make available a critique of the institution of slavery: a critique which is absent from

Behn's novella. Jaher argues that Southerne presents Aboan as an exceptional, non-aristocratic slave, who proves himself Oroonoko's equal, if not his superior, in ability and leadership. In this way, Jaher argues, Southerne subverts the aristocratic justification of slavery grounded in natural inferiority. It is to Aboan moreover, rather than to Oroonoko, that Southerne gives both anti-slavery sentiments and the active role in leading the insurrection. While recognizing that Aboan does not function to advocate total emancipation, Jaher makes a compelling argument for the centrality of this character to contemporary audiences' reception of both the play and its political questioning of the legitimacy of slavery and hereditary determinism.

Laura J. Rosenthal's contribution to the special issue also revisits and seeks to revise understandings of well-known plays. In ' "All injury's forgot": Restoration Sex Comedy and National Amnesia' (*CompD* 42:i[2008] 7–28) Rosenthal focuses predominantly, although not exclusively, on the two popular sex comedies *Marriage à la Mode* and *The Country Wife*. These plays, she argues, explicitly theatricalize the relationship between erotic desire and social organization: features which, she argues, define the sub-genre of the sex comedy. Rosenthal argues that in order to understand the political force, and indeed anxieties, at the heart of these plays, they must be read not, as has been the more recent tendency, for conflicts over individual gendered or class-related freedoms and restrictions but rather for their representation of family, community and nation. The libertine, she suggests, would have been framed and understood by contemporary audiences within the context of the wider family, and therefore society. Working from this basis and drawing on a range of contemporary anti-libertine treatises, Rosenthal further unpacks the ways in which sex comedies explore and test the threat posed by the libertine's desires and class betrayal. 'In the stateroom and in the bedroom', she concludes, 'what transpires ultimately matters less than the subsequent narrative that the community agrees to remember and the transgressions it remembers to forget' (p. 19). Social cohesion, she argues, is the result of strategic acts of oblivion (p. 25), a conclusion which she frames within the context of Charles II's post-Restoration strategy.

Tita Chico's essay 'Gimcrack's Legacy: Sex, Wealth, and the Theater of Experimental Philosophy' (*CompD* 42:i[2008] 29–49), although the last of the essays to focus on Restoration drama in the special issue, is the first of two essays this year which focus on the Royal Society and the figure of the virtuoso. Chico examines two theatrical incarnations of this figure: Gimcrack in Thomas Shadwell's *The Virtuoso* [1676] and Valeria in Susanna Centlivre's *The Basset-Table* [1706]. Chico contextualises the study within contemporary discourse on and histories of both the Royal Society's modest witness and the theatrical virtuoso. By doing so she argues that the dramatic representations in these plays were sites of contestation and clarification over experimental philosophy. She adds further, that they can 'more suggestively alert us to a specific set of associations with sexual desire and the circulation of wealth implicitly bound up with popularization and practice of experimental philosophy' (p. 32). Unpicking this in a detailed analysis of both plays, Chico demonstrates the relationship between experimental philosophy, domestic relations, social status and, by drawing comparisons across both male and female virtuosi, the role of gender identity in navigating these relationships. Moving away from the essays within the special issue of *Comparative Drama*, we also find the virtuoso, the Royal Society and the theatricality of science in Al Coppola's essay. This proves an interesting companion piece to Chico's, particularly with its distinctive political angle. In 'Retraining the Virtuoso's Gaze: Behn's *Emperor of the Moon*, the Royal Society, and the Spectacles of Science and Politics' (*ECS* 41:iv[2008] 481–506), Coppola tackles a play often considered deeply problematic, arguing that the very features considered so are used by Behn, as a committed Tory and in response to the troubling political culture of the late Restoration, to 'identify, stimulate, and ultimately retrain a troubling appetite for uncritical wonder in her audience' (p. 481). Coppola reads the play in the double context of its composition during the Tory Reaction of 1684, and its first performance towards the end of James II's unsettled reign in 1687. Yet he also suggests that *Emperor*'s interrogation of improper spectating is broadly cultural rather than narrowly political. It is, he argues, a critique of the culture of spectacle at the turn of the 1680s, of the Royal Society's role within this and of the enthusiastic virtuoso.

Aphra Behn makes her second appearance this year in Karol Cooper's essay, ' "Too high for souls like mine to hide": Feminine Retreat and Exposure in Aphra Behn's *The Feigned Curtizans*' (*RECTR* 23:iv[2008] 34–45). Through a close reading of the play, with some wider references, Cooper maintains that the notion of the soul was a central feature of Behn's work, and finds that soul rhetoric was used in opposition to an increasingly commercial society: in particular as a way for female characters to possess a unique identity beyond their bodily value. Female bodily value is also the central theme of Felicity Nussbaum's important essay, ' "Real, beautiful women": Actresses and *The Rival Queens*' (*ECLife* 32:ii[2008] 138–58), an essay which serves to remind us of the importance of understanding the period's drama in relation to the materiality of the stage. Drawing on both Jean Christophe Agnew's work *Worlds Apart: The Market and the Theatre in Anglo-American Thought, 1550–1750* [1986] and Natasha Korda's more recent essay 'Labours Lost: Women's Work and Early Modern Theatrical Commerce' (in Holland and Orgel, *From Script to Stage in Early Modern England* [2004]), Nussbaum argues for the importance of recognizing the 'genuine entrepreneurial skill and increasing economic authority' (p. 138) of long eighteenth-century actresses. Focusing upon Nathaniel Lee's tragedy *The Rival Queens*, Nussbaum attributes the popularity of the play across the period, to its actresses and their theatricalized staging of their rivalries, rather than to the performance of Alexander by leading men such as Charles Hart or Thomas Betterton. Instead of being a distraction from the main plot, Nussbaum argues, the actresses' performances were central to the play's popularity with contemporary audiences. Examining prologues and epilogues, as well as the anecdotes and folklore surrounding the play, Nussbaum demonstrates the extent to which these women's perform-ances 'overflowed with social meanings far in excess of their characters' (p. 147), collapsing boundaries between tragic play and comic epilogue, between public and private, and between illusion and life. Paying attention to the material reality of these women, 'who demonstrated hard-won professional achievement and significant economic power', Nussbaum reminds us that their performances shaped 'forms of female subjectivity beyond mere suffering heroines' (p. 147). Katherine R. Kellett also picks up on the theme of female subjectivity this year. In an essay on 'Performance, Performativity, and Identity in Margaret Cavendish's *The Convent of Pleasure*' (*SEL* 48[2008] 419–42) Kellett uses the lenses of queer theory and performance studies to offer an engaging analysis of a play never staged in the Restoration—in part, she argues, as a result of the play's resistance to classification within theatrical conventions. Resistance to classification, Kellett finds, is central to this play, which works both thematically and structurally to reveal the contingency of identity itself. The convent of the title, she demonstrates, 'becomes a rapidly changing environment that transforms with the language that creates it. Its resistance to stabilization—its curiously immaterial space—suggests that the subversive power of identity exists not merely in bodies, but in the discourse that produces those bodies' (p. 421). While Savage identifies the hetero-normative performances of the last two acts as appearing to reinforce patriarchy, she argues that, as a whole, the play's emphasis on the constructed nature of heterosexuality, the expansiveness of performance, and the role of language in the creation of gender roles, offer a challenge to those systems of power working to define and confine women's lives within heterosexual boundaries. Contesting the limits of performance itself, Cavendish's play, Kellett suggests, revels its resistance to assimilation or conformity.

While Kellett's essay examines a problematic play, Elizabeth Savage's ' "For want of Clelia": Re-Placing the Maternal Body in *The Twin-Rivals*' (*CompD* 42:iv[2008] 481–504) turns to problematic characters, continuing this year's focus on understanding drama through the material contexts of staging. The essay analyses the absence of midwives and mothers in Restoration comedy through an examination of the function and problematic power of both Mother Midnight (as performed in drag by the famous Restoration actor William Bullock), and of the unseen mother-to-be, Clelia, in *The Twin Rivals*. In the resistance of both female characters to easy circumscription into and control by the comic world, at the end of the play, Savage suggests that we can find the reason for the widespread absence of such figures across the period's comedies. Contextualizing Mother Midnight and her actions within contemporary discourse on the threatening power of the midwife to usurp proper lineage structures, Savage frames Midnight as the embodiment of fears over midwifery in the period: a character who 'controls, demeans, and even defaces the male body and male authority' (p. 492). Suggesting further that the patrilinear control of female sexuality is only barely maintained at the end of the play, with an impotent comic conclusion failing to adequately punish the character, Savage draws attention to the significance of the use of drag in the staging of the play. 'Character and actor are perpetually disjointed', she argues of famous comedian William Bullock's performance as Mother Midnight, 'producing an intensified comic effect' (p. 500). Functioning to arrest the possible proliferation of meanings associated with the actress's body and therefore the potential seriousness of the character's performance, Bullock's performative presence, Savage reminds us, is central to an understanding of the play.

The material conditions of the stage are the focus of two further works this year, both of which apply detailed analyses of historical sources in order to shed new light on the practical conditions under which theatre operated. Dawn Lewcock's monograph, *Sir William Davenant, the Court Masque, and the English Seventeenth-Century Scenic Stage c.1605–c.1700* offers a chronological study of developments in staging, crossing the conventional boundary of 1660 to demonstrate the influence of Davenant's pre-Restoration staging of masques on both his and others' post-Restoration scenic experimentation. Using dramaturgical and scenographical analyses of a range of plays, framed by a detailed historical understanding of the theatre of the period, chapters 4 to 7 take the reader from Davenant's establishment of Lincoln's Inn Fields through to the end of the century. Across this period, Lewcock suggests, Davenant, and subsequently his successors, experimented with ways of presenting the play as a whole invention (as in a masque), as well as in using scenery to shift the audience's understanding of the passing of time, spatial integrity and simultaneous action. Lewcock credits Davenant with leading a period of theatrical experimentation which cultivated an experience blending the aural and the visual, the actor and the audience. Ultimately, the book argues, the possibilities of the scenic stage were never fully realized in the seventeenth century, owing to both the economic mismanagement of the theatres and the changing political climate. Yet, by the end of the century, the scenic experimentation that Lewcock credits Davenant with leading had impacted both on the writing and on the reception of drama.

Juan A. Prieto-Pablos's essay, 'Admission Prices at the Dorset Garden Theatre: An Analysis of the Duke's Company's Bill for Nell Gwyn's Attendance (1674–1677)' (*TN* 62[2008] 63–75), is the second essay this year to offer an archaeo-historical reading of archival records, and the first of this author's contributions to the year's work. In this essay Prieto-Pablos seeks to answer questions left unanswered by Van Lennep's 1950 transcription of the bill of the title. He does this by examining variations in the prices paid by Nell Gwyn for both operatic and non-operatic performances and by comparing these results to other available data. Although he concludes that the limited data provided by the manuscript and other sources allows no definitive conclusion on admission prices, he nevertheless notes that the manuscript is useful for considering rates over the period. It also, he notes, challenges the idea that attendance rates remained relatively stable over the period. Prieto-Pablos's second contribution this year is notably distinct from his first, being a close reading of a play, albeit an anonymous play referenced only in the bill analysed in his first essay. In 'Ignoramus, *The Woman Turned Bully*, and Restoration Satire on the Common Lawyer' (*SEL* 48[2008] 523–46) Prieto-Pablos makes a convincing case for the merits of this largely neglected play, drawing both on an understanding of the legal and social context in which it appeared and on its relationship to its antecedent, Ruggle's Latin comedy *Ignoramus* (first performed 1615). Arguing that *The Woman Turned Bully* can be read as a re-elaboration of *Ignoramus,* written in response to the Stuart's troubled relations with the law and its practitioners, Prieto-Pablos positions this play as a biting satire which declined in popularity only when the changing political climate of the Exclusion Crisis and Popish Plot demanded new types of Ignoramus.

Two essays this year examine the drama of these years of constitutional crisis. Tracey Miller-Tomlinson's 'Pathos and Politics in John Banks' *Vertue Betray'd or Anna Bullen* (1682)' (*RECTR* 23:i[2008] 46–67) and ' "Seated in the heart": *Venice Preserv'd* Between Pathos and Politics' by Zenon Luis-Martinez (*RECTR* 23:ii[2008] 23–42) both, as their titles suggest, examine the relationship between dramatic pathos and politics, coincidentally also both focusing on plays written in 1682. The arguments made by each are also in accord. Miller-Tomlinson argues that *Vertue Betray'd* 'politicizes affective response in ways that qualify traditional views of seventeenth-century historical drama as degenerating into essentially apolitical romance' (p. 47). She offers a reading of the play which locates effective political action in the affective experience. Taking a compatible approach, in considering *Venice Preserv'd*, Luis-Martinez rejects the conventional reading of this play in terms of either dramatic pathos or Tory opportunism. Instead of being mutually exclusive, the essay argues, the 'aesthetic and emotional universes of *Venice Preserv'd* are inseparable from the play's far-reaching political questions' (p. 26). Our understanding of the pathetic, Luis-Martinez argues, is in need of revision. It must be understood in relation to Restoration experiments with dramatic style and theoretical reflections on tragic form, in which the pathetic can be seen as an aesthetic, rhetorical method and style rather than as a thematic notion. In this context, and drawing on Hobbesian ideas around the relationship between individual interest and the social covenant, Luis-Martinez offers a reading of the play in which the individual and the political are intertwined. Hobbes is also drawn on in Aspasia Velissariou's essay 'The Hobbesian Other in Congreve's Comedies' (*RECTR* 32:i[2008] 68–81). In this Velissariou considers the ways in which Congreve's comedies wrestle with shifting notions of the individual, critiquing the notion of the Hobbesian Other. Looking at a range of Congreve's work Velissariou argues that the playwright's critique of aristocratic degeneration requires more attention than it has received from scholars so far. Finally, this year sees the paperback publication of Susan J. Owen's invaluable *A Companion to Restoration Drama*, providing, at a student-friendly price, twenty-five essays from leading scholars in the field.

(b) Dryden

As critics treat Dryden's *Indian Queen* as the first of his heroic plays, an argument that it is not Dryden's but Howard's commands attention: in 'Sir Robert Howard, John Dryden, and the Attribution of *The Indian Queen*' (*Library* 9:iii[2008] 324–48) David Wallace Spielman emphasizes what should be well known, that this play was published in Howard's *Four New Plays* [1665] and was not included in Dryden's 'Catalogue' of his own works [1691]. In a note explaining the 'Connection' between it and *The Italian Emperor* he says he wrote 'part' of the earlier work. Congreve included it in Dryden's *Dramatic Works* [1717] as having been written by Howard and Dryden, Scott included it in the *Works* [1818] as being mainly Dryden's, and the California editors were sure it was 'essentially' his. H.J. Oliver (*YWES* 44[1965] 227) and Robert D. Hume are almost the only modern scholars who have opposed the attribution to Dryden. It has been suggested that Howard appropriated Dryden's work, but the truth is that Dryden scholars, without adducing new evidence, have appropriated Howard's.

Also concerned with attribution, James A. Winn's 'John Dryden, Court Theatricals, and the "Epilogue to the Faithful Shepherdess"' (*Restoration* 31:ii[2008] 45–54) makes a good case, on circumstantial and stylistic evidence, for thinking that this anonymous epilogue was supplied by the Poet Laureate. It was spoken at a performance of Fletcher's play 'by the little young ladies of the Court' at St James's Palace, home of the Duke and Duchess of York, in 1670. The young ladies revived a good many plays, including *Aureng-Zebe*.

Critics love the Restoration's heady mixture of the erotic and the political. John Denman's '"Too hasty to stay": Erotic and Political Timing in *Marriage à la Mode*' (*Restoration* 31:ii[2008] 1–23) refers to many earlier critiques, in which the play's 'political import' has been 'infrequently grasped', and agrees with Richard Kroll (*YWES* 76[1998] 320 and *YWES* 88[2009] 608–9), for whom it is 'a meditation on the conditions and limitations of Stuart power'. Denman maintains that both erotic and political characters are obsessed with time and timing. If I understand him rightly, marriages and political settlements are necessary, but moments when they seem to transcend time are rare; I found myself meditating on the 'political import' of simultaneous orgasm.

Books Reviewed

Appleby, David J. *Black Bartholomew's Day: Preaching, Polemic and Restoration Nonconformity*. ManUP. [2008] pp. 255. £55 ISBN 9 7807 1907 5612.

Dunan-Page, Anne, and Beth Lynch, eds. *Roger L'Estrange and the Making of Restoration Culture*. Ashgate. [2008] pp. xvii + 236. £60 ISBN 9 7807 5465 8009.

Dutcher, James M., and Anne Lake Prescott, eds. *Renaissance Historicisms: Essays in Honor of Arthur F. Kinney*. UDelP. [2008] pp. 355. $67.50 ISBN 9 7808 7413 0010.

Lewcock, Dawn. *Sir William Davenant, the Court Masque, and the English Seventeenth-Century Scenic Stage c.1605–c.1700*. Cambria Press. [2008] pp. vii + 33. £67.95 ISBN 9 7816 0497 5789.

McDowell, Nicholas. *Poetry and Allegiance in the English Civil Wars: Marvell and the Cause of Wit*. OUP. [2008] pp. 295. £53 ISBN 9 7801 9927 8008.

Owen, Susan J., ed. *A Companion to Restoration Drama*. Blackwell. [2008] pp. v + 456. £26.99 ISBN 9 7814 0517 6101.

Owens, W.R., and Stuart Sim, eds. *Reception, Appropriation, Recollection: Bunyan's Pilgrim's Progress*. Lang. [2008] pp. 253. £31 ISBN 9 7830 3910 7209.

Sambras, Gilles, ed. *New Perspectives on Andrew Marvell.* EPURE. [2008] pp. 194. £16.65 ISBN 9 7829 1527 1218.

Thormählen, Marianne, ed. *English Now: Selected Papers from the 20th IAUPE Conference in Lund 2007.* Centre for Languages and Literature. LundU. [2008] pp. xx + 354. $149.50 ISBN 9 7891 9769 3509.

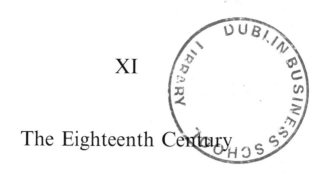

XI

The Eighteenth Century

ELIZA O'BRIEN, ELLES SMALLEGOOR,
SANDRO JUNG AND DAVID E. SHUTTLETON

This chapter has three sections: 1. General and Prose; 2. The Novel; 3. Poetry.
Section 1 is by Eliza O'Brien; section 2 is by Elles Smallegoor and Sandro
Jung; section 3 is by David E. Shuttleton.

1. General and Prose

The motivation behind Zoë Kinsley's *Women Writing the Home Tour,
1682–1812* is that an analysis of accounts of the Home Tour is 'central to our
understanding of the true nature of travel and travel writing, both in the years
being covered and also in the subsequent era of mass tourism' (p. 2).
Representations of otherness at home, national identity and regional diversity
in the accounts that survey England, Wales and Scotland, are addressed here,
drawn from an interesting range of previously unpublished manuscript
sources. Kinsley locates her study of women travel writers in the midst of
the recent turn in criticism that considers travel writing by women in terms
informed by but not restricted to gender: the writer's social class, companions,
geographical location and economics are also factored in. Similarities to and
differences from male travel writers are discussed throughout, but women
writers are the focus here because of the relative neglect of these sources. The
writers surveyed by Kinsley, such as Celia Fiennes, Ann Radcliffe, Hester
Lynch Piozzi and Dorothy Wordsworth, are joined by more obscure writers
such as Mary Morgan, Anne Grant, and Elizabeth Isabella Spence (sourced
from printed travelogues and letters), and the travel journals of Dorothy
Richardson, Elizabeth Diggle's letters, and the writings of Elizabeth Cobbold
(all manuscripts). The chapters are divided into three sections. Part I, 'Travels
and Texts: Considering the Travelogue Form', discusses form, the personal
and subjective yet empirical nature of travelogues, and the organizational
structure that emerges from a Europe-wide systemization from other subjects,
such as linguistics and botany. Part II, 'Perspectives on the Landscape:
Detachment and Destabilization in Home Tour Writing', focuses upon the
relation between print and manuscript, leading to a discussion of aesthetics

Year's Work in English Studies, Volume 89 (2010) © *The English Association; all rights reserved*
doi:10.1093/ywes/maq002

and landscape description and women writers' engagement with preconceived notions of 'feminine' writing and participation in landscape and travel. Part III, 'Travelling Identities: Travel Theory and the Emergence of British Tourism', explores home as other, difference, spectacle, and the rhetoric that expounds and explodes such theories.

In *Refiguring the Coquette: Essays on Culture and Coquetry*, Shelley King and Yaël Schlick have put together a fascinating collection of essays. It is an investigation into the breadth and variety of the figure of the coquette throughout the eighteenth century, structured in three parts, 'dealing first with the constitution of the coquette, then with the moral and disciplinary discourse that traditionally attends her, and finally with the importance of coquetry in the formation of masculinity in the long eighteenth century' (p. 27). When returned to a position of importance in the eighteenth century the figure of the coquette, the editors assert, offers 'a site from which to explore broad, cultural concerns of the period' (p. 13) across a variety of genres. Following on from Peter Cryle and Lisa O'Connell, editors of *Libertine Enlightenment: Sex, Liberty and Licence in the Eighteenth Century* [2004], King and Schlick want to critically recover the coquette in much the same way as the rake and the libertine have been recovered, showing the subject worthy of extended, intensive analysis beyond the familiar representation, and discussing coquetry as the basis for a conceptual framework most usually in relation to gender constructs both male and female, but also as a means of exploring consumption, literature and class. The coquette 'no longer appears an easily definable figure with fixed parameters, and several of these essays themselves problematize the definitional impulse' (p. 27). There is much discussion in each essay about how best to define the term, how it was used in the eighteenth century, and what it signified. The collection is devoted mostly to examining dramatic and fictional texts, but there are some essays here of interest to the general reader. Part I is entitled 'Facades, Performances, and Self-Fashioning: Constructing the Coquette', and contains an essay by Theresa Braunschneider, 'The People that Things Make: Coquettes and Consumer Culture in Early Eighteenth-Century British Satire' (pp. 39–61), which discusses consumer desire and the construction of the figure of the coquette. Part II, 'The Perils and Politics of Femininity: Embodying the Coquette', addresses drama and fiction, but in part III, 'Gentlemen and Macaroni: Coquetry and the Discourses of Masculinity', two essays address the fascinating subject of the male coquette, or coquet, in the eighteenth century. Herbert Klein's 'The Reform'd Male: Coquets and Gentlemen' (pp. 143–63), and 'Garrick's *Male-Coquette* and Theatrical Masculinities' (pp. 164–98) by Leslie Ritchie, show how the development of such a figure is bound up in ideas of male domestication.

An important collection of essays this year was *Everyday Revolutions: Eighteenth-Century Women Transforming Public and Private*, edited by Diane E. Boyd and Marta Kvande. This lively and timely collection interrogates current critical understanding of the bourgeois public sphere and re-examines it in relation to, but also as a challenge to, the Habermasian notion of the same, primarily in its exploration of the public sphere in the late seventeenth and early eighteenth centuries. In doing so it pre-dates Habermas's conception of the beginning of the sphere by some decades, and it explores the permeability of the division between the public and private spheres, using this binary opposition as a starting point for exploration but resisting its attempts to limit study or conception of the public sphere. Awareness of these limits is an important underlying principle of this collection for the editors, who write: 'critical attempts to distance our cultural analysis from the public/ private debate must also rely on the history of the binary itself—how we have used it and how we wish to discard it' (p. 24). Although the main focus of the volume is upon women's fiction, Paula R. Backscheider's 'Hanging On and Hanging In: Women's Struggle to Participate in Public Sphere Debate' (pp. 30–66) provides an excellent point of orientation for women's general involvement in writing and debate, with Aruna Krishnamurthy's essay ' "The Constant Action of our Lab'ring Hands": Mary Collier's Demystification of Work and Womanhood in the Early Eighteenth Century' (pp. 67–93) providing a counterweight to the subsequent essays on Sheridan, Burney, Edgeworth, Austen, Wollstonecraft and, unexpectedly in this company, Defoe.

Another volume of essays this year concerned with debate, influence and participation is *The Atlantic Enlightenment*, edited by Susan Manning and Francis D. Cogliano. This collection of essays results in part from a seminar series and a colloquium held in 2002 at the University of Edinburgh that was devoted to a discussion on the existence of an Atlantic Enlightenment. It is a significant examination of 'the emergence of the Atlantic as an important conceptual paradigm' (p. 3) in Enlightenment studies across literature, culture and philosophy. The awareness of the spatial dimension of the Atlantic in relation to theories of the development of ideas and societies is one that pervades these essays. Space, distance and geography create a distinct flexibility and variety not only in the subjects here discussed but in the methodologies used, chiefly historiographical but also grounded in close readings of texts. As with Boyd and Kvande, novels as literary sources tend to dominate this volume, but Adam Smith and David Hume receive useful new readings. Emma Rothschild's 'David Hume and the Seagods of the Atlantic' (pp. 81–96) discusses Hume's 'Atlantic milieux' (p. 95) and the restless qualities of the *philosophe*'s world, and Peter S. Onuf, in 'Adam Smith and the Crisis of the American Union' (pp. 149–64), offers an interpretation of Smith's *Wealth of Nations* in the context of American independence and emerging nationhood. A useful companion to this volume is Sarah Pearsall's *Atlantic Families: Lives and Letters in the Later Eighteenth Century*. Pearsall investigates the role played by family correspondence in America, Britain, the American colonies and the British Caribbean in keeping families united across vast distances, and uncovers much fascinating detail of conditions and concerns in daily life in this period. Also of interest here is *British and American Letter Manuals, 1680–1810*, edited by Eve Tavor Bannet. This is a four-volume collection of letter manuals, the most popular form of conduct literature in this period, concerned with reading, writing, form and content for both private and professional writers. As such, it is another useful addition to scholars interested in the eighteenth-century print market. A wide variety of British and American publications are reprinted here, and the material is well organized across the volumes in the following order: volume 1, *Academies of*

Complement 1680–1805, volume 2, *Secretaries, 1687–1760*, volume 3, *Complete Letter Writers, 1740–1795*, and volume 4, *The Art of Correspondence, 1770–1810*.

In *Genres of the Credit Economy: Mediating Value in Eighteenth- and Nineteenth-Century Britain* Mary Poovey presents a magisterial new work on credit which addresses the development of the credit economy with that of the book trade. She examines how the classifications which underpin culture and literature change over time, either by design or accident, beginning in the late seventeenth century and finishing in the 1870s. She begins with admirable simplicity, stating that 'one of the functions performed by imaginative writing in general was to mediate value—that is, to help people understand the new credit economy and the market model of value that it promoted' (pp. 1–2), before plunging into a dense and carefully theorized account of value in literary and economic terms. She maps the development of distinctions between fact and fiction, investigating the elevation of the non-imaginative and non-literary forms, such as economic writing, which broke up the sense of literature as it was in the eighteenth century and led to a desperate struggle between fact and fiction in the nineteenth, which affected novels particularly. Of special interest to this section is part V, 'Delimiting Literature, Defining *Literary Value*', whose chapters focus upon the mirroring of the economic division of labour in the literary world. Here Poovey follows the workings of the literary hierarchy to preserve literature from the demands of readers, thereby splitting the literary world into market and art, and investigates the resulting hierarchy of reading that is produced by this split. Concern with generic differentiation follows through to the form of the book. Historical and methodological chapters are sectioned off into interchapters within the main text of literary progression, digression and textual analysis which lends an almost encyclopaedic feel to the book. Beginning with the work of Sir James Steuart and Thomas Bridges, and proceeding via William Cobbett, John Stuart Mill and W. Stanley Jevons to the 'Literary Appropriations' of finance by Dickens, Eliot and Trollope, Poovey's work on the worth of literature and literary scholarship could not be more timely.

In Kate Loveman's *Reading Fictions, 1660–1740: Deception in English Literary and Political Culture* a different kind of value is considered, that of the pleasure of deception. This is a valuable new account of late seventeenth- and early eighteenth-century reading practices and their relation to suspicion and deception. Loveman's guiding principle in this investigation is that readers' interpretative practices were based upon the idea during this period that reading was 'an exercise in detecting falsehoods and avoiding deception' (p. 2), and she explores the political and literary consequences of this exercise. Private and public hoaxes shaped readerships and conditioned audiences. A cultural fascination with shams, coupled with the nature of prose writing being viewed as closer to truth than poetry, meant that the detection of deception in prose, whether in content or in attribution of authorship, became a serious concern. Loveman is careful to avoid reading anachronistically, reminding her readers that what we may view as patently untrue may have been perfectly acceptable as truth to early modern readers. Loveman achieves this by focusing on readers' actual responses, not those merely implied or presumed. In the first chapter, 'Sceptical Reading in the Seventeenth and Early Eighteenth Centuries' (pp. 19–46), careful interpretation and location of contemporary distortions or formulaic references and codes for description enables Loveman to access as closely as possible the contemporary reader's response, setting the framework for her subsequent examination of interpretation and truth. The following seven chapters discuss in turn real-life hoaxes, print, and literary deceptions. Chapter 3, '"Florishing Lyes": Coffee-House Wit in the Restoration" (pp. 61–84), uses jest books, play texts and printed hoaxes. Chapter 5, 'News, Novels and Imposture, 1688–1702' (pp. 109–126), discusses political prose, and chapters 6, 7 and 8 discuss in turn Defoe, Swift and the *Shamela* debate, investigating the relationship between a writer and his readers over a series of publications, such as Swift's satirical writings, in chapter 7, 'Swift's Bites: Eighteenth-Century Raillery in Theory and Practice' (pp. 153–74), and the conditioning of his audience to accept or interpret such writing.

In *Deception and Detection in Eighteenth-Century Britain*, by contrast, Jack Lynch takes as his main focus the critics whose job it was to decide between counterfeit and genuine literary works, such as Edmond Malone, who exposed the Shakespeare forgeries by William Henry Ireland, Richard Bentley, who attacked *Epistles of Phalaris* in 1699, and Samuel Johnson. In such chapters as 'Recognising a Fake When You See One' (pp. 11–30) and 'All Manner of Experience and Observation' (pp. 91–108), Lynch analyses the arguments and discussions that raged throughout the long eighteenth century and pervaded so many aspects of the culture not only in theorizations of what defines fraud but the nature of authenticity itself, or what he calls 'the rhetoric of disproof' (p. vii), discriminating between fraud and the arguments about fraud. Like Loveman, Lynch attests to the importance of careful reading and interpretation of his sources, demanding scholarly evidence as much as the victims of eighteenth-century literary hoaxes do and employing a judicious amount of scepticism when examining such evidence. The result is a non-chronological but well-plotted, informative and subtle account of reading practices, deception and authenticity, whose painstaking analysis is presented in a lively manner that seems to have absorbed much of the playfulness of its subject, without losing any of the seriousness of the issues at stake. The development of the law of evidence and literary criticism is among the subjects that Lynch links to the concept of authenticity, unfolding a view of the eighteenth century that is predicated upon collisions with reality: truth, either mutable or fixed, is defined by its relation to falsehood, fraud, forgery, imposture and deceptions of all kinds, excluding those of a religious or fictional nature. Lynch draws his subjects for analysis broadly from counterfeits which claim to be true, with the familiar Ossian, Mary Toft, Elizabeth Canning, and William Henry Ireland woven into discussions of legal evidence and the work of Geoffrey Gilbert and Jeremy Bentham, philosophical consistency and logic, memory, motive, and wilful credulity. Authenticity is linked to certainty, and as Lynch argues in this perceptive and persuasive study, pursuing authenticity, or combating doubt, is the foundation for much eighteenth-century thought and provides the bedrock for its society.

Authenticity and hoaxing of another kind are discussed in Min Wild's account of the periodical *The Midwife, or Old Woman's Magazine* (1750–3) and its author Christopher Smart, in *Christopher Smart and Satire: 'Mary Midnight' and the Midwife*. Wild's study is devoted to the fictitious writer and editor of *The Midwife*, 'Mary Midnight', and how the figure of the invented persona functioned in the eighteenth-century periodical press and the manner in which it contributed to discussions of authorship, as well as matters of gender, politics and identity. Careful to state her resistance to investigating Smart and Midnight in a series of simple binary oppositions, Wild examines the rhetorical strategies of the periodical, its literary antecedents in the marketplace, and the nature of Smart's conservative politics and his satires, as well as incorporating a discussion of strategic use of Jacobite rhetoric and his critique of Enlightenment philosophy in *The Midwife*. Clearly written and with its argument carefully plotted from chapter to chapter, it provides a straightforward and thoughtful read. Chapter 1, 'Personal Identity and Personae in the Eighteenth-Century Periodical' (pp. 15–42), provides a good general orientation for the specific investigation into 'Mary Midnight' and Christopher Smart that follows, and chapter 4, ' "A Perfect *Swiss* in Writing": Literature and Authorship in the *Midwife*' (pp. 103–32), is of particular interest in relation to current scholarship on attribution of authorship, which has resulted in some important new work this year.

In Thomas Lockwood's 'Did Fielding Write for the *Craftsman*?' (*RES* 59[2008] 86–117), Lockwood overturns Martin Battestin's argument that Fielding wrote for the *Craftsman* by examining Battestin's method for attributing the articles in question, with the addition of contrary evidence which Battestin discounted in his 1989 book, suggesting instead that the author of the essays attributed to Fielding is in fact Nicholas Amhurst, and that Fielding himself never wrote for the periodical. It is a clear, well-argued and rigorous examination of the subject. In a similar vein, in 'After Defoe, before the *Dunciad*: Giles Jacob and *A Vindication of the Press*' (*RES* 59[2008] 487–507) Stephen Bernard investigates the attributed authorship of *A Vindication of the Press* to Defoe and finds instead that Giles Jacob is the more plausible author, through an examination of the world of booksellers, pamphleteering, anonymity and canon formation. This examination is followed by a discussion of how this new attribution may alter Jacob's reputation as one of Pope's dunces.

Another myth is exploded in Ashley Marshall's 'The Myth of Scriblerus' (*JECS* 31[2008] 77–99). This offers a thorough historical investigation of the term and the club itself, examining its applicability as well as its genesis. It banishes some persistent critical misconceptions about the club and its standing in the eighteenth century and provides an orderly investigation into the term and a correction to the scholarly response to it. Also in this volume, Earla Wilputte maps the theories of consciousness, physiology, gender and the passions as they develop though the figure of the Mind Midwife in 'Midwife for the Mind: Delivering the Passions in Aaron Hill's *The Plain Dealer* (1724)' (*JECS* 31[2008] 1–15), charting the progressions and alterations of these theories though Hill's periodical. The June edition of *JECS* is a special volume on slavery, with an introduction by Brycchan Carey, 'Slavery and Antislavery'

(*JECS* 31[2008] 191–6) and a wide range of essays discussing slavery in relation to *Mansfield Park*, *Oroonoko* and the French anti-slavery debate, the letters of Ignatius Sancho, and a special focus on Restoration and eighteenth-century drama, such as Jenna M. Gibbs's contribution, 'Slavery, Liberty and Revolution in John Leacock's Pro-Patriot Tragicomedy, *The Fall of British Tyranny: or, American Liberty Triumphant* (1776)' (*JECS* 31[2008] 241–58). The September volume is also a special edition, this time entitled 'Text, Image and Contemporary Society' with a distinctly European tone, mostly discussing French subject-matter. Of general interest are Penny Brown's 'Capturing (and Captivating) Childhood: The Role of Illustrations in Eighteenth-Century Children's Books in Britain and France' (*JECS* 31[2008] 419–51) and Troy Bickham's 'Defining Good Food: Cookery-Book Illustrations in England' (*JECS* 31[2008] 473–90).

As with cookery books, another unexpected source of literary interest arises in Ala Alryyes, 'War at a Distance: Court-Martial Narratives in the Eighteenth Century' (*ECS* 41[2008] 525–42). This investigation into a minor prose genre, the court-martial narrative and the matrix it occupies between nation, crime, law and rhetorical flourish, opens up a small but valuable field of study in eighteenth-century writing, which is especially useful in relation to the continued expansion of scholarship on crime, law and literature. Also in this volume, Lisa Wynne Smith's ' "An Account of an Unaccountable Distemper": The Experience of Pain in Early Eighteenth-Century England and France' (*ECS* 41[2008] 459–80) provides an investigation into pain narratives, chiefly collections of letters from 1700 to 1740. Not only the theory and practice of medicine in the early eighteenth century but also how it is represented in narrative form is considered here, with the shared vocabulary common to the English and French letter-writers receiving a good examination. In ' "Call No Man Master Upon Earth": Mary Astell's Tory Feminism and an Unknown Correspondence' (*ECS* 21[2008] 507–23), by Sarah Apetrie, previously unknown letters between Mary Astell, the nonjuror George Hickes and an anonymous 'Lady' are used to examine the relation between Astell's conservative religious views and her principle of non-resistance in her published writings with her response to schism and the controversy over nonjurors in private.

The fall edition of *Eighteenth-Century Life* is also concerned with letters, in a special edition devoted to 'The Correspondence of Henry St John and Sir William Trumbull, 1698–1710' (*ECLife* 32:iii[2008] 23–179). It is prefaced by a long introduction (pp. 1–19) to the collection by its editor, Adrian C. Lashmore-Davies, and followed by an index to the letters (pp. 181–8). It is a rich treasure-trove of scholarly interest and careful research and editing. The spring edition of the journal is devoted to the proceedings of the thirteenth international David Nichol Smith Seminar in Eighteenth Century Studies held at the University of Otago, New Zealand. In the introduction Jocelyn Harris and Shef Rogers address the importance of this seminar and the wide variety of subjects covered by it, testifying to the richness of the material and the high level of scholarship (*ECLife* 32:ii[2008] 1–2). Of relevance here in this substantial edition are the following essays. Christina Smylitopoulos's 'Rewritten and Reused: Imagining the Nabob through "Upstart Iconography"' (*ECLife* 32:ii[2008] 39–59) discusses the representation of the Nabob through eighteenth-century graphic satire, focusing upon three main images, the 'Colossus', the 'cit' and the 'equestrian'. In Chris Ackerley's '"The Last Ditch": Shades of Swift in Samuel Beckett's "Fingal" (*ECLife* 32:ii[2008] 60–7) the influence of Swift's early writings upon Beckett receives only a brief mention, but Swift is addressed at greater length by Clive Probyn in 'Blindness and Insight: The World, the Text (of Jonathan Swift) and the Criticism of Edward Said' (*ECLife* 32:ii[2008] 68–80), in a full engagement with writing, power, influence and interpretation. It is an absorbing, lucid piece of scholarship. Ruth Perry investigates the historical factors influencing the establishment and encouragement of folk music and the language of folk music in '"The Finest Ballads": Women's Oral Tradition in Eighteenth-Century Scotland' (*ECLife* 32:ii[2008] 81–97), and Gillian Paku, in 'The Age of Anon: Johnson Rewrites the Name of the Author' (*ECLife* 32:ii[2008] 98–109), examines anonymity and fame in an account of the individualist history of authorship and Johnson's own theories of author, reader and collaboration.

In a particularly rewarding summer edition of *Studies in English Literature* Adam Potkay's 'Recent Studies in the Restoration and Eighteenth Century' (*SEL* 48[2008] 693–729) presents a very useful, wide-ranging and cogent account of recent trends in eighteenth-century criticism, focusing upon the most significant monographs. Potkay views the shifts in criticism and the new paths opened up within the past twenty years, before moving on to a closer analysis of trends beneath the headings 'Public Spheres and Reading Nation', 'The Novel', 'Genres and Themes' and 'Women's Writings'. In 'The Sentimental Satire of Sophia Baddeley' by Amy Cully (*SEL* 48[2008] 677–82) there is an engaging account of *The Memoirs of Mrs Sophia Baddeley* [1787] and the relationship between the actress and her biographer Elizabeth Steele, focusing upon the memoir's place in critical conceptions of gender politics, sensibility, female authorship and satire in private and public writings. Thomas Reinert, in 'Adam Ferguson's Aesthetic Idea of Community Spirit' (*SEL* 48[2008] 613–32), supplies a good addition to recent studies in luxury and virtue. He focuses upon Ferguson's writings which use literary analogies in discussing society, and investigates Ferguson's conception of the aesthetics of society in relation to imaginative fiction. Richard Squibbs, in 'Civic Humorism and the Eighteenth-Century Periodical Essay' (*ELH* 72[2008] 389–413), presents an excellent article which traces the American and British periodical essay from Steel and Goldsmith through Washington Irving and Ralph Waldo Emerson, and maps the ways in which the rhetoric of irony and whimsicality of the essays forms a part of the broader social critique that these essayists offer, as well as a discussion of the forms of civic humanism with which they engage. Chris Roulston's 'Space and the Representation of Marriage in Eighteenth-Century Advice Literature' (*ECent* 49[2008] 25–41) considers social space, the private self and gender from a variety of sources and perspectives related to advice literature, and examines the common thread of anxiety about the control over marriage (or lack thereof) exhibited by such sources. In '"Beings that have existence only in ye minds of men": State Finance and the Origins of the Collective Imagination' (*ECent* 49[2008]

117–39) Robert Mitchell presents a fascinating argument about the role of the print media, principally journalism and pamphlets, in the development of early eighteenth-century theories of imagination in relation to finance. *Studies in Voltaire and the Eighteenth Century* presents its usual wide range of articles of both general and specialized interest, but in a special edition entitled 'Architecture, Cultural History and Luxury in the Eighteenth Century: Selected Papers from the Voltaire Foundation Postgraduate Conference 2007' Stéphane Roy offers a reading of Anglomania in art and literature in relation to bilingual-text prints and engravings, in 'The Art of Trade and the Economics of Taste: the English Print Market in Paris, 1770–1800' (*SVEC* 6[2008] 167–92). In a volume of essays dedicated to John Renwick, Russell Goulbourne analyses the English press coverage of the execution in 1762 of John Calas in 'Voltaire and the Calas Affair in England' (*SVEC* 10[2008] 159–70). He examines translations of Voltaire's writings on the matter, newspapers such as *The London Chronicle, St James Chronicle* and the *Gentleman's Magazine*, as well as the reproduction of a forged letter from Voltaire to D'Alembert, within the context of English and French animosity in the aftermath of the Seven Years War. In the same edition Adrienne Mason provides further discussion of translation in 'Unheard Voices: Two English Translations of Voltaire's *L'Ingénu*' (pp. 237–49) by treating translated texts from 1768 and 1771 as autonomous works, set against a consideration of generic hierarchies in British literature. Finally, *Scriblerian and the Kit-Cats* (*Scriblerian* 40:i/ii[2007–8], 41:i[2008]) has once again has provided two substantial news journals with an extremely broad range of very brief reviews of books and articles from the past few years, covering biography, drama, prose, poetry and ephemera relating to Pope, Swift, Gay and the broad (or perhaps loose) circle of their associates

And so to Johnson. In the winter edition of *Eighteenth-Century Life* Paul Tankard, in 'Johnson and the Walkable City' (*ECLife* 32:i[2008] 1–22), provides a thoughtful account of Johnson and the metropolis and the limits of individual independence, as well as an examination of Johnson's philosophy of walking. Much as a reader encounters Johnson's thoughts 'through miscellaneous encounters' (p. 2) so too, in Tankard's account, does Johnson himself experience the city. In Andrew Barnaby's 'Cringing Before the Law: Milton's Satan, Samuel Johnson and the Anxiety of Worship' from *The Sacred and Profane in English Renaissance Literature*, edited by Mary Papazian (pp. 321–44), Johnson makes an unexpected appearance when he is brought in as support in the eternal debate on the purpose of man's existence. In his discussion of Milton's *Paradise Lost* and the problem of the slippery nature of the representation of God and Satan, and the reasons given for man's existence, Barnaby invokes Johnson's writings on devotion, poetics and the aims of reading sacred history from *Lives of the Poets* to explore his analysis of anxiety and humbling before God. Regarding Johnson's critique of metaphysical poetry as an argument that 'devotional poetry merely embarrasses itself' (p. 30), Barnaby presents an interesting reading of poetry and humiliation in both the reception of *Paradise Lost* and the struggle of Satan himself, but one which is of use to those interested in Johnson's theories of reading and interpretation as well as to scholars of poetry.

Easily the most significant publication this year is Mark Wildermuth's *Print, Chaos and Complexity: Samuel Johnson and Eighteenth-Century Media Culture*, which focuses upon Johnson's non-fiction prose and argues perceptively and with both subtlety and rigour. Following on from the challenges set out by Adrian Johns and David McKitterick in relation to textual stability and authorial intent and their attempts to overthrow notions of fixity regarding pre-1800 print culture, Wildermuth states his purpose as one which, by the recovery of eighteenth-century theories of the relationship between textual stability and instability, re-evaluates Johnson's conception of the mediating force of print and its impact upon society. He writes: 'My argument is that we cannot fully appreciate the connectedness and continuity of Johnson's ideas in these disparate areas [ethics, society and aesthetics] without considering how important print mediation was for Johnson's conception of the dilemmas facing his generation since the beginning of the eighteenth century. I argue that Samuel Johnson, like modern media theoreticians such as Jean Baudrillard, Friedrich Kittler, and Paul Virilio, seeks to understand the impact of contemporary forms of mediation on human epistemology and ethics' (p. 16). Wildermuth examines the ways in which modern theories of mediation have their foundations in the past, but this is a broadly historical and theoretical account, and his approach is not anachronistic. In his consideration of the threatening nature of print, Wildermuth focuses on non-fiction prose 'because my task is to explicate Johnson's most self-conscious attempts to elucidate a philosophy on information culture and complexity' (p. 21). In such chapters as 'Complexity and Mediated Culture in Johnson's Moral Periodical Prose' (pp. 88–108), 'Johnson's Politics in the Milieu of Informatics' (pp. 109–34) and 'Textual Instability, Print, and Complex Dynamics in the Johnsonian Mediated Cultural Milieu' (pp. 25–61), with a chapter discussing Pope's *Essay on Man* as an anticipation of Johnson (pp. 62–87), Wildermuth has furnished us with an ambitious, much-needed study on eighteenth-century mediation and the ways in which print can mediate political theory and practice and encourage or discourage social stability.

With the approach of Johnson's tercentenary come two reissues of Boswell's *Life of Johnson*. Penguin's new, unabridged edition, edited and introduced by David Womersley, is an excellent, scholarly one, with two appendices providing a selection of variants across the first three editions, as well as a comprehensive biographical index. By contrast, the Oxford edition, edited by R.W. Chapman and introduced by Pat Rogers, is the second reissue of the 1980 edition. It contains no new material. Dover has published a straightforward edition of the text of Boswell and Johnson's *A Journey to the Western Isles of Scotland* and *The Journal of a Tour to the Hebrides*, with no supplementary information apart from a map of Scotland. An equally sparse volume is Lyle Larsen's *James Boswell as his Contemporaries Saw Him*. It is a cheerful anthology of brief extracts from Boswell's contemporaries and literary associates, drawn mostly from letters by such luminaries as Fanny Burney, Anna Seward, Peter Pindar, Thomas Grey, David Garrick and Hester Lynch Piozzi, but also from literary reviews and anonymous remarks from the journals of the day. The accounts by Boswell's contemporaries are interspersed with extracts from Boswell's memoirs, and the whole is arranged chronologically in 'Early Years 1740–68', 'Middle Years 1769–85', 'Later Years 1786–95' and 'Postmortem Years 1796–1836', followed by biographical notes of the authors quoted therein. A selection from Johnson's *Dictionary* is offered by Neil Johnson in his compilation *Dr Johnson's Reliquary of Rediscovered Words*, a pocket-sized novelty book consisting of a selection of the more obscure words from the *Dictionary*. More substantial fare is provided by Jeffrey O'Connell and Thomas E. O'Connell in *Friendships Across Ages: Johnson and Boswell; Holmes and Laski*. This interesting account of friendship is structured, cultural and historical divides notwithstanding, upon common themes: close male friendships of long duration; the contrast of youth and age, inexperience and something approaching wisdom; the representation of friendship in journals and letters; a shared background in legal studies (shared further by the authors of this lively book); the opposition of liberal perspectives with conservative ones; and intense sociability. The Holmes and Laski of the title, possibly unfamiliar to eighteenth-century scholars, are Oliver Wendell Holmes, a judge and author of *The Common Law*, who eventually became a senior justice in the American Supreme Court in the early nineteenth century, and his friend Harold Laski, an English émigré first to Canada and then America, a teacher and writer involved in Labour Party politics who ended up at the London School of Economics. Boswell and Johnson, Holmes and Laski are each given a separate chapter, and though the later chapters on father-figures and trouble with women lose some of the vitality of the earlier sections, this offers an enjoyable account of friendship and distinctive characters preserved in their friends' writings, if nothing very new in the way of scholarship. Peter Martin's *Samuel Johnson: A Biography* is a handsome book, with glossy, high-quality illustrations. Its select bibliography consists of mostly bibliographical rather than critical sources. Martin writes at a brisk pace, moving smoothly through necessary historical and social contextual material, and keeps conjecture to a minimum in favour of properly founded fact, with an occasional flourish. In the introduction Martin acknowledges his reservations about bibliographical material, especially that written by Boswell and Johnson's contemporaries, which often manages to reduce the subject to a caricature. Martin intends instead to explore Johnson fully in all his variety and complexity, his personal weaknesses as well as his advanced, liberal attitudes. Martin's intention in this is admirable, but his attempt is not wholly successful.

Nicholas Hudson and Aaron Santesso have edited an excellent collection of essays entitled *Swift's Travels: Eighteenth-Century British Satire and its Legacy*. It is dedicated to Claude Rawson, and inspired by his scholarship and expertise on eighteenth-century satire. In the collection, Swift's satire travels forwards and backwards through the literary tradition, across a broad range of genres. The aim of the volume is the reinvestigation of satire as something that is 'more radical, more troubled, and more ambitious than previously imagined' (p. 1). This reinvestigation is a substantial one. Sixteen essays are divided into three sections. Part I is entitled 'Swift and his Antecedents' and draws on the Renaissance and seventeenth-century models that influenced Swift, from More and Hobbes to Dryden's irony, in essays by David Rosen and Aaron Santesso, Jonathan Lamb and Steven N. Zwicker. Ian Higgins discusses Swiftian satire in relation to political pamphlets and their justification of bloodshed during the revolution, and investigates how closely Swift himself comes at times in his parody of violent justification to justifying bloodshed in an outright manner, in 'Killing No Murder: Jonathan Swift and the Polemical Tradition' (pp. 39–54). Harold Love, in 'Satirical Wells from Bath to Ballyspellan' (pp. 55–73), examines divisive social satire. In part II, 'Swift in his Time', in Barbara M. Benedict's essay, 'Self, Stuff, and Surface: The Rhetoric of Things in Swift's Satire' (pp. 93–107), materiality is deflated, deconstructed and reconstructed again, and so too are language and identity. David Womersley, in 'Swift's Shapeshifting' (pp. 108–23), focuses upon Swift's blurring of language and literary and generic divisions, and the final three essays in this section, by Pat Rogers, Howard Erskine Hill and James McLaverty, discuss Swift's poetry. Part III looks to developments 'Beyond Swift'. Beginning with Nicholas Hudson's contribution, 'Pope and the Evolution of Social Class' (pp. 179–97), this section encompasses two studies on Austen by Peter Sabor and Jenny Davidson and one on Beckett by Marjorie Perloff, a study of Fielding's gallows humour and his deployment of victims and tormentors in the Swiftian mode in 'Fielding's Satire and the Jestbook Tradition: The Case of Lord Justice Page' (pp. 198–216) by Thomas Keymer, and a thoroughly illustrated essay by Ronald Paulson on the theme of cannibalism in Swift's writing as represented in scenes by Hogarth, Goya and Tiepolo, discussing satire, materiality, cruelty and disgust in 'The Hungry Mouth: Eucharistic Parody in Hogarth, Goya, and Domenico Tiepolo' (pp. 251–79).

An equally rich and scholarly essay collection is *Literary Milieux: Essays in Text and Context, Presented to Howard Erskine-Hill*, edited by David Womersley and Richard McCabe. The breadth and variety of Erskine-Hill's scholarly interests (which comprise a lengthy bibliography at the beginning of the collection) is mirrored by the variety of subjects addressed here in sixteen essays. The period covered is broadly eighteenth-century in scope, but there are essays on patronage in Elizabethan and Jacobean Ireland by Richard McCabe, and discussions of Shakespeare by Tom McFaul, David Womersley and David Nokes. The majority of the essays deal with poetry, beginning with Alastair Fowler's 'Poetry and Politics: Some Reflections' (pp. 23–9) and followed by Paul Hammond on Dryden, essays by Julian Ferraro, Robert Douglas-Fairhurst, Hester Jones, Claude Rawson, George Rousseau and Valerie Rumbold on Pope, and Peter McDonald on Wordsworth. Fiction is addressed by Thomas Keymer in 'Materialism, Mechanism, and the Novel' (pp. 307–33). The print market, Whig propaganda and satire are represented here by Niall MacKenzie's essay on a Jacobite song, *A Welcome to the Medal* [1711] in what he calls 'double-edged writing', meaning texts that embody the polarized sense of their own context and can be read in either one way or its opposite, picking up on what Erskine-Hill called the 'twofold vision' of such texts, and presenting an intricate reading of anti-Jacobite polemics, in 'Double-Edged Writing in the Eighteenth Century' (pp. 140–68). Robert J. Mayhew considers the uses to which Pope's correspondence has been put in discussions of Pope, landscape and gardening, suggesting that we should not use them to extract a ready-made theory of landscape but that Pope was rather using landscape as a means to 'bridge the social distance' between himself and his correspondents (p. 201), in 'Self-Fashioned Prospects: Pen, Print, and the Presentation of Landscape in the Correspondence of Alexander Pope' (pp. 187–204).

Prospects of a different kind are presented in *Brilliant Women: Eighteenth-Century Bluestockings* by Elizabeth Eger and Lucy Peltz. Intended as a companion-piece for the National Portrait Gallery's exhibition of the same name in 2008, this is a beautifully illustrated work, with many full-page colour reproductions and some smaller inset etchings and pictures. The exhibition was structured around Richard Samuel's *Portraits in the Characters of the Muses in the Temple of Apollo (The Nine Living Muses of Great Britain)* [1778], which depicted Elizabeth Carter, Anna Letitia Barbauld, Angelica Kaufmann, Elizabeth Sheridan, Charlotte Lennox, Hannah More, Elizabeth Montagu, Elizabeth Griffith and Catharine Macaulay. Eger and Peltz have contributed two essays each. The essays by Eger, 'The Bluestocking Circle: Friendship, Patronage and Learning' (pp. 20–55) and 'The Bluestocking legacy' (pp. 126–51) and Peltz, 'Living Muses: Constructing and Celebrating the Professional Woman in Literature and the Arts' (pp. 56–93) and '"A Revolution in Female Manners": Women, Politics and Reputation in the Late Eighteenth Century' (pp. 94–125) are notable for their discussion of literary sources. In a year that saw many publications on eighteenth-century art and cultural exchange, few offered much in the way of literary engagement, but Eger and Peltz incorporate readings of written as well as visual representations, and provide useful discussions of the world of the professional woman of letters in the mid- to late eighteenth century The volume is completed by a short but succinct list of further reading, and though the essays are not in-depth studies of the subject, as befits an exhibition companion-piece, it provides an excellent literary and visually entrancing introduction to the world of bluestockings. The work of Hannah More undergoes an important recovery in Nicholas D. Smith's *The Literary Manuscripts and Letters of Hannah More*. This is a wonderful addition to textual scholarship and an important reference work for those interested in the writings of Hannah More and her circle. It consists of a catalogue of all known and many newly discovered letters by More in both public and private collections, as well as a catalogue of drama, prose and verse manuscripts, including those translated by and attributed to More. Publication details are provided where possible or relevant. Smith's lengthy introduction (pp. 1–120) provides well-organized accounts of his discoveries and investigations into the libraries and repositories here surveyed under the following sub-headings: Provenance, Verse, Epitaphs, Ann Yearsley, The Book of Fame, Lost and Misattributed Poetical Manuscripts, Prose, Drama, Library and Annotated Books, Extra-Illustrated Copy of *Florio*, Letters, Facsimiles, Miscellaneous, Portraits, Personal Relics and Commemorative Items, Moriana. There is also a bibliography of recent More criticism, a first-line index of manuscript verse, and a full list of repositories. The catalogue of letters is intended as 'a checklist of letters for a projected edition of More's extant correspondence in British and North American repositories' (p. 79), which will doubtless be a much-anticipated publication.

In Devoney Looser's *Women Writers and Old Age in Great Britain,*
1750–1850, also discussed in Chapter XII, Anna Letitia Barbauld, Fanny
Burney, Catherine Macaulay and Hester Lynch Piozzi, among many others,
are examined in the context of the literary marketplace and the effects, either
perceived or actual, of ageing upon the careers of women writers. Looser
discusses the pressures upon and choices available to older writers and how
these affected the types of literature produced by them as their careers
progressed. Utilizing much new biographical and literary material from
archival sources, as well as developing current critical understanding of the
print market, book reception and audience demands, Looser's investigation is
a welcome contribution to cultural and literary studies in the long eighteenth
century. A more general introduction is provided by Paul Goring's *Eighteenth-*
Century Literature and Culture, suitable for undergraduates and focusing upon
1688–1789. It is structured thematically, and its four chapters are systematically laid out, covering 'Historical, Cultural and Intellectual Context',
'Literature in the Eighteenth Century', 'Critical Approaches' and 'Resources
for Independent Study'. The chapter on 'Critical Approaches' is particularly
useful, as it gives an overview of current critical debates, and there is also a
helpful glossary of literary terms and concepts.

   Theory and Practice in the Eighteenth Century: Writing Between Philosophy
and Literature, edited by Alexander Dick and Christina Lupton, is an
invaluable collection of essays. The editors note in their introduction that in
the eighteenth century 'questions posed by each [philosophy and literature]
were the condition of possibility for the other' (p. 9), and this is the principle
that underpins this collection. It is divided into two parts, 'Writing/
Philosophy' and 'Knowing Literature', although the content throughout,
even in part II, is closely bound up in philosophical analysis and interpretation. Part I contains essays by Jonathan Kramnick, Joseph Chaves, Mark
Blackwell, John Richetti, Maureen Harkin and Alexander Dick on Hume,
Smith, Reid, Shaftesbury and Locke, with an intriguing opener by Nicholas
Hudson on Derrida and empiricism. Part II continues the investigation into
Hume with essays by Adam Budd and Eva Dadiez, and Nancy Yousef
presents an account of Rousseau's philosophy in the context of *La Nouvelle*
Héloïse, but there is also a discussion of Wordsworth by Adam Potkay. Essays
by Jonathan Sadow and Brian Michael Norton complete the volume. The
originality and subtlety of this variety of readings of philosophical texts, and
their application to current as well as eighteenth-century conceptions of
literature, reading and writing, render this collection an important one for
scholars working in this area.

   The ongoing work by John McVeagh of editing Defoe's *Review 1704–13* for
Pickering & Chatto sees the appearance this year of volume 6, covering the
years 1709 and 1710. This large volume contains a lengthy introduction and
substantial endnotes, revealing yet more facets of Defoe's journalism and
granting ever greater insights into the early print market, and Defoe's social,
political and literary interests. Also from Pickering & Chatto this year are two
more additions to the series Eighteenth-Century Political Biographies, on
subjects whose often labyrinthine political allegiances are greatly in need of
sustained investigation. In *A Political Biography of Delarivier Manley* Rachel

Carnell has produced the first full-length biography of her subject, informed by new scholarship and biographical research to present a full investigation into the political background and allegiances of Manley's writing under the Tory government. Her early life and education, her relationship with her father and her own elevation to celebrity and notoriety are carefully considered and fully discussed. Similarly, David Oakleaf, in *A Political Biography of Jonathan Swift*, offers very necessary analysis of Smith's political sympathies and his Tory and Whig contacts. Swift's engagement with Irish politics, the politics of the Church, his individual subjectivity and political ideologies receive full, thorough examination and clarification.

Claude Rawson has edited a celebratory collection of essays on Fielding in *Henry Fielding (1797–1754), Novelist, Playwright, Journalist, Magistrate: A Double Anniversary Tribute*. The 'double anniversary' of the title is explained by the 250th anniversary of Fielding's death in 1754 and the tercentenary of his birth in 1707. Following on from Rawson's *Cambridge Companion to Henry Fielding* in 2007, which paid due attention to Fielding's writings on law, crime and society, and to his journalism as well as his novels and dramas, Rawson has gathered a very wide range of essays that deepen present evaluations of Fielding's work and pose some exciting challenges for the field, which stem from the conference held at Yale in 2004. While some of the material here is necessarily summative of Fielding's life and works, there is much in these thirteen essays that is new and exciting, showing how rich and rewarding Fielding studies is at present. The volume is in four sections. Part I, 'Plays and Novels', begins with Thomas Lockwood's 'Fielding from Stage to Page' (pp. 21–39), which traces the development of the Shamela figure from Fielding's early dramas. She is refitted for the novel genre after the publication of Richardson's *Pamela*, but is distinctly present in a series of plays Fielding wrote for Catherine Clive between 1732 and 1735. Drama features again in Joseph Roach's ' "The Uncreating World": Silence and Unspoken Thought in Fielding's Drama' (pp. 40–57), and Thomas Keymer investigates the Machiavellian strain in Fielding's writing, especially his journalism and satire during the Walpole years, in 'Fielding's Machiavellian Moment' (pp. 58–91). Keymer uncovers a subject of great complexity that has fallen out of favour with critics in recent decades, despite some interesting work having been undertaken on the subject in earlier studies. The crude version of Machiavellian statecraft embodied by Walpole at the hands of writers and critics receives a full investigation here, with the persistent influence of Machiavelli upon Fielding long after the writing of *Jonathan Wild*, also discussed. Jonathan Wild appears again in Claude Rawson's 'Avatars of Alexander: Jonathan Wild and the Tyrant Thug, from Voltaire to Brecht' (pp. 91–154). In Rawson's reading of violence and the bloody displays of power by kings, exalted Homeric culture is undermined, or rather exposed for the vicious cruelty that it really is, and Rawson follows what he calls the 'avatars' of the bloody Homeric heroes into Shakespeare, Brecht and beyond. The contemporary distinction between the poetic goodness of Homer's Achilles and the moral goodness which he lacks is not a subtlety which Jonathan Wild makes in his reading, though Fielding, Rawson suggests, does. The last essay in this section is Simon Dickie's '*Amelia*, Sex, and Fielding's

Woman Question' (pp. 155–62), which discusses gender, sexual morality and the perennial problem of Amelia's nose. Dickie considers the rarity of Amelia as a moral and sexual female exemplar in Fielding's fiction, a character who nevertheless embodies Fielding's ambiguity about women and female virtue and his fascination with erring females who are always defined by sexuality even when striving most sincerely to preserve their modesty. Part II, 'Relationships and Collaborations', begins with 'Henry and Sarah Fielding: A Literary Relationship' (pp. 165–72) by Linda Bree, who unpicks the tangled relationships between the Fieldings, their works and their collaborations and influences, uncovering useful new material and interpretations of their domestic relationship as well as at the hands of Henry's contemporary critics. In 'Fielding, Hogarth and Evil: Cruelty' (pp. 173–200) Ronald Paulson examines Hogarth's *The Four Stages of Cruelty* [1751] and looks at cruelty in Fielding and Gay, considering the different forms (personal, political, economic or official) and how their representation is related to suffering and sin. Frédéric Ogée, in '"O, Hogarth, had I thy pencil": Delineations of an Alleged Friendship' (pp. 201–30), follows on smoothly from Paulson in a discussion of classical models and the attack upon social hierarchies, investigating the emerging epistemological status of representations in image as well as in print.

Part III, 'Laws, Politics and Ideas', begins with Pat Rogers's 'Poacher and Gamekeeper: Fielding, the Law, and the Novels' (pp. 233–56), which analyses the seeming contradictions in Fielding's life, as a figure who engages with the law from very different positions in public and private as his career progresses. Rogers suggests that Fielding's unsuitable early life befits his later role as magistrate better than any other training could possibly do. In 'Fielding, Politics, and "Men of Genius"' (pp. 257–70) Bertrand A. Goldgar examines Fielding's rapid changing of sides in the political sphere, from the Opposition to becoming a supporter of Walpole, as Frederick Ribble has recently proved. Goldgar considers the reasons for this switch, discerning a 'deep disenchant-ment with partisan political writing' (p. 269) in Fielding's journalism and periodical writings. Guyonne Leduc's 'Was Fielding a Prefeminist?' (pp. 271–92) historicizes some of the themes from Dickie's earlier essay by contextualizing the debate about gender and the woman question of the seventeenth and early eighteenth centuries, drawing more on Fielding's journalism than the novels, but again coming back to the persistently problematic *Amelia*. In part IV, 'Afterlife', Angela J. Smallwood explores the echoes of *Joseph Andrews* and Fielding's early plays in Elizabeth Inchbald's 1791 drama *Next Door Neighbours*, discussing the shared philosophical heritage of Godwin, Holcroft and Fielding, in 'Jacobites and Jacobins: Fielding's Legacy in the Later Eighteenth-Century London Theatre' (pp. 295–313). Finally, 'Fielding's Legacy in Fiction' (pp. 314–24) by Robert Alter completes the volume, examining the complete assimilation of Fielding by those who followed him, such as Stendhal, as well as investigating all those who, like George Eliot and Henry James, do not seem to borrow but are nonetheless informed as much by what Fielding didn't do, in his rejection of forms from Defoe and Richardson, as by what he did.

Defoe is well served this year by the *Cambridge Companion to Daniel Defoe*, edited by John Richetti. This excellent new collection of thirteen essays illustrates Richetti's claim in the introduction that Defoe, not Pope or Swift, is the 'most important writer of the first thirty years of the English eighteenth century' (p. 2) by virtue of the exemplary discussion of the breadth and variety of Defoe's writing, political interests and cultural engagement. 'The journalist and polemicist without peer, the criminologist, the urbanist, the proto-feminist, the early theorist of globalism and imperialism, the poet and satirist, moralist and social critic, the promoter of Britain's mercantile power and prophet of its future imperial glories, to say nothing of the creator of memorable fictions—Defoe fits all these descriptions and works in all these fields' (p. 3). It opens with Paula Backscheider's broad discussion of Defoe's corporeal body and his presence or absence in his writing, in 'Defoe: The Man in the Works' (pp. 5–25), Backscheider writes: 'To assemble the writings by Defoe that might be called autobiographical is to become intensely aware of the ways he could dramatize, reinterpret, obscure, falsify, and mask his life' (p. 20), and thus sets the tone for the subsequent investigations in the writer and his writing. As befits a *Companion* the range of essays is wide, but the following selection is of interest to this section. In 'Defoe's Political and Religious Journalism' (pp. 25–44) Maximillian E. Novak sets out the political and social context for Defoe's journalism in newspapers and pamphlets, detailing the breadth of Defoe's involvement with as many as twelve newspapers at a time. He considers Defoe's attempts to control and influence opinion and be understood as he wished to be, not to be left open to interpretation. In 'Defoe, Commerce, and Empire' (pp. 45–63), Srinivas Aravamudan examines early globalization and empire expansion in relation to Defoe, looking at his writings on free and restricted trade, and his views on private trade as a solution to governmental interference and force. This then moves into discussion of fiction, but also of travel and trade writings. Following essays by Hal Gladfelder and Deidre Shauna Lynch on Defoe's fiction, Pat Rogers's in-depth study of *Tour thro' the Whole Island of Great Britain* [1724–6] in 'Defoe's *Tour* and the Identity of Britain' (pp. 102–20) examines statistics, source books, and changes to transport, which works well with a subsequent chapter by Cynthia Wall, 'Defoe and London' (pp. 158–82). There is a good selection of maps, and Defoe's London is re-created, full of variety and contradiction, using *A Journal of the Plague Year* [1722] among other texts. John McVeagh's 'Defoe: Satirist and Moralist' (pp. 200–15) is primarily concerned with Defoe's verse satires but moves into a brief but relevant discussion of Defoe's later prose writing and its moral specifics. The remaining essays by Ellen Pollak, Michael Seidel, John Richetti and J. Paul Hunter discuss Defoe's fiction.

2. The Novel

Inger Sigrun Brodey's *Ruined by Design: Shaping Novels and Gardens in the Culture of Sensibility* offers an important contribution to the growing areas of scholarship on sensibility, ruins, and cultural and literary fragmentariness. In

four chapters, Brodey outlines the ambivalence of the ruin and fragmentation—in terms of both 'natural' and artificially constructed follies—in
eighteenth-century Britain, Germany and France. She consults a range of
critical works on landscape gardening, the perception and cultural construction of ruins and the ways in which criticism of the ruin's architecture and
meaning draws on the rhetoric of sensibility to encompass its subjective
appeal. In a historically grounded examination of the syntax of the incomplete
and its aesthetic and psychological possibilities, she argues convincingly that
the ambivalence of the ruin as both a symbol of historic and public
authenticity and also as a space for private contemplation is reflected and
imaginatively reworked in the discourse of sensibility. Drawing on Elizabeth
Wanning Harries's groundbreaking work on the fragment in the eighteenth
century, she identifies the democratizing impulses in ruination and sensibility
in different genres ranging from garden manuals to imaginative writing, and
knowledgeably guides the reader through her case studies of, among others,
Sterne's *Sentimental Journey* and Goethe's *Werther*. She aligns ' "anti-
narrative" techniques that interrupt narration for the sake of immediacy,
intimacy, authenticity, or the appearance of virtue' (p. 73) with spectators'
discontinuous ways of seeing and consuming ruins. Her argument branches
out into detailed discussions of language theories about the possibility of
representing feeling accurately and coherently, exploring the widely perceived
'gaps between sign and meaning or between language and thought' (p. 67), and
accounts of the picturesque reading of ruins as offering a particular
opportunity for spectatorial and emotional participation. Using the inter-
relatedness of ruin discourse and sensibility and charting the European
developments in gardens and their changing and ambivalent symbolism, she
succeeds in providing pervasive interpretations of texts such as Sterne's
Sentimental Journey and Goethe's *Werther* by offering an in-depth contextualization of the garden and ruin as meaningful ideological loci. By the end
of the book she has produced an insightful interdisciplinary study of 'the
novelistic "rhetoric of ruins" ' (p. 86) and the concerns of European sensibility
with 'a tension between completion and incompletion, monument and ruin,
narrative and anti-narrative impulses, and the desire to construct system
versus the desire to particularize experience' (p. 86).

Omitted from last year's *YWES* and also addressing eighteenth-century
concerns with fragmentation and unity is Judith Broome's *Fictive Domains:
Body, Landscape, and Nostalgia, 1717–1770*, a study that investigates the
phenomenon of nostalgia, initially a medical term denoting physical illness
caused by homesickness but gradually evolving into a cultural mindset which
indulges in 'fantas[ies] of restoration' (p. 104), be they of a glorious past, an
immutable social order or a unity of body and soul. Broome adopts an
ideological approach to the culture of nostalgia in the eighteenth century,
arguing that it intensifies in the period as a result of profound social, economic
and geographical changes; contemporary authors, she argues, construct
'imaginary places to turn to' (p. 17) in order to serve a 'conservative interest
in preserving the status quo' (p. 15). The first three chapters explore different
expressions of 'masculine nostalgia' (p. 138) in the writings of Samuel
Richardson, Alexander Pope, Jean-Jacques Rousseau and Oliver Goldsmith,

showing that they place 'the burden of nostalgia' (p. 70) consistently on female characters, whose bodies, gardens and homes are turned into the loci of tradition, 'nature' and stability. Broome's chapter on *Clarissa* and *Sir Charles Grandison* investigates how categories of health and illness intersect with gender, arguing that Richardson 'constructs illusions of wholeness and permanence' to counter fragmentation and the 'contradictions' (p. 32) of the modern world. Considering previous critics' speculation about the cause of Clarissa's death, Broome suggests that it is best understood in the context of nostalgia, as the heroine displays longing for a past in which her body was still 'innocent' (p. 41). She also stresses the performative nature of longing, focusing on the contrasting visual spectacles of Clarissa's peaceful decline and Mrs Sinclair's agitated death (which Broome interestingly compares to accounts of childbirth). Sir Charles Grandison's health is juxtaposed to the numerous suffering bodies of female and Italian characters. Chapters on Pope's poem 'Eloisa to Abelard', Rousseau's *Julie, ou La Nouvelle Héloïse* and Goldsmith's *The Deserted Village* and *The Vicar of Wakefield* are devoted to literary treatments of desire, the sentimental body and the picturesque; in each chapter Broome draws attention to the ways in which these texts help imagine a particular kind of authorship, one whereby the author is foregrounded as a figure who can recover a lost unity of body and mind through the act of writing. Goldsmith, she contends, clearly positions himself as a 'writer of loss' (p. 126). The final chapter, on Sarah Scott's *Millenium Hall*, considers the possibility of 'feminine nostalgia' (p. 137) as an alternative cultural mindset, but ultimately concludes that, in this novel at least, it has paternalistic qualities and is therefore 'uneven' (p. 149). Broome ends with a note for modern readers, saying that we can learn from eighteenth-century ideological constructions of the past and concluding that, in this time of rapid change, 'we have a responsibility to acknowledge all of our past, and to look critically at our own nostalgia' (p. 158).

Kate Loveman's *Reading Fictions, 1660–1740: Deception in English Literature and Political Culture* is a history of seventeenth- and early eighteenth-century reading habits and 'explores the literary and political consequences of the sense, common in this period, that skilled interpretation of narratives was an exercise in detecting falsehoods and avoiding deception' (p. 2). One of its principal aims is 'to situate the "rise of the novel" within a broader history of reading' (p. 2) and to examine 'reading behaviour through the theme of deception' (p. 4). Loveman charts the production and consumption of 'sham' literature, read and discussed socially in the environment of coffee houses, and identifies mechanisms of justification on the part of the author of the sham and strategies of detecting falsehoods on the part of the reader that would be deployed in the fictions of Defoe, Swift, Richardson and Fielding. Tracing various developments from 'witty shamming' to 'political deceptions' (p. 15), involving the religious debates on Protestantism and the supposed dangers of Jacobitism, Loveman knowledgeably explains how 'concepts of shamming helped individuals to define and comprehend the evolving political crisis' (p. 16). Her insightful chapter on Defoe draws on her elaborately developed conceptualization of shamming and discusses not only *Robinson Crusoe*, *Moll Flanders* and *Roxana*, but also his satirical *The Shortest Way with the Dissenters* and *The Review*. She comments that party writers were repeatedly charged with deceiving their readers, and Defoe's works, especially *The Shortest-Way with the Dissenters*, offered a satirical sham that many initially read as an authentic document by a Jacobite High Churchman, but which were subsequently denounced as libellous and irreligious. Although Defoe professed specific ends for his fictions, he was frequently confronted with responses—such as Charles Gildon's on *Robinson Crusoe*—challenging his claims to the truthful writing of 'history'. However, it is the very appeal of false stories being suspected by their readers that engaged the readers in a 'game' with the author by which both could play on the polysemy of terms such as 'sham', 'banter' and 'lie'. Readers had become accustomed 'to scrutinize the truth-content of novelistic narratives' (p. 145) and demonstrated a developed awareness of the syntax of sham literature with which they approached texts such as *Gulliver's Travels* or the corrective to sensibility, *Shamela*. By relating the seventeenth-century tradition of shams to the rise of the novel, Loveman pursues an innovative approach to the reading practices of eighteenth-century imaginary writing and offers a new perspective on the strategies adopted by authors to justify their fictions.

Elizabeth Kraft's *Women Novelists and the Ethics of Desire, 1684–1814: In the Voice of Our Biblical Mothers* is an original, gender-centred study that highlights the ethical dimensions of the long eighteenth-century novel. Building upon genealogies of the novel by Ros Ballaster, Nancy Armstrong and Margaret Doody, setting up a critical dialogue with Emmanuel Lévinas and Luce Irigaray, and invoking a variety of biblical female voices, Kraft examines prose fiction from Aphra Behn to Frances Burney in order to demonstrate, amongst other things, that female novelists 'recognized the ethical danger posed to women by the cultural privileging of the passive female object of desire' (p. 6). The main argument of chapter 1, 'Matriarchal Desire and Ethical Relation', is that Old Testament narratives highlighting the ethics of sexual desire provide a valuable backdrop against which to examine the amatory fiction of Behn, Delarivier Manley and Eliza Haywood. Biblical matriarchs such as Sarah, Rebekah and the female speaker in the Song of Songs, Kraft contends, come to embody 'union without possession' (p. 15), that is, a sexual, chiasmic union whereby *both* lovers recognize each other's difference and subjectivity. Their narratives give expression to female presence and desire and provide it with divine sanction. Kraft acknowledges that early eighteenth-century novels of amorous intrigue are highly sceptical of reciprocal love and its transcendent qualities, but argues that they investigate it as an idea to be cherished and are therefore 'at their core ethical' (p. 22). Chapter 2, 'Men and Women in the Garden of Delight', reads Behn's *Love-Letters Between a Nobleman and his Sister* alongside the Song of Songs, examining the use of pastoral language and imagery and tracing the development from 'libertine irony' in part 1 to the 'dark cynicism' (p. 48) of the more overtly political part 3, in which 'the garden of delight has been transformed into a prison of personal power' (p. 50). Chapter 3, 'Sexual Awakening and Political Power', discusses Behn's 'History of the Nun' and Manley's *The New Atalantis*. The biblical female voices invoked here are those of Deborah, Jael and Rachav, but the established parallels are not always as persuasive as in the previous chapter. While the notion of Deborah as 'the paradigm of the woman in a political world' (p. 56) serves well for an examination of both Behn and Manley's role as politically engaged women writers, the connection between Jael's actions—she violently murders an enemy to her people—and Isabella's violation of her Catholic vows in Behn's work is somewhat strained. Kraft's subsequent analysis of Manley's complex, anxious treatment of party politics and the 'insatiability of female desire' (p. 67) is perceptive, but it is also, at times, too allusive and would have been more persuasive if specific historical events were discussed in more detail. Chapter 4, 'Hieroglyphs of Desire', focuses on the importance of signs, images and allegory in processes of identity construction and cultural assimilation, setting up Queen Esther and Zipporah as 'biblical paradigms' (p. 87) to examine respectively Manley's *Adventures of Rivella* and Haywood's *Love in Excess*. The chapter also stresses Haywood's centrality as a transitional figure in the development of the novel, presenting *Betsy Thoughtless* as a work that registers the growing contemporary discomfort with female subjectivity. Chapter 5, 'His Sister's Song', first highlights Miriam's obscure role as singer in Moses' Song at the Sea, suggesting that Moses is, in fact, singing his sister's song. Kraft then investigates the novels of Samuel Richardson and Sarah Fielding, arguing that the former is representative of a mid-century literary and cultural trend whereby female desire is increasingly articulated by men. In chapter 6, 'The Forgotten Woman', Kraft investigates 'the ethical paradigm of mutuality and reciprocity' (p. 145) through the figure of the suffering woman, loosely associating three female pairs: Sarah and Hagar, mother and 'prototype' (p. 136) of Israel, Laura Glenmorris and Elizabeth Lisburne in Charlotte Smith's *The Young Philosopher*, and Juliet/Ellis Granville and Elinor Joddrel in Frances Burney's *The Wanderer*. The final chapter, 'The Lot Motif and the Redaction of Double Desire', examines Elizabeth Inchbald's *A Simple Story* in the light of Lot's incestuous relationship with his daughters.

Also focusing on female desire is Katherine Binhammer's 'The Whore's Love' (*ECF* 20[2008] 507–34), which adopts an original approach to the eighteenth-century figure of the sentimental prostitute, arguing for a new feminist perspective that acknowledges its 'contribution to the history of love rather than the history of commerce or illicit sex' (p. 509). Examining the role of the penitent prostitute in a range of Magdalen narratives, including the anonymous novel *The Histories of Some of the Penitents in the Magdalen House* [1760], Binhammer shows how some of them complicate conventional victimizations of the whore, giving voice to woman's affective choices and 'erotic agency' (p. 513).

A number of eighteenth-century novels feature in Nicola Lacey's *Women, Crime and Character: From Moll Flanders to Tess of the D'Urbervilles*, a study on the topic of female criminality that grew out of a series of Clarendon lectures held in 2007. Lacey, a feminist legal theorist, is interested in cultural and legal 'mechanisms of responsibility-attribution' (p. xi) and their relationship to the criminalization of women in the eighteenth and nineteenth centuries. Because of its didacticism, its generic hybridity, and its concern with questions of femininity as well as the culture and language of law, Lacey argues, the novel offers valuable insight into changing definitions of selfhood, character and responsibility. She also usefully reminds us that 'the novel-reading classes were precisely those in whose hands law enforcement, at almost every level, lay; hence their perceptions mattered fundamentally to the administration of the system and to outcomes within it' (p. 90). Drawing on legal, social and literary history, and engaging with the writings of Ian Watt, Michael McKeon and Dror Wahrman, Lacey traces the 'shifting relationship between informal codes of norms such as the "cult of sensibility" and the formal system of criminal justice' (p. xii), discussing novels such as Defoe's *Moll Flanders* and *Roxana*, Fielding's *Joseph Andrews*, Richardson's *Pamela* and *Clarissa*, Burney's *Cecilia*, and Godwin's *Caleb Williams*. Literary critics should not expect extensive or fresh analyses of these novels; rather, they are highlighted as documents that register and mediate the gradual disappearance of the autonomous, sexually active, and clever female offender Moll, who, Lacey observes, is 'superseded in the annals of literary female offenders in the realist tradition by heroines like Tess' (p. xi). As a book that draws strong parallels between this literary change and the development of the modern criminal process, this is a valuable contribution to the still expanding field of law and literature studies.

Pickering & Chatto have begun publishing the fifth and final set of volumes of *The Works of Daniel Defoe* (general editors W.R. Owens and P.N. Furbank), namely *The Novels of Daniel Defoe*. Five of the ten volumes were issued this year. The introduction to volume 1, *The Life and Strange Surprising Adventures of Robinson Crusoe*, and volume 2, *The Farther Adventures of Robinson Crusoe*, edited by W.R. Owens, covers topics such as political economy, cannibalism, colonialism and anti-Chinese sentiment, and concludes with a discussion of the novel's afterlife, stressing its ongoing, ubiquitous cultural appeal. The copy-text of both volumes is based on the first editions, but a number of fascinating plates are reproduced that were included in later editions. The introduction to volume 3, *Serious Reflections during the Life and Surprising Adventures of Robinson Crusoe*, edited by G.A. Starr, states that 'instead of being regarded as an anticlimactic final instalment', the text 'should be recognized as a fascinating early draft of a significant body of writing that Defoe produced in the later 1720s' (p. 1). Starr shows how Defoe's contemplative essays contain an exciting combination of seriousness and humour and points to Defoe's paradoxical and ambivalent treatment of topics such as solitude and honesty, providing useful historical context where necessary. Ultimately, he argues, *Serious Reflections* represents an 'exercise in retroactive self-fashioning' whereby the 'esteemed' Crusoe 'plead[s] on Defoe's behalf' (p. 20). The introductory material to volume 4, *Memoirs of a Cavalier*, edited by N.H. Keeble, addresses issues of authorship and authenticity, showing how Defoe constructs an engaging fictional narrative by creatively manipulating primary source material such as Jean le Clerc's biography of Richelieu and *The Swedish Intelligencer*. Despite its heavy reliance on a variety of sources, Keeble argues, the text's unity and coherence are ensured by the 'experiential consistency' (p. 19) and clear narrative voice of the protagonist. Furbank's introduction to volume 5, *The Life, Adventures, and Pyracies, of the Famous Captain Singleton*, is a lengthy critical synopsis of the plot. The volume includes an appendix offering a (probably fictional) account of real-life figure John Freeman, employee of the Royal African Company and likely model for the character of the white naked Englishman in the novel.

Questions of genre inform Nicholas Seager's '"A Romance the likest to Truth that I ever read": History, Fiction, and Politics in Defoe's *Memoirs of a Cavalier*' (*ECF* 20.4[2008] 479–505), which characterizes Defoe's work as a 'moderate corrective' (p. 480) to early eighteenth-century partisan debates about the English civil war. An article also written by Seager is 'Lies, Damned Lies, and Statistics: Epistemology and Fiction in Defoe's *A Journal of the Plague Year*' (*MLR* 103:iii[2008] 639–53). He explains the function of statistical data in *A Journal* by analysing it in the context of the eighteenth-century novel's investment in the discourse of probability. Considering Defoe's literary investment in Enlightenment individualism, Melissa Mowry's historicist and well-researched study 'Women, Work, Rearguard Politics, and Defoe's *Moll Flanders*' (*ECent* 49[2008] 97–116) trenchantly argues that *Moll* 'ambitiously rewrites the economic and political terms of England's seventeenth-century past' (p. 98). Maximillian E. Novak, 'The Cave and the Grotto: Realist Form and Robinson Crusoe's Imagined Interiors' (*ECF* 20.3[2008] 445–68), is an excellent and lucid article arguing that 'it is through his use of the imagery associated with the cave and the grotto, those classic locales of daydream and psychological landscape, that Defoe solidifies *Robinson Crusoe*'s position as a realist text' (p. 446). Novak first investigates and discards the possibility that Crusoe's cave functions as a site of Christian conversion or a place of 'awakening knowledge' (p. 454) as in Baltasar Gracian's *El Criticon* [1681], arguing that the hero is no wilful 'saintly hermit' (p. 451) nor an innocent youth. He then examines Defoe's representation of the grotto in the context of Italian and Islamic literary and pictorial traditions, indicating that even though the author uses the site metaphorically he continues to remind the reader of its materiality.

Also examining imagined interiorities are Kathleen Lubey's 'Erotic Interiors in Joseph Addison's imagination' (*ECF* 20.3[2008] 415–44), William H. Wandless's 'Secretaries of the Interior: Narratorial Collaboration in Sarah Scott's *Millenium Hall*' (*ECF* 21.2[2008–9] 259–81) and Ariane Fennetaux's 'Women's Pockets and the Construction of Privacy in the Long Eighteenth Century' (*ECF* 20.3[2008] 307–34). Lubey suggests that Addison's 'theory of imaginative engagement' (p. 420) may help us understand how novelists such as Richardson and Fielding employ erotic discourse to find a balance between the 'aesthetically pleasurable and the morally responsible' (p. 443), while Wandless develops and extends earlier studies of Scott's novel, uncovering the author's strategic positioning of the anonymous male narrator and the 'remarkably undervalued' (p. 262) female character Mrs Maynard, who, Wandless argues, are made to 'work in tandem to realize Scott's pedagogical ambitions' (p. 272). Adopting a material culture approach and examining a range of eighteenth-century novels from Defoe's *Moll Flanders* to Burney's *Camilla*, Fennetaux draws attention to the dynamics of 'female interiority' (p. 308) in the period.

Examining Eliza Haywood's *The Tea Table* and *Love in Excess* in the context of Lockean and Hobbesian philosophy, Joseph Drury's 'Haywood's Thinking Machines' (*ECF* 21.2[2008–9] 201–28) challenges the ways in which critics such as William B. Warner, Jonathan Brody Kramnick and Helen Thompson have assessed novelistic interiority in Haywood's fiction, arguing that they share a 'problematic interest in representing [it] as somehow free of the conventional moral didacticism that came to dominate later eighteenth-century fiction' (p. 202). The dynamics between altruism and interest are the subject of Charles H. Hinnant's 'Gifts and Wages: The Structures of Exchange in Eighteenth-Century Fiction and Drama' (*ECS* 42:i[2008] 1–18), which contends that novels and plays of the period, such as Manley's *New Atalantis*, Smollett's *Roderick Random* and Behn's *The Lucky Chance* reflect 'not an antithesis between gifts and commodities, but between gifts, favors or alms, and wages' (p. 4). He tentatively concludes that the opposition between altruism and interest did not so much rise with the emergence of a market-driven economy, as scholars have suggested, as 'within the framework of an aristocratic ideology' (p. 16). Adam Poole's short article 'The Narrative Function of John Belford in Samuel Richardson's *Clarissa*' (*Expl* 67:i[2008] 37–9) argues that, after the eponymous heroine and Lovelace, Belford is 'the single most important correspondent' in *Clarissa* as he 'harmonizes' the novel's 'disparate voices' (p. 38) and comes to occupy the position of omniscient narrator, thus acting as a 'channel' (p. 39) for Richardson's moral didacticism. Lynn Shepherd's engaging article ' "Our family has indeed been strangely discomposed": Samuel Richardson, Joseph Highmore and the Conversation Piece in *Clarissa*' (*JECS* 31:iii[2008] 451–72) suggests that Richardson's literary imagination may have been affected by the fact that he had his portrait painted after the publication of *Pamela*. The painting was a conversation piece of his family, and Shepherd notes how, interestingly, in the sequel to *Pamela*, the term 'conversation piece' suddenly occurs, and Pamela's pictorial description of groups of conversing people corresponds to the genre's characteristics. The article itself, though, focuses on Richardson's second novel *Clarissa*, in which Shepherd sees the conversation piece reoccur, but now as 'a powerful metaphor for the articulation of authority and feeling within the family' (p. 452).

Stuart Sim's *The Eighteenth-Century Novel and Contemporary Social Issues: An Introduction* aims to familiarize students and general readers with the complexities of eighteenth-century fiction by drawing on current social issues, thereby increasing the 'public profile' (p. 1) of the literature of the period. He notes that the novels are characterized by their 'cultural subversiveness', their 'engagement with social issues' and 'the exploration of moral dilemmas' which recommend them for discussion in the light of current critical and social debates. The range of Sim's book is impressive, since he charts the novelistic tradition of the long eighteenth century, starting with Aphra Behn's *Oroonoko* and concluding with a discussion of Hogg's *Private Memoirs of a Justified Sinner*. The remaining texts he introduces are *Robinson Crusoe*, *Gulliver's Travels*, *Pamela*, *Tom Jones*, *Tristram Shandy*, *The Mysteries of Udolpho*, *Caleb Williams*, *Waverley* and *Frankenstein*. Subjects dealt with comprise, among others, race, evangelicalism, multiculturalism and social difference, sexual abstinence, family values and fundamentalist terrorism. Each chapter is divided into three parts—a general exposition of 'The Issue', a detailed contextualization of the novel and a 'Conclusion'. Sim explores a variety of pertinent themes such as race in his chapter on *Oroonoko* and introduces the 'Big Brother' contestants Jade Goody and Shilpa Shetty to put into relief racial prejudice and perceptions of race today. Students are thereby introduced to the complex field that the author then explains in a textual reading of Behn's narrative. He addresses the question of whether the protagonist should be regarded as 'a walking advertisement for the benefits of Western cultural imperialism' (p. 11) and offers a sensitive reading that sheds light on the author's ambivalent negotiation of racial difference, slavery and the noble savage. The following chapter on *Robinson Crusoe* is embedded within the discourse of Evangelical Christianity, explained in terms of its influence on and prominence in American political life. The secularists' scepticism of 'political' evangelicalism and 'intelligent design' (p. 23) are then—not always seamlessly—related to Robinson's Puritan spiritual narrative. Sim concludes that 'Crusoe's career helps us to appreciate the mind-set and outlook of the born-again, but, even more interestingly, it reveals some of the glaring gaps in the theology' (p. 32). Sexual politics and the current debate for sexual abstinence are at the centre of the chapter on *Pamela* and are also relevant to Sim's discussion of *The Mysteries of Udolpho* and the different notions of the family. Emily St Aubert grows up in a family that nurtures her, but after being adopted by her aunt and Signor Montini is transferred into a context that reads the 'family unit' as 'prison' (p. 107). Drawing on popular concerns, this introduction establishes useful connections between important contemporary themes and shows their relevance for an understanding of the novels discussed. Students should find this book useful and enlightening. Also noteworthy for undergraduates is the publication by Lutterworth Press of a new edition of George Watson's *The Story of the Novel* (first published by Macmillan in 1979) which is a lucid and compact introductory study of the form and history of the novel genre.

The growing popularity of ecocriticism is palpable in Emily Smith's 'Frances Brooke's Vandalism: Carving Sexual Resistance on Trees in *The History of Emily Montague*' (in Boyd and Kvande, eds., pp. 94–115), which analyses the different ways in which characters of Brooke's epistolary novel 'read' and survey the English and Canadian landscape. While heroine Arabella's father employs 'sexual and imperial styles' (p. 98), and Rivers is engaged in the language of domestic ideology, Bell and Emily 'articulate themselves through the natural world rather than through stylized signs', thus transforming the natural environment into a potential space of female 'dissent' (p. 113). Constructions of female authority and female obedience are under consideration in Marta Kvande's 'Frances Burney and Frances Sheridan: Epistolary Fiction and the Public Sphere' (in Boyd and Kvande, eds., pp. 159–87), which argues that Sheridan's *Sidney Bidulph* and Burney's *Evelina* 'draw attention to the labour involved in creating and maintaining the boundary between public and private' (p. 183).

Oxford University Press has published the thirteenth and final volume of the Wesleyan Edition of Fielding's non-dramatic writings: Henry Fielding, *The Journal of a Voyage to Lisbon, Shamela, and Occasional Writings*, edited by Martin C. Battestin, with special mention of the late Sheridan W. Baker, Jr and Hugh Amory. The impressive volume is presented as an 'anomalous collection' (p. vi) of eighteen prose texts, all based on the first edition where possible, and includes twenty-six illustrations (the majority of which are title pages), and three appendices containing writings attributed to Fielding, notes on the text and a documentary supplement to *The Journal of a Voyage*. Relevant for this section are *Shamela* (pp. 133–95), Fielding's preface to Sarah Fielding's *The Adventures of David Simple* (pp. 339–54) and the preface and Letters XL–XLIV of her sequel *Familiar Letters between the Principal Characters in David Simple* (pp. 462–513); each text is extensively annotated and preceded by a brief introduction that gives valuable insight into its composition, production and reception.

A conference celebrating Henry Fielding's 300th anniversary resulted in the publication of J.A. Downie, ed., *Henry Fielding in Our Time: Papers Presented at the Tercentenary Conference*. A considerable part of this excellent collection of articles focuses on the author's novels. Moving beyond the dichotomy between mythic and historicist readings of *Tom Jones*, Scott Black's 'The Adventures of Love in *Tom Jones*' thoughtfully examines the ways in which this work of fiction 'occupies the space of romance' (p. 36). John J. Burke Jr's readable 'Fielding's Epic Combat with Milton in *Tom Jones*' reminds us of our problematic modern use of the generic label 'novel' when discussing eighteenth-century prose fiction, before juxtaposing the distinctive epic qualities of *Tom Jones* to those of *Paradise Lost*. In 'Fielding's Disruptive Heterosexuality', Gerald J. Butler argues that Fielding's conceptualization of virtue in *Tom Jones* and *Amelia* is inextricably linked to the satisfaction of sexual desire. Robert L. Chibka's 'Henry Fielding, Mentalist: Ins and Outs of Narration in *Tom Jones*' is an engaging and thought-provoking article challenging Fielding's reputation as a novelist uninterested in 'cognitive, ruminative, or affective events' (p. 102). George A. Drake's 'Ritual in *Joseph Andrews*' reads the novel alongside Richard Graves's *The Spiritual Quixote* in order to demonstrate the transformative potential of Parson Adams's 'humiliations and degradations' (p. 143). James Evans, 'Writing London in *Tom Jones*', explores literary and cultural spaces in Fielding's novel, focusing in particular on the author's representation of the West End and the ways in which he probes the performativity of urban living. Regina Janes, 'Fielding and the Case of the Misguided Reader', assesses (and celebrates) the fallible, 'all-too-human, dying author-narrator' (p. 185) in *Tom Jones*, while Christopher D. Johnson's 'Well Bless His Heart: Teaching Fielding in the American South' considers the values of introducing Fielding to evangelical students, suggesting that his comic novels encourage them to scrutinize 'the significance of the things in this life' (p. 196). E.M. Langille's 'Fielding, La Place's *Histoire de Tom Jones* and *Candide*' further explores the parallels between the 1750 French translation of *Tom Jones* and Voltaire's philosophical tale (as discussed in *YWES* 88[2009]). Roger D. Lund, 'The Problem with Parsons: *Joseph Andrews* and the "Contempt of the Clergy" Revisited', politicizes Fielding's ambivalent treatment of clergymen, examining it in the context of contemporary debates about the public reputation of the clergy between 'High-Church reactionaries and Low-Church radicals' (p. 259). Christina Lupton's 'Marriage as a Literary Problem in Fielding's *Amelia*' is a somewhat dense but thoughtful article on Fielding's literary treatment of marriage and novel-reading, arguing that *Amelia* is a 'metanarrative' that does not so much reflect upon the reality of wedlock as upon 'the paradox that the language of fiction and of marriage embody (or codify) as relations to reality' (p. 298). Finally, Brian McCrea's 'Fielding's "Omniscient" Narrator: Romances, Newspapers and the Partial Magic of True History' cogently argues that Fielding's 'I' has not yet been fully explored, stating that 'we need to study, how he makes his narrators [. . .] the voice of the community' (p. 313).

The University Press of Kentucky has published a scholarly edition of Charlotte Lennox's *Henrietta* as part of its Eighteenth-Century Novels by Women series (general editor Isobel Grundy), edited by Ruth Perry and Susan Carlile. Based on the 1761 second-edition text, this fine edition is especially useful for undergraduates new to both the period and the eighteenth-century novel; the annotations provide insight into cultural allusions and contemporary vocabulary while the introduction illuminates Lennox's place in literary history, placing her firmly between Richardson and Fielding on the one hand and Frances Burney and Jane Austen on the other. Perry and Carlile also provide compelling biographical details that help readers see what a prolific and spirited woman writer Lennox was. In addition, the edition includes a chronology, a note on the text highlighting the significant changes Lennox made to the first edition, a seventeen-page appendix indicating variants between the 1758 and 1761 editions, a second appendix listing corrections made by the editors for the sake of clarity, and a bibliography.

Also valuable for students and scholars of Lennox and the eighteenth-century novel is the new critical edition of Lennox's *Sophia*, edited by Norbert Schurer and published by Broadview. Apart from a chronology, textual variants and a bibliography, there is much additional material to explore in this carefully annotated edition: an introduction that considers the extent to which *Sophia* (one of the first novels written for serial publication) is a conventional sentimental novel, brief 'notes' on relevant aspects of English culture such as 'female property and education', reproductions of illustrations to the novel, a selection of contemporary reviews, excerpts from Lennox's periodical *The Lady's Museum*, and a section that covers the subjects of 'Sentimentalism and Moral Philosophy', elucidated by extracts from the work of David Hume, Henry MacKenzie and Mary Alcock, amongst others.

Lee F. Kahan, 'Fathoming Intelligence: The "Impartial" Novelist and the Passion for News in Tobias Smollett's *Ferdinand Count Fathom*' (*ECF* 21.2[2008–9] 229–57), takes issue with the idea that Smollett's novel lacks narrative coherence, arguing that the author functions as a unifying factor and that the plot represents a kind of metafictional, generic struggle between the fleeting, fragmented and fashion-prone periodical (as embodied by Fathom) and the enduring, elevated novel and its ideal, discerning reader (as embodied by Monimia and Renaldo). A small part of John Richardson's 'Imagining Military Conflict during the Seven Years' War' (*SEL* 48[2008] 585–611) is devoted to Sterne's *Tristram Shandy*, which is considered as 'a comic analysis' (p. 588) of the difficulties of representing military conflict and martial heroes. Richardson also discusses the novel in his article 'Sterne's Patriotic Shandeism' (*EIC* 58[2008] 20–42), which considers the extent to which *Tristram Shandy* reinforces contemporary views of the English national character, suggesting that its author complemented the conventional qualities of 'bravery, unchangeableness and (occasionally) common sense' with 'extreme singularity' (p. 27).

Published in the Continuum Reception Studies series, Lana Asfour's *Laurence Sterne in France* is well placed, and complements the collaborative volume *The Reception of Laurence Sterne in Europe* [2004]. The book's aim is to supersede Francis Brown Barton's 1911 study of Sterne's influence in eighteenth-century France and to use the methods and theories of modern reception studies, drawing especially on the work of Wolfgang Iser, Hans Robert Jauss and Gérard Genette. The result is a book, divided into three sections, 'Criticism', 'Translations' and 'Fiction', which offers a record of painstaking research on the periodical press and the reviews that assessed Sterne's work on its initial publication in France, the construction of his critical reputation and his elevation to a canonical figure whose work would serve as a stimulus to Diderot's *Jacques le fataliste*. She also adds a useful appendix of 'Articles on Sterne in French Periodicals, 1760–1800', an important bibliographical resource for further studies of individual aspects of Sterne's French reception. Asfour situates the reception of Sterne's works within neoclassical contexts of imitation and originality and offers much useful information on the ideological positions of the review journals in which assessments of Sterne appeared. She pays attention to French generic debates on modes such as the burlesque and satire and argues that Sterne's readers appreciated his modes in ways that other nations did not. As evidence, she introduces detailed discussions of the translations of the author's works, explicating at the same time in what ways the translation of an English author was theorized by French critics. As her account ends with the year 1800, she has charted the major developments in aesthetic, novelistic and translation theory that defined the reception and adaptation of Sterne's work in France. However, she notes (in my view unnecessarily) that she has resisted the 'impossible task' of 'attempting to describe or objectify' the reception of Sterne's texts, insisting that 'the focus has been on the debates of the period, through which are revealed the richness of and contradictions within the recipient culture' (p. 126). Notwithstanding this reservation, Asfour's book is an accomplished contribution to Elinor Shaffer's larger project of 'The Reception of British Authors in Europe' and sets a high standard for any investigation of the reception of an eighteenth-century British author in France.

Albert J. Rivero and George Justice, eds., *The Eighteenth-Century Novel*, volumes 6–7: *Essays in Honour of John Richetti*, was not received in time for review this year, so will be covered with material from 2009.

3. Poetry

With the notable exception of Alexander Pope, this year was marked by continued attention to the work of traditionally overlooked figures, notably women and labouring-class poets. Attention was also paid to the often neglected Scottish-born and educated poets David Mallet, who gains a modern biographer, and James Grainger, who has been credited with inventing a new genre, the West Indian georgic. An emerging trend was registered by a number of studies concerned with how the poetry of the period portrays the natural environment and in particular represents human–animal interaction. Pope himself gets drawn into these concerns in an important essay by John Sitter (to be discussed below) which, in seeking to provide a corrective dose of scholarly historicism to recent claims regarding Romantic poetry's monopoly on ecological awareness, offers a reading of *An Essay on Man* as crucial evidence. At its best, such work, by feeding off a characteristically eclectic body of 'green' theory and practice, is starting to engender some genuinely new critical insights into the poetry of this period.

Of the canonical poets, Alexander Pope was particularly well served this year by an important body of six essays by leading scholars published as part of the tribute volume *Literary Milieux: Essays in Text and Context Presented to Howard Erskine-Hill*, edited by David Womersley and Richard McCabe. For reasons of space I will not be providing a very detailed account of each individual essay, but the following summaries, presented in the order in which they appear in the volume, aim at indicating the range and content of what, when read in sequence, amounts to a significant collective contribution to Pope studies.

Julian Ferraro's essay, 'Pope, Pen and Press', provides a scholarly, critical reconstruction of Pope's protracted composition of *An Epistle From Mr. Pope, to Dr. Arbuthnot* [1735], as far as this can be ascertained from the extant but geographically dispersed manuscript material directly relating to the writing process. Ferraro's lucid, forensic account is accompanied by an appendix which prints for the first time the entire 260-line autograph draft poem opening 'And of Myself Too...' as it survives in draft (with authorial revisions). Although these verses make no mention of Arbuthnot nor of William Cleland (who is frequently claimed to have been the original addressee), they are usually cited as forming the basis, when revised and expanded, for the original draft of the *Epistle to Arbuthnot*. As Ferraro's close reading indicates, this draft tells us a lot about how the poet reconfigured his early ideas to create a greater degree of intimacy as the 'irascible tone of the Pope's original "Bill of Complaint" is steadily replaced by a more sophisticated exposition, in which he introduces a play of different voices ... [a] play achieved not only by the introduction of an interlocutor—or series of interlocutors—but also by a series of subtle shifts in the tone of Pope's own account of his character and conduct' (p. 130). Ferraro's meticulous mapping of these shifts will be of interest to anyone concerned with the mechanics of Pope's self-fashioning.

George Rousseau's engagingly erudite essay, 'Pope, Rhapsody, and Rapture: "You grow correct that once with Rapture writ"', can usefully be read as a companion piece to his contribution to last year's *Cambridge Companion to Pope* (*YWES* 88[2009] 646), in so far as it addresses the poet's engagement with medical ideas, more specifically the overlaying of traditional notions of the passions by the new 'doctrine of the nerves' articulated most influentially by the anatomist Thomas Willis, the medically trained philosopher John Locke, and Pope's friend, the medical practitioner and popular medical author George Cheyne. Out of necessity Rousseau is required to revisit, albeit in summary, territory he has covered more extensively in his earlier work where he has drawn our attention to the importance of the conceptual language of contemporary neurology for reading eighteenth-century literature, including poetry. But Rousseau's title is drawn from Pope's 1737 *Epilogue to the Satires*, and at the heart of this new essay is an examination of the shifting, problematic meanings of 'rhapsody' and 'rapture' available to the poet and his critics. In so doing Rousseau takes a typically impressive long view, ranging from Homer to Coleridge, while taking in Shaftesbury and John Dennis along the way. Observing that '[a]natomy and physiology, "the arts of the body" as called by Martinus Scriblerus—were branches of natural philosophy near-invalid Pope had good reason to cultivate' (p. 182), Rousseau asks us to consider how the new physiology might have enabled the poet to sustain an 'aesthetics of rhapsody' when the term was in fact losing force. This is a lively essay that unapologetically raises almost as many question as it answers but in so doing deliberately invites the pursuit of fresh paths of contextual enquiry. Rousseau's contribution is followed by Robert J. Mayhew's essay, 'Self-Fashioned Prospects: Pen, Print, and the Presentation of Landscape in the Correspondence of Alexander Pope', which does not directly address the poetry, but is of interest as a reassessment of this subject.

Hester Jones's contribution to the same volume, '"Religion blushing veils her sacred fires": Pope and the Veil of Faith', is concerned with how matters of faith inform the poet's oeuvre. This wide-ranging essay examines the pervasive religious tropes evident in *The Dunciad* (from which her title is derived) and a number of other poems, including 'An Essay on Man', 'To A Lady', the 'Universal Prayer', 'Messiah', 'Epistle to Miss Blount', 'A Prayer to God 1715' and Pope's translation of 'Hymn to St Francis Xavier'. She also examines Pope's declarations of faith in his private correspondence and reconsiders the possible influence of the distinctive spirituality of the French mystic Madame Guyon and her champion Archbishop Fénelon. Jones finds Pope 'consistently engaged in defining the relation in his understanding of Catholic Christianity between true wit and true faith' while his 'relation to any theological position is usually more contrapuntal than antithetical, and always concerned to open up the possibilities of a position rather than close them down' (pp. 209, 222).

The contribution of Robert Douglas-Fairhurst to the same volume is equally comprehensive in approach. In 'Alexander Pope: "Renown'd in Rhyme"', Douglas-Fairhurst is prompted by ideas first broached by Hugh Kenner to present his own reflections upon Pope's 'sensitivity to the relationship between rhyme and time' (p. 233). There is an underlying ethical dimension to these formalist concerns. Drawing upon John Henry Newman's notion of 'credences', his term for the common ways of thinking that provide our moral bearings, Douglas-Fairhurst's thoughtful analysis rests upon his general observation that 'the rhyme-words of a language emerge over a far longer time as the irreducible residue of cultural development, its audible tea-leaves' (p. 236). He concludes that Pope had a 'humane and perceptive understanding of rhyme—not as a mere jingle of words, but as the sound of our consciousness of time, our consciousness in time' (p. 255)

In literary studies the most unassuming titles can sometimes hide the richest fruits, but when the author is Claude Rawson we are unlikely to be deceived. His title 'The Sleep of the Dunces' for his contribution to this volume bucks a long-standing trend in academic literary studies for elaborate titles, but as we might well expect this truly erudite, beautifully choreographed critical essay is a small masterpiece of its kind. Meditating upon the manner in which the Miltonic reverberations 'of Night Primeval, and of Chaos old' have perhaps drawn undue attention away from 'the ignoble particulars' of 'sleep' in *The Dunciad*, Rawson presents a magnificently rich and lively analysis of how tropes associated with 'night' and 'sleep' function throughout the multiple versions of the work he considers to be Pope's *Waste Land* (p. 258). T.S. Eliot is just one of an array of writers with whom Rawson is able to forge ever-enriching verbal comparisons; Homer, Euripides, Virgil, Dante, Milton, Rochester, Garth, Blackmore and Shelley (in 'Peter Bell') are all brought into play here without once losing focus on the central goal of elucidating Pope's vision of cultural catastrophe and apocalyptic 'uncreation'. Along the way our attention is also drawn to the comparative use of the mock-heroic in John Gay's *The Beggar's Opera* and Henry Fielding's *Jonathan Wild* (they appeared in 1728 and 1743, the years which witnessed the first and final versions of *The Dunciad*) and Swift's precise role in promoting what is often thought of as Pope's most Swiftian poem. In short, this essay, the work of a major scholar at the height of his critical powers, is essential reading for anyone with an interest in comprehending Pope's most controversial and complex poem.

Last but not least is an intriguing essay, 'Dulness's Obscure Vowel: Language, Monarchy, and Motherhood in Pope's *The Dunciad in Four Books*' by Valerie Rumbold. Building upon the work of Simon Alderson and others on Pope's use of iconic, imitative versification and how this represents an engagement with contemporary debates over the relationship of words to things and the power of the poet, Rumbold sets out on a forensic exploration of Pope's use of phonaesthetic effects in *The Dunciad in Four Books* of 1743 by comparing these with the practical examples of the meaning of English sounds posited by the seventeenth-century grammarian John Wallis (as translated and frequently incorporated into later textbooks, notably Charles Gildon and John Brightwood's *A Grammar of the English Tongue* [1711]). As Rumbold herself observes, despite any 'Lockean or Saussurean scepticism as modern readers we may bring to Wallis's discussions of the alleged meanings of English sound, his analyses remain aesthetically compelling' (p. 285). And indeed we are inclined to agree that reading 'Pope, with Wallis's analysis in mind is also a salutary reminder that his poetry, so often discussed in terms of its continental and classicising influences, has at its heart, especially where its action or metaphor is essentially physical, a deeply felt relation to a core of the oldest English words' (p. 285). A brief example of how this operates at the level of a single-word is in the couplet 'Instructive work! Whose wry-mouthed portraiture | Display'd the fates her confessors endure' (2: 145–6); as Rumbold notes, 'according to Wallis, initial "wr" represents "Crookedness or Distortion", an inference supported by the group "Wry, wreath, wrest, wrestle, wring, etc"' (p. 285). In a similar vein Rumbold goes on to disclose further and more complex patterns of related word-clusters, before identifying one particular vowel sound 'that is particularly important in orchestrating some of the poem's most characteristic effects ... [T]he sound in question being what Wallis, locating it in the word "mumble", calls "the Obscure (*u*)"' (p. 290). Finding that Pope tends to place words employing this sound in close association with Dulness—words such as 'Plunge', 'Mud', 'Suck' (and 'suckle'), 'lull' (and 'lullaby)—Rumbold observes how, when taken 'together, the referents of these 'Obscure (*u*)' words map onto the lower rather than the high, the physical rather than the intellectual; and they connect in particular with things that are sloppy, viscous and potentially revolting in their transgression of defined boundaries' (p. 291). But what is particularly engaging for me about this essay is that, having mapped the preponderance of this particular sound (as labelled by Wallis), Rumbold's account then pans out into an equally rich exploration of the contexts for comprehending the politicized iconography of motherhood, nursing and infantilism at work in the poem. The result is a rewarding essay that in moving between close linguistic analysis and broad cultural contexts—notably a shift in conceptions of maternal and queenly authority—ably fulfils the parameters signalled in this volume's subtitle: 'Text and Context'.

In his article 'The Rhetoric of Disclosure in James Thomson's *The Seasons*; or, On Kant's Gentlemanly Misanthropy' (*ECent* 49[2008] 1–24) Denis Desroches addresses the frequent charges of unreadability owing to incoherent fragmentation, contrivance and portentousness levelled by modern readers against this omnium gatherum of a poem. His own analysis takes off from the observation that as a focus for discussions of such topics as class relations, geopolitics and Enlightenment philosophy, Thomson's poem has come to 'foreground a critical practice that sees *The Seasons* not as a poem at all, but a dense site of discursive exempla from which certain passages can be strip-mined and made to serve certain ends' (p. 2). Desroches also notes how current academic journalistic conventions, which militate against citing more then twenty lines of verse, have effectively served to reinforce a critical approach that, in charging *The Seasons* with incoherence, 'brings into sharp relief the constraints of our own reading and interpretative practices' (p. 3). Instead Desroches successfully shifts attention away from any purported lack of 'logical rigor' to a more positive exploration of 'rhetorical rigor', specifically what he explicates as Thomson's 'rhetoric of gentlemanly exposure' (p. 3). To achieve this Desroches brings together Marx's conception of 'the societal individual' and John Barrell's work on eighteenth-century conceptions of landscape as, in effect, idealized models of civil society viewed from the perspective of a 'gentleman' whose role (as influentially defined by Richard Steele), is simply to 'shine in the world'. Within this broadly historicist framework Desroches convincingly reads *The Seasons* as Thomson's attempt to 'be that curiously disposed individual of the early to mid- eighteenth century whose social function was not to function at all, but to observe, and in observing be eminently observable himself' (p. 7). Through four variant exercises in close reading, Desroches demonstrates the reach and ultimate limits of this 'rhetoric of exposure' as enacted in short exemplary passages from the poem, whereby 'images of darkness and light, concealing and revealing—the play of "light and shade"—are manipulated in order to generate a sense of the gentleman's ability, in comprehending the workings of the world, to present those working to the reader in a revelatory rather than strictly didactic or even discursive fashion' (pp. 7–8). Citing Kant's notion of a 'sublime misanthropy' in *The Critique of Pure Reason*, whereby the gentleman's world comes to be 'irrevocably changed by this sense of reflection' (p. 21), Desroches finally draws attention to how Thomson is ultimately unable to 'speak, properly speaking, of the sun, of light, of God' but repeatedly seeks to retreat into the rural shade. This is a sophisticated work of rhetorical analysis; one that serves to bring a sense of coherence back to the poem without seeking to impose any anachronistic or simplistically formalist straitjacket.

An even more neglected mid-century descriptive poem is re-evaluated in Beccie Puneet Randhawa's essay, 'The Inhospitable Muse: Locating Creole Identity in James Grainger's *The Sugar Cane*' (*ECent* 49[2008] 67–85). As she rightly observes, James Grainger's didactic poem, first published at London in 1764, has often repulsed modern readers disturbed by the ethical implications of aestheticizing the sugar cane 'at the expense of anaesthetizing the suffering bodies of the slaves who must tend it' (p. 70). More recently the poem has drawn attention from post-colonialist literary historians who, without wishing to set aside Grainger's disconcerting, blatantly self-contradictory shifts from apologist to ameliorist positions, have been concerned with his invention of the West Indian georgic. Randhawa contributes to this project of reassessment by arguing that the poem has 'a more stark and deliberate function: the repudiation of claims of cultural inferiority and degeneracy' typically levelled at the Creole by the mother country (p. 70). She opens with a famous anecdote—of which we have several versions—to the effect that when Grainger, having travelled all the way from St Kitt's to London to see his poem through the press, read it out to members of Johnson's Literary Club he was met with howls of laughter when he reached the line 'Now, Muse, let's sing of rats'. Randhawa uses this story of failed hospitality as a springboard for a reading of the poem that draws upon Peter Hulme's identification of a pattern of exotic and colonial hospitality as well as more abstract conceptions of the ethics of hospitality available in Kant and Lévinas (as read by Derrida). This helpful theoretical framework enables Randhawa to explore 'the complex structures of gratitude, generosity and reciprocity' (p. 71) informing what she identifies as Grainger's attempt to contest established, stereotypical images of the Creole class-faction as peculiarly vicious, luxurious, cruel and degenerate. On this reading Randhawa suggests that the 'monumental awkwardness' of the poem, as evident from its initial, mocking reception in London, rests in the manner in which the poem's 'ideological motivations internalize the very same anxiety of "belonging" and overseas acceptance which the colonial West Indian Creole craved, as a cultural outsider' (p. 68). In Randhawa's hands this approach generates new insights into Grainger's attempts to reconfigure the planter as country-house host, and to recast slavery 'in terms of hospitality, where mutual gratitude and benevolence take the place of enslaved brutality' (p. 78). Her close reading of tropes associated with hospitality is particularly rewarding when she applies her conceptual lens to the objects of Grainger's own medical gaze: the worms and other tropical parasites which figure in the verse as unwanted guests that eat away at their host. But the essay also represents a missed opportunity in so far as it fails to take on board one glaring aspect of Grainger's bid for cultural approval amongst his London-based literary hosts: his status as a Scotsman. Randhawa's unqualified references to 'England' and 'English' throughout her discussion of Grainger's negotiations of his Creole status soon begin to grate if one considers the specifically Scottish perspective registered throughout *The Sugar Cane* (in, for example, Grainger's approval of Scottish-produced linen and his dubious comparison between the relatively comfortable lot of West Indian slaves and that of Scottish miners). As a Scotsman in London, Grainger was already an outsider beholden to hospitality before he ever left for the West Indies. He initially went there in his role as a surgeon-physician, and as such formed part of a Scottish diaspora that made up a culturally significant proportion of the West Indian (Creole) colonialist population. His return, poem in hand, to the climate of intense scotophobia pervading London in the mid-1760s as whipped up by Lord Bute's opponents, must have merely highlighted this doubly marginalized position. To overlook this internal-colonialist context for reading *The Sugar Cane* is a regrettable oversight in what is otherwise a potentially rewarding approach to this intensely problematic poem.

In *David Mallet, Anglo-Scot: Poetry, Patronage, and Politics in the Age of Union*, Sandro Jung presents the first modern, scholarly account of Grainger's compatriot David Mallet (1703?–1765). Mallet who, by anglicizing his name from the original 'Malloch', effectively sacrificed being claimed by future generations as a Scottish writer, was a successful poet, dramatist and Patriot propagandist. Adept at what we might now term literary 'networking', Mallet was a well-known figure in mid-century London, where he associated with the likes of James Thomson, Aaron Hill and Alexander Pope, but outside specialist literary circles he has largely sunk into oblivion. Jung, who is no doubt correct to hold Samuel Johnson—who simply condemns Mallet as a 'party-hack' in the *Lives of the Poets*—largely responsible for the subsequent neglect and distortion of Mallet's achievements, deliberately sets out to put the record straight. This act of scholarly recovery and reappraisal is presented as a deliberate intervention in the current re-examination of the eighteenth-century poetical landscape. Jung is particularly concerned with how Mallet negotiated a mid-century climate in which patronage, politics and poetical self-fashioning are inextricably interlinked. The result is a solid and readable critical biography. It is well supported by archival evidence, including ample reference to Mallet's somewhat fragmentary extant correspondence and his recently recovered notes and drafts relating to the account of the duke of Marlborough that he was compiling at the time of his death. Jung also provides detailed contextual readings of Mallet's most significant works, including his descriptive poem *The Excursion*, his once popular foray into the Thomsonian sublime. And yet Mallet, whose Scottish origins remain veiled in the fog he himself appears to have woven to disguise his family's Jacobite allegiances, remains a somewhat elusive figure. For all that Jung can recover of Mallet's literary ambitions and social connections, we gain hardly any sense of a personal life. But this is no fault of his new biographer, who must be commended for all his scholarly efforts; rather, it is a reflection of glaring gaps in the historical record and Mallet's own facility for evading detection.

One of Mallet's earliest popular successes as a poet was the literary ballad 'William and Margaret', first published by Aaron Hill in *The Plain Dealer* in 1724. In a comprehensive essay entitled ' "The Finest Ballads": Women's Oral Traditions in Eighteenth-Century Scotland' (*ECLife* 32:ii[2008] 81–97), Ruth Perry is more specifically concerned with women's role in a native Scottish song and ballad tradition. Perry does not offer any original primary research, but this well-informed essay does provide a valuable overview of the field, paying particular attention to the role of women as producers and custodians of this rich Scottish oral tradition.

In his journal essay, 'Eighteenth-Century Ecological Poetry and Ecotheology' (*R&L* 40:i[2008] 13–37), John Sitter issues a robust and much-needed historicist corrective to a growing tendency amongst the more flabby followers of Jonathan Bate and Karl Kroeber to associate the origins of ecological consciousness exclusively with Romanticism when in fact, as Sitter himself ably demonstrates, 'the idea that poetry is a special discourse that might reunite mind and nature was current at least a century earlier' (p. 14). The essay opens with an informed exploration of the common ground between our current, if still somewhat diffuse, conceptions of ecotheology (including Arne Neass's influential model of 'deep ecology') and the tenets of eighteenth-century physicotheology as exemplified in John Derham's popular *Physicotheology; or, a Demonstration of the Being and Attributes of God, from his Works of Creation* [1713]. As Sitter demonstrates, such a comparison opens up 'the possibility of sympathetic ecotheological reading of eighteenth-century poetry' before presenting a series of illustrative close readings, starting with a comparison between two rhetorically similar passages from Wordsworth's 'Two-Part Prelude' of 1799 (I.269–74, starting 'Was it for this. . .') and James Thomson's *Seasons* ('Autumn', 1184–8, starting 'Was it then for This. . .'), in which he reveals that is it the latter, rather than Wordsworth, who shows the most ecological awareness (pp. 12–13). There follows an engaging analysis of the figurative use of the term 'peopled' in early eighteenth-century poetry when describing social phenomena in the animal world such as swarms of bees, flocks of birds, or schools of fish. Here Sitter draws upon an early study of *The Language of Natural Description in Eighteenth-Century Poetry* from 1949 by John Arthos, who identified 'peopled' as belonging to a network of terms familiar to anyone who knows the poetry of the period: 'Band, Breed, Brood, Choir, Citizen, Crew, Flock, Fry, Herd, Host, Inhabitants, Kind, Legion, Nation, Race, Seed, Shoal, Squadron, Train, Tribe, Troop'. But as Sitter observes, while a modern ecocritic might be tempted to dismiss such tropes as blatant anthropocentrism, in practice, as in Thomson's description of poultry as 'household feathery people', the actual employment of such language raises important questions regarding 'the eighteenth-century tendency to use "people" to refer both to animals *and* humans—a usage which seems to die out in the early nineteenth century' (p. 18). Here Sitter suggests the 'fact that a broader range of meaning for "people" was open to eighteenth-century poets than most nineteenth-century poets deserves more attention than it has received' (p. 18).

Sitter also addresses the now commonplace argument that Romanticism marks the birth or rebirth of 'green' consciousness, what he wittily refers to as not merely the 'greening of Romanticism' but the uncritical 'Romanticization of greenness' (p. 13). Such claims have largely relied upon a familiar grand narrative, largely derived from Max Weber, that insists that a combination of Cartesian philosophy and the scientific revolution of the seventeenth century produced a 'disenchanted' and 'mechanistic' view of Nature. Doubting whether 'this narrative is true in relation to general European history', in the second half of his essay Sitter addresses how the actual use of the term 'Imperial Race' as applied to 'Man' illustrates how any such claim certainly oversimplifies the line 'between organic and mechanistic metaphors' active in eighteenth-century poetry (p. 20). In particular, he devotes much of the latter half of this enlightening account to addressing Pope's use of the term in *An Essay on Man*, where it typically 'suggests human kinship with other animals and responsibility for them' (p. 21). This groundbreaking essay fully justifies Sitter's concluding declaration that 'ours is a moment when vigorous reconsideration of the traditions of nature poetry before Romanticism would help reanimate both literary and religious discussion' (p. 33).

Ecocriticism is a broad church, but although she is writing from a somewhat different critical perspective some of Sitter's demands are ably met by Anne Milne in her book-length study, *'Lactilla Tends her fav'rite Cow': Ecocritical Readings of Animals and Women in Eighteenth-Century British Labouring-Class Poetry*. In a lucid introduction Milne sets out her concerns with 'representations of nature, natural genius, and instrumentality' (p. 17). She positions her critical project firmly in relation to historicist studies of eighteenth-century labouring-class women's poetry as prompted by the work of Richard Green, Donna Landry, Mary Waldron and others while also displaying a well-informed, practical engagement with ecocriticism (Kate Soper, Steve Baker and others) and related theoretical ideas, notably Gilles Deleuze and Félix Guattari's explorations of the human–animal interface. The ensuing relatively short but rewarding study is arranged into thematic chapters, each focused around the close reading of a significant work by one of five women poets. A very brief summary will give a sense of the coverage. The first chapter, addressing 'Ideologies of Domestication in Mary Leapor's "Man the Monarch"', makes original reference to contemporary textbooks on the domestication of animals. In the second, entitled 'Gender, Class and the Beehive; Mary Collier's "The Woman's Labour" as Nature Poem', Milne considers notions of women as industrious. Drawing upon contemporary manuals on bee-keeping (and how to construct bee-boxes) she offers some intriguing new insights into what by now is a much-read poem. The third chapter, entitled ' "We saw an heifer stray": Ecological Interconnection and Identification in Elizabeth Hands's "Written, originally extempore, on seeing a Mad Heifer run through the Village where the Author lives" ', examines the problem of unpicking 'interlocking oppressions'. The fourth, 'The Silence of the Lambs: Rapture and Release in Ann Yearsley's "Written on a Visit" ', considers how Yearsley negotiates notions of 'wildness' and 'hyper-docility' directly relevant to the poet's own concerns with independence. The title of Milne's final chapter—'Dogs and the "Talking Animal Syndrome" in Janet

Little's "From Snipe, a Favourite Dog, To His Master"'—might be said to speak for itself. Although most of the texts Milne discusses are now available in modern editions, she sensibly provides several less accessible poems in an appendix preceding a full bibliography.

Animals are also a central concern of Ingrid H. Tague in her essay on 'Dead Pets: Satire and Sentiment in British Elegies and Epitaphs for Animals' (*ECS* 41[2008] 57–80). This practical exercise in genre criticism suggests the value of employing minor poetry to explore cultural trends, in this instance shifting attitudes towards animals. As Tague observes, for our modern notion of pets to be possible a society has to have reached a certain level of luxury that can tolerate the keeping of animals that do not contribute as food or by their labour. It is also necessary that there are physical barriers separating the domestic realm from other parts of the household where livestock are kept. Qualifying previous claims that 'pets' (a term originally accorded tame, hand-reared lambs) are essentially a nineteenth century development, Tague uses occasional poetry to reveal how they effectively emerge as a distinct concept earlier in the eighteenth century. At the heart of this account is an analytical survey of the many elegies and epitaphs on dead pets that were increasingly produced as the century proceeded; one that ranges from Thomas Gray's suave 'Ode on the Death of a Favourite Cat' to many obscure, far less sophisticated examples. A significant number were merely witty, comic literary exercises, *jeux d'esprit* inspired by such classical models as Catullus's elegy for Lesbia's sparrow and Ovid's for Corinna's parrot, but as Tague shows, this ephemeral poetic material reveals the many 'ways people used animals to think about humans' place in the world' (p. 292). In the early half of the century poetic allusions to pets tended to be satirical, as in Pope's *The Rape of the Lock*, where lap-dogs invoke contemporary associations between women, fashion and pet-keeping; 'Pets—specially lapdogs, monkeys and parrots—could be seen as useless luxuries, just as women themselves were useless; women's love of pets proved their misplaced values as well as their susceptibility to the whims of fashion' (p. 293). Elsewhere female pets function as objects of male jealously, often through the invocation of blatantly sexual innuendo. On the other side of the equation Tague considers how 'parrots, lapdogs and monkeys lent themselves to easy parallels with other satirical targets, especially fops and beaus who were supposedly the primary distractions of fashionable women' (p. 294). But such comparisons are not always purely comical; by enabling the exploration of conceptual boundaries between the animal and the human, the natural and the domesticated, they could also fulfil a moral purpose. Dogs often raise questions over loyalty, fidelity and trustworthiness, while caged birds are particularly problematic for inviting questions of power relations, a theme that takes on particular resonance amongst proto-feminist women poets towards the end of the century. Animal deaths often invite reflections on human mortality, but as Tague observes, while many verifiers insist upon the traditional Christian notion that humans are supposedly unique in their capacity to reason and hence make moral judgements, some were drawn to consider—often by taking their cue from the Pythagorean concept of metempsychosis—the possibility that their pets had souls. Tague identifies a marked increase in the individuality accorded pets towards the close of the century, as pet-keeping gradually came 'to symbolize all that was best in the human spirit, and mourning the loss of a pet could be seen as praiseworthy rather than ridiculous' (p. 302).

Attention is drawn to two related studies: Julie Prandi's book *The Poetry of the Self-Taught: An Eighteenth-Century Phenomenon*, is only marginally relevant here in as much as she addresses a considerable amount of German poetry and her range of reference extends into the Romantic era. But it is worth noting for her opening discussion of what is at stake in using the term 'self-taught' poet and for the attention she pays to the careers and poetry of Mary Barber, Mary Collier, Stephen Duck and Mary Leapor. Covering some similar ground, Kirsten Juhas's *'I'll to my Self, and to My Muse Be True': Strategies of Self-Authorization in Eighteenth-Century Women Poetry* [*sic*], is a doctoral thesis, as awarded by the Westflische Wihelms University, Munster, in 2007. Despite the infelicity of her title, Juhas presents a fluent, well-illustrated account of how women poets of the period (again extending into the 1790s) negotiated predominantly masculine conceptions of the power of the pen. Topics covered include how they invoked the Muse (specifically a self-consciously 'domestic muse'), adopted ironic slatternly or mad poses and, in poems on 'The Nightingale', adapted the myth of Philomela.

Finally, on rather different tack we have Aaron Santesso's substantial essay '"Playful" Poetry and the Public School' (*ECLife* 32:ii[2008], 57–80) addressing the poetic exercises traditionally encouraged at Westminster School. Although the historical range of this account extends backwards into the seventeenth century, it does have some relevance here for the attention it pays to Latin and English acrostics and anagrams appearing in school anthologies published well into the early eighteenth century.

Books Reviewed

Asfour, Lana. *Laurence Sterne in France*. Continuum. [2008] pp. 182. £65 ISBN 9 7808 2649 5426.

Bannet, Eve Tavor, ed. *British and American Letter Manuals, 1680–1810*. 4 vols. P&C. [2008] pp. 1,712. £350 ISBN 9 7818 5196 9180.

Battestin, Martin C., ed. *The Journal of a Voyage to Lisbon, Shamela, and Occasional Writings*. The Wesleyan Edition of Henry Fielding. Clarendon. [2008] pp. 804. £166 ISBN 9 7801 9926 6753.

Boswell, James, and Samuel Johnson. *A Journey to the Western Isles of Scotland and The Journal of a Tour to the Hebrides*. Dover. [2008] pp. vii + 406. pb $11.95 ISBN 9 7804 8645 5549.

Boyd, Diane E., and Marta Kvande, eds. *Everyday Revolutions: Eighteenth-Century Women Transforming Public and Private*. UDelP. [2008] pp. 287. $58.50 ISBN 9 7808 7413 0072.

Brodey, Inger Sigrun. *Ruined by Design: Shaping Novels and Gardens in the Culture of Sensibility*. Routledge. [2008] pp. 274. £70 ISBN 9 7804 1598 9503.

Broome, Judith. *Fictive Domains: Body, Landscape, and Nostalgia, 1717–1770*. BuckUP. [2007] pp. 191. $42.59 ISBN 9 7808 3875 6348.

Carnell, Rachel. *A Political Biography of Delarivier Manley*. Eighteenth Century Political Biographies. P&C. [2008] pp. xi +306. £60 ISBN 9 7818 5196 8572.

Chapman, R.W., ed. *Life of Johnson*. by James Boswell, introd. Pat Rogers. 3rd edn. OUP. [2008] pp. xxxvi + 1,492. pb £16.99 IBSN 9 7801 9954 0211.

DeMaria, Robert. *British Literature, 1640–1789: An Anthology*. 3rd edn. Blackwell. [2007] pp. xxxviii + 1,135. £24.99 ISBN 9 7814 0511 9283.

Dick, Alexander, and Christina Lupton, eds. *Theory and Practice in the Eighteenth Century: Writing Between Philosophy and Literature*. P&C. [2008] pp. ix + 313. £60 ISBN 9 7818 5196 9388.

Downie, J.A., ed. *Henry Fielding in Our Time: Papers Presented at the Tercentenary Conference*. CSP. [2008] pp. 380. $59.99 ISBN 9 7818 4718 9875.

Eger, Elizabeth, and Lucy Peltz. *Brilliant Women: Eighteenth-Century Bluestockings*. NPG [2008] pp. 159. £18.99 ISBN 9 7818 5514 3890.

Goring, Paul. *Eighteenth-Century Culture and Literature*. Continuum. [2008] pp. 168. hb £55 ISBN 9 7808 2648 5649, pb £11.99 ISBN 9 7808 2648 5656.

Hudson, Nicholas, and Aaron Santesso. *Swift's Travels: Eighteenth-Century British Satire and its Legacy*. CUP. [2008] pp. xii + 304. £50 ISBN 9 7805 2187 9552.

Johnson, Neil. *Dr Johnson's Reliquary of Rediscovered Words*. Marius Press. [2008] pp. xii + 180. £25 IBSN 9 7818 7162 2348.

Juhas, Kirsten. *'I'll to My Self, and to My Muse Be True': Strategies of Self-Authorization in Eighteenth-Century Women Poetry*. Lang. [2008] pp. 313. pb $74.95 ISBN 9 7836 3158 1421.

Jung, Sandro. *David Mallet, Anglo-Scot: Poetry, Patronage, and Politics in the Age of Union*. UDelP. [2008] pp. 211. $48.50 ISBN 9 7808 7413 0058.

King, Shelley, and Yaël Schlick. *Refiguring the Coquette: Essays on Culture and Coquetry*. BuckUP. [2008] pp. 228. $49.50 ISBN 9 7808 3875 7109.

Kinsley, Zoë. *Women Writing the Home Tour, 1682–1812*. Ashgate. [2008] pp. x +286. £50 ISBN 9 7807 5465 6630.

Kraft, Elizabeth. *Women Novelists and the Ethics of Desire, 1684–1814: In the Voice of Our Biblical Mothers*. Ashgate. [2008] pp. viii + 200. £55 ISBN 9 7807 5466 2808.

Lacey, Nicola. *Women, Crime, and Character: From Moll Flanders to Tess of the D'Urbervilles*. OUP. [2008] pp. xiv + 164. $45 ISBN 9 7801 9954 4363.

Larsen, Lyle. *James Boswell as his Contemporaries Saw Him*. FDUP. [2008] pp. 256. $55 ISBN 9 7808 3864 1712.

Looser, Devoney. *Women Writers and Old Age in Great Britain,1750–1850*. JHUP. [2008] pp. 252. $55 ISBN 9 7808 0188 7055.

Loveman, Kate. *Reading Fictions, 1660–1740: Deception in English Literary and Political Culture*. Ashgate. [2008] pp. x + 222. £50 ISBN 9 7807 5466 2372.

Lynch, Jack. *Deception and Detection in Eighteenth-Century Britain*. Ashgate. [2008] pp. xiii + 218. £55 ISBN 9 7807 5466 5281.

Manning, Susan, and Francis D. Cogliano, eds. *The Atlantic Enlightenment*. Ashgate. [2008] pp. xiii + 209. £50 ISBN 9 7807 5466 0408.

Martin, Peter. *Samuel Johnson: A Biography*. W&N. [2008] pp. xvi + 522. £25 ISBN 9 7802 9760 7199.

McVeagh, John, ed. *Defoe's Review 1704–13, vol. 6: 1709–10*. P&C. [2008] pp. 832. £195 ISBN 9 7818 5196 9081.

Milne, Anne. *'Lactilla Tends her fav'rite Cow': Ecocritical Readings of Animals and Women in Eighteenth-Century British Labouring-Class Poetry*. BuckUP. [2008] pp. 173. $52.50 ISBN 9 7908 3875 6928.

Oakleaf, David. *A Political Biography of Jonathan Swift*. Eighteenth-Century Political Biographies. P&C. [2008] pp. ix + 266. £60 ISBN 9 7818 5196 8480.

O'Connell, Jeffrey, and Thomas E. O'Connell. *Friendships Across Ages: Johnson and Boswell; Holmes and Laski*. Lexington. [2008] pp. viii + 193. $60 ISBN 9 7807 3912 0247.

Owens, W.R., and P. N. Furbank, eds. *The Novels of Daniel Defoe*. vols. 1–5. P&C. [2008] pp. 1,600. $750 ISBN 9 7818 5196 7483.

Papazian, Mary A., ed. *The Sacred and Profane in English Renaissance Literature*. UDelP. [2008] pp. 377. $75 ISBN 9 7808 7413 0256.

Pearsall, Sarah. *Atlantic Families: Lives and Letters in the Later Eighteenth Century*. OUP. [2008] pp. x + 294. £50 ISBN 9 7801 9953 2995.

Perry, Ruth, and Susan Carlile, eds. *Henrietta*. by Charlotte Lennox. UKL. [2008] pp. 290. $60 ISBN 9 7808 1312 4902.

Poovey, Mary. *Genres of the Credit Economy: Mediating Value in Eighteenth- and Nineteenth-Century Britain*. UChicP. [2008] pp. x + 511. hb $30.50 ISBN 9 7802 2667 5329, pb $12.50 ISBN 9 7802 2667 5336.

Prandi, Julie. *The Poetry of the Self-Taught: An Eighteenth-Century Phenomenon*. Lang. [2008] pp. 202. $68.95 ISBN 9 7814 3310 2516.

Rawson, Claude, ed. *Henry Fielding (1797–1754), Novelist, Playwright, Journalist, Magistrate: A Double Anniversary Tribute*. UDelP. [2008] pp. 337. $45. ISBN 9 7808 7413 9310.

Richetti, John. *The Cambridge Companion to Daniel Defoe*. CUP. [2009] pp. xiv + 248. £45 ISBN 9 7805 2185 8403.

Schurer, Norbert, ed. *Sophia*. by Charlotte Lennox. Broadview. [2008] pp. 266. $18.95 ISBN 9 7815 5111 6419.

Sim, Stuart. *The Eighteenth-Century Novel and Contemporary Social Issues: An Introduction*. EdinUP. [2008] pp. 213. £15.99 ISBN 9 7807 4862 6007.

Smith, Nicholas D. *The Literary Manuscripts and Letters of Hannah More*. Ashgate. [2008] pp. xxvi + 245. £50 ISBN 9 7807 5466 2709.

Watson, George. *The Story of the Novel*. Lutterworth. [2008] pp. 166. £17.50 ISBN 9 7807 1883 0946.

Wild, Min. *Christopher Smart and Satire: 'Mary Midnight' and the Midwife.*
Ashgate. [2008] pp. viii + 231. £50 ISBN 9 7807 5466 1931.

Wildermuth, Mark E. *Print, Chaos and Complexity: Samuel Johnson and
Eighteenth-Century Media Culture.* UDelP. [2008] pp. 197. £33.50 IBSN 9
7808 7413 0324.

Womersley, David, ed. *The Life of Samuel Johnson.* by James Boswell.
Penguin. [2008] pp. lx + 1,245. pb £18.99 ISBN 9 7801 4043 6624.

Womersley, David, and Richard McCabe, eds. *Literary Milieux: Essays in
Text and Context, Presented to Howard Erskine-Hill.* UDelP. [2008] pp. 371.
$80 ISBN 9 7808 7413 9907.

XII

Literature 1780–1830: The Romantic Period

ORIANNE SMITH, LUKE WRIGHT, FELICITY JAMES, DAVID STEWART, JASON WHITTAKER, CHRISTOPHER MACHELL AND JEREMY DAVIES

This chapter has five sections: 1. General; 2. Prose; 3. The Novel; 4. Poetry; and 5. Drama. Section 1 is by Orianne Smith; section 2 is by Luke Wright; section 3 is by Felicity James; section 4 is by David Stewart, Jason Whittaker and Christopher Machell; section 5 is by Jeremy Davies.

1. General

Romanticists will be pleased to know that several excellent books were published this year in the category of general Romanticism. Devoney Looser's *Women Writers and Old Age in Great Britain, 1750–1850* is a groundbreaking study of the late careers of women writers during this period. Authors such as Catharine Macaulay, Frances Burney, Hester Lynch Piozzi, Maria Edgeworth and Anna Letitia Barbauld all continued to actively publish around or beyond what was called the 'grand climacteric' at age 63 (p. 9). Yet, as Looser reveals, their ongoing efforts to publish past their 'prime' often had severe repercussions. Many were insulted by critics who derided them as relics with little or nothing to say of importance to the current generation. The most famous (or infamous) case was, of course, John Wilson Croker's scathing description of Barbauld as an old 'lady author' who dashes 'down her shagreen spectacles and her knitting needles' (p. 136) to save the empire in *Eighteen Hundred and Eleven* [1812]. The critical reception of this poem by Barbauld's contemporaries has received a great deal of scholarly attention, but what has not been addressed, as Looser points out, is the ageism behind Croker's commentary.

The introduction to *Women Writers and Old Age in Great Britain* provides an overview of what 'old' meant for British women writers from 1750 to 1850. As Looser notes, unlike their male counterparts, whose advanced age was generally thought of as a positive marker of increased wisdom, women writers who continued to publish in their later years had to contend with negative

Year's Work in English Studies, Volume 89 (2010) © *The English Association; all rights reserved*
doi:10.1093/ywes/maq003

stereotypes of old women as especially prone to garrulity, querulousness and dwindling mental capacity. Older women writers who wanted to preserve their reputations, literary or otherwise, were compelled to position themselves as grandmotherly authors of 'classics'. Chapter 1 provides two contrasting case studies to illustrate this point: the case of Maria Edgeworth, who conformed to societal expectations, and the case of Frances Burney, who did not, and the subsequent rise and fall, respectively, of their popularity amongst their readers. Catharine Macaulay's irate response in an unpublished letter to a less than glowing review of her last full-length published work, *Letters on Education* [1790] is discussed in chapter 2 in the context of Macaulay's determination to salvage her reputation as an ageing female historian. Interestingly, some women writers contributed to the stereotyping of older women. Chapter 3 points to the fact that Jane Austen, although an 'old maid' herself, represented old maids like Miss Bates in *Emma* as silly and inconsequential beings. In chapter 4, Looser suggests that Hester Lynch Piozzi's late friendship with the youthful actor William Augustus Conway was one of several innovative attempts to manage her posthumous career. In addition to debunking the myth (perpetuated by her well-meaning niece, Lucy Aiken) that Barbauld was so horrified by the reception of *Eighteen Hundred and Eleven* that she never published again, chapter 5 argues for the importance of Barbauld's later work as an editor and a literary critic. The final chapter attests to the tenacity of Jane Porter in her repeated efforts to secure a royal pension that would honour her literary achievements and provide for her in her old age. Through a series of nuanced readings, Looser reveals how each of these women writers approached old age on their own terms, against and amidst the explicit ageism of many of their contemporaries. The volume concludes with the suggestion that our knowledge of literary history could be enriched by further research on the challenges that ageing women faced during this period, and gestures to other examples of women authors whose decisions later in life could benefit from a more sustained analysis.

Another book published this year that charts new territory in Romanticism is Andrea K. Henderson's *Romanticism and the Painful Pleasures of Modern Life*. Henderson's monograph interrogates the ways in which ideas of mastery and subjection influenced Romantic aesthetics. This wide-ranging and ambitious study argues that the underlying power relationships—particularly the idealization of, and suffering for, objects of desire—in Romantic literature, art, architecture and garden design are the result of the failure of the modern world to deliver on its promise of increased economical and political power. As Henderson demonstrates, this Romantic agony is apparent in the works of writers as different as Frances Burney, William Hazlitt, John Keats and Byron, each of whom represents suffering and willing submission as an opportunity for self-discovery or self-expression. The first chapter, intriguingly entitled 'Finance and Flagellation', provides an overview of how early eighteenth-century accounts of commercial enterprises, including joint-stock companies, focused on the connections between speculation, desire and suffering. As Henderson notes, the eroticism of finance capitalism is apparent in William Hogarth's engravings—*South Sea Scheme* and *The Lottery* [1721]—as well as in Joseph Addison's representation of Lady Credit and

Daniel Defoe's *Roxana*. Burney's four novels—the subject of the next chapter—trace the progress of the intersection of desire and consumerism in the late eighteenth century and the Romantic period. The movement from representations of sadism in Burney's earlier works to representations of masochism in *Camilla* [1796] and *The Wanderer* [1814] reveals an increasing emphasis on the pleasures of unfulfilled desire. Taking up Joanna Baillie's defence of the picturesque, the following chapter argues that the two major aesthetic categories in the Romantic period, the picturesque and the sublime, reflect two different Romantic models of desire: the desire to master and the desire for subjection. The next chapter reveals the connection between eroticized subjection and political critique in the self-representations and literary work of William Hazlitt, Byron and Caroline Lamb. Henderson suggests that the fascination that these writers and others had with the idea of sexual subjection reflected, on a smaller and more manageable scale, their ambivalence about institutional hierarchies and economic inequities at a time of extreme political instability. The final chapter discusses how urban and suburban life created the desire for what Henderson describes as a 'synoptic aesthetic' or 'a taste for the sensation of completeness within a small space' (p. 42). This tendency to enrich or thicken a confined space was promoted by landscape designers such as Humphry Repton and John Claudius Loudon. Later, this synoptic aesthetic was replaced by a more modern aesthetic of the ephemeral. This was apparent, as Henderson persuasively argues, in the paintings of John Constable and J.M.W. Turner. Caught between these two paradigms, the later poems of Keats and Coleridge articulate a sense of mourning or loss about the transience of objects even as they celebrate their beauty (as in the case of Keats) or resign themselves to erotic self-abasement (as in the case of Coleridge).

Another very good book published this year, Elizabeth A. Dolan's *Seeing Suffering in Women's Literature of the Romantic Era*, explores the aesthetic and sociopolitical implications of Romantic suffering from a gendered perspective. As Dolan argues, vision was the dominant mode for understanding suffering in this period. While many (predominantly male) Romantic writers sought to transcend the visual world, because of the longstanding tradition of associating women with bodies, Romantic women writers often represented a physical, embodied mode of vision and suffering in their literary work. *Seeing Suffering* demonstrates how Mary Wollstonecraft, Charlotte Smith and Mary Shelley deliberately drew upon, and experimented with, contemporary aesthetic and scientific visual methods in order to make visible the underlying social structures of suffering. The effect of representations of illness on women's literary authority is the subject of part I. The first chapter discusses Charlotte Smith's representation of women's melancholic suffering in her *Elegiac Sonnets*. By focusing on their bodies, Smith invoked a mid-eighteenth-century model of embodied melancholy that implicitly challenged the Romantic tendency to separate the body from the mind. As Dolan points out, this process enabled Smith to claim literary authority at a time in which literary genius was fast becoming the special province of the male poet and his attempts to transcend the body. The next chapter reveals the connections between contemporary accounts of the contagious eye disease ophthalmia and the yellow, watery eyes of the creature that provokes Victor's initial reaction of disgust and terror in *Frankenstein*. Dolan persuasively argues that the creature's diseased eyes, which beg for a sympathetic response, and Victor's revulsion, is a metaphor for the colonial experience and the consequences of imperial desire.

The next section of *Seeing Suffering* reveals how women writers use vision as a therapeutic measure to bring the isolated sufferer back into the community. Chapter 3 compares the picturesque aesthetics of Mary Wollstonecraft's travel narrative, *Letters from Norway*, with Romantic-era medical treatises that extolled the healing benefits of travel. As Dolan demonstrates, the impetus for Wollstonecraft's trip was not simply to complete Gilbert Imlay's business or for her own pleasure; it was an effort to cure her melancholy and ease her emotional pain by taking advantage of the healthful benefits of a change of scenery. Charlotte Smith's belief in the 'therapeutic value of the botanical gaze' (p. 102) is the subject of chapter 4. Dolan argues that Smith, a lifelong botanizer, prescribed botany as the means to heal melancholy and to suggest that the Linnaean system of classification exemplified a type of language that could provide a more nuanced articulation of suffering. Chapter 5 concludes this section on healing and vision with a discussion of the political elements of Mary Shelley's last published work, the epistolary travel narrative, *Rambles in Germany and Italy, in 1840, 1842, and 1843*. Like Wollstonecraft's *Letters from Norway*, *Rambles* includes a pointed description of the restorative effects of viewing picturesque landscapes. What Shelley sees in Italy becomes a touchstone for her personal grief as well as her political hopes for Italy. The tremendous personal losses that Shelley sustained twenty years before with the deaths of her husband and four children, and her struggles to overcome these losses, are associated with the struggles of the Italian Risorgimento and inscribed on the landscape.

The final section on social justice returns to a discussion of Smith and Wollstonecraft and their efforts to help others to see suffering. In what Dolan describes as 'fictional ethnographies' (p. 17), these two women writers focus on the social conditions of suffering. Chapter 6 explores the didactic nature of Wollstonecraft's *Original Stories* [1788] and Smith's children's work *Rural Walks* [1795]. Unlike other didactic works written during the eighteenth century that simply emphasized acts of charity to the poor, these two children's books focus specifically on the lives of the poor. By inviting children to see the effects of poverty, these two writers reveal the underlying economic and social iniquities that contributed to these scenes of misery and financial distress. The last chapter of *Seeing Suffering* argues that Wollstonecraft's unfinished novel, *Maria, or the Wrongs of Woman* [1798], expands her critique of poverty in her children's work to the suffering of women in England. As Dolan notes, *Maria* provides up to twenty-seven fictional case studies of women from all classes who suffer oppression in a male-dominated society that refuses to see them as social equals.

Robert Miles's *Romantic Misfits* explores the politics of inclusion and exclusion during the Romantic period from another angle. As this illuminating and thoughtful study shows, the concept of the Romantic misfit is essentially a truism: Romanticism itself is in many ways a celebration of the misfit—or the singular genius who eschews the crowd—yet some misfits have fared better than others over the years. *Romantic Misfits* is an attempt to trace the origin of the canonization of the big six by discussing a series of case studies of those who fit 'Romanticism' and those who did not. The first chapter focuses on the colourful story of the Romantic forger W.H. Ireland. Ireland, who forged a series of Shakespearian documents, including letters, a title deed, annotated books supposedly from Shakespeare's library and a manuscript draft of *King Lear*, from 1795 to 2 April 1796, also forged a Romantic identity for himself. Unlike Wordsworth (the subject of the following chapter) who successfully negotiated the forces of print culture by tamping down his original radical style, Ireland's flamboyant flaunting of propriety cost him his reputation, making him, according to Miles, 'the original Romantic misfit' who didn't fit (p. 19). As Miles points out, Wordsworth's early radicalism was revealed in the Gothicism of works such as *Adventures on Salisbury Plain* and *The Borderers*. Chapter 2 argues that the ideological turn in Wordsworth's career occurred when he abandoned the Gothic style in his later works. Another shady character (Count Cagliostro) and another successful poet (Samuel Coleridge) are paired in chapter 3 in a discussion of Thomas Carlyle's essays on these two Romantic figures. Interesting, Carlyle focuses not on their differences, but on their shared adherence to 'transcendental quackery' (p. 99) as a way to establish the authenticity of his own ideological perspective. From the point of view of Carlyle, a late Romantic writing on the verge of the Victorian period, the fake count Cagliostro and Coleridge with his interest in mesmerism are equally suspect: they too are Romantic misfits. What the first few chapters of *Romantic Misfits* demonstrate is that the canon wars were already being waged during the Romantic era, as authors, vying for coveted positions at the centre, underscored the counterfeit or suspicious qualities of their competitors.

The second half of Miles's book reveals that the debate about the 'fitness' of individuals in the terms of institutionalized Romanticism was expanded during the Romantic era to include other categories such as genres, Dissenters and women writers. Chapter 4 discusses the Romantic novel as a generic misfit. As Miles reminds us, the singularity of paring down the Romantic canon to six male poets is even more remarkable when we take into account that one of the literary achievements of the eighteenth century was the rise of the novel, and that the novel once again ascended to the heights of respectability in the Victorian period. Miles argues persuasively that the reason why the Romantic novel was marginalized was that it was perceived as a continuation of an eighteenth-century form—a form that posited a rational, political public sphere at odds with the Romantic subjectivity and introspection of Wordsworth's nature poetry, for instance. As literary tastes changed, the popularity of the novel—or what Miles calls 'the philosophical romance' (p. 6) waned. The last chapter points to the tremendous influence of Rational Dissent on early Romanticism and its subsequent exclusion, and discusses the career of Anna Letitia Barbauld as a case study of the rise and fall of Dissenting ideology.

Two noteworthy collections of essays were published this year in the category of General Romanticism. *Frankenstein's Science: Experimentation and Discovery in Romantic Culture, 1780–1830*, edited by Christa Knellwolf and Jane Goodall, situates Shelley's novel within the scientific and literary debates of her day. Most scholarship on *Frankenstein* has focused primarily on its critique of masculinity and scientific hubris. As the editors point out, the persistent belief in the anti-Promethean message of this novel undercuts the complexity of Shelley's project. To summarize *Frankenstein* simply as a commentary on the dangers of scientific hubris is a generalization that does not take into account what constituted 'science' in the Romantic period. Shelley's novel was in fact created during an exciting period in which radical politics and scientific exploration were not mutually exclusive, giving rise to bold and sometimes controversial experiments in the sciences with electricity, anatomy and medicine. As *Frankenstein's Science* demonstrates, Shelley's representation of Victor Frankenstein and his creature are shaped and influenced by the rich historical context of Enlightenment and Romantic science.

The collection of essays opens with Patricia Fara's overview of popular scientific publications published during Shelley's childhood as well as eighteenth-century novels with a scientific bent such as *Gulliver's Travels* that influenced Shelley's depiction of scientific innovation. The next essay, by Judith Barbour, provides insight into the kinds of scientific conversations that were taking place in the Godwin household as Shelley was growing up. The *Juvenile Library*, a serialized encyclopaedia published by Godwin after 1807, prompted discussion on the revolutionary possibilities of replacing the model of the 'great chain of being' with a new radical ordering based on the Linnaean classification of plants. In the following chapter, Christa Knellworth compares Shelley's exploration of geographical, cultural and social boundaries with contemporary Romantic philosophers such as F.W.J. Schelling and his attempts to map the inner geography of the human mind. The debates in the 1820s concerning animal experimentation and vivisection are the subject of Anita Guerrini's essay, which points to the central role that representations of animals played in critical analyses of the consequences of industrialization. Melinda Cooper probes the connections between the creature's description as a monster in *Frankenstein* and the rise of teratology—the scientific explanation of the existence of monsters—as an exciting new branch of contemporary science in the Romantic era. As Cooper notes, it can hardly be coincidental that one of the first medical practitioners who introduced comparative anatomy was a close friend of the Shelleys. As Joan Kirkby reminds us in her essay, what was considered 'science' in Shelley's day included Mesmerism, the teachings of Swedenborg and spiritualism. Kirkby argues that Victor Frankenstein's obsession with reanimating the dead should be considered alongside discussions of the presence of spirits and the boundaries between life and death by philosophers such as Immanuel Kant and Arthur Schopenhauer. Jane Goodall argues that Shelley's novel should be read in the context of the contemporary research on electricity and its potential as a life science. In his essay, Allan K. Hunter focuses on the cultural anxieties surrounding evolution in the Romantic period that are represented by the description of the creature in *Frankenstein* as possessing preternatural learning abilities and extreme endurance. Ian Jackson expands the discussion on the influence of contemporary electrical experiments on Shelley's novel by pointing out that the most spectacular of these experiments were on human and animal bodies (much like the hybrid body of the creature). As Jackson suggests, Victor Frankenstein bears more than a passing resemblance to the young Percy Shelley and his enthusiasm for experimental natural philosophy. The cultural anxieties surrounding the popular culture of collecting natural history specimens are compared to Victor's obsessive pursuit of nature in Christine Cheater's insightful essay, which includes a fascinating discussion of how an obsessive preoccupation with their work affected the lives of two prominent contemporary collectors. The last essay, by Robert Markley, reveals the afterlife of 'Frankenstein's science' in H.G. Wells's *The War of the Worlds*, arguing that the crucial difference between Shelley's dystopian vision and that of Wells is that Wells points to the bleak possibility that evolution is utterly indifferent to the hopes and dreams of humankind. Yet, as Markley points out, the seeds for Wells's apocalyptic perspective were already present in the tensions between the human characters in *Frankenstein* and the introduction of a new, potentially superior, species, as well as in Mary Shelley's own apocalyptic novel, *The Last Man*. *Romantic Science* will be of interest not only to scholars of the Romantic period, but also to scholars working on the history of science, cultural history and philosophy.

Charlotte Smith in British Romanticism, expertly edited by Jacqueline Labbe, acknowledges Smith's significance in the Romantic canon with a very fine collection of essays written by Smith scholars. The sections of this book on Smith's poetry and novels are reviewed elsewhere, but the last section, entitled 'Private Theatricals and Posthumous Lives', falls under the rubric of General Romanticism. These five essays deepen our understanding of the range of Smith's literary output, as well as the ways in which her literary work shaped and was shaped by other Romantic-era and Enlightenment writers. Diego Saglia's ' "This Village Wonder": Charlotte Smith's *What Is She?* and the Ideological Comedy of Curiosity' (pp. 145–58) probes the connections between Smith's comedy and her novels. Saglia focuses in particular on the shared theme of geographically and culturally situated curiosity as a negative force that results in the persecution or potential destruction of a heroine. In 'Recovering Charlotte Smith's Letters: A History, with Lessons' (pp. 159–73), Judith Phillips Stanton describes her struggles to get Smith's letters published—a journey that began in 1977 as a graduate student and ended in 2002. Stanton's personal narrative as a female scholar working on a female Romantic is refreshingly candid in detailing her frustrations with the publishing process and her excitement when new letters were unearthed. Many of us will sympathize too with Stanton's disconcertment when she discovers that the letter-writing Smith was not necessarily the Smith with whom we are acquainted, and calls Smith an 'obsessed, obsessive harpy' (p. 162). Putting a human face on the academic process is an unusual move, but Stanton does it with such grace and good humour that Stanton's essay is likely to be one of the more memorable essays in this collection.

The final three essays explore the dialogical relationship between Smith and the literary world in which she moved. Stuart Curran's essay, 'Charlotte Smith: Intertextualities' (pp. 175–88), reveals Smith's intense engagement with other writers and works of literature, past and present, in her novels.

In 'Charlotte Smith, Women Poets and the Culture of Celebrity' (pp. 189–202), Stephen C. Behrendt provides an illuminating overview of the responses to Smith's poetry from her contemporaries and her successors. As Behrendt demonstrates, these responses, which persisted for several decades after her death, contributed to the myth-making regarding her psychological and physical state that Smith had initiated in her deeply personal prefaces to her novels. The last essay, by Louise Duckling, '"Tell my name to distant ages": The Literary Fate of Charlotte Smith' (pp. 203–17), explores Smith's literary reputation in a series of nineteenth-century anthologies and dictionaries. What is revealed is that Smith succeeded all too well in interjecting her personal woes into her public persona: her life gradually yet steadily eclipses her work in these nineteenth-century assessments of her literary merit, giving rise to the stereotypical image of the complaining Smith that has only recently been called into question.

This year witnessed the publication of two volumes of Pierre M. Conlon's monumental bibliography of the publications of the Ancien Régime, leading up to its demise and the French Revolution, *Le Siècle des Lumières: Bibliographie chronologique*. These volumes (numbers 26 and 27) include a list of known authors who published during the tumultuous year of 1789, and a volume of supplementary material from 1716 to 1789 that pertains to the fall of the French monarchy. Although the publication explosion during the French Revolution has been well documented by other bibliographers, Conlon's bibliography is an indispensable resource for scholars of British Romanticism who are interested in tracing the seeds of the civil unrest that led to revolution and regicide across the Channel.

Two essays published this year in *Studies in Romanticism* conclude this section: Darren Howard's 'Necessary Fictions: The "Swinish Multitude" and *The Rights of Man*' (*SiR* 47[2008] 161–80) and Tim Fulford's 'British Romantics and Native Americans: The Araucanians of Chile' (*SiR* 47[2008] 225–54). Darren Howard's essay discusses the marked increase in published pleas on behalf of animals at the end of the eighteenth century. In addition to surveying the arguments for animals largely written in didactic literature for children, Howard traces Jeremy Bentham's emphasis on suffering to the cult of sensibility in the eighteenth century. Howard argues that this historical trajectory opened up the possibility of thinking of humans as one type of animal amongst many. In his essay, Tim Fulford provides an intriguing discussion of how the exclusion of the British in the eighteenth century from any knowledge of Spanish America prompted resentment and fantasies regarding the vast wealth and riches garnered by Spain from its colonies.

2. Prose

The year 2007 saw the appearance of two substantially important primary sources: Coleridge's translation of Goethe's *Faustus* and a large number of previously unpublished writings of William Hazlitt (though both appeared *very* late in 2007). I will begin with the Coleridge *Faust*, follow that with all the other material on Coleridge, then discuss Wu's edition of Hazlitt, and finally move on to a discussion of a relevant monograph, and other articles.

Faustus from the German of Goethe translated by Samuel Taylor Coleridge, edited by Frederick Burwick and James C. McKusick [2007], is a work that was reviewed in last year's *YWES*, but the fact that debate over its attribution to Coleridge persisted over the course of 2008, to the point where Burwick felt it necessary to publish an article defending their attribution (reviewed in section 4 below), makes me convinced that it is appropriate for me to throw my hat into the ring.

This edition really is a marvellous piece of detective work. The editors have built upon the suspicions of Paul M. Zall that Coleridge made a translation of the *Faust* and that it survives. In fact Coleridge started it for John Murray in 1814, and this is agreed by everyone. But as with so much of Coleridge's life's work he failed to complete it. Or so we thought. In fact he *did* complete it six years later and published it with Thomas Booseley anonymously. As the simile the editors begin their excellent introduction with illuminates: like Poe's 'Purloined Letter' it was in plain sight all the time.

The volume contains the Coleridge translation, a section of Madame de Staël's *Germany*, which the editors argue increased the market for the *Faust* in England, two further translations of sections of *Faust* which are tied to the series of twenty-six engraved plates by Retsch that were included in the Booseley edition, the John Anster translation of the full *Faust* which some argue (possibly convincingly) that Coleridge worked from in 1814 (thought the editors argue compellingly that the sections of the work translated in 1820 are Coleridge and Coleridge alone) and a final translation by Lord Francis Levenson-Gower. The book is a one-volume comprehensive tutorial on Coleridge's relationship to Goethe and the entire question of whether or not he completed a translation of *Faust*.

The entire work is quite compelling; unless one is a conspiracy theorist, one can be left in no doubt whatsoever that Coleridge did complete his translation. More importantly, when one reads the poetry one sees that it could only be Coleridge's voice. The technical poetic ability with metre and rhyme, combined with perfectly Romantic diction, are simply too good to be anyone else other than Swinburne—and seeing that he was not born until three years after Coleridge died he is an unlikely candidate. Furthermore McKusick has gone to the remorseless detail of putting the entire translation through a piece of software which conducted stylometric analysis of the length of words, punctuation and diction. This provides a quantitative buttress to the interpretation that Coleridge completed the translation, and this is an impressive undertaking which must have been hard graft. I must say, though, that I was convinced long, long before I read the stylometric analysis. I previously thought it unnecessary, because to the eye and ear of any Coleridge scholar the translation could only have come from Coleridge—but McKusick's choice now clearly was much less investigating a new technology and much more donning a flak jacket.

Frankly the debate has begun to remind me of the 'Earl of Oxford' nonsense conspiracy theory surrounding Shakespeare. This is so because, were it not Coleridge who made the translation, there is an unidentified,

German-speaking (which was rare in the period) Romantic poet who has a vision of the sound of language equivalent to that of Coleridge and Wordsworth. Byron is ruled out in an article discussed below, and it damn well was not Wordsworth. I may disagree with the reasons which Burwick and McKusick posit for Coleridge's choice to remain anonymous, very slightly (though I think them plausible), in that I do not think he would have felt his theological authority following the publication of the *Lay Sermons* and *Aids to Reflection* threatened by translating Goethe's *Faust* (he was far, far too arrogant for that), and instead propose the less complex argument that he chose anonymity because he needed the money. Yes, he wanted to complete the project he started—but I see the money as the motivation. I believe the simple explanation for anonymity is that he was terrified he would lose the Booseley money to Murray in a law suit if he put his name to the translation because of his un-repaid advance from Murray—which he surely would have.

What this volume contributes to the greater understanding of Coleridge is, in my opinion, two-pronged. First, it brings into question the presumption that Coleridge was entirely a serial abandoner of projects. I do not for a moment wish to be seen to suggest anything like a position which argues against the plain fact that Coleridge had a near-pathological inability to complete projects from start to finish. But, much as my own argument that the *opus maximum* is in fact a complete but unpolished work entitled *On the Divine Ideas* which was written over a large number of years, in other words it was a project that he came back to over and over (see 'On The Divine Ideas: The Systematic Theology of Samuel Taylor Coleridge' (in J.W. Barbeau, ed., *Coleridge's Assertion of Religion* [2006]), McKusick and Burwick's demonstration that Coleridge did complete his translation of *Faust*, but six years after he first gave up on it, may lead all of us to be slightly wary of the absolute presupposition that any apparently unfinished work was abandoned. Like the Purloined Letter and *On the Divine Ideas*, the finished work was indeed, and others may be, staring us directly in the face like the pieces of a jigsaw puzzle; I am not making any particular suggestions as to possibilities, but merely saying that possibilities may exist. Second, I believe that Coleridge's translation of *Faust* gives us an even greater appreciation for what a superb technician he actually was. There is a fine and extensive discussion of the poetics in the introduction, and it contains a selected history of their reception by contemporary critics. Coleridge's use of couplets, often in trimeter, is particularly impressive and moving. Coleridge may have largely ceased writing his own poetry around 1805, but this volume shows us that he surely retained his full-throated voice later in life, and probably with better technical skill. He may have lost his muse, in the classic comment, but when he borrowed Goethe's he was still the absolute master and visionary of the Romantic voice in English verse.

Overall McKusick and Burwick have accomplished something rare: they have opened new doors for the community's understanding of Coleridge, and have provided us with a new complete work from which to work. It is beyond question that this edition will produce derivative literature—it already has— and probably at least one or two monographs. It is a work which every Coleridgean would enjoy having on his or her shelves.

James P. Rasmussen's article 'Reading the Prophets prophetically in Coleridge's *Confessions*' (*ERR* 19[2008] 403–20) argues that in *Confessions of an Inquiring Spirit* Coleridge sees reading the Bible as 'a prophetic creation of meaning' (p. 403) and specifically argues against the interpretations of Jerome McGann and Tilottama Rajan, who take the view that *Confessions of an Inquiring Spirit* holds that the Bible must be read in historical context. This article is worth reading because of its emphasis on pneumatology within *Confessions*, and because of Rasmussen's discussion of the influence of Schleiermacher and other German hermeneutitians on Coleridge, but unfortunately its premise is mistaken. Certainly *Confessions of an Inquiring Spirit* is a text which has pneumatology at its core, but Rasmussen badly misunderstands the Pentad of Operative Christianity that Coleridge makes clear is the key to reading the book: the synthesis of the Pentad is the preacher, and it is in the preacher's preaching that the 'prophetic creation of meaning' takes place, not the individual's reading of the Bible. McGann may be correct in his interpretation for the wrong reasons (using works by Coleridge from the very early stage of his career to interpret *Confessions,* which I believe is always a dangerous paradigm and practice because Coleridge's mind and views changed drastically over his life—though mind you Coleridge does argue for an historicist practice of reading the Bible in the *Lectures on Revealed Religion* which were written in 1795), but correct McGann is nonetheless.

Patrick Wright, in 'Coleridge's Translucence: a Failed Transcendence' (*RaVoN* 50[2008] 32 paras) argues that Coleridge's aesthetics and philosophy, and the theological writings derivative of them, come from a world-view that was substantially derivative of what he sees as Coleridge's bipolar disorder. He also argues that Coleridge's thought is proleptic of psychoanalysis. Now I have, at various conferences, heard Coleridge diagnosed with ADD, ADHD, Asperger's syndrome and dyslexia. I find none of these diagnoses productive in helping the community of scholars to deal with the received Coleridge texts: and I am very far indeed from a New Critic. This article is psycho-biography, and I happen to dislike psycho-biography intensely. Those scholars who do not will find it fascinating. The principal problem with the article in my view is that in order to push his bipolar disorder interpretation Wright is forced to diminish the influence of dialectical Idealist philosophy on Coleridge—and he does this by using the verb form 'purloined' to describe the relationship. If this is accurate then Fichte purloined from Kant, Schelling purloined from Fichte, and Hegel purloined from the lot. The simple fact of the matter is that it is uncontroversial and universally accepted that Coleridge's dialectical philosophy is both derivative of his reading of German Idealism and different from it. Idealism's dialectic is the source of Coleridge's philosophical world-view, and a pneumatological approach to the Trinity the foundation of this theology of transcendence, not a mental disorder which we have absolutely no way of demonstrating that he suffered from or did not suffer from. As I have said, I was predisposed to dislike this interpretation because I dislike psycho-biography, but those who do like this hermeneutic will indeed find this article of great interest.

Mark L. Barr's 'The Common Law Illusion: Literary Justice in Coleridge's *On the Constitution of the Church and State*' (*CL* 35[2008] 120–43) sees the text of *OTCCS* as giving a pseudo-legal (my phrase) function to the clerisy. I am uncomfortable with the idea that Coleridge saw the clerisy as having a quasi-judicial (Barr's term) function. National trustees (Barr's term), Coleridge undoubtedly saw them as being; but Coleridge is fairly clear that they were guardians of the national education and the national 'treasure trove' (my term) of knowledge. The clerisy were guardians of erudition. The article is interesting because of its stress on the legal ramifications of *On the Constitution of the Church and State*, which are all too often overlooked. Barr sees Coleridge's coming of age in the 1790s as the genesis of his interest in the law, and this is probably uncontroversial. But as I have stated above, I find using the early works of Coleridge, especially the very early ones, to illuminate the mature texts a very dangerous, and often misguiding, practice. Barr is certainly not wrong-headed either to highlight the legal nature of *On the Constitution of the Church and State*, nor Coleridge's lifelong interest in the law: far from it in both cases, but he does perhaps go a step too far in his discussion of the clerisy. In Coleridge's scheme the clerisy would have educated the men who went on to hold judicial functions, but they did not hold even a pseudo-legal function *themselves*.

Comments about great detective work similar to the ones I made about the Coleridge *Faust* can be made about Duncan Wu's two-volume edition of *New Writings of Hazlitt*—though there will be less controversy here. This too is a marvellous piece of detective work. In preparation for his biography of Hazlitt, Wu has traced the writings of Hazlitt which appeared in periodicals. Wu seeks to make the point that Hazlitt was first and foremost a journalist, and to add a journalistic skeleton to the already fleshed-out portrait of Hazlitt as a professional essayist which is most commonly encountered.

Wu's excellent introduction is a mini-biography in itself and contains a very good and concise description of the methods of journalism used on both sides of the turn of the nineteenth century, particularly at the *Morning Chronicle* where Hazlitt began working as a parliamentary reporter in 1812. I suppose Wu's central point in the introduction, and in publishing the collection, is that it was Hazlitt's career as a journalist which led him to theatre reviewing, which led him to other essay writing etc. It is a strongly argued interpretation, and no one knows more about Hazlitt than Wu. I doubt this view will become controversial. The work contains 205 pieces of journalistic writing from the period between the years 1809 and 1830 previously unattributed to Hazlitt (and those which are untitled have been given a parenthetical title by Wu). It also contains nine early versions of formal essays, including early versions of 'On the Love of Life' and 'On Patriotism'. Finally Wu has included twenty-nine pieces of writing which he considers to be questionable attributions, some of which are mere single-paragraph comments from newspapers.

Of particular interest to readers of this article will be the pieces of writing which concern other Romantics: such as a later review of Wordsworth's *Poetical Works* from 1827, Hazlitt's most detailed discussion of Coleridge's poetry, a series of late musings on Coleridge, and attacks on Southey as Poet Laureate. But, what this rather marvellous collection gives any person interested in the Romantic period is a contemporary intellectual chronicle of issues and events both artistic and political by one of the great social commentators and public intellectuals of the era. Furthermore, both volumes have very fine indexes which the reader may use to point him or herself to any particular issue or individual in the era; these are genuinely first-rate.

In a sense there is very little critiquing to do of this publication, because both it and the Coleridge *Faust* contain excellent introductions by very senior editors and provide the wider world of scholarship of the Romantics with new material on which to work. Both open windows previously bricked in, as if prompted by the repeal of the window tax, and allow light into the scholarship from an aspect which has been dead dark for decades. Neither book is inexpensive, but both are well worth the money.

Continuum's *International Faust Studies: Adaptation, Reception, Translation*, edited by Lorna Fitzsimmons, is pricy at £75 for the cloth edition. It contains fifteen discrete articles of merit and a good index. Inspired by the bicentenary of Goethe's *Faust*, the collection is interdisciplinary and broad-ranging. It addresses the impact and influence of the Faust legend in literary traditions around the world. The fifteen articles are arranged into five sections: 'Anteriorities', '*Faust* in Context', '*Faust*: Romantic Intertexts', 'Asia' and 'The Americas, Europe, Africa and Britain'. What I love about this collection is the breadth of its scope. Beginning with an absolutely fascinating discussion by Arnd Bohm arguing that Alexander the Great could have been one of Goethe's historical role models for the figure of Faustus, through Richard Ilgner discussing the prevalence of the Faust legend as a model for fiction written in Canada in the period of the 1980s and up to Paul Malone discussing the employment of the legend in rock musicals in an article entitled 'They Sold their Soul for Rock and Roll', fascinating and fresh interpretation unfolds page after page. I had no idea that Faust has a recent history of production in China, and who would? But Antje Budde's article on that subject engages the intricate anthropological nuances of how the legend translates into a non-Christian culture elegantly.

Coupled with innovative interdisciplinary scholarship is innovative criticism of the Goethe texts. These include but are not limited to the following pieces. An article by Burwick on his edition of the Coleridge translation (which is a different version of the introduction to the edition discussed above—one might have wished a defence of it but the book clearly went into production too early for the backlash of criticism of attribution to appear). Ehrhard Bahr writes theologically acutely of the issues of conflict which arise from the author's choice to use the book of Job as framework for the *Faust* fragment of 1790, and Fred Parker gives a lovely description of how Byron was influenced by Goethe despite his lack of knowledge of the German language (Matthew Lewis had translated it for him orally).

I see this collection as being of genuine value to both *Faust* specialists and the general community of literary scholarship. It would be an excellent text for use in a graduate seminar, and will allow those teaching undergraduates to select specific essays to use in their courses. I am far, far, from an expert on *Faust*, but reading this book made me feel a good deal closer to one. Frankly, the contributors and editor have achieved what they envisioned in the project: a bicentennial monument to Goethe. This was not easy to achieve, and the achievement was effected by producing a fifteen-link chain without a single weak link. Do read this book.

Mark Lussier's article 'Scientific Objects and Blake's Objections to Science' (*WC* 39[2008] 120–2; also discussed below) argues that Blake's objections to both the imprecision of scientific instruments and the practice of sundering the investigator using them from the investigation itself are proleptic of concerns and discussions taking place in the community of scientists today. He is undoubtedly correct. Lussier is well versed in the vocabulary of natural philosophy of the late eighteenth century, and gives accurate and concise summaries of various scientific debates from the period of Blake's lifetime. He is equally well versed in late twentieth-century philosophy of science debates—though I would have liked to see him mention Michael Polanyi's work (but perhaps this is my fixation). The article is uncontroversial, and it is more of an observation than an argument, but it is an observation well grounded in both Blake's poetry and art, and perhaps even more firmly grounded in postmodern philosophy of science. Lussier is both correct and careful to leave this piece as an observation and to avoid making a meta-argument about ultimate reality which would be speculative. As it stands it is a convincing and concise article that serves as an admirable summary of the state of play in postmodern philosophy of science to scholars of literature who may be either unfamiliar with it or in search of a précis of it to provide to their students.

Erinç Özdemir's 'Hidden Polemic in Wollstonecraft's *Letters from Norway*: A Bakhtinian Reading' (*SiR* 47[2008] 321–49; also discussed in section 3 below) discusses letters that Wollstonecraft wrote while living in Scandinavia following her departure from France. This article is very much literary theory imposed on a text, or a set of texts (a paradigmatic reading of a set of texts), but it is done well. For example: 'Still, assessing the work from a contemporary point of view, we cannot but find it interesting that as a text embodying Enlightened humanism, rationalism and feminism, and what we have come to perceive as masculine Romanticism, [*Letters*] is predominantly an expression of Sensibility incorporating some of the main discursive and stylistic elements and characteristics of sentimental literature.' I am delighted to see the epistolary form being taken seriously, and though it might be going a bit too far to call the letters travel writing, since they were intended for a private rather than public audience, I will admit that it might not be going too far either. That issue is ancillary though: Özdemir's real point is that the collection of letters forms a multi-genera work as a whole, and he is probably correct—if nothing else it is now available to the entire scholastic community. This is a long article, and one section of it deals with how the letters give us an autobiographical insight into Wollstonecraft's life (this fact, though indisputable, is hardly surprising). In short, anyone with an interest in Wollstonecraft would find this article of interest whether or not he or she is particularly interested in the imposition of literary theory on texts—in other words in performing paradigmatic readings. Those who are both interested in Wollstonecraft and themselves literary theorists and paradigmatic practitioners will adore it.

'Jacobinism in India, Indianism in English Parliament: Fearing the Enlightenment and Colonial Modernity with Edmund Burke' by Sunil Agnani (*CulC* 68[2008] 131–62), gives a postcolonial, post-Eurocentric reading of Burke, by linking Burke's fear of Indian nationalism with his fear of Jacobinism. This is not forced; he quotes Burke writing of both in the same passages and Burke clearly saw them as linked or intertwined within the greater polity. Agnani's argument is that Burke did not think in a Eurocentric way, and part of his point is to attempt to employ Burke to explode the idea of a 'colonial lag time' where ideas arose in Europe and then spread out to the various empires: 'My contention is that colonialism in the Enlightenment was both more complex and more contradictory than we presently understand it to have been' (p. 132). This article is good intellectual history, and though it may be driven by a political agenda (and please note I say *may*) it is not driven in a heavy-handed way, nor does the interpretation of the Burke texts seem in any way to force an agenda upon them. Agnani concludes the article: 'In more ways than one we can see that the emergence of a colonial modernity is not simply a peripheral element helpful in understanding the beginnings of modernity in Europe, rather it is constitutive of the very language used to describe and name that modernity.' Historians have been moving in the direction of seeing English polity of the eighteenth century in a less Eurocentric light for well over a decade; this article is an example that cultural studies is moving in that direction as well—which is no bad thing. Though this is a long article, it is well written, and well footnoted, and very definitely *not* heavy going—he writes very, very well. It is well worth the time it takes to read it.

3. The Novel

Romantic prose fiction is coming into its own. While there is a long tradition of work on individual novelists in the period, the last few years have marked a new consideration of the genre of the Romantic novel—elusive, frustrating, and fragmented as it is. Two publications this year point the way for future development of this critical trend, in research and teaching. The first is the collection of essays edited by Jillian Heydt-Stevenson and Charlotte Sussman, *Recognizing the Romantic Novel: New Histories of British Fiction, 1780–1830*. This is an excellent study: these diverse essays not only shed light on a range of authors—from Austen and Scott to Hays, Opie, Brockden Brown and Sophia Lee—but also show up some of the problems of categorizing the Romantic-era novel. A strong piece by Michael Gamer, for instance, explores the 'rise of the (reprinted) novel', identifying the role of collections by, amongst others, Anna Laetitia Barbauld and Walter Scott, in creating early novelistic canons. As well as its discussion of contemporary responses to the Romantic novel, the collection as a whole—and, in particular, the editors' thoughtful preface and first chapter—takes stock of the work done over the course of the last decade and re-examines critical approaches to Romantic prose fiction. As the editors point out, these have generally followed two main trends, often interlinked: first, the recovery and rereading of authors who have been largely forgotten, and, secondly, the foregrounding of political and cultural contexts which helps us to understand the implications of the Romantic fiction we *do* know well. The essays in this volume largely tend towards the second category, but there are also insights into less well-known novelists, and less widely read novels by familiar authors. Two good chapters on Frances Burney, for example, examine her less frequently read fiction to make a case for the author as a more sceptical, critical voice than is often recognized. Helen Thompson's 'Burney's Conservatism: Masculine Value and "the Ingenuous Cecilia"' argues that *Cecilia, or Memoirs of an Heiress* [1782] refutes the idea of the humanizing, pacifying influence of domestic fiction. In *Cecilia*, she argues, with its savage, 'semi-barbarous' places and menfolk, we can detect Burney's Enlightenment critique. Suzie Asha Park's '"All agog to find her out": Compulsory Narration in *The Wanderer*' also foregrounds Burney as an interrogative and challenging novelist. Focusing on the heroine's reticence in *The Wanderer: or, Female Difficulties* [1814], Park argues that we might read the novel as questioning the 'Romantic belief in freedom of expression', and as an exploration of the limits and pressures of female expression in particular.

The essays not only present the Romantic novel as a challenging, questioning form—they also, at times, challenge one another. A series of pieces on Austen, for instance, adopt strikingly different critical approaches. Saree Makdisi, in 'Austen, Empire and Moral Virtue', firmly ties *Mansfield Park* to 'the blood and sweat of imperial conquest' (p. 192), in an informed model of criticism which borrows from but also extends Edward Said's argument in *Culture and Imperialism*. Makdisi argues that slavery and imperialism are too often conflated, and calls for a more detailed reading of Romantic subjectivity in relation to Romantic imperialism—one which defines Austen's novel as a grim-sounding 'triumph of the ideology of duty, self-denial, humility, internalized self-regulating discipline, frugality' and relentless productivity (p. 200). What Makdisi sees as Fanny's one-track, self-regulatory zeal is read by Miranda Burgess in the following essay, 'Fanny Price's British Museum: Empire, Genre, and Memory in *Mansfield Park*', in terms of Austen's subtle depiction of an individual's consciousness. Makdisi tends to close down the self-questioning, ambiguous aspects of Austen's narrative; Burgess's chapter nicely suggests an alternative approach which, similarly, reads *Mansfield Park* as an 'exemplary opportunity for investigating the mediation of empire' in both the individual mind and in the novel, but argues that its treatment of memory and history allows 'a questioning of Britain's imperial history' (p. 231). Burgess calls attention to the ways in which Austen's novel includes and mixes other genres, quoting from poetry and discussing the picturesque, for example: this aspect of her argument then informs the subsequent piece, Mary L. Jacobus's 'Between the Lines: Poetry, *Persuasion*, and the Feelings of the Past'. Jacobus's Austen is a thoroughly Romantic novelist, who knowingly uses the poetry of Scott and Byron as a way of registering and responding to questions of history and nation. All three pieces work well together—arguing and productively differing with one another.

There are many other connections and conversations in the volume. The two final pieces, Ina Ferris's exploration of James Hogg in light of Gothic novels and 'secret histories', and Ian Duncan's 'Sympathy, Physiognomy, and

Scottish Romantic Fiction' both, in different ways, contextualize Hogg and demonstrate his engagement in historical and ethical debate. Duncan reads *The Private Memoirs and Confessions of a Justified Sinner* within the context of eighteenth-century discourse on the desire to enter into another person's thoughts and feelings—a discourse which he traces through the language of sympathy in Smith and Hume, and, perhaps more surprisingly, through physiognomy. He argues that Hogg's work mounts a critique of the Smithian model of sympathy, and sets this alongside Walter Scott's *Redgauntlet*—another recognition of the '"Romantic" crisis of an Enlightenment project' (p. 287). Ferris, calling attention to the way in which the title of Hogg's novel is so often reduced to *Confessions*, reminds us of the importance of 'private memoirs' and history to our understanding of it. Placing Hogg's work in a broader context of the historical and national explorations undertaken by the Gothic genre, Ferris reads his 'prankish text' as bringing 'to culmination the gothic novel's scandalous relation to the historiographic enterprise' (p. 282). This, in turn, looks back to an earlier chapter in the volume, Markman Ellis's 'Enlightenment or Illumination: The Spectre of Conspiracy in Gothic Fictions of the 1790s'. Ellis examines three interlinking ideas: the rise of the Gothic novel, the publication of English translations of Kant, and the 'media event' of the Illuminati conspiracy. All three, he argues, shed light on British Romantic responses to the Enlightenment—a key theme of the whole collection.

As such, this volume is a highly useful intervention in the field. The two opening chapters are of especial importance in assessing current critical debate on the novel. The editors, Heydt-Stevenson and Sussman, reflect in the first chapter on the bibliographical work of Peter Garside, showing the dominance of the novel as a form in the period, and then take us through the multiplicity of sub-genres which might be included in this form—wild, passionate experimentations in 'the gothic, the historical novel, the national tale, the oriental tale, the radical or "Jacobin" novel, and the novel of manners' (pp. 13–14). They show connections and 'interpenetrations' between these sub-genres, and between the novel and other forms in the period, to make the case for understanding the Romantic novel 'as a field, not simply a heterogeneous mass of fictional forms' and for tracing the common preoccupations and aims of these different Romantic experiments. Laura Mandell in the subsequent chapter then shows how we can trace one particular narrative—the 'philosophical romance' which resists the conventional marriage plot—through different strands of Romantic fiction. The revolutionary, 'queer', domestic arrangements in, say, *Emma Courtney* and *Adeline Mowbray*, won't fit into the model of a good eighteenth-century novel, and have perhaps contributed to our difficulty in judging Romantic fiction. Yet the alternative social bonds of the Romantic-era novel, as Mandell, Heydt-Stevenson and Sussman argue, force us 'to understand different kinds of communal imagining' (p. 21).

The second important publication in the field this year is *The Cambridge Companion to Fiction in the Romantic Period*, edited by Richard Maxwell and Katie Trumpener—significant not simply in terms of content, but because it represents a development in how Romantic fiction is being taught and studied. As Maxwell and Trumpener comment, for most of the era, 'British novels and tales were ugly ducklings; their swanlike qualities would be mostly recognized in retrospect', a retrospect which is still unfolding. 'The process of discovery', as they note, 'is still in progress, with new candidates for revaluation offered on a surprisingly regular basis' (p. 4). This collection therefore is in some ways a chart of the major critical discoveries and explorations of the last few decades—of regional and provincial fictions, of new forms of working-class fiction, of fiction by women, and of book history and the literary marketplace. The essays are not simply a student resource—although that is one of their primary functions—they also represent a guide to some of the most exciting scholarship in this field, and work alongside *Recognizing the Romantic Novel* as a gauge of the current high standard in Romantic fiction criticism.

The editors of the *Cambridge Companion* set the tone for this strong collection, beginning with a historiography of fiction in the period by Richard Maxwell. This outlines several retrospective moments when the history of Romantic fiction has been considered seriously—one in 1785, with Clara Reeve's *The Progress of Romance*; one just after the First World War, with R.W. Chapman's editions of Austen and J.M.S. Tompkins's *The Popular Novel in England 1770–1800* [1932]; and the last over the closing decades of the twentieth century, with the rise of critical studies such as Gary Kelly's, and bibliographies and studies of book data. Maxwell skilfully positions this *Companion* volume in relation to this history of critical thinking, showing how we are still struggling to gain purchase on the influence and power of Romantic fiction and its forgotten practitioners. Further details on publishing and the marketplace, with an introductory guide to understanding copyright and retail pricing, are given by William St Clair's essay, and Deidre Shauna Lynch explores Gothic fiction and its self-conscious relationship with the reader with reference to chapbook frontispieces and illustrations. Gary Kelly's essay also gives a good summary of the cheap print forms encountered by working-class readers, with plenty of illustrations of chapbooks and 'blue books', outlining the type of market Hannah More's Cheap Repository Tracts were attempting to tap into, and alerting readers to the type of repackaging carried out by firms such as J. Bailey, in whose hands Mary Wollstonecraft's novel becomes the *Life of Jemima; or, The Confessions of an Unfortunate Bastard, Who, by the Antipathy of Her Parents, Was Driven to Every Scene of Vice and Prostitution*! Close attention is paid to the geography of Romantic fiction: Richard Maxwell's second essay details the French origins of the historical novel, showing the cosmopolitan, European reach of British fiction, and the mongrel roots of a range of novels from Jane Porter to Edward Bulwer-Lytton. Martha Bohrer's following piece on provincial fiction usefully discusses the ways in which fiction by Mary Russell Mitford, Maria Edgeworth, George Crabbe and John Galt attempts to capture and report on the idiosyncrasies of the local, linking these to the observations of the natural by Gilbert White and Thomas Bewick. James Watt's 'Orientalism and Empire' gives an introduction to little-known works such as Phebe Gibbes's 1789 epistolary novel, *Hartly House, Calcutta* as well as the orientalism of William Beckford and Mary Shelley, suggesting how we might approach and understand 'the slipperiness of so much of the fiction dealing with the East in this period' (p. 130). This attention to different racial others and the consequences of imperial power is echoed by Ina Ferris's discussion of the Irish novel 1800–29, and the piece by Ian Duncan—whose full-length study, *Scott's Shadow* [2007] was discussed last year—on Scotland and the novel. Paul Keen outlines some of the political arguments and uses of fiction in the period, and this political aspect is further explored by Jill Campbell in her analysis of women writers and the woman's novel, with its account of the dangers faced by women readers, especially susceptible, as Addison and Steele warned, to 'Romances, Chocolate, and the like Inflamers'. She focuses particularly on Mary Wollstonecraft, Mary Shelley, and patterns of influence which she describes as 'maternal transmission'. Katie Trumpener's lively piece on child reading in the Romantic era reminds us of the enduring power of chapbooks on poets from Coleridge to John Clare, hiding away in 'woods and dingles of thorns' to read on Sundays. She outlines the ideological battleground fought over by writers and publishers of didactic and imaginative children's literature, and gives a good introduction to the juvenile fiction of Maria Edgeworth. Formal considerations are addressed by Marshall Brown, whose essay 'Poetry and the Novel' tackles the difficulty of generic categorization by looking at the position of poetry in novels by Charlotte Smith and Walter Scott. Ann Wierda Rowland's essay 'Sentimental Fiction' gives an overview of the Shaftesburian philosophy behind fictional treatments of sympathy in the period, helping students towards an understanding of sentimentality as a 'rhetorical tradition for the reading and representation of the self' (p. 204). The book concludes with a guide to further reading, and the pieces—clear, varied, and well chosen—should prompt students to explore the full-length works of their contributors.

Two good collections which deal with the concept of Romantic transnationalism include thought-provoking pieces on the novel in the period. *Transnational England: Home and Abroad, 1780–1860*, edited by Monika Class and Terry F. Robinson, reproduces on its cover Joshua Reynolds's beautiful painting, *Mrs Baldwin in Eastern Dress*, and this alluring and luxurious image forms the starting point for the volume's exploration of cross-cultural relations. In their introduction, Class and Robinson imaginatively analyse the different pressures and narratives at work in the picture, and give a lucid account of recent critical approaches to imperial expansion, global exchange and cosmopolitanism. This makes the book a valuable contribution to the field and its essays range across transnational responses to areas as diverse as drama, biblical exegesis and culinary practices: of particular relevance to this section are Beccie Puneet Randhawa's discussion of the West Indian characters in Edgeworth's *Belinda* and John C. Leffel's chapter on Austen. Randhawa draws out the ways in which Edgeworth's Creole characters—'a simultaneous and uneasy embodiment of colonizer and colonized' (p. 189)—expose and unsettle the whole notion of 'home' in her novel. Leffel's piece opens with the image of Austen's aunt, Philadelphia Austen, arriving in Madras aboard the *Bombay Castle* in 1752, bound for the colonial marriage market; he goes on, adroitly, to tease out attitudes to this practice through an etching by Gillray, a farce by Edward Topham, Mariana Starke's comedy *The Sword of Peace; or, A Voyage of Love* [1788], and Austen's unfinished juvenile novel *Catharine, or The Bower*. Whereas Topham and Starke view the practice and its participants with suspicion, Austen, argues Leffel, critiques the Indian marriage market and empathizes with the commodified, exploited women involved. The essay references Makdisi's 'Austen, Empire and Moral Virtue', discussed above, and provides a stimulating response to it, seeing in Austen's early work an interrogation of 'Britain's imperial conduct on English domesticity' and an exploration of 'the gendered terms of colonialism' (p. 228).

A similarly thoughtful collection, *Romantic Border Crossings*, edited by Jeffrey Cass and Larry Peer, explores the growth, and difference, of critical approaches to the transnational. Like Class and Robinson, this volume, too, responds to events such as the 2004 NASSR conference on cosmopolitanism, organized by Jeffrey Cox and Jillian Heydt-Stevenson (Cass's introduction quotes their discussion of the conference in *ERR* 16[2005], although it does not seem to appear in the bibliography). There is a nice sense, then, of the works discussed this year being in dialogue. The collection offers three essays which focus specifically on the Romantic-era novel. Valerie Henitiuk's 'To Be and Not To Be: The Bounded Body and Embodied Boundary in Inchbald's *A Simple Story*' focuses on the figure of Matilda as an 'agent of protest' (p. 43). Imprisoned in her father's house, Matilda's 'insistently liminal existence' nevertheless poses a challenge to patriarchal authority, argues Henitiuk. Miriam L. Wallace discusses the porous boundaries of political categorizations in her piece, 'Crossing from "Jacobin" to "Anti-Jacobin": Rethinking the Terms of English Jacobinism'. Wallace highlights the difficulty of defining novels such as Charles Lloyd's *Edmund Oliver* [1798], Elizabeth Hamilton's *Memoirs of Modern Philosophers* [1800] and Charles Lucas's *The Infernal Quixote* [1801]: novels such as these, she argues, 'continue the project of the radical fictions they ostensibly critique' (p. 112). Generic boundaries form the focus of Bronwyn Rivers's 'Genre Crossings: Gothic Novels and the Borders of History'. Like Ina Ferris's essay in *Recognizing the Romantic Novel*, discussed earlier, Rivers makes the case for the Gothic novel as engaged not only with history but also with issues of historiography, offering a close reading of Radcliffe's *The Italian* to support her argument.

The Romantic-era novel also featured prominently in three books already discussed in the first section. Devoney Looser's *Women Writers and Old Age in Great Britain, 1750–1850* includes case studies of Edgeworth and Burney, and of Austen, showing the power of prejudice against the woman writer perceived as elderly. *Seeing Suffering in Women's Literature of the Romantic Era*, by Elizabeth A. Dolan, argues for new modes of 'seeing', and treating, suffering in the period, analysing a range of writing by Wollstonecraft and Charlotte Smith, and novels including *Frankenstein*. Robert Miles's *Romantic Misfits* includes an intriguing chapter on the Romantic novel as a kind of 'generic misfit' itself (p. 133).

Although there were few book-length studies of individual authors this year, there were some excellent articles, with Walter Scott, as ever, one of the most popular subjects. 'I have read all W. Scott's novels at least fifty times', Byron wrote in his Ravenna journal for 1821, lavishing praise on this 'Scotch Fielding': 'wonderful man! I long to get drunk with him'. From Byron's exuberant celebration to Hazlitt's frustrated admiration, Scott's dialogues and differences with other writers provided good material for two imaginative articles this year. Susan Oliver's 'Crossing "Dark Barriers": Intertextuality and Dialogue between Lord Byron and Sir Walter Scott' (*SiR* 47[2008] 15–35) details a 'remarkable poetic dialogue' between the two writers, 'comprising references and counter-references, borrowings, inversions, parodies, pastiches and more straight-forward homage, constructed around tales of cultural encounter on inherently unstable peripheries' (pp. 16–17). Her reading of the parallels between *Don Juan* and *Tales of my Landlord*—both, she shows, fuelled by an 'ironic cynicism'—is especially involving, and while she shows the deep importance of Scott's poetry to Byron, she concludes that 'there is finally a crossing of generic boundaries that shows him positing Scott's novels as the voice of a future that incorporates some of the best of the past' (p. 33). Meanwhile, Stephen Burley's 'Hazlitt's Preface to *Political Essays* and Walter Scott's *Old Mortality*' (*N&Q* 55[2008] 437–9) is a small piece rich in its implications for our understanding of the ways in which Scott was read and used. Burley points out the direct parallel between Hazlitt's opening sentence in the preface to his highly provocative *Political Essays* and Major Bellenden's statement at the siege of Tillietudlem Castle: 'I am no politician.' Drawing out the wider political context of the previously unnoticed allusion, Burley reflects on the long dialogic relationship between the two writers, and convincingly shows how and why Hazlitt was setting himself in opposition to Scott.

Meanwhile, John Lurz, in 'Pro-Visional Reading: Seeing Walter Scott's *The Heart of Mid-Lothian*' (*LIT* 19[2008] 248–67), reconsiders the relationship between reading and seeing in the novel. Lurz calls attention to the ways in which we as readers are invited to think about seeing in the novel—from Effie's concealed pregnancy to Madge Wildfire's defiant exclamation to Butler and Sharpitlaw, 'I am as weel worth looking at as ony book in your aught.' Lurz suggests that by 'claiming a certain kind of "force" for visual communication, *The Heart of Mid-Lothian* attempts to broaden the very idea of communicative power itself' (p. 249). Gary Dyer, in 'The Transatlantic Pocahontas' (*NCC* 30[2008] 301–22) takes a transatlantic perspective on Scott. We too often overlook, he says, the two-way currents of influence, eastward as well as westward, and the way in which 'certain American texts and American stories were pivotal at certain moments' (p. 302). One of these is the Pocahontas story: Scott was certainly interested in the tale, as Dyer shows using carefully garnered evidence. Transmuted to the Middle Ages, the myth helps to shape *Ivanhoe*, suggests Dyer, and then, in its new form, goes on to re-cross the Atlantic and inform Catharine Maria Sedgwick's seventeenth-century romance *Hope Leslie* [1827]. Yet he warns us to be wary of straight-forward 'celebration of boundary-crossing' (p. 315), and unpacks both novels to suggest that 'hybridity is a troubling ideal . . . power relations are such that mixing is seldom an equal, cooperative affair' (p. 316). Although he is at times slightly aggressive in his discussion of other transatlantic-minded critics—his summary footnote dismissal of Richard Gravil's thoughtful work as narrowly canonical, to cite one instance—Dyer's piece is not only of interest to Scott studies, but also an interesting intervention in the rapidly expanding field of transatlantic studies in the Romantic period. In '"Which is the merchant here? And which the Jew?": Friends and Enemies in Walter Scott's Crusader Novels'

(*SiR* 47[2008] 437–52), David Simpson also explores the complex portrayal of other races and religions in Scott, and the way in which the conversion narrative operates both in *Ivanhoe* and *The Talisman*. If Dyer sees *Ivanhoe* as retelling the Pocahontas myth, Simpson foregrounds the novel as a rewriting of *The Merchant of Venice,* and goes on to explore the wider context of 'tolerance or welcoming of the other' in Scott's work; in particular, he reads the Crusader novels, with their 'creative attention and affection' for Rebecca and Saladin, Jew and Arab, as a plea for open-mindedness which is repeatedly frustrated. Despite their 'nod toward a potential coming reconciliation of Saxon and Norman', he concludes, the Crusader novels 'are masterful portrayals of the refusal of hospitality; and they offer a very gloomy account of the consequences of that refusal' (p. 452).

Simpson urges us to read Scott's works as 'novels for our time'; so too does Amy Witherbee in 'Habeas Corpus: British Imaginations of Power in Walter Scott's *Old Mortality*' (*NLH* 39[2008] 355–67). Witherbee takes as her starting point the figure of Scott wandering, fascinated, over the Waterloo battlefield, picking over remnants of the recent past, and musing on the power of Napoleon. She links this to recent philosophical discussions of power and sovereignty; in particular, Giorgio Agamben's history of Western politics and Western sovereignty. She argues that Scott was equally fascinated by the emergence of modern political subjectivity: the post-Waterloo *Old Mortality*, she suggests, not only reflects the evolution of Scottish nationalism but also 'directly invokes a foundational moment in British sovereignty' (p. 357) in its attention to habeas corpus. Just as Scott explored the nature of sovereign power through his portrayal of the past, Witherbee concludes, we too might benefit from 'looking back at the subtle and sometimes conflicting figures through which our cultures imagined power into being' (p. 365). Lyndsay Lunan, in 'Uses of Scott and Burns' (in Lunan, Macdonald and Sassi, eds., *Re-visioning Scotland: New Readings of the Cultural Canon*), reads the two authors as 'complicit in the authoring of a national mythology', albeit in different ways. On one level their differences may be seen to represent a conflict: Burns she sees as representing 'the interiorisation of Scotland, while Scott is responsible for its exteriorisation' (p. 16); the peasant cotter of Lockhart's *Life of Robert Burns* [1828] is set against the grand tartan spectacle, stage managed by Scott, of George IV's Edinburgh visit in 1822. But on the other hand, argues Lunan, although Scott and Burns do form a kind of binary of Scottish literary identity, they should not be understood as 'static opposing monoliths' (p. 27) but as 'symbolic representations of a dynamic process of cultural negotiation in Scottish literature'.

Finally, two very thorough articles take a broadly bibliographical perspective on Scott, revealing the intricate details of nineteenth-century book publishing and purchasing. Ross Alloway's 'Cadell and the Crash' (*BoH* 11[2008] 125–47) builds on some painstaking archival work to provide a fuller picture of the collapse of Archibald Constable and Co., focusing on the publishing house's chief financial officer, Robert Cadell and the 1825–6 financial crisis. Alloway suggests that the role of Cadell has been persistently marginalized, 'limiting our understanding of this pivotal event in British publishing history' (p. 127). Rather than the scheming businessman presented in, say, Eric Quayle's *The Ruin of Sir Walter Scott* [1968] or John Sutherland's 1995 *The Life of Walter Scott*, Alloway sets out, through a meticulous examination of accounts and correspondence, to rehabilitate Cadell's reputation and show how his 'business acumen nearly saved Scott' (p. 128). In 'The Baron's Books: Scott's *Waverley* as a Bibliomaniacal Romance' (*Romanticism* 14[2008] 245–58), Peter Garside explores 'book consciousness' in Scott—not exactly allusiveness, or intertextuality, but instead 'an awareness of the materiality of books' (p. 246). He gives an insight into the creation of *Waverley* through a close study of Scott's book-buying, marginalia, and avid collecting practices, and discusses these in the context both of existing collections in Abbotsford Library and 'bibliomania' in the early nineteenth century.

The theme for the 2008 JASNA AGM, and therefore for *Persuasions: Journal of the Jane Austen Society of North America* (30[2008]), was 'Austen's Legacy: Life, Love, and Laughter'. Claudia L. Johnson's piece asks whether the Austen 'legacy business—and I do mean business' has gone too far. Could we do with a little less Austen? Her gently satirical take on the Janeite legacy— she is, after all, finishing her own study of it, *Jane Austen's Cults and Cultures*—sets the questioning tone for this collection. Jocelyn Harris sets Austen alongside Samuel Johnson to explore different kinds of 'author-love', and Joan Klingel Ray discovers the different natures of Victorian Austen, from arch anti-Janeite Mark Twain to the perceptive, feminist readings of Margaret Oliphant. Staying in the nineteenth century, there is a good essay by Janine Barchas on the ways in which *North and South* might rework *Pride and Prejudice*, and, conversely, on the later 'Cranfordization' of Austen's novel. Oliphant's *Miss Marjoribanks* is read by Amy J. Robinson in light of *Emma*, and Edith Lank details the Austen family intrigue revealed in the marginalia of an edition of Lord Brabourne's 1884 *Letters*. There are also several contributions focusing on twentieth-century legacies: Nora Foster Stovel reads Carol Shields's debt to Austen, with emphasis on their treatment of social rituals, moral subjects, humour and family, amongst other themes, and Juliette Wells discusses Ian McEwan's use of an epigraph from *Northanger Abbey* in *Atonement*, which he has described as his 'Jane Austen novel', and which, like Austen's work, places moral questions at the heart of fiction. A different sort of Austenian legacy is evoked by Sarah Parry, Archive and Education Officer at Chawton House Library, who discusses the 'Pemberley effect' of the Austen 'brand' on the fortunes of country houses such as Lyme Park and Basildon Park. The issue also contains a number of other lively articles and notes, including pieces on Austen's writing desk and letters, on *Sense and Sensibility*, *Emma* and *Twelfth Night*, and on Austen's allusions to Richardson. Helena Kelly's discussion of game and game laws in *Mansfield Park*, Brian Southam's reading of Englishness in *Emma*, Rana Tekcan's editorial note on a Turkish edition of *Pride and Prejudice*, and Laurie Kaplan's analysis of *Lost in Austen* particularly stand out. The idea of Austen's legacy was even more broadly interpreted in *Persuasions On-Line* (29[2008])—here her influence was traced through the works of authors as diverse as James Fenimore Cooper, L.M. Montgomery ('Jane of Green Gables'? speculates Miriam Rheingold Fuller), Virginia Woolf and Susanna Clarke, author of

Jonathan Strange & Mr. Norrell. In addition to these readings of Austen's literary descendants, there are discussions of film adaptations of the novels, as well as Austen's presence in the classroom, marketplace (Deirdre Gilbert discusses Austen 'from Egerton to Kindle') and popular culture. As Brandy Foster puts it in her winningly entitled 'Pimp My Austen: The Commodification and Customization of Jane Austen', an 'Austen' identity now exists which, to some extent, 'subsumes all of the divergent customizations and *genre-fications* into the Jane Austen brand'. A slightly different perspective was offered in the second issue of *Persuasions On-Line* (28:ii[2008]), which takes 'Global Jane Austen' as its theme and offers some excellent and original readings of transnational Austen: *Emma* in light of August von Kotzebue and *Mansfield Park* in relation to Macartney; Jane Austen in Japan, in Turkey and in Spanish adaptations; Austen and contemporary US 'Christian romance'. Pieces on the presence of the French revolutionary wars in contemporary adaptations (by Gillian Dow), and on a South Indian version of *Sense and Sensibility* (by R.N. Simhan) are complemented by a piece on 'Appropriating Austen: Localism on the Global Scene', by Linda Troost and Sayre Greenfield. The different journal issues together form a strong contribution to work on the cultural significance and impact of Austen, a burgeoning critical field in its own right. Worth mentioning, too, in this context, is Fiona Brideoake's 'The Republic of Pemberley: Politeness and Citizenship in Digital Sociability' (*19* 7[2008]), which takes an intriguing post-Habermasian perspective on the nature of online communities. Brideoake pays particular attention to *The Republic of Pemberley* website, which, she says, 'elaborates its extravagant appreciation of Austen's works within the Habermasian rhetoric of eighteenth-century Bluestocking feminism'. Beginning with a detailed contextual discussion of bluestocking culture, she then moves on to read the negotiations and boundaries, the unspoken constraints and hierarchies of the online community. 'Both forms of virtual community', Brideoake argues, 'reproduce the sociable strictures they ostensibly suspend, underscoring the ongoing importance of attending to the operations of power within even the most apparently inclusive of social formations' .

The wider community evoked in *Emma* is contextualized in different ways by Laura Mooneyham White in 'Beyond the Romantic Gypsy: Narrative Disruptions and Ironies in Austen's *Emma*' (*PLL* 44:iii[2008] 305–27) and Robert James Merrett in 'The Gentleman Farmer in *Emma*: Agrarian Writing and Jane Austen's Cultural Idealism' (*UTQ* 77[2008] 711–37). What are the gypsies doing in *Emma*? Mooneyham White traces the 'literary fad' of the gypsy through eighteenth-century literature and suggests the way in which the novel, often ironically, uses the romance traditions associated with their presence. *Emma*'s match-making, for instance, might be compared to gypsies' fortune-telling; the mystery surrounding Harriet's parentage might be compared to the repeated threat that gypsies in romances steal children (as Michael Kramp has pointed out, both Harriet and the gypsies are 'natural', their status uncertain). Mooneyham traces all mentions of and allusions to gypsies through the novel, and concludes that they do not simply bring romance traditions into Highbury, but allow Austen to engage in 'a concise critique and refiguring of the romantic tradition of the gypsy narrative as a whole', casting light on the characters, themes and preoccupations of the novel with marginality and imagination. Merrett, on the other hand, turns back to the central figures in *Emma* and reads the novel in light of controversies in agrarian writing about the gentleman farmer. He explores these in George Crabbe's poem 'The Gentleman-Farmer', and, further back, in Richardson, Fielding, Goldsmith and Smollett, as well as Adam Smith's *Wealth of Nations*, before returning to *Emma* and showing how Knightley represents Austen's ideal of the sociable, productive and humane gentleman farmer. He concludes with a mention of Emma teasing Knightley with her thoughts about his conversation with Robert Martin, concerning 'business, shows of cattle, or new drills...the dimensions of some famous ox': 'these and other agricultural topics', says Merrett, 'will fill her married life', which seems rather a heavy punishment for our heroine.

Two pieces adopted a more philosophical approach to Austen. In 'Form Affects Content: Reading Jane Austen' (*P&L* 32[2008] 315–29), E.M. Dadlez attempts to investigate the impact of form on readers, closely comparing two recent adaptations of *Persuasion* with the novel itself, and rereading D.A. Miller's comments on Austen's style in the toothpick-case episode in *Sense and Sensibility*. 'There is a kind of active, imaginative participation involved in our response to figures of speech and symbols and imagery', Dadlez notes, 'that turns reading into a collaboration' (p. 323). She concludes that in Austen 'apparent trivialities are seldom what they seem, either in content or in form' (p. 328): something which might not come as a surprise to the majority of Austen readers. Wendy S. Jones, in '*Emma*, Gender, and the Mind-Brain' (*ELH* 75[2008] 315–43), explores the nature of sympathy in *Emma*: the novel, she argues, is about perception, and proper ways of seeing and unseeing, which she sets alongside concepts of gender, Hume's theories of sympathy and Reynolds's aesthetic theories. She concludes by 'reading *Emma* neurologically' and speculating on the nature of readerly sympathy, which she sees as taking place at a physical level as 'the emotional components of our neural maps become active' (p. 338). Three small pieces in *The Sewanee Review* offer a nice demonstration of this readerly sympathy at work, focusing on Austen's style in appreciative detail. '*Emma*: Jane Austen's Errant Heroine', by Eugene Goodheart (*SR* 116[2008] 589–604) also takes a cue from D.A. Miller in its close reading of Austen's prose, analysing the nature of community in the novel, and suggesting that Emma should be seen as, perhaps, 'irredeemable in her autonomy' (p. 604). Edwin M. Yoder, 'Otelia's Umbrella: Jane Austen and Manners in a Small World' (*SR* 116[2008] 605–11), discusses issues of courtesy and good behaviour in the novels, calling attention to 'Jane Austen's jeweler's eye for social gesture' (p. 608). Finally, Dawn Potter's 'In Defense of Dullness or Why Fanny Price Is My Favorite Austen Heroine' (*SR* 116[2008] 611–18) makes a spirited case for a flawed Fanny Price, moody, shy, fumbling, awkward—but nevertheless appealing to the reader because of the way she can come to terms with the tedium of her world and take a 'rigorous interest in her own private longings and equivocations' (p. 618).

Meanwhile, Austen's sources were scrutinized from different angles. In 'Jane Austen and "Modern Europe"' (*N&Q* 55[2008] 23–5) Peter Knox-Shaw works to gloss a reference Austen made in September 1813, 'Fanny & I are to go on with Modern Europe together': R.W. Chapman, followed by other scholars, has suggested that this might be a reference to John Bigland's *Letters on the Modern History and Political Aspect of Europe* [1804]. Knox-Shaw suggests that it was instead *The History of Modern Europe* by William Russell (1741–93)—'closer in title, better known and more topical at the time'—and examines some of the implications of this reading for Austen's view of history and Europe. In 'From Pammydiddle to Persuasion: Jane Austen Rewriting Eighteenth-Century Literature' (*ECLife* 32[2008] 29–38) Olivia Murphy travels back to Austen's early story 'Jack and Alice' to show her juvenile allusions and borrowings—her parodies of Johnson, her use of Frances Brooke's novel *The Excursion,* and her lively satire of *Sir Charles Grandison*. Moreover, Murphy argues, these preoccupations—particularly Austen's Richardsonian parodies—continued to inform her fiction throughout her life, from the juvenilia to *Persuasion*. Austen not only demonstrated 'affectionate familiarity' with eighteenth-century fiction's characters, language, and ideological basis, concludes Murphy, but also 'resisted these to the same extent that she deployed them for her own uses' (p. 37). Susan Harlan, in '"Talking" and Reading Shakespeare in Jane Austen's *Mansfield Park*' (*WC* 39[2008] 43–6), discusses Henry Crawford's dramatic reading of *Henry VIII,* which so enthrals Fanny. Crawford, says Harlan, 'appropriates Shakespeare's language as a vehicle by which he performs himself'. Like Crawford, Harlan argues, Austen also appropriates Shakespeare for performative purposes, 'imbuing his play with a "meaning" or "sense" that is uniquely novelistic' (p. 43).

Appropriation of Austen herself formed the subject of Lisa Hopkins's *Relocating Shakespeare and Austen on Screen*. This is a lively discussion of a very wide range of Austen adaptations, which imaginatively sets the marketing and presentation of her work alongside Shakespeare films. 'Where Shakespeare films go, it seems, Austen films follow' (p. 12) argues Hopkins, discussing the intertextual and cultural connections between them, and noting that adaptations of both have become a genre in their own right. The chapters create some unusual connections: the first explores these English icons lazing on the West Coast of America, setting Baz Luhrmann's *Romeo + Juliet* alongside the delightful 'Valley party' interpretation of *Emma* offered by Amy Heckerling's *Clueless*. In chapter 2, the action has shifted eastwards, to James Ivory's *Jane Austen in Manhattan* and Michael Almereyda's *Hamlet*; chapter 3 continues to move east, exploring British films *In the Bleak Midwinter,* directed by Kenneth Branagh, and Sharon Maguire's *Bridget Jones Diary,* and the way in which, in both films, 'England is identified with reality and America with illusion' (p. 80). Anglo-Indian films *Shakespeare Wallah* and *Bride and Prejudice* are discussed in chapter 4, alongside the Indian adaptation of *Sense and Sensibility, Kandukondain Kandukondain*—in India, Hopkins shows, 'Shakespeare and Austen adaptations...take on a life and logic of their own' (p. 129). She closes with a discussion of modern adaptations, and the hijacking of Austen's biography and image, turning a sharp eye on films such as *Becoming Jane,* with its 'slushily suggestive' romantic dialogue, and the new 'portrait' commissioned by Wordsworth Editions which has given the 'very, very dowdy' Austen 'a bit of a make-over, with make-up and hair extensions'

(p. 145). Roberta Grandi also offers a close reading of how novel might be translated into film in 'The Passion Translated: Literary and Cinematic Rhetoric in *Pride and Prejudice* (2005)' (*LFQ* 36[2008] 45–51), which discusses the 'filmic grammar' of Joe Wright's version of Austen.

There was a welcome reissue from Palgrave Macmillan of Tony Tanner's 1986 *Jane Austen*, which has become a teaching staple—lucid and accessible, but also provocative. This edition comes with a preface by Marilyn Gaull and a note on the text by John Wiltshire. Gaull gives a short biography of Tanner and nicely places his role as an Austen critic against a backdrop of twentieth-century revaluations of Austen, and of a changing America in the 1960s and 1970s. In Tanner's contemporary readings, as she shows, Austen becomes an author not of complacent, stable social values, but with 'individual lives as a succession of liminal experiences', dispersed and drifting families (p. xv). Kathryn Sutherland's 2002 edition of J.E. Austen-Leigh's *A Memoir of Jane Austen* was also reissued this year, retaining its excellent introduction and notes. Another useful teaching tool is Gregg A. Hecimovich's *Emma*, a Continuum Reader's Guide, which offers students guidance on close reading, free indirect discourse, word games and social games in the text, as well as a discussion of various film adaptations.

Mary Shelley prompted a good deal of work, most of it, as usual, centred on *Frankenstein*. The most significant contribution to *Frankenstein* studies has already been covered in the first section: *Frankenstein's Science: Experimentation and Discovery in Romantic Culture, 1780–1830*, edited by Christa Knellwolf and Jane Goodall. This sets out to readdress the notion of science in the novel, offering a close look at scientific debates and controversies, 'the cross-fertilisations between radical politics and the dramas of scientific exploration' (p. 2). The collection evokes the vigour and excitement of the research being undertaken by Erasmus Darwin and the Lunar Men (whose theories of evolution—and revolution—are discussed in an essay by Allan K. Hunter) and the showmanship of electrical experimentation, with its revolutionary charge (the subject of essays by Jane Goodall and Ian Jackson). Some highly interesting contexts are outlined, including Patricia Fara's contribution on the scientific education of girls, which deals not only with introductory texts for girls such as Jane Marcet's *Conversations on Chemistry*, but also with contexts such as Ludvig Holberg's *A Journey to the World Underground* [1742], narrated by Niels Klim, once widely read but now 'virtually unknown outside Scandinavia' (p. 23). Amongst other pieces, Christa Knellwolf explores Schelling's ideas on 'the possibility of obtaining metaphysical insight' (p. 51); Anita Guerrini outlines anti-vivisection and vegetarian debates of the 1820s; Melinda Cooper describes comparative anatomy, 'the science of teratology' and 'Shelley's vision of the monstrous' (p. 87). The apparent omission of reference to Sharon Ruston and her work on vitalism was a slight disappointment here.

Peter Melville, in 'Monstrous Ingratitude: Hospitality in Mary Shelley's *Frankenstein*' (*ERR* 19[2008] 179–85), explores the relationship between hospitality and hostility in the novel. In examples such as Frankenstein rejecting his duties as host towards the 'hideous guest' Melville sees a repeated pattern in which 'scenes of hospitality' are couched in a 'language of failure'

(p. 182). His consideration of the De Lacey's 'lovely guest' Safie and her father, whom, as a 'mistreated foreigner', Melville compares to the creature, are particularly striking. In 'Safie/*Saphie*: Mungo Park's *Travels in the Interior Districts of Africa* and the De Lacey Episode in *Frankenstein*' (*ANQ* 21[2008] 45–50), D.S. Neff also addresses the question of Safie's origins from a slightly different perspective. Given that the Shelleys had read Park's *Travels*—albeit with some reservations on Mary's part about Park's prejudices—could Safie look back to Park's discussion of 'certain charms or amulets called *saphies*, which the Negroes constantly wear about them' (p. 46)? Neff discusses the almost 'magical' powers of Safie in this context, and, on a deeper level, shows how Mary Shelley's uncertainty about Park's treatment of non-Christians might have shaped her novel.

Disgust at the 'unearthly ugliness', the 'filthy mass', of Frankenstein's creature, and shame over its creation, are at the heart of the novel, argues James C. Hatch in 'Disruptive Affects: Shame, Disgust, and Sympathy in *Frankenstein*' (*ERR* 19[2008] 33–49). Using the work of the American psychologist Silvan Tomkins on the nature of shame and disgust, Hatch suggests that *Frankenstein* 'places sympathy into conflict with the power of affect' (p. 43). This, Hatch claims, complicates 'ethical readings' of the novel, which draw on Adam Smith and Enlightenment concepts of sympathy. In 'Imperial Vision in the Arctic: Fleeting Looks and Pleasurable Distractions in Barker's Panorama and Shelley's *Frankenstein*' (*RaVoN* 52[2008]) Laurie Garrison compares the perspective afforded by Walton's frame narrative of his doomed Arctic voyage to the popular panoramas exhibited in Henry Aston Barker's Leicester Square Rotunda: these, she says, 'provided a mode of viewing that was particularly conducive to supporting imperial endeavor'. Garrison puts a close reading of the gaps and distractions in Walton's narrative alongside a discussion of the panoramas (a pictorial key to one of these survives and is helpfully reproduced here) to suggest that Shelley's portrayal of the uncertain, unreliable navigator Walton amounts to a critique of imperial vision, especially as manifested in the these exploitative and problematic Arctic explorations of the early nineteenth century. Coverage of expeditions and debates in the *Quarterly Review*, where *Frankenstein* itself was also reviewed, supports her parallel.

In 'The Shelleys and the Idea of "Europe"' (*ERR* 19[2008] 335–50) Paul Stock argues that both *Frankenstein* and Percy Shelley's *Laon and Cythna* are particularly concerned with the meanings of 'Europe' and 'European'. After all, it is as 'an European' that we first catch a glimpse of Frankenstein himself, scudding across the Arctic wastes, and his actions have obvious correlations with revolutionary upheavals. The novel, Stock therefore suggests, offers 'an uneasy analysis of what defines and shapes "the European"', and he goes on to explore this in light of *Laon and Cythna*, intended to be, as Shelley told his publisher, 'the beau ideal as it were of the French Revolution' (p. 337). Stock asks what constitutes this revolutionary 'beau ideal' and indeed what a European 'beau ideal' might look like: he concludes with an interesting speculation about the ways in which the Shelley circle's sexual mores might have been considered by outsiders as 'unEuropean'. Meanwhile Michael Rossington also considered the Shelleys' perspectives on Europe in 'Rousseau and Tacitus: Republican Inflections in the Shelleys' *History of a Six Weeks' Tour*' (*ERR* 19[2008] 321–33). The volume, shaped from diary and letters across a long period, blends 'literary allusion, travel narrative, historical reference and political commentary' to comment on Europe past and present, and, particularly, on 'the records of classical, feudal and eighteenth-century struggles between liberty and tyranny' (p. 322). Rossington especially focuses on the classical allusions of the volume, and the central importance of Tacitus: Shelley's reading of Tacitus, he shows, may be placed in a long republican tradition, which may also be linked to the volume's passionate interest in Rousseau. Both Tacitus and Rousseau, he argues, help to contribute to the volume's promotion of 'alternative values to imperial ambition and consequent violent conflict' (p. 329); they help the Shelleys to counter 'the records of the "reality" of what happened with "imaginings" of a historically-informed kind' (p. 330).

The reworking and reimagining of history is also the central idea of two good essays about Mary Shelley's other works—again paying attention to the wider, European, context. Lisa Vargo's thoughtful article 'Mary Shelley, *Corinne*, and "the Mantle of Enthusiasm"' (*ERR* 19[2008] 171–7) shows the interplay between Shelley and de Staël. *Corinne* shaped Shelley's travels in Italy; the novel also, Vargo shows, informs Shelley's concepts of freedom, and her own literary and biographical treatment of the inspired and enthusiastic woman. Moreover, Shelley and de Staël are bound together by their common interest in Godwin's writing, and their Godwinian conviction that 'emancipation arises from conversation' (p. 171). Vargo traces the Shelley–de Staël conversation through unusual sources—such as Shelley's accounts of the improvisator Tommaso Sgricci in her letters and journals—into *Valperga* and Shelley's 1839 *Lives of the Most Eminent Literary and Scientific Men of France*, which ends with a portrait of de Staël as a 'young and brilliant improvisatrice'. Shelley herself, suggests Vargo, is 'a kind of unacknowledged *improvisatrice* who rewrites history into possibility' (p. 174). Shelley's attention to the narrative possibilities of history is also the focus of Theresa M. Kelley's 'Romantic Temporality, Contingency, and Mary Shelley' (*ELH* 75[2008] 625–52). Taking Michael Serres's discussion of historical time as unfixed, chaotic and 'percolating' as her starting point, Kelley discusses 'contingency in late-eighteenth and early-nineteenth-century thought'—with especial attention to revolutionary hopes and disappointments—and fictional contingency in *Valperga*. History and time in this novel form not a linear sequence, but may instead act—as in Vargo's reading—to offer different narrative possibilities. 'By breaking up the march of history, however briefly', Kelley argues, '*Valperga* creates a space for imagining other worlds and outcomes' (p. 627). Exploring Shelley's two fictional characters, Euthanasia and Beatrice, in interesting detail, Kelley suggests that although they, and their fate, do reflect Shelley's view of revolutionary failures, the novel does also imagine 'an emancipatory future imagined and chastened by its past' (p. 646). There was also an article on *Mathilda*: Katherine A. Miller, '"The remembrance haunts me like a crime": Narrative Control, the Dramatic, and the Female Gothic in Mary Wollstonecraft Shelley's *Mathilda*' (*TSWL* 27[2008] 291–308), attempts a definition of the female Gothic narrative, often seen as offering a conservative depiction of gender. However, Miller instead puts forward a reading of Shelley's female Gothic which privileges resistance and creativity. Mathilda, she urges, should be seen as a 'consummate actress and storyteller', who 'exerts a covert power through staged passivity' (p. 303). More generally, she suggests that the dramatic elements of *Mathilda* are part of a wider pattern of performance and artistry in nineteenth-century female Gothic texts which actually works to asserts feminine agency.

Mary Wollstonecraft features in Erinç Özdemir's 'Hidden Polemic in Wollstonecraft's *Letters from Norway*: A Bakhtinian Reading' (*SiR* 47[2008] 321–49; also discussed in section 2 above). Özdemir discusses the impossibility of pinning down Wollstonecraft's genre or style in this work, which she describes as a 'fusion of sentimental and Romantic discourses . . . in turn fused with a discourse of reason' (p. 321). Özdemir reads these different discourses in the *Letters* in light of Bakhtin's concepts of 'hidden polemic' and 'hybridization', and suggests that their 'fusion' reveals Wollstonecraft's efforts—often conflicted and contradictory—to balance her own Romantic and sentimental subjectivity. Christine Chaney, in 'The "Prophet-Poet's Book"' (*SEL* 48[2008] 791–9), also explores the power of Wollstonecraft's 'hybrid' text, tracing its long reach through the work of Elizabeth Barrett Browning and Virginia Woolf. Chaney's reading of the *Letters* is also informed by Bakhtin, as she explores the possibilities afforded by Wollstonecraft's adoption of the 'literary self-portrait's hybrid discourse'. These gave Barrett Browning a model for 'a life narrative that could operate polemically in the public sphere' (p. 793), and informed her own genre-defying *Aurora Leigh*. The complex self-representation at work in *Letters*, Chaney argues, provides both Barrett Browning and, through her, Woolf with a way of exploring 'narrative subjectivity' and—ultimately—their own potential as women artists.

Mary A. Waters follows up her study of *British Women Writers and the Profession of Literary Criticism, 1789–1832* [2004] with *British Women Writers of the Romantic Period: An Anthology of their Literary Criticism*. Of interest for this section are the substantial extracts from Barbauld's essay and prefaces from *The British Novelists*, showing Barbauld deftly defending the pleasures of the novel form: 'We cut down the tree that bears no fruit, but we ask nothing of a flower beyond its scent and colour' (p. 31). Charlotte Smith, Mary Hays and Elizabeth Inchbald are also represented, and the collection stretches as far as Maria Jane Jewsbury and Harriet Martineau: this is a useful teaching selection, nicely presented. Leya Landau's 'The Metropolis and Women Novelists in the Romantic Period' (*Romanticism* 14[2008] 119–32) also calls attention to ways in which women writers of the period might be viewed together, this time considering the representation of London in fiction. The London which appears in novels such as Burney's *The Wanderer* and Jane Porter's *Thaddeus of Warsaw* [1803] is, Landau argues, a new city—not part of an eighteenth-century city/country dialectic, but discussed in relation to contemporary history, changing national identity and gender.

There was strong work on individual women writers, notably the collection *Charlotte Smith in British Romanticism*, edited by Jacqueline Labbe, already mentioned in section 1; this review will deal with the essays on the novels. Admittedly, it goes against the grain in some ways to be reviewing simply the novels section of the collection—as Labbe points out in her introduction, 'for the first time in one volume we read of her as novelist, poet, playwright, letter-writer—and literary icon' (p. 2). The volume as a whole allows us to see how Smith's keen poetic attentiveness to textual and linguistic detail plays into her novels—and how she pushes at the boundaries of the form. Barbara Tarling explores political history in *Desmond, Old Manor House, The Young Philosopher* in her essay ' "The Slight Skirmishing of a Novel Writer": Charlotte Smith and the American War of Independence'. She shows Smith's 'prolonged and progressive engagement with the politics of revolution' (p. 71) through representations of the American War of the 1770s, which are used to critique the 1790s. This is territory usually associated with Walter Scott, and the historical novel as defined by Lukács; Tarling shows exactly how Smith is using it beforehand, citing, for example, the way in which Desmond hears, and then himself relates, the enlightened French aristocrat Montfleuri's account of the war while himself witnessing the 'Fête de la Fédération'. The 'fictive authority' of Montfleuri's and Desmond's accounts is set alongside the second-hand, unreliable histrionics of Burke. Tarling traces Smith's responses to Burke through her subsequent novels, showing how Smith continued to hold the American War of Independence as an important ideal. *The Young Philosopher* is also the subject of A.A. Markley's essay, discussing Smith's correspondence with Godwin, and tracing her relationship with him, and his work, in the late 1790s. In particular, she explores what Smith might have borrowed from Godwin's use of narrative in *Caleb Williams*, and Mary Wollstonecraft's rewriting of this to create individual speakers in *The Wrongs of Woman*. The concerns of the 1790s, so vividly shown in works such as *The Emigrants* [1793], are shown in the subsequent essay by Amy Garnai to have existed well into the 1800s: moreover, argues Garnai, they revise Smith's 'earlier conception of cosmopolitanism'. Garnai discusses how *The Letters of a Solitary Wanderer* [1800] presents a landscape of displacement and loss, where 'transnational border crossings imply, more than the movement *towards* heterogeneity, hybridity and an idea of universal citizenship, a movement *away from*—in escape from—despotism, intolerance and tyranny' (p. 108). Katherine Astbury's contribution explores *The Banished Man* in French translation, suggesting that it was 'adapted to conform more naturally with aesthetic and political concerns across the Channel' (p. 129). Subtle choices of footnote and phrasing by its translator Louis-Antoine Marquand in 1797, as Astbury shows, alter Smith's original portrait of the revolution and make it more palatable to a French audience. Labbe herself discusses Smith in relation to Burney and Austen—hers is a 'tale of three Willoughbys: Sir Clement, George and John', and, more generally, a discussion of continuities across characters and novels. Labbe pays particular attention to *The Old Manor House* and *Mansfield Park*: Austen, she argues, has a 'dynamic commitment' to Smith, and she shows how both authors take the novel of the 1790s forward into the nineteenth century.

Related to the way in which this collection places Smith's novels in relation to other genres, Ingrid Horrocks, in ' "Her Ideas Arranged

Themselves": Re-Membering Poetry in Radcliffe' (*SiR* 47[2008] 507–27), discusses Radcliffe's work as part of the 'phenomenon of the blended novel', which incorporates poetry, verses and lyrical moments into the text to make up 'a distinctly 1790s form of heteroglossia' (p. 507). Like Mary Jacobus's work on the poetry of *Persuasion*, mentioned above, Horrocks suggests the central importance of verse to *Udolpho*. She reads its poems in thoughtful and illuminating ways to suggest both 'a story of consolation and community' at work in the novel (p. 524), and Radcliffe's plea for imaginative freedom—a plea which takes on special significance in the 1790s. Marilyn L. Brooks, 'Mary Hays's *The Victim of Prejudice*: Chastity ReNegotiated' (*WW* 15[2008] 13–31), also foregrounds the culture and rhetoric of the 1790s, beginning with a discussion of Hays's radical challenge to the notion of chastity, and her desire to 'isolate virtue, as active choice, from chastity, as precept or habit' (p. 16). This was a topic on which Hays had written in the *Monthly Magazine*; she returned to the issue in *The Victim of Prejudice* [1799], which traces the effect of the fallen woman on the subsequent generation—as Brooks shows, acting out Hays's interest in cause and effect.

'Text and Textile in Sydney Owenson's *The Wild Irish Girl*' by Julie Donovan (*Éire* 43[2008] 31–57) explores Owenson's materialist thinking in more ways than one. For Donovan, the materialism of *The Wild Irish Girl* functions not only in terms of Locke, but also through the preoccupation with textiles and clothing in the novel, which become a trope through which Irish nationalism might be reappropriated and transformed. Illustrated not only with close readings but also with images of Irish linen manufacture—spinning, reeling, and bleaching, 'beetling, scotching and hackling the flax'—Donovan's article offers a witty and well-contextualized rereading of the novel, and an original view of Owenson's own self-fashioning. Another good perspective is offered by Christopher Nagle in 'Pleasures and Perils of Sensibility' (*WC* 39[2008] 49–52), who places *The Wild Irish Girl* against de Staël's *Corinne* as a way not only of exploring cross-cultural connections between Sensibility and Romanticism, but also of investigating the vexed nature of home in the work of both these women writers. Meanwhile, Frances Botkin, in 'Burning Down the [Big] House: Sati in Sydney Owenson's *The Missionary*' (*Colloquy: Text Theory Critique* 15[2008] 36–51), explores Owenson's treatment of female agency through a reading of the figure of Luxima, whose attempt of sati disrupts and resists colonial power. Ultimately, however, Botkin concludes, Owenson's novel skirts the issue of sati, and reproduces 'essentialist stereotypes' (p. 48).

Maria Edgeworth's Anglo-Irish identity was the focus of several articles this year. Following Marilyn Butler's lead, who some years ago called for a more subtle reading of Edgeworth's association with the Anglo-Irish ascendancy, Clara Tuite argues, in 'Maria Edgeworth's Déjà-Voodoo: Interior Decoration, Retroactivity, and Colonial Allegory in *The Absentee*' (*ECF* 20[2008] 385–413), that we should foreground the Irishness and Irish sympathies of her fiction. Tuite's catchy title comes courtesy of a fridge magnet purchased in the NYPL gift shop: 'déjà-voodoo', she says, is a good way of describing 'Edgeworth's allegorical practice, which meets the act of imperial anachronizing with the spell of Irish cultural memory', an 'oppositional form of Irish memory work' or 'retro-activity' (pp. 385–6). She discusses this in relation to Edgeworth's 'exuberant satire' of Regency fashion and sociability in *The Absentee*: a novel of generic negotiations, where fashionable life meets the historical and national tale, and where, Tuite argues, interior decoration becomes the ground for 'a narrative of colonial mimicry and exile' (p. 386). In '"Homage to the empty armour": Maria Edgeworth's *Harrington* and the Pathology of National Heritage' (*ELH* 75[2008] 439–69), Natasha Tessone similarly urges a reconsideration of Edgeworth's Irish sympathies, reading *Harrington*'s treatment of Jewishness against an Anglo-Irish background. Tessone calls attention to Edgeworth's embarrassment about the novel's ending, calling it 'an Irish blunder': what, Tessone asks, is specifically Irish about Edgeworth's 'blundering' in this novel? She reads the novel's 'double-edged critique of anti-Semitism and England's heritage politics, its sympathetic characterization of Jewish figures, and, finally, its failure to fully carry out its progressive vision' (p. 442) alongside Edgeworth's subtle explorations of Irish identity, and the *Essay on Irish Bulls*. Julia M. Wright, in '"Wel gelun a gud?": Thomas Sheridan's *Brave Irishman* and the failure of English' (*ISR* 16[2008] 445–60), also discusses the *Essay on Irish Bulls*, setting it in dialogue with Thomas Sheridan's farce *The Brave Irishman: or, Captain O'Blunder*. Both works explore the nature of Irish linguistic difference, but, Wright argues, 'they are diametrically opposed on the capacity of the English language ... to serve as an instrument of education and social change' (p. 3): she suggests that Sheridan has a more flexible attitude to the Irish language.

Similarly, two articles on Maturin both called attention to the complexities of his Anglo-Irish identity. Jim Hansen, in 'The Wrong Marriage: Maturin and the Double-Logic of Masculinity in the Unionist Gothic' (*SiR* 47[2008] 351–69), focuses on the figure of the 'wrong marriage', calling particular attention to Maturin's little-known first Gothic romance, *The Fatal Revenge; or, The Family of Montorio* [1807]. For Hansen, the trope of the 'wrong marriage' comes to embody all the conflicted loyalties of Maturin's position, political and literary. Neither anti-Unionist Irish rebel nor Unionist Irish Tory, a Gothic novelist who borrows from his female predecessors but exhibits anxiety about the Radcliffean model of fiction, Maturin and his work may be read in the context of 'the connected nationalist and gender double-binds that underwrite post-1798 Irish cultural politics' (p. 354). In 'Melmoth Affirmed: Maturin's Defense of Sacred History' (*SiR* 47[2008] 121–45), Ashley Marshall also foregrounds Maturin's Anglo-Irish background, this time in the context of religion. Citing Terry Eagleton's comment that *Melmoth the Wanderer* is driven not by 'metaphysics but money', Marshall argues that the importance of religion has been persistently sidelined in Maturin criticism, and redefines *Melmoth* as 'Puritan gothic'. Philosophical and religious principle, Marshall claims, is central to the novel, and she supports this with a detailed reading of biblical allusion and Christian typography in the work, setting this in the context of the rise of sectarian Catholic nationalism in Ireland at the time that *Melmoth* was written.

4. Poetry

In this section Jason Whittaker covers Blake; Christopher Machell covers work on Shelley and women poets, except Anna Barbauld; David Stewart covers general work, Barbauld and all other poets.

Study of Romantic poetry remains transfixed by questions of canonicity. The canon has expanded, but it has done so in an oddly ambivalent way. Writers are revived, but often without enthusiasm. This section will show, as usual, study of a wide variety of 'new' poets; but the old big six still far outstrip the rest. The new canon has met with a degree of uncertainty, continuing to inhabit obscure corners of research libraries, shunning the bright strip-lights of the classroom. And with the increasing availability of these minor poets in free online editions, the role of the teaching anthology has begun to change. Accordingly, Michael O'Neill and Charles Mahoney's *Romantic Poetry: An Annotated Anthology* is something of a sign of the times. Texts from 'Tintern Abbey' to *Thalaba the Destroyer* are widely available, so the demand for a comprehensive anthology has, to an extent, been superseded. This anthology makes a claim for itself not in its coverage but in its selection. The anthology covers those poets most typically taught (the big six male poets plus the wee four women poets, Barbauld, Smith, Hemans and Landon), and of those ten poets far fewer poems are covered than in other comparable anthologies. Substituted instead are extensive headnotes to each poet and to each individual poem. Some notes are quite modest (two paragraphs for 'Anecdote for Fathers'), others substantial enough to be called short essays (two full double-column pages for the fifty-four lines of 'Kubla Khan'). The editors have a particular commitment to the role that an appreciation of poetic form can play in critical understanding, and it is on account of this formal detail that the anthology is so valuable. Introductory headnotes elucidate the subtleties of each poem's craft, while footnotes comment on line endings, rhyme patterns and other features of the text. Some comments are so brilliantly incisive as to deserve separate publication, such as this account of the metre of *Christabel*: 'each line seems like a stealthy event' (p. 207). Without question, this is by far the best way that any reader could be introduced to these poets, and the anthology is careful not to suggest that an attention to poetic detail precludes other types of investigation. Understanding how a poem creates meaning, however, is the vital first step, and for this reason *Romanticism: An Annotated Anthology* will doubtless be the standard teaching anthology for many years.

The Cambridge Companion to British Romantic Poetry, edited by James Chandler and Maureen N. McLane, is likewise suggestive of the increasing importance of poetic form in Romantic studies. There is in existence a *Cambridge Companion to British Romanticism*, but this volume is emphatically a study of poetry, not history, if a study of poetry which steers just as far clear of a dehistoricized formalism. It is a remarkably sprightly, confident volume; subtle and deft in its understanding of canonical and non-canonical poetics, and cutting-edge precisely in so far as it pays revitalized attention to the cultural significance of these questions. Jeffrey Cox's chapter sets the scene well. Cox provides a survey of all of the poetry published in 1820, considering as he does so the cultural 'battlefield' (p. 26) in which volumes by Keats and

Shelley defined themselves. A number of the chapters reinvestigate the familiar by considering the greatly enriched context of the non-canonical (or the 'pantheon' which Cox identifies) that recent scholarship has identified. Ann Weirda Rowland places poetry and novels in mutual dialogue, '[defining] themselves in and through each other' (p. 118). Tim Fulford's 'Poetry, Peripheries and Empire' opens up a context of the multiplicitous by which one may better understand an apparently singular canon, complementing Andrew Elfenbein's study of the standardization of English in the period, which reveals the way in which poetry made use of 'a mosaic arising from collective experiences of a variety of Englishes from throughout Great Britain' (p. 78). A number of chapters pay particular attention to questions of form, most notably Susan Stewart's. Stewart brilliantly shows how a focus on form informs particular Romantic poems, but also provides an important sense of the variety of ways in which Romantic poets borrowed and adapted earlier forms. This is an exciting collection. Much of the historicizing work in Romantic poetry has been rather dry, tending to leave the poetry behind in the search for ever more contexts to add to that familiar formulation, 'Romantic poetry and...'. If this non-reactionary return to the first part of that equation does truly represent the future, the study of Romantic poetry will be significantly enlivened.

Perhaps the most important, and certainly the most elegant, general book on Romantic poetry this year is Maureen N. McLane's *Balladeering, Minstrelsy, and the Making of British Romantic Poetry*. Importantly, this is a book with a serious commitment to poetics. Yet as McLane herself points out, it is a work of scholarship, with all the dryness that term brings with it, but it is one that benefits immensely from a careful attention to the details of poetry. McLane understands that studying popular culture is inevitably to place oneself in the position of Walter Scott talking to James Hogg's disapproving mother. And indeed those Romantic ballad collectors and antiquarians, including Scott, who offered Romantic readers collections of ballad material surrounded by scholarly annotation, loom large in a book that subtly threads its way between questions of originality, authenticity, inheritance and orality. The book provides us with much new information about balladeering and minstrelsy, but its real strength lies in a subtle theorization of the history of scholarly and poetic appropriation of the traditional. More broadly, the book's real ambition lies in its attempt to address a question common to Wordsworth and Coleridge: 'What is poetry?' The answer, given all of this surrounding scholarly apparatus, is one that is determined by poetry's mediation. Scott's decision to *print* border ballads dismayed Mrs Hogg, and McLane's book is in this sense remarkably timely given our own culture's obsession with the effect of technology on poetry. This is a dense and a long book, but McLane's complication of a series of theoretical, historical and poetic narratives is rendered with a light wit that makes the book consistently compelling. There are chapters which explore the relationship between poetry and music (ballads were always multi-media constructs); Beattie and Scott are discussed in connection with minstrelsy, showing the ways in which minstrelsy dramatizes the relationship between poetry and history; Wordsworth's minstrel poems suggest his attempts to reimagine the socio-poetics of minstrelsy, though John Clare's work, arising from a less certain 'social and economic position' leads to an investigation of the material from 'more urgently critical angles' (p. 165). This is a passionate book, but also a careful one. Theoretically sophisticated yet attuned to the detail of poetics, it ought to prove inspirational to a wide range of scholars of Romantic poetry.

Bridget Keegan's *British Labouring-Class Nature Poetry, 1730–1837* is a significant development in the un-enclosed field of labouring-class poetry. Keegan has played her part in recent scholarly efforts, led by John Goodridge, to expand the canon of these poets, and her book benefits from the recent recovery of many hundreds of labouring-class poets. Keegan zooms in on one particular area, and a central one at that: nature. Writers such as John Clare, Ann Yearsley and Robert Bloomfield had a connection with the land quite different to that of Wordsworth or Keats because they worked on it. But this relationship has its own difficulties. Eco-criticism tends to value those writers who understand human and natural things in a non-hierarchical manner. But farming is cultivation; the land is used for human ends. Eco-criticism has an uneasy relationship with such writers, and Keegan is herself uneasy about the 'usefulness' of this critical methodology to understand such writers. Yet, despite their worryingly georgic understanding of nature, her poets tend to come off well ecologically. Bloomfield is a central figure in the book, and in his poetry 'the idea of sustainability is apparent in the poem's subject matter as well as its design' (p. 12), much like the poets who followed him such as Clare, David Service, William Holloway and Joseph Holland. Keegan's focus not simply on what Bloomfield says but also on how he says it is suggestive of her approach. A central focus is the poetry's ideological significance, but she also makes a key claim for its aesthetic sophistication. Prospect poems and garden poems are in the thick of eighteenth-century convention, but Keegan convincingly shows how subtly the likes of Yearsley, John Learmont and others manipulate those conventions for their own political ends. The strength of Keegan's study is its literary awareness. These poets emerge as careful readers of their literary heritage as much as they are new voices on the literary scene. More conventional than their Romantic contemporaries, that embeddedness in literary heritage is the ground of the startling perspectives they offer.

M.M. Mahood's *The Poet as Botanist* is a hugely enjoyable book born of a lifetime's careful study of plants and poets. She studies five poets (three of them Romantic) who are both poets and botanists, but immerses these chapters in a profusion of illustrative examples from poetical history. The book opens in fine style with a discussion of depictions of the primrose from the Renaissance leading up to Wordsworth and Charles Darwin. Erasmus Darwin's extraordinary poetical rendering of Linnaeus provides an uneasy second chapter. Darwin shares his grandson's empathy with the plant kingdom, but Mahood is too honest and too skilful a critic to allow Darwin much credit as a poet. Yet there are important lessons to be learned in his curious method, not least in the fact that he is a botanist first and a poet second. George Crabbe finds empathy, as might be expected, in weeds, most particularly those which tenaciously cling on to the earth, attempting to repopulate barren land rendered infertile by the incursion of the sea.

Crabbe's botanical knowledge lends his poetry an emotional charge and a vivid excitement that often threaten to overcome the looming dreariness. The best chapter in the book is on Clare. Mahood is splendidly subtle here, delicately evoking the precision with which Clare views the natural world, producing a wonderful 'blend of the exact and the evocative' (p. 133). Clare's poems are sociable in that they understand the villagers' ways of understanding plants, but also sociable in the sense that they understand 'the interdependence of life forms' (p. 138).

In a new study of Romantic correspondence, *Romanticism Gendered: Male Writers as Readers of Women's Writing in Romantic Correspondence*, Andrea Fischerová asks whether the gender of female writers influenced how male Romantic writers read their works. Fischerová's aim is 'to find evidence for the thesis that women writers were respected by male Romantic writers'. Fischerová argues that letters are often mistakenly read as simply 'additional points of reference' but that in her study, letters are 'treated as the dominant information material' (p. 2). *Romanticism Gendered* is split into two main sections, the first dealing with the conceptual challenges behind reading letters as dominant texts, the second section analysing 'the attitudes of the individual readers—Byron, Coleridge, Keats, Scott, Shelley, and Wordsworth—to women's writings' (p. 22). Fischerová argues that the letter in the Romantic period becomes a legitimate literary genre in its own right. She spends some time suggesting how we can categorize letters as texts that claim 'both literariness and authenticity', and subsequently dedicates a subsection of chapter 1 to considering the significant attributes of the letter form. Chapter 2 moves from the theoretical groundwork laid in chapter 1 to consider direct evidence of Fischerová's claims. She begins by examining the dramatist Susannah Centlivre (1669–1723), whose plays enjoyed continuing popularity in the Romantic era, alongside Ann Radcliffe. In the second section of this chapter, Fischerová concentrates on Wordsworth, Byron, Coleridge and Shelley as male readers of women's writing. Fischerová concludes by stating that 'a picture of a gendered Romanticism has been created, represented here by writing men reading works of women' (p. 269). Indeed, given the extensive evidence she offers, it would be difficult to disagree, and her suggestion that a study focusing on the correspondence of Romantic women would complement her own study is a welcome one.

In his chapter, 'States of our Captivity: Nature, Terror and Refugia in Romantic Women's Literature' (in Gomez, Teresa and Aranzazu Usandizaga, *Inside Out: Women Negotiating, Subverting, Appropriating Public and Private Space*, pp. 273–96), Stephen E. Hunt explores Romantic female engagement with the natural world. Hunt focuses on Mary Robinson, Charlotte Smith, Helen Maria Williams and Mary Wollstonecraft, suggesting that not enough 'attention has been paid to appreciation of scenery...in Romantic women's literature' (p. 274). David Wheeler's 'Placing Anna Seward: The "Genius of Place," Coalbrookdale, and "Colebrook Dale"' (*NPEC* 5:i[2008] 30–40) was not available for review and will be covered next year.

'"Soundings of Things Done": The Poetry and Poetics of Sound in the Romantic Ear and Era', a special issue of *Romantic Circles Praxis Series* convened by Susan Wolfson, considered sound in Romantic poetry. Wolfson's

'Sounding Romantic: The Sound of Sound' (*RCPS* [2008] 34 paras) picks up on the paradox that the Romantic obsession with silence required vocal articulation. Moreover, poets including Wordsworth, Coleridge, Southey, Blake, Keats, Shelley and Byron played on the resonance of the word 'sound', investigating the conversational nature of poetic creation as they did so. James Chandler's 'The "Power of Sound" and the Great Scheme of Things: Wordsworth Listens to Wordsworth' (*RCPS* [2008] 20 paras) is a superb consideration of early and late Wordsworth and his response to an emerging scientific discourse of sound. The late poem 'The Power of Sound' echoes and alludes to earlier poetry, particularly the 'Intimations' ode. That echo sounded tinny to late Wordsworth: Chandler shows how he found his earlier understanding of sound and silence theologically dubious. Garrett Stewart's 'Phonemanography: Romantic to Victorian' (*RCPS* [2008] 69 paras) investigates the 'sub or cross-lexical phonic charge' in Keats, Shelley and Wordsworth and, in a philosophically complex argument, demonstrates their influence on Victorian novelists, especially Eliot, Dickens and Hardy. In 'Captivation and Liberty in Wordsworth's Poems on Music' (*RCPS* [2008] 17 paras) Adam Potkay investigates the relationship between music and the will. Music tends to overpower the conscious mind, but Wordsworth was just as interested in its capacity to bring communities together. Accordingly, music is part of a counter-reaction to an emergent commercial order.

There were two other articles of general interest on Romantic poetry. Michael Wiley's 'Romantic Amplification: The Way of Plagiarism' (*ELH* 75[2008] 219–40) discusses what is something of a hot topic in Romantic studies: plagiarism. Recent work by Tilar Mazzeo and Margaret Russett has considered this in some detail, and Wiley adds to this by reminding us of Wordsworth, Coleridge and Southey's response to the wrong kind of appropriation as a kind of 'moral turpitude'. Judith Hawley's 'Grub Street in Albion: or, Scriblerian Satire in the Romantic Metropolis' (*Romanticism* 14[2008] 81–93) shows that, despite the city's insistent modernity, urban poetry of the Romantic period remained stubbornly Augustan, retaining the Juvenalian and Horatian satiric modes that Dryden, Pope and Johnson naturalized in Britain. Hawley's fine piece discusses poetry by the likes of Leigh Hunt, William Gifford and James and Horace Smith, showing how such urban satire is, appropriately, palimpsestic. Also of general interest was Peter J. Kitson, 'The Romantic Period, 1780–1832', a superb contribution to Paul Poplawski's *English Literature in Context* (pp. 306–402). The section is aimed at undergraduates, and any undergraduate who read and absorbed the information presented here would be thoroughly prepared for any seminar. Kitson deftly manages a tough job. He tells the traditional story in detail (the movement from an agrarian to an industrialized economy and a poetical turn against that society towards the transcendental imagination), but he subtly probes and problematizes that narrative with alternative discourses: slavery, orientalism and the rise of the periodical press among others. The section ends with a series of exemplary readings of Romantic-period texts that put that contextual information into practice, offering students a model for criticism.

Anna Letitia Barbauld might well be a central figure in Romanticism these days, yet she remains, like many women poets, oddly marginal too. Students of

Barbauld will benefit enormously from one of the most remarkably learned publications in any area of Romantic poetry this year, William McCarthy's *Anna Letitia Barbauld: Voice of the Enlightenment*. It is a huge volume, densely printed with over a hundred pages of scrupulous notes. It needs to be. Barbauld lived from 1743 to1825, and her life intersected with the literary and political lives of an astonishing range of figures from the eighteenth century and the Romantic period. The central prop of her intellectual life was her participation in the networks of Protestant dissent, surely the most vital literary and intellectual culture of this period. McCarthy ably discusses the different strands of dissent that formed the community in which Barbauld lived with a deft touch. Despite her shyness and her status as a woman, those networks fostered an astonishingly confident, articulate and wide-ranging cultural voice. She castigated a government that refused (repeatedly) to repeal the Test and Corporation Acts that debarred all but members of the Church of England from holding offices of state. In her pioneering *Lessons for Children* she took the lessons of enlightened dissent into education, promoting a plain speaking style that McCarthy characterizes eloquently: 'Language seems to bloom from the pages of *Lessons* as if it were a new creation. Each word seems new minted, freshly imbued with meaning' (pp. 194–5). These books produced perhaps her most significant influence, but they had their critics too. Coleridge, Lamb and Southey all denounced them as deadeningly rational, something McCarthy puts down to jealousy in male writers dwarfed by a greater woman. It is certainly pleasant to think so, and the political animus in apostates like Southey against his former co-radicals is often cynical and nasty. Yet if one cannot help but feel that Lamb had a point, and that the imagination ought to be allowed a certain play, McCarthy is nonetheless surely right to insist on the vitality of those Enlightenment thinkers who saw things differently. Her masterpiece may well be *Eighteen Hundred and Eleven*, a poem that seems rather too pessimistic for an Enlightenment Dissenter with her faith in progress, reason and providence. McCarthy subtly unpacks these tensions, with a keen eye for the many and varied intertexts of a 'learned poem, thick with literary and historical references' (p. 475). Despite its dystopian ring, it remains fearless in telling truth to power and utterly committed to those Dissenting ideals which compelled Barbauld to offer such a dire warning. McCarthy gives us an image of a life that remained heroically true to a set of principles that shaped modernity. This extraordinarily packed, fluidly written biography ought to influence scholars across Romantic studies.

Barbauld's astonishing intellectual range is demonstrated in McCarthy's biography, and her lasting significance as a Dissenting thinker and as an author of children's literature is pleasantly underscored by the editors of a fine collection of essays on children, literature and war: *Under Fire: Childhood in the Shadow of War*, edited by Elizabeth Goodenough and Andrea Immel. The editors conclude the collection with Barbauld and John Aiken's 'Things by Their Right Names' (pp. 255–7), 'the first anti-war story for children in English' (p. 16). Sharon Ruston's 'Natural Rights and Natural History in Anna Barbauld and Mary Wollstonecraft' (in Ruston, ed., *Literature and Science*, pp. 53–71) explores the way that Barbauld and Wollstonecraft subtly manipulated the discourse of animal rights to argue for, respectively, the rights of Dissenters and equality for women. This illuminating account shows just how wide the intellectual horizons of these two polymaths were. Barbauld's 'A Mouse's Petition' receives particular attention.

The year 2008 saw a considerable number of publications on Blake, almost certainly a continuation of the flurry of activity that surrounded the celebrations of the 250th anniversary of his birth the previous year, the most significant single publication being *Blake and Conflict*, a collection of essays from a 2006 conference of the same name. Sarah Haggarty and Jon Mee propose a way for dealing with Blake's contrary visions in a time of conflict as a series of conversations (with particular reference to Jean-Luc Nancy's notion of the inoperative community), although they recognize that this runs the danger of denying or even sanctioning violence in Blake's work, drawing on William Keach's critique of a masculinist will to power that is found in his art and poetry. Conflict in Blake's art and writings is dealt with here in terms of interweaving dialogues between religion, politics and the visual arts, beginning with Saree Makdisi's 'Blake and the Ontology of Empire', which builds on the orientalist critique found in his previous work (including *William Blake and the Impossible History of the 1790s*), examining how Blake 'refuses Orientalism' because he rejects 'the logic of individualism predicated on an opposition to otherness' (p. 12) which had become ingrained in a Western discourse that bound together orientalism, imperialism and Western subjectivity founded on moral virtue as the basis for the self-regulating self. Blake's God, by contrast, is an open one, and his task (evident, for example, in his reading of Paine's *Age of Reason*) is to recover an 'unperverted Bible' of love and forgiveness. Makdisi's thoughtful essay goes very well with Angus Whitehead's contribution, ' "A wise tale of the Mahometans": Blake and Islam, 1819–26', which takes a fascinating look at the Islamic community which was becoming increasingly visible in early nineteenth-century London. The study of Blake's relationship to Islam has started, finally, to become more noticeable among scholarly articles, providing a minor counterpoint to Blake's obvious engagement with Christianity, of various types, and Judaism. Blake's direct references to Islam are, to say the least, fleeting, and Whitehead draws attention to differing interpretations of Blake's orientalism (such as Makdisi's outlined briefly above, or Larrissy's more critical interpretation of Blake in thrall to orientalist attitudes). Whitehead draws on three late references to Islam by Blake, in a conversation with Crabb Robinson, the visionary head of 'Mahomet', and his depiction of the prophet in Dante's *Inferno*, presents positive representations of Islam. A similarly meticulous approach to the historical record is provided in David Worrall's 'Blake, the Female Prophet and the American Agent: The Evidence of the 1789 Swedenborg Conference Attendance List', which builds on previous research conducted by Worrall into the 1789 conference to identify some of the radical (and sometimes shadowy) figures encountered by Blake, such as Dorothy Gott, author of *The Midnight Cry*, and Colborn Barrell.

Susan Matthews's 'Impurity of Diction: The "Harlot's Curse" and Dirty Words' focuses on the role of prostitution as an essential corollary to the formation of polite society and the figure of the virtuous woman. Blake, argues Matthews, uses diction transformatively to celebrate female sexuality rather than to transmit dominant ideas of his day (her comments on our assumptions in locating sexuality in 'corporeality' rather than 'spirituality', and thus failing to appreciate the complexity of Blake's opinions, are particularly pertinent here). It is Blake's dialogic, indeed often ambivalent, relations with Christianity that are covered in the following two essays: David Fallon's '"She cuts his heart out at his side": Christianity and Political Virtue' considers attitudes to civic virtue which, in humanist thinking, tended to be held in opposition to traditional Christian virtues, but not in the line of 'Commonwealthmen' writers such as Milton, Harrington and (later) Richard Price with which Blake was aligned by Gilchrist and others. Fallon sees Blake as demonstrating 'evident affiliations' with civic humanism, but making 'distinctive alterations to produce the type of citizenship he valorized' (p. 97). Haggarty, in 'From Donation to Demand? Almsgiving and the "Annotations to Thornton"', places Blake's annotations to Thornton's *Lord's Prayer Newly Translated* in the ongoing separation of virtuous gift-giving from economics during the long eighteenth century, remarking that Blake's own ideas are often contradictory and even incoherent without a more profound understanding of the gift. One contributor to the debate around economics and charity was William Godwin, who also features in Jon Mee's '"A little less conversation, a little more action": Mutuality, Converse and Mental Fight', which considers the role of conversation in the liberal public sphere as an alternative to commonly perceived French despotism at the time. Mee identifies two cultures of conversation: one polite and consensual, the other 'capacious enough to include contention and dispute' (p. 129). Considering the importance of the latter to Dissenting traditions, Mee starts from Blake's satire on conversation in *An Island in the Moon* through his illuminated books, seeing in this 'aspect of the everyday world' a 'utopian possibility for the future' (p. 139). Sibylle Erle's 'Shadows in the Cave: Refocusing Vision in Blake's Creation Myth' reinterprets the metaphor of the cave to refer fairly specifically to Blake's account of sight and the eye, particularly in relation to empirical philosophers such as Locke and Newton.

This discussion of the science of optics is a serendipitous link to the final three essays of the collection, which deal with various aspects of Blake's visual arts. Mark Crosby's 'A Minute Skirmish: Blake, Hayley and the Art of Miniature Painting' concentrates on that minute particular of Blake's artistic career, the miniature paintings he conducted in Felpham, as a site of conflict with his patron William Hayley, Blake's technique often being at odds with Hayley's instruction and presaging the disputes that were to come later. Luisa Calè, in 'Blake and the Literary Galleries', contrasts the rivalries of the illustrated book market with those of the literary galleries, such as the ones established by Fuseli and Boydell, the latter dealt with most notably, of course, in Morris Eaves, *Counter-Arts Conspiracy*. Blake's work for Young's *Night Thoughts* especially, Calè argues, demonstrates how he was 'experimenting with different book formats in an attempt to access the literary-gallery market' (p. 204), from which he had only ever received minor commissions. Finally, Morton Paley's 'Blake's Poems on Art and Artists' looks at his various texts from 1798 to 1811, such as the annotations to the works of Joshua Reynolds and the *Descriptive Catalogue* but also his verse on contemporaries, that deal with art and artists. Although the prose writings have received considerable scholarly attention, Paley argues that the occasional poetry should not be dismissed as doggerel but examined both as satire and 'as expressions of Blake's views about art, artists and the art market' (p. 210).

The other substantial publication of 2008 was G.E. Bentley Jr's *William Blake's Conversations: A Compilation, Concordance, and Rhetorical Analysis*, a typically scholarly and careful work which, in this instance, offers a comprehensive overview of Blake's conversation as recorded by others and also rhetorical and linguistic analyses drawn from Blake's poetry. Thus, for example, Bentley argues that Blake's various imperfect rhymes are not necessarily the result of a 'tin ear' as was often argued by his earlier (particularly nineteenth-century) readers, but rather in many cases offer some insight into Blake's dialect and pronunciation: 'I conclude that Blake's rhymes are far truer when pronounced in his way than I had previously assumed. It was not his rhymes were astray; the fau't was mine' (p. xxvi). A considerable amount of the introduction is thus given over to a fairly exhaustive list of Blake's various pronunciations and rhymes, although the more interesting sections are really to be found at the beginning and the end of the book, where Bentley offers some general observations on Blake's status as a conversationalist, in particular—as Mary Lynn Johnson points out in her introduction, as an entertaining speaker who combined 'novel thoughts and eccentric notions...with such jocose hilarity and amiable demeanour' (p. xv). While noting that many of the conversations are not entirely reliable sources as to Blake's opinions, Bentley continues with a collection of all known conversations by Blake, as well as the few known samples of Catherine and his two brothers, as well as an extensive concordance and list of sources that will be invaluable for anyone seeking information on what Blake thought outside his own writings. Most of the book is taken up with the list of known conversational snippets, as well as a truly fascinating concordance that will doubtless prove to be a pleasant way of passing the time (whether it is considering his remark that Edward Irving was 'a highly gifted man...a sent man' or his various ironic comments on devils) as well as inspiring further research. It is this element of the collection as a catalogue and concordance that will be the most enduring element of this book, although Bentley also provides some extremely useful insights that do capture traces of Blake's speech as it influenced his own verse.

An altogether stranger book is David Whitmarsh-Knight's *William Blake's Jerusalem Explained*, a companion to his website, based on his 1984 dissertation, *William Blake's The Four Zoas Explained* (<http://www.thefourzoas.com>). This book, published in revised version in 2008 from an online version that had previously been made available in 2005, is certainly ambitious. Fred Dortort, in *The Dialectic of Vision: A Contrary Reading of William Blake's Jerusalem* [1998], rightly observed that critics have tended to pick and choose those elements of Blake's final, most difficult epic that suit their arguments, and that it is rare for any commentator to attempt to view *Jerusalem* as a whole. Whitmarsh-Knight certainly considers the whole text, with a more or less line-by-line exegesis that has as its main aim the desire to show that 'Blake's work is beautifully structured with a clear story-line or plot'

(p. 13). Put simply, I am unconvinced, and the overall effect is reminiscent of reading Ellis's and Yeats's companion volumes to Blake's poetry which formed part of their 1893 critical edition: like them, Whitmarsh-Knight has approached Blake with his own system 'which the world shall have whether they will or no', as Blake wrote of his own Bible of Hell. To be fair to the author, the introduction does offer a stripped-down, rather clear account of what could count as a story-line in *Jerusalem*, and if the subsequent 600 pages do rather become bogged down in detail there are, nonetheless, flashes of inspiration. The unfortunate effect, however, is that the line-by-line approach (familiar from a rather old-fashioned form of biblical exegesis) does mean that the overall shape of his argument has disappeared by the time the reader has struggled through the book.

Two useful collections of Blake's work were reissued in new editions in 2008. David Fuller's *William Blake: Selected Poetry and Prose*, is an updated version in the Longman Annotated Texts series that first appeared in 2000. This stands alongside the publication of the third edition of W.H. Stevenson's *Blake: The Complete Poems* in 2007, both of which will provide valuable information to students setting out on a more intensive reading of Blake. In addition, Mary Lynn Johnson and John E. Grant's *Blake's Poetry and Designs* was also published as a second edition in the Norton Critical Editions series. More extensive in its selection of Blake's original writings than Fuller's collection, where the Norton is particularly useful for new students is in terms of a selection of criticism at the end of the volume, ranging from Robert Hunt's scathing 1809 review to twenty-first-century critics such as Saree Makdisi and Julia Wright. Another book to be noted, which did not arrive in time for review, is Ed Thanhouser's *Urizen Wept: William Blake and the Sublime in Milton: A Poem*. Beginning from the perceived difficulties of Blake's writing (and also Blake criticism), Thanhouser appears to claim that this was intentional on Blake's part in order to emphasize the role of the sublime in his work, an approach which has previously been adopted by Jon Mee in his *Dangerous Enthusiasm* [1991] and with considerable sophistication in Peter Otto's *Blake's Critique of Transcendence* [2000].

Blake: An Illustrated Quarterly included the annual round-up of sales recorded by Robert Essick in 'Blake in the Marketplace, 2007' (*Blake* 41[2008] 140–63), with a high volume of sales continuing at similar levels to those of 2006. Important sales included copy N of *Visions of the Daughters of Albion* and eight plates from copy Y of *Songs of Innocence*, while the most important discovery was a series of eight colour prints, part of *A Small Book of Designs* and including prints taken from *The Book of Urizen* and *The Marriage of Heaven and Hell*. The first part of volume 42, meanwhile, included G.E. Bentley Jr's annual checklist of Blake publications for 2007 (*Blake* 42[2008] 4–45).

Of the various articles and minute particulars published in *Blake* during 2008, the first substantial article, 'Tate Reveals Nine New Blakes and Thirteen New Lines of Verse' (*Blake* 42[2008] 52–72), by Martin Butlin and Robin Hamlyn, provides an account of the new pictures by Blake that were on display in Tate Britain at the end of 2007. The printed images, finished in watercolour, were given by Catherine Blake to Frederick Tatham, but were unknown to Blake scholars until recently. A series of aphorisms was also produced to accompany the illustrations of figures such as Urizen and Ugolino. In ' "This Extraordinary Performance": William Blake's Use of Gold and Silver in the Creation of his Paintings and Illuminated Books' (*Blake* 42[2008–9] 84–108), Angus Whitehead provides a careful and scholarly account of this frequently alluded to but rarely examined feature of Blake's art, by means of which he achieved some of his most dramatic and lustrous effects.

The winter edition of *Studies in Romanticism* included two papers on Blake, Paul Miner's 'Blake's "Tyger" as Miltonic Beast' (*SiR* 47[2008] 479–505) and Talissa J. Ford's ' "Jerusalem is scattered abroad": Blake's Ottoman Geographies' (*SiR* 47[2008] 529–48), the latter of which is probably the more significant. Ford reads Blake's accounts of the 'events of geography' that took place as a result of eighteenth- and early nineteenth-century imperialism as examples of cultural practice more than spatial 'things', itself not necessarily a remarkable innovation when reading Blake, but an idea used here very carefully when dealing with the exploration of the Holy Land and eastern Mediterranean by figures such as William Rae Wilson and François-René de Chateaubriand. The role of Britain in the governance of Britain, still limited by the Ottoman empire during the early nineteenth century, contributed greatly to certain elements of British imperial ambitions—spurred on in part by the example of the Islamic empire of the Ottomans. As such, Blake's engagement with the Anglo-Israelists is, suggests Ford, a more sceptical proposition than commonly assumed if we see in the motif of the Polypus a critical evaluation of imperial ambitions, whereby 'with the potential for a planetary connection that arises from the interconnectivity of all life, we wind up instead with the dangerous and homogenizing proliferation of the Polypus' (p. 546). An important omission, and one which Ford addresses but does not entirely resolve to the satisfaction of her argument, is an address to the Muslims: while I agree with her that a study of Blake's relation to Islam is urgently required, I am not sure that the omission of Muslims in the four addresses that punctuate *Jerusalem* indicates much more than Blake's relative ignorance on the subject. Turning to Miner, his essay explores the ways in which Blake's use of Miltonic imagery and language in 'The Tyger' is reiterated throughout his other prophetic works, most notably in *The Four Zoas* and *The Book of Los* as part of 'arcane reconstructions of Milton's texts' (p. 488). One ostensible function of this paper, the reconstruction of the Miltonic beast, tends to be lost at times in a more general network of Miltonic allusions, and as a central trope the tyger itself appears attenuated and distorted to fit into Miner's real concern, which is a mapping of Milton's hell throughout Blake's verse. Indeed, there is such a wealth (one might say patchwork) of allusions that even this argument is in danger of becoming lost in the details, although when he turns to the 'Redemption and Judgement of this sublime beast' from page 500 onwards, the tyger does return centre stage. His final argument, that '[a]lthough the "Tyger" initially is constructed by Milton's Satan, this fiery best of *Experience*, ultimately, is handed over to Blake's Christ' (p. 504) rests on certain assumptions—I am by no means convinced, despite the mass of allusion, that the tyger can definitively be identified with Satan—but 'Blake's

"Tyger" as Miltonic Beast' is extremely interesting as one demonstration of how networks of Miltonic imagery operate throughout Blake's poetry.

While 'Blake's "Tyger"' dealt with John Milton in a more general sense, a number of articles in 2008 concentrated on *Milton* more specifically. The most interesting was Roger Whitson's 'Applied Blake: *Milton*'s Response to Empire' (*ILS* 9:ii[2008] 87–101) which, beginning from Saree Makdisi's passing association of Blake with Spinoza in *William Blake and the Impossible History of the 1790s* [2003] follows a more substantial reading of Blake in terms of Michael Hardt and Antonio Negri's *Empire* [2000] and *Multitude: War and Democracy in the Age of Empire* [2004]. The most significant aspect of Whitson's article is to deliberately read Blake outside a restrictive historical framework of the 1790s, as Hardt and Negri read Spinoza and (more provocatively) St Francis of Assisi, in order to give 'new relevance' to the new historicist project of the 1990s. Whitson emphasizes the importance of such new historicist readings, particularly the work of Clark and Worrall, but by exploring this notion of Blake applied to the global struggles of the twenty-first century suggest that his 'insistence [on] the building of Jerusalem in the present...can totally change every aspect of the hard material reality that many historicists are too quick to preserve' (p. 98). Jared Richman, in 'Milton Re-membered, Graved and Press'd: William Blake and the Fate of Textual Bodies' (*ERR* 19[2008] 385–401), follows a more traditional relation between authorial anxiety and Blake's 're-membering' of Milton's republican and theological legacy: while it is a careful and decent reading of ways in which Milton was reactivated for a generation of radicals at the time of the French Revolution and Napoleonic Wars, there is little in the essay itself that is particularly radical.

Milton the poem has a slightly more minor role to play in Kathleen Lundeen's 'A Wrinkle in Space: The Romantic Disruption of the English Cosmos' (*PCP* 4[2008] 1–19), which is generally more concerned with the effects of Newtonian physics on Blake as a preparation for conflicting notions of cosmology. While Lundeen's essay is more wide-ranging than Whitson's and Richman's in terms of considering Blake's works, it is of course in *Milton* that some of Blake's most extensive reflections on the nature of cosmology are to be found, particularly his notion of space as comprised of vortices; Lundeen has little to say on Descartes on this subject, which would have also offered a link between the 'postmodern' physics she alludes to and alternatives to Newtonian, mechanistic science in Blake's day. To her credit, Lundeen draws attention to the fact that 'Blake's attempt to redraw the cosmos and inaugurate a new scientific method was a failure' (p. 16), though like many subsequent commentators on Blake she appears to give him more direct credit for later, more 'elastic' conceptions of the universe which he really does not—in scientific circles at least—deserve. In 'Self-Annihilation/Inner Revolution: Blake's *Milton*, Buddhism, and Ecocriticism' (*R&L* 40:i[2008] 39–57), Mark Lussier continues to extend the scope of work he has undertaken both to extend an appreciation of Romantic poetry with regard to Buddhism, and the relation of Blake to reception outside traditionally received ideas. The appeal of Blake to Buddhism has long been a minor strand of Blake studies (at least in North America and Europe—in Japan, a perception of the relations between the two has been evident since the work of Soetsu Yanagi in the early twentieth century at least). Here, Lussier reads Blake's critique of Selfhood in the light of Buddhist practice that, equally importantly, has significant repercussions for ecological thinking in that it describes 'an interconnected subject beyond selfhood': by transforming the power of imagination to expand into one or contract to behold multitudes, 'Blake approaches as close to eastern forms of enlightenment as any western poet or writer' (p. 54).

Two papers provide historicist contexts for some of Blake's later works. 'Voices in the Wilderness: Satire and Sacrifice in Blake and Byron' (*ByronJ* 36:ii[2008] 117–29) by Matt Green begins with the notable response by Blake to Byron's *Cain* to suggest further parallels beyond *The Ghost of Abel*. His general reading of Blake as operating within satirical generic frameworks that could suggest potential crossovers between Blake and Byron (the only living poet to be named in Blake's published works, as Green points out) is not entirely convincing. However, when moving on to a reading of *The Ghost of Abel* as providing a critical but extremely sympathetic amendment of Byron's anger at orthodox theories of sacrifice and atonement, Green offers an extremely perceptive and engaging reading of Blake's later texts. Sibylle Erle's 'Blake, Colour and the Truchsessian Gallery: Modelling the Mind and Liberating the Observer' (*RaVoN* 52[2008]) concentrates on the specific event of Blake's visit to the Truchsessian collection in 1804 as the starting point for a discussion of his notions of optics and perception in contrast to the empiricist theories of Newton and Locke in particular. From Ruskin onwards (and in contrast to Robert Hunt), critics have generally been receptive to Blake's use of colour, and Erle demonstrates that this was more than an intuitive response by Blake but also represented an awareness and understanding of theoretical models of perception and colour that were circulating during his lifetime. Rejecting models of *camera obscura* and *tabula rasa*, Blake instead opts for a constant renewal of connection and stimulation when viewing his images that thus delays (mechanical) interpretation.

'Writ(h)ing Images: Imagination, the Human Form, and the Divine in William Blake, Salman Rushdie, and Simon Louvish' (*ES* 89:i[2008] 94–117) by Axel Stähler considers depictions of the divine in the works of Louvish and Rushdie in relation to Blake's *Illustrations of the Book of Job* rather than, as is more typical, *The Marriage of Heaven and Hell*. By exploring 'ambivalent strategies of resistance' in the three artists, Stähler's particularly original contribution to reception studies of Blake lies in his extended discussion of Louvish's *The Days of Miracles and Wonder* [1997] and that novel's probing of 'the interrelation of fundamentalism and literature' (p. 109). There are a few oddities in Stähler's critical treatment of Blake (such as relying on Keynes for textual references rather than the standard Erdman edition), and his reading of Blake is thus occasionally at fault, but the dialogue that is implicit between Blake and the later writers and explicit between Rushdie and Louvish is a fascinating addition to those interested in the use of Blake's texts by later authors.

Of the final two articles to be considered for 2008, Peter Crisp's 'Between Extended Metaphor and Allegory: Is Blending Enough?' (*L&L* 17:iv[2008] 291–308] uses 'A Poison Tree' to discuss the mental spaces constructed by fictional situations, dealing with the minutiae of those moments when an extended metaphor develops into allegory to constitute blended spaces, a notion from cognitive psychology and linguistics where an integrated space is created via inputs from different mental patterns to create emergent structures. Julie Joosten's 'Minute Particulars and the Visionary Labor of Words' (*ERR* 19[2008] 113–18) is a short article that in some ways can be seen as a complement to Crisp in that it is concerned with the structural and formal conditions of language as 'essential to Blake's constructions of a liberated poetics'.

The year 2008 was a busy one for the William Blake Archive. It began with the addition of Blake's illustrations to Milton's *Paradise Lost*, a group of twelve watercolours acquired by the Reverend Joseph Thomas in 1807. This was followed, in March, with copy A of *Milton*, from the British Museum, being included alongside copy C, as well as the Thomas Butts 1808 set of Milton illustrations to accompany the Thomas versions in April, as well as those commissioned by John Linnell in 1822 being added in July. The year thus provided a wealth of materials for scholars interested in studying Blake's relations with John Milton, while other inclusions on the archive consisted of more copies of *The Marriage of Heaven and Hell* (K, L and M), *The Book of Thel* (L and R) and Blake's engraved illustrations to John Gabriel Stedman's *Narrative, of a Five Years' Expedition, against the Revolted Negroes of Surinam*.

In anticipation of 2009's Homecoming Year, work on Robert Burns in 2008 finds a new home in the Romantic section of *YWES*. Burns, indeed, is peculiarly difficult to position, publishing all of his work in and around the beginnings of the Romantic period, yet seeming more of a precursor than a member of the visionary company. But, as much of this year's work on the poet suggests, Burns is taking an increasingly prominent place in accounts of the period. A number of contributions this year were interested in Burns's legacy. The most Romantic of these was Nigel Leask's '"Across the Shadow Line": Robert Burns, Scottish Romanticism and the English Canon', which forms one-half of Leask and Alan Riach's *Stepping Westward*. Leask provides a superb meditation on Scottish and English nationalism and literature that is informed by postmodern and postcolonial thinking leading into the indicative example of the afterlife of Burns. Leask insists on the importance of James Currie's biography ('nearly all English responses to Burns in the romantic period are reactions ... to Currie's Burns', p. 22), particularly for Currie's account of the constraints placed on Burns's poetry by the poet's circumstances. The Preface to *Lyrical Ballads* is recast as 'an excited response to Burns' (p. 25), while Byron's mobility is shown to have a precursor in his fellow Scot, both of whom challenge 'the organic stability of Anglo-British identity' (p. 28). Lyndsey Lunan's 'National Myths and Literary Icons: The Uses of Scott and Burns in Scottish Literature' (in Lunan et al., eds., pp. 13–29) examines what she sees as a 'Burns–Scott dialectic' (p. 14) in a complex investigation of the way that Scottish writers, notably labouring-class poets like William Motherwell and Robert Tannahill, but principally Hogg and Carlyle, position themselves along that perceived borderline. The two writers serve as models of centre and periphery, authority and challenge, and Lunan's chapter seeks ultimately to muddy that cultural distinction.

Ferenc Morton Szasz's *Abraham Lincoln and Robert Burns: Connected Lives and Legends* expands the range of Burns's influence across the Atlantic. It is a timely book, coming in the year before the 250th anniversary of Burns's birth and the 200th anniversary of Lincoln's, and it is the timelier given Barack Obama's consciously Lincolnian self-image and Scotland's 'Homecoming' national realignment, a series of events that seeks to bring Scotland and America closer together. Burns and Lincoln share a great deal, as Szasz makes clear: most significantly their intermittently synecdochal relationship with their nations. Szasz does a lot more than simply list parallels, numerous though they are. Lincoln was a fan of Burns at a time when Burns was widely beloved by Americans, standing in for a sense of the 'covenanted nation' as an ideal that derived from Scottish cultural paradigms. For Szasz, Burns and, more widely, Scotland, should be understood as integral to the development of Lincoln and, more widely, America. Szasz expertly tracks Burns's vast popular influence in early America before showing just how significant his poetry was to the future president. The argument stretches a little here (Lincoln only quoted Burns twice), but Szasz shows how Lincoln 'borrowed *themes* rather than precise phrases' (p. 57) and even took up the standard Habbie in his fledgling verse. The book then expands its horizons, looking to Lincoln's broader interest in Scottish figures and the development of remarkably similar national cults that, indeed, criss-crossed between the two countries. The book gets a little sentimental at times (one hears too often how 'timeless' the two men's writing is), but this is a significant contribution to the study of Burns and Lincoln, Scotland and America.

One book which will prove invaluable to Burnsians seeking to discover the Romantic and post-Romantic afterlives of the poet is *The G. Ross Roy Collection of Robert Burns: An Illustrated Catalogue*, compiled by Elizabeth A. Sudduth with the assistance of Clayton Tarr. This remarkable collection, housed at the University of South Carolina, contains 5,000 items directly related to Burns, including an extraordinary array of editions, manuscripts, paintings, critical books, music and much else. One is struck by the extraordinarily diverse ways in which Burns has been received. The collection contains material from Soviet-era Russian translations of 'A man's a man' to invitations to Burns suppers at the Brooklyn Freemasons' Kilwinning Lodge, and much else in between. In 1873, by no means an untypical year, nine separate editions of Burns's poetical works were published, some of which the collection holds multiple copies of in different bindings. This splendidly presented, beautifully illustrated catalogue will prove a central resource to Burnsians.

Penny Fielding's *Scotland and the Fictions of Geography: North Britain, 1760–1830* contains an important chapter on Burns, 'Burns, Place and Language' (pp. 40–70). The book as a whole seeks to destabilize understandings of Romanticism that associate it with the local. Burns is an icon of the local but his poetry also, for Fielding, demonstrates the interpenetration of the local and the global even as it constructs a northern/southern division. The description of Burns as a 'genius' by his early critics has often seemed a rather embarrassing example of the tendency to sentimentalize and de-intellectualize the poet. But, as Ronnie Young argues in a fine piece, 'Genius, Men, and Manners: Burns and Eighteenth-Century Scottish Criticism' (*SSR* 9:ii[2008] 129–47), the situation is rather more complex. Burns is not simply the victim of an anglocentric Edinburgh elite. Rather, Burns himself inhabited a variety of positions in relation to genius, including both Ossianic and Augustan conceptions of human nature. It is also worth mentioning an excellent piece on a Burnsian poet, the Airdrie poet William Yates, 'In Search of William Yates of Airdrie, Contemporary of Burns' (*SSR* 9:i[2008] 27–48), by Ian Reid.

Certainly worth mentioning, although perhaps of minor scholarly interest, is *A Night out with Robert Burns: the Greatest Poems*, arranged by Andrew O'Hagan. O'Hagan offers a pleasant greatest hits, arranged under four headings: 'The Lasses', 'The Drinks', 'The Immortals' and 'The Politics', prefaced by an introduction which details O'Hagan's personal journey and lightly discusses the debates over the nature of Burns in contemporary culture and also including a fine standard Habbie appreciation by Seamus Heaney. Burns, for O'Hagan, is multiple: the choice between the sentimental and the radical Burns is a false one, he argues. But he also seeks to question those notions of Burns, and to prompt reassessment. Each poem is prefaced by a short commentary. These are by turns funny, touching and provocative. 'Handsome Nell' comes with O'Hagan's story of his own daughter's birth, while the 'Address to the Deil' is prefaced by a quotation from the US Deputy Under Secretary of Defense for Intelligence, who informs a religious group in Oregon that the real enemy is 'a guy named Satan' (p. 122). Prefacing 'The Slave's Lament' with an anti-Vietnam war quote by Muhammed Ali is exciting stuff, if it tends to lack subtlety: the 'coward slave' of 'Is there for honest poverty' is, for Burns, assuredly a coward. But this is to nit-pick. This is a fine, lively collection from a writer well able to appreciate Burns's many appeals.

There were three excellent collections of essays on Byron's poetics this year, plus a collection on *Byron at the Theatre*, discussed in section 5 below. *Liberty and Poetic Licence: New Essays on Byron*, edited by Bernard Beatty, Tony Howe and Charles E. Robinson, represents a major step forward in the study of Byron. The volume as a whole is concerned to trace 'a magic line, a decorous line increasingly unrecognisable to his contemporaries' (p. 7) between two contraries that fascinated Byron throughout his career, liberty and licence. Byron never simply chose one or the other; rather, he sought to find paths between extremes. The sixteen contributors trace that line in remarkably diverse ways. Michael O'Neill discusses *Childe Harold's Pilgrimage*, examining the division between poetic freedom and a sense of fatedness in the poem. The concluding image of the ocean celebrates mutability, but it also 'finally establishes the bounds of human freedom' (p. 48). Gabrielle Poole's discussion of *Mazeppa* shows how different ideas of freedom 'interact, ally themselves, and clash' (p. 72), so much so that she concludes by warning against unitary interpretations of the poem. Byron's influence on nineteenth-century geologists is explored by Ralph O'Conner, Gavin Hopps considers Byron's freedom from grammatical rule, and both Katharine Kernberger and Peter Graham discuss Byronic selfhood, caught between free will and determinism. Drama is featured strongly in the volume, with essays by Alan Rawes on *Marino Faliero* and Jonathon Shears on *Sardanapalus*. Rawes unearths what he sees as a long-running theme in Byron's thinking, an interest in aristocracy, while Shears sees *Sardanapalus* as offering an aesthetic or imaginative, rather than a political, freedom. Peter Cochran looks at three early works published alongside *Hours of Idleness*, discovering an uncertain probing of the limits of freedom at Southwell. Tom Mole discusses *The Bride of Abydos* in the context of an aversion to being looked at and of looking back. Andrew M. Stauffer considers *Don Juan*'s revision of the tale of 'Inkle and Yarico', and sexual liberty is also discussed by Jonathan Gross. Joan Blythe elucidates the Miltonic precedents of *Cain*, John Clubbe discusses Byron's obsession with Napoleon, Tony Howe deftly unravels the complex involvement of Johnson in the Bowles–Pope controversy, and Timothy Webb rounds off the volume in fine style with a chapter on the links between publication and freedom.

Byron: Heritage and Legacy, edited by Cheryl A. Wilson, contains eighteen essays on Byron that were originally delivered at the August 2001 Byron Conference. Many collections of essays begin as conference proceedings, but most seek to hide the fact. This volume, however, takes the brave decision to push this history to the forefront. The papers were delivered in Manhattan one month before 9/11 directly opposite the World Trade Center. This historical coincidence shadows the collection as a whole, and the book concludes with some unabashedly emotional responses to the event. Regardless, this is a strong and varied contribution to Byron studies, one which seeks to evaluate both Byron's cultural inheritance and his continuing afterlife, both of which were markedly cosmopolitan. Nora Liassis explores a remarkable series of cross-currents between Byron, Cyprus and the American Court of Appeals, and an unlikely link between Byron and Tom Stoppard allows Paul M. Curtis to call attention to 'Byron's unprecedented internationalism' (p. 42), a point driven home in contributions on Byron's Canadian, American and Bulgarian afterlives. Marilyn Gaull contributes an astonishing article that covers dinosaurs, DNA and Godzilla. Others consider Byron's inheritance from Latin and Hebraic sources. Catherine Addison contributes a thoughtful piece on Byron's use of ottava rima, a decision which had literary-historical as well as formal implications. A final section looks to literary inheritors. Shobhana Bhattacharji provides a highly welcome discussion of Childe Harold's relationship with Elizabeth Bennet, and another unlikely connection is found in Christine Kenyon Jones's discussion of Byron's similarity to Charles Darwin and their mutual inheritance from William Paley. There are further contributions on Wordsworth, Heine and angry Victorians such as the Brownings, Carlyle and Tennyson. This is a fine collection of short pieces which, as Bernard Beatty points out in his introduction, 'Byron would have approved of' (p. 4).

A great many critics were interested in the afterlives of the Romantic poets this year, augmenting a recent trend. The most beautifully produced of these was *Byron: The Image of the Poet*, edited by Christine Kenyon Jones. The volume arises from an exhibition at the National Portrait Gallery in 2002–3 entitled 'Mad, Bad and Dangerous: The Cult of Lord Byron'. The volume offers over forty images, including twenty-two colour plates, amply suggestive of the multiplicity with which scholars are faced. Kenyon Jones presents a subtle and learned introduction and seven fine essays. Germaine Greer focuses on Richard Westall's 1813 portrait, showing how 'Byronism' pre-dates Byron: his distinctive pose is enabled by the fact that, as a history painter rather than a portrait painter, Westall modelled Byron in an Apollonian tradition. The Apollo Belvedere also influenced Byron's posture in the Sands portrait, further determining perceptions of the Byronic during Byron's lifetime, as Annette Peach shows. Tom Mole brilliantly discovers an affinity between Bart Simpson and Byron in his contribution. When attempting to create a memorable visual presentation, the fewer lines used the better, so the 'Byronic' image became less and less close to the physical poet. Geoffrey Bond, a collector of Byron memorabilia, describes a Greek medal struck in Byron's honour, and Peter Cochran merrily deconstructs the many and varied television and film representations of the noble poet. Kenyon Jones, like Mole, is interested in Byron's body, but she uses the external image to turn back to the poetry, particularly in 'the association between his physique and the physical characteristics of his verse' (p. 99). Bernard Beatty also focuses on the literary, subtly investigating Byron's understanding of the icon. The book offers a varied account of a variety of Byrons, and it is all the truer to the poet and his images for that. Byron's celebrity received further attention this year in Mark Schoenfield's 'Private Souvenirs: Exchanges among Byron's Southwell Set' (*WC* 38[2008] 30–4). Schoenfield considers the habits of exchanging tokens amongst Byron's friends at Southwell, which he visited occasionally between 1804 and 1807, and the later repercussions when these tokens entered the public sphere following Byron's death. Gilles Soubigou's 'French Portraits of Byron, 1824–1880' (*ByronJ* 36[2008] 45–55) discusses the cultural transmission of a 'distinctive idea of Byron in French art' (p. 45) which moved from the heroic to the comic, 'a touching dandy and an archetypal British eccentric' (p. 52).

Others discussed Byron's afterlives in different ways. Richard Cronin contributed an essay on Byron and Clough, discussed in Chapter XIII. Sarah Wootton's 'The Changing Faces of the Byronic Hero in *Middlemarch* and *North and South*' (*Romanticism* 14[2008] 25–35) also considers Byron's literary legacy. Women writers in the period importantly reinterpreted the Byronic hero, but Wootton stays clear of the more typical embodiments, such as Rochester and Heathcliff. The Byronic figure's extremes of mood allowed the 'ideological indeterminacy' (p. 33) that underpins these novels by Eliot and Gaskell, and in modern film and television adaptations the hero continues to flourish. William Galperin's 'Lord Byron, Lady Byron, and Mrs Stowe' (in McGill, ed., *The Traffic in Poems: Nineteenth-Century Poetry and Transatlantic Exchange*, pp. 125–38) looks at the transatlantic controversy generated in the 1850s by Harriet Beecher Stowe's moralizing in taking sides with Lady Byron against Teresa Guiccioli's well-received memoir. The myth that Byron was too poetical for the life domestic was fostered as a direct counter-response to Stowe, and Galperin uncovers this controversy while re-examining the Turkish tales' rather different depictions of domesticity. Byron's reception history received a further boost in '*In Memoriam* XIII and *The Corsair*' (*N&Q* 55[2008] 34–7), in which Kirstie Blair spots a hitherto unnoticed allusion to Byron by Tennyson. Andrew M. Stauffer's 'The First Printing of a Byron Poem in America' (*N&Q* 55[2008] 31–2) notes that the appearance of 'The First Kiss of Love', in the *Lady's Weekly Miscellany* of New York in 1808, was in fact Byron's first transatlantic trip.

A special issue of *Studies in Romanticism*, entitled *Byron's Scots and Byron's Scotland*, edited by Hermione de Almeida, provided rich pickings. The articles are not, however, hindered by parochialism. This was a period, as de Almeida points out, in which Scots were increasingly at the forefront of the British empire, a cosmopolitanism in tune with Byron's concerns. The essays are not, then, attempts to 'claim' Byron as a Scot, but to 'evoke an even larger, worldly and world-wide, context' (p. 13). Susan Oliver's 'Crossing "Dark Barriers": Intertextuality and Dialogue between Lord Byron and Sir Walter Scott' (*SiR* 47[2008] 15–35) begins in an unlikely locale: the East. Unlikely, that is, until one remembers how frequently the Highland line was figured as an uncertain border between Britain and a disturbing other. Oliver mounts a subtle and attentive analysis of the intertextual interplay between the two writers, noting in particular an uncanny combination of Gothic and oriental elements. Michael P. Steier's ambitious 'Transgressing the Borders of *English Bards and Scotch Reviewers*' (*SiR* 47[2008] 37–52) persuasively suggests that the combination of English and Scottish literary traditions lies at the heart of Byron's cosmopolitanism. Like Oliver, he is interested in the crossing of boundaries, but Steier figures these boundaries in cultural terms, concluding with a discussion of Byron's interpretation of the legacy of Burns. David Hill Radcliffe's 'Byron and the Scottish Spenserians' (*SiR* 47[2008] 53–74) investigates the old Enlightenment topics of progress, civilization and cultural consumption and their relevance to *Childe Harold*. Radcliffe hears the influence of Scott's *Don Roderick* and Campbell's *Gertrude of Wyoming* in its discussion of the progress of genius. Byron mixed cosmopolitanism with nostalgia for an oddly kitsch version of Scotland, and Peter W. Graham investigates this in 'Byron and Expatriate Nostalgia' (*SiR* 47[2008] 75–90). Homesickness becomes connected to urbanity as Byron combined knowledge gained on his travels with memories of Aberdeenshire. The collection closes with Geoffrey Bond's 'The John Murray Archive at the National Library of Scotland' (*SiR* 47[2008] 91–9), which describes some of the treasures to be found (Byronic and otherwise) in this fabulous new acquisition. Byron's Scottish links were also discussed in a fine piece by Roderick S. Speer, 'Scotland in Byron's Life and Poetry' (*KSR* 22[2008] 31–45). Speer discusses the importance of Aberdeen and the Highlands, but he also, like Oliver, investigates his links with Scott. Byron was a 'fanatical reader of the Waverley novels' (p. 39), culminating in a rousing quotation from *Old Mortality* as he set off for Greece.

Byron's theatricalism is something of a commonplace these days, but Jonathon Shears does much to suggest why this is such a central aspect of his poetic method in 'Byron's Aposiopesis' (*Romanticism* 14[2008] 183–95). 'Aposiopesis', the rhetorical habit of interrupting oneself, is central to the way in which *Don Juan* engages the reader as if he or she were watching a play, exploring the significance of the technique for Byron's sense of what happens when 'discourse breaks down' (p. 184). In a complex, lucid piece entitled

'Byronic Measures: Enacting Lordship in *Childe Harold's Pilgrimage* and *Marino Faliero*' (*ELH* 75[2008] 1–26), Bo Earle builds on the work of Jerome Christensen to investigate the nature of the performative in Byron's poetry. Earle's work has affinities with Derrida, specifically in an interest in writing and repetition. Barbara Schaff's 'Italianised Byron—Byronised Italy' (in Pfister and Hertel, eds., *Performing National Identity: Anglo-Italian Cultural Exchange*, pp. 103–21) examines the two-way cultural interchange between Byron and the home he adopted upon exile from Britain in 1816. Byron saw in Italy a theatricality that he embraced, but the poet's own theatrical gestures of national belonging have been embraced in Italy. The Ligurian coastline invites tourists to experience a Byronism which is, as Schaff shows, a 'complete fabrication' (p. 118), if an oddly appropriate fake.

Andrew M. Stauffer's 'The Career of Byron's "To the Po"' (*KSJ* 57[2008] 108–25) considers one of Byron's shorter pieces. The poem, written under the shadow of his developing relationship with Teresa Guiccioli, has been the topic of some debate regarding how it came into print and when Byron wrote it. Stauffer addresses these issues, offering new interpretations in both cases. But the greatest strength of the article is the use Stauffer puts these facts to in opening up the poem, discovering in the end that the two textual versions 'incarnate the divided nature of the poem' (p. 125). Christopher Hands, in 'Byron's Conversation with Shelley' (*EIC* 58[2008] 143–61), enters the debate over Byron's 'materialist' rejection of 'Romantic' (and perhaps Shelleyan) idealism. Far from a simple rejection of materialism, *Don Juan* represents, appropriately in such a conversational poem, 'considered equipoise' (p. 159). The poem engages Shelley in debate, admonishing with one hand, admiring with the other. Mark Sandy uses Nietzsche to open up Byron's thinking about history and himself in ' "The Colossal Fabric's Form": Remodelling Memory, History, and Forgetting in Byron's Poetic Recollections of Ruins' (*RaVoN* 51[2008] 23 paras). Sandy's subtle piece discovers that Byron's desire to forget paradoxically results in remembering. This process prompts his reflections on the nature of his own posthumous subjectivity. Sheila A. Spector's 'The Liturgical Context of the Byron–Nathan *Hebrew Melodies*' (*SiR* 47[2008] 393–412) builds on a recent revival of interest in Byron's *Hebrew Melodies*. She seeks to explain a missing context: Anglo-Jewish identity. The music was supplied by Isaac Nathan, an English Jew, and the songs depend directly on Jewish liturgical precedents. But the effect, Spector argues, was often to ironize those precedents. Stephen Cheeke's excellent 'Byron and the Horatian Commonplace' (*ByronJ* 36[2008] 5–17) subtly threads through the class and political implications of Byron's invocation of the classics. Hazlitt saw in it an unthinking display of a classical education, but, as Cheeke shows, Byron was deeply ambivalent about this classical inheritance and his use of such commonplaces is always interested in their common, or communal nature. Byron's use of the 'desultory rhyme' of the Italian ottava rima has been the subject of a great deal of attention, and Maria Schoina pushes this further in 'Revisiting Byron's Italian Style' (*ByronJ* 36[2008] 19–27). Schoina uncovers a number of other precedents and influences such as his contemporary Ugo Foscolo, shedding light on the 'political dissidence' (p. 25) encoded in that style. Colin Jager's 'Byron and Romantic Occidentalism' (*RCPS* [2008]

35 paras) builds on Akeel Bilgrami's recent essay 'Occidentalism: The Very Idea'. The idea of a rehabilitated Occident is an intriguing one, but, as Jager's subtle essay shows, Byron's *The Giaour* suggests some of the limitations of that theory.

Bernard Beatty's 'The Glory and the Nothing of a Name' (*ByronJ* 36[2008] 91–104) elegantly weaves through Byron's meditations on names and naming. He begins with 'Churchill's Grave: A Fact Literally Rendered', which recognizes Charles Churchill as comet-like, blazing but passing into nothingness. *Manfred* prompts similar concerns, but the opposition between 'glory' and 'nothing' is finally overcome in the person of Aurora Raby in *Don Juan*. 'The Fixed and the Fluid: Identity in Byron and Shelley' (*ByronJ* 36[2008] 105–16) by Michael O'Neill weighs up the different approaches to selfhood in Byron and Shelley. The two poets, as O'Neill subtly demonstrates, engage in a complex interchange with each other's ideas of transcendence, earthliness and nothingness. Byron's connection with Shelley was also discussed by Alexander Bubb in 'Mary and Percy Shelley and Lord Byron's interest in Cataclysm Theories' (*KSR* 22[2008] 46–52). Bubb explores the Newtonian roots of an interest in theories of apocalypse that the Shelleys picked up and passed on to Byron. Matthew J.A. Green's 'Voices in the Wilderness: Satire and Sacrifice in Blake and Byron' (*ByronJ* 36[2008] 117–29) looks at Byron's *Cain* and Blake's response to it, *The Ghost of Abel*. Both, for Green, 'situate themselves within a community of letters' (p. 117) and we can better understand that situation with an examination of their shared inheritance of Menippean satire. Scholars of Byron and Leigh Hunt will welcome the publication of Timothy Webb's 'Leigh Hunt to Lord Byron: Eight Letters from Horsemonger Lane Gaol' (*ByronJ* 36[2008] 131–42). Webb reprints, with ample annotation, eight recently rediscovered letters Hunt wrote to his new noble friend when serving time for his satire on the Prince Regent. Andrew Nicholson's 'Intercepted Letters: Byron, Hobhouse, Hoppner and the Trial of the Queen' (*ByronJ* 36[2008] 29–44) presents some fascinating new information about Byron's intervention from abroad in the Queen Caroline affair. Roderick S. Speer and Kim Nielsen comment on a little-known elegy Byron wrote for his cousin, Peter Parker, who died in the American war of 1812 in '"Gallant Parker! Glory and Greece!": Lord Byron and Captain Sir Peter Parker' (*ByronJ* 36[2008] 57–62). Andrew Stauffer's 'Two Rediscovered Byron Letters' (*ByronJ* 36[2008] 143–6) reprints letters from Byron to E.D. Clarke, Professor of Mineralogy at Cambridge.

It takes some courage to begin a book by declaring one's topic to be 'arguably the most offensive, despised, and ridiculed dandy of the Regency period' (p. 1), but John Stewart does so of Sir James Webster-Wedderburn in *Byron and the Websters: The Letters and Entangled Lives of the Poet, Sir James Webster and Lady Frances Webster*. Stewart has no qualms about taking sides, and he is assuredly on the side of Lady Frances, the wronged woman caught between a profligate fool and a 'pernicious' poet. She had an affair not only with Byron, but also with Wellington, and made herself one of the most talked-about women in Europe. The book deals liberally in the atmosphere of scandal and intrigue, and will be principally of biographical interest to Byronists and scholars of Regency culture. Stewart's scholarship is sound, and he has amassed a great deal of illuminating information about three fascinating figures from the John Murray archives and elsewhere. Michael J. Franklin's 'Jousting for the Honour of Greece and "A Certain Miss Prosyne": Baron Byron and Gally Knight Clash over Costume, Correctness, and a Princess' (*MLR* 103[2008] 330–49) merrily discusses Byron's early admiration and subsequent loathing for Henry Gally Knight. Knight had out-Byroned Byron in his travels, and this combined with some personal politics ensured Byron's distaste. Franklin cleverly unpacks the complexities of a lengthy cat-fight.

Mina Gorji's *John Clare and the Place of Poetry* gracefully and elegantly combines a number of the most significant strands in recent Romantic criticism. Her understanding of Clare is influenced by the history of the book, studies in print culture, an interest in his social class and his place in Romantic-period literary culture. Gorji combines all of these elements with a surefooted and subtle attention to the details of Clare's poetry, and the book that results is likely to prove a touchstone in studies of Clare for some time. The book begins with a discussion of Clare's 'artfully artless' adaptation of modes of allusion to the poets, resulting in a 'subtle act of literary positioning' (p. 30). Clare frequently alluded to Gray's *Elegy*, and in doing so both engaged with and distanced himself from an emergent brand: 'the labouring-class poet'. Gorji's focus on Clare's 'witty, rather than unwitting' (p. 2) style takes issue with a tradition that sees him either as a victim or an enemy of a literary establishment that patronized a lower-class entrant. Yet this not only underestimates Clare's self-consciousness as a poet, it also flattens the complexity of the contemporary literary and cultural scene. Indeed Gorji's understanding of the complexities of Clare's sites of reception is one of the real strengths of the book. There are chapters on Clare's revisions and reinterpretations of Spenser and pastoral and his allusions to eighteenth-century poets, notably Burns and Shenstone. A final chapter considers 'To the Snipe', 'one of Clare's finest and most searching poems about home and homelessness' (p. 97) in great detail. It is a fine chapter with which to conclude as Gorji brings together strands discussing different types of place (social, cultural, literary, printed, physical, intertextual) debunking the notion of Clare as an 'artless peasant poet' (p. 99). The Clare that emerges is as subtle as he is complex: Gorji provides a powerful case for a reassessment of his work.

Clare was, as usual, well served by a number of articles in the ever sprightly *John Clare Society Journal*. Scott McEathron, in 'Clare, John Atkin, and *The Parish*' (*JCSJ* 27[2008] 5–23) does some sterling work with the correspondence of John Atkin, Clare's first epistolary admirer. Atkin, himself a (decidedly minor) poet, is far from loveable in his eager solicitation of patronage, yet he offers in some respects an 'exaggerated version' of Clare. Scott Hess's 'John Clare, William Wordsworth, and the (Un)Framing of Nature' (*JCSJ* 27[2008] 27–44) builds on John Barrell's seminal work, further investigating the ways in which Clare's meticulous narrators reject picturesque notions of perspective. Specifically, Clare rejects the notion of 'framing' landscapes, and in doing so, as so often, produces an 'environmental aesthetic' (p. 28). Tom Bates clears up the background to a portrait of the poet in 'On the Portrait of John Clare by Henry Behnes' (*JCSJ* 27[2008] 45–58). Simon Kövesi has, excitingly, found a review of Clare unknown to scholars, which he presents in 'An Uncatalogued Review of *Poems Descriptive: Dublin Inquisitor*, January 1821' (*JCSJ* 27[2008] 73–80). Sarah Weiger's '"Shadows of Taste": John Clare's Tasteful Natural History' (*JCSJ* 27[2008] 59–71) discusses Clare's response to Elizabeth Kent's *Flora Domestica*. His natural history was distinctive, but distinctly appealing, 'accounting for and celebrating the peculiarities of taste among birds, flowers, insects and men' (p. 59). Kent, the sister-in-law of Leigh Hunt, received some further welcome attention in a fine article by Daisy Hay, 'Elizabeth Kent's Collaborators' (*Romanticism* 14[2008] 272–81). Kent's *Flora Domestica*, a handbook for the suburban gardener, is not simply a piece of ephemera. Rather, as Hay subtly shows, it 'exemplifies the central philosophical tenets of the Hunt circle' (p. 280), though one that was, importantly, written after Hunt left the circle for Italy.

Timothy Morton provides a powerful eco-critical theorization of the concept of 'place' in 'John Clare's Dark Ecology' (*SiR* 47[2008] 179–93). Ecology and Clare's nature poetry have clear links, but Morton is remarkably original in discovering an investigation of place in Clare's 'depression' poems. These poems are 'retroactively corrosive' on Clare's corpus, showing how his sense of place was always unsettled by the recognition that he was writing 'for another' (p. 191). Theresa Adams's 'Representing Rural Leisure: John Clare and the Politics of Popular Culture' (*SiR* 47[2008] 371–92) studies a 'carnivalesque revision of georgic: georgic turned upside down' (p. 372). But popular culture, depoliticized by enclosure, becomes simply a memory for labourers, not a lived reality, and Clare's poetry mourns the loss.

Andrew Keanie's *Hartley Coleridge: A Reassessment of his Life and Work* is by turns enchanting and infuriating, qualities Hartley Coleridge himself embodied. Keanie offers a book that is part biography and part claim for Hartley's significance as a poet, and he does so with at times all too evident enthusiasm for his subject and impatience with a critical establishment that has failed to admit the younger Coleridge. Keanie claims Hartley as a key figure in Romantic poetry, and he does so by contrast with the canonical poets. 'Whereas Byron and Shelley left roadkills behind them as they zipped along the fast-lane', he argues, 'Hartley was easy on everyone' (p. 52). Such a sentence is typical of Keanie's style: witty, lively and effusive, but always teetering on the brink of excess. Hartley, he argues, offers an alternative poetics to the major Romantic poets, one whose 'eccentric and erratic improvisation' and 'lack of homogeneity' (p. 89) is less certain, less grand and less stable than that offered by Byron, Shelley or his father. The observation that his 'eloquence bubbles and flows too lightly to be siphoned off profitably by any political party' (p. 143) is key. Hartley emerges from Keanie's study as a poet who is actively and purposefully lightweight, a poet whose poetry requires a different understanding of literary quality to be appreciated. Yet Keanie seems a little unsure about this at times. Hartley is claimed as a poet of the quotidian, but Keanie values this as an attempt to find 'the lost lineaments of the most high in the most low' (p. 17); this is not a poetry of 'frippery' (p. 20). And yet it is by virtue of his very non-seriousness, his creation of a poetics of waste and luxury, that Hartley often seems most compelling. True, this shades into some worryingly Skimpolian territory at times ('Hartley never even thought about how his rent was paid for him, or who paid it', p. 168). But when Keanie ceases attempting to make Hartley into a canonical Romantic poet and places his work alongside that of writers like George Darley and Thomas Hood, he seems the more valuable for his part in a tradition of serious non-seriousness. If the book disappoints it is only because it promises so much. Hartley Coleridge deserves our attention, often precisely because he fails to be 'Romantic'.

The 'afterlives' of the Romantic poets has been a central topic this year, and attention to the Coleridgean variety was given a welcome boost by a sprightly collection edited by James Vigus and Jane Wright, *Coleridge's Afterlives*. The collection ranges across a hundred years of criticism, from Coleridge's death in 1834 until the publication of I.A. Richards's *Coleridge on Imagination* in 1934. As John Beer remarks aptly in his Afterword, the quality which unites the collection 'above all is its ambiguity' (p. 252). Indeed, the image of the poet-philosopher presented in these diverse essays owes much to Seamus Perry's notion of a paradoxically creative uncertainty in Coleridge. Coleridge appeals to his often reluctant inheritors in spite of himself; as Perry puts it with regard to T.S. Eliot in his own contribution, Eliot comes not so much to an appreciation of Coleridge as 'a deepening exploration of contradictions and perplexities common to them both' (p. 229). The collection moves chronologically. James Vigus focuses on the importance of information about print runs and edition sizes in investigating how Coleridge's work would have reached a wider audience. Lynda Pratt makes an excellent case for Joseph Cottle's 1837 biography as a 'subversive' text, which insists on the importance of Bristol, unsettles class distinctions and recognizes Coleridge's collective creativity, rather than his status as autonomous genius. Frederick Burwick, in 'De Quincey on Coleridge', sheds new light on the complex interplay between the two. Stephen Prickett considers Julius Hare's absorption of Coleridgean Germanic ideas concerning plurality, unity and the fragmentary. Anthony John Harding's excellent chapter places Coleridge as a 'chameleon' (p. 81) in gender, a fact which often coloured his Victorian reception. Daniel Sanjiv Roberts shows how Coleridge's writings on the clerisy were taken up as a form of 'spiritualized nationalism' (p. 108) in India. In a fascinating piece, Laura Dassow Walls shows how Emerson's ultimate rejection of Coleridge was so affected by an earlier attachment that he '[assimilated] Coleridge's ideas so thoroughly they became part of his own nature and thence, part of American literary and cultural history' (p. 125). Daniel Karlin makes a series of only partially successful attempts to find a later Ancient Mariner in Gaskell, Beckett and Conrad, while Jane Wright's subtle and intriguing chapter explores the distinction between art and ethics in a critical tradition from Coleridge to Wilde. Ross Wilson examines Walter Pater's charge of absolutism against Coleridge's dissemination of German thought, and Paul Hamilton also discusses the influence of Coleridge's Germanic interests as they relate to Turner, Ruskin and I.A. Richards. Douglas Hedley further considers philosophy, finding in R.G. Collingwood's philosophy an apparently unconscious Coleridgean influence which sneaks into his thought via Ruskin.

The subject of Coleridge's influence was considered widely this year. Saeko Yoshikawa elegantly explores the connections between Edward Thomas and

Coleridge, particularly with regard to their parallel exploration of the West Country, in 'The Abounding Honeysuckle: Edward Thomas, S.T. Coleridge, and the Quantock Hills' (*ColB* 32[2008] 32–40). Those natural images which nourished Coleridge provided the same role for Thomas as he explored the same ground through Coleridge's eyes. Cristina Flores's '"That Marvellous Coleridge": The Influence of S.T. Coleridge's Poetry and Poetics in Miguel de Unamuno (1864–1936)' (*ColB* 32[2008] 41–7) finds that, like Thomas, de Unamuno sought to 'revive within him' a Coleridgean 'symphony and song'. Nils Clauson's 'Arnold's Coleridgean Conversation Poem: "Dover Beach" and "The Eolian Harp"' (*PLL* 44[2008] 276–304) argues that, whereas Arnold's debt to the other Romantic poets is well known, his debt to Coleridge ought to be acknowledged. 'Dover Beach', he argues, adopts the structure and the voice of Coleridge's conversation poems. Another Victorian poet's connections with Coleridge were examined by Robin L. Inboden in 'Damsels, Dulcimers, and Dreams: Elizabeth Barrett's Early Response to Coleridge' (*VP* 46[2008] 129–50). Barrett, Inboden argues was, intriguingly, as much drawn to the masculine as to the feminine aspects of Coleridge's poetry. Edgar Allen Poe, however, despite some obvious affinities with the poet of *The Ancient Mariner*, ultimately came to recognize too great a difference from the theorist of the 'one life', as Alexander Schlutz argues in 'Purloined Voices: Edgar Allen Poe Reading Samuel Taylor Coleridge' (*SiR* 47[2008] 195–224).

Morton D. Paley's *Samuel Taylor Coleridge and the Fine Arts* is an elegant piece of scholarship by a distinguished Coleridgean. The book offers a narrative of Coleridge's evolving relationship with the fine arts. It is not so much a work of criticism (there is little by way of argument) as a scholarly biography of one aspect of Coleridge's life. As such, its primary value for scholars (beyond the sheer pleasure of reading this fine volume) is as a kind of sourcebook by means of which future scholars can benefit from Paley's formidable knowledge of art, artists and Coleridge's voluminous writings on the subject. The story begins with Sir George Beaumont, who awakened a latent interest in artistic ways of seeing in Coleridge, planting seeds which would grow and develop in Italy in 1805. Paley is particularly strong on Coleridge's relationship with Washington Allston. This relationship, Paley's account suggests, was in its own way as significant as that between Coleridge and Wordsworth. Allston taught Coleridge to see with new eyes: 'always . . . a sensitive describer of landscape, he was now alive to an artist's way of viewing it' (p. 39). Throughout the notebooks are scattered wonderful ekphrastic poetic prose works which Coleridge produced in response to Allston's work, and Paley's deep knowledge of artistic method does much to uncover their full significance. Coleridge's knowledge of art holdings in Britain is thoroughly documented before an excellent account of his opinions on the history of art, including his responses to contemporary artists, importantly Blake. Coleridge is revealed as a remarkably subtle appreciator of the fine arts: witty, self-mocking, at times conventional, at others visionary, but always Coleridgean. Inevitably, 'the ideational precedes the artistic' (p. 136), and Paley is particularly strong on the way imagination underpins his conception of the connections between the arts with regard to key terms such as the picturesque and the beautiful. Coleridge's inquisitive, enthusiastic voice rings out of these pages: Paley's book is an important reminder of just how central art was to Coleridge's thought.

Coleridge's supernaturalism is a subject that is perhaps rather oftener taught than it is discussed by scholars, but George S. Erving's 'The Politics of Matter: Newtonian Science and Priestleyan Metaphysics in Coleridge's "Preternatural Agency"' (*ERR* 19[2008] 219–32), goes some way to remedying the lack. Erving places Coleridge's contribution to Southey's *Joan of Arc* in the context of his Unitarian thinking, showing how Coleridge's interest in the supernatural arises out of his theologico-political interests. Priestleyan Unitarianism is also a central feature in William A. Ulmer's 'Answering *The Borderers* in "The Rime of the Ancient Mariner"' (*ERR* 19[2008] 233–46). Ulmer discovers a web of intersecting philosophical ideas between Wordsworth and Coleridge: *The Ancient Mariner* borrows Wordsworth's answer to Godwin's necessitarianism, giving it in turn a Unitarian slant. But Coleridge finds *The Borderers* so compelling in part because Wordsworth leaned so heavily on his own criticism of Godwin. Gregory Leadbetter's 'Liberty and Occult Ambition in Coleridge's Early Poetry' (*ColB* 32[2008] 1–9) examines the conflict between Coleridge's Dissenting political commitments and his poetical pursuit of metaphysical knowledge between 1794 and 1797, complicating understandings of his Unitarian radicalism. Poems such as 'The Eolian Harp' and 'Religious Musings' tend towards an interest in the unknown, which brought warnings from more committed Unitarians such as Barbauld and Lamb.

The connection between Coleridge's poetry and his journalism received further attention in Heidi Thomson's '"Merely the emptying out of my desk": Coleridge about Wordsworth in the *Morning Post* of 1802' (*ColB* 31[2008] 73–89). Thomson shows the odd combination of private and public in poems such as the 'Dejection' ode and 'The Keep-Sake', in which Coleridge displays an obsession with Wordsworth and discovers a 'socially sanctioned public outlet for his feelings' (p. 74). Dewey H. Hall's '"From Steep to Steep": Poetic Indebtedness in Coleridge and Shelley' (*ColB* 31[2008] 102–11) tries to move beyond the plagiarism debates that concern Coleridge's 'Hymn before Sun-Rise, in the Vale of Chamouny', instead arguing that, just as Coleridge 'amplifies' Frederica Brun's precursor, so Shelley's 'Mont Blanc' is an 'extension, adaptation, or modification' (p. 111) of Coleridge. In 'Wordless Words: Children, Language and Nature's Ministry in "The Nightingale: A Conversation Poem"' (*ColB* 32[2008] 10–17), Samantha Harvey explores Coleridge's complex understanding of the childlike mind and its perception of the natural world. The 1798 version of the poem seems discordant, but Harvey shows how subtly its form carries its philosophical content. Justin Shepherd's '*Fears in Solitude*: Private Places and Public Faces' (*ColB* 32[2008] 18–24) uses Auden to open up the continuity behind the apparent conflict between private and public in *Fears in Solitude*. The poem might be considered, Shepherd argues, as a meditation on the impossibility of combining those two spheres; in doing so he makes a strong claim for its value as a poem, not simply a political polemic. '"Thickening, deepening, blackening": Starlings and the Object of Poetry in Coleridge and Dante' (*ColB* 32[2008] 55–62), by Peter Anderson, rather wonderfully finds a poetics of starlings, birds whose murmuring movement seems to gesture towards something before language.

Coleridge was well known for promising that things would be finished in the future; Francis O'Gorman's 'Coleridge, "Frost at Midnight", and Anticipating the Future' (*Romanticism* 14[2008] 232–44) shows how this habit was in fact a fundamental part of the way he thought about poetry. The effect of necessity on human lives was in conflict with an interest in whether one could 'try, however illusorily, to control the direction of the future through the assertion of a flawed individual will' (p. 233), a conflict he pursued in 'Frost at Midnight'. Frederick Burwick also considers the conversation poems in 'Coleridge's Conversation Poems: Thinking the Thinker' (*Romanticism* 14[2008] 168–82). The poems, when read in sequence, reveal, for Burwick, a conflict between '"blank" perception and the mind's own constitutive role' (p. 179); even when idly musing, thought must be going on beneath the surface. Coleridge revised his 'Monody on the Death of Chatterton' repeatedly from 1785 until his own death in 1834; it should be considered, thus, as far more than a sentimental response to a literary fad, as Heidi Thomson argues in 'A Connection between Chatterton and Wordsworth in Two Coleridge Poems' (*ECLife* 32[2008] 110–19). It remains, she argues, a deeply 'eighteenth century' poem through all its manifestations, but it is also a central intertext for another tributary verse, Coleridge's 'To William Wordsworth', as both poems contain a reproach for a poet that Coleridge had once worshipped. James Mulvihill's '"Like a Lady of a Far Countrée": Coleridge's "Christabel" and the Fear of Invasion' (*PLL* 44[2008] 250–75) examines this 'fragmentary Gothic puzzler' (p. 250) afresh, arguing that contemporary debates (to which Coleridge contributed), about the threat of English Jacobinism explain the air of mystery. Geraldine, the enemy within who has crossed over the threshold with the assistance of one seduced by her mystery, is connected to threats of a fear of invasion. Debra Channick offers a rather more poetical take on the poem in her '"A logic of its own": Repetition in Coleridge's "Christabel"' (*RaVoN* 50[2008] 27 paras). Channick notices the formally disjointed nature of the poem, but in a subtle argument shows how that incoherence has its own coherence. Thematically, formally and psychologically, the poem uses repetition to investigate states of paralysis and creativity.

The debate generated by Frederick Burwick and James McKusick's edition of Coleridge's *Faustus* continued in 2008. Scepticism as to the authorship was rife. Joyce Crick's review (*ColB* 32[2008] 70–84) finds the editors' certainty presumptuous ('the question is not closed until new and conclusive evidence comes along', p. 84). Hugh Craig reviews the stylometric analysis that the editors perform (*ColB* 32[2008] 85–8), and the evidence that Craig's analysis offers tends to support Crick's rather more tentative approach. Burwick answers such critics, adducing some additional circumstantial evidence in 'On Coleridge as Translator of *Faustus from the German of Goethe*' (*ERR* 19[2008] 247–52). Waka Ishikura's 'Coleridge's Poetic Ally—Sir William Rowan Hamilton' (*ColB* 32[2008] 63–9) provides an interesting piece of scholarship on a figure rarely noticed by Coleridge's biographers, William Rowan Hamilton. Hamilton, a mathematician, was consistently inspired by Coleridge's poetry both as a poetaster and as a mathematician. Barry Hough and Howard Davies presented important new archival material detailing Coleridge's activity in Malta in 1805 in 'Coleridge as Public Secretary in Malta: The Surviving Archives' (*ColB* 31[2008] 90–101).

Richard Marggraf Turley has done much to enhance the reputation of Barry Cornwall lately, and he continues the job in fine style in '"Breathing human passion": Keats, Cornwall, Shelley and Popular Romanticism' (*ERR* 19[2008] 253–73). Cornwall's verse sold far better than that of his canonical colleagues, but their critical fortunes seem to have increased in inverse proportion to his. Intriguingly, this attempt to reclaim Cornwall is decidedly not based on his literary merits, but on his ability to act as a thermometer of taste; then as now, both his success and his failure are a result of his fashionability. Marggraf Turley continued this work in '"Slippery Steps on the Temple of Fame": Barry Cornwall and Keats's Reputation' (*KSR* 22[2008] 64–81). The article begins by conclusively naming Cornwall as the author of the positive review of Keats's 1820 volume printed in the *Edinburgh Magazine*. But Marggraf Turley goes beyond this, showing how the association of Cockney poetry with fine phrases at first damned Keats, then Cornwall, before mounting a defence of Cornwall's technique and showing how perceptive a reader of Keats he was.

Brandy Ryan's '"Echo and Reply": The Elegies of Felicia Hemans, Letitia Landon, and Elizabeth Barrett' (*VP* 46[2008] 249–77) presents an interesting discussion of female Romantic elegists, arguing that 'the writing published between 1780 and 1830 reveals that the sensibility usually relegated to the domestic and private realm—the feminine—becomes a tool that accomplished male poets...discuss, evaluate, and adopt' (p. 250). Ryan concludes by asserting that Hemans, Landon and Barrett transfer the potential 'empty echo' of elegiac poetry and give it a 'full voice'. In her chapter 'States of Exile' (in McGill, ed., pp. 15–36), Tricia Lootens discusses Felicia Hemans's 'Landing of the Pilgrim Fathers of New England', a poem centred on the landing site of British pilgrims arriving in Massachusetts. Lootens provides an intriguing analysis of the poem as a 'thoroughly transatlantic work', commenting that 'it seems less ironic than inevitable that the most popular of all Plymouth Rock poems should have been written by a British woman' (p. 15). Aimée Boutin's 'Transnational Migrations: Reading Amable Tastu with Felicia Hemans' (*RomS* 26:iii[2008] 210–20) discusses the poetess Amable Tastu's appropriation of the works of Felicia Hemans. Boutin posits that 'The realities of poetic production in the nineteenth century...contradict the myth of Romantic originality' (p. 211). Moreover, Boutin presents an intriguing defence of the importance of 'dialogue in "poetess poetics"' (p. 212).

Another poet who seems to be undergoing something of a revival is Thomas Hood, and complementing Sara Lodge's monograph, reviewed last year, is Rodney Stenning Edgecombe's *A Self-Divided Poet: Form and Texture in the Verse of Thomas Hood*, missed in 2006. For Edgecombe, Hood is 'self-divided' between two poetical impulses: serious poetry and light verse. Hood does indeed appear (twice) in W.H. Auden's *Oxford Book of Light Verse*, and one of the strengths of this book is to seriously investigate Auden's term. Hood came into his own in the bourgeois space of the literary annuals, and the type of verse he produces celebrates this 'Cockney' realm of tea-drinking milliners and paltry pianofortes. Light verse is distinct from mock-heroic in that description of the apparently low is not held up to be laughed at. And yet this book is not wholly celebratory. Hood became famous as a punster, but for Edgecombe that punning is often simply dextrous, not meaningful, a 'verbal perfume to hide a faint staleness in the matter to which it has been applied' (p. xvii). Like Hartley Coleridge, he is a poet who 'skates across the surface of poetry instead of plumbing its depths' (p. xxi). Edgecombe is pleasingly ambivalent about this quality of his verse. In a series of very learned chapters which take in such splendid texts as the *Odes and Addresses to Great People* (co-authored with J.H. Reynolds) and the poem that might well be his masterpiece, 'Miss Kilmansegg and Her Precious Leg', Edgecombe subtly unwraps the verse itself and discusses its literary antecedents. That poem (along with 'The Song of the Shirt') might be his most serious even in its frivolity, and as Edgecombe shows throughout this book, those two impulses often sit in uneasy rivalry. His 'Keatsian' odes, for example (which Edgecombe shows to be not all that Keatsian) have their own dextrous sparkle that undermines any grandeur. This is certainly the most thorough discussion of Hood's verse we have. It is not quite a call for a recognition of Hood's greatness, but then nor is it (like Lodge's book) a call to appreciate his historical indicativeness, whatever his poetry's quality. It is a subtle and comprehensive, if somewhat elegiac, book. Edgecombe also contributed two short pieces on Hood. In 'Hood, Dickens, Auden and Churchyard Revels' (*N&Q* 55[2008] 43) he shows that the mixing of death and play in Dickens and Auden (two writers who admired Hood) has a source in Hood's *Hero and Leander*. 'A Possible Hapax Legomenon in a Letter by Thomas Hood' (*N&Q* 55[2008] 28–9) explains a detail in one of Hood's letters.

Jennifer N. Wunder's *Keats, Hermeticism and the Secret Societies* asks readers to shake hands, roll up their right trouser leg and become one of the elect. Wunder has found something new not simply to Keats studies but to Romanticism as a whole: the secretive, mysterious culture of Freemasonry, Rosicrucianism and other hermetic societies. Despite there being no direct references to such societies in Keats's writings, this culture provides, Wunder argues, a key aspect of Keats's philosophy and his cultural position. For this culture was not confined to a small elect: pamphlets, books and numerous articles were published on the societies, their rituals and their philosophies. One of the more fascinating parts of the book is her account of those major cultural figures with direct links to Masonic activity in the long eighteenth century. It is a list as extraordinary in its length as in its breadth, containing almost every major Scottish literary figure, and politically catholic enough to include both Thomas Paine and George Canning. Wunder goes beyond simply explicating this context to suggest that it underpins Keats's approach to religion. This is an approach unusual to Keats studies, which has been dominated for fifty years by a materialist (rather than a Neoplatonic) understanding of his approach to the world. Wunder proposes a third way: rather than either a mystical or a rational Keats, we might imagine him as influenced by a Masonic position which facilitated the combination of these extremes. Wunder shows how frequently Keats uses hermetical terms in his work, particularly in *Endymion*, and certainly there are 'points of contact' (p. 20) between Keats and these societies. It is doubtful how far scholars will agree that that contact was a significant one, and certainly there are questionable moments. The *Quarterly Review* criticized Keats's 'obscurity', a term that could well be read in Masonic terms: but surely the more relevant interpretation is that Keats is being accused of incompetence as a poet. The paranoiac spirit of Dan Brown does tend to descend on the book at times, which is unfortunate, as much of it offers a lively and learned treatment of a neglected literary-historical culture and a significant return to the question of Keats's religious beliefs.

Jack Siler's *Poetic Language and Political Engagement in the Poetry of Keats* addresses an issue central in Keats studies since Z's notorious claim in *Blackwood's Magazine* that 'Keats belongs to the Cockney School of Politics, as well as the Cockney School of Poetry'. In recent years the issue has divided critics between those who wish to find a politics for Keats, and those who see Keats creating art which maintains autonomy from the everyday. Siler's intention is to have his cake and eat it. Keats both 'drives the unique role of poetry to the point of seeing it . . . as an end in itself' while also pursuing 'social and political possibilities for poetic language, to make poetry count for something other than itself' (p. 1). Intriguingly, Siler focuses his argument around Peter Burger's *Theory of the Avant-Garde*, suggesting that Keats's understanding of mimesis corresponds with much later developments in aesthetic thinking about the relationship between art and life. The argument that follows is remarkably miscellaneous, incorporating medical, philosophical and aesthetic elements. This range costs the book a cohesive argument. It is often far from clear quite what position the book holds, or in what respects it offers an original contribution. The discussion of previous criticism takes too long, but fails to address the major recent interventions in the field: the bibliography contains only three books published in the last ten years, and misses much relevant scholarship on politics and poetry. Much of that scholarship has sharpened perceptions of the cultural background to Keats's poetry, but Siler has not benefited from this. To describe the *Annals of the Fine Arts* as 'radical' (p. 32) is inaccurate, but it also misses precisely what is interesting about that journal in the cultural and political field in which Keats operated. Discussion of Keats's sonnet on Leigh Hunt's release from prison is similarly simplistic: the 'politics' of the poem surely consists in something rather more complex than the breezy sentiment, worryingly reminiscent of 1960s pop lyrics, that 'song can get us through times with no money better than money can get us through times with no song' (p. 38). The introduction of Burger's work is illuminating, and there are a number of intriguing close readings of Keats's verse. But these bright points are not sufficiently numerous to make this a major addition to Keats studies.

Adam R. Burkey MD's 'Parkinson's Shaking Palsy: The "Aspen-malady" of John Keats' (*KSJ* 57[2008] 128–37) shows how Keats's association of the word 'palsy' with shaking makes certain his acquaintance with James Parkinson's *Essay on the Shaking Palsy* [1817]. Burkey uses this information to discuss some of the implications this has for Keats's verse. Saturn's stooping posture in *Hyperion* may be explained with reference to Parkinson, while Keats's failure to complete *The Fall of Hyperion* may have less to do with his own illness and more with 'a failed concept of health' (p. 137). Keats's connections with science were also explored by Kelly Grovier in '"Paradoxes of the Panoscope": "Walking" Stewart and the Making of Keats's Ambivalent Imagination' (*RaVoN* 52[2008] 19 paras). Grovier picks up on John 'Walking' Stewart's pseudo-scientific notion of a panoscope, which would allow the viewer to glimpse the continual interchange between life and death. Keats's ambivalence about these states was, for Grovier, influenced by such thinking, and it became a source of both comfort and anxiety in his later poetry.

Derek Lowe's subtle 'Wordsworth's "Unenlightened Swain": Keats and Greek Myth in "I stood tip-toe upon a little hill"' (*KSJ* 57[2008] 138–56) begins with Wordsworth's condemnation of Keats's 'Hymn to Pan' as 'a Very pretty piece of paganism'. This incident has recently been read as a politically motivated attack on the younger, radical poet by the disappointing apostate. But, Lowe shows, investigating Keats and Hunt's understanding of a key passage in *The Excursion*, the riposte from Wordsworth was unexpected. Keats misunderstood Wordsworth's position, taking Wordsworth's call for restraint as a licence for imaginative freedom. In a fine piece entitled 'Early William Carlos Williams—"Bad Keats"?' (*CQ* 37[2008] 195–223), Irene Hsiao explores William Carlos Williams's early obsession with Keats. Williams himself saw Keats as a mawkish adolescent influence he shook off (just as Keats saw Leigh Hunt's influence), but as Hsiao shows, in some fine close readings, that influence persisted, particularly in the notion of negative capability. Sarah Wootton's '"Into her dream he melted": Women Artists Remodelling Keats' (*RaVoN* 52[2008] 19 paras) further develops understandings of Keats's posthumous reputation. Wootton moves beyond Pre-Raphaelite renderings of the narrative poems to explore the way women artists reworked the same material. The Glasgow artist Jessie Marion King provides the culmination of a fine piece. Laura Wells Betz's 'Keats and the Charm of Words: Making Sense of *The Eve of St Agnes*' (*SiR* 47[2008] 299–319) notes the way in which the 'enchanting' nature of Keats's 'perfect' musical style has seemed to allow critics to suspend their critical faculties in pure appreciation. Charm, she suggests in a very elegant essay, is Keats's own philosophical intervention, choosing the senses over ideas. Rodney Stenning Edgecombe provided two short pieces on Keats this year. 'Some Potential Corrections to, and Amplifications of, the *Endymion* Annotations in the Longman Keats' (*KSR* 22[2008] 82–90) clarifies some points of reference with regard to Keats's appreciation of art in *Endymion*, while 'Keats, Opie, and the "Ode on a Grecian Urn"' (*KSR* 22[2008] 91–4) ably discusses John Opie's notions of beauty and truth, establishing their influence on the famous closing lines of Keats's ode. Melissa Lloyd's 'Keats's Embodied Cognition: *The Tempest*, Synaesthesia and Contemporary Brain Science' (*KSR* 22[2008] 98–111) finds a link between Keats's obsessive habit of allusion to *The Tempest* and his knowledge of cognitive science from his medical training, showing how these two unlikely bedfellows shaped his poetic method.

Despite a sizeable poetic output, Charles Lamb is rarely considered in this section. One of the particular strengths of Felicity James's *Charles Lamb, Coleridge and Wordsworth: Reading Friendship in the 1790s* is that it reminds us that Lamb was indeed remarkably comfortable in verse, not to mention the sentimental novel and drama. This is the first major monograph on Lamb since Jane Aaron's *A Double Singleness* [1991], and James offers a timely and intellectually rigorous reassessment of the early (pre-Elian) part of Lamb's career. Central to the book is sociability. James shows how Lamb develops a theory of creative communality in conversation primarily with Coleridge, but as part of a wider circle including Charles Lloyd, Robert Southey and William Godwin and other Unitarians, Dissenters and radicals. James describes a series of sociable networks in which Lamb was involved: with Coleridge and Lloyd, with Wordsworth, with his sister Mary and finally with his readers. Sociability underpins Lamb's literary methods as he uses echo and allusion to create communal links between himself and other writers and readers. *Rosamund Gray* is placed in a mutually supportive intertextual relationship with Wordsworth, while Lamb's remarkable drama *John Woodville* is discussed with reference to his development of a mode of 'dense literary allusiveness' (p. 168). The disappointment following the dissolution of the relationship between Lamb, Lloyd and Coleridge allows Lamb to forge a new communal relationship: with his readers. Whereas Coleridge started to turn from a dubious 'reading public', Lamb 'retains faith in the sustained power of sympathy between writer(s) and reader' (p. 71). James's prose is particularly pleasurable: sharply precise, but often merrily sprightly in a way that Lamb himself would surely have endorsed. This book achieves two important aims: it adds greatly to our knowledge of contexts to Lamb's work, but it also makes a major claim for Lamb's significance as a writer who learns from Coleridge and Wordsworth (and from whom they learn), but who deviates from their conception of the literary too. Lamb emerges from James's treatment as a deft, subtle and modest thinker, and a writer whose importance to Romanticism may lie precisely in this odd combination of centrality and marginality.

Thomas Moore, a poet once known principally on account of his *Irish Melodies*, has enjoyed something of a revival of fortunes in recent Romantic criticism, with interest developing in his oriental epic *Lalla Rookh* and his brilliant political satires. That interest took a marked boost this year with the publication of a major new biography, Ronan Kelly's *Bard of Erin: The Life of Thomas Moore*. Kelly's title is a significant one. The Moore that Romanticists have been interested in recovering seems one at odds with the sentimentalist beloved of James Joyce and the Victorians, but Kelly is careful to demonstrate just how significant the melodious, kitsch nationalism was. The biography is particularly strong in investigating the many and varied ways in which Moore has shaped a version of Ireland that remains, to an extent, current. 'Erin', after all, like Caledonia or Albion, is a place that exists only textually, 'both more and less than Ireland' (p. 6). And those melodies, however dubious their nationalism, had a strong political kick, part of Moore's life-long protest against the government in favour of Catholic Emancipation. Formally, they deserve attention too, and Kelly has a sharp ear for their subtleties. They do not simply 'lilt': 'in performance, a note can be held over several notes' (p. 163), and accordingly the meaning changes. The satires receive a rich appreciation as Moore's style brilliantly shifts from the Juvenalian to a 'freer, fresher, determinedly demotic' (p. 213) metropolitan style. Kelly follows the likes of Nigel Leask in seeing an Irish allegory in *Lalla Rookh*'s orientalism, but he is not a partisan critic. Moore's political protest was serious enough, but it was wildly simplistic, 'essentializing the Irish nation as Catholic' (p. 291).

Given Moore's non-sectarian Dublin background, he really should have known better. The Moore that emerges is protean, but also often confusedly mixed, a fit companion for his friend and erstwhile duelling-companion Byron. Kelly has drawn on a sophisticated and wide-ranging array of sources, making the cultural world in which Moore lived and which he satirized easily comprehensible. The complexities and subtleties in Moore, his poetry and his politics that Kelly elucidates will surely make *The Bard of Erin* the first point of call for a new generation of Moore scholars. Moore's *Lalla Rookh* was also discussed in J.C.M. Nolan's 'In Search of an Ireland in the Orient: Tom Moore's *Lalla Rookh*' (*NewHibR* 12:iii[2008] 81–98). Nolan wants Moore criticism to move away from the nationalism of the *Irish Melodies* towards the underground nationalism of Moore's oriental epic. This poem has not had the effect that the *Melodies* have had, but, for Nolan, it offers an alternative Ireland that ought to have attention paid to it.

In addressing 'some of the controversies, legends, and misinformation that became assimilated into Shelley's life story' (p. xii) James Bieri's *Percy Bysshe Shelley: A Biography* presents a new and definitive biography of the Romantic poet. In his preface, Bieri tells us that his background in clinical psychology has informed his interpretation of Shelley's life and literature, an approach that has yielded some intriguing interpretations. The biography is divided into two sections, the first dealing with Shelley's youth, and the second his years in exile. The first chapter introduces the reader not only to Shelley's father Timothy, but also to his grandfather and namesake Bysshe Shelley, a man whose aristocratic ruthlessness and paternal tyranny, Bieri suggests, informed both his son's strict approach to child-rearing, and subsequently his grandson's future rebellion against authority. Bieri's psychoanalytical approach is strongly in evidence in chapter 3, in which he suggests that Shelley's close and protective relationship with his younger sisters informed his future 'concern for equal rights for women' (p. 31). Chapter 7 examines Shelley's emergent identity as a radical poet, and makes some rather interesting analogies to the political radicalism of the mid-twentieth century. Bieri offers a comparison between Shelley's 'political awareness and radicalism at Eton' and the activism of many 'youths of the Vietnam War period', both of which had their roots in belonging to 'affluent, politically aware parents'. Bieri's subtle yet persuasive perspective complements nicely his account of the friendship and politics that Shelley and Thomas Jefferson cultivated while they studied at Oxford, 'a lethargic, conservative intellectual community' (p. 93). The first chapter of part II, ominously entitled 'The Dark Autumn of Suicides', begins by chronicling in harrowing but compelling detail the circumstances of Godwin's stepdaughter Fanny Imlay's suicide, and Shelley's subsequent feelings of guilt over her death. If this section of Bieri's biography becomes darker as it moves towards its (and Shelley's) inevitable end, it remains as enjoyable and accessible to read as the chapters on Shelley's early years. The scholarship on display is formidable throughout, adhering closely to Bieri's mission statement to provide the new definitive biography of the Romantic poet.

Alan Weinberg and Timothy Webb bring us a new collection of essays on Shelley, *The Unfamiliar Shelley*, aiming 'to provide a sense of the neglected range of Shelley's writing ... and to cover a number of phases in his writing career' (p. 3). Their superb introduction concisely foregrounds the material the volume covers, including Shelley's early prose and verse work, incomplete fragments and critically neglected satires such as his burlesque drama on the 1820 Caroline affair, *Swellfoot the Tyrant*. Chapter 14 deals specifically with that play in an essay by Timothy Morton. Morton discusses the relationship between Shelley's representation of the Burkean 'Swinish Multitude' and the author's own vegetarianism within a burgeoning culture of animal rights, the birth of the RSPCA and recent animal cruelty legislation. The chapter certainly fulfils the wider aim of the volume in presenting a largely unfamiliar Shelley. The variety of material covered in this volume is both wide and fresh. Michael Bradshaw discusses Shelley's poetic fragments, asserting that 'the fragment remains an entity in its own right' (p. 21), Christopher R. Miller discusses Queen Mab's character as a 'framing device', something which 'scholars have tended to look past ... to take note of the ideas contained therein' (p. 69) and in an illuminating chapter on Shelley's Neapolitan–Tuscan poetics, Michael Rossington discusses how 'Sonnet II. / Political Greatness' analyses the paradoxical term 'voluntary servitude'. It is a timely volume, and the thorough and innovative scholarship it contains ought to push the study of Shelley into further unlikely if fascinating areas.

Editors Susanne Schmid and Michael Rossington bring us *The Reception of P. B. Shelley in Europe*, a collection of essays examining the consumption of Shelley's works in Europe in the nineteenth and twentieth centuries. *The Reception of Shelley* is the latest in the Continuum series on the reception of nineteenth- and twentieth-century writers in Europe, edited by Elinor Shaffer. The editors of this volume posit that 'the eventual translation and dissemination of [Shelley's] writings in Europe ... represent a vitally important stage in the fulfilment of his literary theory' (p. 4). As Schmid and Rossington explain, the volume aims 'to map out and explain Shelley's diverse European readerships, the vagaries of his European reputations' (p. 6). Indeed, the diversity of Shelley's readerships determines the diversity of the essays in this volume. For example, Jorge Bastos da Silva's chapter on Shelley's reception in Portugal observes that the Romantic poet has 'left no deep mark in the fabric of Portuguese literature, either in the nineteenth or the twentieth century'. Moreover, Shelley in Portugal is consumed 'mainly in a university context': he is 'a writer for academics' (p. 121). In contrast, Rachel Polonsky examines Shelley's significant political influence in Russia, beginning with an analysis of the Russian poet Anna Akhmatova, who 'had been out of official favour ... since 1925' (p. 229). In 1936 Akhmatova began an ultimately aborted translation of Shelley's *The Cenci*, which coincided with her re-entering the publishing world from which she had been absent for eleven years. Polonsky asks whether there is 'any significance in the fact that Akhmatova was contemplating a translation of Shelley's revenge drama at the very time when ... her poetic voice was moving into a new register ... in which to address the subject of Stalin's tyranny' (p. 230). Such highlights give a flavour of a vast, if not comprehensive, volume that excitingly probes Shelley's reception in a dizzyingly broad range of languages, from Catalan and Greek to Bulgarian and Romanian. The range exhibited in its eighteen chapters demonstrates that the history of Shelley's reception in Europe has yet to be fully mapped, but this volume goes a considerable way to achieving that aim.

Shelley's afterlives are also considered in a fine piece by Diane Long Hoeveler, 'The Literal and Literary Circulation of Amelia Curran's Portrait of Percy Shelley' (*WC* 38[2008] 27–30). The portrait formed the model for Jeffrey Aspen's as it is discussed in Henry James's *The Aspen Papers*. James, for Hoeveler, shows how 'the obsessive power of literary and scholarly desire' attempts to seize and resurrect 'fetishized and dead male Romantic poets' (p. 27) for the masculine literary tradition. Michael Rossington reconsiders the politics of Shelley's *History of a Six Weeks' Tour*, co-authored with Mary Shelley, in 'Rousseau and Tacitus: Republican Inflections in the Shelleys' *History of a Six Weeks' Tour*' (*ERR* 19[2008] 321–33), discovering a new element: republicanism. The travel book's focus on ruins and landscape train attention on a history of tyranny and monarchy, suggesting, for Rossington, that Shelley's interest in the Tacitean tradition may have been much more extensive than previously thought. The Shelleys' interests in Europe are further considered in 'The Shelleys and the Idea of "Europe"' (*ERR* 19[2008] 335–49) by Paul Stock. Stock's fine piece considers *Frankenstein* and *Laon and Cythna*, analysing the way in which 'Europe' becomes a remarkably capacious term in the Shelley circle: a less ideal version of 'America' and a site of moral and sexual fluidity. Michael Demson's 'The Disobedient Disciple: Shelley's Divergence from Godwin's Guidance on History and Political Practice' (in Lussier and Matsunaga, eds., *Engaged Romanticism: Romanticism as Praxis*, pp. 113–27) explores Shelley's movement, through 'Queen Mab', 'Alastor' and 'The Revolt of Islam', away from Godwin's influence. Shelley became increasingly interested in other historians' ideas of social progress, and in doing so was ultimately disappointed by his early tutor and father-in-law.

Michael Gamer's 'Shelley Incinerated' (*WC* 38[2008] 23–6) considers the attempts to shape the Shelley myth by the likes of Trelawny, Hunt and Mary Shelley, placing their efforts in the context of contemporary print culture and what Jeffrey Cox has theorized as the habit in Romantic writers of forming themselves into groups in opposition to others. Michael O'Neill makes an eloquent call for not simply reinterpretation of past writers, but also reconsideration of past criticism of those writers, in 'A.C. Bradley's Views of Shelley's Poetry and Poetics' (*Romanticism* 14[2008] 36–46). Much of the value of Bradley's subtle and thoughtful engagement with Shelley lies, for O'Neill, in the 'tactful' way in which Bradley does not turn Shelley into a 'mouthpiece' for his own convictions. George C. Grinnell's 'Ethics in the Face of Terror: Shelley and Biometrics' (*RECPS* 30[2008] 332–51) argues that the response to terror must be more responsible than the anger found in many governments. Shelley's 'On the Medusa of Leonardo da Vinci' is just such a response, for Grinnell, a response to Peterloo that understands the alterity of terror. Of biographical interest is Dana M. Lawton-Balejko's 'A Lost Shelley Letter in Boston College's Francis Thompson Archive' (*KSJ* 57[2008] 25–31), which prints and discusses a letter to Richard Hayward, Godwin's solicitor, shedding new light on Shelley's monetary transactions in 1815. A timely piece by Roman Sympos, 'Enchanted Archive: Influence, Dissemination and Media Transformation in Shelley's "Ode to the West Wind"' (*RaVoN* 50[2008] 18

paras), understands the 'dead leaves' of 'Ode to the West Wind' in reference to
Shelley's concerns over textual transmission. The ode's references to Dante
and Virgil suggest a recognition of the unstable nature of textual mediation in
a period when the scroll was being replaced by the book. This in turn becomes
a reflection on Shelley's own textual moment, providing a fitting insight into
our own culture's anxieties about printed and digital media. Ann Wroe's
'Good Self, Bad Self: The Struggle in Shelley' (*RaVoN* 51[2008] 31 paras)
provides an elegant understanding of Shelley's conflicted understanding of the
relation between the soul and the body. For all his disdain for a soul/body
duality, Shelley often registered a proto-Yeatsian sense of being tied to a dying
animal. As Wroe shows, this allowed Shelley to explore ideas of liberation and
empathy. Eric Gidal's '"O Happy Earth! reality of Heaven!": Melancholy and
Utopia in Romantic Climatology' (*JEMCS* 8[2008] 74–101) offers a
fascinating analysis of Shelley's 'utopian vision' that incorporates both
political and environmental harmony. Gidal posits that 'today's readers may
or may not sympathize with [Shelley's] political and aesthetic motivations', but
argues that the poet's 'association of climate change with earthly happiness
offers us a tragically misguided vision that should raise questions about
Romantic affiliations with modern environmental imperatives' (p. 75). In
'Panoptic Perspectives in Shelley's "Mont Blanc": Collapsed Distance and the
Alpine Sublime' (*Expl* 67:i[2008] 30–3), Joan Reiss Wry insightfully argues
that 'Shelley's experience of "astonishment" and his cognitive response to
sublimity are noticeably different in "Mont Blanc" from those of his
contemporaries' (p. 30), concluding that Shelley 'creates a panopticon that
brings the natural world into focus even as it opens a lens into the infinite'
(p. 33).

Jacqueline M. Labbe's 'Smith, Wordsworth and the Model of the Romantic
Poet' (*RaVoN* 51[2008] 18 paras) reconsiders the notion of Romantic poetic
subjectivity, moving away from a notion of sincerity towards a more
performative model. Charlotte Smith and Wordsworth, in *Beachy Head* and
The Prelude, self-reflexively interrogate and question their own status as poets.
In the end, a poet is most interesting when he or she is least solidly defined.
Labbe's '"The absurdity of animals having the passions and the faculties of
man": Charlotte Smith's Fables (1807)' (*ERR* 19[2008] 157–62) examines
Smith's rejuvenation of the fable. In both her *Natural History of Birds* and
Beachy Head she turns to fabulists such as Aesop and La Fontaine, but moves
beyond her source material, producing work of a darkly disturbing nature.
Angus Whitehead's 'An Allusion to ". . . All the Ghosts in the Red Sea . . ." in
Charlotte Smith's *The Old Manor House* (1794)' (*N&Q* 55[2008] 28–9)
discusses Smith's allusion to the practice in exorcisms of banishing
mischievous ghosts to the Red Sea. Whitehead suggests that in preferring
the vengeance of malevolent ghosts to the discovery of his lover Monimia,
Orlando 'reveals the extent of his fears for her' (p. 29).

Southey studies have revived remarkably of late, largely owing to the
splendid efforts of Lynda Pratt and Tim Fulford. The first major scholarly
edition of his early poetry was produced under their care in 2004, while their
online edition of over 7,000 letters will be published in 2009. They reflect on
this process of 'putting Southey back together again' (p. 187) in a fine article,

'Editing Robert Southey for the twenty-first century' (*ERR* 19[2008] 187–97). They claim for him a strong sense of literary quality (he was 'the foremost radical poet of the day', p. 189) but recognize also his 'frustrating' qualities. No 'Bloomian strong predecessor', he was a 'precursor' who opened new ground upon which later poets built stronger foundations having learned from his mistakes.

Paul H. Fry's *Wordsworth and the Poetry of What We Are* is one of the more remarkable books published this year. The book offers an original thesis. Rather than, as Hazlitt put it, finding in nature only a reflection of his over-inflated ego, Wordsworth's most powerful insight is 'the exhilarated feeling of unity inspired by the indifference, the lack of meaning, in all registers of nonhuman being' (p. 21). Wordsworth discovers what Fry calls an 'ontic' oneness in nature: all things, including rocks and stones and trees, and humans, exist on the same level, sharing a fundamental 'nonhumanity'. This produces an ontological, and not a political, 'levelling'. Indeed, Fry's work offers itself as avowedly non-political, much in contrast to the dominant theme in Wordsworth criticism. Both ecological and new historicist criticism miss the point of Wordsworth's non-human humanism: Fry positions himself as 'neither red nor green but gray, not dull gray but gleaming at times the way rocks...gleam at times' (p. 73). Fry begins by distinguishing Wordsworth from his two most significant early critics, Coleridge and Jeffrey. *The Prelude*, Fry argues, is 'a poem that compulsively quarrels with Coleridge' (p. 130), but the roots of that disagreement are deeper and earlier than previously thought. Despite convincing themselves that they agreed with each other, there is a fundamental lack of fit between a Coleridgean imagination (which seeks to *create* unity) and a Wordsworthian imagination (which *discovers* unity). Jeffrey is an example of a different strain of misunderstanding, a 'Regency voice' that sees value in the natural world only in that it may 'enliven metaphors for human feelings' (p. 42). Wordsworth swerves from these positions, creating verse that compulsively finds value in an almost deadening minerality in all things. The book covers work early and late, including at its centre a superb pair of chapters on *The Prelude* and *The Excursion*. It is particularly welcome to read such fine, attentive criticism of *The Excursion*. Indeed Fry's greatest strength is his subtle weighing up and elucidation of Wordsworth's poetry. The book is philosophically adept but also critically subtle, often offering superb close readings of individual lines. It is a fresh, even jaunty excursus which everywhere speaks of Fry's abiding enthusiasm for his subject.

Late Wordsworth is beginning to receive its share of attention, diminishing if not dispelling the myth of what Harold Bloom called the 'longest dying in poetic history'. James M. Garratt's *Wordsworth and the Writing of the Nation* is in this tradition, if rather ambivalently. He pays far more attention to post-Great Decade Wordsworth, but he does caution us: 'this should not be taken as a call for greater appreciation of the later Wordsworth' (p. 8). This later period is central to his study because it was the period in which Wordsworth was most strenuously active in creating and defining his own self-image. He became a public writer, and in doing so he was, Garratt argues, increasingly interested in *writing* that public. More particularly, his efforts at self-definition precisely mirrored attempts to define the nation. Garratt mounts a remarkably persuasive new-historical 'context' to the writing: the efforts of cartographers and ethnographers to map Britain. The comically inept work of Thomas Larcom is particularly telling. He attempted to capture that nation in microscopic detail, but was continually defeated in his attempt to produce imperial abstraction by the prevalence of local detail. Wordsworth, as Garratt points out, is a poet who seems both too abstract and too particular, but this might be conceived of as a strength. Garratt follows Benedict Arnold in understanding that imperial mapping as manifested in the census, the map and the museum. Wordsworth was interested in all three, and his idea of himself and his idea of the nation often intersected. He was himself a 'national treasure', and just as his attempt to understand himself was torn between discordant detail and abstract unity, so his sense of the nation he was writing was an unstable phenomenon. Garratt pays welcome attention to a period of Wordsworth's career that is perversely understudied given that it was precisely this period in which Wordsworth's canonical status was achieved. His historicizing is subtle and cogent, but the book's real strength is its explanation of the paradoxes of Wordsworth's poetry and public persona.

It has been a good year for editions. *Lyrical Ballads*, the collection that, in many accounts, launched Romanticism, has often been reprinted, but never in a wholly satisfactory edition. The aesthetic whole that the 1798 edition offered, beginning with the 'Ancyent Marinere' and ending at 'Tintern Abbey', is something one would not like to tamper with. And yet the 1800 edition, with its 'Preface', its 'Hart-Leap Well' and its 'Lucy Gray', adds elements of central significance that a good edition could not be without. Michael Gamer and Dahlia Porter, in yet another splendid Broadview edition, have provided the solution that scholars and students have longed for. This remarkable volume provides both the 1798 and 1800 volumes in full. But more than this; in eight appendices, they provide an astonishing wealth of extra material. There are twenty-one reviews of the two editions, the extra material that Wordsworth added in 1802, important correspondence involving Joseph Cottle, Charles Lamb, Charles James Fox and others, commentary on the volume by Wordsworth, Hazlitt and Coleridge, a list detailing how Coleridge and Wordsworth dispersed the poems under different heading in subsequent editions, full texts of poems Coleridge intended for *Lyrical Ballads*, a splendid 'Further Reading' list and even maps of the world, Britain and the Lake District showing where the poems were situated. A simple but effective introduction combines an account of the publishing and personal histories behind the two collections as well as reminding us that the poems retain their vitality aesthetically and morally as 'invitations to think' (p. 21). Two of the most important appendices are those which detail the prose and poetic sources for the *Lyrical Ballads*. These, in combination with the editors' apt footnotes to the poem, allow the reader to map both how closely the volume was intertwined with its historical moment and also how startlingly new it was. This is a volume that will surely become a standard in the field, a vital tool in teaching and scholarship, and more than one could possibly have hoped for.

An excellent discussion of the Bartholomew Fair section of Book VII of *The Prelude* is found in Benjamin P. Myers's 'Wordsworth's Financial

Sublime: Money and Meaning in Book VII of *The Prelude*' (*SCRev* 25[2008] 80–90). The fair was one in which everything was for sale and anything had a price; Myers considers this to be the fact that Wordsworth responded to most strongly, creating a 'financial sublime' out of the frenzied activities of the commercial revolution. Alberto Gabriele's rather ambitious 'Visions of the City of London: Mechanical Eye and Poetic Transcendence in Wordsworth's *Prelude*, Book 7' (*ERR* 19[2008] 365–84) reconsiders the supposed 'failure of vision' in the account of London, arguing instead that Wordsworth engages with contemporary artistic innovations and attempts to capture the fragmentation of experience. This is a welcome reappraisal of the poem, particularly in giving so much respect to Wordsworth's experimental method. There were two fine pieces on *The Prelude* in the *Charles Lamb Bulletin*. George Soule, in 'John Wordsworth's Death and the End of *The Prelude*' (*ChLB* 141[2008] 2–12), speculates that Wordsworth needed a low to counterbalance the highs of Snowdon, and that he found precisely that in early 1805 with the death of his brother Jonathan. Katherine Calloway returns to an old issue in 'Wordsworth's *The Prelude* as Autobiographical Epic' (*ChLB* 141[2008] 13–19): is *The Prelude* properly an epic, or is it autobiography? The question, she argues, misses the point: the poem 'resolves itself into *both* an epic narrative and an autobiography' (p. 13). David Chandler's 'The Importance of *The Three-Part Prelude*' (*EIC* 58[2008] 193–209) considers the many revisions and reworkings of *The Prelude* that have recently come to light. Jonathan Wordsworth reported seventeen distinct versions; Chandler proposes the importance of another. This three-part poem, which Wordsworth worked on between 1801 and 1803, is significant, Chandler suggests, in part because it was a 'failure, a wrong turn' (p. 206), which led Wordsworth to reconsider the relationship between outer and inner that he lost in this version. A chapter of E.L. Risden's *Heroes: Gods and the Role of Epiphany in English Epic Poetry* (a book which makes a strong claim for the ongoing significance of the epic genre) treats *The Prelude*. Wordsworth's epic straddles the internal and the external, and Risden places, at times a little simplistically, Wordsworth's epiphanic spots of time in an epic tradition.

Welcome attention was given to *The Excursion* in Jonathan Farina's '"The mighty commonwealth of things": The Deep Characters of Knowledge in Wordsworth's *Excursion*' (*WC* 38[2008] 11–15). Farina picks up on the particular emphasis Wordsworth gives to material 'things' in the poem, subtly investigating his philosophical understanding of the material and the immaterial. The later poetry was also considered by Michael Timko in 'Superstition, the National Imaginary, and Religious Politics in Wordsworth's *Ecclesiastical Sketches*' (*WC* 38[2008] 16–19). Timko shifts the terms of debate away from enthusiasm towards a post-Reformation opposition to Catholic superstition, showing how Wordsworth's fears over the proposed Catholic Emancipation Bill are shadowed in *Ecclesiastical Sketches* with an attraction to the mysteries of Britain's Catholic past. Wordsworth's later poetry has long been an embarrassment to critics; his 'Ode to Duty', however, is worse still, a late (conservative) poem written in the Great Decade. Yet the apparent choice between imagination (early) and duty (late) is a false one, as Jacob Risinger points out in 'Wordsworth's Imaginative Duty' (*Romanticism*

14[2008] 207–18). From the first, as he argues, imagination and duty were, for Wordsworth, essentially connected.

Marilyn Gaull subtly explores the contemporary and subsequent references in two familiar phrases of Wordsworth's in '"Things forever speaking" and "Objects of all thought"' (*WC* 38[2008] 52–5), comparing and contrasting 'things' and 'objects'. The subject is pursued by Charles J. Rzepka in 'To Be a Thing: Wordsworth's "A slumber did my spirit seal" and the Paradox of Corporealization' (*WC* 38[2008] 56–61). Rzepka's elegant article carefully and quietly opens up an oft-studied poem, concluding ultimately that Wordsworth's poem reflects simply on what it is to be. The same poem is considered by M.D. Walhout in 'Sealed Eyes and Phantom Lovers: The First Line of "A Slumber did my Spirit Seal"' (*WC* 38[2008] 93–101). Walhout discusses the poetic precedents for 'sealing', suggesting that William Hayley and Charlotte Smith are the most likely precursors for Wordsworth's striking image. Adam Potkay's 'Wordsworth and the Ethics of Things' (*PMLA* 123[2008] 390–404) provided the prompt for these essays. In it Potkay, building on Spinoza and Heidegger, argues for a position close to that maintained by Paul Fry, such that Wordsworth produces an ecological ethics based on his understanding of an ontological oneness shared with all things. Anne Ferry's *By Design: Intention in Poetry* includes two fine, elegant chapters on Wordsworth, '*Thing* and *Things*: Wordsworth, Stevens, Ashbery' (pp. 83–107) and 'Optical Illusions: Wordsworth and his Inheritors' (pp. 108–30), which meditate on similar topics. The first investigates the ground between transcendence and immanence covered by that key term, 'thing'. He, like his inheritors, seems caught, Coleridge-like, between the concept and the object, between imagination and reality. The second extends the discussion of the distinction between vision and visionary, placing the discussion in the context of an evolving scientific discourse of sight. The book as a whole is concerned with the subtle changes that signal conscious poetic intention, and here Wordsworth's modest uncertainty about that distinction is subtly revealed.

Dewey W. Hall's 'Wordsworth and Emerson: Aurora Borealis and the Question of Influence' (*RaVoN* 50[2008] 16 paras) considers the remarkable transatlantic cross-currents between Wordsworth and Emerson. This is a matter of light, and electricity, for Hall. Emerson's *The Poet* was influenced by Faraday, but also by the Preface to *Lyrical Ballads*. Inspiration for both poets is at once terrestrial and celestial. Robin Jarvis places Wordsworth's oddly neglected 'Stepping Westward' in a context that is literary, biographical and geographical in 'Madoc in Scotland: A Transatlantic Perspective on "Stepping Westward"' (*ERR* 19[2008] 149–56). Wordsworth's grief for his brother, his recent reading of Southey's American epic *Madoc* and fears over national security all put pressure on the poem, introducing an unlikely transatlantic perspective that Jarvis convincingly makes a case for.

Evasion has been a key trope in Wordsworth studies for more than two decades, most notably in discussions of 'Tintern Abbey'. The kind of criticism which sought to accuse Wordsworth of ideological sneakiness in the poem has been largely supplanted, but, as John Hughes shows in his excellent article 'The Poetics of Orphanhood: Wordsworth's "Salisbury Plain", "The Vale of

Esthwaite" and "Tintern Abbey"' (*Romanticism* 14[2008] 219–31), even the work of critics such as Nicholas Roe and David Bromwich has maintained the habit. Hughes proposes that the poem ought to be considered as therapeutic, considered with the 'speaker's struggle, inevitably linguistic, with his own obscurity to himself' (p. 220). Brian Bates's 'Activating "Tintern Abbey" in 1815' (in Lussier and Matsunaga, eds., pp. 69–81) picks up on Wordsworth's decision to change the title of the poem in 1815 from 'Lines Written' to 'Lines Composed'. This has typically been taken to signify a movement away from the physical act of writing towards a more spontaneous, oral form of creativity, but Bates argues that, placed in context, it is part of an attempt to enter the book-selling marketplace. The poem is also considered in Scott Hess's '"Tintern Abbey's" Environmental Legacy' (in Lussier and Matsunaga, eds., pp. 82–99). Hess reassesses the claims of the likes of Jonathan Bate that the poem is eco-friendly by insisting that ecology be understood in terms of 'cultural and social practices' (p. 83). In the end, Hess concludes, Wordsworth is less interested in these than in the individual consciousness. Bruce Matsunaga takes a slightly different view in 'The Nature of Ecology in Wordsworth's Early Poetry' (in Lussier and Matsunaga, eds., pp. 100–12). Matsunaga uses the work of D.W. Winnicott to explore the epistemological process that Wordsworth engages in. Wordsworth has lessons for contemporary 'deep ecologists' in recognizing the interrelation of natural objects and seeing nature as an independent subject.

Mary Jacobus's '"Distressful Gift": Talking to the Dead' (in Halsey and Slinn, eds., *The Concept and Practice of Conversation in the Long Eighteenth Century, 1688–1848*, pp. 40–64) unlocks Wordsworth, Blanchot and Derrida's understanding of speech. The chapter begins with Wordsworth's grief over his brother's death. With that death, Wordsworth realized that conversations were always connected with death: not an exchange, but an intimation of silence. Jacobus's 'The Ordinary Sky: Wordsworth, Blanchot, and the Writing of Disaster' (*RCPS* [2008] 23 paras) begins with the observation of the glinting sun on a wet road that underpinned two early works towards 'The Ruined Cottage', both of which were gestures towards psychic suffering. Jacobus links these sights to Blanchot and Derrida, suggesting the troubling autobiographical implications of ordinary sights which cover over unrecognized trauma.

Robert Hale builds on the work of Joshua Gonsalves in 'Wordsworth's "The Mad Mother": The Poetics and Politics of Identification' (*WC* 38[2008] 108–14). The tension between the mother and the balladeer changes as Wordsworth continued to revise his corpus. Where, initially, the balladeer sympathizes with the mother, later editions separated the two voices until, finally, the balladeer controls the mother. Markus Poetzsch's 'Vying for "Brilliant Landscapes": Claude Mirrors, Wordsworth, and Poetic Vision' (*WC* 38[2008] 114–20) shows how the Claude Mirror and the poetic seer were competing figures, both attempting to defamiliarize the familiar. 'Wordsworth's resistance to the picturesque', he argues, is 'a strategic and targeted reaction to Gilpin's technological circumvention of poetic imagination' (p. 115). Wordsworth, unlike Coleridge, seems at odds with Germany, but as Alan G. Hill demonstrates in 'Wordsworth's Reception in Germany: Some Unfamiliar Episodes and Contacts, 1798–1849' (*RES* 59[2008] 568–81), by the 1820s things began to change. The *Ecclesiastical Sonnets* were an influence on Baron Bunsen, and more generally his account of visionary power began to attract new, post-Enlightenment readers. Fiona Stafford's 'Plain Living and Ungarnish'd Stories: Wordsworth and the Survival of Pastoral' (*RES* 59[2008] 118–33) uncovers, in remarkably subtle ways, the importance of paying attention to the detail of Wordsworth's 'Michael', a poem that is, she argues, itself a meditation on the significance of the minute. Yet close attention to detail does not come at the expense of an interest in wider concerns. Wordsworth, Stafford argues, revitalizes the pastoral to explore the health of the nation. Wordsworth famously aimed to 'create the taste by which he would be judged', and in the later 1810s a rash of paratexts seemed increasingly to manipulate and control the reader's reading of his work. It was, argues Brian Bates's 'J.H. Reynolds Re-echoes the Wordsworthian Reputation: "Peter Bell", Remaking the Work and Mocking the Man' (*SiR* 47[2008] 273–97), a tactic that J.H. Reynolds ruthlessly and brilliantly undermined in his parodic 'Peter Bell'.

5. Drama

Introducing *'Utopianism and Joanna Baillie'*, a collection in the *Romantic Circles Praxis Series*, Regina Hewitt looks to the return of utopianism in political philosophy for a new way to understand Baillie's dramatic project. Utopian thinking is increasingly seen as a way of constructing standpoints for critique rather than as the production of schematic blueprints for future societies. In its ambitious speculation about how personal, affective transformation might bring about social change, and its concern with procedural as well as substantive justice, Baillie's *Introductory Discourse* to her *Series of Plays* on the passions has significant affinities, Hewitt argues, with the new utopianism, such that contemporary sociology would gain from recognizing her as an important predecessor. The essay that Hewitt contributes to the volume, 'Joanna Baillie's Ecotopian Communities' (*RCPS* [2008] 43 paras), provides an important step towards framing an ecocritical perspective on Baillie's drama. Drawing upon Joseph Meeker's *The Comedy of Survival*, she reads Baillie's comedies as texts that treat sociability as evolutionary rather than teleological, or developmental rather than designed. Presenting complex characters emphatically shaped by their circumstances, they envisage 'somber and tentative adaptations' towards successful dwelling in community. In particular, *The Second Marriage* and *The Alienated Manor* 'deal explicitly with the "recoding" of natural and cultural spaces, public and private spheres'.

In the rest of the volume, Thomas McLean provides a new chronology of Baillie's letters, which supplies fresh information about the dating of 200 letters in the standard collected edition and incorporates the details of some 240 others not included there. Robert C. Hale describes Baillie's *Poems* of 1790 as sympathetic to the spirit of the French Revolution, and sees the book's pastoral scenes as essentially egalitarian. William D. Brewer discusses Baillie's two tragedies on fear, *Orra* and *The Dream*. Superstitious fear brings about reversals in gender roles, giving Orra bursts of physical strength and reducing General Osterloo to helpless tears. Our imagination humanizes us, Baillie shows, but can destroy us when it grows too vivid. Marjean D. Purinton analyses three Baillie comedies—*The Match*, *Enthusiasm* and *The Second Marriage*—in relation to the construction of gender in medical science and pseudo-science. Elsewhere, Gioia Angeletti, in 'Scottish Women Playwrights: Gender and Performativity in Romantic Theatre' (in Lunan, Macdonald and Sassi, eds., pp. 31–49), looks beyond Baillie to discuss metatheatrical plays by three other female Scottish dramatists of the period: Jean Marshall's sentimental comedy *Sir Harry Gaylove*, Christian Carstairs's bizarre, manic *The Hubble-Shue*, and *Sardanapalus*, in which Mary Diana Dods reflects on her own disruption of gender roles.

Byron at the Theatre, the latest in a series of volumes on Byron edited by Peter Cochran, pays particular attention to his neoclassical aesthetics, most notably in Bernard Beatty's 'Untrammelled Will and Suppressed Reason: Byron's Neo-Classical Theatre' (pp. 163–74). For Beatty, Romantic drama privileges characters above their historical contexts and appeals to the sympathy of its audience in order finally to affirm the innocence of its criminal heroes. In this respect, Byron's oriental tales are similar to the dominant drama of his day, but his neoclassical tragedies are the very opposite— Racinean rather than Corneillean. The neoclassical tragedies implicitly 'despise' the contemporary theatre because it cannot allow for 'a restriction which is external to consciousness but which...foreground[s] responsibility and culpability rather than innocence in the tragic protagonists' (p. 174). It is in *Manfred*, Beatty says, that Byron's emphasis shifts from the individualistic will to the restrictive force of history. The collection opens with a pair of essays by Peter Cochran that give a vivid conspectus of early nineteenth-century theatrical culture. 'Byron and Drury Lane' (pp. 1–35) describes Byron's snobbish ignorance of professional stagecraft, while 'Byron, Alfieri and the Writing of Plays' (pp. 36–58) recovers the influence on Byron of Vittorio Alfieri, whose tragedy *Mirra*, Byron said, 'threw me into convulsions'. *Sardanapalus* and the two Venetian tragedies are indebted to Alfieri, but for Cochran the influence was not an especially helpful one, because Alfieri too was more interested in the idea of drama than the practical challenge of writing for performance. Elsewhere in the collection, Malcolm Kelsall discusses atavistic masculinity in Baillie and Byron, and then engages in a sweeping polemic against 'the feminist approach to Baillie' (p. 74); Irina Shiskova proposes that in *Faust* Goethe sought 'to purify and save [Byron's] image in the eyes of his admirers and foes' (p. 83); and Monika Coghen argues that Byron found it politically tempting to forgo Gothic dramatic devices in his historical tragedies, but ultimately could not resist the appeal of a Shakespearian Gothic mode. Other essays explore *The Two Foscari*, *The Deformed Transformed*, and Rudolf Nureyev's ballet version of *Manfred*.

Another essay by Peter Cochran, 'Byron Tries to Reform the London Stage' (in Cochran, ed. *Byron in London*, pp. 114–30), describes in more detail Byron's involvement with Drury Lane Theatre: his authorship of its reopening address in 1812, and his membership of its inept management committee in

1815. Marjean D. Purinton's 'Watches and Watching Time in British Romantic Comedy' (*WC* 39[2008] 46–9) associates tropes of timekeeping, belatedness and wasted time in stage comedies by Baillie, Elizabeth Inchbald and Fanny Burney, among others, with the development of watch-making and the regimentation of time in industrial production. A short but very stimulating essay by Christoph Bode, 'Crossing and Re-Crossing Borders: The Ethical Aporia of Anomy in Wordsworth's *The Borderers*' (*ZAA* 56[2008] 317–24), reads Wordsworth's *The Borderers* as a reflection upon the problems of acting ethically in situations where no common moral law or standard exists to guide us. Wordsworth presents a world in which 'we are ethically called upon to act for ourselves…while at the same time we never have all the information that is necessary and prerequisite for responsible action' (p. 320).

Celestine Woo's *Romantic Actors and Bardolatry: Performing Shakespeare from Garrick to Kean* covers similar ground to Reiko Oya's *Representing Shakespearean Tragedy*, discussed here last year. Woo describes the ways in which David Garrick, John Philip Kemble, Sarah Siddons and Edmund Kean served as 'shapers and catalysts of discourse' about Shakespeare (p. 2), focusing not on their performances as such but on the understandings of Shakespeare that they promoted and made use of. She is especially concerned with the growth of a mass popular culture of Shakespeare appreciation, and in this respect Garrick is the book's hero. Woo describes his innovations in 'marketing Shakespeare to the middle class' (p. 29), and this commercial nous is seen appreciatively as the basis for his contributions to theatre practice and to Shakespearian textual scholarship. Garrick and Siddons, Woo writes, served the public as proxies for Shakespeare himself, whereas Kemble and Kean achieved greatness by their ability to represent 'the current mood of society' (p. 134). The chapter on Kemble stresses his political conservatism and his success in inculcating a nationalistic 'appropriation' of Shakespeare, while that on Siddons argues that her lofty dignity effected a challenge to rigid constructions of gender. The last, on Kean, sees him as 'a star actor who embodied the pleasure of private reading' (p. 139). He became an emblem for interiorized characterology, even though his own dramatic theory turned instead on the importance of honed set-piece flourishes. Uttara Natarajan offers a rewarding examination of the relationship between Kean and Romantic aesthetics in 'Hazlitt and Kean' (*HazlittR* 1[2008] 17–26). Natarajan analyses Hazlitt's great sequence of reviews of Kean's Shakespearian performances in 1814 and 1815, and shows that 'Hazlitt finds that the unity of Shakespeare's sublime characterizations is too frequently undermined by the variety of Kean's dramatic resources' (p. 19). The very brilliance of Kean's representations emphasizes the split between the playwright's original conception and its reproduction on stage. Hazlitt does not, though, share Coleridge's and Lamb's dubiety about the staging of Shakespeare. Instead, he endorses Kean on the basis of the high Romantic ideal of the 'attempt, which, in failing, retains something of the infinitude of its object' (p. 26).

Michael Gamer and Robert Miles's 'Gothic Shakespeare on the Romantic Stage' (in Drakakis and Townshend, eds., *Gothic Shakespeares*, pp. 131–52) offers both an incisive account of the complex relationship between

Englishness, Shakespeare and the rise of Shakespeare-inspired German sensation drama, and a detailed reading of William Henry Ireland's Shakespeare forgery *Vortigern*. The play is seen as a multidirectional political allegory, at once Jacobite and staunchly Protestant, both Jacobin and invested in a fantasy of transcendent English nationhood. In its handling of the mythic relationships between Scots, Britons and Saxons, it tries 'to represent British history as at once inevitable, tragic and providential' (p. 148). In 'The Personating of Queens: Lady Macbeth, Sarah Siddons, and the Creation of Female Celebrity in the Late Eighteenth Century' (in Moschovakis, ed. *Macbeth: New Critical Essays*, pp. 240–57), Laura Engel links Sarah Siddons's regal self-presentation both to that of Queen Charlotte and to her performances as Lady Macbeth. If Siddons's portrayal of her most famous role was always understood in dialogue with her own public image as the era's most acclaimed female actor, then her 'Remarks on the Character of Lady Macbeth' might be 'seen as conveying Siddons's subtle musings on the physical and emotional price she paid for her extraordinary fame' (p. 252). Judith Pascoe reflects on Siddons's voice and 'the way in which that voice was cultivated, rehearsed, consumed and memorialized' (p. 3) in 'Sarah Siddons, Theatre Voices and Recorded Memory' (*ShS* 61[2008] 1–12). Via a discussion of Wordsworth's 'The Solitary Reaper', Pascoe analyses the detailed notes on Siddons's performances made by George Bell. Bell was concerned with the effect Siddons had on her audiences at the time; other recording strategies, though, raised the possibility of transcribing a performance so as to make it possible to re-create it at a later date, and in doing so anticipated the phonograph's mechanical reproduction of sound.

Political theatre was the other main concern this year. Jon Mee sheds new light on Robert Merry's politics in '*The Magician No Conjuror*: Robert Merry and the Political Alchemy of the 1790s' (in Davis and Pickering, eds., *Unrespectable Radicals? Popular Politics in the Age of Reform*, pp. 41–55). Merry—who in the early 1790s was trying to forge a career as 'the English poet of the French Revolution' (p. 42)—may have intended his Covent Garden comic opera partly as a satire on Pitt, which would help to explain its relative failure. The post-revolutionary turbulence left him more a radical than a Whig; spied upon, he retreated to the United States. In 'Remembering Elizabeth Inchbald's *The Massacre*: Romantic Cosmopolitanism, Sectarian History, and Religious Difference' (*ERR* 19[2007] 1–18), Michael Tomko reads Inchbald's tragedy in the context of her Catholicism and of the contested British responses to the French clergy who fled to England after the 1792 September Massacres. The play asks us to imagine a cosmopolitan community in which internecine hatreds can be overcome without local identities having to be abandoned, but also warns us how easily such tolerance can fall prey to mistrust. Fredrick Burwick's 'Gateway to Heterotopia: Elsewhere on Stage' (in Cass and Peer, eds., pp. 27–39) discusses the 'documentary' dramas that staged re-enactments of sensational recent crimes, and compares them to a wide range of plays—by Inchbald, Richard Sheridan, Felicia Hemans, Byron and others—that were set in foreign countries but could be understood as commenting on local current affairs.

Between the outbreak of the Peninsular War in 1808 and the destruction of the liberal constitutional settlement in 1823, Spanish affairs were central to the European political imagination. Diego Saglia's 'Spanish Stages: British Romantic Tragedy and the Theatrical Politics of Spain, 1808–1823' (*ERR* 19[2008] 19–32) shows that during this period Spain was so useful to dramatists as a way of exploring racial, cultural and religious politics, as well as dealing indirectly with contemporary Britain, that reviewers voiced 'regular complaints about the excessive number of plays about Spain' on the London stage (p. 25). Saglia analyses four historical tragedies set in Spain and intended for the patent theatres: Coleridge's *Remorse*, Richard Lalor Sheil's *The Apostle* and *Bellamira*, and Lord John Russell's *Don Carlos*. *Remorse* receives the most attention: Coleridge's revisions of *Osorio* were affected by his views of the Peninsular War and in particular by his ambivalent attitude towards the nationalistic fervour that the Spanish displayed. Marjean D. Purinton's 'Teaching Orientalism through British Romantic Drama: Representations of Arabia' (in Cass and Peer, eds., pp. 135–46) shows how plays of the period— among them Richard Cumberland's *The Arab* and Hannah More's *Sacred Dramas*—might provoke students to reflect upon orientalism and the construction of racial otherness. David Worrall supplies the year's most absorbing discussion of this theme, in 'Islam on the Romantic Period Stage: Hyder Ali, Tippoo Saib and Beyond the Captivity Narrative' (in Davis and Pickering, eds., pp. 167–84). The British campaigns in India against Hyder Ali and his son Tippoo Saib, which lasted throughout the final third of the eighteenth century, generated all the racist and jingoistic stage propaganda that one would expect. Twenty years later, though, the Royal Coburg Theatre staged two remarkable plays, William Barrymore's *El Hyder* [1818] and H.M. Milner's *Tippoo Saib* [1823], that presented their protagonists as heroic Islamic patriots. 'With one dramatic stroke', Worrall writes, the radical and racially tolerant faction of the London theatre world 'totally reversed almost a generation of East India Company propaganda' (p. 169).

Books Reviewed

Beatty, Bernard, Tony Howe, and Charles E. Robinson, eds. *Liberty and Poetic Licence: New Essays on Byron*. LiverUP. [2008] pp. viii + 244. £44.95 ISBN 9 7808 0532 3589 7.

Bentley, G. E. Jr. *William Blake's Conversations: A Compilation, Concordance, and Rhetorical Analysis*. Mellen. [2008] pp. xlix + 297. £74.95 ISBN 9 7807 7344 8483.

Bieri, James. *Percy Bysshe Shelley: A Biography*. JHUP. [2008] pp. xi + 832. £60 ISBN 9 7808 0188 8601.

Burwick, Frederick, and James C. McKusick, eds. *Faustus from the German of Goethe: Translated by Samuel Taylor Coleridge*. OUP. [2007] pp. 343. £98 ISBN 9 7801 9922 9680.

Cass, Jeffrey, and Larry Peer, eds. *Romantic Border Crossings*. Ashgate. [2008] pp. xii + 225. £55 ISBN 9 7807 5466 0514.

Chandler, James, and Maureen N. McLane, eds. *The Cambridge Companion to British Romantic Poetry*. CUP. [2008] pp. xxi + 303. pb £15.99 ISBN 9 7805 2168 0837.

Class, Monika, and Terry F. Robinson, eds. *Transnational England: Home and Abroad, 1780–1860*. CambridgeSP. [2008] pp. xiv + 283. £39.99 ISBN 9 7814 4380 196.

Cochran, Peter, ed. *Byron in London*. CambridgeSP. [2008] pp. viii + 280. £35 ISBN 9 7818 4718 5457.

Cochran, Peter, ed. *Byron at the Theatre*. CambridgeSP. [2008] pp. ix + 218. £35 ISBN 9 7818 4718 4276.

Conlon, Pierre M. *Le Siècle des Lumières: Bibliographie chronologique*. vol. 26 [1789]. Librairie Droz S.A. [2008] pp. xx + 510. £92. ISBN 9 7826 0001 2256.

Conlon, Pierre M. *Le Siècle des Lumières: Bibliographie chronologique*. vol. 27, 2nd supplement: *1716–1789*. Librairie Droz S.A. [2008] pp. xvii + 251. £74. ISBN 9 7826 0001 2584.

Davis, Michael T., and Paul A. Pickering, eds. *Unrespectable Radicals? Popular Politics in the Age of Reform*. Ashgate. [2008] pp. xii + 224. £55 ISBN 9 7807 5465 6197.

Dolan, Elizabeth A. *Seeing Suffering in Women's Literature of the Romantic Era*. Ashgate. [2008] pp. viii + 249. £55. ISBN 9 7807 5465 4919.

Drakakis, John, and Dale Townshend, eds. *Gothic Shakespeares*. Routledge. [2008] pp. xvii + 243. hb £65 ISBN 9 7804 1542 0662, pb £20 ISBN 9 7804 1542 0679.

Edgecombe, Rodney Stenning. *A Self-Divided Poet: Form and Texture in the Verse of Thomas Hood*. CambridgeSP. [2006] pp. xxii + 230. £39.99 ISBN 1 8471 8070 1.

Ferry, Anne. *By Design: Intention in Poetry*. StanfordUP. [2008] pp. 229. £49.50 ISBN 9 7808 0475 7997.

Fielding, Penny. *Scotland and the Fictions of Geography: North Britain, 1760–1830*. CUP. [2008] pp. ix + 235. £55 ISBN 9 7805 2189 5149.

Fischerová, Andrea. *Romanticism Gendered: Male Writers as Readers of Women's Writing in Romantic Correspondence*. CambridgeSP. [2008] pp. xi + 308. £39.99 ISBN 9 7818 4718 6812.

Fitzsimmons, Lorna, ed. *International Faust Studies: Adaptation, Reception, Translation*. Continuum. [2008] pp. 299. £75 ISBN 9 7818 4706 0044.

Fry, Paul H. *Wordsworth and the Poetry of What We Are*. YaleUP. [2008] pp. xvi + 240. £35 ISBN 9 7803 0012 6488.

Fuller, David. *William Blake: Selected Poetry and Prose*. Pearson. [2008] pp xii + 376. £12.99. ISBN 9 7814 0920 4139.

Gamer, Michael, and Dahlia Porter, eds. *Lyrical Ballads 1798 and 1800 by Samuel Taylor Coleridge and William Wordsworth*. Broadview. [2008] pp. 552. pb £9.99 ISBN 9 7815 5111 6006.

Garrett, James M. *Wordsworth and the Writing of the Nation*. Ashgate. [2008] pp. x + 214. £55 ISBN 9 7807 5465 7835.

Goodenough, Elizabeth, and Andrea Immel, eds. *Under Fire: Childhood in the Shadow of War*. WSUP. [2008] pp. x + 289. pb £25.50 ISBN 9 7808 1433 4041.

Gorji, Mina. *John Clare and the Place of Poetry*. LiverUP. [2008] pp. xi + 224. £65 ISBN 9 7818 4631 1635.

Haggarty, Sarah, and Jon Mee. *Blake and Conflict*. Palgrave. [2008] pp. 256. £50 ISBN 9 7802 3057 3871.

Halsey, Katie, and Jane Slinn, eds. *The Concept and Practice of Conversation in the Long Eighteenth Century, 1688–1848*. CambridgeSP. [2008] pp. xxvi + 215. £34.99 ISBN 1 8471 8497 9.

Hecimovich, Gregg A. *Austen's 'Emma'*. Continuum. [2008] pp. 119. pb £11.99 ISBN 9 7808 2649 8489.

Henderson, Andrea K. *Romanticism and the Painful Pleasures of Modern Life*. CUP. [2008] pp. xi + 295. £52 ISBN 9 7805 2188 4020.

Heydt-Stevenson, Jillian, and Charlotte Sussman, eds. *Recognizing the Romantic Novel: New Histories of British Fiction, 1780–1830*. LiverUP. [2008] pp. 345. £65 ISBN 9 7818 4631 1628.

Hopkins, Lisa. *Relocating Shakespeare and Austen on Screen*. Palgrave. [2008] pp. 192. £50 ISBN 9 7802 3057 9552.

James, Felicity. *Charles Lamb, Coleridge and Wordsworth: Reading Friendship in the 1790s*. Palgrave. [2008] pp. xiii + 265. £45 ISBN 9 7802 3054 5243.

Johnson, Mary Lynn, and John E. Grant. *Blake's Poetry and Designs*. Norton. [2008] pp. xxvi + 628. $19.99 ISBN 9 7803 9392 4985.

Jones, Christine Kenyon, ed. *Byron: The Image of the Poet*. UDelP. [2008] pp. xiii + 129. £40.50 ISBN 9 7808 7419 9976.

Keanie, Andrew. *Hartley Coleridge: A Reassessment of his Life and Work*. Palgrave. [2008] pp. xiv + 196. £40 ISBN 9 7814 0397 4372.

Keegan, Bridget. *British Labouring-Class Nature Poetry, 1730–1837*. Palgrave. [2008] pp. xi + 220. £45 ISBN 9 7802 3053 6968.

Kelly, Ronan. *Bard of Erin: The Life of Thomas Moore*. PenguinI. [2008] pp. viii + 624. £25 ISBN 9 7818 4488 1437.

Knellwolf, Christa, and Jane Goodall, eds. *Frankenstein's Science: Experimentation and Discovery in Romantic Culture, 1780–1830*. Ashgate. [2008] pp. x + 225. £55 ISBN 9 7807 5465 4476.

Labbe, Jacqueline, ed. *Charlotte Smith in British Romanticism*. P&C. [2008] pp. 288. £60 ISBN 9 7818 5196 9456.

Leask, Nigel, and Alan Riach. *Stepping Westward*. ASLS. [2008] pp. 96. pb £9.95. ISBN 9 7809 4887 7841.

Looser, Devoney. *Women Writers and Old Age in Great Britain, 1750–1850*. JHUP. [2008] pp. 252. $55 ISBN 9 7808 0188 7055.

Lunan, Lindsey, Kirsty A. Macdonald, and Carla Sassi, eds. *Re-Visioning Scotland: New Readings of the Cultural Canon*. Lang. [2008] pp. xix + 166. pb £25.20 ISBN 9 7836 3155 0632.

Lussier, Mark, and Bruce Matsunaga, eds. *Engaged Romanticism: Romanticism as Praxis*. CambridgeSP. [2008] pp. vii + 267. £34.99 ISBN 1 8471 8914 8.

Mahood, M.M. *The Poet as Botanist*. CUP. [2008] pp. xi + 269. £50 ISBN 9 7805 2186 2363.

Maxwell, Richard, and Katie Trumpener, eds. *The Cambridge Companion to Fiction in the Romantic Period*. CUP. [2008] pp. xviii + 294. hb $90 ISBN 9 7805 2186 2523, pb $29.99 ISBN 9 7805 2168 1087.

McCarthy, William. *Anna Letitia Barbauld: Voice of the Enlightenment.* JHUP. [2008] pp. xxiv + 725. £32 ISBN 9 7808 0189 0161.

McGill, Meredith L., ed. *The Traffic in Poems: Nineteenth-Century Poetry and Transatlantic Exchange.* RutgersUP. [2008] pp. ix + 264. £62.95 ISBN 9 7808 1354 2294.

McLane, Maureen N. *Balladeering, Minstrelsy, and the Making of British Romantic Poetry.* CUP. [2008] pp. xii + 295. £55 ISBN 9 7805 2189 5757.

Miles, Robert. *Romantic Misfits.* Palgrave. [2008] pp. 256. £50 ISBN 9 7814 0398 9932.

Moschovakis, Nick, ed. *Macbeth: New Critical Essays.* Routledge. [2008] pp. xi + 363. £65 ISBN 9 7804 1597 4042.

O'Hagan, Andrew, ed. *A Night out with Robert Burns: The Greatest Poems.* Canongate. [2008] pp. xxviii + 222. pb £7.99 ISBN 9 7818 4767 1127.

O'Neill, Michael, and Charles Mahoney, eds. *Romantic Poetry: An Annotated Anthology.* Blackwell. [2008] pp. xxix + 471. pb £19.99 ISBN 9 7806 3121 3161.

Paley, Morton D. *Samuel Taylor Coleridge and the Fine Arts.* OUP. [2008] pp. xiv + 276. £45 ISBN 9 7801 9923 3052.

Pfister, Manfred, and Ralf Hertel, eds. *Performing National Identity: Anglo-Italian Cultural Exchange.* Rodopi. [2008] pp. 328. £46.43 ISBN 9 7890 4202 3147.

Poplawski, Paul, ed. *English Literature in Context.* CUP. [2008] pp. xx + 685. £18.99 ISBN 9 7805 2183 9921.

Risden, E.L. *Heroes, Gods and the Role of Epiphany in English Epic Poetry.* McFarland. [2008] pp. 204. £35.95 ISBN 9 7807 8643 5418.

Ruston, Sharon, ed. *Literature and Science.* Brewer. [2008] pp. xi + 176. £30 ISBN 9 7818 4384 1784.

Schmid, Susanne, and Michael Rossington, eds. *The Reception of P.B. Shelley in Europe.* Continuum. [2008] pp. xi + 391. £150 ISBN 9 7808 2649 5877.

Siler, Jack. *Poetic Language and Political Engagement in the Poetry of Keats.* Routledge. [2008] pp. xi + 121. £50 ISBN 0 4159 5602 1.

Stewart, John. *Byron and the Websters: The Letters and Entangled Lives of the Poet, Sir James Webster and Lady Frances Webster.* McFarland. [2008] pp. x + 214. pb £35.95 ISBN 9 7807 8643 2400.

Sudduth, Elizabeth A., and Clayton Tarr, eds. *The G. Ross Roy Collection of Robert Burns: An Illustrated Catalogue.* USCP. [2008] pp. xx + 456. £53.95 ISBN 9 7815 7003 8297.

Sutherland, Kathryn, ed. *A Memoir of Jane Austen and Other Family Recollections by James Edward Austen-Leigh.* OUP. [2008] pp. 352. pb £8.99 ISBN 9 7801 9954 0778.

Szasz, Ferenc Morton. *Abraham Lincoln and Robert Burns: Connected Lives and Legends.* SIUP. [2008] pp. xii + 242. £23.95 ISBN 9 7808 0932 8550.

Tanner, Tony. *Jane Austen.* Palgrave. [2007] pp. 312. pb £20.50 ISBN 9 7802 3000 8243.

Thanhouser, ed. *Urizen Wept: William Blake and the Sublime in Milton: A Poem.* VDM. [2008] pp. 116. £32 ISBN 9 7836 3904 9824.

Vigus, James, and Jane Wright, eds. *Coleridge's Afterlives.* Palgrave. [2008] pp. xvi + 269. £50 ISBN 9 7802 3000 8281.

Waters, Mary A. *British Women Writers of the Romantic Period: An Anthology of their Literary Criticism.* Palgrave. [2008] pp. 240. £18.99 ISBN 9 7802 3020 5772.

Weinberg, Alan M., and Timothy Webb, eds. *The Unfamiliar Shelley.* Ashgate. [2008] pp. vii + 369. £60 ISBN 9 7807 5466 3904.

Whitmarsh-Knight, David. *William Blake's Jerusalem Explained.* William Blake Press. [2008] pp. 610. $45. ISBN 9 7814 3482 1010.

Wilson, Cheryl A. *Byron: Heritage and Legacy.* Palgrave. [2008] pp. xiii + 255. £42.50 ISBN 9 7802 3060 0294.

Woo, Celestine. *Romantic Actors and Bardolatry: Performing Shakespeare from Garrick to Kean.* Lang. [2008] pp. xiii + 209. £34 ISBN 9 7814 3310 1632.

Wu, Duncan, ed. *New Writings of William Hazlitt.* 2 vols. OUP. [2007] vol. 1: pp. 507 ISBN 9 7801 9923 5735, vol. 2: pp. 553. vol. 1 vol. 2 ISBN 9 7801 9923 5742. £139.

Wunder, Jennifer N. *Keats, Hermeticism and the Secret Societies.* Ashgate. [2008] pp. 203. £55 ISBN 9 7807 5466 1863.

XIII

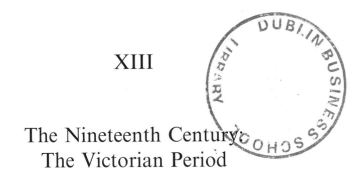

The Nineteenth Century: The Victorian Period

WILLIAM BAKER, ANNA BARTON, JANE WRIGHT,
ALEXIS EASLEY AND DAVID FINKELSTEIN

This chapter has five sections. 1. Cultural Studies and Prose; 2. The Novel; 3. Poetry; 4. Drama; 5. Publishing and Periodical History. Sections 1 and 2 are by William Baker; section 3 is by Anna Barton and Jane Wright; section 4 is by Alexis Easley; section 5 is by David Finkelstein.

1. Cultural Studies and Prose

(a) General

One of the most interesting books on the Victorians published during 2008 is Isobel Armstrong's *Victorian Glassworlds: Glass Culture and the Imagination 1830–1880*. Armstrong's premise is that glass was central to Victorian culture, although it is 'an antithetical material' (p. 11). Glass was everywhere, from windows, mirrors and greenhouses to telescopes, cameras and so on. Armstrong sees 'a period through glass'. Her book is divided into three sections. In the first, there is 'a series of case studies in the making and breaking of glass, production and conflict'. She uses 'the periodical genre of the glass factory visit'. The second Armstrong builds 'round the glassworlds of the panel, the conservatory and the window, and the exhibition'. In a third section she 'moves from fabric to images, and brings the lens of high science together with the optical toys that derived from the same technologies'. This delightfully designed book contains eighty-eight black and white illustrations and a superb coloured jacket illustration of an enamelled glass vase by Kate Hardy. Armstrong writes that 'throughout, Victorian glassworlds provide a material and conceptual site for nineteenth-century modernisms to play out their concerns. Victorian glassworlds produced a many-faceted poetics of glass' (p. 16): just one of the many superb observations in this fascinating book.

Another highlight of the year is Andrew Murphy's *Shakespeare for the People: Working Class Readers, 1800–1900*. Murphy draws upon

Year's Work in English Studies, Volume 89 (2010) © The English Association; all rights reserved
doi:10.1093/ywes/maq004

autobiographies, many unpublished manuscript materials and other evidence to explore the nineteenth-century working-class readership and interest in Shakespeare. He draws a compelling and absorbing picture of the educational, publishing and reading contexts for the fascination amongst the working classes with Shakespeare. There are two highly informative appendices: 'Autobiographers by Year of Birth' (pp. 207–17) and 'Autobiographers Listed Alphabetically' (pp. 218–20). In addition to a most helpful bibliography, there is an extensive index (pp. 237–57). A distinguished Victorianist published and unpublished essays are found in George Levine's *Realism, Ethics and Secularism: Essays on Victorian Literature and Science*. Their focus is in fact Victorian literature and science and Levine's work illuminates both. The only negative is the lack of a bibliography. A reissue with a new preface by the author of a highly influential and important study of the Victorians first published in 1966 is to be found in Steven Marcus's *The Other Victorians: A Study of Sexuality and Pornography in Mid-Nineteenth-Century England*. Marian Wilson Kimber's 'Mr. Riddle's Readings: Music and Elocution in Nineteenth-Century Concert Life' (*NCStud* 21[2007] 163–81) treats an interesting and neglected subject. First, Kimber 'surveys the varied performance settings in which nineteenth-century audiences enjoyed elocution combined with music'. Secondly, she 'examines the increase of this activity on the concert stage at the end of the century owing to the emergence of famed elocutionists with composers who wrote for them'. Thirdly, the decline of such performances are traced (pp. 163–4). In his *The Lotus and the Lion: Buddhism and the British Empire*, J. Jeffrey Franklin provides a fascinating account of the growth and development of Victorian and Edwardian perceptions of Buddhism. This interest witnessed the literary reaction of writers from Rudyard Kipling and D.H. Lawrence to H.P. Blavansky, Thomas Henry Huxley and F. Max Müller. Of especial relevance to students of late nineteenth-century and Edwardian literature are Franklin's first three chapters and his fourth one, 'Buddhism and the Empire of the Self in Kipling's *Kim*' (pp. 128–76). There are two appendices: 'Selective Chronology of Events in the European Encounter with Buddhism' (pp. 209–12) and 'Summary of Selected Buddhist Tenets' (pp. 213–18). There are detailed notes, bibliography and index (pp. 219–73).

Diane Mason's *The Secret Vice: Masturbation in Victorian Fiction and Medical Culture* examines medical writings on masturbation and then looks at their impact upon Victorian pornography and authors such as J.S. LeFanu, Charles Dickens, Oscar Wilde and Bram Stoker. Novels discussed range from *Edwin Drood* and *Our Mutual Friend* to *Dracula* and *The Picture of Dorian Gray*. Mason is not adverse to elaborate footnote documentation: for instance her final chapter contains 100 notes (pp. 151–9). The sixth part of Pickering & Chatto's *Lives of Victorian Literary Figures* continues with volumes devoted to *Lewis Carroll, Robert Louis Stevenson, and Algernon Charles Swinburne by their Contemporaries* in facsimile edition. Tom Hubbard, Rikky Rooksby and Edward Wakeling provide extensive, informative preliminary introductions and detailed headnotes on each of the pieces by Victorian contemporaries that they have selected. All three extend their extracts well into the last century. The only caveat to this excellent series is that the individual editors are not given the opportunity to provide indexes. The volumes are sturdily and attractively bound; the facsimiles are reproduced as well.

Michael Faraday (1791–1867) today tends to be perceived as a Victorian although his formative years were not, as Alice Jenkins clearly shows in *Michael Faradays' Mental Exercises: An Artisan Essay-Circle in Regency London*, her edited collection of the essays and poems produced by Faraday's circle of artisans, who formed a self-help group during the second decade of the nineteenth century. Jenkins explains in her introduction that 'In the summer of 1818, Michael Faraday, then approaching his twenty-seventh birthday and employed as Chemical Assistant in the Royal Institution in London, persuaded four male friends to join him in forming a self-help writing group.' She adds that 'The MS book of essays and poems that this group produced is held in the archive of the Royal Institution and is printed here for the first time, and in full' (p. 1). She provides annotations to the text in footnote documentation with introductory material. There is in addition a useful index (pp. 247–50) to this helpful volume.

Sybil Oldfield's *Jeanie, an 'Army of One': Mrs Nassau Senior, 1828–1877, the First Woman in Whitehall* is an extensive biography of probably the first woman civil servant, and by any account a formidable personality, Mrs Nassau Senior (1828–77). The sister of Thomas Hughes, author of *Tom Brown's Schooldays* [1857], her achievements included co-founding the British Red Cross during the Franco-Prussian War, pioneering social work with Octavia Hill, advocating considerable improvement in the conditions and education of pauper girls, and so on. Her friendship with George Eliot is documented in a remarkable series of letters which were sold at Sotheby's London auction rooms in December 2000 and published with annotations and commentary in William Baker and Ira B. Nadel's *Redefining the Modern: Essays on Literature and Society in Honor of Joseph Wiesenfarth* ([2004] pp. 89–114). Notable features of Sybil Oldfield's book are the thirty-seven illustrations and her 'What Happened to the Others in the Story?', the 'Checklist of Reviews and Notices of Mrs. Senior's *Report*, 1874' on the effect of the education system on pauper girls (printed as the third appendix and not the second one as stated on the contents page of this reviewer's copy) and *The Times* obituary of 'the late Mrs. Nassau Senior, 29 March 1877' (pp. 298–307). The fourth appendix, 'Published References to "Mrs. Nassau Senior"' (pp. 308–15), is thorough up to the start of the present century and then has some noted omissions indicated above. The book was 'reprinted with corrections, 2009' (p. 10). However, these are limited.

Philip Davis's *Why Victorian Literature Still Matters* is part of the Blackwell Manifestos series in which 'critics make timely interventions to address important concepts and subjects' (p. ii). Davis's 'little book is [his] version of what Victorian literature has meant for [him] not as an academic subject but as a form of being' (p. 2). Refreshingly, Davis revels in 'realism' (p. 5) and 'his exploration of what he enjoys ranges over various works written by diverse authors such as Dickens, George Eliot, Elizabeth Gaskell, Hardy (a brief diversion on his poems, see for instance pp. 96–7) and George MacDonald; references to John Stuart Mill are dotted around, as is the name of John Henry Newman. There is consideration of Ruskin (for example, pp. 123–9), and

Tennyson (pp. 106–11), plus a perfunctory, dismissive reference to Thackeray (p. 82). Trollope receives much better treatment, as does Carlyle. Davis has some interesting things to say and writes clearly.

Light, vision and power in nineteenth-century Britain are the subjects of Chris Otter's fascinating and well-documented *The Victorian Eye: A Political History of Light and Vision in Britain, 1800–1900*, which 'argues that the ways in which streets, houses, and institutions were lit, and the ways in which people saw within them, have a political history'. Otter persuasively shows 'that the nineteenth-century history of light and vision is best analyzed as part of the history of freedom, in its peculiarly and specifically British form' (p. 1). Otter's book is replete with innumerable black and white illustrations of subjects ranging from a 'Court with shared facilities' and a 'Narrow alley, without sunlight' (pp. 65–6) to a 'Gaslit printing machine room' (p. 202), and 'Man lying in the Strand, Westminster' (p. 246). Otter draws upon a plethora of Victorian documents and reports to illuminate his subject: hopefully he or somebody will now write a monograph applying his political history to literary images of light and vision in Britain over the course of the nineteenth century.

Elisabeth Kehoe's biography *Ireland's Misfortune: The Turbulent Life of Kitty O'Shea* is remarkable value, running to over 600 pages. Kitty O'Shea's (1846–1921) relationship with the Irish politician and leader Charles Stewart Parnell ruined his career. Kehoe goes over the story of O'Shea's life, background, divorce and its consequences—she died in poverty in 1921—the revelation of Parnell's relationship with her, the wife of one of his parliamentary colleagues and mother of two. She married a spendthrift who initially turned a blind eye to her relationship with Parnell. Kehoe reveals much of the social background and environment of the last years of the nineteenth century and the Edwardian age. She does not, however, reveal much that is new or throws light on the Parnell–O'Shea tangled web of relationships and motivations. Julie Melnyk, *Victorian Religion: Faith and Life in Britain*, is a clearly written and readable account of its subject. Chapters encompass 'the changing relationship of church and state, the history of various denominations, a typical clergyman's career, religious practice in ordinary people's lives, movements for philanthropy and reform, religion's impact in literature, women's role in religious life' and also a good explanation of 'the causes and consequences of various challenges to religious faith' (p. xi). There are two very useful explanatory appendices on 'The Thirty-Nine Articles' and 'The Creeds' (pp. 157–77).

In addition to chapters on S.T. Coleridge and Wordsworth, David Amigoni writes on Darwin, reactions to Darwin, Samuel Butler and Edmund Gosse. Non-fictional prose and novels by Alfred Russell Wallace, Herbert Spencer and Grant Allen, amongst others, are also analysed in his *Colonies, Cults and Evolution: Literature, Science and Culture in Nineteenth-Century Writing* [2007]. 'By examining the multiple faces of "culture" in nineteenth-century writing, especially the writing of evolutionary theory', Amigoni demonstrates 'that some of the most active interpretative devices in the cultural discourses of the present—defamiliarization, hybridity, mimicry, cybernetics' have their roots in nineteenth-century non-fictional prose and novels (p. 3). For instance, in chapter 6 Amigoni discusses Gosse's *Father and Son* 'as an early twentieth-century text on self-culture that looks back to the moment of the publication of the *Origin*, and charts a connection between the progress of evolutionary thought and the trajectory of artistic self-fashioning' (p. 30). Mayhew, Dickens's *Our Mutual Friend* and Gissing's *The Nether World* are just a few of the diverse texts utilized by Michelle Allen in a fascinating account of the resistance to reform of the London sanitary system. Her well-written monograph, *Cleansing the City: Sanitary Geographies in Victorian London*, focuses upon the disruption, chaos and confusion caused by proliferation processes and throws light upon her choice of selected novels and prose works.

Jim Endersby, in his informative *Imperial Nature: Joseph Hooker and the Practices of Victorian Science*, identifies 'three themes ... as dominating our understanding of much of Victorian science—the reception of Darwinism, the consequences of empire, and the emergence of a scientific profession'. These 'were all central to [the] life and work' of Joseph Dalton Hooker (1817–1911). 'Analysing his life forces us to reconsider these central issues' (p. 3). Whilst Endersby's account 'ranges across Hooker's entire career ... in order to focus on [Hooker's] effort to establish himself and his discipline [Endersby concentrates his] account on its early decade, prior to his becoming director of Kew in 1865' (p. 7). The reader thus learns much about the middle years of the nineteenth century, the situation of scientists, the social role they played, and perceptions of them. As Norman Vance observes in his foreword to Greg Morse's *John Betjeman: Reading the Victorians*, this 'fine, wide-ranging study of the formation and achievement of John Betjeman breaks new ground by exploring the complexity and imaginative richness of his evolving Victorianism' (p. v). Morse traces Betjeman's debt not only to Victorian poetry but to architecture and other elements of Victorianism.

Shanyn Fiske, in *Heretical Hellenism: Women Writers, Ancient Greece, and the Victorian Popular Imagination*, seeks 'to dismantle the prevalent notion that knowledge of and appreciation for Greek literature, history and philosophy were restricted in the nineteenth century to upper-class men who were formally schooled in Greek and Latin, [who] believed they were rightful inheritors to ancient legacy [and who] regarded their classical knowledge as a basis of cultural authority' (p. 4). Classical learning and awareness of the classics was, as Fiske well demonstrates, not confined to one gender. Through her thorough analysis of the Victorian performance of *Medea*, Charlotte Brontë's interest in Greek concerns through translation, George Eliot's fictional representations of classical concerns in *Romola* and *Middlemarch*, and others such as Amy Levy, Fiske creates a convincing case. The latter half of Fiske's fascinating monograph revolves around the early career of the distinguished Jane Harrison, who studied the classics at Newnham College, Cambridge, and who in spite of resistance made highly significant contributions to our knowledge of the ancient world in, for instance, her *Prolegomena to the Study of Greek Religion* [1903] and *Themis* [1912].

Mary Rosner's 'Domestic Imperialism in Several Victorian Texts: Contact Zones at Home' (*VN* 113[2008] 88–105) discusses various texts. These range from M.E. Braddon's 1852 novel *Lady Audley's Secret* to accounts of various Victorian trials found for instance in H. Maudsley's 'The Suicide of George Victor Townley' (*Journal of Mental Science* 11[1865] 66–83), and the reports of

'Recent Trials on Lunacy' (*Journal of Psychological Medicine and Mental Pathology* 7[1854] 572–625). Kevin Swafford's 'Science, Technology and the Aesthetics of Everyday Life: H.G. Wells's response to John Ruskin and William Morris in *A Modern Utopia*' (*VN* 113[2008] 77–87) assesses the impact upon H.G. Wells's *A Modern Utopia* [1904] of Ruskin's *Unto This Last* [1864] and 'the brilliance and personality of William Morris' (p. 77). Chris Hagerman's enthralling 'Secret Ciphers, Secret Knowledge: The Classics in British India, ca. 1800–1900' (*VN* 113[2008] 3–21) examines 'the profound connections among classical knowledge, elite status, the imperial ethos, and cultural power symbolized by ... a scrap of paper' (p. 19) hidden in a 'quilt which was in turn secreted inside ... [a] walking stick' containing 'ancient Greek script' with a secret cipher during an 1857 siege of an Imperial outpost. 'The secret message in this way was conveyed to a relief column and its commanding officer' (pp. 3–4). Another example cited by Hagerman is the dying words of one Quentin Battye, 'the second in command of the Guides Cavalry during the 1857 siege of Delhi'. The words were in 'the spirit of self-abnegation, patriotism eulogized by Horace' (p. 13).

Douglas Mao writes in his introduction to his *Fateful Beauty: Aesthetic Environments, Juvenile Development, and Literature 1860–1960* that 'this book describes how a vast array of arguments, speculations, and practices converged, in the last part of the nineteenth century and the first part of the twentieth, around the matter of the growing human organism's molding by surroundings and circumstances' (p. 1). In order to illustrate this, Mao, in a somewhat verbose work, draws upon writings by Oscar Wilde, Walter Pater and other late Victorians. The first five pages of *Fateful Beauty* are for instance preoccupied with the significance of a remark on 'wallpaper which must lead a boy to crime; you should not have such incentives to sin lying about your drawing rooms' found in lectures Wilde gave on an 1882 North American lecture tour and published in his 'The Decorative Arts'. In other words, Mao's is a very clever book, perhaps at times too clever. Jerome Meckier indicates in his foreword to Cynthia DeMarcus Manson's interesting *The Fairy-Tale Literature of Charles Dickens, Christina Rossetti, and George MacDonald: Antidotes to the Victorian Spiritual Crisis* that Manson 'surveys the many literary and pictorial representations of Sleeping Beauty in both elite and popular culture throughout the nineteenth-century' (p. iii). Specifically, Manson focuses upon *Great Expectations*, Christina Rossetti's 'Goblin Market' and George MacDonald's '*Sleeping Beauty* revision, the prose fairy-tale "The Light Princess" [that] first appeared as one of several thought-provoking stories interpolated in his 1864 novel *Adela Cathcart*' (p. 79). Manson's textual explication runs to under 100 pages; her notes, bibliography and index take just over forty pages: whether the high publisher's price tag for such a production is justified is open to question. William Gray's *Death and Fantasy: Essays on Philip Pullman, C.S. Lewis, George MacDonald and R.L. Stevenson* is a collection of essays containing an examination of George MacDonald's *Lilith* [1895] and a comparison of MacDonald and Stevenson, plus a consideration of 'The Incomplete Fairy Tales of Robert Louis Stevenson' (pp. 43–51). There are also chapters on 'Pullman, Lewis, MacDonald and the Anxiety of Influence' (pp. 85–102) and 'Witches' Time in Philip Pullman, C.S. Lewis and George MacDonald' (pp. 103–14). Unfortunately, there is no index.

Victorian Studies contains much of interest for students of cultural studies and prose, including Clair Wintel's 'Career Development: Domestic Display as Imperial, Anthropological, and Social Trophy' (*VS* 50[2008] 279–88); Erika Rappaport's 'Imperial Possessions, Cultural Histories and the Material Turn' (*VS* 50[2008] 289–96); Jed Mayer's 'The Expression of the Emotions in Man and Laboratory Animals' (*VS* 50[2008] 399–417); Joseph Nugent's 'The Sword and the Prayerbook: Ideals of Authentic Irish Manliness' (*VS* 50[2008] 587–613); Theodore M. Porter's 'The Objective Self' (*VS* 50 [2008] 641–7); Jennifer Tucker's 'Objectivity, Collective Sight, and Scientific Personae' (*VS* 50 [2008] 648–57); Amanda Anderson's 'Epistemological Liberalism' (*VS* 50 [2008] 658–65); and Lorraine Daston and Peter Galison's 'Response: *Objectivity* and its Critics' (*VS* 50[2008] 666–77). *Nineteenth-Century Studies* contains Anú King Dudley's 'The Role of the Obstetrical Supporter in the Medicalization of Childbirth' (*NCStud* 21[2007] 47–66) and Wendy Jean Katz's 'Fancy Painting, Street Children, and the Fast Men of the Pavé' (*NCStud* 21[2007] 85–126). Mention too should be made of the inaugural issue of the peer-reviewed *Neo-Victorian Studies* which is online at < http:// www.neovictorianstudies.com > .

Catherine Maxwell's *Second Sight: The Visionary Imagination in Late Victorian Literature* concentrates on a variety of writers 'from the later Victorian period, some canonical, some non-canonical, whose works, in addition to poetry, encompass a variety of literary forms such as the essay, the short story, and the novel'. Furthermore, their work is seen through the lens of 'a number of forms of imaginative vision used by' the writers, 'all of whom are deeply indebted to Romantic influences' (p. 1). Maxwell chooses Dante Gabriel Rossetti, Walter Pater, Vernon Lee, Eugene Lee Hamilton, Theodore Watts-Dunton and Thomas Hardy. On the canonical writers Rossetti and Pater, Maxwell's aim is 'to bring new perspectives and new readers to works that occupy a crucial position in the literature of the late Victorian period' (p. 10). Both are less neglected than Maxwell claims. The discovery in *Second Sight* is the poet Eugene Lee Hamilton (1845–1907) whose sonnets were highly praised by Edith Wharton and more recently by Philip Hobsbaum. Further, Maxwell's attention to the work of Theodore Watts-Dunton (1836–1914), and especially his best-selling novel *Aylwin* [1898], is most welcome (pp. 171–96). Hardy's 'profound interest in specters, shades and shadows' is the focus of the final chapter. There is an extensive, enumerative listing of references at the end of the book (pp. 232–51) followed by a useful index (pp. 253–60).

Alexandra Warwick and Martin Willis in their 'Introduction: Defining Victorian' write that 'Each of the contributors to *The Victorian Literature Handbook* have, in their own ways, offered a definition of Victorian and the *Handbook* as a whole describes a number of the many connotations of that term' (p. 4). Contributions include: Alexandra Warwick's 'The Historical Context of Victorian Literature' (pp. 27–43); Kirsty Bunting and Rhian Williams, ed., 'Literary and Cultural Contexts' (pp. 44–88); Kirstie Blair, Michael Helfand, Priti Joshi, Grace Moor and Tamara Wagner on 'Case

Studies in Reading Literary Texts' (pp. 89–115); Miriam Elizabeth Burstein, Martin Danahay, Carol Margaret Davison and Solveig C. Robinson's 'Case Studies in Reading Critical Texts' (pp. 116–46); Alexandra Warwick, ed., 'Key Critical Concepts and Topics' (pp. 147–62); Jane E. Thomas's 'Changes in the Literary Canon' (pp. 163–76); Martin Willis's 'Changes in Critical Approaches' (pp. 177–89); Laurie Garrison's 'Interdisciplinarity in Victorian Studies' (pp. 190–203); and Ruth Robbins's 'Mapping the Future of Victorian Studies' (pp. 204–15). These contributions are followed by a useful listing of further reading arranged by topics such as 'General Introduction to Victorian Literature and Culture', 'Children and Childhood' and so on (pp. 217–32). Mark Bennett contributes an appendix: 'A Survey of Victorian Literature Curricula' (pp. 233–42), to what is a most interesting and useful collection.

Christopher Stray's edition of *An American in Victorian Cambridge* continues his fascinating work in the seemingly unimportant by-ways of Victorian culture. In this case, he has edited and introduced Charles Astor Bristed's account of the five years he spent at Cambridge during the 1840s. Bristed (1820–74), a grandson of the multi-millionaire John Jacob Astor II, gained his first degree at Yale and then went to Trinity College, Cambridge, in 1840, graduating in 1845. As Patrick Leary notes in his foreword to Stray's edition, 'No cultural history of the relationship between' British and American 'societies, from the nineteenth century to the present, can afford to ignore Bristed's account of his years at Cambridge' (p. 10). Stray's introduction (pp. xiii–xxx), replete with an extensive, enumerative bibliography (pp. xxxi–xxxiv), is both detailed and informative, especially on Bristed's life and Cambridge during the 1840s. The edition itself is helpfully annotated and nicely printed, and the work concludes with 'Charles Astor Bristed 1820–1874. An Annotated Bibliography' (pp. 390–412) and a most helpful index (pp. 413–22). In short, this is a very useful and illuminating volume which is highly recommended to students of Victorian England, and the University of Exeter Press ought to be congratulated on its publication.

John Plotz's *Portable Property: Victorian Culture on the Move* focuses upon economics and the novel and the significance of property which can be moved around, in novels by George Eliot and Thomas Hardy and prose work by William Morris and others. Kevin A. Morrison's fascinating 'Spending a Penny at Rothesay; or, How One Lavatory Became a Gentleman's Loo' (*VLC* 36:i[2008] 79–94) contains two figures illustrating late Victorian Rothesay on the Isle of Bute. For Morrison, 'although luxurious lavatories were constructed as an extension of official efforts begun at midcentury to address hygienic concerns arising from the realities of bodily waste, they are also privileged spaces in which modes of identity are forged and fantasies are stimulated' (p. 81). Drawing upon theorists such as Foucault and on late Victorian newspaper accounts, Morrison reveals much about the late Victorian gentleman's lavatory and Rothesay. Unfortunately, there is no photograph of a lavatory used 'in its broadest sense to describe a structure that includes urinals and waste closets' (p. 91). Neither is there mention of the pioneering work of E.P. Hennock on urban sanitation conducted in the late 1950s and subsequently (see for instance his 'The Urban Sanitary Movement in England and Germany, 1838–1914: A Comparison' (*Continuity and Change*

15:ii[2000] 269–96). Maha R. Atal's 'G.W.M. Reynolds in Paris 1835–1836: A New Discovery' (*N&Q* 55[2008] 448–53) sheds fresh light upon the activities of the prolific journalist and novelist G.W.M. Reynolds.

Christina Bashford's *The Pursuit of High Culture: John Ella and Chamber Music in Victorian London* reveals much about the Victorian cultural scene. The focus is the London concert manager John Ella (1802–88), who was deeply involved in a musical union from 1845 to 1881. This was 'a concert society devoted to the promotion of chamber music in general'. Ella rose 'from provincial, artisan-class obscurity to become a figure of power and influence in London musical life and high society, a successful concert manager and entrepreneur, and a relentless and successful proselytizer for the highest of musical art' (p. 1). Bashford's account ranges from Ella's Leicester roots, his 'Successes, Frustrations, Ambitions, 1828–44' (pp. 56–114), the establishment of the musical union to his 'Endings (1880–8) and Legacy' (pp. 332–56). There are five appendices, ranging from 'Sample Programmes for the Musical Union and Musical Winter Evenings' (pp. 357–60) and 'Analysis of Repertoire at the Musical Union and Musical Winter Evenings' (pp. 361–3) to a listing of 'Performers at the Musical Union and Musical Winter Evenings' (pp. 364–8), followed by details of 'Performers in the Musical Union's Annual Director's Matinées' (pp. 369–70) and 'Performers at the Musical Winter Evenings/ Musical Union Soirées' (p. 373). There is even an appendix on 'Musical Union Audience Statistics' (p. 374). The select bibliography of primary and printed sources (pp. 377–80) contains details which form the foundation for Bashford's study of the John Ella Collection at the University of Oxford Faculty of Music Library. A detailed index (pp. 381–410) concludes this important, well-written and fascinating glimpse into an unfortunately neglected area of Victorian life and culture.

A special issue of *CVE* (66[2007]) is devoted to the subject of 'Victorian Representations of War' and is edited with a useful introduction by Gilles Teulié (*CVE* 66[2007] 15–33). It is divided into five sections: The first contains four essays on the subject of 'Mythifying Wars': Tri Tran's 'Behind the Myth: The Representation of the Crimean War in Nineteenth-Century British Newspapers, Government Archives and Contemporary Records' (*CVE* 66[2007] 53–82); Michael Anton Budd's 'From Heroic Retribution to Civilized Violence: Victorian Images of War and the Making of General Gordon' (*CVE* 66[2007] 83–110); Luisa Villa's 'The Breaking of the Square: Late Victorian Representations of Anglo-Sudanese Warfare' (*CVE* 66[2007] 111–28); and Dorothea Flothow's 'Images of War in Late Victorian War and Adventure Novels for Children' (*CVE* 66[2007] 129–49). Flothow's essay contains a useful alphabetical listing of primary texts (pp. 145–8). Part II focuses upon 'Eye-Witnessing Wars' and contains four contributions: Alison Fletcher's ' "To us the war is a spectacle": Domestic Consumption of the Crimean War in Victorian Britain' (*CVE* 66[2007] 153–76); Ludmilla Omundsen's 'Living in the Making of History! Two Victorian Female Travellers' Representations of the 1879 Anglo-Zulu War' (*CVE* 66[2007] 177–94); Clair Bowen's 'Memorising the Mutiny: Felice Beato's Lucknow Photographs' (*CVE* 66[2007] 195–210); Laïli Dor's 'Conflicting Visions of War: Winston Churchill and Rudyard Kipling's Evocation of the

Boer War' (*CVE* 66[2007] 211–28); and Antoine Capet's 'The Happy Warrior: Winston Churchill and the Representation of War, 1895–1901' (*CVE* 66[2007] 229–52).

Part III focuses upon 'Opposing Centre and Periphery' and has four entries: Flaminia Nicora's 'The Crack in the Cornerstone: Victorian Identity Conflicts and the Representation of the Sepoy Mutiny in Metropolitan and Anglo-Indian Novels' (*CVE* 66[2007] 255–72); Martine Piquet's '*Shoot Straight, You Bastards!* Australians in the Boer War: The Breaker Morant Case' (*CVE* 66[2007] 272–88); Françoise Lejeune's 'Representations of the First Colonial "Civil War" in Victoria's Reign: The Canadian Rebellions in the English Press (1837–1838)' (*CVE* 66[2007] 289–316) and Tamara Wagner's 'Fighting Another's War: Imperialist Projections on the Victorian Novel's Continent' (*CVE* 66[2007] 317–36). Part IV concentrates on 'Voicing Wars' and contains four entries: Stéphanie Prévost's 'Dean Farrar's "Divine Crusade" and Victoria's "Little Wars"' (*CVE* 66[2007] 339–56); Michael Snape's 'British Military Chaplaincy in Early Victorian India' (*CVE* 66[2007] 257–388); Marty Gould's 'Insurrection and Integration: The Indian "Mutiny" of 1857 and the Theatrical Renegotiation of Ethnic Alterities' (*CVE* 66[2007] 389–412); and Matthew Bevis's 'Warring Claims: Victorian Poetry and Conflict' (*CVE* 66[2007] 413–48). Part V focuses upon 'Waging War on Wars' and has five entries: Marianne Camus on 'Waterloo in *Vanity Fair* or the Art of not Representing War' (*CVE* 66[2007] 451–66); Françoise Orazi on 'The Pro-Boer Representation of War and the Origins of New Liberalism' (*CVE* 66[2007] 467–82); Eleonora Sasso's '"The Road of War" and "The Path of Peace": William Morris's Representation of Violence' (*CVE* 66[2007] 483–96); Stéphane Guy's '"A Hollow Sham": The Representation of War in Bernard Shaw's Victorian Plays' (*CVE* 66[2007] 497–518) and Annie Escuret's '*Les Dynastes* de Thomas Hardy: Une poétique spectrale à l'oeuvre contre la guerre' (*CVE* 66[2007] 519–38).

Christian Auer's 'L'Impossible désappartenance: Le Paysan des Hautes Terres d'Écosse et les *clearances* du dix-neuvième siècle' ['A Sense of "Disbelonging": the Peasantry of the Scottish Highlands and Clearances of the Nineteenth Century'] (*CVE* 67[2008] 91–102) draws upon contemporary work and mid-Victorian Scottish sources such as the *Inverness Journal* for 1845 to examine the notion of the clan as perceived in the Highlands. Isabelle Cases' '"Appartenir aux classes populaires": L'Exemple du pub sans l'Angleterre victorienne' ['Belonging to the Lower-Classes: The Example of the Pub in the Victorian Period'] (*CVE* 67[2008] 103–14) explores the way in which the middle classes started to move away from the pub, which they considered not to be respectable enough, and traces the way in which the pub became a largely lower-class institution. Cases interestingly draws upon works by George Sims and Henry Mayhew. Win Hayes's 'Early Swimming Clubs: A Question of Class' (*CVE* 67[2008] 115–27) divides Victorian clubs into three types: those that included the upper and middle classes, secondly the middle-class managers or owners of factories combined with groups involved in the running of organizations; thirdly, working-class individuals. Interestingly, Hayes draws upon minute books of the Associated Metropolitan Swimming Clubs (p. 123) and early issues of *The Swimmer* first published in April 1886

(p. 124). Gilbert Pham-Thanh's ' "Qu'ouir (ou plus...) dans dix (ou plus!) dandies *queer* (ou plus?): Traverser l'épreuve de l'extérieur" ' [' "Queer dandies to the test: keeping in, bumping into, coming out, crossing over and what not" '] (*CVE* 67[2008] 189–99) examines the concept of the 'dandy' (p. 190) in the works of Frances Catherine Gore, Benjamin Disraeli, Thomas Henry Lister, Oscar Wilde and others. Thi Tran's 'Violence et syndicalisme dans le port de Londres en 1912' ['Violence, Terror and the Trade Union Movement in the Port of London in 1912'] (*CVE* 67[2008] 349–64) utilizes contemporary parliamentary papers, Home Office records and contemporary press accounts found in for instance the *Daily Graphic*, the *East End News*, the *East London Advertiser* and the *East London Observer* to illuminate the period following the great miners' strike of early 1912. Abby Franchitti's illustrated 'The *"Envers du décor"* of Suffragette Imagery: Anti-Suffrage Caricature' (*CVE* 67[2008] 439–55) focuses upon the use of caricature in the anti-suffrage campaign of the late Victorian and Edwardian periods. Franchitti provides a useful bibliography listing archives, newspapers and secondary sources (p. 455).

Victorian Literature and Culture (36:i[2008]) includes Sarah Bilston's 'Queens of the Garden: Victorian Women Gardeners and the Rise of the Gardening Advice Text' (*VLC* 36:i[2008] 1–19). Amongst the many revealing details new to the present reviewer was the fact that the first lawn mower was patented in 1830. Bilston examines the growth of many gardening magazines and manuals stimulated by advances in printing press technology and distribution and aimed at the burgeoning market of the middle-class amateur gardener. Julie E. Fromer's fascinating ' "Deeply Indebted to the Tea-Plant": Representations of English National Identity in Victorian Histories of Tea' (*VLC* 36:ii[2008] 531–47) focuses upon book-length tea history, a genre blurring the boundaries between fiction and non-fiction, advertisements and travelogues, personal recollections and attempts at scientific treatises. Many of these histories, which appeared throughout the nineteenth century, were in fact funded by the tea industry, which attempted to create a taste for its product. Paul Young's 'The Cooking Animal: Economic Man at the Great Exhibition' (*VLC* 36:ii[2008] 569–86) uses *The Times* and other contemporary sources to analyse the achievement of the celebrated French chef Alexis Soyer and especially his efforts at the York banquet given by the mayor of York to celebrate the upcoming Great Exhibition of 1851. Emphasis is placed by Young upon the especially cosmopolitan international flavour of Soyer's cooking. Deborah Mutch's 'Intemperate Narratives: Tory Tipplers, Liberal Abstainers, and Victorian British Socialist Fiction' (*VLC* 36:ii[2008] 471–87) focuses upon attitudes towards the consumption of alcohol by the British working class during the last two decades of the nineteenth century. Mutch deals with the influence and power of the temperance movement and the impact of British socialists, who argued that the workers, to use Friedrich Engel's words in his *The Condition of the Working Class in England*, 'were being hypocritically inculcated by self-interested capitalists' (p. 402).

Janice Schroeder's 'Self-Teaching: Mary Carpenter, Public Speech, and the Discipline of Delinquency' (*VLC* 36:i[2008] 149–61) treats a neglected area of scholarship, the study of 'women's public speech in the 1850s and 60s' and in particular 'one of the most prolific female public speakers of mid-nineteenth-century England, Mary Carpenter (1807–77)' (p. 149). Examining Carpenter's career, Schroeder wishes to demonstrate that 'Carpenter's discovery of her public voice was inseparable from her articulation of a new form of professional female selfhood, which in turn informed those voiceless "non-selves"—poor children—whom she both identified and identified with in her reform work' (p. 151). Schroeder's discussion draws upon Carpenter's *Reformatory Schools for the Children of the Perishing and Dangerous Classes and for Juvenile Offenders* [1851], *Voices of the Spirit and Spirit Pictures* [1877] and 'Women's Work in the Reformatory Movement' (*English Woman's Journal* 1[1858] 289–95). *Victorian Review* (*VR* 34:i[2008]) contains 'A Forum on Material Objects', with a preface by Elaine Freedgood (pp. 9–12). This is followed by Samantha Matthews's 'Album' (*VR* 34:i[2008] 13–16); Stephanie Snow's 'Anaesthetic Inhaler' (*VR* 34:i[2008] 17–21); Michael T. Clarke's 'Andrometer' (*VR* 34:i[2008] 22–8); Vanessa Warne's 'Artificial Leg' (*VR* 34:i[2008] 29–33); John M. Picker's 'Atlantic Cable' (*VR* 34:i[2008] 34–7); Talia Schaffer's 'Berlin Wool' (*VR* 34:i[2008] 38–42); Julie Rugg's 'Cemetery' (*VR* 34:i[2008] 43–6); Katharine Anderson's 'Coral Jewellery' (*VR* 34:i[2008] 47–51); Jennifer Blair's 'Fire Escape' (*VR* 34:i[2008] 52–5); Anne Clendinning's 'Gas Cooker' (*VR* 34:i[2008] 56–61); Christopher Kent's 'Gentleman's Coat' (*VR* 34:i[2008] 62–6); Lara Kriegel's 'Lace' (*VR* 34:i[2008] 67–70); Jim Cheshire's 'Stained Glass' (*VR* 34:i[2008] 71–4); and Colette Colligan's 'Stereograph' (*VR* 34:i[2008] 75–82).

Meilee Bridges' account in her 'The Eros of Homeros: The Pleasures of Greek Epic in Victorian Literature and Archaeology' (*VR* 34:ii[2008] 165–84) encompasses prose and poetry in its discussion of the nineteenth-century reception of Homer's work. She draws upon Richard Claverhouse Jebb's 1884 *Fortnightly Review* article on 'Homeric Troy', Robert Browning, accounts of Schliemann's discoveries, Walter Pater and others. She concludes that 'Even for classically trained scholars like Jebb, both Homer and his songs must remain elevated in the Victorian cultural imaginary, not excavated from the dust of the ground—they must survive not as physical remains but as immortal and sublime figures of the imagination' (p. 181). J. Michael Walton's 'Dionysus: The Victorian Outcast' (*VR* 34:ii[2008] 185–200) focuses upon translations of the classical tragedies which 'took off' (p. 186) during the Victorian period. Walton writes that 'between 1837 and 1901 there were at least twenty-six new *Agamemnons* with which to compare "The Browning Version" of 1877' (p. 186). Donald E. Hall's 'Teaching Victorian Pornography: Hermeneutics and Sexuality' (*VR* 34:ii[2008] 19–22) is part of a forum on 'Teaching the Victorians' (other contributors include Kirstie Blair, Gail Turley Houston, Jennifer Green-Lewis, Lorraine Janzen Kooistra and Julianne Smith (*VR* 34:ii[2008] 9–69)). Hall's contribution is followed by a short but valuable 'Selected Annotated Bibliography on Pornography and Pedagogy' by Andrew Urban (*VR* 34:ii[2008] 23–5). *Victorians Institute Journal* (*VIJ* 36[2008]) contains Suzanne Rintoul's 'Intimate Violence and the Tenuous Boundaries of Class in Victorian Street Literature' (*VIJ* 36[2008] 79–102). Rintoul considers in depth 'narratives of intimate violence in Victorian street literature [which] often depict either working-class couples or illicit affairs between impoverished women and wealthy gentleman' (p. 79). She also discusses representations of intimate violence and the representation of fallen women. 'Street literature' Rintoul defines as 'broadsides, pamphlets, and newspapers that were affordable to members of the working classes and sold in individual copies' (p. 98). K. Mays's 'Domestic Spaces, Readerly Acts: Reading(,) Gender, and Class in Working-Class Autobiography' (*NCC* 30:ii[2008] 343–68), in spite of its pretentious title, is quite illuminating. Mention should be made of issue 4:iii of *Nineteenth-Century Gender Studies* which is available at < www.ncgsjournal.com >. This issue contains some interesting essays on *The Saturday Review*, Wilkie Collins's *Man and Wife*, Anne Brontë's *The Tenant of Wildfell Hall*, and Charlotte Brontë's *Villette* and *Jane Eyre*.

(b) Prose

Daniel Bivona's 'Poverty, Pity, and Community: Urban Poverty and the Threat to Social Bonds in the Victorian Age' (*NCStud* 21[2007] 67–83) draws upon passages in Dickens's *Bleak House*, the journalist James Greenwood, especially the articles collected in his *Unsentimental Journeys* and *The Wilds of London* [1874], W.T. Stead's *The Bitter Cry of Outcast London* and other work. Such writings are used to 'provide some evidence of an accelerating movement away from a reliance on the ethics of pity and toward the psychological exteriorization of the poor in discourse' (p. 79). Jacqueline Young, in her 'Rewriting the Boxer Rebellion: The Imaginative Creations of Putnam Weale, Edmund Backhouse, and Charles Welsh Mason' (*VN* 114[2008] 7–28), considers the re-creation of three early twentieth-century depictions of the Boxer Rebellion: Putnam B.L. Weale's edited *Indiscreet Letters from Peking* (9th edition [1906]), and his *Wang the Ningh: The Story of a Chinese Boy* [1920]; J.O.P. Bland and E. Blackhouse's *China Under the Empress Dowager* [1912]; and Charles Welsh Mason's *The Chinese Confession of Charles Welsh Mason* [1924]. She concludes that 'all had very personal reasons for not producing, like writers up to the present day, readable, speculative novels of the rebellion but instead crafting apparently fictional chronicles that were firmly rooted in the fictional worlds of their own imagination' (p. 26). Sarah Hackenberg's 'Alien Image, Ideal Beauty: The Orientalist Vision of American Slavery in Hiram Powers's *The Greek Slave*' (*VN* 114[2008] 30–49) considers the considerable impact of the American sculptor Hiram Powers's 'statue of a naked, white woman in chains ... in England' (p. 31).

Accounts of their journeys in forums such as the *Journal of the Royal Geographical Society* are discussed by Adrian S. Wisnicki in 'Charting the Frontier: Indigenous Geography, Arab-Nyamwezi Caravans and the East African Expedition of 1856–59' (*VS* 51:i[2008] 103–37). Wisnicki focuses in particular upon the writings of Richard Burton and John Speke. Drawing upon various prose texts, Joanna Bourke, in her 'Sexual Violence, Marital Guidance and Victorian Bodies: An Aesthesiology' (*VS* 51[2008] 419–36), 'examines some of the emotional rules encoded in grammars of representation and framed within law and prescriptive marital advice literature, regarding the expression of male sexual aggressivity within the bedroom' (p. 419). Grace Kehler's 'Gothic Pedagogy and Victorian Reform Treatises' (*VS* 51[2008] 437–56) 'considers the work of bodily affect in three Victorian reform treatises about the industrial working classes: Kay's *The Moral and Physical Condition of the Working Classes Employed in the Cotton Manufacture in Manchester*, Chadwick's *Report on the Sanitary Condition of the Labouring Population of Great Britain*, and Engels's *The Condition of the Working Class in England* (p. 437).

In spite of its unwieldy title, *Rethinking Postcolonialism: Colonialist Discourse in Modern Literatures and the Legacy of Classical Writers*, Amar Acheraiou makes some interesting observations. The work 'analyses colonialist discourses in modern literary and nonliterary texts and explores key philosophical concepts in forming colonialism'. Acheraiou's study is divided into two. First, there is 'discussion of the ways in which classical writings influenced colonialist discourse', and secondly 'examination of the relationship between modernist literature and empire' (p. 3). Such a framework provides an interesting foundation for insight into various authors, including H. Rider Haggard and Rudyard Kipling. Drawing upon pamphlets, newspapers, trial transcripts, estate papers and missionary records as well as novels, Tim Watson, in his *Caribbean Culture and British Fiction in the Atlantic World, 1780–1870*, examines Caribbean nineteenth-century culture from the perspective of 'the centrality of subaltern religious life', and 'Creole realism' (p. 10). He focuses upon the writings of Simon Taylor, the colonial politician, bookkeeper and planter, Maria Edgeworth's *Belinda*, the work of Charles White Williams, Samuel Ringgold Ward and others before focusing upon the 1865 Jamaican rebellion and 'its impact in Britain' (p. 13), represented for instance by George Eliot's *Felix Holt*. Watson writes clearly and brings an interesting perspective to bear upon his subject.

Mark Bostridge's interestingly written and lengthy biography *Florence Nightingale: The Making of an Icon* opens with an account of 'the expected imminent arrival' of the second child of William Nightingale in the spring of 1820. Bostridge draws upon the 'massive collection[s]' of Nightingale papers in various repositories to tell her tale and to illuminate many facets of Victorian life. As Bostridge observes 'previously unknown letters continue to materialize' and 'war was Florence Nightingale's lifeblood' (pp. 4–6). Bostridge successfully sifts through the wealth of documentation to produce an eminently readable and richly illuminating account of the subject's life and importance. Heidi Hansson's *New Contexts: Re-framing Nineteenth-Century Irish Women's Prose* contains eight essays. Hansson, in a clearly written introduction, states that the essays in the collection 'bring new critical and theoretical perspectives to bear on Irish nineteenth-century women's writing' (p. 16). She also explains why such writing has been neglected. The contributions include Jacqueline Belanger's '"Improvement in a Nation's Blessing": Elizabeth Hamilton's *The Cottagers of Glenburnie* in Ireland' (pp. 17–34); Riana O'Dwyer's 'Travels of a Lady of Fashion: The Literary Career of Lady Blessington (1789–1849)' (pp. 35–54); Maria Lindgren Leavenworth's 'The Art of Bookmaking: Selina Bunbury's Northern Journeys' (pp. 55–77); Margaret Kelleher's '"Factual Fictions":

Representations of the Land Agitation in Nineteenth-Century Women's Fiction' (pp. 78–91); and Elisabeth Wennö's 'Hybridization as a Literary and Social Strategy: Mrs. Hungerford's *Molly Bawn*' (pp. 92–108). The editor, Heidi Hansson, contributes an essay on 'Patriot's Daughter, Politician's Wife: Gender and Nation in M.E. Francis's *Miss Erin*' (pp. 109–24). The final two contributions are: Tina O'Toole's 'Ireland: The *Terra Incognita* of the New Woman Project' (pp. 125–41) and Julie Anne Stevens's 'The Art of Politics in Somerville and Ross's Fiction with Emphasis on their Final Collection of Stories, *In Mr. Knox's Country*' (pp. 142–60). There then follows an alphabetically arranged, enumerative bibliography (pp. 161–75), notes and references (pp. 176–99) and a useful index (pp. 201–8). Clearly, some of the essays contain less theoretical rhetoric than others, and in such a diverse collection *YWES* readers will find some of more relevance than others to their interests.

Sharmila Sen's 'The Saracen's Head' (*VLC* 36:ii[2008] 407–31), looks at the significance of melons or 'an idea of homeland contained in a mouthful' for an understanding of Victorian India. Particular attention is paid to *Curry Rice (or Forty Plates); or The Ingredients of Social Life at 'Our' Station in India*, 'a book of lithographs and satiric vignettes of life in a British station in India, drawn and composed by [George Franklin] Atkinson in 1859' (p. 407). Kate Thomas's 'Alimentary: Arthur Conan Doyle and Isabella Beeton' (*VLC* 36:ii[2008] 375–90) examines the relationship between Arthur Conan Doyle and Isabella Beeton. Thomas reminds her readers that 'The First Sherlock Holmes story "A Study in Scarlet"' (p. 375) appeared in the 1887 edition of *Beeton's Christmas Annual*. The association between the two 'raises the ... question: what were the relationships between the mass market, the culinary, and the production of judgment and refinement in the nineteenth century' (p. 376) and *Beeton's Book of Household Management* [1859–61]. Thomas uses the work of Conan Doyle and Mrs Beeton to explore her question, paying particular attention to culinary metaphors. For Thomas, 'with [their] characters literally chewing over and chewing out Beeton in order to restore and reproduce middle-class domestic felicity, it is clear how Doyle and Beeton are both "alimentary"—writers whose somewhat pre-digested guides provide nourishment and maintenance to the middle classes' (pp. 387–8). Suzanne Daly and Ross G. Forman's 'Introduction: Cooking Culture: Situating Food and Drink in the Nineteenth Century' (*VLC* 36:ii[2008] 363–73) explores the current implications of Isabella Beeton's observations in her *Book of Household Management* that 'Dining is the privilege of civilization' (p. 363), and those of other Victorian writers on cookery.

Turning to individual prose writers, studies of Arnold's prose include Paul Goetsch's German study of Arnold's *Culture and Anarchy* in his 'Arnolds, Hebraism "und, Hellenism"'. Ein kulturkritisches Thema des spätviktorianischen Romans' (in Horatschek, Bach, Glomb and Horlacher, eds., *Literatur und Lebenskunst. Reflexionen zum guten Leben im britischen Roman vom Viktorianismus zur Postmoderne*, pp. 17–40). The relationship between Matthew Arnold and the American journalist George Washburn Smalley (1833–1916), drawing upon published and hitherto unpublished correspondence, is the subject of Steven Sansom's ' "The regrets which darken last days": Final Years of the Matthew Arnold–George Smalley Connection' (*NCP* 35:ii[2008] 133–62). Not lacking in interest is Kevin McLaughlin's 'Culture and Messianism: Disinterestedness in Arnold' (*VS* 50[2008] 615–39). Judith Johnston's excellent account of 'Sarah Austin and the Politics of Translation in the 1830s' (*VR* 34:i[2008] 101–13), focuses upon the work of Sarah Austin, 'an early Victorian translator of note' whose 'translations from the German in the decade between 1831 and 1841 were especially significant in introducing German intellectual thinking and writing into England' (p. 101).

Another study with Isabella Beeton as its focus is Helen Day's 'A Common Complaint: Dining at the Reform Club' (*VLC* 36:ii[2008] 507–30). Day demonstrates the way in which *Mrs. Beeton's Book of Household Management* drew upon previous narratives of etiquette and cookery books aimed at the bourgeois market that attempted to persuade their readers of the importance of household management. In Margaret Beetham's 'Good Taste and Sweet Ordering: Dining with Mrs. Beeton' (*VLC* 36:ii[2008] 391–406), Pierre Bourdieu is quoted as observing in his *Distinction: A Social Critique of the Judgment of Taste* [1984] that 'in order to understand the workings of culture "in the restricted, normative sense" we must not only relate our discussion to the broad anthropological meanings of the concept, we must also relate it to "taste" in the physical sense'. We must, he argues, bring 'the elaborated taste for the most refined objects ... back into relation with the elementary taste for the flavours of food' (p. 94). Beetham uses this to illuminate passages in Beeton's *Book of Household Management*. She also discusses the various textual incarnations of Beeton's publication and draws attention to the fact that it 'was conceived and brought to life in the context of a flourishing family publishing business' (p. 396).

The spring 2008 edition of the *George Borrow Bulletin* contains the following: 'Badajoz: In Search of Borrow's Gypsies' by David Fernández de Castro (translated by Peter Missler) (*GBB* 36[2008] 3–15); 'When George Borrow Met Spanish *Romania*' by Ignasi Xavier Adiego (*GBB* 36[2008] 15–28); 'Gypsy Luke Project (2)—Further Results' by Peter Missler (*GBB* 36[2008] 29–35); 'Another Early Borrovian! Franz Liszt and the *Gipsy in Music*' by Ann M. Ridler (*GBB* 36[2008] 35–40); 'Three Glorious Johns' by Roger Savage (*GBB* 36[2008] 40–6), which focuses on Borrovian connections in Ralph Vaughan Williams's 'Romantic Ballad Opera' *Hugh the Drover* (p. 40); 'A Friendship Made in Oulton: Borrow and Edward Fitzgerald' by Clive Wilkins-Jones (*GBB* 36[2008] 46–62); '*The Rings of Saturn* and George Borrow' by Dennis Burton (*GBB* 36[2008] 63–71), in which Burton explores connections between W.G. Sebald's (1944–2001) work published in 1995 and Borrow; and the following 'Notes and Queries': (1) 'A Postscript on Borrow's Failed Attempt to Become a Magistrate' by Anne M. Ridler (*GBB* 36[2008] 71–2); (2) 'George Borrow and the Oulton Paris "Vestry"' by Ivan Bunn (*GBB* 36[2008] 72–6); (3) 'A Further Postscript on Borrow and Peto' by Ivan Bunn (*GBB* 36[2008] 76); (4) 'The Piano Forte, a Further Note by Ivan Bunn'(*GBB* 36[2008] 76–7); (5) 'The Borrows at Shrewsbury and Borrow's Second Tour of Wales' by Anne M. Ridler' (*GBB* 36[2008] 77–86); (6) 'Another Musical Borrovian, a Note from CuChullaine O'Reilly of the Long Riders' Guild' (*GBB* 36[2008] 86–7), relating to three songs 'based on Borrow's works ... by an American named George Harris ... published in New York in 1925 by G. Schirmer' (p. 86).

The autumn 2008 issue of the *George Borrow Bulletin* contains: 'Celebrating Richard Ford' (*GBB* 37[2008] 5–9); '"Wherever I chance to be for the time": Defining Bohemia with George Borrow and George Augustus Sala' by Kedrun Laurie (*GBB* 37[2008] 9–24), examining 'the contrasts between Borrow's and Sala's versions of Bohemia' (p. 9); 'Fresh Light on Borrow in London in 1830' by Ann M. Ridler (*GBB* 37[2008] 25–9), which publishes for the first time four Borrow letters; 'Notes and Queries': (1) 'A Further Note on the Ford Gypsy *Luke*, by Tom Bean' (*GBB* 37[2008] 29–30); (2) 'A Further Note on "Three Glorious Johns" from John Hentges' (*GBB* 37[2008] 30–1), adding to Roger Savage's note in volume 36 of the *Bulletin*; (3) 'Experience, Observation and Imagination—An Editorial Reflection by Ann Ridler' (*GBB* 37[2008] 31–3); (4) 'George Borrow at Tregaron: Some Bibliographical Notes from Ken Barrett' (*GBB* 37[2008] 33–5). Peter Missler writes an extensive review of *George Borrow in Portugal*, ed. António Ventura (introduction and notes), original texts translated by Manuel Ruas (Lisbon: Livros Horizonte [2006]; ISBN 9 7224 1404 6) (*GBB* 37[2008] 36–45). The autumn issue for 2008 concludes with Ann M. Ridler's 'Report and Proceedings of the George Borrow Society's Meeting at Clonmel, Co. Tipperary, Republic of Ireland Tuesday 30 September—Friday 3 October 2008' (*GBB* 37[2008] 61–7). This is followed by four papers given at the meeting: 'Borrow in Clonmel' by Michael Ahern (*GBB* 37[2008] 67–73); '"Old and Crazy": The Ship that Bore the Borrows to Ireland' by Colm Kerrigan (*GBB* 37[2008] 73–81); 'Romancing the Romancer: Borrow and W.G. Dowsley' by Martin Murphy (*GBB* 37[2008] 82–90), an account of Dowsley's (1871–1947) 1925 novel, *Travelling Men*, fictionalizing Borrow as a boy; and 'More than Just "A Speech Spoken": Borrow's Interest in Irish Literature and History' by Anne M. Ridler (*GBB* 37[2008] 90–102), followed by the same author's '"Croppies Lie Down"—Two Versions Compared' (*GBB* 37[2008] 102–4).

A notable edition published during 2008 is Marie Mulvey-Roberts', with the assistance of Steve Carpenter, three-volume *The Collected Letters of Rosina Bulwer Lytton*. Well-annotated, with detailed biographical notes, these volumes contain the correspondence of Rosina Bulwer Lytton (née Rosina Doyle Wheeler), who subsequently became the embittered wife of the very difficult Edward Bulwer Lytton. The annotations and the letters throw much light upon her plight, her background, those who supported her, her enemies, her tangled relationships with her children, from whom she was eventually parted, the horrible habit of incarcerating difficult wives in asylums provided you had enough money to do so, and so much more on nineteenth-century upper-crust society. Mulvey-Roberts and Steve Carpenter are to be congratulated on an enormous task: their edition is an invaluable one. A.D. Harvey has an interesting note on 'Richard Burton in the Crimean War' (*N&Q* 55[2008] 476–80).

Carlyle Studies Annual for 2008 opens with David Southern's '"That unhappy War of yours": Eight Letters from Samuel Laurence to Old Friends in New York City, 1861–1875' (*CStA* 24[2008] 5–35), which provides considerable new information on close friends and acquaintances of the

Carlyles and especially Samuel Laurence (1812–84), the eminent portrait painter. Owen Dudley Edwards, in 'Carlyle and Catholicism, Part II: G.K. Chesterton and *Past and Present*' (*CStA* 24[2008] 37–62), considers in detail Carlyle's influence upon Chesterton. There is an appendix: 'G.K. Chesterton's 1904 Introduction to *Sartor Resartus*' (pp. 63–6). One cannot resist brief citations from Chesterton: 'And of all Carlyle's works, *Sartor Resartus* is that which is most marked and filled with this quality of wild fancy, which was his real contribution to the letters of the Victorian time.' Chesterton opens his introduction with the sentence '*Sartor Resartus* is probably the most brilliant of Carlyle's books; certainly it is the most Carlylean' (p. 63). George F. Seelinger and Brent E. Kinser's 'Revisiting Thomas Carlyle and Mathematics' (*CStA* 24[2008] 67–75) considers the relevance today of Carlyle's early interest in mathematics. David R. Sorensen's ' "A Flowing Light-Fountain": Thomas Carlyle, John Ruskin, and the Architecture of Heroism in *The Stones of Venice*' (*CStA* 24[2008] 77–84) considers the influence of the first volume of Ruskin's *The Stones of Venice* upon Carlyle. David Taylor's ' "There is subject for further enquiry here": Vernon Lushington and Thomas Carlyle' (*CStA* 24[2008] 85–99) explores the complicated relationship between Carlyle and his friend and editor, 'the lawyer and positivist Vernon Lushington (1832–1912)' (p. 85). Nora Foster's ' "Free of Formulas": Innovation, Prophecy, and Truth in Thomas Carlyle's *The French Revolution*' (*CStA* 24[2008] 101–15) assesses the twentieth-century reception of Carlyle's work. For Foster, 'Postmodern readers ... can value the *French Revolution* for its bold refusal to ignore the importance of personal human experience in history, for Carlyle's narrative works in unique ways to create emphatic impressions of historical reality' (p. 114). Marie Laniel's 'Revisiting a Great Man's House: Virginia Woolf's Carlylean Pilgrimages' (*CStA* 24[2008] 117–32) treads some familiar ground in her reconsideration of Carlyle's impact on Virginia Woolf. *Carlyle Studies Annual* 24[2008] reprints an essay by the late Benedict Kiely, who died in 2007 (first published in the *Irish Ecclesiastical Record*, 5th series, 67[April 1946] 223–31): 'Comment on Carlyle' (*CStA* 24[2008] 134–44). Kiely's conclusion is moving. He does not gloss over 'the limitations of [Carlyle's] philosophy ... his bigotry and bitterness, his nervous inability to reason from cause to effect'; however, Kiely 'remember[s] in his favour that he was angry at injustice, and when the poor cried out in the streets he was not deaf to the voice of their suffering' (p. 144).

The 'Miscellanies' section of *Carlyle Studies Annual* 24[2008] prints 'A Newly Discovered Account of the Death of Jane Welsh Carlyle' (*CStA* 24[2008] 147–8), a transcription of 'Mark Twain's Notes on the Death of Thomas Carlyle' followed by copies of Twain's holographs (*CStA* 24[2008] 150–3), an extract from 'The Memoirs of Constance Cary Harrison (1843–1920)' under the title 'J.R. Thompson and Thomas Carlyle' (*CStA* 24[2008] 154–8), a note on 'Collecting the Letters of J.A. Froude' (*CStA* 24[2008] 158–62), and '*An Afterword*: "Give Carlyle his due": Goldwin Smith, Thomas Carlyle, and *The Bystander*' (*CStA* 24[2008] 162–75). *Carlyle Studies Annual* 24[2008] concludes with detailed reviews. There is an announcement on the inside back cover for *The Letters of Francis Jeffrey to Thomas and Jane Welsh Carlyle*, edited by William Christie. The present writer has not seen this volume but it ought not to go unnoted. John B. Lamb's 'The Paper Age: Currency Crisis and Carlyle' (*PSt* 30:i[2008] 27–44) discusses Carlyle's *The French Revolution* and the way in which it reflects contemporary anxieties concerning paper money and the gold standard. Such concerns are placed in the context of a historical crisis of values: political, moral and economic. Lamb also considers the ways in which Carlyle uses such symbols in British society and contrasts them with the speculation and inflation that occurred in revolutionary France. The transformation of bank notes into gold was for Carlyle symptomatic of the decay of traditional forms of society and represented the decay of traditional values. Catherine Heyrend's 'De la campagne écossaise aux milieux aristocratiques londoniens: Le Déracinement de Thomas Carlyle?' ['From Rural Scotland to Aristocratic London: Thomas Carlyle's Uprooting?'] (*CVE* 67[2008] 129–45) retreads the well-known truism that the Carlyles always felt alienated in Victorian London and that the sense of uprooting from their Scottish background is reflected in their work.

Andrew C. Long's 'A Refusal and Traversal: Robert Cunninghame Graham's Engagement with Orientalism in *Mogreb-el-Acksa*' (*NCL* 63[2008] 376–410) examines Cunninghame Grahame's 'fin-de-siècle Morocco travelogue *Mogreb-el-Acksa*' (p. 376). The great *Correspondence of Charles Darwin*, published by Cambridge University Press, rolls on with the appearance of volume 16, part 1, covering January–June 1868, and part 2, covering July–December 1868. The volumes are dedicated to the memory of the founding editor of the Darwin Correspondence Project, Frederick Henry Burkhardt (1912–2007) (Part I, x). An extensive introduction to the volumes is followed by acknowledgements, a list of provenances, a detailed note on editorial policy, a table of the Wedgwood and Darwin families up to 1868 and a listing of abbreviations (pp. xix–xlvi); then follows the fully annotated text of the letters. The second part contains six appendices encompassing such topics as 'Translations', 'Chronology', 'Diplomas', 'Presentation Lists for *Variation*', 'Darwin's *Queries about Expression*' and 'Reviews of *Variation*'. There are also listings of 'Manuscript Alterations and Comments', a very useful 'Biographical Register and Index to Correspondents', a bibliography, notes on manuscript sources and an extremely detailed index (pp. 913–1,252). The inside front and back matter in both volumes contains tables of relationships. The texts are accompanied by black and white illustrations of key figures that appear in the correspondence. Once again, the editors have produced a monumental edition worthy of its great subject.

Perhaps the most useful of responses to Darwin covered in this review are to be found in Eve-Marie Engels and Thomas F. Glick's edited, two-volume *The Reception of Charles Darwin in Europe*. These volumes are part of the Athlone Critical Traditions series: 'The Reception of British and Irish Authors in Europe'. The series editor is Elinor Schaffer. The first volume contains, in addition to Thomas F. Glick and Eve-Marie Engels' 'Timeline: European Reception of Charles Darwin' (pp. xxvi–lxxi), an informative 'Editors' Introduction' (pp. 1–22). Contributions include Eve-Marie Engels's 'Darwin's Philosophical Revolution: Evolutionary Naturalism and First Reactions to his Theory' (pp. 23–53); Paul White's 'Correspondence as a Medium of Reception and Appropriation' (pp. 54–65); Greta Jones's 'Nation and Religion: The Debate about Darwinism in Ireland' (pp. 66–78); Mario A. di Gregorio's 'Under Darwin's Banner: Ernst Haeckel, Carl Gregenbaur and Evolutionary Morphology' (pp. 79–97); Dirk Backenköhler's 'Only "Dreams from an Afternoon Nap"? Darwin's Theory of Evolution and the Foundation of Biological Anthropology in Germany 1860–75' (pp. 98–115); Helmut Pulte's 'Darwin's Relevance for Nineteenth-Century Physics and Physicists: A Comparative Study' (pp. 116–34); Anto Leikola's 'Darwinism in Finland' (pp. 135–45); Peter C. Kjoergaard, Niels Henrick Gregersen and Han Henrik Hjermitslev's 'Darwinizing the Danes, 1859–1909' (pp. 146–55); Thore Lie's 'The Introduction, Interpretation and Dissemination of Darwinism in Norway during the Period 1860–90' (pp. 156–74); Bart Leeuwenburgh and Janneke van der Heide's 'Darwin on Dutch Soil: The Early Reception of his Ideas in the Netherlands' (pp. 175–87); Raf de Bont's '"Foggy and Contradictory": Evolutionary Theory in Belgium, 1859–1945' (pp. 188–98); Tómǎs Hermann and Michael Šimunek's 'Between Science and Ideology: The Reception of Darwin and Darwinism in the Czech Lands, 1859–1959' (pp. 199–216); Ken Kalling and Erkei Tammiksaar's 'Descent versus Extinction: The Reception of Darwinism in Estonia' (pp. 217–29); Vincas Būda and Alina Irena Šveistvte 'The Ideas of Charles Darwin in Lithuania: Contributions by Emigrant Authors during the Years of Occupation' (pp. 230–43); Daniel Schümann's 'Struggle for or against Participation? How Darwinism Came to Partitioned Poland in the 1860s and early 1870s' (pp. 244–58); and Vítězslav Orel and Margaret H. Peaslee's 'The Echo of Darwin in Mendel's Brno' (pp. 259–68).

Volume 2 focuses upon 'The Reception of Darwin in Southern and South-East Europe' (p. 17). It includes Patrick Tort's 'The Interminable Decline of Lamarckism in France' (pp. 329–53); Rainer Brömer's 'Many Darwinisms by Many Names: Darwinism and Nature in the Kingdoms of Italy' (pp. 375–85); Francisco Pelayo's 'Darwinism and Paleontology: Reception and Diffusion of the Theory of Evolution in Spain' (pp. 386–99); Agusti Camós's 'Darwin in Catalunya: From Catholic Intransigence to the Marketing of Darwin's Image' (pp. 400–12); Mariano Artigas, Thomas F. Glick and Rafael A. Martínez's 'Darwin and the Vatican: The Reception of Evolutionary Theories' (pp. 413–29); Sándor Soós's 'The Scientific Reception of Darwin's Work in Nineteenth-Century Hungary' (pp. 430–40); Katalin Mund's 'The Reception of Darwin in Nineteenth-Century Hungarian Society' (pp. 441–62); Victoria Tatole's 'Notes on the Reception of Darwin's Theory in Romania' (pp. 463–79); Thomas Junker's 'The Eclipse and Renaissance of Darwinism in German Biology (1900–1950)' (pp. 480–501); Yasha Gall and Mikhail B. Konashev's 'The Reception of Darwin's Theory of Evolution in Russia: 1920s to 1940s' (pp. 502–21); Eduard I. Kolchinsky's 'Darwinism and Dialectical Materialism in Soviet Russia' (pp. 522–52) and Thomas F. Glick's 'Miquel Crusafont, Teilhard de Chardin and the Reception of the Synthetic Theory in Spain' (pp. 553–68). There is a useful bibliography at the end of both volumes, and the second volume contains an extensive index (pp. 613–59) covering the contents of both volumes. Obviously, some of the essays are more clearly written than others. All in all, Engels and Glick's volumes are important additions to our study of Darwin's reception.

Peter W. Graham's *Jane Austen and Charles Darwin: Naturalists and Novelists* is a detailed comparison of the two. Graham's conversation between them ranges from empiricism, their circumstances, their acute observations and analysis of courtship rituals to their mutual awareness that microscopic change was a reflection of transition in the wider universe. Graham's analysis illuminates and sheds fresh light upon the prose of both of his subjects. Martha S. Vogeler's *Austin Harrison and the English Review* is a detailed, extensive study of the political and literary journalist Austin Harrison (1873–1928), paying particular attention to his editorship of *The English Review*, which he took over in 1910. As editor, he considerably expanded its coverage, publishing articles on women's suffrage, parliamentary reform, Irish Home Rule, the threat from Germany and much more. Harrison focuses upon the years 1910–23 and also traces the complex relationship between Austin and his father Frederick Harrison. Fascinating light is thrown upon Harrison's friendships with Frank Harris, Aleister Crowley and others, including George Gissing and Bernard Shaw. Vogeler does indeed, as she intends, make 'the case for giving [Austin Harrison] a place in the wider cultural and political life of his time' (p. 294).

Dennis Shrubsall sheds some light upon a very neglected writer in his 'W.H. Hudson, Author and Naturalist, (1841–1922)' (*N&Q* 55[2008] 522). The Rivendale Press in High Wycombe continues to produce publications of the highest quality, focusing upon the late Victorians and Edwardians. Damian Atkinson's edition of *The Letters of William Ernest Henley to Robert Louis Stevenson* is no exception. Henley (1849–1903) is chiefly remembered today, if at all, as a minor poet, his journalism and editorship forgotten. The advocate of Rodin and Whistler, amongst others, in the *Magazine of Art*, he published Kipling, J.M. Barrie, Alice Meynell, H.G. Wells and Robert Louis Stevenson in his *National Observer*. He initially met Robert Louis Stevenson in the Edinburgh Infirmary in 1875 when Henley was a patient. They became friends and correspondents. Atkinson's meticulously edited and annotated edition of Henley's letters to Stevenson extend from March 1875 through their collaboration on four plays to May 1894 and their falling out. Henley's letters illuminate their relationship and his literary milieu. Deborah Fratz's 'The Powers of Deafness: Harriet Martineau's Disabled Subject as Sociological Observer' (*VIJ* 36[2008] 47–78) is a detailed examination of Martineau's *Life in the Sick Room* [1884] and 'Letter to the Deaf' [1834]. Fratz also considers Martineau's novel *Deerbrook* [1839]. She concludes that '*Deerbrook* succeeds as a seminal, early Victorian work of realist fiction, a solid domestic novel about middle-class women in love and how adversity strengthens individuals and their relationships', adding that, 'for Martineau, the realist genre seemed to curtail the imaginative work of figuring professional careers for either women or the disabled' (p. 68). John Stuart Mill and Harriet Taylor are the main concern of Hilary Fraser's 'The Morals of Genealogy' (*Raritan* 27:iv[2008] 115–32). Fraser concludes that 'perhaps illusion is an important part, a necessary part, of reality. Things happen, in truth, and myths are made of them, and the truths and the myths somehow live together in the human heart' (p. 132).

Lauren M.E. Goodlad's '"Character worth speaking of": Individuality, John Stuart Mill, and the Critique of Liberalism' (*VIJ* 36[2008] 7–46) is a detailed reading of John Stuart Mill's concept of 'liberalism' with particular reference to his *On Liberty* [1859] and other works. Goodlad makes interesting comparisons with twentieth-century American perceptions of 'liberalism'. Volume 32 is the supplementary volume of the monumental edition published by the Oxford University Press of *The Letters and Diaries of John Henry Newman* and contains more than 500 letters omitted from the previous volumes. There are also twelve appendices, covering differing accounts of Newman's funeral, obituary notices from a wide range of newspapers reflecting the atheist, the vegetarian, the *Church Times* and even *The Rod and the Gun*, reminiscences of Newman, and the text of a journal maintained by Newman reflecting his detailed attention to his administrative tasks and dates (pp. 507–660). The additional letters date from 1830 and extend beyond his Anglican period to the last days of Newman's life. Editor Francis J. McGrath's annotations are detailed, thorough and provide the model of scholarly annotation. There are twelve black and white illustrations, seven of which relate to Newman's death, the funeral service, the cortège and his final resting place (pp. 498–503). This superb supplement concludes with a 'List of Letters by Correspondents' (pp. 661–77), a listing of 'Memoranda and Other Documents' (pp. 677–9), a listing of 'Letters to Newman and Others' (pp. 679–80), and a very useful, annotated, extensive index of persons and places (pp. 681–731). McGrath notes in his preface that 'one more task now remains to bring this unique series to a close—namely, the compilation of an index volume for the whole thirty-two volumes'. All students of nineteenth-century Britain, prose, religion and so much more owe a debt of gratitude to McGrath, his predecessor Gerald Tracey, and the publisher for these magnificent volumes. Devon Fisher's 'John Henry Newman and the Spirit of Old Rome' (*NCP* 35:ii[2008] 109–32) concentrates on Newman's travel writing. This 'reveals that travel and development were one and the same for Newman and that his physical travel to Rome in 1833 in many ways proved to be the original moment of his 1845 conversion' (p. 109). In short, Newman's travel writing forces us to reconsider his later conversion. Last but by no means least in this rich year for Newman studies, Dwight A. Lindley III writes on 'Newman's Romantic Meta-Rhetoric in *An Essay in Aid of a Grammar of Assent*' (*Renascence* 41:i[2008] 39–50).

The spring issue of the *Pater Newsletter* contains the extremely useful and important analysis of Pater 'Resources' (*PaterN* [2008] 23–51). This encompasses 'A Walter Pater Web bibliography' compiled by Leslie Higgins (p. 23), followed by accounts of primary sources, secondary sources, related topics, philosophical topics, literary topics, 'Pater's "Circles" Sidney Colvin to Oscar Wilde' (pp. 35–41), 'Queer Studies and Literature, Homosexuality in History to Queer Studies Resources' (p. 41), 'Victorian Literature and Culture: From the BBC to the Victorian Web' (p. 43), and 'Library Information, Electronic Books to Virtual Libraries' (pp. 47–51). *CVE* 68[2008] is entirely devoted to 'Studies in Walter Pater'. In addition to Bénédicte Coste's introduction (*CVE* 68[2008] 13–22) there are ten contributions. These include: Geoffrey Sadock on 'The Contemporary Critical Reception of Walter

Pater: Retrospective and Proleptical Views' (*CVE* 68[2008] 23–45), which includes a table attempting 'to objectify Walter Pater research in the computer age using the search engine' (p. 41); Martine Lambert-Charbonnier's 'Pater's Scholar and the Hypertext' (*CVE* 68[2008] 47–61); Margaux Poueymirou's 'Walter Pater's *Anders-Streben*: As Theory and as Practice' (*CVE* 68[2008] 63–85), a discussion of 'Walter Pater's Seminal Essay "The School of Giorgione" (1877)' (p. 63); J.B. Bullen's 'Pater and Contemporary Visual Art' (*CVE* 68[2008] 87–104), this is accompanied by two black and white illustrative figures; Julia Straub's '"Diaphaneité" and Dante: A New Perspective on Pater's Early Essay' (*CVE* 68[2008] 105–22); Morito Uemura's '"Diaphaneité": Pater's Enigmatic Term' (*CVE* 68[2008] 123–34); Jean-Baptiste Picy's 'Pater's *Poikilia*—Auto-références, métaphors et impressions dans *Platon et la Platonisme* (1893)' (*CVE* 68[2008] 135–54) accompanied by two illustrative colour figures; Anne-Florence Gillard-Estrada's 'The Resurrected Youth and the Sorrowing Mother: Walter Pater's Uses of the Myths of Dionysus and Demeter' (*CVE* 68[2008] 155–80); John Coates's 'Marius' "Grammar of Assent": Pater's Dialogue with Newman' (*CVE* 68[2008] 181–203); and Bénédicte Coste's 'Pater: De la décadence à l'euphuisme' (*CVE* 68[2008] 205–27). All in all, then, these essays are worthy tributes to their subject. Stefano Evangelista's fascinating 'A Revolting Mistake: Walter Pater's Iconography of Dionysus' (*VR* 34:ii[2008] 201–18) examines Pater's 'A Study of Dionysus' published in the *Fortnightly Review* in December 1876. Evangelista focuses upon Pater's friendship with Simeon Solomon (1840–1905) in a consideration of the context of Pater's 'Dionysus'. The article is accompanied by two very useful black and white illustrations (pp. 200, 205) which include Simeon Solomon's *Bacchus* now at the Birmingham Museum and Art Gallery (p. 205).

Billie Andre Inman's elaborately entitled 'How Walter Pater Might Have Countered Charges that He Misused Sources: A Dialogue Between Graduate Student Walter Pater and Professor Samantha Marks at Great State University, USA, in 2003, with an Addendum' (*NCP* 35:ii[2008] 163–82), is an intriguing, clever interaction between early twenty-first-century attitudes and those of Pater's time. According to current notions, Pater might well have been regarded as a plagiarist. He would not have found the current environment conducive to his creativity. However, his treatment of sources was not really an issue to his contemporaries. They were aware that translations and editions made 'silent revisions'. Inman perceptively comments that 'Pater's attitudes towards sources and techniques of using them created in his works a profound intertextuality that is essential to his remarkable style' (p. 172). This survey of a very fertile year in Pater studies should not omit Gabriel Roberts's '"Analysis leaves off": The Use and Abuse of Philosophy in Walter Pater's *Renaissance*' (*CQ* 37[2008] 407–25).

The magisterial *Correspondence of Dante Gabriel Rossetti* continues. The 'Publisher's Note on the Completing Editors and their Contributions' to volume 6, covering the years 1873–4, notes that 'The texts of the letters, dating, ordinance, and head notes in volumes 3 to 9 are the work of the Editor, William E. Fredeman, although since his death in July 1999 new letters have turned up and been inserted, some letters have been re-dated and relocated, and some textual emendations have been made by the completing editors' (p. vii). In other words, Roger C. Lewis, Jane Cowan, Roger W. Peattie, Allan Life and Page Life have completed what William E. Fredeman began for volume 6. Roger C. Lewis, Jane Cowan, Anthony Harrison and Christopher Newall have completed what he began for volume 7, covering the years 1875–7. The sixth volume contains thirty-one black and white illustrations and three full-page colour plates. In addition to an 'Editorial Statement, Editorial Principles, Description of Letter Entries and Stylistic Conventions' (pp. xi–xvii) and a 'Listing of Abbreviations' (pp. xxi–xl), which in itself contains an extensive bibliography of primary and secondary materials, there are the texts of 'Recently Located Letters Not Included in the Earlier Volumes' (pp. 1–4). Each year is prefaced by a listing of Rossetti's 'Major Works of the Year' and a brief 'Summary of the Year's Letters' followed by an extensive 'Chronology' (pp. 7–13). The letters themselves are replete with extensive annotations. There are in volume 6 three appendices: Roger C. Lewis writes on 'Rossetti's Relations with the Morrises 1868–75' (pp. 583–7); Allan Life gives an account of 'The Oil Versions of Rossetti's *Proserpine*' (pp. 588–604); and Allan and Page Life write on 'Monna Innominata Alexa Wilding' (pp. 605–45).

The seventh volume covers the years 1875–7 and follows the pattern laid down by the previous volumes. 'Recently Located and Re-dated Letters not Included in the Earlier Volumes' (pp. 1–4) includes a six-paragraph letter addressed to William Bell Scott dated 8 May [1863] concerning Scott's rejection by the Royal Academy (pp. 1–2). The 'Major Works of the Year' include 'Proserpina' and the oil *La Bella Mano*. The 'Summary of the Year's Letters' notes that Rossetti 'remained in London until mid-October, 1875, when he went to Aldwick Lodge near Bognor'. Throughout the year, the extent of his dissatisfaction with [the art dealer Charles August Howell] increased' (p. 7). The letters begin with one to Walter Theodore Watts-Dunton, dated 2 January 1875 (p. 11), and conclude with an undated letter to Frederick James Shields written on an unspecified Friday evening (p. 478). The final specifically dated letter in volume 7 is to the art collector and shipping magnate Frederick Richards Leyland, dated 20 December 1877. Again, there is much of interest in this volume; however, its value will certainly increase once a detailed index to the volumes appears. The publishers D.S. Brewer, the Modern Humanities Research Association and the printers the Cromwell Press, Trowbridge, Wiltshire, are to be congratulated on producing such magnificent volumes.

D.M.R. Bentley's ' "Of Venus and of Cupid,—Of Strange Old Tales" in the Work of D.G. Rossetti' (*VR* 34:ii[2008] 83–102) usefully illuminates its subject's use of the classics.

In a vintage year also for Ruskin studies may be found Jeremy Tambling's '*Fors Clavigera*: Outside Chances, Posthumous Letters' (*English* 57:ccix[2008] 213–32). Tambling gives a clear reading of Ruskin's *Letters to the Workmen and Labourers of Great Britain*, published between 1871 and 1874. Amongst the issues Tambling discusses are those relating to the perception of Ruskin's letters as 'posthumous' and his examination of 'what in them resists that sense that they are free from the founding authority of the father, and so are controlled by chance' (p. 213). Tambling also pays attention to the ramifications of 'the meaning of their title' and their language. He usefully draws upon the work of Jacques Derrida to provide commentary upon Ruskin's text. Van Akin Burd's 'Ruskin and his "Good Master," William Buckland' (*VLC* 36:ii[2008] 299–315) publishes and discusses the implications of a letter from John James Ruskin to his son's Christ Church, Oxford, tutor, the Reverend William Buckland (1784–1856). The letter, dated 4 November 1837, helps in comprehending 'the importance of Buckland's lectures in Ruskin's conception of geology in his later debates with the evolutionists' (p. 299).

Andrew Leng's important 'Ruskin's Rewriting of Darwin: *Modern Painters 5* and "The Origin of Wood"' (*PSt* 30:i[2008] 64–90) argues that Ruskin's *Modern Painters 5* [1860] is an extensive, although coded, rewriting of Darwin's *The Origin of Species* [1859]. Leng argues that it is necessary for us to rethink our understanding of both and of the ways in which the Victorians reacted to Darwin. Ruskin's *Modern Painters 5* is an elaborate alternative account concentrating upon the origins of wood, as opposed to Darwin's image of the great tree representing natural selection. Ruskin's book concludes with an apocalypse in which Protean dragons similar to those that had recently been resurrected at nearby Crystal Palace Park, triumph. The spring 2008 issue of *Nineteenth-Century Prose* is entirely devoted to John Ruskin. As Sharon Arvonofsky Weltman observes in her 'Introduction: Reinterpreting Ruskin' (*NCP* 35:i[2008] 1–12) 'over a century after [Ruskin's] death, scholars still have plenty of work to do in interpreting this complicated and important figure' (p. 2). She notes that 'the variety of articles in this special issue on John Ruskin attests not only to the diversity of Ruskin's interests but also to the range of approaches and topics in Ruskin studies now' (p. 3). Elizabeth Helsinger, in 'Ruskin and the Aesthetics of Color' (*NCP* 35:i[2008] 13–36), considers Ruskin's perceptions of colour, comparing them with Baudelaire's. For both, what is 'peculiarly modern about color produced across or through obscurity is its power to move modern spectators hyper-conscious of their own exiles and longings' (p. 29). Alison Milbank on the other hand, in her 'Ruskin's Grotesque: *Praeterita* as Dantesque Journey to be Read' (*NCP* 35:i[2008] 37–57), compares Ruskin to his admirer Proust who translated him into French. For Milbank, *Praeterita* is 'a journey into memory to recover a lost self ... a recovery of the world of phenomena'. Like Proust, Ruskin, too, focuses upon 'objects as the fish-hooks upon which memories may be secured' (p. 38). David E. Hanson, in his 'Ruskin, Dante and the Dark Waters of *Praeterita*' (*NCP* 35:i[2008] 58–93), examines the drafts for *Praeterita* to show that Ruskin's truncation and reorganization do not exemplify 'eruptions of a deranged mind' but instead the 'earned pleasure of practtirition' enabling the author and reader to transverse 'Dantean suffering and contrition' (p. 62), in order to experience 'Paradisiacal works with Rosie [La Touche]' and to come to terms with his own memory (p. 85). Francis O'Gorman, in 'Ruskin and Fame' (*NCP* 35:i[2008] 94–112), discusses the *Praeterita* drafts in order to show that 'in a volume written over two decades ... Ruskin was at times uncertain of what the purpose was at all' (p. 103).

Sara Atwood's ' "Riveder le stelle": *Fors Clavigera* and Ruskin's Educational Experiment' (*NCP* 35:i[2008] 113–34) turns attention to another Ruskin work, his longest, spanning 'ninety-six letters and fourteen years'. Atwood argues that '*Fors* has a pattern and a structure ... held together and sustained by the very threads of thought and information that many critics found so rambling' (p. 115). Atwood writes that the work operates 'as a teaching text rather than as a passive exposition of Ruskinian philosophy' (p. 130). Amelia Yeates's 'Ruskin, Women's Reading and Commodity Culture' (*NCP* 35:i[2008] 135–60) considers Ruskin's perception of the woman reader and women's reading. For Ruskin, reading 'forms a locus where the major areas of his thinking—aesthetics, education and political economy—come together' (p. 135), seen for instance in Ruskin's description in *Fors Clavigera* of the behaviour of two young American girls 'on a train journey from Venice to Verona' (p. 148). Ruskin's attack in the second volume of *The Stones of Venice* on paintings by the Spanish artist Bartolomé Esteban Murillo (1617–82) forms the entire focus of Miles Mitchard's 'Race and Radicalism: Ruskin and Murillo' (*NCP* 35:i[2008] 161–80). On the other hand, aesthetics are not the primary concern of Supritha Rajan's 'Sacred Commerce: Rites of Reciprocity in Ruskin' (*NCP* 35:i[2008] 181–99). She focuses on Victorian anthropology and political economy as expressed in Ruskin's works, such as *Time and Tide*, *Unto This Last* and *Munera Pulveris*, arguing that 'Ruskin presents labor as a sacrificial ritual in which individuals experience communality and affirm the sacrosanct nature of the social body by coordinating their actions in a system of reciprocal self-sacrifice' (pp. 182–3).

Jed Mayer's 'Ruskin, Vivisection and Scientific Knowledge' (*NCP* 35:i[2008] 200–22), is one of two articles in the issue dealing with Ruskin's relationship to Victorian science. For Mayer, 'while Ruskin's role in the developing discourses of environmentalism and eco-criticism is beginning to receive due acknowledgment, his similar role in animal rights advocacy has been given little attention, despite its pivotal role in his critique of modernity' (pp. 207–8). Mayer sees Ruskin's opposition to the practice of vivisection as the main factor in his decision to resign his Oxford professorship. Comparing Ruskin's attitudes to vivisection to those of his contemporaries, Mayer concludes that 'Ruskin's approach constitutes a middle ground that could have found a more moderate audience than the polarizing voices that were heard instead on the subject' (p. 9). The relationship between Ruskin and Darwin is the subject of the final essay in this notable issue of *NCP*. George Levine's 'Ruskin, Darwin and the Matter of Mind' (*NCP* 35:i[2008] 223–49) is replete with insights. For example, 'For the most part, Ruskin's brilliant use of metaphor and his application of myth to the material world works in a reverse way—that is, to transform the material into the metaphor, into the mythic' (p. 245). Levine concludes his discussion of the similarities and differences between Ruskin and Darwin: 'Darwin's last book was, in effect, about worms' defecation, upon which our world is built. Ruskin, alas, increasingly lost his power to function in a world that was built that way' (p. 247)—magnificent stuff, worthy of Ruskin and Darwin! Mention should be made of the online *The Eighth Lamp: Ruskin Studies Today* 1:ii. This bi-annual, double-blind refereed journal devoted only to Ruskin may be accessed through

< http://www.oscholars.com/ >. Elizabeth Brewster and Amanda Flynn's 'My Dear Alice: A Newly Discovered Letter from John Ruskin' (*N&Q* 55[2008] 453–7) throws an interesting light upon Ruskin's relationships. Kevin A. Morrison's 'Myth, Remembrance and Modernity: From Ruskin to Benjamin via Proust' (*CL* 60:ii[2008] 125–40) contains an extensive discussion of Ruskin's prose and observations on the nature of the 'aesthetic redemption of ordinary experience' (p. 125) to be found in his work.

Roslyn Jolly's 'Nympholepsy, Mythopoesis and John Addington Symonds' (*VR* 34:ii[2008] 149–64) is a welcome addition to discourse on Symonds. Jolly's lens is Symonds's 'Byronic sense of nympholepsy as the vision of an ideal but unreachable wholeness and harmony of soul [which] infuses some of John Addington Symonds's most striking travel writing, particularly the opening essays of his two collections of the 1870s, *Sketches in Italy and Greece* (1874) and *Sketches and Studies in Italy* (1879)' (p. 151). Jolly also perceptively considers Symonds's 'Amalfi, Paestum, Capri' [1879], which 'provides a sophisticated analysis of the mythopoeic sense as "the apprehension of primeval powers akin to man, growing into shape and substance on the borderland between the world and the keen human sympathies it stirs in us"' (p. 161). Angus Whitehead's 'Mary Seacole's Wonderful Adventures of Mrs Seacole in Many Lands (1857): H V an Identification' (*N&Q* 55[2008] 439–40) contains a fascinating piece of arcane information. George Bernard Shaw spans two centuries and his genius cannot be limited to one period. A useful addition to Shaw studies is to be found in Ronald Ford's collection, *The Letters of Bernard Shaw to the Times, 1898–1950*. Shaw was a great letter-writer and 'The five decades of letters collected in this volume evidence not only Shaw's tireless productivity ... but the interests he took in current events of all kinds, from medicine and theatre to politics and economics.' Michel Pharand adds in his foreword: 'Nothing, it appears, was unimportant for Shaw, and his views on topical matters as they appeared in *The Times* form a fascinating portrayal of the socio-political and literary controversies and debacles of the first half of the twentieth century'. The volume contains 169 letters, of which 109 'have never before been published beyond the pages of *The Times*' (p. ix). Shaw pontificates upon subjects such as naval flogging, women's rights, capital punishment, copyright law, censorship, the atomic bomb, English pronunciation and other subjects. An appendix contains a listing of 'Previously Published Letters to *The Times*' (pp. 305–7) and a detailed index (pp. 308–16), which serves in some way to replace needed footnote annotation; however, groups of letters are followed by helpful commentary on the part of Ronald Ford.

2. The Novel

(a) General

Andrew H. Miller, in his *The Burdens of Perfection: On Ethics and Reading in Nineteenth-Century British Literature*, examines ideas of perfectionism related to morality with specific reference to Jane Austen's *Pride and Prejudice*,

Dickens's *Dombey and Son* and *Great Expectations*, and, especially, George Eliot's *Daniel Deronda*, where he seems to be especially fascinated with the character of Gwendolyn Harleth. Miller brings out well the relative diversity of perceptions revealed in these novels. Somewhat ironically, his readings, especially of attitudes to Gwendolyn Harleth, might have benefited from analysis of Yiddish readers' reactions to a character whom, in late nineteenth-century and early twentieth-century journals, they regarded as thoroughly immoral. George Levine, in his *How to Read the Victorian Novel*, uses *The Pickwick Papers* to illuminate the origins of the Victorian novel, Thackeray's *Vanity Fair* to analyse the realistic novel, Charlotte Brontë's *Jane Eyre* and Dickens's *David Copperfield* to discuss the Bildungsroman and Wilkie Collins's *The Woman in White* as his example of the sensation novel. In his final chapter, George Eliot's *Middlemarch* is examined as the representative Victorian novel. Levine as usual has refreshing things to say about Victorian novels and this book is highly recommended.

An extensive review essay that should not go unnoticed is Silvana Colella's 'Trading Insights: Political Economy, Finance, and Literature' (*NCStud* 21[2007] 223–35). Colella discusses in detail six recent publications: Margaret Schabas, *The Natural Origins of Economics*; Catherine Gallagher, *The Body Economic: Life, Death and Sensation in Political Economy and the Victorian Novel*; Brian P. Cooper, *Family Fictions and Family Facts: Harriet Martineau, Adolphe Quetelet, and the Population Question in England, 1798–1859*; James Taylor, *Creating Capitalism: Joint-Stock Enterprise in British Politics and Culture, 1800–1870*; Francis O'Gorman, ed., *Victorian Literature and Finance*; and Gail Turley Houston, *From Dickens to 'Dracula': Gothic, Economics and Victorian Fiction*. For Colella, all of these books 'develop interesting lines of investigation. How they do so varies' (p. 234), and she is worth reading to understand what the differences are and what needs to be investigated. Transformations in the social and economic status of women during the 1860s, 1870s and 1880s provide a framework for Jennifer Hedgecock's *The Femme Fatale in Victorian Literature: The Danger and the Sexual Threat*. Rosa Dartle in *David Copperfield*, Mary Elizabeth Braddon's *Lady Audley's Secret*, Collins's *Armadale* and Hardy's *Tess* are the works that receive Hedgecock's fullest attention. Hedgecock is at her best when specifically discussing her chosen texts rather than engaging in conversation with some fairly dense theoretical writing.

Alison Case and Harry E. Shaw's *Reading the Nineteenth-Century Novel: Austen to Eliot* is intended as a guide to the nineteenth-century novel, although it is unclear which audience the authors are addressing. Chapters are devoted to discussions of *Pride and Prejudice*, *Persuasion*, *Waverley*, *Wuthering Heights*, *Jane Eyre*, *Vanity Fair*, *Mary Barton*, *Bleak House*, *The Warden*, *Barchester Towers*, *Lady Audley's Secret* and *Middlemarch*. Clearly with such a diverse group of novels, although they are treated as representative instances of the nineteenth-century novel, some discussions are more illuminating than others. A welcome feature is close attention to specific novel passages. There is a helpful appendix: 'Free Indirect Discourse' (pp. 199–205), which could have been more useful with more specific examples. On the whole, this is a useful volume but one that retreads familiar territory, and its further reading (pp. 212–19) contains significant glaring omissions.

Suzanne Daly's 'Spinning Cotton: Domestic and Industrial Novels' (*VS* 51[2008] 272–8) shows how Gaskell's *Wives and Daughters* and Disraeli's *Sybil* 'reveal how gendered dress codes in domestic novels position Indian textiles as markers to virtue and good taste, whereas industrial novels frequently evince a concern with cotton as a commodity and the cotton mill as a space in need of benevolent reform' (p. 272). Lisa Surridge's 'The Plot Thickens: Toward a Narratological Analysis of Illustrated Serial Fiction in the 1860s' (*VS* 51[2008] 65–101) uses 'Mary Elizabeth Braddon's sensational *Eleanor's Victory* and Elizabeth Gaskell's realist *Wives and Daughters*' to argue 'that illustration richly complicates the linear development of plot and plays a key role in constituting and negotiating the generic interplay of sensation and realism' (p. 65). Surridge's clearly written account is accompanied by twenty-seven interesting black and white illustrations from serialized fiction. Jason Marc Harris writes in the opening sentence of the second paragraph of the first chapter of his *Folklore and the Fantastic in Nineteenth-Century British Fiction* that 'How nineteenth century writers initiate, revise and transform preternatural folklore material into narratives of the literary fantastic is the substantive focus' of his work (p. 1). Novelists discussed include Charles Dickens, George Eliot, Neil Gunn, George MacDonald, and Robert Louis Stevenson. Elizabeth Sabiston's *Private Sphere to World Stage from Austen to Eliot* focuses on six women novelists—Jane Austen, Charlotte and Emily Brontë, Elizabeth Gaskell, Harriet Beecher Stowe and George Eliot—in an attempt to demonstrate 'the relationship between the self-reflexive novel and the emerging female text and voice' (p. 3). Sabiston concentrates on *Jane Eyre* and *Wuthering Heights*, various novels of Elizabeth Gaskell and shifting gender roles in *Daniel Deronda*. Her fifth chapter is entitled ' "Iron of Slavery in Her Heart": The Literary Relationship of Elizabeth Gaskell with Harriet Beecher Stowe' (pp. 131–50).

Elizabeth A. Bridgham, in her *Spaces of the Sacred and Profane: Dickens, Trollope and the Victorian Cathedral Town*, argues for 'an expanded understanding of Dickens and Trollope as city writers by increasing the types of cities and, indeed, of representation of Victorian geographical spaces that require literary analysis' (p. 3). In spite of being somewhat prolix, Bridgham genuinely illuminates Dickens's and Trollope's fictional versions of cathedral towns, showing that both 'turn a critical eye to cathedral towns' successes and failings', examining their 'religious and aesthetic potential and the ways in which they fall short of this potential' (p. 154). Ken Newton's *Modern Literature and the Tragic* contains intelligent, detailed readings of Thomas Hardy's *Tess of the d'Urbervilles* and *Jude the Obscure* and Trollope's *The Warden* and other novels. These are read with 'a crucial consideration' in mind, as well as 'the emergence of a cultural context in the latter half of the nineteenth century which provided the basis for a new conception of the tragic that is grounded in pessimism about life and the nature of the world'. To illustrate this, Newton draws upon Schopenhauer and Darwin, and also discusses 'Shaw's reasons for rejecting Darwinism in favour of Lamarckian evolutionary theory'. For Newton, Shaw's 'rejection of Darwinism was on philosophical rather than scientific grounds'. Newton asserts that 'There seems little doubt that Schopenhauerian philosophy and Darwinian evolutionary theory are central to Hardy's tragic representation of life in his fiction' (pp. 64–5). Discussion of Hardy and Trollope is preceded by one on George Eliot, who anticipated their concerns. She 'often shows how trivial acts can inadvertently have major consequences, thus emphasizing a lack of proportion in the nature of things with the implications that concepts of order such as justice in an absolute sense become purely human constructs' (p. 69), as in *The Mill on the Floss* for example.

Sahin Kuli Khattak's *Islam and the Victorians: Nineteenth Century Perceptions of Muslim Practices and Beliefs* largely draws upon fiction for her interesting analysis of the depictions of Islam by Victorian writers. Her concern is with British perceptions of Muslims and Islam both in the Ottoman empire and the Indian colonies. For Khattak, 'misrepresentation is generally manifest' (p. 11). Most of the literature was indeed hostile to Islam. Her most interesting discussions encompass Charles Dickens, Charlotte Brontë and George Eliot's representations, or rather misperceptions, of Islam. In her final chapter, Khattak actually discusses the Islamic concepts that she feels were misrepresented. She herself admits in her 'Afterword' that what is needed is greater 'detailed theological delving into works and concepts that form the fundamentals of Islam and or disparate Muslim nationalities' (p. 140). Daniel Novak's monograph, *Realism, Photograph and Nineteenth-Century Fiction* appears in the series Cambridge Studies in Nineteenth Century Literature and Culture. Novak provides an account of the complex relationship between photography and literary realism during the Victorian era. He draws upon readings and writings about photography and their relationship to the works of Charles Dickens, George Eliot and Oscar Wilde. Contrary to other critics who have made out the case for photography as defining what would constitute realism for literary fiction, Novak argues that photography in itself was associated with that which was considered unreal, in other words, with fiction and products of the literary imagination. For Novak, manipulation is an essential part of nineteenth-century realism and is dependent upon typicality rather than perfect reproduction. In his 'After-Image: Surviving the Photograph', which concludes his book, Novak writes, 'This book has worked to recover a *Victorian* theory of the photographic—a theory, in many ways, of ghostly and fictional bodies, who seem to flicker into a kind of spectral abstraction ... This spectral image of the Victorian photography continues to haunt contemporary discourse through the figures and metaphors we continue to apply to technology' (p. 151). His study is illustrated with many black and white photographs and is certainly an important addition not only to our readings of individual novelists, but to our consideration of Victorian realism.

Arlene Young's '"Petticoated Police": Propriety and the Lady Detective in Victorian Fiction' (*Clues* 26:iii[2008] 15–28) examines nineteenth-century stories and articles that have female detectives. Young's focus is the figure of the Victorian female sleuth and class and gender politics. Young's analysis encompasses interpretations of the cultural content of the text and the images from the stories she selects. A modern novel set in the Victorian period is the subject of Lewis C. Roberts, 'Discipline and Detection: The Domestic Power of Women in Anne Perry's *Highgate Rise*' (*Clues* 26:iii[2008] 29–41). Anne Perry (b. 1938) is a convicted murderer who has written fascinating novels. Her detective fictions set in the Victorian period focus upon women's domestic power, criminal investigations and social reform. In *Highgate Rise* [1991] Roberts argues that Perry can only offer the marriage of Thomas and Charlotte Pitt as any kind of solution to the violence inherent in Victorian society and our own. Troy J. Bassett's useful *At the Circulating Library: A Database of Victorian Fiction, 1837–1901* is available at < http://www .victorianresearch.org/atcl/index.php >. According to the website, 'This project aims to catalogue information about Victorian authors, publishers, and novels.' It 'encompasses all the three-volume novels written during the period: over 5000 titles written by some 1600 authors and published by 130 publishers appearing in *The English Catalogue of Books* and other sources. ATCL can be browsed by author, title, publisher, or year. In addition, users can do keyword searches on author names and book titles' (email posted by Troy Basset on Victoria Listserv, 6 January 2009). Jacqueline Fromonot's 'Pérégrinations at pérégrinismes dans le roman britannique de XIXᵉ siècle: Casuistique du détour par la langue étrangère' [Peregrination and Peregrinism in the British 19th-Century Novel: A Casuistry of the Detour Abroad in a Foreign Language'] (*CVE* 67[2008] 161–73) draws upon passages in Dickens, Thackeray, George Eliot and Trollope to examine the role of peregrinism in Victorian novels generally and in their novels in particular. Natalie Saudo's '"Knocking on Mrs Grundy's door with a bomb of dynamite": Peur(s) desfemmes dans quelques *New Woman Novels* des années 1893–1895' [Wholesome Fear(s) *New Woman* Novels 1893–1895'] (*CVE* 67[2008] 305–22) draws upon Sarah Grand's *The Heavenly Twins*, Arabella Kenealy's *Dr. Janet of Harley Street*, an anonymous novel entitled *A Superfluous Woman* and Grant Allen's *The Woman Who Did* in order to highlight the sense of fear in them and the way in which they illuminate Thomas Hardy's *Jude the Obscure*.

Tara Moore's 'Starvation in Victorian Christmas Fiction' (*VLC* 36:ii[2008] 489–505) focuses upon Christmas literature and its narratives, which spoke to the national concern with the fear of famine and starvation. Moore considers narratives by, amongst others, Charles Dickens, the neglected Benjamin Farjeon, August and Henry Mayhew, the creators of *Punch* and Mary Elizabeth Braddon, which focused upon hunger, and especially starvation, during the Christmas period. John R. Reed's 'Fighting Words: Two Proletarian Military Novels of the Crimean Period' (*VLC* 36:ii[2008] 331–42) is a valuable addition to the discussion of the work of the neglected Anglo-Irish novelist Charles Lever (1806–72) and other forgotten nineteenth-century authors. Reed examines the *Confessions of Harry Lorrequer* [1839] as the first of 'a string of popular novels about the army, with young officers as their heroes' produced by Lever. Other works in 'this subgenre' are described (p. 331), including works by Hawley Smart, G.W.M. Reynolds, Pierce Egan (the younger) and others. Reed's 'object . . . is to show how Reynolds and Egan voiced common complaints about the army in narratives that betray their purpose because they cannot escape the fictional convention that makes their stories attractive to a general audience' (p. 332). Two novels discussed in detail are Pierce Egan, Jr's *Clifton Grey: Or, Love and War: A Tale of the Present Day* [1854] and Reynolds's *The Soldier's Wife* [1853]. Bradley Deane's 'Imperial Barbarians: Primitive Masculinity in Lost World Fiction' (*VLC* 36:i[2008] 205–25) concentrates upon 'tales and forgotten cities, rediscovered races, civilization and continents submerged beneath the sea or the ground, the hidden vestiges of ancient empires' and specifically upon the 'over 200 such stories … published in Britain between 1871 and the First World War'. Focusing upon stories by Rudyard Kipling, Rider Haggard and Arthur Conan Doyle, Deane argues that 'the genre minimizes difference to represent barbarians not as the object of disgust or even of intractably ambivalent envy, but as the models of a new imperial masculinity' (pp. 206–7). A fascinating comparative analysis is found in Kathleen Conway's 'The Discourse of Secrets: Reflection and Growth in *Jane Eyre* and *Middlemarch*' (*VN* 113[2008] 22–34) in which she argues that in both 'secrets become a means to reflection and growth' (*VN* 114[2008] 36).

(b) Authors

There is nothing to report for 2008 on W. Harrison Ainsworth. However, R.M. Ballantyne received some attention. John Miller's 'Adventures in the Volcano's Throat: Tropical Landscape and Bodily Horror in R.M. Ballantyne's *Blown to Bits*' (*VR* 34:i[2008] 115–30) analyses the relationship between Ballantyne's novel, published in 1889, and the catastrophic 1883 volcanic eruption 'that wiped an island from the globe and produced meteorological effects from which no part of the earth was immune' (p. 83). Miller concludes his account: 'in the terms of Freudian psychology, *Blown to Bits* provides a condensed image, saturated with longing and unease, profoundly evocative of the ambivalence at the heart of colonial discourse' (p. 128).

Mary Elizabeth Braddon's *Lady Audley's Secret* [1862] is the subject of Emily E. Auger's 'Male Gothic Detection and the Pre-Raphaelite Woman in *Lady Audley's Secret*' (*Clues* 26:iii[2008] 3–14). Auger's focus is upon the Gothic characteristics of Mrs Braddon's novel, and in particular the locked room, the locked trunk motifs and Lady Audley's Pre-Raphaelite portrait. This is revealed as both a clue and an established fact in the detective's examination of Lady Audley's fraudulent upper-class mobility. Laurie Garrison's 'The Seduction of Seeing in M.E. Braddon's *Eleanor's Victory*: Visual Technology, Sexuality, and the Evocative Publishing Context of Once a Week' (*VLC* 36:i[2008] 111–30) contains a detailed discussion of Braddon's neglected sensation novel *Eleanor's Victory* [1863]. Garrison's perspective is 'the Victorian fascination with the influence of technology', Mrs Braddon's continual 'construction of multiple forms of sexuality' within the context 'of the periodical *Once a Week*' (pp. 111–12). Garrison's account includes George du Maurier's engravings accompanying the *Once a Week* text. As Daniel Martin explains in the opening sentence of his 'Railway Fatigue and the Coming-of-Age Narrative in *Lady Audley's Secret*' (*VR* 34:i[2008] 131–54),

'This essay reads Mary Elizabeth Braddon's *Lady Audley's Secret* through the "railway time" of the 1860s in order to situate Victorian anxieties about railway travel within the context of competing social discourses about the fatigued and nervous modern body.' Martin is also 'interested in how the novel reveals the inherent contradiction in contemporary dialogues about railway travel' (p. 131). Rachel A. Bowser, in 'Shattered Dials and Mute Objects: The Surfaces of *Lady Audley's Secret*' (*Genre* 41[Spring/Summer 2008] 75–94) focuses 'on the novel's efforts to "look beyond" its own surfaces and expose the fragile resolution such efforts produce' (p. 75). Bowser's is a subtle reading showing that the novel is much more complicated than we think. Elizabeth Adams's 'Professional Authorship: M.E. Braddon and Mary' (*N&Q* 55[2008] 467–9) is of interest.

Using a feminist new historicist approach, Sue Thomas, in her *Imperialism, Reform, and the Making of Englishness in Jane Eyre*, examines *Jane Eyre* from the perspectives of imperialism, slavery and race. Her final two chapters focus upon the neglected 1848 stage adaptation of the novel and an 1859 Caribbean parallel text. Thomas's work is largely theoretical, but nonetheless interesting. Julia Sun-Joo Lee's 'The (Slave) Narrative of *Jane Eyre*' (*VLC* 36:ii[2008] 317–29) takes issue with Susan Meyer, who argues in her *Imperialism at Home* [1996] that Charlotte Brontë's 'critique of British slavery and British imperialism' in *Jane Eyre* is based upon 'the West Indies' (p. 71). Sun-Joo Lee argues that it is 'more likely ... that Brontë was thinking not of West Indian slavery, but of American slavery' (p. 317). Lee finds considerable affinities between *Jane Eyre* and Frederick Douglass's *The Narrative of the Life of Frederick Douglass as An American Slave*, first published in 1845. Kevin A. Morrison's 'The Politics of Pain in Charlotte Brontë's *Shirley*' (*NCStud* 21[2007] 19–32) examines 'two notions of freedom' in *Shirley* demonstrating that 'the novel vacillates between' the two 'exploring the contradictory aspects of both, as it attempts to specify and ameliorate social inequality within the framework of early to mid nineteenth-century classical liberalism with its emphasis on individual interests ... and the triumph of the modern commercial and industrial economy'. The first notion 'involves basic rights' and the second 'suggests that justice and liberty have been obtained when the subject is free from distress' (p. 20). Jacqueline Banerjee's 'Charlotte Brontë's "Pain Pressed" Pilgrimage and its Critical Reception' (*VN* 114[2008] 69–92) concludes her account of Victorian and subsequent reactions to Charlotte Brontë's work: 'using pain in the service of art requires self-discipline. [Her] great and continuing popularity suggests that the reading public has always appreciated this, and listens as little now to critical carping as it has done in the past' (p. 90).

There are eleven individual contributions to Sandra Hagan and Juliette Wells's collection *The Brontës in the World of the Arts*. In their introduction (pp. 1–10), the editors outline previous work that has made it 'possible to investigate new and hitherto unexplored aspects of the Brontës involvement with the arts, as well as the artistic responses to their own works' (p. 3). In the first contribution, the pioneer in the field, Christine Alexander, in her 'Educating "The Artist's Eye": Charlotte Brontë and the Pictorial Image' (pp. 11–29), 'attempts to trace Jane [Eyre's] experience of art as a representation of Charlotte Brontë's own education and artistic trajectory, and by extension that of all young women of the period whose lives were circumscribed by convention'. Alexander adds that 'In the process, the essay will provide a survey of the type of visual art that influenced the Brontë family in their formative years' (p. 11). The essay is accompanied by eleven black and white illustrations drawn largely by Charlotte Brontë's artistic hand. Richard J. Dunn's 'Out of the Picture? Branwell Brontë and *Jane Eyre*' (pp. 31–44) focuses upon 'the influence of Branwell Brontë's aesthetics and his efforts towards a professional career upon the mature writing of his sister Charlotte' (p. 4). This contribution too is accompanied by black and white illustrations, in this instance five largely from Branwell's drawings. Antonia Losano's focus in 'Anne Brontë's Aesthetics: Painting in *The Tenant of Wildfell Hall*' (pp. 45–66) is on the implication of Helen's professional work as an artist as depicted in the novel. Juliette Wells, on the other hand, in '"Some of your accomplishments are not ordinary": The Limits of Artistry in *Jane Eyre*' (pp. 67–80), examines Charlotte Brontë's presentation of the amateur, accomplished artist rather than the professional one in *Jane Eyre*. Wells concludes: 'In adapting her own experience as an artist into *Jane Eyre* … Brontë replaces professional aspirations with social and personal ones, and substitutes gratified desire for gratified ambition' (p. 80).

Meg Harris Williams, in her 'The Hieroglyphics of Catherine: Emily Brontë and the Musical Matrix' (pp. 81–99), focuses on 'the way in which Brontë's musicality relates to the aesthetic evolution of emotionality' in *Wuthering Heights* and the association between this and 'some psychoanalytic and philosophical ideas about symbol-formation' (p. 82). Juliette Wells with Ruth A. Solie, in '*Shirley*'s Window on a Musical Society in Transition' (pp. 101–23), rather than focusing as Williams does 'on music as a force both organizing and suggestive' instead examines 'the implication of music actually made and heard in … *Shirley*' (p. 6). In her 'It "might give me with a world of delight": Charlotte Brontë and the Pleasures of Acting' (pp. 125–47), Anne W. Jackson locates Lucy's 'contradictory responses to staged theater … in the context of performance theory' (p. 6). Consumption, dress and fashion are the central concerns of Sara T. Bernstein's '"In this same gown of shadow": Functions of Fashion in *Villette*' (pp. 149–67). Illustrations for editions are discussed in Sandra Hagan's 'An Uneasy Marriage: Edmund Dulac, Lucy Snowe, and the Illustrative *Villette*' (pp. 169–95). Her essay is accompanied by six illustrations taken from the single-volume 1922 Dent edition of *Villette*. Patsy Stoneman's 'Jane Eyre's Other: The Emergence of Bertha' (pp. 197–211) pays attention to twentieth- and early twenty-first-century artistic perceptions of Bertha: these 'owe as much to feminist and postcolonial interpretations as to the original novel' (pp. 8–9). In the final contribution to this important addition to Brontë studies, Linda Lister writes on 'Music of the Moors: The Voices of Emily Brontë and Cathy in Opera and Song' (pp. 213–35). Her essay on operatic and song versions of *Wuthering Heights* concludes with her own song settings from Emily and Charlotte Brontë (pp. 230–3). *The Brontës in the World of the Arts* concludes with an alphabetically arranged, enumerative bibliography (pp. 237–49): there is also an index (pp. 251–6).

Of interest to students of Brontë are the following: Mary Summers's 'Mary Taylor's Response to the *Journal et Lettres* of Eugénie de Guérin' (*BS* 33:i[2008] 1–8); Kathryn Miele's 'Do Unto Others: Learning Empathy in *Agnes Grey*' (*BS* 33:i[2008] 9–19); Christine Colón's 'Beginning Where Charlotte Left Off: Visions of Community in Anne Brontë's *The Tenant of Wildfell Hall*' (*BS* 33:i[2008] 20–9); Paola Tonussi's 'From *Werther* to *Wuthering Heights*: Possible *Convergences*' (*BS* 33:i[2008] 30–43); Graeme Tytler's 'Master and Servants in *Wuthering Heights*' (*BS* 33:i[2008] 44–53); Kristina Bedford's 'Patrick Brontë's Lost Landlords' (*BS* 33:i[2008] 54–7); and Ann Dinsdale's 'Recent Acquisitions at the Brontë Parsonage Museum' (*BS* 33:i[2008] 58–64). *Brontë Studies* July 2008 issue includes: Maddalena de Leo's 'Charlotte Brontë's Use of Italian Culture and Language in her Later Juvenilia' (*BS* 33:ii[2008] 87–90); Sharon Connor's '"Loneness" in the Letter of Charlotte Brontë' (*BS* 33:ii[2008] 91–6); Stephen Whitehead's 'Arthur Bell Nicholls: A Reassessment' (*BS* 33:ii[2008] 9–108); Lee A. Talley's '*Jane Eyre*'s Little-Known Debt to the *Methodist Magazine*' (*BS* 33:ii[2008] 109–19); Cassandra Fell's '*Jane Eyre* and Jenny Lind' (*BS* 33:ii[2008] 120–35); Rebecca White's '"Fresh Eyre"? How Original is Sandy Welch's Televised *Jane Eyre?*' (*BS* 33:ii[2008] 136–47); Ken Hiltner's '*Shirley* and the Luddites' (*BS* 33:ii[2008] 148–58); and Michael Walker's 'Two Eminent Victorian Surgeons' (*BS* 33:ii[2008] 159–68).

Brontë Studies 33:iii[2008] contains much of interest. Jamie S. Crouse's '"This shattered prison": Confinement, Control and Gender in *Wuthering Heights*' (*BS* 33:iii[2008] 179–91), focuses upon 'the recurrent plot device confinement, both physical and psychological, as a means of establishing power over others and its consequences in *Wuthering Heights*'. This is 'explored within the nineteenth-century social framework of traditional gender roles' (p. 179). Crouse writes clearly and on the whole eschews too much complex critical jargon, concluding that 'while Emily Brontë envisions a unity for Catherine and Heathcliff, and freedom from the confines of traditional gender roles, this reality, she shows, does not exist in this life, only perhaps in the next' (p. 190). Laura Inman's '"The Awful Event" in *Wuthering Heights*' (*BS* 33:iii[2008] 192–202), focuses upon the dominating narrative theme of death in *Wuthering Heights*. For Inman, 'Emily Brontë's own experience with death serves in part to explain the focus on death in the novel, and in particular, the presence of numeric symbols of death, which have gone unnoticed by critics'. Further, her poetic proclivity is the basis for understanding why *Wuthering Heights* is a veritable meditation on death (p. 192). James Phillips's 'Marriage in *Jane Eyre*: From Contract to Conversation' (*BS* 33:iii[2008] 203–17) tends to state the obvious: '*Jane Eyre* contends that marriage is irreducible to a contract; it must be sustained by the conversation of equals. Yet the marriage of equals that the novel's conclusion describes between Jane and Rochester cannot be confused with the legal entrenchment of sexual inequality in early nineteenth-century marriage laws' (p. 203). For Phillips, 'Jane needs others, not in order to complete herself, not in order to know herself, but in order to recreate herself' (p. 214), and Phillips clearly indicates that *Jane Eyre* 'is presented as Jane's autobiography, but of course it is not that. It is a work of fiction.' Further, its author 'often seems unsure if she wants to be a writer of fiction' (p. 215). Such observations have interesting ramifications.

In ' "I heard her murmurs": Decoding Narratives of Female Desire in *Jane Eyre* and *Secresy*' (*BS* 33:iii[2008] 218–31), Nicole Plyler Fisk reads *Jane Eyre* 'as a companion text to Eliza Fenwick's *Secresy* (1795)' thereby offering a fresh perspective on Charlotte Brontë's novel (p. 218). Sarah Fermi's 'A Trip to Yorkshire—1842' (*BS* 33:iii[2008] 232–41) publishes a letter dating from 'the time of the Chartist riots during the general strike of August, 1842'. The letter 'reveals details of upper middle-class social life in the West Riding of Yorkshire in the Brontë era and sheds light on a prominent local family well known to the Brontës by reputation, a family related to several others with whom the Brontës had a personal connection' (p. 232). In his 'The Rout of the Reverend Redhead: Gaskell and Longley' (*BS* 33:iii[2008] 242–4), Brian Wilks draws 'attention to the account that the Bishop of Ripon gave his wife of the tale of the Reverend Redhead's experience at the mercy of Haworth villagers objecting to his appointment as their minister'. Wilks notes that 'This version pre-dates and differs from Mrs. Gaskell's account in her *Life of Charlotte Brontë*' (p. 242). James Ogden's most helpful 'A Brontë Reading List: Part 2' (*BS* 33:iii[2008] 245–55), is 'the second part of an annotated bibliography of essays, mostly in scholarly and critical journals, 2000–2007' (p. 245). The first part appeared in *BS* 33:ii[2007] 157–64 (see *YWES* 88[2009] 808). An item of interest too is Bob Duckett's 'New Landmarks in Brontë Bibliography' (p. 256) (*Library Review* 57:i[2008] 67–73).

Alan H. Adamson, a very distant relative, has produced a fascinating account of *Mr. Charlotte Brontë: The Life of Arthur Bell Nicholls* (1819–1906), who married Charlotte Brontë. Drawing upon existing scholarship and family material in his own possession, and 'with the exception of *My Dear Boy* by Margaret and Robert Cochrane', published in 1999, Adamson's 'is the only account of Arthur's life with the focus on him, rather than on Charlotte or Patrick Brontë, Mrs. Gaskell or George Smith'. Adamson's work is divided into three sections. The first part concentrates upon 'Arthur's early development in Ireland' and what he refers to as 'certain traumatic experiences in these early Irish years [that] influenced Arthur's psychological and intellectual formation and ... affected his religious outlook'. The second part of his study examines 'the critical sixteen years of his curacy at Howarth' and the third part focuses on 'the third period of his life from 1861 to 1906 more fully than has previously been done' (pp. xii–xiv). Adamson's text contains fascinating family photographs and a family tree. Katie R. Peel's 'The "thoroughly and radically *incredible*" Lucy Snowe: Performativity in Charlotte Brontë's *Villette*' (*VIJ* 36[2008] 231–44) examines closely the Vashti passage in *Villette* as 'a key to reading Lucy's transgression through performance' (p. 232). Peel concludes that 'Lucy appeals to the reader to challenge the normative ... Lucy ... is queer, and her final "Farewell" is a hope addressed to a queer reader' (p. 247).

Anna-Margaretha Horatschek's ' "I care for myself. [...] I will keep the law": Ethische Implikationen der Selbstsetzung in Charlotte Brontë's *Jane Eyre* (1849) und John Fowles' *The French Lieutenant's Woman* (1969)' (in Horatschek et al., pp. 63–82) is an interesting comparative study written in

German. William Leung 'explores the characterization of Edgar Linton in Emily Brontë's *Wuthering Heights*' (*English* 57:ccvii[2008] 4–38). Augustin Trapenard's 'L'Étrangeté d'une langue étrangère (dé)familiariser l'expérience belge d'Emily Brontë' ['A Strange Foreign Language: (De)familiarizing Emily Brontë's Belgian Experience'] (*CVE* 67[2008] 201–16) treads familiar ground in its examination of Charlotte and Emily Brontë's 1842 stay in Brussels and the creative transformation of the experience. Charlotte Borie's 'La Correspondence de Charlotte Brontë: Coulisses du style et de l'écriture' ['The Letters of Charlotte Brontë: Behind and Around the Scene of Style and Writing'] (*CVE* 67[2008] 367–77) explores a stylistic change in Brontë's letters following her development as a professional novelist. Melissa Fegan's *Wuthering Heights: Character Studies*, directed at the British undergraduate market, is part of the Continuum Character Studies series that 'aims to promote sophisticated literary analysis through the concept of character' (p. ix). Fegan's clearly written account opens with an analysis of the roles of Lockwood and Nelly Dean in Brontë's novel, then looks at its ' "narrative structures" [and] the first generation of Earnshaws and Lintons'. She then proceeds to examine 'the second generation of the same families' before proceeding to a detailed analysis of the characters of Heathcliff and Catherine and the final generation (pp. 10–11). Fegan is to be commended for her lack of pretentiousness, and clearly written, helpful prose. She provides an annotated, useful guide to further reading (pp. 117–19), an enumerative bibliography (pp. 121–4) and a helpful index (pp. 125–30). This text is not for those looking for incomprehensible theoretical approaches. Gwen Hyman's ' "An infernal fire in my veins": Gentlemanly Drinking in *The Tenant of Wildfell Hall*' (*VLC* 36:ii[2008] 451–69) is a valuable addition to our understanding of Anne Brontë's novel by showing how much it is 'sodden with drink'. She writes that 'this startlingly explicit novel is a troubled and troubling anatomy of upper-crust drunkenness, obsessed with issues of control and productivity, of appetites and class, as they play out across the body of its prime spot, the wealthy playboy Arthur Huntingdon'. Additionally, Arthur's drinking is 'emblematic of the increasingly untenable role of the landed gentleman in Victorian culture, and the dire consequences of his appetites suggest the possibility of a radically social revisioning across that gentleman's prone, overstuffed body' (p. 451). Finally, of interest is Monica Germana's 'Plagiarising the Etrick Shepherd: A Note on the Manuscript of Charlotte Brontë's *Tales of the Islanders*' and Winifred Gerin's *Emily Brontë*' (*N&Q* 55[2008] 461–3). Adrian Radu's 'Cosmic Order and Setting as Spiritual and Geographical Entity in Emily Brontë's *Wuthering Heights*' (StudUBBPhil 50:iv[2005] 29–37) focuses upon the novel's setting and makes some refreshing observations.

Usually treated as a post-Edwardian figure, in *Chesterton and the Romance of Orthodoxy: The Making of GKC, 1874–1908*, William Oddie explores Chesterton's spiritual and imaginative development from his adolescence during the 1870s to the earliest decade of the last century. Oddie draws upon unpublished letters and notebooks and examines Chesterton's stories and what Oddie regards as his masterpiece, *Orthodoxy* [1908]. The value of this work primarily lies not only in the interpretations of Chesterton but in its use of hitherto unpublished materials. Elmar Schenkel's 'The Character of a Headstand: Eccentric Hedonism in the Narrative Works G.K. Chestertons' (in Horatschek et al., eds., pp. 237–50) provides a different perspective upon Chesterton. It is good to see a contribution on the anonymous publication of Caroline Clive's (1801–73) crime novel *Paul Ferroll: A Tale*, with its depiction of a violent murder. First published in July 1855, as Adrienne E. Gavin explains in a 'Note on the Text' to her splendid Valancourt Books edition, a second edition followed in October, 'a third edition with concluding notice in December the same year and the fourth in March 1856' (p. xxxix). Gavin's edition is based on the fourth edition. She also provides a clearly written, detailed critical revelation in her introduction (pp. vi–xxxii), 'Suggested Further Reading' and a 'Chronology of Caroline Clive' (pp. xxxiv–xxxvii), plus useful explanatory notes following the text of the novel (pp. 230–43). Two appendices contain extracts from reviews of the various 1855 edition of *Paul Ferroll*, and a third appendix contains Clive's response to the critical reviews of her novel (pp. 244–56). Gavin's is a valuable edition and Valancourt Books too should be congratulated on its publication. Interestingly, Gavin draws attention to an unpublished 1989 University College London doctoral dissertation by Charlotte Lennox-Boyd, 'The Literary Career of Caroline Clive (1801–1873)' (p. 230).

Hoping to emulate his friend Dickens, Collins went on an American tour from September 1873 until March 1874. Susan Hanes's *Wilkie Collins's American Tour, 1873-4* is the first book on the subject. She has searched innumerable Canadian and American sources, newspaper accounts of the tour, and reviews of Collins's public readings. In addition, she has drawn upon her own discoveries of previously unpublished Collins letters and visited the places he visited. Hanes confirms twenty-five readings by Collins in twenty-two different locations, and her book has five extremely useful appendices. The first provides a synopsis of his reading, of his supernatural story 'The Dream Woman' which he enlarged for his American tour. The second is a dated tabular record of his performances and reactions to them. The third, arranged by days and dates, is an account of his itinerary. The fourth an alphabetically arranged list of attendees at two New York dinners in his honour. The fifth contains press portraits from contemporary newspapers of his physical description. Replete with fascinating details, this is a very important addition to our understanding of Wilkie Collins. William Baker, Andrew Gasson, Graham Law and Paul Lewis's *The Collected Letters of Wilkie Collins: Addenda and Corrigenda (4)*, published as a separate pamphlet by the Wilkie Collins Society, 'is the fourth in the series of annual updates to *The Public Face of Wilkie Collins: The Collected Letters*, published in four volumes by Pickering & Chatto in 2005'. The fourth 'Addenda and Corrigenda' contains forty new letters including 'items from auction or dealer's catalogues, libraries and collections which had previously been overlooked' (p. 1). Of considerable interest are a number of hitherto unpublished letters Collins wrote to William D. Booth, the Wall Street lawyer specializing in intellectual property matters.

Graham Law and Andrew Maunder produce a clearly written account of Wilkie Collins's life and career in their *Wilkie Collins: A Literary Life*, part of

Palgrave Macmillan's Literary Lives series. Drawing cleverly upon recent editions of their subject's correspondence and reconstruction of his library revealing his reading preferences, they trace the trajectory of a writer. Law and Maunder reveal how Collins eventually removed himself from the shadow of his religiously obsessed father, his beloved mother and the influence of Dickens to find his individual voice in highly successful novels. His entangled relations with the opposite sex, struggles with 'steadily deteriorating health' issues (p. 174) and a lack of fictional and dramatic success clouded his final years. Law and Maunder's biography places Collins in the context of the social and literary world of mid-Victorian Britain. There is too a useful 'Chronology of Collins's Life and Writings' (pp. x–xvii) in this highly recommended volume. Constance Collin's ' "The arrival of a foreigner and a stranger at my aunt's house": L'étrange et l'étranger dans *The Moonstone* (1868) de Wilkie Collins' (*CVE* 67[2008] 149–60) argues that Wilkie Collins 'turns Victorian representations upside down and poses the problem of definition and identity' in *The Moonstone* (p. 13). Laurence Talairach-Vielmas's ' "You don't suspect me of doing anything wrong, do you?": Peurs, soupçons et paranoïa dans *The Woman in White* de Wilkie Collins' ['Fears, Suspicions and Paranoia in Wilkie Collins's *The Woman in White*'] (*CVE* 67[2008] 323–36), uses a passage in a sermon by the archbishop of York cited in the *North British Review*, 43 [September 1865] concerning sensation novelists—that they wish 'to persuade people that in almost every one of the well-ordered houses of their neighbours there was a skeleton shut up in some cupboard' (p. 204)—as a foundation for an exploration of *The Woman in White*. John R. Reed's 'Law and Narrative Strategy in Wilkie Collins's *The Law and the Lady*' (*VIJ* 36[2008] 217–30) is a detailed, well-written account of the 'intriguing qualities' of Collins's novel. Reed writes: 'The text of the novel self-reflexively plays with its own relationship to the texts contained within its narrative, calling attention to the way in which written accounts transform oral accounts in a manner that makes them more serviceable in the tracing of a mystery—either in a law court or informally by a determined investigator' (p. 228). John Glendening, in 'War of the Roses: Hybridity in *The Moonstone*' (*DSA* 39[2008] 281–304), argues that '*The Moonstone* examines and enacts hybridity ... through the many references to roses and their cultivation that appear throughout the novel' (p. 281).

One of the most insightful critical voices of the late twentieth and early twenty-first centuries, Barbara Hardy, in *Dickens and Creativity*, draws upon Dickens's observations in his letters concerning the creative process and applies them to the various storytellers in his works. She also with great insight examines Shakespeare's influence on Dickens and Dickens's impact on subsequent writers. In addition, in clear prose Hardy provides a concise summary of all of his works. Virginia Zimmerman, in her *Excavating Victorians*, uses the ideas of Paul Ricoeur to read *Little Dorrit* and *Our Mutual Friend*. Her book is concerned with the exploration of diverse cultural reactions to developments in geology and archaeology in nineteenth-century Britain. She places Dickens and the work of others within this context. Jan Alber's *Narrating the Prison: Role and Representation in Charles Dickens' Novels, Twentieth-Century Fiction and Film*, 'investigates the ways in which

Charles Dickens' mature fiction, prison novels of the twentieth century, and prison films narrate the prison' (p. 1). Alber pays particular attention to film adaptations of *Little Dorrit*, *A Tale of Two Cities*, and *Great Expectations*. The distinguished Dickensian David Paroissien has edited the very valuable *Companion to Charles Dickens*. This has thirty-six chapters in five parts with thirty-six contributors. The first part, 'Perspectives on Life' (pp. 1–61), focuses on biography and autobiography and includes contributions by Michael Allen, Nicola Bradbury, the editor and Catherine Peters. The second part, 'Literary/Cultural Contexts' (pp. 63–156), has essays on 'The Eighteenth-Century Legacy' (pp. 65–80); 'Dickens and the Gothic' (pp. 81–96); 'Illustrations', profusely illustrated in black and white (pp. 97–125); 'The Language of Dickens' (pp. 126–41); and 'The Novels and Popular Culture' (pp. 142–56). The third part, 'English History Contexts' (pp. 157–93), has nine essays, ranging from 'Dickens as Reformer' (pp. 159–73) to 'Dickens and the Law' (pp. 277–93). Part IV focuses upon 'The Fiction', and there are individual essays on fifteen of the novels. The final part, 'Reputation and Influence', has three essays focusing on the subject. There is in addition an extensive index (pp. 501–15). The overall quality of the essays, not surprisingly given their authors, is high, and it would be invidious to single out one essay rather than another. Each is followed by a brief list of references and further reading. There is also throughout an eschewal of theoretical discourse.

Approaches to Teaching Dickens's Bleak House is a further addition to the generally excellent Approaches to Teaching World Literature series edited by Joseph Gibaldi. The editors of the *Bleak House* volume, John O. Jordan and Gordon Bigelow, do not depart from the format of the volumes in the series. Jordan and Bigelow contribute part I, 'Materials' (pp. 17–27), giving information on 'Editions', 'Bibliographies', 'Reference Works and Other Resources', 'Visual, Audiovisual and Electronic Materials', and so on. This is followed with the second part of the book devoted to 'Approaches' to *Bleak House* and divided into four sections: 'Victorian Contexts' (pp. 31–70); 'Teaching Specific Scenes, Patterns, or Problems' (pp. 71–112); 'Intertextual Approaches' (pp. 13–156); and 'Specific Teaching Contexts' (pp. 157–97). An appendix to this useful volume is devoted to 'A *Bleak House* Chronology' (pp. 199–200). There are twenty-five contributors to *Approaches to Teaching Dickens's Bleak House*, which concludes with the alphabetically arranged listing of works cited (pp. 211–26), and an index of names (pp. 227–30). *Dickens Studies Annual* features Carolyn Denver's 'The Gamut of Emotions from A to B. *Nickelby's* "Histrionic Expedition"' (*DSA* 39[2008] 1–16). Denver argues that 'In *Nicholas Nickelby*, Charles Dickens develops a new technique for his representation of complex, conflicted, deeply interior human emotions' (p. 1). James Buzard, in his 'Enumeration and Exhaustion: Taking Inventory in *The Old Curiosity Shop*' (*DSA* 39[2008] 17–41), believes that the novel 'makes a crisis in Dickens early career' and that it 'became a metafictional reflection on the condition of his own creativity' (p. 17). Buzard's article is accompanied by eight illuminating black and white illustrations. Lisa Hartsell Jackson's 'Little Nell's Nightmare: Sexual Awakening and Insomnia in Dickens's *The Old Curiosity Shop*' (*DSA* 39[2008] 43–58), applies Freudian ideas to illuminate Little Nell: she 'is drawn to wander, in part, by her budding sexuality' (p. 43). Igor Webb writes on 'Charles Dickens in America: The Writer and Reality' (*DSA* 39[2008] 59–96). For Webb, 'Dickens's disenchanted first visit to the United States in 1842 occasioned a new departure in his writing' (p. 59). Mark M. Hennelly Jr's 'Dickens's Daniel-Plato Complex: *Dombey* and *Bleak House*' (*DSA* 39[2008] 97–126) is accompanied by four black and white illustrations. Hennelly argues that 'through his canon, Dickens significantly adapts the writing on the wall from Daniel, often haunted by Plato's "Allegory of the Cave" wall in *The Republic*, to illustrate spectral "truths" requiring the reader's comparable intertextual interpretation' (p. 97). Natalie Kapetanios Meir, in her ' "What would you like for dinner?": Dining and Narration in *David Copperfield*' (*DSA* 39[2008] 127–47), is concerned with the question raised in the novel 'regarding the adoption and implementation of shared paradigms for social behavior' (p. 127); the article is accompanied by three black and white illustrations.

Dickens's blending, 'as a synthesis in ... the visual and aural' thereby inviting 'a gendered role-reversal for female and male characters and readers to assume power and envision empathetic action' (p. 149), concerns Kimberly L. Brown in her ' "When I kissed her cheek": Theatrics of Sexuality and the Framed Gaze in Esther's Narration of *Bleak House*' (*DSA* 39[2008] 149–75). Keith Easley, in his 'Self-Possession in *Great Expectations*' (*DSA* 39[2008] 177–222), summons the work of Mikhail Bakhtin 'on the authoring of heroes' as a way 'of reading *Great Expectations*' and consequently doing 'justice to Dickens's sense of the dynamic relationship between author/reader and characters' (p. 177). 'Representation of visits to the [Paris] morgue in Dickens's *Uncommercial Traveller* and in Browning's dramatic monologue "Apparent Failure" ' are the subjects of Britta Martens's 'Death as Spectacle: The Paris Morgue in Dickens and Browning' (*DSA* 39[2008] 223–48). Martens's contribution is accompanied by two not very explicit or informative black and white illustrations. Bert Hornback, a distinguished Victorianist, makes an interesting contribution largely focused on 'Mortimer Lightwood' (*DSA* 39[2008] 249–60) and other characters in *Our Mutual Friend*. Daniel Pollack-Pelzner, in his 'Reading and Repeating *Our Mutual Friend*' (*DSA* 39[2008] 261–79), explores 'how the historical drama of Boffin plot's critical reception repeats the representation of its development and interpretation within the novel' (p. 261). In a review essay Natalie B. Cole considers 'Dickens and Gender: Recent Studies, 1992–2007' (*DSA* 39[2008] 305–79). The essay concludes with Cole's useful enumerative, alphabetically arranged 'Dickens and Gender: Recent Studies, 1992–2007' (*DSA* 39[2008] 379–96). This is followed by Timothy Spurgin's equally useful review of 'Recent Dickens Studies, 2006' (*DSA* 39[2008] 397–441), accompanied by a listing of works cited (pp. 442–446)—enumerative and alphabetically arranged. The volume concludes with a helpful index (*DSA* 39[2008] 447–54).

True to form, the *Dickensian* offers much of interest. Juliet Johns's ' "People mutht be amuthed?": Reflections on Chatham's "Dickens World" ' (*Dickensian* 104:i[2008] 5–21) argues that 'Dickens's posthumous assimilation by respectable culture has perhaps blunted his symbolic ability, at least in the public imagination, to radically test perceived cultural hierarchies and oppositions.' For Johns, 'Dickens World forces us to think about Dickens and our cultural landscape afresh' (pp. 18–19). She is referring to 'Dickens World, at the former naval yards in Chatham, [which] cost £62 million and has been nearly forty years in the planning' (p. 5). Michael Irwin's 'The Bright Side of Death: Dickens and Black Humour' (*Dickensian* 104:i[2008] 22–31) considers Dickens's sadistic characters, such as 'the coldly cruel— Murdstone, Gowan or Drummle ... remaining unwaveringly detestable' (p. 27). Toru Sasaki's 'Edmund Wilson's "The Two Scrooges" Reconsidered" (*Dickensian* 104:i[2008] 32–43) concurs with Philip Collins's observation in his *Dickens and Crime* ([1962], p. 307) that he pores over Edmund Wilson's *The Wound and the Bow: Seven Studies in Literature* [1941] ' "with continual delight and benefit" ' (p. 41). The summer 2008 *Dickensian* opens with Robert C. Hanna's 'The Search for Fanny Dickens's Handwriting' (*Dickensian* 104:ii[2008] 101–10). Hanna's article is accompanied by an illustration of the handwriting he is discussing (p. 108). John Drew's 'Dickens on "Poor Hood": A New Article' (*Dickensian* 104:ii[2008] 111–22) reprints with commentary a book review which he attributes to Dickens from *The Daily News*, 29 January 1846, p. 2. Valerie Kennedy's 'Dickens and Savagery at Home and Abroad— Part I' (*Dickensian* 104:ii[2008] 123–39) considers 'the concept of savagery [which] is highly significant in both Dickens's journalism and his fiction' (p. 123). Perhaps the most interesting contribution to this issue is Angus Easson, Margaret Brown, Leon Litvack and Joan Dicks, 'The Letters of Charles Dickens: Supplement IX' (*Dickensian* 104:ii[2008] 140–58). New letters include Dickens to Lady Duff Gordon, 3 February 1846 (pp. 145–7) and Dickens to Frederick Dickens, 10 October 1850 (pp. 147–8). There is also a letter to Sir Joseph Olliffe, 24 August 1856, of which previously only the envelope was known to exist (pp. 157–8). Obituaries in this issue include Lucinda Hawksley's obituary of Elizabeth Dickens (1912–2008) (pp. 188–9) and Michael Slater's obituary of Richard D. Altick (1915–2008), 'the great Victorian scholar' (pp. 189–90).

The winter issue of the *Dickensian* opens with Peter R. Lewis's 'Dickens and the Staplehurst Rail Crash, 9 June 1865' (*Dickensian* 104:iii[2008] 197–203). The author teaches materials engineering and is thus able to authoritatively throw much light on the accident. His article is accompanied by two illustrations, including a 'detail from a contemporary photograph taken at the time by a local resident' (p. 200). Michael Slater's 'New Ternan Material at the Senate House Library, London' (*Dickensian* 104:iii[2008] 204–5) is illustrated by F. Guidi's photograph of Ellen Ternan '(?late 1860s)' (p. 194). Valerie Kennedy's 'Dickens and Savagery at Home and Abroad—Part II' (*Dickensian* 104:iii[2008] 206–22) focuses upon 'Dickens and the Child as Victim or Potential Savage' (pp. 206–12), 'Dangerous Adult Savages' (pp. 212–14) and 'Savagery as Critique' (pp. 215–17). In her conclusion, Kennedy points to the complicated nature of 'Dickens's view of savagery' (p. 217). Robert Terrell Bledsoe and Michael Slater's fascinating illustrated 'Alfred Dickens and the Mystery of the Maltese Cross' (*Dickensian* 104:iii[2008] 223–8) recounts their '30 July 2007 [visit] to Trinity Cemetery in the far north of Manhattan Island ... to visit the grave of Dickens's sixth child and fourth son Alfred' (p. 223). Bledsoe and Slater 'set out to trace the history of the grave and gravestone in order to find out just who it who gave the order for the cross to be carved on it' (p. 225). Robert C. Hanna's 'Solutions to Riddles Contributed to Ellen Beard's Album' (*Dickensian* 104:iii[2008] 229–30) provides solutions to the '20 riddles inscribed in the album belonging to Ellen Beard, sister of Thomas Beard, Dickens's friend and doctor' (p. 229). J.P. Vander Motten and Katrine Daemen-De Gelder's 'Dickens and Servaas de Bruin (1821–1901): Two Unpublished Letters' (*Dickensian* 104:iii[2008] 231–5) contains the text with commentary of two Dickens letters from 17 January and 4 March 1857 which they found 'included in a collection of various autographs preserved in the Royal Archives, The Hague' (p. 231). Both are included 'in Supplement X of the Letters in this issue (see pp. 241–42)' (p. 231). Angus Easson, Margaret Brown, Leon Litvack and Joan Dicks again contribute the invaluable 'The Letters of Charles Dickens: Supplement X' (*Dickensian* 104:iii[2008] 236–46). Highlights, in addition to the two letters to Servaas de Bruin, include a letter to Frederick Dickens dated 9 September 1841 (pp. 237–8), a letter in French to Friedrich Heinrich Geffcken (1830–96), the diplomat and jurist (pp. 244–5) and even a short note to Wilkie Collins dated 17 October 1857 from the 'Office of Household Words'. Issues contain reviews of recent books, conference reviews and obituaries where necessary, and 'Fellowship Notes and News' (pp. 265–7). There is also a useful index to volume 104 and an illustrations listing compiled by Michael Roberts.

The first issue of *Dickens Quarterly* for 2008 contains Christine Alexander's 'The Juvenilia of Charles Dickens: Romance and Reality' (*DQu* 25:i[2008] 3–22); Leslie Simon's 'Archives of the Interior: Exhibitions of Domesticity in *The Pickwick Papers*' (*DQu* 25:i[2008] 23–36); Nancy Metz's 'Italy: The Sequel' (*DQu* 25:i[2008] 37–45); plus extensive reviews of recent work and Elizabeth Bridgham's 'The Dickens Quarterly Checklist' (*DQu* 25:i[2008] 65–9). The second issue of *Dickens Quarterly* for 2008 contains Rodney Stenning Edgecombe's 'The Heroine of Quiet Service in *Dombey and Son*' (*DQu* 25:ii[2008] 73–89); Deborah A. Thomas's ' "Don't let the bastards grind you down": Echoes of *Hard Times* in *The Handmaid's Tale*' (*DQu* 25:i[2008] 90–7); I.E. McManus's 'Charles Dickens: A Neglected Diagnosis' (*DQu* 25:ii[2008] 98–106); Robert Garnett's 'The Mysterious Mourner: Dickens's Funeral and Ellen Ternan' (*DQu* 25:ii[2008] 107–17); reviews and Elizabeth Brigham's informative 'The Dickens Quarterly Checklist' (*DQu* 25:ii[2008] 136–41). In the third issue of the *Dickens Quarterly*, Norbert Lennartz writes on 'Charles Dickens Abroad: The Victorian Smelfungus and the Genre of the Unsentimental Journey' (*DQu* 25:iii[2008] 145–61), a very clear account of Dickens's Italian encounters. Jerome Meckier's '*The Three Clerks* and *Rachel Ray*: Trollope's Revaluation of Dickens Continued' (*DQu* 25:iii[2008] 162–71) focuses upon Trollope's *The Three Clerks* and *Rachel Ray* and the ways in which both 'challenge Dickens as a social realist' (p. 166). Anna Moya and Gemma López's ' "I'm a wild success": Postmodern Dickens/Victorian Cuarón' (*DQu* 25:iii[2008] 172–89) is largely a consideration of Alfonso Cuarón's adaptation of Twentieth Century Fox's *Great Expectations* [1998], produced by Art Linson, written by Mitch Glacer, and with Ethan Hawke and Gwyneth Paltrow. David Parker's 'Dickens's Death: The Peckham Conjecture' (*DQu* 25:iii[2008] 190–3) considers the story that 'Dickens fell ill, it is said, not as Forster tells, while eating dinner with Georgina Hogarth, on 8 June 1870 at Gad's Hill Place, but earlier in the day at Windsor Lodge, the house occupied by Ellen Ternan in Peckham' (p. 190). Issue number iv opens with Catherine Waters's '"Fairy Palaces" and "Wonderful Toys": Machine Dreams in *Household Words*' (*DQu* 25:iv[2008] 215–31). This is a consideration not of the better-known attack by Dickens 'on industrialism in *Hard Times*' but on 'the factory tourist tales he published alongside it in *Household Words* [that] reveal a more mixed response to the industrial developments of his day' (p. 228). Jennifer Gribble's 'The Bible in *Great Expectations*' (*DQu* 25:iv[2008] 232–40) focuses upon the implications of biblical allusions in the novel and their relevance to its contradictory conclusions. Logan Delano Browning's 'Changing *Notes* into *Pictures*: An American Frame for Dickens's Italy' (*DQu* 25:iv[2008] 241–9) concentrates on the largely neglected, early *American Notes*. This issue, in common with others, concludes with Elizabeth Bridgham's very useful 'Dickens Quarterly Checklist', divided into 'Primary Sources', 'Secondary Sources', 'Recent Dissertations', 'Web Sites of Note' and 'Miscellaneous' (*DQu* 25:iv[2008] 268–73).

Various aspects of Dickens receive treatment in *Studies in English Literature*. Danielle Coriale, in her 'Sketches by Boz, "So frail a machine"' (*SEL* 48[2008] 801–12), argues that the young Dickens expressed anxiety concerning the publication of sketches by Boz and tried to impose structure to create the illusion of textual stability and authorial control. Michael Hancher's 'Grafting *A Christmas Carol*' (*SEL* 48[2008] 813–27) draws attention to the hybrid elements of *A Christmas Carol* and to Dickens's concern over piracy of the work. Daniel Stout's 'Nothing Personal: The Decapitation of Character in *A Tale of Two Cities*' (*Novel* 41:i[Fall 2007] 29–52) focuses upon Stout's perception 'of the indifference to individual distinction ... as a widespread feature of [*A Tale of Two Cities*] and the French Revolution it imagines' (p. 29). Luc Bouvard's '*Nicholas Nickelby*, Adaptation, Rehearsal and Catharsis' (*CVE* 67[2008] 379–91) explores the concept of theatricality in *Nicholas Nickelby* and late twentieth-century cinematic adaptations of the novel. Michael Kramp's 'From Race to Lore to Domestic Utility: Sissy Jupe as a Functional Stylized Gypsy' (*VIJ* 36[2008] 193–216) considers Dickens's depiction of gypsies in *Hard Times* and the necessity in the novel of 'the functional utility of Sissy's preserved exotic otherness' (p. 208). In spite of Kramp's convoluted style, he has some useful insights to make on Dickens's text.

Robert Douglas-Fairhurst provides the introduction and notes to the Oxford World's Classics *Great Expectations*, edited by Margaret Cardwell. There are four appendices: 'The Original Ending' (pp. 443–4); 'Dickens's Working Notes' (pp. 444–8); '*All the Year Round* Instalments and Chapter-Numbering in Different Editions' (pp. 449–51); and 'The 1861 Theatrical Adaptation' (pp. 452–7). These are followed by Douglas-Fairhurst's detailed 'Explanatory Notes' (pp. 458–820). Lynn Cain's *Dickens, Family, Authorship: Psychoanalytic Perspectives on Kinship and Creativity* draws extensively upon the linguistic and psychoanalytic work of Kristeva and Lacan. Cain's focus is four novels written between 1843 and 1853: *Martin Chuzzlewit, Dombey and Son, David Copperfield* and *Bleak House*. In spite of thickets of abstruse prose,

Cain has some interesting insights. L.T. Castillo's 'Natural Authority in Charles Dickens's *Martin Chuzzlewit* and the Copyright Act of 1842' (*Nineteenth-Century Literature* 62[2008] 435–64) sheds much light upon the various texts of *Martin Chuzzlewit*. Laurence W. Mazzeno's *The Dickens Industry Critical Perspectives 1836–2005* is a clearly written, historically based account of different critical perspectives to Charles Dickens. Beginning with the Dickens phenomenon of the 1836 to 1870 period, Mazzeno moves through the subsequent anti-Victorian period and the birth of the Dickens industry. There are chapters on reactions during and after the Second World War, Dickens and the mainstream of academic criticism from 1960 to 1969, the state of play around the 1970s and after, Dickens in the age of theory from 1980 to the end of the last century, and Dickens and traditional criticism during that period. Mazzeno also covers the opening years of the present century. This is a first-rate work revealing much about the academic profession and its assumptions, as well as Charles Dickens.

Karl Ashley Smith, in his *Dickens and the Unreal City: Searching for Spiritual Significance in Nineteenth-Century London*, writes that 'In the London of his novels, Dickens constructs a symbolic microcosm of the universe which allows him to explore imaginatively the process by which things come about, sometimes in ways harmonious with his declared convictions, sometimes in ways that diverge from them' (p. 10). Essentially, Smith reads Dickens's novels through a religious lens. For instance, 'Despite ... misgivings about the hated doctrine of Original sin ... Dickens clearly feels that Christ's death has enabled Betty Higden [in *Our Mutual Friend*] to accept and transcend her own' (p. 21). Smith examines the relationship between Dickens's use of traditional religious symbolism and the realities depicted in his work. Jenny Hartley's *Charles Dickens and the House of Fallen Women* tells the story of Dickens's establishment in the autumn of 1847 of Urania Cottage. In Shepherd's Bush this was a hostel for destitute young women who came from workhouses, prisons, the streets and police courts. Some were petty thieves, prostitutes or simply homeless. The finances came from Dickens's millionaire friend Angela Burdett Coutts, and her letters to Dickens provide a major source for Hartley's narrative. Last but by no means least, of interest is the prolific Rodney Stenning Edgecombe's 'A Sketch by Boz and the Nightmare Aria in Gilbert's *Iolanthe*' (*N&Q* 55[2008] 480–1).

The year 2008 was a very thin one for Conan Doyle studies. The exception is Stella Pratt-Smith's 'The Other Serpents: Deviance and Contagion in "The Speckled Band"' (*VN* 113[2008] 54–66), which investigates 'from an impertinent perspective [how] instability relates to ['The Speckled Band"s] inconsistent and pervasive associations between colonial influence, deviance and contagion' (p. 54). To turn to George Eliot, Moira Gatens's 'Gender and Genre: Marian Evans, George Henry Lewes and "George Eliot"' (*Angelaki* 13:ii[2008] 33–44) 'considers the couple comprised by Marian Evans (1819–80)—better known as George Eliot—and her partner in life, George Henry Lewes (1817–78) alongside the theorization of the genre of the English realist novel in the nineteenth century'. Gatens 'consider[s] some of the rules and conventions that govern various kinds of coupling: between Marian Evans and G.H. Lewes, between gender and genre, and between George Eliot and the realist novel' (p. 33). As is to be expected from Moira Gatens, this is a clever essay. She concludes that ' "George Eliot" might ... be understood as a potent multiplicity that through the genre of the realist novel expressed the powers and the longings, the curiosity and the wisdom, the passion and the imagination, of the fertile coupling of Marian Evans and George Henry Lewes' (p. 41). Kimberly J. Stern's 'A Common Fund: George Eliot and the Gender Politics of Criticism' (*PSt* 30:i[2008] 45–62) reconsiders George Eliot's reviewing in the *Westminster Review* not in terms of the reviews being preludes to her novels but in the context of nineteenth-century women's writing. Stern argues that in her reviews George Eliot considers the woman writer to be an important contributor to literary culture and as the originator and gatekeeper of periodical criticism. Stern also examines George Eliot's gender politics and argues that she may be considered as a forerunner of the modern feminist critic. For Stern, there are close affinities between feminist history and prose tradition. Nancy Henry's *The Cambridge Introduction to George Eliot* 'provides an introduction to Eliot's life, reading and historical milieu' (p. viii). There are chapters on the 'Life' (pp. 1–13), 'Historical Contexts' (pp. 14–29) and 'Literary Influences' (pp. 30–40). Individual works are discussed (pp. 41–103), and the 'Afterlife' (pp. 104–14). There is an enumerative further reading section (pp. 120–2) and an index (pp. 123–9). K.M. Newton continues his raid upon the text of *Daniel Deronda* in his 'George Eliot and the Bushmen' (*N&Q* 55[2008] 45–6), in which he throws some light upon a sentence in chapter 28 of the novel.

The *George Eliot Review* (39[2008]) includes Graham Handley's '*Scenes* and After' the thirty-sixth George Eliot Memorial Lecture, 27 October 2007 (*GER* 39[2008] 7–17); Gregory Tate's 'George Eliot's Poetry of the Soul (Prize Essay)' (*GER* 39[2008] 18–26); Toni Griffiths's ' "Acting Out" in *Daniel Deronda*' (*GER* 39[2008] 27–34) and Annemarie Frank's '*Daniel Deronda*: The Cultural Imperative of Religion' (*GER* 39[2008] 35–44). Handley's lecture is yet another outstanding contribution to Victorian studies from this eminent and rather neglected authority. Tate's essay is brief, but anything on George Eliot's poetry is welcome. His focus is mainly on her conception of poetry with a few observations on *The Spanish Gypsy* and 'The Legend of Jubal'. Toni Griffiths also contributes an all-too-short paper illustrating 'the way in which psychoanalytic perspectives can help us to understand the effect which a complex literary text like *Daniel Deronda* has on the reader' (p. 27). Annemarie Frank's focus is upon the ways in which '*Daniel Deronda* differs strikingly from [George Eliot's] earlier works in the presentation of its protagonists and her innovative use of the literary genres of realism and romanticism' (p. 35). There are the usual short reviews. Mention should be made of Jonathan Ouvry and Gabriel Woolf's remarks in 'Celebration for Kathleen and Bill Adams' (*GER* 39[2008] 63–6) to mark their retirement from the George Eliot Fellowship which they so devotedly served for forty years. The text is printed of Roger Simmonds's address at the George Eliot birthday luncheon, 25 November 2007: 'The Toast to the Immortal Memory' (*GER* 39[2008] 71–5). There is an interesting contribution from John Burton: 'Reflections on *Scenes Revisited*: A Festival Celebrating the 150th Anniversary of *Scenes of Clerical Life*' (*GER* 39[2008] 76–8) as well as Kathleen Adams's final report to the

George Eliot Fellowship (*GER* 39[2008] 19–82), and Maiko Ohtake's 'Japanese Branch Report' (*GER* 39[2008] 83–5).

George Eliot–George Henry Lewes Studies contains two very important, extensive contributions. The first, Avrom Fleishman's 'George Eliot's Reading: A Chronological List' (*GEGHLS* 54–5[2008] 1–106) was reissued in a corrected version as a separate supplement to the 2008 *GEGHLS*. The second contribution is Martin Raitiere's 'Did Herbert Spencer Have Epilepsy? Some Links Involving John Hughlings-Jackson, G.H. Lewes, and George Eliot' (*GEGHLS* 54–5[2008] 107–47). Donald Hawes contributes his annual succinct, well-written 'Articles on George Eliot in 2007: A Selective Survey' (*GEGHLS* 54–5[2008] 148–54), and this is followed by reviews of recent books on George Eliot and G.H. Lewes. Ansgar Nünning's 'Experiments in Life: Formen un Funktionen der narrative Inszenierung von Lebenswissen und Lebenskunst in George Eliots Romanen aus der Sicht einer lebenswissensch-aftlich orientierten Literaturwissenchaft' [Experiments in Life: Form and Function of Narrative Scenes. Life and Literature in George Eliot's Novels from the perspective of her knowledge of life orientated towards literary study] (in Horatschek et al., eds., pp. 83–118) makes many perceptive points. Lana L. Dalley's 'The Economics of "A Bit o' Victual", or Malthus and Mothers in *Adam Bede*' (*VLC* 36:ii[2008] 549–67) draws affinities between George Eliot's early novel and an essential element in the debate between T.R. Malthus and his followers and their suggestion that foolish, economically strained marriages were related to an unrealized desire to commit infanticide as the married couples would probably be unable to feed their children. Malthus and his followers classified child murder as one of the key checks to population, regarding it as amongst the worst kinds of immorality and misery. Dalley applies Malthusian concerns about sex, the family, responsibility and dependence to her reading of *Adam Bede* and argues that it is not without significance that George Eliot's novel is set in the year 1799, a year following the initial publication of Malthus's *An Essay on the Principle of Population*. Daniel S. Malachuk's '*Romola* and Victorian Liberalism' (*VLC* 36:i[2008] 41–57) considers Henry James's critique of *Romola*. Writing in 1861 as the novel appeared in *The Cornhill*, James wrote of it as 'a very beautiful story, but ... quite worthless ... as a picture of life in the fifteenth century' (p. 41). Malachuk considers *Romola* within the context of a tradition of Victorian liberal discourse about the function of virtue in a political climate otherwise primarily concerned with the fuller realization of individual freedoms. He looks at a similar problem in the Florentine republic. Malachuk also examines Eliot's treatment of the concept of freedom in *Romola* in contrast to how the late fifteenth-century republics perceived women. In doing so he makes some illuminating observations about *Romola*.

Jill L. Matus's 'Historicizing Trauma: The Genealogy of Psychic Shock in *Daniel Deronda*' (*VLC* 36:i[2008] 59–78) usefully 'explores how George Eliot came to represent in Gwendolen the hallmarks of the way we define trauma. Its aim is not simply to demonstrate that Gwendolen is a traumatized subject, but to tease out the discursive strands which George Eliot drew together and to place her representation in the context of an emergent cultural and scientific discourse of psychic wounding and its effects on memory and consciousness, a discourse that arguably helped to produce the way we understand trauma today' (p. 60). In doing so, Matus makes interesting observations concerning our reading of Gwendolen Harleth; however, some of Matus's observations have a familiar ring. Josh Epstein's ' "Neutral Physiognomy": The Unreadable Faces of *Middlemarch*' (*VLC* 36:i[2008] 131–48) 'argue[s] that Eliot's novel expresses misgivings not only about wrong physiognomic readings but about the very ideological grounding and epistemological implications of physiognomy' (p. 132). Epstein's wordy article is accompanied by illustrations from Johann Casper Lavater's *Essays on Physiognomy, Designed to Promote the Love and Knowledge of Mankind* [1784–98], and in places also retreads familiar territory. Kevin A. Morrison's ' "The mother tongue of our imagination": George Eliot, Landscape-Shaped Subjectivity, and the Possibility of Social Inclusion' (*VR* 34:i[2008] 83–100) is the winner of *VR*'s best graduate student paper award. Morrison is concerned with 'contextualizing *The Mill on the Floss* within debates on national belonging' (p. 97).

Social mistakes are the keynote of Kent Puckett's *Bad Form: Social Mistakes and the Nineteenth-Century Novel*. Puckett focuses upon Flaubert's *Madame Bovary*, Henry James's *The Princess Casamassima*, and George Eliot's *Middlemarch* as his central illustrations of the gaffe, the *faux pas*, the social errors. His reading of the dense text of *Middlemarch* exposes the mistakes of its characters in George Eliot's intricately woven fabric. In his third chapter, 'Looking Good: Style and its Absence in George Eliot', Puckett observes, for instance, the characteristics common to Dorothea Brooke and the hero of *Felix Holt, the Radical*. He writes that 'In both cases, characters are distinguished by a lack of style that expresses personal resignation as well as recognition of the structural and historical limits of convention.' Pickett notes that Dorothea's 'sartorial austerity is meant to provide a point of functional contrast to the various fashion-hungry characters who populate *Middlemarch*' (pp. 84–6). Puckett is far from the first to make such an observation; however, such points are worth restating, especially as he provides a theoretical underpinning from the writings of D.W. Winnicott, Slavoj Žižek and others. Antonie Gerard van den Broek's splendid edition of George Eliot's relatively neglected yet important lengthy poem *The Spanish Gypsy* contains an informative preface and introduction (pp. ix–lv). The former, by the consultant editor William Baker, provides a survey of the background for the work, the location of George Eliot's notebooks containing the sources she draws upon and a brief account of critical reactions to *The Spanish Gypsy*. Van den Broek's introduction assesses these at length and conveys a powerful case for a revaluation of the poem's importance. The editor comments that 'it merits close attention and investigation, since its themes and characters are integrated to Eliot's moral and imaginative vision, a mirror of her ongoing idealism' (p. lv). The text is clearly laid out and followed by 'George Eliot's Notes' (pp. 269–71). There are four appendices: 'Notes on the Spanish Gypsy and Tragedy in General' (pp. 273–7); 'Eliot's Notes on Gypsies' (pp. 279–88); 'Eliot's Notes on Spain' (pp. 289–302: these were initially edited by Andrew Thompson); and 'Eliot's Notes on the Inquisition' (pp. 303–12: initially discovered by the consulting editor). These are followed by van den Broek's extensive, thorough, useful 'Editorial Notes' (pp. 313–36) and listing and description of 'Textual Variants' (pp. 337–441) which concludes this invaluable edition. Pickering & Chatto are to be congratulated in publishing one of George Eliot's hitherto least available but nevertheless highly significant texts.

Anna Despotupoulou's '"The Abuse of Visibility": Domestic Publicity in Late Victorian Fiction' (in Gomez Reas and Usandizaga, eds., *Inside Out: Women Negotiating, Subverting, Appropriating Public and Private Space*, pp. 87–106), compares and contrasts *Daniel Deronda* and Henry James's *The Wings of the Dove*. Despotopoulou argues that 'by employing diction related to the public sphere when assessing the female characters' inner concerns' both writers 'exhibit their anxiety about the abuse of privacy and the redefinition of the female self in relation to commodities' (p. 87). In addition to close textual reading, Despotopoulou usefully draws upon the ideas of Jürgen Habermas. Finally, mention should be made of Alice Jenkins's 'George Eliot, Geometry and Gender' (*E&S* 61[2008] 72–90). Jenkins highlights 'the ways in which Victorian culture ascribed contradictory, over-determined and yet very powerful gender coding to Euclidean geometry' (p. 72). She concludes that 'Maggie's epiphany rehabilitates geometry and its yearning towards abstraction and perfection, finding—however briefly—a way of making them serve a generous moral purpose, freeing them from aridity and using them to make the individual and the circumstantial world into a unity' (p. 88). Jenkins's essay could have been enriched by drawing upon materials in the reconstructions of George Eliot's and George Henry Lewes's library, where Jenkins would have found material on Euclidean geometry.

The *Gaskell Society Journal* contains material of considerable interest, and the 2008 issue is no exception (although somebody ought to check the proof-reading on its cover page which states erroneously that the 2008 issue is 'volume 20'!). This issue begins with a listing of 'Gaskell on the Internet' (*GSJ* 22[2008] iii]). Walter E. Smith's 'A Trip to Scarborough and Some Letters: An Informal Remembrance of John Geoffrey Sharps' (*GSJ* 22[2008] 1–9) is a tribute by one great Gaskell bibliographer to another, accompanied appropriately by a photograph (see p. 6). There is also a picture of Sharps at work on the cover page: he would not have approved of the misprint! Mary Jeanette Moran's '"A Word or Two hear about Myself": Narrating Subjectivity and Feminist Ethics' (*GSJ* 22[2008] 10–21) concludes that 'Through Mary's presence as narrator and character, *Cranford* indicates how qualities traditionally associated with femininity can foster a system of ethical relationships in which the interaction between self and other recognizes both the uniqueness and connectedness of each party' (p. 19). Lindsy Lawrence's 'Gender Play "At our social table": The New Domesticity in the *Cornhill* and Elizabeth Gaskell's *Wives and Daughters*' (*GSJ* 22[2008] 22–41) demonstrates Gaskell and her illustrator du Maurier's 'flexible domesticity' by focusing 'on the interplay between the non-fiction articles of the *Cornhill*, the 1864 instalment of *Wives and Daughters*, and du Maurier's illustration for this instalment' (p. 23). The article is accompanied by an illustration from du Maurier (p. 35). John Beer's clearly written 'Elizabeth Gaskell's Legacy from Romanticism' (*GSJ* 22[2008] 42–55) reflects upon 'the particular characteristics of the years 1830 to 1850, and what could be thought of as their distinctive quality' (p. 42). Beer is particularly illuminating in his discussion of 'Elizabeth Gaskell's relationship with the English language', which he considers 'unusually complex, even torturous' (p. 52). Alan Shelston also tackles a large topic in his 'Education in the Life and Work of Elizabeth Gaskell' (*GSJ* 22[2008] 56–71).

Carol A. Bock adds to our biographical knowledge in her 'Elizabeth Gaskell's "Useful" Relatives: Katharine and Anthony Todd Thomson and the Society for the Diffusion of "Useful Knowledge"' (*GSJ* 22[2008] 72–85). Michael F. Dixon writes on '"A very nice American"—Gaskell's enigmatic Mr. Collier' (*GSJ* 22[2008] 86–95), shedding light on Elizabeth Gaskell's 4 September 1865 'unannounced visit from an American Unitarian minister, a "Mr. Collier"' (p. 86). Robert Poole's '"A poor man I know": Samuel Bamford and the Making of *Mary Barton*' (*GSJ* 22[2008] 96–115) is very informative on the radical Samuel Bamford (1788–1872). Tatsuhiro Ohno's 'Statistical Analysis of the Structure of *North and South*: in the Quest for the Standard Interpretation' (*GSJ* 22[2008] 116–44) uses statistical analysis to examine 'which of the two major plots is the more representative of the novel's theme' (p. 116). Rebecca White's '"A joke spoken in a rather sad tone": *Cranford*, Humour and Heidi Thomas's Television Adaptation' (*GSJ* 22[2008] 145–60) discusses the BBC adaptation of *Cranford*, written by Heidi Thomas and shown in 2007. This is also the subject of Alan Shelston's review (*GSJ* 22[2008] 161–2). This issue concludes with most useful reviews, a report on the Gaskell Society Conference held at Canterbury Christ Church University, 27–30 July 2007, and there are other matters of interest concerning local Gaskell societies. Benjamine Toussaint-Thiriet's 'Le Sentiment d'appartenance dans *North and South* d'Elizabeth Gaskell' ['The Sense of Belonging in Elizabeth Gaskell's *North and South*'] (*CVE* 67[2008] 79–90) examines a major theme of *North and South*, the sense of belonging. Jill Rappoport, in her 'Conservation of Sympathy in *Cranford*' (*VLC* 36:i[2008] 95–110), focuses upon *Cranford*'s (1851–3) depiction of 'a community of shabby-genteel women who support each other, in the virtual absence of men, through gift practices'. Rappoport uses Mrs Gaskell's novel as an example of 'mid-century works that treat sympathetic exchange in a sustained manner and on an expanded scale, writing women's charity in terms of sympathy and sisterhood rather than coin' (p. 95). Melissa Jenkins's lengthy '"His crime was a thing apart": Elizabeth Gaskell Writes a Fathers' Life' (*VIJ* 36[2008] 245–74) draws upon many of Gaskell's texts in order to show the ways in which a November 1856 letter from Patrick Brontë influenced her *Life of Charlotte Brontë* and her final novel *Wives and Daughters*. Last but by no means least, Nancy Weyant's 'Annual Bibliographical Supplements' to her 1992–2001 *Annotated Guide to Secondary Language Sources on the Life and Works of Elizabeth Gaskell* is updated every six months. See < http://library.bloomu.edu/weyant > and < http://www.nancyweyant.com/index.php/pages/GaskellBibliography-Intro.html > .

Danielle Coriale's '*Gaskell's Naturalist*' (*Nineteenth-Century Literature* 63[2008] 346–75) is an extensive study of *Mary Barton* [1848] situating it 'within early Victorian discourses about natural history by studying the figure of the working-class naturalist Job Legh' (p. 346)

To turn to Gissing, Lewis D. Moore's *The Fiction of George Gissing: A Critical Analysis* examines Gissing's fiction from three main perspectives: Gissing's social imagination; his personal imagination; and his cultural imagination. Moore's focus is on Gissing's use of his imagination rather than on the works being autobiographical. Clearly, the author is very familiar with the breadth of Gissing's work and writes with considerable insight. Christine Huguet's 'Figures de l'exil dan *New Grub Street* de George Gissing' ['George Gissing's Fictional Elaboration on Exile in *New Grub Street*'] (*CVE* 67[2008] 67–77) considers exclusion in Gissing's fiction with particular reference to *Born in Exile* [1892], *New Grub Street* [1891] and Gissing's essay 'The Hope of Pessimism'. Jean Gregorek, in 'The Odd Man: Masculinity and the Modern Intellectual in George Gissing's *Born in Exile*' (*NCStud* 21[2007] 199–216), argues that 'critics have neglected to see' in Gissing's work 'the intimate connections the novel constructs between [its] themes and the issues generated by the presence of the New Women in the text'. The novel's theme has been frequently noticed: 'the ambiguous social status of the (implicitly male) Victorian intellectual and its painstaking account of the social psychology of (implicitly male) exclusion' but not its 'return to the Woman Question' (p. 199). The novel can be read 'as an indictment of the Victorian social structure', as a revelation of 'the subtle strategies of class prejudice motivated by a concern to justify existing economic privilege' and also 'as an anatomy of the production of modernist gender ideology' (p. 213). In spite of the preponderance of critical jargon, however, Gregorek has some useful insights into Gissing's complex novel.

Two volumes bound in a single volume, *Spellbound George Gissing*, edited by Christine Huguet, is a '*Festschrift* . . . written by eleven critics from different countries who, on behalf of all lovers of Gissing, wish to honour [Pierre] Coustillas, the doyen of Gissing scholars and his wife Hélène' (vol. 1, p. 5). The first volume consists of introductory material on Gissing by the editor, Christine Huguet, followed by examples of Gissing's narrative art taken from his short stories (pp. 25–205). Huguet provides an introduction to each, and where appropriate there are the original periodical illustrations. 'Phoebe's Fortune', as Huguet explains, 'was written in early November 1883 and published four months later in *Temple Bar* with significant editorial alterations'. She presents a 'bilingual edition' with the English text and, on the opposite recto page, 'a German translation by the writer's lifelong friend Edward Bertz'. The translation 'emerged in 1891 with Gissing's complete approval out of a combination of the original manuscript and the bowdlerized serial text' (p. 55). The second volume, 'A Twenty-First Century Reappraisal' (p. 5), consists of twelve contributions: Dianna Maltz's 'Romantic Idylls and Market Realities: Continental Europe in Gissing's "Gretchen"' (pp. 7–22); Bouwe Postmus's 'The Popularity of the Picturesque: Oliver Bell Bunce and Gissing's "An English Coast-Picture"' (pp. 23–35); Markus Neacey's 'The Textual History of "Phoebe's Fortune": Towards a Third Version of Gissings' Story via Eduard Bertz's German Translation' (pp. 37–62); Robert Selig's '"Lou and Liz": Ironic Echoes of Popular Culture' (pp. 63–80); John Sloan's '"The Day of Silence": Gissing and the Victorian Celebration of Death' (pp. 81–92); Barbara Rawlinson's '"A Midsummer Madness"' (pp. 93–8);

Christine Devine's '"By the Kerb": Too Radical' (pp. 99–108); Constance Harsh's '"The Foolish Virgin" and the One Thing Needful' (pp. 109–18); David Grylls's 'Addicted to Newsprint: "Spellbound"' (pp. 119–32); M.D. Allen's 'Chesney Wold and "A Daughter of the Lodge": The Death of the Feudal Spirit' (pp. 133–46); and Christine Huguet's 'The Pig and Whistle; or, Kindliness Rewarded' (pp. 147–62). There is also an appendix: 'Chronology of Gissing's Short Stories' (pp. 167–73).

The following 2008 issues of the *Gissing Journal* have come to our attention. *GissingJ* 44:iii[2008] contains M.D. Allen's report on 'The Third International George Gissing Conference (27–28 March 2008, Lille, France): A Personal Response' (*GissingJ* 44:iii[2008] 1–5); William Greenslade's 'The *Festschrift*' (*GissingJ* 44:iii[2008] 6–11); Anthony Petyt's 'The Gissings' Wakefield Circle: VI—The Ash Family' (*GissingJ* 44:iii[2008] 12–25); Markus Neacey and Wulfhard Stahl's '"His favourite work,—education": The Letters of Eduard Bertz to Heinrich Rehfeldt, 1880' (*GissingJ* 44:iii[2008] 26–52). *GissingJ* 44:iv[2008] contains M.D. Allen's 'Margaret Bedford Gissing, *Pendennis*, and the Manchester Debacle' (*GissingJ* 44:iv[2008] 1–8); Richard Dennis's 'Cornwall Mansions: The Rise and Fall of 7K and its Neighbours' (*GissingJ* 44:iv[2008] 9–25) and Marcus Neacey's 'St. Ruth: George Gissing's Drill-Sergeant in War and Peace' (*GissingJ* 44:iv[2008] 26–46). Audrey Fessler, in '"The boy was a girl": Reconstructing Gender and Class to Deconstruct Differences in Sarah Grand's *The Heavenly Twins*' (*VN* 113[2008] 38–53), in spite of her theory-laden title, provides an interesting account of the 'stand-alone novella, *The Tenor and the Boy: An Interlude*, which the pioneering feminist author had sought but failed to publish fourteen years earlier'. She then 'enfolded' the novella into her 'best selling, triple-decker novel *The Heavenly Twins* (1893)' (p. 38).

The *Hardy Review* (10:i[2008]), in addition to extensive book reviews, contains an editorial by its editor, Rosemary Morgan (*HR* 10:i[2008] 1–7), and Jeanie Smith's 'Checklist' (*HR* 10:i[2008] 8–11) of recent work in Hardy studies. A regular feature of the journal is an online discussion of a particular Hardy poem, and on this occasion the text is Hardy's 'Proud Songsters'. The discussion of this poem may be found on pp. 12–36. This is followed by two poems stimulated by a reading of Hardy by Bill Morgan, 'Among the Family Photos' and 'Reading at Night' (*HR* 10:i[2008] 37–8). A 'London Letter: Reprints for the first time *The Critic's* account of this meeting of the London literati of the 1890s' (*HR* 10:i[2008] 39–42). This largely consists of Arthur Waugh's account of 'the quarterly dinner of the Omar Khayám Club' (p. 39). There follows another forum, again compiled and edited by Rosemary Morgan, on Hardy's 'The Impercipient' (*HR* 10:i[2008] 43–67). Another poem follows, Isobel Robin's 'Paper Ghosts' (*HR* 10:i[2008] 68). William A. Davis's '"Irreconcilables," "Reclaimables," and "First Falls": Lady Mary Jeune and the Fallen Woman in *Tess of the d'Urbervilles*' (*HR* 10:i[2008] 69–82) focuses upon Lady Mary Jeune (1845–1931) essays on the fallen woman and Hardy's reactions to them. In her editorial to (*HR* 10:ii[2008]) Rosemary Morgan draws attention to the purpose of the *Hardy Review*, 'first and foremost ours is a celebration of Thomas Hardy and of those of his followers who so treasure his literary endowment that they are prepared to give freely of their time, and generously of their scholarly expertise—in trust and appreciation to The Thomas Hardy Association' (p. 104). Richard Nemesvari provides a 'Report on the Thomas Hardy Association's LIFE Page' (*HR* 10:ii[2008] 105–6), 'Two Uncollected Items: "Femininity in Literature" (Constance Goddard Dubois)' "Two Early Illustrations to *The Mayor of Casterbridge*' (pp. 107–9) provides the text of Dubois's letter to *The Critic* originally published on 11 November 1893 (pp. 310–11) relating to Hardy. It is followed by a commentary and illustrations (p. 108–9). 'A Thomas Hardy Association Discussion Group: The Poem of the Month', compiled and edited by Rosemary Morgan (*HR* 10:ii[2008] 110–17) focuses on reactions to Hardy's 'Four in the Morning'. This is followed by notes relating to a previous 'Poem of the Month' discussion on 'Proud Songsters' and Hardy's 'The Melancholy Hussar' (pp. 118–19). Ross C. Murfin's 'Prestidigitations of Discourse: The Problem(s) with *Tess of the d'Urbervilles*' (*HR* 10:ii[2008] 120–1) essentially reflects upon its author's perception that he 'now see[s] all of Hardy's novels as structurally troubled and internally conflicted' (p. 120).Thierry Goater's ' "The Letter Killeth": The Text as Fetish in *Jude the Obscure*' (*HR* 10:ii[2008] 129–37) reflects that 'Hardy's last novel is made strange for the reader through its fetishization of texts and signs' (p. 136). Ilaria Mallozzi's 'Reflections on Water and Time: Hardy and Brodsky in Venice' (*HR* 10:ii[2008] 138–46), a usefully illustrated essay, draws parallels 'between Thomas Hardy and the Russian poet Joseph Brodsky': the idea 'comes from Brodsky's own essay on Hardy's collection entitled "Wooing the Inanimate" ' found in Brodsky's collection on *Grief and Reason* published in 1995 (p. 138). Keith Callis's 'The American Intoxication: Discontinuity, Vision and Tragic Experience in *Tess of the d'Urbervilles*' (*HR* 10:ii[2008] 147–71) is a lengthy essay dealing with the 'American motif' (p. 147) in Hardy's work and with specific reference to *Tess of the d'Urbervilles*. In addition to two poems stimulated by reading Thomas Hardy, the issue concludes with useful detailed book reviews.

Ken Ireland's 'Trewe Love at Solentsea? Stylistics vs. Narratology in Thomas Hardy' (in Watson, ed., *The State of Stylistics*, pp. 61–73) is one of the rare applications of a comparison of stylistic and narratological approaches to Hardy's short story 'An Imaginative Woman'. Stefan Horlacher's ' "…and he took it *literally*"—Literatur als Instrument der Lebenskunst: Konzeptionen (in)adäquater Lektüre in Thomas Hardy's Roman *Jude the Obscure*' [Literature as an Instrument of an Art Form: concepts in an adequate reading of Thomas Hardy's *Jude the Obscure*] (in Horatschek et al., eds., pp. 139–74) should not be ignored. In 'Thomas Hardy, *Two on a Tower*: Vers une rédéfinition cosmique de l'appartenance' [Thomas Hardy's *Two on a Tower*: Towards a Sense of Cosmic Belonging'] (*CVE* 67[2008] 55–66) Laurence Estanove focuses on *Two on a Tower* [1882] and Hardy's depiction of the relationship between the microcosm and the macrocosm in the novel. Yvonne Bezrucka's '*The Well-Beloved*: Thomas Hardy's Manifesto of "Regional Aesthetics" ' (*VLC* 36:i[2008] 227–45) considers Hardy's *The Well-Beloved* 'first published in serial instalments (from 1 October to 17 December 1892) with illustrations by Water Paget … in *The Illustrated London News* … It then appeared in book form, with substantial revisions, as *The Well-Beloved: A Sketch of a Temperament* in 1897, and was, in fact, the last of Hardy's novels to appear (*Jude the Obscure* being published in 1895)'. For Bezrucka, 'of fundamental importance is the fact that Hardy wrote the novel twice', heralding his transition to an almost exclusive focus upon poetry' (pp. 227–8). Patricia Pulham's 'From Pygmalion to Persephone: Love, Art, Myth in Thomas Hardy's *The Well-Beloved*' (*VR* 34:ii[2008] 219–40) is an intertextual study of Hardy's poem 'Rome: The Vatican: Sala delle Muse', composed in 1887 and published in 1902, and his novel *The Well-Beloved* [1897]. Pulham writes: 'love, art and mythology' are introduced in the poem and later developed in Hardy's *The Pursuit of the Well-Beloved* [1892] and in his subsequent novel (p. 220). Anna Henchman looks at 'Hardy's Stargazers and the Astronomy of Other Minds' (*VS* 51[2008] 37–64). Providing examples from many of Hardy's works, Henchman shows that he 'compares the act of observing another person to the scientific practice of observing the stars in order to reveal structural obstacles to accessing other minds. He draws on astronomy and optics to underscore the discrepancy between the full perceptions one has of one's own consciousness and the lack of such sensory evidence for the consciousness of others' (p. 37). In short, Henchman looks at Hardy's interest in astronomy and optics. In so doing, fresh light is thrown upon his writings, such as *Two on a Tower* [1882], *The Woodlanders* [1887] and *The Return of the Native* [1878].

There are few items to report on Rider Haggard. An interesting reading of *She* is found in the first chapter of Carey J. Snyder's *British Fiction and Cross-Cultural Encounters: Ethnographic Modernism from Wells to Woolf*. Snyder's 'Explorer Ethnography and Rider Haggard's African Romance, *She*' (pp. 23–58) isolates the ethnographic elements of the novel and places it in the context of a conversation with the developing practice of fieldwork ethnographers. Snyder also discusses Mary Kingsley in a similar context. Stanwood S. Walker's ' "Backwards and backwards ever": Charles Kingsley's Racial-Historical Allegory and the Liberal Anglican Revisioning of Britain' (*Nineteenth-Century Literature* 62[2008] 339–79) focuses on Kingsley's novels of the 1850s *Alton Locke*, *Hypatia* and *Westward Ho!* and draws attention to 'the various ambivalences and inconsistencies with which Kingsley's thought and writings are so patently rife'. Walker argues that these 'actually constituted some of their apparent strengths in his own day (or were at least inseparable from those strengths)' (p. 339).

The *Richard Jefferies Society Newsletter* [Spring 2008] contains snippets of information of interest to readers of Richard Jefferies, including a report accompanied with photographs of the damage done to Jefferies' favourite mulberry tree by freak storms in September 2007 (p. 14) and observations with photographs on 'Jefferies' Grave at Broadwater Cemetery, Worthing' (pp. 15–17). Mention, too, should be made of Hugoe Matthews and Phyllis Treitel's *Richard Jefferies: An Index of Themes, Thoughts and Observations*. The work includes a basic index to the major elements in Jefferies' published work, a word index and passages containing Jefferies' personal statements or observations that relate to his central themes. The subject index focuses upon topics such as nature and man, farming and religion, and focuses upon Jefferies' non-fictional writings. All in all, this is yet another invaluable contribution to Richard Jefferies scholarship by Hugoe Matthews and Phyllis Treitel.

Cinematic aspects of Kipling's short story 'Mrs. Bathurst' are the focus of Élodie Raimbault's 'Écran magique et prégnance du hors champ: L'Art du cadrage dans "Mrs. Bathurst" de Kipling' ['Magic Screen and Off-Screen Intensity: Framing as an Art in "Mrs. Bathurst" by Kipling'] (*CVE* 67[2008] 407–19). Jean Fernandez's 'Hybrid Narratives: The Making of Character and Narrative Authority in Rudyard Kipling's "His Chance in Life"' (*VLC* 36:ii[2008] 343–59) examines Kipling's short story 'His Chance in Life' found in *Plain Tales from the Hills* [1888], indicating that hybridity plays a crucial role in the story. 'The narrative illogic of "His Chance in Life," its display of narrative voice', Fernandez writes, 'plagued by self-contradiction, inconsistency, and irony, all suggest that in India, hybrid/ity narratives could expose the irrationality of the Imperial project' (p. 355). Peter Havholm begins his *Politics and Awe in Rudyard Kipling's Fiction* with a description of his initial boyhood encounter with Kipling's work and of his continuing enthusiasm for Kipling. Havholm writes: 'Efforts to exonerate or shield Kipling from the ethical criticisms lodged against him are not convincing', and that Kipling's 'politics infuse his art from the beginning, and his politics from the beginning are those his father and mother developed in Bombay and Lahore in the 1870s'. Havholm uses 'Uncovenanted Mercies', the final tale in 'Kipling's last published collection' to demonstrate the 'integration of policies with narrative' in his work. Havholm spends much time on *Kim*, a work he perceives as essentially 'ambivalent' (pp. 5–6). There is much engagement in Havholm's monograph with critical responses to his subject; there is also a deep knowledge and engagement with Kipling's work, his journalism, short stories, fiction and other prose. A caveat is that Havholm's prose is often dense. U.C. Knoepflmacher's 'Kipling's "Mixy" Creatures' (*SEL* 48[2008] 923–33) is a clever piece drawing attention to Kipling's irony with a special relation to hybrid figures in the *Just So Stories* and *Kim*.

Rudyard Kipling's early stories are the subject of Inna Lindgrén's interesting '*Plain Tales from the Hills* as Emergent Literature' (*NJES* 6:ii[2007] 83–104). Lindgrén correctly points out that 'Kipling is now ... seen as a major world figure, but the community he originally represented is no longer one [with] which many people can or want to be associated' (p. 104). The *Kipling Journal* contains Paul March-Russell's '*Rewards and Fairies* and the Neo-Romantic Debt' (*KJ* 82:cccxxvi[2008] 6–13); Charlotte Joergensen's 'Synthesis and Fragmentation: Panoramic Visuality in *Kim*' (*KJ* 82:cccxxvi[2008] 14–21); Debra D. Wynn's 'Traffics and Re-discoveries: Rudyard Kipling Collections at the Library of Congress' (*KJ* 82:cccxxvi[2008] 22–31); George Simmer's 'Kipling and Shell-Shock: The Healing Community' (*KJ* 82:cccxxvi[2008] 32–9); Daniel Karlin's '"Tin Fish": Two Texts, Two Readings' (*KJ* 82:cccxxvi[2008] 40–7); Elodie Raimbault's 'Finding One's Way Through *Actions and Reactions*' (*KJ* 82:cccxxvi[2008] 48–55); Carolyn Oulton's '"Ain't goin' to have any beastly Erickin'": The Problem of Male Friendship in *Stalky & Co.*' (*KJ* 82:cccxxvi[2008] 56–61), and 'If any Question Why He Died: John Kipling and the Myths of the Great War' (*KJ* 82:cccxxvi[2008] 62–8); John Walker's 'The Kipling Library: Sale of Surplus

Books' (*KJ* 82:cccxxix[2008] 7); K. St John Damstra's 'Attacking the Boers in the Style of Kipling Sahib' (*KJ* 82:cccxxix[2008] 10–25); Alastair Wilson's '"Mrs. Bathurst"—A Sequel?' (*KJ* 82:cccxxix[2008] 27–37); Maurice Pennance's 'How the Fox Got a Bushy Tale' with an illustration by Benjamin Pennance (*KJ* 82:cccxxix[2008] 38–41); and Jamie Paris's 'On Kipling's Ambivalence Towards War in "Mary Postgate"' (*KJ* 82:cccxxix[2008] 42–59). Unfortunately, numbers 327 and 328 have not reached us in order to be mentioned.

Charles Allen's highly readable *Kipling Sahib: India and the Making of Rudyard Kipling, 1865–1900* focuses primarily on its subject's younger years from 1865 to 1900. These are the years of Kipling's Indian childhood, his abandonment in an alien England, his return to India and his coming to maturity. Allen also writes on the Indian experience of Lockwood and Alice, Kipling's parents. The contradictions inherent in Kipling may be seen in his childhood, cosseted by servants, his farewell words spoken to his mother in Hindustani, years of relative impoverishment, strong discipline and narrow confines in the old country. The Kipling who returned to India in 1882 was full of suppressed tensions to be creatively transformed. The strength of Allen's biography is in its illustrations, the depiction of lost colonial worlds, and the revelation of contradictions and paradoxes that underlie his subject's great fictional and poetic achievement. David Sergeant's 'Kipling's Compositional Practice in Two Manuscripts' (*N&Q* 55[2008] 465–7) sheds light upon a relatively unexplored area of Kipling studies.

A welcome addition to studies of the neglected Vernon Lee is found in Catherine Delyfer's 'Être et paraître dans *Miss Brown* de Vernon Lee' ['Being and Seeming in Vernon Lee's *Miss Brown*'] (*CVE* 67[2008] 393–406). This discusses Vernon Lee's first novel *Miss Brown* [1884], arguing that 'through the description of the career of Anne Brown, this anti-*bildungsroman* particularly exposed the social, political, intellectual and sexual exploitation of female models and muses' (p. 19). Sophie Mantrant's 'A mourir de peur/ rire: *The Great God Pan* d'Arthur Machen (1894)' ['Frighteningly Funny: *The Great God Pan* (1894) by Arthur Machen'] (*CVE* 67[2008] 291–304) is a welcome addition to writings on the neglected Arthur Machen. 'The aim of this article is to highlight the semantic, structural and stylistic ingredients used to arouse dread or anxiety' in Machen's first major success, *The Great God Pan* (p. 16). Claire Wrobel's 'A Neo-Gothic Novel: Arthur Machen's *The Three Impostors*' (*CVE* 67[2008] 337–48) is also a welcome discussion of Machen's long-neglected 1895 Gothic novel. Catherine Lanone's '"But in that room, in that presence, I was invertebrate": La Peur de l'autre dans *The Beetle* de Richard Marsh' (*CVE* 67[2008] 281–90) is a useful discussion of Marsh's depiction of terror in his 1897 novel *The Beetle*. Thomas Prasch's 'Eating the World: London in 1851' (*VLC* 36:ii[2008] 587–602) is a detailed account of Henry Mayhew's 'Comic instant novel about the transformation of London in the year of the Great Exhibition', *The Adventures of Mr. and Mrs. Sandboys and Family, Who Came Up To London to 'Enjoy Themselves' and to See the Great Exhibition* [1851]. Prasch's fascinating essay uses Mayhew's parodic fiction to reveal 'the metropolis's new cosmopolitanism, its internationalized palate' (pp. 587, 598).

An addition to studies of another critically neglected writer is found in Fabienne Gaspari's ' "La Peur de desire": *A Mummer's Wife* et *Esther Waters* de George Moore' [' "The Fear of Desire": *A Mummer's Wife* and *Esther Waters* by George Moore'] (*CVE* 67[2008] 253–67). Gaspari explores Moore's use of industrialization and urbanization in the two novels to demonstrate their effect upon their central characters. Bruce Durie's 'Dick Donovan, the Glasgow Detective, and his Creator, James Edward (Joyce Emerson Preston) Muddock' (*Clues* 26:ii[2008] 23–38) is a rare article focusing upon the obscure late Victorian writer James Edward Muddock, aka Dick Donovan, aka Joyce Emerson Preston Muddock, author of, amongst other works *Only a Woman's Heart: The Story of a Woman's Love: A Woman's Sorrow*, published by George Newnes in 1894. Durie argues that Muddock's Glasgow-based detective Dick Donovan was the real progenitor of the protagonist-narrator genre of serial detective fiction which was extremely popular prior to his eclipse by Arthur Conan Doyle and Sherlock Holmes. Durie shows that extant biographical information about Muddock is either incorrect or misleading largely due to the writer's own inventions and obfuscations. The University of South Carolina Press reprints William North's (1824/5–54) *The City of Jugglers* [1850] from the first edition now in the Department of Rare Books and Special Collections at the university. Patrick Scott notes in an informative 'About this Book and its Author' that 'only three surviving copies are recorded in WorldCat, with only two listed in libraries in North America'. Scott writes that the work 'is one of the most original novels of the mid-Victorian period; it is also the most elusive book by one of the nineteenth-century's most elusive authors'. Its setting is the London of 1848, the year of European ferment and social unrest (p. v).

In a thin year for Margaret Oliphant studies, Andrea Kaston Tange, in her 'Redesigning Femininity: *Miss Marjoribanks's Drawing-Room of Opportunity*' (*VLC* 36:i[2008] 163–86), argues that the novel 'raises complex questions about how' the place of women is defined and limited. Tange focuses upon the character of Lucilla in the novel, emphasizing her 'contradictory position' (p. 178) and the manner in which this illustrates Oliphant's own social dilemma and career: 'while one might gain some measure of influence by exploiting the "Power" of one's sanctioned cultural position, ultimately, Oliphant's world, like Lucilla's, had "no sphere" to fully accommodate an intellectual and energetic woman' (p. 182). In a delightfully illustrated account, Heather A. Evans's 'Kittens and Kitchens: Food, Gender and *The Tale of Samuel Whiskers*' (*VLC* 36:ii[2008] 603–23) writes about Beatrix Potter's Edwardian fiction. The centre of Evans's attention is the 1906 novel *The Tale of Samuel Whiskers, or The Roly-Poly Pudding* published by Frederick Warne & Co. in 1908 and the role food, eating and cookery play in it and other work by Beatrix Potter. There have been signs of a revival of interest in Charles Reade. Although it is not evident from the title of her essay, Christine L. Krueger's '*Vox Populi, Vox Vulgari*: Pro Se Representation in Victorian Popular Legal Culture' (*NCStud* 21[2007] 27–137) is concerned with Charles Reade's *Griffith Gaunt* [1865–6] and *Hard Cash* [1863]. Reade's novels and others, for instance Trollope's *Phineas Redux* [1873–4], are read in the context of the 1836 Prisoner's Counsel Act, which allowed defendants legal representation and its consequences. S. Walsh's '"Arithmetic of Bedlam!"': Markets and Manhood in Charles Reade's *Hard Cash*' (*Nineteenth-Century Literature* 63[2008] 1–40) is a detailed analysis of Reade's neglected novel.

It is pleasing to see an article discussing the work of Anne Thackeray Ritchie (1837–1919). Amanda Holton's 'Resistance, Regard and Rewriting: Virginia Woolf and Anne Thackeray Ritchie' (*English* 57:ccvii[2008] 42–64) 'discusses the literary relationship of the novelist and memoirist, Anne Thackeray Ritchie ... and her step-niece Virginia Woolf. Ritchie's influence was a highly significant one' (p. 42). R. Dury's 'Stevenson in Italy and in Italian' (*SSR* 9:i[2008] 61–78) is a detailed assessment of the time Robert Louis Stevenson spent in Italy and of his reception in Italian. In his 'Murder and the Supernatural: Crime in the Fiction of Scott, Hogg and Stevenson' (*Clues* 26:ii[2008] 10–22), Christopher MacLachlan traces the development of crime fiction with especial relevance to the work of Sir Walter Scott, James Hogg and Robert Louis Stevenson. MacLachlan perceives Scott as viewing murder as deeply culturally embedded. For Hogg, the emphasis is upon the consequences of murder for the community and the individual. Stevenson, on the other hand, whilst concentrating upon the traumatic effect of crime, highlights the individual and the psychological rather than Hogg's emphasis on the supernatural.

An addition to the Signet Classics editions would not be of interest to *YWES* readers. A notable exception is the reissuing of *Treasure Island* containing an excellent new introduction by Patrick Scott. He perceptively writes that in composing *Treasure Island* 'Stevenson discovered for himself a new kind of fiction with many of the features we now think of as modern: shorter and more dense than the sprawling Victorian three-decker, avoiding any explicit and intrusive authorial voice, narrated by a participant' and, Scott adds, 'puzzling and indeterminate in its ending, conscious of the way previous stories or ways of talking underlie perceptions we think new' (p. xviii). The 1883 Cassell & Company first edition text is followed by a useful enumerative 'Selected Bibliography' divided into 'Prose Works' (p. 201), 'Collected Editions' and 'Biography and Criticism' (pp. 202–4). This Signet edition is remarkable value for its low retail price and hopefully is widely available outside the USA.

The year 2008 was a fertile one for Bram Stoker studies. Meilee D. Bridges's 'Tales from the Crypt: Bram Stoker and the *Curse of the Egyptian Mummy*' (*VIJ* 36[2008] 137–66) illuminates Bram Stoker's depiction of 'The reanimated figure of the embalmed Egyptian [that] stalks the pages of more than thirty Victorian and Edwardian novels, short stories, poems, and plays haunting readers' imaginations in the way that only the undead can' (p. 137). Bridges takes into account Stoker's revision of his *The Jewel of the Seven Stars* in the 1912 edition: the novel was first published in 1903. On a similar note, Aviva Briefel looks at 'Hands of Beauty, Hands of Horror: Fear and Egyptian Art at the Fin de Siècle' (*VS* 50[2008] 263–71) and sheds interesting light on Bram Stoker's *The Jewel of Seven Stars* [1903]. Briefel 'examines the gothicization of Egyptian manual productions in late-Victorian mummy narratives'. She shows that 'these narratives often isolate the mummy's hand as a signifier of craftsmanship' and contends 'that the horror of the mummy's hand emanates from its ambiguous position as an artifact that is itself a means of production' (p. 263). Kate Hebblethwaite's introduction to the Penguin Classics edition of one of Bram Stoker's less available novels, *The Jewel of the Seven Stars*, emphasizes its concern with Egyptian regeneration, and late Victorian interests in the Orient, and its perceived savagery and apparent moral degradation. Hebblethwaite also provides a chronology and list of further reading. She chooses the text of the first edition published by William Heinemann in June 1903.

An important addition to Bram Stoker studies is *Bram Stoker's Notes for Dracula. A Facsimile Edition*, annotated and transcribed by Robert Eighteen-Bisang and Elizabeth Miller, with a foreword by Michael Barsanti. Bram Stoker's initial notes and outline for *Dracula* [1897], originally auctioned at Sotheby's London in 1913, were purchased by a New York book dealer, James Drake. They re-emerged in the 1930s and 1940s in the Charles Scribner's Sons New York inventory. In 1976 the Rosenbach Museum and Library acquired them from the Philadelphia bookseller Chares Sessler. Robert Eighteen-Bisang, the collector and expert on Dracula and vampire literature, and Elizabeth Miller have now produced a remarkable edition of the 'handwritten plot notes, handwritten research notes, and typewritten research notes' (p. 7) replete with extensive page-by-page black and white facsimiles of the notes on the verso page and transcriptions with extensive annotation on the recto page. An 'Overview' discusses the significance of the notes in terms of their relevance to 'Narrative Time', 'The Construction of the Plot' and other features (pp. 275–89). There follows an exposition on 'The Myth of *Dracula*' (pp. 291–4). There are nine appendices to this excellent volume, including 'Bram Stoker: A Brief Biography' (pp. 299–300); 'Bram Stoker: A Brief Bibliography' (pp. 301–3); and 'Bram Stoker's Library' (pp. 313–14). There is even a detailed 'Index of Bram Stoker's Original Notes' (pp. 325–7) followed by an 'Index of Editors' Annotations' (pp. 328–31). Gordon Bigelow's '*Dracula* and Economic History' (*ClioI* 38:i[2008] 39–60) argues that Stoker's novel 'is concerned with the question whether a modernity conceived in terms of market capitalism promises an authentic human freedom or merely an evolving form of servitude, and its representation of sexual difference is integral to this concern' (p. 39).

Sadly, another thin year to report for William Makepeace Thackeray studies. Peter J. Capuano's 'At the Hands of Becky Sharp: (In)Visible Manipulation and *Vanity Fair*' (*VIJ* 36[2008] 167–92) examines 'Thackeray's representation of [Becky Sharp's] hands' and he attempts 'to demonstrate [that] the partial invisibility of Becky's hands is a deliberate and fundamental aspect of *Vanity Fair*'s thematic and formal design' (p. 167). The text is accompanied by illustrations from the original serialization and a fascinating page from *Punch* (p. 188). However, as refreshing as it is to see an article on Thackeray, there is a good deal of special pleading in Capuano's reading. A welcome addition to yet another thin year in Thackeray studies is Julia Kent's 'Thackeray's "Marriage Country": The Englishness of Domestic Sentiment in *Vanity Fair*' (*NCC* 30:ii[2008] 127–46). Anthony Trollope's *The Way We Live Now* [1875] is the focus for Tamara S. Wagner's 'Speculators at Home in the Victorian Novel: Making Stock-Market Villains and New Paper

Fictions' (*VLC* 36:i[2008] 21–40). Melmot's origins become increasingly irrelevant to those he does business with. Close enquiry is shirked and Wagner argues that the aristocratic would-be investors who scramble for a seat on one of his boards are guilty of not only nourishing a fraudulent financier whose background as a swindler they are well aware of, but also for building on unclear attitudes to those they perceive to be successful in speculation. Instability related to speculation is embodied conveniently by an international man of mystery and can easily be exorcised by his self-destruction. Laurent Bury's 'Intrusion et exclusion dans les romans politiques de Trollope' ['Intrusion and Exclusion in Trollope's Political Novels'] (*CVE* 67[2008] 43–54) focuses upon the sense of belonging and exclusion in two of Trollope's political novels *The Prime Minister* [1876] and *The Duke's Children* [1880]. Zubair S. Amir's ' "So delightful a plot": Lies, Gossip and the Narration of Social Advancement in *The Eustace Diamonds*' (*VLC* 36:i[2008] 187–204) treads familiar ground in its discussion of 'one of the most inveterate and gifted liars in Victorian fiction, Lizzie Eustace ... [who] is also one of the most enigmatic'. For Amir, 'Driven both by her social ambition and by her desire to retain the Eustace family diamonds—a necklace given to her by her late husband but claimed by his relatives as an heirloom—Lizzie depends on deceit to achieve her ends throughout the novel'. He continues, 'Yet, her reliance on mendacity becomes perplexingly excessive, confusing not only her sycophantic companion, Julia Macnulty, but most of the story's other characters as well' (p. 187). One of the few individual studies devoted to Trollope and which was not picked up in the 2007 review, is Margaret Markwick's interesting *New Men in Trollope's Novels: Rewriting the Victorian Male*. In her study, Markwick includes analysis of 'Victorian Manliness' (pp. 15–36); 'Men in Fiction' (pp. 37–60); 'Telling Masculinities' (pp. 61–82); 'Sex and the Single Man' (pp. 117–40); 'Husbands, Fathers, Sons' (pp. 141–74) and Trollope's use of 'Smoking Rooms: Bawdy Jokes' (pp. 175–98).

Joseph Bristow's *Oscar Wilde and Modern Culture* and his twelve contributors are concerned with Wilde's literary reputation. Accompanied by thirty-five black and white illustrations, a good deal of *Oscar Wilde and Modern Culture* is concerned with 'the ways in which radical writers, political campaigners, experimental artists, and risk-taking dramatists addressed aspects of Wilde's legacy not long after his turn-of-the-century death' (p. xiii). Contributors include: Lucy McDiarmid's 'Oscar Wilde, Lady Gregory, and Late-Victorian Table-Talk' (pp. 46–62); Daniel A. Novak's 'Sexuality in the Age of Technological Reproducibility: Oscar Wilde, Photography and Identity' (pp. 63–95); Erin Williams Hyman's '*Salomé* as Bombshell, or How Oscar Wilde Became an Anarchist' (pp. 96–109); Richard A. Kaye's 'Oscar Wilde and the Politics of Posthumous Sainthood: Hofmannsthal, Mirabeau, Proust' (pp. 110–32); Yvonne Ivory's 'The Trouble with Oskar: Wilde's Legacy for the Early Homosexual Rights Movement in Germany' (pp. 133–53); Julie Townsend's 'Staking *Salomé*: The Literary Forefathers and Choreographic Daughters of Oscar Wilde's "Hysterical and Perverted Creature" ' (pp. 154–79); Lizzie Thynne's ' "Surely you are not claiming to be more homosexual than I?" Claude Cahun and Oscar Wilde' (pp. 180–208); Laurel Brake's 'Oscar Wilde's

An Ideal Husband and W. Somerset Maugham's *The Constant Wife: A Dialogue'* (pp. 209–33); Leslie J. Moran's 'Transcripts and Truth: Writing the Trials of Oscar Wilde' (pp. 234–58); Francesca Coppa's 'The Artist at Protagonist: Wilde on Stage' (pp. 259–84); Matt Cook's 'Wilde Lives: Derek Jarman and the Queer Eighties' (pp. 285–304); and Oliver S. Buckton's 'Oscar Goes to Hollywood: Wilde, Sexuality and the Gaze of Contemporary Cinema' (pp. 305–37). The book concludes with a select bibliography (pp. 339–42). There is a detailed index (pp. 347–55) and a very useful, annotated 'Chronology' (pp. xxxv–xlii). The aim of Florina Tufescu's *Oscar Wilde's Plagiarism: the Triumph of Art over Ego* is 'to settle the last remaining dispute in the field of Wilde studies, to remove the last objections to Wilde's canonization' (p. 1), and this relates to the issue of plagiarism. For Tufescu, 'plagiarism, as practiced by Wilde, is life-giving and not mind-numbing, the assertion of the absolute modernity of beauty' (p. 141). Whether or not readers accept this argument and defence is a personal matter. It is certainly argued with verve and vigour. Oliver Tearle's 'Dorian Gray's Schoolbooks' (*N&Q* 55[2008] 463–5) should not be ignored when reviewing the year's work in Wilde studies.

Tamara Wagner's 'Depressed Spirits and Failed Crisis Management: Charlotte Yonge's Sensationalisation of the Religious Family' (*VIJ* 36[2008] 275–302) is a welcome addition to critical studies of the neglected Charlotte Yonge. Wagner's focus is Yonge's *The Trial; or, More Links of the Daisy Chain* [1864], which forms the novelist's 'most extensive venture into literary sensationalism' (p. 275). Wagner pays particular attention to Yonge's fictional depiction of 'prevailing treatments of what is currently termed depression'. For Wagner, Yonge's novels 'simultaneously underscore the complexities of religious fiction by domestic women writers and the alternative approaches to low spirits [they] can offer beyond the promotion of particular articles of faith' (p. 297). Last but by no means least, drawing upon letters, diaries, manuscripts and Anglo-American newspaper reports, Meri-Jane Rochelson's *A Jew in the Public Arena: The Career of Israel Zangwill* is a highly significant addition to works on Zangwill's fiction, drama and prose writings. Rochelson draws upon her extensive knowledge of the life and work of Zangwill and its context. Divided into nine chapters, Rochelson's is an indispensable work for studying Zangwill and for an analysis of late Victorian and Edwardian literature and culture. She provides a very useful descriptive 'Chronology of Israel Zangwill's Life and Work' (pp. xvii–xxvi). Rochelson's well-written work demonstrates that she is the leading authority on Zangwill.

3. Poetry

In this section Anna Barton reviews works about the Brontës, Arthur Hugh Clough, Edward FitzGerald, Gerard Manley Hopkins, Tennyson, Michael Field and other writers of the *fin de siècle*. Jane Wright reviews works about Arnold, the Brownings, the Rossettis and other Pre-Raphaelites, and work by Anna Barton.

The ever-expanding canon of Victorian poetry received a major boost this year with the publication of Herbert Tucker's *Epic: Britain's Heroic Muse 1790–1910*. It is difficult to do justice to the scope of Tucker's study in a brief review, but all those interested in poetry in the long nineteenth century would do well to consult this impressive work of scholarship. Tucker argues for the vital significance of epic throughout this period, recovering shoals of minor and neglected epic writers and treating their lengthy—and in many cases fairly terrible—poems with relish. He views epic, crucially, as a form always concerned with collective, communal, and in many cases national or imperial, claims, suggesting that poets and readers were 'predisposed to conceive the entire epic transaction in collectively affiliative terms' (p. 26). His emphasis is primarily historicist, and war and reform inspire many of the poems he discusses, as do religious and historical concerns. Early chapters treat long poems by Keats, Byron, Scott and Wordsworth, among others, while for Victorianists the key chapters are likely to be those dealing with Tennyson, Barrett Browning and Browning. But it must be noted that Tucker never restricts himself to discussion of any one major poet: rather, the works of these poets are reconceptualized by being located in the broader context of hundreds of other epics dealing with similar themes or deploying similar forms. Familiar poems take on new guises in this light, while Tucker reveals a wealth of unfamiliar poems to the reader. The length of Tucker's study is certainly off-putting to the casual reader, but his prose is always lively and entertaining, and *Epic* contains many of his characteristically brilliant close readings. Few scholars could fail to find interest and inspiration in this work.

Another contribution to the growing canon was Florence Boos's edited anthology, *Working-Class Women Poets in Victorian Britain*. Boos divides her authors into 'Rural Poets', 'Factory Poets' and 'Lyricists and Feminists', with the Scottish poet Janet Hamilton standing alone at the start of the volume. Poets covered here range from the relatively well known (Eliza Cook, Ellen Johnston) to the less familiar (Isabella Chisholm, Mary MacDonald MacPherson). Boos includes prose extracts and helpful introductions to each poet, plus portraits and photographs and a comprehensive bibliography. This is a very valuable collection, which follows Pickering & Chatto's editions of labouring-class poets in widening our appreciation of the field of Victorian working-class writing.

Matthew Arnold's poetry, once again this year, received only a small amount of attention. Both Kate Campbell's *Matthew Arnold* from the Northcote Writers and their Work series, and Stefan Collini's *Matthew Arnold: A Critical Portrait* (reissued from the 1994 edition) contain a chapter that deftly addresses Arnold's work as a poet. Campbell's book, as a whole, emphasizes Arnold's publicist career as he grappled with ideas of modernity, and so places the poetry in this light, seeing in it a picture of the self-absorbed modern consciousness that Arnold went on to reject. Collini's study (well known by now) traces the language of a number of Romantic concerns and highlights some of the ways that Arnold's poems, as (differently) his prose, reveal 'the quality of having a deeper preoccupation than their ostensible subjects' (p. 34). Nils Clausson's article, 'Arnold's Coleridgean Conversation Poem: "Dover Beach" and "The Eolian Harp"' (*PLL* 44:iii[2008] 276–304), provides a long discussion of the possible forms of indebtedness of 'Dover Beach' to the Coleridgean conversation poem, and 'The Eolian Harp' in particular. Clausson rightly notes the shared conversational voice, natural setting, flight of imagination, and final concern with faith in each poem; that last, of course, constituting one of the greater differences between the two, in terms of content of belief, if not in terms of its role in the poetic structure. Looking back again to the Romantics, Mark Sandy, in '"Echoes of that Voice": Romantic Resonances in Victorian Poetic Birdsong' (in Radford and Sandy, eds., *Romantic Echoes in the Victorian Era*, pp. 155–73), has brief remarks on the continued Romantic force of echoes of, or references to, literary birds and bird song in Arnold's 'Dover Beach', 'Philomela', and 'To Marguerite—Continued'. The chapter also contains some fine, brief remarks on this topic in poems by Charlotte Smith ('The Return of the Nightingale') and John Clare ('The Nightingale's Nest') and notes Clare's greater (perhaps more Victorian) emphasis on the bird's condition and habitat than on its symbolic function.

'Matthew Arnold's "The Buried Life"' (*ANQ* 21:i[2008] 42–4), by Francis O'Gorman, highlights a more contemporary connection, between Arnold's poem and Richard Chevenix Trench's 'The Descent of the Rhone' [1835]. When Arnold's poem closes 'And then he thinks he knows | The hills where his life rose, | And the sea where it goes', it may be glancing at Trench's description of the thought-weary human 'Weighing whither this life tends, | For what high and holy ends | It was lent us, whence it flows, | And its current whither goes'. However, where Trench's metaphorical life-river, his poem suggests, goes on to the 'sea'/'eternity', Arnold's poem recasts the metaphor to emphasize the uncertainty of that Christian stay, and the final secularity of human endeavour. Looking neither to forebears nor contemporaries, but onwards toward modernism, C.D. Blanton, in 'Arnold's Arrhythmia' (*SEL* 48[2008] 755–67), reads in 'Empedocles on Etna' a figuration of the kind of 'crisis of reading' that constituted Arnold's ultimate move away from poetry to prose. Blanton considers that while the disruptions and difficulties of 'Empedocles on Etna', in both form and content, actually succeed in catching up the arrhythmic quality of modernity that he (in a different sense) so descried elsewhere, Arnold's famous preface of 1853 (and indeed his prose at large) might be better understood through attention to its unity of tone rather than through attempts to prescribe the consistency of its meaning. In a broad sense, such a view of the prose is common. But, by reading 'Empedocles on Etna' as a successful expression of the literary-critical position, and the prose (the preface) as poetic in method, Blanton also asserts a specific and interesting role for Arnold in the development of central modernist values and practices. Molly Clark Hillard moves us from a modern to a postmodern Arnold in '"When desert armies stand ready to fight": Re-reading McEwan's *Saturday* and Arnold's "Dover Beach"' (*PAns* 6[2008] 181–206), which argues that the moment in McEwan's novel when Daisy Perowne recites 'Dover Beach' to her attacker 'constitutes a moment of neo-Victorianism' (p. 183). In a considered article that turns on the theme of misreading, Hillard makes the case for broadening the definition of neo-Victorian so that it might accommodate any textual recognition of the contemporary resonances of the Victorian period.

Michael L. Ross, 'On A Darkling Planet: Ian McEwan's *Saturday* and the Condition of England' (*TCL* 54:i[2008] 75–96) also considers McEwan's Victorian inheritance, making brief reference to Arnold in an article the primary focus of which is on comparisons with other Condition of England novels.

Unavailable in 2006, *The Treatment of Themes of Mortality in the Poetry of the Brontë Sisters* by Yana Rowland is one of two monographs published in recent years to focus exclusively on the Brontës as poets. Although it recognizes the need for a reappraisal of the Brontë's poetic corpus, Rowland's dense, theoretical study gains little from a comparison with Janet Gezari's fine, concise consideration of Emily Brontë's poetry, *Last Things: Emily Brontë's Poems* (reviewed last year). It is more ambitious in scope than *Last Things*, dealing with each of the Brontë sisters in turn in three linked sections that all identify a thematic preoccupation with mortality, a theme that Rowland approaches from a bewildering variety of theoretical angles. Rowland is well versed in the 'ontophilosophy and existential ethics' (p. 11) of Heidegger, Lévinas, Derrida and Bakhtin, but she fails to communicate her knowledge to the reader with any clarity so that the poems (of which the book deals with an impressive range) are often lost within the argument.

Despite this recent flurry of monographs, the poetry of the Brontës remains an under-researched area. The potential relevance of their work to current critical concerns is indicated by a small number of articles, two of which are included in *Sublimer Aspects: Interfaces Between Literature, Aesthetics, and Theology* [2007], edited by Natasha Duquette. The first of these, Susan R. Bauman's '"How Shall *I* Appear?": The Dialogue of Faith and Doubt in Anne Brontë's Hymns' (pp. 80–98), discusses how Anne Brontë's hymns are able to accommodate faith as well as doubt, the private lyric voice and the public voice of the preacher, albeit within an acceptable feminine form. Bauman identifies a significant influence in the work of Cowper, and pieces together an intertextual dialogue between the life and work of the two poets before going on to survey a selection of Anne's hymns, tracing themes of faith and doubt in works that she characterizes as instructional lyrics of intellectual and emotional struggle. In the same volume, Sandra Hagen again mentions Anne Brontë's hymns in her persuasive essay '"Take my Lips": Frances Ridley Havergal and the Pleasures of Hymnody for Victorian Single Women' (pp. 112–30), which takes the convention of anonymity for published hymns as a starting point for a discussion of their composition by Victorian single women who found a means of covert expression in the self-effacing poetics of hymnody. Hagen employs Foucauldian theories of social scrutiny to argue that the spinster might choose textual invisibility to avoid society's intrusive, disempowering gaze. She explores the 'submissive posture' (p. 119) of Havergal's hymns that nevertheless particularize and perform the self alongside the work of Christina Rossetti and Anne Brontë. Worth mentioning at this point (although it is not concerned with the Brontës) is Cheri Larsen Hoeckley's contribution to the same collection, 'Poetry, Activism and "Our Lady of the Rosary": Adelaide Procter's Catholic Poetics in *A Chaplet of Verses*' (pp. 145–59), which employs Procter's Catholicism and her relationship to early feminism and Victorian philanthropy as grounds for a rereading of *A Chaplet of Verses*, which gains new significance when considered as a whole volume after the model of *Songs of Innocence and of Experience*. Returning to the Brontës, 'No Coward Souls: Poetic Engagement between Emily Brontë and Emily Dickinson' by Michael Moon (in McGill, ed., *The Traffic in Poems: Nineteenth Century Poetry and Transatlantic Exchange*, pp. 231–49) considers the significance of Emily's 'last' poem for Dickinson. Beginning with the fact that the poem was read at Dickinson's funeral, Moon reads the poem as a hymn, in relation to *Wuthering Heights* and in its original context as a Gondal poem. She stresses the importance of these contexts in relation to critical debates about the various possible contexts of Dickinson's brief lyrics.

A lively essay by Yopie Prins, 'Robert Browning, Transported by Meter' (in McGill, ed., pp. 205–30), interestingly tracks the reception of Browning's poetry across the Atlantic, across different media (poetry, music and film), and even across different kinds of transportation (mechanical and metrical), placing its final emphasis on the significance of reading metre as, effectively, a Victorian 'technology' designed (especially by Browning) to transport readers into the future. Browning's American connections also led to valuable explorations of 'Caliban upon Setebos' in particular in 2008. Andrew M. Stauffer, in ' "The King is Cold", by Stoddard, not Browning' (*VLC* 36[2008] 361–2), neatly corrects an earlier note he had written (*VLC* 26:ii[1998] 465–73) which suggested that the poem 'The King is Cold' was by Browning. The poem is now known to have been written by the minor contemporary American writer Richard Henry Stoddard. The mix-up was a consequence of the poem's attribution to Browning in the *New York News* in 1857; however, in 1880 it was belatedly published by Stoddard under his own name. Citing Stauffer's article, Joseph Phelan, in 'Richard Henry Stoddard and the Brownings' (*BSNotes* 33[2008] 58–68) also corrects the misattribution and offers illuminating further discussion of the literary relationship between Browning and Stoddard. Acknowledging the popularity of imitative works, or 'burlesques', among Stoddard's contemporaries, Phelan most interestingly notes the possibility that one of Stoddard's own dramatic poems ('The Witches Whelp' [1852]) might have provided inspiration for 'Caliban upon Setebos'.

Work on Caliban's oft-treated theological musings came in the form of two interesting articles offering different perspectives on the subject. Carol Fry's article, 'Caliban upon the Demiurge: Gnosticism on the Island in "Caliban upon Setebos" ' (*VN* 113[2008] 67–76), elaborates convincingly on the importance of Gnostic thought to Browning's complex theology in the poem. Fry outlines a series of parallels between Gnosticism and Caliban's thinking, elucidating, among other things, the Gnostic belief in both a Demiurge (a conceivable, and not all-powerful, god) and the Pleroma (or Fullness), which have been noted for their relation to Caliban's notions of Setebos and the Quiet, respectively; she also considers, in particular, the Gnostic portrayal of the Demiurge as a jealous god alongside the apparently jealous nature of Setebos. In a richly argued article entitled 'Darwin, Natural Theology, and Slavery: A Justification of Browning's Caliban' (*ELH* 75[2008] 871–97), Joseph Loesberg rightly disputes discussions of the poem which restrictively see Caliban's thinking as either a confused, post-Darwinian attempt to explain God, or, relatedly, as an indirect expression of the importance of accepting a Christian divinity over a natural theological explanation of deity. Caliban's extrapolation from his environment of a spiteful and capricious god, Loesberg argues, has a stronger basis in the conditions of his enslavement—and his consciousness of that enslavement— than it does in other features of Caliban's psychology or in Browning's own religious convictions. Not only aware of himself as one enslaved, but as an independent moral agent caught in a reactive and mediatory condition, what Caliban most starkly presents is the struggle (unresolved within the poem, because unresolvable within Caliban's consciousness) to work out the meaning of his enslavement. Such concerns with the degree or kind of Caliban's awareness also form part of an insightful chapter by Sophie Ratcliffe, in her book *On Sympathy*. Ratcliffe rightly points out that critical uncertainty about whether the poem intends sympathy or satire to be uppermost in our response to Caliban is itself indicative of the poem's central concern with frustrated understanding. Dwelling on the importance, but questioning the actual possibilities of sympathy, Ratcliffe also provides sensitive new readings of poems, including 'Cleon', 'Mr. Sludge, "The Medium"', parts of *The Ring and the Book*, and 'An Epistle Containing the Strange Medical Experiences of Karshish, the Arab Physician'.

In an engaging article on 'Browning on the Romantics on Mont Blanc' (*BSNotes* 33[2008] 3–20), John Woolford elucidates Browning's intricate and humane responsiveness to his Romantic forebears through their presence in his poem 'La Saisiaz' [1878], written in response to the sudden death of his friend Annie Egerton Smith in 1877. The poem, Woolford shows, variously responds to or revises a number of poems by Shelley, Byron, Wordsworth and Coleridge. Whilst revealing his scepticism about Romantic associations between memory and landscape, Browning, Woolford explains, uses this engagement with his forebears to assert the value of memorialization, at once acknowledging his own early Romanticism and, at the same time, offering a fraternal and careful critique of his predecessors. Also exploring Browning's Romantic inheritance, in '"Wandering between Two Worlds": The Victorian Afterlife of Thomas Chatterton' (in Radford and Sandy, eds., pp. 27–37) Julie Crane highlights Browning's interest in Chatterton and speculates on Chatterton's possible presence in 'Mr. Sludge, "The Medium"'. Crane interestingly discusses Chatterton and Sludge as both caught imaginatively between being figures of, on the one hand, harmless creativity and, on the other, immoral fraudulence. Looking to modernist rather than Romantic connections, Matthew Bolton elucidates links between T.S. Eliot's works and those of Browning in '"Not known, because not looked for": Eliot's Debt to Browning' (*YER* 25:ii[2008] 10–19). Focusing on both as 'poets of the psychological monologue', Bolton provides a convincing account of the attractions and difficulties that Browning presented to the younger poet. In so doing, he maps Eliot's reworking of a number of Browning's monologic and dialogic techniques, from increasingly stylistically internalized monologues (such as Prufrock's) to long poems with multiple speakers (comparing *The Ring and the Book* with *The Waste Land*).

The Ring and the Book is also the subject of a significant article by Laura Struve, '"This is no way to tell a story": Robert Browning's Attack on the Law in *The Ring and the Book*' (*LawL* 20:iii[2008] 423–43). Neatly refuting critics who have seen *The Ring and the Book* as a work whose own methods are influenced by nineteenth-century developments in the legal system (a system which moved away from the earlier 'accused speaks' model in which the accused party defended her- or himself without the aid of a legal representative, towards the adversarial model better known today), Laura Struve argues that Browning's poem in fact constitutes an attack on such nineteenth-century developments. Noting the importance of Bentham's theory of legal fictions, but disputing critics who push this kind of influence into Foucauldian analysis, Struve finds that *The Ring and the Book* is a story not about the law as such, or about narrative methods for reaching the truth, but instead about the troubling extension of fiction into the legal system (a process that the nineteenth century seemed to be witnessing), and also, therefore, about the importance, in the end, of making difficult, clear-cut moral choices. In a different vein, David Sassian, in 'The Ritual in "The Novel in *The Ring and the Book*"': Browning, Henry James, Eric Gans' (*VP* 46[2008] 233–47), offers to illuminate *The Ring and the Book*, and Henry James's response to it in his essay 'The Novel in *The Ring and the Book*', through a consideration of literary scholar and cultural anthropologist Eric Gans's notions of the origins of language in acts of collective violence.

In 'Browning's "Home-Thoughts, from the Sea": A Warning against Hubris' (*ANQ* 21:i[2008] 37–42), Warren U. Ober and John H. Panabaker note instances of critical misreading or partial inattention to the poem and argue that it is not a nationalistic or patriotic work, as previous commentary has tended to suggest, but rather a warning against taking too much pride in the British empire, and a subtle reminder of the ephemeral nature of power. They rightly highlight that God and Jove are linked in the poem, not as contrasting figures but as different names for the same deity ('Jehovah, Jove, or Lord!', as Pope has it in his 'Universal Prayer' [1738]), and they argue that the awkward pronunciation of Africa (given a long *a*, to sound 'Africay')—the poem's final word—would have produced a comic effect for Victorian readers which would undermine the poem's already ambivalent piety. They end by comparing the poem to Kipling's 'Recessional'. Adopting Arthur Hallam's description of Tennyson's 'new species of poetry, a graft of the lyric on the dramatic', in 'Browning's Grafts' (*SEL* 48[2008] 769–78) Linda M. Shires reads in some of Browning's letters to Fanny Haworth a dramatic (and self-dramatizing) male voice working out its poetic potential through its sense of opposition to the more lyrical, apparently straightforward voice of a silent female interlocutor. In a note entitled 'Within the Text of Browning's THE GUARDIAN ANGEL' (*Expl* 66:ii[2008] 91–3), Paul Ardoin suggests that the angel described as 'My angel' by the narrator of the poem, and commonly thought to be Elizabeth Barrett Browning, is better read as the spirit of art which can offer comfort in times of trouble.

Work on Elizabeth Barrett Browning also continues to be rich and diverse, and might be defined broadly, this year, by its interest in influence, whether the influence of earlier writers on EBB, or her own influence on other authors, in England or America. In a chapter called 'Elizabeth Barrett Browning and Victorian Versions of Byron and Wollstonecraft: Romantic Genealogies, Self-Defining Memories and the Genesis of Aurora Leigh' (in Radford and Sandy, eds., pp. 123–41), Marjorie Stone argues that the impact of Mary Wollstonecraft's thought on EBB, in both the latter's youth and her maturity, is easily overlooked but is intriguingly linked with EBB's early responses to Byron. Stone explains that, although a strong admirer of Byron, EBB's notes on what she reads record her criticisms of the elder poet's representation of women in terms which recall Wollstonecraft, while her letters hint at links between such thinking and the genesis of *Aurora Leigh*. Christine Chaney, in 'The "Prophet-Poet's Book"' (*SEL* 48[2008] 791–9), also notes the significance of Wollstonecraft as a literary model for EBB in her development of the hybrid form of *Aurora Leigh*. More specifically, Chaney links the associative, thematic workings of Wollstonecraft's and EBB's texts to discussion of *Aurora Leigh*'s much-noted status as a kind of self-portrait. In so doing, she draws fresh attention to the way such self-portraiture constitutes a more socially disruptive form than traditional (male-dominated) autobiographical narrative. Chaney argues that EBB deployed such facets of the poem to support her claim for the female poet's role as a prophet for her society, a society increasingly in need of telling hybrid stories and stories of hybridity.

More Romantic echoes resound in Brandy Ryan's '"Echo and Reply": The Elegies of Felicia Hemans, Letitia Landon, and Elizabeth Barrett' (*VP* 46[2008] 249–77), which reviews recent criticism and explores the particular limits and licences faced and exploited by female elegists, before suggesting that, as the inhibited life led by women could seem itself like a kind of death for the woman poet, the poetry of death offered a special opportunity for the female elegist to connect with her poetic predecessors. EBB has an important and truculent-seeming place in this regard, as she most openly criticizes and rejects features of her female forebears' work. EBB's insistence that poetry should address contemporary life, Ryan argues, emerges in a rebuke to Letitia Landon made in EBB's 'Stanzas Addressed to Miss Landon and Suggested by her "Stanzas on the Death of Mrs. Hemans"' [1835]. EBB, who does not straightforwardly seek sympathetic engagement with her predecessors, questions the value of elegy at all, and so criticizes her female predecessors for entering into that (implicitly male-dominated) tradition rather than establishing a new one. Unlike Hemans or Landon, by refusing to manipulate a tradition and instead rebuking it, EBB might oddly be aligned with a more traditionally masculine position, in so far as she places herself 'in a position of power over her predecessors'. That hopeful position of power can also be seen in four poems which, Beverly Taylor suggests, chart the poet's varied but persistent deployment of child figures in her poems to contest Romantic (specifically Rousseauvian) ideas about the nature and purpose of education. In 'Elizabeth Barrett Browning and the Politics of Childhood' (*VP* 46[2008] 405–27), Taylor argues that, whether offering a feminine alternative to the stuff of masculine legend (as she does in 'Hector in the Garden') or challenging the conventions of a mother's role in her child's education (as in 'A Romance of the Ganges'), EBB used her representations of children to expose the dangers of perpetuating narrow or conservative constructions of gender.

Brent E. Kinser, in ' "A very beautiful tempest in a teapot": Elizabeth Barrett Browning, Thomas Carlyle, and the Annotation of *Aurora Leigh*' (*BSNotes* 33[2008] 21–39), provides commentary on Carlyle's annotations to *Aurora Leigh*, and by this means sheds yet other light on EBB's deft subversion of men's social assumptions. Offering an account of their acquaintance, and of the well-known presence of Carlyle's *Vates* and Hero as Poet to the concerns of *Aurora Leigh*, Kinser notes that Carlyle's amusing annotations (some of which betray his misunderstanding) reveal either an inability or a refusal to recognize the extent to which Aurora successfully wields his own (masculine?) philosophical perspectives, so that the sage actually foregrounds with his comments a further aspect of EBB's literary success.

International relations are also prominent once more in four further pieces on EBB. In an at times slightly confusing essay, 'Elizabeth Barrett Browning's Italian Poetry: Constructing National Identity and Shaping the Poetic Self' (in Hertel and Pfister, eds., *Performing National Identity: Anglo-Italian Cultural Transactions*, pp. 123–36), Fabienne Moine seeks to compare EBB's emotions and physical life with what she calls her allegorized representation of Italy, in works including *Casa Guidi Windows* and *Poems Before Congress*. Arguing for the importance of reading EBB as a political poet, Moine discusses comparisons made between childbirth and the birth of a nation, and suggests that in refusing to write about Italy without overt emotion, EBB sought to perform something of the identity of the passionate Italian political scene. Mary Loeffelholz's chapter, 'Mapping the Cultural Field: *Aurora Leigh* in America' (in McGill, ed., pp. 139–59), explores the ways that once popular, but now largely forgotten, American writers (chiefly Josiah Holland and Lucy Larcom), responded to and adapted *Aurora Leigh*. With an emphasis on the much-desired power of poetry as a successful cultural mediator (a mediator at once of divisions of class, nationality, and sex), Loeffelholz argues for the mediatory role of Holland's and Larcom's poems in presenting that transatlantic hope. Loeffelholz also discusses the way that EBB offered Emily Dickinson a high-art model for poetry by women, and the influence, in this respect, of class and cultural hierarchies in America in shaping the reception of British verse. Exploring a very different international context in 'Sight, Sound, and Silence: Representations of the Slave Body in Barrett Browning, Hawkshaw, and Douglas' (*VN* 114[2008] 51–68), Debbie Bark uses 'The Runaway Slave at Pilgrim's Point' to prompt an insightful discussion of the relation between colour (as a visible signifier) and sound or silence (with their different signifying potentials) in representations or expressions of slave's bodies, suggesting that for EBB (as, differently, for Frederick Douglass and Ann Hawkshaw) sound offers a complex and elusive potential for reconciliation which sight might otherwise counter. The role of sound and silence in EBB's representation of slavery is diversely significant to Sara Hackenberg's 'Alien Image, Ideal Beauty: The Oriental Vision of American Slavery in Hiram Power's *The Greek Slave*' (*VN* 114[2008] 30–49), in which Hackenberg comments on EBB's representation in 'Hiram Power's Greek Slave' of the statue as an incitement to Western women to break their 'white silence'. Amy Billone makes large claims for the intertextual relationship between two more poets in 'Elizabeth Barrett's and Alfred Tennyson's Authorial and Formal

Links' (*SEL* 48[2008] 779–89), which traces parallels in their respective biographies and reviews their opinion of one another, employing selective evidence to prove that Tennyson was Barrett Browning's favourite poet and revisiting claims that her work imitates and responds to Tennyson, focusing in particular on Barrett's response to *In Memoriam*.

Two studies place EBB and Christina Rossetti side by side this year. Maria LaMonaca's *Masked Atheism: Catholicism and the Secular Victorian Home* includes a chapter on *Aurora Leigh* and *Goblin Market*, which argues that Roman Catholicism is influential in both poems on the role of the female figures, in particular, as well as on the versions of transubstantiation that occur in each. Noting EBB's ambivalence about Catholicism, LaMonaca argues that each of the women in *Aurora Leigh* can be connected with Rome, whether positively or negatively; and in *Goblin Market* she finds tropes and ideas that might have been more readily associated with the redemptive power of Roman (not just Anglo-) Catholicism by some of Rossetti's contemporaries. *Desire and Gender in the Sonnet Tradition* by Natasha Distiller contains discussions of EBB's *Sonnets from the Portuguese* and Rossetti's *Monna Innominata*. The book looks at the work of female sonneteers from Mary Wroth to Edna St Vincent Millay and attempts to place them in a 'post-Lacanian framework' in order to shed light on the language of 'Petrarchan subjectivity' (p. 117), and thence to show how each female writer in question reworked, challenged, or cautiously aligned herself with such language. Distiller summarizes the critical background to these sequences, and so tells again a story of the female poet's voice subjected to, and limited by, biographical reading. Examining *Sonnets from the Portuguese*, she suggests that the female speaker successfully presents her desire without asserting a need to dominate her beloved, so that she moves both within and beyond established Petrarchan patterns (an argument presumably borrowed indirectly from sensitive earlier readings by critics including Angela Leighton). 'In fact', Distiller asserts, '*Sonnets from the Portuguese* is highly educated both formally and thematically about the conventions on which it draws and the rules it breaks' (p. 116). However, Distiller also declares that EBB's speaker's words are prompted not by her own desire but by that of the male beloved, that 'far from needing her beloved to be absent, [she] is reliant on his presence, his voice, and his desire, for her own' (p. 116). This oddly ignores many reversals, ironies, and nuances of tone, allusion and image throughout the sequence, and close attention to such literary matters is largely unforthcoming throughout. Without explanation, Distiller decides to work with the sequence of forty-three sonnets that appeared in *Poems* [1850], rather than the final sequence as it was published in 1856. In the chapter on Christina Rossetti, Distiller alleges that Rossetti has been most subject to the dangers of biographical criticism because 'Most of the information available about her is biographical' (p. 123). She then goes on to explore Rossetti's desire to 'write Laura's voice back into the [sonnet] tradition' (p. 124). Her discussion of *Monna Innominata* seems to suggest, however, that Rossetti finally lets go this possibility and instead turns the elusive and inaccessible nature of love in the Petrarchan tradition to account in representing the impossibility of gaining full knowledge of God. There is perhaps an edginess in Distiller's phrasing in both these chapters that in order justly to credit her chosen authors with intelligence requires quite a stark sense of there always being a clear 'system', 'schema', or 'framework' for defining femininity and the gendering of desire. Nevertheless, Distiller's broadest points about the poets' spry challenges to convention remain true enough. Gender has long been a difficult subject to write about, and this book presents some of that difficulty.

The only article on Clough to be published this year, 'Byron, Clough and the Grounding of Victorian Poetry' (*Romanticism* 14:i[2008] 13–24) by Richard Cronin is an astute comparison which begins by discussing the different ways the two poets thought and wrote about travel and tourism, and goes on to read Clough's Dipsychus and his companion Spirit as a pair of bourgeois, post-Byronic, self-conscious tourists. However, rather than proposing Clough's poetry as a straightforward rejection of what was regarded by many Victorians as a stale Romantic aesthetic, Cronin proposes Byron as a solution to Clough's concerns about the unworldliness that had come to characterize Victorian poetry and an alternative to Wordsworth, against whom Clough rebels by exchanging blank verse for the hexameter line.

Unavailable last year, *Michael Field and their World* [2007], edited by Margaret D. Stetz and Cheryl A. Wilson, is the first collection of essays devoted to the work of the Michael Field poets. This impressive compendium of over twenty short essays is an important milestone for Field studies, demonstrating the quantity and range of research that is being carried out on their rich and varied corpus. There remains a good deal of focus on Field's poetic and pseudonymic identity. Rachel Morley's introduction to the volume, 'Talking Collaboratively: Conversations with Michael Field' (pp. 13–20), takes a ficto-critical approach imagining conversations with Bradley and Cooper and incorporating their essay 'Effigies' in order to draw out their interest in their own posthumous reputation. Katharine (J.J.) Pionke also employs personal reflections in her consideration of the Field pseudonym, 'Michael Field: Gender Knot' (pp. 23–8), which seeks to strike a balance between claims that the name was adopted for commercial purposes and claims that it is intrinsic to Bradley and Cooper's authorial identity by arguing that the name, which was adopted for convenience, gained significance for the couple and their work after the fact. Holly Laird considers another of Bradley and Cooper's pseudonymous identities in 'Michael Field as Author of *Borgia*' (pp. 29–38), which looks at the late period of Michael Field's career, during which time they published a series of Roman plays attributed to 'the author of Borgia'. Again, evidence suggests that this new identity was motivated by necessity, but nevertheless presented new opportunities to the couple to 're-double' their double identity. 'Attributing the Substance of Collaboration as Michael Field' by Maria Deguzman (pp. 71–81) considers again the significance of the pseudonym and the possible meaning of its different parts. 'Rethinking Michael Field: The Case for the Bodleian Letters' by Sharon Bickle (pp. 39–47) brings our attention to a collection of letters that pre-date the journal publications of Bradley and Cooper, considering the influence of their literary executor, who excluded private correspondence from the work given over to the British Library. Bickle makes a persuasive case for the power of the archive to frame our understanding of literary identity and offers a brief reassessment of the early lives of Bradley and Cooper and the role played by Emma Cooper, Edith's mother. Two strong contributions by Joseph Bristow and Rhian E. Williams focus on Field's 1893 collection, *Underneath the Bough*. In 'Michael Field's Lyrical Aestheticism: *Underneath the Bough*' (pp. 49–62) Bristow considers Michael Field's relationship with the Scottish critic John Miller Gray and summarizes the publication history of *Underneath the Bough*, which started life as *Songs and Sundry Nocturnes*. Williams offers an astute reading of the opening poem of *Underneath the Bough* in 'Michael Field's Shakespearean Community' (pp. 63–70), arguing that the poem's reference to Shakespeare's birthday allows Field to speak through Shakespeare, suggesting a model of 'community' rather than 'partnership'. Williams suggests that Field's 'song book' presents itself as a self-consciously communal object and discusses the way Shakespeare the sonneteer provides Field with a model of sexually subversive lyric subjecthood with which they could identify. Essays about the world of Michael Field do important work in demonstrating Bradley and Copper's links to their late Victorian moment. 'Penetrating Matthew Arnold' by Ed Madden (pp. 83–95) suggests that the late nineteenth-century shift in representations of Tiresias that focus on his liminal gender and sexuality might originate with Michael Field's representation of Tiresias in 'LII', included in *Long Ago* [1889], which responds to Arnoldian classicism (an expanded version of this essay is included in Madden's *Tiresian Poetics: Modernism, Sexuality, Voice, 1888–2001*). In 'The Dialectics of Conversion: Marius and Michael Field' (pp. 97–105) Kit Andrews discusses the relationship between Field and Pater via their exploration of pagan and Christian aesthetics, and Valerie Fehlbaum explores the similarities between Michael Field and the Hepworth Dixon sisters who moved in similar artistic circles to Bradley and Cooper and produced similarly diverse and various literary and artistic outputs ('Sisters in Life, Sisters in Art: Ella and Marion Hepworth Dixon', pp. 107–15). Bradley and Cooper's public life is the subject of Linda K. Hughes's essay, 'Reluctant Lions: Michael Field and the Transatlantic Literary Salon of Louise Chandler Moulton' (pp. 117–25), which details the relationship between Field and the American poet and journalist and provides an illuminating comparative reading of Field's 'The Sleeping Venus' and Moulton's 'Laus Veneris' in order to reassess Bradley and Cooper's attitude towards their professional celebrity. 'The Sapphic Culture of Michael Field and Radclyffe Hall' by Richard Dellamora (pp. 127–36), which reads Field's Sapphic phenomenology as a precursor of Hall, introduces another clutch of essays dealing with Field's sexuality. Again emphasis is placed on Field's relevance to established critical and theoretical frameworks. 'Michael Field as Dandy Poet' by Elizabeth Primamore (pp. 137–46) argues that Field's poetic identity—a product of the culture of aestheticism and the figure of the dandy—provides a prototype of the female dandy; Brooke Cameron's essay, '"Where twilight touches ripeness amorously": The Gaze in Michael Field's *Sight and Song*' (pp. 147–53), returns to the theme of the gaze in Field's ekphrastic collection, applying Irigaray; in 'Michael Field and the Challenges of Writing a Lesbian Catholicism' (pp. 155–62), Frederick S. Roden considers Catholicism's accommodation of lesbian femininity and proposes Field as representative of a proto-modern

Catholic homosexuality; and in 'Michael Field and Saint Sebastian' (pp. 163–70), Dinah Ward looks at three poems from *Sight and Song* that are based on paintings of St Sebastian in order to question of the visibility of homosexuality in the late nineteenth century. Bradley and Cooper's abiding interest in paganism and their late conversion to Roman Catholicism present inviting paradoxes that are sensitively handled by two essays. 'Keeping Faith: Consistency and Paradox in the World View of Michael Field' by Chris Snodgrass (pp. 171–80) and 'Michael Field's Pagan Aestheticism' by Camille Cauti (pp. 181–90) both draw together the pagan and the Christian through discussions of their traditions of sacrifice. Diana Maltz brings to light an unfamiliar context in her essay 'Katherine Bradley and Ethical Socialism' (pp. 191–201), which describes Bradley's association with socialist people and ideas, her membership of Fellowship of New Life and Guild of St George, her difficult relationship with Ruskin and the impact that this had on her social activism. Four final essays turn to the materiality of Field's work. 'Michael Field's Translations into Verse' by Julie Wise (pp. 203–10) and 'The Concrete Poetics of Michael Field's *Sight and Song*' by Nicholas Frankel (pp. 211–22) return to the claims of objectivity and the theme of objecthood in *Sight and Song*; 'Apian Aestheticism: Michael Field and the Economics of the Aesthetic' by Marion Thain (pp. 223–36) conducts a virtuoso reading of *Wild Honey from Various Thyme* in the contexts of Victorian renegotiations of apian imagery and the economics of late nineteenth-century bee-keeping; and 'Outmoded Dramas: History and Modernity in Michael Field's Aesthetic Plays' by Ana Parejo Vadillo (pp. 237–49) concentrates on Field's use of history and argues that the outmoded nature of their plays achieves a vital alienation that avoids commodification.

Two further essays about Michael Field published in 2008 also focus on their material poetics. 'To Those Who Love Them Best: The Erotics of Connoisseurship in Michael Field's *Sight and Song*', in Krista Lysack's excellent *Come Buy, Come Buy: Shopping and the Culture of Consumption in Victorian Women's Writing*', offers same-sex desire as an alternative economy that emphasizes a pleasure which need not involve ownership. Engaging with recent reassessments of aestheticism's relationship to consumerism, Lysack suggests that the exchange that occurs within the lyrics poses significant questions for the book in which they are published—itself a consumer product. Characteristic of Lysack's book as a whole, the chapter deals incisively with contextual material, providing a detailed and informative account of Bradley and Cooper's experience of the market as writers for the Bodley Head.

A series of four short articles on 'Victorian Materialities', published in *Victorian Studies* following the 2007 North American Victorian Studies Association/Victorian Studies Association of Western Canada conference, begins with 'Michael Field and the Detachable Lyric' by Emily Harrington (*VS* 50[2008] 221–32), which looks at the three published incarnations of Field's 'She was a royal lady born', demonstrating how, in each different material context, the poem contributes to a discussion about detachment and attachment that is central to the work of the lyric and making a sound case for a re-examination of Michael Field's corpus of plays in which a number of their lyrics were originally published. 'Newspaper Poems: Material Texts in the

Public Sphere' by Natalie M. Houston (*VS* 50[2008] 233–42) also calls for the reattachment of Victorian poetry to its print cultural context by conducting a short survey of some poems published in *The London Times*. Like Harrington, Houston is also concerned with the material characteristics of the poems: their position on the newspaper page, the surrounding articles and signature. She directs much-needed attention towards newspaper poems, which, as she shows, are distinct from poetry published in the periodical press and suggest a more significant role for poetry as an 'interpretive framework' (p. 241) for current events. Meredith Martin takes a different approach to poetry and materiality in her article, 'Gerard Manley Hopkins and the Stigma of Meter' (*VS* 50[2008] 243–53), which suggests that the visual marks employed by Hopkins to indicate metrical stress impress the materiality of metre on the reader. Martin's thoughtful reading turns on the idea that metre might be understood as the incarnation of language, and she draws out Hopkins's understanding of words as bodies under stress in *The Wreck of the Deutschland*. Catherine Robson's neat response to the three papers, 'The Presence of Poetry: Response' (*VS* 50[2008] 255–62) leaves little doubt that Victorian poetry is central to the print cultural moment.

'Love Thinking' by Adela Pinch (*VS* 50[2008] 379–97), the only article published in 2008 to deal with Coventry Patmore or George Meredith, is an expansive article that explores the relationship between feeling, thinking and metre in Victorian poetry via judicious focus on a short section and lyric prelude from *The Angel in the House* and the opening of *Modern Love,* which rewrites the interrelationship of sleeping, thinking and kissing suggested by Patmore's earlier poem. Pinch moves out from a demonstration of both poets' apparent scepticism concerning the potential reconciliation of thought and love to discuss the metrical implications of the lyric, which empties thought of content and represents it instead as the ongoing, impulsive action of the mind that constitutes a failure of knowledge and the uncertain struggle for intimacy. The poetry of a rather different relationship is explored by Kathleen Béres Rogers, in 'Maria Jane Jewsbury to Henry Jephson, M.D.: An Undiscovered Poetic Fragment' (*VP* 46[2008] 511–14), which notes the discovery of a handwritten dedication to Dr Henry Jephson of a copy of *Phantasmagoria* [1825], associating Jewsbury with a late eighteenth- and early nineteenth-century tradition of patient poems to doctors and suggests a new ending to her poem 'Winter Welcomed'.

Celebrating his bicentenary in 2008 was Edward FitzGerald, the subject of a special issue of *Victorian Poetry* edited by Erik Gray, whose monograph, *The Poetry of Indifference* [2006], is one of a handful of critical works to return to FitzGerald in recent years. This is another rich and stimulating collection of essays that demonstrates FitzGerald to be a rewarding poet whose work has much to contribute to an understanding of Victorian poetry and popular culture. Gray's introduction, 'FitzGerald and the *Rubáiyát*, in and out of Time' (*VP* 46[2008] 1–14) traces the reception history of the *Rubáiyát*, paying particular attention to the rocky fortunes it suffered in the twentieth century and the controversy surrounding Robert Graves's 1967 translation and making a strong case for the *Rubáiyát*'s cultural significance on the basis of the cultural debate it has elicited over the last century. Following this introduction, 'Accident, Orientalism and Edward FitzGerald as Translator' by Annamarie Drurie (*VP* 46[2008] 37–53) takes up the charge of colonialist appropriation that is commonly levelled against the *Rubáiyát* and mounts a strong defence of FitzGerald's approach to translation by arguing that his composition did not seek to render the Persian original obsolete but that it acknowledged the impossibility of literal translation in its recourse to a liberal translation or imitation that did not pretend to accuracy. Drurie argues that this approach is reflected in FitzGerald's 'aesthetics of accident' (p. 40): its suggestion and subsequent abandonment of certain formal patterns and the persistence of images of the arbitrary throughout. Herbert F. Tucker makes a further contribution to work on the *Rubáiyát* as translation in 'Metaphor, Translation and Autoekphrasis in FitzGerald's *Rubáiyát*' (*VP* 46[2008] 69–86), an agile discussion of the *Rubáiyát*'s self-conscious materiality. Arguing that the poem's metaphorical language often blocks the reader's way to meaning, drawing attention to the textuality of translation, Tucker's suggestive reading ably demonstrates how the translation (or 'rendering', p. 80) creates a physical space of its own that is—to return to Gray's introduction—both within and out of its own time. In 'The Benefits of Reading the *Rubáiyát of Omar Khayyam* as Pastoral' (*VP* 46[2008] 55–67) Giuseppe Albano finds a place for FitzGerald's poem within the structures of retreat and return that characterize pastoral literature. Focusing on the drinking and drunkenness that affect the speaker and his speech, Albano draws out the double implications of drunkenness via a discussion of the complex position occupied by drinking within Sufi culture, and concludes that as pastoral the poem allows a double reading that accommodates both aesthetic pleasure and an interrogation of the human need for retreat. Finally Daniel Karlin returns to the *Rubáiyát*'s print cultural identity, this time from an editorial perspective. 'Editing the *Rubáiyát*: Two Case Studies and a Prospectus' (*VP* 46[2008] 87–103) considers the editorial challenges posed by the multiple editions of FitzGerald's poem, examining a selection of printed and digital solutions.

The year 2008 saw the publication of three monographs on Hopkins. *The Playfulness of Gerard Manley Hopkins* by Joseph F. Feeney takes Hopkins studies in a new direction by looking at his lighter side. Observing that Hopkins has 'long been viewed as serious and anguished', Feeney asserts the conviction that the Jesuit poet-priest was, at the same time 'consistently' and 'compulsively' playful (p. xv), and he undertakes to seek out moments of play in his life and work. Beginning with the life, Feeney provides an anecdotal biography of Hopkins, drawing attention to the young Gerard's love of games, his recourse to whimsy and bathetic or incongruous description in his letters, his comic verses and epigrams, and his eccentricity. The variety of playfulness exhibited here is illuminating, but it suggests a rather elastic understanding of 'play' that is, at times, self-defeating. The second chapter does provide a definition of play, which it takes from Johan Huizinga's *Homo Ludens* [1938] (it is perhaps surprising that Feeney ignores other theories of play—Kantian idealism for example, or theories of the lyric—that might bring his study into more ready conversation with other critical discourses), who identifies play as 'fun', 'creativity', 'contest' and 'style' (p. 46) and the remainder of the book reads Hopkins's poetry in precisely these terms. Approaching the poetry in the same way as he approaches the biography, Feeney looks for moments of playfulness in a chronological account of Hopkins's creative output. This approach is successful up to a point and Feeney makes the reader alive to the possibility that Hopkins's poetry is playful even when it is most serious. At its most convincing, Feeney's discussion of Hopkins's word-play suggests a comparison with Edward Lear that is ripe for further development (Hopkins gave his mother a book of Lear's nonsense verse as a gift). However, at other points, Feeney identifies as play certain elements of Hopkins's poetry that might equally be called paradox, dialect, or simply form, and in his enthusiasm to demonstrate Hopkins's sense of fun, Feeney does not go as far as he might in considering the implications of playfulness for his thought or faith. This will doubtless be the work of future scholars, for whom Feeney's book will provide a valuable starting point.

   The Language of Poetry as a Form of Prayer: The Theo-Poetic Aesthetics of Gerard Manley Hopkins by Francis X. McAloon returns to more familiar territory, employing Hopkins's poetry as a case study in order to explore the spiritual possibilities of non-scriptural texts. McAloon traces the use of Christian poetry by twentieth-century mystics and critics (including his own personal experience), and asks questions about the way poetry mediates religious experience. Defining poetic prayer as the combined work of a particular context and poetic content in the production of a spiritual consequence, he interrupts his discussion at certain points to dwell upon the experience of a particular reader to whom Hopkins's poetry 'ministers' (p. 47). This ministry is approached in three different ways, each of which allows for the transformative possibility of a text. First, McAloon discusses the hermeneutics of the poetic/spiritual encounter via Paul Ricoeur's writing on meaning and interpretation. The following section considers the influence of Ruskin, Duns Scotus, Ignatius of Loyola and Parmenides. Finally McAloon offers a broad introduction to new historicist criticism and a theological critique that attempts to rehouse new historicism within a Christian spiritual context. McAloon's book is therefore not a work of literary criticism—examples from Hopkins's poetry are notable by their scarcity—and his interest in Hopkins is largely as a means to a spiritual end. It is nevertheless a work that demonstrates Hopkins's wide appeal across the disciplines and the enduring power of his poetry.

   Paul Mariani's biography of Hopkins, *Gerard Manley Hopkins: A Life* was unavailable for review this year and will be included next year.

   Recent critical interest in Victorian poetry and religion has given Hopkins studies renewed centrality, and the best of this year's articles suggest a recognizably Victorian Hopkins. 'The Heart's Bower: Emblematics in Gerard Manley Hopkins's *The Wreck of the Deutschland* (1876)' (*VP* 22:i[2008] 32–47) by Aakansha Virkar-Yates is a case in point. Virkar-Yates traces the incorporation of seventeenth-century emblematic practice into the meditative treatises of the Jesuit Counter-Reformation and its links to Herbert and the Oxford Movement and to the Pre-Raphaelite Brotherhood, suggesting that recognition of the emblematics of the *Wreck* might move emphasis away from the body and reframe the poem within a mystical tradition. Maureen Moran's contribution to Adrian Grafe's collection of essays on late Victorian and modern poetry and religion, *Ecstasy and Understanding Religious Awareness in English Poetry from the Late Victorian to the Modern Period*, 'The Heart's Censer: Liturgy, Poetry and the Catholic Devotional Revolution' (pp. 27–45), reads the work of Hopkins alongside poetry by Francis Thompson, Elizabeth Jennings and David Jones, focusing again on the relationship between religious and aesthetic experience via what the essay describes as a late nineteenth-century 'revolution' whereby liturgy was read as poetry and devotional activity understood in terms of the theatrical. Drawing on Newman's reference to the Roman Catholic Church as poet and tracing similar ideas through Pater, Moran explores the poetic performativity of Roman Catholicism in Hopkins's 'The Bugler's First Communion'. A second essay in Grafe's collection, 'Gerard Manley Hopkins as Religious Conduit in Geoffrey Hill, George Mackay Brown and Edwin Muir' (pp. 6–15) by Catherine Phillips, discusses whether Hopkins's religious fervour (as expressed in *The Wreck of the Deutschland*) is transmitted into and retained by three twentieth-century poets. Two articles by Fredric W. Schlatter, SJ, pay detailed attention to Hopkins as a reader of Newman. Schlatter provides a persuasive account of Hopkins's engagement with Newman's rhetoric in 'Hopkins on the Art of Newman's Prose' (*HQ* 35:iii–iv[2008] 75–110), an article that draws together reservations about Newman's prose, particularly *The Grammar of Assent*, set out by Hopkins in essays and letters throughout his life. Dealing with each case in turn, Schlatter pays particular attention to Hopkins' remarks about Newman's style: its lack of 'brilliancy' or rhetorical flare. Comparing these remarks with Newman's own idea of style, Schlatter shows Hopkins to be astute in his recognition of Newman's approach to prose composition, suggesting a fruitful literary relationship, which he continues to explore in 'Hopkins and Newman: Two Disagreements' (*CL* 57:iii[2008] 401–18).

David J. Leigh offers a broader perspective on Hopkins's theology in 'Paradoxes of Redemption in the Poetry of Hopkins' (*HQ* 35:iii–iv[2008] 111–19), which takes the Catholic belief that paradox is one of the three ways to understand and articulate God as the starting point for a discussion of Hopkins's use of paradox in his sermons and poems including the *Wreck* and a selection of the Terrible Sonnets. Work that has, over the last few years, sought to redefine formalism by situating it in relation to the body also provides new ways into Hopkins. These critical opportunities are taken up by another pair of articles: 'Gerard Manley Hopkins and the Kinesthetics of Conviction' (*VS* 51[2008] 7–35), by Susan Chambers, and ' "Beautiful Action": Hopkins and the Perfect Body' (*HQ* 35:i–ii[2008] 3–18), by Duc Dau. Chambers's article offers another thorough, relevant reading of the stresses and interrupted syntax of the *Wreck*, which, she argues, reproduce the experience of strenuous thought. The article focuses on the shift from the psychological to the physical that occurs between parts one and two of the poem and suggests that the psychological is not rendered in opposition to the physical but as a physical mode of experience in itself. Dau reads Hopkins's theorization of the body via Platonic and Aristotelian philosophy and Catholic theology. Drawing on Hopkins's undergraduate essays, Dau balances teleological philosophy, the relationship between form and substance and representations of beauty and virtue in order to make a strong case for the value that Hopkins places on the body, particularly the perfect body of Christ. ' "Strokes of Havoc": Tree-Felling and the Poetic Tradition of Ecocriticism in Manley Hopkins and Gerard Manley Hopkins' (*VP* 46[2008] 487–509) by Marianconcetta Constantini follows on from Jude Nixon's 2006 article which identified Hopkins's father as the author of 'The Old Trees' (published anonymously in 1878) and suggested it as an intertext for 'Binsey Poplars'. Constantini employs a Bloomian model to look again at the relationship between father and son, suggesting that, whereas Manley's poem is written in the conservative Romantic tradition whereby nature offers an emblem of the past, which provides uncertain shelter against the change of the present, Gerard's later poem takes a more objective, scientific approach to ecological concerns. Perhaps the most Victorian Hopkins of all is revealed by another excellent article by Jude V. Nixon, ' "If all had bread": Father Gerard Hopkins, the Condition of England Question and the Poor of Nazareth House' (*HQ* 35:i–ii[2008] 19–46), which breaks new ground, exploring Hopkins's role as chaplain of Nazareth House in Oxford where his work both attested to and influenced his abiding concern for the poor. Because of a lack of biographical evidence in journals and letters, Nixon turns to house registers and funeral records, carrying out careful documentary research that brings valuable insight to Hopkins's early experience as a priest and suggests an interesting comparison between Hopkins and Carlyle. Finally, the *Hopkins Quarterly* contains two shorter articles: 'Wielding Hopkins into Song' (*HQ* 35:i–ii[2008] 120–30) by Kevin Waters, SJ, a composer who considers the challenges and opportunities of Hopkins's unique rhythms and syntax when setting his poetry to music; and 'A Passing of Heroes: Seamus Heaney's "Seeing the Sick" and Hopkins's "Felix Randal" ' (*HQ* 35:i–ii[2008] 47–54) by Arnd Bohm, which strengthens the well-established connection between Heaney and Hopkins in a nicely observed reading of 'Seeing the Sick' and 'Felix Randal', drawing attention to their sidelong attitude to the identity of their subjects, their use of dialect and their representation of the relationship between father and son.

Two new editions of Christina Rossetti's work appeared in 2008. One, published by Penguin Classics (London: Penguin [2008] pp. xlii + 262 Page 78), offers a good selection of the most significant and best-known poems and is a good general introduction for first-time readers to the key preoccupations of Rossetti's work. The volume is edited with an introduction and notes by Dinah Roe, whose introduction explains her desire in this edition to focus on some of Rossetti's neglected devotional poems; accordingly, the notes place helpful emphasis on the significance of biblical influence. A longer edition, including poems and prose, was published by Oxford World's Classics (Oxford: Oxford University Press [2008] pp. xlii + 518), edited with an introduction and notes by Simon Humphries. This edition includes stories, letters and devotional prose, alongside a significant selection of the poems; its introduction offers concise, authoritative accounts of Rossetti's biography, religious life, literary influences, and literary revisions, and the notes offer rich interpretative material (even creative predicaments) to the student, as well as the more standard forms of explanatory and intertextual apparatus.

Humphries is also the author of three notes in *N&Q* this year, which offer not just their local insights, but, collectively, a renewed challenge to criticism on Rossetti to attend with precision to what can at first seem the unanswerable puzzles or superficial features of her poems. In 'Christina Rossetti's "Goblin Market" and Bunyan's Orchard of Beelzebub' (*N&Q* 55[2008] 49–51) Humphries further illuminates the symbolic riches of 'Goblin Market' by noting the importance of Bunyan's *The Pilgrim's Progress* to consideration of the eucharistic purge that Lizzie offers Laura. Humphries neatly affirms the resistance of Rossetti's poem to Christian interpretation by showing how comparison with Bunyan's text reveals a doubleness in the spiritual import of the fruit, and so also emphasizes the importance of *how* worldly things are used, over and above their having any fixed or singular spiritual meaning. Another intertextual illumination is provided in 'Christina Rossetti's "Goblin Market" and Spenser's Malbecco' (*N&Q* 55[2008] 51–4), in which Humphries also suggests the significance of Malbecco, from *The Faerie Queen*, to interpretation of 'Goblin Market'. Malbecco, who dies feeding on 'toades and frogs, his pasture poisonous', and who, now so wasted away, '*Gealosie* is hight', may or may not be associated with Laura in Rossetti's poem. But whether he is or not, Humphries explains, his allusive presence to Laura's loss of 'succous pasture' in the form of Goblin fruits, should encourage more careful reading of the presence of jealousy in Laura's story. And finally, in 'Christina Rossetti's "My Dream" and Apocalypse' (*N&Q* 55[2008] 54–7), Humphries describes how Rossetti's awareness of the beast visions of Daniel and Revelation (from Spenser as well as her biblical reading), and also how the apocalyptic thinking of the priest William Dodsworth, combine suggestively to link 'My Dream' indirectly to Rossetti's concerns about the contemporary events of the Crimean War. Contemporary international contexts are also the concern of 'Goblin Markets: Women Shoppers and the East in London's West End', the opening chapter of Krista Lysack's *Come Buy, Come Buy*. Lysack discusses the relationship between consumer desire and imperialism, identifying female consumers as potentially disruptive participants in the Victorian imperial project and arguing that the poem offers an alternative economy where desire is sustained without cost. In the context of the commodified East and the transformation of shopping into a female leisure activity with particular focus on the opening of Liberty's East India House, Lysack conducts a lively close reading of *Goblin Market*, offering a persuasive alternative to the 'renunciative Rossetti' (p. 17).

Christ's gaze, as a sign at once of the need for repentance and the offer of spiritual renewal, is the subject of an elaborate article by Esther T. Hu, entitled 'Christina Rossetti, John Keble, and the Divine Gaze' (*VP* 46[2008] 175–89). Hu contrasts Keble's depiction in 'St. Peter's Day' of Christ's 'watch' over Peter (with its emphasis on forgiveness) with the greater intimacy and egalitarianism suggested by Rossetti's use of Christ's gaze in her own St Peter poems. The piece contains some nice local remarks about Rossetti's use of rhyme in the St Peter sonnets. Kathryn Ready, in 'Reading Mary as Reader: The Marian Art of Dante Gabriel and Christina Rossetti' (*VP* 46[2008] 151–74), explores how the works of both Christina and Dante Gabriel Rossetti register at once renewed interest in the Virgin Mary and, simultaneously, the 'decline in English culture of the Mary as Reader trope' which celebrates Mary's importance to human comprehension of the Logos. In so doing, Ready rightly notes that Christina's work carefully maintains Mary's inspirational role (at once for all Christians and specifically for women) in the matter of biblical interpretation, whereas Dante Gabriel's (as they do in others ways) seek to reinforce women's subordination and even to deprive them of what spiritual rights and capacities they were otherwise deemed to have.

Dante Gabriel also received some significant attention this year. Family rifts, depression, and illness fill another handsomely produced volume of *The Correspondence of Dante Gabriel Rossetti. The Last Decade, 1873–1882*, volume 7: *Kelmscott to Birchington, 1875–1877*, edited by William E. Fredeman, the seventh of nine volumes, the first of which appeared in 2002. Volume 7 covers January 1875 to December 1877, a period which included the publication, among other things, of 'La Bella Mano' and 'Proserpina' as 'Sonnets for Pictures / Italian and English' in the *Athenæum* (28 August 1875).

The question of translation, not just across languages but across media, informs the most extensive study of the Pre-Raphaelites this year, Elizabeth K. Helsinger's commanding and wide-ranging exploration, *Poetry and the Pre-Raphaelite Arts: Dante Gabriel Rossetti and William Morris*. In this absorbing book, Helsinger reinvigorates possibilities for attending to the interplay between visual and verbal media, and in the process presents a compelling argument for the profound stimulus that the Pre-Raphaelites provided later writers in their hopes to retain and assert the power of the arts for society. It is a timely work in this as in other respects. Focusing on what she calls three influential 'strategies for renewing poetry', Helsinger defines 'acts of attention', 'repetition', and 'translation' as crucial features and, simultaneously, preoccupations of Pre-Raphaelite work which each highlight a specific (and intense) kind of perception. That kind of perception (commonly called 'aesthetic perception') is itself a sensory resource effectively designed by these works to expand the reader's or viewer's receptivity to new and unexpected connections. (The Ruskinian emphasis on this kind of activity as vital for social and cultural health is inevitably strong.) In each of the chapters, Helsinger describes the migration (or 'translation') of one or more features of visual art and experience into the realm of poetry in order to show how Pre-Raphaelite arts (painting and design) offered new perspectives on aesthetic experience which generated or renewed practices of poetic composition. Alongside less well-known works, richly explored, major works discussed in detail include Morris's *The Defence of Guenevere* and *The Earthly Paradise*, and Rossetti's 'The House of Life'. Among the many interesting wider implications of this study, Helsinger's productive remarks on the inspiration that Pre-Raphaelite works provided to modernist and later twentieth-century writers may themselves inspire further reflection on the patterns and renewals stimulated by Pre-Raphaelite arts (pp. 16–23).

Successfully disrupting patterns is the subject of Marianne Van Remoortel's article, 'Metaphor and Maternity: Dante Gabriel Rossetti's *House of Life* and Augusta Webster's *Mother and Daughter*' (*VP* 46[2008] 467–86), which discusses male writers' common use of the female body (birth and motherhood in particular) to describe (men's) acts of literary creativity, before explaining how Augusta's Webster's unfinished collection of sonnets, *Mother and Daughter*, implicitly provides a thoroughgoing critique of such metaphors. After describing Rossetti's almost obsessive deployment of metaphors of birth and maternity in *The House of Life*, and 'Willowwood' and its fascination with metaphoricity, Van Remoortel notes that the role and presence of maternity in Webster's sonnets starkly disqualify the idea of using it metaphorically by calling attention to its alienating physicality and presenting it as the embodiment of an unmediated and preverbal symbiosis. The article offers a compelling case for attending to both *The House of Life* and *Mother and Daughter* as equal 'intertexts' concerned with the role of maternity in the period's literature, and it persuasively asserts Webster's right to parity with Rossetti in terms of literary treatment and achievement. In ' "The wind blows cold out of the inner shrine of fear": Rossetti's Romantic Keats' (in Radford and Sandy, eds., pp. 51–66), Sarah Wootton explores the simultaneous sanctification and commodification of Keats by Rossetti, before offering a carefully poised discussion of how Rossetti exploits Keats in the process of his own self-fashioning. Wootton goes on to put a convincing case for the ultimate problem that Rossetti generated for himself through his complex esteem for the elder poet, suggesting that Rossetti's final inability to make a successful visual engagement with Keats's work attests the creative redundancy of his narcissism and the Romantic poet's final ascendancy. Narcissism in a different guise is also the subject of Todd O. Williams's 'Reading Rossetti's "The Mirror" through Lacan's Mirror Stage' (*Expl* 67:i[2008] 48–51), which offers a brief reading of 'The Mirror' in the light of Lacan's notion of the mirror stage, and notes that, through the woman's disinterest in him, Rossetti's speaker discovers a vacancy within himself which leaves his understanding of his own desires unresolved. Charles Martindale, in 'Dryden's Ovid: Aesthetic Translation and the Ideal of the Classic' (in Lianeri and Zajko, eds., *Translation and the Classic: Identity as Change in the History of Culture*, pp. 83–109), rightly reminds readers that Rossetti anticipates Pound's better-known claim that translations are always also interpretations of what they translate. Rossetti's views on the challenging decisions involved in translating features of form and content together, and the 'inner standing point' (or personal identification with his predecessors) that Rossetti aimed to achieve, provide Martindale with a starting point for describing 'An Aesthetic Theory of Translation' with application to earlier literary translations. Finally, ' "An aching pulse of melodies": Dante Gabriel Rossetti's Poetic Magnetism', a chapter in Catherine Maxwell's *Second Sight*, looks again at the visionary content of Rossetti's poetry, which was attended to by his first admirers, but then sidelined by modern criticism, which has tended to locate Rossetti's worth in the natural detail of his work. Maxwell traces a poetic preoccupation with the mesmeric in an illuminating discussion of two sonnets by Theodore Watts-Dunton that suggest a comparison between Coleridge and Rossetti, casting both as poetic visionaries and isolated victims. She goes on to consider Rossetti's representations of Proserpine and Narcissus, suggesting identification between these figures and the figure of Rossetti as poet via accounts of Rossetti's personal magnetism and his interest in the possibilities of mesmerism, and draws attention to the mesmeric relationships described in

House of Life sonnets. The historical contexts explored by Maxwell in her discussion of Rossetti renew the possibilities of the familiar image of the poetic visionary more generally.

Work on Swinburne in 2008 reflects the poet's diverse literary identities and associations, casting him as scholar, Pre-Raphaelite cousin, parodist and proto-modern and opening out a variety of new avenues for scholarship, which will doubtless have been developed in 2009, the centenary of Swinburne's death. 'Swinburne, "Hertha", and the Voice of Language' (*VLC* 36:ii[2008] 283–97) by Jerome McGann is a densely argued article that considers 'Hertha' [1869] as Swinburne's poetic manifesto. McGann proposes the Vedic tradition—via Muller's 'Comparative Mythology'—as a possible influence on Swinburne's approach to its cultural, philosophical possibilities. Focusing on the poem's use of the first person, McGann suggests that Swinburne follows a Sanskrit model whereby 'I' speaks of a universal identity, allowing poetry to perform the relationship between text, language and being. Richard Frith considers Swinburne's influences closer to home in 'The Defence of Yseult: Swinburne's Queen Yseult and William Morris' (*JWMS* 18:i[2008] 85–95), revisiting the circumstances of the composition of Swinburne's unfinished juvenile poem and offering the poem as an early example of the difference between Morris and Swinburne that would later lead the older poet to criticize his Pre-Raphaelite disciple. Frith traces Swinburne's sources for the Tristram legend and comments on the significance of variations and changes made by Swinburne. He discusses the form of the poem, which Swinburne took from two early poems by Morris, and focuses on the thematic influence of the 'Defence of Guinevere', comparing the two men's loss of faith and attraction to the ideas of courtly love. Nick Freeman brings a fresh perspective to familiar thematic concerns in 'Edward Thomas, Swinburne and Richard Jeffries: "The Dead Oak Tree Bough"' (*ELT* 51:ii[2008] 283–97), which refigures Thomas's relationship with Victorian poetry as one of reconciliation via a close reading of his modern ballad 'The Gallows', which he links to Swinburne because of its thematic treatment of the relationship between pleasure and pain. As Freeman points out, Thomas wrote a critical study of Swinburne in 1912, and this article contributes to the rich vein of criticism that has begun to reassess the early twentieth century's relationship to its Victorian poetic heritage. One of a handful of worthwhile and interesting treatments of parodic representations of the nineteenth-century literary scene to be published this year, 'The "Spasmodic" hoaxes of W.E. Aytoun and A.C. Swinburne' (*SEL* 48[2008] 849–60) by Heather Morton compares Aytoun's 'Firmilian: A Tragedy' with Swinburne's 'The Monomaniac's Tragedy', exploring the ways in which these two hoaxes represent and critique the relationship between periodical reviews and poetry. Morton argues that, whereas Aytoun holds fast to the authority of the reviewer, Swinburne makes fun of both poet and critic, exposing both the silliness of spasmodism and the hypocrisy of anonymous reviewing in ways that suggest Swinburne's early and ongoing awareness of the cultural power relations at work in the Victorian literary world. Robin Fox explores a different sort of playfulness in his article 'Playing by the Rules: Sound and Sense in Swinburne and the Rhyming Poets' (*PL* 32:ii[2008] 217–40), a potentially interesting examination of the meaning that is created by arbitrary rhyme in lyric poetry, which is hampered by Fox's distractingly personal style and his patronizing references throughout to an unnamed 'lady critic' out of whose remarks he constructs a straw-man argument against the significance of rhyme.

One of two monographs to be published on Tennyson in 2008, *Tennyson's Name: Identity and Responsibility in the Poetry of Alfred Lord Tennyson* by Anna Barton, remaps Tennyson's career by attending to the pervasive and influential nature of his concern with names and naming; and in so doing it offers fresh and convincing readings of the major (as well as a number of more minor) poems. The first chapter shows how *Poems by Two Brothers* both draws upon and distances itself from Byron's self-presentation in *Hours of Idleness*, before going on to explore the sometimes talismanic, sometimes disturbing qualities that names have in *Poems, Chiefly Lyrical*. This establishes a number of concerns about the business of 'making a name' for oneself which are developed in different ways as the book progresses. A chapter on 'Inherited Names' examines possible biographical reasons for Tennyson's own particular edginess about giving (and given) names, and includes an insightful reading of *The Princess* (its lyrics and the role of child figures especially) which argues for Tennyson's attempt, in that poem, to accommodate signs of his professional youth within his maturing desire to address the age. The place of names in elegies is central to a chapter which includes readings of *In Memoriam* and *Ode on the Death of the Duke of Wellington*. Examining concerns about the inadequacy of language in the face of death, and the need for simple epitaphs (perhaps just names alone), Barton traces the emergence of the mature Tennysonian voice (and name) reluctantly coupling itself with the emergent identity of a maturing imperial nation. The responsibility that being named bestows is then the subject of a significant new reading of *Maud*, which sets the poem alongside contemporary debates about the pros and cons of anonymous journalism, both literary-critical and political. With *Maud*, Barton explains, we enter a world of horrifying anonymity (the speaker is anonymous, as is his father, his mother, indeed everyone accept Maud) in which the speaker must struggle to keep control of his story. Even Maud, the only (and repeatedly) named figure in the poem, is at risk of seeming an anonymous presence because of the extent to which she becomes a repository for the speaker's own anxieties and obsessions. It is she, Barton nicely argues, who seems to bear the burden of responsibility for everything the speaker says and does, as he shifts his early fear of names into a morbid preoccupation with her one name and all that it comes to mean for him. Placed in this light, the poem looks like a parable of the dangers of literary anonymity and the pains of responsibility; pains which Tennyson felt as the commodification of his own name increased. That commodification, though, would also inflect the more confident way in which Tennyson, Barton suggests, learnt to 'successfully negotiate a place for the material name within the late nineteenth-century world of advertising slogans and branded goods' through *Idylls of the King*. This chapter (chapter 5) reflects on the way that names accrue past associations and carry them into the future, and it convincingly shows that, as the names of the knights of Camelot are increasingly sullied, so too does Camelot more rapidly fall. But by this point Tennyson (still playing out his concern about his own name through these means) can nevertheless, Barton explains, explore the social parameters of names from his now more secure, 'branded' position. The book's final chapter, 'The Name of Old Friends', focuses on the close of Tennyson's career through the lens of his relationship with Edward FitzGerald, and sensitively exposes the delicate complications of finally having a name as powerful as Tennyson had achieved.

Tennyson's Rapture: Transformations in the Dramatic Monologue by Cornelia Pearsall focuses exclusively on Tennyson's dramatic monologues in a series of revisionist readings that bravely challenge received wisdom concerning the speaker's unintentional betrayal of himself to the reader. The title of her study is taken from part 87 of *In Memoriam*, when the mourner recalls listening to Hallam speak at a meeting of the Cambridge Apostles and describes the audience being carried away (rapt) by the speaker's 'rapt oration', a passage that highlights Hallam's potential as a politician and the effective potential of public speech. Pearsall focuses on the series of dramatic monologues with classical subjects that were begun in the wake of Hallam's death—'St Simeon Stylites', 'Ulysses', 'Tithonus' and 'Tiresias'—and argues that each pays political, scholarly and intellectual tribute to his Cambridge friend through effective and transformative oratory. Central to Pearsall's thesis is the identification between Tennyson and his speakers, who are transformed by Pearsall's account into great orators. Tennyson is transformed too, into a poet with a strong political identity whose compositional practice is Whiggish in its work of return and revision. Placing further renewed emphasis on the Cambridge context, Pearsall argues that Tennyson's friendship with Hallam was founded on an intellectual bond that is compared with Hallam's other influential friendship, with W.E. Gladstone. By retracing Tennyson's classical education at Somersby and Cambridge in the light of early nineteenth-century discussions concerning the authenticity of Homeric Troy, Pearsall ably demonstrates the contemporary resonance that Ilion held for Tennyson, Hallam and Gladstone. Pearsall's scholarly account of Victorian classical scholarship makes new sense of the identities and motivations of each of Tennyson's monologists. This is achieved most strikingly in Pearsall's reading of 'Ulysses', who, we are reminded, is gifted with the arts of guile and persuasion and who, having sold a wooden horse to the Trojans, now carries away his mariners by convincing them of a democratic fantasy, using rhetoric that is implicitly compared with Gladstone's compelling public oratory. Tennyson, Pearsall argues, is suspicious of rapture on such a massive scale, but he never doubts the power of speech to achieve it.

Perhaps in an anticipatory lull preceding Tennyson's forthcoming bicentenary year, relatively few articles about Tennyson appeared in 2008. Of these, three focus on the *Idylls of the King*. In 'The Once and Future Sword: Excalibur and the Poetics of Imperial Heroism in *Idylls of the King*' (*VP* 46[2008], 207–29) Jeffrey E. Jackson returns to the pivotal scenes in 'The Morte D'Arthur' in which Bedivere repeatedly fails to return Excalibur to the lake. Building on earlier work that considers the relationship between the *Idylls* and the Victorian marketplace, Jackson looks at instances when swords are rejected or 'stayed' throughout the sequence and suggests that the refusal to bear arms constitutes the rejection of violence, materiality and commercialism. In a thoughtful consideration of the poetics of the long poem, Jackson also considers the sword as metonymy, and writes convincingly of the *Idyll*'s rejection of metonymic poetics in favour of the more expansive and unifying possibilities of epic metaphor. 'Alfred Tennyson's "Vivien" and "Guinevere": Sensation Stories in a Medieval Setting' (in Sikorska, ed., *Medievalisms: The Poetics of Literary Re-reading*, pp. 159–72) by Agnieszka Setecka suggests that Tennyson might have had a rather more forgiving attitude to market economics by drawing parallels between two of the *Idylls* and a genre with unabashedly commercial interests. Setecka considers the changes made by Tennyson to Malory's original in order to discuss the appeal of medievalism to the Victorian reader and identifies a shift away from Malory's chivalric focus towards a focus on love relationships. Her comparison between Tennyson's *Idylls* and sensation fiction, grounded in similarities between subject matter of each, suggests the way that fiction and poetry simultaneously express and expose Victorian ideology. Chene Heady takes the cultural identity of the *Idylls* as the starting point for a comparison with Yeats. ' "I am weary of that foolish tale": Yeats's Revision of Tennyson's *Idylls* and Ideals in "Time and the Witch Vivien" ' (*SiMed* 16[2008] 67–82) reads Yeats's poem against 'Merlin and Vivien'. Its focus remains with Yeats but it nevertheless indicates the significance of Tennyson and the *Idylls* as icons of Britishness against which Yeats was able to formulate his proto-modern Irish nationalism. In contrast, Christy Rieger's essay, 'Tennyson's *The Princess* as Palimpsest: The Oriental Tale and Woman's Nature' (in Lewes, ed., *Double Vision: Literary Palimpsests of the Eighteenth and Nineteenth Centuries*, pp. 105–16), returns to the Eastern inflection of Tennyson's earlier long poem. Relying on the research carried out by John Killham (whose name is unfortunately misspelt throughout) in *Tennyson and The Princess: Reflections of an Age*, she argues that the orientalism of *The Princess* provides a subtext, or 'colonialist palimpsest' (p. 108) for the poem's anti-feminist narrative. The essay explores the poem's voyeurism via Lacanian, postcolonial and queer theory and locates the poem's feminism in its failure fully to assimilate the femininity that it encounters. Nineteenth-century psychology rather than Lacanian psychoanalysis provides the starting point for Scott Dransfield's discussion of disease, metricality and voice in *Maud*: 'The Morbid Meters of *Maud*' (*VP* 46[2008] 279–97). His article provides a helpful contextual account of nineteenth-century medical theories that understood excitable utterance to be a symptom and the modern age to be a cause of nervous disease, before moving on to suggest that *Maud*'s troubling rhythms might represent a diseased nervous system that fails to regulate and control the poem's form and utterance. Finally, in 'Tennyson and the Legacies of Romantic Art' (*Romanticism* 14:i[2008] 1–12) Seamus Perry offers a delightful consideration of the prosaic moments in Tennyson's poetry, in which he identifies a Romantic ambivalence concerning High Art. Perry's article presents a gently persuasive challenge to Marxist critiques of Victorian bourgeois aestheticism via—among other things—a particularly fine reading of Lancelot's apparently bland appreciation of the Lady of Shalott's 'lovely face', which concludes Tennyson's early lyric.

The *Tennyson Research Bulletin* marked the bicentenary of Alfred's older brother Charles Tennyson Turner with a special issue dedicated to his life and work. 'Charles Tennyson Turner: Lyricism and Modernity' by Roger Ebbatson (*TRB* 9:ii[2008] 157–76) frames Tennyson Turner's use of the sonnet form to explore societal contradiction with Adorno's theory of the lyric, which contends that lyric poetry seeks to heal a split between the lyric self and nature. Ebbatson argues that Charles Tennyson Turner might be likened to Adorno's lyric self, lost to or within the social space, and demonstrates the ways in which his sonnets hold themselves in tension with the modern world. Joseph Phelan, in 'Charles Tennyson Turner's Prefatory Sonnets' (*TRB* 9:ii[2008] 177–87) takes a different approach to the modernity of Tennyson Turner's sonnets, suggesting that they are forerunners of late Victorian aestheticism, rewriting Wordsworthian Romantic retreat as a Victorian crisis of will that cultivates a still, imagist focus, pre-empting Pater's 'gem-like flame'. 'Charles Tennyson Turner and his Audience' by Roger Evans (*TRB* 9:ii[2008] 188–200) returns Tennyson Turner to his contemporaries in a clear account of his publishing career. Evans traces Tennyson Turner's sonnet-writing through his years as an undergraduate and helpfully sketches the lively exchange of sonnets that took place between the poet and his Cambridge friends, offering an enlightening account of a career marked by critical recognition in spite of poor sales. Evans dwells briefly on contemporary comparisons made between Charles and his more celebrated brother, a theme which is also taken up in Valerie Purton's 'Two Brothers: A Note on Charles Tennyson Turner's Influence on Tennyson's Poetry' (*TRB* 9:ii[2008] 201–4), a nice piece of manuscript research which suggests that Tennyson composed 'Balin and Balan' around the time of Charles's death, opening up a new reading of the tragic brotherly relationship represented in Tennyson's Arthurian idyll. The special issue also contains a biographical outline of Tennyson Turner and an exhaustive bibliography of his published works, which will be an invaluable resource to critics interested in Tennyson Turner, an interest that this issue suggests would be fruitful and rewarding. Tennyson Turner's identity as a poet who wrote largely for the periodical press means that his work might be of particular value to research into Victorian poetry and print culture to which Katherine Ledbetter's 2007 monograph, *Tennyson and Victorian Periodicals*, made such a significant contribution.

Another less canonical poet is brought to the fore in Gary H. Paterson's monograph, *At the Heart of the 1890s: Essays on Lionel Johnson*, which makes a zealous case for the recognition of Johnson's significance. The introductory biography and bibliography sketch a man of contradictory impulses—contemplativeness and a romantic attachment to the past held in tension with urban dandyism and decadence—and an important figure within the close cultural networks of the *fin de siècle*. Paterson draws particular attention to Johnson's conversion to Rome and his interest in Irish culture, providing grounds for a reconsideration of Johnson in the light of current critical preoccupations. The essays that follow take a straightforwardly historicist, thematic approach to Johnson's poetry. Chapter 2, 'Lionel Johnson and the 1890s', offers a neat elucidation of some aspects of decadent culture and style, identifying Johnson's individualism and pessimism as evidence of a qualified association with the movement. Chapters 3 and 4 focus on Johnson's religious thought and poetry, offering an account of his middle-class Anglican background, his early interest in Buddhism and transcendental philosophy, and his conversion to Rome, considering the influence of Newmanist theology, Arnoldian humanism and the aestheticism of Pater, and stressing the importance of Oxford for Johnson's spiritual and literary development. Chapter 5 makes an illuminating comparison between the Easter poems of Clough and Johnson that reveals something of the two poets' approaches to matters of faith and doubt. Chapters 6 and 7 address more formal concerns, and chapter 7 contributes to other work done in 2008, unearthing the funny-bone of Victorian poetry (see also Feeney, *The Playfulness of Gerard Manley Hopkins*), by identifying moments of satire and fun in a body of work that is best known for the decadent despair of his most anthologized poem, 'The Dark Angel'. As the title acknowledges, the book works as a collection of essays linked by a shared subject rather than as a coherent thesis, and as such it provides an interesting and varied introduction to the poet's life and work, covering a good range of Johnson's poetry and including a substantial amount of material from his letters and journalism.

Although Michael Field dominates the year's work on late Victorian poetry by women, two articles direct attention to a handful of their contemporaries. 'Uncanny Transactions and Canny Forms: Rosamund Marriott Watson's *Marchen*' by Lee O'Brien (*VP* 46[2008] 429–50) returns from recent work on Watson's modernism to consider Watson the Victorian. Dealing specifically with Watson's lyrical folk tales, this lively and engaging article explores Watson's fairy worlds via the Freudian uncanny, arguing that the familiar and unfamiliar are staged simultaneously within the lyric space in Watson's texts, which feminize their Victorian folkloric heritage. Gender politics is also at the heart of 'Politicizing Dance in Late Victorian Women's Poetry' by Cheryl Wilson (*VP* 46[2008], 191–205), which assesses the relationship between the proto-feminism of the New Woman and *fin-de-siècle* aestheticism through readings of poems by late Victorian women poets that focus on representations of dance—a field within the woman's sphere that attracted the interest of the aesthetic movement. Wilson offers persuasive readings of poems by Amy Levy, Katherine Tynan and A. Mary F. Robinson that provide revisionist accounts of the woman in the ballroom, situating their work and the dance that they describe within the aesthetic tradition while at the same time maintaining a commitment to the representation of the experience of 'everyday women'.

Other *fin-de-siècle* poets covered in 2008 include Wilde, Dowson, Henley and Symons. Edward H. Cohen provides grounds for a reassessment of Henley's cultural significance in his article 'The Publication and Reception of W.E. Henley's *A Book of Verses*: "The Diversity of Contemporary Tongues"' (*ELT* 51:ii[2008] 184–203), which brings to light a newly discovered scrapbook kept by Henley's wife, containing records of more than forty reviews of *A Book of Verses* [1888]. Cohen lists the reviews, which include pieces by Theodore Watts Dunton, J.M. Barrie, Alice Meynell, G.B. Shaw and Oscar Wilde, and provides a selection of short extracts alongside a helpful outline of Henley's career and the circumstances that led to the book's publication, particularly the composition of a selection of poems inspired by Henley's twenty-month stay in the Royal Infirmary of Edinburgh. 'From the Beauty of Religion to the Religion of Beauty: Catholicism and Aestheticism in Fin-de-Siècle Poetry' by Claire Masurel Murray (in Duquette, ed., pp. 16–26) usefully brings together different representations of Catholic liturgy in poetry by Dowson, Wratislaw, Wilde, Symons and Gray to make the straightforward argument that in decadent poetry Catholicism becomes a space of aesthetic ritual, which offers respite from the materialism of Victorian Britain. Philip E. Smith's edited collection of essays, *Approaches to Teaching the Works of Oscar Wilde*, includes only one that deals with Wilde's poetry: '"All men kill the thing they love": Romance, Realism, and the Ballad of Reading Gaol' by Joseph Bristow (pp. 230–47). This rich and invigorating introduction to Wilde's best-known poem focuses on its most famous line and the questions that it poses about the relationship between the particular and the abstract. Bristow explores the relationship between the author (who signs himself 'C.3.3') and his subject (C.T.W.) and elucidates the poem's comment on the British penal system, providing a wealth of information about Wilde's own experience of prison life, and includes a literary framework that introduces the possibility of a relationship between crime and art. Rodney Stenning Edgecombe's note, 'Tennyson, Wilde and the Anti-Aubade in *Dombey and Son*' (*N&Q* 55[2008] 38–9) sets out a fascinating web of connections between three Victorian dawns: the dawn of Mr Dombey's wedding, the 'blank dawn' of *In Memoriam* VII and the frightened dawn of Wilde's 'Harlot's House'.

4. Drama

Recent research in the field of Victorian drama highlights the diversity of popular theatre genres, including farce, melodrama and music drama, as well as alternative forms of performance art, such as trapeze acts, poetry readings and *poses plastiques*. Scholars also shed new light on children and nineteenth-century theatre, illuminating their often overlooked roles as celebrities, performers and cultural tropes. This year saw the publication of major scholarly works on Henry Irving and Oscar Wilde. These critical studies enhance understanding not only of the pivotal roles Wilde and Irving played in the history of nineteenth-century drama but also of their crucial influence on twentieth-century theatre and performance. The relationship between performance and national identity received significant critical attention in other contexts as well. Scholars investigated how Anglo-colonial forms of theatre and performance supported and challenged notions of British national identity. They also shed light on the pivotal role of Shakespeare and Ibsen in the formation of Victorian drama and British national identity.

Kathryn Prince's *Shakespeare in the Victorian Periodicals* addresses the significance of theatre journals in the reception history of Shakespearean drama. In her chapter on the *Theatrical Journal*, for example, Prince demonstrates how periodicals promoted the appreciation of unadulterated Shakespeare in the wake of the Theatres Regulation Act of 1843. This act repealed legislation that designated Drury Lane and Covent Garden as the only authorized venues for staging Shakespeare's plays. In the resulting 'free market' for literary commodities, multiple versions of the plays were produced in London. The *Theatrical Journal* aimed to improve theatre-goers' taste by encouraging them to seek out productions that were historically and textually accurate. After the success of the Great Exhibition in 1851, the *Theatrical Journal* encouraged the British public to view 'authentic' Shakespeare productions as an expression of national fidelity. In the next chapter, Prince further develops the link between Shakespeare and British nationalism by examining periodical debates focused on proposals for a national theatre. Within the context of this debate, many journalists focused on the educative value of Shakespeare's plays, which were often neglected or bowdlerized in the commercial theatre market. Of course the movement to establish a 'home' for Shakespeare in a British national theatre would not be successful until the middle of the twentieth century.

Henrik Ibsen's plays, like Shakespeare's, were often invoked in Victorian debates over the future of British theatre. Katherine Kelly's 'Pandemic and Performance: Ibsen and the Outbreak of Modernism' (*SCRev* 25:i[2008] 12–35) explores the rise of 'Ibsenism' in Britain during the last three decades of the nineteenth century. During this period, the publication and staging of Ibsen's plays prompted sexologists, feminists, critics and activists to assess the health of *fin-de-siècle* British society. Within these debates, the metaphor of contagion was often employed by hostile critics, who viewed Ibsenism as a kind of literary infection. Kelly contends that the debate over Ibsenism led to the development of 'counterpublics and counter-discourses aimed at the kind of reforms urged by Ibsen's protagonists' (p. 12). The emergence of counterpublics, she argues, was a crucial precondition for the development of modernism in the early decades of the twentieth century.

Recent scholarship suggests that Victorian actor-manager Henry Irving also played a foundational role in the development of twentieth-century theatre. The centenary of Irving's death in 2005 produced a number of remarkable reassessments of his career. Perhaps none is more ground-breaking than Richard Foulkes's collection of essays, *Henry Irving: A Re-Evaluation of the Pre-Eminent Victorian Actor-Manager*. Foulkes asserts that the aim of his collection is not only to re-evaluate Irving's achievements as a virtuoso Victorian actor-manager but also to assess the impact of his work on twentieth- and twenty-first-century theatre. Contributors to the volume address all aspects of Irving's work in the theatre, including his collaborations with actors and playwrights and his mastery of stagecraft. The collection also includes articles on Irving's relationships with major figures in Victorian theatre, including George Bernard Shaw, Ellen Terry and J.L. Toole. The collection includes essays by Michael Read, Jim Davis, Katharine Cockin, Kristan Tetens, Doug Kirshen, Laurence Senelick, Jeffrey Richards, Jean Chothia, Stephen Cockett, Kenneth DeLong and L.W. Conolly. Taken together, these essays not only make a strong case for the significance of Irving as the 'pre-eminent Victorian actor-manager' but also demonstrate his enduring influence on twentieth-century drama. The volume includes a comprehensive bibliography as well as a CD of incidental music to Henry Irving's *The Merchant of Venice*.

Like Henry Irving, W.S. Gilbert and Arthur Sullivan have been the focus of increased scholarly attention in recent years. Alan Fischler, in his essay 'Dialectics of Social Class in the Gilbert and Sullivan Collaboration' (*SEL* 48[2008] 829–37), examines how the dynamics of social class informed one of the most important partnerships in the history of British theatre. W.S. Gilbert, as a product of bourgeois ideology, wrote libretti that represented the law as a positive force in the lives of his middle-class characters. After all, as Fischler points out, 'Obedience to the law—as embodied not just in statute but also in codes of conduct and morality—was the essence of Victorian middle-class respectability' (p. 832). Gilbert's focus on the 'transformation of lowlifes to bluebloods' in his libretti reflected the interests of Arthur Sullivan, who had grown up in the Lambeth slums and aspired to social acceptance among the British aristocracy (p. 833). The success of Gilbert and Sullivan was thus in part due to the fusion of their separate class positions and aspirations.

Patience [1881] is of course one of the most widely studied of Gilbert and Sullivan's collaborations. Carolyn Williams, in her recently published essay, 'Parody and Poetic Tradition: Gilbert and Sullivan's *Patience*' (*VP* 46[2008] 375–403), examines the opera's incorporation of debates over poetry and poetics in the 1870s, including the controversy surrounding the publication of James Buchanan's 'The Fleshly School of Poetry' [1871]. By parodying both 'aesthetic' and 'idyllic' modes of poetry, embodied by Bunthorne and Grosvenor, the opera questions the validity of both poetic schools. She notes that the 'libretto manages, by implication, to comment on a long nineteenth-century history of Romantic and Victorian poetry, and it shows Gilbert to have been exceptionally well informed about poetic controversy in the decades before *Patience*' (p. 375).

Scholarly interest in the work of Gilbert and Sullivan reflects broader critical fascination with musical drama during the Victorian era. Three chapters of Claire Mabilat's *Orientalism and Representations of Music in the Nineteenth-Century British Popular Arts* focus specifically on orientalist musical stage works in the long nineteenth century. The first chapter provides an overview of general developments in musical genres during this era, and the second chapter focuses on ways in which libretti constructed women as sexually compliant or predatory 'Orientals'. Male 'Others', she argues, were most often represented as sexually rapacious aggressors. Mabilat cites examples from several orientalist productions, including the *Nautch Girl* [1891] and *The Geisha* [1896]. In the next chapter, she analyses images of the 'noble savage' and the 'cruel, scheming Oriental' in musical drama of the period (p. 81). While early in the century there were a large number of 'noble savage' figures in musical drama, by the end of the century, representations of the 'Other' were characterized by 'increased mockery and negative stereotyping', thus reflecting *fin-de-siècle* fears of miscegenation (p. 17).

Two essays published in *Victorian Traffic* (Sue Thomas, ed.) also examine performances of colonial otherness on the Victorian stage. Mandy Treagus's 'Agents or Objects? Maori Performances in Britain' (pp. 124–42), examines the experiences of Maori performers who toured Britain in 1863–4 and 1911. Although they were exploited by promoters, they 'nevertheless expressed their own opinions, forged their own alliances, and ultimately via these found their way back to New Zealand' (pp. 141–2). Anne Collett, in her essay 'Pauline Johnson-Tekahionwake: Trafficking Woman' (pp. 143–62), explores the experiences of a mixed-blood 'Mohawk Princess' who gave performances of her poetry in North America and England during the 1890s. Like the Maori performers, Johnson-Tekahionwake was a victim of a racist exhibition culture, yet she was able to assert some degree of agency and resistance through her performances. Taken together, Treagus's and Collett's essays suggest that 'trafficking' of the colonial celebrity was a form of exploitation, yet such 'traffic' also enabled resistance to prevailing ideologies of race and gender. The next two essays in the collection focus on the experiences of European performers abroad who were able to capitalize on the conventions of celebrity media in order to promote their own careers. Nick Frigo, in 'Oscar's Wild(e) Year in America' (pp. 163–77), demonstrates how Wilde used his time abroad to perfect his performance style. And Peta Tait, in 'Female Pleasure and Muscular Arms in Touring Trapeze Acts' (pp. 178–91), explores how travelling trapeze artists were able to capitalize on the public's desire for 'kinaesthetic pleasures' and sexual titillation.

Performance art indeed assumed diverse forms during the Victorian era. Nicole Anae's 'Poses Plastiques: The Art and Style of "Statuary" in Victorian Visual Theatre' (ADS 52[2008] 112–30), discusses the significance of 'living statues' as a popular form of entertainment in British and colonial contexts. In performances in West End theatres and circus shows, scantily clad actors assumed statue-like poses in imitation of Greek and Roman gods. Poses plastiques were integrated into respectable theatre productions, but they were also associated with scandalous dance-hall spectacles. Anae discusses several practitioners of this art form, arguing that poses plastiques 'tested the very limits of Victorian visual theatre' (p. 112). In her investigation of Australian examples, she examines how notions of collective national identity were expressed in a form of theatre 'without words' (p. 125).

During the Victorian era courtrooms were important sites of performance, both on and off the stage. Susie Steinbach's 'From Redress to Farce: Breach of Promise Theatre in Cultural Context, 1830–1920' (JVC 13:ii[2008] 247–76) examines shifting public reactions to breach of promise legal actions, as reflected on the stage. Focusing primarily on two plays of the period—Trial by Jury [1875], produced by Gilbert and Sullivan, and Bardell v. Pickwick [1871], adapted from an episode in Dickens's Pickwick Papers—Steinbach situates breach of promise plays within the context of legal, social and theatrical developments from 1830 to 1920. Steinbach points out that during the Victorian era jilted fiancés had the right to bring suit against their former lovers, and in the early decades of the century such suits met with public approbation. However, by the 1870s, breach of promise actions were treated as farcical in the popular media. At the same time, breach of promise actions were often the subject of farce—an increasingly popular comic genre on the stage at the end of the nineteenth century. The popularity of breach of promise theatre influenced reportage of actual court cases, which were perceived as being 'artificial' or 'theatrical' (p. 269). Steinbach thus effectively demonstrates how courtroom and stage at the end of the nineteenth century were characterized by a 'productive tension between notions of performance and authenticity' (p. 249).

Melodrama continues to be of keen interest to scholars working in the field of nineteenth-century drama. Katherine Newey's essay, ' "Thus Far and No Farther!": The "Proper Lady" and the Ends of Melodrama' (in Gay, Johnston and Waters, eds., *Victorian Turns, NeoVictorian Returns: Essays on Fiction and Culture*, pp. 50–8), includes discussion of domestic melodramas, the so-called 'she-dramas' performed primarily at the Adelphi Theatre during the 1830s. Newey briefly analyses John Baldwin Buckstone's *Ellen Wareham, Wife of Two Husbands* [1833] and *Agnes de Vere; or, the Wife's Revenge* [1836] as well as Edward Stirling's *Jane Lomax; or the Mother's Crime* [1839]. These seemingly conventional melodramas, she argues, 'offer alternative readings, focused around the central female characters, which represent women as powerful and active' (p. 53). In these works, women characters are governed by conventional melodramatic plot structures that end in marriage or death; nevertheless, 'it is their transgression that generates the plot interest and emotional punch of the plays, and it is their impassioned speaking out that drives the action' (p. 54). Newey links the transgressive potential of melodrama to the development of Victorian fiction, particularly Charlotte Brontë's *Villette*.

In *Wilkie Collins: A Literary Life*, Graham Law and Andrew Maunder include a chapter on Collins's work in the theatre, including his melodramas and adaptations of novels for the stage. Law and Maunder persuasively argue for greater critical appreciation of Collins's dramatic works, which 'demonstrate attempts to master different theatrical techniques … offer scope for reader-identification, and feed anxieties prompted by "real-life" events' (p. 105). Indeed, they argue, Collins's later works can be viewed as forerunners of the well-made play and the problem play, genres which dominated the British stage by the 1880s and 1890s. Law and Maunder also provide insight into Collins's collaborations with Dickens and provide background on several of Collins's most significant productions, including *No Thoroughfare* [1867] and *Black and White* [1869].

Children and Victorian drama also received significant critical attention this year. Anne Varty's *Children and Theatre in Victorian Britain: 'All Work, No Play'* is a comprehensive study of child actors on the stage, including their training, roles and audiences. Children's theatre was of course wildly popular throughout the Victorian era. In 1887 alone it is estimated that 10,000 children worked as actors in pantomime productions (p. 2). As a way of explaining the popularity of children's performances, Varty argues that the child actor served as 'as a vessel for adult fantasy' and ultimately as a means for increasing 'awareness of child as social being' (p. 18). Varty devotes significant attention to the controversies surrounding the employment of children in theatrical productions, including debates leading to the passage of the Prevention of Cruelty to Children Act [1889], which regulated children's work in the theatre industry.

In 'The Drama of Precocity: Child Performers on the Victorian Stage' (in Denisoff, ed., *The Nineteenth-Century Child and Consumer Culture*, pp. 63–78) Marah Gubar provides a revealing reassessment of children's roles in the

Victorian theatre. Rather than viewing the popularity of child performers as an expression of the Victorian obsession with the artless purity of youth, Gubar argues that child actors were usually billed as precocious performers, whose 'prematurely developed skills and much-vaunted versatility enabled them to blur the line between child and adult, innocence and experience' (p. 64). She profiles several child performers and a variety of all-child performances that have been neglected in recent criticism, thus suggesting new directions for research on children and the Victorian stage.

David Haldane Lawrence's 'Performing Working Boys: The Representation of Child Labour on the Pre- and Early Victorian Stage' (*NTQ* 24:ii[2008] 126–40), examines plays produced during the 1830s and 1840s focused on the plight of children employed in urban industries. Through an examination of five plays—*The Factory Girl, The Factory Boy, The Dumb Man (or Boy) of Manchester, The Climbing Boy* and *The Cabin Boy*—Lawrence demonstrates how playwrights of the period idealized the lives of child labourers for a bourgeois audience. This lack of realism was reinforced by the convention of using women actors to play boys' parts on the early Victorian stage. Sentimentalized accounts of the travails of child labourers were linked to social problem fiction of the period, such as Frances Trollope's *The Life and Adventures of Michael Armstrong the Factory Boy* [1840], which is thought to have inspired Thomas Haines's play *The Factory Boy*. Lawrence concludes by noting that the representation of child labourers 'possibly fuelled a popular desire to end the industrial exploitation of children', but was also 'responsible for appeasing bourgeois guilt and inertia over the mistreatment of working children in early- to mid-nineteenth-century Britain' (p. 139).

The plays of Oscar Wilde received a great deal of critical attention this year. In ' "The Brutal Music and the Delicate Text"? The Aesthetic Relationship between Wilde's and Strauss's *Salome* Reconsidered' (*MLQ* 69:iii[2008] 367–89), Petra Dierkes-Thrun argues against the conventional viewpoint that the modernism of Strauss's 1905 music drama is radically different than the decadent symbolism of Wilde's 1892 play. Instead, she argues that Wilde and Strauss shared the goal of inspiring 'corporeal affect and aesthetic intoxication' (p. 379). Indeed, her analysis of the two works demonstrates how our conceptions of 'decadence' and 'modernism' are often inadequate for describing literature during this transitional period. Modernism, she argues, was produced by a dynamic interplay of literary themes and strategies rather than a strictly linear series of stages or developments.

Horst Schroeder, in his essay 'The First Editor of the Four-Act Version of *Earnest*: Hermann Freiherr von Teschenberg' (*Wildean* 32[2008] 8–28), examines history of the German translation of *The Importance of Being Earnest* [1903]. Considered the most authoritative text of the four-act version of the play, Hermann Freiherr von Teschenberg's translation has a colourful history. Schroeder situates Teschenberg's work as a translator within the broader context of homosexual activism in *fin-de-siècle* Berlin, particularly his association with sexologist Magnus Hirschfield (1868–1935) and the Wissenschaftlich-humanitäres Komitee. Schroeder also highlights Teschenberg's connection to Isidore Leo Pavia (1875–1945), who was his collaborator on translations of *Lady Windermere's Fan* and Wilde's other plays. In an appendix to the article, Schroeder includes a translation of Teschenberg's brief 'Reminiscence of Oscar Wilde' [1903], which depicts the great writer as a martyr who 'had been too proud to tell a lie and to play the hypocrite' (p. 25).

Ronald Paul, in his essay ' "[U]ngrateful, discontented, disobedient, and rebellious": Subaltern Voices in the Writings of Oscar Wilde' (*NJES* 7:ii[2008] 19–38), situates Wilde's *Vera; or, The Nihilists* [1880] within the playwright's broader commitment to exploring socially marginalized voices and concerns. Paul argues against critical interpretations that paint Wilde as an apolitical aesthete and depict *Vera* as an expression of 'political quietism' (p. 29). Instead, he argues, the play highlights the 'struggle for freedom and democracy, albeit through a clash of political strategies and personal affections' (p. 29). Vera, in his reading, becomes a feminist prototype who engages in self-assertive political activism. She is thus one of many subaltern voices asserted in Wilde's most overtly political writings.

In an article entitled 'Paul Verlaine and *A Platonic Lament*: Beardsley's Portrayal of a Parallel Love Story in Wilde's *Salomé*' (*ELT* 51:ii[2008] 152–63), Joan Navarre sheds light on the one of Beardsley's most enigmatic illustrations: *A Platonic Lament*. Navarre notes that Jean Cocteau identified the winking jester as a portrait of poet Paul Verlaine. The Young Syrian in the illustration, she points out, is a caricature of Arthur Rimbaud and thus is identified as an object of desire for the Page and, by extension, for Verlaine himself. Consequently, while the play suggests the perils of forbidden love between the Page and the Young Syrian, the illustration alludes to the illicit, stormy relationship between Verlaine and Rimbaud. In this way, Beardsley 'displays an acute appreciation of Wilde's words—specifically, the historical resonances inherent in Wilde's story about the affection of an older man for a younger man' (p. 162).

Two recently published essay collections on Wilde will serve as useful resources for teachers and scholars alike. Joseph Bristow's *Oscar Wilde and Modern Culture: The Making of a Legend* includes a variety of essays that investigate the impact of Wilde's life and works on writers and performers from the late nineteenth century to the present day. Chapters on Wilde's *Salomé* are likely to be of particular interest to scholars of Victorian drama. Erin Williams Hyman, in her essay 'Salomé as Bombshell, or How Oscar Wilde Became an Anarchist' (pp. 96–109), situates the 1896 French production of *Salomé* within the context of anarchist discourse at the *fin de siècle*. Julie Townsend's 'Staking Salomé: The Literary Forefathers and Choreographic Daughters of Oscar Wilde's "Hysterical and Perverted Creature" ' (pp. 154–79), also provides useful context for understanding the play and its cultural resonances. Townsend examines earlier French literary representations of Salomé, demonstrating how Wilde's play engages in a dialogue with these earlier works. In addition, she examines Loïe Fuller's 1907 dance performance, *Tragédie de Salomé*, as a response to representations of Salomé by decadent male writers of the nineteenth century. The volume also includes excellent essays by Laurel Brake, Leslie Moran, Francesca Coppa and Oliver Buckton analysing reinterpretations of Wilde and his plays on stage and screen during the twentieth century. An introductory essay by Joseph Bristow, as well as chapters by Lucy McDiarmid, Daniel Novak, Richard Kaye, Yvonne Ivory, Lizzie Thynne and Matt Cook, complete the collection.

Philip Smith's *Approaches to Teaching the Works of Oscar Wilde* includes a variety of useful resources, including recommendations of primary and secondary materials for classroom use. A substantial portion of the book is devoted to teaching Wilde's comedies, with essays by Sos Eltis, Melissa Knox, Francesca Coppa, Kirsten Shepherd-Barr, Robert Preissle and Alan Ackerman. Although there is substantial attention to the often-taught *Importance of Being Earnest*, the collection includes essays on *Lady Windermere's Fan*, *A Woman of No Importance* and *An Ideal Husband*. Even more impressively, the collection includes five essays on pedagogical approaches to Wilde's *Salomé,* contributed by Eszter Szalczer, Joan Navarre, Beth Tashery Shannon, Petra Dierkes-Thrun and Samuel Lyndon Gladden. An extended focus on *Salomé* is justified, Smith notes, given that it is the 'most engaging and most difficult of Wilde's texts for students' (p. 21). In addition to essays on Wilde's work as a dramatist, Smith's volume includes a wealth of other contextual and pedagogical materials that make his collection an essential resource for teachers working in the field of Victorian drama.

5. Periodicals and Publishing History

Work on Victorian periodical and publishing history continues to meet the levels of quality and quantity seen over the past few years. Particularly striking has been the amount of work published this year that has situated the role of popular culture, social history and readership studies in nineteenth-century periodical and publishing contexts.

A good example of this is Anne Humpherys and Louis James's edited collection, *G.W.M. Reynolds: Nineteenth-Century Fiction, Politics and the Press.* As a radical newspaper proprietor and Chartist agitator, best-selling novelist G.W.M. Reynolds (1814–79) loomed large in the cultural and political life of mid-Victorian Britain. Though little known today, Reynolds's multifarious excursions into novel writing, journalism, periodical publication and radical politics made him a significant voice in articulating working-class culture and interests. During his lifetime his popular novels sold in the hundreds of thousands, his *Reynolds's Newspaper* (1850–1967) had a weekly circulation at its peak of 300,000, and his radical support of working men's rights led Dickens to brand him 'a person notorious for his attempts to degrade the working men of England by circulating among them books of a debasing tendency' (p. 206). Reynolds's career is subject to much scrutiny in this collection, and is characterized by energy and a singular drive to overcome personal and commercial obstacles. The editors of this collection contextualize well Reynolds's multifarious career, first as writer, editor and failed bookseller in Paris, in the 1830s, later as editor of bestselling periodicals (*The London Journal, Reynolds's Miscellany, Reynolds's Newspaper*), and then as author of popular serialized Penny weekly series (*The Mysteries of London* and *The Mysteries of the Court of London*) in the 1840s and 1850s. These issues are amplified in contributions divided into five general sections. These include contributions on: Reynolds's work in France (Sara James, 'G.W.M. Reynolds and the Modern Literature of France', pp. 19–32; Rohan McWilliam, 'The French Connection: G.W.M. Reynolds and the Outlaw Robert Macaire', pp. 33–52); his politics and the periodical press (Andrew King, '*Reynolds's Miscellany*, 1846–1849: Advertising Networks and Politics', pp. 53–74; Michael H. Shirley, 'G.W.M. Reynolds, *Reynolds's Newspaper* and Popular Politics', pp. 75–90; Michael Diamond, 'From Journalism and Fiction into Politics', pp. 91–8; and Antony Taylor, '"Some Little or Contemptible War upon her Hands"', pp. 99–122). Other topics covered include his key serial work *The Mysteries of London*, the subject of pieces by Anne Humpherys, 'An Introduction to G.W.M. Reynolds's "Encyclopedia of Tales"', pp. 123–32; Berry Chevasco, 'Lost in Translation: The Relationship between Eugene Sue's *Les Mystères de Paris* and G.W.M. Reynolds's *The Mysteries of London*', pp. 133–46; Stephen James Carver, 'The Wrongs and Crimes of the Poor: the Urban Underworld of *The Mysteries of London* in Context', pp. 147–60; Juliet John, 'Reynolds's *Mysteries* and Popular Culture', pp. 161–78. There is also room for discussion regarding his place in popular culture (Louis James, 'Time, Politics and the Symbolic Imagination in Reynolds's Social Melodrama', pp. 179–98; Graham Law, 'Reynolds's "Memoirs" Series and "The Literature of the Kitchen"', pp. 199–210; Ellen B. Rosenman, 'The Virtue of Illegitimacy: Inheritance and Belonging in *The Dark Woman* and *Mary Price*', pp. 211–24; and Brian Maidment, 'The Mysteries of Reading: Text and Illustration in the Fiction of G.W.M. Reynolds', pp. 225–46). The collection concludes with a coda on his posthumous reputation (Sucheta Bhattacharya, 'G.W.M. Reynolds: Rewritten in Nineteenth-Century Bengal', pp. 247–58; and Ian Haywood, 'Modernity, Memory and Myth: *Reynolds's News* and the Cooperative Movement', pp. 259–70). Of bibliographical value is a comprehensive list of G.W.M. Reynolds's works prepared by Louis James, as well as a bibliography of selected secondary works, undertaken by Helen Hauser. The avid and enthusiastic tenor of this collection, and the thorough investigation by these pieces of Reynolds's legacy, offer an important addition to studies of nineteenth-century British cultural history, and should be read.

Reynolds is not the only reforming editor to have received exemplary treatment this year. Equally valuable is Edwin Hirschmann's biography, *Robert Knight: Reforming Editor in Victorian India*. Hirschmann's forty-year quest to throw light on Knight's role in Indian press history offers a valuable study of a British liberal who based his working career on promoting and sustaining principles of fairness, justice and equality. It was a career that spanned moments such as the founding of the *Bombay Times* in 1857, its relaunch as the *Times of India* in 1861, the ill-fated attempt to launch the periodical *The Statesman* in London between 1879 and 1881, and the founding and editing of the Calcutta-based *Statesman and Friend of India* from 1877 until his death in 1890. Knight, though embedded within the imperial framework that ruled India, nevertheless spoke out consistently against British excesses, was an early supporter of the Indian National Congress and in the end comes out of this engaging biography as an individual thoroughly assimilated into his adopted country.

India also features in two contributions on the Indo-British publishing firm Thacker, Spink and Co. in Robert Fraser and Mary Hammond, eds. *Books Without Borders*, volume 2: *Perspectives from South Asia*. In 'Book Circulation and Reader Responses in Colonial India' (p. 100–11), David Finkelstein discusses the 1880 transatlantic return voyage from London to Calcutta and back of a London published 'mutiny' novel by the novelist Philip Meadows Taylor. Thacker, Spink and Co. were key retailers of British fiction in the Indian book market, and their background history is sketched out by Finkelstein and more fully developed in Victoria Condie's 'Thacker, Spink and Company: Bookselling and Publishing in Mid-Nineteenth-Century Calcutta' (pp. 112–24). Thacker, Spink and Co. also are discussed in Shafquat Towheed's detailed piece on the production and dissemination of Rudyard Kipling's first short-story collection, 'Two Paradigms of Literary Production: The Production, Circulation and Legal Status of Rudyard Kipling's *Departmental Ditties* and Indian Railway Library Texts' (pp. 125–36). Volume 1 of the essay collection set *Books Without Borders, The Cross-National Dimension in Print Culture*, features an important piece by Sydney J. Shep ('Books Without Borders: The Transnational Turn in Book History', pp. 13–37), suggesting theoretical frameworks and questions that the book history field would do well to consider in a move to broaden research agendas to encompass transnational trends and linkages.

Popular periodical literature is the subject of an interesting piece by Kate Macdonald and Marysa DeMoor, 'Borrowing and Supplementing: The Industrial Production of "Complete Story" Novelettes and their Supplements, 1865–1900' (*PubH* 63[2008] 67–95). The extensive piece complements a similar article by Macdonald featured in the same journal the previous year. Macdonald and DeMoor draw our attention to an unresearched area of publishing and periodical studies, the weekly penny domestic fiction market that flourished in the latter third of the nineteenth century in Britain. The novelette, or cheap periodical that published complete stories rather than serialized fiction, was a particularly robust format catering to the increasing numbers of readers seeking light fiction for daily work commutes on trains and other means of public transport. It is estimated that, between 1865 and 1900, over eighty novelettes or related periodical titles were published in Britain, along with fiction supplements to established periodical sources. Macdonald and DeMoor offer useful primary data on this publishing sub-genre, demonstrating the continuing popularity of such material amongst working-class readers.

Readership remains a strong interest in publications this year. Two new works focus on reader reception of Shakespeare, but angling at the subject from different perspectives. In *Shakespeare in the Victorian Periodicals*, Kathryn Prince draws on textual analysis of periodical material to draw various conclusions about readership reception and contemporary evaluation of Shakespeare's value in didactic, gender-based and critical terms. The section discussing working-class press usage of Shakespeare to reach mass readers covers similar ground to Andrew Murphy's in-depth and richly documented study *Shakespeare for the People: Working-Class Readers, 1800–1900*. The comparison is unbalanced, for Prince's reliance solely on periodical texts pales when viewed against Murphy's nuanced evaluation of Shakespeare's place in British working-class culture as drawn from a wide range of primary and secondary sources, including autobiographies, visual imagery, publishing details and educational textbook material.

Commodities, information systems and their textual reconfigurations in serialized fiction and periodical culture are key themes uniting three interesting works by Richard Menke (*Telegraphic Realisms: Victorian Fiction and Other Information Systems*), John Plotz (*Portable Property: Victorian Culture on the Move*) and Catherine Waters (*Commodity Culture in Dickens's Household Words: The Social Life of Goods*). Menke takes as his starting point the place of new information systems such as the telegraph and the penny post in the work of novelists such as Dickens, George Eliot, Trollope and Gaskell. The study is an ambitious blend of informatics theory, media history concerns and literary criticism, which is only unsatisfactory in its ignoring of print technology advances as another key element of nineteenth-century information and communication infrastructures that also find their way into such texts. John Plotz also chooses an interdisciplinary approach to literary material, in this case focusing on textual manifestations of material culture and material objects (portable property such as dolls, handkerchiefs, items of personal nature), as they appeared in signal serialized texts by George Eliot, Thomas Hardy and William Morris, among others. The work also skims past the idea of examining print culture as enmeshed in technological change, or offering nuanced insight into material contexts affecting such literary conceptions of the Victorian world. Catherine Waters, on the other hand, deftly traces the manner in which Dickens's editing of *Household Words* knowingly engaged with the expansion of commodity culture and cultural consumption of mass-produced products. Her critical attention to the manner in which the journal reflects the changing relationship between people and things in nineteenth-century British society is a valuable addition to the theoretical development of periodical studies work.

A long-awaited volume of essays on children's literature joins another text on Victorian periodical representations of fairy tales in reinvigorating critical study of this area of textual production. *Popular Children's Literature in Britain*, edited by the late Julia Briggs, Dennis Butt and M.O. Grenby, takes as its starting point two distinct definitions of the popular and offers case studies interrogating both definitions. The term 'popular' as denoting works chosen for pleasure, inexpensive, suited to ordinary taste, is contrasted to the term as it denotes commercially successful work. How such terminology can work to reveal what becomes ephemeral and forgotten, as well as what comes to be claimed for posterity as classic texts, is a significant thread running through this extensive and valuable collection. Of interest to nineteenth-century specialists are the following contributions: Kevin Carpenter, 'Robin Hood in Boys' Weeklies to 1914' (pp. 47–68); David Blamires, 'From Madame d'Aulnoy to Mother Bunch: Popularity and the Fairy Tale' (pp. 69–86); George Speaight with Brian Alderson, 'From Chapbooks to Pantomime' (pp. 87–100); Dennis Butts, 'Finding and Sustaining a Popular Appeal: The Case of Barbara Hoffland' (pp. 105–22); Elaine Lomax, 'Telling the Other Side: Hesba Stretton's "Outcast" Stories' (pp. 123–48); Dennis Butts,

'Exploiting a Formula: The Adventure Stories of G.A. Henty' (pp. 149–84); Kimberley Reynolds, 'Rewarding Reads: Giving, Receiving and Resisting Evangelical Reward and Prize Books' (pp. 189–208); and Aileen Fyfe, 'Tracts, Classics and Brands: Science for Children in the Nineteenth Century' (pp. 209–28).

Caroline Sumpter continues the development of new insights into children's literature in *The Victorian Press and the Fairy Tale*. Sumpter draws on media history, print culture and book history studies to make useful arguments regarding the form in which fairy tales were shaped by the outlets they appeared in, and by the knowing efforts of authors working in this field to maximize their commercial appeal. Sumpter's survey takes in a range of periodical texts to develop these issues in lucid form, ranging from shilling monthlies to socialist, left-wing periodicals and modernist little magazines.

The figure of Joseph Norman Lockyer, nineteenth-century editor of *Nature*, crosses two studies of Victorian science periodicals. With 'Nineteenth-Century Popular Science Magazines: Narrative, and the Problem of Historical Materiality' (in Holmes, ed., *Mapping the Magazine: Comparative Studies in Magazine Journalism*), James Mussell contributes a study of narrative strategies in representing science to popular audiences for a collection on magazine journalism. In journals such as *Nature* and *Knowledge: An Illustrated Magazine of Science*, science popularizers sought to walk the fine line between claiming authority as scientific experts and explicating complex scientific information in accessible form.

Lockyer's contemporary William Crookes, editor, chemist, inventor and controversial advocate of occultism and spiritualism, is the subject of William H. Brock's long-gestated biography, *William Crookes (1832–1919) and the Commercialization of Science*. Though billed as a study of Crookes's role in various scientific arenas, the work threads Crookes's life history through examination of his scientific work, including his editorship of various mid-century photography magazines and his long-running stint as editor of *Chemical News* (model for the current format of *Nature*). The work is as thorough as one would expect from an emeritus professor who has spent most of his working life examining areas related to Crookes's scientific interests (spectroscopy, public health, chemical physics).

Elite periodical production is ostensibly the subject of Ann Ardis and Patrick Collier's essay collection *Transatlantic Print Culture, 1880–1940: Emerging Media, Emerging Modernism*. As they note in their introduction, the period between the emergence in the 1880s in Great Britain of the 'New Woman' and 'New Journalism', and modernism's high point of cultural influence in the 1920s saw an avalanche of print periodical publications in transatlantic settings. Between 1885 and 1905, over 7,500 new periodicals were launched in the US alone, with over 250 little magazines founded and in circulation by century's end. In Great Britain there was a similar trend in print journal growth, with more than 50,000 periodicals in circulation by 1922, servicing a wide variety of constituents, from general interest readers to specialist trade and professional groups. While most of this volume is dedicated to early twentieth-century periodical history, there are pieces contextualizing modernist magazine productions within nineteenth-century contexts. Among these can be counted Laurel Brake's thought-provoking essay, 'Journalism and Modernism, Continued: The Case of W.T. Stead' (pp. 149–66), which makes a convincing case for positioning the crusading 'New Journalist' W.T. Stead as a proto-modernist. Though best known for his populist-driven, investigative reportage from the 1880s through to his ill-fated death in the sinking of the *Titanic* in 1910, Stead also produced a series of annuals between 1891 and 1907 aimed at merging transatlantic social concerns with populist-focused yet distinctively modernist critical material. He customized the fiction published to link politics and popular genres ('political romances', 'journalistic fiction'), and drew on the latest technology to produce a modernist-leaning hybridity of texts conjoining diagrams, maps, photographs, engravings, literary fragments, factual treatises and commentary.

In *The New Bibliopolis: French Book Collectors and the Culture of Print, 1880–1914*, Willa Z. Silverman offers an interesting comparative study of the role of French book collectors in promoting European book arts and elite textual production, as well as the role of influential publishers such as Paul Gallimard in developing markets for illustrated books in *fin-de-siècle* France. The study provides useful material against which to compare British efforts in this particular area of book trade studies.

Book trade connections on a trans-regional basis are the subject of John Hinks and Catherine Armstrong's edited collection *Book Trade Connections from the Seventeenth to the Twentieth Centuries*. The volume is the ninth and latest in the Print Network series, developed from an annual conference dedicated to highlighting new research on British book trade history connections. Ably edited, *Book Trade Connections* is an eclectic mix of fine-grained studies and speculative research reports, ranging from the eccentric and ephemeral to more bibliographically focused contributions. Many pieces work well, offering sharp insights into unusual examples of book trade history. Of relevance to nineteenth-century interests is Frank Felsenstein's research report on an incredible archive recently uncovered in a public library attic in Muncie, Indiana ('What Middletown Read: Print Networks in the Nineteenth-Century West', pp. 203–24). The complete history of book borrowings at the Muncie Public Library from 1874 to 1904 is the starting point for an ongoing project appraising the place of texts in the cultural life of what has been called the quintessential midwestern US town, whose growth and development over the twentieth century has been extensively tracked by social historians. Felsenstein's piece is nothing more than a lightly modified conference presentation, offering only a tentative and generally descriptive snapshot of what these new records can tell us about reading habits. This unfinished tone is also present in Paul Smith's descriptive accounting of his past work on oral traditions and their representations in nineteenth-century printed chapbooks of 'mumming' or traditional folk plays ('The Chapbook Mummers Play: Analysing Ephemeral Print Traditions', pp. 181–202). It contrasts with the more rounded and better-explicated companion piece by Eddie Cass on printing histories of Easter focused chapbooks and folk plays in Lancashire, Yorkshire and the Lake District ('The Printing History of the Peace Egg Chapbooks', pp. 161–80). More successful are the core contributions focusing on late seventeenth- and eighteenth-century print culture, of which

Victorianists might find useful Johanna Archbold's detailed mapping of Irish monthly periodicals produced in the 1790s, during the turbulent run-up to the Irish rebellion of 1798 and the Act of Union in 1800 ('Periodical Reactions: The Effect of the 1798 Rebellion and the 1800 Act of Union on the Irish monthly periodical', pp. 135–60). The pieces that are successful demonstrate eloquent and erudite discussion of issues to hand. They ultimately demonstrate how British book history at its best, as John Feather points out in the general survey piece that begins the proceedings, can be trans-regional in nature, incorporating Irish, Scottish and Welsh dimensions to what for many in the past has been seen mainly as a London-focused enterprise.

Scottish publishing history is the subject of several works this year. Antony Kamm contributes a short but heavily illustrated study on *Scottish Printed Books, 1508–2008*, produced in conjunction with a well-received national exhibition on the subject at the National Library of Scotland. It sits well alongside a similar popular account of publishing history, the late Humphrey Carpenter's engaging gallop through the seven generations of publishers who steered a famous London publishing house, *The Seven Lives of John Murray: The Story of a Publishing Dynasty, 1768–2002*. The firm's heads, all named John, could trace their publishing roots to the first John Murray's arrival in London in the late 1760s. Over the next 200 years the firm rose to international eminence, building, in particular during the Victorian period, a reputation as the well-regarded publisher of Jane Austen, Byron, Shelley, Darwin, David Livingstone, Gladstone and many other illustrious nineteenth-century figures. Though the history treads paths well worn by previous studies, Carpenter's work retells the highlights of this firm's activities in fresh prose style.

Thomas F. Bonnell points out Scottish contributions to innovations in the development of poetry anthology markets and texts in *The Most Disreputable Trade: Publishing the Classics of English Poetry 1765–1810*. Using primary sources and a great deal of bibliographical and archival material, Bonnell persuasively argues that Scots publishers such as the Foulis brothers and William Creech were key players in developing significant, affordable editions of British classics and popular poetry anthologies from the 1760s and 1770s onwards. The forms and style they pioneered would be replicated in early nineteenth-century 'pocket libraries' of plays, poetry and canonical texts produced by the likes of Charles Cooke, John Sharpe and Alexander Chalmers.

Irish press history as it touches upon British Victorian sensibilities is noted in two differing pieces covering nineteenth-century journal foundings. In Richard C. Allen and Stephen Regan, eds., *Irelands of the Mind: Memory and Identity in Modern Irish Culture*, Joan Allen contributes a piece on Irish Catholic Press incursions into nineteenth-century Britain ('"Keeping the Faith": The Catholic Press and the Preservation of Celtic Identity in Britain in the Late Nineteenth Century', pp. 32–49). The title is deceptive, for in fact the piece is more an exegesis of the role in press history of Irish newspaper entrepreneur and nationalist figure Charles Diamond. Diamond's launch and editing of key Irish-focused newspapers throughout the 1880s and 1890s would play a significant part in cementing and shaping the identity of Irish emigrants to England, Scotland and Wales. Among the more than forty newspaper titles he had amassed by the time of his death in 1934 could be counted *The Irish Tribune* [1884–97] and the influential *Catholic Herald* [1885–present]. The piece offers promising insight into Diamond's political and social concerns, but could have benefited from more development of the arguments and examples used.

Mark O'Brien offers us a retrospective history of the founding and survival of a bastion of Irish journalism in *The Irish Times: A History*. Ireland's oldest national daily newspaper, founded in 1859 as a representative of unionist political views, would turn in the mid-1950s into a pillar of liberal opinion. Well written and engaging, the work focuses more on the newspaper's twentieth-century history, and is disappointingly sparse in its coverage of nineteenth-century beginnings and development.

An unusual example of transregional and transnational book connections is *Tracing the Connected Narrative: Arctic Exploration in British Print Culture 1818–1860*, Janice Cavell's excellent study of nineteenth-century Arctic exploration narratives. It draws well on a variety of printed and archival sources, and provides a coherent and well-structured narrative explicating the manner in which the various controversies, debates and personalities that dominated this particular area of British expansionist tendencies and desire to explore foreign spaces were constructed in book and journalistic form. Particularly interesting are the questions the work addresses related to authenticity, the place of authority in constructing a public persona for the explorers under discussion, and the process by which debate in the periodical press shaped general public perceptions of these narratives and their protagonists.

Transnationalism of another sort is Richard Freebury's topic in ' "Pirates" or "Honourable Men": British Perceptions of American Attitudes to Literary Property as Reflected in *The Bookseller*, 1858–1891'. (*PubH* 63[2008] 5–66). His work analyses over thirty years' worth of debate and discussion found in the pages of *The Bookseller*, founded in 1858 as the premier monthly trade journal for the British bookselling and publishing trades. As his piece ably shows, between 1858 and the implementation of the Chace Copyright Act of 1891, which brought US copyright practices more in line with those of the UK and international policies, *The Bookseller* documented complex shifts in public stances on the matter. If the 1850s and 1860s were characterized by concern over the unethical appropriation of British works for US publication without adequate compensation, by the 1870s and 1880s the tone of the journal's reports became more conciliatory, acknowledging the manner in which literary success for many writers had been bolstered by public access in the US to inexpensive versions of their work. Literary fame could still lead to literary fortune, and the increasing professionalization of authorship was reflected in this shift in stance.

Journal articles that have appeared this year with relevance to periodical and publishing history studies include the following: Joseph Eaton, 'A New Albion in New America: British Periodicals and Morris Birkbeck's English Prairie, 1818–1824' (*ANCH* 9:i[2008] 19–36); Ross Alloway, 'Cadell and the

Crash' (*BH* 11[2008] 125–48); Catherine Waters, '"Fairy Palaces" and "Wonderful Toys": Machine Dreams in Household Words' (*DQu* 25:iv[2008] 215–31); Rachel Sagner Buurma, 'Ephemeral Forms: E.S. Dallas, Novel Reading, and the New Victorian Review' (*ELN* 46:i[2008] 119–25); Reinhard Zimmermann, 'Law Journals in Nineteenth-Century Scotland' (*Edinburgh Law Review* 12[2008] 9–25); Stevan Vogenauer, 'Law Journals in Nineteenth-Century England' (*Edinburgh Law Review* 12[2008] 26–50); Arlene Young, '"Entirely a Woman's Question"? Class, Gender, and the Victorian Nurse' (*JVC* 13:i[2008] 18–41); Toni Weller, 'Preserving Knowledge through Popular Victorian Periodicals: An Examination of *The Penny Magazine* and the *Illustrated London News*, 1842–1843' (*LH* 24:iii[2008] 200–7); Rhoda Desbordes, 'Representing "Informal Empire" in the Nineteenth Century: Reuters in South America at the Time of the War of the Pacific, 1879–83' (*MedHis* 14:ii[2008] 121–40); Suzanne Rintoul, 'Intimate Violence and the Tenuous Boundaries of Class in Victorian Street Literature' (*VIJ* 36[2008] 79–102); Laurie Garrison, 'The Seduction of Seeing in M.E. Braddon's *Eleanor's Victory*: Visual Technology, Sexuality, and the Evocative Publishing Context of *Once a Week*' (*VLC* 36:i[2008] 111–30); Jennifer M. Regan, '"We Could Be Of Service to other Suffering People": Representations of India in the Irish Nationalist Press, c.1857–1887' (*VPR* 41:i[2008] 61–77); Patrick Scott, 'Body-Building and Empire-Building: George Douglas Brown, the South African War, and *Sandow's Magazine of Physical Culture*' (*VPR* 41:i[2008] 78–94); Andrea Broomfield, 'Rushing Dinner to the Table: The *Englishwoman's Domestic Magazine* and Industrialization's Effects on Middle-Class Food and Cooking, 1852–1860' (*VPR* 41:ii[2008] 101–23); K.G. Valente, '"Who will explain the explanation?": The Ambivalent Reception of Higher Dimensional Space in the British Spiritualist Press, 1875–1900' (*VPR* 41:ii[2008] 124–49); Scott Banville, '*Ally Sloper's Half-Holiday*: The Geography of Class in Late-Victorian Britain' (*VPR* 41:ii[2008] 150–73); Edward Jacobs, 'The Politicization of Everyday Life in *Cleave's Weekly Police Gazette* (1834–36)' (*VPR* 41:iii[2008] 225–47); Megan Ward, '"A charm in those fingers": Patterns, Taste, and the *Englishwoman's Domestic*' (*VPR* 41:iii[2008] 248–69); Kimberley Morse Jones, 'Bibliography of the New Art Criticism of Elizabeth Robins Pennell (1890–95)' (*VPR* 41:iii[2008] 270–87); David H. and Deirdre C. Stam, 'Bending Time: The Function of Periodicals in Nineteenth-Century Polar Naval Expeditions' (*VPR* 41:iv[2008] 301–22); Pamela Fletcher and Anne Helmreich, 'The Periodical and the Art Market: Investigating the "Dealer-Critic" System' in Victorian England' (*VPR* 41:iv[2008] 323–51); Matthew McIntire, 'Odds, Intelligence, and Prophecies: Racing News in the Penny Press, 1855–1914' (*VPR* 41:iv[2008] 352–73); Natalie M. Houston, 'Newspaper Poems: Material Texts in the Public Sphere' (*VS* 50:ii[2008] 233–42); Georgina O'Brien Hill, '"Above the breath of suspicion": Florence Marryat and the Shadow of the Fraudulent Trance Medium' (*WW* 15:iii[2008] 333–47); John Oliphant, '"Touching the light": The Invention of Literacy for the Blind' (*Paedagogica Historica* 44:i–ii[2008] 67–82).

Books Reviewed

Acheraiou, Amar. *Rethinking Postcolonialism: Colonialist Discourse in Modern Literatures and the Legacy of Classical Writers*. Palgrave Macmillan. [2008] pp. 250. £50 ISBN 9 7802 3055 2050.

Adamson, Alan H. *Mr. Charlotte Brontë: The Life of Arthur Bell Nicholls*. McG-QUP. [2008] pp. 188. £18.99 ISBN 9 7807 7353 3653.

Alber, Jan. *Narrating the Prison: Role and Representation in Charles Dickens' Novels: Twentieth-Century Fiction and Film*. Cambria Press. [2008] pp. 295. $94.95 ISBN 1 9340 4360 5.

Allen, Charles. *Kipling Sahib: India and the Making of Rudyard Kipling 1865–1900*. Little, Brown. [2008] pp. 448. £20 ISBN 9 7803 1672 6559.

Allen, Michelle. *Cleansing the City: Sanitary Geographies in Victorian London*. OhioUP. [2008] pp. 232. hb £47.95 ISBN 9 7808 2141 7706, pb £23.95 ISBN 9 7808 2141 7713.

Allen, Richard C., and Stephen Regan, eds. *Irelands of the Mind: Memory and Identity in Modern Irish Culture*. CambridgeSP. [2008] pp. 240. £34.99 ISBN 9 7818 4718 4221.

Amigoni, David. *Colonies, Cults and Evolution: Literature, Science and Culture in Nineteenth-Century Writing*. CUP. [2007] pp. 254. £50 ISBN 9 7805 2188 4587.

Ardis, Ann, and Patrick Collier, eds. *Transatlantic Print Culture, 1880–1940: Emerging Media, Emerging Modernism*. Palgrave Macmillan. [2008] pp. 259. £50 ISBN 9 7802 3055 4269.

Armstrong, Isobel. *Victorian Glassworlds: Glass Culture and the Imagination 1830–1880*. OUP. [2008] pp. 472. $60 ISBN 9 7801 9920 5202.

Atkinson, Damian. *The Letters of William Ernest Henley to Robert Louis Stevenson*. Rivendale Press. [2008] pp. 400. $75 ISBN 1 9072 0111 3.

Baker, William, Andrew Gasson, Graham Law, and Paul Lewis. *The Collected Letters of Wilkie Collins: Addenda and Corregenda (4)*. Wilkie Collins Society. [2008] pp. 32. £2.

Barton, Anna. *Tennyson's Name: Identity and Responsibility in the Work of Alfred Lord Tennyson*. Ashgate. [2008] pp. 166. £55 ISBN 9 7807 5466 4086.

Bashford, Christina. *The Pursuit of High Culture: John Ella and Chamber Music in Victorian London*. Boydell. [2007] pp. xiv + 410. £50 ISBN 9 7818 4383 2980.

Bonnell, Thomas F. *The Disreputable Trade: Publishing the Classics of English Poetry, 1765–1810*. OUP. [2008] pp. 387. £50 ISBN 9 7801 9953 2209.

Boos, Florence, ed. *Working-Class Women Poets in Victorian Britain: An Anthology*. Broadview. [2008] pp. 363. $32.95 ISBN 9 7815 5111 5962.

Bostridge, Mark. *Florence Nightingale: The Making of an Icon*. FS&G. [2008] pp. 672. $35 ISBN 9 7803 7415 6657.

Bridgham, Elizabeth A. *Spaces of the Sacred and Profane: Dickens, Trollope, and the Victorian Cathedral Town*. Routledge. [2008] pp. 192. $95 ISBN 0 4159 7952 8.

Briggs, Julia, Dennis Butts, and M.O. Grenby, eds. *Popular Children's Literature in Britain*. Ashgate. [2008] pp. 342. £55 ISBN 9 7818 4014 2426.

Bristow, Joseph, ed. *Oscar Wilde and Modern Culture: The Making of a Legend*. OhioUP. [2008] pp. xliv + 356. $28.95 ISBN 9 7808 2141 8383.

Brock, William H. *William Crookes (1832–1919) and the Commercialization of Science*. Ashgate. [2008] pp. 556. £65 ISBN 9 7807 5466 3225.

Burkhardt, Frederick, et al., eds. *The Correspondence of Charles Darwin*. vol. 16: part 1: January–June 1868, part 2: *July–December 1868*. CUP. [2008] pp. 1,312. £160 ISBN 9 7805 2151 8369.

Cain, Lynn. *Dickens, Family, Authorship: Psychoanalytic Perspectives on Kinship and Creativity*. The Nineteenth Century. Ashgate. [2008] pp. 202. $99.95 ISBN 9 7807 5466 1801.

Campbell, Kate. *Matthew Arnold*. Northcote. [2008] pp. 132. £12.99 ISBN 9 7807 4630 9469.

Cardwell, Margaret, ed. *Great Expectations*, by Charles Dickens, introd. Robert Douglas-Fairhurst. OUP. [2008] pp. 482. $9.95 ISBN 9 7801 9921 9766.

Carpenter, Humphrey. *The Seven Lives of John Murray: The Story of a Publishing Dynasty, 1768–2002*. Murray. [2008] pp. 370. £25 ISBN 9 7807 1956 5328.

Case, Alison, and Harry E. Shaw. *Reading the Nineteenth-Century Novel: Austen to Eliot*. Blackwell. [2008] pp. 224. $34.95 ISBN 0 6312 3143 9.

Cavell, Janice. *Tracing the Connected Narrative: Arctic Exploration in British Print Culture 1818–1860*. UTorP. [2008] pp. 329. £40 ISBN 9 7808 0209 2809.

Christie, William, ed. *The Letters of Francis Jeffrey to Thomas and Jane Welsh Carlyle*. P&C. [2008] pp. 250. $215 ISBN 9 7818 5196 9821.

Collini, Stefan. *Matthew Arnold: A Critical Portrait*. OUP. [2008] pp. 156. £17 ISBN 9 7801 9954 1881.

Davis, Philip. *Why Victorian Literature Still Matters*. Wiley-Blackwell. [2008] pp. viii + 172. pb £14.99 ISBN 9 7814 0513 5795.

Denisoff, Dennis, ed. *The Nineteenth-Century Child and Consumer Culture*. Ashgate. [2008] pp. 252. £55 ISBN 9 7807 5466 1566.

Dillon, Sarah. *The Palimpsest: Literature, Criticism, Theory*. Continuum. [2007] pp. x + 164. £60 ISBN 9 7808 2649 5457.

Distiller, Natasha. *Desire and Gender in the Sonnet Tradition*. Palgrave. [2008] pp. 232. £45 ISBN 9 7802 3053 5633.

Duquette, Natasha, ed. *Sublimer Aspects: Interfaces Between Literature, Aesthetics, and Theology*. CambridgeSP. [2008] pp. 240. £34.99 ISBN 9 7818 4718 3361.

Eighteen-Bisang, Robert, and Elizabeth Miller, eds. *Bram Stoker's Notes for Dracula: A Facsimile Edition*. McFarland. [2208] pp. 331. $65 ISBN 0 7864 3410 4.

Eliot, George. *Adam Bede*. OUP. [2008] pp. 624. £6.99 ISBN 9 7801 9920 3475.

Endersby, Jim. *Imperial Nature: Joseph Hooker and the Practices of Victorian Science*. UChicP. [2008] pp. 400. £18 ISBN 0 2262 0791 9.

Engels, Eve-Marie, and Thomas F. Glick. *The Reception of Charles Darwin in Europe*, 2 vols. Continuum. [2008] vol. 1: pp. lxxii + 328, vol. 2: pp. x + 659. $395 ISBN 9 7808 2645 8339.

Feeney, Joseph F. *The Playfulness of Gerard Manley Hopkins*. Ashgate. [2008] pp. 206. £55 ISBN 9 7807 5466 0057.

Fegan, Melissa. *Wuthering Heights: Character Studies*. Continuum. [2008] pp. xii + 130. $15.56 ISBN 9 7808 2649 3460.

Fiske, Shanyn. *Heretical Hellenism: Women Writers, Ancient Greece, and the Victorian Popular Imagination*. OhioUP. [2008] pp. 262. $39.95 ISBN 0 8214 1817 3.

Ford, Ronald (collected, and annotated). *The Letters of Bernard Shaw to The Times*. foreword by Michel W. Pharand. IAP. [2007] pp. xii + 316. $32 ISBN 9 7807 1652 9194.

Foulkes, Richard, ed. *Henry Irving: A Re-evaluation of the Pre-eminent Victorian Actor-Manager*. Ashgate. [2008] pp. 212. £55 ISBN 9 7807 5465 8290.

Franklin, J. Jeffrey. *The Lotus and the Lion: Buddhism and the British Empire*. CornUP. [2008] pp. 273. £19.50 ISBN 9 7808 0144 7303.

Fraser, Robert, and Mary Hammond, eds. *Books Without Borders, vol. 1: The Cross-National Dimensions in Print Culture*. Palgrave. [2008] pp. 210. £45 ISBN 9 7802 3021 0295.

Fraser, Robert, and Mary Hammond, eds. *Books Without Borders, vol. 2: Perspectives from South Asia*. Palgrave. [2008] pp. 204. £45 ISBN 9 7802 3021 0332.

Fredeman, William E., ed. *The Correspondence of Dante Gabriel Rossetti: The Last Decade 1873–1882, vol. 6: Kelmscott to Birchington 1873–1874*. Brewer. [2006] pp. xl + 646. £125 ISBN 1 8438 4060 X.

Fredeman, William E., ed. *The Correspondence of Dante Gabriel Rossetti. The Last Decade, 1873–1882, vol. 7: Kelmscott to Birchington 1875–1877*. Brewer. [2008] pp. 428. £125 ISBN 9 7818 4384 1340.

Friedman, Stanley, et al., eds. *Dickens Studies Annual Essays on Victorian Fiction*, vol. 39. AMS. [2008] pp. xii + 454. £162.50 ISBN 9 7804 0418 9396.

Gavin, Adrienne E., ed. *Paul Ferroll: A Tale*, by Caroline Clive. Valancourt Books. [2008] pp. xl + 256. $18.95 ISBN 9 7819 3455 5.

Gay, Penny, Judith Johnston, and Catherine Waters, eds. *Victorian Turns, NeoVictorian Returns: Essays on Fiction and Culture*. CambridgeSP. [2008] pp. 240. £35 ISBN 1 8471 8662 9.

Gómez Reus, Teresa, and Aránzazu Usandizaga, eds. *Inside Out: Women Negotiating, Subverting, Appropriating Public and Private Space*. Rodopi. [2008] pp. 365. £73 ISBN 9 7890 4202 4410.

Grafe, Adrian, ed. *Ecstasy and Understanding Religious Awareness in English Poetry from the Late Victorian to the Modern Period*. Continuum. [2008] pp. 183. £60 ISBN 9 7808 2649 8649.

Graham, Peter W. *Jane Austen and Charles Darwin: Naturalists and Novelists*. Ashgate. [2008] pp. 214. $99.95 ISBN 9 7807 5465 8511.

Gray, William. *Death and Fantasy: Essays on Philip Pullman, C.S. Lewis, George MacDonald and R.L. Stevenson*. CambridgeSP. [2008] pp. 122. $49.99 ISBN 9 7818 4718 8717.

Hagan, Sandra, and Juliette Wells, eds. *The Brontës in the World of the Arts*. Ashgate. [2008] pp. 256. £55 ISBN 0 7546 5752 3.

Hanes, Susan R. *Wilkie Collins's American Tour, 1873 –4.* P&C. [2008] pp. 155. £60 ISBN 9 7818 5196 9685.

Hansson, Heidi, ed. *New Contexts: Re-framing Nineteenth-Century Irish Women's Prose.* CorkUP. [2008] pp. vii + 208. £25 ISBN 9 7818 5918 4165.

Hardy, Barbara. *Dickens and Creativity.* Continuum. [2008] pp. 181. $39.95 ISBN 9 7818 4706 4592.

Harris, Jason Marc. *Folklore and the Fantastic in Nineteenth-Century British Fiction.* Ashgate. [2008] pp. 248. £55.00 ISBN 978-0-7546-5766-8.

Hartley, Jenny. *Charles Dickens and the House of Fallen Women.* Methuen. [2008] pp. xvi + 287. £17.99 ISBN 9 7804 1377 6433.

Havholm, Peter. *Politics and Awe in Rudyard Kipling's Fiction.* Ashgate. [2008] pp. 204. $99.95 ISBN 9 7807 5466 1641.

Hebblethwaite, Kate, ed. *The Jewel of Seven Stars*, by Bram Stoker. Penguin. [2008] pp. 320. £8.99 ISBN 9 7801 4144 2211.

Hedgecock, Jennifer. *The Femme Fatale in Victorian Literature: The Danger and the Sexual Threat.* Cambria Press. [2008] pp. xiv + 230. £61.95. ISBN 9 7816 0497 5185.

Helsinger, Elizabeth K. *Poetry and the Pre-Raphaelite Arts: Dante Gabriel Rossetti and William Morris.* YaleUP. [2008] pp. 352. £30 ISBN 9 7803 0012 2732.

Henry, Nancy. *The Cambridge Introduction to George Eliot.* CUP. [2008] pp. 142. $19.99 ISBN 9 7805 2167 0975.

Hertel, Ralf, and Manfred Pfister. *Performing National Identity: Anglo-Italian Cultural Transactions.* Rodopi. [2008] pp. 332. £46 ISBN 9 7890 4202 3147.

Hinks, John, and Catherine Armstrong, eds. *Book Trade Connections from the Seventeenth to the Twentieth Centuries.* OakK/BL. [2008] pp. 265. £25 ISBN 9 7815 8456 2290.

Hirschmann, Edwin. *Robert Knight: Reforming Editor in Victorian India.* OUP. [2008] pp. 272. £21.99 ISBN 0 1956 9622 0.

Holmes, Tim, ed. *Mapping the Magazine: Comparative Studies in Magazine Journalism.* Routledge. [2008] pp. 156. £70 ISBN 9 7804 1549 4984.

Horatschek, Anna-Margaretha, Susanne Bach, Stefan Glomb, and Stefan Horlacher, eds. *Literatur und Lebenskunst: Reflexionen zum guten Leben im britischen Roman vom Viktorianismus zur Postmoderne.* [Literature and the Art of Life: reflections on the good life in the British novel from the Victorians to the Post-Moderns]. WVT. [2008] pp. 324. €32 ISBN 9 7838 6821 0064.

Hubbard, Tom, Rikky Rooksby, and Edward Wakeling, eds. *Lives of Victorian Literary Figures, vol. 6: Lewis Carroll, Robert Louis Stevenson and Algernon Charles Swinburne by their Contemporaries.* P&C. [2008] pp. 1,213. £275 ISBN 9 7818 5196 9050.

Huguet, Christine, ed. *Spellbound, George Gissing: A Twenty-First Century Reappraisal.* Equilibris. [2008] pp. 384. hb £99 ISBN 9 7890 5976 0073, pb £67 ISBN 9 7890 5976 0080.

Humpherys, Anne, and Louis James, eds. *G.W.M. Reynolds: Nineteenth-Century Fiction, Politics, and the Press.* Ashgate. [2008] pp. 296. £55 ISBN 9 7807 5465 8542.

Jenkins, Alice, ed. *Michael Faraday's Mental Exercises: An Artisan Essay Circle in Regency London.* LiverUP. [2008] pp. 256. £45 ISBN 9 7818 4631 1406.

Jordan, John O., and Gordon Bigelow. *Approaches to Teaching Dickens's Bleak House.* MLA. [2008] pp. vii + 230. $19.75 ISBN 9 7816 0329 0142.

Kamm, Antony. *Scottish Printed Books, 1508–2008.* Sandstone/NLS. [2008] pp. 51. £5.99 ISBN 9 7819 0520 7213.

Kehoe, Elisabeth. *Ireland's Misfortune: The Turbulent Life of Kitty O'Shea.* Atlantic Books. [2008] pp. 608. £19.99 ISBN 9 7818 4354 4869.

Khattak, Shahin Kuli Khan. *Islam and the Victorians: Nineteenth-Century Perceptions of Muslim Practices and Beliefs.* Tauris Academic Studies. [2008] pp. 205. £47.50 ISBN 9 7818 4511 4299.

LaMonaca, Maria. *Masked Atheism: Catholicism and the Secular Victorian Home.* OSUP. [2008] pp. 231. £35 ISBN 9 7808 1421 0840.

Law, Graham, and Andrew Maunder. *Willkie Collins: A Literary Life.* Palgrave Macmillan. [2008] pp. 240. £45 ISBN 9 7814 0394 8960.

Law, Graham, and Andrew Maunder. *Wilkie Collins: A Literary Life.* Palgrave. [2008] pp. 214. £45 ISBN 1 4039 4896 8.

Levine, George. *How to Read the Victorian Novel.* Wiley-Blackwell. [2007] pp. 200. £50 ISBN 9 7814 0513 0554.

Levine, George. *Realism, Ethics and Secularism: Essays on Victorian Literature and Science.* CUP. [2008] pp. x + 284. $99 ISBN 9 7805 2188 5263.

Lewes, Darby, ed. *Double Vision: Literary Palimpsests of the Eighteenth and Nineteenth Centuries.* Lexington. [2008] pp. 296. £45 ISBN 9 7807 3912 5694.

Lianeri, Alexandra, and Vandra Zajko, eds. *Translation and the Classic: Identity as Change in the History of Culture.* OUP. [2008] pp. 440. £70 ISBN 9 7801 9928 8076.

Lysack, Krista. *Come Buy, Come Buy: Shopping and the Culture of Consumption in Victorian Women's Writing.* OhioUP. [2008] pp. 256. £24.50 ISBN 9 7808 2141 8116.

Mabilat, Claire. *Orientalism and Representations of Music in the Nineteenth-Century British Popular Arts.* Ashgate. [2008] pp. 252. £55 ISBN 9 7807 5465 9624.

Madden, Ed. *Tiresian Poetics: Modernism, Sexuality, Voice, 1888–2001.* FDUP. [2008] pp. 402. £72 ISBN 9 7808 3863 9375.

Manson, Cynthia DeMarcus. *The Fairy-Tale Literature of Charles Dickens, Christina Rossetti, and George MacDonald: Antidotes to the Victorian Spiritual Crisis.* Mellen. [2008] pp. 148. $99.95 ISBN 9 7807 7345 1025.

Mao, Douglas. *Fateful Beauty: Aesthetic Environments, Juvenile Development, and Literature 1860–1960.* PrincetonUP. [2008] pp. 332. £24.95 ISBN 9 7806 9113 3485.

Marcus, Steve. *The Other Victorians: A Study of Sexuality and Pornography in Mid-Nineteenth-Century England.* Transaction. [2008] pp. xxii + 292. pb £28.95 ISBN 9 7814 1280 8194.

Markwick, Margaret. *New Men in Trollope's Novels: Rewriting the Victorian Male.* The Nineteenth Century. Ashgate. [2007] pp. 228. $99.95 ISBN 9 7807 5465 7248.

Mason, Diane. *The Secret Vice: Masturbation in Victorian Fiction and Medical Culture*. ManUP. [2008] pp. viii + 184. £55 ISBN 9 7807 1907 7142.

Matthews, Hugoe, and Phyllis Treitel. *Richard Jefferies: An Index of Themes, Thoughts and Observations*. Petton Books. [2008] pp. 264. £15 ISBN 9 7809 5228 1320.

Maxwell, Catherine. *Second Sight: The Visionary Imagination in Late Victorian Literature*. ManUP. [2008] pp. 288. £55 ISBN 9 7807 1907 1447.

Mazzeno, Laurence W. *The Dickens Industry: Critical Perspectives, 1836–2005*. CamdenH. [2008] pp. 288. £40 ISBN 9 7815 7113 3175.

McAloon, Francis X. *The Language of Poetry as a Form of Prayer: The Theo-Poetic Aesthetics of Gerard Manley Hopkins*. Mellen. [2008] pp. 247. £107 ISBN 9 7807 7345 0226.

McGill, Meredith M., ed. *The Traffic in Poems: Nineteenth-Century Poetry and Transatlantic Exchange*. RutgersUP. [2008] pp. 276. £22.50 ISBN 9 7808 1354 2300.

McGrath, Francis J., ed. *The Letters and Diaries of John Henry Newman*, vol. 32: Supplement. OUP. [2008] pp. xvi + 731. £120 ISBN 9 7801 9953 2704.

Melnyk, Julie. *Victorian Religion: Faith and Life in Britain*. Praeger. [2008] pp. 232. £27.95 ISBN 9 7802 7599 1241.

Menke, Richard. *Telegraphic Realism: Victorian Fiction and Other Information Systems*. StanfordUP. [2008] pp. 321. £53.95 ISBN 0 8047 5691 9.

Miller, Andrew H. *The Burdens of Perfection: On Ethics and Reading in Nineteenth-Century British Literature*. CornUP. [2008] pp. 260. £21.95 ISBN 9 7808 0144 6610.

Moore, Lewis D. *The Fiction of George Gissing*. McFarland. [2008] pp. viii + 220. $39.95 ISBN 9780786435098.

Morse, Greg. *John Betjeman: Reading the Victorians*. SussexAP. [2008] pp. 272. $75 ISBN 9 7818 4519 2716.

Mulvey-Roberts, Marie, and with Steve Carpenter, eds. *The Collected Letters of Rosina Bulwer Lytton*. 3 vols. P&C. [2008] pp. 1,200. $520 ISBN 9 7818 5196 8039.

Murphy, Andrew. *Shakespeare for the People: Working Class Readers, 1800–1900*. CUP. [2008] pp. 258. $99 ISBN 9 7805 2186 1779.

Newton, K.M. *Modern Literature and the Tragic*. EdinUP. [2008] pp. 180. £50 ISBN 9 7807 4863 6730.

North, William. *The City of Jugglers; or, Free-Trade in Souls. A Romance of the 'Golden' Age*. USCP. [2008] pp. xvi + 256. $19.95 ISBN 9 7815 7003 8112.

Novak, Daniel A. *Realism, Photography, and Nineteenth-Century Fiction*. CUP. [2008] pp. xvi + 234. £50 ISBN 9 7805 2188 5256.

O'Brien, Mark. *The Irish Times: A History*. FCP. [2008] pp. 312. £30 ISBN 9 7818 4682 1233.

Oddie, William. *Chesterton and the Romance of Orthodoxy: The Making of GKC, 1874–1908*. OUP. [2008] pp. viii + 401. £25 ISBN 9 7801 9955 1651.

Oldfield, Sybil. *Jeanie, an 'Army of One': Mrs. Nassau Senior, 1828–1877, the First Woman in Whitehall*. SussexAP. [2008] pp. 348. $39.95 ISBN 1 8451 9254 0.

Otter, Chris. *The Victorian Eye: A Political History of Light and Vision in Britain, 1800–1910.* UChicP. [2008] pp. 362. hb £34 ISBN 9 7802 2664 0761, pb £13 ISBN 9 7802 2664 0778.

Paroissien, David, ed. *A Companion to Charles Dickens.* Blackwell. [2008] pp. xviii + 516. £110 ISBN 9 7814 0513 0974.

Paterson, Gary H. *At the Heart of the 1890s: Essays on Lionel Johnson.* AMS. [2008] pp. 175. £40 ISBN 9 7804 0464 4697.

Pearsall, Cornelia. *Tennyson's Rapture: Transformation in the Victorian Dramatic Monologue.* OUP. [2008] pp. 397. £40 ISBN 9 7801 9515 0544.

Plotz, John. *Portable Property: Victorian Culture on the Move.* PrincetonUP. [2008] pp. 268. £19.95 ISBN 9 7806 9113 5168.

Prince, Kathryn. *Shakespeare in the Victorian Periodicals.* Routledge. [2008] pp. 180. £65 ISBN 0 4159 6243 9.

Puckett, Kent. *Bad Form: Social Mistakes and the Nineteenth-Century Novel.* OUP. [2008] pp. 192. £23.99 ISBN 9 7801 9533 2759.

Radford, Andrew, and Mark Sandy, eds. *Romantic Echoes in the Victorian Era.* Ashgate. [2008] pp. 250. £55 ISBN 9 7807 5465 7880.

Ratcliffe, Sophie. *On Sympathy.* OUP. [2008] pp. 280. £56 ISBN 9 7801 9923 9870.

Rochelson, Meri-Jane. *A Jew in the Public Arena: The Career of Israel Zangwill.* WSUP. [2009] pp. 368. £32.95 ISBN 9 7808 1433 3440.

Rowland, Yana. *The Treatment of Themes of Mortality in the Poetry of the Brontë Sisters.* PlovdivUP. [2006] pp. 361. ISBN 9 7895 4423 3624.

Sabiston, Elizabeth. *Private Sphere to World Stage from Austen to Eliot.* Ashgate. [2008] pp. x + 214. £55 ISBN 9 7807 5466 1740.

Sikorska, Liliana, ed. *Medievalisms. The Poetics of Literary Re-reading.* Lang. [2007] pp. 229. £30 ISBN 9 7836 3157 2177.

Silverman, Willa Z. *The New Bibliopolis: French Book Collectors and the Culture of Print, 1880–1914.* UTorP. [2008] pp. 312. £48 ISBN 9 7808 0209 2113.

Smith, Karl Ashley. *Dickens and the Unreal City: Searching for Spiritual Significance in Nineteenth-Century London.* Palgrave Macmillan. [2008] pp. 256. £45 ISBN 9 7802 3054 5236.

Smith, Philip E., ed. *Approaches to Teaching the Works of Oscar Wilde.* MLA. [2008] pp. 350. £45 ISBN 9 7816 0329 0098.

Snyder, Carey J. *British Fiction and Cross-Cultural Encounters: Ethnographic Modernism from Wells to Woolf.* Palgrave Macmillan. [2008] pp. 264. pb £42.50 ISBN 9 7802 3060 2915.

Stetz, Margaret D., and Cheryl A. Wilson, eds. *Michael Field and their World.* Rivendale. [2007] pp. 256. £30 ISBN 9 7819 0420 1083.

Stevenson, Robert Louis. *Treasure Island.* introd. Patrick Scott. Signet. [2008] pp. vii + 204. pb £2.79 ISBN 9 7804 5153 0974.

Stray, Christopher, ed. *An American in Victorian Cambridge*, by Charles Astor Bristed. UExeP. [2008] pp. xxxviii + 422. hb £45, pb £16.99 ISBN 9 7808 5989 8256.

Sumpter, Caroline. *The Victorian Press and the Fairy Tale.* Palgrave. [2008] pp. 254. £50 ISBN 9 7802 3051 8056.

Thomas, Sue. *Imperialism, Reform, and the Making of Englishness in Jane Eyre*. Palgrave Macmillan. [2008] pp. 208. £45 ISBN 9 7802 3055 4252.

Thomas, Sue, ed. *Victorian Traffic: Identity, Exchange, Performance*. CambridgeSP. [2008] pp. 327. £40 ISBN 1 8471 8455 3.

Tucker, Herbert. *Epic: Britain's Heroic Muse 1790–1910*. OUP. [2008] pp. 737. £35 ISBN 9 7801 9923 2987.

Tufescu, Florina. *Oscar Wilde's Plagiarism: The Triumph of Art over Ego*. IAP. [2008] pp. viii + 198. £30 ISBN 9 7807 1652 9040.

van den Broek, Antonie Gerard, ed. *The Spanish Gypsy*, by George Eliot. P&C. [2008] pp. lxi + 451. £100 ISBN 9 7818 5196 8473.

Varty, Anne. *Children and Theatre in Victorian Britain: 'All Work, No Play'*. Palgrave. [2008] pp. 306. £50 ISBN 9 7802 3055 1558.

Vogeler, Martha S. *Austin Harrison and the English Review*. UMissP. [2008] pp. xviii + 326. £42.50 ISBN 9 7808 2621 8155.

Warwick, Alexandra, and Martin Willis, eds. *The Victorian Literature Handbook*. Continuum. [2008] pp. 258. £16.99 ISBN 9 7808 2649 5778.

Waters, Catherine. *Commodity Culture in Dickens's Household Words: The Social Life of Goods*. Ashgate. [2008] pp. 184. £50 ISBN 9 7807 5465 5787.

Watson, Greg, ed. *The State of Stylistics*. Rodopi. [2008] pp. xxii + 518. $140 ISBN 9 7890 4202 4281.

Watson, Tim. *Caribbean Culture and British Fiction in the Atlantic World, 1780–1870*. CUP. [2008] pp. 263. $99 ISBN 0 5218 7626 5.

Weyant, Nancy. *Annual Bibliographical Supplements to her 1992–2001 Annotated Guide to Secondary Language Sources on the Life and Works of Elizabeth Gaskell*. Updated every six months. See < http://library. bloomu.edu/weyant and http://www.nancyweyant.com/index.php/pages/ GaskellBibliography-Intro.html >.

Zimmerman, Virginia. *Excavating Victorians*. SUNY. [2008] pp. 231. £40.75 ISBN 9 7807 91472 2798.

XIV

Modern Literature

AARON JAFFE, ANDREW RADFORD, MARY GROVER,
SAM SLOTE, ANDREW HARRISON, BRYONY RANDALL,
NICK BENTLEY, REBECCA D'MONTE,
GRAHAM SAUNDERS, MATTHEW CREASY AND
MARIA JOHNSTON

This chapter has seven sections 1. General; 2 Pre-1945 Fiction; 3. Post-1945 Fiction; 4 Pre-1950 Drama; 5 Post-1950 Drama; 6. Pre-1950 Poetry. 7. Modern Irish Poetry. Section 1 is by Aaron Jaffe; section 2(a) is by Andrew Radford; section 2(b) is by Mary Grover; section 2(c) is by Sam Slote; section 2(d) is by Andrew Harrison; section 2(e) is by Bryony Randall; section 3 is by Nick Bentley; section 4 is by Rebecca D'Monte; section 5 is by Graham Saunders; section 6 is by Matthew Creasy; section 7 is by Maria Johnston.

1. General

The 'modern' takes one of the greediest slices of *The Year's Work in English Studies*. Because it telescopes into the contemporary—at least in this publication—the purview encompasses a century-plus spree of eventful and open-ended literary and cultural history with ever-expanding reference. English studies is already a capacious, elastic category, corroborated by a peek at the offerings in university English departments these days, where all sorts of literary and non-literary, Anglo and non-Anglo things are being 'read' and 'studied'. The work of scholars of English, it seems, is now more a matter of addition (more regions, more texts) than subtraction. Consequently, this reviewer has favoured books that try to reflect this expansive framework while attempting to shed some light on the conceptual conditions that define it.

This section continues, of course, to emphasize the British Isles as a geographical locus for scholarship as well to give special attention to literature as a particular object of study, but it also recognizes that the force of much recent work in the discipline has been to challenge any self-evident equation between English literature and English studies. Outside the reference shelves, it's a rare book that takes on a task as monumental as engaging the range of

Year's Work in English Studies, Volume 89 (2010) © *The English Association; all rights reserved*
doi:10.1093/ywes/maq015

anglophone twentieth-century literature with any claim to diachronic comprehensiveness. Century-spanning, literary-historical arguments are infrequent, overshadowed by an ongoing critical renaissance concerning the century's first decades—the so-called new modernist studies—and its multitude of heady, albeit largely synchronic, concerns. Nevertheless, if the early part of the century anamorphically distorts the image of the rest, there has been a palpable shift within modernist studies towards pressuring the category itself as it gives way to periodizing questions of lateness, post-ness, the contemporary, and the present. Here, the continued actuality and productivity of the disciplinary parameters of modernist studies as such should be noted—despite the recent protestations to the contrary by Susan Stanford Freidman in her 2009 keynote address to the Modernist Studies Association.

The two most obvious areas of general interest—the main ways for modern scholarship to 'go big'—continue to be found, first, in the turn to material culture and the archive, and, second, in attention to geopolitical and global-sociological factors. These tendencies themselves can be seen as impulses of temporal and spatial maximalism—an infinite archival regression and a literary canon expanded world-wide. In E.H. Gombrich's recently translated *A Little History of the World* [2005]—a book written for children in the 1930s—he suggests a fanciful image: the historical archive as a deep well with walls made of stacked documents, lit by falling embers of burning paper: 'Does all this looking down make you dizzy? [L]et's light a scrap of paper, and drop it down into that well. It will fall slowly, deeper and deeper. And as it burns it will light up the sides of the well. Can you see it? It's going down and down. Now it's so far down it's like a tiny star in the dark depths. it's getting smaller and smaller . . . and now it's gone' (p. 2). The moral is as unmistakable as it is ambivalent. Gombrich invites all would-be historicists to make a wish—but the counsel of fairy tales is also not far from view: beware of bottomless pits. More recently, in *Modernism and the Crisis of Sovereignty* the late Andrew John Miller has also cautioned us that utopian desires for an expanded critical framework—a 'postnational' world-wide archive—may be a side-effect of the vertiginous unravelling of community and location through globalization (pp. xx–xxi).

These tendencies necessarily underscore the urgency of criticism and commentary foregrounding scrutiny into their own interpretative conditions. In addition to the utopian desire for a pluralist, post-national world-wide archive, three other vectors of interest inform this year's work, which may pull in various directions: first, a continued injunction to 'return' to the aesthetic and a renewed interest in form, especially involving modernist vernaculars, to evoke Miriam Hansen's term; second, a broader stake in comprehensive forms of media studies and examining the systemic workings of cultural value; and, third, a kind of post post-theory laying down of arms, moving beyond the critical impasses of the much-discussed end of (poststructuralist) theory announced a few years back into new questions, debates and themes. Theory is finally dead; let the theorizing begin anew, without all the baggage (and resistances) of its uneven 1980s and 1990s reception. Stephen Ross's edited collection *Modernism and Theory: A Critical Debate* [2008] (Routledge), for example, registers the important and timely propositions that 'modernism and theory must be thought together' and that 'theory is modernism's key continuation' (pp. 2–3). Theoretical thinking and speculative writing not only have decided preoccupations with and orientations to modernist texts; they also follow distinctively modernist histories. In so far as English studies has been lately dominated by a certain pluralizing, historicist strain, it has often been leveraged on constraining or submerging this discourse.

Andrew John Miller's *Modernism and the Crisis of Sovereignty* provides an excellent example of an ambitious book at the forefront of these several concerns. Among other things, the book tries to push back on overly sanguine versions of global literature, 'pluralistic visions of a literature without boundaries'. Informed by Thomas Hobbes, Carl Schmitt and Giorgio Agamben, it examines W.B. Yeats, Virginia Woolf, and T.S. Eliot as 'postnational' writers, 'who, faced with the proliferation of multiple "social imaginaries", come to conceive of their respective geopolitical situations by means of "provisional strategies" rather than by means of an essentializing vision of national unity centered on the state apparatus' (p. 167). As the author puts it, the modernists were haunted by the contradictions of affiliation and association in a political situation defined by a continuous state of emergency that developed during the First World War. Firm demarcations between war and peace (and between interiority and exteriority) no longer worked; integrity of identity and territory became at once superfluous and unremitting; and, Yeats, Woolf, Eliot and other modernists (whom Miller understands in terms of their 'complexly mediated textual and institutional afterlives') were enmeshed in a perpetual, cosmopolitical crisis of sovereign power, from which we have not yet emerged. The thoughtful discussion of the importance of recognizing situations in which, in Dominick LaCapra's words, 'the interpreter is implicated in the temporal processes interpreted' is worth a look for anyone trying to understand the problems of modern literary history (pp. 7–15). Among the numerous smart things found in this book, two strong chapters on Yeats stand out in particular. Here, Miller provides a visionary reformulation of Yeats's politics and poetics that asks us to reconsider his investment in the invention of the Irish nation in the light of Ireland's 'anomalous geopolitical situation' (recalling Seamus Deane), where he 'found himself compelled to negotiate the permeable boundaries of state and individual sovereignty' (p. 153). Even though the book centres on three well-established literary monuments, Miller's argument usefully maps a new way of conceptualizing the relationship between modernism and politics. This innovative scholar died young in 2009, and will be missed.

David Wills's *Dorsality: Thinking Back through Technology and Politics* (Minnesota) also pursues an inventive, complex, and theoretically attuned project, again drawing significantly on a second look at the theory corpus. Following through on Ross's insistence that modernism and theory be read co-extensively and in mutually illuminating ways, Wills draws together striking juxtapositions of writers and philosophers (Heidegger, Lévinas, Joyce, Broch, Schmitt, Derrida, Benjamin, Sade and Nietzsche) and themes (houses, oceans, walking, throwaway lines, castaways) paying off on the book's Heideggerian sense of poetry doubling back on thinking. From each of these figures, he isolates an arresting, inventive instance of 'dorsality', an embodied reflex leading to speculation about what lies behind the relation between humanity and technology:

> The turn would be the deviation that occurs—naturally as it were—within the seemingly automatic advance of ambulation or locomotion. It turns as it walks. Technology as mechanicity is located—not for the first time but in a particularly explicit way, that is to say, as fundamental relation to the earth as exteriority—in the step.... The particular importance of the privilege I am giving to the turn resides ... in its sense of a departure that is also a detour, a deviation, a divergence into difference. We will imagine the human turning as it walks, deviating from its forward path in order, precisely to move forward, advancing necessarily askew. To repeat: the turn is the deviation from itself by means of which the human, in being or 'moving' simply human, is understood to become technological. (p. 4)

The aphoristic, gnomic style Wills employs may not be everyone's cup of tea, but it leads him to some striking claims. As one reviewer noted, the force of his book is that he 'win[s], perhaps for good, the race backwards to decide when we first became posthuman' by pinning it to our first steps as bipeds (< http://reconstruction.eserver.org/092/willsreview.shtml >). For Wills, this primal lurch as a kind of natural technology points to the paradox that we are most essentially human as we fall back on technologies. Technology—and perhaps, modernity, too, though he does not say this—thus stands not before humanity, but always behind it, over its shoulder, so to speak.

Reading Joyce's *Ulysses* alongside Broch's *Death of Virgil* leads Wills to an engrossing discussion of literature and the ethics of exile and homecoming. 'The throwaway—element and operation of signification within a work of fiction—is', he writes, 'like the castaway, in exile, at a loss for home and country' (p. 88). It is, he explains,

> less about narrative origin and control than about the far more complex and vexed question of the destination and limits of textual signification in general, but it demonstrates how in *Ulysses*...those two effects become intertwined. We no longer have a coherent or homogenous narrative voice directing the outflow of signifying elements; indeed, narratorial effects get caught up within the vagaries of signification in general. Thus when Bloom flings away his wooden pen after writing "I am a", the reader is cast back to the Bloom who, about to throw away his newspaper, has it intercepted by Bantam Lyons...Narratorial voice, and finally signification in general, are thrown away in *Ulysses* to the extent of being cast away, castaways as in Mallarmé's *Throw of the Dice*, shipwrecked, like Ulysses or Odysseus, far from home. (p. 86)

At another point in *Dorsality*, he ties the 'dorsal turn' to this peculiar enterprise of literary criticism itself: 'Commentary comes from after or from behind to put a new face on the work it refers to; it rewrites the natural or creative function as a techno-rhetorical one; and it ruptures the self-identity of the work, exposing it to oceanic drift' (p. 104). Commentary (criticism, analysis, interpretation) serves as a 'natural technology' of the literary, an oceanic drift which lands Bloomian flotsam on our beachheads, whereas 'current historicist approaches to literature inasmuch as they presume a nonliterary literal before and after the textual...cross the ocean to better ignore it' (p. 104).

In *Stalking the Subject: Modernism and the Animal*, Carrie Rohman comes at post-humanities themes differently from Wills but from an approach similarly oblique—namely, animal studies. Rohman identifies animal studies as 'a new discipline surrounding the cultural and discursive significance of animality and its relationship to Western metaphysics and humanist discourses' (p. 1). Animals are more than another trendy literary theme (standing somewhere in queue with other uncanny subjects like cyborgs, ghosts, cannibals, pirates, zombies, and so on) for literary historicists to contemplate changes in 'human assumptions and anxieties', because, according to Rohman, they bring immanent methodological and theoretical matters to the fore, developed elsewhere by Deleuze and Guattari, Derrida, Elizabeth Grosz and Cary Wolfe. '[A]nimal studies', she writes, 'emerges from the legacy of poststructuralism and its attendant analysis of subject-formation, at the same time as its interest in the radically "other" pushes the recent "turn to ethics" in literary studies beyond the familiar boundaries of the human' (pp. 8–9). Following suit, what's strong about her approach is a willingness to interpret literary texts (Charles Darwin, Sigmund Freud, Joseph Conrad, H.G. Wells, D.H. Lawrence, Djuna Barnes) not merely as ideological dress-up—symptoms of repressed and marginalized animality—but as canny, theoretical collaborators, as it were, in rewriting or de-sublimating the discourse of species. The framing of the book's argument in the context of early British modernism is welcome, if largely underexamined. It has something to do with the literary reception of Darwinian science in England and thus the importance of Wells. In his *The Island of Dr. Moreau*, he was 'among the first...to thematize clearly the post-Darwinian uncertainty [about] the human subject's stability in relation to its species status' (p. 64).

Strange things happen to the formation of the 'subject' in the early twentieth century, and, by implication, literary history of this period does not hold with accounts of subject formation that end things unproblematically in the nineteenth century or earlier. New dilemmas about animality are one place in which evidence for this can be seen. Another is in a new prominence for 'eccentricities of public life', as Justus Nieland puts it in the subtitle to his excellent book *Feeling Modern: The Eccentricities of Public Life*, vehicles for minimal subjectivity, mass-mediated expressions of oddballism, and quirky and cranky behaviour launched into the erratic, queer and eccentric orbits of modern public space (or, 'publicness', as he prefers to call it). Nieland's is the last of the four books in this year's work that bear witness to a continued centrality of theory to the ambitions of literary studies. Like several of the others, it engages significantly with Agamben, as it U-turns from many received commonplaces about subjectivity and personhood. Borrowing also from Benjamin, Arendt and Kracauer, the book serves up a heady and surprisingly potable stew of literary and film studies and some really smart revisionist cultural excavation. 'How did modernism understand the demands placed on emotional life by the new, and increasingly mediated, forms of early-twentieth-century public life?' Nieland asks (p. 2). For answers he looks to modernist eccentrics like Wyndham Lewis, Nathanael West, Djuna Barnes and E.E. Cummings; film icons like Charlie Chaplin and Sergei Eisenstein; and visual artists like Joseph Cornell and Marsden Hartley—discussing their responses to such lively arts as vaudeville, cartoons, dance and music hall, and slapstick. From this material, these figures fashioned an alternative language of affect, 'a curious marriage of intimate feeling and impersonality', for coping with the privations of exposed creaturely life (p. 25). In a sense, Nieland addresses much the same landscape as Miller—the state of exception and the fate of the subject of modernist art—but does so employing a far more thoroughgoing account of the scope of modernism's manifold cultural investments. These motives remain idealist to the last. In popular forms, modernism found a way to lead public life to a reparative higher ground based on sentimentalism, sympathy and intimacy. Perhaps, he overplays his hand somewhat when indicting the materialist turn in modernist studies, though: 'modernism's sublunary relocation has seemed particularly pressing to critics and has rewarded them amply with the tasty ironies attending this rebirth into telluric context' (p. 5). Implicated in these sublunary tendencies, *Feeling Modern* shows how sedulously attending to the affective textures of the sublunary arts seriously jacks up their legitimacy. Tasty ironies, indeed. The conceptual heavy lifting needed to teach modernism to come to terms with how it feels requires no less than re-legitimating modern public space.

Yet the discovery by modernist studies of material culture—'modernism's sublunary relocation'—continues apace. If Nieland's book shows the unceasing scholarly potential of studying modernist subjects and subjectivities, Elizabeth Outka's *Consuming Traditions: Modernity, Modernism, and the Commodified Aesthetic* shows further possibilities when attending to modernist objects and commodities. Outka, like Nieland, is worried about overcoming the stubbornly entrenched moral agonistics of high and low. Or, as she has it, the dynamics of authenticity and artifice:

> [W]e are adept at (and often smug about) unmasking the commerce behind the facade: the distressed furniture is not really old, the soft-lit reproduction of the villager's house hides the economic hardships that were found there, and at the very least, that new soft sweater is unlikely to deliver the sophisticated atmosphere from the catalogue. Such exposure is important and ongoing critical work, but the rush to condemn (or at least ironically smirk) has limited a critical investigation of either the history of such marketing or its powerful allures. (p. 5)

Focusing on E.M. Forster, Henry James, H.G. Wells, early Virginia Woolf and other *Literature in Transition* authors, Outka tries to do aesthetic justice to the pervasiveness of the modern allure of authenticity, heritage and nostalgia—especially the way in which these cultural values encode gender trouble and class aspiration—without being smug or smirking, building in this regard on the exemplary work of Jennifer Wicke and Rachel Bowlby. The chapter on Selfridges stands out, a really stellar mixture of cultural history and literary criticism. Outka's interest is both the 'urge to construct, buy, reproduce, package, and sell a range of images and ideas clustered around authenticity' and the 'new literary works that recognized, critiqued, and exploited the phenomenon for innovative literary ends' (p. 5). The paradox, which she dusts off through analysis of department store windows, model towns, ideal homes and suburban sprawl, lies in a message to 'Purchase the right object, build the right building, preserve the right relic, and one might possess an appealing aura of the past, maintain a sense of authentic tradition, and, by one's very participation in the novel production of such spaces and things, simultaneously be new, up-to-date, fashionable' (p. 7).

Both Nieland and Outka in their own ways are keen to formulate new syntheses about modern problems of style and matter, but it makes sense to this reviewer to think about both projects sharing in new efforts to understand the relation between the aesthetic artefact and emerging audience structures, networks which were often expressly non-literary, such as music-hall spectatorship and shop-window gazing. Continuing along these lines brings us to *The Modern Girl Around the World: Consumption, Modernity, and Globalization*, a pioneering collection edited by a research collective of University of Washington professors in the humanities and social sciences (the Modern Girl Around the World Research Group). In this case, the editors pursue a highly original method of cultural phenomenology in order to explore a particularly world-spanning form of the commodity aesthetic: the simultaneous invention and manifold meaning of 'the modern girl' in the 1920s and 1930s. Pursuing two research questions about this modernist vernacular form over a period of years—'How was the Modern Girl global? And what made her so?'—the editors treat the Modern Girl as a 'heuristic device', a means of 'serving to find out or discover' many things about aesthetic culture, globalism, globalization, nationalist and post-nationalist politics, micro- and macro-history, colonialism and postcolonialism, power, gender, modernity and cultural and sociological method itself (pp. 2–3). The topic, and the book's status as a collaboratively edited project, allow for the uncommon combination of detailed analysis and comprehensive claims about what the editors call the 'multidirectional citation' of this vernacular form of modernity, which simultaneously produces actual historical agents all over the globe and conveys ways and means for the consumption of their representations.

Under the rubric of audience structure and communication networks, two other notable books appeared: Ned Schantz's *Gossip, Letters, Phones: The Scandals of Female Networks in Film and Literature* and Stefan Collini's *Common Reading: Critics, Historians, Publics*. Schantz's clever monograph is more modestly sized, but, thematically speaking, it pairs surprisingly well with *The Modern Girl Around the World*. 'Picture an old girls' network', he writes: 'Picture women using whatever resources they have at their disposal to support and promote each other—not in any Utopia or sheltered enclave, but in the modern world as it developed since the eighteenth century' (p. 3). One wonders what kind of historical continuities exist between this old girls' network— convincingly linked to the hidden narrative circuitry of private life, sympathy, gossip and identification wired into the British novel—and the post-literary, global boom of 'it' girl culture discussed by the Modern Girl collective and even more recently in Judith Brown's *Glamour in Six Dimensions: Modernism and the Radiance of Form* (Cornell [2009]). Can one make the case for the latter being leveraged over the ruins of the former? Schantz, for one, won't say, leaping from the aged chestnuts of the English novel canon (*Clarissa, Emma, Middlemarch*) to popular narrative films of more recent provenance (*Pillow Talk, You've Got Mail, The Terminator, Bound*). Here finally, *pace* Friedman's call to arms, is an example of that vaunted modernism without modernism, although Schantz's engagement with Friedrich Kittler, the important theorist of modernism, suggests where one might go to begin connecting the dots about when and where 'the rhythm of modernity bounces its female subject back and forth between the typewriter and the cinema' (pp. 55–6).

Stefan Collini's *Common Reading* is the only book included here that actually covers the purported historical span of this section: 'the literary and intellectual culture of Britain from, roughly, the early nineteenth century to the present' (p. 1). That Collini is an eminent intellectual historian trying to write in a hybrid of academic and non-academic styles is telling; his interests and tone usefully avoid the sticky patches and constitutive myopia of practical criticism. Thus you won't find too many close readings of literary texts. Instead, the author narrows his subject by turning again and again on a single problem: how do writer-intellectuals contribute to the invention of their readership? The book, he explains, could be thought of as recounting the journey of the person (formerly man) of letters in the twentieth century, producing non-academic non-fiction written seriously and thoughtfully for a readership of non-academics. It necessarily touches on, in Collini's words, 'the fate of "general" periodicals, the history of reading, the role of criticism, changing conceptions of "culture", the limitation of biography, and the function of universities' (p. 1). Indeed, form follows function, as Collini himself tries to 'sail a course between the rocks of journalistic superficiality and academic unreadability' in his essays (p. 2). He writes compellingly about the pressing need for legitimate terra firma 'somewhere between the punchy opinionatedness of the newspaper column and the rigorous austerities of the scholarly article' (p. 5). In fact, the book collects a prodigious amount of just this sort of writing, which he has written over the last few years in a variety of reviews and occasional pieces.

In an odd way, the book—the first half, at least—provides a nice companion to Alain Badiou's similarly assembled *Pocket Pantheon: Figures of Postwar Philosophy* (Verso [2009]), refracting twentieth-century intellectual life from another nation. Instead of French public intellectuals like Sartre, Althusser, Lacan, Deleuze, Derrida and Foucault, we get British ones like Connolly, Empson, Rebecca West, Orwell, A.L. Rowse, E.H. Carr, E.P. Thompson and Perry Anderson. Not that we couldn't find British philosophers and psychoanalysts or French literary critics and historians if we had to, but the contrast between the respective elites—the kind of intellectuals which Badiou and Collini pursue respectively—speaks volumes. Above all, for Collini, scribbling critics and historians represent heroic ideal readers who have landed on terra firma—with occasional help from independent means or academic appointments in the US.

One finds a 2001 review of Jonathan Rose's *The Intellectual Life of the British Working Classes* among the topical essays that comprise the second half of the book. Collini worries about the methodological difficulties in writing the history of reading in general: 'How much could we ever know about the practice of this form of solitary vice on a mass scale?' (p. 248). Although he is moved by Rose's accounts of autodidacticism extracted from working-class autobiographies, he is sceptical about the enterprise of representing and generalizing about 'ordinary readers'. '[I]n this age of "access,"' he writes, 'Jude would not have to scrawl on the walls of Christminster'. And now: 'Somewhere, out there, someone is at this moment picking up a book. They may be about to change their life forever, or they may be about to escape from it for a while. The book may be one of the hundreds that are mentioned in [Rose's book], or it may be one of the millions that are not. Who knows: perhaps in another valley someone is even reading *Mrs Dalloway*' (p. 256). It's far more likely, of course, that he or she is reading Dan Brown. To make this point doesn't mean making it smugly— thinking of Outka's warning. It only suggests that reading on a mass scale is a game of numbers and probabilities, and all forms of cultural commentary, particularly as we approach the sheer numinosity of cultural material available from the contemporary context, imply questions of specificity, administration, selection and value.

Can you talk about readers and not talk about what they read? And, if you talk about what they read, are you really talking at all about them? One way to think about consumption is to examine what consumers say about what they consume (Collini, Rose); the other is to examine the ways texts themselves thematize acts of cultural consumption (Nieland, Outka, Schantz, the 'Modern Girl' group). Collini touches on some carry-overs from the modernist era (Aldous Huxley, Edmund Wilson and Rebecca West, for example), but the strength of *Common Reading* lies in its many discussions of the mid-century transition to the contemporary: 'there have certainly been fundamental changes in [education, culture and knowledge] in the last half-century or so: contemporary working-class readers generally have more formal schooling than their predecessors; they have access to vastly more sources of information and entertainment... We live in a less "didactic" society, auto- or otherwise' (p. 256). It is exceedingly difficult for literary critics and historians not to read this transition elegiacally, with apologies to Larkin, everyone young going down the long slide to information and entertainment, endlessly. Yet, Collini, for one, does not hold with those who rail against 'the alleged sorry state of the present' (p. 6).

Last year, this section featured several books foregrounding the mid-century (Peter Kalliney and Marina MacKay). This year, the section will close by highlighting two compelling attempts to write contemporary literary history: Dominic Head's *The State of the Novel: Britain and Beyond* and David James's *Contemporary British Fiction and the Artistry of Space: Style, Landscape, Perception*. Published in the Blackwell Manifestos series, Head's polemical book is simultaneously concerned with discussing promising signs of life in 'serious literary fiction' today and what he sees as the troubles of academic criticism and 'its deepening insularity' (p. 1). The analysis is lively and particularly sharp about the shortcomings of the 'death of the novel' thesis (p. 9) and the methodological problems of contemporaneity (chapter 1).

At times, he is a bit too ready to adopt the blame-theory-first line, as if interest in non-genre literature written by 'serious' novelists was reduced because of a few stylistic excesses committed by and for a few people in English departments (pp. 25–8). If rumours about the death of the novel are premature, surely the death of theory is also frequently exaggerated.

There's something of a Goldilocks effect going on here, too, when Head defines what counts as serious as existing somewhere between *Bridget Jones's Diary* and *Boundary 2*. The Eng. Lit. faculty, above all, is not to be trusted with making critical judgements, it seems:

> What is meant by [the serious literary novel] is the kind of book that is shortlisted for literary prizes; which is to say—looking at the evidence accrued—a narrative written in an ongoing humanist tradition that enlarges readers' social, historical or philosophical perceptions by means of the fictional projection of character and circumstance (usually), and/or through linguistic or formal innovation (not usually overtly). (p. 12)

Head's novelists include Ian McEwan, Monica Ali, Martin Amis, Don DeLillo, J.G. Ballard and John Updike, and topics of general (as opposed to 'merely' academic) interest such as 9/11, transatlanticism, globalism and multiculturalism, literary prize culture, and tourism. Ironically—and Head might agreed with this claim—his book is really an effort to reform the practices of university teachers of post-war fiction. Echoing Collini's call for a stylistic third way, he wants to release this in-group from 'straitjacket of academic professionalism' (p. 27).Head calls for more literary criticism and history addressing mixed audiences of specialists and non-specialists: 'I do think that criticism of the novel is a *secondary* form of writing, in that it responds to aesthetic objects of attention that can very well exist without being analysed; but the analysis uncovers an alternative and complementary insight, of particular value if it can be brought to bear on concerns that have a general social application' (p. 6). Contrast Head's words cited above, about commentary coming 'from after or from behind to put a new face on the work'. James's *Contemporary British Fiction* follows the same 'conviction to write about contemporary fiction rather than contemporary theory' (p. vi) that animates Head. The sleight of hand he has in mind is familiar—and sometimes it's not the word 'theory' but 'film' or 'popular culture' that stands in for the contemporary literary scene in literary criticism. James argues that one way to talk critics down from this disciplinary ledge is to attend to the particular aesthetic spaces of and the particularity of space in contemporary fiction. His third chapter, on Ballard and Sinclair and the impossibilities of navigating urban London, shows the merits of this approach. The illuminating extended analysis of such individual practitioners of the novelistic art include J.G. Ballard, Iain Sinclair, Caryl Phillips, Pat Barker, Adam Thorpe, Trezza Azzopardi and A.L. Kennedy. Such discussion 'aims to communicate something of the vivacity of narrative space as an *event for reading* itself, by which settings become scenes of process and reciprocity, rather than as an aspect of fiction to be described in inert, topographical terms' (p. 7). Grand theory is dead, long live small theory 'that does justice to the singularity of individual practitioners' (p. 6).

Thinking of the various crises of commentary explored in the books of this year's section, Archimedean predicaments abound. Multiple crises of legitimacy are the mainstay of its negative dialectics, as are multiple modernist and neo-modernist hendiadys: war and peace, global and local, present and future, front and back, human and animal, style and matter, subject and object, production and consumption, academic and non-academic, literary and non-literary. It seems these are the most fruitful starting points for contemporary literary critics and scholars. As a closing note, Jonathan Eburne's *Surrealism and the Art of Crime* merits mentioning here, because this book precisely models an argument-driven book that is theoretically and historically rigorous and yet also reworks a synthetic literary history of the century in useful ways. The links to the British framework are admittedly highly tendentious. Certainly surrealism had British exponents such as David Gascoyne, but Eburne's focus is mostly French (there is a discussion of Chester Himes). The book has a fine first sentence: 'The path of surrealism through the twentieth century is littered with corpses' (p. 1). Curating its own archive of irrational European literature and thought—'detective mysteries, crime films, sensationalist journalism, and documents of clinical opinion' which stimulated, provoked and preoccupied them (p. 8)—surrealism was, in Eburne's formulation, 'a synthesis, drawing from avant-garde poetics and aesthetics as from popular literature, from psychoanalysis and criminology, and from journalism and political philosophy' (p. 4). It would be congenial to this reviewer to find more alternative histories in the literature and culture of the twentieth century written along these lines—more of the synthetic, and, thinking of *The Modern Girl Around the World*, more heuristic devices.

2. Pre-1945 Fiction

(a) British Fiction 1900–1930

In 2008 some of the most nuanced research continues to prioritize those writers whose fiction has hitherto been ignored by commentators committed to keeping the canon of Anglo-American literary modernism 'high' and 'narrow'. It is heartening to see more detailed scrutiny of Ford Madox Ford's long and varied literary career, not only as a prolific, experimental novelist but also as an endearingly wayward patron, editor and forthright champion of a younger generation of authors. Moreover, there are searching and stringent reassessments of the politics and aesthetics of gender, focusing specifically on women writers such as May Sinclair, Vernon Lee (Violet Paget), Jean Rhys, Sylvia Townsend Warner, Elizabeth Bowen and Mary Butts. This is attested by the fully updated and revised second edition of Peter Childs's *Modernism*, as part of the New Critical Idiom series, which constructively complicates our perception of this literary period by charting the 'modern movement' in its regional, national and global contexts. Childs, like Jane Garrity in 'Found and Lost: The Politics of Modernist Recovery' (*Mo/Mo* 15[2008] 803–12), canvasses Mary Butts as one of those interwar women writers who had almost vanished through the cracks of literary history, given the strident and hectoring 'celebration of maleness' in 'established modernist criticism' (p. 24). Like Pericles Lewis in *The Cambridge Introduction to Modernism* [2007], Childs crystallizes the principal concepts, influences and patterns of thought with emphatic assurance and without lapsing into obfuscating jargon. He methodically surveys the 'competing' techniques and 'drives' (p. 4) which dominate and structure the diverse writings of both acclaimed figures such as Joseph Conrad, who has generated a vast cottage industry in academic circles, and overshadowed or unfashionable writers, for instance Arthur Machen and Arnold Bennett. Childs's lucid overview recognizes that since the publication of Jed Esty's *A Shrinking Island* [2004], Diana Wallace's *The Woman's Historical Novel* [2005 hb, 2008 pb], Bonnie Kime Scott's *Gender in Modernism: New Geographies, Complex Intersections* [2007] and Kitty Hauser's *Shadow Sites: Photography, Archaeology, and the British Landscape 1927–1955* [2008], critics have sought to privilege a broader and more inclusive comprehension of international modernism.

Mary Butts's fiction and autobiographical writings showcase a lifelong and keen fascination with the findings of feminist classical scholar Jane Ellen Harrison, who features prominently in Kolocotroni and Mitsi, eds., *Women Writing Greece: Essays on Hellenism, Orientalism and Travel*, which gauges representations of the Hellenic world and interrogates the complex role of 'gender in travel and cultural mediation' (p. 5). Martha Klironomos's essay 'British Women Travellers to Greece, 1880–1930' (pp. 135–57) is persuasive in tracing motifs through Harrison's myriad archaeological and topographical texts. Excerpts from Harrison's *Epilogomena to the Study of Greek Religion* [1921] are especially welcome in the subsection on 'Religion and Belief' in Matthews, ed., *Modernism: A Sourcebook*, a substantive anthology of documents which supplies key contextual background for Anglo-American literature between 1900 and 1930. Matthews's editorial acumen in this historically informed collection throws into bold relief how the field of modernist studies has witnessed a dizzying 'succession of critical "revisions", "re-mappings", and "re-thinking" across the past thirty years' (p. 1). Matthews brings misconstrued archival material back into circulation, reflecting how recent scholarship has addressed patterns of consumer capital, technological inventions, visual culture, transnationalist feminism, emigration and global travel.

David Matless's 'A Geography of Ghosts: The Spectral Landscapes of Mary Butts' (*CultGeo* 15[2008] 335–57) analyses Mary Butts's recondite and encrypted cartography of space and place in novels such as *Armed with Madness* [1928]. Thanks largely to Jane Garrity's expert scholarship both in *Step-Daughters of England: British Women Modernists and the National Imaginary* [2003] and Doan and Garrity, eds., *Sapphic Modernities* [2006], Mary Butts's oeuvre has been situated in complex interwar debates about racial purity, the imperial consciousness, nationalistic individualism and bitterly contested ideologies of Englishness. Matless benefits from Garrity's punctilious readings of Butts's occult narrative mappings to show that her fiction, with its stress on a haunted rustic hinterland, mobilizes an increasingly bellicose rhetoric that lauds discernible social differences and a deterministic credo of 'blood' immune to comparative scrutiny or logical criticism.

Joanna Grant's *Modernism's Middle East: Journeys to Barbary* offers a radical 're-mapping' that explores how the ancient civilizations and contemporary existential dilemmas adumbrated by the 'Near' and 'Middle East' were a source of deep concern to anglophone authors in the early twentieth century. Grant's analyses of Wyndham Lewis and Vita Sackville-West demonstrate that 'Orientalist' fantasies were inextricably enmeshed with yearnings to reconfigure both the Western psyche and the generic models it emphasized to best 'represent itself' (p. 8). Such a project, Grant avers, was construed as a core part of a more quixotic enterprise to 'save' Anglo-American culture from neurasthenic torment and decadent excess (p. 15). Grant indicates with particular acuity how Sackville-West's literary efforts to chart the comfortless grandeur of an exotic elsewhere 'fell victim' to the crude and reductive Western stereotypes she sought so strenuously to circumvent.

Like Vita Sackville-West and Mary Butts, Dorothy Richardson has become the beneficiary of sedulous and percipient scholarship in recent years, as attested by Scott McCracken's *Masculinities, Modernist Fiction and the Urban Public Sphere* [2007], which blends urban cultural history, gender studies and critical theory in its assessment of Richardson and the 'New Woman' novelists. Deborah Parsons's modestly concise *Theorists of the Modernist Novel* deals with *Painted Roofs*, the first instalment of what would become Richardson's thirteen-volume novel *Pilgrimage*, as a 'quasi-autobiographical' account of the 'thwarted prospects, trauma, depression, hard work and creative determination' that had epitomized Richardson's own life from the 1890s to 1912 (p. 8). Like Celena E. Kusch in 'Disorienting Modernism: National Boundaries and the Cosmopolis' (*JML* 30:ii[2007] 39–60), Parsons stresses the interlocking regimes of gender, empire and capital in Richardson's corpus, as well as its calibration of a temporality that erodes the concepts of a fully developed and coherent subjectivity, which also throws into sharper relief lesser-known novels such as Rosamond Lehmann's *Dusty Answer* [1927] and Rose Macaulay's mordant satire *Keeping Up Appearances* [1928]. Parson's project raises core questions about how Richardson's protagonist seeks to become an agent of cultural transformation at a time when women were entering the public sphere as suffragists and socialists.

Melinda Harvey's essay, 'Dwelling, Poaching, Dreaming: Housebreaking and Homemaking in Dorothy Richardson's *Pilgrimage*' (in Reus and Usandizaga, eds., *Inside Out: Women Negotiating, Subverting, Appropriating Public and Private Space*, pp. 167–88), scrutinizes the heroine Miriam's 'tentative steps towards gaining access to urban spaces that had been commonly denied to respectable women' (p. 26). Harvey canvasses two 'emblematic sites of female independence', the Bloomsbury bedsit and the turn-of-the-century café (p. 27). Harvey contends that Richardson presents both spaces as affording the heroine a redemptive sense of 'welcoming homeliness' while freeing her from essentialized categories of identification and the stultifying routines of domestic existence (p. 27). Although the 'anonymous bed-sit' (p. 27) vouchsafes Miriam a measure of liberation from the drab, unfinished uniformity of suburbia, it is cosmopolitan café culture which helps her overcome earlier traumas and greatly sharpens her interpersonal and aesthetic capabilities.

Like Darling and Whitworth, eds., *Women and the Making of Built Space in England, 1870–1950* [2007], Scott and Keates, eds., *Going Public: Feminism and the Shifting Boundaries of the Private Sphere* [2004], and Amy G. Richter's *Home on the Rails* [2005], *Inside Out* debunks with intellectual verve the 'well-entrenched assumptions' (p. 23) associated with separate spheres in the field of literary studies. This is nowhere better exemplified than in Laurel Forster's elegantly crafted essay 'Women and War Zones' (pp. 229–48), which appraises May Sinclair's little-known autobiographical text, *A Journal of Impressions in Belgium* [1915].

Sinclair's *Impressions* also features in Wendy Parkins's *Mobility and Modernity in Women's Novels, 1850–1930: Women Moving Dangerously*. Parkins demonstrates that interwar fiction delineates the rich opportunities as well as the grievous limitations on women's agency. The overwhelming bulk of previous assessments of female mobility in a context epitomized by seismic social and political ferment have focused disappointingly on urban contexts in which young women were compelled to self-commodify as a condition of their circulation. Parkins broadens and deepens this scholarly approach to gauge the movements of the female subject beyond the ambit of a metropolitan marketplace which fosters and channels desire. Elizabeth Robins's 1907 suffrage novel *The Convert* is a signal inclusion in this nimble and lively analysis of how women 'may be willing participants in the vanguard of change' or rather 'swept along helplessly' in the ceaseless flux of 'modern life' (p. 3).

Allan Hepburn has edited two new collections of Elizabeth Bowen's writing for Edinburgh University Press. *People, Places, Things* assembles in one handy volume essays that were published in British, Irish and American periodicals during Bowen's lifetime. Some of these essays exist only as typescript drafts and are published here for the first time. *The Bazaar and Other Stories* also brings together some unfinished drafts of fairy tales, social dramas and existential parables. Some of the best short stories here concentrate on the young adult female as a figure of transition and radical indeterminacy entangled in familial or generational strife, or confronting for the first time a modern marketplace which simultaneously enforces and dissipates lopsided social designations. As Hepburn indicates, Bowen's work—as far back as *The Hotel* [1927] and *The Last September* [1929]—scrupulously registers and dissects the encrypted or overt operations of power between generations. Hepburn's excellent edition of the stories enables us to trace the ways in which Bowen's fascination with interstitial cultural allegiances conditions not only her perception of English, Irish and Anglo-Irish national identities, but also her elliptical depictions of camaraderie and burgeoning or thwarted sexuality.

A historical as well as a psychic past of trauma and dislocation—so often the main theme of recent research on Richardson and Bowen—also imbues Vernon Lee's short stories, according to Patricia Pulham's *Art and the Transitional Object in Vernon Lee's Supernatural Tales*. Pulham merges psychoanalytic theory with subtle socio-historical scholarship to weigh a selection of Lee's 'fantastic' tales and how they articulate the overlapping— and 'uncanny'—economies of sex, gender, class and national designation.

Pulham's elegantly structured study benefits from the signal revival of critical interest in this 'transitional' figure of literary modernism, as evidenced by Vineta Colby's *Vernon Lee: A Literary Biography* [2003], Christa Zorn's *Vernon Lee: Aesthetics, History, and the Victorian Female Intellectual* [2003] and Mary Patricia Keane's *Spurious Ghosts: The Fantastic Tales of Vernon Lee* [2004]. More recently, a fine collection of critical essays, *Vernon Lee: Decadence, Ethics, Aesthetics* [2006] and the first annotated edition of selected supernatural stories, *Hauntings and Other Fantastic Tales* [2006] have been published. Pulham affirms Lee's tendency to embed in the layers of these uncanny narratives oppositional, arcane or radically ambivalent forms of female subjectivity. Pulham's discerning account should be scrutinized alongside Catherine Clay's *British Women Writers 1914–1945: Professional Work and Friendship* [2007], and especially Jill R. Ehnenn's *Women's Literary Collaboration, Queerness, and Late-Victorian Culture*, which canvasses the myriad histories and functions of women's literary partnerships, such as that of Vernon Lee and 'Kit' Anstruther-Thomson.

Steve Pinkerton's 'Trauma and Cure in Rebecca West's *The Return of the Soldier* (*JML* 32:i[2008] 1–12) notes that two critical trends have persisted with surprising resilience in scholarship on West's most acclaimed novel: first, the magisterial dismissal, for psychoanalytic as well as purely literary reasons, of amnesiac Chris Baldry's climatic 'cure' (pp. 1–2), and, second, the underestimation of Chris's sweetheart, Margaret Allington. Pinkerton contends that the soldier's cure in fact emerges as a convincing transferential encounter in light of recent advancements in trauma theory, and that Margaret—an intuitive analyst and therapist—is key to Chris's transformation, for better or worse. Pinkerton asks us to reappraise an unduly slighted character, recognizing Margaret's robust agency in the text.

This year also saw the publication of the fifth and final volume of *The Collected Letters of Katherine Mansfield*, edited by Vincent O'Sullivan and Margaret Scott, which covers the almost thirteen months during which she sought more effectual treatment for the tuberculosis that would kill her. Those Mansfield commentators who have queried the apparently freakish resolve which led her to ignore orthodox medical wisdom, as well as the wishes of her spouse and wide circle of friends, for the choice of Gurdjieff's Institute for the Harmonious Development of Man at Fontainebleau, will find in this correspondence a fascinating insight into the thinking and fierce determination behind her decision.

Paul Newland's *The Cultural Construction of London's East End: Urban Iconography, Modernity and the Spatialisation of Englishness*, like Phillips, ed., *A Mighty Mass of Brick and Smoke* [2007] and David L. Pike's *Metropolis on the Styx* [2007], explores how the image of metropolitan space, developed during the late nineteenth century, continues to operate in the twenty-first century as an imaginative zone in which to confront and process biting anxieties concerning the ideology of progressive enlightenment, cool rationality, ethnicity and exotic 'Otherness'. Like Nicholas Freeman's *Conceiving the City* [2007], Newland's breadth of attention is melded with probing, discipline-specific close reading of narrative techniques. Newland brings a welcome focus to Arthur Morrison's novels of working-class struggle in the

East End, such as *The Hole in the Wall* [1902]. He also scrutinizes Ford Madox Ford's representation of the city in the impressionistic 1905 essay *The Soul of London* as a profoundly modern enclave that stubbornly resists totalization.

The twelve new essays collected in Gasiorek and Moore, eds., *Ford Madox Ford: Literary Networks and Cultural Transformations*, project Ford as 'an inveterate chronicler of his life and times' (p. 13), not just in his narrative prose fiction but also in the numerous memoirs and works of literary and cultural commentary. The contributors are highly distinguished in their specialities and each documents with limpid clarity Ford's involvement in and promulgation of various coteries, cliques and artistic movements, such as his dealings with Wyndham Lewis, Ford's complex editorial function at the *English Review*, his distinctive brand of 'Impressionism', and collaboration with disciples. As Gasiorek and Moore demonstrate in their incisive introduction to this collection, Ford's quest for 'continuities', while a notable facet of his thought and authorial practice, should not deflect readers from canvassing his need to identify historical and literary divisions, fractures or conflicts (p. 22). These essays project Ford not just as a partial and canny observer of the seismic socio-political convulsions which define the modern movement, but also as a tireless and heterodox participant in it. The *English Review*, launched in 1908, was an 'integral part' of Ford's effort to refresh literary culture, a 'focal point for organised artistic activity' (p. 24). John Attridge's essay (pp. 29–41) brings out with panache the complex irony of the *English Review*'s efforts to resist insular atavisms and constricting ideologies of Englishness by welcoming contributions from writers of a more cosmopolitan background. As with Max Saunders's incisive essay on 'Ford and Impressionism' (pp. 151–66) there is a strong sense of Ford's 'belief' that literary 'nuclei' were of signal importance to the 'health of the republic of letters' because they fostered the type of spirited 'interchange' that the arts needed if they were to prosper (p. 25).

John Attridge's 'Steadily and Whole: Ford Madox Ford and Modernist Sociology' (*Mo/Mo* 15:ii[2008] 297–315) indicates that social disintegration and cultural ferment have been perceived as trademark themes, among the defining processes of modernity. Employing Matthew Arnold as a touchstone, Attridge frames worries about wholeness and integrity as a complex Victorian bequest, and grounds the discussion of fragmentation concretely in Ford's searching social criticism in *The Soul of London*. Attridge offers a sophisticated and compelling argument; indeed some of his most pointed interventions relate to Ford's unjustly overlooked 1908 supernatural romance *Mr Apollo*, in light of Edwardian sociology's fascination with synthesis.

Damon Marcel DeCoste's '"A frank expression of personality"? Sentimentality, Silence and Early Modernist Aesthetics in *The Good Soldier*' (*JML* 31:i[2007] 101–23) charts the novel's engagement with 'emergent modernism' (p. 101), gauging it not simply as radical in technique but more as a bracing expression of urgent pre-war debates about aesthetics, utility and ethics. Whereas Jeffrey Mathes McCarthy has contended that *The Good Soldier* doggedly defends Vorticism against the competing aesthetics of Bloomsbury, DeCoste argues that Ford's novel actually subverts that very same Vorticist-Imagist strain of modernism with which he was conversant, and to which he so often 'pledged' his 'literary allegiance' (p. 102). DeCoste's astute essay should be read alongside Rose De Angelis's 'Narrative Triangulations: Truth, Identity, and Desire in Ford Madox Ford's *The Good Soldier*' (*ES* 88:iv[2007] 425–46) and Stephen E. Severn's essay on 'Ford Madox Ford's *The Good Soldier*, Creative Writing, and Teaching the Modernist Novel in the Introductory-Level Literature Classroom' (in Irvine, ed., *Teaching the Novel across the Curriculum*, pp. 130–43).

Jennifer Meyer's *Men of War: Masculinity and the First World War in Britain*, like Jon Stallworthy's *Survivors' Songs: From Maldon to the Somme* and Hammond and Towheed, eds., *Publishing in the First World War: Essays in Book History* [2007], illuminates how Ford Madox Ford sought to balance artistic integrity with a patriotic impulse to fashion effective pro-British propaganda. Meyer concentrates on five forms of personal narrative, including men's trench journals written, arranged and illustrated by British and Dominion soldiers for the purpose of fostering unit cohesion. She scrutinizes in particular how conceptualizations of extrovert virility and selfless courage were produced, interrogated and overturned by British Great War servicemen. Like Knights, ed., *Masculinities in Text and Teaching* and Christopher Forth's *Masculinity in the Modern West*, Meyer is especially acute when exploring how specific situations as well as intended audience governed the ways in which masculine identities were declared and calibrated during this fraught era. The first chapter, 'Writing Home', adroitly situates individual constructions against a backdrop of cultural ideals of the fearless warrior hero and the disciplined spouse and father during and after the Great War. Meyer argues that letters home not only operated as 'conduits of news' that 'kept the home front connected and informed' but also as 'spaces' in which men could inspect their own domestic responsibilities as well as the 'martial role of the soldier' (p. 15). Like Robert Hemmings's *Modern Nostalgia*, Meyer's book teases out the relationship between the elegiac backward-looking glance, traumatic loss and autobiographical practice. As a case study of modern nostalgia, Hemmings supplies a salutary alternative to the perception that Siegfried Sassoon's historical and cultural relevance is restricted to the Great War and to the twilight of the British empire.

Peter Havholm's *Politics and Awe in Rudyard Kipling's Fiction* not only offers a sharpened awareness of Kipling's understanding of empire from evidence in Anglo-Indian newspapers and periodicals of the 1880s, but also provides a richly textured explanation for Kipling's post-1891 turn to fantasy, fable and stories written to be enjoyed by children. Havholm explores what has been construed as 'an increasingly strident tone' after Kipling's 'settling permanently in England in 1899' (p. 137). Whereas the bulk of recent Kipling scholarship produces a view of the author as radically and enigmatically ambivalent towards imperialist politics, Havholm presents an author strikingly consistent in his aesthetic, cultural and ideological investments across a long career. Havholm prioritizes a writer of 'hidden simplicities' (p. xi) whose artistic repertoire is devoted to refining an experience of 'wonder and delight' (p. 91) at a world of profound, even exhilarating otherness. But many of Kipling's most memorable fictions, in addition to evoking awe, also trigger an accompanying feeling of deep unease at the racial politics which Havholm avers is only ancillary to our response. Kipling, as Angelia Poon posits in

Enacting Englishness in the Victorian Period: Colonialism and the Politics of Performance, writes existential parables as well as ferocious parodies of 'imperialism' (p. 135). Indeed the colonial encounter, as Gurminder K. Bhambra argues in *Rethinking Modernity: Postcolonialism and the Sociological Imagination* [2007], is 'constitutive' of the very disciplines that articulate or strive to comprehend 'modernity' (p. 16).

William B. Dillingham's *Being Kipling* canvasses Kipling's identity and world-view, as Kipling perceived it, through a probing and unusual examination of *Land and Sea Tales for Scouts and Guides*. Dillingham employs this collection, which is frequently belittled by critics and biographers alike, to afford rare insight into formative events from Kipling's adolescence that influenced his personality and the beliefs which resonate through his mature fiction and poetry. The eight stories, eight poems and three essays of *Land and Sea Tales* are all scrutinized closely both for what they disclose about the sensuous immediacy of Kipling's felt experience, and for their intrinsic aesthetic merit. Dillingham's book should be surveyed alongside Gavin and Humphries, eds., *Childhood in Edwardian Fiction: Worlds Enough and Time*, which is the first book-length scrutiny of the Edwardian fictional cult of childhood, and erodes glib assumptions that the Edwardian period was merely a smug 'continuation' of the 'Victorian age' (p. 4).

McLean, ed., *H.G. Wells: Interdisciplinary Essays* shifts attention away from Wells's earlier 'scientific romances' to focus on his neglected short stories, journalism and science textbooks published between 1900 and 1930, stressing his need for 'art to instigate' meaningful, root-and-branch 'social reform' (p. 2). Bernard Loing's essay on *Love and Mr Lewisham* [1900] discusses how the composition of this unfairly overlooked novel functioned like a 'period of apprenticeship' for Wells in his determination to write a penetrating novel of manners (pp. 76–85). John R. Hammond's essay on 'Wells and the Discussion Novel' (pp. 86–98) argues persuasively that Wells in the later fiction is a far more experimental and formally adventurous novelist 'than he is typically given credit for' (p. 86).

For specialists in the life and work of E.M. Forster and Joseph Conrad, 2008 offered a dizzying variety of book-length monographs, new annotated editions and inventive critical essays. As Tony Davies remarks in *Humanism*, it is Forster's strong 'preference for the dialogical and ironic over the solemnly monological, for scepticism over belief' (p. 40) which appeals to a new generation of literary theorists and cultural commentators. Amar Acheraiou's *Rethinking Postcolonialism: Colonialist Discourse in Modern Literatures and the Legacy of Classical Writers* interrogates postcolonial discourse analysis and posits a new model of interpretation that resituates the historical and ideological resonance of the 'colonial concept'. In chapters on Forster and Conrad he questions key issues, including hybridity, Otherness and territoriality. Acheraiou is convincing when showing that hybridity as both a theoretical tool and a historical construct is not 'a linear, flat narrative of cultural exchange' but a 'twisted, multilayered imperial tale' of 'forced encounters and unequal relationships' (p. 2). However, Acheraiou's contention that Forster and Conrad each held 'an idealised image of Greece' (p. 82) is counterbalanced by enigmatic ambivalence towards ancient Greek culture.

The reading of Forster's 1903 story 'Albergo Empedocle' presents 'ancient Greece as a rampart against modernity's discontents' while at the same time pointing towards its 'impotence' as a fund of 'aesthetic and ideological' rehabilitation (p. 83).

Carey J. Snyder's *British Fiction and Cross-Cultural Encounters: Ethnographism from Wells to Woolf* argues that British modernist writers such as Conrad and Forster read widely in comparative anthropology, conducted their own sporadic 'fieldwork' and thematized the challenges of cultural confrontation in their fiction (p. 25). Snyder brings canonical and popular texts together with travelogues, diaries and ethnographic surveys to show in an interdisciplinary light how anthropological concepts and methods infused the generic and formal experiments of literary modernism. As Snyder avers, compartmentalizing the work of writers like Haggard and Wells as 'too popular', or Forster as too determinedly 'realist', hampers efforts to construe the 'period's pervasive engagement with ethnographic ideas and scenarios' (p. 13). Only two book-length studies take up the connection between British modernism and ethnography per se—Marc Manganaro's *Culture, 1922: The Emergence of a Concept* [2002] and Gregory Castle's *Modernism and the Celtic Revival* [2001]—but these focus exclusively on the modernism of Ireland among the British Isles. Whereas Castle undervalues the 'pervasiveness of the ethnographic imagination in the modern period' (p. 15) Snyder adroitly demonstrates that it shapes an 'emerging global consciousness' (p. 16).

De Lange et al., eds., *Literary Landscapes: From Modernism to Postcolonialism* contains a perceptive essay by Gail Fincham on 'Space and Place in the Novels of E.M. Forster' (pp. 38–57) which raises questions about the function of imagination in the fashioning of regional topographies. Fincham contends that in *Howards End* and *A Passage to India* Forster disavows the belief in that unencumbered and free space celebrated by the earlier tales. In Forster's last two novels, 'the forces' of 'capitalist commodi-fication' and imperialist rapacity 'crowd out the possibilities of the liberal humanist worldview' and its construction of a site whose unkempt profusion offers a safe 'retreat' from metropolitan malaise. Jeremy Hawthorn's essay 'Travel as Incarceration: Jean Rhys's *After Leaving Mr Mackenzie*' indicates how the 'geographical, social, cultural and historical markers' that specify a space out of 'a neutral territory' are 'always inflected by gender'. Using Jean Rhys's novel *After Leaving Mr Mackenzie* Hawthorn demonstrates that the site of Bohemia, a locale that is both spatial and metaphorical, is 'by no means an identical territory for men and women or for rich and poor' (pp. 58–74). For the 'penniless, deracinated, single woman' it becomes a source of existential unease and biting estrangement.

Andrea Zemgulys's *Modernism and the Locations of Literary Heritage* reads E.M. Forster's *Howards End* against the development of a growing heritage industry in England generally and London particularly. Zemgulys posits that Forster found himself in a city that was being fashioned as 'historic' in ways incongruous with his own critical and cultural agenda. Douglas Mao's *Fateful Beauty: Aesthetic Environments, Juvenile Development, and Literature 1860–1960* subjects Forster's *Howards End* to a rigorous critique, addressing, like

H.G. Wells's *Tono-Bungay* and Aldous Huxley's *Crome Yellow*, 'what the great house nurtures' and 'the material circumstances of the artist' (p. 179).

Lago et al., eds., *The BBC Talks of E.M. Forster 1929–1960* details how Forster's radio broadcasts were a remarkable and multifaceted contribution to British cultural history, though they are only infrequently acknowledged by commentators on his life and work. Through these seventy annotated broadcasts, it becomes apparent that Forster used his public profile not only to address literary topics, but also to branch out into moments of incisive social commentary. Of particular note is his 1930 broadcast on the death of his one-time friend D.H. Lawrence, which irradiates Forster's assured grasp of the motifs woven into the verbal texture of *The Plumed Serpent*. As Mary Lago suggested in her 1995 biography, *E.M. Forster: A Literary Life*, the broadcasts provide a 'lens' through which to magnify many of Forster's core aesthetic and sociological concerns. *The BBC Talks* complements Richard E. Zeikowitz's scrupulously annotated edition of *Letters between Forster and Isherwood on Homosexuality and Literature*, which supplies insight into Forster's long struggle to craft a satisfactory ending for his groundbreaking but yet unpublished novel, *Maurice*.

Jay Dickson's vigorously expressed essay, 'E.M. Forster's *The Longest Journey* and the Legacy of Sentiment' (in Hepburn ed., *Troubled Legacies: Narrative and Inheritance*, pp. 163–90), chronicles the accretion of meanings which cluster around the term 'bequest' in the Edwardian period, and especially how the language of legal entitlement functions to adumbrate complex emotional and cultural inheritances (p. 164). Dickson is astute in arguing for 'sudden death as a structural event' in Forster's fiction and its centrality to ascertaining his 'novelistic project' (p. 164). Indeed, Dickson demonstrates that Forster's obsession with plots of entailment and disturbed lines of transmission reaches beyond monetary bequests and tangible landed estates to 'the emotional and ethical legacies left after someone's demise' (p. 164). Dickson concludes that 'as much as [Forster] wanted to accept a literal and figurative patrimony' he also desired to deviate from and probe the yearnings of the 'dead', especially 'in terms of how they themselves wished to be remembered' (p. 164). Overall, Dickson's essay supplies a fresh and energetic appraisal of how concepts of tradition, loyalty and regional affiliation coming from the past imbue the restless redefinition of modern subjectivities.

Jenny Sharpe's essay, 'The Unspeakable Limits of Rape: Colonial Violence and Counterinsurgency' (in Burke and Prochaska, eds., *Genealogies of Orientalism: History, Theory, Politics*, pp. 215–44), shows that *A Passage to India* revolves around a discourse of rape that Sharpe historicizes by sedulously tracing the crime from its provenance in the 1857 Mutiny to the 1919 Amritsar massacre. Sharpe's shrewd analysis reminds us of a problem that continues to vex and divide feminist commentators: how do we pinpoint the 'real crime' in this novel? Is it Adela Quested's accusation or Aziz's 'alleged assault' (p. 32)?

John Stape's probing and eloquent biography *The Several Lives of Joseph Conrad* throws into high relief its subject's restless ability to retool his own aesthetic imperatives, in order to stay ahead of the times. Stape projects a

Conrad grappling with 'a deep sense of otherness' and 'multiple cultural identities', as well as a consummate professional writer eager to consolidate a profitable place in a crowded literary marketplace. Lothe et al., eds., *Joseph Conrad: Voice, Sequence, History, Genre*, is a collection of twelve essays which construe a variety of Conrad's fictions through the lens of 'multiple theoretical perspectives' (p. 1). Essays by James Phelan (' "I affirm nothing": *Lord Jim* and the Uses of Textual Recalcitrance', pp. 41–59) and Gail Fincham (' "To Make You See": Narration and Focalization in *Under Western Eyes*', pp. 60–80), also reveal Conrad's 'tantalizingly complex development of the resources of voice' which is at the core of his seemingly 'paradoxical' capacity 'to engage and enthral the common reader while challenging the theorist' with the artfulness of his 'narrative technique' (p. 9). Indeed, one of the triumphs of this new collection is its confident ability to present Conrad himself as a 'major narrative theorist' through the deployment of 'innovative temporalities and plots' (p. 2). Allan H. Simmons's essay '*The Nigger of the 'Narcissus'*: History, Narrative, and Nationalism' (pp. 141–59) attests that 'Conrad's practice as a writer provides a site both to apply and to text existing theory' (p. 3).

Paul Wake's *Conrad's Marlow: Narrative and Death in Youth, Heart of Darkness, Lord Jim and Chance* follows on from Bernard J. Paris's recent monograph *Conrad's Charlie Marlow* [2005] by taking as its object the four texts narrated by this figure. Whereas Paris adopted a psychological approach to Marlow, Wake finesses a rigorous narratological standpoint, surveying a plethora of theoretical mechanisms while also thoroughly weighing the immense bulk of secondary scholarship devoted to this figure. Wake figures Marlow in terms of the 'liminality that allows him to occupy an ever-shifting position within, and across', the four key texts (p. xi).

Graham MacPhee's essay, 'Under English Eyes: The Disappearance of Irishness in Conrad's *The Secret Agent*' (in MacPhee and Poddar, eds., *Empire and After: Englishness in Postcolonial Perspective*, pp. 101–17), questions the insights into imperialism of 'that self-identified Englishman, Joseph Conrad' (p. 19) by reading the disappearance of the Irish context of political insurgency from one of Conrad's most widely praised novels. MacPhee contends that Conrad's Englishness, far from being idiosyncratic, actually fuses with the potent tendency within nineteenth- and twentieth-century British culture in 'submerging Irish political violence' under the 'banner' of an 'irrational', wayward and 'abstract' attack on civilized virtue (p. 103). David Punter's essay, 'Terrorism and the Uncanny, or, The Caves of Tora Bora' (in Collins and Jervis, eds., *Uncanny Modernity: Cultural Theories, Modern Anxieties*, pp. 201–15), conceives of the Professor in Conrad's *The Secret Agent* as 'an early avatar of the suicide bomber'; without obvious motivation, he seems 'a necessary efflorescence of the inhumanity of the city, a figuration constructed from alienation' (pp. 201–2). Christopher Herbert's *War of No Pity: The Indian Mutiny and Victorian Trauma* situates Mutiny literature in a 'lineage of modern writing' that 'culminates in Mr. Kurtz's encounter' with the 'horror' (pp. 25–6) in *Heart of Darkness*.

Yael Levin's *Tracing the Aesthetic Principle in Conrad's Novels* proposes that Conrad's narratives 'evolve and develop around a central contradiction: shadow, silence and darkness' and other such 'indelible markers of lack' as if they had a formidable presence and intensity (p. 3). Conrad, according to this densely textured account, delights in complicating the 'clear categorical distinction' between 'absence and presence' as revenants of the intangible seem to brush physical objects with spectral fingertips (p. 3). For Levin, the key aesthetic principle in Conrad's fiction is 'the otherwise present'—namely that which stimulates desire and perpetuates it by preventing its satisfaction or fulfilment. The consideration of *The Arrow of Gold* and *Suspense* in this regard is especially impressive. Levin's account of *Lord Jim* should be measured against Thomas Strychacz's *Dangerous Masculinities*, which contains an important chapter on Conrad's novel and its relationship to gender studies.

Knowles, ed., *"My Dear Friend": Further Letters to and about Joseph Conrad* is a 'sequel and supplement' (p. ix) to Knowles's *A Portrait in Letters: Correspondence to and about Conrad* [2006], which has become a companion to the nine weighty volumes of Conrad's own correspondence. Volumes 8 and 9 of *The Collected Letters of Joseph Conrad* were published in December 2007, to coincide with the 150th anniversary of the birth of this Polish seaman turned writer of English literature, and brings to completion a mammoth enterprise that began with the appearance of the first volume in 1983, under the general editorship of Frederick R. Karl and Laurence Davies. The final four volumes have appeared since 2002, though Laurence Davies, reflecting on how it has taken the best part of half a century to garner, catalogue and annotate Conrad's letters, admits in his eloquent introduction to volume 9 that this 'does not pretend to be the final word' on the correspondence.

Knowles benefits from Davies's sterling editorial scholarship, and does a fine job here of restoring 'the quality of exchange, interaction and debate' that characterizes Conrad's correspondence with H.G. Wells, Ford Madox Ford and Arnold Bennett, as well as offsetting 'the inevitable one-sidedness' that results from the tendency of publishing the writer's letters 'in splendid isolation' (p. ix). This present volume also gathers a number of recently discovered letters to and about Conrad, including the important cluster of late letters from John Galsworthy, located by J.H. Stape.

Joseph Conrad: A Personal Record [1912], edited by Zdzisław Najder, J.H. Stape and S.W. Reid, was first serialized in Ford Madox Ford's *English Review* in 1908–9 and represents Conrad's most probing autobiographical work. These reminiscences both chronicle and fictionalize his early life and the first tentative phases of his careers as a writer and as a seaman. *A Personal Record* also operates as a highly effective artistic and political declaration of intent. In this scholarly edition errors introduced by typists and earlier publishers have been corrected to present the text as Conrad intended it. The introduction scrupulously tracks Conrad's myriad sources and provides a lively history of writing and reception. In addition to notes which clarify recondite literary, historical and geographical references, the editors offer four maps and a genealogical table to supplement this explanatory material.

Berthoud et al., eds., *'Twixt Land and Sea* is a most welcome addition to the excellent Cambridge Edition of the Works of Joseph Conrad, which presents new texts of 'The Secret Sharer', 'The Smile of Fortune' and 'Freya of the Seven Isles'. These three stories, drafted while Conrad was working on *Under Western Eyes*, were collected together in 1912 and marked the turning point in

Conrad's professional fortunes. The introduction canvasses the sources for these stories, and supplies a detailed and discerning history of composition, publication and their reception up to our time. Of particular help is an insightful essay and comprehensive textual apparatus which gauges the manifold revisions, excisions and censorship the tales underwent.

Agnes S.K. Yeow's *Conrad's Eastern Vision: A Vain and Floating Appearance* posits that Conrad's Malay Archipelago is an inscrutable, unmoored and notoriously slippery construct which draws attention to the 'discursive collision and collusion' of 'fiction and history' (pp. 1–3). Yeow's central contention that the dialogue between these bitterly contesting voices creates an amorphous discourse is hardly fresh; yet her detailed textual analysis reveals that Conrad stages 'truth' as a conversation between myriad vehicles of meaning and is itself a pernicious illusion. Yeow also demonstrates that, in Conrad's era, the fascination with subjective standpoints was evidenced by the dizzying proliferation of new optical devices and innovative techniques of seeing. In the Eastern tales, Yeow argues, it is the nebulous nature of vision which Conrad underscores as he evokes a milieu which is true to his fleeting impressions yet also 'vaporous', inconclusive, open-ended and tentatively provisional.

Tom Henthorne's *Conrad's Trojan Horses: Imperialism, Hybridity, and the Postcolonial Aesthetic* contends that while abundant scholarship has 'fixed' Conrad as an early modernist, it may be more accurate to measure his work against such early twentieth-century writers as S.K. Ghosh and Solomon Plaatje—postcolonialists who refined canny strategies for camouflaging their anti-imperialist stance when dealing with British publishers. Henthorne posits that as Conrad began to acquire a larger, imperial audience, he refined a strategy of obfuscating his radical politics through deployment of multiple narrators, slyly sardonic irony and free indirect discourse, and other modes that are now inextricably tied to literary modernism. Henthorne's alertness to recent critical responses to Conrad as both a man of, and beyond, his time is impressive. To some degree, Conrad was ready to offer imperialist readers what they required: exotic narratives of adventure and romance. Yet Conrad employs the conventions of populist imperialist genres only to subvert them with malicious glee. In effect, Henthorne concludes, 'he was writing postcolonial novels well before the genre was established' (p. 173).

Alex Segal's 'Deconstruction, Radical Secrecy, and *The Secret Agent*' (*MFS* 54:ii[2008] 189–208) shows that Derrida's preoccupation with secrecy throws into high relief the intermingling of legality, genteel respectability, intrigue and withheld knowledge in Conrad's novel. Segal avers that Derrida and Conrad both evoke what might be termed 'a depthless secret' which allows incompatible interpretative hypotheses to proliferate, so creating an insoluble mystery or a code that cannot be broken (pp. 195–6). However, *The Secret Agent* does not embrace Derrida's notion of a 'democracy to come', nor does it exemplify the endeavour to loosen 'the sway of the Author'. Rather, Segal adeptly concludes, Conrad strives to 'solidify his own identity as a survivor', specially authorized to dissect the tainted underbelly of metropolitan life (p. 204).

Ihor Junyk, 'Beyond the Dialectic: Conrad, Lévinas, and the Scene of Recognition' (*MFS* 54:i[2008] 140–59), interprets *Heart of Darkness* through the lens of Lévinas's ethical philosophy, focusing specifically on two key scenes—Marlow's meetings with Kurtz and the Intended. Conrad, in Junyk's thesis, strives to move beyond the brutality inherent in the Hegelian philosophical tradition, to a viewpoint which places sober self-restraint, respect and responsibility as the first articles of its creed. Of the huge array of article-length submissions on Conrad mention should be given to the following pointed interventions, many of which evince adventurous independence of mind: Douglas Kerr, 'Stealing Victory? The Strange Case of Conrad and Buchan' (*Conradiana* 40:ii[2008] 147–63); Harry Sewall, 'Liminal Spaces in *Lord Jim* and *The Rescue*' (*Conradiana* 40:ii[2008] 109–28); Paul Vlitos, 'Conrad's Ideas of Gastronomy: Dining in "Falk"' (*VLC* 36:ii[2008] 433–49); Daniel Just, 'Between Narrative Paradigms: Joseph Conrad and the Shift from Realism to Modernism from a Genre Perspective' (*ES* 89:iii[2008] 273–86); Fred Solinger, '"Absurd Be—Exploded!": Re-membering Experience through Liminality in Conrad's *Heart of Darkness*' (*Conradiana* 40:i[2008] 61–70); and John Lutz, 'A Rage for Order: Fetishism, Self-Betrayal, and Exploitation in *The Secret Agent*' (*Conradiana* 40:i[2008] 1–24).

(b) British Fiction 1930–1945

Much work in this area has taken an ethical turn. Studies of Greene, Orwell and Waugh tend to focus on the moral universe of the narratives. There is also an increasing number of studies on re-narration, especially in connection with the work of Greene and Orwell. New approaches include studies of the cultural transmission of texts.

However, the only publication to deal exclusively with fiction of this period is an online journal, *Working Papers on the Web*, produced by Sheffield Hallam University. A special edition, entitled 'Investigating the Middlebrow' and edited by Erica Brown, includes essays on authors whose cultural status was the subject of contemporary debate: Gilbert Frankau, Winifred Holtby, Rosamond Lehmann and Elizabeth von Arnim. Brown's introduction offers an incisive overview of the ways in which critics as different as Q.D. Leavis and Virginia Woolf responded to the growth of a print culture which seemed to threaten their constructions of literary value. However, as Brown points out, the 'very selection of novelists Leavis uses to illustrate middlebrow taste demonstrates the instability and subjectivity of the category'. The diversity of the texts discussed by the essayists in this journal volume and the range of critical approaches used demonstrate the value of attending to the reception of interwar texts to help us understand how cultural hierarchies during this period were constructed.

The first essay in the issue, Nicola Humble's 'The Queer Pleasures of Reading: Camp and the Middlebrow' (*WPW* 11[2008] 17 paras), examines the use of camp in depictions of homosexual identity in a range of novels, using the framework for debate set up by Susan Sontag in 'Notes on Camp'. In her discussion of the novels of Nancy Mitford, Rosamond Lehmann, Rachel

Ferguson and, pre-eminently, E.F. Benson she suggests that 'the concept of camp provides one more way of understanding that elaborate dance whereby the middlebrow novel manages to be both populist and snobbish, conservative and radical, inclusive and excluding, sophisticated yet playful—all at the same time'. Not only is Humble's use of Sontag's terms persuasive and the range of insight formidable, but she exhibits two qualities rare in academic discourse: wit and the ability to convey the pleasures of the texts she is analysing.

Though Juliane Römhild's essay on Elizabeth von Arnim, '"Betwixt and Between": Reading von Arnim Writing Elizabeth' (*WPW* 11[2008] 18 paras) does not deal with a text from our period, it raises an issue pertinent to the cultural debates conducted within it: the suspect nature of literary pleasure and readability that accompanied the valorization of an uncompromising high modernism. Römhild demonstrates how von Arnim's fictional Elizabeth exercises the critical independence of just such a woman and in just such a novel that would later be disparaged as 'middlebrow'. In '"Half-amused, half-mocking": Laughing at the Margins in Rosamond Lehmann's Dusty Answer' (*WPW* 11[2008] 17 paras) Sophie Blanch, like Humble, considers the way in which homosexual identity is depicted in Rosamond Lehmann's *Dusty Answer* [1927] (Lehmann's equivocal cultural status having been subtly analysed by Wendy Pollard's recent reception study—*Rosamond Lehmann and her Critics: The Vagaries of Literary Reception* [2004]). Blanch, like Humble, notes that 'humour remains a critical, and critically under-examined, mode of discharging gender anxiety and fragile constructions of class superiority in the inter-war years'. Her essay suggests further uses of George Meredith's and Henri Bergson's theories of comedy in studies of the neglected genre of interwar comedy.

Victoria Stewart, 'Middlebrow Psychology in Gilbert Frankau's Novels of the 1930s' (*WPW* 11[2008] 22 paras), argues that one of the male authors anathematized by Q.D. Leavis as middlebrow, Gilbert Frankau, was experimenting with techniques to represent new ways of understanding unstable subjectivities and mental breakdown, in ways that parallel modernist experiments. Winifred Holtby too attempted to communicate radical ideas to a wide audience. Lisa Regan's essay, 'The Romance of Africa: Gender, Adventure and Imperialism in the Novels of Winifred Holtby' (*WPW* 11[2008] 28 paras), explores how 'Holtby's fiction positions the interwar "middlebrow" novel in critical dialogue with high- and lowbrow representations of Africa as an exotic, distinct and inferior "other"'. Regan discusses the way in which Holtby resists the terms with which 'a large and ever increasing body of competent fiction' read by the 'great intermediate class of novel reading public' was dismissed. Both Stewart's and Regan's studies provide evidence that popular fiction can be read as counter-hegemonic.

There is still scope for more investigation of the cultural status and the narrative strategies of the fiction of Evelyn Waugh, Graham Greene and George Orwell. Though their fiction has proved to have an enduring appeal, the critical work on them sometimes tends to deal with the nature of their non-literary values. Stephen K. Land, in *The Human Imperative: A Study of the Novels of Graham Greene*, describes the nature of the moral universe constructed in Greene's novels: the dynamics of the conflict between hero and antagonists and the way in which these dynamics change in the later novels. He points out that, though the victims of the conflict between hero and antagonist have minor roles in the plot, they function as key moral indicators, their fate providing a moral epiphany for the morally confused protagonist. The attraction of the morally dubious for the hero renders his investigative gaze compromised, but nevertheless shapes the reader's response to the complex moral distinctions constructed by each novel. Land reads the novels as stable constructs and focuses on structure and plot function rather than discourse; several interesting points are made, chief of which is that hero and antagonist become progressively kin during the later novels, thus putting pressure on Greene to create a second antagonist more sinister than the first in order to restore the dynamics of the default plot associated with the thriller genre. Though all the readings are persuasive there are, perhaps, few surprises.

Also concerned with Greene's ethical imperatives, and to some extent a study of re-narration, is Malika Rebai Maamri's 'Cosmic Chaos in *The Secret Agent* and Graham Greene's *It's a Battlefield*' (*Conradiana* 40:ii[2008] 179–92). The links drawn between the two texts are largely thematic: the injustice of official justice and the unreadable and unknowable nature of identity. However, there is a suggestive discussion towards the end of the essay of the debt both authors owe to Lombroso's construction of female deviance. Maamri argues that Guglielmo Ruggero and Césare Lombroso's *The Female Offender* [1895] might be the origin of the contrast between the ways in which male and female criminality are represented in the work of both Conrad and Greene. Whereas the male criminal's aberrant behaviour deviates from a supposedly civilized norm, the female criminal's behaviour is essentially that of a victim who is therefore not considered deviant.

Greene is linked with Waugh in the brief essay by Lynda Prescott in Robert Fraser and Mary Hammond's *Books Without Borders*, volume 1: *The Cross-National Dimension in Print Culture*. This two-volume collection of essays introduces a new dimension to book history and studies of reception by examining the way in which texts acquire new meanings as they are transmitted from one culture to another. Many of these essays offer new avenues of research into cultural transmission at this period. Lynda Prescott's brief essay, 'Greene, Waugh, and the Lure of Travel' (pp. 147–58), explores the way both authors use the notion of 'elsewhere' (discussed by Paul Fussell in *Abroad* [1980]) as an expression of alienation both from an authentic inner identity and from a British culture from which they could derive such an identity. Both authors, of course, used the material gathered for commissioned travel writing in their fiction; Prescott points the way to more extended comparisons of how the differing genres of travel writing and fiction enforce differing kinds of perspective on and engagement with the same observed 'other'.

Greene's fictions, like Orwell's, are now so deeply embedded in our culture that it is not surprising to find studies of the ways in which they have been re-narrated, for example Sander Lee's 'John Drake in Greeneland: Noir Themes in *Secret Agent*' (in Sanders and Skoble, eds., *The Philosophy of TV Noir*, pp. 69–82). However, such studies rarely illuminate much about the original narrative transposed.

In his article '"Noble Bodies": Orwell, Miners, and Masculinity' (*ES* 89:iv[2008] 427–46) Ben Clarke has followed his exemplary *Orwell in Context: Communities, Myths and Values* [2007] with a persuasive account of the way in which Orwell represents miners and mining. Orwell's celebration of the supposedly and traditionally masculine qualities engendered by mining means that such work is figured as elemental rather industrial. Clarke argues that Orwell's 'positive myth of the "archetypal proletarian"... obscures the inequalities and tensions within these communities. It also does not resolve the problem of their being closed structures. The very practices and values that made mining communities cohesive excluded "outsiders", not least Orwell himself'(p. 427). Clarke argues that, although Orwell's homoerotic celebration of miners is shared with Harold Heslop's *Last Cage Down* [1935], Jack Hilton's *English Ways* [1940] and the works of D.H. Lawrence, his utopian fantasy of what he calls, in *The Road to Wigan Pier*, 'the easy completeness' of a miner's family life lacks the acknowledgement contained in the work of Alan Sillitoe and Lawrence that drunkenness and violence often threatened domestic happiness. Nor did Orwell address the gender inequalities upon which his fantasy rested, either within the home or within the mining communities. Orwell's idealizations of mining communities lack the complexity of debates about value and identity traced by writers such as Lawrence, Lewis Jones and Sillitoe; however, his idealizations serve to dramatize the perceived absence of cohesion in the communities to which Orwell felt he might be assigned.

The title of Lorraine Saunders's critical study of Orwell's novels, *The Unsung Artistry of George Orwell: The Novels, from Burmese Days to Nineteen Eighty-Four*, declares its recuperative intent. The literary focus of her critique is welcome and the comparison of Orwell's narrative strategies with Gissing's is illuminating. Her analysis of the subject position of each novel works to weaken the traditional identification of Orwell with his defeated and compromised protagonists. However, it is curious that the pressure on Orwell scholars to be thrown back on to a moral evaluation is felt even within this literary-critical study. It is as though they are constrained by the terms Orwell set himself and which Saunders strives to challenge, terms which derive from Orwell's conviction that the political commitment demanded of the times was bound to compromise literary artistry.

As its title indicates, David Lebedoff's *The Same Man: George Orwell and Evelyn Waugh in Love and War* is not a work of academic scholarship or literary analysis. Its sources are not new and its interests are biographical and ideological. However, its uses for the academic lie in its provocative argument, outlined in the chapter entitled 'The Same Man' (pp. 181–211), that Orwell and Waugh, for all their personal and political differences, promote a similar set of values.

In conclusion, there have been far fewer studies of works from this period than there were in 2007. Not many of the studies that have been published make connections between writers, who remain segregated by gender, genre or cultural status.

(c) James Joyce

The absence of any prevailing theoretical trend in Joyce studies over the past few years has proven to be advantageous in that a number of disparate theoretical and methodological approaches have been allowed to thrive. This present survey will cover two years, 2007–8, in which a number of important works appeared, and while there is no overall critical direction that could be said to be dominant, the number of 'micro trends' in evidence here is encouraging. For example, 2007 saw the publication of a spate of books specifically devoted to *Finnegans Wake*, which until recently had seemed to be neglected when work published on it is compared to the number of books concerning Joyce's other texts. Two of these works on the *Wake* involve genetic criticism, which now seems to be emerging into the mainstream of Joyce and *Wake* criticism, one is a throwback to postcolonial criticism, albeit with a novel angle, and one offers a fresh philosophical, and specifically ethical, reading.

Consolidating more than a decade of pioneering work on genetic studies of the *Wake*, the inelegantly but aptly entitled collection of essays, *How Joyce Wrote Finnegans Wake: A Chapter-by-Chapter Genetic Guide*, presents a survey of the *Wake* from the perspective of the composition of each chapter. As the editors Luca Crispi and Sam Slote note in the introduction, this arrangement is potentially problematic in that the *Wake* was not, in point of fact, written chapter by chapter. To assuage this problem, their introduction summarizes the salient features of the *Wake*'s seventeen-year composition from a chronological perspective, thereby providing an overview for the detailed information that follows in the various chapters. Taken as a whole, the essays in this volume provide a comprehensive account of the creation and development of the *Wake* from a variety of perspectives, thereby illustrating the range and possibilities of genetic criticism. In total, the essays in this collection make a compelling case about how the *Wake* can be better understood by seeing it through its 'work in progress', that is, through its seventeen-year gestation. The editors were also fortunate to be able to discuss the *Wake* manuscripts acquired by the National Library of Ireland in March 2006 and so the information presented is reasonably up-to-date. These new documents show that Joyce's composition practices were more varied than previously assumed. Predictably, some of the contributions are better than others. Particularly notable contributions include Jed Deppman's slow and patient analysis of how chapter II.4 was built up or 'fused' together out of two separate vignettes; Dirk Van Hulle's subtle reading of the genesis and evolution of Book IV; and Finn Fordham's essay, which describes the ways in which the first and last chapters, which were composed at different times, were linked together to form the circular *ricorso* of the *Wake*. *How Joyce Wrote Finnegans Wake* is a major achievement and represents a significant advance in genetic studies.

Finn Fordham, one of the contributors to *How Joyce Wrote Finnegans Wake*, has also written a first-rate full-length study of the *Wake*: *Lots of Fun at Finnegans Wake*. In terms of influence, this book will likely supersede John Bishop's *Joyce's Book of the Dark*, now over twenty years old. Fordham's approach is multi-polar: rather than limit himself to one theoretical method-ology, he deploys seven different theoretical perspectives as a means of not just interpreting the *Wake* but of showing how, through practical exegesis, the *Wake* invites and encourages multiplicity. These different approaches—structural, narrational, theoretical, inspirational, philological, genetic and exegetical—are introduced and discussed in the first chapter and then applied to four brief sample passages from the *Wake*. The readings themselves are nuanced, original and perspicacious, and the book is crisply written. The readings proceed from a genetic perspective by starting with the compositional evolution of the selected passages, but the readings Fordham provides are much more catholic than genetic criticism. Beyond simply providing exegeses of passages of the *Wake*, Fordham presents and illustrates a whole new approach to reading it, one that is generous and sensitive to multiplicity. In a sense, Fordham's book is valuable as a lesson in the ethics of Wakean hermeneutics.

In many ways, complementary to Fordham's book is Philip Kitcher's *Joyce's Kaleidoscope: An Invitation to Finnegans Wake*. Kitcher aims towards a more general interpretative overview of the *Wake* which is developed in the first seven chapters. He then moves on to give a chapter-by-chapter survey of the work that follows from his prolegomenon. In effect Kitcher reads the *Wake* as a work of ethical philosophy and argues that it is vitally preoccupied 'with the assessment and vindication of a human life, a vindication to be achieved, if at all, in retrospect' (p. 12). He thus construes it as a humanist work eminently concerned with the ambiguity and ambivalence of life. While such a reading may seem retrograde, Kitcher argues for it well and with the requisite force and nuance. His book is very much in keeping with an ethical turn that has been taking place in Joyce criticism over the past few years: an awareness that perhaps Joyce's works aren't merely repositories of puzzles for critics and readers to solve and resolve but are instead concerned with promoting a way of life open to and tolerant of ambiguity and plurality. While it is admirable in many ways, I find that Kitcher's underlying thesis is belied by the readings he presents of individual chapters and passages. While overall he is concerned with plurality and an ethics of ambiguity, his readings are, for the most part, strikingly linear and novelistic, as if he were denying ambiguity and complexity at the level of the individual passage while championing ambiguity at the larger level. In this respect I find Fordham's book, with its more eclectic hermeneutics, a better illustration of the thesis Kitcher presents. Nonetheless, this is a significant book and, taken together with Fordham's, advances the state of *Wake* studies.

Len Platt's new book, *Joyce, Race and Finnegans Wake*, follows from much of the recent postcolonial criticism of Joyce—in particular Vincent Cheng's *Joyce, Race, and Empire*—while also offering a substantial new take on the topic. Platt reads the *Wake* as engaging in a sustained negative critique of European racism as promulgated through both the sciences and politics. In this he follows on from Philippe Sollers's famous claim from the 1975 Joyce Symposium in Paris that the *Wake* is 'the most formidably anti-fascist book produced between the two wars'. Platt finds Vico's influence on the *Wake* important because of the way in which Vico promoted the universality and interconnectedness of human life and culture. And so, through this prism of universality, Platt reads every page of the *Wake* as orientated against the promotion of any form of monolithic culture and identity. He also faults much postcolonial criticism of the *Wake* for focusing too much on an Irish context to Joyce's critique of race, thereby being guilty of (or at least susceptible to) the charge of a form of Hibernocentric racism. Like Kitcher's book, and perhaps even more so, Platt does little to problematize issues of plot and character in the *Wake*, preferring to treat them as relatively stable entities in order to educe his chosen theme. Such critical mono-opticality perhaps runs the risk of undermining the theoretical plurality he wishes to reveal and analyse. Of the four major books on the *Wake* to appear in 2007, Platt's is the most reductive in that he continually insists upon one central theme to Joyce's book, even if that theme is plurality. However, this is far from a damning problem and does not necessarily seriously undermine the contribution that Platt makes with this book.

Like Fordham's book, Richard Beckman's *Joyce's Rare View: The Nature of Things in Finnegans Wake* advocates a multifaceted approach to the *Wake*. Beckman's approach is different from Fordham's, although the results are equally playful and incisive. Beckman's analysis can effectively be summed up as variations on a theme, with the theme being the 'rare view'. The idea is that each new perspective affords another 'rare view' of both this particular motif and its variations, as well as of the larger structure of the *Wake*. In this way, Beckman's analysis differs from Clive Hart's motival analysis of the *Wake*—first published in 1962 but inordinately influential on most of the *Wake* criticism that has appeared since—by showing how interpretations of structurality themselves change through shifting motifs. Beckman's readings are minute and attentive, but he is always aware of larger issues and makes a cogent argument about the epistemological implications of Joyce's linguistic experimentation. As with Fordham, Beckman's work exemplifies the virtues of critical plurality.

Each of these five books is significant for *Wake* studies, and the fact that they all appeared in the same year is both unusual and welcome. Of course, other significant books on Joyce were published in 2007. The introductory volume genre remains, as ever, popular, with new titles appearing regularly. One of the finest examples of the general introduction to Joyce is Derek Attridge's *How to Read Joyce*, which is part of Granta's How to Read series. In his introduction Attridge cogently argues the virtues of Joyce's complexity to the end that, rather than impeding a first-time reader's appreciation of Joyce's works, the complexity actually serves it. The readings Attridge presents of passages from Joyce's major works illustrate this principle. His readings of the individual texts begin with brief passages that then lead into discussions of grander themes. These readings are models of elegance and perspicacity. While intended for the beginner, there is much in his readings that could be of use to (supposedly) more advanced critics, at least in terms of being a paradigm of lucid style. In particular, his two chapters on the *Wake* are thorough and engaging. This book is definitely one to recommend for the novice and would be particularly suitable as a secondary text for a course on Joyce.

A strong addition to theoretical approaches to Joyce can be found in Brian Cosgrove's *James Joyce's Negations: Irony, Indeterminacy and Nihilism in Ulysses and Other Writings*. Cosgrove's concern is an issue central to all of Joyce's works—irony. Specifically, Cosgrove construes irony as a 'metaphysical stance' rather than a humble problem of rhetoric, in that the existence of the possibility of irony indicates an insufficiency of the representational capacity of language. The central focus of his argument is that Joycean irony has more in common with the Schlegelian flavour than the Flaubertian. This is not to deny Flaubert influence over Joyce; rather, it serves to emphasize where Joyce differs from his French precursor. Cosgrove claims that the Flaubertian ironic stance is one of detachment and thus implies the artist's bemused superiority. In distinction, the perspective of Joycean irony would be embedded within the chaotic world it ironizes, thereby avoiding the pretence of superiority. This allows for a reading of Joyce that is at once humanistic (Joyce laughs with us, not at us) but also complex, in that this Joycean empathy derives directly from a realization of the negativity of language. Joycean irony is thus Joyce's vehicle for acknowledging, and affirming, the indeterminacy, and even incoherence, of the world. Cosgrove nimbly works his way through Schlegel (and, crucially in this case, Nietzsche, whose influence on Joyce remains something of a lacuna in the secondary literature) in order to show how Joyce's works negotiate systematicity through indeterminacy. Through detailed readings of *Dubliners* and *Ulysses*, Cosgrove examines numerous modalities of the unreliability of linguistic utterance. He also provides thematic investigations through *Ulysses*, such as the issues of stylistic multiplicity and Joyce's encyclopaedic mania and how these implicate broader epistemological issues, such as how a putatively totalizing work relates to and indicates chaos and indeterminacy. Cosgrove's analysis is fresh and insightful about both the theories he applies and, more importantly, the Joycean text.

As part of the increasing productivity of Joyceans in Italy, the Joyce Studies in Italy series continues to publish compelling new work. The latest addition to the series, *Joyce and/in Translation*, edited by Rosa Maria Bollettieri Bosinelli and Ira Torresi, derives from a panel held at the 2006 Joyce Symposium in Budapest. The essays in this collection show the diversity of approaches translation studies makes possible for Joyce criticism. Patrick O'Neill's contribution summarizes his 2005 book *Polyglot Joyce*, where he characterized the material and theoretical implications and additions posed, exposed and imposed by translations. He argues that translations are not merely secondary derivatives that exist alongside an original text which retains supremacy, but rather are interpretations and reinterpretations of an ongoing trans-linguistic process of textuality. Many of the other contributions in this volume share and expand upon O'Neill's premises and provide many fascinating examples and illustrations of what happens when the Joycean texts get translated. Of particular note is Serenella Zanotti's account of early Italian translations of *Ulysses*, Irena Grubica's analysis of the two Croatian translations of *Ulysses* and Fritz Senn's brief survey of the ostensibly simply elements of Joyce's text that can confound translation. Another volume on translation and Joyce is Ida Klitgård's *Fictions of Hybridity: Translating Style in James Joyce's Ulysses*. Klitgård examines the three different Danish translations of *Ulysses* (all by the same translator, Morgens Boisen) for their relative strengths and weaknesses; she pays special attention to the vagaries and problems of rendering stylistic effects across languages. Klitgård writes engagingly, even though a book-length study on the subject of translation can easily devolve into a series of tables of mistranslated or poorly translated words and phrases.

Besides the Joyce Studies in Italy series, Franca Ruggieri has initiated a new series of shorter books devoted to Joyce, the 'piccolo biblioteca Joyciana', also published by Bulzoni. Amongst their offerings is a collection of recent essays by Fritz Senn, *Ulyssean Close-Ups*. Despite the title, the focus is not exclusively on *Ulysses*: the first essay, 'In Full Gait: Aesthetics of Footsteps', traces patterns of walking and gait from *Dubliners* through *Ulysses*. Throughout these essays Senn displays his customary sense of sticking close to the details of the text in order to unweave compelling interpretations. If, as Kitcher proposes in his book on the *Wake*, Joyce teaches us something about how to live—that is, Joyce is a writer primarily concerned with an ethics— Senn is an interpreter most concerned with the ethics of reading, of responding to the nuances and oddities of the text with probity and acumen. In particular, the final essay, 'Authorial Awareness', is important in that it opens the question of how much a reader should account for what the author may or may not have known; while Senn doesn't formally answer this question, he does much in this short piece to elucidate the importance of the issues raised by this problem.

Senn's memoirs of his many years with both Joyce's texts and his fellow-Joyceans—*Joycean Murmoirs*, ably edited by Christine O'Neill— make a compelling addition to his many essays on Joyce. On the one hand, these memoirs serve as an insider's perspective upon the evolution of what is (sometimes derisively) termed the 'Joyce industry' (in which this present review is but one tiny cog). Senn is consistently tactful and avoids straying into the realm of the merely gossipacious. While Senn has been instrumental and influential in the development of this critical cadre right from the start, he is also, as he announces, something of an outsider since he is not a professional academic. On the other hand, he frequently takes the opportunity during his recollections to launch into reflections on and observations about Joyce's texts. His love of Joyce's works is clearly in evidence. The memoirs consist of interviews held with Christine O'Neill, who has done a superlative job of editing the material into thematically aligned chapters (a separate German edition is also available, with some differences in the contents in order to orient the volume to a Swiss German audience).

In terms of providing an insider's account of the development of Joyce criticism, a companion volume to Senn's memoirs can be found in the collected letters of Adaline Glasheen and Hugh Kenner, *A Passion for Joyce*, edited by Edward Burns, who has previously edited Glasheen's correspondence with Thornton Wilder. Like Senn, while both these individuals were instrumental in establishing the 'Joyce industry', both considered themselves outsiders: Kenner's interests were too wide-ranging for him to think of himself as solely a Joycean, and Glasheen was not a professional academic. Their letters provide a fascinating running commentary on this history of Joyce studies from these individuals, revealing various biases (such as a mutual dislike of

Richard Ellmann). In particular, Kenner's letters about the controversy that emerged after the publication of the Rosenbach manuscript of *Ulysses* in 1977 as to whether or not that manuscript provided all the fair-copy text of the first edition of *Ulysses* show that bitter polemic over textual matters is hardly novel in Joyce studies. The letters also provide an interesting window on Kenner's critical creativity as he writes to Glasheen about the books he is writing, first *Joyce's Voices* (first published in 1978) then his *Ulysses* (first published in 1980, revised in 1987). As with his previous volume, Burns's editorial work is beyond impressive: seemingly no detail is left unglossed. His care and attention to the letters of Joyce critics make one realize yet again the deficient state of affairs such critics have to contend with because of the unavailability of a good collection of Joyce's own letters.

Of course the 'Joyce industry' continues to flourish, as is evidenced in the number of conferences devoted to this one author. One of the issues of the large biennial Joyce symposia is that while a broad topic is chosen for the conference, and usually one that is related to the location of that conference, the sheer number of papers means that this rubric is honoured more in the breach than the observance. This means that most symposia tend to lack an overall coherence, which is not necessarily a bad thing in that it allows, at least potentially, for spontaneity. For example, the 2002 symposium in Trieste was designated 'Mediterranean Joyce', and indeed some, but hardly the majority, of the participants delivered papers related to this theme. However, the editors of the conference volume, Sebastian D.G. Knowles, Geert Lernout and John McCourt, chose to entitle the conference proceedings, *Joyce in Trieste: An Album of Risky Readings*, after Margot Norris's plenary address, thereby letting that emerge in 'retrospective arrangement' as the conference theme. Norris's talk, 'Risky Reading of Risky Writing', which is included in the volume, follows from her 2003 book *Suspicious Readings of Joyce's Dubliners*. Norris's argument is that the reader can take responsibility for textual uncertainties by pressing in readings 'against the grain' to see what conclusions and ramifications, however tentative, may emerge. In the 2003 book she focused on *Dubliners*, and in her Trieste paper she applied this tactic to *Ulysses* and the *Wake*. Like Senn and Kitcher, although in a slightly different vector, her argument has broader ethical implications than just hermeneutics since, as she says, 'In life we are often obliged to make judgements in the face of insufficient evidence, limited knowledge, and characters, events, and motivations that are unfathomable' (pp. 37–8). While the other writers collected in this volume don't necessarily practise this idea of 'risky reading'—and the notion of 'risk' is perhaps something of a melodramatic overstatement when it comes to literary criticism—there are a good number of compelling articles. Michael Groden provides a preliminary account of the National Library of Ireland's 2002 acquisition of Joyce manuscripts; while this was cutting-edge in 2002 when he first delivered this paper at the conference, the material is still useful as a survey of the new material. Vike Martina Plock provides an original reading of 'Nausicaa' by linking it back to 'Cyclops' through its manipulation of Irish nationalist hagiography. The collection also includes a brief piece by Hugh Kenner, perhaps his last on Joyce.

Other works that appeared in 2007 are the new edition of Vivian Igoe's guidebook *James Joyce's Dublin Houses and Nora Barnacle's Galway*, a meticulous inventory of Joyce and Nora's numerous residences in Dublin and Galway that is filled with detailed information garnered over many years. At the other end of various different spectrums would be Peter Mahon's book on Joyce and Derrida, *Imagining Joyce and Derrida: Between Finnegans Wake and Glas*. While obviously heavily theory-laden, Mahon's book lacks meticulousness. In his reading of the rapports between the *Wake* and Derrida's *Glas* he neglects to seriously discuss the works of Derrida that actively engage with Joyce's texts. In many ways, Mahon largely ignores the linguistic complexity of *Finnegans Wake*; instead, his reading is thematic and narrative-oriented and so, ultimately, his readings of both Derrida and Joyce tend to be simplistic and reductive. His book is an example of the sort of work that gave deconstruction a bad name in the 1980s.

Beyond the expected arrival of numerous new books of Joyce criticism, the traditional venues, the journals and conferences, keep chugging along. The year 2007 saw the North American conference at the University of Texas–Austin as well as the summer schools in Dublin and Trieste and a workshop at the Zurich Joyce Foundation on cruxes in Joyce's work. The *Joyce Studies Annual* was resurrected, being translocated from Austin to Fordham University in New York, under the editorship of Moshe Gold and Philip Sicker. Highlights include an essay by Margot Norris, again following from her suspicious readings of *Dubliners*, but this time moving into 'possible worlds' theory with a reading of 'Wandering Rocks'. The 2008 issue includes some papers first presented at the 2007 Austin conference by Carol Shloss and Robert Spoo about the litigation between Shloss and the James Joyce Estate over her 2003 biography of Lucia Joyce. In early 2007, a California court upheld Shloss's rights to use copyrighted material in her work. While her victory technically does not set any precedent, it is a heartening result for scholars. In collaboration with Michael Groden and Paul K. Saint-Amour, Shloss and Spoo prepared a list of 'frequently asked questions' about copyright matters affecting Joyce scholars for the *James Joyce Quarterly* (*JJQ* 44[2007] 753–84).

Dublin is seeing a marked increase in Joyce activity. In addition to several annual conferences that began in 2008, including one for postgraduate students that will rotate between University College Dublin, Trinity College Dublin, and the Università Roma III and a research colloquium at UCD, the *Dublin James Joyce Journal (DubJJJ)*, under the editorship of Anne Fogarty and Luca Crispi, was launched in 2008. The inaugural issue contains articles by Christine O'Neill on Niall Montgomery, Cóilín Owens on *Dubliners*, Terence Killeen on Alfred Hunter and Malcolm Sen on Joyce's orientalism.

The range of Joyce books that appeared in 2008 is more eclectic than those from 2007, although a few broad trends can be educed. The multi-contributor introductory volume, as exemplified by the Cambridge Companion series, sees a fresh entry with Richard Brown's *A Companion to James Joyce*. The twenty-five essays are divided into three broad sections. The first looks at Joyce's four major works, the second, 'Contexts and Locations', examines the various cultural resonances that inform Joyce's works, and the third,

'Approaches and Receptions', examines the contexts in which Joyce's works can be and have been examined. The second section is especially interesting in terms of essays devoted to contexts not normally associated with Joyce, especially within an introductory volume, such as Japan and New Zealand, written by, respectively, Eishiro Ito and David Wright. Indeed, essays by John Nash (on Joyce's reception in Ireland) and Mark Wollaeger (on postcolonial theory) do an excellent job of showing how complex the question of Joyce as an Irish writer is and has been for previous generations of readers and critics. The essays in the third section are mostly first-rate In particular, Jean-Michel Rabaté does a very good job in clearly delineating the impact Joyce has had on French theory. Daniel Ferrer provides an elegant introduction to genetic criticism and Katherine Mullin does an excellent job of contextualizing Joyce as a modernist writer through the magazines in which his works were serialized.

The introductory volumes gained another addition with David Pierce's *Reading Joyce*. Unlike the typical introductory book, Pierce's weaves in autobiographical elements: describing what Joyce has meant to him is one of his strategies for trying to entice others to share his enthusiasm. Ever since Alice Kaplan's *French Lessons* the memoir form has acquired some popularity within works of criticism as this has the advantage of conveying an emotional as well as an intellectual response to a work of literary art. (Perhaps Roland McHugh's *The Finnegans Wake Experience* could be seen as a precursor to the hybrid of memoir and critical monograph.) Since Joyce is somewhat of an autobiographical writer—albeit a complex one in terms of the interweave between autobiography and fictionalization—an autobiographical or semi-autobiographical response can certainly be apt. And in the context of Pierce's book I think that he does effectively communicate his enthusiasm to first-time readers. What is potentially very useful is that Pierce spends some time with potential misapprehensions such readers may encounter, using them as potential 'portals of discovery' for the text. He also provides many useful illustrations to his text as a further entrée into Joyce by helping ground the texts within their historical and cultural milieu. Pierce's book is certainly unique within the genre of introductory texts and manages to be both engaging and informative.

A number of comparative studies appeared in 2008, each one with a different theoretical and critical orientation. Perhaps the most striking of these is Dirk Van Hulle's *Manuscript Genetics, Joyce's Know-How, Beckett's Nohow*, which attempts to rephrase the rapport between Beckett and Joyce, thereby moving the comparative study of these two authors to a more nuanced level. As Van Hulle's title indicates, his approach is to this problem is through genetic criticism, and this proves to be an ideal optic for the task at hand since he argues that, for both Joyce and Beckett, 'the composition process is an integral part of what these authors' works convey' (p. 2). Van Hulle is remarkably adroit at showing how practical problems of interpreting Joyce's manuscripts, such as the relative dating of different drafts, implicate broader theoretical issues. For example, his examination of the various possible hypotheses of the sequence in which Joyce wrote the first drafts of what became the first two sections of chapter I.5 of the *Wake* suggests how Joyce himself was a kind of genetic critic of his own work in that he was actively commenting upon his own processes of writing. If Joyce's works are exemplary for genetic criticism, as can be seen in the sheer quantity of work done in this regard over the past twenty years, then, Van Hulle argues, Beckett's writings are likewise relevant. It is in the Beckett section that Van Hulle really breaks new ground. This is clearly a significant work of criticism for Joyce studies, Beckett studies and genetic criticism.

Alistair Cormack's *Yeats and Joyce: Cyclical History and the Reprobate Tradition* maintains that both Yeats and Joyce turned to esoteric philosophy and mysticism—such as Berkeley, Blake, Bruno and Vico—as a means of creating 'a new prolific historical consciousness' (p. 159), thereby effecting a specifically Irish variety of modernism. Cormack's yoking of Yeats and Joyce in a reconfiguration of how modernism might be construed is novel and provocative, albeit not without room for contention. His reading of chapter II.2 of the *Wake* as an earnest—rather than, as has previously been understood, ironic—reworking of Yeats's use of mysticism and esoteric sources in *A Vision* is perhaps exemplary of his whole book. The reading is audacious and original and potentially provides a whole new way of understanding the *Wake*, although at the expense of seeing its humour. Unfortunately, Cormack tends to miss or downplay the ironic in Joyce.

One of many surprising gaps in Joyce scholarship is the absence of a sustained study of Joyce and Proust, two obvious key figures for European modernism. Attempting to redress this lack is Michael O' Sullivan's *The Incarnation of Language: Joyce, Proust and a Philosophy of the Flesh*. Rather than approaching these two authors from the perspective of the issue of memory and recollection—an obvious but still pending analysis—O'Sullivan addresses the issue of incarnation. He makes a distinction between incarnation and embodiment in order to signal a critique of poststructural readings of both Joyce and Proust. As will be familiar to readers of Merleau-Ponty, embodiment redefines the Cartesian split between mind and body, but, O'Sullivan argues, at the expense of valorizing linguistic negativity, as can be evinced in deconstructive readings of Joyce and Proust. And so, instead, he emphasizes incarnation, that is, a consubstantiality of word and flesh. In terms of Joyce's persistent engagement with Catholic theology, such a notion is promising, although O'Sullivan might be missing the mark when he argues that in *Ulysses* only Molly can be said to exemplify the union of flesh and language. His argument is novel and engaged with both the Joycean and the Proustian corpus.

A different approach to Joyce's use and abuse of Catholic theology can be found in Roy Gottfried's new book *Joyce's Misbelief*. In effect, Gottfried reads Joyce's works through Buck Mulligan's comment to Stephen that 'you have the cursed jesuit strain in you, only it's injected the wrong way' (*Ulysses* 1.209). According to Gottfried's analysis, Joyce consistently defines his aesthetic against Catholic dogma, and so he consistently redefines and reorients key concepts of Catholicism, such as *epicleti* and epiphany. In order to rebel, Joyce consistently needs something to rebel *against*. For Gottfried, Joyce's catholicism comes as a reaction from and against Catholicism; that is, Joyce rebels against dogma—any type of dogma, any self-privileging assertion of a univocal truth—by projecting an eclectic array of the partial and fragmented. Gottfried does tread an established critical path, but he provides some original and meticulous close readings of passages, from *Dubliners* to *Ulysses* to the *Wake*. While he attenuates certain concepts—such as schism and heresy—in order to advance his overall argument, his book is a welcome and serious addition to a crucial dimension of Joyce's aesthetic.

Thomas Jackson Rice offers a different definition of Joyce's aesthetic in his new book *Cannibal Joyce*, which, like Gottfried's book, is published as part of the University Press of Florida Joyce series. Rice characterizes Joyce as cannibalistic, not strictly in the sense of flesh-eating, but rather in an alternative meaning of the word 'cannibal': a repurposing of parts from an otherwise non-functional machine. In this way, cannibalism is a type of creativity born out of what is defunct, redigesting it, so to speak. Rice's analysis of Joyce's 'cannibalistic' reappropriation and repurposing consists of three aspects, linguistic, cultural and technological. In this final part of the book, on technology, Rice follows on from his earlier book *Joyce, Chaos, and Complexity* [1997] as well as from work by Louis Armand. An interesting conceptual association can be made between Rice's book and those by Gottfried and O'Sullivan in that all three discuss transubstantiation as a metaphor (or perhaps metonym) for artistic creativity. Rice's insights and readings are novel and provocative even if he is on occasion in danger of attenuating his metaphorical concept of 'cannibalism'.

Proving that it still hasn't been fully digested into the corpus of Joyce criticism, postcolonial criticism remains a potent force, as is evinced in the collection edited by Leonard Orr, *Joyce, Imperialism, and Postcolonialism*. There is no overarching theme to the essays in this collection other than an engagement with various modalities of postcolonial criticism and theory. Jon Hegglund's essay on how Joyce mimes and parodies colonial patterns of epistemological acquisition and codification in 'Ithaca' is one of the stronger contributions. Also of note are essays by Christy Burns and Michael Tratner, both of whom apply a comparative approach to their readings of Joyce by bringing in, respectively, Brian Friel and Salman Rushdie.

Joyce's sole extant play *Exiles* has always been the ugly duckling of his oeuvre; even *Giacomo Joyce* has received more critical attention. In *The Early Joyce and the Writing of Exiles* Nick De Marco attempts to situate *Exiles* within the development of Joyce's aesthetic as a kind of culmination of Joyce's youthful interest in and enthusiasm for Ibsen and his earliest writings on aesthetics. De Marco goes through all of Joyce's early works and notebooks in great detail and traces out a line of artistic egoism in the evolution of Joyce's aesthetics. In this, his book works as a complement to Jean-Michel Rabaté's *James Joyce and the Politics of Egoism* [2001]. While his thesis suffers from the 'Ellmaniacal' mistake of biographical tautology in terms of reading the character of Stephen Dedalus as a figuration of James Joyce, his study is a worthwhile addition.

Rounding out another year's worth of new Joyce criticism is Cóilín Owens's *James Joyce's Painful Case*, a thorough reading of that story from *Dubliners* through a variety of different perspectives, each prompted, Owens argues, by tendencies latent within that text. Although his focus is one story, his readings have implications for all of *Dubliners* and, indeed, for all of Joyce's oeuvre. Owens argues that Joyce concatenates so many diverse perspectives into one single story that it likewise requires a critical plurality to reckon with it. His methodology and readings are elegant and inspire one to imagine similarly multi-perspectival approaches to Joyce's other works.

(d) D.H. Lawrence

D.H. Lawrence criticism and scholarship continue to open up fresh perspectives on his life and works. The year 2008 saw the publication of three monographs, two biographies, two significant chapters in books and five journal articles, plus new volumes of the three specialist Lawrence journals, and new selections of Lawrence's letters and poems.

Keith Sagar's *D.H. Lawrence: Poet* is a welcome addition to the slim body of reliable writings on the poetry. In a prefatory note to the book's lengthy bibliography, Sagar stresses that Lawrence's poetry has certainly not been neglected in critical circles, but there are still surprisingly few book-length studies one could recommend without reservation to interested undergraduates. The only two consistently insightful monographs are Sandra M. Gilbert's *Acts of Attention* [1972] and Holly A. Laird's *Self and Sequence* [1988]. Amit Chaudhuri's more recent *D.H. Lawrence and 'Difference': Postcoloniality and the Poetry of the Present* [2003] is perhaps symptomatic in the way it sets up a promising theoretical framework for approaching the poetry, only to pay seriously flawed attention to specific poems. As both an authority on Lawrence's life and works, and a practising poet, Sagar brings a well-informed and clear-headed, but also refreshingly opinionated, perspective to bear on Lawrence's poetry. His book comprises six chapters, covering the full range of Lawrence's career in verse; the chapters were previously published between 1985 and 2003, but they are presented here in a fully revised and updated form. The title invites us to read it as a kind of riposte to F.R. Leavis's hugely influential *D.H. Lawrence: Novelist*, which helped to secure Lawrence's place in the canon at the expense, perhaps, of undervaluing his achievements in verse. Where Leavis inserted Lawrence the novelist into a 'Great Tradition' of English (or naturalized English) writers whose works are imbued with a high moral seriousness (Jane Austen, George Eliot, Henry James, Joseph Conrad), Sagar sees the mature, post-1920 poetry as departing from native models and following the free-verse example of the American Walt Whitman. In fact, the chapter on 'Lawrence's Debt to Whitman' reflects the particular strengths of Sagar's approach, as he reads Lawrence's early and late poetry against the work of the earlier poet, giving detailed critical consideration to Lawrence's essay on Whitman from *Studies in Classic American Literature*. He notes that Lawrence described one of his early poems as 'Whitmanesque', and, drawing on the insights of Christopher Pollnitz, the editor of the forthcoming Cambridge edition of the poetry, he suggests that this poem may be 'A Still Afternoon in School', in which Lawrence first turned his hand to writing free verse. The 'confused and inept' rhymed opening of this poem gives way to 'an impressive, rapturous free verse coda' (p. 33). Another early poem, 'A Man at

Play on the River', is said to be 'as close to Whitman as Lawrence was ever to get, perhaps a little too close' (p. 34), yet the chapter traces Whitman's formative influence on Lawrence, showing how the several drafts of Lawrence's essay on Whitman in the *Studies* move from treating him 'as a whipping-boy for American democracy' (p. 39), or controversially dismissing him as a sexual pervert foolishly pursuing small girls, to finally acknowledging Whitman's importance as a poet opposed to the dualism of mind and body, 'the first to break the mental allegiance' (p. 41). Sagar argues that the Whitman essay actually tells us remarkably little about 'what Whitman gave Lawrence as a poet'; for this we must turn instead to the essay 'Verse Free and Unfree' (later retitled 'Poetry of the Present'), which is said to echo Whitman's account of his own poetic principles. The real connection between Whitman and the author of *Birds, Beasts and Flowers* lies in their shared use of a complex humour in their verse: 'a tricksy technique for subverting the normal standards of ... readers, luring us, under cover of comedy, beyond the limitations of our usual, narrowly reasonable and secular anthropocentrism' (p. 45). Taking account of the latest research on Lawrence, Sagar has written the kind of book which helps us to see new things in the verse, and to reassess elements which we thought we knew but had never subjected to serious critical examination.

Hilary Hillier's short volume *Talking Lawrence: Patterns of Eastwood Dialect in the Work of D.H. Lawrence* takes a sociolinguistic approach to Lawrence's use of dialect in his Nottingham writings, focusing on the short story 'Odour of Chrysanthemums', the novel *Sons and Lovers* and the plays *A Collier's Friday Night, The Widowing of Mrs. Holroyd, The Merry-go-Round* and *The Daughter-in-Law*. Hillier compares Lawrence's rendition of the dialect in these works with the data she has collected from recent interviews with children from two schools in the area, including Greasley Beauvale Infants School, which Lawrence himself attended. Her work shows the care with which Lawrence recorded features of the language of his home town, and his great sensitivity to the connotative implications of expression and the social codes that non-standard language conveys.

In *Love and Death in Lawrence and Foucault*, Barry J. Scherr sets himself the task of exposing what he sees as the repressive and damaging hegemonic structure of the modern American academy. He rails against the West's 'self-destructive practice of multiculturalism, left-wing political correctness, and the Clintonesque trendy left-wing obliviousness/appeasement/valorization of Third World Terrorists (from Osama bin Laden to Saddam Hussein to North Korea's Kim to Arafat to Mandela)' (p. 1). Scherr views academics like Henry Louis Gates, 'the highest paid "Professor of Humanities" at Harvard University', as thriving on the political culture created by these 'self-destructive' practices. Gates is criticized as 'the most successful—and most blatant and simplistic—player of the "victimhood" card/"race card"' (pp. 201–2); he is referred to as 'a bogus, pretentious sham' (p. 251). However, at the centre of the book is an intensification of Scherr's earlier attack, in *D.H. Lawrence Today* [2004], on what he views as the 'anti-life' theories of Michel Foucault, and on Foucault's openly homosexual lifestyle. In a frankly offensive discussion of Foucault's lifestyle choices, Scherr refers to his '(homo)sexual promiscuity—promiscuity which eventually achieved his death via AIDS' (p. 192). In a short chapter of four pages ('Foucault on Death: A Lawrentian Note'), he views Foucault's analysis of the subject's powerlessness before socio-political structures as unduly negative, and sees his celebration of death as a guarantor of self-realization as denigrating some Lawrentian ideal of 'the God-mystery within us' (p. 194). It is unfortunate to find Lawrence being co-opted into an angry, even bitter, rant against recent trends in American political and academic life. Even those readers who sympathize with Scherr's overriding critique of political correctness will struggle to engage with the angry, homophobic and racist tone of the book. Scherr's rhetoric is monotonous and exhausting. He wields quotation marks like Ursula wields her cane in chapter 13 of *The Rainbow*: they descend on the reader like so many brutal blows, bludgeoning him into submission. Any new insights on offer are sadly lost in the breathless onslaught.

Michael Squires's *D.H. Lawrence and Frieda: A Portrait of Love and Loyalty* is a compact new biography of the writer, concentrating on the emotional dynamics of his relationship with his wife. Squires has access to a large body of Frieda's unpublished correspondence, which lends his writing on the marriage, and on Frieda's nurturing of Lawrence's posthumous reputation, a greater authority and insight than earlier accounts. The book presents their married life as marked by 'commitment and affection shaded with betrayal' (p. 173). It sheds an interesting light on the couple's strained relations with admirers like Dorothy Brett and Mabel Dodge Sterne, and it highlights Lawrence's brief affair with Rosalind Baynes, and Frieda's amorous interactions with John Middleton Murry and the early stages of her affair with Angelo Ravagli, whom she eventually married in 1950. *D.H. Lawrence and Frieda* offers a concise and accessible version of a story which is told at greater length in *Living at the Edge*, the 2002 biography Squires wrote with his own wife, Lynn K. Talbot.

David Ellis, the author of the third and final volume of the Cambridge biography of Lawrence, has written an experimental biography focusing on the author's final illness, death and posthumous life. *Death and the Author: How D.H. Lawrence Died, and Was Remembered* uses Lawrence's response to his tuberculosis, his treatment of the condition, and his death, with its various emotional and legal implications and literary critical legacies, as a central focus around which he gathers a whole series of reflections on final things, drawing on the lives and deaths of other famous consumptive writers such as Keats, Katherine Mansfield, Kafka, Chekhov and George Orwell. The book is broken down into three sections ('Dying', 'Death' and 'Remembrance'), each subdivided into short chapters dealing with issues such as denial, the lure of suicide, famous last words, and the posthumous settling of scores. It contains a wealth of biographical detail on Lawrence, including several very telling anecdotes relating to Lawrence's relations with his mother-in-law, the Baroness Anna von Richthofen, and with his sometime friend and worthy adversary, John Middleton Murry. Indeed, despite its morbid subject-matter, the book is extremely readable and informed throughout by an urbane, dry humour which refuses to sentimentalize things. We are reminded of Lawrence's own comment on Maurice Magnus, an acquaintance who committed suicide to avoid the legal consequences of debt: 'the dead ask only for *justice*: not praise or exoneration' (quoted by Ellis, p. 219). The intelligent, sympathetic but unapologetic clear-sightedness of this book is something which Lawrence himself might have appreciated.

In a chapter entitled ' "When the Indian Was in Vogue": D.H. Lawrence, Aldous Huxley, and Ethnological Tourism in the Southwest', from her *British Fiction and Cross-Cultural Encounters: Ethnographic Modernism from Wells to Woolf* (pp. 157–88), Carey J. Snyder reads Lawrence's writings on New Mexico and the American Southwest in the context of contemporary Southwest tourism and ethnography. Lawrence is said to criticize both the tourist's idealization of the native Indian and the white Indian's pandering to the tourist mentality, but Snyder argues that his own desire to access the primitive Indian psyche—his 'primitivist longing to reconnect with lost origins' (p. 160)—is riven with contradiction, since it uncritically reproduces the Westernized gaze of the ethnographer. Lawrence's hatred of the spectacle of an inauthentic Indian culture staged for Western visitors is felt to overlook the fact that his own writings on the region—and especially on its landscape— echo the idealized discourses on the Southwest intended to draw visitors to the area. Snyder's critical positioning here is interesting, and her engagement with the problems and paradoxes associated with the ethnographic gaze is highly suggestive, but the tone of the chapter in its treatment of Lawrence is peculiarly arch; in the final paragraphs, an implicit dislike of what Snyder clearly sees as Lawrence's colonialist mindset gives way to open hostility. The chapter refers to Lou Witt in *St. Mawr* as 'Lawrence in drag', and it clumsily attacks what it sees as Lawrence's racist attitude towards Tony Luhan, the Indian partner of his Taos host, Mabel Dodge Sterne. Lawrence is said to claim the right to move between cultures while implying that 'Luhan and other Indians jeopardize their identity by crossing over into mainstream American life' (p. 175). The racial issues at stake here are, of course, complicated and delicate; while one can concede the point about Lawrence's blindness to certain features of his own positioning as a Western observer of 'authentic' American Indian culture, it is difficult to imagine what a fully self-aware gaze might be like. Snyder praises Emily Post in the travel narrative *By Motor to the Golden Gate* [1916] for her self-negating awareness of her inability to escape the ignorant and potentially destructive reproduction of the tourist gaze. However, one might question whether this resignation manages to free itself of all traces of Western bias, or (indeed) whether Snyder's own use of the term 'mainstream American life' is as innocent or neutral as she would have us believe.

Andrew Harrison contributed an essay entitled 'Hymns in a Man's Life: The Congregational Chapel and D.H. Lawrence's Early Poetry' to Adrian Grafe, ed., *Ecstasy and Understanding: Religious Awareness in English Poetry from the Late Victorian to the Modern Period* (pp. 46–57). Harrison examines Lawrence's early involvement with the Congregational Church in Eastwood and his painful break with orthodox religion in the autumn and winter of 1907. He explores the tensions involved in the young Lawrence's exile from his mother's beloved chapel through a close consideration of the early poem 'Weeknight Service', and close readings of 'Eastwood—Evening' and 'The

Piano' (early versions of the poems better known as 'The Little Town at Evening' and 'Piano').

Turning to this year's journal articles, in '"I need a master": Sylvia Plath Reads D.H. Lawrence' (*English* 57:ccxviii[2008] 127–44) Sally Bayley seeks to examine 'Lawrence's significant impact on Plath's body of imagery, lexicon and choice of theme' (p. 128). She alludes to an essay Plath wrote on Lawrence while studying at Cambridge, notes Plath's attendance at the second day of the Lady Chatterley trial, and draws sporadically on Plath's annotations of selected Lawrence works in her library, currently held at Smith College. In particular, Bayley suggests that 'Plath's interest in uncanny landscapes, reflected in poems such as "Wuthering Heights", can be traced to her close reading of Lawrence's story "The Woman Who Rode Away"'; she remarks that Plath's 'The Shrike' 'seems to be directly connected to her reading of ... "Sons and Lovers"' (p. 133); she speculates that Plath's 'Dark Wood, Dark Water' 'appears to be a study of gothic landscape akin to the aesthetic of Northern Romanticism, mediated via Lawrence' (p. 137); and she argues that 'Ariel' enacts 'the "new dawn" or self of Lawrence's fable, "The Man Who Died"' (p. 142). These comparative readings might have made for an interesting (if rather disparate and unstructured) short essay on the two writers, but Bayley's ambition to reveal Plath's broader indebtedness to Lawrence's thematic range and lexicon effectively leads her away from the safe shallows of the comparative approach into the deep and murky waters of cultural studies. Bayley discusses Plath's use of the Freudian and Lawrentian vocabularies as if neither was influential in the wider Anglo-American culture of the 1950s and 1960s; she writes as if each note of influence, or each possible allusion, can be traced back to a specific source, or even to an underlining in a personal copy or a marginal annotation. We are informed that 'the language of Plath's "Elm" ... is strikingly similar to the language of Freud's essay, "The Pleasure Principle", with its definition of the death-drive' (p. 135), and that 'Plath's "selfish" involvement with Lawrence continued into her year spent as a Fulbright scholar in Cambridge, 1956–57' (p. 131). In effect, of course, we can hardly be surprised to find Plath's lexicon of the death-drive, or the uncanny, echoing Freud, or her language of the mythical, the primitive, the gothic and the sexual echoing Lawrence. It would have been impossible for anyone studying English literature at Cambridge in the mid-1950s *not* to have been exposed to, and influenced by, Lawrence's writings. In reading *Fantasia of the Unconscious*, Plath was engaging with Lawrence's own osmotic mediation of Freudian ideas in the 1920s; any account of that text's impact on Plath in the 1950s, or of her own engagement with Freudian terms, must necessarily acknowledge the intervening layers of mediation, and respond with a suitably nuanced understanding. In contrast, Bayley's language of 'influence' flattens out the history of ideas into naive assertions of the following type: 'Lawrence draws together the language of Freudian psychoanalysis with a smattering of colour-coded symbolism' (p. 137); 'Both Plath and Lawrence ... are engaged with the experience of the uncanny as it relates to and releases unconscious material' (p. 140). The essay is hamstrung by its weak grasp of cultural and intellectual contexts.

Peter Fjågesund applies an unusual historical lens to the fiction in 'D.H. Lawrence's *Women in Love*: Gerald Crich and Captain Scott' (*ES* 89:ii[2008] 182–94). This essay re-examines the myth surrounding Scott's heroism and selflessness on his ill-fated expedition to the South Pole, 1910–12. Drawing on a range of historical and biographical sources, he suggests that Scott's connection with British imperial ambitions and national pride both before his death in 1912 and during the war years, is drawn upon by Lawrence in his critical depiction of Gerald Crich in *Women in Love*, whose 'soldierly' demeanour and reputation as an explorer of the 'savage regions' of the Amazon in some sense deflates and satirizes British military pride, especially in the final chapters, in which Gerald dies among the snow-capped peaks of the Tyrol. Fjågesund spends much of his article filling in the possible access Lawrence may have had to Scott's private life through his friends Mary and Gilbert Cannan, Compton Mackenzie and Lady Cynthia Asquith; he argues that 'it is likely Lawrence had considerably more information than he would otherwise have received from the press alone of Captain Scott, his wife and the personal intrigues involving them' (p. 190). His observation that contemporary readers of *Women in Love* in 1916 (when its first version was completed) and even 1920 (when it was first published in America) might well have associated Gerald's physical prowess and the manner of his untimely death with Captain Scott is an intriguing possibility. However, his further argument that Lawrence went to the pains of 'collecting relevant biographical material and … sifting it for his artistic needs' (p. 191) is less convincing, as is his contention that the novel's assault on the Scott myth contributed to its refusal by publishers during the war years.

In 'Eros in the Sick Room: Phosphorescent Form and Aesthetic Ecstasy in D.H. Lawrence's *Sons and Lovers*' (*JNT* 38:ii[2008] 135–76), Kimberly Coates reads Lawrence's third novel as staging a search for a new and shifting, organic or 'phosphorescent' idea of aesthetic form, and doing so through its commitment to exploring Paul Morel's radically unstable sexual identity and wavering desire. Coates focuses on the significance of sick-rooms in *Sons and Lovers*, suggesting that they function in the novel as 'queer' spaces which break down 'hetero-normative representations' (p. 136). Paul is said to be attracted to the somewhat masculine Clara Dawes, whose proud and sullen bearing reflects the attitude of her estranged husband, Baxter; Paul achieves a real bond with the husband once he (Baxter) is feminized through illness. Paul moves between the sick-rooms of his mother and Baxter, just as he moves between the masculine woman and the feminine man, suggesting that his sexual identity, like his aesthetic vision as an artist, is caught between different possibilities and various performative acts. We are reminded of the scene from the uncut version of the novel, in which Paul stays overnight at the house of Clara's mother, wearing Baxter's pyjama trousers and trying on Clara's stockings. Coates suggests that 'libidinal crossings that refuse to be contained in predetermined narratives lie at the very heart of *Sons and Lovers*' (p. 140); Lawrence is said to be a writer 'who arguably anticipates post-structuralist notions of identity and sexuality as inherently unstable; a writer who creates a language and style radically at odds with predetermined meanings and fixed categories as they plagued his time and continue to plague our own' (p. 168).

The connection the essay makes between the unstable form of the novel and the transformations in Paul Morel's desire is in places intriguing, but its lengthy engagement with Lawrence's two books on psychoanalysis is opaque and diffuse, and its treatment of Lawrence as a forebear of Judith Butler seems rather opportunistic, eschewing any consideration of Lawrence's modernist radicalism in favour of a celebration of his contemporary 'relevance'.

In '"I am not England": Narrative and National Identity in *Aaron's Rod* and *Sea and Sardinia*' (*JML* 31:iv[2008] 54–70), Bridget Chalk seeks to redress the negative consensus of critical opinion on the formlessness of *Aaron's Rod* and the emptiness of its central protagonist by reading the novel as a conscious departure from the convention-bound and restrictive ideas of selfhood imposed by, on the one hand, the tradition of the *Bildungsroman*, and on the other the ubiquity of the passport as a guarantor of one's physical identity, nationality and moral rectitude. Chalk draws on Lawrence's later essays on the novel, written in the mid-1920s, to argue that the form of *Aaron's Rod* and its characterization represent 'a systematic unravelling of the logic of the *Bildungsroman*' (p. 61). She suggests, however, that his ambitious attempt 'ultimately fails to reconstitute the novel's social purpose from within' (p. 57), since he can only negate the old conventions of character motivation and plot development crucial to the novel genre. By way of contrast, she suggests that the looser and less generically homogeneous form of travel writing gave Lawrence the freedom to transform narrative convention and use episodic structure in a more incisive and compelling manner. The strength of the article lies in its attempt to account for Lawrence's post-war experimentalism without treating him as a proto-postmodernist. Lawrence's narrative style is quite rightly traced back to his resistance to 'the imposition of official identity and the accompanying loss of autonomy in the construction of the self' (p. 55). Unfortunately, the piecemeal and rather too descriptive analysis of the novel is insufficient to support the essay's bold assertions about the 'disarticulation' of identity, or the text's 'disconnected and aimless structure' (p. 63), or 'the destabilization of Aaron's social identity' (p. 58). The essay also builds its argument on a very narrow range of Lawrence's texts, not even alluding to other, equally experimental, post-war novels such as *The Lost Girl*, *Mr Noon* and *Kangaroo*. Indeed, its grip on the rest of Lawrence's oeuvre seems surprisingly weak; for example, there is a striking reference to *Sons and Lovers* and *The Rainbow* as novels which 'trace the development and social integration of a single protagonist' (p. 62), whereas in fact the central thrust of each of these texts is precisely the *failure* of its central protagonist to achieve 'social integration'.

Finally, in 'The Very First Lady Chatterley? Mrs. Havelock Ellis's *Seaweed*' (*ELT* 51:ii[2008] 123–37), Jo-Ann Wallace discusses Edith Ellis's 1898 novel, *Seaweed: A Cornish Idyll*, and raises the 'possibility' that 'it served as one source for D.H. Lawrence's 1928 novel, *Lady Chatterley's Lover*' (p. 131). The description of the novel's fraught publication history is fascinating. Edith Ellis's novel was published by 'The University Press at Watford', but effectively suppressed after a raid on that publisher by Scotland Yard, whose intended target was her husband's (Havelock Ellis's) sexological study, *Sexual Inversion*. It was subsequently reissued in Britain in a substantially

revised (i.e. toned-down) form in 1907 as *Kit's Woman: A Cornish Idyll*, and in
America in 1909 as *Steve's Woman*; T. Werner Laurie published a popular
edition in Britain in 1916. The suppression of *Seaweed* invites comparison with
the still more complex fate of Lawrence's novel in the literary marketplace; its
plot echoes Lawrence's later text at a number of points. In Ellis's novel, a
Cornish tin-miner is paralysed from the waist down; his devoted wife cares for
him, but briefly takes a lover (a ship's mate) whom she meets on one of her
regular trips to the coast to gather seaweed to use as a tonic for her husband's
legs. The physical relationship soon ends, however, because of her spiritual
commitment to her husband, in spite of her husband's willing (indeed
enthusiastic) acceptance of her sexual nature and need for physical fulfilment.
Wallace describes it as a turn-of-the-century 'sex novel', and notes how *Lady
Chatterley's Lover* reads like an 'ironic postwar response' (p. 132) to its
idealistic, spiritual treatment of its sexual theme. In Ellis's novel, the husband's
broadmindedness is rewarded by his wife's spiritual devotion, while in
Lawrence's novel Clifford's readiness to entertain the idea of his wife taking a
lover is subject to his rigorous (and quite brutal) upholding of class
boundaries, and Constance Chatterley must renounce constancy to the
spiritual depravity of her culture in favour of a revitalizing sexual commitment
to Mellors, the gamekeeper. Even if we are not convinced by the argument that
Lawrence actually read the novel (and/or that he learnt about it during his
time in Cornwall between 1915 and 1917), the two novels can be said to emerge
in response to a common English cultural heritage. In reading Ellis's novel
alongside *Lady Chatterley's Lover*, Wallace backs a recent trend of interest
in Lawrence's last novel which seeks to locate it in the culture of
'late-nineteenth-century English progressive idealism' (p. 124).

The *D.H. Lawrence Review* is slowly catching up with its backlog of essays.
The latest double issue, comprising volumes 32 and 33, was published in 2008
but backdated to 2003–4. It contains nine essays, applying a range of textual,
historical and theoretical approaches to their subject. Highlights include David
Game's essay on 'Aspects of Degenerationism in D.H. Lawrence's *Kangaroo*'
(*DHLR* 32–3[2003–4] 87–101) and Ben Stoltzfus's 'Lacan's Knot, Freud's
Narrative, and the Tangle of "Glad Ghosts"' (*DHLR* 32–3[2003–4] 102–14).
Tim Marshall's 'Claiming the Body: "Odour of Chrysanthemums", Death, the
Great War and the Workhouse' (*DHLR* 32–3[2003–4] 19–34) reads the death
of Walter Bates in Lawrence's story in the context, first, of 'cultural practices
surrounding death in the nineteenth century' (p. 19); then of debates around
the ownership of dead bodies following the 1832 Anatomy Act, which 'granted
anatomists legal access to dead bodies remaining unclaimed from workhouses
and hospitals' (p. 27); and finally of tensions during the Great War over the
status of the bodies of dead soldiers, which in 1919, in the face of growing
logistical problems with mass repatriation, were formally declared the
property of the British state. Marshall's approach is attentive both to textual
details in the story and to the historical context of the text's reception: he
describes Lawrence's subtle depiction of Elizabeth Bates's specific social
anxieties, but he also suggests rather convincingly that the first readers of the
short-story volume *The Prussian Officer*, published in November 1914, would

have read 'Odour of Chrysanthemums' as engaging with early wartime debates around the status and fate of soldiers' bodies.

This year the two issues of *Études Lawrenciennes*, volumes 38 and 39, were devoted to the subject of pluralism in Lawrence, collecting essays on 'The One and the Many' and 'A Plurality of Selves and Voices' respectively. Volume 38 contains contributions by (among others) Michael Bell on 'Reflections on the Death of a Porcupine', Noëlle Cuny on *The Lost Girl*, and Stephen Rowley on 'Bavarian Gentians'; the contributors to volume 39 include Earl Ingersoll on Lawrence's friendship with E.M. Forster, Neil Roberts on free indirect discourse in Lawrence and Katherine Mansfield, and Jacqueline Gouirand on screen adaptations of *Lady Chatterley's Lover*.

The *Journal of D.H. Lawrence Studies* (1:iii[2008]), contains James T. Boulton's 'Further Letters of D.H. Lawrence' (*JDHLS* 1:iii[2008] 7–13) and John Worthen's transcription of the 1921 *Hutchinson's Magazine* version of the short story 'Fanny and Annie' (*JDHLS* 1:iii[2008] 57–77), plus essays or notes by Colm Kerrigan, Keith Sagar, John Turner, Howard J. Booth, David Game, Jeff Wallace, and Michael Squires and Lynn K. Talbot. In 'D.H. Lawrence and the Spontaneous Gesture' (*JDHLS* 1:iii[2008] 33–54), John Turner discusses Lawrence's celebration of spontaneity in the personal context of his long-standing inner conflict between depression and creativity, the historical context of the Great War, and the cultural context of the spread of psychoanalytic theories. He notes that the word 'spontaneity' only became an important term for Lawrence after the publication of *The Rainbow*: in *Women in Love* the word is used seventeen times, while it occurs forty-three times in the 1918–19 *Studies in Classic American Literature*, and '24 times in the 20 pages of the 1919 essay "Democracy"' (p. 46). Turner traces Lawrence's use of the term, and the broader implications of 'spontaneity', in his essays on classic American literature, where Lawrence proposed a revision of Freudian ideas, dealing not with 'the repressed unconscious', but with 'the creative unconscious' or 'the hidden spontaneous life of the material body' (p. 48). On the one hand, through his analysis of the American authors Lawrence critiques 'the repressive age in which we live' (p. 47), while on the other he attempts to construct a quasi-scientific account of 'the emotional life of the body' (p. 49). Turner shows how the versatile account of repressed impulses in the essays bears 'eloquent testimony to [Lawrence's] inner liveliness' (p. 52), while their esoteric neurological language is 'strained', revealing 'the difficulty of [his] own struggle to achieve spontaneity' (p. 50).

Among the latest editions of Lawrence's texts, James T. Boulton has edited a new volume of *Selected Letters* for Oneworld Classics. He provides a generous selection from the eight-volume edition of the *Letters* he edited for Cambridge University Press, and includes three additional, recently discovered letters in an appendix: the first to Augusta de Witt, 22 October 1916; the second to Philip Heseltine, 11 June 1917; and the third to Dr Andrew Morland, 9 February 1930. The letters are helpfully divided into seven sections, each prefaced with a few short paragraphs describing the biographical context. The volume also includes a short (25-page) biography of Lawrence, a descriptive list of correspondents, and a full and extremely useful index.

The new Penguin Classics edition of Lawrence's works is completed with the
publication of the *Selected Poems*, edited and introduced by James Fenton. In
his introduction Fenton describes his editorial principles: he selected poems
'from the individual collections made during Lawrence's lifetime' and printed
them 'in the order in which they occur in these collections' (p. xiii).
Unfortunately, he chose to print the texts found in the *Complete Poems*
volume, edited by Vivian de Sola Pinto and Warren Roberts, rather than
reproducing the poems as they appeared in the contemporary collections.
The *Complete Poems* volume is not a critical edition, and it does not always
reproduce the order of poems established in the first editions. However,
editorial reservations aside, Fenton's selection is judicious, and he brings an
infectious enthusiasm to the job. He argues that 'Lawrence's free verse is free
to some purpose. It is powerfully mimetic, and what it imitates is the surge
of the passions, the motions of thought, the rush of the perceptions'. He
reprints all the old favourites: 'Last Lesson of the Afternoon', 'Piano', 'Bat',
'Snake', 'Bavarian Gentians', and 'The Ship of Death'. Yet the reader new to
Lawrence's verse will also be introduced to lesser-known gems such as
'Sorrow' and 'Brooding Grief' from *Amores* [1916] and 'On the Balcony' from
Look! We Have Come Through! [1917]. As we wait for the publication of the
Cambridge edition of the poems, the liveliness of this selection, and its
comparative brevity, may help to win over those readers perturbed by the
1,000 pages of the *Complete Poems*.

(e) Virginia Woolf

The central thesis of Kathryn Simpson's fascinating book *Gifts, Markets and
Economies of Desire in Virginia Woolf* (one of only three monographs
dedicated entirely to Woolf this year) is that 'gift-giving in Woolf's writing
signifies an alternative feminine libidinal economy' (p. 2). Drawing on Mauss,
Rubin and Cixous *inter alia*, Simpson amplifies her thesis at a number of
different levels: in terms of Woolf's own practices of gift-giving, particularly of
books; by close-reading instances of gift-giving in Woolf's work, explicit or
implied; and through exploration of the 'textual generosity' of Woolf's writing,
'in its richness, depth, and associative connections' (p. 6). Her first chapter
continues the recent growth of interest in the previously neglected short essays,
as well as *A Room of One's Own* and *Three Guineas*. Simpson traces a
trajectory in Woolf's non-fiction, arguing that in the mid- to late 1930s 'what
Woolf saw as the damaging ramifications of the increasing commodification of
writing and the pressures of the literary marketplace come into sharper critical
focus' (p. 34). The second chapter discusses 'queering the market' in *Mrs
Dalloway* and associated texts; careful close reading of both actual and
'intended' gift-giving in these texts reveals how the characters 'mov[e] between
gift and market economies, between homoerotic possibility and heterosexual
conformity' (p. 84). A third chapter discusses creative gifts in *To the
Lighthouse*, *Orlando* and *Between the Acts*, and a fourth and final chapter
examines the short fiction, introducing the seductive idea of Woolf's smuggling
'sexual and economic contraband' (p. 131) into these stories. This is a

meticulous and rigorous exploration of the intersecting discourses of desire and economics without ever reducing one to the other and, crucially, never losing sight of the texture of Woolf's prose.

Teresa Prudente's *A Specially Tender Piece of Eternity: Virginia Woolf and the Experience of Time* 'aims at shedding light on the stratified temporality characterizing Woolf's novels' (p. ix): the a-linear temporalities of Woolf's texts (following Ricoeur), and in particular temporalities of eternity and the ecstatic. The first part of the book reads *To the Lighthouse* and *Orlando* especially with reference to 'moments of being'; Prudente concludes that 'the coexistence and interdependence of the two feelings of ecstasy and empti-ness...appear as the climax of Woolf's insistence on the modern subject's divided perception' (p. 63), the roots of which perception can be found in Woolf's handling of time. The second part is 'a specific inquiry into the relationship between ecstasy and writing' (p. xi) focusing particularly on the ineffability of the ecstatic moment; Prudente elegantly expresses the way in which the ineffable engages a foundational problematic of artistic represen-tation: 'The un-representability of ecstasy thus seems to function also as an allegory which suggests the less specific discrepancy between experience and expression' (p. 71). The third part opens out to look at Woolf's novels in context, particularly in relation to Gide's *Les Faux-Monnayeurs*, moving towards a discussion of the novel genre's capacity to handle time.

As the subtitle would suggest, Maria DiBattista's *Imagining Virginia Woolf: An Experiment in Critical Biography* takes an unconventional approach to the biographical form. DiBattista treads a careful path in negotiating her position which, while crucially acknowledging that authors, Virginia Woolf included, are knowable 'primarily and most intimately as figments that exist only in our imagination'—indeed, she bases her entire project on this premise—neverthe-less insists that this knowledge 'is as valuable as it is inevitable' (p. 172). While what drives the work is the inevitable sense that we construct an idea of 'the author' as we read, this 'instinct' (to take up a word of Woolf's) is not converted into a hunt for what might be called the 'real' Woolf. Rather, as DiBattista puts it, 'The subject of this biography is not the historical person who was born in 1882 and died in 1941. The subject is Virginia Woolf, the figment who exists as much in the minds of her readers as in the pages of her books' (p. 9). The result is a highly readable yet serious and novel reading of Woolf through various 'personalities'—the Sibyl of the Drawing Room, the Author, the Critic, the World Writer and the Adventurer (with the Adventurer emerging as the Captain Self, per *Orlando*)—which admirably articulate Woolf's multifaceted writing personae. The discussion of the contrast between Woolf's novelistic voice and her critical one, for example, seems to exemplify Woolf's own view of the true critic as one who can 'seem...to bring to light what was already there beforehand, instead of imposing anything from the outside' (Woolf, quoted in DiBattista, p. 100).

Gabrielle McIntire's *Modernism, Memory and Desire* announces itself as the first monograph devoted to the 'unusual' pairing of T.S. Eliot and Woolf. The book's central thesis is that for both these writers 'representing the past was...a sensuous endeavour that repeatedly turned to the erotic and the corporeal for some of its most authentic elaborations' (p. 2)—in other words, that there is often a desiring, even sexual, charge to their engagement with memory and history. This erudite work is perhaps slightly belated in some of its claims: the suggestion that there is a lack of critical focus on corporeality and sexuality in Woolf is contraindicated by, for example, Simpson's work reviewed here, or Patricia Moran's work on trauma reviewed last year. Similarly, McIntire's appeal for us to see Woolf as 'a thinker of memory and history' chimes directly with, for example, Sanja Bahun's essay this year. Nevertheless McIntire's work adds substantially to thinking about both of these areas. Her careful cross-references across texts, focusing on *Orlando*, *To the Lighthouse*, 'A Sketch of the Past' and *Between the Acts* but including many of the essays, add conviction to her readings of, for instance, the implications of the promiscuity of memory for Woolf. Particularly significant is McIntire's exploration of Woolf's claims not to have read Freud before 1939—claims which, as McIntire demonstrates, are often accepted by Woolf critics but appear thoroughly implausible.

Rosi Braidotti's 'Intensive Genre and the Demise of Gender' (*Angelaki* 13[2008] 45–57) gestures towards the various Deleuzian 'becomings' in Woolf's work, and focuses on Woolf's correspondence with Vita Sackville-West where, as Braidotti puts it, 'The space of the letters is an in-between, a third party that does not fully coincide with either Virginia or Vita, but rather frames the space of their relationship' (p. 50). Elsewhere Braidotti puts it even more emphatically, arguing that 'the apersonal nature of the desire at work here [between Woolf and Sackville-West] does not coincide at all with the individual biographies of the protagonists' (p. 51). This argument relies on 'a sustainable model of an affective, de-personalized, highly receptive subject which quite simply is not one, not there, not that. As Virginia Woolf put it: "I am rooted, but I flow." (*The Waves*, 69)' (p. 46)—a subject easily recognizable to readers of Woolf. While one senses that those without thorough grounding in Deleuzian terminology and thought may sometimes miss some of the nuance in this piece, Braidotti's sensitive reading of the space of the correspondence, and in particular Sackville-West's reaction to her relationship with Woolf's *Orlando*, provides an exciting and productive way to approach the humanity of the participants, without falling back onto potentially simplistic biographical readings.

Megan M. Quigley's 'Modern Novels and Vagueness' (*Mo/Mo* 15[2008] 101–29) argues that vagueness is a central, valued concept in Woolf's theories of language. Quigley deftly explores evidence of Woolf's engagement with Bertrand Russell's alleged formulation of a 'special language' to avoid vagueness and aspiring to the definite, compared with Woolf's own attachment to the vague, in a range of texts including *To the Lighthouse*, *Night and Day* and her BBC broadcast 'Craftsmanship'. Quigley concludes that Woolf posits, *contra* Russell, an ontological, or semantic, vagueness, one which does not come about because of an inadequacy in language to express the definite outlines of the world, but rather is the result of vagueness in the world itself. While Quigley's suggestion that there is an 'overemphasis in literary criticism on classicism and objectivity as characterizing modernist works of art' (p. 123) might itself be overstating the case, nevertheless this piece certainly adds another helpful inflection to our understanding of Woolf's engagement with an uncertain, transitional world.

Sara Crangle's essay 'The Time Being: On Woolf and Boredom' (*MFS* 54[2008] 209–32) similarly reads Woolf through an apparently unpromising concept, though Crangle does not want to rehabilitate boredom as a positive term so much as draw our attention to its literary and philosophical significance. Though the essay begins with boredom in Heidegger and Nietzsche, Crangle's work continues the current flourishing trend in critical work reading Woolf with Levinas. Crangle summarizes her position as 'a sense that the boredom behind Woolf's creative desires—both authorial and fictional—is informed by a longing to abandon the stultifying sameness of selfhood for the endless unknowns of otherness' (p. 211). Key here is Levinas's boredom or 'haunting presence' which, *contra* Heidegger and Nietzsche, 'demands that we continually perceive ourselves in the light of otherness' (p. 215); it is this sense of the indispensable other which resonates so strongly with Woolf. The article weaves together a few key instances or evocations of boredom across Woolf's writing, focusing in particular on *Orlando*; as in much recent work on Woolf class becomes strongly visible as Woolf appears, in part, to perpetuate the traditional distinction between aristocratic melancholy and plebeian boredom. It concludes with an extended reading of the short story 'The Lady in the Looking Glass' which, Crangle argues, 'demonstrat[es] how a bored self remains determined by, and might move toward, the endlessly interesting unknowability of otherness' (p. 227).

Virginia Woolf: Art, Education and Internationalism offers a selection of papers from the seventeenth annual international Woolf conference. As one would expect from the theme, comparative essays feature strongly in this collection, South or Central American writers in particular, with contributions on Woolf and the Mexican writer Rosario Castellanos (Reyes), the Brazilian Clarice Lispector (Smith-Hubbard), and the Chilean María Luisa Bombal (Ayuso). Elizabeth Bowen and Monica Ali are also put into dialogue with Woolf (in Gerend and Smith respectively); as are, in a slightly different way, Judith Butler, Susan Sontag and Arundhati Roy in Kimberley Engdahl Coles's essay; whether explicitly or implicitly, argues Coles, all three of these writers endorse Woolf's call to '"fight with the mind," and', Coles concludes, 'we can, we must, teach others to do the same' (p. 45). Judith Allen's analysis of 'Thoughts on Peace in an Air Raid' concludes with a similarly urgent assertion of the continued relevance of Woolf's essay, whose politics, argues Allen, are articulated not least through its dialogic, conversational mode. To keep talking is, by implication, crucial at a time when, as Allen notes, 'the silencing of women's voices is still with us' (p. 29). (Elsewhere, Marian Eide's '"The Stigma of Nation": Feminist Just War, Privilege, and Responsibility' (*Hypatia* 23[2008] 48–60) also assesses the utility of Woolf's politics in relation to twenty-first-century geopolitics.) Chinese connections appeared in Patricia Laurence's 'Hours in a Chinese Library', focusing on Woolf's correspondence with the Chinese writer Ling Shuha which, according to Laurence, challenges Gayatri Spivak's position that 'the subaltern cannot speak' (p. 14); and in Xiaoquin Cao's brief but fascinating overview of the reception of Woolf in China, which 'began to flourish from the late 1900s' (p. 83). Richard

Zumkhawala-Cook's '*Tae the Lichthoose*: Woolf's Scotland and the Problem of the Local' 'entertains rather than answer[s], the question: why Scotland?' (p. 57) as the setting for this novel, and elegantly suggests that while the characters in the novel 'in the end are shown to be tourists; the novel . . . is not' (p. 62), redeemed by the 'Time Passes' central section and in particular the figure of Mrs McNabb, who Zumkhawala-Cook argues appears as 'the human and humanized embodiment of the Scottish working class, of domestic labor, and of regional identity' (p. 58). Other notable essays are Erica Delsandro's suitably dynamic exploration of aerial perspectives in Woolf; the next instalment of Suzanne Bellamy's work on the Australian scholar Nuri Mass, whose previously unpublished 1942 MA thesis constitutes 'possibly the first [complete study of Woolf's major novels] in the world' (p. 131); and Jane de Gay's plenary address, which explores how the trope of metamorphosis 'plays a key role in Woolf's rejection of nation, her embracing of transnational cultures, and her archaeological journeying down into the past' (p. 139).

The Berkeleyan table of *To the Lighthouse* featured in a number of essays this year. Michel Serres's '*Feux et signaux de brume*: Virginia Woolf's Lighthouse' (*SubStance* 37[2008] 110-31) gravitates towards a philosophical discussion of animism, via a lyrical eulogy to Woolf's novel which, Serres claims, converted him from a realist to an idealist; and which, in opening, he suggests registers the '*superabundant multiplicity of . . . durations*' (p. 111) more precisely than does Proust, whom Woolf was reading while she was writing *To the Lighthouse*. Taking up the invitation to consider Berkeley's question, namely 'what becomes of the things of the world when no one perceives them' (p. 113), he concludes that the novel comes down on the side of the idealists, asserting that 'I see, for my own part, that Virginia Woolf wrote *To the Lighthouse* only in order to describe, passionately, subtly, precisely, intensely, ecstatically, divinely . . . perception: her own and that of the two heroines. And to affirm that it sustains the world' (pp. 122–3). Heidi Storl's 'Heidegger in Woolf's Clothing' (*P&L* 32[2008] 303–14) is a brief but elegant reading of *To the Lighthouse* from a philosopher's perspective as a way of understanding key Heideggerian concepts; it also indicates to Woolf scholars how helpful Heideggerian terminology might be to elucidate the effects of Woolf's prose and her 'sustained meditation on *that-which-is*' (p. 303). Finally, the Berkeleyan table is also present in David Dwan's 'Woolf, Scepticism and Manners' (*TPr* 22[2008] 249–68). Suggesting that 'Woolf's investment in manners is closely related to her distinctive form of scepticism' (p. 249), the first part of Dwan's closely textured essay discusses Woolf's scepticism in relation to Hume's, arguing that the limits of their scepticism can be drawn where they both engage with the role of habits and customs—or, more specifically for Woolf, of manners. Dwan concludes that while manners, for Woolf, add a necessary 'pattern to our world', one must be wary of this pattern becoming 'a fetish and the basis for another form of dogmatism' (p. 263); but while, according to Dwan, 'Woolf certainly acknowledges that manners reflect and sustain structures of domination', this does not ultimately 'mitigate her own snobbish views' (p. 264).

The content of the year's *Woolf Studies Annual* was particularly eclectic—in terms of form and perspective, at any rate, with *Mrs Dalloway* being the main focus of two of the six essays (by Melissa Bagley and Kaley Joyes), and featuring strongly in a third, Patricia McManus's 'The "Offensiveness" of Virginia Woolf: From a Moral to a Political Reading' (*WStA* 14[2008] 91–138). McManus's substantial essay is a sustained challenge to current paradigms of reading Woolf's politics, and begins by directly engaging with Woolf's 'snobbish' views. As McManus observes, commentators tend to deal with Woolf's more politically problematic statements either by dismissing her as a snob or by dismissing the statements as aberrations. For McManus, as for Hermione Lee, from whom McManus takes her cue, this will not do; we must 'swallow Woolf whole' (Lee, quoted in McManus, p. 92). To do this, McManus argues, we must shift from a moral to a political discourse, and in particular we must see Woolf's comments in historical context. She argues that Woolf privileged above all the 'private self', conceived 'not as the inhabitant of a particular realm but as the site of a particular way of knowing, a disembodied, profoundly non-social, epistemological position from which— and only from which—culture, and with culture politics, becomes possible' (p. 101), which we must see as resistance to the increasing 'deprivatisation of areas of life hitherto designated private' (p. 98). McManus demonstrates Woolf's privileging of this 'private' self not only through the more explicit articulations of *Three Guineas* but also, and perhaps most contentiously, through Woolf's use of free indirect discourse, taking *Mrs Dalloway* as an example—though McManus suggests that any of Woolf's novels would have done just as well, since they all 'desire a public composed of privatised readers' (p. 124). McManus's careful weighing up of the factors informing Woolf's politics are summed up in this suggestion: 'That *she had to make a choice* [about which class position to align herself with—namely, her own] was a consequence of structural dynamics outside Woolf's control; that *she made the choice she did* speaks of her own politics, her perception of her class as the most likely agent of reform' (p. 121). Melissa Bagley's 'Nature and Nation in *Mrs Dalloway*' (*WStA* 14[2008] 35–52) also considers the politics of *Mrs Dalloway* but explores the use of biological metaphor in the text to indicate Woolf's critique of the assumption that 'the nation's order and socially or politically formed identities have less to do with a wilful or subconscious engagement of ideology than with biological factors' (p. 35). Bagley identifies a faultline in the discourse of nature and nation which Woolf aims to expose; the patriarchal order replicates and reinforces social structures, including gender, through metaphors of the natural, but 'many kinds of industrial and technological progress tie to a society's ability to work with and overcome the forces of nature' (p. 47), thus rendering these metaphors, and in turn the structures they underpin, unstable. Kaley Joyes's 'Failed Witnessing in Virginia Woolf's *Mrs Dalloway*' (*WStA* 14[2008] 69–90) approaches a different theme in this text, extending critical work on Woolf and trauma to argue that 'Woolf's authentic representation of individual psychological trauma and its cultural context can expose, but not overcome, the innumerable challenges to healing First World War trauma' (p. 69). Social structures are also crucial here: Joyes convincingly argues that, while Rezia and Clarissa are the only characters in the novel to approach Septimus's trauma with anything like 'the dialogic witnessing that can heal psychic wounds' (p. 70), they are ultimately prevented from adequately doing so because of their marginalized social positions.

Mónica G. Ayuso's essay, 'Virginia Woolf in Mexico and Puerto Rico' (*WStA* 14[2008] 1–19), is a more expansive addition to the work on Woolf and Spanish American writers published this year. Encouraged by 'theoretical developments in transnational feminism' (p. 1) and informed by the work of Homi K. Bhabha, Ayuso explores how two contemporary Spanish American writers, Rosaria Castellanos and Rosario Ferré, have read Woolf over the course of their careers. The influence of *A Room of One's Own* and *Three Guineas* appears particularly strong, for perhaps obvious reasons; Ayuso concludes by suggesting that 'Woolf's Outsiders' Society could be said to stretch beyond the spatial boundaries of England to include these two "educated men's daughters," born a generation later and an ocean apart' (pp. 14–15). Heidi Stalla's essay, 'William Bankes: Echoes of Egypt in Virginia Woolf's *To the Lighthouse*' (*WStA* 14[2008] 21–34), also has an international theme, though of a very different sort. This shorter piece investigates a possible model for William Bankes: William John Bankes, a prominent plunderer of Egyptian artefacts in the late eighteenth century, and 'one of the first Europeans to record the temple of Ramses II at Abu Simbel' (p. 27). Stalla notes that Vita Sackville-West wrote to Woolf from Egypt in 1926, while Woolf was composing the novel, and concludes by pointing at a few apparently Egyptian allusions in *To the Lighthouse* (and indeed other novels), the most persuasive of which is the echo of the slave-maker Ramses II in the name 'Ramsay', given that, as Stalla notes, 'Woolf writes frequently about how the English government throughout the greater part of its history has treated women like slaves' (p. 31). Unfortunately, however, the essay's findings are somewhat piecemeal and inconclusive; the intriguing question the essay poses, namely 'what part might William Bankes and the exploration of Egypt play in *To the Lighthouse*?' (p. 27) is not convincingly answered. Finally, Molly McQuade offers a letter to Woolf: entitled 'Life Sentences' (*WStA* 14[2008] 53–67), this creative-critical hybrid picks up and runs with Woolf's reinvention of the sentence, noting that 'your sentence could respond with a freedom that seemed denied to you personally' (p. 54). This engaging piece performs as it observes the work of the sentence—though McQuade admits that 'I prefer the pursuit of paragraphs, not sentences' (p. 53), she nevertheless reveals in darts and flashes some of the techniques Woolf used to (re-)create the sentence, and their effects.

The spring 2008 issue of the *Journal of the Short Story in English* was devoted to Woolf; as Christine Reynier points out in her introduction, the 'cosmopolitanism' of Woolf's short stories is aptly addressed here by thirteen contributors from six different countries. Of particular note were Kate Henderson's 'Fashioning Anti-Semitism: Virginia Woolf's "The Duchess and the Jeweller" and the Readers of *Harper's Bazaar*' (*JSSE* 50[2008] 49–65), offering a truly novel perspective on this text and its depiction of Jewishness by considering the context of its original appearance in what was a fashion magazine as much as a literary publication; Anne McClellan's investigation of the woman scholar figure in 'Adeline's (Bankrupt) Education Fund: Woolf, Woman and Education in the Short Fiction' (*JSSE* 50[2008] 85–101); the elegant use of Deleuze and Guattari and careful attention to textual variants in Oliver Taylor's '"What's 'it'—What do you mean by 'it'?": Lost Readings and Getting lost in "Kew Gardens"' (*JSSE* 50[2008] 121–35) to produce a reading of that story which emphasizes the role of the body; Laura Marcus's dazzlingly wide-ranging exploration of the 'telescope story' in its various manifestations across a range of Woolf's texts, '"In the Circle of the Lens": Woolf's "Telescope" Story, Scene-Making and Memory' (*JSSE* 50[2008] 153–69); and Emilie Crapoulet's illuminating reading of 'The String Quartet' as 'an elaboration of the shortcomings of the verbalisation of music' (p. 212) in 'Beyond the Boundaries of Language: Music in Virginia Woolf's "The String Quartet"' (*JSSE* 50[2008] 201–15).

There was a notable clutch of what one might call compare-and-contrast essays this year. Among the most successful was Rebecca Wisor's 'Virginia Woolf and Vera Brittain: Pacifism and the Gendered Politics of Public Intellectualism' (*StHum* 35[2008] 137–53), using Edward Said's idea of 'cultural marginalization as a necessary precondition for intellectual activity' (p. 139) to 'trace the confluence of [Woolf's and Brittain's] thinking on the subjects of marginalization and intellectualism' (p. 148) and more broadly to implore intellectual historians to pay more attention to the potentially unacknowledged predecessors of today's public intellectuals. Sarah Balkin's 'Regenerating Drama in Stein's *Doctor Faustus Lights the Lights* and Woolf's *Between the Acts*' (*MD* 51[2008] 433–57) subtly negotiates around the question of 'influence', moot in this instance, to offer a perceptive study of the temporality of these texts in relation to their dramaturgical aspects. 'Like Stein', Balkin argues, 'Woolf ends with a return to the beginning and, as Stein, the beginning is one we never saw' (p. 452). Louise A. Poresky's 'Cather and Woolf in Dialogue: *The Professor's House* and *To the Lighthouse*' (*PLL* 44[2008] 67–86), however, sometimes appears to forget its initial caveats about the necessarily speculative basis of any argument that Cather's novel directly influenced Woolf; while some of Poresky's comparisons are intriguing, they risk being undermined by overstated claims such as 'Virginia Woolf takes Cather's novel [with various characteristics also found in *To the Lighthouse*] [and] From all this Woolf creates a novel . . .' (pp. 84–5)—this surely needs to be couched in more cautious terms. In her 'Demolishing the Castle: Virginia Woolf's Reaction to T.S. Eliot's *Murder in the Cathedral*' (*CEA* 70[2008] 46–55), Carol Osborne is in the more secure position of being able to draw on Woolf's recorded responses to Eliot's play; also addressing *Between the Acts*, this essay explores the differences between the two authors' positions on religion in particular. Rather than comparing Woolf's fiction with that of a contemporary, Monica Girard, in 'Virginia Woolf's Suicide Notes: Michael Cunningham's Art of Transposing a Life's Epilogue into a Fictitious Prologue' (in Crinquand, ed., *Last Letters*), explores Michael Cunningham's use of Woolf's real suicide note, plus first-hand accounts of the day of her suicide, in his novel *The Hours*, arguing that he interweaves fictional and 'real' elements to generate 'an illusory representation of Virginia Woolf's death which satisfactorily appears quite real and plausible' (p. 52). Woolf's cosmopolitanism is again to the fore in Caroline Lusin's 'Red Flowers and a Shabby Coat: Russian Literature and the Presentation of "Madness" in Virginia Woolf's

Mrs Dalloway' (*CCS* 5[2008] 289–300), which emphasizes the 'Russian fever' that gripped Great Britain in the early twentieth century, and uses this as the foundation for a clear, sharp and convincing reading of novellas by Gogol and Garshin as intertexts for Woolf's novel. Finally, Pam Fox Kuhlken's 'Clarissa and Cléo (En)Durée Suicidal Time in Virginia Woolf's *Mrs Dalloway* and Agnès Varda's *Cléo de 5 à 7*' (*CLS* 45[2008] 341–69) provides an interesting cross-disciplinary comparison of Woolf's novel and Varda's 1961 film, demonstrating how they are 'more than texts by women about women set in a single day' (p. 341). Kuhlken argues that in both these texts the protagonists escape from masculine *temps*, move through feminine *durée*, but finally move towards an 'androgynous time' in 'an aesthetic black hole conjured into extra-textual existence' (p. 341).

Sanja Bahun also puts Woolf into dialogue with a figure from a different discipline, but attenuates the distinction between Woolf as a writer of fiction and Walter Benjamin as a cultural historian and philosopher to emphasize the 'commensurability of [their] philosophies of history' (p. 100). Her exception-ally fine essay, 'The Burden of the Past, the Dialectics of the Present: Notes on Virginia Woolf's and Walter Benjamin's Philosophies of History' (*ModCult* 3:ii[2008] 100–15), carefully negotiates what is known or can be speculated about Woolf's and Benjamin's knowledge of each other's work; it then produces a highly convincing reading of both the shared subject-matter and, crucially, the 'structural correspondence' of their late work, specifically *Between the Acts* and 'On the Concept of History'. Bahun suggests that neither writer simply proposes a replacement of the linear model of history with a cyclical one; rather, 'their reflections vacillate between the different proposed and rejected models of history' (p. 104). This vacillation is, Bahun argues, reflected in the quality of both writers' prose, characterized by 'the alteration of exuberance and minimalism', and serial composition (p. 110). Bahun's claim that both writers gain from their 'discursive juxtaposition', in that 'Woolf's mature aesthetic politics is placed where it should rightfully abide—in the realm of the philosophy of history—and Benjamin's cogitations on history become actualized in aesthetic performance' (p. 111) is amply justified on the basis of this intervention.

Andrea Zemgulys's *Modernism and the Locations of Literary Heritage* provides an original reading of modernism's literary heritage not so much through texts, but rather the places and spaces that had become, as she puts it, 'newly historic' (p. 4) in the early twentieth century. Chapter 6 considers Woolf's approving engagement with 'literary geography' in her essays, as well as its presence in *Orlando* and *Night and Day*. Like McManus, Zemgulys draws attention to Woolf's approval of the 'impersonal' attitude in reading and writing, and also makes a claim for *Night and Day* as marking 'a turn to Woolf's modernist vision, a turn that does not dismiss "the Victorians" . . . but instead captures their worthy *character*' (p. 178). Marie Lanel's 'Revisiting a Great Man's House: Virginia Woolf's Carlylean Pilgrimages' (*CAnn* 24[2008] 117–31) comes to a similar conclusion, namely that 'Although she had sought to repudiate Carlyle's historical vision, Woolf cannot disown it entirely' (p. 129). In keeping with this current interest in Woolf's Victorian inheritance was this year's Annual Virginia Woolf Birthday Lecture, by Henrietta Garnett.

Published as *Leslie Stephen: A Nineteenth Century Legacy*, Garnett's paper paints a lively portrait of Stephen and 'the different perspectives from which Virginia viewed him as well as...those traits she inherited from him' (p. 3).

A number of books taking a broadly postcolonial perspective featured Woolf to some extent. Laura Winkiel's discussion of Woolf in *Modernism, Race and Manifestos* focuses almost entirely on her non-fiction. Winkiel argues that the essay 'Mr Bennett and Mrs Brown' 'borrows from the manifesto genre several of its revolutionary qualities', but suggests that, by the time of *Three Guineas*, Woolf had come to critique 'an overuse of the manifesto form' (p. 197). *Three Guineas* emerges as a hybrid text which ultimately, in both form and content, 'suggests that impurity and inclusion are the proper attributes of a democratic state' (p. 195). In her immense *Freedom's Empire: Race and the Rise of the Novel in Atlantic Modernity, 1640–1940*, Laura Doyle observes that while 'postcolonial readings of Woolf most often consider her in relation to India', she herself proposes instead that many of Woolf's novels present 'revisionary parables of Anglo-American modernity', detectable if we 'consider the water tropes in her writing as expressions of the colonial legacy more broadly' (p. 413). Doyle also emphasizes the fleeting visibility of a queer sexuality emerging alongside, and in resistance to, the discourse of race and empire which these tropes evoke. Carey J. Snyder's chapter on Woolf in *British Fiction and Cross-Cultural Encounters* persuasively reads *The Voyage Out* through the concept of self-nativizing, which Snyder defines as 'the move to regard one's own culture through the estranging lens of ethnography, such that familiar customs, artefacts and beliefs are rendered strangely visible' (p. 100); she also considers 'Street Haunting' as an instance of self-nativizing participant observation. Drawing also on Woolf's contemporaries Jane Harrison and Ruth Benedict, this chapter is a significant addition to work on the intersections between Woolf's text and ethnography (also this year, see Glenn Willmott's *Modernist Goods: Primitivism, the Market and the Gift* for a brief discussion of Woolf drawing on anthropological and psychoanalytic discourse). Alissa G. Karl also focuses on Woolf's first novel in a chapter of her *Modernism and the Marketplace*. Karl's argument 'that *Voyage* features no native characters who can provide an alternative view renders Woolf's entire text vulnerable to the charge of Anglocentrism' (p. 54) indicates the difference between her position and Snyder's, though Karl goes on to indicate that Woolf does critique patriarchy and imperialism in this text, albeit ambivalently; she states that Woolf's texts 'allow us to trace the strategies and effects of consumer capital as it administers ideological, psychic, political and economic empire' (p. 43).

Jennifer Green-Lewis and Margaret Soltan's chapter on beauty in *Mrs Dalloway*, in their book *Teaching Beauty in DeLillo, Woolf and Merrill*, both explores how that novel seems to view beauty and what it can and cannot achieve, and attempts to identify what is 'beautiful' about Woolf's prose. Part of a larger project which aims to return discussion of the beautiful to academia, and the undergraduate classroom in particular, this chapter is narrated from the position of an instructor leading a class in discussion of Woolf's novel. It offers some attentive close readings of Woolf's prose, and if it comes to any conclusion, it is perhaps that the beauty of her writing has in large part to do with its evocation of correspondences, and its gesture towards a shared experience. The evocation of shared experience is also central G. Douglas Atkins's lively appreciation of Woolf's 'The Death of the Moth' in his (in some ways 'unabashedly old-fashioned', p. xi) collection *Reading Essays: An Invitation*, with Atkins observing 'It is not…individual—certainly not personal—interpretation that emerges here: through Woolf's far-from-clinical eye we see the seen, and share in it' (p. 138).

It is not perhaps surprising that Jack Stewart focuses on *To the Lighthouse* in his chapter on Woolf in *Color, Space, and Creativity: Art and Ontology in Five British Writers*. Beginning with reference to Fry's aesthetic theory, the chapter traces the way in which particular features of visual art (optics, particular colours alone, in pairs or in groups, etc.) function in Woolf's text, though not, Stewart is careful to note, as 'simple color–character equations' but rather through '*transpos[ing]* emotional vibrations into color wavelengths' (p. 41), while the second part of the chapter considers 'gendered and geometric space and the psychology of creativity' (p. 20). Julia Prewit Brown's *The Bourgeois Interior: How the Middle Class Imagines Itself in Literature and Film* also has a chapter on *To the Lighthouse*; she reads Woolf's text as an elegy to the nineteenth-century domestic interior, with a deeper sense of communal loss at its close than in Forster's *Howards End*: 'once [Mrs Ramsay—which Brown misspells as 'Ramsey' throughout] departs from the living, the domestic interior decays' (p. 109).

Janine Uttell's essay, 'Meals and Mourning in Woolf's *The Waves*' (*CollL* 35[2008] 1–19), adds to the growing body of work on Woolf and elegy. Here, Uttell uses Patricia Rae's concept of proleptic elegy to explore the significance of the two communal meals that feature in *The Waves* and argue that not only, as is frequently argued, is the first meal a prefiguration of Percival's death, and thus functions as a proleptic elegy, but 'the second meal is itself, too, a proleptic funeral—for each of the six characters as they near the end of their lives' (p. 14). '"I meant nothing by *The Lighthouse*": Virginia Woolf's Poetics of Negation', by Roberta Rubenstein (*JML* 31[2008] 36–53), systematically reads 'the marked meanings of 'nothing' and its variants' (p. 36) in Woolf's novel, arguing that 'the poetics of negation cues readers to notice the dark places and negative spaces in Woolf's fiction and in her life', but also reminds us that the text is structured by oscillation, concluding that 'Virginia Woolf names, frames and imaginatively negates nothingness' (p. 50).

The two issues of the *Virginia Woolf Miscellany* published this year focused on Woolf and pedagogy (*VWM* 73[2008]), and Woolf and photography (*VWM* 74[2008]). The issue on pedagogy was particularly engaging, with essays addressing topics as diverse as using Woolf as a model in the composition classroom, embracing the 'difficulty' of Woolf's writing and teaching Woolf using GoogleEarth[TM]. The *Virginia Woolf Bulletin* features a previously unpublished review by Woolf entitled 'Some Poetic Plays' (*VWB* 27[2008]), as well as a variety of letters—of particular interest is the correspondence between Woolf and Mrs G.E. Easdales, whose daughter Jean had her poetry published by the Hogarth Press at the age of 17 and went on to write a 'gothic-modernist' narrative poem *Amber Innocent*, published with a dust-jacket by Vanessa Bell (the only one Bell designed for the Press in

1939) (*VWB* 28[2008]). *Mrs Dalloway* was the most written-about novel in this year's three issues; one essay probes the significance of the text's minor characters (including Purvis and the singing beggar) (*VWB* 28[2008] 36–47), and another short piece identifies the song from Tennyson's *The Princess* as key intertext for the first page of Woolf's novel (*VWB* 28[2008] 48–52). Also of note was an intriguing short memoir of growing up at 22 Hyde Park Gate from 1943 (*VWB* 29[2008] 44–50). Finally, there were two particularly interesting titles this year from the growing Bloomsbury Heritage series: Julie Singleton's *A History of Monk's House and Village of Rodmell*, and Diana Gardner's *The Rodmell Papers: Reminiscences of Virginia and Leonard Woolf by a Sussex Neighbour*, published posthumously, and which, as Claire Gardner (the author's niece) says in an introduction, 'gives the reader some more glimpses of [the Woolfs] as they interact with the Rodmell community' (p. 7).

3. Post-1945 Fiction

The year 2008 was reasonably productive in the area of post-1945 fiction, although there were fewer monographs than in previous years. There has, however, been a higher proportion of books that balance an introductory approach aimed at the student market with genuinely new research. This review will begin by looking at four books that were published in 2007, but did not make last year's list.

There were three additions to Manchester University Press's Contemporary British Novelists series in 2007: Dominic Head's *Ian McEwan*, Brian Baker's *Iain Sinclair* and Simon Kövesi's *James Kelman*. Head's book provides a critical insight into the novels of one of the most important contemporary writers and indeed, Head makes great claims for McEwan as the 'most significant of a number of writers (including Martin Amis, Kazuo Ishiguro and Graham Swift) who have resuscitated the link between morality and the novel for a whole generation, in ways that befit the historical pressures of their time' (p. 1). This reading of McEwan as central to contemporary British literary culture is advanced in an interesting introduction that identifies the connection between the novelist and some of the main issues in British society and culture more generally over the last forty years or so, including 'fading colonialism; the dissolution of the British class structure; educational reform; the transformation of family life; and the second wave of feminism' (p. 5). McEwan's exploration of moral dilemmas and situations in his fiction is thus read as mapping similar concerns in public debates at large. For Head, McEwan's concern with the ethics of narrative is a touchstone of his work, although the way in which that has been expressed has developed over his novelistic career from the beginning of the 1970s. Head also sees a link in McEwan to a tradition in the post-war British novel that engages with the sense of an identity crisis in liberal humanism, an influence he traces to McEwan's teachers on the University of East Anglia's pioneering Creative Writing MA, Angus Wilson and Malcolm Bradbury. Perhaps more important for Head is McEwan's connection with Iris Murdoch's exploration of the ethical function of fiction to investigate moral issues, especially during moments of crisis for individual characters. The book is organized into ten chapters, the middle eight of which offer close readings of McEwan's main fiction from *The Cement Garden* [1978] to *Saturday* [2005]. Head deals with one novel in each chapter (except chapter 2, which discusses McEwan's short stories alongside *The Cement Garden*, and chapter 5, which discuses both *The Innocent* and *Black Dogs*), and this allows him the space to provide intriguing and detailed analyses of individual texts. The chapters on *The Child in Time*, *Enduring Love* and *Atonement* are especially astute. Head reads *The Child in Time* as a social condition novel in which McEwan 'reinvents the novel of society in his own terms' by interweaving the public and the private and exploring moral dilemmas that relate to both. *Enduring Love* is discussed as a hybrid form that cleverly produces a philosophical novel of ideas with the pace and narrative drive of a thriller. In chapter 8, Head rightly identifies *Atonement* as McEwan's greatest achievement, concentrating particularly on the way in which the novel explores 'how national myths are inscribed [and] the construction of a literary tradition' (p. 156). The book as a whole provides a fascinating analysis of McEwan's fiction up to 2007.

Brian Baker's *Iain Sinclair* is only the second full-length monograph on this important contemporary British writer (the first was Robert Bond's *Iain Sinclair*, published in 2005 by Salt Publishing). This may be due to the perception that Sinclair's writing is difficult. Baker, however, manages to produce a sophisticated and yet accessible analysis of the author's work. His approach is to relate Sinclair's writing to relevant literary and cultural contexts, and to useful theoretical concepts drawn primarily from post-structuralist and postmodern theory. In a very useful introduction, Baker identifies some of these main contexts and themes, which are then explored in the rest of the book. In particular, he identifies the 1960s countercultural influences on Sinclair's writing—on his early poetry in particular, but also on his later fiction. Baker also cleverly explores one of the central tensions for Sinclair: how to combine the figure of the detached social observer with a writing that, in part, wants to offer a social, political and cultural critique of contemporary Britain. Baker suggests that Sinclair's approach to this tension is through his interest in the anti-psychoanalytic theories of R.D. Laing, who is shown to be an important touchstone for the author's work. Laing's romanticized focus on the radical potential of the idea of madness is shown to be attached for Sinclair to a utopian politics of the counterculture—an idea that features in much of his fiction. Baker is also keen to identify Sinclair's interest in the relationship between textuality and geographical space, linking him to the postmodern geographies of figures such as Edward Soja, Fredric Jameson and Michel Foucault. After the highly informative introduction, the book is divided into seven main chapters, each of which takes a particular theme in Sinclair's writing. The first chapter concentrates mainly on Sinclair's 1970s poetry, while chapter 2 discusses his first novel, *White Chappell, Scarlet Tracings*. Chapter 3 focuses on Sinclair's particular form of social and political critique, and especially on the critique of Thatcherism in *Downriver*. The next chapter traces Sinclair's interest in outsider figures, manifest in his own narrative techniques, and in some of his subjects, such as his non-fiction book on John Clare, *Edge of the Orison*. This theme is further pursued in a detailed reading of *Rodinsky's Room*, a collaboration between Sinclair and Rachel Lichtenstein that focuses on exile and the marginalization of London's East End Jewish community. The fifth chapter, 'The Visual Text', develops the ideas introduced in the introduction on Sinclair's radical and distinctive exploration of the relationship between geographical and textual space. This is focused primarily on *Slow Chocolate Autopsy*, the 1997 book Sinclair published in collaboration with Dave McKean. Chapter 6 details the move of Sinclair's textual geographies to the spaces outside central London, specifically the Millennium Dome and the M25, in *London Orbital: A Walk Around the M25*. The last chapter offers interesting readings of *Radon Daughters*, *Landor's Tower* and *Dining on Stones*. All in all, Baker has produced a wide-ranging, erudite and theoretically informed analysis of Sinclair's work that will set the standard for future Sinclair criticism.

The third book to come out in 2007 in the Contemporary British Novelists series is Simon Kövesi's *James Kelman*, which is a well-informed and engaging analysis of one of Scotland's most important contemporary writers. The book is organized into six chapters, the first of which is a fascinating discussion of some of the main themes in Kelman's writing. Kövesi looks in particular at the critical reception of Kelman's work and the positioning of himself outside what he sees as mainstream British fiction. In particular, Kövesi shows how the representation of the ordinary is political in Kelman's fiction. There is also an excellent discussion of the way in which Kelman approaches issues related to working-class fiction through his manipulation of narrative voice, language and realism. This includes a description of Kelman's careful selection of words in a socio-political context, for example, in an intriguing analysis of the author's replacement of the word 'margarined' for 'buttered' in a draft of one of his novels. Kövesi extrapolates this specific example to tease open some of the tensions inherent in Kelman's representation of working-class life. The rest of the book discusses these issues in relation to Kelman's main novels, with a chapter each given over to *The Busconductor Hines* [1984], *A Chancer* [1985], *A Disaffection* [1989] and *How Late It Was, How Late* [1994]. The final chapter looks at Kelman's two most recent novels *Translated Accounts* [2001] and *Careful in the Land of the Free* [2004]. Interspersed in these chapters is a discussion of Kelman's short stories, plays, and political and critical essays. Throughout, the focus is on the 'interrelated themes... of class, politics, language and masculinity' (p. 30). Although Kövesi is occasionally critical of some of Kelman's writing, the book as a whole celebrates the novelist's control of language and narrative technique, and Kövesi succeeds in achieving one of the stated aims of the book: 'to recover Kelman's work as artful literature, conveyed in a highly crafted and actively resourced language [which] works against the prevalent notion that Kelman's world is the product of a primitivist, passive mimesis assumed by many commentators to be the only tool of the working-class realist' (p. 30).

Sonya Andermahr's edited book *Jeanette Winterson: A Contemporary Critical Guide* includes essays by a number of leading critics of contemporary British fiction. Andermahr has done an excellent editing job on this book, providing an introduction and very helpful synopses at the beginning of each chapter. She also provides a useful introduction that focuses on the two main trends in the overall critical approach to Winterson: her place within (lesbian) feminist discourses, and her engagement with the formal and philosophical aspects of postmodernism. She also contributes a chapter that investigates Winterson's adaptation of the traditional romance narrative to incorporate lesbian relationships, and to attempt to produce romance narratives that loose themselves from fixed gender identities. Lucie Armitt argues that Winterson has gradually moved away from feminist concerns in her fiction, replacing them with a genderless engagement with postmodernism. Helena Grice and Tim Woods also explore Winterson's engagement with postmodern theories, especially in her tendency to deconstruct a series of binary oppositions such as fact/fiction, history/story and male/female. Jane Haslett looks at Winterson's treatment of the body in *The Passion*, *Sexing the Cherry* and *Written on the Body*, drawing on feminist and queer theory. Jennifer Gustar's chapter, 'Language and the Limits of Desire', deploys psychoanalytical models from Freud, Lacan and Kristeva in thoughtful readings of *The Passion* and *Written on the Body*. Ginette Carpenter focuses on the representation of reading in Winterson's fiction, while Michelle Denby looks at the importance of religion in *Oranges Are Not the Only Fruit*, *The Passion* and *Gut Symmetries*. Philip Tew's essay on the representation of male characters and masculinity offers an area that has been lacking in Wintersonian criticism to date. He argues convincingly that although male characters tend to take a background role in Winterson's fiction, they are, nevertheless, treated with a certain amount of sympathy; an approach that splices interestingly with her treatment of female identity and sexuality. Sonia Marie Melchiore extends the discussion by looking at Winterson's writing for film, radio and the stage as well as the BBC adaptation of *Oranges*. Gavin Keulks closes the volume with a critical survey of Winterson's most recent work, arguing that she both pushes postmodern experimentation in terms of form while holding on to more 'realist' concepts such as love and history. The book as a whole is an excellent addition to the critical body of work on Winterson, and although many of the essays address common debates in Wintersonian studies, there are a number of fresh perspectives on her writing.

One of the main monographs to come out in 2008 was Dominic Head's *The State of the Novel: Britain and Beyond*, which, as its title suggests, takes a critical overview of the condition of contemporary British fiction. It would be misleading to describe Head's book as a polemic; nevertheless, he produces an interesting critique of the contemporary novel and its relationship with literary-critical practice. In particular, the book registers his 'impatience with academic literary criticism, and its deepening insularity' in its failure to connect with fiction writers and the broader literary culture. In an engaging introduction, Head sets out his advocacy of 'an access of self-consciousness and a willingness to break out of the systematic institutional straitjacket' into which he considers academic literary criticism finds itself. The introduction goes on to address a number of other concerns in the contemporary literary culture. He challenges the predominant chronological reading of post-war fiction as a gradual decline in the British novel from the 1950s to the 1970s followed by a renaissance in the 1980s and 1990s, countering such a narrative by citing a number of significant novels produced in the mid-1970s. He also rejects the mandarin assumptions of academic critics regarding the 'general reader', stressing that the former should not underestimate the sophisticated reading practices engaged in by the latter, and arguing that 'the well-versed novel reader might be at a parallel level of sophistication to the narratologist' (p. 8). He also analyses the complexities and inconsistencies in defining the 'serious literary novel', citing examples from Nick Hornby and, in an extended analysis, John Banville's *The Sea* as revealing the difficulty of identifying what is both serious and literary about these writers' work. Head pursues these themes in five chapters that are organized around specific issues and offer critical readings of individual novels, some well known, and some less so. Chapter 1 continues to interrogate the idea of a renaissance in British fiction from the 1980s onwards, and addresses what he sees as the false dichotomy between realism and experimentalism deployed in much criticism in the field. The second half of this chapter directs these themes to an analysis of the genre of the 'seaside novel', which he describes as an example of English provincialism, and he discusses work by less well-known novelists such as Stephen Blanchard, Andrew Cowan and Chris Paling. His main argument in this section is that 'the seaside novel of the 1990s distils the essence of social relations post-Thatcher...by revitalizing the prosaic descriptiveness of provincial realism with the reflective tones of confessional narrative' (p. 46). The second chapter explores the place of fiction in broader contemporary culture, assessing the impact the recent culture of prizes and awards has had on literary production. This is discussed through the example of Ian McEwan's *Amsterdam*, which Head claims represents a novel that might almost be said to have been designed to win the Booker Prize, which it did in 1998. The second half of the chapter looks at the way the Booker Prize has produced an ambiguous relationship with fiction on the part of former commonwealth nations despite the number of writers that have won it from some of those countries. Head uses this as a basis to discuss fiction by V.S. Naipaul, J.G. Farrell, Paul Scott, Nadine Gordimer and, in particular, Kiran Desai. Chapter 3 continues to explore postcolonial literature written in English, focusing specifically on issues of representation in Monica Ali's *Brick Lane*, and later exploring it as an example of post-9/11 literature in comparison with Zadie Smith's *White Teeth*, a novel that has a similar cultural setting but a distinctly different tone and outlook. The post-9/11 theme is pursued in the fourth chapter, which includes intriguing readings of Ian McEwan's *Saturday* and Martin Amis's *Yellow Dog* in particular, both of which he reads as metaphorically replaying acts of terror through localized examples of violence. Head's reading of *Saturday* is more convincing in this context than that of *Yellow Dog*, as with the latter the splicing of the novel with Amis's journalistic pieces on terrorism and 'Islamism' seems forced. However, his discussion of *Yellow Dog*'s exploration of masculine violence produces an intriguing reading, whether or not it can be fruitfully described as a post-9/11 novel. There is also discussion of Philip Roth's *American Pastoral* and John Updike's *Terrorist*, which frames the chapter's title, 'Terrorism in Transatlantic Perspective'. The last chapter, 'Global Futures: Novelists, Critics, Citizens', returns to one of Head's main aims in the book—to explore the cultural dialogue between those groups. He does this through analyses of a number of novels by contemporary writers that offer (usually negative) representations of academics and cultural commentators, including Philip Roth's *The Human Stain*, Claire Messud's *The Emperor's Children* and J.M. Coetzee's *Disgrace*. This chapter also returns to the theme of the post-9/11 novel with discussion of Don DeLillo's *Mao II* and *Falling Man* (the former as a pre-9/11 anticipation of the metaphorical power terrorism accumulates in post-9/11 America). In summary, the book produces a mature and thoughtful reflection on the condition of contemporary British fiction and literary criticism, and despite the jumping around in terms of theme the central arguments are established with keen intelligence and supported by insightful readings of individual novels.

Another monograph published this year in the field of contemporary narrative is Gerry Smyth's *Music in Contemporary British Fiction: Listening to the Novel*. This is an engagement in an aspect of literature that has not previously had much attention. Smyth sets out his relationship with other writers and theorists working in the intersection of fiction and music in the introduction. In particular, he makes reference to cultural theorist Jacques Attali's claim that sound (or what he calls noise) is central to human culture. Smyth also discusses the development of word studies and music studies, both of which are influences on his approach. Although Smyth's main aim is to pursue an 'immanent form of analysis, based primarily upon what emerges from the texts themselves' (p. 5), and although his main focus is on the period 1990–2008, the first part of the book sets out a theoretical approach and discusses historical examples of what he calls the 'music-novel' from the eighteenth century to the early 1990s. This part is divided into two chapters, the first of which identifies distinctions in the use of music in literature in terms of inspiration, metaphor and form, and in which he maps out the terrain of the critical debate in each of these areas. The second chapter discusses examples such as Lawrence Sterne's *Tristram Shandy*, Thomas Hardy's *Jude the Obscure* and Colin MacInnes's *Absolute Beginners*. Part II offers readings of individual contemporary British novels in three chapters organized around the themes of different musical genres; the way music is used in different genres of fiction; and the 'uses of music' in fiction. Chapter 3 identifies the way in which popular music, in particular, became a source of serious cultural discourse from the 1980s onwards. He attributes this cultural shift to two factors: first, the resistance to a perceived waning of art music in the period resulted in a number of novelists producing fiction that engaged in cultural debates over music; secondly, the emergence of punk in the 1970s as a moment after which popular music increased its cultural capital. This chapter then goes on to identify the way in which selected novels from the period engage with specific musical genres, for example, folk in *Captain Corelli's Mandolin* by Louis de Bernières; rock in Salman Rushdie's *The Ground Beneath Her Feet*; hip-hop in Zadie Smith's *On Beauty*; and dance in Alan Warner's *Morvern Callar*. The fourth chapter moves the focus from musical genre to fictional genre and, interestingly, carries out the task of observing 'the manner in which music is invoked in relation to the different formal and conceptual concerns' in a range of literary genres (p. 133). It then goes on to discuss a range of genres with respect to specific novels, including graphic fiction in *Horace Dorlan* by

Andrzej Klimowski; fantasy in Terry Pratchet's *Soul Music*; the thriller in *Johnny Come Home* by Jake Arnott; and the crime novel in Ian Rankin's *Exit Music*. The last chapter moves the discussion away from genre and engages with a diversity of social and cultural themes in which the music-novel has been central. These include the use of music to identify historical periods, and in some cases to create a sense of nostalgia; the exploration of the relationship between music and silence; and, lastly, how love and music have often been connected in contemporary British fiction. This chapter includes a short discussion of a number of novels, including Rose Tremain's *Music and Silence*, Hanif Kureishi's *The Buddha of Suburbia*, Jonathan Coe's *The Rotters' Club*, Kazuo Ishiguro's *The Unconsoled* and *Buddha Da* by Anne Donovan. Overall, Smyth's book is a broad survey of this relatively new field, and while it would have been good to have had more detailed readings of individual novels, it succeeds in further opening up a rich area for the study of contemporary fiction that promises to be a feature of much criticism in the future.

Another major series concentrating on contemporary British fiction is Palgrave's New British Fiction, aimed at both literary scholars and students. There have been two books in the series this year, the first of which is Kaye Mitchell's *A.L. Kennedy*. As with all the books in the series, it is organized into three parts, the first of which offers a timeline, which combines important historical and cultural events with relevant biographical details and publishing history pertaining to Kennedy; an introductory chapter that contextualizes her fiction; and a brief biography. The second part offers critical analysis of Kennedy's major works, and the third part includes an interview with the author and a critical survey of the critical reception of Kennedy's work in both the literary media and in academic studies. The introduction picks up on two important contexts for Kennedy, her place as a Scottish writer and her relationship with contemporary women's fiction. Through discussion of Kennedy's comments and other relevant works, such as Alasdair Gray's *Lanark*, Alan Warner's *Morvern Callar*, Irvine Welsh's *Trainspotting* and Janice Galloway's *The Trick is to Keep Breathing*, Mitchell argues that Kennedy distances herself from both a national and a gendered (and in particular a feminist) context, preferring to maintain an outsider status in her writing generally. While avoiding being attached too closely to reductive social categories, Mitchell does stress that Kennedy is interested in exploring the representation of marginalized identity. As she writes: 'What we find in Kennedy's work ... are the suggestions that [the] representation of the culturally and socially marginalized is by no means straightforward, particularly where their interior lives are concerned' (pp. 17–18). Part II looks at Kennedy's major works in a series of three chapters, each of which serves as both an introduction to recurrent themes and approaches in her work, and as a critical reading of individual books. Chapter 3 discusses Kennedy's exploration of marginal identities in two of her early collections of short stories, *Night Geometry and the Garscadden Trains* and *Now That You're Back*, and her first novel *Looking for the Possible Dance*. In this chapter, Mitchell is particularly interested in the way in which identity is represented as unstable in these books, especially in terms of Scottishness and gender. She draws thoughtfully on theoretical perspectives from Homi Bhabha and Franco

Moretti in her analysis of Kennedy's work in this chapter. Chapter 4 concentrates on readings of *So I Am Glad, Original Bliss* and *Everything You Need,* focusing specifically on her reconfiguration of the romance genre wherein romance becomes 'a kind of religion' (p. 69). This is followed in chapter 5 by an intriguing analysis of Kennedy's interest in the inadequacy of language and breakdowns in the communication process as a general theme identified in three of her later works, *Indelible Acts, Paradise* and *Day.* This analysis of individual texts is followed by the transcription of an interview with Kennedy from 2006, and an informative and critically engaged summary of the critical reception of her work. There has been relatively little literary criticism on Kennedy's fiction to date, and this book sets a solid benchmark for future work on a writer who is increasingly becoming an important figure in British fiction.

The second book in this series this year is Stephen Morton's *Salman Rushdie,* which follows the established format of an introductory part with a timeline and biographical reading, which in this case is a discussion of Rushdie's position as a postcolonial writer who has embraced South Asian modernity and migratory narratives. Morton intervenes in the debate on Rushdie by focusing attention away from him as a postmodernist writer to read him in terms of South Asian historical and cultural contexts. As Morton writes, 'to read Rushdie as an avatar of postmodernism is to ignore the ways in which Rushdie's literary style is precisely a response to the historical condition of South Asia's postcolonial modernity from the diasporic standpoint of a British Indian Muslim' (p. 13). The second part of the book takes this broad approach and applies it to Rushdie's major works. This part is divided into six chapters that follow a chronological framework. Chapter 3 discusses *Midnight's Children* and *Shame,* offering a detailed analysis set against the politics of India and Pakistan respectively in the period after the Second World War. Chapter 4 looks at *The Satanic Verses, Haroun and the Sea of Stories* and *East, West.* This might seem at first to be an awkward grouping (other than in terms of chronological proximity), given the varying audiences for these texts; however, Morton makes interesting connections between them based on the way each text achieves a reassessment of Islamic literature and culture, which itself reveals Rushdie's engagement with religious and historical contexts. Chapters 5 and 6 are given over to one novel each, *The Moor's Last Sigh* and *The Ground Beneath Her Feet* respectively, while chapter 7 examines *Fury* and *Shalimar the Clown.* Each of these chapters develops Morton's central reading of Rushdie as a major figure in what he identifies as postcolonial modernity. The last part provides a detailed summary of Rushdie's other writing and his critical reception. The book as a whole is a worthy contribution to Rushdie studies, and Morton achieves the often difficult balancing act of producing an introduction to a writer in a style that is accessible, while engaging with and often advancing the important debates on this central figure in contemporary fiction.

Nick Bentley's *Contemporary British Fiction* also combines an introduction to the area with critical engagement with some canonical writers that have emerged over the period as well as some less well-known writers. The present reviewer is the author of this book so what follows is informative rather than critical. The book is part of Edinburgh University's Critical Guides series and follows the format of the series by including a chronology and an introduction that focuses on the major historical and theoretical contexts for the period. This includes the following section headings: Politics; Class; Gender and Sexuality; Postcolonialism, Multiculturalism and National Identity; Youth and Subcultures; and A Note on Theory. The rest of the book produces critical analyses of fifteen contemporary British novels divided into five chapters. The first of these chapters discusses narrative form and includes critical analysis of Martin Amis's *London Fields*, Alasdair Gray's *Poor Things* and Zadie Smith's *White Teeth*, approaching the former two novels as examples of postmodernist technique, while Smith's novel is read as a return to a realistic mode, echoing nineteenth-century models in a contemporary and multicultural British setting. Chapter 2, 'Writing Contemporary Ethnicities', explores Salman Rushdie's *Shame*, Courttia Newland's *Society Within* and Monica Ali's *Brick Lane*. The third chapter turns its attention to issues of gender and sexuality in studies of Angela Carter's *The Passion of New Eve*, Jeanette Winterson's *Oranges Are Not the Only Fruit* and Nick Hornby's *Fever Pitch*. Chapter 4, 'History, Memory and Writing', explores this range of topics in Graham Swift's *Waterland*, A.S. Byatt's *Possession: A Romance* and Ian McEwan's *Atonement*. The last main chapter focuses on issues of the representation of cultural and literary space in Hanif Kureishi's *The Buddha of Suburbia*, Iain Sinclair's *Downriver* and Julian Barnes's *England, England*. There is a conclusion followed by a number of student resources at the end of the book.

Elizabeth Taylor is a post-war writer who has received relatively little critical attention, and N.H. Reeve's book on her in the Writers and their Work series aims in part to address this lack. Reeve emphasizes the understated style of Taylor's writing and reads her work as tied to the historical context of the three decades after the Second World War, during which most of her fiction was published. This short book concentrates on Taylor's thirteen novels, the analysis of which is arranged in five chapters that take a broadly chronological approach, although the last chapter concentrates solely on Taylor's 1954 novella *Hester Lilly*. The attention given to this novel is warranted by Reeve's claim that it brings together most of the themes in Taylor's fiction: 'the antagonism between an older and a younger woman; the terror of being supplanted; old age, loneliness, repletion and habit; living in a house not properly one's own; a sudden crisis of identity, the dream of transformation— above all, the breaking down of defence, the raw exposure of crumbling and growing: crumbling mostly' (p. 86). Not all of these themes, of course, are present in every Taylor novel, but this synopsis provides a way of approaching many of them. In the previous four chapters, Reeve offers perceptive, if relatively brief, readings of Taylor's fiction. The first two chapters discuss Taylor's 1940s novels, identifying them as concerned with characters that in different ways are coming to terms with the personal upheavals caused by the Second World War. Reeve often refers to Freudian (and to a lesser extent Lacanian) models of psychoanalysis as ways of reading of Taylor, and this works especially well with the gothic sensibilities that Taylor uses in some of her 1940s novels, including *A Wreath of Roses*. Reeve also identifies Taylor's use of intertextual allusion, such as to Charlotte Brontë in *At Mrs Lippincote's* and to Jane Austen's *Northanger Abbey* in *Palladian*. The former of these is particularly convincing as Reeve analyses the thematic use of the attic space in *At Mrs Lippincote's*, where 'To have the key to the attic... is to have the means of guarding the secret places of the self against the danger of unpredictable exposure or trespass' (p. 27). Chapter 3 looks mainly at Taylor's fiction of the 1950s, which Reeve argues shows her developing the 'possibility of longer, more detached views or of a more decisive sense of shift into new conditions' (p. 42), and their interest in the imprisoning effects of power, on both 'those wielding it as much as on those suffering it or drawn into its orbit' (p. 56). This chapter offers readings of *A Game of Hide and Seek*, *The Sleeping Beauty*, *Angel* (Taylor's only historical novel), and *In a Summer Season*. The fourth chapter begins by tracing a certain move in Taylor's 1960s fiction to the influence of her seeing a production of Samuel Beckett's *Happy Days* in 1962. This Beckettian influence is seen particularly in characters attempting to distract themselves from a vacuous world in Taylor's *The Soul of Kindness*, and in an 'increasingly dry and laconic voice [with] sentences and paragraphs pared right down' in *The Wedding Group* (p. 67). This sensibility is continued in explorations of ageing in *Mrs Palfrey at the Claremont* and *Blaming*. Books in the Writers and their Work series tend to bridge the gap between an introduction to a writer's work and a critical engagement with the fiction, and Reeve's book consummately achieves this balance. It is well written, offers intriguing analyses of Taylor's fiction, and succeeds in its aim of reclaiming this much underrated writer.

The Fiction of A.S. Byatt by Louisa Hadley is another addition to Palgrave's Reader's Guides to Essential Criticism series. Hadley provides an accessible and detailed guide to the most important criticism on Byatt to date. In an informative introduction she gives biographical details and publishing history and sets out the key parameters and contexts of Byatt's fiction and other writing. In this she emphasizes the tendency in the early criticism of the novelist's work to compare her to her sister Margaret Drabble, much to the annoyance of Byatt. It was with the success of *Possession: A Romance*, her fifth novel, published in 1990, that Byatt's work started to be taken more seriously in its own right. Hadley identifies three main areas in which Byatt's fiction has been approached: 'the relationship to literary traditions, the role of the artist and women's issues' (p. 5), although she stresses Byatt's ambivalent relationship with all of these issues, citing her work as an example of self-conscious realism which flirts with postmodernism, and her concerns with the position of the artist in general, and not only the female artist. The book as a whole aims to consider 'both the responses to individual texts as well as the wider critical debates surrounding Byatt's oeuvre as a whole' (p. 4). This is achieved in chapters arranged chronologically (in the main) that deal with each of the novels from *Shadow of a Sun* [1964] to *A Whistling Woman* [2002], while also making reference to Byatt's literary criticism, and a final chapter that concentrates on the short stories. Given the prominence of *Possession* in Byatt's output, two chapters are dedicated to it: one on its formal experiments as a dialogue between realism and postmodernism, and one on its engagement with historical contexts. Each of the chapters begins with a section on the immediate reviews, followed by short sections on the main critical responses particular to each text. The first chapter on *Possession*, for example, divides the critical attention it received into the following sections: '*Possession* as a Victorian Novel', '*Possession* as a Postmodern Novel', 'Beyond Postmodernism?', 'Postscript: A Romantic Ending?', 'Byatt on Realism' and 'Woman as Artist'. This division of the criticism into thematic areas is one of the strengths on the book, and reveals Hadley's knowledge of both the main criticism and the contexts in which that criticism was produced.

4. Pre-1950 Drama

There is rather an odd selection of pre-1950 drama books to review this year, including several general works on theatre in the West End, and those on T.S. Eliot and Robert Graves, as well as collected essays on the Grand Guignol. Once more, this period of theatre history seems to be little covered by writers and critics. In this respect, it is salutary to mention Marina MacKay's edited book, *The Cambridge Companion to the Literature of World War II*. In what is always an excellent series, this volume misses an opportunity by (briefly) mentioning French theatre during the Second World War (Jean-Paul Sartre, Jean Anouilh), but not British theatre. Rod Mengham, for example, mentions the film *Cottage to Let* [1941] to illustrate his point about contemporary interest in spies and fifth columnists, but does not seem to be aware that this first appeared as a stage play by Geoffrey Kerr in 1940. Admittedly, the book's remit is wide, covering world literature, but its omission of drama is perhaps typical of the way in which British theatre before 1950 is often overlooked.

Haunted Theatres, by Tom Ogden, is an amusing selection of ghost stories about American, Canadian and British theatres, and also recounts a little of the history of various West End theatres. We learn about the death in 1897 of Victorian actor William Terriss, outside the Adelphi, at the hands of Richard Prince, who envied Terriss his career. As Terriss lay dying outside the stage door, his last words were 'I will be back.' Since then, it is claimed, there have been several sightings in the theatre and surrounding area. The event is marked by a plaque on the wall of the Adelphi, although the building itself was demolished at the end of the nineteenth century, upon which it was given a new identity as the Century theatre, before becoming the Adelphi again. Replaced by an art deco design in 1930, when it had the addition of Royal to its name, it reverted back to its original name ten years later. Another tale is told of Margaret Rutherford and her husband, Stringer Davis, forced by the thick fog outside to spend the night in the dressing room at the Theatre Royal, Haymarket. During the night, she saw the ghost of John Baldwin Buckstone, a nineteenth-century actor-manager, as did Donald Sinden during the run of *The Heiress* in 1949. His appearance is meant to be a good omen, marking the successful run of a show. In a touch of meta-theatre, the Phantom of the Opera made a ghostly appearance during the musical of that name, at Her Majesty's theatre in London in the 1980s. Other ghosts of that theatre include Herbert Beerbohm Tree, who was seen by the entire cast of Sir Terence Rattigan's *Cause Célèbre* in the 1970s. The playhouse itself underwent a number of transformations, having been consumed by fire three times before its present incarnation was built in 1892. There is also the strange story of the jacket in the costume department of the Duke of York's theatre, which actresses insisted was trying to suffocate them, and the apparition of a Victorian actress, Violet Melnotte, who took up ownership of the same theatre, on and off, until she died in 1935. Spectral manifestations continued there throughout the Second World War, when it was badly damaged in bombing raids, becoming less frequent as the theatre underwent a number of changes: it was refurbished by Capital Radio in the late 1970s, and used by the Ambassador Theatre Group chain as its headquarters from the 1980s. The Theatre Royal Drury Lane is purported to be the most haunted theatre in the world: its ghosts include Charles Macklin and Sarah Siddons from the eighteenth century, Edmund Kean's son, Charles, the clown Joseph Grimaldi, and Dan Leno, a music-hall artiste. There is also a figure known as the Man in Grey, who made an appearance in the upper circle as the cast of *The Dancing Years* had a photo call in 1939.

Paul Ibell's *Theatreland*, as its subtitle explains, is a journey through the heart of London's theatre. Charting the history of London's Theatreland, from the Elizabethan period to the present day, there are a number of areas of interest to those who study the theatre of the first half of the twentieth century. We learn, for example, that the Theatre Royal Drury Lane, one of two 'patent houses' allowed by Charles II to stage 'serious' drama during the Restoration, was in danger of closing down in the 1930s, due to dwindling audiences. Ivor Novello was called upon to save 'the Lane', coming up with the extravaganza *Glamorous Night* [1935]. During the war the Entertainments National Service Association (ENSA) had its headquarters there, and the nose cone of a bomb, which crashed through the roof and became buried in the floor, is on display next to a chair taken from the Reichstag at the end of the war by theatre producer Basil Dean. We also hear about the popularity of all-male drag shows which toured in the period immediately after the war, such as *Soldiers in Skirts* and *Forces Showboat*, which stemmed from shows got up by the men in the services while they were away fighting. Ibell says, 'the shows were a way of seeing (and in a curious way celebrating) men in the armed services in a fun, and certainly unthreatening way. This was militarism not as in a Nazi propaganda film, but as in a saucy seaside postcard' (p. 34). This tradition, it is suggested, prompted the careers of performers like Danny La Rue. Ibell has a jaunty, conversational style, and the book zips along at a speedy pace as he covers a range of subjects: the relationship between the Royal Family and the theatre, theatrical dynasties, Americans in London, and so on. There is also an interesting chapter on 'Drama Queens', recounting the amicable but rival-driven friendship between Ivor Novello and Noël Coward, as well as a section on female theatre managers, such as Gladys Cooper, who ran the Playhouse theatre with her husband from 1917 to 1927, and then on her own until 1933, and Lilian Baylis at the Old Vic and Sadler's Wells. Yet while this may be an appealing book it is essentially rather lightweight; there is a lack of considered analysis, which at times can be frustrating, as well as certain antiquated prejudices: Terence Rattigan is described as 'a very old-fashioned writer', for example, whose career was destroyed by John Osborne's *Look*

Back in Anger, when, as critical commentary for some time has observed, the playwrights are not as dissimilar as was once thought.

Richard J. Hand and Michael Wilson provide a coherent investigation of *London's Grand Guignol and the Theatre of Horror*—Guignol being a kind of drama popular during the 1920s, perhaps as a response to the First World War. The book is divided into two sections: the first gives a historical overview of London's Grand Guignol, with information on performance, censorship, reception, critics and its legacy, while the second section consists of ten plays by writers as various as Reginald Berkeley (*Eight O'Clock* [1920]), Christopher Holland (*The Old Woman* [1921]) and Noël Coward (*The Better Half* [1922]). The first Grand Guignol-influenced play was introduced to Britain by José Levy in 1912, with *Seven Blind Men* at the Palladium in London. Like several others that followed, this was adapted from the French. As Hand and Wilson note, 'The Grand Guignol was quintessentially a French form, and more specifically Montmartrean, and whilst it adapted to local conditions as it was exported around the world, it remained resolutely French in its approach to the portrayal of sex and violence in particular' (p. 20). Yet Levy founded a Grand Guignol theatre at the Little Theatre in London, which produced a series of British plays in this style, even if this took place over a very short period of time: from 1920 to 1922. He did this by asking for one-act plays, which would 'present sections of life as it is, gay sometimes, frequently sad, occasionally very horrible, but as it is, without the sugar coating, or saccharine centre of the so-called "popular" play' (p. 24). This had the effect of appealing to new writers such as Noël Coward. The involvement of Sybil Thorndike, her brother Russell, and her husband Lewis Casson also helped to give the plays an air of respectability, as well as attracting other actors and writers. Like the Grand Guignol theatre in Paris, the geographical placement of the Little Theatre added to the overall theatrical effect. Sandwiched between the Strand and the Embankment, it had a 'marginal' place in London's theatreland, being close enough to the West End to draw audiences and yet slightly off the beaten track. It had an established air of rebellion, being originally set up in 1910 by Gertrude Kingston as a place to stage suffrage drama. The Parisian Grand Guignol was more erotic and bloody than its British counterpart, which was tempered by the gentility of West End audiences and the censorship laws of the Lord Chamberlain, and anyone interested in history of stage censorship in Britain would do well to look at the chapter here on this subject. Hand and Wilson note how scripts were sometimes only submitted to the Lord Chamberlain's Office once rehearsals were well under way, in the belief that this would force them to capitulate over any changes, and that the ensuing 'bad publicity' often helped to arouse audience interest. Working in a genre that set itself against the Establishment was seen as a worthy aspiration, as Mervyn McPherson declared in *The Grand Guignol Annual Review 1921*: 'we prefer to be ambitious and, if necessary, to die of too much daring, than complacently to endure the mediocre. This might well be the slogan of the Grand Guignol' (p. 61). In terms of the plays themselves, Christopher Holland's *The Old Women* [1921] stands out. Set in an asylum, peopled by doctors, nuns and madwomen, Holland's play balances comedy, tragedy and horror as the underlying clash between science and religion is played out.

Altogether this is a well- researched book on a fascinating piece of theatre history.

Robert Graves is known particularly for his writing on the First World War, for example *Good-bye to All That*. Steven Trout brings together the original transcript of the 1929 edition, with the essay 'A Postscript to *Good-bye to All That*', and Graves's play *But It Still Goes On* (both 1930). Trout suggests that the essay and play provide a context in which to read the more celebrated work. Maurice Browne, the producer of R.C. Sherriff's *Journey's End* in the West End in 1929, who founded the Chicago Little Theatre before overseeing the beginnings of a drama programme at Dartington Hall, invited Graves to write a war play. *Good-bye to All That* stood in direct contrast to the typical war narratives of the time, which emulated Victorian stylistic elegance, for a fragmentary and rambling 'meta-memoir' (p. xviii). Equally, *But It Still Goes On* was quite different from Sherriff's claustrophobic trench setting and worthy speeches about the conflict between patriotic loyalty and the dangers of life at the Front. Instead, Graves presented Browne with a farce set in London, which satirizes English morality and at time seems almost Ortonesque in its surreal juxtaposition, and brusque treatment, of sexuality and death. Unsurprisingly, especially given its frankness about homosexuality and use of famous people and family members (for example, Siegfried Sassoon appears as a 'closeted homosexual', p. xxxix, and Graves's father as 'an over-rated "novelist and poet"', p. xxx), the play was not staged. Trout sees connections between this play and works by Oscar Wilde and George Bernard Shaw, as well as suggesting that it anticipated characters in Evelyn Waugh's satirical novels of the 1930s. This is an absorbing and original take on Graves, whose despair about the horrors of the First World War punctures the comic surface of the play in a series of disturbing and violent vignettes.

Another literary lion is taken on in John Worthen's 'short biography' of T.S. Eliot, which charts how Eliot had written the vast majority of his poems by 1942, when 'it was his plays that made and retained him a public name' (p. 104). His career in the theatre began in 1933, when E. Martin Browne, an influential figure involved in the revival of religious and poetic drama during this period, asked him to write a pageant to raise money for north London churches. *The Rock* was the result, duly staged in 1934. *Murder in the Cathedral* swiftly followed a year later, again directed by Browne for the Canterbury Festival, before going on to the West End. It was this success that led Eliot away from writing plays like *Sweeny Agonistes*, which he had originally intended, and more towards the poetic drama favoured by Browne. His next play, *The Family Reunion*, was difficult to write, owing to its autobiographical basis, only lasting on the London stage for thirty-eight performances in March 1939. *The Cocktail Party* followed a decade later, first appearing at the Edinburgh Festival, before becoming a success in the West End. This was repeated with *The Confidential Clerk* in 1953, although it was not as profitable as its predecessor. Finally, in 1958, *The Elder Statesman* was staged. Worthen points to Eliot's inability to move beyond verse in his plays, or to be able to create realistic conversations, which made them stilted and artificial. He quotes Virginia Woolf who, on seeing *The Family Reunion*, remarked: 'not a dramatist. A monologist' (pp. 205–6). Worthen concludes that 'The resulting superficiality of the lives with which the plays were concerned sits very oddly with the deep accounts Eliot proffers of how it might be possible to live better' (p. 206). The plays revolve around a spiritual catalyst or crisis, even while they employ the dramatic conventions of the time: the drawing-room setting, the upper-class household, the comic working classes. Worthen suggests Eliot deployed this juxtaposition knowingly, which 'exemplified his conception of the violent intersection of the concerns of the timeless moment with events occurring in time', but for audiences, this resulted merely in 'being on two quite different levels simultaneously' (p. 207). While there are only a few pages in this biography on Eliot's work in the theatre, the comments are illuminating and cogent.

Finally, Sos Eltis brings together a disparate group of writers in her article, 'Bringing Out the Acid: Noël Coward, Harold Pinter, Ivy Compton-Burnett and the Uses of Camp' (*MD* 51[2008] 211–33). In doing this, Eltis manages to provide a fresh perspective on the work of Coward. She expands upon Susan Sontag's theory in 'Notes on "Camp"' [1964], where brief mention is made of Coward's use of 'intentional camp ... which means to be funny, as opposed to "Genuine Camp", which is always naïve and takes itself entirely seriously' (p. 211). Eltis argues that Coward's work embodies the 'essence of camp sensibility', described by Sontag as 'a love of the unnatural, of style and artifice. Rooted in passion, it is the glorification of character' (p. 211). While this is perhaps not true of Coward's more serious plays—*Post Mortem* [1930], *Cavalcade* [1931], *This Happy Breed* [1939]—it can be seen to apply to plays such as *Hay Fever* [1924], *Present Laughter* [1939] and *Blithe Spirit* [1941]. Here the instability of language and meaning rubs against the comic surface, creating a sense of ambiguity. This is furthered by the characters, who construct personae for themselves to act out. There is no real sense of closure at the end of these plays; rather, they display 'the ironic disengagement of camp, operating outside the conventional borders of comedy and tragedy, lacking the emotional and social commitment that gives them meaning' (p. 212).

5. Post-1950 Drama

While being a lean year for major studies there has been activity in other areas. For example 2008 saw the launch of Continuum's Modern Theatre Guides, and there have been re-evaluations on the work of John Osborne and the theatrical landscape of the 1950s; the work of Sarah Kane has been revisited and a theoretical framework established that will assist ongoing debates about documentary theatre.

The most significant monograph produced this year has been Amelia Howe Kritzer's *Political Theatre in Post-Thatcher Britain: New Writing, 1995–2000*. This is a welcome attempt at contextualizing some of the complex developments that have taken place in new writing over the last decade. Whereas Aleks Sierz's *In-Yer-Face Theatre: British Drama Today* [2001] set out to provide a unified reading, of the 1990s by relating the story of a group of young dramatists, including Sarah Kane, Mark Ravenhill and Anthony

Neilson, with broadly unified aims and style, Kritzer's book demonstrates that the millennium saw new theatre writing splintering off into many different styles and themes. The opening chapter provides a broad discussion of the term 'political theatre', before breaking new writing into five thematic chapters. The period of in-yer-face theatre is revisited, and there is a welcome chapter entitled 'Intergenerational Dialogue' which looks at the work of older playwrights such as Caryl Churchill, who has continued to produce innovative work in the millennial decade. Kritzer is able to follow up and develop an ongoing interest that came out of her influential *The Plays of Caryl Churchill: Theatre of Empowerment* [1991] as she looks at millennial and post-millennial work such as *Blue Heart* [1997] *Far Away* [2000] and *A Number* [2002]. Other chapters also start to reflect the difficulty of Kritzer's project as the narrative of British playwriting in recent years has become more fragmented in its aims and approaches. The chapter 'Systems of Power' attempts a hesitant discussion of recent history plays such as Nick Dear's *Power* [2003], and then brings in a number of diverse examples such as Michael Frayn's *Democracy* [2003] and Zinnie Harris's *Further Than the Furthest Thing* [2000]. The chapter 'Issues for Post-Thatcher Britain' also considers aspects of racism, Northern Ireland and questions of political leadership. At times, it becomes difficult to come to firm conclusions about the social and political conditions that are producing these works—a situation not helped by the fact that the plays themselves are often discussed in isolation from each other. While the readings themselves are thoughtful and considered in their analysis, overall the book lacks a sense of cohesion that would make it a definitive study of the last ten years in British theatre writing.

Philip Roberts, *About Churchill: The Playwright and the Work*, is the latest in Faber's excellent series on individual dramatists. In looking at Churchill's work Roberts adopts an approach of largely choosing to ignore the considerable (and growing) amount of academic criticism on the playwright, preferring instead to draw on comments made by those who have worked with Churchill, such as Max Stafford-Clark, David Lan and Stephen Daldry. The volume looks at the plays in a chronological order and considers them in the light of their cultural and historical context. There is also perceptive analysis of recent work such as *Drunk Enough to Say I Love You* [2006]. Of particular scholarly interest is Robert's detailed inclusion of unpublished and unper-formed work that opens up exciting new avenues for those working on Churchill's existing canon.

Caryl Churchill's *Top Girls* [1982] is also the subject of Alicia Tycer's short monograph study in the Continuum Modern Theatre Guides series [2008] The book provides intelligent readings of key scenes from the play and useful cultural and political background, as well as the changing critical views that this landmark play has elicited during a period of over twenty years. Of particular interest is Tycer's analysis of *Top Girls'* reception in America, through several notable, but under-reported, productions of the play. There is also welcome analysis given to the 1995 BBC television adaptation of the play.

In the same series is this reviewer's *Patrick Marber's Closer*, which follows the same format as other volumes in the series by setting out the cultural and political context in which the play was written as well as analysis of key scenes. There is also a production history and discussion of the 2004 film adaptation.

The playwright Peter Gill's *Apprenticeship* is both a partial biography and a cultural and theatrical history. Drawing on a recently discovered diary which Gill kept as young actor rehearsing for the RSC's production of Brecht's *The Caucasian Chalk Circle* [1962], the book is both a personal account of life in post-war Britain and a record of Gill's own reflections on the British cultural and theatrical landscape during the 1960s. *Apprenticeship* is most valuable in its accounts of the Royal Court and some of the abrasive personalities who did so much to shape its reputation during this decade. Although Gill has enjoyed a long relationship with the theatre over the years— both as a director (the book includes an interesting account of his reclamation of D.H. Lawrence's plays at the Court) and as a playwright—his account is untainted by any trace of sentimentality, and he is keen to debunk some of the mythologies that have grown around particular productions or figures. There are also critical accounts (often shaped by bad personal experiences) of the early days of the RSC where Gill was acting, and thoughtful criticisms of its time under Peter Hall. The book contains Gill's own frequently waspish impressions of other venerable institutions such as the National Theatre, and there are also several clear-sighted accounts and analyses of topics ranging from Noël Coward's fortunes during the 1950s to the influence of Brecht on British theatre culture after the Berliner Ensemble visit in 1955.

Theatre of the 1950s also dominates Dominic Shellard's edited collection, *The Golden Generation: New Light on Post-War British Theatre*. The essays, many of which have been written as part of the British Library Theatre Archive Project, are diverse in range and with many based on direct archival research, succeed in allowing fresh perspectives to be reached on some familiar areas. Shellard's essay, 'Stability, Renewal and Change: Gielgud and Olivier in 1957', using the two renowned actors as a case study, presents a convincing reappraisal of 1957 as a 'deeply significant year for British theatre' (p. 91), whereby drama by new wave writers, such as John Osborne's *The Entertainer* [1957], consolidated the promise shown in the watershed year of 1956. Ewan Jeffrey's 'Theatres of Resistance: Michel Saint-Dennis and George Devine' traces through archival sources the complex relationship between the two men and how their work together brought much-needed ideas from Europe into the British theatre during the 1950s. Kate Dorney's chapter, 'Ralph Richardson', also makes use of the archive held at the British Library to trace and evaluate Richardson's long theatrical and film career. Laura White's 'Smashing Open the French Windows: The Acting Profession and British Theatre in the 1960s and 1970s' also traces the changing styles and development of acting technique, drawn in part from interviews conducted with practitioners for the Arts and Humanities Research Council (AHRC) project. The strongest article in the collection is Kate Harris's 'Evolutionary Stages: Theatre and Television 1946–56', which not only traces the complex and frequently suspicious relationship theatre had with television during the years following the Second World War but, in drawing on the BBC Written Archives Centre, also shed new light on the impact of the BBC's screening of extracts from the original Royal Court production of *Look Back in Anger* [1956]. This collection, which is handsomely illustrated with some rare photographs and sketches, is a useful re-evaluation of the early post-war period in British theatre.

Look Back in Anger is also the subject of a short monograph by Aleks Sierz (in many respects the Jimmy Porter of British theatre criticism), in the Continuum Modern Theatre Guides series. The volume is a useful addition to the attention that Osborne's play continues to attract. Sierz not only brings us up to date with current critical debates and controversies about the play, including recent attempts to displace its central place in the narrative that makes up post-war British drama, but also discusses notable recent productions of the play and includes useful extracts from new interviews with actors such as David Tennant. Michael Sheen and Emma Fielding.

Look Back in Anger is also the subject of Luc Gilleman's 'From Coward to Osborne: Or the Enduring Importance of *Look Back in Anger*' (*MD* 51[2008] 104–25) and notes both the rapidity of its canonization immediately after its Royal Court debut and the equal speed with which dissenting views set out to question its importance. Gilleman argues that a British theatre 'obsessed with its own stagnation' during the 1950s, provided the vital conditions in which *Look Back in Anger* was able to 'burst through the defences of the theatrical establishment' (p. 107). Gilleman also draws attention to the fact that the perceived gulf between the 'angry young men' and established playwrights such as Coward and Rattigan was in some respects a false opposition.

The supposed divergence in style and sensibility between Coward's generation and the one that followed is also the subject of Sos Eltis's 'Bringing Out the Acid: Noël Coward, Harold Pinter, Ivy Compton Burnett and the Uses of Camp' (*MD* 51[2008] 211–33), also reviewed in the previous section, which reads a number of Coward's plays against Susan Sontag's influential 'Notes on Camp'. The article also revisits the appreciation that Coward and Pinter showed for each other's work (with Coward describing Pinter's *The Homecoming* [1965] as a 'sort of Cockney Ivy Compton-Burnett' (p. 226)—a reference to Burnett's novels which Eltis expands upon in the article). Eltis argues that both dramatists also share a quality of switching mercurially between different linguistic registers as well as producing work that presents 'a flawless surface that stands in problematic relation to content' (p. 223). Here, Pinter's *The Caretaker* [1960] is offered as an example of 'a more brutal extension of the techniques deployed by Coward's protagonists', or 'camp with the gloves off' (p. 225)

While the subject of documentary theatre continued to be a frequent topic for discussion in theatre journals this year, Will Hammond and Dan Steward's *Verbatim Verbatim: Contemporary Documentary Theatre* is the first book devoted exclusively to the subject. However, this is not a major new study of the area. Instead, it is a volume consisting of a series of interviews with a number of notable British practitioners who have used this particular form. These include directors Max Stafford-Clark, Alecky Blythe and Nicholas Kent as well as the writers David Hare, Robin Soans and Richard Norton Taylor. While the interviews are informative and represent useful source material, the first major study on this important area of theatre has yet to appear.

Elsewhere, a much-needed theoretical approach to the subject of documentary theatre has begun to emerge. Ursula Canton's article, '"We may not know reality, but it still matters": A Functional Analysis of "Factual Elements" in the Theatre' (*ConTR* 18:ii[2008] 318–27), uses Nicholas Wright's *Vincent in Brixton* [2002] and Tanika Gupta's *Gladiator Games* [2005] as examples of a growing number of plays that incorporate documentary, biography and historical material. Canton observes that as yet no satisfactory critical apparatus exists to explain this trend—either as symptomatic of postmodern experiments in the 'real' or as a reflective model of social reality. Canton points out that, with *Vincent in Brixton*, the production was sometimes overly keen to emphasize the veracity of its credentials as 'factual'—such as casting the Dutch actor Jochum ten Haaf to convince British audiences of the play's authenticity (p. 322). In comparison, Canton argues, *Gladiator Games* seems on the surface to be less artfully constructed, in that material taken from the inquiry into the death of Zahid Mubarek is used as verification for the narrative's claims for 'truth', for example the list of citations included in the playtext (p. 323). However, Canton argues that by separating the documented sources and the invented dialogue, shows that artifice is just as much in play.

In the same issue of *Contemporary Theatre Review* (*ConTR* 18:iii[2008] 307–17), Paola Botham brings the work of Jürgen Habermas into the analysis of verbatim drama in her article 'From Deconstruction to Reconstruction: A Habermasian Framework for Contemporary Political Theatre' (*ConTR* 18:iii[2008] 307–17). Here she analyses Habermas's term 'public sphere' as a potential reason for the popularity of this form of theatre in plays such as Jonathan Holmes's *Falujah* [2007], where it provides a means of breaking through audiences' sense of powerlessness against the onslaught of postmodernism (p. 308). Botham argues that, by operating in the public sphere, such plays 'open ... the door to a renewed understanding of political theatre' (p. 310). The article also responds unconsciously to the debate raised in Canton's article about factual and fictional material coexisting in a text by asserting that 'the playwright/editor has a legitimate (and unavoidable) entitlement to add his/her own artistic voice to the verbatim chorus' (p. 313). Botham also recognizes the austerity of much verbatim theatre—exemplified in work staged at the Tricycle such as *The Colour of Justice* [1999] and *Called to Account* [2007]—and argues that it is this very property that allows the form to 'exceed postmodernism's infinite itch for deconstruction' (p. 316).

Botham cites Derek Paget's early pioneering work on the subject as evidence of the public sphere on which verbatim drama operates (p. 312). Paget himself makes a welcome return to his work on the subject in the article 'New Documentarism on Stage: Documentary Theatre in New Times' (*ZAA* 56:ii[2008] 129–41), a reprise of and response to his influential article 'Verbatim Theatre: Oral History and Documentary Techniques', originally published by *New Theatre Quarterly* in 1987. In revisiting this area Paget looks at reasons behind the upsurge of new plays during the period 1990–2007. Particular attention is paid to so-called 'tribunal' and 'verbatim' plays such as David Hare's *The Permanent Way* [2004] and Richard Norton Taylor's *Called To Account*. Paget's article looks at some of the defining features of these offshoots of documentary theatre, and suggests that the popularity for this form comes from its insistence on the veracity of fact because 'faith in facts . . . ha[s] drained away from "post-documentary" cultures in mediatised societies' (p. 141).

Documentary theatre also exercises the 'Backpages' section of *Contemporary Theatre Review* (*ConTR* 18:ii[2008] 272–9), where a range of views are brought together from the universities of London, Glasgow and California in response to the National Theatre of Scotland's production of *Black Watch* [2006]. Some contributions are from those who saw the play in performance and others from those who had only read the play. However, the Anglo-American nature of the feedback is interesting in relation to a play that discusses both the highly nationalistic elements that operate in conflict zones such as Iraq and the Black Watch regiment's involvement in a succession of past colonial wars. The respondents also make interesting comments about the play's attitudes to America, framed through the often disparaging remarks made by the Scottish soldiers. One respondent, David Archibald, calls *Black Watch* '*the* Scottish play about Iraq', but also points out that its concentration on the regiment also 'constructs a one-sided historical narrative . . . that plays down its often brutal imperial past' (p. 279).

Not surprisingly, the centenary of Samuel Beckett's birth in 2006 saw an outpouring of scholarly activity. One of the first edited collections from one of the many conferences that took place around the world in the centenary year is *Beckett at 100: Revolving It All*, edited by Linda Ben-Zvi and Angela Moorjani, which brings together a selection of essays the majority of which were first presented at Trinity College Dublin. The essays encompass Beckett's prose work, but there are also contributions that address particular plays. Several of these concentrate on *Krapp's Last Tape* [1958], and it is interesting to note that, following Harold Pinter's performance as Krapp at the Royal Court in Beckett's centenary year, this play now seems to have displaced both *Waiting for Godot* [1953] and *Endgame* [1957] in the contemporary imagination. Carla Locatelli's 'Projections: Beckett's *Krapp's Last Tape* and *Not I* as Autobiographies' (pp. 68–80) maintains that the play is less an autobiographical excursion than 'Beckett . . . reflecting back to his spectators the voyeuristic dimension of their pathos' (p. 78). Enoch Brater's 'Beckett's Romanticism' (pp. 139–51), argues that Krapp's attempts to record memory and his anti-heroic qualities make him a quasi-romantic hero, yet points out that at the same time, 'Krapp's bulky tape recorder is nonetheless an effective instrument for keeping romanticism in check' (p. 147) within a text that he sees as displaying 'intrusive but intuitive romanticism' (p. 148). Irit Degani-Raz's 'The Spear of Telephus in *Krapp's Last Tape*' (pp. 190–201) concentrates on the central place of the tape recorder in the play, and its function as a modern-day spear of Telephus. Here, the recorder 'inverts and reveals itself to be a damaging tool capable not only of distorting memory but even corrupting the original event itself' (p. 191). Antonia Rodríguez-Gado's 'Re-Figuring the Stage Body through the Mechanical Re-Production of Memory' (pp. 202–16) is also concerned with the use of the tape machine through 'the relationship established between the stage figure of Krapp and the recorded voice of memory' (p. 202). The essay draws attention to the moments where the stage presence of Krapp is compared to his mechanically recorded voice. Other theatre essays in the collection include Herbert Blau's semi-autobiographical 'Apnea and True Illusion: Breath(less) in Beckett' (pp. 35–53), which observes that, from his experience of directing Beckett's work in the 1960s, *Krapp's Last Tape* can claim to be as political as anything written by Brecht. Angela Moorjani's '"Just Looking": Ne(i)ther-World Icons, Elsheimer Nocturnes, and Other Simultaneities in Beckett's *Play*' (pp. 123–38) makes comparisons with artistic representations of the underworld and the instantly recognizable iconography of Beckett's *Play* [1962], where 'the stage image of the three urns, encircled in darkness, echoes a still older mythic underworld' (p. 127). Anna McMullan's 'Beckett's Theater: Embodying Alterity' (pp. 166–76) focuses upon Beckett's first full-length play *Eleutheria* [1947] as a response to the events of the Second World War and the Holocaust. Mariko Hori Tanaka's 'Ontological Fear and Anxiety in the Theater of Beckett' (pp. 246–58), Mary Bryden's 'The Mid-Century Godot: Beckett and Saroyan' (pp. 259–70) and Elin Diamond's 'Beckett and Caryl Churchill along the Möbius Strip' (pp. 285–98) all look at Beckett's various legacies of influence. Finally, Hersh Zeifman's 'Staging Sam Beckett as a Dramatic Character' (pp. 311–18), is a lively essay looking at another aspect of Beckett's afterlife—namely his appropriation as a dramatic figure in Michael Hasting's play *Calico* [2004], Sean Dixon's *Sam's Last Dance* [1997] and Justin Fleming's *Burnt Piano* [1999].

Beckett's *Waiting for Godot* is the subject of Mark and JulietteTaylor-Batty's volume for Continuum's Modern Theatre Guides series. Its major strength is its exploration of the play's French origins, and especially the first production in Paris directed by Roger Blin. The Taylor-Battys' knowledge of French language and culture comes to the fore in their discussion of some of the important differences between the French and English versions that Beckett himself provided, and they argue that 'it is only when he begins to write in French ... that Beckett's unique style really begins to appear, and that he throws off the shackles of the influence of predecessors and contemporaries' (p. 6).

Jonathan Boulter's *Beckett: A Guide for the Perplexed*, also by Continuum Press, looks more widely across Beckett's entire oeuvre and tends to concentrate more on the novels than the plays, although *Waiting for Godot*, *Endgame*, *Not I* [1972] and *Krapp's Last Tape* are covered in some depth. The emphasis is far more on textual analysis than on the historical and cultural contextualization that Batty undertakes with *Waiting for Godot*. Instead, Boulter treats the texts to a range of philosophical and theoretical couplings, such as Beckett with Freud, Lacan and Derrida. However, the book is a considerable achievement in bringing together so lucidly in one volume Beckett's work in both the theatre and the novel.

The work of Sarah Daniels is the focus of Heather's Debling's '"How will they ever heal ... ?": Bearing Witness to Abuse and the Importance of Female Community in Sarah Daniels's *Beside Herself*, *Head-Rot Holiday*, and *The Madness of Esme and Shaz*' (*MD* 51[2008] 259–73, goes some way towards re-evaluating some of Daniels's later plays which look at the effects of the abuse of women, associated mental illness, and the use of testimony as a process of healing. The article also makes a timely contribution to the ongoing debates that have arisen out of trauma studies in other disciplines, with Debling arguing that the presence of female communities in many of the plays discussed is vital in facilitating a coming to terms with past abuse. In these plays, Debling observes, Daniels places the female hysteric centre-stage, not as a male spectacle, but instead as one permitted to 'reveal the testimony recorded on her abused body' (p. 26).

Issues of psychiatry also preoccupy Alicia Tycer in her detailed and illuminating article "'Victim. Perpetrator. Bystander'': Melancholic Witnessing of Sarah Kane's *4.48 Psychosis*' (*TJ* 60:i[2008] 23–36) which looks at the problematic issue of interpreting Sarah Kane's last play through her suicide in 1999 as '"the lost object"', which in turn 'threatens to annul the melancholic ambiguity' (p. 25) of *4.48 Psychosis*, and which Tycer argues has the potential to be both redemptive and enabling for an audience in witnessing 'depictions of psychic trauma' (p. 27). Tycer goes on to argue that *4.48 Psychosis*, with its 'non-linear structure facilitates a trauma-based reading' (p. 27).

The traumatized body is also the subject of Amy Strahler Holzapfel's 'The Body in Pieces: Contemporary Anatomy Theatres' (*PAJ* 30:ii [2008] 1–16). Using Caryl Churchill's *A Number* amongst several other illustrative performances, Holzapfel questions modernism's reaction to the banning of the public spectacle of medical autopsy in early twentieth-century Europe. She argues that the practice has been resurrected through a fascination for the autopsy in television programmes ranging from *MASH* to *Six Feet Under* and *Nip/Tuck*, but also though 'the trajectory of postmodern performance' where 'bodies on stage, while not deceased, are framed as anatomized subjects' (p. 1). In the case of Churchill's *A Number*, gene technology has rendered a series of cloned offspring 'as a mediated pastiche of parts' (p. 1).

Jerzy Limon's 'Waltzing in *Arcadia*: A Theatrical Dance in Five Dimensions' (*NTQ* 24:iii[2008] 222–8) offers a close reading of the final scene in one of Tom Stoppard's most popular plays, and in particular how a series of different time streams are manipulated via different melodies. Stoppard's *Arcadia* [1993] is also the subject of John Fleming's insightful short study of the play for Continuum's *Modern Theatre Guides* [2008]. Drawing on previously unpublished interview material with Stoppard, Fleming's volume traces the history of the play's production and its cultural and historical context—both in its historical setting of the early 1800s alongside Stoppard's ongoing interests in scientific development between past and present. There is also an interesting discussion of the New York production of the play at the Lincoln Centre (pp. 79–83).

'As Long as the Punters Enjoy it' (*NTQ* 24:iii[2008] 260–9) is a long interview conducted by Aleks Sierz with the playwright Tanika Gupta. The discussion looks back at a writing career that began in 1996 and considers two of her most recent plays—the quasi-docudrama *Gladiator Games* [2005] and *Sugar Mummies* [2006], about Western female sex tourism.

Elaine Aston's 'A Fair Trade? Staging Female Sex Tourism in *Sugar Mummies* and *Trade*' (*ConTR* 18:ii[2008] 180–92) is a far more extensive exploration of Gupta's play, alongside analysis of Debbie Tucker Green's *Trade* [2004].The article brings into question the problems that feminism puts forward concerning women's sexual pleasure, against the economic disparity (and with it charges of sexual exploitation) that female sex tourism perpetuates in an international context. Aston sees one way of reading the two plays as a demonstration of the female individualism championed in the post-feminism of 1990s. However, Aston argues that *Sugar Mummies* and *Trade* both also demonstrate that sexual fulfilment ignores 'local, social inequalities and oppressions' (p. 182). The article points towards the need for 'travel romance' as a vital ingredient in female sex tourism, even if the belief is self-delusional (p. 186), and is also critical of *Sugar Mummies* as being prone to avoiding the more 'politicizing possibilities of [Gupta's] subject' (p. 190). In contrast, Aston sees Tucker Green's *Trade* as engaging far more rigorously in what she calls the 'feminist political' (p. 190) and in particular its critique of bourgeois post-feminism.

The theatre director James Macdonald is interviewed by R. Darren Gobert in 'Finding a Physical Language: Directing for the Nineties Generation' (*NTQ* 24:ii[2008] 141–57), where he talks about how different strategies as a director have come into play when working with the very different theatre languages encountered in Caryl Churchill's *Top Girls* and *A Number* [2002] or Martin Crimp's *Fewer Emergencies* [2005] and Sarah Kane's *4.48 Psychosis*.

Kane's last play, as well as Joe Penhall's *Blue/Orange* [2000] and Conor McPherson's *Shining City* [2004], form the core of Ariel Watson's substantial article 'Cries of Fire: Psychotherapy in Contemporary British and Irish Drama' (*MD* 51[2008] 188–210). Watson points out that, while the area of psychoanalysis and theatre has received more attention than psychotherapy theatre (p. 188), psychotherapy has the inherent theatricality of the confessional as well as showing power relationships between patient and therapist. However, Watson points out that Kane and Penhall's concern is 'primarily with [therapy's] failures rather than with its capacity to improve the human condition' (p. 189). This ends in both plays critiquing psychotherapeutic treatments as 'tools for the manipulation and objectification ... of the patient (p. 189).

Crimp's earlier play, *Attempts on her Life* [1997], and Kane's *4.48 Psychosis* also form the basis of David Barnett's 'When Is a Play not a Drama? Two Examples of Postdramatic Theatre Texts' (*NTQ* 93:i[2008] 14–23), in which some of the key ideas in Hans-Thies Lehman's book *Post Dramatic Theatre* [1999] are applied to Crimp and Kane, especially in relation to how their respective plays represent time. Barnett concludes that, by adopting these post-dramatic techniques rather than conventionally representative ones, both 'invite creative approaches to the business of acting and making theatre' (p. 23).

Questions of post-dramatic theatre also occupy Louise LePage's short piece, 'Posthuman Sarah Kane', for the 'Backpages' section of *Contemporary Theatre Review* (*ConTR* 18:iii[2008] 401–3), in which 'contemporary identity' in Kane's work 'is redefined as a kind of insecure *post*human hybrid' (p. 402), either through disruption of space/time, or both, whereby 'self and other are no longer necessarily distinct' (p. 402).

Two articles on Martin Crimp and Sarah Kane are also to be found in Elizabeth Angel-Perez and Alexander Poulain's edited collection *Hunger on*

Stage [2008]. As the title suggests, the volume contains articles that look at representations of hunger, gluttony and starvation in drama throughout various historical periods. Vicky Angelaki's 'Taking a Bite of the Big Apple: Martin Crimp's *The Treatment*' (pp. 257–67) not only argues that the play is central to any consideration of his work, but that it 'is the first step towards a critique of the blatant commodification of art and the manipulation of the author/artist by the art industry for the purposes of financial gain' (p. 328). Aleks Sierz's '"We're all bloody hungry": Images of Hunger and the Construction of the Gendered Self in Sarah Kane's *Blasted*' (pp. 268–79) argues that Sarah Kane's debut 'can be rediscovered as a world which is infused with a series of metaphorical ideas about hunger, feeding and body functions' (p. 269). Sierz produces a comprehensive reading of the play in these terms, together with discussion of how these ideas operate with another overriding concern in her work—the mutilated body.

Ideas concerning subjectivity in Kane's work also form one of the three case studies examining subjectivity within the framework of postmodernism in Karolina Gritzner's '(Post) Modern Subjectivity and the New Expressionism: Howard Barker, Sarah Kane, and Forced Entertainment' (*ConTR* 18:iii[2008] 328–40). As well as examining current debates about postmodernism and performance, Gritzner usefully focuses on the work of Theodor Adorno as her main theoretical model, and argues that 'an Adornian approach to theatre would suggest that the theatrical space can provide conditions for subjective freedom only if the aesthetic principles employed create a world that is sufficiently removed from the social and moral prescriptions of objective reality' (p. 331). Gritzner then traces the ways in which theatre has represented the condition of subjectivity through modernism and postmodernism, using examples including Howard Barker (who fits Adorno's criteria of theatre most closely), Sarah Kane and Forced Entertainment. Gritzner reads Kane's work as more radically experimental than Barker's in its 'responses to the contradictions of late twentieth century global capitalism' (p. 334), and also provides some important questioning of the humanist readings given to date in *Blasted* [1995] (p. 335). Her final two plays, *Crave* [1998] and *4.48 Psychosis*, are also read beyond the common interpretation as 'plays for voices' by placing an emphasis on 'the criticism of the subject [as] the latest turn of reification in global late capitalism' (p. 336).

Sarah Kane's *Blasted* is also the subject of Helen Iball's short monograph for Continuum's Modern Theatre Guides [2008] This is the most ambitious treatment of the play to date in terms of both its analysis and revaluation of the play and its inclusion of new interview material. Iball provides fascinating analysis of the play in terms of the importance that space within the hotel setting provides, and with it the body as another form of space that is marked out. There is also an excellent tracing and reassessment of changing views of the play (which Iball terms its 'afterlife'), both through academic criticism and successive productions. To this end, Iball presents two case studies in 2006 for comparison: Thomas Ostermeier's production at the Schaubühne Berlin (which visited London's Barbican in 2006) and Graeae's UK touring version in the same year. The concluding chapter also puts forward a speculative, but highly relevant, consideration of how future productions of *Blasted* might be reconceived by practitioners.

Several articles this year consider ongoing developments in British playwriting. Harry Derbyshire's 'The Culture of New Writing' in the 'Backpages' section of *Contemporary Theatre Review* (*ConTR* 18:i[2008] 131–4) complements interview material to ask the question 'whether writers [are] being steered ... towards writing the kinds of play that theatre companies wanted to stage' (p. 132). Derbyshire comes to no firm conclusion over the matter, but the diversity of views expressed is of interest. In the same section is an interview with Lisa Goldman (*ConTR* 18:i[2008] 134–7), who since 2006 has been the artistic director of London's Soho theatre. Here she discusses the current state of political playwriting, and displays a scepticism about the current vogue for verbatim theatre, suggesting that it may be seen as 'debate ... poorly dressed in the clothes of theatre' (p. 135). There is a discussion of Philip Ridley's *Leaves of Glass* [2007], which was Goldman's inaugural production at the Soho as its artistic director. There is also a further interview in the same 'Backpages' section with Graham Whybrow, the Royal Court's former literary manager. In 'Looking Back, Looking Forward: Literary Management at the Royal Court' (*ConTR* 18:i[2008] 137–40), Whybrow makes some interesting comments about current trends, such as the vogue for contemporary settings rather than historical ones (p. 138). Whybrow also displays scepticism towards the 'workshopping' process to which many young playwrights find themselves subjected, and discusses the changes in ethos and direction during the time when Stephen Daldry, and later Ian Rickson, ran the Royal Court.

This review of the year's work ends pessimistically with two articles on the current state of British playwriting. Trish Reid's short piece, 'Scottish Arts Council Wields the Axe', in the 'Backpages' section of *Contemporary Theatre Review* (*ConTR* 18:iii[2008] 398–400), discusses the demise of established companies such as 7:84 Scotland as a result of funding cuts, as well as the surprising (and disturbing) news that Glasgow-based company Suspect Culture has suffered the same fate. Reid goes on to assess some of the company's innovative productions, including *Airport* [1996] and *Mainstream* [1999], and speculates that the company's lack of a clear regional identity (in comparison to the worldwide success of National Theatre of Scotland's production of *Black Watch*) may have been the principal reason for its demise.

Aleks Sierz's 'Reality Sucks: The Slump in British New Writing' (*PAJ* 30:ii[2008] 102–7) accuses British theatre of being 'in thrall to a mix of social realism and naturalism whose hegemonic power remains a problem even today' (p. 102). Sierz perceptively puts forward the argument that this situation has come about as a rearguard critical reaction in response to experiments against realism such as Katie Mitchell's production (in a new translation by Martin Crimp) of *The Seagull* [2006]. However, in Sierz's view, this reactionary retreat into the familiar comforts of socio-realism has resulted in new plays that are little more than 'soapy dramas for couch potatoes' (p. 104) with the consequence that, since 2001, 'English new writing has entered first into a crisis and then into a slump' (p. 105). However, Sierz's article is not entirely despondent. For example, it points towards the work of

Dennis Kelly and Debbie Tucker Green as two notable exceptions, and to new appointments such as Dominic Cooke at the Royal Court and Lisa Goldman at the Soho, who have produced notable work including Mike Bartlett's *My Child* [2007] and Hassan Abdulrazzak's *Baghdad Wedding* [2007].

6. Pre-1950 Poetry

'Even now', Jean Moorcroft Wilson observes, 'Private [Isaac] Rosenberg lacks the rank he deserves and his work demands' (p. 1). Her biography, *Isaac Rosenberg: The Making of a Great War Poet: A New Life* is one of two major publications in 2008 that may help to redress this. Wilson traces Rosenberg's life from early experiences in Bristol and the East End of London to his final years in the trenches of the First World War. She pays particular attention to the links between Rosenberg's artistic career and his poetry; to the influence of Yiddish upon the structure and soundscape of his writing; and to the detail of life in the trenches. In addition to documenting his life and acquaintance, she provides thoughtful readings of his war poetry. Without doubt, *The Making of a Great War Poet* will become the standard scholarly biography.

Oxford University Press has also added a collection of Rosenberg's poems, plays and prose to its 21st-Century Oxford Authors series, edited by Vivien Noakes. This derives from her previous complete edition of Rosenberg's poems and plays, providing copious notes on allusions, sources and provenance. There is a useful selection of Rosenberg's letters here, including crucial letters written from the trenches during his final months. Noakes claims to correct various 'misreadings' in the edition of mislaid letters by Rosenberg edited by Jean Lydiard (reviewed in *YWES* 88[2009] 972). The volume also includes notes and essays by Rosenberg on art, mostly written or published during his stay in South Africa before the First World War. The current hardback edition is unlikely to be purchased beyond libraries, but paperback publication might help to secure the wider dissemination of a poet whose work still tends to be underrepresented.

The likely popularity of poets such as Rosenberg often depends upon the availability of reasonably priced, well-edited modern editions. So the publication of Edna Longley's new edition of Edward Thomas's poetry may be good news for his fans. Until now, the most readily available collection of his work has been Faber's partial reprint of R. George Thomas's edition. Longley claims to restore or emend various aspects of Thomas's texts following re-evaluation of the manuscript evidence; the poems have also been reordered into chronological sequence. Longley has edited collections of Thomas's poems previously, but this edition is specifically described as 'The Annotated Collected Poems'. As many pages of detailed notes, including copious material from his prose writings, follow 150 pages of Thomas's poems. Much of this material goes beyond the standard editorial task of supplying textual or contextual information and offers readings of form and detail, sketching broader arguments about Thomas's significance: Longley emphasizes the importance of memory to Thomas, the reflexive treatment of artistic creation in the poems, and the importance of his 'eco-historical' imagination.

The volume, then, is the culmination of a lifetime's work on Thomas and, in effect, combines an edition of Thomas's poetry with a meditation upon his work.

Elsewhere, Nick Freeman contests Thomas's reputation as a war poet by offering a reading of 'The Gallows', in 'Edward Thomas, Swinburne, and Richard Jefferies: "The dead oak tree bough" ' (*ELT* 51:ii[2008] 164–83). After contrasting Thomas with the modernists, Freeman argues persuasively that his poetry responds to late Victorian influences, specifically, the folk ballads collected by Cecil Sharp, the animal stories (and sadistic tendencies) of Richard Jefferies and the poetic forms of Swinburne. These formed, Freeman concludes, an 'eclectic engagement'.

Gabrielle McIntire devotes four out of seven chapters to T.S. Eliot in *Modernism, Memory, and Desire*, her study of Eliot and Virginia Woolf. His bawdy poems about 'King Bolo and his Big Black Bassturd Kween' feature prominently in her argument that, for modernists, 'memory is always already invested and intertwined with writing sexuality, the body, and desire' (p. 2). Although they were written within private letters, McIntire describes the Bolo poems as Eliot's 'most sustained poetic output' (p. 15). She makes much of his suggestion that Wyndham Lewis publish them in *Blast*, but concludes that Eliot became reticent about their publication once he had achieved exposure for less risqué poetry. For McIntire, Eliot's treatment of Bolo's obscene interactions with 'Colombo' present 'a queer pornotropic poetics of colonialism' (p. 28), offering a figure for his dealings with history in his public work. The book divides between reading the scurrilously obscene humour of the Bolo poems with a po face, and searching out innuendo ('cunning passages') elsewhere in Eliot's work. It has, though, the virtue of emphasizing the intense quality of yearning in Eliot's poetry. An unconventional Eliot, 'sexy, dangerous, and crucially *uneven*' (p. 7), replaces the coolly clinical possum, reviled by some critics.

Ed Madden considers similar sexual material in *Tiresian Poetics*, which devotes two chapters to the appearance of Tiresias in *The Waste Land* as a 'figure par excellence' of 'modernist textual and sexual ambiguity' (p. 15). Madden considers Tiresias as 'queer', a site where oracular voice converges with sexual knowledge, evoking strangeness, sexual difference and unease. The first chapter on Eliot concludes that *The Waste Land* is 'a staging of homosexual panic' (p. 127): Tiresias does not transcend sexual difference; instead he represents 'a feminized male' and is used to 'tropologically figure anxieties about the penetrable male body' (p. 124). The second chapter on *The Waste Land* is more wide-ranging, reviewing manuscript drafts, the influence of cinema, the work of Roger Vittoz on neurasthenia, J.G. Frazer, and anal dilators. Its conclusions are broadly similar though: 'Eliot's Tiresias is autobiographically performative' (p. 174) and the footnote about Tiresias added to book publication of the poem represents an attempt to control the revelations this figure threatens about the nature of desire and sexual difference.

John McCombe considers a different seductive figure in 'Cleopatra and her Problems: T.S. Eliot and the Fetishization of Shakespeare's Queen of the Nile' (*JML* 31:ii[2008] 23–38). In the early part of his career Eliot was drawn to

Shakespeare's Cleopatra and her sexuality, McCombe argues, as the subject of Roman imperial power. McCombe repeatedly places Eliot's poetry and criticism in relation to 'colonialist discourse' (p. 33). His allusions to her position in Shakespeare's plays as the object of other people's discourse coincided with parliamentary and journalistic debate about '"the problem" of Egypt' (p. 26). But Cleopatra also echoed Eliot's own sense of himself as an outsider in London, which explains, McCombe suggests, why these references diminish as Eliot came to feel that he had established a critical and literary reputation.

One premise of Leon Surette's comparative study of Eliot and Wallace Stevens, *The Modern Dilemma*, is that previous scholars have failed to compare without weighing the claims of one over the other. Yet this is not completely avoided here, and there is a slight deference to Eliot throughout: his work is usually the first to be considered in any chapter, and more chapters are devoted to specific consideration of his work than to that of Stevens. A central theme is the shared interest these poets took in humanism and, Surette claims, their shared rejection of it. He focuses discussion of this through their respective responses to the work of Ramon Fernandez, but also gives consideration to their interest in the work of Marianne Moore and their responses to the First World War. Surette's most controversial claims are that Eliot underwent a 'brief infatuation' with humanism under the influence of Bertrand Russell and that Stevens was less sympathetic to some aspects of humanism than has been admitted previously. Tendentious in parts, the book remains mainly stimulating and informed.

Chapter 5 of Andrea Zemgulys's *Modernism and the Locations of Literary Heritage* examines Eliot's interest in the city churches of London. Her larger subject is that of 'Heritage', understood as the late Victorian attempt to preserve a particular vision of Britain's past within locations and monuments. This view of the past is, she claims, 'unfashionable' both with the modernists, who found it irredeemably middle-class, and with scholars of modernism, who prefer more urban, technologically driven conceptions of modern space. The chapter on Eliot (pp. 126–44) draws on his outrage over the threat to demolish nineteen city churches. Zemgulys finds an odd but striking model for Eliot's 'historical sense' here, in his commitment to understanding the present through the vestiges of the past. She then discovers allusions to and traces of these churches in *The Waste Land*, claiming that 'they stage its innovations and reveal its art' (p. 135). Her most forcefully argued claim is that the churches are co-opted into a Foucauldian 'heterotopia' within *The Waste Land* and its conjunctions of different times and spaces. They are linked to the crumbling 'towers' of 'What the Thunder Said' and function, in effect, as synecdoche for Eliot's sense of the world that he imagines is under threat and whose destruction *The Waste Land* may relish. Zemgulys does not always convince, but her approach is arresting and her interest in material space which is 'not a determining condition, but subject to the meanings made of it by . . . texts' (p. 4) suggests recent refinements within literary historicism.

Matthew Bolton argues, in '"Not known, because not looked for": Eliot's Debt to Browning' (*YER* 25:ii[2008] 10–19), that Robert Browning's dramatic monologues constitute 'critical touchstones' (p. 18) for Eliot. Browning's influence upon poems such as 'Portrait of a Lady' is so obvious as to have remained hidden, Bolton claims. He cites passing references in Eliot's criticism, allusions and manuscript drafts to show how Eliot 'internalized' Browning (p. 15).

Scholars of Eliot's poetry continue to track down his sources and allusions for *Notes and Queries*. In 'A Possible Source for the Seduction Scene in *The Waste Land*' (*N&Q* 55[2008] 491–2) James Womack traces the encounter between the typist and the 'young man carbuncular' to Aubrey Beardsley's Decadent poem, 'The Three Musicians'. In the same issue, Matthew Peters maps plot elements of *The Bostonians* onto 'The Lovesong of J. Alfred Prufrock'. In addition to the influence of Jules Laforgue, Peters argues, 'a less compacted Jamesian ironic tone' should also be acknowledged (*N&Q* 55[2008] 489–91). Ian Higgins argues that a partial allusion to *Dracula* in 'What the Thunder Said' evokes Stoker's treatment of 'imperial collapse' (p. 500) in '*The Waste Land* and *Dracula*' (*N&Q* 55[2008] 499–500). Similarly, David Boddy, '"The Fire Sermon", but which Fire Sermon?' (*N&Q* 55[2008] 500–1), claims that the 'Fire Sermon' in *The Waste Land* may allude to an annual 'Fire Sermon' at the church of St Magnus Martyr, as well as the Buddhist text Eliot cites in his notes.

In a sub-chapter of *Modernist Goods* (pp. 161–93) Glenn Willmott re-examines the Thunder's question from *The Waste Land*—'What have we given?'—in relation to the notion of 'aboriginal heritages'. This concept designates for Willmott those primitive cultures from outside Western capitalist and imperialist traditions which fascinated modernists like Eliot. Citing Kristeva's abject and the role of the gift in these 'aboriginal heritages', Willmott suggests that Eliot's relation to the primitive cultures which may hold out the vestiges of cohesion or transcendence in *The Waste Land* involves a patina of irony. He participates, Willmott argues, in a 'parodic shamanry' (p. 193).

In *Poetry and Nation Review* Eliot receives praise from Michael Alexander for his capacity 'to write on two levels simultaneously' in a brief article about the influence of Dante upon poetry, 'Poets in Paradise: Chaucer, Pound, Eliot' (*PNR* 34:iii[2008] 12–13). Eliot is also discussed briefly, alongside Thomas Hardy and others, in David Gervais's extended consideration of the forms and values of simplicity in poetry, 'The Condition of Simplicity: Parts One and Two' (*PNR* 34:iv[2008] 42–8 and *PNR* 34:v[2008] 41–7).

Significant amounts of important material relating to Eliot are promised in 2009 and 2010, including the first volumes in a collected edition of his prose. Until then, William Pritchard provides an amiable survey of the highlights of Eliot's uncollected criticism, 'Eliot's Mischievous Prose' (*HopRev* 1:iii[2008] 383–402), which emphasizes his 'sceptical and astringent humour', especially in the earlier essays. Elsewhere, G. Douglas Atkins praises Eliot's capacity to make 'distinctions' (p. 147) in his prose. Atkins's account of 'Tradition and the Individual Talent', in *Reading Essays: An Invitation* (pp. 140–58), places Eliot's essay within a broader framework. Eliot, Atkins argues, transforms the essay-writing tradition by re-evaluating its relation to the individual from within.

Two chapters of Peter Edgerly Firchow's book on British conceptions and misconceptions of Germany, *Strange Meetings*, are relevant to this section of *YWES*. 'Sunlight in the Hofgarden' (pp. 23–55) describes the influence of Munich on T.S. Eliot, D.H. Lawrence and Rupert Brooke. Firchow focuses on the 'Marie' section of 'The Burial of the Dead' and finds the body of Ludwig II of Bavaria at the bottom of the Starnbergersee, a potent figure for Eliot's Fisher King. Brookes' experiences in Munich and linguistic capacities in German, Fisher suggests, were broader and more influential than his reputation as a parochial Georgian poet would indicate. Secondly, 'W.H. Auden and Josef Weinheber' (pp. 219–46) concerns Kirchstetten, the small town that both poets chose as their final resting place. Auden felt drawn there as an antidote to his experiences in Berlin, marred by the rise of Nazism and the Second World War. Despite Weinheber's Nazism, their shared love of Kirchstetten's quiet rural values, Firchow argues, allowed a conciliation between these poets within Auden's later poetry.

Auden and Eliot also receive notable attention in *Ecstasy and Understanding*, Adrian Grafe's collection of essays on religious awareness in modern poetry. David Summers uses Jean-Luc Marion's theories of 'saturated phenomenon' to explore selfhood in *Four Quartets* in relation to the experience of transcendence (pp. 71–83). Drawing upon Paul Ricoeur, Summers maps Eliot's narrative understanding of selfhood onto his use of Dante's *Divine Comedy*: the experience of transcendence in a modern epoch is 'small' by comparison. David Rudrum investigates the apocalyptic imaginings of Eliot's 'The Hollow Men' alongside W.B. Yeats's 'The Second Coming' (pp. 58–70). The modernism of these poems, Rudrum argues, lies in the way they question the notion of apocalypse as an ending. They unfold, he argues 'a bleak, terrible, futureless present . . . fragmentary and partial' (p. 66), reinvigorating religious poetry in the process.

In her account of Auden's conversion to Christianity in the same volume, Kathleen Bell describes his turn from thinking about desire and the body in Freudian terms towards a conception of the body as the locus for a politics and theology of virtue and justice (pp. 84–10). Auden, she argues, was strongly influenced here by the poetry of Charles Williams, as well as the theology of Reinhold Niebuhr. The essay also refers to Hannah Arendt and to 'The Platonic Blow', an uncollected, explicitly pornographic poem attributed to Auden. Also relevant to this section of *YWES* is Andrew Harrison's essay on the poetry of D.H. Lawrence (pp. 46–57). Harrison questions Lawrence's own account of his sharp falling away from religion, describing a more gradual loss of faith that arose from Lawrence's university experiences and the death of his mother. The essay offers readings of two unpublished, early poems that make moving connections between home, chapel and community.

Six years since the previous volume, 2008 saw the next instalment in Edward Mendelson's monumental edition of Auden's complete works, a third volume of his prose, covering the years 1949 to 1955. This material runs from the Page–Barbour Lectures Auden gave at the University of Virginia (published as *The Enchafèd Flood*), through his substantial output as a reviewer to talks given on the BBC in the 1950s (which appear in an appendix). Mendelson's thoughtful and informative introduction marries Auden's prose to his poetry as a forum for trying out ideas, but also traces his engagements with particular authors (including T.S. Eliot), his experiments with form, and key concepts such as his specialized understanding of history. Mendelson's annotations illuminate a significant body of Auden's writings, diverse and challenging in interests and outlook. His work continues to be a triumph of scholarship and editing.

Stephen Bygrave's essay, 'Foucault, Auden and Two New York Septembers' (in Morton and Bygrave, eds., *Foucault in an Age of Terror: Essays on Biopolitics and the Defence of Society*, pp. 215–29), uses Foucault's *The Defence of Society* to explore the 'reactivation' of 'September 1 1939' in the wake of the attacks upon the World Trade Centre on 11 September 2001 (p. 216). Bygrave traces the poem's reception following the attack, but also examines its textual history in relation to public events, from the Second World War to Lyndon Johnson and the Vietnam War. Auden's poem can usefully, Bygrave indicates, be placed by work by Foucault and Habermas to probe the difficulties of achieving a public voice and 'the subjection wrought by power' (p. 228).

James Womack's article 'Auden's Goethe' (*EIC* 58[2008] 333–54) sketches connections between the two poets, from allusions to Goethe in Auden's poetry, to his translations of Goethe and suggestions of a biographical identification with Goethe. As a translator, Womack argues, Auden's engagement with Goethe 'as a human figure rather than an inhuman figurehead' is such that liberties he took in translating constitute a dialogic tribute to Goethe's humanity. In 'Hood, Dickens, Auden and Churchyard Revels' (*N&Q* 55[2008] 43), Rodney Stenning Edgecombe traces the distant affinity between 'gamesome boys' leaping over gravestones in Hood's 'Hero and Leander' and the 'collective indifference to the vanished individual' explored in 'Musée des Beaux Arts'.

Elizabeth Loizeaux also explores 'Musée des Beaux Arts' in *Twentieth Century Poetry and the Visual Arts* as part of her investigation of 'twentieth-century ekphrasis'. For Loizeaux, works of verbal art which evoke the visual arts are uneasy about their own status and caught in a complex of feeling generated by the triangular relationship between poet, object and reader. The poems of ekphrasis which interest her are representative, she claims, of 'continuous and ongoing efforts across the century to break open the possibilities of lyric poetry' (p. 9). The chapter on Auden (pp. 63–79) explores the ethics of being a bystander: she begins with the concept of ekphrasis as an elegy by a living poet for a dead image, before discussing attitudes towards death. It is a wide-ranging chapter, citing responses to Auden's poem from Elizabeth Bishop to Irving Feldman; placing her arguments in context with the work of subsequent poets, such as Seamus Heaney; and exploring the historical context of Auden's poem, especially his experiences as a documentary photographer of the effects of war during the 1930s. Auden, she argues, raises 'the possibility that art may offer a way of attending to death and suffering that can loosen the indifference to others the poem claims as a fact of life' (p. 69).

Sophie Ratcliffe also interrogates Auden's sense of ethical obligation in *On Sympathy*. She devotes one chapter to a close reading of *The Mirror and the*

Sea, his response to *The Tempest* (pp. 123–68). In this ambitious work, dense with literary insight and philosophical observation, Ratcliffe begins by tackling the question of whether it is possible to feel for or with fictional characters. Roughly, she argues that while this *is* a possibility, the limits of such sympathetic feeling form the ethical and religious drift of writings by her three central authors, Browning, Auden and Beckett. The limits of literary sympathies remind us of the limits to our daily dealings with human beings. Prospero, Caliban and Miranda play a significant role here—both within the original dramatic context of *The Tempest* and in the ways that Ratcliffe's chosen authors rework Shakespeare. Allusion, on this account, symbolically registers similarity and difference, proximity and distance between creative minds. Her account of Auden probes his religious thinking in the 1940s and traces verbal and allusive links to Henry James. She understands the dramatic use of cliché in *The Mirror and the Sea* as a development from Browning's dramatic monologues. Cliché, rhyme and facile forms of speech, Ratcliffe argues with poignancy, function as 'parables' about humanity's repeated failure to acknowledge the difference and strangeness of others. Auden, she claims, espoused an exemplary uncertainty.

The year 2008 saw the publication of Thomas Hardy's *'Poetical Matter' Notebook* in a transcription, edited by Pamela Dalziel and Michael Millgate. This notebook dating from the last decade of Hardy's life consists of fragments of poems, recopied notes, rhythmic schemes, fragmentary anecdotes, and excerpts from newspapers. Since the physical copy of the notebook was mislaid in 1952, the present edition is based upon a digitally enhanced copy of a microfilm. The annotations are assiduous yet unobtrusive, and this notebook provides useful insights into the interests and working methods of Hardy's final years.

Tim Dolin devotes a chapter to Hardy's late career as a poet in his slim biography, *Thomas Hardy*. Short and serviceable, the inset panels of information about dates and authors referred to indicate that this volume is intended for A-level students and undergraduates, and it should serve this purpose well.

In 'The Periodical Context of Thomas Hardy's "In the Time of 'The Breaking of Nations"' ' (*N&Q* 55[2008] 58–60), Kevin Morrison asserts the 'interdisciplinary insights of book history' (p. 58) as a tool for resolving critical disagreement about whether the poem presents patriotic sentiment or anti-war feeling. The support of the *Saturday Review* for military conscription, Morrison argues, and its general investment in an optimistic view of the war, mean that Hardy's poem should be read 'as neither for nor against the war but, rather, as multivalent'.

In 'Retaining the Phantom: Desire, Sympathy and the Rhetoric of Elegy' (*THSJ* 4:i[2008] 30–43), Allison Cooper Davis reads 'Thoughts of Phena: At News of her Death' through Peter Sacks's theories of elegy. Citing Petrarch, she argues that Hardy's poem finds consolation by exerting imaginative control over its subject matter (Hardy's cousin, Tryphena Sparks), thus dissolving 'the female'. This reading is then extended to Hardy's later poems about the death of his wife. We should, Cooper Davis argues, 'be sceptical of the elegiac mode itself' (p. 42).

Anne-Lise François also tracks the allusive background to Hardy's poetry in '"Not thinking of you as left behind": Virgil and the Missing of Love in Hardy's *Poems of 1912–13*' (*ELH* 75[2008] 63–88). She traces the implications of Hardy's epigraph to *Poems of 1912–13* beyond its reference to the relationship between Aeneas and Dido to Aeneas's relationship with his wife Creusa and his failure to turn back for her. François finds this a powerful figure for Hardy's relations with his first wife and for understanding 'missing as a mode of love and not simply its lack or failure' (p. 67).

Laurence Estanove draws upon Michel Collet to describe 'the porosity of voices' (p. 33) in Hardy's poetry in '"Voices from things growing in a churchyard": Hardy's Verse on Both Sides of the Grave' (*THSJ* 4:ii[2008] 29–39). The dead speak in Hardy's poems, through gravestones, epitaphs and other less tangible presences. Beyond these horizons, Estanove argues, death is 'teeming with life' (p. 38). In the same issue of the *Hardy Society Journal*, Lakshmi Raj Sharma offers a close reading of 'Afterwards' which has a very different tenor (*THSJ* 4:ii[2008] 40–5). Hardy's poem, Sharma argues, asks for his work to be remembered after his death for the detailed quality of its observation of natural phenomena. E.T.H. Teague also investigates Hardy's noticings in 'Hardy's "Round Moon": An Astronomical Curiosity' (*THSJ* 4:iii[2008] 70–5), measuring Hardy's 'Seeing the Moon Rise' against astronomical records to prove that it preserves a highly specific moment in time.

In a glossy new imprint the *Hardy Review* now incorporates contributions to the Thomas Hardy Association's online discussion group. These usually take the form of a regular 'Poem of the Month' forum, as in discussions of 'Proud Songsters' (*THR* 10:i[2008] 12–36) and 'Four in the Morning' (*THR* 10:ii[2008] 110–17), although the spring volume also reproduces an online discussion of 'The Impercipient' (*THR* 10:i[2008] 43–67). Individual contributions within these sequences tend to be short, so the exchanges recorded are lively, but their content is definitely learned, from lexicological investigations to detailed analysis of the scansion of Hardy's poems. Since each of these discussions involves multiple contributors and does not follow a single line of development it is hard to do them justice in these pages, other than to record that they are usually informative and present an optimistic picture of the current state of Hardy scholarship.

Among the few critical responses to William Empson from 2008, Paul Bové concludes *Poetry against Torture* with a chapter on Empson and the mind (pp. 117–36). Bové finds Empson's intolerance of cruelty and his fierce defence of lucid critical analysis an exemplary antidote to recent attempts by the US government to legitimize torture within the 'war on terror'. Oleg Gelikman's '"Cold Pastoral": Werner Herzog's Version of Empson' (*MLN* 123[2008] 1141–62) begins by examining the ideological structures underpinning documentary film, before shifting to Empson's pastoral and presenting his early film reviews as theoretical precursors to *Some Versions of Pastoral*. Gelickman applies his analysis of Empson's account of social antagonisms and complex ideas compressed into simple forms to a reading of Werner Herzog's *Grizzly Bear*. The structures of Herzog's film, he claims, present Timothy Treadwell as a form of fallen pastoral hero. The essay is an odd journey, but it is not without its insights. In '*Seven Types of Ambiguity* and James Joyce' (*N&Q*

55[2008] 68–72), Matthew Creasy explores the origins of Empson's fascination with *Ulysses* in his university years and uncovers traces of Joyce's influence within the passages chosen for comment in *Seven Types*.

The cover of *Poems in the Porch*, edited by Kevin Gardner, claims that it will prompt a 'radical reassessment of [John Betjeman's] canon'. This is a grand claim for a slim volume of twenty religious poems written for radio broadcast and the fragments of two incomplete poems. In fact, six of these can be found in *Collected Poems* and seven of them have been published previously but not collected. The other poems were to have been published in a volume entitled *Verses from the Vestry*, intended to capitalize upon a previous collection (*Poems in the Porch*), but Betjeman and his publishers considered them too slight.

Despite being a 'self-confessed idler' (p. 77) (or perhaps because of it) Betjeman does, however, earn a chapter in John Bale's *Anti-Sport Sentiments in Literature* (pp. 77–95). Not a work of literary criticism, Bale's book seeks to supplement accounts of hostility towards sport with evidence from the arts. His account of Betjeman draws on his poetry and critical writings for biographical purposes, uncovering negative attitudes towards sport from his schooling to his later dislike for its monotonous public architecture. Nevertheless, Bale observes, Betjeman was not above evoking sport in his poetry for nostalgic purposes. Interestingly, Bale also reveals Betjeman's love of body-surfing. Unfortunately, no copy of Greg Morse's *John Betjeman: Reading the Victorians* had been made available at the time of writing.

The work of Ivor Gurney has received relatively little scholarly treatment in recent years. Pamela Blevins's account of his friendship with Marion Scott, *Song of Pain and Beauty*, is the first biography of Gurney since 1978. Its narrative is largely determined by Gurney's life: Blevins starts with their meeting at the Royal College of Music in 1911, but then explores Gurney's family background and his education, followed by his enlistment and the sudden blooming of poetic activity in the trenches. She charts his erratic mental health from a nervous breakdown before the war to repeated treatments at various mental institutions afterwards, and explores aspects of his ambiguous sexuality, from intense male friendships to his (unrequited) passion for Annie Drummond, a nurse who treated him at the Edinburgh War Hospital. Blevins emphasizes Gurney's musical career as a writer of songs and composer of settings, but also explores Scott's role in fostering this, especially through her activities as a music critic. The book is a work of devotion in two senses: it documents assiduously the friendship between Gurney and Scott, but is also passionate about its subject matter. For a biography, *Song of Pain and Beauty* wears it scholarship openly: it is episodic in presentation, placing notes a little obtrusively at the end of its short chapters, breaking up a narrative that is otherwise absorbing.

In *Modern Nostalgia: Siegfried Sassoon, Trauma and the Second World War*, Robert Hemmings addresses the output of Siegfried Sassoon after the First World War. A nuanced understanding of nostalgia, he argues, is required to defend Sassoon against accusations of self-indulgence. Hemmings duly charts the place of nostalgia within literary history, medical history and the development of psychology. He explores Sassoon's experience of analysis with W.H. Rivers in relation to burgeoning psychoanalytic theories of shell shock and 'war neurosis', before considering his autobiographical poems and prose and his public stance towards the Second World War. Giving due space to Sassoon's critics, Hemmings's approach is unusual: rather than defending Sassoon against accusations of narcissism, he looks to Freudian psychoanalysis to account for it. In spite of Sassoon's declared resistance to the aesthetics of modernism, Hemmings attempts to recoup his work by making it exemplify a series of modern dilemmas, from a problematic relationship to the past to an uncertain sense of selfhood and a fluid sexuality. Nostalgia figures here, with compelling detail, for the trauma of severance and loss, as well as sentiment.

Two biographical studies of Rudyard Kipling were published in 2008 as well as several articles in the specialist journals. William Dillingham's *Being Kipling* attempts to light up important corners of his personality by scrutinizing the rarely considered short stories and poems in *Land and Sea Tales for Scouts and Guides* [1923]. Although the volume is predominantly concerned with Kipling's short stories, it gives significant consideration to several poems too, particularly 'The Junk and Dhow' (pp. 58–60), 'The Last Lap' (pp. 119–22) and 'Ave Imperatrix' (pp. 182–90). Vested in biographical exploration, these readings are highly sensitive to Kipling's use of rhythm and its relation to the ideological currents and counter-currents of his writings. Charles Allen's lively account of the formative influence of Anglo-Indian society upon Kipling, *Kipling Sahib: India and the Making of Rudyard Kipling* offers little in the way of formal analysis of the poems, but does co-opt them into its biographical account. Allen quotes Kipling's poems from their first, newspaper and periodical, sources, tracing early unsigned works. He also supplies interesting contextual information, such as the likely influence of the execution of Private George Flaxman upon 'Danny Deever'.

Jad Adams's article 'Decadent or Hearty? Kipling's Dilemma' (*KJ* 82:cccxxv[2008] 9–27) largely focuses upon Kipling's novel, *The Light that Failed*, but gives some consideration to Kipling's early poetry in its attempt to connect him with the Decadent writings of Arthur Symons, Oscar Wilde and Aubrey Beardsley. George Simmers begins and ends his account of Kipling's response to the notion of shell shock in his short stories with a brief analysis of the poem 'The Mother's Son' (*KJ* 82:cccxxvi[2008] 32–9). Simmers identifies Kipling's faith in the value of sharing stories as one source for the first person in this poem. In the same issue of the *Kipling Journal*, Daniel Karlin offers an insightful analysis of 'Tin Fish' (*KJ* 82:cccxxvi[2008] 40–7). Karlin contrasts the publication of this poem in collected editions of Kipling's poetry with its first, untitled appearance at the head of an article about submarine warfare. Kipling's poem is shown to contain a cruel streak of identification with impassive destruction.

The *Kipling Journal* of September reproduces Patrick Brantlinger's 'Kipling's "White Man's Burden" and its Afterlives' (*KJ* 82:cccxxxviii[2008] 39–58). Originally published in *English Literature in Transition* (*ELT* 50:ii[2007]), this article traces the allusive fortunes of Kipling's poem in the form of parodic responses in the 1890s through to recent writings about the current wars in Afghanistan. Finally, Shamus O.D. Wade poses the question 'Who Was the Better Poet: Kipling or William McGonagall?' without

apparent irony (*KJ* 82:cccxxvii[2008] 40–9). Wade's choice of poetic examples
and biographical anecdotes indicates that he thinks Kipling the lesser man.
Curious.

7. Modern Irish Poetry

This was a bumper year for Thomas Kinsella scholarship. Two studies of
Kinsella's poetry—one by the veteran Kinsella devotee Maurice Harmon and
the other by a young academic Andrew Fitzsimons—were published to
coincide with the poet's eightieth birthday, and both make good use of
material from the Emory archive that is home to the manuscripts. It has long
been a critical commonplace to hold Kinsella up as a notable yet marginalized
Irish poet—David Wheatley's epithet of Kinsella as 'dethroned God' is
emblazoned on the back jacket of Fitzsimons's study—a condition that has
been attributed to various causes, most usually, to the poet's break with
traditional formal procedures in the late 1960s and his move away from
mainstream publishing. Harmon has long been a champion of Kinsella's work;
his 1974 *The Poetry of Thomas Kinsella* was the first of its type. Bizarrely for a
work of critical scholarship, this recent study, *Thomas Kinsella: Designing for
the Exact Needs*, opens with a poem dedicated to his subject which celebrates
their long friendship and by so doing proclaims Harmon's authority as a
Kinsella intimate. The issue of certain scholars having privileged close access
to their subjects is, to my mind, a problematic one. The poet John Berryman
once recalled how the services required by one professor writing a book on
Berryman's poetry were such that Berryman not only answered all of the
scholar's questions for him but even waited on him, pouring his drinks for him
while he typed. It is a humorous anecdote, but it nonetheless raises the
important issue of critical distance. In this instance, it is clear that Harmon is
too close to his subject, and this results in a study that lacks a freshness of
approach and a willingness to criticize or question. Harmon's respectful study
lacks an original synthesizing thesis. Instead it moves chronologically across
Kinsella's oeuvre, book by book, and so forms a basic, largely thematic
guidebook to the poetry for the casual reader. For a study that insists on the
importance of close reading, this almost completely privileges theme over
technique; too often we get only vague references to poetic devices, and these
seem to serve mainly as indicators of Harmon's schoolboy-like adherence to
the dictates of close reading. Harmon fails to provide any real insight into the
way that Kinsella's collections are designed as sequences, as mosaic-like
arrangements, wherein key motifs and images modulate and develop across
the developing oeuvre. Thus we get no meaningful sense of how exactly
Kinsella is 'designing for the exact needs'. Instead, the same themes are
explored ad nauseam with little sense of a rich and intricate expanding poetry.
Furthermore, because each chapter begins with an overview of what will
follow, the commentary quickly becomes repetitive. Indeed, Harmon's
vocabulary could also have done with more variation; the word 'sundering',
for example, is employed three times over as many pages.

Most dismayingly, Harmon refers very infrequently to the work of other Kinsella scholars despite the fact that the book's back cover features an effusive tribute from Derval Tubridy, whose 2001 study of the *Peppercanister Poems* far outweighs Harmon's in its contribution to Kinsella scholarship and on whose scholarship Harmon has clearly relied for his grasp of the poet's later work. The one selling-point that Harmon's study might be seen to have is its inclusion of the translations from Irish. Yet the section on *The Táin* offers little more than a summary of the narrative peppered with large chunks of unanalysed quotation from Kinsella's translation. In the same chapter, on Kinsella's *New Oxford Book of Irish Verse*, little more than an outline of the subjects of the poems is given. The next chapter's focus on *An Duanaire* is more successful in that it at least attends to the fact that these are translations of poetry from one language into another. However, in neither chapter are issues pertaining to the act and art of translation—political, cultural, artistic or otherwise—addressed, and Harmon makes no reference to the translations of the same poems that have been made by others.

The shortcomings of Harmon's study become even more apparent when it is read alongside Fitzsimons's. *The Sea of Disappointment: Thomas Kinsella's Pursuit of the Real*, in its carefully plotted journey through Kinsella's advancing poetics of disappointment and with Kinsella's belief in poetry's access to the real as guiding principle, is far more sophisticated in its understanding of the work, making for a much-needed contribution to Kinsella studies. What Harmon is content to take as a given Fitzsimons sets out to interrogate at a fundamental level. With his probing and well-supported readings of key poems from across the oeuvre, Fitzsimons corrects reductive readings and too-simplistic narratives of the poet's development. Importantly, he illuminates how, contrary to established views, Kinsella was from the first frustrated by traditional formal procedures, and Fitzsimons charts his gradual move into a more organic, though no less crafted, sense of poetic form. The established mode of reading Kinsella's 'abandoned formalism' in the context of what is by now a tired 'formal versus free verse' debate is naive and unhelpful, as Fitzsimons persuasively argues. Related to this is the well-known—although not yet substantially examined—fact that Kinsella had been absorbing the work of American modernist poets long before he actually set foot on American soil; he reviewed Stevens and Pound as early as 1956, for example. Yet there is still more work to be done on this area, as Fitzsimons himself acknowledges in his introduction. Robert Lowell's breakthrough into free verse in the 1950s is summoned at the opening of the third chapter—Lowell memorably characterized his earlier poetic efforts as 'prehistoric monsters'—but one feels that Fitzsimons could have gone further here and considered perhaps the ways in which Lowell's development may be seen as analogous to Kinsella's. Lowell too, far from renouncing the formal 'blessed structures' of his early poetry for a looser free mode, continued to draw on those well-learned tricks of the poetic trade by using 'traditional' forms such as the sonnet. As with Lowell, then, Kinsella *expands* his poetic resource instead of simply abandoning formalism, and Fitzsimons is alert to how Kinsella is a 'measuring artist' to the end. The scope of Kinsella's poetry is laid out; he is a multifaceted, far-reaching poet and not one tied to any single position.

This largeness is missing from Harmon's study. Indeed, unlike the far-sighted Fitzsimons, Harmon seems to have a blind spot when it comes to American poetry. There are a mere two fleeting references to Ezra Pound, while William Carlos Williams—that other great poet who thinks with his poem—is completely absent. Resonances of Wallace Stevens cry out to be attended to in Harmon's reading of 'Carraroe', but Stevens is not once mentioned. Reading Harmon reading Kinsella, the reader would be justified in thinking that Kinsella was writing in a hermetically sealed box with only Jung, Dante and Mahler for company. This is particularly ironic when one considers how Kinsella's advocates lament the poet's isolation in critical narratives of Irish poetry. Even when Harmon invokes staple figures, such as Dante or W.B. Yeats, his comments betray a lack of acuity. Reading Yeats's roll-call of the main players in the Rising in 'Easter 1916' back through Kinsella's 'A Country Walk', Harmon remarks on how, unlike Kinsella who has no 'tolerance for nationalist violence', Yeats 'raises his heroes to heroic status'. Any sensitive reader of Yeats's ambivalent elegy will take issue with this interpretation. Fitzsimons, reading the same lines from 'A Country Walk' understands that there is something far more complex going on between the two poets and has the insight to bring in other critical voices to open up some of these complexities. The strength of Fitzsimons's approach over Harmon's is made evident when Fitzsimons, deeply attuned to the echoes of other writers in Kinsella—such as those of William Blake for whose overlooked influence he makes a case—uncovers the identity of William Skullbullet as Blake. Harmon focuses on the same lines from the same poem yet misses this link completely and is content to take the customary line (which originated with Tubridy) which has Skullbullet as the cartographer William Petty. Unlike Harmon, Fitzsimons makes excellent use of the insights of other critics and engages with and extends the key critical debates over Kinsella's work, arguing back to some of Kinsella's most audible detractors such as Edna Longley. He too has done his homework when it comes to the political, social and cultural contexts out of which Kinsella's poetry of disappointment is shaped. Fitzsimons's exemplary study must now be built on—there is much more to be said about this major Irish poet—and Kinsella's extensive poetics must continue to be examined.

'The critical writing of poets is always an oblique apologia for their own poems', Justin Quinn, a poet himself, asserts, as part of his critique of Kinsella in his new *Cambridge Introduction to Irish Poetry, 1800–2000.* Quinn's agenda in writing this survey of two centuries of Irish poetry is made clear in the book's opening gambit as he poses a number of questions designed to discomfit any reader who might be sitting too comfortably: 'What is Irish poetry?' is the first of the rhetorical spanners thrown in the works. By the end of Quinn's study, these questions still hang in the air—no bad thing by any means—but what has come into focus is the fact that the poetry that constitutes this slippery category is a boundless (or boundary-less) body of work and, what's more, that it has long been so. That the parameters of Irish poetry cannot be fixed by nationality, ideology, creed or class—nationalist ideology is the author's bugbear throughout—is surely well established by now as we sit assuredly in the twenty-first century with our revisionist and transnational spectacles firmly in place. Quinn's concerted effort to leave nationalist frameworks behind and raise complex questions about cultural identity will surely serve to rid undergraduate students of any easy preconceptions, but for the informed reader he too often runs the risk of perpetuating such blinkered views by repeatedly invoking them. Despite the title given to the final chapter, it is clear that Ireland has not disappeared yet, not for this poet-critic anyway. The end result of this approach is that too much Irish poetry—roughly that which comes before the point designated by Selina Guinness as the era of the New Irish Poets—is generally typified as stagnant, conservative and weighed down by ideology. For instance, Ireland's 'overwhelming poetic conservatism' is impressed upon readers who might have mistakenly regarded Kinsella's technique as ground-breaking. In his bid to break with his predecessors and send a 'disappearing Ireland' packing, Quinn does not sufficiently acknowledge his own generation's substantial debts to its enablers and the continuities that exist. Thus, in the final chapter, the linguistic range of David Wheatley's poetry signifies, according to Quinn, 'a movement away from the usual demarcations of Irish poetry', but it is clear from reading across the expanses of Irish poetry from James Clarence Mangan to Wheatley himself—indeed, Wheatley is quite obviously a poetic descendant of Mangan—that there never have been clear demarcations in Irish poetry, that the best of it has always delighted in shape-shifting and boundary-crossing. Elsewhere, Quinn singles out MacNeice as a poet who 'refused to accept the borders of his country as the borders of his world', yet of what poet worth study is this not true?

Quinn is so determined to rehabilitate the reader and push his central thesis that he at times does a disservice to some of the poets under scrutiny. The difficulties of his project—and the attendant frustrations that Quinn must have felt while working through it—are apparent. Having just outlined how our understanding of Kinsella continues to be enlarged in a recent study, it is dismaying for this reviewer to see Quinn holding to the one-dimensional view of Kinsella as a neo-nationalist. Also, Quinn has a hot-headed proclivity to dismiss poets without taking other critical appraisals into account. In this way, despite Quinn's reliance on Antoinette Quinn's scholarship for his discussion of Patrick Kavanagh, he rejects any suggestions of formal radicalism and experimentation in *The Great Hunger*—truculently viewing it as closer in style to Edgar Lee Masters's *Spoon River Anthology* instead of the more usual model of Eliot's *The Waste Land*—which she has persuasively argued for. Quinn, never one to suffer fools, is correct to set the limits of Kavanagh's achievement as a 'handful' of poems—the rest is 'dismal'—nonetheless, more could have been said about that poem's significance in its time and after, instead of only focusing on its obvious and by now well-examined flaws. It is not that Quinn's judgements are wrong, rather that he detracts from his own argument by treating his subjects in such an offhand fashion. Brian Coffey is one of the poets unceremoniously written off—his poetry of 'vagueness and blandness' is barely glanced at—as is Francis Ledwidge, who is cast aside for the more trendy J.M. Synge, while W.R. Rodgers and John Hewitt are deemed to have been valuable only 'for the fact that they existed'. Blanaid Salkeld's poetry is returned 'unsatisfactory' and, as if to confirm its inconsequentiality, the date of publication of her collection *The Fox's Covert* is given incorrectly. But the most blundering error in judgement comes with Nuala Ní Dhomhnaill, whom Quinn views as being inferior to her translator into English, Paul Muldoon. That Quinn deems Muldoon a 'far superior poet' is not the problem here. Rather, Quinn goes on to attribute all of the low points in the translations to Muldoon's 'lack of interest in '[Ní Dhomhnaill's] original', professing how, 'ultimately [Muldoon's] translations amount to a criticism of her limitations'. The degree of negative criticism here is unjustified and, worse, it is wholly unsupported by any readings of her poetry in Irish. What is more, the evidence in favour of Ní Dhomhnaill's achievement as a poet is there, if we need it, in the fact that Muldoon has gone on to translate more of her work; the critically acclaimed *The Fifty-Minute Mermaid* [2007] testifies to the continuing success of their collaborations.

The chapter groupings are not always advantageous. Eiléan Ní Chuilleanáin is among the poets lumped together in the chapter 'Feminism and Irish Poetry', yet it is clear that her work does not belong within such confines and would have fitted much better into, for instance, the chapter on poetry and translation. Again, one wonders why Quinn chooses to perpetuate reductive views and categorizations such as 'Women's Poetry' by herding most of the older Irish poets who happen to be women into one chapter. Medbh McGuckian is another case in point. That said, it remains that this is a valuable and invigorating study and it should be recommended reading for undergraduates everywhere. Its strengths lie in Quinn's remarkable capacity for shrewd and sophisticated close readings of illustrative poems. Quinn is a bracing critic and a vital reader of poetry. Whatever its shortcomings, every reader will find something to argue with here, and so its capacity to stimulate debate must surely stand as a measure of its achievement. Every reader will also learn much along the way. It is, after all, cast as an introduction and it is undeniably a sharply intelligent and eminently readable overview of a perpetually troublesome subject. Quinn's frustrations are the reader's own.

Ireland is well known for its representation of itself in literary terms. Tourists arriving in Dublin airport, before they've even made it as far as the departure point for the literary pub-crawl, are greeted with images of the country's best exports, its writers, and, if they've flown with the national airline, even their seats will have been inscribed with quotations from Irish literary works. It seems to be a uniquely Irish phenomenon. That poetry holds a high office in Ireland was evinced by the establishment of the Chair of Ireland Professor of Poetry in 1998 to 'manifest the value of poetry within our cultural and intellectual life'. *The Poet's Chair: The First Nine Years of the Ireland Chair of Poetry*, edited by Paul Durcan, John Montague and Nuala Ní Dhomhnaill, collects the public lectures given by the first three of these professors of poetry, and each of these essays points up the well-travelled cosmopolitanism and far-reaching nature of Irish poetry. John Montague's contributions focus on his own development as a poet and his formative encounters with American poets and poetry as well as on the hot topic of poetry translation. On the other side of the world, Nuala Ní Dhomhnaill, in her essay 'Kismet', recounts her defining experience of Turkish culture and how by immersing herself in the Turkish language she came to see the artistic possibilities that her own native Irish language made available. This revealing essay does much to remind us of Ní Dhomhnaill's breadth as a writer and as a citizen of the world who is at home in many languages. Paul Durcan, in the book's most engaging and free-wheeling essays, focuses on what would have been at the time three of the more under-rated Irish poets: Anthony Cronin, Harry Clifton and Michael Hartnett. His essay on the latter's 'Sibelius in Silence' restores a key poem to critical attention and is particularly rich in the way that it connects Sibelius's art and dominant themes with those of Hartnett. Overall, this collection makes a strong case for the latitude that Irish poetry enjoys.

Conor McCarthy is no less aware of the extensive reach of Irish poetry across space and time. In *Seamus Heaney and Medieval Poetry* he provides a lucid overview of Heaney's engagement with the literature of the Middle Ages in all of its forms. Moving through *Buile Suibhne, Station Island* and *Beowulf,* McCarthy presents Heaney as a 'great translator', and as a disruptive crosser of national, linguistic and cultural boundaries who problematizes and complicates neat binaries—such as those between England and Ireland and its languages—and too-easy narratives of tradition. In this way, he expands his outlook to consider the implications of Heaney's look to Scotland and so focuses in the final chapter on Robert Henryson's *The Testament of Cresseid.* Heaney's retelling of Henryson's work, and the constellation of other languages and literatures that it involves—Trojan material, Chaucer, Shakespeare—is given due attention here, although the insights into the poetry in this chapter suffer as they give way to other concerns, and too much space is devoted to plot summaries. More on Heaney's translation itself would have been desirable. The scope of the study is large, but rarely does it lose its way. At all times, McCarthy is attuned to the reach of Heaney's work—to the extensiveness of his multivalent word-hoard—and to the enriching mutuality that exists between the original poetry and the translations as he mines key poems from across Heaney's oeuvre for their medieval undertow. Indeed, the medieval is shown to have a contemporary resonance—it is, for Heaney, crucial to our understanding of contemporary reality—particularly in the handling of themes of gender, exile, guilt, responsibility and identity and in his engagement with the Troubles in Northern Ireland. By focusing on Heaney's intimate knowledge and deployment of this range of resources McCarthy illuminates important aspects of his poetry and poetics and makes apparent the multiplicity, intertextuality and hybridity of Heaney's work, thus, in turn, broadening the reader's understanding of the development of poetry through the ages. Of course, much scholarly work has already been done in this area—on Heaney's look to Dante in particular—and McCarthy's debt to scholars such as Bernard O' Donoghue, himself a medievalist, and Neil Corcoran in his essential *The Poetry of Seamus Heaney* [1998] is heavy indeed. However, McCarthy valuably provides the first book-length study of this integral aspect of Heaney's work and so lays the groundwork for further explorations.

Yeats was once described by Louis MacNeice as being 'like a figure from a fancy dress party; he looked wrong in the daylight'. Students coming to Yeats for the first time often display the same resistance to his work when faced with its esoteric obscurities, its 'secret discipline'. In his clearly written and student-friendly study *Yeats's Poetic Codes* Nicholas Grene, himself a lecturer to undergraduates at Trinity College Dublin, provides a useful handbook for student and lecturer alike as, concordance in hand, he undertakes to demystify and decode Yeats by tracing the recurrence of pivotal words across his oeuvre. The most engaging chapter is the first, wherein Grene investigates the significance of Yeats's strategic dating, and misdating, of his poems. This intriguing topic could surely have made for a book-length study in itself. The other most notable chapter is that on voices. When Robert Frost dined with Yeats in 1928 he was struck by how Yeats and George Russell 'took ordinary conversation and lifted it into the realm of pure literature'. Indeed Yeats himself reminded Frost of his own pre-eminence as a poet of conversation: 'You know I was the first poet in modern times to put that colloquial everyday speech of yours into poetry. I did it in my poetic play *The Land of Heart's Desire*.' Grene marks 'The Folly of Being Comforted' out as Yeats's 'first conversation poem', and the chapter explores Yeats's play of voices, in dialogue and in conflict, and argues persuasively that Yeats is a 'great dramatic poet' as opposed to a great 'poetic dramatist'. Again, this chapter seems too short, but the student will find it helpfully suggestive. Not surprisingly, as in chapter after chapter Grene systematically traces the appearance of certain words, the approach grows a little wearying with seemingly endless usages of the same word presenting themselves for comment. Also, what strikes one most in the chapter on Yeats's use of tenses and moods is Grene's lack of attentiveness to matters of poetic form; his tendency to privilege sentence structure over poetic structure leaves much more to be said, and his readings of the poems for their sense only (in the main) means that poetry scholars will not be satisfied and will probably find themselves running off to consult Helen Vendler's *Our Secret Disciple: Yeats and Lyric Form* [2007] to fill this need. Finally, through their attempted decoding all that can be said about Yeats's poems is what we know already; that nothing in Yeats can be fixed. Each word modulates and changes colour across the oeuvre, making for a poetry of shifting symbolism and one that is constantly in flux, in constant change and in conflict. And it is in this, as Grene shows in this diligent guidebook, that the endless pleasure and challenge of the poetry lies.

Isaiah Berlin, writing to a correspondent from Dublin's Shelbourne Hotel in 1938, details in his letter how, at the very moment he writes, there happens to be with him in the same room 'two fishermen from the west of Ireland talking of fish' while just to his right, a 'wonderfully majestic' W.B. Yeats is very audibly 'chanting verse in a corner to a young woman'. A writer of fiction could not convincingly invent such a scenario and the understandably incredulous Berlin himself wondered at the 'absurd and sublime' quality of this chance convergence. Ronald Schuchard's *The Last Minstrels: Yeats and the Revival of the Bardic Arts* presents Yeats in just such a mode as it takes the reader on an absorbing, keenly detailed field trip across the decades of Yeats's profound involvement in promoting the music of human speech and of the poetry that comes out of it. Pronouncing itself a 'reconstruction', the study seeks to recover a crucial aspect of Yeats's poetics that has been neglected and even disparaged by many of Yeats's most esteemed readers. What Yeats called 'the art of the troubadour' is fundamental to his poetics—to what Grene calls his dramatic poetry—and to his development as a writer; it is thus central to the development of modern poetry. This is an inspired subject and one that demanded sustained critical scrutiny of this kind. The early years of what his more sceptical critics termed Yeats's 'cantillating epidemic' are exhaustively traced through London and Dublin, and Yeats's persistence with his theory of an auditory poetics as he shuttles between the two locations inspiring societies of fellow troubadours in each city is strongly felt. It makes for a slow-paced but never tedious reading experience. Every lecture that Yeats gave on the subject of speaking poetry, of the inherent music of the verse, and every performance given to illuminate his developing theory, is assiduously recounted with recourse to witness statements and other carefully investigated source material. Such is the attention to detail in this meticulously researched study that the footnotes often reach De Selbian lengths. Adorned too with high-quality images and photographs, Schuchard's book succeeds in re-creating the period, moment by moment, and resuscitating Yeats's art. However, more in these early chapters on how this theory should impact on our understanding of certain poems would have made for a stronger argument and would also have provided relief from the documentary-based reconstruction that dominates. At times, one senses that Schuchard doesn't want other narratives to get in the way of his own story, as when he makes only passing reference to helpful studies such as Brian Devine's *Yeats: The Master of Sound* [2006] on the question of Yeats's use of Irish metres, the *amhran* and *sean nos* styles of expression. That said, Schuchard's privileging of archival material far outweighs such critical swervings.

The study really takes off when we arrive at 'Minstrels and Imagists' and Yeats shacks up with that other troubadour Ezra Pound. After having carefully traced the early developments, this latter section of the book soars, and we are, in the final chapter, treated to reconstructions of Yeats at the BBC directing his troubadours in the art of saying poetry over the radio. Nor is Schuchard averse to enlivening his jam-packed narrative with some very telling in-jokes from the period. Readers can laugh along with D.H. Lawrence's parodic imitation of Florence Farr's chanting: 'Ping...wa...n...ng', and with Pound wickedly renaming the mage's tower Thoor Bally phallus. Schuchard's thorough, even-handed approach ensures that he leaves nothing out. The abiding image of the poet that emerges, of Yeats 'humming away' to himself as he wrote, beating time with his right hand as he did even on his deathbed—always composing 'in the sequence of the musical phrase'—is a lasting one, and it is for this that the reader is most grateful to Schuchard's hard graft. This study will be indispensable for all readers of Yeats's work and of modern poetry in general, as it casts much-needed light on this unappreciated aspect of Yeats's poetics, crucially making a new Yeats available in a substantial way and deepening our understanding of both Yeats's art and the changes and developments in modern poetry that it brought about.

Another compendious work that sheds light on a lacuna in Irish poetry and Irish studies more broadly is Gerald Dawe's capacious anthology *Earth Voices Whispering: An Anthology of Irish War Poetry 1914–1945*. Appropriately, its title is taken from the poem 'Nocturne' by the Irish modernist poet Thomas MacGreevy. The fact of the involvement of so many Irish in the First World War in particular—an estimated 35,000 were killed—has until recently been part of the nation's history of silence and exclusion, and so this anthology may be seen to be carrying out a larger moral imperative by restoring Ireland's First World War dead to cultural memory and showing the impact of that moment in poetic terms. That its publication was supported by the Military History of Ireland Trust is a mark of its wider cultural significance. For Dawe, it is the work of Francis Ledwidge—a poet who receives short shrift in Quinn's survey—that best embodies the tensions intrinsic to Ireland's 'other' history, as Dawe terms it. Of course the subject has been addressed in a number of historical studies of the period, and recent works of poetry scholarship have also started to investigate it in poetry. Fran Brearton's pioneering study *The Great War in Irish Poetry: W.B. Yeats to Michael Longley* [2000] introduced the subject by attending to the poetry and poetics of six poets predominantly from the north of Ireland, while Jim Haughey's *The First World War in Irish Poetry* [2002] written very much in the wake of Brearton's, takes a more wide-ranging and, it must be said, more diffuse and unfocused view, covering thirty-odd poets, the poetry of too many of whom is far from worthy of such critical attention. Published in 2007, Tim Kendall's tome of essays, *The Oxford Handbook of British and Irish War Poetry* is curiously lacking in its coverage of war poetry from the Republic of Ireland—as Dawe himself noted in his review of the collection for the *Irish Times*, only the Troubles of the latter half of the century are treated—and so Dawe's own anthology neatly fills this gap.

Dawe, in his short, sensitive introduction emphasizes how this is a 'shared history' between Britain, Ireland and the US, and the poetry collected here speaks to this reality. The anthology broadcasts a complex polyphony of voices; a wide range of poets of a diversity of class, race, creed and politics, both combatants and non-combatants, all moved to register their experience in words. Chronologically speaking, we travel from Katharine Tynan to Van Morrison (rounded off with a fitting postscript by Samuel Beckett) as we move through the First World War, the Spanish Civil War, the Second World War and the War of Independence, as well as Ireland's own domestic conflicts. Of course, as is to be expected in such a comprehensive collection, the poetry is also diverse in terms of standard; not all of the poems presented here are first-rate. One is reminded of Marianne Moore's verdict on her famous war poem 'In Distrust of Merits': for Moore it was not poetry at all but merely protest, for, although it functioned as testimony to the intolerableness of war, formally it was not a poem. What emerges most powerfully, however, in the best poetry here, is the fact of war in everyday life and the shadow it casts long after the historic event has taken place. Derek Mahon's punningly entitled 'The Home Front' shows how as a poet born in 1941 he was born into war and has grown up with it. War marks all of our lives, and shapes us, as many of the poems here explore in a myriad ways. One hopes that this anthology will usher in a new critical focus on this period and on the work of unduly neglected poets such as Patrick MacDonogh, Anthony Glavin and, to a lesser extent, MacGreevy himself; his 'De Civitate Hominum' included here is a powerful and troubling meditation on the relation between aesthetics and war, the 'still life' of both. Obviously, the presence of war in Irish poetry does not stop with 1945, as this anthology does. This suggests that a sequel may be required.

Having briefly noted the limitations of Justin Quinn's grouping of Irish women poets under the rubric 'Feminism and Irish Poetry', I now turn to his *Irish Poetry After Feminism*, a diminutive collection of critical essays developed out of papers from a 2006 symposium at the Princess Grace Library. In his deft introduction, Quinn as editor puts forward a number of questions, some of which, when read in the light of the essays that follow, seem to openly challenge certain feminist approaches to poetry and so signal the potential pitfalls of this line of attack. Thus, the problematic relation between poetry and critical theory raises its head. Here too, Quinn rightly takes Eavan Boland to task for her prohibitive stance in her 'Against Love Poetry'; there are more nuanced and advanced conversations about male–female relations to be heard, as Quinn sketches. Having launched a pre-emptive strike in this way, Quinn, with shrewd sleight of hand, exits himself from the proceedings, leaving the contributors to fight it out among themselves as he makes his getaway. Moynagh Sullivan, whose dogmatic essay is positioned first in the book, immediately blacklists Quinn (among others) as an enemy of feminism for his remarks on women's poetry made in the course of a review. Sullivan argues, unconvincingly, for the 'cultural misogynies' evident in Quinn's remarks and goes on to list a litany of such critical abuses against Irish women poets. In the next essay, Peter McDonald responds to Sullivan's 'hermeneutics of gender' with good sense—mindful of the fact that as a male critic he can do no right— by devoting his essay to a scholarly consideration of poetic form and the origins of poetry.

Not surprisingly, the most successful essays are those which, unlike Sullivan's, actually focus on reading poetry and that resist getting mired in the totalizing discourse of feminism; Fran Brearton's reading of Mahon's 'First Principles' is the best example of this. These essays will no doubt trigger further bouts of heated debate, but too many of them through their own practices display the dangers of reading poetry through the immovable rigidities of, in this case feminist, theoretical frameworks. Lucy Collins's essay is in the right spirit; it sees the possibilities, the new 'poetic spaces' that a selection of younger Irish women poets have made for themselves. On the flipside, Selina Guinness imposes a feminist reading on Vona Groarke's 'The Annotated House'—as a poem about female masturbation—that continues to baffle this reader at least. For instance, for Guinness, the phrase 'months heaped in the basement' has 'menstrual undertones'. This seems to me a good example of the theorist distorting the poem to fit their theory. The collection ends on a high point with a refreshing take on the subject, as David Wheatley goes 'in search of the poetry of misogyny' in Samuel Beckett's poetry and wonders 'what might a feminist reading of it look like?' For all of its many moments of interest, what this collection proves is that feminism in Irish poetry studies trails some way behind its American counterpart, and that an informed and wider-ranging debate still needs to be had. We have to learn how to read poetry with theory in a way that opens up possibilities rather than closes them down with prescriptive, predetermined readings.

What is 'the future of Irish poetry'? Richard Tillinghast, himself a noted American poet and critic asks this question in one of the essays in his collection of literary criticism *Finding Ireland: A Poet's Exploration of Ireland's Literature and Culture*. Tillinghast presents himself as a foreign literary correspondent for non-Irish readers while for Irish readers he hopes to 'bring a certain freshness to familiar topics'. Having put forward a number of disclaimers in this way, what follows is a largely uncritical view of Irish culture and literature delivered with more than a hint of nostalgia for his lost Ireland of the mind. Essays on Heaney and Yeats, although clearly the work of an astute and committed reader of poetry, are also at times 'a bit bright-eyed and naïve', to quote Tillinghast on his newly-arrived-in-Ireland self. Apart from his praiseworthy attention to Yeats's versification, these essays deal largely with already familiar areas of enquiry. Conversely, his essay on Derek Mahon's poetry exhibits the advantages of having one practising poet read another. Best of all is his essay on the *Wake Forest Anthology* poets. Here, in an all too-rare moment of taking issue, Tillinghast criticizes Jefferson Holdridge's claim that Irish poetry should be 'impersonal and self-mortifying'. His opinions of the poets here are wise and perceptive.

Despite repeated requests, Liffey Press failed to deliver a review copy of Holdridge's *The Poetry of Paul Muldoon*. However, it is heartening to know that the Muldoon industry is still chugging away and that readers in need of explication are not being left in the dark as the poetry collections continue to mount. Tim Kendall's illuminating and pioneering book-length study of Muldoon's poetry [1996] was met with audible sighs of relief from even the closest of close readers; a grateful Helen Vendler hailed it as just the book for readers who are unable to follow Muldoon's 'Joycean game of baffle the reader' as it would 'at last permit American readers to understand the poet's basic references'. Clair Wills followed suit with her excellent *Reading Paul Muldoon*, and a further two collections of critical essays ensured that Muldoon's readers would not be starved of required reading. Holdridge's book will no doubt be of interest to Muldoon's growing readership in the United States and to readers of his later poetry collections, song lyrics and essays on poetry—Wills's study stops with *Hay* [1998]. From what one can glean from the publicity information, it is clear that Holdridge privileges a broader thematic approach over Wills's and Kendall's keen close readings of individual collections, and so his book will most likely serve best as a general overview and introduction for the uninitiated.

Books Reviewed

Acheraiou, Amar. *Rethinking Postcolonialism: Colonialist Discourse in Modern Literatures and the Legacy of Classical Writers*. Palgrave. [2008] pp. x + 250. £45 ISBN 9 7802 3055 2050.

Allen, Charles. *Kipling Sahib: India and the Making of Rudyard Kipling*. Little, Brown. [2008] pp.426 + xxii. £20 ISBN 978 0 316 72655 9.

Andermahr, Sonya, ed. *Jeanette Winterson: A Contemporary Critical Guide*. Continuum. [2007] pp. x + 177. £14.99 pb ISBN 9 7808 2649 2753.

Angel-Perez, Elizabeth, and Alexandra Poulain, eds. *Hunger on Stage*. Cambridge Scholars Press, Cambridge. [2008] pp. 300. hb £33.24 ISBN 1847185959.

Atkins, Douglas M. *Reading Essays: An Invitation*. UGeoP. [2008] pp. 272. £44.95 ISBN 9 7808 2032 8263.

Attridge, Derek. *How to Read Joyce*. Granta. [2007] pp. 118. pb £7 ISBN 1 8260 7912 0.

Baker, Brian. *Iain Sinclair*. Contemporary British Novelists. ManUP. [2007] pp. 192. hb £50 ISBN 9 7807 1906 9048, pb £15.99 ISBN 9 7807 1906 9055.

Bale, John. *Anti-Sport Sentiments in Literature: Batting for the Opposition*. Routledge. [2008] pp. 201 + xvi. £80 ISBN 978 0 415 42265 9.

Beckman, Richard. *Joyce's Rare View: The Nature of Things in Finnegans Wake*. UFlorP. [2007] pp. 256. $60 ISBN 0 8130 3059 5.

Bentley, Nick. *Contemporary British Fiction*. Edinburgh Critical Guides. EdinUP. [2008] pp. xiv + 245. hb £50 ISBN 9 7807 4862 4195, pb £15.99 ISBN 9 7807 4862 4201.

Ben-Zvi, Linda, and Angela Moorjani, eds. *Beckett at 100: Revolving It All*. OUP. [2008] pp. 334. pb £58 ISBN 9 7801 9532 5485.

Berthoud, J. A., Laura L. Davis, and S.W. Reid, eds. *'Twixt Land and Sea*. CUP. [2008] pp. 688. £55 ISBN 9 7805 2187 1266.

Bhambra, Gurminder K. *Rethinking Modernity: Postcolonialism and the Sociological Imagination*. Palgrave. [2007] pp. viii + 200. pb £20 ISBN 9 7802 3022 7156.

Blevins, Pamela. *Ivor Gurney and Marion Scott: Song of Pain and Beauty*. Boydell. [2008] pp. 331 + xviii. £30 ISBN 978 1 84383 421 2.

Bosinelli, Rosa, Maria Bollettieri, and Ira Torresi. *Joyce and/in Translation*. Bulzoni. [2007] pp. 170. pb €15 ISBN 8 8787 0253 0.

Boulter, Jonathan. *Beckett: A Guide for the Perplexed*. Continuum. [2008] pp. 200. pb £12.99 ISBN 9 7808 2648 1955.

Boulton, James T., ed. *Selected Letters*. by D.H. Lawrence. Oneworld Classics. [2008] pp. 520. £12.99 ISBN 9 7818 4749 0490.

Bové, Paul. *Poetry against Torture: Criticism, History and the Human*. HongKongUP. [2008] pp. 159 + xvi. $59.50 ISBN 978 962 209 926 5.

Brown, Julia Prewitt. *The Bourgeois Interior*. U of Virginia P. [2008] pp. 208. £26.95 ISBN 9 7808 1392 7107.

Brown, Richard. *A Companion to James Joyce*. Blackwell. [2008] pp. 440. £105 ISBN 1 4051 1044 0.

Burke, Edmund, and David Prochaska, eds. *Genealogies of Orientalism: History, Theory, Politics*. UNebP. [2008] pp. xi + 446. pb £22 ISBN 9 7808 0321 3425.

Burns, Edward M., ed. *A Passion for Joyce: The Letters of Hugh Kenner and Adaline Glasheen*. UCDubP. [2008] pp. 433. £68 ISBN 1 9045 5896 5.

Childs, Peter. *Modernism*, 2nd edn. Routledge. [2008] pp. viii + 238. pb £13.99 ISBN 9 7804 1541 5460.

Collini, Stefan. *Common Reading: Critics, Historians, Publics*. OUP. [2008] pp. 376. £26 ISBN 0 1992 9678 2.

Collins, Jo, and John Jervis, eds. *Uncanny Modernity: Cultural Theories, Modern Anxieties.* Palgrave. [2008] pp. 256. £45 ISBN 9 7802 3051 7714.

Cormack, Alistair. *Yeats and Joyce: Cyclical History and the Reprobate Tradition.* Ashgate. [2008] pp. 220. £55 ISBN 0 7546 6028 6.

Cosgrove, Brian. *James Joyce's Negations: Irony, Indeterminacy and Nihilism in Ulysses and Other Writings.* UCDubP. [2007] pp. 256. €60 ISBN 1 9045 5885 9.

Criquand, Sylvie, ed. *Last Letters.* CambridgeSP. [2008] pp. 160. £29.99 ISBN 9 7818 4718 4016.

Crispi, Luca, and Sam Slote, eds. *How Joyce Wrote Finnegans Wake: A Chapter-by-Chapter Genetic Guide.* UWiscP. [2007] pp. 522. £60 ISBN 0 2992 1860 0.

Dalziel, Pamela, and Michael Milligate. *Thomas Hardy's 'Poetical Matter' Notebook.* OUP. [2008] pp. 129 + xxviii. £21 ISBN 978 0 19 922849 2.

Davies, Tony. *Humanism,* 2nd edn. Routledge. [2008] pp. viii + 168. pb £13.99 ISBN 9 7804 1542 0655.

Dawe, Gerald, ed. *Earth Voices Whispering: An Anthology of Irish War Poetry, 1914–1945.* Blackstaff. [2008] pp. 412. £16.99 ISBN 9 7808 5640 8229.

De Lange, Attie, Gail Fincham, Jeremy Hawthorn, and Jakob Lothe, eds. *Literary Landscapes: From Modernism to Postcolonialism.* Palgrave. [2008] pp. xxv + 221. £50 ISBN 9 7802 3055 3163.

De Marco, Nick. *The Early Joyce and the Writing of Exiles.* Aracne. [2008] pp. 203. €12 pb ISBN 8 8548 1885 9.

DiBattista, Maria. *Imagining Virginia Woolf: An Experiment in Critical Biography.* PrincetonUP. [2008] pp. ix + 208. £13.39 ISBN 0 6911 3812 5.

Dillingham, William B. *Being Kipling.* Palgrave. [2008] pp. 256. £42.50 ISBN 9 7802 3060 9112.

Dolin, Tim. *Thomas Hardy.* Haus. [2008] pp. 186. pb £9.99 ISBN 978 1 904950 77 6.

Doyle, Laura. *Freedom's Empire: Race and the Rise of the Novel in Atlantic Modernity, 1640–1940.* DukeUP. [2008] pp. 592. £18.99 ISBN 0 8223 4159 X.

Durcan, Paul, John Montague, and Nuala Ní Dhomhnaill. *The Poet's Chair: The First Nine Years of the Ireland Chair of Poetry.* Lilliput. [2008] pp. 264. pb €20 ISBN 9 7818 4351 0956.

Eburne, Jonathan. *Surrealism and the Art of Crime.* CornUP. [2008] pp. 324. £23.95 ISBN 0 8014 4674 0.

Ehnenn, Jill R. *Women's Literary Collaboration, Queerness, and Late-Victorian Culture.* Ashgate. [2008] pp. xi + 207. £55 ISBN 9 7807 5465 2946.

Ellis, David. *Death and the Author: How D.H. Lawrence Died, and Was Remembered.* OUP. [2008] pp. xvi + 273. £20 ISBN 9 7801 9954 6657.

Fenton, James, ed. *Selected Poems, by D.H. Lawrence.* Penguin. [2008] pp. xxvi + 200. £9.99 ISBN 9 7801 4042 4584.

Firchow, Peter Edgerly. *Strange Meetings: Anglo-German Literary Encounters from 1910 to 1960.* CUAP. [2008] pp. 283 + xvi. $64.95 ISBN 9 780813 215334.

Fitzsimons, Andrew. *The Sea of Disappointment: Thomas Kinsella's Pursuit of the Real.* UCDubP. [2008] pp. 288. €60 ISBN 9 7819 0455 8972.

Fleming, John. *Tom Stoppard's Arcadia*. Continuum. [2008] pp. 124. £10.99 ISBN 978 0 8264 9621 8.

Fordham, Finn. *Lots of Fun at Finnegans Wake*. OUP. [2007] pp. 270. £49 ISBN 0 1992 1586 7.

Forth, Christopher E. *Masculinity in the Modern West: Gender, Civilisation and the Body*. Palgrave. [2008] pp. 256. pb £17.99 ISBN 9 7814 0391 2411.

Fowler, David. *Youth Culture in Modern Britain, 1920–1970: From Ivory Tower to Global Movement. A New History*. Palgrave. [2008] pp. 320. pb £18.99 ISBN 9 7803 3359 9228.

Fraser, Robert, and Mary Hammond. *Books Without Borders*. vol. 1: *The Cross National Dimension in Print Culture*. Palgrave. [2008] pp. xiv + 210. £45 ISBN 0 2302 1029 5.

Gardner, Diana. *The Rodmell Papers: Reminiscences of Virginia and Leonard Woolf by a Sussex Neighbour*. Bloomsbury Heritage. [2008] pp. 48. £6 ISBN 9 7818 9796 7416.

Gardner, Kevin. *Poems in the Porch: The Radio Poems of John Betjeman*. Continuum. [2008] pp. 148. £14.99 ISBN 978 1 84706 328 1.

Garnett, Henrietta. *Leslie Stephen: A Nineteenth Century Legacy*. VWGB. [2008] pp. 23. £4 ISBN 9 7809 5557 1701.

Gasiorek, Andrzej, and Daniel Moore, eds. *Ford Madox Ford: Literary Networks and Cultural Transformations*. Rodopi. [2008] pp. 283. pb £45 ISBN 9 7890 4202 4373.

Gavin, Adrienne E., and Andrew F. Humphries, eds. *Childhood in Edwardian Fiction: Worlds Enough and Time*. Palgrave. [2008] pp. 248. £45 ISBN 9 7802 3022 1611.

Gill, Peter. *Apprenticeship*. Oberon. [2008] pp. 124. £8.99 ISBN 9 7818 4002 8713.

Gottfried, Roy. *Joyce's Misbelief*. UFlorP. [2008] pp. 160. $60 ISBN 0 8130 3167 5.

Grafe, Adrian, ed. *Ecstasy and Understanding: Religious Awareness in English Poetry from the Late Victorian to the Modern Period*. Continuum. [2008] pp. xi + 183. £60 ISBN 9 7808 2649 8649.

Grant, Joanna. *Modernism's Middle East: Journeys to Barbary*. Palgrave. [2008] pp. 224. £45 ISBN 9 7802 3020 9534.

Green-Lewis, Jennifer, and Margaret Soltan. *Teaching Beauty in DeLillo, Woolf and Merrill*. Palgrave. [2008] £42.50 pp. xiii + 224 ISBN 0 2306 0124 3.

Grene, Nicholas. *Yeats's Poetic Codes*. OUP. [2008] pp. 247. £45 ISBN 9 7801 9923 4776.

Hadley, Louisa. *The Fiction of A.S. Byatt*. Readers' Guides to Essential Criticism. Palgrave. [2008] pp. ix + 192. £42.50 hb ISBN 9 7802 3051 7912, pb £13.99 ISBN 9 7802 3051 7929.

Hammond, Will, and Dan Steward, eds. *Verbatim Verbatim: Contemporary Documentary Theatre*. Oberon. [2008] pp. 174. pb £14.99 ISBN 9 7818 4002 6979.

Hand, Richard J., and Michael Wilson. *London's Grand Guignol and the Theatre of Horror*. UExeP. [2007] pp. xi + 291. pb £15.99 ISBN 9 7808 5989 7921.

Hanna, Julian. *Key Concepts in Modernist Literature*. Palgrave. [2008] pp. 224. pb £13.99 ISBN 9 7802 3055 1190.

Harmon, Maurice. *Thomas Kinsella: Designing for the Exact Needs*. IrishAP. [2008] pp. 248. pb €24.75 ISBN 9 7807 1652 9521.

Hauser, Kitty. *Shadow Sites: Photography, Archaeology, and the British Landscape 1927–1955*. OUP. [2008] pp. x + 314. £75 ISBN 9 7801 9920 6322.

Havholm, Peter. *Politics and Awe in Rudyard Kipling's Fiction*. Ashgate. [2008] pp. xi + 187. £55 ISBN 9 7807 5466 1641.

Head, Dominic. *Ian McEwan*. Contemporary British Novelists. ManUP. [2007] pp. 219. hb £50 ISBN 9 7807 1906 6566, pb £14.99 ISBN 9 7807 1906 6573.

Head, Dominic. *The State of the Novel: Britain and Beyond*. Blackwell. [2008] pp. 175. hb £45 ISBN 9 7807 1906 6566, pb £14.99 ISBN 9 7814 0517 0109.

Hemmings, Robert. *Modern Nostalgia: Siegfried Sassoon, Trauma and the Second World War*. EdinUP. [2008] pp. 168. £50 ISBN 9 7807 4863 3067.

Henthorne, Tom. *Conrad's Trojan Horses: Imperialism, Hybridity, and the Postcolonial Aesthetic*. TTUP. [2008] pp. xiv + 234. £55 ISBN 9 7808 9672 6338.

Hepburn, Allan, ed. *The Bazaar and Other Stories*. EdinUP. [2008] pp. vi + 384. pb £16.99 ISBN 9 7807 4863 5726.

Hepburn, Allan, ed. *People, Places, Things: Essays by Elizabeth Bowen*. EdinUP. [2008] pp. x + 480. pb £19.99 ISBN 9 7807 4863 5696.

Hepburn, Allan, ed. *Troubled Legacies: Narrative and Inheritance*. UTorP. [2007] pp. viii + 297. £32 ISBN 9 7808 0209 1109.

Herbert, Christopher. *War of No Pity: The Indian Mutiny and Victorian Trauma*. PrincetonUP. [2008] pp. ii + 352. £25 ISBN 9 7806 9113 3324.

Hillier, Hilary. *Talking Lawrence: Patterns of Eastwood Dialect in the Work of D.H. Lawrence*. Critical, Cultural and Communications Press. [2008] pp. 64. £5 ISBN 9 7819 0551 0184.

Holdridge, Jefferson. *The Poetry of Paul Muldoon*. Liffey Press. [2008] pp. 224. pb €16.95 ISBN 9 7819 0578 5308.

Iball, Helen. *Sarah Kane's Blasted*. Continuum. [2008] pp. 124. pb £10.99 ISBN 9 7808 2649 2036.

Ibell, Paul. *Theatreland: A Journey through the Heart of London's Theatre*. Continuum. [2009] pp. xvi + 240. £25 ISBN 9 7818 4725 0032.

Igoe, Vivian. *James Joyce's Dublin Houses and Nora Barnacle's Galway*. Lilliput. [2007] pp. 186. €13 pb ISBN 1 8435 1082 6.

Irvine, Colin C. *Teaching the Novel across the Curriculum*. Greenwood. [2008] pp. x + 344. £57.95 ISBN 9 7803 1334 8969.

James, David. *Contemporary British Fiction and the Artistry of Space: Style, Landscape, Perception*. Continuum. [2008] pp.1–195. £65 ISBN 18 4706 4949.

Karl, Alissa. *Modernism and the Marketplace: Literary Culture and Consumer Capitalism in Rhys, Woolf, Stein, and Nella Larsen*. Routledge. [2008] pp. 184. £50 ISBN 9 7804 1598 1415.

Kitcher, Philip. *Joyce's Kaleidoscope: An Invitation to Finnegans Wake*. OUP. [2007] pp. 304. £21 ISBN 0 1953 2102 9.

Klitgård, Ida. *Fictions of Hybridity: Translating Style in James Joyce's Ulysses.* UP of Southern Denmark. [2007] pp. 282. kr298 ISBN 8 7767 4193 8.

Knights, Ben, ed. *Masculinities in Text and Teaching.* Palgrave. [2008] pp. 240. £50 ISBN 9 7802 3000 3415.

Knowles, Owen, ed. *'My Dear Friend': Further Letters to and about Joseph Conrad.* Rodopi. [2008] pp. xxxiv + 211. £40 ISBN 9 7890 4202 4649.

Knowles, Sebastian D.G., Geert Lernout, and John McCourt, eds. *Joyce in Trieste: An Album of Risky Readings.* UFlorP. [2007] pp. 254. $60 ISBN 0 8130 3033 3.

Kolocotroni, Vassiliki, and Efterpi Mitsi, eds. *Women Writing Greece: Essays on Hellenism, Orientalism and Travel.* Rodopi. [2008] pp. 264. pb £33 ISBN 9 7890 4202 4816.

Kövesi, Simon. *James Kelman.* Contemporary British Novelists. ManUP. [2007] pp. 204. hb £50 ISBN 9 7807 1907 0969, pb £14.99 ISBN 9 7807 1907 0976.

Kritzer, Amelia Howe. *Political Theatre in Post-Thatcher Britain: New Writing, 1995–2000.* Routledge. [2008] pp. 246. £50 ISBN 9 7814 0398 8294.

Lago, Mary, Linda K. Hughes, and Elizabeth MacLeod Walls, eds. *The BBC Talks of E.M. Forster 1929–1960.* UMissP. [2008] pp. xiv + 477. £55 ISBN 9 7808 2621 8001.

Land, Stephen K. *The Human Imperative: A Study of the Novels of Graham Greene.* AMS. [2008] pp. ix + 286. $87.50 ISBN 0 4046 1595 6.

Lebedoff, David. *The Same Man: George Orwell and Evelyn Waugh in Love and War.* RH. [2007] pp. xv + 264. $26 ISBN 9 7814 0006 6346.

Levin, Yael. *Tracing the Aesthetic Principle in Conrad's Novels.* Palgrave. [2008] pp. xii + 203. £42.50 ISBN 9 7802 3060 9860.

Loizeaux, Elizabeth. *Twentieth-Century Poetry and the Visual Arts.* CUP. [2008] pp. 261 + xii. £48 ISBN 978 0 521 88795 3.

Longley, Edna. *Edward Thomas: The Annotated Collected Poems.* Bloodaxe. [2008] pp. 332. pb £12 ISBN 978 1 85224 746 1.

Lothe, Jakob, Jeremy Hawthorn, and James Phelan, eds. *Joseph Conrad: Voice, Sequence, History, Genre.* OSUP. [2008] pp. xii + 283. £40 ISBN 9 7808 1425 1652.

MacKay, Marina, ed. *The Cambridge Companion to the Literature of World War II.* CUP. [2009] pp. xix + 234. £45 ISBN 9 7805 2188 7557.

MacPhee, Graham, and Prem Poddar, eds. *Empire and After: Englishness in Postcolonial Perspective.* Berghahn. [2007] pp. vii + 211. £30 ISBN 9 7818 4545 3206.

Madden, Ed. *Tiresian Poetics: Modernism, Sexuality, Voice, 1888-2001.* FDUP. [2008] pp. 402. £64.50 ISBN 978 0 8386 3937 5.

Mahon, Peter. *Imagining Joyce and Derrida: Between Finnegans Wake and Glas.* UTorP. [2007] pp. 405. $69 ISBN 0 8020 9249 6.

Mao, Douglas. *Fateful Beauty: Aesthetic Environments, Juvenile Development, and Literature 1860–1960.* PrincetonUP. [2008] pp. x + 319. £50 ISBN 9 7806 9113 3485.

Matthews, Steven, ed. *Modernism: A Sourcebook.* Palgrave. [2008] pp. xxii + 295. pb £18.99 ISBN 9 7814 0399 8309.

McCarthy, Conor. *Seamus Heaney and Medieval Poetry*. B&B. [2008] pp. 195. £45 ISBN 9 7818 4384 1418.

McIntire, Gabrielle. *Modernism, Memory and Desire: T.S. Eliot and Virginia Woolf*. CUP. [2008] pp. ix + 274. £52 ISBN 0 5218 7785 7.

McLean, Steven, ed. *H.G. Wells: Interdisciplinary Essays*. CambridgeSP. [2008] pp. viii + 184. £45 ISBN 9 7818 4718 6157.

Mendelson, Edward. *The Complete Works of W.H. Auden: Prose: Volume III, 1949-1955*. PrincetonUP. [2008] pp. 779 + xxxviii. £35 ISBN 9 7806 9113 3263.

Meyer, Jennifer. *Men of War: Masculinity and the First World War in Britain*. Palgrave. [2008] pp. 232. £55 ISBN 9 7802 3022 2014.

Miller, Andrew John, *Modernism and the Crisis of Sovereignty*. Routledge. [2008] pp. vii-222. £80 ISBN 0 4159 5604 8.

Mitchell, Kaye. *A.L. Kennedy*. New British Fiction. Palgrave. [2008] pp. x + 200. hb £42.50 ISBN 9 7802 3000 7567, pb £9.99 ISBN 9 7802 3000 7574.

Modern Girl Around the World Research Group, ed. *The Modern Girl Around the World: Consumption, Modernity, and Globalization*. DukeUP. [2008] pp. 448. £16.99 ISBN 0 8223 4305 3.

Morse, Greg. *John Betjeman: Reading the Victorians*. Sussex Academic Press. [2008] pp. 272. £49.99 ISBN 9 7818 4519 2716.

Morton, Stephen. *Salman Rushdie*. New British Fiction. Palgrave. [2008] pp. xii + 200. hb £40 ISBN 9 7814 0399 7005, pb £9.99 ISBN 9 7814 0399 7012.

Morton, Stephen, and Stephen Bygrave. *Foucault in an Age of Terror: Essays on Biopolitics and the Defence of Society*. Palgrave. [2008] pp. 234 + x. £50 ISBN 978 0 230 57433 5.

Najder, Zdzisław, J.H. Stape, and S.W. Reid, eds. *Joseph Conrad: A Personal Record*. CUP. [2008] pp. xlix + 227. £75 ISBN 9 7805 2186 1762.

Newland, Paul. *The Cultural Construction of London's East End: Urban Iconography, Modernity and the Spatialisation of Englishness*. Rodopi. [2008] pp. 321. pb £52 ISBN 9 7890 4202 4540.

Nieland, Justus. *Feeling Modern: The Eccentricities of Public Life*. UIllp. [2008] pp.336. £16.99 ISBN 0 2520 7546 3.

Noakes, Vivien. *21ˢᵗ-Century Oxford Authors: Isaac Rosenberg*. OUP. [2008] pp. 456 + xxxvi. £50 ISBN 978 0 19 85340 2.

O'Neill, Christine, ed. *Joycean Murmoirs: Fritz Senn on James Joyce*. Lilliput. [2007] pp. 330. €40 ISBN 1 8435 1125 0.

O'Sullivan, Michael. *The Incarnation of Language: Joyce, Proust and a Philosophy of the Flesh*. Continuum. [2008] pp. 192. £60 ISBN 1 8740 6047 1.

O'Sullivan, Vincent, and Margaret Scott, eds. *The Collected Letters of Katherine Mansfield, vol. 5: 1922–1923*. OUP. [2008] pp. xv + 376. £63 ISBN 9 7801 9818 3990.

Ogden, Tom. *Haunted Theatres*. Globe Pequot Press. [2009] pp. xiii + 287. pb £9.99 ISBN 9 7807 6274 9492.

Orr, Leonard, ed. *Joyce, Imperialism, and Postcolonialism*. SyracuseUP. [2008] pp. 180. $23 ISBN 0 8156 3188 X.

Outka Elizabeth. *Consuming Traditions: Modernity, Modernism, and the Commodified Aesthetic*. OUP. [2008] pp. 232. £30 ISBN 0 1953 7269 7.

Owens, Cóilín. *James Joyce's Painful Case*. UFlorP. [2008] pp. 256. $60 ISBN 0 8130 3193 1.

Parkins, Wendy. *Mobility and Modernity in Women's Novels, 1850–1930: Women Moving Dangerously*. Palgrave. [2008] pp. vi + 224. £45 ISBN 9 7802 3052 5429.

Parsons, Deborah. *Theorists of the Modernist Novel: James Joyce, Dorothy Richardson, Virginia Woolf*. Routledge. [2007] pp. x + 176. pb £12.99 ISBN 9 7804 1528 5438.

Pierce, David. *Reading Joyce*. Pearson Longman. [2008] pp. 365. £16 ISBN 1 4058 4061 3.

Platt, Len. *Joyce, Race and Finnegans Wake*. CUP. [2007] pp. 222. £50 ISBN 0 5218 6884 6.

Poon, Angelia. *Enacting Englishness in the Victorian Period: Colonialism and the Politics of Performance*. Ashgate. [2008] pp. x + 174. £50 ISBN 9 7807 5465 8481.

Prewit Brown, Julia. *The Bourgeois Interior: How the Middle Class Imagines Itself in Literature and Film*. UPVirginia. [2008] pp. 208. £26.95 ISBN 0 8139 2710 2.

Prudente, Teresa A. *Specially Tender Piece of Eternity: Virginia Woolf and the Experience of Time*. Lexington. [2008] pp. 208. £39.95 ISBN 0 7391 2555 9.

Pulham, Patricia. *Art and the Transitional Object in Vernon Lee's Supernatural Tales*. Ashgate. [2008] pp. xxi + 166. £55 ISBN 9 7807 5465 0966.

Quinn, Justin. *The Cambridge Introduction to Modern Irish Poetry, 1800–2000*. CUP. [2008] pp. 260. £47 ISBN 9 7805 2184 6738.

Quinn, Justin, ed. *Irish Poetry After Feminism*. Smythe. [2008] pp. 107. £25 ISBN 9 7808 6140 4674.

Ratcliffe, Sophie. *On Sympathy*. OUP. [2008] pp. 266 + xiv. £50 ISBN 9 7801 9923 9870.

Reeve, N.H. *Elizabeth Taylor*. WTW. Northcote. [2008] pp. xi + 112. pb £12.99 ISBN 9 7807 4631 1554.

Reus, Teresa Gomez, and Aranzazu Usandizaga, eds. *Inside Out: Women Negotiating, Subverting, Appropriating Public and Private Space*. Rodopi. [2008] pp. 368. £58.40 ISBN 9 7890 4202 4410.

Rice, Thomas Jackson. *Cannibal Joyce*. UFlorP. [2008] pp. 208. $60 ISBN 0 8130 3219 9.

Roberts, Philip. *About Churchill: The Playwright and the Work*. Faber. [2008] pp. 304. pb £12.99 ISBN 9 7895 7122 9628.

Rohman, Carrie. *Stalking the Subject: Modernism and the Animal*. ColUP. [2008] pp. 208. pb £19 ISBN 0 2311 4507 1.

Royer, Diana, and Madelyn Detloff, eds. *Virginia Woolf: Art, Education and Internationalism*. Clemson University Digital Press. [2008] pp. vi + 164. $19.95 ISBN 9 7809 7960 6649.

Sagar, Keith. *D.H. Lawrence: Poet*. Humanities-Ebooks. [2008] pp. 188. £15 ISBN 9 7818 4760 0684.

Sanders, Steven, and Aeon J. Skoble, eds. *The Philosophy of TV Noir*. UPKen. [2008] pp. viii + 272. $35 ISBN 9 7808 1312 4490.

Saunders, Graham. *Patrick Marber's Closer*. Continuum. [2008] pp. 118. pb £10.99 ISBN 9 7808 2649 2050.

Saunders, Lorraine. *The Unsung Artistry of George Orwell: The Novels, from Burmese Days to Nineteen Eighty-Four*. Ashgate. [2008] pp. x + 159. £50 ISBN 9 7807 5466 4406.

Schantz, Ned. *Gossip, Letters, Phones: The Scandals of Female Networks in Film and Literature*. OUP. [2008] pp. 200. £40 ISBN 0 1953 3591 0.

Scherr, Barry J. *Love and Death in Lawrence and Foucault*. Lang. [2008] pp. 395. £42 ISBN 9 7808 2049 5408.

Schuchard, Ronald. *The Last Minstrels: Yeats and the Revival of the Bardic Arts*. OUP. [2008] pp. 447. £55 ISBN 9 7801 9923 0006.

Senn, Fritz. *Ulyssean Close-Ups*. Bulzoni. [2007] pp. 111. pb €10 ISBN 8 8787 0230 1.

Shellard, Dominic, ed. *The Golden Generation: New Light on Post-War British Theatre*. BL. [2008] pp. 224. £20 ISBN 9 7807 1234 9475.

Sierz, Aleks. *John Osborne's Look Back in Anger*. Continuum. [2008] pp. 121. £10.99 ISBN 9 7808 2649 012.

Simpson, Kathryn. *Gifts, Markets and Economies of Desire in Virginia Woolf*. Palgrave. [2008] pp ix + 240. £45 ISBN 1 4039 9706 3.

Singleton, Julie. *A History of Monk's House and Village of Rodmell, Sussex Home of Leonard and Virginia Woolf*. Cecil Woolf. [2008] pp. 54. £7 ISBN 9 7818 9796 7461.

Smyth, Gerry. *Music in Contemporary British Fiction: Listening to the Novel*. Palgrave. [2008] pp. ix + 256. £50 ISBN 9 7802 3057 3284.

Snyder, Carey J. *British Fiction and Cross-Cultural Encounters: Ethnographism from Wells to Woolf*. Palgrave. [2008] pp. 264. £45 ISBN 9 7802 3060 2915.

Squires, Michael. *D.H. Lawrence and Frieda: A Portrait of Love and Loyalty*. Deutsch. [2008] pp. 200. £16.99 ISBN 9 7802 3300 2323.

Stallworthy, Jon. *Survivors' Songs: From Maldon to the Somme*. CUP. [2008] pp. xiii + 226. £45 ISBN 9 7805 2172 7891.

Stape, John. *The Several Lives of Joseph Conrad*. Pantheon. [2008] pp. xxvii + 369. $30 ISBN 9 7814 0004 4498.

Stewart, Jack. *Color, Space, and Creativity: Art and Ontology in Five British Writers*. FDUP. [2008] pp. 320. £57.50 ISBN 0 8386 4165 2.

Surette, Leon. *The Modern Dilemma: Wallace Stevens, T.S. Eliot and Humanism*. McG-QUP. [2008] pp. 416 + xii. £27 IBSN 978 0 7735 3363 9.

Taylor-Batty, Mark, and Juliette Taylor-Batty. *Samuel Beckett's Waiting for Godot*. Continuum. [2008] pp. 115. pb £10.99 ISBN 9 7808 2649 5945.

Tillinghast, Richard. *Finding Ireland: A Poet's Explorations of Irish Literature and Culture*. UNDP. [2008] pp. 296. pb $25 ISBN 9 7802 6804 2325.

Trout, Steven, ed. *Robert Graves: Goodbye To All That and Other Great War Writings*. Carcanet. [2007] pp. xxxiii + 371. £45 ISBN 9 7818 5754 6651.

Tycer, Alica. *Caryl Churchill's Top Girls*. Continuum. [2008] pp. 134. £10.99 ISBN 9 7808 2649 5563.

Van Hulle, Dirk. *Manuscript Genetics, Joyce's Know-How, Beckett's Nohow*. UFlorP. [2008] pp. 230. $60 ISBN 0 8130 3200 9.

Wake, Paul. *Conrad's Marlow: Narrative and Death in Youth, Heart of Darkness, Lord Jim and Chance.* ManUP. [2007] pp. viii + 145. £50 ISBN 9 7807 1907 4905.

Wallace, Diana. *The Woman's Historical Novel: British Women Writers, 1900–2000.* Palgrave. [2008] pp. xiii + 269. pb £20 ISBN 9 7802 3022 3608.

Willmott, Glenn. *Modernist Goods: Primitivism, the Market, and the Gift.* UTorP. [2008] pp. 384. £42 ISBN 9 7808 0209 7699.

Wills, David. *Dorsality: Thinking Back through Technology and Politics.* UMinnP. [2008] pp. 200. pb £14 ISBN 0 8166 5345 3.

Wilson, Jean Moorcroft. *Isaac Rosenberg: The Making of a Great War Poet: A New Life.* W&N. [2008] pp. 468. £25 ISBN 978 0 2978 5145 5.

Winkiel, Laura. *Modernism, Race and Manifestos.* CUP. [2008] pp. ix + 256. £52 ISBN 0 5218 9618 5.

Worthen, John. *T.S. Eliot: A Short Biography.* Haus. [2009] pp. vi + 330. £16.99 ISBN 9 7819 0659 8358.

Yeow, Agnes S.K. *Conrad's Eastern Vision: A Vain and Floating Appearance.* Palgrave. [2008] pp. 252. £50 ISBN 9 7802 3054 5298.

Zeikowitz, Richard E. *Letters Between Forster and Isherwood on Homosexuality and Literature.* Palgrave. [2008] pp. 208. £42.50 ISBN 9 7802 3060 6753.

Zemgulys, Andrea. *Modernism and the Locations of Literary Heritage.* CUP. [2008] pp. viii + 247. £50 ISBN 9 7805 2188 9247.

XV

American Literature to 1900

MICHAEL COLLINS, CLARE ELLIOTT, ANNE-MARIE FORD AND THERESA SAXON

This chapter has two sections: 1. General; 2. American Literature to 1900. Section 1 is by Theresa Saxon; section 2 is by Michael Collins, Clare Elliott and Anne-Marie Ford.

1. General

American Literature continues to provide important scholarly resources, as well as articles of interest to the general reader, in the 'Book Reviews' and 'Brief Mentions' sections of the quarterly publication. This year, articles have also appeared on a diverse range of nineteenth-century literary and cultural issues. For example, 'The Republican Mammy? Imagining Civic Engagement in *Dred*' by Elizabeth Duquette (*AL* 80:i[2008] 1–28) explores Stowe's 1856 publication for expressions of the potential for individual impact on political change in social and institutional structures. 'The Unsentimental Woman Preacher of *Uncle Tom's Cabin*' by Dawn Coleman (*AL* 80:ii[2008] 265–92) features Stowe's most notorious work of 1852, which looks at religious rhetoric and social power, and the relationship between the cultural practice of sermonizing and narrative practice. 'Self-Abasement and Republican Insecurity: *Paul Fane* in its Political Context' by David Grant (*AL* 80:iii[2008] 443–69), is explored more fully in section 2 of this chapter. '"That damned mob of scribbling siblings": The American Romance as Anti-Novel in *The Power of Sympathy* and *Pierre*' by Elizabeth Dill (*AL* 80:iv[2008] 707–38) examines William Brown Hill's 1789 production alongside Melville's troubled and troubling novel of 1852—both located here as anti-novelistic challenges to the specificities of genre and narrative structure in relation to sensationalism, sentimentalizing narratives and incest. '"The best of me is there": Emerson as Lecturer and Celebrity' by Bonnie Carr O'Neill (*AL* 80:iv[2008] 739–67) traces Emerson's attitude towards his own status as poetic 'celebrity'.

The full and detailed bibliographical listings of books, articles, review essays, notes and dissertations of the annual publication *Modern Language*

Year's Work in English Studies, Volume 89 (2010) © *The English Association; all rights reserved*
doi:10.1093/ywes/maq005

Association International Bibliography also consistently proves a useful resource for scholars. *American Literary Scholarship: An Annual* constitutes an exhaustive bibliographical survey of the year's critical writing—part I dealing with American literary greats, and part II providing a chronological view of the year's output. Editor David J. Nordloh, and the team of contributing scholars, cover extensive ground in this valuable resource, which includes sections on Emerson, Thoreau, Fuller and Transcendentalism; Hawthorne; Melville; Whitman and Dickinson; Mark Twain; Henry James; Wharton and Cather, as well as providing a general guide to scholarship on nineteenth-century literature. This year's edition [2008] covers critical material published in 2006. *American Literary History* continues to offer a substantial scope of resources for students and specialists in American literature. This year [2008], volumes 1 and 2 form a special anniversary issue: 'Twenty Years of American Literary History'. A series of reflexive articles considers nineteenth-century writers in relation to the complexities of 'American Literary History'. Essays, throughout the year, continue to address the multicultural and interdisciplinary studies of nineteenth-century literature.

2. American Literature to 1900

George Boulukos's *The Grateful Slave: The Emergence of Race in Eighteenth-Century British and American Culture* takes a transatlantic interest in the eighteenth-century trope of the 'grateful slave' and attacks directly the problem of the concept of slavery. Boulukos identifies a 'paradoxical state of voluntary slavery' from the outset, in order to suggest that this could be achieved (and achieved hypothetically in eighteenth-century fiction) through an emotional, and natural, relationship of gratitude. The study focuses on the eighteenth-century English-speaking world, and locates the historical phenomenon of voluntary slavery within it, claiming that the concept of the grateful slave has been overlooked in traditional literary research despite its obvious links with the justification of racial oppression, slavery and colonialism. The argument clearly outlines the 'evolution' of the notion of the grateful slave. Chapter 1 begins helpfully with a prehistory of the term and looks to the seventeenth century's negotiation 'between the practice of white supremacy in the middle passage and the colonies and the metropolitan discourse insisting on the unity of humankind'. It goes on to argue that seventeenth-century slave-trading captains, who wrote many of the accounts of West Africa from 1680 to 1740, adopted 'sentimental representations of African slaves and of colonial violence'. By doing so, their desire to appear sentimentally engaged (to their metropolitan readers) was often at odds with the treatment of the enslaved that their accounts recorded. Boulukos locates this as the embryonic stage of that 'fictional grateful slave trope' that would reach its maturity in the eighteenth century, and he identifies Defoe's *Colonel Jack* as the text which gives life to this idea in 1722. All of this is very convincing and only strengthened in chapter 2, when Boulukos reminds readers that *Colonel Jack* is 'self-consciously set at a moment when racial categories are inchoate and are developing differently in various parts of the

Atlantic world' and that Defoe uses the possibility of 'sympathy' to 'theorize a justification of the legal and practical differences that were institutionalized at the end of Bacon's rebellion'. The emergence of an emphasis on racial difference in slavery is presented alongside the discussion of racial difference in the novel, with chapter 4 dealing with that period of transition in approaches to race during the 1780s, which served to enhance the rhetoric of grateful slavery and 'happy slaves'. The argument is remarkably well sustained, with some finely interlaced historical and literary analysis, culminating in a powerful and resonant counter-example: Olaudah Equiano's resistance to the trope of the grateful slave in *The Interesting Narrative*. It is an instance of the exceptional case proving a rule, completing an evolution from grateful to faithful slaves and on to 'mammies' and martyrs. With its meticulous research and eloquent prose, Boulukos's book will be crucial reading for scholars of race and slavery in the eighteenth-century Atlantic world.

A work on slavery worthy of inclusion here is Glenda Carpio's *Laughing Fit to Kill: Black Humor in the Fictions of Slavery*, which sets out to argue that slaves adopted humour in an effort to counteract normative white perception. Carpio argues that in doing so, an alternative self-perception was constructed, one which still persists in the writings, performances and visual art of contemporary black Americans, and one which continues to depend on that psychological tool of humour. Carpio cites one slave aphorism which succinctly supports this argument: 'Got one mind for white folk to see / 'Nother for what I know is me'. This wry knowledge exemplifies Carpio's point: 'For black Americans, humor has often functioned as a way of affirming their humanity in the face of its violent denial.' The study is interdisciplinary, tackling the creative outpourings of black comedians, writers and artists. Although the material stretches well into the twentieth century, with a chapter on Richard Pryor's comedy performances, the kernel of the argument is slavery itself and the function of humour in the fictions of slavery. For example, Pryor's groundbreaking stand-up act and *Chappelle's Show* are discussed alongside the ironic nineteenth-century fiction of William Wells Brown and Charles W. Chesnutt. Both the clarity of Carpio's prose and the nature of the territory help make this otherwise heavily theoretical study accessible and engaging, and so it will make an excellent tool for teaching advanced students in American Studies.

It would be unusual to undertake any consideration of nineteenth-century American literature without discussing the familiar theme of nature. The biographical encyclopaedia *Early American Nature Writers*, edited by Daniel Patterson, admirably represents the diversity of early American writing while claiming, 'Of all national literatures, no other is more responsive to its physical place on Earth than American literature.' According to Patterson, the American imagination has always returned to the continent as its primary muse, at once as a basis for new epistemologies and as a guide for human culture. The entries range over the lives and work of more than fifty authors, a 'motley group' including 'explorers, naturalists, sportsmen, travellers, farmers, preachers, essayists, philosophers, artists, editors, musicians, educators, poets, and carpenters'. Although the seventeenth century is amply covered by entries on John Bartram (1699–1777), William Byrd II (1674–1744), Louis Hennepin

(1640–*c*.1701) and Francis Higginson (*c*.1586–1630), Patterson's definition of the term 'early' tends, perhaps misleadingly, to include a glut of late eighteenth and nineteenth-century writing, and even (somewhat confusingly) some twentieth-century figures such as Florence Merriam Bailey (1863–1948). Nonetheless, the volume should serve as an excellent resource for students of nineteenth-century America, as well as those interested in the history of contemporary national debates in ecology and environmental theory, particularly with reference to canonical nineteenth-century nature writers such as Ralph Waldo Emerson, Thomas Jefferson and Henry David Thoreau. There are particularly valuable biographical essays on all three figures. All of the entries are contributed by a scholar in the field and are usefully combined with a primary and secondary bibliography. Taken as a whole, the contents emerge self-consciously out of an academic school of ecocriticism, which lends a freshness of tone to the coverage of more familiar authors while still rehearsing the biographical 'facts' effectively. One might have hoped for either a thematic or chronological (rather than merely alphabetized) organization of material, but the editor's instructive introduction and valuable additional bibliography are undoubted assets to an encyclopaedia that will make an excellent teaching tool for undergraduate study and an important resource for students.

Nineteenth-Century Black Women's Literary Emergence: Evolutionary Spirituality, Sexuality, and Identity, edited by Sallyann Ferguson, forms an important contribution to the study of African American women's writing, which has been overshadowed elsewhere by that of their male counterparts. There seems to be a general neglect of nineteenth-century women writers in America when it comes to anthologies and categorical literary criticism, and so Ferguson's work on marginalized women writers is both timely and corrective. The collection of ten texts by ten authors, including Jarena Lee, Harriet Jacobs and Elizabeth Keckley, spans a variety of genres: the essay, the novella, the short story, spiritual narratives and drama. Helpfully, the editor considers these texts in the context of the turbulent history of the mid-nineteenth century of the United States and, illuminatingly, it includes antebellum and postbellum fugitive slave narratives. As with Patterson's volume, this collection uses nature as the focal point for the study of each of the ten works. Nature is considered as the veil behind which the Founding Fathers hid in the successful bid to exclude a large proportion of the American population from the freedom of the Constitution, the 'genetic causes of [their] victimization' being nature's 'mistake'. Ferguson plays on the centrality of nature and the natural in these collected writings and focuses on African women's 'chronological primacy' in human history. As such, she makes their narratives a significant starting point for *all* American literature—and, indeed, literature per se. Her introduction to the anthology explores the binary of nature and nation, according to which nature is figured to encompass the entire human family, while nation is an artificial construct of racist, sexist 'Eurocentric Man', who seeks to remove himself from any African connection through a sustained 'quest for white supremacy'. This collection attempts to return to nature in an effort to forgo that false construction called 'nation' which has so effectively obscured several of the writers featured in this anthology. It makes for a fascinating collection, and scholars and students of African American studies, American literature and gender studies will all benefit from Ferguson's selection.

Joe Lockard's *Watching Slavery: Witness Texts and Travel Reports* deals precisely with the voyeurism of seventeenth-century slave-trading captains who wrote accounts of West Africa sentimentalizing slaves and the violence of slavery. By examining travel accounts, fiction, poetry and legal texts, Lockard analyses accounts of the authors' encounters with slavery in America. He begins his discussion of what he calls the 'witness literature of slavery' at the auction block, and extends that discussion to the social role of witness in resisting slavery. The study is primarily concerned with the failure of witness literature to achieve any sufficiently transformative effect and thus to avoid the violence of the Civil War. Apart from a final chapter on William Still and the success of African American witness literature, his study asks penetratingly why witness literature remained overwhelmingly limited in aspiration. Lockard does not undermine the importance of that literature, but rather questions whether imaginative writing can ever undertake revolutionary ends through peaceful tactics: 'To examine failure in the witness literature of slavery does not detract from its political power, but rather explores questions concerning the capacity of rhetorical and imaginative witness to achieve goals of liberation by peaceful means.' He locates this failure as a symptom of a greater failure, and to understand that we must return once more to nature. *Watching Slavery* identifies the shortcomings of political discourse to achieve a peaceful resolution to the sectional contest over slavery as the consequence of the larger problem: the 'inability of the white-authored literature of slavery, as a corpus, to witness the equal humanity of African peoples'. For witness literature to succeed where the Civil War would later fail, the white-authored literature of slavery would first have to recognize nature's unity rather than, as Sallyann Ferguson terms it, 'nature's mistake'. Lockard's work engages with antebellum America in an attempt to understand the role of witness literature in political action not only then but now, in contemporary America.

No discussion of slavery in the United States would be complete without mention of the early 'terrorist' (and the figure arguably most responsible for the commencement of the Civil War) John Brown. Bruce Ronda's *Reading the Old Man: John Brown in American Culture* is a long awaited addition to the varied body of criticism on Brown. Where W.E.B. Du Bois's famous biography *John Brown* [1909] celebrated him as an American hero who rid the United States of the evil of slavery, most late twentieth-century criticism focused on Brown as a terrorist who slaughtered women and children. David Reynolds's 2006 biography, *John Brown, Abolitionist: The Man Who Killed Slavery, Sparked the Civil War, and Seeded Civil Rights*, challenged other recent scholarship on Brown that portrays him as a blood-thirsty 'madman'. Reynolds claimed that it is misleading to romanticize Brown, yet equally misleading to identify him with modern terrorism. Noting this binary in Brown scholarship, Ronda's more recent work refuses to categorize him either as a liberator and martyr or as a madman, offering instead a complex, multifaceted account of a complex character. This book gives a full and vivid account of the Harpers Ferry raid which cost Brown his life.

More interestingly, it takes a look at Brown from the perspective of nineteenth-century writers such as Thoreau and Melville. Although this is an eclectic piece, challenging critical misrepresentations of Brown by offering new and varied representations of the controversial figure, it seems surprising that the author fails to discuss Ralph Waldo Emerson's relationship with Brown. Fascinatingly, Emerson spoke out passionately in support of Brown and his family after the raid on Harpers Ferry, and in fact went so far as to house Brown for a time, when many other abolitionists had abandoned him. For these reasons, Emerson arguably deserves a chapter here, too.

Charles W. Chesnutt's *The Marrow of Tradition* earned praise from William Dean Howells as a work of great power, when it was first published in 1901. Continued interest in Chesnutt's writing has prompted a republishing of *The Marrow of Tradition*, a captivating novel which was in the vanguard of literary challenges to racial stereotypes, and tells the tragic story of two families, set in the American South, during the post-Reconstruction period. The narrative climaxes in a race riot, based on the 1898 riots in Wilmington, North Carolina, and is especially compelling because Chesnutt relied on eyewitness accounts to help create an authentic setting. He began his literary career writing local-colour stories, many of which were published in the *Atlantic Monthly*; these, too, were greatly admired by Howells, who wrote enthusiastically in the *Atlantic* of May 1900, 'he sees his people very clearly, very justly, and he shows them as he sees them ... He touches all the stops, and with equal delicacy in stories of real tragedy and comedy and pathos. ... He has sounded a fresh note, boldly, not blatantly, and he has won the ear of the more intelligent public.' Chesnutt was to prove an inspiration for the writers of the Harlem Renaissance, and remains important as a writer of local colour, capturing, as he did, the sights, sounds and customs of both southern and northern African American communities. Amongst his contemporary writers, Chesnutt stands tall as a fine and forceful stylist, who handled dialects in a lively manner, and created a wide range of non-stereotypical characters. That this, his most popular novel, is a fictionalized retelling of the Wilmington race riots, engineered by white supremacists and an inflammatory press, simultaneously explores the social and political themes that prevailed in the southern states at the turn of the twentieth century, and is, therefore, a powerful and significant text for all students of American culture and history.

Students of feminist literature will be delighted with the appearance of Janet Beer's *The Cambridge Companion to Kate Chopin*. Split into four sections covering Chopin's life, *At Fault*, race and ethnicity, and feminist theory and postcolonial New Orleans, the collection brings together eleven new essays by established scholars. Emily Toth provides a lively account of Chopin's life, while Donna Campbell places Chopin firmly in her nineteenth-century context and makes a convincing argument for seeing *At Fault* as a social-problem novel. Pamela Knights' 'Kate Chopin and the Subject of Childhood' argues that Chopin considered children as readers as well as subjects in her fiction, reminding us of the controversy surrounding the publication of *The Awakening* in 1899 (a work deemed suitable only for 'more mature minds'). Urging readers to return to the complexities of Louisiana's racial and ethnic mix, Susan Castillo focuses on *At Fault* and short stories from *Bayou Folk* to address the position of black women in Chopin's work. Likewise, Katherine Joslin's 'Kate Chopin on Fashion in a Darwinian World' examines the dynamism of ethnicity and gender in nineteenth-century Louisiana, especially as they were inflected by class consciousness. In 'The Awakening and New Woman Fiction' Ann Heilmann considers Chopin's fiction in relation to broader developments in Anglo-American writing, as well as in French literature, the European adultery novel and the sensation novels of Louisa May Alcott, Mary Braddon and Wilkie Collins. Her essay concludes that The Awakening is part of a constellation of thematic concerns, which illuminate cultures in which 'married women held no legal rights over their bodies'. In addition to feminist readings, Michael Worton's 'Reading Kate Chopin through Contemporary French Theory' interestingly concludes that Chopin's 'work is less a manifesto of emancipation than a multi-faceted exposition of quests for enduring relationships'. Elizabeth Nolan's 'The Awakening as Literary Innovation: Chopin, Maupassant and the Evolution of Genre' acknowledges Maupassant's influence on Chopin's work but also attempts to consider the kaleidoscopic ways in which her writing engages with Romanticism, Transcendentalism, literary realism, naturalism and New Woman fiction, while also anticipating feminism and experimental modernism. Similarly, Avril Horner's 'Kate Chopin, Choice and Modernism' argues that Chopin's work, particularly The Awakening, achieves a formal pluralism that directly anticipates Woolf, Joyce, Lawrence and Mansfield. The complexities of the French culture of Louisiana are the focal point of Helen Taylor's essay, '"The Perfume of the Past": Kate Chopin and Post-Colonial New Orleans', which goes so far as to suggest that The Awakening is Chopin's ultimate rejection of Creole society. Finally, Bernard Koloski provides an overview of Chopin's critical reception, crediting her biographers Per Seyersted and Emily Toth with resurrecting the work and effectively establishing Chopin studies. While Beer's Cambridge Companion will be a valuable resource for undergraduates in particular, its high-quality scholarship guarantees a much wider readership.

Kate Chopin in the Twenty-First Century: New Critical Essays, edited by Heather Ostman, is divided into three sections, 'Reading "Culture" in Chopin's Works'; 'Religion, Race, Class, and Gender in the Shorter Texts'; and 'Issues of Privilege in The Awakening'. In the first section, a provocative essay by Donna and David Kornhaber deals with class status in New Orleans at the turn of the century, while Jane F. Thrailkill's 'Chopin's Lyrical Anodyne for the Modern Soul' examines At Fault and a selection of short stories to confront Chopin's definition of culture, extending that term to include music, novels, religion and sex. 'Chopin in Vogue: Establishing a Textual Context for A Vocation and A Voice' reminds us of the cultural significance of Vogue as the early publisher of Chopin's stories and makes the interesting point that Chopin's experiment in literature paralleled the magazine's own aim of representing women in a variety of different, often challenging, social roles. The second section of the collection deals with religion, race, class and gender. Garnet Ayers Batinovich claims plausibly that religion is the primary source of female oppression in Chopin's work, detecting an anti-Catholic undertone in At Fault that helps to illuminate a parallel anti-Christian theme in

The Awakening. Lisa A. Kirby focuses on two Chopin stories to explore how they question nineteenth-century expectations of gender marriage against local colour and community. Meredith Frederich's 'Extinguished Humanity: Fire in Kate Chopin's "The Godmother"' discusses the symbolism of fire and how Chopin uses this to better understand humanity and its loss. The third and final section of the collection turns to *The Awakening* and offers some new readings of that most famous novel. Rebecca Nisetich's 'From "Shadowy Anguish" to "The Million Lights of Sun"': Racial Iconography in *The Awakening*' encourages the reader to consider the largely overlooked issue of race in the novel, and its nuanced depiction throughout Chopin's work. Li-Wen Chang's '*The Awakening*: Chopin's Reading of Women and Economics in Ourland' uses 'Thorstein Veblen's socio-psychological economic theory and Charlotte Perkins Gilman's analysis of marital economics' to examine the novel in which the economics of marriage are shown to eventually overpower Edna Pontellier. Overall, this makes for a particularly interesting collection, with attention given to a post-Katrina interpretation of Chopin's work.

In John Lysaker's *Emerson and Self Culture* Emerson's interest in John Brown makes an important appearance, which is shown to be symptomatic of a metamorphosis in his later years into a less familiar and more challenging character than many might think they know. Lysaker returns to Emerson as a pure philosopher, as opposed to the airy Transcendentalist that much contemporary criticism claims him to be. This is a relatively new area in Emerson studies, pioneered mainly by Stanley Cavell, in which Emerson is examined as a serious thinker and rigorous ethicist. Lysaker uses Emerson almost as a teaching tool to better understand one's own self-culture. He has an excellent chapter on 'The Genius of Nature', which recalls Emerson's own well-known essay 'Nature' of 1836, and offers a philosophical discussion of what Emerson termed there the 'NOT-ME'. Although it will be of most interest to philosophers (and philosophically informed cultural historians), it is difficult not to be impressed by Lysaker's thorough engagement with Emerson's vast oeuvre. His varied readings of the journals as well as the essays provide a fresh approach to the idea of Emerson and self-culture, which literary critics will appreciate and which will enrich Emerson scholarship.

Eyes Upside Down: Visionary Filmmakers and the Heritage of Emerson by P. Adams Sitney examines the work of eleven American avant-garde filmmakers: Stan Brakhage, Robert Beavers, Hollis Frampton, Jonas Mekas, Marie Menken, Ian Hugo, Andrew Noren, Warren Sonbert, Su Friedrich, Ernie Gehr and Abigail Child. Sitney's study approaches the work of these filmmakers as the inheritors of an Emersonian tradition as explored by John Cage, Charles Olson and Gertrude Stein. This work supposes a reconsideration of American culture as it blends a reading of sixty years of film, from the Second World War, with the nineteenth-century poetics of Emerson. This will find a place in the libraries of committed Emersonians and Americanists in general, as well as avant-garde film scholars.

Leland S. Person's *The Cambridge Introduction to Nathaniel Hawthorne* is an excellent guide for the novice student, subdivided usefully into sections: Hawthorne's life; his contexts; the short fiction; the four novels; and Hawthorne's critics. Chapter 2, on Hawthorne's contexts, will be of benefit to undergraduates interested in learning more about crucial historical terms (Puritanism and Transcendentalism) while there are also contributions on feminism, race and nineteenth-century manhood. An incredibly detailed account of Hawthorne's short fiction is given in comprehensive sections devoted to fifteen of the shorter texts. Chapter 4's analyses of Hawthorne's novels and chapter 5's sections on biography and criticism will serve new readers well, and the excellent third chapter on Hawthorne's short fiction also helps to distinguish this fine critical introduction.

Religion plays a key role in Roberta Weldon's *Hawthorne, Gender, and Death: Christianity and its Discontents*, which opens with a convincing consideration of death and its consolations as 'the most necessary of necessary fictions'. Weldon sets up the terms for reading Hawthorne's well-documented literary representations of death and death-denial alongside his representations of gender relations. Assured pronouncements such as the following punctuate Weldon's prose: 'In Hawthorne's fiction, death is primarily male work', a statement qualified by: 'To make death yield meaning, the male protagonist is frequently willing to overlook, reject, and sacrifice women.' To deny the realities of the destruction of death and instead to make it (constructively) 'yield meaning' is for Weldon (and Hawthorne) a gendered affair. Chapter 1 of Weldon's work places male death anxiety at the heart of *The Scarlet Letter* with Dimmesdale's death and Hester's complicity in the preservation of the male social order. In chapter 2, she returns to the consolation of faith in mid-nineteenth-century New England but focuses on the forces that threatened such consolation: scientific theory, Darwinian principles, materialism, commercialism. Here, she reads Hawthorne as adopting the literary persona of the anxious secular man of his time, attempting to live without that 'necessary fiction' of faith. In chapters 3, 4 and 5, Weldon offers stimulating readings of Hawthorne's other novels. In *The House of the Seven Gables*, the secular world of Hawthorne's creation scrutinizes the idea of eternal life, and what results is a 'domestic Gothic horror story'. In *The Blithedale Romance*, the dead body of Zenobia becomes entangled with the body politic of the secular state, and Weldon offers *The Marble Faun* as 'the most complete exploration of the patriarchal system in Hawthorne's fiction'. Weldon's work returns to the problem of nineteenth-century Christian culture's denial of death and the ways in which consolations of dying affect how we live, with moral and ethical consequences.

Since the institutionalization of a more self-reflexive Americanist criticism in the 1980s, the ideology of American Romanticism has been the subject of much debate among critics. Many of the most influential works concerned with exploring the Romantic imagination of writers such as Hawthorne and Melville (Duke University Press's New Americanist series in particular) have been highly critical of these authors' literary endeavours to establish a neutral space of reflection, free from the influence of the market and history, from which to question the assumed nature of truth or reality in nineteenth-century America. Such a process, it has often been noted, is seen as inherently bourgeois, masculine and elitist. Taking issue with this, Peter West's *The Arbiters of Reality: Hawthorne, Melville and the Rise of Mass Information Culture* begins assertively by reclaiming the importance of this Romantic detachment as a tool to critique the fabricated realities created through antebellum journalism. For West, romance is an artfully deployed 'mode of storytelling that carefully, even obsessively, invoked and rejected the truth claims of those cultural practices responsible for commodifying the real and peddling it before the mass public'. *The Arbiters of Reality* suggests that much postmodern scholarship, which has consistently 'treated "reality" as a word that is always to be put inside of quotation marks', is bland and apolitical. Instead, West's book has, at its heart, a Romanticism of its own, but is never naive. It is quite refreshing in our contemporary climate of scepticism. In chapters that resurrect the ebullient print cultures of antebellum Salem, Boston and New York as lenses through which to close read American Romantic fiction, West aims to show how Hawthorne and Melville's Romantic beliefs concerning the essential truth behind perceptions allowed them to articulate a position that was resistant to more mainstream visions of American destiny as the triumph of individualism and capitalist acquisition. The first three chapters on Hawthorne's work, particularly how the New England writer used and adapted popular news stories as a source for his more subversive fictions, are well researched and enlightening. However, it is in chapters 3, 4 and 5, on Melville and New York City, where the book's greatest strengths are to be found. Chapter 4 ('Zachary Taylor and the American Telegraph in Melville's New York') is a fascinating account of how the use of telegraphic communication during the Mexican–American War enhanced antebellum Americans' desire for objective reportage. West shows that, even as this desire was courted and propagated by the emergent news media, Melville's short fiction from the 1840s and 1850s serves to expose this dream of objectivity as a mask of imperialism and white supremacist ideology. Underpinned by strong close reading and an admirable directness, this is a valuable book and a good introduction to scholarship on Melville and Hawthorne's literary and social contexts.

Maria A. Windell's 'Sanctify Our Suffering World with Tears: Transamerican Sentimentalism in *Joaquin Murieta*' (*NCL* 63[2008] 170–96) brings to our attention the first novel by a Native American writer. *The Life and Adventures of Joaquin Murieta, the Celebrated Californian Bandit*, published under the name Yellow Bird (John Rollin Ridge, the mixed-race novelist), is Ridge's 1854 dime novel. Windell's article outlines how its critical treatment has hitherto been concerned with Ridge's outrage at US management of the Cherokee and his anger at the divisions within the Cherokee nation, which destroyed his family. The 'unapologetically masculinist sensibilities' in such criticism overlook, she argues, how the author's treatment of women reflects either the importance of male characters or, more generally, minority populations. In this commendable article Windell reconsiders the situation of women in the novel by developing a plausible argument for rethinking its account of heroism.

Benjamin Fisher's *Cambridge Introduction to Edgar Allen Poe* has a helpful chapter on the context of slavery pertinent to several of the works reviewed this year (as well as the work of Poe more narrowly). Nature, Fisher argues, is Poe's most important vehicle for Gothic fantasy, as a discussion of 'The Raven' sets out in detail. Slim as it is, the volume will benefit students and general readers alike, providing an introduction to the life and writings of Poe before moving into a discussion of his experiments with form and genre. It considers the major works (*The Fall of the House of Usher*, 'The Raven', *The Murders in the Rue Morgue*) as well as giving an overview of various theories of Poe and his work.

In 1968, upon reading Henry Thoreau's *Journal*, John Cage claimed to see 'any idea I've ever had worth its salt'. Cage's line recalls Emerson's famous boast from *Self-Reliance* [1841] that 'in every work of genius we recognize our own rejected thoughts; they come back to us with a certain alienated majesty'. Jannika Bock's *Concord in Massachusetts, Discord in the World* deals with Cage's discovery of Thoreau and the profound effect the nineteenth-century writing was to have on his compositions and on his life as he began to read his own thoughts reflected back at himself. Bock's work offers a re-examination of the writings of Thoreau and Cage (as well as his visual art and musical compositions), juxtaposing their texts in order to illustrate Cage's enduring interest in Thoreau's life and works. Although Bock uses the radio broadcast *Lecture on the Weather* as one famous example of Cage's musical salute to Thoreau, the main argument concerns Cage's poems and lectures. Indeed, Bock makes careful explorations of Cage's poetic lines, which draw directly from Thoreau's *Journal*. The title of this work divides attention between Thoreau's work in Concord Massachusetts and Cage's discordant compositions known worldwide. The author then subdivides the work into three main areas: the juxtaposition of the written works of Thoreau and Cage; intertextuality in Thoreau and Cage; and a new approach to Cage's aesthetics. Bock's offerings on the writings of Thoreau will not illuminate his work for Thoreau scholars. Indeed, chapter 3 opens with a 'definition' of Transcendentalism, which is an adequate but thin retelling of that well-known story of the formation of Transcendentalist culture. Where the book does venture into new ground is in the latter section. This is where it will be interesting to Americanists and scholars of American poetry in particular. Bock quite rightly claims that, until now, Cage's written works have been reviewed as supplementary to understanding his musical compositions. In fact, Cage's poetry has been anthologized in several published collections, and Bock is correct to consider it primarily in terms of its own merit. The study ends with interesting readings of several poems, drawing out their references to Thoreau. The reader is left, then, with a clearer understanding of Cage as an American *poet* to be considered alongside Thoreau, whom he so ardently admired.

In recent years, Twain's travel writing has received renewed attention in scholarship. Especially strong examples of this trend are Thomas Ruys Smith's *River of Dreams: Imagining the Mississippi Before Mark Twain* (LSUP [2007]) and Jeffrey Alan Melton's *Mark Twain, Travel Books and Tourism* (UAlaP [2002]). This is, in part, a consequence of the interests of new historicism since the 1980s in anecdote, historical incident and marginalia, which has established travel writing as a valuable resource of desirable cultural material. Harold H. Hellwig's *Mark Twain's Travel Literature: The Odyssey of a Mind*, is the latest addition to this body of work. However, Hellwig takes a different route through Twain's travelogues by attempting to approach them from a phenomenological perspective. According to the author, this involves 'the study of experiences from the first-person point of view, particularly the structures of consciousness'. This should provide an interesting view of Twain's work, particularly in terms of biographical detail, but is actually the book's primary failing. In order to achieve his aims, Hellwig employs a methodology based upon outdated 'structuralist principles' that enable the author to make the universal claim that all of Mark Twain's writing, whether fiction, letters or journalism, is informed by the same set of codes, themes and ideas about travel. Since Hellwig's methodology is so peculiarly outdated, it is appropriate, therefore, that he is fascinated by Twain's use of nostalgia, claiming that it 'takes place in a realm of timelessness ... it becomes an attempt to defeat time'. There is a certain irony in that through his use of older structuralist traditions, Hellwig is doing the same. The theoretical implications of his methodology are that, regardless of the material Hellwig is analysing (chapters 3 to 7 concern 'Innocents Abroad', 'Roughing It', 'A Tramp Abroad', 'Life on the Mississippi' and 'Following the Equator' respectively), the cultural specificities of each work are disregarded in favour of broad, atemporal claims about Twain's 'mind'. Indeed, there is little sense (barring an appendix of 'Travel Books Probably Read and Owned By Mark Twain') that Twain was engaged, in any serious way, with other authors or traditions. The 'probably' in this appendix is telling, and bespeaks a larger tendency in the books towards uncertain expression produced, not unsurprisingly, by the task of trying to recreate Twain's thought processes ('the codes ... that appear consistently in this body of work') as though they were coherent across his lifetime.

The general problems of the author's methodology mar insights that might have been interestingly restructured to comprise a study of how Twain's thoughts on the exercise of composition manifest themselves in his fiction. Of particular interest are chapters 2 and 8, which deal, respectively, with the influence of Twain's early experiences as a riverboat pilot on his memory and writing, and travel on the construction of identity in *The Adventures of Tom Sawyer* and *The Adventures of Huckleberry Finn*. For a book that proclaims to take Twain's travel writing as seriously as his fiction it is a serious problem that only in writing about that fiction does the book make any truly valuable interventions into the scholarship surrounding one of nineteenth-century America's finest literary stylists.

By resituating Walt Whitman within the textures of his own period (the turbulent 1830s, 1840s and 1850s, the groundswell of abolition and the lead up to the Civil War), Jason Stacy's *Walt Whitman's Multitudes: Labor Reform and Persona in Whitman's Journalism and the First 'Leaves of Grass', 1840–1855* provides an excellent account of the poet's mid-century experience. In doing this, Stacy brings to life the period's national history, which shaped Whitman's poetry and his poetics so dramatically. His consideration of Whitman's journalism offers new approaches to his poetry, while at the same time the journalism itself brings to life the social history of the mid-nineteenth century. Stacy draws attention to Whitman's important involvement in the politic discourse of his day and sheds new light on the poetic personas emerging from the 1855 edition of *Leaves of Grass*. The book is divided clearly into chronological sections, each of which expresses one of Whitman's given 'personas' or occupations at the time: artisan, schoolmaster, editor and bard. Identifying these various selves gives the reader a fresh insight into Whitman's period and his writing. This work will be of great benefit to anyone interested in Whitman's life and times but also to political and social historians, replete as it is with the decisive acts of his century as seen through the eyes of its most important journalist.

In *Worshipping Walt: The Whitman Disciples*, Michael Robertson evangelizes on the merit and, indeed, the necessity, of reading *Leaves of Grass* as a life-changing spiritual tract rather than 'just as a book of poetry'. He resists the urge, which those disciples of Whitman indulged, to consider *Leaves of Grass* only as a spiritual guidebook, and instead allows for the aesthetic, historical and political readings of *Leaves* to underpin his work. For instance 'Whitmanite' fervour is somewhat accounted for in its late nineteenth-century context of a secularized (or poly-religious) modernity. However, despite Robertson's careful attention to such matters, this work unashamedly places the weight of religion—emphatically not quasi-spirituality—at the heart of Whitman's undertaking. In writing *Leaves*, he argues, 'one deep purpose underlay the others, and has underlain it and its execution ever since—and that has been the religious purpose'. This book succeeds in three main ways. First, by aligning himself (somewhat) with the nine Whitman disciples whom the book explores, Robertson provides a captivating account of Whitman's personal magnetism, and the humility of those who felt drawn to him, without resorting to gossipy anecdote or speculative asides. Instead, the disciples themselves are permitted dignity and stature. Anne Gilchrist's (widow of William Blake's biographer) veritable stalking (moving children and furniture from England to Philadelphia in pursuit of Walt's affections) is recounted as follows: 'The spirit could only have come from Anne, who was able to make the about-face from infatuated would-be-lover to friend.' She makes this transformation, we are told, 'with extraordinary facility and grace'. The accounts of the nine chosen disciples (William O'Connor and John Burroughs, Anne Gilchrist, R.M. Bucke, John Addington Symonds, Edward Carpenter, Oscar Wilde, J.W. Wallace and Horace Traubel) remind us of the immediacy with which some nineteenth-century readers took to *Leaves* and the myriad ways in which it 'spoke' to those readers. For Symonds the collection was a code, which he spent two decades of correspondence with Whitman grappling to understand, about love between men. For Gilchrist it served as a personal love letter from Walt summonsing her to leave England and live a new, free life in the United States.

David Grant's 'Self-Abasement and Republican Insecurity: *Paul Fane* in its Political Context' (*AL* 80[2008] 443–69) revisits that American man of letters Nathaniel Parker Willis and his 1857 novel, *Paul Fane*. Grant makes a sound argument for the political significance of *Paul Fane*, which was 'conceived, written, serialized, and finally released in the pivotal years for the Republican party, 1854 to 1856, when its diagnosis of the nation's problems became the dominant view in the North'. Grant discusses the growing familiarity of the American public with writers who became identified with the anti-slavery movement, and he cites Lowell, Bryant, Read, Whittier, Stowe and Curtis as examples. Although *Paul Fane* makes no direct reference to slavery, Grant makes a sound argument for reading Willis's novel and its illustration of 'the relationship between a fledgling America and an established Europe' alongside the emergence of the new party. Grant argues concisely that in the political and cultural discourse in the first half of the nineteenth century, Europe had 'represented a paradoxically internal threat to American integrity', and that *Paul Fane* deals with the same rhetorical territory. This is an interesting piece on the history of that time as well as an instructively original study of *Paul Fane*.

Books Reviewed

Adams Sitney, P. *Eyes Upside Down: Visionary Filmmakers and the Heritage of Emerson*. OUP. [2008] pp. vii + 417. pb £17.99 ISBN 9 7801 9533 1158.

Beer, Janet, ed. *The Cambridge Companion to Kate Chopin*. CUP. [2008] pp. v + 184. pb £17.99 ISBN 9 7805 2170 9828.

Bock, and Jannika. *Concord in Massachusetts, Discord in the World: The Writings of Henry Thoreau and John Cage*. Lang. [2008] pp. vii + 273. pb £36 ISBN 9 7836 3158 4132.

Boulukos, and George. *The Grateful Slave: The Emergence of Race in Eighteenth-Century British and American Culture*. CUP. [2008] pp. viii + 280. £50 ISBN 9 7805 2188 5713.

Carpio, Glenda R. *Laughing Fit to Kill: Black Humor in the Fictions of Slavery*. OUP. [2008] pp. xi + 287. hb £41 ISBN 9 7801 9530 4701.

Chesnutt, Charles W. *The Marrow of Tradition*. DodoP. [2008] pp. 256. pb £11.99 ISBN 9 7814 0992 3992.

Ferguson, Sallyann, ed. Nineteenth-Century Black Women's Literary Emergence: Evolutionary Spirituality, Sexuality, and Identity. Lang. [2008] pp. xliv + 305. pb £17.50 ISBN 9 7814 3310 1571.

Fisher, Benjamin F. *The Cambridge Introduction to Edgar Allan Poe*. Cambridge Introductions to Literature. CUP. [2008] pp. viii + 136. pb £10.99 ISBN 9 7805 2167 6915.

Hellwig, Harold H. Mark Twain's Travel Literature: The Odyssey of a Mind. McFarland. [2008] pp. 227. pb £31.50 ($35) ISBN 9 7807 8643 8514.

Lockard, Joe. *Watching Slavery: Witness Texts and Travel Reports*. Lang. [2008] pp. xii + 213. £50 ISBN 9 7808 2049 5422.

Lysaker, John T. *Emerson and Self-Culture*. IndUP. [2008] pp. xi + 226. pb £17.99 ISBN 9 7802 5321 9718.

Ostman, Heather, ed. *Kate Chopin in the Twenty-First Century: New Critical Essays*. CambridgeSP. [2008] pp. vii + 162. £29.99 ISBN 1 8471 8647 5.

Patterson, Daniel, ed. *Early American Nature Writers: A Bibliographical Encyclopaedia*. Greenwood. [2008] pp. xi + 433. £70 ISBN 9 7803 1334 6804.

Person, Leland S. *The Cambridge Introduction to Nathaniel Hawthorne*. CUP. [2008] pp. v + 144. pb £12.99 ISBN 0 5216 7096 9.

Robertson, Michael. *Worshipping Walt: The Whitman Disciples*. University Presses of California, Columbia and Princeton. [2008] pp. viii + 350. £19.95 ISBN 9 7806 9112 8085.

Ronda A, Bruce. *Reading the Old Man: John Brown in American Culture.* UTennP. [2008] pp. xvii + 218. £27.30 ISBN 9 7815 7233 6209.

Stacy, Jason. Walt Whitman's Multitudes: Labor Reform and Persona in Whitman's Journalism and the First 'Leaves of Grass', 1840–1855. Lang. [2008] pp. vii + 168. £32.40 ISBN 9 7814 3310 1533.

Weldon, Roberta. *Hawthorne, Gender and Death: Christianity and its Discontents.* Palgrave Macmillan. [2008] pp. x + 203. £42.50 ISBN 9 7802 3060 2908.

West, Peter. *The Arbiters of Reality: Hawthorne, Melville and the Rise of Mass Information Culture.* OSUP. [2008] pp. 229. £28 ($44.95) ISBN 9 780 8142 1088 8.

XVI

American Literature: The Twentieth Century

JAMES GIFFORD, JAMES M. DECKER, MICHAEL BOYD AND AMY M. FLAXMAN

This chapter has six sections: 1. Poetry; 2. Fiction 1900–1945; 3. Fiction since 1945; 4. Drama; 5. African American Writing; 6. Native, Asian American, Latino/a and General Ethnic Writing. Section 1 is by James Gifford; section 2 is by James M. Decker; section 3 is by Michael Boyd; section 4 is by Amy M. Flaxman; section 5 is by James M. Decker; section 6 is by James M. Decker.

1. Poetry

The year 2008 brought several reissues of critical works as well as critical editions of twentieth-century poetry. Heather Cass White's editorial work on *A-Quiver with Significance: Marianne Moore 1932–1936*, published by ELS Editions, is particularly strong, and the book's facsimile production of Moore's works from 1932 to 1936 will surely return attention to Moore's poetic practices. White's detailed records of each variant of the included poems provides the necessary resources for continuing work on Moore, and her introduction adroitly draws critical attention to the importance of these first and subsequent variants as well as the possibilities for further work. This kind of critical edition is new for ELS Editions, and their 2008 titles (with attractive and readable design by Jason Dewinitz) suggest more useful work to come. New Directions has also reissued Kenneth Patchen's *The Walking-Away World* and *We Meet* in affordable trade editions. Both volumes integrate Patchen's original artwork and picture poems, the former consisting entirely of black and white facsimiles. *The Walking-Away World* carries an introduction, 'Looking at Kenneth Patchen', by the cartoonist Jim Woodring, and *We Meet* is prefaced by Devendra Banhart. Both write cogently for a lay audience, and attracting work from such celebrities demonstrates New Directions's interest in continued development of a general audience for Patchen's works.

The clear standout in critical reissues in 2008 is Haun Saussy, Jonathan Stalling, and Lucas Klein's edition of Ernest Fenellosa's and Ezra Pound's

Year's Work in English Studies, Volume 89 (2010) © *The English Association; all rights reserved*
doi:10.1093/ywes/maq006

The Chinese Character as a Medium for Poetry. This critical reissue of a work that shows Pound's own idiosyncratic editorial work presents significant challenges, but the editors and designers have more than met the demands. Fordham University Press has also invested significant work in the appearance of the book, which is attractive and suitable to the original character of the publication. The original text has received extensive attention in Pound criticism, and this new edition has already been widely reviewed in largely favourable terms—Saussy, Stalling and Klein, in their editorial matter, cover the existing scholarship and detail the utility of this critical edition exhaustively. It is certainly a book that will receive wide use in Pound scholarship and modernist studies in general, if the other 2008 texts on Pound and Fenellosa are any indication of the degree of continuing interest. These works on Pound follow the year after the first volume of A. David Moody's major biography of the poet. The continued high pace in Pound criticism is striking. In *Ezra Pound's Chinese Friends: Stories in Letters*, Zhaoming Qian adds to this his critical edition of 162 letters between Pound and Chinese scholars over a period of forty-five years, and this ties directly to his well-received previous works on Pound. The problems with Pound's sense of Chinese characters and languages have been a thorn for critics, and as Qian demonstrates, Pound's idiosyncratic incorporations into the Cantos were anything but ill informed. Perhaps the most useful element Qian contributes is his clear timeline of how much Chinese writing Pound was capable of understanding at any given time and what resources he drew from for that understanding. While a more extensive critical introduction could be desired, especially given the need to clear the critical debate that has amassed on this topic, Qian remains content as an editor to point to the most overt answers given by his work and leave the remainder for critics to respond to. By integrating periodic commentaries into the body of the book itself, between authors, periods or topics, Qian also manages to contextualize each critical revision implicit in the preceding materials. The detailed, yet not cumbersome, editorial apparatus makes the text useful and easy to interpret. The appendix containing Pound's 'Ezra Pound's Typescript for "Preliminary Survey" (1951)' will also give scholars a specific instance in which to apply the information and chronology in the letters. This is a volume that is certain to appear in the secondary literature for many years.

Garrick Davis provides a similarly useful compendium of the New Criticism in general, in *Praising it New: The Best of the New Criticism*, which will likely attract interest from the same audience, especially those taking part in the new modernist studies. Davis's volume draws together modernist critical texts not commonly available together in one or even a few volumes, such as Pound's 'How to Read', John Crowe Ransom's 'Criticism, Inc.', and R.P. Blackmur's 'Religious Poetry in the United States'. The standard New Critical essays of T.S. Eliot, Cleanth Brooks, Randall Jarrell, Hugh Kenner and Yvor Winters are, of course, granted significant space in the volume, all of which combines to provide a convenient collected text with enough breadth and redirection of scholarly attention to serve as both a textbook in the classroom and a fresh resource for established scholars. Although New Criticism has lost its fashionable appeal, Davis's works allows the reader to use this volume as both a collection of scholarship and an overview of a paradigmatic vision of the period.

Reissues of criticism were also prominent in 2008. John Xiros Cooper's exceptional *T.S. Eliot and the Ideology of Four Quartets* and A. David Moody's *Tracing T.S. Eliot's Spirit: Essays on his Poetry and Thought* have both been reprinted in affordable trade editions by Cambridge University Press more than a decade after their first appearance in the mid-1990s. Both texts are standards in criticism and are frequently cited, so their easier availability is welcome. Most modernist and T.S. Eliot scholars are already very familiar with both books, but they continue to offer a compelling contribution to scholarship and very useful resources for the classroom. The reissue of Moody's *Tracing T.S. Eliot's Spirit* seems to have been intended as a serendipitous companion to his excellent first volume of his biography of Ezra Pound; the two works in tandem demonstrate Moody's major contributions to modernist studies as a whole. Russell Kirk's standard biography-cum-critical study, *Eliot and his Age: T.S. Eliot's Moral Imagination in the Twentieth Century*, has been re-released in a comparably inexpensive edition by ISI Books. Kirk's approach has dated significantly over the past four decades, but his close relationship with Eliot and care as a reader continue to be useful for emerging scholars and as an important representation of the shifting trends in critical work. Cambridge has also reissued Linda A. Kinnahan's more recent *Poetics of the Feminine: Authority and Literary Tradition in William Carlos Williams, Mina Loy, Denise Levertov, and Kathleen Fraser*. Kinnahan's influence can be seen in the subsequent work over the past fourteen years on Loy, Levertov, and Fraser, so this fresh presentation of her monograph is good to find and will be a great convenience to researchers. Academic work on Levertov, in particular, has developed substantially since 1994, so Kinnahan's work is now somewhat dated; however, much of her thesis and critical intervention still have merit as necessary polemics to established and ongoing criticism, which makes the book surprisingly fresh.

A number of late arrivals from 2007 also merit attention. Daniel Katz's *American Modernism's Expatriate Scene: The Labour of Translation* begins with two chapters on Henry James's prose but leads into an extended discussion in the rest of the volume that is mainly focused on American poets, including a final chapter on the less studied prose of the poets John Ashbury, James Schuyler and Jack Spicer. This movement across the century and between prose and poetry works well and gives Katz significant leeway in developing his analysis of the unique traits of American expatriatism (both within and outside North America). In this sense, Katz's use of 'translation' is both literal and figurative in the 'carrying across' of any act of translation. The metaphor is largely developed from his work on Pound and the explicit continuation of the Poundian tradition in the New York school, but the more literal concern is the transatlantic development of American writing, from which English writers and writing cannot be fully distinguished. Katz's chapter on 'Pound and Translation' is the strongest in the book and will be of interest to Pound scholars, especially having come at the same time as the new release of *Pound and Fenellosa* by Fordham University Press. Katz is preoccupied with Pound's notion of phanopoeia in relation to his interest in Chinese poetry, such that the translation between sign and signifier is reduced. This is then turned back to Pound's own works, in which Katz retraces the influence of Chinese characters in Pound's attempts to translate specific images into poetic text while relying on a syntax that alludes to Chinese emphases and idiosyncrasies. The unification of phanopoeia and ideograms that Katz articulates leads him to adroit interpretations of Pound's poetry and poetic theorization. In some respects, this reading is most effective moving from James to Pound, and from Pound to the New York school poets (who travelled much less), in which the transatlantic movement is secondary to the role of translation and moving across in the figurative form of the works themselves; the inclusion of Gertrude Stein and Wyndham Lewis is, in contrast, an overt development of the specifically transatlantic nature of this succession of poetic ideas. While this works, it does leave the chapter on Stein and Lewis somewhat aloof from the remainder of the book. In this sense, the final summation of the volume turns to the distinctly American space Katz finds in mid-century poetry, in which Europe no longer figures as a point of origin.

Michael O'Neill's *The All-Sustaining Air: Romantic Legacies and Renewals in British, American, and Irish Poetry since 1900* covers a remarkable range, though its American focus is primarily on T.S. Eliot and Wallace Stevens (the materials on Auden date primarily prior to 1939). O'Neill's discussion of Roy Fisher in the final chapter certainly invites further consideration of William Carlos Williams and Robert Duncan, though the former only appears in the chapter on Paul Muldoon. The discussion of Eliot as a counter-Romantic develops from longstanding critical regard for the origins of modernism in Romanticism. In this regard, O'Neill draws significantly on Christopher Ricks, A. David Moody, whose work was reissued this year, and Eliot's own critical work on the Romantics. The most convincing part of O'Neill's argument, which is developed out of yet departs from this previous criticism, is based in Eliot's rebuttal of the Romantics paired with his constant appropriation of their phrasing. From Eliot's injunction to cure Romanticism by analysing it, O'Neill draws the breakdown in Eliot's analysis: his rearticulation and repetition of Romanticism in the very poets he derogates. The Romantic version of the *The Waste Land* and each of the *Four Quartets*, 'East Coker' in particular, that this reconsideration generates is impressive. The obsessive returns to Romantic articulations in poetic phrase and critical analogy to which O'Neill draws attention are compelling and prompt the reader to question if the 'New' in Eliot's strong readings is in fact an unconscious ventriloquism of the tradition he sought to forever alter. Provocatively, O'Neill concludes his discussion of Eliot with the ubiquitous phrase from 'The Frontiers of Criticism' that 'When the poem has been made, something new has happened, something that cannot be wholly explained by *anything that went before*. That, I believe, is what we mean by "creation"', to which he immediately juxtaposes John Keats's insistence that 'That which is creative must create itself' (p. 82). He turns the same close attention to Stevens and unravels his intense usurpation and rearticulation of Percy Bysshe Shelley, Keats and Byron. Shelley is tied to Stevens more than any other poet in O'Neill's articulation, and a particularly Nietzschean perspective on Shelley's anarchist rejection of rulers and gods sits behind many of the descriptions. This tie has been established in criticism of Stevens's work for quite some time, and a more intricate development from Stevens's criticism would strengthen O'Neill's contentions here, in particular since the thematic unity is clear. The transatlantic lives of several of the other poets in O'Neill's volume may also appeal to scholars at work on American poetry, in particular the materials on Auden immediately prior to his emigration, as well as Paul Muldoon and Roy Fisher due to their significant American residences.

The 2007 release of Nicola Shaughnessy's *Gertrude Stein* in the Writers and their Work series provides a good reference for undergraduate students and those in need of a quick timeline and direct critical views. The book is broken into clear thematic sections, although the subsections on specific texts are not listed in the table of contents. As a book primarily intended for a reference audience, this is some hindrance, though Shaughnessy's writing is clear, concise, and leads readers into the complexity of Stein's prose and poetry without losing them in a flood of detail. Standard critical problems such as Cubism, Stein's style and thematic preoccupations, and the dialogues in her later dramas are dealt with succinctly in order to give a full overview to young scholars, and in this way the book succeeds. Readers familiar with the other myriad titles in the Writers and their Work series will find familiar approaches and brief coverage here. Naomi Pasachoff's *A Student's Guide to T.S. Eliot* performs a similar service, but its audience is more clearly that of high school students or perhaps college freshmen with no previous experience in significant literary studies. That said, as a biography-in-little and as a quick overview, the volume stands out for its clarity and the author's clear comprehension of Eliot's works as a whole. It is likely not suitable for undergraduate classrooms but would provide a handy resource for those new students too abashed to ask for a rudimentary overview. The summary given of the various drafts of *The Waste Land* is impressive for a work of this kind, and its clarity would be a productive model for most introductory lectures. The same holds true for its overview of *Four Quartets*, in which Pasachoff again adeptly manages complex moments in the text for a reader otherwise unlikely to notice them.

Several 2007 books appeared through the Manchester University Press, and the most provocative among them is likely David Herd's *Enthusiast! Essays on Modern American Literature*. Herd's argument begins with a polemical misprision of Ralph Waldo Emerson's contention that the retrospective nature of American culture in 1836 constitutes the origin of modern American literature, in tandem with his intention to engender 'enthusiasm' in American literature, a quasi-religious experience of awe akin to a Joycean epiphany. This notion is echoed overtly in Herd's contention that 'what this book offers is a portrait of the writer as an enthusiast' (p. 18). This sense of enthusiasm, however, places Herd's work in conflict with bureaucracy and in particular the bureaucratic forces of modern academic institutions. This brings a good deal of liveliness to his investigations and also allows for a critical sleight of hand that unifies his highly diverse series of writers, Thoreau, Melville, Pound, Moore, O'Hara and Schuyler. Herd is not placing them in a common sense of enthusiasm nor fitting them into a critical spectrum of literary concerns with enthusiasms; instead, he asks how these authors can be seen if they are regarded through their enthusiasm. The general transition from the nineteenth to the twentieth century parallels a transition in Herd's work from prose to poetry, and this critical move merits more attention than it receives in the book itself. That said, the later chapters on Pound and Moore are particularly rich in close readings and strong critical moves to reconsider both poets through their enthusiasm. This leads to a reconsideration of current debates in the scholarship on both authors: for Pound in relation to economics and distribution, and for Moore in relation to her revisions to better 'Display' or pass along the traits of her poetic works. The epistemological focus in Herd's discussion of O'Hara makes new contributions, and his chapter on James Schuyler is particularly welcome. The chapters are disjointed at times, and there are several moments at which Herd slips into referring to them as articles, which may be indicative of their initial form. It seems unlikely that readers will attend to the book in a specific effort to grapple with American 'enthusiasm' *per se*, but the careful readings he offers of each modern poet will repay attention from scholars.

In *Tiresian Poetics: Modernism, Sexuality, Voice, 1888–2001*, Ed Madden also takes a thematic approach to surveying modernist American literature, in his case what he calls 'Tiresian poetics'. The more specific issues at stake in his analyses are the liminal space between conflicting notions of sexuality, knowledge and identity. The major focus, however, relates to using queer theory to investigate the unstable nature of gender, desire and identity in works by Michael Field, T.S. Eliot, and Djuna Barnes, as well as Austin Clarke. Madden's interpretation of Eliot takes up two chapters in the volume, and this is clearly the centrepiece. There is a clear forward motion of texts leading to Eliot's *The Waste Land* and following it in allusion and response. The year 1922 may be a watershed, but the volume need not have adopted this central vision, and the work on Barnes would merit expansion, in particular Madden's discussion of her long poems from the 1960s. The book's central concern with essentialist identities, most particularly but not exclusively sexual identities, works well in a productive tension with its insistence on stylistic instability and recurrent imagery of sexual abjection. The most particularly useful contribution is Madden's careful analysis and articulation of each author's allusions to Tiresias and sexual transgression in general, homosexual transgression in particular. Whether this is through retracing Barnes's allusions to Eliot or Eliot's allusions to Sappho, the care taken in unpacking each reference and its potential uses in a critical reading is impressive. The combination of traditional explication and theoretical investigation through queer theory is innovative if not entirely fresh, and follows on several recent works on Barnes, Eliot and Clark in this vein.

Alan Filreis offers one of the most provocative analyses of mid-century American poetry this year in *Counter-Revolution of the Word: The Conservative Attack on Modern Poetry 1945–1960*. The University of North Carolina Press at Chapel Hill has produced a highly readable and attractive volume that complements the contents, but Filreis's adept handing of the stylistic and political conflicts in American modern poetry holds attention without the need for such support. Perhaps the most impressive feature is Filreis's ability to move between locales and movements while maintaining a continuity of theme and focus. This balance between critical interpretations of primary texts and socio-historical overview of the networks and circumstances that gave rise to these particular works is impressive, as is the seamless overlapping between American and British poetry networks that is evidenced in the volume. Filreis's sense of modern and revolutionary poetry is fairly well contained, primarily indicating his interest in the conservative reactionary rebuttal of stylistic innovations (particularly those associated with syntax) and politics of the left (nearly exclusively Marxist). This tension is made clear in Filreis's opening sentence, which both opens the field of his work (a much-needed opening in criticism) and forecloses on the potential range of alternative avant-gardes and political views: '*Counter-Revolution of the Word* is about conservatives' attempt to destroy the modernist avant-garde in the anticommunist period after World War II' (p. ix). This is hastily qualified by an acknowledgement that this avant-garde was 'not ideologically of a kind' though aesthetically unified. However, this opening presages a continually present perspective in which this aesthetic unity aligns with Marxist visions of social organization, and that also casts anti-communist perspectives as inherently conservative. Filreis's readings and critical interventions in the established discourse are both adroit and executed with impressive adeptness, but the range of anarchist poets who 'were not ideologically of a kind' with the communist poets is surprisingly understated, as is the conservatism/fascism kinship at several moments. Robert Duncan, Kenneth Rexroth, Kenneth Patchen, Mac Low, Ezra Pound and other self-identifying (at one time or another) anarchists or anti-authoritarians occupy a major portion of the book's critical argument, but their anarchism is largely elided or overlooked. This does nothing to diminish Filreis's analysis of the anti-communist forces that worked contrary to the American avant-garde, but it does replicate the anti-communist vision in which communist and anarchist politics and aesthetic practices are indistinguishable as simply an Other. Much of this perspective appears to develop from the social vision established by the Auden generation, and Auden is an important figure in this volume, after whom the social voice of poetry that could 'speak' in its propagandist vein or 'show' in its poetics was reductively identified as either conservative or revolutionary: the avant-garde and formal innovation being the latter and the classical tradition and individualist lyricism the former. The aesthetic conflict is certainly caught in this polarity between right and left, but the mode of aesthetic innovation is multiple. This point is perhaps made most clearly when Filreis draws specifically on Herbert Read's work on education through art and American surrealism in general. Read's outspoken anarchism, with a brief period of communist sympathies while organizing the introduction of surrealism to England, is well known and comprises a major preoccupation in his critical writings, especially those in relation to aesthetics. The so-called 'Open Form' of English surrealism, in which complex interpretative responsibility is shared rather than authoritarian, is well documented, and bridges American and English movements involving several of the poets Filreis examines: David Gascoyne's work with Kenneth Patchen, Henry Miller's bridge between Herbert Read and Robert Duncan, Kenneth Rexroth's detailed interest in and distribution of British anarchist poets, the anarchist Circle poets of Berkeley and so forth. The classification of other more traditional poets, such as Robert Graves, as voices of conservative censorship is also potentially misleading, though the aesthetic break between lyricism and innovation in these polarities is still a genuine interest. Laura Riding Jackson's absence is also notable. However, this perspective casts the folk movement as anti-communist, which is surely not the case, and likewise negates the individualist impetus behind much of the avant-garde's formal innovations. Rather than a binary opposition, a four-part division of political sensibilities may have afforded much more nuance for revolutionary instances of lyricism and traditional poetic forms, as well as differing perspectives on experimentalism based on collectivist or anti-authoritarian world-views. All of this is to say that Filreis's *Counter-Revolution of the Word* is highly stimulating and sure to provoke a great deal of critical response. The intervention the book enacts into patriotic and depoliticized histories of American poetry (conducted in the mid-century but concerned with poetic productions from both the nineteenth and twentieth centuries) is excellent and much needed for the ongoing development of late modernist studies. Filreis's blending of historical and literary analysis makes a strong model for future work, and the book is an excellent resource both for those who differ from and those who agree with its ideological premise.

G. Matthew Jenkins's *Poetic Obligation: Ethics in Experimental American Poetry after 1945* displays a similar breadth and concern with poetic movements built from stylistic innovation through to politics. His basic premise develops from Plato's banishment of poetry from the scope of ethical philosophy and the turn contrary to this in the late nineteenth and early twentieth centuries in which philosophy became more open to literary and poetic inspiration, in particular with regard to ethics. This position grants Jenkins considerable opportunities for theoretical and literary analysis, most frequently in relation to war and Eros. He takes the book through thematic and topical foci, loosely dividing the Objectivists, Embodiment and Sexualities into six chapters that deal with George Oppen, Charles Reznikoff, Edward Dorn, Robert Duncan, Susan Howe and Lyn Hejinian. Nearly all of these authors have enjoyed renewed critical attention in the past few years, so Jenkins's contribution is timely. The topical divisions feel arbitrary across the book since each poet's works wander between these concerns fairly freely, though this does not mar the reading experience. Moving through all six authors taking up Jenkins's ethical and political concerns works well, and the divisions make the book accessible either in pieces based on the reader's interests or as a whole. In addition to Jenkins's work, the University of Iowa Press published James E. von der Heydt's *At the Brink of Infinity: Poetic Humility in Boundless American Space*, which complements Jenkin's focus on ethics and pursues earlier American poetry. Von der Heydt's preoccupations are clearly with Emily Dickinson, Robert Frost, Elizabeth Bishop, Ralph Waldo Emerson and James Merrill; however, his discussion of pragmatism and anti-authoritarian figures such as Henry David Thoreau suggests interests beyond the ecological focus of his work that would interact well with David Kadlec's *Mosaic Modernism: Anarchism, Pragmatism, Culture*. In many respects, the book offers a dissenting voice for the conservatism aligned with Frost and lyricism in general by Filreis, and von der Heydt's period focus on the late nineteenth and early twentieth centuries suggests alternative ways of reading the mid-century critical revisions to poetry's ethics.

With regard to American modernist poetry, 2008 was impressive in its diversity. Modernism in general continues to enjoy a publishing boom among university presses and periodicals, and continued attention to poetry forms a significant component in this trend; 2009 has exhibited the same development. In *Between Positivism and T.S. Eliot: Imagism and T.E. Hulme*, Flemming Olsen draws attention to T.E. Hulme's influence on imagist poetry as well as his development from the general positivist perspectives in the sciences and realist narrative in the Victorian era through to distinctly modernist notions of a hyper-real or perspectival work. Though Olsen focuses primarily on Hulme and the zeitgeist of his critical moment, the volume is useful for recontextualizing Ezra Pound's and H.D.'s roles in imagism after Hulme as well as the intellectual traditions from which they broke. The latter is, by and large, the main strength of the volume, which is far more concerned with the intellectual milieu than with close readings of specific texts. While Olsen's breadth has merit and utility, the book is hindered by the lack of an index to allow easier access to this breadth, and by printing errors that begin on the first page. Three volumes from Verlag Dr Müller give similar overviews of modernist authors. Sister Barbara Sudol's *Mystical Elements in the Poetry of T.S. Eliot: T.S. Eliot's Poetry from 1909–1942* builds from the basic contention that 'Eliot did have profound mystical moments in his life' and that the reader can come to understand mystical enlightenment through reading Eliot's mystical poetry. The telos of development from Eliot's early works to *Four Quartets* is the dominant theme in the book, and the primary preoccupation is with Christian mysticism, often to the exclusion of modernist aesthetics and the political context of the projects in which Eliot was engaged prior to his conversion. Sudol's readings are undeniably useful in articulating the sources and preoccupations of Eliot's works after 1927, but as a whole the volume tends to be reductive. The book is most productive when she is exploring the Christian allusions and terminology of *Four Quartets*, but even here too much time is given over to established biographical facts about Eliot that are not necessary to the critical enterprise at hand. Doris Kraler-Bergmann has a similarly narrow focus in her very brief monograph *Sylvia Plath's Lyrical Responses to Works of Art: A Portrait of the Artist(s)*. Kraler-Bergmann's primary argument begins with Plath's poems for *ARTnews* and their continuation in other poems concerned with the visual arts and ekphrasis. This, in tandem with her attention to Plath's keen interest in the visual arts throughout her life, allows Kraler-Bergmann to draw attention to what she convincingly presents as a critical myopia. However, the great brevity of the book leaves the reader wondering if it could reasonably have been condensed into a single article in a periodical. Iain Landles brings a more refreshing text to Verlag Dr Müller's catalogue. His *Case for Cummings: A Reaction to the Critical Misreadings of E.E. Cummings* is robust and clear in its language, carrying the enthusiasm (if one can borrow from Herd's volume) of a young reader without the concomitant mawkishness. Editing in the book, including paragraph indentations, is minimal, and it seems unlikely the volume was edited after the author's submission. As early as the fourth page, the author identifies the text in hand as 'this dissertation'. As a dissertation, and a good one, this book succeeds, but as an independent volume of criticism it would have been improved by extensive trimming by an editor's blue pen while retaining (and compressing) the energy that makes the sound critical commentary appealing. Moving through Bloom's *Anxiety of Influence* to Paul de Man's *Blindness and Insight* and Christopher Norris's *Deconstruction*, much of the critical terrain of this book demonstrates the author's familiarity with the requisite works for someone entering the profession rather than the critical works necessary for the book itself; this shows the work's origins in a thesis far more than the inadvertently dropped word 'dissertation'. Such passages could be cut entirely without reducing the value of the book and its genuine merit. The primary contention of Landles's volume, that Cummings has been inappropriately fixed in criticism through the perspective of a 'late' Cummings who makes sense of the 'early' Cummings, is sound and will surely make a contribution to scholarship. The extensive discussion of Cummings's *The Enormous Room* and its self-conscious emphasis on discourse, often read through Bakhtin here, convincingly demonstrates the primary thesis the Cummings's early works cannot be read reliably from the perspective of his later productions and their critical contexts.

Noriko Takeda has published a second volume continuing from her *A Flowering Word: The Modernist Expression in Stéphane Mallarmé, T.S. Eliot, and Yosano Akiko*, which was published, also by Peter Lang, in 2000. *The Modernist Human: The Configuration of Humanness in Stéphane Mallarmé's Hérodiade, T.S. Eliot's Cats, and Modernist Lyrical Poetry* continues, eight years later, her project to link Eliot and Mallarmé. The critical context for this work is somewhat dated and draws very largely from critics who were contemporary to Eliot. There is much merit to the enthusiasm of this perspective, and Takeda remains true to her thesis that the poetics of both authors reflect a commitment to a particular vision of humanism, but more ties to contemporary criticism and a more nuanced approach to the problem of the lyric in modernism as a whole would have given the volume more utility to scholars. She is strongest when outlining Eliot's prototypes in Edward Lear, William Blake, Charles Baudelaire and Lewis Carroll. Further development of this lineage and Eliot's purposes in appropriation and allusion would have extended the book's scope in more specifically critical ways. The secondary criticism is used more extensively with regard to Mallarmé, and Takeda's work here will likely interest academics in this field.

Sussex Academic Press produced *Aristotle and Modernism: Aesthetic Affinities of T.S. Eliot, Wallace Stevens, and Virginia Woolf* by Edna Rosenthal, and her capacious project to 'expose the Aristotelian under-pinnings of literary modernism' through Eliot, Stevens and Woolf allows for a useful reconsideration of the latter two authors. The middle chapter, on Stevens, is likely to be of the greatest interest. As she acknowledges, 'Stevens' improbable Aristotelianism is my limiting case precisely because the dis-agreement on his poetics appears to straddle a more fundamental—broader, deeper and older—critical divide.' This chapter is the most adept in managing dissenting voices in the existing criticism while drawing their discord to an agreement over shared principles of transcendental 'inspiration' subjected to the poet's labour and work in a tradition. Beginning with Hugh Kenner and J. Hillis Miller, Rosenthal develops to Jeffrey Perl and Marjorie Perloff, finally moving on to Stevens and Eliot themselves to demonstrate how a return to the primary text is capable of resolving the critical disjunctions she identifies. The eventual contention that Eliot's aesthetics are compatible with Friedrich Schlegel's sense of Romanticism as a development of classicism, and that Stevens's fundamental poetry is compatible with Eliot's classicism, is convincing in her terms, though still likely to give rise to productive dispute.

Josephine Park presents a compelling pairing of American visions of Asia and Asian American visions of America in her *Apparitions of Asia: Modernist Form and Asian American Poetics*. As the title suggests, this is not simply a clever pairing of politicized perspectives caught in the neocolonial gaze outward from an imperial power but also a careful exploration of the genuine formal commonalities and mutual influences replete in modernist and mid-century literature. Park begins with Walt Whitman and Ernest Fenellosa as the first to establish a distinctly American literary orientalism, and from this moves to Pound's responses to both authors. Her work would have benefited from access to Qian's editorial work on Pound's Chinese correspondents also released this year, and one can hope such developments will appear in the periodical literature. The section on Pound ends by avoiding the developments of the late 1930s and ultimately aligns him in a position of what Amin Malak might call 'ambivalent affiliations'. The subsequent turn to Gary Snyder opens with an immediate demonstration of his invocation of Chinese allusions via direct citation and discussion of Pound. Snyder's own ambivalent affiliations are made clear for any unfamiliar readers, though his equally complex appropriation of Whitman's nostalgic vision of access to the Orient, which in turn becomes knowledge of the Same through the exploration of its projection on the Other. Via the Orient, Snyder finds his position in America. While this could have developed into a modernist genealogy of the Beats, it instead takes Park to the burdens felt by Asian American poets who inherited this orientalist tradition for their work in an overlapping tradition of texts. In this section, Park relies less on previous scholarship and develops not only her unique critical revisions but also much-needed presentations of the otherwise often overlooked Asian American poetic heritage. This 'ill fitted heritage', as Park describes it, is the point at which the book breaks off, presenting a series of reconciliations as well as ambivalences over continuing development. In this sense, both sets of poets inherited a tradition with which they struggle in a typically modernist fashion, and the Asian American poets are presented as struggling with another problem of traditional newness. This second half of the book is significantly shorter and introduces many readers to less familiar figures in American poetry. The brevity and clear introduction of the poetic heritage to a likely new audience work well and suggest several opportunities for further critical work.

Critical work on Sylvia Plath continued apace in 2008: in addition to Kraler-Bergmann's book already mentioned above, Jo Gill's *The Cambridge Introduction to Sylvia Plath* appeared, as did Anita Helle's edited collection, *The Unraveling Archive: Essays on Sylvia Plath*. The persistent interest in Plath's writings, especially for the classroom, is an obvious factor in each of these works. Gill's guide is oriented to undergraduate readers but would certainly give a valuable overview to any reader. Her presentation of Plath's prose works apart from *The Bell Jar* demonstrates that her readership expectations extend beyond the typical classroom. Gill's focus on the variant publications and the restored edition of *Ariel*, as well as on Plath's correspondence, demonstrates her capacious sense of audience, which includes both postgraduate and professorial readers. Gill's approach to the variants is largely through a historical/chronological and biographical context, which allows her to carefully read the primary text. A more theorized sense of the role of variants could have expanded the book in this area, but it is certainly not necessary for the reader in search of a primer. As a primer, the book excels and exceeds expectations for detail and nuance in reading, in particular with regard to Plath's less complex works. Helle's collection, *The Unraveling Archive*, takes an archival approach, but the specific aims vary from chapter to chapter. The general trend here is to consider the 'right' and 'wrong' manuscripts based on faithfulness to a particular copy-text. The notion of an eclectic text put forward by Jerome McGann in the early 1980s would have informed the more textually oriented chapters; this also appears to have been Helle's intention from her discussion in the introduction, which draws on Jacques Derrida's *Archive Fever* and refers to the provocative work put forward recently by Ben Alexander. Tracy Brain's chapter, 'Unstable Manuscripts: The Indeterminacy of the Plath Canon', opens the volume; it concludes by invoking McGann's notion of the eclectic text, but in many respects this would have been a stronger beginning than ending. Brain's work is by far the most engaging for a reader interested in the textual and archival problems posed by Plath's oeuvre, and her readers here would likely not have an extensive textual background given the still fresh developments going on in Plath criticism, but as the most important textual chapter in the volume, a greater emphasis on contemporary theories of editorial work would have been appreciated. Kate Moses' 'Sylvia Plath's Voice, Annotated' also presents fresh readings and new information, but Brain does stand out in this section. The second, and by far the largest, component of the volume is concerned solely with the archive in the more figurative sense: memory and the politics of commemoration. These chapters present a more diverse series of readings of Plath's works than would normally be expected in a volume with a titular dedication to archival study (for which Plath is still a much-overlooked author in many respects, despite recent work), but for Plath scholars the collection as a whole is surely a strong contribution. Lynda K. Bundtzen's chapter, 'Poetic Arson and Sylvia Plath's "Burning the Letters"', makes much of the violence of burning textual artefacts, and a good deal of her work relates to paralleling the poetic materials with an autobiographical time-frame for Plath's composition. Surprisingly little, however, is said of the provocative description early in the chapter of Smith College's Mortimer Rare Book Room, which holds several Plath manuscripts composed on the back of Hughes's works. Although no mention of this is made elsewhere in the book, such manuscripts abound, including a good-sized collection in the McPherson Library's Special Collections at the University of Victoria. Plath and Hughes had a habit of reusing each other's manuscripts, recto/verso, but there is little close attention here to determining the order of composition. Had Plath taken Hughes's manuscripts (recto), it would be unlikely that she would have crossed out her own draft after completion (verso), and such cross-outs appear in the Plath manuscript holdings elsewhere. The opposite, with Hughes using Plath's (recto) drafts, crossing them out, and drafting his own material (verso) seems far more likely. The other conflict here is with alternating type and script by each poet. Such complexities could contribute much to discussions of the politics and biographical contexts of Plath's and Hughes's composition methods, but it would entail the kind of careful scholarship seen in Lawrence Rainey's reconstruction of the various typescripts of T.S. Eliot's *The Waste Land* in 'Eliot Among the Typists' (*Mo/Mo* 12[2005] 27–84). This form of careful archival and editorial scholarship has yet to fully develop in Plath criticism, and there are no major innovations that will revise our view of Plath's cultural and familial contexts in Helle's volume. It is, however, a valuable contribution to general Plath scholarship and begins the much-needed discussion of the range of Plath manuscripts and typescripts available.

Bethany Hicok's *Degrees of Freedom: American Women Poets and the Women's College, 1905–1955* contains a strong chapter on Plath as well. The same focus on biographical alignment of the poetic works and the restoration of her own vision for *Ariel* prior to Hughes's editorship recurs here, but Hicok's focus on the educational background that led to Plath's works is innovative. The archival work involved in Hicok's reconstruction of Plath's time at Smith College is significant and should present new information and interpretative opportunities for scholars, in particular the work on Plath's own records of her education. The New Critical focus of her professors and her own acquisition of works by the New Critics during her studies is put to good use here, and Plath's struggle with these influences is convincing. The tension over positive female role models in poetry is palpable, and Hicok works this in tandem with the McCarthy fear of lesbianism, which she retraces through Plath's poetry and journals. A more striking critical turn is hinted at here as well, though Hicok only intimates that Plath's thematic and stylistic decisions reflect her attempt at a revision to the New Criticism and a proposition with regard to alternative critical ventures. The same thematic foci are repeated in the volume as a whole. The major chapters are dedicated to Marianne Moore and Plath, two chapters each, with another on Elizabeth Bishop and one on 1930s poetry in general, which is also largely concerned with Bishop. This scope is compelling, and the volume's general argument with regard to the importance of the educational experiences of American female poets is hard to challenge. The only weakness is the division of the book between two major poets, which makes the other inclusions seem more minor than they need be, Bishop in particular. The chapter on the journal *Con Spirito* takes up its avant-garde intentions and the network that developed around it. These two topics, networks and revisions to the established modernist discourse, merit expansion, and the development of a theory of poetry that Hicok proposes here is compelling. Elizabeth Bishop's revisionary reading of Eliot in the journal, as the book details, demonstrates the 'strong' poetess's misprision of her predecessors. Harold Bloom's influence seems implicit here, but the argument with regard to a belated form of modernist writing and a distinctly

American women's poetry deriving from the educational background of the major poets makes good sense. As Hicok retraces Bishop's revisions to Eliot's 'Tradition and the Individual Talent' and Gerard Manley Hopkins, it seems increasingly possible to suggest that the network surrounding the authors in her volume constitutes an inadvertent movement in American poetry. Arising from common material conditions, this seems more than reasonable. This development is most closely tied to Bishop when Hicok reads her works closely. That each chapter moves from social to critical context and finally to a close reading of the works is useful for both research and lecture preparation; however, as a whole, the book ends with only a short coda. A larger critical project within which the book as a whole might fit seems wanting, though amply prepared for. That 'Women's colleges provided an important cultural and critical space for American women poets and played a central role in their poetic development' is indisputable by the end of Hicok's book, but the cultural paradigms and poetic movements developing from this demonstrated fact still offer other scholars a useful continuation of Hicok's work.

Elizabeth Willis's edited collection *Radical Vernacular: Lorine Niedecker and the Poetics of Place* does much to establish Niedecker's importance to multiple movements in American poetry, and the book itself challenges critics to continue working on this overlooked poet. Willis is surprisingly convincing in her argument for Niedecker's contributions, and Michael Davidson's opening chapter sets the regional tone that the volume takes up repeatedly. However, Eleni Sikelianos's 'Life Pops from a Music Box Shaped Like a Gun: Dismemberments and Mendings in Niedecker's Figures' is perhaps the most provocative chapter. Sikelianos presents Niedecker's works in relation to the major armed conflicts during her life. As is noted at several points in the volume, Niedecker has been most strongly aligned with Louis Zukovsky, and the resistance to war, and the dismembered and broken nature of her war images comes as no surprise. Their extent, however, is a reminder. One unclear topic in the volume is Niedecker's politics, and the current tensions over various forms of ecoregionalism, in particular left-libertarian ecoregionalism and ecofeminism, are not resolved here; yet Niedecker's importance to these debates seems certain in view of the analyses put forward in this book. In response to the book's title, which 'vernacular' seems clear even while which 'radical' remains less fully developed. While one could hope such questions could be resolved in a volume with such a specific focus, the need to cover critical ground that is not yet fully established is also constantly visible. For this reason, the book is particularly useful: it establishes Niedecker's importance and the nature of the discussions that are likely to continue to develop with regard to her works and the New York Objectivists in general. At the same time, it provides an invaluable resource for scholars still unfamiliar with the still growing body of critical work on Niedecker. The recurrent gestures towards previous essays on Niedecker by Marjorie Perloff and Peter Nicholls (both from 1996) point to the strength as well as relative scarcity of critical work. Most importantly, the volume directs attention to not only the value of work on Niedecker but also the importance of her work to other poets and the work already established around them.

Planets on Tables: Poetry, Still Life, and the Turning World by Bonnie Costello stands out as an exceptional book this year. Her writing is genuinely enjoyable to read, yet its critical insights and theoretical scope are impressive. Opening with a direct disruption to the politics of poetry, using the usual suspects of Adorno, Yeats and Auden, Costello returns attention to the social life of each work, rather than the private world of their individual 'planets'. In so doing, she positions her discussion of the 'still life' works of poetry and their painterly qualities within a broader discussion of the tension between aesthetic and social imperatives in twentieth-century American poetry in general. In some respects, the book reminds one of Jack Stewart's *Color, Space, and Creativity: Art and Ontology in Five British Writers*, but the careful excavation of the texts is more firmly established here. The deftness with which Costello moves from Leon Trotsky to Edna St Vincent Millay or George Oppen is impressive, especially since her common argumentative thread remains clear throughout. The solution to competing imperatives in this charged poetic and political climate emerges, for Costello, as the quotidian, which re-establishes a private/public dichotomy such that 'Still life is, then, one of many ways the arts find to bring the distant near and to relate to the world and public events within the private life'. In this sense, the quotidian arises from material conditions, yet the poetic vision of such conditions and their politics is inevitably seen from the vantage of personal daily life. From this premise, Costello develops five chapters, one each on Wallace Stevens, William Carlos Williams, Elizabeth Bishop, Joseph Cornell and Richard Wilbur. In each chapter, the same clarity of writing and keenness of attention are present, and even while dealing with texts familiar to most scholars Costello finds new perspectives that will hold attention.

Another volume from 2008 that stands out as deserving particular attention (and likely to draw significant responses) is Anita Patterson's *Race, American Literature and Transnational Modernisms*. The general perspective of the volume derives from new modernist studies, with Edgar Allan Poe and Derek Walcott as outliers in the book as a whole. The central, and most elaborate, chapters are concerned with mainstream modernist figures such as T.S. Eliot, Ezra Pound, Langston Hughes, Wilson Harris and those closely related in criticism, such as Walt Whitman, Jules Laforgue and Jacques Roumain. Much of the critical perspective here derives from Paul Giles, James Clifford and Simon Gikandi, and in this regard there are no new theoretical perspectives that drive Patterson's most recent work to differ from her previous volumes. However, the main critical intervention of the volume does not attempt a new critical paradigm in this regard. Instead, it draws attention to the transnational networks involved in what has already been established in critical studies of race and colonialism in modernist American literature. In essence, as networks emerge as an influential way to align works and writers, the traditional racial and national bodies that identify them are minimized. In many respects, this makes sense in a period of increasing international migration, and it would seem a necessary revision given the bi-national and racially diverse nature of the authors Patterson selects. Nonetheless, the polemical value of this stance is important. To argue that Eliot's works are defined by their interest in French symbolist poetry and American national literary heritage seems commonplace, but to then use this breadth as a lever against the received narratives of poets of specific nationalist schools or movements is still relatively new. Such practices have become increasingly explicit since the late 1990s, but Patterson does much to make them a subject of discussion themselves. Historical studies of the reception of various modernisms as they migrate around the globe have grown in number, but Patterson's contention that such migrations return and that the varying modernisms are themselves born from previous transnational movements is useful. The productive blending of biographical studies of literary networks of influence and allusion with critical readings of the works in their social context (in tandem with Patterson's acumen for postcolonial theory) points to a developing trend in transnational modernisms in general, though more prominently with regard to prose. In a more traditional sense, Patterson's reconstruction of the sequence of influence between Laforgue, Eliot and Hughes (which is in many respects the core of the book) will e sure to interest scholars working each of these authors individually.

Benzi Zhang takes a kindred approach to networks of influence that deny singular views of national schools or movements. His volume, *Asian Diaspora Poetry in North America* is more theoretically oriented than Patterson's work—repeatedly having recourse to Julia Kristeva, notions of liminality, identity and so forth—but it is also more attached to a sense of ethnicity in its network of authors. Both American poetry and poetry itself are secondary to Zhang's development of the critical problems of diaspora, identity, and borders. For instance, Joy Kogawa, a Canadian writer known almost exclusively for her prose writings, appears in the volume exclusively in relation to her poetic works, even as Maxine Hong Kingston appears in the same sections through recourse to her prose. In this regard, a broader sense of literary work rather than only poetry would have been helpful, especially since several of the authors work in both poetry and prose, and they also develop the same critical concepts in both areas of work. It is too much to ask, but the focus on blurred notions of place and the overlapping of place and identity also offer opportunities to connect with multiple diasporic literatures, perhaps most easily Jewish and Greek works from the same periods. Regardless, Zhang's most immediate contribution in this cogent study is his timely presentation of authors and works that ought to be more familiar to scholars and critics working in twentieth-century American literature. Several have become widely read through programmes meant to instil 'diversity' in undergraduate education (both Kingston and Kogawa fit here), but Zhang's insistence on reading these authors as part of a diaspora consistently returning to the same theoretical issues and resolving the same problematics in their works presents them in a new light. Like Patterson's work, Zhang's seeks to move these authors into a general discussion of twentieth-century works drawing on dispersed networks of influence and distribution. As a comparatist, Zhang is also very strong at presenting works from diverse cultural backgrounds with a sense of their mutual circumstances of material production, and in this sense his focus on diasporic writing and the problems arising from its conditions is pertinent to the broad range of works on which he draws. The book is also commendable for drawing attention to such poets as Cyn Zarco, Rita Wong and Arthur Sze, who are known locally but too often fail to appear in broader studies of North American writing.

Lesley Wheeler's *Voicing American Poetry: Sound and Performance from the 1920s to the Present* rounds out 2008 in this review. The subjects are more traditional in Wheeler's work, but her focus on the genealogy of American poetic performance is extraordinarily informative and suggests very useful reimaginings of specific works. Wheeler plays off the distinction between voice in the text itself and the voice of performance, in particular when these two are in conflict for a variety of possible reasons. This productive tension is not used reductively, with only one form of voice lending authenticity. Instead, Wheeler points to the growing sense of individual voice in the text itself, often entirely independent of the commodity of poetic performance. She is careful in balancing the shifting performance practices for different periods and different poets (often constantly changing) in order to forward her thesis that the material conditions of production and distribution influence the nature of the work of art. In many respects, her nuanced excavation of the cultural context of works performed live (by both poets and professional readers), those transmitted by radio or via recordings, and the nature of 'voice' figuratively in the printed text would seem to immediately point to Theodor Adorno's notion of the work of art in the age of mass production and the potential for pseudo-individualization. Neither Adorno nor Walter Benjamin appears in the text; nor does critical theory's contribution to analyses of the material production and dissemination of mass culture. Relatively little in the way of cultural studies enters the book, which is more specifically rooted in modernist studies. This is the only surprising critical lacuna. Nonetheless, as a history and nuanced reading of the varying traditions in poetry performance in America over the past century, Wheeler's work is certain to become a standard reference. It is also lucid and remarkable in its range and historical detail.

2. Fiction 1900–1945

David H. Evans contends, in *William Faulkner, William James, and the American Pragmatic Tradition*, that, contra the critical consensus, Faulkner was a pragmatist rather than an idealist. Evans focuses on James's new 'conception of truth', which he views as fundamentally narratival. While acknowledging Faulkner's 'guileless countryman' pose, Evans argues that approaching the writer via a philosophical approach is profitable, especially given his obsession with time. Seeing a convergence between Jamesian and Faulknerian temporality, Evans argues that Faulkner exhibited a 'commitment to constant change'. This change represented itself in a tension between Emersonian optimism and a past that reveals 'a process of ongoing degradation, its moral stability a dubious and delusive mirage'. Faulkner's style, which employs a 'deferred period', enacts James's critique of the 'absolute mind', which adheres to the 'great transcendental metaphor ... a grammatical sentence'. Evans suggests that Faulkner's pragmatism manifests itself via an awareness of the confidence man and his ability to create community where none existed before and demonstrate that 'truths are *made*, not found'. Further, Evans avers that Jamesian 'verification' competes with previous conceptions of time that oppose subjective and objective time, and places both ideas on a continuum similar to one used by Faulkner in his narratives. Evans applies his theory to three of Faulkner's novels, *The Hamlet*, *Absalom, Absalom!*, and *Go Down, Moses*. Through his lens of pragmatism, Evans remarks that readers need to downplay Faulkner's Gothicism and scrutinize the way that his books 'celebrate the unfinished openness of human life and the possibility of fabricating new futures'.

Theresa M. Towner's *The Cambridge Introduction to William Faulkner* offers a concise overview of Faulkner's life and major works. Towner does a nice job of relating Faulkner's various experiences, such as during the First World War and in Hollywood. While she primarily summarizes Faulkner's life, Towner does offer some effective quotations, such as one he delivered at his Nobel Prize ceremony: 'I feel that this award was not made to me as a man but to my work—a life's work in the agony and sweat of human spirit, not for glory and least of all for profit, but to create out of the materials of the human spirit something which did not exist before.' The bulk of the book provides brief discussions of Faulkner's novels and stories, from *Soldier's Pay* and *Mosquitoes* to *Light in August* and *The Reivers*. Towner's prose and analysis are fairly light, as exemplified by this comment on *The Sound and the Fury*: 'Yes, there are two Quentins in this novel; and yes, one of them is a girl.' However, Towner does make some prescient comments, such as her point that in *The Town* Flem will be watched by a 'coalition that understands the measures he is willing to take as he moves toward [a] publicly respectable place'. Another section of the book concerns 'contexts', and informs readers about how Faulkner responded to contemporary and historical events in his fiction. Towner shows, for instance, that Faulkner wrote letters to the editors of several papers and in 1947 considered himself the best contemporary American writer after Thomas Wolfe. The book's final section examines Faulkner's critical reception. Designed for undergraduates, the work provides a serviceable, if brief, look at Faulkner.

In *Faulkner and Welty and the Southern Literary Tradition*, Noel Polk collects a number of essays on a variety of topics concerning Faulkner and Welty, from war and communism to domestic violence and alienation. Polk explains that he is more interested in pursuing the minor chords of both writers instead of investigating the larger themes more typically studied in a book-length work. The title essay examines how Faulkner's 'epic' concerns compare with Welty's 'domestic' ones. In the next chapter, Polk discusses the Luxembourg garden scene in *Sanctuary*, which he views as a 'setting culturally at odds with the rest of the novel's location in the rural and unsophisticated' South. In the Snopes trilogy, Polk sees that masculine identity 'defines and destroys itself at one end or the other of the continuum between [the] hard and soft phallus'. Other essays trace racism in *Go Down, Moses*, family in Welty's fiction, and the 'domestic darkness' of Welty's *The Ponderable Heart*. In general, the essays have a meandering, oral feel to them. While they often make interesting observations, they frequently are too laconic at the holistic level.

While previous examinations of Ernest Hemingway's high school career have illuminated readers' understanding of his evolution as a writer and a man, none do so with the thoroughness of Morris Buske's *Hemingway's Education, a Re-examination: Oak Park High School and the Legacy of Principal Hanna*. Buske, who taught at Oak Park High and who had unprecedented access to Hemingway materials, recontextualizes the school's curriculum and explains how principal John Calvin Hanna implemented a series of broad—if short-lived—reforms, at the centre of which was an 'emphasis on both composition and English literature'. In his first chapter, Buske demonstrates how, influenced by Charles W. Eliot, Hanna (who left after Hemingway's first year) updated antiquated reading lists and urged teachers in all disciplines to assign writings. Buske then discusses Hemingway's first year, the only one for which none of his compositions is extant. However, several of Hemingway's sister's themes exist, which offer a sense of the topics expected—a heavy dose of mythology. The next chapter, on Hemingway's sophomore year, offers more specifics, including the assertion that Fannie Biggs was the first to encourage Hemingway to become a writer. The chapter on Hemingway's junior year, in addition to revealing the syllabus for English III, examines Hemingway's revisions of a composition and notes that this was the year that the young man—in his own words—decided to embark on his 'career of study'. Buske recounts Hemingway's senior year and discusses an untitled story, probably influenced by *Heart of Darkness*, that deals with the Spanish–American War. The book contains a multitude of early photographs of Hemingway and his Oak Park environment, and an appendix publishes some of Hemingway's high school compositions—with titles such as 'Brooks' and 'How to Hike'—for the first time. A sample of the prose reveals a young Hemingway striving to build tension for his audience: 'I felt the rush of the canoe like a runaway horse, the fending off of black rocks with my short cant hook handle, that awful moment when we jammed and I heard the ribs crack.' In all, Buske's short book offers some exciting new material to consider with respect to Hemingway's development.

Mark P. Ott's *A Sea of Change: Ernest Hemingway and the Gulf Stream, a Contextual Biography* also culls under-studied primary material from a Hemingway archive, this time the Hemingway collection at the JFK Library in Boston. A renowned fisherman, Hemingway kept detailed fishing logs full of 'short, precise, representational descriptions of what he observed on the Gulf Stream', which Ott employs to 'explain the stylistic transformation' between the publication of *A Farewell to Arms* and *The Old Man and the Sea*. Discussing Hemingway's first encounters with deep-sea fishing, Ott contends that for Hemingway, the Gulf Stream 'allows one to heighten one's own human experience through intimate contact with nature'. Ott argues that the Gulf Stream holds tremendous symbolic power for Hemingway, both as an atemporal, mythic space and as a locus of human struggle with nature. Ott amply quotes Hemingway's logs and explains that they reveal both how Hemingway matured from a novice fisherman to a world-class one and how he 'is creating a document that is meant to teach the reader why things happened rather than merely record their occurrence'. Additionally, Ott investigates Hemingway's aesthetics and considers various labels such as realism, naturalism and modernism. Ott closely reads both *To Have and Have Not* and *The Old Man and the Sea* and indicates that, in these books, Hemingway learns what is underneath the iceberg. According to Ott, both in philosophy and form, Hemingway became more precise and immediate.

Teaching Hemingway's The Sun Also Rises, comprising seventeen essays edited by Peter L. Hays, offers pedagogical approaches to one of Hemingway's most taught novels. Hays's introduction enumerates the reasons for the need for a book on teaching the novel: obscure topical references, a distant historical milieu, the Hemingway myth, and esoteric knowledge (such as bullfighting). Hays's contributors aim towards a variety of settings, from secondary schools and two-year colleges to research universities, and they tackle a host of concerns, ranging from anti-Semitism and alcohol to masculinity and values. Unlike essays in similar volumes, those in Hays's book supplement their discussion of classroom practice with reading schedules, study questions, paper topics and the like, all of which will provide immediate assistance to teachers. Additionally, the various chapters provide a wealth of strategies, such as reading passages aloud so that students may '*hear* the cosmopolitan cacophony', looking for 'echo scenes', critiquing the Hemingway code, and employing logotherapy to show how various characters find (or don't find) meaning in their lives. The essays provide the personal reflection that typifies volumes of this sort, but they also offer theoretically informed discussions. For instance, Amy Vondrak's essay applies gender theory and 'the ramifications of phallic masculinity' to Brett and Jake, while Thomas Smyth considers a Marxist approach (among others) and suggests demonstrating to students how Jake 'use[s] economic power to create a masculine identity not based on sexuality'. Some of the essays—such as Ellen Andrews Knodt's concentration on active learning—explore a single general approach, while others—such as Lawrence R. Broder's essay on intertextuality—present a series of topics. The book's contributors also actively seek to inject student voices into the discourse, and they frequently cite student comments and papers. In all, the volume presents a fresh look at Hemingway's classic.

Citing the impact of the burgeoning film industry on Fitzgerald, Guatam Kundu's *Fitzgerald and the Influence of Film: The Language of Cinema in the Movies* explores the writer's visual and aural elements and links them to cinematic techniques. Kundu claims that 'visual categorization' is both a hallmark of Fitzgerald's thematic concerns and a centrepiece of his narrative strategy, which 'create[s] a visualized world that is both recognizable and yet more vivid, intense, and dramatically charged than actuality'. Kundu further suggests that Fitzgerald borrows from a cinematic vocabulary. For instance, in *This Side of Paradise*, Kundu suggests the staccato form recognized by many readers in fact mimics the discontinuous 'frames' of a movie as it offers a 'series of *partialized* views' that fill various 'establishing shots' with a series of close-ups. Kundu stops short of suggesting that Fitzgerald's adoption of conventions analogous to filmic ones was conscious; he employs them 'in abundance' nonetheless. The host of cinematographic techniques utilized by Fitzgerald includes panning, close-ups, flashbacks, freeze frames, and dissolves. Kundu demonstrates that Fitzgerald also makes use of montage, 'sound track'-like verbal equivalents, and colour/lighting. Besides *This Side of Paradise*, Kundu concentrates on *The Great Gatsby*, *Tender Is the Night* and *The Love of the Last Tycoon*.

Keith Gandal's *The Gun and the Pen: Hemingway, Fitzgerald, Faulkner and the Fiction of Mobilization* examines the effects of failing to serve overseas in combat positions during the First World War on three key American novelists. Focusing on *The Sun Also Rises*, *The Great Gatsby* and *The Sound and the Fury*, Gandal writes that the 'famous sense of woundedness, diminishment, and loss in these works ... stems not principally from the disillusionment or the alienation from traditional values ... but ... from personal rejection by the U.S. army'. The new scientific approach to the military and its concomitant meritocracy, Gandal contends, shocked and 'emasculated' the three writers and allowed educated ethnic soldiers to enter the traditionally affluent, Anglo-Saxon realm of officer training. To support his thesis, Gandal examines archival documents pertaining to the authors' military service. Discussing Fitzgerald's Jay Gatz, Gandal suggests that the writer modelled him on 'ethnic' officers who outperformed him in the military—a fact that made Fitzgerald bitterly include Gatz's fabrication of his educational background. Gandal contextualizes such promotions, however, through discussion of the army's use of intelligence testing. Gandal speculates that Faulkner's Benjy was derived partially from the writer's interest in such testing's efforts to eliminate the 'feeble minded' from the ranks. In addition, Gandal discusses the impact of the army's rhetoric of 'clean' sexual health—and its ineffective effort to steer American soldiers away from prostitutes and 'charity girls'— which made a major impression on the three writers, who infused issues of sexuality throughout their novels. For instance, Gandal suggests that Hemingway's Jake Barnes, who frequents prostitutes, offers a sophisticated, ironic alternative to the 'sentimental moralism' of the American army. Gandal adds a final chapter that discusses Djuna Barnes, Nathanael West and Henry Miller in relation to the relatively explicit anti-venereal disease campaign.

Considering John Dos Passos's diminished critical reputation, Jun Young Lee writes in *History and Utopian Disillusion: The Dialectical Politics in the Novels of John Dos Passos* that the writer's turn towards conservatism coupled with a New Critical abhorrence of his political radicalism alienated two key audiences that could have championed him. Building on the work of Barbara Foley, however, Lee argues that Dos Passos 'exposes the problems and absurdities of the modern capitalist society by dialectical totalization, thereby trying to evoke a utopian impulse as a reaction to the present dystopia, the modern capitalist society'. Lee begins the book with an overview of various dialectical paradigms, including those proffered by Hegel, Marx, Althusser, Benjamin and Feuerbach. His next chapter focuses on American capitalism, paying particular attention to the notion of American exceptionalism and the dark side of Jazz Age prosperity, such as the fact that the top 1 per cent of families 'earned as much as 42 percent of the low-income families'. Such disparities, Lee argues, galvanized Dos Passos in his view that America oppressed its workers. Lee then looks at how Dos Passos turned his political consciousness to his early fiction. Examining *One Man's Initiation: 1917*, and *Three Soldiers* and *Manhattan Transfer*, Lee traces how Dos Passos's use of juxtaposition is limited in the first two novels by its reliance on 'bohemianism and radical individualism' and in the latter by its muted treatment of 'the underlying social and historical causes' of capitalist alienation. Lee privileges the *USA* trilogy as Dos Passos's signature achievement in dialectical mediation and his orientation towards 'impersonality, objectivity, and collectivity'. In these novels, Lee argues, Dos Passos finally expunges the romantic protagonists who tacitly clashed with the ideology of themes. Further, in the trilogy Dos Passos's modern chronicle-like montage eschews closure and invites readers to engage in a consideration of American capitalism. Ultimately, Lee observes that Dos Passos 'articulate[es] a utopia [by] rely[ing] on images of the present utopia, unfulfilled needs, and the dissatisfaction of the existing order in a dialectical way'.

Suggesting that Djuna Barnes prefigured many elements of poststructuralism and feminism, Diane Warren writes in *Djuna Barnes' Consuming Fictions* that the writer creates a 'tension between autonomy and cultural constraint' in her fiction. In pursuing her ideas, Warren employs a number of theorists, including Bakhtin, Mulvey, Kristeva, Cixous and Butler. Warren claims that Barnes's adoption of carnivalesque techniques 'emphasises the anti-hierarchical but also . . . raises questions about the limits of subversions'. Reviewing the diverse criticism of Barnes, Warren asserts that 'Barnes' subtle and ambivalent texts retain the ability to unsettle their readers' ethical responses'. Making use of Barnes's journalism, Warren primarily discusses *Ryder*, *Ladies Almanack*, *Nightwood*, *The Antiphon* and *Spillway*, arguing that Barnes refuses to exchange one hierarchical cultural code for another, and that instead she 'complicates the question of verifiability'. According to Warren, Barnes 'challenges the role of the reader/spectator' and its 'constructed nature'. Further, the writer, in examining taboo topics such as lesbianism, employs radical intertextuality and polyphony. As a whole, Barnes's writing is 'uncontainable' in its interrogation and satirizing of contemporary issues of gender, technology and psychoanalysis, among others.

The 2008 volume of the *Thomas Wolfe Review* contained a number of interesting articles on the Southern author and his works, including Paula Gallant Eckard's 'Narrative, Work, and Grief in Thomas Wolfe's *The Lost Boy*' (*TWR* 32[2008] 7–21), which focuses on the narrative implications of the labour involved in grieving. Gallant observes that the novella investigates how narratives 'express the unexpressible and . . . speak to the paradox and burden that death creates for the living'. Cash Wiley compares Wolfe and Charles W. Chesnutt in 'What Do Charles Chesnutt and Thomas Wolfe Have to Tell us about North Carolina?' (*TWR* 32[2008] 22–33), an article that looks at the autobiographical elements of their musings on their childhood state. Wiley notes that 'when both Chesnutt and Wolfe chose to accurately and realistically portray the violence, racism, and class struggles of their region, they were challenged by a literary establishment that preferred a safer, more agreeable view of the South'. In his Thomas Wolfe Student Prize-winning essay, 'Paper Doll Matinee: Thomas Wolfe's Theatre' (*TWR* 32[2008] 62–9), Chris Prewitt disputes the characterization of Wolfe as a 'failed' playwright, arguing that critical and popular acceptance are not the only criteria that one should employ to judge the plays' success. Prewitt claims not that the plays themselves function at the highest artistic level but that the techniques Wolfe employed enabled him to 'create fiction of the highest calibre with the ability to re-create memory, making every moment of his life a dramatic production and every soul he encountered a character, allowing audiences to relive the moment, and staging an autobiographical matinee'. Hiroshi Tsunemoto presents the intriguing theory that Wolfe, renowned for his prodigiously expansive novels, was a 'haiku-minded poet' in 'Thomas Wolfe's Haiku World' (*TWR* 32[2008] 94–100). Tsunemoto notes Wolfe's predilection for natural imagery and suggests that many of his sentences, while not conforming to the syllabic requirements of the form, 'are so sophisticated that there is a spiritual kinship between him and the poetic practitioners of Japanese haiku'.

At first blush (and perhaps second blush) Gertrude Stein, the radical modernist, and Edith Wharton, the committed realist, seem polar opposites, but in *The Making of Americans in Paris: The Autobiographies of Edith Wharton and Gertrude Stein*, Noel Sloboda discovers that 'they iterate comparable views on identity, autobiography, and, most significantly, what landmarks define the terrain of the early twentieth century'. In his first chapter, Sloboda examines the problems inherent in studying autobiography, including the unreliability of memory, the inadequacy of language, and the limits of persona. Sloboda grounds this discussion of autobiography in Wharton's *A Backward Glance* and Stein's *The Autobiography of Alice B. Toklas*, and he suggests that both books 'undermine the authenticity of the figure[s] designated as [themselves]'. The book's second chapter investigates the context surrounding the production of both books and attempts to demonstrate why both women tackled autobiographical projects when they did. Sloboda charges that the pair were less interested in discussing past accomplishments than they were in strengthening their position in the publishing world. Over the next three chapters, Sloboda explains that Wharton and Stein employed popular models in crafting their stories, and that their overlapping subjects (Paris, Henry James, and the First World War) fed the appetite of a public increasingly interested in autobiography. With respect to Paris, the writers fed an increasing appetite for literary tourism (spurred on by the Depression) by drawing on their more esoteric pre-war experiences in Paris. As for James, Sloboda argues that Wharton and Stein 'take advantage of him as a commodity of the literary marketplace'. In discussing their war experiences, Sloboda asserts that despite being known for their boundless imaginations, neither woman transcends the standard 'conversion narrative' that traced how they overcame disorientation and pitched in to help the Cause. Sloboda concludes that both writers, regardless of their reputations, 'integrate elements from fashionable literary modes ... and transform themselves to suit the tastes and expectations of the common reader'.

Wharton gets treated—along with Hamlin Garland, Frank Norris, Theodore Dreiser and Willa Cather—in a different, and less flattering, way in Donald Pizer's *American Naturalism and the Jews: Garland, Norris, Dreiser, and Cather*. In this very short book, Pizer, generally regarded as the foremost expert on naturalism, tackles the anti-Semitic writings of some of the most important American writers of the late nineteenth and early twentieth centuries. Central to Pizer's analysis is the paradox that anti-Semitism, 'with its underlying atavistic hate and fear of the stranger/outsider', could coexist with 'the more enlightened character of their values, writings, and activities' in other arenas, such as poverty and women's rights. Pizer first investigates Garland, who, though he 'lacked the rabid vehemence of the full-scale anti-Semite' and never attacked Jews in his public writings, 'express[ed] a nonactivist anti-Semitism' that ignored or downplayed the more full-throated prejudice of figures such as Henry Ford and Mary Elizabeth Lease, a fact that suggests the writer felt the Jews to be a growing problem. In contrast to Garland's genteel anti-Semitism, Norris's is perfectly vicious, and, according to Pizer, reveals a 'full and intense commitment to a belief that views other races both as inferior and as a threat to the Anglo-Saxon racial makeup'. Unlike the racialist arguments of Norris, who died before such anti-Semitism took on explosive political dimensions, those pursued by Dreiser were largely economic and based in stereotypes of Hollywood Shylocks. Interestingly, Dreiser held to his views even when challenged by the likes of Mike Gold and when Hitler's ascendance made public anti-Semitism anathema. Pizer discusses Wharton and Cather in a single chapter, and observes that neither writer dealt with Jewish issues in the public manner of their male contemporaries. However, in their fictive portraits of Jews, both Wharton and Cather, Pizer alleges, divulge a 'foundation of patrician distrust of the supposed Jewish emphasis on the economic in all matters'. In each case, Pizer closes, the writers in question failed to note the gap between their quest for social justice and that sought after by the Jews, and they also neglected the impact of environmental determinism on their own perceptions.

Willa Cather's Francophilic tendencies are examined in Stéphanie Durrans's *The Influence of French Culture on Willa Cather*. Durrans observes of Cather's canon that 'There is hardly a novel without a character of French extraction at its center or, at least, appearing at a pivotal moment.' Despite having an 'imperfect' mastery of spoken French, Cather could read it well, and she adored French culture. Nevertheless, Durrans observes that Cather never claimed to have been directly influenced by her favourite French authors—such as Flaubert, Sand and Balzac—although Durrans posits that the impact went far beyond simple allusions and was 'discursively encoded' in Cather's work. Durrans examines a number of Cather's texts, including *O Pioneers!*, *Death Comes for the Archbishop* and *The Professor's House*, and explores a variety of topics, such as the femme fatale, historiography, and Romanticism. Durrans alleges that Cather adopts the deep structure of several key writers in her novels, as when she utilizes Zola in *O Pioneers!* as a 'subtext . . . [that] could . . . be seen as a way of undermining the foundations of her own text by questioning the actual relevance of Romantic visions of love in the real world'. Durrans ably shows parallel after parallel between various of Cather's French influences and the American writer's work. From *Song of the Lark*'s echoes of George Sand's strategy of 'conciliat[ing] art and love through a twist in the plot' to the 'web of intertextual relationships' in *A Lost Lady*, Cather troped on the thematic and aesthetic concerns of her French literary mentors. Durrans charges that Cather transports the French scene to the Nebraskan plains and 'makes [her] text a space of interaction and integration that still preserves the integrity of her models'.

David Porter, in his *On the Divide: The Many Lives of Willa Cather*, examines the conflicting and evolving ways in which Cather represented herself in her fiction, in her marketing activities and in private. Porter points out that Cather had a 'penchant for playing roles' and 'lived on different planes'. He sees the primary split as being between an iconic, somewhat remote, image and that of a 'tireless and savvy go-getter'. The former representation is Cather-as-Artist, far removed from petty quotidian concerns, while the latter reveals a scrappy businesswoman concerned with sales and promotion. Porter looks closely at dust-jacket blurbs and other, often anonymous, material and suggests that because of stylistic similarities to known texts, Cather wrote the copy. Porter notes that the earliest promotional materials divulge Cather's insecurities and seem 'amateurish and overdone'. A decade later, however, shows a much more confident Cather who is more restrained in her language but more ambitious in her claims. By 1940 the transformation is complete, and Porter suggests that the various blurbs 'offer important glimpses of how Cather wished to present herself'. Porter also looks at how Cather interacted with close friends Sarah Orne Jewett and Mary Baker Eddy, remarking that she saw in the women various parts of herself (containing 'very different values'), which she transcribed fictionally. Porter notes the 'contrasting pulls' of the two women and demonstrates how they manifest themselves in various of her works. Porter examines Cather's key works through the context of the divided self, and concludes that 'her capacity to see her own different and often warring sides ... is at the heart of her ability as a novelist to create characters so torn, so fascinating, so profoundly human'.

Cather is also the subject of John J. Murphy and Merril Maguire Skaggs's edited volume *Willa Cather: New Facts, New Glimpses, Revisions*. The book brings together twenty-one essays that mine the new Drew University Cather archive. The materials in the collection, based on 'the most important private collection of Catheriana in America', contains thousands of letters, Cather's handwritten corrections to her collected works and other rare gems. The editors divide the book into five sections, dealing respectively with Cather's relationship with the Menuhin family, her apprentice work, correspondence, fragmented texts and biography. Among the contributors are numerous Cather experts, including Joseph Urgo, Timothy Bintrim, David Porter and Janis P. Stout. The topics, driven by the Drew collection, range from Cather as illustrator and Cather as existentialist to the typescript of *Sapphira and the Slave Girl* and Cather's ballet training. One of the more important discoveries occurs in Suzi Yost Schulz and John A. Yost's essay, in which they demonstrate that Beatrix Florance—the addressee of several letters in the archive—'most probably served as the prototype for the character of Lucy Gayheart'. Murphy and Ann Romines both examine a four-page fragment, 'Cécile', that Cather rejected for inclusion in *Shadows on the Rock*. Another significant find in the archive is a unique typescript of *Sapphira and the Slave Girl*, which two contributors, Laura Winters and Charles W. Mignon, discuss in their essays. No doubt future scholars will benefit from these early looks at the new materials, and the book is an important synthesis of the collection.

The fifth volume of *Nexus: The International Henry Miller Journal* contains numerous articles on the infamous author. Miller's relationship with Herbert Read is recounted in James Gifford's 'Surrealism's Anglo-American Afterlife: The Herbert Read and Henry Miller Network' (*Nexus* 5[2008] 36–64). Examining the correspondence between the men, Gifford posits that the letters 'outline a neglected literary network that revises the accepted history of Anglo-American Surrealism's rapid rise and premature expiration'. Looking at Miller's crucial essay, D.A. Pratt's 'On Reading Henry Miller's *The World of Sex*' (*Nexus* 5[2008] 65–134) compares the extensive changes between the 1940 and 1957 redactions and lobbies for the primacy of the earlier version: 'the original text is simply stronger, virtually sentence by sentence—better worded, better described, and generally better in meaning'. Karl Orend recounts an unexamined incident in Miller's life—the ghost-writing of an academic thesis—in his 'Sex Dreams, Cancer, and Nightmares—Joseph Millard Osman, Anonymous Friends, the *Tribune* Crowd, and Henry Miller's Unknown Book' (*Nexus* 5[2008] 135–49). Orend opines that Miller infused the thesis with his own thoughts and that it reveals 'clear links to the social writing contained in *Moloch* ... and *The Mezzotints*'. An application of Foucault to Miller serves as the basis of Laraine Rungo's '"Between Ideas and Living": A Foucaultian Reading of Henry Miller' (*Nexus* 5[2008] 215–39). Rungo argues that Foucault's concept of author-function 'reveals the subversive nature of Miller's narrative style'. Garen Torikian compares *The Colossus of Maroussi* with *Big Sur and the Oranges of Hieronymus Bosch* in 'Finding the Bad in the Good: Miller's Greece and Big Sur Made Whole' (*Nexus* 5[2008] 247–58). Writing that both books divulge 'many characters hostile to Miller's sanity', Torikian observes that such figures 'are presented not as condemnations, but as warnings of what happens to those who do not trust themselves first'. The much-discussed topic of sexuality forms the basis of Phillip Mahoney's '*Tropic of Cancer* and Sexual Discourse: A "Critical Hole"' (*Nexus* 5[2008] 259–71). Mahoney notes that the novel prompts a situation in which the book 'both obeys the wider historical imperative to discuss sex and, paradoxically, creates a situation in which it becomes all the more necessary to talk about it'. Eric D. Lehman debates Welch Everman's application of Jean François Lyotard to Miller's writings in 'Henry Miller and Jean François Lyotard: The Aesthetics of the "Inhuman" in *Tropic of Cancer*' (*Nexus* 5[2008] 272–84). Lehman reverses Everman's contention that Miller embodies Lyotard's notion of the sublime, arguing that 'statements by Miller and Lyotard undermine ... Everman's claim that the narrator's task is the capturing of the sublime and the theoretical support for it'.

3. Fiction since 1945

Daniel Cordle's *States of Suspense: The Nuclear Ages, Postmodernism and United States Fiction and Prose* is about 'the ways in which various nuclear states of suspense that pertained between 1945 and 2005 inflected United

States fiction and prose'. More specifically, he works from the idea that suspense defines this period, and he defines suspense in relation to nuclear disaster or 'anticipation of disaster rather than disaster itself'. The first part of the book is devoted primarily to defining terms for his study as well as examining fiction from the Cold War era. It is in the second part of the book that Cordle turns to more contemporary fiction. Thomas Pynchon's *Gravity's Rainbow* and Paul Auster's *In the Country of Last Things* are examined in relation to the idea of the nuclear-threatened city. Additionally, Cordle looks at depictions of the nuclear-threatened family in works like Don DeLillo's *White Noise*. Cordle addresses, also, the nuclear-threatened planet in works like Kurt Vonnegut's *Cat's Cradle*. In the final chapters, Cordle examines the political nature of fiction in the nuclear age. Using texts like Tim O'Brien's *The Nuclear Age*, he explores the political dimensions of fiction in an age where the individual is represented as 'lost and powerless within such large and impenetrable systems'. Ultimately, Cordle's study aims to uncover the 'cultural effects of nuclear technology'; what he finds is the use of suspense in fiction and prose of the era.

According to Jay Prosser's introduction to the collection of essays entitled *American Fiction of the 1990s: Reflections of History and Culture*, fiction in the 1990s is 'vital, energized, and prolific in good part from being hooded into the decade—from reflecting and refracting American culture and history'. The collection is organized in five parts. The essays comprising part I deal with transnational borders, ethnicity and cultural translation. Part II looks at the role race plays in fiction in the 1990s; part III looks at historical narratives; part IV examines sexual imagery. The final portion of the collection examines postmodern technology, ending with Stephen J. Burn's essay, 'The End of Postmodernism: American Fiction at the Millennium'. Prosser is explicit in his attempt to position this collection of essays as a progressive step forward for New American studies. The 1990s, he claims, 'saw the emergence of approaches that question the mythologization surrounding old ideas of America as pastoral and the function of the frontier to advance history'. This newer way of thinking about American studies takes account of the 'international and global dimension of American literature and culture' and 'questions American innocence—ideals of America and the contemporary as exceptional'. It is in the context of New American studies that Prosser offers the fifteen essays contained in the pages of this collection.

John Duvall begins the introduction to *The Cambridge Companion to Don DeLillo* by arguing for the importance of DeLillo as a novelist and establishing the focus of this collection as being to 'provide the reader with an overview of DeLillo's achievement as a novelist, taking up the author's poetics and themes, as well as providing a more in-depth coverage of his best-known and most frequently taught novels'. The twelve essays contained in this book are divided into four parts. Part I deals with DeLillo's 'Aesthetic and Cultural Influences', part II looks at the author's early fiction, while part III looks at his major novels. Part IV is devoted to 'Themes and Issues'. Duvall's subtitle for the introduction of the volume, 'The Power of History and the Persistence of Mystery', reveals his preoccupation with how DeLillo's work intersects with history. 'DeLillo's final significance', Duvall writes, 'may lie in the way that, while he recognizes the power of history, he insists on the novel as a counterforce to the wound of history through the persistence of mystery'. Joseph Conte, in writing the conclusion to the collection, returns to DeLillo's look at history, by making connections between DeLillo's work and the fall of the towers on September 11, as well as the Cold War.

As the title aptly implies, Andrew Tate's *Contemporary Fiction and Christianity* examines the manner in which themes of Christianity appear in contemporary fiction. His book begins with a clear indication that he will 'focus on the surprising and sometimes prophetic friction generated by the antagonistic but animated relationship between the contemporary novel and Christian theology'. Tate does just this in the seven short chapters of this volume, and in doing so he looks at authors like Updike, DeLillo, Irving and Maine. According to Tate, postmodernism represents a 'post-secular' culture and, as such, its fiction includes 'questions of religious reading, the return of the miraculous; the heretical impulse and the significance of apocalyptic visions'. The chapters of the book, in fact, are loosely organized around these issues. Tate's conclusion arrives at the insight that 'the contemporary novel has become a space in which sacred and secular concerns converge in surprising ways'.

In his book *Colonialism and the Emergence of Science Fiction*, John Rieder synthesizes two areas of English studies—the early history of science fiction and the 'history and discourses of colonialism'. The most obvious insight implied by such a synthesis is, even by the author's standards, not the most innovative one. Rieder writes that the 'thesis that colonialism is a significant historical context for early science fiction in not an extravagant one'. However, Rieder aims his scholarship not at identifying the connection between colonialism and science fiction, but to the questions of 'how and to what extent the stories engage colonialism'. Further, he does this in order to determine 'how early science fiction lives and breathes in the atmosphere of colonial history and its discourses, how it reflects or contributes to ideological production of ideas about the shape of history, and how it might, in varying degrees, enact a struggle over humankind's ability to reshape it'. Rieder's analysis encounters such issues as the colonial gaze, the appropriation of wealth and the construction of race.

4. Drama

Two exemplary monographs in the University of Michigan's Modern Dramatists series were released this year, one on Edward Albee and another on Suzan-Lori Parks.

The monograph on Edward Albee, still creative at 80, was written by Toby Zinman, Professor of English at University of the Arts in Philadelphia and also the theatre critic for the *Philadelphia Inquirer*. Zinman writes in a very lively style: 'Each of the plays has its own essay, facilitating access for the reader who, having seen a production or read a script, wants to know more. I imagine these essays as the basis of a silent dialogue between us.' The author also wants the reader to know that her reluctance to choose a particular kind of reading of the plays, i.e. feminist, Marxist, etc., 'echoes Albee's firm views' as illustrated in his 'Read Plays?'.

Along with the essential elements for a study of Albee—complete with a bibliography and chronology—she offers the reader an engaging trip through the development of Albee's work: 'Edward Albee's career began with shocking play, shocking in both its content and its redefinition of realism; *The Zoo Story* would radically alter American Theater in the second half of the twentieth century. And it is splendid that nearly half a century later, *The Goat* shocked audiences and critics again.' Albee's latest accomplishment is a prequel to *Zoo Story* but is yet unpublished.

The author of the second volume, Deborah Geis, Associate Professor at De Pauw University, is already known for her contribution to *Approaching the Millennium: Essays on Tony Kushner's Angels in America*, reviewed here in 2006. In the present monograph, she covers, in very readable prose, the wide-ranging accomplishments of Ms Parks. She discusses the major plays and puts them in context.

The insights given us in *The Selected Letters of Thornton Wilder*, compiled and edited by Jackson Bryer and Robin Gibbs Wilder, are invaluable. Bryer is a veteran of the sorting and annotating of letters; his skills can be seen in the excellent edition of *The Selected Letters of Eugene O'Neill* and the very popular *Dear Scott, Dearest Zelda: The Love Letters of F. Scott Fitzgerald and Zelda Fitzgerald*. Gibbs Wilder is a niece by marriage of Thornton Wilder and knew him well. As an independent scholar with a Ph.D. in history she is very well suited for the role she plays in this collection. The letters give us a glimpse into the world that Wilder inhabited—letters include those to famous people as well as more intimate letters to members of his family. Apparently, the playwright shines through in this correspondence, for there are snippets of dialogue and descriptions of scenes that foretell his talent of writing for the stage. The collection is divided into sections covering ten years each—for the historian and the casual reader alike. Included as well is a complete index for those seeking a quote or a literary connection. In addition to the obvious stature of Thornton Wilder, the fascinating subjects of his correspondence, and the pleasant read of the letters collected in this book, we must also acknowledge the important step Bryer and Gibbs Wilder have made in the study of the playwright with this present volume—it being only the third collection of Wilder's correspondence. The two previous collections are narrower in scope—*The Letters of Gertrude Stein and Thornton Wilder* [1996] and *A Tour of the Darkling Plain: The Finnegans Wake Letters of Thornton Wilder to Adaline Glasheen* [2001].

This year we have, finally, a very helpful and illuminating critique of *Spalding Gray's America* written by William Demastes. As a man whose friendship with Gray developed over the years and was continued through a correspondence, Demastes brings his scholarly abilities together with his readable style and special insights and offers a book really worth reading. Not researched in detail for this book is the typical biographical information; that is left to Kathie Russo, Spalding Gray's widow, who is at work on just such a book. Instead, Demastes explores the man and his work as a unified artistic creation.

Continuum, in its Modern Theatre Guide series, has brought out *Tony Kushner's Angels in America* which, putting the cart before the horse, has us realize the happy occasion of this epic masterpiece's inclusion in the curriculum of theatre programmes. As is true to the series, this book gives a critical introduction to the play while also exploring aspects of the text in performance and production. Ken Nielsen, a Ph.D. candidate at CUNY—Graduate Center, has put together a thorough and intelligent companion to Tony Kushner's groundbreaking play.

Arthur Miller: 1915–1962 is simply titled and, simply put, the long-awaited biography of Arthur Miller by scholar Christopher Bigsby. Bigsby is a well-known and established authority on Miller as well as a novelist—so that along with accurate and informed data we have a compelling read. As Arthur Millerites are aware, this is not the first exploration of their favourite author's work by Bigsby, who should be a favourite author of the group in his own right by this point. His other titles include *Remembering Arthur Miller* [2005], *Arthur Miller and Company* [1990], *The Oxford Companion to Arthur Miller* [1997] and of course *Arthur Miller: A Study* [2005]. The significance of the latest volume of Bigsby's increases even more when we realize that, as a close friend of the playwright for over thirty years, the scholar has been able to base *Arthur Miller:1915–1962* on interviews and conversations that he had with the playwright and also on an archive put at his disposal on Miller's death in 2005.

Stone Tower: The Political Theater of Arthur Miller, written by Jeffrey D. Mason and published by the University of Michigan Press, concentrates on Miller as a political playwright. The book opens with a detailed discussion of Miller's testimony in 1956 before the House Committee on Un-American Activities. Mason goes on to a critique of Miller's essays and then a discussion of the playwright's response to certain themes as expressed in his dramas, including the Holocaust, the treatment of women and certain elements of male domination. In conclusion, he considers *Resurrection Blues* and proposes that Miller's angst over authority and power was unresolved.

Palgrave's Modern Dramatists series has brought out an expanded edition of Neil Carson's *Arthur Miller*. The revised and expanded edition of this popular 'handbook to Miller' now includes Miller's entire canon, including dramatic and non-dramatic texts. The late plays are discussed within the context of what is now Miller's complete body of work.

Ira Nadel has written *David Mamet: A Life in the Theater*, which is both a biography and an appreciation of the man and his work. He includes in his discussion the playwright's family life, but also makes certain to explore the influence that his Jewish upbringing, life in Chicago, and views on masculinity have had on his writing. Nadel offers us this telling quote from Mamet: 'The prevailing attitude was that if you could not express yourself correctly, you were dead meat. My father put an almost pathological emphasis on semantics ... There was a best word for everything and God help you if you didn't use it.'

Beyond the Golden Door: Jewish American Drama and Jewish American Experience is part of Palgrave's Studies in Theatre and Performance series. Written by Julius Novick—Professor Emeritus of Drama Studies at SUNY–Purchase and theatre critic for the *Village Voice*, this thought-provoking book considers the contribution of American dramatists of the twentieth century who were born Jewish. Included in the discussion are early works such as Raphaelson's *The Jazz Singer* and Elmer Rice's pieces, as well as Clifford Odets and Gertrude Berg's *Me and Molly*. A chapter is also devoted to Arthur Miller's Jewish characters. Jules Pfeiffer and Paddy Chayefsky share a chapter with Jon Robin Baitz, and Neil Simon is covered most extensively. A further chapter is devoted to musicals (*Fiddler on the Roof*, *Rags*, *Falsettos*). The 1980s and 1990s are represented by Alfred Uhry, Wendy Wasserstein and Tony Kushner, among others.

The author discusses from the start the significance of the Jewishness of each writer to his work: 'The American theater has not lacked for dramatists who were Jewish, but they are seldom thought of as "Jewish dramatists." One important reason for this is that until well after World War Two, Jewish American playwrights seldom concerned themselves exclusively, or primarily, or even occasionally with Jewish protagonists and Jewish themes.' The author is forthright about his opinions 'I reject the idea, tenaciously held in some quarters, that a writer who is a member of a minority group has some kind of moral duty to be always the representative of that minority group.'

African American Theater: A Cultural Companion by Glenda Dickerson is an excellent interactive guide for classroom use. The author brings a knowledge of both history and art to this survey of theatrical works from 1850 to the present. An emphasis is placed on the social realities which affected both the dramatists and various elements of the production process. The final pages are a discussion of how the past informs the work of August Wilson and Suzan-Lori Parks. Engrossing illustrations and an ample reference list are included.

At last there is a comprehensive volume available that pays tribute to and gives voice to the accomplishments of some previously unsung but highly influential creative people: they are the subject of *American Women Stage Directors of the Twentieth Century*, written by Anne Fliotsos and Wendy Vierow. Each director is given her own space—that is, ten pages of biographical and directing data as well as commentary by the subjects themselves which elucidate their individual/idiosyncratic processes as well as the business of stage directing in general. The volume includes basic information never before available in one place as well as sparkling gemlike tidbits from creative minds.

Three other books are also of note. *The New Music Theater: Seeing the Voice, Hearing the Body* by Eric Salzman and Thomas Desi is a comprehensive study of the musical. The authors divide their book into four parts, the first of which discusses music and sound, while the second examines the notion of spectacle. The third part examines the *mise-en-scène*, while the final section offers a theory and history of musical theatre. The book excludes opera, and defines 'new music theater' as 'theater that is music driven ... where, at the very least, music, language, vocalization, and physical movement exist, interact, or stand side by side in some kind of equality but performed by different performers and in a different social ambience than works normally categorized as operas'. The second book, *Poetics of Difference and Displacement: Twentieth-Century Chinese–Western Intercultural Theatre*, written by Min Tian and published by Hong Kong University Press, examines its subject from China's first theatrical contact with Europe to its contemporary incarnation. Tian shows the reciprocal nature of Chinese and Western theatre, from the importance of Asian theatre, to modernists such as Pound and Brecht, to the transformative introduction of Western realism into Chinese drama. The book takes as its premise the idea that intercultural theatre involves 'a process of displacement and re-placement of culturally specified and differentiated theatrical forces, rejecting any universalist and essentialist presumptions'. Finally, once again the *New York Theater Review*, edited by Victoria Linchong and others, was published by the stalwart Black Wave Press. The 2008 edition was exemplary, covering the under-represented alternative theatres and playwrights of New York.

5. African American Writing

Lauri Ramey, consulting with Paul Breman (publisher of the Heritage series), offers an important collection of essays on under-studied African American poets in her *The Heritage Series of Black Poetry, 1962–1975: A Research Compendium*. Ramey contextualizes Breman's 'unlikely venture' and explains how he desired to 'connect the past and the present of African American poetry' by publishing the work of forebears, established figures, and new voices. The project resulted in twenty-seven volumes of African American poetry. Among the poets published were Audre Lorde, Ishmael Reed, Dolores Kendrick and Robert Hayden. The book combines academic essays, memoirs and rare poetry from the series. In the first section, essays range from Melba Joyce Boyd's rumination on Dudley Randall and Edward A. Scott's discussion of Samuel Allen to Joanne V. Gabbin's study of Kendrick and Ramey's own essay on Ray Durem. The memoir section includes contributions from Breman, Sonia Sanchez, Clarence Major, Ebele Oseye and others. In the poetry section, Durem, Lorde, Mukhtarr Mustapha, Ron Fair and several others appear. A sample from Nkemka Asika's 'To Be Whole Again': 'Don't let them take away your spirit | The beautiful part of you | Fight them, the poet'. The book also contains original 'statements' by several of the authors, including Lorde, who writes, 'But what is in my blood and skin of riches, of brown earth and noon-sun, and the strength to love them, comes from the roundabout journey from Africa through sun islands to a stony coast'. In all, Ramey's book should deliver on its promise to 'stimulate further reading and research'.

Lauri Ramey discusses the aesthetic impact of slave spirituals and songs on later African American poetry in *Slave Songs and the Birth of African American Poetry*. Arguing that previous discussions of the genre ignore their poetic influence and that the African American 'high art' canon tends to omit the songs altogether, Ramey contends that many of the songs reveal innovative formal structures and that it is difficult to locate African American poets who have *not* been influenced by them. In her next chapter, Ramey examines how Romantic and modernist poetry heralded a return to the 'primitive', a privileging of authentic voice, and a renewed emphasis on the performative. For Ramey, the omission of slave songs from the major anthologies, even those purporting to be inclusive, is problematic. Ramey next demonstrates how slave songs parallel the theological concerns of some of the most revered lyric poetry and 'embody a permeable boundary between the sacred and secular and an intimate relationship between these two realms of experience'. Using 'free-floating imagery', the songs conjoin disparate 'conceptual spaces' in a manner similar to poets such as George Herbert and Gerard Manley Hopkins. Disputing earlier charges that the songs lack originality, Ramey next explains how the spirituals employed Old Testament stories not imitatively but selectively, seizing mainly on those elements that 'derive a sense of power, purpose, and identity in the present'. Ramey concludes with a compelling argument that the omission of slave songs from the American literary canon is an injustice.

In his *Deans and Truants: Race and Realism in African American Literature*, Gene Andrew Jarrett also examines the political dimensions of the African American canon. Re-examining the recurrent debate within (and without) African American critical circles over authenticity and whether those writers who chose not to focus on explicit racial politics deserve canonization, Jarrett demonstrates how later African American critics echoed William Dean Howells's supposition that writers of African descent—such as Paul Laurence Dunbar—should exclusively tackle racial topics. While Howells fed into a demand for 'minstrel realism', later Black Arts critics such as Amiri Baraka called for African American writers to pursue 'the pragmatic ethos and aesthetic of racial realism'. Jarrett thoroughly discuss the role of Alain Locke, who frequently serves as a political lightning rod—for both sides of the debate. For Jarrett, Locke represents a paradox of sorts, benefiting from mentoring in 'white' institutions yet calling for artists to reject such influence. Jarrett does an admirable job of examining the cultural moment surrounding the production of African American literature and criticism. For example, comparing the symposia of *The Crisis* and *The Messenger*, Jarrett notes that the results differed radically over whether racial difference or cultural similarity marked African Americans. While the critics created categories, the writers, Jarrett observes, stubbornly refused to get in line. From Dunbar, Zora Neale Hurston and George Schuyler to Frank Yerby, James Baldwin and Toni Morrison, African American authors who stray from prescribed topics frequently receive an icy silence from the critics. Jarrett ultimately suggests, however, that breaking the 'hermeneutical circle' is possible.

Examining how various writers employed jazz as a way to interrogate American cultural anxieties, Paul McCann's *Race, Music, and National Identity: Images of Jazz in American Fiction, 1920–1960* looks at Langston Hughes, Rudolph Fisher, Claude McKay and Ralph Ellison, and as well as Caucasian authors such as F. Scott Fitzgerald and Jack Kerouac. McCann demonstrates that initial uses of—and responses to—jazz tended to be negative, which he ascribes to a tendency for early audiences to see the genre as embodying a cultural decadence sparked by the First World War. McCann looks at various popular discussions of jazz to bolster his examination of fictional and poetic renderings of jazz. For instance, he remarks that many critics associated jazz with primitivism, a phenomenon defined in blatant racial terms as 'a vulgar artifact of the African American musical tradition'. McCann points out that jazz was generally neglected in American literature until white bands such as the New Orleans Rhythm Kings started to appropriate improvisational techniques, a phenomenon seen as a cultural 'decay'. He further speculates that a post-war desire for isolationism (which competed with a wish for international power) also fuelled depictions of jazz as a primitive movement divorced from Western artistic traditions. Consequently, jazz was often portrayed as a 'social threat to Anglo-European assumptions regarding artistic credibility'. African American authors, such as Hughes, resisted such characterizations and offered images of jazz that were empowering and implicitly critical of American society. As jazz became more ensconced in the public consciousness, particularly after the 1938 publication of Dorothy Baker's *Young Man with a Horn*, negative portraits of jazz clashed with more positive ones that coded jazz as a subversive critique of American conformity and racial prejudice. Ralph Ellison, for instance, showed how the improvisation of jazz was conducive to the discovery of one's 'authentic self' despite 'the corrupting influence of ['mainstream'] culture'. For white Beat writers, moreover, jazz took on a talismanic quality, a password for underground hipsterism. By the late 1950s, McCann claims, jazz 'enjoy[ed] classical status', but was still often seen as owing more to primitivism than intellectualism.

A balanced treatment of Langston Hughes's biography and methodology is the goal of Jonathan Scott's *Socialist Joy in the Writing of Langston Hughes*, which claims that the writer 'cannot in the end be understood by critical approaches that depend on equilibrium, completion, and continuity'. Scott first considers a wide range of postcolonial theory on the concept of exile, ultimately claiming that he 'acknowledges a different trajectory in postcolonial studies, an alternative line of critical inquiry and writing that rejects the despair and sense of loss typically associated with European exile precisely by welcoming exile's collective political possibilities and realigning them with the process of liberatory cultural resistance in the hemisphere as a whole'. Joy, then, rather than mourning, lies at the heart of Hughes's artistic methodology and its cross-cultural references. Remarking on Hughes's amazing cross-generic production (he wrote in over a dozen different modes), Scott states that 'this eclecticism, in fact, is one of the main features of the New Negro movement as a whole: an approach to cultural work that sees culture itself as a many-fronted way of life and thus asserts black culture's central place in all aspects of American social and political development and change'. Nevertheless, Scott is careful to contextualize Hughes's prolific writings, and he recounts the negative reception (both within and without the African American critical community) that the writer often received, noting that the source of the vitriol was often Hughes's tendency to reject simplistic nationalism in favour of an exploration of the nuanced, contradictory impulses within American culture—particularly with respect to race. Scott notes that, as a poet, Hughes created a 'place of ideological tension in which aesthetic hierarchies are rigidly class-based compared to the popular-democratic song, where social class is often announced loudly and proudly'. Hughes articulated his critique of American ideology via images of literal and metaphorical mestizos rather than in the rhetoric of pluralism. Scott also analyses Hughes's journalism, including his 'Simple' stories, in which 'everyday life was posed as a political problem'. Scott feels that, as Hughes aged, 'the task was to attract workers to socialism with an advanced artistic technique and a steady diet of aesthetic forms and structures that raised their standards while meeting their desires and reflecting their own way of seeing and feeling the world'. In assessing the totality of Hughes's career, Scott finds that 'While not a resolution of the contradictions between cultural nationalism, integrationism, and socialism, Hughes's concept of the North American mestizo served as a powerful countermyth to the cold war ideology of American pluralism, recast lately as "multiculturalism".'

Langston Hughes and Richard Wright—as well as Theodore Dreiser and James T. Farrell—feature prominently in Mary Hricko's *The Genesis of the Chicago Renaissance: Theodore Dreiser, Langston Hughes, Richard Wright, and James T. Farrell*. Hricko claims that as the momentum of the Harlem Renaissance began to wane, many key African American writers found Chicago an attractive destination because of its rising tide of activism. According to Hricko, this second Chicago Renaissance (the first is generally defined as occurring from 1890 to 1920), unlike the predominantly African American-led Harlem Renaissance, fostered a cross-racial artistic atmosphere. Hricko looks at the journalistic background of the four writers and also discusses their association with communism/socialism and the literary mode of naturalism, which she views as being focused on 'the role of social conditions'. Hricko employs a broadly biographical approach in the four chapters devoted to the writers. Rather than performing extended close readings of exemplary texts, Hricko looks at the men's journalism and points out Chicago themes in their various narratives. For instance, of Dreiser she writes, 'More than any element derived from Dreiser's Chicago fiction is the sense of individualism from the restrictive nature of the greater community.' Regarding Hughes, Hricko remarks that 'Chicago nurtured Hughes's social-political conscious.' In her chapter on Wright, Hricko cites the University of Chicago's sociology department and communist party as major influences on Wright's artistry. Finally, Hricko notes of Farrell, contra Dreiser and Hughes, that Chicago 'is a place of destruction that fragments the individual's experience toward alienation and unfulfillment'.

María Eugenia Cotera, in *Native Speakers: Ella Deloria, Zora Neale Hurston, Jovita González and the Poetics of Culture*, looks at how three women of colour merged high academic culture with folkways and feminist sensibilities. Cotera notes that all three women were 'no doubt shaped by the continuous though ever-changing mechanisms of empire and colonialism' yet managed to critique these superstructures via their writing and studies in folklore and anthropology, as well as in their activism. While committed to their academic pursuits, the women, Cotera remarks, all saw possibility within the realm of fiction, where they focused on gender politics. Aware of the 'discursive corral' in which women of colour from diverse backgrounds are often herded, Cotera desires to explore the 'borderlands of difference', a critical manoeuvre that allows her to discuss similarities without homogenizing Native Americans, African Americans and Chicanas. Cotera notes in

particular that critics tend to minimize differences between Deloria and
Hurston, a fact that leads a to a 'unidimensional vision of their contributions
to cultural politics'. Mindful, then, of the writers' unique perspectives, Cotera
suggests that the women—in pursuing anthropological concerns—'were
acutely aware of the ways in which their ethnographic and literary
representations might be deployed to ends not confined to scientific or
aesthetic realms'. Cotera also notes that each woman frequented both
intellectual urban centres and 'unsophisticated' rural areas. Supplementing
the published record with correspondence and unpublished manuscripts,
Cotera concludes that the trio of authors invented 'a new kind of storytelling
practice that fully and formally incorporates their experiences as women of
color working at the margins of mainstream institutions, feminist imaginings,
and nationalist/tribalist politics'.

With *Ralph Ellison: A Biography*, Arnold Rampersad delivers the
magisterial telling of Ralph Ellison's life. Drawing on scores of unpublished
and hitherto unexamined documents, Rampersad paints a balanced picture of
an extraordinarily talented writer who rankled many within the African
American community with his ambivalent response to the civil rights
movement. Charting Ellison's rise to fame with the publication of *Invisible
Man* and the subsequent 'tangled mess of fears and doubts' that prevented him
from finishing his work in progress, Rampersad takes care to juxtapose his
subject with the wider cultural upheavals of the twentieth century. Rampersad
deftly demonstrates how Ellison was viewed as 'cold and stingy' to some and 'a
man of grace, intelligence, wit, and courage' to others, a dichotomy that often
split along racial lines. Ellison's justly celebrated triumph over his bleak
Oklahoma City circumstances, his time at the Tuskeegee Institute, his musical
training, and his composition and publication of the literary marvel *Invisible
Man* all receive ample space in the biography, but Rampersad unearths many
new facts, such as Ellison's mother's practice of giving him magazines
discarded by her employers. Rampersad traces Ellison's seven-year effort to
compose *Invisible Man* and points out the book's various stylistic and thematic
innovations, including its rejection of sociological aesthetics. Writing that 'To
[Ellison], sociology typically reduces, compresses, and distorts knowledge.
Intrinsically it lacked what it claimed to possess, a capacity for deep human
understanding', Rampersad establishes that Ellison developed an early
antipathy for 'anthropological' approaches to the problem of race, which no
doubt contributed to his clash with writers of the Black Arts movement, whom
he regarded as crudely ideological. He would, for instance, dismiss Leroi Jones
(Amiri Baraka) as ignoring the 'poetry and ... ritual' in the blues and
extracting only the politics. For his part, Jones thought Ellison a 'snob'.
Rampersad thus fully discusses Ellison's strained relationship with African
American writers immersed in the struggle for civil rights, but he also reveals
an Ellison who was aware of its import and who voiced his opinions, such as
during a 1954 speech at Tuskegee, where Ellison deplored the forced ignorance
born of segregation and stood while his young audience 'erupted in applause'.
Rampersad also has fulsome praise for Ellison's non-fiction, such as *Shadow
and Act*. However, the latter part of the book concentrates on Ellison's failed
attempt to recapture his fictional success amongst a life of accolades, academic

work, travel and parties. Following the success of *Invisible Man*, Ellison almost immediately embarked on the creation of a second novel, but despite some amazing fragments (which would later be edited into *Juneteenth*), he never finished it, a fact that Rampersad ascribes to a number of factors, not the least of which were a fire that destroyed a draft of the book (though Rampersad claims that Ellison overestimated the number of lost pages) and Ellison's status as a 'Black literary patrician'. Rather than write more novels, Ellison was feted (by the white literary establishment and factions within the African American community) and disparaged (by younger, more radical African American literati). Rampersad also cites the death of Ellison's friend Albert Murray as a major reason for Ellison's malaise, fiction-wise (of course, Ellison left a considerable body of non-fiction). In all, Rampersad offers an extremely detailed account of Ellison's life and avoids hagiography without disparaging the writer in the process.

Elisabeth Petry, daughter of Ann Petry, published *At Home Inside: A Daughter's Tribute to Ann Petry*, a biography/memoir of her late mother. Petry culls her very private mother's extant journals for never-before-published insights. Becoming a character in the book, Petry explains that her mother strongly discouraged investigations into her past and erected impediments to intimacy even with her closest relatives. Petry uses a brisk narrative style to recount her mother's story, from her manipulation of her basic biographical details (such as her birth date) to her discomfort with fame. Petry extracts generous portions of her mother's journal, which she italicizes. These lend insight into Ann Petry's gift for detail as well as her thoughts on a variety of subjects, such as her observation that people of African descent were individuals 'of great open spaces' who, after being enslaved and enduring the Middle Passage, now are 'trapped [in the cities]—in concrete—brick—steel—old-law tenements—one toilet in the hall for 25–30 people'. Petry also describes her mother's eccentric daily habits, including her hoarding of papers (but not clothing). Anecdotes about the circumstances surrounding the publication of *The Street*, moreover, add to our understanding of that novel. Petry further reveals her mother's bravery in facing the end of her life. In all, Petry's book is a delightful, if somewhat wistful, portrait of Ann Petry.

In *Toni Morrison and the Idea of Africa*, La Vinia Delois Jennings investigates Toni Morrison's complex use of African symbolism, an approach often falsely attributed to an interest in postmodernism. Jennings identifies Morrison's use of oral tropes as particularly African, and she further notes that the Nobel winner frequently probes survival strategies inspired by the Middle Passage and adopts a 'Creole' outlook that necessarily blends many different African cultures. Noting that most critics view Morrison through a Western/Christian framework, Jennings suggests that it would be more profitable to interpret her works via the 'socio-religious directives of the cross within the circle and the philosophies of Voudoun, Candomblé, and their two African-based pantheons of gods, respectively the loa and the orixás'. In this way, readers may witness how Morrison traces the links between African Americans and their African forebears. In subsequent chapters, Jennings looks at a specific African philosophy as it applies to Morrison's work. For example, she explores the evolution of the scholarship surrounding Western and Central

African religious traditions as they survived the Middle Passage, and observes that Morrison looked to the Caribbean and its version of Dahomey's Vodun (especially as it relates to the Kongo Yowa) for her creolized aesthetic. Jennings discovers the cross-within-a-circle symbol in at least five of Morrison's novels, from the early *Sula* to the later *Paradise*. Jennings ranges widely in her discussion of African and Caribbean culture and applies her findings on such topics as animism (to *Tar Baby*), living-dead ancestors (to *Song of Solomon*), and sacrifice (to *Sula*).

Justine Tally offers another perspective on Morrison in her *Toni Morrison's Beloved: Origins*, which employs Foucault's theories to 'excavate' Enlightenment conceptions of humanity based in 'scientific racism'. Tally posits that Morrison knew of Foucault's ideas and integrated them into her writing process as she drafted *Beloved*, her 'counter-slave narrative'. She also notes that Sethe's story parallels one recounted by Foucault in *Moi, Pierre Rivière, ayant égorgé ma mère, ma sœur et mon frère*. In offering her critique of Age of Reason racism, Morrison 'enacts Foucault's theory that the Enlightenment episteme of knowledge is literally inscribed on Sethe's body'. In performing her act of Foucauldian archaeology, Morrison—according to Tally—must negotiate the 'disremembrance' of the Middle Passage, a traumatic series of genocidal acts marked by silence that 'continues to call for redress'. Additionally, Tally examines how Morrison recasts various classical myths such as Dionysus and Artemis within the novel. Further, Morrison employs a variety of Egyptian myths to counterbalance and interrogate classic Greek and Roman ones.

6. Native, Asian American, Latino/a and General Ethnic Writing

Lee Schweninger's *Listening to the Land: Native American Literary Responses to the Landscape* examines the persistent stereotype of Native Americans as the ultimate 'green' advocates and seeks to correct an over-reductive image with cogent analysis. Beginning with a series of passages from ecologically minded writers such as Louise Erdrich, Paula Gunn Allen, and Louis Owens, Schweninger observes that these expressions of 'deep and ethical regard for the land' often feed into naive ethnic constructions that rely on notions of 'special' relationships with the earth. A review of the conflicting scholarship on the question reveals diverse ideas of Native environmentalism, with some arguing that early Native Americans were fairly poor stewards of 'megafauna', and Sherman Alexie mocks the Noble Savage imagery by citing the unfortunate squalor of some reservations—though Schweninger points out that Alexie perpetuates such ideas elsewhere in his oeuvre. Schweninger also examines the globalizations present in Euro-American popular culture—such as *Dances with Wolves* and *The Last of the Dogmen*—that present Natives as 'living in some sort of natural paradise'. Schweninger then applies his analysis to numerous Native writers who represent 'a broad historical and geographical range', including N. Scott Momaday, Louise Erdrich, Vine Deloria Jr, and Gerald Vizenor. In such writers, as with Alexie above, Schweninger finds a complex interaction of internalized stereotypes, spiritual and practical environmental concerns, and resistance to simplistic caricatures of 'Indian wisdom'.

Penelope Myrtle Kelsey argues, in *Tribal Theory in Native American Literature: Dakota and Haudenosaunee Writing and Indigenous Worldviews*, that much recent scholarship on Native American literatures leans too heavily on Euro-American biases and ignores concerns particular to various Native traditions and communities. These biases tend to collapse—naively—distinct Native cultures into a monolithic entity. Kelsey reviews competing theoretical frameworks, such as those offered by Craig Womack and Elvira Pulitano, and the tensions between Native scholars and those advocating broader postcolonial approaches. For her part, Kelsey rejects Euro-Western theory because it is 'primarily focused on what Native American literature can tell the dominant society about itself'. Instead, while 'not denying the interplay of multiple traditions in Native American literature', she contends that the importance of tribal strategies and conventions to the literature necessitates the use of Native epistemologies rather than 'culturally inappropriate' ones that may, in fact, replicate cultural violence. Kashaya writers and Ojibwe writers employ different strategies and should thus be examined accordingly. Tribal-specific approaches will, Kelsey argues, help 'identify ... unique features' of the various texts. In line with her theoretical conception, Kelsey examines a smaller body of Dakota and Haudenosaunee texts, such as those by Zitkala Ša, Charles Eastman and Ella Deloria, and draws on indigenous background to illuminate their meanings.

Exploring attempts to quash Native American performances, Joshua David Bellin suggests, in *Medicine Bundle: Indian Sacred Performance and American Literature 1824–1932*, that American literature and culture nevertheless absorbed key elements of Native oral texts and rituals. Bellin looks at the evolution of American attitudes towards Native American performance, specifically that related to medicine, and shows how such outlooks 'profaned [sacred texts and] stripped [them] of [their] sacred qualities' in order to present a 'titillating, totemic' commodity that banked on the myth that the original practitioners had been wiped out entirely. Drawing on a wide range of historical information, such as the Indian Removal Act, New Echota, and Indian 'boarding schools', Bellin looks at texts such as George Catlin's *Letters and Notes* in order to explain the changing cultural landscape that allowed hitherto feared and reviled practices to be appropriated and packaged for family audiences. Bellin looks at a variety of writers, including William Apess, Black Elk and Wovoka. The cultural exchange between sacred performances and secular ones such as Buffalo Bill's Wild West show reveals that neither Native Americans nor Euro-Americans 'can escape the other's presence'. Bellin claims that the examination of Indian performance 'assumed a unique prominence in American print culture ... the key to Indian character'. Native identities (and perceptions thereof) were 'tested, contested, and forged anew' within this crucible.

Bringing together a dozen major scholars of Native American literature, including Janice Acoose, Craig S. Womack, Daniel Heath Justice, Cheryl Suzack and Lisa Brooks, *Reasoning Together: The Native Critics Collective* engages in a collective critical enterprise that, while not a dialogue in the truest sense, enables readers to see a broad range of approaches and issues. The collective aim of the book is for the scholars 'to reflect on the history of their discipline', a field of study that has burgeoned only within the last few decades. Womack provides a lengthy introduction that contextualizes the field and outlines key moments and issues. Interestingly Womack, in describing the book's process, in which the contributors engaged in debate with each other during drafting, comments that it is 'easier to talk about' the communal nature of Native texts than it is to '*perform* community'. The authors tackle both historical issues, such as the Indian Self-Determination Act, and emergent ones, such as neoconservative calls for anti-gay legislation. Suzack, for instance, uses Winona LaDuke's *Last Woman Standing* to investigate how gender impacts collective and individual identity, and confronts previous critics who discounted feminism's usefulness for Native studies. In another essay, Tol Foster argues that 'generalized theories have done real damage to Native communities' and asserts that 'an emphasis on the historical and cultural archives' will be more productive in illuminating Native texts. Employing a far different mode, Robert Warrior looks at Joy Harjo's erotic poetics and suggests that her work stands as a counterpoint to cerebral academic discourse and symbolizes 'embodiment' and a commitment to freeing Native theory from its own disproportionate sense of abstraction. The authors occasionally comment on the other contributors, but generally the book maintains the feel of a critical anthology rather than a collaborative work.

In *Exiles on Main Street: Jewish American Writers and American Literary Culture*, Julian Levinson revisits a number of familiar figures, from Emma Lazarus and Waldo Frank to Anzia Yezierska and Irving Howe, and considers how they (and their characters) 'reshape their identities as Jews in the face of the radical newness called America'. Levinson builds on Sacvan Bercovitch's conception of the Jew as outsider and suggests that Jewish writers often take on the role of 'prophetic outsider' by merging indigenous Judaic sources with typical American habits. In the book's first section, Levinson notes a disparity between Jewish males and females, observing that the men evince a sadness, while the women are joyous. For Levinson, the tone evident in writers such as Abraham Cahan is 'wistful' and 'mournful', while that in authors such as Mary Antin is one of 'celebration' and affirmation, a difference that he attributes to competing traditions, the first stemming from talmudic studies and the second from a more 'spiritualized' Judaism that reflects Transcendentalist influences. Levinson's second section also notes a schism in Jewish writing, this time between increased social mobility and a 'pervasive new sense of unease'. Levinson asserts that, for writers such as Ludwig Lewinsohn, Jewishness served more as a set of mores and an 'allegory for the amelioration of injustice' than as an 'affirmation of racial or ethnic continuity'. Levinson's third section deals with the issues surrounding the Yiddish tradition and how it injects 'an older stratum of Jewish existence' into the contemporary debate. In the final section, Levinson looks at the post-Second World War era and its blend of 'high and low registers' and proud post-immigrant Jewishness. Levinson concludes that the writers he considers demonstrate that the pattern of 'Jewish life transforms and persists just at the moment it seems to be dissolving'.

While 'ethnic' literatures are often viewed 'as the [primitive] antithesis' to the more experimental modes of modernism, in *African, Native, and Jewish American Literature and the Reshaping of Modernism*, Alicia Kent contends that 'writers from these communities developed their own strategies of self-representation, strategies that experiment with genre and narrative form to reflect the conditions of modernity specific to their cultural and racial experiences'. Kent sees this experimentation occurring on three planes, the spatial, temporal and rhetorical, as 'ethnic' writers alter their relationships with home, repair ruptures with the past, and negotiate generic frontiers. After outlining her theoretical framework, Kent devotes a chapter each to African American, Native American, and Jewish American writers. In the first of these, she examines Charles Chesnutt and Zora Neale Hurston, two authors who frequently employed pre-modern settings and characters in their work. Discussing the modernist 'break' or revision of the past, Kent remarks that for writers of African descent, this phenomenon took place far earlier, with the forced brutality of the Middle Passage rather than the First World War. In examining the effects of this disjuncture, Kent examines the cultural context of such events as the Great Migration from the south, minstrelsy, and the increase in lynchings, and she demonstrates that the propensity for the earliest African Americans to produce non-fiction and autobiographies stemmed from a need to grapple with those who would deny their identity as humans. Artists such as Chesnutt, however, 'challenged the anthropological project' and used fiction as a 'place to imagine the unimaginable'. Hurston, working later, moves back to anthropological concerns, but with a difference: she want to 'represent a collective diasporic voice, to bring the folk in the text'. In discussing Native American writers, Kent also investigates the cultural background, showing, for instance, how Native Americans were also mocked in minstrel shows and how they were used by advertisers and others as the essence of the primitive. Kent asserts that Mourning Dove, by employing 'an alternative to the genres Native writers were expected to use, [adopted] a kind of literary experimentalism, in which she makes writing "new" to reflect the different Okanogan ontological and epistemological paradigms'. Of D'Arcy McNickel, Kent observes that, mirroring the generic experimentation of mainstream modernists, he 'creates a narrative that links Salish and Euro-American cultures, mixes oral and written forms, commingles scientific and fictional representations, and crosses boundaries between anthropological and literary discourses while remaining distinctly Native'. In the chapter on Jewish writers, Kent first looks at widespread anti-Semitism and then shows how Abraham Cahan fails to merge his modernist aspirations with his anthropological tendencies. Kent indicates, however, that Anzia Yesierska is better able to 'engage in an intertextual dialogue with Modernist writers of the period, both in . . . thematic focus on nostalgia for a lost past and in the formal experimentation'. Kent sums up her investigation by suggesting that the groups she looks at 'adapted [to modernism] by transforming the very genres that labeled them traditional and primitive. Focusing on their literary solutions to the rhetorical contexts that have depicted them as not modern changes the shape of Modernism both descriptively and prescriptively.'

Josephine Park, in *Apparitions of Asia: Modernist Form and Asian American Poetics*, examines the cross-cultural exchange between both modernist appropriators of 'Asian' motifs and aesthetics and Asian American poets who sought to resist and modify such orientalist readings. In looking at Ezra Pound's poetic obsession with the East, and China in particular, Park claims that the poet reveals two aspects of orientalism: one that 'sets apart difference' and one that 'enshrines a shared ideal'. Park reads a number of poems by Pound, Jack Kerouac, Gary Synder and others who make use of Asian aesthetics. In addition, she notes the paradox that, however inspiring traditional Asian forms were for many Caucasian American poets, for Asian Americans such as Albert Saijo and Lawson Fusao Inada, conventions such as those surrounding haiku proved limiting, even crippling because of orientalist expectations. Park digresses from her study of poetry per se in rehearsing the well-known battle for authenticity staged between playwright Frank Chin and novelist/memoirist Maxine Hong Kingston, a debate that mirrors some of the orientalist charges levelled against Pound and others. Park pays particular attention to the poetry of Theresa Hak Kyung Cha and Myung Mi Kim, whom she claims employ modernist techniques, in an instance of influence begetting influence. For Cha, this results in a 'disintegration of memory' and a 'subtle critique of the modern lyric', while Kim tackles the 'open wound of history' and ironically uses imagism to reinvest meaning in the invisible.

A more general approach is offered by Bella Adams in her *Asian American Literature*, which offers a literary history of her subject. In her first chapter, Adams offers a chronology of Asian American literature as well as an overview of significant periods such as the 1960s and 1970s, when Frank Chin's 'combative rhetoric' and Trinh T. Minh's 'polemics' consciously subverted previous stereotypes perpetuated by Euro-Americans. Adams ranges widely in her topics, rehearsing the impact of 'relocation' camps on Japanese American writers, discussing the perceived communism of Chinese American writers, exploring the realist ambivalence (or caution) of mid-century Asian writers, and mentioning the hybrid forms that melded Asian and American literary traditions. This last theme, in particular, interests Adams, who also affords much space to the debate between the 'androcentric' ethos of Chin, Shawn Wong and others and the emergent feminism of Maxine Hong Kingston, Amy Ling, and others, a struggle that Lisa Lowe observes allows for the 'erasure of particularity on the basis of unity'. Adams also surveys several major theoretical debates among critics of Asian American literature, including the politically charged nature of the label 'Asian American literature' itself, which tends to collapse differences, homogenize diverse cultures, and 'commodify' ethnicity. However, Adams opines that Asian American literature is a viable category, as it 'help[s] to render ... identity heterogeneous through the depiction of demographic and ideological diversity'. As she studies the various eras and debates within Asian American literature, Adams proffers readings of many key figures, including Gish Jen, Amy Tan, Bharati Mukherjee and John Okada.

Readers will discover a far narrower scope in Wenying Xu's *Eating Identities: Reading Food in Asian American Literature*, which presents the notion that cuisine produces meaning and identity within various Asian American cultures. For Xu, food reveals a host of political and cultural issues, including those concomitant with gender rituals, sexuality and diaspora. However, Xu finds the psychological aspect of food to be its most powerful influence on identity formation. Xu exemplifies her thoughts on her various sub-topics by interpreting key texts, including Frank Chin's *Donald Duk*, David Wong Louie's *The Barbarians Are Coming*, Monique Truong's *The Book of Salt* and Li-Young Lee's poetry. Grounding her comments in the contemporary theory of critics such as bell hooks and Helen Vendler, Xu makes a number of prescient observations regarding food and identity formation, noting, for instance, that Chin's character Donald's 'masculinization and ethnicization are partially made possible through an embedded discourse of food/appetite [that] becomes actualized by ridiculing women as well as by excluding their participation in food production', a phenomenon that relies on a distinction between professional and domestic cooking. Ironically, Xu later explains that the latter mode typically evinces a warm 'evocation of the maternal', a fact that helps serve to 'emasculate' Asian men involved in the food industry. Xu, who in her introduction advocates the supposedly *passé* practice of close reading, supports her readings very well, as when she reads Mei Ng's *Eating Chinese Food Naked* and cites several passages in which Nick's questionable manners reveal him to be selfish despite his good-guy exterior. Xu convincingly argues that, while eating may appear to represent an innocuous, private act, it is pregnant with cultural and psychological meaning.

In her *Threshold Time: Passage of Crisis in Chicano Literature*, Lene M. Johannessen discusses the concept of the Borderland and how it functions with respect to Bakhtin's notion of the threshold chronotype, in which a crisis is represented as a compelled crossing of a threshold. The violence and tension of the space serves as a 'point of gravitation for discourse', and orient Chicano/a literature and its multi-temporal aesthetic. Johannessen applies this concept to a number of nineteenth- and twentieth-century Chicano/a writers, including María Amparo Ruíz de Burton, Tomás Rivera, and Richard Rodriguez. Among other concerns, Johannessen discusses the convention of double-voiced narration, assimilation, fragmentation, memory and dispossession. While, in the nineteenth century, the Borderland developed as a reaction to an emergent crisis, as Chicano/a writing gained a foothold it transformed into a refuge and even an empowering space. Johannessen ultimately views the Borderland as an invigorating, therapeutic realm that writers employ to negotiate identity.

Books Reviewed

Acoose, Janice, et al. *Reasoning Together: The Native Critics Collective.* UOklaP. [2008] pp. 451. pb $24.95 ISBN 978 0 8061 3887 4.

Adams, Bella. *Asian American Literature*. EdinUP. [2007] pp. 224. $70 ISBN 978 0 7486 2272 1.

Bellin, Joshua David. *Medicine Bundle: Indian Sacred Performance and American Literature 1824–1932*. UPennP. [2008] pp. 272. $55 ISBN 978 0 8122 4034 0.

Bigsby, Christopher. *Arthur Miller*. HarvardUP. [2008] pp. 776. $35 ISBN 978 0 6740 3505 4.

Breyer, Jackson R., and Robin Gibbs Wilder, eds. *The Selected Letters of Thornton Wilder*. HC. [2008] pp. 768. $39.95 ISBN 978 0 0607 6507 0.

Buske, Morris. *Hemingway's Education, a Re-examination: Oak Park High School and the Legacy of Principal Hanna*. Mellen. [2007] pp. 142. $99.95 ISBN 978 0 7734 5218 4.

Carson, Neil. *Arthur Miller: 1915–1962*. 2nd edn. Palgrave. [2008] pp. 160. pb $33 ISBN 978 0 2305 0718 2.

Cass White, Heather, ed. *A-Quiver with Significance: Marianne Moore 1932–1936*. ELS. [2008] pp. xxx + 137. pb CAN$22 ISBN 978 1 5505 8380 9.

Cooper, John Xiros. *T.S. Eliot and the Ideology of Four Quartets*. CUP. [2008] pp. xi + 235. pb £19.99 ISBN 978 0 5210 6091 5.

Cordle, Daniel. *States of Suspense: The Nuclear Age, Postmodernism and United States Fiction and Prose*. ManUP. [2008] pp. 224. $79 ISBN 978 0 7190 7712 5.

Costello, Bonnie. *Planets on Tables: Poetry, Still Life, and the Turning World*. CornUP. [2008] pp. xvii + 205. $29.95 ISBN 978 0 8014 4613 9.

Cotera, María Eugenia. *Native Speakers: Ella Deloria, Zora Neale Hurston, Jovita González and the Poetics of Culture*. UTexP. [2008] pp. 300. $60 ISBN 978 0 2927 1868 3.

Davis, Garrick, ed. *Praising It New: The Best of the New Criticism*. OhioUP. [2008] pp. xxviii + 332. $36.95 ISBN 978 0 8040 1108 2.

Demastes, William W. *Spalding Gray's America*. Limelight. [2008] pp. 276. pb $19.95 ISBN 978 0 8791 0360 4.

Dickerson, Glenda. *African American Theater: A Cultural Companion*. Polity. [2008] pp. 256. pb $24.95 ISBN 978 0 7456 3443 5.

Durrans, Stéphanie. *The Influence of French Culture on Willa Cather*. Mellen. [2008] pp. 280. $119.95 ISBN 978 0 7734 5239 7.

Duvall, John N., ed. *The Cambridge Companion to Don DeLillo*. CUP. [2008] pp. 224. pb $29.95 ISBN 978 0 5216 9089 7.

Evans, David H. *William Faulkner, William James, and the American Pragmatic Tradition*. LSUP. [2008] pp. 289. $40 ISBN 978 0 8071 3315 9.

Fenellosa, Ernest, and Ezra Pound. *The Chinese Character as a Medium for Poetry*. ed. Haun Saussy, Jonathan Stalling and Lucas Klein. FordUP. [2008] pp. xiv + 216. $25 ISBN 978 0 8232 2868 3.

Filreis, Alan. *Counter-Revolution of the Word: The Conservative Attack on Modern Poetry 1945–1960*. UNCP. [2008] pp. xxiii + 422. $40 ISBN 978 0 8078 3162 5.

Fliotsos, Anne, and Wendy Vierow. *American Women Stage Directors of the Twentieth Century*. UIllP. [2008] pp. 488. $60 ISBN 978 0 2520 3226 8.

Gandal, Keith. *The Gun and the Pen: Hemingway, Fitzgerald, Faulkner and the Fiction of Mobilization*. OUP. [2008] pp. 288. $55 ISBN 978 0 1953 3891 X.

Geis, Deborah R. *Suzan-Lori Parks.* UMichP. [2008] pp. 184. pb $18.95 ISBN 978 0 4720 6946 2.

Gill, Jo. *The Cambridge Introduction to Sylvia Plath.* CUP. [2008] pp. xiii + 152. pb £11.99 ISBN 978 0 5216 8695 2.

Hays, Peter L., ed. *Teaching Hemingway's The Sun Also Rises.* KentSUP. [2007] pp. 403. $39.95 ISBN 978 0 8733 8954 9.

Helle, Anita. Ed. *The Unraveling Archive: Essays on Sylvia Plath.* UMichP. [2007] pp. 277. pb $25 ISBN 978 0 4720 6927 9.

Herd, David. *Enthusiast! Essays on Modern American Literature.* ManUP. [2007] pp. 212. £50 ISBN 978 0 7190 7428 8.

Hicok, Bethany. *Degrees of Freedom: American Women Poets and the Women's College 1905–1955.* BuckUP. [2008] pp. 218. $51.50 ISBN 978 0 8387 5693 5.

Hricko, Mary. *The Genesis of the Chicago Renaissance: Theodore Dreiser, Langston Hughes, Richard Wright, and James T. Farrell.* Routledge. [2008] pp. 229. $95 ISBN 978 0 4159 5792 3.

Jarrett, Gene Andrew. *Deans and Truants: Race and Realism in African American Literature.* UPennP. [2008] pp. 240. $47.50 ISBN 978 0 8122 3973 3.

Jenkins, G. Matthew. *Poetic Obligation: Ethics in Experimental American Poetry after 1945.* UIowaP. [2008] pp. xv + 263. $42.50 ISBN 978 1 5872 9635 2.

Jennings, La Vinia Delois. *Toni Morrison and the Idea of Africa.* CUP. [2008] pp. 260. $95 ISBN 978 0 5218 8504 3.

Johannessen, Lene M. *Threshold Time: Passage of Crisis in Chicano Literature.* Rodopi. [2008] pp. 208. $60 ISBN 978 9 0420 2332 5.

Katz, Daniel. *American Modernism's Expatriate Scene: The Labour of Translation.* EdinUP. [2007] pp. 197. £50 ISBN 978 0 7486 2526 0.

Kelsey, Penelope Myrtle. *Tribal Theory in Native American Literature: Dakota and Haudenosaunee Writing and Indigenous Worldviews.* UNebP. [2008] pp. 190. $45 ISBN 978 0 8032 2771 2.

Kent, Alicia. *African, Native, and Jewish American Literature and the Reshaping of Modernism.* Palgrave. [2008] pp. 241. $75 ISBN 978 1 4039 7797 7.

Kinnahan, Linda A. *Poetics of the Feminine: Authority and Literary Tradition in William Carlos Williams, Mina Loy, Denise Levertov, and Kathleen Fraser.* CUP. [2008] pp. xi + 285. pb £21.99 ISBN 978 0 5211 0157 8.

Kirk, Russell. *Eliot and his Age: T.S. Eliot's Moral Imagination in the Twentieth Century.* ISI. [2008] pp. xxxi + 408. pb $18 ISBN 978 1 9338 5953 9.

Kraler-Bergmann, Doris. *Sylvia Plath's Lyrical Response to Works of Art: A Portrait of the Artist(s).* Verlag Dr Müller. [2008] pp. 88. pb £32 ISBN 978 3 6390 3464 6.

Kundu, Guatam. *Fitzgerald and the Influence of Film: The Language of Cinema in the Movies.* McFarland. [2008] pp. 203. pb $35 ISBN 978 0 7864 3134 2.

Landles, Iain. *The Case for Cummings: A Reaction to the Critical Misreading of E.E. Cummings.* Verlag Dr Müller. [2008] pp. 353. £54 ISBN 978 3 6390 9250 9.

Lee, Jun Young. *History and Utopian Disillusion: The Dialectical Politics in the Novels of John Dos Passos.* Lang. [2008] pp. 228. $70.95 ISBN 978 0 8204 8642 6.

Levinson, Julian. *Exiles on Main Street: Jewish American Writers and American Literary Culture*. IndUP. [2008] pp. 254. $24.95 ISBN 978 0 2533 5081 7.

Linchong, Victoria. *New York Theater Review 2008*. BlackWaveP. [2008] pp. 336. pb $19.95 ISBN 978 0 6152 0056 7.

Madden, Ed. *Tiresian Poetics: Modernism, Sexuality, Voice, 1888–2001*. FDUP. [2008] pp. 402. $80 ISBN 978 0 8386 3937 5.

Mason, Jeffrey D. *Stone Tower: The Political Theater of Arthur Miller*. UMichP. [2008] pp. 328. $54.50 ISBN 978 0 4721 1650 9.

McCann, Paul. *Race, Music, and National Identity: Images of Jazz in American Fiction, 1920–1960*. FDUP. [2008] pp. 192. $42 ISBN 978 0 8386 4140 7.

Moody, A. David. *Tracing T.S. Eliot's Spirit: Essays on his Poetry and Thought*. CUP. [2008] pp. 195. pb £14.99 ISBN 978 0 5210 6096 6.

Murphy, John J., and Merrill Maguire Skaggs, eds. *Willa Cather: New Facts, New Glimpses, Revisions*. FDUP. [2008] pp. 345. $65 ISBN 978 0 8386 4135 4.

Nadel, Ira. *David Mamet: A Life in the Theater*. Palgrave. [2008] pp. 304. $26.95. ISBN 978 0 3122 9344 5.

Nielsen, Ken. *Tony Kushner's Angels in America*. Continuum. [2008] pp. 136. $90 ISBN 978 0 8264 9503 6.

Novick, Julius. *Beyond the Golden Door: Jewish American Drama and Jewish American Experience*. Palgrave. [2008] pp. 200. pb $26.95 ISBN 978 0 2306 1966 5.

Olsen, Fleming. *Between Positivism and T.S. Eliot: Imagism and T.E. Hulme*. UPSouthernDenmark. [2008] pp. 193. £30.99 ISBN 978 8 7767 4283 6.

O'Neill, Michael. *The All-Sustaining Air: Romantic Legacies and Renewals in British, American, and Irish Poetry since 1900*. OUP. [2007] pp. 208. £51 ISBN 978 0 1982 9928 7.

Ott, Mark P. *A Sea of Change: Ernest Hemingway and the Gulf Stream, a Contextual Biography*. KentSUP. [2008] pp. 151. $29 ISBN 978 0 8733 8923 9.

Park, Josephine. *Apparitions of Asia: Modernist Form and Asian American Poetics*. OUP. [2008] pp. 208. $55 ISBN 978 0 1953 3273 3.

Pasachoff, Naomi. *A Student's Guide to T.S. Eliot*. Enslow. [2008] pp. 160. pb $27.93 ISBN 978 0 7660 2881 4.

Patchen, Kenneth. *The Walking-Away World*. ND. [2008] pp. xi + 274. pb $18.95 ISBN 978 0 8112 1757 6.

Patchen, Kenneth. *We Meet*. ND. [2008] pp. xvi + 282. pb $18.95 ISBN 978 0 8112 1758 3.

Patterson, Anita. *Race, American Literature, and Transnational Modernisms*. CUP. [2008] pp. vi + 241. £47 ISBN 978 0 5218 8405 1.

Petry, Elisabeth. *At Home Inside: A Daughter's Tribute to Ann Petry*. UMP. [2008] pp. 208. $30 ISBN 978 1 6047 3100 1.

Pizer, Donald. *American Naturalism and the Jews: Garland, Norris, Dreiser, and Cather*. UIllp. [2008] pp. 88. $30 ISBN 978 0 2520 3343 4.

Polk, Noel. *Faulkner and Welty and the Southern Literary Tradition*. UMP. [2008] pp. 207. $50 ISBN 978 1 9341 1084 1.

Porter, David. *On the Divide: The Many Lives of Willa Cather*. UNebP. [2008] pp. 372. $50 ISBN 978 0 8032 3755 3.

Prosser, Jay, ed. *American Fiction of the 1990s: Reflections of History and Culture*. Routledge. [2008] pp. 249. $120 ISBN 978 0 4154 3566 8.

Qian, Zhaoming, ed. *Ezra Pound's Chinese Friends: Stories in Letters*. OUP. [2008] pp. xxvi + 242. pb £21 ISBN 978 0 1992 3860 6.

Ramey, Lauri. *Slave Songs and the Birth of African American Poetry*. Palgrave. [2008] pp. 216. $75 ISBN 978 1 4039 7569 8.

Ramey, Lauri, ed., with Paul Breman. *The Heritage Series of Black Poetry, 1962–1975: A Research Compendium*. Ashgate. [2008] pp. 327. $99.95 ISBN 978 0 7546 5782 5.

Rampersad, Arnold. *Ralph Ellison: A Biography*. Vintage. [2007] pp 657. $35 ISBN 978 0 3754 0827 4.

Rieder, John. *Colonialism and the Emergence of Science Fiction*. WesleyanUP. [2008] pp. 200. $70 ISBN 978 0 8195 6873 2.

Rosenthal, Edna. *Aristotle and Modernism: Aesthetic Affinities of T.S. Eliot, Wallace Stevens, and Virginia Woolf*. SussexAP. [2008] pp. 152. £55 ISBN 978 1 8451 9171 9.

Salzman, Eric, and Thomas Desi. *The New Music Theater: Seeing the Voice, Hearing the Body*. OUP. [2008] pp. 416. $39.95 ISBN 978 0 1950 9936 2.

Schweninger, Lee. *Listening to the Land: Native American Literary Responses to the Landscape*. UGeoP. [2008] pp. 224. $59.95 ISBN 978 0 8203 3058 2.

Scott, Jonathan. *Socialist Joy in the Writing of Langston Hughes*. UMissP. [2008] pp. 265. $39.95 ISBN 978 0 8262 1677 9.

Shaughnessy, Nicola. *Gertrude Stein*. Northcote. [2007] pp. xiv + 130. pb £12.99 ISBN 978 0 7463 0906 3.

Sloboda, Noel. *The Making of Americans in Paris: The Autobiographies of Edith Wharton and Gertrude Stein*. Lang. [2008] pp. 195. $67.95 ISBN 978 1 4331 0104 1.

Sudol, Sister Barbara. *Mystical Elements in the Poetry of T.S. Eliot: T.S. Eliot's Poetry from 1909–1942*. Verlag Dr Müller. [2008] pp. 179. £45 ISBN 978 3 6390 7725 4.

Takeda, Noriko. *The Modernist Human: The Configuration of Humanness in Stéphane Mallarme's Hérodiade, T.S. Eliot's Cats, and Modernist Lyrical Poetry*. Lang. [2008] pp. 166. £42.50 ISBN 978 0 8204 8828 8.

Tally, Justine. *Toni Morrison's Beloved: Origins*. Routledge. [2008] pp. 174. $95 ISBN 978 0 4153 2045 3.

Tate, Andrew. *Contemporary Fiction and Christianity*. Continuum. [2008] pp. 161. $120 ISBN 978 0 8264 8907 9.

Tian, Min. *Poetics of Difference and Displacement: Twentieth-Century Chinese-Western Intercultural Theatre*. HongKongUP. [2008] pp. 282. $59.50 ISBN 978 9 6220 9907 6.

Towner, Theresa M. *The Cambridge Introduction to William Faulkner*. CUP. [2008] pp. 124. $70 ISBN 978 0 5218 5546 2.

Von Der Heydt, James E. *At the Brink of Infinity: Poetic Humility in Boundless American Space*. UIowaP. [2008] pp. xviii + 242. $42.50 ISBN 978 1 5872 9628 4.

Warren, Diane. *Djuna Barnes' Consuming Fictions*. Ashgate. [2008] pp. $99.95 ISBN 978 0 7546 3920 7.

Wheeler, Lesley. *Voicing American Poetry: Sound and Performance from the 1920s to the Present.* CornUP. [2008] pp. 235. pb $19.95 ISBN 978 0 8014 7442 2.

Willis, Elizabeth. *Radical Vernacular: Lorine Niedecker and the Poetics of Place.* UIowaP. [2008] pp. xxiii + 306. $39.95 ISBN 978 1 5872 9698 7.

Xu, Wenying. *Eating Identities: Reading Food in Asian American Literature.* [2007] UHawaiiP. pp. 206. pb $30 ISBN 978 0 8248 3195 0.

Zhang, Benzi. *Asian Diaspora Poetry in North America.* Routledge. [2008] pp. xvi + 177. £60 ISBN 978 0 415 95717 6.

Zinman, Toby. *Edward Albee.* UMichP. [2008] pp. 176. pb $18.95 ISBN 978 0 4720 6919 5.

XVII

New Literatures

FEMI ABODUNRIN, MRIDULA NATH CHAKRABORTY,
LEIGH DALE, ELIZABETH HICKS, RICHARD J. LANE,
IRA RAJA, TONY SIMOES DA SILVA, PAUL SHARRAD,
CHRIS TIFFIN AND NELSON WATTIE

This chapter has six sections: 1. Africa; 2. Australia; 3. Canada; 4. The Caribbean; 5. India and Sri Lanka; 6. New Zealand. Section 1 is by Femi Abodunrin and Tony Simoes da Silva; section 2 is by Leigh Dale and Chris Tiffin; section 3 is by Richard Lane; section 4 is by Elizabeth Hicks and Paul Sharrad; section 5 is by Mridula Nath Chakraborty and Ira Raja; section 6 is by Nelson Wattie.

1. Africa

(a) General

Some significant items from 2007 are noted here as they were unavailable for review in time for the previous volume. Tejumade Olaniyan and Ato Quayson, eds., *African Literature: An Anthology of Criticism and Theory*, chronicles the evolution of African literature as 'a propelling force in the growth of more global studies such as postcolonial literary and cultural studies' (p. 1). However, the editors lament that while the continent's literature has grown in volume and reputation in the past few decades, African literary criticism and theory have attained far more modest degrees of recognition and success, especially in Europe and North America, even though 'literary and critical production are not discrete entities but in a relationship both supportive and critical [and of] mutually affective intimacy' (p. 1). The present volume is the first anthology of its kind, and its goal is 'to redress the glaring lack, construct an easily accessible "home" for the canonical statements of African literary criticism and theory, and thereby help foster a more vigorous discursive tradition' (p. 1). The book attempts not only to foster methodological work but to serve a pedagogical purpose in making the major critical texts available to the classroom (p. 2). Thus it is organized into a wide array of themes predominant in African literary discourse, with selections in each section from

Year's Work in English Studies, Volume 89 (2010) © *The English Association; all rights reserved*
doi:10.1093/ywes/maq019

different points of view to 'emphasize the history, production, circulation, circumstances, and preoccupations of modern African literary discourse that underscore the uniqueness of the tradition as well as its linkages and similarities to and with other traditions' (p. 2). According to the editors, the 'socially-oriented issues' of African literature offer new and interesting insights into literary-theoretical issues in general and help break down stereotypes of theory being inaccessible and irrelevant to everyday life (pp. 2–3).

The anthology is divided into thirteen parts. Parts I and II, entitled 'Backgrounds' and 'Orality, Literacy, and the Interface', comprise eight and five essays respectively. Alain Ricard's 'Africa and Writing' (pp. 7–15); Albert S. Gerard's 'Sub-Saharan Africa's Literary History in a Nutshell' (pp. 16–21); Bernth Lindfors's 'Politics, Culture, and Literary Form' (pp. 22–30); Russell G. Hamilton's 'African Literature in Portuguese' (pp. 31–7); Anissa Talahite's 'North African Writing' (pp. 38–45); Jonathan Ngate's 'A Continent and its Literatures in French' (pp. 46–53); Simon Gikandi's 'African Literature and the Colonial Factor' (pp. 54–9); and V.Y. Mudimbe's 'African Literature: Myth or Reality' (pp. 60–4) address the varied cultural and historical provenance of what Alain Ricard has described as the 'African chapter in the history of writing' (p. 7). According to Ricard, the 'exclusivist school' of criticism has seen early voices 'as graphic artists more than as writers or inventors' (p. 11), but from an 'inclusivist position we can safely say that the African chapter in the history of writing is probably one of the longest in human history and that the obsession with orality—what Leroy Veil and Landeg White (1991) call 'the invention of oral man'—is 'more an ideological and political posture than a well-informed theoretical stand' (p. 14). Similarly, Albert S. Gerard's characteristically lucid contribution asserts that 'the introduction of the writing skill to Africa was by no means a consequence of western colonisation' (p. 16). Sub-Saharan Africa has a lengthy literary history, ranging from substantial amounts of poetry in Arabic written in the Islamized areas of black Africa, to the written art practised in the oldest Christian country on the continent, Ethiopia. The European influence merely 'found its proper place in initiating the third phase in a historical process that has lasted for nearly 2,000 years' (p. 16). Lindfors's contribution, on the other hand, like those of Hamilton and Ngate, reopens the age-old debate on writing in colonial languages, and contends that 'an African author who chooses to write in a colonial language—particularly English or French—will be able to reach a much wider audience both at home and abroad and will not be prevented from articulating mature ideas that the church, state or school finds offensive' (p. 22). Hamilton ('African Literature in Portuguese') points out that Portuguese was the first European language to reach sub-Saharan Africa, and that 'as a consequence of this early presence, African writing in Portuguese appeared before anything comparable in English, French, and other European languages' (p. 31). Ngate's article sees writing by francophone Africans as a second wave, following colonial texts on Africa and Africans. Gikandi and Mudimbe look at how African literary criticism has been 'a process of inventing and organising African literature' and Gikandi regards his own intervention as 'both an hypothesis and a wish' (p. 60). Mudimbe attempts to formulate 'the perspectives from which commentaries on and analyses of African discourses could become means of understanding African experiences from a more productive viewpoint' (p. 60). The production of a modern African literature in the crucible of colonialism is Gikandi's focus. He argues that, 'from the eighteenth century onwards, the colonial situation shaped what is meant to be an African writer, shaped the language of African writing, and overdetermined the culture of letters in Africa' (p. 54). Talahite's equally seminal overview of 'North African Writing' is discussed in the relevant sub-section below.

Part II contains Liz Gunner's 'Africa and Orality' (pp. 67–73); Abiola Irele's 'Orality, Literacy, and African Literature' (pp. 74–82); Isidore Okpewho's 'Oral Literature and Modern African Literature' (pp. 83–91); Mary E. Modupe Kolawole's 'Women's Oral Genres' (pp. 92–6); and Harold Schenb's 'The Oral Artist's Script' (pp. 97–100). It examines the epistemic features of orality and what Okpewho has described as 'the many ways in which writers have engaged in the transfer of styles from the oral tradition to the written text' (p. 65). The valorization of the written word and the widespread perception of orality as 'the absence of literacy' has, according to Gunner, neglected the fact that 'orality needs to be seen in the African context as the means by which societies of varying complexity regulated themselves, organized their present and their past, made formal spaces for philosophical reflections, pronounced on power, questioned and in some cases contested power, and generally paid homage to "the word"' (p. 67). Irele's contribution examines orality's uneasy relation to literacy. He notes that structural linguistics in general and literary theory in particular, as well as the direct impact of the work of Milman Parry, Albert Lord and the Chadwicks, prompted 'a reassessment of the literate tradition of Western civilization itself', and contributed to 'a broadened awareness of literature and thus created the conditions for a scholarly investigation of African orality not merely in a purely linguistic framework, as in the early phase of Africanist studies, but also from a literary and artistic perspective' (p. 74). Okpewho's essay examines 'the various ways in which modern African writers have made their contribution toward this vindication of traditional African culture' (p. 83), through translation, adaptation and exploitation. Besides their utilization of European languages in translation to bring out the poetic quality and the charm of the original, perhaps the most intense and skilful level of exploitation of African oral tradition can be found in the work of Wole Soyinka: 'In a number of his plays and in some of his poems and definitely in both his novels, he has borrowed heavily from traditional mythology for the construction of characters and situations. He is principally indebted to Yoruba mythology, especially that aspect of it that narrates the relationships between the divinities, and so contains for Soyinka the basic elements of the Yoruba outlook on life' (p. 90). Similarly, in her exploration of 'Women's Oral Genres', Kolawole focuses on 'unfolding oral genres that are tools of women's self-enhancement in African orature' (p. 93). According to Kolawole, contrary to existing myths and theories, women's voices remain audible, especially in satirical songs and poetry, which are women's domain: 'Egungun satirical songs among the Yoruba, Hausa women's court poetry, Nzema Maiden songs in Ghana, Impongo solo among the Ila and Tonga of Zambia, Akan dirges and Nnwonkoro in Ghana, Galla lampoons, Kamba grinding (work) songs, are specific female oral genres' (p. 92). Finally, Schenb's contribution examines South African oral artists' script, and the ways in which 'performance gives the images their context, and gives the members of the audience a ritual experience that bridges past and present, shaping their lives' (p. 97).

Entitled 'Writer, Writing, and Function' and 'Creativity in/and Adversarial Contexts', parts III and IV of the anthology comprise the various responses of creative writers across the continent to the idea that literature has a social function. Chinua Achebe's 'The Novelist as Teacher' (pp. 103–6) and 'The Truth of Fiction' (pp. 107–14); Nadine Gordimer's 'Three in a Bed: Fiction, Morals, and Politics' (pp. 115–21); Naguib Mahfouz's 'Nobel Lecture' (pp. 122–5); Njabulo S. Ndebele's 'Redefining Relevance' (pp. 126–31); and Albie Sachs's 'Preparing Ourselves for Freedom' (pp. 132–8) are clear testimonies that many of the continent's accomplished writers are also some of its finest critics. Achebe's seminal essay is a classic example of the notion that the African writer and his or her European counterpart inhabit different worlds: 'We have learnt from Europe that a writer or an artist lives on the fringe of society' (p. 103) as opposed to the African being 'a teacher' enmeshed in social affairs. Gordimer's 'Three in a Bed' analogy describes fiction as holding together politics, morality and storytelling. Achebe similarly asserts, 'we invent different fictions to help us out of particular problems we encounter in living' (p. 108). For him, the truth of literature 'does not enslave it...Its truth is not like the canons of an orthodoxy or the irrationality of prejudice and superstition' (p. 114). Similarly, Mahfouz's Nobel lecture underscores the importance of science, literature and sublime human values in the service of mankind. He speaks from his own peculiar position of being 'born in the lap of these two civilizations (Pharaonic and Islamic)' (p. 123), and offers his own conviction that 'Truth and justice will remain for as long as Mankind has a ruminative mind and a living conscience' (p. 123).

'The adversarial contexts' of African literature, on the other hand, portray postcolonial pathologies of all kinds, including religious fundamentalism and an ever-widening inequality between Africa and the world, against which 'African literature and literary studies propose another theory...and the flowering of the creative muse' (p. 139). Wole Soyinka's 'A Voice That Would not be Silenced' (pp. 141–3); Micere Githae Mugo's 'Exile and Creativity: A Prolonged Writer's Block' (pp. 144–9); Jack Mapanje's 'Containing Cockroaches (Memories of Incarceration Reconstructed in Exile)' (pp. 150–6); Ngugi wa Thiong'o's 'Writing Against Neo-Colonialism' (pp. 156–64); Breyten Breytenbach's 'The Writer and Responsibility' (pp. 165–71); Nawal El Saadawi's 'Dissidence and Creativity' (pp. 172–7); Zoe Wicomb's 'Culture Beyond Color? A South African Dilemma' (pp. 178–82); Nuruddin Farah's 'In Praise of Exile' (pp. 183–5); and Dambudzo Marechera's 'The African Writer's Experience of European Literature' (pp. 186–91) examine, from different cultural, political and critical standpoints, writers' experiences as political prisoners in the numerous gaols of the postcolonial state. Soyinka's critical exploration of the assassinated Algerian journalist, poet and fiction writer, Tahar Djaout underscores the deadliness of 'the life and death discourse of the twenty-first century [which] is unambiguously the discourse of fanaticism and intolerance' (p. 142). Advocating an 'empowering discourse' that would respond to the 'experience of a woman writer, also a single parent, faced with the challenges of exile under unique circumstances' (p. 144), Mugo's essay dramatizes how the pangs of exile caused a 'prolonged writer's block'. The Malawian writer Jack Mapanje agrees with Mugo that some writers 'only needed someone in some authority to consider your poem, your book, your thoughts and ideas subversive, rebellious, or merely radical, for you to be in trouble' (p. 150). Ngugi divides the African historical experience into three distinct phases: 'the age of the anti-colonial struggle, the age of independence; and the age of neo-colonialism' (p. 157). Writing against neocolonialism entails that the writer 'must be part of the song the people sing as once again they take up arms to... complete the anti-imperialist national democratic revolution they had started in the fifties, and even earlier' (p. 164). Breytenbach and Wicomb focus on the peculiar condition of the writer in South Africa, while El Saadawi's account examines the interfaces between dissidence and creativity from the perspective of the Arabic language: 'For me the word struggle in Arabic (*alnidal*) sheds most light on the meaning of dissidence. The *dissident* in Arabic (*al-munadil*) means the fighter who cooperates with others to struggle against oppression and exploitation, whether personal or political' (p. 172, original italics). Farah, Breytenbach, Wicomb and El Saadawi are discussed in the relevant subsections that follow. Parts V, VI and VII are entitled 'On Nativism and the Quest for Indigenous Aesthetics: Negritude and Traditionalism' (pp. 193–278), 'The Language of African Literature' (pp. 278–322) and 'On Genres' (pp. 323–407).

Part VIII, 'Theorizing the Criticism of African Literature' (pp. 409–60), commences a discussion of the nature and character of the critical traditions that have been applied to the study of African literature, and leads, in parts IX to XIII, respectively, to focuses on 'Marxism' (pp. 461–510), 'Feminism' (pp. 511–91), 'Structuralism, Poststructuralism, Postcolonialism, and Postmodernism' (pp. 593–680), 'Ecocriticism' (pp. 681–723) and 'Queer, Postcolonial' (pp. 725–64), and the application of these theories to African literature. Part VIII rehearses the issues in establishing the criticism of the continent's literature: who has the right to write about African matters, the proper relationship to Western critical tradition, how to maintain 'a strictly formal approach that would be sensitive to the intertextual relations among texts and the processes of defamiliarization that help to delimit African literary writing from the non-literary sphere as such' (p. 409). In it we find Eldred D. Jones's 'Academic Problems and Critical Techniques' (pp. 411–13); Rand Bishop's 'African Literature, Western Critics' (pp. 414–21); Kenneth W. Harrow's 'A Formal Approach to African Literature' (pp. 422–6); Ambrose Kom's 'African Absence, a Literature without a Voice' (pp. 427–31); Biodun Jeyifo's 'The Nature of Things: Arrested Decolonization and Critical Theory' (pp. 432–43); Christopher L. Miller's 'Reading through Western Eyes' (pp. 444–8); Olakunle George's 'Inherited Mandates in African Literary Criticism: The Intrinsic Paradigm' (pp. 449–54); and Florence Stratton's 'Exclusionary Practices in African Literary Criticism' (pp. 456–60). Part IX examines how a Marxist theoretical framework has been differently applied to African literature, both as a 'default interpretation as pertaining to social relations within specific national entities' and as a broader class struggle within the processes of 'decolonization and cross-cultural contact' (p. 461). Omafume F. Onoge's 'Towards a Marxist Sociology of African Literature' (pp. 463–75); Ngugi wa Thiong'o's 'Writers in Politics: The Power of Words and the Words of Power' (pp. 476–83); Amilcar Cabral's 'National Liberation and Culture' (pp. 484–91); Agostinho Neto's 'Concerning National Culture' (pp. 492–5); and Ayi Kwei Armah's 'Masks and Marx: The Marxist Ethos vis-à-vis African Revolutionary Theory and Praxis' (pp. 496–510) are critical examinations of what the editors have described as the 'the dialectical interplay between society-as-context and literature-as-product' (p. 461). Ten out of the eleven articles in the 'Feminism' section are written by women writers themselves, as opposed to critics of their work, and their application of 'the restored (absent) detail of womanhood in all its range—sex, maternality, domestic labour, the bearing of cultural knowledge—serves to secure a different kind of critical enterprise from that which ignores these vectors of feminist identity' (p. 511). The essays include Ama Ata Aidoo's 'To Be an African Woman Writer: An Overview and a Detail' (pp. 513–19); Nawal El Saadawi's 'The Heroine in Arab Literature' (pp. 520–5); Flora Nwapa's 'Women and Creative Writing in Africa' (pp. 526–32); Lauretta Ngcobo's 'African Motherhood: Myth and Reality' (pp. 533–41); Molara Ogundipe-Leslie's 'Stiwanism: Feminism in an African Context' (pp. 542–50); Buchi Emecheta's 'Feminism with a Small 'f'!' (pp. 551–7); Yvonne Vera's 'Writing Near the Bone' (pp. 558–60); Carole Boyce Davies's 'Some Notes on African Feminism' (pp. 561–9); Obioma Nnaemeka's 'Bringing African Women into the Classroom: Rethinking Pedagogy and Epistemology' (pp. 570–7); Uzo Esonwanne's 'Enlightenment Epistemology and the Invention of Polygyny' (pp. 578–84); and Ato Quayson's 'Feminism, Postcolonialism and the Contradictory Orders of Modernity' (pp. 585–91). The essays in Part XI are focused on 'how to understand the coupling of key terms—Africa and the West, structuralism and poststructuralism, postcolonialism and postmodernism—where the conjunctive "and" masks a wide range of possible mutualities and antagonisms' (p. 593). Sunday O. Anozie's 'Genetic Structuralism as a Critical Technique: Notes Toward a Sociological Theory of the African Novel' (pp. 596–8); Abiola Irele's 'In Praise of Alienation' (pp. 599–607); Biodun Jeyifo's 'In the Wake of Colonialism and Modernity' (pp. 608–13); Simon Gikandi's 'Poststructuralism and Postcolonial Discourse' (pp. 614–20); Robert J.C. Young's 'Subjectivity and History: Derrida in Algeria' (pp. 621–7); Anne McClintock's 'The Angel of Progress: Pitfalls of the Term "Post-colonial"' (pp. 628–36); Tejumola Olaniyan's 'Postmodernity, Postcoloniality, and African Studies' (pp. 637–45); Ato Quayson's 'Postcolonialism and Postmodernism' (pp. 646–53); Kwame Anthony Appiah's 'Is the Post- in Postmodernism the Post- in Postcolonial?' (pp. 654–64); Lewis Nkosi's 'Postmodernism and Black Writing in South Africa' (pp. 665–9); and Karin Barber's 'African-Language Literature and Postcolonial Criticism' (pp. 670–80) all problematize, from different critical and theoretical positions, the application of these theoretical strands to African literature. Parts XII and XIII of the anthology are focused on fairly new branches of African literary criticism, 'Ecocriticism' and 'Queer, Postcolonial' respectively. These frameworks link literature to environmental change and the representation of alternative sexualities and offer important ways of connecting to some of the burning social questions in Africa today. 'What is clear from all four pieces is the need for a close reading of African texts to see how they might be made available for a close reading of the alternative sexualities that are in evidence all across the continent, from gay bars in Accra to the after-effects of homosexual relations of the male dormitory system in apartheid South Africa, where migrant men lived in the cities separated from their wives, girlfriends and families for long periods and had to explore different sexualities from what was assumed to be the norm' (p. 725). Chris Dunton's '"Wheyting be dat?": The Treatment of Homosexuality in African Literature' (pp. 727–35); Gaurav Desai's 'Out of Africa' (pp. 736–45); Juliana Makuchi Nfah-Abbenyi's 'Toward a Lesbian Continuum? Or Reclaiming the Erotic' (pp. 746–52); and Brenna Munro's 'Queer Futures: The Coming-Out Novel in South Africa' (pp. 753–64) cover the 'queer, postcolonial' in the criticism of African literature. William Slaymaker's 'Echoing the Other(s): The Call of Global Green and Black African Responses' (pp. 683–97); Byron Caminero-Santangelo's 'Different Shades of Green: Ecocriticism and African Literature' (pp. 698–706); Juliana Makuchi Nfah-Abbenyi's 'Ecological Postcolonialism in African Women's Literature' (pp. 707–14); and Rob Nixon's 'Environmentalism and Postcolonialism' (pp. 715–23), on the other hand, foreground the emerging terrain of African ecocriticism and the interface between its theory and praxis. *African Literature: An Anthology of Criticism and Theory* has lived up to the bidding of its editors, the highly readable essays providing a detailed overview of African literary-critical and theoretical tradition. It will most certainly enable students and scholars to approach the field with less trepidation.

C.L. Innes's *Cambridge Introduction to Postcolonial Literatures in English* sets out to examine 'some of the writing that has emerged during the past century from the numerous and complex range of postcolonial societies which were formerly part of the British Empire' (p. vii). Although it does ask how writers 'have been thought about under the aegis of postcolonial studies, and...what varying meanings postcolonial literature may have in different contexts' (p. vii), the book focuses on the literary texts rather than the theories. It was the establishment of the British Commonwealth and courses in Commonwealth literature in English departments in various universities in Britain that first organized these literatures under one discursive formation: 'Later, such courses would also be introduced in Australia, Canada, India, Sri Lanka and the various African countries, though emphasis was more often on the country's own writers, rather than a comparative study or survey, and there was often considerable opposition to the introduction of such courses' (pp. 3–4). Kenyan writer Ngugi wa Thiong'o complained, for example, 'about the absence of any reference to writing by Africans in English departments in Kenya and Uganda, and describes his own struggle to introduce African literature courses at the University of Nairobi' (p. 4). The subsequent amalgamation of Commonwealth literary studies, Black studies and Third World studies produced contemporary postcolonial literary studies, and, according to Innes, 'accounts for its peculiar features and debates within the discipline', one that tries to cover 'a wide range of European settler colonies as well as predominantly indigenous and former slave colonies' (p. 5). Its theory is equally complex. Innes argues that, 'While Bhabha, Said and Spivak, and more recently Kwame Anthony Appiah, Paul Gilroy, Edouard Glissant and Stuart Hall, have most strongly influenced the critics of postcolonial literatures, it is Fanon who has perhaps most influenced writers—particularly in Africa and the Caribbean, and particularly in the earlier phases of resistance to colonization and the creation of a national consciousness' (p. 12). Concentrating on literary texts from several areas which represent different histories of colonial and postcolonial relationships, the nine major chapters and the conclusion are 'designed in part to enable a sense of the diversity of texts and approaches as well as contexts, and an awareness that no one framework is adequate to all' (p. 13). Chapters 2 and 3, entitled 'Postcolonial Issues in Performance' (pp. 19–36) and 'Alternative Histories and Writing Back' (pp. 37–55), examine the role of theatre in various African and Irish contexts and its construction of 'alternative and subaltern histories' as a ground for cultural nationalism and a 'response to the colonial and Hegelian insistence on a lack of "native" history' (p. 15). In *The Wretched of the Earth*, Fanon valorized drama over poetry or the novel 'as the best means of raising the consciousness of people involved in an anticolonial struggle' (p. 19), and Innes notes how Wole Soyinka and John (Pepper Clark) Bekederemo combined West African dramatic traditions with ancient and contemporary European drama to create theatre in English that worked a nationalist programme but with international reach (p. 22). Similarly, under the shadow of Fanon's chapter on 'National Consciousness' Innes examines how male and female writers differently take up and rewrite a series of colonial narratives, from Shakespeare through Conrad to Defoe. While Chinua Achebe's *Things Fall Apart* [1958] and *Arrow of God* [1964] could be described as contesting a colonialist mentality, the Ghanaian novelist Ama Ata Aidoo's *Our Sister Killjoy* [1977] seeks 'to use the language, the literary forms, the technology of the colonizer, to bring them (Sissie and Aidoo) back home to an Africa which is not merely a literary or metaphorical construct, but their home—an Africa whose physical reality welcomes and challenges them' (p. 51). Autobiographical writing is yet another means of writing a national history 'which is not defined within the terms of the colonialist version of history' (p. 15), and chapter 4 (pp. 56–71) explores writing the self in postcolonial texts. Chapters 5, 6 and 7 are entitled 'Situating the Self: Landscape and Place' (pp. 72–96), 'Appropriating the Word: Language and Voice' (pp. 97–118) and 'Narrating the Nation: Form and Genre' (pp. 119–36) respectively. Chapter 8, 'Rewriting her Story: Nation and Gender' (pp. 137–60), focuses on the gendering of landscape and its consequences for women writers, and chapter 9, entitled 'Rewriting the Nation: Acknowledging Economic and Cultural Diversity' (pp. 161–76), is a critical articulation of the sense of disillusion expressed by authors such as Ayi Kwei Armah, Ngugi wa Thiong'o, Arundhati Roy and Salman Rushdie. Finally, focusing specifically on Britain, chapter 10, 'Transnational and Black British Writing: Colonizing in Reverse' (pp. 177–96), explores 'the particular relationships of postcolonial writers within the "heart of empire"' (p. 17). Innes's lucid and rigorously theorized book is an excellent introduction to 'postcolonial literatures in

English'. It presents characteristically recondite critical and theoretical issues with a disarming simplicity and clarity.

Femi Abodunrin's *Blackness: Culture, Ideology and Discourse* was first published in Germany in 1996 under the Bayreuth African Studies series; a second, expanded, edition was published in 2008. Abodunrin's book-length study examines what Olu Obafemi, in his foreword to this second edition, has described as 'the often misperceived homogeneity of the experiences of (and strategies of articulating them) of postcolonial peoples in identifying the two main contexts of self-definitions' (p. xi). The study distinguishes between those postcolonial peoples with a concrete metaphysical cosmos and pre-colonial heritage which can be reconstructed and harmonized with postcolonial reality (Africa, India, the indigenous people of the South Pacific, North America, New Zealand and Australia) and those 'postcolonial regions that have no cultural backcloth from which to reconstruct and thus have to engage in acts of subversion of the colonialist mythic imagination through 'the counter-culture of the imagination' (the Caribbean and the non-indigenous people of New Zealand, Australia, and Canada) (p. xi). Focusing on nine writers from Africa and across the black diaspora, Abodunrin grapples with 'issues of ideology—Negritude, humanism and materialism' (pp. xi–xii). Fresh amplification and enlargement of the theoretical postulations of the first edition have, according to Obafemi, 'produced an entirely new book' that ranges from Chinua Achebe's early critiques of colonialist Eurocentric misperceptions to more contemporary works by Akachi Adimora Ezeigbo and the martyred literary/revolutionary figure Ken Saro-Wiwa (p. xii).

(b) West Africa

Aderemi Raji-Oyelade and Oyeniyi Okunoye (eds.), *The Postcolonial Lamp: Essays in Honour of Dan Izevbaye*, is a volume of essays in honour of one of the foremost critics of African literature and culture, Daniel S. Izevbaye. Attending to the formal structure and texture of the literary artefact, Izevbaye has bequeathed to the contemporary reading of African literatures what Biodun Jeyifo has described as 'the thoroughness or astuteness with which a literary scholar reads individual works' (p. 3) and a critical methodology that emphasizes an adequate grasp of theory and a sense of the cultural history of the text. In their lucid introduction to the volume, entitled 'Daniel S. Izevbaye: The Scholar-Critic as Illuminant' (pp. xii–xxi), the editors use M.H. Abrams's metaphor of the mirror and the lamp to assess Izevbaye's forty-plus seminal essays. The postcolonial lamp confers authority on the critic, 'without any attempt to invest him or her with the power of infallibility' (p. xiv).

The vast majority of contributors to the volume are former students. Part I opens with Biodun Jeyifo's captivating 2006 public lecture in honour of Izevbaye entitled 'For Dan Izevbaye: Literature and its "Others" in the Developing World' (pp. 3–18) and J.O.J. Nwachukwu-Agbada's 'D.S. Izevbaye: Critic of a Dual Mandate' (pp. 19–30). Jeyifo was a student of Izevbaye's who later encountered him as a senior colleague at Ibadan. He sees Izevbaye's career coinciding with 'the phenomenal *irruption* of [African] literature on the stage of world cultural history' in the space of a single generation (p. 9). His publications are 'telling indices of liberation from intellectual servitude to the colonizers and their imperial literary-critical traditions' (p. 11). Jeyifo divides Izevbaye's oeuvre into two categories, the exegetical essays and the metacritical essays, the latter group dealing with 'the institution of criticism in its relation to literature... and with temporal and formal patterns in the new African literature' (p. 12). Jeyifo regards Izevbaye's metacritical essays as some of the best that we have in African literature, precisely because 'he happens to be one of our finest exegetical critics' (p. 13). Nwachukwu-Agbada describes Izevbaye as a critic of two worlds: he has been tagged a Eurocentric scholar but 'In fact his writings are often directed towards the founding of African critical standards. In most of his essays, Izevbaye often draws attention to what is African in a piece of African work, contrasts it with what he has observed in the literature of the West, and makes a case for African critical concepts and criteria' (p. 21).

Part II of the volume comprises Pius Adesanmi's 'Africa, India and the Postcolonial: Notes Toward a Praxis of Infliction' (pp. 33–57), Aderemi Raji-Oyelade's 'Bondages of Bonding: The Challenge of Literary Criticism in the New Age' (pp. 58–70) and Oyeniyi Okunoye's 'Modern African Poetry as Counter-Discursive Practice' (pp. 71–89)—all centred on theory either broadly or as applied to African writing. The penultimate part III of the volume comprises essays that are concerned with the critical enterprise and poetics, or what Wole Ogundele has described as the critical legacies of the revolution that Nigeria's literature in English underwent between the late 1970s and the mid-1980s: 'During this period, a group of young poets and not-so-young critics emerged, who quarrelled loudly with the established ones and formulated in the process a new poetic that combined rejection of the pre-war poetry with a justification of their own evolving one' (p. 129). It includes Osita Ezeliora's 'Elegy for the Mystery Cocks: Modern African Literature and the Making of its Classics' (pp. 93–128), Wole Ogundele's 'An Appraisal of the Critical Legacies on the 1980s Revolution in Nigerian Poetry in English' (pp. 129–46), Wale Oyedele's 'Reflections on the Nature of Canonical Activity and its Black Paradigms' (pp. 147–64), Dele Layiwola's 'The Hero in Yeatsian Dramaturgy' (pp. 165–78) and Sola Olorunyomi's 'Orality as Text in Mutation' (pp. 179–89). Finally, part IV is made up of essays that are preoccupied with textual exegesis in its various forms. Harry Garuba's 'The Poetics of Possibility: A Study of Femi Osofisan's *The Chattering and The Song* and *Morountodun*' (pp. 193–206), Wumi Raji's 'Urban Dislocation and Post-Colonial Transformation in the Plays of Femi Osofisan' (pp. 207–18) and Muhammed O. Badmus's 'The Popular Theatre and the Radical Aesthetics: The Example of Femi Osofisan' (pp. 219–36) focus on different aspects of Osofisan's dramaturgy. Laura Moss's ' "Scarring Public Memory": Displacement, Hybridity, and Wole Soyinka's *Beatification of Area Boy*' (pp. 237–46) and Gbemisola Remi Adeoti's 'Gynocentric Aesthetics and Dramatic Politics in Nigerian Drama: A Reading of Tess Onwueme's *The Reign of Wazobia* and J.P. Clark's *The Wives' Revolt*' (pp. 247–64) examine the poetic representation of a hybrid space in Soyinka's 'Lagosian Kaleidoscope' and what Adeoti has described as the gynocentric polemics and aesthetics recoverable in the plays of Onwueme and Clark (p. 247). Chima Anyadike's 'The Cracks in the Wall and the Colonial Incursion: *Things Fall Apart* and *Arrow of God* as Novels of Resistance' (pp. 265–78), Akachi Ezeigbo's 'Discordant Tongues: Language and Power in Ken Saro-Wiwa's *Sozaboy*' (pp. 279–87), Lekan Oyegoke's 'Retrying Ali A. Mazrui's *The Trial of Christopher Okigbo*' (pp. 288–99), Jane Bryce's '"He said, she said": Gender and the Metanarrative of Nigerian Identity Construction' (pp. 300–24), Jude Aigbe Agho's '"Living in the Fast Lane": A Comparative Study of Amma Darko's *Beyond the Horizon* and May Ifeoma Nwoye's *Fetters and Choices*' (pp. 325–36), Isidore Diala's 'Andre Brink and Malraux' (pp. 337–54), Ismail Bala Garba's '"The Lost Language of Enlightenment": *Return to Algadez* and the New Nigerian Writing' (pp. 355–70) and Ademola O. Dasylva's 'Identity and Memory in Omoboyede Arowa's Oriki Performance in (Yoruba) Ekiti Dialect' (pp. 371–96) focus on familiar and not-so-familiar fictional texts in the Nigerian and African contexts, and vibrancy of the African oral traditions. The volume closes with 'Text of Interview with D.S. Izevbaye' by Aderemi Oyelade-Raji and Oyeniyi Okunoye (pp. 397–403).

(c) East and Central Africa

Tina Steiner's 'Navigating Multilingually: The Chronotope of the Ship in Contemporary East African Fiction' (*ESA* 51:ii[2008] 49–58) examines the 'intriguing conception of an Indian Ocean culture of compromise and a relational multilingualism against its literary representations in the fiction of Jamal Mahjoub, the Anglo-Sudanese writer, and Abdulrazak Gurnah, the Zanzibar-born writer now residing in Britain' (p. 50), and is part of *English Studies in Africa*'s special issue on 'The Story of the Voyage'. Michael Titlestad's introduction, 'Voyages and Stories: Considering the *Wager*' (*ESA* 51:ii[2008] 1–8), contextualizes Philip Edwards's *The Story of the Voyage: Sea Narratives in Eighteenth-Century England* [1994] from which the special issue takes its title, 'as did the colloquium held at the Wits Institute for Social and Economic Research (WISER) in October 2008 at which earlier versions of these articles were presented' (p. 1). Steiner examines Mahjoub's 1998 novel *The Carrier* and Gurnah's 2001 novel *By the Sea* against the backdrop of Amitav Ghosh's travelogue and history of the Indian Ocean and situates 'Ghosh's perhaps somewhat idealized picture of the Indian Ocean in relation to Gilroy's *Black Atlantic*, where he mentions the chronotope of the ship as the maker for black humanity' (p. 50). While Mahjoub's novel critiques the Eurocentric traveller's tale by selecting non-Western Rashid as its protagonist, sending him to 'a savage Europe which is contrasted with the civilized African and Mediterranean spaces with which Rashid is familiar' (p. 53), Gurnah's novels in general portray merchant voyages, stressing 'an interlinked history, not necessarily harmonious but one in which the ship was an important connector' (p. 55). Mahjoub's *The Carrier* 'rewrites the history of science by insisting on a shared history in which Greek, Arabic, and North African scientists influence each other' (p. 53). One of Steiner's primary conclusions is that Mahjoub and Gurnah are writers 'for whom large themes—of language and translation, memory, science and alternative subjectivities—are part of ordinary, complex and intersecting paths across the sea. ... The chronotope of the sea in these two East African novels needs to be understood as both a marker of circularity (the south–east–south connection) of the Indian Ocean World and a marker for transnational migrations to the North' (p. 57).

Despite the obvious appeal for postcolonial studies of work and authorship that blur boundaries, enact hybridity and challenge national constructs, Asian African writing remains a relatively quiet field. Perhaps for this reason the critic who ventures therein is energized with the originality of the writing to produce work of equal status. In 'East African Literature and the Politics of Global Reading' (*RAL* 39:i[2008] 1–23), Peter Kalliney writes one of this year's most challenging and rewarding critical essays in the area of eastern and southern African studies. Focusing essentially on M.G. Vassanji's *The Gunny Sack*, Kalliney argues that 'bringing academic accounts of globalization into dialogue with novels like *The Gunny Sack* may create a space wherein scholars can make transparent their narrative politics' (p. 4). Drawing on critiques that postcolonial studies has exhausted its political significance because of an over-privileging of textuality, Kalliney juxtaposes some of globalization studies, to 'postcolonial theory's ... sophisticated understanding of narrative in historical context and as a political instrument' (p. 4). Discussing what he calls a 'double discourse of value' in operation upon 'postcolonial fiction, and other so-called minority literatures', he writes: 'We weigh their literary merits and aesthetic value as we would with any piece of literature. But in addition to that, we have placed an extra political expectation on minority literature.' And he asserts: 'in order to gain entry into the cultural center, [minority literatures] must incessantly rehearse conditions of subordination and exclusion' (p. 18). While it is arguable that the very category of 'minority literature' is unhelpful in accounting for the value of writing such as *The Gunny Sack*, Kalliney's essay offers a provocative intervention into an academic field where the politics of cultural production, professional performance and aesthetic value continually vie with each other for supremacy.

(d) Southern Africa
Also as part of *English Studies in Africa*'s special issue on 'The Story of the Voyage', Carl Thompson, 'The *Grosvenor* Shipwreck and the Figure of the Female Crusoe: *Hannah Hewit, Mary Jane Meadows*, and Romantic-Era Feminist and Anti-Feminist Debate' (*ESA* 51:ii[2008] 9–20) and Michael Titlestad, '"The Unhappy Fate of Master Law": George Carter's *A Narrative of the Loss of the Grosvenor, East Indiaman* (1791)' (*ESA* 51:ii[2008] 21–37), present critical analysis of 'the textual afterlife of the wreck of the *Grosvenor*, East Indiaman, which ran aground on the shores of South Africa in 1782' (p. 6). Thompson's essay examines the wreck's literary legacy, which extends from the 1790s until the present day. Thompson seeks to 'reconstruct this now forgotten, but not unimportant episode in Romantic-era print culture. And in so doing ... suggest[s] that one of the more intriguing literary legacies of the *Grosvenor* shipwreck is that it may have led, by way of Dibdin's *Hannah*

Hewit, to the imagining of new forms of female heroism and agency' (p. 10). *Mary Jane Meadows* [1802], Thompson argues, is a necessary addition to the *Grosvenor* 'canon': it is 'an anonymous reworking of Dibdin's novel...apparently in a spirit of critique as well as of plagiarism. The result is a fiction that is arguably more effective than Dibdin's original' (p. 10). Similarly, Titlestad explores the South African literary legacy of the wreck and notes that it 'was reworked into a lengthy sentimental vignette by Charles Dickens in an essay on shipwreck that he wrote for *Household Words'*. Titlestad traces the interest in the death of Master Law back to 'George Carter's *A Narrative of the Loss of the* Grosvenor, *East Indiaman*' (p. 21). Meg Samuelson's ' "Lose your mother, kill your child": The Passage of Slavery and its Afterlife in Narratives by Yvette Christiansë and Saidiya Hartman' (*ESA* 51:ii[2008] 38–48) is a critical examination of 'the sea as an archive in which the afterlife of slavery continues to surface' as encoded in Christiansë's *Unconfessed: A Novel* [2006] and Saidiya Hartman's autobiographical journey along the Atlantic slave route in *Lose Your Mother* [2007]. Slavery 'is encoded in their narratives as a chronotope from which to profitably—or rather *un*profitably—engage a present in which racial capitalism continues to produce and shape its subjects on both sides of the Atlantic, and in which the legacies of Cape slavery persist in troubling the liberatory narratives of the "new" South Africa' (p. 45). There are some articles on *Moby-Dick* and one connecting Australia and *The Rime of the Ancient Mariner*, but it is Kevin Goddard's ' "Like circles on the water": Melville, Schopenhauer and the Allegory of Whiteness' (*ESA* 51:ii[2008] 84–92) that connects to Africa. It explores how 'aspects of the role whiteness as a racial marker may be seen to play in a future South Africa' (p. 84). Using some personal observations, mixed with a reading of Melville's *Moby-Dick* and Schopenhauer's *The World as Will and Representation*, Goddard's essay is an attempt 'to step outside the realm of racial classification itself, [and] to explore the possibility of a world beyond racialized confines' (p. 84).

To return to the Olaniyan and Quayson anthology of criticism and theory, Southern Africa is represented by Breyten Breytenbach's 'The Writer and Responsibility' (pp. 165–71), Zoe Wicomb's 'Culture Beyond Color? A South African Dilemma' (pp. 178–82), Lewis Nkosi's 'Postmodernism and Black Writing in South Africa' (pp. 665–9) and Brenna Munro's 'Queer Futures: The Coming-Out Novel in South Africa' (pp. 753–64). Breytenbach's essay, which is an address to the Dutch PEN Centre, is placed in the 'Creativity in/and Adversarial Contexts' section. If, according to Breytenbach, 'there is no easy solution to the dilemma South Africa poses, neither for me as a non-Black exile, nor for you as sympathetic Dutch writers' (p. 171), Wicomb elaborates on the complexity of the South African condition, 'which the New South Africa, frightened by its own newness, invokes almost as often as it does the imagined community of nation', but sees that very complexity as guaranteeing the life of oral and print literary culture (p. 178). She sets out some of the different problems of adaptation for each racial group: 'we have all become rather perversely attached to apartheid. How will black people, long accustomed to dispossession and deprivation, adjust to a new condition of not being racial victims? Our chant of we-the-oppressed-black-majority with it moral upper hand has at times a curious ring of comfort, since it absolves us from taking responsibility for our own condition, precisely because our more assertive cries have never had any perlocutionary effect' (p. 179). If Wicomb considers language to be the shared commonality 'which a writer will comfortably use and abuse to her own advantage' (p. 179), it is that same linguistic medium that Lewis Nkosi argues has created an unmendable split between black and white writing in South Africa: 'This split . . . will find no ready analogy in the difference between, say, Afrikaans and English literatures, a division which is only comparable to the difference between regional literatures in the United States, especially between southern and northern, and between rural and urban writing, a difference which is largely a matter of constellation of certain themes and preoccupations' (p. 665). The colonial status of black writing in South Africa produced a 'view of black writing as wilful *sui generis* and naturally resistant to any attempt to bring it into fruitful contact with other contemporary movements in world literatures. . . . In any event, where theory counts for so much—as seems to be the case with current artistic movements—it cannot be an accident that most works that are tuned into contemporary aesthetics movements are by white rather than black writers' (p. 668). Finally, Brenna Munro argues that, while the whole notion of gay modernity might have been scripted by the West, 'the terms of this modernity are being revised by queer Africans. Emerging black South African writer K Sello Duiker does just that. In his novels *Thirteen Cents* (2000) and *The Quiet Violence of Dreams* (2001) he appropriates and transforms the coming-out novel, thus engaging with both Western notions of gay identity and the official African national coming-out narrative' (p. 754).

Perhaps it is to be expected that South African studies should be strongest in South Africa, and much of the work in this review focuses on South African literature, often emerging from academic institutions in that country. Indeed, even when it is produced out of British or American academia, essays are regularly written by exiled South Africans. Thematically the focus remains overwhelmingly on South Africa's apartheid past and the way it haunts the present and the future. Although working from within literary studies, many critics adopt a quasi-archaeological methodology that positions the work of imagination as a 'dig' to be excavated in search of proof of South Africa's enduring inability to shake off the horrors of the apartheid period. The work of the Truth and Reconciliation Commission (1993–7) and its representation in fiction writing bulk large in much of the work under review. Other dominant themes are a growing concern with animals' well-being (evidence of the appeal of what might be termed 'the animal turn' in postcolonial studies); less obvious, the 'spiritual turn' (Michael Chapman, *CW* 20:ii[2008] 67–73) attracts a number of critical explorations; the African city attracts a number of essays. The writing of J.M. Coetzee, Zakes Mda and Doris Lessing dominates studies of single authors. It should be noted too that E'skia Mphahlele passed away in 2008, and an obituary in *Current Writing* (*CW* 20:ii[2008] i–ii) offers an overview of the work of one of the quiet giants of South African letters.

Edited by Merete Falck Borch, Eva Rask Knudsen, Martin Leer and Bruce Clunies Ross, *Bodies and Voices: The Force-Field of Representation and Discourse in Colonial and Postcolonial Studies* brings together the proceedings of the EACLALS conference held in Copenhagen in 2002. The essays are organized primarily by geographical region, and Southern Africa is well represented. In 'Martyred Bodies and Silenced Voices in South African Literature Under Apartheid' (pp. 3–15) André Viola notes the apartheid regime's obsession with 'large-scale engineering in order to segregate the corporeal envelopes of its inhabitants', and writes that 'In [South African] literature, numerous voices arose to testify to the ruthlessly treated black body' (p. 3). Viola is especially interested in the ghostly energy of bodies in the work of fiction, absence-presences that return again and again 'as a substitute for the silenced voice of the land' (p. 3). Of J.M. Coetzee's *The Age of Iron* he says: 'The suggestion is manifestly that the children's trampled bodies carry such weight that they cannot be constrained, and will rise up again some day' (p. 9). Discussing two works by Nadine Gordimer, 'Six Feet of the Country' [1956] and *The Conservationist* [1984], he detects in her treatment of black bodies a shift of vision for the future. In *The Conservationist* he writes: 'Not only does [Gordimer] reinstate the excluded body in the social sphere, but, although it is voiceless, she entrusts it with was a momentous message at the time' (p. 10). That 'message' is one that Viola argues makes the various works he examines the ideal supplement, in a Derridean sense, to the work of history and archival memory. In 'Postcolonial *Disgrace*: (White) Women and (White) Guilt in the 'New South Africa' (pp. 17–31), Georgina Horrell centres her discussion on Coetzee's *Disgrace* [2000], stating that 'The body inscribed in Coetzee's text is not a "tabula rasa": it is the body of a white woman.' She goes on to undertake 'an investigation of whiteness and the embodied, gendered implications of *Disgrace*' (p. 20). Work such as Horrell's would have been quite novel in 2002, but the passing of time has seen an avalanche of critical material on this novel, most of which has highlighted its 'embodied, gendered implications'. Horrell concludes by stating that it is not her intention to find either the novel or its author guilty of racism or sexism; rather, her essay 'trace[s] a moment in white postcolonial writing that is attempting to negotiate the existential term for a humiliating present and a dark, disrupted future' (p. 30). Somewhat ironically, such vocabulary places the essay within a body of thinking in which white victimhood is the real issue in post-apartheid South Africa, an issue to which I return below. Benaouba Lebdai, 'Bodies and Voices in Coetzee's *Disgrace* and Bouraoui's *Garçon Manqué*' (pp. 33–43), draws on novels by a South African and an Algerian novelist to examine the social imaginary of two deeply scarred societies. Like Viola and Horrell, Lebdai sees the work of fiction and 'the depiction of [the] "corporeality" of characters' (p. 33) as bearing traces of history and mirroring the material conditions of a society. The essay offers interesting responses to the novels, often closely supported by textual evidence, but just as often the novels are retold rather than critically examined.

Apart from Lessing (see below), the other main focus of 2008 was the work of J.M. Coetzee. Both have been awarded the Nobel Prize, and that no doubt boosts the body of criticism their writing receives. However, it is tempting to trace such attention also to their status as white writers working out of an Africa to which the white person has an increasingly tenuous claim. Julie Mullaney's ' "This is dog country": Reading off Coetzee in Alex Miller's *Journey to the Stone Country*' (*PcT* 4:iii[2008] 1–18) is original, engaging and rewarding in its comparison of two outstanding writers whose fiction repeatedly returns to the haunting of settler societies in South Africa and Australia. Miller's work in particular has long been concerned, almost obsessively so, with a patient and courageous uncovering of the multiple layers of history, memory and culture through which the (white) Australian self has come to define being and belonging. Although much of his earlier writing reflected a similar concern, this is less the case in Coetzee's recent work. In *Disgrace*, however, Coetzee offers up one of the bleakest takes on the possibility of (white) belonging in post-apartheid South Africa. For Mullaney, 'Miller's nod to Coetzee...expands into a creative acknowledgement of a shared legacy, as both writers divulge a common set of difficulties in addressing the fabric of postcolonial settler cultures, where questions of complicity, responsibility and restorative justice now take centre stage' (p. 1).

Noam Gal's 'A Note on the Use of Animals for Remapping Victimhood in J.M. Coetzee's *Disgrace*' (*AfI* 6:iii[2008] 241–52) 'aims to join a growing group of studies about the nature of Nature in Coetzee's late works, some of which focus primarily on dogs' (p. 241). Commenting on one of the novel's most significant moments, Gal writes: 'The facile and swift killing of the dogs aligns them with Lurie and his daughter as innocent and defenceless victims, while it simultaneously endows the attackers with an aura of pure evil, that of villains who commit a forbidden act and deviate from any acceptable human values'. Since 'the dogs are not part of the political turmoil of post-apartheid South Africa', Gal proposes, they represent total innocence. Given the novel's 'replacement of the human with the animal' (p. 243), the killing of the dogs becomes the means by which white people are allowed a way out of the ethical dilemma of postcolonial South Africa; they are (like the dogs, newly rendered innocent and incomprehensibly victimized. Gal concludes his dense and subtle reading of the novel by stating that 'Lurie's existential process in the novel...is of becoming a healed victim, fully human, historically and morally re-established, an ex-victimizer' (p. 252). This is a persuasive reading of the novel, and of Lurie's character. However, the discussion would have been enriched by some recognition that dogs in South Africa have been trained from birth to hate black people, made into killing weapons in a state apparatus that controlled and remade the meaning and purpose of language and things. The newly discovered focus on animals in Coetzeean studies must work free of its Eurocentric standpoint. Might it be useful to consider the love of dogs and animals more generally as a variation of the many responses to Gayatri Spivak's cranky question on the right to voice, a debate that remains topical? Perhaps it is easier to speak on behalf of, or for, a creature presumed to be oppressed but unlikely to challenge the critic's desire to be good. That said, the debate on the representation of dogs and other four-legged creatures has emerged with growing intensity and indeed subtlety.

Yet another piece on Coetzee, this time exploring the theme of colonial violence through a close reading of *Waiting for the Barbarians* [1980] and *Diary of a Bad Year* [2007], is Robert Spencer's 'J.M. Coetzee and Colonial Violence' (*Interventions* 10:ii[2008] 173–87). This is a difficult essay to assess, as the author is adamant that either Coetzee's novels or the essay, or all of them, have the ability to proffer 'the necessary corrective to torture: an egalitarian and unabashedly humanist moral code based on our shared vulnerability to physical pain' (p. 174). I was less than persuaded that the essay had succeeded in 'offer[ing] an example of a form of literary criticism appropriate to an era that has demonstrated the manifest durability and even intensification of imperial ideologies and practices' (Abstract, p. 173). This kind of claim is the reason so much postcolonial criticism is seen as posturing and/or vicariously living off the suffering of others. Spencer concludes: 'human rights is where poetry becomes the law, where the imaginative sympathy engendered by writers like Coetzee is embodied in our actions and institutions' (p. 186). Elizabeth S. Anker works in this spirit in 'Human Rights, Social Justice, and J.M. Coetzee's *Disgrace*' (*MFS* 54:ii[2009] 233–67), a challenging essay with real flashes of brilliance, Anker takes on Coetzee's novel with the care and perspicuity of the forensic detective, and the reading stands out in a field already groaning under the weight of Coetzee scholarship. She makes no claims as to the unique agency of her essay, offering up instead a quietly intelligent, confident and deeply rewarding engagement with Coetzee's notoriously elusive writing.

'African City "Textualities"' is the focus of a special issue of the *Journal of Postcolonial Writing* (*JPW* 44:i[2008]), guest-edited by Ranka Primorac, who states that 'this special issue seeks to align itself with a growing body of literature celebrating the diversity and creativity of African cities outside the narrow and centralizing notions of both "Africa" and "modernity"' (p. 1). Primorac herself contributes an essay, 'The Modern City and Citizen Efficacy in a Zambian Novel' (*JPW* 44:i[2008] 49–59), that examines the representation of Lusaka in a novel by Sekeloni S. Banda to explore how 'it links Zambia's capital city to social change and the ongoing national debate to with citizen efficacy in the democratic process' (p. 49). Commenting on *Dead Ends'* intertwining of diverse genres, ranging from the classic detective novel to the hard-boiled thriller, she places the novel as a cultural and political contribution both to Zambia's 'social imaginary' (p. 56) and to writing in Southern Africa concerned with the place of citizen in the postcolonial African nation. The collection includes a number of other essays that focus on Southern Africa textual narratives. Meg Samuelson's 'The Urban Palimpsest: Representing Sophiatown' (*JPW* 44:i[2008] 63–75) is primarily an examination of a range of representations of the suburb of Johannesburg renamed Triomf (Triumph) by the apartheid regime and since then known once again as Sophiatown. Reading across written and filmic narratives, Samuelson combines a thorough and extensive knowledge of her subject with a confident and incisive critical analysis. Despite its somewhat repetitive structure, the essay fully conveys Sophiatown's long and fraught history of violence, dispossession and resistance that resonates with South African history as a whole. The figure of woman expresses the irrepressible force of Sophiatown, for 'while the urban modernity Sophiatown represented and inspired may have been razed by bulldozers, it has not been erased' (p. 69). In the broader setting of South African literary studies, often characterized by political statements showing critics' urgent desire to reassert their relevance in post-apartheid South Africa, Meg Samuelson's essay is a powerful demonstration of how literary criticism can articulate a political point through detailed, nuanced analysis of selected texts.

The following issue of the *Journal of Postcolonial Writing* includes a couple more essays intended for the earlier volume. In 'Ivan Vladislavić and the Possible City' (*JPW* 44:iv[2008] 333–44), James Graham reads the South African author's *Portrait with Keys: The City of Johannesburg Unlocked* [2006] to argue that Vladislavić offers up a different picture, less bleak than the common image of Johannesburg. Drawing on urban development theory and some of the work done on Johannesburg's transformations post-apartheid, Graham endorses what he believes is Vladislavić's emphasis on a more optimistic vision of the city's future. He writes: 'To read Vladislavić's portrait of Johannesburg is therefore to be opened to the possibility of profoundly different social systems *coexisting* in the same space' (p. 342). Graham's reading is informed and topical, but much too optimistic. The claim that Vladislavić's book disavows a *flâneur* aesthetic fails to account for the dangerous erotics of the book (in the sense of Georges Bataille's understanding of erotics as a play with death). The strength of Vladislavić's narrative is precisely its almost hysterical claim to survival in a city renowned for its unspeakable levels of violence. Indeed, Graham allows that the Johannesburg Vladislavić depicts serves as a comment on the residual presence of a divided Johannesburg in post-apartheid South Africa.

Also in *JPW*, Jane Poyner's 'Writing Under Pressure: A Post-Apartheid Canon?' (*JPW* 44:ii[2008] 103–14) undertakes a survey of recent South African literature, tracing the multiple forces of change unleashed initially by resistance to apartheid and then by an attempt to deal with its imprint on the fabric of the Rainbow Nation. 'In the tradition of engaged writing', she notes, 'contemporary South African novelists have pointed up the need both to bear witness to the past in order to build a better future and also to regard the promises of truth and reconciliation in the "Rainbow Nation" with a politically urgent and measured scepticism' (p. 112). This is an important assertion and one pursued with critical acuity and energy by Louise Bethlehem in *Skin Tight: Apartheid Literary Culture and its Aftermath* [2006], though Poyner makes no reference to this work. Poyner's essay reflects the growing concern among cultural and literary scholars to capture the new thematic, political and critical paradigms in Southern African studies in English.

Cheryl Stobie's 'Sisters and Spirits: the Postcolonial Gothic in Angelina N. Sithebe's *Holy Hill*' (*CW* 20:ii[2008] 26–36) argues that 'the most useful lens through which to analyse Sithebe's doubled representations is that of the postcolonial Gothic' (p. 26). This she does in her essay through a close reading of the novel that borrows application of the Gothic to postcolonial studies by critics such as David Punter. She asserts that 'If the Gothic is generally received as discomfiting and destabilizing, then the postcolonial Gothic is doubly so—and this effect is amplified when gender is also factored in' (p. 28). Of *Holy Hill* she says that 'it is not following the line of anti-Catholicism found in early Gothic fictions'; rather, 'it shows the difficulties involved in reconciling or even juxtaposing two different belief systems' (p. 31). In the kind of conclusion that has become almost de rigueur in South African literary criticism, she notes that 'The end of the novel offers no easy hope, but neither does contemporary South African society' (p. 34). Michael Wessels's 'Religion and the Interpretation of the /Xam Narratives' in the same issue (*CW* 20:ii[2008] 44–58) is one of two essays he published on this material, the other appearing in the *Journal of Southern African Studies*, '"The Story in which the Children are Sent to Throw the Sleeping Sun into the Sky": Power, Identity and Difference in a /Xam Narrative' (*JSAS* 34:ii[2008] 479–94). Wessels's essay in *Current Writing* is a fascinating examination of a single /Xam narrative, 'A Visit to the Lion's House'. The discussion juxtaposes a number of different responses to the story and assesses its role in the perpetuation of 'the idea that the Khoisan had no religion and, consequently, no right to land or humane treatment' (p. 44). However, Wessels warns against a tendency 'to regard the Bushmen [*sic*] as spiritual man, the embodiment of authentic, natural man' (p. 54). He goes on: 'What is important, in my view, is an enquiry into how /Xam categories of the supernatural, the secular, the profane and sacred are produced and reproduced in the discursive fields of the narratives' (p. 55). The theme of religion that frames many of the contributions to *Current Writing* 20:ii is discussed in 'Modern Prophets Produce a New Bible: Christianity, Africanness and the Poetry of Nontsizi Mgqwetho' (*CW* 20:ii[2008] 77–86), by Duncan Brown. Following a brief discussion on the little critical work on poet and intellectual Mgqwetho, which includes an essay by former South African president Thabo Mbeki (p. 78), Brown counters a 'secular/nationalist approach' (p. 79) with one that reads Mgqwetho's work from the perspective of 'the growing field of postcolonial biblical scholarship', especially 'in view of her own considerable interest in reading the Bible' (p. 79). This is a persuasive attempt at making sense of a writer whose own position and those of fluid political discourses of nationalism and identity do not always gel easily. Michael Chapman's contribution to the same journal is entitled 'Postcolonial Studies: A Spiritual Turn' (*CW* 20:ii[2008] 67–73) and this forcefully argued piece brings into play two key threads in postcolonial studies. The first is the relatively recent turn the essay's title detects, one which saw 'Ashcroft, Griffiths and Tiffin in the second edition of *The Post-Colonial Reader* (2006)—a standard reference book in university literature syllabuses— add a section in their Introduction on "The Sacred"' (p. 68). Noting a tendency to collapse religion and spirituality, Chapman stresses a 'focus . . . on a spiritual dimension in the postcolony or, more particularly, in postcolonial studies' (p. 68). Following a persuasive 'case-study' of a powerful utterance by a Khoi man on being expelled from his land by the apartheid regime, Chapman writes: 'The agonised words capture the dilemma of a person caught between his bitter resentment of historical dispossession and his belief in a just, albeit mysterious God' (p. 69). He concludes that 'the challenge [for the postcolonial literary curriculum] is to find an ethical and aesthetic language of response that, in the same social space, can value both the fiction of, say, Salman Rushdie and ! Kaha's voice of spiritual invocation' (p. 71).

Sally-Ann Murray's essay, 'On Ivan Vladislavić on Willem Boshoff on Conceptual Art' (*CW* 20:i[2008] 16–28), captures something of the mood of criticism in the 'transitional period'—a phrase used to denote the ongoing post-apartheid period. Like Mda, Ivan Vladislavić attracts a fair dose of critical attention, vying for critical space with the ever-growing body of research on J.M. Coetzee's writing. 'Vladislavić has become well known as a creator of clever, artful fiction' and 'has acquired a reputation as an influential contributor to public debates around South African art and art criticism' (p. 18). Murray's essay focuses on a book Vladislavić wrote on fellow South African artist Willem Boshoff and reads it as a form of self-reflexive writing in which 'Ivan Vladislavić—or perhaps the persona "Ivan Vladislavić"' emerges 'as an artist of idea' (p. 17). The real force of Murray's essay is its great intellectual verve and curiosity. To read Murray reading Vladislavić writing on Boshoff is to engage in a genuinely challenging act of criticism. Dirk Klopper's 'In Pursuit of the Primitive: Van der Post's *The Lost World of the Kalahari*' (pp. 38–46) approaches the book from a travel-writing theoretical perspective. At the heart of Klopper's essay are two questions: whether it is possible to demarcate a terrain of the native that is not already constituted by the terms established by modernity; and what means are available to the traveller, and to the travel writer, who enters the space of the 'the foreign and the strange' (p. 39) as an agent of modernity. His answer, arrived at through a close analysis of Van der Post's book, argues for a dynamic relationship between the categories 'primitive' and 'modern', one in which both terms are placed in constant and productive interaction. 'If Van der Post knows the Bushmen better than they know themselves, this is because they exist in him as his own primitive self' (p. 43). Hilary P. Dannenberg picks up some of these concerns about self and other, and the politics of the contact zone in 'Nadine Gordimer's *The Pickup* and the Desert Romance Tradition in Post/Colonial Anglophone Tradition' (pp. 69–82). Dannenberg juxtaposes Gordimer's novel to 'a colonial text in the tradition [of the desert romance], E.M. Hull's *The Sheik*, in order to show in detail exactly how Gordimer's *The Pickup* constitutes a multiple inversion and reworking of the paradigms of earlier narrative traditions' (p. 70). In setting the scene for a reading of Gordimer's work by analysing Hull's narrative, Dannenberg observes that Hull's character Hassan 'turns out not to be an Arab at all but of European lineage', linking *The Sheik* [1919] 'to the logic of traditional colonial romance in the manner of Rudyard Kipling's *Kim* and also of Edgar Rice Burroughs's *Tarzan* stories' (p. 72). Strangely, by this logic no one of Arab descent living in Europe can be considered European. Such exclusionary racial binaries are the stuff of colonial romance, but perpetuation of them into the present without critical question raises problems. How, and why, is cultural and ethnic hybridity a bonus in postcolonial writing but an impossibility for Hassan? Reading Dannenberg with Klopper's piece in mind, I wondered how the representation of the Libyan desert in *The English Patient* [1992], also co-opted by Dannenberg into the tradition of desert romance novel, can be such a potent sign of ethical engagement with the (space of) the other while Van der Post usually gets taken to task for his equally romanticized view of the Kalahari. Dannenberg's romanticization of the Libyan desert is crucial to a reading that demonizes *The Sheik* in order to elevate *The Pickup*, but the argument is slight. After all, Julie Summers's growing connection with the family of the Arab character Ibrahim in Gordimer's story might equally be read as a reiteration of the colonial romance. Julie, one might suggest, undergoes a phase of 'going native', something that Ibrahim seems well aware of. The presumption that Ibrahim is deluded by the American Dream while Julie can see through it has all the hallmarks of white South African liberalism; *they* just can't get it without the wise counsel of the white person. The novel's treatment of Ibrahim's intense desire to leave for the USA, of all places, becomes a key element in its articulation of an anti-Americanism that is typical of much writing that posits a critique of neoliberalism, which is what *The Pickup* also is. However unwittingly, the novel's comment on the brain drain from Africa and other developing locations presumes that 'the natives' owe it to their peoples and states to stay put, while the rest of *us* flow freely in modernity.

The Pickup [2001] and the concern with globalization and neoliberalism are taken up by Tony Simoes da Silva in 'Paper(less) Selves: The Refugee in Contemporary Textual Culture' (*Kunapipi* 30:i[2008] 58–72). Simoes da Silva argues that the refugee's growing visibility in novels and films, but also through the authoring or co-authoring of personal narratives of survival, positions the 'refugee subjectivity' as a perfect symbol of the zeitgeist of the twenty-first century. Working through Zygmunt Bauman and Giorgio Agamben, Simoes da Silva positions the refugee 'as modernity's underbelly, a subject position inextricable to a political unconscious where it both challenges and gives new meanings to the function of the nation-state' (p. 58). The author aims to complicate readings of refugees as invariably helpless victims of political and historical upheaval and focuses rather on some of the ways in which a refugee subjectivity manifests itself. 'For all the danger and alienation they experience, [refugees] live meaningful existences parallel to, even central to, mainstream society' (p. 72). The essay makes reference also to South Africa-based Angolan writer, Simão Kikamba, whose work was published in English by Kwela Books, and to a novella by South African author Patricia Schonstein Pinnock, *Skyline* [1999].

Vuyiswa Ndabayakhe and Catherine Addison write, in 'Polygamy in African Fiction' (*CW* 20:i[2008] 89–98), that 'If debate about polygamy is often strangely absent from the media and society in African countries, this is certainly not the case in fictional works from this continent, which very frequently explore the issue of marriage' (p. 89). In a strongly—even passionately—argued essay, Ndabayakhe and Addison offer an informed overview of the body of writing in favour of and against polygamy, highlighting the pressures brought to bear on these discourses by colonial and postcolonial politics. The essay undertakes a thematic and formal analysis of a number of literary works to argue that "[s]o many stories showing polygamy as the cause of African women's suffering would seem to most critics a sufficient damning indictment of the institution" (p. 94). Yet this is a somewhat simplistic view; polygamy is proscribed in most Western societies yet women continue to experience violence and oppression. Polygamy may be 'a stumbling block in the path to female emancipation and self-expression' (p. 96) but its end will require a little less critical naivety.

Zakes Mda's work also was the focus of a series of essays, often concerned with *The Heart of Redness* [2000]. Derek Alan Barker's learned discussion about whether Mda's writing is or should be seen as 'magical realist' is both endlessly fascinating and irritatingly pedantic. 'Escaping the Tyranny of Magic

Realism? A Discussion of the Term in Relation to the Novels of Zakes Mda' (*PcT* 4:ii[2008] 1–20) is also the kind of work likely to make it to every study of Mda for years to come; critics far more than readers are fascinated by the temptation to throw writers into the right box, or electronic folder. Zakes Mda's work is the focus of another essay in *CW* (20:i[2008] 105–13), "The Man, the Woman and the Whale: Exploring the politics of the Possible in Zakes Mda's *The Whale Caller*" this one by Ralph Goodman. Concerned with the enduring power of racial constructions in post-apartheid South Africa, the essay reads *The Whale Caller* as a text about ' "desire", "knowledge", "power" and "reason", as well as the psychic "demons" and "monsters" who turn out to be much more complex than these words denote' (p. 111). While it offers an insightful analysis of Mda's text, the real value of Goodman's essay is the way in which the novel is 'allowed to speak' to and with the reader through the critic, Goodman being merely a medium rather than an insufferable expert.

In 'Between Nature and Culture: The Place of Prophecy in Zakes Mda's *The Heart of Redness*' (*CW* 20:ii[2008] 92–102), Dirk Klopper focuses on Mda's use of a historical event as the key theme in the novel and especially on his reliance on the work of historian Jeff Peires (*The Dead Will Arise* [1989]) in order to do so. Klopper reads the novel within this socio-historical context and examines its 'depiction of a society negotiating the tensions between traditional practices and modernising imperatives' (p. 93). However, he examines not the figure of Nongqawuse, the young girl whose story Peires's book tells and whose actions were responsible for the defeat of the amaXhosa in the nineteenth century, but two other characters in the novel, Qukezwa and Camagu. Following a brief but detailed discussion of 'the emergence of the figure of the prophet in Xhosa society' (p. 94), Klopper goes on to state that 'Qukezwa experiences and interprets nature in ways that open the cultural symbolic to what lies beyond its current signifying capacity, reaching beyond the known to give sense to the possible' (p. 99).

Mda's debt to Peires in *Heart of Redness* is cause for a mini-kerfuffle when Andrew Offenburger accuses Mda of plagiarizing *The Dead Will Arise*. In a brutally forensic but thoroughly substantiated act of literary criticism, Offenburger shows, in 'Duplicity and Plagiarism in Zakes Mda's *The Heart of Redness*' (*RAL* 39:iii[2008] 164–99), that Mda's take on poetic licence at times does cross over into more complicated levels of borrowing. After first setting out his case through a close comparison between the texts, Offenburger goes on to discuss the act of subversive 'writing back' that characterizes much postcolonial fiction and plagiarism, situating Mda's novel against Yambo Ouologuem's *Le Devoir de Violence* and Calixthe Beyala's *Le Petit Prince de Belleville*. According to Offenburger, while both these works have emerged from years of negative criticism and even opprobrium as novels that manage to convey their respective authors' sense of artistry, the same cannot be said of Mda's novel. Zakes Mda himself was given the opportunity to respond to the piece (and did so seemingly unaware of the identity of his accuser; he refers to the author of the essay as 'he or she'). In 'A Response to "Duplicity and Plagiarism in Zakes Mda's *The Heart of Darkness* by Andrew Offenburger"' (*RAL* 39:iii[2008] 200–3) Mda points out the obvious fact that his novel is dedicated to Peires and that the latter's book is acknowledged in *The Heart of*

Redness as the key source for the novel; Offenburger himself makes this point. Mda also notes that the other major influence in the imagining of the novel was his own familial and ethnic oral tradition of storytelling. Ultimately Mda's quiet and measured piece serves as a powerful counterweight to Offenburger's essay, but it fails to rebut its core thesis.

The work of South African poet P.J. Philander is little known, a combination of the passage of time and changing literary fashions. Philander was a 'Coloured' South African poet who wrote in Afrikaans, and the kind of verse he produced has little to say to the New South Africa. Hein Willemse's essay, 'Integrity and Ambivalence: The Case of the South African Poet P.J. Philander's Epic Poem, *Zimbabwe*' (*RAL* 39:i[2008] 125–48), proposes that *Zimbabwe* was a complex response to the imaginative engagement with the socio-political setting of Southern Africa that epitomized a certain way of dealing and responding to Africa as something foreign to South Africa. As he writes, 'South African education policies, under the successive apartheid regimes, actively discouraged knowledge of or identification with countries to the north of the Limpopo River' (p. 125). Willemse offers a brief but thorough account of the myth of origin that surrounded the ruins of Great Zimbabwe until the early twentieth century and which ascribed it to the Phoenicians because Africans were supposed incapable of building such a structure. Quoting at length from the poem, Willemse seeks to trace a tension that he believes it articulates between a dominant settler standpoint, to return to Bhabha, and 'the tale of an abortive colonization—mainly brought about by the settlers' insularity, their inability to read the signs of history, and their failure to survive through strategic compromise' (p. 141). Willemse's reading places Philander as a 'political moderate' trapped in an environment that demanded unambiguous political stances. This is a predicament shared in part by a fellow, younger South African writer, the white Mark Behr, whose first novel was initially written in Afrikaans and then translated by him. Cheryl Stobie's 'Fissures in Apartheid's "Eden": Representations of Bisexuality in *The Smell of Apples* by Mark Behr' (*RAL* 39:i[2008] 70–86) chooses to read bisexuality in the days of apartheid as a figuration of the stress it placed on individuals. 'The bisexual figure of Dad reveals that the white male Afrikaner, and by extension apartheid South Africa, cannot live up to the onerous strictures at its heart' (p. 81). Stobie's thoughtful response to the novel and to its political setting illustrates a kind of literary criticism that is richly enhanced by a close engagement with critical theory. She offers a close critical reading that is generous in the way it reaches out to the text and uncompromising in its observations on the novel's ambivalent politics. As she writes at one point: 'Reading *The Smell of Apples* is . . . much like wearing bifocal lenses: one sees what the young Marnus sees, then, with a quick shift of perspective, one sees what the boy, enclosed in a false education, cannot see' (p. 78). The strength of this essay is precisely its ability to make the reader, too, occupy Manus's position, and that of his father, or of a white South African man in apartheid South Africa.

This focus on ever-shifting binaries that seeks to envision a post-binary world-view even as it recognizes the impossibility of such a stance is picked up by Pallavi Rastogi in a close reading of Indian South African author Ahmed

Essop. In 'Citizen Other: Islamic Indianness and the Implosion of Racial Harmony in Postapartheid South Africa' (*RAL* 39:i[2008] 107–24) Rastogi laments the passing of a close political solidarity amongst non-whites in the New South Africa, arguing that Indians in particular now bear the brunt of much of the distrust felt by South Africa's ever larger black population, in which unemployment figures usually hover above 40 per cent. Rastogi's thesis is built on the kind of semi-sociological study that remains especially strong in Southern African studies. For Rastogi, Essop's work shows that it is especially 'South African Indian Muslims... [who] are subject to another level of alterity, furthering the neurosis of an identity already fractured by centuries of otherness' (p. 108). The essay concludes with a bleak premonition that post-apartheid South Africa's failure to properly integrate South African Indians 'compels us then to question its very "legitimacy" as a *truly* postcolonial nation' (p. 122).

Ronit Frenkel, in 'Performing Race, Reconsidering History: Achmat Dangor's Recent Fiction' (*RAL* 39:i[2008] 149–65), sets out to 'argue that Dangor narrates a complex and nuanced alternative to dominant under-standings of South Africa, moving away from a bifurcated logic of black and white, good and bad, past and present into a byzantine and intricate conception' (p. 150). Although one might point out that the term 'byzantine' is already part of a dichotomous way of seeing and knowing that positioned (and positions) 'the Orient' as a site and a source of mystery and outright confusion, as Edward Said stressed repeatedly, the essay offers a persuasive response to Dangor's fictions. Frenkel underlines the force of 'narratives of ambiguity [that] reflect what was suppressed during apartheid, while also revealing the resurfacing of these repressed narratives, in a postapartheid present' (p. 156), and in this way it speaks to the 'archaeological' impulse in South African studies noted above. In this new paradigm it has become de rigueur to adopt a Janus-like standpoint where the present has almost no future, merely a past haunting backwards into further rehearsals of trauma and despair. Frenkel is not immune from this, and in part the essay responds to novels that are obsessed with the past, as in *Bitter Fruit*'s treatment of the TRC's work. But it is arguable that critics too often adopt a default position that forces the work of fiction into what has become such a dominant critical paradigm. Significantly, despite the attention to a splintering of dichotomies, work such as Frenkel's makes no allusion to theoretical contributions to black (and other) identities found in the writing of Stuart Hall or Paul Gilroy.

Michael Green's 'Translating the Nation: From Plaatje to Mpe' (*JSAS* 34:ii[2008] 325–42) takes a rather different tack, though the comparison it undertakes remains concerned with apartheid and its aftermath. As he notes, the 'aim here...is to identify ways in which the trope of translation as both a literal and a figurative activity operates within notions of nationalism developed in radically different discursive environments' (p. 327). In an extensively researched discussion on the politics, and indeed the poetics of cultural translation in a society as multilingual as South Africa, Green brings into play the dynamic ways in which language, culture and nationalism operate. Plaatje's use of English as a medium, he says, reflects the writer's 'commitment to the multilingual nature of the nation' and 'a reciprocal attitude to translation that runs directly counter to the almost standard assumption of translation as a violation that operates in postcolonial translation studies' (p. 331). Green's essay offers a response genuinely attuned to the complexity of power and cultural relations in the postcolonial moment.

Also in *JSAS* (34:iii[2008] 575–90), Barbara Caine's '"A South African Revolutionary, but a Lady of the British Empire": Helen Joseph and the Anti-Apartheid Movement' makes no effort to smooth the contradictions in Joseph's personal and political attitudes; rather, Caine exposes them precisely in order to create a multilayered portrait of Joseph's ongoing negotiation of her position as a white woman and as a Christian working in a Marxist movement committed to state secularism. Caine writes: 'The tenor of Joseph's relationships was always problematic: her demands could be unreasonable and her demeanour difficult. She sought acceptance, but often eschewed intimacy' (pp. 590–1). However, she was warmly embraced by the Nelson Mandela, whose description of her Caine adopts as the title of her essay, and Winnie Mandela and many other ANC operatives would call her 'the mother of the struggle' (p. 591). The shift away from literature seen in Caine's essay is one reflected also in Aaron L. Rosenberg's 'Making the Case for Popular Songs in East Africa: Samba Mapangala and Shaaban Robert' (*RAL* 39:iii[2008] 99–120). Rosenberg's intellectually engaging discussion makes the case that music 'is one of the most widely communicated forms of verbal art on the continent' and as such it offers a pertinent site for study of the performance of postcolonial identities. This is an obvious but often overlooked point. Like Green, Rosenberg identifies in literature a residual colonial standpoint that popular cultural forms such as music can overcome more successfully. In a compelling essay, Rosenberg undertakes a detailed comparison between Mapangala and Robert, concluding that, in spite of their 'different geographies and chronologies, [they] are both engaged in constructing and breathing life into communities of self and collective identity that exceed, supersede, and explode conventional notions of nation and ethnicity as expressed through Eurocentric models of identity' (p. 117). There are some odd moments in the essay—why use Pratt (p. 108), given the wealth of analysis on postcolonial 'writing back' from a literary perspective?—and a tendency to continually defer the argument by tackling relatively minor issues, but on the whole this is a strong contribution to critical studies of contemporary African urban identities.

In 'Toward an African Ecocriticism: Postcolonialism, Ecology and *Life & Times of Michael K*' (*RAL* 39:i[2008] 87–106) Anthony Vital adopts an ecocritical focus and reads J.M. Coetzee's novel in order to propose that 'Ecocriticism, if it is to pose African questions and find African answers, will need to be rooted in local (regional, national) concern for social life and its natural environment.' Crucially, he argues, 'It will need, too, to work from an understanding of the complexity of African pasts, taking into account the variety of responses to currents of currents of modernity that reached Africa from Europe initially, but that now influence Africa from multiple centers, European, American, and now Asian, in the present form of the globalizing economy' (p. 88). I quote at length because it strikes me that Africa emerges here as merely a *tabula rasa* recipient of the various waves of an outside modernity. As the essays collected in the 'Symposium on Engaging Modernities: Cultural and Intellectual Trajectories from East and Southern Africa' (*JCL* 43:i[2008] 79–133) show, that was hardly ever the case. Vital's essay is caught between a desire to argue that the novel constitutes a critique of 'colonial discursive inscription' and seeing it as part of the modernizing project. While his reading of *Life & Times of Michael K* makes some incisive observations, ultimately the essay falls back into a simplistic romanticization of Nature that is, as if by default, the position of much ecocritical thinking. I wonder if a reading of popular fiction or fiction in general produced elsewhere in Africa would yield this kind of anguished attempt at squeezing the love of nature from the words on the page. Vital suggests that 'if it is possible to link conservation and empire, it is also possible to perceive a new kind of concern for the environment emerging in the post-colonial era, one attuned to histories of unequal development and varieties of discrimination, including, of course, racism and sexism' (p. 90). Yet the critical discourses it engages with trace their genealogy to Wordsworth, Rousseau and other European literary figures rather than to non-Western figures. The work of Kwame Appiah and Vandana Shiva, for example, might have much to teach contemporary literary studies. Vital's analysis of how Coetzee fails to make his novel 'speak Nature' is passionate and clearly well intentioned, but it is hard to see why Coetzee or anyone else should have to come up with the goods for critics 'wanting to make a world different from the one (set in motion circa 1492) in which they are caught' (p. 102). Could we quibble over that date too?

The ethical turn in postcolonial literary studies resurfaces in Irene Visser's essay, 'How to Live? Guilt and Goodness in Rian Malan's *My Traitor's Heart*' (*RAL* 39:iii[2008] 149–62). Malan wrote his book after returning from the USA, where he lived for many years, to post-apartheid South Africa. In a powerful narrative of introspection that ranges between self-mocking exhibitionism and trenchant political critique, Malan takes to task the meaning of whiteness in South Africa. As an Afrikaner returning to a country haunted by the horrors committed in his name, 'the impediment to a free and fulfilling existence for Malan is his sense of guilt, of betrayal and complicity', Visser notes (p. 149). Her essay goes against much of the criticism that has placed Malan's memoir as a self-indulgent and second-rate work of self-pleading, revealing it rather as the flawed but also courageous and imaginative narrative it is.

In ' "There's got to be a man in there": Reading Intersections between Gender, Race and Sexuality in South African Magazines' (*AfI* 6:iii[2008] 275–91), Nadia Sanger undertakes a detailed analysis of a series of contemporary magazines according to their readership. In addition to the usual focus on gender, the research also considers the race of the intended readerships. In broad terms, all magazines attract a 'rainbow' readership, as is to be expected in the Rainbow Nation, but percentages vary from one publication to another. This is a peculiarly South African essay that would have benefited from a brief account of the hypocritical censorship rules under apartheid. Then, the breasts of naked white women in magazines were decorated with appropriately placed stars, while black women's breasts could be purchased in the form of postcards available from cosmopolitan Johannesburg to the most backward *dorp* in the back of beyond. As it is, Sanger's case comes across as rather derivative, given all the work following John Berger's *Ways of Seeing* [1972] about the packaging of women's (and men's) bodies in the popular media. Yet *Ways of Seeing* does not even rate a mention here, despite claims that some, if not all, the women depicted in these magazines are framed within well-established patterns of objectification of the female body. Again, writing about how one 'construction not only hypervisibilizes black women as the "other" or the "African" but simultaneously presents white (hetero)femininity as normative and "empty" through its apparent lack of "culture", "ethnicity" and exoticism' (p. 289), she might well have referred to Edward Said's influential study, *Orientalism* [1978], or to similarly significant writings such as Reina Lewis's *Gendering Orientalism* [1995].

The *Journal of Commonwealth Literature* dedicated another symposium to what it termed 'Engaging Modernities: Cultural and Intellectual Trajectories from East and Southern Africa' (*JCL* 43:i[2008] 79–150), comprising three essays. The first essay, by Bhekizizwe Peterson, entitled 'Sol Plaatje's *Native Life in South Africa*: Melancholy Narratives, Petitioning Selves and the Ethics of Suffering' (*JCL* 43:i[2008] 79–95), sets out to challenge conventional readings of the novel as a derivative work marked by colonial mimicry. Peterson argues that *Native Life* should be read as showing how the 'new African intelligentsia . . . negotiated the complex and convoluted demands of a colonial existence' (p. 80). Drawing on postcolonial readings of the function of education in the colonial process, Peterson proposes that the novel be read as a savvier engagement with the constrained political conditions in which it was produced. *Native Life*, he says, was bearing witness to and recording for posterity the deleterious effects of the Native Lands Act of 1912. 'Speaking to us across a century', he writes, 'Plaatje compels us to reflect on humankind's disturbing ability to remain unmoved by the suffering of others' (p. 94). Not unlike Peterson, Khwezi Mkhize uses 'Citashe's Apostrophe—"Zimkile! Mfo wohlanga": The Unfinished "Preface" to an African Modernity' (*JCL* 43:i[2008] 97–114) to attack frameworks placing African writers and intellectuals under a foreign lens. However unwittingly, critics have failed fully to understand 'Zimkile!' because many have worked with imperfect or incomplete translations of the poem, or read it through a model that privileges the 'political urgency' of the work of art. As Louise Bethlehem persuasively argues in *Skin Tight* [2006], the weight of 'political urgency' on South African writing and criticism has led to some narrow and simplistic work. Mkhize reads Citashe's poem as a foundational work for a textual black culture in South Africa and for a black political consciousness as well. This is a lucid and thoroughly challenging essay. In a brilliant performance of argument Mkhize totally inhabits the discussion of the fraught understanding of modernity in Africa and of African modernity. As he puts it: 'Citashe's call to stately arms (the pen), readily draws on a double-voicedness that transgresses colonial meanings through ambiguity, slippage and mimetic subservience' (p. 104). As he closes the discussion, Mkhize suggests that I.W.W. Citashe's 'anxieties, which were the result of the unfulfilled promises of modernity, necessitated that the present and the future be a time of radical openness' (p. 112). The third essay, by Grace Musila, is discussed below.

Sabrina Brancato's argument in 'Afro-European Literature(s): A New Discursive Category?' (*RAL* 39:iii[2008] 2–13) is a provocative one, if not entirely original. Drawing on what she perceives as a growing visibility of Afro-European cultural production and the strength of an attendant critical discipline, Brancato surveys of some of the most significant Afro-European writers at work in non-anglophone Europe. While this is an important task likely to lead others to expand on it, Brancato's critical position is too often simplistic. To speak of Buchi Emecheta as an Afro-European writer requires that one recognize also her dual status as a Nigerian writer, one seen as a founding force within African women's writing. Similarly Nigerian Chica Unigwe may live in Europe, but her work reflects a clear and often poignant exilic perspective; Unigwe writes first of all as a modern Nigerian woman (and we can debate the meaning of 'modern'). Incidentally, her work may indeed be poorly known in Europe, but it is inaccurate to say that little is available in English; much of it is, though increasingly she publishes in other European languages (Dutch). Brancato's essay would have benefited greatly from a reading of Lynn Innes's comprehensive study of Afro-European writing across centuries.

Along with the 'spiritual turn' and 'the ecological turn', postcolonial studies have also recently taken on a concern with trauma and the usefulness of trauma theory for discussions of colonization. This is hardly surprising when we consider that Frantz Fanon trained as a psychoanalyst and both novelists Kenyan Ngugi wa Thiong'o and Barbadian George Lamming, among so many others, have stressed in their work the lasting effects of colonialism in the colonized psyche. *Studies in the Novel* devoted an entire issue to this theme, co-edited by Stef Craps and Gert Buelens. As might be expected, the enduring impact of colonialism, apartheid and racism means that Southern African literary narratives account for half the essays in the collection. Making close use of Roseanne Kennedy's earlier writing, Mairi Emma Neeves's 'Apartheid Haunts: Postcolonial Trauma and Lisa Fugard's *Skinner's Drift*' (*SNNTS* 40:i–ii[2008] 108–26) explores Fugard's fragmented narrative structure to argue that her constantly "shifting points of view...challenge...and sub-vert...the isolating power of trauma' (p. 116). The concept of a traumatic memory that Fugard explores in her novel is one identified by Shane Graham in '"This text deletes itself": Traumatic Memory and Space-Time in Zoe Wicomb's *David Story*' (*SNNTS* 40:i–ii[2008] 127–46). Graham makes the case that too often in South African literary studies the work of the Truth and Reconciliation Commission is insufficiently analysed, and argues specifically for a critique of the use of trauma theory because its emphasis on the 'the "talking cure" paradigm' which the TRC favoured 'is inadequate in itself for the complex dynamics that emerged from and shaped South Africa's revolutionary transition due to that paradigm's tendency toward a depoliti-cized individualist psychology' (p. 129). Leaving aside whether what happened in post-apartheid South Africa can be described as 'revolutionary', Graham overlooks the obvious, if admittedly naive, approach the TRC adopted, one in which each individual story was to be woven into a narrative of collective trauma. Graham's essay offers a painstakingly detailed reading of Wicomb's novel; it combines perspicuous criticism with narrow critique that overplays the importance of the imaginative or critical work in the creation of a politics of material reparation. Finally, in 'The Past in the Present: Personal and Collective Trauma in Achmat Dangor's *Bitter Fruit'* (*SNNTS* 40:i–ii[2008] 146–54) Ana Miller again picks up on the disseminated focalization of narrative as a technique that allows for multiple viewpoints to emerge and for counternarratives to operate. Dangor's novel, with its intense dramatization of the haunting of the past in the daily existence of a couple in post-apartheid South Africa, brings Miller to say that it 'represents the damaging psychological effects of repressed and silenced trauma, but it also raises numerous difficulties that surround the articulation and communication of trauma' (p. 154). It too resists, or at least complicates, the TRC's emphasis on the narrativization of trauma as part of a national healing process. Miller's essay is part of a wider attitude within contemporary South African literary studies that the TRC 'did not get it right', that some novelists and filmmakers are starting to redress this flaw and that the critic finally can put it right. Miller's essay is much too thoughtful to be lumped in this group, for as she notes, individuals deal with trauma in completely diverse ways. Besides, 'Although the novel focuses on personal traumas, these are set against the background of collective traumatic experiences' (p. 152). She brings into relief the way in which 'Literature can individualise and differentiate generalized experiences to foreground heterogeneity, complexity, and ambiguity' (p. 154) without seeking to arrogate for itself the sole ability to do so.

The title of Maurice Taonezvi Vambe's 'Changing Nationalist Politics in African Fiction' (*AfI* 6:iii[2008] 227–39) is slightly misleading, as the essay focuses pretty much exclusively on Zimbabwean writing. The case Vambe makes is persuasive and while not entirely original, as he acknowledges, it is especially topical in the context of Zimbabwe's current crisis. Vambe is interested in the ongoing dialogue, or contestation between nation, national consciousness and literary narration, terms that he defines via the work of Simon Gikandi, Homi Bhabha and, less persuasively, Terry Eagleton. It is a pity that Abdulrazak Gurnah's insightful discussion of nationalism in europhone African writing, in the *Financial Times* in 2007, is not mentioned in this discussion, as it set out an exemplary template for the kind of work Vambe does here. That said, the value of Vambe's essay rests in his close readings of selected Zimbabwean novels. As a Zimbabwean scholar long based in South Africa, Vambe's work betrays a real sense of urgency and personal engagement with the material, something that often sharpens his critical and political standpoints. Yet, just as often the novels are read as if the writers intended them exclusively as challenges to 'official descriptions' (p. 228) and Vambe repeatedly ascribes to the selected novelists political views and intentions that the novels do not support in the same straightforward manner.

Also writing on Zimbabwe, in '"Mortgaged Futures": Trauma, Subjectivity and the Legacies of Colonialism in Tsitsi Dangarembga's *The Book of Not*' (*SNNTS* 40:i–ii[2008] 86–101) Rosanne Kennedy places the second novel by Dangarembga in a critical dialogue with the work of Frantz Fanon. In a wide-ranging and stimulating discussion that combines trauma and postcolonial theories and the critic's ability to rise to the challenge of the work of imagination. Kennedy has previously co-edited with Jill Bennett a collection of essays on the overlap between trauma and postcolonial studies entitled *World Memory: Personal Trajectories in Global Time* [2003], and her present essay is part of a larger attempt to expand on the possibilities trauma theory offers for a rethinking of contemporary postcolonial culture.

In the cities issue of the *Journal of Postcolonial Writing* (*JPW* 44:i[2008]) Grace Musila contributes 'Remapping Urban Modernities: Julie Ward's Death and the Kenyan Grapevine' (*JPW* 44:i[2008] 37–47), returning to the theme she explores in another essay she published in 2008, the death of British tourist Julie Ward in 1988 (*JCL* 43:i[2008] 115–34; discussed below). Musila now discusses the climate of rumour and innuendo that grew in the aftermath of Ward's death, and the Kenyan police's inability to ascertain its cause. Musila writes that 'To understand the amount of interest that Julie Ward's death was able to mobilize in the Kenyan grapevine, it is imperative to place it within the Kenyan socio-political and its social imaginaries as related to the [former Kenyan president] Moi state' (p. 39). In the context of a deeply secretive government that perpetrated constant acts of violence on its people, the unresolved death of a white foreigner served as a catalyst to a fecund culture of claim and counter-claim and in turn led to a new phase in debates about modernity as inherently European and colonial, and tradition as endemic to Africa. In the context of *JPW*'s thematic focus, Musila's essay foregrounds the evolving dialectic between rural and urban spaces in contemporary Kenya, and by implication in Africa more generally. Although the essay makes its case with some persuasiveness, greater attention to the function and power of rumour in postcolonial settings would have supported the attention it demands should be given to context and history in order to avoid 'the essentialising of Africa' (p. 43) that the journal issue seeks to challenge.

The focus shifts to literary historiography with an energetic discussion of a number of books produced in response to the murder of Julia Ward in the Maasai Mara in 1988. In 'Between the Wildebeest, Noble Savages and Moi's Kenya: Deceit and Cultural Illiteracies in the Search for Julie Ward's Killer(s)' (*JCL* 43:i[2008] 115–34) Grace Musila's sustained dissection of the commodification of the Maasai, a people who 'have enjoyed a longstanding monopoly of the role of East Africa's noble savages', points out how a people 'believed to have successfully resisted Western modernity have now become an iconic marker of [modern] Kenya, the tourist paradise' (p. 123). Their involvement in Ward's death revives 'a certain [colonial] discursive archive on Africa' (p. 116) that continues to inflect relations between British (and by implication Western) people and Kenyans, here an obvious emblem for Africans. By default, Musila offers a scathing critique of the enduring power of whiteness, an invisible visible discourse that also determines how critics have continued to operate. Musila is less persuasive when she argues that, in their dealings with both the Kenyan police and legal system and with the father of Julie Ward, who undertook his own investigations and went on to write one of the books Musila critiques, the Maasai took advantage of their liminal position to avoid having to engage the apparatus of modernity. There is a certain irony in the way in which an essay that articulates such a powerful attack on the colonial romance itself falls into the trap of romanticizing a shrewd and wily Maasai, at one with the past but just as easy with the present and presumably the future. However, it would be churlish to conclude on this note, for Musila's essay is a sophisticated and incisive critique of the ethnographic gaze in travel writing, in the tourism industry's role in creating 'exotic locations', but also in much cultural criticism.

In the *Bodies and Voices* collection already mentioned, Chantal Zabus's 'From "Cutting Without Ritual" to "Ritual Without Cutting": Voicing and Remembering the Excised Body in African Texts and Contexts' (in Borch et al., eds., pp. 45–67) is historically contextualized, theoretically provocative and critically insightful. Her discussion of 'Female Genital Cutting', rephrased in the essay as 'female excision', contextualizes the practice in (post)colonial and anti-colonial discourses in pre-independence Kenya and in Egypt, making the case that the practice of female excision is complex and always subsumed within strong political discourses and social forces. Echoing a concern explored by much of the writing collected in *Bodies and Voices*, Zabus argues that 'Literature remains a privileged place where women's voices are heard, all the more so in women's experiential texts. "Voicing" acquires its full dimension when the Western-illiterate or semi-educated teller recounts her experience of infibulation to an amanuensis, that is, a person, often a Western woman, who transcribes from dictation' (pp. 63–4). Ironically, perhaps because of its difficult content and theoretical framework, the essay foregrounds an issue that inflects earlier essays as well, the politics of editorial touch. Admirably light in handling others' stories, it is vexing in the case of Maya Garcia Vinuesa's reading of Yvonne Vera's *Butterfly Burning* in 'A Woman's Body on Fire' (in Borch et al., eds., pp. 69–79). Although well-intentioned, the essay is riddled with mistakes. The name of Vera's main character, for example, appears in three different spellings, once on the same page, and the racial situation in Southern Rhodesia is described as 'apartheid' without any qualifications (p. 69). Clearly, the author is responsible for ensuring that such details are correct, and that pronouns are not left dangling in search of a noun, but a heavier editorial hand would have ensured that what is in essence an interesting discussion was not seriously undermined by poor expression and structure.

Also writing on Vera, Jessica Murray claims that her 'works can be read as examples of testimony: as texts which, though fictional, nevertheless provide testimonial evidence of the trauma experienced by the characters and by the broader Zimbabwean society' (p. 1) in 'Tremblings in the Distinction between Fiction and Testimony' (*PcT* 4:ii[2008] 1–19). This is hardly a novel idea: as far back as 2004 Terence Ranger, perhaps still the pre-eminent scholar on Zimbabwean history, credited Vera's fiction with making him rethink his own interpretation of history. As Ranger stressed, in the context of Robert Mugabe's hijacking of the writing of the nation's history, Vera's fiction served as a counternarrative that both challenged and corrected Zimbabwe's dominant narrative. Nevertheless, Murray's reliance on the work of Jacques Derrida, notably in *Demeure: Fiction and Testimony* [2000], provides an interesting reading of a quintessentially African writer within a broader theoretical and critical framework. I wondered, though, about her description of Zimbabwe as 'a post-conflict society' (p. 17).

Following the award to Doris Lessing of the Nobel Prize in literature, a
conference at Leeds Metropolitan University in 2007 sought to address her
work in the context of the author's African background and the *Journal of
Commonwealth Literature* dedicated a symposium to some of the papers
presented (*JCL* 43:ii[2008]). In the words of the guest editors and conference
organizers Susan Watkins and Claire Chambers, 'critics have been, until
comparatively recently, reluctant to see Lessing as a postcolonial' (p. 3), so the
essays collected here seek to complicate conventional profiles of Lessing as a
'mother figure' of contemporary Western feminism by looking at her work
with reference to her time in Rhodesia. As in *Bodies and Voices*, many of the
works in *JCL* explore a question that has long haunted postcolonial studies,
Gayatri C. Spivak's 'Can the Subaltern Speak?' [1988]. This symposium adds
some interesting twists to answers provided so far. Yet can Lessing ever be
seen as speaking *for* or indeed *to* Zimbabwe? Is anything gained by reading
Lessing as a Zimbabwean writer? The editors believe so and state that 'As we
write this Editorial, the political and economic situation in Zimbabwe is
worsening. Lessing's work provides an important "backstory" for these
developments, suggesting *the* ways in which discourses about land and its
reapportionment are actually derivative of British colonial rule' (p. 9, emphasis
added). Even without that definitive article this seems much too ambitious a
claim. In many ways it is precisely through this insistence by largely white
critics working outside Zimbabwe (and often outside Africa, too) that their
work provides the perfect explanation of Mugabe's brutal actions that allows
him to get away with as much as he does. I wonder what makes the story of
whiteness such a powerful foil for the suffering of black Zimbabweans? In
'"Alone in a Landscape": Lessing's African Stories Remembered' (*JCL*
43:ii[2008] 99–115), Dennis Walder asserts that 'Lessing's dilemma is the vexed
one of all white settler writings, viewed from the post-colonial perspective.
How much is it possible to represent the Other?' (p. 109). Walder proposes that
the key to Lessing's 'mythic country' can be traced to her childhood in
Rhodesia 'in solitary communing with nature rather than with people' (p. 100),
however unwittingly confirming the view that for the white person Africa has
always been about nature rather than people. At the heart of Walder's reading
is a concern with the way Lessing re-signifies nostalgia as a powerful way of
looking forward rather back to the past. He writes: 'Her awareness of the
dangers of colonial fantasizing about the African soul, combined with her
sense of the socio-political realities of her corner of Africa, enable her to
distance herself from the limitations of personal nostalgia, although she has
been criticized for drawing on European cultural memories and their implicit
racism in doing so" (p. 108). Walder concludes by asserting that there are
many different types of nostalgia and that Lessing's is not a wasted emotion.
Nostalgia is also the main idea behind Victoria Bazin's 'Commodifying the
Past: Doris Lessing's *The Golden Book* as Nostalgia Narrative' (*JCL*
43:ii[2008] 117–31). Like Walder, Bazin seeks to read Lessing against the
critical mainstream, as it were, highlighting in the quintessentially postmodern
The Golden Book, 'the realist fragment embedded within the novel' (p. 117).
She states that 'A more historicized critical engagement with Lessing's
depictions of colonial Africa (the former Rhodesia) is required' since for

Lessing, 'artistic breakthrough comes with the awareness of the present not as a moment as a fixed point but rather as a process' (p. 119). For Bazin this is best encapsulated in the incident at the Mashopi Hotel ('the Mashopi hotel narrative thread', p. 121), a moment in the book that she believes constitutes not only 'a representation... of war-time Rhodesia, but also a metonym for a form of British colonialism that relates to post-war Englishness as it was tenuously reconfigured in the period after World War II' (p. 120). Commenting on Lessing's own interest in John Osborne's *Look Back in Anger* [1958], Bazin concludes: '*The Golden Notebook* then looks backwards to its literary precursors in a gesture of recognition and emulation, as well as forwards to the formal experiments of what would come to be known as postmodernism' (p. 130).

Christine W. Sizemore focuses on Lessing's convoluted and fraught 'standpoint', a term she uses here in its Bhabhaesque inflection. For Sizemore, in '*In Pursuit of the English*: Hybridity and the Local in Doris Lessing's First Urban Text' (*JCL* 43:ii[2008] 133–44), this is a position informed by Lessing's colonial, feminist and communist backgrounds. In a lively and detailed discussion of the novel, Sizemore shows how the book foregrounds Lessing's effort to come to grips with the reality of a London, and an England, which she knew as a (colonial) fiction. *In Pursuit of the English* is read here as a crucial stage in the transfiguration of the English colonial into the outsider in England: 'As she comes to know the people in her neighbourhood, Doris realizes that she must adjust her search for the "two grails" ': ' "England" [and 'the English']... and the "Working Class" as if they were universals' (p. 134). Referring to Lessing's alter ego in the work, she writes: 'Doris has to revise her understanding and experience of class' (p. 137). Sizemore is especially good at showing how Lessing's 'hybrid vision... overlays London geography with African images both visual and aural' (p. 140).

Although each of these essays makes some contribution to Lessing criticism, Julie Cairnie's 'Rhodesian Children and the Lessons of White Supremacy: Doris Lessing's "The Antheap" ' (*JCL* 43:ii[2008] 145–56) is perhaps the most original. Cairnie picks up on the story's concern with a relationship between two young boys, one white and the other black, to discuss the effects of discourses of race, gender, class and sexuality. At the core of this essay is a 'focus on boys and formation of masculinities (or "growing manhood"), as Tommy puts it in "The Antheap")' that underlines a belief that 'An understanding of the formation of white masculinities is critical to understanding the formation of Rhodesia and its de-formation' (p. 147). Cairnie's thesis is not unique in the link it establishes between heteronormative sexuality and racial discourses of superiority. However, the reading she offers is carefully and effectively situated within a broader concern in Southern Rhodesia with the creation and perpetuation of dominant white identities. In sharp contrast to the earlier essays, Cairnie argues that ' "The Antheap" never engages in nostalgia. It is, after all, written with a sense of presence and immediacy; and its chronological trajectory is not simply the end-point of the boys' story, but their unwritten future' (p. 153). Unfortunately Cairnie too cannot avoid taking a shot at Robert Mugabe's reign by noting yet again that Lessing's story 'points out childhood's mutability, its lack of fixity. In her story, this lends the boys' future a degree of hope but in Mugabe's Zimbabwe we may wonder if childhood, with its future trajectory, has any substantive meaning at all' (p. 154). Well, it does, whatever white critics and memoirists might think; it will surprise many people, but black children will go on being children.

Robin Visel's reading of *The Grass Is Singing* offers an interesting premise, that the novel may be read 'within the genre of Zimbabwean literature of Chimurenga, of resistance, in which violence is interpreted through ritual and the personification of natural forces' (p. 157). Visel's essay, ' "Then Spoke the Thunder": *The Grass is Singing* as a Zimbabwean Novel' (*JCL* 43:ii[2008] 157–66), is extensively researched and argued with ease and critical insight. She ranges across a wide body of critical theories, of criticism of the novel and of Lessing's work as a whole. However, despite the brilliant performance of argument, I was never persuaded that *The Grass Is Singing* is a Zimbabwean novel, nor that it engages in any meaningful way in the Chimurenga. Perhaps that does not matter.

(e) North Africa

Roy Armes's *Postcolonial Images: Studies in North African Film* is a book-length study of the political and cultural contexts of North African films that begins with a contextualization of the intricate links between the 'Novel, Film and Imperialism': 'Just as the continuity of imperial dominance from nineteenth to twentieth century (though now with a new dominating power and an added range of victims) is undeniable, so too is the Hollywood film's role as successor to the European novel as purveyor of the kind of narratives we so crave' (p. 3). Although Edward Said's detailed analysis, in his seminal *Culture and Imperialism*, of the nineteenth-century novel and its close affinity with contemporary European imperialism makes no mention of film, according to Armes, 'a connection remarkably similar to that linking the novel and European colonialism can be posited between the Hollywood movie and US twentieth-century imperialism' (p. 2). Likewise, French films shot in North Africa carry colonialist exclusions and distortions.

The preponderance of films focusing on settler-dominated Algeria coincided with the advent of scripts focusing 'exclusively on Europeans and rendering North Africans invisible' (p. 5). By contrast, Maghreb cinemas have illustrated the complex relationship between colonialism and nationalism with clarity, and, according to Armes, Maghreb filmmakers have always worked towards creating a true indigenous film production: 'Many, like the Algerian Merzak Allouache, saw their task as to tell stories in a simple way, to avoid the "heavy machinery" of big international production and to sweep away the "classical structures of cinema"' (p. 7). Thus the post-independence filmmakers and the national cinemas born in the late 1960s are part and parcel of 'the new sense of national identity which is seeking new forms of expression' (pp. 7–8). Besides being 'members of a Westernized bilingual elite of the kind found throughout the postcolonial world' (p. 9), the Maghrebian filmmakers are almost all men, and 'With only one director born in the 1970s, the dearth of younger filmmakers is even more striking than the paucity of women directors' (p. 10). Armes's rigorously theorized study is divided into two parts: part I, entitled 'Histories', comprises five chapters covering decades from the 1960s. Part II is a study of 'Themes and Styles' and the new importance of women directors: 'Today hybridity is a universal phenomenon and it is possible to posit "the exemplary status of the immigrant as the 'central figure' of a modernity that deprives everyone of familiar landmarks, forcing everyone to adopt new codes' (p. 184).

As mentioned earlier, Olaniyan and Quayson, eds., *African Literature*, includes articles on North African writing. Anissa Talahite's 'North African Writing' (pp. 38–45); Naguib Mahfouz's 'Nobel Lecture' (pp. 122–5) and Nawal El Saadawi's 'Dissidence and Creativity' (pp. 172–7) are choice essays focusing on what Talahite describes as a literature that 'offers a perspective that cannot be strictly confined within the geographical boundaries of North Africa. From a linguistic and cultural point of view, it is part of Arabic literature, a category that includes the literature from countries both of North Africa and the Middle East' (p. 38). The Berber culture and language that preceded the introduction of Arab culture also exert a significant influence, and a more recent birth of a new literature that originated from the experience of French colonialism in the former colonies of the Maghreb (Morocco, Algeria and Tunisia), have created, according to Talahite, a complex literary scene (p. 39). Mahfouz's Nobel lecture reinforces this sense of the heterogeneity of North African writing, and draws on both the Pharaonic and Islamic civilizations, from his own peculiar perspective as an Egyptian and Arab writer: 'It was my fate, ladies and gentlemen, to be born in the laps of these two civilizations, and to absorb their milk, to feed on their literature and art. Then I drank the nectar of your rich and fascinating culture' (p. 123). Focusing on the whole notion of 'Dissidence' and how it affects creativity, on the other hand, El Saadawi argues that, from both a historical and a contemporary perspective, there is an urgent need to 'Demystify Words'. The Arab word for 'dissidence', El Saadawi proposes, means the fighter who co-operates with others to struggle against oppression and exploitation, whether personal or political: 'If we wanted to translate these ideas into postmodern language, we might say that the deheroization of self and other is at the core real dissidence; of radical ethics, an aesthetics of creativity, or of critical ontology of self or other. Real dissidence avoids lapsing into the reverse essentialism of a cult of self or the other. It avoids one-way reflexive self-monitoring by including the other in this process. It is thus that the analytical links between ourselves and our social context are maintained' (p. 177).

2. Australia

(a) General
This year saw a consolidation of interest in the commercial aspects of Australian publication (labelled 'cultural materialism') including enthusiastic calls for the application of statistical analysis to publishing history. The Mark

Davis debate on the recent decline of Australian literary publishing spluttered to life again in articles that were mostly written in the final year of the Howard conservative government, although it is by no means clear that the advent of a Labor government will have much effect on those publishing conditions. Poetry again shows itself as a vital if uneconomic force, with many articles and three full-length books of criticism appearing, the best of which was Philip Mead's *Networked Language: Culture and History in Australian Poetry*. Eco-poetics continues to define itself, sometimes by claiming resonance with Aboriginal writing and sensibility. A useful article that attempts to lay out the field is that by Libby Robin discussed below. The year also saw Australian criticism looking outwards to other cultures and literatures, with books and articles concerned with Australia's representation of and relationships with China, Japan, Italy, Britain and Russia.

Peter Craven's 'Criticism and Fiction in Australia' (*Overland* 192[2008] 65–70) and Ken Gelder's 'Criticism and Fiction in Australia' (*Overland* 192[2008] 71–6) are two sides of a debate held at the Sydney Writers' Festival that revisits the broad question of value in literature, revealing some of the interesting politics of Australian criticism in the process. Craven advocates a confident Arnoldian position which affirms that 'the right to appreciate the finest writing that has been written . . . is one of the most fundamental things our democracy can give to a human being' (p. 66) and accuses Gelder of preferring classification and description to judgement. Gelder responds by rejecting any narrow quest for value in a 'vertical canon', since 'the cultural field these days is horizontal and promiscuous, not vertical and monogamous' (p. 72). Of particular interest is where their broadly opposing positions lead them on writers like Frank Moorhouse and J.M. Coetzee. In the following issue, Susan Lever contributes a coda to the debate using the same title (*Overland* 193[2008] 64–7). However, she vastly extends its range, lobbing grenades at unexpected targets in the manner of a matriarch at her ninetieth birthday party who is expected just to say thank you and instead tells the assembled family unpalatable home truths about themselves with perfect lucidity and sweetness. *Inter alia*, Lever tells us that Australian novels suitable for undergraduate teaching need to be 'about 150 pages long, demonstrate multiple narrative voice and transitional modernism, with a bit of adventure and the grounds for some postcolonial reading' (p. 64); Australian writers have no confidence in their audience (p. 65); Australian literary writers don't know much about 'the ordinary politics of working life' (p. 66) or for that matter about Australia since they don't watch enough television (p. 66); literary criticism requires scholarship, not research (p. 67) and Australian literary academics should spend less time writing grant applications to do unnecessary research and more time actually writing literary criticism (p. 67). In an aside on the problems of publishing criticism, Lever extols the publishing paradigm used for the *Journal of the Association for the Study of Australian Literature* which issues a hard copy for its members, but provides the content for free download via the Australian National Library. She claims that while only 300 hard copies are produced, all the articles are downloaded more than 200 times a month.

Libby Robin, in 'The Eco-Humanities as Literature: A New Genre' (*ALS* 23:iii[2008] 290–304), claims that responses to the science of climate change constitute a new genre of thought and writing in which the dichotomies of science and humanities and the human and the natural are exploded. She argues that Australia differs from the US in that Australia has never fetishized wilderness in the way that the North Americans did, always taking a predominantly acquisitive and utilitarian attitude to Australian nature as 'working landscape' (p. 300). Even had more attention been paid to Aboriginal views of land, this would not have encouraged a sense of wilderness since Aborigines value close connection to and involvement with country. A poetics of nature must have a non-rational imaginative dimension and a particularity (p. 299), so an Australian literature of the environment will not simply mirror its English or American predecessors. The current climate crisis makes the extreme climate of Australia and imaginative writings of it potentially paradigmatic for much of the world. CA Cranston shows the sort of application this theory can produce in 'Wet, in the Mindscape of the Dry: Water Tanks as Nature/Culture Signifiers' (in Devine and Crewe-Volpp, eds., *Words on Water: Literary and Cultural Representations*, pp. 23–38). Cranston believes that modern urban behaviour has been influenced by cultural and historical forces. Specifically, despite recent droughts, Australian suburbanites are reluctant to install (galvanized iron) water tanks because (1) galvanized iron is associated with the celebration of the heroic, dry Outback and hence it would be somehow unpatriotic actively to harvest water; (2) iron as a house-cladding material is associated with poverty and lower-class housing compared to the 'successful' materials of clay-brick, concrete block and stucco, and even timber; (3) for at least some Australians iron is associated with migrant camps and thus is a marker of exclusion and non-assimilation. Despite these contraindications, Cranston notes that some modern architecture is reprising corrugated iron as a cladding material (even, in one example, to the point of incorporating a fake water tank into a new home). This is a huge argument for which the literary examples supplied are grossly inadequate, but the article is interesting as a model of how literature and practical ecology may be increasingly brought together. One aspect of ecocriticism involves a philosophical repositioning of the human in the natural world. Another aspect is a more domestic meditation on how we relate sensuously to the natural on a daily basis. A good example of this type of criticism is Anne Collett's 'The Extraordinary in the Ordinary: Kate Llewellyn's Self-Portrait of a Lemon' (*Antipodes* 22:ii[2008] 111–15), which grounds some of Llewellyn's poems about lemons in sweeping arcs of contextualization through Llewellyn's garden journals, Collett's childhood memories of her father's orchard, a fairy story involving the missing element of piquancy supplied by salt (paralleling lemon), and Llewellyn's formal experiments with the Persian ghazal. The result is a surprisingly coherent and lambent analysis. Tony Hughes d'Aeth's 'Islands of Yesterday: The Ecological Writing of Barbara York Main' (*Westerly* 53[2008] 12–26) discusses the approach of a Western Australian writer who supplemented her scientific credentials with a more emotional element in her writing. However, she 'does not forsake the scientific paradigm so much as hybridise it', avoiding 'the obverse of pure instrumental knowledge, which is aestheticism' (p. 20). D'Aeth contrasts York Main's second book *Twice Trodden Ground* [1971] with the

slate of shire histories of the Western Australian wheat belt that celebrate
pioneer endeavours to clear scrub for wheat farming and build a rural social
infrastructure. In this book, d'Aeth claims, York Main manages to fuse two
systems, that of 'thoughts, feeling, memories and sense experience' and 'the
biological system of the vestigial bushland' (p. 22). Rather surprisingly, the
article concludes with a quotation from T.S. Eliot, who came to believe that
long tenure of land and mutual adaptation of landscape and human occupants
produced the 'happiest' nations (p. 24). Emily Bitto, in '"Simple Facts of
Light and Stone": The Eco-Phenomenology of Anthony Lawrence' (*ALS*
23:iii[2008] 251–63), argues that this well-published but rather neglected poet
has troubled critics with a too-present sense of self in his poems about the
natural world. However, this self actually shows Lawrence's sophisticated
ecological sense as he takes up contemporary questions of how humans
interact with environment. Far from being prescriptive, his approach can be
described as 'eco-phenomenological' (p. 257) since it acknowledges that
Nature is not known by the poet, but only experienced. The self–Nature nexus
is adroitly explored in half a dozen poems to show that Lawrence is 'a
distinctive and interesting ecopoetic presence in Australian poetry' (p. 262).

Veronica Brady's *The God-Shaped Hole: Responding to the Good News in
Australia* is a volume of short essays and addresses which are as much about
social and political relations in Australia as they are about spirituality and the
numinous in Australian fiction and poetry. Most of the pieces are too short to
more than gesture towards an argument, but the two essays that focus on
Andrew McGahan's *The White Earth* give the author a little more scope.
'Borders, Identity and Australia' (pp. 41–9) moves from the reminder that
'border' can indicate proximity and rapprochement as well as division to two
recent novels, *The White Earth* and Kate Grenville's *The Secret River*. Brady
argues that the views of McGahan's settler protagonist, McIvor, reflect those
of the One Nation political movement of the mid-1990s, seeking national
strength and unity through a triumphalist 'might is right' philosophy and view
of history. This masculine view is undermined at the end of the novel by the
more questioning stance of McIvor's nephew, William, who realizes that
owning the land will bring obligation rather than self-affirmation. Brady seems
to find *The White Earth* a touchstone for modern political attitudes since she
also uses it to comment on the Cronulla riots of 2005. 'After Cronulla: The
Defense of *The White Earth*' (pp. 81–7) discusses the phenomenon of the riots
and the reluctance of mainstream political leaders to admit that the
disturbances were racially or at least ethnically motivated. She relates this to
McIvor's attempted dominance and possession of the land, denying the
shadows and memories that its violent history had engendered. Other essays,
such as 'The Poetics of Place: Judith Wright's "At Cooloola"' (pp. 51–60) and
'An Incident in the Culture Wars: Judith Wright's "Haunted Land"'
(pp. 61–70), remind us that Wright had a strong sense of the land as bearing
dark reminders of guilty deeds. In 'The Dragon Slayer: Patrick White and
History' (pp. 33–40), Brady goes back to White's early novel *The Living and
the Dead* to argue that his modernist anti-realism was not a retreat from
reality, but rather an attempt to comprehend the spiritual that energized and
explained it. If Brady's lectures and talks seem slighter than the articles we are

used to from her, John Kinsella's pieces in *Contrary Rhetoric: Lectures on Landscape and Language* are full-length lectures that have translated to the printed page remarkably well. This collection ranges across historico-critical studies (early Western Australian poets Henry Clay and Elizabeth Deborah Brockman); unusually thematized literary criticism (Michael Dransfield as a landscape poet caught between city and country); postmodern cultural analyses (the mailbox in Australian, British and US consciousness); revisions of the Australian legend (Baynton's 'The Chosen Vessel'); and an essay on Australian pastoral. The only false note in the book is the essay on Brockman. Like so many other critics who have recuperated forgotten writers, Kinsella overvalues the skills of his quarry and somehow discerns a 'religious poet of complexity and ambiguity', a genuine 'landscape poet' and a 'deeply psychological poet' (p. 80) whose 'prosody is modern and complex' (p. 93) in what is really pretty awful verse.

Anita Heiss and Peter Minter, eds., *Macquarie PEN Anthology of Aboriginal Literature*, contains an introduction, 'Aboriginal Literature' (pp. 1–8), that traces the writing history of Aborigines alongside their political history since 1788. This significant anthology contains a wide variety of materials, from early letters and petitions to modern poetry, fiction, memoirs, song lyrics, political speeches, essays and journalism. Heiss also contributes an essay, 'Aboriginal Children's Literature: More than Just Pretty Pictures', to Bernadette Brennan's *Just Words* (pp. 102–17) which describes a range of recent children's books by Aboriginals and discusses their educational and cultural importance. Carole Ferrier, '"Disappearing Memory" and the Colonial Present in Recent Indigenous Women's Writing' (*JASAL* special issue[2008] 37–55), maps the emergence of Aboriginal women's writing since Monica Clare's *Karobran* in 1978. She explores the reasons for the preference for autobiographical realism in the early writing, but sees that early realism as coincident with 'self-constructions [of the authors] as moral and respectable' (p. 41). That mould was broken by Ruby Langford Ginibi, whose warts-and-all self-depiction in *Don't Take Your Love to Town* refused to adopt a moral pose for a white audience. Personal experience was increasingly supplemented by historical research, leading to the emergence of the motif of 'going back to land to recover lost history' (p. 39). Ferrier argues that one of the most frustrating aspects of Aboriginal existence is the inability (or refusal) of whites to listen to them. The latter half of the paper concentrates on two recent novels, Vivienne Cleven's *Her Sister's Eye* and Alexis Wright's *Carpentaria*. Ferrier's account shows how both novels move away from realism, use fire as a cataclysmic purifier in the action, incorporate positive views of male Aboriginal figures, employ humour and satire of authority as modes of resistance, and pursue hope by evoking 'other frames of reference and notions of time, of past, present and future' (p. 49).

Heather Kerr and Lawrence Warner edited *Projections of Britain in the United States of America, Australia and New Zealand 1900–1950*, the proceedings of a conference held at the University of Adelaide in 2004. Graham Tulloch's 'Walter Murdoch, Scottish Australian English Professor, on Britain' (pp. 63–70) shows how insidiously England or Britain remained an inescapable reference point for this widely published critic, no matter how much he tried to identify with and promote Australian literature. Bruce Bennett's 'Under Cover: Projections of British and Australian Secret Intelligence' (pp. 25–35) is a much more ambitious piece, not only sketching the history of Australian espionage from the earliest encounters of British and French ships off the Australian coast, but also showing that Australians had a role in some of the great British spy scandals of the twentieth century, including journalists like Philip Knightley investigating Kim Philby. Bennett argues that the presentation of Philby by Knightley and others may have been influenced by Australians' ambivalent attitude to Ned Kelly. Bennett covers an even earlier period in his 'Politics and Spying: Representations of Pre- and Early Australia' (*Antipodes* 22:i[2008] 17–22). This essay describes aspects of the navigational scramble to locate, map and occupy fertile areas of Terra Australis Incognita, and the attempts to gather intelligence that went with that competition. In Sheila Fitzpatrick and Carolyn Rasmussen's *Political Tourists: Travellers from Australia to the Soviet Union in the 1920s–1940s* there are two essays on Australian writers' visits to the Soviet Union in the 1930s: Jeff Sparrow's 'Guido Baracchi, Betty Roland and the Soviet Union' (pp. 122–45) and John McNair's '"Comrade Katya": Katharine Susannah Prichard and the Soviet Union' (pp. 146–69). Sparrow's article says little about Roland's playwriting, but in a fascinating, forensic way documents the inconsistencies in her different accounts of her visit to the Soviet Union and explains them in relation to her personal relationships and her increasing revulsion from Stalinism. McNair does not generate the same investigative excitement as Sparrow, but he discusses the lifetime engagement with Russia of a more significant Australian writer, including her extensive publishing success in the USSR. *Australians in Italy: Contemporary Lives and Impressions*, edited by Bill Kent, Ros Pesman and Cynthia Troup, is the record of a symposium at Prato in Italy which contains a couple of pieces of literary interest, the more important of which is Bruce Bennett's 'More than a Love Affair: Australian Writers and Italy' (06.1–06.11). Bennett canvasses a range of Italian connections, from Italian characters in novels by Katharine Susannah Prichard, Eve Langley and Desmond O'Grady, to Australian writers musing on the impact of classical art and culture or writers travelling in Italy and recording their impressions, to Australian writers such as David Malouf living in Italy and setting fiction there. The short survey is more impressionistic than systematic, but Bennett's wonderful eye for the apt quotation makes the paper surprisingly suggestive. The book, incidentally, announces its e-birth by paginating for digital access, rather than in a continuous sequence across the volume. Continuing an Italian theme, Gaetano Rando's 'Images of Sicily and Australia in the Narratives of Venero Armanno and Antonio Casella' (*Antipodes* 22:ii[2008] 155–61) introduces the work of these two authors, who have written a dozen novels between them. Rando concentrates on the cultural nexus and the effects of both time and locale that complicate the characters' identity formation, suggesting that the novels 'propose a multiple conceptualisation of Australia that defines it also as a Sicilian space' (p. 159).

We recorded last year that discussion of the decline of Australian literature publishing had tailed off. That observation proved to have been premature. Nathan Hollier's 'Between Denial and Despair: Understanding the Decline of

Literary Publishing in Australia' (*SoRA* 40:i[2007] 62–77) assembles bleak statistics and dire prognostications before helpfully dividing earlier commentators in the debate into Adam Smith marketeers, Marxist nationalists, and Keynesian interventionists. The final section, 'What Is To Be Done?', is rather short on suggestions, mentioning a newly formed association of small publishers (wonderfully named SPUNC Inc.) and enjoining 'pessimism of the intellect and optimism of the will' (p. 74). Possibly galled by being enrolled in Hollier's list of Keynesian interventionists, Mark Davis responds with 'Literature, Small Publishers and the Market in Culture' (*Overland* 190[2008] 4–11). Having noted with satisfaction that there is now a much more general awareness in Australian literary criticism of the impact of publishing conditions and settled a few scores with critics of his earlier arguments, Davis dismisses neo-protectionism as an aid to Australian literature. He then points out that none of the previous debate has really faced the fundamental question, 'What is literature for?' (p. 6). His own confident answer is that it is neither a necessary aid to nationalism, nor an inherent marker of superior taste, nor a secular religion, but an expressive form that can 'play out (often very) complex ideas, metaphors, evocations of belief, states of being, narratives of events, people, places and selves, at length, in an accessible form that is relatively affordable to make and consume' (p. 7). Having established that literature is worth preserving, most of the essay argues that since literature is no longer the dominant cultural form it once was, the real hope for Australian literature is in small publishers simply because they prove that market economy models are not adequate to explain their existence, since they 'represent precisely the sort of selflessness and civic purpose' that isn't supposed to occur in an economy of 'rational self-interest' (p. 10). Hollier returns to the issue in 'This Art Business' (*Overland* 191[2008] 57–63) to redeclare himself against market models of literary culture because of the lack of diversity that results. Although he argues that the continued existence of small publishers is not a valid cause for optimism since their existence is precarious, he and Davis seem to be fiercely agreeing on most points. A novelist, Wayne Macauley, in 'The Other Way' (*Meanjin* 67:ii[2008] 157–63), argues that neo-protectionism is the solution. Commercial publishers have lost interest in Australian literary fiction, but the slack can be taken up by small presses with adequate subsidies or even by government-subsidized self-publication. Macauley points out that the Australia Council Theatre Board funds the writing *and production* of plays which is analogous to the writing *and publication* of fiction. Despite the prejudice against self-publication, assessment of quality by funding bodies should be no more difficult for new fiction than it is for new drama. Also from the coalface, Louise Swinn, Kate Freeth and Zoe Fattner's 'A Lovely Form of Madness: Small Presses in Australia' (*Island* 114[2008] 27–37) is an enthusiastic perspective on small press publishing from people involved in it. The article includes a list of Australian small presses, and directs readers to the Small Press Association's website, < www.spunc.com.au > . From a more iconoclastic perspective, Jenny Lee, in 'The Trouble with Books' (*Overland* 190[2008] 17–21), brushes aside sentimental attachment to the well-made codex to declare that the electronic book is already here and the questions are simply whose reading device will come to dominate and how we will be charged for content. The piece is largely a response to Emmy Hennings's 'Shares and Share Alike' in the same issue (*Overland* 190[2008] 12–16), which looks at what has happened in digital music distribution and asks whether digital book publishing will make the same mistake of being over-restrictive. Both writers agree that the Amazon Kindle's stand-alone proprietary software system 'is not the way [for publishers] to go' (p. 20).

Katherine Bode, in 'Beyond the Colonial Present: Quantitative Analysis, "Resourceful Reading" and Australian Literary Studies' (*JASAL* special issue[2008] 184–97), makes an enthusiastic call for a more statistical approach to Australian literary studies, fearing that the current focus on analysis of individual authors impedes 'a cultural materialist overview' (p. 185), props up an elitist literary canon (p. 186), neglects 'the interoperability of literature with other forms of communication' (p. 188), shuts off Australian literary studies from 'the inherent internationalism of literary culture' (p. 189), fails to 'meet the demands . . . of the new technology' (p. 190), prevents literary scholars from participating in public debates 'around reading and literature in Australia' (p. 192), limits access to research funding (p. 193), and encourages individual study which impedes the 'collaborative research (both disciplinary and interdisciplinary)' that is 'central to the enhancement, production and communication of new knowledge' (pp. 193–4). A supporting example for Bode's argument is supplied in the same issue by Jason Ensor in 'Reprints, International Markets and Local Literary Taste: New Empiricism and Australian Literature' (*JASAL* special issue[2008] 198–218), which explains a research project on patterns of Australian fiction publishing, manipulating data drawn from AustLit. Commencing with an assertion of the importance of place, and acknowledging the definitional difficulty in 'Australian novel' Ensor recounts that he performed 88 advanced searches on AustLit to locate and segment (by year, place of publication etc.), 19,000 first-edition Australian novels and a further 15,000 reprints and translations. He then manipulated this data to extract patterns of publishing. Samples given in the article include graphs of new Australian novels produced in Australia versus those produced in the UK over more than a century; new novels over a twenty-year period, from the major pulp fiction publishers graphed against those from other publishers; a list of publishers of the greatest number of new Australian novels; a century of new Australian novels omitting the major pulp publishers graphed by place (UK against Australia); reprinted and translated Australian novels graphed by place (UK, Australia and Other Countries) and year; a list of the novels most often reprinted in Australia; a list of the novels most often reprinted or translated outside Australia; a list of the authors most often reprinted or translated outside Australia; a list of the novels most often reprinted in Australia 1950–75; a list of the novels most often reprinted outside Australia 1950–75; and a list of the novels most often reprinted outside Australia 1990–2005. These examples begin to suggest the range of ways in which the data can be used. This is a significant project and the techniques developed may well correct some misconceptions about the broad course of Australian publishing, but the questions and caveats crowd in: publishing is not the same as selling or reading; not all publishers flag their reissues in the same way; a reprint event does not indicate the number of copies reprinted, and so forth. Moreover, a statistical approach is vulnerable to inaccuracy. According to Figure 6, *Such Is Life* was by a big margin the most reprinted Australian novel in the period from 1890 to 2005, appearing in 1903, not being reprinted until 1999 and then being reprinted twenty-six times between that year and 2005. The column entry should read '1903–2004'; it takes only two incorrect digits in '1999 to 2004' to create nonsense.

Bode gives an example of her own statistical research in 'Graphically Gendered: A Quantitative Study of the Relationships between Australian Novels and Gender from the 1830s to the 1930s' (*AuFS* 23:lviii[2008] 435–50). This essay also draws its data from the AustLit database, underlining the growing importance to the field of that particular resource. Bode attempts a more ambitious argument than Ensor, trying to test the claims of the feminist revision of Australian literary history with its emphasis on the devaluing of women writers in the nineteenth century and their dominance in the 1930s. Bode has interesting facts, but they are limited since her primary data (like Ensor's) consists of the raw number of new novels in any one year without any differentiation between 'literary' novels and formula ones, without any reference to size of print run or reprint life, and without any apparent awareness that in the nineteenth century the bulk of Australian fiction was serialized in newspapers and only a small proportion appeared in book form anyway. This is very primitive data to support an argument about literary reputation and influence. Bode's attempt to compare the Australian experience with the English one is also problematic because she uses Gaye Tuckman's research on the Macmillan archive to generalize across English publishing. A third paper depending on statistical analysis is Toni Johnson-Woods's 'The Promiscuous Carter Brown' (*JASAL* special issue[2008] 163–83). This paper sketches out the publication history of this prolific detective series, with much emphasis on translations, especially into European languages. The paper notes reasons why the compilation is difficult: titles of the books change with reprinting, occasionally two different novels have the same title, and the variable translation of titles means that it is often difficult to ascertain without inspecting the copy closely what novel it translates. Johnson-Woods reiterates that the Carter Brown books are Australia's most exported and most translated literary property.

Beth Driscoll's 'How Prizes Work in the Literary Economy' (*HEAT* NS 18[2008] 175–92) derives from research in the archive of the Man Booker Prize and consequently focuses more on that and other European prizes than it does on Australian ones. Nevertheless, it makes a good case for the paradox of the literary prize which holds out the guarantee of excellence and exclusivity even as it deliberately employs populist marketing strategies such as celebrity announcements of the longlist and shortlist. The article offers curious *aperçus*, such as the list of prizes for which a new novel written in Melbourne today could be entered, and the fact that both the Booker and the Nobel prizes for literature were instituted in part in the name of social redemption—the Booker McConnell sugar company having been erstwhile slavers in the Caribbean, and Alfred Nobel seeking to expiate the guilt he felt for having invented dynamite. Literary prizes are also the starting point for Nicholas Hasluck in

'Thought Crimes and Other Themes in Commonwealth Literature' (*Quadrant* 52:v[2008] 36–43). From his experience as a literary judge and arts administrator Hasluck surveys some recent prizewinners, including J.M. Coetzee's *Disgrace*, Kate Grenville's *The Secret River* and Peter Carey's *The Unusual Life of Tristan Smith*, within a humanistic framework that draws on John Stuart Mill, Justice Holmes of the US Supreme Court and George Orwell on the vital importance of society's expressing and testing new ideas.

Robert Dixon and Veronica Kelly's *Impact of the Modern: Vernacular Modernities in Australia 1870s–1960s* is the edited collection of papers of a conference on that theme in Brisbane in 2006. Devoted to many branches of Australian popular culture, the book reflects the project of situating Australian literature in European and international contexts, specifically 'international modernity' (p. xiv). The editors' introduction, 'Australian Vernacular Modernities: People, Sites and Practices' (pp. xiii–xxiv) lays out a double set of tensions explored in the book between internationalism and national paradigms and between high and low (vernacular) modernism. Deborah Jordan, in ' "Written to tickle the ears of the groundings in garden cities": The Aesthetic of Modernity: Vance and Nettie Palmer and the *New Age*' (pp. 91–108), argues that the critical concentration on the Palmers as literary nationalists means that their commitment to international modernism has been completely overlooked. The paper offers plenty of evidence of Vance Palmer's admiration for A.L. Orage and his circle, while showing that Nettie was already working on the French Symbolists before the modernist movement really became established. Later, Nettie became less interested in what modernism had to offer as she sought a more intense engagement with the land and history of Australia. The same writer offers a more ponderous piece, ' "All that my love and I / Strive till after we die": The Courtship Letters of Vance and Nettie Palmer, 1909–1914' (*JASAL* special issue[2008] 75–91), to argue that this, the 'finest series of courtship letters ever likely to be archived in Australia' (p. 76), 'is vital in understanding the conceptual basis of the creative work of Vance and Nettie Palmer' (p. 75). Despite a clever manoeuvre in comparing the sequence to courtship letters between the Barrett Brownings and between the Dowell O'Reillys, Jordan's short account doesn't succeed in making the letters seem coherent enough to be the significant context for the creative work that she claims, while they seem far too cerebral to be either inspiringly passionate or playfully fun, so we await the forthcoming edition of them, in which the claims made here may be justified at greater length.

Susan Sheridan, in '*Australian Letters* and Postwar Modernity' (*ALS* 23:iii[2008] 264–78), writes a straightforward but rich and subtle account of an Adelaide magazine that created a distinctive space and seemed able to predict new styles and new writers with considerable skill. Staffed by Max Harris, Geoffrey Dutton and Rosemary Wighton, the journal was eclectic, anti-academic and successful despite having no institutional or membership support. Part of its success was matching up artistic endeavour and what would these days be called lifestyle concerns. 'A literary magazine that carried advertising for Penfolds wines, TAA airlines and John Martins department store, as well as for the *Times Literary Supplement*, ABC subscription concerts and book publishers, was unique' (p. 273). One of the magazine's most successful experiments was to commission a number of paintings from different Australian painters to reproduce with particular poems. Sheridan argues that although it was criticized for a lack of direction and for editorial enthusiasm rather than rigour, the magazine was a leader in its time, and today seems far more modern than any of its contemporaries. In 'Virgin Sock-Washers and Tweed Jackets' (*Southerly* 68:ii[2008] 177–92) Adrienne Sallay surveys the short-story explosion of the 1970s and its importance for the women's movement at the time. The article gives particular attention to the role of Vicki Viidikas in 'the beginnings of post-modernism in Australia' (p. 184). Leonie Kramer's 'Censorship, Liberty and Licence' (*Quadrant* 52:vii–viii[2008] 17–19) is a brief anecdotal account of her various brushes with censorship, the most important being her tenure on the Australian censorship board (National Literature Board of Review) in 1971–2 when Don Chipp was minister. She explains that the board was not set up to ban books but rather to reprieve books of literary merit that the Customs Department had already judged should be banned. Shortly after the Whitlam government's election, the Attorney General Lionel Murphy disbanded the board. Murphy was, Kramer believes, 'responsible for the rapid change in . . . community standards' (p. 19) of the 1970s as liberty dissolved into licence.

Ralph Spaulding's 'Joyce Eyre and Australian Literature at the University of Tasmania' (*ALS* 23:iv[2008] 463–73) describes the introduction of Australian literature into the curriculum. Spaulding has been able to track down evidence of curriculum and even exam papers to present a sense of how the emerging discipline was framed, and hazards some suggestions about the critical influences the principal lecturer followed. Paul Eggert's 'Australian Classics and the Price of Books: The Puzzle of the 1890s' (*JASAL* special issue[2008] 130–57) is a lengthy essay on the role of book availability in canon formation. The question the paper explores is why *The Recollections of Geoffry Hamlyn*, *His Natural Life*, and *Robbery Under Arms* established themselves as a proto-canon in the 1890s. Without discounting the feminist argument of gender bias, he proposes that the marketing strategies of publishers contributed, and that the timely release of cheap editions of these novels cemented their position, while other publishers (notably George Bentley) were reluctant to enter the cheap end of the market. So in part writers such as Catherine Martin simply had the wrong publisher to be marketed successfully at that time. In the same issue of *JASAL*, Robert Dixon responds with 'Australian Literature and the New Empiricism: A Response to Paul Eggert, "Australian Classics and the Price of Books"' (*JASAL* special issue[2008] 158–62). Dixon welcomes Eggert's approach, seeing it as an application of William St Clair's methodology in *The Reading Nation of the Romantic Period*, then overstates Eggert's argument to claim his position is antithetical to that of Susan Sheridan and the 1980s feminists. Neither position, Dixon claims, can arrive at a fair account of reading at the time while it limits itself to Australian literature. What critics should be pursuing are 'the broader questions about reading *literature in Australia*' (p. 162), citing approvingly recent attempts in this direction by Elizabeth Webby and Tim Dolin. Neatly intersecting with these papers is Alison Rukavina's '"This is a wonderfully comprehensive business": The Development of the British–Australian and International Book

Trades, 1870–1887' (*S&P* 32:ii[2008] 69–94). This is a study of Edward Petherick's work as London manager of the Melbourne firm, George Robertson. Drawing heavily on Petherick's papers at the Australian National Library, the essay shows that by the 1880s the Australian book market was extremely attractive to British publishers, and that Robertson had established dominance in the trade by opening an office in London. Petherick was an enterprising manager who did much good work identifying the most efficient shipping routes, establishing contacts with English, continental and American publishers and booksellers, and even forging a publishing partnership between Robertson and Richard Bentley & Son. The article is full of interesting sidelights including Petherick helpfully reporting a Christchurch NZ bookseller for stocking American piracies of Bentley titles, the cost of telegrams between Australia and the UK in the 1880s, and the fact that books for Australia were shipped in zinc-lined containers.

In this print-on-demand age when even university presses are producing books so inherently nasty that one fears one would catch a social disease from them were it not for the antiseptic white of their paper, it is a pleasure to see that Horden House can actually make a beautiful book and sell it for a reasonable price. Nathan Garvey's *The Celebrated George Barrington: A Spurious Author, the Book Trade, and Botany Bay* is a biography of the convict formerly credited with the 'True Patriots All' prologue, but it is a biography in the special sense that Barrington 'lived' through the many accounts of his life that were circulated while he pursued a flamboyant career as a pickpocket in England and continued to propagate after he was transported to Botany Bay. So famous had Barrington been, largely through the speeches he made during his various trials, that after he was transported a lively publishing industry ran for thirty years plagiarizing books and issuing them in his name. The most famous of these, *A Voyage to New South Wales* [1795], was lifted from a number of books, especially John Hunter's *An Historical Journal of the Transactions at Port Jackson and Norfolk Island*. Although Barrington was a notorious thief, he had nothing to do with the extensive set of plagiarisms done in his name, nor any of their reprints and translations. Garvey provides a full descriptive bibliography of the 'Barrington Books' that runs to more than eighty pages. In a more modern take on the question of literary fraud, Simon Caterson, in 'The Ethics of Literary Hoaxes' (*Quadrant* 52:vi–vii[2008] 99–101), argues that authors should 'tell the truth about the things that readers can reasonably expect to be true' (p. 100), and that the dissembling of a Norma Khouri is a betrayal of the intimacy created by authorial language. Literary forgery can also have massively deleterious consequences, as in the case of *The Protocols of the Learned Elders of Zion* produced by the tsarist secret police around 1905, exposed as fraudulent in 1921, co-opted by the Nazis to justify their eugenicist policies in the 1930s, and still avidly read in Middle Eastern countries.

Van Ikin and Keira McKenzie compiled the 'Annual Bibliography for Australia 2007' (*JCL* 43:iv[2008] 5–30). As usual this gives a selective list of both creative and critical works, with an emphasis on poetry and fiction. It is prefaced by a thirteen-page introduction that provides a narrative of the year's highlights including succinct indications of the level of enthusiasm of reviews.

Apparently house style, since it is true for all the national bibliographies included in the issue, the general criticism is curiously arranged alphabetically by title. Ron Blaber contributes the annual survey of non-fiction to *Westerly* (53[2008] 76–92), arranged under a number of quasi-thematic headings, 'Country', 'Plays, Prams and Poetry', 'Distant Lives and the Need for Belonging' and 'The Tycoon, the Judge, and the Politician'. Of note is the way he sees a book of indigenous memoirs and stories, *Heartsick for Country: Stories of Love, Spirit and Creation*, edited by Sally Morgan, Tjalaminu Mia and Blaze Kwaymullina, as offering a viewpoint from which white attempts to identify with the land can be examined. Roger Bourke contributes the survey of Australian fiction for 2007–8 to *Westerly* (53[2008] 50–8). Bourke judges Alex Miller's *Landscape of Farewell* the stand-out work of a strong year for fiction. He notes also a couple of novels from established writers that had a very long gestation: Tim Winton's *Breath* (his first novel for seven years) and Matthew Condon's *The Trout Opera*, which Condon says took him more than a decade to write. Two first novels that Bourke finds very promising are Alice Nelson's *The Last Sky* and David Cohen's *Fear of Tennis*. The companion piece on poetry, 'Making the Leap: Australian Poetry 2007–2008', is contributed by Meriel Griffiths (*Westerly* 53[2008] 130–45). In keeping with the 'looking outwards' theme noted in the introduction to this essay, Griffiths leads off with a note on *Over There: Poems from Singapore and Australia*, edited by John Kinsella and Alvin Pang. Griffiths is delighted also by the twin annual anthologies *Best Australian Poetry* and *Best Australian Poems*, which are selling well. She finds the strength of poetry publishing in Australia well attested by the fifty-five collections and anthologies that were submitted to *Westerly* during the year. Faye Christenberry compiled the annual 'Bibliography of Australian Literature and Criticism Published in North America—2007' for *Antipodes* (22:ii[2008] 178–92). In the global age of Google, Bookfinder and Amazon it is hard to understand the rationale for a bibliography whose delimiters are place of issue, especially if the item is issued by an international publisher like Rodopi or Manchester University Press that is clearly headquartered elsewhere but happens to maintain a US office. Also, the definition of 'Australian' is puzzling when the listing includes such names as Janet Frame, Ruth Dallas, Keri Hulme, Albert Wendt, Patricia Grace and so forth. Nevertheless, the *Antipodes* bibliography is useful for following the North American publications of Australian novelists and poets, for its listing of reviews, and for its locating and listing of articles in general journals that carry critical material on Australian writers only infrequently. James Doig and Milan Smiljkovic admit that their 'A Checklist of Australian Fantastic Literature to 1960' (*StAWF* 1[2008] 51–89) is a work in progress, and that there are definitional problems galore in what to include. Nevertheless they make a modest start in cataloguing a set of sub-genres that seem to enjoy unending popularity, and no doubt the checklist will at some stage morph into an updatable electronic form. After twenty years John Hay, John Arnold, Kerry Kilner and Terence O'Neill bring their monumental bibliography to completion with *The Bibliography of Australian Literature: P–Z*. This is an author-based, four-volume work spun off from the increasingly indispensable AustLit database. It totally supersedes Miller and Macartney's 1956 compilation and will probably be the last attempt at a comprehensive hardcopy bibliography of Australian literature that the world will see. The bibliography confines itself to the traditional literary genres, fiction, poetry and drama, and seeks to list every author who has published a book in those genres. Non-fiction is selectively included for those authors who are already listed by virtue of publishing at least one book in the core genres. There is no listing of criticism apart from a referral to AustLit or other sources. Given that the work has a cut-off date of 2000 and that it does not include criticism, many who have access to AustLit will feel that they do not need to consult these volumes, but there are many tasks for whic*. *BAL* is quicker and more convenient if there is a copy to hand. The seventy-page index of pseudonyms means that we can now discard our Nesbitt and Hadfields, also.

(b) Prose

Ouyang Yu's *Chinese in Australian Fiction 1888–1988* is the belated publication from a Ph.D. thesis completed in 1994. It opens with a very handy summary of the history of Australian–Chinese relations, and of Chinese immigration to Australia, then moves on to sketch out its theoretical parameters, which comprise a not very sophisticated form of race analysis— 'racism does have its usefulness as a valid theoretical approach' (p. 43). There is a positive racism as well as a negative racism, but the result in either case is stereotyping of the Chinese characters portrayed, and a failure to individualize them or to portray them as on a level, and hence able to interact, with Western characters. The book then analyses Australian fiction in three tranches, 1888–1901, 1902–1949 and 1950–1988, arranging its material in each section in descending order of racist unspeakableness. In the first section the *Bulletin* writers, William Lane and the other invasion novelists are pilloried, with the Anglo-Australian Hume Nisbet singled out as the only writer of the time to show a more sympathetic view of Chinese people. But even then Nisbet's achievement is thought to be limited, since it is simply the addition of 'positive orientalism' or the ascription of idealized characteristics to the Chinese characters, which equally preclude meaningful interracial contact. This section usefully reminds us of how bitterly racist the labour movement of early federation was, and how even people like Mary Gilmore who would later become admirers of emergent communist China were violently opposed to Chinese immigration into Australia fifty years earlier (p. 134). Ouyang finds that fundamentally racist stereotypes continued into his second period with a similar sense that the Anglo-Australian writers were less likely to be contemptuously dismissive. He also notes an increase in positive idealized portrayals, as 'Chinese with white hearts'. These portrayals, however, are limited by their sense of approval being accorded on the basis of the degree to which the character approximates European values and behaviours. A gender differential also enters the discourse, male Australian writers being more likely to depict female Chinese characters as attractively exotic than female Australian writers do. Just as Hume Nisbet had stood out as the least typical writer of the first period, George Johnston emerges as more sympathetic to the

Chinese in novels such as *High Valley* and *The Long Road*. Johnston visited China as a war correspondent and depicted the Chinese with sympathy, albeit he was harshly critical of their Kuomintang rulers. The account of the representation gains a new dimension after the victory of the Communists and the playing out of the Cold War. Leftist writers, especially those who visited China, were likely to portray Chinese characters more positively and to set fiction in China itself. But even when they are writing sympathetically, Ouyang argues, Australian writers find it hard to break out of standard depictions of the Chinese. He identifies several ways in which Christopher Koch's Billy Kwan (in *The Year of Living Dangerously*) embodies older stereotypes: his otherness, his facility as intermediary, his 'eccentricity, his knack for entertaining, his childlike devotion to Hamilton, his secretiveness, and his desire for revenge' (p. 320). Two recent developments have improved the climate for fictional representation of the Chinese: the rise of China as a political and economic power, and the emergence of Asian Australian writers such as Brian Castro and Don'o Kim. The result of these two factors has been for the first time an interiorization of a Chinese view and an assignment of active roles to Chinese characters that are not just those of clever intermediary or convenient martyr. Ouyang points out that Castro's *Birds of Passage* [1983] is the first Australian fiction that portrays a Chinese character actively defending himself to the point of killing a white man in an honourable, as opposed to a treacherous, way (p. 357). For a book appearing in 2008, Ouyang's cut-off date of 1988 seems a little early given that he might have found significant changes in the last twenty years and avoided the rather grumpy note on which the survey ends. The book risks becoming a catalogue of stereotype-spotting, but its sheer scope, its range across popular as well as more canonical literature, and its convincing presentation of the longevity of the stereotypes make it a valuable study. The thirty-five-page bibliography of Australian fiction containing Chinese characters could be greatly extended (possibly as a collaborative wiki-project), but should be treated with caution as it includes publishers such as 'Redmond Bentley & Co.' and a South Australian publisher, Eagle Press, that will be a surprise to Brunton Stephens scholars.

It seems extraordinary that books on Australian perceptions of the Chinese and of Japan should appear almost simultaneously, but Megumi Kato's *Narrating the Other: Australian Literary Perceptions of Japan* invites comparison with Ouyang's longer study. Kato finds that the Japanese have been puzzling to the Australian consciousness, not fitting easily into the category of inferior non-white because of the apparent sophistication of their culture. Although there was a significant Japanese presence in Australia from the nineteenth century, it was associated with the pearling industry in the far north and north-west of the country (p. 15) and never entered mainstream Australian consciousness in the way that the Chinese on the goldfields and on the edge of cities had. The Japanese, also, had been less easy to dominate and dismiss. Kato notes that Japan's Westernization in the nineteenth century was undertaken voluntarily rather than being forced upon it, and that (less honourably) in the Second World War work camps Japan became the only Eastern nation ever to have enslaved whites in a substantial way. The book makes the point that representation is of crucial and long-lasting importance for international relations. Studies like this or Ouyang's throw up a different set of writers' names from the usual Clarkes, Lawsons, and Henry Handel Richardsons; the earliest writers to describe or set fiction in Japan were James Hingston (a Melbourne journalist), Douglas Sladen (by then returned to England after his Australian sojourn) and Carlton Dawe (a South Australian who moved to Britain). Rosa Praed's Japanese novel *Madam Izàn* has almost never been referred to in critical discussions but it gets a guernsey here. All of these writers find that well-intentioned rapprochement can go only so far and that there are racist taboos, often on both sides. Kato's chapter on invasion novels of the early twentieth century explains the historical background that fostered them, but also makes the point that the fiction was a way of keeping alive the suspicion of the Japanese. These novels, Kato argues, seldom individualize the Japanese, referring to them as a sort of corporate mass biding its time before swooping in to overcome and occupy an insouciant Australia. Some of the best writing in the book occurs in the discussion of the war fiction, which is divided into a number of chapters concerned with jungle fighting, Australian prisoner-of-war experiences and Japanese prisoner-of-war and Occupation experiences. Presumably because of the greater amount of material, the treatment becomes less author-centred and more thematic. Thus a section might explore the motif of Australian soldiers discovering the humanity of the Japanese jungle soldier with illustrative moments from half a dozen different texts. The war theme is continued in a further chapter on books discussing the Cowra breakout and the postwar occupation of Japan; not surprisingly, Hal Porter features here. The final chapter deals with a miscellany of individual works from the 1980s and 1990s which increasingly manage to avoid the stereotypes of the past and suggest more pluralist views in Australia, but because of that very disparity they are difficult to summarize neatly. The book has a useful timeline of events and publications of Japanese/Australian relevance and a bibliography, but surprisingly, no index.

Katherine Bode's *Damaged Men Desiring Women: Male Bodies in Contemporary Australian Women's Fiction* shows this critic working in a very different mode from her work discussed in the 'General' section above. After having discerned a trend towards the portrayal of 'wounded men' in early twenty-first-century fiction by women, Bode's distinctive disregard for precedent or reputation informs an eclectic selection of works by largely new or lesser-known writers: Georgia Blain, Fiona Capp, Mireille Juchau, Sarah Miles, Wendy Scarfe and Gillian Watkinson. Eschewing a simple thematic or theoretically monocular approach, Bode develops an interlinked series of readings which engage with the culturally and structurally problematic ways in which these novels reverence the damaged male body to develop a subtle argument about the ways in which representations of damaged men are used to recuperate heterosexual men as ethical subjects. Unexpectedly, Bode argues that Wendy Scarfe, a writer who has tended to self-publish, has offered a much more critical story of masculinities in her novel *Miranda* than is found in work by writers and publishing houses that enjoy a much higher reputation for literary fiction.

Susan Lever's *David Foster: The Satirist of Australia* is a balanced and well-written coverage of a novelist who creates problems for critics and readers alike. With highly wrought prose and a set of zany ideas, Foster has looked like a very unaccommodating novelist indeed, but Lever defends him as belonging to a 'ratbag tradition harking back to Xavier Herbert, Miles Franklin and Joseph Furphy' (p. 202). Lever traces the development of his thought and explicates his novels in order, explaining why this Miles Franklin award-winner has not been more generally celebrated. She portrays him as preoccupied with a masculinist tradition of Australian culture which he sees as essentially sterile because it is not grounded in contact with the natural world. In fact, Foster has come to see the masculine impulse which has led to much violence, perversion and destruction since white settlement as destroying civilization, and as an impediment to the spiritual. He comes to propose voluntary castration as a way of arriving at spiritual enlightenment. These are extreme ideas, which help to explain not only the limited popularity of this writer, but also the difficulty Lever has in discussing him as a satirist. She admits that his satirical approach is not the normal 'mock folly and vice in order to reform it' (p. 4) model based upon a stable and coherent position. The problem with the label seems to be that while Foster has the comic touches and the penchant for exaggeration that one associates with satire, he is too distrustful of communal politics and too interested in arcane ideas to call the social world to account on an agreed agenda of rational social behaviour. Moreover, Lever argues, satire has morphed under postmodernism into a more freewheeling form of engagement (p. 32). In Foster's case this is marked by 'exuberant inventiveness' (p. 56) and 'performance' (p. 89) which 'may have no program for reform' (p. 73), which raises the question of whether it can still be called satire. Lever cites examples of Foster's talks and performances at literary festivals and conferences to show that the challenges he throws out are consistently difficult for all forms of audience.

Carole Ferrier's '"Never forget that the Kanakas are men": Fictional Representations of the Enslaved Black Body' (in Borch et al., eds., pp. 205–23) is a historically well-grounded exploration of the representation of cross-race sexual relations in a number of novels, including Jean Devanny's *Cindie*, Faith Bandler's *Wacvie*, Nancy Cato's *Brown Sugar* and David Crookes's *Blackbird*. Ferrier detects a continuing silence about aspects of race and sex in colonial Queensland despite the work of historians like Ray Evans, Kay Saunders and Peter Corris, but notes that these fictions 'have engaged with material that was not centrally visible in the general consciousness' (p. 221). Frances Devlin-Glass's 'A Politics of the Dreamtime: Destructive and Regenerative Rainbows in Alexis Wright's *Carpentaria*' (*ALS* 23:iv[2008] 392–407), which won the inaugural Laurie Hergenhan Prize is a tightly written explication of the mode of Wright's novel, showing that its 'magical realism' is not a soft escape to the imaginary in the face of science, progress and development, but rather a world-view in which the specificity of the natural is underpinned by an ecologically based cosmology. This makes the mode equally available for celebration of the natural and for Rabelaisian satire. Devlin-Glass follows others in preferring the term 'supervital' for what is normally described as supernatural or sacred in Aboriginal culture because it links the supernatural with the natural rather than opposing them. Devlin-Glass also contributes 'The Eco-Centric Self and the Sacred in Xavier Herbert's *Poor Fellow My Country*' (*JASAL* 8[2008] 45–63), which is a sympathetic discussion of Herbert's 1974 opus pointing out that while the novel can be attacked for its heavy didacticism, Herbert's social vision was quite advanced for its day, and that the novel develops a concept of self that is situated in ecological frameworks. By accentuating the connections between the sacred and the ecological Herbert shows a 'self-realising individual in no way separable [from] or discretely related to the sentient ecosystem in which he finds himself' (p. 59). Annalisa Oboe's 'Metamorphic Bodies and Mongrel Subjectivities in Mudrooroo's *The Undying*' (in Borch et al., eds., pp. 225–35) is a bravura reading of the Gothic body in Mudrooroo's *The Undying*. Running a complex argument that includes embodiment in narrative and the Ovidian transform-ation of George the narrator into his totemic animal, Oboe reads the vampiric theme as signalling European abjection and consumption of the indigene. She argues that the breadth of cultural and historical reference and the triumphant indeterminacy of George's subjectivity show that George's narrative control maintains him as a survivor. Diana Schwerdt contributes to Anna Haebich and Baden Offord, eds., *Landscapes of Exile*, a discussion of a fictionalization of the refugee experience which has been close to the surface of Australian consciousness for the last ten years. 'The "Third Space" as Void: Exile and Self-Destruction in Eva Sallis's *The Marsh Birds*' (pp. 135–48) opens with reference to the positive views of exile and cultural hybridity of Edward Said and Homi Bhabha, especially Bhabha's 'third space' which represents the potential developments that cultural hybridity implies. Schwerdt shows, however, a much bleaker view of the asylum experience where the negotiation that would be required to create a third space is not allowed to develop. Instead, the protagonist of Sallis's novel faces a series of reductive and disorienting episodes that destroy his memory and even his sense of self, resulting in his death. Schwerdt argues that the novel is a stinging criticism of current Australian refugee policy, but also that it raises large questions about the role of cultural pluralism in modern Australia. A more positive view of exile is explored in J.V. D'Cruz and William Steele's 'Recognising Home in David Martin's Additive Exile: The Necessary Other that Puts Us into Relation' (in Haebich and Offord, eds., pp. 157–71). 'Additive exile' is David Martin's term for the view that it is possible for the trans-national to belong to multiple places and, rather than becoming paralysed by nostalgia and loss of the past, to find possibilities in both places and allegiances. A deft reading of a number of Martin's texts develops this idea. Catherine Padmore's 'Future Tense: *Dead Europe* and Viral Anti-Semitism' (*ALS* 23:iv[2008] 434–45), is a little more self-regarding than one might wish in pointing out the ambiguities in Tsiolkas's project of exposing anti-Semitism through examining some of the novel's technical strategies.

Robert Dixon's 'Ghosts in the Machine: Modernity and the Unmodern' (*JASAL* 8[2008] 121–37) explicates Gail Jones's 2006 novel *Dreams of Speaking*, particularly around the paradox that while in one sense modernity implies a dismissal of the past, the past obstinately continues to obtrude in part through the very globalizing technologies that have apparently allowed modernity to escape from it. The arc of the novel is from an academic pursuit of the 'poetics of modernity' to a contemplation of the 'ethics of friendship' (p. 121). In 'Visual Art and Bourgeois Forms in Shirley Hazzard's Fiction' (*Southerly* 68:i[2008] 13–23) Brigitta Olubas argues that Hazzard's fiction has consistently combined a lambent portrayal of the inner life with a sharp and often satirical view of the world of public affairs. Olubas finds a correlative for this, if not an actual influence, in the paintings of the Dutch Masters, especially Vermeer, whose suggestive oppositions of the worlds of merchants and soldiers correspond to the meeting-point of public and private that Hazzard has explored across all her fiction. Hazzard's method is discussed further by Olubas in 'Anachronism, Ekphrasis and the "Shape of Time" in *The Great Fire*' (*ALS* 23:iii[2008] 279–89), which meditates on a number of dissonances in Hazzard's 2003 novel. The novel itself as a fundamentally temporal form may seem to be inherently disjoined from a more visual and digital age, but Olubas is struck by a series of incidents or motifs in the novel in which time seems to be frozen or emblematized by a painterly scene. Such scenes imply a narrative method and even an aesthetic that conjoin the visual and the temporal. From this premise, many apparently incidental aspects of the novel can be seen to operate in some sort of ekphrastic mode, whether it is the Vermeer-like interiors, the downed warplane in Yunan, or the letters which transport frozen moments of memory and desire around the world. The subtle argument leads Olubas to see the novel developing 'relations of continuity, reflection, and ultimately, generosity' (p. 284). Helen O'Reilly's 'Linda's Linoleum: Visual Imaging in Eleanor Dark's *Prelude to Christopher*' (*Southerly* 68:i[2008] 95–103) argues that in Dark's first published novel patterns and colour effects structure the text more significantly than plot and characterization. Two patterning motifs are especially important: the geometric linoleum in Linda's kitchen and the painting of her by D'Aubert. The second part of the essay uses a comparison with Nabokov to characterize Dark as a 'synaesthete' (p. 100), although providing this label does not add much to the analysis of the effects in the novel.

Dorothy Jones, in 'Bottling the Forbidden Fruit: Marion Halligan's Fiction' (*ALS* 23:iii[2008] 318–27), finds that Halligan's fiction has been neglected because of its focus on the quotidian and the domestic typified by its prevalent food and food imagery. However, food reveals its ambivalence in replaying the myths of the Hesperides, Tantalus and especially the Garden of Eden. The serpents in Halligan's fiction run the spectrum of marital infidelity, the male 'taboo' (p. 324) of femininity, violence and murder. Jones neatly teases out the intertextual breadth and symbolic depth of a number of stories, notably *The Apricot Colonel* [2006]. Michael Ackland's ' "What a history is that? What an enigma…?": Imagination, Destiny and Socialist Imperatives in Christina Stead's *Seven Poor Men of Sydney*' (*Southerly* 68:iii[2008] 189–212) is a straightforward, even old-fashioned, but admirably lucid reading of Christina Stead's first novel. Ackland sees the novel as a contest of ideas mirroring Stead's own desire to explore a socialist vision but not being prepared to be bound by the party line on how socialist fiction should be written. A feature of the argument is Ackland's explanation of why the English Romantic model of expanded imagination underpinned by 'natural piety' is not available to

Stead's characters. In 'The Uncanny in Barbara Baynton's "Scrammy 'And"
and Christina Stead's "The Triskelion"' (*Southerly* 68:ii[2008] 144–52),
William Lane applies Freud's theory of the uncanny to short stories by
Baynton and Stead with some success, although he does not claim that we
learn more about each story from its being compared to the other. In 'Power,
Vanishing Acts and Silent Watchers in Janette Turner Hospital's *The Last
Magician*' (*JASAL* 8[2008] 107–20), Maureen Clark scrutinizes the level of
agency realized by socially marginalized characters in Hospital's novel,
notably the Lucy/Lucia narrator and the titular magician Charlie Chan.
Noting the potential agency of characters who watch but are themselves
unnoticed by society, Clark finds a comparable active-passive agency in the
photographs that allows the major characters to 'assuage anxiety and take
possession of a material, if still insecure, social space' (p. 119).

When Craig Munro published the *First UQP Story Book* in 1981 he was
quite chuffed that it brought together for the first time 'The Drover's Wife'
stories by Henry Lawson, Murray Bail and Frank Moorhouse. In 'The
Drovers' Wives' (*Southerly* 68:ii[2008] 193–208) Mandy Sayer shows how far
this self-conscious 'tradition' has expanded with additional stories by Barbara
Jefferis, Anne Gambling, Chris Eipper and Sayer herself. Sayer argues
that what started as a quintessential expression of the male bush tradition
has been co-opted as a tool of feminist critique. Nicholas Dunlop returns
to Peter Carey's early short stories in 'Cartographic Conspiracies: Maps,
Misinformation, and Exploitation in Peter Carey's "American Dreams"'
(*Antipodes* 22:i[2008] 33–9). The argument depends on a rather risky
conflation of 'model' and 'map' and on burying the story under an avalanche
of postcolonial and semiotic theory, but it achieves its best moments in
exploring the tensions between synchronicity and diachronicity in the story. In
2007, thirty-five years after her first book of poetry, Rhyll McMaster
published a novel which Eileen Cheong discusses in 'Reclaiming Identity in
Rhyll McMaster's *Feather Man*' (*Hecate* 34:ii[2008] 127–35). Cheong introduces it as a book that struggled to find a publisher but then received better
than modest acclaim when it did appear. Her very plotty account of the novel
shows the protagonist being abused by a succession of males, even (potentially) by the final 'good' one, Paul. Cheong concludes: 'McMaster reminds us
that Sooky's eventual identity must be independent of men—for even the most
"fond", "benign" and "indulgent" (p. 132) of men must want something of
your soul in return' (p. 135).

Mark Kipperman's 'White Settler/Big City: Mimicry and the Metropolis in
Fergus Hume's *The Mystery of a Hansom Cab*' (*Antipodes* 22:ii[2008] 129–36)
draws on Robert Dixon and Andrew McCann plus Homi Bhabha to offer a
reading of the ambiguity of aspirational experience at the centre of Hume's
famous nineteenth-century murder mystery, arguing that 'modernity is
characterised by a nauseating fear of dislocation, hypocrisy, and a corruption
that crosses oceans in space, generations in time, and the borders of classes and
nations' (p. 133). Len Platt, in '"Altogether better-bred looking": Race and
Romance in the Australian Novels of Rosa Praed' (*JASAL* 8[2008] 31–44),
argues that Praed is obsessed with race and needs to be seen in the context of
European attitudes to race. He traces the history of race ideas from the

sixteenth century. In a reflection of both Haggard and Kipling, Praed defends aristocracy, and in doing so reveals a eugenicist streak in which the old aristocrats of culture give way to the new aristocrats of nature. She depicts the Celts as a wayward and ill disciplined form of the Coming Man. Platt applies this paradigm to Praed's view of the Aborigines to show that she was not so forward-looking as has been claimed. The racism that underpinned Praed's and other contemporary views was soon to be overtaken by a more structuralist sense of language and anthropology and hence a rejection of scientific race theory. Praed's biographer, Patricia Clarke, contributes to Haebich and Offord, eds., *Landscapes of Exile*, 'A Paradox of Exile: Rosa Praed's Lifelines to her Australian Past' (pp. 19–30), in which she proposes that Praed's escape from 'eucalyptic cloisterdom' to the bright literary lights of London was an exile as much as it was a liberation. Clarke discusses the ways in which Praed continued to draw on family for material for her books and how she continued to value her Australian memories throughout her life. The article contains a convenient list of Praed's twenty or so Australian books grouped by the parts of Queensland in which they are set. Robyn Emerson revisits one of the most popular twentieth-century Australian girls' stories in 'Requiem for *A Little Bush Maid*' (*Southerly* 68:i[2008] 59–73). Emerson argues that, despite the long-lived popularity of Mary Grant Bruce's novel and its many sequels, and despite the elimination of the worst of racist attitudes and the successive repackaging of the work as a heritage novel or a tale for the pony club set, the modern Australian child cannot relate to the story. It and the other Billabong books may, however, have a future if reborn in a television series.

(c) Poetry

Philip Mead's *Networked Language: Culture and History in Australian Poetry* does have a chapter on digital poetry, but the 'networked' of the title invokes a much broader sense of contextualizing poetry. Moving right away from the verbal icon of New Criticism, Mead seeks not only to see poetry in the historical and social context of its genesis, but also to take account of its accretive relationships down to the time of its reading. With gestures to Pierre Bourdieu, Mead makes the 'understanding' (a favourite word) of poetry a product of its linguistic patterns and their interpretation, its bio-historical genesis, the economic and cultural circumstances of the country at the time it was produced, its critical reception since production, its relation to other poetry in Australia and abroad, and its relation to other arts, government policy, publishing technology and so forth. If this inclusiveness seems to promise the ultimate multi-layered history of Australian poetry, Mead stops well short of that, but he has certainly availed himself of the whole range of approaches in what is a deeply interesting if selective collection of essays. This, he tells us, is not an order-from-chaos project, remapping the dominant patterns of Australian poetry; rather, he aims 'to write about poetry in Australia, both past and present, in ways that hopefully refocus attention on a cultural expression that hasn't been understood as well as it might have been'

(p. 21). The book is not interested so much in picking fights with existing interpretations as in exploring overlooked contexts of the writing which inevitably make those interpretations seem premature or thin. Kenneth Slessor may well have been on the edge of the Lindsay vitalist movement as literary historians keep telling each other, but he was also an engaged film critic for much of his journalistic life, and Mead is able to show how influential this was on the form of his own poetry. The readings of 'Last Tram' and 'Five Bells' that result are especially convincing. The Ern Malley poems have been rising steadily in the canon of (legitimate) Australian poetry, and are today represented in national anthologies. As Mead notes, the fictitious Malley has even been proposed as 'Australia's national poet' (p. 92). Mead contrasts the hoax with the pastiche practice of continental modernists, but also discusses at length the dynamics of the obscenity trial brought against Max Harris to show how the legal establishment was prosecuting poetry (or more properly, poetic obscurity) as much as indecency. Symptomatic of the book's rich byways, there is an extended reading of the relation of the 'Prince of Tyre' poem to Shakespeare's *Pericles*. The essay on Judith Wright seeks to remind readers of Wright's extensive career as an activist in a number of social and environmental areas as well as her status as an extra-academy intellectual partnered with the philosopher Jack McKinney. The book concludes with an essay on two ethnic poets, Greek Australian Π.Ο., and Aboriginal Lionel Fogarty. The essay explores the linguistic dimensions of identity and social politics, finding that although their respective projects produce difficult poetry that has not been given much attention, both writers forge 'a poetic space where the diversities of politics and identity . . . are able to be articulated and represented' (p. 454).

Noel Rowe's *Ethical Investigations: Essays on Australian Literature and Poetics* is a posthumous collection edited by Bernadette Brennan that won the ASAL Walter McCrae award in 2009. In these reprinted essays, Rowe addresses a number of specific questions with clarity and a forensic sense of the relationship between language and ethics. There is a bias in the subject matter towards Catholic poets, with James McAuley and Francis Webb being especially well represented. Although predominantly about poetry (Rowe published four books of poems himself) one of the best essays in the book is a patient and incisive investigation of 'honesty' in Hal Porter's autobiography, and the way that the question of truth was treated by Porter's biographer, Mary Lord, and subsequent critics. The essay on Les Murray's poems about his mother also pursues questions of guilt and blame in a careful and revealing way. John Kinsella's *Disclosed Poetics: Beyond Landscape and Lyricism* [2007] disavows attempting a defence of poetry, but aims to clarify 'what constitutes place, and why and how we write about it' (p. xi). The book proposes time as a fusing agent, since 'landscape is part of time and the lyric is a representational grounding of time' (p. xii). Kinsella offers 'not an analysis, but a stretching out of the poetic line. It is commentary; but interactive commentary. It is a conversation between text, reader, place and poet' (p. xii). 'Stretching out the poetic line', 'interactive commentary' and 'conversation' turn out to mean 'unstructured discussion' as the promise of the orderly contents pages is constantly disappointed. The book finds its triumphant unity, however, in the author's self-presentation. It may not be a defence of poetry, but it is certainly an *apologia pro vita sua*.

As well as the books discussed, poetry was the focus of two conferences in 2007, one celebrating the centenary of A.D. Hope's birth, and the other on Christopher Brennan and Mallarmé. Selected papers from both were published in a meaty special issue of *Southerly*. Henry Weinfield's '"Thinking out afresh the whole poetic problem": Brennan's Prescience; Mallarmé's Accomplishment' (*Southerly* 68:iii[2008] 10–26) starts from Brennan's brief essay on Mallarmé, and goes on to analyse closely Mallarmé's essay 'Crise de vers' to account for what Brennan saw to admire in Mallarmé. Katherine Barnes's 'Hearths and Windows: Christopher Brennan's Interlude Poems and the Question of Modernism' (*Southerly* 68:iii[2008] 39–55) chooses the 'Interlude' poems from Brennan's *Poems (1913)* to argue that attempts to co-opt the poem to modernism are misguided. On various grounds she sees the respective techniques of T.S. Eliot and Brennan as quite different. The persistent 'rupture' (p. 53) implied by the layout of the sections in Brennan's *Poems* is not the modernist one of a dissociated consciousness, but rather a stage in an ultimately cohesive myth. Barnes finds better comparisons (and precursors) for Brennan's practice in Mallarmé and Keats. It is almost sixty years since G.A. Wilkes published his five-part study 'New Perspectives on Brennan's Poetry' in *Southerly*, so there is a special interest in seeing him return to this author in 'False Starts and Winding Ways: Christopher Brennan's "Vigil"' (*Southerly* 68:iii[2008] 81–107). The essay is a careful explication and assessment of a poem first published by Brennan in 1916, but written in the mid-1890s. Retracing the evolution of the text in the manuscript record and using correspondence to and from Dowell O'Reilly, J. Le Gay Brereton and A.G. Stephens, Wilkes is able to retrace what the poem was intended to do in the early design for 'The Labour of the Night' and to argue why it was superfluous to the cycle that was finally published as *Poems*. Wilkes's cautious suggestion is that the second part of 'Vigil' may be a parody of the first.

Walter Kirsop's 'Christopher Brennan's Reading' (*Southerly* 68:iii[2008] 229–43) is not a straightforward summary of what Brennan read and how it most obviously affected his poetry, but more a review essay or history of previous attempts to describe sections of Brennan's reading in this way, counterpointed by an account of Brennan's habits in acquiring, annotating, and sharing books and the posthumous fate of sections of his library. Kirsop calls for a full catalogue of the dispersed library and its annotations as being just as needed as a good edition of Brennan's letters. Chris Wallace-Crabbe's 'A.D. Hope: The Wicked Little Poems' (*Southerly* 68:iii[2008] 31–6) was apparently first read at a conference on Hope, and it has made no adjustment to print, totally eschewing footnotes and running an annoying Senior Common Room tone: 'What, we might very well ask, can be the final difference between transvaluation and mischief?' (p. 36). The argument seems to be that Hope's habitual urbane rationality is punctuated by mischievous and self-indulgent moments when sex or satire cut sharply and unexpectedly across the tone of the poem, but scholars who don't happen to know Hope's entire corpus by heart will find it a chore to follow the argument through. Ann

McCulloch's 'A.D. Hope, the Life and the Art: Let It Rip' (*Southerly* 68:iii[2008] 264–81) offers personal insights into Hope's intellectual predilections from his biographer. The 'let it rip' of the title points to Hope's belief that life was to be accepted and one's past not to be regretted. This does not entail any stoic passivism since Hope was a constant interventionist through his satire. In fact, he believed that poetry created something that was a tribute to life rather than a reflection of it. Hence Hope finds more to agree with in Nietzsche than in Freud about the relationship of one's past to one's present. The essay includes a couple of unpublished poems from the notebooks, and concludes by quoting a witty sketch of life, 'Card Game', from Hope's final volume that is well worth looking at.

Ruth Morse's 'Elegies for Odysseus: Mimicry, Pastiche, Poetry, A.D. Hope and Derek Walcott' (*Southerly* 68:iii[2008] 60–78) is a large argument about 'europhone' culture's desire to reprise the epic and attempts by Walcott and Hope to effect this. Hope is the junior player in the argument, which is laid out in very general terms: 'Historically there has been pressure on the poets of new nations to provide their artificial states with a foundation epic at once forward-looking and culturally unifying, to forge a new language, in which to express transcendent new forms' (p. 73). For various historical reasons—the article is very aware of the poet being a hostage of fortune—'Hope could not do...what Walcott or Seamus Heaney can' (p. 74), and he is criticized for misogyny far more than Walcott is, even though the latter is 'much less interested in women' (p. 71). The interest of the article is in the broad cultural history it sketches and in the occasional sparky aside: 'I suspect that *Voss* is going to come to seem a cranky, willed effort. *A Fringe of Leaves*, however, may well survive in a line which runs through *Robinson Crusoe* to *The Enchanted Isle* and back to *The Tempest*' (p. 74). Like Susan Lever quoted earlier, Morse also declares herself against 'the retreat from aesthetic judgment which has been so characteristic of the critical movements of the last thirty years' (p. 60). If Morse has her eye on the large canvas, Henry Weinfield, in 'A.D. Hope's "The Death of the Bird": Between Romantic Symbol and Modernist Anti-Symbol' (*Southerly* 68:iii[2008] 161–71), has his on the individual lines of what he regards as 'one of the great lyric poems in English of the twentieth century' (p. 161). He argues that Hope's bird is not a Romantic symbol in the manner of Keats's nightingale or Shelley's skylark because it really exists; the issue is the sort of universe in which it exists. Weinfield argues that this universe is fundamentally benign, despite its apparent cold detachment at the bird's death. 'The Craft of Making and Breaking: Responses to Tradition/s in A.D. Hope and Agha Shahid Ali' (*Southerly* 68:iii[2008] 284–93) is a brief comparison by Santosh K. Sareen and Ipsita Sengupta of A.D. Hope with a Kashmiri poet. Both are seen to be decentred from their national traditions, 'formophiles' (p. 286), and 'unashamed of what Amitav Ghosh calls the "bardic register"' (p. 287). Although the pigeonholing of Hope seems a little dated (and is challenged by other essays in the same issue), the article gives an interesting insight into how Hope (and for that matter Australian literature) appeared to Indian scholars in 2007 when the paper was originally read.

Toby Davidson, in 'Francis Webb in Western Australia' (*Westerly* 53[2008] 115–26), is a little cross about the apparent lack of critical interest in Webb. The article squeezes what juice it can from letters Webb wrote while visiting the West for a few weeks in 1951 as a guide to reading the poetry. One hermeneutical focus point is Webb's complaint about the rapacity of the flies if they had a wound to attack, and his admission that 'my dial and mitts were knocked about in a tumble in Mandurah' (p. 118). Davidson is forced to admit that while it is possible that Webb's psychological condition landed him in a serious fight, nothing can be proved. Also with a biographical slant, Helen Hewson's ' "Music Ever!": John Shaw Neilson's Encounter with Paul Verlaine' (*Southerly* 68:iii[2008] 213–27) shows just how much exposure Neilson, the 'half-blind recluse of the Mallee' (p. 222) as Nettie Palmer called him, had to European Symbolist ideas and poetry through publications connected with A.G. Stephens and Bernard O'Dowd. In particular, O'Dowd's publication of a translation of Paul Verlaine's short manifesto 'Ars Poetica' in *The Heart of the Rose*, which advocated poetic music above all, seems to have influenced Neilson profoundly. In ' "Our own way back": Spatial Memory in the Poetry of David Malouf' (*JASAL* 8[2008] 92–106), Emily Bitto argues that Malouf's concept of memory involves a spatial dimension as well as a temporal one. Imaginative writing is a reinhabiting of experience in a more adequate way. These ideas are demonstrated in a series of poems dealing with Moreton Bay, before the article turns to collective memory as opposed to individual memory and Malouf's postcolonial project of validating and making valuable non-European experience. Elizabeth Allen's 'The Ghost of Icarus' (*Southerly* 68:i[2008] 176–90) is primarily a discussion of Rosemary Dobson's use of paintings in her poetry, which she describes as a haunting. This is not the haunting of a recriminatory guilty history as in Judith Wright, or the Freudian uncanny of displaced memory, but rather an artistic pressure to understand and react to some earlier work of art. The article has some good things to say about Breugel's painting of Icarus, and Dobson's response to it in 'The Bystander'. Werner Senn's 'Voicing the Body: The Cancer Poems of Philip Hodgins' (in Borch et al., eds., pp. 237–49) starts with the observation from Susan Sontag that a terminally ill cancer patient is habitually depicted as reduced by fear and humiliation and thus incapable of any form of self-assertion. By a close reading of his poems, Senn shows that Philip Hodgins found a variety of tones and positions to oppose that reduction during his twelve-year terminal illness. Sometimes bitter, sometimes detached and satirical, sometimes almost exuberant, Hodgins 'succeeded in demonstrating an exemplary sanity, emotional balance and poetic control' (p. 248).

Ross Chambers's ' "Isn't there a poem about this, Mr de Mille?": On Quotation, Camp and Colonial Distancing' (*ALS* 23:iv[2008] 377–91) is a lithe and subtle reading of John Forbes's commissioned bicentenary poem 'On the Beach' that argues that the poem picks up much of the excitement of the decade while it mocks the historical achievements and the nationhood that Forbes had been commissioned to celebrate. Forbes also questions the laureate role of the poet, his ambivalence and diffidence reflected in the way the suite of poems substitutes suggestion, question and intertextuality for a clear expression of a celebratory position. Stuart Cooke's 'Singing up Country in the

Poetry of Judith Wright and Pablo Neruda' (*ALS* 23:iv[2008] 408–21) brings together two 'world poets' (p. 408) linked by their sense of nature and history and their political praxis. The essay offers more about Neruda than it does about Wright, but the comparisons and refracted comments, especially about the impact of Heidegger on the two poets, are mildly rewarding. In a very readable piece, 'Erocide is Painless: Insensation in Les Murray's *Fredy Neptune*' (*ALS* 23:iv[2008] 422–33), Robert Savage reads Fredy's inability to feel as an externalization of Murray's sense of sexual rejection as a teenager. 'Erocide' is Murray's own coinage for an experience he claims is more pervasive than that of gays and rape victims put together. Savage shows how Murray has refocused the incident that inspired the poem—the burning of women by a mob in Siamanto in the Armenian genocide—from visual to tactile, and points out the dangers in appropriating it to semi-autobiographical purposes. Keith McKenry, in '"Sweet Mary of Kilmore": Discrimination in Australian Folk Song Scholarship' (*ALS* 23:iv[2008] 474–80), discusses different versions of a deceived-and-abandoned-woman ballad, arguing that Russel Ward's omission of it from his compilation is symptomatic of a gender bias in such research. McKenry includes texts of the quite dissimilar Irish and Australian versions. As an item of *curiosa*, Michael Farrell's 'The Black or Unfair Image: Reading Ned Kelly's *Babington Letter* as a Sonnet' (*JASAL* 8[2008] 7–16), about a letter from Ned Kelly to a police sergeant, may turn out to be a Sokal-type test of what modern journals can be persuaded to publish, although its author has not yet formally declared it to be a hoax.

(d) Drama

Jonathan Bollen, Adrian Kiernander and Bruce Parr's *Men at Play: Masculinities in Australian Theatre since the 1950s* uses plays in performance to chart evolving ideas of masculinity in Australia from the 1950s to the 1990s. Starting with formulations of 'masculinity', the book gives examples from different types of plays (musicals, realistic drama) to demonstrate the way in which stage presentation, including dialogue, silences, styles of acting and violence, reveals underlying ideas of what maleness is and what sort of behaviour is provoked by it. The argument is enriched on occasion by considering alternative versions of the text in drafts and prompt copies such as the ending of *Summer of the Seventeenth Doll* (p. 48). Themes such as inarticulacy, violence, bullying, indigenous masculinity, masculinity and war, multicultural masculinity, gay masculinity and masculinity and parenting structure the chapters. The final chapter does not focus on an aspect of behaviour, however, but rather on a locale, considering the beach as a special locus for performing masculinity. This is not the sort of book that struggles with difficult language to discover its message in conveying it. The motifs, categories and sub-categories all seem to have been clearly worked out in advance, the discussions of the plays are taut and economical, and the exposition is written with remarkable lucidity. In Chris Mead's *What Is an Australian Play? Have We Failed our Ethnic Writers?* the author summarizes an investigation into the production of new plays and the rise and fall of new theatre groups, some of which are ethnic or indigenous, in Australia, the UK and New Zealand. He finds that while there has been some institutional support for the performance of plays, and a degree of community support for the groups that perform them, there are no programmes to support ethnic and indigenous playwrights. The plays that have been performed are often ensemble-developed in production rather than developed from a script. Mead does not believe that the playscript is dead, however, and he calls for mainstream theatre companies to seek out indigenous scripts more actively to supplement their repertoire, since diversity of offerings is the leading audience preference. Currently mainstream theatre companies limit themselves to monitoring fringe and suburban productions, following up any that seem to be particularly successful. The new Playwriting Australia National Playwriting Festival could help identify indigenous playwrights who would profit from a formal training programme in writing scripts. The monograph mentions a number of recent productions and indigenous theatre groups whose activities (and even existence) might be difficult to track down from other sources.

Joanne Tompkins's 'Adapting Australian Novels for the Stage: La Boite Theatre's Versions of *Last Drinks*, *Perfect Skin*, and *Johnno*' (*ALS* 23:iii[2008] 305–17) offers a readable account of the issues that can be encountered in adaptation from novel to stage. The novels in the title are by Andrew McGahan, Nick Earls and David Malouf respectively. Among the issues raised are attempts to incorporate the audience more actively into the story, simplification yet increasing focus in distilling for the stage, and four properties of the stage that can be deployed in place of verbal exposition: stage setting, performance, 'responses and emotions...perceived by the audience' (p. 307) although not 'articulated or illustrated by the actors' (p. 307), and doubling of characters as a method of highlighting themes. Tompkins refers closely to performances at Brisbane's La Boite theatre to illustrate aspects of adaptation.

Melissa Bellanta, in 'The Larrikin's Hop: Larrikinism and Late Colonial Popular Theatre' (*ADS* 52[2008] 131–47), argues that the larrikin was an iconic figure at the end of the nineteenth century, ranking with the suffragette and the shearer. As a result of social disorderliness, including a notorious gang rape case in Sydney in 1886, the larrikin became a figure of fear to the middle classes, but a semi-comic version had a significant presence on the variety-hall stage, combining flash dressing and a love of mischief. Glen McGillivray, in 'Mis-recognised Knowledges: National Identity and the Unreliable Narrator in Jack Hibberd's *A Stretch of the Imagination* and Josephine Wilson's *The Geography of Haunted Places*' (*ADS* 52[2008] 69–84), seeks to recuperate the latter play which was dismissed in some quarters as 'performance art' rather than true drama. His method of doing this is to argue its similarity to Hibberd's play, both being monologues but, more significantly, both being produced at times when political trends in the country were moving away from positions that had existed for some time. The 'drama' of *Geography* needs to be understood in that context. Jasna Novakovic's 'The Dialectic of Myth and Politics in *The Knight of the Long Knives* by Dorothy Hewett' (*Southerly* 68:i[2008] 139–49) is an attempt to resuscitate a play Dorothy Hewett wrote on the Whitlam sacking that has never been performed. However, the invocation of frameworks of nature cults, the avant-garde and Shakespeare is not enough to persuade us that this truly is 'a unique attempt in Australian theatre history at uniting life and art' (p. 147). Michael Connor's 'Follies Bizarre: Australia's Political Theatre' (*Quadrant* 52:iii[2008] 22–8) is a breathtaking attack on left theatre in Australia which he sees as headed by Stephen Sewell and which he describes as foul-mouthed, dealing in stereotypes not characters, historically amnesiac, politically naive, consumed by hate, constantly attacking the sort of people who read *Quadrant*, contemptuous of real Australians, numbingly boring, published by Currency Press, set as texts by schools and universities supported by the ABC and overall constituting 'a state-funded assault on the principles of liberal democracy' (p. 22). Connor argues that leftist writers have become 'vanity liberals' who see themselves as brave dissidents but who are in fact followers of the mob. The vehemence of this article suggests that drama criticism in Australia may have drifted a little away from F.R. Leavis's 'common pursuit of true judgement'.

3. Canada

(a) General

Aiming at a transcultural understanding of literature produced by the different language communities in Canada, Reingard M. Nischik, ed., *History of Literature in Canada: English-Canadian and French-Canadian* is a comprehensive collection of essays. Critical of previous literary histories, Nischik notes that the term 'Canadian literature' is in itself problematic since it can lead to historical surveys that exclude or downplay French Canadian or Anglo-Canadian literary history. Instead, *History of Literature in Canada* is an ambitious attempt at providing extensive coverage of both literatures, with six chronological divisions: I. Beginnings; II. The Literature of New France, 1604–1760; III. The Literature of British Canada, 1763–1867; IV. From the Dominion to the Territorial Completion of the Nation, 1867–1918; V. The Modern Period, 1918–1967; and VI. Literature from 1967 to the Present. The thirty-five chapters are concise and clearly written, with a relatively small amount of material on pre-modern Canadian literatures. Guy Laflèche writes three chapters on the literature of New France with a brief 'Historical Background', and two more detailed chapters, 'Literature on New France' and 'Colonial Literature in New France', where 'literature' necessarily includes travel and exploration writing, missionary reports, historical accounts and the extensive *Relations des Jésuites de la Nouvelle-France* [1632–72] as well as poetry and correspondence. The second section has a historical overview by Dorothee Scholl and two chapters, Gwendolyn Davies's 'English-Canadian Colonial Literature' and Dorothee Scholl's 'French-Canadian Colonial Literature under the Union Jack'. Coverage to the modern period is concluded in the third section with Tracy Ware's 'English-Canadian Literature, 1867–1918: The Making of a Nation' and Fritz Peter Kirsch's 'French-Canadian Literature from National Solidarity to the École littéraire de Montréal'. For the modern period and literature to the present, chapters divide along national and genre lines, with essays on politics and literature, poetry, the novel, the short story, theatre and drama, socio-political and cultural developments, literary theory and criticism, and broader movements such as modernism, postmodernism, 'canons of diversity', First Nations, Inuit and Métis literature, orality, transculturalism and migrant writing. The final chapter, by Andrea Oberhuber, covers 'The Institutionalization of Literature in Quebec'. What makes this volume unique is its juxtaposition of material on English and French Canadian writing; while the resulting chapters are in themselves quite short, reading them in relation to one another tells a larger, more culturally diverse, story. For example, the role of anthologies in the literatures of the immigrant experience in Georgiana Banita's 'Canons of Diversity in Contemporary English-Canadian Literature' can be compared with Gilles Dupuis's chapter on migrant literature in Quebec: 'Transculturalism and *Écritures Migrantes*'. Similarly, the role of orality in Eva Gruber's 'Literature of the First Nations, Inuit, and Métis' can be compared with Ursula Mathis-Moser's 'Orality and the French-Canadian Chanson'. The resulting holistic understanding of Canadian literary history embraces diversity and difference, but also acknowledges some shared cultural experiences.

Two books that approach indigenous literature from apparently opposing perspectives are Deena Rymhs's *From The Iron House: Imprisonment in First Nations Writing* and Eva Gruber's *Humor in Contemporary Native North American Literature: Reimagining Nativeness*. Incarceration serves as a place and a trope in Rymhs's study, which is divided between prison and residential school writing. Key authors in the first section include Leonard Peltier, James Tyman and Yvonne Johnson; in the second section, on the residential school, the authors are Basil Johnston, Tomson Highway and Jane Willis. The Native residential school system is regarded as 'prefiguring' (p. 3) the prison system in Canada, and Rymhs also examines the reserve as a site in which Canadian aboriginals are physically segregated and trapped in poverty, their territory having been 'curtailed' (p. 5). This is a Foucauldian approach to territorial and psychological containment and punishment, examining 'the multiple and often overlapping sites of discipline that define delinquency and that naturalize the power to punish' (p. 11). Rymhs pays close attention to genre and the adaptation of indigenous modes of writing to the spaces of incarceration. For example, the chapter on Leonard Peltier looks at his resistance to a Christian juridical discourse and his alternative modes of Native testimony, whereas life stories are the focus when examining writing by Tyman and Johnson. The fourth chapter, on 'Prison Collections and Periodicals', concerns an important genre of indigenous writing that can be difficult to access outside penal institutions. Exploring the question of audience and how this question affects the written text, Rymhs notes that prison writing allows indigenous peoples to 'transcend' (p. 73) their imprisonment. The chapter also covers issues of orality as it is expressed in prison writing. The Foucauldian notion of incarceration and other societal mechanisms of control is offered as one of the reasons why the residential school experience parallels that of prisons; Rymhs also argues that Native authors themselves makes the comparison. The two most successful chapters that explore incarceration as a trope cover Tomson Highway's *Kiss of the Fur Queen* and the notion that the residential school is 'a distanced zone' (chapter 6; p. 102), and the notion, in relation to Jane Willis's *Geniesh: An Indian Girlhood*, that the autobiographical mode is mimetic of a Western desire for individualism and containment (chapter 8). Gruber also focuses on a Native mode of writing that is often passed over in silence: that of humour. Self-reflective Native humour can offer a shared cultural response to postcolonial indigenous identity, one which goes beyond romantic stereotypes or notions of tragic victimhood. Gruber examines North American Native humour, which necessarily crosses the colonial border lines between America and Canada. The first chapter provides a historical and conceptual overview of the topic, while subsequent chapters offer substantial readings under the following headings: 'Reimagining Nativeness through Humour: Concepts and Terms'; 'Expressing Humour in Contemporary Native Writing: Forms'; and 'Humour at Work in Contemporary Native Writing: Issues and Effects'. While many of the close readings focus on the works of Thomas King, a large number of other humorous texts and interludes are also covered. The first main chapter on concepts and terms is probably the most useful to critics working in this area, including a definition of Native humour: 'humour created by Native people that reflects and shapes aspects of Native as well as Euro-American life and culture' (p. 40). Control of identity involves controlling the production of Native images: alternative images and re-inhabiting stereotypes to counter 'clichéd misrepresentations' (p. 29) from within. An intriguing notion put forward by Gruber is that Native humour is a mode of defamiliarization, where 'humour figures as the agent of imaginative subversion and is instrumental in a regeneration of Nativeness' (p. 35). Formally, Gruber notes that there are similarities with the Euro-American humorous tradition, although idiosyncrasies include trickster humour and the use of 'Red English' (p. 41). Gruber pays close attention to the fact that humour is entertaining, and that the reimagination of Native identity is facilitated by this fact; humour is theorized as being in itself a mode that critiques master-narratives and embedded, often racist, notions of indigenous identity. In summary, while there is not space to evaluate all of the close readings that follow in the book, Gruber's study is groundbreaking and makes an important contribution to the topic.

Wide-ranging critical responses to the question of engaging with Canadian literature 'from a distance' are gathered in Charlotte Sturgess and Martin Kuester's edited collection *Reading(s) from a Distance: European Perspectives on Canadian Women's Writing*. While the bulk of the twenty essays are close readings of a particular author or text, four critics consider the broader critical implications of the topic: Coral Ann Howells, 'Complex Transactions: Reading from a Distance'; Larissa Lai, 'Brand Canada: Oppositional Politics, Global Flows, and A People to Come'; Mary Condé, 'Relations: Mother Countries and Negotiating Identities in Contemporary Canadian Women's Fiction'; and Reingard M. Nischik, 'Multiple Challenges: The Canadian Artist Story and Gender'. Howells charts the European interest in Canadian women's writing starting with Frances Brooke's *The History of Emily Montague*, which appeared in 1769 (not the date given in Howells's essay), but she also observes that, until recently, Canadian national identity was effaced in favour of textual criticism per se. Early examples of European

Canadian literature initiatives, such as the 1983 Strasbourg Conference on the English Canadian Short Story, and early critical collections in Europe, are shown to follow close-reading rather than identity-politics interpretative strategies. Howells argues that it was not until the 1990s that European critics moved on to examine 'a specifically Canadian imaginary' (p. 16). Lai regards her involvement in anti-racist identity politics in Canada as positively informing her own creative writing, and her critical conception of Canadian literature. She refers to Hegel's master/slave narrative, and Deleuze's notion of 'a people to come' (p. 31), to theorize Canadian identity within globalization. Different mother–daughter relations, including the fact that Queen Elizabeth II appears as a symbolic mother for Canada in much fiction, are theorized by Condé as a central concern within Canadian women's writing; she also compares and contrasts Canada–US literary relations with those of Canada and the UK. Nischik argues that the Canadian artist story is important for Canadian women writers, and for readers in Germany, who approved of alternative feminist narratives. Nischik reads key short stories through three critical categories: gender-affliction, gender-consciousness and gender-affirmation. Gender and genre are further addressed by Katalin Kürtösi, 'Women Playing Women in Sharon Pollock's *Blood Relations*'; Anca-Raluca Radu, 'Writing Women: Masks and Masquerade in Short Stories by Alice Munro'; and Jutta Zimmermann, 'The "New Sentimentalism" in Recent Canadian Fiction: The Example of Ann-Marie MacDonald's *The Way the Crow Flies*'. Zimmermann's essay helps with critical understanding of the shift away from more experimental novels in Canadian literature to fiction that utilizes 'a more traditional narrative form and structure' (p. 112). Postmodern historiographic metafiction no longer dominates, but an interest in historical narratives remains. Zimmermann argues that the parallels with the sentimental literary tradition from the eighteenth and nineteenth centuries reveal a similar mode in Canada, where there is a new concern with 'ethics, spirituality, and religion', yet this 'does not preclude an explicitly political preoccupation with national identity' (p. 113). The new sentimentalism is thus driven by a dissatisfaction with relativist postmodern theory and literature. Comparative approaches are also highly productive in Brigitte Glaser's 'Women and War: Representations of Histories of Violence in Contemporary Canadian Fiction' and Barbara Korte's 'Women's Views of Last Men: Mary Shelley's *The Last Man* and Margaret Atwood's *Oryx and Crake*'. Glaser examines four contemporary novels: Sandra Birdsell's *The Rußländer* [2001], Frances Itani's *Deafening* [2003], Jane Urquhart's *The Stone Carvers* [2001], and Kerri Sakamoto's *One Million Hearts* [2003]. She shows that women writers in Canada often focus on war through an indirect treatment, with a concern with the lasting impact of war. Korte provides an excellent overview of Mary Shelley's *The Last Man* [1826], which she sees as a generic model—the last-man narrative—for cultural critique, one which Atwood draws on and reworks in new ways, notably with her representation of genetic technologies in *Oryx and Crake* [2003]. This essay provides another important way of exploring eschatological tropes in contemporary Canadian fiction.

Knowledge concerning the beginnings of the Anglo-Canadian canon is enhanced with a collection of essays edited by Jennifer Chambers, *Diversity and Change in Early Canadian Women's Writing*. Where authors covered have received in-depth critical attention prior to the publication of this volume, the contributors examine their less frequently studied works, or adopt a new critical approach. The first main essay, by Kathryn Carter, called 'Neither Here Nor There: Mary Gapper O'Brien Writes "Home," 1828–1838', examines the hybrid genre of the journal letter and the practicalities of pre-postal service delivery routes, to map colonial Canada in dynamic new ways, especially in relation to the unsettling of notions of home and domesticity. David Copeland, in 'Finding the Words: Form and Language in *Canadian Crusoes*', describes Catharine Parr Traill's *Canadian Crusoes: A Tale of the Rice Lake Plains* [1852], a book sometimes known by its third edition title, *Lost in the Backwoods*. Copeland reveals how *Canadian Crusoes* synthesizes botanical observation with didactic children's literature as a way of representing the pioneer experience, more famously achieved by Traill via her use of the epistolary form in *The Backwoods of Canada* [1836]. Similarly, Cecily Devereux explores less well known books by Duncan in her essay 'Colonial Space/Imperial Identity: How Sara Jeannette Duncan Navigated Victorian Canada, Americanization, and the Empire of the Race by Herself'. Devereux observes the paradox that Duncan is known primarily for her Canadian novel *The Imperialist* [1904], while the bulk of her fiction is situated outside Canada, in India, Europe and the US; she argues that Duncan had a more complex, imperial notion of her own identity. Another aspect of Duncan's identity, the femininity expressed in her interviews, is the subject of Jessica Langston's '"*I Inquired Rather Delicately*": Femininity as Strategy in Sara Jeannette Duncan's Interviews'. Duncan's excessive gender performance is interpreted by Langston as a way of critiquing essentialism. In Jennifer Chambers's 'A Woman's Will: The Dissonance between Life and Art in May Agnes Fleming's Formulaic Domestic Fiction', stereotypical gender performances are shown to be exceeded through resisting the generic constraints of formula fiction; this is mainly achieved by showing the differences between women's identities in the domestic sphere versus the workforce. Chambers closely analyses Fleming's novels *The Actress' Daughter* [posthumously published in 1886] and *Lost for a Woman* [1880]. Gender stereotypes in Canada were being debated and reconsidered in a wide range of women's writing on social reform at the beginning of the twentieth century, and it was through collective action that feminism was immeasurably strengthened, explored by Katja Thieme in '"The grim fact of sisterhood": Female Collectivity in the Works of Agnes Maule Machar, Nellie L. McClung, and Mabel Burkholder'. The final three essays in the book take a biographical approach, with Katherine Sutherland's 'Re-evaluating the Literary Reputation of Isabella Valancy Crawford'; Moira Day's '"The larks, still bravely singing, fly": Clara May Bell's *Psyche* and Women Upholding "the Bright Torch" of the Arts at the University of Alberta 1914–1918'; and Benjamin Lefebvre's 'The Fitness of Things: *Anne of Green Gables*, Social Change, and L.M. Montgomery's "Discerning Extraordinary Observer"'. Sutherland's essay is a useful survey of critical attitudes to Crawford, and she resituates Crawford's work in relation to three contexts: that of 'national literature, female sexuality and aboriginal culture' (p. 125). Tracing the remnants of a now lost musical comedy, the drama *Psyche*, Day provides an unusual approach to early women's writing, offering a model for related future research. Finally, Lefebvre's reading of a Canadian classic posits two types of implied reader of the novel, creating a doubled narrative voice: one for the youth audience, and one for a more sophisticated, mature audience 'invited to provide a writerly reading of the novel, to add his or her own perspective in order to *produce* the text's meaning' (p. 174). Overall, this collection of essays provides critics with new avenues of research, not just exploring alternative texts by early women writers, but modelling exciting new critical approaches.

A book of essays edited by Smaro Kamboureli brings together essays by one of Canada's most significant critics and translators, Barbara Godard, the title demonstrating Godard's range: *Canadian Literature at the Crossroads of Language and Culture*. Kamboureli notes in her introductory interview how Godard has 'been instrumental in introducing theory' into Canadian critical discourse as well as being a leading translator 'generating a vibrant dialogue between Anglophone Canadian literature and Quebec writers, especially women' (p. 17). The interview with Godard offers biographical and historical insights into the institutional development of a more theoretical approach to the arts in Canada, and explores Godard's focus on issues of gender in translation as well as 'the dynamic interactions between hegemonic systems and subaltern subversions of them' (p. 43) in the act of translating between cultures. Godard's essays that follow are theoretically complex, yet always readable. In 'Structuralism/Post-Structuralism: Language, Reality, and Canadian Literature', Godard argues that Canadian critics absorbed forty years of European theory in one decade, bringing together German critical theory and French structuralism and poststructuralism in a unique Canadian hybrid, the study of which 'is an exercise in comparative literature' (p. 55). Godard is careful to distinguish Canadian and American versions of poststructuralism, showing how the Yale school, for example, differs from Robert Kroetsch's and Stephen Scobie's initial deconstructionist approaches. In 'Critical Discourse In/On Quebec', Godard shows how theory is 'pluralist' (p. 88); for example, a body of writing has emerged, mainly within feminism, to challenge critical and societal orthodoxies. Godard specifically mentions Nicole Brossard and Madeleine Oeullette-Michalska, who produce what Brossard has called '*fiction/theory*' (p. 90). 'The Politics of Representation: Some Native Canadian Women Writers' is an essay that reveals that literary criticism and more popular modes of discourse, such as journalism, have different ways of conceiving Canadian First Nations writing, with Godard arguing that popular discourses often express a coded, but still present, racism. The essay that follows, 'Deterritorializing Strategies: M. Nourbese Philip as Caucasianist Ethnographer', demonstrates Godard's sophisticated handling of theoretical language as a way of engaging with immigrant aesthetics. Godard argues forcibly that 'emigration makes language deterritorialized' which can lead to 'a break or rupture with power, forms, norms, hierarchies' (p. 167). Two different ways of approaching the comparative literatures of Canada are 'Canadian? Literary? Theory?' and 'Writing Between Cultures', where both are in effect concerned with hybrid forms in Canadian literary theory, especially in its dependence upon translation and reading ethically. Canadian literature exists in 'field(s) of relational differences' (p. 181) just as the fact that a 'country in transition necessitates a consideration of literature not in terms of identity but of relationality' (p. 202). In 'Notes from the Cultural Field: Canadian Literature from Identity to Commodity', Godard examines Northrop Frye, Harold Innis and other major Canadian critical and cultural theorists. The importance of translation is again addressed in 'A Literature in the Making: Rewriting and the Dynamism of the Cultural Field', while the wide-ranging essay, 'Relational Logics: Of Linguistic and Other Transactions in the Americas', contains useful analysis of Marshall McLuhan's role in the understanding of the social imaginary, and a fascinating section on 'theorizing languages as ecology' (p. 336), with reference to critic Pierre Nepveu among others.

Re-examining the critical methodology of autoethnography, Eleanor Ty and Christl Verduyn, in their edited collection of essays *Asian Canadian Writing Beyond Autoethnography*, cover literary work produced in the last decade by Canadians of Asian heritage. Ty and Verduyn argue that Asian Canadian writing has not only become 'more experimental in form, theme, focus, and technique' (p. 3), it has also become more self-reflective, interrogating older models of ethnic identity, such as multiculturalism. In other words, Asian Canadian writing has moved beyond autoethnography, calling into question some of the essentialist notions still embedded in its convergence of purportedly postmodern ethnography and autobiography. The comprehensive critical and literary-historical overview in the editors' introduction is a useful document for researchers in this area, as well as providing summaries of the essays in the book. Almost all of the contributors reflect upon their critical methodology, and not just the opening section on 'Theoretical Challenges and Praxis', two of the most comprehensive essays in this regard being Eva C. Karpinski's '"Do not exploit me again and again": Queering Autoethnography in Suniti Namjoshi's *Goja: An Autobiographical Myth*', and Smaro Kamboureli's 'The Politics of the Beyond: 43 Theses on Autoethnography and Complicity'. Karpinski maps out the problem that virtually all of the contributors have with autoethnography: that it is a methodology deploying binary discourses that can reinscribe hierarchy and essentialism. She suggests that feminist approaches can go beyond this reinscription, alongside theoretical accounts of liminality and hybridity, all of which she finds in Namjoshi's *Goja*, a text which 'experiments with mythopoiesis' situating the subject in 'the spaces of radical otherness through spectacular displays of discursive heteroglossia, combining Western and Asian traditions, Christian, Hindu, and Greek symbolism' (p. 228). In her '43 Theses', Kamboureli goes into detail concerning the boundaries and paradoxes of autoethnography, which she notes is a double discourse, complicit with the problems of representing otherness, but performatively revealing these problems, rather than trying to construct a progressive system of knowledge. To move beyond such a hegemonic epistemology is to perform, and to read, 'autoethnography otherwise' (p. 57), also the title to Paul Lai's essay in the book, where he notes that such a process places ideological demands upon the reader and the discursive and cultural field within which such texts are produced and received. Many of the critics in this volume are highly sceptical of the popularity of the autobiographical genre within the Asian Canadian literary marketplace. Larissa Lai, in her essay 'Strategizing the Body of History: Anxious Writing, Absent Subjects, and Marketing the Nation', is critical of autobiographies and memoirs, since she believes that marginalized subjects can be buried deeper in the autobiographical text, mainly by their narratives being received by, and incorporated into, nationalist discourse, thus displacing and ignoring more profound trauma. Using different genres as a way of evading such marginalization is the subject of Pilar Cuder-Domínguez's 'The Politics of Gender and Genre in Asian Canadian Women's Speculative Fiction: Hiromi Goto and Larissa Lai'. Speculative fiction can provide enough distance from the ethnographic, Cuder-Domínguez argues, to allow for a questioning and unsettling of questions of ethnicity and identity. Another related writing strategy is to occupy multiple identities at the same time, explored by Joanne Saul in her essay ' "Auto-hyphen-ethno-hyphen-graphy": Fred Wah's Creative-Critical Writing'. Once more, this is a case of avoiding binary modes of representation, which Wah successfully achieves in his multiple reconfigurations of diasporic identity.

(b) Fiction

A comprehensive survey of Laurence's writing necessarily includes her African novels and criticism; in Nora Foster Stovel's *Divining Margaret Laurence: A Study of her Complete Writings*, the discussion of the ways in which her African-focused writing influences her Canadian novels is a key contribution to scholarship. Stovel argues that it is the 'African experience' that enabled Laurence to become 'a great Canadian novelist' (p. 7) because Laurence could more broadly begin to understand Canada's postcolonial status and the position of women within a patriarchal culture. The chapter on Laurence's poetry translations also reveals the ways in which this project influenced her Canadian fiction. Stovel suggests that Laurence's novel *The Stone Angel* [1964] is not just her first Canadian novel, but also her last African novel, the transition between these two worlds being embedded in the text at multiple levels, for example with the protagonist's name, Hagar, being both a name from the Bible and a Somali word meaning 'thornbush' (p. 15). Travel is a major part of Laurence's life, but it is also a key trope in her writing. Exploring Laurence's travel narratives, collected and published as *Heart of a Stranger* [1976], is important because in them she worked out some of the themes of her fiction. It is Stovel's chapters on Laurence's writing about, or set in, Africa, that are the most compelling: chapter 4 covers Laurence's translation of Somali poetry and prose; chapter 5 covers her critical monograph *Long Drums and Cannons: Nigerian Dramatists and Novelists, 1952–1966* [1968]; and chapter 6 examines her African travel writing and novels. Useful observations include revealing how Somali poetic devices inform Laurence's prose writing, such as the heavy use of alliteration in Somali poetry, the use of character-ization in Somali long narrative poems, and moral elements which are central in Somali literature in general. Stovel notes how Laurence's early draft of *This Side Jordan* [1960] opposed complex indigenous characters with such strong anti-imperialism that her white characters became 'caricatures' (p. 139); she also argues that the 'true hero' of the novel is 'Ghana itself' (p. 140). Chapters 7 to 11 cover more familiar territory, starting with Laurence's Manawaka cycle; chapter 12 is perhaps the most intriguing, examining Laurence's unfinished novel sharing the same title as her memoirs, *Dance on the Earth*. Stovel analyses the text in relation to Laurence's entire works, speculating how this ambitious novel, that in part answered back to Laurence's more religious critics, would have been completed. After examining Laurence's children's fiction, the penultimate chapter looks at her memoirs, and the book concludes with a chapter, appropriately, on closure in Laurence's work.

Two books on Lucy Maud Montgomery take opposing approaches to the critical use of biographical information. Irene Gammel, in *Looking for Anne: How Lucy Maud Montgomery Dreamed Up A Literary Classic*, questions biographical information as part of her critical sleuthing, while Elizabeth Waterston's *Magic Island: The Fictions of L.M. Montgomery* interweaves biographical and critical observations with the overriding notion that the biographical can illuminate the critical. Waterston suggests that contemporary research has filled the significant gaps in the record of Montgomery's life, and therefore each text by Montgomery can be considered 'in the light of new reflections on her experience, her times, her reading, and her professional intentions' (p. 7). This critical approach depends on notions of intentionality and the ability of the critic to separate outer and inner life, for example, Waterston's suggestion that character and plot 'come from Montgomery's experiences of other people' while 'the tone of the telling comes from her own nature' (p. 15). The book as a whole usefully places each major publication in relation to significant events in Montgomery's life, with some close textual reading. Gammel, however, is far more sceptical about biographical information; while Montgomery was a committed journal writer, Gammel notes that 'she was also ruthless in burning and discarding old letters, documents, diaries, and notebooks' (p. 14), leaving the critic with highly edited versions of her creative life. Gammel proposes to focus on the period in which *Anne of Green Gables* was being developed (1903–8), by examining unconventional sources and sites of information, in particular, an image of the American model Evelyn Nesbit, which 'became the model for Anne's face' (p. 16), and three textual sources: the poem 'To Anne' published in *Godey's Lady's Book* in 1893, the character 'Charity Ann' from a story published in *Godey's Lady's Book* in 1892, and the character 'Lucy Ann' from a story published in *Zion's Herald* in 1903. Interestingly, Gammel argues that the ur-text for all of the orphan Ann stories so popular in the period was James Whitcomb Riley's *Little Orphant Annie*, a nursery rhyme published in 1885. Gammel suggests that this lineage signifies that *Anne of Green Gables* is not dependent upon Kate Douglas Wiggin's *Rebecca of Sunnybrook Farm* [1903] as critics have argued. In summary, while these two books occupy opposing methodological positions with regard to biographical criticism, they both offer sophisticated analytical insights into Montgomery's texts and writing life.

Ian Rae, in *From Cohen to Carson: The Poet's Novel in Canada*, suggests that the reason why so many of Canada's novelists start as poets is that there is a 'reciprocal relation between the contemporary long poem and novel' (p. 3);

Rae also calls this 'a serial relation' (p. 6). The rhetorical strategies developed in narrating poetry become crucial in the experimental and lyrical approach to prose writing in Canada. Rae focuses on Leonard Cohen's *The Favourite Game* [1963], Michael Ondaatje's *Coming Through Slaughter* [1976], George Bowering's *A Short Sad Book* [1977], Daphne Marlatt's *Ana Historic* [1988], and Anne Carson's *Autobiography of Red: A Novel in Verse* [1998]. Rae regards Ondaatje as a key author because he draws on Sheila Watson and Leonard Cohen, the latter being linked with, and drawing deeply on, A.M. Klein, especially his genre-crossing novel *The Second Scroll* [1951]; Rae therefore concludes his book with a study of Ondaatje's *The English Patient* [1992]. One of the most fascinating sections in the book's introduction on genre is 'Poetry, Narrative, and Electronic Media', which examines McLuhan's research into the relationship between poetry and the novel, with emphasis upon McLuhan's *Through the Vanishing Point: Space in Poetry and Painting* [1968]. McLuhan's notion of electronic media illuminates 'the compositional practices' (p. 16), Rae asserts, of the authors in question. The redefinition of the serial novel in Bowering's work also provides a key anchor in Rae's rereading. Bowering rejects the 'plot-driven realist serial' in favour of a new mode of prose writing 'based on the serial poem', where he 'created continuity between discrete sections of narrative by developing them recursively around motifs, which in his work tend to be phrases and syntactic constructions (or other formal constraints), as much as visual images' (p. 138). Rae also looks closely at the aesthetics of serial film, music, and photography throughout his study.

A new collection of essays edited by Sarah A. Appleton, *Once Upon a Time: Myth, Fairy Tales and Legends in Margaret Atwood's Writings*, examines the ways in which the mythological substrate of Atwood's writing is used as a way of exploring more complex adult issues and ideas. Dystopian intertexts and Jungian archetypes are explicated in Appleton's 'Myths of Distinction; Myths of Extinction in Margaret Atwood's *Oryx and Crake*', while Carol Osborne, in 'Mythmaking in Margaret Atwood's *Oryx and Crake*', focuses on Atwood's post-apocalyptic vision. Osborne sees Atwood's myth-making as functioning on three levels: the therapeutic; as a warning device; and as a self-reflexive interrogation of contemporary meaning-making through language and modern myth. Two essays explore Atwood's use of the Penelope myth: Shannon Hengen's 'Staging Penelope: Margaret Atwood's Changing Audience' and Coral Ann Howells, '"We can't help but be modern": *The Penelopiad*'. Hengen looks at the transposition of Atwood's work into the different media of film, opera and drama, and explores the way in which such media draw upon Atwood's performative language and provide a communal feminist experience. In a wide-ranging essay on Atwood's use of myth throughout her writing career, Howells calls *The Penelopiad* 'Atwood's Gothic version of *The Odyssey*' (p. 58); she argues that Atwood challenges patriarchal mythological narrative and, in the case of Penelope, claims the 'right to tell a different story' (p. 64). Imagery, and photographic images are a constituent part of Atwood's magical realism, argues Sharon Wilson in 'Fairy Tales, Myths, and Magic Photographs in Atwood's *The Blind Assassin*', in which she closely interprets five key structural images in Atwood's novel. Another structural analysis is Karen Stein's 'It's About Time: Temporal Dimensions in Margaret Atwood's *Life Before Man*', here examining the novel's juxtaposition of mythic and realist narratives. Stein argues that the surface of *Life Before Man* is realist, with a mythic subtext 'in which the characters act out a cyclic pattern of birth, death, and rebirth, following the cycle of the year' (p. 96). After an interesting section on Atwood's affinities with modernist authors, Stein shows how the novel's critique of realism functions via time. Theodore F. Sheckels, 'No Princes Here: Male Characters in Margaret Atwood's Fiction', re-examines the 'male characters shoved into the background' (p. 115) of Atwood's work. Sheckels suggests that fairy tales and myth connect these characters through the motif of the rescuing prince, with five suggested categories: dark princes, shadowy princes, comic princes, sad princes and unfinished princes. Fact and fiction come together in an apparently mythological story by Atwood concerning a Tasmanian species that Shuli Barzilai discovered was true, narrated in her 'Unfabulating a Fable, or Two Readings of "Thylacine Ragout"'. The final essay, Kathryn VanSpanckeren's 'Atwood's Female Crucifixion: "Half-Hanged Mary"', is reviewed below in the poetry section.

A significant contribution to Atwood scholarship is Simone Drichel's 'Regarding the Other: Postcolonial Violations and Ethical Resistance in Margaret Atwood's *Bodily Harm*' (*MFS* 54[2008] 20–49), which argues that postcolonial criticism should engage more thoroughly with ethical readings, in this case via the work of Emmanuel Levinas. Drichel initially examines *Bodily Harm* through Sartre's concept of the gaze, and the way in which Atwood's novel explores the postcolonial 'doubling of identity' whereby the Canadian settler is both colonizer and colonized (p. 29). The hostage section of the novel is read through Levinas, whereby the character Rennie is involved in regarding the face of the Other (the character Lora), and the Levinasian gifts of touch and regard. Finally, Drichel shows how postcolonial critics have largely misunderstood the ethical complexities of *Bodily Harm*. Atwood's resistance to dualistic notions of subjectivity is the subject of Sofia Sanchez-Grant's 'The Female Body in Margaret Atwood's *The Edible Woman* and *Lady Oracle*' (*JIWS* 9[2008] 77–92), where food and the body are perceived as languages that can be manipulated and recoded. Another way in which Atwood explores the mind/body dualism is through psychological trauma and its bodily effects, which Bethan Jones discusses in 'Traces of Shame: Margaret Atwood's Portrayal of Childhood Bullying and its Consequences in *Cat's Eye*' (*CS* 20[2008] 29–42). A particularly astute part of the essay is the intertextual tracing of Atwood's and Shakespeare's characters called Cordelia, thereby 'mapping the intersection between literatures of contemporaneity and of the Elizabethan age' (p. 34). Jones not only examines *King Lear* in this context, but also Cordelia's appearances in *Julius Caesar* and *Macbeth*, suggesting that Atwood's Cordelia has a dysfunctional relationship with her father, yet 'it serves as an underlying source for her adverse treatment of Elaine' (p. 36). Two key essays on *The Handmaid's Tale* are Lauren A. Rule's 'Not Fading into Another Landscape: Specters of American Empire in Margaret Atwood's Fiction' (*MFS* 54[2008] 627–53) and Deborah A. Thomas's '"Don't let the bastards grind you down": Echoes of *Hard Times* in *The Handmaid's Tale*'

(*DQu* 25[2008] 90–7). North American identity is the subject of Rule's essay, and the way in which Atwood writes fiction with landscapes 'haunted by US imperialism' (p. 628). Looking at Atwood's short story 'Death by Landscape' alongside *The Handmaid's Tale*, Rule notes how frontier spaces were historically feminized and that this makes North American landscape a territory of gendered power relations; Atwood's critique of Romantic modes of representing landscapes is explored well, especially her revision of ekphrasis and her reworking of Wordsworth's Lucy poems in her short story. Thomas approaches *The Handmaid's Tale* via its parallels with Dickens's *Hard Times*, the main one being that both novels feature women oppressed by totalitarian systems of control. The long list of 'common elements' (p. 95) shared by the two novels cannot be a coincidence, suggests Thomas, and the detailed proof provides the groundwork for exploring further this intriguing creative substrate of Atwood's work. Atwood's *Oryx and Crake* continues to get significant coverage, with three key essays being Pilar Cuder Domínguez's 'Margaret Atwood's Metafictional Acts: Collaborative Storytelling in *The Blind Assassin* and *Oryx and Crake*' (*RCEI* 56[2008] 57–68), Barbara Korte's 'Margaret Atwood, *Oryx and Crake* (2003)' (in Peters, Stierstorfer and Volkmann, eds., *Teaching Contemporary Literature and Culture*, vol. 2: *Novels, Part I*, pp. 21–36), and Barbara Korte's 'Fundamentalism and the End: A Reading of Margaret Atwood's *Oryx and Crake* in the Context of Last Man Fiction' (in Stierstorfer and Kern-Stähler, eds., *Literary Encounters of Fundamentalism: A Casebook*, pp. 151–63). Domínguez finds parallels between *The Blind Assassin* and *Oryx and Crake*, in particular 'the dynamics of storytelling' as related to 'the literary act' and 'the writing triangle' of author, reader and novel as mediator (p. 58). Bakhtin's theory of chronotopes serves to explain Atwood's use of the writing triangle, a chronotope that Domínguez calls 'the lovers' room' (p. 59): a parallel, internal counter-discourse. Both novels also utilize the narrative structure of 'framing text and embedded tale' (p. 62). Domínguez argues that these narrational strategies are part of Atwood's postmodernism. Korte summarizes and contextualizes *Oryx and Crake* in her overview of the novel, while in 'Fundamentalism and the End' she situates the novel in the genres of apocalyptic writing and the nineteenth-century 'last man' narrative. The sophisticated point made in this essay is that apocalyptic writing is as suspicious of fundamentalism as modernity, and this is illuminated with reference to Mary Shelley's *The Last Man* [1826], and Olaf Stapledon's *Last and First Men* [1930] among other novels. Korte also situates the core idea of *Oryx and Crake* in A.S. Neill's *The Last Man Alive* [1970], as well as the biographical backdrop of 9/11. Fundamentalism and modernity are regarded as 'dialectically interwoven' in *Oryx and Crake*, whereby the 'terrorism depicted in Atwood's novel is directed against but also emerges from an unlimited belief in technology and economic liberalism' (p. 157).

A comprehensive introduction to Ondaatje's internationally famous novel is provided by Jutta Zimmerman's 'Michael Ondaatje, *The English Patient* (1992)' (in Peters et al., eds., pp. 425–42). Zimmerman contextualizes the novel before comparing novel and film as a good place to begin literary analysis. The essay is particularly strong on narrative structure and techniques, as well as spatial form and free indirect discourse, making this a good starting point for understanding *The English Patient*'s complexity. At a deeper level, Rachel D. Friedman's 'Deserts and Gardens: Herodotus and *The English Patient*' (*Arion* 15[2008] 47–83) rereads the critical debate about the different endings of the novel and film versions, arguing that the centrality of Herodotus in the novel needs further consideration. The importance of nomadic identity, and different conceptions of home and nostalgia for home, are related by Friedman to the opposition of the desert and the garden in the novel: 'The entire novel of desert wandering is thus framed by scenes in a garden' (p. 72). Friedman suggests that the novel is attempting to find a non-oppressive identity that goes beyond this binary opposition. A productive comparative approach to Ondaatje's fiction is Carla Comellini's 'Bodies and Voices in Michael Ondaatje's *The English Patient* and *Anil's Ghost*' (in Borch et al., eds., pp. 187–95), where the antinomies of body and spirit are analysed. Substantial new research on *Anil's Ghost* is produced by Victoria Burrow in 'The Heterotopic Spaces of Postcolonial Trauma in Michael Ondaatje's *Anil's Ghost*' (*SNNTS* 40[2008] 161–77), where the notion that there is a turning away from trauma, from a developed world perspective, is explored in Ondaatje's text. Burrow argues that Ondaatje occupies the perspectives of the developing and developed worlds, and therefore he can map the heterotopia, or place of otherness, in a unique way. In the process of explicating the text, Burrow also develops Michel Foucault's theory of the heterotopia and applies it to postcolonial and trauma studies in general. Frank Davey's extensive critique of Ondaatje in his *Post-National Arguments: The Politics of the Anglophone-Canadian Novel since 1967* [1993] is answered in Robert David Stacey's 'A Political Aesthetic: Michael Ondaatje's *In the Skin of a Lion* as "Covert Pastoral"' (*ConL* 49[2008] 439–69). William Empson's concept of 'covert pastoral' is applied to Ondaatje, the term defined as that which 'represents a missed opportunity to read a work of pastoral in terms of its appropriate modality' (p. 446). It is in response to the reception and misinterpretation of a text, here the criticism arguing that *In the Skin of a Lion* fails politically, that Empson's theory is so usefully deployed.

Rohinton Mistry gets good coverage in three essays: Caroline Herbert's '"Dishonourably Postnational"? The Politics of Migrancy and Cosmopolitanism in Rohinton Mistry's *A Fine Balance*' (*JCL* 43[2008] 11–28), Eli Park Sorensen's 'Excess and Design in Rohinton Mistry's *A Fine Balance*' (*Novel* 41[2008] 342–63), and Bindu Malieckal's 'The Bangladeshi Genocide in Rohinton Mistry's *Such a Long Journey*' (*AteneaPR* 28[2008] 75–91). Herbert achieves a nuanced reading of Mistry's short story 'Lend Me Your Light' [1987], as well as *A Fine Balance*, by applying to these texts the concept of 'double duty' or accountability to homeland and migrant country. Mistry is shown to be problematizing the notion of migrant postnational space. Literary realism is the dominant mode of postcolonial writing, according to Sorensen, yet it is not often given more than thematic treatment by postcolonial critics. Sorensen rereads *A Fine Balance* and its realist mode in light of Georg Lukác's theory of the novel, rejecting postcolonial notions of good and bad realism derived from Benedict Anderson's notion of the realist novel 'embodying "homogeneous, empty time"' (p. 358). Bindu takes a historical approach to contextualize the political and social unrest narrated in Mistry's *Such a Long Journey*, with some useful materials for scholars new to this text and the history of the Bangladeshi genocide.

Contemporary Fiction and Christianity by Andrew Tate, has one chapter (ch. 6) with a Canadian focus: '"How clear is your vision of heaven?": Douglas Coupland at the End of the World'. He notes how Coupland is 'absorbed' by eschatology, and makes the astute observation that his novels are punctuated with 'persistent rumours of grace' (p. 107). Coupland's 'endism' (a term used by James Annesley in his *Blank Fictions* [1998]) is Adventist, argues Tate, which unlike much postmodernist apocalyptic fiction, promises 'revelation' (p. 108). Coupland's fiction, open to the ultimate arrival of the other, is messianic in this postmodern sense, where novels such as *Girlfriend in a Coma* feature redemptive suffering as part of a bigger sacred story. Tate covers Coupland's exploration of chronological and kairotic time, as well as messianic time, and concludes with a section on resurrection imagery. This is a comprehensive analysis of Coupland's fiction, revealing the complexities and subtleties of Coupland's eschatological and messianic vision. Questions of genre are considered in Cinda Gault's 'Marian Engel's *Bear*: Romance or Realism?' (*CanL* 197[2008] 29–40). Interpreting the novel as romance leads to an optimistic notion of female and national identity; interpreting the novel as realism, however, '*Bear* becomes an engagement with the historical and gendered circumstances that make the story seem strategically non-triumphant' (p. 30).

Vancouver's urban spaces are important for Asian Canadian fiction, with new insights in this field by Marie Lo, in 'The Currency of Visibility and the Paratext of "Evelyn Lau"' (*CanL* 199[2008] 100–17), and Glenn Deer, in 'Remapping Vancouver: Composing Urban Spaces in Contemporary Asian Writing' (*CanL* 199[2008] 118–44). Lo examines the paratextual narratives that surround Lau's texts, positioning her within the social concept of the model minority, and how Lau operates with and subverts this indirectly racist concept (it was used initially as a critique of African American under-achievement). Asian Canadian spatial consciousness is a major part of the Vancouver landscape. Deer relates this consciousness to issues of ethnicity and urban regeneration, examining Coupland's *City of Glass* [2000], before covering Asian Canadian texts: Madeleine Thien's *Simple Recipes* [2001], Nancy Lee's *Dead Girls* [2002], Kevin Chong's *Baroque-a-nova* [2001] and Larissa Lai's *Salt Fish Girl* [2002]. This new generation of Asian Canadian writers is critical of Vancouver's urban spaces, their characters being excluded in many respects from mainstream society, yet also able to create complex identities precisely because of the malleability of Vancouver's ever morphing urban landscape. Racialized and sexualized spaces are the subject of Yu-Hsiang Fu Bennett's 'Dystopic Here, Utopic There: Spatial Dialectics in SKY Lee's *Disappearing Moon Café*' (*NTU* 19[2008] 61–80). Bennett develops a theory of spatial dialectics, which is a 'utopic site' (p. 75) outside normative sexual and political relations. References to Canadian First Nations in Asian Canadian writing are analysed in Marie Lo's 'Model Minorities, Models of Resistance: Native Figures in Asian Canadian Literature' (*CanL* 196[2008] 96–112). Lo notes how, within Asian Canadian writing, Canadian First Nations writers are seen as models of resistance, and relationships between Asian Canadian and First Nations characters enable a remodelling of identity that is outside the model minority or 'yellow peril' paradigms. A paper related to this emphasis upon spatiality and identity in Asian Canadian writing is Julie Spergel's '"Space Invasion": Jewish Canadian Women Writers and the Reshaping of Canadian Literature' (*RCEI* 56[2008] 43–56), which examines gender and ethnicity in spatial Jewish Canadian chronotopes.

Rudy Wiebe's work continues to receive excellent coverage, with significant essays by Malin Sigvardson, 'Regenerative Knitting: Work and Hope in Rudy Wiebe's Mennonite Triptych' (*MQR* 82[2008] 161–73), Susan Birkwood, 'From "Naked Country" to "Sheltering Ice": Rudy Wiebe's Revisionist Treatment of John Franklin's First Arctic Narrative' (*Nordlit* 23[2008] 25–38), and Janne Korkka, 'Facing Indigenous Alterity in Rudy Wiebe's Early Writing' (in Huttunen, Ilmonen, Korkka and Valovirta, eds., *Seeking the Self—Encountering the Other: Diasporic Narrative and the Ethics of Representation*, pp. 72–90). Sigvardson develops a highly sophisticated theological and phenomenological reading of Wiebe's three Mennonite novels, *Peace Shall Destroy Many* [1962], *The Blue Mountains of China* [1970] and *Sweeter Than All the World* [2001], with the focus on Mennonite concepts of work and hope, which Sigvardson argues 'are phenomena that are close to the kinetic and kinaesthetic materiality of Wiebe's fiction' (p. 163). Phenomenological directedness or intentionality is shown to be part of the pre-subjective strata of Wiebe's novels, alongside the material embodiment of work and hope. This reading is an important contribution to Wiebe studies. Differences between Dene and British culture are the main focus of Birkwood's essay, which clearly describes this opposition in Wiebe's historiographical metafiction. Taking an ethical approach to questions of representation of the other in Wiebe's work, Korkka suggests that Levinas's theories can help critics get beyond the Mennonite/First Nations opposition used to categorize his work.

Intertextual relationships between fiction and the wider literary and extra-literary canon are approached by three critics: Richard Ilgner, 'Faust and the Magus Tradition in Robertson Davies' *The Rebel Angels*' (in Fitzsimmons, ed., *International Faust Studies: Adaptation, Reception, Translation*, pp. 205–15), Marta Dvorak, 'Resurgences of the Extra-Textual and Metatextual in Jane Urquhart's *The Stone Carvers*' (*Com* 31[2008] 22–7), and Catherine Lanone, 'Mourning/Mocking Browning: The Resurgence of a Romantic Aesthetics in Jane Urquhart's *The Whirlpool* (1986)' (*Com* 31[2008] 8–21). The recovery of the holistic in Davies's work is shown to be integrally bound up with Goethe's Faust narrative, which Ilgner unravels in detail through specific comparative analysis. Dvorak shows how inscriptions, carvings, and monuments are part of the extra-textual architecture and landscape of Urquhart's aesthetic, while Lanone examines Urquhart's negotiation of the British Romantic heritage. Other essays of note relating to mainstream Canadian women's fiction include Corinne Bigot's '"And now another story surfaced": Re-emerging Voices, Stories, and Secrets in Alice Munro's "Family Furnishings"' (*Com* 31[2008] 28–35), Lorna Hutchinson's

'Uncovering the Grotesque in Fiction by Alice Munro and Gabrielle Roy' (*SCL* 33[2008] 187–210), Elke D'Hoker, 'Moments of Being: Carol Shields's Short Fiction' (*SCL* 33[2008] 151–68), and Isla Duncan's 'Margaret Laurence's *A Jest of God* as a Work of Simultaneous Narration' (*SCL* 33[2008] 136–50).

Two less well known Maritime authors, Susan Kerslake and Lesley Choyce, are the focus of David Creelman's 'Swept Under: Reading the Stories of Two Undervalued Maritime Writers' (*SCL* 33[2008] 60–79), in which the role of small presses and innovative writing techniques is shown to contribute to critical perception. Creelman also notes that these authors produce work that 'resists the signifying codes that typically define the Maritime region'. Reception studies are put to work to understand the opposite situation in Danielle Fuller's 'The Crest of the Wave: Reading the Success Story of Bestsellers' (*SCL* 33[2008] 40–59), while the practices of reading Maritime literature within Canada are more widely explored in Tony Tremblay's ' "Lest on too close sight I miss the darling illusion": The Politics of the Centre in "Reading Maritime"' (*SCL* 33[2008] 23–39). Breaking the boundaries of regionalism are authors Paul Bowdring and Michael Winter, in Paul Chafe's 'Beautiful Losers: The *Flâneur* in St. John's Literature' (*NF&LS* 23[2008] 115–38), and Wayne Johnston in Fevronia Novac's 'Paternal Authority in Wayne Johnston's *The Navigator of New York*' (*NF&LS* 23[2008] 171–84).

(c) Poetry

A special issue of *Capilano Revier* is on Sharon Thesen, with a range of short reflective essays, creative and critical responses to her work and an interview with Daphne Marlatt. In Andrea Actis's ' "Alive and watching": Sharon Thesen and the Eighth Type of Ambiguity' (*CapR* 3[2008] 28–35), ambiguity and ethics are shown to be essential partners in Thesen's poetry. Three essays examine different aspects of Thesen's *The Good Bacteria*: Colin Browne's ' "How much of Heaven has gone from Earth?": Sharon Thesen's "The Good Bacteria Suite"' (*CapR* 3[2008] 48–58), Andrew Klobucar's 'She Who Destroys Light: Sharon Thesen's *The Good Bacteria* and the Organic Imagination' (*CapR* 3[2008] 104–10), and Kent Lewis's 'As Above, So Below: Parallax in Sharon Thesen's *The Good Bacteria*' (*CapR* 3[2008] 114–18). Juxtapositions are explored by Browne, who delineates the ways in which the mundane and the transcendent are at times opposed, and at others merge in Thesen's work, such as her use of the word 'hauling' that appears in an Emily Dickinson poem. Intertexts are important to Thesen: Browne examines the role of Robert Bringhurst's *A Story as Sharp as a Knife: The Classical Haida Mythtellers and their World* [1999] on the rhythms of Thesen's poetry, while Klobucar is interested in Coleridge's influence on her work. Derrida's reading of the pharmakon, that which is both poison and cure, is used by Lewis to explicate Thesen's contradictions and pairing of opposites. Lewis notes that Thesen's poems make a 'double gesture' (p. 115) whereby contradictions are deconstructed. Thesen's intermixing of high and popular culture is the subject of Mary Di Michele's biographical reflections in 'Your Own Heart a Satire' (*CapR* 3[2008] 132–7). Shared experiences are also narrated in Thea Bowering's 'Sharon Thesen: Poem in Memory, and Growing Up There' (*CapR* 3[2008] 42–7). Other significant essays in this special issue cover the role of Whitman in Thesen's work in Jenny Penberthy's 'Canine Kin: Sharon Thesen's "Animals"' (*CapR* 3[2008] 140–5), the role of fire in Canadian poetry in Nancy Holmes's 'Report from the Savage Fields: Sharon Thesen's "The Fire"' (*CapR* 3[2008] 97–103) and Thesen's romantic irony in Meredith Quartermain's 'Irony's Rhyme' (*CapR* 3[2008] 146–54). While most of the critical essays in this special issue are very short, they are insightful, witty and creative, offering academic and personal reflections on Thesen's work.

Lori Emerson is the guest editor of a special issue of *Open Letter* celebrating the work of poet bpNichol. The issue has many short, creative and critical responses to bpNichol's work, such as John Havelda's 'And Torture One Poor Word a Thousand Ways' (*OpL* 5[2008] 79–80), which discusses his own use of paragrams in relation to bpNichol's extensive use of them in *The Martyrology* (6 volumes [1972–87]). Significant longer essays include analysis of 'a theory of simultaneity' (p. 10) in Rob Winger's '"a magician explaining his best trick"': Postcard Poetics from bpNichol's "You Too, Nicky"' (*OpL* 5[2008] 10–24), observing not only that the Japanese poetic diary form *utanikki* structures Nichol's work, but that *utanikki* is also important for the genesis of the Canadian long poem. Kevin McPherson Eckoff's 'Organ Donor: Transplanting my Eye/I into bpNichol's *Selected Organs*' (*OpL* 5[2008] 25–32), is a theoretical, self-reflexive account of an engagement with Nichol's aesthetic, interweaving theories of the body with biographical readings of the text. Gaston Bachelard's theories of space inform Debby Florence's discussion of Nichol's 'language space' (p. 110) in '"Axe-cessing the Void": bpNichol's Activity of Language' (*OpL* 5[2008] 110–14), especially the notion of a daydream as creating a phenomenological space of memory. Of note is Geoffrey Hlibchuk's '"Hazardous Connections": A Consideration of bpNichol's Poetics of Chain' (*OpL* 5[2008] 81–90).

The journal *Tish* played an important part in the poetry of the 1960s, as Lance La Rocque reveals in 'The Other Side of Utopia: The Opacity of Perception in the Poetry of the First Run of *Tish*, 1961–63' (*SCL* 33[2008] 49–76). However, La Rocque notes a difference between the utopian register of the prose writings in the journal and the actual poetry produced in the first run, where the 'mood shifts; perceptions and locus withhold their treasures, evoking a gloomy sensibility' (p. 50). La Rocque traces this difference to the *Tish* poets' sense of alienation from the technological modern city of Vancouver which, ironically, is constitutive of their subjectivities, leading to a 'phenomenological' (p. 73) poetics.

Trauma studies continue to develop, with essays by Kathryn VanSpanckeren, 'Atwood's Female Crucifixion: "Half-Hanged Mary"', which is the concluding essay in Appleton, ed., *Once Upon a Time* (reviewed above in the fiction section), and Robert Hemmings, 'Of Trauma and Flora: Memory and Commemoration in Four Poems of the World Wars' (*UTQ* 77[2008] 738–56). VanSpanckeren notes that the poem 'Half-Hanged Mary' brings together central themes in Atwood's work: 'uncanny women, patri-archal violence against females, [and] female struggles for survival and autonomous identity' (p. 152). VanSpanckeren argues further that the poem questions, from a feminist perspective, the Christian doctrine of redemptive sacrifice through setting up parallels between Christ and Atwood's ancestor, Mary Webster, who survived her sacrificial ordeal. VanSpanckeren's analysis of the three rough drafts of the poem held at the Thomas Fisher Rare Book Library at the University of Toronto is highly useful for scholars interested in how Atwood's manuscripts are edited and developed, and she describes the evolution of the poem 'from personal narrative to mythic revisioning' (p. 170). Canadian war poet John McCrae is one of four poets analysed by Hemmings, who criticizes the notion that the poppy is a symbol memorializing only the Canadian experiences of the First World War. Hemmings suggests that critics should pay more attention to McCrae's literary background, and that it was through his knowledge of aesthetics that he could successfully partake of and recode the 'language of flowers' (p. 740) developed in nineteenth-century literature, revealing the traumatic darkness that underlay the poetic experience of the war. A related essay on racist trauma is Jordana Greenblatt's 'Something Sadistic, Something Complicit: Text and Violence in *Execution Poems* and *Thirsty*' (*CanL* 197[2008] 80–95), where poets George Elliott Clarke and Dionne Brand are shown to approach extreme violence in different ways, yet both 'involve the reader' (p. 81) in the violence of the text. Clarke's *Execution Poems* offer an aesthetic of linguistic beauty to negate extreme violence, whereas Brand involves the reader in interpretative choices, leading to an aesthetic of hope.

The importance of the ocean for Maritime poetry is discussed in Wanda Campbell's '"Every sea-surrounded hour": The Margin in Maritime Poetry' (*SCL* 33[2008] 151–70), where sea poetry is posited as 'the quintessential marginal poetry' (p. 152). After covering a wide range of critical notions of the sea in Maritime aesthetics, Campbell focuses on four poets: Deirdre Dwyer, Harry Thurston, Lesley Choyce and Anne Compton. Campbell argues that these poets share an interest in the sea as a site in which memory and hope intersect. More mundane objects can be found in Catherine Bates's 'Messing with the Archive: Back Doors, Rubbish and Traces in Robert Kroetsch's *The Hornbooks of Rita K*' (*SubStance* 37[2008] 8–24), in which she ponders the different modes of selection or deselection that lead to objects being awarded value or status as worthy of archiving, and how this in turn helps with a reading of Kroetsch's heterogeneous and unorthodox text. Another highly unorthodox text that foregrounds methods of con-struction is the subject of Robert David Stacey's 'Toil and Trouble: On Work in Christian Bök's *Eunoia*' (*CanPo* 62[2008] 64–79). Defending the playfulness and seriousness of Bök's quadruple vocalic lipograms (where one or more letters of the alphabet are excluded from the poetic text), Stacey regards these poems as reflective of twenty-first-century Canadian consumer culture. Linguistic constraint, Stacey suggests in contrast to many critics of *Eunoia*, creates an aesthetic relationship with labour and the politics of literary production.

(d) Drama

An overview of Canadian drama and evolutionary theories provides a useful approach to plays concerning biological differences. Craig Walker's '"Hopeful Monsters and Doomed Freaks": Evolutionary Overtones in Canadian and American Drama' (in Maufort and De Wagter, eds., *Signatures of the Past: Cultural Memory in Contemporary Anglophone North American Drama*, pp. 15–30), begins by comparing and contrasting American and Canadian history and culture before turning to Ann-Marie MacDonald's *Belle Moral* ([2005]; originally called *The Arab's Mouth*), a play about biological abnormality. Using geneticist Richard Goldschmidt's category of the 'hopeful monster' (p. 18), Walker applies theories of macro-evolution to ponder the question of why so many American plays feature 'doomed freaks' (p. 20), compared with the more positive Canadian theatrical experience of the 'hopeful monster'. Plays discussed in answering this question include Jodi Essery's *Fathom* [2007], Wendy Lill's *Chimera* [2007] and Damien Atkins's *Lucy* [2007]. Questions of national differences also occur in Erica Kelly's '"This is not where we live": The Production of National Citizenship and Borderlines in Sharon Pollock's *The Komagata Maru Incident*' (*SCL* 33[2008] 257–71). The way in which Pollock focuses on certain historical characters and downplays the role of other officials involved in this immigration incident in Vancouver is important for her construction of border spaces. Kelly argues that Pollock has effaced the political nature of the Ghadr supporters who attempted entry into British Canada as part of their political project to end British rule in India, thereby effacing 'Canada's own role in the production of Empire' (p. 266). However, this selective storytelling is still important in unsettling the boundaries of nation-states and revealing the history of racism in Canada.

Time and memory are explored in Mary Blackstone's '"Prior was here": Renegotiating a Role for the Ghost of Cultural Memory in Four Cree Plays' (in Maufort and De Wagter, eds., pp. 179–95), and Kirsty Johnson's 'Performing an Asylum: *Tripping through Time* and *La Pazzia*' (*ThTop* 18[2008] 55–67). Collective experiences and memories are shared through theatre, which Blackstone argues relates to First Nations storytelling through being oral and social. Blackstone examines different approaches to indigenous memory and performance in Tomson Highway's *The Rez Sisters* [1988] and *Dry Lips Oughta Move to Kapuskasing* [1989], Daniel David Moses' *Almighty Voice and his Wife* [1991] and Damon Badger Heit's *Broken Bones* [2006]. Highway's focus on personal and collective memory is related to his use of tribal and polemical language, whereby, as Blackstone notes, 'Highway focuses principally on retrieving and renegotiating intragroup memory in order to unify the aboriginal community around traditional cultural beliefs' (p. 184). In comparison, Moses dramatizes conflicted intergroup memory, and Heit situates cultural memory 'as a point of transit between past, present and future, between the social and the personal, between collective and individual expression' (p. 190). Social history is approached from a different perspective by Johnston in her analysis of two Workman Theatre Project productions which engage with issues of mental illness.

The Workman Theatre Project, as Johnston explains, is an innovative and productive group working with people with mental illness; in the case of the plays *Tripping through Time* [1993] and *La Pazzia* [1999], the links with the Queen Street Division of the Centre for Addiction and Mental Health are analysed through performance techniques. An interesting link with Canadian pioneer author Susanna Moodie, who visited and wrote about the institution, is discussed. The associated concept of patient dignity and the medical practitioners and patients involved in the institution is the subject of *La Pazzia*.

Reid Gilbert and Ann Wilson edit an issue of *Canadian Theatre Review* on the intersection of performance and consumption with the title 'Consuming Performance: Intersections of Theatre, Bars and Restaurants' (*CTR* 134[2008]). In 'Dinner Theatre' (*CTR* 134[2008] 3–11), Susan Bennett argues that not much critical activity has taken place in this area since Robert Wallace's call to action in the editorial to *CTR* 44[1985]. Bennett provides information about Stage West Calgary and its strategies for reaching a broader audience, before discussing non-franchise dinner theatres in other parts of Canada. Sarah Banting, in 'Eating at the Buffet of Love: "Consummating" *Tony n' Tina's Wedding* in Vancouver' (*CTR* 134[2008] 12–17), argues that the co-performances between actors and audience in *Tony n' Tina's Wedding* are created through the shared consumption of food. Notions of production and consumption are problematized by J. Paul Halferty in 'Performing the Construction of Queer Space' (*CTR* 134[2008] 18–26), which reads 'the bar as a kind of script' (p. 19), in part through the theories of Michel de Certeau, where the patron of queer bars actively performs varied roles, occupying different subject/object positions. Alexis Lazaridis Ferguson, in 'Uses of Disorder and the Citizen Spectator' (*CTR* 134[2008] 27–31), discusses Sennett's notions of space and class segregation in contemporary cities, and his concept of 'survival communities' (p. 28) which involves societal re-engagement. Ferguson applies these ideas to alternative performance events, such as *Assembly*, where Vancouver's Radix Theatre re-created a bar in a hotel conference room to facilitate a communal theatrical experience. Another Radix event is discussed in Parie Leung's 'Diner Theatre: A Site-Specific Exploration of Life, Death, Consumption and Survival in Radix's *Box and Box*²' (*CTR* 134[2008] 32–8). *Box* was produced in Vancouver's Templeton Diner in 1999, creating an existential state of limbo for performers and spectators as a way of addressing eschatological questions. Leung examines the adaptations of this piece when it toured in Victoria and Toronto. In Dustin Scott Harvey's 'Théâtre à la Carte!' (*CTR* 134[2008] 39–42), spectator choice is taken to extremes with the Gary Williams *Café DaPoPo* theatre event in a Halifax diner. Williams offers the audience a menu with different theatrical performances available as part of this monthly production, mixing popular and more mainstream forms of entertainment in a space in which diners can see other performances that are simultaneously occurring. Harvey makes an interesting comparison with second-generation internet applications such as YouTube, MySpace and Facebook. The final essay is a reflective piece on the role of the Ship Inn, St John's, in encouraging and sustaining creative performance arts. The script is 'Assembly: A Surreal

Self-Improvement Seminar', a collective creation by Emelia Symington Fedy et al. (*CTR* 134[2008] 47–67).

The various processes involved in theatrical devising, or collaboration and performance development, is the subject of *CTR* 135[2008], edited by Bruce Barton and Ker Wells. The issue is composed of two sequences of essays: first, mainly collaborative pieces (or pieces reflecting on collaboration), and second, single-author essays. Examples of the former include the process of devising Leaky Heaven's *Bone in her Teeth* in Steven Hill and Heidi Taylor's 'Devising Disaster: Leaky Heaven Circus and *The Raft of the Medusa*' (*CTR* 135[2008] 6–10), an email exchange between theatre ensemble Ben Stone, Susan Leblanc-Crawford and Alex McLean, in 'Flirting with Zuppa Circus' (*CTR* 135[2008] 11–13), followed by Roberta Barker's 'Crossing the River: Zuppa Circus's *Penny Dreadful*' (*CTR* 135[2008] 14–16), and two essays on the Old Trout Puppet Workshop, the first by the workshop members, called 'To Be Honest, We Devised Theatre Companies Are Kind of Like Gangs' (*CTR* 135[2008] 17–19), the second by Vanessa Porteous, 'Fear and Bon-Bons: Devising *Pinocchio* with the Old Trout Puppet Workshop' (*CTR* 135[2008] 20–2). The dynamic process of collaboration is expressed in the French phrase *ça bouge* ('it moves'), given a more nuanced translation by Craig Walker, 'Staging the Impossible: SaBooge Theatre' (*CTR* 135[2008] 23–7), where both the word and this theatre ensemble signify 'impertinently restless, intellectually dynamic and indefatigably industrious' (p. 23). Responses from SaBooge members are written by Jodi Essery, Kayla Fell and Andrew Shaver. Two essays look at One Reed Theatre Ensemble: Evan Webber, with Frank Cox-O'Connell, Megan Flynn, Daniel Mroz and Marc Tellez, 'All Seams: Some Information from One Reed Theatre Ensemble' (*CTR* 135[2008] 28–30), and Janne Cleveland, 'Telling an Old Story in a New Way: One Reed Theatre Ensemble Devises an Alternative Perspective on a Conflicted History' (*CTR* 135[2008] 31–3). Webber et al. make the interesting observation that 'If the search for text/objects' in the devising process for *Nor the Cavaliers Who Come With Us* 'was like a noisy field trip, then making the performance material was more like a visit to the library, or the laboratory' (p. 29). Cleveland approaches the historical background of *Nor the Cavaliers Who Come With Us* more closely, noting that the ensemble manage to create what Artaud called 'non-linear exploration of colonization' (p. 32). The second sequence of short critical and reflective pieces is extensive, published under the following headings: Site(s); Perception(s); Crossing(s); Training(s); Memor(ies). Essays are by Kate Cayley, 'Devised Theatre and the Unstable Audience' (*CTR* 135[2008] 49–51); Jerry Wasserman, 'Collective Creation on the West Coast' (*CTR* 135[2008] 52–4); Estelle Shook, 'Making Theatre with Horses' (*CTR* 135[2008] 55–7); Pil Hansen, 'The Reflection Forums at Moving Stage Lab' (*CTR* 135[2008] 58–60); Michelle Newman, 'Notes on Falling and Flying' (*CTR* 135[2008] 61–3); Michael Devine, 'Talons of Desire: BoxWhatBox and *Hawks* in Southern Serbia' (*CTR* 135[2008] 64–6); Kim Renders. 'In the Room the Women Come and Go, Talking of Growing Old' (*CTR* 135[2008] 67–9); Heather Fitzsimmons Frey, 'Cultivating Process' (*CTR* 135[2008] 70–2); Yvette Nolan, 'Dramaturging the Process' (*CTR* 135[2008] 73–5); Diana

Belshaw, 'Empowering Actors: Devised Theatre Training at Humber College' (*CTR* 135[2008] 76–8); Lisa Wolford Wylam, 'Devising Twenty-First Century Approaches to Actor Training in Central Canada' (*CTR* 135[2008] 79–81); Maiko Bae Yamamoto, 'All That Remains' (*CTR* 135[2008] 82–4); Ker Wells, Varrick Grimes, Elizabeth Rucker, Alex McLean and Jane Wells, 'Number Eleven, in Particular' (*CTR* 135[2008] 85–108); and Bruce Barton, 'Forwards: The Theatre Centre's Residence Program' (*CTR* 135[2008] 109–12). The script is 'Icaria' by Number Eleven Theatre, Varrick Grimes, Alex McLean, Jane Wells, and Ker Wells (*CTR* 135[2008] 91–108).

A major contribution to regional theatre scholarship is the 'Alberta Theatre' issue of *CTR*, edited by Anne Nothof. Interviews are by Moira Day, 'John Murrell at the Banff Centre' (*CTR* 136[2008] 5–10); Mieko Ouchi, 'Translating Alberta' (*CTR* 136[2008] 50–3), in conversation with Toyoshi (Yoshi) Yoshihara; and Shelley Scott, 'Interview with Playwright Ron Chambers' (*CTR* 136[2008] 65–8). Critical essays begin with Ken Cameron's discussion of the Edmonton International Fringe Festival in his 'Jesters, Rabbits and Mavericks' (*CTR* 136[2008] 11–16), with analysis of the problematic and challenging transition from material produced at the Fringe and longer-term development in theatre companies. The advantages in playwrights having a permanent base are explored by Conni Massing in 'Alberta Playwrights-in-Residence: Home on the Stage' (*CTR* 136[2008] 17–19). Massing gives examples of the high creativity and productivity rates of playwrights who hold residence positions, but also ponders the downside of potential burnout or creative restrictions in fitting in with particular theatre company aesthetics. Three different approaches to play development are James MacDonald's 'Developing a National Drama at the Citadel' (*CTR* 136[2008] 20–5), Marty Chan's 'Phoenix Rising' (*CTR* 136[2008] 26–9) and Lynda Adams's 'Creation Explosion in Central Alberta' (*CTR* 136[2008] 30–3). Recounting in some detail the development of the play *Vimy*, MacDonald includes information on Citadel's script development, blocking, staging, and preliminary set designs, in a comprehensive essay on the topic. Citadel's dramaturge Vern Thiessen and artistic director Bob Baker also feature in Chan's essay, which looks at artistic risk-taking merging opera and theatre. The small community can punch above its weight in theatrical terms according to Adams; she narrates the development of *The Dada Play* in Red Deer, Alberta, revealing how theatre can synthesize creative, artistic revivals in such locations. Alternative media, performance spaces, and non-mainstream practices are all important factors in the vitality of Alberta theatre, discussed in essays by Allan Boss, 'CBC Radio Drama in Alberta: Featuring Wild Rose Writers' (*CTR* 136[2008] 34–9), Kirsty Johnson, 'MoMo on the Edge: Calgary and Mixed Ability Dance Theatre' (*CTR* 136[2008] 40–4), Scott Sharplin, 'Fifty Years of Walterdale' (*CTR* 136[2008] 45–9), Diane Bessai, 'Dramatic Initiatives at the University of Alberta' (*CTR* 136[2008] 54–61) and James Dugan, 'Gwen Pharis Ringwood at the University of Calgary' (*CTR* 136[2008] 62–4). The script is by Ron Chambers, '17 Dogs' (*CTR* 136[2008] 69–102).

4. The Caribbean

(a) General

Diaspora continues to supply a methodological framework for discussing Caribbean writing. One instance is Christine Chivallon's investigation 'On the Registers of Caribbean Memory of Slavery' (*CulS* 22:vi[2008] 870–91). The article focuses on the French Caribbean and is not literary but provides a useful mapping of differences between francophone and anglophone theories of diasporic identity and a discussion of problems inhering in constructivism. It builds a model for regional identity in which multiple narratives born of the break with Africa and fragmentation of community under slavery signify not lack of origin located in lost collective memory, but the grounds for 'a multiply-segmented culture, producing several, collective orientations simultaneously' (p. 872). That this diasporic focus is not just confined to Caribbean studies is evident in Mark Shackleton's collection, *Diasporic Literature and Theory—Where Now?* In amongst essays on Gloria Anzaldúa, Michael Ondaatje, Salman Rushdie and Kazuo Ishiguro, John McLeod, in 'Diaspora and Utopia: Reading the Recent Work of Paul Gilroy and Caryl Phillips' (pp. 2–17), weighs up the melancholic, past-directed side of diaspora theory against its celebratory utopian aspect. He dismisses Jonathan Sell's depiction of Zadie Smith as creating a present freed of historical hang-ups and of Caryl Phillips as being tied to 'sombre, unproductive retrospection', pointing out the subtle moments of hope in the latter (as seen in *A Distant Shore* [2003]) as a 'non-idealized illustration of diaspora ethics...linked to the practices of everyday life' (p. 3), and approving of those (Benita Parry, Avtar Brah) who insist on specifics of 'vernacular' material existence informing abstractions of theory. In this context, he assesses Paul Gilroy's *After Empire* [2004] as admirably working with popular culture's subversions of nation and race to envision multicultural community, but projecting a too idealistic vision. Joel Kuortti samples some postcolonial teaching from Canada, the US and the UK (plus one instance from Australia) to see how diasporic movements have affected curricula. He concludes that breaking down the Anglocentric canon has allowed an alternative postcolonial one to emerge. The sample is rather small and calls for a more extensive project (availability of texts is one factor that needs more attention, and differences between universities in the West Indies and UK/North America could be examined) but it is clear that within the sample provided Afro-diasporic writers dominate the scene, and Walcott, Kincaid, Naipaul, Césaire and Jean Rhys feature in the nineteen most popular writers listed. Kuortti notes that most of the writers are men, and Sandra Courtman, '"Lost Years": The Occlusion of West Indian Women Writers in the Early Canon of Black British Writing' (pp. 57–77), takes up Jean Rhys's almost disappearance until her sudden rediscovery and leap to 'canonical' standing with *Wide Sargasso Sea* to ask which other women from the Caribbean have been overlooked in the history of West Indian writing. Focusing on the years of postwar migration to Britain, she challenges the scholarly opinion that most women remained tied to orality and the home, taking up Joyce Gladwell, Beryl Gilroy and Lucille Iremonger as instances of women engaged with writing, and noting that many women (Merle Collins, Merle Hodge, Marina Maxwell, Claudia Jones, Pearl Connor-Mogotsi) worked in a range of textual modes (political writing, journalism, drama, dance, folklore) that didn't figure in more limited constructions of the literary guarded by men, both black and white. Courtman draws attention to other 'creole' writers like Rhys (Rosalind Ashe, Joan Riley, Phyllis Shand Allfrey) and to writers who worked in popular culture genres, seeing them all as forerunners of the visible literary presence of Caribbean women today. There is a useful table of publications by year, covering 1948–1979, noting the genres. Mark Shackleton, 'Resisting Terminal Creeds: The Trickster and Keeping the Field of Diaspora Studies Open' (pp. 180–95), closes the collection by returning to the big picture of diaspora theory to look for new ways of thinking through tensions mapped in the opening essays. The trickster crosses boundaries and expresses the diasporic desires of 'cultural survival, cultural adaptation and resistance' (p. 180). Literary treatments of tricksters, from indigenous writers in North America and New Zealand and from Africa and the Caribbean, are cited. (The relevance here is of course Anansi, and mention is made of Agard, Brodber, Bennett, Brathwaite, Melville, Salkey and Senior.) It is a quick rounding off that rather too readily subordinates texts/writers to academic theoretical interest, but the idea of an indigenous diaspora (at least in a sense of displaced consciousness, if not also dispersal from homelands) deserves further elaboration.

African roots and echoes constitute a central interest in other work, and this topic also enables a wider field of study via connections to the US. Sylvia Xavier, 'Crosstown Jakes in 1920s Manhattan: Racial Formations in John Dos Passos' *Manhattan Transfer* and Claude McKay's *Home to Harlem*' (*MFS* 54:iv[2008] 715–43), looks at depictions of the 'New Negro' soldier returning from the war. The writers use a modernist primitivism to produce working-class attacks on bourgeois values. The novels show gradations of prejudice in order to demonstrate the pervasive presence of racism, but (following Toni Morrison's *Playing in the Dark*) Xavier sees Dos Passos presenting 'racial ambiguity' whereas McKay's protagonist performs 'racial audacity'.

Dorothea Fischer-Hornung, '"Keep alive the powers of Africa"': Katherine Dunham, Zora Neale Hurston, Maya Deren, and the Circum-Caribbean Culture of Vodoun' (*AtStud* 5:iii[2008] 347–62), discusses Dunham's *The Dances of Haiti* and Deren's *Divine Horsemen: The Living Gods of Haiti* in connection with Zora Neale Hurston's explorations of Vodoun in Haiti and Hoodoo in Louisiana through in the *Journal of American Anthropology* and her novels *Mules and Men* and *Tell My Horse*. Hurston's linking of US and Caribbean practices is matched by Deren's use of Haitian Vodoun to express her interest in 'altered states of the (un)conscious through film' (p. 13). Dunham sees herself as a potential mediator between African culture in Haiti and North America. The three women are connected through their 'diasporic style' and 'commitment to something very old and very new in the cultures of the extended Caribbean' (p. 14).

In '"The progress of the heat within"': The West Indies, Yellow Fever, and Citizenship in William Wells Brown's *Clotel*' (*SLJ* 41:i[2008] 1–19) Kelly

Wisecup argues that Brown uses yellow fever in New Orleans to make connections between fever and revolution (via the Haitian American revolutionary Picquilo), black and white communities, Haiti and the US South. These 'destabilize antebellum geographies of bodies, race and nation' (p. 2). Fever makes 'southerners both American and Caribbean' (p. 16).

Adam Rothman's 'Lafcadio Hearn in New Orleans and the Caribbean' (*AtStud* 5:ii[2008] 265–83) explores the work of the Graeco-Irish writer during his 1870s–1880s 'tropical phase' in Louisiana and the Caribbean. Hearn celebrated the cultural diversity of the Creole world and saw connections between New Orleans Creoles and Caribbean societies. Rothman gives an overview of Hearn's life before focusing on his first novella, *Chita* [1888], about a young orphaned Creole girl. He then turns to *Two Years in the French West Indies* [1890] and Hearn's Martinican novella *Youma* [1890], whose central figure of the family's nurse symbolizes the era of slavery. The tropical texts are brought together in a synchronic map using Jameson's modified application of Greimas's semiotic square.

'Toward a Definition of Caribbean American Regionalism: Contesting Anglo-America's Caribbean Designs in Mary Seacole and Sui Sin Far' by Sean X. Goudie' (*AL* 80:ii[2008] 293–322) uses the trope of hospitality to discuss the influence of Caribbean–US relations on writing which he classifies as Caribbean American Regionalism. He focuses on two migrant working women of colour writing in the late nineteenth century: Jamaican Creole healer and boarding house operator Mary Seacole and Eurasian writer Sui Sin Far (the pen-name of Edith Maude Eaton). Both women critiqued US dominance in the Caribbean during that period, exposing 'the (in)hospitality of industry and the industry of (in)hospitality' (p. 298).

An extensive treatment of connections between the US, the Caribbean and the world can be found in Daphne Lamothe, *Inventing the New Negro: Narrative, Culture, and Ethnography*. The book focuses on Zora Neale Hurston, Franz Boas, W.E.B. Du Bois, James Weldon Johnson, Sterling Brown and Katherine Dunham to show how ethnography provided new ways of representing African American culture in literary and artistic form.

Black diaspora and postcolonial frameworks also encourage work across the three major languages of the region. In francophone studies, Haiti received a lot of attention in 2008 (*SmAx* 27[2008] was a special issue entitled *Haiti Now!*, guest-edited by Charles Forsdick, Martin Munro and Elizabeth Walcott-Hackshaw). Here and elsewhere Patrick Chamoiseau and Edwige Danticat were the most prominent names. For example, Andy Stafford, in 'Patrick Chamoiseau and Rodolphe Hammadi in the Penal Colony: Photo-Text and Memory-Traces' (*PcS* 11:i[2008] 27–38), explores a photo-essay documenting the 1993 visit to the remains of the Iles du Salut penal colony off the French Guyanese coast. Stafford provides a historical overview of the site, perceiving Chamoiseau's essay as 'interested in the forgotten of history' (p. 30). Rather than seamlessly blending prose with images throughout, the text begins with the essay and then presents Hammadi's photographs as a related but autonomous unit. Stafford argues that the photo essay is a 'key text in Francophone, postcolonial and memory studies' (p. 33). Work across the various languages of the region is also reflected in Fernando Cordobés's two-part survey of anglophone Caribbean writing in Spanish (*CuadHam* 695[2008] 49–59 and 696[2008] 43–50).

As with the Lafcadio Hearn article, several works consider the colonial 'prehistory' of Caribbean literature. Carl Plasa in '"Conveying away the *Trash*": Sweetening Slavery in Matthew Lewis's *Journal of a West India Proprietor, Kept during a Residence in the Island of Jamaica*' (*RoN* 50[May 2008]) analyses a journal entry describing Matthew Lewis's 1834 visit to a sugar mill which, in Plasa's opinion, reveals sugar-making as 'an allegory for the making of the *Journal*'. He states that, even though Lewis portrays himself as an enlightened slave-owner, 'the task of eliminating the marks of racial violence from his portrayal of the estate itself proves...difficult'. Jean Marsden, in 'Performing the West Indies: Comedy, Feeling, and British Identity' (*CompD* 42:i[2008] 73–88), examines two plays exploiting England's fascination with its colonies: Richard Cumberland's *The West Indian* [1771] and George Colman the Younger's *Inkle and Yariko* [1787]. These 'sentimental' comedies produced a shared colonialist subjectivity in playwright and audience through representations of English benevolence. Marsden employs Raymond Williams's term 'structures of feeling' to generate her analysis. Rezzan Kocaöner Silkü, in 'Wonderful Adventures: Transcending Liminality and Redefining Identity in Mary Jane Grant Seacole's Autobiography' (*ArielE* 39:i–ii[2008] 113–28), discusses the autobiography of Seacole, born of a Creole mother and Scottish father in Kingston, Jamaica. In Silkü's view, the autobiography enables Seacole to 'give voice to the Other' (p. 115) and negotiate a new space for herself as 'a mediator between the black and white cultures by redefining her identity in terms of Englishness rather than blackness' (p. 126).

The move towards a wider cultural studies approach continues to shift attention beyond literary print. For example, Jennifer Thorington Springer, '"Roll it Gal": Alison Hinds, Female Empowerment and Calypso' (*MFRT* 8:i[2008] 93–129), looks at how Hinds recovers that musical form from its sexist representation of women's bodies. *SmAx* 25[2008] contains several responses to Krista A. Thompson's *An Eye for the Tropics*, which discusses photographic images from nineteenth- and twentieth-century Jamaica and the Bahamas. Leon Wainwright, in 'Solving Caribbean Mysteries: Art, Embodiment and an Eye for the Tropics' (*SmAx* 25[2008] 133–44), discusses the representation of the Caribbean in postcards and paintings, showing how it created a 'tropical picturesque' that interpellated viewers as colonial subjects but 'not without discomfort and difference' (p. 141). He assesses Thompson's book against art from Trinidad. Beth Fowkes Tobin, in 'Caribbean Subjectivity and the Colonial Archive' (*SmAx* 25[2008] 145–56), questions whether exotic images of the tropics in colonial photography can be made to reveal subaltern black histories and examines how Thompson's book shows the problems of historians using postcards to reconstruct the past and how it attempts to include local responses to such images. In 'The Picturesque, Miss Nottage and the Caribbean Sublime' (*SmAx* 25[2008] 157–68), Richard J. Powell uses selected images and examples to argue that, via Thompson's analysis, we can find a regional aesthetic countering the colonial sublime with melodrama and public show. In the same issue, Nadi Edwards, moves from visual to musical culture in 'Notes on the Age of Dis: Reading Kingston through Agamben' (*SmAx* 25[2008] 1–15). Agamben's idea of 'bare life' (*homo sacer*) informs a discussion of dance-hall lyrics to depict Kingston as dystopia. Edwards focuses on Brathwaite's 'Trench Town Rock' and makes connection to the Holocaust, Abu Ghraib and Guantánamo. The *Journal of Caribbean Studies* (*JCSt* 36:i[2008]) is all about cinema, while *JCSt* 36:ii[2008] includes articles on both cinema and music. Unfortunately, after a long career promoting Black Studies and editing the *Journal of Caribbean Studies*, O.R. Dathorne passed away in 2007.

One book that seems to bring together all of these interests and trends is *Caribbean Without Borders: Literature, Language and Culture*, edited by Dorsia Smith, Raquel Puig and Ileana Cortés Santiago from conference presentations at the University of Puerto Rico, 2007. French, Spanish and English, literature and language studies, Bob Marley and Afro-Puerto Rican Dance all rub shoulders; Claude McKay is placed 'in dialogue' with Fyodor Dostoyevsky, and the Caribbean takes in the New York stage (J. Robinson's 1792 play *The Yorker's Stratagem or, Banana's Wedding*). Other chapters look at Cristina García's novel about Chinese workers who fought against Spain in Cuba (*Monkey Hunting* [2003]), narrative structure and language register in Sam Selvon, ghosts as signs of possibility in Wilson Harris's *The Ghost of Memory* [2006], the 'Wet Poetries' of Lorna Goodison and Olive Senior, the Caribbean built environment (urban Basseterre read against spatiality in *Beka Lamb* and *Crick Crack Monkey*), women writers (Paule Marshall, Zee Edgell, Michelle Cliff and Elizabeth Nunez-Harrell) and 'the strategy of memory'. The importance of the volume lies in its spread of content. Within anglophone literary studies, with the exception of the move into mixing literature and human geography and a few less attended-to texts, this quite readable collection offers little that hasn't been said. However, Tatiana Tagirova's linking of Russia's cultural cringe (relative to France and Germany before the revolution) to the racial cultural politics of McKay's novels seems well worth exploring in more detail and across a wider range of postcolonial writers than the Harlem Renaissance people studied already.

(b) Journal Articles

Postcolonial Text is an online quarterly coming originally from the Association for Commonwealth Language and Literature Studies. Its 2008 issues included Cynthia James's critical survey (*PcT* 4:iv[2008]) of Trinidad editor and writing teacher Anson Gonzalez's recent poetry. *Proseleela* [2007], *Chela Quest* [2005] and *Crossroads of Dream* [2003] are read via autobiographical criticism (Sandra Pouchet Paquet, Jerome Bruner and Jens Brockmeier) to show the various forms of haiku, prose poem, fable and memoir are arranged as a struggle with earthly pleasures and social crises on a path towards spiritual enlightenment. Links are made to Wordsworth, Brathwaite and Walcott, and the composing of a disciple persona is connected to Gonzalez's attachment to the ECKANKAR religious group and to Hindu elements in Trinidad's cultural mix.

PcT 4:ii[2008] has Lorna M. Burns reading Wilson Harris's *Jonestown, The Mask of the Beggar* and *The Ghost of Memory* under the heading 'Creolization and the Collective Unconscious'. Drawing partly on Derek Attridge's idea of the 'singularity' of the new as exceeding existing models, she traces aspects of creolization theory, noting its basis in colonial relocation and its spread to wide cultural meanings such as Brathwaite's, Glissant's and Harris's usage as 'potentiality for the generation of genuinely original forms' (pp. 2–4) that don't synthesize but open up to the new along a shifting relational boundary between 'culture's discourse and the unknown' (p. 6). Alchemy is Harris's metaphor for such creolization, and he employs Jungian devices (the archetype of the Homeric beggar) to signify movement (often through revisiting past violence—as in Jonestown or the London killing of a Brazilian following the 2005 bombings) towards unrealizable wholeness figured in references to art reaching beyond its own limits. Burns suggests Harris's vision connects to Spinoza.

The same issue contains a study of 'the non-native native' in V.S. Naipaul's *A Bend in the River* by Joseph Walunywa. The problematic nature of an immigrant community, itself resulting from colonial pressures but holding economic power in African societies, is resolved by the protagonist moving to a centre of global import. However, although Naipaul does present the negative view of Africa criticized by Achebe, he is not Salim, and the book also critiques neocolonialism in showing Salim's shortcomings and his disillusion on arriving in Europe, though he ends by subscribing to 'utopian globalization' (pp. 18–19). Walunywa reviews East Indian settlement in Africa, traces Salim's story, charts connections to Conrad and Virgil and surveys critical responses to the book. The novel reflects Naipaul's own ambiguous position as critic of colonialism co-opted into the machinery of First World cultural production, but the article ends by siding with Achebe.

A Bend in the River is also the subject of Imraan Coovadia's article in *PcT* 4:i. He tracks Naipaul's interest in Virgil to the misquotation of the *Aeneid* in Trinidad and Tobago's colonial past and in the African setting of the novel. This seems (against the evidence) to propose a benign mixing of peoples. Naipaul enacts a power struggle with the reader by withholding information, and making jokes, cryptic Latin allusions and provocative political comments to establish authority in a work that 'returns obsessively to the scene of authority's collapse' (p. 2). Polarized responses to Naipaul's work are partly the result of a deliberate textual strategy, as seen in the evocation of disgust (strange meals) and fear (random violence) and the reference to other written texts within the novel that implicitly contrast with an ideal of literary elegance and ironic sophistication.

Giselle A. Rampaul uses callaloo as a vehicle for reading Robert Antoni's *Divina Trace* (*PcT* 4:i[2008]). It represents the 'eclectic and unconventional' mix of forms as well as heterogenous West Indian (and in particular, Trinidadian) identity. The text, however, distorts things and refuses simple fusion, as we see in the contradictions embodied in the genealogies and various cultural affiliations of the mysterious Magdalena. The text illustrates Glissant's 'poetics of relating' and Bakhtin's heteroglossia (pp. 4–6). The book works with mirror images, but fragments and tangles language to distort reflections and break up binaries. The reader is implicated in this process, which melds human and monkey, deformity and form.

Stef Craps, 'Linking Legacies of Loss: Traumatic Histories and Cross-Cultural Empathy in Caryl Phillips's *Higher Ground* and *The Nature of Blood*' (*SNNTS* 40:i–ii[2008] 191–202), reads the two novels as setting up different stories of trauma to address each other, in keeping with Cathy Caruth's argument that despite differences of circumstance experiencing trauma can itself provide a source of connection across cultures.

Anna S. Blumenthal, 'Claire Harris's "Where the Sky is a Pitiful Tent": How Two Women Respond after Witnessing Political Torture' (*JCL* 43.ii[2008] 85–95), examines the different rhetorical strategies adopted by women to cope with trauma. Harris works with 'collage' and contrapuntal voices to convey the conflicted nature of life, and in 'Sky' draws on Rigoberta Menchu to dramatize two responses to violence, one objectifying and public in prose, the other poetic, emotional and personal (a model taken from Belenky et al., *Women's Ways of Knowing* [1986]). Neither is completely adequate since each includes refusals to see some aspects of the violence, but the ironic interweaving of speakers suggests a composite potential for recovery and strength.

'The Melancholic Structure of Memory in Dionne Brand's *At the Full and Change of the Moon*' (*JCL* 43:i[2008] 57–75), by Maureen Moynagh, depicts Brand turning away from black diaspora as the 'incorporation of loss' by refiguring Freudian 'pathological melancholy' vested in the haunting subject of slavery into a diagnosis of the pathology of 'racist disavowal' that refuses to 'accommodate the dead' in modernity itself. Moynagh uses Glissant's figure of loss as a foundational beginning for New World diasporic black society, and works with Dominick LaCapra and Cathy Caruth and others to show how specific historical events (here a mass suicide of enslaved workers on a Trinidad plantation) have a ghostly psychic life beyond their moment. Melancholy serves as 'counter-memory', keeping lost history alive, ultimately to envision a utopian politicized conversion of it into a mourning that the post-slavery literature of metropolitan modernity remains unable to realize.

This article continues a tradition of 'Middle Passage' scholarship that, as noted above, wrestles with issues of memory and rupture. Theories and practice in textual memory have taken on a particular valency in postcolonial studies generally and provide the theme for number 26 of *Small Axe*. Most of its content falls outside the anglophone writing ambit, but Patricia Saunders, 'Defending the Dead, Confronting the Archive: A Conversation with Marlene Nourbese-Philip' (*SmAx* 26 12:ii[2008] 63–79), discusses the poetry sequence *Zong!* This recounts the murder of 150 Africans thrown overboard by slavers and examines subsequent legal action in which the deaths were treated merely as damage to property despite Granville Sharp's attempt to make it a murder case. The work asks how the story of the dead can be told and seeks to explode history and discourse from the inside, from the bones, breaking up language to get to a visceral telling by not telling.

How to speak the unspeakable is also the focus of Isabel Alonso-Breto, who uses a linguistics and translation studies framework to consider embodied speech and the paradox of 'Translating English into English in a Case of

Symbolic Translation: Language and Politics through the Body in Marlene Nourbese Philip's "She Tries her Tongue, Her Silence Softly Breaks"' (in, Muñoz-Calvo, Buesa-Gómez and Ruiz-Moneva, eds., *New Trends in Translation and Cultural Identity*, pp. 21–34).

SmAx 25[2008] contains several articles on literary culture as well as the work on other media already mentioned. Curdella Forbes's 'Fracturing Subjectivities: International Space and the Discourse of Individualism in Colin Channer's *Waiting in Vain* and Jamaica Kincaid's *Mister Potter*' (*SmAx* 25 12:i[2008] 16–37) makes an interesting theoretical intervention in suggesting a particular kind of individualist writing from the Caribbean. Commonwealth literature is often read as a literature of community, even when it is diasporic, but some 'private, personal and underworld' texts affirm community by challenging it. The international movement of peoples de-links community from individuals. 'If Channer unravels diasporic community and global relationality by patching them into a projection of the individual self, Kincaid [shows] an intensely concentrated struggle between two narratives of self that destroy each other' (p. 31). The US is the uncanny subtext of both books. Shirley Toland-Dix, in 'The Hills of Hebron: Sylvia Wynter's Disruption of the Narrative of the Nation' (*SmAx* 25[2008] 57–76) performs a feminist reading of Wynter's only novel *The Hills of Hebron* [1962], appearing at Jamaica's independence from Britain, asserting that Wynter was the 'only Anglophone Afro-Caribbean woman novelist to appropriate the epic narrative of the nation' (p. 5). The novel informs Wynter's subsequent critical essays, which treat the abuse of black women as part of the broader issue of racism. Toland-Dix claims that Wynter's feminism is not overt and distrusts a movement dominated by privileged white women. Corinna McLeod, in 'Constructing a Nation: Jamaica Kincaid's *A Small Place*' (*SmAx* 25[2008] 77–92), argues that the book, like Antigua, is difficult to define. She states that the text's metafictional doubleness allows Kincaid to play 'the dual role of insider and outsider' and 'destabilizes the reader/author paradigm' (p. 80). This is tied to a 'virulent attack on tourism' (p. 87) as a colonialist construction of the island. Michael O. West, in 'Seeing Darkly: Guyana, Black Power, and Walter Rodney's Expulsion from Jamaica' (*SmAx* 25 [2008] 93–104), uses recently discovered records to shed light on the 1968 'Rodney affair'. Then a UWI lecturer, Rodney was expelled from Jamaica after attending a Black Power conference in Canada. West regards the affair as significant not only in Guyana's subsequent sympathies for Black Power but in the wider history of that movement.

Norval (Nadi) Edwards, in 'Tradition, the Critic and Cross-Cultural Poetics: Wilson Harris as Literary Theorist' (*JWIL* 16:ii[2008] 1–30), discusses Harris's move 'away from cultural nationalist investments in language as coterminous with culture, nation and identity' to the 'mythopoeic and post-historical' (pp. 1–2). Edwards charts central themes across three books of Harris's essays written between 1951 and 1982, noting their 'imagistic associations, intuitive leaps, and conceptual denseness' (p. 3) that resist social realism in favour of the carnivalesque (p. 10) and visionary. Major commentators (James, Drake, Rohlehr, Wynter, Slemon) are canvassed and differences from deconstruction noted (p. 17). Harris has reshaped Standard

English 'by compounding and subverting semantic and syntactic rules' (pp. 23–5). Edwards concludes that Romanticism and modernism combine in Harris's work but operate to undo the sovereign subject (p. 26).

Laura Selph, 'The Teacher's Quest: Performance and Pedagogy in Earl Lovelace's *Salt*' (*JWIL* 16:ii[2008] 31–61), continues the critical rediscovery of this novel, taking Eric Williams and Shalini Puri's *The Caribbean Postcolonial* [2004] as an instance of debates about national identity and the unitary Enlightenment subject to demonstrate the formal complexity of *Salt*. Clearly a national allegory in its content, Selph argues (borrowing Bhabha's pedagogical national linear temporality versus performative recursive temporality) that the novel's performance (seen via myriad allusions to popular culture) 'ruptures' the nationalist model. Within the story, Alford moves from Anglophile teacher to nationalist potential demagogue to someone more sensitive to subaltern experience (due to Bango's intervention). This refusal of nationalist linearity is not matched by the quest mode of the book, but its multiple beginnings and repetitions enact a performative 'ongoing process of overlapping scenarios' (p. 47) not unlike Gilroy's antiphonal metaphor for relational identities. A vision of nationalist multicultural creolité sits with Lovelace's 'argument . . . for reparations to descendants of slaves' (p. 58), culminating in the novel's performative call to march: an 'anticlimax, provocation, opening' (p. 59). This is a careful, clear and compelling piece of theorized close reading.

Bhoendradatt Tewarie interviews V.S. Naipaul on his visit to Trinidad and Tobago in 2007 (*JWIL* 16:ii[2008] 62–74). Naipaul contrasts his ahistorical child's view of the island with his present eye, changed by the years of writing. He stresses the importance of *Miguel Street* and his consciousness of 'ways of looking and how every way changes the configuration of the world' (p. 65). The process of writing *Biswas*, his first travel book, and the drive/struggle to keep going: to 'do the work' (p. 68), plus problems of being misunderstood by metropolitan critics before postcolonial experience became valued, are mentioned. But good critics can show a writer what he has done. Naipaul claims he does not judge small places without history but rather the history that has left them 'without a guiding idea' (p. 73), and argues for a moral point to writing.

The last article in *JWIL* 16:ii[2008] is 'A Note on Some Rhetorical Traditions in Michael Smith's Poetry' by Eric Doumerc (75–89). After a quick review of Smith's career and his reputation as a performance/ dub poet, Doumerc shows links to Jamaican deejay work (e.g. U-Roy), Rastafarian style, Louise Bennett and the 'street conversation' convention of comic/satiric dramatic monologue.

In the subsequent issue, Andrew Armstrong considers 'Writing and Reading: Intertextuality and the Anxieties of Interpretation in Mark McWatt's *Suspended Sentences*' (*JWIL* 17:i[2008] 1–19). He brings out in some detail (with nods to Wilson Harris, Harold Bloom and Paul Ricoeur) the complex narrative structuring, allusions to Guyana's landscape, wordplays, references to paintings and so on that link indigenous storytelling and postmodern techniques, 'profane and ritual . . . epistemological and teleological' (pp. 2, 4) and interrogate the operations of memory. The whole becomes 'a complex meditation on acts of representation and reading' (p. 11). There are interesting comments on the need for and difficulty of atonement symbols and *Bildung* in the Caribbean.

Lorna Burns writes on 'Landscape and Genre in the Caribbean Canon: Creolizing the Poetics of Place and Paradise' (*JWIL* 17:i[2008] 20–41). Through poetry from James Grainger to Walcott, she charts the colonialist inscription of the Caribbean as Eden in order to bring together the ecocritical idealation of nature and the region's violent history. Burns contrasts Glissant's revision of untamed nature as creolizing possibility with Benitez-Rojo's shift away from landscape to the chaotic city, positioning Marson and Césaire as forerunners to their reworking of paradisal tropes and seeing a 'rhizomatic poetics of creolization' working out of historical legacies and into current writing.

Richard W.L. Clarke follows with 'Lamming, Marx, Hegel' (*JWIL* 17:i[2008] 42–53). This focuses on George Lamming's critical output, particularly 'The Negro Writer and his World', which Clarke believes is informed by Hegel's master–slave dialectic. He discusses Lamming's view that the negro writer writes for three concentric 'worlds': himself, his community and the wider population. Lamming's Marxist underpinning means that he strives to understand the postcolonial situation in economic terms. He also argues that the church and the law 'revolve around the privileging of one skin colour and the demonisation of the other' (p. 43).

Raphael Dalleo, 'Bita Plant as Literary Intellectual: The Anticolonial Public Sphere and *Banana Bottom*' (*JWIL* 17:i[2008] 54–67), canvasses critiques of populist triumphalist readings of *Banana Bottom*, arguing book and author cannot resolve the European–Jamaican folk binary because of McKay's middle-class origins. He goes on to show that class as internally divided about the future and the book as dramatizing a tussle between literary intellectuals and technocratic professionals. Gossip operates as a pervasive demotic 'counterpublic' but is unreliable and even dangerous. The novel seeks a more reliable public sphere and posits 'the literary intellectual, sympathetic to the people' as the best guide to a future nation (p. 62).

The online journal *Anthurium* 6:ii[2008] contains several articles on Caribbean writing. Alison J. Donnell, in 'Welsh and West Indian, "like nothing . . . seen before": Unfolding Diasporic Lives in Charlotte Williams' *Sugar and Slate*' (*Anthurium* 6:ii[2008] 51 paras.) discusses the 2002 autobiography of the half-Welsh, half-Afro-Caribbean writer. The book is structured in three geographical sections—Africa, Guyana and Wales—reflecting the writer's travels. It tells of Welsh involvement in the West Indies as plantation owners, describing 'Welsh and West Indian bodies connected by suffering'. Donnell believes that Williams's memoir refuses to fit the mould of diasporic theory, black Atlantic criticism or women's autobiography. 'Maps of Memory and the Sea in Dionne Brand's *At the Full and Change of the Moon*' (*Anthurium* 6:ii[2008] 21 paras.) by Michael Laramee examines 'the interplay of water/ocean/sea with collective history and individual memory' in several texts. He asserts that Brand's writing is the product of her 'base' as 'woman, Black and lesbian', tied to her representations of areas of the Caribbean she terms 'Nowhere' and 'Door of No Return'. Melva Persico, in 'Intertextuality and "The Joker": Tirso de Molina's *The Trickster of Seville* and Derek Walcott's

The Joker of Seville' (*Anthurium* 6:ii[2008] 29 paras.), begins by posing the question of whether intertextuality is an adaptation of an earlier work or whether it reveals 'influences from one or more previously existing works within a text'. She discusses Molina's and Walcott's 1630 and 1978 versions of the Don Juan tale. Walcott, rather than mimicking the earlier play, 'imaginatively amplified structure, themes and characterization' to portray the ills of Caribbean society. Roberto Strongman's article, 'A Caribbean Response to the Question of Third World National Allegories: Jameson, Ahmad and the Return of the Repressed' (*Anthurium* 6:ii[2008] 44 paras.), foregrounds the debate surrounding Fredric Jameson's assertion that all Third World texts are national allegories. While allegory is a 'powerful anticolonial discursive mechanism', Strongman also asks whether, if the literature is indeed allegorical, this is because of First World control of the publication industry. He discusses the Caribbean literary theme of the denial of the subjectivity of the repressed and refers to the 'uneasy tension' between postcolonial and Caribbean studies arising from the fear that the former could possibly 'erase the specificity of Caribbean culture and history'. This is a carefully argued paper positing a different kind of Third World allegory with implications beyond the Caribbean.

David McInnis, in 'Re-orienting the Gothic Romance: Jean Rhys, Tayeb Salih, and Strategies of Representation in the Postcolonial Gothic' (*ArielE* 39:iii[2008] 85–106), links the Gothic tropes of the doppelgänger and xenophobia to postcolonial anxieties about loss of identity. Rhys's *Wide Sargasso Sea* is an example of postcolonial Gothic romance, showing 'the prominent Gothic fascination with liminal states, borders and the sublime' (p. 13). Antoinette exemplifies this liminality, existing as she does 'in the margins of race, and on the border of European whiteness and Caribbean indigenousness' (p. 16).

Rhys is also the subject of 'Jean Rhys's Postmodern Narrative Authority: Selina's Patois in "Let Them Call It Jazz"' (*CollL* 35:ii[2008] 20–37), by Kristin Czarnecki, who examines Rhys's 1962 depiction of a mulatta from Martinique whose move to London is marred by homelessness and mistreatment. The article sees Selina's use of patois as transforming her marginalized voice into 'one of authority' (p. 21). It cites examples of dialect writing by other twentieth-century writers such as T.S. Eliot, concluding that Rhys's use of patois foregrounds her own liminality and quest to establish a 'postmodern narrative authority' (p. 34).

Françoise Lionnet, 'Continents and Archipelagoes: From *E Pluribus Unum* to Creolized Solidarities' (*PMLA* 123:v[2008] 1503–15), employs the US motto to discuss creolization through the lens of France and the US. France's racial problems show the traditional model of democratic belonging as unsuccessful. Further, American communal society is seen by many French as divisive because its differentialist racial discourse has been associated with anti-Semitism and anti-immigrant rhetoric. According to Lionnet, Caribbean writers regard 'the one' as a globe, a 'world in which there is total ongoing creolization without exception' (p. 1508). This is reflected in the openness of the Creole language and underwritten by 'creolized solidarities and [an] archipelagic epistemology' (p. 1511).

Velma Pollard's 'The Americas in Anglophone Caribbean Women Writers: Bridges of Sound' (*ChE* 15:ii[2008] 179–88) articulates ways in which diasporic connections are established through sound in some Caribbean poetry. It considers sound (and its absence) in Olive Senior's 'Hurricane Story, 1951' and a poem by Nancy Morejon. It then shifts focus to Paule Marshall's *Praisesong for the Widow*, a poem about an African American woman who leaves her Caribbean cruise to 'join in the singing and dancing, the sounds and the movements of Africa' (p. 183). Erna Brodber's poem *Louisiana* features a taped interview. The article concludes that in these texts 'sound is the medium which facilitates the two-way flow' (p. 188) between the US South and the Caribbean.

Olive Senior's short stories are the focus of an interview with Hyacinth Simpson (*Wasafiri* 53[2008] 10–15), which begins with a transnational focus. Senior's own life finds an echo in her characters 'caught between two worlds', though she sees this as both the generic source of narrative and a specific Jamaican crisis of striving for 'personal space' in which to attain the social amenities of democratic society. She locates her own imagination firmly in her Jamaican roots and talks at length about technique: finding the right narrative voice to speak to a reader, working from an image towards a story, learning how to punctuate prose conveying oral patwa narrative and how to contextualize for non-Jamaicans without compromising authenticity.

Lewis R. Gordon, in 'Some Pitfalls in Contemporary Caribbean Consciousness: Thinking Through the Americas Today' (*CIEHL* 9[2008] 81–9), offers a personal reflection on Gordon's middle name—Ricardo—which has disappeared and reappeared throughout his life according to circumstances. Fluctuations of ethnic marking are seen in Corsica as France shored up its centre—Paris. The article argues the continuing relevance of Frantz Fanon to contemporary events such as the 'War on Terror' and problems in postcolonial Africa. Gordon concludes by asserting that in Latin America the most disadvantaged are black and first peoples.

In 'Swearing at—Not by—History: Obscenity, Picong and Irony in Derek Walcott's Poetry' (*CollL* 35:ii[2008] 104–25) Jason Lagapa regards Caliban's attitude to language as an aid to understanding Derek Walcott's poetic use of profanity. Citing examples of Walcott's 'ironic poetics' (p. 123) from 'The Schooner *Flight*' and *Omeros*, the article explores the idea that the poet uses obscenity in order to reassert the history of the Caribbean.

Another reading of *Omeros* comes from Martin McKinsey. 'Missing Sounds and Mutable Meanings: Names in Derek Walcott's *Omeros*' (*Callaloo* 31:iii[2008] 891–902) works with the power and ambiguities of colonial naming (as discussed by Pratt, Bhabha, Bentson and Ngugi) to defend Walcott against critiques that his characters remain framed by the nomenclature of slavery. Their loss of the link to Africa is akin to Saussure's empty signifier, and Achilles' descent to the underworld to meet Alofabe recognizes African roots but challenges originary authenticity. Change occurs through repetitions across time, and names modulate to allow for black Greeks delinked from imposed slave names. Another reading of the Homeric connection can be found in Joe Moffett's 'On Chapter XLV of Derek Walcott's *Omeros*' (*NConL* 38:ii[2008] 6–8). Aaron Eastley also engages with Walcott's use of Homer in

'Contemporizing *Black Athena*: Walcott's *Odyssey* and the Articulation of Classical–Postcolonial Alliances' (*Sargasso* 1[2007–8] 39–56). Eastley likens the 'dispossessed and misapprehended Odysseus' in Walcott's 1992 play with the upsetting of 'rightful ownership of cultural and intellectual capital in the modern Western world' effected by Martin Bernal's Afrocentric reworking of history in *Black Athena* [1987] (p. 39). Surveying the criticisms of the book, he notes how, irrespective of its validity, it turns Europe's self-interested justification of natural priority around and mirrors the 'writing back' of postcolonials raised on a diet of the Western classics. Eastley uses Stuart Hall and comparisons with Joyce and Soyinka to validate creative appropriations that reject essentialist notions of ownership of culture and show Walcott's engagement in the play and essays with 'black' claims to 'white' traditions.

In the previous number of *Callaloo*, Brittnay Buckner interviews Jamaica Kincaid in 'Singular Beast: A Conversation with Jamaica Kincaid' (*Callaloo* 31:ii[2008] 461–9). Kincaid eschews a 'fixed understanding' of the writing process, letting the work find its own rhythm (p. 461). Being critical is not to be angry, and Kincaid doesn't just write to 'honour her black people'. She takes 'the bastard view' in which honour comes from telling the truth. She was driven to write by being poor in New York and advises young black writers to think that there is no one else but them and that they are the exception, concluding with the mantra: the 'truth is your best friend' (p. 469).

Rosamond S. King, in 'Re/Presenting Self & Other: Trans Deliverance in Caribbean Texts' (*Callaloo* 31:ii[2008] 581–99), finds the terms 'transgender, transvestite and transsexual' problematic and just uses *trans* to refer to 'a broad identity that includes the varieties of strategies people use to choose, inhabit, or express a gender other than that which society assigns to their body' (p. 582). She analyses three novels—*Cereus Blooms at Night* (Shani Mootoo), *No Telephone to Heaven* (Michelle Cliff) and *Sirena Selena vestida de pena* (Mayra Santos-Febres), noting that in Caribbean fiction 'trans' characters are employed to re/present conventional gender, as tools to deliver conventional characters to their better selves, and as 'tortured or benevolent angels' (p. 583). In the small societies of the Caribbean, 'trans' characters are stuck with binaries that leave them marginalized (p. 598).

The last issue for 2008 begins with an introductory essay improbably but interestingly linking Walcott to global economics. Michael Collins, 'Politics as the Art of Equivalent Say: Reflections on Derek Walcott and W. Arthur Lewis, China and St Lucia' (*Callaloo* 31:iv[2008] 1000–10), sees poet and economist alike as striving to give the dots on the map 'equivalent say' to major powers like China and permit them to resist stereotypes of tropical torpor and poverty. Collins notes V.S. Naipaul's early inspiration from Walcott's work.

David Farrier, '"The Other is the Neighbour": The Limits of Dignity in Caryl Phillips's *A Distant Shore*' (*JPW* 44:i[2008] 403–14), uses Levinas and Agamben to assess 'the camp' as marking the limit of the refugee's claim to citizenship and the dignity of the migrant/asylum-seeker as vital to the fluid movements of modern society. Place and belonging in an English village are made complex by postwar global awareness and a nostalgia for cultural uniformity that is challenged by what England fought against. Characters explore how dignity as decorum 'occupies a limit and place of tension' (p. 407) in Levinas's 'proximity of the Other'. Solomon's death exemplifies Agamben's *homo sacer*: killed but not sacrificed, challenging the responsibility of neighbour Dorothy and the community he partially inhabits as an illegal immigrant. (The camp migrant's dream of England as a Foucauldian heterotopia bears comparison to Rhys's England for Antoinette.) Farrier mentions Phillips's subterfuge to enter Sangatte migrant camp to report on conditions, realizing Agamben's point that testimony confesses to what cannot be spoken of save by those who cannot speak.

In the same issue Véronique Bragard, ' "Uncouth Sounds" of Resistance: Conradian Tropes and Hybrid Epistemologies in Pauline Melville's *The Ventriloquist's Tale*' (*JPW* 44:i[2008] 415–26), notes how *Heart of Darkness* has provoked writers like Achebe, Coetzee and Wilson Harris. Melville sets up another Kurtz (Father Napier) and another voyage into the (Guyanan) interior, and her Amerindians 'become a creative response to Conrad's portrayal of the "uncouth sounds" of babbling Africans' (p. 415). Melville also reprises Evelyn Waugh's *A Handful of Dust* to provide a metacritique, injecting a Harris-like visionary ending and turning Conrad's journey upriver into one that connects with ancestors and nature. Miscegenation, incest and magic challenge colonialist boundaries, while missions, anthropologists, miners and loggers threaten indigenous life.

The following number takes us again to Walcott's *Omeros* as 'The Refiguration of the Caribbean Eden' (*JPW* 44:ii[2008] 127–37), by Maik Nwosu. Sea imagery unites Caribbean place with global history, colonial conquests with tourism, memory with memory washed away. The article reads characters (the four Homers, Seven Seas, Ma Kilman) against literary sources (Melville, Milton) and historical allusions (particularly slavery) to chart a 'bridging process' (p. 134) in part founded in nature and shamanic healing, and follows Gikandi's opinion that Walcott, even as he works against Western history, remains trapped in European modernism. He 'points to a desire for rootedness through a mythic passageway that signals both a spiritual return [and] a new consciousness' (p. 136).

Kerry-Jane Wallart's 'Einstein, Evelyn Waugh and the Wapisiana Indians: Ventriloquism and Eclipses in Pauline Melville's *The Ventriloquist's Tale*' (*CE&S* 31:i[2008] 36–47) sketches the complex plot and its inclusion of 'back story' to Waugh's Guyana visit and its function of unleashing a flood of indigenous hi/story. 'Even as the Wapisiana can ventriloquize the cries of animals...the narrator mimics the...voices of the Indians living in the hinterland' (p. 37), suggesting Bakhtinian carnival. However, the book is so polyphonic that even if the voices can be tracked back to one narrator, that figure is an unreliable trickster, mixing myth and realism, Einsteinian relativity and Darwinian evolution, science and magic as unresolved oppositions. 'Characters...are united by...bewilderment' in a 'neo-baroque' world owing much to Wilson Harris (p. 40). Pre-Babel indigenous utterance (never actually heard) becomes a performativity without meaning save in itself, and is set against T.S. Eliot's meaning-full poetry and the author's avoidance of local creole. The book echoes Benitez-Rojo's entropic vision rather than 'writing back' in some utopian national/postcolonial manner.

Patricia Donatien-Yssa finds 'Resurgence and Creative Resistance in Shani Mootoo's *Cereus Blooms at Night*' (*CE&S* 31:i [2008] 93–102). Mootoo's novel is a catharsis that connects to Caribbean literature in its 'counter-discursive style...closely linked to the notions of memory and history, and to the denunciation of colonisation' (p. 93). She also echoes Caribbean critiques of women's voicelessness but queers the previous models. Brutality, actual, historical and symbolic, permeates the book's content and style until the suffering Chandin becomes abusive too and radical creativity is required to break the cycle (figured in Mala's schizophrenia and gardening—though this too is a kind of prison until she is saved by androgynous Tyler's therapeutic reconstruction of the past). Mootoo employs an 'aesthetics of trauma' to speak out Caribbean legacies of violence.

Kathleen Gyssels, in 'Scarlet Ibises and the Poetics of Relation: Perse, Walcott and Glissant' (*CE&S* 31:i [2008] 103–16), suggests that Glissant's ideal of a Caribbean 'poetics of relation' seems refuted by lack of continued dialogue between him and Walcott and across the various languages of the region, but they have a common—critical—interest in Perse and Césaire, and all of them employ bird imagery as a mark of migratory connection. Multiple languages, like bird cries, become a productive net rather than a barrier. Gyssels offers close readings of texts from each writer and closes with a passing critique of the Nobel Prize as too anglophone-biased.

(c) Books

Annalisa Oboe and Anna Scacchi edited *Recharting the Black Atlantic: Modern Cultures, Local Communities, Global Connections*, an impressive volume on migration and identity in the Caribbean seen through history, literature and the arts. The chapter by Franca Bernabei, '"What We All Long For": Dionne Brand's Transatlantic Metamorphoses' (pp. 109–27), deftly discusses Trinidad Canadian Brand's work, beginning with the non-fictional *A Map to the Door of No Belonging*. The 'door' refers to the ports where slaves were shipped to the Americas, 'a metaphor for black uprooting' (p. 112). *What We All Long For*, a novel set in Toronto, tells of four young people (Vietnamese, Italian/Jamaican, Nova Scotian and Jamaican) who seek distance from their parents' ethnicity. Brand paints Toronto as a cosmopolitan city that enlivens the protagonists, and ultimately the novel 'significantly reconfigures the relationship between the local and the global' (p. 116). Itala Vivan's chapter, 'The Iconic Ship in the Atlantic Dialogue of Black Britain' (pp. 225–37), examines the role as signifier of the *Empire Windrush*, whose 492 Caribbean immigrants to London in 1948 marked 'the beginning of what is now called Black Britain' (p. 225). The ship becomes an icon of migration in Andrea Levy's *Small Island*. Black British culture opened up a new Englishness at the hands of architects, artists and writers. British identity now includes the struggle for freedom of articulation of young black British generations. Dorothea Fischer-Hornung's chapter, 'Transbodied/ Transcultural: Moving Spirits in Katherine Dunham's and Maya Deren's *Caribbean*' (pp. 197–211), examines representations of Haiti and the culture of voodoo in Maya Deren's *Divine Horsemen* and Katherine Dunham's *The Dances of Haiti*, viewing the dancing body as a 'syncretic signifier' (p. 197). Dunham, an African American dancer and performer and one-time student of anthropology, influenced dances in the 1955 film *Mambo*. Deren's films of voodoo dancers in Haiti circulated after her death. Elvira Pulitano's chapter, 'Re-Mapping Caribbean Land(Sea)Scapes: Aquatic Metaphors and Transatlantic Homes in Caryl Phillips's *The Atlantic Sound*' (pp. 301–18), explains that Phillips, a native of St Kitts who migrated to England aged 4 months, has redefined his 'home' as a point in the Atlantic, between England, Africa and North America. The 'sound' of Phillips's title encompasses both the voices in the cities linked to the slave trade—Elmina, Charleston and Liverpool—and those silenced on the journey. The book's ending suggests that 'there is no ultimate promised land' for 'Africans in the diaspora' (p. 316). Paul Giles, in 'Narratives of Traversal: Jamaica Kincaid and the Erasure of the Postcolonial Subject' (pp. 365–77), discusses how postcolonialism and Kincaid's poetics have come to be characterized by 'narratives of traversal, a two-way process involving reciprocal interactions between different territories' (p. 365). Contradictions in postcolonial theory are due to its failure 'to deal convincingly with U.S. culture' (p. 366), and postcolonialism needs to take into account 'the issue of a common heritage, a common planet' (p. 375).

Thomas Glave's anthology, *Our Caribbean: A Gathering of Lesbian and Gay Writing from the Antilles*, makes a more specific regional intervention that connects to such global concerns. He collects fiction, non-fiction, poetry and memoir by gay, lesbian, bisexual and transgender authors from between 1956 and 2005, some of which is in translation. Apart from worrying over what languages to use and how best to denote the groups represented, Glave makes an important addition to the growing number of studies of non-hetero Caribbean life by proving that its literature 'actually existed and could exist' (p. 1).

Wider aspects of translation are canvassed in *Cultures of Translation*, edited by Klaus Stierstorfer and Monika Gomille. Gomille's 'Translating the Caribbean: Issues of Literary and Postcolonial Translation' (pp. 3–18) argues that V.S. Naipaul's *The Enigma of Arrival* [1987] connects its English setting to the Caribbean via his translation of the image of the ruined estate. In the novel, de Chirico's painting of a ship and a Mediterranean port, from which the title is derived, represents the journey from the Old to the New World and is a metaphor of 'cultural translation' (p. 7). The narrator's walking 'translates' his identity by way of mapping the land and inhabiting its story (p. 12).

Rita Felski also works a broad topic in *Rethinking Tragedy*. In this collection, David Scott, 'Tragedy's Time: Postemancipation Futures Past and Present' (pp. 199–217), suggests that in a present devoid of emancipationist prospects 'the anticolonial mode of narrativizing the past in the present as Romance' is no longer valid (p. 203). In his 1963 edition of *The Black Jacobins* [1938], C.L.R. James added six paragraphs at the beginning of chapter 13. Scott proposes two contributing factors to James's revision: the collapse of revolutionary hopes after the Second World War and the disintegration 'of James's hopes for a meaningful decolonisation of the Anglo-Creole Caribbean' (p. 209). Scott reads the novel's protagonist, the revolutionary Toussaint L'Ouverture, as Hamlet rather than Caliban, the six additional paragraphs in the novel revealing that 'postemancipation futures may not follow straightforwardly... upon the pasts of slavery' (p. 214).

Aaron C. Eastley parallels Martin McKinsey's article in 'Lifting "The Yoke of the Wrong Name": How Walcott Uses Character Names to Negotiate a Positive Afro-Caribbean Diasporic Identity in *Omeros*' (in Cancel and Woodhull, eds., *African Diasporas: Ancestor, Migrations and Borders*, pp. 70–9). *Omeros* addresses 'issues of identification and healing within the context of the Caribbean and its history of African slavery' (p. 71). Eastley argues that the Greek-named characters Achille and Philocrete show that assimilation can result in alienation from the African past, but that Walcott's play on the slaves' names reveals an 'Afro-Caribbean syncretic identity which appropriates and re-articulates' both African and European elements (p. 78).

Russell West-Pavlov, in 'David Dabydeen, *The Intended* (1991)' (in Peters et al., eds., pp. 123–38), assesses the novel's potential as a pedagogical tool. A biographical sketch of the Guyanese-born Dabydeen puts him in the 'second wave' of black British writers seeking cultural pluralism. The 'ambiguities and polyvalences of a literary artefact' (p. 124) make *The Intended* valuable in prompting students' discussions of their own situations within the framework of an 'emancipatory educational politics' (p. 135). West-Pavlov explores the novel's engagement with *Heart of Darkness*, its use of colour dualism, and its movement from 'the crippling space of the colonizer/colonized... to the empowering space of the ex-colony/metropolis' (p. 133). The analysis concludes with a select bibliography.

Dunja M. Mohr's *Embracing the Other: Addressing Xenophobia in the New Literatures in English* includes Russell West-Pavlov's '"Daft Questions": Xenophobia, Teaching, and Social Semiosis in Caribbean-British Fiction. Using Intertextuality and Narratology to Analyze a Text by David Dabydeen' (pp. 49–60). This repeats material from the article reviewed above. Lawrence Volkmann's chapter, entitled 'The Quest for Identity in Benjamin Zephaniah's Poetry' (pp. 245–63), asks whether poetry performed by West Indians in Britain, generally spoken in creole, can be considered as belonging to the Caribbean literary canon. Citing Homi Bhabha and bell hooks, Volkmann asks how this literature is read by white European readers. The chapter incorporates illustrations of Zephaniah himself, his book covers and emblem, discussing his preference for making his poetry accessible via the internet and performance. 'Speak' and 'Neighbours' show how Zephaniah's poetry pits a white perspective against a black one so the reader occupies an active role, with the poet 'as a partner, if not guide, in this quest for identities' (pp. 258–60). Sissy Helff's 'Desired Exotica: Gendered Spaces in Queer West Indian Diasporic Fiction' (pp. 279–92) begins with Foucault's concept of heterotopia and the connection between real and imagined spaces. It then discusses orientalist myth-making, with mention of Edward Said and Terry Goldie. Helff argues that West Indian queer literature 'concentrates on the representation of the domestic sphere and its public/private dichotomy' (pp. 283–4). *Cereus Blooms at Night* [1990] by Shani Mootoo perceives the ancestral house as patriarchal, the garden as matriarchate and the Alms house as a site for overcoming xenophobia and homophobia.

Jahlani Bongo-Niaah, 'Grafting a New History: Rastafari Memory Gems Articulating a "Hermeneutics of Babylon"' (in Opoku-Agyemang, Lovejoy, and Trotman, eds., *Africa and Trans-Atlantic Memories: Literary Manifestations of Diaspora and History*, pp. 343–69) describes the Rastafarian movement, in particular its musicians (here, Mortimer Planno, Bob Marley and four Dance Hall musicians), as articulating 'a knowledge and system of action towards developing the consciousness of a redeemed/liberated African' (p. 343).

Margaret Heady's *Marvelous Journeys: Routes of Identity in the Caribbean Novel* parallels the development of the Caribbean novel of identity from modernist to postmodernist consciousness with a progression from marvellous realism to magic realism. It works primarily with francophone writing and Alejo Carpentier, but will be useful for studies of English texts that use the marvellous to explore being in, yet not of, an expanded West.

Washed by the Gulf Stream: The Historical and Geographical Relation of Irish and Caribbean Literature also makes use of Carpentier in a project that compares postcolonial regions to avoid 'centre-margin' constructs. Despite its title, the book is a comparison of literary texts centred on the figure of James Joyce. Author Maria McGarrity is part of the editorial team for the journal *Anthurium* and has also worked for the *James Joyce Literary Supplement*, so is well placed to bring Ireland and the Caribbean into productive juxtaposition. She does this elegantly on a basis of island studies (Diana Loxley, Rod Edmond and Vanessa Smith, Felipe Fernández-Armesto), trauma theory (Cathy Caruth), and archetypal symbols (Elias Canetti is quoted) as well as diaspora theory (all the 'usual suspects', especially Glissant). Careful to acknowledge the specific differences of each postcolonial site and the dangers of 'big picture' comparative work (the Gulf Stream here is a multi-stranded, multi-directional set of connections, not a singular tie, p. 113), McGarrity usefully resituates Jean Rhys and Alejo Carpentier alongside the Irish tradition of Great House novels (also haunted by fire and decay), links Walcott and Joyce via attention to the several key 'washing' scenes in narratives of errantry that destabilize fixed origins and identities, and distinguishes between Frank McCourt and Jamaica Kincaid on the one hand, and George Lamming and Joyce on the other in their 'exile' from the 'diseased body' of the mother island, escape overseas or creative separation enabling recovery. E.A. Markham's poetry also receives attention. Once or twice there is a sense of the brush being a bit too broad or too quickly applied, but the book is a pleasure to read and full of fresh details.

Race, American Literature and Transnational Modernisms by Anita Patterson employs a transnational approach to link American modernism and black postcolonial writing. Patterson observes many similarities between St-John Perse and T.S. Eliot, and connects them to Whitman as poets of landscape. In chapter 3, analysis shifts to Langston Hughes, tracing his literary journey through Paris and the West Indies, and his life-long friendship with Haitian writer Jacques Roumain, both of whom admired Baudelaire and Laforgue. Chapter 4 asserts that 'the dense intertextual and historical relations between Harris and Eliot are hard to miss' (p. 130) and analyses Wilson Harris's *Eternity to Season*, in particular its evocation of Amerindian civilizations and the frontier. Chapter 5 shows Derek Walcott claiming the legacy of Perse, Poe, Eliot, Pound and others. The book concludes that Caribbean poetry 'needs to be understood within the larger contexts of transamerican modernism and the multilingual, diasporic, New World contexts of imperialism' (p. 184).

Cristina Bacchilega, in 'Extrapolating from Nalo Hopkinson's *Skin Folk*: Reflections on Transformation and Recent English-Language Fairy-Tale Fiction by Women' (in Benson, ed., *Contemporary Fiction and the Fairy Tale*, pp. 178–203), argues that Hopkinson's stories work towards the 'creolization of the fairy tale on a number of levels, from the cultural to the linguistic and the sociohistorical' (p. 188). One way in which they do so is through their sense of orality. All fifteen stories focus on women and depict 'the inner transformation of an individual' (p. 183). The text is web-like, with each story linked in a story cycle. Hopkinson writes 'from a context of blackness and Caribbeanness' to produce 'postmodern, feminist and postcolonial phantasmagoria' (pp. 196–7), similar to the work of Angela Carter and others.

Kathleen Gyssels and Bénédicte Ledent, eds., *The Caribbean Writer as Warrior of the Imaginary* / *L'Ecrivain caribéen, guerrier de l'Imaginaire*, gathers together work in both French and English. In the section 'Creative Writers/ Auteurs' Wilson Harris, 'The Mystery of Timelessness' (pp. 25–30) advocates a change to the form of the novel to escape stylistic restrictions imposed by European standards on writers from other cultures. He quotes examples (including his own *Four Banks of the River of Space*) countering this problem with 'a sense of curious timelessness' (p. 26), and calls for a 'profound cross-culturality' (p. 27). Caryl Phillips, in 'Give Me Your Tired, Your Huddled Masses' (pp. 31–47), reflects on his thirteen-year residence in New York. He appreciates its cultural diversity but feels that September 11 has restricted its range of vision. The remainder of the book is entitled 'Critical Perspectives/Perspectives critiques'. Wendy Knepper, 'The *Émerveillé*: Initiating the Warrior of the Imaginary' (pp. 51–72), examines the post-1995 writing of Patrick Chamoiseau. 'Is the Caribbean Becoming a Crispy Chicken?', by Michiel Van Kempen (pp. 169–77), begins with extracts from interviews with Patrick Chamoiseau and Dutch Poet Laureate Gerrit Komrij, and questions whether 'Caribbeanness' is disappearing under global capitalism, but shows an increased use of creole in literature. Hena Maes-Jelinek, 'Wilson Harris's Multi-Faceted and Dynamic Perception of the Imaginary' (pp. 179–88), shows how many of Harris's essays are about the imagination and concludes that, rather than espousing 'art for art's sake', Harris's fiction 'compares the power of imagination and art... to stimulate social change' (p. 187). Patricia Murray summarizes the themes of Harris's essays and fiction as landscape, Amerindian concepts of identity, and the 'tracing of under-explored indigenous routes in the Caribbean/Americas' (p. 194). In 'A Caribbean and Universal Self: Wilson Harris as "Warrior of the Imaginary"' (pp. 189–202), she focuses on myth and archetype in *The Dark Jester*, which recounts the conquest of Peru, re-enacting history in order to heal through 'guerrilla' acts of the imagination (pp. 189–201). Abdennebi Ben Beya, 'A

Caribbean Contribution to a Global Ethic: Relation and Singular Pluralities' (pp. 235–48), looks at the work of Frantz Fanon and Édouard Glissant, arguing that Caribbean thinkers challenge oppression through an ethic of cultural diversity. Kathie Birat, in '"Neither 'written' nor 'spoken'": The Ambiguities of Voice in the Fiction of Caryl Phillips' (pp. 287–306), explores the interplay between writing and voice, describing his definition of voice as 'individual utterance and collective story' (p. 295). Phillips's short stories gain meaning when read as a single narrative. Characters' voices contrast with the written narrative in which they are embedded, reflecting the problems of reconstructing a history of slavery. In 'Caribbean Autobiographies as Weapons in Identity Construction: Jamaica Kincaid's *Annie John*' (pp. 307–19) Manuela Coppola discusses Kincaid's 'non-conventional autobiography skilfully playing with fact and fiction' (p. 308) via parody and metafictional techniques. Comparison with *Lucy* [1990] shows that in *Annie John* too, the protagonist identifies with Lucifer. Mother-figures, despite symbolizing death and deceit, nevertheless stimulate the daughters' creativity. Doris Hambuch, 'Caribbean Warriors in Canada: Dionne Brand as a Representative' (pp. 321–32), fixes on Verlia's joining the Black Power movement in Brand's first novel, *In Another Place, Not Here*, to argue a militancy consistent with Brand's essays and coinciding with the increase in hostility in Toronto towards multiculturalism at the time. Rhona Hammond's chapter, 'Towards What? Walcott and the Dynamics of Change' (pp. 333–43), begins with a quotation from *Omeros* about the hero's powerlessness in the face of change. In the poet's output between 1979 and 1997 Hammond finds comparisons with the work of Chamoiseau and Naipaul. Walcott responds to change in his own way, through 'humanism, creation, and imagination' (p. 326). '"You t'ink hero can dead—til de las' reel?"': Perry Henzell's *The Harder They Come* and Sergio Corbucci's *Django*' (pp. 397–409), by Maria Cristina Fumagalli, looks at connections between Henzell's 1972 film and Thelwell's 1980 novel based on it, and the 'spaghetti western' *Django* [1966]. The western turns Henzell's protagonist, Ivan, into a 'warrior of the imagination' (p. 398), and the film's message is that the system can be beaten. '"Fighting Injustice and Insubordination": Mutabaruka's Return to the Motherland' (pp. 411–36) is a discussion by Mutabaruka and Werner Zips of the film of Mutabaruka's performance at the third Panafest in Ghana in 1997. In 'Waging the War from the Outside: The Writers of the West Indian Diaspora and their Role in the Future of the Caribbean' (pp. 453–65), Bénédicte Ledent reflects on the role and responsibility of Caribbean writers, beginning with Chamoiseau's use of poetics against oppression. She notes the difficulty in defining the Caribbean writer these days, and argues that writers of the anglophone Caribbean diaspora can all be considered 'Warriors of the Imaginary' through their 'retrieval of silenced history and a critical appraisal of contemporary Caribbean life' (p. 462).

Bodies and Voices, edited by Merete Borch, Eva Rask Knudsen, Martin Leer and Bruce Clunies-Ross, also reviewed in section 1(d) above, contains three papers that deal with the Caribbean. 'Postcolonial Education and Afro-Trinidadian Social Exclusion', by Derren Joseph (pp. 285–307), provides a historical overview of the education system in Trinidad and Tobago, and presents a case study of a 1970 educational initiative, SERVOL (Service Volunteers for All). This provided a means for young people unsuited to formal education to 'develop their skills through community service, followed by vocational training and formal certification' (p. 304). Giselle Rampaul, in 'Voice as Carnivalesque Strategy in West Indian Literature: Sam Selvon's *The Lonely Londoners* and *Moses Ascending*' (pp. 309–19), maintains that Carnival subverts dominant discourse and gives voice to the common man, and applies Merle Hodge's term 'calypso narrative' to the novels' use of humour in their attacks on authority. Rampaul discusses the oral nature of Selvon's writing, its juxtaposition of British Standard English and creole, and its use of profanity and sexual language. 'The Representation of Oppressed (Corpo)Realities: Cripples, Dwarfs and Blind Men in the Plays of Edgar Nkosi White' (pp. 321–30) examines the work of the Monserrat-born playwright. Author Nuria Casado Gual takes his major theme to be 'the effects of white-on-black oppression' (p. 321) and shows how White's characters are crippled not only physically but also by racism. The article concludes that, ironically, the crippled characters represent 'wholeness through their own imperfection' (p. 329).

As European nations once insulated from global movements of people suddenly find themselves multicultural, so postcolonial theory takes on a new relevance. Finland funded four research projects on 'ethical inquiry and postcolonial thought', and again diaspora is the idea that binds them. Huttunen et al., eds., *Seeking the Self—Encountering the Other*, is informed by Levinas and Deleuze and contains sections on 'The Ethics of Encounter', 'Strategies for Representing the Self and the Nation', 'Bodies as Borders' and 'Rewriting the Home in Diaspora'. Within this wide-ranging compilation, Caribbean entries continue the interest in gender and sexualities found in other work in this chapter. Julie E. Moody-Freeman, '"Un/Silencing" African Diasporic Women's Voices: Contesting Power and Silence in Paule Marshall's *Daughters*' (pp. 52–71) makes heavy work of delineating the nexus between rape in the narrative and colonial history, a commonplace in many works and their analyses. The piece reflects the whole collection's failing, which is to bury texts under a thick layer of critical reference, so that it seems the project is not to understand Caribbean writing and culture, but rather to subordinate them to the theoretical interests of the scholars writing. Elina Valovirta, for example, adopts Eve Kosofsky Sedgwick's ideas on 'reparative reading' to examine not so much how novels avoid the tendency in queer studies to emphasize negative oppression, as to see how the universal theorized reader might use them 'to conceptualize the ethical dimension of the text–reader relationship' (p. 184). '"Caribbean Passion" as a Reparative Practice: The Hyper-Sexual and the Asexual Woman in the Fiction of Opal Palmer Adisa and Erna Brodber' (pp. 182–97) does make some interesting observations on 'a politics of sensuality both physical and spiritual' (p. 184) in books presenting two quite different modes of sexuality (though the types identified are by no means new in Caribbean fiction or its scholarship, and the tropics as a place of passion of any kind is not exactly a liberatory postcolonial motif).

Sometimes one feels the tendency in postcolonial studies to treat the area of focus as a pathology in need of a cure (often by scholars from the First World).

The Caribbean seems particularly prone to this academic temptation because of the trauma of slaving history, and one wonders how productive salvation by literary scholarship can be and whether the contemporary Caribbean might require new modes of analysis (see Maureen Moynagh on Dionne Brand above). Kaisa Ilmonen turns to a new area of focus but reproduces the old discourse in 'Healing the Traumas of History: (Trans)Sexual Diasporas in Caribbean Literature' (pp. 229–46). As in Rosamond King's 'trans' article, she finds that queer characters in Mootoo, Scott and Cliff occupy roles of 'healer, helper and mediator' (p. 229) but fails to see that narratives of 'good' minority figures helping central characters to discover their selfhood are the stuff of colonial romance and do not necessarily work 'to heal the traumas of history caused by Eurocentric binary thinking' (p. 230). There's a too easy slippage from gender-bending to destabilizing black–white race relations, and a transsexual male who teams up with a transsexual female surely confirms heteronormativity? The ideas of a 'sexual diaspora' and new conceptions of home, though, are interesting contributions. Under the rubric of 'rewriting the home', Maria Mårdberg and Helena Wahlström consider 'Parenthood in the African Diaspora: Caryl Phillips' *Crossing the River*' (pp. 291–310). They show how the novel, while it emphasizes the ruptures of slave and diasporic history, explores possibilities of 'family' connections beyond the biological. Within the frame of masculinity studies, the chapter notes that African men have experienced fatherhood under very different circumstances' to whites (p. 292) and so Phillips recasts Africa as fatherland rather than sustaining or mourning mother. Mothers, on the other hand, struggle to keep home as a site of resistance against anomie and racism. Phillips's interest in survival ultimately offers only brief comfort, and his masculinist revision erases the idea of an African motherland to leave only loss. Joel Kuortti, 'Over the Black Water: Silenced Narratives of Diaspora in Ramabai Espinet's *The Swinging Bridge*' (pp. 311–32), is more text-centred than other chapters, using the story of Indian indentured diaspora to Trinidad (here women's stories) as another example of trying to fill the gaps and breaks of history. Disrupting the master-narrative is also effected in this novel, too, by inserting non-hetero-sexual figures, though neither women nor homosexuals seem to prosper. The novel itself, however, is a productive intervention in structures of power.

India is replete with anthologies of critical essays on postcolonial topics and Jasbir Jain and Supriya Agarwal have added to them, editing *Writers of the Caribbean Diaspora: Shifting Homelands, Travelling Identities* (Sterling). This book did not arrive in time for review and will be dealt with next in the next volume.

Another volume that remains unsighted is Mamadou Kandji's edited collection, *Women's Studies, Diasporas and Cultural Diversity* (Presses Universitaires de Dakar). It contains an essay by Adama Coly on 'The West Indian Woman as Scapegoat in Jean Rhys's *Wide Sargssso Sea* (1966) and Sonny Ladoo's *No Pain Like This Body* (1972)' (pp. 145–62). Another is *Displacements and Transformations in Caribbean Cultures* edited by Lizabeth Paravisini-Gebert and Ivette Romero-Cesareo (University Press of Florida) which contains two relevant pieces: Kevin Meehan's. '"To shake this nation as nothing before has shaken it": C.L.R. James, Radical Fieldwork, and

American Popular Culture' (pp. 77–99) and 'Moving Metaphors: The Representations of AIDS in Caribbean Literature and Visual Arts' by Ivette Romero-Cesareo (pp. 100–26).

Literary studies per se cannot attain full cogency without some 'para--literary' scholarship. 'History of the book' research has been making valuable contributions in recent years and Robert Fraser contributes to this with 'School Readers in the Empire and the Creation of Postcolonial Taste' (in Fraser and Hammond, eds., *Books Without Borders*, volume 1: *The Cross-National Dimension in Print Culture*, pp. 89–106). He discusses the impact of Nelson's *West Indian Readers* on a generation of West Indian writers—seen, for example, in V.S. Naipaul's *The Enigma of Arrival*. Fraser gives a brief history of the use of these readers in the Caribbean and describes their contents and adaptations to the local contexts. Influences on other writers are tracked and he concludes that the Nelsons 'planted seeds in the fertile soil of a vibrant culture, thereby helping in the long run to yield up a literature' (p. 104).

Also important to literary analysis are studies of language amongst Caribbean peoples. Peter Patrick in 'British Creole: Phonology' (in Kortmann, Upton and Schneider, eds., *Varieties of English 1: The British Isles*, pp. 253–68) analyses Creole as spoken by those born in Britain of Caribbean descent. Creole is spoken across ethnic groups, predominantly by the working class. Patrick refers to previous research on consonants, prosody and intonation, and uses a sample word list as spoken by a subject, in order to analyse vowel sounds.

Pronunciation samples are provided on CD-ROM in Edgar Schneider's edited collection, *Varieties of English 2: The Americas and the Caribbean*. The book is divided into two parts, the first of which covers phonological variation, and the second morphology and syntax. The sections dealing with the Caribbean are divided into the following geographical locations: the Bahamas, Jamaica, smaller islands, Barbados, Trinidad and Tobago, and Suriname. At the end of the first section is a useful synopsis by Schneider, which 'attempts to survey and systematize the phonetic and phonological variability' in the region (p. 383). Consistency across the contributions is based on responses to a given list of features reliant on Wells's system of lexical sets. Chapters provide exercises and study questions for use in conjunction with the CD-ROM, as well as a reference list, and there is an extensive bibliography.

Opening mention of work consolidating the literary archive by delving into early writings, and of the diasporic connections that increasingly confound taxonomical attempts to define writers and their work by nation or region, lead us to two more books. Tim Watson's *Caribbean Culture and British Fiction in the Atlantic World, 1780–1870*. Watson investigates Jamaica's 'creole realism' by focusing on the letters of Simon Taylor, a wealthy Creole. He compares them with Maria Edgeworth's 1810 novel *Belinda*, this showing 'its principals' "humanity"' towards 'the animate and inanimate objects under their protection', while Taylor's letters complain that 'the idea of humanity was being used against the planters like a weapon' (p. 42). Chapter 2 looks at two texts by Charles White Williams: an 1826 travelogue and the novel *Hamel* [1827], pro-slavery texts which reveal 'the hidden worlds of the enslaved

Jamaicans themselves' (p. 12). Then Watson analyses the career of minister, activist and writer Samuel Ringgold Ward, who became involved in the Morant Bay rebellion of 1865. Chapter 4 focuses on the impact of the rebellion in Britain, through a discussion of George Eliot's novel *Felix Holt* [1865]. The author concludes that the ordinary people of the Caribbean were placed at the centre of history, first through romance and later via realism.

Before Windrush: Recovering an Asian and Black Literary Heritage Within Britain, edited by Pallavi Rastogi and Jocelyn Fenton Stitt, works the same revisionary project. Four chapters focus on the Caribbean. In chapter 1, 'Gender in the Contact Zone: West Indian Creoles, Marriage, and Money in British Women's Writing, 1786–1848' (pp. 15–48), Jocelyn Fenton Stitt demonstrates how Romantic-era British women writers employed the West Indies in their critiques of imperialism and slavery and 'recognized the dangers when the values of the colonial world' and West Indian creoles 'were brought into the British domestic space' (p. 16). Charlotte Brontë's *Jane Eyre*, Lucy Peacock's 'The Creole' [1786], Mary Hays's *Emma Courtney* [1796], Maria Edgeworth's *Belinda* [1801], Amelia Opie's *Adeline Mowbray* [1805] and Helena Wells's *Constantia Neville* [1800] are the texts discussed. In chapter 2, 'Maiden Voyage: Slavery, Domesticity, and Trans-Atlantic Resistance in *The History of Mary Prince*' (pp. 49–71), Michelle Taylor argues for Prince's text to be positioned within trans-Atlantic literary history and culture. Prince exercises 'insurgent domesticity' to gain control over her story and life within the economy of slavery. 'A Virtuous Nurse and a Pícara: Mary Seacole's Self-Characterization in *Wonderful Adventures of Mrs. Seacole in Many Lands*' (pp. 72–87), begins by presenting the accepted image of Seacole as a heroic Creole nurse in the Crimean War. Stoyan Tchaprazov points out, however, that Seacole presented herself in a less flattering light, and he examines her writing as picaresque. In chapter 8, 'C.L.R. James: Knowing England Better than the English' (pp. 198–222), W.F. Santiago-Valles connects research on revolutions for writing *The Black Jacobins* [1938] to James's involvement in radical British politics and his membership of the African Bureau, a group formed by exiled Caribbean and African intellectuals in London in the 1930s.

(d) Single-Author Studies

Tracey Walters has edited *Zadie Smith: Critical Essays*, which champions a two-way relationship between British and Caribbean literature: on the one hand, the British ancestry of many Caribbean writers has long been emphasized; on the other, while novels such as Zadie Smith's *White Teeth* are classified as British, they have a decidedly Caribbean flavour. Chapter 5, by Raphael Dalleo, 'Colonization in Reverse: *White Teeth* as Caribbean Novel' (pp. 91–104), argues that Smith's novel may also be considered as Caribbean because of its characters (their language and clothing), settings and tropes. He highlights Smith's irony and humour and maintains that she shows us a 'London that is British and Caribbean and South Asian and American all at the same time' (p. 93). In chapter 6, '"Gimme Shelter": Zadie Smith's *On Beauty*' (pp. 107–21), Susan Alice Fischer connects Smith's text to Zora Neale

Hurston's *Their Eyes Were Watching God* and her study of voodoo *Tell My Horse*. Fischer explores Smith's association of the goddess Erzulie with the character of Victoria, stating that it 'adds a much-needed dimension to understanding Victoria's sexuality and its transformative power in the novel' (p. 115). In chapter 8, 'From the Dispossessed to the Colonized: From Samuel Selvon's *The Lonely Londoners* to Zadie Smith's "Hanwell in Hell"' (pp. 141–55), Sharon Raynor claims that, while the alienation of Smith's characters arises from their marginal isolation, Selvon's West Indian immigrants are busy trying to find a home in London.

Laurence Breiner has produced a detailed study of someone eulogized at his death as a playwright but whose influence was primarily from a lifetime of writing poetry. *Black Yeats: Eric Roach and the Politics of Caribbean Poetry* concentrates on Roach's problematic construction of himself as poet via close readings arranged into the major periods of his production (1930s, 1950s and his late and brief recovery in the 1970s) and set against the cultural and political movements of these times. Breiner describes his role as 'curatorial' (p. 10) and he has done sterling work in bringing together and making sense of poems scattered between Trinidad and London, newspapers and BBC tapes, and the early literary magazines that generated the Caribbean literary tradition. Roach worked (like Yeats) with idealized images of rural peasantry converted into symbols for regional consciousness and a 'grammar of metaphors' (p. 98). This left him ambiguously positioned (*from* the farmers of Tobago but not *of* them, celebrating their survival but aware of their brute realities), and his emphasis on poetic craft teetered between its evanescence and transcendence, Miltonic inflation and local observation, just as his characters oscillated between rooted ancestors and escapist adventurers. Ultimately, poetic vision and poet alike were defeated by the failure of federation, urbanization and the new politicized performance verse from Jamaica. Close reading of poems that the critic admits are unsuccessful can become wearisome, but Breiner shows the development and gives a sense of the overall importance of Roach's project, and he writes clearly with his own entertaining turns of phrase. The book has a good index and useful bibliography. It is an important addition to the scholarly picture of Caribbean poetry.

Frank Rosengarten's *Urbane Revolutionary: C.L.R. James and the Struggle for a New Society* is a wide-ranging and thoroughly researched volume. Rosengarten explains that he was motivated to write the book for several reasons: the failure of Soviet socialism; the problems faced by revolutionary movements in Africa, Asia and Latin America; and his own interest in thinkers such as James who questioned the ability of Marxism to solve problems of human experience. He employs biographical details and unpublished material such as letters. The volume is divided into two parts. Part I, entitled 'Marxism and Johnsonism', relates to the pseudonym used by James in the early 1940s. Chapter 1 traces James's early life in Trinidad and his arrival in England in 1932, where racism moved him towards Marxism, the method used to analyse the Haitian Revolution in *The Black Jacobins* [1938]. Chapter 2 discusses the British Trotskyist groups to which James belonged and charts his incorporation of Hegelian thought into his writings. Chapter 3 describes

James's 1934–6 membership of the Independent Labour Party (ILP). It also reveals that, in the 1950s, James broke with Leninism and shows how this is evident in his writing. Chapter 4 is an in-depth examination of the Johnson–Forest Tendency (JFT) group (1941–7), its title formed from the aliases of James and Raya Dunayevskaya, It also discusses Constance Webb and Selma Deitch, who became James's second and third wives. Chapter 5 tells how James's theoretical support of gender equality was not always evident in his treatment of the women in his own life. However, in the later part of his life he was changed by the women's liberation movement. Chapter 6 shows James responding enthusiastically to the anti-Stalinist upheavals in Europe. It also describes his admiration for Castro. In part II, entitled 'National-Popular Politics', James's trip to Ghana in 1957 is assessed. His life from 1958 to 1966 falls into three distinct phases: from Trinidad in 1958 to the London move in 1962; his stay in London until 1965; life back in Trinidad till the end of 1966, during which he founded the Workers and Farmers Party, and edited *We the People*. Chapter 8 analyses *A History of Pan-African Revolt* [1938]. Part III looks at James's fictional and literary-critical output from the late 1920s to the 1960s. This expresses the same revolutionary thought as his other writings but shows James's 'flair for reproducing the vernacular English spoken by his mainly proletarian and plebian characters' (p. 157). In chapter 10 Rosengarten sets out two of James's principles: the creative autonomy of art and literature over officialdom, and the close relationship between literature and society. It traces debts to Gramsci and Benjamin and analyses James's treatment of European Romanticism and ancient Greek civilization. Chapter 11 focuses on James's criticism on Herman Melville. James's believed that great works like *Moby-Dick* 'are great precisely and only because they take their inspiration from the literary history of a national culture' (p. 205). Chapter 12 discusses James's belief in art for the masses and his writing on popular culture. Chapters 13 and 14 expand on Rosengarten's belief that, in *The Black Jacobins* and *Beyond a Boundary*, James found a language and expression that satisfied 'both a literarily sophisticated and a broad popular audience' (p. 219).

The other 'grand old man' of Caribbean writing, Wilson Harris, is given book-length treatment in Raja Sekhar Patteti's *The Fiction of Wilson Harris: A Study in West Indian Discourse* (Prestige). Sarah Lawson Welsh has also written a monograph on Grace Nicholls as part of the British Council series. These books did not arrive in time for comment and will, we hope, be covered in the next volume.

(d) Dissertations

Although there will have been many theses on Caribbean writing completed in other countries, these are the ones listed in *Dissertation Abstracts International*, this descriptor still meaning predominantly work from the USA.

Gretchen Elizabeth Kellough, *Tisseroman: The Weaving of Female Selfhood within Feminine Communities in Postcolonial Novels*, a Ph.D. thesis at Northwestern University, examines feminine community in Buchi Emecheta, Maryse Condé, Myriam Warner-Vieyra, Calixthe Beyala and Edwidge

Danticat. The term *tisseroman* is employed to describe the novels' many voices.

Jill Toliver Richardson's *Narratives of Displacement: The Evolution of the Caribbean-American Transnational Narrative*, a Ph.D. thesis at the City University of New York, compares three generations of American writers originally from the Spanish-, French-, and English-speaking Caribbean, analysing their depictions of the transnation and transnational identity. Paule Marshall's *Brown Girl, Brownstones* and Piri Thomas's *Down These Mean Streets* represent the 1930s to 1950s. Jamaica Kincaid's *Lucy* and Julia Alvarez's *How the García Girls Lost their Accents* are set during the 1960s to 1980s. Edwidge Danticat's *Breath, Eyes, Memory*, Junot Díaz's *Drown*, Loida Maritza Pérez's *Geographies of Home*, Abraham Rodriguez's *Spidertown* and Angie Cruz's *Soledad* represent the 1980s to the present. Postcolonial, diaspora, and globalization theory are used to examine the various ways in which these writers imagine home.

Barbara L. Shaw's *(Re)mapping the Black Atlantic: Violence, Affect, and Subjectivity in Contemporary Caribbean Women's Migration Literature*, a Ph.D. thesis at the University of Maryland, College Park [2007], examines migrant protagonists and the books as cultural products which migrate between economies. The study urges that the Caribbean be considered part of the Americas, but also that American studies come to embrace the complex relationships between the Caribbean, the United States and Britain.

Juan Carlos Canals, *Warriors of the Imaginary in the Contemporary Caribbean (1946–2002): George Lamming (Barbados), Ana Lydia Vega (Puerto Rico), and Patrick Chamoiseau (Martinique)*, a Ph.D. thesis at the University of Puerto Rico [2007], uses Chamoiseau's term 'warrior of the imaginary' to examine struggles in the Antilles during the second half of the twentieth century as the confrontation between militant Antillean literature and (neo)colonial forms of domination.

Veronica J. Austen, *Inhabiting the Page: Visual Experimentation in Caribbean Poetry*, a Ph.D. thesis at the University of Waterloo (Canada) [2007], explores the aesthetic and social implications of inscription and visual design in Shake Keane, Claire Harris, Marlene Nourbese Philip, Kamau Brathwaite and LeRoy Clarke. It unites postcolonial literary criticism and contemporary debates about visual poetic practice in North America.

Lisa Eleanor Nadia Outar, *Stopovers and Homelands: Twentieth- and Twenty-First-Century Representations of Indianness in Caribbean Literature and Popular Culture*, a Ph.D. thesis at the University of Chicago [2007], explores novels by George Lamming, Edgar Mittelholzer, V.S. Naipaul and Earl Lovelace; short stories by Shani Mootoo, Neil Bissoondath and Sasenarine Persaud; and the musical form of chutney soca. It analyses conceptions of creolization in Trinidad, Guyana, Barbados and Martinique, showing that Indianness in the Caribbean is at a crossroads between the diasporic model, which views the various groups as bound to their homelands, and the creole view, which would have them combine to form a new culture.

Laura Selph, *Performing the Caribbean Nation: Chamoiseau, Lovelace, and Kincaid*, a Ph.D. thesis at the University of Oregon [2007], describes how Caribbean cultural identity is often regarded as diasporic and fails to take into account questions of self-determination. However, Patrick Chamoiseau's *Texaco*, Earl Lovelace's *Salt* and Jamaica Kincaid's *A Small Place* have revised the concept of the nation by utilizing performance to combine the diaspora paradigm with one that addresses a politics of self-determination.

Dora Ysabel Marron Romero, *Sacred Powers: Women and African-Derived Religions in 20th Century Caribbean Narrative*, a Ph.D. thesis at the University of Miami [2007], examines Maryse Condé's *Moi, Tituba sorcière... Noire de Salem* [1986], Mayra Montero's *Del rojo de su sombra* [1992], Simone Schwartz-Bart's *Pluie et vent sur Télumée Miracle* [1972] and Erna Brodber's *Louisiana* [1994], each of which offers a different treatment of African-derived religions. The study maintains that this kind of religion enables the major characters in the novels—all women—to use their healing powers to gain an authority generally denied to them by mainstream Christianity and secular society.

Carrie K. Barker, *Genealogy and Decolonization: The Historical Novel of the Twentieth Century Caribbean*, a Ph.D. thesis at New York University, discusses twentieth-century historical novels (de Lisser, Reid and Cliff of Jamaica, Rhys of Dominica, and Mittelholzer of Guyana, written in English; Savane/Salavina and Chamoiseau of Martinique, Schwarz-Bart and Condé of Guadeloupe, written in French; González Ginorio, Muñoz and Ferré of Puerto Rico, written in Spanish). It applies Georg Lukács's argument regarding the effect of political and economic factors on the nineteenth-century European historical novel to the Caribbean context, discussing the novels in terms of decolonization.

5. The Indian Subcontinent and Sri Lanka

(a) Books

Only two single-author studies were located this year—on Vikram Seth and Nissim Ezekiel—but they were unavailable for review. Other work registered a strong presence of thematic criticism, especially monographs foregrounding the permeability of literary texts to social and political realities. Three clear areas of scholarship emerge as common concerns: the domestic space of the home as a site for probing questions of modernity, history and the nation; the contentious yet immensely productive relationship between literature and history; and finally, issues of minority belonging, both in the context of national cultures in the subcontinent as well as in the diaspora. The year was notable for bringing sophisticated theoretical analysis to bear upon close readings of literary texts. Although prominent writers such as Salman Rushdie, Arundhati Roy and Vikram Seth continued to be the chief focus of scholarship, a number of less well-known authors and their works also became the subject of some astute analysis.

Dirk Wiemann's *Genres of Modernity: Contemporary Indian Novels in English* focuses on two privileged metonymies of modernity: time and home (p. 14). Through close readings of a range of novels which foreground multiple, deviant ways of being modern, such as Salman Rushdie's *Midnight's*

Children, Shashi Tharoor's *The Great Indian Novel*, Vikram Chandra's *Red Earth and Pouring Rain*, Kiran Nagarkar's *Cuckold* and Vikram Seth's *A Suitable Boy*, Wiemann argues that the basic gesture of postcolonial literature and theory is to 'first expose the physical, political, juridical, epistemic violence that modernity entails; then "trace the itinerary of the silencing" of that which is excluded from the folds of the (allegedly) universally modern; and finally—in sermon mode—take positive recourse to that which was silenced and cannot be spoken within the folds of the dominant.' (p. 6). Wiemann's analysis of the above novels, especially his fascinating discussion of Kiran Nagarkar's *Cuckold*, highlights their status as ironic, self-conscious, dissident national allegories which together demonstrate a multiplicity of aesthetic strategies for disclaiming the universalism claimed by Walter Benjamin's notion of homogenous empty time, taken up by Benedict Anderson as a condition of possibility for the modern nation as imagined community (p. 7). The Indian novel, Wiemann argues, disrupts the mainstream account of the 'rise of the novel' wherein the novel, having first 'risen' autonomously in parts of Europe, proliferated beyond its boundaries in what was merely an imitative reproduction of the modular form. Drawing upon the scholarship of Franco Moretti, Meenakshi Mukherjee and Shivarama Padikkal, Wiemann argues that the late nineteenth-century emergence of the novel in India exemplified a complex 'compromise' instead of mere derivation (p. 43). At the same time, however, he is aware that interrogating the universalism of Time proposed in the narrative of entrenched modernity takes more than the assertion of 'locally diverse modes of appropriating the globally dispersed "input" from the centre'. What Moretti, Mukherjee and Padikkal fail to consider, in Wiemann's view, is the extent to which the notion of the centre itself is constituted by an entanglement with its alleged Other (p. 42). In thus seeking to establish the porosity of the 'centre', Wiemann lays open to questioning the purportedly 'autonomous' development of the English novel itself even as he disputes any understanding of culture in merely 'national' terms (p. 50).

The second half of this enormously rewarding study addresses critical interventions, in theory and fiction, in the representation and ideological functions of the category of the domestic figured as a semi-autonomous sphere of belonging which is never fully dissociated from the larger framework of the nation (p. 209). As part of the grand dichotomy of private and public, domesticity and intimacy form constitutive moments of the classically modern imaginary. This dichotomy, however, gets subverted in the novels of Amit Chaudhuri, Amitav Ghosh and Arundhati Roy through the notion of 'a public domesticity' drawn from postcolonial feminism which exposes the home not as the haven of intimacy but rather the site of production of citizen/subjects (p. 291). While the above three writers are examined individually in separate chapters, Wiemann also attends to the formulations of home in contemporary Indian 'domestic' fiction by Shashi Deshpande, Githa Hariharan and Vikram Chandra (p. 183). Punctuating his discussion of an essay by Libby Martin and Chandra Talpade Mohanty, 'What's Home Got To Do With It?', with short excursuses from the above instances of domestic fiction, Wiemann shows how the home is itself produced and reinforced by discourses that assign home its functions and ideals. Thus, the multiple reproductive functions of wife/daughter-in-law within the home may be articulated as pure intimacy, but in so far as these also serve to establish the home as a site of the (re)production of labour power, of normalized gendered citizen/subjects, cultural continuity, and, in the case of minority and diasporic frameworks, as a line of defence against cultural assimilation, 'intimate' responsibilities are ultimately social in nature (p. 190).

The domestic space is also the focus of analysis in Geetanjali Singh Chanda's *Indian Women in the House of Fiction*. Like Wiemann, Chanda also situates the domestic in continuation with and reproductive of the larger frame of the nation into which home is inserted: 'Attitudinally, the haveli reproduces, in microcosm, the Indian social structure of kinship patterns, where the clan or the family is privileged over the individual unit' (p. 61). But while, for Wiemann, the concept of home as the site of the symbolic production of national culture interferes with the polarity of inside/outside in a historically specific manner (Wiemann, p. 206), Chanda's focus on the domestic space is ultimately neither historically specific nor interested in the 'outside' aspect of the inside/outside polarity. Chanda begins by arguing that the architectural style of the 'haveli' is the prototype for the urban Indian home (p. 28). Drawing on the feminist contention that the physical rules and boundaries of a place imperceptibly shape social behaviour, Chanda claims that the spatial organization of a haveli results in a structural muting of its female inhabitants (p. 29). However, she continues, the segregated zenana spaces of the haveli also contain the potential for being transformed into an empowering 'woman-space'—a site of female friendships which frequently transgress the boundaries of caste, class and age, even if these are sustained less by political strategy than a personal, subjective empathy linking women to one another (p. 36). Chanda then proceeds to trace a 'shift' in location from haveli to bungalow in Indian English women's novels which impels their protagonists to negotiate between the ideologies of what the psychologist Alan Roland has called a 'we-self', socially approved if not enforced, as a behavioural code, and an 'I-self' which comes with the promise of greater freedom (p. 97). Yet, even as the bungalow marks a change in dwelling and perspective from the extended family grouping to a nuclear and individual focus, the pressure to conform to older patterns of living associated with the haveli continues to be felt, not just in the bungalow setting but also in the as yet uncharted space of urban apartment living. Finally, the book offers a discussion of the nation itself as an imagined domestic space of a house, homes in diaspora and 'extra-domestic spaces' such as women-only homes.

Although Chanda cautions that the zenana should not be seen as a totally 'free space' where women meet as equals, the thrust of her analysis ends up eliding differences of class and caste. Even more problematic is her attempt to track the change in dwelling from haveli to bungalow in Indian English women's novels in terms of a symbolic shift from the extended family grouping to a narrowing of family ties associated with an individualist way of life (p. 92). Thus Attia Hosain's *Sunlight on a Broken Column* and Rama Mehta's *Inside the Haveli* 'capture the haveli, a pan-Indian dwelling, at a specific moment of its disintegration if not demise' (p. 61). Given the enormous explicatory burden which the dwelling in general and the haveli in particular is made to carry in Chanda's reading, it is curious that her only attempt to suture the dwelling into the larger social text consists of a generic reference to 'patriarchal oppression'. Relying on repetition more than evidence, Chanda's bold and intriguing thesis is finally unable to show the ways in which homes are always also mapped onto a social grid. In her intense focus on the 'inside' (of the haveli as well as the text) her analysis fails to sufficiently acknowledge not just the ways in which the dichotomy of inside and outside has historically circumscribed the lives of women but how homes are also sites for the production of a national culture, and achieve their political symbolism precisely by virtue of its removal from the public.

Notions of inside and outside are not just formative of gender norms; they also play a constitutive role in conceptions of literary history and the processes of canon formation. Although the title of Chanda's book, *Indian Women in the House of Fiction*, raises exciting possibilities for re-evaluating the place of Indian women's writing in English within the larger frame of the postcolonial literary canon, it is not one that she really explores at any length. It falls to Paul Sharrad to challenge the formative role of the inside/outside dichotomy in the construction of literary history. Sharrad's *Postcolonial Literary History and Indian English Fiction* takes on the precise task of formulating a commonly accessible rhetorical/theoretical model for reconceptualizing the place of Indian English writing within the corpus of contemporary Indian literary expression in such a way as to do away with the notions of inside and outside. At the level of textual analysis, Sharrad finds the metaphor of the fold to be more productive than the more critically celebrated figure of Deleuze and Guattari's rhizome. A fold is a useful concept with which to comprehend individual works as well as a heuristic offering some ways of thinking about the relationship of the anglophone novelist to the multilingual national, and now transnational, communities of modern India (p. 248). To the extent that the form of each fold is unique, it allows for difference rather than mere diversity. And to the extent that the cloth is the same (though even there the threads and weave may vary) it does not call for a surrendering of the idea of historical continuity (p. 256). Sharrad's theoretical remodelling of literary history thus allows for meaningful relationships to be established across disparate literatures without resort to linear and hierarchized concepts such as 'influence' and without having to process texts against a canonical historical mainstream (pp. 258–9). Through a fascinating discussion linking G.V. Desani's *All About H. Hatterr*, Thomas Carlyle's *Sartor Resartus*, I. Allan Sealy's *Trotter Nama* and Rushdie's *Midnight's Children*, Sharrad is able to show how his envisaging of literary history as a spatial network of texts which may be unrelated by historical and geographical specificities but which have trace connections through time and space may lead to the Eurocentric canon becoming estranged to itself, necessitating the dispensing of the temporal sequence entirely (p. 34). While this does not render centre–margin models wholly redundant, it does dispense with an overdetermined canonical structuring wherein everything new and different must be placed in relation to an established tradition (p. 37).

Apart from problematizing the notion of literary history, Sharrad's book is also concerned with the engagement of Indian English fiction (and the critical debates around it), with national history. Through close readings of the novels of Anita Desai, Arundhati Roy, Namita Gokhale, Raj Kamal Jha, Akhil Sharma, Ranga Rao, Mukul Kesavan, Jhumpa Lahiri and Bharati Mukherjee, among others, Sharrad is able to illustrate the vital significance of history as a theme in the national as well as globalized context. However, history in these texts is not assigned its traditional status as an objective and factual account to be transcribed more or less accurately into fiction. Rather, it is itself seen as textually constructed, just as texts are historically situated and produced. Viewed from this perspective, the dichotomies of inside and outside, private and public, not only overlap but also interfuse, especially since these are equally part of the project of building nation and national culture (p. 14). For Sharrad, the critical significance of history to Indian English fiction derives not from its traditional status as a bastion of truth but from its capacity for absorbing the challenges to its assimilative authority. Unravelling the fabric of history involves altering the ways in which texts are seen to connect with society and readers are seen to connect with texts—connections that are more than just mimetic referentiality (p. 244).

History also remains a vital theme in H.S. Komalesha's *Issues of Identity in Indian English Fiction: A Close Reading of Canonical Indian English Novels*. Komalesha's study, however, is less interested in challenging the assimilative power of history than it is in a more straightforward tracing of Indian English novelists' deployment of history as the 'creative raw material' for developing their major themes. Komalesha's rather bald sketch of the chief thematic concerns in Indian writing in English includes nation, partition and postcolonial debunking of the nation (p. 98). In this account, people's imagining of identity in India in the 1930s was largely associated with the nation as defined through its culture and religion: 'In fact, there was nothing beyond nation and religion to which these people could relate themselves' (p. 66). With the efforts of the Indian National Congress, religion gradually gave ground to the nation, and competing versions of nationalism became the defining factors of the period. Gandhi emerged during this phase as a pan-Indian symbol of India's non-violent heritage to become an undisputed leader of the masses as also a major character in the literature of the time (p. 97).

As the second significant theme in Indian writing in English, Komalesha discusses the partition and 'the dangerous alliance between nation and religion' as represented in the novels of Manohar Malgonkar, Bhabhani Bhattacharya and Khushwant Singh. The trauma of 1947, he argues, resulted in people searching for 'more contemporaneous markers of identity that would no longer confine their sentiments to nation' (p. 127). So it was up to the next generation of writers, such as Rushdie, Ghosh, Tharoor, Roy and others, to explore the possibility of what Komalesha identifies as his third theme, namely, the creation of 'a new identity leaving behind the concept of identity called nation that had once sustained writers such as Raja Rao, R.K. Narayan, Venkataramani, Mulk Raj Anand and others'.

For Komalesha, early twentieth-century interest in history derives from the twin desires for a creative liberation from the tyrannies of history and to recover a past that enables a reconstruction of the present. In the decades leading up to independence, the representational configuration of History, Nation and Nationalism creates an interesting literary dynamic of decolonization which may be distinguished from that of the post-1980s generation of writers who 'basically employ history to problematize their sense of belonging' (p. 28). Although Komalesha's analysis allows for generational differences in the literary deployment of history, his focus on history as 'creative raw material' is finally unable to account for the complex processes of mediation by which history is deployed in fiction. The reader comes away from this study with the impression that these macro categories of identity promoted by the Indian National Congress in an attempt to construct a 'unified pan Indian identity' were never contested in Indian writing in English until the 1980s generation of Rushdie, Ghosh, Tharoor and Roy. In sum, Komalesha's account of identity is painted in such broad brush strokes that the final picture fails to capture the complex negotiation of identity which takes place on a daily basis. His understanding of the relationship between literature and history likewise presumes a transparency that is critically unsustainable.

A more productive enquiry into the processes by which literary texts accommodate history may be found in Benazir Durdana's *Muslim India in Anglo-Indian Fiction*. Based on her close readings of three Anglo-Indian novels—Philip Meadows Taylor's *Confessions of a Thug*, Rudyard Kipling's *Kim* and E.M. Forster's *A Passage to India*—Durdana identifies a pattern of noticeable difference between the historical presence of Muslims in India, both as rulers and British subjects, and the image of them that developed during the years of British domination (p. 22). While she finds the three Anglo-Indian authors to be fairly unambiguous in their recording of exterior features, the deeper they penetrate into issues of personality and questions of religious faith the greater seems to be the discrepancy between their writing and the sources which serve as their creative models (pp. 17–18). As Durdana notes, Muslim characters in British fiction routinely display a mindless, heartless rigidity which finally contributes to an understanding of Islam as the kind of faith that inspires passion but deadens compassion and rationality (p. 21). Durdana's study analyses the specific nature of such representations and explores the hidden and manifest drives that cause Anglo-Indian fiction to cast Islam in these terms (p. 21).

Writing from within the tradition of colonial discourse analysis, Durdana nonetheless challenges many of the Saidian assumptions in *Orientalism*. Unlike Said, who views Islam and India as distinct categories, Durdana recognizes the significance of the fact that from the fifteenth century onwards Islam not only found an increasingly strong foothold in India to become its second most populous religion, but also absorbed certain distinct characteristics of the indigenous cultures of India. Durdana's analysis strives to trace the tension between Indian Muslims and their British colonizers to unpack marked local complexities that are missing from the West's experience of Islam in the land of its birth (p. 5). Durdana argues that when the British colonial power looked upon the decaying Mughals in India it saw its own image: as a precursor in the imperial race, the Muslim community in India displayed all the symptoms of success, indulgence, decadence and defeat, generating what she calls the 'anxiety of fraternity' in the hearts of the wary British (p. 8). In her thesis, it is this psychological drama that gets played out in the aesthetic re-creation of Islamic identity in Anglo-Indian fiction (pp. 154–5).

Moving on from colonial fiction to the much wider stage of postcolonial literary and cultural production is Kavita Daiya's *Violent Belongings: Partition, Gender, and National Culture in Postcolonial India*. Daiya's book pursues an interdisciplinary enquiry into South Asian ethnic violence and related mass migration in and after the partition of 1947. Contrary to the view that the violence of partition was a unique aberration, Daiya argues that it was a formative moment that consolidated particular narratives about citizenship, belonging and gendered ethnicity in postcolonial India (p. 22) as well as critically shaping the contemporary diasporic discourse in South Asian American and British Asian communities about ethnicity, gender and racial discrimination (p. 15). The postcolonial legacy of partition, she argues, is evident in the tense struggle over the production of secular national culture in the subcontinent, the discourses that debate the place of religion in India and in the historical interpretation of justice and minority belonging (p. 2). Through an intense engagement with South Asian literature and cinema, Daiya reveals how partition enabled the cultural ethnicization and gendering of belonging in the nation, which in turn became articulated with the ambivalent ethnicization of citizenship by the Indian state, leading to the contemporary popular Hindu nationalist minoritization of non-Hindus, especially Muslims, in India (p. 15).

Given the official account of the partition refugees' seamless assimilation into Indian national life, the book is notable for its attention to the cultural story of the role of violence and refugees in shaping national histories—a story which has largely been marginalized in the focus on oral testimony and elite history in Indian historiography in general, and early partition historiography as well (p. 25).

Readers will also welcome Daiya's attempt to open up the discussion of partition violence by exploring the violence done to the sexual male body, which remains elided in the contemporary historical investigation of gender and nationalism (p. 28). Examining a range of literary texts from the subcontinent and the diaspora, Daiya shows how the violence done to male bodies played a critical, symbolic role in the production of nationalist sentiment in the public imagination. Daiya's discussion of the representation of women's experience of partition violence and displacement in literature, political documents and oral histories also breaks new ground by making visible the forms of sexual violence whose origins were not communalistic or nationalist, and which were therefore inassimilable into the history and discourse of national modernity.

Literature from the diaspora is also the subject of an edited collection by Neil Murphy and Wai-chew Sim, *British Asian Fiction: Framing the Contemporary*. In an interesting move, Murphy and Sim stretch the category British Asian to include not just writers from South Asia but also those from other parts of Asia, including Japan, Hong Kong and Malaysia. This expansion allows them at once to recognize the changing shape of British literature and access the presence of 'new structures of feeling' which have emerged as a consequence of and in tandem with Britain's post-imperial status.

The twenty essays included in this volume focus on a varied group of authors including Salman Rushdie, Kazuo Ishiguro, Timothy Mo, Hanif Kureishi and their younger contemporaries, such as Sunetra Gupta, Atima Srivastava, Monica Ali and Hari Kunzru. Focused primarily on the formal and aesthetic features of fictional works, many of these short and incisive pieces also make judicious use of critical theory, while contributing to our understanding of the range of British and affiliated identities and cultural contexts.

Among the essays that deserve individual mention is Sharanya Jayawickrama's 'Narrative as Lifeline' (pp. 141–62). In her account of A. Sivanandan's *When Memory Dies* Jayawickrama notes how memory in this novel is figured as falling rain that nourishes stories from the ground, and creates a desire in the narrator to return to the past, to the things that connect him to his country and to 'tell its story'. Needless to say, the narrator of *Memory* tells 'no one story' but rather relates the details of lives connecting and intersecting across generations (p. 149). However, unlike a number of other British Asian writers who deploy the narrative strategy of retrieving memory as alternative history in order to counter unidimensional narratives of identity that threaten to circumscribe their lands of origin, Sivanandan's strategy of imagining community through alternative narratives also involves the creation of a viable black political identity in Britain.

While Jayawickrama's essay focuses on the uses of memory in negotiating the dynamics of multi-ethnic belonging and affiliation in Britain, Leila Neti's discussion of Meera Syal's *Anita and Me* (pp. 97–118), turns to language and speech. In her essay 'Siting Speech', Neti suggests that the primacy of sight in the racial ordering of difference has become increasingly complicated by technologies that enable communication via non-visual modes, privileging the uses of speech and language as tools for subverting the dominant culture's expectations and presuppositions (p. 101). Syal's second novel is the subject of Dave Gunning's essay, 'Cultural Conservatism and the Sites of Transformation in Meera Syal's *Life Isn't All Ha Ha Hee Hee*' (pp. 119–40). Gunning argues that Syal's interrogation of the simplistic representations of British Asian communities and personhood ultimately moves towards an affirmation of the value of 'traditional' cultures to her protagonists, but not without acknowledging the limits to which this acceptance should stretch (p. 121). Alan Robinson's discussion of Hari Kunzru's *Transmission* (pp. 77–96) takes us away from questions of history, identity and belonging to an instance of postmodernist writing informed by literary and cultural theory. Kunzru's novel probes the nature of self and 'reality' in an economically and culturally networked world driven by the two main forces of Westernized modernity: globalized capitalism and instrumental rationality (p. 82). Although *Transmission* depicts no alternative to the monolithic capitalist system, it doesn't suggest that the system is either invulnerable or all-pervasive (p. 93)—a view instantiated by the novel's ideological critique of social control and its recourse to an ending wherein the narrator's socially constructed self is allowed to disappear without a trace in an affirmative half-belief that an alternative to Westernized modernity might exist, although its location remains unclear (p. 95).

As a novel that addresses the 'epistemological crisis of scientific procedure' Romesh Gunesekera's *Reef* also lends itself to a poststructuralist analysis. Yet, as Gerd Bayer's reading shows (pp. 273–88), the focus of Gunesekera's novel derives less from a postmodernist questioning of the truthfulness of scientific findings and more from the vast margin of error and chaos with the collection of data that leads to such results. This reluctance to buy wholesale into the postmodernist agenda is also evident in Cordula Lemke's reading of Gunesekera's most recent novel, *Heaven's Edge* (pp. 289–308). Lemke draws our attention to the novel's simultaneous straddling of two different positions regarding postmodernism: Marc the protagonist's means of gaining agency by way of telling stories depends on a postmodernist understanding of language in which storytelling and agency determine each other. At the same time the novel also recognizes that the oscillating movements of language can be suddenly halted by death, and that storytelling may be denied a place in the hierarchy of cultural discourses competing for attention in a terror-stricken world.

As an index of the tremendous socio-cultural diversity in contemporary British Asian writing, the collection also includes an essay by Kenneth Chan on the work of Timothy Mo, who may be credited with having initially opened up the British literary establishment to immigrant writing, especially from China (pp. 237–54). In a more meta-critical mode, Tamara Wagner parodies, with reference to Ooi Yang-May's *The Flame Tree*, the recognizable stereotypes and clichés in diasporic writing (pp. 163–82), Wendy O'Shea Meddour discusses the failure of existing interpretative discourse on Hanif Kureishi's *The Buddha of Suburbia* (pp. 33–54), and Ruth Maxey's essay on Monica Ali's *Brick Lane* probes the politics of the critical reception of immigrant literature in the British academy (pp. 217–36).

Critical writing on literature from the South Asian diaspora also features in Mark Shackleton's edited volume, *Diasporic Literature and Theory—Where Now?* The first of the two articles grouped under a subheading of 'Diasporas of Violence and Terror' is Neelam Srivastava's 'Decolonizing the Self: Gandhian Non-Violence and Fanonian Violence as Comparative "Ethics of Resistance" in *Kanthapura* and *The Battle of Algiers*' (pp. 86–103). Srivastava's essay (which appears to be slightly at odds with its context of diaspora studies), examines the different arguments for social action and/or self-reformation as part of revolutionary anti-colonial change. Thus Fanon argued for a purifying popular violence to counter colonial violence while the elite pan-African socialists took the opposite stand of supporting Gandhian non-violence. While Fanon drew on a tradition of anti-fascist thought (Améry, Agamben and Benjamin) in which one asserts/finds one's humanity in rising up against state violence, for Gandhi internal spiritual purification was the first step towards bringing about external change. Drawing upon Gandhian ethics, *Kanthapura* shows the interaction of personal, mental change with public action not only in its story of village caste reform and anti-British protest, but also in the author's break with standard patterns of English and novelistic prose. On the other hand, the film *Battle for Algiers* adopts Fanonian views, showing the circuits of violence that allow us to sympathize with a violent Algerian populace. The article doesn't advance our knowledge of either text or set of ideas, though it does interestingly claim that both theorists locate violence within the colonized self (p. 99), noting an unusual passage from Gandhi and suggesting that his internal reform towards ahimsa is itself an act of violence that engages in an ethics of violent action.

In the second article, 'Anti-Americanism and U.S. Imperialism in Salman Rushdie's *Fury*' (pp. 104–18), Stephen Morton notes the diaspora politics in Thatcher's Britain that drive *The Satanic Verses* and analyses Professor Malik Solanka, the central character of *Fury*, as similarly torn between love of liberal democracy and a comfortable lifestyle and loathing of the wealth and smug imperialism of America. Morton tracks anti-American rhetoric from early times, linking it to Neil Lazarus's binary of decolonizing hope and post-independence despair in countries now experience neo-imperialist interventions. The reading is backed by Rushdie's journalism on Bush's America, Appadurai's ideas on diaspora and Jameson's thoughts on postmodern suppression of affect. Solanka's rage is fuelled by the contradictions of diasporic experience, the demand for but containment of ethical critique from an intelligentsia, and urban modernity in which computer games stand in for political action. More than a personal venting of frustration, *Fury* allows Rushdie to ask questions about the political and ethical possibilities of diasporic affect, especially for the liberal intellectual who wants to condemn Third World failings without falling into First World complicity, or to rail against First World imperialism while living in the heart of the beast.

(b) Journal Articles
A very interesting year in which international debates in studies in the humanities ran counter to articles specifically on Indian subcontinental and Sri Lankan literature. The big picture of English studies in international journals was: ongoing concerns over the continuing hegemony of English as a global language, the concept of English as lingua franca and the acquisition of English through linguistic (not literary) methods; the absolute insistence on translation as the only way to argue for the viability and sustenance of a world literature; renewed engagements with modernity and the question of the 'new', especially in relation to literary historiography; and the provocative turn towards European postcoloniality.

Despite the focus of this section on subcontinental Indian and Sri Lankan literature, it would be remiss of me not to mention some special symposia that took up the above-mentioned concerns, without which scholarship in the region would remain uncontextualized and unmediated. What becomes clear is that the question of the general application of the English language simply cannot be removed from English literary scholarship in an age of globalized higher education/research and in a market dominated by interrogations of the very relevance of literature and commodity-driven publishing regimes.

World Englishes 27:iii–iv[2008] devoted four papers to 'Intelligibility and Cross-Cultural Communication in World Englishes' with Braj B. Kachru taking 'The First Step: The Smith Paradigm for Intelligibility in World Englishes' (*WEn* 27:iii–iv[2008] 293–6). He discusses the usefulness of

Larry Smith's coining of EIL (English as an international language) in order to complicate earlier distinctions between methodologies in EFL (English as a foreign language) and ESL (English as a second language). Yamuna Kachru adapted to linguistics what has been relevant to contemporary disciplines for some time now, i.e. the notions of 'Cultures, Contexts and Interpretability' in the same issue (*WEn* 27:iii–iv[2008] 309–19).

The debate continued in another forum with David Crystal's updates on the current statistics of English, and, to his own 1985 question, 'How many millions use English?' he cautiously answered, 'Two thousand million?' (*EnT* 24:i[2008] 3–6). His estimate sparked off a lively exchange on the Indian Association of Commonwealth Literature and Language Studies listserv, reminding us of the close connection between language as literal as well as a concept-metaphor, to use Gayatri Chakravorty Spivak's useful formulation. Rajend Mesthrie, in the same issue (*EnT* 24:i[2008] 28–32), commenting on Braj B Kachru's seminal 1988 piece, 'The Sacred Cows of English', rehearsed the 'culture bomb' effect of 'English circling the globe'. R.K. Agnihotri (*EnT* 24:iv[2008] 51–64) crystallized the 'Continuing Debates over the Native Speaker: A Report on a Symposium on English in India and Indian English' by responding to how English now definitely had 'a definable place in the language ecology of India' (p. 52).

The above discussions on the language found resonance in a special issue of the *European Journal of English Studies* (*EJES* 12:i[2008]), wherein Bessie Dendrinos, Mina Karavanta and Bessie Mitsikopoulou, in 'Introduction: Theorizing New English(es): The Double Contingency of Postcoloniality and Globality' (*EJES* 12:i[2008] 1–14), appealed against the vilification of English, asked that attention be paid to the structural conditions of its empowerment, and made the case for 'praxes of translation' to operate as 'critical interruptions' in the 'dissemination' and 'practices of New English(es)' (p. 5). Rajagopalan Radhakrishnan, 'Is Translation a Mode?' (*EJES* 12:i[2008] 15–31), argued that the very idea of 'New Englishes' might potentially be an attempt to tame the clamorous Many in favour of an universalizing One, and that for translation to be truly inter- and intra-lingual, the politics of globalization as 'a language' should be intimately understood.

The argument for multiplicity continued in the pages of *Philosophy and Literature* (*P&L* 32[2008]) when Patrick Colm Hogan spoke 'Of Literary Universals: Ninety-Five Theses' (*P&L* 32[2008] 145–60) and Ihab Hassan hinted towards 'twelve perspectives' in response to his own question, 'how many ways are there of questioning theory in our age?' in 'Literary Theory in an Age of Globalisation' (*P&L* 32[2008] 1–10). Alexander Beecroft came up with six modes of configuration in 'World Literature Without a Hyphen: Towards a Typology of Literary Systems' (*NLR* 54[Nov./Dec. 2008] 87–100), where he took up, among others, the 'Sanskrit example' of Sheldon Pollock to explain the circulation of literatures within cosmopolitan literary systems. Beecroft was responding to two recent theses by Pascale Casanova and Franco Moretti that chart *Weltliteratur*, and his binary continuities offer much food for thought in mapping out the current relationship between literature and its environment: epichoric to panchoric, vernacular to national, regional to global.

But the most provocative, and Babel-ian, interventions, predictions and prescriptions, came from an almost 500-page discussion of 'Literary History in the Global Age' in a special issue of *New Literary History* (*NLH* 39:iii[2008]). Many of the essayists engaged with Casanova and Moretti and with the contemporary political and cultural demands of literary histories. While Fredric Jameson announced the End of the New, Hans Ulrich Gumbrecht asked if we would continue to write histories of literature. Brian Stock returned to interpretative pluralism and Walter F. Veit to uses of comparative literary history. Nadia Al-Bagdadi and Wai Chee Dimock performed feats of planetary literary history in the context of Arabic and Egyptian traditions respectively. Rey Chow again dreamt of intercultural equivalence in translation, while Emily Apter mused upon the untranslatables in world systems. Hayden White and Jonathan Arac provided commentaries on each of these seventeen essays, not one of which engaged at any length or depth with the two purported giants of current global history, India and China—with considerable literary histories of their own!

It is in the above context that I situate my review of work done in journals on subcontinental Indian and Sri Lankan literature in 2008. A work that performs beautifully what these theorists have suggested above is a most fascinating example of archival research, 'A New Wave of Indian Inspiration: Translations from Urdu in Malay Traditional Literature and Theatre' (*IML* 36:civ[2008] 115–53). Vladimir Braginsky and Anna Suvorova examine the well-documented Indo-Malay cultural interface in the late nineteenth century to gesture towards understandings of its earlier stages, for example in Malacca in the fifteenth and sixteenth centuries or Aceh in the seventeenth. Englobing translation, intertextuality, historiography, materiality and transculturation in all their fertile possibilities, they examine how translation-adaptations from Urdu (informed by Hindustani and Persian) brought to life not only half a dozen literary works—*Hikayat Gul Bakawali*, *Syair Indra Sebaha*, *Hikayat Sultan Butamam*, *Hikayat Ganja Mara*—in the Malay world, but also led to the creation of the Wayang Bangsawan theatre. This translation activity was made possible by the introduction of the lithographic press and lending libraries, combined with travelling Parsi theatre troupes from India, hosted and brokered by the influential Indo-Malay community. This work suggests how similar projects might be undertaken to broaden our understanding of older routes of cross-fertilizations in global circuits.

A second exemplar in this scale of world literature research was offered by Emily T. Hudson in 'Time that Ripens and Rots all Creatures: Temporality and its Terrors in the Sanskrit Mahābhāratā' (*SLI* 41:ii[2008] 41–62). What this essay lacks in rhetorical flourish it makes up in close textual analysis of the concept of time in the Sanskrit epic. In a year when literary critics obsessed about the end of history, Hudson provided an intimate, and at the same time expansive, look at the framing narrative device in an epic that 'moves back and forth in time as well as into "simultaneous meanwhiles"', thereby making a case for its sustained contemporary study (p. 53). Her literary analysis could be connected in exciting ways to contemporary theorizations of temporality and spatiality in history.

In similar vein, but more sketchy, was Alex Padamsee's argument for 'Uncertain Partitions: "Undecidability" and the Urdu Short Story' (*Wasafiri* 23:i[2008] 1–5). Taking up Gyanendra Pandey's concept of 'undecidability' and Alok Bhalla's notion of 'bewilderment', Padamsee argues that the question of narrative is central to understanding the unnarratibility of partition in the subcontinent. He suggests that that the fragmentary and 'traumatic aspect' of the short story serves content well, refusing the trajectory of narration and the teleology of nationalism implicit in partition historiography. One would like to see an extended discussion of Padamsee's idea (derived from the work of Sukeshi Kamra, Tai Yong Tan and Gyanesh Kudaisya). It could further be opened up to the other complicated partition story (of Bengal), which has not yet received the same canonical status.

Another example of form and content working in creative tension was showcased in Dohra Ahmad's 'The Home, the World and the United States: *Young India*'s Tagore' (*JCL* 43:i[2008] 23–41). Ahmad looks at how Nobel laureate Rabindranath Tagore, who by the end of the 1990s was seen as 'the ultimate model of a non-sectarian humanism utterly immune to the allure of the nation-state' (pp. 26–7), was actually put to selective use in the service of a long-distance nationalism in Lala Lajpat Rai's exilic New York periodical, *Young India* [1918–20]. Rai's vision of an inclusive, transnational, dynamic, diverse and unabashedly utopian polity had to actively exclude the dissent of Tagore, who had declared his distance from and disenchantment with the idea of the nation by the time *Young India* started appearing in the counter-culture and little magazine press of New York. The article starts with an examination of Rai's investment in the iconic nationalism of a geopolitical entity yet to be born, but then veers off into a discussion of Tagore's condemnation of the same in *Ghare Baire*. It usefully locates Tagore as a figure who became the victim of his own reputation as world seer and prophet, and whose persona, rather than his lyric poetry, became the embodiment of Indian cultural and national identity.

Asha Nadkarni, again in an American context, takes us from *Young India* to *Mother India* in ' "World-Menace": National Reproduction and Public Health in Katherine Mayo's *Mother India*' (*AQ* 60:iii[2008] 805–27). Tracing closely the connection between British imperial policies in the early twentieth century and American commercial expansionist interests in India, Nadkarni shows Mayo's rhetorical movement from metaphor to metonymy to represent Mother India as both minatory, multitudinous menace and incapable of (national) reproduction. Published only seven years after *Young India* folded, Mayo's *Mother India* paints as catastrophic India's claim on self-rule when filtered through the 'pathological body politic' (p. 818) harbouring a 'democracy of disease' that can only be monstrously delivered (p. 810). Nadkarni persuades us that, in employing specifically the clinical language of hygiene and contagion, Mayo betrays deep ambivalence in the project of modernity's global circulation of goods and bodies, and instead she wants to hold on to a kind of 'medicalized nativism' that will prevent/police the transmission of material culture from a threateningly promiscuous and sexually suspect Hindu country. In fact, Hinduism's sinister and unhealthy appeal in the US is the hinge on which Mayo's depiction of an at-risk nation turns. In a cogent, sleight-of-hand argument, Nadkarni proves that it is precisely because Indian and US women are placed on a continuum of motherhood that Mayo's vision of 'manifest domesticity' mirrors back upon itself, implicating both nations in practices of 'world-menace' (p. 805).

As if flouting Mayo's injunction that women's place is at home, Nupur Chaudhuri gives an account of 'Krishnobhabini Das's *Englande Bangamohila*: An Archive of Early Thoughts on Bengali Women's Nationalism and Feminism' (*JWH* 20:i[2008] 197–216). Chaudhuri shows how Krishnobhabini's travel narrative in England questioned both the imperial feminist vision of Indian women as inferior and challenged it on the home grounds of patriarchy. Thinking comparatively about the place of 'woman' in country and community led Krishnobhabini to write about English feminists such as Mary Carpenter, Florence Nightingale and Lady Baker in relation to her compatriots. While the essay offers an important sketch of a woman in her times, it never questions how Krishnobhabini might be implicated within the project of nation-making precisely through the appellation of Bangamahila. It would be useful to complicate the speaking position of a caste Hindu woman's account of herself by emphasizing the 'literary' in addition to the historical in Krishnobhabini's text, i.e. by paying close attention to the construction of the genre of the travelogue itself with its connotations of insider/outsider positions and its ethnographic gaze.

Offering just such a thick analysis is Ellen Brinks's 'Gendered Spaces in *Kamala: The Story of a Hindu Child-Wife*' (*NCC* 30:ii[2008] 147–65). Published nine years after Krishnobhabini's travel narrative, Krupabai Satthianadhan's 1894 novel of social reform for women complicates anthropologies of high-caste Hindu women's lives through her unique strategic perspective as an Indian Christian feminist. Allegedly the first novel in English by an Indian woman, *Kamala* offers a view into domestic, wild and gender-segregated spaces in which reform from within may be affected, in addition to external judicial intervention. Brinks locates this novel specifically in the context of the debates of the 1880s and 1890s on the question of child marriage and the 1891 Age of Consent Act controversy in India. *Kamala* widens the discussion beyond the narrow legal scope of biological age to offer a vision of companionate marriage, thereby delivering a scathing critique of a cruel and conjugally confining joint family system. Brinks makes a suggestion exciting for feminist scholarship: since the figure of embodied maternity is so threatening and dangerous for women in an exogamous social sphere, the prospect of stepping out of a generational matrix offers Kamala, the eponymous protagonist of the novel, the gift of education, one that continues in perpetuity. And lest this move be co-opted by any liberal feminist agenda of (solitary) self-emancipation, Brinks concludes her essay with an examination of the socio-psychological spaces outside domesticity that provide rich mediations in the project of 'knowing' and 'knowledge of' the self. Writing the female body, a favourite trope and trajectory of first-wave discourse, is achieved in *Kamala* not in a room of one's own, but in public, if gender-segregated, spaces that commit to the necessity of engagement with others like and unlike oneself.

Moving on to a contemporary site, Anuradha Ramanujan offers an astute textual analysis and theoretical explication of two narrative representations of the 'dacoit queen' in 'The Subaltern, the Text and the Critic: Reading Phoolan Devi' (*JPW* 44:iv[2008] 367–78). She raises questions of textual authority, contending figurations, conflicting ideologies and editorial mediations in 'feminist' life-stories that carry the burden of witnessing, oral testimonial and resistance. Ramanujan uses the trope of 'betrayal' to untie the double bind of alliance formation and appropriation attending feminist workings across difference. Employing Mala Sen's biography, *India's Bandit Queen: The True Story of Phoolan Devi* [1991], on which Shekhar Kapur's film is loosely based, and the personal testimonial, *I, Phoolan Devi* [1996], Ramanujan furthers the challenge to middle-class feminist assumptions which treat rape in essentialist terms as a 'women's issue', unmediated by considerations of caste, class and religion. By destabilizing both the 'object' of heteropatriarchy and the notion of an authentic identity-constitution through pain/trauma, Ramanujan's readings of these texts continue with ongoing vexed questions in feminist enquiry around speech/subjectivity and differential locations of power.

Pamela Butler and Jigna Desai continue from where Ramanujan's essay concludes with the problematic of self-positioning and native informancy in particular genre and pedagogical situations. 'Manolos, Marriage and Mantras: Chick-Lit Criticism and Transnational Feminism' (*MFRT* 8:ii[2008] 1–31) considers the sub-genre of South Asian popular novels that construct neoliberal subjectivity through the prisms of consumption, marriage and realism. Instead of reading transnational chick lit as representative instantiations of a racialized, marginalized and/or exoticized polity, Butler and Desai use transnational feminist *critique* as a reading method to uncover the political economy of race, nation and migration. They eschew white feminism's normative reading of chick lit as symptomatic of an apolitical postfeminism in the US, and instead foreground neoliberal feminism's emphasis on choice and consumption as the problematic of contemporary female agency. Reading Kavita Daswani's *For Matrimonial Purposes* [2004] and *The Village Bride of Beverly Hills* [2005] and Sonia Singh's *Goddess for Hire* [2004], they ask if women-of-colour chick lit might offer productive illuminations on relations of power operant in the global arena. Butler and Desai conclude that instead of simply being reduced to white chick lit's little sister, women-of-colour chick lit should be engaged with as a site that throws up for examination markers of white privilege, capital and citizenship as well as one that delightfully subverts the genre fiction through disindentificatory processes. But there is a troubling conflation of the figure of the woman of colour with the metropolitan migrant woman in this article that evades the issue of the complicity of the latter within global publishing and transmission regimes. I am not entirely convinced of the extent to which migratory, racialized tropes and figures can really disrupt the neoliberal feminist narrative that Butler and Desai critique.

Kavita Daiya addresses this complication in 'Home and the Nation: Women, Citizenship and Transnational Migration in Postcolonial Literature' (*JPW* 44:iv[2008] 391–402). Reading the representation of migrant women and refugees in the fiction of Nadine Gordimer and Amitav Ghosh, Daiya looks at how the celebratory rhetoric of globalization and postcolonial nationalisms is mediated via gendered subalternity. She makes an especially compelling argument through the icon of the female foetus in Ghosh's *Circle of Reason*, which critiques the notion of any deterritorialized nationality or idea of fluid, contemporary global citizenship. In illuminating the political limits of subjective imagination, Ghosh's characters go against Arjun Appadurai's formulation of agency in imagined worlds and signal the failure of modern migrations. Similarly, Gordimer's illegal female migrants travelling through Kruger Park in 'The Ultimate Safari' are likened to the wildlife that surrounds them, indicating their double subalternity as black and stateless. Even though this is a short essay, and relies a little too heavily on secondary criticism to provide its theoretical backbone, it does some important work in bringing to the fore the violence associated with contemporary transnationality, a state that Daiya demonstrates is riven with the contradictions of oppression and opportunity for those who are caught within it and trying to make a life despite it. In making her point using disenfranchised, deterritorialized women in postcoloniality who make a bid to and claim for agency, Daiya understands the extremely fraught conditions of possibility of female entrepreneurship in the increasingly corporate world of instrumental and institutionalized migrancy.

Maria-Sabina Draga Alexandru makes the opposite point in 'Performance, Performativity, and Nomadism in Vikram Chandra's *Red Earth and Pouring Rain*' (*CLS* 45:i[2008] 24–39). She characterizes NRI (Indians living abroad) writers as operating in 'maximum freedom' through permanent contact and a distant positioning reflected in their commuting life patterns—a cyclical existence that she adduces from Rosi Braidotti's nomadic subjectivity. She also uses Deleuze and Guattari's principle of multiplicity to understand the performance of this nomadism in Chandra's adaptation of Indian oral narratology for his 1995 novel. Even though the essay offers an intriguing and enabling model for understanding Chandra's rhizomatic plotline, it suffers from an unwieldy and unrelated framework that includes the work of theorists as diverse as J.L. Austin, J. Hillis Miller, Ralph Yarrow, Andrew Parker and Eve Kosofsky Sedgwick. This essay comes into its own only in the second half, after Alexandru declares her thesis: that Chandra's performative use of the oral tradition makes his text a nomadic one.

Richard Brock continues with the theme of peregrination in 'An "Onerous Citizenship": Globalization, Cultural Flows and the HIV/AIDS Pandemic in Hari Kunzru's *Transmission*' (*JPW* 44:iv[2008] 379–90). In the hands of Arjun Mehta, Kunzru's protagonist, a software retrovirus becomes the medium through which to understand one of the most profound fears of our times: contagion and dis-ease/death as the inevitable result of the transcultural and transnational movements of people, ideas and capital across the globe. Reading *Transmission* as an AIDS allegory, Brock goes on to examine the implications of such a reading in terms of the critique it offers of an unrestrained globality, as well as the subversion it effects of established First World discourses on the pandemic. Pushing further the position of theorists of globalization that HIV/AIDS be understood as its symptom, he suggests that indeed there is a mutual metaphorical dependency between the two. This is a richly imaginative paper, invoking Arjun Appadurai's concept of 'scapes'.

Brock relentlessly addresses the financescapes, technoscapes and ethnoscapes imbricated in the mesh of a postnational, transcultural world.

Citizenship remains a troubled site of analysis in Caroline Herbert's '"Dishonourably Postnational?": The Politics of Migrancy and Cosmopolitanism in Rohinton Mistry's *A Fine Balance*' (*JCL* 43:ii[2008] 11–28). Taking its title from Timothy Brennan's observation that the figure of the cosmopolitan often suffers 'the taint of being dishonourably postnational' (p. 13), the essay uses the trope of detachment and distance to comprehend migrant engagement with a geopolitical entity called nation. The essay takes up R. Radhakrishnan's formulation of the 'double duty' of national accountability in relation to diasporic subjectivity to read Mistry's migrants. At the beginning of the essay, Herbert warns against conflating the figures of the migrant and the cosmopolitan, but she herself soon collapses authorial biography and characters' lives, migrancy and the diasporic existence of Parsis in India. Denying the literary work its own imaginative logic, Herbert imposes a template of cookie-cutter postcolonial and diasporic theory upon Mistry's texts to arrive at a reductionist interpretative frame.

Rashna B. Singh offers a much more persuasive reading of the thousand-year-old Zoroastrian domicile in 'Traversing Diacritical Space: Negotiating and Narrating Parsi Nationness' (*JCL* 43:ii[2008] 29–47). She sees in Parsi ambivalence a complex process of negotiation with their historical and geographical contingency of arrival and settlement in India. She too uses R. Radhakrishnan's work, but to understand how the term 'Indian' is unmoored from its central position when marginal characters in the fiction of Bapsi Sidhwa, Rohinton Mistry and Thrity Umrigar come to occupy a speaking position within its national imaginary. Their perceived partial participation in the imagined fabric of the nation becomes a means of unsettling any majoritarian claims that the other, dominant, India might have. In fact, by such a (supposed) reticence in being 'Indian', the Parsi community denies the viability of a completely Hindu-identified India. The very variance of this group from other, more assimilated, ones in the subcontinent becomes an argument against any totalizing, monocultural sense of an Indian identity or sensibility. Its explicit 'Westernized' presence becomes yet another ingredient in the melting-pot that India truly is, argues Singh, following the work of Homi Bhabha on hybridity.

Looking at another minority community is Ralph Crane's 'Contesting the Can(n)on: Revisiting *Kim* in I. Allan Sealy's *The Trotter-Nama*' (*JPW* 44:ii[2008] 151–8). Crane traces the uneasy concern for pedigree in Sealy's saga on the Anglo-Indians to Kipling's quintessential Raj novel, using the latter's words from 'His Chance in Life': 'One of these days, this people [Anglo-Indians] ... will turn out a writer or a poet; and then we shall know how they live and what they feel.' The 'Borderline folk' of Kipling's description find their voice and vision in seven generations of the Trotters, who narrate their own Anglo-Indian history of the subcontinent by writing themselves into every major moment of British Indian history. Unlike the Parsis though, theirs is a history completely mediated by British imperialism and thus rewrites that canon with close postcolonial attention to the very events that defined them. The most interesting angle of analysis Crane introduces is in unpacking the term 'Anglo-Indian' and working with the broadest definition possible, thereby including both Kipling and Sealy in it. This section of the essay deserves further attention as it opens up the question of intertextuality and inheritance in world literature itself.

On the subject of Sri Lanka, it was a lean year for scholarship on Michael Ondaatje. Robert David Stacey's 'A Political Aesthetic: Michael Ondaatje's *In the Skin of a Lion* as "Covert Pastoral"' (*ConL* 49:iii[2008] 439–69) stands out for both his forceful analysis of the novel as well as sharper argument about genre. He starts with critiques of the novel that fault it for exploiting, rather than empowering its working-class Torontonian subjects, silenced in official histories of Canadian culture. Citing Paul Alpers's passing reference to *The English Patient* in his comprehensive study *What Is Pastoral?* [1996], Stacey argues that it is precisely the pastoral mode that permits the earlier novel to frame the political and economic disempowerment of its subjects within the narrative of the nation (a case that has also been made for Chang Rae-Lee's *A Gesture Life* in the American context). Stacey understands *In the Skin of a Lion*'s sympathetic treatment of an urban industrial proletariat as an example of William Empson's 'covert pastoral', where the artist's relationship to his subjects is knowingly and aesthetically explored through a paradigm of power. Possibilities of reciprocity and recognition are opened up in a pastoral, Stacey contends—a view that Marxist critics in particular are quick to refute as dangerously idealizing and escapist. Nailing the argument to the blowing up of the waterworks, Stacey concludes that *In the Skin of a Lion* refuses any heroic denouement because it honours, after all, the labour of the hands that went into the building. In giving up the master claim to his artistic and aesthetic licence, Stacey claims, Ondaatje recognizes the constraints of history and the utter irrefutability and irreducibility of the past, which has a reality that transcends the power of the novelist, however revolutionary and revisionary his politics might be.

Attention to genre continued across the Bay of Bengal in Michael Perfect's 'The Multicultural Bildungsroman: Stereotypes in Monica Ali's *Brick Lane*' (*JCL* 43:iii[2008] 109–20). Before making his own argument, Perfect catalogues scholarship on the controversial aspects of the novel, most particularly the charge that Ali perpetuates cultural stereotypes about Islamic subjects in postcolonial nations. Perfect wonders whether novels of this kind can indeed act as 'forums' whose postmodern metatextuality absolves them from the charge of cultural commodification. His response instead is to hail Ali's novel as a realist Bildungsroman based on the fact that she relied on Naila Kabeer's sociological treatise *The Power to Choose* for models for her most abject characters. Despite the promise of the title, Perfect's essay succumbs to the same 'profound unease' that has characterized other responses that read difference in a deterministic way in *Brick Lane*.

Finally, Salman Rushdie continues to attract scholarship, five articles in my count, attesting to his serious and significant hold on current postcolonial imagination. Alex Stähler develops the concept of prophetic encounter in *The Satanic Verses* with 'Writ(h)ing Images: Imagination, the Human Form, and the Divine in William Blake, Salman Rushdie, and Simon Louvish' (*ES* 89:i[2008] 94–117). He argues that, rather than the *Marriage of Heaven and Hell*, it is William Blake's last major work, the illustrations to the biblical book of Job, that provides the foil to *The Satanic Verses*. He brings in Simon Louvish's *The Days of Miracles and Wonders* [1997] as a response to and extrapolation of Rushdie's novel, and argues that these three texts read together offer the opportunity for a renewed examination of the interrelation of fundamentalisms and literature in our contemporary times. He concludes that the imaginative process at best offers ambivalent strategies of resistance.

Neil ten Kortenaar's 'Fearful Symmetry: Salman Rushdie and Prophetic Newness' (*TCL* 54:iii[2008] 339–61) and Stephen Morton's '"There were collisions and explosions. The world was no longer calm": Terror and Precarious Life in Salman Rushdie's *Shalimar the Clown*' (*TPr* 22:ii[2008] 337–55) both take up the issue of 'newness' in Rushdie's novels. Kortenaar starts with the question of the arrival of newness into the world in order to then explore the politics of postcolonial literature, which are both a specific geopolitical and historical development and a highly successful market strategy. He argues that Rushdie, as a believer in his own prophetic genius, posits postcolonial migrancy and originality in the literary marketplace as the harbingers of such newness.

Morton places the publication of *Shalimar the Clown* in the context of Rushdie's call for a reformation of Islam in the aftermath of the London bombings of 7 July 2005. He traces the itinerary of US foreign policy in South Asia from the Bretton Woods Agreement to the war in Afghanistan and offers the thesis that Rushdie, in his writings, occupies an ambivalent position with regard to these international developments vis-à-vis Islam. Rushdie foregrounds the struggle in Kashmir in his 2005 novel so as to offer a parallel ethical challenge to contemporary superpowers who engineered the Cold War and the 'War on Terror'. Morton argues that Rushdie demands a non-partisan response to the political, military and technological forces of postcolonial modernity in the valley and compels a consideration of the precarious life of Kashmir(is). If *Midnight's Children* is the paradigmatic Third World text that Fredric Jameson characterizes as national allegory, then *Shalimar the Clown* stages the impossibility of any kind of Kashmiriyat. If the fall of Saladdin Chamcha and Gibreel Farishta from the wreckage of Air India flight 420 above the English Channel signals the experience of postcolonial migration, then the fate of the non- or trans-national peoples in Kashmir shifts the focus away from the transformative potential of migration. Newness in this context needs to be imagined differently.

Caroline Herbert features again with '"No longer a memoirist but a voyeur": Photographing and Narrating Bombay in Salman Rushdie's *The Ground Beneath Her Feet*' (*JPW* 44:ii[2008] 139–50). She looks at Rushdie's photographer-narrator as a mediator between aesthetics and politics and as a voice of protest against the changing face of the erstwhile inclusive ethos of Bombay. Beginning with Susan Sontag's conceptualization of photographs as bearers of connectedness between memory and reality, Herbert reads Rushdie's 1999 novel as radical renegotiation of the relationship between the cosmopolitan migrant artist and his remembered (if lost) homeland. The tension between distance and intimacy, participation and passivity determines any national narrative history for such an intellectual. The increasingly fundamentalist climate in the city turns the erstwhile writer and/or protagonist into a voyeur, with all the attendant associations the word invokes. This transformation in perspective is marked by the fixing of the narrator's identity in religious rather than in secular terms. Herbert persuasively argues that photography, as a practice of possession and dispossession, then becomes the preferred mode of understanding and recording a changing land- and mindscape.

Nicole Weickgenannt looks at another deliberate narrative strategy of Rushdie's in 'The Nation's Monstrous Women: Wives, Widows and Witches in Salman Rushdie's *Midnight's Children*' (*JCL* 43:ii[2008] 65–83). She offers a timely reading of the function of misogyny and the monstrous female figures in his 1981 novel. Weickgenannt places Rushdie's female characters in the context of the construction of Indian womanhood in Indian nationalist discourses. She suggests that, as cultural repositories of tradition, Indian women are denied the same status as the men with respect to Westernization and modernization. In fact, given that the nationalist movement mobilizes women's strength while trying to contain their threatening potential, women can only be depicted as a national menace. The idea of the monstrous power of women is further illustrated in the demonization of the Indira Gandhi figure and Parvati, which uses the stereotypes of the widow and the witch. Taking a different stance from some feminist critiques of *Midnight's Children*, Weickgenannt argues that Rushdie deliberately uses misogyny and monstrosity to critique the role of the nation-state vis-à-vis gender and patriarchy in post-independence India.

I conclude this review with one of the most knowledgeable reading pleasures of the year: Tabish Khair's 'Indian Pulp Fiction in English: A Preliminary Overview from Dutt to Dé' (*JCL* 43:iii[2008] 59–74). This kind of survey has long been overdue in the sub-genre of subcontinental pulp fiction and Khair offers more than a preliminary overview, on both substantive and formal grounds. Khair documents the tremendous versatility of Indian bhasha languages in translating and transforming from European novels and Victorian pulp as well as transliterating between our own scripts. But given that pulp fiction is the medium of the masses, Khair problematizes the definition of English pulp fiction in a nation where fewer then 4 per cent (his estimate) speak the language. I am tempted to cite almost every statistic and genre formulation he offers, but I will desist, saying only that this is a tour de force that brings together many of the issues in English language and their intimate connection to literature in the subcontinent that I highlighted earlier. Connecting moments of inception to processes of dissemination, i.e. the muse and the market, Khair flourishes the felicitous turn of phrase that is the highlight of the best of subcontinental scholarship in English. Beginning with nineteenth-century historical romances, and tracing the influences on detective fiction, science fiction and fantasy fiction, Khair finally arrives at Shobha Dé, glamorous model-wife-mother-socialite-columnist, whose spectacular foray into the realm, he believes, coincides with the 'rise of Rushdie' and of a certain kind of Indian urban middle class. Khair correctly points out that Dé's oeuvre transmogrifies her clichéd narratives into acute reflections of the crosscurrents of change in the great Indian middle class. From Dé, Khair moves on to the equally fascinating figure of Sujata Massey, who situates her Japanese American detective within a self-consciously topical and cosmopolitan space and bends the genre once again.

In all, feminist critique was strong in the subcontinent and brought into scholarly limelight necessary texts and archives of increasing relevance in the region. In terms of Indian writing in English, the canonical writers continued to command respect and attention, but not enough work was done on less well-known but significant and emerging writing. Exciting translation work came into being, but again, not enough of it, despite the growing sense in world literature of avenues unexplored.

6. New Zealand

(a) Books
Recent volumes have traced the development of literary biography in New Zealand, a major genre for about a decade, seemingly reflecting a concern for the individual writer above the more theoretical, often nationalistic general-izations of earlier years. In 2008 this development seems to have turned inward, in the sense that there are more autobiographies than biographies to record.

Fiona Kidman, author of some twenty volumes, including novels, short stories and poems, published the first volume of her autobiography, *At the End of the Darwin Road* in 2008. As she admits herself, the early chapters, covering her childhood and a variety of jobs in her youth, show little indication of why she was to be so successful in later life, becoming one of the first New Zealand women to make her living as a writer. Much of it was due to sheer determination and a willingness to take on any kind of commission: journalism, scriptwriting and much more. From the point of view of cultural history, the later chapters are full of matter that reveals how writers' lives were run. For those more interested in Kidman herself, the earlier chapters have much to say about the borderline between fact and fiction. In telling her story she quotes from the novels and indicates what personal events gave rise to their incidents. But the novels are rarely simply a description of fact. Kidman describes how her earliest letters to her mother resulted in her removal from boarding school, which amounted to a discovery that "writing worked" (p. 49). From this point on her urge to write seems to have been unstoppable. Prizes for juvenilia encouraged the trend. From a broader perspective, Kidman's memoirs tell us much about writers of the time. Sometimes, it seems, her life was lived entirely within the literary world; we see a constant series of parties and other social contacts with writers such as Lauris Edmond, Witi Ihimaera, Phoebe Meikle, Denis Glover, Alistair and Meg Campbell and many more, but Kidman also worked vigorously in organizations relating to her writing, such as PEN, the New Zealand Book Council and the Writers in Schools movement. Married to a Maori, she naturally took an interest in the 'Maori Renaissance' of the 1970s and 1980s, but like Michael King, she discovered that non-Maori people, no matter how deep their sympathy, were not always welcomed by those who wanted to develop their own indigenous voices. Historians interested in these matters will find anecdotes and moments of insight in this book but will have to look beyond it for a deeper analysis of the issues.

Greg McGee's memoir, *Tall Tales (Some True)*, also reveals much of the writing life in New Zealand, but from a different perspective and in a very different tone. He employs a brash, sometimes colloquial or even coarse style to tell a masculine tale of writing for theatre and television. Inevitably McGee's one undisputed success, the play *Foreskin's Lament* [1980], occupies a lot of the territory, but since his tales are not always chronological, the play, its production and its aftermath crop up in various parts of the book. The story of the play's journey past sceptical directors, through workshops where it seemed no longer to belong to its author and onto the stage for the resonant first production has much in common with similar odysseys, but in this case it is told with panache and it is, after all, about a play that acquired iconic status almost as soon as it was seen by an audience. McGee clearly has pleasure in the telling, but there are also tales of very hard times and—like Kidman—of indifference from and rejection by entrepreneurs. McGee came close to being a professional rugby player and also acquired, somewhat reluctantly, qualifications as a lawyer. His memoir vividly evokes life in these varied professions from the viewpoint of someone deeply involved in them, yet distanced and (self-)critical as well. There is also much to be learned about the ups and downs of writing for television, and the most exciting passages are those connected with a mini-series on the Erebus aircraft disaster and its terrible aftermath of intrigue and cover-up. How an investigative writer researches such material and the damaging effects it can have on him and his subjects is revelatory. This is not literary criticism, but it tells inhabitants of the ivory tower very clearly what it is like to live precariously as a writer. Closer to the interests of present readers may be the detailed accounts of scriptwriting techniques resulting from the working of a vigorous intelligence on raw experience.

The most conventional of these autobiographies and the one that tells us least about the development of the writer's mind is Barbara Anderson's *Getting There*. Anderson was a 'late starter' as a novelist, and most of her book concerns her life as a wife and mother. Every life is unique, of course, but this one is told in the tone of an upper-class lady and is so lacking in originality (though nicely written) that one feels one has read it all before. In the last chapter Anderson's career as a writer is outlined and we learn of the enthusiastic responses of agents, publishers and critics to her books. All this is externalized, however, and reveals nothing of the inner development towards aesthetic or philosophical understanding.

Despite its title, Elizabeth Knox's *The Love School: Personal Essays* is another writer's memoir, more elegantly written than any of those mentioned above and also more introverted, tracing the development of the writer as a fantasist rather than as a social being, yet rich as well in information about Knox's relationships with family, friends and colleagues. While the others are responses to the question of what it means to be a New Zealand writer, Knox seems to respond more to the question: What does it mean to be a writer at all? This is in keeping with the general tendency in her fiction to ignore purely national issues. In her earliest, more autobiographical work, the level is sub-national—the focus is a specific, narrowly defined locality. In her later work it is supra-national, often set in other countries or, more accurately, in countries of the mind. *The Love School* explains this phenomenon more clearly than any critic could do. The long opening section describes 'the Game' played by the Knox siblings, who, like the Brontës, invented lands inhabited and ruled by extraordinary characters. At various points in their later lives the game was continued, sometimes with the participation of privileged friends. Knox's first (unpublished) novel was about a family with imaginary friends (p. 107). The tendency to take invented figures as seriously as, or more seriously than, the people of 'real life' continues throughout her writing career. Her first published novel, *After Z-Hour*, was inspired by hearing her father speak for the first time of his experiences in the war, but since she did not share that experience her imagination built on the small amount of information he supplied (p. 183). Knox remarks, 'I follow the wandering eye of my imagination and write with the freedom of my insignificance' (p. 202). In a later section of the book (pp. 284–305) she provides excerpts from her diary, all relating to writing and amounting to a rich illustration of her methods and creative thoughts. The book is rounded off with an equally interesting account of how she and various people close to her read. Without a doubt this is the fullest account of a writer's mind and mental processes ever written in New Zealand.

This group of autobiographies is rounded off by yet another well-researched and informative biography: Joanna Woods's *Facing the Music: Charles Baeyertz and the Triad*. Baeyertz was an extraordinary, indefatigable and opinionated polymath who edited his own magazine, *The Triad*, from 1893 to 1915, writing the majority of its content himself. As a writer on many subjects but predominantly on music, Baeyertz was a force to be reckoned with. From 1909 he engaged Frank Morton as co-editor, and it was Morton who was responsible for many of the polemical and uncompromising literary reviews in the magazine. There were other notable contributors of poetry and fiction, their names being a good summary of New Zealand writing at the turn of the century. Woods covers the life of Baeyertz and of the journal with both enthusiasm and critical understanding, making her book a major contribution to cultural history in a period that is relatively unfamiliar to modern readers.

Janet Wilson's short book *Fleur Adcock* is also partly biographical although basically a study of Adcock's poetry, in keeping with the conventions of the Writers and their Work series, to which it belongs. Wilson is often good at analysing individual poems but even better in her overview of the changing themes and their interrelationships through Adcock's distinguished career. Born in New Zealand but spending most of her childhood and early adolescence in England before returning to New Zealand and then, having completed her studies in Classics, returning to England again, Adcock's allegiances and affinities are understandably mixed. Although she has insisted on her Englishness since settling in London in 1963, she has never ceased pursuing her New Zealand interests in her life and work. Wilson analyses this duality with considerable subtlety and traces it in the poetry, although her

argument is sometimes obscured by her ready acceptance of certain theoreticians and their jargon. Questions of 'home' and 'diaspora' are treated in
detail, but Adcock's growing interest in gender issues, travel, ecology and
genealogy are given due consideration in later chapters. Wilson has a clear
view of this complex poet and it is a pity that she does not always convey it
with complete clarity in her own language.

In his MA thesis, now published as *Alternative Small Press Publishing in
New Zealand*, Michael O'Leary offers a perspective on New Zealand literature
that is new to academic studies. In his usage, 'alternative' essentially means
'non-commercial', although he points out that some publishers (such as Steele
Roberts, who actually published the present book) occupy the middle ground,
taking up many titles that the larger publishers ignore but still managing, just,
to survive as a commercial venture. O'Leary traces small press publishing back
to the very origins of writing and distribution in New Zealand. The first item
printed in the country was a six-page tract, *Catechism in Maori*, hand-printed
and distributed by the Reverend W. Yate in 1830. On several levels it could be
called a disaster, but even in this it might be said to found the small press
tradition. In fact standards have varied from the rough and ready to the
extremely elegant with high aesthetic pretensions (and prices). O'Leary divides
the historical overview into three periods: 1830 to 1930, a century of practical
work and tentative exploration; 1930 to 1970, when 'New Zealand publishing
came of age in a literary sense'; and after 1970, a period 'which has seen an
explosion of small press publishers experimenting with many different forms of
typology, technology and literary production' (p. 12). Methods of distribution
have varied from door-to-door sales to hiring professional distribution
companies. The term 'vanity publishing' is discounted by O'Leary, who
claims that virtually all publishing in New Zealand is of that kind in some way,
considering that the 'commercial' publishers accept large state or university
subsidies for their work or for individual items, and he argues that New
Zealand literature would barely exist if it depended entirely on commercial
sales. He is critical of the lack of academic attention to many of the books in
the field he is covering, due to 'various policies of exclusion', and highlights, in
particular, a number of 'glaring omissions' from *The Oxford Companion to
New Zealand Literature* (p. 61). In general, he makes a good case for a more
inclusive definition of New Zealand literature. A very useful part of his book is
a list of the 'alternative small' presses he considers important from a literary
point of view together with a bibliography of their publications, including
names that will be familiar to any reader of the country's literature. This is a
thought-provoking contribution to matters of definition in the field.

The first opportunity for New Zealand writers to devote time to their work
without financial pressure was the Robert Burns Fellowship at Otago
University, granted to the novelist Ian Cross in 1959. The history of this
award, *Nurse to the Imagination: 50 Years of the Burns Fellowship*, has been
compiled by Lawrence Jones in the form of introductions to each of the
winners and an excerpt from the work they wrote while holding the
fellowship. The list of fellows is (mostly) impressive and includes such
luminaries as 'the three Maurices': Duggan, Shadbolt and Gee. Janet Frame,
James K. Baxter, Witi Ihimaera, Sam Hunt, Owen Marshall and Michael King

are some of the other names that shine on the list. Jones is an experienced and knowledgeable commentator, and the book can be read as an excellent introduction to some of the leading writers of the country or as an anthology of work mainly relating to Dunedin. The standard of the Fellows is not uniformly high, but there is much in this book to make its reader want to read more.

For more than twenty years a reassessment of Robin Hyde has been under way, a rehabilitation, its proponents rightly say, after neglect and worse by her own generation of masculinist nationalists, such as Curnow, Glover and Fairburn. The fight is not yet over, partly because the tradition of masculinism still has vocal advocates, but it is surprising to realize that *Lighted Windows: Critical Essays on Robin Hyde*, edited by Mary Edmond-Paul, is the first ever collection of essays on this writer, who is now widely (but not universally) seen as author of one of the founding classics of the modern New Zealand tradition. It is an excellent book of a consistently high standard and adds much to our understanding of Hyde's place in the story of her country's literature. In her introduction Edmond-Paul summarizes the false (because uninformed) image of Hyde propagated by her contemporaries and later writers, and then the changing image of Hyde since the 1980s. It was not only a lack of information about Hyde's short but complicated life and about her many unpublished works that coloured the original image but also the version of national literature that became the conventional standard, with which Hyde's writing was incompatible. The editor and several of the contributors make it clear that story of Hyde's reception is therefore inseparable from the story of New Zealand's (especially literary New Zealand's) view of itself. No less than her male colleagues, Hyde was trying to define the nature of New Zealand life and culture after the disappointment of the casual indifference of Britain to the dominion's enormous contribution to the war against Germany and Austro-Hungary, but her definition differed quite radically from that of the others. It was the international rise of feminism that spurred the rehabilitation of Hyde in the 1980s. But the extensive publication and republication of her work made it clear to discerning readers that she had much to say to men as well as to women and brought about a general realization that her work was greater (both in extent and in substance) than had previously been realized. The collection of works in various genres and the creation of definitive texts has been fundamental to all of this, and Michele Leggott's exhaustive and painstaking work, especially on Hyde's poems, has been crucial. Several of the contributors to this volume are in effect summarizing theses they wrote under Leggott's supervision. After the introduction, the volume opens with three essays on *Wednesday's Children* [1937], now widely viewed as Hyde's finest, 'most intelligent' novel. In 'Turning the Tables: Domesticity and Nationalism in *Wednesday's Children*' (pp. 29–39) Michelle Elleray introduces major themes of the entire book and explains that preconceptions of 'realism' carried over from Hyde's masculine contemporaries can only lead to a distorted understanding of Hyde, who uses levels of imagery, symbolism and sheer fantasy that break the realist mould. In 'Running Ever out of Reach: Carnival and Fantasy on Wednesday's Island' (pp. 41–52) Renata Casertano brings a European understanding of the carnivalesque to illuminate this novel. In Carnival the social conventions that govern daily life are lifted, even reversed, providing relief from the unspoken tensions created by conventional repression and revealing alternative ways of organizing society and conducting life on a personal level. Wednesday's island in the Hauraki Gulf, which her family and friends believe is real but which is actually a fantasy, performs a similar function for New Zealand society. A more political dimension of the novel is discussed by Nadine Attewell in 'No Alternative: Robin Hyde and the Politics of Loss' (pp. 53–66). Wednesday's home-making on her island implies processes of nation-building, and the 'incursion' of a stranger, Mr Bellister, brings about changes and perceptions not unlike those resulting from the invasion of Maori society by strangers from Europe. Hyde provides an astute presentation of New Zealand masculine society in its extreme form in a duology of novels based on the life of a returned soldier she interviewed in prison while herself living in a similarly authoritarian institution, a mental hospital. This is examined by Alex Calder in 'Violence and the Psychology of Recklessness: Robin Hyde's *Passport to Hell*' (pp. 67–72). Starkie, the protagonist of *Passport to Hell* and *Nor the Years Condemn*, is an extraordinarily courageous soldier and a man who shows deep loyalty, affection and even love for his fellow soldiers, but who is also criminally insubordinate and sometimes almost stupidly reckless. Calder shows how Hyde presents Starkie as a unified figure whose positive and negative characteristics come from the same source and have been shaped by a life in tightly disciplined institutions: Marist school, workplace, orphanage, army, prison. The implication is that all New Zealand men are shaped by conformity or non-conformity with such backgrounds. In 'Other Pastures: Death, Fantasy and the Gothic in Robin Hyde's Short Stories' (pp. 73–88) Alison Jeffrey extends the argument about Hyde's non-realistic elements, in this case concentrating on the short stories, a comparatively neglected yet very extensive part of Hyde's prolific output. Jeffrey's thesis, that, far from being varieties of escapism, death, fantasy and the Gothic 'challenge injustices and give voice to aspects often silenced in Western, patriarchal, capitalist culture' (p. 73), is backed up with the analysis of a wide range of finished and unfinished stories. A major contribution, even in this excellent collection, is Diana Bridge's knowledgeable essay on Hyde's China: 'China, Imagined and Actual, in Robin Hyde's *The Godwits Fly*, Two Journal Entries and the "China" Poems' (pp. 89–106). She shows that Hyde was interested in China before she actually went there. The Chinese community in New Zealand figures in *The Godwits Fly* and Arthur Waley's popular translations of Chinese poetry were eagerly absorbed by Hyde and applied to various themes in her work. This provided a basis for her perceptions when she visited Shanghai and was taken by her compatriot, Rewi Alley, to see the battlefields of the war being conducted against Japan. Her reporter's keen sense of observation was combined with her experience as an outsider and her background knowledge to form some of her most effective poems. At the same time a different tradition also informed her work, and this is discussed in Megan Clayton's 'Thoroughly Modern Malory: Robin Hyde's Poetic Ciphers and Camelot Codes' (pp. 107–18). The Arthurian legends fascinated Hyde and provided images of loyalty and betrayal which she could apply to experiences in her own life and the world around her. Susan Ash takes a different approach in 'Archival Poetics: Michele Leggott reads Robin Hyde' (pp. 119–26). She is interested in the driving force that makes Leggott's editorial work so perfectionist and concludes that Leggott is constructing a character, almost as a novelist does, the person behind the poems, and that she does so because of the affinities between Robin Hyde as a disabled woman, an outsider in a male-driven world and herself, also a fine poet who is disabled (by increasing blindness). The apparently objective approach of the archivist and editor assumes a creative dimension. In 'When Iris Meets Eve: An Australasian Friendship' (pp. 127–41) Brigid Magner views the relationship between Hyde (i.e. Iris Wilkinson) and Eve Langley partly as an embodiment of the cultural relationship between New Zealand and Australia. The two women shared attitudes to their literary aspirations, child-bearing and the sense of antipodean exile. Both were also excluded by masculine coteries. Hyde's period in a mental health institution has been referred to briefly already and it is discussed in more detail by Alison Hunt in 'Angel-Guarded Liar in a Pleasant Quiet Room: Robin Hyde's Experiences in the New Zealand Mental Health System of the 1930s' (pp. 143–50). In 1933 Hyde was admitted voluntarily to Auckland Mental Hospital after a suicide attempt. From a modern perspective the treatment was not remarkable; the main impression is that Hyde concealed much of significance from her doctor and was given an opportunity to recuperate at leisure rather than being forced to undergo in-depth analysis and therapy. In 'Novitia the Anti-Novice: Robin Hyde's Parliamentary Reports' (pp. 151–62), Nikki Hessell discusses yet another neglected genre in Hyde's work. As a 'lady reporter' Hyde seems to have played the political ingénue, expressing a distanced, satirical and puzzled view of proceedings—in keeping, Hessell suggests, with the sceptical attitude of her putative readers to the ritual exercise of power in parliament. In a concluding, richly suggestive essay, 'Interviews with a Ghost: Visiting Gunnersbury/Revisiting *Dragon Rampant*' (pp. 163–76), Jolisa Gracewood offers a total reassessment of Hyde's book about her experiences in China. Most readers, I suspect, have shared James Bertram's view, quoted here, that this book is 'fragmentary and chaotic, and not very easy to follow', but Gracewood is able to argue convincingly that this is due to a deliberate strategy reflecting the confusion and constant disruption of the traveller's experience and, more importantly, she demonstrates that it coheres on the level of imagery and symbolism much more than a 'realistic' reading might suggest. This rounds off the themes of the book as a whole very nicely. For example, Hyde's references to her English-made shoes gradually falling apart, which might seem like a piece of whimsy, can be related to her awareness that the English basis of New Zealand life was in tatters, while its position in relation to Asia in general and China in particular was strengthening, at least on a cultural level. The fact that her visit was a diversion gladly taken on a journey towards England (where she was to commit suicide) is characteristic of her own turning away from the 'Home' tradition and her belief that New Zealand should follow her in that. She was ahead of her time in picturing (rather than arguing) the position of her country in relation to Asia, and if we read *Dragon Rampant* in this way its structure is more apparent and it becomes easier to follow.

(b) Journals

The 2008 volume of the *Journal of New Zealand Literature* opens with a tribute to the distinguished literary editor Robin Dudding, who died on 21 April 2008, shortly before the award ceremony for an honorary doctorate from the University of Auckland. He was editor from 1958 to 1966 of *Mate*, a leading literary journal of its time, and this work persuaded Charles Brasch to appoint him as editor of *Landfall* when Brasch retired from that position at the end of 1966. When he was dismissed from *Landfall* by the Caxton Press for 'late delivery', Dudding founded his own journal, *Islands* and, significantly, most well-known writers shifted their allegiance to his new enterprise. When *Islands* ceased publication in 1987, Dudding had completed thirty years as a literary editor—he also worked as a book editor for Auckland University Press. In his tribute, Peter Simpson writes that 'Dudding will be remembered with affection and gratitude by the writers he served and by the country whose literature he did so much to consolidate and nourish' (p. 15).

Even in his title, 'Cathedral Rock: Allen Curnow's Italy' (*JNZL* 26[2008] 16–40), Alex Calder hints at the New Zealand baggage Curnow carried when he visited Italy late in life: Cathedral Rock is a surf-casting spot near Karekare and the perceptions of Florence's cathedral in the poem 'In the Duomo' are blended with that site and the activities around it so that a kind of palimpsest results. This interweaving of places and also of events—for example the slaughter of the Pazzi family by the Medicis after one of the Medicis had been killed in the cathedral is associated with the assassination of Aldo Moro—is typical of the series of poems relating to Italy that Calder analyses. He is able to draw out many interrelationships between these poems and earlier phases of Curnow's work, adding considerably to our understanding and appreciation of this poet. Compared with this, Sarah Shieff's examination of Frank Sargeson's relationship to Italy, 'Risotto with Pipis: Frank Sargeson in Italy' (*JNZL* 26[2008] 41–58), is shallower, but she is able to argue that Sargeson's visit to Italy on his two-month hike through Europe did not result—as a superficial reading might suggest—in his rejection of the European experience as too overwhelming for his sensibilities, but rather in a kind of compromise in which he recognizes and is even saddened by the provinciality of his home but also accepts and explores it. The article that follows this is by Valérie Baisnée and considers 'To Ibiza: Separation and Recreation in Janet Frame's Island Narrative' (*JNZL* 26[2008] 59–72). It exemplifies the risks people take in trying to bridge the gap between theorizing at a relatively abstract level and analysing the actual practice of a writer. Theoretical ideas about islands taken from Eric Fougère, Mario Tome, Tom Conley and Gilles Deleuze are imposed on certain narratives of Frame which are supposed to exemplify them but were written, surely, for quite different purposes. The oft-belaboured Freudian 'heimlich' (uncanny) is dragged out again as a way to dress up banal insights into Frame's narratives. Indeed, stripped of the theoretical *Überbau*, what Baisnée has to say about Frame's writing is commonplace. Similar doubts are awakened by Patrick West's contribution 'Theoretical Allegory/Allegorical Theory: (Post-)Colonial Spatializations in Janet Frame's *The Carpathians* and Julia Kristeva's *The Old Man and the Wolves*' (*JNZL* 26[2008] 73–94).

His opening claim that Frame criticism can be categorized in three classes—postcolonial readings, applications of Julia Kristeva's psychoanalysis and combinations of these two—seems to slight a vast amount of scholarship that studies Frame without any reference to *these* frames (including Baisnée's article just discussed). He says that the second group is smaller than the first, and the footnote reveals that it has indeed only one representative: Howard McNoughton. This makes it hard to accept the following point that the third group is even smaller than the second, and indeed the footnote refers to two scholars, Patrick West himself and Janet Wilson. All this can disconcert the reader before the argument really begins. West prepares his argument at the outset with the words: 'This article argues that spatiality subtends the operations of both theory and allegory, and also that allegory has always already slipped inside the sleeve of theory' (p. 75). How does 'spatiality' here relate to 'spatializations' in the title? If 'theory' refers to Kristeva, 'allegory' must refer to Frame, but this assumes more than many a reader will be willing to do, namely that *The Carpathians* should be read as allegory. This point needs arguing, but West takes us further regardless. West has it that allegory is 'always' embodied in theory (if that is what 'slipping inside the sleeve of' actually means). Such 'always' propositions are the very stuff of theory but they tend to do injustice to the particularity of literary narrative. Sure enough, the following discussion focuses on such weighty things as the Memory Flower and the Gravity Star while leaving aside the narrative motion that bears them along. It is refreshing to move on to the next article, Christopher Burke's 'Turning the Inside Out: Pre-Liberation Literary Worlds in the Works of Frank Sargeson, James Courage and Bill Pearson' (*JNZL* 26[2008] 95–117), which provides some genuinely new insights into the works he discusses and relates them to each other fluently. Burke is concerned with 'pre-liberation' homosexual (gay, queer) writers and the masking techniques they used to be able to write with reasonable honesty in a country that criminalized their sexuality. Burke is able to uncover a variety of techniques in his subjects borrowed from other 'non-normative' issues and applied to a sometimes implicit but often remarkably explicit attack on 'herteronormative regimes of power' (p. 96). This interesting account of reactions to homophobia is followed by an account of aspects of sinophobia, in particular the depictions of Chinese bodies as monstrous, in Kathy Ooi's 'Uncanny Embodiments: The "Lost Chinaman" Hoax and Syd Stevens's *The Image of Ju Lye*' (*JNZL* 26[2008] 118–35). Ooi reminds us that in late nineteenth- and early twentieth-century cartoons and writing, 'Chinese bodies were portrayed as filthy, disease-ridden, mindless beings stupefied by opium' (p. 120). While they were scorned for the dreadful conditions in which they lived (of necessity), they were also feared for their apparent ability to survive where others presumably couldn't. The alarmist reports that New Zealand society would be overrun by huge numbers of Chinese were added to a fear that this ability to survive would lead to their dominance over 'white' New Zealand. They were seen as not really human: Ooi quotes a remark by Charles Ferrall that the prominent teeth of Chinese in cartoons made them look something like rodents. This animalism was supported by *The Lost Chinaman: A Complete Story* [1927] describing a hoax perpetrated by the author, Charles Magnus. A sheep's carcase was dressed to resemble a missing Chinese man and was thought to be his body until the official post-mortem was carried out. The story was taken up in *The Image of Ju Lye*, a play written for the Alexandra Blossom Festival by Syd Stevens in 1960 (revived in 1961 and 1972). The play is replete with sinophobic comments, such as: 'A man can't even walk down the street without getting his feet tangled up with Chinamen' (quoted on p. 124). As Ooi remarks: 'The play constructs the prank as a worthy gesture and makes little attempt to critique it or consider its effect on the Chinese' (p. 127). In fact it is implicitly praised as drawing the (Pakeha) community together. To this day, the play and the incident it portrays are seen as an essential element of local history in Alexandra. This is followed by Ann Pistacchi's 'Te Whare Tapa Wha: The Four Cornerstones of Maori Health and Patricia Grace's *Dogside Story*' (*JNZL* 26[2008] 136–52), which considers Grace's novel explicitly as a political rather than an aesthetic artefact and uses concepts from community health issues and specifically from a report of the Health and Disability Commissioner to discuss character motivation. This issue of *JNZL* is rounded off by six substantial reviews of recent books in New Zealand studies.

Irene Visser's article, 'Exclusion and Revolt in Witi Ihimaera's *Whale Rider*' (*CE&S* 30:ii[2008] 63–74), departs from the more conventional view of the story as an assertion of the power of local myth to restore strength and cohesion to a small, decimated community by treating it as an example of 'feminist revolt'. For this purpose she calls on Julia Kristeva's extension of Freud's ideas about myth to give it social rather than individual psychological significance. On this reading Paikea's breach of tradition is an assertion of the feminine element against its exclusion by representatives of the tradition, notably her grandfather. While connecting with the force of the tradition—the power of the 'whale rider' to (re-)originate the community—the girl breaches that part of it that has acted as an exclusion of the feminine. Another article on Ihimaera, Otto Heim's 'The Interplay of the Local and the Global in Witi Ihimaera's Revisions' (*JPW* 43:iii[2007] 310–22), explores his attempts to resurrect and recast some of his older works after reaching a belief that they supported colonialism in a way he had not intended. The melancholy fact is that novels that appealed to a wide range of readers have been rendered less accessible in this process, largely because the simple narration of 'showing' has been blended, sometimes clumsily, with a didactic 'telling' in an attempt to continue to employ the Maori locale while adapting to the world of globalization. Heim analyses these processes with commendable patience but is unable to defend the writer, in the end, against the charge that his efforts to bridge the local and the global have despoiled the aesthetic effects of the original stories. All this could be seen as an attempt by Ihimaera to connect with the younger world of 'Generation X', where cultural nationalism, obversely reflected in his early work, has been vanishing into the distance in a country that provides little comfort or security to those burdened with student debt and too few opportunities for the employment that could relieve them of it. Patrick Evans astutely examines one literary manifestation of this situation in ' "Men's Fungible Memories": Hallucinated History in Carl Shuker's *The Method Actors*' (*JPW* 43:iii[2007] 311–36). Shuker is one example among many of younger New Zealand writers who have simply (or seemingly) abandoned an interest in their country's affairs by setting their fictions anywhere but there. *The Method Actors* [2005] is set mainly in an expatriate community of Americans, Australians, New Zealanders, Canadians, Dutch, Indonesians and other people living in Tokyo. Its protagonist is a historian attempting and failing to grasp imaginatively certain moments of the past, and especially the so-called 'Rape of Nanking', which becomes implicitly a locus for all violations of a people and a culture by the military forces of another. Rather than penetrating Japanese society or blending its characteristics 'globally' into their own, the characters are lost and confused at the interface between cultures, and the protagonist's efforts grow more confused the further they are driven. Evans analyses this material as well as Shuker's own position with a clarity some of the other essays discussed above could benefit from.

(c) Other

A brief overview of university history is offered by Nicholas Reid in *The University of Auckland: The First 125 years*. It is probably intended for new staff or perhaps students and includes a glance at the poets and novelists who have been or still are on the staff. There is also a summary account of some of the library's treasures.

Janet Frame's novel *Towards Another Summer* was published in 2008, forty-five years after it was written. A hint of why publication was so long delayed is conveyed by Geoffrey Moorhouse in 'Cold Comfort', an article for the *Guardian* [5 July 2008]. It appears that the novel is a fictional account of a weekend spent with Moorhouse and his first wife in February 1983. The Thirkettles, a fictional couple with two children who give the protagonist, Grace Cleave, a weekend in their home, are virtually portraits of the Moorhouse family. In his article Moorhouse traces some of the points of identity and also turns the tables by painting a portrait of Frame as seen by the Moorhouses. When asked why she did not publish the novel during her lifetime, Frame said that it was 'too personal', but, as Moorhouse points out, it is no more personal than practically all her fiction, based as it is on her inner life, and there is nothing to offend the Moorhouses, even though they feel a little regretful at some of the details conveyed in the novel (such as the physical and apparent emotional coldness of their home).

Hong Kong is Pacific rim area where English-language literary life is more extensive than many realize. This is partly because of the inaccessibility of many relevant works. It is fortuitous, therefore, that an online literary journal is now available: *Cha*. Tammy Ho Lai-ming, a co-editor of *Cha* has given an account of its origins and strategies on the Asia and Pacific Writers' Network: < www.apwn.net >.

Books Reviewed

Abodunrin, Femi. *Blackness: Culture, Ideology and Discourse,* 2nd edn. Dokun Publishing House. [2008] pp. 452. $46.95 ISBN 1 5922 1074 0.

Anderson, Barbara. *Getting There: An Autobiography*. VUP. [2008] pp. 334. NZ$50 ISBN 9 7808 6473 5904.

Appleton, Sarah A., ed. *Once Upon a Time: Myth, Fairy Tales and Legends in Margaret Atwood's Writings*. CambridgeSP. [2008] pp. 186. $59.99 ISBN 9 7818 4718 8643.

Armes, Roy. *Postcolonial Images: Studies in North African Film*. IndUP. [2007] pp. 278. £12.95 ISBN 0 2532 1744 X.

Benson, Stephen, ed. *Contemporary Fiction and the Fairy Tale*. WSUP. [2008] pp. 216. $29.95 ISBN 9 7808 1433 2542.

Bode, Katherine. *Damaged Men Desiring Women: Male Bodies in Contemporary Australian Women's Fiction*. VDM Verlag. [2008] pp. 286. €79 ISBN 9 7838 3643 6612.

Bollen, Jonathan, Adrian Kiernander, and Bruce Parr, eds. *Men at Play: Masculinities in Australian Theatre Since the 1950s*. Rodopi. [2008] pp. xii + 215. €50 ISBN 9 7890 4202 3574.

Borch, Merete Falck, Eva Rask Knudsen, Martin Leer, and Bruce A. Clunies Ross, eds. *Bodies and Voices: The Force-Field of Representation and Discourse in Colonial and Post-Colonial Studies*. Rodopi. [2008] pp. xl + 459. €100 ISBN 9 7890 4202 3345.

Brady, Veronica. *The God-Shaped Hole: Responding to the Good News in Australia*. ATFP. [2008] pp. xiii + 128. A$22.95 ISBN 9 7819 2069 1875.

Breiner, Laurence A. *Black Yeats: Eric Roach and the Politics of Caribbean Poetry*. Peepal Tree. [2008] pp. 312. pb £16.99 ISBN 9 7818 4523 0470.

Brennan, Bernadette, ed. *Just Words? Australian Authors Writing for Justice*. UQP. [2008] pp. xvi + 200. A$32.95 ISBN 9 7807 0223 6389.

Cancel, Robert, and Winifred Woodhull, eds. *African Diasporas: Ancestor, Migrations and Borders*. African Literature Association 14. AWP. [2008] pp. 464. $55 ISBN 9 7815 9221 6499.

Chambers, Jennifer, ed. *Diversity and Change in Early Canadian Women's Writing*. CambridgeSP. [2008] pp. 218. $69.99 ISBN 9 7818 4718 7321.

Chanda, Geetanjali Singh. *Indian Women in the House of Fiction*. Zubaan. [2008] pp. 348. Rs595 ISBN 9 7881 8988 4109.

Daiya, Kavita. *Violent Belongings: Partition, Gender, and National Culture in Postcolonial India*. TempleUP. [2008] pp. 274. $54.50 ISBN 1 5921 3743 1.

Devine, Maureen, and Christa Grewe-Volpp, eds. *Words on Water: Literary and Cultural Representations*. WVT. [2008] pp. vi + 206. €22.50 ISBN 9 7838 6821 0491.

Dixon, Robert, and Veronica Kelly, eds. *Impact of the Modern: Vernacular Modernities in Australia 1870s–1960s*. USydP. [2008] pp. xxiv + 308. A$49.95 ISBN 9 7819 2089 8892.

Durdana, Benazir. *Muslim India in Anglo-Indian Fiction*. Writers Ink. [2008] pp. 304. Taka500 ISBN 9 8470 1150 0003.

Edmond-Paul, Mary, ed. *Lighted Windows: Critical Essays on Robin Hyde*. UOtagoP. [2008] pp. 226. NZ$40 ISBN 9 7818 7737 2582.

Felski, Rita, ed. *Rethinking Tragedy*. JHUP. [2008] pp. viii + 368. $65 ISBN 9 7808 0188 7390.

Fitzpatrick, Sheila, and Carolyn Rasmussen. *Political Tourists: Travellers from Australia to the Soviet Union in the 1920s–1940s*. MelbourneUP. [2008] pp. xv + 312. A$49.95 ISBN 9 7805 2285 5333.

Fitzsimmons, Lorna, ed. *International Faust Studies: Adaptation, Reception, Translation*. Continuum. [2008] pp. 320. £75 ISBN 9 7818 4706 0044.

Fraser, Robert, and Mary Hammond, eds. *Books Without Borders*, vol 1: *The Cross-National Dimension in Print Culture*. Palgrave Macmillan. [2008] pp. 224. $80 ISBN 0 2302 1029 5.

Gammel, Irene. *Looking for Anne: How Lucy Maud Montgomery Dreamed Up a Literary Classic*. Key Porter Books. [2008] pp. 312. $21.48 ISBN 9 7815 5263 9856.

Garvey, Nathan. *The Celebrated George Barrington: A Spurious Author, the Book Trade, and Botany Bay*. Horden House Rare Books. [2008] pp. viii + 327. A$64 ISBN 9 7818 7556 7546.

Glave, Thomas. *Our Caribbean: A Gathering of Lesbian and Gay Writing from the Antilles*. DukeUP. [2008] pp. 416. $89.95 ISBN 9 7808 2234 2081.

Godard, Barbara. *Canadian Literature at the Crossroads of Language and Culture*, ed. Smaro Kamboureli. NeWest. [2008] pp. 412. $36.95 ISBN 9 7818 9712 6363.

Gruber, Eva. *Humor in Contemporary Native North American Literature: Reimagining Nativeness*. CamdenH. [2008] pp. 266. $70 ISBN 9 7815 7113 2574.

Gyssels, Kathleen, and Bénédicte Ledent, eds. *The Caribbean Writer as Warrior of the Imaginary / L'Ecrivain caribéen, guerrier de l'imaginaire*. Cross/Cultures 101. Rodopi. [2008] pp. xviii + 487. $140 ISBN 9 7890 4202 5530.

Haebich, Anna, and Baden Offord, eds. *Landscapes of Exile: Once Perilous Now Safe*. Lang. [2008] pp. ix + 273. €41.10 ISBN 9 7830 3911 0902.

Hay, John, John Arnold, Kerry Kilner, and Terence O'Neill, eds. *The Bibliography of Australian Literature: P–Z*. UQP. [2008] pp. xxvi + 994. A$175 ISBN 9 7807 0223 6891.

Heady, Margaret. *Marvelous Journeys: Routes of Identity in the Caribbean Novel*. Caribbean Studies 16. Lang. [2008] pp. 127. $61.95 ISBN 9 7808 2047 6100.

Heiss, Anita, and Peter Minter, eds. *Macquarie PEN Anthology of Aboriginal Literature*. A&UA. [2008] pp. xix + 260. A$39.95 ISBN 9 7817 4175 4384.

Huttunen, Tuomas, Kaisa Ilmonen, Janne Korkka, and Elina Valovirta, eds. *Seeking the Self—Encountering the Other: Diasporic Narrative and the Ethics of Representation*. CambridgeSP. [2008] pp. xxii + 364. $59.99 (£39.99) ISBN 9 7818 4718 6319.

Innes, C.L. *The Cambridge Introduction to Postcolonial Literatures in English*. CUP. [2007] pp. 295. pb $26.99 ISBN 1 5922 1458 4.

Jones, Lawrence, ed. *Nurse to the Imagination: 50 Years of the Robert Burns Fellowship*. UOtagoP. [2008] pp. 250. NZ$45 ISBN 9 7618 7737 2650.

Kato, Megumi. *Narrating the Other: Australian Literary Perceptions of Japan*. MonashUP. [2008] pp. x + 234. A$37.95 ISBN 9 7818 7692 4591.

Kent, Bill, Ros Pesman, and Cynthia Troup, eds. *Australians in Italy: Contemporary Lives and Impressions.* MonashUP. [2008] pp. xi + 248. A$37.95 ISBN 9 7809 8036 1681.

Kerr, Heather, and Lawrence Warner, eds. *Projections of Britain in the United States of America, Australia and New Zealand 1900–1950.* Lythrum. [2008] pp. vii + 72. A$24.95 ISBN 9 7819 2101 3188.

Kidman, Fiona. *At the End of the Darwin Road: A Memoir.* RH (Vintage). [2008] pp. 272. NZ$34.99 ISBN 9 7818 6941 9948.

Kinsella, John. *Disclosed Poetics: Beyond Landscape and Lyricism.* ManUP. [2007] pp. xii + 249. £55 ISBN 9 7807 1907 5582.

Kinsella, John. *Contrary Rhetoric: Lectures on Landscape and Language.* Fremantle Press. [2008] pp. 336. A$29.95 ISBN 9 7819 2136 1050.

Knox, Elizabeth. *The Love School: Personal Essays.* VUP. [2008] pp. 367. NZ$35 ISBN 9 7808 6473 5928.

Komalesha, H.S. *Issues of Identity in Indian English Fiction: A Close Reading of Canonical Indian English Novels.* Lang. [2008] pp. 196. pb £29 ISBN 9 7830 3911 1121.

Kortmann, Bernd, Clive Upton, and Edgar W. Schneider, eds. *Varieties of English 1: The British Isles.* MGruyter. [2008] pp. xxix + 512. pb $29.95 ISBN 9 7831 1019 6351.

Lamothe, Daphne. *Inventing the New Negro: Narrative, Culture, and Ethnography.* UPennP. [2008] pp. 240. $55 ISBN 9 7808 1224 0931.

Lever, Susan. *David Foster: The Satirist of Australia.* Cambria. [2008] pp. xvi + 246. $94.95 ISBN 9 7819 3404 3981.

Maufort, Marc, and Caroline De Wagter, eds. *Signatures of the Past: Cultural Memory in Contemporary Anglophone North American Drama.* Peter Lang GmBh. [2008] pp. 314. $54.95 ISBN 978 90 5201 4548.

McGarrity, Maria. *Washed by the Gulf Stream: The Historic and Geographic Relation of Irish and Caribbean Literature.* UDelP. [2008] pp. 196. $40 ISBN 9 7808 7413 0287.

McGee, Greg. *Tall Tales (Some True): Memoirs of an Unlikely Writer.* PenguinNZ. [2008] pp. 313. NZ$37 ISBN 9 7801 4300 9139.

Mead, Chris. *What Is an Australian Play? Have We Failed Our Ethnic Writers?* Currency. [2008] pp. xiv + 81. $21.99 ISBN 9 7809 8028 0272.

Mead, Philip. *Networked Language: Culture and History in Australian Poetry.* ASchP. [2008] pp. vii + 540. A$28.50 ISBN 9 7817 4097 1973.

Mohr, Dunja M., ed. *Embracing the Other: Addressing Xenophobia in the New Literatures in English.* Cross/Cultures 95. Rodopi. [2008] pp. xvii + 341. $108 ISBN 9 7890 4202 3772.

Muñoz-Calvo, Micaela, Carmen Buesa-Gómez, and Maria Angeles Ruiz-Moneva, eds. *New Trends in Translation and Cultural Identity.* CambridgeSP. [2008] pp. ix + 459. $67.99 ISBN 9 7818 4718 6539.

Murphy, Neil, and Wai-chew Sim, eds. *British Asian Fiction: Framing the Contemporary.* Cambria. [2008] pp. xvi + 418. £79.95 ISBN 9 7816 0497 5413.

Nischik, Reingard M., ed. *History of Literature in Canada: English-Canadian and French-Canadian.* CamdenH. [2008] pp. 605. $90 ISBN 9 7815 7113 3595.

Oboe, Annalisa, and Anna Scacchi, eds. *Recharting the Black Atlantic: Modern Cultures, Local Communities, Global Connections*. Routledge. [2008] pp. ix + 423. $108 ISBN 9 7804 1596 1110.

Olaniyan, Tejumade, and Ato Quayson, eds. *African Literature: An Anthology of Criticism and Theory*. Blackwell. [2007] pp. 774. £91 ISBN 9 7805 2180 8132.

O'Leary, Michael. *Alternative Small Press Publishing in New Zealand*. Steele Roberts. [2008] pp. 152. NZ$49.99 ISBN 9 7818 7744 8164.

Opoku-Agyemang, Naana, Paul E. Lovejoy, and David V. Trotman, eds. *Africa and Trans-Atlantic Memories: Literary and Aesthetic Manifestations of Diaspora and History*. AWP. [2008] pp. vii + 477. $34.95 ISBN 9 7815 9221 6338.

Ouyang, Yu. *Chinese in Australian Fiction 1888–1988*. Cambria. [2008] pp. xix + 531. $139.95 ISBN 9 7816 0497 5161.

Paravinisi-Gebert, Lizabeth, and Ivette Romero-Cesareo, eds. *Displacements and Transformations in Caribbean Cultures*. UPFlorida. [2008] pp. xii + 252. $59.95 ISBN 9 780 8130 3218 4.

Patterson, Anita. *Race, American Literature and Transnational Modernisms*. Caribbean Studies in American Literature and Culture 155. CUP. [2008] pp. 248. $84 ISBN 9 7805 2188 4051.

Peters, Susanne, Klaus Stierstorfer, and Laurenz Volkmann, eds. *Teaching Contemporary Literature and Culture, Volume 2: Novels, Part 1*. WVT. [2008] pp. 292. €24.50 ISBN 9 7838 6821 0859.

Rae, Ian. *From Cohen to Carson: The Poet's Novel in Canada*. McG-QUP. [2008] pp. 388. $95 ISBN 9 7807 7353 2762.

Raji-Oyelade, Aderemi, and Oyeniyi Okunoye, eds. *The Postcolonial Lamp: Essays in Honour of Dan Izevbaye*. Bookcraft. [2007] pp. 418. €19.95 ISBN 9 7820 3070 8.

Rastogi, Pallavi, and Jocelyn Fenton-Stitt, eds. *Before Windrush: Recovering an Asian and Black Literary Heritage within Britain*. CambridgeSP. [2008] pp. vi + 233. $52.99 (£34.99) ISBN 9 7818 4718 4138.

Reid, Nicholas. *The University of Auckland: The First 125 Years*. AucklandUP. [2008] pp. 105. NZ$39.99 ISBN 9 7818 6940 4130.

Reid, Verna. *Women Between: Construction of Self in the Work of Sharon Butala, Aganetha Dyck, Mary Meigs and Mary Pratt*. UCalgaryP. [2008] pp. 359. $39.95 ISBN 9 7815 5238 2424.

Rosengarten, Frank. *Urbane Revolutionary: C.L.R. James and the Struggle for a New Society*. UPMissip. [2008] pp. xiii + 282. $50 ISBN 9 7819 3411 0263.

Rowe, Noel. *Ethical Investigations: Essays on Australian Literature and Poetics*, ed. Bernadette Brennan. Vagabond. [2008] pp. 240. A$30 ISBN 9 7809 8051 1314.

Rymhs, Deena. *From the Iron House: Imprisonment in First Nations Writing*. WLUP. [2008] pp. 146. $65 ISBN 9 7815 5458 0217.

Schneider, Edgar W., ed. *Varieties of English 2: The Americas and the Caribbean*. MGruyter. [2008] pp. xxix + 800. pb $29.95 ISBN 9 7831 1019 6368.

Shackleton, Mark, ed. *Diasporic Literature and Theory—Where Now?* CambridgeSP. [2008] pp. xiv + 199. £34.99 ISBN 9 7814 4380 0136.

Sharrad, Paul. *Postcolonial Literary History and Indian English Fiction.* Cambria. [2008] pp. 320. £64.95 ISBN 9 7816 0497 5604.

Smith, Dorsia, Raquel Puig Campos, and Ileana Cortés Santiago, eds. *Caribbean Without Borders: Literature, Language and Culture.* CambridgeSP. [2008] pp. xiii + 245. £34.99 ISBN 9 7814 4380 0396.

Stierstorfer, Klaus, and Monika Gomille, eds. *Cultures of Translation.* CambridgeSP. [2008] pp. xi + 186. $52.99 ISBN 9 7818 4718 6959.

Stierstorfer, Klaus, and Annette Kern-Stähler, eds. *Literary Encounters of Fundamentalism: A Casebook.* Winter, Heidelberg UP. [2008].

Stovel, Nora Foster. *Divining Margaret Laurence: A Study of her Complete Writings.* McG-QUP. [2008] pp. 406. $95 ISBN 9 7807 7353 4377.

Sturgess, Charlotte, and Martin Kuester, eds. *Reading(s) from a Distance: European Perspectives on Canadian Women's Writing.* Wiβner-Verlag. [2008] pp. 263. €26.80 ISBN 9 7838 9639 6181.

Tate, Andrew. *Contemporary Fiction and Christianity.* Continuum [2008] pp. 176. £24.99 ISBN 9781441161758.

Ty, Eleanor, and Christl Verduyn, eds. *Asian Canadian Writing: Beyond Autoethnography.* WLUP. [2008] pp. 330. CAN$38.95 ISBN 9 7815 5458 0231.

Walters, Tracey L., ed. *Zadie Smith: Critical Essays.* Lang. [2008] pp. viii + 221. pb $34.95 ISBN 9 7808 2048 8066.

Waterston, Elizabeth. *Magic Island: The Fictions of L.M. Montgomery.* OUPC. [2008] pp. 248. $24.95 ISBN 9 7801 9543 0035.

Watson, Tim. *Caribbean Culture and British Fiction in the Atlantic World, 1780–1870.* CUP. [2008] pp. xv + 263. $90 ISBN 9 7805 2187 6261.

Wiemann, Dirk. *Genres of Modernity: Contemporary Indian Novels in English.* Rodopi. [2008] pp. 344. pb £69 ISBN 9 7890 4202 4939.

Wilson, Janet. *Fleur Adcock.* Northcote/British Council. [2007] pp. 141. £12.99 ISBN 9 7807 4631 0403.

Woods, Joanne. *Facing the Music: Charles Baeyertz and the Triad.* UOtagoP. [2008] pp. 247. NZ$ 39.99 ISBN 978 1 877372 55 1.

Theses*

Austen, Veronica J. *Inhabiting the Page: Visual Experimentation in Caribbean Poetry.* Ph.D. University of Waterloo (Canada). [2007].

Barker, Carrie K. *Genealogy and Decolonization: The Historical Novel of the Twentieth Century Caribbean.* Ph.D. New York University. [2008].

Canals, Juan Carlos. *Warriors of the Imaginary in the Contemporary Caribbean (1946–2002): George Lamming (Barbados), Ana Lydia Vega (Puerto Rico), and Patrick Chamoiseau (Martinique).* Ph.D. University of Puerto Rico, Rio Piedras (Puerto Rico). [2007].

Kellough, Gretchen Elizabeth. *Tisseroman: The Weaving of Female Selfhood within Feminine Communities in Postcolonial Novels.* Ph.D. Northwestern University [2008].

Outar, Lisa Eleanor Nadia. *Stopovers and Homelands: Twentieth- and Twenty-First-Century Representations of Indianness in Caribbean Literature and Popular Culture.* Ph.D. University of Chicago. [2007].

Richardson, Jill Toliver. *Narratives of Displacement: The Evolution of the Caribbean–American Transnational Narrative.* Ph.D. City University of New York. [2008].

Romero, Dora Ysabel Marron. *Sacred Powers: Women and African-Derived Religions in 20th Century Caribbean Narrative.* Ph.D. University of Miami.[2007].

Selph, Laura. *Performing the Caribbean Nation: Chamoiseau, Lovelace, and Kincaid.* Ph.D. University of Oregon. [2007].

Shaw, Barbara L. *(Re)mapping the Black Atlantic: Violence, Affect, and Subjectivity in Contemporary Caribbean Women's Migration Literature.* Ph.D. University of Maryland, College Park. [2007].

* All theses appear in *Dissertation Abstracts International* [2008].

XVIII

Bibliography and Textual Criticism

WILLIAM BAKER

Notably absent from this year's account is *Studies in Bibliography*, which is becoming increasingly late in its production. So we begin in alphabetical order of title with *The Beckford Society Annual Lectures, 2004–2006*, edited by Richard Allen. They contain David Watkin's 'Thomas Hope, Designer, Collector, Patron: New Links with Beckford' (*BSAL* [2008] 3–18). Watkin, Professor of the History of Architecture and a Fellow of Peterhouse, Cambridge, considers 'the many links between Beckford and Hope' (p. 4): both were 'early pioneers of the oriental taste' (p. 15). Kim Sloan's '"Amusements of solitude" and "talismans of transport": William Beckford and Landscape Painting in Britain and Abroad' (*BSAL* [2008] 19–52) is the Beckford Society's tenth annual lecture delivered on Thursday, 17 November 2005 at the Travellers Club, 106 Pall Mall, London SW1 (p. 19). Her account is accompanied by interesting black and white illustrations. In her lecture, Sloan hopes 'to make clear ... how crucial and elemental the role of patrons was in this key early Romantic period in the evolution of British landscape in watercolours—how mutually dependent artists and patrons were, not just on a commercial level in the demand and supply of works of art, but in the development of each other's vision and taste' (p. 47). It is accompanied by seventy-two footnotes. Rictor Norton's 'Oddities, Obituaries and Obsessions: Early Nineteenth-Century Scandal and Social History Glimpsed through William Beckford's Newspaper Cuttings' (*BSAL* [2008] 53–72) also has the same number of footnotes and constitutes the Beckford Society's eleventh annual lecture delivered on Thursday, 16 November 2006, also at the Travellers Club (p. 53). For Norton, 'Beckford's scrapbooks provide a handy shortcut to the gay history of this period, and they illustrate the depth of social intolerance during this era. They are valuable for the light they shine both on society and on Beckford's personal life' (p. 69). All in all, publications of the Beckford Society are worth acquiring and may be obtained for £5 in the UK and £6 outside the UK. The price includes postage. Enquiries should be sent to < Sidney.Blackmore@btinternet.com >.

Blake: An Illustrated Quarterly (42:i[Summer 2008]) contains G.E. Bentley Jr's 'William Blake and his Circle: A Checklist of Publications and Discoveries in 2007' (*Blake* 42:i[2008] 4–52). He has received assistance from Hikari Sato

Year's Work in English Studies, Volume 89 (2010) © *The English Association; all rights reserved*
doi:10.1093/ywes/maq007

for Japanese publications. Bentley's account is exceedingly detailed, including three Dutch items, six Flemish ones, nineteen Japanese, six Spanish and scholarship in eleven other non-English-speaking countries. Nineteen doctoral dissertations are also recorded, including one from the University of Madrid and Seoul, South Korea, as well as universities in English-speaking countries. Bentley remarks that 'There were extensive public celebrations of Blake's anniversary. Probably the most lastingly notable of these were two editions of *Jerusalem* published on the same day, Blake's 250th birthday' (p. 4).

The Book Collector is replete with fascinating material. Each issue begins with an extensive review article and there are the usual detailed 'News and Comment', 'Sales, Catalogues, and Exhibitions' and 'Book Review' features in each of quarterly issues. The spring *BC* (57:i[2008]) is largely devoted to a celebration of the sixtieth anniversary of the Folio Society and opens with an essay on the history of its significance (*BC* 57:i[2008] 11–20). Alan Bennett continues the tribute with 'Pictures at an Exhibition: Words Spoken at the Opening of the Exhibition in the King's Library at the British Museum to Celebrate the Folio Society's 60th Anniversary in October 1997' (*BC* 57:i[2008] 37–40). Sue Bradbury, editor-in-chief of the Folio Society, reflects upon her experiences in her 'Words as Well as Music' (*BC* 57:i[2008] 42–52). Neal Street's 'The Designer as Impresario' (*BC* 57:i[2008] 53–8) considers the typography used in the society's productions. Geoffrey Beare's well-illustrated 'Artists as Illustrators' (*BC* 57:i[2008] 59–77) is 'a very limited and partial survey of what the Folio Society has achieved in illustration over the past 60 years'. Bryan Forbes's 'My Tutankhamen Moment' (*BC* 57:i[2008] 79–84) considers what Folio Society productions have meant to him. Mirjam M. Foot's 'A Patron of Bookbinding' (*BC* 57:i[2008] 85–94) reflects upon the society's bindings and is accompanied with some interesting illustrations. David Knott's 'An Edition Binding by George Portbury of Exeter for *A New Treatise on Tillage Land*, 1796' (*BC* 57:i[2008] 97–104) is the hundredth contribution to *BC*'s distinguished series, English and Foreign Bookbindings. In the obituaries in this first issue for 2008, James Fergusson examines the life and work of the bookseller Peter Jolliffe (1947–2007) and Nicholas Barker writes on the life and work of Maud Rosenthal (1909–2007).

The summer issue opens with a lengthy review of 'Shakespeare's World Pictured' (*BC* 57:ii[2008] 191–208) of Heather Wolfe's edition of *The Trevelyon Miscellany of 1608*, which is an introduction to the Folger Shakespeare Library's MS V. b. 232 published in Seattle and London by the University of Washington Press in 2007 and in a collector's edition with '50 copies bound in green velvet, in clam-shell box [and] Limited Edition, 950 copies bound in full cloth'. The fifty copies are priced at $3,500 each and the limited edition at $750 each (p. 208). B.J. McMullin's '"The Cambridge Affair": The Ged-Fenner Stereotyping Venture' (*BC* 57:ii[2008] 217–46) assesses 'the nature and extent of William Ged's contribution to the development of the process of stereotyping in Britain'. Modern preoccupation with this 'effectively began with John Carter's study in 1960'. McMullin concludes that 'My own interpretation of the available evidence is that Ged, disillusioned by the experience, simply picked up his tools and went home, that the failure of the venture was due to the machinations of at least two of the partners, not to the failure of Ged's process' (pp. 217, 246). If *YWES* browsers wish to learn more, they'd better read the whole article! David Batterham's 'Robert Partridge—the Quest for a Corvo Forger' (*BC* 57:ii[2008] 249–54) relates Batterham's meeting with Robert Partridge, an obsessive collector of Corvo, amongst others. G. Thomas Tanselle's 'Additions to the Bibliography of Mitchell Kennerley' (*BC* 57:ii[2008] 255–61) is a record based on his own collection of Kennerley items and adds to Daniel Boice's *The Mitchell Kennerley Imprint* 'published in 1996 as a volume in the Pittsburgh Series in Bibliography' (p. 255). Antony Griffiths's 'An Agreement for Dorat's "Fables" 1773' (*BC* 57:ii[2008] 263–77) introduces and explains the background to the French text which follows 'of the deed drawn up between Dorat and Monory—6 September 1775' (p. 273). Dorat was 'the best-selling author of the day' and Monory a leading Parisian publisher (p. 264). Obituaries include Nicolas Barker writing on 'the bibliographer's bibliographer' Dan Laurence (1920–2008), 'born Daniel Hyman Goldstein in the Bronx in 1920' (pp. 302–3), and Robin Meyers on 'Gavin Bridson (1936–2008)', whose 'bibliographical output in graphic art printing and natural history illustration was prodigious' (pp. 303–5).

The autumn 2008 *BC* opens with 'The Law in Manuscript' (*BC* 57:iii[2008] 335–48). This is an extensive review of Sir John Baker and Anthony Taussig's compilation *A Catalogue of the Legal Manuscripts of Anthony Taussig*, published as part of the Selden Society Supplementary Series in 2007. John Saumarez Smith's 'Dropping Books with Larry McMurtry' (*BC* 57:iii[2008] 367–70) focuses upon the serious bookselling activities of the novelist and provides a glimpse of his 'magnificent private library' (p. 370). Susan J. May's 'The Piccolomini Library: A Monument to Christian Neoplatonism and Early Reform' (*BC* 57:iii[2008] 371–99), accompanied by nine full-page colour figures (pp. 381–8), is a detailed account of 'The Piccolomini Library ... a commemoration of the life of Pope Pius II, a monument to humanism, but also a reminder of a pre-Reformation movement towards reform' (p. 399). This is followed by an all-too-brief account of 'The Dispersal of the Collections of Bent Jeul-Jensen [1922–2006]' (*BC* 57:iii[2008] 400–1), the great collector. There is one obituary in this issue. Nicolas Barker writes on Robert Henry Harling (1910–2008), who worked with Ian Fleming and, in addition to distinguished war work redesigning 'the ailing *Daily Sketch* for Lord Kensley' (p. 448), was also a prolific author.

The final issue for 2008 opens with reflections by David McKitterick on 'Cardiff: An End or a Beginning?' (*BC* 57:iv[2008] 483–500). McKitterick reflects upon the trend of 'Library de-accessioning' (p. 484) and the activities of 'the City of Cardiff Library [which] has been throwing out nineteenth- and twentieth-century books for years' (p. 487). Mark Crosby's 'William Blake's Annotations to Milton's "Paradise Lost"' (*BC* 57:iv[2008] 513–48) provides a fascinating description of one of the 'three books from the collection of the guest curator, Michael Phillips' exhibited at 'the opening of the William Blake Exhibition at Tate Britain in November 2000 ... either owned or annotated by William Blake' (p. 513). The article is accompanied by thirteen black and white illustrations. Thomas R. Adams's 'Defining Americana: The Evolution of John Carter Brown' (*BC* 57:iv[2008] 549–72) is an account by Thomas

Randolph Adams, who died on 1 December 2008, of the evolution of the great library upon which he had such a formative influence. John Saumarez Smith writes on 'Tools of Execution: The Library Sales of Robert J. Vanderbilt and Howard Colvin' (*BC* 57:iv[2008] 573–6). 'Richard Hood, Vellum Binder' (*BC* 57:iv[2008] 577–86) is the subject of P.J.M. Marks's account, accompanied by three black and white illustrations. Christian Coppens contributes 'English and Foreign Bookbindings 101', writing on 'Fancing Fencing: Fencers Bound to Bindings' (*BC* 57:iv[2008] 587–90). Accompanied by two black and white illustrations, this deals with examples of the collecting of fencing books. There are two obituaries. Nicolas Barker writes on 'Milo Cripps, 4th Lord Parmoor (1929–2008)'. Parmoor 'by chance rather than will [took] over the management of Bernard Quaritch, the long-established antiquarian booksellers and publishers in 1972' (p. 617). Christian Galantaris writes on 'Pierre Berès (1913–2008)' (pp. 620–3), the 'Bookseller, publisher, art expert' (p. 620).

The eleventh volume of *Book History*, edited by Ezra Greenspan and Jonathan Rose, contains much of interest to readers of this chapter of *YWES*. In her 'The Cost of Doing Scribal Business: Prices of Manuscript Books in England, 1300–1483' (*BoH* 11[2008] 1–33), Joanne Filippone Overty focuses on the evidence provided by 'quantitative analyses of the book trade during the period 1300–1483' (p. 1). Evidence is drawn in tabular form from 'Books Valued at Hereford Cathedral Library, 1300–1400, in Pence' (table 1, pp. 4–5), the 'Production Costs, London Bridge Antiphoners' (table 2, p. 6) and the 'Production Costs, Peterhouse Manuscripts, Fifteenth Century' (table 3). The fourth table records the 'Production Costs, *Evangeliarium*, Collegiate Church of St. George, c. 1379–85'. There is also a graph of 'Manuscript valuations from Oxford and Hereford, 1300–1483' (p. 11). There are three appendices: 'Appendix A: Inventory of Books Valued at Merton College, Oxford, and Hereford Cathedral Library, c. 1300–1340'; 'Appendix B: Inventory of Books Valued at Merton College, Oxford, c. 1360'; and 'Appendix C: Books Valued at Oxford University by Thomas Hunt, University Stationer (c. 1483)' (pp. 14–25). There is a problem, however. Overty draws upon largely secondary sources. For instance, her third and fourth tables and part of appendix A, appendix B and appendix C are drawn from works published in 1931 and 1885. Unless the present reviewer has missed something, I cannot find any detailed analysis or questioning of these printed sources. There are fifty-nine notes to Overty's essay.

Margaret Schotte's ' "Books for the Use of the Learned and Studious": William London's *Catalogue of Most Vendible Books*' (*BoH* 11[2008] 32–58) contains a very detailed account with extensive notation of a provincial bibliographical text produced between 1657 and 1660. Mark R.M. Towsey's ' "Patron of Infidelity": Scottish Readers Respond to David Hume, c. 1750–1820' (*BoH* 11[2008] 89–124) draws upon selected, hitherto largely unpublished responses to Hume's work uncovered in the National Register of Archives for Scotland. Ross Alloway's 'Cadell and the Crash' (*BoH* 11[2008] 125–48) also draws upon materials at the National Library of Scotland and assistance from the Bank of Scotland to illuminate the cashflow problems which so severely affected Sir Walter Scott and the firm of Constable during the 1825–6 financial crisis.

David Faflik's 'Authorship, Ownership, and the Case for *Charles Anderson Chester*' (*BoH* 11[2008] 149–68) focuses upon a 'little-known pamphlet novel *Life and Adventures of Charles Anderson Chester* (1849)' noted by Roger Butterfield 'in his 1955 bibliography for the Philadelphia writer George Lippard' (p. 149). Information concerning Lippard's pamphlet novel eluded Butterfield and others; however, Faflik has uncovered much. Lize Kriel's 'From Private Journal to Published Periodical: Gendered Writings and Readings of a Late Victorian Wesleyan's "African Wilderness"' (*BoH* 11[2008] 169–98) draws upon the 1891 private journal of Owen Watkins. He was the leader of a group who 'in the winter of 1891 ... embarked on an expedition that would stretch the influence of Wesleyan Methodist Christianity far across the northern boundary of the Transvaal' (p. 171). Accompanied by seven illustrations taken from *Wesleyan Missionary Notices*, it reveals much about the expedition and the transformation of a diary record into publication.

Janice Cavell's 'In the Margins: Regimental History and a Veteran's Narrative of the First World War' (*BoH* 11[2008] 199–220) also utilizes hitherto unpublished materials to document previously recorded matter. The focus is upon the annotations by W.H.R. McQuaid to S.G. Bennett's *The 4th Canadian Mounted Rifles, 1914–1919* (Toronto: Murray Printed Company [1926]). A participant, McQuaid adds a fresh perspective on 'Bennett's narrative, with its focus on the two contrasting poles of annihilation at Sanctuary Wood and courageous perseverance at Passchendaele'. This 'gave a profound meaning to even the limited and dearly bought military victory achieved by the 4th CMR in October 1917... McQuaid's individual emotional and psychological needs' resulted in very interesting responses to Bennett's account (p. 215). Robert Franciosi's 'Designing John Hersey's *The Wall*: W.A. Dwiggins, George Salter, and the Challenges of American Holocaust Memory' (*BoH* 11[2008] 245–74), in common with Cavell, deals with highly traumatic experiences, but of course on a larger scale. In Franciosi's words, this 'work of great size and ambition, *The Wall* posed a formidable and unprecedented challenge to Hershey's publisher'—the house of Knopf—'how to present and market a novel whose very subject, despite acts of heroic resistance, is ultimately a story of mass death, a story American audiences were particularly unprepared to face, not just in 1950 but over the ensuing decades' (p. 248). The article is accompanied by nine revealing, stark black and white illustrations of the typeface, the spine and front cover design, the jacket design, the front flap and other materials, and draws upon the Salter Collection at the Wing Foundation and the Newberry Library in Chicago, George Salter being the jacket designer. Franciosi is to be commended for his incredible research in a deeply moving article.

Trysh Travis's 'The Women in Print Movement: History and Implications' (*BoH* 11[2008] 275–300) is essentially a review article dealing with recent publications focusing upon feminist movements and book history in the United States and to some extend Canada at the end of the twentieth century. The final contribution is that of Matt Cohen writing on 'The History of the Book in New England: The State of the Discipline' (*BoH* 11[2008] 301–24). Again, this may be regarded as a review essay concentrating on recent work in book history, focusing on a specific American region, that of New England. There are other essays which may be of interest to *YWES* readers in this issue of *Book History*. Nicole Howard writes on 'Marketing Longitude: Clocks, Kings, Courtiers, and Christiaan Huygens' (*BoH* 11[2008] 59–89) and Mary A. Nicholas and Cynthia A. Ruder write on 'In Search of the Collective Author: Fact and Fiction from the Soviet 1930s' (*BoH* 11[2008] 221–44).

The *Book and Magazine Collector* (*BMC* [2008]) issues contain much of interest, with coloured illustrations accompanying each article. Mike Ashley's 'Kipling in the Magazines' (*BMC* 290[2008] 25–39) celebrates the centenary of Rudyard Kipling's receipt of the Nobel Prize by examining his magazine appearances. Mike Gent's 'Elvis Presley in Print' (*BMC* 290[2008] 40–56) deals with another age and culture and concludes with a listing of 'Collectible Elvis Publications' (pp. 55–6). The bibliography accompanying David Howard's 'The Books of Dick Francis' (*BMC* 290[2008] 58–69) lists innumerable first editions, omnibus editions, short stories, uncollected short stories and others, including the biography of Lester Piggott. There are apparently four biographies of Dick Francis in existence, one dealing with his career as a steeplechase jockey. Sarah V. Buckley focuses upon 'The Children's Books and School Stories of L.T. Meade' (*BMC* 290[2008] 72–87), and her UK bibliography of Meade's children's books (pp. 84–7) reveals that Mead was prolific. Andrew Payne's 'Northwest Passage 1818 to 1860' (*BMC* 290[2008] 90–104) focuses upon the literature describing the major nineteenth-century expeditions trying to find a way through the Arctic Ocean and a shorter trade route to the Far East. Some of the early works cited by Payne are indeed expensive, for instance Frederick William Beechey's *Narrative of a Voyage to the Pacific and Behring's Strait ... in the years 1825, 1826, 1827, 1828*, published by Henry Colburn and Richard Bentley in 1831, is valued between £2,000 and £3,000.

David Blake's 'The Detective Novels of Colin Watson' (*BMC* 291[2008] 24–31) is the opening article of the February issue and contains a useful 'Colin Watson UK/US Bibliography' (p. 31). Rupert Neelands's 'Soldier Poets of the Great War' (*BMC* 291[2008] 34–57) is accompanied by illustrations from the Imperial War Museum and a letter from Robert Graves dated 24 July 1960 'stating slightly inaccurately that "24 July was the day I died officially—my twenty-first birthday"' (p. 45). Neelands's bibliography is restricted to works by Rupert Brooke, Robert Graves, Siegfried Sassoon, who fetches the highest prices, and Charles Sorley (p. 57). Mike Ashley, in his 'Joseph Conrad' (*BMC* 291[2008] 61–73), commemorates the 150th anniversary of its subject's birth: Conrad was born on 3 December 1857. Ashley's bibliography of Conrad's works (pp. 73–5) reveals that Conrad is expensive to collect. The highest-priced item is *The Nigger of the Narcissus: A Preface* in a privately printed limited edition of 100 copies published in 1902 at £3,000 plus. David Howard's 'Patrick Leigh Fermor' (*BMC* 291[2008] 76–84) celebrates the work and achievements of a Second World War hero and his contributions to travel literature. A neglected, prolific Victorian writer is the subject of Richard Dalby's 'The Crime and Detective Stories and other Adult Novels of L.T. Meade' (*BMC* 291[2008] 87–98). The bibliography at the conclusion of

Dalby's article is by no means confined to Meade's crime fiction, but also lists, with publishers and estimated prices, her 'Other Adult Novels' (pp. 96–8).

The first essay in the March issue, Jonathan Scott's 'New Collectables' (*BMC* 292[2008] 12–15) asses what is worth collecting. Mark Valentine's 'Olivia Manning: A Centenary Tribute' (*BMC* 292[2008] 24–9) pays homage to 'the author of two fine trilogies of 20th-century fiction' (p. 25) and contains a 'Complete UK Bibliography' (p. 29). This reveals that Manning was not a prolific writer who does not, surprisingly, command high prices. David Ashford and Norman Wright's 'Mike Hubbard' (*BMC* 292[2008] 32–44) is the twenty-seventh of *BMC*'s series on 'Great British Comic Artists': the illustrations are at times worth screwing up the eyes to view. There is even a 'Mike Hubbard Price Guide' (p. 44). Mike Ashley devotes his attention to the prolific 'Upton Sinclair' (*BMC* 292[2008] 46–64), whose bibliography contained in the 'Price Guide' concluding the essay is fairly extensive (pp. 59–64). Norman Wright and David Ashford's 'One Hundred Years of Billy Bunter' (*BMC* 292[2008] 66–79) revels in 'an iconic anti-hero who is still universally recognized and cherished one hundred years after his first appearance in print' (p. 67). There is a selected 'Frank Richards Greyfriars Bibliography' (pp. 78–9). David Blake writes on 'The Detective Fiction of Patricia Moyes' (*BMC* 292[2008] 82–102). Richard Dalby's 'Theodore Sturgeon: Grand Master of Fantasy, Science and Sorcery' (*BMC* 292[2008] 91–102) focuses upon 'one of the best loved of all science fiction writers' (p. 90).

The April issue leads with Jonathan Scott's 'New Collectables' (*BMC* 293[2008] 12–15), which focuses upon culinary books. Mike Ashley's 'Weird Tales' (*BMC* 293[2008] 24–37) focuses largely upon Canadian and British reprint editions of the American fantasy magazine *Weird Tales*. Some of the prices cited in his 'Weird Tales Price Guide' for the early issues of the American fantasy magazine are relatively high: for instance, the March 1923 first issue will cost between £2,500 and £3,000. Robin Healey's 'Fifty Valuable Non-Fiction Books in Britain from 1500 to the Present' (*BMC* 293[2008] 42–65) is rather generalized. It begins with Dame Juliana Berners's *The Boke of Hawkynge and Huntynge and Fysshynge*. The 1518 third edition is priced in excess of £130,000. It concludes with John Locke's *Two Treatises on Civil Government* [1690] which will set its buyer back between £20,000 and £30,000. Andrew Thomas's 'Alan Bennett' (*BMC* 293[2008] 68–83), in addition to fascinating illustrations, provides a UK bibliography for this popular writer (pp. 82–3). The rather pretentiously entitled 'The Library in the Body: Collecting Bibliomysteries' (*BMC* 293[2008] 86–101) is authored by 'betweenthelines'. Essentially the author is examining what he/she regards as a 'fascinating bywater of crime fiction' (p. 86). Amongst the authors cited are John Creasey and Robert Barnard. There is an accompanying selected bibliography (pp. 99–101) arranged chronologically in order of publication, beginning with Angus B. Reache's *Clement Lorimer, or The Book with the Iron Clasps*. With twelve illustrations by George Cruikshank, published by David Bogue in 1849, a copy in the original cloth is much more desirable than a rebound one. The article concludes with seven cheaply priced items by Marianne Macdonald.

The May issue celebrates 'Ian Fleming: Book Collector'(*BMC* 294[2008] 22–33) in an assessment by Jonathan Scott. It is followed by Richard Dalby's 'Signed and Inscribed Ian Fleming' (*BMC* 294[2008] 34–5), concluding with a listing of forty-four items in chronological order that 'were the cream of Fleming's collection of 1,000 + titles' (pp. 36–7). Graham Andrews writes on 'The American Rivals of James Bond' (*BMC* 294[2008] 40–55). David Ashford and Norman Wright focus on 'Philip Mendoza' (*BMC* 294[2008] 56–66) in 'Great British Comic Artists No. 28: Elizabeth Goudge' (*BMC* 294[2008] 68–79) Nicola Lisle examines the work of 'one of the most acclaimed female writers of post-war Britain' (p. 68). Richard Dalby contributes 'Jack Williamson: Grand Master of Science Fiction: A Centenary Tribute' (pp. 82–97). Paul Willetts interviews the now out-of-fashion 'Alan Sillitoe' (*BMC* 294[2008] 98–104) and the interview concludes with an 'Alan Sillitoe UK Bibliography' (pp. 105–6).

The June issue contents page contains an interesting misprint, being dated April 2008 rather than June 2008! Mike Ashley writes on 'Conan Doyle in the Strand' (*BMC* 295[2008] 28–43). This is followed by a listing of 'All of Conan Doyle's contributions to the English edition of *The Strand* grouped by volume, but with individual issues cited' (pp. 43–6). In Graham Andrews's 'The American Rivals of James Bond: Part 2' (*BMC* 295[2008] 48–59) the illustrations contain some fairly garish front covers. There is an extensive selected US/UK bibliography of the 'American Rivals of James Bond' (pp. 59–64). Richard Dalby provides a well-written account of 'Thomas Fuller: Divine, Historian & Antiquary' (*BMC* 295[2008] 68–77). I suspect that the prices given for Fuller's copies are on the lower end of the scale, in other words, the buyer would be fortunate indeed to obtain the first edition of Fuller's *The Historie of the Holy Warre*, published in Cambridge by T. Buck in 1639, for under £600. David Howard's 'The Travel Books of Wilfred Thesiger' (*BMC* 295[2008] 78–88) provides useful illustrations of the traveller's travels and a 'Wilfred Thesiger UK Bibliography' (p. 88). David Howard's 'R.D. Wingfield's "Inspector Frost" Books: The 80th Anniversary' (*BMC* 295[2008] 90–7) focuses upon the books rather than David Jason's TV portrayal of the 'slovenly insubordinate policeman' (p. 91). The same writer focuses upon 'William Boyd' (*BMC* 295[2008] 98–106).

The July 2008 issue leads with an article by Stephen Honey with a US/UK bibliography on 'Joseph Wambaugh: Laureate of the LAPD' (*BMC* 296[2008] 28–39). It is accompanied by illustrations of some fairly garish dust-jackets. Nick Hogarth's 'Dickens' Landscapes' (*BMC* 296[2008] 42–61) is the consequence of 'the opening of Dickens Land, an indoor theme park based on his work and situated in Chatham, Kent, the area often seen as the heart of the real Dickens land ... Hogarth highlights the importance of place in Dickens' novels and goes in search of a growing sub-stratum of Dickensian books' (p. 42). Amply illustrated, there is an extensive 'Dickens Land Bibliography' (pp. 55–9) followed by an informative listing of a 'Select Dickens Gazetteer' (p. 60). Hogarth values a four-volume 1861–2 set in good condition of Henry Mayhew's *London Labour and the London Poor* at between £400 and £600. This is probably a gross underestimate, even though a facsimile paperback edition in four volumes was published in Dover in 1968.

Nicola Lisle provides 'Anita Brookner: An 80th Birthday Tribute' (*BMC* 296[2008] 64–73). This tribute to a very fine stylist and novelist is most welcome and probably overdue. Given Brookner's importance, the prices of her first editions seem most reasonable. The same could not be said of the subject of Mark Valentine's 'E.W. Hornung: Creator of Raffles, The Gentleman Crook' (*BMC* 296[2008] 74–83). Valentine's article concludes with 'W.W. Hornung—Complete UK Bibliography' (p. 83): the Raffles books in particular seem expensive. Norman Wright and David Ashford's '70 Years of the Beano' (*BMC* 296[2008] 86–[100]) will recall for some *YWES* readers their childhood. Indeed, 'As Britain's best-loved comic celebrates its platinum anniversary, Norman Wright and David Ashford look at the key characters in the comic's history and consider why *The Beano* has enjoyed such a remarkably long and successful run' (p. 87).

Rosaline Parker writes on 'Aleister Crowley' (*BMC* 297[2008] 26–35). Her article is accompanied by a lengthy 'Aleister Crowley—Bibliography' (pp. 32–5) revealing that Crowley's earliest poetry commands extremely high prices. David Howard's 'The Books of Kazuo Ishiguro' (*BMC* 297[2008] 36–44) is an instructive account of the author of the Booker prize-winning *The Remains of the Day* [1989] and other significant books. It concludes with a UK bibliography (p. 44) revealing that Ishiguro (b. 1954) is not over-prolific, being the author of six novels, several short stories and a screenplay to date. Mark Valentine writes on 'Frank Kingdon-Ward Himalayan Explorer' (*BMC* 297[2008] 46–54), the UK bibliography of Kingdon-Ward's works reveals that his first publication, *On the Road to Tibet*, published in Shanghai in 1910, is a highly priced commodity. Jonathan Scott writes on the better-known 'Stephen King' (*BMC* 297[2008] 56–73): the US/UK bibliography accompanying the article extends for seven pages and is accompanied by some fairly evocative illustrations (pp. 66–73). 'Betweenthelines' writes on 'The Theme of the Crime: A New Approach to Collecting Crime Fiction' (*BMC* 297[2008] 74–80). Arnold Wesker, who was knighted in 2006, is the subject of an essay by William Baker (*BMC* 297[2008] 84–101), accompanied by some illustrations of Wesker rarities from the author's own collection and a UK bibliography (pp. 99–101). Mark Valentine's 'The MS in a Red Box: The Strange Case of an Anonymous Book and the Mystery that Followed' (*BMC* 297[2008] 113–17) recounts a mysterious episode in 1903 when 'the publisher John Lane received a parcel through the post at his London offices in Vigo Street, under the sign of The Bodley Head'. The parcel contained the manuscript of a novel. However, 'the manuscript had no sign of the author, and no title, and there was no accompanying letter' (p. 113).

Jonathan Scott, in his feature 'New Collectables' (*BMC* 298[2008] 12–17) writes on the Scorpion Press. His article includes 'Scorpion Press publications in author alphabetical order' (pp. 15–17). The Irish poet Derek Mahon received the David Cohen Prize for Literature 'regarded as the premiere honour for writers in the UK and ... awarded for a lifetime's achievement'. Mahon is the subject of John Dunne's article (*BMC* 298[2008] 28–38) accompanied by interesting dust-jacket photographs. There is a very useful 'Derek Mahon UK and Eire Bibliography' (pp. 37–8), revealing that a copy in very good condition, first issued in wrappers, of Mahon's first publication

Twelve Poems [1965] is valued at between £300 and £400. Andrew Thomas writes on the journalist Jeffrey Bernard (*BMC* 298[2008] 40–6) and focuses on the 'career of a writer who never actually wrote a book and was constitutionally unable to apply himself to the task of doing so' (p. 40). Most of the photographs accompanying the article show the subject with a glass in his hand! David Howard writes on 'The Crime Novels of Minette Walters' (*BMC* 298[2008] 48–55) and there is an accompanying UK bibliography (p. 55).

William Somerset Maugham is coming back into fashion with the publication of recent biographies by Selena Hastings and Jeffrey Meyers and the release of the latest film version of *The Painted Veil*. Mike Ashley, in his 'W. Somerset Maugham' (*BMC* 298[2008] 58–71), reconsiders, 'probably the most popular of British novelists and short-story writers and certainly among the highest paid' (p. 59). The price guide to Maugham (pp. 67–71) reveals that although he is out of critical fashion, he can still command reasonably high prices, especially in the case of his earlier novels. Richard Dalby writes on 'Early Books on China' (*BMC* 298[2008] 72–9). This is followed by David Ashford and Norman Wright, 'Great British Comic Artists No. 28: Ron Smith' (*BMC* 298[2008] 80–97). Ashford and Wright remind us that Smith provided the illustrations for comics such as the *Adventure*, the *Wizard* and the *Hotspur*. The 'Ron Smith Price Guide' extends for five pages and is a useful guide to British popular comics all published by the Amalgamated Press. Rikky Rooksby contributes a fascinating account of 'Ralph Vaughan Williams, on the 50th Anniversary of his Death on 26 August 1958' (*BMC* 298[2008] 98–107), accompanied by revealing photographs. The 'Ralph Vaughan Williams—UK Bibliography' reveals an active industry in 'Critical Studies on the Music of Ralph Vaughan Williams' (p. 107).

David Howard's 'The Travel Books of Bill Bryson' (*BMC* 299[2008] 28–38) comes accompanied by some rather garish illustrations, especially the opening one with Bryson, seaside railings, the pier and seagulls swooping on his fish and chips. Richard Dalby's 'M.M. Kaye: A Centenary Tribute' (*BMC* 299[2008] 40–8) is devoted to 'the undisputed doyenne of the Indian historical novel' (p. 40). The UK bibliography reveals that M.M. Kaye mainly produced crime and detective novels rather than the novel for which she is best known, partly through its television adaptation, *The Far Pavilions* [1978]. David Howard's 'The Books of Beryl Cook' (*BMC* 299[2008] 50–60) celebrates the life and work of the painter and illustrator of the foibles of British working-class life. Mike Ashley's 'Beatrice Grimshaw: Queen of the South Seas' (*BMC* 299[2008] 62–71) celebrates 'one of the best-selling woman writers in the world' (p. 63). Her bibliography (pp. 70–1) shows that from the last decade of the nineteenth century through to the late 1930s she was fairly prolific, although 'she died in poverty in 1953' (p. 63). Mark Valentine writes on 'Frank Baker: A Centenary Tribute' (*BMC* 299[2008] 73–80). Baker 'had a great success with his 1940 novel *Miss Hargreaves*, about two young men who invent a poet for fun, giving her all sorts of unlikely attributes. The snag is that she then seems to come to life' (p. 73). Baker's (1908–82) work has now disappeared into obscurity. For Valentine, it and Baker's autobiography 'deserves to be better appreciated for [their] closely observed and compelling cast of real characters

... subtle and inventive handling of fantasy and humour, and that constant sense of being in the company of a keen, curious and sensitive mind' (p. 80).

Another forgotten figure, George Richmond Samways, who 'died at the age of 101 on 8 August 1996' (p. 83) is the subject of an article by David Whitehead (*BMC* 299[2008] 82–93). Samways's chief claim to fame is his contribution to the *Greyfriars Holiday Annuals*, the *Greyfriars Herald St. Jim's Gazette*. 'Great British Comic Artists No. 30' (*BMC* 299[2008] 94–106) is the subject of David Ashford and Norman Wright's essay on Frank Humphris: 'Of all the British artists who have tackled the Western comic strip, there are few who have equalled Frank Humphris, not simply for his ability, which was substantial, but most of all for his unsparing attempts at historical accuracy' (p. 94).

'Alice and her imitators ... For a book that's often called "inimitable," *Alice* has a surprisingly large number of imitators. Nick Hogarth sifts the evidence and wonders whether today's distortions of Alice will take over from the real thing' (p. 24). Hogarth's account (pp. 24–40) contains a six-page 'Collecting Carrolliana: Alice and her Imitators Bibliography' (*BMC* 300 [2008] 34–42). Andrew Thomas's 'Dowsing' (*BMC* 300[2008] 44–56) discusses the literature of 'the ancient practice of dowsing ... or divining' (p. 45) and contains 'Books on Dowsing—Bibliography' (pp. 55–6). Nicola Lisle assesses 'A Hundred Years of Mills & Boon' (*BMC* 300[2008] 74–83) and concludes with 'Mills and Boon—Selected UK Bibliography' (pp. 81–3). 'George Bellaris was the pseudonym adopted by the banker Harold Blundell (1902–85) for his 58 novels written between 1941 and 1980. Less well known are the four books written under his other bye line Hilary Landon' (p. 84). David Blake writes on 'George Bellaris: The Banker of Crime' (*BMC* 300[2008] 84–92). 'George Bellaris—UK/US Bibliography' (pp. 90–2) reveals that Blundell was prolific: his archival material is now at the John Rylands Library, University of Manchester. Richard Dalby's 'Alexander Solzhenitsyn (1918–2008)' (*BMC* 300[2008] 94–105) considers the great Russian author's life and work, and the bibliography enumerates his work translated into English (pp. 104–5)

The December 2008 issue contains regular features, such as 'In the Sale Rooms', which opens all the other *BMC*s. The opening article is Richard Dalby's 'Kenneth Grahame's *The Wind in the Willows*: A Centenary Tribute' (*BMC* 301[2008] 18–30), which is accompanied by a UK/US bibliography and some fine illustrations. Barry Forshaw writes on the prolific American writer 'James Lee Burke' (*BMC* 301[2008] 32–40). Richard Dalby provides 'John Milton (1608–1674): A Quartercentenary Tribute' (*BMC* 301[2008] 42–53). David Howard pens 'The Books of Timothy Mo' (*BMC* 301[2008] 54–63), including a UK bibliography revealing that 'never prolific, his 30 years as a novelist have produced just six books' (p. 54). For those *YWES* readers who are punsters, Andrew Thomas's 'Jockeys' (*BMC* 301[2008] 66–79) will be of interest. Jeff Brooks's 'Classics Illustrated' (*BMC* 301[2008] 82–8) is an account of the history of the graphic novel series Classics Illustrated. Derek Collett provides an illuminating account of 'Nigel Balchin' (*BMC* 301[2008] 90–102) with a UK bibliography (p. 102).

The Christmas 2008 issue, in addition to heralding a new producer for the journal, contains Mark Valentine on 'Kenneth Gandar-Dower

(1908–44): Explorer and Eccentric' (*BMC* 302[2008] 18–24). Rosalie Parker writes on the great Margaret Atwood (*BMC* 302[2008] 26–37). The accompanying bibliography (pp. 34–7) reveals that Atwood is prolific, and draws attention also to her poetry. David Howard gives an account of 'The Books of James Herriot' (*BMC* 302[2008] 40–9). Jonathan Scott contributes '100 Great Collectables: Part One' (*BMC* 302[2008] 52–67). Each is accompanied by an illustration. Scott's number 100 is Ronald Searle's *Down with Skool* [1953] and his fiftieth collectable is H.P. Lovecraft's *The Outsider and Others* [1939]. According to Scott, the Searle in fine condition will cost £30 and the Lovecraft between £1,000 and £1,500. Richard Dalby gives an account of Willy Pogány: Artist and Master Designer of the Christmas "Books Beautiful"' (*BMC* 302[2008] 70–87). The bibliography of Pogány's illustrated books extends over five pages. Peter Berresford Ellis, who uses the pseudonym Peter Tremayne for his fiction writing, writes interestingly on 'A Reflection of Ghosts: The Life of Dorothy Macardle 1889–1958' (*BMC* 302[2008] 90–103).

James E. May's *The Eighteenth-Century Intelligencer* (edited for the East-Central American Society for Eighteenth-Century Studies) appeared with its usual three numbers for 2008, new series, volume 22 (nos. 1–3: January, May and September, separately paginated). The first number begins with 'The Publication History of Lord Chesterfield's Letters to his Godson' by Christopher Mayo (*ECIntell* 22:i[2008] 1–16), who is editing Chesterfield's letters. Confusion has long occurred between Chesterfield's first series of letters to his illegitimate son and this second to his 'distant cousin, godson, adopted son, and heir', another Philip. The manuscripts have also been confusingly archived, but Mayo distinguishes the materials and reattributes '*Letters from a Celebrated Nobleman* from Lord Bolton to Lord Chesterfield', while attributing '41 newly located letters to Chesterfield'. One of these is reproduced here. Three appendices offer 'Passages Expurgated from Chesterfield's Letters to his Godson', 'Unpublished Passages from the Final Draft of Chesterfield's Letter Delivered, after his Death, to his Godson' and 'Identification of Letters and Fragments in Letters from a Celebrated Nobleman'. Scott Paul Gordon contributed 'Lehigh University Press' (*ECIntell* 22:i[2008] 16–19), an account of the press he directs, emphasizing its eighteenth-century studies publications and noting its innovative projects series, Digitized Scholarly Editions. Various reviews, announcements, obituary notices and other 'news' precedes an index for *ECIntelligencer* volumes 19–21[2005–7].

The May number begins with 'The Mighty Cavern of the Past' (*ECIntell* 22:ii[2008] 1–8), the 2007 EC/ASECS Presidential Address, by Kevin Joel Berland, a survey of literature on caves and contemporary conjectures about their origins and relation to earthquakes and of early tourist literature for caves. In 'ECCO and the Future of Eighteenth-Century Studies' (*ECIntell* 22:ii[2008] 8–13), Corey E. Andrews offers complaints, reflections and proposals in the face of the growing importance of ECCO, that is, the Eighteenth Century Online Collection from Gale Cengage, a proprietary database found 'too expensive for many medium-sized universities and small colleges', for which Gale 'has no immediate plans to offer a subscription service for individual scholars who haven't got ECCO'. Andrews encourages these scholars 'to create their own digital archives, producing searchable texts in a non-proprietary format for universal use' (p. 13). He also suggests some myths about or exaggerations of ECCO's utility. In 'The Gerald Coke Handel Collection at the Foundling Museum' (*ECIntell* 22:ii[2008] 13–19), Katharine Hogg, the collection's librarian, introduces to scholars this library at 40 Brunswick Square, London. She first sketches Handel's support for the home to abandoned children, as through benefit concerts. Hogg's next focus is Gerald Coke (1907–90), who collected Handel material for over sixty years and whose collection of libretti, manuscripts, books and the like is now in the Foundling Museum. The museum displays its treasures to visitors, but scholars can work on the materials, aided by a new online catalogue (see < www.foundlingmuseum.org.uk >). The next article is another survey of resources, 'Eighteenth-Century Imprints in the Art Research Library of the National Gallery of Art, Washington' (*ECIntell* 22:ii[2008] 20–22), by Dr John P. Heins, a cataloguer at the library. Established with the National Gallery of Art in 1941, 'the Art Research Library has developed into a major art research center with substantial resources benefiting not only the Gallery's curatorial staff, but also visiting scholars and members of the general public with an interest in art-historical research' (p. 20). Among its 350,000 books, periodicals and documents on the history, theory and criticism of art and architecture are over 2,000 pre-1800 titles, including over 250 eighteenth-century auction catalogues, plus the holdings of the Department of Prints and Drawings, which also collects books. Books in Italian and French make up nearly half the early holdings.

In a review essay entitled 'Discovering and Cataloguing Franklin's Books' (*ECIntell* 22:ii[2008] 25–30), treating Kevin J. Hayes's revision of Edwin Wolf, II's *The Library of Benjamin Franklin* [2006], Yvonne Noble begins by recollecting Wolf's project in the late 1950s, when she was on the staff creating that first catalogue of Franklin's library. The new catalogue, like the first, 'brings together titles that have been identified through provenance, by shelfmarks, inscriptions, annotation, lists like Benny Bache's, the Nannie T. Bache sale catalogue, accession records of Philadelphia institutions, records of individuals who bought heavily from Dufief, and writings by and to Franklin and his family in Franklin Papers files and elsewhere'. Surprisingly, a full four-fifths of Franklin's copies of these titles have been located, although this leaves 'approximately 750 potentially to be found' (pp. 28–29). Bibliographical and textual work reviewed in the May issue include *Tobias Smollett, Scotland's First Novelist: New Essays in Memory of Paul-Gabriel Boucé*, edited by O.M. Brack Jr [2007], reviewed by Christopher D. Johnson (pp. 31–34); Richard B. Sher's *The Enlightenment and the Book: Scottish Authors and their Publishers in Eighteenth-Century Britain, Ireland, and America* [2007], reviewed by O.M. Brack Jr. (pp. 34–37); Steve Newman's *Ballad Collection, Lyric and the Canon: The Call of the Popular from the Restoration to the New Criticism* [2007], reviewed by Corey Andrews (pp. 37–39); *The Cambridge Companion to Frances Burney*, edited by Peter Sabor [2007], reviewed by Mascha Gemmeke (pp. 39–43); and William Baker's *Critical Companion to Jane Austen: A Literary Reference to her Life and Work* [2008], reviewed by Ellen Moody (pp. 43–46).

The September issue begins with an textual and attribution study by O.M. Brack Jr, 'Samuel Johnson's 'Life of Boerhaave': Texts New and Old' (*ECIntell* 22:iii[2008] 1–10). Brack tracks additions and partial reprintings follow the first publication in the *Gentleman's Magazine* (January through April 1739), as in Robert James's *Medicinal Dictionary* [1743], both attributed solidly to Johnson. But he rules against Johnson's responsibility for a version reprinted with alterations in the *Universal Magazine* for February and March 1752 and for 'Passages', a short abstract of the 'Life' published in the *London Chronicle*, 12–14 December 1758. Brack also finds that in 'only three significant places in the 'Life of Boerhaave' does Johnson add information and reflections that do not seem to have a direct basis in his source (Schultens's *Oratio academica in memoriam Hermanii Boerhaavii*)' (p. 6). In '*Eighteenth-Century Audio*' (*ECIntell* 22:iii[2008] 11–13), Marie E. McAllister describes a new internet site that 'indexes every recording of an eighteenth-century poem located to date' (p. 11), and also hosts about fifty original recordings made by undergraduates at Martha Washington University (< http://ecaudio.umwblogs.org >). Reviews of note include Peter M. Briggs's review of W.B. Gerard's *Laurence Sterne and the Visual Imagination* [2006] (pp. 18–20); Mary Jane Chaffee's of Claire Brock's *The Feminization of Fame, 1750–1830* [2006] (pp. 28–31); and Elizabeth Powers's—within a review essay—of Elizabeth Eger and Lucy Pelz, eds., *Brilliant Women: 18th-Century Bluestockings* [2008], published by Yale University Press (pp. 34–36), in part as a catalogue for the exhibition with that title at the National Portrait Gallery in London.

Three issues of the interesting *Journal of Scholarly Publishing* have come to attention published in 2008. Beth Luey's 'A Different Kind of Profession: The Council of Editors of Learned Journals Keynote Address, MLA Convention 2006' (*JScholP* 39:ii[2008] 93–108) is based upon her keynote address to the 2006 meeting of the Council of Editors of Learned Journals in which she sensibly discusses the qualities necessary in journal editing. Elizabeth Le Roux and Francis Galloway's 'Assessing the Demand for Scholarly Publishing in South Africa' (*JScholP* 39:ii[2008] 109–27) is based upon 'an exploratory study ... undertaken to assess the demand for scholarly publishers based in South Africa but serving the continent as a whole'. Contrary to expectations, the survey 'explodes the myth of the African publisher as the site of last resort for academic authors' (p. 109). Jean-Pierre V.M. Hérubel's 'Historical Scholarship, Periodization, Themes and Specialization: Implications for Research and Publication' (*JScholP* 39:ii[2008] 144–55) asserts that 'within the scholarly communication system, historical scholarship represents a burgeoning and evolving intellectual topography'. The author's 'discussion attempts to frame historical research and scholarship within a contextual disciplinary environment where specialization and the use of historical periodization and discrete themes reflect necessary conditions of historical research and scholarship' (p. 144). The eminent indexer Hazel K. Bell, in her 'Editors and Copy Editors in Fiction: Taking a Carpet-Sweeper to the Jungle' (*JScholP* 39:ii[2008] 156–67), 'considers the various types of editors and copy editors presented in fiction: the conscientious, the compulsive, the stereo-typical, the Cinderellas, the ruthless, the arrogant, and the power-abusers'

(p. 156). This fascinating article draws upon material from P.D. James, Herman Wouk, Barbara Pym and Margaret Atwood amongst others. In his 'Sinners Well Edited' (*JScholP* 39:ii[2008] 168–73), Adam A.J. Deville cogently argues that 'It is not possible to blame "technology" for the inability of many academics to write well, because most of today's faculty were trained before the advent of cell phones and computers' (p. 168). William W. Savage Jr's 'The Transom: Too Many Cookbooks Spoil the Stupor' (*JScholP* 39:ii[2008] 181–5) takes the devil's advocate line, arguing that 'really good manuscripts' do find a publisher rather than 'fail to find a place on some press's seasonal list because they were crowded out by cookbooks' (p. 184).

Margaret Stieg Dalton's 'The Publishing Experiences of Historians' (*JScholP* 39:iii[2008] 197–240) contains the results of a questionnaire aimed at obtaining 'the views of scholars on the so-called crisis of the scholarly monograph'. The major conclusions include the sense that 'the refereeing process is considered essential and that it accomplishes its purposes successfully; that there exists widespread reluctance to publish in a format that is available only electronically; that the emphasis on the bottom line in university presses has had an impact on the topic historians have chosen to investigate and so on' (p. 197). 'Appendix A' consists of the questionnaire, which was extensive, and it also includes responses (pp. 225–40). Historical scholarship but with relevance to scholarship in English studies is also the subject of Jean-Pierre V.M. Herubel's 'Acknowledging Clio's Lesser Children: The Importance of Journals for Historical Research and Scholarship' (*JScholP* 39:iii[2008] 241–56). The author's 'discussion has attempted to articulate the importance of history journals, their proliferation, and their place within the larger spectrum of scholarly publication in history' (p. 254). Another useful but short article is Stephen K. Donovan's 'Publication and Diversity' (*JScholP* 39:iii[2008] 294–300), which all too briefly considers the multiplicity of 'the range of potential outlets for academic publishing' (p. 294). All of us can benefit from another short article, this time by Brian Martin entitled 'Writing a Helpful Referee's Report' (*JScholP* 39:iii[2008] 301–6). Martin concludes 'a helpful report is orientated towards building on strengths and improving weak points' (p. 304). Based in Australia, he does not take into account cultural differences say between Britain and the United States of America. These are also not considered in his follow-up 'Surviving Referees' Reports' (*JScholP* 39:iii[2008] 307–11).

Robert Hauptman's 'Authorial Ethics: How Writers Abuse their Calling' (*JScholP* 39:iv[2008] 323–53) 'offers theoretical grounding and details of specific cases from the humanities (life-writing), social sciences (psychology), and hard sciences (biomedicine)' on 'the many ethical arrogations that can occur' (p. 323). There is an un-annotated, alphabetically arranged appendix containing a 'Bibliography on Authorial Ethics' (pp. 348–53). Unfortunately, Hauptman does not consider the instances of eminent readers for distinguished university presses who, for instance, might wish to retain their own high position on the pedestal by detracting from the labours of those whom they consider to be potential rivals. Hopefully, that can be a subject for another article in the *Journal of Scholarly Publishing*. Counterfactuality is the subject of David Henige's 'The Alchemy of Turning Fiction into Truth

Calling' (*JScholP* 39:iv[2008] 354–72). Each issue of the *Journal of Scholarly Publishing* contains short essays by William W. Savage Jr, who plays the role of devil's advocate in various matters. See for instance his 'The Transom: The Man who Wrote Himself to Death' (*JScholP* 39:iii[2008] 312–17) and 'The Transom Vanity Fare Calling' (*JScholP* 39:iv[2008] 428–34).

JScholP (40:i[2008]) leads with Cecile M. Jagodzinki's 'The University Press in North America: A Brief History' (*JScholP* 40:i[2008] 1–20), which is an all too brief account. Jagodzinski concludes that 'despite the financial pressures ... university presses continue to represent a significant proportion of book publishing in the United States'. Indeed, 'between 1995 and 2005, the number of new titles issued by university presses increased 14 per cent' (p. 16). Rebecca Ann Bartlett's 'University Presses 2008: A Snapshot in Time' (*JScholP* 40:i[2008] 21–39) is a compilation of a forum conducted by an eminent *Choice* editor on university presses. It includes observations by Holly Carver, director of the University of Iowa Press, Malcolm Litchfield, director of Ohio State University Press, Penny Kaiserlian, director of the University of Virginia Press, Pat Soden, director of the University of Washington Press, Sheila Leary, director of the University of Wisconsin Press and Phil Pochoda, director of the University of Michigan Press. It is followed by Rebecca Ann Bartlett and Tom Radko's compilation of 'Significant University Press Titles for Undergraduates, 2007–2008' (*JScholP* 40:i[2008] 40–65), arranged in alphabetical order of university presses, beginning with Akron and concluding with Yale. Hooman Estelami, Albert N. Greco and Robert M. Wharton's 'The Scholarly Book Buyer's Decision Process: A National Survey of University Faculty Members in the United States' (*JScholP* 40:i[2008] 66–96) 'reports on a national survey of university faculty members in the United States regarding the factors that influence their purchases of scholarly books' (p. 66). They conclude that 'The primary decision factor in the purchase of scholarly books for research use is the content of the book, as reflected in the topic, content, and reputation of the author. Factors such as publication date, price, length of book, and publisher are far less relevant in determining book purchase decisions' (p. 91). In a fairly detailed article, Sanford G. Thatcher, 'On the Author's Addendum' (*JScholP* 40:i[2008] 97–115), explores the implications of the ' "take back the copyrights" ' movement within universities in reaction to the so-called serials crisis in scholarly publishing' (p. 97). As usual, William W. Savage Jr contributes a provocative essay, in this instance, 'The Transom in Hoc Gizmo Vinces' (*JScholP* 40:i[2008] 116–22), which in spite of its slick title is in effect a warning about the perils of digitalization. Each issue also contains useful reviews, some of which are relevant to readers of *YWES*.

The Library continues to produce on a regular basis articles of considerable interest. Alison Wiggins's 'What Did Renaissance Readers Write in their Printed Copies of Chaucer?' (*Library* 9:i[2008] 3–36) contains a fascinating survey of marginalia and readers' markings in fifty-four copies of Chaucer printed during the Renaissance. Wiggins's conclusions are of considerable interest, revealing from the evidence that Chaucer's eminence influenced and was a source of inspiration for his Renaissance readers. Judith Milhous and Robert D. Hume's 'One Hundred and Thirty-Seven Neglected English Play Manuscripts in the British Library (c. 1770–1809), Part I' (*Library* 9:i[2008]

37–61) examines Coventry Patmore's 1864 presentation at the British Museum of 137 play manuscripts and fragments primarily submitted to R.B. Sheridan for Drury Lane production, covering the period 1776–1809. Of these 109 are not recorded by Allardyce Nicoll in his *Handlists of English Drama*. B.J. McMullin's 'Machine-Made Paper, Seam Marks, and Bibliographical Analysis' (*Library* 9:i[2008] 62–88) clearly examines the production of machine-made paper in the British Isles before the middle of the 1830s. The focus is upon the implications of the construction of the Fourdrinier paper-making machine. Henk Dragstra's 'Between Customer and Court: *A Brief Abstract of the Genealogie and Race of All the Kynges of England and its Lost Source*' (*Library* 9:ii[2008] 127–57) discusses Godet's lengthy series of portraits of English monarchs to the middle of the sixteenth century, starting with William the Conqueror. Some of these accounts are in Dutch, and Dragstra is concerned to examine the accuracy of the Dutch translations and their sources. His article sheds considerable light upon attitudes to English monarchs during the middle of the sixteenth century. Judith Milhous and Robert D. Hume's 'One Hundred and Thirty-Seven Neglected English Play Manuscripts in the British Library (c. 1770–1809), Part II' (*Library* 9:ii[2008] 158–96) focuses upon those plays not recorded by Allardyce Nicoll.

Arthur Freeman's 'Everyman and Others, Part I: Some Fragments of Early English Printing, and their Preservers' (*Library* 9:iii[2008] 267–305) is concerned with the collection and identification of the printed fragments of early English and the ways in which they contributed to printing history and to the establishment of literary texts. The first part of his two-part essay is concerned with the chronology of the preservation of artefacts, and encompasses late seventeenth-century antiquarians such as John Bagford, the so-called 'new bibliographers' of the earliest years of the last century, and figures such as Sir John Fenn, Philip Bliss, J.O. Halliwell-Phillipps, Henry Bradshaw, E. Gordon Duff, Robert Proctor and a host of others. Paul Dyck's ' "A New Kind of Printing": Cutting and Pasting a Book for a King at Little Gidding' (*Library* 9:iii[2008] 306–33) is a detailed description of the Ferrar family harmonized gospel, which they made at Little Gidding for King Charles I in around 1635. Specific attention is paid in Dyck's account to the textual materials utilized in the book's creation, the identification of the specific editions used, and the work's layout and apparatus. David Wallace Spielman's 'Sir Robert Howard, John Dryden, and the Attribution of *The Indian-Queen*' (*Library* 9:iii[2008] 334–48) examines the question of who wrote *The Indian-Queen*, first performed in 1664: was it Sir Robert Howard or John Dryden? Spielman demonstrates that the case for attributing the work solely to Dryden has no factual basis and that Dryden did not claim the work. Spielman concludes that the evidence comes down in favour of Howard as the principal author.

The Library 9:iv opens with Daniel Wakelin and Christopher Burlinson's 'Evidence for the Construction of Quires in a Fifteenth-Century English Manuscript' (*Library* 9:iv[2008] 383–96). This is an account of conservation work recently carried out at St John's College, Cambridge, MS S.54 relating to a collection of Middle English carols and lyrics from the late fifteenth century and revealing 'that what had seemed to be separate bifolia were in fact quadrifolia, with further evidence suggesting that the quadrifolia derived from octofolia, or pages created by folding sheets three times and only then cutting them apart' (abstract). Arthur Freeman's 'Everyman and Others, Part II: The Bandinel Fragments' (*Library* 9:iv[2008] 397–427) focuses less on personalities than on a collection assembled by the librarian at the Bodleian Bulkeley Bandinel (1781–1861). Of the fragments in the collection, eight are taken from books not in the STC: a fascinating discovery. Oliver Pickering's note on 'Two Pynson Editions of the Life of St. Katherine of Alexandria' (*Library* 9:iv[2008] 471–8) focuses upon the activities of Richard Pynson and his printing of a fragmentary life of St Katherine. Utilizing fragments in a book in Ripon Cathedral Library, Pickering sheds new light on the make-up and type-ornaments of Pynson's printing efforts. As usual, each issue of *The Library* contains short but comprehensive reviews of recent work in bibliography, textual history, and the history of the book.

Library History continues to publish articles of interest to *YWES* readers. Archie L. Dick's ' "Blood from Stones": Censorship and the Reading Practices of South African Political Prisoners, 1960–1990' (*LH* 24:i[2008] 1–22) draws upon 'The jail diaries, authorized biographies, autobiographies, prison memoirs, interviews, and prison letters of more than fifty political prisoners and two prison censors' in order 'to describe the reading practices of South African political prisoners' (p. 1). He concludes: 'There is little doubt that some of the prisoners were voracious readers', for instance Dennis Goldberg read 365 books annually. Dick's essay concludes with an appendix, 'List of South African Political Prisoners Mentioned in the Article' (pp. 14–17). There are 144 accompanying notes. Katrina M.L. Sked and Peter H. Reid's 'The People behind the Philanthropy: An Investigation into the Lives and Motivations of Library Philanthropists in Scotland between 1800 and 1914' (*LH* 24:i[2008] 48–63) is an examination of Scottish library philanthropists during the nineteenth and early twentieth centuries. An appendix contains 'Brief Biographical Information for Each of the Philanthropists' (pp. 59–60), and there are eighty-seven accompanying notes. Renae Satterley, 'The Libraries of the Inns of Court: An Examination of their Historical Influence' (*LH* 24:iii[2008] 208–19), is a discussion of London's Inns of Court libraries extending from the fifteenth to the eighteenth centuries. She concludes that the libraries of the Middle Temple, the Inner Temple, Lincoln's Inn and Gray's Inn 'are historically significant not only because of their links to their development of law in England, but also because they are excellent examples of Renaissance and Stuart libraries, and highlight what the educated gentry were reading (and annotating)' (p. 218). Clearly, there is much more work to be done in this area. J. Bydder's 'Fact and Fiction in English-Language Thrillers with Russian Characters: The 1930s' (*LH* 24:iv[2008] 253–61) is a survey of thriller fiction written during the 1930s revealing the concerns and the prejudices of the period reflecting a 'fear of Communism rather than of the Soviet people' (p. 253). Novelists surveyed include John Le Carré, Dorothy Sayers, W.E. Johns, Nevil Shute, John Buchan, Michael Annesley and Graham Greene among others, for example H.C. ('Sapper') McNeile. Finally, P. Rafferty's 'Identifying Diachronic Transformations in Popular Culture Genres: A Cultural-Materialist Approach to the History of

Popular Literature Publishing' (*LH* 24:iv[2008] 262–72), a rather pretentiously titled paper, is an attempt to propose 'a methodology through which to examine the history of generic novels' (p. 262). A table is provided of 1980s 'Troubles Thrillers' (p. 269).

Notes & Queries, thank goodness, proceeds on its informative way through the centuries. Kevin J. Hayes, 'More Books from Poe's Library' (*N&Q* 55[2008] 457–9), is a detailed account mainly drawn from the library catalogue of the nineteenth-century Philadelphia autograph collector John Gribbel. His collection was auctioned in New York in 1940 and contained Poe items, some of which had been owned by Poe's parents. These include 'copies of the two-volume 1802 Harrisburg, Pennsylvania edition of Susanna Rowson's *Charlotte Temple: A Tale of Truth*, the first bestseller in American literature' (p. 457). Other works that Poe owned include 'a copy of *The Prose Remains of Henry Kirke White of Nottingham*' dated 1824. This contains a short story 'Melancholy Hours, No. 12' that anticipates Poe's 'A Descent into the Maelström' (p. 459). George Monteiro's 'Unrecorded American Printings of Henry James' (*N&Q* 55[2008] 463) indicates that James's 'The Story of a Masterpiece' appeared in serial form in 1888 'in *The Evening News*, a newspaper published in San Jose, California'. Monteiro also notes 'a printing in the Chicago *Daily Inter Ocean*' for 1892 of James's 'The Real Thing' (p. 463). Arthur Sherbo continues to produce fascinating articles. His '*Delta*, an Almost Forgotten "Little Magazine"' (*N&Q* 55[2008] 486–9) reveals unlisted reviews of, amongst others, the *Collected Poems of Wallace Stevens*, *D.H. Lawrence: Selected Literary Criticism*, essays on William Faulkner, on Robert Frost, on Hemingway, Edith Wharton, and Iris Murdoch's *The Bell*. Other authors whose reviews went unnoted include Ezra Pound, William Empson, Tennyson, E.M. Forster, Donald Davie and William Carlos Williams. Melissa Edmundson's 'Complicating Kitty: A Textual Variant in Rebecca West's *The Return of the Soldier*' (*N&Q* 55[2008] 492–3) focuses upon the characterization of Kitty in Rebecca West's *The Return of the Soldier* [1918] and in particular 'a textual variant which occurs in later editions' of the novel (p. 492).

The important *Papers of the Bibliographical Society of America* (*PBSA* 102[2008]) continues to contain material of great interest and significance, and of the highest quality. Kess Boterbloem's 'The Genesis of Jan Struys's *Perillous Voyages* and the Business of the Book Trade in the Dutch Republic' (*PBSA* 102:i[2008] 5–28) sheds light upon 'the publication of writings by seafarers' (p. 6) and their distribution. 'Approximately twenty-five Dutch, French, German, and English editions and translations' of Jan Struys's *Perillous Voyages*, first published in 1676 with the first English publication in 1683, were 'issued in the century after its first publication' (p. 11). Pat Rogers and Paul Baines's 'The Attribution of Books to Publishers: Edmund Curll and the *Memoirs* of John Macky' (*PBSA* 102:i[2008] 29–60) is of more direct interest, and, as usual with these distinguished authors, they throw much light upon eighteenth-century book trade history. In this case, they illuminate 'the bookseller Edmund Curll (1683–1747) ... a representative figure in the book trade [and] his working methods' (p. 30). Troy J. Bassett's 'The Production of Three-Volume Novels in Britain, 1863–97' (*PBSA* 102:i[2008] 61–76) attempts to 'indicate how many three-volume novels were produced during the nineteenth-century' (p. 63). Bassett's study draws upon the *Publishers' Circle* and *The English Catalogue of Books* as well as other sources. Bassett's article is accompanied by two tables and three figures. The two tables show 'Three-Volume Novel Titles, 1884–97' and 'New Three-Volume Novel Titles, 1863–97' (p. 65). The three figures illuminate 'New Three-Volume Novel Titles, 1863–97' (p. 66), 'New Fiction Titles, 1870–94' and 'New Fiction Titles, 1870–94' (pp. 69–70). Bassett's article is full of illuminating information such as, for instance, the fact that 'in the peak year of production, 1883, nineteen publishers accounted for the 155 three-volume novels produced that year' (p. 71). Laura Rattray's 'Cinematic License: Editorial Imprints on the Hollywood Novels of Horace McCoy' (*PBSA* 102:i[2008] 77–94) focuses upon a forgotten American novelist and screenwriter Horace McCoy and his Hollywood activities.

Goran Proot and Leo Egghe's 'Estimating Editions on the Basis of Survivals: Printed Programmes of Jesuit Plays in the *Provincia Flandro-Belgica* before 1773, with a Note on the "Book Historical Law"' (*PBSA* 102:ii[2008] 149–74) begins with the question 'Is it possible to estimate the total number of editions of a corpus of published work that have ever been produced on the basis of surviving copies? That is the question this contribution deals with' (p. 149). Noel Waite's '"The Best Holidays on the Globe": Charles Francis, American Typothetae, and the Federation of New Zealand Master Printers' (*PBSA* 102:ii[2008] 175–96) 'can be read as a self-contained exposition on the formation and national federation of Master Printers' Associations in New Zealand from 1901 to 1921'. On the other hand, Waite has 'tried to locate this critical activity in the development of a national print culture in an international context that speaks to a global history of communications' (p. 175). Maura Ives's 'Jean Ingelow in the *Youth's Magazine*' (*PBSA* 102:ii[2008] 197–220) examines the specific periodical publications of the neglected nineteenth-century author Jean Ingelow. David Alan Richards's 'Kipling and the Bibliographers' (*PBSA* 102:ii[2008] 221–34) discusses Kipling's complex relationship with his bibliographers.

MacD. P. Jackson's 'The Authorship of *A Lover's Complaint*: A New Approach to the Problem' (*PBSA* 102:iii[2008] 284–313) returns once again to the very thorny, complex issue of the Shakespeare canon. Jackson thinks 'that Vickers, Bate, and Rasmussen are wrong, that Thorpe was right, and that the poem [*A Lover's Complaint*] should be retained within the Shakespeare canon' (p. 285). Jackson's *modus operandi* was to 'enter into the *LION* search box every unusual spelling in *LC* as it is printed in the *Sonnets* quarto of 1609' (p. 287). He relates his evidence, admits that 'The *LION* database is not perfect, and no doubt [he has] been guilty of a few oversights here and there' (p. 306) and concludes that *A Lover's Complaint* 'shares more rare phrases and collocations with Shakespeare's plays than with those of any other dramatist [it] exhibits some arresting lexical links to the Shakespeare canon ... has the same Chinese-boxes narrative structure as Shakespeare's *The Phoenix and the Turtle*, and ... was published under the full name of William Shakespeare'. Its exclusion from the Shakespearian canon 'strikes' Jackson 'as incredible'

(p. 313). This is certainly a thought-provoking article and not the last on the subject.

Another interesting article dealing with the Elizabethan and Jacobean canon is Meg Powers Livingston's 'Repetition Brackets: Plus or Minus? A Reinterpretation of the Evidence in *The Woman's Prize* and *A Wife for a Month*' (*PBSA* 102:iii[2008] 315–39). Livingston 'revisits two opposing theories that attempt to explain a particular category of textual anomalies called repetition brackets, which occur occasionally in some manuscript and print versions of early modern plays'. Livingston uses 'two plays from the Beaumont and Fletcher canon [to] demonstrate that one of the theories, which posits restored cuts as an explanation, better accounts for the textual confusion in these plays, and consequently may provide a new tool for assessing censorship practices in the period' (p. 315). Mention should be made briefly of Marvin J. Heller's 'The Bear Motif in Seventeenth- and Eighteenth-Century Hebrew Books' (*PBSA* 102:iii[2008] 341–61). John A. Dussinger's 'Another Anonymous Compilation from Samuel Richardson's Press: *A Select Manual of Devotions for Sick Persons* (1733)' (*PBSA* 102:iii[2008] 363–85) draws upon the author's work on the Cambridge edition of the correspondence of Samuel Richardson. It is accompanied by two appendices. The first contains the 'Sources of *A Select Manual of Devotions* (1733)' (pp. 383–4) and the second appendix lists the *Meditations Collected from the Sacred Books* [1750] and 'Psalms for the Sick', *A Select Manual of Devotions* [1733] (p. 385).

John Bidwell's 'Biographical Dictionaries of the Book Trades' (*PBSA* 102:iv[2008] 421–44) was in fact the *PBSA*'s 'Presidential Address'. Bidwell speaks 'about book people—printers, publishers, booksellers, and members of the allied trades engaged in book production—papermakers, typefounders, bookbinders, and illustrators', just to mention a few (p. 421). Another side of the book business is described in Adam G. Hooks's 'Booksellers' Catalogues and the Classification of Printed Drama in Seventeenth-century England' (*PBSA* 102:iv[2008] 445–64), which opens with an arresting quotation from Graham Greene's *The Complaisant Lover*: 'You wouldn't understand how important a bookseller's catalogue is ... One has to know what to put in and what to leave out' (1959 London edition, William Heinemann, p. 21; cited p. 445). Sarah Howe's 'The Authority of Presence: The Development of the English Author Portrait, 1500–1640' (*PBSA* 102:iv[2008] 465–99) is accompanied by seven illustrations of authors, eight figures illustrating various elements of portrait publication, three tables containing data for author portrait incidents (pp. 491–2) and a ninety-item appendix listing 'the author-portrait containing books that are the basis of [Sarah Howe's] investigations' (pp. 493–9). Hannah Sullivan's 'Modernist Excision and its Consequences' (*PBSA* 102:iv[2008] 501–19) begins with Hemingway's description of 'his principles of composition'. Sullivan explores 'the bibliographical consequences of Hemingway's principle, with particular attention to the genesis of *The Sun Also Rises*'. She argues that 'revision through omission and deletion is not a compositional strategy unique to Hemingway' but also can be applied to Ezra Pound, Marianne Moore, T.S. Eliot and James Joyce' (pp. 501–2).

The final issue of *PBSA* for 2008 contains a supplement 'Book Catalogues, Tomorrow and Beyond. Proceedings of the 2008 Conference Sponsored by the

Grolier Club and the Bibliographical Society of America' (*PBSA* 102:iv[2008] 543–80). This consists of five papers. Eric Holzenberg's 'A Conference on Book Catalogues, Tomorrow and Beyond' (*PBSA* 102:iv[2008] 543–6); Wm. P. Barlow Jr's 'On the Private Collecting of Book Catalogues' (*PBSA* 102:iv[2008] 547–55); Christian Coppens's 'A Consensus of Publishers' and Booksellers' Catalogues up to 1600: Some Provisional Conclusions' (*PBSA* 102:iv[2008] 557–65); Maria Hutchison's 'Book Transaction Data at AbeBooks: Opportunities and Challenges' (*PBSA* 102:iv[2008] 567–72) and G. Thomas Tanselle's 'Some Thoughts on Catalogues' (*PBSA* 102:iv[2008] 573–80). There is a detailed index to volume 102 (pp. 581–98) and each issue contains succinct and useful book reviews. The editor of *BSA* 102, T.H. Howard-Hill, is once again to be congratulated on producing four such fascinating issues which are replete with important information for scholars of the book and *YWES* readers.

Publishing History (*PubH* 63[2008]) contains two articles. In the first, Richard Freebury draws upon his current work on *The Bookseller* in his detailed ' "Pirates" or "Honourable Men": British Perceptions of American Attitudes to Literary Property as Reflected in *The Bookseller*, 1858–1891' (*PubH* 63[2008] 5–66). Freebury's article contains 300 notes! In the second article, Kate MacDonald and Marysa DeMoor write on 'Borrowing and Supplementing: The Industrial Production of "Complete Story" Novelettes and their Supplements, 1865–1900' (*PubH* 63[2008] 67–95). The author's conclude that their 'study of the novelettes' reveals that an 'unknown readership was buying unknown fiction by unknown writers' (p. 86).

Publishing History (*PubH* 64 [2008]) contains two articles of relevance to *YWES* readers. Gerald S. Greenberg's 'David A. Randall: Newspaper Publisher, Bookseller and Author in Columbus, Ohio, 1845–1875)' (*PubH* 64[2008] 5–32) and Richard Freebury's 'Competitive Trade or Learned Profession: British Attitudes to Bookselling and Booksellers' Prices as Reflected in *The Bookseller*, 1858–1891' (*PubH* 64[2008] 33–76). Greenberg draws upon forgotten, unused Midwest archives to illuminate the life and work of David A. Randall. Richard Freebury again draws upon his work with *The Bookseller* to reflect upon 'British Attitudes to Bookselling and Booksellers Prices' (p. 33). This time he has only 162 notes, but curiously both his articles omit previous work on *The Bookseller* found for instance in volume 3 of Alvin Sullivan's *British Literary Magazines* ([1984], pp. 49–54).

The *Rare Book Review* has now ceased publication: perhaps the glossy, trendy nature of its illustrations somehow alienated advertisers. This is mere speculation. R.M. Healy's account of Felix Dennis's rare book collection, entitled 'The Wizard of Oz' (*RBR* 35:i[2008] 20–5), leads the February/March issue and is accompanied by some mildly pornographic illustrations. Dennis possesses copies of the first edition of *Moby-Dick* amongst other treasures. Stephen Ratcliffe's 'Search for a Star' (*RBR* 35:i[2008] 34–7) provides an interesting account of the activities of Cosway bindings. These 'are books bound in full morocco leather with a portrait miniature (sometimes more than one), painted on ivory and inset into the binding and protected by a thin sheet of glass' (p. 34). In this instance, the illustrations accompanying the account are entirely appropriate. Joe McCann's 'Don't Believe the Hype' (*RBR*

35:i[2008] 46) is an all too short account largely drawn from the modern firsts field of why some authors and editions are much more expensive than others and why some authors fetch much higher prices than others. The indefatigable Sandra Hindman, in 'A Gentle Madness?' (*RBR* 35:i[2008] 48–53), examines why some people obsessively pursue manuscripts.

Roger Dobson's 'Machen's Labyrinth' (*RBR* 35:ii[2008] 12–13) commemorates the sixtieth anniversary of the 'death of the master of mystery' Arthur Machen (p. 12). Stanley Campbell's 'Devil May Collect' (*RBR* 35:ii[2008] 20–6) discusses the collecting activities of Ian Fleming. The editors can't resist, of course, illustrating the article with the obvious! However, Campbell's account is accompanied by an extremely useful 'Buying & Selling Ian Fleming (b 1908 d 1964)', which is in effect an annotated bibliography of Fleming's output (p. 26). Chris Saunders's 'Children of the Evolution' (*RBR* 35:ii[2008] 28–31) is an exploration of 'the continuing importance of the Father of Natural Selection' (p. 28). Rob Larson's 'Krash! Kapow! Ker-ching!' (*RBR* 35:ii[2008] 36–9) contains a useful discussion of the rise in prices and popularity of comic books. Tom Congalton's 'Rare Books as Investments' (*RBR* 35:ii[2008] 40–1) retreads a well-examined field relating to pricing and the economics of the book trade. Joe McCann's 'Recollections and Jollifications' (*RBR* 35:ii[2008] 46–7) pays tribute to the book collector Peter Jolliffe (1947–2007), who specialized in modern firsts. Australia's oldest museum, the Australian Museum Research Library, is the subject of Matthew Stephens's 'A Cabinet of Paper Curiosities' (*RBR* 35:ii[2008] 48–51).

The June/July 2008 issue (*RBR* 35:iii) focuses upon the London book fairs and especially on 'the discovery of [Shelley's] *Poetical Essay on the Existing State of Things* (1811)' (p. 6). R.M. Healey's 'The Rimbaud of Cwmdonkin Drive' (*RBR* 35:iii[2008] 28–33) is a review and discussion with the Dylan Thomas collector Jeff Towns of a new film exploring 'Dylan Thomas's life, loves and near death' (p. 28). It concludes with a useful 'Buying & Selling Dylan Thomas (b 1914 d 1953)' (p. 33). Chris Saunders' 'Eye of the Tyger' (*RBR* 35:iv[2008] 32–7) 'celebrates the innocence and experience of Albion's greatest artist'—William Blake (p. 32). Saunders's article is usefully accompanied by illustrations from Blake. Steward Bennett's 'Cataloguing the Uncatalogued' (*RBR* 35:iv[2008] 40–4) is an interesting account of Bennett's discovery of 'pre-1801 English books in OCLC or COPAC that aren't in ESTC' (p. 41). Nicola Lisle's 'The Money Train' (*RBR* 35:iv[2008] 48–51) contains a useful account of Edith Nesbit and concludes with 'Buying & Selling Edith Nesbit (b 1858 d 1924)' (p. 51). Colin Steele's 'Not the End of the Discworld' (*RBR* 35:v[2008] 22–7) examines the work of Terry Pratchett and concludes with the helpful 'Buying & Selling Terry Pratchett (b 1948)' (p. 27). Charlotte Luxford's 'A Group of One's Own' (*RBR* 35:v[2008] 28–32) retreads familiar territory in its exploration of 'love and loss in Virginia Woolf's intimate circle' (p. 29). R.M. Healey's 'Over and Out' (*RBR* 35:v[2008] 36–9) consists of an interview with Sebastian Carter on the occasion of the 2008 'closure of The Rampant Lions Press and the retirements of its owner' (p. 36). Angela Jackson's 'Birthday Present' (*RBR* 35:vi[2008] 8–10) contains a glimpse into the Ted Hughes archive acquired by the British Library for £500,000. Margaret Willes's 'The Enigmatic Bibliophile' (*RBR* 35:vi[2008]

12–13) assesses the collecting activities of Charles Winn (1795–1874), an obsessive collector who 'in the 1850s … turned his attention to acquiring Shakespeareana' (p. 12). Philip W. Errington's 'That Sort of Bear' (*RBR* 35:vi[2008] 26–9) is an assessment of the influence of E.H. Shepard (1879–1876), who illustrated *Winnie-the-Pooh* and other works. Stanley Campbell's 'Tales of the Riverbank' (*RBR* 35:vi[2008] 42–6) examines the life and achievement of Kenneth Grahame and includes 'A Guide to Collecting *The Wind in the Willows*' and 'Buying & Selling Kenneth Grahame (b 1859 d 1932)' (pp. 45–6).

The December/January 2009 issue is the last of *The Rare Book Review*. Overall, the magazine contained useful book chat, information on auction houses, dealers and personalities in the book trade, including collectors, auctioneers and buyers. It never really found a happy medium between an appeal to a mass market, reflected in its occasional pornographic entries, and an appeal to the serious book collector. Items such as its auction diary and its reviews will be missed, as will the serious articles and insights that it provided.

The Bulletin of the Bibliographical Society of Australia and New Zealand has been retitled *Script & Print*, but as noted in last year's account (*YWES* 88 [2009] 1230), we shall continue to refer to it by its former abbreviation. Omitted last year was (*BSANZB* 31:ii[2007]). This item includes Paul Eggert's 'Textual Criticism and Folklore: The Ned Kelly Story and *Robbery Under Arms*' (*BSANZB* 31:ii[2007] 69–80), which was a revised version of the paper he gave at the Annual Conference of the Bibliographical Society of Australia and New Zealand in 2003 in Canberra. In his opening paragraphs, Eggert reflects upon the importance of textual criticism. He applies the ramification of textual criticism to 'Rolf Boldrewood's bushranger classic of the 1880s *Robbery Under Arms*' (p. 70) and concludes with a consideration of Peter Carey's 'impressive novel *A True History of the Kelly Gang*'. For Eggert, 'Carey has done what Boldrewood so innovatively achieved in the 1880s: the invention, or, really, the reinvention of the bushranger's voice' (pp. 79–80). This article is yet another addition to Eggert's impressive achievements. It is pleasing to know that the present writer may have contributed to this in a small way at the University of Kent in England in the late 1970s when Eggert noticeably walked out of a lecture he was giving which emphasized George Eliot's textuality. As Eggert subsequently confessed, the implications for a D.H. Lawrence literary critic at the time were too extensive to take too much of!

Paul Watt's 'The Catalogue of Ernest Newman's Library: Revelations about his Intellectual Life in the 1890s' (*BSANZB* 31:ii[2007] 81–103) reveals much about the interests of the great musicologist and journalist Ernest Newman and draws upon the sale on 10–11 December 1959 at Hodgson & Co. in London of Newman's extensive library. An appendix contains 'Extracts from the Catalogue of Sale Relating to Specific Items and Related Material discussed in the Article' (p. 97). Watt sensibly says in his conclusion that 'Looking over the catalogue of a writer's library in search of clues to their life is … an exercise that yields both predictable and surprising results' (p. 96). Rebecca-Anne De Rozario's 'Don't Steal a Book by its Cover: *The Book Thief* and Who Reads It' (*BSANZB* 31:ii[2007] 104–16) is accompanied by four full-page black and white illustrations. It focuses on 'how one particular book, in its various covers, articulates the generations of its readership and, furthermore, reproduces and celebrates the tactile nature of bibliography within its diverse covers' (p. 104).

BSANZB 32:iii[2008] contains Keith Maslen's 'Our Part to Name: The Early Book Trade of Dunedin, New Zealand' (*BSANZB* 32:iii[2008] 133–43): the title explains the content. Nathan Garvey's 'A Dynasty of the Margins of the Trade: The Bailey Family of Printers, ca. 1740–1840, Part I' (*BSANZB* 32:iii[2008] 144–62) considers an important and neglected subject, how 'smaller family firms operate[d] in the shadows of the more prominent booksellers, who as many accounts would have it, dominated the trade to the point that their careers were synonymous with the history of the trade itself' (p. 144). B.J. McMullin's 'Patterned Book Cloth: A Review Essay' (*BSANZB* 32:iii[2008] 163–75) is an extensive review essay accompanied by two illustrations of Andrea Krupp's *Bookcloth in England and America 1823–1850* (Oak Knoll Press/British Library/Bibliographical Society of America [2008]). Regarding Krupps as 'a splendid edition', McMullin acknowledges her work 'as the basis of an industry standard … for the description of the surface appearance of book cloth, of no matter what period' (p. 163).

The great enumerative and descriptive bibliographer T.H. Howard-Hill's 'W.J. Cameron and the Universal Catalogue of British Literature' (*BSANZB* 32:iv[2008] 197–211) is the lead article. Howard-Hill considers the achievement of William James Cameron (1926–1989). 'Cameron directed at the University of Western Ontario a Hand-Printed Books Project'. A New Zealander who completed his Ph.D. at the University of Reading in 1957, he taught at McMaster University in Hamilton, Ontario, from 1964 and 'died of a stroke in his home on 18 April 1989' (p. 204). Howard-Hill reviews his career and achievement, concluding that 'Cameron has his place in the bibliographical history of three nations—New Zealand, Australia and Canada—a considerable achievement that we should remember' (p. 211). Rebecca-Anne C. Do Rozario considers 'Fforde's Book Upgrades: Downloaded Errata and Metafictional Cancellation' (*BSANZB* 31:ii[2008] 212–18). In plain English, this considers the interesting subject of electronic upgrades for novels maintained on an author's website. B.J. McMullin in his '*PBSA* Turns One Hundred' (*BSANZB* 31:ii[2008] 219–32) considers the achievements of the publications of the *Papers of the Bibliographical Society of America* which celebrated its centenary 'with the beginning of volume 101 in 2007' (p. 219). As usual, McMullin makes perceptive observations, for instance commenting on 'the relative slowness of American bibliographers to concern themselves with bibliographical analysis' (p. 228). One would have wished for more on the individual editors of the journal. However, McMullin's article is most welcome and timely. He concludes that 'The only threat to *PBSA* may well result from the development of new forms of access that make print on paper an uneconomic medium' (p. 232). Mark R. Godburn's 'The Earliest Dust Jackets—Lost and Found' (*BSANZB* 31:ii[2008] 233–9) gives an account of a dust-jacket from an English annual, *Friendship's Offering for 1830*, which recently turned up in the Bodleian Library. This pre-dates the existing 'earliest known dust jacket ... [for] *The Keepsake* for 1833' (p. 233). Two illustrations are included, and there is an appendix of 'Important books in jackets that are unlocated today'. These range from Edward Falkener, ed., *Daedalus* [1860] to a New York-published edition in 1884 by [John E. Wheelock] of 'Don Juan' which 'has a sealed-wrapping jacket, the latest one known' (p. 239). *Script & Print* contains interesting and often critical reviews. This issue is no exception. For instance, J. McL. Emmerson's 'Pamphlets and Pamphleteering: A Review Essay' (*BSANZB* 31:ii[2008] 239–45) discusses 'Joad Raymond: *Pamphlets and Pamphleteering in Early Modern Britain*' and 'Alexandra Halasz: *The Marketplace of Print: Pamphlets and the Public Sphere in Early Modern England*', both published by Cambridge University Press in 2006.

Subscribers may also find included in issues an offprint of Roger E. Stoddard's *What Can a Librarian Do?* This was the 'Keynote address for the Bibliographical Society of Australia and New Zealand conference "Hunters and Gatherers: Building Collections of Books" 16 October 2004' published by the Center for the Book at Monash University in 2004. There is a preface (pp. 3–4) by Wallace Kirsop. Basically, Stoddard gives a fascinating account of the few days he spent in Vienna every other year from 1994 until 2002 'during a tour of Germanophone book dealers' (p. 1). The lecture concludes with kabbalistic wisdom! (*BSANZB* 32:i[2008] 5) is a special issue, *Transitus: Medieval and Renaissance Manuscripts in Australia and New Zealand*, edited by James Lowry, Margaret Manion and Patrick Spedding. Margaret Manion's 'Medieval and Renaissance Manuscripts in Australia: Resources, Research and Opportunities' (*BSANZB* 32:i[2008] 7–20) is a useful overall survey. Lawrence Warner's 'The University of Sydney *Statuta Angliae* (RB Add. MS 39) and the 45,011 Parish Churches: England's Most Poplar Urban Myth, ca. 1327–1606' (*BSANZB* 32:i[2008] 21–35) describes in detail the fourteenth-century English manuscript. Bernard J. Muir's 'Interrogating a Witness: The Case for MS Crouch 10' (*BSANZB* 32:i[2008] 36–48) describes 'a twelfth-century witness of questionable origins and obscured subsequent peregrinations' today housed at the Ballart Fine Art Gallery (pp. 36–7). Christopher de Hamel's 'The Bohun Bible Leaves' (*BSANZB* 32:i[2008] 49–63) focuses upon 'two large fourteenth-century Latin Bible leaves in the Reed Collection in the Dunedin Public Library' (p. 49). An appendix lists 'Known leaves from the Bohun Bible' (pp. 60–3). De Hamel's is a description of 'no fewer than 166 other leaves from the manuscript' (p. 49) that have become known to De Hamel in the past few years. This issue is accompanied by eight full-page, colour illustrations of leaves described in the articles. Alison Rukavina's ' "This is a wonderfully comprehensive business": The Development of the British–Australian and International Book Trades, 1870–1887' (*BSANZB* 32:ii[2008] 69–94) draws upon the correspondence of Edward Petherick, who was George Robertson's distribution manager based in London from 1870 to 1887 as a source of information on the 'viable and lucrative' Australian book market. Rukavina's article is accompanied by two black and white illustrations. Ian Morrison's 'The Writings of Theresa Tasmania: Notes on an Investigation into a Nineteenth-Century Literary Pseudonym' (*BSANZB* 32:ii[2008] 95–105) concerns the 'recent discovery of Theresa Tasmania's writings pre-dating' 1868 (p. 96). Morrison further assesses the evidence for 'identifying Lucy Anna Edgar' (1838–?) 'as Theresa Tasmania' (p. 103). Morrison supplies as an appendix 'Known Writings of Theresa Tasmania' (pp. 104–5). This particular edition of *Script & Print* is noteworthy for some detailed reviews: see pages 106–24. Another article of interest is Paul Goetsch's 'Shakespeare und die englische Rezeption des Stoizismus' (in Neymeyr, Schmidt and Zimmermann, *Stoizismus in der europäischen Philosophie, Literatur, Kunst und Politik*, vol. 2, pp. 673–710). This should not go ignored as it contains a useful account of the perception of Shakespeare's relationship to stoicism in English and German literature.

To turn to books. R.C. Alston's *A Bibliography of the English Language from the Invention of Printing to the Year 1800* continues with volume 21, which essentially contains additions to the previous volumes. In all, Alston adds 2,380 items, leaving 'about another 100,000 titles to check before this project can be regarded as complete' (p. xix). In the section on 'The Future' in his introduction, Alston notes that he has 'agreed to donate the project and its future development to the Institute of English Studies in the School of Advanced Study, University of London' (p. xviii) and plans the final volume to be the twenty-second one. In other words, one to go. We can only hope that he lives to complete his wonderful task of producing, to cite the subtitle, 'A Systematic Record of Writings on English, and on Other Languages in English, Based on the Collection of the Principal Libraries of the World'.

The latest volume in the important *Bibliography of Australian Literature*, general editors John Arnold and John Hay, with Kerry Kilner and Terence O'Neill as associate editors, covers K through O up to the year 2000. In addition to a useful explanatory introduction (pp. ix–xii), there is a 'Sample Entry and Users Guide' (pp. xv–xvii), an appendix, 'Excluded and Relocated Authors and Titles (K–O)' (pp. 601–2), an 'Index of Pseudonyms and Variant Names' (pp. 603–56), and an 'Index of Titles' (pp. 657–750). Author entries contain basic biographical details such as date of birth and date of death, bibliographical details of works, brief comments, sources where known of papers, and additional information. In short, *The Bibliography of Australian Literature* is indispensable.

Nicholas Basbanes, the author of *A Gentle Madness* [1999] and other works on the obsession of book-collecting and the personalities who indulge in it, has now written *A World of Letters: Yale University Press, 1908–2008*. This is the centenary history of the press, which has published more than 8,000 volumes over a century. Basbanes's history is chronological, although he does focus upon the press's acquisition of Eugene O'Neill's famous *Long Day's Journey Into Night*, which in fact is their all-time best seller. Basbanes also spends quite a bit of space on the controversy ignited in 1965 by the publication of *The Vineland Map*. Yale University Press has a trade division in addition to an academic side, and Basbanes pays attention to this aspect of its achievements. It did after all publish E.H. Gombrich's *A Little History of the World* [2005], which has sold more than 150,000 copies.

The Oxford Wesleyan Edition of Fielding's non-dramatic writings is completed with the publication of Martin C. Battestin's edition of *The Journal of a Voyage to Lisbon, Shamela* and *Occasional Writings*. The occasional writings include every work of Fielding excluded from the twelve previously published volumes of the non-dramatic writings. Battestin's choice for 'the copy-text for each work is its first edition, or first appearance in print, these being the printings closest to the manuscript and therefore most likely to transmit the author's accidentals'. His textual apparatus records the alterations of accidentals and substantives. However, typographical errors remain unrecorded and have been corrected. There are other regularizations of similar matter, including punctuation fonts (p. xx). There are three appendices (pp. 681–782). The first focuses on 'Writings Attributed to Fielding', the second on 'The Texts' and the third contains a 'Documentary Supplement to *The Journal of a Voyage to Lisbon*'. This magnificent volume concludes with an extensive index (pp. 783–803), and there are over twenty-six accompanying illustrations to the text.

Peter Beal's *A Dictionary of English Manuscript Terminology, 1450–2000* is a superb and important work. As he writes in his preface, it 'was originally inspired by John Carter's *ABC for Book Collectors* (first published in 1952). What he had done for books it seemed reasonable to do for manuscripts'. As Beal explains, his 'dictionary evolved from an estimated 250 entries into 1,500 or more (counting 600 cross references), and as brief definitions grew longer, and as the boundaries of John Carter's book were abandoned, it became clear that the main principle of selection operating here was my own interests and knowledge' (p. viii). Indeed, Beal's knowledge and interests are extensive and extremely helpful. The text is accompanied by ninety-five illustrations. It begins with 'Abbreviation', an entry which extends to four erudite paragraphs (pp. 1–4) and is accompanied by an illustration from 'An autograph letter signed by Lord Burghley, to the Earl of Essex, 21 May 1597 in Burghley's characteristic cursive italic hand, with a proliferation of abbreviations' (pp. 2–3). The book concludes with a clearly written paragraph explanation of 'Year Books' (p. 451). Beal's is a wonderful work and should be in every library and scholar's collection. It even concludes with a helpful select bibliography (p. 452–80).

Hazel K. Bell is the doyenne of indexers. Her clearly-written and informative *From Flock Beds to Professionalism: A History of Index-Makers* is an extensive account of her profession. As David Crystal comments in his preface, 'having read Hazel Bell's book, I am sad that I did not know its contents before. I knew most of the names it contains ... but I was unprepared for the range, diversity and sheer brilliance of the personalities lying behind the names' (p. xiii). Bell moves from an introductory section on the 'Methods, Training, Remuneration, Social and Personal Characteristics' (pp. 3–18) of indexers to accounts of what she describes as 'Lone Workers' (pp. 21–230). She begins with Bernardo Machiavelli and his 'indexes to Livy 1428–1500' (pp. 21–2) and concludes with an entry on 'Michael Robertson Continental indexer b. 1954' (pp. 229–30). Many of the entries are written by Bell, but other entries, for instance those on Machiavelli and others, have their source in *The Indexer*. For instance the Machiavelli entry belongs to Hans H. Wellisch. Following these entries are items on 'Banding Together' (pp. 233–300) with accounts of the Index Society and *The Indexer*. There are listings of 'Editorials in *The Indexer*, 1958–95' (p. 303) and 'Obituaries in *The Indexer*, 1958–95' (p. 305) followed by 'Chronology of Print-Only Indexing' (pp. 307–9). This important book concludes with a listing of references (pp. 311–16), acknowledgements (pp. 317–19) and of course an extensive index (pp. 321–33), which should provide a model to us all.

The three volumes of *The Short Fiction of Ambrose Bierce: A Comprehensive Edition*, edited by S.T. Joshi, Lawrence I. Berkove and David E. Schultz, 'is the first edition of Ambrose Bierce's fiction to be based upon consultation of manuscripts and early printed sources. It is also the first edition to include the totality of Bierce's output of short fiction'. The volumes contain 249 items; of these, 'one story ("Alasper") is unpublished, 58 have not been previously reprinted from the newspapers and magazines in which they originally appeared, and 74 have not been reprinted since their appearance in Bierce's early volumes of 1873–74' (vol. 1, p. xxv). The conclusion to each volume contains a listing of 'Selected Textual Variants' (see vol. 1, pp. 461–98; vol. 2, pp. 865–92; vol. 3, pp. 1213–23). The problem is that there is no clear explanation of the principles of the listing of the textual variants. With this and other minor caveats, Joshi and his fellow editors have produced a thorough and scholarly edition with useful introductions and notations. The third volume contains three useful appendices. The first deals with 'Variant Texts' (pp. 1139–75), the second with 'Bierce on his Fiction' (pp. 1177–85), the third with 'Supplementary Texts' (pp. 1187–1205). These are followed by 'Texts by Others' (pp. 1207–12) and there is a detailed bibliography (pp. 1225–8), a listing of 'Bierce's Civil War Stories Arranged Chronologically' (p. 1229), an 'Alphabetical Listing of Bierce's Fiction' (pp. 1231–4), an 'Index to Bierce's Fiction' (pp. 1235–56) and a general index (pp. 1257–75).

Note should be made of two recent Broadview anthologies of British Literature, edited by Joseph Black et al.: *The Twentieth Century and Beyond*, volume 6A: *From 1900 to World War II* and *The Twentieth Century and Beyond*, volume 6B: *From 1945 to the Twenty-First Century*. Both are attempts to compete in a highly competitive market and especially with the Norton anthologies. Both contain comprehensive and sensibly annotated materials. A selection problem with twentieth-century and beyond materials is of course the issue of copyright. This seems not to detract from the significance of the materials found in these volumes, which should be useful for both graduate and undergraduate usage on both sides of the Atlantic. The price is reasonable and the binding sturdy, although the squat format is rather curious.

A very useful bibliography published in 2005 should not go unmentioned. As John R. Roberts, in his foreword to Jacob Blevins's *An Annotated Bibliography of Thomas Traherne Criticism, 1900–2003* writes, 'This comprehensive, fully annotated enumerative bibliography of critical studies of the life and works of Thomas Traherne will provide scholars, critics, and students of this often enigmatic seventeenth-century writer with an immensely useful research tool. It will be helpful also to those interested in early modern English poetry and prose in general and English intellectual history' (p. i). Blevins's *Annotated Bibliography* is descriptive rather than evaluative. The starting point is 1900 and the concluding date is 2003. Most book reviews are excluded, although important review articles are included. Items in French, German, Japanese, Italian and other languages are included in addition to English. There are two appendices, one listing doctoral dissertations (pp. 153–60) and the second listing primary texts (pp. 161–6). There are two indices, an 'Author Index' (pp. 167–70) and a 'Subject Index' (pp. 171–5). In spite of the high price being charged for this work, it is exceedingly useful and should be widely available.

Jorge Luis Borges's 'The Library of Babel' is the base text for William Goldbloom Bloch's *The Unimaginable Mathematics of Borges' Library of Babel*. This is an exploration and explication of Borges's complexity. In his preface Bloch writes that 'there are three main themes woven into [his] book. The first one digs into the Library, peels back layers uncovering nifty ideas, and then runs with them for awhile. The second thread' focuses upon 'the mathematics behind [Borges'] ideas'. Bloch's 'third focus is on literary aspects of the story and Borges' (pp. xii–xiv). There is certainly much to think about here, and *YWES* readers should not be put off by the multiple mathematical illustrations which litter the text. There are detailed notations, a most helpful glossary and an extremely useful 'Annotated Suggested Readings' (pp. 157–80). These are followed by an alphabetically arranged evaluative bibliography and a very helpful index (pp. 181–92). Indeed, in the index the listing of contents under 'Books' in fact indicates much of the interest of Bloch's fascinating book: 'contents of'; 'description of'; 'distinct number of'; 'first page of'; 'grain-of-sand'; '"infinitely thin"'; 'lack of organization in distribution'; 'number of'; 'orderings of'; 'shelving pattern of'; 'short description of'; 'spine of'; 'thickness of' (p. 187).

Asa Briggs's latest work, *A History of Longmans and their Books 1724–1990: Longevity in Publishing*, continues his interest in institutional history and in particular the firm of Longmans. He edited *Essays in the History of Publishing in Celebration of the 250th Anniversary of the House of Longman, 1724–1974*, published by Longman in 1974, containing essays by diverse hands covering differing perspectives on the activities of the publishing house. Briggs's connection, as he explains in his fifth appendix, 'Life Span, an Autobiographical Note' (pp. 561–85), goes back a long way. His history, however, is not a hortatory one. It concludes in 1990, or four years 'before the House of Longman ceased to exist as an independent business'. This, Briggs confesses, was 'an event which took [him] by surprise and for which [he] was not prepared'. It became finally in 1994 part of 'a conglomerate' which it had in effect been since 1968. Briggs stops in 1990 mainly because the Pearson Archive—'Longman had become part of the multi-product Pearson conglomerate'—was 'inaccessible' to him (p. 3).

Briggs, in his 'Prologue: Longevity' (pp. 1–27), notes that during the 270 years of Longmans' existence the firm had at least 'twenty-eight imprints' (p. 4). Chapters encompass 'The Creation of a Business, 1724–1797' (pp. 29–87), and 'The Dynamics of Growth' (pp. 89–147), which focuses upon 'the dynamics of the eighteenth-century book trade' (p. 89). The fourth chapter, 'Publisher, Authors and Readers, 1797–1842' (pp. 149–227) concentrates upon a great period in Longmans' fortune and fame. 'Leviathan, 1842–1879' (pp. 229–91) is concerned with the period after the death of Thomas Norton III in 1842 and 1879, when 'the mid-Victorian years were indubitably over' (p. 290). Chapter 6, 'Publishers, Readers and Authors, 1879–1918' (pp. 293–375), takes the history through the years of the First

World War, a period that 'changed little in the routines of Paternoster Row'. Chapter 7 describes a period of 'Continuity and Change, 1918–1968' (pp. 377–439). These years witnessed the destruction of Longmans' Paternoster Row building in January 1941 during the London Blitz, the 1968 Pearson amalgamation and the move in the same year to the Burnt Mill building at Harlow. A chapter on 'Recalling Yet Restructuring, 1968–1976' (pp. 441–83) is followed by 'Profile of an Enterprise, 1976–1990' (pp. 485–553). These are the years in which Tim Rix was the chief executive and, from 1984, chairman. The final chapter, 'Epilogue: Posterity' (pp. 535–41), places Longman within a general historical perspective including transformations in book prices, book trade history and book historiography. There are four very informative appendices: 'A Note on Sources' (pp. 543–6); a listing of the 'Succession of Imprints of the House of Longman 1724–1990' (p. 547); a chronological tabulation of 'The Longman Family' (pp. 548–9); a 'Time Span 1724–1990' (pp. 551–60) and Briggs's autobiographical sketch. The index (pp. 567–87) is useful but cursory, and on occasions not over-helpful. For example, under 'Paternoster Row (London)' (p. 581), there are page references but no indication on which pages the reader will find the record of its destruction.

Mention should be made of the eleventh volume of the projected seventeen-volume *The Complete Works of Robert Browning with Variant Readings and Annotations*, edited by Michael Bright. This volume contains the text with a complete record of variants and extensive explanatory notes of two lengthy Browning poems from the 1870s, *Fifine at the Fair* and *Red Cotton Night-Cap Country*. This is not the appropriate place and there is not space to comment at length on the textual controversies surrounding the competitive editions of Browning's poetry, except to say that Bright's edition is exceedingly well documented.

John Bryant's *Melville Unfolding: Sexuality, Politics, and the Versions of Typee: A Fluid-Text Analysis, with an Edition of the Typee Manuscript* focuses upon a description of the various incarnations of Herman Melville's *Typee*. As Bryant observes in his opening sentence, 'This book about a fluid text is itself a fluid text because it has evolved through several versions.' Melville revised *Typee* extensively, and there are a 'thousand revision cites in the manuscript'. These are examined by Bryant, who 'devised a reading text of the manuscript that provides the final wording Melville intended by his many revisions'. Interestingly, Bryant shows how a digital edition of *Typee* would have been inadequate, and how government funding was not forthcoming for his plan to develop 'an online site that would allow readers to inspect digital images of the manuscript and my transcription simultaneously, and to use a version of my reading text to hyperlink to the revision sequences and narratives I had composed'. However, eventually the University of Virginia Press came to the rescue and a fluid text edition can be found at < http://rotunda.upress.-virginia.edu:8100/index.php?page_id=Home >. This still was unsatisfactory as 'it does not provide the creature comforts of a book, which in [the author's] view is the better venue for the kind of theorizing and critical analysis I was beginning to perform based on findings in the manuscript' (p. v–vii). Consequently, the present book is the result. In short, Bryant's monograph provides a fascinating insight not only into the fluid text of Melville's *Typee*, but also into contemporary ways of dealing with such fluidity, digital and otherwise.

The late, eminent biographer Humphrey Carpenter's (1946–2005) story of the John Murray publishing dynasty was commissioned in 2002 and remained incomplete when its author died. It has finally been published under the title *The Seven Lives of John Murray: The Story of a Publishing Dynasty, 1768–2002*, edited by Candida Brazil and James Hamilton, with additional material by James Hamilton. First published in 2008, it appeared a year later in paperback. Carpenter, Brazil and Hamilton brilliantly depict the history of a great publishing house. The brief, four-paragraph 'Epilogue' (pp. 310–11) is sad to read. This describes the moving of the Murray archive from Albemarle Street to the National Library of Scotland in Edinburgh, where it is now housed. The concluding paragraph reads that 'The library has remained at Albemarle Street, as have the paintings and the artefacts, and as have' the remaining descendants of the Murray dynasty, 'although they have never actually lived there. And also remaining at number 50 is all the intangible evidence that binds together the history of the publishing dynasty and its house' (p. 311). There is an appendix containing two short scenarios constituting 'Scenes from a Silent Movie together with a further imaginary scene by Humphrey Carpenter' focusing upon 'The House of Murray, 1860–1892' in other words, a period when it was at its greatest (pp. 312–17). The book concludes with a 'Dramatis Personae: Chronology of the Murrays' (pp. 318–19). There are detailed notes to this wonderful and informative book, which has a bibliography and a detailed index.

The second edition of Mary Carruthers's classic *The Book of Memory: A Study of Memory in Medieval Culture*, first published in 1990, offered its author 'an opportunity to rethink, recast, correct and generally reassess the conclusion [she] offered in 1990' (p. ix). She focuses upon two themes which were not emphasized in the earlier edition. First, the 'issues of memory and forgetting, particularly in relation to historical narratives of various sorts and to monuments' (p. x), and, secondly, another matter to which the first edition gave much too short a shrift: the place of 'rote memorization—memorizing by heart—in the edifice of an ancient and medieval education' (p. xii). Carruthers further acknowledges that most of the post-1989 'work has come from historians of various kinds' including 'of literature both in Latin and in vernaculars—but some as well has come ... from psychologists, anthropologists, neuroscientists, and computer designers' (p. xiv).

Mention should be made of the first supplement to Marvin L. Colker's great *Trinity College Library Dublin: Descriptive Catalogue of the Mediaeval and Renaissance Latin Manuscripts* [1991]. This consists of two parts. The first part contains a 'Description of Mediaeval and Renaissance Latin Manuscripts Acquired, from 1990 to 2003, by the Manuscripts Department of Trinity College Library Dublin' (pp. 11–154). The second part consists of 'Addenda and Corrigenda, Chiefly Bibliographical Additions to Marvin L. Colker, *Trinity College Library Dublin, Descriptive Catalogue of the Mediaeval and Renaissance Latin Manuscripts*' (pp. 155–6), a 'Key to Short References' (pp. 157–62) and 'Addenda and Corrigenda for the Catalogue of 1991' (pp. 163–219).

A foremost intellectual historian of today, Stefan Collini's essays, which have previously appeared in the *Times Literary Supplement*, the *London Review of Books* and elsewhere, are now collected together in his *Common Reading*. 'Substantially, these essays explore aspects of the literary and intellectual culture of Britain, from the early twentieth century to the present.' The collection of essays is divided into two parts: the first part focuses on 'Writing Lives' and the essays 'are largely exercises in intellectual portraiture, attempts to characterize, evaluate, and situate their subjects'. Subjects extend from Cyril Connolly, V.S. Pritchett, William Empson and E.P. Thompson to Roger Scruton. In the second part, 'Reading Matters', 'the focus shifts more to the nature of the diverse publics for whom these figures wrote, and to the cultural traditions and institutional frameworks within which they operated' (p. 1). So there are sections headed ' "The Great Age": The Idealizing of Victorian Culture' (pp. 211–20) and, to take one other instance, 'The Completest Mode: The Literary Critic as Hero' (pp. 257–67). Collini writes well and always has something interesting to say in what is essentially a work of reference and literary history.

The latest volume, in this instance number 15, of Kevin L. Cope's expensive but very useful *1650–1850: Ideas, Aesthetics, and Inquiries in the Early Modern Era*, contains seven essays, a special feature and extensive book reviews that are edited by Scott Paul Gordon. In the articles, Steven Minuk discourses on 'The "Sincere hand and faithful eye" of Marvell's *Last Instructions to a Painter*' (pp. 3–22); Deborah Needleman Armintor discusses ' "From this time, I shall survey myself in the glass with a sort of philosophical pleasure": Newton and Narcissism in *Sir Isaac Newton's Philosophy Explain'd for the Use of the Ladies*' (pp. 23–36); Kenneth Chong discusses 'Faith and Reason, Warning the Read in *The Pilgrim's Progress*' (pp. 37–61); Katherine O'Donnell examines a neglected area in 'Edmund Burke, *Cúrteanna Éigse*, and Literary Clubs' (pp. 63–74); Pramod K. Nayar's 'The Rhetoric of Ruin: William Hodges's India' (pp. 75–106) has as its foundation William Hodges's profusely illustrated account of his travels, *Travels in India during the years 1780, 1781, 1782 and 1783*, which was first published in 1793, with a second and corrected edition appearing a year later and reprinted in New Delhi by Munshiram Manoharlal in 1999. Arnd Bohm returns to more familiar territory in his 'Unnatural Conjugation in *Tristram Shandy*, Book VII' (pp. 107–54). The equally suggestive title, 'A Concordance of Bosoms: Reconstructing Lewis's *Monk*', is the subject of Frederick S. Frank's contribution (pp. 155–80). This concludes with, believe it or not, a 'Table: A Grand Census of Bosoms' (pp. 170–80).

These articles are appropriately followed by a special feature edited and introduced by Philip Smallwood, 'Critical Voices: Humor, Irony, and Passion in the Literary Critics of the Long Eighteenth Century' (pp. 183–334). Following Smallwood's interesting introduction (pp. 183–8) may be found: Tom Mason's 'Abraham Cowley's Amiability' (pp. 189–218); David Roberts's ' "Almost impossible in praise" Dedicatory Criticism in English Dramatic Texts of the Seventeenth Century' (pp. 219–41); Cedric D. Reverand II's 'The

Epic Dryden Never Wrote' (pp. 243–71); Min Wild's '"The bottom of all things": Christopher Smart's Old Crone of Criticism' (pp. 271–92); Philip Smallwood's 'Voice and Laughter in Johnson's Criticism' (pp. 293–314) and Adam Rounce's 'Joseph Warton's Enthusiasms' (pp. 315–34). Scott Paul Gordon's 'Book Reviews' section covers twenty-one books, beginning with Blair Hoxby's review of Balachandra Rajan's *Milton and the Climates of Reading* (Toronto: University of Toronto Press [2006]; pp. 335–9) and concludes with Alison Hickey's review of another eminent scholar-critic's work, Jack Stillinger's *Romantic Complexity: Keats, Coleridge, and Wordsworth* (Urbana: University of Illinois Press [2006]; pp. 410–15). There is in addition an 'Addenda and Corrigenda' (pp. 417–18) and a name-based index (pp. 419–27). So something of interest for scholars and textual critics yet again in this volume.

The seventy-fifth anniversary of the Association of Research Libraries is celebrated with a sumptuously illustrated book containing collection profiles with highlights and collection overviews of the 118 of the 123 libraries who are members. Entries in Philip N. Cronenwett, Kevin Osborn and Samuel A. Streit's edited *Celebrating Research* begin with the W.S. Hoole Special Collections Library at the University of Alabama Libraries and details of the David Walker Lupton African American Cookbook Collection (pp. 28–9), and conclude with the Sterling Memorial Library at Yale University Library and an illustration from its great map collection (pp. 262–3). A description of each of the libraries is accompanied by an illustration from its collection. The Thomas W. Baldwin Collection at the University of Illinois at Urbana-Champaign Library Rare Book and Manuscript Library is accompanied by illustrations of an 'Elizabethan manuscript. c. 1550' and sixteenth-century 'Elizabethan school texts' (p. 119). The Lilly Library at Indiana University Libraries Bloomington illustration is from the annotated typescript of Orson Welles's '*Voodoo Macbeth*': the words 'SMOKE POT' and 'RAISE HELL WITH EVERYthing', amongst other comments, are scrawled in red crayon across the typescript (p. 120). As Nicolas Baker points out in his informative introduction (pp. 13–25), 'the variety of the material covered in the profiles of their collections selected by 118 of ARL's members for this volume is in itself remarkable' (p. 15).

There are twenty-one chapters in the *Companion to Emblem Studies* edited by Peter M. Daly. Of especial interest is Stephen Rawles 'Emblem Bibliography' (pp. 1–41), which 'is mainly concerned with descriptive or analytical bibliography of printed books rather than secondary bibliographies ... bibliographies of modern editions, or with manuscript material', although a listing of 'important secondary bibliographies' is listed in a footnote (p. 25). Rawles's bibliography is highly selective and divided into seven sections: 'General Works of Bibliography Concerning the Emblem' (pp. 32–4); 'Emblem Bibliographies on Specific Subjects or Groups' (pp. 34–5); 'Emblem Books by Country' (pp. 35–6); 'Author-Specific Bibliographies and Catalogues' (pp. 36–8); 'Library-Specific Catalogues' (pp. 38–9); 'Printers' (pp. 39–40); and by 'City' (pp. 40–1). The editor Peter M. Daly contributes four chapters: 'Emblems: An Introduction' (pp. 1–25); 'Emblem Theory: Modern and Early Modern' (pp. 43–78); 'The Emblem in Material Culture' (pp. 411–56); and 'The *Nachleben* of the Emblem in Some Modern Logos, Advertisements, and Propaganda' (pp. 489–518). He also compiles a 'Selective Bibliography for Further Reading' (pp. 519–602). There are contributions on the emblem in various countries. These range from France and French-speaking countries, German-speaking regions, Hungary, the Low Countries, Poland, Russia, Scandinavia and Spain to the United Kingdom and America. There is a detailed listing of the black and white illustrations provided in the text (pp. 603–8), detailed notes on the contributors (pp. 609–15) and an extensive index (pp. 617–32). This is the twentieth volume in the AMS Studies in the Emblem series, and contains items of considerable interest not merely to students of the emblem.

Marlies K. Danziger's *James Boswell: The Journal of his German and Swiss Travels, 1764*, is the first volume in the Yale Research Series of Boswell's journeys covering his travels through the German–Swiss territories from mid-June 1764. Following a stay in Utrecht to study law, it extends to New Year's Day 1765, when Boswell crossed the Alps to continue his European tour in Italy, Corsica and France. Danziger's extensive introduction clearly explains editorial procedures and annotations. She restores the original spelling, punctuation and paragraphs and Boswell's French passages. This is another invaluable volume in the continuing research edition of the private papers of James Boswell.

Audrey Ekdahl Davidson (1930–2006) was a distinguished musicologist, and *Aspects of Early Music and Performance* 'represents a sampling of her interests' (p. vii). It contains her essays on 'Five Settings of Songs Attributed to Sir Philip Sidney' (pp. 101–22), 'Milton's Economiastic Sonnet to Henry Lawes' (pp. 123–32) and 'George Herbert and the Celestial Harmony' (pp. 133–54). John Davies, Nigel Jenkins, Menna Baines and Peredur I. Lynch's *The Welsh Academy Encyclopedia of Wales* restricts its biographical entries 'to the dead, celebrity often proving transitory, but the living may nevertheless gain entry "by the back door": it would be bizarre, for instance, to treat pop music without mention of Shirley Bassey, or devolution without reference to Ron Davies' (p. xviii). The detailed 'Introduction and Acknowledgments' (pp. xvii–xxii) explains the inclusions and exclusions in the encyclopedia from persons to topics to topography and so on. The encyclopedia begins with a short pictorially illustrated entry on 'A Oes Heddwch? (Is there peace?)' (p. 1) and concludes with Alfred Eckhart Zimmern, the academic and author, Ernest Zobole, the painter, and the film *Zulu*. Somewhat ironically, neither Zimmern or Zobole was born in Wales! There is an all too short but interesting and informative entry on 'Literature' (pp. 464–8), and some writers receive separate entries, such as Bernice Rubens (1928–2004) (p. 781). All in all, a very worthwhile volume.

Gary Day's stimulating *Literary Criticism: A New History* 'is not just concerned with the relation between criticism and the language of economics. It also focuses, from the Renaissance onwards, on English criticism' (p. 6). Day's first chapter focuses upon the concept of 'criticism' (p. 10) having its origins in the Greeks and Romans, and the lengthy chapter covers 'the issues and ideas on which modern criticism is based' (p. 61). Day's second chapter is devoted to 'Medieval Criticism' (pp. 65–110), his third chapter to 'English

Renaissance Criticism' (pp. 111–55), his fourth chapter to the 'English Enlightenment and Early Romantic Criticism' (pp. 156–206), his fifth chapter to 'English Romantic, Moral and Aesthetic Criticism' (pp. 207–56), and his sixth chapter to the contentious modern period: 'Institutionalising English Criticism: Men of Letters, Modernism, Tradition and Theory' (pp. 257–315). There is a very useful bibliography (pp. 316–34) and index (pp. 335–44). If Day's book could be reissued in paperback form it would provide a very good textbook for graduate classes studying the history of literary criticism.

Christopher De Hamel provides an introduction to *Book of Beasts: A Facsimile of MS Bodley 764*. He writes: 'The medieval illuminated manuscript Bestiary, now MS Bodley 764 in the Bodleian Library in Oxford, dates from the middle of the thirteenth century and is of extreme importance and beauty.' De Hamel adds that 'A Bestiary means a book of beasts, but it goes beyond animals alone. Bodley 764 has 135 pictures of animals, including birds, reptiles and fish' (p. 5). The facsimile contains wonderful coloured illustrations. It is expensive but worth every penny to experience almost the real thing.

Jan Tschichold (1902–74) is regarded as one of the greatest and most influential typographers of the last century. Cees W. de Jong's *Jan Tschichold: His Life, Work and Legacy* contains 278 colour examples of Tschichold's work (331 illustrations in all) covering many aspects of Tschichold's life, work and legacy. In Britain, he is chiefly known as the designer for the important Penguin Book title pages and covers which were so pervasive in the middle years of the twentieth century. In addition to de Jong's introduction (pp. 13–22), there are very informative and detailed accounts by Alston W. Purvis on 'Tschichold and the New Typography' (pp. 23–154); Martijn F. le Coultre on 'Tschichold and Poster Design' (pp. 155–256); Richard B. Doubleday on the 'Resurgence of Classical Design' (pp. 257–98); and Hans Reichardt and Cees W. de Jong on the 'Perfectly Legible and Readable' (pp. 299–342). These accounts are accompanied by an 'Index of Names' (pp. 343–6) and a short 'Selected Literature and Source List' (pp. 347–51). The amount of information contained in the essays and the lavish illustrations drawing upon archival photographs, many published here for the first time, reveal the influences upon their subject, his diverse career, his important poster work and, for Penguin Books, his creation of the typeface Sabon. In short, de Jong's collection is an indispensable accompaniment to our knowledge of twentieth-century typography and, given its price, represents remarkable value.

Brian Dibble's *Doing Life: A Biography of Elizabeth Jolley* (1923–2007) provides a fascinating account of the writer who blossomed late. Her publishing career began when she was in her fifties in Australia, but her earlier life was spent in England and Scotland. Dibble had total access to the writer's private papers and the book contains much that is important about mid-twentieth-century publishing history, including an extensive enumerative bibliography of Jolley's works which is indebted to Barbara Milech and Brian Dibble's *Elizabeth Jolley—A Bibliography, 1965–2007*. This is available online from the Elizabeth Jolley Research Collection, John Curtin Prime Ministerial Library, Curtin University of Technology, Perth, WA, at < http://john.curtin.edu.au/jolley > . There is in addition a detailed listing of 'Elizabeth Jolley—Archival Material' including letters (pp. 316–19).

Sarah Dillon's *The Palimpsest: Literature, Criticism, Theory* begins with Thomas De Quincey's explanation of the concept of palimpsest in an article of the same name published in *Blackwood's Magazine* in 1845. Essentially, Dillon's work explores the palimpsest metaphor through examining its history, its use by De Quincey, D.H. Lawrence, Arthur Conan Doyle, Umberto Eco, H.D., Ian McEwan and others. There is, in addition to notation at the end of each chapter, an extensive alphabetically arranged enumerative 'Bibliography' (pp. 147–59) and a rather brief index (pp. 161–4). The study also draws attention the theoretical work by Freud, Saussure, Barthes, Derrida and others on the subject, including a fine essay by Josephine McDonagh who, in her 'Writings on the Mind: Thomas De Quincey and the Importance of the Palimpsest in Nineteenth-Century Thought' (*PSt* 10:i [1987] 207–24) 'offers the only previous sustained study of its significance' (p. 3). The two illustrative figures accompanying the text exemplify its range. The first is from *Fragments of the Iliad of Homer from a Syriac Palimpsest* [1851] (p. 22) and the second is from D.H. Lawrence's college notebook (p. 45).

Martin J. Duffell's *A New History of English Metre* fills an important gap, as he points out in his introduction: 'Almost a hundred years have passed since George Saintsbury produced his great three-volume *History of English Prosody*, and in that time there have been many changes in the ways that poets versify, and even more in the methods critics use to approach texts.' Further, although I think that Duffell is exaggerating in implying a bias on Saintsbury's part which may not have been present, 'no author today would want to continue in the elitist and chauvinistic tone of Saintsbury's three volumes, typified by the constant use of the terms "doggerel" and "foreign" as pejoratives to apply to any line that offends the author's personal taste and any research that conflicts with his own views'. The last volume of Saintsbury's work was published in 1910, and his was not the only consideration of English metrics written during the last two decades of the nineteenth century and first decade of the twentieth. Indeed, Duffell describes the period as 'a Golden Age of English metrics'. Duffell's aim 'is to provide teachers and students of English literature with a historical account of how poets have versified in English right up to the present day'. His 'second aim is to familiarize this literary audience with some of the latest linguistic research into metre and to compare the traditional explanation of how various types of line are crafted with the metrical analyses offered by a number of modern writers' (pp. 3–4). These are ambitious aims: whether they succeed or not must remain subjective. There is no doubt that Duffell's *A New History of English Metre* contains a lot of important basic information. It concludes with 'Statistical Tables' (pp. 239–56), a bibliography (pp. 257–74) and an extensive index (pp. 275–90).

Volume 99 of English Literary Studies' Important Editions and Monographs is James Gifford's edition of Lawrence Durrell's *Panic Spring: A Romance*, which was originally published under the pseudonym of Charles Norden by Faber & Faber in 1937. James A. Bringham's 'Afterword' contextualizes the novel, placing it amongst Durrell's early works and with Richard Pine's introduction discusses the significance of *Panic Spring* to

Durrell's oeuvre and his development as a writer. The annotations and commentary reveal that *Panic Spring* is, in the words of Stefan Herbrechter in his back-cover endorsement of the edition, 'an important missing link, accentuating the continuity of Durrell's aesthetic and ideological development as a writer and as an influential cultural figure between the wars and beyond'.

Volume 100 of ELS is an edition of Lawrence Durrell's first novel, *Pied Piper of Lovers*. This was first published in 1935 by Cassell & Company. Drawing heavily upon Durrell's own life, the novel depicts the Anglo-Indian childhood of Walsh Clifton and his attempt to reconcile what may be called 'mother India' and 'father England'. Clearly, leaving India was a trauma and deeply affected the rest of his life. The novel also depicts London and Bloomsbury in the 1920s. Owing to the personal revelations, Durrell did not allow republication during his lifetime and the novel became very obscure. Gifford writes in his introduction that 'Durrell's difficulty with this tension between race and nationality, marking as they do the frail fabric of identity, is made palpable, yet its resolution is elusive. This difficulty drives Durrell's later work just as readily as it directs our interpretive ventures' (p. xvi).

The great Dreiser edition continues with Clare Virginia Eby's edition of 'Dreiser's fourth published novel *The Genius* of 1915'. As she indicates in her 'Editorial Principles and Copy-Text' 'this edition is not offered as a definitive text ... Rather, it is presented as an important version of Dreiser's book, a text that Dreiser named *The Genius* and completed in 1911, before the significant revisions that were incorporated in the novel published four years later. This edition thus presents Dreiser's novel as it existed at a crucial moment in its long history of composition.' In fact, Eby uses as a copy-text 'the 1911 holograph manuscript' found at the Annenberg Rare Book and Manuscript Library at the University of Pennsylvania (p. 856). The text is followed by a 'List of Abbreviations' (pp. 749–50), essays on 'The Composition of *The Genius:* The 1911 Version to Print' (pp. 751–61), 'The Intellectual and Cultural Background to *The Genius*: The 1911 Version to Print' (pp. 762–91) and extensive 'Historical Notes' (pp. 792–852). The 'Textual Commentary' is divided into two: 'Editorial Principles and Copy-Text' (pp. 855–6) and 'Textual Notes' (pp. 857–72). These are followed by 'Textual Apparatus' (pp. 873–4) and 'Selected Emendations' (pp. 875–94). There are various appendices (pp. 895–907) and a useful index (pp. 908–52). Eby's edition will become the standard one to use.

Owen Dudley Edwards's magisterial *British Children's Fiction in the Second World War* was reviewed in *YWES* 88[2009] 1257. The publication of paperback edition of this important work should be mentioned in passing. The binding is sturdy, the computer-generated typesetting easy on the eye and there are eleven accompanying illustrative figures. Andrew Elgar and Peter Sedgwick have edited a second edition of *Cultural Theory: The Key Concepts*. Entries obviously vary in length; however, this second edition includes many new entries, including ones on 'colonialism', 'cyberculture', 'globalization', 'terrorism' and 'visual studies' amongst others. All in all, a useful reference work. Elizabeth Evenden's *Patents, Pictures and Patronage: John Day and the Tudor Book Trade* is an extensive study of probably the most important English printer of the later sixteenth century, John Day. It opens by placing

Day within the context of the sixteenth-century printing industry, his early activities in the book trade, and then examines his important productions. Evenden concludes that 'Day showed himself as worthy of patronage, not just because of his skills in the art of printing; he showed the English elite—in particular, William Cecil, Robert Dudley and Matthew Parker—the true propaganda potential of the printing press' (p. 179). There is a select 'Bibliography of Manuscript and Printed Primary Sources' (pp. 189–205) followed by 'Secondary Sources' (pp. 206–14), and an index (pp. 215–20). It seems churlish to quibble about such a clearly written and fine scholarly study, which is highly recommended. However, an important omission is work done at Northern Illinois University by Kimberly van Kampen on John Day based upon her own unique personal collection of his books.

Irving E. Fang's *Alphabet to Internet: Mediated Communication in our Lives*, a large-format (28 x 21.5 cm thick) book by an emeritus professor from the School of Journalism and Mass Communications at the University of Minnesota, is essentially an attempt to describe the history of writing or, in the language of the book, 'Mediated Communication' (p. 5). The first chapter 'traces writing from tokens at burial sites and scratches on jars in ancient Sumer to the output of Greek writing, and the application of writing in the great Asian empires' (p. 8). The final chapter 'tries to find points of cohesion across a vast landscape. It considers the astonishing range of communication choices we now have, and what we give up in social cohesion to get them' (p. 10). In the margins are trendy quotes from gurus such as Marshall McLuhan (p. 82) and, to name one other, Bernard Lewes (p. 339). The book is thoroughly documented and there is an extensive bibliography (pp. 389–406) with an index (pp. 407–20). 'A Timeline of Communication and Culture' begins in 4500 BCE (p. 421) and concludes in 2007, the final entry reading '17-year old Ashley Qualls earns millions via MySpace.com business' (p. 560). This volume is probably aimed at undergraduate classes in North American universities in communication: good luck.

The fourth volume of *The Edinburgh History of the Book in Scotland* focuses upon 'Professionalism and Diversity, 1880–2000'. The opening sentence of the editors David Finkelstein and Alistair McCleery's clearly written introduction essentially sums up what the individual essays in the volume describe: 'Publishing and the spread of books in Scotland between 1880 and 2000 has followed a trajectory linked to economic and political realities: from economic success derived from the industry's integration into British overseas markets in the nineteenth and early twentieth centuries, to its decline, merger, restructuring and redevelopment within a globalised marketplace and a devolved regional political structure' (p. 1). Well illustrated and documented, the volume is divided into six sections, each containing individual contributions, all of a high standard: '1. The Publishing Infrastructure: 1880–1980' (pp. 13–91); '2. Production, Form and Image' (pp. 92–181); '3. Publishing Policies: The Literary Culture' (pp. 182–294); '4. Publishing Policies: The Diversity of Print' (pp. 295–384); '5. Authors and Readers' (pp. 385–454); and '6. The Future of the Book in Scotland' (pp. 455–77). These are followed by details of the twenty-nine contributors (pp. 478–83), an extensive, enumerative, alphabetically arranged bibliography (pp. 484–502), and a detailed index (pp. 503–24). Particularly helpful are the editors' brief overviews to each of the respected sections in this important reference work.

Robert D. Fleck's *Books about Books: A History of Bibliography of Oak Knoll Press, 1978–2008* celebrates the thirtieth anniversary of a press devoted to bibliography and represented by 320 books published between 1978 and 2008: the press is still actively producing. 'A History of the Press, 1978–2008' (pp. 3–54), accompanied by black and white illustrations, is followed by a bibliography, 'an attempt to list every identifiable printing of each Oak Knoll Press publication' (p. 57). The first publication recorded is the reprinting of the original edition of 1880 of F.C. Bigmore and C.W.H. Wyman's *A Bibliography of Printing*, published in 1978 (p. 59) and the final book recorded is Steven Abbott's *Gore Vidal: A Bibliography*, published in 2008 (p. 209). This fascinating volume concludes with an extensive index listing author and title (pp. 211–32).

Robert Fraser admits in his preface to *Book History through Postcolonial Eyes. Rewriting the Script* that 'No one person can—or will soon—write a comprehensive history of the book from a postcolonial point of view'. His intention in his 'modest volume is to set a course by which others may later choose to steer'. Fraser perceives the book 'in the broadest meaning of the term, especially insofar as it draws upon the parallel communicative modes of spoken expression and script'. There is also 'an ulterior motive' at work 'which is to explain book history to postcolonial theorists, and postcoloniality to book history' (pp. ix–x). Divided into three parts, Fraser's chapters range from 'The Problematics of Print' (pp. 3–26), which draws upon material in the 'faded Georgian splendor of the Asiatic Society on Kolkata, or else amid the austere postmodern architecture of the Rare Books Room of the British Library' (p. 4), 'Transmitting the Word in Africa' (pp. 78–101), to 'Licensed Snoopers and Literary Protestors' (pp. 144–63), which is basically an account of attempts at civil control of newspaper editors with examples drawn from Calcutta, the Cape of Good Hope and rural Bengal. Fraser's study concludes with a useful bibliography (pp. 189–201) and index (pp. 202–10).

Nathan Garvey writes in his *The Celebrated George Barrington: A Spurious Author; the Book Trade, and Botany Bay*: 'This is a book about the "Barrington" books, the main aim of which is to describe and clarify a body of work that has long been regarded as a curiosity of early Australian literature.' Garvey continues, 'In a broader sense, it is also an inquiry into the print cultures of the late eighteenth and early nineteenth centuries, and, more particularly, the somewhat shadowy world of popular publishing in this period' (p. 9). Of Irish origins, George Barrington (*c.*1758–1804), was transported for theft to New South Wales in 1791. His activities acquired mythical status. Edgar Allen Poe cites him 'as a definitive example of the fundamental amorality of genius' (p. 2). Books which 'he had nothing whatsoever to do with' (p. 3) were attributed to him. Garvey's lengthy initial chapter, 'The Prince of Pickpockets' (pp. 11–71), considers Barrington's 'rise to fame and notoriety' (p. 7). The second chapter, 'The *Lives* of George Barrington' (pp. 73–102) outlines the publishing history of the biographies of

Barrington that appeared following 'his transportation sentence in 1790' (p. 7). 'Under a Deceptive Mask: Barrington as Author', the third chapter (pp. 102–66), is an examination of 'the fraudulent use of Barrington's name in the publication of a number of works from 1795' (p. 8). An 'Epilogue' (pp. 167–72) succinctly assesses the significance of the Barrington myth. It is followed by extensive 'References' (pp. 173–221) documenting the text. Garvey then provides an extensive descriptive 'Bibliography of the "Barrington" Books Published in the Period 1790–1840' (pp. 223–313). Garvey's fascinating, well-produced and illustrated book concludes with a select bibliography (pp. 315–17) and a useful, detailed index (pp. 319–27).

Bertrand A. Goldgar and Ian Gadd's edition of Swift's *English Political Writings, 1711–1714* is yet another addition to *The Cambridge Edition of the Works of Jonathan Swift.* Following a chronology (pp. xv–xxiii) and an extensive list of abbreviations (pp. xxiv–xxix), the forty-three-page introduction (pp. 1–43) is extensive and clearly written, placing the texts in their political, social, historical and textual context. The texts are fully annotated at the foot of the page and are followed by 'Textual Introduction and Accounts of Individual Works' (pp. 327–518). This monumental edition concludes with an enumerative, alphabetically arranged bibliography of primary and secondary works (pp. 519–28) and an index (pp. 529–46).

Brief mention should be made of Paul Goetsch's study in German of the English and American reception of the Faust myth. Goetsch's *Machphantasien in englischsprachigen Fust-Dichtungen: Funktiongeschichtliche Studien* focuses upon Marlowe's *Doctor Faustus*, Oscar Wilde's *The Picture of Dorian Gray*, H.G. Wells's *The Island of Dr. Moreau* and other work, including writings by Dorothy Sayers, I.A. Richards, Malcolm Lowry and Joseph Conrad to mention a few. There is of course an extensive discussion of the Faust myth applied to Shakespeare's *Macbeth*. Goetsch's enumerative, alphabetically arranged bibliography (pp. 287–98) is very useful for its listing of critical discussions of the myth. These discussions are placed under their author, so for example under Thomas Carlyle there are references to C.F. Harold's *Thomas Carlyle and German Thought, 1819–1934* (New Haven [1934]) and L. Metzger's '*Sartor Resartus*: A Victorian Faust' (*CL* 13[1961] 316–31). In addition, there is an extensive, separate, author-based index (pp. 299–303).

Another item of interest by Paul Goetsch is his 'The English Oak: The Changing Fortunes of a Political Icon' (*Symbolism* 8 [2008] 279–321). Goetsch surveys references and allusions to the oak in many periods in English literature post-1660. The emphasis is upon 'those meanings attributed to the oak that define Englishness or aspects of English politics deemed important by one or more political groups ... the fortunes of the oak depend largely on historical development and peculiarly national circumstances' (p. 279). Authors discussed range from Michael Drayton, Abraham Cowley, John Evelyn, Edmund Waller and John Dryden in the seventeenth century to Alexander Pope, Edward Young, James Thomson, William Cowper and Tobias Smollett in the eighteenth century. Subsequent literary figures include William Blake, Leigh Hunt, S.T. Coleridge, William Wordsworth, Scott, Byron, Shelley and, amongst the Victorians, James Froude, Tennyson, Carlyle, Disraeli and others.

Jeff Gomez chooses to open his *Print Is Dead: Books in our Digital Age* with a quote from Tom Stoppard, 'One of the questions that haunts me—it's a question for philosophers and brain science—is, if you've forgotten a book, is that the same as never having read it?' Gomez's book has a tripartite structure. In the first part, he 'shows how publishing leads to change'. In the second part, he describes 'the current conditions in terms of what's happening in other industries and what brought us culturally to this point'. And in the third part he discusses 'the issues going forward in terms of what life will be like in a digital world for writers, readers and publishers'. He avoids the issue, for instance, of 'what digital reading will mean to libraries or universities' or 'the debate over Google's plan to scan books and libraries'. His book is also New York-orientated, although he recognizes 'that the debate over the future of the book is a global discussion' (pp. 6–7). Given the contemporary nature of Gomez's issues, his book has relevance to the here and now; whether it will be anything more than of historical significance in a peripheral debate, only time will tell.

Mina Gorji's critical assessment of John Clare, *John Clare and the Place of Poetry*, does deal, although too briefly, with the thorny and controversial issue of editing Clare. She writes, 'The way in which Clare has been edited contributes to the prevailing image of him as unliterary and as a marginal figure outside literary culture.' For Gorji, 'By leaving the poems unpunctuated, and restoring dialect words as well as variant and non-standard spellings which had been edited out of early published versions, the Oxford Clarendon edition offers what it claims is an authentic Clare.' However, contemporary editions of his work enhance 'our appreciation of Clare's poetry and its place in literary culture of his day'. Further, contemporary 'volumes were part of a collaborative effort between poet, friends and publishers, and the language, style and form of the poems, together with the paratextual material, the titles, epigraphs and prefaces, placed Clare in a number of distinct literary communities'. Her discussion of Clare's 'The Nightingale's Nest' is particularly interesting in this respect (pp. 8–9, and see pp. 9–11).

Paul Gravett's *Graphic Novels: Everything You Need to Know* is a companion to the world of the graphic novel. As Gravett points out in his opening chapter, suitably entitled 'Things to Hate about Comics', the graphic novel is very difficult to define and 'The word graphic does not have to mean disturbing, extreme, and in your face, shown in hard outlines, grotesque caricatures, or lurid coloring' (p. 8). His book provides lots of answers to the question 'So what are graphic novels?' (p. 9). In spite of the jocular and trendy style, much can be gained from Gravett's well-illustrated account, first published in 2005.

Douglas Gray's *Later Medieval English Literature* presents the unfashionable analysis by a single author of a literary period. The modern trend is to examine historical periods of literature through the perspectives of various authors. Gray clearly marks out his territory in his opening sentence: 'This study aims to present students and readers with a guide to the literature written in English from the death of Chaucer to the earlier sixteenth century' (p. vi). He does this superbly in clear, concise, non-pretentious prose. His book is divided into five sections. The first is introductory (pp. 3–156), the second deals with prose (pp. 157–306), the third with poetry (pp. 307–440), the fourth with Scottish writing (pp. 441–566) and the fifth focuses upon drama (pp. 567–702). Gray displays his learning lightly, and this wonderful volume concludes with a detailed index (pp. 703–11).

Imtiaz H. Habib writes, in his introduction to his *Black Lives in the English Archives, 1500–1677*, that 'it is the contention of this book that the substantial archival evidence of black people in England between 1501 and 1676 ... contributes significant, irreversible, and hitherto unavailable materialities to current understanding of racial discourse in sixteenth- and seventeenth-century England'. He adds, 'These records mark the empirical intimacy of the English construction of the racial other, and of the national-imperial drive that is its most immediate occasion, both parallel to and independent of such formations in the travel literature of the period.' By these, Habib has in mind the writings of John Mandeville, Leo Africanus, William Towerson, Richard Eden, Richard Hakluyt and Samuel Purchas, amongst others (pp. 9–10). The first chapter examines 'Early Tudor Black Records' (pp. 19–62), the second 'Elizabethan London Black Records' (pp. 63–120), the third 'Black Records of Seventeenth-Century London' (pp. 121–92), the fourth 'Black People Outside London, 1558–1677' (pp. 193–238), and the fifth 'Indians and Others' (pp. 239–60). An important appendix to Habib's significant monograph consists of a 'Chronological Index of Records of Black People, 1500–1677' (pp. 273–368).

Louisa Hadley's book on *The Fiction of A.S. Byatt* concludes with a helpful, enumerative bibliography of Byatt's books, interviews and reviews of her work (pp. 163–71). Daniel Hahn and Nicholas Robins, eds., *The Oxford Guide to Literary Britain and Ireland*, is an updated version of a classic work which was first published in 1997 and constitutes a gazetteer of upward of 2,000 locations in Britain and Ireland which have literary associations. Arranged geographically, the focus ranges from a village, a town or a city to a specific house or place where authors gained inspiration. Margaret Drabble, John Sutherland and others contribute features on writers who are specifically associated with places, such as the Brontës, Thomas Hardy, Walter Scott and James Joyce. This is a valuable reference work, but given its size and format, hardly one which can be carried around in a rucksack.

The fifth incarnation of James L. Harner's indispensable *Literary Research Guide: An Annotated Listing of Reference Sources in English Literary Studies* reassesses each of the works included in the fourth edition [2002] and evaluated reference sources, print and electronic, that appeared after May 2001. Harner further notes in his 'Prefaces' that 'readers of earlier editions will notice some major changes in the fifth edition: the inclusion of far more electronic resources and the wholesale deletion of entries for scholarly journals and background studies as well as the section on encyclopedias in the "Literature-Related Topics and Sources" division'. He adds, 'the reason for the electronic additions is obvious: the proliferation of bibliographic databases, text archives and other outlying resources'. In short, 'in numerical terms' Harner has 'deleted 236 entries, added 78 and revised 482. The *Guide* now includes 1,059 entries; refers to 1,555 additional books, articles, and electronic resources in annotations and headnotes; and cites 723 reviews'. Harner favours 'subscription-based resources or those sponsored by a professional organization or university'. Further, according to Harner, 'the electronic version of the guide will be updated regularly' (p. x). The present writer has used the various incarnations of Harner for decades in his Bibliography and Methods of Research course which is compulsory for all MA and Ph.D. students in the Department of English at Northern Illinois University. Quite simply, Harner's book is indispensable for graduate study in English. It has a detailed index of names (pp. 759–78), index of titles (pp. 779–814) and subject index (pp. 815–26). Noticeable and revealing is the fact that some bibliographical studies stand the test of time. The names of E. Arber (two items) G.E. Bentley (one item), E.K. Chambers (four items), W.W. Greg (three items), H. Jenkinson (two items), A.W. Pollard and G.R. Redgrave (one item), and J. Sabin (one item) are just names from yesteryear who cannot be dismissed or thrown away. This illustrates a fact that great work will survive. Harner's is not only a record of the present but also a monument to the past.

Robert Hauptman's *Documentation: A History and Critique of Attribution, Commentary, Glosses, Marginalia, Notes, Bibliographies, Works-Cited Lists, and Citation Indexing and Analysis* thoroughly discusses various systems of literary documentation. These range from marginalia, footnotes, illustration and the University of Chicago to MLA and other citation systems, including their histories. He thoroughly examines their negatives and positives. 'Documentation is a study and critique of the apparatus that traditionally validates and enhances scholarly (and, infrequently, creative) works. It has been limited to the text and its parentheses, marginalia, notes and bibliographic listings' (p. 200). There is an extensive alphabetically arranged, enumerative bibliography and a thorough index (pp. 209–29) to this very welcome account of a neglected subject. Hauptman's text is accompanied by many black and white illustrations: these are especially helpful in the 'Marginalia' chapter (pp. 71–111).

There are three editions to record of the magnificent *The Collected Works of James Hogg* under the general editorship of the late Douglas S. Mack and Gillian Hughes. In the first, an edition of Hogg's *Midsummer Night Dreams and Related Poems*, Gillian Hughes and Meiko O'Halloran have completed the work of the eminent Hogg scholar Jill Rubenstein who died in August 2002 in the middle of her work on this edition. Their work represents the first complete edition of *Midsummer Night Dreams and Related Poems* since 1822, when it appeared in Hogg's *Poetical Works*. It contains a detailed, annotated text of the ten poems based upon the 1822 edition and Hogg's notes as a copy-text. Hogg's notes are also included and there are two appendices. The first concentrates on a 'MS Fragment of "The Field of Waterloo. A Poem"' and the second on 'Hogg's MS Notes to *The Pilgrims of the Sun*' (pp. 153–8).

The second edition is the third and final volume of the *Collected Edition of Hogg's Letters*. This final edition encompasses the years 1832 to 1835. In 1832 Hogg makes his first visit to London and is lionized. He explores possibilities of writing in American periodicals and deals with the claims made on his time as a celebrity author. A circle of young disciples compensates for the loss of dear old friends. He also casts a satirical look at what he regards as an age of cheap periodicals and political reform. A useful appendix contains 'Notes on

Correspondents' (pp. 304–59). This is followed by 'Notes on the Texts' (pp. 360–8), a useful and necessary glossary (pp. 369–72) and there is a very useful index.

The third edition to record is Suzanne Gilbert's edition of Hogg's first major collection of poetry, *The Mountain Bard*, published in 1807. In 1821 he published a revised edition. Gilbert's edition prints for the first time the 1807 collection, the surviving pre-1807 version of poems and the complete 1821 version. The complex evolving history of the work, its place within eighteenth-century antiquarian ballad-collecting projects and Romanticism, are fully discussed in her introduction, as are the editorial principles.

Nadine Holdsworth and Mary Luckhurst's *A Concise Companion to Contemporary British and Irish Drama* contains welcome detailed entries on British and Irish drama since 1979. The work is divided into four parts: part I explores 'National Politics and Identities' (pp. 5–84); part II, 'Sites, Cities and Landscapes' (pp. 85–146); part III, 'The Body, Text and the Real' (pp. 147–222); and part IV, 'Science, Ethics and New Technologies' (pp. 223–82). There are contributions from Helen Freshwater, Claire Gleitman, Sarah Gorman, David Higgins, Nadine Holdsworth, Mary Luckhurst, Tom Maguire, D. Keith Peacock, Dan Reballato, Heike Roms, Ken Urban, Geoff Willcocks and Fiona Wilkie.

Peter Holliday's *Edward Johnston: Master Calligrapher* re-examines the work and legacy of the master calligrapher, typeface designer and creator of the lettering and branding for the London underground, Edward Johnston (1872–1944). In addition to providing details of the craft community at Ditchling in Sussex, it includes fascinating information on the people associated with it, such as Eric Gill, David Jones, Bernard Leach and others who had a profound impact upon English lettering and calligraphy during the twentieth century. Superbly produced by the British Library and Oak Knoll Press, the volume is replete with illustrations.

Brief mention should be made of the publication of Andrew Hook's classic *Scotland and America: A Study of Cultural Relations, 1750–1835*, first published in 1975. This new edition contains a fresh preface by the author, an updated bibliography, and a foreword by the eminent historian of Scottish–American relations, Richard Sher. Hook writes superbly well, with wit and erudition. Valerie Hotchkiss and Fred C. Robinson's *English in Print: From Caxton to Shakespeare to Milton* contains descriptions of over a hundred early English books now at the Rare Books and Manuscript Library at the University of Illinois, Urbana-Champaign, and the Elizabethan Club at Yale University. It is profusely illustrated with over 130 full-colour images. This catalogue, based on an exhibition held at New York's Grolier Club between 14 May and 26 July 2008, begins with William Caxton and concludes with John Milton's *Areopagitica* [1644]. Shakespeare, although no evidence has come to light of him being a printer or a dramatist overly concerned with the publication of his own dramas, has central pride of place.

Originally 'organized alphabetically by topic, and comprising more than 700 entries written by 60 eminent scholars', the three-volume *Greenwood Encyclopedia of Latino Literature*, edited by Nicolás Kanellos, provides 'the birth and death dates of authors, when available, as well as other relevant biographical, bibliographical, stylistic, and cultural information'. Further, with 'general and thematic articles, most authors are placed within their historical, literary, and cultural contexts' (p. xxv). The entries begin with 'Aboy Benítez, Juan (1876–1901)', 'A young Puerto Rican novelist who lost his life in the collision and sinking of a Staten Island ferry boat' (pp. 1–2) and concludes with the Venezuelan journalist, political figure and writer, 'Zumeta, César (1850–1955)' (p. 1308). Obviously, with such a quantity of entries, the level is bound to vary, but on the whole, these four volumes contain much useful information, and the fourth volume has an enumerative bibliography (pp. 1309–16) and an extensive index to the four volumes (pp. 1317–52).

Don W. King's account of a great poet Ruth Pitter, *Hunting the Unicorn: A Critical Biography of Ruth Pitter*, contains an enumerative bibliography of her poetry publications, BBC radio broadcasts, BBC Brains Trust appearances, essays, interviews, letters and journals and audio recordings, plus critical reviews, essays and books about her (pp. 319–33). Andrea Krupp's *Bookcloth in England and America 1823–1850*, with a preface (pp. vii–viii) by Sue Allen encompasses the introduction of bookcloth and its earliest usage (pp. 1–12), bookcloth grain nomenclature (pp. 13–15) and observations on various cloth grain patterns (pp. 16–21). There are three appendices. The first itemizes grain patterns with date range and frequency and supplies cross-references to previous nomenclature (pp. 22–32). The second and third appendices contain a catalogue of 248 nineteenth-century bookcloth grains and include actual-size images of the various grains (pp. 33–100). The accompanying illustrations are in colour and demonstrate the ribbon-embossed patterns. This clearly is an important work.

The great American book designer, typographer and artist Bruce Rogers (1870–1957) was the subject of an exhibition held at the Thomas Fisher Rare Book Library at the University of Toronto from 24 September to 21 December 2007. This exhibition was largely based upon the collection of Rogers's materials amassed by Thomas Schweitzer, and now appears as a catalogue by Richard Landon entitled *Humane Letters: Bruce Rogers, Designer of Books and Artist. With an Introductory Essay on Collecting Bruce Rogers by Thomas T. Schweitzer*. In his essay 'The Joys and Sorrows of Collecting Bruce Rogers' (pp. 19–32), Schweitzer describes the problems and challenges involved in collecting Rogers. Some of these problems may be seen in Rogers's entry in *Who Was Who 1951–1960* revealing his transatlantic connections. In addition to his work for the Riverside Press in Cambridge, Mass., from 1895 to 1912, Rogers worked as the printing adviser to Cambridge University Press in the UK, to the Harvard University Press and, from 1928, as an independent designer of books. These included the Oxford Lectern Bible of 1935. His fascination with T.E. Shaw (T.E. Lawrence) led to his *The Odyssey*, translated by T.E. Shaw [1931] and two volumes of *Letters of T.E. Shaw to Bruce Rogers* published in 1933 and 1936. So great was Rogers's reputation that the University Printer at Cambridge University Press printed a *Report on the Typography of the Cambridge University Press Prepared in 1917 at the Request of the Syndics by Bruce Rogers and now Printed in Honour of his Eightieth Birthday* at Christmas, 1950. Landon's catalogue includes fifty-two Rogers productions. Title pages and other illustrations of Rogers's work, with the number of copies printed, are included in colour with fascinating and detailed accompanying illustration, revealing much about the Anglo-American printing and publishing world of the first half of the twentieth century. This book reveals that Bruce Rogers was truly, to use Richard Landon's words in his preface, 'a great book designer' (p. 7).

The eminent scholar of the 1890s, Mark Samuels Lasner, has yet again provided an important addition to our knowledge of the period. His *The Bookplates of Aubrey Beardsley*, is largely based upon his own collection currently on loan to the University of Delaware Library. Following Lasner's brief introduction (pp. 7–12), is a list of short titles (pp. 13–14) and then a checklist. The first is of 'Bookplates Designed by Beardsley' (pp. 15–24) and the second and larger section of the book 'Bookplates Adapted from Beardsley's Designs' (pp. 25–104). There is in addition a brief index (pp. 105–7). Essentially, this book describes and illustrates for the first time the forty plates made from Beardsley's works. Those who utilized Beardsley included a Hungarian composer, the eccentric Aleister Crowley, an eminent lawyer and others.

Barbara Tepa Lupack and Alan Lupack's *Illustrating Camelot* contains a comprehensive and well-illustrated study of Arthurian illustration found in the revival of interest in the Arthur legend in the nineteenth century. Analysis ranges from the illustrated editions of Tennyson's *Idylls of the King*, to exceedingly popular children's retellings of Malory's *Morte d'Arthur*, to work in areas other than literature, such as Julian Margaret Cameron's photographic portraits, Russell Flint's watercolours and Gustave Doré's engravings. The authors have given us a fascinating, informative and well-produced book. Brendan Lynch's *Parsons Bookshop: At the Heart of Bohemian Dublin 1949–1989* is a succinctly well-written account of a central Dublin bookshop which flourished from 1949 to 1989. It was frequented by such luminaries as Brendan Behan, Patrick Kavanaugh and Flann O'Brien. Lynch's account is peppered with some fascinating anecdotes and personal reminiscences. Jack Lynch's *Deception and Detection in Eighteenth-Century Britain* focuses upon James Macpherson, William Henry Ireland, Thomas Chatterton and others. Lynch's focus is upon readings of how contemporary eighteenth-century readers and critics perceived forgery and misrepresentation, rather than seeing the activities of his central figures through a late twentieth-century lens.

Cheryl Alexander Malcolm and David Malcolm's *A Companion to the British and Irish Short Story* contains forty-nine chapters. These are divided into two parts. The first covers the years 1880–1945 and includes for instance chapters by Patrick Lonergan on 'Irish Short Fiction: 1880–1945' (pp. 51–64) and Jopi Nyman on 'The Detective and Crime Story: 1880–1945' (pp. 65–80). Part II covers the period 1945 to the present and, like the first part, is divided into 'Topics and Genres' and 'Readings of Individual Authors and Texts'. For instance, Cheryl Alexander Malcolm writes on 'The Anglo-Jewish Short Story since the Holocaust' (pp. 330–41) and Michael Meyer on 'Feminist Voices: Women's Short Fiction after 1945' (pp. 342–55). Individual readings of authors and texts include Michael Parker on 'Alan Sillitoe: "The Loneliness of the Long Distance Runner"' (pp. 409–15), Robert Ellis Hosmer Jr on 'The Short Stories of Elizabeth Taylor' (pp. 416–22), John Kenny on 'William

Trevor: Uncertain Grounds for Assured Art' (pp. 480–7) and, to take one more instance from many, Peter Clanfield on 'James Kelman: *Greyhound for Breakfast*' (pp. 532–40). Obviously, with so many contributors there is bound to be a range of quality in the entries, but overall this is fairly high and they are of considerable interest.

Nicole Matthews writes in the introduction to her collection of essays with Nickianne Moody, *Judging a Books by its Cover: Fans, Publishers, Designers and the Marketing of Fiction*: 'This collection argues that book covers—the wrapping of image, typography and puff prose that surrounds the written contents of a book—really matter' (p. i). Matthews and Moody's collection is divided into four parts. The first part consists of four essays by diverse hands on the subject of 'Approaches to the Book Cover'. Alistair McCleary writes on 'The Paperback Evolution: Tauchnitz, Albatross and Penguin' (pp. 3–18), Angus Phillips on 'How Books Are Positioned in the Market: Reading the Cover' (pp. 19–30), Val Williamson on 'Relocating Liverpool in the 1990s: Through the Covers of Regional Saga Fiction' (pp. 31–42) and Nickianne Moody on 'Empirical Studies of the Bookshop: Context and Participant Observation in the Study of Selling and Marketing of Science Fiction and Fantasy' (pp. 43–62). Part II focuses on 'What Makes a Book Popular?' and contains Elizabeth Webby's 'Literary Prizes, Production Values and Cover Images' (pp. 63–70), Clair Squires's 'Book Marketing and the Booker Prize' (pp. 71–82) and Susan Pickford's 'Jerome K. Jerome and the Paratextual Staging of Anti-Elitism' (pp. 83–94). Part III, ' "The Record of the Film of the Book": Cultural Industries and Intertextuality', contains Gerry Carlin and Mark Jones's 'Pop Goes the Paperback' (pp. 95–106), Rebecca N. Mitchell's ' "Now a Major Motion Picture": The Delicate Business of Selling Literature through Contemporary Cinema' (pp. 107–16) and Alexis Weedon's 'In Real Life: Book Covers in the Internet Bookstore' (pp. 117–28). The final part, 'Translating Covers: Moving Audiences and the Marketing of Books', contains Melissa Sky's 'Cover Charge: Selling Sex and Survival in Lesbian Pulp Fiction' (pp. 129–46), Chris Richards's 'Addressing "Young Adults"? The Case of Francesca Lia Block' (pp. 147–60) and the final contribution, by Pamela Pears, on 'Images, Messages and the Paratext in Algerian Women's Writing' (pp. 161–71).

Andrew Maunder, who has written fine studies of Victorian literature, has compiled an excellent reference work. His *The Facts on File Companion to the British Short Story* is an approximately 350,000-word compendium on its subject. Following a most informative introduction (pp. v–xvi), Maunder begins with alphabetically arranged entries, starting with a critical account of *The Acid House* by Irving Welsh from 1994 (pp. 1–2) and concluding with an entry on Israel Zangwill (pp. 476–7). Appendices include a glossary (pp. 479–506) and an alphabetically arranged, enumerative bibliography of studies 'devoted exclusively to the British short story' (pp. 507–8). In addition there is a list of contributors (pp. 501–11) and an extensive index (pp. 513–28). Clearly with so many different hands at work, writing over 450 entries, length and quality are going to vary. However, overall the standard is high. A notable exception is any mention of the work of Leonard Merrick (1864–1934), who wrote innumerable short stories, many of which were highly praised by his contemporaries. However, it is pleasing to see entries on younger writers, such as Toby Litt (pp. 244–5).

Shakespeare's Book: Essays in Reading, Writing and Reception consists of a series of essays designed to challenge the idea that Shakespeare was not interested in books or book culture. It 'examines Shakespeare's works in relation to [their] different contexts of production and reception' (p. 13). In their introduction the editors Richard Meek, Jane Rickard and Richard Wilson challenge perceived notions in ' "Th'world's volume": Printer, Page and the Literary Field' (pp. 1–28). The book is divided into three parts. The first consists of four essays on 'Books': Patrick Cheney writes on ' "An index and obscure prologue": Books and Theatre in Shakespeare's Literary Authorship' (pp. 29–58); Helen Smith on ' "A man in print"? Shakespeare and the Representation of the Press' (pp. 59–78); Richard Meek on ' "Penn'd speech": Seeing and Not Seeing in *King Lear*' (pp. 79–102) and Richard Wilson on ' "A stringless instrument": *Richard II* and the Defeat of Poetry' (pp. 102–22).

The second part has three entries and is devoted to 'Texts': Gabriel Egan writes on 'Foucault's Epistemic Shift and Verbatim Repetition in Shakespeare' (pp. 123–39); Duncan Salkeld on ' "As sharp as a pen": *Henry V* and its Texts' (pp. 140–64) and E.A.J. Honigmann on 'Shakespeare's Deletions and False Starts, Mark 2' (pp. 165–86). The third part has four entries and is devoted to 'Readers': George Donaldson writes on 'The First Folio: "My Shakespeare"/ "Our Shakespeare": Whose Shakespeare?' (pp. 187–206), Jane Richard on 'The "First" Folio in Context: The Folio Collections of Shakespeare, Jonson and King James' (pp. 207–32), Stanley Wells on 'A New Early Reader of Shakespeare' (pp. 233–40) and John Lyon on ' "Too long for a play": Shakespeare Beyond Page and Stage' (pp. 241–54). Lukas Erne's 'Afterword' (pp. 255–66) focuses upon textuality and the printing of Shakespeare's plays. All in all, a very worthwhile volume, although some of the essays contain more jargon than others.

Jon Millington's *William Beckford: A Bibliography* is a delightfully produced, printed and bound volume reflecting well on its publishers, the Beckford Society, and its author. The Beckford Society was created in 1995 in order to promote interest in the accomplishments of William Beckford (1760–1844), noted for his authorship of *Vathek*. Since its publication in 1786 the novel has appeared in 165 editions and in twenty different languages. Beckford also created one of the most important architectural monuments of the Gothic revival, Fonthill Abbey. John Piper's lithograph of the abbey is used as the dust-jacket illustration for the present volume. Beckford collected books and works of art, he travelled, built, wrote and was a landscape gardener. The bibliography is divided into two parts, the first devoted to Beckford's life and the second to literature. The first part has nine sections: 'Accounts of Beckford's Life' (pp. 23–43), 'Aspects of Beckford' (pp. 44–66) including 'Character', 'Politics', 'Religion', 'Sexuality'—interesting books and articles on homosexuality, sexual ambiguity, and bisexuality are listed here (pp. 57–60)—'Slavery', 'Wealth' and so on. These are followed by material on the Beckford 'Family' (pp. 67–78). There are books and articles listed on 'Contemporaries' (pp. 79–97), beginning with Jane Austen and concluding with James Wyatt. There are in addition listings on 'Fonthill' (pp. 98–160), including 'Other Fonthills' extending from Ireland to the USA, Tasmania and Lisbon (pp. 159–60), 'Beckford's Tower and Bath' (pp. 161–96) now restored and maintained by a preservation trust, 'Landscape Gardening' (pp. 197–203), Beckford's 'The Collection' (pp. 204–34) encompassing his library, ceramics, furniture, gold and silver, paintings and drawings, sculpture, stained glass, works of art and sales. The ninth section is devoted to 'Exhibitions' (pp. 235–47). The second part has eight sections. The first, 'Beckford's Works: First Editions', notes that 'Most of these entries also appear, together with later editions and related articles in the succeeding section' (pp. 251–6). A separate section, 11, is devoted to '*Vathek* and *The Episodes*: Editions' (pp. 257–74). This encompasses versions in English, French, German, Italian, Portuguese, Russian, Spanish and 'Other Languages', beginning with Catalan and concluding with Turkish (interestingly nothing in Arabic, Hebrew or Yiddish). The section concludes with 'Abridgements' and 'Extracts from *Vathek*' (pp. 272–4). The twelfth section lists '*Vathek* and *The Episodes*: Criticism' (pp. 275–306). By far the most extensive section contains 'Books' (pp. 279–96) and, also alphabetically arranged by author, 'Articles' (pp. 297–306). The next section, 13, itemizes 'Travel' (pp. 307–29). This is followed by items about 'Beckford's Other Works' (pp. 330–44), and then 'Literary Studies' (pp. 345–51). Section 16 lists, with all-too-brief annotations, 'Works Influenced by Beckford' (pp. 352–66). Amongst the 'Principal Novels' noted are Susan Sontag's *The Volcano Lover: A Romance* (p. 353). Authors included in 'Other Fiction, Poems and Sketches' (pp. 353–66) extend from Benjamin Disraeli (*Contarini Fleming*) and Thomas Hardy (*Jude the Obscure*) to Herman Melville (*White Jacket*). The final section, 17, lists 'Bibliographies' (pp. 367–73). An extensive index (pp. 374–410) and an index to Beckford's writings (p. 411) follows. References are to pages. Curiously, Millington's *William Beckford: A Bibliography* lacks enumeration. The arrangement is on occasion repetitious; annotation is inconsistent and mostly perfunctory. As Millington notes in his introduction, his 'bibliography covers works published up to the end of 2005 and concentrates on those printed in English and other European languages'. The author should be commended for his common sense, represented for instance by his comment: 'Actual website addresses are not given in this work because they change or go out of date so rapidly' (p. 12). The book is typeset in Sabo, designed by Humphrey Stone and superbly printed and bound by Biddles of King's Lynn, Norfolk. *William Beckford: A Bibliography* is clearly a labour of love. It should be purchased by all libraries and collections with material on English culture and society.

Kaye Mitchell's monograph on *A.L. Kennedy* contains a primary and secondary annotated bibliography (pp. 165–75). Of particular interest are Kennedy's newspaper articles chiefly written for the *Guardian*. The primary bibliography is essentially enumerative and the secondary bibliography contains brief content annotations. The third edition of the *MLA Style Manual and Guide to Scholarly Publishing* updates the 1985 first edition and the 1998 second edition. The main additions are in fact documentation relating to the new technologies. As MLA documentation is standard, this useful and well-presented book will remain an indispensable guide until a fourth edition is produced.

The second volume of *The Cambridge History of the Book in Britain*, edited by Nigel J. Morgan and Rodney M. Thomson, deals with the period 1100–1400 and is profusely illustrated. In the first section Christopher De Hamel writes on 'Books and Society' (pp. 3–21) and Rodney M. Thomson and Nigel J. Morgan write on 'Language and Literacy' (pp. 22–40). The following section contains essays by Pamela Robinson, M.B. Parkes, the editors, Michael Gullick and Nicholas Hadgraft, Rodney M. Thomson and M.A. Michael on various aspects of 'Book Production' (pp. 41–196). The final section is devoted to twelve chapters on various aspects of 'Readership, Libraries, Texts and Contexts' (pp. 197–487). It would be invidious to single out any individual contributions from those written by Richard Sharpe, Jeremy Catto, Jan Ziolkowski, Michael Twomey, Nigel Ramsay, Nigel Morgan, Alan J. Fletcher, Anne Hudson, Alexandra Barratt, Tony Hunt, Julia Boffey and A.S.G. Edwards, Daniel Huws, Geoffrey Martin and Rodney M. Thomson, Nigel Ramsay, Charles Burnett, Peter Murray Jones, Nicolas Bell and, last but by no means least, Martin Kauffmann. All are of outstandingly high quality and will provide an important record of documentation and interpretation for years to come. The volume concludes with a list of abbreviations (pp. 488–91), an extensive bibliography (pp. 492–564), a general index (pp. 567–99) and an index of manuscripts (pp. 600–15), plus an extensive eighty-two pages of illustrations.

Heather Cass White's edition of Marianne Moore's *A-Quiver with Significance: Marianne Moore, 1932–1936*, contains all the facsimile versions of the poems Marianne Moore published between 1932 and 1936, the period generally recognized to be her greatest. As the editor writes in her preface, 'The present volume is an argument for the uniqueness of Marianne Moore's achievement during the years 1932 to 1936, and the importance of reading her poetry from those years in its earliest published form' (p. xi). In addition to the poems, variants are included, and the volume concludes with 'A Note on the Illustrations' to *The Pangolin and Other Verse* (pp. 127–30), '*Marianne Moore* 1925–1941: A Timeline' (pp. 131–6), a listing of works cited (p. 137) and an index of poems (p. 138).

John Mullan's *Anonymity: A Secret History of English Literature* was first published by Faber & Faber in 2007. A rather splendid dust-jacket, which unfortunately will no doubt be removed when the volume enters libraries, illustrates well its subject: anonymity. Mullan's concern is with hidden identity in English literature. As Mullan writes in his introduction, 'it is not obvious to today's readers that publication and secrecy might go together, but so they once did' (p. 3). For Mullan, anonymity is pervasive in English literature, encompassing such names as Spenser, Donne, Marvell, Defoe, Swift, Fanny Burney, Jane Austen, Byron, William Makepeace Thackeray, Lewis Carroll, Tennyson, George Eliot, Sylvia Plath and Doris Lessing, to name just a few! In a lively style, Mullan discusses their work and others, considering the reasons behind anonymity and its consequences. Replete with extensive footnotes (pp. 298–336), an extensive bibliography (pp. 337–51) and a useful index (pp. 353–74), this is a very useful reworking of a not unfamiliar subject.

Nora Nachumi's *Acting Like a Lady: British Women Novelists and the Eighteenth-Century Theater* is a study of Restoration and eighteenth-century fiction and theatre with a special emphasis upon theatrical history, and focuses upon the representation of gender. The work 'assumes that the experiences of actual women color—and are colored by—culturally prevalent images about female nature'. It concludes with an appendix listing 382 female novelists who wrote between 1660 and 1818. 'At least 135, or one third of this number, were involved in the theater' (p. xviii). The distinguished literary historian and book collector James G. Nelson is the author of the highly important trilogy *The Early Nineties: A View from the Bodley Head* (Harvard University Press [1971]), *Elkin Mathews: Publisher to Yeats, Joyce, Pound* (University of Wisconsin [1989]) and *Publisher to the Decadents: Leonard Smithers in the Careers of Beardsley, Wilde, Dowson* (Penn State University Press [2000]), amongst other seminal works focusing on the last decades of the nineteenth century and early years of the twentieth century. The CD-ROM *The Private Library of James G. Nelson: Books, Manuscripts, Prospectuses, Flyers, Catalogs and Related Items* records bookplates, books, manuscripts, prospectuses, flyers, catalogues and related items. The collection consists of some 2,000 items and is primarily but not exclusively 'an imprint collection—that is, a library of books bearing the imprint, or "style" of a publishing house'. The concentration is upon three firms: The Bodley Head, Elkin Mathews and Leonard Smithers). 'However, the collection also can be described as a nineties collection since all three firms were active in London during that colorful decade which featured such well-known figures in the arts as Oscar Wilde and Aubrey Beardsley' (CD-ROM p. 6). But it is not limited to those figures and extends to materials from the pre-Raphaelite and aesthetic periods into the modernist era, to include fascinating materials on W.B. Yeats, James Joyce, Ezra Pound and others. The descriptions are largely based upon two exhibitions of these materials held at the Special Collections at the University of Wisconsin at Madison and the University of Kentucky at Lexington. This magnificent repository for further study of individual authors, the period, publishing history and so much else has been donated to Columbia University, where future scholars will be able to consult its riches. Literary scholars and book historians are once again deeply indebted to James G. Nelson, the doyen of the *fin de siècle*.

An important monograph has been produced by Ralph Norris. His *Malory's Library: The Sources of The Morte Darthur* contains the first monograph analysis of the sources of Sir Thomas Malory's *Morte Darthur* to appear since 1921, and is the first detailed study since the publication of Vinaver's three-volume edition of Malory in 1947. Norris's study 'focuses mainly on the less familiar subject of the minor sources of Malory's work'. Although his emphasis is on the 'minor sources', he also inevitably discusses the so-called 'major sources' (p. 6) and attempts 'a complete list of Malory's sources' (pp. 163–4); he admits in a somewhat contradictory fashion that 'there appears to be no such thing as a typical minor source for Malory' (p. 164). There is an appendix, 'Analogues to Malory's "Love and Summer Passage"' (pp. 169–72), and the listing of works cited (pp. 173–84) includes manuscripts and incunables as well as texts and critical works. There is also an extensive index (pp. 185–199). On the negative side, there are some typographical errors, footnotes which are incomplete, and citations which are misspelled, and Malory's sources for 'The Tale of Sir Gareth' and 'The Healing of Sir Urry' episode have eluded him.

Volume 23 of *Spenser Studies: A Renaissance Poetry Annual* contains items of interest for all students of Spenser, his contemporaries, and the Renaissance. Of particular interest to students of bibliography and textual studies are two articles dealing with marginalia in copies of *The Faerie Queene*. Tianhu Hao's 'An Early Modern Male Reader of *The Faerie Queene*' (*SSt* 23[2008] 257–60) describes the annotations in a copy of the 1609 edition now at the Columbia University's Rare Book and Manuscript Library. Anne Lake Prescott, on the other hand, describes 'Two Copies of the 1596 *Faerie Queene*: Annotations and an Unpublished Poem on Spenser' (*SSt* 23[2008] 261–71). These copies are 'badly damaged or partial copies' that she 'recently acquired' (p. 261). Her article is accompanied by two illustrations (pp. 272–3). Hao's and Prescott's are but two of fifteen other fascinating articles to be found in this indispensable volume for students of the great Edmund Spenser.

Oyekan Owomoyela's *The Columbia Guide to West African Literature in English since 1945* is a detailed introduction to the literary traditions of Gambia, Sierra Leone, Liberia, Ghana and Nigeria. The focus is West African literature in English, and the work is divided into three parts: the first part focuses upon 'The Literary and Cultural Context of West African Literature in English' (pp. 1–50); the second part focuses upon 'West African Literature A–Z' (pp. 51–182) and part III is devoted to 'Writers and Selected Works' (pp. 183–94). There is in addition a detailed index (pp. 195–215). M.B. Parkes's beautifully produced quarto-size *Their Hands before our Eyes: A Closer Look at Scribes, The Lyell Lectures Delivered at the University of Oxford 1999* provides an indispensable account of the history of handwriting. Divided into four sections, the first focuses upon 'Scribes in their Environments' (pp. 3–53), the second on 'Scribes at Work' (pp. 57–145), the third part is devoted to 'Glossary, Indexes and Select List of Printed Works' and contains a 'Select Glossary of Technical Terms Applied to Handwriting' (pp. 149–55), an 'Index of Scribes Referred to by Name or Pseudonym' (pp. 157–60), an 'Index of Manuscripts Cited' (pp. 161–9), a 'Select List of Printed Works Cited' (pp. 172–84) and an extremely helpful general index (pp. 185–8). Following this are sixty-nine black and white plates that are referred to in Parkes's text. Hopefully, this book will be reissued in paperback form so that it can be used as a classroom text. Parkes writes clearly and informatively. We should all be grateful for his work, which illuminates our understanding of the history of handwriting and our knowledge of the historical period from which handwriting emerged.

David Pearson's important *Books as History: The Importance of Books Beyond their Texts* is written in an age of great transformation, in which the very existence of the book is being questioned. Pearson's focus is the importance of the books beyond their texts, and he draws attention to the manner in which they have been printed, their bindings, annotations within them if they exist, vandalism and so on. In other words, Pearson focuses upon the book as an artefact. His is an important, timely and well-written account of an important subject. The first volume of Donald Pizer's *A Picture and a Criticism of Life: New Letters: Theodore Dreiser* consists of a selection from Dreiser's previously unpublished letters. Thomas P. Riggio, the general editor of the Dreiser Edition, points out in his preface that 'Theodore Dreiser was an inveterate correspondent, writing an estimated 20,000 letters over the span of a half-century' (p. xi) and only 1,300 have been previously published. Although a few of the letters included in Pizer's edition 'have appeared in various journals and books', the majority have not (p. xxxv). The carefully edited text consists of introductory headnotes on the letters' background and context where appropriate, and there are detailed, very helpful annotations to what is an important addition to the ongoing edition of Dreiser's works.

Gill Plain and Susan Sellers's *A History of Feminist Literary Criticism* is divided into three sections: the first deals with 'Pioneers and Protofeminism' (pp. 5–100); the second focuses upon 'Creating a Feminist Literary Criticism' (pp. 101–208) and part III focuses upon 'Poststructuralism and Beyond' (pp. 209–335). There is a 'Postscript: Flaming Feminism' by Susan Gubar (pp. 336–41). Other contributors range from Helen Wilcox writing on 'Feminist Criticism and the Renaissance in the Seventeenth Century' (pp. 27–45), Jane Goldman on 'The Feminist Criticism of Virginia Woolf' (pp. 66–84) and Claire Colebrook on 'Feminist Criticism and Poststructuralism' (pp. 214–34). There are also contributions from Caroline Dinshaw, Susan Manly, Elizabeth Fallaize, Mary Eagleton, Helen Carr, Linda Anderson, Arlene R. Keizer, Caroline Gonda, Calvin Thomas, Madelon Sprengnether, Judith Still, Chris Weedon, Heather Love and Stacy Gillis in addition to the editors. The standard of the contributions is uniformly high.

Paul Poplawski is an authority on D.H. Lawrence and has also written the excellent *A Jane Austen Encyclopedia* [1998] and edited *The Encyclopedia of Literary Modernism* [2003]. He has now edited *English Literature in Context*, which includes extensive entries chronologically arranged: Valerie Allen on 'Medieval English, 500–1500' (pp. 1–109); Andrew Hiscock on 'The Renaissance, 1485–1660' (pp. 110–210); Lee Morrissey on 'The Restoration and Eighteenth Century, 1660–1780' (pp. 211–305); Peter J. Kitson on 'The Romantic Period, 1780–1832' (pp. 306–402); and Maria Frawley on 'The Victorian Age, 1832–1901' (pp. 403–518). The editor writes on 'The Twentieth Century, 1901–1939' (pp. 519–92) and John Brannigan on 'The Twentieth Century, 1939–2004' (pp. 593–663). There is also an index (pp. 664–84). The entries follow the same formula: chronology; historical overview; literary overview, texts and issues; readings; reference. Poplawski has edited a clearly written, very useful reference work.

Between the 1570s and the early eighteenth century, *The Whole Booke of Psalmes* witnessed over a thousand editions. Beth Quitslund's *The Reformation in Rhyme: Sternhold, Hopkins and the English Metrical Psalter* is the first monograph devoted entirely to the history, 'the composition and early reception of this volume' (p. 5). It also traces the changes which the work underwent during the centuries, revealing a social, historical, political and religious transformation. There are four appendices: 'Chronological Bibliographies' (pp. 275–8); 'Non-Psalm Contents of the 1562 *Whole Booke of Psalmes*' (pp. 279–82); 'Authorship and the Development of the English Metrical Psalter' (pp. 283–92); and 'Attribution and Misattribution in the 1562 *Whole Booke of Psalmes*' (pp. 293–8). There is an extensive enumerative bibliography, an index to biblical passages and a general index (pp. 299–321).

Brave New Words: The Oxford Dictionary of Science Fiction, edited by Jeff Prucher, is a historical dictionary replete with entries on everything relating to the genre of science fiction. Science-fiction works, the language of science fiction, the creators of science fiction and so much more are contained within this dictionary, which is an expansion of the Oxford English Dictionary Science Fiction Citations Project, 'which has been collecting citations for science fiction terminology since 2001 (online at www.jesseword.com/sf)' (p. ix). Entries encompass various citations of a word's usage, from its earliest known appearance. Evidence is taken from science-fiction novels and short stories, mainstream publications, fanzines, screenplays, newspapers, comics, songs and of course the internet. These illuminate words such as 'spacesuit' with its apparent 1929 first usage, 'blast off' (1937) and, to take another instance, 'robot' from 1920, although 'death ray' dates from 1915 and 'science fiction' has been used since 1851.

John D. Rateliff's *The History of the Hobbit. J.R.R. Tolkien*, part 2: *Return to Bag-End* presents for the first time in two volumes the complete text of the original manuscript of Tolkien's *The Hobbit*. Rateliff provides an extensive commentary and record of the innumerable alterations made to the story by Tolkien prior to and after its publication. There are detailed annotations, an essay on the date of composition and Tolkien's subsequent revisions. Appendices include: '*The Denham Tracts*' (pp. 841–54); 'Tolkien's Letter to *The Observer*' (pp. 855–65); 'The *Devergatal* (the Dwarf Names)' (pp. 866–71); and 'Tolkien's Correspondence with Arthur Ransome' (pp. 872–79). There is in addition an extensive index (pp. 881–905).

Regina Schneider, in her *Sidney's (Re)Writing of the Arcadia*, hopes 'to elucidate the ways in which the *Arcadia*'s internal diversity was intentional rather than accidental and to show how Sidney both transformed existing literary conventions for his own purposes and developed his own narrative techniques in the course of writing and rewriting the *Arcadia*'. Schneider's work depends upon her examination of the manuscript version, *c.*1580; the text in the 1590 printed version; and 'the combined version of 1593'. She aims 'to reestablish a new text that represents its chronological development more accurately than the hybrid edition of 1593 with its illusion of continuation and closure'. She then examines 'the four different stages in the development of this text—the Eclogues, the *Old Arcadia*, the revision process as preserved in the 1593 edition, and the *New Arcadia* of 1590' in order to 'demonstrate how each stage is marked by the influence of one genre in particular' (p. xix). In other words, Schneider interweaves textual, source and critical study in what is a densely argued monograph. William Sherman's *Used Books: Marking Readers in Renaissance England* is the work of a scholar who has 'caught the marginalia bug' (p. xii). His study examines concepts of marginalia focusing upon the Renaissance. Chapters are devoted to 'Books, bodies and symbols ... Women, memory and household management ... Reading and religion ... Navigation and exploration ... Politics and law' (p. xx). Sherman writes clearly and is not afraid to acknowledge his debt to previous scholars. His book contains extremely informative and useful illustrative figures.

Mention should be made of Willa Z. Silverman's *The New Bibliopolis: French Book Collectors and the Culture of Print, 1880–1914*. Her 'Introduction: The New Bibliopolis' contains a fascinating discourse on 'What Is the History of Bibliophilia?' (pp. 6–8). Although Silverman's focus is 'book collecting in France from the early Third Republic to the onset of the First World War' (p. 5), her observations still have relevance to students of the history of the book in the English-speaking world. Geoffrey Sutton has compiled a *Concise Encyclopedia of the Original Literature of Esperanto*. The language was initiated by L.L. Zamenhof (1859–1917) in an idealistic attempt at communication between different languages and cultures. Sutton's is a record of the creative writing in Esperanto by bilingual speakers from diverse countries who have chosen to write in the language because of its virtues. Sutton's work is divided into 'The Original Literature of Esperanto 1887–2007 with Biographies, Dates, Descriptions of Work and Concise Bibliographies in Chronological Order' (pp. 21–576), 'Outline of Esperanto's Linguistic Structure and Creative Capabilities' (pp. 577–602) and bibliographies (pp. 603–70). There are also appendices on 'Esperanto Culture—Summary', 'Associated Reference Works in Literature and Linguistics and Allied Disciplines' and 'Libraries and Further Information', followed by an extensive index (pp. 675–727).

Carol Taffe's *Ireland through the Looking Glass: Flann O'Brien, Myles na gCopaleen and Irish Cultural Debate* is the first monograph to thoroughly study the work of the Irish journalist and comic writer Brian O'Nolan (1911–66) who wrote under the nom de plume Flann O'Brien. The bibliography contains a listing of the author's books, unpublished materials, serial journalism, occasional articles and stories, translations and reviews. It also provides a useful guide to manuscript collections of twentieth-century post-independence Irish collections and an extensive secondary bibliography of writings about the period (pp. 251–66). In addition there is an extensive index (pp. 266–74) and detailed, useful notations to references to the text found at the end of the book (pp. 209–50). Taffe's study firmly places O'Nolan's work within its specifically Irish context and consequently illuminates the cultural and publishing history of independent Ireland in the middle years of the twentieth century. Marianne Thormählen's edited *English Now: Selected Papers from the 20th IAUPE Conference in Lund 2007* is dedicated to the memory of William Speed Hill (1935–2007), the eminent bibliographer and editor of the important journal *Text*. The selection of papers of those given at the 20th Triennial Conference of the International Association of University Professors of English, which took place at Lund University, 6–10 August 2007, was based upon recommendations from the thirty-seven conference chairs. Amongst the fascinating papers, of particular interest to students of bibliography and textual studies is Alexis Weedon's 'Textual Production and Dissemination in Book History: A Case Study of Cross-Media Production between the Wars' (pp. 318–31), which is concerned with the use of 'quantitative measures to increase our understanding of a book's origins and influence' (p. 318). Weedon focuses in particular upon

'Baroness Orczy, A.E.W. Mason and Elinor Glyn' as 'three examples of cross-media production between the wars' (pp. 321–30).

The first volume of Pierre Walker and Greg Zacharias's *The Complete Letters of Henry James, 1872–1876* heralds the beginning of what promises to be a great scholarly edition that has obtained from various foundations and institutions 'a commitment to the editing, annotation, and publication of an edition of more than ten thousand Henry James letters' (p. xi). Following Millicent Bell's extensive and well-written 'Introduction: The Passage to Europe' (pp. xv–lvii), there is a listing of 'Symbols and Abbreviations' (p. lix) and a detailed chronology, beginning on 11 May 1872 and concluding on 8 July of the following year (pp. lxi–lxix). An 'Errata' page lists four errata in the volume (p. lxxi). The first letter published is from Henry James to his mother and father, dated 20 May 1872, written on the steamship *Algeria*, which left New York for Liverpool on 11 May 1872 (p. 3). The final letter in the volume is written to Mary Lucinda Holton James (1847–1922), who married Henry James's younger brother, nicknamed 'Bob' (1846–1910), written on 8 July 1873 from Berne, Switzerland. There is a very informative 'Biographical Register' of recipients and other people mentioned in the letters (pp. 337–61). This is followed by 'Genealogies' (pp. 364–6) and a 'General Editors' Note' (pp. 367–77) which opens with the sensible observation that the editors 'intend *The Complete Letters of Henry James* to be as useful to as broad a range of readers as possible, given the limitations of print reproduction' (p. 367). This very valuable volume concludes with a listing of works cited (pp. 379–87) and a most helpful index (pp. 389–410).

Larissa P. Watkins's *Burnsiana* commemorates the 250th anniversary of the birth of Robert Burns in 2009. The Masonic Temple, the Supreme Council of the Ancient & Accepted Scottish Rite, Southern Jurisdiction, USA, based in Washington, DC, has produced a bibliography of its William R. Smith Burnsiana Collection. Oak Knoll have acted as distributors of the 8.5 x 11-inch book replete with small black and white reproductions of, mainly, engravings and paintings (these are listed on pp. 135–9: 'Illustration/Engraving Credits'). The problem with the review copy sent to me by the distributors Oak Knoll is that page 111 is followed by the 'Geographical Index' to the first chapter (pp. 143–55). There is then a 'Publisher Index' to the first chapter (pp. 157–61), a 'Publisher Index' to the second chapter (pp. 163–5) and the third and fourth chapters (pp. 167–70). Something has gone amiss in the production stage of Larissa P. Watkins's bibliography. Neither she nor the Masons seem to have been well served by the distributors and producers of the volume. Essentially *Burnsiana* is a pleasant memento to an interesting nineteenth-century collection that seems not to have been added to since the collector William R. Smith's death in 1912. The publication announced from the Oak Knoll Press claims that Smith's collection is unparalleled and that 'it is the second largest compilation of Burns materials in the world, ranking only behind the collection maintained in the Mitchell Library in Glasgow, Scotland'. The announcement further claims that 'In terms of American material about Burns, the library of Supreme Council' in Washington 'has the world's largest collection'. These are contentious claims, especially as the collection appears to be frozen in time. The G. Ross Roy collection at the

Thomas Cooper Library at the University of South Carolina, Columbia, has a Kilmarnock edition not found in the William R. Smith Collection. In addition, it has the unique Merry Muses, original manuscripts and probably five times as many editions of Burns as those listed in the Smith Collection. The publication of its catalogues published by the University of South Carolina Press and the Thomas Cooper Library in April 2009, compiled by Elizabeth Sudduth's introduction and annotation by the eminent Burns scholar and collector G. Ross Roy and colour illustrations, is eagerly awaited. Some idea of its riches may be gleaned from the 51-page *Robert Burns: An Exhibition February 1971* catalogue and introductory note by G. Ross Roy, held at the Swen Franken Parson Library and Northern Illinois University. Of course, the Ross Roy Collection was augmented during the last years of the twentieth century and opening decade of the twenty-first.

A sumptuous volume worthy of its subject is to be found in *The Robert J. Wickenheiser Collection of John Milton at the University of South Carolina*. Robert J. Wickenheiser was formerly Professor of English and University President at Mount St Mary's University, Maryland (1987–1993) and St Bonaventure University (1994–2003). This is a heavily bound book with the endpapers containing illustrations of the collection at the Wickenheiser home. There are extensive descriptions of the individual items of the collection and notes and abbreviations with sections on 'The Collection and its Origins' (pp. 1–32), 'Descriptive Listing of Editions' (pp. 33–678); 'Descriptive Listing of Miltoniana Divided Chronologically by Centuries' (pp. 679–750); 'John Milton in Select Anthologies (Chronologically Listed)' (pp. 751–64); 'Original Drawings, Illustrations, Engravings and Other' (pp. 765–92); 'John Martin (1789–1854): Mezzotint Illustrator' (pp. 793–800); 'Ephemera and Objets d'Art' (pp. 801–10); 'Photographs of Additional Select Items' (pp. 811–18); appendix, 'Recent Additions of Note' (pp. 819–20); bibliography (pp. 821–6), and an alphabetical, enumerative index (pp. 827–39). The descriptions are not only the work of the owner but also of Patrick Scott, the eminent and extremely knowledgeable director of Rare Books and Special Collections and Professor of English at the University of South Carolina at Columbia.

Mark E. Wildermuth's *Print, Chaos and Complexity: Samuel Johnson and Eighteenth-Century Media Culture* focuses upon Samuel Johnson's non-fiction. Wildermuth's aim 'is to show how eighteenth-century awareness of the interplay between fixity and instability in print helps us contextualize and comprehend the role print played in developing Johnson's awareness of the ways in which print mediation impacted human beings ethically, socially, and aesthetically as users of signs' (p. 16). Admittedly, Wildermuth's prose is exceedingly prolix; however, he does have some very useful insights into Samuel Johnson's non-fictional prose. Margaret Willes writes in her introduction to her *Reading Matters: Five Centuries of Discovering Books*: 'This book sets out to examine how people bought and acquired books over the past 500 years' (p. xiii). She focuses upon the relationships between readers and the volumes they read. Chapters range from a study of a great, late sixteenth-century book lover, Bess of Hardwick and the Cavendish family (pp. 1–27), to Samuel Pepys (pp. 28–55), provincial libraries in the late seventeenth and the eighteenth centuries (pp. 56–82), Thomas Jefferson (pp. 83–108), the reading of distinguished architect Sir John Soanes (pp. 109–35), 'Fact and Fiction in Georgian Britain' (pp. 136–67), Charles Winn (pp. 168–92) and an obscure nineteenth-century bibliophile, 'The Common Reader: Books for Working Men and Women' (pp. 193–232), and she concludes, interestingly enough, with a chapter on those two great, twentieth-century characters, Denis and Edna Healey, which she entitles 'Children of the Revolution: The Books of Denis and Edna Healey' (pp. 233–62). There is a very useful appendix on 'Equivalent Values of the Pound' showing 'changes in the value of money... giving the amount of money required at November 2007 to purchase goods bought at £1,' revealing that in 1800 £1 was the 2007 equivalent of £35.41 (p. 263). How much it is worth today, one daren't think. There are extensive notes to each chapter and a detailed, enumerative listing of further reading plus a useful index (pp. 264–95). There are seven full-page colour plates and eighty-three black and white illustrations in this extremely interesting and well-written study by a former editor at various London publishing houses and publisher at the National Trust.

A useful reference work is the critical study by Raymond Leslie Williams, *The Columbia Guide to the Latin American Novel since 1945*, offering 'many features of a literary history of the modern Latin American and Caribbean novel as well as several features of an encyclopedia'. The work is organized into two parts. The first part consists 'of a four-part history of the Latin American novel from 1945 to 2005'. The second part contains entries arranged alphabetically covering the letters A through Z 'that succinctly explain the novelistic tradition of specific nations, topics, authors, and the content of selected individual novels'. The work is completed by an annotated bibliography of studies on the Latin American and Caribbean novel. 'Most of the novels described, analyzed or mentioned ... were written in Spanish, and many ... have been translated into English' (p. vii). The pages are double-columned and the entries rarely exceed a page. In other words, reasonably short. However, they are informative and clearly written. Williams's work is more of a guide than a comprehensive reference work to the subject.

Richard Wires's fascinating account, *The Politics of the Nobel Prize in Literature: How the Laureates Were Selected, 1901–2007*, provides information which surprisingly has not been produced previously and deals, as its title suggests, with the politics of the Nobel Prize in literature. It avoids personal details, although in the case of the great Graham Greene, for instance, there are eight references to his being among those who should have been awarded the prize and a hint of perhaps one of the main reasons why he never received it. Wires's is a fascinating, well-written study and includes two appendices: 'Laureates in Chronological Order' and 'Laureates in Alphabetical Order' (pp. 249–52).

David Womersley and Richard McCabe's *Literary Milieux: Essays in Text and Context Presented to Howard Erskine-Hill* includes sixteen essays largely focused on the eighteenth century, 'presented in honour of the distinguished scholar Howard Erskine-Hill, emeritus professor of Literary History at Cambridge University' (p. 7). Following the editors' preface (pp. 7–12), there is 'Howard Erskine-Hill: A Bibliography' (pp. 13–19). This is enumerative, and includes his thesis on Pope, his books, his monographs and editions, articles, reviews, published letters, the obituaries he wrote, translations and poetry. Finally in this year's review, the Cornell Wordsworth series is a majestic one. The publication of the complete *Excursion* is an edition of the longest poem published by Wordsworth during his lifetime. The editors Sally Bushell, James A. Butler and David Garcia have somewhat controversially chosen as their copy-text the corrected second issue of the poem from 1814. Their main reason for doing so seems to be the absence of printer's manuscripts for the complete poem. Printed verbal and non-verbal variants and extensive editorial annotation, accompanied by photographic illustrations, are also included in this edition, which is bound to be an important one in the history of editions of Romantic poetry.

Note

The writer wishes to thank Professors James E. May and Patrick Scott for their help with this chapter.

Books Reviewed

Alston, R.C. *A Bibliography of the English Language from the Invention of Printing to the Year 1800*. vol. 21, part 1: Addenda Volumes I–X; vol. 21, part 2: Addenda Volumes XI–XVIII; vol. 21, part 3: Addenda Facsimiles. Smith Settle Yeadon. [2008] parts 1 and 2, pp. xl + 856; part 3, no pagination. $148.81 ISBN 9 7809 0229 6015.

Arnold, John, and John Hay, eds. *The Bibliography of Australian Literature, K–O to 2000*. UQP. [2007] pp. 751. $142 ISBN 9 7807 0223 5986.

Basbanes, Nicholas. *A World of Letters: Yale University Press, 1908–2008*. YaleUP. [2008] pp. 240. $26 ISBN 9 7803 0011 5987.

Battestin, Martin C., ed. *Henry Fielding's The Journal of a Voyage to Lisbon, Shamela and Occasional Writings*. Clarendon. [2008] pp. 804. $270 ISBN 9 7801 9926 6753.

Beal, Peter. *A Dictionary of English Manuscript Terminology, 1450–2000*. OUP. [2008] pp. 480. $125 ISBN 9 7801 9926 5442.

Bell, Hazel K. *From Flock Beds to Professionalism: A History of Index-Makers*. OakK. [2008] pp. 340. $95 ISBN 9 7815 8456 2283.

Black, Joseph, et al., eds. *The Broadview Anthology of British Literature: The Twentieth Century and Beyond, vol. 6A: From 1900 to World War II and The Twentieth Century and Beyond; vol. 6B: From 1945 to the Twenty-First Century*. Broadview. [2008] pp. 1,590. $60 ISBN 9 7815 5111 8697.

Blevins, Jacob. *An Annotated Bibliography of Thomas Traherne Criticism, 1900–2003*. Mellen. [2008] pp. 188. $99.95 ISBN 0 7734 6023 3.

Bloch, William Goldbloom. *The Unimaginable Mathematics of Borges' Library of Babel*. OUP. [2008] pp. 192. $19.95 ISBN 0 1953 3457 4.

Briggs, Asa. *A History of Longmans and their Books, 1724–1990: Longevity in Publishing*. [2008] pp. 624. $110 ISBN 9 7815 8456 2344.

Bright, Michael, ed. *The Complete Works of Robert Browning with Variant Readings and Annotations*. vol. 11. OhioUP/Baylor University. [2008] pp. 504. $70 ISBN 9 7808 2141 8390.

Bryant, John. *Melville Unfolding: Sexuality, Politics, and the Versions of Typee: A Fluid-Text Analysis, with an Edition of the 'Typee' Manuscript*. UMichP. [2008] pp. 464. $75 ISBN 9 7804 7211 5921.

Bushell, Sally, James A. Butler, and David Garcia, eds. *The Excursion*. by William Wordsworth. CornUP. [2007] pp. 1,256. $99.95 ISBN 9 7808 0144 6535.

Carpenter, Humphrey. *The Seven Lives of John Murray: The Story of a Publishing Dynasty 1768–2002*. Murray. [2008] pp. xiv + 370. £12.99 ISBN 9 7807 1956 5335.

Carruthers, Mary. *The Book of Memory: A Study of Memory in Medieval Culture*. CUP. [2008] pp. 519. $90 ISBN 0 5218 8820 4.

Cass White, Heather, ed., introd. and notes. *A-Quiver with Significance: Marianne Moore, 1932–1936*. ELS. [2008] pp. xxx + 138. $22 ISBN 1 5505 8380 8.

Colker, Marvin. *Trinity College Library Dublin: Descriptive Catalogue of the Mediaeval and Renaissance Latin Manuscripts Supplement One*. FCP. [2008] pp. 220. $75 ISBN 9 7818 4682 0953.

Collini, Stefan. *Common Reading*. OUP. [2008] pp. 376. $50 ISBN 9 7801 9929 6781.

Cope, Kevin L., ed. *1650–1850: Ideas, Aesthetics, and Inquiries in the Early Modern Era*. vol. 15. [2008] pp. xiv + 427. $163.50 ISBN 9 7804 0464 4154.

Cronenwett, Philip N., Kevin Osborn, and Samuel A. Streit, eds. *Celebrating Research*. Association of Research Libraries. [2008] pp. 312. $99.99 ISBN 1 5940 7769 X.

Daly, Peter M. *Companion to Emblem Studies*. AMS. [2008] pp. xii + 632. $225 ISBN 0 4046 3720 5.

Danziger, Marlies K., ed. *James Boswell: The Journal of his German and Swiss Travels, 1764*. EdinUP/YaleUP. [2008] pp. 490. $75 ISBN 9 7807 4861 8064.

Davidson, Audrey Ekdahl. *Aspects of Early Music and Performance*. AMS. [2008] pp. xi + 220. $92.50 ISBN 9 7804 0464 6011.

Davies, John, Nigel Jenkins, Menna Baines, and Peredur I. Lynch, eds. *The Welsh Academy Encyclopedia of Wales*. UWalesP. [2008] pp. 1,107. $99 ISBN 9 7807 0831 9536.

Day, Gary. *Literary Criticism: A New History*. EdinUP. [2008] pp. viii + 344. £50 ISBN 9 7807 4861 5636.

De Hamel, Christopher. *Book of Beasts: A Facsimile of MS Bodley 764*. Bodleian. [2008] pp. 280. $250 ISBN 1851243178.

De Jong, Cees W., ed. *Jan Tschichold: His Life, Work and Legacy*. T&H. [2008] pp. 352. £39.95 ISBN 9 7805 0051 3989.

Dibble, Brian. *Doing Life: A Biography of Elizabeth Jolley*. UWAP. [2008] pp. 352. $32 ISBN 9 7819 2140 1060.

Dillon, Sarah. *The Palimpsest: Literature, Criticism, Theory.* Continuum. [2008] pp. x +164. $120. ISBN 9 7808 2649 5457.

Dudley Edwards, Owen. *British Children's Fiction in the Second World War.* EdinUP. [2009] pp. viii + 744. pb £29.99 ISBN 9 7807 4861 6503.

Duffell, Martin J. *A New History of English Metre.* DavidB. [2008] pp. 230. $89.50 ISBN 9 7819 0598 1915.

Eby, Clare Virginia, ed. *The Genius.* by Theodore Dreiser. UIllP. [2008] pp. 952. $95 ISBN 9 7802 5203 1007.

Elgar, Andrew, and Peter Sedgwick. *Cultural Theory: The Key Concepts.* Routledge. [2008] pp. 447. $26.95 ISBN 9 7804 1539 9395.

Evenden, Elizabeth. *Patents, Pictures and Patronage: John Day and the Tudor Book Trade.* Ashgate. [2008] pp. xii + 220. $99.95 ISBN 9 7807 5465 4803.

Fang, Irving E. *Alphabet to Internet: Mediated Communication in our Lives.* Rada Press. [2008] pp. 560. $95 ISBN 9 7819 3301 1905.

Finkelstein, David, and Alistair McCleery, eds. *The Edinburgh History of the Book in Scotland, vol. 4: Professionalism and Diversity, 1880–2000.* EdinUP. [2007] pp. xx + 524. £105 ISBN 9 7807 4861 8293.

Fleck, Robert D. *Books about Books: A History of Bibliography of Oak Knoll Press, 1978–2008.* OakK. [2008] pp. 232. $25 ISBN 9 7815 8456 2481.

Fraser, Robert. *Book History through Postcolonial Eyes: Rewriting the Script.* Routledge. [2008] pp. xiv + 210. $37.95 ISBN 9 7804 1540 2941.

Garvey, Nathan. *The Celebrated George Barrington: A Spurious Author; the Book Trade, and Botany Bay.* Horden House Rare Books. [2008] pp. viii + 328. $60 ISBN 9 7818 7556 7546.

Gifford, James, ed. *Panic Spring: A Romance.* by Lawrence Durrell, introd. Richard Pine, afterward James A. Bringham. ELS. [2008] pp. xxxiv + 238. $25 ISBN 1 5505 83816.

Gifford, James, ed. and introd. *Pied Piper of Lovers,* by Lawrence Durrell, afterword James A. Bringham. ELS. [2008] pp. xvii + 282. $25 ISBN 1 5505 83824.

Goldgar, Bertrand A., and Ian Gadd, eds. *The Cambridge Edition of the Works of Jonathan Swift: English Political Writings, 1711–1714.* CUP. [2008] pp. xxx + 546. $150 ISBN 9 7805 2182 9298.

Goetsch, Paul. *Machphantasien in englischsprachigen Fust-Dichtungen: Funktiongeschichtliche Studien.* Ferdinand Schöningh, Paderborn, Germany. [2008] pp. 303. No price available. ISBN 9 7835 0676 4997.

Gomez, Jeff. *Print Is Dead: Books in our Digital Age.* Macmillan. [2008] pp. 300. $24.95 ISBN 9 7802 3052 7164.

Gorji, Mina. *John Clare and the Place of Poetry.* LiverUP. [2008] pp. 224. $95 ISBN 9 7818 4631 1635.

Gravett, Paul. *Graphic Novels: Everything You Need to Know.* Collins Design. [2005] pp. 192. $29.95 ISBN 0 0608 2425 5.

Gray, Douglas. *Later Medieval English Literature.* OUP. [2008] pp. 712. $130 ISBN 9 7801 9812 2180.

Habib, Imtiaz H. *Black Lives in the English Archives, 1500–1677.* Ashgate. [2008] pp. xvi + 416. $99.95 ISBN 9 7807 5465 6951.

Hadley, Louisa. *The Fiction of A.S. Byatt.* Palgrave Macmillan. [2008] pp. 192. $22.95 ISBN 9 7802 3051 7929.

Hahn, Daniel, and Nicholas Robins, eds. *The Oxford Guide to Literary Britain and Ireland*. OUP. [2008] pp. xii + 270. $60 ISBN 0 1986 1460 8.

Harner, James L. *Literary Research Guide: An Annotated Listing of Reference Sources in English Literary Studies*. MLA. [2008] pp. xvii + 826. $37.50 ISBN 9 7808 7352 8085.

Hauptman, Robert. *Documentation: A History and Critique of Attribution, Commentary, Glosses, Marginalia, Notes, Bibliographies, Works-Cited Lists, and Citation Indexing and Analysis*. McFarland. [2008] pp. 240. $35 ISBN 9 7807 8643 3339.

Hogg, James. *The Collected Letters of James Hogg, vol. 3: 1832 to 1835*. EdinUP. [2008] pp. 450. $75 ISBN 9 7807 4861 6756.

Hogg, James. *Midsummer Night Dreams and Related Poems*. ed. the late Jill Rubenstein, completed by Gillian Hughes with Meiko O'Halloran. EdinUP. [2008] pp. cii + 235. £60 ISBN 9 7807 4862 4409.

Hogg, James. *The Mountain Bard*. ed. Suzanne Gilbert. EdinUP. [2007] pp. 384. $33.56 ISBN 9 7807 4862 0067.

Holdsworth, Nadine, and Mary Luckhurst. *A Concise Companion to Contemporary British and Irish Drama*. Blackwell. [2008] pp. 295. $95.95 ISBN 1 4051 3053 9.

Holliday, Peter. *Edward Johnston: Master Calligrapher*. BL/OakK. [2007] pp. xxii + 387. $49.95 ISBN 1 5845 6198 X.

Hook, Andrew. *Scotland and America: A Study of Cultural Relations, 1750–1835*. Humming Earth. [2008] pp. 292. $30 ISBN 1 8462 2017 3.

Hotchkiss, Valerie R., and Fred C. Robinson. *English in Print: From Caxton to Shakespeare to Milton*. UIllP. [2008] pp. 234. $65 ISBN 9 7802 5203 3469.

Joshi, S.T., Lawrence I. Berkove, and David E. Schultz, eds. *The Short Fiction of Ambrose Bierce*. vols. 1–3. UTennP. [2008] vol. 1, pp. 497, vol. 2, pp. 500, vol. 3, pp. 500. $50 each; vol. 1 ISBN 9 7815 7233 5363, vol. 2 ISBN 9 7815 7233 5370, vol. 3 ISBN 9 7815 7233 5387.

Kanellos, Nicolás. *The Greenwood Encyclopedia of Latino Literature*. Greenwood. [2008] pp. xxxvi + 1,360. $299.95. ISBN 0 3133 3970 8.

King, Don W. *Hunting the Unicorn: A Critical Biography of Ruth Pitter*. KSUP. [2008] pp. 360. $55 ISBN 9 7808 7338 9471.

Krupp, Andrea. *Bookcloth in England and America 1823–1850*. OakK. [2008] pp. 102. $35 ISBN 9 7815 8456 2139.

Landon, Richard. *Humane Letters: Bruce Rogers, Designer of Books and Artist. With an Introductory Essay on Collecting Bruce Rogers by Thomas T. Schweitzer. An Exhibition at the Thomas Fisher Rare Book Library, University of Toronto, 24 September–21 December 2007*. University of Toronto Library. [2007] pp. 112. CAN$30 ISBN 9 7807 7276 0630.

Lasner, Mark Samuels. *The Bookplates of Aubrey Beardsley*. Rivendale. [2008] pp. 108. $25 ISBN 1 9042 0110 5.

Lupack, Barbara Tepa, with Alan Lupack. *Illustrating Camelot*. Brewer. [2008] pp. 288. $60 ISBN 9 7818 4384 1838.

Lynch, Brendan. *Parsons Bookshop: At the Heart of Bohemian Dublin 1949–1989*. Liffey Press, Dublin, Ireland. [2006] pp. 252. $27.95 ISBN 9 7819 0578 5117.

Lynch, Jack. *Deception and Detection in Eighteenth-Century Britain*. Ashgate. [2008] pp. 218. $99.95 ISBN 9 7807 5466 5281.

Malcolm, Cheryl Alexander, and David Malcolm. *A Companion to the British and Irish Short Story*. Blackwell. [2008] pp. 571. $199.95 ISBN 9 7814 0514 5374.

Matthews, Nicole, and Nickianne Moody, eds. *Judging a Book by its Cover: Fans, Publishers, Designers and the Marketing of Fiction*. [2007] pp. xxix + 192. $99.95 ISBN 9 7807 5465 7316.

Maunder, Andrew. *The Facts on File Companion to the British Short Story*. FOF. [2007] pp. 511. $85 ISBN 0 8160 5990 X.

Meek, Richard, Jane Rickard, and Richard Wilson. *Shakespeare's Book: Essays in Reading, Writing and Reception*. ManUP. [2008] pp. 288. $84.95 ISBN 9 7807 1907 9054.

Millington, Jon. *William Beckford: A Bibliography*. Beckford Society, The Timber Cottage, Crockerton, Warminster, Wiltshire, BA12 8AX. [2008] pp. 416. £52 ISBN 0 9537 8363 4.

Mitchell, Kaye. *A.L. Kennedy*. Palgrave Macmillan. [2008] pp. 180. £9.99 ISBN 9 7802 3000 7567.

MLA Style Manual and Guide to Scholarly Publishing. MLA. [2008] pp. xxiv + 340. $32.50 ISBN 9 7808 7352 2977.

Morgan, Nigel J., and Rodney M. Thomson, eds. *The Cambridge History of the Book in Britain, vol. 2: 1100–1400*. CUP. [2008] pp. xxiv + 616. $190 ISBN 9 7805 2178 2180.

Mullan, John. *Anonymity: A Secret History of English Literature*. PrincetonUP. [2007] pp. 374. $22.95 ISBN 9 7806 9113 9418.

Nachumi, Nora. *Acting Like a Lady: British Women Novelists and the Eighteenth-Century Theater*. AMS. [2008] pp. xxvi + 345. $94.50 ISBN 9 7804 0464 8503.

Nelson, James G. *The Private Library of James G. Nelson: Books, Manuscripts, Prospectuses, Flyers, Catalogs and Related Items*. Private distribution. [2008] pp. 537. CD-ROM.

Neymeyr, Barbara, Jochen Schmidt, and Bernhard Zimmermann. *Stoizismus in der europäischen Philosophie, Literatur, Kunst und Politik*. Band 2: Berlin. Walter de Gruyter [2008] pp. 1307. $263.15 ISBN 978-3-11-020405-6.

Norris, Ralph. *Malory's Library: The Sources of The Morte Darthur*. Brewer. [2008] pp. 200. $90 ISBN 9 7818 4384 1548.

Oram, William A., Anne Lake Prescott, and Thomas P. Roche Jr. *Spenser Studies: A Renaissance Poetry Annual*. vol. 23. AMS. [2008] pp. viii + 322. $110 ISBN 9 7804 0419 2335.

Owomoyela, Oyekan. *The Columbia Guide to West African Literature in English since 1945*. ColUP. [2008] pp. 216. $85 ISBN 9 7802 3112 6861.

Parkes, M.B. *Their Hands before our Eyes: A Closer Look at Scribes. The Lyell Lectures Delivered at the University of Oxford 1999*. Ashgate. [2008] pp. xx + 190 + 69 plates. $124.95. ISBN 9 7807 5466 3379.

Pearson, David. *Books as History: The Importance of Books Beyond their Texts*. OakK. [2008] pp. 208. $49.95 ISBN 9 7815 8456 2337.

Pizer, Donald, ed. *A Picture and a Criticism of Life: New Letters, vol. 1: Theodore Dreiser*. UIllP. [2008] pp. 392. $60 ISBN 9 7802 5203 1069.

Plain, Gill, and Susan Sellers. *A History of Feminist Literary Criticism.* CUP. [2007] pp. 352. $130 ISBN 0 5218 5255 2.

Poplawski, Paula, ed. *English Literature in Context.* CUP. [2008] pp. 685. $34.95 ISBN 9 7805 2154 9280.

Prucher, Jeff, ed. *Brave New Words: The Oxford Dictionary of Science Fiction.* OUP. [2007] pp. 384. $35 ISBN 9 7801 9530 5671.

Quitslund, Beth. *The Reformation in Rhyme: Sternhold, Hopkins and the English Metrical Psalter, 1547–1603.* Ashgate. [2008] pp. x + 322. $114.95 ISBN 9 7807 5466 3263.

Rateliff, John D. *The History of the Hobbit. J.R.R. Tolkien, part 2: Return to Bag-End.* HoughtonM. [2007] pp. 467 [469–905]. $35 ISBN 0 6189 6847 4.

Schneider, Regina. *Sidney's (Re)Writing of the Arcadia.* AMS. [2008] pp. 238. $86 ISBN 9 7804 0462 3432.

Sherman, William H. *Used Books: Marking Readers in Renaissance England.* UPennP. [2008] pp. 259. $45 ISBN 9 7808 1224 0436.

Silverman, Willa Z. *The New Bibliopolis: French Book Collectors and the Culture of Print, 1880–1914.* UTorP. [2008] pp. 312. $75 ISBN 9 7808 0209 2113.

Sutton, Geoffrey. *Concise Encyclopedia of the Original Literature of Esperanto.* Mondial. [2008] pp. x + 728. $66 ISBN 9 7815 9569 0906.

Taffe, Carol. *Ireland through the Looking Glass: Flann O'Brien, Myles na gCopaleen and Irish Cultural Debate.* CorkUP. [2008] pp. x + 274. £30 ISBN 9 7818 5918 4424.

Thormählen, Marianne, ed. *English Now: Selected Papers from the 20th IAUPE Conference in Lund 2007.* LundU. [2008] pp. xx + 354. $46 ISBN 9 7891 9769 3509.

Walker, Pierre A., and Greg W. Zacharias, eds. *The Complete Letters of Henry James.* MLA. [2008] pp. 391. $90 ISBN 9 7808 0322 5848.

Watkins, Larissa P. *Burnsiana.* OakK. [2008] pp. 240. $65 ISBN 9 7815 8456 2467.

Wickenheiser, Robert J. *The Robert J. Wickenheiser Collection of John Milton at the University of South Carolina.* published in co-operation with the Thomas Cooper Library, University of South Carolina. USCP. [2008] pp. xvi + 840. $90 ISBN 9 7815 7003 7283.

Wildermuth, Mark E. *Print, Chaos and Complexity: Samuel Johnson and Eighteenth-Century Media Culture.* UDelP. [2008] pp. 197. $48.50 ISBN 0 8741 3032 8.

Willes, Margaret. *Reading Matters: Five Centuries of Discovering Books.* YaleUP. [2008] pp. 295. $30 ISBN 0 3001 2729 4.

Williams, Raymond Leslie. *The Columbia Guide to the Latin American Novel since 1945.* ColUP. [2007] pp. 400. $67 ISBN 9 7802 3112 6885.

Wires, Richard. *The Politics of the Nobel Prize in Literature: How the Laureates Were Selected, 1901–2007.* Mellen. [2008] pp. 269. $109.95 ISBN 9 7807 7344 9572.

Womersley, David, and Richard McCabe, eds. *Literary Milieux: Essays in Text and Context Presented to Howard Erskine-Hill.* University of Delaware Press. [2008] pp. 371. $80 ISBN 9 7808 7413 9907.

YWES Index of Critics

YWES Index of Authors and Subjects